Fromm

W9-BIY-496

POSTCARDS

FROM

EUROPE

Summer visitors can gaze on fields of sunflowers as they drive through southern France.
See chapter 6. © Bob Krist.

The Acropolis in Athens—ancient symbol of "the glory that was Greece." See chapter 8.
© Kindra Clineff.

The Louvre and I. M. Pei's controversial glass pyramid reflect the convergence of old and new in Paris. See chapter 6. © Bob Krist.

Magnificent Chambord, the largest château in the Loire Valley. See chapter 6. © Kevin Galvin.

Marie Antoinette played shepherdess at this quaint hamlet, part of the Petit Trianon in Versailles. See chapter 6. © Kindra Clineff.

The Arc de Triomphe has witnessed some of France's proudest moments and some of its more humiliating defeats. See chapter 6. © Kevin Galvin.

The quieter side streets of popular Montmartre are worth seeking out for their views over the Paris rooftops. See chapter 6. © Bob Krist.

Walking the cobblestone streets of Stockholm's Gamla Stan (Old Town) at night is a trip back in time. See chapter 17. © Bob Krist.

Restaurant-lined rue des Bouchers in Brussels' historic heart. See chapter 2. © Kevin Galvin.

"Checkmate." Men playing chess relax in Budapest's thermal baths. See chapter 9. © Catherine Karnow.

Medieval castles, Gothic cathedrals, cobblestone streets and tranquil canals hauntingly evoke Bruges' past. See chapter 2. © Kevin Galvin.

The Vltava River winds through historic Prague, one of Europe's most vibrant and beautiful cities. See chapter 3. © Anthony Cassidy/Tony Stone Images.

Baroque Salzburg's alpine setting is on the banks of the Salzach River. See chapter 1. © Kevin Galvin.

Amsterdam's graceful cityscape is lined with canals, bridges, and 17th-century town houses. See chapter 12. © Kevin Galvin.

In Holland, watery expanses are punctuated by scenic windmills. See chapter 12. © Michael Defreitas.

*Capped by Brunelleschi's dome—
an amazing architectural feat—
the Duomo dominates Florence's
skyline. See chapter 11.
© Kevin Galvin.*

*Olive trees and grapevines dot Tuscany's rolling hills in the heart of Italy. See chapter 11.
© Jean Miele/The Stock Market.*

In Florence, visitors are no longer allowed to climb the fragile Leaning Tower of Pisa. See chapter 11. © Massimo Mastrorillo/The Stock Market.

The maritime province of the Algarve is dotted with hundreds of Portugal's finest beaches. See chapter 14. © Foto World/The Image Bank.

Hiking Dingle Peninsula on the lush Emerald Isle. See chapter 10. © M. Timothy O'Keefe.

St. Paul's Cathedral in London is a monument to beauty and tranquillity. See chapter 5. © Kelly/Mooney Photography.

Rich in history, Edinburgh Castle is one of the highpoints of a visit to Scotland. See chapter 15.
© Kindra Clineff.

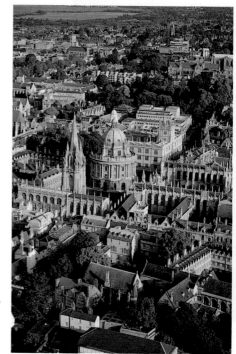

In Oxford, the towers and spires of one of the world's great universities rise majestically skyward. See chapter 5.
© Chris Donaghue.

Seville's glorious 14th-century El Alcázar has been the residence of Spanish monarchs since the days of Ferdinand and Isabella. See chapter 16. © *Ric Ergenbright.*

Neuschwanstein Castle's gothic turrets rise from the rugged Bavarian Alps. See chapter 7.
© Jeff Hunter/The Image Bank.

Frommer's® 2000

Europe

with Online Directory by Michael Shapiro

MACMILLAN • USA

MACMILLAN TRAVEL

Macmillan General Reference USA, Inc.
1633 Broadway
New York, NY 10019

Find us online at **www.frommers.com**

ISBN 0-02-862995-7
ISSN 1091-9511

Editor: Margot Weiss
With special thanks to David Gibbs, Justin Lapatine, and Leslie Wiggins.
Production Editor: Carol Sheehan
Photo Editor: Richard Fox
Design by Michele Laseau
Staff Cartographers: John Decamillis, Roberta Stockwell
Front cover photo: Ramsau in Bavaria, Germany
Page creation by Melissa Auciello-Brogan, Bob LaRoche, Sean Monkhouse, and Angel Perez

SPECIAL SALES

Contents

12   The Netherlands   765

13   Norway   796

14   Portugal   823

List of Maps

ABOUT THE AUTHORS

Darwin Porter, a native of North Carolina, was assigned to write the very first edition of a Frommer's guide devoted solely to one European country. Since then, he has written many best-selling Frommer's guides to all the major European destinations. In 1982 he was joined in his research efforts by **Danforth Prince,** formerly of the Paris bureau of the *New York Times,* who has traveled and written extensively about Europe.

Alan Crosby has lived and worked as a journalist in Prague for the past 6 years. He is co-author of *Frommer's Prague & the Best of the Czech Republic.*

Robert Emmet Meagher, a dual citizen of Ireland and the United States, is professor of humanities at Hampshire College in Amherst, Massachusetts. The author of more than a dozen books, plays, and translations, he has lived and worked in Ireland, twice holding visiting professorships at Trinity College Dublin.

George McDonald has lived in Amsterdam and Brussels as a former editor of the Sabena Belgian World Airlines and deputy editor of the KLM Royal Dutch Airlines in-flight magazines. He is now a freelance journalist and travel writer, and has written extensively about the Netherlands and Belgium for international magazines and guidebooks.

Sherry Marker's love of Greece began when she majored in classical Greek at Harvard. She has studied at the American School of Classical Studies in Athens and studied ancient history at the University of California at Berkeley. Author of a number of guides to Greece, she has published articles in the *New York Times, Travel & Leisure,* and *Hampshire Life.* She has written books on a variety of subjects, including a history of London for young adults. She is co-author of *Frommer's Greece.*

Hana Mastrini is a native of the western Czech spa town of Karlovy Vary who became a veteran of "Velvet Revolution" as a student in Prague in 1989. She began contributing to Frommer's guides while helping her husband John better understand his new home in the Czech Republic.

John Mastrini is a former television news anchor from the United States. He has lived in Prague since 1989, where he works as a journalist and media consultant. He is co-author of *Frommer's Prague & the Best of the Czech Republic.*

AN INVITATION TO THE READER

In researching this book, we discovered many wonderful places—hotels, restaurants, shops, and more. We're sure you'll find others. Please tell us about them, so we can share the information with your fellow travelers in upcoming editions. If you were disappointed with a recommendation, we'd love to know that, too. Please write to:

Frommer's Europe 2000
Macmillan Travel
1633 Broadway
New York, NY 10019

AN ADDITIONAL NOTE

Please be advised that travel information is subject to change at any time—and this is especially true of prices. We therefore suggest that you write or call ahead for confirmation when making your travel plans. The authors, editors, and publisher cannot be held responsible for the experiences of readers while traveling. Your safety is important to us, however, so we encourage you to stay alert and be aware of your surroundings. Keep a close eye on cameras, purses, and wallets, all favorite targets of thieves and pickpockets.

WHAT THE SYMBOLS MEAN

✪ Frommer's Favorites

Our favorite places and experiences—outstanding for quality, value, or both.

The following abbreviations are used for credit cards:

AE	American Express	EURO	Eurocard
CB	Carte Blanche	JCB	Japan Credit Bank
DC	Diners Club	MC	MasterCard
DISC	Discover	V	Visa
ER	EnRoute		

FIND FROMMER'S ONLINE

Arthur Frommer's Budget Travel Online (**www.frommers.com**) offers more than 6,000 pages of up-to-the-minute travel information—including the latest bargains and candid, personal articles updated daily by Arthur Frommer himself. No other Web site offers such comprehensive and timely coverage of the world of travel.

Introduction: Planning a Trip to Europe

Irresistible and intriguing, the ever-changing Europe of today offers you more excitement, experiences, and travel memories than ever. In compiling this volume for today's time-pressed traveler, we've tried to do two things: open the door to Europe's famous cities—their art and architecture, restaurants and theater, hotels and history—and guide you to all the experiences that no one would want to miss on even a cursory visit. So although this guide has to skim the highlights, we've also tossed in offbeat destinations and adventurous suggestions that lead to surprises and delights around every corner. In other words, we've tried to capture something of the best—the very essence of Europe—into one carry-along edition.

EUROPE TODAY

The day of traveling across Europe with a single currency and no border formalities is not here yet, but changes—including the introduction of the euro—are underway. However, what attracts visitors, the rich culture and histories in which each of Europe's myriad countries and regions are so strongly steeped, remains the same. From the splendor of a Greek temple towering above the arid Sicilian landscape to the majestic peaks of the Alps, from the sound of flamenco in a Madrid tavern to the blasting of a brass band in Munich's Hofbräuhaus—one Europe it may be on the map (and now on the bankbooks), but on the ground, it's still a Europe of countless facets and proud, distinct, and diverse heritages. There's no other place on earth where you can experience such enormous cultural changes by driving from one mountain valley to the next, where in only a few miles you're likely to encounter not only a different language but different food, architecture, and culture as well.

If you've come to pay your respects to the past, you're on the right continent. Over the past 3,000 years, Europe has seen some of the greatest intellectual and artistic developments the world has ever known. The European landscape is dense with the museums, cathedrals, palaces, and monuments that serve as repositories for much of this past glory. But the good news is that the continent is still in a dynamic, creative mode; artistic and cultural ferment are still very much part of the present, and Europe still helps set the trends in fashion, industrial design, cinema, technology, music, literature, and science. The dynamic European environment is all about life, innovation, entertainment, and, of course, food, which exists side by side with the artistic and cultural grandeur of the past.

Europe

Norwegian Sea

North Atlantic Ocean

Bergen •

NORWAY

GRAMPIAN
Aberdeen •

TAYSIDE
Perth •

North Sea

DENMARK

Belfast •

Edinburgh

IRELAND
Dublin •

DINGLE PENINSULA
KERRY COUNTY

Liverpool •

U. K.
COTSWOLDS Oxford
Bath •
STONEHENGE ■
Salisbury •
London •

THE NETHERLANDS

Hamburg •

Amsterdam

GERMANY

Bruges •
BELGIUM
Brussels •
Liège •
• Bonn

Frankfurt •

LUX.

English Channel

• Le Havre

Rothenburg ob der Tauber •

• Paris

Strasbourg • Augsburg

LOIRE VALLEY

Munich •

BAVARIAN ALPS

FRANCE

Bern • Innsbruck •

SWITZERLAND

Bay of Biscay

Geneva • **BERNER OBERLAND**

• Bordeaux

Milan •

Bilbao •

Arles • **PROVENCE**
Marseille • Nice •

MONACO
Florence

• Porto

Côte d'Azur

TUSCANY

PORTUGAL

• Madrid

ANDORRA

Barcelona •

CORSICA

• Lisbon

SPAIN

ALGARVE
Córdoba •
Seville • Valencia •

ANDALUSIA
• Granada

• Malaga

Costa del Sol

SARDINIA

Cagliari •

Mediterranean Sea

0 ___ 155 Miles
0 ___ 155 Kilometers

E-0001

2

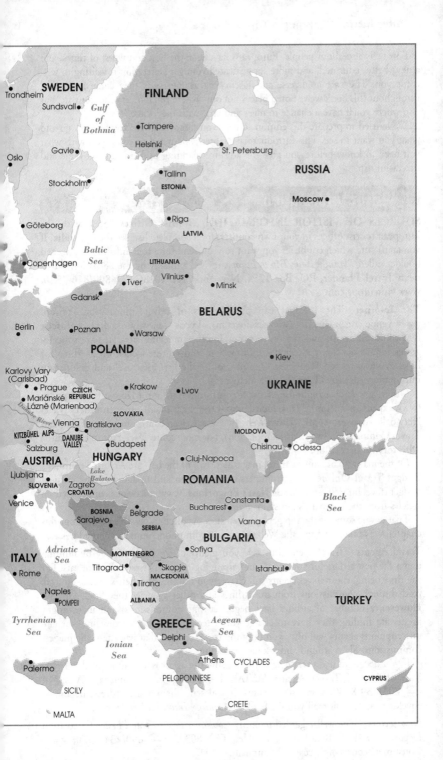

Europe is also about people. Europeans have seen the best and worst of times, and a new, better educated, and more sophisticated younger generation is waiting to welcome you. They are as diverse and fascinating as the lands they come from, and throughout this book we've noted places not only where you'll meet other tourists, but also where you'll have a chance to meet and chat with the locals.

We've tried to prepare this edition to help you discover where you want to go and what you want to see. This introductory chapter is designed to equip you with what you need to know before you go—the advance-planning tools for an enjoyable and successful trip.

1 Visitor Information

SOURCES OF VISITOR INFORMATION   Tourist Offices   Start with the European tourist offices in your own country; for a complete list, see the Appendix. If you aren't sure which countries you want to visit, send for a free, information-packed booklet called *Planning Your Trip to Europe,* revised annually by the 28-nation **European Travel Planner,** P.O. Box 1754, New York, NY 10185 (☎ **800/816-7530;** www.visiteurope.com).

The Internet   The Internet can provide lots of travel information. **Yahoo!** (www.yahoo.com), **Excite** (www.excite.com), **Lycos** (www.lycos.com), **Infoseek** (www.infoseek.com), and the other major Internet indexing sites all have subcategories for travel, country/regional information, and culture—click on all three for links to travel-related Web sites. One of the best hotlists for travel and destination information is Excite's **City.Net** (www.city.net).

Other good clearinghouse sites for information are **Microsoft's Expedia** (www.expedia.msn.com), **Travelocity** (www.travelocity.com), the **Internet Travel Network** (www.itn.com), **TravelWeb** (www.travelweb.com), and the **European Travel Commission** (www.visiteurope.com). For more sources, see Frommer's Online Directory on page 1086.

Of the many, many online travel magazines, two of the best are **Arthur Frommer's Budget Travel Online** (www.frommers.com), written and updated by the guru of budget travel himself, and **Condé Nast's Epicurious** (www.epicurious.com), based on articles from the company's glossy magazines.

That covers some of the top general Web sites. As often as possible throughout this chapter, we've included specific Web sites along with phone numbers and addresses.

Travel Agents   Travel agents can save you plenty of time and money by hunting down the best airfare for your route and arranging for rail passes and rental cars. For the time being, most travel agents still charge you nothing for their services—they're paid through commissions from the airlines and other agencies they book for you. However, a number of airlines have begun cutting commissions, and increasingly, agents are finding they have to charge you a fee to hold the bottom line—or else unscrupulous agents will offer you only the travel options that bag them the juiciest commissions. Shop around and ask hard questions.

If you decide to use a travel agent, make sure the agent is a member of the **American Society of Travel Agents (ASTA),** 1101 King St., Alexandria, VA 22314 (☎ **703/739-8739;** www.astanet.com). If you send them a self-addressed stamped envelope, ASTA will mail you the booklet *Avoiding Travel Problems* for free.

Newsletters   The well-regarded monthly *Consumer Reports Travel Letter,* Circulation Department, P.O. Box 53629, Boulder, CO 80322 (☎ **800/234-1970;** www. ConsumerReports.org), costs $39 annually.

Travel Bookstores   If you live outside a large urban area, you can order maps or travel guides from bookstores specializing in mail- or phone-order service. Some of these are **Book Passage,** 51 Tamal Vista Blvd., Corte Madera, CA 94925 (☎ **800/ 321-9785** or 415/927-0960; www.bookpassage.com); and **Forsyth Travel Library,** 1780 E. 131st St., P.O. Box 480800, Kansas City, MO 64148-0800 (☎ **800/ FORSYTH;** www.forsyth.com). And of course, there's **Amazon**'s huge online bookstore (www.amazon.com).

Canadians can contact **Ulysses Travel Bookshop,** 4176 rue St-Denis, Montréal, PQ H2W 2M5 (☎ **514/843-9447**), or 101 Yorkville Ave., Toronto, ON M5R 1C1 (☎ **416/323-3609**).

2 Entry Requirements & Customs

PASSPORTS   Safeguard your passport in an inconspicuous, inaccessible place like a money belt. If you lose your passport, visit the nearest consulate of your native country as soon as possible for a replacement. Passport applications can be downloaded from the Internet sites listed below.

U.S. Citizens   If you're applying for a first-time passport, you need to do it in person at one of 13 passport offices throughout the United States; a federal, state, or probate court; or a major post office (although not all post offices accept applications; call the number below to find the ones that do). You need to present a certified birth certificate as proof of citizenship, and it's wise to bring along your driver's license, state or military ID, and social security card as well. You also need two identical passport-sized photos (2 in. by 2 in.), taken at any corner photo shop (not one of the strip photos, however, from a photo-vending machine).

For people over 15, a passport is valid for 10 years and costs $60 ($45 plus a $15 handling fee); for those 15 and under, it's valid for 5 years and costs $40. If you're over 15 and have a valid passport that was issued within the past 12 years, you can renew it by mail and bypass the $15 handling fee. Allow plenty of time before your trip to apply; processing normally takes 3 weeks but can take longer during busy periods (especially spring). For general information, call the **National Passport Agency** (☎ **202/647-0518**). To find your regional passport office, call the **National Passport Information Center** (☎ **900/225-5674;** travel.state.gov).

Canadian Citizens   You can pick up a passport application at one of 28 regional passport offices or most travel agencies. The passport is valid for 5 years and costs $60. Children under 16 may be included on a parent's passport, but need their own to travel unaccompanied by the parent. Applications, which must be accompanied by two identical passport-sized photographs and proof of Canadian citizenship, are available at travel agencies throughout Canada or from the central **Passport Office, Department of Foreign Affairs and International Trade,** Ottawa, ON K1A 0G3 (☎ **800/567-6868;** www.dfait-maeci.gc.ca/passport). Processing takes 5 to 10 days if you apply in person, or about 3 weeks by mail.

Traveler's Tip

Make two photocopy collages of your important documents: the first page of your passport (the page with the photo and identifying information), driver's license, and other ID. Leave one copy at home with a family member or friend, and carry the other with you (separate from the originals!).

U.K. Citizens   As a member of the European Union (EU), you need only an identity card, not a passport, to travel to other EU countries. However, if you already possess a passport, it's always useful to carry it. To pick up an application for a regular 10-year passport (the Visitor's Passport has been abolished), visit your nearest passport office, major post office, or travel agency. You can also contact the **London Passport Office** at ☎ 020/7271-3000 or search its Web site at www.open.gov.uk/ukpass/ukpass.htm. Passports are £21 for adults and £11 for children under 16.

Irish Citizens   You can apply for a 10-year passport, costing IR£45, at the **Passport Office,** Setanta Centre, Molesworth Street, Dublin 2 (☎ 01/671-1633; www.irlgov.ie/iveagh/foreignaffairs/services). Those under age 18 and over 65 must apply for a IR£10 3-year passport. You can also apply at 1A South Mall, Cork (☎ 021/272-525) or over the counter at most main post offices.

Australian Citizens   Apply at your local post office or passport office or search the government Web site at www.dfat.gov.au/passports/. Passports for adults are A$126 and for those under 18 A$63.

New Zealand Citizens   You can pick up a passport application at any travel agency or Link Centre. For more info, contact the **Passport Office,** P.O. Box 805, Wellington (☎ 0800/225-050). Passports for adults are NZ$80 and for those under 16 NZ$40.

CUSTOMS   Import Restrictions   Returning **U.S. citizens** who have been away for 48 hours or more are allowed to bring back, once every 30 days, $400 worth of merchandise duty-free. You'll be charged a flat rate of 10% duty on the next $1,000 worth of purchases. Be sure to have your receipts handy. On gifts, the duty-free limit is $100. You cannot bring fresh foodstuffs into the United States; tinned foods, however, are allowed. For more information, contact the **U.S. Customs Service,** 1301 Constitution Ave. (P.O. Box 7407), Washington, DC 20044 (☎ 202/927-6724) and request the free pamphlet *Know Before You Go.* It's also available on the Web at www.customs.ustreas.gov/travel/kbygo.htm.

   U.K. Citizens returning from a European Community (EC) country will go through a separate Customs Exit (called the "Blue Exit") especially for EC travelers. In essence, there is no limit on what you can bring back from an EC country, as long as the items are for personal use (this includes gifts), and you have already paid the necessary duty and tax. However, customs law sets out guidance levels. If you bring in more than these levels, you might be asked to prove that the goods are for your own use. Guidance levels on goods bought in the EC for your own use are 800 cigarettes, 200 cigars, 1kg smoking tobacco, 10 liters of spirits, 90 liters of wine (of this, not more than 60 liters can be sparkling wine), and 110 liters of beer. For more information, contact **HM Customs & Excise,** Passenger Enquiry Point, 2nd Floor Wayfarer House, Great South West Road, Feltham, Middlesex, TW14 8NP (☎ 020/8910-3744; or consult their Web site at www.open.gov.uk.

   U.K. citizens returning from a non-EC country have a customs allowance of 200 cigarettes; 50 cigars; 250g of smoking tobacco; 2 liters of still table wine; 1 liter of spirits or strong liqueurs (over 22% volume); 2 liters of fortified wine, sparkling wine, or other liqueurs; 60cc (ml) perfume; 250cc (ml) of toilet water; and £145 worth of all other goods, including gifts and souvenirs. People under 17 cannot have the tobacco or alcohol allowance. For more information, contact **HM Customs & Excise,** Passenger Enquiry Point, 2nd Floor Wayfarer House, Great South West Road, Feltham, Middlesex, TW14 8NP (☎ 020/8910-3744; from outside the U.K. 44/181-910-3744), or consult their Web site at www.open.gov.uk.

   For a clear summary of **Canadian** rules, write for the booklet *I Declare,* issued by **Revenue Canada,** 2265 St. Laurent Blvd., Ottawa, ON K1G 4KE (☎ 613/993-0534).

Canada allows its citizens a $500 exemption, and you're allowed to bring back duty-free 200 cigarettes, 2.2 pounds of tobacco, 40 imperial ounces of liquor, and 50 cigars. In addition, you're allowed to mail gifts to Canada from abroad at the rate of Can$60 a day, provided they're unsolicited and don't contain alcohol or tobacco (write on the package "Unsolicited gift, under $60 value"). All valuables should be declared on the Y-38 form before departure from Canada, including serial numbers of valuables you already own, such as expensive foreign cameras. *Note:* The $500 exemption can be used only once a year and only after an absence of 7 days.

The duty-free allowance in **Australia** is A$400 or, for those under 18, A$200. Personal property mailed back should be marked "Australian goods returned" to avoid payment of duty. Upon returning to Australia, citizens can bring in 250 cigarettes or 250 grams of loose tobacco, and 1,125ml of alcohol. If you're returning with valuable goods you already own, such as foreign-made cameras, you should file form B263. A helpful brochure, available from Australian consulates or Customs offices, is *Know Before You Go.* For more information, contact **Australian Customs Services,** GPO Box 8, Sydney NSW 2001 (☎ 02/9213-2000).

The duty-free allowance for **New Zealand** is NZ$700. Citizens over 17 can bring in 200 cigarettes, or 50 cigars, or 250 grams of tobacco (or a mixture of all three if their combined weight doesn't exceed 250 grams); plus 4.5 liters of wine and beer, or 1.125 liters of liquor. New Zealand currency does not carry import or export restrictions. Fill out a certificate of export, listing the valuables you are taking out of the country; that way, you can bring them back without paying duty. Most questions are answered in a free pamphlet available at New Zealand consulates and Customs offices: *New Zealand Customs Guide for Travelers,* Notice no. 4. For more information, contact New Zealand Customs, 50 Anzac Ave., P.O. Box 29, Auckland (☎ 09/359-6655).

VISAS   Countries covered in this guide do not require visas for U.S. or Canadian citizens for stays shorter than 90 days.

DRIVING PERMITS   Although a valid U.S. state driver's license usually suffices, it's wise to carry an **International Driving Permit,** which costs $12 and can be obtained from any AAA branch if accompanied by two passport-size photos.

3 Money

Traveler's checks, while still the safest way to carry money, are going the way of the dinosaur. The aggressive evolution of international computerized banking and consolidated ATM networks has led to the triumph of plastic throughout Europe—even if cold cash is still the most trusted currency. Odds are you can saunter up to an ATM in the dinkiest Sicilian village with your bankcard or PIN-enabled Visa and get some local cash out of it. Never rely on credit cards and ATMs alone, however. Although most hotels and many restaurants throughout Europe accept plastic, smaller towns and cheaper places are still wary, and occasionally the phone lines and computer networks used to verify your card can go down and render your plastic useless. Always carry some local currency, and some traveler's checks for insurance.

ATMs   Plus, Cirrus, and other networks work on many ATMs in Europe, giving you local currency and drawing it directly from your checking account. This is the fastest, easiest, and least expensive way to change money. You take advantage of the bank's bulk exchange rate (better than anything you'll get on your own exchanging cash or traveler's checks) and, unless your home bank charges you for using a non-proprietary ATM, you won't have to pay a commission. Make sure the PINs on your bank- and credit cards will work in Europe; you usually need a four-digit code (six digits often

Phoning Around

To make a phone call **from the United States to Europe,** dial the international access code, **011,** then the **country code** for the country you're calling, then the **city code** for the city you're calling, and then the regular telephone number. For an operator-assisted call, dial **01,** then the country code, then the city code, and then the regular telephone number; an operator then comes on the line.

The following are the codes for the countries and major cities covered in this guide. They are the codes you use to call from overseas or from another European country; if you're calling from within the country, see the "Telephone" entry in the "Fast Facts" section for each city. (*Two notes:* First, Copenhagen and all areas within Monaco have no city code; the code is built into all phone numbers. Second, the 0181 and 0171 city codes in London are in the process of being replaced. Both new and old codes are in effect April 1999, and by April 2000, the old codes will have been phased out. We have used the new codes throughout this edition. All numbers now begin with 020—drop the initial zero when dialing from outside the U.K.—followed by a 7 if the number was a 0171 number and an 8 if the number was a 0181 number.)

Austria	**43**	**France**	**33**
Salzburg	662	Nice	4
Vienna	1	Paris	1
Belgium	**32**	**Germany**	**49**
Brussels	2	Berlin	30
The Czech Republic	**420**	Munich	89
Prague	2	**Greece**	**30**
Denmark	**45**	Athens	1
Copenhagen	none	**Hungary**	**36**
England	**44**	Budapest	1
London	20		

won't work). Keep in mind that you are usually able to access only your checking account, not savings, from ATMs abroad.

Both the **Cirrus** (☎ 800/424-7787; www.mastercard.com/atm) and **Plus** (☎ 800/843-7587; www.visa.com/atms) networks have automated ATM locators that list the banks in each country that accept your card, or just search out any machine with your network's symbol emblazoned on it. Europe is getting to be like America—a bank on virtually every corner—and increasingly, most are globally networked. You can also get a cash advance through Visa or MasterCard (contact the issuing bank to enable this feature and get a PIN), but note that the credit card company will begin charging you interest immediately, and many have begun assessing a fee every time. American Express card cash advances are usually available only from AMEX offices, which you'll find in every European city.

CREDIT CARDS   Most middle-bracket and virtually all first-class and deluxe hotels, restaurants, and shops in Europe accept major credit cards—American Express, Diners Club, MasterCard, and Visa (not Discover). Some budget establishments accept plastic; others do not. The most widely accepted cards these days are Visa and MasterCard, but it pays to carry American Express too. Note that you can now often choose to charge credit card purchases at the price in euros or in the local currency;

Ireland	353	Portugal	351
Dublin	1	Lisbon	1
Italy	39	Scotland	44
Florence	55	Edinburgh	131
Rome	6	Spain	34
Venice	41	Barcelona	3
Monaco	377	Madrid	1
Monte Carlo	none	Sweden	46
The Netherlands	31	Stockholm	8
Amsterdam	20	Switzerland	41
		Geneva	22

The easiest and cheapest way to **call home from abroad** is with a **calling card.** On the road, you just dial a local access code (almost always free) and then punch in the number you're calling plus the calling-card number. If you're in a non–touch-tone country, just wait for an English-speaking operator, who will put your call through. The "Telephone" entry in the "Fast Facts" for each city gives the AT&T, MCI, and Sprint access codes for that country. Your calling card will probably come with a wallet-sized list of local access numbers in each country. You can also call any one of those companies' numbers to make a **collect call** as well; just dial it and wait for the operator.

When it comes to **dialing direct,** calling from the United States to Europe is much cheaper than the other way around, so whenever possible, have friends and family call you at your hotel rather than you calling them. To dial direct back **to the US and Canada from Europe,** the international access code is often, but not always, 00; the country code is 1, and then you punch in the area code and number. For **Australia** and **New Zealand,** the access code is also 00; the country codes are 61 and 64, respectively.

since most European currencies are now locked together, the dollar amount always comes out the same, but it could help you comparison-shop.

TRAVELER'S CHECKS   Most large banks sell traveler's checks, charging fees of 1% to 2% of the value of the checks. AAA members can buy American Express checks commission-free. Traveler's checks are great travel insurance because if you lose them—and have kept a list of their numbers (and a record of which ones were cashed) in a safe place separate from the checks themselves—you can get them replaced at no charge. Hotels and shops usually accept them, but you get a lousy exchange rate. Use traveler's checks to exchange for local currency at banks or American Express offices. Personal checks are next to useless in Europe.

   American Express (☎ **800/221-7282;** www.americanexpress.com) is one of the largest issuers of traveler's checks, and theirs are the most commonly accepted. They also sell checks to holders of certain types of American Express cards at no commission. **Thomas Cook** (☎ **800/223-7373** in the U.S. and Canada, 020/7480-7226 in London, or 609/987-7300 collect from other parts of the world; www.thomascook.com) issues MasterCard traveler's checks. **Citicorp** (☎ **800/645-6556** in the U.S. and Canada, or 813/623-1709 collect from anywhere else in the world; www.citicorp.com) and many other banks issue checks under their own name or under

What's Up with the Euro?

In 1999, the euro single European currency was launched in Austria, Belgium, Finland, France, Germany, Ireland, Italy, Luxembourg, the Netherlands, Portugal, and Spain. The other countries covered in this guide, including the Czech Republic, Denmark, England, Greece, and Sweden, among others, are not under the euro umbrella. However, for the life of this edition, you will continue to trade in the old currency of all the countries covered—that is, the peseta for Spain, the escudo for Portugal, the lire for Italy, the deutsch mark for Germany, and so forth. Although the actual paper notes and coins won't be introduced until January 1, 2002—and the national currencies won't be fully phased out until July 1, 2002—banks and stock exchanges are obligated in the meantime to carry out all non-cash transactions in euros, and you can make your credit card purchases in euros. This allows you to more easily compare the cost of something in Paris to the same item's cost in Rome, without having to juggle conversion rates for francs, lire, and dollars. This is good news for travelers, and even better news for Europe's economic strength as their markets can now compete on an even footing.

The symbol of the euro is a stylized *E*, which actually looks like an uppercase *C* with a horizontal double bar through the middle; its official abbreviation is "EUR.". At press time the Euro had fallen 12% since its introduction in January, and had almost reached a 1:1 conversion rate with the American dollar.

MasterCard or Visa. Get checks issued in dollar amounts (as opposed to, say, French francs) as they are more widely accepted abroad.

WIRE SERVICES   **American Express MoneyGram,** Wadsworth St., Englewood, CO 80155 (☎ **800/926-9400**), allows friends back home to wire you money in an emergency in less than 10 minutes. Senders should call AMEX to learn the address of the closest outlet that handles MoneyGrams. Cash, credit card, or the occasional personal check (with ID) are acceptable forms of payment. AMEX's fee is $40 for the first $500 with a sliding scale for larger sums. The service includes a short telex message and a 3-minute phone call from sender to recipient. The beneficiary must present a photo ID at the outlet where the money is received.

CURRENCY EXCHANGE   Although currency conversions in this guide were accurate at press time, European exchange rates fluctuate. For up-to-date rates, look in the business pages or travel section of any major U.S. newspaper, check online at the **Universal Currency Converter** (www.xe.net/currency), or call **Thomas Cook** (see "Traveler's Checks," above).

It's more expensive to purchase foreign currency in your own country than it is once you've reached your destination. But it's a good idea to arrive in Europe with a bit of the local currency—at least enough to get you from the airport to your hotel, so you can avoid the bad rates you get at airport currency exchanges. Bring along about $30 to $50 in the local currencies of every European city you'll be visiting (call around to the major branches of local banks in your hometown to find the best rate).

While traveling, either withdraw local currency from an ATM (see "ATMs," above) or convert your cash or traveler's checks at a bank whenever possible—banks invariably give better rates than tourist offices, hotels, travel agencies, or exchange booths. You lose money every time you make a transaction, so it's often better to convert large sums at once (especially in flat-fee transactions). The rates for converting traveler's checks are usually better than those for cash, but you get the best rates by withdrawing money from an ATM with your bank or credit card.

VALUE-ADDED TAX (VAT)   All European countries charge a value-added tax (VAT) of 15% to 33% on goods and services—it's like a sales tax that's already included in the price. Rates vary from country to country, although the goal in EU countries is to arrive at a uniform rate of about 15%. Citizens of non-EU countries can, as they leave the country, get back most of the tax on purchases (but not services) if they spend above a designated amount (usually $50 to $200) in a single store.

Regulations vary from country to country, so inquire at the tourist office when you arrive to find out the procedure; ask what percentage of the tax is refunded, and if the refund is given to you at the airport or mailed to you later. Look for a **TAX FREE SHOPPING FOR TOURISTS** sign posted in participating stores. Ask the storekeeper for the necessary forms, save all your receipts, and, if possible, keep the purchases in their original packages. Save all your receipts and VAT forms from each EU country to process all of them at the **"Tax Refund"** desk in the airport of the last country you visit before flying home (allow an extra 30 minutes or so at the airport to process forms).

4 When to Go

Europe is a continent for all seasons, offering everything from a bikini beach party on the Riviera in summer to the finest skiing in the world in the Alps in winter.

Europe has a continental climate with distinct seasons, but there are great variations in temperature from one part to another. Northern Norway is plunged into Arctic darkness in winter, but in sunny Sicily the climate is usually temperate—although snow can fall even on the Greek islands in winter, and winter nights are cold anywhere. Europe is north of most of the United States, but along the Mediterranean they see weather patterns more along the lines of the U.S. southern states. In general, however, seasonal changes are less extreme than in most of the United States.

The peak travel period and tourist **high season**—when all tourist facilities are strained—lasts from mid-May to mid-September, with the most tourists hitting the continent from mid-June to August. In general, this is the most expensive time to travel, except in Austria and Switzerland where prices are actually higher in winter during the ski season. And since Scandinavian hotels depend on business clients instead of tourists, lower prices can often be found in the fleeting summer months when business clients vacation and a smaller number of tourists take over.

You'll find smaller crowds, relatively fair weather, and often lower prices at hotels in the **shoulder seasons** from Easter to mid-May, and from mid-September to mid-October. **Off-season** (except at ski resorts) is November to Easter, with the exception of the Christmas season (December 25 to January 6). Much of Europe, Italy especially, takes the month of August off, and August 15 to August 30 is vacation time for many locals, so expect the cities to be devoid of natives, but the beaches packed.

CLIMATE Britain & Ireland   Everyone knows that it rains a lot in Britain and Ireland. Winters are rainier than summers; August and September to mid-October are the sunniest months. Summer daytime temperatures average in the low to mid-60s Fahrenheit, dropping to the 40s on winter nights. Ireland, whose shores are bathed by the Gulf Stream, has a milder climate and the most changeable weather—a dark, rainy morning can quickly turn into a sunny afternoon, and vice versa. The Scottish Lowlands have a climate similar to England's, but the Highlands are much colder, with storms and snow in winter.

What Time Is It, Anyway?

Based on U.S. eastern standard time, Britain, Ireland, and Portugal are 5 hours ahead of New York City; Greece is 7 hours ahead of New York. The rest of the countries in this book are 6 hours ahead of New York. For instance, when it's noon in New York, it's 5pm in London and Lisbon; 6pm in Paris, Copenhagen, and Amsterdam; and 7pm in Athens. The European countries now observe daylight saving time. The time change doesn't usually occur on the same day or in the same month as in the United States.

If you plan to travel to Ireland or continental Europe from Britain, keep in mind that the time will be the same in Ireland and Portugal, 2 hours later in Greece, and 1 hour later in the other countries in this guide.

Scandinavia   Summer temperatures above the Arctic Circle average in the mid-50s, dropping to the mid-teens during the dark winters. In the south, summer temperatures average around 70°F, dropping to the 20s in winter. Fjords and even the ocean are often warm enough for summer swimming, but rain is frequent. The sun shines 24 hours a day in midsummer above the Arctic Circle, where winter brings semi-permanent twilight. Denmark's climate is relatively mild by comparison, with moderate summer temperatures and winters that can be damp and foggy, with temperatures in the mid-30s.

Northern Europe   In the Netherlands, the weather is never extreme at any time of year. Summer temperatures average around 67°F and the winter average is about 40°F. The climate is rainy, with the driest months from February to May. Mid-April to mid-May the tulip fields burst into color. The climate of northern Germany is very similar. Belgium's climate is moderate, varying from 73°F in July and August to 40°F in December and January. It does rain a lot, but the weather is at its finest in July and August.

France & Germany   The weather in Paris is approximately the same as in the U.S. mid-Atlantic states, but like most of Europe, there's less extreme variation. In summer the temperature rarely goes beyond the mid-70s. Summers are fair and can be hot along the Riviera. Winters tend to be mild, averaging in the 40s, although it's warmer along the Riviera. Germany's climate ranges from the moderate summers and chilly, damp winters in the north to the mild summers and very cold, sunny winters of the alpine south.

Switzerland & the Alps   The alpine climate is shared by Bavaria in southern Germany, and the Austrian Tyrol and Italian Dolomites—winters are cold and bright and spring comes late, with snow flurries well into April. Summers are mild and sunny, although the alpine regions can experience dramatic changes in weather any time of year.

Central Europe   In Vienna and along the Danube Valley the climate is moderate. Summer daytime temperatures average in the 70s, falling at night to the 50s. Winter temperatures are in the 30s and 40s during the day. In Budapest, temperatures can reach 80°F in August and 30°F in January. Winter is damp and chilly, spring is mild, and May and June are usually wet. The best weather is in the late summer through October. In Prague and Bohemia, summer months have an average temperature of 65°F, but are the rainiest, whereas January and February are usually sunny and clear, with temperatures around freezing.

Southern Europe   Summers are hot in Italy, Spain, and Greece, with temperatures in the high 80s Fahrenheit, or even higher in some parts of Spain. Along the Italian Riviera, summer and winter temperatures are mild, and except in the alpine regions, Italian winter temperatures rarely drop below freezing. The area around Madrid is dry and arid, and summers in Spain are coolest along the Atlantic coast, with mild temperatures year-round on the Costa del Sol. Seaside Portugal is very rainy, but has a temperature range between 50°F and 75°F year-round. In Greece there's sunshine all year, and winters are usually mild, with temperatures around 50° to 55°F. Hot summer temperatures are often helped by cool breezes. The best seasons to visit Greece are mid-April to June and mid-September to the end of October, when the wildflowers bloom and the tourists go home.

5 Special-Interest Vacations

CYCLING   Cycling tours are a good way to see Europe at your own pace. Some of the best are conducted by the **Cyclists' Tourist Club,** 69 Meadrow, Godalming, Surrey, England GU7 3HS (☎ **01483/417-217;** www.ctc.org.uk). **Holland Bicycling Tours, Inc.,** P.O. Box 6485, Thousand Oaks, CA 91359 (☎ **800/852-3258;** fax 805/495-8601; e-mail: hbhr50a@prodigy.com), leads 8-day bicycle tours throughout Europe. **Experience Plus** (☎ **800/685-4565;** www.xplus.com) runs bike tours across Europe, and **Cicilsmo Classico,** 13 Marathon St., Arlington, MA 02174 (☎ **800/866-7314;** fax 781/641-1512; www.ciclismoclassico.com), is an excellent outfit running tours of Italy.

HIKING   Wilderness Travel, 1102 9th St., Berkeley, CA 94710 (☎ **800/ 368-2794;** www.wildernesstravel.com), specializes in walking tours, treks, and inn-to-inn hiking tours of Europe, as well as less strenuous walking tours. **Sherpa Expeditions,** 131A Heston Rd., Hounslow, Middlesex, England TW5 ORD (☎ **020/ 8577-2717;** www.sherpa-walking-holidays.co.uk), offers both self-guided and group treks through off-the-beaten-track regions of Europe; they are represented in the United States by **Himalayan Travel, Inc.,** 110 Prospect St., Stamford, CT 06901 (☎ **800/225-2380**). Two long-established, somewhat upscale walking tour companies are **Butterfield & Robinson,** 70 Bond St., Suite 300, Toronto, ON M5B 1X3 (☎ **800/678-1147;** fax 416/864-0541; www.butterfield.com), and **Country Walkers,** P.O. Box 180, Waterbury, VT 05676-0180 (☎ **800/464-9255;** fax 802/ 244-5661; www.countrywalkers.com).

Most European countries have associations geared toward aiding hikers and walkers. In England it's the **Ramblers' Association,** 1–5 Wandsworth Rd., London SW8 2XX (☎ **020/7339-8500;** www.ramblers.org.uk); in Italy contact the **Club Alpino Italiano,** 7 Via E. Fonseca Pimental, Milan 20127 (☎ **02/205-7231;** www.cai.it); for Austria, try the **Österreichischer Alpenverein (Austrian Alpine Club),** Wilhelm-Greil-Strasse 15, Innsbruck, A-6020 (☎ **0512/595470;** www. alpenrerein.at); in Norway, it's the **Norwegian Mountain Touring Association,** Storgata 3, Box 7, Sentrum 0101 Oslo (☎ **22-82-28-22;** fax 22-82-28-55; www. smnodnt.ck).

HORSEBACK RIDING   One of the best companies out there is **Equitour,** P.O. Box 1262, Dubois, WY 82513 (☎ **800/545-0019,** or 307/455-3363; fax 307/ 455-2354; www.ridingtours.com), with 5- to 7-day rides through many of Europe's most popular areas, such as Tuscany and the Loire Valley.

HOME EXCHANGES   Intervac U.S., P.O. Box 590504, San Francisco, CA 94159 (☎ **800/756-7440** or 415/435-3497; www.intervac.com), is part of the largest worldwide home-exchange network, with a special emphasis on Europe. It publishes four catalogs a year, listing homes in more than 36 countries. Members contact each other directly. Listing fees vary from country to country; contact them for complete details and costs.

EDUCATIONAL/STUDY TRAVEL   The best (and one of the most expensive) of the escorted cultural tour operators is **IST Cultural Tours** (☎ 800/833-2111; www.ist-tours.com), whose tours are first-class all the way and are accompanied by a certified expert in whatever field the trip focuses on. If you missed out on study abroad in college, the brainy **Smithsonian Study Tours** (☎ 202/357-4700; www.si.edu/tsa) may be just the ticket, albeit a pricey one. The cheaper alternative is **Smithsonian Odyssey Tours** (☎ 800/258-5885), run by Saga International Holidays (these trips cost less because you stay in 3- or 4-star hotels rather than deluxe). Also contact your alma mater or local university to see if they offer summer tours open to the public and guided by a professor specialist.

The **National Registration Center for Studies Abroad (NRCSA),** P.O. Box 1393, Milwaukee, WI 53203 (☎ 414/278-7410; www.NRCSA.com), and the **American Institute for Foreign Study (AIFS),** 102 Greenwich Ave., Greenwich, CT 06830 (☎ 800/727-2437 or 203/869-9090; www.AIFS.com), can both help you arrange study programs and summer programs abroad.

The biggest organization dealing with higher education in Europe is the **Institute of International Education,** with headquarters at 809 United Nations Plaza, New York, NY 10017-3580 (☎ 212/984-5400; www.iie.org). A few of its booklets are free, but for $42.95, plus $5 postage, you can buy the more definitive *Vacation Study Abroad.* To order publications, check out the IIE's online bookstore at www.iie.org; call ☎ 800/445-0443 or 301/617-7804; fax 301/206-9789; or write to the Institute of International Education, P.O. Box 371, Annapolis Junction, MD 20701-0371.

A clearinghouse for information on European-based language schools is **Lingua Service Worldwide,** 211 E. 43rd St., Suite 1303, New York, NY 10017 (☎ 800/ 394-LEARN or 212/867-1225; fax 212/983-2590; www.itctravel.com; e-mail: itctravel@wordlnet.att.net).

CULINARY SCHOOLS   **Cuisine International,** P.O. Box 25228, Dallas, TX 75225 (☎ 214/373-1161; fax 214/373-1162; www.cuisineinternational.com), brings together some of the top independent cooking schools and teachers based in various European countries so you can book your week-long culinary dream vacation.

Italian Cuisine in Florence, Via Trieste 1, 50139 Firenze (☎ 055/480041; e-mail: mirel@boxl.tin.it), provides several gourmet classes in regional as well as Nouva Cucina. Most courses are 5 days, but short workshops for larger groups are also available. The **International Cooking School of Italian Food and Wine,** 201 E. 28th St., New York, NY 10016-8538 (☎ 212/779-1921; fax 212/779-3248), offers courses from May to October in Bologna, the "gastronomic capital of Italy."

Le Cordon Bleu, rue Léon-Delhomme 8, 75015 Paris (☎ 800/457-2433 in the U.S., or 01-53-68-22-50), was established in 1895 as a means of spreading the tenets of French cuisine to the world at large. They have many programs outside their flagship Paris school.

6 Health & Insurance

HEALTH   You'll encounter few health problems traveling in Europe. The tap water is generally safe to drink (except on trains and elsewhere it is marked as non-drinking water), the milk pasteurized, and health services good to superb. You will, however, be eating foods and spices your body isn't used to, so you might want to bring along Pepto-Bismol tablets in case indigestion or diarrhea strikes.

If you worry about getting sick away from home, you may want to consider **medical travel insurance** (see below). In most cases, however, your existing health plan will provide all the coverage you need. Be sure to carry your identification card in your wallet.

If you suffer from a chronic illness, consult your doctor before your departure. For conditions like epilepsy, diabetes, or heart problems, wear a **Medic Alert Identification Tag** (☎ **800/825-3785;** www.commedicalert.org), which immediately alerts doctors to your condition and gives them access to your records through Medic Alert's 24-hour hotline. Membership is $35, plus a $15 annual fee.

Pack prescription medications in your carry-on luggage. Carry written prescriptions in generic, not brand-name form, and dispense all prescription medications from their original labeled vials. This helps foreign pharmacists fill them—and customs officials approve them. If you wear contact lenses, pack an extra pair in case you lose one.

Contact the **International Association for Medical Assistance to Travelers (IAMAT)** (☎ **716/754-4883** or 416/652-0137; www.sentex.net/~iamat). This organization offers tips on travel and health concerns in the countries you'll be visiting and lists many local English-speaking doctors. When you're abroad, any local consulate can provide a list of area doctors who speak English. If you do get sick, you might want to ask the concierge at your hotel to recommend a local doctor.

Many European hospitals are partially socialized, and you'll usually be taken care of speedily, often at no charge for simple ailments. If you have to be admitted, most health insurance plans and HMOs will cover, at least to some extent, out-of-country hospital visits and procedures. However, most make you pay the bills up front at the time of care, and reimburse you after you've returned and filed all the paperwork. Members of Blue Cross/Blue Shield can now use their cards at select hospitals in most major cities worldwide (☎ **800/810-BLUE** or www.bluecares.com/blue/bluecard/wwn for a list of participating hospitals).

INSURANCE Comprehensive insurance programs, covering basically everything from trip cancellation and lost luggage, to medical coverage abroad and accidental death, are offered by the following companies: **Access America,** 6600 W. Broad St., Richmond, VA 23286-4991 (☎ **800/284-8300**); **Travelex Insurance Services,** P.O. Box 9408, Garden City, NY 11530-9408 (☎ **800/228-9792**); **Travel Guard International,** 1145 Clark St., Stevens Point, WI 54481 (☎ **800/826-1300;** www.travelguard.com); and **Travel Insured International,** P.O. Box 280568, East Hartford, CT 06128-0568 (☎ **800/243-3174;** www.travelinsured.com). British travelers can try **Columbus Travel Insurance,** 17 Devonshire Square, London EC2M 4SQ (☎ **020/7375-0011** in London; www.columbusdirect.com).

Medicare covers only U.S. citizens traveling in Mexico and Canada. Two companies specializing in accident and medical care are **MEDEX International,** P.O. Box 5375, Timonium, MD 21094-5375 (☎ **888/MEDEX-00** or 410/453-6300 outside the U.S. and Canada; fax 410/453-6301; www.medexassist.com); and **Travel Assistance International (Worldwide Assistance Services, Inc.),** 1133 15th St. NW, Suite 400, Washington, DC 20005 (☎ **800/821-2828** or 202/828-5894; fax 202/828-5896).

For information on **car renter's insurance,** see "By Car" under "Getting Around," below.

7 Tips for Travelers with Special Needs

TIPS FOR TRAVELERS WITH DISABILITIES Europe won't win any medals for handicapped-accessibility, but in the past few years its big cities have made an effort to accommodate travelers with disabilities. *A World of Options,* a 658-page book of resources for travelers with disabilities, covers everything from biking trips to scuba outfitters. It costs $35 ($30 for members) and is available from **Mobility International USA,** P.O. Box 10767, Eugene, OR, 97440 (☎ **541/343-1284,** voice and TDD; www.miusa.org). Annual membership for Mobility International is $35, which includes their quarterly newsletter, Over the Rainbow. In addition, **Twin Peaks Press,** P.O. Box 129, Vancouver, WA 98666 (☎ **360/694-2462**), publishes travel-related books for people with disabilities.

The **Moss Rehab Hospital** (☎ **215/456-9600**) has been providing friendly and helpful phone advice and referrals to travelers with disabilities for years through its **Travel Information Service** (☎ **215/456-9603;** www.mossresourcenet.org).

You can join **The Society for the Advancement of Travel for the Handicapped (SATH),** 347 Fifth Ave. Suite 610, New York, NY 10016 (☎ **212/447-7284;** fax 212-725-8253; www.sath.org) for $45 annually, $30 for seniors and students, to gain access to their vast network of connections in the travel industry. They provide information sheets on travel destinations, and referrals to tour operators who specialize in traveling with disabilities. Their quarterly magazine, *Open World for Disability and Mature Travel,* is full of good information and resources. A year's subscription is $13 ($21 outside the U.S.).

Travelers with disabilities might also want to consider joining a tour that caters specifically to them. One of the best operators is **Flying Wheels Travel,** 143 West Bridge (P.O. Box 382), Owatonna, MN 55060 (☎ **800/535-6790**). They offer escorted tours and cruises, with an emphasis on sports, as well as private tours in minivans with lifts. Other reputable specialized tour operators include **Access Adventures** (☎ **716/889-9096**), which offers sports-related vacations; **Accessible Journeys** (☎ **800/TINGLES** or 610/521-0339), for slow walkers and wheelchair travelers; **The Guided Tour, Inc.** (☎ **215/782-1370**); **Wilderness Inquiry** (☎ **800/728-0719** or 612/379-3858); and **Directions Unlimited** (☎ **800/533-5343**).

You can get a copy of *Air Transportation of Handicapped Persons* by writing to Free Advisory Circular No. AC12032, Distribution Unit, U.S. Department of Transportation, Publications Division, M-4332, Washington, DC 20590.

Vision-impaired travelers should contact the **American Foundation for the Blind,** 11 Penn Plaza, Suite 300, New York, NY 10001 (☎ **800/232-5463**), for information on traveling with seeing-eye dogs.

For British Citizens   The **Royal Association for Disability and Rehabilitation (RADAR),** Unit 12, City Forum, 250 City Rd., London EC1V 8AF (☎ **020/7250-3222**), publishes three holiday "fact packs." The first provides general information, including planning and booking a holiday, insurance, finances, and useful organizations and holiday providers. The second outlines transportation and rental equipment options. The third deals with specialized accommodations.

Another good service is the **Holiday Care Service,** Imperial Building, 2nd Floor, Victoria Road, Horley, Surrey RH6 7PZ (☎ **01293/774-535;** fax 01293/784-647), a national charity that advises on accessible accommodations for the elderly and persons with disabilities. Annual membership costs £30.

TIPS FOR FAMILIES   Europeans expect to see families traveling together. Europe is a multigenerational continent, and you sometimes see the whole clan traveling around. Also, Europeans tend to love kids. You'll often find a child guarantees you an even warmer reception at hotels and restaurants.

At **restaurants,** ask waiters for a half portion to fit junior's appetite. If you're traveling with small children, three- and four-star hotels may be your best bet—**babysitters** are on call so you can take the occasional romantic dinner, and such hotels have a better general ability to help visitors access the city and its services. But even cheaper hotels can usually find you a sitter. Traveling with a pint-sized person usually means pint-sized rates. An **extra cot** in the room won't cost more than 30% extra—if anything—and most museums and sights offer **reduced-price** or free admission for children under a certain age (which can range from 6 to 18). Kids almost always get discounts on plane and train tickets, too.

Several books on the market offer tips to help you travel with kids. Two, *Family Travel* (Lanier Publishing International) and *How to Take Great Trips with Your Kids* (The Harvard Common Press), are full of good general advice that can apply to travel anywhere. Another reliable tome, with a worldwide focus, is *Adventuring with Children* (Foghorn Press).

Family Travel Times is published six times a year by TWYCH (Travel with Your Children; ☎ **888/822-4388** or 212/477-5524), and includes a weekly call-in service for subscribers. Subscriptions are $40 a year for quarterly editions. A free publication list and a sample issue are available by calling or sending a request to the above address.

Families Welcome!, 92 N. Main, Ashland, OR 97520 (☎ **800/326-0724** or 541/482-6121), a travel company specializing in worry-free vacations for families, offers "City Kids" packages to certain European cities.

The University of New Hampshire runs **Familyhostel** (☎ **800/733-9753**), an intergenerational alternative to standard guided tours. You live on a European college campus for the 2- or 3-week program, attend lectures, seminars, go on lots of field trips, and do all the sightseeing—all of it guided by a team of experts and academics. It's designed for children (aged 8 to 15), parents, and grandparents.

TIPS FOR GAY & LESBIAN TRAVELERS   Much of Europe has grown to accept same-sex couples over the past few decades, and in most countries homosexual sex acts are legal. To be on the safe side, do a bit of research and test the waters for acceptability in any one city or area. As you might expect, smaller towns tend to be less accepting than cities. Gay centers include parts of London, Paris, Berlin, Milan, and Greece. The **International Gay & Lesbian Travel Association (IGLTA),** (☎ **800/448-8550** or 954/776-2626; fax 954/776-3303; www.iglta.org), links travelers up with the appropriate gay-friendly service organization or tour specialist. With around 1,200 members, it offers quarterly newsletters, marketing mailings, and a membership directory that's updated quarterly. Membership often includes gay or lesbian businesses but is open to individuals for $150 yearly, plus a $100 administration fee for new members. Members are kept informed of gay and gay-friendly hoteliers, tour operators, and airline and cruise-line representatives. Contact the IGLTA for a list of its member agencies, who will be tied into IGLTA's information resources.

General gay and lesbian travel agencies include **Family Abroad** (☎ **800/999-5500** or 212/459-1800; gay and lesbian); **Above and Beyond Tours** (☎ **800/397-2681;** mainly gay men); and **Yellowbrick Road** (☎ **800/642-2488;** gay and lesbian).

There are also two good, biannual English-language gay guidebooks, both focused on gay men but including information for lesbians as well. You can get the *Spartacus International Gay Guide* or *Odysseus* from most gay and lesbian book stores, or order them from **Giovanni's Room** (☎ **215/923-2960**) or **A Different Light Bookstore** (☎ **800/343-4002** or 212/989-4850). Both lesbians and gays might want to pick up a copy of *Frommer's Gay & Lesbian Europe* ($21.95) or *Gay Travel A to Z* ($16). *The Ferrari Guides* (www.q-net.com) is another good series of gay and lesbian guidebooks.

Out and About, 8 W. 19th St. #401, New York, NY 10011 (☎ **800/929-2268** or 212/645-6922), offers guidebooks and a monthly newsletter packed with good information on the global gay and lesbian scene. A year's subscription to the newsletter costs $49. *Our World,* 1104 North Nova Rd., Suite 251, Daytona Beach, FL 32117

(☎ **904/441-5367**), is a slicker monthly magazine promoting and highlighting travel bargains and opportunities. Annual subscription rates are $35 in the United States, $45 outside the United States.

TIPS FOR SENIORS   Don't be shy about asking for discounts, but always carry some kind of identification, such as a driver's license, that shows your date of birth. Also, mention that you're a senior citizen when you first make your travel reservations. Many hotels offer seniors discounts, and in most cities, people over the age of 60 qualify for reduced admission to theatres, museums, and other attractions, and discounted fares on public transportation.

Members of the **American Association of Retired Persons (AARP),** 601 E St. NW, Washington, DC 20049 (☎ **800/424-3410** or 202/434-2277), get discounts not only on hotels but on airfares and car rentals, too. AARP offers members a wide range of special benefits, including *Modern Maturity* magazine and a monthly newsletter.

Grand Circle Travel is also one of the hundreds of travel agencies specializing in vacations for seniors (347 Congress St., Suite 3A, Boston, MA 02210 (☎ **800/221-2610** or 617/350-7500)). Many of these packages, however, are of the tour-bus variety, with free trips thrown in for those who organize groups of 10 or more. Seniors seeking more independent travel should probably consult a regular travel agent. **SAGA International Holidays,** 222 Berkeley St., Boston, MA 02116 (☎ **800/343-0273**), offers inclusive tours and cruises for those 50 and older. SAGA also sponsors the more substantial "Road Scholar Tours" (☎ **800/621-2151**), which are fun-loving but have an educational bent.

If you want something more than the average vacation or guided tour, try **Elderhostel** (☎ **877/426-8056;** www.elderhostel.org) or the University of New Hampshire's **Interhostel** (☎ **800/733-9753**), both variations on the same theme: educational travel for senior citizens. On these escorted tours, the days are packed with seminars, lectures, and field trips, and the sightseeing is all led by academic experts. **Elderhostel,** 75 Federal St., Boston, MA 02110-1941 (☎ **877/426-8056;** www. elderhostel.org), arranges study programs for those aged 55 and over (and a spouse or companion of any age) in the United States and in 77 countries around the world, including Asia, Africa, and the South Pacific. Most courses last about 3 weeks and many include airfare, accommodations in student dormitories or modest inns, meals, and tuition. Write or call for a free catalog, which lists upcoming courses and destinations. **Interhostel** takes travelers 50 and over (with companions over 40), and offers 2- and 3-week trips, mostly international. The courses in both these programs are ungraded, involve no homework, and often focus on the liberal arts. They're not luxury vacations, but they're fun and fulfilling.

Although these **specialty books** on the market are U.S.-focused, they do provide good general advice and contacts for the savvy senior traveler. Thumb through *The 50+ Traveler's Guidebook* (St. Martin's Press), *The Seasoned Traveler* (Country Roads Press), or *Unbelievably Good Deals and Great Adventures That You Absolutely Can't Get Unless You're Over 50* (Contemporary Books). Also check out your newsstand for the quarterly magazine *Travel 50 & Beyond.*

TIPS FOR STUDENTS   The best resource for students is the **Council on International Educational Exchange,** or CIEE. They can set you up with an ID card (see below), and their travel branch, **Council Travel Service** (☎ **800/226-8624;** www. ciee.com), is the biggest student travel agency operation in the world. It can get you discounts on plane tickets, rail passes, and the like. Ask them for a list of CTS offices in major cities so you can keep the discounts flowing (and aid lines open) as you travel.

From CIEE you can get the student traveler's best friend, the $18 **International Student Identity Card (ISIC).** It's the only officially acceptable form of student identification, good for cut rates on rail passes, plane tickets, and other discounts. It also provides you with basic health and life insurance and a 24-hour help line. If you're no longer a student but are still under 26, you can get a **GO 25** card from the same people, which gets you the insurance and some of the discounts (but not student admission prices in museums).

In Canada, **Travel CUTS,** 200 Ronson St., Ste. 320, Toronto, ONT M9W 5Z9 (☎ **800/667-2887** or 416/614-2887; www.travelcuts.com), offers similar services. **Campus Travel,** 52 Grosvenor Gardens, London SW1W 0AG (☎ **020/7730-3402;** www.campustravel.co.uk), opposite Victoria Station, is Britain's leading specialist in student and youth travel.

TIPS FOR WOMEN TRAVELERS   Several Web sites offer women advice on how to travel safely and happily. The **Executive Woman's Travel Network** (www.delta-air.com/womenexecs/) is the official woman's travel site of Delta airlines and offers women tips on staying fit while traveling, eating well, finding special airfares, and dealing with many other feminine travel issues. **WomanTraveler** (www.womantraveler.com) is an excellent guide that suggests places where women can stay and eat in various destinations. The site is authored by women and includes listings of women-owned businesses, such as hotels, hostels, etc.

Several books on the market cater to the concerns of the female traveler. Look into the *Virago Women's Travel Guides,* $14.95. The series is excellent but new, and covers only three cities to date: London, San Francisco, and Amsterdam. *Safety and Security for Women Who Travel,* by Sheila Swan Laufer and Peter Laufer, is well worth $12.95, and *Adventures in Good Company: The Complete Guide to Women's Tours and Outdoor Trips* at $16.95 is a very good resource.

TIPS FOR SINGLE TRAVELERS   Many people prefer traveling alone, save for the relatively steep cost of booking a single room, which usually costs well over half the price of a double. **Travel Companion** (☎ 516/454-0880) is one of the nation's oldest roommate finders for single travelers. Register with them and find a trustworthy travel mate who will split the cost of the room with you and be around as little, or as often, as you like during the day.

Several tour organizers cater to solo travelers as well. **Experience Plus** (☎ **800/685-4565;** fax 907/484-8489) offers an interesting selection of single-only trips.

Travel Buddies (☎ **800/998-9099** or 604/533-2483) runs single-friendly tours with no singles supplement. **The Single Gourmet Club** (133 E. 58th St., New York, NY 10022; ☎ **212/980-8788;** fax 212/980-3138) is an international social, dining, and travel club for singles, with offices in 21 cities in USA and Canada, and one in London.

You might also want to research the *Outdoor Singles Network* (P.O. Box 781, Haines, AK 99827). An established quarterly newsletter (since 1989) for outdoor-loving singles, ages 19 to 90, the network will help you find a travel companion, pen-pal, or soulmate within its pages. A 1-year subscription costs $45, and your own personal ad is printed free in the next issue. Current issues are $15. Write for free information or check out the group's Web site at www.kcd.com/bearstar/osn.html.

8 Getting There

FLYING FROM NORTH AMERICA

Most major airlines charge competitive fares to European cities, but price wars break out regularly and fares can change overnight. For a list of the major North American and European national airlines and their toll-free numbers and Web sites, see the Appendix.

Tickets tend to be cheaper if you fly mid-week or off-season. **High season** on most airline routes is usually June to mid-September—the most expensive and most crowded time to travel. **Shoulder season** is April through May, mid-September to October, and December 15 to 24. **Low season**—featuring the cheapest fares—is November to December 14 and December 25 through March.

You can get the best fares simply by planning ahead and buying low-cost advance-purchase (APEX) tickets. Usually APEX tickets must be purchased 14 to 21 days in advance, and your stay in Europe must last between 7 and 30 days. The downside is that an APEX ticket locks you into those dates and times, with penalties for changing them.

A more flexible, but more expensive, option is the regular economy fare, which allows for a stay shorter than the 7-day APEX minimum. You're also usually free to make last-minute changes in flight dates and to have unrestricted stopovers.

TIPS FOR GETTING THE BEST AIRFARES

BUDGET TRAVEL AGENCIES   Before venturing into the realm of consolidators, virtual travel agents, and courier services, try simply calling up a travel agency that specializes in budget travel. An agency like **Council Travel** (☎ **800/2-COUNCIL;** www.ciee.org), a student travel specialist, always has the scoop on the latest cheap fares, and you don't have to be a student, under 26, or a teacher to use it (although you'll save even more if you are).

In addition, **Cheap Tickets** (☎ **800/377-1000, 1-800/FLY-4-LESS,** and **1-800/ FLY-CHEAP**) all specialize in finding the lowest fares out there. You can often get discounted fares on short notice without all the advance-purchase requirements.

CONSOLIDATORS   Consolidators, also known as bucket shops, act as clearing-houses for blocks of tickets on regularly scheduled flights that airlines discount during slow periods. One of the biggest U.S. consolidators is **Travac,** 989 Sixth Ave., New York, NY 10018 (☎ **800/TRAV-800** or 212/563-3303; www.travac.com). Also try **TFI Tours International,** 34 W. 32nd St., New York, NY 10001 (☎ **800/ 745-8000**).

In the United Kingdom, **Trailfinders** (☎ **020/7937-5400** in London) is a consolidator that offers access to tickets on major European carriers. There are many bucket shops around Victoria Station and Earls Court in London. **CEEFAX,** an information service included on many home and hotel TVs, runs details of package holidays and flights to continental Europe and beyond.

CHARTER FLIGHTS   In a strict sense, charters book a block of seats (or an entire plane) months in advance and then resell the tickets to consumers. Always ask about restrictions: You might have to purchase a tour package and pay far in advance, and pay a stiff penalty—or forfeit the ticket entirely—if you cancel. Charters are sometimes canceled when the plane doesn't fill. In some cases, the charter company offers you an insurance policy in case you need to cancel for a legitimate reason (hospitalization or death in the family).

Council Travel, 205 E. 42nd St., New York, NY 10017 (☎ **800/226-8624** or 212/822-2800; www.ciee.org), arranges charter seats on regularly scheduled aircraft. One of the biggest charter operators is **Travac** (see "Consolidators," above). For Canadians, good charter deals are offered by **Martinair** (☎ **800/627-8462;** www. martinair.com) and **Travel CUTS** (☎ **888-450-2887;** www.travelcuts.com), which also has an office at 295A Regent Street in London (☎ **020/7255-2082**).

REBATORS   These outfits will book you any ticket at the regular fare, and then pass along part of their commission from the airline to you—although many also assess a fee. Most rebates run 5% to 25%, minus a $25 handling fee, so you really don't save any money unless the ticket costs over $600. Rebators aren't travel agents, but they sometimes offer services such as land arrangements and car rentals.

Specializing in clients in the Midwest, **Travel Avenue,** 10 S. Riverside Plaza, Suite 1404, Chicago, IL 60606 (☎ **800/333-3335** or 312/876-6866; www.travelavenue. com), offers cash rebates on every ticket over $300. Another major rebator is **The Smart Traveller,** 3111 SW 27th Ave. (P.O. Box 330010), Miami, FL 33133 (☎ **800/ 448-3338** or 305/448-3338), offering discounts on packaged tours.

INTERNET DEALS

It's possible to get some great deals on airfare, hotels, and car rentals via the Internet. The sites highlighted below are worth checking out (also see Frommer's Online Directory, at the back of the book), especially since all services are free. Always check the lowest published fare, however, before you shop for flights online.

Arthur Frommer's Budget Travel (www.frommers.com): Home of the Encyclopedia of Travel and Arthur Frommer's *Budget Travel* magazine and daily newsletter, this site offers detailed information on 200 cities and islands around the world, and up-to-the-minute ways to save dramatically on flights, hotels, car reservations, and cruises.

The best part of **Microsoft Expedia's** (www.expedia.com) travel site is the "Fare Tracker": You fill out a form on the screen indicating that you're interested in cheap flights from your hometown, and once a week they'll e-mail you the best airfare deals on up to three destinations.

Several major airlines offer a free e-mail service known as **E-Savers,** via which they send you their best bargain airfares on a regular basis. The catch? These fares are usually available only if you leave the very next Saturday (or sometimes Friday night) and return on the following Monday or Tuesday. If you'd prefer not to get 20 or so different e-mails every week, sign up with www.smarterliving.com, which consolidates all the individual e-savers into one convenient mailing.

TRAVELING BY PACKAGE OR ESCORTED TOUR

PACKAGE TOURS   Package tours are not the same thing as escorted tours. They are simply a way of buying your airfare and accommodations at the same time and getting an excellent rate on both. Your trip is your own. In many cases, a package that includes airfare, hotel, and transportation to and from the airport costs you less than the hotel alone if you booked it yourself. The downside is that many stick you in large, international-style hotels (which in Europe are often outside the historic center); you do get a good rate for that sort of hotel, but with a little more work (and the hotel reviews in this book), you can easily find a mid-range pension or friendly little B&B on your own for the same price or less and right in the heart of the action.

All major airlines flying to Europe sell vacation packages (see the Appendix for a list of airline toll-free numbers and Web sites). The best place to start looking for independent packagers is the travel section of your local Sunday newspaper and national travel magazines. **Central Holidays** (☎ **800/611-1139;** www.centralholidays.com) is one of the best and most reputable package-tour operators. **Liberty Travel** (many locations; check your local directory, since there's not a central 800 number; www. libertytravel.com) is one of the biggest packagers in the Northeast, and usually boasts a full-page ad in Sunday papers. **American Express Vacations** (☎ **800/241-1700;** www.americanexpress.com/travel) and **Kemwel** (☎ **800/678-0678;** www.kemwel. com) are both reputable options.

FLY/DRIVE TOURS   Fly/drive holidays, which combine airfare and car rental, are increasing in popularity and are a lot cheaper than booking both airfare and car rental independently. They are available mainly through major European airlines.

ESCORTED GROUP TOURS With a good escorted group tour, you'll know ahead of time just what your trip will cost, and you won't have to worry about your transportation, luggage, hotel reservations, communicating in foreign languages, and other nuts-and-bolts requirements of travel—there's an experienced guide who takes care of all that and leads you through all the sightseeing. The downside of a guided tour is that you trade much of the freedom and personal free time that independent travel grants you, and you often see only the canned, postcard-ready side of Europe through the tinted windows of a giant bus. You get to *see* Europe, but rarely do you get the chance to really know it. Consult a good travel agent for the latest offerings and advice.

Two of the top escorted tour operators are **American Express Vacations,** which offers the most comprehensive tours to Europe, and **Kemwel** (for both, see "Package Tours," above). If you want a tour that balances independent-style travel and plenty of free time with all the pluses of a guided tour, try the very popular itineraries offered by **Europe Through the Back Door,** 120 Fourth Ave. North, P.O. Box 2009, Edmonds, WA 98020-2009 (☎ **425/771-8303;** www.ricksteves.com), run by Rick Steves, of public television's "Travels in Europe" fame.

GETTING TO THE CONTINENT FROM THE U.K.

BY TRAIN Many different rail passes and discounts are available in the U.K. for travel in continental Europe. One of the most complete overviews on the subject is available from **Rail Europe Special Services Department,** 10 Leake St., London SE1 7NN (☎ **0990/848-848**), or **Wasteels,** Platform 2, Victoria Station, London SW1V 1JT (☎ **020/7834-7066**). Wasteels, and also the London Branch of **Campus Travel,** 52 Grosvenor Gardens, London SW1W OAG (☎ **020/7730-3402;** www. usitcampus.co.uk), are particularly well-versed in information about discount travel as it applies to persons under 26, full or part-time students, and senior citizens.

The most prevalent option for younger travelers, the **EuroYouth passes,** are available only to travelers under 26 and entitle the pass holder to unlimited second-class rail travel in 26 European countries. If you're a senior citizen and a full-time resident of the U.K., you might want to ask about the **Rail Europe Senior Pass.** Priced at £5 ($8.25), it entitles the holder to discounts of up to 30% on many European rail lines on routes that traverse international boundaries. A prerequisite for acquiring the card is that the applicant must already have a British Senior Citizen rail card, which is available only to full-time residents of the U.K. who pay £16 ($26.40) and present proof of their full-time residency in the U.K. at any BritRail ticket office.

BY CHUNNEL The *Eurostar* train shuttles between London and both Paris and Brussels; the trip time is less than 3 hours (compared to 10 hours on the traditional train-ferry-train route). **Rail Europe** (☎ **800/94-CHUNNEL;** www.raileurope.com) sells tickets on the *Eurostar* between London and Paris or Brussels (both $149 one-way).

You can phone for *Eurostar* reservations (☎ **0990/300-003** in London, 01-44-51-06-02 in Paris, and 800/EUROSTAR in the U.S.; www.eurostar.com). *Eurostar* trains arrive and depart from Waterloo Station in London, Gare du Nord in Paris, and Central Station in Brussels.

BY FERRY/HOVERCRAFT **Brittany Ferries** (☎ **01705/892-200;** www.brittany-ferries.com) is the largest British ferry/drive outfit. It sails from the southern coast of England to five destinations in Spain and France. From Portsmouth, sailings reach St-Malo and Caen; from Poole, Cherbourg. From Plymouth, sailings go to Santander in Spain.

P&O Channel Lines (☎ 0990/980-980; www.posl.com) operates car and passenger ferries between Portsmouth and Cherbourg (three departures a day; 5 to 7 hours); between Portsmouth and Le Havre, France (three a day; 5½ hours); and between Dover and Calais, France (25 sailings a day; 1¼ hours).

Stena Sealink (☎ 01233/315-455), carries both passengers and vehicles. This company is represented in North America by BritRail (☎ 800/677-8585, or 212/575-2667 in New York). Stena offers conventional ferryboat service between Harwick, England, to the hook of Holland for $87 per person round-trip.

Unless you're interested in a leisurely sea voyage, passengers without cars might be better off using the quicker, and slightly cheaper, Hoverspeed (☎ 01304/240-241; www.hoverspeed.co.uk). Hoverspeeds make the 35-minute crossing between Calais and Dover 7 to 15 times per day, with the more curtailed schedule in winter. Prices are £25 ($41.25) for adults on foot or £14 ($23.10) for children. Vehicle fares range from £78 to £139 ($128.70 to $229.35). Prices are one-way or 5-day return.

BY CAR   Many car-rental companies won't let you rent a car in Britain and take it to the Continent, so always check ahead. There are many "drive-on, drive-off" car-ferry services across the Channel; see "By Ferry/Hovercraft," above. There are also Chunnel trains that run a drive-on/drive-off service every 15 minutes (once an hour at night) for the 35-minute ride between Ashford and Calais.

BY COACH   Although travel by coach is considerably slower and less comfortable than train travel, if you're on a budget you might opt for one of **Eurolines's** regular departures from London's Victoria Coach Station to destinations throughout Europe. Contact Eurolines at 52 Grosvenor Gardens, Victoria, London SW1W OAU (☎ 020/7730-8235 or 01582/404511; www.eurolines.co.uk).

9 Getting Around

BY TRAIN

In Europe, the shortest—and cheapest—distance between two points is lined with railroad tracks. European trains are less expensive than those in the United States, far more advanced in many ways, and certainly more extensive. Modern high-speed trains make the rails faster than the plane for short journeys, and overnight trains get you where you're going without wasting valuable daylight hours—and you save money on lodging to boot.

Europe has a rainbow of train classifications that range from local milk runs that stop at every tiny station to high-speed bullet trains that cruise at 130 m.p.h. between major cities.

Many high-speed trains throughout Europe, including the popular EC (EuroCity), IC (InterCity), and EN (EuroNight) trains, require that you pay a supplement in addition to the regular ticket fare. It's included when you buy regular tickets, but not in any rail pass, so check at the ticket window before boarding; otherwise, the conductor will sell you the supplement on the train—along with a fine.

Seat reservations are also required on some of the speediest of the high-speed runs—any train marked with an *R* on a printed train schedule. Reservations range from $15 up to $50 or more (when a meal's included). You can almost always reserve a seat within a few hours of the train's departure, but to be on the safe side, you'll probably want to book your seat a few days in advance. You need to reserve any sleeping couchette or sleeping berth, too.

With two exceptions, there's no need to buy individual train tickets or make seat reservations before you leave the States. However, on the high-speed *Artesia* run

(Paris-Turin and Milan) you must buy a supplement—on which you can get a substantial discount if you have a rail pass, but only if you buy the supplement in the States along with the pass. It's also wise to reserve a seat on the *Eurostar,* as England's frequent "bank holidays" (long weekends) book the train solid with Londoners taking a short vacation to Paris.

The difference between first- and second-class seats on European trains is minor—a matter of 1 or 2 inches of extra padding and maybe a bit more elbow room. European train stations are usually as clean and efficient as the trains, if a bit chaotic at times. In stations you will find posters showing the track number and timetables for regularly scheduled runs that pass through (departures are often on the yellow poster). Many stations also have tourist office outposts and hotel reservations desks; banks with ATMs; and newsstands where you can buy phonecards, bus and metro tickets, maps, and local English-language event magazines.

You can get much more information about train travel in Europe and get automated schedule information by fax, by contacting **Rail Europe** (☎ **800/438-7245;** www.raileurope.com). If you plan on doing a lot of train travel, consider purchasing the *Thomas Cook European Timetable* ($27.95 from travel specialty stores or order it at ☎ **800/FORSYTH**). Each country's national railway Web site, which includes schedules and fare information, occasionally in English, is hotlisted at Mercurio (mercurio.iet.unipi.it).

RAIL PASSES   The greatest value in European travel has always been the rail pass, a single ticket that allows you unlimited travel (or travel on a certain number of days) within a set period of time. If you plan on going all over Europe by train, purchasing a rail pass will end up being much less expensive than buying individual tickets. Plus, a rail pass gives you the freedom to hop on a train whenever you feel like it, and there's no waiting in ticket lines. For more focused trips, you might want to look into national or regional passes, or just buy individual tickets as you go.

The granddaddy of passes is the **Eurailpass,** covering 17 countries (most of western Europe except Britain). It has been joined by the **Europass,** which covers 5 to 12 countries (depending on what sort of version you buy); this pass is mainly for travelers who are going to stay in the heart of western Europe.

Rail passes are available in either **consecutive-day** or **flexipass** versions (in which you have, say, 2 months in which to use 10 days of train travel). Consecutive-day passes are best for those taking the train frequently (every few days), covering a lot of ground, and making many short train hops. Flexipasses are for folks who want to range far and wide but plan on taking their time over a long trip, and intend to stay in each city for a while.

If you're under age 26, you can opt to buy a regular first-class pass or a second-class youth pass; if you're 26 or over, you're stuck buying a first-class pass. Passes for kids 4 to 11 are half-price, and kids under 4 travel free.

Countries Honoring Train Passes

Eurail Countries: Austria, Belgium, Denmark, Finland, France, Germany, Greece, Hungary, Ireland, Italy, Luxembourg, the Netherlands, Norway, Portugal, Spain, Sweden, Switzerland.
Europass Core Countries: France, Germany, Switzerland, Italy, Spain.
Europass Add-on "Zones": Austria/Hungary, Belgium/Netherlands/Luxembourg, Greece (including the ferry from Brindisi, Italy), Portugal.
Note: Great Britain isn't included in any pass.

The rates quoted below are for 1999; they rise each year.

- **Eurailpass:** Consecutive-day Eurail passes cost $554 for 15 days, $718 for 21 days, $890 for 1 month, $1,260 for 2 months, or $1,558 for 3 months.
- **Eurail Flexipass:** Good for 2 months of travel, during which you can travel by train for 10 days (consecutive or not) for $654, or 15 days for $862.
- **Eurail Saverpass:** A Saverpass is good for two to five people traveling together. The Saverpass costs $470 per person for 15 days, $610 for 21 days, $756 for 1 month, $1,072 for 2 months, or $1,324 for 3 months.
- **Eurail Saver Flexipass:** This is the flexipass for two to five people traveling together. The Saver Flexipass costs $556 per person for 10 days within 2 months, or $732 per person for 15 days within 2 months.
- **Eurail Youthpass:** This is the second-class rail pass for travelers under 26. It costs $388 for 15 days, $499 for 21 days, $623 for 1 month, $882 for 2 months, or $1,089 for 3 months.
- **Eurail Youth Flexipass:** Only for travelers under 26, this pass allows for 10 days of travel within 2 months for $458, or 15 days in 2 months for $599.
- **Europass:** If your trip will focus on the core of western Europe—specifically France, Germany, Switzerland, Italy, and Spain—Eurail is wasteful spending. Go for the Europass, which gives you 5, 6, 8, 10, or 15 days of train travel in those five countries for 2 months. You can expand the scope of your pass by purchasing add-on "zones"—Austria/Hungary; Belgium/Netherlands/Luxembourg; Greece (including the ferry from Brindisi, Italy); and Portugal. The base pass ranges in price from $348 for 5 days to $728 for 15 days. The pass is also linked to associate countries, including Austria/Hungary, Benelux (Belgium, the Netherlands, and Luxembourg), Greece, and Portugal. If Greece is a country you choose, the pass even includes the ferry crossing from Brindisi in Italy. Associate countries extend the geographical reach of your pass, and the length of your pass remains the same. You can add one associate country for $60 or two associate countries for $100.
- **Europass Youth:** The Europass Youth is good in second-class only and is for travelers under 26. This pass grants 5, 6, 8, 10, or 15 days of unlimited train travel in France, Germany, Italy, Spain, and Switzerland, with 2 months to complete your travel. The cost is $233 for 5 days, $253 for 6 days, $313 for 8 days, $363 for 10 days, and $513 for 15 days. It costs $45 to add one associate country or $78 to add two associate countries (see Europass, above).
- **EurailDrive Pass:** This pass offers the best of both worlds, mixing train travel and rental cars (through Hertz or Avis) for less money than it would cost to do them separately (and one of the only ways to get around the high daily car-rental rates in Europe when you rent for less than a week). You get 4 rail days and 2 car days within a 2-month period. Prices (per person for one adult/two adults) vary with the class of the car: $399/$339 economy class, $439/$359 compact, and $459/$369 mid-sized. You can add up to 5 extra rail and/or car days. Extra rail days are $59 each; car days cost $61 each for economy class, $80 compact, and $90 mid-sized. You have to reserve the first car day a week before leaving the States, but can make other reservations as you go (always subject to availability). If there are more than two adults, the extra passengers get the car portion free, but must buy the 4-day rail pass for $280.
- **Eurodrive Pass:** This is a similar deal, but it's good for Europass countries only (and no add-on zones) and for shorter trips. It's good for 3 rail days and 2 car days within a 2-month period. Prices (per person for one adult/two adults) are $345/$284 economy class, $379/$304 compact, and $399/$314 mid-sized. You

can add up to 7 extra rail days at $45 each, and unlimited extra car days for $59 to $89 each, depending on the class of car.

There are also national rail passes of various kinds, regional passes such as ScanRail (Scandinavia), BritRail (covering Great Britain), and the European East Pass (good in Austria, Czech Republic, Slovakia, Hungary, and Poland). Some types of national passes you have to buy in the United States, some you can get on either side of the Atlantic, and still others you must buy in Europe. Remember, seniors, students, and youths can usually get discounts on European trains—in some countries just by asking, in others by buying a discount card good for a year (or whatever). Rail Europe or your travel agent can fill you in on all the details.

As for Eurail and its offshoots, you have to buy them in the United States (they are available from some major European train stations, but are up to 10% more expensive). You can buy rail passes from most travel agents, but the biggest supplier is **Rail Europe** (☎ 800/438-7245; www.raileurope.com), which also sells most national passes, save a few minor British ones. A recommendation is to contact Rick Steve's **Europe Through the Back Door** (☎ 425/771-8303; www.ricksteves.com). He sells all Europe-wide and all national rail passes and sends a free video and guide on how to use rail passes with every order. Plus, he doesn't tack on the $10 handling fee all other agencies do.

BritRail (☎ 888/BRITRAIL; www.britrail.com) specializes in rail passes in Great Britain, and **DER Tours** (☎ 800/782-2424; www.dertravel.com) is a Germany specialist that also sells other national passes (except French and British ones).

BY CAR

Many rental companies grant discounts if you **reserve in advance** (usually 48 hours) from your home country. Weekly rentals are almost always less expensive than day rentals. Three or more people traveling together can usually get around cheaper by car than by train (even with rail passes).

Train Trip Tips

To make your train travels as pleasant as possible, remember a few general rules:

- Hold on to your train ticket after it's been marked or punched by the conductor. Some European railroad systems require that you present your ticket when you leave the station platform at your destination.

- While you sleep—or even nap—be sure your valuables are in a safe place; you might temporarily attach a small bell to each bag to warn you if someone attempts to take it. If you've left bags on a rack in the front or back of the car, consider securing them with a small bicycle chain and lock to deter thieves, who consider trains happy hunting grounds.

- Few European trains have drinking fountains and the dining car may be closed just when you're at your thirstiest, so take a bottle of mineral water with you. As you'll soon discover, the experienced European traveler comes loaded with hampers of food and drink and munches away throughout the trip.

- If you want to leave bags in a train station locker, don't let anyone help you store them in it. A favorite trick among thieves is feigned helpfulness, then pocketing the key to your locker while passing you the key to an empty one.

When you reserve a car, be sure to ask if the price includes the EU value-added tax (VAT), personal accident insurance (PAI), collision-damage waiver (CDW), and any other **insurance options.** If not, ask what these extras cost, because at the end of your rental, they can make a big difference in your bottom line. The CDW and other insurance might be covered by your credit card if you use the card to pay for the rental; check with the card issuer to be sure.

If your credit card doesn't cover CDW, **Travel Guard International,** 1145 Clark St., Stevens Point, WI 54481-9970 (☎ **800/826-1300;** www.travel-guard.com), offers it for $5 per day. Avis and Hertz, among other companies, require that you purchase a theft-protection policy in Italy.

The main car-rental companies include **Avis** (☎ **800/331-1212;** www.avis.com); **Budget** (☎ **800/527-0700;** www.budgetrentacar.com/); **Europcar** (known as Dollar in the U.S.; ☎ **800/800-6000;** www.europcar.com); **Hertz** (☎ **800/654-3131;** www.hertz.com); and **National** (☎ **800/227-7368;** www.nationalcar.com).

U.S.-based companies that specialize in European car rentals are **Auto Europe** (☎ **800/223-5555;** www.autoeurope.com); **Europe by Car** (☎ **800/223-1516,** or 212/581-3040 in New York; www.europebycar.com); and **Kemwel Holiday Auto** (☎ **800/678-0678;** www.kemwel.com). Europe By Car and Kemwel also offer a low-cost alternative to renting for periods longer than 15 days: **short-term leases,** in which you technically buy a fresh-from-the-factory car and then sell it back when you return it. All insurance is included, from liability and theft to personal injury and CDW, with no deductible.

European drivers tend to be more aggressive than their American counterparts, and gas is generally expensive. Never rent a car just to drive around a European city—the drivers and traffic patterns can drive anyone crazy, parking is difficult and expensive, and the public transportation is usually excellent anyway. Never leave anything of value in the car overnight, and nothing visible any time you leave the car (this goes double in Italy, triple in Naples).

MAPS   AAA supplies good maps to its members. **Michelin maps** (☎ **800/423-0485;** www.michelin-travel.com) are made for the tourist. The maps rate cities as "uninteresting" (as a tourist destination); "interesting"; "worth a detour"; or "worth an entire journey." They also highlight particularly scenic stretches of road in green, and have symbols pointing out scenic overlooks, ruins, and other sights along the way.

BY PLANE

Although trains remain the cheapest and easiest way to get around in Europe, air transport options have improved drastically in the past few years. Intense competition with rail and ferry companies has slowly forced airfares into the bargain basement. **British Airways** (☎ **800/AIRWAYS;** www.britishairways.com) and other scheduled airlines now fly regularly from London to Paris for only £91 to £103 ($150.15 to $169.95) round-trip, depending on the season. Lower fares usually apply to midweek flights and carry advance-purchase requirements of 2 weeks or so.

The biggest airline news in Europe is the rise of the **no-frills airline** modeled on American upstarts like Southwest. By keeping their overheads down through electronic ticketing, forgoing meal service, and flying from less popular airports, these airlines are able to offer low, low fares. Most round-trip tickets cost from $60 to $160. This means now you can save lots of time, and even money, over long train hauls, especially from, say, London to Venice, or from central Europe out to peripheral countries such as Greece or Spain. Budget airlines include **EasyJet** (☎ **44-870/600-000;** www.easyjet.com), and British Airway's subsidiary **Go** (☎ **44-1279/666-388**) in

The Rules of the Road: Driving in Europe

- Drive on the right except in England, Scotland, and Ireland, where you drive on the left.
- *Do not ride* in the left lane on a four-lane highway; it is truly only for passing.
- If someone comes up from behind and flashes their lights at you, it's a signal for you to slow down and drive more on the shoulder so that they can pass you more easily (two-lane roads here routinely become three cars wide).
- Except for the German Autobahn, most highways do indeed have speed limits of around 60 to 80 m.p.h. (100 to 135kmph).
- Remember, everything's measured in kilometers here (mileage and speed limits). For a rough conversion, 1km = 0.6 miles.
- That gas may look reasonably priced, but remember the price is per liter, and 3.8 liters = 1 gallon, so multiply by four to estimate the equivalent per-gallon price.

England; **Ryanair** (☎ 353/1609-7800 in Ireland; 44-541/569-569 in England) in Ireland; **Debonair** (☎ 44-541/500-300) in Munich; **Air One** (☎ 39-6/488-800 or toll free in Italy 1478/48-880; www.air-one.com) in Italy; and **Virgin Express** (☎ 32-2/752-0505; www.virgin-express.com), an offshoot of Virgin Air, in Belgium. Be aware, though, that the names might change because these small airlines are often economically vulnerable and can fail or merge with a big airline. Still, as quickly as one disappears, another will take off.

Lower airfares are also available throughout Europe on **charter flights** rather than regularly scheduled ones. Look in local newspapers to find out about them. Consolidators cluster in cities like London and Athens.

Flying across Europe on regularly scheduled airlines can destroy a budget and be super expensive. Whenever possible, book your total flight on one ticket before leaving. For example, if you're flying from New York to Rome, but also plan to visit Palerno, Florence, and Turin, have the total trip written up on one ticket. Don't arrive in Rome and book separate legs of the journey, which costs far more when it's done piecemeal.

Sometimes national carriers offer remarkable deals to non-European residents, which cuts down costs of flying within Europe. For example, **Lufthansa** offers a "Discover Europe" package of three flight coupons, which vary in price, depending on the nation of origin. Another bargain is **Alitalia's** "Europlus." First, you have to book a transatlantic flight, perhaps from New York to Rome. After that, and for only $299, you can purchase a package of three flight coupons. This entitles you to fly on any three flights anywhere in Europe served by Alitalia (not just Italy). You can also purchase unlimited additional tickets, one way, for another $100 per ticket.

Another fine deal is offered in London by **Go Fly Limited** (☎ 84-56-05-43-21 in London; www.go-fly.com), a subsidiary of British Airways. Go Fly offers 40% off standard round-trip air fares. There is a 2-night minimum stay. Sample round-trip air fares from London are as follows: Edinburgh £40 ($66); Copenhagen £60 ($99); Rome £70 ($115.50); and Lisbon £70 ($115.50).

American citizens can call **Eurair** (☎ 888/387-2479 or 512/404-1291; www.eurair.com) for their Europe flight pass serving 20 countries, 13 airlines, and 62 European cities. It costs only $90 each to travel one-way between these cities.

Because discount passes are always changing on air routes within Europe, it's best to check in with **Air Travel Advisory Bureau** in London (☎ **020/7636-5000;** www.atab.co.uk). This bureau offers a free service directory to the public for suppliers of discount airfares from all major U.K. airports.

BY BUS

Bus transportation is readily available throughout Europe; it sometimes is less expensive than train travel and covers a more extensive area, but can be slower and much less comfortable. European buses, like the trains, outshine their American counterparts, but they're perhaps best used only to pick up where the extensive train network leaves off. There is one major bus company serving all the countries of Western Europe (no service to Greece). It is **Eurolines,** whose central booking number is in London (☎ **0990/143219**). The staff at this number can make reservations and quote prices. They have the latest schedules for all bus routes.

10 Tips on Accommodations

Traditional European hotels tend to be simpler than American ones and emphasize cleanliness and friendliness over amenities. For example, even in the cheapest American chain motel, free cable is as standard as indoor plumbing. In Europe, however, few hotels below the moderate level even have in-room TVs.

Unless otherwise noted, all hotel rooms in this book have **private bathrooms.** However, the standard European hotel bathroom might not look like what you're used to. For example, the European concept of a shower is to stick a nozzle in the bathroom wall and a drain in the floor. Shower curtains are optional. In some cramped private bathrooms, you'll have to relocate the toilet paper outside the bathroom before turning on the shower and drenching the whole room. Another interesting bathroom fixture is the "half tub," in which there's only room to sit, rather than lie down. The half tub usually sports a shower nozzle that has nowhere to hang—so your knees get very clean and the floor gets very wet. Hot water may be available only once a day and not on demand—this is especially true with shared bathrooms. Heating water is costly, and many smaller hotels do it only once daily, in the morning.

TIPS FOR GETTING THE BEST ROOM AT THE BEST RATE

The *rack rate* is the maximum rate a hotel charges for a room. It's the rate you'd get if you walked in off the street and asked for a room for the night. Hardly anybody pays these prices, however, and there are many ways around them. Below are some suggestions for getting the most for your money:

- **Don't be afraid to bargain.** Get in the habit of asking for a lower price than the first one quoted. Most rack rates include commissions of 10% to 25% or more for travel agents, which many hotels cut if you make your own reservations and haggle a bit. Always ask politely whether a less expensive room is available than the first one mentioned, or whether any special rates apply to you. You may qualify for corporate, student, military, senior citizen, or other discounts. Be sure to mention membership in AAA, AARP, frequent flyer programs, or trade unions, which could entitle you to special deals, too.
- **You don't have to take the first room they show you.** Ask to see several. Open and close windows to see how well they shut out noise. Always ask for a corner room. They're usually larger, quieter, and closer to the elevator. They often have more windows and light than standard rooms, and they don't always cost more. When you make your reservation, ask if the hotel is renovating; if it is, request a

---

Traveler's Tip

If you call a hotel from home to reserve a room in advance, ***always follow up with a confirmation fax.*** Not only is it what most hotels prefer, but it is printed proof that you've booked a room. Keep the language simple; state your name, number of people, what kind of room (make sure you say "double with one bed" or "double with two beds"), how many nights you'd like to stay, and the starting date for the first night. Remember: Europeans abbreviate dates day/month/year, not month/day/year.

---

room away from the renovation work. Many hotels now offer nonsmoking rooms; if smoke bothers you, by all means ask for one. Inquire, too, about the location of the restaurants, bars, and discos in the hotel—they could all be a source of irritating noise.

- **Rely on a qualified professional.** Certain hotels give travel agents discounts in exchange for steering business their way, so if you're shy about bargaining, an agent may be better equipped to negotiate discounts for you.
- **Dial direct.** When booking a room in a chain hotel, call the hotel's local line, as well as the toll-free number, and see where you get the best deal. A hotel makes nothing on a room that stays empty. The clerk who runs the place is more likely to know about vacancies and often grants deep discounts to fill up.
- **Remember the law of supply and demand.** Resort hotels are most crowded and therefore most expensive on weekends, so discounts are usually available for mid-week stays. To the contrary, business hotels in downtown locations are busiest during the week; expect discounts over the weekend. Avoid high-season stays whenever you can: Planning your vacation just a week before or after official peak season can mean big savings.
- **Look into group or long-stay discounts.** If you come as part of a large group, you should be able to negotiate a bargain, since the hotel can then guarantee occupancy in a number of rooms. Likewise, when you're planning a long stay in town (usually from 5 days to a week) you'll qualify for a discount. As a general rule, you get 1 night free after a 7-night stay.
- **Avoid excess charges.** When you book a room, ask whether the hotel charges for parking. Most hotels have free, available space, but many urban or beachfront hotels don't. Also, find out before you dial whether your hotel imposes a surcharge on local or long-distance calls. A pay phone, however inconvenient, may save you money.
- **Consider a suite.** If you are traveling with your family or another couple, you can pack more people into a suite (which usually comes with a sofa bed), and thereby reduce your per-person rate. Remember that some places charge for extra guests, and some don't.
- **Book an efficiency.** A room with a kitchenette allows you to grocery shop and eat some meals in. Especially during long stays with families, you're bound to save money on food this way.
- **Investigate reservation services.** These outfits usually work as consolidators, buying up or reserving rooms in bulk, and then dealing them out to customers at a profit. They do garner special deals that range from 10% to 50% off; remember, however, these discounts apply to rack rates, inflated prices that people rarely end up paying. You're probably better off dealing directly with a hotel, but if you don't

like bargaining, this is certainly a viable option. Most of them offer online reservation services as well. Some of the more reputable providers are **Accommodations Express** (☎ 800/950-4685; www.accommodationsxpress.com); **Hotel Reservations Network** (☎ 800/96HOTEL; www.180096HOTEL.com); **Quikbook** (☎ 800/789-9887, includes fax on demand service; www.quikbook. com); and **Room Exchange** (☎ 800/846-7000 in the U.S., 800/486-7000 in Canada). Online, try booking your hotel through **Arthur Frommer's Budget Travel** (www.frommers.com), and save up to 50% on the cost of your room. **Microsoft Expedia** (www.expedia.com) features a "Travel Agent" that directs you to affordable lodgings.

USING A HOTEL BOOKING SERVICE

When you arrive in town, a desk in either the train station or at the tourist office acts as a central hotel reservations service for the city. Tell them your price range, where you'd like to be in the city, and sometimes even the style of hotel, and they'll use a computer database to find you a room in town.

The advantages of booking services are that they do all the room-finding work for you—for a nominal fee—and they always speak English, whereas individual hoteliers may not. When every hotel in town seems to be booked up—during a convention or festival, or perhaps just in high season—they can often find space for you at inns that aren't listed in the guidebooks or other main sources. On the downside, hotels in many countries often charge higher rates to people booking through such a service.

1

Austria

By Darwin Porter & Danforth Prince

With the fall of the Iron Curtain and the subsequent reintegration of Eastern Europe, Austria once again stands at the continental cross-roads, much as it did in the heyday of the Austro-Hungarian Empire. Its capital, Vienna, stranded during the postwar years on the edge of Western Europe, is reclaiming its position as an important international city.

The country offers a lot to do, from exploring historic castles and palaces to skiing on some of the world's finest alpine slopes or hiking in the Danube Valley.

1 Vienna & the Danube Valley

Vienna still retains much of the glory and grandeur of the empire's heady days. Museum treasures from all over Europe, baroque palaces through which Maria Theresa and her brood wandered, the lively music of Johann Strauss, Gustav Klimt's paintings, the concert halls, the unparalleled opera—it's all still here, as if the empire were still flourishing.

Tourism is growing as thousands arrive every year to view Vienna's great art and architecture, to feast on lavish Viennese pastries, to go exploring in the Vienna Woods, to sail down the Danube, to attend Vienna's balls, operas, and festivals, and to listen to the "music that never stops."

Visitors today face a newer and brighter Vienna, a city with more joie de vivre and punch than it's had since before the war. There's also a downside: Prices are on the rise. They haven't reached the height of the Ferris wheel at the Prater, but they're climbing there.

Only in Vienna

Cruising the Danube (Donau)   Johann Strauss took a bit of poetic license in calling the Donau "The Blue Danube," as it's actually a muddy green. To take a cruise, try the legendary DDSG, **Blue Danube Shipping Company,** Donaureisen, Handelskai 265 (☎ **01/727-50-0**), which offers mostly 1-day trips from Vienna. Along the way, you'll pass some of the most famous sights in eastern Austria, including Krems and Melk.

Watching the Lippizaner Stallions   Nothing evokes imperial Vienna more than the Spanish Riding School, which specializes in "dressage," a severely disciplined art originally taught to riders in Vienna by La Guérinière, who fled here to escape the French Revolution. The white stallions, a result of crossbreeding between Spanish thoroughbreds and Karst (Arabian) horses, are the finest equestrian performers on Earth. Riders, wearing brown dress coats, with doeskin breeches and two-corner hats, put the horses through their incredible demonstrations, with the public admitted to watch.

Heurigen Hopping in the Vienna Woods   When the *heurigen,* wine taverns that celebrate the arrival of each year's new wine, or *heuriger,* place a symbolic pine branch over their doors, the Viennese rush to the taverns to drink the new wine and feast on country dishes such as local ham, bacon and lentils, and roast pork. Grinzing is the most visited area. The light, white wine, served chilled, is made from a medley of grapes harvested in the vineyards of the Wienerwald, or Vienna Woods. Shaded by hazels and birches in centuries-old courtyards, often with a panoramic view of the Danube Valley, the Viennese taste the results of each new harvest, turning the occasion into a festival.

Exploring the Hapsburgs' Lifestyle   The Hapsburgs were one of the great dynastic ruling families of Europe, and even today you can see the grandeur of their former lifestyle. Their winter palace, Hofburg, was the seat of an imperial throne that once governed the Austro-Hungarian Empire until its demise in 1918. The sprawling palace complex reads like an architectural textbook, dating from 1279 with subsequent additions through the 18th century. You can also visit their summer palace, Schönbrunn, with its 1,441 rooms. The great baroque architect, J. B. Fischer von Erlach, modeled his plans on those of Versailles.

Biking Along the Danube   The Lower Danube Cycle Track has been called a "velocipede's Valhalla." The most exciting villages and stop-offs along the Danube are linked by a riverside bike trail between Vienna and Naarn. As you bike along, you can take in the attractions, ranging from castles to medieval towns, with latticed vineyards adding to the scenery. You can rent bikes from the train or ferry stations, and the Vienna tourist office can supply route maps.

Strolling on the Kärntnerstrasse   The center of the Inner City and the heart of Viennese life is the pedestrian-only Kärntnerstrasse (or "Carinthia Street," in English), one of Europe's liveliest shopping streets. At any time of the day or night, people can be seen parading along this street paved by purchases, taking in the new window displays of fabulous merchandise. Street performers during the day are always out to amuse; vaudeville isn't dead in Vienna. When you tire of all that, you can retreat to one of the cafe terraces for some people watching.

Attending a Concert by the Vienna Boys' Choir   In this city steeped in musical traditions and institutions—everybody from Mozart to Johann Strauss the Elder to Richard Strauss to Wagner—one group has distinguished itself among all others. It's the Vienna Boys' Choir, or *Wiener Sängerknaben,* with origins going back to the 12th century. Created by Maximilian I, the choir was attached to the Hofmusikkapelle at the Hofburg, where it still performs. The choir sings mass at the Hofburgkapelle on Sundays and holidays, except in July and August. The voices are among the purest in all of Europe, and hearing these talented children is reason enough to buy a ticket to Vienna.

Experiencing the Majesty of St. Stephan's Cathedral   It's been suggested that without Dompfarre St. Stephan, Vienna would "lose its soul." Its vast roof is exactly twice the height of its walls. The Viennese regard this monument with great affection, calling it *Der Steffl.* One of its chief treasures is the Wiener Neustadt altarpiece in carved wood, painted and gilded, in the Virgin's Choir. In all, the cathedral is one of Europe's great Gothic structures, crowned by a 450-foot steeple.

Vienna

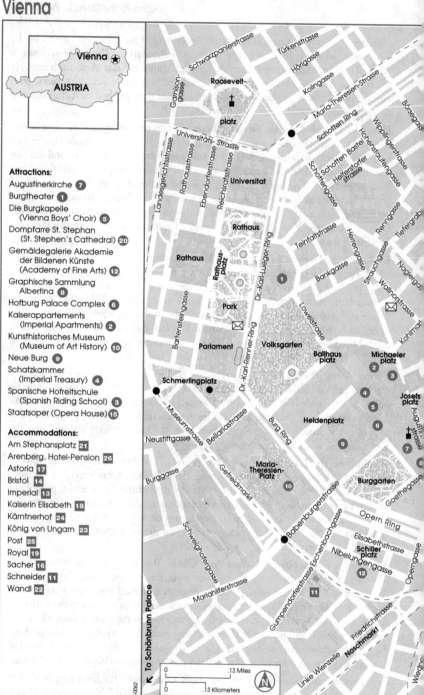

34

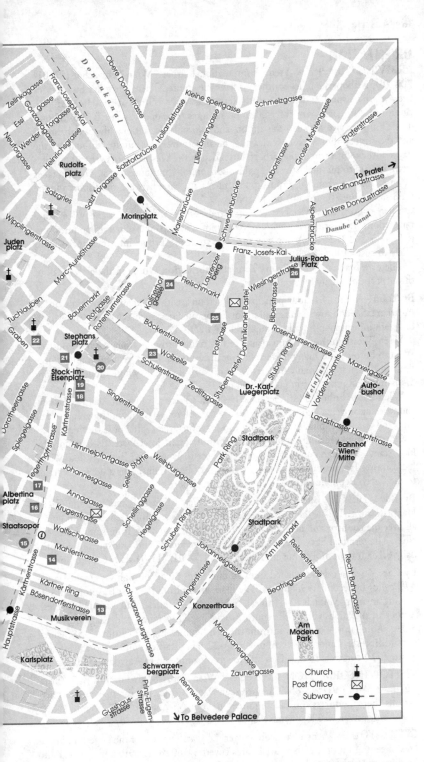

ORIENTATION

ARRIVING   By Plane   Vienna's international airport, **Wien Schwechat** (☎ 01/700-70), is about 12 miles southeast of the city center. There is regular **bus service** between the airport and the City Air Terminal (Wien Mitte), at the Hotel Hilton. Buses run 24 hours a day every 20 to 60 minutes. The one-way fare is 70S ($5.60). There's also service between the airport and two railroad stations, the Westbahnhof and the Südbahnhof, with buses leaving the airport every 30 minutes throughout the day. For the return trip to the airport, buses depart the Westbahnhof every 30 minutes from 5:30am to midnight (reaching the Südbahnhof 15 minutes later). The trip takes 20 to 25 minutes from the airport to the Inner City. Fares between the airport and the train station are 70S ($5.60) per person.

There's also **train** service between the airport and the Wien Nord and Wien Mitte rail stations. Trains run daily 5:07am to 9:30pm. The trip takes about 45 minutes, and the fare is 34S ($2.70). A one-way **taxi** ride from the airport into the Inner City is likely to cost 410S ($32.80).

There's a branch of the **Vienna Tourist Information Office** in the arrival hall of the airport open daily 8:30am to 9pm.

By Train   Vienna has four principal rail stations, with frequent connections to all Austrian cities and towns and to all major European cities, such as Munich and Milan. For train information for all stations, call ☎ 01/17-17.

Wien Westbahnhof, Europaplatz, is for trains arriving from western Austria, Western Europe, and many Eastern European countries. It has frequent train connections to all major Austrian cities. Trains from Salzburg arrive two per hour daily from 5:40am to 8:40pm; the trip takes 3¼ hours.

Wien Südbahnhof, Südtirolerplatz, has train service to southern Austria, the new countries of Slovenia and Croatia (formerly part of Yugoslavia), and Italy. It also has links to Graz, the capital of Styria, and to Klagenfurt, the capital of Carinthia.

Other stations include **Franz-Josef Bahnhof,** Franz-Josef-Platz, used mainly by local trains, although connections are made here to Prague and Berlin. **Wien Mitte,** Landstrasser Hauptstrasse 1, is also a terminus of local trains, plus a depot for trains to the Czech Republic and trains to Schwechat Airport.

By Bus   The **City Bus Terminal** is at the Wien Mitte rail station, Landstrasser Hauptstrasse 1. This is the arrival depot for Post buses and Bundesbuses from points all over the country, and also the arrival point for private buses from some European cities. The terminal has lockers, currency-exchange kiosks, and a ticket counter open daily 6:15am to 6pm. For bus information, call ☎ 01/711-01 daily 6am to 9pm.

By Car   Vienna can be reached from all directions by major highways (called *autobahnen*) or by secondary highways. The main artery from the west is Autobahn **A-1,** coming in from Munich (291 miles), Salzburg (209 miles), and Linz (116 miles). Autobahn **A-2** arrives from the south, from Graz (124 miles) and Klagenfurt (192 miles). Autobahn **A-4** comes in from the east, connecting with Route **E-58,** which runs to Bratislava and Prague. Autobahn **A-22** takes traffic from the northwest, and Route **E-10** connects to the cities and towns of southeastern Austria and Hungary.

VISITOR INFORMATION   The official **Wien Tourist-Information** is at Kärntnerstrasse 38 (☎ 01/513-88-92), open daily 9am to 7pm. You can make room reservations here. Address postal inquiries to the Vienna Tourist Board, Obere Augartenstrasse 40, 1025 Vienna (fax 01/211-14-57).

CITY LAYOUT   Vienna has evolved over the years into one of the largest metropolises of central Europe, with a surface area covering 160 square miles. It's divided into 23 districts (*bezirke*), each identified with a Roman numeral.

The size and shape of **Bezirke I,** the **Inner City,** roughly correspond to the original borders of the medieval city. Other than the Cathedral of St. Stephan, very few medieval buildings remain. Many of the buildings were reconstructed in the baroque or neoclassical style, and others are modern replacements of buildings bombed during World War II. As Austria's commercial and cultural nerve center, the central district contains dozens of streets devoted exclusively to pedestrian traffic. The most famous of these is **Kärntnerstrasse,** which bypasses the Vienna State Opera House as it runs south from the center.

The Inner City is surrounded by the **Ringstrasse,** a circular boulevard about 2½ miles long whose construction between 1859 and 1888 was one of the most ambitious (and controversial) examples of urban restoration in the history of central Europe. Confusingly, the name of this boulevard changes many times during its encirclement of the Inner City. Names that apply to it carry the suffix *-ring:* for example, Opernring, Schottenring, Burgring, Dr.-Karl-Lueger-Ring, Stubenring, Parkring, Schubertring, and Kärntner Ring.

Surrounding the Ringstrasse are the **inner suburban districts** (Bezirkes II through IX). They contain most of the villas and palaces of Vienna's 18th-century nobility amid complexes of modern apartment houses and the 19th-century homes of middle-class entrepreneurs. The **outer suburban districts** embrace a wide range of residential, industrial, and rural settings.

Northeast of the center, beyond the Danube Canal, is the **Second District,** with the famous amusement park, the Prater. East of the center, in the **Third District,** you'll find the art treasures and baroque setting of the Belvedere Palace. West of the center is Schönbrunn Palace.

GETTING AROUND   By Public Transportation   Vienna Transport (*Wiener Verkehrsbetriebe*), with its network of facilities covering hundreds of miles, can take you where you want to go—by U-Bahn (subway), tram (streetcar), or bus. Vienna Public Transport has **Information Centers** located at Karlsplatz, open Monday to Friday 7am to 6pm and on Saturday, Sunday, and holidays 8:30am to 4pm; on Stephansplatz, open Monday to Friday 6:30am to 6:30pm and on Saturday and Sunday 8:30am to 4pm; and on Praterstern, open Monday to Friday 7am to 6:30pm. There are centers at each of the larger Metro stations, too. For information, call ☎ 01/79-09-105.

Vienna has a **uniform fare,** allowing the same tickets to be used on all means of transportation as well as on the **Schnelbahn (Rapid Transit)** of the Austrian Federal Railways in the Vienna area and on some connecting private bus lines. A single (one-ride) ticket costs 20S ($1.60); that's also the price for two rides by a child. Children under 6 ride free.

It's wise to buy your tickets in advance at a *tabak-trafik* (tobacconist shop) or at an advance-sales office in one of the three public transport information centers (see above for locations). All advance-sales offices are open Monday 6am to noon, Tuesday and Wednesday 6:30am to 12:30pm, and Thursday and Friday 12:30 to 6:30pm. Most buses and streetcars do not have conductors, which means that you must have the correct change, 20S ($1.60), when you buy your ticket aboard or from a vending machine at the station. A ticket bought from a machine is stamped with the date and time of purchase. Tickets purchased in advance must be stamped before you start your ride by the machine on conductorless streetcars or at the platform barriers of the underground or Stadtbahn. Once a ticket is stamped, it can be used for one trip in one direction, including transfers.

By Bus & U-Bahn (Subway)   You can ride directly into the Inner City from the suburbs or outlying districts on the U-Bahn U1 or on city bus no. 1A, 2A, or 3A. The

U-Bahn runs daily 6am to midnight; buses operate Monday to Saturday 6am to 10pm, and Sunday 6am to 8pm.

By Tram   More and more tram routes are being phased out in favor of buses or the U-Bahn, but trams are still in heavy use within the center of Vienna, especially lines 1 and 2. Trams are also in use between the Westbahnhof and Burgring (take line 58), and between the Westbahnhof and the Südbahnhof (take line 18). Finally, line D runs between the Südbahnhof and the Ring. Trams operate between 5:30am and 12:30am.

By Taxi   Taxi stands are marked by signs, or you can call for a radio cab by phoning ☎ 31-300, 60-160, 81-400, 91-011, or 40-100. Fares are indicated on an official taxi meter. The basic fare is 27S ($2.15), plus 14S ($1.10) per kilometer. There's an extra charge of 16S ($1.30) for luggage carried in the trunk. For rides after 11pm, and for trips on Sunday and holidays, there's a surcharge of 10S (80¢). If you call for a radio cab, additional charges apply.

By Car   Major car-rental companies operating in Vienna include **Avis,** Opernring 1 (☎ **800/654-3001** in the U.S., or 01/587-62-41 in Vienna); **Budget Rent-a-Car,** City/Hilton Air Terminal (☎ **800/472-3325** in the U.S., or 01/714-6565 in Vienna); and **Hertz,** in the Marriott Hotel, Parkring 12A (☎ **800/654-3001** in the U.S., or 01/513-38-41 in Vienna).

By Bike   Vienna has more than 155 miles of marked bike paths within the city limits. In July and August, many Viennese, encouraged by city officials, leave their cars in the garage and ride bikes. Specially marked cars of the U-Bahn transport bikes free in July and August, Monday to Friday 9am to 3pm and after 6:30pm until the trains stop running, and on weekends from 9am until the trains stop running. All other times, you pay half the regular U-Bahn fare to take a bike on the U-Bahn.

Rental stores abound at the Prater amusement park and along the banks of the Danube Canal, which is the favorite spot for most Viennese to go biking. One of the best is **Copacagrana,** Reichsbrücke, on the Donauinsel (☎ **01/23-65-18-57**), which is open from May to October daily from 9am to 9pm. Or you can rent from a kiosk in the **Westbahnhof** (☎ **01/58-00-329-85**), between May and October every day from 8am to 7pm. The Vienna Tourist Board can also supply a list of rental shops and more information about bike paths throughout the city. Bike rentals begin at around 200S ($16) a day.

Traveler's Tip

The **Vienna Card** gives you access to all public modes of transportation (subway, bus, and tram) within Vienna—as well as discounts in city museums, shops, and restaurants—for a single, **discounted price.** A 24-hour network pass costs 50S ($4) and is good for a full day of public transport. A 72-hour network pass sells for 130S ($10.40). For 180S ($14.40), you can buy a versatile **3-day strip ticket,** which can be used for 3 separate days of travel; a rail attendant punches the ticket each day it is used. Vienna Cards are easy to find throughout the capital, or you can purchase one outside Vienna over the telephone with a credit card (☎ **01/ 798-44-00-28**).

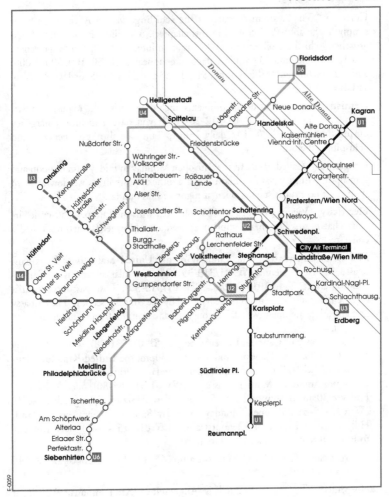

Fast Facts: Vienna

American Express The most convenient office is at Kärntnerstrasse 21–23 (☎ **01/515-40**), near Stock-im-Eisenplatz, open Monday to Friday 9am to 5:30pm, and Saturday 9am to noon.

Bookstores **Gerold & Co.,** Graben 31 (☎ **01/533-50-14**), is a good bookstore in Vienna for English-language publications. You can also try **Shakespeare & Company,** Sterngasse 2 (☎ **01/535-50-53**), especially for English-language magazines.

Business Hours Most shops are open Monday to Friday 9am to 6pm, and Saturday 9am to noon, 12:30pm, or 1pm. On the first Saturday of every month, the custom is for shops to remain open until 4:30 or 5pm. The tradition is called *langer Samstag.*

Currency   The Austrian currency is the **schilling,** written ASch, AS, Ös, or simply S (the abbreviation used in this chapter). A schilling is made up of 100 groschen (which are seldom used). Coins are minted as 5, 10, and 50 groschen, and 1, 5, 10, 20, and 50 schilling. Banknotes appear as 20, 50, 100, 500, 1,000, and 5,000 schilling. At this writing, $1 = 12.4S and £1 = 20.3S, or 1S = 8¢. Also, 1EUR=13.7S.

Dentists/Doctors   For dental problems, including during the night or on Saturday and Sunday, call ☎ **01/512-20-78.** If you have a medical emergency during the night, call ☎ **141** daily 7pm to 7am. See also "Emergencies" and "Hospitals," below.

Drugstores   Called *apotheke,* they are open Monday to Friday 8am to noon and 2 to 6pm, Saturday 8am to noon. Each apotheke posts in its window a list of shops that take turns staying open at night and on Sunday.

Electricity   Vienna operates on 220 volts AC, with the European 50-cycle circuit. That means U.S.-made appliances need a transformer (sometimes called a converter).

Embassies/Consulates   The Embassy of the **United States** is at Boltzmanngasse 16, 1090 Vienna (☎ **01/313-39**). The consular section is at Gartenbaupromenade 2–4, 1010 Vienna (☎ **01/313-39**). Lost passports, tourist emergencies, and other matters are handled by the consular section. The embassy and consulate are open Monday through Friday from 8:30am to noon and 1 to 3:30pm.

The Embassy of **Canada,** Laurenzerberg 2 (☎ **01/531-38**), is open Monday to Friday 8:30am to 12:30pm and 1:30 to 3:30pm; the **United Kingdom,** Jauresgasse 12 (☎ **01/716-13-53-38**), open Monday to Friday 9:15am to noon and 2 to 4pm; **Australia,** Mattiellistrasse 2–4 (☎ **01/512-85-80**), open Monday to Friday 8:30am to 1pm and 2 to 5:30pm; **New Zealand,** Springsiedelgasse 28 (☎ **01/318-85-05**), open Monday to Friday 8:30am to 5pm; and **Ireland,** Hilton Center, Landstrasser Hauptstrasse 2 (☎ **01/715-42-47**), open Monday to Friday 9 to 11:30am and 1:30 to 4pm.

Emergencies   Call ☎ **122** to report a fire, ☎ **133** for the police, or ☎ **144** for an ambulance.

Hospitals   The major hospital is **Allgemeines Krankenhaus,** Währinger Gürtel 18–20 (☎ **01/404-00**).

Internet Access   **Café Stein,** Wahringerstrasse 6–8, 1090 (☎ **01/319 7241**), is a cybercafe across from the University of Vienna. It has six Macintosh stations for customers to use. A half hour of Internet access costs 50S ($4). Its Web site is www.cafe-stein.co.at/stein/. Open daily from 7am to 1am.

Lost Property   A lost-property office, **Zentrales Fundamt,** is maintained at Wasagasse 22 (☎ **01/313-44-92**), open Monday to Friday 8am to 3pm. Items found on trains are taken to the central lost-property office at the Westbahnhof. Items left on buses and streetcars are passed on to the Wasagasse office after 3 days. If you miss something as soon as you get off the bus, you can pick it up (provided it's returned) at Wiener Stadtwerke (Verkehrsbetriebe; ☎ **01/790-94-35-00**) without waiting 3 days.

Post Office   Addresses for them can be found in the telephone directory under "Post." Post offices are generally open for mail services Monday to Friday 8am to noon and 2 to 6pm. The central post office, the Hauptpostamt, is at Fleischmarkt

19 (☎ **01/515-09-0**), and most general post offices are open daily 24 hours a day.

Taxes   Vienna imposes no special city taxes, other than the national value-added tax that's tacked on to all goods and services. The tax depends on the item, but can range up to 34% on luxury goods, and 21% on car rentals.

Telephone   The **country code** for Austria is **43**. The **city code** for Vienna is **1**; use this code when you're calling from outside Austria. If you're within Austria, use **01**. The toll-free international access codes are: **AT&T** ☎ 022-903-011; **Sprint** ☎ 022-903-014, **MCI** ☎ 022-903-012.

WHERE TO STAY

If you're looking for a place near the Vienna airport, the **Novotel Wien Airport,** Flughafen Wien, Schwechat (☎ **01/70107-0;** fax 01/707-3239), is a bland but clean chain hotel, little more than a sleeping factory for people arriving late or meeting early morning flights. The cost is 1,850S ($148) for a double, and parking is free. It's only a 5-minute walk to the check-in point for your flight.

VERY EXPENSIVE

✪ **Hotel Bristol.** Kärntner Ring 1, 1015 Vienna. ☎ **800/325-3535** in the U.S., or 01/ 515-160. Fax 01/515-16-550. www.luxurycollection.com/bristol. 146 units. A/C MINIBAR TV TEL. 3,600–5,600S ($288–$448) double; from 7,000S ($560) suite. AE, DC, MC, V. Parking 300S ($24). U-Bahn: Karlsplatz. Tram: 1 or 2.

This six-story landmark is a superb choice, with a decor evoking the full power of the Hapsburg Empire. When it was constructed in 1894 next to the State Opera, it was the ultimate in luxury, and the addition of black-tiled bathrooms and modern conveniences have helped maintain its high standard. Bedrooms are sumptuously appointed. The club floor offers luxurious comfort, with period furnishings complimenting the hotel's *fin de siècle* architecture. In the late '90s, this landmark was acquired by the luxury division of ITT Sheraton, and every year a different floor of the hotel is completely renovated. The Bristol's restaurant, the Korso, is one of the best in Vienna, and the modern Rôtisserie Sirk and the elegant Café Sirk are also meeting places for gourmets.

Hotel Imperial. Kärntner Ring 16, 1015 Vienna. ☎ **800/325-3589** in the U.S., or 01/ 50-110-0. Fax 01/501-10-410. 160 units. A/C MINIBAR TV TEL. 5,500–7,600S ($440–$608) double; from 14,000S ($1,120) suite. AE, DC, MC, V. Parking 450S ($36). U-Bahn: Karlsplatz.

This hotel is Vienna's grandest and most "imperial" looking, lying 2 blocks from the State Opera and 1 block from the Musikverein. The hotel was built in 1869 as the private residence of the duke of Württemberg. It was converted into a private hotel in 1873, and in the mid-1990s, it joined the luxury group of ITT Sheraton. Everything is outlined against a background of polished red, yellow, and black marble; crystal chandeliers; Gobelin tapestries; and fine rugs. The rooms are soundproof and generally spacious with firm mattresses and marble bathrooms. Courtyard rooms are more tranquil but lack views. The elegant restaurant, Zur Majestät, has a turn-of-the-century atmosphere and offers traditional Austrian dishes done with a light touch.

Hotel Sacher. Philharmonikerstrasse 4, 1010 Vienna. ☎ **01/514-56.** Fax 01/51-45-78-10. www.sacher.com. E-mail: hotel@sacher.com. 108 units. A/C MINIBAR TV TEL. 3,900–7,000S ($312–$560) double; from 11,200S ($896) suite. AE, DC, MC, V. Parking 390S ($31.20). U-Bahn: Karlsplatz. Bus: 4A. Tram: 1, 2, 62, 65, D, or J.

The glory of the Hapsburg era is still evoked as you walk through the public rooms here. The red velvet, crystal chandeliers, traditional wallpaper, and brocaded curtains are reminiscent of Old Vienna. The hotel is popular with groups, however, and the heavy traffic is taking a toll. Although the hotel has its die-hard admirers, if you're going truly grand, the Imperial and Bristol are superior. Many rooms, especially those near the top, are small (and have cramped bathrooms), but most accommodations are generous in size and often have sitting areas and medium-size marble bathrooms. Those facing the opera house have the best views, and inside rooms tend to be dark.

EXPENSIVE

Hotel am Stephansplatz. Stephansplatz 9, 1010 Vienna. ☎ **01/534-05-0.** Fax 01/534-05-711. E-mail: hotel@stephansplatz.co.at. 60 units. MINIBAR TV TEL. 2,160–2,360S ($172.80–$188.80) double. Rates include breakfast. AE, DC, MC, V. Parking 350S ($28). U-Bahn: Stephansplatz.

Walk out the door and you're facing the front entrance to Vienna's cathedral if you stay in this hotel, with its unadorned circa 1956 facade. The location is unbeatable, although a lot of other Viennese hotels have more charm than this one and a more helpful staff. Nevertheless, the place has many winning qualities and is not overrun with groups on package tours. Some bedrooms contain painted reproductions of rococo furniture and references to imperial Austria. Most accommodations, however, are rather sterile and functional, and 10 are equipped with showers only instead of tub baths. The most interesting units overlook the facade of the cathedral, and the more tranquil ones open onto an inner courtyard. Lack of air-conditioning could be a problem here in midsummer, as guests must open their windows onto Stephansplatz, which is noisy until late at night. The hotel's dining choice, Domcafé, serves everything from drinks and snacks to full-fledged meals.

Hotel Astoria. Kärntnerstrasse 32–34, 1015 Vienna. ☎ **01/515-77-0.** Fax 01/515-77-82. www.verkehrsbuero.at/hotel. E-mail: astoria@atnet.at. 108 units. MINIBAR TV TEL. 2,400S ($192) double; 3,800S ($304) suite. Rates include breakfast. AE, DC, MC, V. Parking 300S ($24). U-Bahn: Stephansplatz.

Hotel Astoria is for nostalgia buffs who want to recall the decadent last days of the Austro-Hungarian Empire. A first-class hotel, the Astoria has a desirable location on the shopping mall close to St. Stephan's Cathedral and the State Opera. Decorated in a slightly frayed turn-of-the-century style, the hotel offers well-appointed and traditionally decorated bedrooms. The interior rooms tend to be too dark, and singles are just too cramped. Of course, it has been renovated over the years, most recently in 1996, but the old style has been respected. The management offers a good standard at a decent but not cheap price.

✪ **Hotel Kaiserin Elisabeth.** Weihburggasse 3, 1010 Vienna. ☎ **01/515-260.** Fax 01/515-267. 63 units. MINIBAR TV TEL. 2,450S ($196) double; 2,750S ($220) suite. Rates include buffet breakfast. AE, DC, MC, V. Parking 350S ($28). U-Bahn: Stephansplatz.

This hotel of yellow stone is conveniently located only 1 block from St. Stephan's. The interior offers Oriental rugs on well-maintained marble or wood floors. The soundproof rooms have been considerably updated since Richard Wagner, Franz Liszt, and Edvard Grieg each spent a night here. Although some parts of the building date from the 14th century, you're likely to see an up-to-date decor of polished wood, clean linen, and perhaps another Oriental rug in your room. The tiled bathrooms are a little small.

Hotel König von Ungarn. Schulerstrasse 10, 1010 Vienna. ☎ **01/515-840.** Fax 01/515-848. 32 units. A/C MINIBAR TV TEL. 2,290S ($183.20) double; 2,690S ($215.20) suite. Rates include breakfast. AE, DC, MC, V. Parking 200S ($16). U-Bahn: Stephansplatz.

In a choice site on a narrow street near the cathedral, this hotel has been in business for more than 4 centuries, and is Vienna's oldest continuously operated accommodation.

It's an evocative, intimate, and cozy retreat in an early 17th-century building, once a *pied-à-terre* for Hungarian noble families visiting the Austrian capital. Mozart reportedly lived here in 1791. The interior is filled with interesting architectural details, and the King of Hungary restaurant—under separate management—is one of the city's finest. Newly renovated bedrooms have low-key luxury, traditional decor, and modern convenience, along with some Biedermeier decorative touches. Try for the two with balconies.

MODERATE

Hotel-Pension Arenberg. Stubenring 2, 1010 Vienna. ☎ **800/528-1234** in the U.S. or 01/512-52-91. Fax 01/513-93-56. www.bestwestern.com. E-mail: arenberg@ping.at. 23 units. A/C TV TEL. 1,480–1,850S ($118.40–$148) double; 1,780–2,150S ($142.40–$172) suite. Rates include breakfast. AE, DC, MC, V. Parking 252S ($20.15). U-Bahn: Schwedenplatz.

This genteel but unpretentious pension occupies the second and third floors of a six-story apartment house set in an upscale neighborhood on Ringstrasse. It offers soundproof bedrooms, a bit on the small side, outfitted in an old-world style with Oriental carpets, conservative furniture, and interesting art. One enthusiastic reader found it full of old-world charm, and said the English-speaking staff couldn't have been more delightful and helpful. "On your second visit they treat you like family," the reader wrote.

Hotel Royal. Singerstrasse 3, 1010 Vienna. ☎ **01/515-68-0.** Fax 01/513-96-98. 82 units. MINIBAR TV TEL. 1,650–2,000S ($132–$160) double; 2,800S ($224) suite. Rates include breakfast. AE, DC, MC, V. U-Bahn: Stephansplatz.

The lobby of this nine-story hotel less than a block from St. Stephan's Cathedral contains the piano on which Wagner composed *Die Meistersinger von Nürnberg*. Each room is furnished differently, in a style influenced by 19th-century Italy, with some good reproductions of antiques and an occasional original. Try for a room with a balcony and a view of the cathedral. Corner rooms with spacious foyers are also desirable, although those facing the street tend to be noisy. The on-site restaurant, Firenze, serves Tuscan food, of course.

Hotel Schneider. Getreidemarkt 5, 1060 Vienna. ☎ **01/588-380.** Fax 01/588-38-212. E-mail: schneider@hotels.or.at. 70 units. MINIBAR TV TEL. 1,720–2,200S ($137.60–$176) double. Rates include buffet breakfast. AE, DC, MC, V. Parking 250S ($20). U-Bahn: Karlsplatz.

This hotel stands in the center of Vienna between the State Opera and the famous Nasch Market. It's a modern five-story building with panoramic windows on the ground floor and a red-tile roof. The interior is warmly decorated with some 19th-century antiques and comfortably upholstered chairs. Many musicians, singers, actors, and other artists are loyal regulars. This is one of Vienna's better small hotels, with firm beds, tile bathrooms, and good housekeeping. Families are especially fond of the place because each of the suites contains kitchenettes.

INEXPENSIVE

Hotel Kärntnerhof. Grashofgasse 4, 1010 Vienna. ☎ **01/512-19-23.** Fax 01/513-22-28-33. E-mail: kaerntnerhof@netway.at. 44 units. 1,200–1,720S ($96–$137.60) double; 2,250–2,800S ($180–$224) suite. Rates include breakfast. AE, DC, MC, V. Parking 200S ($16). U-Bahn: Stephansplatz.

Only a 4-minute walk from the cathedral, Kärntnerhof advertises itself as a family-oriented hotel. The public rooms are tastefully decorated with Oriental rugs, well-upholstered chairs and couches with cabriole legs, and an occasional 19th-century portrait. The bedrooms are more modern, usually with the original parquet floors and striped or patterned wallpaper set off by curtains. The tiled bathrooms glisten.

✪ **Hotel Post.** Fleischmarkt 24, 1010 Vienna. ☎ **01/51-58-30.** Fax 01/515-83-808. 107 units (77 with bathroom). TV TEL. 860S ($68.80) double without bathroom; 1,420S ($113.60) double with bathroom; 1,100S ($88) triple without bathroom; 1,740S ($139.20) triple with bathroom. Rates include buffet breakfast. AE, DC, MC, V. Parking 220S ($17.60). Tram: 1 or 2.

Hotel Post lies in the medieval slaughterhouse district, today an interesting section full of hotels and restaurants. The dignified front is constructed of gray stone, with a street-level facade of black marble. The manager is quick to tell you that both Mozart and Haydn frequently stayed in a former inn at this address, although the current structure is only about a century old. In 1996 and 1997, all the furnishings in the rooms were replaced and upgraded. The well-maintained bedrooms are streamlined and functional.

Hotel Wandl. Petersplatz 9, 1010 Vienna. ☎ **01/53-45-50.** Fax 01/53-455-77. E-mail: reservation@hotelwandl.com. 138 units (134 with bathroom). TV TEL. 1,200S ($96) double without bathroom; 1,650–1,950S ($132–$156) double with bathroom. Rates include breakfast. AE, DC, MC, V. Parking 420S ($33.60). U-Bahn: Stephansplatz.

Despite a discreet 1997 renovation, staying at this hotel is like stepping into a piece of family history—it has been under the same ownership for generations. Built around 1700, the establishment has views of the steeple of St. Stephan's from many of its windows, which often open onto small balconies. The breakfast room is a high-ceilinged two-toned room with hanging chandeliers and lots of ornamented plaster; the bedrooms are quite spacious, and the bathrooms are small but adequate. Room service is available 24 hours a day.

WHERE TO DINE
ON OR NEAR KÄRNTNERSTRASSE
Very Expensive

✪ **Drei Husaren.** Weihburggasse 4. ☎ **01/512-10-92.** Reservations required. Main courses 255–395S ($20.40–$31.60); menu dégustation (6 courses) 920S ($73.60); set-price 4-course business lunch 390S ($31.20). AE, DC, MC, V. Daily noon–3pm and 6pm–1am. U-Bahn: Stephansplatz. VIENNESE/INTERNATIONAL.

Just off Kärntnerstrasse, this enduring favorite—a Viennese landmark since it opened in 1935—serves inventive and classic Viennese cuisine. Against a background of Gypsy melodies, you'll dine on freshwater salmon with pike soufflé, mussel soup, breast of guinea fowl, an array of sole dishes, and such old-time favorites as *Tafelspitz* (boiled beef). The chef specializes in veal, including his deliciously flavored *Kalbsbrücken Metternich*. The place is celebrated for its repertoire of more than 35 hors d'oeuvres, which are rolled around the dining room on four separate trolleys. Every diner pays a supplemental music charge of 50S ($4).

König von Ungarn. Schulerstrasse 10. ☎ **01/512-53-19.** Reservations required. Main courses 220–350S ($17.60–$28); set-price menu 340–450S ($27.20–$36) at lunch, 490–700S ($39.20–$56) at dinner. AE, DC, MC, V. Sun–Fri noon–2:30pm and 6–10:30pm. U-Bahn: Stephansplatz. Bus: 1A. VIENNESE/INTERNATIONAL.

This beautifully decorated restaurant is inside the famous hotel of the same name. The restaurant itself has operated since the 1600s, the present management dating from 1979. Food is well prepared and traditional—don't come here for experimental cooking. You dine under a vaulted ceiling surrounded by crystal, chandeliers, antiques, and marble columns. If you're in doubt about what to order, try the *Tafelspitz*, a savory boiled-beef specialty elegantly dispensed from a trolley. Other menu choices, which change seasonally, include venison in a Chinese mushroom sauce, a ragoût of seafood with fresh mushrooms, grilled sea bass with crabmeat sauce and a spinach-flavored strudel, or tournedos with a mustard-and-horseradish sauce. The service is superb.

Sacher Hotel Restaurant. Philharmonikerstrasse 4. ☎ **01/514-560.** Reservations required. Main courses 180–610S ($14.40–$48.80). AE, DC, MC, V. Daily noon–2:30pm and 6–11pm. U-Bahn: Karlsplatz. AUSTRIAN/VIENNESE/INTERNATIONAL.

This has long been an enduring favorite for pre- or post-opera dining. It seems like all celebrities who come to Vienna are eventually spotted in the Red Bar with its adjacent dining room, where live piano music is presented every evening from 7pm to midnight, or in the brown-and-white Anna Sacher Room, the site of many a high-powered meal. There's no better place in Vienna to sample the restaurant's most famous dish, *Tafelspitz*, the Viennese boiled-beef platter that was an emperor's favorite. The chef serves it here with a savory, herb-flavored sauce. Other excellent dishes include fish terrine, Styrian-style lamb chops with cream cabbage, veal steak with morels, and rib steak with onions. For dessert, there's the world-renowned *Sachertorte*, said to have been created in 1832 by Franz Sacher while he served as Prince Metternich's apprentice.

Expensive

✪ **Plachutta.** Wollzeile 10. ☎ **01/512-1577.** Reservations recommended. Main courses 202–305S ($16.15–$24.40). DC, MC, V. Daily 11:30am–11:15pm. U-Bahn: Stubentor. VIENNESE.

Few restaurants have built such a culinary shrine around one dish. Here it's *Tafelspitz*, the boiled-beef dish that was the favorite of Emperor Franz Joseph throughout his prolonged reign. Whichever of the ten versions you order, it invariably comes with sauces and garnishes that transform a dull-sounding dish into a delectable culinary traipse through yesteryear. Two of the cuts of beef most often associated with the dish include *Schulterscherzel* (shoulder of beef) and *Beinfleisch* (shank of beef). Regardless of the cut you specify, your meal is accompanied by hash-browned potatoes, chives, and horseradish with chopped apples.

Moderate

Dö & Co. Akademiestrasse 3. ☎ **01/512-64-74.** Reservations recommended for tables. Main courses 115–245S ($9.20–$19.60). AE, DC, MC, V. Mon–Fri 10:30am–7:30pm; Sat 10am–6pm. U-Bahn: Karlsplatz. DELI.

This sophisticated delicatessen is next to the State Opera. Depending on the season, the asparagus might have been flown in from Paris or Argentina, and the shellfish from the North Sea or the Bosphorus. Sprawling glass cases are laden with rich displays of pâtés, seafood salads, and Viennese pastries. You can take your purchases to go or sit at one of the tiny, somewhat-cramped tables near the entrance.

Zum Schwarzen Kameel. Bognergasse 5. ☎ **01/533-81-25.** Main courses 160–280S ($12.80–$22.40). MC, V. Mon–Fri 9am–8pm; Sat 8:30am–4pm. U-Bahn: Schottentor. Bus: 2A or 3A. INTERNATIONAL.

This restaurant has been in the same family since 1618. A delicatessen against one of the walls sells wine, liquor, and specialty meat items, although most of the action takes place in the cafe, which on Saturday mornings is packed with Viennese recovering from a late night with massive doses of caffeine. The restaurant beyond the cafe, with only 11 tables, is a perfectly preserved art nouveau room. Specialties include herring filet Oslo, potato soup, tournedos, Roman *saltimbocca* (veal with ham), and daily fish specials, along with the more traditional veal gulasch and *Tafelspitz* (boiled beef).

Inexpensive

Augustinerkeller. Augustinerstrasse 1. ☎ **01/533-10-26.** Main courses 110–180S ($8.80–$14.40); glass of wine 29–32S ($2.30–$2.55). AE, MC, V. Daily 11am–midnight. U-Bahn: Stephansplatz or Karlsplatz. AUSTRIAN.

Augustinerkeller, in the vaulted basement of the part of the Hofburg complex that shelters the Albertina Collection, has served wine, beer, and food since 1857. It attracts a lively group of patrons from all walks of life, and sometimes they get boisterous, especially when the *schrammel* music goes late into the night. It's one of the best values for wine tasting in Vienna. Aside from the wine and beer, the establishment serves simple food, including roast chicken on a spit, roast pork shank, *Schnitzel,* and Viennese *Tafelspitz* (boiled beef).

✪ **Buffet Trzesniewski.** Dorotheergasse 1. ☎ **01/512-32-91.** Reservations not accepted. Sandwiches 9S (70¢); pastries 20S ($1.60). No credit cards. Mon–Fri 8:30am–7:30pm; Sat 9am–5pm. U-Bahn: Stephansplatz. SANDWICHES.

Everyone in Vienna knows about this place, from the most hurried office worker to the city's elite hostesses. Franz Kafka lived next door and used to come in for sandwiches and beer. Its current incarnation is unlike any buffet you may have seen, with six or seven cramped tables and a rapidly moving line jostling for space next to the glass countertops. Indicate to the waitress the kind of sandwich you want, and if you can't read German signs, just point. Most people come here for the delicious finger sandwiches, which include 18 combinations of cream cheese, egg and onion, salami, mushroom, herring, green and red peppers, tomatoes, lobster, and many more.

✪ **Gulaschmuseum.** Schulerstrasse 20. ☎ **01/512-1017.** Reservations recommended. Main courses 75–152S ($6–$12.15). MC, V. Mon–Fri 9am–midnight; Sat–Sun 10am–midnight. U-Bahn: Wollzeile or Stephansplatz. AUSTRIAN/HUNGARIAN.

If you thought that gulasch was available in only one form, think again. This restaurant celebrates at least 15 varieties of it. Each version is a Hungarian culinary tradition redolent with the taste of that country's most distinctive spice, paprika. The Viennese adopted this dish from their former "colony" centuries ago, and have long ago made it their own. You can order versions of gulasch based on roast beef, veal, pork, fried chicken livers, and even all-vegetarian versions made with potatoes, beans, or mushrooms. Boiled potatoes and rough-textured brown or black bread usually accompany your choice. An excellent beginning is a Hungarian dish referred to as the national crêpe of the Magyars, Hortobágy palatschinken, stuffed with minced beef and paprika-flavored cream sauce.

Wiener Rathauskeller. Rathausplatz 1. ☎ **01/405-12-190.** Reservations required. Main courses 100–250S ($8–$20); Vienna music evening with dinner (Tues–Sat at 8pm) 410S ($32.80). AE, DC, MC, V. Mon–Sat 11:30am–3pm and 6–11pm. U-Bahn: Rathaus. VIENNESE/INTERNATIONAL.

City halls throughout the Teutonic world have traditionally maintained restaurants in their basements, and Vienna is no exception. Although its famous Rathaus was built between 1871 and 1883, its cellar-level restaurant wasn't added until 1899. Today, in half a dozen richly atmospheric dining rooms, with high vaulted ceilings and stained-glass windows, good and reasonably priced food is served. The chef's specialty is a Rathauskellerplatte for two, consisting of various cuts of meat, including a veal schnitzel, lamb cutlets, and pork médaillons. One section of the cellar is devoted every evening to a Viennese musical *soirée* beginning at 8pm. Live musicians ramble through the world of operetta, waltz, and *Schrammel* music—suitable entertainment as you dine.

Zwölf-Apostelkeller. Sonnenfelsgasse 3. ☎ **01/512-67-77.** Main courses 78–145S ($6.25–$11.60). AE, DC, MC, V. Daily 4:30pm–midnight. Closed 3 weeks in July. Bus: 1A. Tram: 1, 2, 21, D, or N. VIENNESE.

Rows of wooden tables stand under vaulted ceilings, with lighting partially provided by streetlights set into the masonry floor. It's so deep that you feel you're entering a dungeon. Sections of this old wine tavern's walls predate 1561. This place is popular with students who love its low prices and proximity to St. Stephan's. In addition to beer and wine, the establishment serves hearty Austrian fare. Specialties include roast pork with dumplings, Hungarian goulash soup, a limited number of vegetarian dishes, and a *Schlachtplatte* (hot black pudding, liverwurst, pork, and pork sausage with a hot bacon-and-cabbage salad).

NEAR FLEISCHMARKT
Moderate
Griechenbeisl. Fleischmarkt 11. ☎ **01/533-19-77.** Reservations required. Main courses 165–225S ($13.20–$18); set-price menu 270–445S ($21.60–$35.60). AE, DC, MC, V. Daily 11am–1am (last orders at 11:30pm). Tram: N. U-Bahn: Schwedenplatz. AUSTRIAN.

Griechenbeisl was established in 1450 and is still one of the leading restaurants of Vienna. It has a labyrinthine collection of dining areas on three different floors, all with low vaulted ceilings, smoky paneling, wrought-iron chandeliers, and Styrian-vested waiters who scurry around under large trays of food. As you go in, be sure to see the so-called inner sanctum, with signatures of such former patrons as Mozart, Beethoven, and Mark Twain. The food is hearty, ample, and solidly bourgeois. Menu items include deer stew, both Hungarian and Viennese goulash, sauerkraut garni, *Wiener Schnitzel,* and venison steak.

Wein-Comptoir. Bäckerstrasse 6. ☎ **01/51-21-760.** Reservations recommended. Main courses 130–290S ($10.40–$23.20). AE, DC, MC, V. Mon–Sat 6pm–midnight. U-Bahn: Stephansplatz. AUSTRIAN/INTERNATIONAL.

This is one of the most charming wine-tavern restaurants in the Old Town. You can sample a wide selection of wines, mostly Austrian, on the street level, or descend into the brick-vaulted cellar, where tables are arranged for meals. Here, waiters run up and down the steep steps, serving not only wine but also standard Austrian and international fare. Since most dishes are cooked to order, prepare yourself for a long wait. Full meals might include breast of venison in a goose-liver sauce, *Tafelspitz* (boiled beef), or breast of pheasant with bacon, and such vegetarian dishes as spinach dumplings with fresh Parmesan and hot butter sauce.

NEAR STADTPARK
Very Expensive
Steirereck. Rasumofskygasse 2. ☎ **01/713-31-68.** Reservations required. Main courses 248–395S ($19.85–$31.60); 3-course set-price lunch 395S ($31.60); 5-course set-price dinner 880S ($70.40). AE, V. Mon–Fri 10:30am–3pm and 7pm–midnight. Closed holidays and weekends. Bus: 4. Tram: N. VIENNESE/AUSTRIAN.

Steirereck means "corner of Styria," which is exactly what Heinz and Margarethe Reitbauer have created in the rustic decor of this intimate restaurant. Near the Danube Canal, southeast of Bahnhof Wien Mitte, it is considered by some Viennese to be the best in the city. The Reitbauers offer both traditional Viennese dishes and "new Austrian" selections. You might begin with a caviar-semolina dumpling, roasted turbot with fennel (served as an appetizer), or the most elegant and expensive item of all, goose-liver *Steirereck*. Enticing main courses are asparagus with pigeon and saddle of lamb for two diners. The menu is wisely limited and well prepared, changing daily depending on the fresh produce available at the market.

Moderate
Kardos. Dominikaner Bastei 8. ☎ **01/512-69-49.** Reservations recommended. Main courses 108–220S ($8.65–$17.60). AE, DC, MC, V. Tues–Sat 11am–2:30pm and 6–11pm. Closed Aug. U-Bahn: Schwedenplatz. HUNGARIAN/SLOVENIAN/BALKAN.

This restaurant specializes in the strong flavors and mixed grills of the Great Hungarian Plain, turning out such traditional specialties as *Palatschinken Hortobagy,* fish soup in the style of Lake Balaton, piquant little rolls known as *grammel* seasoned with minced pork and spices, and a choice of grilled meats. In an atmospheric cellar, the restaurant is decorated with bold colors and Hungarian accessories, sort of Gypsy *schmaltz.* There's sometimes a strolling violinist during the winter months.

COFFEEHOUSES & CAFES

✪ **Café Demel.** Kohlmarkt 14. ☎ **01/533-55-16.** Daily 10am–7pm. U-Bahn: Stephansplatz. Bus: 1A or 2A.

The windows of this much-venerated establishment are filled with fanciful spun-sugar creations of characters from folk legends. Perhaps Lady Godiva's 5-foot tresses shelter a miniature village of Viennese dancers. You can most definitely expect to see St. Nicholas at Christmastime. Inside you find a splendidly baroque Viennese landmark with black marble tables, cream-colored embellished plaster walls, elaborate half paneling, and crystal chandeliers covered with white milk-glass globes. Dozens of different pastries are offered every day, including cream-filled horns (*Gugelhupfs*). Coffee costs 50S ($4), and those tempting cakes begin at 50AS ($4).

Café Dommayer. Dommayergasse 1. ☎ **01/877-54-65.** Mon–Sat 7am–midnight. Tram: U4 (green line) to Schönbrunn.

One of the city's most atmospheric cafes, not far from Schönbrunn Palace, this is where both Johann Strausses (father and son alike) played waltzes for members of Vienna's *grande bourgeoisie.* Established in 1787 by a local writer, the cafe still has an old-world style, with Biedermeier accessories set amid silver samovars, formally dressed waiters (many of whom are short-tempered), and a chic and very Viennese clientele. A special Viennese coffee costs 38S ($3.05).

Café Landtmann. Dr.-Karl-Lueger-Ring 4. ☎ **01/532-06-21.** Daily 8am–midnight. Tram: 1, 2, or D.

One of the Ring's great cafes, this spot has a history dating to the 1880s. Overlooking the Burgtheater, it has traditionally drawn a mixture of politicians, journalists, and actors. It was also Freud's favorite. The original chandeliers and the pre-war chairs have been refurbished. We highly suggest spending an hour or so here, chatting, perusing the newspapers, sipping on coffee, or planning the day's itinerary. A large coffee costs 42S ($3.35), and full meals are available. A set-price lunch costs 110S ($8.80). Meals are served daily from 11:30am to 3pm and 5 to 11pm.

SEEING THE SIGHTS OF VIENNA

The Inner City (*Innere Stadt*) is the tangle of streets from which medieval Vienna grew. Much of your exploration will be confined to this area, encircled by the boulevards of "The Ring" and the Danube Canal. The main street of the Inner City is **Kärntnerstrasse,** most of which is a pedestrian mall. The heart of Vienna is **Stephansplatz,** the square on which St. Stephan's Cathedral sits.

SIGHTSEEING SUGGESTIONS FOR FIRST-TIME VISITORS

If You Have 1 Day   Begin at **St. Stephan's Cathedral,** and from here, branch out for a tour of the enveloping Inner City, or Old Town. But first climb the tower of the cathedral for a panoramic view of the city (you can also take an elevator to the top). Stroll down **Kärntnerstrasse,** the main shopping artery, and enjoy the 11am ritual of coffee in a grand cafe, such as the **Café Imperial.** In the afternoon, visit **Schönbrunn,** seat of the Hapsburg dynasty. Have dinner in a typical Viennese wine tavern.

If You Have 2 Days   On the second day, explore other major attractions of Vienna, including the **Hofburg,** the **Imperial Crypts,** and the **Kunsthistorisches Museum.** In the evening, attend an opera performance or some other musical event.

If You Have 3 Days   On your third day, try to attend a performance of either the **Spanish Riding School** (Tuesday through Saturday) or the **Vienna Boys' Choir** (singing at masses on Sunday). Explore the **Belvedere Palace** and its art galleries; stroll through the **Naschmarkt,** the city's major open-air market; and cap the day by a visit to one or more of Vienna's cabarets, wine bars, or beer cellars.

If You Have 4 Days   On day 4, take a tour of the **Vienna Woods** and then visit **Klosterneuburg Abbey,** the major abbey of Austria. Return to Vienna for an evening of fun.

EXPLORING THE HOFBURG PALACE COMPLEX

The winter palace of the Hapsburgs, the Hofburg (☎ 01/587-55-54), with its vast, impressive courtyards, sits in the heart of Vienna. To reach it (you can hardly miss it), head up Kohlmarkt to Michaelerplatz 1, Burgring. You can also take the U-Bahn to Herrengasse, or else tram no. 1, 2, D, or J to Burgring.

This complex of imperial edifices, the first of which was constructed in 1279, grew and grew as the empire did, so that today the Hofburg Palace is virtually a city within a city. The palace, which has withstood three major sieges and a great fire, is called simply *die Burg,* or "the palace," by Viennese. Of its more than 2,600 rooms, fewer than two dozen are open to the public.

✪ **Schatzkammer (Imperial Treasury).** Hofburg, Schweizerhof. ☎ **01/533-79-31.** Admission 80S ($6.40) adults; 50S ($4) children, senior citizens, and students. Wed–Mon 10am–6pm.

The Schatzkammer is the greatest treasury in the world. It's divided into two sections: the Imperial Profane and the Sacerdotal Treasuries. One part displays the crown jewels and an assortment of imperial riches, and the other contains ecclesiastical treasures. The most outstanding exhibit in the Schatzkammer is the imperial crown, which dates from 962. It's so big that, even though padded, it was likely to slip down over the ears of a Hapsburg at a coronation. Studded with emeralds, sapphires, diamonds, and rubies, this 1,000-year-old symbol of sovereignty is a priceless treasure. Also on display is the imperial crown worn by the Hapsburg rulers from 1804 to the end of the empire. You'll see the saber of Charlemagne and the holy lance from the 9th century. Among great Schatzkammer prizes is the Burgundian Treasure seized in the 15th century, rich in vestments, oil paintings, gems, and robes.

✪ **Kaiserappartements (Imperial Apartments).** Michaeler Platz 1. ☎ **01/533-75-70.** Admission 80S ($6.40) adults, 60S ($4.80) students under 25, 40S ($3.20) children 6–15, free for children under 6. Daily 9am–4:30pm.

On the first floor of the Hofburg complex are the Kaiserappartements, where the emperors and their wives and children lived. To reach these apartments, you enter through the rotunda of Michaelerplatz. The apartments are richly decorated with tapestries, many from Aubusson. The Imperial Silver and Porcelain Collection descends directly from the Hapsburg household and provides an insight into their court etiquette. Most of these pieces are from the 18th and 19th centuries. Leopoldinischer Trakt, or Leopold's apartments, date from the 17th century. These Imperial Apartments seem more closely associated with Franz Joseph than with any other emperor, a result of his incredibly long reign.

☼ Hofmusikkapelle Wien (Vienna Boys' Choir). Die Burgkapelle, (Palace Chapel), Hofburg (entrance on Schweizerhof). ☎ **01/533-99-27.** Tickets, 60–350S ($4.80–$28). Masses (performances) held only Jan–June and mid-Sept until the end of Dec, Sun and holidays at 9:15am.

Construction of this Gothic chapel began in 1447 during the reign of Emperor Frederick III, but it has been massively renovated since. From 1449 it was the private chapel of the royal family. Today the Burgkapelle is the home of the Hofmusikkapelle Wein, an ensemble consisting of the Vienna Boys' Choir and members of the Vienna State Opera chorus and orchestra. Written applications for reserved seats should be sent at least 8 weeks in advance; use a credit card, and do not send cash or checks. For reservations, write to Verwaltung der Hofmusikkapelle, Hofburg, 1010 Vienna. If you didn't plan in advance, a limited number of tickets are sold at the Burgkapelle box office every Friday from 3 to 5pm on. Get there early, as the line starts forming before the box office even opens. For those with strong legs and empty wallets, standing-room tickets are free.

Neue Burg. Heldenplatz. ☎ **01/521-770.** Admission to Hofjagd and Rüstkammer, Musikinstrumentensammlung, and Ephesos-Museum, 30S ($2.40) adults, 15S ($1.20) children. Hofjagd and Rüstkammer, Musikinstrumentensammlung, and Ephesos-Museum, Wed–Mon 10am–6pm.

The last addition to the Hofburg complex was the Neue Burg, or New Château. Construction started in 1881 and continued until work was halted in 1913. The palace was the residence of Archduke Franz Ferdinand, the nephew and heir apparent of Francis Joseph, whose assassination at Sarajevo set off the chain of events that led to World War I. The arms and armor collection is second only to that of the Metropolitan Museum of Art in New York. It's in the **Hofjagd and Rüstkammer,** on the second floor of the New Château. On display are crossbows, swords, helmets, and pistols, plus armor, mostly the property of the emperors and princes of the House of Hapsburg. Another section, the **Musikinstrumentensammlung** (☎ **01/521-77-470**), is devoted to musical instruments, mainly from the 17th and 18th centuries, with some from the 16th. In the **Ephesos-Museum (Museum of Ephesian Sculpture),** Neue Burg 1, Heldenplatz, with an entrance behind the Prince Eugene monument (☎ **01/521-77-0**), you'll see the Parthian monument, the most important relief frieze from Roman times ever found in Asia Minor.

Graphische Sammlung Albertina. Augustinerstrasse 1. ☎ **01/53-483.** Admission 45S ($3.60) adults, 20S ($1.60) students, free for children under 11. Tues–Sun 10am–5pm.

The development of graphic arts since the 14th century is explored at this Hofburg museum. Housing one of the world's greatest graphics collections, the museum was named for a son-in-law of Maria Theresa. The most outstanding treasure in the Albertina is the Dürer collection, although what you usually see are copies—the originals are shown only on special occasions. See, in particular, Dürer's *Praying Hands,* which has been reproduced throughout the world.

Augustinerkirche. Augustinerstrasse 3. ☎ **01/533-70-99.** Guided tour, 10S (80¢) contribution. To arrange a visit, contact the church office, Pfarre St. Augustin, Augustinerstrasse 3, or the music office (☎ 01/533-69-63). The most convenient—and dramatic—time to visit is Sun 11am, when a high mass is celebrated, with choir, soloists, and orchestra.

This church was constructed in the 14th century as part of the Hofburg complex to serve as the parish church of the imperial court. In the latter part of the 18th century it was stripped of its baroque embellishments and the original Gothic features were revealed. The Chapel of St. George, dating from 1337, is entered from the right aisle. The royal weddings of Maria Theresa and François of Lorraine (1736), Marie

Antoinette and Louis XVI of France (1770), Marie-Louise of Austria to Napoléon (1810, but by proxy—he didn't show up), and Francis Joseph and Elizabeth of Bavaria (1854) were all held here.

✪ **Spanische Hofreitschule.** Michaelerplatz 1, Hofburg. ☎ **01/533-90-32.** Regular performances, 250–900S ($20–$72) seats, 200S ($16) standing room. Training performances with music, 250S ($20). (Children under 3 not admitted, but children 3–6 attend free with adults.) Training session, 100S ($8) adults, 30S ($2.40) children. Regular performances, Apr–June and Sept, Sun 10:45am, most Weds 7pm. Training performances with music, Mar and Oct–Dec, Sun at 10:45am; Apr–June and Sept, Sat at 10am.

The Spanish Riding School is in the white, crystal-chandeliered ballroom in an 18th-century building of the Hofburg complex, designed by J. E. Fischer von Erlach. We always marvel at the skill and beauty of the sleek Lippizaner stallions as their adept trainers put them through their paces in a show that hasn't changed for 4 centuries.

Reservations for performances must be made in advance, as early as possible. Order your tickets for the Sunday and Wednesday shows in writing to Spanische Reitschule, Hofburg, 1010 Vienna (fax 01/535-01-86), or through a travel agency in Vienna. (Tickets for Saturday shows can be ordered only through a travel agency.) Tickets for training sessions with no advance reservations can be purchased at the entrance Innerer Burghof-In der Burg.

Lippizzaner Museum. Reitschulgasse 2, Stallburg. ☎ **01/526-41-84-30.** Admission 50S ($4) adults, 35S ($2.80) children. Daily 9am–6pm. U-Bahn: Stephansplatz.

The latest attraction at Hofburg Palace is this newly opened museum near the stables of the famous white stallions. This permanent exhibition begins with the historic inception of the Spanish Riding School in the 16th century and extends to the stallions' near destruction in the closing weeks of World War II. Exhibits, including paintings, historic engravings, drawings, photographs, uniforms and bridles, plus video and film presentations, bring to life the history of the Spanish Riding School, offering an insight into the breeding and training of these champion horses. Visitors to the museum can see through a window into the stallions' stables while they are being fed and saddled.

OTHER TOP ATTRACTIONS IN THE INNER CITY

✪ **Dompfarre St. Stephan (St. Stephan's Cathedral).** Stephansplatz 1. ☎ **01/515-52.** Cathedral, free; tour of catacombs, 40S ($3.20) adults, 15S ($1.20) children under 14. Guided tour of cathedral, 40AS ($3.20) adults, 15AS ($1.20) children under 14. North Tower, 40AS ($3.20) adults, 15AS ($1.20) children under 15; South Tower, 30S ($2.40) adults, 20S ($1.60) students, 10S (80¢) children under 15. Evening tours, including tour of the roof, 130S ($10.40) adults, 50S ($4) children under 15. Cathedral, daily 6am–10pm except times of service. Tour of catacombs, Mon–Sat at 10, 11, and 11:30am, and 2, 2:30, 3:30, 4, and 4:30pm; Sun at 2, 2:30, 3:30, 4, and 4:30pm. North Tower Apr–Sept daily 9am–6pm, Oct–Mar daily 8:30am–5pm. South Tower daily 9am–5:30pm. Guided tour of cathedral Mon–Sat at 10:30am and 3pm, Sun 3pm. Special evening tour Sat 7pm (May–Sept). Bus: 1A, 2A, or 3A. U-Bahn: Stephansplatz.

A basilica built on the site of a Romanesque sanctuary, the cathedral was founded in the 12th century in what was, even then, the town's center. Stephansdom was virtually destroyed in a 1258 fire that swept through Vienna, and toward the dawn of the 14th century the ruins of the Romanesque basilica gave way to a Gothic building. The cathedral suffered terribly in the Turkish siege of 1683, then stood in peace until the Russian bombardments of 1945. Reopened in 1948 after restoration, the cathedral is today one of the greatest Gothic structures in Europe, rich in wood carvings, altars, sculptures, and paintings. The steeple, rising some 450 feet, has come to symbolize the very spirit of Vienna. You can climb the 343-step south tower, which dominates the

Viennese skyline and offers a view of the Vienna Woods. Called *Alter Steffl* (Old Steve), the tower with its needlelike spire was built between 1350 and 1433. The North Tower (Nordturm), reached by elevator, was never finished to match the South Tower, but was crowned in the Renaissance style in 1579. The view from here sweeps over the city and the Danube.

Gemäldegalerie Akademie der Bildenden Künste (Academy of Fine Arts). Schiller-platz 3. ☎ **01/58-816.** Admission 50S ($4) adults or children. Tues–Sun 10am–4pm. U-Bahn: Karlsplatz.

It's a sin to leave Vienna without going to the painting gallery in the Academy of Fine Arts to see the *Last Judgment* triptych by the incomparable Hieronymus Bosch. In this work, the artist conjured up all the demons of the nether regions for a terrifying view of the suffering and depravity of humankind. There are many 15th-century Dutch and Flemish paintings and several works by Botticelli and Lucas Cranach the Elder. The academy is also noted for its 17th-century art by Van Dyck, Rembrandt, and a host of other artists.

✪ **Kunsthistorisches Museum (Museum of Fine Arts).** Maria-Theresien-Platz, Burgring 5. ☎ **01/525-24-0.** Admission 100S ($8) adults, 70S ($5.60) students and senior citizens, free for children under 11. Tues–Sun 10am–6pm. U-Bahn: Mariahilferstrasse. Tram: 52, 58, D, or J.

Across from the Hofburg Palace, this huge building houses many of the fabulous art collections gathered by the Hapsburgs as they added new territories to their empire. A highlight is a fine collection of ancient Egyptian and Greek art. The museum also has works by many of the greatest European masters, such as Velázquez and Titian.

ATTRACTIONS OUTSIDE THE INNER CITY

✪ **Schönbrunn Palace.** Schönbrunner Schlossstrasse. ☎ **01/811-13.** Admission 120S ($9.60) adults, 105S ($8.40) students under 25, 60S ($4.80) children 6–15, free for children under 6. Apartments, Apr–Oct daily 8:30am–5pm; Nov–Mar daily 9am–4:30pm. U-Bahn: U4 (green line) to Schönbrunn.

A Hapsburg palace of 1,441 rooms, Schönbrunn was designed and built between 1696 and 1712 by those masters of the baroque, the von Erlachs, who were ordered to create a palace whose grandeur would surpass that of Versailles. However, Austria's treasury, drained by the cost of wars, would not support the ambitious undertaking, and the original plans were never carried out.

When Maria Theresa became empress she changed the original plans, and the Schönbrunn we see today is her conception, with its delicate rococo touches designed for her by Austrian Nikolaus Pacassi. It was the imperial summer palace during Maria Theresa's 40-year reign, from 1740 to 1780, the scene of great ceremonial balls and lavish banquets, and the fabulous receptions held here during the Congress of Vienna.

The State Apartments are the most stunning. Much of the interior ornamentation is in 23½-karat gold. Of the 40 rooms you can visit, particularly fascinating is the grandest rococo salon in the world, the "Room of Millions," decorated with Indian and Persian miniatures.

Österreichische Galerie Belvedere. Prinz-Eugen-Strasse 27. ☎ **01/795-57.** Admission 60S ($4.80) adults, 30S ($2.40) children. Tues–Sun 10am–5pm. Tram: D to Schloss Belvedere.

Belvedere Palace was designed by Johann Lukas von Hildebrandt, who was the last major Austrian baroque architect. Built as a summer home for Prince Eugene of Savoy, the Belvedere consists of two palatial buildings. The pond reflects the sky and palace buildings, which are made up of a series of interlocking cubes, and the interior is dominated by two great, flowing staircases.

Unteres Belvedere (Lower Belvedere), with its entrance at Rennweg 6A, was constructed from 1714 to 1716, and contains the Gold Salon, one of the palace's most beautiful rooms. It also houses the Barockmuseum (Museum of Baroque Art). Oberes Belvedere (Upper Belvedere) was started in 1721 and completed in 1723. It contains the Gallery of 19th- and 20th-Century Art, with an outstanding collection of the works of Gustav Klimt (1862–1918); be sure to see his extraordinary *Judith*. The Museum of Medieval Austrian Art is in the Orangery.

ORGANIZED TOURS

Wiener Rundfahrten (Vienna Sightseeing Tours), Stelzhamergasse 4–11 (☎ 01/712-468-30; U-Bahn: Landstrasse Wien Mitte), offers some of the best organized tours of Vienna and its surroundings. Tours depart from a signposted area in front of the Vienna State Opera House, and include running commentary in both German and English.

CITY TOURS   The historical city tour costs 390S ($31.20) for adults and is free for children 12 and under. It's ideal for visitors who are pressed for time and yet want to be shown the major (and most frequently photographed) monuments of Vienna. It takes you past the historic buildings of Ringstrasse—the State Opera, Hofburg Palace, museums, Parliament, City Hall, Burgtheater, the University, and the Votive Church—into the heart of Vienna. Tours leave the State Opera daily at 10:30 and 11:45am and at 3 and 4:30pm.

The company's **"Grand City Tour,"** a bus tour with commentary that includes an exterior view of the Belvedere Palace and a walk through Schönbrunn Palace, departs daily from the State Opera House at 9:15am and 2:15pm. From April to November, an additional tour is offered at 10:15am. The tour costs 390S ($31.20) for adults and 160S ($12.80) for children under 12.

TOURS OUTSIDE THE CITY   Looking to travel farther afield? Vienna Sightseeing's bus tour to the **"Vienna Woods and Mayerling"** includes a tour of Baden, a spa once favored by the Hapsburg aristocracy, and a stop at Mayerling, site of the still-unexplained death of Crown Prince Rudolf, the only son of Austria's last emperor, Franz Joseph. The tour is long on schmaltz and nostalgia and costs 480S ($38.40) for adults and 160S ($12.80) for children.

If you're interested in visiting **Budapest,** once the co-capital of the Austro-Hungarian empire, the company offers a full-day bus tour there daily between April and October. The tour departs at 8am, returns at 8:30pm, and includes lunch and a 3-hour bus tour of Budapest's most prominent monuments. The cost is 1,290S ($103.20) for adults and 800S ($64) for children. Between November and March, the day trip to Budapest is offered only on Tuesday, Thursday, and Saturday.

THE SHOPPING SCENE

Vienna is known for some excellent goods, including petit-point items and hand-painted porcelain. Also popular is *loden,* the boiled and rolled wool fabric made into overcoats, suits, and hats, as well as knitted sweaters. The most famous shopping streets are in the city center (First District), including **Kärntnerstrasse, Graben, Kohlmarkt,** and **Rotensturmstrasse.** Other shopping streets include Mariahilfer-strasse, Favoritenstrasse, and Landstrasser Hauptstrasse.

Albin Denk, Graben 13 (☎ 01/512-44-39), is the oldest continuously operating porcelain store in Vienna, in business since 1702. You'll see thousands of objects from Meissen, Dresden, and other regions.

The state-owned auction house, **Dorotheum,** Dorotheergasse 17. (☎ 01/515-60-0), is the oldest in Europe, dating from 1707, when it was founded by

Emperor Joseph I as an auction house where impoverished aristocrats could fairly—and anonymously—sell their heirlooms. Today the Dorotheum is also the scene of many art auctions. If you're interested in what's being auctioned off, you give a small fee to a *sensal*, one of the licensed bidders, and he or she will bid in your name. Auctions are usually conducted every Monday to Saturday at 2pm, although in particularly busy periods, additional auctions might be held at 11am and at 3pm. Viewings of the pieces about to go on the block are possible every Monday to Friday from 10am to 6pm, and every Saturday from 9am to 5pm.

Loden Plankl, Michaelerplatz 6 (☎ **01/533-80-32**), established in 1830 by the Plankl family, is the oldest and most reputable outlet in Vienna for traditional Austrian clothing. You'll find Austrian loden coats, shoes, trousers, dirndls, jackets, lederhosen, and suits for men, women, and children. The building, located opposite the Hofburg, dates from the 17th century.

The three-floor ✪ **Ö.W. (Österreichische Werkstatten),** Kärntnerstrasse 6 (☎ **01/ 512-24-18**), sells hundreds of handmade art objects from Austria. Some 200 leading artists and craftspeople throughout the country organized this cooperative to showcase their wares. It's easy to find, only half a minute's walk from St. Stephan's Cathedral.

VIENNA AFTER DARK

The best source of information about what's happening on the cultural scene is *Wien Monatsprogramm,* distributed free at tourist information offices and at many hotel reception desks. *Die Presse,* the Viennese daily, publishes a special magazine in its Thursday edition outlining the major cultural events for the coming week. It's in German, but might still be helpful.

THE PERFORMING ARTS

TICKETS TO THE AUSTRIAN STATE THEATERS   Tickets and information for the four state theaters—the Staatsoper (State Opera), Burgtheater (National Theater), Volksoper, and the Akademietheater—can be obtained by calling a central office, ☎ **01/514-44-29-59,** Monday through Friday 8am to 5pm. The major season is from September to June. For all four theaters, box-office sales are made only 1 month before each performance at the **Bundestheaterkasse,** Goethegasse 1 (☎ **01/ 51-44-40**), open Monday to Friday 8am to 6pm, Saturday 9am to 2pm, and Sunday and holidays 9am to noon. Credit- and charge-card sales can be arranged by calling ☎ **01/513-15-13** Monday to Friday 10am to 6pm, Saturday and Sunday 10am to noon. Tickets for all state theater performances, including the opera, can also be obtained by writing to the **Österreichischer Bundestheaterverband,** Goethegasse 1, 1010 Vienna; orders must be received at least 3 weeks in advance of the performance to be booked. You can also fax for information and ticket requests at 01/514-44-2969.

Opera & Classical Music

Music is at the heart and soul of Viennese culture. This has been true for centuries, and the city continues to lure composers, musicians, and music lovers. Vienna's operas are presented in the quintessential opera house, one of the three most important in the world. Besides the world-renowned Vienna Philharmonic, Vienna is home to three other major orchestras: the Vienna Symphony, the ÖRF Symphony Orchestra, and the Niederösterreichische Tonkünstler. The Wiener Sympohniker (Vienna Symphony) performs in the **Konzerthaus,** Lothringerstrasse 20 (☎ **01/712-12-11**), a major concert hall with three auditoriums, also the venue for chamber music and other programs.

In summer when the state theaters are closed, the Vienna Opera Festival presents performances and movie screenings of highlights from past opera seasons. The venue is the plaza in front of City Hall, and everything is free.

Wine Tasting in the *Heurigen*

Heurigen are the Viennese wine taverns often celebrated in operettas, films, and song. *Heurigen* are found on the outskirts of Vienna, principally in Grinzing (the most popular district) and in Sievering, Neustift, Nussdorf, or Heiligenstadt. **Grinzing** lies at the edge of the Vienna Woods, a 15-minute drive northwest of the center. Take tram no. 38 to Grinzing.

Only 20 minutes from Vienna, ✪ **Weingut Wolff,** Rathstrasse 50, Neustift (☎ **01/440-37-27**), is one of the most enduring and beloved of Heurigen. Although aficionados claim the best Heurigen are "deep in the countryside" of Lower Austria, this one comes closest to offering an authentic experience near Vienna. In summer a flower-decked garden set against a backdrop of ancient vineyards beckons. You can really fill up here, with some of the best wursts (sausages) and roast meats (especially the delectable pork), as well as freshly made salads. Find a table under a cluster of grapes and sample the fruity young wines, especially the Chardonnay, Sylvaner, and Gruner Veltliner. The tavern is open from Monday to Saturday from 2pm to 1am and Sunday from 11am to 1am, with main courses ranging from 80 to 220S ($6.40 to $17.60).

Altes Presshaus, Cobenzigasse 15 (☎ **01/320-02-03**), was established in 1527, the oldest continuously operating *Heurige* in Grinzing, with an authentic cellar you might ask to visit. The place has a genuine, smoked-stained character with wood paneling and antique furniture. The garden terrace blossoms throughout the summer. Meals cost 150 to 350S ($12 to $28), with glasses of wine beginning at 30S ($2.40). Try such *Heurigen*-inspired fare as smoked pork shoulder, roast pork shank, sauerkraut, potatoes, and dumplings. Open March to December daily, 4pm to midnight.

Staatsoper (Vienna Opera). Opernring 2. ☎ **01/514-44-29-60.** Tickets 120–2,300S ($9.60–$184). Tours 2 to 5 times daily, 40S ($3.20) per person; tour times are posted on a board outside the entrance. U-Bahn: Karlsplatz.

When the opera was bombed into a shell in World War II, the Viennese made its restoration their top priority, despite other pressing needs, finishing it in time for the country's celebration of independence from occupying forces in 1955. A repertoire of some 40 works is performed every season, with the Vienna Philharmonic in the pit and leading international stars on the stage. In their day, Gustav Mahler and Richard Strauss worked here as directors. The new year usually starts off with a gala performance of *Die Fledermaus.*

Wiener Philharmoniker (Vienna Philharmonic). Karlsplatz 6. ☎ **01/505-81-90.** U-Bahn: Karlsplatz.

When the prestigious Philharmonic is not traveling throughout the world, its home is the **Musikverein.** Built between 1867 and 1869, the suitably ornate concert hall is the site of the famous New Year's Day concert, broadcast internationally.

Theater

For performances in English, head to **Vienna's English Theatre,** at Josefsgasse 12 (☎ **01/402-12-60** or 01/402-82-84; U-Bahn: Rathaus).

Burgtheater (National Theater). Dr.-Karl-Lueger-Ring 2. ☎ **01/514-44-2959.** Tickets 180–480S ($14.40–$38.40). Tram: J. Bus: 13A.

Burgtheater produces classical and modern plays. Even if you don't understand German, you might want to attend a performance here, especially if a familiar Shakespeare play is being staged. This is one of Europe's premier repertory theaters; it's the dream of every German-speaking actor to appear here.

NIGHTCLUBS, CABARETS, BARS & CASINOS

✪ **Loos American Bar.** Kärntnerdurchgang 10. ☎ **01/512-3283.** No cover. U-Bahn: Stephansplatz.

This very dark, sometimes mysterious bar was designed by the noteworthy architect Adolf Loos in 1908. Today it welcomes singles and couples who tend to be bilingual and very hip, and more often then not, part of the arts and media scene. Walls, floors, and ceilings are sheathed in layers of dark marble and black onyx, making it one of the most expensive small-scale decors in the city. The bartender's specialties include 15 kinds of martinis, plus 11 kinds of Manhattans.

Rhiz Bar Modern. Llerchenfeldergürtel, 37–38 Stadtbahnbögen. ☎ **01/409-2505.** No cover. U-Bahn: Josefstädterstrasse.

Hip, multicultural, and sophisticated, this bar is where you should head when you've had your fill of Vienna's Hapsburg nostalgia and crystal chandeliers. Mozart definitely didn't play here. It's nestled into the vaulted, turn-of-the-century niches created by the trusses of the U-6 subway line, abut 2½ miles west of St. Stephan's cathedral, a few blocks west of the Ring. Here, within the once-grimy architecture of the Industrial Revolution, a team of entrepreneurs have installed stainless-steel ventilation ducts, a sophisticated stereo system, and a TV camera that constantly broadcasts images of its trendy clientele over the Internet every night between 10pm and 3am. (Its home page is www.rhiz.org.)

St. Urbani-Keller. Am Hof 12. ☎ **01/533-91-02.** No cover. U-Bahn: Stephansplatz or Herrengasse.

Named after the patron saint of wine making, this historic cellar has been open since 1906. Many of the artifacts inside, from the German Romantic paneling to the fanciful wrought-iron lighting fixtures, were designed by one of Austria's most famous architects, Walcher von Molthein. The cellar has brick vaulting dating from the 13th century and sections of solid Roman walls you can admire while listening to the nightly folk music. Open Monday to Friday 11am to 11pm and Saturday and Sunday 4 to 10pm. Watch your step on the way up or down.

Volksgarten. Entrances from the Heldenplatz and from Burgring 1. ☎ **01/533-05-180.** Cover 70S ($5.60) for the evergreen music (8pm–2am nightly), 80–150S ($6.40–$12) for the disco music (nightly 11pm–4am). U-Bahn: Volkstheatre.

This is the largest and most diverse entertainment complex within Vienna's Ring. You'll find a series of restaurants, bars, and clubs within a labyrinth of rooms and outdoor spaces that form one happy-go-lucky maze. Many visitors prefer the area with the evergreen music, where everything from Tyrolean or Bavarian oom-pah-pah music alternates with rock from the 1950s to the 1970s. A restaurant on the premises is open continuously from 11am to midnight.

Casino Wien. Esterházy Palace, Kärntnerstrasse 41. ☎ **01/512-48-36.** No cover. You need to show your passport to enter. Tram: 1, 2, or D.

Set on the city's main shopping thoroughfare, a 5-minute walk from the Bristol Hotel, this is the only casino in Vienna. You'll find tables for French and American roulette, blackjack, poker, a dice game known as 7-11, and chemin de fer, as well as the ever-present slot machines and a bar. Men are encouraged to wear jackets and ties. Open daily 11am to 3am, with the gaming tables available at 3pm.

Gay Bars

Alfi's Goldener Spiegel, Linke Wienzeile 46 (entrance on Stiegengasse; ☎ **01/ 56-66-608**), is one of the most popular gay spots in Vienna, attracting a lot of foreigners. It's a combination restaurant and bar. Food items, which include well-seasoned and well-prepared versions of Wiener schnitzel, are served Wednesday to Monday from 7pm to 2am.

Alte Lampe, Heumühlgasse 13 (☎ **01/567-34-54**), is the oldest gay bar in Vienna, established in the 1960s. Today's patrons listen to the same schmaltzy piano music that has been played here for years. Open daily 9pm to 4am.

Frauencafé, Langegasse 11 (☎ **01/406-37-54**), is exactly what its name would imply: a politically conscious cafe for lesbian and (to a lesser degree) heterosexual women who appreciate the company of other women. Established in 1977 in cramped quarters in a century-old building, it's filled with magazines, newspapers, modern paintings, and a clientele of Austrian and foreign women. Open Tuesday through Saturday; in summer from 8pm to 1am, and in winter from 7pm to 1am.

DAY TRIPS ALONG THE DANUBE

KLOSTERNEUBURG   On the northwestern outskirts of Vienna, this old market town is the site of **Klosterneuburg Abbey (Stift Klosterneuburg),** Stiftsplatz 1 (☎ **02243/411-0**), the most historically significant abbey in Austria. It's visited not only for its history but for its art treasures, including the world-famous enamel altar of Nikolaus of Verdun, a work dating back to 1181. The monastery also boasts the largest private library in Austria, with more than 1,250 handwritten books and many antique paintings.

The monastery can be visited only as part of guided tours; most are conducted in German with occasional brief translations into English. They're given daily from 9am to noon and 1:30 to 4:30pm. The cost is 60S ($4.80) for adults or children.

Getting There   Motorists can take Route 14 northwest of Vienna, following the south bank of the Danube. Otherwise, take the U-Bahn from the Westbahnhof heading for Heiligenstadt, where you can then board a bus marked Klosterneuburg.

HERZOGENBURG MONASTERY   Founded in the early 12th century by a German bishop from Passau, this Augustinian monastery, 3130 Herzogenburg (☎ **02782/ 83312-0**), lies 7 miles south of Traismauer and 10 miles south of the Danube.

The present complex of buildings that form the church and the abbey was reconstructed in the baroque style. That master of baroque, Fischer von Erlach, designed some of it. Outstanding features include the high altar, painted by Daniel Gran, and the series of 16th-century wood paintings. The monastery is known for its library containing more than 80,000 works.

Entrance costs 50S ($4) for adults, 10S (80¢) for students, and 40S ($3.20) for those over 65. You can wander around alone or participate in a guided tour, departing daily at 9, 10, and 11am, and at 1, 2, 3, 4, and 5pm. The attraction is open only April to October daily from 9am to 6pm. There's a wine tavern in the complex serving Austrian specialties and wine made from local grapes.

Getting There   From Vienna, head west of the city via Autobahn A-1, following the signs to Salzburg and Linz, exiting at the signposted turnoff for Heiligenkreuz.

KREMS   In the eastern part of the Wachau on the left bank of the Danube lies Krems, a city some 1,000 years old. Krems is a mellow town of courtyards, old churches, and ancient houses in the heart of vineyard country, with some partially preserved town walls. Just as the Viennese flock to Grinzing and other suburbs to sample new wine in *Heurigen,* so the people of the Wachau come here to taste the vintners' products, which appear in Krems earlier in the year.

The most interesting part of Krems today is what was once the little village of Stein. Narrow streets are terraced above the river, and the single main street, **Steinlanderstrasse,** is flanked with houses, many from the 16th century. **Grosser Passauerhof,** Steinlanderstrasse 76, is a Gothic structure decorated with an oriel. Another house, at Steinlanderstrasse 84, once the imperial tollhouse, combines Byzantine and Venetian elements among other architectural influences.

Pfarrkirche St. Veith (parish church) stands in the center of town at the Rathaus, reached by going along either Untere Landstrasse or Obere Landstrasse. Rich with gilt and statuary, it's the town's most visible church and the ecclesiastical centerpiece of the local parish.

Wein Stadt Museum Krems (Historical Museum of Krems), Körnermarkt 14 (☎ 02732/801-567), is in a restored Gothic-style Dominican monastery. It has a gallery displaying the paintings of Martin Johann Schmidt, a noted 18th-century artist better known as Kremser Schmidt. Admission is 40S ($3.20) for access to both areas of the museum. The museum is open March to November, Tuesday to Sunday 1 to 6pm.

Getting There   Krems is 50 miles west of Vienna and 18 miles north of St. Pölten. From Vienna, drive north along Autobahn A-22 until it splits into three roads near the town of Stockerau. Once there, drive due west along Route 3, following the signs into Krems.

Trains depart from both the Wien Nord Station and from the Wien Franz-Josefs Bahnhof for Krems every 2 hours daily from 5am until around 8:30pm. Many are direct, although some require a transfer in the railway junctions of Absdorf-Hippersdorf or St. Pölten. The trip takes 1 to 1½ hours. Call ☎ 01/17-17 for schedules.

During the warm-weather months, between mid-May and late September, **river cruisers** owned by the DDSG-Donaureisen Shipping Line depart westward from Vienna every Sunday at 8:30am en route to Passau, in Germany. They arrive upstream in Tulln around 11:15am, and then continue westward to Krems, arriving there around 1:40pm. For more information, call the shipping line in Vienna (☎ 01/588-800) or the tourist office in either Tulln (Albrechtsgasse 32; ☎ 02272/658-36) or Krems (Undstrasse 6; ☎ 02732/82676).

DÜRNSTEIN   Less than 5 miles west of Krems is the loveliest town along the Danube, Dürnstein, which draws throngs of tour groups in summer. Terraced vineyards mark this as a Danube wine town, and the town's fortified walls are partially preserved.

The **ruins of a castle fortress,** 520 feet above the town, are linked to the Crusades. Here Richard the Lion-Hearted of England was held prisoner in 1193. You can visit the ruins if you don't mind a vigorous climb (allow an hour). The castle isn't much, but the view of Dürnstein and the Wachau is more than worth the effort.

The 15th-century **Pfarrkirche (parish church)** also merits a visit. The building was originally an Augustinian monastery, reconstructed in the baroque style; the church tower is the finest baroque example in the whole country.

Getting There   Motorists can take Route 3 west from Krems. **Train** travel to Dürnstein from Vienna requires a transfer in Krems (see above). In Krems, trains depart approximately every 2 hours on routes that parallel the northern bank of the Danube on their way to Linz. These departures connect with trains from Vienna. Call ☎ 01/17-17 in Vienna for information.

The Danube Valley

About eight **buses** a day travel between Krems and Dürnstein, some of which coordinate with the arrival time of one of the many daily trains from Vienna. The bus trip between Krems and Dürnstein takes 20 minutes.

MELK   Finally, you arrive at one of the greatest sights in Austria, or in the words of Empress Maria Theresa, "If I had never come here, I would have regretted it." Some 55 miles west of Vienna, on the right bank of the Danube, Melk marks the western terminus of the Wachau, lying upstream from Krems.

Melk's major attractions are the **Melk Abbey,** Dietmayerstrasse 1 (☎ **02752/ 523-12**), one of the finest baroque buildings in the world, and the **Stiftskirche** (abbey church).

The rock-strewn bluff where the abbey stands overlooking the river was once the seat of the Babenbergs, who ruled Austria from 976 until the Hapsburgs took over. A center of learning and culture, the abbey's influence spread all over Austria, a fact familiar to readers of the *The Name of the Rose* by Umberto Eco. Most of the design of the present abbey was by the baroque architect Jakob Prandtauer. Its marble hall, called the Marmorsaal, contains pilasters coated in red marble. Despite all this adornment, the abbey takes second place in lavish glory to the **Stiftskirche,** the golden abbey church, damaged by fire in 1947 but now almost completely restored.

The abbey is open daily, with tours leaving at 15- to 20-minute intervals from 9am to 5pm (until 4pm October to March). Guides make efforts to translate into English a running commentary that is otherwise German. Adults pay 70S ($5.60) for guided tours and 55S ($4.40) for unguided tours; children 45S ($3.60) and 30S ($2.40).

Getting There Trains leave frequently from Vienna's Westbahnhof to Melk, with two brief stops; the trip takes about 1 hour. If you're going by car, take Autobahn A-1 55 miles west from Vienna.

2 Salzburg & Environs

A baroque city on the banks of the Salzach River, set against a mountain backdrop, Salzburg is the beautiful capital of the province of Land Salzburg. The city and the river were named after its early residents who earned their living in the salt mines. In this "heart of the heart of Europe," Mozart was born in 1756, and the composer's association with the city attracts hordes of tourists, and their dollars, to the area.

The **Old Town** lies on the left bank of the river, where a monastery and bishopric were founded in 700. From that start, Salzburg grew in power and prestige, becoming an archbishopric in 798. Under the prince-archbishops, the city became known as the "German Rome." Responsible for much of its architectural grandeur are those masters of the baroque, Fischer von Erlach and Lukas von Hildebrandt.

"The City of Mozart," "Silent Night," and *The Sound of Music*—Salzburg lives essentially off its rich past. Site of the world's snobbiest summer musical festival, it is a front-ranking cultural mecca for classical music year-round. Salzburg is set among alpine peaks and embraces both banks of the Salzach River, the perfect backdrop to perpetuate its romantic image.

One of Europe's greatest tourist capitals, most of Salzburg's day-to-day life spins around promoting its music and its other connections. Although *The Sound of Music* was filmed way back in 1964, this Julie Andrews blockbuster has become a cult attraction and is definitely alive and well in pre-millennium Salzburg. Ironically, Austria was the only country in the world where the musical failed when it first opened. It played for only a single week in Vienna, closing after audiences dwindled.

Only in Salzburg

Listening to Mozart It is said that at any time of the day or night in Salzburg, somebody somewhere is playing the music of Wolfgang Amadeus Mozart. It might be at a festival, an open-air concert, or, more romantically, an orchestra in a belle époque theater. Regardless, the sound of music drifting through the air of Salzburg is likely to have been created by this child prodigy. Mozart during most of his short life had little means of support, and regrettably he isn't around today to grow rich on the royalties. In spite of the success of *The Magic Flute* late in 1791, his career ended in obscurity. Try to arrange to hear the biggest "rock star" of the 18th century on his home turf where he knew such acclaim and so much pain. Where to go to hear this musical genius? A better question might be where not to go.

Cafe Sitting A time-honored tradition in this city of art and culture. Find a cafe table on Mozartplatz and, while nibbling on your strudel, enjoy the strains of a string orchestra. The coffeehouse is a Salzburg institution; you can sit for hour after hour talking to friends, reading magazines or newspapers supplied by the cafe, or even writing your memoirs. Of course, you can order coffee, too, in at least 20 or 30 different versions, everything from jet black to *weissen ohne* (with milk). Even the drinking water served with your coffee is the best in Europe: It comes ice-cold from the Alps.

Shopping Getreidegasse This is the main shopping street of Salzburg, one of the liveliest in Europe. With its towering, five- and six-story Altstadt houses, it's more like a movie set. But that merchandise in the jam-packed stores is real, albeit expensive. At any time of the day or night, people can be seen parading along the street, taking in the new window displays of fabulous things from all corners of the globe. The scene lasts well into the night.

Wandering Through Mirabell Gardens   You can live out a baroque fantasy by wandering through Fischer von Erlach's gardens on the right bank, with their classical statues and reflecting pools. It makes you wish you'd lived in a more elegant era. These are the gardens where Julie Andrews and her seven charges *do-re-mi*-ed in *The Sound of Music*. The most enthralling section is the Dwarf's Garden, with its 12 statues of the little Danubian dwarfs. The gardens were built in 1606 by archbishop Wolf Dietrich as a setting for the sumptuous Mirabell Palace he had constructed for his mistress Salome Alt and their brood of 10.

Attending a Performance of *Everyman*   This annual event, staged at the time of the Salzburg Festival near the cathedral at Domplatz, is an adaptation of Hoffmannsthal's morality play. It's been holding audiences spellbound for decades.

Touring the Hohensalzburg Fortress   For your sightseeing highlight, visit the largest medieval fortress in central Europe, dating from 1077. The fortress towers 400 feet above the Salzach River on a rocky dolomite ledge. Once the residence of the powerful archbishop rulers of Salzburg, it was also a siege-proof haven against invaders. A sinister part is the torture chamber, which once echoed with screams of the unfortunate. Some 100 tiny steps carry you to a lookout post for a panoramic view of Salzburg and the distant Alps.

ORIENTATION

Salzburg is only a short distance from the Austrian-German frontier, so it's convenient for exploring many of the nearby attractions of Bavaria (see chapter 7, "Germany"). On the northern slopes of the Alps, the city is at the intersection of traditional European trade routes and is well served today by air, Autobahn, and rail.

ARRIVING   By Plane   The **Salzburg Airport,** Innsbrucker Bundesstrasse 95 (☎ 0662/8580), lies 2 miles southwest of the city center. It has regularly scheduled air service to all Austrian airports, as well as to Frankfurt, Amsterdam, Brussels, Berlin, Dresden, Düsseldorf, Hamburg, Paris, and Zurich. Major airlines serving the Salzburg Airport are **Austrian Airlines** (☎ 0662/85-45-11), **Lauda Air** (☎ 0662/85-63-64), **Air France** (☎ 0662/17-89), **Lufthansa** (☎ 0662/809-080), and **Tyrolean** (☎ 0662/85-45-33).

Bus no. 77 runs between the airport and the main rail station of Salzburg. The bus departs every 30 minutes during the day, and the trip takes 20 minutes and costs 20S ($1.60) one-way. A taxi takes about 15 minutes, and you're likely to pay at least 150S ($12).

By Train   Salzburg's main rail station, the **Salzburg Hauptbahnhof,** Südtirolerplatz (☎ 0662/8887-3163), is on the major rail lines of Europe, with frequent arrivals not only from all the main cities of Austria, but also from European cities such as Munich. Between 5:05am and 8:05pm, trains arrive every 30 minutes from Vienna (trip time: 3½ hours). There are eight daily trains from Innsbruck (trip time: 2 hours). For central rail information, call ☎ 0662/17-17. Trains also arrive every 30 minutes from Munich (trip time: 2½ hours).

From the train station, buses depart to various parts of the city, including the Altstadt. Or you can walk from the rail station to the Altstadt in about 20 minutes. Taxis are also available, and the rail station has a currency exchange and storage lockers.

By Car   Salzburg is 209 miles southwest of Vienna and 95 miles east of Munich. It's reached from all directions by good roads, including Autobahn **A-8** from the west (Munich), **A-1** from the east (Vienna), and **A-10** from the south. **Route 20** comes into Salzburg from points north and west, and **Route 159** serves towns and cities from the southeast.

VISITOR INFORMATION   The **Salzburg Information Office,** at Mozartplatz 5 (☎ **0662/88987-330**), is open July through September daily 9am to 8pm and off-season Monday to Saturday 9am to 6pm. The office makes hotel reservations for a 7.2% deposit plus a 30S ($2.40) booking fee for two people, and provides information. To reach it, take bus no. 5, 6, or 51 into the center. There's also a tourist information office on Platform 2A of the Hauptbahnhof, Südtirolerplatz (☎ **0662/88887-340**).

CITY LAYOUT   Most of what visitors come to see lies on the left bank of the Salzach River in the **Altstadt** (Old Town). If you're driving, you must leave your car in the modern part of town—the right bank of the Salzach—and descend on the Altstadt by foot, as most of it is for pedestrians only.

The heart of the inner city is **Residenzplatz,** with the largest and finest baroque fountain this side of the Alps. On the western side of the square stands the **Residenz,** palace of the prince-archbishops, and on the southern side of the square is the **Salzburg Cathedral (Dom).** To the west of the Dom lies **Domplatz,** linked by archways dating from 1658.

On the southern side of Max-Reinhardt-Platz and Hofstallgasse, edging toward **Mönchsberg**—a mountain ridge slightly less than 2 miles long—stands the **Festspielhaus,** or Festival Theater, built on the foundations of the 17th-century court stables.

GETTING AROUND   By Bus/Tram   A quick, comfortable service is provided by city buses through the center of the city from the Nonntal parking lot to Sigmundsplatz, the city-center car park. Fares are 20S ($1.60) for one ride for an adult, 11S (90¢) for children 6 to 15; those under 6 travel free. *Be warned:* Buses stop running at 11pm.

By Taxi   You'll find taxi ranks scattered at key points all over the city center and in the suburbs. The **Salzburg Funktaxi-Vereinigung** (radio taxis) office is at Rainerstrasse 27 (☎ **0662/8111**). To order a taxi in advance, call that number. Taxi fares start at 30S ($2.40).

Traveler's Tip

The **Salzburg Card** not only entitles visitors to use of **public transportation,** but also acts as an **admission ticket** to the city's most important cultural sights and institutions. With the card, tourists can visit Mozart's birthplace, the Hohensalzburg fortress, the Residenz gallery, the world-famous water fountain gardens at Hellbrunn, the Baroque Museum in the Mirabell Garden, and the gala rooms in the Archbishop's Residence. The card can also be used to take in sights outside town, such as Hellbrunn Zoo, the open-air museum in Grossingmain, an excursion to the salt mines of the Dürnberg, or a trip in the gondola at Untersberg. With the card, you get a brochure with maps and sightseeing hints. The cards are valid for 24, 48, or 72 hours and cost 200S ($16), 280S ($22.40), and 300S ($24) respectively. Children up to 15 years of age receive a 50% discount. The pass can be purchased from Salzburg travel agencies, hotels, tobacconists, and municipal offices.

Salzburg

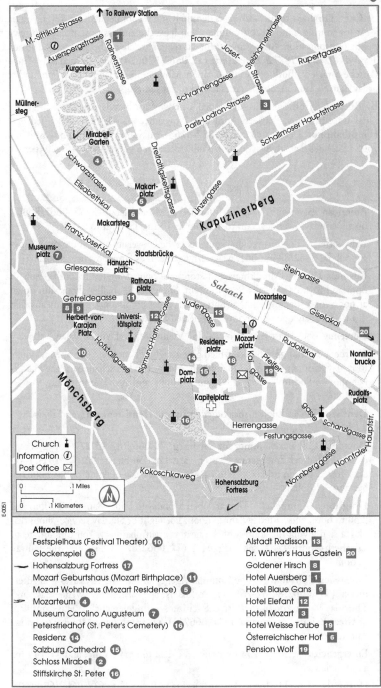

Church ✝
Information ⓘ
Post Office ✉

0 _____ .1 Miles
0 _____ .1 Kilometers

Attractions:
Festspielhaus (Festival Theater) ⑩
Glockenspiel ⑱
Hohensalzburg Fortress ⑰
Mozart Geburtshaus (Mozart Birthplace) ⑪
Mozart Wohnhaus (Mozart Residence) ⑤
Mozarteum ④
Museum Carolino Augusteum ⑦
Petersfriedhof (St. Peter's Cemetery) ⑯
Residenz ⑭
Salzburg Cathedral ⑮
Schloss Mirabell ②
Stiftskirche St. Peter ⑯

Accommodations:
Alstadt Radisson ⑬
Dr. Wührer's Haus Gastein ⑳
Goldener Hirsch ⑧
Hotel Auersberg ①
Hotel Blaue Gans ⑨
Hotel Elefant ⑫
Hotel Mozart ③
Hotel Weisse Taube ⑲
Österreichischer Hof ⑥
Pension Wolf ⑲

By Car Driving a car in Salzburg is definitely not recommended. However, you need a car for touring Land Salzburg, unless you have the endless time needed to rely on public transportation. Arrangements for car rentals are always best if made in advance. Try **Avis** (☎ **0662/877278**) or **Hertz** (☎ **0662/876674**), both located at Ferdinand-Porsche-Strasse 7. Both offices do business Monday to Friday 8am to 6pm and Saturday 8am to 1pm. A 21.2% tax is added to car rentals.

By Bike City officials have developed a network of bicycle paths, which are indicated on city maps. Between April and November, bicycles can be rented at the **Hauptbahnhof,** Desk 3 (☎ **0662/8887-3163**), on Südtirolerplatz. The cost is about 150S ($12) per day, unless you have a rail ticket; then you pay 90S ($7.20) per day.

Fast Facts: Salzburg

American Express The office is located at Mozartplatz 5–7 (☎ **0662/8080**), open Monday to Friday 9am to 5:30pm and Saturday 9am to noon.

Baby-sitters English-speaking students at the University of Salzburg often babysit; call ☎ **0662/8044-6001.** Make arrangements as far in advance as possible.

Business Hours Most shops and stores are open Monday to Friday 9am to 6pm and Saturday, usually 9am to noon. Some of the smaller shops shut down at noon for a lunch break. Salzburg observes *langer Samstag,* which means that most stores stay open until 5pm on selected Saturdays.

Currency See "Fast Facts: Vienna" in "Vienna & the Danube Valley," above.

Currency Exchange Banks, which give a slightly better rate, are open Monday to Friday 8am to noon and 2 to 4:30pm. Money can be exchanged at the Hauptbahnhof on Südtirolerplatz daily, 7am to 10pm, and at the airport daily, 9am to 4pm.

Dentists For an English-speaking dentist, call **Dentistenkammer,** Faberstrasse 2 (☎ **0662/87-34-66**).

Doctors Call **ärztekammer für Salzburg** (☎ **0662/87-13-27**). For emergencies, the **Medical Emergency Center,** Paris-London-Strasse 8A (☎ **141**), is on duty from 7pm on Friday to 7am on Monday; it's also open on public holidays. See also "Hospitals," below.

Drugstores (Apotheke) They are open Monday to Friday 8am to 12:30pm and 2:30 to 6pm, and Saturday 8am to noon. For night or Sunday service, shops display a sign giving the address of the nearest open pharmacy. You can also go to **Elisabeth-Apotheke,** Elisabethstrasse 1 (☎ **0662/87-14-84**), near the railway station.

Embassies/Consulates The Consular Agency of the **United States** is at Altermarkt (☎ **0662/84-87-76**). The office is open Monday, Wednesday, and Thursday 9am to noon to assist U.S. citizens with emergencies. The Consulate of **Great Britain,** Altermarkt 4 (☎ **0662/84-81-33**), is open Monday to Friday 9am to noon.

Emergencies Call ☎ **133** for police, ☎ **122** to report a fire, and ☎ **144** for an ambulance.

Hospitals **Unfahl Hospital** is on Dr.-Franz-Rehrl-Platz (☎ **0662/65-80-0**), and **Krankenhaus und Konvent der Barmherzigen Brüder** is at Kajetanerplatz 1 (☎ **0662/80-88-0**).

Internet Access   Das Computerhaus Inter-Cafe is at Rainbergstrasse 3A (☎ **0662/844-377**; e-mail: feedback@syscon.co.at). Open daily 9am to midnight.

Lost Property   Fundamt/Bundespolizeidirektion, the lost-and-found bureau, is supervised by the Salzburg Polizei at Alpenstrasse 90. Call ☎ **0662/6383-2330** for information, but only Monday to Friday 8:30am to 4:30pm. You can show up in person at the office Monday to Friday 8:30am to 1:30pm.

Post Office   The main post office is at Residenzplatz 9 (☎ **0662/844-1210**), open Monday through Friday 7am to 7pm and Saturday 8 to 10am. The post office at the main railway station is open 24 hours a day.

Telephone   The **country code** for Austria is **43**. The **city code** for Salzburg is **662**; use this code when you're calling from outside Austria. If you're within Austria, use **0662**. For the toll-free international access codes see "Telephone" under "Fast Facts: Vienna."

WHERE TO STAY
ON THE LEFT BANK (ALTSTADT)
Very Expensive
Altstadt Radisson. Rudfolkskai 28 & Judengasse 15, 5020 Salzburg. ☎ **800/333-3333** in the U.S., or 0662/848-571. Fax 0662/848-571-6. 60 units. MINIBAR TV TEL. 2,500–5,000S ($200–$400) double; 5,500–9,700S ($440–$776) suite. Rates include buffet breakfast. AE, DC, MC, V. Parking 300S ($24).

This is not your typical Radisson property—in fact, it's a rather radical departure for the chain in style and charm. Dating from 1377, this is a luxuriously and elegantly converted Altstadt inn, with a second entrance on Judengasse. Its closest rival in town is the old-world Goldener Hirsch, to which it finishes second. The old and new are blended perfectly here, and the historic facade conceals top-rate comforts and amenities. The cozy antique-filled lobby sets the tone. Most guests are housed in the main building, which is approached along old hallways. In a structure this large, bedrooms naturally vary greatly in size, but all have a certain charm and sparkle. The rooms are exceedingly comfortable with some of the city's best beds, along with elegant bathrooms outfitted with fluffy towels and hair dryers. Overlooking the river, the Restaurant Symphonie is one of the best hotel dining rooms in the city.

✪ **Goldener Hirsch.** Getreidegasse 37, 5020 Salzburg. ☎ **800/325-3589**, or 0662/8084. Fax 0662/8485-178-45. www.austria.at/goldener-hirsch. E-mail: goldhirsch@aalpin.co.at. 70 units. A/C MINIBAR TV TEL. 3,300–7,300S ($264–$584) double; from 5,700–8,200S ($456–$656) suite. Higher rates reflect prices at festival time (the first week of April and mid-July to Aug). AE, DC, MC, V. Valet parking 250S ($20). Bus: 55.

The award for the finest hotel in Salzburg goes to the Goldener Hirsch, steeped in legend and with a history going back to 1407, although it was last renovated in 1997. Near Mozart's birthplace, the hotel is composed of four medieval townhouses, three of which are joined in a labyrinth of rustic hallways and staircases. The fourth, called "The Coppersmith's House," is across the street, containing 17 charming and elegant rooms, each with a marble bathroom and lots of space. All rooms are beautifully furnished and maintained. The hotel is home to two of the most important restaurants of Salzburg. The hotel's charm and personal service are outstanding.

Expensive
Hotel Elefant. Sigmund-Haffner-Gasse 4, 5020 Salzburg. ☎ **0662/84-33-97.** Fax 0662/84-01-0928. 36 units. MINIBAR TV TEL. 1,700–1,970S ($136–$157.60) double. Rates include buffet breakfast. AE, DC, MC, V. Parking 100S ($8). Bus: 1, 2, 5, 6, or 51.

Near the Rathaus in the Old Town, in a quiet alley off Getreidegasse, is this well-established, family-run hotel. It's one of the most ancient buildings in Salzburg—more than 700 years old—but was last renovated in 1992. In the lobby you'll see a pink-and-white marble checkerboard floor as well as a 400-year-old marquetry cabinet. The well-furnished and high-ceilinged bedrooms have safes and hair dryers. One of our favorite rooms is the vaulted Bürgerstüberl, where high wooden banquettes separate the tables.

Moderate

Hotel Blaue Gans. Getreidegasse 41–43, 5020 Salzburg. ☎ **0662/84-13-17.** Fax 0662/84-13-179. 45 units. TEL. 1,250–1,550S ($100–$124) double. Rates include breakfast. AE, DC, MC, V. Parking 162S ($12.95). Bus: 1 or 2.

Set only a short walk from the much, much more expensive Hotel Goldener Hirsch, the "Blue Goose," housed in a 500-year-old building, has been some kind of an inn for more than 400 years. Bedrooms were renovated in stages between 1995 and 1998. Each is cozy and comfortable and, in many cases, contains a TV. All have good beds with firm mattresses. On the premises is the Stadtgasthof Blaue Gans, which functions as a cafe, a beer hall, and a cozy, traditional bistro.

Inexpensive

Hotel Weisse Taube. Kaigasse 9, 5020 Salzburg. ☎ **0662/84-24-04.** Fax 0662/84-17-83. www.weissetaube.co.at/hotel. E-mail: wollner@weissetaube.co.at. 33 units (31 with bathroom). MINIBAR TV TEL. 980–1,680S ($78.40–$134.40) double (all with bathroom). Rates include breakfast. AE, DC, MC, V. Parking garage 120S ($9.60). Bus: 5, 51, or 55.

The reception area of "The White Dove" lies behind a stone-trimmed, wrought-iron and glass door a few steps from Mozartplatz. The hotel is in the pedestrian area of the Old Town, but you can drive up to it to unload baggage. Constructed in 1365, Weisse Taube has been owned by the Haubner family since 1904. Some of the public rooms contain the original massive ceiling beams, but the bedrooms were renovated in the 1990s and are comfortably streamlined, with traditional furnishings, including frequently changed mattresses. The hotel has an elevator, a TV room, and a bar.

Pension Wolf. Kaigasse 7, 5020 Salzburg, ☎ **0662/84-34-530.** Fax 0662/84-24-234. 15 units. TV TEL. 980–1,630S ($78.40–$130.40) double. Rates include breakfast. AE. Tram: 5, 6, 51, or 55.

Ideally located near Mozartplatz, this place dates from 1429. A stucco exterior with big shutters hides the rustic and inviting interior, which is decorated with a few baroque touches. The often sunny bedrooms have recently been renovated, and many new bathrooms have been installed, making this a more inviting choice than ever. Beds have firm mattresses, but the rooms are a bit cramped, as are the bathrooms. Still, this pension represents very good value for high-priced Salzburg. Since the hotel is usually full, even in off-season, reservations are imperative.

ON THE RIGHT BANK

Very Expensive

Österreichischer Hof. Schwarzstrasse 5–7, 5020 Salzburg. ☎ **800/223-6800** in the U.S. and Canada, or 0662/889-77. Fax 0662/889-77-551. 127 units. A/C MINIBAR TV TEL. 2,600–5,900S ($208–$472) double; from 6,900S ($552) suite. Rates include buffet breakfast. AE, DC, MC, V. Parking 320S ($25.60). Bus: 1, 5, 29, or 51.

Built originally as the Hotel d'Autriche in 1866 on the right bank of the Salzach River, this hotel over the years has survived the toils of war and frequent renovations. A new era began when the Gürtler family, owners of the famous Hotel Sacher in Vienna, took over in 1988. A tremendous year-long renovation has turned the "ÖH," as guests fondly call it, into a jewel amid the villas on the riverbank. The cheerful rooms are well furnished, quite spacious, and individually decorated; most have high ceilings. Try to reserve one of the bedrooms overlooking the river. Drinking and dining facilities are available, including the Roter Salon, an elegant dining room facing the river, and the Zirbelzimmer, an award-winning wood-paneled restaurant.

Moderate

Dr. Wührer's Haus Gastein. Ignaz-Rieder-Kai 25, 5020 Salzburg. ☎ **0662/62-25-65.** Fax 0662/62-25-659. 16 units. MINIBAR TV TEL. 1,400–2,000S ($112–$160) double; from 2,200–2,400S ($176–$192) suite. Rates include breakfast. MC, V. Parking garage 200S ($16). Bus: 49.

This prosperous-looking Teutonic villa was built as a private home in 1953, amid calm scenery on the bank of the Salzach River. Guests appreciate the spacious flowering garden, a nice spot for breakfast or afternoon tea. The interior is sparsely but pleasantly furnished, with conservative pieces and Oriental carpets. Bedrooms—often quite large—contain cozy Salzburg furniture crafted by regional artisans. Many accommodations have private balconies.

✪ **Hotel Auersperg.** Auerspergstrasse 61, 5027 Salzburg. ☎ **0662/889-44-0.** Fax 0662/889-44-55. E-mail: hotel.auersperg@magnet.at. 63 units. MINIBAR TV TEL. 1,140–2,140S ($91.20–$171.20) double; 2,090–2,980S ($167.20–$238.40) suite. Rates include breakfast. AE, DC, MC, V. Free parking. Bus: 15 from the train station.

This traditional family-run hotel consists of a main structure, a less expensive adjoining annex, and its own sunny gardens. The guest rooms are especially inviting—warm, cozy, of generous size, with excellent beds and well-equipped bathrooms. Modern furnishings, big windows, and chintz covers create a harmonious decor in the individually decorated rooms. There is an old-fashioned charm wherever you go, from the reception hall with its 19th-century molded ceilings to the antique-filled drawing room. The hotel also has a good restaurant, bar, sauna, and steam bath. Its fitness center is on the top floor with a roof terrace offering panoramic views of Salzburg.

Hotel Mozart. Franz-Josef-Strasse 27, 5020, Salzburg. ☎ **0662/87-22-74.** Fax 0662/87-00-79. E-mail: hotel-mozart.sbg@magnet.at. 33 units. MINIBAR TV TEL. 1,460–1,860S ($116.80–$148.80) double. Rates include breakfast. AE, DC, MC, V. Closed Jan–Feb. Free parking. Bus: 15, 27, or 29.

Mozart is a comfortable, family-run hotel that's a 10-minute walk from the train station and only 5 minutes from the Linzergasse pedestrian area and the famous Mirabell Garden. It greets visitors with a buff-colored stucco six-story facade. Bedrooms are often sunny and have all the standard amenities, including duvet-covered twin beds with firm mattresses and medium-sized tiled bathrooms equipped with hair dryers and good towels. The hotel, with its careful service and courteously attentive staff, contains many thoughtful touches, such as drawings of the old city of Salzburg.

WHERE TO DINE

Two special desserts you'll want to sample while here are the famous *Salzburger nockerln,* a light mixture of stiff egg whites, and the elaborate *Mozart-Kugeln,* with bittersweet chocolate, hazelnut nougat, and marzipan. You'll also want to try the beer from one of the numerous Salzburg breweries.

ON THE LEFT BANK (ALTSTADT)

Very Expensive

Goldener Hirsch. Getreidegasse 37. ☎ **0662/8084-861.** Reservations required. Main courses 290–420S ($23.20–$33.60); 5-course set-price menu 690S ($55.20). AE, DC, MC, V. Daily noon–2:30pm and 6:30–9:30pm. Bus: 55. AUSTRIAN/VIENNESE.

The best restaurant in Salzburg's best hotel attracts the brightest luminaries of the international music and business community. It's staffed with a superb team of chefs and waiters who preside over an atmosphere of elegant simplicity. Specialties include parfait of smoked trout in a mustard-dill sauce, saddle of venison in a cranberry cream sauce, veal in saffron sauce, roast filet of char with dill mustard and asparagus, *Tafelspitz* (boiled beef), and roast duck in its own gravy. Dishes are impeccably prepared and beautifully served.

Expensive

✪ **Alt-Salzburg.** Bürgerspitalgasse 2. ☎ **0662/84-14-76.** Reservations required. Main courses 128–295S ($10.25–$23.60); set-price menu 480–560S ($38.40–$44.80). AE, DC, MC, V. Mon 6–11:30pm; Tues–Sat 11:30am–2pm and 6–11:30pm (till midnight in August). Closed Feb 3–16. Bus: 1, 15, or 49. AUSTRIAN/INTERNATIONAL.

This restaurant, one of the most venerated in the city, offers a retreat into old-world elegance. It's a bastion of formal service and refined cuisine. The building, located right in the town center, dates from 1648 and has a wood-ceilinged room, crafted to reveal part of the chiseled rock of the Mönchsberg. Main dishes include lamb chops in red wine sauce; filet of river char sautéed with tomatoes, mushrooms, and capers, leaf spinach, and potatoes; and saddle of venison with morel-flavored cream sauce with red cabbage and dumplings.

Purzelbaum. Zugallistrasse 7. ☎ **0662/84-88-43.** Reservations required. Main courses 245–285S ($19.60–$22.80); 4-course set-price menu 540S ($43.20). AE, DC, MC, V. Mon 6–11pm; Tues–Sat noon–2pm and 6–11pm. Bus: 55. AUSTRIAN/VIENNESE.

In a residential neighborhood, this restaurant is near a duck pond at the bottom of a steep incline leading up to Salzburg Castle. The three dining rooms contain marble buffets from a French buttery and an art nouveau ceiling. Menu items change according to the inspiration of the chef, and include venison in red wine sauce, sole meunière, beefsteak cooked in a savory casserole or grilled and served with pepper sauce, and the house specialty, scampi Grüstl, composed of fresh shrimp with sliced potatoes and baked with herbs in a casserole.

Moderate

Café Winkler. Mönchsberg Terrace, Mönchsberg. ☎ **0662/847-738.** Reservations recommended for meals, not for cafe items. Main courses 190–295S ($15.20–$23.60). AE, DC, MC, V. Tues–Sun noon–2pm and 6–10pm. Limited food items available Tues–Sun 2–6pm. Also open Mon (same hours) during Salzburg Festival. Access via the Mönchsberg elevator. INTERNATIONAL.

Set on a rocky plateau (the Mönchsberg Terrace) high above the city, the Winkler was built sometime during the 1950s and has been drawing tourists like a magnet ever since. Ringed with large expanses of glass, it offers the best panoramas in Salzburg. The table next to you will likely be filled with bus tour members snapping photos of the city's baroque spires. The menu here is broad enough to satisfy someone who wants a full Austrian meal or merely a caffeine fix. The menu includes a gratin of scampi, filet steaks with peppercorns or with mushroom sauce, or saddle of venison with a sauce made from seasonal berries. The food is surprisingly good for such a touristy place.

Inexpensive

Festungsrestaurant. Hohensalzburg Schloss, Mönchsberg 34. ☎ **0662/84-17-80.** Reservations required July–Aug. Main courses 115–225S ($9.20–$18). MC, V. June–Sept daily 10am–10pm; Apr–May and Oct, Wed–Sun 10am–8pm; Nov–Mar, Wed–Sun 10am–5pm. Funicular from the Old Town. SALSBURG/AUSTRIAN.

Since the Middle Ages, this pair of solid and venerable dining rooms has been dispensing food and drink to archbishops, priests, servants, travelers, and, during wartime, to soldiers and their commanders. The compound is poised 400 feet above the Altstadt and the Salzach River, with a panoramic view over the spires and cupolas of the city and its nearby alpine peaks. In warm weather, tables are set up in nearby gardens. The menu offers well-flavored and time-tested cuisine that includes *Salzburger Bierfleische,* a gulasch-like stew, and a succulent version of *Salzburger Schnitzel,* a pork scallop stuffed with mushrooms, bacon, and tomatoes.

✪ **Humboldtstube.** Gstättengasse 6. ☎ **0662/843-171.** Reservations recommended. Main courses 85–128S ($6.80–$10.25); set menus 82–115S ($6.55–$9.20). AE, DC, MC, V. Daily 11am–1am. Bus: 1 or 2. AUSTRIAN.

This restaurant's charm lies in its allegiance to virtually every aspect of old-fashioned Austria, including its decor and cuisine. In a building dating from 1492, the dining room is entirely sheathed in old paneling and accented with noncommittal paintings. A staff of hardworking, and sometimes harassed, women carry heaping platters that remind older Austrians of their childhood. Examples include gulasch soup; Weiner schnitzels or pork schnitzels; roasted beef with onions; noodles flavored with ham, cheese, mushrooms, herbs, and onions; and the dessert, Salzburger knockerl. Your strained arteries will appreciate the well-supplied salad bar.

Krimpelstätter. Müllner Hauptstrasse 31. ☎ **0662/43-22-74.** Reservations recommended. Main courses 68–135S ($5.45–$10.80). No credit cards. Tues–Sat 11:45am–2pm and 6–10pm (and on Mon, May–Sept). Closed 3 weeks in Jan. Bus: 49 or 95. SALZBURGIAN/AUSTRIAN.

Originally constructed as an inn back in 1548, this is an enduring Salzburg favorite, with chiseled stone columns supporting vaulted ceilings and heavy timbers. In summer a beer garden, full of roses and trellises, attracts up to 300 visitors at a time. If you want a snack, a beer, or a glass of wine, head for the paneled door marked *Gastezimmer* in the entry corridor. If you're looking for a more formal and quiet meal, three cozy antique dining rooms sit atop a flight of narrow stone steps. The same menu is offered in each of the different areas, a hearty Land Salzburg regional cuisine featuring homemade sausages, spinach noodles, and wild game dishes.

Sternbräu. Griesgasse 23. ☎ **0662/84-21-40.** Main courses 80–140S ($6.40–$11.20); set-price menu 140–200S ($11.20–$16). No credit cards. Daily 9am–11pm. Bus: 2, 5, 12, 49, or 51. AUSTRIAN.

This place seems big enough to have fed half the Austro-Hungarian army, with a series of rooms that follow one after the other in varying degrees of formality. The Hof-bräustübl is a rustic fantasy with masonry columns, hand-hewn beams, and wood paneling. You can also eat in the chestnut tree–shaded beer garden, usually packed on a summer's night, or under the weathered arcades of an inner courtyard. Daily specials, served by a battalion of aproned waiters, include such typical Austrian dishes as Wiener and chicken schnitzels, trout, cold marinated herring, Hungarian goulash, and hearty regional soups. You come here for hearty, filling portions—not for any refinement in cuisine.

✪ **Stiftskeller St. Peter (Peterskeller).** St.-Peter-Bezirk 1–4. ☎ **0662/84-12-680.** Reservations recommended. Main courses 100–250S ($8–$20). AE, MC, V. Daily 11am–midnight. Bus: 29. AUSTRIAN/VIENNESE.

Legend has it that Mephistopheles met with Faust in this tavern established by Benedictine monks in A.D. 803. In fact, it's the oldest restaurant in Europe, housed in the abbey of the church that supposedly brought Christianity to Austria. Aside from a collection of baroque banqueting rooms, there's an inner courtyard with vaults cut from rock, a handful of dignified wood-paneled rooms, and a brick-vaulted cellar with a tile floor and rustic chandeliers. In addition to the wine from the abbey's vineyards

(*Prelaten*, a young, fruity white wine, is the most popular), the tavern serves good home-style Austrian cooking, including braised oxtail with mushrooms and fried polenta, and braised veal knuckle with anchovy sauce. Other menu items include *Tafelspitz* (boiled beef) and *Bauernpfandl*, a succulent version of pork filet stuffed with mushrooms and served with spaetzle.

ON THE RIGHT BANK
Moderate
Hotel Stadtkrug Restaurant. Linzer Gasse 20. ☎ **0662/87-35-45.** Reservations recommended. Main courses 90–217S ($7.20–$17.35); set-price menu 130–400S ($10.40–$32). AE, DC, MC, V. Wed–Mon noon–3pm and 6–11pm. Bus: 27 or 29. AUSTRIAN/INTERNATIONAL.

Across the river from the Altstadt, on the site of what used to be a 14th-century farm, this restaurant occupies a structure rebuilt from an older core in 1458. In the 1960s, a modern hotel was added in back. The old-fashioned dining rooms in front now serve as one of the neighborhood's most popular restaurants. In an antique and artfully rustic setting, illuminated by gilded wooden chandeliers, you can enjoy hearty, traditional Austrian cuisine, such as cream of potato soup "Old Vienna" style, braised beef with burgundy sauce, roast duckling with bacon dumplings and red cabbage/apple dressing, and glazed cutlet of pork with caraway seeds and deep-fried potatoes.

Inexpensive
Zum Fidelen Affen. Priesterhausgasse 8. ☎ **0662/877-361.** Main courses 95–140S ($7.60–$11.20). No credit cards. Mon–Sat 5pm–midnight. Bus: 1 or 2. AUSTRIAN.

On the eastern edge of the river near the Staatsbrücke, this is the closest thing in Salzburg to a loud, animated, and jovial pub with food service. It's in one of the city's oldest buildings, dating from 1407, and caters to an eclectic bar crowd. Management's policy is to allow only three reserved tables on any particular evening; the remainder are given to whoever happens to show up. Menu items are simple, inexpensive, and based on regional culinary traditions. A house specialty is a gratin of green (spinach-flavored) noodles in cream sauce with strips of ham. Also popular are seasonal meat and mushroom casseroles, and at least three different kinds of main-course dumplings flavored with meats, cheeses, herbs, and various sauces. Everyone's favorite drink here is Trumer pils beer.

CAFES
✪ **Café-Restaurant Glockenspiel.** Mozartplatz 2. ☎ **0662/84-14-03-0.** Summer, daily 9am–midnight (food served until 11pm); rest of the year, daily 9am–8pm (food served until 6pm). Closed second and third weeks of Nov and Jan. Bus: 55.

This is the city's most popular cafe, with about 100 tables with armchairs out front. You might want to spend an afternoon here, particularly when there's live chamber music. You can't miss the glass case filled with every caloric delight west of Vienna. Coffee starts at 35S ($2.80), and comes in many varieties, including Maria Theresa, which contains orange liqueur.

✪ **Café Tomaselli.** Altermarkt 9. ☎ **0662/84-44-88.** Mon–Sat 7am–9pm; Sun and holidays 8am–9pm. Closed 5 days in Jan. Bus: 2, 5, 6, 51, or 55.

Established in 1705, this cafe opens onto one of the most charming cobblestoned squares of the Altstadt. Aside from the summer chairs placed outdoors, you'll find a high-ceilinged room with many tables, small crystal lighting fixtures, and lots of conversation among the *haute bourgeoisie* crowd. A waiter brings a pastry tray filled with 40 different kinds of cakes. Other menu items include omelets, wursts, ice cream, and a wide range of drinks. Pastries begin at 25S ($2), and the most elaborate cakes cost 38AS ($3.10). Coffee costs 36S ($2.90) for a mélange.

SEEING THE SIGHTS IN THE CITY OF MOZART

The Old Town lies between the left bank of the Salzach River and the ridge known as the **Mönchsberg,** which rises to a height of 1,650 feet. The main street of the Altstadt is **Getreidegasse,** a narrow little thoroughfare lined with five- and six-story burghers' buildings. Most of the houses along the street are from the 17th and 18th centuries. Mozart was born at no. 9 (see "More Attractions," below). Many lacy-looking wrought-iron signs are displayed, and a lot of the houses have carved windows.

You might begin your tour at **Mozartplatz,** lined with outdoor cafes. From here you can walk to the even more expansive **Residenzplatz,** where torchlight dancing is staged every year, along with outdoor performances.

SIGHTSEEING SUGGESTIONS FOR FIRST-TIME VISITORS

If You Have 1 Day   Start slowly with a cup of coffee at the **Café-Restaurant Glockenspiel** on Mozartplatz. Then from the Altstadt, take the funicular to the **Hohensalzburg Fortress** for a tour. After lunch in an old tavern, visit **Mozart's birthplace** on Getreidegasse, and stroll along the narrow street. Later, visit the **Residenz.**

If You Have 2 Days   In the morning of your second day, explore the **Dom** and the **cemetery of St. Peter's.** Take a walking tour through the **Altstadt.** In the afternoon, explore **Hellbrunn Palace,** 3 miles south of the city.

If You Have 3 Days   On day 3, visit the many attractions of Salzburg you've missed so far: the **Mönchsberg,** the **Mozart Wohnhaus,** and the **Museum Carolino Augusteum** in the morning. In the afternoon, see the **Mirabell Gardens** and **Mirabell Palace** and at least look at the famous **Festspielhaus** (Festival Hall), dating from 1607; tours are sometimes possible.

If You Have 4 or 5 Days   On day 4, head for some of the sights in the environs of Salzburg. Go to **Gaisberg** in the morning, which at 4,250 feet offers a panoramic view of the Salzburg Alps. After lunch, head for **Hallein,** the second-largest town in Land Salzburg, for a look at its salt mines. On day 5, take the **"Sound of Music Tour"** (see "Organized Tours," below) and visit the places where this world-famous musical was filmed. Return to Salzburg in time to hear a Mozart concert, if one is featured (as it often is).

THE TOP ATTRACTIONS

✪ **Residenz.** Residenzplatz 1. ☎ **0662/80-42-26-90.** Admission to Residenz state rooms, 70S ($5.60) adults, 40S ($3.20) students 16–18 and senior citizens, 25S ($2) children 6–15, free for children under 6. Residenz Gallery, 70S ($5.60) adults, 25S ($2) students 16–18 and senior citizens, free for children under 16. Combined ticket to state rooms and gallery, 95S ($7.60). May–Oct and Dec, daily 10am–5pm; Jan–Apr and Nov, Mon–Fri 10am–5pm. Bus: 5 or 6.

This opulent palace, just north of Domplatz in the pedestrian zone, was the seat of the Salzburg prince-archbishops after they no longer needed the protection of the gloomy Hohensalzburg Fortress of Mönchsberg. The Residenz dates from 1120, but work on its series of palaces began in the late 1500s and continued until about 1796. The lavish rebuilding was originally ordered by Archbishop Wolfgang ("Wolf") Dietrich. The Residenz fountain, from the 17th century, is one of the largest and most impressive baroque fountains north of the Alps. The child prodigy Mozart often played in the Conference Room for guests. More than a dozen state rooms, each richly decorated, are open to the public via guided tour. On the second floor you can visit the **Residenzgalerie Salzburg** (☎ **0662/84-04-51**), an art gallery founded in 1923, now containing European paintings from the 16th to the 19th centuries, displayed in 15 historic rooms.

Glockenspiel (Carillon). Mozartplatz 1. ☎ **0662/80-42-27-84.**

The celebrated glockenspiel with its 35 bells stands across from the Residenz. You can hear this 18th-century carillon at 7am, 11am, and 6pm. Visits are no longer allowed within the Glockenspiel.

✪ Salzburg Cathedral. South side of Residenzplatz. ☎ **0662/84-11-62.** Cathedral, free; excavations, 30S ($2.40) adults, 20S ($1.60) students and children 6–15, free for children under 6; museum, 70S ($5.60) adults, 25S ($2) students and children 6–15, free for children under 6. Cathedral, daily 8am–8pm (until 6pm in winter); excavations, Easter to mid-Oct daily 9am–5pm; museum, May 16–Oct 26 daily 10am–5pm. Bus: 1.

Located where Residenzplatz flows into Domplatz, this cathedral is world-renowned for its 4,000-pipe organ. The original foundation dates from A.D. 774, superseded in the 12th century by a late-Romanesque structure that was destroyed by fire in 1598. Prince-Archbishop Wolf Dietrich commissioned a new cathedral, but his overthrow prevented the completion of the project. The Italian architect Santino Solari built the present cathedral, which was consecrated in 1628 by Archbishop Paris Count Lodron.

Hailed by some critics as the "most perfect" northern Renaissance building, the cathedral has a marble facade and twin symmetrical towers. The mighty bronze doors were created in 1959. The interior is richly baroque with elaborate frescoes, the most important of which, along with the altarpieces, were designed by Mascagni of Florence. In the crypt, traces of the old Romanesque cathedral have been unearthed.

The treasure of the cathedral and the "arts and wonders" the archbishops collected in the 17th century are displayed in the **Dom Museum** (☎ **0662/84-41-89**), entered through the cathedral. The **cathedral excavations** (☎ **0662/84-52-95**), entered around the corner (left of the Dom entrance), show the ruins of the original foundation.

Stiftskirche St. Peter. St.-Peter-Bezirk. ☎ **0662/844-578.** Free admission. Daily 6am–8pm.

Founded in A.D. 696 by St. Rupert, whose tomb is here, this is the church of St. Peter's Abbey and Benedictine Monastery. Once a Romanesque basilica with three aisles, the church was completely overhauled in the 17th and 18th centuries in elegant baroque style. The west door dates from 1240. The church is richly adorned with art treasures, including some altar paintings by Kremser Schmidt.

Petersfriedhof (St. Peter's Cemetery). St.-Peter-Bezirk. ☎ **0662/84-45-78-0.** Tours 12S (95¢). Catacombs, May–Sept daily 10am–5pm every 60 minutes; Oct–Apr daily 10:30am–4pm. Bus: 1.

This cemetery lies at the stone wall that merges into the rock of the Mönchsberg. Many of the aristocratic families of Salzburg lie buried here, as well as many other noted persons, including Nannerl Mozart, sister of Wolfgang Amadeus. You can also see the Romanesque Chapel of the Holy Cross and St. Margaret's Chapel, dating from the 15th century. *Warning:* Tours of the catacombs in theory follow the hours outlined above; however, they may not be offered for almost any reason.

Hohensalzburg Fortress. Mönchsberg 34. ☎ **0662/84-24-30-11.** Admission (excluding guided tour but including museum) 35S ($2.80) adults, 20S ($1.60) children 6–19, free for children under 6. Admission and conducted tours 70S ($5.60) adults, 20S ($1.60) ages 6–19, free for children under 6. Conducted 50-minute tours of the interior are offered daily,

Apr–June 9:30am–5pm; July–Oct 9:30am–5:30pm; and Nov–Mar 10am–4:30pm. Fortress and museums, Apr–June and Oct daily 9am–6pm; July–Sept daily 8am–7pm; and Nov–Mar daily 9am–5pm. The funicular from Festungsgasse (☎ **0662/84-26-82**) runs every 10 minutes during daylight hours and the round-trip costs 69S ($5.50) for adults, 37S ($2.95) for children 6–16, free for children under 6. If you're athletic, you can reach the fortress on foot from Kapitelplatz by way of Festungsgasse or from the Mönchsberg via the Schartentor.

The stronghold of the ruling prince-archbishops before they moved "downtown" to the Residenz, this fortress towers 400 feet above the Salzach River on a rocky Dolomite ledge. The massive fortress crowns the Festungsberg and literally dominates Salzburg. Work on Hohensalzburg began in 1077 and was not finished until 1681. This is the largest completely preserved castle left in central Europe. The elegant state apartments, once the courts of the prince-archbishops, are on display.

The **Burgmuseum** contains a collection of medieval art. Plans and prints tracing the growth of Salzburg are on exhibit, as well as instruments of torture and many Gothic artifacts. The **Rainermuseum** has displays of arms and armor. The beautiful late-Gothic St. George's Chapel, dating from 1501, is adorned with marble reliefs of the apostles.

MORE ATTRACTIONS

⊙ Mozart Gerburtshaus (Mozart's Birthplace). Getreidegasse 9. ☎ **0662/84-43-13.** Admission 70S ($5.60) adults, 55S ($4.40) students, 20S ($1.60) children. Daily 9am–6pm.

The house where Wolfgang Amadeus Mozart was born on January 27, 1756 houses exhibition rooms and the apartment of the Mozart family. The main treasures are the valuable paintings (such as the well-known oil painting—left unfinished—by Joseph Lange, *Mozart and the Piano*) and the original instruments: the violin Mozart used as a child, his concert violin, his viola, fortepiano, and the clavichord.

Schloss Mirabell (Mirabell Palace). Off Makartplatz. ☎ **0662/8072-0.** Free admission. Staircase, daily 8am–6pm. Marmorsaal, Mon, Wed, and Thurs 8am–4pm; Tues and Fri 1–4pm. Bus: 1, 5, 6, or 51.

This palace and its gardens were originally built as a luxurious private residence called Altenau. Prince-Archbishop Wolf Dietrich had it constructed in 1606 for his mistress and the mother of his children, Salome Alt. Not much remains of the original grand structure. Lukas von Hildebrandt rebuilt the schloss in the first quarter of the 18th century, and it was modified after a great fire in 1818. The official residence of the mayor of Salzburg is now in the palace, which is like a smaller edition of the Tuileries in Paris. The ceremonial marble Barockstiege-Englesstiege, "angel staircase," with sculptured cherubs, carved by Raphael Donner in 1726, leads to the Marmorsaal, a marble and gold hall used for concerts and weddings. Chamber music concerts are staged here.

Museum Carolino Augusteum. Museumsplatz 1. ☎ **0662/841-134-0.** Admission 40S ($3.20) adults, 30S ($2.40) seniors over 60, 15S ($1.20) students and children 6–19, free for children under 6. Tues 9am–8pm; Wed–Sun 9am–5pm. Bus: 1, 49, or 95.

Several collections are brought together under one roof in this museum that reflects Salzburg's cultural history. The archaeological collection contains the well-known Dürnberg beaked pitcher, as well as Roman mosaics. Some 15th-century Salzburg art is on view, and there are many paintings from the Romantic period, as well as works by Hans Makart, who was born in Salzburg in 1840.

Mozart Wohnhaus (Mozart Residence). Makartplatz 8. ☎ **0662/88-43-13.** Admission 70S ($5.60) adults, 55S ($4.40) students, 20S ($1.60) children 15 and under. June–Sept daily 10am–5pm; Oct–May daily 10am–4pm. Bus: 1 or 5.

In 1773 the Mozart family moved from the cramped quarters of Mozart's birthplace, and young Mozart lived here with his family until 1780. In the rooms of the former Mozart family apartments, a museum documents the history of the house and the life and work of Wolfgang Amadeus.

But this is not the original house. Destroyed by bombing in 1944, it was rebuilt according to the specifics of an 1838 engraving and reopened on January 26, 1996—the eve of Mozart's birthday anniversary. A mechanized audio tour in six languages with relevant musical samples accompanies the visitor through the rooms of the museum.

Mönchsberg. ☎ 0662/6205-51-180. Express elevators leave from Gstättengasse 13, daily 9am–11pm; round-trip fare 27S ($2.15) adults, 14S ($1.10) children 6–15, free for children under 6.

West of the Hohensalzburg Fortress, this heavily forested ridge extends for some 1½ miles above the Altstadt and has fortifications dating from the 15th century. Several vistas can be seen, and a panoramic view of Salzburg is possible from Mönchsberg Terrace just in front of the Grand Café Winkler.

THE MIRABELL GARDENS

Mirabell Gardens, off Makartplatz, are on the right bank of the river. Laid out by Fischer von Erlach and now a public park, these baroque gardens are studded with statues and reflecting pools, making the gardens a virtual open-air museum. Some of the marble balustrades and urns were also designed by von Erlach. There's also a natural theater. Be sure to visit the bastion with fantastic marble baroque dwarfs and other figures, located by the Pegasus Fountains in the lavish garden west of Schloss Mirabell. From the garden, you have an excellent view of the Hohensalzburg Fortress. Admission is free, and the gardens are open daily from 7am to 8pm from June through September. The rest of the year, hours are daily from 7am to dusk. Bus: 1, 5, 6, or 51.

ORGANIZED TOURS

The best tours are offered by **Salzburg Panorama Tours,** Mirabellplatz (☎ **0662/88-32-11-0**), which is the Gray Line company for Salzburg. The original, and somewhat cultish, *"Sound of Music* **Tour"** combines the Salzburg city tour with an excursion to the lake district and the places where the film was shot. The English-speaking guide shows you the historical and architectural landmarks of Salzburg, as well as part of the Salzkammergut countryside. The 4½-hour tour departs daily at 9:30am and 2pm and costs 350S ($28).

You must take your passport along for any of three trips into **Bavaria** in Germany. One of them, called the **"Eagle's Nest Tour,"** takes visitors to Berchtesgaden and on to Obersalzberg, where Hitler and his elite followers had a vacation retreat. The 4½-hour tour departs daily at 9am, May 15 to October 31, and costs 550S ($44). Among other tours offered, **"The City & Country Highlights"** takes in historic castles and the surrounding Land Salzburg landscape. The 5-hour tour departs daily at 1pm and costs 550S ($44). Bookings are possible at the bus terminal at Mirabellplatz/St. Andrä Kirche (☎ **0662/87-40-29**). Tour prices are the same for all ages.

THE SHOPPING SCENE

Salzburg obviously doesn't have Vienna's wide range of merchandise. However, if you're not going on to the Austrian capital, you might want to check out some of the shops recommended below. Good buys in Salzburg include souvenirs from Land Salzburg, dirndls, lederhosen, petit point, and all types of sports gear. **Getreidegasse** is a main shopping thoroughfare, but you'll also find some intriguing little shops on **Residenzplatz.**

Established in 1871, **Drechslerei Lackner,** Badergasse 2 (☎ **0662/84-23-85**), offers both antique and modern country wood furniture. Among the new items are chests, chessboards, angels, cupboards, crèches, candlesticks, and most definitely chairs.

Musikhaus Pühringer, Getreildegasse 13 (☎ **0662/84-32-67**), established in 1910, sells all kinds of classical musical instruments, as well as a large selection of electronic instruments (including synthesizers and amplifiers). You'll find classical and folk-music CDs and tapes, plus many classical recordings, especially those by Mozart. The store is only a few buildings away from the composer's birthplace.

One of the best places in town to buy local Austrian handcrafts and original regional clothing is **Salzburger Heimatwerk,** Am Residenzplatz 9 (☎ **0662/ 84-41-10**). Items for sale include Austrian silver and garnet jewelry, painted boxes, candles, wood carvings, copper and brass ceramics, tablecloths, and alpine patterns for cross-stitched samplers. Another section sells dirndls and the rest of the regalia native to the land and still donned during commemorative ceremonies and festivals.

Wiener Porzellanmanufaktur Augarten Gesellschaft, Alter Markt 11 (☎ **0662/ 84-07-14**), might very well tempt you to begin a porcelain collection. The origins of this world-class manufacturer go back 275 years, when it started as one of several branches of the Meissen porcelain manufacturers in Germany. Today, its product is legendary and its patterns, including *Wiener Rose, Maria Theresia,* and the highly distinctive *Biedermeier,* are well known to thousands of Austrian matriarchs who recognize them from their own wedding days. The company also produces such historical pieces as the black-and-white demitasse set created by architect-designer Josef Hoffman.

SALZBURG AFTER DARK
THE PERFORMING ARTS

It's said that there's a musical event—often a Mozart concert—staged virtually every night in Salzburg. To find the venue, visit the Salzburg tourist office, Mozartplatz 5 (☎ **0662/88987-330**), for a free copy of *Veranstaltungen,* a frequently updated pamphlet listing all major—and many minor—local cultural events.

The major ticket agency affiliated with the city of Salzburg is next to Salzburg's main tourist office, at Mozartplatz 5. The **Salzburger Ticket Office** (☎ **0662/ 84-03-10**) is open Monday to Friday 10am to 6pm (until 7pm in midsummer) and Saturday 9am to noon.

If you don't want to pay a ticket agent's commission, you can go directly to the box office of a theater or concert hall. However, many of the best seats may have already been sold, especially those at the Salzburg Festival.

CONCERTS & OTHER ENTERTAINMENT

Besides the venues listed below, you can attend a concert in dramatic surroundings in the Fürstenzimmer (Prince's Chamber) of the **Hohensalzburg Fortress.** Guest musicians of international renown perform on occasion. The box office, at Adlgasser-Weg 22 (☎ **0662/82-58-58**), is open daily 9am to 9pm. Performances are daily from mid-May to mid-October, at either 8 or 8:30pm, and tickets are 360 to 420S ($29.15 to $34). For more information, call ☎ **0662/843430-11.**

Festspielhaus. Hofstallgasse 1. ☎ **0662/8045.** Tickets 100–4,000S ($8–$320). The higher cost is for the best seats at the Salzburg Festival; average but good seats run 550–950S ($44–$76). Bus: 1, 5, or 6.

The rich collection of concerts that make up the Salzburg Festival's program are presented in several different concert halls scattered throughout Salzburg. The largest is

How to Get Tickets to the Salzburg Festival

One of the premier music attractions of Europe, the **Salzburg Festival** celebrated its 79th season in 1999. Composer Richard Strauss founded the festival, aided by director Max Reinhardt and writer Hugo von Hofmannsthal. Details on the festival are available by writing to Salzburg Festival, Hofstallgasse 1, 5020 Salzburg, Austria (☎ **0662/8045-579**).

Festival tickets are in great demand, and there never are enough of them. Don't arrive expecting to get into any of the major events unless you've booked your tickets far ahead. Travel agents can often get tickets for you, and you can also go to branches of the Austrian National Tourist Office at home or abroad.

An annual event is Hofmannsthal's adaptation of the morality play *Everyman*, which is staged (in German) outside the cathedral in Domplatz.

Subject to many exceptions and variations, and excluding ticket agent commissions, drama tickets generally run 200 to 2,500S ($16 to $200). Opera tickets can begin as low as 600S ($48), ranging upward to 4,200S ($336).

the Festspielhaus, which contains two permanent theaters, in close proximity to other festival venues. Within the Festspielhaus complex, you'll find the **Grosses Haus** (Big House), seating 2,170, and the **Kleines Haus** (Small House), which with a seating capacity of 1,323 isn't really that small. There's also the **Felsenreitschule,** an outdoor auditorium with a makeshift roof. Originally built in 1800 as a riding rink, it's famous as the site where scenes from *The Sound of Music* were filmed. Information and tickets are available either at the Festspielhaus (see above) or through the **Kulturvere-iningung** ticket office at Waagplatz 1A, near the tourist office (☎ **0662/84-45-01**). Their services are available Monday to Friday 9:30am to 5pm.

Mozarteum. Schwarzstrasse 26 and Mirabellplatz 1. ☎ **0662/87-31-54.** Tickets 250–800S ($20–$64); the best seats run 1,200–2,500S ($96–$200). Bus 1, 5, 6, or 51.

On the right back of the Salzach River, near Mirabell Gardens, this is the major music and concert hall of Salzburg. All the big orchestra concerts, as well as organ recitals and chamber-music evenings, are offered by the Mozarteum. In the old building at Schwarzstrasse are two concert halls, the Grosser Saal and the Wiener Saal. In the newer building on Mirabellplatz, concert halls include the Grosses Studio, the Leopold-Mozart Saal, and the Paumgartner Studio. The box office is open Monday to Thursday 9am to 2pm and Friday 9am to 4pm. Performances are at 11am or 7:30pm.

BEER GARDENS & THE CASINO

✪ **Augustiner Bräustübl.** Augustinergasse 4. ☎ **0662/43-12-46.** Bus: 27.

Regardless of the season, you'll have one of your most enjoyable and authentic evenings in Salzburg at this bierstube and biergarten that has been dispensing oceans of beer since it was established in 1622. Depending on the weather, the city's beer-drinking fraternity gathers either within the cavernous interior, where three separate rooms each hold up to 400 people, or in the leafy, chestnut-shaded garden. The excellent beer, brewed on the premises, is served Monday to Friday 3 to 11pm and Saturday and Sunday 2:30 to 11pm. Throughout the year, the staple here is Märzen beer, which costs 28S ($2.25) for a brimming half-liter.

Stiegelbräu Keller. Festungsgasse 10. ☎ **0662/84-26-81.**

To get here, you have to negotiate a steep cobblestoned street that drops off on one side to reveal a panoramic view of Salzburg. Set immediately below the Hohensalzburg Fortress, and established in the early 1800s, part of this place is carved into the rocks of Mönchsberg mountain. The staff here is preoccupied with supplying large volumes of the local brew (Steigelbräu) and food to enthusiastic locals. If the weather permits, head for the leafy garden; otherwise, sip your suds in the cavernous interior. Mugs of beer, costing 35S ($2.80) each, are supplemented with small to enormous platters of such traditional bierkeller food as sausages and schnitzels. Open daily May to September, from 10am to midnight.

Within a separate room, folkloric **"Sound of Music" dinner shows** are offered. They are presented May to September, daily 7:30 to 10pm. A three-course meal plus the show costs 520S ($41.60). If you prefer to skip the dinner, you can show up at 8:15pm and pay 360S ($28.80), which includes the show, dessert, and coffee.

Casino Salzburg Schloss Klessheim. 5071 Walzsezenheim. ☎ **0662/854-4550.** Cover 260S ($20.80); includes 300S ($24) worth of casino chips.

Occupying the Schloss Klessheim, a baroque palace, this is the only year-round casino in Land Salzburg. On the premises is a stylish restaurant plus bars. Monday night is poker night. You must show some form of identification—a driver's license or a passport—and except during the hottest months of summer, men are encouraged to wear jackets and ties. The complex is open daily 3pm to 3am. To get here, drive west along Autobahn A-1, exiting at the Schloss Klessheim exit, about a mile west of the center of Salzburg. Also, the casino maintains a flotilla of red-sided free shuttle buses that depart from the rocky base of the Mönchsberg every hour on the half-hour, daily 2:30pm to midnight.

DAY TRIPS FROM SALZBURG

SCHLOSS HELLBRUNN   This early 17th-century palace was built as a hunting lodge and summer residence for Prince-Archbishop Markus Sittikus. The **Hellbrunn Zoo,** also here, was formerly the palace's deer park. The palace **gardens,** some of the oldest baroque formal gardens in Europe, are known for their trick fountains. As you walk through, take care—you might be showered from a surprise source when you least expect it. Some 265 figures in a mechanical theater move by hydraulics to the music of an organ, also powered by water. The rooms of the schloss are furnished and decorated in 18th-century style. See, in particular, the **banquet hall** with its trompe l'oeil painting. The gardens are at Fürstenweg 37, Hellbrunn (☎ **0662/820-372-16**). Admission is 30S ($2.40) for adults and 25S ($2) for children. Open April and October daily 9am to 4:30pm; May, June, and September daily 9am to 3:30pm; July and August daily 9am to 10pm.

Getting There   Bus 55 from Salzburg runs here in 18 minutes. By car, leave Salzburg along Route 341 to the southeast for about 3 miles. Near Rudolfsplatz, turn right at the signpost for Hellbrunner Strasse; the street leads to the castle.

✪ **DÜRNBERG SALT MINES (SALZBERGWERK HALLEIN)**   These salt mines (☎ **06245/83511-0**) are the big lure at Hallein, south of Salzburg. On guided tours, you walk downhill from the ticket office to the mine entrance, and then board an electric mine train that takes you deep into the caverns. From here, you go on foot through galleries, changing levels by sliding down polished wooden slides, and then exit on the train that brought you in. An underground museum traces the history of salt mining back to remote times.

Tours lasting 1½ hours are conducted April to October daily 9am to 5pm and November to March daily 11am to 3pm. Admission is 195S ($15.60) for adults, 95S

($7.60) for children between 6 and 15, 65S ($5.20) for children between 4 and 6, and free for children 3 and under.

Getting There   Hallein is connected to Salzburg, 10 miles away, by both train and bus. From Hallein there's a cable railway to Dürnberg. By car, take A-10 south to Hallein; a modern road from there leads to a large parking lot near the mine's ticket office.

✪ **EISRIESENWELT**   Some 30 miles south of Salzburg by train is this "World of Ice Giants," the largest known **ice caves** in the world. One of the region's most unusual geological oddities, Eisriesenwelt lies in the Pongau basin, on the western cliffs of the Hochkogel, towering over the Salzach Valley. The caves stretch for about 26 miles, although only a portion of that length is open to the public. You'll see fantastic ice formations at the entrance, extending for half a mile. The climax of this chilly underworld tour is the spectacular "Ice Palace."

The ice caves, open between May and October, must be visited as part of an organized tour. Two-hour supervised tours begin at hourly intervals every day between 9:30am and 3:30pm, with more frequent departures offered during July and August when the caves are open until 4:30pm. For more information, call ☎ **06468/5248.** Tours begin at a mountain outpost set 5,141 feet above sea level. From here, you walk to the nearby entrance to the caves. The tour, with the cable car (see below) included, costs 200S ($16) for adults, and 95S ($7.60) for children 4 to 14.

Getting There   To reach the Eisriesenwelt, head for the village of Werfen, a center for exploring the ice caves. From Salzburg, A-10 south leads to Werfen; the caves are signposted. If you go by train to Werfen, you can take a taxi bus marked EISRIESENWELT, which departs for the ice caves at 15-minute intervals from Werfen's Hauptplatz (main square). The round-trip fare is 70S ($5.60) per person. Some hardy travelers opt to hike the steep road, a strenuous 3½-mile, uphill trek that rises abruptly from 1,600 to 3,000 feet. The bus deposits you at the same point you'll reach if you're traveling by car. From the parking lot, a cable car hauls you uphill to the caves' entrance. Once again, some hardy travelers choose to hike uphill to the caves' entrance, although this is recommended only if you have lots of time and lots of energy.

BERCHTESGADEN   Although it's in Germany, Berchtesgaden is one of the most popular day trips, about 14 miles south of Salzburg. Berchtesgaden is situated below the many summits of Watzmann Mountain (8,900 feet at the highest point). According to legend, these mountain peaks were once a king and his family who were so evil that God punished them by turning them into rocks.

Many visitors expect to see one of Hitler's favorite haunts, since the name Berchtesgaden is often linked with the Führer and the Nazi hierarchy. This impression is erroneous. Hitler's playground was actually at Obersalzberg (see below). Berchtesgaden itself is an old alpine village with ancient winding streets and a medieval marketplace and castle square.

The **Schlossplatz** is partially enclosed by the castle and the **Stiftskirche (Abbey Church),** dating from 1122, a Romanesque foundation with Gothic additions. The church interior contains many fine works of art; the high altar has a painting by Zott dating from 1669. The **Königliches Schloss Berchtesgaden** (☎ **08652/20-85**) is now a museum mainly devoted to the royal collection of sacred art, including wood sculptures by the famed artists Veit Stoss and Tilman Riemenschneider. You can also explore a gallery of 19th-century art. Admission is 7DM ($4) for adults and 3DM ($1.70) for children 6 to 16 (free for children under 6). From Easter to September, hours are Sunday to Friday 10am to 1pm and 2 to 5pm. Off-season, hours are Monday to Friday 10am to 1pm.

On the opposite side of the square from the church is a 16th-century arcade that leads to **Marktplatz,** with alpine houses and a wooden fountain from 1677 (restored in 1860). Some of Berchtesgaden's oldest inns and houses border this square.

Salzbergwerk Berchtesgaden, Bergwerkstrasse 83 (☎ **08652/6-00-20**), lies at the eastern edge of town. These salt mines have been worked since 1517; the deposits are more than 990 feet thick and still being processed today. Older children will especially enjoy donning protective miner's clothing for the guided tours that begin with a ride into the mine on a small wagon-like train. After nearly a half-mile ride, visitors explore the rest of the mine on foot, sliding down a miner's chute and riding on the salt lake in a ferry. The highlight of the tour is the "chapel," a grotto containing unusually shaped salt formations eerily illuminated. The 1½-hour tour can be taken any time of the year, in any weather. Admission is 19.50DM ($11.10) for adults and 9.50DM ($5.40) for children 4 to 14. The mines are open May to October 15 daily 9am to 5pm. In the off-season, hours are Monday to Saturday 12:30 to 3:30pm.

Getting There   Trains run every hour during the day from Salzburg to Berchtesgaden; you have to change trains at Freilassing. Frequent **buses** also travel from Salzburg to Berchtesgaden. Motorists take Route 20 south of Salzburg (the route is signposted all the way).

۞ OBERSALZBERG   The drive from Berchtesgaden to Obersalzberg at 3,300 feet is along one of Bavaria's most scenic routes. Here Hitler settled down in a rented cottage while he completed *Mein Kampf.* After he came to power in 1933, he bought Haus Wachenfeld near the hamlet of Hintereck and had it remodeled into his residence, the Berghof. Obersalzberg became the holiday center for Nazis leaders, including Martin Bormann and Hermann Göring.

A major point of interest is the **Kehlstein,** or Eagle's Nest, which can be reached only by a thrilling bus ride up a 4½-mile-long mountain road that was blasted out of solid rock, an outstanding feat of construction and engineering when begun in 1937. To reach the spot, you must enter a tunnel and take a 400-foot elevator ride through a shaft to the summit of the Kehlstein Mountain. Here you can enjoy the panoramic view and explore the rooms of the Nazi leadership's original teahouse, which includes Eva Braun's living room. Of the many buildings that once made up Hitler's lavish holiday compound, this is the only one that wasn't bombed into oblivion by Allied troops near the end of the war. It's open daily 9am to 5pm.

Getting There   For information about trips to Kehlstein, call ☎ **08652/54-73.** RVO **buses** (local buses based in Berchtesgaden) run from the Berchtesgaden Post Office 2½ miles uphill to Obersalzberg-Hintereck; the round-trip journey costs 5.80DM ($3.30). From Hintereck, a special mountain bus carries you another 4 miles uphill to the Kehlstein parking lot. The bus departs Hintereck every half-hour. The ticket price of 20DM ($11.40) includes the elevator ride from the Kehlstein parking lot up to the teahouse itself.

3 Innsbruck & the Tyrol

Land of ice and mountains, dark forests and alpine meadows full of spring wildflowers, Hansel and Gretel villages, summer holidays, and winter sports—that's Tyrol.

Skiers flock here in winter for a season that runs from mid-December to the end of March. It's been a long time since the eyes of the world focused on Innsbruck for the Winter Olympics of 1964 and 1976, but the legacy lives on in the ski conditions and facilities on some of the world's choicest slopes.

This spectacular alpine region also offers travelers a host of other outdoor activities year-round, such as wonderful hiking and mountain climbing, glacier tours, and trout fishing. July and August bring the most visitors to the province, many of them North Americans, so reservations are essential.

Only in the Tyrol

Strolling Through Innsbruck's Altstadt (Old Town)   All tours of the medieval center begin at the Goldenes Dachl, or "Golden Roof," a three-story balcony on a late-Gothic mansion capped with 2,657 gold-plated tiles. Emperor Maximilian I used the balcony as a royal box to watch tournaments in the square below. From this central point you can wander around at leisure—each street holds sightseeing highlights, shops, and cafes.

Standing on Top of the Hungerburg   This mountain plateau 2,860 feet above Innsbruck is the most beautiful spot in the Tyrol, a province known for its stunning views. To stand here on a summer night, watching the fountains and the floodlit buildings of Innsbruck below, is worth the trip to Austria. In the unlikely event you're not satisfied with this view, you can take a cable railway even higher to the Seegrube and the Hafelekar at 7,655 feet for a sweeping view of alpine peaks and glaciers. Mountain scenery rarely gets more spectacular than this.

Skiing on the Arlberg   Serious skiers head for the Arlberg, with peaks that top the 9,000-foot mark. Its vast network of lifts, cableways, and runs stretch for miles, and a world-renowned ski school will introduce you to skiing as you'll rarely encounter it elsewhere. A good base for this adventure is St. Anton am Arlberg, on the eastern side of the Arlberg, 71 miles west of Innsbruck. St. Anton's is virtually the cradle of alpine skiing.

Hiking in the Alps   From June through September, hikers and climbers flock to the area around Innsbruck for the walks and climbs of a lifetime. Hikers can take cable-car lifts to trails that cross lofty plateaus. The Innsbruck tourist office distributes a free brochure filled with tips about the best trails. For those who'd like to learn to climb, the **Alpine Schule,** In der Stille 1, 6161 Natters (☎ **0512/546-000**), offers lessons.

Doing the Ski Circus at Kitzbühel   At one of the most famous resorts in Tyrol, you can ski downhill for more than 50 miles. There are runs for every skill level. Because the terrain is so ideal, numerous championship ski events are held here, including a World Cup event each January. The "circus" is an intricately linked and carefully planned combination of runs, cable railways, and lifts, designed to give you one of the greatest ski experiences of a lifetime.

Experiencing Alpine Après-Ski Life   Many visitors flock here not for the skiing but the après-ski life, an institution unto itself. Each resort from Innsbruck to Seefeld has its own peculiar flavor and joie de vivre, and you'll quickly find the spot suitable for you. Notices of the "big events" of the evening are posted around the resorts, and visitors quickly learn what's "hot" on any given night. Hockey games, holiday parties, sleigh trips into secluded valleys, and toboggan rides are also part of the never-ending après-ski life.

INNSBRUCK

Although Innsbruck is a city with a long imperial past, still remarkably vivid, most visitors don't come for the history, but for the mountains. Alpine peaks surround

Innsbruck, protecting it from the cold winds of the north (we've seen vegetable gardens growing in January).

Today, Innsbruck's beauty, especially its medieval town center, is protected by town planners who ensure that any new structures built in the inner city harmonize with the pre-existing Gothic, Renaissance, and Baroque buildings. It is only to the east and west along the Inn River that modern urban development unfolds far from the center. Visitors can take countless excursions into the environs; at the doorstep of Innsbruck lie some of the most beautiful drives in Europe. Head in any direction, up any valley, and you'll be treated to mountains and alpine beauty almost unmatched anywhere else, including Switzerland.

Innsbruck is easily reached from Salzburg (118 miles to the northeast) and from Munich (99 miles to the north), but it's a long, 304-mile haul west of Vienna.

ORIENTATION

ARRIVING   By Plane   Innsbruck's airport, **Flughafen Innsbruck-Kranebitten,** Fürstenweg 180 (☎ **0512/22525**), is 2 miles west of the city. It offers regularly scheduled air service from each of the major airports of Austria and from most of Europe's major cities. The region's local carrier, **Tyrolean Airways** (☎ **0512/2222**), is by far the most visible and aggressively marketed carrier at this airport, so much so that the only other regularly scheduled flights Tyrolean co-manages are with **Austrian Airlines** (☎ **0512/582-9850**). The airport also receives a handful of charter flights from throughout Europe.

From the airport, **bus line F** leads to the center of the city. Tickets cost 21S ($1.70). A taxi ride takes about 10 minutes and costs from 100S ($8).

By Train   Innsbruck is connected with all parts of Europe by international railway links. Arrivals are at the **Hauptbahnhof,** Südtirolerplatz (☎ **0512/17-17** for all rail information). Frequent trains pull in here from all major European and Austrian cities. There are at least 10 daily trains from Munich (trip time: 2 hours) and about a dozen from Salzburg (trip time: 2 to 3½ hours, depending on the route).

By Bus   Bus service to all Austrian cities is provided by both **Postal Buses** and **Federal Railway Buses.** You can take a bus from Salzburg, although the train is more efficient. For central information about bus routings through Tyrol, call ☎ **0512/58-51-55.**

By Car   If you're driving down from Salzburg in the northeast, take Autobahn **A-8** west, which joins Autobahn **A-93** (later it becomes the A-12), heading southwest to Innsbruck. This latter Autobahn (A-93/A-12) is the main artery in from Munich. From the south, you can take the Brenner toll motorway.

VISITOR INFORMATION   The **tourist office** at Burggraben 3 (☎ **0512/59850**) is open Monday to Friday 8am to 6pm and Saturday 8am to noon. It will supply you with a wealth of information, as well as a list of inexpensive private rooms for rent in Innsbruck. On the first floor of the same building is **Innsbruck-Information** (☎ **0512/5356**), which arranges tours, sells concert tickets, and makes hotel reservations. It's open Monday to Saturday 8am to 6pm, Sunday 9am to 6pm.

CITY LAYOUT   This historic city is divided by the Inn River into left- and right-bank districts. Two major bridges cross the Inn, the **Universitätsbrücke** and the **Alte Innsbrücke (Old Inn Bridge).** Many of the attractions, including the Hofkirche and the Goldenes Dachl, are on the right bank. If you arrive at the Hauptbahnhof, take Salurner Strasse and Brixener Strasse to Maria-Theresien-Strasse, which will put you into the very heart of Innsbruck.

The **Altstadt** is bounded on the north by the Inn River and on the south by Burggraben and Marktgrabben. The main street of this historic district is **Herzog-Friedrich-Strasse,** which becomes **Maria-Theresien-Strasse,** the axis of the post-medieval new part of town. The Altstadt becomes strictly pedestrian after 10:30am (wear good shoes on the cobblestoned streets).

GETTING AROUND   A network of three **tram** and 25 **bus** lines covers all of Innsbruck and its environs. Single tickets in the central area cost 21S ($1.70), and a booklet of four tickets goes for 54S ($4.30). For information about various routes, call the **Innsbrucker Verkehrsbetriebe** (☎ 0512/7102). Tickets can be purchased at the Innsbruck tourist office (see above), tobacco shops, and vending machines.

Postal buses leave from the Central Bus Station, adjacent to the Hauptbahnhof on Sterzinger Strasse, for all parts of Tyrol. The station is open Monday to Friday 7am to 5:30pm and Saturday 7am to 1pm. For information about bus schedules, call ☎ 0512/58-51-55.

Taxi stands are in all parts of town, or you can call for a radio car (☎ 0512/5311). You can take a ride in a horse-drawn cab, starting in front of Tiroler Landestheater, Rennweg. The cost for a 30-minute ride is 320S ($25.60).

Bikes can be rented at the Hauptbahnhof, the main rail station. The cost is 150 to 200S ($12 to $16) per day. If you carry a Eurail or Interrail pass, the charge is only 90 to 160S ($7.20 to $12.80) per day. You can return bikes to any rail station in Austria if you don't plan to come back to Innsbruck. Bicycle rentals are available only from April to early November.

For exploring Tyrol by car, try either **Avis,** Salurner Strasse 15 (☎ 0512/57-17-54), open Monday to Friday 7:30am to 6pm, Saturday 8am to noon, and Sunday 9am to noon; or **Hertz,** at Südtirolerplatz 1 (☎ 0512/58-09-01), across from the Hauptbahnhof, open Monday to Friday 7:30am to 6pm and Saturday 8am to 1pm (closed Sunday). Prices at both agencies fluctuate throughout the year, depending on special promotions and supply and demand. Remember that you always get a cheaper rental rate if you reserve your car from North America through either company's toll-free reservation network.

Fast Facts: Innsbruck

American Express   The office at Brixnerstrasse 3 (☎ 0512/58-24-910) is open Monday to Friday 9am to 5:30pm and Saturday 9am to noon.

Currency Exchange   The best place to exchange is at the tourist office (see "Visitor Information," above).

Dentists/Doctors   The tourist office (see "Visitor Information," above) can supply a list of private English-speaking dentists and doctors in the Innsbruck area. Or you can contact the **University Clinic,** Anichstrasse 35 (☎ 0512/504).

Drugstores   In the heart of Innsbruck, **St.-Anna Apotheke,** Maria-Theresien-Strasse 4 (☎ 0512/58-58-47), is open Monday to Friday 8am to 12:30pm and 2:30 to 6pm, and Saturday 8am to noon; it also posts addresses of other pharmacies open on weekends or late at night.

Emergencies   In case of trouble, call ☎ 133 for the police, ☎ 122 for a fire, or ☎ 144 for an ambulance.

Hospitals   Try the **University Clinic,** located at Anichstrasse 35 (☎ 0512/504).

Innsbruck

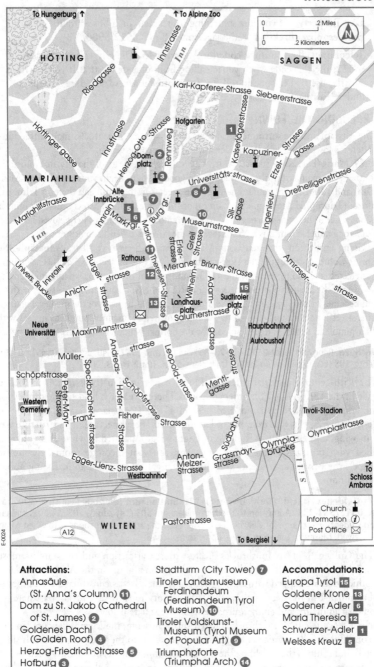

Attractions:

Annasäule
(St. Anna's Column) 11

Dom zu St. Jakob (Cathedral
of St. James) 2

Goldenes Dachl
(Golden Roof) 4

Herzog-Friedrich-Strasse 5

Hofburg 3

Hofkirche 8

Stadtturm (City Tower) 7

Tiroler Landsmuseum
Ferdinandeum
(Ferdinandeum Tyrol
Museum) 10

Tiroler Voldskunst-
Museum (Tyrol Museum
of Popular Art) 9

Triumphpforte
(Triumphal Arch) 14

Accommodations:

Europa Tyrol 15

Goldene Krone 13

Goldener Adler 6

Maria Theresia 12

Schwarzer-Adler 1

Weisses Kreuz 5

Lost Property If you lose something (other than on a bus or train), go to the **Bundespolizeidirektion,** Kaiserjägerstrasse 8 (☎ **0512/5900**).

Telephone The **country code** for Austria is **43.** The **city code** for Innsbruck is **512;** use this code when you're calling from outside Austria. If you're within Austria, use **0512.** For the toll-free international access codes see "Telephone" under "Fast Facts: Vienna."

EXPLORING THE TOWN

The Altstadt and the surrounding alpine countryside are Innsbruck's main attractions. Often it's fascinating just to wander around and people-watch.

✪ **Maria-Theresien-Strasse,** which cuts through the heart of the city from north to south, is the main street of Innsbruck and a good place to begin your exploration. Many 17th- and 18th-century houses line this wide street. On the south end there's a **Triumphpforte (Triumphal Arch),** modeled after those in Rome. Maria Theresa ordered it built in 1765 to honor her son's marriage and to commemorate the death of her beloved husband, Emperor Franz I. From this arch southward, the street is called Leopoldstrasse.

Going north from the arch along Maria-Theresien-Strasse, you'll see **Annasäule (St. Anna's Column)** in front of the 19th-century Rathaus (the present town hall). The column was erected in 1706 to celebrate the 1703 withdrawal of invading Bavarian armies during the War of the Spanish Succession. Not far north of the Annasäule, the wide street narrows and becomes Herzog-Friedrich-Strasse, running through the heart of the medieval quarter. This street is arcaded and flanked by a number of well-maintained burghers' houses with their jumble of turrets and gables; look for the dormer windows and oriels.

Hofburg. Rennweg 1. ☎ **0512/58-71-86.** Guided tour 55S ($4.40) adults, 20S ($1.60) students, 10S (80¢) children under 12. Daily 9am–5pm. Tram: 1 or 3.

The 15th-century imperial palace of Emperor Maximilian I was rebuilt in rococo style in the 18th century on orders of Maria Theresa. Later it held sad memories for the empress, for her husband died here in 1765. The palace, flanked by a set of domed towers, is a fine example of baroque secular architecture. The structure has four wings and a two-story Riesensaal (Giant's Hall), painted in white and gold and filled with portraits of the Hapsburgs. You can visit the state rooms, the house chapel, the private apartment, and the Riesensaal on a guided tour, lasting about half an hour.

✪ **Goldenes Dachl (Golden Roof) Maximilianeum.** Herzog-Friedrich-Strasse 15. ☎ **0512/581-111.** Admission to the Maximilianeum 50S ($4) adults, 20S ($1.60) children and students. No charge for viewing the Goldenes Dachl, and no restrictions as to when it can be viewed. Museum, Tues–Sun 10am–6pm. Tram: 1 or 3.

"The Golden Roof" is Innsbruck's greatest tourist attraction and certainly its most characteristic landmark. It's a three-story balcony on a house in the Altstadt; the late-Gothic oriels are capped with 2,657 gold-plated tiles. It was constructed for Emperor Maximilian I in the beginning of the 16th century to serve as a royal box where he could sit in luxury and enjoy tournaments in the square below.

In 1996, the city of Innsbruck added a small museum, the Maximilianeum, to the second floor of the municipal building that's attached to the Goldenes Dachl. Inside, you'll find exhibits that celebrate the life and accomplishments of the Innsbruck-based Hapsburg emperor, Maximilian I, whose rule extended from the end of the Middle Ages to the dawn of the German-speaking Renaissance. Look for costumes, silver chalices and coins, portraits, and a video that depicts his life and times.

With the same ticket, you can also visit the **Stadtturm (City Tower),** Herzog-Friedrich-Strasse 21 (☎ **0512/57-59-62**). Formerly a prison cell, the tower dates from the mid-1400s and stands adjacent to the Rathaus. From its top, you can look out over the city rooftops to the mountains beyond.

Museums & Churches

Hofkirche. Universitätsstrasse 2. ☎ **0512/58-43-02.** Admission 20S ($1.60) adults, 15S ($1.20) students, 10S (80¢) children under 15. Mon–Sat 9am–5:30pm. Tram: 1 or 3.

The most important treasure in the Hofkirche is the empty tomb of Maximilian I. This elegant marble sarcophagus is a great work of the German Renaissance. It has 28 bronze 16th-century statues depicting Maximilian's real and legendary ancestors surrounding the kneeling emperor, with 24 marble reliefs on the sides showing scenes from his life.

Dom zu St. Jakob (Cathedral of St. James). Domplatz 6. ☎ **0512/58-39-02.** Free admission. Winter daily 7:30am–6:30pm; summer daily 7:30am–7:30pm. Closed Fri noon–3pm. Tram: 1 or 2.

Designed and rebuilt from 1717 to 1724 by Johann Jakob Herkommer, the Dom has a lavishly embellished baroque interior, partly the work of the Asam brothers. A chief treasure is the *Maria Hilf (St. Mary of Succor)*, painted by Lucas Cranach the Elder, on the main altar.

Tiroler Landesmuseum Ferdinandeum (Ferdinandeum Tyrol Museum). Museumstrasse 15. ☎ **0512/59-489.** Admission 60S ($4.80) adults, 20S ($1.60) children. May–Sept daily 10am–5pm, Thurs 10am–5pm and 7–9pm; Oct–Apr Tues–Sat 10am–noon and 2–5pm, Sun 10am–1pm. Tram: 1 or 3.

This museum has a gallery showing the works of Flemish and Dutch masters and also traces the development of popular art in the Tyrolean country. You'll also see the original bas-reliefs used in designing the Goldenes Dachl.

Tiroler Volkskunst-Museum (Tyrol Museum of Popular Art). Universitätsstrasse 2. ☎ **0512/58-43-02.** Admission 40S ($3.20) adults, 25S ($2) students, 15S ($1.20) children. Mon–Sat 9am–5pm; Sun 9am–noon. Tram: 1 or 3.

This popular art museum is in the Neues Stift, or New Abbey, and adjoins the Hofkirche on its eastern side. It contains one of the largest and most impressive collections of Tyrolean artifacts, ranging from handcrafts, furniture, Christmas cribs, and national costumes to religious and profane popular art.

Zoos & Views

Alpenzoo. Weiherburggasse 37. ☎ **0512/29-23-23.** Admission 70S ($5.60) adults, 50S ($4) students, 35S ($2.80) children 6–15, 20S ($1.60) children 4–6. Daily 9am–6pm (5pm in winter). Bus: 2 (May 15–Sept only). Tram: 1 to the Hungerburgbahn (cog railway) or drive north on Höhenstrasse.

From this zoo, lying on the southern slope of the Hungerburg plateau, you get a panoramic view of Innsbruck and the surrounding mountains. The zoo contains animals indigenous to the Alps, plus alpine birds, reptiles, and fish. There are more than 800 animals belonging to over 140 different and sometimes rare species, including otters, eagles, elk, rabbits, vultures, wildcats, bison, and wolves.

ENJOYING THE GREAT OUTDOORS

Five sunny, snow-covered **ski areas** around the Tyrol are served by 5 cableways, 44 chairlifts, and several ski hoists. The area is also known for bobsled and toboggan runs and ice-skating rinks.

In summer you can play tennis at a number of courts, golf on either a 9- or an 18-hole course, and go horseback riding, mountaineering, gliding, swimming, hiking, or shooting.

The Most Beautiful Spot in Tyrol

The ✪ **Hungerburg mountain plateau** (2,860 feet) is the most beautiful spot in Tyrol, affording the best view of Innsbruck, especially on summer nights when much of the city, including fountains and historic buildings, is floodlit. You can drive to the plateau, or take a cog railway, the Hungerburgbahn, which departs from a point about a half-mile east of the center of Innsbruck, at the corner of Rennweg and Kettenbrücke. (To reach the cog railway's departure point from Innsbruck's center, take tram no. 1 or bus C.) In summer, the cog railway departs at 15-minute intervals daily from 9am to 8pm, then runs at 30-minute intervals until 10:30pm. The rest of the year, it operates at 30-minute intervals daily from 8:30am to dusk (between 5 and 6pm). Round-trip fares on the cog railway cost 55S ($4.40) for adults and 30S ($2.40) for children. For schedules and information, call ☎ **0512/ 58-61-58.**

Once you arrive at the Hungerburg plateau, you can progress even farther into the alpine wilds via the **Nordkette cable car.** Designed as a skier-friendly gondola suspended high above the rocky terrain, it will carry you up to the **Seegrube** and the **Hafelekar** (7,655 feet), for a sweeping view over the Tyrolean peaks and glaciers. Hill climbers and rock climbers appreciate this route which leads to a labyrinth of mountain trails; for skiers, it's the departure point for dozens of downhill runs. Throughout the year, the Nordkette cable car runs daily, at 20-minute intervals, from 8:30am to 5:30pm. A round-trip between Innsbruck and Hafelekar costs 225S ($18) for adults and 110S ($8.80) for students and children under 16.

The **Hofgarten,** a public park containing lakes and many shade trees, lies north of Rennweg.

For information on all sports activities, contact the tourist office (see "Visitor Information," above).

ORGANIZED TOURS

The best way to get a quick and convenient overview of Innsbruck is to take a 2-hour **bus tour** of the city's major monuments. Tours depart from a clearly marked point in front of the city's main railway station on the Südtirolerplatz and cost 160S ($12.80) per adult or 70S ($5.60) for those under 16. The experience includes multilingual running commentary on the city's history and architectural highlights, and a 20-minute walk through the heart of the old city. April to September, tours depart at 10am, noon, and 2pm; October to March, one tour a day departs at noon.

If you're really crunched for time, there's a 1-hour bus tour of the city, with no time spent walking, that provides only a very basic introduction. Hours vary, according to demand, but since the 1-hour tour costs 130S ($10.40), almost as much as the 2-hour tour, most visitors opt for the latter. For information on either tour, contact the **Innsbruck Tourist Information Office** at Burggraben 3 (☎ **0512/5356**).

THE SHOPPING SCENE

You'll find a large selection of Tyrolean specialties and all sorts of skiing and mountain-climbing equipment. Stroll around **Maria-Theresien-Strasse, Herzog-Friedrich-Strasse,** and **Museumstrasse,** ducking in and making discoveries of your own.

Lodenbaur, Brixner Strasse 4 (☎ **0512/58-09-11**) is devoted to regional Tyrolean dress, most of which is made in Austria. There's a full array for men, women, and children.

One of the best stores in Innsbruck for handcrafted sculpture and pewter, carved chests, and furniture is **Tiroler Heimatwerk,** Meraner Strasse 2 (☎ **0512/58-23-20**). The store carries textiles, lace, bolts of silk, and dress patterns for those who want to whip up their own dirndls. The elegant decor includes ancient stone columns and vaulted ceilings.

Using old molds discovered in abandoned Tyrolean factories, **Zinnreproduktionen Rudolf Boschi,** Kiebachgasse 8 (☎ **0512/58-92-24**), produces fine reproductions of century-old regional pewter at reasonable prices. Mr. Boschi also reproduces rare pewter objects acquired from auctions throughout Europe. Look for a copy of the 18th-century pewter barometer emblazoned with representations of the sun and the four winds. The work is done in a nearby foundry south of Innsbruck.

WHERE TO STAY
Very Expensive
Hotel Europa Tyrol. Südtirolerplatz 2, 6020 Innsbruck. ☎ **800/223-5652** in the U.S., or 0512/5931. Fax 0512/58-78-00. 140 units. MINIBAR TV TEL. 2,200–3,400S ($176–$272) double; 4,200–5,800S ($336–$464) suite. Rates include breakfast. AE, DC, MC, V. Parking 150S ($12).

Opposite Innsbruck's railway station, this elegant hotel has a formal paneled lobby with an English-style bar, accents of green marble, and Oriental rugs. The rooms and suites are handsomely furnished, with all the modern conveniences and Tyrolean or Biedermeier-style decorations. Each tasteful unit has a marble bathroom with a hair dryer. The restaurant Europa Stüberl, the finest in Innsbruck, is recommended in "Where to Dine," below.

Expensive
🔾 **Romantikhotel-Restaurant Schwarzer Adler.** Kaiserjägerstrasse 2, 6020 Innsbruck. ☎ **0512/58-71-09.** Fax 0512/56-16-97. www.tiscover.com/romantikhotel-schwarzer-adler. E-mail: romantikhotel-innsbruck@netway.at. 28 units. MINIBAR TV TEL. 1,700–2,200S ($136–$176) double; 2,100–2,900S ($168–$232) suite. Rates include breakfast. Half-board 310S ($24.80) per person extra. AE, DC, MC, V. Parking 120S ($9.60). Tram: 1 or 3.

The hotel lies behind an antique, stuccoed facade with shutters and a big-windowed tower. Its owners, the Ultsch family, have furnished the interior in an authentic and charming Austrian style. Aged paneling, vaulted ceilings, hand-painted regional furniture, antiques, and lots of homey clutter make for a cozy and inviting ambience. The original Tiroler Stube has a history going back 4 centuries, and the K. u K. (Kaiser und König) Restaurant has won awards for its modern Austrian cuisine.

Moderate
🔾 **Hotel Goldener Adler.** Herzog-Friedrich-Strasse 6, 6020 Innsbruck. ☎ **0512/ 57-11-11.** Fax 0512/58-44-09. 37 units. MINIBAR TV TEL. 1,600–2,100S ($128–$168) double; from 2,860S ($228.80) suite. Rates include breakfast. AE, DC, MC, V. Parking 196S ($15.70). Tram: 1 or 3.

Even the phone booth near the reception desk of this 600-year-old hotel is outfitted in antique style, concealed behind an old panel. Famous guests have included Goethe, Mozart, and the violinist Paganini, who cut his name into the windowpane of his room. The handsome rooms in this family-run hotel sport leaded windows with stained-glass inserts, travertine floors, ornate carved Tyrolean furniture, and chandeliers with figures carved from rams' horns. All the rooms have private safes, firm mattresses, and well-maintained bathrooms that come in a variety of sizes.

Hotel Maria Theresia. Maria-Theresien-Strasse 31, 6020 Innsbruck. ☎ **800/528-1234** in the U.S., or 0512/5933. Fax 0512/57-56-19. 107 units. MINIBAR TV TEL. 1,500–2,200S ($120–$176) double; 2,200–2,800S ($176–$224) suite. Rates include American breakfast. AE, DC, MC, V. Parking 140S ($11.20). Tram: 1 or 3.

This Best Western hotel with its elegantly classic facade is on Innsbruck's famous shopping street a few blocks away from the winding alleys of the old town. A striking oil portrait of the empress herself hangs in the reception area. The helpful staff will do everything possible to make you feel comfortable. Most of the recently redecorated rooms are medium-size and have firm mattresses. The marble-floored bathrooms are tiny but equipped with good towels and a hair dryer. Restaurant Tyrol serves a local and international cuisine.

Inexpensive
City-Hotel Goldene Krone. Maria-Theresien-Strasse 46, 6020 Innsbruck. ☎ **0512/58-61-60.** Fax 0512/580-18-96. www.touringhotels.at. E-mail: r.pischl@tirol.com. 37 units. TV. 890–1,200S ($71.20–$96) double; from 1,400–1,600S ($112–$128) suite. Rates include breakfast. AE, MC, V. Parking 100S ($8). Bus: A, H, K, or N. Tram: 1.

Near the Triumphal Arch on Innsbruck's main street, this green-and-white baroque house offers three-star comfort: modern, well-maintained rooms; an elevator; soundproof windows; and a Viennese-inspired coffeehouse/restaurant, the Café, where a salad buffet is set up daily 11:30am to 2pm. The cafe/restaurant is open Monday to Saturday 7am to 11pm.

Gasthof-Hotel Weisses Kreuz. Herzog-Friedrich-Strasse 31, 6020 Innsbruck. ☎ **0512/59479.** Fax 0512/59-47-990. E-mail: hotel.weisses.kreuz@eunet.at. 39 units (30 with bathroom). TEL. 820–860S ($65.60–$68.80) double without bathroom; 1,040–1,220S ($83.20–$97.60) double with bathroom. Rates include breakfast. AE, MC, V. Parking 100S ($8). Tram: 1 or 3.

This atmospheric, historic inn in the center of Innsbruck has been altered over the years to keep abreast of shifting tastes and requirements. An elevator now carries guests up the two flights to the reception area. Bedrooms, often under beamed ceilings, have been modernized and frequently renovated, with stylish but simple furnishings, including good beds. In 1769, 13-year-old Wolfgang Mozart and his father, Leopold, stayed here. The hotel's facade is graced by an extended bay window, stretching from the second to the fourth floor.

WHERE TO DINE
Expensive
Europa Stüberl. In the Hotel Europa Tyrol, Brixner Strasse 6. ☎ **0512/5931.** Reservations required. Main courses 95–320S ($7.60–$25.60); set-price menus 350–460S ($28–$36.80). AE, DC, MC, V. Daily 11am–2pm and 6:30–11pm. AUSTRIAN/INTERNATIONAL.

This distinguished restaurant, with a delightful Tyrolean ambience, serves both the hotel guests and the general public. Traditional regional and creative cooking is the chef's specialty. Fresh Tyrolean trout almost always appears on the menu, and meat dishes range from red deer ragoût to saddle of venison to such exotica as fried jelly of calf's head Vienna style with a lamb's tongue salad. Many dishes are served for two people, including roast pike-perch with vegetables and buttery potatoes, and Bresse guinea hen roasted and served with an herb sauce. There's also a heaping platter known as a Europastüberl Rindl that contains portions of sirloin steak, veal cutlet, calves' liver, and venison sausage garnished with fresh vegetables and sauerkraut. Smaller appetites appreciate such main course regulars as Tyrolean dumplings stuffed with bacon, spinach, and cheese, and served with sauerkraut. Many of the seasonal specialties change every 2 weeks.

✪ **Restaurant Goldener Adler.** Herzog-Friedrich-Strasse 6. ☎ **0512/57-11-11.** Reservations recommended. Main courses 150–275S ($12–$22); set–price menus 90–100S ($7.20–$8). AE, DC, MC, V. Daily 11:30am–10:30pm, with a limited menu 2–6pm. Tram: 1 or 3. AUSTRIAN/TYROLEAN/INTERNATIONAL.

Richly Teutonic, and steeped in the decorative traditions of the Tyrolean Alps, this beautifully decorated restaurant has a deeply entrenched reputation and a loyal following among local residents. There are four separate dining rooms, each elaborately paneled and filled with antique accessories. The menu includes good, hearty fare that warms you right up—the chefs aren't into delicate subtleties. Examples include Tyrolean bacon served with horseradish and farmer's bread; carpaccio of filet of beef with Parmesan and olive oil; cream of cheese soup with croutons; and *Tyroler Zopfebraten,* a flavorful age-old specialty consisting of strips of veal steak served with herb-enriched cream sauce and spinach dumplings. A well-regarded and time-tested specialty is *Adler Tres:* spinach dumplings, stuffed noodles, and cheese dumplings, all in a brown butter sauce with melted mountain cheese.

Moderate

Altstadtstüberl. Riesengasse 13. ☎ **0512/58-23-47.** Reservations recommended. Main courses 75–290S ($6–$23.20). AE, DC, MC, V. Mon–Sat 11am–3pm and 5:30–midnight. Tram: 1 or 3. AUSTRIAN.

In a building whose walls date from 1360, this is one of the most solidly reliable, moderately priced restaurants in Innsbruck. There's a salad buffet and a satisfying roster of international dishes (steaks, salads, roast lamb, and pastas), as well as old-time Austrian favorites, including *Tafelspitz* (boiled beef) with horseradish sauce; *Wiener Schnitzel;* rack of lamb, and a frequently changing selection of homemade pastries. Try the *Kaiserschmarrn,* a doughy crêpe filled with a slow-cooked mixture of plum and apricot marmalade enhanced with raisins, cut into bite-sized portions, and served with a compote of apples.

Hirschen-Stuben. Kiebachgasse 5. ☎ **0512/58-29-79.** Reservations recommended. Main courses 150–245S ($12–$19.60); set-price lunch 90–250S ($7.20–$20). DC, MC, V. Tues–Sat 11am–2pm; Mon–Sat 6–10pm. Tram: 1 or 3. AUSTRIAN/ITALIAN.

Beneath a vaulted ceiling in a house built in 1631, Hirshchen-Stuben is charming, well established, and well recommended. Down a short flight of stairs from the street, you'll find hand-chiseled stone columns, brocade chairs, and a warm ambience. The food is well prepared and the staff is helpful, polite, and efficient. Menu items include steaming plates of pasta, fish soup, monkfish in a tomato-basil sauce, and sliced veal in cream sauce Zurich style.

Inexpensive

Restaurant Ottoburg. Herzog-Friedrich-Strasse 1. ☎ **0512/57-46-52.** Reservations recommended. Main courses 95–250S ($7.60–$20); 2-course set-price lunch 98S ($7.85). AE, DC, MC, V. Daily 11am–3pm and 5–11pm. Closed Tues Oct–June. Tram: 1 or 3. AUSTRIAN/INTERNATIONAL.

This historic restaurant was originally established around 1745 and occupies two floors of a 13th-century building that some historians say is the oldest in Innsbruck. Inside are four intimate and atmospheric dining rooms with a "19th-century neo-Gothic decor." Dishes include venison stew, "grandmother's mixed grill," fried trout, and three varieties of roasts.

Stiegl-Bräu Innsbruck. Wilhelm-Greil-Strasse 25. ☎ **0512/58-43-38.** Main courses 130–250S ($10.40–$20). No credit cards. Daily 10am–midnight (last orders at 11pm). Tram: 1 or 3. AUSTRIAN/INTERNATIONAL.

One of the most reliable and atmospheric of the cost-conscious restaurants of Innsbruck, this animated beer hall/restaurant is owned by a Salzburg-based brewery (Stiegl-Bräu) that has been making beer since 1492. There are two crowded and well-used dining rooms and an outdoor beer garden that's open only in summer. Menu items are described by the hardworking staff as "the people's food," and include rib-sticking versions of braised beef, braised veal, hearty stews, Irish mutton, lamb and pork chops, sausages, and schnitzels that are often accompanied with braised cabbage or sauerkraut and dumplings.

INNSBRUCK AFTER DARK

The major venue for **performing arts** is the **Landestheater,** Rennweg 2 (☎ 0512/52074). The 150-year-old theater offers a variety of programs. The box office is open Monday to Saturday 8:30am to 8:30pm and Sunday 5:30 to 8:30pm, and performances usually begin at 7:30 or 8pm. Tickets cost 85 to 460S ($6.80 to $36.80) for operettas and opera, 70 to 390S ($5.60 to $31.20) for theater. Concerts are often presented at the Kunstpavillon in the **Hofgarten** in summer.

Bars, Clubs & Folk Music

In summer, the outdoor bar at **Club Filou,** Stiftsgasse 12 (☎ 0512/58-02-56), blossoms with ivy-covered trellises and parasols. Inside you'll find an intimate hangout filled with Victorian settees and pop art. In a separate, very old room is the disco, with a ceiling supported by medieval stone columns and ringed with a high-tech steel balcony. Tall drinks (such as Tom Collins), in both the cafe and disco, begin at around 68S ($5.45); a beer costs 38S ($3.05). The cafe is open daily 6pm to 4am; the disco is open daily 9pm to 4am. Food is available until 3am.

If you want to try an amazing martini, go to **Sparkling Cocktails,** Innstrasse 45 (☎ 0512/28-78-80), where virtually any kind of mixed drink or cocktail, including an almost lethal zombie, can be crafted by the highly experienced staff. Drinks range from 68 to 125S ($5.45 to $10) and are served Monday to Saturday 7pm to 2am.

Young people hang out at **Treibhaus,** Angerzellgasse 8 (☎ 0512/58-68-74), a combination cafe, bar, and social club. Within its battered walls, a changing roster of art exhibitions, cabaret shows, and protest rallies are presented, daily from 10am to 1am, with live music at erratic intervals. Cover for live performances is 180 to 250S ($14.40 to $20).

Goethe Stube, Restaurant Goldener Adler, Herzog-Friedrich-Strasse 6 (☎ 0512/57-11-11), offers authentic folk music programs throughout the Christmas-New Year's season, Easter, and the winter season. There's no cover, but a one-drink minimum; a large beer costs 40S ($3.20); meals start at 200S ($16). Open daily 7 to 11:30pm.

ST. ANTON AM ARLBERG

A modern resort has grown out of this old village on the Arlberg Pass that was the scene of ski history in the making. At St. Anton (elev. 4,225 feet), Hannes Schneider developed modern skiing techniques and began teaching tourists how to ski in 1907. The Ski Club Arlberg was born in 1901, and in 1911 the first Arlberg-Kandahar Cup competition was held. Before his death in 1955, Schneider saw his ski school rated as the world's finest. Today the school is still one of the world's largest and best, with about 300 instructors (most of whom speak English). St. Anton am Arlberg in winter is quite fashionable, popular with the wealthy and occasional royalty—a more conservative slice of the rich and famous than you see at other chic ski resorts.

There's so much emphasis on skiing here that few seem to talk of the summertime attractions. In warm weather, St. Anton is tranquil and bucolic. A riot of wildflowers blooming in the fields and meadows announces the beginning of spring.

St. Anton is 372 miles west of Vienna and 62 miles west of Innsbruck.

ESSENTIALS

ARRIVING   By Train   Because of St. Anton's good rail connections to eastern and western Austria, most visitors arrive by train. St. Anton is an express stop on the main rail lines crossing over the Arlberg Pass between Innsbruck and Bregenz. Just to the west of St. Anton, trains disappear into the Arlberg tunnel, emerging almost 7 miles later on the opposite side of the mountain range. About one train per hour arrives in St. Anton from both directions. Trip time from Innsbruck is 75 to 85 minutes, depending on the train; from Bregenz, around 85 minutes. For local rail information, call ☎ **05446/24020.**

By Bus   The town is the point of origin for many bus travelers who travel from St. Anton on to such other resorts as Zürs and Lech. There is no local number to call for bus information.

By Car   Motorists should take Route 171 west from Innsbruck.

VISITOR INFORMATION   The **tourist office** is in the Arlberghaus in the center of town (☎ **05446/22690**). It's open July to mid-September, Monday to Friday 8am to noon and 2 to 6pm, Saturday to Sunday 10am to noon; May to June and mid-September to November, Monday through Friday 8am to noon and 2 to 6pm; December to April, Monday through Friday 8am to 6pm, Saturday 9am to noon and 1 to 7pm, and Sunday 10am to noon and 3 to 6pm.

HITTING THE SLOPES IN ST. ANTON

Perfect snow and treeless slopes make this area an ideal spot for skiing. The ski fields of St. Anton stretch over a distance of some 6 square miles. Beginners stick to the slopes down below, while more experienced skiers head to the runs from the Galzig and Valluga peaks. A cableway will take you to **Galzig** (6,860 feet), where there's a self-service restaurant. You go from here to **Vallugagrat** (8,685 feet), the highest reachable station. The peak of the **Valluga,** at 9,220 feet, commands a panoramic view. St. Christoph is the mountain annex of St. Anton.

Other major ski areas include the **Gampen/Kapall,** an advanced-intermediate network of slopes, whose lifts start just behind St. Anton's railway station; and the **Rendl,** a relatively new labyrinth of runs to the south of St. Anton that offers many novice and intermediate slopes.

OTHER ACTIVITIES & ATTRACTIONS

There are many other cold-weather pursuits than just skiing, such as ski jumping, mountain hikes, curling, skating, tobogganing, and sleigh rides, plus après-ski on the quiet side.

Ski und Heimat Museum (Skiing and Local Museum), in the Arlberg-Kandahar House (☎ **05446/2475**), traces the development of skiing in the Arlberg, as well as the history of the region from the days of tribal migrations in and around Roman times. The museum, in the imposing structure at the center of the Holiday Park in St. Anton, is open from December through April on Monday through Saturday 2:30pm to midnight. From mid-June to late September, it's open Thursday through Tuesday 10am to 6pm (closed the rest of the year). Admission is 20S ($1.60) for adults and 10S (80¢) for children.

WHERE TO STAY & DINE

✪ **Hotel Schwarzer Adler.** 6580 St. Anton am Arlberg. ☎ **800/528-1234** in the U.S., or 05446/22440. Fax 05446/224462. E-mail: schwarzer.adler@st-anton.at. 50 units. TV TEL. Winter 2,000–4,600S ($160–$368) double; summer 1,000–2,000S ($80–$160) double. Rates include half-board. AE, DC, MC, V. Closed May–June and Oct–Nov. Free parking.

This hotel has been owned and operated by the Tschol family since 1885. The beautiful building in the center of St. Anton was constructed as an inn in 1570 and became known for its hospitality to pilgrims crossing the treacherous Arlberg Pass.

The 400-year-old frescoes on the exterior were discovered during a restoration and have been faithfully restored to their original grandeur.

The hotel has a rustic-yet-elegant interior, with blazing fireplaces, painted Tyrolean baroque armoires, and Oriental rugs. There are handsomely furnished and well-equipped bedrooms in the main hotel, plus 13 slightly less well-furnished (but less expensive) rooms in the annex, which is across the street above the Café Aquila. There's a sauna and a fitness center, and the hotel's restaurant is well known for its excellent cuisine.

Raffl-Stube. In the Hotel St. Antoner Hof, St. Anton am Arlberg. ☎ **05446/2910.** Reservations required. Main courses 200–325S ($16–$26); set-price menu 1,000–1,200S ($80–$96). AE, DC, MC, V. Daily 11am–2pm and 7–10:30pm. Closed mid-Oct to mid-Dec and mid-Apr to mid-June. AUSTRIAN.

This isn't the most visible or flamboyant restaurant in St. Anton, but it's one of the coziest. Containing only a half-dozen tables, it occupies an enclosed corner off the lobby of one of the resort's most prominent hotels. Because of its small scale and emphasis on well-prepared food, it can get very exclusive. Reservations are essential, especially if you're a non-resident. Overflow diners are offered a seat in a spacious but less special dining room across the hall. The hotel has long enjoyed a reputation for its cuisine, but somehow the food in the stube tastes even better. Quality ingredients are always used, and the kitchen prepares such tempting specialties as roast goose liver with salad; cream of parsley soup with sautéed quail eggs; filet of salmon with wild rice; and trout "prepared as you like it," along with the ever-popular fondue bourguignonne.

MORE DINING   If you can't secure a reservation at Raffl-Stube, don't despair. St. Anton has plenty of other less expensive options, usually hotel dining rooms open to non-guests. You can get classic Austrian dishes at the historic **Hotel Alte Post Restaurant** (☎ **05446/25530**) and the first-rate **Hotel Kertess Restaurant** (☎ **05446/2005**), located high on a slope in the suburb of Oberdorf. For superb international cuisine, head to the medieval **Hotel Schwarzer Adler Restaurant** (☎ **05446/22440**). Although none of these hotels have a street address, they are all signposted at various places in town, so you should have no trouble finding them.

SEEFELD

Seefeld, 15 miles northwest of Innsbruck, is one of Austria's "big three" international winter-sports spots (St. Anton and Kitzbühel being the other two). Seefeld hosted the 1964 and 1976 Nordic events for the Olympic Winter Games and the 1985 Nordic Ski World Championships. The fashionable resort lies some 3,450 feet above sea level on a sunny plateau.

ESSENTIALS

ARRIVING   By Train   More than a dozen trains per day arrive from Innsbruck (trip time: around 40 minutes). There's also train service from Munich and Garmisch-Partenkirchen, Germany. For rail information, call ☎ **05212/2438.**

By Bus   Buses depart daily from Innsbruck's Hauptbahnhof; trip time is around 45 minutes. For bus information, call ☎ **0512/58-51-55** in Innsbruck.

By Car   From Innsbruck, head west along Route 177 until you reach the junction with Route 313; at that point, turn north.

VISITOR INFORMATION   The **Seefeld tourist office** is at Klosterstrasse 43 (☎ **05212/2313**). It's open mid-September to mid-December and March to mid-June, Monday to Saturday 8:30am to 12:15pm and 3 to 6pm; other months, Monday to Saturday 8:30am to 6:30pm.

HITTING THE SLOPES & OTHER ACTIVITIES

SKIING   Skiers are served by one funicular railway, two cable cars, three chairlifts, and 14 drag lifts. The beginner slopes lie directly in the village center. The base stations of the lifts for the main skiing areas (known as **Gschwandtkopt** and **Rosshutte/Seefelder Joch**) are at most half a mile away from the center, and are serviced by free daily nonstop bus service. There are 124 miles of prepared **cross-country tracks.**

OTHER WINTER ACTIVITIES   Other winter activities offered here include curling, horse-drawn sleigh rides, outdoor skating (ice-skating school, with artificial and natural ice rink), horseback riding, indoor tennis (Swedish tennis school), tube sliding (you slide on rubber inner tubes—lying down or sitting), indoor golf facilities, parasailing, bowling, squash, hiking (60 miles of cleared paths), fitness studio, swimming, and saunas.

SUMMER ACTIVITIES   Summer visitors can enjoy swimming in three lakes, in a heated open-air swimming pool on Seefeld Lake, or at the Olympia indoor and outdoor pools. Other summer sports include tennis on 18 open-air and 8 indoor courts (Swedish tennis school), horseback riding (two stables with indoor schools), and golf on the 18-hole course, which has been rated by golf insiders as one of the 100 most beautiful courses in the world. Hiking on 124 miles of walks and mountain paths, cycling, minigolf, parasailing, and rafting can also be enjoyed.

A GOOD PLACE TO STAY

✪ **Hotel Klosterbräu.** Klosterstrasse 30, 6100 Seefeld. ☎ **05212/26210.** Fax 05212/ 3885. www.klosterbraeu.com. E-mail: info@klosterbraeu.com. 136 units. MINIBAR TV TEL. Winter 3,000–3,800S ($240–$304) double, from 4,000S ($320) suite; summer 2,400–2,800S ($192–$224) double, from 3,600S ($288) suite. Rates include board. AE, DC, MC, V. Closed Apr–May and Oct–Nov. Parking 150S ($12).

The town's most unusual and elegant hotel is constructed around a 16th-century cloister. The dramatic entrance is under a thick stucco arch. Inside, soaring vaults are supported by massive columns of the same porous stone that built Salzburg (you can

---

Side Trips to Bavaria

While you're based in Seefeld, it's relatively easy to explore parts of Bavaria in Germany. You may or may not get to see little **Wildmoos Lake.** It can, and sometimes does, completely vanish in a day or so, and then all you may find are cows grazing on what has become meadowland. However, the lake will come back just as suddenly, and if conditions are right, it will be deep enough for swimmers. Wildmoos Lake comes and goes more frequently than Brigadoon.

Wildmoos Lake is a 5-minute drive west from Seefeld (it's signposted from the center of town). Cars are not permitted on the drive until after 5pm. Buses run from the center of Seefeld several times a day. Or, it's a 10- to 15-minute walk from the center of town.

The little German town of **Mittenwald,** one of the highlights of Bavaria, can also be easily explored on a day trip from Seefeld. (For more on Mittenwald see chapter 7, "Germany.") It's best to take the train from Seefeld, which departs hourly until 9pm (trip time: 1 hour). Two buses per day also make the trip, although the traffic is so congested the bus trip often takes twice as long as the train. Contact the tourist office for the bus schedule.

still see prehistoric crustaceans embedded in the stone). The luxurious decor includes thick carpeting, Oriental rugs, antiques, and beautifully furnished paneling. The well-furnished and elegant bedrooms are encased in a towering chalet behind the front entrance.

Restaurants on the premises include a country-style Bräukeller, a rustic Tyrolean room, and a more formal dining room where guests sit below ancient ceiling vaults. Dishes include international and Austrian specialties. The person at the next table might be a vacationing celebrity traveling incognito. À la carte dinners go for 350 to 600S ($28 to $48), and reservations are necessary.

In the evening, Die Kanne is a nightclub, and a daily afternoon tea dance in winter allows the hotel guests to meet one another. There are indoor and outdoor swimming pools, a sauna, health club, solarium, golf, tennis, mountain climbing, and skiing within walking distance.

A GOOD PLACE TO DINE

Sir Richard. Innsbruckerstrasse 162. ☎ **05212/2093.** Reservations required. Main courses 190–310S ($15.20–$24.80). DC, MC, V. Daily 11:30am–2pm and 6:30–10pm. Closed 2 weeks in Nov and Tues in winter. AUSTRIAN/ITALIAN.

On the southern outskirts of town, this restaurant creates an elegant ambience of year-round Christmastime, with masses of flowers, dozens of burning candles, and immaculately pressed linen. Entrees are presented on delicate china by an attentive staff. You might begin your meal with watercress soup, followed by one of the lamb, veal, or fish dishes, often accompanied by masterful sauces. Even the fresh leafy salads have just the right degree of tartness. For a taste of Italy, try one of the pastas or risottos, complemented by a glass of one of the many Italian reds. Everything on the short menu is mouth-watering, made with the freshest of ingredients.

THE KITZBÜHEL ALPS

Both hard-core skiers and the rich and famous are attracted to this ski region. The Kitzbühel Alps are covered with such a dense network of lifts that they now form the largest skiing complex in the country, with a series of excellent runs. The action centers on the town of Kitzbühel, but there are many satellite resorts that are much less expensive, including St. Johann in Tyrol.

Kitzbühel is, in a sense, a neighbor of Munich, 81 miles to the northeast, whose municipal airport is the entry point for most wintertime visitors.

Edward, prince of Wales (you may remember him better as the duke of Windsor), may have put Kitzbühel on the international map with his 1928 "discovery" of what was then a town of modest guesthouses. His return a few years later with Mrs. Simpson caused the eyes of the world to focus on this town, and the "upper crust" of England and other countries soon followed. At the time of this 20th-century renaissance, however, Kitzbühel was already some 8 centuries old, and a settlement has been here much, much longer than that.

ESSENTIALS

ARRIVING   By Train   Kitzbühel sits astride the main train lines between Innsbruck and Salzburg, receiving one express train and about two local trains per hour from both of these cities. Trip time from Innsbruck is about 1 hour; from Salzburg, around 2½ hours. For rail information, call ☎ **05356/64055.**

By Bus   Two buses travel daily from Salzburg's main railway station to Kitzbühel (trip time: around 2¼ hours). Nine local bus lines run into and up the surrounding valleys. A bus runs every 30 to 60 minutes between Kitzbühel and St. Johann in Tyrol (trip time: 25 minutes). For information, call ☎ **05356/627-15.**

By Car Kitzbühel is 62 miles east of Innsbruck. From Innsbruck, take Autobahn A-12 east to the junction with Route 312 heading to Ellmau. After bypassing Ellmau, continue east to the junction with Route 161, which you take south to Kitzbühel.

VISITOR INFORMATION The **tourist office** is at Hinterstadt 18 (☎ 05356/ 621-55). In the winter ski season and in July and August, it is open Monday through Friday 8:30am to 6:30pm, Saturday 8:30am to noon and 4 to 6pm, and Sunday 10am to noon and 4 to 6pm. In off-season, hours are Monday through Friday 8:30am to 12:30pm and 2:30 to 6pm and on Saturday 8:30am to noon. In winter, call ☎ **182** for snow reports.

SEEING THE SIGHTS IN TOWN

The town has two main streets, both pedestrian walkways: **Vorderstadt** and **Hinterstadt.** Kitzbühel has preserved its traditional architecture, at least along these streets. You'll see three-story stone houses with oriels and scrollwork around the doors and windows, heavy overhanging eaves, and Gothic gables.

The **Pfarrkirche (parish church)** was built from 1435 to 1506 and renovated in the baroque style in the 18th century. The lower part of the **Liebfrauenkirche (Church of Our Lady)** dates from the 13th century, the upper part from 1570. Between these two churches stands the **Ölbergkapelle (Ölberg Chapel)** with a 1450 "lantern of the dead" and frescoes from the latter part of the 16th century.

In the **Heimatmuseum,** Hinterstadt 34 (☎ **05356/645-88**), you'll see artifacts from prehistoric European mining eras and the north alpine Bronze Age, a winter-sports section with trophies of Kitzbüheler skiing greats, and exhibits detailing the town's history. The museum is open Monday to Saturday 9am to 12:30pm; admission is 30S ($2.40) for adults and 5S (40¢) for children and students.

HITTING THE SLOPES & OTHER OUTDOOR ACTIVITIES

SKIING In winter the emphasis in Kitzbühel, 2,300 feet above sea level, is on skiing, and facilities are offered for everyone from novices to experts. The ski season starts just before Christmas and goes until late March. With more than 62 lifts, gondolas (cable cars), and mountain railroads on five different mountains, Kitzbühel has two main ski areas, the **Hahnenkamm** (renovated in 1995) and the **Kitzbüheler Horn.** Cable cars are within easy walking distance, even for those in ski boots.

The linking of the lift systems on the Hahnenkamm has created the celebrated ✪ **Kitzbühel Ski Circus,** which makes it possible to ski downhill for more than 50 miles, with runs that suit every skill level. Numerous championship ski events are held here; the World Cup event each January pits the world's best skiers against the toughest, fastest downhill course, a stretch of the Hahnenkamm specifically designed for speed. Its name, *Die Streif,* is both feared and respected among skiers. A ski pass costing 2,000S ($160) entitles the holder to use of all the lifts that form the Ski Circus.

Skiing has been a fact of life in Kitzbühel since 1892, when the first pair of skis was imported from Norway and intrepid daredevils began to slide down the snowy slopes at breakneck speeds. Many great names in skiing have since been associated with Kitzbühel, the most renowned being Toni Sailer, a native of the town, who was the triple champion in the 1956 Winter Games in Cortina.

OTHER WINTER ACTIVITIES There are many other winter activities: ski-bobbing, ski jumping, ice skating, tobogganing, hiking on cleared trails, curling, and hang gliding, as well as such indoor activities as tennis, bowling, and swimming. The children's ski school offers training for the very young. And don't forget the lively après-ski scene, with bars, nightclubs, and dance clubs rocking from when you come off the slopes until the wee hours.

The Scoop on Ski Passes

Ski passes and the costs of chair lifts can be purchased on the spot at ski resorts in Austria, but this invariably leads to higher costs. Savvy skiers usually arrive with a ski package, booked through a travel agent, that includes the cost of their hotel, plus a ski pass that also covers the cost of major chair lifts.

If purchased individually, ski passes at the same resort often carry different price tags throughout the winter season, depending on snow conditions. Of course, they're the most expensive during two peak periods: the Christmas season through New Year's and the month of February. They are often lower at the beginning and end of the ski season, when snow conditions aren't at their best. A typical ski pass is likely to cost around 2,000S ($160) for adults or 1,000S ($80) for children for a 1-week period. It's also possible to purchase a 1-day pass. Costs usually range from 385S ($30.80) to 410S ($32.80) for adults or around 200S ($16) for children. You can rent skis at all Austrian resorts. Downhill equipment rental usually runs from 170S ($13.60) to 500S ($40) per day, with snowboards averaging 180S to 350S ($14.40–$28).

SUMMER ACTIVITIES   Kitzbühel has plenty of summer pastimes too, including walking tours, visits to the **Wild Life Park** at Aurach (about 2 miles from Kitzbühel), tennis, horseback riding, golf, squash, brass band concerts in the town center, cycling, and swimming. There's an indoor swimming pool, but we recommend going to the **Schwarzsee** (Black Lake), a peat lake about a 15-minute walk from the center of town. Here you'll find bathing spots, boats to rent, fishing, windsurfing, a water-ski school, and restaurants.

One of the region's most exotic collections of alpine flora is clustered into the jagged and rocky confines of the **Alpine Flower Garden Kitzbühel,** where species of gentian, gorse, heather, and lichens are found on the sunny slopes of the Kitzbüheler Horn. Around 6,000 feet above sea level, the garden—which the municipality of Kitzbühel owns and maintains as an incentive to midsummer tourism—is open late May to early September daily 8:30am to 5:30pm. It's at its most impressive June to August. Admission to the garden is free, and many visitors opt to view it by taking the Kitzbüheler Horn gondola (cable car) to its uppermost station and then descending on foot via the garden's labyrinth of footpaths to the gondola's middle station. The **Kitzbüheler Horn gondola** (☎ **05356/6951**) departs from Kitzbühel at 20-minute intervals daily throughout the summer and winter months from 8:30am to 5:30pm; a round-trip ticket is 180S ($14.40).

WHERE TO STAY

Hotel Bruggerhof. Reitherstrasse 24, 6370 Kitzbühel. ☎ **05356/62806.** Fax 05356/644-7930. 25 units. TV TEL. Winter 1,500–1,840S ($120–$147.20) double; summer 1,160–1,300S ($92.80–$104) double. Rates include half-board. AE, DC, V. Free parking. Closed Apr to mid-May and mid-Oct to Dec 15.

About a mile west of the town center, near the Schwarzsee, is this countryside chalet with a sun terrace. Originally a 1920s farmhouse, the interior has massive ceiling beams, some carved into Tyrolean patterns, and a corner fireplace. In 1960 it was expanded and enlarged into the hotel you see today, a three-star choice that's family-oriented, cozy, and well maintained. The dining room is graced with wooden ceilings and wrought-iron chandeliers. Rooms are comfortable and cozy, decorated in an alpine style, with firm beds and somewhat cramped bathrooms. A whirlpool, steam bath, and solarium are just a few of the amenities guests enjoy year-round; tennis and miniature golf facilities are available in summer.

✪ **Hotel Zur Tenne.** Vorderstadt 8–10, 6370 Kitzbühel. ☎ **05356/644440.** Fax 05356/ 64803-56. 50 units. MINIBAR TV TEL. Winter 2,400S ($192) double, 3,050S ($244) suite for three; summer 1,750S ($140) double, 1,950S ($156) suite for three. Rates include breakfast. Half-board 480S ($38.40) per person extra in winter; 300S ($24) in summer. AE, DC, MC, V. Free parking outdoors; 100S ($8) in covered garage nearby.

This hotel combines Tyrolean *Gemütlichkeit* (friendliness and coziness) with urban style and panache. The staff show genuine concern for their clientele at this hotel created in the 1950s when three 700-year-old houses were joined into one unit. Accommodations come in a wide range of sizes—each elegantly furnished, often with canopied beds. Each unit has a firm mattress, fairly large bathrooms, and often French doors leading to private patios or balconies. The hotel sports the most luxurious health complex in town, complete with a tropical fountain, two hot tubs, a sauna, and a hot and cold foot bath. The elegant Zur Tenne Restaurant serves an international cuisine.

WHERE TO DINE

Florianistube. In the Gasthof Eggerwirt, Gaensbachgasse 12. ☎ **05356/62437.** Reservations recommended. Main courses 110–150S ($8.80–$12). AE, MC, V. Daily 11am–2pm and 6–10pm. Closed Nov 1–Dec 6 and Easter to end of May. INTERNATIONAL.

Named after St. Florian, patron saint of the hearth, this restaurant is in one of the resort's less ostentatious guesthouses, and it welcomes outsiders. The menu is comprehensive for such a stube-type place; it might include typical Austrian or Tyrolean dishes, as well as tournedos with mushroom sauce, spaghetti with clam sauce, or fondue bourguignonne. For something really local, order *Bauernschmaus,* a heaping hot platter of smoked pork, roast pork, pork sausages, sauerkraut, potatoes, and dumplings. In summer, a lunch or dinner buffet is served outside under the trees of the rear garden.

Wirtshaus Unterberger-Stuben. Wehgasse 2. ☎ **05356/66127.** Reservations recommended. Main courses 160–340S ($12.80–$27.20); set-price menus 420–850S ($33.60–$68). No credit cards. Daily noon–1:30pm and 6:30–10:30pm. Closed June and Nov and Tues in summer. INTERNATIONAL.

Throughout the 1980s, this was the preferred hangout for the rich and famous. Although the trendy may have moved elsewhere, the place still has a lot of prestige, and you're likely to be served one of your finest meals in Tyrol. If it's on the menu, try the poppyseed soufflé. Specialties, from the many countries that once belonged to the Austrian Empire, include terrine of roast chicken liver with a salad of wild mushrooms and filet of pike-perch with mountain herbs and baby vegetables. The restaurant is open for snacks, coffee, and drinks 9am to midnight, but meals are served only during lunch and dinner hours (see above).

2 Belgium

by George McDonald

Modest, unassuming Belgium has never been a country to boast of its charms. Although all eyes are focused on Brussels's glow as the "capital of Europe," there's another Belgium of medieval castles, Gothic cathedrals, cobblestone streets, and tranquil canals waiting in the shadows. In one of Europe's smaller countries, the timeless beauty of Bruges and Ghent are accessible even to the most hurried visitor.

1 Brussels

In many ways, this city symbolizes Europe's endeavor to unite. After centuries of occupation by Spanish, French, and Austrian empires, whose power struggles tore Europe apart, the city now hosts the bureaucratic empire trying to bring it all together. Headquarters of the European Union (EU), NATO, and scores of other governmental organizations, Brussels is a bastion of officialdom, a hatchery for the regulations that govern and often annoy the rest of Europe.

Bruxellois are more than a little ambivalent about their city's transformation into a power center. At first, the waves of Eurocrats seemed to bring a new cosmopolitan air to a slightly provincial city, but as old neighborhoods were leveled to make way for office towers, people wondered whether Brussels was losing its soul. After all, Brussels doesn't only mean business. This city inspired surrealism and worships comic strips, prides itself on handmade lace and chocolate, and serves each of its artisanal beers in a unique glass.

Fortunately, not all of Brussels's individuality has been lost in this transition, and although the urban landscape has suffered from wanton overbuilding, the city's spirit survives in traditional cafes, bars, bistros, and restaurants. Whether elegantly art nouveau or eccentrically festooned with posters, curios, and knickknacks, these centuries-old establishments provide a warm, convivial ambience that is peculiarly Belgian.

These imaginatively decorated interiors reflect the importance residents attach to culinary pleasure. The city's diverse populations—French-speaking Walloons and Dutch-speaking Flemings—have their differences, but they both love a good meal. In this, they are joined by the Euro and international minorities. From crisp "French" fries and waffles on the streetcorner to succulent Flemish and Walloon specialties, it's hard to eat badly in Brussels.

Only in Brussels

Strolling into the Grand-Place   There's nothing in Brussels quite like your first look at the timeless perfection of this historic, cobbled square, bordered by gabled guild-houses and the Gothic tracery of the Hôtel de Ville (Town Hall) and Maison du Roi (King's House).

Shooting *Manneken-Pis*   With a camera, naturally. Nobody seems able to resist this statue of a gleefully piddling little boy. Should you be any different?

Meeting with Brueghel and Magritte   The Historic section of the Royal Fine Arts Museums has paintings by Brueghels such as *The Fall of Icarus* and *Winter Landscape With Ice Skaters,* along with works by Rubens, Bosch, Van Dyck, Jordaens, and others. Go underground to the Modern section for works by Magritte, Delvaux, Ensor, Rops, Alechinsky, and others.

Pigging Out on Belgian Chocolates   Devilish handmade Belgian pralines are so addictive they should be sold with a government health warning. Try Wittamer in place du Grand Sablon.

Enjoying Art Nouveau   Brussels considers itself the world capital of this colorful, sinuous style. Local architect Victor Horta (1861–1947) was its foremost practitioner, and his work can be seen in many buildings around town.

Shopping at the Galeries Royales St-Hubert   Opened in 1847, the world's first shopping mall is a light, airy triple gallery enclosing boutiques, bookshops, cafes, restaurants, and a theater and cinema.

Strolling Around Europe   Mini-Europe, that is—a collection of emblematic buildings from the European Union's 15 member nations. They include the Leaning Tower of Pisa, Big Ben, the Acropolis, the Arc de Triomphe, and the Brandenburg Gate, all in beautifully rendered 1:25-scale detail.

Drinking Brussels Beer at Le Falstaff   A fanciful mix of art nouveau, art deco, and rococo, Falstaff boasts some of the most self-important waiters in the land as well as an amazing selection of Belgian beers. Ask them, deferentially, for a typical Brussels brew, such as *gueuze.*

ORIENTATION

ARRIVING   By Plane   In addition to the national carrier **Sabena, Brussels National Airport,** at Zaventem, 14.5km (9 miles) from the city center, is served by most major European airlines and many other international carriers. Direct trains to Brussels's three main stations (Gare du Nord, Gare Centrale, Gare du Midi) run from 5:43am to 11:14pm; one-way fare is 140BF ($4) in first-class and 90BF ($2.55) in second. You can buy tickets at all railway stations. Trip time to Gare du Nord is 20 minutes, and trains have wide corridors and extra space for baggage.

   Taxi fare is around 1,200BF ($34.30) to the city center.

By Train   Brussels is served by high-speed Eurostar trains from London, and the Thalys from Paris, Amsterdam, and Cologne, in addition to slower Eurocity (EC) and Intercity (IC) international services. For schedule and fare information for Belgium and abroad, call ☎ **0900/10-366.** Tickets are sold at all stations and through travel agents. There are timetables at all stations; main stations have information and reservation counters.

   If you are arriving from another European country, you will probably want to get out at **Gare Centrale,** Carrefour de l'Europe 2; **Gare du Midi,** rue de France 2 (the Eurostar and Thalys terminal); or **Gare du Nord,** rue du Progrès 86.

Brussels

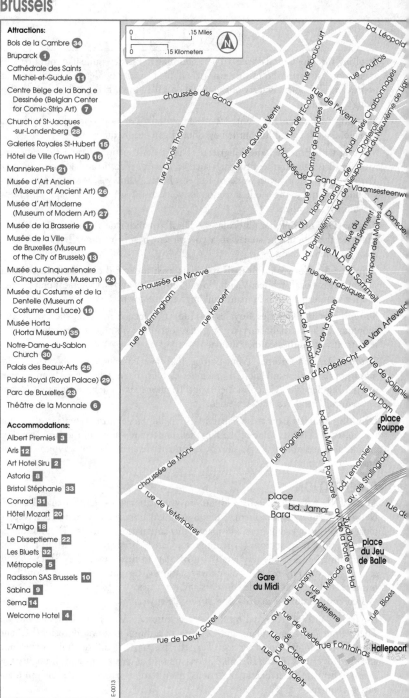

Attractions:

Bois de la Cambre 34

Bruparck 1

Cathédrale des Saints Michel-et-Gudule 11

Centre Belge de la Bande Dessinée (Belgian Center for Comic-Strip Art) 7

Church of St-Jacques -sur-Londenberg 28

Galeries Royales St-Hubert 15

Hôtel de Ville (Town Hall) 16

Manneken-Pis 21

Musée d'Art Ancien (Museum of Ancient Art) 26

Musée d'Art Moderne (Museum of Modern Art) 27

Musée de la Brasserie 17

Musée de la Ville de Bruxelles (Museum of the City of Brussels) 13

Musée du Cinquantenaire (Cinquantenaire Museum) 24

Musée du Costume et de la Dentelle (Museum of Costume and Lace) 19

Musée Horta (Horta Museum) 35

Notre-Dame-du-Sablon Church 30

Palais des Beaux-Arts 25

Palais Royal (Royal Palace) 29

Parc de Bruxelles 23

Théâtre de la Monnaie 6

Accommodations:

Albert Premies 3

Aris 12

Art Hotel Siru 2

Astoria 8

Bristol Stéphanie 33

Conrad 31

Hôtel Mozart 20

L'Amigo 18

Le Dixseptieme 22

Les Bluets 32

Métropole 5

Radisson SAS Brussels 10

Sabina 9

Sema 14

Welcome Hotel 4

E-0013

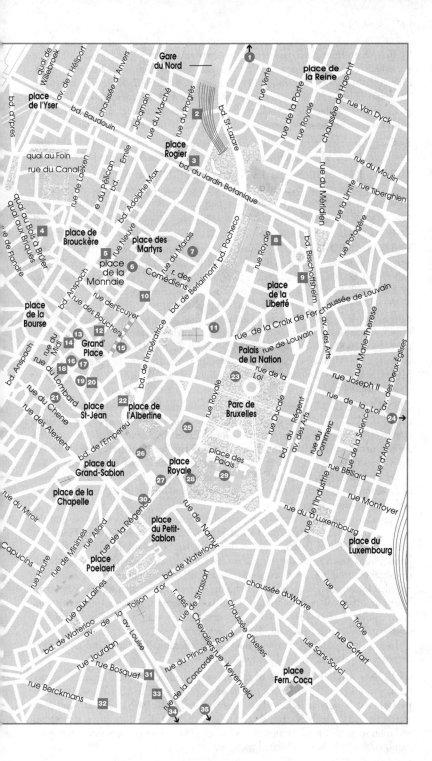

By Bus Eurolines has a daily return service from London's Victoria Coach Station. For schedule and fare information on this and services from other European cities, contact Eurolines (☎ **0990/808080** in Britain, ☎ **02/203-07-07** in Belgium). Most international buses arrive in **rue Fonsny** beside Gare du Midi; some stop at city center locations around **place de Brouckère.** Belgium has few useful regional bus services, as trains do most of the work; those that do exist usually stop at **Gare du Nord.**

By Car Major expressways to Brussels are the A7 (E19) from Paris, A10 (E40) from Oostende, A1 (E19) from Amsterdam, and A3 (E40) from Aachen and Cologne.

By Boat P&O North Sea Ferries (☎ **0148/237-7177**) has a daily car ferry service from Hull in northern England to Zeebrugge; overnight journey time is 14 hours. **Hoverspeed** (☎ **0990/595-522**) has a frequent (five to seven times daily) fast-catamaran car ferry service from Dover in England to Ostend; journey time is under 2 hours.

VISITOR INFORMATION Tourist Information Brussels (T.I.B.) on the ground floor of the Hôtel de Ville (Town Hall), Grand-Place, 1000 Brussels (☎ **02/ 513-89-40**; fax 02/514-45-38) sells a comprehensive visitors' booklet, *Brussels Guide & Map,* for 70BF ($2); makes same-day hotel reservations; organizes paid-for guided walking tours in summer; and has multilingual guides who can be engaged by the hour or day. It is open from April to December, daily 9am to 6pm; January to March, Monday to Saturday 9am to 6pm. The **Belgian Tourism Center,** rue du Marché-aux-Herbes 63, 1000 Brussels (☎ **02/504-03-90;** fax 02/504-02-70), is open from June to September, Monday to Saturday 9am to 7pm, Sunday 9am to 6pm; October to March, Monday to Saturday 9am to 6pm, Sunday (Apr, May, Oct) 9am to 6pm or (Nov to Mar) 1 to 5pm.

CITY LAYOUT Most main attractions are inside the heart-shaped inner ring-road, roughly 2.4km (1.5 miles) in diameter, that follows the line of the old city walls. Small cobblestoned streets cluster around the **Grand-Place.** Two nearby well-traveled lanes are restaurant-lined **rue des Bouchers** and **petite rue des Bouchers.** A block west of the Grand-Place, the classical colonnaded **Bourse** (Stock Exchange) stands at the center of Brussels's nightlife zone. A few blocks north is the **National Opera** on place de la Monnaie. The city's busiest shopping street, **rue Neuve,** starts from this square and runs north for several blocks.

"Uptown," southeast of the center and literally atop a hill, is where you find the second great square, **place du Grand-Sablon,** as well as the **Royal Fine Arts Museums** and **Royal Palace.** Head southwest across boulevard de Waterloo to place Louise, from which a chic shopping street, **av. Louise,** extends south and a slightly less fashionable shopping street, **av. de la Toison d'Or,** runs northeast. Both are surrounded by attractive side streets, containing typical Belgian architecture. East of av. Louise and south of av. de la Toison d'Or is **Ixelles district,** near the **University,** with many casual, inexpensive restaurants, bars, and cafes. Northeast of Ixelles, the modern European Union district surrounds **place Schuman.**

To make navigating challenging, maps list street names in French and Dutch. For consistency and ease, I've used the French names.

GETTING AROUND Maps of the integrated public transport network (métro, tram, and bus) are free from the tourist office, offices of the **S.T.I.B. public transportation company** at Galerie de la Toison d'Or 20 (☎ **02/515-20-00**), and from métro stations **Porte de Namur, Rogier,** and **Gare du Midi.** All stations and most bus and tram stops have public transportation maps. The full system operates 6am to midnight, after which there's a limited night-bus system.

By Métro (Subway)   Although not extensive, this fast and efficient system covers important city center locations and reaches the suburbs. You can identify stations by signs with a white letter M on a blue background.

By Bus & Tram   Urban vehicles are yellow; stops are marked with red-and-white signs. Stop them by extending your arm as they approach. Tickets, which can also be used on the métro, cost 50BF ($1.45) for a single (called a "direct"); 240BF ($6.85) for a five-journey ticket bought from the driver; 340BF ($9.70) for a ten-journey ticket available from métro stations; and 130BF ($3.70) for a 1-day ticket valid on all urban services.

Insert your ticket into the orange machines inside buses and trams and at métro platforms. Your ticket must be inserted each time you enter a new vehicle, but as it permits multiple transfers within a 1-hour period, during that time only one journey is canceled by the electronic scanner.

By Taxi   Minimum rate is 95BF ($2.70) during the day, 170BF ($4.85) at night, increasing by 38BF ($1.10) per kilometer inside the city and 76BF ($2.15) per kilometer beyond city limits. You need not add a tip unless there has been extra service, such as helping with heavy luggage. All taxis are metered, and *cannot be hailed in the street;* there are taxi stands on many principal streets. Call **ATR** (☎ 02/647-22-22), **Autolux** (☎ 02/411-12-21), **Taxis Bleus** (☎ 02/268-00-00), or **Taxis Verts** (☎ 02/349-49-49).

By Car   At rush hour (an hour either side of 9am and 5pm), it is almost impossible to move on main roads inside the city and on the R0 outer ring-road. Do yourself a favor: Leave the car at a car park.

Fast Facts: Brussels

American Express   The AMEX office is at bd. du Souverain 100, 1000 Brussels (☎ 02/676-21-11). It's open Monday to Friday 9am to 1pm and 2 to 5pm.

Business Hours   Banks are open Monday to Friday 9am to 1pm and 2 to 4:30 or 5pm. Shopping hours are Monday to Saturday 9 or 10am to 6 or 7pm. Some stores, such as bakers and news vendors, open earlier, and some open the same hours on Sunday. Many stores stay open on Friday until 8 or 9pm.

Currency   The exchange rate used in this chapter is $1 = 35 Belgian francs (BF) or 1BF = 3¢. Also, 1EUR = 40.3BF and £1 = 61.4BF.

Currency Exchange   Banks offer the best rates, but exchange offices in railway stations come close. If you carry American Express traveler's checks, change them at **American Express** (see above), where there's no commission charge. Hotels and street bureaux de change offer poorer rates and may charge high commissions, but are open in the evenings and on weekends. **Thomas Cook,** Grand-Place 4 (☎ 02/513-28-45), has reasonable rates. There are many ATMs around town, connected to Cirrus and Plus, and identified by "Bancontact" and "Mister Cash" logos. You must have a 4-digit PIN to access the ATMs.

Dentists/Doctors   For emergency medical service around the clock, call ☎ 02/479-18-18; ask for an English-speaking doctor. For emergency dental service, call ☎ 02/426-10-26 or 02/428-58-58.

Embassies   The **U.S. Embassy** is at bd. du Regent 27, 1000 Brussels (☎ 02/508-21-11); **Australian Embassy,** rue Guimard 6–8, 1040 Brussels (☎ 02/231-05-00); **Canadian Embassy,** av. de Tervuren 2, 1040 Brussels

(☎ **02/741-06-11**); **Irish Embassy,** rue Froissart 89, 1040 Brussels (☎ **02/230-53-37**); **New Zealand Embassy,** bd. du Regent 47, 1000 Brussels (☎ **02/512-10-40**); **South African Embassy,** rue de la Loi, 1040 Brussels (☎ **02/285-44-00**); and **United Kingdom Embassy,** rue Arlon 85, 1040 Brussels (☎ **02/287-62-11**).

Emergencies   For an ambulance, call ☎ **100;** for police assistance, ☎ **101;** for fire, ☎ **100.**

Internet Access   Try @**Internem,** bd. Général Jacques 68, 1050 Ixelles (☎ and fax **02/649-45-09;** www.internem.be), a Vietnamese restaurant and cybercafe; open daily noon to midnight.

Lost Property   Contact Brussels National Airport baggage office (☎ **02/723-60-11**) if you have lost property aboard an aircraft; for property lost in the airport, contact **Brussels Terminal Company** (☎ **02/753-68-20**). Main railway stations have lost property offices (☎ **02/555-25-25**); for métro, tram, or bus, contact **S.T.I.B.,** av. de la Toison d'Or 15 (☎ **02/515-23-94**).

Post Office   The office at **Gare du Midi,** av. Fonsny 48a (☎ 02/534-11-40), is open 24 hours a day. Others are open Monday to Friday 9am to 5pm; closed weekends and public holidays (the main office at the **Centre Monnaie** shopping center, place de la Monnaie [☎ **02/226-21-11**], is also open Saturday 9am to 1pm).

Safety   Brussels is generally safe, but there's a rise in crime, much of it drug related, particularly pickpocketing, theft from cars, and muggings in métro station foot tunnels. Tourists are targets of pickpockets on the métro and in tourist areas such as the Grand-Place.

Telephone   Belgium's country code is **32.** Brussels's city code is **2;** use this code when calling from outside Belgium. In Belgium, use **02.**

A local call costs 15BF (45¢) for 3 minutes. To make international calls, use a Belgacom telecard, available at Belgacom offices and many news vendors for 200BF ($5.70), 500BF ($14.30), or 1,000BF ($28.55); or walk 1 block north of Gare Centrale to the Belgacom office at bd. de l'Impératrice 17 (☎ **02/540-61-11**), open daily 8am to 10pm. It costs 130BF ($3.70) for a 3-minute call to the United States and 120BF ($3.45) with a telecard. To make a collect or calling card call from a pay phone, deposit 10BF (30¢) and dial one of the following access numbers to reach an American operator or an English-language voice prompt: **AT&T** (☎ **0800/10-010**), **MCI** (☎ **0800/10-012**), and **Sprint** (☎ **0800/11-605**).

WHERE TO STAY

The business of Brussels is business, a fact reflected in the cost and nature of available accommodations. Hotels in the upper price range offer a wealth of facilities for business travelers—conference rooms, fax machines, and efficient, though impersonal, service. At every level, hotels fill up during the week and empty out on weekends and in July and August when the Eurocrats leave. In off-peak periods, rates can drop as much as 50% from those quoted below; be sure you're quoted the correct rates, which include VAT and service.

The **T.I.B.** office in the Grand-Place (☎ **02/513-89-40**) and the **Belgian Tourist Office** at rue du Marché-aux-Herbes 63 (☎ **02/504-03-90**) make reservations for the same day, if you go in person, for a small fee (deducted by the hotel from its room rate). T.I.B. publishes an annual *Hotel Guide* with listings by price range, and can provide complete information on hostels and call to find out if space is available. **Belgian Tourist Reservations,** bd. Anspach 111, 1000 Brussels (☎ **02/513-74-84;** fax 02/513-92-77), reserves hotel rooms throughout Belgium and often gets substantial discounts. Hotels with unsold rooms sell them well below advertised prices through this office.

An alternative to hotels is a bed-and-breakfast. Brussels has several good B&B organizations: **Bed & Breakfast Taxistop,** rue du Fossé-aux-Loups 28, 1000 Brussels (☎ **02/223-22-31;** fax 02/223-22-32); **Bed & Brussels,** rue V. Greyson 58, 1050 Brussels (☎ **02/646-07-37;** fax 02/644-01-14); and **New Windrose,** av. Paul Dejaer 21a, 1060 Brussels (☎ **02/534-71-91;** fax 02/534-71-92). All will send you a list of host families (the Windrose includes a profile of the families) and rates. Booking fee is 500BF ($14.30) per reservation; rates vary from 1,500BF to 2,200BF ($42.85 to $62.85) for a double.

The **Sheraton Brussels Airport,** Luchthaven Brussel Nationaal (facing Departures), 1930 Zaventem, Belgium (☎ **800/325-3535** in the U.S. and Canada, or 02/725-10-00; fax 02/725-11-55; www.sheraton.come), couldn't be more convenient to the airport without being on the runway. You find all the comfort you would expect of a top-flight Sheraton. Doubles cost 12,400BF to 13,400BF ($354.30 to $382.85) per night.

VERY EXPENSIVE

Conrad. av. Louise 71, 1050 Brussels (at place Stéphanie). ☎ **02/542-42-42.** Fax 02/542-42-00. www.brussels.conradinternational.com. E-mail: bruhc—rm@hilton.com. 269 units. A/C MINIBAR TV TEL. 15,000BF ($428.55) double; suites 32,000BF ($914.30) and way up. AE, DC, MC, V. Parking 490BF ($14). Métro: Louise.

Big, bright, and fancy, the Conrad has spacious rooms and luxurious furnishings that vary from room to room yet maintain a classic stance. His-and-her bathrobes, trouser presses, hair dryers, and ice makers grace the rooms, and bathtubs are huge. Service and amenities are all you would expect from a hotel in its price category—24-hour room service, sports and fitness center, wheelchair access, parking garage. The French restaurant La Maison du Maître offers all the refinements of haute cuisine; Café Wiltshire maintains a less formal tone.

Métropole. place de Brouckère 31 (close to Centre Monnaie), 1000 Brussels. ☎ **02/217-23-00.** Fax 02/218-02-20. www.metropolehotel.be. E-mail: info@metropolehotel.be. 410 units. MINIBAR TV TEL. 12,500BF ($357.15) double; 18,000BF ($514.30) suite. Rates include buffet breakfast. AE, DC, JCB, MC, V. Parking 500BF ($14.30). Métro: Brouckère.

This 19th-century hotel, with ornate marble-and-gilt interior and lavish public rooms, is several blocks from the Grand-Place. Spacious guest rooms have classic furnishings and some modern luxuries, including heated towel racks, hair dryers, and trouser presses. Amenities include a relaxation center with sauna, Turkish bath, Jacuzzi, solarium, and flotation tank. Elegant L'Alban Chambon caters to the sophisticated diner; extravagant Victorian Café Métropole caters to the sophisticated cafe hound. There's a heated sidewalk terrace with an uninspiring view of a busy street.

Radisson SAS Brussels. rue du Fossé-aux-Loups 47 (close to Gare Centrale). ☎ **800/333-3333** in the U.S. and Canada, or ☎ 02/219-28-28. Fax 02/219-62-62. www.radisson.com/brussels.be. E-mail: sales@bruzh.rdsas.com. 281 units. A/C MINIBAR TV TEL. 13,000BF ($371.45) double; suites from 19,000BF ($542.85) and way up. AE, CB, DC, MC, V. Parking 770BF ($22). Métro: Gare Centrale or De Brouckère.

In modern harmony with its neighborhood a few blocks from the Grand-Place, this upscale chain hotel incorporates part of the medieval city wall. Large rooms are decorated in a variety of styles, including Scandinavian, Asian, and Italian. Personal answering machines in each room are a nice touch. Amenities include a health club and sauna. The fine Sea Grill specializes in fish; the Atrium serves Belgian and Scandinavian specialties; and Henry J Bean's, an American-style bar and grill, is popular with locals and expats.

EXPENSIVE

✪ **Astoria**. rue Royale 103 (near Colonne du Congrès), 1000 Brussels. ☎ **800/SOFITEL** in the U.S. and Canada, or ☎ 02/227-05-05. Fax 02/217-11-50. E-mail: info.bxl.astoria@ sofitel.be. 118 units. A/C MINIBAR TV TEL. 5,500BF ($157.15) double; 18,000BF ($514.30) suite. AE, CB, DC, MC, V. Valet parking 600BF ($17.15). Métro: Botanique.

The minute you walk into the belle époque foyer, you are transported to a more elegant age. This hotel dates from 1909, a few years before Europe's age of innocence ended with World War I, and its plush style recalls the panache of that vanished heyday. Rooms are attractively furnished in a way that's in keeping with the hotel's character, although not extravagantly so, and include the latest fixtures and fittings, such as marble bathrooms, wall-mounted hair dryers, and two telephones.

Bristol Stéphanie. av. Louise 91–93, 1050 Brussels. ☎ **02/543-33-11.** Fax 02/538-03-07. 142 units. A/C MINIBAR TV TEL. 10,200BF ($291.45) double; suites from 18,500BF ($514.30) and way up. AE, DC, MC, V. Parking 350BF ($10). Métro: Louise.

This sleekly modern hotel looks like it was built for the 21st century. Every feature, from lobby design and fittings to furnishings in the kitchenette suites, is streamlined, functional, and representative of the very best in avant-garde planning. It's in a pretty section of avenue Louise, one of the city's most select shopping streets, and has an indoor swimming pool and parking garage. The Gourmet Restaurant has an international menu that includes Norwegian specialties.

✪ **L'Amigo**. rue de l'Amigo 1–3 (behind the Bourse), 1000 Brussels. ☎ **02/547-47-47.** Fax 02/513-52-77. www.hotelamigo.com. E-mail: hotelamigo@hotelamigo.com. 185 units. MINIBAR TV TEL. 8,900–11,500BF ($254.30–$328.55) double; suites from 15,500BF ($442.85) and way up. Rates include continental breakfast. AE, DC, JCB, MC, V. Parking 490BF ($14). Métro: Bourse.

In Brussels slang, an "amigo" is a prison, and indeed, a prison once stood here. Don't worry; any resemblance to the former accommodations is nominal. Within a brick exterior, an austere Spanish Renaissance lobby is decorated with stone floors and Flemish tapestries. Understated Old European refinement permeates the stately corridors, and guest rooms are lushly outfitted with fine furniture, Oriental rugs, and framed paintings. Although the restaurant is unremarkable and fitness buffs have to go elsewhere to exercise, the hotel provides world-class comforts. Two-thirds of rooms have air conditioning; all have hair dryers.

MODERATE

✪ **Albert Premier**. place Rogier 20 (beside Gare du Nord), 1210 Brussels. ☎ **02/ 203-31-25.** Fax 02/203-43-31. 285 units. MINIBAR TV TEL. 3,000–5,000BF ($85.70–$142.85) double. Rates include buffet breakfast. DC, MC, V. Limited parking available on street. Métro: Rogier.

With a fully renovated interior behind its graceful 19th-century facade, this hotel has retained its popularity and cachet through the mixed fortunes of the square on which it stands. This once elegant, then seedy, neighborhood on the edge of the city center has been turned around and is now a business and administrative area. Rooms are minimalist in terms of facilities, yet modern, comfortable, and attractively decorated. There's a fine restaurant on the premises.

Aris. rue du Marché-aux-Herbes 78–80, 1000 Brussels (off Grand-Place). ☎ **02/514-43-00.** Fax 02/514-01-19. 55 units. A/C TV TEL. 6,500BF ($185.70) double. Rates include buffet breakfast. DC, JCB, MC, V. Limited parking available on street. Métro: Gare Centrale.

What this shiny, ideally positioned hotel lacks in personality it makes up for in amenities. Rooms are impersonal but well outfitted. All have full bathrooms with hair dryers and toiletries, double-glazed windows, firm beds, and a private safe. Charming it isn't, but you'll have all the comforts of home, including air-conditioning.

Art Hotel Siru. place Rogier 1 (beside Gare du Nord), 1210 Brussels. ☎ **02/203-35-80.** Fax 02/203-33-03. 101 units. MINIBAR TV TEL. 3,900–6,200BF ($111.45–$177.15) double. Rates include buffet breakfast. AE, DC, MC, V. Parking 425BF ($12.15). Métro: Rogier.

The Siru is a fascinating hotel in what was once a rundown area that's rapidly undergoing gentrification. The Siru's owner persuaded 100 Belgian artists, including some of the country's biggest names, to "decorate" each of the stylishly modern and well-equipped rooms with a work on travel. Given the unpredictable nature of reactions to modern art, some clients apparently reserve the same room time after time, while others have asked for a room change in the middle of the night. It is not easily forgotten.

Le Dixseptième. rue de la Madeleine 25, 1000 Brussels (off place de l'Albertine). ☎ **02/502-57-44.** Fax 02/502-64-24. 24 units. MINIBAR TV TEL. 6,600BF ($188.55) studio; 9,800–13,600BF ($280–$388.55) suite. AE, DC, MC, V. Limited parking available on street. Métro: Gare Centrale.

This is a delightful spot close to the Grand-Place in a neighborhood of restored houses. Its rooms are as big as the suites in many hotels, and some have balconies. All are in 18th-century style, with wood paneling and marble chimneys, and are named after Belgian painters from Brueghel to Magritte. Two beautiful lounges are decorated with carved wooden medallions and 18th-century paintings.

Sema. rue des Harengs 6–8, 1000 Brussels (close to Grand-Place). ☎ **02/514-07-60.** Fax 02/548-90-39. 11 units. TV TEL. 4,500BF ($128.55) double. Rates include buffet breakfast. AE, DC, MC, V. Limited parking available on street. Métro: Gare Centrale.

This hotel is small and modern, yet warmly inviting. The cozy lobby is up a flight of stairs, and from there an elevator takes you to your room. Gleaming wood floors, white walls, and bright bedspreads create a cheerful setting in quite large guest rooms. Windows are double-glazed to keep out noise, and bathrooms have hair dryers and toiletries.

INEXPENSIVE

Hôtel Mozart. 23 rue du Marché-aux-Fromages, 1000 Bruxelles (close to Grand-Place). ☎ **02/502-66-61.** Fax 02/502-77-58. 47 units. TV TEL. 3,000BF ($85.70) double. Rates include continental breakfast. AE, DC, MC, V. Limited parking available on street. Métro: Gare Centrale.

Go a flight up from street level, and guess which famous composer's music wafts through the sparkling lobby? Salmon-colored walls, plants, and old paintings create a warm, intimate ambience that's carried into the rooms. Although furnishings are blandly modern, colorful fabrics and exposed beams lend each room a rustic originality. Several are duplexes with a sitting room underneath the loft bedroom. Top rooms have a great view.

Les Bluets. rue Berckmans 124, 1060 Brussels (close to Porte de Hal). ☎ **02/534-39-83.** Fax 02/534-39-83. E-mail: bluets@eudoramail.com. 10 units. TV TEL. 2,650BF ($75.70) double. Rates include continental breakfast. MC, V. Limited parking available on street. Métro: Hôtel des Monnaies.

In a house dating from 1864, you'll find a fine old family hotel with a proprietress who looks on her guests almost as members of the family. Each room is different, but all have high ceilings and unusual antiques and knickknacks. The effect is more that of a comfortable country house than a hotel. All rooms have hair dryers.

Sabina. rue du Nord 78, 1000 Brussels. ☎ **02/218-26-37.** Fax 02/219-32-39. 24 units. TV TEL. 2,500BF ($71.45) double. Rates include buffet breakfast. AE, DC, MC, V. Limited parking available on street. Métro: Madou.

This small hostelry is like a private residence, presided over by hospitable owners. A grandfather clock in the reception area and polished wood along the restaurant walls give it a warm, homey atmosphere. Rooms vary in size, but all are comfortable and simply, yet tastefully, done in modern style and pastel tones, with twin beds side-by-side against a laminate headboard. Three rooms have kitchenettes for 100BF ($2.85) extra; all have hair dryers.

✪ **Welcome.** Quai au Bois-à-Brûler 23, 1000 Brussels (at the Marché-aux-Poissons). ☎ **02/219-95-46.** Fax 02/217-18-87. www.hotelwelcome.com. E-mail: info@hotelwelcome.com. 6 units. A/C MINIBAR TV TEL. 2,400–3,400BF ($68.55–$97.15) double. DC, MC, V. Free parking. Métro: Ste-Catherine.

It would be hard to imagine a smaller hotel (it's the city's smallest), or one that will leave you with fonder memories. It has such fiercely loyal regulars that the hotel is often fully booked—admittedly not a difficult feat—so you should reserve far ahead. The enthusiastic couple who own it, Michel and Sophie Smeesters, have created bright, cheerful guest rooms and a superb attached seafood restaurant, La Truite d'Argent (see "Where to Dine," below).

WHERE TO DINE

It's almost impossible to eat badly in a city where streets are named after food markets: rue du Marché-aux-Fromages, rue du Marché-aux-Herbes, rue du Marché-aux-Porcs, and rue du Marché-aux-Poulets recall open-air cheese, herb, pork, and chicken stalls that once lined the streets. This gastronomic obsession has spawned 2,000 restaurants, meaning you'll have no problem eating well at a reasonable price.

Most of the city's favorite dishes are based on local products, with the notable exception of its beloved mussels, served in ingenious variations from September through the winter, which come from Zeeland in the Netherlands.

Belgium is renowned for 400 brands of beer produced by hundreds of small breweries; Belgian chefs use beer in their sauces the way French chefs use wine. Beef, chicken, and fish are often bathed in a savory sauce based on the local *gueuze* and *faro* brews. Beer is the perfect accompaniment to the sturdy Flemish dishes you find on menus around town: *waterzooï,* fish or chicken stew with a parsley-and-cream sauce; *stoemp,* a purée of vegetables and potatoes with sausage, steak, or chop; *paling in 't groen* (eel in a grass-green sauce); *ballekes* (spicy meatballs); and *hochepot* (stew). Belgians deserve credit for perfecting a culinary quintet of cheese, waffles, fried potatoes, chocolate, and beer—no visit to Brussels is complete without a generous sampling of each.

VERY EXPENSIVE

✪ **Comme Chez Soi.** place Rouppe 23. ☎ **02/512-29-21.** Reservations required for dinner. Main courses 1,250–2,975BF ($35.70–$85); menus 2,150–4,950BF ($61.45–$141.45). AE, DC, MC, V. Tues–Sat noon–2pm and 7–10pm (closed July and Christmas/ New Year holidays). Métro: Anneessens. FRENCH.

This is the stellar end of the culinary spectrum, with unforgettable French cuisine presented in an art nouveau setting. An expedition inside the hallowed portals of this restaurant, which sports three Michelin stars, will surely be the culinary highlight of any trip to Brussels. The name means "Just Like Home" and, although the food is a long way from what most people eat at home, the welcome from Master Chef Pierre Wynants is warm. His standards are high enough for the most rigorous tastebuds on earth.

La Maison du Cygne. Grand-Place 9. ☎ **02/511-82-44.** Reservations recommended on weekends. Main courses 950–1,600BF ($27.15–$45.70); set-price menu 2,200BF ($62.85). AE, DC, MC, V. Mon–Fri noon–2:15pm and Mon–Sat 7pm–midnight (closed 3 weeks in Aug). Métro: Gare Centrale or Bourse. FRENCH.

This grande dame of Brussels restaurants has one Michelin star and overlooks the Grand-Place from the former Butchers' Guildhouse. "The House of the Swan's" service, though a tad stuffy, is as elegant as the polished walnut walls, bronze wall sconces, and green velvet. Because of its location, Cygne is usually crowded at lunchtime, but dinner reservations are likely to be available.

La Sirène d'Or. place Ste-Catherine 1a ((at the Marché-aux-Poissons). ☎ **02/513-51-98.** Main courses 800–1,200BF ($22.85–$34.30); set-price menus 890–1,300BF ($25.45–$37.15). AE, DC, MC, V. Wed–Sat noon–2pm and 6–10pm. Métro: Ste-Catherine. SEAFOOD/FRENCH.

In the colorful Fish Market, beside the now-vanished harbor where fishing boats used to tie up right in the heart of Brussels, this restaurant's specialties are, not surprisingly, seafood. Chef Robert Van Duüren was once chef to the Prince of Liège, now King Albert II of Belgium, so the menu's dishes have that royal touch. The setting is dark wood walls, overhead beams, velvet-seated chairs, and Belgian lace curtains. Specialties are grilled turbot with ginger and *bouillabaisse* Grand Marius (a garlicky mixed fish soup).

EXPENSIVE

De l'Ogenblik. Galerie des Princes 1. ☎ **02/511-61-51.** Main courses 600–900BF ($17.15–$25.70); menu du jour 2,000BF ($57.15). AE, DC, MC, V. Mon–Sat noon–2:30pm and 7pm–midnight (Fri, Sat to 12:30am). Métro: Gare Centrale or Bourse. FRENCH/BELGIAN.

In the elegant surroundings of the Galeries Royales St-Hubert, this restaurant offers good taste in a Parisian bistro setting. It often gets busy, but the ambience in the two-level, wood-and-brass dining room is convivial, if a little too tightly packed. Look for garlicky seafood and meat dishes.

✪ **La Quincaillerie.** rue du Page 45 (at rue Américaine). ☎ **02/538-25-53.** Main courses 640–960BF ($18.30–$27.45); menu du jour 1,750BF ($50). AE, CB, DC, MC, V. Mon–Fri noon–2:30pm and 7pm–midnight; Sat–Sun 7pm–midnight. Tram: 81, 82, 91, or 92 to chaussée de Charleroi. FRENCH.

In Ixelles, a part of the city where good restaurants are as common as streetlights, this spot stands out, even though it may be a little too aware of its own modish good looks and a shade pricey. The setting is a traditional former hardware store, with wood paneling and masses of wooden drawers. It's busy enough to get the waitstaff harassed and absent-minded, yet they are always friendly. Specialties include *escalope du saumon rôti au gros sel* (salmon in roasted rock salt) and *canette laquée au miel et citron vert* (baby duck with a crust of honey and lime).

La Truite d'Argent. quai aux Bois-à-Brûler 23 (at the Marché-aux-Poissons). ☎ **02/219-95-46.** Main courses 720–1,080BF ($20.55–$30.85); set-price menu 1,250BF ($35.70). AE, DC, MC, V. Mon–Fri noon–2:30pm and 7–11:30pm. Métro: Ste-Catherine. FRENCH/SEAFOOD.

Enthusiastic owners Michel and Sophie Smeesters positively insist on delivering savory seafood specialties. "Superb" is the best word to describe the menu-dishes, which include meat choices. All are prepared from fine ingredients, and the presentation is exquisite, so pleasing to the eye you might hesitate to destroy the image by eating it. You can dine on a sidewalk terrace on the Fish Market in good weather.

MODERATE

✪ **Brasserie de la Roue d'Or.** rue des Chapeliers 26 (off Grand-Place). ☎ **02/514-25-54.** Main courses 550–850BF ($15.70–$24.30); menu du jour 1,650BF ($47.15). AE, DC, MC, V. Daily noon–12:30am. Métro: Gare Centrale or Bourse. BELGIAN/GRILLS/SEAFOOD.

This welcoming, high-ceilinged brasserie has an art nouveau and Magritte decor that includes lots of dark wood, mirrors, and marble-topped tables. An extensive menu caters to just about any appetite, from grilled meats to a good selection of cooked salmon and other seafood, as well as old Belgian favorites like *stoemp*. An extensive wine, beer, and spirits list is enjoyed by the loyal local following. The colorful owner, Jef De Gelas (who also owns 't Kelderke, listed below), is known locally as the "King of Stoemp."

L'Amadeus. rue Veydt 13. ☎ **02/538-34-27.** Main courses 1,000BF ($28.55). AE, DC, MC, V. Tues–Sun noon–3pm, 6pm–2am; Mon 6pm–2am. Métro: Louise. MODERN BELGIAN.

The postmodern chic of this winebar/restaurant is a refreshing change from traditional Belgian style. Its candlelit interior is so dim you would think they're hiding something, but the cooking is nothing to be ashamed of. The menu includes such vegetarian treats as vegetarian lasagne and ricotta and spinach tortellini, and for meat eaters, caramelized spare ribs and several salmon dishes, all accompanied by delicious home-made nut bread. The Sunday brunch is all-you-can-eat for 670BF ($19.15) and includes smoked fish, cheese, eggs, bread, cereal, juice, and coffee.

Le Falstaff. rue Henri-Maus 17–25 (beside the Bourse). Telephone, prices, and credit card details not available at press-time. Métro: Bourse. BELGIAN.

Shock and horror reverberated through the city in 1999 when this legendary art nouveau tavern went bankrupt. Happily, it was soon announced that the business had been taken over by a French company, who planned to reopen Falstaff under new management. Details were still being worked out as this edition of Frommer's went to press, but we have been assured that visitors will again be able to enjoy Falstaff's stunning decor and reasonably priced brasserie food, which is why we're including it.

Le Falstaff Gourmand. rue des Pierres 38 (close to the Bourse). ☎ **02/512-17-61.** Main courses 480–720BF ($13.70–$20.55); menu 1,000BF ($28.55). AE, DC, MC, V. Tues–Sun 11:30am–3pm and 7–11pm (except Sunday evening). Métro: Bourse. BELGIAN/FRENCH.

Le Falstaff brasserie on rue Henri Maus across from the Bourse is widely renowned as a classic art nouveau bar and eatery. Around the corner, its sister establishment has a different but equally notable style. Service is attentive, prompt, and friendly, and it's surprising that more people don't take advantage of its charms. First-class Belgian and French-oriented dishes include one of the best deals in Brussels: a three-course *menu gourmand*, which includes an apéritif, glass of wine with the starter, and a small pitcher of wine with the main course.

✪ **Le Joueur de Flûte.** rue de l'Epée 26 (beside the Palais de Justice). ☎ **02/513-43-11.** Reservations required. Set-price menu 1,200BF ($34.30). MC, V. Mon–Fri 7–11pm. Métro: Louise. FRENCH.

Dining in this tiny restaurant is nothing if not straightforward—take it or leave it. There is only one menu, with a couple of variations for the main course. Don't let that, or the fact that it serves only 16 diners each evening, put you off. Owner and chef Philippe Van Cappelen has had more than a passing acquaintance with

Michelin stars in his time, and now he likes to keep it small, simple, and friendly. Van Cappelen cooks whatever he feels like cooking, and it's just about guaranteed to be delicious.

Le Marmiton. rue des Bouchers 43 (off Grand-Place). ☎ **02/511-79-10.** Main courses 480–720BF ($13.70–$20.55); menu du jour 695BF ($19.85). AE, DC, MC, V. Daily noon–3pm and 6–11:30pm (12:30am on weekends). Métro: Gare Centrale or Bourse. BELGIAN/FRENCH.

A warm and welcoming environment, hearty servings, and a commitment to satisfying customers are hallmarks here. On a menu that emphasizes fish, the seafood cocktail starter is a heap of shellfish and crustaceans substantial enough to be a main course, and the sole is excellent. Meat dishes are available, too. The menu is complemented by an excellent wine list selected by the Portuguese/Belgian owner and chef, whose love of his own cooking shows in his waistline and in the attention he devotes to his customers.

INEXPENSIVE

In 't Spinnekopke. place du Jardin-aux-Fleurs 1. ☎ **02/511-86-95.** Main courses 400–780BF ($11.45–$22.30); plat du jour 295BF ($8.45). AE, DC, MC, V. Mon–Fri noon–3pm and 6–11pm; Sat 6pm–midnight. Métro: Bourse. BELGIAN.

At this Brussels institution founded in 1762, hardy standbys of Belgian cuisine, such as *stoemp* and *waterzooï*, are given all the care and attention they deserve, from kitchen staff and diners alike. You dine in a tilted, wood-floored building at simple tables, and more likely than not squeezed into a small space. But getting caught "In the Spider's Web" is worth it.

La Grande Porte. 9 rue Notre-Seigneur (4 blocks west of place du Grand-Sablon). ☎ **02/512-89-98.** Main courses 395BF–525BF ($11.30–$15). V. Mon–Fri noon–3pm and 6pm–2am; Sat 6pm–4am. Bus 20, 48. BELGIAN.

Paper lanterns, marionettes, old posters, and fashionably "distressed" walls create a comfortable, relaxed space to enjoy several Flemish specialties. Near the working-class Marolles district, the food is simple, plentiful, and hearty. A lunch of *ballekes, waterzooï,* or *stoemp* with sausage will fill you up for the rest of the day and most of the night.

L'Auberge des Chapeliers. rue des Chapeliers 1–3 (off Grand-Place). ☎ **02/513-73-38.** Main courses 300BF–635BF ($8.55–$18.15); menus 605BF–820BF ($17.30–$23.45). AE, DC, MC, V. Mon–Thur noon–2pm and 6–11pm; Fri noon–2pm and 6–midnight; Sat noon–3pm and 6pm–midnight; Sun noon–3pm and 6–11pm. Métro: Gare Centrale. BELGIAN.

Bistro food has been served up in this 17th-century building, the former Hatmakers' Guildhouse, for more than a quarter of a century. Popular with locals who live and work in the area, as well as with tourists fortunate enough to find it, it can be crowded at the height of lunch hour, so it's a good idea to come just before noon or just after 2pm. There are traditional Belgian dishes, many cooked in beer, and mussels on the menu, and servings are more than ample.

✪ **'t Kelderke.** Grand-Place 15. ☎ **02/513-7344.** Main courses 360–450BF ($10.30–$12.85); plat du jour 390BF ($11.15). AE, DC, MC, V. Daily noon–2am. Métro: Gare Centrale or Bourse. BELGIAN.

Despite being on the Grand-Place, this is far from being a tourist trap. As many Bruxellois as tourists pack the long wooden tables in the brick-arched cellar. Great traditional Belgian fare, with little in the way of frills, is served from the open kitchen. Try specialties such as stoemp with *boudin* (sausage), *carbonnades à la Flamande* (Flemish beef stew), *lapin à la gueuze* (rabbit in Brussels beer), and big steaming pans filled with Zeeland mussels.

SEEING THE SIGHTS
SIGHTSEEING SUGGESTIONS FOR FIRST-TIME VISITORS

If You Have 1 Day   Spend the day exploring the historic Center. Beginning with the magnificent **Grand-Place**, visit the 15th-century **Town Hall**, the **Museum of the City of Brussels**, and the **guildhouses**, before moving on to *Manneken-Pis*, the **Cathedral of Sts-Michel-et-Gudule**, and the 19th-century **Royal St Hubert Galleries** for some serious shopping (or window shopping). Buy a bag of chocolates at Wittamer on the **Place du Grand-Sablon** and browse the antiques shops around the square before heading over to tranquil **Place du Petit-Sablon** for a rest. After a dinner that should include mussels (if the month of your visit has an "r" in it), spend the evening checking out one or more of Brussels's famed cafes.

If You Have 2 Days   On the second day, explore Belgian art and architecture in their many permutations. Begin with Brueghel and Rubens at the **Musée d'Art Ancien** and then move into the 20th century with Magritte and Delvaux at the **Musée d'Art Modern** next door. While you're in the neighborhood, take a look at the neo-classical harmony of the **Place Royale** and the monumental **Royal Palace.** At the **Belgian Center for Comic-Strip Art,** you can follow the adventures of comic-book heroes and admire the art nouveau architecture of this restored warehouse. Continue your art nouveau explorations by strolling the side streets off **avenue Louise.**

If You Have 3 Days   On the third day get up early and stop by the **flea market** in the place du Jeu de Balle. Then, head out to the attractions park, **Bruparck,** on the city's northern edge. Bruparck includes Mini-Europe and the Océade water theme park. Nearby are the spheres at the **Atomium** and a panoramic view of the city from the viewing deck. For your last night in Brussels, have dinner or drinks in one of the **guild hall restaurants** that overlook the Grand-Place. The illuminated square is even more beautiful at night than during the day.

BRUSSELS'S HISTORIC SQUARES & STREETS

GRAND-PLACE   Ornamental gables, medieval banners, gilded facades, sunlight flashing off gold-filigreed rooftop sculptures, and a general impression of harmony and timelessness—there's a lot to take in all at once when you first enter the Grand-Place (*Grote Markt* in Dutch). Once the pride of the Hapsburg Empire, the Grand-Place has always been the very heart of Brussels. Characterized by Jean Cocteau as "a splendid stage," it's the city's theater of life.

Your tour should include a visit to the gothic **Hôtel de Ville (Town Hall);** the neogothic **Maison du Roi (King's House)**—despite its name it has never been a royal palace—which houses the **Musée de la Ville de Bruxelles** (Brussels City Museum); and the **Musée de la Brasserie (Brewers Museum),** housed in the beautiful old brewers' guildhouse at Grand-Place 10.

PLACE DU GRAND-SABLON   Considered classier than the Grand-Place by the locals—although busy traffic diminishes the cafe-terrace experience—the Grand-Sablon is lined with gabled mansions. This is antiques territory, and many of those mansions house antiques shops or private art galleries, with pricey merchandise on display. The dealerships have spread into neighboring side streets, and on Saturday and Sunday mornings an excellent antiques market sets up its stalls in front of **Notre-Dame du Sablon Church.** This flamboyantly Gothic edifice, with no fewer than five naves, was paid for by the city's Guild of Crossbowmen in the 15th century. The statue of Minerva in the square dates from 1751. Take bus 34, 95, or 96 from the Bourse.

PLACE DU PETIT-SABLON   Just across rue de la Régence, the Grand-Sablon's little cousin is an ornamental garden with a fountain and pool, a magical little retreat from the city bustle. The 48 bronze statuettes adorning the surrounding wrought-iron fence symbolize Brussels's medieval guilds, and two statues commemorate Counts Egmont and Hornes, beheaded in 1568 for protesting the extravagant cruelties of the Council of Blood, the Spanish Inquisition's enforcement arm in the Low Countries. Take bus 34, 95, or 96 from the Bourse.

PLACE ROYALE   Meeting point of rue de la Régence and rue Royale, streets on which stand many of the city's premier attractions, the square is graced by an equestrian statue of Duke Godefroi de Bouillon, leader of the First Crusade. Its inscription describes him as the "First King of Jerusalem," a title Godefroi himself refused, accepting instead that of "Protector of the Holy Places" (which amounted to the same thing). Also in Place Royale is the neoclassical **Church of St-Jacques-sur-Coudenberg.** Take bus 71 from Brouckère.

MUSEUMS, CHURCHES & MONUMENTS

Manneken-Pis. Corner of rue du Chêne and rue de l'Etuve. Métro: Gare Centrale or Bourse.

Brussels's favorite little boy gleefully does what a little boy's gotta do, more often than not watched by a throng of admirers snapping pictures. Children especially seem to enjoy his bravura performance. This is not the original statue, which was prone to theft and anatomical "maltreatment" and was removed for safekeeping. Louis XV of France began the tradition of presenting colorful costumes to "Little Julian" to make amends for Frenchmen having kidnapped the statue in 1747; the outfits are housed in the Musée de la Ville de Bruxelles in the Grand-Place.

✪ **Hôtel de Ville (Town Hall).** Grand-Place. ☎ **02/279-43-55.** Admission 80BF ($2.30) for guided tours only. Apr–Sept Tues 11:30am and 3:15pm, Wed 3:15pm, Sun 12:15pm; Oct–Mar Tues 11:30am and 3:15pm, Wed 3:15pm. Métro: Gare Centrale or Bourse.

The spectacular Gothic hall in the Grand-Place is open for visits when Brussels's council of aldermen is not in session. You should begin with the exterior, however, particularly the sculptures on the facade, many of which are 15th- and 16th-century jokes. Inside are superb 16th- to 18th-century tapestries; one depicts the duke of Alba, whose cruel features reflect the brutal oppression he and his Council of Blood imposed on Belgium; others are scenes from the life of Clovis, first king of the Franks. The aldermen meet in a plush, mahogany-paneled room surrounded by mirrors—presumably so that each party can see what underhand maneuvers the others are up to.

Palais Royal (Royal Palace). place des Palais. ☎ **02/551-20-20.** Free admission. July 22 to late Sept Tues–Sun 10:30am–4:30pm. Métro: Parc or Arts-Loi.

Work on the palace began in 1820, and it was given a grandiose Louis XVI-style facelift in 1904. King Albert II has his offices here, but he and Queen Paola do not live there. It is also used for state receptions. You can visit the ornate throne room, which has magnificent chandeliers, and other public rooms.

Cathédrale des Sts-Michel-et-Gudule. parvis Ste-Gudule. ☎ **02/217-83-45.** Free admission to church; crypt 40BF ($1.15). Daily 7am–6pm. Métro: Gare Centrale.

Victor Hugo considered this magnificent church to be the "purest flowering of the Gothic style." Begun in 1226, it was officially dedicated as a cathedral only in 1961. The 16th-century Hapsburg Emperor Charles V took a personal interest in its decoration, donating the superb stained-glass windows. In recent years its stonework has been undergoing cleaning and restoration, and the dazzlingly bright exterior makes a superb sight. Inside, spare decoration focuses attention on its soaring columns and arches.

Musées Royaux des Beaux-Arts de Belgique. rue de la Régence 3. ☎ **02/508-32-11.** Admission 150BF ($4.30) adults, 50BF ($1.45) children. Ancient Art Museum Tues–Sun 10am–noon and 1–5pm; Modern Art Museum Tues–Sun 10am–1pm and 2–5pm. Tram: 92, 93, or 94 to place Royale.

Musée d'Art Ancien (Museum of Ancient Art): Brueghel and Rubens are the stars of the show, but the greater history of Belgian painting is well represented. The collection includes international masters, with works by Van Gogh and the French impressionists. Guided tours are available on request.

Musée d'Art Modern (Museum of Modern Art): Next-door neighbor to the Museum of Ancient Art, the Museum of Modern Art has an emphasis on underground works—if only because the museum's eight floors are all below ground level. Magritte is well represented; so are Delvaux, De Braekeleer, Dalí, Permeke, and many others. Guided tours are available on request.

Musée de la Ville de Bruxelles (Brussels City Museum). Grand-Place. ☎ **02/279-43-50.** Admission 100BF ($2.85) adults, 80BF ($2.30) children 5–15, free for children under 5. Mon–Thurs 10am–12:30pm and 1:30–5pm (Oct–Mar until 4pm); Sat–Sun 10am–1pm. Métro: Gare Centrale or Bourse.

In the neogothic Maison du Roi, the displays cover Brussels through the ages, including its traditional arts and crafts of tapestry- and lace-making. Among its most fascinating exhibits are old paintings and scale reconstructions of the historic city center, particularly those showing the riverside ambience along the now-vanished River Senne. Pride of place goes to more than 500 costumes—including an Elvis costume—donated to *Manneken-Pis*.

Musée Horta (Horta Museum). rue Américaine 25. ☎ **02/543-04-90.** Admission 150BF ($4.30) on weekdays; 200BF ($5.70) on weekends. Tues–Sun 2–5:30pm. Tram: 81, 82, 91 or 92.

Brussels owes much of its rich art nouveau heritage to Victor Horta, a resident architect who led the development of the style. His home and an adjoining studio are now a museum. Restored to their original condition, they showcase his use of flowing, sinuous shapes and colors, in both interior decoration and architecture.

Musée du Cinquantenaire (Cinquantenaire Museum). Parc du Cinquantenaire. ☎ **02/741-72-11.** Admission 150BF ($4.30). Tues–Fri 9:30am–5pm; Sat–Sun 10am–5pm. Métro: Schuman.

Formerly known as the Royal Museums of Art and History (Musées Royaux d'Art et d'Histoire), the monumental Cinquantenaire traces the story of civilization, particularly but not exclusively European civilization. Departments include archeology, antiquity (which has a giant model of Imperial Rome), and European decorative arts.

Musée du Costume et de la Dentelle (Museum of Costume and Lace). rue de la Violette 6. ☎ **02/512-77-09.** Admission 100BF ($2.85) adults, 80BF ($2.30) children 5–16, free for children under 5. Mon–Sat 10am–12:30pm and 1:30–5pm (Oct–Mar until 4pm); Sat–Sun 2–4:30pm. Métro: Gare Centrale or Bourse.

In a city famous for its lace, no visit would be complete without seeing the marvelous antique creations in this museum near the Grand-Place. Besides examples of historic Belgian lace, the museum displays costumes, including dress from the 16th to the 19th centuries.

Centre Belge de la Bande Dessinée (Belgian Center for Comic-Strip Art). rue des Sables 20. ☎ **02/219-19-80.** Admission 200BF ($5.70). Tues–Sun 10am–6pm. Métro: Gare Centrale.

Called the "CéBéBéDé" for short, the center displays such popular cartoon characters as Lucky Luke, Thorgal, and, of course, Tintin, yet does not neglect the likes of

Superman, Batman, and the Green Lantern. Grown-ups love it as well. As icing on the cake, it's housed in a Victor Horta building, the Magasins Waucquez, which was slated for demolition when the center took it over.

PARKS & GARDENS

The **Parc de Bruxelles** borders rue Royale, between Parliament and the Royal Palace. Once the hunting preserve of the dukes of Brabant, it is now a landscaped garden. In 1830, Belgian patriots confronted Dutch troops here during the War of Independence. Though not that large, the park manages to contain everything from carefully trimmed borders to rough patches of trees and bushes, and has fine views along its main axes. The métro stop is Parc or Arts-Loi.

Brussels' big public park, the **Bois de la Cambre,** begins at the top of av. Louise in the city's southern section. This is the lung of the city, and it gets pretty busy on sunny weekends. Its centerpiece is a small lake with an island in the center reached by an electrically powered pontoon. Some busy roads run through the park and traffic moves fast on them, so be careful with children. Take tram 92 or 93 from Parc de Bruxelles.

Kids especially enjoy the sights at **Bruparck,** on the city's northern edge, at bd. du Centenaire, Laeken. There's nothing else quite like the **Atomium** (☎ 02/474-89-77), a cluster of giant spheres built for the 1958 World's Fair that represent the atomic model of an iron molecule enlarged 165 billion times. You can wander around inside the spheres; the sight from the viewing deck is marvelous. The Atomium is open April to August 9am to 8pm; September to March 10am to 6pm. Admission is 200BF ($5.70) for adults, 150BF ($4.30) for children 3 to 12, and free for children under 1m 20cm (47 inches); look out for reduced-rate combined tickets if you're also planning to visit Mini-Europe and the Océade.

Adults and kids alike get a kick out of strolling around the landmarks of **Mini-Europe** (☎ 02/478-05-50), which include Big Ben, the Leaning Tower of Pisa, the Seville Bull Ring, as well as more modern emblems of continental achievement, such as the Channel Tunnel and the Ariane rocket (which actually takes off, kind of). As the scale is 1:25, everyone feels like giants. It's open in July and August from 9:30am to 8pm; before and after this period, Mini-Europe opens progressively later and closes progressively earlier; it's closed January and February. Admission is 395BF ($11.30) adults, 295BF ($8.45) children 12 and under, and free for children under 1m 20cm (47 inches). Métro: Heysel. Mini-Europe is next to the **Océade** water leisure center.

ORGANIZED TOURS

Three-hour coach tours are available from **De Boeck Brussels City Tours,** rue de la Colline 8 (☎ 02/513-77-44). Each tour costs 790BF ($22.55) for adults and 395BF ($11.30) for children. Bookings can be made through most hotels, and arrangements can be made for hotel pick-up. Regular tours operate throughout the year, and private tours can also be arranged.

Chatterbus, rue des Thuyas 12 (☎ 02/673-18-35), operates a daily 3-hour tour, June 15 to September 15, starting at 10am from the Galeries Royales St-Hubert, next to rue du Marché-aux-Herbes 90, a few steps from the Grand-Place. The walking tour covers the historic center, followed by a bus ride through areas most tourists never see. You hear about life in Brussels and get a better feel for the city. The price is 300BF ($8.55).

ARAU, the Workshop for Urban Research and Action, bd. Adolphe Max 55 (☎ 02/219-33-45), is a committee of concerned Brussels residents who give 3-hour themed coach tours, including "Surprising Parks and Squares," "Brussels 1900 Art Nouveau," "Grand-Place and Its Surroundings," and "Alternative Brussels." Advanced reservations are advised. Prices are 600BF ($17.15). Tours operate on a rotating basis on Saturdays from March to November, and private group tours can be arranged throughout the year.

All tours are given in English, among other languages.

THE SHOPPING SCENE

Don't look for many bargains in Brussels. As a general rule, the upper city around av. Louise and Porte de Namur is more expensive than the lower city around rue Neuve and the shopping galleries on place de la Monnaie and place Brouckère. (For shopping hours, see "Business Hours" under "Fast Facts: Brussels," above.) A useful source of information is the weekly English-language magazine *The Bulletin,* which keeps tabs on shopping trends, reviews stores, and carries advertising.

Galeries Royales St-Hubert is one of Europe's oldest shopping malls, a light and airy arcade hosting boutiques, cafe terraces, and street musicians playing classical music. Opened in 1847, architect Pierre Cluysenaer's Italian neo-Renaissance gallery has a touch of class and is well worth a stroll through, even if you have no intention of looking in a shop window. The elegant triple gallery—Galerie du Roi, Galerie de la Reine, and Galerie des Princes—forerunner of city arcades such as London's Burlington, is near the Grand-Place, between rue du Marché-aux-Herbes and rue de l'Ecuyer, and split by rue de Bouchers. There are accesses on each of these streets. Take the Métro to Gare Centrale or Bourse.

At the **Flea Market** on place du Jeu-de-Balle, a large square in the Marolles district, you can find some exceptional decorative items, many recycled from the homes of the "recently deceased," as well as unusual postcards, clothing, and household goods. Everything from antiques to junk, from North African clothes to Soviet chic, is sold here. The market is held daily 7am to 2pm.

Every weekend, place du Grand Sablon hosts a fine **Antiques Market.** Salesmanship is low-key, interest pure, prices not unreasonable, and quality of merchandise—including silverware, pottery, paintings, and jewelry—high. The market is open Saturday 9am to 6pm and Sunday 9am to 2pm.

The Grand-Place has a Flower Market, daily 7am to 2pm, and a weekly Bird Market, with many varieties of birds for sale. Nearby, at the top end of rue du

---

Where to Buy Belgian Chocolates & Lace

Belgian chocolates are rightly famous worldwide. **Neuhaus,** Galerie de la Reine 25 (☎ **02/502-59-14;** métro: Gare Centrale or Bourse), sells exquisite hand-made chocolates. **Wittamer,** place du Grand-Sablon 12 (☎ **02/512-37-42;** tram 92 or 93), makes some of the world's best handmade pralines, and their rolls, breads, pastries, and cakes have been winning fans since 1910. **Dandoy,** rue au Beurre 31 (☎ **02/511-81-76;** métro: Bourse), is for cookies-'n'-cakes fans. Try traditional Belgian specialties such as spicy *speculoos* cookies and *pain à grecque.*

Manufacture Belge de Dentelle, Galerie de la Reine 6–8 (☎ **02/511-44-77;** métro: Gare Centrale or Bourse), specializes in top-quality handmade Belgian lace. Another good lace store is **Maison Antoine,** Grand-Place 26 (☎ **02/512-48-59;** métro: Gare Centrale or Bourse), in a former guildhouse where Victor Hugo lived in 1852. The quality is superb, service friendly, and prices reasonable.

In case you want
to see the world.

**At American Express, we're here to make your journey
a smooth one. So we have over 1,700 travel service locations in over 130 countries ready to help. What else
would you expect from the world's largest travel agency?**

do more

Travel

**Call 1 800 AXP-3429 or visit
www.americanexpress.com/travel**

In case you want to be welcomed there.

We're here to see that you're always welcomed at establishments everywhere. That's why millions of people carry the American Express® Card – for peace of mind, confidence, and security, around the world or just around the corner.

do more

In case you're running low.

We're here to help with more than 190,000 Express Cash locations around the world. In order to enroll, just call American Express at 1 800 CASH-NOW before you start your vacation.

do more   AMERICAN EXPRESS

Express Cash

And in case you'd rather be safe than sorry.

We're here with American Express® Travelers Cheques. They're the safe way to carry money on your vacation, because if they're ever lost or stolen you can get a refund, practically anywhere or anytime. To find the nearest place to buy Travelers Cheques, call 1 800 495-1153. Another way we help you do more.

do more

Travelers Cheques

Marché-aux-Herbes, in the Agora, the weekend Crafts Market has lots of fine little specialized jewelry and other items, most of which are inexpensive.

Forget computer games and Disney stores—if you need to buy a gift for the kids, take home some Tintin mementos from **Boutique de Tintin,** rue de la Colline 13 (☎ 02/514-45-50).

Don't miss **De Boe,** rue de Flandre 36 (☎ 02/511-13-73; métro: Ste-Catherine), a small shop near the Fish Market, with heavenly aromas of roasted and blended coffee, a superb selection of wines in all price categories, and an array of specialty crackers, nuts, spices, teas, and gourmet snacks, many of which come in tins that make them easy to pack.

Among shops selling fashionable clothing and accessories, try **Delvaux,** Galerie de la Reine 31 (☎ 02/512-71-98; métro: Gare Centrale or Bourse), a local company making and selling some of the best, and priciest, handbags and leather goods in Belgium. **Olivier Strelli,** av. Louise 72 (☎ 02/511-21-34; métro: Louise), is owned by the top-rated Belgian fashion designer, whose line is strong on elegant, ready-to-wear items.

For the most books and magazines in English, visit **Waterstone's,** bd. Adolphe Max 71 (☎ 02/219-27-08; métro: Rogier), a branch of the British bookstore chain.

BRUSSELS AFTER DARK

The city offers a full range of evening activities, including dance, opera, classical music, jazz, film, theater, and discos. For an exhaustive listing of events, consult the "What's On" section of the English-language weekly *The Bulletin.*

PERFORMING ARTS

La Monnaie. place de la Monnaie ☎ 02/229-12-11. Métro: Brouckère.

The superb Théâtre Royal de la Monnaie, founded in the 17th century, is home to the **Opéra National** and the **Orchestre Symphonique de la Monnaie.** The resident ballet company is Belgian choreographer Anna Theresa de Keersmaeker's **Group Rosas.**

Music & Theater

The **Palais des Beaux-Arts,** rue Royale 10 (☎ 02/507-84-66; métro: Parc), is home to the Belgian National Orchestra. The **Cirque Royal,** rue de l'Enseignement 81 (☎ 02/218-20-15; métro: Parc), formerly a real circus, is used for music, opera, and ballet.

Theaters concentrate on French- and Dutch-language plays, many adapted from English, with occasional English-language performances. **Théâtre Royal du Parc,** rue de la Loi 3 (☎ 02/512-23-39; métro: Parc), is a magnificent edifice occupying a corner of the Parc de Bruxelles opposite Parliament. Most performances of classic and contemporary drama and comedies here are in French. (At the time of this writing, the theater had been heavily damaged by fire, and its future is uncertain.)

Traditional Bruxellois marionette theater is maintained in an old cafe, **Théâtre Toone VII,** Impasse Schuddeveld, Petite rue des Bouchers 6 (☎ 02/217-27-53; métro: Gare Centrale or Bourse). Often treating sophisticated subjects, puppet master José Géal presents adaptations of classic tales in the local dialect, Brussels Vloms, as well as in English, French, Dutch, and German.

THE CLUB & MUSIC SCENE

Brussels is not as noted for nightlife as some neighboring capitals—dining out being the most popular local activity. However, nightlife is alive and well, and if its range is smaller than that of bigger cities like London and Paris, the quality is not.

Impressions

You can get tickets for all venues from the **Central Booking Office** (☎ **0800/ 21-221**) and from individual box offices, or reserve them against a credit card for pick-up the night of the performance.

Cabarets & Discos

Chez Flo. rue au Beurre 25. ☎ **02/513-31-52.** Dinner and floor-show 1,475–2,950BF ($42.15–84.30); the highest price includes a half-bottle of champagne per person. Show begins at 8pm. Métro: Bourse.

A bit of a hoot, this transvestite cabaret and dinner show is outrageous and comfortable at the same time.

Griffin's Night Club. Royal Windsor Hotel, rue Duquesnoy 5. ☎ **02/505-55-55.** Open Tues–Sat 10pm–4 or 5am. No cover.

A fashionable, well-dressed kind of disco with a varied taste in musical styles and periods.

Le Fuse. rue Blaes 208. ☎ **02/511-97-89.** Cover varies: Sat techno evenings, Pussy Lounge and La Démence free from 10–11pm, thereafter 300BF ($8.55). Open Tues–Sun 10pm–5am. Bus: 20 or 48.

This is the place if only techno will do. On the first Friday of every month, it reinvents itself as the women-only Pussy Lounge, and every Sunday as the men-only La Démence.

Le Show Point. place Stéphanie 14. ☎ **02/511-53-64.** No cover. Mon–Sat 10pm–dawn (show begins at 12:30am). Métro: Louise.

Brussels isn't Paris when it comes to putting on Moulin Rouge–type shows, but Show Point adopts a similar approach. From 10pm until dawn, showgirls, scantily clad or wearing fanciful costumes, strut their stuff in a variety of fetching choreographies. Drinks cost 1,000BF ($28.55).

Le Sparrow. rue Duquesnoy 16. ☎ **02/512-66-22.** Cover 320BF ($9.15), includes a drink. Thurs–Sat 10pm–dawn. Métro: Gare Centrale.

This disco always seems on the verge of going out of style, yet never quite gets there, even if it has lost the wildness of its younger days. A location off the Grand-Place helps. So does an up-to-date approach to music—techno, house, trip-hop, garage, whatever.

Jazz & Blues

Jazz has taken a hit in recent years, with some of the city's best-loved spots closing down.

L'Archiduc. rue Antoine Dansaert 6. ☎ **02/512-06-52.** Sunday jazz cover 400–500BF ($11.45–$14.30). Daily 4pm–4am. Métro: Bourse.

Very chi-chi and not the friendliest of scenes, this art deco bar serves up a sophisticated program of jazz on weekends, usually beginning at 5pm. A stylish crowd lounges about in the blue light and nods appreciatively at the mellow sounds.

Marcus Mingus Jazz Spot. Impasse de la Fidelité 10 (off rue des Bouchers). ☎ **02/ 502-02-97.** Open Mon–Sat 7:30pm–2am. Cover 200BF ($5.70) Wed, 300BF ($8.55) Fri–Sat. Métro: Gare Centrale or Bourse.

A popular new jazz cafe that attracts top local performers and an occasional international name. Concerts begin a couple hours after opening time. There's a jam session on Thursday.

Belgian Brews

Be warned: Belgian beers are stronger than those of the U.S.—alcohol content can be as high as 12%. Try a rich, dark Trappist ale brewed by monks from Chimay, Orval, Rochefort, Westmalle, and Westvleteren monasteries. Brussels is well known for its *lambic* beers, which use naturally occurring yeast for fermentation, are often flavored with fruit, and come in bottles with champagne-type corks. Unlike any other beer, they're more akin to a sweet sparkling wine. *Gueuze,* a blend of young and aged lambic beers is one of the least sweet. If you prefer something sweeter, try raspberry-flavored *framboise* or cherry-flavored *kriek. Faro* is a low-alcohol beer, sometimes sweetened or lightly spiced.

THE BAR SCENE

Now you're talking. Bars are where Brussels really dwells. The city's cafes and bars run the gamut from art nouveau palaces to convivial local watering-holes. Don't leave without lingering a few hours in one, savoring Belgium's incredible variety of beers.

A la Morte Subite. rue Montagne-aux-Herbes Potagères 7. ☎ **02/513-13-18.** Métro: Gare Centrale.

Although its name means "Sudden Death," don't worry. You'll probably survive in this fine old cafe, which appeals to an eclectic cross-section of society, from little old ladies to bank managers, dancers and musicians from the top cultural venues, and students. Decor consists of stained-glass motifs, old photographs, paintings and prints on the walls, and plain wooden chairs and tables. Specialties are traditional Brussels beers: gueuze, faro, and kriek, as well as abbey brews such as Chimay, Maredsous, and Grimbergen. The staff's attitude takes a little getting used to, especially if you need more than 3 seconds to decide what you want. If you can be decisive, you'll have a friend for life—or at any rate, for the evening.

Halloween. rue des Grands-Carmes 10. ☎ **02/514-12-56.** Métro: Bourse.

The decor is enough to give you the creeps: Gargoyles, devils, and other assorted creatures from the darker recesses of the human mind create a disturbing ambience in what is an unforgettable bar inhabited mostly by the young and the trendy.

Le Cirio. rue de la Bourse 18. ☎ **02/512-13-95.** Métro: Bourse.

Many customers look like they've made their pile across the road at the Stock Exchange and retired here in a state of genteel splendor. That's Le Cirio, a quiet, refined place to sip your drink, in surroundings that make the exercise seem worthwhile.

Le Falstaff. rue Henri Maus 17. ☎ **02/511-87-89.** Métro: Bourse.

Waitstaff at the city's most stylish cafe are widely considered to have an attitude problem. Yet the main problem here is finding a seat, so popular is it. Opened in 1904, Falstaff's art nouveau is enlivened with a dash of art deco.

Le Fleur en Papier Doré. rue des Alexiens 53. ☎ **02/511-16-59.** Métro: Bourse.

This bar calls itself a "temple of surrealism," but old prints, plates, horns, porcelain, and knickknacks on the walls are more evocative of a cozy hunting lodge than a room Magritte might have painted—although it's said that he and other surrealists used to hang out here. Now painters, poets, and an after-theater crowd sip beer, munch on snacks, and enjoy the relaxed atmosphere. On weekend nights, there's an accordian player; poetry readings are held upstairs several times a month.

A DAY TRIP TO WATERLOO

The battle that ended Napoléon's empire was fought several miles south of Waterloo on a stretch of rolling farmland that remains much as it was on June 18, 1815. Before touring it, you should study a 360° panoramic mural and see a short movie of the battle at the **Centre du Visiteur,** route du Lion 252–254, Braine L'Alleud (☎ 02/385-19-12). To survey the battlefield climb the nearby **Butte du Lion** (Lion Mound), a pyramid-like hill behind the center. These three sites are open daily from April to September, 9:30am to 6:30pm; October, 9:30am to 5:30pm; November to February, 10:30am to 4pm; March, 10am to 5pm. Viewing the audiovisual show costs 200BF ($5.70) for adults, 170BF ($4.85) for students and seniors, 135BF ($3.85) for children ages 6–12, free for children under 6; Panorama tickets cost 110BF ($3.15), 80BF ($2.30), and 60BF ($1.70) respectively; Lion Mound tickets 40BF ($1.15), 40BF ($1.15), and 20BF (55¢). Combined tickets for all three cost 300BF ($8.55), 250BF ($7.15), and 190BF ($5.45). A waxworks museum as well as the farms that played a crucial role in the battle are only a short stroll from the Visitor's Center.

You can fill in details of the battle at the **Wellington Museum,** chaussée de Bruxelles 147, Waterloo (☎ 02/354-78-06), a former inn where Wellington wrote his victory dispatch. The museum is open April through September daily from 9:30am to 6:30pm; October to March daily 10:30am to 5pm. Admission is 100BF ($2.85) adults, 80BF ($2.30) seniors and students, 40BF ($1.15) for children ages 6–12, and free for children under 6.

GETTING THERE   Bus "W" leaves on the half hour and the hour from a bus terminal on av. de Stalingrad, a block south of place Rouppe. It stops at both the museum and the visitor center. By car, take the N5 south through the Bois de la Cambre and Forêt de Soignes.

2 Bruges & Ghent

Both Flemish cities are showcases of medieval art and architecture, yet each has a distinctive character that makes visiting them a complementary experience. Walking around Bruges is like taking a step back in time. This almost perfectly preserved medieval city, with graceful squares, such as the Markt and Burg, and historic architecture, is a sight in itself. Ghent is austere but more authentic, with a forbidding castle and three-towered cathedral. Some of the northern Renaissance's most outstanding paintings hang in the cities' museums and churches, most notably in Bruges' Church of Our Lady and Groeninge Museum, and Ghent's St. Bavo's Cathedral.

BRUGES (BRUGGE)

From its 13th-century origins as a cloth manufacturing town to its current incarnation as a tourism magnet, Bruges seems to have changed little. As in a fairy tale, swans glide down the winding canals and the stone houses look like they're made of gingerbread. Even though modern glass-fronted stores have taken over the ground floors of ancient buildings, and the swans scatter before tour boats chugging along the canals, Bruges has managed the transition from medieval to modern with remarkable grace. The town seems revitalized rather than crushed by the tremendous influx of tourists that pour in each season. Even more amazing is the warm welcome that the populace extends to its visitors. Tourism is an economic necessity, of course, but the people who

Bruges

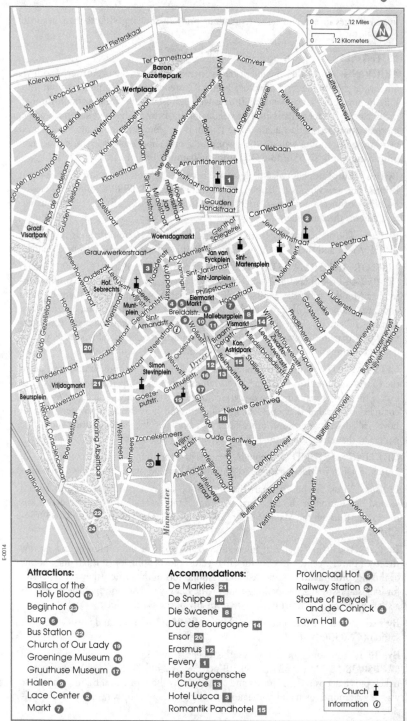

Attractions:

Basilica of the
  Holy Blood ⑩
Begijnhof ㉓
Burg ⑥
Church of Our Lady ⑲
Groeninge Museum ⑯
Gruuthuse Museum ⑰
Hallen ⑨
Lace Center ②
Markt ⑦

Accommodations:

De Markies ㉑
De Snippe ⑱
Die Swaene ⑧
Duc de Bourgogne ⑭
Ensor ⑳
Erasmus ⑫
Fevery ①
Het Bourgoensche
  Cruyce ⑬
Hotel Lucca ③
Romantik Pandhotel ⑮

Provinciaal Hof ⑤
Railway Station ㉔
Statue of Breydel
  and de Coninck ④
Town Hall ⑪

Church ✝
Information ⓘ

121

live in Bruges love it and take tremendous pride in showing visitors their beautiful town.

ESSENTIALS

ARRIVING By Train Frequent trains arrive from Brussels and Antwerp (both via Ghent), and from the ferry ports of Ostend (Oostende) and Zeebrugge. A train from Lille in northern France connects Bruges with Eurostar trains from London through the Channel Tunnel to Paris and Brussels. Look for Brugge, the town's Flemish name, on the station destination boards. The station is on Stationsplein, about 1 mile south of town, a 20-minute walk to the town center or a short bus or taxi ride. For train information, call ☎ **050/38-23-82** from 6:30am to 10:30pm.

By Bus Eurolines has twice-daily service between London and Brussels, stopping at Bruges. For reservations in Britain, contact Eurolines (☎ **0990/808080**). There are Eurolines connections from many European cities via Brussels. Bruges's main bus station adjoins the train station.

By Car The main expressways to Bruges are the E40/A-10 from Brussels and Ghent, the E17/A-14 and then E40/A-10 from Antwerp, and the E40/A-10 from Ostend.

VISITOR INFORMATION The **Tourist Office,** at Burg 11, 8000 Bruges (☎ **050/44-86-86;** fax 050/44-86-00; www.brugge.be/brugge), is open April to September Monday to Friday 9:30am to 6:30pm, Saturday and Sunday 10am to noon and 2 to 6:30pm; October to March Monday to Friday 9:30am to 5pm, Saturday and Sunday 9:30am to 1pm and 2 to 5:30pm. The friendly and efficient office has brochures that outline walking, coach, canal, and horse-drawn cab tours, as well as detailed information on many sightseeing attractions and cultural events.

CITY LAYOUT Bruges has two "hearts" in side-by-side monumental squares called the **Markt** and the **Burg.** Narrow streets fan out from these squares, and a network of canals threads its way through every section of this small city. The center is almost encircled by a canal that opens at its southern end into the **Minnewater** (Lake of Love), filled with swans and other birds and bordered by the **Begijnhof** and a fine park. On the outer side of the Minnewater is the train station.

GETTING AROUND Although street signs and transport information are in Dutch, English is widely spoken, so you should have no problem getting directions.

By Bus Most city buses depart the bus station beside the train station, or from a second bus station at the big square called 't Zand, west of the Markt. Several bus routes pass through the Markt. For city and regional bus information, call ☎ **059/56-53-53.**

By Car You'll find it all but impossible to use a car in the confusing and narrow streets of the city center. Leave your car at your hotel parking lot (if it has one), at one of the big, prominently signposted underground lots in the center (they get expensive for long stays), or at a free parking zone by the railway station, south of the center. It's a short walk into the heart of the city from any of the parking lots.

By Taxi There are taxi stands at the Markt (☎ **050/33-44-44**) and outside the train station (☎ **050/38-46-60**).

By Bike You can rent a bike at the Baggage Department of the train station (☎ **050/38-58-71**) for 325BF ($9.30) per day or 250BF ($6.95) with a valid train ticket, plus a deposit. Some hotels and several shops also rent bikes. Biking is a terrific way to get around town and to the nearby village of Damme by way of beautiful canalside roads.

By Boat   Going around by tour boat is another great way to see Bruges, especially on a fine day. The view from those open-top boats is unforgettable. See "Boat Trips & Other Organized Tours," below.

EXPLORING HISTORIC BRUGES

Walking is by far the best way to see Bruges, whose town center is traffic-free. Wear good walking shoes, as those charming cobblestones can be hard going. Begin at the Markt, with its 13th–16th-century **Belfort (Belfry)** and **Hallen (Hall)**, Markt 7 (☎ 050/44-87-11). The Belfry's octagonal tower soars 272 feet (84 meters) and holds a magnificent 47-bell carillon. Climb the 366 steps to the Belfry's summit for a panoramic view of Bruges and the surrounding countryside all the way to the sea. Much of the city's commerce was conducted in the Hallen in past centuries. Today it is used as an exhibition center by local art dealers. The Belfry and Hall are open daily April to September 9:30am to 5pm, and October to March, 9:30am to 12:30pm and 1:30 to 5pm. Admission is 100BF ($2.85) for adults, 50BF ($1.45) for children.

The **sculpture group** in the center of the Markt depicts two Flemish heroes, butcher Jan Breydel and weaver Pieter de Coninck, who led an uprising in 1302 against the wealthy merchants and nobles who dominated the guilds, and then went on to an against-all-odds victory over French knights in the Battle of the Golden Spurs later that same year. The large neogothic **Provinciaal Hof** dates from the 1800s and houses the government of West Flanders province.

An array of beautiful buildings, a virtual trip through the history of architecture, stands in the **Burg,** a public square just steps away from the Markt. Here the Count of Flanders, Baldwin "Iron Arm," built a fortified castle (burg), around which grew the village that developed into Bruges.

The **Stadhuis (Town Hall),** Burg 11 (☎ 050/44-87-11), is a beautiful Gothic structure built in the late 1300s, making it the oldest town hall in Belgium. Don't miss the upstairs **Gotische Zaal (Gothic Room),** with its ornate decor and wall murals depicting highlights of Bruges's history. The Town Hall is open April through September daily 9:30am to 5pm; October through March 9:30am to 12:30pm and 2 to 5pm. Admission is 60BF ($1.70) for adults, 20BF (55¢) for children. The price includes entry to the neighboring Renaissance **Hall of the Brugse Vrije (Hall of the Liberty of Bruges),** which has been restored to its 16th-century condition. It has a superb black marble fireplace decorated with an alabaster frieze and topped by a carved oak chimney-piece with statues of Emperor Charles V and his illustrious grandparents: Emperor Maximilian of Austria, Duchess Mary of Burgundy, King Ferdinand II of Aragon, and Queen Isabella I of Castile.

Next to the Town Hall is the richly decorated, Romanesque **Heilige-Bloedbasiliek (Basilica of the Holy Blood),** Burg 10 (☎ 050/33-67-92). Since 1149 this has been the repository of a cloth fragment holding what is said to be the blood of Christ, brought to Bruges after the Second Crusade by the Count of Flanders. Every Ascension Day (June 1 in 2000), in the Procession of the Holy Blood, the bishop carries the relic through the streets, accompanied by costumed residents acting out Biblical scenes. The relic is kept in the basilica museum inside a rock-crystal vial, which is in a magnificent gold-and-silver reliquary. The basilica is open April through September daily 9:30am to noon and 2 to 6pm; October through March daily 10am to noon and 2 to 4pm (closed Wednesday afternoon). Admission to the basilica is free; to the museum, it's 40BF ($1.15) for adults, 20BF (55¢) for children.

Through the centuries, one of the city's most tranquil spots has been the ✪ **Begijnhof,** Wijngaardstraat (☎ 050/33-00-11), and so it remains today. *Begijns* were religious women, similar to nuns, who accepted vows of chastity and obedience but drew the line at poverty. Today, the begijns are no more and the Begijnhof is occupied by Benedictine nuns who keep the begijns' traditions alive. Their tree-sprinkled lawn, surrounded by little whitewashed houses, makes a marvelous place to escape from the hurly-burly of the outside world. The Begijnhof is open March through November daily 10am to noon and 1:45 to 5pm (April through September weekends until 5:30pm); December through February Monday, Tuesday, and Friday 11am to noon; Wednesday and Thursday 2 to 4pm. Admission to the Begijn's House is 60BF ($1.70) for adults, 30BF (85¢) for children; the courtyard is permanently open and admission free.

It took two centuries (13th to 15th) to build ✪ **Onze-Lieve-Vrouwekerk (Church of Our Lady)**, Mariastraat (☎ 050/34-53-14), and its soaring 122-meter-high (396-foot) spire can be seen from a wide area around the city. Among the many art treasures housed inside are its beautiful marble *Madonna and Child* by Michelangelo (one of his few works to be seen outside Italy); a painting of the *Crucifixion* by Anthony Van Dyck; and impressive side-by-side bronze tomb sculptures of Charles the Bold, who died in 1477, and Mary of Burgundy, who died in 1482. The church is open April through September Monday to Saturday 10 to 11:30am and 2:30 to 5pm (Saturday until 4pm), Sunday 2:30 to 5pm; October through March Monday to Saturday 10 to 11:30am and 2:30 to 4:30pm (Saturday until 4pm), Sunday 2:30 to 4:30pm. Admission to the church and the *Madonna and Child* altar is free; to the chapel of Charles and Mary, 60BF ($1.70) for adults, 30 (85¢) for children.

The ✪ **Groeninge Museum**, Dijver 12 (☎ 050/44-87-11), is one of Belgium's leading fine arts museums, with a collection that covers painting in the Low Countries from the 15th to the 20th century. Its Flemish Primitives Gallery holds 30 works by such painters as Jan van Eyck (portrait of his wife, Margerita van Eyck), Rogier van der Weyden, Hieronymus Bosch (*The Last Judgment*), and Hans Memling. Works by Magritte and Delvaux are also on display. The museum is open April to September daily 9:30am to 5pm; October through March Wednesday to Monday 9:30am to 12:30pm and 2 to 5pm. Admission is 200BF ($5.70) for adults, 100BF ($2.85) for children.

In a courtyard next to the Groeninge is an ornate mansion where Flemish nobleman and herb merchant Louis de Gruuthuse lived in the 1400s. Now the **Gruuthuse Museum**, Dijver 17 (☎ 050/44-87-11), it has thousands of antiques and antiquities, including paintings, sculptures, tapestries, lace, weapons, glassware, and richly carved furniture. It is open April through September daily 9:30am to 5pm; October through March Wednesday to Monday 9:30am to 12:30pm and 2 to 5pm. Admission is 130BF ($3.70) for adults, 70BF ($2) for children, 250BF ($7.15) for families with children under 18.

A popular attraction, needless to say, is the **Kantcentrum (Lace Center)**, Peperstraat 3a (☎ 050/33-00-72). Bruges lace is famous the world over, and there's no lack of shops offering you the opportunity to take some home. At the center, the ancient art of making lace is passed on to a new generation, while you get a firsthand look at artisans making many of the items sold in the city's lace shops. The center is open Monday to Saturday 10am to noon and 2 to 6pm (Saturday until 5pm). Lace-making demonstrations are in the afternoon. Admission is 60BF ($1.70) for adults, 40BF ($1.15) for children.

BOAT TRIPS & OTHER ORGANIZED TOURS

If you'd like a trained, knowledgeable guide to accompany you, the tourist office can provide one for 1,500BF ($42.85) for the first 2 hours, 750BF ($21.45) for each additional hour. In July and August, join a daily guided walking tour at 3pm from the tourist office for 150BF ($4.30); free for children under 14.

Make sure you take an ✪ **open-top canal boat tour** while in Bruges; it's a fine way to view the city. Departure points are marked with an anchor icon on tourist office maps.

Boats operate from March to November daily 10am to 6pm; December to February on weekends, school holidays, and public holidays 10am to 6pm (unless the canals are frozen). A half-hour cruise costs 170BF ($4.85) for adults, 85BF ($2.45) for children over 4. Wear something warm for cold or windy weather.

Another lovely way to tour Bruges is by **horse-drawn carriage.** From March to November, they are stationed in the Burg (Wednesday in the Markt); a 30-minute ride costs 900BF ($25.70) per cab, and 450BF ($12.85) for each additional 15 minutes.

Sightseeing Lines coach tours (50 minutes) depart hourly every day from the Markt; first bus at 10am, last bus at 7pm in July and August, and at 4, 5, or 6pm in other months. Fares are 380BF ($10.85) for adults, 250BF ($7.15) for children; call ☎ **050/31-13-55.**

Get out of town to the Flanders countryside on a **Back Road Bike Co.** bicycle tour (☎ **050/34-30-45**), with options for 18km, 30km, and 40km (11, 18, and 25 mile) tours. Call ahead to book; meeting and departure point is the Burg.

WHERE TO STAY

Bruges's hotels fill up fast. Don't arrive without a reservation, especially in summer. If you do, the tourist office has a reservation service; you can also book in advance here and in tourist offices throughout the country. Accommodations are less heavily booked during the week than on weekends.

Expensive

De Snippe. Nieuwe Gentweg 53, 8000 Bruges. ☎ **050/33-70-70.** Fax 050/33-76-62. 9 units. MINIBAR TV TEL. 5,500–7,500BF ($157.15–$214.30) double. Rates include full breakfast. AE, CB, DC, MC, V. Limited parking available on street.

In an early 18th-century building in the town center, De Snippe offers luxurious and spacious rooms. Many of them have fireplaces, and all are furnished with restrained elegance. De Snippe has long been known as one of Bruges's leading restaurants (see "Where to Dine," below).

Die Swaene. Steenhouwersdijk 1, 8000 Bruges. ☎ **050/34-27-98.** Fax 050/33-66-74. E-mail: dieswaene@unicall.be. 22 units. MINIBAR TV TEL. 5,800–7,200BF ($165.70–$205.70) double; 8,950–10,950BF ($255.70–$312.85) suite. Rates include buffet breakfast. AE, DC, JCB, MC, V. Parking 300BF ($8.55).

This small hotel overlooking a city center canal has been called one of the most romantic in Europe. All of the comfortable rooms are elegantly and individually furnished. The lounge was the Tailors' Guild Hall, from 1779. The restaurant, whose specialty is seafood, has won favorable reviews from guests and critics alike, and there's a sauna and indoor swimming pool.

✪ **Romantik Pandhotel.** Pandreitje 16, 8000 Bruges. ☎ **050/34-06-66.** Fax 050/34-05-56. 24 units. MINIBAR TV TEL. 4,990–5,990BF ($142.55–$171.15) double; 6,990–7,490BF ($199.70–$214) family rooms and suites. Rates include buffet breakfast. AE, DC, MC, V. Limited parking available on street.

Close to the Markt, this lovely 18th-century mansion surrounded by plane trees is an oasis of tranquility. Although it provides modern conveniences, such as hair dryers, its exquisite, old-fashioned furnishings lend special grace to the comfortable rooms. Guests praise Mrs. Chris Vanhaecke-Dewaele highly for her hospitality and attention to detail.

Moderate

De Markies. 't Zand 5, 8000 Bruges. ☎ **050/34-83-34.** Fax 050/34-87-87. 18 units. TV TEL. 2,900–3,200BF ($82.85–$91.45) double. Rates include buffet breakfast. AE, CB, DC, MC, V. Parking in nearby lot 350BF ($10).

For those who want to experience Bruges's old-world charm without surrendering modern comforts or their wallet, this is a good bet. Its position on a corner of the big square, 't Zand, makes it convenient for exploring the old center. The spacious rooms are decorated in black, salmon, and green, with modern furnishings.

✪ **Duc de Bourgogne.** Huidenvettersplein 12, 8000 Bruges. ☎ **050/33-20-38.** Fax 050/34-40-37. 10 units. TV TEL. 3,700–5,300BF ($105.70–$151.45) double. Rates include continental breakfast. AE, CB, DC, MC, V. Limited parking available on street.

This is a small, elegant hotel in a 17th-century canal-side building. Fairly large guest rooms are luxuriously furnished and decorated, with antiques scattered throughout. A good restaurant on the ground floor overlooks the canal (see "Where to Dine," below).

Erasmus. Wollestraat 35, 8000 Bruges. ☎ **050/33-57-81.** Fax 050/33-47-27. E-mail: erasmus@ap.be. 9 units. MINIBAR TV TEL. 3,750–5,000BF ($107.15–$142.85) double. Rates include buffet breakfast. AE, CB, MC, V. Limited parking available on street.

Just steps away from the Belfry, this cozy hotel is set in a picturesque little square alongside a canal in the town center. All rooms have writing desks and attractive, modern furnishings, as well as coffeemakers and hair dryers.

✪ **Het Bourgoensche Cruyce.** Wollestraat 41–43, 8000 Bruges. ☎ **050/33-79-26.** Fax 050/34-19-68. 8 units. TV TEL. 3,500–4,900BF ($100–$140) double. Rates include continental breakfast. AE, DC, MC, V. Parking in nearby lot 350BF ($10).

Opening onto a lovely inner courtyard, right in the middle of town (the Belfry is just 100 yards away), this tiny family-run hotel epitomizes the Bruges experience. Rooms are quite large with contemporary furnishings; modern bathrooms have hair dryers. Best of all is the hospitality of the proprietors, who also oversee one of the best restaurants in town on the ground floor (see "Where to Dine," below).

Inexpensive

✪ **Ensor.** Speelmansrei 10. ☎ **050/34-25-89.** Fax 050/34-20-18. 12 units. TEL. 1,960–2,190BF ($56–$62.55) double. Rates include breakfast. AE, MC, V. Limited parking available on street.

If you want to open your window and know right away you're in Bruges, get a room here overlooking the canal. Although most units are relatively large, and all come with bright, modern bathrooms, it's the canal view at a budget price that makes this hotel a standout. There's a radio in every room, and an elevator.

Fevery. Collaert Mansioenstraat 3, 8000 Bruges. ☎ **050/33-12-69.** Fax 050/33-17-91. E-mail: hotelfevery.brugge@unicall.be. 11 units. TV TEL. 2,000–2,400BF ($57.15–$68.55) double. Rates include buffet breakfast. AE, CB, MC, V. Free parking.

Centrally located near the Markt, this small hotel has comfortable rooms that are beautifully furnished in modern style, with a small table and chairs. Rooms are being enlarged in 1999 and 2000. There's a downstairs bar and dining room, and baby-sitting can be arranged.

Hotel Lucca. Naaldenstraat 30, 8000 Bruges. ☎ **050/34-20-67.** Fax 050/33-34-64. 17 units, 13 with bathroom. TEL. 1,950BF ($55.70) double without bathroom; 2,500BF ($71.45) double with bathroom. Rates include buffet breakfast. AE, MC, V, DC. Limited parking available on street.

Built in the 14th century by a wealthy merchant from Lucca, Italy, the high ceilings and wide halls of this mansion convey a sense of luxury. The rooms are in excellent condition and sport pine furnishings and pretty flowered wallpaper. The rooms with private bathrooms also have TV. Breakfast is served in a cozy medieval cellar.

WHERE TO DINE
Very Expensive

De Karmeliet. Langestraat 19. ☎ **050/33-82-59.** Reservations required. Main courses 750–1,250BF ($21.45–$35.70); set-price menus 2,600–3,200BF ($74.30–$91.45). AE, DC, V. Tues–Sat noon–2pm and 7–9:30pm; Sun 7–9:30pm except June to Sept. Closed Jan, last week of Aug, first week of Sept. BELGIAN/FRENCH

In 1996 chef Geert Van Hecke became the first Flemish chef to be awarded three Michelin stars. He has described his award-winning menu as "international cuisine made with local products" that aims to combine French quality with Flemish quantity. The result is outstanding, and the decor is as elegant as the fine cuisine deserves.

De Snippe. Nieuwe Gentweg 53. ☎ **050/33-70-70.** Reservations required. Main courses 850–1,350BF ($24.30–$38.55). AE, DC, MC, V. Tues–Sat noon–2:30pm; daily 7–10pm. FLEMISH/FRENCH.

In the 18th-century mansion hotel of the same name, the restaurant enjoys a well-earned reputation as one of Bruges's finest regional choices. Try the crayfish creations, scampi, or sliced wild duck.

Expensive

Duc de Bourgogne. Huidenvettersplein 12. ☎ **050/33-20-38.** Reservations required. Main courses 600–900BF ($17.15–$25.70); set-price menus 1,275–2,150BF ($36.45–$61.45). AE, CB, DC, MC, V. Tues 7–9pm; Wed–Sun noon–2pm and 7–9pm. Closed Jan, July. FRENCH.

This large dining room, overlooking a canal illuminated at night, is a Bruges classic. The menu is lengthy; the set-price lunch menu changes daily, and the set-price dinner every 2 weeks. Specialties include veal filets in a port sauce.

't Bourgoensche Cruyce. Wollestraat 41–43. ☎ **050/33-79-26.** Reservations required. Main courses 550–850BF ($15.70–$24.30); 3-course set-price meal 1,400BF ($40) at lunch, 2,200BF ($62.85) at dinner. AE, DC, MC, V. Thurs–Mon noon–2:30pm and 7–9:30pm. Closed Nov. CONTINENTAL.

You'd be hard put to find a better location, finer food, or a friendlier welcome. The rustic charm of this small dining room overlooking a canal in the town center is only one intimation of the culinary delights in store. Its regional specialties are perfection, and the menu, reflecting the best ingredients available, includes superb seafood dishes.

Moderate

De Stove. Kleine Sint-Amandsstraat 4. ☎ **050/33-78-35.** Main courses 540–725BF ($15.45–$20.70); set-price menu 1,350BF ($38.55). AE, DC, MC, V. Fri–Tues noon–1:45pm and 6:30–9:30pm. FLEMISH/SEAFOOD.

This small restaurant seats only 20 in a rustic atmosphere that is a touch more modern than is usual for Bruges. The seafood specialties are well worth a try, particularly the Flemish fish stew.

Graaf van Vlaanderen. 't Zand 19. ☎ **050/33-31-50.** Main courses 375–450BF ($10.70–$12.85). AE, DC, MC, V. Fri–Wed noon–2pm and 6–9pm. STEAK/SALADS.

This reasonably priced restaurant in a small hotel near the railway station has an extensive menu and a decor that relies heavily on mirrors and plants. The food is equally simple, featuring minute steak (steak so thin it cooks in a minute) and French fries, spaghetti, and salads.

Kasteel Minnewater. Minnewater 4. ☎ **050/33-42-54.** Main courses 400–750BF ($11.45–$21.45); menu du marché 980BF ($28); menu gastronomique (tasting menu) 1,600BF ($45.70). V. Daily noon–2:30pm and 7–10pm. FRENCH/SEAFOOD.

With a superb location near the Begijnhof, and a terrace on the Minnewater (Lake of Love), this château-style restaurant exudes an easygoing charm and offers fine food.

It's particularly rewarding to end up here after a long day of sightseeing through the city.

Inexpensive

Brasserie Erasmus. Wollestraat 35. ☎ **050/33-57-81.** Main courses 300–750BF ($8.55–$21.45). AE, CB, MC, V. Tues–Sun 11am–midnight. FLEMISH.

This small, popular restaurant is a great stop after viewing the cathedral and nearby museums. It serves a large variety of dishes, including a very good *waterzooï* with fish and *lapin à la bière* (rabbit in a beer sauce). About 150 different brands of beer are also offered here.

't Koffieboontje. Hallestraat 4. ☎ **050/33-80-27.** Main courses 350–650BF ($10–$18.55). AE, DC, MC, V. Daily noon–11pm. SEAFOOD/FLEMISH.

The bright and stylishly modern interior here strikes a noticeable contrast to the often dark ambience of many Bruges restaurants. An extensive menu is equally cheery, featuring good, but not fancy, seafood specialties like lobster and salmon, and such Belgian staples as mussels, steak, and sole.

GHENT (GENT)

At the confluence of the Rivers Leie and Scheldt, Ghent was the seat of the powerful counts of Flanders, whose great castle, built in 1180, still stands as a gloomy reminder of their dominance.

For years the city was considered by tourists to be a poor relation of Bruges, only to be visited if there was time at the end of a trip. That's no longer true. The old town has been spruced up to attract more visitors, and Ghent has never looked so good. Although it's larger and more citified than Bruges, its center has enough cobblestoned streets, meandering canals, and 16th-century Flemish architecture to make it nearly as magical as its more famous sister.

ESSENTIALS

ARRIVING   By Train   Ghent is 32 minutes by train from Brussels. The main railway station, **Sint-Pieters** (☎ **09/222-44-44**), is on Maria Hendrikaplein, a mile or so south of the city center; trams 1, 10, 11, and 12 go directly from there into town.

By Bus   The bus station (☎ **09/210-94-91**) adjoins Sint-Pieters railway station. Try to avoid the bus; it is slow and requires changes.

By Car   You get there on the E40/A-10 from Brussels, E17/A-14 from Antwerp, and E40/A-10 from Bruges and Ostend.

VISITOR INFORMATION   The **Tourist Office** is at Predikherenlei 2, 9000 Ghent (☎ **09/225-36-41;** fax 09/225-62-88), open Monday to Friday 8:30am to noon and 1 to 4:30pm. More convenient for personal visits is the **Infokantoor (Inquiry Desk)** in the cellar of the Belfry, Botermarkt 17a, 9000 Ghent (☎ **09/ 266-52-32;** fax 09/224-15-55), open April to October daily 9:30am to 6:30pm; November to March 9:30am to 4:30pm.

CITY LAYOUT   **Korenmarkt** is the city's heart. The most important sights, including the **Town Hall, St. Bavo's Cathedral,** and **Belfry,** lie within half a mile of here. The **River Leie** winds through the center and connects with the **River Scheldt** and canals that lead to a busy port area. Citadel Park, the location of the **Fine Arts Museum,** is near Sint-Pieters railway station.

GETTING AROUND   Ghent has an excellent tram and bus system, with many lines converging at Korenmarkt. Walking is the best way to see the city center and

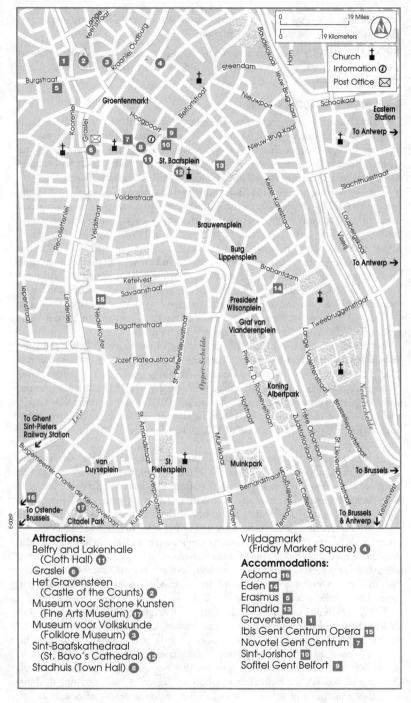

Ghent

Attractions:
Belfry and Lakenhalle
  (Cloth Hall) ⑪
Graslei ⑥
Het Gravensteen
  (Castle of the Counts) ②
Museum voor Schone Kunsten
  (Fine Arts Museum) ⑰
Museum voor Volkskunde
  (Folklore Museum) ③
Sint-Baafskathedraal
  (St. Bavo's Cathedral) ⑫
Stadhuis (Town Hall) ⑧

Vrijdagmarkt
  (Friday Market Square) ④

Accommodations:
Adoma ⑯
Eden ⑭
Erasmus ⑤
Flandria ⑬
Gravensteen ①
Ibis Gent Centrum Opera ⑮
Novotel Gent Centrum ⑦
Sint-Jorishof ⑩
Sofitel Gent Belfort ⑨

experience at a human pace its effortless combination of history and modernity. Beyond the center, use public transportation.

SPECIAL EVENTS   The last week of July witnesses the **Gentse Feesten (Ghent Festivities),** a time of music, dancing, and generally riotous fun and games throughout the city.

EXPLORING HISTORIC GHENT

The city's historic monuments have a solemnity that gives them a somewhat forbidding look. In the case of the Castle of the Counts of Flanders, it was meant to look this way because Ghent's citizens were so often in revolt against their overlord. The "Three Towers of Ghent"—St. Bavo's Cathedral, the Belfry, and St Nicholas Church—form an almost straight line pointing toward St Michael's Bridge.

The best starting point is **Sint-Baafskathedraal (St. Bavo's Cathedral),** Sint-Baafsplein (☎ **09/223-10-46**). Within this 14th-century cathedral's plain Gothic exterior lies a splendid baroque interior and some priceless art. A 24-panel altarpiece, *The Adoration of the Mystic Lamb,* completed by Jan van Eyck in 1432, is St. Bavo's showpiece. Other treasures include Rubens's *The Conversion of St. Bavo,* painted in 1624, in the Rubens Chapel in the semicircular ambulatory behind the high altar. The cathedral is free and open daily from 8:30am to 6pm except during religious services. The Adoration of the Mystic Lamb altar and the Crypt are open April to October Monday to Saturday 9:30am to noon and 2 to 6pm, Sunday 1 to 6pm; November to March Monday to Saturday 10:30am to noon and 2:30 to 4pm, Sunday 2 to 5pm. Admission is 60BF ($1.70) for adults, 50BF ($1.45) for children.

Just across the square from the cathedral are the 14th-century ✪ **Belfry and Lakenhalle (Cloth Hall),** Sint-Baafsplein (☎ **09/223-99-22**), which together form a glorious medieval ensemble. From the Belfry, great bells have rung out Ghent's civic pride down through the centuries, and a 54-bell carillon does so today. The 1425 Cloth Hall was the gathering place of medieval wool and cloth merchants. You can visit the Belfry with a guide and with the aid of an elevator. Tours leave Tuesday through Sunday at hourly intervals from 2:10 to 5:10pm. Tickets cost 100BF ($2.85) for adults, 30BF (85¢) for children 7 to 16 (under 7 free).

Crouching like a gray stone lion over the city, the grim-looking **Het Gravensteen (Castle of the Counts),** Sint-Veereplein (☎ **09/225-93-06**), was clearly designed by the counts of Flanders to send a message to rebellion-inclined Gentenaars: Keep your thoughts to yourself; better still, don't have any at all. Surrounded by the waters of the River Leie, the castle was begun by Philip of Alsace, Count of Flanders, fresh from the Crusades in 1180. If its 6-foot-thick walls, battlements, and turrets failed to intimidate attackers, the counts could turn to a well-equipped torture chamber, some of which can be seen in a small museum in the castle. The view from the ramparts of the central keep, the donjon, is worth the climb. The castle is open daily April to September 9am to 6pm; October to March daily 9am to 5pm. Admission is 200BF ($5.70), free for children under 12. Call ahead if you would like a guided tour.

The ✪ **Stadhuis (Town Hall)** at the corner of Botermarkt and Hoogpoort (☎ **09/223-99-22**) has what you might call a split personality. A plain Renaissance facade fronts Botermarkt, while a garishly ornamented Gothic side faces Hoogpoort. Work began in 1518 and continued until the 18th century, and centuries of changing tastes and the availability or lack of money are reflected in the building's many styles. In its **Pacificatiezaal (Pacification Room),** the Pacification of Ghent was signed in 1567, declaring the Low Countries' repudiation of Spanish rule and their intention to permit religious freedom. Guided tours leave from May to October, Monday to Thursday at 2pm from the tourist office in the Belfry "Raadskelder." Tickets cost 100BF ($2.85) for adults, 30BF (85¢) for children.

The **Museum voor Schone Kunsten (Fine Arts Museum),** in Citadel Park, Nicolaas de Liemaeckereplein 3 (☎ 09/222-17-03), is home to ancient and modern masterpieces, including works by Rubens, Van Dyck, and Bosch, along with moderns such as James Ensor and Constant Permeke. The museum is open Tuesday to Sunday 9:30am to 5pm. Admission is 100BF ($2.85), free for children under 12.

In a group of former city center almshouses from the 1300s, the **Museum voor Volkskunde (Folklore Museum),** Kraanlei 65 (☎ 09/223-13-36), displays authentic replicas of rooms where craft skills were practiced around 1900. There is an attached marionette theater (check with the museum for the performance schedule). The museum is open April to October daily 9am to 12:30pm and 1:30 to 5:30pm; November to March Tuesday to Sunday 10am to 12:30pm and 1:30 to 5pm. Admission is 100BF ($2.85) adults, 50BF ($1.45) children 12 to 18, free for children under 12.

A row of gabled **guildhouses** built along Graslei between the 1200s and 1600s, when the waterway was Ghent's harbor, form a perfect ensemble of colored facades reflected in the waters of the River Leie. To view them as a whole, cross the bridge over the Leie to Korenlei, and walk along the bank past each one. These buildings once housed the craftsmen, tradespeople, and merchants who formed the commercial core of the city. This is an ideal spot to snap a picture capturing the essence of Ghent.

The **Vrijdagmarkt (Friday Market Square)** is a popular meeting spot today, and was a popular rallying point in times past. A statue of Jacob Van Arteveld is a tribute to the leader of a revolt in the 1300s, and its base is adorned by the shields of some 52 guilds. The square is now a major shopping area and the scene of a lively street market every Friday. A short distance away, smaller **Kanonplein** is guarded by a gigantic cannon known as Mad Meg (Dulle Griet), which thundered away in the 1400s in the service of Burgundian armies.

BOAT RIDES & OTHER ORGANIZED TOURS

A boat ride along the canals is an ideal way to see the city's highlights. From April to October, open and covered boats leave every 30 minutes, daily from 10am to 7pm from the Graslei and Korenlei; narration is in several languages. The trip lasts about 35 minutes; the fare is 160BF ($4.55) for adults, 80BF ($2.30) for children under 12. Call ☎ 09/282-92-48 for more information.

Qualified guides (☎ 09/233-07-72) lead private walking tours Monday to Friday at a charge of 1,500BF ($42.85) for the first 2 hours, 600BF ($17.15) for each additional hour.

Horse-drawn carriages leave from Sint-Baafsplein and Korenlei daily from 10am to 7pm, from Easter to October. A half-hour ride costs 800BF ($22.85).

WHERE TO STAY

The tourist office provides a free "Hotels and Restaurants" booklet and makes hotel reservations for a returnable deposit. Considering its popularity, Ghent has fewer hotels than might be expected, and those in the city center are often full at peak times, so try to book ahead.

Very Expensive

Novotel Gent Centrum. Gouden Leeuwplein 5, 9000 Ghent. ☎ **800/221-4542** or ☎ 09/224-22-30. Fax 09/224-32-95. www.hotelweb.fr. 121 units. A/C MINIBAR TV TEL. 5,050BF ($144.30) double; 6,050BF ($172.85) suite. AE, DC, MC, V. Limited parking available on street.

This modern hotel near the Town Hall is within easy walking distance of all the city's major sights. A modern edifice has been designed to fit, more or less, into its ancient surroundings. Guest rooms are nicely furnished and have individual heating controls. The facilities are all you'd expect from a top hotel, with light, airy public rooms and a garden terrace.

Expensive

Sofitel Gent Belfort. Hoogpoort 63, 9000 Ghent. ☎ **09/233-33-31.** Fax 09/233-11-02. E-mail: sofitel_gent@unicall.be. 128 units. A/C MINIBAR TV TEL. 8,000BF ($228.55) double; 14,650BF ($418.55) suite. AE, DC, MC, V. Parking 150BF ($4.30).

Ghent's top hotel has an enviable position across from the Town Hall and within easy distance of the main tourist attractions. The big rooms are furnished in a modern, efficient style, and come with hair dryers. The hotel is bright and modern and has been designed to at least partly fit with its venerable surroundings.

Moderate

✪ **Erasmus.** Poel 25, 9000 Ghent. ☎ **09/224-21-95.** Fax 09/233-42-41. 12 units. TV TEL. 3,500–4,200BF ($100–$120) double; 5,000BF ($142.85) suite. Rates include buffet breakfast. AE, MC, V. Limited parking available on street.

Each room is different in this converted 16th-century house, but all are plushly furnished with antiques and ornamented with knickknacks. The rooms have high oak-beam ceilings, and the bathrooms are luxuriously modern. Some rooms have leaded-glass windows, some overlook a carefully manicured inner garden, and some have elaborate marble fireplaces. Breakfast is served in an impressive room that would have pleased the Counts of Flanders.

Gravensteen. Jan Breydelstraat 35, 9000 Ghent. ☎ **09/225-11-50.** Fax 09/225-18-50. www.gravensteen.be. E-mail: hotel@gravensteen.be. 46 units. MINIBAR TV TEL. 3,990–4,700BF ($114–$134.30) double; 4,615–5,240BF ($131.85–$149.70) suite. Rates include full breakfast. AE, DC, MC, V. Parking 150BF ($4.30).

A short walk from Graslei and the Castle of the Counts, this lovely mansion was built in 1865 for a Ghent textile baron. You enter through the old carriageway, made up of ornamented pillars and an impressive wall niche occupied by a marble statue. The attractive rooms look out on the moated castle in front; those to the back have city views. A top-floor "Belvedere" offers magnificent views of the city. There's no dining room, but plenty of good restaurants are within walking distance.

Ibis Gent Centrum Opera. Nederkouter 24–26, 9000 Ghent. ☎ **09/225-07-07.** Fax 09/ 223-59-07. 134 units. TV TEL. 3,345BF ($95.55) double. Rates include buffet breakfast. AE, DC, MC, V. Parking 300BF ($8.55).

Rooms in this modern hotel between the city center and the railway station are bright and comfortably furnished. There's a nice bar, and although there's no restaurant, several good ones are nearby. The hotel offers good accommodations at moderate rates. A major renovation program was undertaken in 1997 and 1998.

✪ **Sint-Jorishof (also known as Cour St-Georges).** Botermarkt 2, 9000 Ghent. ☎ **09/ 224-24-24.** Fax 09/224-26-40. www.hotelbel.com/cour-st-georges.htm. E-mail: cour.st. georges@hotelbel.com. 28 units. TV TEL. 3,700–4,400BF ($105.70–$125.70) double. Rates include full breakfast. AE, DC, MC, V. Parking 150BF ($4.30).

In the city center opposite the town hall, this historical treasure has been a quality inn since 1228. If you stay here you'll be in good company, historically speaking: Mary of Burgundy, Charles V, and Napoléon have all spent the night. Try to get a room in the old building rather than in the modern annex across the street. Decor in the pleasant and comfortable rooms is traditional, and the rates are low for such a prime site. Reserve as far ahead as possible.

Inexpensive
Adoma. Sint-Denijslaan 19, 9000 Ghent. ☎ **09/222/65-50.** Fax 09/245-09-37. 15 units. TV TEL. 2,100BF ($60) double. Rates include continental breakfast. MC, V. Free parking.

Conveniently located behind Sint-Pieters train station, this recently renovated hotel has taken a major leap upward in its style and facilities, without sacrificing its reasonable rates. Spacious rooms, brightly decorated with modern furnishings, add up to a comfortable, though not luxurious, experience.

✪ **Eden.** Zuidstationstraat 24, 9000 Ghent. ☎ **09/223-51-51.** Fax 09/233-34-57. 28 units. TV TEL. 2,400–3,200BF ($68.55–$91.45) double. Rates include buffet breakfast. MC, V. Free parking.

Not far from the center, this is a nice hotel for its price range. The decor is pleasantly modern, and each room has a tapestry on the wall. Although most bathrooms are small, each has at least a toilet and shower, and some have full bathrooms.

Flandria. Barrestraat 3, 9000 Ghent. ☎ **09/223-06-26.** Fax 09/233-77-89. 27 units. 1,400–1,800BF ($40–$51.45). MC, V. Rates include continental breakfast.

Some rooms are better than others at this super-budget hotel, so ask to see the room first. Decor is minimal, but the rooms are clean and the staff is friendly.

WHERE TO DINE
Ghent restaurants keep Flemish culinary traditions alive and well, and prices are generally well below those in Brussels. A helpful, free "Hotels and Restaurants" booklet published by the tourist office lists prominent restaurants in all price brackets.

Very Expensive
Jan Breydel. Jan Breydelstraat 10. ☎ **09/225-62-87.** Main courses 675–1,150BF ($19.30–$32.85). AE, DC, MC, V. Tues–Sat noon–2pm and 7–10pm; Mon 7–10pm. SEAFOOD/FLEMISH.

Top honors go to this exquisite restaurant on a quaint street near the Castle of the Counts. Its interior is a garden delight of greenery, white napery, and light woods. Dishes are as light and airy as the setting, with delicate sauces and seasonings enhancing the fresh ingredients. Seafood and regional specialties are all superb.

✪ **'t Buikske Vol.** Kraanlei 17. ☎ **09/225-18-80.** Reservations recommeneded on weekends. Main courses 495–895BF ($14.15–$25.55); set-price menus 975–1,650BF ($27.85–$47.15). AE, V. Mon, Tues, Thurs, Fri noon–2pm and 7–9:30pm; Sat 7–9:30pm. BELGIAN/FRENCH.

This is one of the city's gems, thanks to chef Peter Vyncke's insistence on the best ingredients, served in a cozy, intimate atmosphere. You can't go wrong with the salmon in butter sauce, but for more adventure, try the *filet de biche* (doe steak) or the *terrine de faison* (grilled pheasant). It isn't open much, but when it is, it does the business.

Moderate
Auberge de Fonteyne. Gouden Leeuwplein 7. ☎ **09/221-69-26.** Main courses 350–700BF ($10–$20). MC, V. Mon–Fri noon–2:30pm and 6pm–midnight; Sat noon–2am; Sun noon–2pm. MUSSELS/FLEMISH.

It might seem difficult for the food to equal the extravagant good looks of this art deco restaurant, but it comes pretty close. Waterzooï (a stew of fish or chicken with a parsley and cream sauce) is a favorite here, as are heaps of the big Zeeland mussels that Belgium loses its collective cool over.

Graaf van Egmond. Sint-Michielsplein 21. ☎ **09/225-07-27.** Main courses 475–695BF ($13.55–$19.85). AE, DC, MC, V. Daily noon–3pm and 6–11pm. FRENCH/FLEMISH.

In a marvelous 13th-century townhouse on the River Leie, the restaurant serves Flemish dishes such as *carbonnade flamande* (beef stew) and *asparagus à la flamande*, along with French creations. If you can get a window seat, there's a spectacular view of the towers of Ghent.

Guido Meerschaut. Kleine Vismarkt 3. ☎ **09/223-53-49.** Main courses 320–495BF ($9.15–$14.15); set-price menu 880BF ($25.15). AE, DC, MC, V. Tues–Sat noon–2:30pm and 6–10:30pm. SEAFOOD/FLEMISH.

Guido also owns a fish shop in the Fish Market, so it's no surprise that he specializes in seafood. Well-prepared fish fresh from the North Sea is served in a simple yet elegant room painted with scenes from Fish Market history. Dover sole, sole Ostendaise, a variety of cod, herring, and other fish dishes predominate, along with North Sea shrimp, oysters, and mussels prepared in a variety of ways.

't Klok Huys. Corduwaniersstraat 65. ☎ **09/223-42-41.** Reservations recommended on weekends. Main courses 375–750BF ($10.70–$21.45). AE, MC, V. Daily noon–2:15pm and 6–11pm. BELGIAN.

This local favorite is in the heart of the Patershol, an old district that is becoming known for its many small restaurants. Named "the clock house" for the 30 clocks that adorn the yellow walls, it has the same owner as the celebrated 't Buikske Vol and also provides excellent cuisine, but at a lower price. Flemish dishes such as waterzooï and beef carbonnade are on the permanent menu; a blackboard lists the more elaborate daily specials. They might include endive wrapped in ham and coated in a cheese sauce, or a plate of fresh poached fish battered in a buttery, herb sauce with a hint of nutmeg.

Inexpensive

Amadeus. Plotersgracht 8. ☎ **09/225-13-85.** Reservations required. Spare rib dinner 450BF ($12.85). No credit cards. Mon–Thur 7pm–midnight; Fri–Sat 6pm–midnight; Sun noon–3pm and 6pm–midnight. RIBS/CONTINENTAL.

Amadeus is for the confirmed meat eater—ribs, to be precise. Sure, there are vegetarian and fish plates available, but all Ghent comes here for the all-you-can-eat spare rib dinner. A slab of perfectly cooked ribs is served on a tray with a choice of delicious sauces and a baked potato. If you're up to it, you can order another and another and another. A bottle of wine is on the table, and you pay for what you drink from it. The decor is sumptuously art nouveau with burnished wood, mirrors, and colored glass, and the ambience is fun and relaxed.

Ghent After Dark

PERFORMING ARTS Opera is performed in the 19th-century **De Vlaamse Opera,** Schouwburgstraat 3 (☎ 09/225-24-25), October through mid-June. For non-premier performances, tickets cost 250 to 2,500BF ($7.15 to $71.45). Most performances begin at 8pm, with occasional 3pm matinees. It's best to book ahead. Ghent venues for puppet shows are the **Museum of Folklore,** Kraanlei 65 (☎ 09/223-13-36); **Taptoe Teater,** Forelstraat 91c (☎ 09/223-67-58); and **Magie,** Haspelstraat 39 (☎ 09/226-42-18). Check with the tourist office for performance schedules during your visit.

BARS & TAVERNS In typical Flemish fashion, Ghent's favorite after-dark entertainment is frequenting atmospheric cafes and taverns. You'll have a memorable evening in any one you choose. **De Witte Leeuw,** Graslei 6 (☎ 09/233 3733), has a 17th-century setting and more than 300 varieties of beer. At **Dulle Griet,** Vrijdagmarkt 50 (☎ 09/224-24-55), if you deposit one of your shoes, you'll be given a glass of potent Kwak beer in the wooden frame that a Kwak glass needs to stand up—you might need artificial support as well if you drink too many Kwaks. The smallest building on Graslei is the former Toll House, now a nice little tavern called **Het Tol-huisje,** Graslei 10 (☎ **09/224-30-90**).

Groentenmarkt, near the Castle of the Counts, makes for a pretty good pub-crawl in an easily navigable area. Try **Het Waterhuis aan de Bierkant,** Groentenmarkt 9 (☎ **09/225-06-80**), which has more than 100 different Belgian beers, including locally made Stopken. A couple of doors along is **'t Dreupelkot,** Groentenmarkt 12 (☎ **09/224-21-20**), a specialist in deadly little glasses of jenever (a stiff spirit similar to gin). Ask owner Paul to recommend one of his 100 or so varieties, or walk straight in and boldly ask for a 64-proof Jonge Hertekamp or a 72-proof Pekèt de Houyeu; if they don't knock you down, you may be up for an 8-year-old 100-proof Filliers Oude Graanjenever or a 104-proof Hoogspanning. Across the tramlines is **Het Galgen-huisje,** Groentenmarkt 5 (☎ **09/233-42-51**), a tiny and, perforce, intimate place popular with students.

3

The Czech Republic

by John Mastrini, Hana Mastrini & Alan Crosby

If you have time to visit only one Eastern European city, the place to go is Prague. The quirky Czech capital, often called "baroque Disneyland" because of its fairy-tale architecture, is a perfect end-of-millennium destination. Here you'll encounter the triumphs and tragedies of the past 10 centuries spiked with the peculiarity of the post-Communist reconstruction.

But Prague isn't the Czech Republic's only draw. Visitors are again flocking to west Bohemia after some of the world's best-known spas were restored to their Victorian-era splendor.

1 Prague & Environs

by John & Hana Mastrini

Almost 75 years after native-son Franz Kafka's death, Prague's mix of the melancholy and the magnificent, the shadows and the fog of everyday life, set against some of Europe's most spectacular architecture, still confounds all who live or visit here. Its tightly wound brick paths have felt the hooves of kings' horses, the jackboots of Hitler's armies, the heaving tracks of Soviet tanks, and the shuffle of students in passive revolt. The 6-centuries-old Charles Bridge is today jammed with visitors and venture capitalists looking for memories or profits from a once-captive city now enjoying yet another renaissance. (Too bad mindless graffiti now blights many a glimpse of this otherwise magnificent city.)

A turbulent past and promising future gives Prague its eclectic energy, while its baroque and Renaissance atmosphere provides its gravity.

Only in Prague

Strolling Across Charles Bridge   The silhouettes of the statues lining the crown jewel of Czech heritage hover like ghosts in the still of the sunrise skyline. Early in the morning you can stroll across the bridge without encountering the crowds that'll be there by midday. At dusk, the statues are the same, but the odd light play seems to have transformed the bridge and the city beyond. Late at night, "Peace, Love, and Spare Change" describes the scene, as musicians, street performers, and flower people come out to commune with the bridge and each other.

Proceeding Down the Royal Route   The downhill jaunt from Prague Castle, through Malá Strana (Lesser Town), across Charles Bridge to Old Town Square, is a day in itself. The trip recalls the route of the Bohemian Kings; today it's lined with quirky galleries, shops, and cafes.

Spending a Moment with the Children of Terezín   On display at the Ceremonial Hall of the Old Jewish Cemetery are sketches drawn by children held at the Terezín concentration camp. These drawings are a moving lesson in the Nazi occupation of Czechoslovakia.

Getting Lost in Staré Město   Every week a new cafe or gallery seems to pop up along the narrow winding streets of Staré Město (Old Town). Prague is best discovered by getting lost, and Old Town's impossible-to-navigate streets are made for it.

Wandering Around the Practice Halls   During hotter weather, many windows of rehearsal rooms scattered throughout Staré Město (Old Town) and Malá Strana (Lesser Town) are open. Lucky wanderers might stumble on a free concert amid the ancient alleys.

Enjoying an Afternoon in the Letná Beer Garden   Nice weather sends Czechs in search of open air and affordable beer. The tree-covered Letná Chateau (Letenský zámeček) garden on the Letná plain is a hidden treasure that serves up a local favorite brew from Velké Popovice called *Kozel* (Goat), as well as a great city view.

Experiencing Beer and Oompah-Pah at U Fleků   A more raucous and touristy beer gathering can be found at the U Fleků beer hall in New Town. You can wash down traditional Czech dishes with U Fleků's own dark home brew, accompanied by traditional drinking music.

Picnicking on Vyšehrad   Of all the parks where you could go for a picnic, the citadel above the Vltava, which guards the south end of the old city, is the most calm and interesting. Its more remote location means less tourist traffic, and the gardens, city panoramas, and national cemetery provide pleasant walks and poignant history.

Taking a Trip to Karlštejn Castle   A 30-minute train ride south is the most visited Czech landmark outside Prague. Built by King Charles IV (Karel IV in Czech, the namesake of Charles Bridge) in the 14th century to protect the crown jewels of the Holy Roman Empire, this Romanesque hilltop bastion fills the image of the castles of medieval lore.

ORIENTATION

ARRIVING   By Plane   Newly rebuilt **Ruzyně Airport** (☎ **02/2011 1111**) is 12 miles west of the city center. You'll find a bank for changing money (usually open daily 7am to 11pm), telephones, and several car-rental offices.

Plenty of **taxis** line up in front of the airport. The fancy cars parked in front of the terminal cost about twice the price of the rickety Škoda and Lada taxis off to the right. ČSA, the Czech national airline, has a **shuttle bus** to and from Náměstí Republiky in downtown Prague, which runs every 30 minutes from 5:30am to 9:00pm. The ČSA main office, at V Celnici 5 (☎ **02/2010 4111**), is about 5 blocks from the Náměstí

Traveler's Tip

Most of Prague's taxi drivers will take advantage of you; getting an honestly metered ride from the airport is close to impossible. The fare from the airport to Wenceslas Square should be no more than about 450Kč ($13). If you pay only twice this, consider yourself lucky.

Prague

Attractions:
Bertramka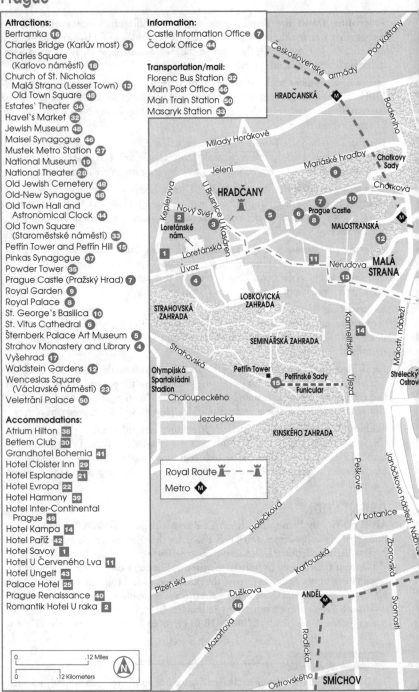
Charles Bridge (Karlův most) 31
Charles Square
  (Karlovo náměstí) 18
Church of St. Nicholas
  Malá Strana (Lesser Town) 13
  Old Town Square 45
Estates' Theater 34
Havel's Market 32
Jewish Museum 48
Maisel Synagogue 46
Mustek Metro Station 27
National Museum 19
National Theater 28
Old Jewish Cemetery 48
Old-New Synagogue 48
Old Town Hall and
  Astronomical Clock 44
Old Town Square
  (Staroměstské náměstí) 33
Petřín Tower and Petřín Hill 15
Pinkas Synagogue 47
Powder Tower 35
Prague Castle (Pražský Hrad) 7
Royal Garden 9
Royal Palace 8
St. George's Basilica 10
St. Vitus Cathedral 6
Šternberk Palace Art Museum 5
Strahov Monastery and Library 4
Vyšehrad 17
Waldstein Gardens 12
Wenceslas Square
  (Václavské náměstí) 23
Veletrǎní Palace 50

Accommodations:
Atrium Hilton 38
Betlem Club 30
Grandhotel Bohemia 41
Hotel Cloister Inn 29
Hotel Esplanade 21
Hotel Evropa 22
Hotel Harmony 39
Hotel Inter-Continental
  Prague 49
Hotel Kampa 14
Hotel Paříž 42
Hotel Savoy 1
Hotel U Červeného Lva 11
Hotel Ungelt 43
Palace Hotel 25
Prague Renaissance 40
Romantik Hotel U raka 2

Information:
Castle Information Office 7
Čedok Office 44

Transportation/mail:
Florenc Bus Station 32
Main Post Office 46
Main Train Station 50
Masaryk Station 33

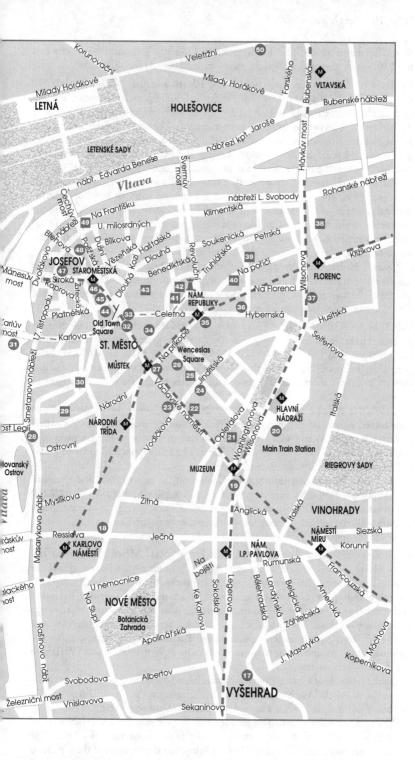

Republiky metro station. The shuttle costs 95Kč ($2.90). You can also take **city bus no. 119,** which goes to the Dejvická metro station (Line A) for 12Kč (35¢).

By Train   Of the two central rail stations, **Hlavní nádraží,** Wilsonova třída 80, Praha 1 (☎ 02/2461 1111), is the grander and more popular; however, it's also seedier. The basement holds a 24-hour luggage-storage counter charging 15Kč (50¢) per bag up to 33 lbs per day (counted from midnight). The nearby lockers aren't secure and should be avoided. Beneath the main hall are surprisingly clean public showers that are a good place to refresh yourself for just 40Kč ($1.20); they're open Monday to Friday 6am to 8pm, Saturday 7am to 7pm, and Sunday 8am to 4pm. On the second floor is the train information office (marked by a lowercase *i*), open daily 6am to 10pm. From the main train station it's a 5-minute stroll to the "top" end of Wenceslas Square or a 15-minute walk to Old Town Square. Metro Line C connects the station to the rest of the city. Metro trains depart from the lower level, and city-center no-transfer tickets, costing 8Kč (25¢), are available at the newsstand near the metro entrance. Taxis line up outside the station day and night.

   Nádraží Holešovice, Partyzánská at Vrbenského, Praha 7 (☎ 02/2422 4200), usually serves trains from Berlin and other points north. Although it isn't as centrally located as the main station, its more manageable size and position at the end of metro Line C make it almost as convenient.

VISITOR INFORMATION   Those arriving by train at either of the two primary stations (Hlavní or Holešovice—see above) will have the greatest success finding information from **AVE Ltd.** (☎ 02/2422 3226 or 02/2422 3521; fax 02/5731 2984; e-mail: ave@avetravel.cz; www.avetravel.cz), an accommodations agency that also distributes printed information. The two train station offices are open daily 6am to 10pm.

   Čedok, Na Příkopě 18, Praha 1 (☎ 02/2419 7111), once the country's official state-owned visitors bureau, is now a traditional travel agency. Like others in town, it prefers selling tickets and tours to dispensing free information. The company also books rail tickets and accepts major credit cards. The office is open Monday to Friday 8:30am to 6pm and Saturday 9am to 1pm.

   The city's **Cultural and Information Center,** on the ground-floor of the remodeled Municipal House (Obecní dům), Náměstí Republiky 5, Praha 1 (☎ 02/2200 2100; fax 02/2200 2636; e-mail: od@monet.cz), is a new attempt at visitor-friendly relations, offering advice, tickets, souvenirs, refreshments, and rest rooms. It's open daily 9am to 5pm.

CITY LAYOUT   The **River Vltava** bisects Prague. **Staré Město (Old Town)** and **Nové Město** (New Town) are on the east (right) side of the river, while the **Hradčany** (Castle District) and **Malá Strana** (Lesser Town) are on the west (left) bank.

   Bridges and squares are the most prominent landmarks. **Charles Bridge,** the oldest and most famous of those spanning the Vltava, is at the epicenter and connects Old Town with Lesser Town and the Castle District. Several important streets radiate from Old Town Square, including fashionable **Pařížská** to the northwest, historic **Celetná** to the east, and **Melantrichova,** connecting to **Wenceslas Square (Václavské náměstí)** to the southeast.

   On the west side of Charles Bridge is **Mostecká,** a 3-block-long connection to **Malostranské náměstí,** Malá Strana's main square. Hradčany, the Castle District, is just northwest of the square, while a second hill, **Petřín,** is just southwest.

   When reading maps or searching for addresses, keep in mind that *ulice* (abbreviated ul.) means "street," *třída* means "avenue," *náměstí* (abbreviated nám.) is a "square" or "plaza," a *most* is a "bridge," and *nábřeží* is a "quay." In Czech, none of these terms is

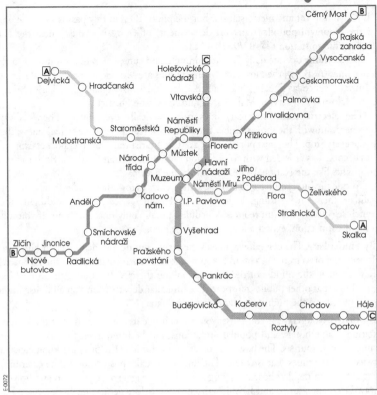

capitalized. In addresses, street numbers follow the street name (like Václavské nám. 25). Each address is followed by a district number, such as Praha 1 (*Praha* means "Prague" in Czech).

GETTING AROUND   By Metro, Bus & Tram   Prague's communist-built public transport network is a vast—and usually efficient—system of subways, trams, and buses. You can ride a maximum of four stations on the metro or 15 minutes on a tram or bus, without transfers, for 8Kč (25¢); children 5 and under are free. This is usually enough for trips in the historic districts. Rides of more than four stops on the metro, or longer tram or bus rides, with unlimited transfers for up to 1 hour after your ticket is validated, cost 12Kč (35¢). You can buy tickets from coin-operated orange machines in metro stations or at most newsstands marked TABÁK or TRAFIKA. Hold on to your ticket (which you must validate at the orange or yellow stamp clocks in each tram or bus when you get on board or at the entrance to the metro) during your ride—you'll need it to prove you've paid if a ticket collector asks.

If you're caught without a valid ticket, you have to pay a 200Kč ($6) fine to a plain-clothes ticket controller on the spot. Make sure he or she shows you a very official-looking badge. Oversized luggage (larger than carry-on size) requires a single trip ticket for each piece. You may be fined 400Kč ($12) for not having tickets for your luggage.

A **1-day pass** good for unlimited rides is 70Kč ($2.10), a **3-day pass** 180Kč ($5), a **7-day pass** 250Kč ($8), and a **15-day pass** 280Kč ($9). If you're staying for more than 2 weeks, buy a **monthly pass** for 380Kč ($12). You can buy the day passes at the

"DP" windows at any metro station, but the photo ID monthly pass is available only at the Dopravní podnik (transport department) office on Na bojišti, near the I. P. Pavlova metro station (☎ **02/9619 1111**).

Metro trains operate daily 5am to midnight and run every 3 to 8 minutes. On the three lines (A, B, C), the most convenient stations are Můstek, at the foot of Václavské náměstí (Wenceslas Square); Staroměstská, for Old Town Square and Charles Bridge; and Malostranská, serving Malá Strana and the Castle District.

The **electric tram** (streetcar) lines run practically everywhere. There's always another tram with the same number traveling back. You never have to hail trams; they make every stop. The most popular, no. 22 (the "tourist tram" or "pickpocket express") has become less crowded with the addition of the no. 23 tram in 1998. Both run past top sights like the National Theater and Prague Castle.

To ride the **bus,** you have to buy the same tickets as for other modes in advance and validate them on boarding. Regular bus and tram service stops at midnight, after which selected routes run reduced schedules, usually only once per hour. If you miss a night connection, expect a long wait for the next.

By Funicular   The cog railway makes the scenic run up and down Petřín Hill every 15 minutes or so from 9:15am to 8:45pm, with an intermediate stop at the Nebozízek Restaurant in the middle of the hill overlooking the city. It requires the same 12Kč (35¢) ticket as other public transport. The funicular departs from a small house in the park just above the middle of Újezd in Malá Strana.

By Taxi   Avoid taxis! If you must, you can hail one in the streets or in front of train stations, large hotels, and popular attractions, but be forewarned that many drivers simply gouge tourists. The best fare you can hope for is 17Kč (50¢) per kilometer, but twice or three times that isn't rare. The rates are usually posted not on the exterior of the car but on the dashboard, making it too late to haggle once you're in and on your way. Negotiate a price and have it written down before getting in. Better yet, go on foot or by public transport. Somewhat reputable companies with English-speaking dispatchers are **AAA Taxi** (☎ **02/2432 2432** or 02/1080); **RONY Taxi** (☎ **02/692 1958** or 02/430 403 or 02/1073); and the unfortunately named **ProfiTaxi** (☎ **02/ 1035**). Get a receipt (and send it to the mayor).

By Car   Driving in Prague is not worth the money or effort. The roads are frustrating and slow, and parking is minimal and expensive. If you want to rent a car to explore the environs, try **Europcar/InterRent,** Pařížská 28, Praha 1 (☎ **02/2481 0039**), open daily 8am to 8pm. Also there's **Hertz,** Karlovo nám. 28, Praha 2 (☎ **02/291 851** or 02/290 122), and **Budget,** at Ruzyně Airport (☎ **02/316 5214**) and in the Hotel Inter-Continental, náměstí Curieových, Praha 1 (☎ **02/231 9595**).

Local Czech car-rental companies sometimes offer lower rates than the big international firms. Try **SeccoCar,** Přístavní 39, Praha 7 (☎ **02/800 647**).

Fast Facts: Prague

American Express   For travel arrangements, traveler's checks, currency exchange, and other member services, visit the city's sole office at Václavské nám. 56 (Wenceslas Square), Praha 1 (☎ **02/2280 0251;** fax 02/2221 1131). It's open daily from 9am to 7pm. To report lost or stolen cards, call ☎ **02/2280 0800.**

Business Hours   Most **banks** are open Monday to Friday 8:30am to 6pm, but some also open Saturday 9am to noon. Business **offices** are generally open Monday to Friday 8am to 6pm. **Pubs** are usually open daily 11am to midnight.

Most **restaurants** open for lunch noon to 3pm and for dinner 6 to 11pm; only a few stay open later.

Currency   The basic unit of currency is the **koruna** (plural, **koruny**) or **crown,** abbreviated **Kč.** Each koruna is divided into 100 **haléřů** or **hellers.** Notes, each of which bears a forgery-resistant metal strip and a prominent watermark, are issued in 20, 50, 100, 200, 500, 1,000, 2,000, and 5,000 koruny denominations. Coins are 10, 20, and 50 hellers and 1, 2, 5, 10, 20, and 50 koruny. At this writing, \$1 = approximately 33Kč and £1 = 54Kč, or 1Kč = 3¢. Also, 1EUR = 36.5Kč

Currency Exchange   Banks generally offer the best exchange rates. Don't hesitate to use a credit or debit card to draw cash for the best rates. **Komerční banka** has three convenient Praha 1 locations with ATMs accepting Visa, MasterCard, and American Express: Na Příkopě 33, Národní 32, and Václavské nám. 42 (☎ **02/2442 1111** central switchboard for all branches). The exchange offices are open Monday to Friday 8am to 5pm, but the ATMs are accessible 24 hours.

Doctors/Dentists   If you need a doctor or dentist and your condition isn't life-threatening, you can visit the **Polyclinic at Národní,** Národní 9, Praha 1 (☎ **02/2207 5120;** for emergencies, ☎ 02/0600 111; operator 02/140 533) during walk-in hours, 8am to 5pm. Dr. Stránský is an Ivy League–trained straight-talking physician. For **emergency medical aid,** call the **Foreigners' Medical Clinic,** Na Homolce Hospital, Praha 5 (☎ **02/5292 2146** or 02/5292 2191 after hours).

Embassies   The **U.S. Embassy** is at Tržiště 15, Praha 1 (☎ **02/5732 0663**). The **Canadian Embassy** is at Mickiewiczova 6, Praha 6 (☎ **02/2431 1108**). The **U.K. Embassy** is at Thunovská 14, Praha 1 (☎ **02/5732 0355**). The **Australian Honorary Consul** is at Na Ořechovce 38, Praha 6 (☎ **02/2431 0743**). The **Embassy of Ireland** is at Velvyslanectví Irska, Tržiště 13, Praha 1 (☎ **02/ 5753 0061**).

Emergencies   You can reach Prague's **police** and **fire** services by dialing ☎ **158** from any phone. To call an **ambulance,** dial ☎ **155.**

Hospitals   Particularly welcoming to foreigners is **Nemocnice Na Homolce,** V úvalu 84 (Motol), Praha 5 (☎ **02/5292 2146** or 02/5292 2191 after hours). The English-speaking doctors can also make house calls.

Internet Access   The best of the cybercafes in Prague is **Terminal Bar** at Soukenická 6, three blocks from Nám. Republiky on the yellow line (☎ **02/ 2187 1999**), where about a dozen twin-seater workstations are available for 100Kč (\$3.05) an hour for non-members (charged by the quarter hour with a 15-minute minimum).

Luggage Storage/Lockers   The **Ruzyně Airport Luggage Storage Office** never closes and charges 30Kč (90¢) per item per day. Left-luggage offices are also available at the main train stations, **Hlavní nádraží** and **nádraží Holešovice.** Both charge 15Kč (50¢) per bag (up to 33 lbs) per day (counted from midnight) and are technically open 24 hours, but if your train is departing late at night, check to make sure someone will be around. Luggage lockers are available in all of Prague's train stations, but they're not secure and should be avoided.

Pharmacies   The most central pharmacy (*lékárna*) is at Václavské nám. 8, Praha 1 (☎ **02/2422 7532**), open Monday to Friday 8am to 6pm. The nearest emergency (24-hour) pharmacy is at Palackého 5, Praha 1 (☎ **02/267 814**).

If you're in Praha 2, there's an emergency pharmacy on Belgická 37 (☎ 02/ 258 189).

Taxes   A 22% **value-added tax (VAT)** is built into the price of most goods and services rather than being tacked on at the register. (A plan to lower the VAT on hotels and resturants to 5% was under consideration in 1999 but not yet approved by press time). Most restaurants include VAT in the prices stated on their menus. If they don't, that fact should be stated somewhere on the menu.

Telephone   The **country code** for the Czech Republic is **420**. The **city code** for Prague is **2**; use it if you're calling from outside the country. If you're within the Czech Republic but not in Prague, use **02**. If you're calling within Prague, simply leave off the code and dial the regular phone number.

For **directory assistance** in English, dial (without a charge) **0149**. For **information on services** and rates, dial **0139**. Dial tones are continual high-pitched beeps that sound something like busy signals in America. After dialing a number from a pay phone, you might hear a series of very quick beeps that tell you the line is being connected. Busy signals sound similar to dial tones only quicker.

There are two kinds of **pay phones.** One accepts coins and the other operates only with a phonecard, available from post offices and news agents in denominations ranging from 50Kč to 500Kč ($1.50 to $15). The minimum cost of a **local call** is 3Kč (10¢). Coin-op phones, if they work, have displays telling you the minimum price for your call. They don't make change, so don't load more than you have to. You can add more coins as the display gets near zero. The more efficient phonecard telephones deduct the price of your call from the card. If you're calling home, get a phonecard with plenty of points, as calls run about 42Kč ($1.30) per minute to the United States and 25Kč (50p) to the United Kingdom. Hotels usually add their own surcharge, sometimes as hefty as 100% to 200%, which may surprise you when you're presented with the bill. Ask before placing any call from a hotel. Charging to your phone credit card from a public telephone is often the most economical way to call home.

To charge a call to your calling card, dial **AT&T USA Direct** (☎ 00/ 420-001-01), **MCI CALL USA** (☎ 00/420-001-12), or **Sprint Express USA** (☎ 00/420-871-87). Canadians can connect with **Canada Direct** at ☎ 00/ 420-00 1-51, and Brits can connect with **BT Direct** at ☎ 00/420-044-01 or **Mercury Call UK** at ☎ 00/420-044-50. From a pay phone in the Czech Republic, your local phone card is debited only for a local call.

Tipping   At most restaurants and pubs, locals just round the bill up to the nearest few koruny. When you're given good service at tablecloth places, a 10% tip is proper. Washroom and cloakroom attendants usually demand a couple of koruny, and porters in airports and rail stations usually receive 20Kč (60¢) per bag. Taxi drivers should get about 10%, unless they've already ripped you off.

WHERE TO STAY

Prague's full-service hotels have had to tighten their efficiency in the face of heavier international competition, but room rates still top those of many similar or better quality hotels in Western Europe. Pensions with limited services are cheaper than hotels, but compared with similar western B&Bs, they're pricey. The best budget accommodations are rooms in private homes or apartments. But if you require just a roof over your head, Prague has several relatively clean hostels; most seem to be temporary affairs, so for the latest, contact **AVE Ltd.** (see below).

Expect to pay between 750Kč and 1,500Kč ($23 and $45) for a single and between 1,500Kč and 6,000Kč ($45 and $182) for an apartment for two. Rental agencies include my favorite, **AVE Ltd.** (☎ **02/2422 3226** or 02/2422 3521; fax 02/5731 2984 or 02/2461 7113; e-mail: ave@avetravel.cz; www.avetravel.cz), located at Ruzyně airport; at the main train station, Hlavní nádraží; and at the north train station, nádraží Holešovice. There's also the **Prague Accommodation Service,** Haštalská ul. 7, Praha 1 (☎ **02/231 0202;** fax 02/231 6640); **Top Tour,** Rybná 3, Praha 1 (☎ **02/232 1077;** fax 02/2481 1400); and the former-Communist bureau **Čedok,** at Na Příkopě 18, Praha 1 (☎ **02/2419 7111;** fax 02/232 1656).

STARÉ MĚSTO (OLD TOWN) & JOSEFOV

Very Expensive

Grandhotel Bohemia. Královdvorská 4, Praha 1. ☎ **02/2480 4111.** Fax 02/232 9545. www.austria-hotels.co.at/austria-hotels/grandhotel-bohemia. E-mail: grand-hotel-bohemia@austria-hotels.icom.cz. 78 units. A/C MINIBAR TV TEL. 13,068Kč ($396) double; from 19,140Kč ($580) suite. Breakfast is included. AE, DC, MC, V. Metro: Náměstí Republiky.

Opened in 1994, the Bohemia is sophisticated and comfortable, and if you don't care about being overcharged, it's certainly the place to stay. In this wonderfully restored art nouveau–style hotel, the extravagant, gilded public areas are impressive and quite different from the contemporary guest rooms. The bright and cheerful accommodations aren't large, but are fitted with extras like trouser presses, faxes, and answering machines. Use the unspectacular restaurant only as a matter of convenience. There's also a small cafe.

Hotel Intercontinental Prague. nám. Curieových 43/5, Praha 1. ☎ **02/2488 1111.** Fax 02/2481 0071. www.interconti.com. E-mail: prague@interconti.com. 364 units. A/C MINIBAR TV TEL. From 10,700Kč ($325) double; from 13,200Kč ($400) suite. Rates include buffet breakfast. Children under 10 free in parents' room. AE, DC, MC, V. Metro: Staroměstská.

The upper suites have hosted luminaries such as Michael Jackson, Madeleine Albright, and, so legend has it, terrorist Carlos the Jackal. The 1970s design has been updated with a glittering modern fitness center and an atrium restaurant. The standard guest rooms aren't very large but are comfortable, with decent but not exceptional upholstered furniture, computer ports, and marble baths. A riverside window might give you a glimpse of the castle or the metronome at the top of Letná park across the river.

Expensive

✪ **Hotel Paříž.** U Obecního domu 1, Praha 1. ☎ **02/2219 5195.** Fax 02/2422 5475. www.hotel-pariz.cz. E-mail: booking@hotel-pariz.cz. 92 units. TV TEL. 7,920–8,910Kč ($240–$270) double; from 9,600Kč ($290) suite. Rates include breakfast. AE, CB, DC, MC, V. Metro: Náměstí Republiky.

At the edge of náměstí Republiky and across from the Municipal House, the Paříž provides a rare glimpse back into the gilded First Republic. Each light fixture, etching, and curve at this art nouveau landmark recalls the days when Prague was one of the world's richest cities. For a glimpse of the hotel's atmosphere, rent the film *Mission Impossible;* you can see Tom Cruise plotting his revenge from within one of the fine suites. The rooms are some of the most comfortable in Prague, with modern updates of art deco accents.

Hotel Ungelt. Štupartská 1, Praha 1. ☎ **02/2482 8686.** Fax 02/2482 8181. www.interacta.cz/accol.htm. 9 units. TV TEL. 6,330Kč ($192) 1-bedroom suite for 2 guests; Mar, July, Aug 5,740Kč ($174). 8,640Kč ($262) two-bedroom suite for 3 or 4 persons; Mar, July, Aug 7,820Kč ($237). Rates include breakfast. AE, MC, V. Metro: Staroměstská or Náměstí Republiky.

The three-story Ungelt offers airy, spacious suites. Each contains a living room, a full kitchen, and a bath. The bedrooms have standard-issue beds and not-too-attractive upholstered couches, but do boast luxurious accents like huge chandeliers and antique dressers; some have magnificent hand-painted ceilings. One of my editors and his family raved about the location and spaciousness, especially with two small boys in tow.

Moderate

✪ **Betlem Club.** Betlémské nám. 9, Praha 1. ☎ **02/2421 6872.** Fax 02/2421 8054. 22 units. MINIBAR TV TEL. 3,400Kč ($103) double. Rates include breakfast. No credit cards. Metro: Národní třída.

This small hotel offers a great location on a cobblestoned square across from where Protestant firebrand Jan Hus once preached. The rooms are decorated with bland modern pieces but are comfortable and fairly priced. One great advantage is that if you come by car, the Betlem lets you park in spots in front of the hotel, a rarity for this parking-deficient city.

Inexpensive

✪ **Hotel Cloister Inn/Pension Unitas.** Bartolomějská 9, Praha 1. ☎ **02/232 7700.** Fax 02/232 7709. www.cloister-inn.cz. E-mail: cloister@cloister-inn.cz. Pension has 32 units (none with bathroom). 1,200Kč ($36) double. Hotel side has 25 doubles with ensuite showers for 3,400Kč ($103). Both rates include breakfast (a more extensive buffet on the hotel side). No credit cards accepted from pension guests but AE, MC, V accepted from hotel guests. Metro: Národní třída.

Between Old Town Square and the National Theater, the Unitas/Cloister Inn is half a pension and half a hotel, housed in a building that was formerly a convent before the secret police coverted it into holding cells. It sounds ominous, but the Unitas offers sparse, clean accommodations in the old cells at an unbeatable price for the location. Proprietor Jiří Tlaskal has taken over managment from the secret police and the Sisters of Mercy (the nuns, not the rock group). George (in English, as he prefers) has refurbished the hotel side with smart colors and comfortable Scandinavian furniture. For a bizzare treat in the pension, you might like to stay down in Cell P6, once occupied by dissident playwright Václav Havel, a frequent "guest" of the secret police and now president of the country.

NOVÉ MĚSTO (NEW TOWN)

Very Expensive

Hotel Hilton Atrium. Pobřežní 1, Praha 8. ☎ **02/2484 1111.** Fax 02/2484 2378. www.hilton.com. E-mail: sales_prague@hilton.com. 788 units. A/C MINIBAR TV TEL. 9,690Kč ($293) double; from 12,350Kč ($374) suite. Breakfast 570Kč ($17) extra, but included in executive suite. AE, CB, DISC, MC, V. Metro: Florenc.

The Atrium was built in a galleria style seemingly out of place in Prague, and its rooms are relatively cushy and functional, somewhat like those in a better-than-average U.S. motel. The building is packed with amenities, including a tennis club, pool, fitness center, and casino. The location of this modern mammoth just outside the central city isn't ideal, but the overpriced hotel Mercedes are ready to take you where you want, and the service is pure Hilton.

Palace Hotel. Panská 12, Praha 1. ☎ **02/2409 3111.** Fax 02/2409 3135. www.hotel-palace.cz. E-mail: palhoprg@mbox.vol.cz. 124 units. A/C MINIBAR TV TEL. From 9,880Kč ($299) double; from 11,970Kč ($363) suite. Rates include breakfast. AE, DC, MC, V. Metro: Můstek.

Now surpassed in overall comfort by only the Savoy in Hradčany, the Palace is a top, upscale, central-city offering, a block from Wenceslas Square, although if given the choice, the Paříž has far more character. Still, the Palace's delicately colored guest rooms are some of the largest and most modern luxury accommodations in Prague, with Italian marble bathrooms. Two rooms for the disabled are available.

Expensive

Hotel Esplanade. Washingtonova 19, Praha 1. ☎ **800/444-7462** in the U.S. or 02/2421 1715; 800/181-535 in the U.K. Fax 02/2422 9306. 74 units. TV TEL. 8,400Kč ($254) double; from 8,950Kč ($271) suite. Rates include breakfast. AE, MC, V. Metro: Muzeum.

Located on a side street at the top of the square, the Esplanade began life as a bank and the offices of an Italian insurance company. The rooms are bright and airy, some with standard beds, others with French provincial headboards and tables, and others with extravagant canopies. Number 101 is over the top with antique wooden chairs, intricate inlaid tables, and a fascinating embossed wall covering. You might be put off by having the main train station across the street, but an honest-looking doorman says the hotel is safe. Just the same, be advised not to stroll alone in the neighborhood at night.

Prague Renaissance. V Celnici 7, Praha 1. ☎ **02/2182 1111.** Fax 02/2182 2200. www. renaissancehotel.com. E-mail: Ren_Prg_Business@compuserve.com. 315 units. A/C MINIBAR TV TEL. 5,681Kč ($172) double; from 6,631Kč ($200) suite. Breakfast (American buffet) is 437Kč ($13) extra. AE, CB, DC, MC, V. Metro: Náměstí Republiky.

The Renaissance, opened in 1993, has the standard comforts of most top-level business hotels. It's around the corner from the central bank and caters to conferences and entrepreneurs. Suites on the top floor are spacious and have walk-in closets and sizable bathrooms. A few standard rooms are wheelchair-accessible.

Moderate

Hotel Harmony. Na Poříčí 31, Praha 1. ☎ **02/232 0016** or 02/232 0720. Fax 02/231 0009. 60 units. MINIBAR TV TEL. 3,510Kč ($106) double; from 3,770Kč ($114) suite. Extra bed 850Kč ($26). Rates include breakfast. AE, MC, V. Metro: Náměstí Republiky or Florenc.

The orange-and-blue industrial upholstery and built-in beds aren't particularly attractive but are fairly comfortable. Framed prints of Czech landscapes dot the walls. The neighborhood is a jumble of newspaper offices and local shops, with not a lot to see, but the trams that run past will whisk you into Old Town. There are two restaurants, but neither is recommended.

Inexpensive

Hotel Evropa. Václavské nám. 25, Praha 1. ☎ **02/2422 8117.** Fax 02/2422 4544. 87 units (20 with bathroom), 3 suites. 2,160Kč ($65) double without bathroom, 3,400Kč ($103) double with bathroom; from 4,700Kč ($142) suite. Rates include continental breakfast. AE, MC, V. Metro: Můstek.

The statue-studded exterior is still one of the most striking landmarks on Wenceslas Square, but unlike other early century gems, it hasn't been polished and continues to get duller. The rooms are aging and most don't have bathrooms; some are just plain shabby. The best choice is a room facing the square with a balcony, but all are falling into various levels of disrepair. Still, this is an affordable chance to stay in one of Wenceslas Square's once-grand addresses.

MALÁ STRANA (LESSER TOWN)

Expensive

Hotel U Červeneho Lva. Nerudova 41, Praha 1. ☎ **02/537 239** or 02/538 192. Fax 02/ 538 193. www.hotel-lev.cz. E-mail: hotel.lev@sms.paegas.cz. 8 units. MINIBAR TV TEL. 6,400Kč ($194) double; from 7,800Kč ($236) suite. Rates include breakfast. AE, MC, V. Metro: Malostranská.

Near Prague Castle, the 15th-century burgher house "At the Red Lion" is squeezed among the crafts shops and cafes on the main road leading up to Hradčany. The suites with period ceilings have a double bed in the bedroom and two twins in the living room. All the rooms in the Red Lion are smallish, but the hardwood floors, open-beam ceilings, and the gorgeous antique furniture make up for the lack of space. The staff is courteous and sophisticated. If your room faces the street, with the windows open you'll hear the patter of tourists' feet or revelling pub closers. Some Frommer's readers have complained that the noise is nearly impossible during warm months, so ask for a back room.

Moderate

Hotel Kampa. Všehrdova 16, Praha 1. ☎ **02/5732 0404.** Fax 02/5732 0262. www.euroagentur.cz. E-mail: hotel.kampa@mbox.vol.cz. 85 units. TEL. 3,550Kč ($107) double. Rates include breakfast. AE, MC, V. Metro: Malostranská; then the no. 12, 22, or 23 tram to the Hellichova stop.

The Kampa has a choice location on a quiet winding alley off the park, giving you quick access to Malá Strana and Charles Bridge. The rooms smack of Communist chintz, but they're comfortable if you don't expect first-class surroundings. The best rooms boast a park view, so request one when booking or checking in.

HRADČANY
Very Expensive

Hotel Savoy. Keplerova 6, Praha 1. ☎02/2430 2430. Fax 02/2430 2128. www.hotel-savoy.cz. E-mail: savhoprg@mbox.vol.cz. 61 units. A/C MINIBAR TV TEL. From 8,740Kč ($265) double; from 11,970Kč ($363) suite. Rates include breakfast. AE, DC, MC, V. Tram: 22 or 23.

Prague's finest new hotel, opened in 1994, belongs to the company that manages the more venerable Palace on Wenceslas Square. Behind the massive Foreign Ministry, Černín Palace, and a few blocks from the castle, it welcomes you with a tastefully modern lobby. The guest rooms are richly decorated and boast every amenity, as well as spacious marble bathrooms. The beds are consistently huge, a rejection of the central-European twin-beds-shoved-together look. The pleasant staff provides attention to detail a cut above most hotels here. The Savoy's Hradčany Restaurant is also one of the finest dining rooms in town (see "Where to Dine," below).

Expensive

✪ **Romantik Hotel U raka.** Černínská 10, Praha 1. ☎ **02/2051 1100.** Fax 02/2051 0511. www.romantikhotels.com. E-mail: uraka@login.cz. 6 units. 6,200Kč ($188) double; 7,200Kč ($218) suite. Rates include breakfast. AE, MC, V. Tram: 22 or 23.

Hidden among the stucco houses and cobblestoned streets of a pristine medieval neighborhood on the far side of Prague Castle is this most pleasant surprise. In a ravine below the Foreign Ministry gardens, the old-world farmhouse has been lovingly reconstructed. This is the quietest getaway you could imagine in tightly packed Prague. The rustic rooms have heavy wooden furniture, open-beam ceilings, and exposed brick. The much-sought-after suite has a fireplace and adjoins a private garden, making it a favorite for honeymooners.

WHERE TO DINE

The true Czech dining experience can be summed up in three native words: *vepřo, knedlo, zelo*—pork, dumplings, cabbage. If that's what you want, try most any *hostinec* (Czech pub). Most offer a hearty *guláš* or pork dish with dumplings and cabbage for about 80Kč to 150Kč ($2.40 to $4.55). After you wash it down with Czech beer, you won't care about the taste or your arteries.

It's a big world.

And we've got the network to cover it.

Global connection with the AT&T Network

AT&T direct service

Enjoy going to the corners of the earth? We're with you. With the world's most powerful network, **AT&T Direct®** Service gives you fast, clear connections from more countries than anyone,* and the option of an English-speaking operator. All it takes is your AT&T Calling Card or credit card.† And the planet is yours.

FOR A LIST OF **AT&T ACCESS NUMBERS**, TAKE THE ATTACHED WALLET GUIDE.

For Travelers
who want more than
the Official Line

Also Available:

Macmillan Publishing USA

Traveler's Tip

Beware: Some restaurants gouge customers by charging exorbitant amounts for nuts or other seemingly free premeal snacks left on your table. Ask before you eat.

At most restaurants, menu prices include VAT. Tipping has become more commonplace in restaurants where the staff is obviously trying harder; rounding up the bill to about 10% or more is usually adequate.

STARÉ MĚSTO (OLD TOWN) & JOSEFOV
Expensive

✪ **Bellevue.** Smetanovo nábřeží 18, Praha 1. ☎ **02/2422 7614.** Reservations recommended. Main courses 400–600Kč ($12–$18); set-price menu 1,190Kč ($36). AE, DC, MC, V. Daily noon–3pm and 5:30–11pm; Sun brunch 11am–3pm, then 7pm–11pm. Metro: Staroměstská. INTERNATIONAL/WILD GAME.

In short, when in Prague, go to the Bellevue, just a few dozen steps from Charles Bridge on the Old Town side of the river. The intelligent menu boasts choice beef, nouvelle sauces, well-dressed fish and game, delicate pastas, and gorgeous desserts. Poached Norwegian salmon glistens in a light herb sauce and prawns dance on a piquant garlic glaze. Several wild game options stand out, like Fallow deer with oysters and mushrooms. The consistent food and presentation and the pleasant and perfectly timed service make the Bellevue an evening to remember.

V zátiší. Liliová 1, Praha 1. ☎ **02/2422 8977.** Reservations recommended. Main courses 395–695Kč ($12–$21); set-price menu 775Kč–1,075Kč ($23.50–$32.50). AE, DC, MC, V. Mon–Sun noon–3pm and 5:30–11pm. Metro: Národní třída. INTERNATIONAL.

V zátiší (still life) has a casual elegance, like the living room of a beachfront Mediterranean villa with cushy, upholstered, wrought-iron chairs and plenty of artfully arranged flora. Here, you'll find several fish and game choices, and a scampi that never disappoints. The dessert selections often echo those at the Bellevue, which is run by the same restaurant group, but a flaming vodka-doused Siberian palačinka one snowy Christmas Eve here stands out in my memory. Maybe one of the helpful waiters will convince the chef to do it again.

Moderate

La Provence. Štupartská 9, Praha 1. ☎ **02/232 4801.** Reservations recommended. Main courses 150–400Kč ($4.50–$12). AE, MC, V. Daily noon–midnight. Metro: Náměstí Republiky. FRENCH.

A French country wine cellar meets urban kitsch. The din of the crowd allows you to discuss private matters without too much eavesdropping. La Provence offers a wide array of French provincial dishes, as well as tangy Italian pastas and the spiciest scampi in Prague. Salads, from Caesar to Niçoise, are large and fresh; they come with fresh French bread and garlic butter. Weekends often attract drag queens from the Banana Cafe upstairs for a funky lip-synch floor show.

Reykjavik. Karlova 20, Praha 1. ☎ **02/2222 1218.** Main courses 190–450Kč ($5.75–$13.60). AE, DC, MC, V. Daily 11am–midnight. Metro: Staroměstská. SEAFOOD/STEAKS.

On one of the busiest pedestrian intersections, Reykjavik is a safe choice just off Charles Bridge. Decorated like a clubby brasserie, it offers a consistent line-up of Icelandic salmon and steaks flown in every day from the north country. During the summer, you can dine on a platform out in front as the throngs pass by on Karlova Street on their way to Charles Bridge or Old Town Square.

Inexpensive

Klub architektů. Betlémské nám. 5a, Praha 1. ☎ **02/2440 1214.** Reservations recommended. Main courses 110–130Kč ($3.30–$3.95). AE, MC, V. Daily 11:30am–midnight. Metro: Národní třída. CZECH/INTERNATIONAL.

Across the courtyard from Jan Hus's Bethlehem Chapel, this eclectic clubhouse for the city's progressive architects is the best non-pub value in Old Town. Sitting in the stone celler, among industrial swag lights, you can choose from baked chicken, pork steaks, pasta, stir-fry chicken, and even vegetarian burritos. Wicker seats and torches set up in the courtyard make for an enjoyable summer night, although the alfresco menu is limited.

✪ **Pivnice Radegast.** Templová 2, Praha 1. ☎ **02/232 8069.** Main courses 55–120Kč ($1.65–$3.60). AE, MC, V. Daily 11am–midnight. Metro: Můstek or Náměstí Republiky. CZECH.

The raucous Radegast dishes up Prague's best pub *guláš* in a single narrow vaulted hall, where the namesake Moravian brew seems to never stop flowing from its taps. Around the corner from a bunch of popular bars, the Radegast attracts a good mix of visitors and locals and a young upwardly mobile crowd.

Pizzeria Rugantino. Dušní 4, Praha 1. ☎ **02/231 8172.** Individual pizzas 90–150Kč ($2.75–$4.55). No credit cards. Mon–Sat 11am–11pm; Sun 6–11pm. Metro: Staroměstská. PIZZA.

The wood-fired stoves and handmade dough result in a crisp, delicate crust, a perfect platform for a multitude of cheeses, vegetables, and meats. The Diabolo with fresh garlic bits and very hot chiles goes nicely with a cool iceberg salad and a pull of Krušovice beer. The constant buzz, no-smoking area, and heavy childproof wooden tables make this place a family favorite.

✪ **U medvídků.** Na Perštýně 7, Praha 1. ☎ **02/2422 0930.** Main courses 80–250Kč ($2.40–$8). AE, MC, V. Daily 11am–11pm. Metro: Národní třída. CZECH.

Bright and noisy, the House at the Little Bears serves a better-than-average *vepřo, knedlo, zelo* with two-color cabbage. The pub, on the right after entering, is much cheaper and more lively than the bar to the left. It's a hangout for locals, German tour groups, and foreign journalists in search of the original Czech Budweiser beer, *Budvar*. In high season, an oompah band plays in the beer wagon.

NOVÉ MĚSTO (NEW TOWN)
Moderate

✪ **Restaurant U Čížků.** Karlovo nám. 34, Praha 2. ☎ **02/2223 2257.** Reservations recommended. Main courses 180–330Kč ($5–$10). AE, MC, V. Daily noon–10pm. Metro: Karlovo náměstí. CZECH.

One of the city's first private restaurants, this cozy cellar cum hunting lodge on Charles Square can be recognized by the long line of German tour buses outside. The fare is purely Czech, and the massive portions of game, smoked pork, and other meats will stay with you for a while. The traditional Starý český talíř (local meat, dumplings, and cabbage) is about as authentic Czech as it gets. The still excellent value earns this pioneer a star.

Inexpensive

Café Louvre. Národní třída 20, Praha 1. ☎ **02/297 223.** Reservations not accepted. Main courses 100–200Kč ($3.05–$6). AE, DC, MC, V. Daily 8am–11pm. Metro: Můstek. CZECH/ INTERNATIONAL.

This big breezy upstairs hall, the artsy restaurant fomerly known as Gany's, is great for a coffee, an inexpensive pretheater meal, or an upscale game of pool. A fabulous art

Kavárna Society

Cafe life is back in a big way in Prague, now that the Slavia and the Municiple House Kavárna have returned. From dissident blues to high society, these are the places where nonpub Praguers spend their afternoons and evenings, sipping coffee and smoking cigarettes while reading, writing, or talking with friends.

The ✪ **Kavárna (Cafe) Slavia,** Národní at Smetanovo nábřeží 2, Praha 1 (☎ **02/2422 0957;** metro: Národní třída), reopened in 1997, after a half-decade sleep, prolonged by a Boston real estate speculator who was sitting on the property. President Havel (a Slavia regular when it was the dissident hangout) intervened, and after a long legal battle, the Slavia returned on the Velvet Revolution's eighth anniversary. "A small victory for reason over stupidity," Havel called it. The restored crisp art deco room recalls the Slavia's 100 years as the meeting place for the city's cultural and intellectual crowd. You'll still find a relatively affordable menu of light fare served with the riverfront views of Prague Castle and the National Theater. Open daily 8am to midnight.

The quaint **Café Milena,** Staroměstské nám. 22, Praha 1 (☎ **02/2163 2609;** metro: Staroměstská), is managed by the Franz Kafka Society and named for Milena Jesenská, one of the writer's lovers. The draw is a great view of the Orloj, the astronomical clock with the hourly parade of saints on the side of Old Town Square's city hall. It's open daily 10am to 10pm, and no credit cards are accepted.

Of all the beautifully restored spaces in the Municipal House, the **Kavárna Obecní dům,** náměstí Republiky 5, Praha 1 (☎ **02/2200 2763;** metro: Náměstí Republiky), might be its most spectacular room. Lofty ceilings, marble accents and tables, an altarlike mantle, huge windows, and period chandeliers provide the awesome setting for coffees, teas, and other drinks, along with pastries and light sandwiches. A true turn-of-the-century afternoon. It's open daily 7:30am to 11pm, and no credit cards are accepted.

The newer Bohemians have made Velryba, at Opatovická 24 on a small side street near narodní třída, the late 20th century version of the Slavia. Here, cheap pasta salads mix with clove cigarette smoke and pop art. It's very difficult to get a table more than a few minutes after noon as the students and young intellectuals homestead. It's open 11am to 2am, and no credit cards are accepted.

nouveau interior, with huge original chandeliers, buzzes with local coffee talk, the shopping crowd, business lunches, and students. Starters include smoked salmon, battered and fried asparagus, and ham au gratin with vegetables. Main dishes range from trout with horseradish to beans with garlic sauce. Avoid the always-overcooked pastas and stick to the basic meats and fish. In the snazzy billiards parlor in back, you can have drinks and light meals served.

MALÁ STRANA
Expensive
Circle Line Brasserie. Malostranské nám. 12, Praha 1. ☎ **02/530 308.** Reservations recommended. Set-price menu 1,000Kč ($30). AE, MC, V. Mon–Sat 6–11pm. Metro: Malostranská. FRENCH/INTERNATIONAL.

The Circle Line has jumped track from a primarily seafood draw to a fuller French-oriented international menu. The setting still has a breezy casual ease despite its frequently buttoned-up crowd from the nearby embassies. While the Hollywood directors' chairs feel a bit cheap, the food continues to impress. Starters include rich duck foie gras lightly fried with peaches, as well as sauteed oysters and artichokes. Main courses range from straightforward baked chicken in herbs to poached turbot with slices of Prague ham.

✪ **U Malířů Maltézské nám.** 11, Praha 1. ☎ **02/5732 0317.** Reservations recommended. Main courses 430–990Kč ($13–$30); set-price menu 1,690Kč ($52). AE, DC, MC, V. Daily 7–10pm. Metro: Malostranská. FRENCH.

The owners of U Malířů have given in to the pressure of competition and are now offering a more affordable chance to sample the finer attributes of a Parisian kitchen. Surrounded by Romance-age murals and gorgeously appointed tables in three intimate dining rooms, you're faced with some tough choices. Creamy scallops ragoût swim in light vanilla sauce, pike perch comes with truffles, rack of lamb is glazed in tarragon, and an exotic set of quail chicks bathe in Armagnac. If you want a truly old-world evening of elegant romance and French specialties, U Malířů is finally getting to be worth it.

Moderate

Avalon Bar & Grill. Malostranské nám. 12, Praha 1. ☎ **02/530 308.** Main courses 120–250Kč ($4.45–$9.25). AE, MC, V. Daily 11am–1am. Metro: Malostranská. AMERICAN.

Avalon still provides the same retreat from Central European stodginess that it did when it opened in 1994. The well-stacked club leads the sandwiches, but there's also grilled chicken, burgers, potato skins, and buffalo wings, plus many takes on fresh salads with pasta and seafood.

U modré kachničky. Nebovidská 6, Praha 1. ☎ **02/5732 0308.** Reservations recommended. Main courses 290–390Kč ($9–$12); set-price menu 1,000Kč ($30). AE, MC, V. Daily noon–4pm and 6:30–11:30pm. Metro: Malostranská. CZECH/WILD GAME.

The "Blue Duckling," on a narrow Malá Strana street, tries (and often succeeds) at turning traditionial Czech food into Bohemian cuisine, but sometimes its results fall short. A series of small dining rooms with vaulted ceilings and playfully frescoed walls is packed with antique furniture and pastel-flowered linen upholstery. The menu is loaded with wild game and quirky spins on Czech village favorites. Try the Malá Strana Templar's Sword, a skewer sampling several domesticated and wild meats.

Inexpensive

Bohemia Bagel. Újezd 16, Praha 1. ☎ **02/531 002.** Bagels and sandwiches 20–135Kč (60¢–$4.10). No credit cards. Daily 8am–midnight. Tram: 6, 9, 12, 22, or 23 to Újezd stop. BAGELS/SANDWICHES.

Bohemia Bagel emerged in 1997 at the base of Petřín Hill as the answer to the lazy-morning bagel-less blues. The roster of golden-brown, hand-rolled, stone-baked bagels is stellar. Plain, cinnamon raisin, garlic, or onion provide a sturdy but tender frame for Scandinavian lox and cream cheese or jalapeño-cheddar cheese (on which you can lop Tex-Mex chili for the Sloppy Bagel). The cushioned wooden booths in an earthy contemporary setting are comfortable.

HRADČANY
Expensive

Hradčany Restaurant. In the Hotel Savoy, Keplerova 8, Praha 1. ☎ **02/2430 2430.** Reservations recommended. Main courses 490–600Kč ($14.80–$18). AE, MC, V. Daily noon–11pm. Tram: 22 or 23, 2 stops past Prague Castle. INTERNATIONAL.

Matching the crisp English setting of the Savoy Hotel in which it resides, the Hradčany is the most elegant choice this side of the castle. The menu lists a variety of beef, pork, and seafood, including succulent poached salmon and lean sliced veal in herb cream sauce. There are also surprises, such as herb-stuffed tortellini and prawns in avocado mousse. The service sets the standard for Prague, and the new lunch sitting is sure to attract a solid crowd to this jewel beyond the castle gates.

Inexpensive

Saté Grill. Pohořelec 3, Praha 1. ☎ **02/2051 4552**. Main courses 55–200Kč ($1.70–$6). No credit cards. Daily 11am–10pm. Tram: 22 or 23. INDONESIAN.

A lunchtime savior near the castle, the Saté has made quite a business out of its simple Indonesian dishes at simple prices. The unassuming Saté storefront on the same side as the Swedish embassy doesn't scream out to you, so look closely. The pork saté comes in a peanut sauce along with a hearty noodle Migoreng. The casual atmosphere eagerly welcomes foot-dragging visitors in search of a bite and a rest.

IN VINOHRADY

Inexpensive

Radost F/X é. Bělehradská 120, Praha 2. ☎ **02/2425 4776**. Main courses 80–200Kč ($2.40–$6). MC, V. Daily 11am–5am. Metro: I. P. Pavlova. VEGETARIAN.

En vogue and vegetarian, Radost is a clubhouse for hip New Bohemians. The veggie burger is well seasoned and substantial on a grain bun, and the soups, like lentil and onion, are light and full of flavor. The dining area is a dark rec room of upholstered armchairs, chaise lounges, couches from the 1960s, and coffee tables from which you eat. Too cool.

NEAR VYŠEHRAD

Moderate

Le Bistro de Marlene. Plavecká 4, Praha 2. ☎ **02/291 077**. Reservations recommended. Main courses 340–530Kč ($10–$16). AE, MC, V. Mon–Fri noon–2:30pm and 7pm–10:30pm; Sat 7pm–10:30pm; Sun closed. Metro: Vyšehrad. FRENCH.

On a residential street near Vyšehrad park, Marlene's is packed with locals and visitors in search of the finest casual French cuisine in town. Chef Marlene Salomon has kept the menu short and simple, focusing on high-quality meats and produce. Many starters are recommendable, including flan aux champignons (mushrooms). Of the main courses, roast leg of lamb and steak curry are delicate and well prepared.

SEEING THE SIGHTS

In Prague, you'll get the most enjoyment from a slow, aimless wander through the city's heart. If you have the time and energy, absorb the grand architecture of Prague Castle and the Old Town skyline (best from Charles Bridge) at sunrise and then at sunset. You'll see two completely different cities.

Except for the busy main streets, where you may have to dodge traffic, Prague is ideal for walking. Actually, walking is really the only way to explore Prague. Most of the town's oldest areas are walking zones, with motor traffic restricted.

SIGHTSEEING SUGGESTIONS FOR FIRST-TIME VISITORS

Prague is the perfect city to discover simply by getting lost in the center. If you have only a couple of days, though, do what visiting kings and potentates do on a short visit: Walk the **Royal Route** from the top of the Hradčany hill (tram no. 22 or 23 or a taxi is suggested for the ride up unless you're very fit). Tour **Prague Castle,** and then stroll across **Charles Bridge** on the way to the winding alleys of **Old Town (Staré Město).** There, explore the varied sights of **Old Town** and the **Jewish Quarter (Josefov).**

If you're lucky enough to have more time, check out Malá Strana (Lesser Town), and visit the **National Art Gallery at Šternberk Palace** and the **Strahov Monastery** with its ornate libraries. For a great respite from the crowded city, visit the old southern citadel over the Vltava, **Vyšehrad,** where you get a completely different view of the city you've just explored.

PRAGUE CASTLE & CHARLES BRIDGE

Dating from the 14th century, ✪ **Charles Bridge (Karův most),** Prague's most celebrated structure, links Prague Castle to Staré Město. For most of its 600 years, the 1,700-foot-long span has been a pedestrian promenade, although for centuries walkers had to share the concourse with horse-drawn vehicles and trolleys. Today, the bridge is filled with hordes walking among folksy artists and street musicians.

The best times to stroll across the bridge are in early morning or around sunset, when the crowds have thinned and the shadows are more mysterious, but you'll be crisscrossing the bridge throughout your stay.

✪ **Prague Castle (Pražský Hrad).** Hradčanské nám., Hradčany, Praha 1. ☎ **02/ 2437 3368.** Grounds, free. Combination ticket to 4 main castle attractions (St. Vitus Cathedral, Royal Palace, St. George's Basilica, Powder Tower), 100Kč ($3.05) adults, 50Kč ($1.50) students without guide; 150Kč ($4.55) adults, 100Kč ($3.05) students with English-speaking guide. Ticket is valid 3 days. Castle, daily 9am–5pm (to 4pm Nov–Mar). Metro: Line A to Malostranská, then tram 22 or 23, up the hill, two stops.

The huge hilltop complex known collectively as **Pražský Hrad** encompasses dozens of towers, churches, courtyards, and monuments. A visit could easily take an entire day or more. Still, you can see the top sights—St. Vitus Cathedral, the Royal Palace, St. George's Basilica, the Powder Tower, plus Golden Lane—in the space of a morning or an afternoon.

St. Vitus Cathedral (Chrám sv. Víta), constructed in A.D. 926 as the court church of the Přemyslid princes, was named for a wealthy 4th-century Sicilian martyr and has long been the center of Prague's religious and political life. The key part of its Gothic construction took place in the 14th century under the direction of Mathias of Arras and Peter Parléř of Gmuend. In the 18th and 19th centuries, subsequent baroque and neo-Gothic additions were made. In 1997, Pope John Paul II visited Prague to honor the 1,000th anniversary of the death of 10th-century Slavic evangelist St. Vojtěch. He conferred the saint's name on the cathedral along with St. Vitus's, but officially the Czech state calls it just St. Vitus.

The ✪ **Royal Palace (Královský palác),** in the third courtyard of the castle grounds, served as the residence of kings between the 10th and the 17th centuries. Vaulted Vladislav Hall, the interior's centerpiece, was used for coronations and special occasions. Here Václav Havel was inaugurated president. The adjacent Diet was where the king met with advisers and where the supreme court was held. You'll find a good selection of guidebooks, maps, and other related information at the entrance.

St. George's Basilica (Kostel sv. Jiří), adjacent to the Royal Palace, is Prague's oldest Romanesque structure, dating from the 10th century. It was also Bohemia's first convent. No longer serving a religious function, the building now houses a museum of historic Czech art.

Golden Lane (Zlatá ulička) is a picturesque, fairy-tale street of tiny 16th-century servants' houses built into the castle fortifications. The houses now contain shops, galleries, and refreshment bars. In 1917, Franz Kafka lived briefly at no. 22.

The **Powder Tower (Prašná věž a.k.a. Mihulka)** forms part of the northern bastion of the castle complex just off the Golden Lane. Originally a gunpowder storehouse and a cannon tower, it was turned into a laboratory for the 17th-century alchemists serving the court of Emperor Rudolf II.

GETTING TICKETS   Tickets are sold at the **Prague Castle Information Center** (☎ **02/2437 3368**), in the second courtyard after passing through the main gate from

Hradčanské náměstí. The center also arranges tours in various languages and sells tickets for individual concerts and exhibits.

OTHER TOP ATTRACTIONS

The Jewish Museum. Maisel Synagogue, Maiselova 10 (between Široká and Jáchymova 3), Praha 1. ☎ **02/2481 0099.** Combined admission to all museum parts 450Kč ($14) adults, 330Kč ($10) students. May–Oct tours for groups of 10 or more on the hour starting 9am (last tour 4pm). Nov–Apr tours leave whenever enough people gather in same language. Metro: Staroměstská.

The Jewish Museum is the organization managing all the Jewish landmarks in Josefov, which forms the northwest quarter of Old Town. The organization offers guided package tours as part of a comprehensive admission price, with an English-speaking guide. The package includes the **Ceremonial Hall, Old Jewish Cemetery, Old-New Synagogue, Pinkas Synagogue, Klaus Synagogue, Maisel Synagogue,** and the newly refurbished **Spanish Synagogue.**

The Maisel Synagogue is used as the exhibition space for the Jewish Museum. Most of Prague's ancient Judaica was destroyed by the Nazis during World War II. Ironically, those same Germans constructed an "exotic museum of an extinct race," thus salvaging thousands of objects, such as the valued Torah covers, books, and silver now displayed at the Maisel Synagogue.

✪ **Old-New Synagogue (Starovová synagoga).** Červená 3. ☎ **02/2481 0099.** Admission 200Kč ($6) adults, 100Kč ($3) students. Sun–Fri 9am–6pm. Metro: Staroměstská.

First called the New Synagogue to distinguish it from an even older one that no longer exists, the Old-New Synagogue, built around 1270, is Europe's oldest Jewish house of worship. Jews have prayed here continuously for more than 700 years, carrying on even after a massive 1389 pogrom in Josefov that killed over 3,000 Jews. It was interrupted only between 1941 and 1945 because of the Nazi occupation. The synagogue is also one of Prague's largest Gothic buildings, with vaulted ceilings and Renaissance-era columns.

✪ **Old Jewish Cemetery (Starý židovský hřbitov).** U Starého hřbitova 3A. ☎ **02/2481 0099.** Admission 250Kč ($8) adults, 190Kč ($6) students. Sun–Fri 9am–6pm. Metro: Staroměstská.

Dating from the mid-15th century, this is one of Europe's oldest Jewish burial grounds, 1 block from the Old-New Synagogue. Because the local government of the time didn't allow Jews to bury their dead elsewhere, graves were dug deep enough to hold 12 bodies vertically, with each tombstone placed in front of the last. The result is one of the world's most crowded cemeteries: a 1-block area filled with more than 20,000 graves. Among the most famous persons buried here are the celebrated Rabbi Loew (died 1609), who created the legendary Golem (a clay "monster" to protect Prague's Jews), and banker Markus Mordechai Maisel (died 1601), then the richest man in Prague and protector of the city's Jewish community during the reign of Rudolf II. The adjoining **Ceremonial Hall** at the end of the path is worth a look for the heart-wrenching drawings by children held at the Terezín concentration camp during World War II (see "Day Trips from Prague," below, for more on Terezín). Also worth seeing is the newly reopened Spanish Synagogue at Vězeňská 3, down Široká street from the Old-New Synagogue, with exhibitions of more contemporary Jewish history in Prague.

Šternberk Palace Art Museum (Šternberský palác). Hradčanské nám. 15, Praha 1. ☎ **02/3335 7332.** Admission 70Kč ($2.10) adults, 40Kč ($1.20) students/children. Tues–Sun 10am–6pm. Metro: Malostranská then tram 22 or 23 two stops up the hill to the Prague Castle stop.

Famous Squares

The most celebrated square, **Old Town Square (Staroměstské náměstí),** is surrounded by baroque buildings and packed with colorful craftspeople, cafes, and entertainers. In ancient days, the site was a major crossroad on central European merchant routes. In its center stands a memorial to Jan Hus, the 15th-century martyr who crusaded against Prague's German-dominated religious and political establishment. Unveiled in 1915, on the 500th anniversary of Hus's execution, the monument's most compelling features are the asymmetry of the composition and the fluidity of the figures.

The **Astronomical Clock (orloj)** at **Old Town Hall (Staroměstská radnice)** performs a glockenspiel spectacle daily on the hour from 8am to 8pm. Originally constructed in 1410, the clock has long been an important symbol of Prague.

Wenceslas Square (Václavské náměstí), a former horse market, has thrice been the focal point of riots and revolutions—in 1918, 1968, and 1989.

The jewel in the National Gallery crown, the gallery at Šternberk Palace, adjacent to Prague Castle's main gate, displays a wide array of European art throughout the ages. It features 6 centuries of everything from oils to sculptures. The permanent collection is divided chronologically into pre–19th-century art, 19th- and 20th-century art, and 20th-century French painting and sculpture. The collection includes a good selection of cubist works by Braque and Picasso. Temporary exhibits, such as Italian Renaissance bronzes, are always on show.

Veletržní Palace. Dukelských hrdinů 47, Praha 7. ☎ **02/2430 1111.** Admission 80Kč ($2.40) adults, 40Kč ($1.20) students. Tues–Sun 10am–6pm (Thurs to 9pm). On Thurs after 5pm, admission 40Kč ($1.20) for all exhibitions. Metro: Vltavská or tram 17.

This remodeled 1925 palace now holds the bulk of the National Gallery's collection of 20th-century works by Czech and other European artists. Three atrium-lit concourses provide a comfortable setting for some catchy and kitschy Czech sculpture and multimedia works. Alas, the best cubist works by Braque and Picasso, Rodin bronzes, and other primarily French pieces are relegated to a poorly lit section on the second floor. Several sections are devoted to peculiar but thought-provoking works from Czech artists that prove creativity still flowed under the weight of the Iron Curtain. Many traveling foreign temporary exhibits are shown on the first floor.

MORE ATTRACTIONS

Bertramka (Museum W.A. Mozart). Mozartova 169, Praha 5. ☎ **02/543 893.** Admission 50Kč ($1.50) adults, 30Kč (90¢) students. Daily 9:30am–6pm. Tram: 2, 6, 7, 9, 14, or 16 from Anděl metro station.

Mozart loved Prague, and when he visited he often stayed with the family who owned this villa, the Dušeks. Now a museum, the villa contains displays that include his written work and harpsichord. There's also a lock of Mozart's hair, encased in a cube of glass. Much of the Bertramka villa was destroyed by fire in the 1870s, but Mozart's rooms, where he finished composing *Don Giovanni,* miraculously remained untouched.

The Estates' Theater (Stavovské divadlo). Ovocný trh 1, Praha 1. ☎ **02/2421 5001.** Metro: Můstek.

The theater was completed in 1783 by the wealthy Count F. A. Nostitz. Mozart staged the premier of *Don Giovanni* here in 1787 because he felt that the conservative patrons in Vienna didn't appreciate him or his passionate and often shocking work. "Praguers understand me," Mozart was quoted as saying. Czech director Miloš Forman returned to his native country to film his Oscar-winning *Amadeus,* shooting the scenes of Mozart in Prague with perfect authenticity at the Estates' Theater.

The theater doesn't have daily tours, but tickets for performances—and the chance to sit in one of the elegant private boxes—are usually available. Tour events are occasionally scheduled, and individual tours can be arranged by calling the city heritage group **Pražská vlastivěda** at ☎ **02/2481 6184.**

✪ **Strahov Monastery and Library (Strahovský klášter a knihovna).** Strahovské nádvoří 1, Praha 1. ☎ **02/2051 6654.** Admission 40Kč ($1.20) adults, 20Kč (60¢) students. Tues–Sun 9am–noon and 1–5pm. Tram: 22 or 23 from Malostranská metro station.

The second oldest monastery in Prague, Strahov was founded high above Malá Strana in 1143 by Vladislav II. It's still home to Premonstratensian monks, a scholarly order closely related to the Jesuits, and their dormitories and refectory are off-limits. What draws visitors are the monastery's ornate libraries, holding more than 125,000 volumes.

Cathedral of St. Nicholas (Chrám sv. Mikuláše). Malostranské nám., Praha 1. Free admission. Daily 9am–5pm. Metro: Malostranská, then tram 22 or 12 one stop to Malostranské nám.

This church is critically regarded as one of the best examples of the high baroque north of the Alps. K. I. Dienzenhofer's 1711 design was augmented by his son Kryštof's 260-foot-high dome, which has dominated the Malá Strana skyline since its completion in 1752. Prague's smog has played havoc with the building's exterior, but its gilded interior is stunning. Gold-capped marble-veneered columns frame altars packed with statuary and frescoes.

Parks & Gardens

From **Vyšehrad,** Soběslavova 1 (☎ **02/296 651**), legend has it that Princess Libuše looked out over the Vltava valley toward the present-day Prague Castle and predicted the founding of a great state and capital city. Vyšehrad was the seat of the first Czech kings of the Přemyslid dynasty before the dawn of this millennium.

Today, the fortifications remain on the rocky cliffs, blocking out the increasing noise and confusion below. Within the confines of the citadel, lush lawns and gardens are crisscrossed by dozens of paths, leading to historic buildings and cemeteries. Vyšehrad is still somewhat of a hidden treasure for picnics and romantic walks, and from here you'll see one of the city's most panoramic views. Take tram no. 3 from Karlovo náměstí to Výtoň south of New Town.

The **Royal Garden (Královská zahrada)** at Prague Castle, once the site of the sovereigns' vineyards, was founded in 1534. Dotted with lemon trees and surrounded by 16th-, 17th-, and 18th-century buildings, the park is laid out with abundant shrubbery and fountains. Enter from U Prašného mostu street north of the castle complex.

In Hradčany, the castle's **Garden on the Ramparts (Zahrada na Valech),** below the castle with a gorgeous city panorama, was reopened in spring 1995 after being thoroughly refurbished. The park is open Tuesday to Sunday 9am to 5pm. Part of the excitement of **Waldstein (Wallenstein) Gardens (Valdštejnská zahrada)** is its location, behind a 30-foot wall on the back streets of Malá Strana. Inside, elegant, leafy gravel paths, dotted by classical bronze statues and gurgling fountains, fan out in every direction.

Letná (metro: Vltavska, then tram no 1; 3 stops to Sparta stop) was the only place flat and open enough to have a big military parade, so the Communists made use of it. Pope John Paul II (twice) and Michael Jackson have played here since the revolution. Praguers and tourists love Letná because of its great overlooks on the city side and the wide open spaces for jogging and meditating. There are plenty of trees to rest under on hot summer days, and the beer garden next to the Letenske zamecek villa serves up one of the favorite local lagers, Kozel (Goat), during the high season.

A SPECIAL GROUP TOUR

If you're traveling in a large group and really want a unique sightseeing experience, why not rent your own classic trolley? With enough people, it really can be affordable, thanks to the **Historic Tram Tour (Elektrické dráhy DP),** Patočkova 4, Praha 6 (☎ and fax **02/312 3349**).

If you send a fax with details 1 day ahead, the city transport department can arrange a private tour using one of the turn-of-the-century wooden trams that once traveled on regular lines through Prague. Up to 24 people can fit in one car, which sports wooden-planked floors, cast-iron conductor's levers, and the "ching-ching" of a proper tram bell.

It costs 2,940Kč ($89) per hour. Up to 60 people can fit into a double car for 3,780Kč ($114) per hour. You can also order a cold smorgasbord with coffee, beer, champagne, a waiter to serve, and an accordion player. You can choose the route the tram takes—the no. 22 route is best.

THE SHOPPING SCENE

Czech porcelain, glass, and cheap but well-constructed clothing draw hoards of day-trippers from Germany. Private retailers have been allowed to operate here only since late 1989, but many top international retailers have already arrived. Shops lining the main route from Old Town Square to Charles Bridge are also great for browsing. For clothing, porcelain, jewelry, garnets, and glass, stroll around **Wenceslas Square** and **Na Příkopě,** connecting Wenceslas Square with náměstí Republiky.

For glass and crystal, try **Moser,** Na Příkopě 12 (☎ **02/2421 1293**), Prague's most prestigious crystal shop, which opened in 1857. Even if you're not buying, the inimitable old-world shop is definitely worth a browse. A second shop is at Malé nám. 11.

At **Cristallino,** Celetná 12 (☎ **02/261 265**), you'll find a good selection of stemware and vases in traditional designs. The shop's central location belies its excellent prices. At **Pavilon,** Vinohradská 50 (☎ **02/2209 7111**), a new four-tiered galleria, fashion junkies can browse in stores from Lacoste to Diesel, have their hair done, buy some Timberlands, and bring home a hunk of bacon from the Belgian Butcher.

Havelský trh (Havel's Market), Havelská ulice, Praha 1 (Metro: Můstek), is on a short street running perpendicular to Melantrichova, the main route connecting Staroměstské náměstí with Václavské náměstí. This open-air market (named well before a Havel became president) features dozens of private vendors selling seasonal home-grown fruits and vegetables. Other goods, including flowers and cheese, are also for sale. Since this place is designed primarily for locals, the prices are exceedingly low by Western European standards. The market is open Monday to Friday 7am to 6pm.

PRAGUE AFTER DARK

Prague's nightlife has changed completely since the Velvet Revolution—for the better if you plan to go clubbing, for the worse if you hope to sample the city's classical offerings. Still, seeing *Don Giovanni* in the Estates' Theater, where Mozart first premiered it, is worth the admission. Ticket prices, while low by Western standards, have become prohibitively high for the average Czech. However, you'll find the exact reverse in the rock and jazz scene. Dozens of clubs have opened, and world-class bands are finally adding Prague to their European tours.

Turn to the ***Prague Post*** for listings of cultural events and nightlife around the city; it's available at most newsstands in Old Town and Malá Strana.

Once in Prague, you can buy tickets at theater box offices or from any one of dozens of agencies throughout the city center. Large centrally located agencies (take the metro to Můstek for all) are **Prague Tourist Center,** Rytířská 12, Praha 1 (☎ 02/2421 2209), open daily 9am to 8pm; **Bohemia Ticket International,** Na Příkopě 16, Praha 1 (☎ 02/2421 5031); and **Čedok,** Na Příkopě 18, Praha 1 (☎ 02/2481 1870).

THE PERFORMING ARTS

Although there's plenty of music year-round, the symphonies and orchestras all come to life during the ✪ **Prague Spring Music Festival,** a 3-week series of concerts featuring the country's top performers, as well as noted guest conductors, soloists, and visiting symphony orchestras. The festival runs May 12 to June 2. Tickets for concerts are 250Kč to 2,000Kč ($7.60 to $60).

The Czech Philharmonic Orchestra and Prague Symphony Orchestra usually perform at the **Rudolfinum,** náměstí Jana Palacha, Praha 1 (☎ 02/2489 3352; metro: Staroměstská). The Czech Philharmonic is the traditional voice of the country's national pride, often playing works by Dvořák and Smetana; the Prague Symphony ventures into more eclectic territory. Tickets range from 100Kč to 600Kč ($3.05 to $18).

In a city full of spectacularly beautiful theaters, the massive pale-green **Estates' Theater (Stavovské divadlo),** Ovocný trh 1, Praha 1 (☎ 02/2421 5001; metro: Můstek), is one of the most awesome. Built in 1783 and site of the premiere of Mozart's *Don Giovanni* (conducted by the composer), the theater now hosts many of the classic productions of European opera and drama. Simultaneous English translation, transmitted via headphone, is available for most plays. Tickets cost 200Kč to 1,000Kč ($6 to $33).

Lavishly constructed in the late-Renaissance style of northern Italy, the gold-crowned **Národní divadlo (National Theater),** Národní 2, Praha 1 (☎ 02/2491 4129; metro: Národní třída), overlooking the Vltava River, is one of Prague's most recognizable landmarks. Completed in 1881, the theater was built to nurture the Czech National Revival—a grassroots movement to replace the dominant German culture with that of native Czechs. Today, classic productions are staged here in a larger setting than at the Estates' Theater, but with about the same ticket prices.

The National Theater Ballet performs at the National Theater. The troupe has seen most of its top talent go West since 1989, but it still puts on a good show. Some critics have complained that Prague's top company has been performing virtually the same dances for many years and they're in serious need of refocusing. Choreographer Libor Vaculík has responded with humorous and quirky stagings of off-the-wall ballets such as *Some Like It Hot* and *Psycho.* Tickets cost 200Kč to 600Kč ($6 to $18).

Laterna Magika, Národní třída 4, Praha 1 (☎ 02/2491 4129; metro: Národní třída), is a performance-art show in the new wing of the National Theater. The multimedia show, which combines live theater with film and dance, was once considered on the radical edge. The shows are not for those easily offended by nudity. Tickets are 400Kč ($12).

THE CLUB & MUSIC SCENE

Prague's club and music scene is limited but lively. Local acts still have a garage-band sound, but are adding more sophisticated numbers to their gigs. Many venerable jazz groups who toiled in the underground caverns are finding a new audience in visitors who stumble on their clubs. It is no longer a huge shock to see well-known Western bands playing a couple of sets in Prague.

Rock & Dance Clubs

Club Lavka. Novotného lávka 1, Praha 1. ☎ 02/2421 4797. www.lavka.cz. Cover 50Kč ($1.50), ticket prices for performing art 120–150Kč ($3.60–$4.55). AE, MC, V. Always open. Metro: Staroměstská.

At Lávka, straightforward dance hits attract one of Prague's best-looking young crowds. Because of its location next to the Staré Město foot of Charles Bridge, it also attracts a lot of less well-dressed visitors. Open 24 hours, the club is one of the nicest in town, offering a large bar, a good dance floor, and fantastic outdoor seating in warm months.

Radost F/X. Bělehradská 120, Praha 2. ☎ **02/2251 3144.** Cover usually 50Kč ($1.50). No credit cards. Metro: I. P. Pavlova.

Popular with a mixed gay and model crowd, Radost F/X is built in the American mold. In a subterranean labyrinth of nooks and crannies there's a pulsating techno-heavy dance floor with good sightlines for wallflowers. Radost, extremely stylish and self-consciously urban, is open daily 9pm to 5am.

Roxy Experimental Space. Dlouhá 33, Praha 1. ☎ **02/2481 0951.** Cover 100–150Kč ($3–$4.50). No credit cards. Cafe noon–midnight; club 10pm–6am. Metro: Náměstí Republiky.

One of the city's most unusual venues, Roxy is a subterranean theater with a wrap-around balcony overlooking a concrete dance floor. The club is ultra-downscale and extremely popular on Friday and Saturday. Persian rugs and lanterns soften the atmosphere but don't improve the lousy acoustics. Acid jazz, funk, techno, ambient, and other danceable tunes attract an artsy crowd after midnight. Several live acts are also featured here each month, with music ranging from Czech acid jazz to Allanah Miles.

Jazz Clubs

AghaRTA Jazz Centrum. Krakovská 5, Praha 1. ☎ **02/2221 1275.** Cover 60–100Kč ($1.80–$3.05). Metro: Muzeum.

Upscale by Czech standards, the AghaRTA regularly features some of the best music in town, from standard acoustic trios to Dixieland, funk, and fusion. Hot Line, the house band led by AghaRTA part-owner and drummer extraordinaire Michael Hejuna, regularly takes the stage with its keyboard-and-sax Crusaders-like sound. Bands usually begin at 9pm. The club is open Monday to Friday 5pm to 1am and Saturday and Sunday 7pm to 1am.

Reduta Jazz Club. Národní 20, Praha 1. ☎ **02/2491 2246.** Cover usually 100Kč ($3.05). Metro: Národní třída.

This is a smoky subterranean room that looks exactly like a jazz cellar should. An adventurous booking policy, which even included a saxophone gig with a U.S. president in 1994, means that different bands play almost every night. Music usually starts around 9pm. It's open 9pm to midnight.

PUBS & BARS

You'll experience true Czech entertainment in only one kind of place—a smoky local pub serving some of the world's best beer. Remember to put a cardboard coaster in front of you to show you want a mug, and never wave for service, as the typically surly waiter will just ignore you.

Chapeau Rouge/Banana Café. Jakubská 2, Praha 1. No phone. Metro: Staroměstská.

Hidden on a small Old Town back street, this loud and lively, if slightly seedy, place has twin bars, plank floors, and a good sound system playing contemporary rock. They have four types of beer on tap and feature regular drink specials. Open daily noon to 5am, it's busy and fun—if you avoid the headache-inducing concoctions from the frozen drink machine.

U Fleků. Křemencova 11, Praha 2. ☎ **02/2491 5118.** Metro: Národní třída.

Originally a brewery dating back to 1459, U Fleků is Prague's most famous beer hall, and one of the only pubs that still brews its own beer. This huge place has a myriad of timber-lined rooms and a large, loud courtyard where an oompah band performs. Tourists come here by the busload, so U Fleků is avoided by disparaging locals who don't like its German atmosphere anyway. The pub's special dark beer is excellent, however, and not available anywhere else. Open daily 9am to 11pm.

U Zlatého tygra. Husova 17, Praha 1. ☎ **02/2222 1111.** Metro: Staroměstská or Můstek.

One of the most famous Czech pubs, At the Golden Tiger was a favorite watering hole of President Havel and the late writer Bohumil Hrabal. Particularly smoky, and not especially tourist friendly, this place is a one-stop education in Czech culture. Havel and President Bill Clinton joined Hrabal for a traditional Czech pub evening here during Clinton's 1994 visit to Prague. It's open daily 3pm to 10:30pm.

GAY & LESBIAN BARS

For details on the gay and lesbian community, call the **SOHO Infocentrum** at ☎ **02/2422 0327.** For a stylish place to dance, try **Radost F/X** (see "The Club & Music Scene," above).

"A" Klub Milíčova 32. Praha 3. No phone. Cover 25Kč (75¢). Metro: Flora, then tram 9.

Lesbians should look for this sharply decorated bar, covered with the works of female artists and sporting cushy chairs and couches. Friday's are only for women. Men are allowed on other nights, but only in the company of a woman. There's dancing and relaxed chat here daily 6pm to 6am.

Fire Club. Seifertova 3, Praha 3. No phone. No cover. Metro: Hlavní nádraží.

Just across the tracks from the main train station is the Fire Club, which used to be the rock palace Alterna Komotovka. It has been transformed into a wild pink-and-neon cavern serving an almost exclusively gay crowd, offering original Budweiser on tap. It's open Friday and Saturday 9pm until whenever they feel like closing.

CASINOS

Prague has many casinos, most offering blackjack, roulette, and slot machines. House rules are usually similar to those in Las Vegas. **Casino Palais Savarin,** Na Příkopě 10 (☎ **02/2422 1636;** metro: Můstek), occupying a former rococo palace, is the city's most beautiful game room, open daily 1pm to 4am. Other recommended casinos are **Casino de France,** in the Hotel Hilton Atrium, Pobřežní 1 (☎ **02/2481 0988**), open daily 2pm to 6am; and **Casino U Nováků,** Vodičkova 30 (☎ **02/2416 2427**), open daily 1pm to 5am.

DAY TRIPS FROM PRAGUE
KARLŠTEJN CASTLE By far the most popular day trip from Prague, this medieval castle, 18 miles southwest of Prague, was built by Charles IV in the 14th century to safeguard the crown jewels of the Holy Roman Empire. As you approach the castle, which has been restored to its original state, little can prepare you for your first view: a spectacular Disney-like castle perched high on a hill, surrounded by lush forests and vineyards. The **Holy Rood Chapel** is famous for the more than 2,000 precious and semiprecious inlaid gems that adorn its walls, and the **Chapel of St. Catherine** was King Karel IV's private oratory. (*Warning:* Both chapels were closed for a short time last year; it might be worth checking ahead to make sure that they will be open during your visit.) Both the **Audience Hall** and the **Imperial Bedroom** are impressive, despite being stripped of their original furnishings.

Admission is 100Kč ($3.05) for adults and 50Kč ($1.50) for children. It's open daily May, June, and September 9am to noon and 12:30 to 6pm; July and August 9am to noon and 12:30 to 7pm; and November and December 9am to noon and 1 to 4pm.

The best way to get to Karlštejn is by **train** (there's no bus service). Most trains leave from Prague's Smíchov Station (at the Smíchovské nádraží metro stop) hourly throughout the day and take about 45 minutes to reach Karlštejn. The one-way second-class fare is 22Kč (65¢). You can also **drive:** Leave Prague from the southwest along Highway 4 in the direction of Strakonice and take the Karlštejn cutoff, following the signs (and traffic!).

KUTNÁ HORA   A medieval town that grew fantastically rich from the silver deposits beneath it, Kutná Hora, 45 miles east of Prague, is probably the second most popular day trip. The town's ancient heart is quite decayed, making it hard to believe that this was once the second most important city in Bohemia.

The main attraction is the enormous **St. Barbara's Cathedral (Chrám sv. Barbory)** at the southwestern edge of town. The cathedral's soaring arches, dozens of spires, and intricate designs raise expectations that the interior will be just as impressive—and you won't be disappointed. On entering (you have to enter from the side, not the front), you see several richly decorated frescoes full of symbols denoting the town's two main industries of mining and minting. Admission is 40Kč ($1.20) for adults and 20Kč (65¢) for children. It's open Tuesday to Sunday 9am to noon and 1 to 5pm.

When you leave the cathedral, head down the statue-lined **Barborská street,** where you'll pass the early **Baroque Jesuit College** built in the late 17th century.

A visit to Kutná Hora isn't complete without a trip to ✪ **Kostnice,** the "bone church." It's located a mile down the road in Sedlec; those who don't want to walk can board a local bus on Masarykova street; the fare is 6Kč (20¢). From the outside, Kostnice looks like most other Gothic churches. But once you go inside, you know this is no ordinary church. All the decorations, designed by František Rint, are made from human bones. The bones came from victims of the 14th-century plague and the 15th-century Hussite wars; both events left thousands of dead, who were buried in mass graves. As the area developed, the bones were uncovered, and the local monks came up with this idea.

Admission is a bargain at 25Kč (75¢) for adults and 10Kč (30¢) for children. It's open July and August, daily 9am to noon and 1 to 5pm; the rest of the year, Tuesday to Sunday 9am to noon and 1 to 4pm.

The **bus** departs from the terminal at Prague's Želivského metro station and takes about an hour. The 50-minute **drive** from Prague is relatively easy. Take Vinohradská ulice, which runs due east from behind the National Museum at the top of Wenceslas Square, straight to Kutná Hora. Once out of the city, the road turns into Highway 333.

TEREZÍN (THERESIENSTADT)   The name Terezín (*Theresienstadt* in German) occupies a unique place in the atrocious history of Nazism. This former Austro-Hungarian imperial fortress turned concentration camp, 30 miles northwest of Prague, witnessed no gas chambers, mass machine-gun executions, or medical testing; it was used instead as a transit camp. About 140,000 people passed though Terezín's gates; many died here, and more than half ended up at the death camps of Auschwitz and Treblinka.

Terezín will live in infamy for the cruel trick played by SS chief Heinrich Himmler. On June 23, 1944, three foreign observers came to Terezín to find out if the rumors of Nazi atrocities were true. They left under the impression that all was well, duped by a carefully planned "beautification" of the camp. So the observers wouldn't think the camp was overcrowded, the Nazis transported some 7,500 of the sick and elderly to

Auschwitz. The trick worked so well that the Nazis made a film of the camp while it was still "self-governing," called *A Town Presented to the Jews from the Fuehrer.* Terezín was liberated by Russian forces on May 10, 1945, 8 days after Berlin had fallen to the Allies.

Today, Terezín stands as a memorial to the dead and a monument to human depravity. Once inside the **Major Fortress,** you'll immediately be struck by its drab, plain streets. Just off the main square lies the **Museum of the Ghetto,** chronicling the rise of Nazism and life in the camp. English pamphlets describing the exhibits are provided. Admission is 50Kč ($1.50) for adults and 25Kč (75¢) for children. A ticket to enter both the Major and Minor Fortresses is 100Kč ($3.05) for adults and 50Kč ($1.50) for children. The Major Fortress is open daily 9am to 6pm. The **Minor Fortress** is about a 10-minute walk from the Major Fortress over the Ohře River. Just in front of the fortress's main entrance is the **National Cemetery (Národní hřbitov),** where the bodies exhumed from the mass graves were buried. As you enter the main gate, the sign above it, *Arbeit Macht Frei* ("Work Sets One Free"), sets a gloomy tone. You can walk through the prison barracks, execution grounds, workshops, and isolation cells.

Terezín is a 45-minute **drive** from Prague, on the main highway that leads north out of Prague and goes to Berlin via Dresden. Six **buses** leave daily from Florenc Bus Station (metro line C) for the 1-hour trip. The Prague-based **Wittman Tours** (☎ 02/ 2481 2325) offers a bus tour to Terezín that costs 950Kč ($28.70), 550Kč ($16.60) for students. Call for times.

2 West Bohemia & the Spas

by Alan Crosby

The Czech Republic is composed of two regions: Bohemia and Moravia. The bigger of the two, Bohemia, occupying the central and western areas of the country, has for centuries been caught between a rock (Germany) and a hard place (the Austrian Empire). Bohemia was almost always in the center of regional conflicts, both secular and religious. But the area also flourished, as witnessed by the wealth of castles that dot the countryside and the spa towns that were once the playgrounds of the rich and famous.

Although Bohemia is historically undivided, there are clear-cut distinctions in the region's geography that make going from town to town easier if you "cut" Bohemia into sections. This section focuses on west Bohemia, home to the country's spa towns. It's also one of the few regions in the Czech Republic where a full-blown tourist infrastructure is already in place. Its main towns—Karlovy Vary (Carlsbad), Mariánské Lázně (Marienbad), and to a lesser extent Plzeň and Cheb—offer a wide array of accommodations, restaurants, and services. All are constantly being reconstructed, renovated, and restored.

A relatively inexpensive network of trains and buses covers the region. West Bohemia is generally rougher terrain, so only serious cyclists should consider touring the area on two wheels. For those with a car, the highways can range from top-notch, such as the newly built Prague-Plzeň motorway, to an asphalt horror ride such as the Prague–Karlovy Vary route. Roads generally are much slower than in Western Europe, so leave yourself plenty of time. Gas stations are constantly springing up, so stops for food and fuel are rarely hard to come by. Please note that if you drive the D-5 (Prague-Plzeň) and D-1 (Prague-Brno) highways, your car must display the country's highway sticker; these stickers, which you can buy at most every gas station and border crossing, cost 800Kč ($24.25) and save you from being hassled by the police.

Most towns are distant enough that you should drive from one to another. However, if you'd rather stay in one place and make day trips, I'd recommend staying in Karlovy Vary and then taking excursions from there. The **Kur-Info Vřídelní Kolonáda,** 360 01 Karlovy Vary (☎ **017/322 9312** or **322 4097;** fax 017/246 67) can provide information on bus trips to Mariánské Lázně and other regional sights.

Only in West Bohemia

Relaxing at Karlovy Vary and Mariánské Lázně These two spas are excellent examples of what was once central Europe's resort area. You can enjoy hot springs that offer everything from drinking samples to body treatments.

Drinking the Original Pilsner Pilsner Urquell and Budvar, two of the world's best and most famous beers, come from Bohemia, from the city of Plzeň in the west and České Budějovice in the south, respectively.

Touring Český Krumlov Bohemia's second largest castle is one of the most celebrated in Europe.

KARLOVY VARY (CARLSBAD)

The discovery of Karlovy Vary (Carlsbad), 75 miles west of Prague, by Charles IV reads something like a 14th-century episode of *The Beverly Hillbillies.* According to local lore, the king was out huntin' for some food when up from the ground came a-bubblin' water (although discovered by his dogs, not an errant gunshot). Knowing a good thing when he saw it, Charles immediately set to work building a small castle, naming the town that evolved around it Karlovy Vary (Charles's Boiling Place). The first spa buildings were built in 1522, and before long, notables like Albrecht of Wallenstein, Russian Czar Peter the Great, and later Bach, Beethoven, Freud, and Marx all came to take the waters.

After World War II, East Bloc travelers (following in the footsteps of Marx, no doubt) discovered the town, and Karlovy Vary became a destination for the proletariat. On doctor's orders, most workers enjoyed regular stays of 2 or 3 weeks, letting the mineral waters ranging from 43.5° to 72° Celsius (110.3° to 161.6° Fahrenheit) from the town's 12 spas heal their tired and broken bodies. Even now, most spa guests are there by doctor's prescription.

But most of the 40-plus years of communist neglect—they even excised most of the social aspect of spa-going and turned it into a science—have been erased by a barrage of renovators who are restoring almost all the spa's former glory. Gone is the statue of Yuri Gagarin, the Russian cosmonaut. Gone are almost all the crumbling building facades that used to line both sides of the river. In their place now stand restored buildings, cherubs, caryatids, and more.

Nearly 100,000 people travel annually to the spa resort to sip, bathe, and frolic. Most enjoy the 13th spring, a hearty herb-and-mineral liqueur called Becherovka, more than the 12 nonalcoholic versions. Czechs will tell you that all have medicinal benefits.

ESSENTIALS

ARRIVING **By Train** *At all costs, avoid the train from Prague,* which takes over 4 hours on a circuitous route. If you're arriving from another direction, Karlovy Vary's main train station is connected to the town center by bus no. 13.

By Bus Frequent express buses make the trip from Prague's Florenc station to Karlovy Vary's náměstí Dr. M. Horákové in about 2½ hours. Buses leave from platform 21 or

Bohemia

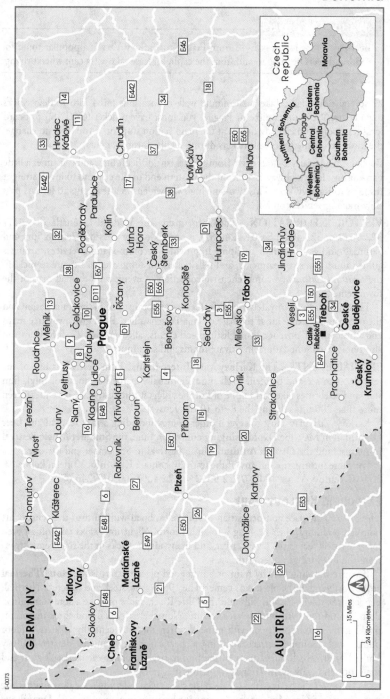

Warning to Drivers

Be warned that highway E-48 from Prague to Karlovy Vary is a popular route for reckless drivers heading to and from the capital. Please take extra care when driving.

---

22 several times daily. Take a 10-minute walk or local bus no. 4 into Karlovy Vary's town center. Note that unlike in Prague, you must have a ticket (6Kč/20¢) to board local transport. You can buy tickets at the main station stop, or, if you have no change, the kiosk across the street sells tickets during regular business hours.

By Car The nearly 2-hour drive from Prague isn't difficult but can be at times a little hair-raising. Take highway E-48 from the western end of the city and follow it straight through to Karlovy Vary. This two-lane highway widens in a few spots to let cars pass slow-moving vehicles on hills.

VISITOR INFORMATION **Kuri-Info,** inside the Vřídelní kolonáda (☎ **017/ 322 9312** or 322 4097; fax 017/246 67), is open Monday to Friday 7am to 5pm and Saturday and Sunday 9am to 3pm. It provides accommodation services, arranges guided tours and spa treatments, and sells tickets for some events. Be sure to pick up the *Cultural Calendar,* a comprehensive collection of events with a small map of the town center.

There are also two privately run **Info-Centrum** booths: one in the train station and the other in a parking lot at the base of Jana Palacha ulice. Both give away free maps and a brochure of current cultural listings and events called *Promenáda.* Info-Centrum also books accommodations in private rooms and sells tours.

SPECIAL EVENTS The **Karlovy Vary International Film Festival** is one of the few places to see and be seen. Each summer (usually at the beginning of July), film stars and celebrities take part in one of Europe's biggest film festivals. Six venues screen more than 200 films during the 8- to 10-day festival.

Karlovy Vary plays host to several other events, including a **jazz festival** and **beer Olympiad** in May, the **Dvořák singing contest** in June, the **Summer Music Festival** in August, and the **Dvořák Autumn Music Festival** in September and October.

For more information on any of the festivals, contact **Kur-Info,** Vřídelní kolonáda, 360–01 Karlovy Vary (☎ **017/322 9312** or 322 4097; fax 017/246 67).

EXPLORING KARLOVY VARY

The town's slow pace and pedestrian promenades, lined with turn-of-the-century art nouveau buildings, turn strolling into an art form. Nighttime walks take on an even more mystical feel as the sewers, river, and many major cracks in the roads emit steam from the hot springs underneath.

If you're traveling here by train or bus, a good place to start is the **Hotel Thermal** at the north end of the old town's center. The 1960s glass, steel, and concrete Thermal, between the town's eastern hills and the Ohře River, sticks out like a sore communist thumb amid the 19th-century architecture. Nonetheless, you'll find three important places here: its outdoor pool with mineral water, the only centrally located outdoor public pool; its upper terrace, boasting a spectacular view; and its theater, Karlovy Vary's largest, which holds many of the film festival's premier events. Look at it, and then turn and walk away. Try not to picture it again.

As you enter the heart of the town on the river's west side, you'll see the ornate white wrought-iron **Sadová kolonáda** adorning the beautifully manicured park **Dvořákovy sady.** Continue following the river, and about 100 meters later you'll encounter the

Mlýnská kolonáda, a long, covered walkway housing several Karlovy Vary springs, which you can sample 24 hours a day. Each spring has a plaque beside it telling which mineral elements are present and the temperature of the water. Bring your own cup or buy one just about anywhere to sip the waters since most are too hot to drink from your hands. Remember, some springs are rather hot.

When you hit the river bend, the majestic **Church of St. Mary Magdalene** sits perched atop a hill, overlooking the **Vřídlo,** the hottest spring in town. Built in 1736, the church is the work of Kilian Ignac Dientzenhofer, who also created two of Prague's more notable churches—both named St. Nicholas. Housing Vřídlo, which blasts water some 50 feet into the air, is the glass building where the statue of Soviet astronaut Gagarin once stood. (Gagarin's statue has since made a safe landing at the Karlovy Vary airport.) Now called the **Vřídelní kolonáda,** the structure, built in 1974, houses several hot springs you can sample for free. The building also holds the Kuri-Info information center and several kiosks selling postcards, stone roses, and drinking cups.

Heading away from the Vřídelní kolonáda are Stará and Nová Louka streets, which line either side of the river. Along **Stará (Old) Louka** you'll find several fine cafes and glass and crystal shops. **Nová (New) Louka** is lined with hotels and the historic town's main theater, currently under reconstruction.

Both streets lead to the **Grandhotel Pupp.** After a massive reconstruction, the Pupp is once again the crown jewel of the town. Gone are the effects of nearly 50 years of communism (it was temporarily called the Grand Hotel Moskva); once again, splendor radiates from its restored facade. Regardless of capitalism or communism, the Pupp remains what it always was: the grand dame of hotels in the area. Once catering to nobility from all over central Europe, the Pupp still houses one of the town's finest restaurants, the Grand, and its grounds are a favorite with the hiking crowd. The reconstruction has also brought with it a plethora of designer shops catering to those who just don't know what to wear.

If you still have the energy, atop the hill behind the Pupp stands the **Diana Lookout Tower.** Footpaths leading through the forests eventually spit you out at the base of the tower, as if to say, "Ha, the trip is only half over." The five-story climb up the tower tests your stamina, but the view of the town is more than worth it. For those who aren't up to the climb just to get to the tower, a cable car runs to the tower every 15 minutes or so.

THE SHOPPING SCENE

Crystal and porcelain are Karlovy Vary's other claims to fame. Dozens of shops throughout town sell everything from plates to chandeliers.

Ludvík Moser founded his first glassware shop in 1857 and soon became one of the country's foremost names in glass. Now his name can be found in almost every store along the river. Many of the stores will pack and ship your purchases either back to Prague or all the way home. I recommend comparison shopping as prices can sometimes vary greatly for similar items.

WHERE TO STAY

Private rooms used to be the best places to stay in Karlovy Vary for both quality and price, but this is changing as more and more hotels renovate and raise standards—as well as prices. Private accommodation can still provide better value, but it takes a little extra work. If you want to arrange a room, try the **Info-Centrum** (see "Visitor Information," above). Expect to pay about 500Kč to 1,000Kč ($15 to $30) for a single and 750Kč to 1,200Kč ($23 to $36) for a double.

Spa Cures & Treatments

Most visitors to Karlovy Vary come specifically to get a spa treatment, a therapy that lasts 1 to 3 weeks. After consulting with a spa physician, guests are given a regimen of activities that may include mineral baths, massages, waxings, mud packs, electrotherapy, and pure oxygen inhalation. After spending the morning at a spa or sanatorium, guests are then usually directed to walk the paths of the town's surrounding forest.

The common denominator of all the cures is an ample daily dose of hot mineral water, which bubbles up from 12 springs. This water definitely has a distinct odor and taste. You'll see people chugging it down, but it doesn't necessarily taste very good. Some thermal springs actually taste and smell like rotten eggs. You might want to take a small sip at first.

You'll also notice that almost everyone in town seems to be carrying "the cup," basically a mug with a built-in straw that runs through the handle. Young and old alike parade through town with their mugs, filling and refilling them at each new thermal water tap. You can buy these mugs everywhere for as little as 50Kč ($1.50) or as much as 500Kč ($15); they make a quirky souvenir. *Be warned:* None of the mugs can make the hot springs taste any better!

The minimum spa treatment lasts 1 week and must be arranged in advance. A package traditionally includes room, full board, and complete therapy regimen; the cost varies from about $40 to $100 per person per day, depending on the season and facilities. Rates are highest from May to September and lowest from November to February. For information and reservations in Prague, contact **Čedok,** Na příkopě 18 and Václavské nám. 24, Praha 1 (☎ **02/2419 7111;** fax 02/2421 0502). Many hotels also offer spa and health treatments, so ask when you book your room. Most will happily arrange a treatment if they don't provide it directly.

Visitors to Karlovy Vary for just a day or two can experience the waters on an "outpatient" basis. The **State Baths III** (☎ 017/256 41) welcomes day-trippers with mineral baths, massages, saunas, and a cold pool. It's open for men on Tuesday, Thursday, and Saturday and for women on Monday, Wednesday, and Friday 7:45am to 3pm. **Vojenský lázeňský ústav,** Mlýnské nábřeží 7 (☎ **017/ 311 9111**), offers similar services and costs about 500Kč ($15) per day.

Some of the town's major spa hotels accommodate only those who are paying for complete treatment, unless their occupancy rates are particularly low. The hotels I've listed below accept guests for stays of any length.

Grandhotel Pupp. Mírové nám. 2, 360 91, Karlovy Vary. ☎ **017/310 9111.** Fax 017/322 4032. 110 units. MINIBAR TV TEL. 5,445Kč ($165) double deluxe; 7,165Kč ($215) studio deluxe; 10,500Kč ($315) apt; 13,333Kč ($400) Imperial apt; 27,830Kč ($835) Presidential apt. Breakfast not included (extra $11). AE, DC, MC, V.

Well known as one of Karlovy Vary's best hotels, the Pupp, built in 1701, is also one of Europe's oldest. While the hotel's public areas ooze with splendor and charm, the guest rooms aren't as consistently enchanting. The best rooms tend to be those that face toward the town center and are on the upper floors; these rooms have good views and sturdy wooden furniture. The hotel's Grand Restaurant serves up as grand a dining room as you'll find, with the food to match (see "Where to Dine," below).

Hotel Dvořák. Nová Louka 11, 360 21, Karlovy Vary. ☎ **017/322 4145.** Fax 017/ 322 2814. 79 units. MINIBAR TV TEL. 3,500–5,400Kč ($106–$164) double. AE, DC, MC, V.

Now part of the Vienna International hotel/resort chain, the Dvořák has improved immensely over the past year or two, especially in terms of service. If the Pupp has the history and elegance, the Dvořák has the facilities, including a well-equipped fitness center, a sauna, and an indoor pool.

Hotel Embassy. Nová Louka 21, 360 01, Karlovy Vary. ☎ **017/322 1161-5.** Fax 017/ 322 3146. 11 units. TV TEL. 2,730–3370Kč ($82–$102) double; 3,000–3,666Kč ($90–$110) double deluxe; 3,500–4,335Kč ($105–$130) apt. Breakfast and parking included. AE, V.

This family-run hotel manages to evoke the turn of the century with elegantly decorated rooms. Although smaller than those at the Pupp, the rooms are impeccably furnished with windows that overlook the river. The restaurant downstairs is where a lot of movers and shakers at the Karlovy Vary film festival get away from the glitz and get down to business.

Parkhotel Pupp. Mírové nám. 2, 360 91, Karlovy Vary. ☎ **017/310 9111.** Fax 017/ 322 4032. 114 units. MINIBAR TV TEL. 3300Kč ($100) double; 4,300Kč ($130) apt. Breakfast not included (extra $8). AE, DC, MC, V.

This is how the other half live at the Pupp. At four stars, this wing of the Grandhotel Pupp is housed within the same complex as its five-star cousin, but a world apart in terms of frills—and price. Still, the rooms are large and all of the same facilities are available; the views are just less spectacular.

WHERE TO DINE

Embassy. Nová Louka 21. ☎ **017/322 1161.** Reservations recommended. Main courses 145–895Kč ($4.40–$27.10). AE, V. Daily 10am–11pm. CZECH/CONTINENTAL.

On the ground floor of the hotel with the same name, the Embassy restaurant has two sides—a pub on one side and an intimate dining room on the other. On a cold day the pub works wonders with a hearty goulash soup. But the dining is the Embassy's hidden treasure. What the meals lack in flair, they more than make up for with sophistication. Salmon with a delicate dill sauce or beef with a surprisingly light mushroom sauce are two of the choices that set this restaurant apart.

Grand Restaurant. In the Grandhotel Pupp, Mírové nám. 2. ☎ **017/310 9111.** Reservations recommended. Main courses 240–1,100Kč ($7.30–$33). AE, V. Daily noon–3pm and 6–11pm. CONTINENTAL.

It's no surprise that the Grandhotel Pupp has the nicest dining room in town, an elegant affair with tall ceilings, huge mirrors, and glistening chandeliers. A large menu gives way to larger portions of salmon, chicken, veal, pork, turkey, and beef in a variety of heavy and heavier sauces. Even the trout with mushrooms is smothered in butter sauce.

Hospoda U Šejka. Stará Louka 10. No phone. Main courses 99–214Kč ($3–$6.50); beer 20Kč (60¢). MC, V. Daily 11am–11pm. CZECH.

A new addition to the pub scene, U Šejka plays on the tried and true Good Soldier Svejk tourist theme. Luckily the tourist trap goes no further, and once inside, you find a refreshingly unsmoky although thoroughly Czech atmosphere. Locals and tourists alike rub elbows while throwing back some fine lager and standard pub favorites, such as goulash and beef tenderloin in cream sauce.

✪ **Promenáda.** Tržiště 31. ☎ **017/322 5648.** Reservations highly recommended. Main courses 139–498Kč ($4.20–$15.10). AE, V. Daily noon–11pm. CZECH/CONTINENTAL.

This intimate spot may not be as elegant as the Grand, but for Karlovy Vary residents, it has become one of *the* places to dine. Across from the Vřídelní kolonáda, the Promenáda serves the best food around, offering a wide selection of generous portions. The daily menu usually includes well-prepared wild game, but the mixed grill for two or the chateaubriand, both flambéed at the table, are the chef's best dishes.

MARIÁNSKÉ LÁZNĚ (MARIENBAD)

When Thomas Alva Edison visited Mariánské Lázně in the late 1800s, he proclaimed, "There is no more beautiful spa in all the world." The town is 29 miles southwest of Karlovy Vary and 100 miles west of Prague.

While the spa town stands in the shadow of the Czech Republic's most famous spa town, Karlovy Vary, it wasn't always that way. First mentioned in 1528, the town's mineral waters gained prominence at the end of the 18th century and the beginning of the 19th. Nestled among forested hills and packed with romantic and elegant pastel hotels and spa houses, the town, commonly known by its German name, Marienbad, has played host to such luminaries as Goethe (where his love for Ulrika von Levetzow took root), Mark Twain, composers Chopin, Strauss, and Wagner, as well as Freud and Kafka. England's Edward VII found the spa resort so enchanting he visited nine times and even commissioned the building of the country's first golf club.

ESSENTIALS

ARRIVING   By Train   The express train from Prague takes just over 3 hours, costing 165Kč ($4.85) for first class; 110Kč ($3.25) for second class. Mariánské Lázně train station, Nádražní nám. 292 (☎ **0165/625 321**), is south of the town center; take bus no. 5 into town.

By Bus   The 3-hour bus trip from Prague costs 120Kč ($3.65). The Mariánské Lázně bus station is adjacent to the train station on Nádražní náměstí; take bus no. 5 into town.

By Car   Driving from Prague, take E-50 through Plzeň to Stříbro—about 14 miles past Plzeň—and head northwest on highway 21. The clearly marked route can take up to 2 hours. From Karlovy Vary, the trip is about 50 miles. Take highway 20 south and then turn right onto highway 24 in the town of Bečov.

VISITOR INFORMATION   Along the main strip lies **Infocentrum KaSS,** Dům Chopin, Hlavní 47, 353 01, Mariánské Lázně (☎ and fax **0165/622 474** or 0165/5892). In addition to dispensing advice, the staff sells maps and concert tickets and can arrange accommodations in hotels and private homes. It's open Monday to Friday 7am to 7pm and Saturday and Sunday 9am to 6pm.

SPECIAL EVENTS   Mariánské Lázně honors one of its frequent visitors, Chopin, with a yearly festival devoted to the Polish composer and his works. The **Chopin Festival** usually runs for 8 to 10 days near the end of August. Tickets range from 70Kč to 1,500Kč ($2.10 to $45.45).

Each June, the town also plays host to a **classical music festival** featuring many of the Czech Republic's finest musicians, as well as those from around the world. For more information or ticket reservations for either event, contact **Infocentrum KaSS** (see "Visitor Information," above).

Patriotic Americans can show up on **July 4** for a little down-home fun, including a parade and other flag-waving special events commemorating the town's liberation by U.S. soldiers in World War II.

Taking the Waters at Mariánské Lázně

When walking through the town, it's almost impossible to miss the **Lázeňská Kolonáda,** just off Skalníkovy sady. From Hlavní třída, walk east on Vrchlického ulice. Recently restored to its former glory, the eye-catching cast-iron and glass colonnade is adorned with ceiling frescoes and Corinthian columns. Built in 1889, it connects a half-dozen major springs in the town center; this is the focal point of those partaking in the ritual. Bring a cup to fill or, if you want to fit in with the thousands of guests who are serious about their spa water, buy one of the porcelain mugs with a built-in straw that are offered just about everywhere. Do keep in mind that the waters are used to treat internal disorders, so the minerals may act to cleanse the body thoroughly. You can wander the colonnade any time; water is distributed daily 6am to noon and 4 to 6pm.

For a relaxing mineral bubble bath or massage, make reservations through the **Spa Information Service,** Mírové nám. 104, 353 29, Mariánské Lázně (☎ **0165/ 655 555** or 655 550; fax 0165/655 500). Also ask at your hotel about spa treatments and massages they offer or can arrange. Treatments cost from 300Kč ($9.10) and up.

More to See & Do

There's not much town history, since Mariánské Lázně officially came into existence only in 1808, but engaging brevity is what makes the two-story **Muzeum hlavního města (City Museum),** Goetheovo nám. 11 (☎ **0165/622 740**), recommendable. Chronologically arranged displays include photos and documents of famous visitors. Goethe slept in the upstairs rooms in 1823, when he was 74 years old. If you ask nicely, the museum guards will play an English-language tape that describes the contents of each of the rooms. You can also request to see the museum's English-language film about the town. Admission is 20Kč (60¢), and it's open Tuesday to Sunday 9am to 4pm.

You can also take a walk in the woods. The surrounding **Slavkovský les (Slavkov Forest)** has about 70 kilometers of marked footpaths and trails through the area's gentle hills.

The **Mariánské Lázně Golf Club** (☎ **0165/624 300**), a 6,195-meter, par-72 championship course, lies on the edge of town. The club takes pay-as-you-play golfers, and a fully equipped pro shop rents clubs. Greens fees are 1,200Kč ($36.35) and club rental is 500Kč ($15.15).

Where to Stay

The main strip along **Hlavní třída** is lined with hotels, many with rooms facing the colonnade. If you feel comfortable about doing this, I suggest walking the street and shopping around for a room; most hotels charge from 2,000Kč to 3,500Kč ($61 to $106) for a double May to September. Off-season prices can fall by as much as half.

For private accommodations, try **Palackého ulice,** running south of the main spa area.

Hotel Golf. Zádub 55, 353 01 Mariánské Lázně. ☎ **0165/622 651.** Fax 0165/622 655. 28 units. MINIBAR TV TEL. 2,220–3,540Kč ($67–$107) double; 4,230–5,460kč ($127–$164) suite. Rates include breakfast. AE, DC, MC, V.

One of the more luxurious hotels, the Golf isn't actually in town but across from the golf course about 2 miles down the road leading to Karlovy Vary. This hotel is busy, so reservations are recommended. The English-speaking staff delivers on their pledge to cater to every wish. The rooms are bright and spacious, with an excellent restaurant and terrace on the first floor. Not surprisingly, the staff can help arrange a quick 18 holes across the street. The hotel has also recently opened its own spa center. In the winter, the golf course is used freely by cross-country skiers.

✪ **Hotel Koliba.** Dusíkova 592, 353 01 Mariánské Lázně. ☎ **0165/625 169.** Fax 0165/763 10. 10 units. MINIBAR TV TEL. 1,200–1,470Kč ($36–$45) double. AE, MC, V.

Away from the main strip but still only a 7-minute walk from the colonnade, the Koliba is a rustic hunting lodge set in the hills on Dusíkova, the road leading to the golf course and Karlovy Vary. The rooms are very comfortable. The hotel offers a wide array of spa and health treatments, which cost extra. A small hill directly outside the hotel, serviced by two ski lifts, is perfect for teaching the children how to ski or for a romantic cross-country skiing weekend.

Hotel Palace. Hlavní třída 67, 353 01 Mariánské Lázně. ☎ **0165/622 222.** Fax 0165/624 262. 45 units. MINIBAR TV TEL. 2,150–3,570 Kč ($65–$108) double; 2,810–5,100 ($85–$155) suite. AE, DC, MC, V.

The 1920s Palace is a beautiful art nouveau–style hotel just 300 feet from the colonnade. Although the rooms are not tremendously spacious, they are comfortable and tastefully, almost regally, decorated with turn-of-the-century furniture and lavish curtains and chandeliers. In addition to a good Bohemian restaurant with one of the nicest terraces in town, the hotel contains a cafe, wine room, and snack bar.

Hotel Villa Butterfly. Hlavní třída 72, 353 01 Mariánské Lázně. ☎ **0165/6201.** Fax 0165/626 210. 94 units. MINIBAR TV TEL. 2,100–3,300Kč ($64–$100) double; 3,250–5,400Kč ($98–$164) suite; 4,500–7,200Kč ($136–$218) apt. Rates include breakfast. AE, DC, MC, V.

The Butterfly has upgraded its rather ordinary rooms into 94 first-rate spacious living quarters. In fact, from the front hall to the fitness room and down to its underground parking, the Butterfly has really taken off. Oddly enough, the renovations, which must've cost a lot, have had a reverse effect on the hotel's prices, now a good 15% lower. An English-speaking staff and a good selection of foreign-language newspapers at the reception are added bonuses, as is one of the better cups of coffee in town at the ground floor cafe.

Hotel Zvon. Hlavní třída 68, 353 01 Mariánské Lázně. ☎ **0165/622 015.** Fax 0165/623 245. 79 units. MINIBAR TV TEL. 1,720–6,720Kč ($52–$202) double; 2,370–8,460Kč ($72–$204) suite. Prices depend on the season. AE, DC, MC, V.

Next door to the Palace, in a prime spot directly across from the colonnade, the Zvon lacks a bit of the panache that its smaller neighbor has, but it still ranks as one of the town's nicer hotels. Ask for a room that faces out over the Kolonada. Not only is the view spectacular, the rooms on this side tend to be larger and brighter.

WHERE TO DINE

Churchill Club Restaurant. Hlavní třída 121. No phone. Main courses 120–400Kč ($3.65–$12.10). MC, V. Daily 11am–11pm. CZECH.

A lively bar atmosphere makes the Churchill one of the few fun places to be after dark. Don't let the name fool you—the food is traditional Czech with few surprises, which is both good and bad. A large selection of beers also sets the Churchill apart from other places along the main strip.

✪ **Hotel Koliba Restaurant.** Dusíkova 592. ☎ **0165/625 169.** Reservations recommended. Main courses 85–385Kč ($2.60–$11.65). No credit cards. Daily 11am–11pm. CZECH.

Like the hotel it occupies, the Koliba restaurant is a shrine to the outdoors. The rustic dining room, centered on an open fire grill, boasts a hearty rustic atmosphere that goes perfectly with the restaurant's strength: wild game. Check the daily menu to see what's new or choose from the wide assortment of specialties *na roštu* (from the grill), including wild boar and venison. The second room off the dining area makes for a great lunch stop, especially on a cold winter day when the fireplace is roaring.

Restaurant Fontaine. In the Villa Butterfly, Hlavní třída 72. ☎ **0165/626 201.** Main courses 90–290Kč ($2.75–$8.80). AE, DC, MC, V. Daily 6–11pm. CZECH/INTERNATIONAL.

The restaurant has undergone a major transformation for the better. The dining room is large but remains quiet, although a little too well lit. Bow-tied waiters serve traditional Bohemian specialties, like succulent roast duck, boiled trout, and chateaubriand, as well as some inventive variations such as shark.

PLZEŇ (PILSEN)

Some 400 years ago, a group of men formed Plzeň's first beer-drinking guild, and today, beer is probably the only reason you'll want to stop at this industrial town 55 miles southwest of Prague. Alas, the town's prosperity and architecture were ravaged during World War II, leaving few buildings untouched. The main square, náměstí Republiky, is worth a look, but after that, there's not much to see.

ESSENTIALS

ARRIVING   By Train   It's more comfortable taking the train to Plzeň than the bus, although a lot slower now that the motorway connects the city to Prague. A fast train from Prague gets you to Plzeň in just under 2 hours. Trains between the two cities are plentiful and fit most every schedule. The train fare costs 84Kč ($2.55) first class or 56Kč ($1.70) second. To get from the train station to town, walk out the main entrance and take Americká street across the river, and then turn right onto Jungmannova, which leads to the main square.

By Bus   The bus from Prague takes about an hour and costs 69Kč ($2) but tends to be cramped. If you do take the bus, head back into town along Husova to get to the square.

By Car   A newly finished highway makes the drive between Prague and Plzeň, one of the few worry-free trips a motorist can make in the country. Go west from Prague on D-5 and 40 minutes later you'll be there.

VISITOR INFORMATION   The **City Information Center Plzeň,** náměstí Republiky 41, 301 16 Plzeň (☎ **019/723 6535;** fax 019/722 4473), is packed with literature to answer travelers' questions. A helpful, multilingual staff will also point you in the right direction. Open Monday to Friday 10am to 5pm and Saturday and Sunday 10am to 3:30pm.

SPECIAL EVENTS   If you're an American, or speak English, being in Plzeň in May is quite an experience. On May 8, Gen. George S. Patton was forced to halt his advance after liberating the area, in accordance with an Allied agreement to stop. The Russians were then allowed to "free" Prague, as agreed. Forty years of communist oppression, however, means that the town now celebrates May 8 or **Liberation Day** with a vengeance. Although the celebrations have cooled some from the heady days just after the Velvet Revolution of 1989, you'll still be fêted and praised into the wee hours, as the city's people give thanks to the forces that ended Nazi occupation.

Anxious to capitalize on its beer heritage and always happy to celebrate, Plzeň has started its own Oktoberfest, called **Pivní slavnosti.**

EXPLORING PLZEŇ

Founded in 1295 by Přemysl King Václav II, Plzeň was, and remains, western Bohemia's administrative center. Václav's real gift to the town, however, was granting it brewing rights. As a result, more than 200 microbreweries popped up in almost every street-corner basement. Realizing the brews they were drinking had become mostly inferior by the late 1830s, rebellious beer drinkers started demanding quality from their brewers. "Give us what we want in Plzeň, good and cheap beer!" became the battle cry. By 1842, the brewers had combined their expertise to produce a superior brew through what became known as the Pilsner brewing method.

Plzeňský Prazdroj (Pilsner Breweries), at U Prazdroje 7, will interest anyone who wants to learn more about the brewing process. It's actually made up of several breweries, pumping out brands like Pilsner Urquell and Gambrinus, the most widely consumed beer in the Czech Republic. The 1-hour tour of the factory (which has barely changed since its creation) includes a 15-minute film and visits to the fermentation cellars and brewing rooms. The tour is at 12:30pm Monday to Saturday. It costs 30Kč (90¢) Monday to Friday and 50Kč ($1.50) Saturday; the price includes a dozen beer-oriented postcards and a tasting of some freshly brewed beer (for details on other tours available, call ☎ **019/706 2017**).

If you didn't get your fill of beer facts at the brewery, the **Pivovarské muzeum (Beer Museum)** (☎ **019/722 4955**; fax 019/723 5574), is 1 block away on Veleslavínova. Inside this former 15th-century house, you'll learn everything there is to know about beer but were afraid to ask. In the first room, once a 19th-century pub, the guard winds up an old German polyphone music box from 1887 that plays the sweet though scratchy strains of Strauss's *Blue Danube*. Subsequent rooms display a wide collection of pub artifacts, brewing equipment, and mugs. Most displays have English captions, but ask for a more detailed museum description in English when you enter. Admission is 25Kč (75¢), and it's open daily from May to September 10am to 6pm; October through April, Tuesday to Sunday 10am to 6pm.

Now full of more brewing knowledge than you might have wanted, proceed to the main square to see what's hopping (sorry, I couldn't resist). Dominating the center is the Gothic **Cathedral of St. Bartholomew,** boasting the tallest steeple in the Czech Republic at 333 feet. Inside the church, a beautiful marble Madonna graces the main altar.

You'll see an Italian flair to the first four floors of the 16th-century **Town Hall** and in the *sgrafitto* adorning its facade. Later on, more floors were added, as well as a tower, gables, and brass flags, creating the illusion that another building had just fallen on top of the original. In front of the town hall, a 1681 **memorial** commemorates victims of the plague.

Just west of the square on Sady pětatřicátníků lies the shattered dreams of the 2,000 or so Jews who once called Plzeň home. The **Great Synagogue,** the world's third largest, was built in the late 19th century. Sadly, its doors remain locked, although funds are being raised to support urgent repairs.

WHERE TO STAY

For private rooms that are usually outside the town center but a little cheaper, try **Čedok** at Sedláčkova 12 (☎ **019/723 7419;** fax 722 3703), open Monday to Friday 9am to noon and 1 to 5pm (to 6pm in summer) and Saturday 9am to noon. Expect to pay about 500Kč to 1,000Kč ($15 to $30) for a double.

Hotel Central. Náměstí Republiky 33, 305 28 Plzeň. ☎ **019/722 6757** or 722 6059. Fax 019/722 6064. 50 units. TV. 1,200Kč ($36) double. AE, MC, V.

This rather sterile building is across from St. Bartholomew's Church and has generously given itself a four-star rating. The surly staff notwithstanding, the hotel is clean and quiet for such a central location. The rooms are very plain, but the beds are surprisingly comfortable. With few choices around, you could do worse than the Central.

Interhotel Continental. Zbrojnická 8, 305 34 Plzeň. ☎ **019/723 6479.** Fax 019/ 722 1746. 55 units (20 with shower only, 25 with bathroom). TV TEL. 1,460Kč ($44) double with shower only; 2,150Kč ($65) double with bathroom; 3,700Kč ($112) deluxe double. AE, MC, V.

About a block from the old town square, the modern Continental is considered by locals to be one of the best in town, but keep in mind that there's not much to choose from. Spacious, comfortable rooms are outfitted with velvet-covered furniture and blue-tiled bathrooms.

WHERE TO DINE

Městařská Beseda. Smetanovy sady 13. ☎ **019/723 6667.** Main courses 49– 170Kč ($1.50–$5.15). MC, V. Sun–Thurs 10am–11pm; Fri–Sat 10am–midnight. CZECH/ CONTINENTAL.

The high ceilings and wall murals add a touch of elegance to this large restaurant frequented by the theater crowd. The prices are reasonable for the center, but the meals are unimaginative. It's a great place to stop for a late-evening coffee and some strudel or for a nightcap.

Pilsner Urquell Restaurant. U Prazdroje 1 (just outside the brewery gates). No phone. Main courses 65–229Kč ($2–$7). AE, MC, V. Mon–Sat 10am–10pm. CZECH.

This isn't a visitor-oriented pub; in the same building that houses the brewery's management, the pub has remained true to its beer suppliers by cooking hearty basic Czech meals, although it has become a little pricey.

Restaurace Na Spilce (At the fermenting cellar). U Prazdroje (just inside the brewery gates). ☎ **019/706 2754.** Main courses 35–239Kč ($1.05–$7.25). AE, MC, V. Mon–Thurs 11am–10pm; Fri–Sat 11am–11pm; Sun 11am–9pm. CZECH.

The Na Spilce looks like a 600-seat tourist trap, but the food is quite good and reasonably priced. The standard *řízký* (schnitzels), goulash, and *svíčková na smetaně* (pork tenderloin in cream sauce) are hearty and complement the beer that flows from the brewery. If you've got a big appetite or just can't decide, try the Plzeňská Bašta, with ample servings of roasted pork, smoked pork, sausage, sauerkraut, and two kinds of dumplings.

CHEB (EGER) & FRANTIŠKOVY LÁZNĚ

As with Plzeň, few people who travel through Cheb, 105 miles west of Prague and 25 miles southwest of Karlovy Vary, actually stop and look around. From the outside, that's understandable, but it's too bad. The center of Cheb is one of the more architecturally interesting places in west Bohemia, and its history is fascinating as well.

A former stronghold for the Holy Roman Empire on its eastern flank, Eger, as it was then known, became part of Bohemia in 1322. Cheb stayed under Bohemian rule until it was handed to Germany as part of the 1938 Munich Pact. After World War II, it returned to Czech hands, when most of the area's native Germans, known as Sudeten Germans, were expelled for their open encouragement of the invading Nazis. This bilingual, bicultural heritage can be seen in the town's main square, which could easily sit on either side of the border if it weren't for the Czech writing on the windows. These days, the Germans have returned, but only for a few hours at a time, many for the town's thriving sex trade and cheap alcohol. Don't be surprised to see women around almost every corner looking to ply their trade. Still, Cheb is worth exploring for its melange of architectural styles, the eerie Jewish quarter Špalíček, and the enormous Romanesque Chebský Hrad (Cheb Castle).

Only about 20 minutes up the road from Cheb is the smallest of the three major west Bohemian spa towns, **Františkovy Lázně.** Although it pales in comparison to Karlovy Vary and Mariánské Lázně, Františkovy Lázně has taken great strides in the past few years to try to erase the decline it experienced under communism. There's not much to see save for the **Spa Museum,** which holds an interesting display of bathing artifacts, but it's a much quieter and cleaner place to spend the night than Cheb.

To get to Františkovy Lázně from Cheb by car, take E-49. The trip takes about 20 minutes. You can also take a taxi; just agree with the driver before you get in that the fare won't be more than 250Kč ($7.60).

ESSENTIALS

ARRIVING   By Train   Express trains from Prague usually stop in Cheb, as do several trains daily from Karlovy Vary. Cheb is on a main train route, so it's easy to catch many international connections here. The train takes 3½ hours and costs 165Kč ($5) first class and 110Kč ($3.35) second.

By Bus   Cheb is a long bus ride from Prague, and I suggest avoiding taking the bus if possible. It's more manageable to take the bus from Karlovy Vary to Cheb.

By Car   Cheb is located on E-48, one of the main highways leading to Germany. If you're driving from Prague, take the same route as you would to Karlovy Vary, which eventually brings you to Cheb. The drive takes about 2½ hours.

VISITOR INFORMATION   You'll find maps, guidebooks, lodging, and even a currency exchange (at a fairly steep price, so use it only if desperate) at the **Informační Centrum Goetz & Hanzlík,** náměstí Přemysla Otakara II (☎ **0166/459 480;** fax 0166/459 291). Open Monday to Sunday 9:30am to 6pm.

EXPLORING CHEB

The main square, **náměstí Krále Jiřího z Poděbrad,** attracts most of the attention, and is a good place to begin a tour of the old town. Although it has been overrun with touristy shops and cafes that serve mediocre German fare, the square still shines with Gothic burgher houses and the baroque **old town hall (stará radnice).** At its south end, the **statue of Kašna Roland,** built in 1591, is a former symbol of capital punishment, reminding people of the strength justice can wield. At the other end of the square stands the **Kašna Herkules,** a monument to the town's former strength and power. Next to it is a cluster of 11 timber houses, called **Špalíček.** These houses used to be owned by Jews in the early 14th century, but a fervently anti-Semitic clergy in the area incited such hatred against the Jews that they were forced into an alley now called ulička Zavražděných (Murder Victim's Lane), where they were unceremoniously slaughtered in 1350.

Across from Špalíček is the **Cheb Museum** (☎ **0166/422 246**), where another murder took place almost 300 years later—that of Albrecht von Wallenstein in 1634. On the upper level a display vividly depicts the assassination. The museum's first floor displays many 20th-century paintings from which you can trace the town's slow demise. Admission is 20Kč (60¢), and it's open Tuesday to Sunday 9am to noon and 1 to 5pm.

The old town of Cheb is also packed with several churches. The most interesting is **St. Nicholas,** around the corner from the museum. It's a hodgepodge of architecural styles: Romanesque tower windows, a Gothic portal, and a baroque interior.

TOURING CHEB CASTLE

An excellent example of Romanesque architecture is **Cheb Castle,** in the northeast part of the old town. Overlooking the Elbe River, the late 12th-century castle is one of central Europe's largest Romanesque structures.

The castle's main draws are its **chapel of Sts. Erhard and Ursala** and the **Černá věž (Black Tower).** The two-tiered early Gothic chapel has a somber first floor where the proletariat would congregate, while the emperor and his family enjoyed the much cheerier and brighter second floor with its Gothic windows. Alas, there are no tours of the castle, and the English text provided at the entrance does little to inform you. Admission is 50Kč ($1.50). It's open Tuesday to Sunday: June to August 9am to noon and 1 to 6pm, May and September 9am to noon and 1 to 5pm, and April and October 9am to noon and 1 to 4pm. Closed November to March.

Across the courtyard from the chapel stands the **Černá věž (Black Tower).** From its 60-foot-high lookout, you can see the best views of the town. The tower seems dusty and smeared with pollution, but its color isn't from the emissions of the Trabants and Škodas that drive through the streets. Rather, the tower is black because it's actually made from lava rocks taken from the nearby Komorni Hurka volcano (now dormant).

WHERE TO STAY
In Cheb

Hotel Hvězda. Náměstí Krále Jiřího z Poděbrad 4, 350 01 Cheb. ☎ **0166/422 549.** Fax 0166/422 546. 44 units. TV TEL. 1,150Kč ($35) double. AE, MC, V.

Overlooking the rather noisy main square, the Hvězda is a lone star in the Cheb hotel universe. The small but clean rooms make it bearable, and the staff tries to make your stay comfortable. If you can't stay in Františkovy Lázně and don't want to drive farther, this is really the only hotel I'd recommend in town.

In Františkovy Lázně

Hotel Tři lilie. Jiráskova 17, 351 01 Františkovy Lázně. ☎ **0166/542 415.** Fax 0166/542 044. 32 units. TV TEL. 3,100Kč ($94) double; 4,500Kč ($136) suite. AE, MC, V.

In 1808, Goethe stayed here, and he knew what he was doing. The Three Lilies is worth the extra money since it's the only luxury hotel in the area. Cheb needs a nice hotel like this. You can relax here; the spotless, spacious, well-appointed rooms block out any noise. The staff is very attentive and can arrange spa treatments, massages, and other health services. On the main floor is a nice, but a bit pricey, bar and restaurant.

Interhotel Slovan. Národní třída 5, 351 01 Františkovy Lázně. ☎ **0166/542 841-2.** Fax 0166/542 843. 25 units. TV TEL. 900–1,650Kč ($27–$50) double. AE, MC, V.

This hotel isn't as elegant as the Three Lilies just down the main street, but it's a nice place nonetheless. The rooms are a little plain and small, but for the money, they're one of the best bets in town. The only drawback is a staff that at times forgets the customer is paying for service.

WHERE TO DINE
In Cheb

Restaurace Fortuna. Náměstí Krále Jiřího z Poděbrad 29. ☎ **0166/422 110.** Main courses 95–189Kč ($2.90–$5.75). No credit cards. Daily 10am–2am. CZECH.

If you need to have one last schnitzel before leaving, this is as good a place as any. The food is uniformly good but not great, with most Czech specialties accounted for. It's one of the only restaurants open late, and a terrace right on the main square lends to its appeal.

Staročeská Restaurace. Kamenná 1. No phone. Main courses 65–225Kč ($1.95–$6.80). No credit cards. Daily 10am–10pm. CZECH/CHINESE.

This restaurant serves much the same fare as all the other restaurants on or around the square, but what caught my eye were the few Chinese meals offered. The *kuře*

Kung-Pao (Kung pao chicken) was a good spicy alternative to the sausages, meat, and dumplings most of the other diners were having.

In Františkovy Lázně

Restaurace Interhotel Slovan. Národní třída 5. No phone. Main courses 85–199Kč ($2.60–$6.05). No credit cards. Daily 8am–10pm. CZECH.

Be prepared for more heavy central European cuisine, with all four Czech food groups—meat, potatoes, dumplings, and cabbage—well represented. The fish dishes tend to be a lighter meal than the pork cutlet smothered in cheese and ham, but both proved excellent. Oddly, the service at the restaurant is markedly better than at the hotel.

ČESKÉ BUDĚJOVICE

This fortress town was born in 1265, when Otakar II decided that the intersection point of the Vltava and Malše rivers would be the perfect site to protect the approaches to southern Bohemia. Although Otakar was killed at the battle of the Moravian Field in 1278, and the town subsequently ravaged by the rival Vítkovic family, the construction of České Budějovice continued, eventually taking the shape originally envisaged.

Today, České Budějovice, the hometown of the original Budweiser brand beer, is now more a bastion for the beer drinker than a protector of Bohemia. But its slow pace, relaxed atmosphere, and interesting architecture make it a worthy stop, especially as a base for exploring southern Bohemia or for those heading on to Austria.

ESSENTIALS

ARRIVING   By Train   Daily express trains from Prague make the trip to České Budějovice in about 2½ hours. The fare is 147Kč ($4.45) first class or 98Kč ($2.95) second class.

By Bus   Several express buses run from Prague's Florenc station each day, taking 2 hours and costing 109Kč ($3.20).

By Car   Leave Prague to the south via the main D-1 expressway and take the cutoff for Highway E-55, which runs straight to České Budějovice. The trip takes about 1½ hours.

VISITOR INFORMATION   Tourist Infocentrum, náměstí Přemysla Otakara II 2 (☎ 038/680 2005; fax 038/594 80), provides maps and guidebooks and finds lodging.

SPECIAL EVENTS   Each August, České Budějovice hosts the largest **International Agricultural Show,** the country's massive "state fair."

EXPLORING THE TOWN

You can comfortably see České Budějovice in a day. At its center is one of central Europe's largest squares, the cobblestoned **náměstí Přemysla Otakara II.** The square contains the ornate **Fountain of Sampson,** an 18th-century water well that was once the town's principal water supply, plus a mishmash of baroque and Renaissance buildings. On the southwest corner is the **town hall,** an elegant baroque structure built by Martinelli between 1727 and 1730. On top of the town hall, the larger-than-life statues by Dietrich represent the civic virtues: justice, bravery, wisdom, and diligence.

One block northwest of the square is the **Černá věž (Black Tower),** visible from almost every point in the city. Its 360 steps are worth the climb to get a bird's-eye view in all directions. The most famous symbol of České Budějovice, this 232-foot-tall

Keeping Up with the Schwarzenbergs: Visiting a 141-Room English Castle

Only 8 kilometers north from České Budějovice lies **Hluboká nad Vltavou.** The distance is short enough to make a pleasant bike trip from the city or a quick stop on the way to, or coming from, Prague, Třeboň, or Tábor. The castle is open from April to October Tuesday to Sunday from 10am to 5:30pm. Tours in English run at 11am and 2 and 4pm and cost 80Kč ($2.40).

Built in the 13th century, Hluboká has undergone many face-lifts over the years, but none that left as lasting an impression as those ordered by the Schwarzenberg family. As a sign of the region's growing wealth and importance in the mid-19th century, the Schwarzenbergs remodeled the 141-room castle in the neo-Gothic style of England's Windsor Castle. Robin Leach would be proud; no expense was spared. The Schwartzenbergs removed the impressive wooden ceiling from their residence at Český Krumlov and reinstalled it in the large dining room. Other rooms are equally garish in their appointments, making a guided tour worth the time, even though only about a third of the rooms are open to the public.

To complete the experience, the **Alšova Jihočeská Galerie (Art Gallery of South Bohemia),** in the riding school at Hluboká, houses the second-largest art collection in Bohemia, including many interesting Gothic sculptures from the area.

If you're driving to Hluboká from České Budějovice, take Highway E-49 north and then Highway 105 just after leaving the outskirts of České Budějovice. For cyclists or drivers who prefer a slower, more scenic route, take the road that runs behind the brewery; it passes through the village of Obora.

16th-century tower was built as a belfry for the adjacent **St. Nicholas Church.** This 13th-century church, one of the town's most important sights, was a bastion of Roman Catholicism during the 15th-century Hussite rebellion. You shouldn't miss the church's flamboyant white-and-cream 17th-century baroque interior.

TOURING A BEER SHRINE

On the town's northern edge sits a shrine for those who pray to the gods of the amber nectar. This is where it all began, where **Budějovicky Budvar,** the original brewer of Budweiser brand beer, has its one and only factory. Established in 1895, Budvar draws on more than 700 years of Bohemian brewing tradition to produce one of the world's best beers. Contact Budvar n.p., Karolíny Světlé 4, České Budějovice (☎ 038/ 770 5111 or ☎/fax 770 5337).

Four trolley buses—nos. 2, 4, 6, and 8—stop by the brewery; this is how the brewery ensures that its workers and visitors reach the plant safely each day. The trolley costs 6Kč (20¢) to the brewery. You can also hop a cab from the town square for about 100Kč to 150Kč ($3.35 to $4.45).

Tours can be arranged by phoning ahead, but only for groups. If you're traveling alone or with only one or two other people, ask a hotel concierge at one of the bigger hotels (I suggest the Zvon) if he or she can put you in with an already scheduled group. Failing that, you might want to take a chance and head up to the brewery, where, if a group has arrived, another person or two won't be noticed.

WHERE TO STAY

Several agencies can locate reasonably priced private rooms. Expect to pay between 400Kč and 1,000Kč ($12 to $30) per person, in cash. **Tourist Infocentrum** (see "Visitor Information," above) can point you toward a wide selection of conveniently located rooms and pensions.

Hotel Malý Pivovar (Small Brewery). Ulice Karla IV 8–10, 370 01 České Budějovice. ☎ **038/731 3285.** 30 units. MINIBAR TV TEL. 1,800Kč ($55) double; 2,200–2,890Kč ($67–$88) suite. Rates include breakfast. AE, MC, V.

Around the corner from the Zvon, a renovated 16th-century microbrewery combines the charms of a B&B with the amenities of a modern hotel. The rooms are bright and cheery, with antique-style wooden furniture. Exposed wooden ceiling beams lend a farmhouse feel in the center of town. It's definitely worth consideration if being directly on the square (you're only 30 meters from it) isn't a problem.

Hotel Zvon. Náměstí Přemysla Otakara II 28, 370 42 České Budějovice. ☎ **038/731 1384.** Fax 038/731 1385. 75 units. MINIBAR TV TEL. 2,060–2,430Kč ($62–$74) double; 2,750–2,950Kč ($83–$89) triple; 2,595–3,700 ($79–$112) suite. AE, MC, V.

Location is everything for the city's most elegant hotel, which occupies several historic buildings on the main square. The upper-floor rooms have been renovated and tend to be more expensive, especially those with a view of the square. Others are relatively plain and functional. The views from those in front, however, can't be topped. Rooms facing the square on the upper floors aren't only brighter, they're larger and nicer, too. Try to avoid the smaller rooms, usually reserved for tour groups. There's no elevator, but if you don't mind the climb, stay on the fourth floor. One of the biggest changes here in recent years has been the staff, which seems to be learning that guests like respect and quality treatment.

WHERE TO DINE

Masné Krámy (Meat Shops). Krajinská 29. ☎ **038/32 652.** Main courses 59–175Kč ($1.80–$5.30). No credit cards. Daily 10am–11pm. CZECH.

If you've pledged not to go to any "tourist traps," you might make an exception for this one housed in an historic building. Just northwest of náměstí Přemysla Otakara II, labyrinthine Masné Krámy occupies a series of drinking rooms on either side of a long hall, and is a must for any serious pub-goer. The inexpensive and filling food is pure Bohemia, including several pork, duck, and trout dishes. Come for the boisterous atmosphere or what's possibly the best goulash in the Czech Republic.

Rybářský Sál. In the Hotel Gomel, třída Míru 14. ☎ **038/731 390.** Main courses 130–590Kč ($3.95–$17.90). AE, DC, MC, V. Mon–Thurs 11am–10pm; Fri–Sat 11am–11pm. CZECH/INTERNATIONAL.

The Rybářský Sál is a popular restaurant known for four freshwater fish: carp, trout, perch, and pike. Chicken Kiev and other "turf" dishes are also served. The dining room is modern and minimally decorated with hanging fishnets. If the menu isn't your taste, try the **Myslivecký Sál** in the same hotel for wild game and more meat-laden dishes at similar prices.

ČESKÝ KRUMLOV

If you have time for only one day trip, consider making it Český Krumlov, 96 miles south of Prague. One of Bohemia's prettiest towns, Krumlov is a living gallery of elegant Renaissance-era buildings housing charming cafes, pubs, restaurants, shops, and galleries. In 1992, UNESCO named Český Krumlov a World Heritage Site for its historic importance and physical beauty.

Consider yourself warned: Word has spread about Český Krumlov. Summer season can be unbearable, as thousands of visitors blanket its medieval streets. If possible, try to visit in the off-season—I suggest autumn to take advantage of the colorful surrounding hills—when the crowds recede, the prices decrease, and the town's charm can really shine. Who knows? You might even hear some Czech!

Bustling since medieval times, the town, after centuries of embellishment, is exquisitely beautiful. In 1302, the Rožmberk family inherited the castle and used it as their main residence for nearly 300 years. Looking out from the Lazebnický bridge, with the waters of the Vltava below snaking past the castle's gray stone, you'll feel that time has stopped. At night, with the castle alight, the view becomes even more dramatic.

Few deigned to change the appearance of Český Krumlov over the years, not even the Schwarzenbergs, who usually had an unrestrained flair for opulence. At the turn of the 19th century, several house facades in the town's outer section were built, as were inner courtyards. Thankfully, economic stagnation in the area during communism meant little money for "development," so no glass-and-steel edifices, like the Hotel Thermal in Karlovy Vary, jut out to spoil the architectural beauty. Instead, a medieval impression reigns supreme, now augmented by the many festivals and renovations that keep the town's spirit alive.

ESSENTIALS

ARRIVING   By Train   The only way to reach Český Krumlov by train from Prague is via České Budějovice, a slow ride that deposits you at a station relatively far from the town center. It takes 3½ hours; the fare is 165Kč ($5) first class or 110Kč ($3.35) second class.

By Bus   The nearly 3-hour bus ride from Prague usually involves a transfer in České Budějovice and costs 129Kč ($3.80). The bus station in Český Krumlov is a 15-minute walk from the town's main square.

By Car   From Prague, it's a 2-hour drive along E-55.

VISITOR INFORMATION   On the main square, the **Information Centrum,** náměstí Svornosti 1, 381 00 Český Krumlov (☎ and fax **0337/711 183**), offers a complete array of services from booking accommodations to ticket reservations for events, as well as a phone and fax service. It's open daily 9am to 8pm in July and August, and 9am to 6pm the rest of the year.

SPECIAL EVENTS   After being banned during communism (a little too feudalistic for Gottwald), the **Slavnost pětilisté růže (Festival of the Five-Petaled Rose)** has made a triumphant comeback. It's held each year on the summer solstice. Residents of Český Krumlov dress up in Renaissance costume and parade through the streets. Afterward, the streets become a stage with plays, chess games with people dressed as pieces, music, and even duels "to the death."

Český Krumlov also plays host to a 2-week **International Music Festival** every August, attracting performers from all over the world. Performances are held in nine spectacular venues. For information or ticket reservations, contact the information center's ticket hotline at ☎ **0337/711 650.**

EXPLORING ČESKÝ KRUMLOV

Bring a good pair of walking shoes and be prepared to wear them out. Český Krumlov not only lends itself to hours of strolling, but its hills and alleyways demand it. No cars, thank goodness, are allowed in the historic town, and the cobblestones keep most other vehicles at bay. The town is split into two parts—the **Inner town** and **Latrán**, which houses the castle. They're best tackled separately, so you won't have to crisscross the bridges several times.

Begin at the **Okresní Muzeum (Regional Museum)** (☎ **0337/711 674**) at the top of Horní ulice. Once a Jesuit seminary, the three-story museum now contains artifacts and displays relating to Český Krumlov's 1,000-year history. The highlight of this mass of folk art, clothing, furniture, and statues is a giant model of the town that offers a bird's-eye view of the buildings. Admission is 30Kč (60¢), and it's open Tuesday to Sunday from 10am to 12:30pm and 1 to 6pm.

Across the street is the **Hotel Růže (Rose),** which was once a Jesuit student house. Built in the late 16th century, the hotel and the prelature next to it show the development of architecture; Gothic, Renaissance, and rococo influences are all present. If you're not staying at the hotel, don't be afraid to walk around and even ask questions at the reception desk.

Continue down the street to the impressive late Gothic **St. Vitus Cathedral.** Be sure to climb the church tower, which offers one of the most spectacular views of both the Inner Town and the castle across the river.

As you continue down the street, you'll come to **náměstí Svornosti.** For such an impressive town, the main square is a little disappointing, with few buildings of any character. The **Radnice (Town Hall),** at náměstí Svornosti 1, is one of the few exceptions. Its Gothic arcades and Renaissance vault inside are exceptionally beautiful in this otherwise rundown area. From the square, streets fan out in all directions. Take some time just to wander through them. You might want to grab a light snack before crossing the bridge.

As you cross the bridge and head toward the castle, you'll see immediately to your right the former **hospital and church of St. Jošt.** Founded at the beginning of the 14th century, it has since been turned into apartments. Feel free to snoop around, but don't enter the building.

One of Český Krumlov's most famous residents was Austrian-born artist Egon Schiele. He was a bit of an eccentric who, on more than one occasion, raised the ire of the town's residents (many were distraught with his use of their young women as his nude models); his stay was cut short when residents' patience ran out. But the town readopted the artist in 1993, setting up the **Egon Schiele Foundation and the Egon Schiele Centrum** in Inner Town, Široká 70–72, 381 01, Český Krumlov (☎ **0337/711 224;** fax 0337/711 191). Back across the river from the castle, it documents his life and work, housing a permanent selection of his paintings as well as exhibitions of other 20th-century artists. Admission depends on the exhibitions being displayed. It's open daily 10am to 6pm.

For a different perspective on what the town looks like, take the stairs from the **Městské divadlo (Town Theater)** on Horní ulice down to the riverfront and rent a boat from **Maláček boat rentals** at 50Kč ($1.50) per hour. Always willing to lend his advice, the affable Pepa Maláček will tell you what to watch out for and where the best fishing is (no matter how many times you say that you don't want to fish!).

SEEING THE ČESKÝ KRUMLOV CHÂTEAU

Reputedly the second-largest castle in Bohemia (after Prague Castle), the **Český Krumlov Château** was constructed in the 13th century as part of a private estate. Throughout the ages, it has passed to a variety of private owners, including the Rožmberk family, Bohemia's largest landholders, and the Schwarzenbergs, the Bohemian equivalent of *Dynasty*'s Carrington family.

From the entrance, by the bear moat, you'll begin the long climb up to the **castle.** Greeting you is a round 12th-century tower—painstakingly renovated and re-opened in 1998—with its Renaissance balcony. You'll pass over the moat, now occupied by two brown bears. Beyond it is the **Dolní Hrad (Lower Castle)** and then the **Horní Hrad (Upper Castle).**

Perched high atop a rocky hill, the château is open from April to October only, exclusively by guided tour. Visits begin in the rococo **Chapel of St. George,** continue through the portrait-packed **Renaissance Hall,** and end with the **Royal Family Apartments,** outfitted with ornate furnishings that include Flemish wall tapestries and European paintings. Tours last 1 hour and depart frequently. Most are in Czech or German, however. If you want an English-language tour, arrange it ahead of time by calling ☎ **0337/711 465** (fax 0337/711 687).

The tour costs 100Kč ($3.05) for adults and 50Kč ($1.50) for students. The castle hours are Tuesday to Sunday: May to August 7:45am to noon and 12:45 to 4pm, September 8:45am to noon and 12:45 to 4pm, and April and October 8:45am to noon and 12:45 to 3pm. The last entrance is 1 hour before closing.

Once past the main castle building, you can see one of the more stunning views of Český Krumlov from **Most Na Plášti,** a walkway that doubles as a belvedere over the Inner Town. Even farther up the hill lies the castle's riding school and gardens.

Most visitors don't realize that beyond this part of the castle they can have one of the Czech Republic's finest dining experiences at ✪ **Krčma Markéta,** Latrán 67 (☎ **0337/712 195**). To get there, walk all the way up the hill through the castle, past the Upper Castle and past the Castle Theater. Walk through the raised walkway and into the Zámecká zahrada (Castle Garden), where you'll eventually find this Renaissance pub. Going inside is like leaving this century. There's no need for plates here, as meals are served on wooden blocks. Drinks come in pewter mugs.

Although owners have come and gone, the atmosphere and good times are still the same. There's no menu—just go up to the spit and see what's roasting; usually there's a wide variety of meat, including succulent pork cutlets, rabbit, chickens, and pork knees, a Czech delicacy. The waiter/cook will bring bread and a slab of spiced pork fat (considered a good base for drinking), but don't worry—refusing to eat it won't raise anyone's ire. Instead, wait until the entree comes. Yes, that obligatory smattering of cabbage is all the vegetables you're going to get. Vegetarians need not apply. Krčma Markéta is open daily 6 to 11pm. Reservations are recommended. Main courses are 80Kč to 200Kč ($2.40 to $6.05). No credit cards are accepted.

WHERE TO STAY

Hotels are sprouting up, or are getting a "new" old look; Pension and Zimmer Frei signs line Horní and Rooseveltova streets and offer some of the best values in town. For a comprehensive list of area hotels and help with bookings, call or write to the Infocentrum listed above.

Moderate

Hotel Růže (Rose Hotel). Horní 153, 381 01 Český Krumlov. ☎ **0337/711 141** or 0337/ 2245. Fax 0337/711 128. 73 units. MINIBAR TV TEL. 1,530–3,420Kč ($46–$104) double; 1,800–4,230Kč ($55–$128) small suite; 2,700–4,950Kč ($82–$150) large suite. Rates include breakfast. AE, MC, V.

Once a Jesuit seminary, this stunning Italian Renaissance building has been turned into a well-appointed hotel. Comfortable in a big-city kind of way, it's packed with amenities and is one of the top places to stay in Český Krumlov. But for all of the splendor of the building, you may find the Růže a bit of a disappointment. The rooms, although clean and spacious, look as though they were furnished from a

Sears warehouse in the U.S. Midwest. The promise of a Renaissance stay dissipates quickly.

Inexpensive

Hotel Konvice. Horníul. 144, 381 01 Český Krumlov. ☎ **0337/711 611.** Fax 0337/711 327. 10 units. 1,050Kč 1,300Kč ($39) double; 1,600–2,500Kč ($48–$76) suite. Rates include breakfast. No credit cards.

If you can get a room with a view out the back, take it immediately. The rooms themselves are small but clean and comfortable, with nice parquet floors and well-appointed bathrooms. As you overlook the river and the castle on the opposite bank, you'll wonder why anyone would stay at the Růže just a few doors up.

✪ **Pension Anna.** Rooseveltova 41, 381 01 Český Krumlov. ☎ **0337/711 692.** 6 units. 800–1,000Kč ($24–$30) double; 1,100–1,300Kč ($33–39) suite. Rates include breakfast. No credit cards.

Along "pension alley," this is a comfortable and rustic choice. What makes this pension a favorite is the friendly management and the homey feeling you get as you walk up to your room. Forget hotels—this is the kind of place where you can relax. The owners even let you buy drinks and snacks at the bar downstairs and take them to your room. The suites, with four beds and a living room, are great for families and groups.

Pension Na louži. Kájovská 66, 381 01 Český Krumlov. ☎ and fax **0337/712 880.** 7 units. 1,000Kč ($30) double; 1,200Kč triple ($36). Breakfast included. No credit cards.

Smack-dab in the heart of the Inner Town, the small Na louži, built in 1459 and decorated with early 20th-century wooden furniture, is full of charm. The only drawback is beds with footboards that can be a little short for those over 6 feet tall. Don't worry about the noise—the pub downstairs is not open late!

✪ **Pension Ve Věži (In the Tower).** Latrán 28, 381 01 Český Krumlov. ☎ **0337/711 742.** 4 units (none with bathroom). May–Sept 1,400Kč ($42) double; 1,800Kč ($55) quad. Oct–Apr 750Kč ($23) double; 1,200Kč ($36) quad. Rates include breakfast. No credit cards.

A private pension in a renovated medieval tower just a 5-minute walk from the castle, Ve Věži is one of the most magnificent places to stay in town. It's not the accommodations themselves that are so grand—none has a bathroom and all are sparsely decorated—it's the wonderful ancient ambience. Advance reservations are always recommended.

WHERE TO DINE

Hospoda Na louži. Kájovská 66. ☎ **0337/711 280.** Main courses 49–129Kč ($1.50–$3.90). No credit cards. Daily 10am–10pm. CZECH.

The large wooden tables encourage you to get to know your neighbors in this Inner Town pub, located in a 15th-century house. The atmosphere is fun and the food above average. If no table is available, stand and have a drink; the seating turnover is pretty fast, and the staff is accommodating. In summer, the terrace seats only six, so dash over if a seat becomes empty.

Restaurant Na Ostrově (On the island). Na ostrově 171. ☎ **0337/711 699.** Main courses 60–245Kč ($1.80–$7.40). No credit cards. Daily 11am–11pm. CZECH.

In the shadow of the castle and, as the name implies, on an island, this restaurant is best on a sunny day when the terrace overflows with flowers, hearty Czech food with plenty of chicken and fish dishes, and lots of beer. The staff is very friendly and very slow—usually only two waiters work a shift. This is a great place to relax and enjoy the view.

Restaurant Eggenberg. Latrán 27. ☎ **0337/711 761.** Main courses 80–195Kč ($2.40–$5.75). MC, V. Daily 10am–11pm. CZECH.

Located in the former cooling room of the local Eggenberg Brewery, this is one of the few big beerhalls in town, with some of the freshest draft anywhere. Traditional meat-and-dumplings–style Czech food is augmented by vegetarian dishes.

Rybářská Bašta Jakuba Krčína. Kájovská 54. ☎ **0337/712 692.** Reservations recommended. Main courses 90–310Kč ($2.75–$9.40). AE, MC, V. Daily 7am–11pm. CZECH.

One of the town's most celebrated restaurants, this place specializes in freshwater fish from surrounding lakes. Trout, perch, pike, and eel are sautéed, grilled, baked, and fried in a variety of herbs and spices. Venison, rabbit, and other game are also available, along with the requisite roast beef and pork cutlet.

4 Denmark

by Darwin Porter & Danforth Prince

In this chapter, we've concentrated on Copenhagen, Denmark's capital, and have added a few important side trips that can be taken in a day or two. The name for Copenhagen came from the word *køben-havn,* meaning "merchants' harbor." This city grew in size and importance because of its position on the Øresund (the Sound) between Denmark and Sweden, guarding the entrance to the Baltic. From its humble beginnings, Copenhagen has become the largest city in Scandinavia, home to 1.5 million people. It's the seat of the oldest kingdom in the world.

Copenhagen

Copenhagen is a city with much charm, as reflected in its canals, narrow streets, and old houses. Its most famous resident was Hans Christian Andersen, whose memory still lives on. Another of Copenhagen's world-renowned inhabitants was Søren Kierkegaard, who used to take long morning strolls in the city, planning his next essay; his completed essays eventually earned him the title "father of existentialism."

But few modern Copenhageners are reading Kierkegaard today, and neither are they as melancholy as Hamlet. Most of them are out having too much fun. Copenhagen epitomizes a Nordic *joie de vivre,* and the city is filled with a lively atmosphere, good times (none better than at the Tivoli Gardens), sex shows, countless outdoor cafes, and all-night dance clubs. Of course, if you come in winter, the fierce realities of living above the 55th parallel set in. That's when Copenhageners retreat inside their smoky jazz clubs and beer taverns. The fun goes on: It's just not outdoors.

Modern Copenhagen still retains some of the characteristics of a village. If you forget the suburbs, you can cover most of the central belt on foot, which makes it a great tourist spot. It's almost as though the city were designed for pedestrians, as evidenced by its Strøget (strolling street), Europe's longest and oldest walking street.

Only in Copenhagen

Reliving the Past at Dragør　On Copenhagen's doorstep, this seafaring town once flourished as a bustling herring port on the Baltic. Life, however, passed it by, and for that we can be grateful because it looks much as it used to, with half-timbered ocher-and-pink 18th-century cottages—all with thatched or red-tiled roofs. The entire village is under the protection of the National Trust of Denmark. In a 35-minute ride from the Danish capital, you can be delivered back in a time capsule.

Biking in Copenhagen & Zealand   Copenhagen vies with Amsterdam as the biking capital of Europe. It's a flat city, with lots to see, and with motorists who tend to be more bike-conscious and considerate toward bikers than drivers in many other European cities. You can pedal beside canals, past palaces and grand antique buildings, and even out into the countryside to see some of the highlights of Zealand, the island on which Copenhagen lies. If the idea of an extended bike trip in Denmark appeals to you, contact **Bike Denmark,** 1A Olaf Poulsens Allee, 3480 Fredensborg (☎ **48-48-58-00**); or its North American sales agent, **ScanAm World Tours,** 933 Route 23, Pompton Plains, NJ 07444 (☎ **800/545-2204**). Their specialty is self-guided bike tours through Zealand, Funen, and the sheltered (less-windy) eastern coast of Jutland. For more information on this company, check out their Web site at www.bikedenmark.com.

Spending a Day & a Night at the Tivoli   These pleasure gardens are worth the air ticket to Copenhagen. They're not Disneyland, but these 150-year-old gardens are unique. They're a little bit of everything: open-air dancing, restaurants, theaters, concert halls, an amusement park . . . and, oh yes, gardens as well. From the first bloom of spring until the autumn leaves start to fall, they're devoted to harmless fun, often of the type enjoyed back in the belle époque days. The gardens are worth a visit anytime, but are best at twilight when the lights begin to glint among the trees.

Shopping for Danish Designs   The simple but elegant lines that became fashionable in the 1950s have made a comeback—nowhere more so than in Denmark. Danish modern in chairs, glassware, and even buildings has returned. "Old Masters" such as Arne Jacobsen, Hans Wegner, and Poul Kjærhom are celebrated, and their designs from the 1940s and 1950s are sold today in antique stores. Wegner is now viewed as the grand old man of Danish design, noted for his sculptural teak chairs. Younger designers have followed, creating everything from chairs, desks, and furnishings to table settings and silverware. For the best display of Danish design, walk along pedestrian-only Strøget, Copenhagen's major shopping street. The best single showcase is **Illums Bolighus** at Amagertorv 10 (☎ **33-14-19-41;** Bus: 28, 29, or 41).

Visiting the Palaces   At Copenhagen's Christianborg Palace, the queen officially receives guests in the Royal Reception Chamber, where you must don slippers to protect the floors. The complex also contains the Parliament House and the Supreme Court. From 1441 until the fire of 1795, this was the official residence of Denmark. You can tour the richly decorated rooms, including the Throne Room and banqueting hall. Below you can see the well-preserved ruins of the 1167 castle of Bishop Absalon, founder of Copenhagen. The other monument of note is Rosenborg Castle, founded by Christian IV in the 17th century. This red-brick Renaissance castle remained a royal residence until the early 19th century, when it was converted into a museum. It still houses the crown jewels, and its collection of costumes and royal memorabilia is unequaled in Denmark.

Viewing the Beer People's Art   The cultural capital of Europe in 1996, pre-millennium Copenhagen remains a rich treasure trove of art. The Glyptotek, behind the Tivoli Gardens, was founded by Mr. Carlsberg Beer himself, Carl Jacobsen, in the 19th century. It contains everything from the Egyptians to Rodin and van Gogh, Manet to Monet to Renoir—and especially Gauguin.

ORIENTATION

ARRIVING   By Plane   When you arrive at **Kastrup Airport** (☎ 31-54-17-01), 7¼ miles from the center of Copenhagen, you can reduce costs by taking an SAS coach to the city terminal; the fare is 35DKK ($5.05). A taxi to the city center costs around 130DKK ($18.85). Even cheaper is a local bus, no. 250S, leaving from the international arrivals terminal every 15 to 20 minutes for the Town Hall Square in central Copenhagen and costing 15DKK ($2.15). Launched in 1998, air-rail links for the first time have connected the airport with the Central Railway Station in the center of Copenhagen. The ride takes only 11 minutes, costing 16.40DKK ($2.40). **SAS** (☎ 800/221/2350) is the major carrier to Copenhagen. **TWA** (☎ 800/ 221-2000) also flies to Copenhagen daily from New York's JFK airport. **Delta** (☎ 800/241-4141) has daily nonstop flights from JFK in New York at comparable prices to those offered by SAS and TWA.

By Train   Trains from the continent arrive at the **Hoved Banegård (Central Rail-road Station),** in the very center of Copenhagen, near the Tivoli and the Rådhus-pladsen. For rail information, call ☎ 33-14-17-01. The station operates a luggage-checking service, but room bookings are available only at the tourist office (see "Visitor Information," below). You can exchange money at **Den Danske Bank** (☎ 33-12-04-11), open daily 7am to 8pm.

   From the Central Railroad Station, you can connect with **S-tog,** the local subway, with trains leaving from platforms in the terminus itself. Ask at the information desk near Tracks 5 and 6 about which train you should board to reach your destination.

By Bus   Buses from Zealand or elsewhere in Denmark also pull into the Central Railroad Station (see "By Train," above). For bus information, call ☎ 36-45-45-45.

By Car   If you're driving from Germany, a car-ferry takes you from Travemünde to Gedser in southern Denmark. From Gedser, get on E-55 north, an express highway that delivers you to the southern outskirts of Copenhagen. If you're coming from Sweden and crossing at Helsingborg, you land on the Danish side at Helsingør. From here, take express highway E-55 south to the northern outskirts of Copenhagen.

By Ferry   Most ferryboats land at Havnegade at the end of the south side of Nyhavn, a short walk to the center of Copenhagen. Taxis also wait here for ferry arrivals. Most arrivals are from Malmö, Sweden; ferries from continental Europe usually land in South Zealand. **Hydrofoils** (☎ 33-12-80-88) arrive hourly during the day from Malmö, Sweden. The trip takes 40 minutes and costs from 20 to 50DKK ($2.90 to $7.25).

VISITOR INFORMATION   The **Copenhagen Tourist Information Center,** Bernstorffsgade 1 (☎ 33-11-13-25), is across from Tivoli's main entrance. It's open September 16 through April, Monday to Friday 9am to 4:30pm and Saturday 9am to 1:30pm; May through June and September 1 through 15, daily 9am to 9pm; and July through August, daily 8am to 11pm.

CITY LAYOUT   The heart of Old Copenhagen is a maze of pedestrian streets, bor-dered by Nørreport Station to the north, Town Hall Square (Rådhuspladsen) to the west, Kongens Nytorv to the east, and the Inderhavnen (Inner Harbor) to the south. One continuous route, **Strøget,** the world's longest pedestrian street, goes east from Town Hall Square to Kongens Nytorv and is made up of five streets: Frederiks-berggade, Nygade, Vimmelskaftet, Amagertorv, and Østergade. Strøget is lined with shops, bars, restaurants, and sidewalk cafes in summer. **Pistolstraede,** a narrow street about a 3-minute walk west of Kongens Nytorv, is a maze of galleries, restaurants, and boutiques, all housed in restored 18th-century buildings.

Fiolstraede (Violet Street), a dignified street with antiques shops and bookshops, cuts through the university (Latin Quarter). If you turn into Rosengaarden at the top of Fiolstraede, you'll come to **Kultorvet** (Coal Square) just before you reach Nørreport Station. Here you join the third main pedestrian street, **Købmagergade** (Butcher Street), which winds around and finally meets Strøget on Amagertorv.

At the end of Strøget you approach **Kongens Nytorv** (King's Square), the site of the Royal Theater and Magasin, the largest department store in Copenhagen. This puts you at the beginning of **Nyhavn,** the former seamen's quarter that has been gentrified into an upmarket area of expensive restaurants, apartments, cafes, and boutiques. The government of Denmark is centered on the small island of **Slotsholmen,** connected to the center by eight bridges. Several museums, notably Christiansborg Castle, are found here.

The center of Copenhagen is **Rådhuspladsen** (Town Hall Square). From here it's a short walk to the Tivoli Gardens, the major attraction, and the Central Railroad Station, the main railroad and subway terminus. The wide boulevard, **Vesterbrogade,** passes by Tivoli until it reaches the Central Railroad Station. Another major street is named after Denmark's most famous writer, **H. C. Andersens Boulevard,** running along Rådhuspladsen and the Tivoli Gardens.

GETTING AROUND   A joint zone fare system includes Copenhagen Transport buses and State Railway and S-tog trains in Copenhagen and North Zealand, plus some private rail routes in a 25-mile radius of the capital, enabling you to transfer from train to bus and vice versa with the same ticket.

A *grundbillet* (basic ticket) for both buses and trains costs 11DKK ($1.60). You can buy 10 tickets for 70DKK ($10.15). Children under 12 ride for half-fare; those under 5 go free on local trains, and those under 7 go free on buses. For 70DKK ($10.15), you can purchase a ticket allowing 24-hour bus and train travel through nearly half of Zealand; a 72-hour ticket is available for 150DKK ($21.75). These tickets are half-price for children 7 to 11; free for children under 7.

The **Copenhagen Card** entitles you to free and unlimited travel by bus and rail throughout the metropolitan area (including North Zealand), 25% to 50% discounts on crossings to and from Sweden, and free admission to many sights and museums. The card is available for 1, 2, or 3 days and costs 140DKK ($20.30), 255DKK ($36.95), and 320DKK ($46.40), respectively. Children 11 and under are given a 50% discount. For more information, contact the Copenhagen Tourist Information Center (see "Visitor Information," above).

Students who have an **International Student Identity Card (ISIC)** are entitled to a number of travel breaks in Copenhagen. A card can be purchased in the United States at any Council Travel office; for the office nearest you, call ☎ **800/ GET-AN-ID.**

For information about low-cost train and plane trips, go to **Waastels,** Skoubogade 6 (☎ **33-14-46-33**), in Copenhagen. Hours are Monday to Friday 9am to 7pm, Saturday 10am to 3pm. Wasteels specializes in inexpensive travel by plane within Europe, and they are also the experts on special youth fares.

Eurailpasses and Nordturist Pass tickets are accepted on local trains in Copenhagen.

By Bus   Copenhagen's well-maintained buses are the least expensive method of getting around. Most buses leave from Rådhuspladsen. A basic ticket allows 1 hour of travel and unlimited transfers within the zone where you started your trip. For information, call ☎ **36-45-45-45.**

By S-tog (Subway)   The S-tog connects heartland Copenhagen with its suburbs. Use of the tickets is the same as on buses (above). You can transfer from a bus line to an S-train on the same ticket. Eurailpass holders generally ride free. For more information, call ☎ **33-14-17-01** between 6:30am and 11pm.

By Car   It's best to park your car in any of the dozens of city parking lots, and then retrieve it when you're ready to explore the capital's environs. Many car parks are open 24 hours a day; a few others tend to close between 1 and 7am. Some close on Saturday afternoon and on Sunday during non-peak business hours when traffic is presumably lighter. Costs tend to range from 11 to 20DKK ($1.60 to $2.90) per hour or 55 to 85DKK ($8 to $12.35) per 24 hours. Two of the most centrally located car parks are **Industriens Hus,** H. C. Andersens Blvd. 18 (☎ **33-91-21-75**), which is open Monday to Friday 7am to 12:45am and Saturday and Sunday 9am to 12:45am; and the more reasonable **Statoil,** Israels Plads (☎ **33-14-37-76**), which is open around the clock.

By Taxi   Watch for the *fri* (free) sign or green light to hail a taxi. Be sure the taxis are metered. **Københavns Taxa** (☎ **35-35-35-35**) operates the largest fleet of cabs. Tips are included in the meter price: 22DKK ($3.20) at the drop of the flag and 10DKK ($1.45) per kilometer thereafter, Monday to Friday 6am to 6pm. From 6pm to 6am and all day and night on Saturday and Sunday, the cost is 11DKK ($1.60) per kilometer. Basic drop-of-the-flag costs remain the same, however. Many drivers speak English.

By Bicycle   To reduce pollution from cars, Copenhageners ride bicycles. You can rent a bike at **Københavns Cyklebors,** Gothersgade 157, next to the botanical gardens (☎ **33-14-07-17**) for 40DKK ($5.80) per day or 185DKK ($26.85) per week. Shop hours are Monday to Friday, 8:30am to 5:30pm and Saturday, 10am to 1:30pm.

Fast Facts: Copenhagen

American Express   Its office is more limited in Copenhagen than within equivalent capitals of Europe, as it offers facilities only for foreign exchange and customer service for Amex cardholders who lose their cards or need travel checks. Their temporary office is a small premises at Nørregade 7A, 3rd floor (☎ **33-12-23-01**), although it's likely that a new address, with the same phone, will be operational before the millennium. In the meanwhile, any individual wanting the services of a travel agent can contact Amex's affiliate, **Profile Travel,** Gamie Kongevej 2 (☎ **77-33-55-66**), open Monday to Friday 9am to 5pm, and on Saturday 9am to noon (to 2pm between May and August).

Business Hours   Most **banks** are open Monday to Friday 9:30am to 4pm (Thursday until 6pm). **Stores** are generally open Monday to Thursday 9am to 5:30pm, Friday 9am to 7 or 8pm, and Saturday 9am to 2pm; most are closed Sunday.

Currency   The Danish currency is the **krone** (crown), or **DKK** in its plural form, made up of 100 **øre.** Banknotes are issued in 50, 100, 500, and 1,000DKK. Coins come in 25 and 50 øre, and 1, 2, 5, 10, and 20DKK; the 1-, 2-, and 5-krone coins have a hole in the center. The rate of exchange used in this chapter was $1 = 6.78DKK or 1DKK = 15¢. Also, 1EUR = 7.4DKK and £1 = 11.33DKK.

Currency Exchange   Banks are generally your best bet to exchange currency. When banks are closed, you can exchange money at **Forex** (☎ **33-11-29-05**) in the Central Railroad Station, daily 8am to 9pm, or **The Change Group**

(☎ **33-93-04-55**), Østergade 61, Monday to Saturday 9am to 10pm and Sunday 9am to 8pm.

Dentists & Doctors   For emergency dental treatment, go to **Tandlaegevagten,** Oslo Plads 14 (☎ **35-38-02-51**), near Østerport Station and the U.S. Embassy. Open Monday to Friday 8am to 9:30pm and Saturday, Sunday, and holidays 10am to noon. Be prepared to pay in cash. To reach a doctor, dial ☎ **33-93-63-00,** Monday to Friday 9am to 5pm, or ☎ **38-88-60-41** after hours. The doctor's fee is payable in cash. Virtually every doctor speaks English.

Embassies   The embassy of the **United States** is at Dag Hammarskjölds Allé 24, 2100 København (☎ **35-55-31-44**); the embassy of the **United Kingdom,** at Kastelsvej 36—40, 2100 København (☎ **35-44-52-00**); the embassy of **Canada,** on Kristen Berniskowsgadei, 1105 København K (☎ **33-12-22-99**); the embassy of **Ireland,** at Østbanegade 21, 2100 København (☎ **31-42-32-33**); and the embassy of **Australia,** Strandboulevarden, 2100 København (☎ **39-29-20-77**). There is no **New Zealand** embassy.

Emergencies   Dial ☎ **112** for the fire department, the police, or an ambulance, or to report a sea or air accident. Emergency calls from public phone kiosks are free (no coins needed).

Post Office   For information about the Copenhagen post office, call ☎ **33-33-89-00.** The main post office, where you can pick up your general delivery letters, is Tietgensgade 35—39, 1704 København (☎ **33-33-89-00**), open Monday to Friday 11am to 6pm, Saturday 10am to 1pm. The post office at the Central Railroad Station is open Monday to Friday 8am to 10pm, Saturday 9am to 4pm, and Sunday 10am to 4pm.

Telephone   The **country code** for Denmark is **45,** and this two-digit number precedes any call that's intended for Denmark dialed from another country. Danish phones are fully automatic. Dial just the 8-digit number, for there are no city area codes. At public phone booths, use two 50-øre coins or a 1-krone or 5-krone coin only. Don't insert coins until your party answers. You can make more than one call on the same payment if your time hasn't run out. Available at post offices, phone cards cost 30DKK ($4.35), 50DKK ($7.25), and 100DKK ($14.50). Remember that it can be expensive to phone from your hotel room. Emergency calls are free. To make phone calls or send faxes or telexes, go to the **Telecom Denmark** at the Central Railroad Station (☎ **33-14-20-00**), open Monday to Friday 8am to 10pm and Saturday and Sunday 9am to 9pm. The toll-free international access codes are: **AT&T** ☎ 8001-0010, **Sprint** ☎ 800-10-877, **MCI** ☎ 8001-0022.

WHERE TO STAY
NEAR KONGENS NYTROV & NYHAVN
Very Expensive

Hotel d'Angleterre. Kongens Nytorv 34, 1050 København. ☎ **800/44-UTELL** in the U.S., or 33-12-00-95. Fax 33-12-11-18. E-mail: anglehot@remmen.dk. 130 units. A/C MINIBAR TV TEL. 2,075–2,900DKK ($300.90–$420.50) double; from 3,450DKK ($500.25) suite. AE, DC, MC, V. Parking 150DKK ($21.75). Bus: 1, 6, or 9.

At the top of Nyhavn, this seven-story hotel, built in 1755 and extensively renovated in the 1980s, is the premier choice for Denmark (though a bit staid and stodgy). The rooms are beautifully furnished with art objects and the occasional antique. They vary in size, but each has a good bed with a firm mattress; the marble bathrooms

Copenhagen

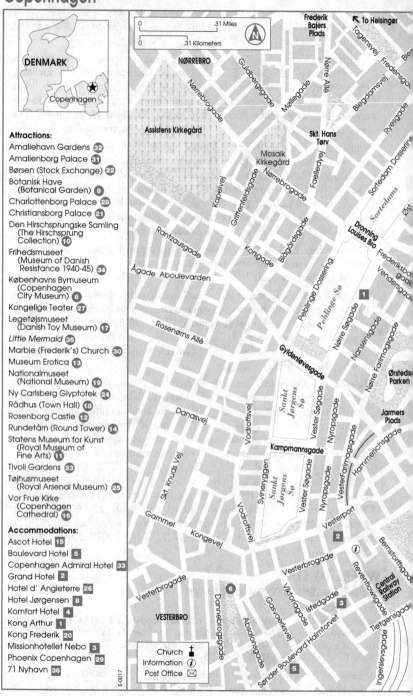

DENMARK

Copenhagen

Attractions:
Amaliehavn Gardens ③②
Amalienborg Palace ③①
Børsen (Stock Exchange) ②②
Botanisk Have
  (Botanical Garden) ⑨
Charlottenborg Palace ②⑧
Christiansborg Palace ②①
Den Hirschsprungske Samling
  (The Hirschsprung
  Collection) ⑩
Frihedsmuseet
  (Museum of Danish
  Resistance 1940-45) ③④
Københavns Bymuseum
  (Copenhagen
  City Museum) ⑥
Kongelige Teater ②⑦
Legetøjsmuseet
  (Danish Toy Museum) ⑰
Little Mermaid ③⑤
Marble (Frederik's) Church ③⓪
Museum Erotica ⑬
Nationalmuseet
  (National Museum) ⑲
Ny Carlsberg Glyptotek ②④
Rådhus (Town Hall) ⑱
Rosenborg Castle ⑫
Rundetårn (Round Tower) ⑭
Statens Museum for Kunst
  (Royal Museum of
  Fine Arts) ⑪
Tivoli Gardens ②③
Tøjhusmuseet
  (Royal Arsenal Museum) ②⑤
Vor Frue Kirke
  (Copenhagen
  Cathedral) ⑯

Accommodations:
Ascot Hotel ⑮
Boulevard Hotel ⑤
Copenhagen Admiral Hotel ③③
Grand Hotel ②
Hotel d' Angleterre ②⑥
Hotel Jørgensen ⑧
Komfort Hotel ④
Kong Arthur ①
Kong Frederik ②⓪
Missionhotellet Nebo ③
Phoenix Copenhagen ②⑨
71 Nyhavn ③⑥

E-0017

192

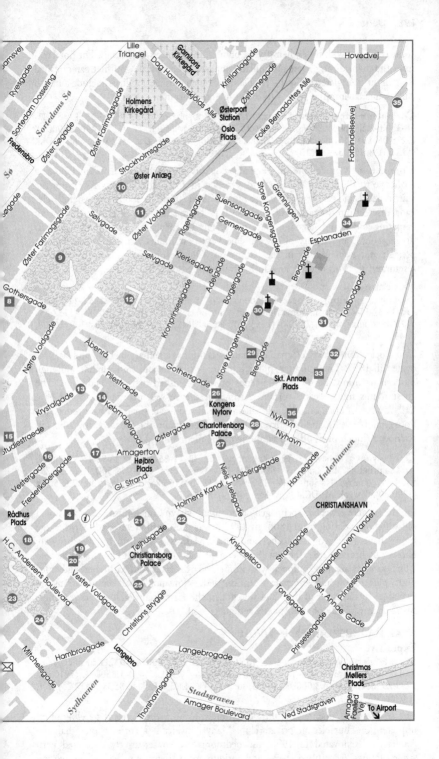

come complete with robes, hair dryers, phones, thick towels, and scales. The hotel features the main dining room, Wiinblad, along with an upscale gourmet eatery called Restaurant d'Angleterre. Both serve Danish/French cuisine. Facilities include a health club, sauna, swimming pool, Turkish bath, and solarium.

✪ **Phoenix Copenhagen.** Bredgade 37, 1260 København. ☎ **33-95-95-00.** Fax 33-33-98-33. E-mail: phoenix@vip.cybercity.dk. 212 units. MINIBAR TV TEL. 1,490–2,390DKK ($216.05–$346.55) double; from 2,800DKK ($406) suite. AE, DC, MC, V. Parking 90DKK ($13.05). Bus: 1, 5, 9, or 10.

More than any other hotel in Copenhagen, this top-of-the-line newcomer poses a challenge to the nearby d'Angleterre. Opened in 1991, the Phoenix rose from the ruined neoclassicism of a royal house built in the 1700s. The rooms are tastefully elegant, discreet interpretations of Louis XVI. Beds are large with firm mattresses; wool carpeting and chandeliers add grace notes. The Italian marble bathrooms have hair dryers, robes, and plenty of towels. The very best rooms also have faxes, trouser presses, and even phones in the bathrooms. On the premises is a Danish/French restaurant, the Von Plessen, and an English-inspired pub, Murdoch's.

Moderate

Copenhagen Admiral Hotel. Toldbodgade 24–28, 1253 København. ☎ **31-11-82-82.** Fax 33-32-55-42. E-mail: admiral@hotel.dk. 366 units. TV TEL. 950–1,210DKK ($137.75–$175.45) double; from 1,750DKK ($253.75) suite. AE, MC, V. Free parking. Bus: 1, 9, 10, 28, or 41.

Two blocks from Nyhavn Canal, this hotel was built as a granary in 1787 and last renovated in 1997. The building still features thick timbers and stone arches, although modern partitions have created a series of well-furnished first-class bedrooms. The guest rooms might lack a certain charm, but they're well maintained. Some have harbor views or open onto French balconies. Bathrooms are small but have bidets, tile floors, marble walls, and hair dryers. The hotel restaurant, the Pinafore, specializes in seafood. A lunch plate offers a sampling of the menu's fish dishes.

✪ **71 Nyhavn.** Nyhavn 71, 1051 København. ☎ **33-11-85-85.** Fax 33-93-15-85. E-mail: arp@isa.dknet.dk. 82 units. MINIBAR TV TEL. Mon–Thurs 1,350–1,550DKK ($195.75–$224.75) double; Fri–Sun 950–1,150DKK ($137.75–$166.75) double; suite 2,695DKK ($390.80) all week. AE, DC, MC, V. Free parking. Bus: 650.

On the corner between Copenhagen harbor and Nyhavn Canal, this hotel is a restored old warehouse dating from 1804. In 1997 it was thoroughly renovated. Most of the rooms have a view of the harbor and canal. Mattresses are firm but the beds are narrow; bathrooms are rather small and contain hair dryers; most have a stall shower. The best units are also equipped with ironing boards, faxes, and bathrobes, and computer plugs are available at the reception desk. Nonsmoking accommodations are available. In the cellar of the 1804 warehouse, the Restaurant Pakhuskælderen offers rustic charm, plenty of atmosphere, and good food.

NEAR RÅDHUSPLADSEN & TIVOLI

Expensive

Kong Frederik. Vester Voldgade 25, 1552 København. ☎ **800/44-UTELL** in the U.S., or 33-12-59-02. Fax 33-93-59-01. 110 units. MINIBAR TV TEL. 1,450–1,650DKK ($210.25–$239.25) double; from 3,000DKK ($435) suite. AE, DC, MC, V. Parking 85DKK ($12.35). Bus: 1, 6, or 28.

The smallest of Copenhagen's ultra-chic hotels, Kong Frederik has the feeling of an unpretentious but elegant private club. Many consider it a cozier choice than the Angleterre. Renovated in 1996, the bedrooms are conservatively decorated with striped fabrics, overstuffed chairs, and antique prints. Bathrooms have good lighting and hair dryers. The Queen's Restaurant is recognized for its fine cuisine and excellent service. As is typical of the region, seafood is widely featured.

Moderate

Ascot Hotel. Studiestraede 61, 1554 København. ☎ **33-12-60-00.** Fax 33-14-60-40. www. dkhotellist.dk. E-mail: hotel@ascothotel.dk. 143 units. TV TEL. 920–1,390DKK ($133.40–$201.55) double; 1,090–2,090DKK ($158.05–$303.05) suite. Rates include buffet breakfast. AE, DC, MC, V. Free parking. Bus: 14 or 16.

On a side street, about a 2-minute walk from Town Hall Square, sits one of Copenhagen's best small hotels. The Ascot was built in 1902 and was enlarged and modernized in 1994. The furniture is rather standard; the finest units open onto the street, although the rooms in the rear get better air circulation and more light. Bathrooms are large and tiled and have a good supply of towels. The firm mattresses are renewed as frequently as needed. Facilities include a small gymnasium.

Grand Hotel. Vesterbrogade 9A, 1620 København. ☎ **31-31-36-00.** Fax 31-31-33-50. 151 units. MINIBAR TV TEL. 1,295–1,695DKK ($187.75–$245.75) double; 2,195–2,795DKK ($318.25–$405.30) suite. Rates include buffet breakfast. AE, DC, MC, V. Bus: 1, 6, 16, 27, 28, or 29.

Built in 1880, this surprisingly elegant landmark hotel near the Central Railroad Station was most recently renovated in 1997. Rooms are tastefully furnished and well maintained with excellent, sleep-inducing beds. Bathrooms are superior—large, marble-clad, and furnished with a goodly assortment of towels and a hair dryer. The Grand Bar overflows in summer onto a sidewalk cafe, and Oliver's Restaurant serves freshly prepared Danish specialties.

Komfort Hotel. Løngangstræde 27, 1468 København. ☎ **33-12-65-70.** Fax 33-15-28-99. E-mail: principal@euroconnect.dk. 201 units. TV TEL. 1,250DKK ($181.25) double; additional bed 225DKK ($32.65). Rates include buffet breakfast. AE, DC, MC, V. Parking 90DKK ($13.05). Bus: 1, 5, or 6.

In the heart of Copenhagen, close to the Town Hall, the Komfort Hotel offers good value. In just 2 minutes, you can walk over to the Tivoli Gardens. All its medium-sized bedrooms are furnished in modern Danish design and contain good, firm mattresses. However, the overall look, including the small but well-maintained private bathrooms, is somewhat motel-like. Towels are a bit skimpy, so ask for extras. The hotel's restaurant, Hattehylden, serves traditional Danish food, or try the John Bull Pub, the oldest English pub in the city. There's even a pool room.

Kong Arthur. Nørre Søgade 11, 1370 København. ☎ **33-11-12-12.** Fax 33-32-61-30. www.dk.hotellist.dk/kongarthur.htm. E-mail: hotel@kongarthur.dk. 107 units. MINIBAR TV TEL. 750–1,145DKK ($108.75–$166) double; 2,700DKK ($391.50) suite. Rates include buffet breakfast. AE, DC, MC, V. Free parking. Bus: 5, 7, or 16.

An orphanage when it was built in 1882, this good-value hotel sits behind a private courtyard next to the tree-lined Peblinge Lake. A new wing with more spacious rooms, including 20 for nonsmokers, was added in 1993. Each of the comfortably furnished and carpeted bedrooms has an in-room VCR and safe. Bathrooms are medium-sized and contain hair dryers and an adequate assortment of towels. The hotel's Restaurant Brøchner is recommended for its reasonably priced Danish and French cuisine, and a Japanese restaurant serves full meals from a sushi bar.

Inexpensive

Boulevard Hotel. Sønder Blvd. 53, 1720 København. ☎ **33-25-25-19.** Fax 33-25-25-83. 20 units (none with bathroom). TV TEL. 500DKK ($72.50) double. No credit cards. Bus: 10.

Simple and plain but well kept, this five-story hotel is about a 10-minute walk from the main rail station. Renovated in the late 1980s from an older core, it's unpretentious and unassuming, with bright, acceptably decorated rooms. Beds have been slept in by many guests, but are reasonably comfortable if a bit narrow. Each has a sink with hot and cold running water; the toilets and showers are in rooms off the central corridors. Breakfast is the only meal served.

Missionshotellet Nebo. Istedgade 6, 1650 København. ☎ **33-21-12-17.** Fax 33-23-47-74. www.nebo.dk. E-mail: nebo@email.dk. 150 units (72 with bathroom). TV TEL. 600DKK ($87) double without bathroom; 840DKK ($121.80) double with bathroom; extra bed 200DKK ($29). AE, DC, MC, V. Parking 25DKK ($3.60). Bus: 1, 6, 16, 28, or 41.

This hotel near the rail station is a quiet retreat, with a tiny lobby and a lounge that opens onto a side courtyard. The small rooms are clean and up-to-date, though Spartan; they're furnished in a Nordic functional style. Some beds are comfortable, but others have mattresses that sag in the middle. There are bathrooms on all floors.

ON HELGOLANDSGADE & COLBJØRNSENSGADE

Copenhagen's main accommodations street is near the Central Railroad Station, where Helgolandsgade runs parallel to Colbjørnsensgade. The many moderately priced hostelries here can be booked through a central office at Helgolandsgade 4 (☎ **31-31-43-44**). Adjacent to the **Triton Hotel,** it's operated jointly by the Triton and the well-recommended **Absalon Hotel.** Admittedly, most callers phoning this service are siphoned off to either of those hotels, but if space in those hotels is full, lodgings are found in other decent and acceptable hotels in the neighborhood. Calls are accepted only between the hours of 9am and 5pm daily; outside this time frame, the number is diverted to other uses.

A GAY HOTEL

Hotel Jørgensen. Rømersgade 11, 1362 København. ☎ **33-13-81-86.** Fax 33-15-51-05. 24 units; 13 dormitory rms (72 beds). TV TEL. 580DKK ($84.10) double; 115DKK ($16.65) per person in dormitory. Rates include breakfast. MC, V. Parking free overnight. Bus: 14 or 16.

In 1984 the Jørgensen was transformed into Denmark's first gay hotel. A white stucco establishment, it's on a busy boulevard in the central city, with a patronage mainly of gays and lesbians, although straights are welcome. The rooms are conventional and have dormitory-style beds. Family rooms house four to five people, and the 12 rooms accommodate 6 to 14 each. Rental of either requires guests to provide their own sheets or sleeping bag. Breakfast is the only meal served.

WHERE TO DINE

That national institution, the *smørrebrød* or open-faced sandwiches, is introduced at lunch. Literally, this means "bread and butter," but the Danes stack this sandwich as though it were the Leaning Tower of Pisa—then they throw in a slice of curled cucumber and bits of parsley or perhaps sliced peaches or a mushroom for added color.

NEAR KONGENS NYTROV & NYHAVN
Very Expensive

✪ **Kong Hans Kaelder.** Vingårdsstraede 6. ☎ **33-11-68-68.** Reservations required. Main courses 265–335DKK ($38.40–$48.55); set-price menu 465–725DKK ($67.45–$105.10). AE, DC, MC, V. Mon–Sat 6pm–midnight. Closed Dec 24–26. Bus: 1, 6, or 9. INTERNATIONAL.

This vaulted Gothic cellar, once owned by King Hans, may be the best restaurant in Denmark. Its most serious competition comes from Kommandanten, which many discriminating palates hail as the best. Located on "the oldest corner of Copenhagen," it has been carefully restored and is now a Relais Gourmand. A typical three-course lunch would be smoked salmon from the restaurant's own smokery with aquavit and grain mustard, salmis of mallard duckling with spätzle, and then caramelized vanilla creme with pears. At dinner, you might choose lobster consommé with basil and ravioli, young pigeon with jasmine rice galette, a selection of Danish and French cheeses, finished with Valrhona chocolate in variations with citrus fruit marmalade.

Expensive

✪ **Kommandanten.** Ny Adelgade 7. ☎ **33-12-09-90.** Reservations required. Main courses 240–270DKK ($34.80–$39.15); set-price menu 580DKK ($84.10). AE, DC, MC, V. Mon–Fri noon–2pm; Mon–Sat 6–10pm. Bus: 1 or 6. INTERNATIONAL.

Built in 1698 and the former residence of the military commander of Copenhagen, Kommandanten is the epitome of Danish chic and charm, famously decorated in shades of blue and silver. The menu offers a mouth-watering array of classical dishes mixed with innovative selections, a medley of strong yet subtle flavors. The finest seasonal ingredients are used, and the menu changes every 2 weeks. You might be offered the grilled catch of the day, breast of duck with port-wine sauce, grilled turbot with spinach sauce, or gratinée of shellfish; or oxtails removed from the bone and served with fried lobster, purée of potatoes and parsley, and a lobster cream sauce.

Moderate

Café Lumskebugten. Esplanaden 21. ☎ **33-15-60-29.** Reservations recommended. Main courses 168–250DKK ($24.35–$36.25); 3-course set-price lunch 275DKK ($39.90); 4-course set-price dinner 465DKK ($67.45). AE, DC, MC, V. Mon–Fri 11am–10:30pm; Sat 5–10:30pm. Bus: 1, 6, or 9. DANISH.

This restaurant is a clean, well-managed bastion of Danish charm, with an unpretentious elegance. It was established in 1854 as a rowdy tavern for sailors by a now-legendary matriarch named Karen Marguerita Krog. Today, a tastefully gentrified version of the original beef hash is still served. Two glistening-white dining rooms are decorated with antique ships' models, oil paintings, and pinewood floors. The food and service are excellent. Menu specialties include Danish fish cakes with mustard sauce and minced beetroot, fried platters of herring, sugar-marinated salmon with mustard-cream sauce, and a symphony of fish with saffron sauce and new potatoes.

Inexpensive

Ida Davidsen. Store Kongensgade 70. ☎ **33-91-36-55.** Reservations not necessary. Sandwiches 45–150DKK ($6.50–$21.75). DC, MC, V. Mon–Fri 9am–4pm (last order). Bus: 1 or 9. SANDWICHES.

This restaurant has flourished within the Danish psyche since 1888 when the forebears of its present owner, Ida Davidsen, established a sandwich shop. Today, five generations later, the family matriarch and namesake is known as the "smørrebrød queen of Copenhagen" selling a greater variety of open-faced sandwiches (177 kinds) than anyone else in Denmark. If you opt for a sandwich here, you'll be in good company: Her fare has even been featured at royal buffets at Amalienborg Castle. You'll select your choice by pointing to it in a glass-fronted display case, after which a staff member carries it to your table. Naturally, there's a vast selection to choose from, including types made with salmon, lobster, shrimp, smoked duck with braised cabbage and horseradish, liver pâté, ham, herring, and boiled egg.

NEAR RÅDHUSPLADSEN & TIVOLI

Moderate

Restaurant Flyvefisken. Lars Bjørnstr. 18. ☎ **33-14-95-15.** Reservations recommended at dinner. Lunch platters 60–100DKK ($8.70–$14.50); dinner main courses 95–150DKK ($13.75–$21.75); set-price dinners 148–210DKK ($21.45–$30.45). DC, MC, V. Mon–Sat noon–3pm and 5:30–10:30pm. Bus: 5. DANISH/THAI.

The decor of this restaurant is authentically Danish, complete with colors of the national flag, thick wooden tables, and paneling. And indeed, the lunch you order is likely to focus on smørrebrød (open-faced sandwiches), different preparations of herring, grilled steaks with fried onions, and freshly made salads. But beginning at 5:30pm, the culinary venue changes radically, and the fiery cuisine of Thailand becomes the norm. Expect strong curries and lemongrass, the hot fish soups of Bangkok, grilled lamb, sharkmeat in basil sauce, chicken with cashews and fiery peppers, steaming cupfuls of green and black tea, and bottles of Singha beer. It's a marvelous change of pace from typically Danish fare.

Inexpensive

✪ **Riz Raz.** Kompagnistræde 20 (at Knabrostræde). ☎ **33-15-05-75.** Reservations not necessary. Vegetarian buffet 59DKK ($8.55) per person; main courses 79–150DKK ($11.45–$21.75). DC, MC, V. Daily 11:30am–midnight. Bus: 5 or 6. MEDITERRANEAN.

Bustling and unpretentious, this decidedly un-Danish hideaway offers the best all-vegetarian buffet in Copenhagen. You help yourself from a sprawling network of buffet tables laden with each of the vegetarian specialties of the Mediterranean world, including Morocco, Egypt, Lebanon, Greece, and Italy, all for a price that by Scandinavian standards is highly reasonable. Carry your selections to a warren of small dining rooms, each of which leads—railroad style—into the next. There's additional seating outdoors during nice weather, or upstairs. Expect a medley of virtually every vegetable known to humankind, prepared either *au naturel,* or as part of a marinated fantasy that might include the antipasti of Italy, the hummus of Lebanon, or an array of long-simmered casseroles inspired by the cuisines of the Moroccan highlands.

NEAR ROSENBORG SLOT

Very Expensive

St. Gertruds Kloster. Hauser Plads 32. ☎ **33-14-66-30.** Reservations required. Set-price menus 340–750DKK ($49.30–$108.75); children's menu 90DKK ($13.05); main courses 215–268DKK ($31.15–$38.85). AE, DC, MC, V. Daily 4–11pm. Closed Dec 25–Jan 1. Bus: 4E, 7E, 14, or 16. INTERNATIONAL.

Near Nørreport Station and south of Rosenborg Castle, this is the most romantic restaurant in Copenhagen. There's no electricity in the labyrinth of 14th-century underground vaults, and the 1,500 flickering candles, open grill, iron sconces, and rough-hewn furniture create an elegant medieval ambience. The chefs display talent and integrity, their cuisine reflecting precision and sensitivity. Every flavor is fully focused; each dish balanced to perfection. At dinner, you might start with a pâté of fresh foie gras with a Madeira glacé and duck bacon or king prawn sautéed in parsley butter and served in red curry cream with honey-preserved apples and shallots, then move on to a combination of three kinds of fish with crayfish tails, mild curry jus, and a ratatouille of vegetables and rice.

AT GRÅBRØDRETORV

Moderate

Bøf & Ost. Gråbrødretorv 13. ☎ **33-11-99-11.** Reservations required. Main courses 125–175DKK ($18.15–$25.40); set-price meals 95DKK ($13.75) at lunch, 235DKK ($34.05) at dinner. DC, MC, V. Mon–Sat 11:30am–10:30pm. Closed Jan 1 and Dec 24–25. Bus: 5. DANISH/FRENCH.

"Beef & Cheese" is housed in a 1728 building, and its cellars come from a medieval monastery. In summer a pleasant outdoor terrace overlooks Gray Friars Square. Specialties include lobster soup, fresh Danish bay strips, a cheese plate with six selections, and entrecôte with various sauces and butters and a baked potato. Seasonal dishes rotate in and out of the menu, making good use of regional mushrooms, fish, and game.

Inexpensive

Pasta Basta. Valkendorfsgade 22. ☎ **33-11-21-31.** Reservations recommended. Main courses 67–145DKK ($9.70–$21.05). No credit cards. Sun–Wed 11:30am–3:30am; Thurs–Sat 11:30am–5:30am. Bus: 5. ITALIAN.

Its main attraction is a loaded table of cold antipasti and salads, which many diners believe is one of the best values in town. The restaurant is divided into half a dozen cozy dining rooms, each with a decor inspired by ancient Pompeii. Menu choices include at least 15 kinds of pasta (all made fresh on the premises), raw marinated filet of beef (carpaccio) served with olive oil and basil, a platter with three kinds of Danish caviar (whitefish, speckled trout, and vendace, all served with chopped onions, lemon, toast, and butter), and fresh mussels cooked in a dry white wine with pasta and creamy saffron sauce. Late nights are often lively, so if you can't sleep and you're hungry, this can be an entertaining option.

Peder Oxe's Restaurant/Vinkaelder Wine Bar. Gråbrødretorv 11. ☎ **33-11-00-77.** Reservations recommended. Main courses 69–159DKK ($10–$23.05); set-price lunch 69–89DKK ($10–$12.90). DC, MC, V. Daily 11:30am–midnight. Bus: 5. DANISH.

In the Middle Ages this was the site of a monastery, but the present building dates from the 1700s. The restaurant/wine bar was established in the 1970s and is still popular among young people. A salad bar is included in the price of the main course, but it's so tempting that many prefer to enjoy it alone for 69DKK ($10) per person. Dishes include lobster soup, Danish bay shrimp, open-faced sandwiches, hamburgers, and fresh fish. The bill of fare, though standard, is well prepared.

AT CHRISTIANSBORG

Very Expensive

Krogs Fiskerestaurant. Gammel Strand 38. ☎ **33-15-89-15.** Reservations required. Main courses 228–395DKK ($33.05–$57.30); set-price menu 385DKK ($55.80) for 3 courses, 435DKK ($63.05) for 5 courses. AE, DC, MC, V. Mon–Sat 11:30am–4pm and 5:30–10:30pm. Bus: 2, 10, or 16. SEAFOOD.

Classically elegant and opposite the old fish market, this restaurant's premises were built in 1789 as a fish shop. The canal-side plaza where fishers moored their boats is now the site of the outdoor dining terrace. Converted into a restaurant in 1910, the establishment serves very fresh seafood in a single large room tastefully decorated in an antique style with old oil paintings and rustic colors. The well-chosen menu includes lobster soup, bouillabaisse, natural oysters, mussels steamed in white wine, and sautéed turbot with corn cassoulet. Each dish is impeccably prepared and filled with flavor. A limited selection of meat dishes is also available.

Expensive

Nouvelle. 34 Gammel Strand. ☎ **33-32-04-00.** Reservations recommended. Main courses 225–295DKK ($32.65–$42.80); 3-course set-price lunch menu 275DKK ($39.90); 4-course set-price dinner 485DKK ($70.30). AE, DC, MC, V. Mon–Fri 11:30am–3pm and 6–10pm; Sat 7:30–9pm. Closed Dec 22–Jan 6. Bus: 28, 29, or 41. DANISH.

Set in one of the oldest surviving houses in Copenhagen, a prosperous-looking villa built around 1700, this restaurant lies upstairs from the also-recommended and less expensive Thorvaldsen (see below). Chefs here are known for their finesse in creating modern adaptations of traditional Danish favorites. You'll dine in one of three elegantly rustic dining rooms whose windows overlook a nearby canal and whose ambience was created to emulate the interior of an upscale Danish country *kro* (inn). Menu items change with the season and the inspiration of the chefs, but might include herring in puff pastry with caviar; turbot served in a fruity gewürztztraminer sauce; filet of veal with truffle sauce; and an unusual starter known as "egg nouvelle," which is a simple boiled egg with a significant difference: It's stuffed with a mousseline of lobster and accompanied with a dollop of Sevruga caviar. A thrilling dessert specialty is an assortment of three sherbets: white chocolate, blackberries plus their liqueur, and pear.

Moderate

Fiskekaelderen. Ved Stranden 18. ☎ **33-12-20-11.** Reservations recommended. Main courses 145–265DKK ($21.05–$38.40); 3-course set-price menu 325DKK ($47.15). AE, DC, V. Mon–Fri noon–3pm and 5–10pm; Sat–Sun 6–10pm. Bus: 1, 6, or 10. SEAFOOD.

Although the building dates from 1750, Fiskekaelderen was opened in 1975 and is today the best seafood restaurant in Copenhagen. The restaurant prides itself on very fresh fish either imported from the Mediterranean or caught in the waters of the North Atlantic. Warmly nautical in decor, it has a bubbling lobster tank and an ice table displaying the fish of the day. Try the lobster bisque with fish and lobster roe, Danish fish soup, stuffed sole poached in white wine and glazed with hollandaise sauce, fried plaice with potatoes, or fricassée of three types of fish in saffron-flavored bouillon with noodles. Some beef dishes, such as Charolais sirloin, are also served.

Inexpensive

Thorvaldsen. 34 Gammel Strand. ☎ **33-32-04-00.** Reservations recommended. Main courses 60–135DKK ($8.70–$19.60). AE, DC, MC, V. Mon–Sat 11:30am–4pm. Bus: 28. DANISH.

Part of the success of this artfully simple Danish bistro derives from its association with Nouvelle, one of Copenhagen's most talked-about modern restaurants (see above). Open only for lunch, it lies on the street level of the circa 1700 mansion it occupies, adjacent to a canal. Named after the 18th-century merchant who occupied the site originally, it features a single blue and white dining room, and menu specialties that taste best when accompanied with beer, aquavit, or any selection from the copious wine list that it shares with its more famous counterpart upstairs. Menu items include a tasty version of traditional herring in cream and onion sauce, filet of eel simmered with white beans and onions, and an all-Danish platter whose four components change with the seasons.

IN TIVOLI

Food prices inside Tivoli are about 30% higher than elsewhere. Try skipping dessert at a restaurant and picking up a less expensive treat at one of the many stands. Take bus no. 1, 6, 8, 16, 29, 30, 32, or 33 to reach the park and either of the following restaurants. *Note:* These restaurants are open only from May to mid-September.

Very Expensive

Divan II. Vesterbrogade 3. ☎ **33-12-51-51.** Reservations recommended. Main courses 265–345DKK ($38.40–$50.05); set-price meal 295DKK ($42.80) at lunch, 385–585DKK ($55.80–$84.80) at dinner. AE, DC, MC, V. Daily 11am–midnight. DANISH/FRENCH.

One of the finest restaurants in Tivoli was established in 1843, the same year as Tivoli itself, and despite its designation as Divan II, it's nonetheless older than its nearby competitor, the less formal Divan I. Service is almost unrelentingly impeccable in a garden setting where the cuisine is among the most urbane in the Danish capital. Examples include fried filet of salmon served with a turbot bisque and tomato-and-basil concassé, a paupiette of filet of sole with lobster mousseline with fried oyster mushrooms and a turbot bisque, and monkfish médaillons sautéed with veal bacon and served with fricassée of morels. Dinners here are elaborate, memorable, and highly ritualized.

Expensive

Restaurant P.H. Vesterbrogade 3, Tivoli. ☎ **33-75-07-75.** Reservations recommended. Main courses 155–245DKK ($22.45–$35.55); set-price lunch 145DKK ($21.05); set-price dinners 185–398DKK ($26.85–$57.70). AE, DC, MC, V. Daily noon–10:30pm (last order). DANISH/FRENCH.

One of the most upscale and elegant restaurants within Tivoli bears the initials of Paul Hemmingsen (1894–1967), an architect, interior designer, and writer, whose works are known to virtually every Dane. A relative newcomer to the Tivoli restaurant scene, where owners and venues change only very, very rarely, the restaurant has gained a flash of fame since it was established in the late 1990s, thanks to intelligent cuisine and a freshness of image that older, more jaded restaurants within Tivoli might have lost. You'll dine in a modern-looking building that Hemmingsen designed, within a sunflooded, cheerfully modern decor. Menu items are based on French and Danish traditions, with touches of Asian pepper and spice to heat things up just a bit. The menu intelligently draws upon fine Danish culinary traditions without the heaviness. The chefs seem capable of preparing everything well. Opt for the North Sea turbot, with white asparagus and spring cabbage, or if you want something rooted in the old kitchens of Denmark, try the Danish veal cutlet with a panade of ham and shallots served with potato baked in a calf's tail confit and a creamy morel sauce.

EXPLORING COPENHAGEN
SIGHTSEEING SUGGESTIONS FOR FIRST-TIME VISITORS

If You Have 1 Day   Take a walking tour through the heart of the old city, which will give you time to recover from jet lag. Spend the late afternoon at Christiansborg Palace on Slotsholmen island where the queen of Denmark receives guests. Early in the evening head to the Tivoli.

If You Have 2 Days   On day 2, visit Amalienborg Palace, the queen's residence. Try to time your visit to witness the changing of the guard. Continue beyond the palace to *The Little Mermaid* statue. In the afternoon, see the art treasures of Ny Carlsberg Glyptotek. At night, seek out a local tavern.

If You Have 3 Days   In the morning of the third day, journey to Rosenborg Castle, summer palace of King Christian IV, and then wander through the park and gardens. Have lunch at one of the restaurants lining the canal at Nyhavn, the traditional seamen's quarter of Copenhagen. In the afternoon, go to Rundetårn (Round Tower) for a panoramic view of the city, and if time remains, stop in at the National Museum and Denmark's Fight for Freedom Museum.

If You Have 4 Days   Head north to Louisiana, the modern-art museum, and continue on to Helsingør to visit Kronborg Castle, famously associated with Shakespeare's *Hamlet*. Return by train to Copenhagen in time for a stroll along the Strøget, Europe's longest walking street. For dinner, visit the village of Dragør.

If You Have 5 Days   On the fifth day, visit Frilandsmuseet, at Lyngby, a half-hour train ride from Copenhagen. Have lunch at the park. Return to Copenhagen and take a walking tour along its canals. If time remains, tour the Carlsberg brewery. Pay a final visit to the Tivoli to cap your adventure in the Danish capital.

THE TIVOLI GARDENS

✪ **Tivoli Gardens.** Vesterbrogade 3. ☎ **33-15-10-01.** Admission 11am–1pm, 35DKK ($5.05) adults, 20DKK ($2.90) children under 12; 1–9:30pm, 45DKK ($6.50) adults, 20DKK ($2.90) children; 9:30pm–midnight, 30DKK ($4.50) adults, 20DKK ($2.90) children. Rides 20DKK ($2.90) each. Daily 11am–midnight. Closed mid-Sept to Apr. Bus: 1, 16, or 29.

Copenhagen's *Little Mermaid*

The one statue *everybody* wants to see in Copenhagen is the life-size bronze of *Den Lille Havfrue*, inspired by Hans Christian Andersen's *The Little Mermaid*, one of the world's most famous fairy tales. The statue, unveiled in 1913, was sculpted by Edvard Eriksen and rests on rocks right off the shore. The mermaid has been attacked more than once, losing an arm in one misadventure, and decapitated as recently as January 6, 1998.

In summer, a special "Mermaid Bus" leaves from Rådhuspladsen (Vester Voldgade) at 10:30am and then at half-hour intervals until 5:30pm. On the "Langelinie" bus there's a 20-minute stop at *The Little Mermaid*. If you want more time, take bus no. 1, 6, or 9.

Since it opened in 1843, this 20-acre garden and amusement park in the center of Copenhagen has been a resounding success, with its thousands of flowers, merry-go-round of tiny Viking ships, games of chance and skill (pinball arcades, slot machines, shooting galleries), and Ferris wheel of hot-air balloons and cabin seats. There's even a playground for children.

An Arabian-style fantasy palace, with towers and arches, houses more than two dozen restaurants in all price ranges, from a lakeside inn to a beer garden. Take a walk around the edge of the tiny lake with its ducks, swans, and boats.

A parade of the red-uniformed Tivoli Boys Guard takes place on weekends at 6:30 and 8:30pm, and their regimental band gives concerts Saturday at 3:30pm on the open-air stage. The oldest building at Tivoli, the Chinese-style Pantomime Theater, with its peacock curtain, stages pantomimes in the evening.

THE TOP MUSEUMS

Don't worry about not understanding the explanations in the museums; virtually all have write-ups in English.

✪ **Ny Carlsberg Glyptotek.** Dantes Plads 7. ☎ **33-41-81-41.** Admission 30DKK ($4.35) adults, free for children under 16. Free admission Wed and Sun. Tues–Sun 10am–4pm. Bus: 1, 2, 5, 6, 8, or 10.

The Glyptotek, behind the Tivoli, is one of Scandinavia's most important art museums. Founded by 19th-century art collector Carl Jacobsen, the museum comprises two distinct departments: modern works and antiquities. The modern section has both French and Danish art, mainly from the 19th century. Sculpture, including works by Rodin, is on the ground floor, and works of the Impressionists and related artists, including van Gogh's *Landscape from St. Rémy*, are on the upper floors. Egyptian, Greek, and Roman art are on the main floor; Etruscan and Greek art are found on the lower floor. The Egyptian collection is outstanding; the prize is a prehistoric rendering of a hippopotamus. A favorite of ours is the Etruscan art display. In 1996, the Ny Glyptotek added a French Masters' wing, with an extensive collection of masterpieces.

Statens Museum for Kunst (Royal Museum of Fine Arts). Sølvgade 48–50. ☎ **33-74-84-94.** Admission 30–50DKK ($4.35–$7.25) adults, free for children under 16. Tues and Thurs–Sun 10am–5pm; Wed 10am–8pm. Bus: 10, 14, 43, or 184.

Reopening in the autumn of 1998 after a major restoration, this well-stocked museum houses painting and sculpture from the 13th century to the present. There are Dutch golden-age landscapes and marine paintings by Rubens and his school, plus portraits by Frans Hals and Rembrandt. The Danish golden age is represented by Eckersberg, Købke, and Hansen. French 20th-century art includes 20 works by Matisse. In the Royal Print Room are 300,000 drawings, prints, lithographs, and other works by such artists as Dürer, Rembrandt, Matisse, and Picasso.

Den Hirschsprungske Samling (The Hirschsprung Collection). Stockholmsgade 20. ☎ **35-42-03-36.** Admission 25DKK ($3.60) adults; free for children under 16; 40DKK ($5.80) for special exhibitions. Wed 11am–9pm; Thurs–Mon 11am–4pm. Bus: 14, 42, or 43.

This collection of Danish art from the 19th and early 20th centuries is in Ostre Anlaeg, a park in the city center. Heinrich Hirschsprung (1836–1908), a tobacco merchant, created the collection and it has been growing ever since. The emphasis is on the Danish golden age, with such artists as Eckersberg, Købke, and Lundbye, and on the Skagen painters, P. S. Krøyer and Anna and Michael Ancher. Some furnishings from the artists' homes are exhibited.

Nationalmuseet (National Museum). Ny Vestergade 10. ☎ **33-13-44-11.** Admission 30DKK ($4.35) adults, free for children under 16. Tues–Sun 10am–5pm. Closed Dec 24–25 and 31. Bus: 1, 2, 5, 6, 8, 10, 28, 29, 30, 32, 33, 34, or 35.

A gigantic repository of anthropological artifacts, this museum is divided primarily into five departments. The first section focuses on prehistory, the Middle Ages, and the Renaissance in Denmark. These collections date from the Stone Age and include Viking stones, helmets, and fragments of battle gear. Especially interesting are the *lur* horn, a Bronze Age musical instrument, among the oldest instruments in Europe, and the world-famous "Sun Chariot," an elegant Bronze Age piece of pagan art. The Royal Collection of Coins and Medals contains various coins from antiquity. The Collection of Egyptian and Classical Antiquities offers outstanding examples of art and artifacts from ancient civilizations.

Frihedsmuseet (Museum of Danish Resistance, 1940–45). Churchillparken. ☎ **33-13-77-14.** Free admission. May–Sept 15 Tues–Sat 10am–4pm, Sun 10am–5pm; Sept 16–Apr Tues–Sat 11am–3pm, Sun 11am–4pm. Bus: 1, 6, or 9.

On display here are relics of torture and concentration camps, the equipment used for the wireless and illegal films, British propaganda leaflets, satirical caricatures of Hitler, information about both Danish Jews and Danish Nazis, and the paralyzing nation-wide strikes. An armed car, used for drive-by shootings of Danish Nazi informers and collaborators, is on the grounds.

Frilandsmuseet (Open-Air Museum). Kongevejen 100. ☎ **45-85-02-92.** Admission 30DKK ($4.35) adults, free for children. Free admission on Wed. Easter–Sept Tues–Sun 10am–5pm; Oct 1–18 Tues–Sun 10am–4pm. Closed Oct 19–Easter. S-tog: From Copenhagen Central Station to Sorgenfri (leaving every 20 minutes). Bus: 184 or 194.

This reconstructed village in Lyngby, on the fringe of Copenhagen, captures Denmark's one-time rural character. The "museum" is nearly 90 acres; a 2-mile walk around the compound reveals a dozen authentic buildings—farmsteads, windmills, fishers' cottages. Exhibits include a half-timbered 18th-century farmstead from one of the tiny windswept Danish islands, a primitive longhouse from the remote Faroe Islands, thatched fishers' huts from Jutland, tower windmills, and a potter's workshop from the mid-19th century.

Museum Erotica. Købmagergade 24. ☎ **33-12-03-11.** Admission 59DKK ($8.55). May–Sept daily 10am–11pm; Oct–Apr Mon–Fri 11am–8pm, Sat 10am–9pm, Sun 10am–8pm. Bus: 1, 16, or 29.

Opened in the summer of 1992, this is the only museum in the world where you learn about the sex lives of such famous people as Freud, Nietzsche, and Duke Ellington.

Founded by Ole Ege, a well-known Danish photographer of nudes, it's within walking distance of the Tivoli and the Central Railroad Station. In addition to revealing a glimpse into the sex lives of the famous, it presents a survey of erotica around the world and through the ages. The exhibitions range from "the tame to the tempestuous"—from Etruscan drawings and Chinese paintings to Greek vases depicting a lot of sexual activity.

Tivoli Museum. Vesterbrogade 3. ☎ **33-15-10-01.** Admission 20DKK ($2.90) adults, 10DKK ($1.45) children. Apr 24–Sept 13 daily 11am–6pm; off-season Tues–Sun 10am–4pm. S-tog to Central Station.

Some 150 years of Europe's most famous amusement park are revealed in this offbeat museum spread across three floors. Models, films, 3-D displays, pictures, posters, and original artifacts reveal how the Danes and their foreign visitors have been having fun over the decades. Opening in 1993, the museum was an instant hit with Tivoli devotees. It's a great idea to come here if you have only one chance to visit Copenhagen in a lifetime, and the Tivoli has shut down for the year at the time of your visit. Legendary performers, which have included everyone from Marlene Dietrich to a flea circus that ran for 65 years, are revealed. Children will delight in the rides of yesterday (some good enough to recycle today).

Tøjhusmuseet (Royal Arsenal Museum). Tøjhusgade 3. ☎ **33-11-60-37.** Admission 20DKK ($2.90) adults, 5DKK (75¢) children 6–17, free for children under 6. Tues–Sun noon–4pm. Closed Jan 1 and Dec 24–25 and 31. Bus: 1, 2, 5, 6, 8, 10, 28, 29, 30, 32, 33, 34, or 35.

This museum features a fantastic display of weapons used for hunting and warfare. On the ground floor—the longest vaulted Renaissance hall in Europe—is the Canon Hall, stocked with artillery equipment from 1500 up to the present day. Above the Canon Hall is the impressive Armory Hall with one of the world's finest collections of small arms, colors, and armor. The building was erected during the years 1598 to 1604.

THE ROYAL PALACES

✪ **Amalienborg Palace.** Slotsplads. ☎ **33-12-21-86.** Admission 35DKK ($5.05) adults, 5DKK (75¢) children 5–15, free for children under 5. Jan–Apr Tues–Sun 11am–4pm; May daily 11am–4pm; June–Aug daily 10am–4pm; Sept–Oct daily 11am–4pm; Nov–Dec 13 Tues–Sun 11am–4pm; Dec 26–31 daily 11am–4pm. Closed Dec 14–25. Bus: 1, 6, 9, or 10.

These four 18th-century French-style rococo mansions have been the home of the Danish royal family since 1794, when Christiansborg burned. Visitors flock to witness the changing of the guard at noon when the royal family is in residence. A swallowtail flag at mast signifies that the queen is in Copenhagen and not at her North Zealand summer home, Fredensborg Palace.

The Royal Life Guard in black bearskin busbies like the hussars leaves Rosenborg Castle at 11:30am and marches along Gothersgade, Nørrevold, Frederiksborggade, Købmagergade, Østergade, Kongens Nytorv, Bredgade, Sankt Annæ Plads, and Amaliegade to Amalienborg. After the event, the guard, still accompanied by the band, returns to Rosenborg Castle via Frederiksgade, Store Kongensgade, and Gothersgade.

In 1994 some of the official and private rooms in Amalienborg were opened to the public for the first time. The rooms, reconstructed to reflect the period 1863 to 1947, belonged to members of the reigning royal family, the Glücksborgs, who ascended the throne in 1863. The highlight is the period devoted to the long reign (1863–1906) of King Christian IX and Queen Louise.

✪ **Christiansborg Palace.** Christiansborg Slotsplads, Prins Jørgens Gård 1. ☎ **33-92-64-92.** Admission to Royal Reception Rooms, 37DKK ($5.35) adults, 10DKK ($1.45) children; parliament, free; castle ruins, 20DKK ($2.90) adults, 5DKK (75¢) children. Reception Rooms,

May and Sept, guided tours Tues–Sun at 11am and 3pm; June–Aug, guided tours daily at 11am, 1pm, and 3pm; Oct–Apr, guided tours Tues, Thurs, and Sun at 11am and 3pm. English-language tours given only mid-June to late Sept, Tues, Thurs, Sat, Sun 10am–4pm. Ruins, May–Sept Tues–Fri and Sun 9:30am–3:30pm. Closed Oct–Apr. Bus: 1, 2, 6, 8, or 10.

This granite-and-copper palace on the Slotsholmen—a small island that has been the center of political power in Denmark for more than 800 years—houses the Danish parliament, the Supreme Court, the prime minister's offices, and the Royal Reception Rooms. A guide leads you through richly decorated rooms, including the Throne Room, banqueting hall, and Queen's Library. Before entering, you're asked to put on soft overshoes to protect the floors. Under the palace, visit the well-preserved ruins of the 1167 castle of Bishop Absalon, founder of Copenhagen.

Rosenborg Castle. Øster Voldgade 4A. ☎ **33-15-32-86.** Admission 45DKK ($6.50) adults, 10DKK ($1.45) children under 15. Palace and treasury (royal jewels), June–Aug, daily 10am–4pm; May and Sept to mid-Oct, daily 11am–3pm; mid-Oct to Apr 30, Tues, Fri, and Sun 11am–2pm. S-tog: Nørreport. Bus: 5, 10, 14, 16, 31, 42, 43, 184, or 185.

This red-brick Renaissance-style castle houses everything from narwhal-tusked and ivory coronation chairs to Frederik VII's baby shoes—all from the Danish royal family. Its biggest draws are the dazzling crown jewels and regalia in the basement Treasury, where a lavishly decorated coronation saddle from 1596 is also shown. Try to see the Knights Hall (Room 21), with its coronation seat, three silver lions, and relics from the 1700s. Room 3 was used by founding father Christian IV, who died in this bedroom decorated with Asian lacquer art and a stucco ceiling.

CHURCHES & OTHER ATTRACTIONS

Frederikskirke. Frederiksgade 4. ☎ **33-15-01-44.** Free admission to church; 20DKK ($2.90) adults, 10DKK ($1.45) children to dome. Church, Mon, Tues, Thurs, Fri 11am–2pm; Wed 11am–6pm; Sat 11am–4pm; Sun noon–4pm. Dome, Oct–May Sat–Sun 11am–12:45pm; June–Sept daily 11am–12:45pm. Bus: 1, 6, or 9.

This 2-centuries-old church, with its green copper dome—one of the largest in the world—is a short walk from Amalienborg Palace. After an unsuccessful start during the neoclassical revival of the 1750s in Denmark, the church was finally completed in Roman baroque style in 1894. In many ways, it's more impressive than Copenhagen's cathedral.

Vor Frue Kirke (Copenhagen Cathedral). Nørregade. ☎ **33-14-41-28.** Free admission. Mon–Fri 9am–5pm. Bus: 5.

This Greek Renaissance-style church, built in the early 19th century near Copenhagen University, features Bertel Thorvaldsen's white marble neoclassical works, including *Christ and the Apostles.* The funeral of Hans Christian Andersen took place here in 1875, and Søren Kierkegaard's in 1855.

Rådhus (Town Hall). Rådhuspladsen. ☎ **33-66-25-82.** Admission to Rådhus, 30DKK ($4.35); clock, 10DKK ($1.45) adults, 5DKK (75¢) children. Guided tour, Rådhus, Mon–Fri 3pm, Sat 10am; tower, Mon–Sat at noon. Bus: 1, 6, or 8.

Built in 1905, the Town Hall has impressive statues of Hans Christian Andersen and Niels Bohr, the Nobel Prize–winning physicist. Jens Olsen's famous **World Clock** is open for viewing Monday to Friday 10am to 4pm and Saturday at noon. The clockwork is so exact that the variation over 300 years is 0.4 seconds. Climb the tower for an impressive view.

Rundetårn (Round Tower). Købmagergade 52A. ☎ **33-73-03-73.** Admission 15DKK ($2.15) adults (14 and older), 5DKK (75¢) children 5–13. Tower, Sept–May Mon–Sat 10am–5pm, Sun noon–5pm; June–Aug Mon–Sat 10am–8pm, Sun noon–8pm. Observatory, Sept 26–Mar 20 Tues–Wed 7–10pm. S-tog: Nørreport. Bus: 5, 7E, 14, 16, or 42.

This 17th-century public observatory, attached to a church, is visited by thousands who climb the spiral ramp (no steps) for a panoramic view of Copenhagen. The tower is one of the crowning architectural achievements of the Christian IV era. Peter the Great, in Denmark for a state visit, galloped up the ramp on horseback.

Botanisk Have (Botanical Garden). Gothersgade 128. ☎ **35-32-22-22.** Free admission. Apr–Sept daily 8:30am–6pm; Oct–Mar daily 8:30am–4pm. S-tog: Nørreport. Bus: 5, 7, 14, 16, 24, 40, or 43.

Planted from 1871 to 1874, the Botanical Gardens, across from Rosenborg Castle, are at a lake that was once part of the city's defensive moat. Special features include a cactus house and a palm house, which seem even more exotic in the far northern country of Denmark. An alpine garden contains mountain plants from all over the world.

ORGANIZED TOURS

BUS & BOAT TOURS   For orientation, try the 1½-hour **City Tour** (2½ hours with a visit to a brewery) that covers major scenic highlights, such as *The Little Mermaid*, Rosenborg Castle, and Amalienborg Palace. On workdays, tours also visit the Carlsberg brewery. Tours depart May 30 to September 13 daily at 1pm and cost 125DKK ($18.15) for adults, 20DKK ($2.90) for children.

The **City and Harbor Tour,** a 2½-hour trip by launch and bus, departs from Town Hall Square. The boat tours the city's main canals, passing *The Little Mermaid* and the Old Fish Market. It operates May 30 to September 13 daily at 1pm. Tours cost 165DKK ($23.90) for adults, 30DKK ($4.35) for children under 12.

Shakespeare buffs will be interested in an afternoon excursion to the castles of North Zealand. The 7-hour tour explores the area north of Copenhagen, including visits to Kronborg (Hamlet's Castle), a brief trip to Fredensborg, the Queen's residence, and a stopover at Frederiksborg Castle and the National Historical Museum. Tours depart from the Town Hall Square, May 2 to October 16 Wednesday, Saturday, and Sunday at 10:15am. The cost is 335DKK ($48.55) for adults, 40DKK ($5.80) for children.

One of the most appealing of the guided tours departing from Copenhagen is the **Hans Christian Andersen Tour,** which involves a 10-hour bus transit from the Danish capital to the verdant island of Funen. It departs every Wednesday and Sunday between June and September at 8:30am from Rådhusplads. The cost of 480DKK ($69.60) includes the bus transit from Copenhagen through Zealand, over the recently completed High Bridge spanning the Great Belt, to Odense, birthplace of Hans Christian Andersen. The price of lunch and the cost of access to the museums and castles visited en route, is extra. Visits along the way include Egeskov Castle, built in 1554, and the house and museum of the fabled storyteller himself. Advance reservations are necessary. For more information about these tours, contact **Copenhagen Excursions** at ☎ **32-54-06-06,** or **Vikingbus** at ☎ **32-55-44-22.**

GUIDED WALKS   English-language guided walking tours of Copenhagen are offered from the beginning of May until September 15 at 40DKK ($5.80) for adults and 20DKK ($2.90) for children. Contact the Copenhagen Tourist Information Center, Bernstorffsgade 1 (☎ **33-11-13-25**).

THE SHOPPING SCENE

Customers refer to the two owners of the **The Amber Specialist,** Frederiksberggade 28 (☎ **33-11-88-03;** bus: 28, 29, or 41) as "The Amber Twins." These blonde-haired ladies specialize in "the gold of the north." This stone—really petrified resin—

originated in the large coniferous forests that covered Denmark some 35 million years ago.

Boghallen, Rådhuspladsen 37 (☎ **33-11-85-11;** bus: 2, 8, or 30), is a big store carrying many books in English (including translations of Danish works) as well as a wide selection of travel-related literature, including maps. The shop is at Town Hall Square.

One of Denmark's top department stores, **Illum's,** Østergade 52 (☎ **33-14-40-02;** bus: 1, 6, 9, or 10), is on the Strøget. Take time to browse through its vast world of Scandinavian design. There's a restaurant and a special export cash desk at street level. The elegant **Magasin,** Kongens Nytorv 13 (☎ **33-11-44-33;** bus: 1, 6, 9, or 10), is the biggest department store in Scandinavia. It offers an assortment of Danish designer fashion, glass and porcelain, and souvenirs. Goods are shipped abroad tax-free.

In the Royal Copenhagen retail center, legendary ✪ **Georg Jensen,** Amagertorv 6 (☎ **33-11-40-80;** bus: 1, 6, 8, 9, or 10), is known for its fine silver. For the connoisseur, there's no better address—this is the largest and best collection of Jensen hollowware in Europe. Jewelry in traditional and modern design is also featured. One department specializes in seconds produced by porcelain and glassware manufacturers. In the Royal Copenhagen retail center, **Holmegaards Glasvaerker,** Amagertorv 6 (☎ **33-12-44-77;** bus: 1, 6, 8, 9, or 10), is the only major producer of glasswork in Denmark. Its Wellington pattern, created in 1859, is available once again. The Holmegaard glasses and Regiment Bar set reflect solid craftsmanship.

A center for modern Scandinavian and Danish design, **Illums Bolighus,** Amagertorv 10, on Strøget (☎ **33-14-19-41;** bus: 28, 29, or 41), is one of Europe's finest showcases for household furnishings and accessories of every kind. The store also sells fashions and accessories for women and men. There's even a gift shop. ✪ **Royal Copenhagen** and **Bing & Grøndahl Porcelain,** Amagertorv 6 (☎ **33-13-71-81;** bus: 1, 2, 6, 8, 28, 29, or 41 for the retail outlet or 1 or 14 for the factory), was founded in 1775. Royal Copenhagen's trademark, three wavy blue lines, has come to symbolize quality in porcelain throughout the world. The factory was a royal possession for a century before passing into private hands in 1868 and has turned out a new plate each year since 1908; most of the motifs depict the Danish countryside in winter.

Established in 1926, **Kunsthallens Kunstauktioner,** Gothersgade 9 (☎ **33-32-52-00;** bus: 1, 6, 9, or 10), is Europe's leading dealer in the pan-European school of painting known as COBRA (*Co*penhagen, *Br*ussels, and *A*msterdam). These works, produced from 1948 to 1951, were an important precursor of abstract expressionism. The gallery holds 12 auctions yearly, 8 with modern art; the others concentrate on the 19th century. At **Sweater Market,** Frederiksberggade 15 (☎ **33-15-27-73;** bus: 2, 8, or 30), take your pick from Scandinavian and Icelandic top-grade sweaters, hats, and scarves, handknit in 100% wool. There's also a large selection of Icelandic wool jackets and coats.

COPENHAGEN AFTER DARK

In Copenhagen, a good night means a late night. On warm weekends hundreds of rowdy revelers crowd Strøget until sunrise, and jazz clubs, traditional beer houses, and wine cellars are routinely packed. The city has a more serious cultural side as well, exemplified by excellent theaters, operas, and ballets. **Half-price tickets** for some concerts and theater productions are available the day of the performance from the ticket kiosk opposite the Nørreport rail station, at Nørrevoldgade and Fiolstræde; it's open Monday to Friday noon to 7pm and Saturday noon to 3pm. On summer evenings there are outdoor concerts in Fælled Park near the entrance, near Frederik V's Vej; inquire about dates and times at the Copenhagen Tourist Office.

THE PERFORMING ARTS

Det Kongelige Teater (Royal Theater). Kongens Nytorv. ☎ **33-69-69-69.** Tickets, 60–600DKK ($8.70–$87), half price for seniors 67 and over and those under 26 (1 week before a show begins). Box office Mon–Sat 1–8pm; telephone hours Mon–Sat 1–7pm. Bus: 1, 6, 9, or 10.

The Royal Theater, which dates from 1748, is home to the renowned **Royal Danish Ballet,** one of the world's premier ballet companies performing all over the globe, and the **Royal Danish Opera.** Because the arts are state-subsidized in Denmark, ticket prices are comparatively low, and some seats may be available at the box office the day before a performance. The season runs from August to May.

NIGHTCLUBS

Fellini. Hammeritchsgade 1. ☎ **33-93-32-39.** Cover 50DKK ($7.25). Bus: 2, 6, 9, or 43.

This is Copenhagen's most luxurious and upscale nightclub, with a distinctly international theme. Set in, but independent from, the SAS Royal Hotel, it's a flashback to the disco era, complete with a lit dance floor and mirror ball hemmed in by two bars. Thursday and Friday, there's dancing to soul and disco music, and Saturday is party night, featuring such musical themes as Latin salsa, eclectic African, or house music. It's open Thursday to Saturday 10pm to 5am. The age range is from 30 to 40, and dress is stylish but casual.

Lekitch/The Fever. Gothersgade 8F, Bolthensgaard. ☎ **33-93-74-15.** Cover 50DKK ($7.25) after midnight. Bus: 1, 6, or 9.

Discos come and go with alarming frequency in the Danish capital, but this remains one of the hotter, more popular venues for a late-night crowd of 25- to 35-year-olds, some of whom are avid fans of whatever musical innovation has just emerged in London or Los Angeles. The decorative themes derive from the 1960s cult classic *A Clockwork Orange.* Looking for insights into the heady world of the Danish arts? Head for the club's lower level, where luminaries from ballet, high fashion, and other fields are likely to be gossiping. The club is open Thursday to Saturday from 11pm to 5am.

A ROCK & POP VENUE

Den Røde Pimpernel. Kattasundit 4. ☎ **33-12-20-32.** No cover Tues–Thurs; 40DKK ($5.80) Fri–Sat.

Relocated in the very heart of the city, the Scarlet Pimpernel, with its lively atmosphere, is a good place for people watching and dancing to an odd mix of contemporary pop and old-time evergreen ensembles. There's a bit of an attitude; the clientele is admitted only after being inspected through a peephole. The club is open Tuesday to Saturday 9pm to 8am.

JAZZ & BLUES CLUBS

Copenhagen JazzHouse. Niels Hammingsensgade 10. ☎ **33-15-26-00.** Cover 40–70DKK ($5.80–$10.15). S-tog: Nørreport.

This place rocks and rolls, offering an all-purpose venue that plays—depending on the night of the week—everything from live jazz concerts to late-night disco. There's dancing to every possible kind of electronically amplified music every Wednesday to Sunday between 11pm and at least 3am. The quality and breed of jazz depends entirely on whomever is scheduled to appear on any particular evening. Live music tends to begin around 8:30pm. There's a cafe on the premises and tableside seating for up to 300 jazz fans at a time.

Mojo Blues Bar. Løngangsstraede 21C. ☎ **33-11-64-53.** No cover Sun–Thurs; 40DKK ($5.80) Fri–Sat. Bus: 2, 8, or 30.

This is one of the leading blues clubs in Scandinavia. Softly lit by candle and globe lamps, Mojo seats about 90 people at wooden tables and chairs and on a long bench along one wall. On weekends, which are often standing-room only, up to 125 people cram through the door. Most come for the live blues performed mainly by Danish groups, although German, American, and British bands sometimes take the stage. It's open daily 8pm to 5am.

A DANCE CLUB

Baron & Baroness. Vesterbrøgade 2E. ☎ **33-16-01-01.** Cover 50DKK ($7.25) for disco only. Bus: 250E or 350E.

Set a short walk from Tivoli, this is a relatively upscale nightclub whose decor incorporates faux-medieval crenellations, attracting a crowd that's a bit more prosperous and mature than nearby competitors catering only to teenagers. Full meals cost from 150 to 250DKK ($21.75 to $36.25), and on nights when there's no disco, solo musicians play fiddle, piano, harmonica, or whatever. The bars here are open nightly from 6pm till at least 3am; the restaurant from 6pm to 11pm. Disco, featured one floor above the street restaurant, is offered only on Thursday to Saturday, from 10pm till dawn.

BARS

Det Lille Apotek, at Stor Kannikestraede 15 (☎ **33-12-56-06;** bus: 2, 5, 8, or 30), is a good spot for English-speaking foreign students to meet their Danish contemporaries. Although the menu varies, keep an eye out for the prawn cocktail and tenderloin. The main courses run from about 88 to 128DKK ($12.75 to $18.55) at dinner. The kitchen is open daily 11:30am to 5pm, Sunday to Thursday from 5:30 to 10pm, and Friday to Saturday 5:30 to 11:30pm. The bar is open daily 11am to midnight (closed December 24 to 26).

Frequented by celebrities and royalty, the ✪ **Library Bar,** in the Hotel Plaza, Bernstorffsgade 4 (☎ **33-14-92-62;** bus: 6), was rated by the late Malcolm Forbes as one of the top five bars in the world. In a setting of antique books and works of art, you can order everything from a cappuccino to a cocktail. The setting is the lobby level of the landmark Plaza, commissioned in 1913 by King Frederik VIII. The bar was designed and built as the hotel's ballroom, and Oregon pine was used for the paneling. The oversized mural of George Washington and his men dates from 1910. It's open Monday to Saturday 11:30am to 1am and Sunday 11:30am to midnight.

Nyhavn 17, Nyhavn 17 (☎ **33-12-54-19;** bus: 1, 6, 27, or 29), is the last of the honky-tonks that used to make up the former sailors' quarter. This cafe is a short walk from the patrician Kongens Nytorv and the d'Angleterre luxury hotel. In summer you can sit outside. On Tuesday to Saturday evenings, there's free entertainment from a solo guitarist or guitar duet. It's open Sunday to Thursday 10am to 2am and Friday to Saturday until 4am.

Built in 1670, **Hvids Vinstue,** Kongens Nytorv 19 (☎ **33-15-10-64;** bus: 1, 6, 9, or 10), is a wine cellar that's a dimly lit safe haven for an eclectic crowd, with many patrons—both theater-goers and actors and dancers—drawn from the Royal Theater across the way. In December only, a combination of red wine and cognac is served. It's open Monday to Saturday from 10am to 1am; closed Sunday in July and August.

GAY & LESBIAN CLUBS

Café Babooshka. Turensensgade 6. ☎ **33-15-05-36.** Bus: 5, 7, or 16.

This is Copenhagen's premier lesbian bar, owned and managed by women. Near the Ørsteds Parken and Gyldenløvesgade, it welcomes men, gay and straight, but primarily identifies itself as a spot where lesbians can be themselves. After 8pm the cafe-style format is transformed into a disco. There's no cover, and Friday and Saturday nights are reserved for women only. The place is open Sunday to Thursday 4pm to 1am, and Friday to Saturday 4pm to 2am.

Pan Society. Knabrostræde 3. ☎ **33-13-19-48.** Bus: 28, 29, or 41.

This nationwide organization established in 1948 for the protection and advancement of gay and lesbian rights is headquartered at a 19th-century yellow building off the Strøget. A dance club occupies three of its floors, and a modern cafe's on the ground floor. Every night is gay night, although a lot of straights come here because the music is good. The cafe is open daily from 8pm to 5am. The dance club, however, is open on Wednesday from 11pm to 3am, Thursday 10pm to 4am, Friday and Saturday 10pm to 5am, and Sunday 11pm to 3am. Admission to the dance club is 55DKK ($8).

GAMBLING

Danish authorities allowed the country's first fully licensed casino, **Casino Copenhagen,** in the SAS Scandinavia Hotel, Amager Blvd. 70 (☎ **33-96-59-65;** bus: 5, 11, 30, or 34), to open just after Christmas 1990. Today gamblers play such popular games as roulette, baccarat, punto banco, blackjack, and slots. The operation is overseen by Casinos of Austria, Europe's largest casino operator. It's open daily 2pm to 4am. The cover is 80DKK ($11.60).

DAY TRIPS FROM COPENHAGEN

DRAGØR Visit the past in this old seafaring town on the island of Amager, 3 miles south of Copenhagen's Kastrup Airport. It's filled with well-preserved half-timbered ocher-and-pink 18th-century cottages with steep red-tiled or thatched roofs; many are under the protection of the National Trust.

Dragør (pronounced *Drah-wer*) was a busy port on the herring-rich Baltic Sea in the early Middle Ages, but when fishing fell off, it became just another sleepy waterfront village. After 1520, Amager Island and its villages—Dragør and Store Magleby—were inhabited by the Dutch, who brought their own customs, Low-German language, and agricultural expertise to Amager, especially their love of bulb flowers. In Copenhagen, you still see wooden-shoed Amager selling their hyacinths, tulips, daffodils, and lilies in the streets.

A rich trove of historic treasures is found in the **Amager Museum,** Hovedgaden 4–12, Store Magleby (☎ **32-53-93-07;** bus: 30, 33, or 350S), outside Dragør. The exhibits reveal the affluence achieved by the Amager Dutch, with rich textiles, fine embroidery, and luxuries such as carved silver buckles and buttons. The interiors of a Dutch house are especially interesting, showing how these people decorated their homes and lived in comfort. Admission is 20DKK ($2.90) for adults, 10DKK ($1.45) for children. It's open April to September, Wednesday through Sunday noon to 4pm; October to March, Wednesday and Sunday noon to 4pm.

The exhibits at the harborfront **Dragør Museum,** Havnepladsen 2–4 (☎ **32-53-41-06;** bus: 30, 33, or 350S), show how the Amager Dutch lived from prehistoric times to the 20th century. Farming, goose breeding, seafaring, fishing, ship piloting, and ship salvage are delineated through pictures and artifacts. Admission is 20DKK ($2.90) for adults, 10DKK ($1.45) for children. It's open May to September Tuesday to Friday 2 to 5pm, Saturday and Sunday and holidays noon to 6pm; closed October to April.

Getting There Dragør is a 35-minute trip on bus no. 30, 33, or 73E from Rådhuspladsen (Town Hall Square) in Copenhagen.

LOUISIANA   Established in 1958, the ✪ **Louisiana Museum of Modern Art,** Gl. Strandvej 13 (☎ **49-19-07-19**), is idyllically situated in a 19th-century mansion on the Danish Riviera surrounded by a sculpture park, opening directly onto the Øresund. It's 20 miles north of Copenhagen. Paintings and sculptures by modern masters (Giacometti and Henry Moore, to name two) are displayed, as well as the best and most controversial works of modern art. The museum name came from the first owner of the estate, Alexander Brun, who had three wives, each named Louise. Admission is 55DKK ($8) for adults, 15DKK ($2.15) for children 4 to 16, and free for children under 4. It's open Thursday to Tuesday 10am to 5pm and Wednesday 10am to 10pm; closed December 24, 25, and 31.

Getting There   Humlebaek, the nearest town to Louisiana, can be reached by train from Copenhagen (København–Helsingør). Two trains an hour leave from the main station in Copenhagen (trip time 40 minutes). Once you're at Humlebaek, follow signs to the museum, a 15-minute walk.

HELSINGØR (ELSINORE)   Helsingør (*Elsinore* in English) is visited chiefly for "Hamlet's Castle." Aside from its literary associations, the town has a certain charm: a quiet market square, medieval lanes, and old half-timbered and brick buildings, remains of its once-prosperous shipping industry. The **Tourist Office,** at Havnepladsen 3 (☎ **49-21-13-33**), is open Monday to Friday 9:30am to 5pm and Saturday 10am to 1pm.

There's no evidence that Shakespeare ever saw this sandstone-and-copper Dutch Renaissance-style castle, full of intriguing secret passages and casemates, but he made **Kronborg Slot,** Kronborg (☎ **49-21-30-78**), famous in *Hamlet.* According to 12th-century historian Saxo Grammaticus, though, if Hamlet had really existed, he would have lived centuries before Kronborg was erected (1574–85). Over the years some famous productions of the Shakespearean play have been staged here, the castle's bleak, austere atmosphere providing a good foil for the drama.

During its history (1785–1922), the castle has been looted, bombarded, gutted by fire, and used as a barracks. The starkly furnished Great Hall is the largest in northern Europe. The church, with its original oak furnishings and the royal chambers, is also worth exploring. Admission to the castle is 30DKK ($4.35) for adults, 10DKK ($1.45) for children 6 to 14. It's open May to September, daily 10:30am to 5pm; October and April, Tuesday to Sunday 11am to 4pm; November to March, Tuesday to Sunday 11am to 3pm; closed Christmas Day. Guided tours are given every half hour October to April. In summer you can walk around on your own. The castle is half a mile from the rail station.

Getting There   Once you reach Helsingør, 25 miles north of Copenhagen, you're deposited in the center of town and can cover all the major attractions on foot. There are frequent trains from Copenhagen, which take 50 minutes. Some 30 buses leave Copenhagen daily for the 1-hour trip to Helsingør.

5 England

by Darwin Porter & Danforth Prince

London may no longer be the capital of a global empire, but it is the city of the moment—lively, fast-paced, and teeming with action. London is defined by its fascinating contradictions: It is both home to an overwhelming jumble of antiquity and the world's trend-setter for the latest music, fashion, and food (the cuisine is better than ever). As stimulating as London is, however, you'll want to tear yourself away to visit legendary Stonehenge on the Salisbury Plain, Oxford University, and the unspoiled stone-built villages of the Cotswolds. The classic city of Bath is not just a museum of the past, with echoes ranging from the Romans to 18th-century Jane Austen, but a vibrant, fashionable city of today, renowned for its shopping and architectural monuments.

1 London

Dr. Samuel Johnson said, "When a man is tired of London, he is tired of life, for there is in London all that life can afford." In this section, we'll survey a segment of that life: ancient monuments, literary shrines, museums, walking tours, Parliament debates, royal castles, waxworks, palaces, cathedrals, and parks.

Only in London

Enjoying a Traditional English Tea Having a "cuppa" in London is a classic experience. Try the Goring Hotel, 15 Beeston Place, SW1 (☎ **020/7396-9000**), dating from 1910. From the lounge, you'll have a view of a small garden as you enjoy finger sandwiches, the hotel's special Ceylon blend tea, scones, and the chef's famous "light fruit cake," offered from a trolley.

Attending West End Theater London is the theater capital of the world, with more plays produced here than anywhere else. The live stage offers a unique combination of variety, accessibility, and economy—and perhaps a look at next year's Broadway hit.

Studying the Turners at the Tate Upon his death in 1851, J. M. W. Turner bequeathed his personal collection of 19,000 watercolors and some 300 paintings to the people of Britain. He wanted his finished works, some 100 paintings, displayed under one roof. For 125 years, Turner's wish was unfulfilled. The expansion of the Clore Gallery changed this. The artist lived and died on the Thames's banks in Chelsea and painted the river in its many changing moods.

Shopping at Harrods   This vast emporium in Knightsbridge, spread over 15 acres, proclaims as its motto *Omnia Omnibus Ubique*—"everything for everyone, everywhere." They mean it, too. Want an elephant? Go to Harrods: In 1975 someone called Harrods at midnight and ordered a baby elephant to be delivered to the home of the governor of California, Ronald Reagan. The animal arrived safely, albeit a bit bewildered. You can even arrange your funeral at the store.

Dining at Rules   Rules, at 35 Maiden Lane, WC2 (☎ **020/7836-5314**), dates from 1798, when it was first established as an oyster bar. It may, in fact, be London's oldest restaurant. Long a venue for the theatrical elite and literary *beau monde,* it still serves the same dishes that delighted Edward VII and his mistress, Lillie Langtry. Charles Dickens liked the place so much he had a regular table. If it's feathered or furred, it's likely to be served here.

Doing a Pub Crawl   Americans bar hop, Londoners strike out on pub crawls. With thousands of pubs within the city limits, you would be crawling indeed if you tried to have a drink in each of them. Many pubs today are only for "lager louts," with Formica, loud jukeboxes, and an obsessive concern with football (soccer) scores. But traditional pubs remain, especially in central London, with their long mahogany bars, dark wood paneling, and Victorian curlicue mirrors to make it worthwhile to go on a crawl and partake of pub grub. And the grub's gotten much better!

Spending a Rainy Day at the British Museum   It shelters one of the most comprehensive collections of art and artifacts in the world. Everything is here, from the finest assembly of Islamic pottery outside the Muslim world to the Elgin Marbles. Just when you think you've seen everything, you might stumble into the room displaying sculptures from the Mausoleum at Halicarnassus, one of the Seven Wonders of the Ancient World. Even if it's not raining, you'll savor a visit here.

ORIENTATION

GETTING THERE   By Plane   Heathrow Airport, west of London, in Hounslow (☎ **020/8759-4321**), one of the world's busiest airports, is divided into four terminals, each relatively self-contained. Terminal 4 handles many of the long-haul and transatlantic operations of British Airways, but most U.S. airline flights arrive at Terminal 3. Terminals 1 and 2 receive the intra-European flights of several European airlines. There is an Underground (subway) connection from Heathrow Central to the center of London; the 50-minute trip costs £3.30 ($5.45). Airbuses will also take you to central London in about an hour; they cost £6.10 ($10.05) for adults and £4.10 ($6.75) for children. A taxi usually costs from £25 to £30 ($41.25 to $49.50), but might be higher. For more information about train or bus connections, call ☎ **020/7222-1234.**

The British Airport Authority now operates a **London-Heathrow Express** (☎ **0845/600-1515**), a 100-mile-an-hour train service running every 15 minutes daily from 5:10am until 11:40pm between Heathrow and Paddington Station in the center of London. Trips cost £10 ($16.50) each way for economy class, rising to £20 ($33) for first-class. Children ages 5 to 15 go for half the fare (free for those 4 and under). The trip takes only 15 minutes each way between Paddington and Terminals 1, 2, and 3, or 20 minutes from Terminal 4. The trains have special areas for wheelchairs. From Paddington, passengers can connect to other trains or hail a taxi. You can buy tickets on the train or at self-service machines at Heathrow Airport (also available from travel agents). At Paddington, a bus link, Hotel Express, takes passengers from

Paddington to a number of hotels in central London, costing £2.05 ($3.40) for adults, £1.05 ($1.75) children 5 to 15 (free 4 and under). This service has already revolutionized travel to and from the airport, much to the regret of London cabbies.

Gatwick (☎ **01293/535353** for flight information), a smaller and more remote airport, lies 25 miles south of London, in West Sussex. Charter flights as well as many scheduled flights arrive here. Trains leave for London every 15 minutes during the day and every hour at night; they cost £9 ($14.85) for adults and half-price for children aged 5 to 15 (under 5 free). There is also an express Flightline bus (no. 777) from Gatwick to Victoria Station in central London that departs every half hour from 6:30am to 8pm and every hour from 8 to 11pm; it costs £7.50 ($12.40) per person. A taxi from Gatwick to central London usually costs £50 to £60 ($82.50 to $99); however, you must negotiate a fare with the driver before you get into the cab. The London meter does not apply since Gatwick lies outside the Metropolitan Police District.

By Train   Most trains originating in Paris and traveling through the Chunnel pull in at **Waterloo Station.** Visitors from Amsterdam arrive at the **Liverpool Street Station,** and those journeying south by rail from Edinburgh disembark at **King's Cross Station.** All are connected to London's vast bus and Underground network, and have phones, restaurants, pubs, luggage-storage areas, and London Regional Transport Information Centres.

By Car   If you're taking a car across the channel, you can quickly connect with a motorway into London. London is encircled by a ring road. Determine which part of the city you want to enter and follow the signs there. But you should confine your driving in London to the *bare minimum;* before you arrive, call your hotel for advice on where to park. Be warned—parking is scarce and expensive. Most important driving tip in England: *Remember to drive on the left.*

VISITOR INFORMATION   The **Britain Visitor Center,** 1 Regent St., London SW1 4NX (☎ **020/7808-3808;** Tube: Piccadilly Circus), houses the British Tourism Authority as well as the national tourist boards of England, Ireland, Scotland, and Wales. The center can change money and book accommodations, travel, and theater tickets. Open Monday through Friday 9am to 6:30pm, Saturday and Sunday 10am to 4pm, with extended Saturday hours June through September.

For a full information pack on London, write to the London Tourist Board, 26 Grosvenor Gardens, SW1 WODU.

CITY LAYOUT   For our purposes, London begins at **Chelsea,** on the north bank of the river, and stretches for roughly 5 miles north to **Hampstead.** Its western boundary runs through Kensington, while the eastern boundary lies 5 miles away, at Tower Bridge. Inside this 5-by-5-mile square, you'll find all the hotels and restaurants and nearly all the sights that are usually of interest to visitors.

The logical, although not geographical, center of this area is **Trafalgar Square,** which we'll take as our orientation point. Stand here facing the steps of the imposing National Gallery; you're looking northwest. That is the direction of **Piccadilly Circus**—the real core of tourist London—and the maze of streets that makes up **Soho.** Farther north runs **Oxford Street,** London's gift to moderately priced shopping, and still farther northwest lies Regent's Park and the zoo.

At your back (that is, south) runs **Whitehall,** which houses or skirts nearly every British government building, including the official residence of the prime minister at **10 Downing Street.** In the same direction, a bit farther south, stand the Houses of Parliament and Westminster Abbey.

Flowing southwest from Trafalgar Square is the table-smooth **Mall,** flanked by parks and mansions and leading to Buckingham Palace, the queen's residence. Farther along in the same direction lie **Belgravia** and **Knightsbridge,** the city's plushest residential areas, and south of them is chic **Chelsea,** plus **King's Road,** where the punks used to hang out; today it's principally an upscale boulevard for shopping.

Due west stretches the superb and high-priced shopping area bordered by **Regent Street** and **Piccadilly Street** (as distinct from the Circus). Farther west lie the equally elegant shops and even more elegant homes of **Mayfair.** Then comes **Park Lane,** with its deluxe hotels. On the other side of Park Lane is **Hyde Park,** the biggest park in central London and one of the largest in the world.

Charing Cross Road runs north from Trafalgar Square, past **Leicester Square,** and intersects with **Shaftesbury Avenue.** This is London's theater land. A bit farther along, Charing Cross Road turns into a browser's paradise, lined with shops selling new and secondhand books. At last it funnels into **St. Giles Circus.** This is where you enter **Bloomsbury,** site of the University of London, the British Museum, and erstwhile stamping ground of the famed "Bloomsbury group," led by Virginia Woolf.

Northeast lies **Covent Garden,** known for its Royal Opera House; today it's a major shopping, restaurant, and cafe district.

Follow **The Strand** eastward from Trafalgar Square and you'll come to **Fleet Street.** Beginning in the 19th century, this corner of London became the most concentrated newspaper district in the world. **Temple Bar** stands where The Strand becomes Fleet Street, and only here do you enter the actual City of London, or "the City." Its focal point and shrine is the Bank of England on **Threadneedle Street,** with the Stock Exchange next door and the Royal Exchange across the street. In the midst of all the hustle and bustle rises **St. Paul's Cathedral,** Sir Christopher Wren's monument to beauty and tranquility.

At the far eastern fringe of the City looms the **Tower of London,** shrouded in legend, blood, and history and permanently besieged by battalions of visitors.

Beyond the City lies the **East End,** traditionally one of London's poorest districts, which was nearly obliterated by Hitler's bombs. The East End has always been filled with legend and lore; it's also the home of the Cockney, London's most colorful character. Today, many immigrants make their home in this area, providing even greater richness.

GETTING AROUND   By Public Transportation   Both the Underground (subway) and bus systems are operated by London Transport. Travel Information Centres are found in the Underground stations at King's Cross, Hammersmith, Oxford Circus, St. James's Park, Liverpool Street Station, and Piccadilly Circus, as well as in the British Rail stations at Euston and Victoria and in each of the terminals at Heathrow Airport. They take reservations for London Transport's guided tours and have free Underground and bus maps and other information. A **24-hour telephone information** service is available by calling ☎ **020/7222-1234.**

London Transport, Travel Information Service, 55 Broadway, London SW1H 0BD, also offers **Travelcards** for use on the bus, Underground, and British Rail service inside Greater London. Available in a number of combinations for adjacent zones, Travelcards can be purchased for periods of 7 days to 1 year. A Travelcard allowing travel in two zones for 1 week costs £16.60 ($27.40) for adults and £5.50 ($9.05) for children.

For shorter stays in London, a **1-Day Off-Peak Travelcard** can be used on most bus, Underground, and British Rail services throughout Greater London Monday through Friday after 9:30am and at any time on weekends and bank holidays. The

London Underground

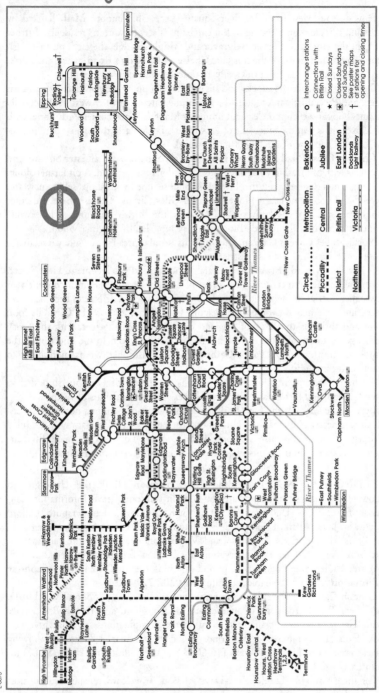

216

Travelcard is available at Underground ticket offices, Travel Information Centres, and some newsstands. A two-zone card costs £3.50 ($5.75) for adults, £1.80 ($2.95) for children ages 5 to 15; children 4 and under ride free.

By Underground (Subway)   Known locally as "the tube," all Underground stations are clearly marked with a red circle and blue crossbar. You can find your station on the large diagram displayed on the wall, which has an alphabetical index. By following the colored bands, you can see at a glance where—or whether—you have to change and how many stops until your destination.

You can transfer as many times as you like as long as you stay in the Underground. The flat fare for one trip within the central zone is £1.30 ($2.15). Trips from the central zone to destinations in the suburbs range from £1.30 to £4.40 ($2.15 to $7.25) in many cases.

By Bus   The comparably priced bus system is almost as good as the Underground, and you'll have a better view of the city. To find out about current routes, pick up a free bus map at one of the London Regional Transport's Travel Information Centres listed above.

Fares vary according to the distance traveled. Generally, the cost is 50p to £1.20 (85¢ to $2), less than tube fares. If you travel for two or three stops, the cost is 60p ($1); longer runs within zone 1 are charged 90p ($1.50). If you want to be warned when to get off, simply ask the driver or conductor. Call the 24-hour hotline (☎ **020/ 7222-1200**) for schedules and fares.

By Taxi   For a radio cab, phone ☎ **020/7272-0272** or 020/7253-5000. The minimum fare is £1.40 ($2.30) for the first third of a mile or 1 minute and 51 seconds, with increments of 20p (35¢) thereafter, based on distance or time. Each additional passenger is charged 40p (65¢). Passengers pay 10p (15¢) for each piece of luggage in the driver's compartment and any other item more than 2 feet long. Surcharges are imposed after 8pm and on weekends and public holidays. All these tariffs include VAT, and fares usually increase annually. It's recommended that you tip 10% to 15% of the fare.

By Car   Rent a car in London only if you plan to take excursions into the environs. Because of impenetrable traffic and parking difficulties, it's virtually impossible to see London by car.

By Bicycle   One of the most popular bike rental shops is **On Your Bike,** 52–54 Tooley St., London Bridge, SE1 (☎ **020/7378-6669;** tube: London Bridge), open Monday through Friday 9am to 6pm, Saturday 9:30am to 5:30pm, and Sunday 11am to 4pm. The 10-speed sports bikes, with high seats and low-slung handlebars, cost £15 ($24.75) per day or £60 ($99) per week and require a £200 ($330) deposit.

Fast Facts: London

American Express   The main office is at 6 Haymarket, SW1 (☎ **020/ 7930-4411;** tube: Piccadilly Circus). Full services are available Monday through Friday 9am to 5:30pm, Saturday 9am to 4pm. At other times—Saturday 4pm to 6pm and Sunday 10am to 5pm—only the foreign-exchange bureau is open.

Baby-sitters   The best is **Childminders,** 6 Nottingham St., London W1M 3RB (☎ **020/7935-3000;** tube: Baker Street). You pay £5.50 ($9.05) per hour in the daytime and £4 to £5 ($6.60 to $8.25) per hour at night. There is a 4-hour minimum, and hotel guests are charged a £5 ($8.25) booking fee each time they use a sitter.

Business Hours   Banks are usually open Monday through Friday 9:30am to 3:30pm. **Pubs and bars** are open Monday through Saturday 11am to 11pm, Sunday noon to 10:30pm. Many pubs observe these extended Sunday hours; others prefer to close during the late afternoon (3 to 7pm). **Stores** are generally open 9am to 5:30pm, and until 7pm on Wednesday or Thursday. Most central shops are open on Saturday from 9am to 1pm.

Currency   **The basic unit of currency is the **pound sterling (£), which is divided into 100 pence (p). There are 1p, 2p, 10p, 20p, 50p, and £1 and £2 coins; banknotes are issued in £1, £5, £10, £20, and £50 denominations. The rate of exchange used in this chapter was $1 = 61p or £1 = $1.65. Also, 1EUR = 65p.

Dentists & Doctors   **For dental emergencies, call **Eastman Dental Hospital (☎ 020/7915-1000; tube: King's Cross). Some hotels have doctors on call. In an emergency, contact **Doctor's Call** (☎ 020/8900-1000). **Medical Express,** 117A Harley St., W1 (☎ **020/7499-1991;** tube: Regent's Park), is a private British clinic that's not part of the free British medical establishment. It's open Monday through Friday from 8am to 6pm and on Saturday from 9:30am to 2:30pm.

Drugstores   **In Britain they're called "chemist shops." **Bliss The Chemist, 5 Marble Arch, W1 (☎ **020/7723-6116;** tube: Marble Arch), is open daily 9am to midnight. Every London neighborhood has a branch of **Boots,** Britain's leading chain.

**Electricity   **It's 220-volt, 50-cycle AC, instead of 110-volt, 60-cycle AC, as in the United States, so visitors need to bring adapters for electric appliances.

Embassies & High Commissions   **The **U.S. Embassy is at 24 Grosvenor Sq., W1 (☎ **020/7499-9000;** tube: Bond Street). However, for passport and visa information, go to the U.S. Passport and Citizenship Unit, 55–56 Upper Brook St., London, W1 (☎ **020/7499-9000,** ext. 2563 or 2564; tube: Marble Arch). Hours are Monday through Friday 8:30am to noon and 2 to 4pm (on Tuesday the office closes at noon). The **Canadian High Commission,** MacDonald House, 38 Grosvenor Sq., W1 (☎ **020/7258-6600;** tube: Bond Street), handles visas for Canada. It's open Monday through Friday from 8 to 11am only. The **Australian High Commission,** at Australia House, Strand, WC2 (☎ **020/ 7379-4334;** tube: Charing Cross or Aldwych), is open Monday through Friday 9:30am to 3:30pm. The **New Zealand High Commission,** at New Zealand House, 80 Haymarket at Pall Mall, SW1 (☎ **020/7930-8422;** tube: Charing Cross or Piccadilly Circus), is open Monday through Friday 10am to noon and 2 to 4pm. The **Irish Embassy,** at 17 Grosvenor Place, SW1 (☎ **020/ 7235-2171;** tube: Hyde Park Corner), is open Monday through Friday 9:30am to 1pm and 2:15 to 5pm. The **South African High Commission,** South Africa House, Trafalgar Square, WC2 (☎ **020/7451-7299;** tube: Charing Cross), is open Monday to Friday 10am to noon and 2 to 4pm.

Emergencies   **In London, for police, fire, or an ambulance, dial ☎ **999.

Hospitals   **Emergency care 24 hours a day, with the first treatment free under the National Health Service, is offered by Royal Free Hospital, Pond Street, NW3 (☎ **020/7794-0500; tube: Belsize Park), and University College Hospital, Gower Street, WC1 (☎ **020/7387-9300;** tube: Warren Street).

Internet Access   Café Internet, 22–34 Buckingham Palace Rd., SW1 (☎ **020/ 7233-5786;** e-mail: cafe@cafeinternet.co.uk), is open daily 10am to 11pm.

London's New Area Codes

New London area codes took effect in April 1999, but through April 2000, both the old codes and the new code will be in effect. In the new system, one code, **020,** will replace the old 0171 and 0181 codes. 020 is then followed by an eight-digit number beginning with either a 7 or an 8 (7 for a number that had a 0171 code, 8 for a number that had a 0181 code). We have used the new codes throughout this edition. When calling from outside the United Kingdom, you need to dial **004420** followed by the eight-digit phone number. If you're within the United Kingdom but not in London, use 020 followed by the new eight-digit number. If you're calling within London, simply leave off the code and dial only the eight-digit number.

Luggage Storage & Lockers   Lockers can be rented at Heathrow and Gatwick and at all major rail stations. Check the Yellow Pages for private companies that offer long-term storage.

Post Office   The Main Post Office is at 24 William IV St., WC2N 4DL (☎ **020/7484-9307;** tube: Charing Cross). It operates as three separate businesses: inland and international postal service and banking, philatelic postage stamp sales, and the post shop, selling greeting cards and stationery (all open Monday through Saturday 8am to 8pm).

Taxes   The British government levies a 25% tax on gasoline ("petrol"). In 1994, Britain imposed a departure tax: £10 ($16.50) for flights within Britain and the European Union or £20 ($33) for passengers flying elsewhere, including to the United States. This tax is generally written into the price of your ticket.

Telephone   To call London from the United States, dial the international code **44** (Britain's country code) and either 171 or 181, or 208 or 207 (see "London's New Area Codes") and then the 7-digit local telephone number. To call outside London, dial the international code 44 and then the exchange code and the local telephone number. Pay phones take either coins or phonecards, readily available at most newsstands and sold in denominations from £1 ($1.60) to £20 ($32). The cost of a local call is 10p for the first 2 minutes. Phones don't give change, so stick to the 10p coins. The toll-free international access codes are: **AT&T** ☎ 0800-013-0011, **Sprint** ☎ 0500-890-877, **MCI** to call using BT ☎ 0800-89-0222, to call using C&W ☎ 0500-89-0222.

WHERE TO STAY

In most of the places listed, a service charge ranging from 10% to 15% will be added to your bill. The British government also imposes a VAT (value-added tax) that adds 17.5% to your bill. If you're looking for moderately priced and clean accommodations near the airport, try the **Renaissance London Heathrow Hotel,** Bath Rd., Houndslow TW6 2AQ (☎ **020/8759-6311;** fax 020/8897-1113).

MAYFAIR
Very Expensive
✪ **Brown's Hotel.** 29–34 Albemarle St., London W1A 4SW. ☎ **020/7493-6020.** Fax 020/7493-9381. www.brownshotel.com. 118 units. A/C MINIBAR TV TEL. £265 ($437.25) double; from £420 ($693) suite. VAT extra. AE, DC, MC, V. Tube: Green Park.

Brown's, the quintessential London hotel, was opened by a former manservant of Lord Byron in 1837, the year Queen Victoria ascended the throne. Today, Brown's occupies some 14 historic houses on two streets just off Berkeley Square. Bedrooms, many quite small, are traditionally furnished with old-fashioned comfort, luxurious mattresses,

London Accommodations

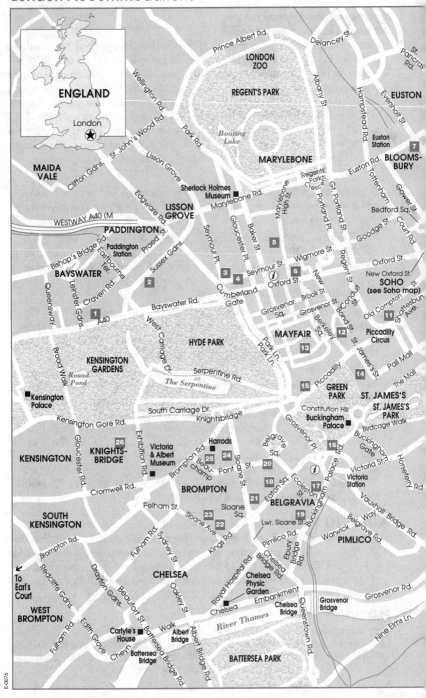

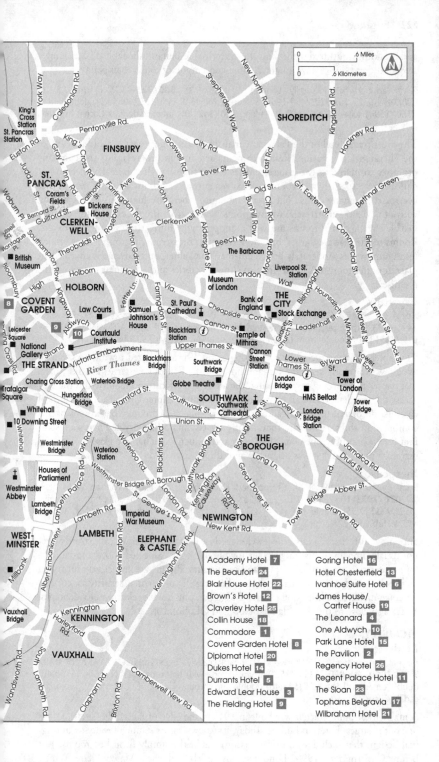

Academy Hotel **7**
The Beaufort **24**
Blair House Hotel **22**
Brown's Hotel **12**
Claverley Hotel **25**
Collin House **18**
Commodore **1**
Covent Garden Hotel **8**
Diplomat Hotel **20**
Dukes Hotel **14**
Durrants Hotel **5**
Edward Lear House **3**
The Fielding Hotel **9**

Goring Hotel **16**
Hotel Chesterfield **13**
Ivanhoe Suite Hotel **6**
James House/
 Cartref House **19**
The Leonard **4**
One Aldwych **10**
Park Lane Hotel **15**
The Pavilion **2**
Regency Hotel **26**
Regent Palace Hotel **11**
The Sloan **23**
Tophams Belgravia **17**
Wilbraham Hotel **21**

and beautifully outfitted bathrooms. In the formal restaurant, the table d'hôte changes frequently, and dishes have a lighter, more contemporary touch than before.

Park Lane Hotel. Piccadilly, London W1Y 8BX. ☎ **800/325-3535** in the U.S., or 020/7499-6321. Fax 020/7499-1965. 305 units. MINIBAR TV TEL. £260 ($429) double; from £360 ($594) suite. AE, DC, MC, V. Parking £26 ($42.90). Tube: Hyde Park Corner or Green Park.

The most traditional of the Park Lane mansions was almost entirely sold in 1996 to the Sheraton Corporation. Refurbishments are now in progress, but the company promises to maintain the hotel's quintessential British style. Some 150 accommodations were recently redecorated. Its silver entrance, still an art deco marvel, has been used in many films. The accommodations here are luxurious and spacious, with new, deluxe mattresses. Many rooms have marble fireplaces, and the original marble-sheathed bathrooms are well-equipped with fluffy towels and hair dryers. Rooms to the rear are darker, but more tranquil. Brasserie, the ground-floor French restaurant, serves moderately priced cuisine. The Palm Court Lounge is an excellent place for afternoon tea. There are also fitness facilities and a business center on the premises.

Expensive

Hotel Chesterfield. 35 Charles St., London W18 LX. ☎ **020/7491-2622.** Fax 020/7491-4793. E-mail: reservations@chesterfield.viewinn.co.uk. 110 units. A/C MINIBAR TV TEL. £190 ($313.50) double; from £350 ($577.50) suite. AE, DC, MC, V. Tube: Green Park.

This hotel was constructed by connecting a trio of brick-fronted townhouses, one of which was for many years the London home of the Earl of Chesterfield. Inside, original plaster moldings, glossy paneling, the air of Victorian respectability, and the easy access to Berkeley Square all contribute to the hotel's allure. Upstairs, a labyrinth of carefully decorated hallways lead to the well-decorated bedrooms. Bathrooms have a combination shower and tub, robes, fluffy towels, and a hair dryer. There's a restaurant on the premises, open daily for lunch and dinner, and a bar in a glass-roofed conservatory that fills what was originally an outdoor courtyard.

Inexpensive

Ivanhoe Suite Hotel. 1 St. Christophers Place, Barrett St. Piazza, London W1M 5HB. ☎ **020/7935-1047.** Fax 020/7224-0563. www.scoot.co.uk/ivanhoe-suite-hotel/. 8 units. TV. £79 ($130.35) double; £89 ($146.85) triple. Rates include continental breakfast. AE, DC, MC, V. Tube: Bond St.

Shopping buffs flock to this little jewel tucked away in a part of town off Oxford Street not usually known for its hotels. This townhouse hotel is located above a restaurant, on a pedestrian street of boutiques and restaurants. Rooms are attractively furnished and recently redecorated, each with a sitting area, its own entry, security video, and beverage-making facilities along with a fridge/bar, plus a wide selection of videotapes. You're also close to the shop-flanked New and Old Bond streets.

PICADILLY

Moderate

Regent Palace Hotel. 12 Sherwood St., near Piccadilly Circus, London W1A 4BZ. ☎ **020/7734-7000.** Fax 020/7734-6435. 950 units (none with bathroom). TV TEL. £94 ($150.40) double on Fri and Sat; £54 ($86.40) double Sun through Thurs. AE, DC, MC, V. Tube: Piccadilly Circus.

A major focal point since it was built in 1915 at the edge of Piccadilly Circus, this is one of the largest hotels in Europe. Today, it's known for its staunch loyalty to an original design, that includes no private bathrooms in the simply furnished rooms. Just before Christmas of 1998, London's most celebrated chef, Marco Pierre White, opened The Titanic on the ground floor, a plebian plunge (for him) into moderately priced dining. The restaurant's phone number is ☎ **020/7437-1912.**

St. James's
Expensive

Dukes Hotel. 35 St. James's Place, London SW1A 1NY. ☎ **800/381-4702** in the U.S., or 020/7491-4840. Fax 020/7493-1264. www.dukeshotel.co.uk. 81 units. A/C TV TEL. £200 ($330) double; from £310 ($511.50) suite. AE, DC, MC, V. Parking £32 ($52.80). Tube: Green Park.

Dukes provides elegance without ostentation. Along with its nearest competitors, The Stafford and 22 Jermyn Street, it attracts the urbane guest who's looking for charm, style, and tradition in a hotel. Since 1908 it has stood in a quiet courtyard off St. James's Street, offering well-furnished rooms equipped with satellite TV, private bar, and luxurious beds. Marble-clad bathrooms have soft towels and hair dryers. Dukes Restaurant is small and elegant, serving both classic British and continental cuisine.

Bloomsbury
Moderate

Academy Hotel. 17–21 Gower St., London WC1E 6HG. ☎ **800/678-3096** in the U.S., or 020/7631-4115. Fax 020/7636-3442. 48 units. TV TEL. £125–£145 ($206.25–$239.25) double; £185 ($305.25) suite. AE, DC, MC, V. Tube: Tottenham Court Rd. or Goodge St.

Right in the heart of London's publishing district, the Academy's tacky modern rears its ugly head here and there, but many of the original architectural details were preserved when these three 1776 Georgian row houses were joined. The hotel was substantially upgraded in the 1990s, with a bathroom added to every bedroom—whether there was space or not. Grace notes include the glass panels, colonnades, and the intricate plaster work on the front of the building. Rooms are decorated rather blandly, but they are well cared for. Facilities include an elegant bar, a library room, a secluded patio garden, and a restaurant serving French and continental food.

Covent Garden
Very Expensive

One Aldwych. 1 Aldwych, London WC2B 4BZ. ☎ **800/447-7462** in the U.S., or 020/7300-1000. www.onealdwych.co.uk. E-mail: sales@onealdwych.co.uk. 105 units. A/C MINIBAR TV TEL. £265–£320 ($437.25–$528) double; from £395 ($651.75) suite. AE, DC, MC, V. Tube: Covent Garden or Charing Cross.

Of the many hotels that compete for five-star ratings, London's newest offers Zen-like tranquility and simplicity. It was originally erected in 1907 as the stately headquarters for the (now-defunct) *Morning Post.* Before its reinauguration as a hotel in 1998, the interior was stripped and gutted and refashioned by teams of London's most sought-after designers and decorators. Bedrooms are artfully outfitted with simple lines, raw silk curtains, and rich color schemes of sage, purple, burnt orange, and deep reds, and equipped with luxurious mattresses, computer modems, and electrical outlets that can handle both North American and European currents. Deluxe bathrooms have hair dryers, robes, and fluffy towels. There's an all-day cafe and bistro, Indigo, that serves California-inspired cooking daily, plus the more formal Axis, featuring modern British and Pacific Rim cuisine. On the premises is a state-of-the-art health club and a pool almost 60 feet long.

Expensive

Covent Garden Hotel. 10 Monmouth St., London WC2H 9HB. ☎ **020/7806-1000.** Fax 020/7806-1100. 50 units. A/C MINIBAR TV TEL. £175–£195 ($288.75–$321.75) double; £260–£350 ($429–$577.50) suite. AE, MC, V. Parking: £30.50 ($50.30). Tube: Leicester Sq. or Covent Garden.

Originally built as a French-directed hospital around 1850, the premises lay derelict and empty for many years until it was converted in 1996 into one of the most charming boutique hotels in London. Across from Neal's Yard and behind a bottle-green facade that evokes a 19th-century storefront, the site also contains two charming restaurants. Upstairs, soundproof bedrooms are lushly outfitted with Asian fabrics, many of which are elaborately adorned with hand-embroidered designs. Their decorative trademark? Each room contains a clothier's mannequin. The bedrooms also contain great mattresses, thick towels, and a hair dryer.

Moderate

The Fielding Hotel. 4 Broad Court, Bow St., London WC2B 5QZ. ☎ **020/7836-8305.** Fax 020/7497-0064. 26 units (24 with bathroom). £95–£120 ($156.75–$198) double with bathroom. AE, DC, MC, V. Tube: Covent Garden.

One of London's more eccentric hotels, the Fielding is cramped, quirky, and quaint, but an enduring favorite nonetheless. Next to the Bow Street Magistrates Court and almost opposite the Royal Opera House, the hotel lies on a pedestrian street still lit by 19th-century gas lamps. Covent Garden, with its pubs, shops, markets, restaurants, and street entertainment, is just outside your door. The hotel is named after the novelist Henry Fielding of *Tom Jones* fame, who lived in Broad Court with his brother. Rooms and bathrooms are definitely small and old-fashioned, and very few rooms have anything approaching a view. Floors dip and sway, and the furnishings and fabrics have known better times, but the loyalists love its rickety charm. When sterile modern has got you down, step back into England of yesteryear.

VICTORIA

Expensive

✪ **Goring Hotel.** 15 Beeston Place, Grosvenor Gardens, London SW1W 0JW. ☎ **020/7396-9000.** Fax 020/7834-4393. www.goringhotel.co.uk. E-mail: reception@goringhotel.co.uk. 75 units. TV TEL. £195–£235 ($321.75–$387.75) double; from £260 ($429) suite. AE, DC, MC, V. Parking £25 ($41.25). Tube: Victoria Station.

Located just behind Buckingham Palace, this is our premier choice for the Victoria area. The charm of a traditional English country home is reflected in the paneled drawing room, where fires crackle in the ornate fireplaces. The well-furnished rooms here are called apartments; some units are air-conditioned, and all have unbelievably comfortable beds. The refurbished marble bathrooms have extra-long tubs, bidets, fluffy towels, and hair dryers. Try to get a room overlooking the garden. The Goring is one of the best places in London for afternoon tea, and its restaurant offers the area's finest traditional English dishes. Guests have free use of a nearby health club.

Moderate

Tophams Belgravia. 28 Ebury St., London SW1W 0LU. ☎ **020/7730-8147.** Fax 020/7823-5966. www.tophams.com. E-mail: Tophams_Belgravia.compuserve.com. 43 units (23 with bathroom). TV TEL. £120–£130 ($198–$214.50) double without bathroom; £140–£155 ($231–$255.75) double with bathroom; £230 ($379.50) suite. AE, DC, MC, V. Tube: Victoria Station.

Tophams came into being in 1937, when five small row houses were interconnected. Even after complete renovations in 1997, the hotel has retained its country-house flavor, complete with flower-filled window boxes and informal reception rooms decorated with pretty chintzes and antiques. All guest rooms have firm mattresses, hair dryers, satellite TV, and hot beverage–making facilities; the finest of the bunch also have ensuite bathrooms and four-poster beds. The best feature of this hotel, however, is its proximity to public transportation: It's only a 3-minute walk from Victoria Station.

✪ **Windermere Hotel.** 142–144 Warwick Way, London SW1V 4JE. ☎ **020/7834-5163.** Fax 020/7630-8831. www.windermere_hotel.co.uk. E-mail: windermere@compuserve.com. 23 units (20 with bathroom). TV TEL. £75 ($123.75) double without bathroom; £93–£100 ($153.45–$165) double with bathroom; £120 ($198) triple with bathroom; £130 ($214.50) quad with bathroom. AE, CB, MC, V. Tube: Victoria.

This award-winning small hotel is an excellent choice for those who want to be near Victoria Station. The Windermere was built on the site of the old Abbot's Lane, which linked Westminster Abbey to its abbot's residence—all the kings of medieval England trod here. This fine example of early Victorian classical design offers lots of English character. All of the refurbished rooms are comfortably furnished and have such amenities as satellite TV, coffeemakers, and comfortable mattresses. Most rooms have a small private bathroom equipped with a hair dryer and a set of medium-sized towels; public corridor bathrooms are also adequate and well maintained. The ground-floor rooms facing the street tend to be noisy at night. The hotel's "The Pimlico Room" is a very popular restaurant.

Inexpensive

Collin House. 104 Ebury St., London SW1W 9QD. ☎ **020/7730-8031.** Fax 020/ 7730-8031. 13 units (8 with bathroom). £70 ($115.50) double without bathroom; £73 ($120.45) double with bathroom. Rates include English breakfast. No credit cards. Tube: Victoria Station.

This mid-Victorian townhouse is a good, clean bed-and-breakfast, where everything is well maintained. There are a number of family rooms. The main bus, rail, and underground terminals are all about a 5-minute walk from the hotel.

✪ **James House/Cartref House.** 108 Ebury St. and 129 Ebury St., London, SW1W 9QD. ☎ **020/7730-7338** for James House, **020/7730-6176** for Cartref House. Fax 020/7730-7338. 21 units (12 with bathroom). £62 ($102.30) double without bathroom; £73 ($120.45) double with bathroom; £78 ($128.70) quad without bathroom; £104 ($171.60) quad with bathroom. AE, MC, V. Tube: Victoria Station.

Hailed by many publications, including the *Los Angeles Times,* as one of the top 10 B&Bs in London, James House and Cartref House (across the street), deserve the accolades. Derek and Sharon James run both properties, and are the finest hosts in the Victoria Station area. They are constantly refurbishing, so everything looks state of the art. Each room is individually designed, and some of the large rooms have bunk beds suitable for families. The generous English breakfast will have you skipping lunch. Don't worry about which house you're assigned; both are equally nice.

CHELSEA
Moderate

Blair House Hotel. 34 Draycott Place, London SW3 2SA. ☎ **020/7581-2323.** Fax 020/7823-7752. 11 units. TV TEL. £105–£115 ($173.25–$189.75) double. Rates include continental breakfast. AE, DC, MC, V. Tube: Sloane Sq.

This comfortable hotel is a good, reasonably priced choice in the heart of Chelsea. The old-fashioned building, of architectural interest, has been modified and completely refurbished, with every comfortable room sporting hair dryers and tea- or coffee-making equipment. The quieter rooms are in the back.

The Sloane. 29 Draycott Place, London SW3 2SH. ☎ **020/7581-5757.** Fax 020/7584-1348. 12 units. A/C TV TEL. £140 ($231) double; £225 ($371.25) suite. AE, DC, MC, V. Tube: Sloane Sq.

Set within a red-brick Victorian-era townhouse that has been richly and tastefully renovated in recent years, this hotel combines a decor of 19th-century antiques with modern comforts, and a desirable Chelsea location near Sloane Square. The bedrooms are decorated with some wonderful pieces of furniture. The front desk will quote you a price if you can't go home without one. A bar with a panoramic view on the top floor serves a limited menu if you need a snack before trying the dozens of restaurants within the surrounding neighborhood. (There's also 24-hour room service.) Staff is accommodating, pan-European, and tactful.

Wilbraham Hotel. 1–5 Wilbraham Place (off Sloane St.), London SW1X 9AE. ☎ **020/ 7730-8296.** Fax 020/7730-6815. 46 units. TV TEL. £100–£106 ($165–$174.90) double. No credit cards. Nearby parking £12 ($19.80). Tube: Sloane Sq.

This dyed-in-the-wool British hotel is set on a quiet residential street just a few hundred yards from Sloane Square. Within the three Victorian townhouses that have been joined together, the slightly faded but well-maintained bedrooms are traditionally furnished and have fireplaces and leaded windows. Expect sagging beds. On the premises is an attractive, old-fashioned lounge.

KNIGHTSBRIDGE
Expensive
The Beaufort. 33 Beaufort Gardens, London SW3 1PP. ☎ **800/888-1199** in the U.S or Canada, or 020/7584-5252. Fax 020/7589-2834. www.thebeaufort.co.uk/index.htm. 28 units. TV TEL. £200 ($330) double; £325 ($536.25) junior suite for 2. Rates include continental breakfast. AE, DC, MC, V. Tube: Knightsbridge.

One of London's finest boutique hotels has an elegant townhouse atmosphere, with personal service providing the ultimate in tranquility. Only 200 yards from Harrods, it sits behind two Victorian porticoes and an iron fence. Each of the modern and graceful, if exceedingly small, bedrooms features at least one painting by a London artist and plush carpeting. Units contain excellent mattresses, fax machines, and trouser presses. The adequate bathrooms are equipped with hair dryers. Light meals are available from room service.

Claverley Hotel. 13–14 Beaufort Gardens, London SW3 1PS. ☎ **800/747-0398** in the U.S., or 020/7589-8541. Fax 020/7584-3410. 29 units. TV TEL. £120–£190 ($198–$313.50) double; £190 ($313.50) junior suite. Rates include English breakfast. AE, DC, MC, V. Tube: Knightsbridge.

Located on a quiet cul-de-sac, this tasteful hotel, one of the neighborhood's very best, is just a few blocks from Harrods. It's a small, cozy place accented with Georgian-era accessories. The lounge has the feel of a country house. Most rooms have Victorian-inspired wallpaper, wall-to-wall carpeting, and comfortably upholstered armchairs. Two singles are without bathrooms.

SOUTH KENSINGTON
Moderate
Regency Hotel. 100 Queen's Gate, London SW7 5AG. ☎ **800/223-5652** in the U.S., or 020/7370-4595. Fax 020/7370-5555. 209 units. A/C MINIBAR TV TEL. £147 ($242.55) double; from £215 ($354.75) luxury suite. AE, DC, MC, V. Parking: £24 ($39.60). Tube: South Kensington.

The Regency—close to museums, Kensington, and Knightsbridge—takes its name from the historical period of the Prince Regent, later George IV. Located on a street lined with Doric porticoes, six Victorian terrace houses were converted into one stylish, seamless whole. The hotel's restaurant, the Pavillion, serves moderately priced international dishes. At your disposal are the Regency Health Club (with steam rooms, minigym, saunas, and a sensory-deprivation tank), plus a business center.

LANCASTER GATE
Moderate

Commodore. 50 Lancaster Gate, London W2 3NA. ☎ **020/7402-5291.** Fax 020/7262-1088. www.commodore/hotel.com. 90 units. MINIBAR TV TEL. £105–£115 ($173.25–$189.75) double; £150 ($168) suite. Rates include breakfast. AE, DC, MC, V. Tube: Lancaster Gate.

Although it's been here for 25 years, the Commodore is enjoying renewed success as travelers have rediscovered the charm of its eclectically shaped rooms set within the verdant, tree-lined neighborhood of Lancaster Gate. About a quarter of the rooms in the adjoining townhouses are split-level, with a sleeping gallery set at the top of a short flight of stairs. Overall, the decor is comfortable and cozy in the refurbished rooms with excellent mattresses and recently renovated bathrooms. There's a bar and a restaurant on the premises.

PADDINGTON
Inexpensive

The Pavilion. 34–36 Sussex Gardens, London W2 1UL. ☎ **020/7262-0905.** Fax 020/7262-1324. www.msi.com.mt/pavilion. 27 units. TV TEL. £90 ($148.50) double. Rates include breakfast. AE, DC, MC, V. Parking £5 ($8.25). Tube: Edgwater Road.

Until the early 1990s, this was a rather dull, ordinary-looking B&B—that is, until a team of fashion industry entrepreneurs took over and radically redecorated the rooms, turning it into an idiosyncratic little hotel. The result is a theatrical and often outrageous decor that's much appreciated by the many fashion models and music-industry people who regularly make it their temporary home in London. Behind a blackened 1830s Victorian façade, the hotel offers rooms without any particular frills, but each has a distinctive decorative style. Examples include a "kitsch 70s" room ("Honky-Tonk Afro"), an oriental bordello theme ("Enter the Dragon"), and some with 19th-century ancestral themes. One Edwardian-style room, a gem of emerald brocade and velvet, is called "Green with Envy." Each rather small room (especially by the standards of Amazonian runway walkers) contains tea-making facilities. Breakfast is the only meal served.

ST. MARYLEBONE
Expensive

The Leonard. 15 Seymour St., London W1H 5AA. ☎ **020/7935-2010.** Fax 020/7935-6700. E-mail: the.leonard@dial.pipex.com. 31 units. TV TEL. £180 ($297) double; £225–£390 ($371.25–$643.50) suite. AE, DC, MC, V. Tube: Marble Arch.

In 1996, a team of savvy entrepreneurs acquired a quartet of adjacent 17th-century townhouses and combined them into this tasteful hotel near Marble Arch. The individually decorated and wallpapered bedrooms have double-glazed windows to keep out street noise and excellent mattresses. Marble-countered bathrooms are equipped with combination shower and tub and fluffy towels. Some rooms have working fireplaces, but all are equipped with a VCR and a hi-fi stereo system. There's no restaurant on the premises, but a 24-hour cafe near the reception area serves sandwiches and simple meals. There's also a small-scale exercise room on the top floor.

Moderate

Durrants Hotel. George St., London W1H 6BJ. ☎ **020/7935-8131.** Fax 020/7487-3510. 92 units. TV TEL. £135 ($222.75) double; £175 ($288.75) family room; £250 ($412.50) suite. AE, MC, V. Tube: Bond St.

Established in 1789 off Manchester Square, this historic hotel, with its brown-brick facade ornamented with Georgian details, is a snug, cozy, and traditional retreat—almost like a poor man's Browns. The establishment's oldest bedrooms face the front and have slightly higher ceilings than the newer ones. Even the most recent accommodations, however, have elaborate cove moldings and very comfortable furnishings. Many also contain air-conditioning and minibars. The pub is a neighborhood favorite.

Inexpensive

Edward Lear Hotel. 28–30 Seymour St., London W1H 5WD. ☎ **020/7402-5401.** Fax 020/7706-3766. www.edlear.com. E-mail: edwardlear@aol.com. 36 units (5 with bathroom). TV TEL. £60 ($99) double without bathroom; £79.50–89.50 ($127.20–$143.20) double with bathroom; £105 ($168) suite. Rates include English breakfast. MC, V. Tube: Marble Arch.

This popular budget hotel is made all the more desirable by the bouquets of fresh flowers in the public rooms. It's 1 block from Marble Arch in a pair of brick townhouses dating from 1780. The western house was once home to poet and artist Edward Lear, whose illustrated limericks adorn the sitting room walls. Steep stairs lead up to the cozy, if fairly small, bedrooms. The only major drawback is that this is an extremely noisy part of London, so ask for rooms in the rear.

WHERE TO DINE

All restaurants and cafes in Britain are required to display the prices of their food and drink so that the customer can see before entering the eating area. Charges for service and any minimum charge or cover must also be made clear. The prices shown must include 17.5% VAT. Most restaurants add a 10% to 15% service charge to your bill, but if nothing has been added, leave a 12% to 15% tip.

MAYFAIR

Very Expensive

✪ **Chez Nico at Ninety Park Lane.** 90 Park Lane, W1. ☎ **020/7409-1290.** Reservations required (2 days in advance for lunch, 10 days for dinner). Set-price 3-course lunch £33 ($54.45); à la carte dinner £54 ($89.10) for 2 courses, £66 ($108.90) for 3 courses. AE, DC, MC, V. Mon–Fri noon–2pm; Mon–Sat 7–11pm. Closed 10 days around Christmas/New Year's. Tube: Marble Arch. FRENCH.

Nico Ladenis is one of the most talked-about chefs in Great Britain—and certainly the only one who is a former oil company executive, economist, and self-taught cook. As befits any three-star Michelin restaurant, diners here are treated to a memorable experience, including the very best of postnouvelle cuisine, in which classical cooking is creatively adapted to local fresh ingredients. The menu changes frequently, according to Nico's inspiration. Specialties include a warm salad of foie gras on toasted brioche with caramelized orange, or a Bresse pigeon rivaled only by Gavroche. Desserts are sumptuous.

Le Gavroche. 43 Upper Brook St., W1. ☎ **020/7408-0881.** Reservations required, as far in advance as possible. Main courses £28–£38 ($46.20–$62.70); set-price lunch £39 ($64.35); menu exceptionnel £85 ($140.25). AE, MC, V. Mon–Fri noon–2pm and 7–11pm. Tube: Marble Arch. FRENCH.

Le Gavroche has long stood for quality French cuisine, perhaps the finest in Great Britain, although Michelin gives it only two stars as opposed to Chez Nico's three (see above). It's the creation of two Burgundy-born brothers, Albert and Michel Roux. Service is faultless, the ambience chic and formal without being stuffy. The menu changes constantly, depending on what fresh produce is available and, more important, the chefs' inclinations. Their wine cellar is among London's most interesting. Try, if featured, soufflé Suissesse, *papillote* of smoked salmon, or *tournedos gratinés aux poivres* (pears).

Expensive

L'Oranger. 5 St. James's St. SW1A. ☎ **020/839-3774**. Reservations recommended. Set-price lunches £19.50–£23.50 ($32.15–$38.80); set-price dinner £33.50 ($55.30). AE, DC, MC, V. Mon–Fri noon–3pm; Mon–Sat 6–11:15pm. Tube: Green Park. CONTINENTAL.

This bistro-cum-brasserie occupies a large, rectangular, high-ceilinged space in an affluent neighborhood near the bottom of St. James's Street, and as such, manages to elevate a Gallic brasserie into an artfully upscale dining experience. Amid touches of paneling and burnt-orange paint, masses of flowers and uniformed waiters, you'll appreciate the exquisitely choreographed set menus of executive chef Kamel Benamar, whose abilities have been praised by a clientele described as "people who have made it" by London pundits. The menus are likely to include foie gras poached in a red Pessac wine sauce, and pan-fried filet of sea bass with zucchini, tomatoes, basil, and a black-olive vinaigrette. Other staples might include crispy filets of cod with bouill-abaisse sauce and new potatoes, and braised leg of rabbit in Madeira sauce with whole cloves of yellow garlic *en confit* and braised cabbage.

PICCADILLY & LEICESTER SQUARE

Very Expensive

✪ **Oak Room/Marco Pierre White.** In Le Méridien Piccadilly, 21 Piccadilly, W1. ☎ **020/7437-0202**. Reservations required as far in advance as possible. Set-price lunch £29.50 ($48.70); set-price menu gourmand £80–£90 ($132–$148.50). AE, MC, V. Mon–Fri noon–2:15pm; Mon–Sat 7–11:15pm. Closed Christmas. Tube: Piccadilly Circus. MODERN BRITISH.

Put simply, "MPW" is the best chef in London. The only difference is he has moved from the Hyde Park hotel in Knightsbridge to the glamorous surroundings of Le Méridien Piccadilly. He serves London's finest cuisine in the city's most beautiful dining room, restored to its original oak and gilt splendor and filled with art.

Creative, sophisticated, and bold, this daring chef claims he never apprenticed in France, beyond the 2 weeks spent eating in Paris restaurants. Unlike major competitors making names for themselves by reinterpreting English cuisine, White remains a French classicist who refuses to Anglicize or even diversify his cooking. We're talking Bresse pigeon in a classic sauce thickened with bird's blood, just as they did in France in 1898. His menu dazzles with its caramelized wing of skate with winkles (edible sea shells) or his filet of sea bass with fennel, and certainly his braised pig's trotters. One diner claimed that White makes the world's greatest mashed potatoes, which were "sieved, puréed, and squeezed through silk stockings." White vies with Nico Ladenis as the most temperamental chef in London, but he's clearly a magician. If you can, catch his show.

Expensive

Coast. 26B Albemarle St., W1X 3FA. ☎ **020/7495-5999**. Reservations required. Main courses £13.50–£22.50 ($22.30–$37.15). AE, MC, V. Mon–Sat noon–3pm and 6pm–midnight; Sun noon–3:30pm and 6–11pm. Tube: Piccadilly Circus. MODERN INTERNATIONAL.

This place is so cutting edge, so 21st-century, that you get the feeling it tries just a bit too hard to maintain its avant-garde image as one of the hippest restaurants in London. It is set in a former automobile showroom, with lots of parquet woodwork and lighting fixtures that protrude like bug-eyes from their settings (they have also been called breastlike protuberances). Food is eclectic and international. Chef Terry is an original, truly innovative—some say too innovative. Yet flavor is paramount, especially in the lightness of the fish dishes. Terry tempts with his pressed terrine of wood pigeon, pan-fried foie gras, celery root, and prunes, and his baked plum tomato with Langhirano Parma ham and basil oil. Then it's on to Irish Glen Arm salmon on pomme purée with roasted shallots and a lentil red wine sauce.

Moderate

Atlantic Bar & Grill. 20 Glasshouse St., W1 ☎ **020/7734-4888.** Reservations required. Main courses £13–£18 ($21.45–$29.70); set-price lunch £14.90 ($24.60), including 2 glasses of wine. AE, MC, V. Mon–Fri noon–2:45pm; Mon–Sat 6pm–3am; Sun 6–10:30pm. Tube: Piccadilly Circus. MODERN BRITISH.

A titanic eatery installed in a former art deco ballroom off Piccadilly Circus, this 160-seat restaurant draws the trendy to a most untrendy part of London. When it opened in the spring of 1994, it was named "restaurant of the year" by *Good Food Guide.* It still draws a resurgent yuppie crowd making a comeback from their '80s heyday, although graying a bit at the temples. Even Madonna still shows up. Classically trained executive chef Richard Sawyer is at the helm, serving the world's most sublime potato and chive hash, which seems incidental to the accompanying smoked salmon. Try the delectable Helbridean salmon in a creamy champagne sauce with summer sorrel, or most definitely, the hickory-smoked Aberdeen Angus beef filet with a green Szechuan peppercorn sauce. The menu changes every 2 months but is always strong on seafood.

SOHO

Expensive

Mezzo. 100 Wardour St., W1. ☎ **020/7314-4000.** Reservations required for Mezzonine. Mezzonine main courses £15–£20 ($24.75–$33); Mezzo 3-course dinner £40 ($66). £5 ($8.25) cover at Mezzo Thurs–Fri after 10:30pm. AE, DC, MC, V. Mezzo: daily noon–2:30pm; Mon–Thurs 6pm–midnight; Fri–Sat 6pm–3am; Sun 6–11:30pm. Mezzonine: daily noon–2:30pm; Mon–Thurs 5:30pm–1am; Fri–Sat 5:30pm–3am; Sun 5:30–11:30pm. Tube: Tottenham Court Rd. MODERN BRITISH/INTERNATIONAL.

This all-out blockbuster, the latest creation of entrepreneur Sir Terence Conran, is a 750-seat Soho eatery, dubbed the biggest restaurant in Europe. The owners are still hoping for immortality in the *Guinness Book of World Records.* The mammoth space has been split into several separate restaurants, including the Mezzonine upstairs, serving Thai/Asian cuisine with a European flair. Downstairs is the swankier Mezzo, which can seat 400 at a time in an atmosphere that evokes pre-war Hollywood. There's even a Mezzo Café, stocked with sandwiches and drinks.

Mezzonine serves dishes such as marinated salmon with ginger, star anise, and shallots; and roast marinated lamb with yogurt and cumin on flat bread. In the basement, more ambitious dishes are prepared by 100 chefs working behind glass. Here a modern British menu includes shoulder of lamb slow-roasted and enlivened with lemon zest and anchovies.

Quo Vadis. 26–29 Dean St., W1. ☎ **020/7437-9585.** Reservations required. Main courses £13–£27.50 ($21.45–$45.40); set lunches £14.75–£19.75 ($24.35–$32.60). AE, MC, V. Sun–Fri noon–3pm; Mon–Sat 6–11pm; Sun 6–10:30pm. Tube: Leicester Sq. or Tottenham Court Rd. MODERN BRITISH.

Wealthy and sophisticated Brits, as well as prominent members of the Tory party, enjoy the irony that this hyper-trendy restaurant occupies the former apartment house of the Communist patriarch, Karl Marx. He'd never recognize the stylish, postmodern ode to cutting-edge art you'll see today. Many rubberneckers bypass the restaurant altogether and head upstairs to the bar. Here Damien Hirst, the same controversial artist whose cow carcass in formaldehyde wowed the London art scene in the early 1990s, has positioned a severed cow head and a severed bull's head, in separate aquariums filled with preservatives. Although the restaurant is associated with culinary superstar Marco Pierre White, don't expect that this temperamental chef will actually be garnishing the edges of whatever you happen to order. The actual nectar and ambrosia you get will be prepared by his designated underling, Jeremy Hollingsworth. This is one of the flashiest restaurants in London, although its detractors call it flash-in-the-pan. And the food? Although competent and highly appealing, it finishes a distant second to the social blitz generated by the clientele, the setting, and the vagaries of fashion.

Moderate

Dell'Ugo. 56 Frith St., W1. ☎ **020/7734-8300.** Reservations required. Main courses £8–£12 ($13.20–$19.80). AE, DC, MC, V. Mon–Fri noon–3pm; Mon–Sat 7pm–midnight. Tube: Tottenham Court Rd. MEDITERRANEAN.

One of Soho's finest, this multistory restaurant serves immensely popular cuisine at affordable prices. Legions of young Soho suits have claimed it as their favorite spot, but this noisy, modern landmark doesn't please everybody. Critics claim there's too long a wait between courses and dishes are overly contrived. However, we've found the robust Mediterranean dishes packed with flavor and based on the finest of ingredients. The ground floor "caff" offers bar snacks throughout the day, from tapas to meze. Both the restaurant and separated bistro change their à la carte choices often. Start with the goat's cheese in a spicy tomato vinaigrette. For a main course we recommend the linguini with langostine or the rosemary-skewered lamb with charred eggplant. Grilled seafood dishes are moist and delectably seasoned.

The Ivy. 1–5 West St., WC2. ☎ **020/7836-4751.** Reservations required. Main courses £9.75–£23 ($16.10–$37.95); Sat–Sun lunch £17.50 ($28.90). AE, DC, MC, V. Daily noon–3pm and 5:30pm–midnight (last order). Tube: Leicester Sq. ENGLISH/FRENCH.

Effervescent and sophisticated, the Ivy has been intimately associated with the West End theater district since it was established in 1911. Meals are served until very late, ideal for after the theater. With its ersatz 1930s look, the Ivy is fun and humming. The menu appears deceptively simple, but the fresh ingredients are skillfully prepared. Dishes include white asparagus with sea kale and truffle butter; seared scallops with spinach, sorrel, and bacon; and salmon fish cakes.

Ming. 35–36 Greek St., W1. ☎ **020/7734-2721.** Main courses £7.50–£18 ($12.40–$29.70); 2-course, set-price dinner £15 ($24.75); 3-course, set-price dinner £20 ($33). AE, MC, V. Mon–Sat noon–11:45pm. Tube: Tottenham Court Rd. CANTONESE/PEKINESE.

In bustling Soho, this winning Chinese restaurant lies on Shaftesbury Avenue behind the Palace Theatre. The chefs in the kitchen, Mr. Bib and Mr. Bun (we're not making this up), welcome you to their Far East outpost, gaily decorated in green and pink. This is no chop suey and chow mein joint. Many of the recipes have real flair. Fish, especially prawns and squid, are prepared in delectable ways, as are a number of tofu combinations. Cauliflower, sautéed in butter and flavored with bits of chili and slivers of spring onions, is an unusual appetizer. You might follow with spiced and peppered duck breast, or simmered chicken with ginger and orange. Mussels in black bean sauce are worth a return visit, as is a whole sea bass cooked Thai style.

Soho Spice. 124–126 Wardour St., W1. ☎ **020/7434-0808.** Reservations recommended. Main courses £9.50–£14 ($15.65–$23.10); set menus £15.95–£22.95 ($26.30–$37.85). AE, MC, V. Sun–Wed noon–midnight; Thurs noon–1am; Fri–Sat noon–3pm. Tube: Tottenham Court Rd. SOUTH INDIAN.

One of Central London's most stylish Indian restaurants combines a sense of media and fashion chic with the flavors and scents of Southern India. You might opt for a drink at the cellar-level bar before heading to the large street-level dining room decorated in the saffron, cardamom, bay, and pepper hues prevalent within Soho Spice's piquant cuisine. The wait staff, dressed in similarly vivid uniforms, will propose choices from a wide array of dishes, including slow-cooked Indian *tikkas* with lamb, chicken, fish, or all-vegetarian. The cuisine will satisfy traditionalists, but has a modern, nouveau-Soho flair. The presentation takes it a step above typical Indian restaurants.

Inexpensive

Chuen Cheng Ku. 17 Wardour St., W1. ☎ **020/7437-1398.** Reservations recommended on weekend afternoons. Main courses £7–£18 ($11.55–$29.70); set-price menus £9.50–£32 ($15.65–$52.80). AE, DC, MC, V. Daily 11am–11:45pm. Closed Dec 24–25. Tube: Piccadilly Circus or Leicester Sq. CHINESE.

This is one of the finest of Soho's "New China." This large restaurant on several floors seats 400 diners and is noted for its Cantonese food and its long and interesting menu. Specialties are paper-wrapped prawns, rice in lotus leaves, steamed spareribs in black-bean sauce, and shredded pork with cashew nuts, all served in generous portions.

BLOOMSBURY
Moderate

Chiaroscuro. 24 Coptic Street, WC1. ☎ **020/7636-2731.** Reservations recommended. Main courses £9–£17 ($14.85–$28.05); set-price menus £13.50 ($22.30). AE, MC, V. Mon–Fri noon–3pm; Mon–Sat 6–11:45pm. Tube: Tottenham Court Rd. or Holborn. MODERN BRITISH/ PAN-PACIFIC.

This recommended restaurant, created by rising star Sally James, who's assisted by her husband Carl, lies near the British Museum. Dining rooms are on three floors of a Georgian townhouse; the restaurant also includes a playroom to amuse the kids while their parents dine. The frequently changing menu reads like a tour de force of culinary Scotland, Spain, Greece, Japan, and Thailand. Dishes include a purée of parsley with a tapenade of black olives, served with lemon butter on foccaccio; a tempting platter of mixed antipasti; steamed mussels with grilled chicken and chorizo sausage with french fries and *rouille* sauce; and a shredded confit of duck with rustic summer salad, lentils, and bacon.

Villandry. 170 Great Portland St., W1. ☎ **020/7631-3131.** Reservations recommended. Main courses £11–£14 ($18.15–$23.10). AE, MC, V. Mon–Sat noon–3pm and 7–10pm; food store Mon–Sat 8am–8pm. Tube: Great Portland St. INTERNATIONAL/CONTINENTAL.

Food lovers and gourmands flock to this combination food store, delicatessen, and restaurant, where racks of the finest meats, cheese, and produce in the world are displayed and changed virtually every hour, and where some of the finest of the merchandise is quickly and almost whimsically transformed into menu choices within the restaurant. The setting is an oversized Edwardian-style storefront north of Oxford Circus. The interior is artfully minimalist and immaculate—sort of a pared-down temple to the glories of fresh produce and esoteric foodstuffs. Ingredients change here so frequently that the menu is rewritten twice a day—during our latest visit, the menu included such perfectly crafted dishes as breast of duck with fresh spinach and a gratin of baby onions; boiled haunch of pork with blood sausages, mashed potatoes, kale, and mustard sauce; filets of black codfish with prosciutto, radicchio, and creamed lentils; and pan-fried turbot with deep-fried celery, artichoke hearts, and hollandaise sauce.

Inexpensive

Wagamama. 4 Streatham St., WC1. ☎ **020/7323-9223.** Reservations not accepted. Main courses £9–£11 ($14.85–$18.15). MC, V. Mon–Sat noon–11pm; Sun 12:30–10pm. Tube: Tottenham Court Rd. JAPANESE.

Wagamama is very hot. We couldn't really understand the fuss, but the long line up the stairs and out the door of this popular Japanese noodle house attests to our minority opinion. It's noisy and overly crowded, and you'll have to wait on a long, if fast-moving, line for a spot at one of the picnic tables filled with fellow patrons happily (and noisily) slurping up huge bowls of noodles and broth. Using hand-held computers, the wait-staff transmits your order (along with 1,200 others a day) back to the hysterical open kitchen. This fun noodle joint lies in a basement just off New Oxford Street. All dishes on the menu are built around ramen noodles with your choice of chicken, beef, or salmon served with *gyoza,* a light pancake filled with vegetables. Vegetarian dishes are also available, but skip the so-called Korean-style dishes. The philosophy here is one of "positive eating & positive living."

COVENT GARDEN & THE STRAND
Expensive
Rules. 35 Maiden Lane, WC2. ☎ **020/7836-5314.** Reservations recommended. Main courses £13.95–£17.95 ($23–$29.60). AE, DC, MC, V. Daily noon–11:30pm. Tube: Covent Garden. ENGLISH.

London's most quintessentially British restaurant was established in 1798 as an oyster bar, and its framed memorabilia celebrates the apex of the British Empire. Around the turn of the century, Edward VII, portly future king of England, used to come here with his infamous mistress, Lillie Langtry. Their signed portraits still embellish the yellowing walls, along with that of Charles Dickens, who crafted several of his novels here. You can order such classic dishes as jugged hare, Aylesbury duckling in orange sauce, and game dishes (but only from mid-August to February or March).

Moderate
Belgo Centraal. 50 Earlham St., WC2. ☎ **020/7813-2233.** Reservations required for the restaurant. Main courses £8.95–£18.95 ($14.75–$31.25); set menus £6–£13 ($9.90–$21.45). AE, DC, MC, V. Mon–Sat noon–11:30pm; Sun noon–10:30pm. Closed Christmas. Tube: Covent Garden. BELGIAN.

Chaos reigns supreme in this audacious and cavernous basement where mussels mariniére with frites and 100 Belgian beers are the raison d'être. Take a freight elevator down past the busy kitchen into a converted cellar that has been divided into two large eating areas. One is a beer hall seating about 250. The menu here is the same as in the restaurant, but reservations aren't needed. Reservations are required for the restaurant side, which has three nightly seatings: 5:30, 7:30, and 10pm. Although tons of mussels are the big attraction here, you can also opt for fresh Scottish salmon, roast chicken, a perfectly done steak, or one of the vegetarian specialties. Gargantuan plates of wild boar sausages arrive with *stoemp,* a Belgian version of mashed spuds and cabbage.

Porter's English Restaurant. 17 Henrietta St., WC2. ☎ **020/7836-6466.** Reservations recommended. Main courses £7.95–£8 ($13.10–$13.20); set-price menu £16.50 ($27.20). AE, DC, MC, V. Mon–Sat noon–11:30pm; Sun noon–10:30pm. Tube: Covent Garden or Charing Cross. ENGLISH.

Porter's specializes in classic English meat pies. Main courses are so generous that the menu eliminates appetizers. The traditional bangers-and-mash plate is featured daily. With whipped cream or custard, the hot or cold "puddings" include bread-and-butter pudding or steamed syrup sponge. Although the English call all desserts puddings, at Porter's they are in fact puddings in the American sense.

FLEET STREET
Inexpensive
Ye Olde Cheshire Cheese. Wine Office Court, 145 Fleet St., EC4. ☎ **020/7353-6170.** Main courses £7.95–£13.25 ($13.10–$21.85). AE, DC, MC, V. Daily noon–2:30pm and 6–9:30pm. Drinks and bar snacks available daily 11:30am–11pm. Tube: St. Paul's or Blackfriars. ENGLISH.

Dating from the 13th century, this is the most famous of the old City chophouses and pubs. It claims to be the spot where Dr. Samuel Johnson entertained admirers with his acerbic wit. Later, many of the ink-stained journalists and scandalmongers of 19th- and early 20th-century Fleet Street made it their "local." Within, you'll find six bars and two dining rooms. The house specialties include "ye famous pudding"—steak, kidney, mushrooms, and game—and Scottish roast beef, with Yorkshire pudding and horseradish sauce.

THE CITY
Moderate

✪ **Café Spice Namaste.** 16 Prescot St., E1. ☎ **020/7488-9242.** Reservations required. Main courses £8.95–£14.95 ($14.75–$24.65). AE, DC, MC, V. Mon–Fri noon–3pm and 6:15–10:30pm; Sat 6:30–10pm. Tube: Tower Hill. INDIAN.

This is our favorite Indian restaurant in London, where the competition is stiff. It's cheerfully housed in a landmark Victorian hall near Tower Bridge, lying just east of the Tower of London. The chef, Cyrus Todiwala, is a Parsi and former resident of Goa, where he learned many of his culinary secrets. He concentrates on spicy southern and northern Indian dishes with a strong Portuguese influence. As a novelty, Todiwala occasionally even offers a menu of emu dishes; when marinated, the meat is rich and spicy and evocative of lamb. Many patrons journey here just for the complex chicken curry known as *xacutti*. The homemade chutneys alone are worth the trip; our favorite is made with kiwi. All dishes come with fresh vegetables and Indian bread. With all the exotic ingredients, the often time-consuming preparation, the impeccable service, the warm hospitality, and the spicy but subtle flavors, this is hardly a curry hash house.

WESTMINSTER
Moderate

Tate Gallery Restaurant. Millbank, SW1. ☎ **020/7887-8877.** Reservations required 2 days in advance. Main courses £10–£16 ($16.50–$26.40); 2-course set-price lunch £16.75 ($27.65); 3-course set-price lunch £18.50 ($30.55); afternoon tea £4.95–£7.95 ($8.15–$13.10); £15 ($24.75) minimum per person. AE, MC, V. Mon–Sat noon–3pm and Sun noon–4pm; Mon–Sat 3–5pm for afternoon tea. Tube: Pimlico. Bus: 77 or 88. ENGLISH.

The Tate restaurant is particularly attractive to wine lovers, offering what may be the best bargains for superior wines to be found anywhere in the country. It is especially strong on Bordeaux and Burgundies. If you're looking for food instead of (or in addition to) wine, the restaurant specializes in French cuisine. The menu changes every month and might include duck prepared in a variety of ways or lamb or veal dishes.

CHELSEA
Moderate

Blue Bird. 350 King's Rd., SW3. ☎ **020/7559-1142.** Reservations recommended. Set lunch Mon–Fri £12.75–£15.75 ($21.05–$26); main courses £9.75–£30 ($16.10–$49.50). AE, DC, MC, V. Mon–Fri noon–3:30pm and 6–11:30pm; Sat 11am–4pm and 6–11:30pm; Sun 11am–4pm and 6–11pm. Tube: Sloane Sq. MODERN BRITISH/PACIFIC RIM.

Called a *restaurant de gare*—a railway station restaurant—this enormous echoing space resounds every night with clinking silverware and peals of laughter. Although there's a cafe, an upscale delicatessen, and a housewares store on the street level, the heart and soul of this place is the restaurant one floor up. The upscale menu emphasizes savory, cooked-to-the-minute cuisine, with a wood-burning stove used to roast everything from lobster to game. A breathtakingly immense shellfish bar stocks on ice every crustacean you can think of, and a bar off to one side does a thriving business with the Sloane Square subculture. Perennial favorites include the veal scallopine layered with prosciutto, white beans, and sage, as well as pasta and fresh seafood specials.

Afternoon Tea in London: Where to Have a Cuppa

Brown's Hotel. 29–34 Albemarle St., W1. ☎ **020/7493-6020.** Reservations not accepted. Afternoon tea £17.95 ($29.60). AE, DC, MC, V. Daily 3–5:45pm. Tube: Green Park.

The lounge is decorated with English antiques, wall panels, oil paintings, and floral chintz, much like a private English country estate. Give your name to the concierge upon arrival; arrangements will be made for you to be seated on clusters of sofas and settees or at low tables. The regular afternoon tea includes a choice of 10 different teas, plus sandwiches, scones, and pastries.

Claridge's. Brook St., W1. ☎ **020/7629-8860.** Reservations recommended. Jacket and tie for men. High tea £18 ($29.70). AE, DC, MC, V. Daily 3–5pm. Tube: Bond St.

Claridge's teatime rituals manage to persevere through the years with as much pomp and circumstance as the British Empire itself. A portrait of Lady Claridge gazes beneficently from the paneled walls as a choice of 17 kinds of tea is served ever-so-politely.

Georgian Restaurant. On the fourth Floor of Harrods Department Store, 87–135 Brompton Rd., SW1. ☎ **020/7581-1656.** High tea £13.75 ($22.70) per person. AE, DC, MC, V. Mon–Sat 3:45–5:30pm (last order). Tube: Knightsbridge.

A flood of visitors is somehow gracefully herded into a high-volume but nevertheless elegant teatime venue, which is in a fourth-floor room that's so long its staff refers to it as "the Mississippi River." The list of teas available—at least 50—is sometimes so esoteric that you might feel that you're choosing a vintage bottle of wine instead of a cup of tea.

The Orangery. In the gardens of Kensington Palace, W8. ☎ **020/7376-0239.** Reservations not accepted. Pot of tea £2 ($3.30); summer cakes and puddings £1.90–£4.25 ($3.15–$7). MC, V. Apr–Sept 10am–6pm; Oct–Mar 10am–4pm. Tube: Kensington High St. or Queensway.

Set about 50 yards north of Kensington Palace, this tearoom occupies a long and narrow garden pavilion (The Orangery) built in 1704 by Queen Anne as a site for her tea parties. Rows of potted orange trees bask in sunlight, and tea is served amid Corinthian columns, ruddy-colored bricks, and a pair of Grinling Gibbons wood carvings.

English Garden. 10 Lincoln St., SW3. ☎ **020/7584-7272.** Reservations required. Main courses £11.50–£18.75 ($18.95–$30.95); set-price lunch £16.75 ($27.65). AE, DC, MC, V. Mon–Sat 12:30–2:30pm and 7:30–11:30pm; Sun 12:30–2pm and 7–10:30pm. Closed Dec 25–26. Tube: Sloane Sq. ENGLISH.

In this historic Chelsea townhouse, the Garden Room on the ground floor has whitewashed brick with panels of large, stylish flowers. Gothic-inspired rattan chairs and candy-pink tablecloths complete the scene. With the domed conservatory roofs and banks of plants, this is a metropolitan restaurant par excellence. Every component of our last meal here was well prepared and proportioned. Tasty old-fashioned dishes include Arbroath smokie fishcake, saddle of venison and "potted" cabbage, and roast rump of lamb with butter beans and bacon. Save room for the mango fool with macaroons or the white chocolate cheesecake, each delectable.

KNIGHTSBRIDGE
Expensive
Zafferano. 15 Lowndes St., SW1. ☎ **020/7235-5800.** Reservations required. Set menus £26.50–£36.50 ($43.70–$60.20). AE, MC, V. Mon–Sat noon–2:30pm and 7–11pm. Tube: Knightsbridge. ITALIAN.

There's something honest and satisfying about this restaurant, where decor consists of little more than ochre-colored walls, immaculate table linens, and a bevy of uniformed staff members who diligently attend to their duties. Much of the allure derives from a sophisticated and modernized interpretation of Italian cuisine, which includes such dishes as ravioli of pheasant with black truffles, rabbit with Parma ham and polenta, sea bream with spinach and balsamic vinegar, and monkfish with almonds. Joan Collins claimed the chefs produce "culinary fireworks," but found the bright lighting far too harsh. The owners pride themselves on one of the most well-rounded collections of Italian wine in London: You'll find as many as 20 different vintages each of Brunello and Barolos, and about a dozen vintages of Sassecaia.

KENSINGTON
Moderate
Joe's. 126 Draycott Ave., SW3. ☎ **020/7225-2217.** Reservations required. Main courses £10–£17.50 ($16.50–$28.90). AE, DC, MC, V. Mon–Sat noon–3pm and 7–11pm; Sun 10am–5pm. Tube: South Kensington. MODERN BRITISH.

This is one of three London restaurants established by fashion designer Joseph Ettedgui, who has enticed well-known names from the British fashion, music, and entertainment industries to this fun and glamorous spot. You can enjoy such dishes as crab-crusted halibut, breast of duck with roasted root vegetables, char-grilled swordfish with cracked wheat and salsa verde (green sauce), or tiger prawns and monkfish kabobs with a sesame balsamic dressing. It's safe but a bit unexciting. Brunch is served on Sunday, which is the cheapest way to enjoy this place. The atmosphere can be both laid-back and stuffy, just as Kensington trend-setters prefer it.

Pasha. 1 Gloucester Rd., SW7. ☎ **020/7589-7969.** Reservations recommended. Main courses £10–£17 ($16.50–$28.05). AE, DC, MC, V. Daily noon–3pm and 7–11:30pm. Tube: Gloucester Rd. MOROCCAN.

You'll find virtually every kind of ethnic restaurant in London, but few equal the zest and style of this re-creation of a medina palace in Marrakesh. Within a pair of dining rooms outfitted with rich upholstery, flickering candles, belly-dancing music, and artifacts from the Sub-Sahara, you'll enjoy regional and time-honored specialties that once were the domain only of cherished family guests. Examples include a crispy lamb salad with pomegranate and mint, grilled sea bass with warm hummus and parsley salad, chicken *merguez* (spicy sausage) tagine with a coriander; and chargrilled skewered chicken with green chili salsa. And if you have a fondness for the semolina specialty of North Africa (couscous), you'll have at least three different kinds to choose from.

SOUTH KENSINGTON
Expensive
Bibendum/Oyster Bar. 81 Fulham Rd., SW3. ☎ **020/7581-5817.** Reservations required in Bibendum; not accepted in Oyster Bar. Main courses £17–£23 ($28.05–$37.95); 3-course set-price lunch £28 ($46.20); cold seafood platter in Oyster Bar £22 ($36.30) per person. AE, DC, MC, V. Bibendum, Mon–Fri 12:30–2:30pm and 7–11:15pm, Sat 12:30–3pm and 7–11:15pm, Sun 12:30–3pm and 7–10:15pm; Oyster Bar, Mon–Sat noon–11:30pm, Sun noon–3pm and 7–10:30pm. Tube: South Kensington. MODERN FRENCH/MEDITERRANEAN.

This fashionable eatery occupies two floors of an art deco masterpiece. Built in 1911, it formerly housed the British headquarters of the Michelin tire company. Bibendum, the more visible restuarant, is located one floor above street level in a white-tiled room whose stained-glass windows, streaming sunlight, and chic clientele create an attractive atmosphere. The menu is known for its freshness and simplicity, and includes roast quail flavored with Marsala and thyme, braised oxtail with prunes and almonds, and *ris de veau* (sweetbreads) with black butter and capers. Simpler meals and cocktails are available in the street-level Oyster Bar.

The Collection. 264 Brompton Rd., SW3. ☎ **020/7225-1212.** Reservations recommended. Main courses £11–£16 ($18.15–$26.40); set-price menu £35 ($57.75). AE, DC, MC, V. Daily noon–3pm and 6:30–11pm. Tube: South Kensington. INTERNATIONAL.

Few restaurants have tethered themselves as tightly to the aesthetics and preoccupations of the fashion industry as this temple to voyeurism and the vanities. It occupies an echoing warehouse, where tones of taupe and mushroom compete for attention with touches of silver and a 30-foot underlit catwalk (the only access to the place). Don't worry about a snobbish chill: Manager Julian Shaw, a celebrity in his own right, is one of the most adept and humorous in London, skilled at dealing with big-ticket, big-ego fashion moguls. Yummy menu items include crispy duck with *yaki soba* noodles; sesame-crusted tuna steak with sweet potatoes and *bok choi;* sea bream with cilantro; and pan-fried calves' liver with sage and onions. This place also has a great bar scene.

Hilaire. 68 Old Brompton Rd., SW7. ☎ **020/7584-8993.** Reservations recommended. 2-course set-price lunch £19.50 ($32.15); 3-course set-price lunch £23.50 ($38.80); 3-course set-price dinner £34 ($56.10); 4-course set-price dinner £37 ($61.05); dinner main courses £13.50–£21.50 ($22.30–$35.50). AE, DC, MC, V. Mon–Fri 12:15–2:30pm; Mon–Sat 6:30–11:30pm. Closed bank holidays. Tube: South Kensington. CONTINENTAL.

Hilaire is a jovially cramped restaurant, housed in what was originally a Victorian storefront. Chef Bryan Webb prepares a mixture of classical French and *cuisine moderne* at what has become one of London's most stylish restaurants. The menu always reflects the best of the season's offerings, but main courses have included rack of lamb with tapenade and wild garlic, saddle of rabbit, and grilled tuna with Provençal vegetables.

NOTTING HILL GATE
Moderate

Achy Ramp. 150 Notting Hill Gate, W11. ☎ **020/7221-2442.** Reservations required Fri–Sat; otherwise strongly recommended. Main courses £13.50–£16.50 ($22.30–$27.20). AE, DC, MC, V. Daily noon–2:45pm and 6:45–10pm. Tube: Notting Hill Gate. MODERN EUROPEAN.

The theme of this "medical chic" restaurant will remind you either of a harmless small-town pharmacy or an underground chemist's lab. That ambiguity is richly appreciated by the arts-conscious crowd that flocks here, partly because they're interested in what Damien Hirst (*enfant terrible* of London's contemporary art world) has created and partly because the place can be a lot of fun. The drink menu lists lots of highly palatable martinis as well as a somewhat questionable concoction known as a Cough Syrup (cherry liqueur, honey, and vodka over ice). Bottles of pills, bar stools whose seats are shaped like aspirin, and painted representations of Fire, Water, Air, and Earth decorate this spot favored by minor celebs and party people. Upstairs in the restaurant the hospital theme is a lot less pronounced, but nonetheless subtly omnipresent. Menu items include such dishes as a carpaccio of sea bass; lamb cooked with celery, spinach, and herb juices; fisherman's pie; home-salted cod and eggplant pie; and roasted duck with white peaches and French fries.

SEEING THE SIGHTS

London is not a city to visit hurriedly. It's so vast, so stocked with treasures, that it would take a lifetime to explore it thoroughly. Even a quick visit to London, however, gives you a chance to see what's creating the hottest buzz in shopping and nightlife as well as the city's time-tested treasures.

SIGHTSEEING SUGGESTIONS FOR FIRST-TIME VISITORS

If You Have 1 Day   No first-time visitor should leave London without visiting **Westminster Abbey.** See **Big Ben** and the **Houses of Parliament,** and then walk over to see the Changing of the Guard at **Buckingham Palace** if it's being held. Have dinner at a restaurant in **Covent Garden;** we like Porter's English Restaurant. For a nightcap, head over to the **Red Lion,** 2 Duke of York St. (☎ **020/7930-2030**), in Mayfair, a Victorian pub.

If You Have 2 Days   Devote a good part of your second day to exploring the **British Museum,** one of the world's biggest and best. Spend the afternoon visiting the **Tower of London** and seeing the collection of crown jewels (but expect slow-moving lines). Cap your day by boarding one of the **London Launches** to experience the city from the river. For dinner try one of London's landmark restaurants such as **Rules,** 35 Maiden Lane.

If You Have 3 Days   In the morning of your third day, go to the **National Gallery,** facing Trafalgar Square. Then enjoy an afternoon at **Madame Tussaud's Waxworks.** Take some time to stroll through **St. James's** and try to catch a cultural performance at the **South Bank Centre,** site of the Royal Festival Hall, or a play or musical on **West End.**

If You Have 4 Days   In the morning of your fourth day, head for the **City,** the financial district in the East End. Here you'll tour Sir Christopher Wren's **St. Paul's Cathedral.** Spend a few hours strolling the City and visit a few of its many metropolitan attractions. In the late afternoon, head down **King's Road** in Chelsea to shop the many and varied boutiques.

If You Have 5 Days   On your fifth day, explore the **Victoria and Albert Museum** in the morning, and then head to the **Tate Gallery** for lunch at its restaurant. Finally, see where history was made during the dark days of World War II; visit the **Cabinet War Rooms** at Clive Steps (see "Official London," below), where Churchill directed the British operations against the Nazis. In the evening, attend the theater.

THE TOP ATTRACTIONS

✪ **Tower of London.** Tower Hill, on the north bank of the Thames, EC3. ☎ **020/ 7709-0765.** Admission £10.50 ($17.35) adults, £7.90 ($13.05) students and senior citizens, £6.90 ($11.40) children, free for children under 5. Family ticket for 5 members (but no more than 2 adults) £31 ($51.15). Apr–Oct Mon–Sat 9am–5pm, Sun 10am–5pm; Nov–Mar Sun–Mon 10am–4pm; Tues–Sat 9am–4pm. Closed Dec 24–26 and Jan 1. Tube: Tower Hill. Boats: From Westminster Pier.

This ancient fortress continues to pack in visitors attracted by its macabre associations with all the legendary figures who were imprisoned or executed here. The fortress is actually a compound, in which the oldest and finest structure is the White Tower, begun by William the Conqueror. Here you can view the Armouries, which dates from the reign of Henry VIII. A display of instruments of torture and execution recalls some of the most ghastly moments in the history of the Tower. To see the **Jewel House,** where the crown jewels are kept, go early in the day, especially during summer, before the long lines form. A palace once inhabited by King Edward I in the late 1200s was opened to visitors for the first time in 1993. Above Traitor's Gate, it is the only surviving medieval palace in Britain. Free 1-hour tours are given by guides in period costumes every 30 minutes, starting at 9:30am from the Middle Tower near the main entrance. The tour includes the Chapel Royal of St. Peter ad Vincula (St. Peter in Chains). The last guided walk starts about 3:30pm in summer, 2:30pm in winter.

✪ **Westminster Abbey.** Broad Sanctuary, SW1. ☎ **020/7222-7110.** Free admission to cloisters. Abbey, £5 ($8.25) adults, £3 ($4.95) students, £2.50 ($4.15) children 11–18 (free 10 and under). Family ticket (2 adults, 2 children) £16 ($26.40). Mon–Fri 9am–3:45pm; Sat 9:15am–1:45pm and 3:45–4:45pm. Tube: Westminster or St. James's Park.

In 1065 the Saxon king, Edward the Confessor, founded a Benedictine abbey and rebuilt the old minster church on this spot, overlooking Parliament Square. The first English king crowned in the abbey was Harold in 1066, before he was killed at the Battle of Hastings later that same year. The man who defeated him, Edward's cousin, William the Conqueror, was also crowned at the abbey; the coronation tradition has continued to the present day, broken only twice (Edward V and Edward VIII). The **abbey** is the site of state occasions, including the September 1997 funeral of Diana, Princess of Wales, which led to a 25% increase in visitors to the abbey. The essentially early English Gothic structure seen today owes more to Henry III's plans than to those of any other sovereign, although many architects, including Wren, have contributed to the abbey. Built on the site of the ancient lady chapel in the early 16th century, **Henry VII Chapel** is one of the loveliest in Europe, with its fan vaulting, Knights of Bath banners, and Torrigiani-designed tomb of the king. You can also visit the most hallowed spot in the abbey, the **shrine of Edward the Confessor** (canonized in the 12th century). In the saint's chapel is the **Coronation Chair,** made at the command of Edward I in 1300. Another noted spot is the **Poets' Corner,** to the right of the entrance to the Royal Chapel, with monuments to Chaucer, Shakespeare, "O Rare Ben Johnson" (his name misspelled), Samuel Johnson, the Brontë sisters, Thackeray, Dickens, Tennyson, Kipling, even the American Longfellow.

A guided tour of the abbey lasts about 1½ hours and costs £3 ($4.95) in addition to the entrance fee. For advance bookings, call ☎020/7222-7110. Or enjoy a personal audio tour, an Audioguide renting for £2 ($3.30).

The **cloisters** of the abbey are open daily 9am to 6pm, charging no admission. Other attractions to visit on site are the **Chapter House, Pyx Chapter,** and the **museum of Westminster relics,** open daily 10:30am to 4pm, charging £2.50 ($4.15) for adults and £1.30 ($2.15) for children. The **College Garden** is open only on Tuesday and Thursday 10am to 6pm. It's free but you're invited to make a donation.

Houses of Parliament. Westminster Palace, Old Palace Yard, SW1. ☎ **020/7219-4272** for the House of Commons, or ☎**020/7219-3107** for the House of Lords. Free admission. House of Lords, open to the public Mon–Wed from 2:30pm; Thurs from 3pm; also some Fridays (check by phone); closings depend on specific debate. House of Commons, open to the public Mon–Tues 2:30–10:30pm; Wed 9:30am–10:30pm; Thurs 11:30am–7:30pm; also some Fri (check by phone). Join line at St. Stephen's entrance. Tube: Westminster.

These Houses, the assemblies that effectively trimmed the sails of royal power, are the stronghold of Britain's democracy. Both Houses (Commons and Lords) are situated in the former royal Palace of Westminster, the king's residence until Henry VIII moved to Whitehall. The present Houses of Parliament were built in 1840, but the Commons chamber was bombed and destroyed by the Luftwaffe in 1941. However, the 320-foot tower that houses Big Ben remained standing and the "symbol of London" continues to strike its chimes. Except for the Strangers' Galleries, the two Houses of Parliament are closed to tourists. To be admitted to the Strangers' Galleries, join the public line outside the St. Stephen's entrance; often there is a delay before the line is admitted.

London Attractions

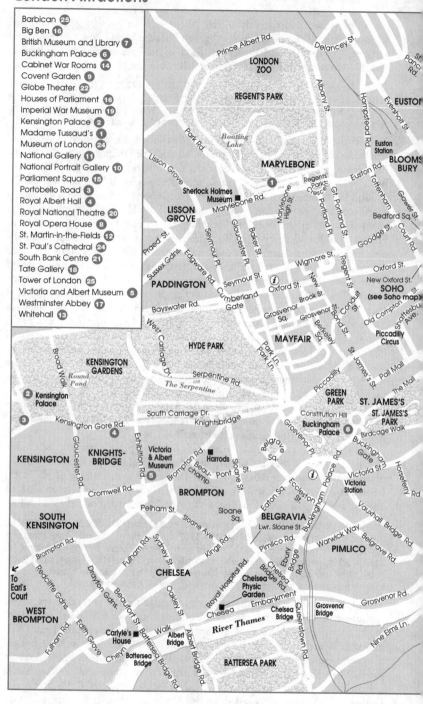

Barbican 25
Big Ben 16
British Museum and Library 7
Buckingham Palace 6
Cabinet War Rooms 14
Covent Garden 9
Globe Theater 22
Houses of Parliament 16
Imperial War Museum 19
Kensington Palace 2
Madame Tussaud's 1
Museum of London 24
National Gallery 11
National Portrait Gallery 10
Parliament Square 15
Portobello Road 3
Royal Albert Hall 4
Royal National Theatre 20
Royal Opera House 8
St. Martin-in-the-Fields 12
St. Paul's Cathedral 24
South Bank Centre 21
Tate Gallery 18
Tower of London 25
Victoria and Albert Museum 5
Westminster Abbey 17
Whitehall 13

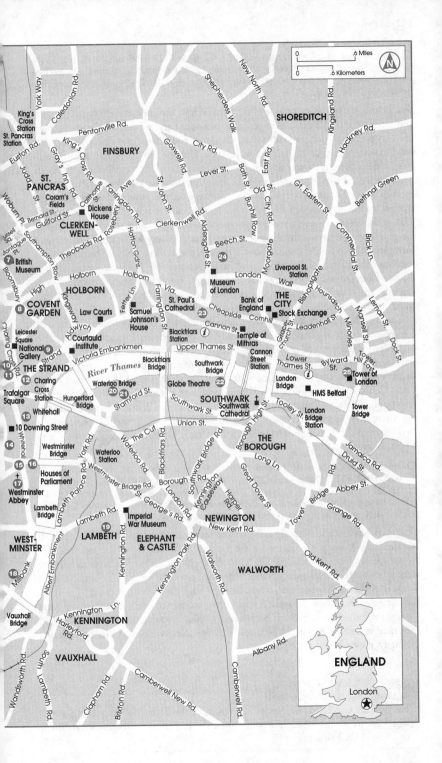

✪ **British Museum.** Great Russell St., WC1. ☎ **020/7323-8599** or 020/7636-1555 for recording. Free admission. Mon–Sat 10am–5pm; Sun noon–6pm (the galleries start to close 10 min. earlier). Closed Jan 1, Good Friday, early May, and Dec 24–26. Tube: Holborn, Tottenham Court Rd., or Russell Sq.

The British Museum shelters one of the world's most comprehensive collections of art and artifacts, including countless treasures of ancient and modern civilizations. Even on a cursory first visit, be sure to see the Asian collections (the finest assembly of Islamic pottery outside the Islamic world), the Chinese porcelain, the Indian sculpture, and the prehistoric and Romano-British collections. The overall storehouse splits basically into the national collections of antiquities; prints and drawings; coins and medals; and ethnography. The Assyrian Transept on the ground floor displays the winged and human-headed bulls and lions that once guarded the gateways to the palaces of Assyrian kings. From here you can continue into the angular hall of Egyptian sculpture to see the Rosetta stone, whose discovery led to the deciphering of hieroglyphs. Also on the ground floor is the Duveen Gallery, housing the Elgin marbles, now the subject of much controversy. The *Sutton Hoo* Anglo-Saxon burial ship, discovered in Suffolk, is, in the words of an expert, "the richest treasure ever dug from English soil." The Portland Vase, one of the most celebrated possessions of the British Museum, was found in 1582 outside Rome.

The British Museum will celebrate the millennium by creating London's first covered public square at the center of its world-famous neoclassical building. By autumn of 2000 the museum's inner courtyard, hidden for 150 years, will be transformed into the Great Court, a two-acre square spanned by a spectacular glass roof. The court will house a center for education, galleries, and more exhibition space. At the heart of the Great Court, the Reading Room will be restored and reopened in 2000 as home to a new public reference library. Following the transfer of the British Library to another site, more space has opened up on Great Russell Street. In time the ethnography collections from the Museum of Mankind will be returned to the original home site in Bloomsbury.

✪ **Buckingham Palace.** At the end of The Mall (the street running from Trafalgar Sq.). ☎ **020/7839-1377.** Palace tours £10 ($16) adults to age 60, £7.50 ($12) adults over 60, £5 ($8.25) children under 17. (*Warning:* These ticket prices, or even the possibility of public admission to Buckingham Palace, are subject to change.) State apts. open Aug–Sept daily 9:30am–4:30pm. Tube: St. James's Park, Green Park, or Victoria.

This massively graceful building is the official residence of the queen, and you can tell whether Her Majesty is at home by the Royal Standard flying at the masthead. In spring 1993, Queen Elizabeth II agreed to allow visitors for the first time to tour her state apartments and picture galleries. The palace will be open to the public for 8 weeks in August and September, when the royal family is away on vacation. The tours include not only the state apartments, but also a number of other rooms used by King George IV and designed by John Nash in the 1800s, including the Throne Room and the grand staircase. The queen's picture gallery has some world-class masterpieces that are rarely, if ever, seen by the public.

The Plundering Empire

For decades Greece has demanded the return of the Elgin Marbles, calling it "war loot." Greece claims the Elgin Marbles as part of its heritage, although so far Britain has refused their demands.

Buckingham Palace's most famous spectacle is the **Changing of the Guard.** The new guard, marching behind a band, comes from either the Wellington or Chelsea Barracks and takes over from the old guard in the forecourt of the palace. When this martial ceremony occurs is the subject of mass confusion—*when* it happens, it begins at 11:30am. In theory, that is supposed to be from mid-April to July and on alternate days the rest of the year. It can be canceled in bad weather and during major state events. Call ☎ **0839/123-411** for the latest information. You should always check locally to see if one of the world's most famous military rituals is likely to be staged during your visit.

Madame Tussaud's. Marylebone Rd., NW1. ☎ **020/7935-6861.** Admission £9.75 ($16.10) adults, £7.45 ($12.30) senior citizens, £6.60 ($10.90) children under 16. Combination tickets, including the new planetarium, £12 ($19.80) adults, £9.25 ($15.25) seniors, £8.50 ($14) children under 16. Mon–Sat 10am–5:30pm. Tube: Baker St.

In 1770, an exhibition of life-sized wax figures was opened in Paris by Dr. Curtius. He was soon joined by his niece, Strasbourg-born Marie Tussaud, who learned the secret of making lifelike replicas of the famous and the infamous. During the French Revolution, the head of almost every distinguished victim of the guillotine was molded by Madame Tussaud or her uncle. An enlarged Grand Hall continues to house years of old favorites, as well as many of today's heads of state and political leaders. In the Chamber of Horrors, you can have the vicarious thrill of walking through a Victorian London street, where special effects include the shadowy terror of Jack the Ripper. Planetarium shows begin at 12:20pm daily, and are presented every 40 minutes.

✪ **Tate Gallery.** Beside the Thames on Millbank, SW1. ☎ **020/7887-8725.** Free admission, except special exhibitions varying from £3–£5 ($4.95–$8.25). Daily 10am–5:50pm. Tube: Pimlico. Bus: 77A, 36, C10, or 88.

The Tate houses two collections: British paintings from the 16th century on, and England's finest collection of modern art, domestic and foreign. Try to schedule at least two visits—the first to see the museum's comprehensive exhibit of the works of J. M. W. Turner, the drawings of William Blake, and the pre-Raphaelites; and the second to take in the modern collection. Only a portion of the collections can be displayed at any one time.

Note: The Tate's famous modern art collection is scheduled for relocation in May 2000 to the imposing former Bankside Power Station on the banks of the Thames opposite St. Paul's Cathedral. Hours and price of admission have not yet been set for the new **Tate Gallery of Modern Art,** Bankside, SE1 (☎ **020/7887-8729**).

✪ **National Gallery.** On the north side of Trafalgar Sq., WC2. ☎ **020/7839-3321.** Free admission. Daily 10am–6pm (9pm Wed). Closed Jan 1, Good Friday, and Dec 24–26. Tube: Charing Cross, Embankment, or Leicester Sq.

In an impressive neoclassical building, the National Gallery houses a comprehensive collection of Western paintings, representing all the major schools from the 13th to the early 20th centuries. The 1991 Sainsbury wing houses the large collection of Sienese, Venetian, and Florentine masters. Of the early Gothic works, the *Wilton Diptych* (French or English school, late 14th century) is the rarest treasure; it depicts Richard II being introduced to the Madonna and child by John the Baptist and the Saxon king, Edward the Confessor. The 16th-century Venetian masters and the northern European painters are well represented, including Pieter Brueghel the Elder's Bosch-influenced *Adoration*.

✪ **St. Paul's Cathedral.** St. Paul's Churchyard, EC4. ☎ **020/7236-4128.** Cathedral, £4 ($6.60) adults, £2 ($3.30) children 6–16. Galleries, £3.50 ($5.75) adults, £1.50 ($2.45) children. Guided tours £3.50 ($5.75), recorded tours £3 ($4.95), free for children 5 and under.

Sightseeing Mon–Sat 8:30am–4pm; galleries Mon–Sat 10am–4:15pm. No sightseeing Sun (services only). Tube: St. Paul's.

It was during the Great Fire of 1666 that the old St. Paul's was razed, making way for a new Renaissance structure designed by Sir Christopher Wren and built between 1675 and 1710. The classical dome of St. Paul's dominates the City's square mile. Inside, the cathedral is laid out like a Greek cross; it houses few art treasures but has many monuments, including a memorial chapel to American service personnel who lost their lives in World War II. Encircling the dome is the Whispering Gallery, where vocal discretion is advised. Wren lies in the crypt, along with the Duke of Wellington and Lord Nelson.

✪ **Victoria and Albert Museum.** Cromwell Rd., SW7. ☎ **020/7938-8500.** £5 ($8.25) for adults, £3 ($4.95) for students and senior citizens, free for children under 18. Mon noon–5:45pm; Tues–Sun 10am–5:45pm. Tube: South Kensington.

This is the greatest museum in the world devoted to the decorative arts. It's also one of the liveliest and most imaginative museums in London—where else would you find the quintessential "little black dress" as part of a permanent collection? The medieval collection houses such treasures as the Early English Gloucester candlestick. The largest collection of Renaissance sculpture outside of Italy is on display here, including works by Donatello and Bernini. The cartoons by Raphael, conceptual designs for the Sistine Chapel, are owned by the Queen and exhibited here.

The museum also has the greatest collection of Indian art outside India, plus Chinese and Japanese galleries. Don't miss the Dress Collection, featuring wince-inducing corsets through the ages.

Kensington Palace. The Broad Walk, Kensington Gardens, W8. ☎ **020/7937-9561.** Guided tour £8.50 ($14) adults, £6.70 ($11.05) seniors and students, £6.10 ($10.05) children, £26.10 ($43.05) family ticket. June–Sept daily 10am–5pm; off-season Wed–Sun 10am–3pm. Tube: Queensway or Bayswater on north side of gardens; High St. Kensington on south side.

Once the residence of British monarchs, Kensington Palace hasn't been the official home of reigning kings since George III. Originally named Nottingham Palace, the complex dates from about 1605, but was redesigned by Sir Christopher Wren in 1689. Since the end of the 18th century, the palace has been home to some members of the royal family, and the State Apartments are open for tours.

The palace is now the London home of Princess Margaret as well as the Duke and Duchess of Kent. Of course, it was once the home of Diana, Princess of Wales, and her two sons (Harry and William now live with their father at St. James's Palace, where Diana's body lay in the Chapel Royal during the week before her funeral). Kensington Palace is best known for the millions and millions of flowers placed in front of it during the days following Diana's death. Newly restored, the State Apartments and Ceremonial Dress Collection today display trompe l'oeil murals by William Kent and ceremonial robes belonging to Queen Mary and George V. Visitors are guided through a series of theme rooms, including even a tailor shop stocked with materials used in court dress. One section includes a collection of state-occasion dresses, hats, and shoes worn by queens in the past 50 years. In the State Apartments, 15 rooms, including the restored King's Gallery and the Cupola Room, where Queen Victoria was baptized, are permanently opened to the public.

MORE SIGHTS
Official London

Whitehall and Cabinet War Rooms. Entrance to the War Rooms is by Clive Steps at the end of King Charles St., SW1, off Whitehall near Big Ben. ☎ **020/7930-6961.** Admission

Remembering Princess Diana

Princess Diana is buried on a picturesque island on the Oval Lake at Althorp, the Spencer family estate at Great Brington in Northamptonshire. You won't have access to the gravesite or the island, but you can view the island from across the lake. Admission is £9.50 ($15.65) adults, £7.50 ($12.40) seniors, and £5 ($8.25) children.

You must book tickets long in advance by calling ☎ **01604/592-020** or writing **Althorp Admissions,** c/o Wayhead, The Hollows, St. James's Street, Nottingham, NG1 6FJ. A special train and bus service will be operated by Virgin Trains; since details weren't set at press time, call ☎ **0345/484-950.**

At Althorp, Earl Spencer, Diana's brother, has opened a $5 million shrine to the late princess, including a museum, a gift shop, and a cafe. The museum contains, among other exhibits, letters she wrote as a schoolgirl, the stunning silk dress she wore as a bride at Westminster Abbey, and the high-fashion outfits she later appeared in to the delight of paparazzi. Some exhibits are almost embarrassingly personal, such as a toy rabbit with an ear missing. You can also see poignant films of her as a carefree child dancing in the gardens and later on a ride with her sons, William and Harry. The men in her life—Prince Charles, James Hewitt, and even Dodi al Fayed—are notable only by their absence from the museum.

£4.80 ($7.90) adults, £2.40 ($3.95) children. Apr–Sept daily 9:30am–6pm (last admission 5:15pm); Oct–Mar daily 10am–5:30pm. Closed Christmas and holidays. Tube: Westminster or St. James's.

Whitehall, the seat of the British government, developed on the grounds of Whitehall Palace, which was turned into a royal residence by Henry VIII after snatching it from its former occupant, Cardinal Wolsey. Whitehall extends south from Trafalgar Square to Parliament Square. Along it you'll find the Home Office, the Old Admiralty Building, and the Ministry of Defence.

Visitors today can see the **Cabinet War Rooms,** the bombproof bunker suite of rooms, just as they were left by Winston Churchill at the end of World War II. You can see the Map Room with its huge military wall maps; the Atlantic map is a mass of pinholes (each hole represents at least one convoy). Next door is Churchill's bedroom-cum-office, which has two BBC microphones over which his famous broadcasts stirred the nation.

More Museums

Imperial War Museum. Lambeth Rd., SE1. ☎ **020/7416-5000.** Admission £4.70 ($7.75) adults, £3.70 ($6.10) senior citizens and students, £2.35 ($3.90) children; free daily 4:30–6pm. Open daily 10am–6pm. Closed Dec 24–26. Tube: Lambeth North or Elephant & Castle.

Constructed around 1815, this large domed building, the former Bethlehem Royal Hospital for the Insane (or Bedlam), houses collections relating to the two world wars and other military operations. There are four floors of exhibitions, including a vast area of historical displays, two floors of art galleries, and a dramatic re-creation of London at war during the blitz.

Museum of London. 150 London Wall, EC2. ☎ **020/7600-3699.** Admission £5 ($8.25) adults; £3 ($4.95) children, students, and senior citizens; £12 ($19.80) family ticket. Tues–Sat 10am–5:50pm; Sun noon–5:50pm. Tube: St. Paul's, Barbican, or Moorgate.

In London's Barbican district near St. Paul's Cathedral, the Museum of London traces the history of London from prehistoric times to the postmodern era through relics, costumes, household effects, maps, and models. Anglo-Saxons, Vikings, Normans—all the invaders are here, displayed on two floors around a central courtyard.

Galleries

National Portrait Gallery. St. Martin's Place, WC2. ☎ **020/7306-0055.** Admission £4 ($6.60) adults; £3 ($4.95) seniors, students, and children ages 12–18; children 11 and under free. Mon–Sat 10am–5:45pm; Sun noon–5:45pm. Tube: Charing Cross or Leicester Sq.

The National Portrait Gallery was founded in 1856 to collect the likenesses of famous British men and women. Today the collection is the most comprehensive of its kind in the world and constitutes a unique record of those who created the history and culture of the nation. A few paintings will catch your eye, including Sir Joshua Reynold's portrait of Samuel Johnson ("a man of most dreadful appearance"). You'll also see a portrait of William Shakespeare, which is claimed to be the most "authentic contemporary likeness" of its subject of any work yet known, and the portrait of the Brontë sisters, painted by their brother Branwell. The most recent addition to the gallery includes portraits of British sports figures, a tribute to athletic icons of past and present generations—everything from the Chariots of Fire athletes of the 1920s to the superstars of today.

The Millennium Approaches

British Airways London Eye. Jubilee Gardens, SE1. ☎ **020/7487-0294.** Admission £6.95 ($11) adults, £5.30 ($9) seniors/students, £4.80 ($8) children under 16. Tube: Embankment or Waterloo.

Opening in December 1999, this extraordinary Ferris wheel is the world's highest observation wheel. Protected from the elements inside 32 high-tech capsules, passengers rise slowly to a height of 450 feet and receive a 30-minute slow-moving "flight" over the heart of the capital, complete with commentary and bird's-eye views that are "usually only accessible by helicopter or aircraft."

Millennium Dome. Greenwich, SE10. Admission and hours weren't set at press time, but check with the LTB (see "Visitor Information," above) or the Millennium Web site **www. LondonMillenniumCity.com.** Tube: North Greenwich.

With 14 themed zones arranged around a central performance area, the controversial Millennium Dome opens on January 1, 2000. At the dome's center, a thrice-daily show (created by Mark Fisher and Peter Gabriel) with 200 performers and stunning visual effects will "propel visitors through the story of humanity." Among the zones are **Body,** a walk through the world's largest representation of the human form, with a chance to see how the body works; **Spirit,** the opportunity to explore the values underpinning our society; and **Mind,** a look at the latest developments in understanding the human brain.

LONDON'S PARKS

London's parklands easily rate as the greatest "green lung" system of any large city. One of the biggest is **Hyde Park.** With the adjoining Kensington Gardens, it covers 636

To Vent or Not to Vent

Speakers' Corner in the northeast corner of Hyde Park is one of the most bizarre sights in London. Political activists, evangelists, and every crackpot in Britain who wishes to be heard can hop on a soapbox and speak their minds every Sunday from 11am to dusk. Democracy in action has never been so colorful!

acres of central London with velvety lawn interspersed with ponds, flower beds, and trees. **Kensington Gardens** is home to the celebrated statue of Peter Pan with the bronze rabbits that toddlers are always trying to kidnap. East of Hyde Park, across Piccadilly, stretch **Green Park** and **St. James's Park,** forming an almost-unbroken chain of landscaped beauty. This is an ideal area for picnics—hard to believe it was once a festering swamp near the leper hospital. **Regent's Park,** north of Baker Street and Marylebone Road, was designed by the 18th-century genius John Nash to surround a palace that never materialized. The **open-air theater** and the **London Zoo** are in this most classically beautiful of London's parks.

ORGANIZED TOURS

One of the most popular bus tours is called **"The Original London Sightseeing Tour,"** where London unfolds from a traditional double-decker bus, with live commentary by a guide. The 1½-hour sightseeing tour costs £12 ($19.80) for adults and £6 ($9.90) for children under 16. The tour plus Madame Tussaud's costs £21 ($34.65) for adults and £12 ($19.80) for children. You can buy tickets on the bus or from any London Transport or London Tourist Board Information Centre, where you can receive a discount. Departures are from various convenient points within the city. For information or ticket purchases on the phone, call ☎ **020/8877-1722.**

Touring boats operate on the Thames all year and can take you to places within Greater London and beyond. Main embarkation points are Westminster Pier, Charing Cross Pier, and Tower Pier, a system that lets you, for instance, take a "water taxi" from the Tower of London to Westminster Abbey or a more leisurely cruise from Westminster to Hampton Court Palace or Kew Gardens. Several companies operate motor launches, offering panoramic views of one of Europe's most historic waterways en route. For information and reservations, there are specific numbers: the **Westminster/ Greenwich** service at ☎ **020/7930-2062; Hampton Court** service at ☎ **020/ 7930-2062;** and **Tower** service, ☎ **020/7237-5134.** Westminster Pier is on Victoria Embankment, SW1.

Hands down, the best regularly scheduled walking tours of London are offered by ✪ **The Original London Walks** (☎ **020/7624-3978**). Over 100 tours are offered each week, ranging from ghost walks to one that features sites related to the Beatles. The guides are superb and include prominent actors and actresses, as well as the man many consider to be the foremost authority on Jack the Ripper. This is a great way to discover London's underappreciated East End. Walks cost £4.50 ($7.45) for adults or £3.50 ($5.75) for students and senior citizens. Children under 15 join the tours for free. No reservations are needed; call the number above for walk times and starting locations.

THE SHOPPING SCENE
THE TOP SHOPPING STREETS & NEIGHBORHOODS

There are several key streets that offer some of London's best retail stores—or simply one of everything—compactly located in a niche or neighborhood, perfect for strolling and shopping.

THE WEST END   As a neighborhood, the West End includes the tiny Mayfair district and is home to the core of London's big-name shopping. Most of the department stores, designer shops, and multiples (chain stores) have their flagships in this area.

The key streets are **Oxford Street** for affordable shopping (start at Marble Arch tube station if you're ambitious, or Bond Street station if you just want to see some of it), and **Regent Street,** which intersects Oxford Street at Oxford Circus (tube: Oxford Circus).

There are several branches of the private-label department store **Marks & Spencer,** but the Marble Arch store (on Oxford Street) is the flagship, and worth shopping for the high-quality goods. There's a grocery store in the basement and a home furnishings department upstairs.

Regent Street has fancier shops—more upscale department stores (including the famed **Liberty of London**), multiples (**Laura Ashley**), and specialty dealers—and leads all the way to Piccadilly.

In between the two, parallel to Regent Street, is **Bond Street.** Divided into New and Old, Bond Street (tube: Bond Street) also connects Piccadilly with Oxford Street and is synonymous with the luxury trade. Bond Street has had a recent revival and is the hot address for all the international designers.

Burlington Arcade (tube: Piccadilly Circus), the famous glass-roofed, Regency-style passage leading off Piccadilly, is lined with intriguing shops and boutiques specializing in fashion, jewelry, Irish linen, cashmere, and more.

Just off Regent Street (actually, tucked right behind it) is **Carnaby Street** (tube: Oxford Circus), which is also having a comeback. Although it no longer dominates the world of pace-setting fashion as it did in the 1960s, it's still fun to visit, especially for teens wanting cheap souvenirs, a purple wig, or a little something in leather. There's also a convenient branch of **Boots The Chemist** here.

For a total contrast, check out **Jermyn Street,** off Regent Street south of Piccadilly, a tiny 2-block-long street devoted to high-end men's haberdashers and toiletries shops; many have been doing business for centuries. Several hold royal warrants (for doing business with Buckingham palace), including **Turnball & Asser,** where HRH Prince Charles has his pj's made.

The West End leads to the theater district, passing through two more shopping areas: the still-not-ready-for-prime-time **Soho,** where the sex shops are slowly being turned into cutting-edge designer shops, and **Covent Garden,** which is a masterpiece unto itself. The original marketplace has overflowed its boundaries and eaten up the surrounding neighborhood, creating an area where you can easily get lost, but it's fun to just wander and shop. Covent Garden is especially mobbed on Sundays.

KNIGHTSBRIDGE & CHELSEA This is the second-most famous of London's retail districts because it's the home of **Harrods,** 87–135 Brompton Rd., Knightsbridge (☎ **020/7730-1234;** tube: Knightsbridge). Harrods is London's—indeed Europe's—top department store. The sheer range, variety, and quality of merchandise is dazzling; be sure not to miss the delicatessen and food halls. The store has been refurbished to restore it to the elegance and luxury of the 1920s and 1930s. A small street nearby, **Cheval Place,** is home to designer resale shops.

Walk toward Museum Row and you'll soon find **Beauchamp Place** (tube: Knightsbridge), pronounced "Beecham." The street is only 1 block long, but it features the kinds of shops where young British aristos buy their clothing.

Head out at the **Harvey Nichols** end of Knightsbridge, away from Harrods, and shop your way through the designer stores on **Sloane Street** (Hermés, Armani, **Prada,** and the like), then walk past Sloane Square and you're in an altogether different neighborhood: King's Road.

King's Road (tube: Sloane Square), Chelsea's main thoroughfare, will forever remain a symbol of London in the Swinging Sixties. Today, King's Road is a lineup of markets and "multistores," large or small conglomerations of indoor stands, stalls, and booths within one building or enclosure.

Chelsea doesn't begin and end with King's Road. If you choose to walk the other direction (southwest) from Harrods along Brompton Road, you connect to a part of Chelsea called **Brompton Cross,** another trendy area for designer shops made popular when Michelin House was rehabbed by Sir Terence Conran for **The Conran Shop** 81 Fulham Rd., SW 3 (☎ 020/7589-7401).

Also check out **Walton Street,** a tiny, serpentine street running from Brompton Cross back toward the museums. About 2 blocks of this 3-block street are devoted to fairy-tale shops, where m'lady goes to buy aromatherapy, needlepoint, or costume jewelry or meet with her interior designer.

Finally, don't forget all those museums right there in the corner of the shopping streets. They all have great gift shops.

KENSINGTON & NOTTING HILL **Kensington High Street** (tube: High St. Kensington) is the most recent hangout for teens who have graduated from Carnaby Street and are now setting street fashion trends. While there are a few staples of basic British fashion on this strip, most of the stores feature clothes that stretch, are very, very short, or very, very tight.

From Kensington High Street, you can walk up **Kensington Church Street,** which, like Portobello Road, is one of the city's main shopping avenues for antiques. Kensington Church Street dead-ends into the Notting Hill Gate tube station, which is where you would arrive for shopping in **Portobello Road.** The dealers and the weekend market are 2 blocks beyond.

THE TOP MARKETS

THE WEST END The most famous market in all of England, **Covent Garden Market** (☎ 020/7836-9136; tube: Covent Garden), offers several different markets daily from 9am to 5pm (we think it's most fun to come on Sunday). **Apple Market** is the fun, bustling market in the courtyard, where traders sell . . . well, everything. Many of the items are what the English call collectible nostalgia; they include a wide array of glassware and ceramics, leather goods, toys, clothes, hats, and jewelry. Some of the merchandise is truly unusual. This becomes an antique market on Mondays. Meanwhile, out back is **Jubilee Market** (☎ 020/7836-2139), which is also an antique market on Mondays. Every other day of the week, it's sort of a fancy hippie-ish market with cheap clothes and books. Out front there are a few tents of cheap stuff, except again on Monday, when antique dealers take over here, too.

St. Martin-in-the-Fields Market (tube: Charing Cross) is good for the young and hip who don't want to trek all the way to Camden Market (see below) and can be satisfied with imports from India and South America, crafts, and some local football souvenirs. It's located near Trafalgar Square and Covent Garden; hours are Monday through Saturday 11am to 5pm, and Sundays noon to 5pm.

NOTTING HILL Whatever you collect, you'll find it at the **Portobello Market** (tube: Notting Hill Gate). It's mainly a Saturday happening, from 6am to 5pm. (You needn't be here at the crack of dawn; 9am is fine. You just want to beat the tour bus crowd.) Once known mainly for fruit and vegetables (still sold here throughout the week), Portobello in the past 4 decades has become synonymous with antiques. But don't take the stallholder's word for it that the fiddle he's holding is a genuine Stradivarius left to him in the will of his Italian great-uncle; it might just as well have been nicked from an East End pawnshop.

The market is divided into three major sections. The most crowded is the antique section, running between Colville Road and Chepstow Villas to the south. (*Warning:* There's a great concentration of pickpockets in this area.) The second section (and the oldest part) is the "fruit and veg" market, between Westway and Colville Road. In the third and final section there's a flea market, where Londoners sell bric-a-brac and lots of secondhand goods they didn't really want in the first place. But looking around still makes for an interesting Saturday.

NORTH LONDON If it's Wednesday, it's time for **Camden Passage** (☎ 020/ 7351-5353; tube: Angel) in Islington, where each Wednesday and Saturday there's a very upscale antique market. It starts in Camden Passage and then sprawls into the streets behind. It's on Wednesdays from 7am to 2pm and Saturdays from 9am to 3:30pm.

Don't confuse Camden Passage with **Camden Market** (very, very downtown). Camden Market (tube: Camden Town) is for anyone into body piercing, blue hair (yes, still), vintage clothing, or amazing people watching. Serious vintage collectors might want to explore during the week, when the teen scene isn't quite so overwhelming. Market hours are 9:30am to 5:30pm daily, with some parts opening at 10am.

LONDON AFTER DARK

Weekly publications such as *Time Out* and *Where*, available at newsstands, give full entertainment listings and have information on restaurants, clubs, and theaters. You'll also find listings in daily newspapers, notably *The Times* and *The Telegraph*.

THE PERFORMING ARTS

If you want to see specific theatrical performances—especially hit ones—purchase your tickets in advance. The best way to do this is to buy your ticket from the theater's box office. Often you can call in advance; many theaters accept bookings by telephone if you give your name and credit-card number when you call. You can also make theater reservations through ticket agents, such as **Keith Prowse/First Call,** Suite 1000, 234 W. 44th St., New York, NY 10036 (☎ 800/669-8687 or 212/398-1430, or **020/7836-9001** in London). The fee for booking a ticket in the United States is 35%; in London, it's 25%.

Theater

Globe Theater. New Globe walk, Bankside, SE1. ☎ 020/7928-6406. Tours £5 ($8.25) adults, £4 ($6.60) students and seniors, and £3 ($4.95) children. Performance tickets and schedules vary; call for details. Tours daily 9:15am–12:15pm. Tube: Mansion House.

A recent addition to London's theater scene is the replica of Shakespeare's Globe Theatre. Performances are staged on the theater's original site as they were in Elizabethan times: without lighting, scenery, or such luxuries as cushioned seats or a roof over the audience.

Royal Shakespeare Company (RSC). Barbican Centre, Silk St., Barbican, EC2. ☎ 020/ 7638-8891 (box office). Barbican Theatre, £6–£26.50 ($9.90–$43.70); The Pit, £11–£18.50 ($18.15–$30.55) matinees and evening performances. Tube: Barbican, Moorgate, or Liverpool St.

One of the world's finest theater companies is based in Stratford-upon-Avon and here at the Barbican Centre. The central core of the company's work remains the plays of William Shakespeare, but it also presents a wide-ranging program. There are three different productions each week in the Barbican Theatre, a 1,200-seat main auditorium with excellent sight lines throughout, thanks to a raked orchestra; and the Pit, the small studio space where much of the company's new writing is presented.

Fringe Benefits

Some of the best theater in London is performed on the "fringe"—at the dozens of so-called fringe theaters that usually attempt more adventurous productions than the established West End theaters; they are also dramatically lower in price and staged in more intimate surroundings. Check the weekly listings in *Time Out* for schedules and showtimes.

Royal National Theatre. South Bank, SE1. ☎ **020/7452-3000.** Tickets £10–£25 ($16.50–$41.25); midweek matinees, Sat matinees, and previews cost less. Ticket purchases Mon–Sat 10am–11pm. Tube: Waterloo, Embankment, or Charing Cross.

Occupying a prime site on the South Bank of the River Thames, the Royal National Theatre is the flagship of British theater. Home to one of the world's greatest stage companies, the National houses three theaters. The largest, named after Lord Olivier, is reminiscent of the Greek amphitheater with 1,200 seats fronting its fan-shaped open stage.

Classical Music & Opera

London Coliseum. London Coliseum, St. Martin's Lane, WC2. ☎ **020/7632-8300** for reservations. Tickets £5–£12 ($8.25–$19.80) balcony, £12.50–£32 ($20.65–$52.80) upper circle, £22.50–£49.50 ($37.15–$81.70) dress circle, £37–£49.50 ($61.05–$81.70) stalls. About 100 discount balcony tickets sold on the day of performance. Tube: Charing Cross or Leicester Sq.

The London Coliseum, built in 1904 as a variety theater and converted into an opera house in 1968, is London's largest and most splendid theater. The **English National Opera,** one of the two national opera companies, performs a wide range of works, from great classics to Gilbert and Sullivan to the new and experimental, staged with flair and imagination.

Royal Albert Hall. Kensington Gore, SW7. ☎ **020/7589-8212.** Tickets £8–£150 ($13.20–$247.50). Tube: South Kensington, Kensington High St., or Knightsbridge.

Since 1941, the hall has been the annual setting for the BBC Henry Wood Promenade Concerts ("The Proms") from mid-July to mid-September. A British tradition since 1895, the variety of programs are outstanding, often presenting newly commissioned works for the first time.

South Bank Centre, Royal Festival Hall. On the South Bank, SE1. ☎ **020/7960-4242.** Tickets £5–£35 ($8.25–$57.75). Box office 10am–9pm. Tube: Waterloo or Embankment.

Across Waterloo Bridge rise three of the most comfortable and acoustically perfect concert halls in the world: Royal Festival Hall, Queen Elizabeth Hall, and the Purcell Room. Within their precincts, more than 1,200 performances a year are presented.

THE CLUB & MUSIC SCENE

Nightclubs & Cabarets

Bagley's Studios. King's Cross Freight Depot, off York Way, N1. ☎ **020/7278-2777.** Cover £10–£20 ($16.50–$33). Guaranteed openings Fri–Sun 10pm–7am. Otherwise, openings depend on whatever promoter wants to book the space. Tube: King's Cross.

The premises are vast, echoing, a bit grimy, and reminiscent of a warehouse that might have held munitions during the dark days of World War II. Set in the bleak industrial landscapes behind King's Cross Station, its interior is radically transformed 3 nights a week into one of London's most animated rave events. It's scattered over two floors, each the size of an American football field, and subdivided into three rooms, each with its own ambience and sound system. Wander around for the room that best fits your vibe—and energy level.

Rock

Barfly Club. At the Falcon Pub, 234 Royal College St., NW1. ☎ **020/7482-4884.** Cover £7–£11 ($11.55–$18.15). Nightly 7:30pm–2 or 3am, with most musical acts beginning at 8:15pm. Tube: Camden Town.

Set in a dingy residential neighborhood in north London, this is a deceivingly traditional-looking pub that's distinguished by the nightly roster of rock bands who come in from throughout the UK for bouts of beer and high-energy music. A recorded announcement supplies the schedule, along with explicit instructions on how to reach it through a warren of narrow streets. You're likely to get virtually anything here—all part of the fun and adventure.

The Rock Garden. 6–7 The Piazza, Covent Garden. ☎ **020/7836-4052.** Open Sun–Thurs 5pm–2am, until 3am Fri and Sat. Cover £5–£10 ($8.25–$16.50); diners enter free. Tube: Covent Garden.

A long-established venue for rock, blues, and indie bands, it maintains a bar and a stage in the cellar and a restaurant on the street level. The cellar area, known as The Venue, has hosted such bands as Dire Straits, The Police, and U2 before they became more famous (and more expensive to see). The cover charge isn't imposed until 10pm Friday and Saturday, or until 8pm otherwise.

Jazz & Blues

100 Club. 100 Oxford St., W1. ☎ **020/7636-0933.** Cover Fri £8 ($13.20); Sat £8 ($13.20) members, £9 ($14.85) nonmembers; Sun £6 ($9.90). Tube: Tottenham Court Rd. or Oxford Circus.

The reasonably priced 100 Club is a serious rival to the city's upscale jazz clubs. Its host of bands includes the best British jazz musicians, as well as many touring Americans. Rock, R&B, and blues are also presented. It's open Monday through Friday 8:30pm to 3am, Saturday 7:30pm to 1am, and Sunday 7:30 to 11:30pm.

Ronnie Scott's. 47 Frith St., W1. ☎ **020/7439-0747.** Cover Mon–Thurs £15 ($24.75), Fri–Sat £20 ($33). Tube: Tottenham Court Rd., Leicester Sq., or Piccadilly Circus.

Mention the word *jazz* in London and people immediately think of Ronnie Scott's, long the citadel of modern jazz in Europe, and where the best English and American groups are still booked. In the Main Room you can either stand at the bar or sit at a table, where you can order dinner. The Downstairs Bar is more intimate. On weekends the separate Upstairs Room has a disco called Club Latino. Open Monday through Saturday 8:30pm to 3am.

Dance Clubs & Discos

Camden Palace. 1A Camden High St., NW1. ☎ **020/7387-0428.** Cover £5 ($8.25) Tues; no cover Wed; £7–£10 ($11.55–$16.50) Fri; £15–£20 ($24.75–$33) Sat. Tube: Camden Town or Mornington Crescent.

Camden Palace is housed inside what was originally a theater built around 1910. It draws an over-18 crowd that flocks there in various costume and mood according to the night of the week. Since it offers a rotating style of music, it's best to phone in advance to see if that evening's lineup appeals to your taste. Open Tuesday and Wednesday 10pm to 2am, Friday 10pm to 4am, and Saturday 9pm to 7am.

Equinox. Leicester Sq., WC2. ☎ **020/7437-1446.** Cover £5–£12 ($8.25–$19.80); £3 ($4.95) students. Tube: Leicester Sq.

The Equinox has nine bars, the largest dance floor in London, and a restaurant modeled along the lines of a 1950s American diner. Virtually every kind of dance music, save rave, is featured here. It's open Monday through Thursday 9pm to 3am and Friday and Saturday 9pm to 4am.

Hippodrome. Leicester Sq., WC2. ☎ **020/7437-4311.** Cover £2.50–£12 ($4.15–$19.80). Tube: Leicester Sq.

This is one of London's greatest (and most touristy) discos, an enormous place where light and sound envelop you from all directions. Revolving speakers even descend from the roof to deafen you in patches, and you can watch yourself on closed-circuit video. The Hippodrome is open Monday to Saturday 9pm to 3am.

Ministry of Sound. 103 Gaunt St., SE1. ☎ **020/7378-6528.** Cover £10 ($16.50). Tube: Elephant & Castle.

Removed from the city center, this club-of-the-minute is popular with the local set and relatively devoid of tourists. It has a big bar and an even bigger sound system that blasts garage and house music to the enthusiastic crowds on two dance floors or relaxing in the cinema room. Be warned that the door policy is selective. Open Friday 10:30pm to 6am, and Saturday midnight to 9am.

Wag Club. 35 Wardour St., W1. ☎ **020/7437-5534.** Cover £5–£10 ($8.25–$16.50). Tube: Piccadilly Circus or Leicester Sq.

This popular dance club hides behind an innocuous-looking brick facade. The club covers two floors, one decorated with Celtic designs and colorful renditions of medieval tarot cards, the other in bright primary colors, with huge black-and-white canvases. White fur fabric sculptures adorn the walls; high-tech lighting illuminates the dance floor. The music alternates between live bands and recorded music. Call to see what's happening any given night. Open Tuesday to Thursday 10pm to 3am, Friday 10pm to 4am, and Sunday 10pm to 5am.

Comedy

The Comedy Store. 1A Oxendon St., off Piccadilly Circus. ☎ **01426/914433.** Cover £11 ($18.15) Tues–Wed, £12 ($19.80) Thurs–Fri and Sun, £13 ($21.45) Sat. Shows 8pm to midnight. Reservations accepted through Ticketmaster at ☎**020/7344-4444;** club opens 1½ hours before each show.

The Comedy Store is London's most visible showcase for both established and emerging comic talent. Even if the performers are unfamiliar to you, you can still enjoy the spontaneity of live British comedy. Visitors must be over 18 years of age.

The Gay & Lesbian Scene

The most reliable source of information on gay clubs and activities is the **Gay Switchboard** (☎ 020/7837-7324), a line that's always busy. The staff runs a 24-hour service for information on places and activities catering to homosexual men and women. Offering similar help for women is **Lesbian Line** (☎ 020/7251-6911), which is staffed Tuesday to Thursday 7 to 10pm and Monday and Friday 2 to 10pm.

The Box. 32–34 Monmouth St. (at Seven Dials), WC2. ☎ **020/7240-5828.** Tube: Covent Garden/Leicester Sq.

Adjacent to one of Covent Garden's best-known traffic junctions, Seven Dials is a Mediterranean-style bar. Gay men outnumber gay women, although the venue is too sophisticated and blasé to care about sexual definitions. Year-round, the place defines itself as a "summer bar," throwing open its doors and windows to a cluster of outdoor tables that attracts a crowd at the slightest hint of warmth. Open Monday through Saturday 11:30am to 11:30pm and Sunday noon to 6pm.

The Edge. 11 Soho Sq., W1. ☎ **020/7439-1313.** No cover. Tube: Tottenham Court Rd.

Few bars in London exemplify tolerance, humor, and sexual diversity as well as this one. You'll get the idea the moment you enter; the first two floors are painted in intertwined shades of red and blue, with accessories that change with the season. The clientele ranges from the ostentatiously gay to Randy Andy types slumming on a pub crawl away from the Royal Palace. Open Monday through Saturday noon to 1am and Sunday 2 to 10:30pm.

Heaven. The Arches, Craven St., WC2. ☎ **020/7930-2020.** Cover £4–£10 ($6.60–$16.50). Tube: Charing Cross or Embankment.

This London landmark club is within the vaulted cellars of Charing Cross Railway Station. Black inside and reminiscent of a very large air-raid shelter, Heaven is one of England's biggest and best-established gay clubs. It's divided into four different areas, each connected by a labyrinth of stairs and catwalks, and hallways. The club features different theme nights, where, depending on the night of the week, gay men, gay women, or mostly heterosexuals predominate. Call before you go if you want to hear what's going on. Open Monday and Wednesday 10:30pm to 3am, Friday and Saturday 10:30pm to 6am.

Substation Soho. 1A Dean St., W1. ☎ **020/7287-9608.** Cover £3–£8 ($4.95–$13.20). Tube: Tottenham Court Rd.

Catering to the tastes and whims of gay nightclubbers, this sprawling, and sometimes packed, space features three bars, a dance floor with rotating DJs, video screens, pool tables, and a wide open attitude and environment. About 80% of the clients are gay men aged 18 to 50; the remainder are women, both gay and straight, who appreciate the joint's tolerant sense of permissiveness. It's open Tuesday to Thursday 10:30pm to 3:30am, Friday 10pm to 5am, and Saturday 10pm to 6am.

The Pub Scene

Nag's Head. 10 James St., WC2. ☎ **020/7836-4678.**

This is one of London's most famous Edwardian pubs. In days of yore, patrons had to make their way through lorries of fruit and flowers to drink here. But when the market moved, 300 years of British tradition faded away. Today, the pub is patronized mainly by young people. The draft Guinness is very good.

Red Lion. 2 Duke of York St. (off Jermyn St.), SW1. ☎ **020/7930-2030.**

This little Victorian pub with its early-1900s decorations and 150-year-old mirrors, has been compared in spirit to Édouard Manet's painting *A Bar at the Folies-Bergére.* On Saturday, homemade fish-and-chips are also served. Wash down your meal with Ind Coope's fine ales or the house's special beer, Burton's, an unusual brew made of spring water from the Midlands town of Bourton-on-Trent.

Salisbury's. 90 St. Martin's Lane, WC2. ☎ **020/7836-5863.**

Glittering cut-glass mirrors reflect the faces of English stage stars (and hopefuls) sitting around the curved buffet-style bar here.

Shepherd's Tavern. 50 Hertford St., W1. ☎ **020/7499-3017.**

This is one of the focal points of the all-pedestrian shopping zone of Shepherd's Market. The street-level bar is cramped but congenial; many of the regulars recall this tavern's popularity with the pilots of the Battle of Britain.

CASINOS

There are at least 25 casinos in the West End alone, with many more scattered throughout the suburbs, but we can't make specific recommendations. Under a new law, casinos aren't allowed to advertise or appear in a guidebook. It isn't illegal to gamble, only to advertise a gambling establishment. Most hall porters can tell you where you can gamble in London. You will be required to become a member of your chosen club, and then you must wait 24 hours before you can play at the tables, strictly for cash. The most common games are roulette, blackjack, punto banco, and baccarat.

DAY TRIPS FROM LONDON

✪ **HAMPTON COURT PALACE**   On the north side of the Thames, 13 miles west of London in East Molesey, Surrey, this 16th-century palace of Cardinal Wolsey (☎ **020/ 8781-9500**) can teach us a valuable lesson: Don't try to outdo your boss, particularly if he happens to be Henry VIII. The rich cardinal did just that, then lost his fortune, power, and prestige, and ended up giving this lavish palace to the Tudor monarch. Henry took over, eventually outdoing the Wolsey embellishments. Although the palace enjoyed prestige and pomp in Elizabethan days, it owes much of its present look to William and Mary—or rather to Sir Christopher Wren, who designed and had the Northern (or Lion) Gates built. Today, you can wander through the apartments, filled with porcelain, furniture, paintings, and tapestries. The Renaissance Gallery is graced with some of the best art, mainly paintings by old masters on loan from Queen Elizabeth II.

The gardens—including the Great Vine, King's Privy Garden, Great Fountain Gardens, Sunken Gardens, Board Walk, Tiltyard, and Wilderness—are open daily year-round 7am to dusk (but not later than 9pm) and can be visited free except for the Privy Garden, for which admission is £2 ($3.30), unless you pay for a palace ticket. The cloisters, courtyards, state apartments, great kitchen, cellars, and Hampton Court exhibition are open April to October, Monday 10:15am to 6pm and Tuesday to Sunday 9:30am to 6pm. From November to March, hours are Monday 10:15am to 4:30pm, and Tuesday to Sunday 9:30am to 4:30pm. The Tudor tennis court and banqueting house are open the same hours as above, but only from mid-March to mid-October. Admission to all these attractions is £10 ($16.50) for adults, £7.60 ($12.55) for students and senior citizens, and £6.60 ($10.90) for children 5 to 15 (free for children under 5). A family ticket costs £29.90 ($49.35) (2 adults and up to 3 children).

You can get to Hampton Court by bus, train, boat, or car. London Transport buses no. 111, 131, 216, 267, and 461 make the trip, as do Green Line Coaches (ask at the nearest London Country Bus office for routes 715, 716, 718, and 726). Frequent trains from Waterloo Station (Network Southeast) go to Hampton Court Station. If you have the time (about 4 hours), boat service is offered to and from Kingston, Richmond, and Westminster.

✪ **WINDSOR CASTLE**   When William the Conqueror ordered a castle built on this spot, he began a legend and a link with English sovereignty that has known many vicissitudes, the most recent being a 1992 fire. The state apartments display many works of art, porcelain, armor, furniture, three Verrio ceilings, and several 17th-century Gibbons carvings. Several works by Rubens adorn the King's Drawing Rooms. Of the apartments, the grand reception room, with its Gobelin tapestries, is the most spectacular.

Queen Mary's Doll's House is a palace in perfect miniature. The Doll's House was given to Queen Mary in 1923 as a symbol of national goodwill. The house, designed by Sir Edwin Lutyens, was created on a scale of 1 to 12. It took 3 years to complete and involved the work of 1,500 tradesmen and artists.

St. George's Chapel is a gem of the Perpendicular style, sharing the distinction with Westminster Abbey as burial place of English monarchs (Victoria is a notable exception). The present St. George's was founded in the late 15th century by Edward IV on the site of the original Chapel of the Order of the Garter (Edward III, 1348).

Admission is £10 ($16.50) for adults, £7.50 ($12.40) for students and senior citizens, and £5 ($8.25) for children 16 and under; family ticket £22.50 ($37.15) (2 adults and 2 children). The castle at Castle Hill is open March through October daily 10am to 5pm; November through February, daily 10am to 4pm. Lying 21 miles west of London, Windsor Castle (☎ **01753/831118**) can be reached in 50 minutes on a train from Paddington Station.

2 Oxford, the Cotswolds & Stratford-upon-Avon

One of England's most picturesque areas is the Cotswolds and the country around Shakespeare's birthplace, Stratford-upon-Avon. After visiting London, many move on to visit the ancient university city of Oxford and the still untouched Cotswold villages that, despite attracting healthy amounts of tourism, retain their authentic character as sleepy old wool towns. Both time and tradition beckon you on to these places.

Only in the Heart of England

The Oxford Colleges   Every Oxford student has his or her favorite college—usually the one he or she attends. All 36 are worth seeing, although some are more impressive than others. Our favorite is University College or "Univ," as it is popularly known. It's the oldest building foundation in Oxford, dating from 1249, and legend has it that it was founded by Alfred the Great, although few scholars seriously believe that. There's even a memorial here to the poet Shelley, who was expelled by the college.

The Romance of Oxford   Walk down the long sweep of The High, one of the most striking streets in England. Have a mug of cider in one of the old student pubs, and listen to the sounds of May Day, when the choristers sing in Latin from Magdalen Tower. Hear the Great Tom bell from Tom Tower, whose 101 peals traditionally signal the closing of the college gates. Crane your neck to check out the towers and spires rising majestically, or skinny dip at Parson's Pleasure. And, in this home of one of the world's great universities, find a tiny, dusty bookstall where you can pick up a valuable first edition.

Town Hopping in the Cotswolds   Less than 100 miles west of London are the rolling limestone uplands of the Cotswold Hills. This is picture-postcard England, with villages built from honey-colored stone, bearing names like Upper and Lower Slaughter, Bourton-on-the-Water, and Moreton-in-Marsh. The Cotswolds stretch northeast in a curving 60-mile arc, all the way from the elegant city of Bath to the Bard's Stratford-upon-Avon. The most glamorous Cotswold towns are Broadway and Chipping Campden.

The World of Shakespeare   Five of the most important buildings connected with the Bard are, miraculously, still standing. Shakespeare's birthplace, a modest half-timbered and gabled Tudor house, is virtually the spiritual center of Stratford. Other Tudor buildings include Anne Hathaway's Cottage and Mary Arden's House. You can even visit Shakespeare's grave at Holy Trinity Church.

The Bard's Tales   No theater seems to equal the Royal Shakespeare Theatre. Over the years, the greatest Shakespearean actors in the world, from Lord Laurence Olivier or Sir John Gielgud on down, have performed here. At its riverside location, and under the patronage of the queen, this theater opened on April 23, 1932, on the Bard's birthday. Shakespeare is the only fare; the season runs from April 17 to October 5.

Downing a Pint with the Actors at the Dirty Duck   This pub, the most famous in Stratford, is called the Black Swan. But over the years actors appearing in local Shakespearean productions have nicknamed it "the Dirty Duck." In the old days you might have shared a pint with Olivier, Gielgud, Glenda Jackson, or several with Peter O'Toole. Today it's likely to be Emma Thompson, Kenneth Branagh, or Derek Jacobi. Stratford players have made this their home since the 18th century. As for the food, it's not at all as bad as legend has it.

Oxford

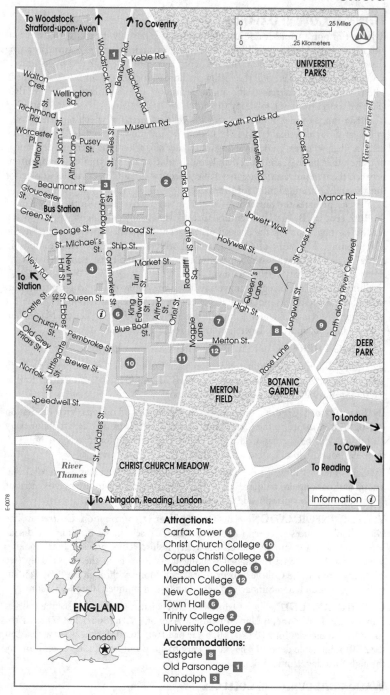

Attractions:
Carfax Tower ④
Christ Church College ⑩
Corpus Christi College ⑪
Magdalen College ⑨
Merton College ⑫
New College ⑤
Town Hall ⑥
Trinity College ②
University College ⑦

Accommodations:
Eastgate 8
Old Parsonage 1
Randolph 3

ENGLAND

London

E-0078

TOWN & GOWN: OXFORD

Believe it or not, Oxford is not just home to what is possibly the world's most prestigious university. Unlike Cambridge, to which it is often compared, Oxford is a true city of business and commerce. But if Oxford isn't entirely dominated by its university, the college spires are still the reason the hordes, including tour buses, flock here. The fast-flowing pedestrian traffic might seem more like the streets of London than what we expect from not-so-sleepy Oxford.

At any time of the year you can tour the colleges, many of which represent jewels in England's architectural crown. The Oxford Information Centre (see "Visitor Information," below) offers guided walking tours daily throughout the year. Just don't mention the other place (Cambridge), and you shouldn't have any trouble. Comparisons between the two universities are inevitable, of course, Oxford being better known for the arts and Cambridge more for the sciences.

The city predates the university—in fact, it was a Saxon town in the early part of the 10th century. By the 12th century, Oxford was already growing in reputation as a seat of learning, much to the chagrin of Paris. The first colleges were founded in the 13th century. The story of Oxford is filled with local conflicts: The relationship between town and gown wasn't as peaceful as it is today, and riots often flared over the rights of the university versus the town.

Ultimately, the test of a great university lies in the caliber of the people it turns out. Oxford can name-drop a mouthful: Roger Bacon, Sir Walter Raleigh, John Donne, Sir Christopher Wren, Samuel Johnson, William Penn, Lewis Carroll, Harold Macmillan, Graham Greene, and T. E. Lawrence, just to name a select few.

GETTING THERE   Oxford is 54 miles northwest from London.

By Train   Trains from Paddington Station reach Oxford in 1¼ hours. Service is every hour. A cheap, same-day round-trip ticket costs £12.40 ($20.45); call **British Rail** at ☎ **0345/484-950** for more detailed information.

By Bus   **Oxford Citylink** provides coach service from London's Victoria Station (☎ **020/7824-0056**) to the Oxford bus station. Coaches usually depart about every 20 minutes during the day from gate 10; the trip takes approximately 1¾ hours. A same-day round-trip ticket costs £7 ($11.55).

By Car   Take M-40 west from London and follow the signs; allow a leisurely hour. Traffic and parking are a disaster in Oxford; you might want to use one of the four "Park and Ride" lots just outside the city.

VISITOR INFORMATION   The **Oxford Tourist Information Centre,** at The Old School, Gloucester Green (☎ **01865/726871**), sells maps, brochures, and souvenirs, as well as the famous Oxford University T-shirt. It also provides hotel booking services for £2.50 ($4.15). Guided walking tours leave from the center daily (see "Walking Around the Colleges," below). It's open Monday through Saturday 9:30am to 5pm year-round, and Sunday and bank holidays in summer 10am to 3:30pm.

GETTING AROUND   Since Oxford is relatively flat, a good way to see the colleges is by bicycle. **Bike Zone,** 6 Lincoln House Market St. (☎ **01865/728877**), rents 15-speed hybrid bicycles for £10 ($16.50) a day or £16 ($26.40) for the week with a £50 ($82.50) refundable deposit. The staff is very friendly and helpful. It's open Monday through Saturday 9am to 5:30pm.

WALKING AROUND THE COLLEGES

The best way to get a running commentary on the important sightseeing attractions is to go to the Oxford Information Centre. **Two-hour walking tours** through the city and the major colleges leave daily at 11am and 2pm, and cost £4.50 ($7.45) for adults and £2.50 ($4.15) for children. The tours do not include New College or Christ Church.

OVERVIEW   For a bird's-eye view of the city and colleges, climb **Carfax Tower** (☎ **01865/792653**), located in the city center. This structure is distinguished by the clock and figures that strike the quarter hours. Carfax Tower is all that remains from St. Martin's Church, where William Shakespeare once stood as godfather for William Davenant, who also became a successful playwright. A church stood on this site from 1032 until 1896. The tower used to be higher, but was lowered after 1340, following complaints from the university to Edward III that townspeople threw stones and fired arrows at students during town-and-gown disputes. Admission is £1.20 ($2) for adults, 60p ($1) for children. The tower is open April through October daily from 10am to 5:30pm; November through March, it's open Monday to Saturday from 10am to 3:30pm.

CHRIST CHURCH   Begun by Cardinal Wolsey as Cardinal College in 1525, Christ Church (☎ **01865/276492**), known as the House, was founded by Henry VIII in 1546. Facing St. Aldate's Street, Christ Church has the largest quadrangle of any college in Oxford. Tom Tower houses Great Tom, the 18,000-pound bell referred to earlier. It rings at 9:05pm nightly, signaling the closing of the college gates. The 101 times it peals signifies the number of students in residence at the time of the college's founding.

The college chapel was constructed over a period of centuries, beginning in the 12th century. The cathedral's most distinguishing features are its Norman pillars and the vaulting of the 15th-century choir. In the center of the great quadrangle is a statue of Mercury mounted in a fish pond. The college and cathedral can be visited daily 9am to 5:30pm. The entrance fee is £3 ($4.95) for adults and £2 ($3.30) for children.

MAGDALEN COLLEGE   Pronounced *Maud*-lin, Magdalen College, High Street (☎ **01865/276000**), was founded in 1458 by William of Waynflete, bishop of Winchester and later chancellor of England. Its alumni range from Wolsey to Wilde. Opposite the botanic garden, the oldest in England, is the bell tower, where the choristers sing in Latin at dawn on May Day. The reflection of the 15th-century tower is cast upon the waters of the Cherwell below. On a not-so-happy day, Charles I—with his days numbered—watched the oncoming Roundheads from this tower. The 15th-century chapel is worth a visit, despite its many latter-day trappings. Ask when the hall and other places of special interest are open. The grounds of Magdalen are the most extensive of any Oxford college; there's even a deer park. You can visit Easter to September daily 2 to 6pm; off-season, daily 2 to 5pm. Admission is £2 ($3.30), but it's charged only from Easter to September.

MERTON COLLEGE   Founded in 1264, Merton College, Merton Street (☎ **01865/276310**), is among the three oldest colleges at the university. It stands near Corpus Christi College on Merton Street, the sole survivor of Oxford's medieval cobbled streets. Merton College is noted for its library, built between 1371 and 1379 and said to be the oldest college library in England. There was once a tradition of keeping some of its most valuable books chained. Now only one book is secured to illustrate that historical custom. Among the library's treasures is an astrolabe (an astronomical instrument used for measuring the altitude of the sun and stars) thought to have belonged to Chaucer. You pay £1 ($1.65) to visit the ancient library, as well as the Max Beerbohm Room (the satirical English caricaturist who died in 1956). The library and college are open Monday through Friday from 2 to 4pm and Saturday and Sunday from 10am to 4pm (closed for 1 week at Easter and Christmas).

A favorite pastime is to take **Addison's Walk** through the water meadows. The stroll is named after former alumnus, Joseph Addison, the 18th-century essayist and playwright noted for his contributions to the *The Spectator* and *The Tatler*.

UNIVERSITY COLLEGE University College, High Street (☎ **01865/276602**), is the oldest one at Oxford, dating back to 1249, when money was donated by an ecclesiastic, William of Durham (the old claim that the real founder was Alfred the Great is more fanciful). The original structures have all disappeared, and what remains today is essentially 17th-century architecture, with Victorian as well as more contemporary additions. For example, the Goodhart Quadrangle was added as late as 1962. The college's most famous alumnus, Shelley, was "sent down" for collaborating on a pamphlet on atheism. However, all is forgiven today, as the romantic poet is honored by a memorial erected in 1894. The hall and chapel of University College can be visited daily during vacations from 2 to 4pm for a charge of £1.50 ($2.45) for adults, 60p ($1) for children. Chapel services are held daily at 4 and 6pm.

NEW COLLEGE New College, New College Lane, off Queen's Lane (☎ **01865/279555**), was founded in 1379 by William of Wykeham, bishop of Winchester and later lord chancellor of England. His college at Winchester supplied a constant stream of students to New College. The first quadrangle, dating from before the end of the 14th century, was the first quadrangle to be built in Oxford, and created an architectural precedent for the other colleges to follow. In the antechapel is Sir Jacob Epstein's remarkable modern sculpture of *Lazarus* and a fine El Greco painting of St. James. One of the treasures of the college is a *crosier* (pastoral staff of a bishop) belonging to the founding father. In the garden, you can stroll among the remains of the old city wall. The college (entered at New College Lane) can be visited Easter to September daily from 11am to 5pm; off-season, daily from 2 to 4pm. Admission is £1 ($1.65).

THE SHOPPING SCENE

Alice's Shop. 83 St. Aldate's. ☎ **01865/723793.**

In its way, Alice's Shop might have played a more important role in English literature than any other shop in Britain. Set in a 15th-century building, it was a general store during the period that a professor of mathematics named Charles Dodgson (a.k.a. Lewis Carroll) was composing a little story called *Alice in Wonderland.* The store is believed to have been the model for important settings in the book. Today, the place is a favorite stop of Lewis Carroll fans, who gobble up commemorative pencils, chess sets, party favors, bookmarks, and in rare cases, original editions of some of Carroll's works.

Bodleian Library Shop. Old School's Quadrangle, Radcliffe Sq., Broad St. ☎ **01865/277216.**

This shop specializes in Oxford-derived souvenirs for those with academic pretensions or hard-core Rob Lowe fans. (Remember *Oxford Blues?*) There are more than 2,000

Punting: A Sport & a Pastime

At **Punt Station,** Cherwell Boathouse, Bardwell Road (☎ **01865/515978**), you can rent a punt (a flat-bottomed boat maneuvered by a long pole and a small oar) for £8 to £10 ($13.20 to $16.50) per hour, plus a £40 to £50 ($66 to $82.50) deposit. Rates are comparable at Magdalen Bridge Boathouse. Punts are rented from March to mid-June and late August to October, daily from 10am until dusk; from mid-June to late August, when a larger inventory of punts is available, it's open daily 10am to 10pm.

objects available, including books describing the history of the university and its various colleges, pewter and crystal paperweights, and Oxford banners and coffee mugs.

Castell & Son (The Varsity Shop). 13 Broad St. ☎ **01865/244000.**

Castell & Son is the best outlet for clothing emblazoned with the Oxford logo or heraldic symbol. Objects include both whimsical and dead-on-serious neckties, hats, T-shirts, sweatshirts, pens, bookmarks, beer and coffee mugs, and cuff links.

Magna Gallery. 41 High St. ☎ **01865/245805.**

Magna is one of the best-respected antiquarian galleries in Oxford, with engravings, maps, and prints made between 1550 and 1896. The shop also stocks general topography, botanical prints, caricatures, and maps of Oxford and Oxfordshire.

Once a Tree. 99 Gloucester Green ☎ **01865/793558.**

Few other shops in England glorify trees and wood products as artfully as this shop. A member of a rapidly blossoming chain, it stocks wood-carved objects that range from the functional and utilitarian (kitchen spoons and breadboards) to the whimsical and exotic (carved wooden flowers, chunky jewelry, boxes, bowls, mirror frames, furniture, and mantelpieces).

The Oxford Collection. 1 Golden Cross Courtyard, off Cornmarket. ☎ **01865/247414.**

You'll find Oxford souvenirs here, such as glass beer steins etched with the university's logo and a wool cardigan-like sweater with brass buttons bearing the university crest.

WHERE TO STAY

The **Oxford Tourist Information Centre,** Gloucester Green, opposite the bus station (☎ **01865/726871**), operates a year-round room-booking service for a fee of £2.50 ($4.15), plus a refundable deposit. The center has a list of accommodations, maps, and guidebooks.

Expensive

Eastgate Hotel. 23 Merton St., The High, Oxford, Oxfordshire, OX1 4BE. ☎ **01865/ 248244.** Fax 01865/791681. 43 units. TV TEL. £130–£155 ($214.50–$255.75) double; from £155 ($255.75) suite. AE, DC, MC, V. Bus: 7.

The Eastgate stands opposite the ancient Examination Halls, next to Magdalen Bridge, within walking distance of Oxford colleges and the city center. Recently refurbished, it offers modern facilities while retaining in the public rooms the atmosphere of an English country house. The comfortably furnished rooms have hot beverage–making equipment. The Shires Restaurant offers roasts and traditional English fare, complemented by a choice of wines.

✪ **Old Parsonage Hotel.** 1 Banbury Rd., Oxford OX2 6NN. ☎ **01865/310210.** Fax 01865/311262. 30 units. MINIBAR TV TEL. £145–£170 ($239.25–$280.50) double; from £195 ($321.75) suite. Rates include English breakfast. AE, DC, MC, V. Bus: 7.

This extensively renovated hotel near St. Giles Church and Keble College is so old (1660) that it looks like an extension of one of the ancient colleges. Originally a 13th-century hospital named Bethleen, it was restored in the early 17th century. Oscar Wilde once lived here and is famed for the remark, "Either this wallpaper goes, or I do." The bedrooms are individually designed but not large. The marble bathrooms are air-conditioned, with their own phone extensions and hair dryers. All suites and some bedrooms have sofa beds. The bedrooms open onto the private gardens, and 10 are on the ground floor.

The Randolph. Beaumont St., Oxford, Oxfordshire OX1 2LN. ☎ **800/225-5843** in the U.S. and Canada, or 01865/247481. Fax 01865/791678. 109 units. TV TEL. £155–£185

($255.75–$305.25) double; from £275 ($453.75) suite. AE, DC, MC, V. Parking £10 ($16.50). Bus: 7.

Since 1864, the Randolph, with its striking arched stone entrance, has overlooked St. Giles, the Ashmolean Museum, and the Cornmarket. The hotel illustrates how historic surroundings can be combined with modern conveniences to create elegant accommodations. The furnishings are traditional, and all rooms have a private bathroom, hair dryer, and hot beverage–making facilities. While some rooms are quite large, others are a bit cramped. The double glazing on the windows seems inadequate to keep out the midtown traffic noise. In this price range, we'd opt first for the Old Parsonage before checking in here. The hotel's Spires Restaurant offers both time-tested English and modern cuisine in a high-ceilinged Victorian dining room. There's also a wine bar.

Moderate
Oxford Moat House. Godstow Rd., Wolvercote Roundabout, Oxford, Oxfordshire OX2 8AL. ☎ **01865/489988.** Fax 01865/310259. 155 units. TV TEL. £98–£139 ($161.70–$229.35) double. AE, MC, V. Closed Dec 24–Jan 2. Bus: 60.

As one of the Queens Moat Houses group, this hotel adheres to the principles of motel design, with an emphasis on spacious, glassed-in areas and streamlined bedrooms. Patronized mainly by motorists, it's at the northern edge of Oxford 2 miles from the center, hidden from the traffic at the junction of A-40 and A-34. Each refurbished room features a color TV, pay-for-view movies, trouser press, and hot beverage–making equipment. The Moat House has a swimming pool, squash courts, sauna, solarium, and snooker (billiards) room. Its Oxford Blue Restaurant serves a standard English menu.

Inexpensive
River Hotel. 17 Botley Rd., Oxford OX2 0AA. ☎ **01865/243475.** Fax 01865/724306. 21 units, 19 with bathroom. TV TEL. £45–£60 ($74.25–$99) double without bathroom; £67.50 ($111.40) double with bathroom. Rates include breakfast. MC, V. Bus: 4C or 52.

This hotel lies about a quarter mile west of Oxford's commercial core, and charges less than many of its competitors that are just a bit more central. It was originally built around 1900 by a respected local craftsman whose casement windows and flower boxes are still in place. About a quarter of the accommodations are across the street in a comfortable stone-sided annex. There's a bar on the premises, a simple restaurant, and cozy furnishings within the bedrooms. Three singles without bathrooms rent for £39 ($64.35). Each contains a tea-maker.

Tilbury Lodge Private Hotel. 5 Tilbury Lane, Eynsham Rd., Botley, Oxford, Oxfordshire OX2 9NB. ☎ **01865/862138.** Fax 01865/863700. 9 units. TV TEL. £55–£68 ($90.75–$112.20) double; £75–£85 ($123.75–$140.25) double with 4-poster bed. Rates include English breakfast. MC, V. Bus: 42, 45, 45A, 45B, or 109.

On a quiet country lane about 2 miles west of the center of Oxford, this small hotel is less than a mile from the railway station. Eddie and Eileen Trafford accommodate guests in their well-furnished and comfortable bedrooms. The most expensive room has a four-poster bed. The guesthouse also has a Jacuzzi and welcomes children. If you don't arrive by car, Eddie can pick you up at the train station.

WHERE TO DINE
Very Expensive
✪ **Le Manoir aux Quat' Saisons.** Great Milton, Oxfordshire OX44 7PD. ☎ **01844/ 278881.** Fax 01844/278847. Reservations required. Main courses £30–£35 ($49.50–$57.75); lunch menu du jour £32 ($52.80); lunch or dinner menu gourmand £69 ($113.85). AE, DC, MC, V. Daily noon–2:15pm and 7:15–10:15pm. Take Exit 7 off M-40 south and head along

A-329 toward Wallingford; look for signs for Great American Milton Manor about a mile later. FRENCH.

Some 12 miles southeast of Oxford, Le Manoir aux Quat' Saisons offers the finest cuisine in the Midlands. The gray- and honey-colored stone manor house was originally built by a Norman nobleman in the early 1300s. The connection with France has been masterfully revived by the Gallic owner and chef, Raymond Blanc. You can enjoy such highly creative specialties as quail eggs, spinach, Parmesan, and black truffle ravioli in a rosemary *jus;* light crab bisque with ginger and lemongrass; or braised boned oxtail filled with shallots and wild mushrooms in a Hermitage red-wine sauce with purée of parsnips. Each dish is an exercise in studied perfection.

The gabled house was built in the 1500s, improved and enlarged in 1908. An outdoor swimming pool, still in use, was added much later. Inside, there are 19 luxurious bedrooms, each decorated boudoir style with lots of flowery draperies, ruffled canopies, color TV, phone, private bathroom, and high-quality antique reproductions; the cost is £195 to £425 ($321.75 to $701.25) for a double.

Expensive

Elizabeth. 82 St. Aldate's St. ☎ **01865/242230.** Reservations recommended. Main courses £13.75–£18.75 ($22.70–$30.95); lunch £17 ($28.05). AE, DC, MC, V. Tues–Sat 12:30–2:30pm and 6:30–11pm; Sun 7–10:30pm. Closed Easter weekend and Christmas week. Bus: 7. FRENCH/CONTINENTAL.

Portraits of Elizabeth II hang near the entrance of this stone-sided house opposite Christ Church College, where a well-trained staff serves beautifully presented French dishes. The larger of the two dining rooms is decorated with Goya and Velázquez reproductions and exudes a restrained kind of dignity; the smaller room is devoted to *Alice in Wonderland*–inspired designs. The kitchen is at its best with chicken royale, Scottish steaks, several different fish served in white-wine or lemon-butter sauce, and Basque *pipérade* (omelet with sweet peppers).

Moderate

Cherwell Boathouse Restaurant. Bardwell Rd. ☎ **01865/552746.** Reservations recommended. Main courses £9–£17 ($14.85–$28.05); set-price dinner from £19.50 ($32.15); Sun lunch £17.50 ($28.90). AE, DC, MC, V. Tues 6–11:30pm; Wed–Sat noon–2pm and 6–11:30pm; Sun noon–2pm. Closed Dec 24–30. Bus: Banbury Rd. FRENCH.

This Oxford landmark on the River Cherwell is owned by Anthony Verdin. The cooks change the menu every 2 weeks to take advantage of the availability of fresh vegetables, fish, and meat. In summer, the restaurant also seats on the terrace. The chefs turn out the best roast pheasant in Oxford, and other dishes, including a loin of free-range pork in a creamy tarragon and green peppercorn sauce, are as delicately handled. A very reasonable, even exciting, wine list complements the dishes.

Inexpensive

Munchy Munchy. 6 Park End St. ☎ **01865/245710.** Reservations recommended. Main courses £4.50–£8.75 ($7.45–$14.45). MC, V. Tues–Sat noon–2pm and 5:30–10pm. Closed 2 weeks in Sept and 3 weeks in Dec. Bus: 52. SOUTHEAST ASIAN/INDONESIAN.

Some Oxford students, who frequent this restaurant near the station, claim that it offers the best food value in the city. Main dishes depend on what's available in the marketplace, and there are no appetizers. Ethel Ow is adept at herbs and seasoning, as reflected in such dishes as king prawns sautéed with turmeric, coriander, and a purée of apricots; or a spicy lamb with eggplant, Szechuan red pepper, star anise, and crushed yellow bean sauce. Indonesian and Malaysian dishes are popular. Sometimes, especially on Friday and Saturday, long lines form at the door. Children 5 and under are not permitted on Friday and Saturday evenings.

A Day Trip from Oxford: Blenheim Palace

Just 8 miles northwest of Oxford stands the extravagantly baroque Blenheim Palace (☎ **01993/811325**), England's answer to Versailles. Blenheim is the home of the 11th duke of Marlborough, a descendant of John Churchill, the first duke, who was an on-again, off-again favorite of Queen Anne's. In his day (1650–1722), the first duke was the supreme military figure in Europe, having defeated the forces of Louis XIV at Blenheim, a village on the Danube River. The lavish palace of Blenheim was built for the duke as a gift from the queen. It was designed by Sir John Vanbrugh, who was also the architect of Castle Howard; the landscaping was created by the famous 18th-century landscape gardener, Capability Brown.

The palace is loaded with riches: antiques, porcelain, oil paintings, tapestries, and chinoiserie. North Americans know Blenheim as the birthplace of Sir Winston Churchill. His birth room is included in the palace tour, as is the Churchill exhibition, four rooms of letters, books, photographs, and other memorabilia. Today the former prime minister lies buried in Bladon Churchyard, near the palace.

Blenheim Palace is open mid-March to October, daily from 9am to 4:45pm. Admission is £7.80 ($12.85) for adults, £5.75 ($9.50) for seniors and children 16 to 17, £3.80 ($6.25) for children 5 to 15 (free for children 4 and under).

If you're driving, take the A-34 northwest from Oxford; otherwise, the no. 20 Gloucester Green bus (☎ **01865/772250**) leaves Oxford from the Gloucester Green about every 30 minutes during the day for the half-hour trip.

PUBS WITH PEDIGREE

Bear Inn. Alfred St. ☎ **01865/721783.** Snacks and bar meals £2–£6 ($3.30–$9.90). No credit cards. Mon–Sat noon–11pm; Sun noon–3pm and 7–10:30pm. Bus: 2A or 2B. ENGLISH.

A short block from The High, overlooking the north side of Christ Church College, this is the village pub, an Oxford tradition since the 13th century. Its swinging inn sign depicts the bear and ragged staff, old insignia of the earls of Warwick, who were among the early patrons. Some former owners developed a peculiar habit: clipping neckties. Around the lounge bar you'll see the remains of thousands of ties, which have been labeled with their owners' names. For those of you wearing neckties, who want to leave something behind, a thin strip from the bottom of your tie will be cut off (with your permission, of course).

Turf Tavern. 4 Bath Place (off Holywell St.). ☎ **01865/243235.** Main dishes £2.95–£5.95 ($4.85–$9.80). MC, V. Mon–Sat 11am–11pm; Sun noon–3pm and 7–10:30pm. Bus: 52. ENGLISH.

This 13th-century tavern lies on a very narrow passageway near the Bodleian Library. Thomas Hardy used the place as the setting for *Jude the Obscure*. During his student days at Oxford, Bill Clinton was a frequent visitor. At night, the nearby old tower of New College and part of the old city wall are floodlit, and in warm weather you can sit in any of the three gardens that radiate outward from the pub's central core. For wintertime warmth, braziers are lighted in the courtyard and in the gardens.

BOURTON-ON-THE-WATER

Its numerous fans describe it as the quintessential Cotswold village, with a history going back to the Celts. Residents fiercely protect the heritage of their 15th- and

16th-century architecture even as the Cotswold tour bus hordes descend on their town. Populated since Anglo-Saxon times, Bourton-on-the-Water developed into a strategic outpost along the ancient Roman road, Fosse Way, that traversed Britain from the North Sea to the St. George's Channel. During the Middle Ages, its prosperity came from wool, which was shipped all over Europe. During the Industrial Revolution when the greatest profits lay in finished textiles, the town became little more than a backwater producer of raw wool. Never "modernized," its traditional appearance remains preserved. The "Venice of the Cotswolds" is a great place to stop for lunch and a stroll along the riverbanks.

ESSENTIALS

GETTING THERE   By Train   Trains make the 2-hour trip from Paddington Station in London to nearby Moreton-in-Marsh; call ☎ **0345/484950** for schedules. From Moreton-in-Marsh, Pulhams Bus Company (☎ **0990/808080**) runs buses for the 15-minute (6-mile) journey to Bourton-on-the-Water. Trains also run from London to Cheltenham or Kingham; while somewhat more distant than Moreton-in-Marsh, both towns also have bus connections into Bourton-on-the-Water.

By Bus   National Express coaches (☎ **0990/808080**), from Victoria Coach Station in London, travel to both Cheltenham and Stow-in-the-Wold. From either of those towns, Pulhams Bus Company (see above) operates about four buses per day into Bourton-on-the-Water.

EXPLORING THE TOWN

A handful of minor museums can be visited within the town, each of which grew up from idiosyncratic collections amassed over the years by local residents. They include the **Cotswold Motor Museum** (☎ **01451/821255**), the **Bourton Model Railway Exhibition and Toy Shop** (☎ **01451/820686**), and **Birdland** (described below). But these museums don't compare with the evocative history of Bourton-on-the-Water itself.

The **Model Village at the Old New Inn,** High St. (☎ **01451/820467**), was constructed by a local hotel owner, Mr. Morris, to while away some of the doldrums of the Great Depression. His scale model (1:9) is big enough to allow viewers to walk through a re-creation of the town. If you opt to visit this place, you won't be alone: The Queen of England has marveled at the site's workmanship and detailing, and Ford Motor Company used it as the centerpiece of an ad campaign for its compact Fiesta (that is, a small-scale car photographed within a small-scale village). Admission costs £1.50 ($2.45) for adults, £1.20 ($2) for senior citizens, and £1 ($1.65) for children. It's open daily 9am to 6pm or until dusk in summer; daily 10am to 4pm in winter.

About a mile east of Bourton-on-the-Water, on the banks of Windrush River, is **Birdland,** Rissington Road. (☎ **01451/820480**). Established in 1958 on 8½ acres of

Back Roads to Bourton-on-the-Water

If you have a car, the best way to get a feel for the scenic beauty of the Cotswalds is to ditch the main routes in favor of the back roads. From Oxford, follow A-40 northwest to Buford, the gateway to the Cotswolds, and then follow the signs to Great Barrington, about 4 miles away, by turning left onto an unclassified road just north of the bridge over the Windrush River. After passing through Great Barrington's double row of Cotswold cottages, continue west toward Windrush. From here, take an unnumbered road northwest to Sherborne, and, once here, go another 6 miles north to Bourton-on-the-Water.

field and forests, this handsomely designed homage to ornithological splendors houses about 1,200 birds representing 361 species. Included is the largest and most varied collection of penguins in any zoo, with glass-walled tanks that allow observers to appreciate their agile underwater movements. Birdland has a picnic area and a children's playground in a wooded grove. Admission is £4 ($6.60) for adults, £3 ($4.95) for senior citizens, and £2.25 ($3.70) for children ages 4 to 14. Birdland is open April to October, daily 10am to 6pm; November to March, daily 10am to 4pm.

WHERE TO STAY & DINE

Old Manse Hotel. Victoria St., Bourton-on-the-Water, Cheltenham, Gloucestershire GL54 2BX. ☎ **01451/820082.** Fax 01451/810381. 16 units. TV TEL. Sun–Thurs £60–£80 ($99–$132) double, £85–£100 ($140.25–$165) suite; Fri–Sat £72–£96 ($118.80–$158.40) double, £120 ($198) suite. Rates include English breakfast. AE, DC, MC, V.

An architectural gem reminiscent of Nathaniel Hawthorne's *Mosses from an Old Manse*, this hotel in the town center sits by the slow-moving river that wanders through the village green. Although built of Cotswold stone in 1748, with chimneys, dormers, and small-paned windows, it has been modernized. The recently refurbished bedrooms are cozily comfortable with soft beds and fine linen. The bathrooms are small, but efficiently organized. Dining is a treat in the Le Jardin du Vin, which serves dinner daily from 6:30 to 9:30pm. Typical dishes include Dover sole, stuffed Bibury trout, and roast English lamb. Sometimes roast pheasant is featured.

Old New Inn. High St., Bourton-on-the-Water, Cheltenham, Gloucestershire GL54 2AF. ☎ **01451/820467.** Fax 01451/810236. 17 units (6 with bathroom). TV. £64 ($105.60) double without bathroom; £76 ($125.40) double with bathroom. Rates include English breakfast. MC, V.

This landmark inn draws hungry and weary travelers into a warm embrace of old-fashioned comforts and solid English cuisine. On the main street, overlooking the river, it's a good example of Queen Anne design (the miniature model village in its garden was referred to earlier). The comfortable rooms have homelike furnishings and soft beds. Nonresidents are welcome for meals, with lunches priced at £15 ($24.75) and dinner costing from £20 ($33). Spend an evening in the redecorated pub lounge playing darts and chatting with the villagers over a pint.

EN ROUTE TO STOW-ON-THE-WOLD

If you've ended your walk in Upper Slaughter, you can take the B-4068 directly northeast to Stow-on-the-Wold, our next stop. However, if you're back in Bourton-on-the-Water, you can head northeast on A-429, which in just a short time delivers you to Stow.

STOW-ON-THE-WOLD

This Cotswold market town remains unspoiled, despite the busloads of tourists who stop off en route to Broadway and Chipping Campden. Stow-on-the-Wold may not be the Cotswold lover's favorite—Chipping Campden takes that honor—but we find it even more delightful as it has a real town atmosphere, lying 9 miles southeast of Broadway, 10 miles south of Chipping Campden, 4 miles south of Moreton-in-Marsh, and 21 miles south of Stratford-upon-Avon. The town is the loftiest in the Cotswolds, built on a *wold*, or rolling hill, about 800 feet above sea level. In its open market square you can still see the stocks where offenders in the past were jeered at and pelted with rotten eggs by indignant townspeople. Today the square teems with pubs and outdoor cafes. Off the square, you can wander at leisure through some of the narrowest alleyways in Britain.

The Cotswolds

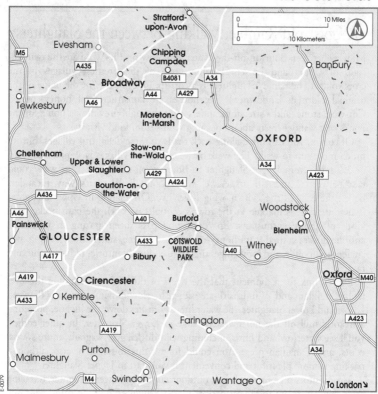

History buffs: The final battle of the English Civil War, between the Roundheads and the Royalists, took place in Stow-on-the-Wold. This is a good base for exploring the Cotswold wool towns, as well as Stratford-upon-Avon.

ESSENTIALS

GETTING THERE   By Train   From London, take a train to Moreton-in-Marsh (see below) from London's Paddington Station, a service that runs several times a day. From Moreton-in-Marsh, continue by a Pulhams bus for the 10-minute ride to Stow-on-the-Wold.

By Bus   National Express (☎ **0990/808080**) coaches also run daily from London's Victoria Coach Station to Moreton-in-Marsh, where a Pulhams Bus Company coach goes the rest of the way to Stow-on-the-Wold. Several Pulhams coaches also run daily to Stow-on-the-Wold from Cheltenham.

VISITOR INFORMATION   The **Tourist Information Centre,** at Hollis House, The Square (☎ **01451/831082**), is open April through October, Monday to Saturday from 9:30am to 5:30pm and Sunday 10:30am to 4pm; November through March, Monday to Saturday 9:30am to 4:30pm.

ANTIQUES HEAVEN

Don't be fooled by the hamlet's sleepy, country-bucolic setting: Stow-on-the-Wold has developed over the past 20 years into the antique buyer's mecca of Britain, and as such has at least 60 merchandisers scattered throughout the village and its environs. Some

A Cotswold Ramble: Walking Between the Slaughters

Midway between Bourton-on-the-Water and Stow-on-the-Wold are the twin villages of Upper and Lower Slaughter, two of the prettiest villages in the Cotswolds. (The name "Slaughter" is a corruption of *de Scoltre,* the name of the original Norman landowner.) The houses are constructed of honey-colored Cotswold stone, and a stream meanders right through, providing a home for the ducks that wander freely about, begging scraps from kind visitors.

Of course, you can drive along back roads to these delightful villages, but it's much more fun to walk. The walk between the two villages is 1 mile each way, or 2½ miles from Upper Slaughter to Bourton-on-the-Water. Your walk could take between 2 and 4 hours. A well-worn footpath, **Warden's Way,** meanders beside the edge of the swift-moving River Eye. Originating in Upper Slaughter (where its start is marked at the town's central car park), the path beckons all kinds of nature enthusiasts. En route, you pass sheep grazing in meadows, antique houses crafted from honey-colored local stone, stately trees arching over ancient millponds, and footbridges that have endured centuries of foot traffic and rain.

Don't think for a moment that the rivers of this region (including the Eye, Colne, Diklar, and Windrush) are sluggish, slow-moving streams: Between Upper and Lower Slaughter, the water literally rushes down the incline, powering a historic mill on the northwestern edge of Lower Slaughter. In quiet eddies, you'll see waterfowl and birds, including wild ducks, gray wagtails, mute swans, coots, and Canadian geese. You could follow this route in reverse, although parking is more plentiful and convenient if you start in Upper Slaughter.

Most visitors prefer to end their outdoor ramble in Lower Slaughter, retracing their steps upstream to the car park at Upper Slaughter. But you could continue your walk for another 1½ miles to Bourton-on-the-Water. To extend your trip, follow Warden's Way across the A-429 highway, which is identified by locals as Fosse Way. Your path will leave the river's edge and strike out across cattle pastures in a southerly direction. Most of the distance from Lower Slaughter to Bourton-on-the-Water is tarmac covered; it's closed to motor traffic, but ideal for trekkers or bikers. Watch for bird life, and remember that you're legally required to close each of the several gates that stretch across the footpath.

Warden's Way enters Bourton-on-the-Water through the hamlet's northern edges. The first landmark you'll see will be the tower of St. Lawrence's Anglican Church. From the base of the church, walk south along The Avenue (one of the hamlet's main streets) and end your Cotswold ramble on the Village Green, directly in front of the War Memorial.

visitors thrill at the chance to rummage at random through the town's various venues, dusty and otherwise. For those who do, here is a selection of the town's most interesting and unusual.

In four showrooms inside an 18th-century building on the town's main square, **Anthony Preston Antiques, Ltd.,** The Square (☎ 01451/831586), specializes in English and French furniture, including some large pieces such as bookcases, and decorative objects such as paperweights, lamps, paintings on silk, and more.

Baggott Church Street, Ltd., Church Street (☎ 01451/830370), is the smaller, and perhaps more intricately decorated, of two shops founded and maintained by a well-regarded local antiques merchant, Duncan ("Jack") Baggott. The shop has four showrooms loaded with furniture and paintings from the 17th to the 19th centuries. More eclectic and wide-ranging in its inventory is **Woolcomber House,** Sheep Street (☎ 01451/830662), the second of Baggott's two shops, which contains about 17 rooms. Serious buyers and wholesalers of antiques usually ask for access to the bulging inventories of antique furniture stocked in a warehouse that's about 50 feet from this shop. It's understood that purchases are usually made in bulk and shipped as part of containers to other antique stores around the world.

Covering about half a block of the town center, **Huntington's Antiques, Ltd.,** Church Street (☎ 01451/830842), has one of the largest stocks of quality antiques dating from the Middle Ages through the 17th century, and informal (country "vernacular") pieces from the Middle Ages to the end of the 18th century. Wander at will through 10 ground-floor rooms, and then climb to the second floor, where a long gallery and additional showrooms bulge with refectory tables, unusual cupboards, and much more.

WHERE TO STAY & DINE

Fosse Manor Hotel. Fosse Way, Stow-on-the-Wold, Cheltenham, Gloucestershire GL54 1JX. ☎ **01451/830354.** Fax 01451/832486. 22 units. TV TEL. £118 ($194.70) double; £170 ($280.50) suite. Rates include English breakfast. "Bargain Breaks" (2-night minimum required): £65–£95 ($107.25–$156.75) per person, including half-board. AE, CB, DC, MC, V. Take A-429 1¼ mi. south of Stow-on-the-Wold.

Although lacking the charm of the Grapevine (see below), Fosse Manor is a close second. With its stone walls and neogothic gables almost concealed by strands of ivy, the hotel lies near the site of an ancient Roman road that used to bisect England. From some of the high stone-sided windows, you can enjoy a view of a landscaped garden with a sunken lily pond, flagstone walks, and an old-fashioned sundial. The interior is conservatively modernized with such touches as a padded and upholstered bar and a dining room where dinners cost £24 ($39.60). The bedrooms are homelike, with matching fabrics and wallpaper.

Grapevine Hotel. Sheep St., Stow-on-the-Wold, Cheltenham, Gloucestershire GL54 1AU. ☎ **800/528-1234** in the U.S. and Canada, or 01451/830344. Fax 01451/832278. 22 units. TV TEL. £74–£114 ($122.10–$188.10) per person. Rates include breakfast. "Bargain Breaks" (2-night minimum): £69–£119 ($113.85–$196.35) per person, including half-board. AE, DC, MC, V.

The Grapevine, facing the village green, mixes urban sophistication with reasonable prices, rural charm, and intimacy. Although it's the best inn in the town, it doesn't have the charm and grace of Wyck Hill House on the outskirts. The Grapevine was named after the ancient vine whose tendrils shade and shelter the beautiful conservatory restaurant. Each bedroom has tasteful furnishings, a hair dryer, and a tea- and coffeemaker. Six rooms offer a minibar. Full meals feature English, French, and Italian cuisine.

✪ **Wyck Hill House.** Burford Rd., Stow-on-the-Wold, Cheltenham, Gloucestershire GL54 1HY. ☎ **01451/831936.** Fax 01451/832243. 32 units. TV TEL. £130 ($214.50) double; £210 ($346.50) suite. Rates include English breakfast. AE, DC, MC, V. Drive 2½ miles south of Stow-on-the-Wold on A-424.

Parts of this otherwise Victorian country house, which sits on 100 acres of grounds and gardens, date to 1720. One wing of the manor house rests on the foundations of a Roman villa, uncovered in the course of recent restoration. Now the area's showcase country inn, Wyck Hill House offers well-furnished bedrooms in the main hotel, the coach-house annex, or the orangery. Excellent food is also served, with a two-course lunch costing £13.95 ($23) and a three-course lunch going for £16.95

A Side Trip to Bibury

Most visitors in a rush head north from Burford to Stow-on-the-Wold and Broadway (see below). But if you have the time, you can dip south and in less than an hour you'll be in Bibury. From Burford, go southwest along the A-433 to reach one of the loveliest spots in the Cotswolds.

The utopian romancer of Victoria's day, the poet William Morris, called it England's most beautiful village. It is matched only by Painswick for its scenic village beauty and purity. Both villages are still unspoiled by modern invasions. On the banks of the tiny Coln River, Bibury is noted for Arlington Row, a group of 15th-century gabled cottages, which is protected by the National Trust. You can admire the cottages from the outside; you're not, however, supposed to peer into the windows, as they are still people's homes.

The main thing to do here is to wander around enjoying the village scene. If you're dying to see a museum, check out the **Cotswold Country Museum** (☎ **01451/860715**), located in a former mill, with an impressive collection of old carts and industrial machines. Rooms show how locals lived and worked in the 19th century. Admission is £1.50 ($2.45) for adults, £1.25 ($2.05) for senior citizens, and 75p ($1.25) for children. Open mid-March to mid-November, Monday to Saturday 10am to 4pm, Sunday 1 to 4pm; off-season, Saturday and Sunday 10am to dusk.

If you'd like to stay in Bibury, the finest hotel and restaurant in the village is **The Swan,** Bibury, Gloucestershire GL7 5NW (☎ **01285/740695;** fax 01285/ 740473). This cozily overstuffed hotel offers charming and tasteful bedrooms with antique furniture, as well as TV and telephones. On the premises is an informal brasserie, with outdoor seating in the hotel's courtyard. A more formal restaurant, with crystal chandeliers and heavy damask curtains, specializes in modern British food. Rates are £150 to £220 ($247.50 to $363) double occupancy and include English breakfast. AE, MC, and V are accepted.

($27.95). Dinners are à la carte, averaging £32.50 to £48 ($53.65 to $79.20) per meal.

EN ROUTE TO MORETON-IN-MARSH

From Stow-on-the-Wold you can continue directly north along A-429 into Moreton-in-Marsh in 15 minutes. Or you can take a detour and visit the two "Swells"—Lower Swell, a mile west of Stow on B-4068, and Upper Swell, a mile from Lower Swell on an unnumbered but signposted road. Like the Slaughters, they are charming and unspoiled 18th-century villages lying on back roads. From these two villages, you can take side roads north to Bourton-on-the-Hill en route to Moreton-in-Marsh 7 miles away.

MORETON-IN-MARSH

Moreton-in-Marsh, near many interesting villages, is an important center for rail passengers headed for the Cotswolds. It is also a lively market town that comes alive on Tuesdays when farmers and craftspeople from the surrounding area come in to sell their goods. The town is 4 miles north of Stow-on-the-Wold, 7 miles south of Chipping Campden, and 17 miles south of Stratford-upon-Avon. Don't take the name "Moreton-in-Marsh" too literally; "marsh" derives from an old word meaning "border," so you won't have to wade through any wetlands on your visit.

The town, which once lay on the ancient Fosse Way, is itself the central attraction, rather than specific sights or museums. Look for the 17th-century Market Hall and the old Curfew Tower, and then walk down the shop-flanked High (the main street), where Roman legions trudged centuries ago. The Market Hall on High Street is a Victorian Tudor structure from 1887. The Curfew Tower on Oxford Street dates from the 1600s (in the 19th century, its bell rang daily). However, far more alluring are the antique shops along the wide Fosse Way. Moreton-in-Marsh doesn't rival Stow-on-the-Wold in shopping, but everybody seems to be a shopkeeper here.

ESSENTIALS

GETTING THERE   By Train   You can take a train from London Paddington Station, arriving in about 2 hours. For schedules and information, call ☎ **0345/484950.**

By Bus   National Express coaches run from London's Victoria Coach Station to Moreton-in-Marsh daily, taking about 1¼ hours. Call ☎ **0990/808080** for details.

VISITOR INFORMATION   The nearest tourist office is at Stow-on-the-Wold (see above).

WHERE TO STAY

Manor House Hotel. High St., Moreton-in-Marsh, Gloucestershire GL56 0LJ. ☎ **800/ 876-9480** in the U.S., or 01608/650501. Fax 01608/651481. 40 units. TV TEL. £90–£125 ($148.50–$206.25) double; £135 ($222.75) suite. Rates include English breakfast. AE, DC, MC, V.

The town's best choice, the Manor House comes complete with a host of idiosyncrasies: its own ghost, a priest's hiding hole, a secret passage, and a moot room used centuries ago by local merchants to settle arguments over wool exchanges. This formal yet gracious house is located on the main street. From the rear you can see the marks of a number of different architectural periods. A pretty garden is hidden behind vine-covered walls. The bedrooms are tastefully furnished, often with antiques or fine reproductions. Many have great old desks set in front of window ledges, with a view of the garden and ornamental pond. The hotel has a heated indoor pool, a spa bath, and a sauna.

White Hart Royal Hotel. High St., Moreton-in-Marsh, Gloucestershire GL56 0BA. ☎ **01608/650731.** Fax 01608/650880. 19 units. TV TEL. £65–£70 ($107.25–$115.50) double. Rates include English breakfast. AE, MC, V.

A mellow old Cotswold inn once graced by Charles I (in 1644), the White Hart provides modern amenities within an old-fashioned atmosphere. It long ago ceased to be the premier inn of the town, but it's still a good, comfortable place to spend the night. The well-furnished bedrooms all have comfortable beds and a few antiques intermixed with basic 20th-century pieces.

WHERE TO DINE

Marsh Goose. High St. ☎ **01608/652111.** Reservations recommended. Lunch main courses £10–£15 ($16.50–$24.75); 3-course set-price lunch £15.50 ($25.60); on Sun £21 ($34.65); 4-course set-price dinner £27 ($44.55). AE, DC, MC, V. Tues–Sun 12:30–2:30pm; Tues–Sat 7:30–9:45pm. MODERN BRITISH.

In a highly competitive area of England, the food here ranks at the top, with creative seasonal cuisine that showcases the talents of chef Sonya Kidney. Despite its country-house elegance, this is very much an outpost of young and sophisticated Londoners. The unusual cuisine is modern British, with good doses of Caribbean style thrown in. Examples include pan-fried scallops served with artichoke hearts, lime dressing, and strips of smoked goose breast; grilled médaillons of monkfish on celery root purée; and

---

Insider's Tip

In summer, Shakespeare is performed on the Theatre Lawn; there is nothing as memorable as watching *A Midsummer's Night Dream* on a balmy July evening in the middle of the Cotswolds.

---

roast Barbary duck with sautéed pear, cassis sauce, and parsnip crisps. A favorite dessert is the hot dark chocolate soufflé with white chocolate sauce.

CHIPPING CAMPDEN

Historian G. M. Trevelyan described Chipping Campden's High Street as "the most beautiful village street now left in the island." The Cotswold stone houses built along High Street by rich wool merchants of the Middle Ages have been so well preserved that even today the town remains a medieval gem. On the northern edge of the Cotswolds, Campden, a Saxon settlement, was mentioned as early as the *Domesday Book,* a survey of England compiled for William the Conqueror around 1086. Its church dates from the 15th century, and its old market hall, composed of 14 stone arches, is the loveliest in the Cotswolds. Look also for its almshouses, which, along with the market hall, were built by a wealthy wool merchant, Sir Baptist Hicks, whose tomb is in the church.

Regardless of how often the English visit the Cotswolds, Chipping Campden remains a favorite destination. Off the main road, it's in striking distance of many major points of interest. Unfortunately, this means that double-decker buses frequently run through here on their way to Oxford or Stratford-upon-Avon. It lies 36 miles northwest of Oxford, 12 miles south of Stratford-upon-Avon, and 93 miles northwest of London.

ESSENTIALS

GETTING THERE   By Train   Trains depart from London's Paddington Station for Moreton-in-Marsh; the trip takes approximately 2 hours. Call ☎ **0345/484950** for schedules. At Moreton-in-Marsh, a bus operated by Castleway's travels the 7 miles to Chipping Campden five times a day. Many visitors opt for a taxi from Moreton-in-Marsh to Chipping Campden.

By Bus   The largest nearby bus depot is Cheltenham, which receives service several times a day from London's Victoria Coach Station. From Cheltenham, however, bus service (by Barry's Coaches) is infrequent and uncertain, departing at the most only three times per week. Call Gloucester's coach station at ☎ **01452/527516** for schedules.

VISITOR INFORMATION   The summer-only **Tourist Information Centre** is at Noel Court, High Street (☎ **01386/841206**), open daily from 10am to 6pm.

WHERE TO STAY & DINE

✪ **Cotswold House Hotel.** The Square, Chipping Campden, Gloucestershire GL55 6AN. ☎ **01386/840330.** Fax 01386/840310. 15 units. TV TEL. £120–£160 ($198–$264) double; £170 ($280.50) 4-poster room. Rates include English breakfast. AE, DC, MC, V.

A stately, formal Regency house dating from 1800, right in the heart of the village opposite the old wool market, Cotswold House sits amid 1½ acres of tended, walled garden with shaded seating. It's the best place to stay in town. Note the fine winding Regency staircase in the reception hall. The medium-sized to spacious bedrooms are furnished in themes ranging from Gothic to French to military; all are incredibly comfortable. You can dine in the restaurant, which serves first-class English and French food in a formal, elegant dining room, or in Forbes Brasserie.

Noel Arms Hotel. High St., Chipping Campden, Gloucestershire GL55 6AT. ☎ **800/528-1234** in the U.S. and Canada, or 01386/840317. Fax 01386/841136. 26 units. TV TEL.

£89–£99 ($146.85–$163.35) double; half-board £139 ($229.35) per person. Children up to 10 stay free in parents' room. Rates include English breakfast. AE, DC, MC, V.

This old coaching inn has been famous in the Cotswolds since the 14th century, although it long ago lost its supremacy to the Cotswold House. In 1651, Charles II rested here after his defeat at the Battle of Worcester. Tradition is kept alive in the decor, with fine antiques, muskets, swords, and shields. There's a private sitting room for residents, but you might prefer the lounge with its 12-foot-wide fireplace. Twelve bedrooms date from the 14th century; the others, comfortably furnished and well appointed, are in a more sterile modern wing built of Cotswold stone. The oak-paneled Gainsborough Restaurant offers an extensive menu, with an international wine list. Typical English dishes, such as venison and mushroom pie or roast prime sirloin of beef with Yorkshire pudding, are featured.

BROADWAY

The most overrun and tourist-trodden town of the Cotswolds is also one of the most beautiful and glamorous, hence its enduring popularity. Broadway, the showcase village of the Cotswalds, has a wide High Street flanked with lovely honey-colored stone buildings, remarkable for their harmonious design. Overlooking the Vale of Evesham, it's a major stop for bus tours and is mobbed in summer. However, it still manages to retain its charm in spite of the tourist invasion. Many of the Cotswolds' prime attractions, as well as Shakespeare country, lie within easy reach of Broadway, which is 15 miles southwest of Stratford-upon-Avon, 5 miles west of Chipping Campden, and 93 miles northwest of London.

ESSENTIALS

GETTING THERE   By Train   Connections are possible from London's Paddington Station via Oxford. The nearest railway stations are at Moreton-in-Marsh (7 miles away) or at Evesham (5 miles away). Call ☎ **0345/484950** for schedules. Frequent buses arrive from Evesham, but you'll have to take a taxi from Moreton.

By Bus   From London's Victoria Coach Station, one coach daily runs to Broadway, taking 2½ hours. Call ☎ **0990/808080** for details.

By Car   From Chipping Campden, take the B-4081 southwest to the junction with A-44, at which point you cut northwest to Broadway. The town is entered via B-4632.

VISITOR INFORMATION   The **Tourist Information Centre,** 1 Cotswold Court (☎ **01386/852937**), is open March through December, Monday to Saturday 10am to 1pm and 2 to 5pm.

WHERE TO STAY

Broadway Hotel. The Green, Broadway, Hereford and Worcester WR12 7AA. ☎ **01386/ 852401.** Fax 01386/853879. 18 units. TV TEL. £70–£95 ($115.50–$156.75) double. Rates include English breakfast. AE, DC, MC, V.

One of the most colorful places in town is this converted 15th-century house located right on the village green. Formerly used by the abbots of Pershore, the hotel combines the half-timbered look of the Vale of Evesham with the stone of the Cotswolds. The owners have comfortably modernized the Broadway without sacrificing any of its old-world charm. All the pleasantly furnished rooms have hot-beverage facilities and central heating. In an attractive dining room, an attentive staff serves good, if not spectacular, fare.

Dormy House. Willersey Hill, Broadway, Hereford and Worcester WR12 7LF. ☎ **01386/ 852711.** Fax 01386/858636. 49 units. TV TEL. £142 ($234.30) double; £170 ($280.50) 4-poster room; £182 ($300.30) suite. Rates include English breakfast. AE, DC, MC, V. Closed Dec 24–28. Free parking. Take A-44 2 miles southeast of Broadway.

This manor house high on a hill above the village boasts panoramic views in all directions. Its great location has made it a favorite place for a meal, afternoon tea, or lodgings. The owners transformed it from a sheep farm, furnishing the 17th-century house with a few antiques, good soft beds, and full central heating; they also extended these amenities to an old adjoining timbered barn, which they converted into studio rooms, with open-beamed ceilings. The Tapestry Restaurant (see "Where to Dine," below) serves excellent cuisine, and the cellar houses a superb selection of wines.

✪ **Lygon Arms.** High St., Broadway, Hereford and Worcester WR12 7DU. ☎ **01386/852255.** Fax 01386/858611. 65 units. TV TEL. £163–£180 ($268.95–$297) double; from £260 ($429) suite. VAT extra. Rates include continental breakfast. AE, DC, MC, V. Free parking.'

This many-gabled guesthouse basks in its reputation as one of the greatest Old English inns. In the rear the inn opens onto a private garden, with 3 acres of lawns, trees, flower borders, stone walls with roses, and nooks for tea or sherry. Today, the charming cluster of antique-laden public rooms evoke a quainter past. Many but not all the rooms are also decorated with antiques; a new wing offers a more modern environment. Each room is furnished with a hair dryer and trouser press. Meals are served in the oak-paneled Great Hall, with a Tudor fireplace, a vaulted ceiling, and a minstrels' gallery.

WHERE TO DINE

Tapestry Restaurant. In Dormy House, off the A-44, Willersey Hill, Broadway. ☎ **01386/852711.** Reservations recommended. Lunch main courses (Mon–Sat) £7.95–£9.75 ($13.10–$16.10); set-price Sun lunch £18.50 ($30.55); dinner main courses £14.80–£22 ($24.40–$36.30); table d'hôte menus (dinner only) £27.50–£34 ($45.40–$56.10). AE, DC, MC, V. Sun–Fri noon–2pm; Mon–Sat 7–9:30pm; Sun 7–9pm. MODERN BRITISH.

Two miles from the center of Broadway, beside the highway leading to Moreton-in-Marsh and Oxford, is one of the most charming and well-managed restaurants in the district. It has an elegant but less stringent formality than the Lygon Arms. The setting is as pastoral as a landscape by Constable. You'll dine in a room ringed with Cotswold stone or in an adjacent glass-sided (and nonsmoking) conservatory. Chef Alan Cutler creates imaginative dishes and presents them with a stylish flair. For an appetizer, we tried the seared escalope of Scottish smoked salmon on caper and horseradish butter sauce. Main courses include pheasant, grouse, and partridge with a bread sauce parfait and rich game sauce; and saffron-laced tagliatelle with deep-fried vegetables in tempura batter and Provençale sauce. The cellar houses a superb collection of wines.

STRATFORD-UPON-AVON

William Shakespeare, of course, was born here. Little is known about his early life, and many of the stories connected with Shakespeare's days in Stratford are largely fanciful, invented to amuse the vast number of literary fans who make the pilgrimage. David Garrick, the actor, really launched the shrine in 1769 when he organized the first of the Bard's commemorative birthday celebrations.

Tourist magnets include the Royal Shakespeare Theatre and the Swan Theatre, where the Royal Shakespeare Company performs its long season (November to September). Visitors too often rush back to London after a performance. Despite the crowds, Stratford's literary pilgrimage sights merit a visit. The town today aggressively hustles the Shakespeare connection, a bit suffocatingly so; everybody seems in business to make a buck off the Bard.

The town is virtually overrun by visitors in the summer; the crowds dwindle in winter, when you can walk the streets and seek out the places of genuine historic

Owlpen Manor: A Journey to Brigadoon

As beautiful as Bibury is, there is a place even lovelier. It's the hamlet of ✪ **Owlpen Manor** near Dursley, lying immediately to the south of Painswick off the beaten track. "Owlpen in Gloucestershire" has been called the British version of Brigadoon, an English Shangri-la. Even Prince Charles, who lives nearby at Highgrove, called it "the epitome of an English village," with its population of 35 lucky souls.

The hamlet centers on a medieval church, an Elizabethan manor, and a collection of stone-built cottages, all honey colored. In the center you can stroll through the gardens of the triple-gabled manor, constructed between 1450 and 1720. Visits are possible daily April through October from 2 to 5pm, costing £4.25 ($7) to see inside the antique-filled house or else just £3 ($4.95) to stroll through the beautifully kept grounds. There's also a restaurant on site, Cyder Press, serving typically English food.

Insider's Tip: You can actually rent one of these cottages if you fall in love with the Cotswolds and want to hang out for a while. Several have been luxuriously converted into guest accommodations, including a studio flat in the old Tithe Barn and our favorite, "Summerfield Cottage," which opens onto a murmuring brook. This fairytale hamlet is overseen by Nicholas Mader, a descendant of Sir Geoffrey and Lady Mader, fabled Pre-Raphaelite art patrons. For information about visits to the manor and its grounds, the village itself, or cottage rentals, call ☎ **01453/860261.** In the United States, you can call The London Connection at ☎ **801/393-9120** for more information. Weekly rentals range from £225 to £800 ($371.25 to $1,320), although you can sometimes slip in for a 2-day break, costing £85 ($140.25) for two people.

From Broadway, head south on A-46 to Painswick and then south on A45—signposted Stroud—until you come to the junction on A419. At that point, turn south on B-4066 in the direction of Uley and follow the signposts to Owlpen Manor.

interest without losing a limb. Stratford is 91 miles northwest of London and 40 miles northwest of Oxford.

ESSENTIALS

GETTING THERE   By Train   Amazingly, considering the demand, there are no direct trains from London to Stratford-upon-Avon. However, from London's Paddington Station you can take the train to Leamington Spa, and then change trains for Stratford-upon-Avon. The journey takes about 3 hours and costs £22 ($36.30) for the round-trip ride. For schedules and information, call ☎ **0345/484950.**

By Bus   Eight **National Express** (☎ **0990/808080**) coaches a day leave from Victoria Station; the trip takes 3¼ hours. A single-day round-trip ticket costs £14.50 ($23.90), except Friday when the price is £17.50 ($28.90).

By Car   From Broadway, continue northeast along A-46 directly into Stratford-upon-Avon.

VISITOR INFORMATION   The **Tourist Information Centre,** Bridgefoot (☎ **01789/293127**), can provide any details you might want to know about the Shakespeare houses, theater, and other attractions, and can assist you in booking rooms. It's open March to October, Monday to Saturday from 9am to 6pm, and Sunday from 11am to 5pm. In the off-season, hours are reduced to Monday through Saturday from 9am to 5pm.

THEATER

✪ **Royal Shakespeare Company** has a major showcase in Stratford-upon-Avon, the Royal Shakespeare Theatre, Waterside, Stratford-upon-Avon CV37 6BB (☎ **01789/295623**), on the banks of the Avon. Seating 1,500 patrons, the theater season runs from November to September. In an average season, five Shakespearean plays are staged.

Opened in 1986, the Swan Theater seats 430 on three sides of the stage, as in an Elizabethan playhouse. It is connected to its older counterpart and shares the same box office, address, and phone number. The Swan presents about five plays in a season.

It's important to reserve tickets in advance, which you can book by phone or from a travel agent. In New York, try Edwards and Edwards (☎ **800/223-6108**) or Keith Prowse (☎ **800/669-8687**); a service charge will be added. You can also call the theater box office (payment by major credit card) at the number listed above; it's open Monday to Saturday from 9am to 8pm, closing at 6pm on days with no performances. Seat prices range from £6.50 to £46 ($10.75 to $75.90). A small number of tickets are always held for sale on the day of a performance. You can pick up your ticket on the day it is to be used, but you can't cancel once your reservation is made unless 2 full weeks' advance notice is given.

SHAKESPEARE PILGRIMAGE SIGHTS

Besides the attractions on the periphery of Stratford, there are many Elizabethan and Jacobean buildings in town that are administered by the Shakespeare Birthplace Trust. One ticket, which costs £10 ($16.50) for adults, £5 ($8.25) for children, and £9 ($14.85) for seniors and students, lets you visit the five most important sights. You can buy tickets at any of the Trust properties.

✪ **Shakespeare's Birthplace.** Henley St. ☎ **01789/204016.** Admission £5.50 ($9.05) adults, £2.75 ($4.55) children. Mar 20–Oct 19, Mon–Sat 9am–5pm, Sun 9:30am–5pm; off-season, Mon–Sat 9:30am–4pm, Sun 10am–4pm. Closed Dec 23–26.

The son of a glover and whittawer (leather worker), the Bard was born on St. George's day (April 23) in 1564 and died 52 years later on the exact same date. Filled with Shakespeare memorabilia, including a portrait and furnishings from the writer's time, the Trust property is a half-timbered structure, dating from the first part of the 16th century. The house, bought by public donors in 1847, is preserved as a national shrine. You can visit the oak-beamed living room, the bedroom where Shakespeare was probably born, a fully equipped kitchen of the period (look for the "baby-minder"), and a Shakespeare Museum, illustrating his life and times.

✪ **Anne Hathaway's Cottage.** Cottage Lane, Shottery. ☎ **01789/204016.** Admission £4 ($6.60) adults, £2 ($3.30) children. Mar 20–Oct 19, Mon–Sat 9:30am–5pm, Sun 10am–5pm; off-season, Mon–Sat 9:30am–4pm, Sun 10am–4pm. Closed Dec 23–26. You can walk across the meadow to Shottery from Evesham Place in Stratford (pathway marked), or take a bus from Bridge St.

In the hamlet of Shottery, 1 mile from Stratford-upon-Avon, is the thatched, wattle-and-daub cottage where Anne Hathaway lived before her marriage to Shakespeare. It's the most interesting of the Trust properties, and the most unchanged. The Hathaways were yeoman farmers, and the cottage provides a rare insight into the life of such a family in Shakespeare's day. Many original furnishings, including the courting settle (love seat) and utensils, are preserved inside the house, which was occupied by descendants of Shakespeare's wife's family until 1892.

New Place/Nash's House. Chapel St. ☎ **01789/204016.** Admission £4 ($6.60) adults, £2.50 ($4.15) children. Mar 20–Oct 19, Mon–Sat 9:30am–5pm, Sun 10am–5pm; off-season, Mon–Sat 10am–4pm, Sun 10:30am–4pm. Closed Dec 23–26. Walk west down High St.; Chapel St. is a continuation of High St.

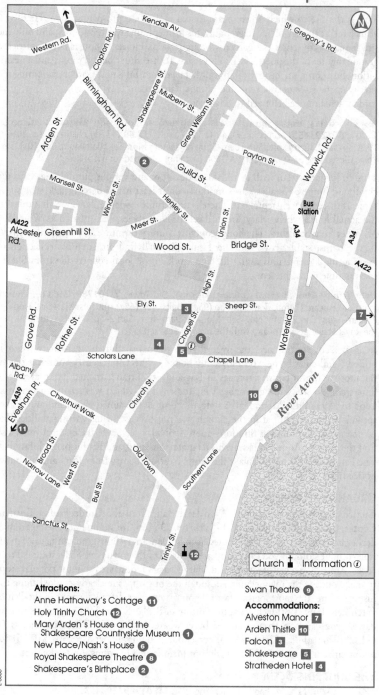

Stratford-upon-Avon

Attractions:
Anne Hathaway's Cottage **11**
Holy Trinity Church **12**
Mary Arden's House and the
  Shakespeare Countryside Museum **1**
New Place/Nash's House **6**
Royal Shakespeare Theatre **8**
Shakespeare's Birthplace **2**

Swan Theatre **9**

Accommodations:
Alveston Manor **7**
Arden Thistle **10**
Falcon **3**
Shakespeare **5**
Stratheden Hotel **4**

Church **✝** Information **ⓘ**

This is the site to which Shakespeare retired in 1610, a prosperous man. He died 6 years later, at the age of 52. Regrettably, his former home was torn down, and only the site remains. You enter the gardens through Nash's House (Thomas Nash married a granddaughter of the poet). Nash's House has 16th-century period rooms and an exhibition illustrating the history of Stratford. The delightful Knott Garden, adjoining the site, is in the style of a fashionable Elizabethan garden. New Place has its own great garden, which once belonged to Shakespeare.

Mary Arden's House and the Shakespeare Countryside Museum. Wilmcote. ☎ **01789/293455.** Admission £4.40 ($7.25) adults, £2.40 ($3.95) children. Mar 20–Oct 19, Mon–Sat 9:30am–5pm, Sun 10am–5pm; off-season, Mon–Sat 10am–4pm, Sun 10:30am–4pm. Closed Dec 23–26. Take the A-3400 (Birmingham) road for 3½ miles.

This Tudor farmstead, with its old stone dovecote and various outbuildings, was the childhood home of Shakespeare's mother—or at least it was determined to be so by some 18th-century entrepreneur. There is no definite evidence, however, that this was the actual home where Mary Arden dwelled. Nonetheless, it's situated at Wilmcote, 3½ miles from Stratford. The house contains country furniture and domestic utensils. In the barns, stable, cowshed, and farmyard you'll find an extensive collection of farming implements illustrating life and work in the local countryside from Shakespeare's time to the present.

Holy Trinity Church (Shakespeare's Tomb). Old Town. ☎ **01789/266316.** Church, free; Shakespeare's tomb, donation 60p (95¢) adults, 40p (65¢) students. Mar–Oct, Mon–Sat 8:30am–6pm, Sun 2–5pm; Nov–Feb, Mon–Sat 9am–4pm, Sun 2–5pm. Walk 4 minutes past the Royal Shakespeare Theatre with the river on your left.

In an attractive setting near the Avon River is the parish church where Shakespeare is buried ("and curst be he who moves my bones"). The 13th-century church is one of the most beautiful parish churches in England, its entrance framed by an avenue of lime trees. To see Will's grave, head for the chancel, which was reconstructed from 1465 to 1491 in the Perpendicular style, the tomb lit by stained-glass windows. Shakespeare's prominent burial in the church was not because of his writing abilities. He earned this stellar tomb as Stratford-upon-Avon's lay-rector. In the chancel you'll also find the grave of Anne Hathaway, his daughter, Susanna, and her husband, John Hall. The Parish Register here displays the Bard's baptismal entry from 1564 and his burial notice from 1616.

ORGANIZED TOURS

Guided tours of Stratford-upon-Avon leave daily from the **Guide Friday Tourism Center,** Civic Hall, Rother Street (☎ **01789/294466**). In summer, open-top double-decker buses depart every 15 minutes from 9:30am to 5:30pm. You can take a 1-hour ride without stops, or you can get off at any or all of the town's five Shakespeare's Properties. Anne Hathaway's Cottage and Mary Arden's House are the most popular stops to make outside the town center. Although the bus stops are clearly marked along the historic route, the most logical starting point is on the sidewalk in front of the Pen & Parchment Pub, at Bridgefoot, at the bottom of Bridge Street. Tour tickets are valid all day, so you can hop on and off the buses wherever you want. The tour price is £8 ($13.20) for adults, £2.50 ($4.15) for children under 12, and £6.50 ($10.75) for senior citizens or students. Tickets do not include cost of admission to the sites.

THE SHOPPING SCENE

Arbour Antiques, Ltd. Poet's Arbour, Sheep St. ☎ **01789/293453.**

This shop sells antique weapons, used for both warfare and sport, from Britain, Europe, and, in some cases, India and Turkey. If you've always hankered after a full suit of English armor, this place can sell you one.

Dianthus. 1 Centre Craft Yard, off Henley St. ☎ **01789/292252.**

More than any other pottery studio in Stratford, Dianthus benefits from an intimate knowledge of Pacific Rim ceramics, with emphasis on unique creative statements in stoneware. In spacious quarters, three potters display their technique on potter's wheels.

National Trust Shop. 45 Wood St. ☎ **01789/262197.**

You'll find textbooks and guidebooks describing places of interest in and around Stratford, descriptions of National Trust properties throughout England, stationery, books, china, pewterware, and even toiletries, each inscribed, embossed, or painted with logos that evoke some aspect of English tastes and traditions.

Pickwick Gallery. 32 Henley St. ☎ **01789/294861.**

Everything here is a well-crafted work of art produced by copper or steel engraving plates or printed by means of a carved wooden block. Look for the satirical engravings by William Hogarth, lampooning Parliamentary corruption during the late 18th century.

Shakespeare Bookshop. 39 Henley St. ☎ **01789/292176.**

Set in an antique house across from the Shakespeare Birthplace Center, this is the region's premier source for textbooks and academic treatises on the Bard and his works. It has books for all levels of interest and readership, from picture books to the weighty tomes that will please a Ph.D.

Trading Post. 1 High St. ☎ **01789/267228.**

Scattered over three floors of an Elizabethan house said to have been occupied by one of Shakespeare's daughters as an adult, Trading Post offers a jammed and slightly claustrophobic assortment of gift items that lean toward the kitschy and nostalgic. Included in the roster of items are doll's houses and furnishings, a scattering of small, easy-to-transport antiques, and memorabilia of your visit to the Midlands.

WHERE TO STAY
Very Expensive
✪ **Welcombe Hotel.** Warwick Rd., Stratford-upon-Avon, Warwickshire CV37 ONR. ☎ **01789/ 295252.** Fax 01789/414666. 68 units. TV TEL. £175 ($288.75) double; £200–£275 ($330–$453.75) suite. Rates include English breakfast. AE, DC, MC, V. Take A-439 1½ miles northeast of the town center.

For a formal, historic hotel, there is none better in Stratford. The Welcombe is housed in one of England's great Jacobean country estates, a 10-minute ride from the heart of Stratford-upon-Avon. Its keynote feature is an 18-hole golf course. The home once belonged to Sir Archibald Flower, the philanthropic brewer who helped create the Shakespeare Memorial Theatre. Converted into a hotel, it is surrounded by 157 acres of grounds and has a formal entrance on Warwick Road, a winding driveway leading to the main hall. The public rooms are heroic in size, with high mullioned windows providing views of the park. Regular bedrooms—some big enough for tennis matches—are luxuriously furnished; those in the garden wing, although comfortable, are small.

Expensive

Alveston Manor Hotel. Clopton Bridge, Stratford-upon-Avon, Warwickshire CV37 7HP. ☎ **800/225-5843** in the U.S. and Canada, or 01789/204581. Fax 01789/414095. 106 units. TV TEL. £120–£145 ($198–$239.25) double; from £260 ($429) suite. AE, DC, MC, V.

This black-and-white timbered manor is perfect for theatergoers. It's just a 2-minute walk from the Avon off B-4066. If the Welcombe, on the outskirts, has cornered the deluxe trade, the Alveston—along with the Shakespeare (see below)—are tied for the most atmospheric choices within the town itself. The hotel is crowned with chimneys and gables, and has everything from an Elizabethan gazebo to Queen Anne windows. Mentioned in the *Domesday Book,* the building predates the arrival of William the Conqueror. The rooms in the manor house will appeal to those who appreciate old slanted floors, overhead beams, and antique furnishings. Some triples or quads are available in the modern section, which is connected by a covered walk through the rear garden. The rooms here have built-in pieces and a color-coordinated decor; 20 are set aside for nonsmokers.

Shakespeare. Chapel St., Stratford-upon-Avon, Warwickshire CV37 6ER. ☎ **800/225-5843** in the U.S. and Canada, or 01789/294771. Fax 01789/415411. 67 units. TV TEL. £150 ($247.50) double; £180 ($297) suite. Children up to 16 stay free in parents' room. AE, DC, MC, V.

This hotel has snatched up the premium name in town. Filled with historical associations, the original core of this hotel dates from the 1400s. It's been called both the Four Gables Hotel and the Five Gables Hotel. In the 1700s a demure facade of Regency brick was added to conceal the intricate timber framing, but in the 1880s, with a rash of Shakespearean revivals, the hotel was restored to its original Tudor look. Today it is rivaled within Stratford only by Alveston Manor. Residents can relax in the post-and-timber-studded public rooms, within sight of fireplaces and playbills from 19th-century productions of Shakespeare's plays. The bedrooms are named in honor of noteworthy actors, Shakespeare's plays, or Shakespearean characters. The oldest are capped with hewn timbers, and all have modern comforts. Even the newer accommodations are at least 40 to 50 years old and have rose-and-thistle patterns carved into many of their exposed timbers.

Moderate

Arden Thistle Hotel. 44 Waterside, Stratford-upon-Avon, Warwickshire CV37 6BA. ☎ **01789/294949.** Fax 01789/415874. 63 units. TV TEL. £122 ($201.30) double. AE, DC, MC, V.

Theatergoers flock to this hotel across the street from the main entrance of the Royal Shakespeare and Swan theaters. Its red brick main section dates from the Regency period, although over the years a handful of adjacent buildings were added, including an uninspired modern extension. The interior was completely refurbished after the hotel was purchased by the Thistle chain in 1993, and today there is a well-upholstered lounge and bar; a dining room (Bards) with bay windows; a covered garden terrace; and comfortable but narrow bedrooms with trouser presses, hair dryers, and hot-beverage facilities.

Falcon. Chapel St., Stratford-upon-Avon, Warwickshire CV37 6HA. ☎ **01789/279953.** Fax 01789/414260. 73 units. TV TEL. £105 ($173.25) double; £125 ($206.25) suite. AE, DC, MC, V.

The Falcon blends the old with the new. At the rear of a black-and-white timbered inn, licensed a quarter of a century after Shakespeare's death, is a more sterile 1970 bedroom extension, joined by a glass-covered passageway. In the heart of Stratford, the inn faces the Guild Chapel and the New Place Gardens. The recently upgraded bedrooms in the older section have oak beams, diamond leaded-glass windows, some antique furnishings, and good reproductions. Each room includes an electric trouser press and hot-beverage facilities, but not enough soundproofing to prevent you from hearing what BBC show your neighbor is watching next door.

Inexpensive

Sequoia House. 51–53 Shipston Rd., Stratfor-upon-Avon, Warwickshire CV37 7LN. ☎ **01789/268852.** Fax 01789/414559. 24 units, 20 with bathroom or shower. TV TEL. £75 ($123.75) double without bathroom; £82.50 ($136.15) double with bathroom. Rates include English breakfast. AE, DC, DISC, MC, V.

This hotel has its own beautiful garden on three-quarters of an acre conveniently located across the Avon opposite the theater. Renovation has vastly improved the house, which was created from two late Victorian buildings. The rooms, which are some of the most comfortable in town for their price range, have firm mattresses, small but tidy bathrooms, and beverage-makers. Guests can relax in a lounge that has a licensed bar and an open Victorian fireplace. The hotel also has a private parking area.

Stratheden Hotel. 5 Chapel St., Stratford-upon-Avon, Warwickshire CV37 6EP. ☎ **01789/297119.** 9 units. TV TEL. £60–£66 ($99–$108.90) double. Rates include English breakfast. MC, V.

First mentioned in a property deed in 1333, this hotel lies a short walk north of the Royal Shakespeare Theatre. The Stratheden, built in 1673 (and today the oldest remaining brick building in the town center), has a tiny rear garden and top-floor rooms with slanted, beamed ceilings. It has improved in both decor and comfort with the addition of fresh paint, new curtains, and good beds. The dining room, with a bay window, has an overscale sideboard that once belonged to the "insanely vain" Marie Corelli, an eccentric novelist, poet, and mystic, and a favorite author of Queen Victoria.

WHERE TO DINE

Box Tree Restaurant. In the Royal Shakespeare Theatre, Waterside. ☎ **01789/293226.** Reservations required. Matinee lunch £18.50 ($30.55); dinner £28 ($46.20). AE, MC, V. Thurs–Sat noon–2:30pm; Mon–Sat 5:45pm–midnight. FRENCH/ITALIAN/ENGLISH.

This restaurant, right in the theater itself, is surrounded by glass walls that provide an unobstructed view of the Avon and its swans. During intermission a snack feast of smoked salmon and champagne is offered. There's a special phone for reservations in the theater lobby. Many dishes are definitely Old English (apple and parsnip soup); others reflect a continental touch. By flickering candlelight, choose among Dover sole, wild boar sausage, pheasant suprême, or roast loin of pork. Homemade desserts are likely to include crème brûlée, an old-time favorite at the Box Tree. Better food can be had at other places, such as Hussain's, but none is as convenient for theatergoers.

Greek Connection. 1 Shakespeare St. ☎ **01789/292214.** Reservations recommended. Main courses £11.95–£16.95 ($19.70–$27.95). DC, MC, V. Daily noon–2:30pm in summer; daily 5:30–10pm year-round. GREEK.

This restaurant occupies a high-ceilinged building that dates from 1854 and originally served as a Methodist chapel. Today, authentic Greek food is accompanied by live music and dancing nightly. Chefs George and Spiros serve up such favorites as *moussaka* (freshly minced meat embedded in layers of eggplant, zucchini, and potatoes with a dome of creamy béchamel) and stuffed grape leaves. Many patrons say that ordering the mezedakia is the best option; you get a wide sampling of Greek hors d'oeuvres and won't have to choose only one from the enticing menu.

A Day Trip from Stratford to Warwick Castle

Perched on a rocky cliff above the Avon, Warwick Castle is a stately late-17th-century–style mansion surrounded by a magnificent 14th-century fortress. The castle was described by Sir Walter Scott in 1828 as "that fairest monument of ancient and chivalrous splendor which yet remains uninjured by time." The first significant fortifications were built by Ethelfleda, daughter of Alfred the Great, in 914. Two years after the Norman Conquest in 1068, William the Conqueror ordered the construction of a motte and bailey castle. The castle mound is all that remains today of the Norman castle.

The Beauchamp family, earls of Warwick, is responsible for the appearance of the castle today, and much of the external structure remains unchanged from the mid-14th century. The staterooms and Great Hall house fine collections of paintings, furniture, arms, and armor. The armory, dungeon, torture chamber, ghost tower, clock tower, and Guy's tower create a vivid picture of the castle's turbulent past and its important role in the history of England. Visitors can also see the Victorian rose garden, a re-creation of an original design from 1868 by Robert Marnock.

On Castle Hill, Warwick Castle (☎ 01926/406600) is open daily 10am to 5pm. Admission is £9.25 ($15.25) for adults, £5.60 ($9.25) for children 4 to 16, £6.65 ($10.95) for senior citizens and students (free for children 3 and under), and £26 ($42.90) for family of 4.

Trains run frequently between Stratford and Warwick, and a Midland Red Bus leaves every hour (no. 18 or X16) during the day; the trip takes 15 to 20 minutes. Motorists should take A-46 north from Stratford.

Hussain's. 6A Chapel St. ☎ 01789/267506. Reservations recommended. Main courses £5.75–£12.95 ($9.50–$21.35). AE, DC, MC, V. Daily noon–2pm and 5pm–midnight. INDIAN.

Dining here has been compared to a visit to a private Indian home, and this is definitely one of the brighter spots on an otherwise bleak culinary landscape. The well-trained, alert staff welcomes guests, advising them about special dishes. Against a setting of pink crushed-velvet paneling, you can select from an array of northern Indian dishes. Herbs and spices are blended imaginatively in the kitchen to create a distinctive flavor. Many tandoori dishes are offered, along with various curries. Hussain's is across from the Shakespeare Hotel and historic New Place.

Shepherd's Garden Restaurant. In the Stratford House Hotel, 18 Sheep St. ☎ 01789/268288. Reservations recommended. Lunch £4.95–£13.95 ($8.15–$23); dinner main courses £8–£13.95 ($13.20–$23). AE, DC, MC, V. Mon–Sat 10am–9:15pm. ENGLISH/FRENCH.

Light and airy, this restaurant has a skylit conservatory look and a loyal clientele of local residents, including directors and actors from the nearby theaters, who drop by for simple lunches and more elaborate dinners. Lunches are served in a lounge-style setting, which spills out during nice weather onto a walled outdoor patio. Evening meals are accented with cascading vines and potted plants. The English and French cuisine might include a terrine of salmon and scallops, grilled goat's cheese with marinated peppers, chicken livers pan-fried in whisky, filets of chicken with herbs, and *boeuf bourguignonne*. Vegetarian dishes are likely to include macaroni with cheese and leeks, and a fricassée of wild mushrooms. It's standard, but reliable and solid fare.

PUBS

Black Swan. Waterside. ☎ **01789/297312.** Reservations required for dining. Main courses £7–£17 ($11.55–$28.05); bar snacks £1.50–£4.50 ($2.45–$7.45). MC, V (restaurant only). Pub, Mon–Sat 11am–11pm, Sun noon–3pm and 7–10:30pm; restaurant, Tues–Sun noon–2pm, Mon–Sat 6–11:30pm. ENGLISH.

Affectionately known as the "Dirty Duck," this has been a popular hangout for Stratford players since the 18th century. The wall is lined with autographed photos of past patrons, such as Lord Laurence Olivier. The front lounge and bar echoes with intense conversation. In the spring and fall an open fire blazes. In the Dirty Duck Grill Room, typical English grills are featured, although no one ever accused the Dirty Duck of serving the best food in Stratford. Main dishes include braised kidneys or oxtails, roast chicken, or honey-roasted duck.

Garrick Inn. 25 High St. ☎ **01789/292186.** Main courses £5–£11 ($8.25–$18.15). MC, V. Meals daily noon–8:30pm; pub, Mon–Sat 11am–11pm, Sun noon–10:30pm. ENGLISH.

Near Harvard House, this black-and-white timbered Elizabethan pub from 1595 has an unpretentious charm. It's named after David Garrick, one of England's greatest actors. The front bar, decorated with tapestry-covered benches, an old oak refectory table, and an open fireplace, is filled with locals. The back bar has a circular fireplace with a copper hood and mementos of the triumphs of the English stage. The specialty is homemade pies, such as steak and ale, steak and kidney, or chicken and mushroom.

3 Stonehenge & Bath

Many visitors with limited time head for the "West Countree" of England, where they explore its two major attractions: Stonehenge—the most important prehistoric monument in Britain—and Bath, England's most elegant city, famed for its architecture and its hot springs. If you have the time, you might also visit Salisbury Cathedral and the other prehistoric sites in the area, at Avebury and Old Sarum.

Only in Stonehenge & Bath

Seeing Stonehenge at Twilight   The mysteries of Stonehenge exert a powerful draw on people the world over. How and why the monumental stones were arranged here becomes an even bigger riddle from up close; their origin dates back some 3,500 to 5,000 years. But only the silent Salisbury Plain knows for sure.

Taking Afternoon Tea at the Pump Room   The best way to return to the glory of Beau Nash's elegant 18th-century Bath is to come here for afternoon tea. Tradition dictates that first you sip the foul-tasting waters of the hot springs. After that, you can sweeten your palate with afternoon tea and freshly baked cakes as you listen to violin music.

Tasting Gingerbread at the American Museum   If you ever wondered what made George Washington grow up not to tell lies, it was probably the spice in his mother's gingerbread. You can still taste that gingerbread, baked fresh every day based on her old recipe, at the American Museum at Claverton Manor on Bathwick Hill, 2½ miles outside Bath. This was the first American museum established outside the United States, and it remains the best. There's everything here from a copy of Washington's flower garden at Mount Vernon to a Conestoga wagon.

Enjoying a Summer Afternoon Cruise   The Kennet and Avon Canal, just outside of Bath, is lined with leafy banks. The canal links the Thames River at Reading in the east with the docks of the city of Bristol in the west. Long neglected, this 1810 canal has been redredged and its more than 100 locks restored to their former glory. In all, some 90 miles of navigable canal is open to the public once again. They are now filled with pleasure craft and waterbuses that ply the waters between Bath and Folly Swing Bridge, the most romantic part of the canal. Hop aboard *Scenic I* running on the hour daily from 11am to 7pm, upstream from Pulteney Weir opposite Parade Gardens. Check with tourist information for more details about other boat trips.

Spending a Morning at Bath Abbey   Before this 1499 church was constructed, both a Saxon abbey and a Norman cathedral had stood on the site. A sunny morning is the best time to view it; the light pours through the sparkling panes of glass in the towering clerestory windows, providing natural illumination for the fan vaulting, one of the purest forms of English Perpendicular architecture.

Downing a Pint at the Saracen's Head   This is the oldest pub in Bath, dating from 1713. Back when it was an inn, Charles Dickens boarded here in 1835. Saracen's Head, 42 Broad St. (☎ **01225/426518**), no longer puts up overnight guests, but still welcomes visitors for a pint under its beamed ceilings and original plasterwork. You'd be assured of a warm welcome at this unpretentious place. It's cozy and filled with chatty, friendly locals.

STONEHENGE

Standing enigmatically on the Salisbury Plain is the renowned monument of Stonehenge, a stone circle believed to be anywhere from 3,500 to 5,000 years old. This circle of lintels and megalithic pillars is the most important prehistoric monument in Britain. You'll find it 2 miles west of Amesbury at the junction of A-303 and A-344/ A-360, about 9 miles north of Salisbury.

ESSENTIALS

GETTING THERE   By Car   To reach Stonehenge from London, head in the direction of Salisbury, 90 miles to the southwest. Take the M-3 to the end of the run, continuing the rest of the way on A-30. Once at Salisbury, after stopping to view its cathedral (see below), head north on Castle Road from the center of town. At the first roundabout or traffic circle, take the exit toward Amesbury (A-345) and Old Sarum. Continue along this route for 8 miles and then turn left onto A-303 in the direction of Exeter. Stonehenge is signposted, leading you up the A-344 to the right. In all, it's about 12 miles total from Salisbury.

By Train or Bus   You can also reach Stonehenge by train and bus from London. A Network Express train departs hourly from Waterloo Station in London bound for Salisbury; the trip takes 2 hours. Buses also depart four or five times per day from London's Victoria Station, heading for Salisbury; the trip takes 2½ hours. Once at Salisbury, you can take a Wilts & Dorset bus (☎ **01722/336855** for schedules), which runs several vehicles daily, depending on demand, from Salisbury to Stonehenge. This company's buses depart from the train station at Salisbury, heading directly to Stonehenge; the trip takes 30 minutes and a round-trip passage costs £4.25 ($7) for adults, £2.10 ($3.45) for children under 14. Use Salisbury (see below) as a refueling stop.

Stonehenge Traveler's Tip

We like to visit Stonehenge at twilight, when the last of the photo-snapping bus hordes have departed. Amid relative calm, you can ponder the monument's occult origins. The setting rays of sunshine reflect off the ancient stones and seem to heighten their mystery.

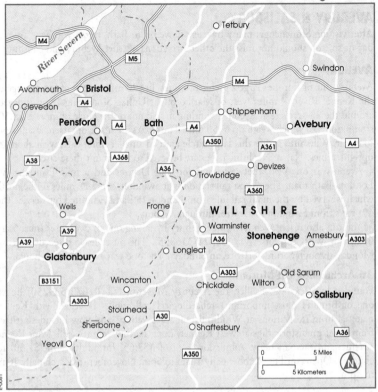

EXPLORING STONEHENGE

Despite its familiarity, visitors cannot help but be impressed when they first see Stonehenge. It is an astonishing engineering feat. The boulders, the bluestones in particular, were moved many miles, possibly from as far away as southern Wales, to this site.

The widely held view of the 18th- and 19-century romantics that Stonehenge was the work of the Druids is without real foundation. The boulders, many weighing several tons, are believed to have predated the arrival in Britain of the Celtic Druidic cult. Recent excavations continue to bring new evidence to bear on the origin and purpose of this prehistoric circle. Controversy has always surrounded the site, especially since the publication of *Stonehenge Decoded* by Gerald S. Hawkins and John B. White, which maintains that Stonehenge was an astronomical observatory—that is, a Neolithic "computing machine" capable of predicting eclipses.

The site is now surrounded by a fence to protect it from vandals and souvenir hunters. Your ticket permits you to go inside the fence, all the way up to a short rope barrier about 50 feet from the stones. In spring 1996, a full circular tour around Stonehenge began; a modular walkway has been introduced to cross the archaeologically important area that runs between the Heel Stone and the main circle of stones. This lets you complete a full circuit of the stones, an excellent addition to the well-received audio tour.

Admission to Stonehenge (☎ **01980/623108**) is £3.90 ($6.45) for adults, £2 ($3.30) for children, and £2.90 ($4.80) for students and seniors. It's open March 16 to May 31 and September 1 to October 15 daily 9:30am to 6pm; June 1 to August 31 daily 9am to 7pm; and October 16 to March 15 daily 9:30am to 4pm.

AVEBURY & SALISBURY

After visiting Stonehenge, many travelers move on to Bath, but if you have an extra day or so, you should not miss the other attractions nearby, Avebury and Salisbury.

AVEBURY

Avebury, one of Europe's largest prehistoric sites, lies 20 miles north of Stonehenge on the Kennet River, 7 miles west of Marlborough. Unlike Stonehenge, you can walk around the 28-acre site at Avebury, winding in and out of the circle of more than 100 stones, some of which weigh up to 50 tons. The stones are made of sarsen, a sandstone found in Wiltshire. Inside this large circle are two smaller ones, each with about 30 upright stones. Native Neolithic tribes are believed to have built these circles.

Avebury is on A-361 between Swindon and Devizes and a mile from the A-4 London–Bath road. The closest rail station is at Swindon, some 12 miles to the north, which is served by the main rail line from London to Bath. A limited bus service (no. 49) runs from Swindon to Devizes through Avebury.

You can also reach Avebury from Salisbury by taking one of two buses (nos. 5 and 6) run by Wilts & Dorset (☎ **01722/336855**). The buses leave three times a day Monday through Saturday (twice on Sunday). The one-way trip takes 1½ hours.

An Archaeological Museum

Founded by Alexander Keiller, the **Avebury Museum** (☎ **01672/539250**) houses one of Britain's most important archaeological collections. It began with Keiller's material from excavations at Windmill Hill and Avebury, and now includes artifacts from other prehistoric digs at West Kennet, Long Barrow, Silbury Hill, West Kennet Avenue, and the Sanctuary. Admission is £1.60 ($2.65) for adults, 80p ($1.30) for children. Open April to October daily 10am to 6pm; November to March daily 10am to 4pm.

SALISBURY

Long before you enter Salisbury, the spire of the cathedral comes into view, just as John Constable painted it many times. Salisbury lies in the Avon River Valley, and is a fine place to stop for lunch and a look at the cathedral on your way to Stonehenge.

For driving directions, see above. Salisbury can be reached by bus from the Victoria Coach Station in London. There is also direct rail service from London from Waterloo Station. Call ☎ **0345/484950** for schedules and information.

Salisbury Visitor Information is at Fish Row (☎ **01722/334956**).

✪ Salisbury Cathedral.

You can search all of England, but you'll find no better example of the early English, or pointed, style than the magnificent Salisbury Cathedral. Construction was begun as early as 1220 and took 38 years to complete; this was rather fast in those days since it was customary for a cathedral building to require at least 3 centuries. The soaring spire was completed at the end of the 13th century. Despite an ill-conceived attempt at renovation in the 18th century, the architectural integrity of the cathedral has been retained.

The cathedral's 13th-century octagonal chapter house (note the fine sculpture), which is especially attractive, possesses one of the four surviving original texts of the Magna Carta, along with treasures from the diocese of Salisbury and manuscripts and artifacts belonging to the cathedral. The beautiful cloisters and exceptionally large close, with at least 75 buildings in its compound (some from the early 18th century and others predating that), dramatically set off the cathedral.

Attractions Near Salisbury

Old Sarum. Castle Rd., 2 miles north of Salisbury off A-345.

Old Sarum is believed to have been an Iron Age fortification known to the Romans as *Sorbiodunum*. Much later, Saxons also used the fortification. The Normans built a cathedral and a castle here in what was then a medieval walled town. Parts of the old cathedral were taken down to build the city of New Sarum (Salisbury).

For information, call ☎ **01722/335398.** Admission is £1.90 ($3.15) for adults, £1.40 ($2.30) for senior citizens, and £1 ($1.65) for children. Open April to September, daily 10am to 6pm; off-season, daily 10am to 4pm. Bus nos. 3, 5, 6, 7, 8, and 9 out of Salisbury run every 20 minutes to the site.

Wilton House. About 2½ miles west of Salisbury in the town of Wilton on A-30.

Wilton House, one of England's great country estates, is the home of the earls of Pembroke. Originally built in the 16th century, it has undergone many alterations, most recently in Victoria's day. It's noted for its 17th-century staterooms by the celebrated architect Inigo Jones. It is believed that Shakespeare's troupe might have entertained here. Preparations for the D-day landings at Normandy were laid out here by Eisenhower and his advisors, with only the silent Van Dyck paintings in the Double Cube room as witnesses.

The house displays paintings by Sir Anthony Van Dyck, Rubens, Brueghel, and Reynolds. A dynamic film introduced and narrated by Anna Massey brings to life the history of the family since 1544, the year it was granted the land by Henry VIII. You then visit a reconstructed Tudor kitchen and Victorian laundry plus "The Wareham Bears," a unique collection of some 200 miniature dressed teddy bears.

Growing on the 21-acre estate are giant cedars of Lebanon, the oldest of which were planted in 1630. The Palladian Bridge was built in 1737 by the ninth earl of Pembroke and Roger Morris. There are rose and water gardens, riverside and woodland walks, and a huge adventure playground for children.

For information, call ☎ **01722/746729.** Admission is £7 ($11.55) for adults, and £4.50 ($7.45) for children 5 to 15 (under 5 free). To enter the grounds only costs £4 ($6.60) for adults, and £2.75 ($4.55) for children. Open April through October, daily 11am to 6pm (last admission at 5pm).

The cathedral at The Close in Salisbury (☎ **01722/555120**) is open May to August daily 8:30am to 8:15pm; September to April daily 8am to 6:30pm. To visit the cathedral costs £3 ($4.95) for adults, £2 ($3.30) students and seniors, £1 ($1.65) children, or £6 ($9.90) family of four. Guided tours are offered Monday through Saturday from 11am to 2pm and cost £2.55 ($4.10).

Where to Dine

Harper's Restaurant. 6–7 Ox Row, Market Sq. ☎ **01722/333118.** Reservations recommended. Main courses £5.50–£12.50 ($9.05–$20.65); set-price 3-course menu £9.50 ($15.65). AE, DC, MC, V. Mon–Sat noon–2pm and 6–9:30pm; Sun 6–9pm (June–Sept only). ENGLISH.

The chef-owner of this place prides himself on specializing in homemade and wholesome "real food." The pleasantly decorated restaurant is on the second floor of a red brick building at the back side of Salisbury's largest parking lot, in the town center. You can order from two different menus, one featuring cost-conscious bistro-style platters, including beefsteak casserole with "herbey dumplings." A longer menu includes all-vegetarian pasta diavolo or spareribs with French fries and rice.

Salisbury Haunch of Venison. 1 Minster St. ☎ **01722/322024.** Main courses £6.95–£11.95 ($11.45–$19.70); bar dishes for lunches, light suppers, and snacks £4.50–£8 ($7.45–$13.20); set menus £7.95–£12.50 ($13.10–$20.65). AE, DC, MC, V. Daily noon–3pm; Mon–Sat 7–9:30pm; pub, Mon–Sat 11am–11pm, Sun noon–3pm and 7–11pm. Closed on Christmas and Easter. ENGLISH.

Right in the heart of Salisbury, this creaky-timbered 1320 chophouse serves excellent dishes, especially English roasts and grills. Stick to what it's known for, and you'll rarely go wrong. Tasty grilled venison sausages in a Dijon mustard sauce is a nice starter; follow with the time-honored house specialty: roast haunch of venison with gin and juniper berries. Many other classic English dishes are served, such as a medley of fish and shellfish, and grilled Barnsley lamb chops with "bubble and squeak" (cabbage and potatoes).

Silver Plough. White Hill, Pitton, near Salisbury. ☎ **01722/712266.** Reservations recommended. Main courses £7–£15 ($11.55–$24.75); bar platters £4.50–£7.50 ($7.45–$12.40). AE, DC, MC, V. Restaurant, daily noon–2:30pm; Mon–Sat 7–10pm, Sun 7–9pm; pub, Mon–Sat 11am–3pm and 6–11pm, Sun noon–3pm and 7–10:30pm. Closed Dec 25–26 and Jan 1. Take A-30 for 5 miles east of Salisbury; it's at the southern end of the hamlet of Pitton. ENGLISH.

Built as a stone-sided farmhouse 150 years ago, the Silver Plough is now a charming country pub with an attached restaurant. Snacks available in the bar include ratatouille au gratin and grilled sardines with garlic butter and freshly baked bread. In the somewhat more formal dining room, the chef prepares such dishes as fresh Dorset mussels in a white wine, garlic, and cream sauce; sliced breast of duck in cracked pepper or orange sauce; and roast guinea fowl in a sharp strawberry sauce. The Silver Plough has known many famous visitors, but the management prefers to stick to its quiet, country atmosphere and concentrate on making its guests feel at home.

EN ROUTE TO BATH

From Stonehenge, follow the sign south to the A-303 heading west. Continue past Chicklade until you come to the junction of A-350 heading directly north. Take this route toward Warminster, where you can connect with the A-36 into Bath. You'll enter at the southern tier of the city.

BATH

In 1702 Queen Anne made the trek from London, 115 miles west to the mineral springs of Bath, thereby launching a fad that was to make the city England's most celebrated spa.

The most famous personage connected with Bath's growing popularity was the 18th-century dandy Beau Nash. The master of ceremonies of Bath, Nash cut a striking figure. In all the plumage of a bird of paradise, he was carted around in a sedan chair, dispensing (at a price) trinkets to courtiers and aspirant gentlemen. This polished arbiter of taste and manners succeeded in making dueling déclassé.

The 18th-century architects John Wood the Elder and his son envisioned a proper backdrop for Nash's activities. These architects designed a city of honey-colored stone quarried from nearby hills, a feat so substantial and lasting that Bath today is the most harmoniously laid-out city in England. The city became a popular spot for leading political and literary figures, including Dickens, Thackeray, Nelson, and Pitt, and most important, of course, Jane Austen. Canadians may already know that General Wolfe lived on Trim Street, and Australians might want to visit the house at 19 Bennett St. where their founding father, Admiral Phillip, lived.

The city of Bath has had two lives. Long before its Georgian and Victorian popularity, it was known to the Romans as *Aquae Sulis*. The foreign legions founded the baths here (which can be visited today) to ease their rheumatism in the curative mineral springs.

Remarkable restoration and careful planning have ensured that Bath retains its handsome look today, although it does have somewhat of a museum appearance, with the attendant gift shops in place. Prices, stimulated by massive tourist invasion, tend to be high, but Bath remains one of the high points of the West Country.

ESSENTIALS

GETTING THERE   By Train   At least one train an hour leaves London's Paddington Station bound for Bath during the day; the trip takes 70 to 90 minutes. For schedules and information, call ☎ **0345/484950.**

By Bus   One National Express coach leaves London's Victoria Coach Station every 2 hours during the day for the 2½-hour trip. For schedules and information, call ☎ **0990/808080.**

By Car   Coming from London, drive west on M-4 to the junction with A-4, on which you continue west to Bath.

VISITOR INFORMATION   The **Bath Tourist Information Centre,** at Abbey Chambers, Abbey Church Yard (☎ **01225/477101**), opposite the Roman Baths, is open May to September, Monday to Saturday 9:30am to 6pm and Sunday 10am to 4pm; off-season, Monday to Saturday 9:30am to 5pm and Sunday 10am to 4pm.

GETTING AROUND   One of the best ways to explore Bath is by bike. You can rent one from **Somerset Valley Bike Hire** (☎ **01225/442442**), behind the train station. It's open daily from 9am to 6pm, charging £14 to £25 ($23.10 to $41.25) per day, depending on the type of bike. Deposits range from £20 to £75 ($33 to $123.75).

SPECIAL EVENTS   For 17 days in late May and early June each year the city is filled with more than 1,000 performers. The **Bath International Music Festival** focuses on classical music, jazz, and new music from orchestras, soloists, and artists from all over the world. Opening night celebrations are complete with fireworks. Bath also offers the best in walks, tours, and talks, plus free street entertainment. For more information, contact the **Bath Festivals Box Office,** 2 Church St., Abbey Green, Bath BA1 1NL (☎ **01225/463362**).

EXPLORING BATH

In addition to the attractions listed below, you'll want to visit some of the buildings, crescents, and squares in town. The **North Parade** (where Oliver Goldsmith lived) and the **South Parade** (where English novelist and diarist Frances Burney once resided), the work of John Wood the Elder, are the architectural idealization of harmony. The younger Wood designed the elegant half-moon row of townhouses, the **Royal Crescent.** One of the most beautiful squares is **Queen Square,** which displays the work of Wood the Elder. Both Jane Austen and Wordsworth once lived here. Also of interest is **The Circus,** built in 1754, as well as the shop-lined **Pulteney Bridge,** designed by Robert Adam and often compared to the Ponte Vecchio of Florence.

Bath Abbey. Orange Grove. ☎ **01225/422462.** Free admission; donation requested £1.50 ($2.45). Heritage Vaults £2 ($3.30) adults, £1 ($1.65) students, children, and senior citizens.

Abbey, Apr–Oct Mon–Sat 9am–6pm; Nov–Mar Mon–Sat 9am–4:30pm; year-round, Sun 1–2:30pm and 4:30–5:30pm. Heritage Vaults, Mon–Sat 10am–4pm.

Built on the site of a much larger Norman cathedral, the present-day abbey is a fine example of the late Perpendicular style. When Queen Elizabeth I came to Bath in 1574, she ordered a national fund set up to restore the abbey. The interior and its many windows plainly illustrate why the abbey is called the "Lantern of the West." Note the superb fan vaulting, with its scalloped effect. Beau Nash was buried in the nave and is honored by a simple monument totally out of keeping with his flamboyant character. In 1994, the Bath Abbey Heritage Vaults opened on the south side of the abbey. This subterranean exhibition traces the history of Christianity at the abbey site since Saxon times.

Pump Room and Roman Baths. Abbey Church Yard. ☎ **01225/477785.** Admission £6.70 ($11.05) adults, £4 ($6.60) children. Apr–Sept daily 9am–6pm; Oct–Mar Mon–Sat 9:30am–5pm, Sun 10:30am–5pm. Evenings in Aug 8–10pm.

Founded in A.D. 75 by the Romans, the baths were dedicated to the goddess Sulis Minerva; in their day they were an engineering feat. Even today, still fed by Britain's most famous hot-spring water, they're among the finest Roman remains in the country. After centuries of decay, the original baths were rediscovered during Queen Victoria's reign. The site of the Temple of Sulis Minerva has been excavated and is now open to view. The museum displays many interesting objects from Victorian and more recent archeological digs (look for the head of Minerva). Coffee, lunch, and tea, usually with music from the Pump Room Trio, can be enjoyed in the 18th-century pump room, overlooking the hot springs. There's also a drinking fountain spouting hot mineral water; it tastes horrible, but is supposedly beneficial.

No. 1 Royal Crescent. 1 Royal Crescent. ☎ **01225/428126.** Admission £4 ($6.60) adults, £3 ($4.95) children, £8 ($13.20) family ticket. Mar–Oct Tues–Sun 10:30am–5pm; Nov–Feb Tues–Sun 10:30am–4pm (last admission 30 min. before closing). Closed Good Friday.

The interior of this Bath townhouse has been redecorated and furnished by the Bath Preservation Trust in late 18th-century style. The house is located at one end of Bath's most magnificent crescent, west of the Circus.

American Museum. Claverton Manor, Bathwick Hill. ☎ **01225/460503.** Admission £5 ($8.25) adults, £4.50 ($7.45) students and senior citizens, £2.50 ($4.15) children. Late Mar to late Oct, Tues–Sun 2–5pm. Bus: 18.

Some 2½ miles outside Bath is the first American museum established outside the United States. In a Greek Revival house (Claverton Manor), the museum sits on extensive grounds high above the Avon valley. Authentic exhibits of pioneer days have been shipped over from the States. On the grounds is a copy of Washington's flower garden at Mount Vernon and an American arboretum. A permanent exhibition in the New Gallery displays the Dallas Pratt Collection of Historical Maps.

ORGANIZED TOURS

The **Heart of England Tourist Board** (☎ 01905/763436) and the **West Country Tourist Board** (☎ 01392/276351) have details of numerous guided tours within their regions. The staff can arrange outings with registered guides ranging from short walks to luxury tours that include accommodations in stately homes.

Free, 1¾-hour walking tours are conducted throughout the year by the Mayor's Honorary Society (☎ 01225/477786). Tours depart from outside the Roman Baths Monday to Friday at 10:30am and 2pm, Sunday at 2:30pm, and Tuesday, Friday, and Saturday at 7pm. A slightly different tour by Bath Parade Tours, costing £3.50 ($5.75) per person, leaves Saturday at 2:30pm from outside the Roman Baths. Reservations aren't needed for either tour.

Jane Austen Tours take you in the footsteps of the author and her characters. These tours leave Saturday from the Abbey Lace Shop, York Street (☎ **01225/436030**), and cost £3 ($4.95) per person. You'll be told the time to meet when you make a reservation.

To tour Bath by bus, you can choose among several tour companies; some have open-top buses leaving from the Tourist Information Centre, which supplies details of changing schedules and prices. Among the best bus tours is **Patrick Driscoll/Beau Nash Guides,** Elmsleigh, Bathampton, BA2 6SW (☎ **01225/46210**); these tours are more personalized than most. Another good outfitter is **Sulis Guides,** 2 Lansdown Terrace, Weston, Bath BA1 4BR (☎ **01225/429681**).

THE SHOPPING SCENE

Bath has the finest shopping possibilities outside London. Here is a sampling to get you started.

Bath Stamp & Coin Shop. 12–13 Pulteney Bridge. ☎ **01225/463073.**

This is the largest seller of antique coins and stamps in Bath, with hundreds of odd or unusual numismatics from throughout England and its former empire. Look also for antique Venetian glass and a scattering of English antiques.

Beaux Arts Gallery. 13 York St. ☎ **01225/464850.**

The most important gallery of contemporary art in Bath, it specializes in well-known British artists. The gallery occupies a pair of interconnected, stone-fronted Georgian houses, set close to Bath Abbey.

Rossiter's. 38–41 Broad St. ☎ **01225/462227.**

This very English version of a department store offers four floors of merchandise. They'll ship any of the Royal Doulton, Wedgwood, or Spode to anywhere in the world. Look especially for the displays of ginger jars, vases, and clocks manufactured by Moorcroft, and perfumes by London-based Floris.

Walcot Reclamation. 108 Walcot St. ☎ **01225/444404.**

This sprawling and dusty storeroom sells 19th-century architectural artifacts. The 20,000-square-foot warehouse is located a quarter-mile northeast of Bath. Anything can be shipped.

Whittard of Chelsea. 10 Union Passage. ☎ **01225/447787.**

The most charming and unusual shop in Bath, Whittard of Chelsea supplies everything you'll need to duplicate the dearly held tea-drinking ritual. If you want an exotic tea to wow your friends back home, ask for Monkey-Picked Oolong, a Chinese tea from plants so difficult to reach that leaves can be gathered only by trained monkeys.

WHERE TO STAY
Very Expensive

✪ **Bath Spa Hotel.** Sydney Rd., Bath, Avon BA2 6JF. ☎ **01225/444424.** Fax 01225/444006. 98 suites. MINIBAR TV TEL. Sun–Thurs £169–£195 ($278.85–$321.75) double; Fri–Sat £179–£199 ($295.35–$328.35) double; week-long £239–£429 ($394.35–$707.85) suite for 2. AE, DC, MC, V. Free parking. East of the city off A-36.

This restored 19th-century mansion, which lies at the end of a tree-lined drive on 7 acres of landscaped grounds, is a 10-minute walk from the center of Bath. It is an even more stunning addition to the Bath hotel scene than the Royal Crescent. The drawing room of this former home of an English general has been restored, and the log-burning fireplaces, elaborate moldings, oak paneling, and staircases create a warm country-house charm. The rooms, most quite spacious, are handsomely furnished with the best English furniture and well-chosen and coordinated fabrics. The hotel features an indoor swimming pool, gymnasium, tennis court, health and leisure spa, beauty treatment rooms, and an English croquet lawn.

The premier hotel restaurant, which serves continental cuisine, is called Vellore House, the name the former owner here gave his home. You'll find immaculate service and superb food and wine; a set-price dinner is served from 7 to 10pm daily. A second restaurant, the Alfresco Restaurant, offers a Mediterranean-style menu. In summer, guests can dine outside in an informal garden with a fountain.

Fountain House. 9–11 Fountain Buildings, Lansdown Rd., Bath, Avon BA1 5DV. ☎ **01225/ 338622.** Fax 01225/445855. 14 units. MINIBAR TV TEL. £140–£220 ($231–$363) 1-bedroom suite for 2; £200–£246 ($330–$405.90) 2-bedroom suite for 4. Rates include continental breakfast. AE, DC, MC, V. Parking £15 ($24.75).

On the northern edge of the city center, this hotel comprises three Georgian neo-classical, natural stone-fronted structures dating from 1735. British entrepreneur Robin Bryan created the all-suite hotel that has been favorably compared to the most prestigious in England. There are no public rooms. Each suite has original or reproduction antiques, at least one bedroom, a sitting room, private bathroom, and all the accoutrements you'd expect in such an elegant hotel. The hotel stands within 100 yards of Milsom Street, the city's main shopping and historic thoroughfare. It doesn't serve a formal breakfast; rather, breakfast is delivered in a basket to your door.

Priory Hotel. Weston Rd., Bath, Avon BA1 2XT. ☎ **01225/331922.** Fax 01225/448276. 29 units. TV TEL. £160 ($264) standard double; £190–£230 ($313.50–$379.50) deluxe room for 2. Rates include English breakfast. AE, DC, MC, V. Free parking.

Converted from one of Bath's Georgian houses in 1969, the Priory is on 2 acres of formal and award-winning gardens with manicured lawns and flower beds, a swimming pool, and a croquet lawn. The hotel reopened, vastly refurbished and improved, in the spring of 1997; if anything, it is more inviting than ever. It's not as overly commercial as the Francis, but is less expensive than the Bath Spa or Royal Crescent, while offering a similar townhouse aura. The bedrooms are individually decorated and furnished with antiques; our personal favorite is Clivia (all rooms are named after flowers or shrubs), a nicely appointed duplex in a circular turret.

The restaurant consists of three separate dining rooms, one in a small salon in the original building; the others have views over the garden. The menu is varied and reflects seasonal availability. Grouse, partridge, hare, and venison are served in season, as is the succulent lamb roasted with herb-flavored bread crumbs. A three-course dinner is offered, and on Sunday, traditional roasted meats are featured.

Queensberry Hotel. Russel St., Bath, Avon BA1 2QF. ☎ **800/323-5463** in the U.S., or 01225/447928. Fax 01225/446065. 22 units. TV TEL. £120–£190 ($198–$313.50) double. Rates include continental breakfast. MC, V. Parking 50p (85¢) per hour.

Although hardly as grand as the addresses previously considered, this place derives much of its beauty from the many original fireplaces, ornate ceilings, and antiques, which the creators of the property, Stephen and Penny Ross, have preserved. The Marquis of Queensberry commissioned John Wood to build this house in 1772. Each of the three interconnected townhouses that form this hotel was constructed in the early Georgian era. Today each bedroom has antique furniture and carefully chosen upholstery. Open since 1988, the Queensberry has become one of Bath's most popular hotels. You can dine at the exceptional Olive Tree, offering contemporary English cuisine (see "Where to Dine," below).

✪ **Royal Crescent Hotel.** 16 Royal Crescent, Bath, Avon BA1 2LS. ☎ **800/457-6000** in the U.S., or 01225/823333. Fax 01225/339401. 46 units. TV TEL. £190–£290 ($313.50–$478.50) double; from £380 ($627) suite. AE, DC, MC, V. Free parking.

Standing proudly in the center of the famed Royal Crescent, this Georgian colonnade of townhouses was designed by John Wood the Younger in 1767. Before the arrival of the Bath Spa, it was long regarded as Bath's premier hotel. Crystal chandeliers, period furniture, and paintings add to the rich adornment. The bedrooms, including the Jane Austen Suite, are often lavishly furnished with four-poster beds and Jacuzzi baths. Each bedroom also offers such comforts as a trouser press, hair dryer, bathrobes, fruit plates, and other special touches. Excellent English cuisine is served in the Dower House Restaurant. Reservations are essential for rooms or meals. The continental cuisine is imaginative, with ever-so-polite and formal service.

Expensive

Francis Hotel. Queen Sq., Bath, Avon BA1 2HH. ☎ **800/225-5843** in the U.S. and Canada, or 01225/424257. Fax 01225/319715. 94 units. TV TEL. £124–£144 ($204.60–$237.60) double; £179–£199 ($295.35–$328.35) suite. AE, DC, MC, V. Free parking.

An integral part of Queen Square, and the first major design by John Wood the Elder, architect and creator of Bath's most prestigious buildings, the 18th-century Francis seems overly commercial and touristy today. Originally consisting of six private residences dating from 1729, the Francis was opened as a private hotel by Emily Francis in 1884 and has offered guests first-class service for more than 100 years. Many of the well-furnished and traditionally styled bedrooms overlook Queen Square—named in honor of George II's consort, Caroline. The public rooms feature some 18th-century antiques, a cocktail bar, and the Edgar Restaurant, which offers both British and international food.

Moderate

Pratt's Hotel. South Parade, Bath, Avon BA2 4AB. ☎ **01225/460441.** Fax 01225/448807. 46 units. TV TEL. £95 ($156.75) double. Rates include English breakfast. Children under 15 stay free in a room shared with 2 adults. AE, DC, MC, V. Parking £8.50 ($14).

Once the home of Sir Walter Scott, Pratt's, which has functioned as a hotel since 1791, is conveniently located for sightseers. Several elegant terraced Georgian townhouses were joined together to make a comfortable hotel that has small to spacious rooms (typical for a former private home) with nice, but utilitarian furnishings. In the hotel are warm, cheerful lounges, a bar, and a high-ceilinged dining room. Well-conceived English and French cuisine is served in the dining room.

Inexpensive

✪ **Apsley House Hotel.** 141 Newbridge Hill, Bath, Avon BA1 3PT. ☎ **01225/336966.** Fax 01225/425462. 9 units. TV TEL. £70 ($115.50) double; £80–£105 ($132–$173.25) suite. Rates include English breakfast. DC, MC, V. Free parking. Take A-4 to Upper Bristol Rd. and fork right at the traffic signals into Newbridge Hill.

This charming and stately building, just a mile west of the center of Bath, dates back to 1830 and the reign of William IV. It's set in its own gardens, with a square tower, arched windows, and a walled garden with south views. In 1994 new owners refurbished the hotel, filling it with country-house chintzes and antiques borrowed from the showrooms of an antique store they own. (Some hotel furniture is for sale.) The bedrooms are comfortably furnished and filled with fine fabrics and attractive accessories.

Dukes' Hotel. 53–54 Great Pulteney St., Bath, Avon BA2 4DN. ☎ **01225/463512.** Fax 01225/483733. 23 units. TV TEL. £65–£95 ($107.25–$156.75) double; £75–£115 ($123.75–$189.75) family room. Rates include English breakfast. AE, CB, DC, MC, V. Free parking. Bus: 18.

A short walk from the heart of Bath, this building dates from 1780. It has been completely restored and both its bedrooms and public rooms have been rather elegantly furnished and modernized. Many of the original Georgian features, including cornices and moldings, have been retained. Amenities include electric trouser presses and hair dryers. Guests can relax in a refined drawing room or the cozy bar. A traditional English menu is also offered.

Laura Place Hotel. 3 Laura Place, Great Pulteney St., Bath, Avon BA2 4BH. ☎ **01225/463815.** Fax 01225/310222. 8 units. TEL. £68–£88 ($112.20–$145.20) double; £110 ($181.50) family suite. Rates include English breakfast. AE, MC, V. Free parking. Bus: 18 or 19.

Built in 1789, this hotel won a civic award for the restoration of its stone facade. On the corner of a residential street overlooking a public fountain, it's only a 2-minute walk from the Roman Baths and Bath Abbey. The hotel has been skillfully decorated with antique furniture and fabrics evocative of the 18th century. Rooms are exceedingly cozy and comfortable in the best tradition of English B&Bs.

Number Ninety Three. 93 Wells Rd., Bath, Avon BA2 3AN. ☎ **01225/317977.** 4 units. TV. £38–£55 ($62.70–$90.75) double; £60–£75 ($99–$123.75) triple. Rates include English breakfast. AE, MC, V. Bus: 3, 13, 14, 17, 23, or 33.

This well-run guesthouse is a traditional British B&B: small but immaculately kept and well maintained. Its owner is a mine of local information. The elegant Victorian house serves a traditional English breakfast, and it is within easy walking distance from the city center, rail, and National Bus stations. Evening meals are available by prior arrangement. Parking can be difficult in Bath, but the hotel can advise you.

Sydney Gardens Hotel. Sydney Rd., Bath, Avon BA2 6NT. ☎ **01225/464818.** Fax 01225/484347. 6 units. TV TEL. £75 ($123.75) double. Rates include English breakfast. AE, MC, V. Free parking.

This spot recalls the letters of Jane Austen, who wrote to friends about the long walks she enjoyed in Sydney Gardens, a public park just outside the city center. In 1852, an Italianate Victorian villa was constructed here immediately adjacent to the gardens. Three rooms have twin beds and the other three have 5-foot-wide double beds. Each room is decorated with an English country-house charm. Amenities include hair dryers and beverage-making facilities. Only breakfast is served. There's also a footpath running beside a canal. No smoking.

Nearby Places to Stay

Homewood Park. Hinton Charterhouse, Bath, Avon BA3 6BB. ☎ **01225/723731.** Fax 01225/723820. 21 units. £135–£210 ($222.75–$346.50) double; £275 ($453.75) suite. Rates include English breakfast. AE, DC, MC, V. Free parking. Take A-36 (Bath-Warminster Rd.) 6 miles south of Bath.

This small, family-run hotel, set on 10 acres, was built in the 18th century and enlarged in the 19th. Overlooking the Limpley Stoke Valley, it's a large Victorian house with grounds adjoining the 13th-century ruin of Hinton Priory. Each bedroom is luxuriously decorated and furnished with taste and charm. Most rooms overlook the gardens and grounds or offer views of the valley. You can play tennis and croquet in the garden. Riding and golf are also available nearby. Guests can enjoy beautiful walks through the Limpley Stoke Valley.

However, most visitors come here for the French and English cuisine, which is prepared with skill and flair. The dining room faces south, overlooking the gardens.

Hunstrete House. Hunstrete, Pensford, near Bristol, Avon BS39 4NS. ☎ **01761/490490.** Fax 01761/490732. 23 units. TV TEL. £160–£195 ($264–$321.75) double; £230–£260 ($379.50–$429) suite. Half-board £210–£230 ($346.50–$379.50) double; £280 ($462) suite for 2. Rates include English breakfast. AE, DC, MC, V. Free parking. Take A-4 about 4 miles west of Bath, then A-368 another 4½ miles toward Weston-super-Mare.

This fine Georgian house, which has earned Relais & Châteaux distinction, is situated on 92 acres of private parkland. Six units are in the Courtyard House, attached to the main structure and overlooking a paved courtyard with an Italian fountain and flower-filled tubs. Swallow Cottage, which adjoins the main house, has its own private sitting room, double bedroom, and bathroom. Units in the main house are individually decorated. There is a heated swimming pool in a sheltered corner of the walled garden. Part of the pleasure of staying at Hunstrete is the contemporary and classic cuisine served in the dining room.

✪ Ston Easton Park. Ston Easton, Somerset BA3 4DF. ☎ **01761/241631.** Fax 01761/241377. 27 units. TV. £175–£245 ($288.75–$404.25) double; £265–£295 ($437.25–$486.75) suite; £270–£375 ($445.50–$618.75) state room. Children under 7 not accepted. AE, DC, MC, V. Free parking. 12 miles south of Bath, signposted from A-39 south.

From the moment you pass a group of stone outbuildings and the century-old beeches of the 30-acre park, you know you've come to a very special place. The mansion was created in the mid-1700s from the shell of an existing Elizabethan house. In 1977, after many years of neglect, Peter and Christine Smedley acquired the property and poured money, love, and labor into its restoration. Now it's one of the great country hotels of England. A pair of carved mahogany staircases is ringed with ornate plaster detailing, and the place is replete with antiques. Tasteful bedrooms are filled with flowers. A gardener's cottage houses two separate suites, and the stateroom is regal with a four-poster bed in the large bedroom and a private seating area.

A sunflower-colored formal dining room displays museum-quality oil portraits, grandeur, and exquisite attention to detail. The chef prepares superb food from an imaginative menu.

WHERE TO DINE
Moderate

Hole in the Wall. 16 George St. ☎ **01225/425242.** Reservations recommended Mon–Fri and required on Sat. Main courses at lunch £5.50 ($9.05); main courses at dinner £15 ($24.75); 3-course set dinner £16.50 ($27.20). AE, MC, V. Mon–Sat noon–2pm and 6–11pm. MODERN ENGLISH/FRENCH.

After an unsuccessful interlude as an Italian restaurant, this renovated Georgian town-house reopened in 1994, signaling the rebirth of what was among the most famous restaurants in Britain during the 1970s. Its owners are Gunna and Christopher Chown, whose successful restaurant in Wales has already received critical acclaim. The pair of interconnected dining rooms are accented with polished copper pots, darkened ceiling beams, whitewashed walls, and a large fireplace. The menu choices change frequently, according to the chef's inspiration and ingredient availability, but dishes might include a warm salad of monkfish with Parma ham and exotic mushrooms; summer mushroom cutlet; braised lamb shank with roasted potatoes, garlic, and tomatoes; braised pork tenderloin wrapped in bacon with a brandy cider and applesauce; and chocolate sorbet along with various warm and cold puddings. The house that accommodates the restaurant was built of honey-colored Bath stone around 1790.

Moon and Sixpence. 6A Broad St. ☎ **01225/460962.** Reservations recommended. Main courses £11–£15 ($18.15–$24.75); set-price lunch £8.95–£12.95 ($14.75–$21.35); 2-course lunch buffet in the wine bar £5.95 ($9.80); set-price dinner £16.95–£21.95 ($27.95–$36.20). AE, MC, V. Daily noon–2:30pm and 5:30–10:30pm (until 11pm Fri–Sat). INTERNATIONAL.

One of Bath's leading restaurants and wine bars, the Moon and Sixpence occupies a stone building east of Queen Square, with an extended conservatory and sheltered patio. Situated just off Broad Street, it has a cobbled passageway that leads you past a fountain into its courtyard.

The food might not be the equal of that served at more acclaimed choices, including the Hole in the Wall, but the value is unbeatable. At lunch a large buffet with a selection of hot and cold dishes is featured in the wine bar section. In the upstairs restaurant overlooking the bar, full service is offered. Main courses might include such dishes as filet of lamb with caramelized garlic, or médaillons of beef filet with a bacon, red wine, and shallot sauce. Look for the daily specials on the continental menu.

Olive Tree. In the Queensberry Hotel, Russel St. ☎ **01225/447928.** Reservations recommended. Main courses £12.75–£15 ($21.05–$24.75); set-price 3-course lunch £15.50 ($25.60); set-price 3-course dinner £21 ($34.65). MC, V. Mon–Sat noon–2pm and 7–10pm; Sun 7–9:30pm. MODERN ENGLISH/MEDITERRANEAN.

In the basement of this previously reviewed hotel, Stephen and Penny Ross operate one of the most sophisticated little restaurants in Bath. Stephen uses the best and freshest local produce. The menu is changed to reflect the season, often with game and seafood specialties. You might begin with a Provençal fish soup with *rouille* and croutons, or eggplant and mozzarella fritters with a sweet red pepper sauce—unless the grilled scallops with noodles and pine nuts tempt you instead. Then you could move on to Gressingham duck breast lightly grilled with shallots and kumquats, or loin of venison with wild rice and morels delicately flavored with a tarragon sauce. Stephen is also known for his great desserts; they might include a hot chocolate soufflé or an apricot and almond tart.

Popjoy's Restaurant. Sawclose. ☎ **01225/460494.** Reservations recommended. Main courses £12–£17 ($19.80–$28.05); set-price 3-course lunch £10.50 ($17.35). AE, DC, MC, V. Mon–Sat noon–2pm and 6–11pm. BRITISH/INTERNATIONAL.

This restaurant is named after Bath's most famous English Regency couple, Beau Nash and his mistress, Julianna Popjoy. In the circa 1720 Georgian home, where the couple entertained their friends and established the fashions of the day, two dining rooms are located on separate floors. Dishes display inventiveness and solid technique. Menu choices include terrine of duck and chicken liver wrapped in bacon with a tomato coulis; watercress and potato soup; sautéed lamb kidneys with crispy smoked bacon; braised lamb shoulder with a sage and garlic stuffing; and tagliatelle with leeks and cream sauce.

Inexpensive

Beaujolais. 5 Chapel Row, Queen Sq. ☎ **01225/423417.** Reservations recommended. Set-price 2-course lunch £9 ($14.85); set-price 2-course dinner £13.50 ($22.30); dinner main courses £10.90–£14.50 ($18–$23.90). AE, MC, V. Daily noon–2:30pm and 7–11pm. FRENCH.

Every year, Beaujolais, the best-known bistro in Bath, seems to increase its loyal following. Established in 1973, it is the oldest restaurant in Bath under its original ownership. Diners are drawn by the good, honest cooking and good value. Begin perhaps with a salad of warm scallops or rabbit terrine served with chutney. Main dishes include an excellent grilled loin of lamb topped with a crispy julienne of ginger and leeks. House wines are modestly priced. One area of the restaurant is reserved for nonsmokers, and people with disabilities (wheelchair access), children (special helpings), and vegetarians will all find comfort here.

Woods. 9–13 Alfred St. ☎ **01225/314812.** Reservations recommended. Main courses £11–£13.50 ($18.15–$22.30); set-price lunches £5–£7 ($8.25–$11.55); set-price dinners

Day Trips from Bath: Longleat House & Stourhead

LONGLEAT HOUSE   Between Bath and Salisbury, Longleat House, Warminster, in Wiltshire (☎ **01985/844400**), owned by the seventh marquess of Bath, lies 4 miles southwest of Warminster, off A-36, and 4½ miles southeast of Frome on A-362. The first view of this magnificent Elizabethan house, built in the early Renaissance style, is romantic enough, but the wealth of paintings and furnishings in its lofty rooms is dazzling. From the Elizabethan great hall to the library, state rooms, and grand staircase, the house is filled with beautiful tapestries and paintings. The library contains the finest private collection in the country. The Victorian kitchens are open, and various exhibitions are mounted in the stable yard.

Events are staged frequently on the grounds. The Safari Park has a vast array of animals in open parklands, including Britain's only white tiger. The Maze, the longest in the world, was added to the attractions by the current marquess. It has more than 1½ miles of paths; the first part is comparatively easy, but the second is pretty complicated.

Admission is £5 ($8.25) for adults, £4 ($6.60) for children; admission to Safari Park is £6 ($9.90) for adults, £4.50 ($7.45) for children. Special exhibitions and rides require separate admission tickets. Passport tickets for all of Longleat's attractions cost £13 ($21.45) for adults and £10 ($16.50) for children, including admission to the Butterfly Garden, Simulator Dr. Who Exhibition, Postman Pat's Village, Adventure Castle, and more. It's open mid-March to September daily 10am to 6pm; October to Easter daily 10am to 4pm. The park itself is open mid-March to October 31, daily 10am to 6pm (last cars are admitted at 5:30pm or sunset).

STOURHEAD   After a visit to Longleat, you can drive 6 miles down B-3092 to Stourton, a village just off the highway 3 miles northwest of Mere (A-303). A Palladian house, Stourhead (☎ **01747/841152**) was built in the 18th century by the banking family of Hoare. The magnificent gardens, blending art and nature, became known as *le jardin anglais.* Set around an artificial lake, the grounds are decorated with statues, temples, bridges, islands, and grottoes. The gardens are open daily 9am to 7pm (or until dusk), and cost £4.50 ($7.45) for adults and £2.50 ($4.15) for children from March to October. Off-season tickets cost £3.50 ($5.75) for adults and £1.50 ($2.45) for children. The house is open March 30 to October 30, Saturday through Wednesday noon to 5:30pm. Admission is £4.50 ($7.45) for adults and £2.50 ($4.15) for children. A combination ticket to both attractions goes for £8 ($13.20) for adults or £3.80 ($6.25) for children.

£10.50–£14 ($17.35–$23.10). AE, MC, V. Mon–Sat noon–2:30pm and 6–10:30pm; Sun noon–4pm. Closed Dec 25–26. ENGLISH/FRENCH/ASIAN.

Named after John Wood the Younger, the architect of Bath's famous Assembly Room that lies across the street, this restaurant in a Georgian building is run by horse-racing enthusiast David Price and his French-born wife, Claude. Diners can opt for the set-price menu or choose among the seasonally changing à la carte dishes noted on a chalkboard. Good bets include pear and parsnip soup; smoked chicken salad with Stilton and avocado; pan-fried cod roe; and a perfectly prepared breast of chicken with tomatoes, mushrooms, red wine, and tarragon.

BATH AFTER DARK

Theatre Royal, located next to the new Seven Dials development at Sawclose (☎ 01225/448844; for credit-card bookings, call 01225/448861), was restored in 1982 and refurbished with plush seats, red carpets, and a painted proscenium arch and ceiling. Now the most beautiful theater in Britain, it has 940 seats, a small pit, and grand tiers rising to the upper circle. A **studio theater** at the rear of the main building opened in 1996. The theater publishes a schedule of forthcoming events, which usually include West End shows. It operates but 6 to 8 weeks a year. Prices vary, but tickets generally begin at £9 ($14.85).

Beneath the theater, reached from the back of the stalls or by a side door, are the theater vaults, where you will find a bar and a restaurant, serving an array of dishes from soup to light à la carte meals.

France   6

by Darwin Porter & Danforth Prince

France presents visitors with an embarrassment of riches—no other country concentrates such a diversity of sights and scenery into so compact an area. This chapter explores that diversity: Paris and the Ile de France; the Loire Valley in the northwest with its châteaux and vineyards; Provence, in the southwest, with its ancient culture; and the lush semitropical coast of the Mediterranean, the French Riviera, and the Côte d'Azur.

1 Paris

Today, Paris is in many ways less French and more international. Those Parisians who were born and bred in the city and who have French ancestry have accepted that they might one day become a minority in their own hometown, as waves of immigrants from the far stretches of the former empire, including Vietnam and North Africa, flood their gates. And with the millions of visitors pouring in annually from all over the world, you can no longer separate Paris from its visitors—they have virtually become one and the same.

Legendary Paris style and chic are changing, too. Unless you frequent upscale watering holes, you'll see very few Parisians dressed quite as alluringly and formally as they did a few years ago. Many young Parisians have adopted the casual attire of their American counterparts. And although the old haute couture houses have experienced rough times, prêt-à-porter designers are flourishing.

The late president François Mitterrand wanted to leave an architectural legacy to rival or surpass that of the autocratic "Sun King," Louis XIV. Mitterrand's dream was to make Paris the undisputed capital of the European Union. To do that, he virtually painted Paris in gold (well, gilt at least), cleaned the Louvre's facade, spruced up the Champs-Elysées, and ran up a $6-billion tab as he built, restored, and recast. The most controversial of these projects was I. M. Pei's metal-and-glass pyramid entrance for the Louvre, a design selected by Mitterrand himself.

Thanks to Mitterrand, a more glamorous Paris is the stage on which lovers walk arm in arm along the Seine, children scamper about in the Tuileries, cafes fill with animated conversation, and women dance the cancan at the Moulin Rouge.

Only in Paris

Strolling Along the Seine   Painters like Sisley, Turner, and Monet have all fallen under the Seine's spell. Romantic couples continue to stroll along its banks, and anglers still cast their lines here. The *clochards* still seek a home for the night under its bridges, and on its banks the *bouquinistes* still peddle postcards, perhaps some 100-year-old pornography, or a tattered edition of an old history of Indochina. Some athletic visitors walk the full 7-mile stretch of the river, but you might want to confine your stroll to central Paris, passing the Louvre, Notre-Dame, and the Pont Neuf.

Window-Shopping Along the Faubourg St-Honoré   In the 1700s this was home to the wealthiest of Parisians; today it's home to the stores that cater to them. Even if you don't buy anything, you'll enjoy some great window-shopping with big names such as Hermès, Larouche, Courrèges, Cardin, Saint Laurent, and Lagerfeld.

Spending a Languid Afternoon in a Cafe   The Parisian cafe is an integral part of life. Even if it means skipping a museum, spend some time at a cafe. Whether you have one small coffee or the most expensive cognac in the house, nobody will hurry you and you can see how the French really live.

Attending an Opera or a Ballet   In 1989, the acoustically perfect Opéra Bastille was inaugurated to compete with the *grande dame* of Paris's musical scene, the Opéra Garnier. The recent renovation of the Garnier has returned it to its rococo splendor. A night here beneath a ceiling by Chagall will take you back to the Second Empire. Whether it be for a performance of Bizet or Tharp, check out these two major Paris landmarks. Dress with pomp and circumstance.

Discovering Hidden Montmartre   This district is the most touristy part of Paris. However, far removed from the area's top draw, Sacré-Coeur, another neighborhood unfolds—that of the true Montmartrois. Arm yourself with a good map and wander any of the back streets away from the souvenir shops. Seek out such streets as rue Lepic (refresh yourself at the Lux Bar, no. 12), rue Constance, rue Tholozé (with a view over the rooftops), lively rue des Abbesses, and rue Germain-Pilon. None is famous, none receives hordes of visitors, but each is flanked with buildings whose detailing shows the pride and care that permeates Paris's architecture. You'll discover dozens of other streets on your own.

Checking Out the Marchés   A daily Parisian ritual is ambling through one of the open-air markets to purchase fresh food to be consumed that day—some ripe and creamy Camembert or a pumpkin-gold cantaloupe at its peak when consumed before sundown. Even if you're staying in a hotel with no kitchen facilities, you can gather supplies for a picnic in one of the city's parks. The vendors arrange their wares into a mosaic of vibrant colors. Our favorite market is on rue Montorgueil, beginning at rue Rambuteau, 1er (Métro: Les-Halles).

ORIENTATION

GETTING THERE   By Plane   Paris has two major international airports: Aéroport d'Orly, 8½ miles south, and Aéroport Roissy—Charles de Gaulle, 14 miles northeast of the city. The Air France bus that travels between Orly and Roissy airports departs at 20-minute intervals daily between 6am and 11pm. The trip takes 50 minutes and costs 75F ($12.75).

At **Charles de Gaulle (Roissy) Airport** (☎ **01-48-62-22-80**), foreign carriers use Aérogare (terminal) 1, and Air France flys into Aérogare 2. From Aérogare 1, you take a moving walkway to the passport checkpoint and the Customs area. The two terminals are linked by a shuttle bus (*navette*). The **free shuttle bus** connecting Aérogare 1 with Aérogare 2 also transports passengers to the Roissy rail station, from which fast RER trains leave every 15 minutes heading to such Métro stations as Gare-du-Nord, Châtelet, Luxembourg, Port-Royal, and Denfert-Rochereau. A typical train fare from Roissy to any point in central Paris is 49F ($8.35). Passengers arriving on chartered flights from virtually anywhere tend to arrive at Terminal T-9, a relatively simple facility without the architectural drama of either of the other two aerogares. It lies immediately next to the RER station, a short walk from Aerogare 1, and as such, is accessible by the above-mentioned shuttlebus network.

You can also take an **Air France shuttle bus** to central Paris for 60 to 70F ($10.20 to $11.90). It stops at the Palais des Congrès (Port e Maillot), and then continues on to place de l'Etoile, Gare de Montparnesse, and Gare de Lyon, where subway lines can carry you farther along to any other point in Paris. That ride, depending on traffic, takes between 45 and 55 minutes. The shuttle departs about every 12 minutes between 5:40am and 11pm. Another option is the **Roissybus,** which departs from the airport daily from 5:45am to 11pm and costs 45F ($7.65) for the 45- to 50-minute ride. Departures are about every 15 minutes from 6am to 11pm daily, and the bus takes you near the corner of rue Scribe and place de l'Opéra in the heart of Paris.

A **taxi** from Roissy into the city costs about 300F ($51). From 8pm to 7am, fares are 40% higher. Long queues of both taxis and passengers form outside each of the airport's terminals, but are surprisingly orderly.

Orly Airport (☎ 01-49-75-15-15) also has two terminals—Orly Sud (south) for international flights and Orly Ouest (west) for domestic flights. They're linked by a free shuttle bus. **Air France buses** leave from Exit K of Orly Sud and from Exit D of Orly Ouest every 12 minutes between 5:45am and 11pm, heading for Gare de Montparnasse and Gare des Invalides. The fare for the trip is 45F ($7.65). At Exit J arrival level in Orly Ouest and Exit H, Platform 4, in Orly Sud, you can board an **Orly bus** to Denfert-Rochereau in central Paris. Expect to pay 30F ($5.10).

An alternative method for reaching central Paris involves taking a **free shuttle bus** that leaves both of Orly's terminals at intervals of about every 8 minutes for the nearby Métro and RER train station (Pont-de-Rungis/Aéroport-d'Orly), from which RER trains (Line B) make the 30-minute ride into the city center. The train fare to Les Invalides, for example, is 57F ($9.70).

A **taxi** from Orly to the center of Paris costs about 225F ($38.25), more at night. Don't take a meterless taxi from Orly Sud or Orly Ouest—it's much safer and usually cheaper to hire a metered cab from the lines, which are under the scrutiny of a police officer.

Returning to the airport, buses leave the Invalides terminal heading either to Orly Sud or Orly Ouest every 15 minutes, taking about 30 minutes.

By Train   There are six major train stations in Paris: **Gare d'Austerlitz,** 55 quai d'Austerlitz, 13e (servicing the southwest with trains to the Loire Valley, the Bordeaux country, and the Pyrénées); **Gare de l'Est,** place du 11-Novembre-1918, 10e (servicing the east, with trains to Strasbourg, Nancy, Reims, and beyond to Zurich, Basel, Luxembourg, and Austria); **Gare de Lyon,** 20 bd. Diderot, 12e (servicing the southeast with trains to the Côte d'Azur, Provence, and beyond to Geneva, Lausanne, and Italy); **Gare de Montparnasse,** 17 bd. Vaugirard, 15e (servicing the west with trains to Brittany); **Gare du Nord,** 18 rue de Dunkerque, 15e (servicing the north with trains to Holland, Denmark, Belgium, and the north of Germany); and **Gare St-Lazare,** 13 rue d'Amsterdam, 8e (servicing the northwest with trains to Normandy and London).

For general train information or to make reservations, call ☎ **08-36-35-35-35** if your destination takes you from Paris to anywhere else in France or Europe. If your ride will be limited to Paris and its suburbs, call ☎ **01-53-90-20-20** instead.

Buses operate between the stations, and each of these stations has a Métro stop. Taxis are also available at every station at designated stands. *Note:* The stations and surrounding areas are usually seedy and frequented by pickpockets, hustlers, hookers, and drug addicts. Be alert, especially at night.

By Bus   Most buses arrive at **Gare Routière Internationale du Paris-Gallieni,** 28 av. du Général-de-Gaulle, Bagnolet (☎ **08-36-69-52-52;** Métro: Gallieni). The eastern suburb of Bagnolet is a 35-minute Métro ride from central Paris.

By Car   Driving a car in Paris is definitely *not* recommended. Parking is difficult and traffic dense. If you do drive, remember that Paris is encircled by a ring road called the *périphérique.* The major highways into Paris are the **A-1** from the north (Great Britain and Benelux); the **A-13** from Rouen, Normandy, and other points of northwest France; the **A-109** from Spain, the Pyrénées, and the southwest; the **A-7** from the French Alps, the Riviera, and Italy; and the **A-4** from eastern France.

VISITOR INFORMATION   The city's main **tourist information office** is at 127 av. des Champs-Élysées, 8e (☎ **01-49-52-53-54**), where you can get information about Paris and its provinces. Between April and October, the office is open daily from 9am to 8pm, with an annual closing on May 1. Between November and March, the office is open daily from 11am to 6pm, with an annual closing on December 25. Although the above-mentioned address is the largest tourist information post in the city, it's supplemented with an additional branch in the base of the Eiffel Tower (open only between May and October, Monday to Saturday from 8am to 8pm), and in the arrivals hall of the Gare de Lyon (open year-round, Monday to Saturday, from 8am to 8pm). Any of the above-mentioned tourist offices can give you free copies of the 50-page English-language leaflets *Time Out* and *Paris Users' Guide.*

CITY LAYOUT

Paris is surprisingly compact. Occupying 432 square miles (6 more than San Francisco), it's home to more than 10 million people. The River Seine divides Paris into the **Right Bank (Rive Droite)** to the north and the **Left Bank (Rive Gauche)** to the south. These designations make sense when you stand on a bridge and face downstream, watching the waters flow out toward the sea—to your right is the north bank; to your left the south. Thirty-two bridges link the Right Bank and the Left Bank, some providing access to the two small islands at the heart of the city, **Ile de la Cité**—the city's birthplace and site of Notre-Dame—and **Ile St-Louis,** a moat-guarded oasis of sober 17th-century mansions.

Between 1860 and 1870 Baron Georges-Eugène Haussmann, at the orders of Napoléon III, forever changed the look of Paris by creating the legendary *grands boulevards:* St-Michel, St-Germain, Haussmann, Sébastopol, Magenta, Voltaire, and Strasbourg.

The "main street" on the Right Bank is the **avenue des Champs-Élysées,** beginning at the Arc de Triomphe and running to **place de la Concorde.** Haussmann also created avenue de l'Opéra and the 12 avenues that radiate starlike from the Arc de Triomphe, giving it its original name, place de l'Etoile (*étoile* means "star"). It was renamed place Charles-de-Gaulle following the general's death; today it's often referred to as **place Charles-de-Gaulle-Etoile.**

ARRONDISSEMENTS IN BRIEF   The heart of medieval Paris was the **Ile de la Cité** and the areas immediately surrounding it. As Paris grew, it absorbed many of the

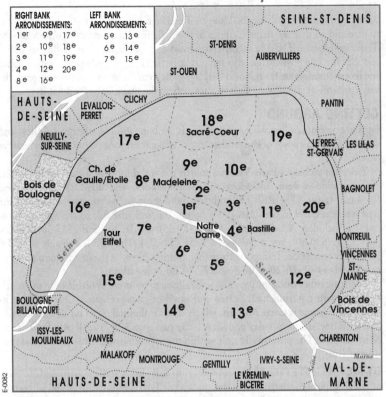

SEINE-ST-DENIS

RIGHT BANK ARRONDISSEMENTS:
1er 9e 17e
2e 10e 18e
3e 11e 19e
4e 12e 20e
8e 16e

LEFT BANK ARRONDISSEMENTS:
5e 13e
6e 14e
7e 15e

ST-DENIS

AUBERVILLIERS

ST-OUEN

HAUTS-DE-SEINE

LEVALLOIS-PERRET

CLICHY

PANTIN

NEUILLY-SUR-SEINE

Ch. de Gaulle/Étoile

Bois de Boulogne

17e

18e Sacré-Coeur

19e

LE PRES-ST-GERVAIS

LES LILAS

9e

8e Madeleine

10e

2e

BAGNOLET

16e

1er

3e

11e

20e

7e

Notre Dame

4e Bastille

MONTREUIL

Tour Eiffel

6e

VINCENNES ST-MANDE

5e

12e

Seine

Bois de Vincennes

15e

BOULOGNE-BILLANCOURT

14e

13e

ISSY-LES-MOULINEAUX

VANVES

CHARENTON

Marne

MALAKOFF

MONTROUGE

GENTILLY

IVRY-S-SEINE

Seine

VAL-DE-MARNE

LE KREMLIN-BICETRE

HAUTS-DE-SEINE

E-0082

once-distant villages, and even today each of these *arrondissements* (districts) retains a distinct character. They're numbered from 1 to 20, starting at the center around the Louvre and progressing in a clockwise spiral. The key to finding any address in Paris is looking for the arrondissement number, rendered as a number followed by either *e* or *er* (1er, 2e, and so on). If the address is written out more formally, you can tell what arrondissement it's in by looking at the postal code. For example, the address might be written with the street name and then "75014 Paris." The last two digits, 14, indicate that the address is in the 14th arrondissement, Montparnasse.

On the Right Bank, the **1er** is home to the Musée du Louvre, place Vendôme, rues de Rivoli and St-Honoré, Palais Royal, and Comédie-Française—an area filled with grand institutions and grand stores; at the center of the **2e** is the Bourse (stock exchange), making it the city's financial center; most of the **3e** and the **4e** is referred as the Marais, the old Jewish quarter that in the 17th century was home to the aristocracy—today it's a trendy area of boutiques and restored mansions as well as the center of Paris's gay and lesbian community. On the Left Bank, the **5e** is known as the Latin Quarter, home to the Sorbonne and Panthéon and associated with the intellectual life that thrived in the 1920s and 1930s; the **6e**, known as St-Germain-des-Prés, stretches from the Seine to boulevard du Montparnasse, and is associated with the 1920s and 1930s—as well as being a center for art and antiques, it boasts the Palais and Jardin du Luxembourg within its boundaries. The **7e**, containing both the Tour Eiffel and Hôtel des Invalides, is a residential district for the well heeled.

Back on the Right Bank, the **8e** epitomizes monumental Paris: with the triumphal avenue des Champs-Élysées, the Élysées Palace, and the fashion houses along avenue

Montaigne and the Faubourg St-Honoré. The **18e** is home to Sacré-Coeur and Montmartre and all that the name conjures of the bohemian life, painted most notably by Toulouse-Lautrec. The **14e** incorporates most of Montparnasse, including its cemetery, but the **20e** is where the city's famous lie buried in Père-Lachaise and where today the recent immigrants from North Africa live. Beyond the arrondissements stretch the vast *banlieue,* or suburbs, of Greater Paris, where the majority of Parisians live.

GETTING AROUND

Paris is a city for strollers whose greatest joy is rambling through unexpected alleys and squares. Given a choice of conveyance, try to make it on your own two feet whenever possible.

You can purchase a **Paris-Visite,** a tourist pass valid for 3 or 5 days on the public transportation system, including the Métro, buses, and RER (Réseau Express Régional) trains. (The RER has both first- and second-class compartments, and the pass lets you travel in first-class.) As a bonus, the funicular ride to the top of Montmarte is included. A 1-day pass costs 55F ($9.35); a 2-day pass 90F ($15.30); a 3-day pass 120F ($20.40), and a 5-day pass 175F ($29.75). The card is available at RATP (Régie Autonome des Transports Parisiens), tourist offices, or the main Métro stations; call ☎ **01-44-68-20-20** or 08-36-68-77-14 for information.

There are other discount passes as well, although most are available only to French residents with government ID cards and proof of taxpayer status. One available to temporary visitors is **Carte Mobilis,** which allows unlimited travel on all bus, subway, and RER lines during a 1-day period. A 1-day pass costs 30F ($5.10). Ask for it at any Métro station. The pass is valid only within the 20 arrondissements—not in the suburbs of Paris.

BY MÉTRO   The Paris Métro (subway) runs daily from 5:30am to around 1:15am, at which time all underground trains reach their final terminus at the end of each of their respective lines. (Be alert that their arrivals in the underground stations of central Paris might be as much as an hour before the end of their run.) The subways are reasonably safe at any hour, but beware of pickpockets. Transfer stations are known as *correspondances.* Note that some transfers require long walks (Châtelet is the most notorious), but most trips require only one transfer. On the urban lines, it costs the same to any point. One ticket costs 8F ($1.35).

BY BUS   Buses are much slower than the subway. Most run from 7am to 8:30pm (a few operate to 12:30am, and 10 operate during the early-morning hours). Service is limited on Sunday and holidays. Bus and Métro fares are the same and you can use the same *carnet* tickets on both. Most bus rides (including all of those that begin and end within the 20 arrondissements of Paris) require one ticket, but some destinations between the arrondissements of Paris and some of the city's suburbs require up to, but never more than, two.

If you intend to use the buses a lot during your stay in Paris, pick up an **RATP bus map** at their office on place de la Madeleine, 8e, at any tourist information office, or at RATP headquarters, 52–54 quai de la Rapée, 12e (☎ **01-44-68-20-20**). For detailed information on bus and Métro routes, call ☎ **08-36-68-41-14.**

Traveler's Tip

When purchasing Métro tickets, a *carnet* is the best buy—10 tickets for 52F ($8.85).

BY TAXI   The flag drops at 14F ($2.40), and you pay 3.36F (55¢) per kilometer. At night, expect to pay 5.45F (95¢) per kilometer. On airport trips, you're not required to pay for the driver's empty return ride. Should you get tied up in a traffic jam and have a long wait, a basic charge of 120F ($20.40) per hour is assessed, or 60F ($10.20) per 30 minutes of waiting time. Tip 12% to 15%—the latter usually elicits a *merci*. For radio cabs, call ☎ **01-45-85-85-85,** 01-42-70-41-41, or 01-42-70-00-42—note that you're charged from the point where the taxi begins the drive to pick you up.

BY CAR   Don't even consider driving in Paris, unless you're a battle-hardened veteran of urban guerilla tactics. The streets are narrow and parking is next to impossible.

BY BICYCLE   Paris-Vélos, 2 rue du Fer-à-Moulin, 5e (☎ **01-43-37-59-22;** Métro: Censier-Daubenton), rents by the day, weekend, or week, charging from 100 to 160F ($17 to $27.20) per weekday, from 160 to 220F ($27.20 to $37.40) Saturday and Sunday, and from 450 to 600F ($76.50 to $102) for a week. Deposits of 1,000 to 2,500F ($170 to $425) are required. Bikes are rented Monday through Saturday 10am to 12:30pm and 2 to 7pm.

BY BOAT   The **Batobus** (☎ **01-44-11-33-44),** a series of 150-passenger ferryboats with big windows suitable for viewing the passing riverfronts, operate every day between April and mid-October along the Seine, stopping at five points of tourist interest. You can board at the Eiffel Tower, Musée d'Orsay, Louvre, Notre-Dame, or the Hotel de Ville docks. Transit between each stop costs 20F ($3.40), and departures are about every 30 minutes from 10am to 7pm.

Fast Facts: Paris

American Express   The largest travel service in the world operates a 24-hour-a-day hotline from its administrative headquarters in the Paris suburb of Reuil-Malmaison (☎ **01-47-77-70-00).** Don't expect to walk in for help, as it's geared only for telephone handling of emergency questions such as lost cards. The day-to-day services, such as tours and money-changing, are available at affiliates in central Paris. They include an Amex branch at 11 rue Scribe, 9e (☎ **01-47-77-47-61;** Métro: Opéra) and a smaller affiliate at 38 av. Wagram, 8e (☎ **01-42-27-58-80;** Métro: Ternes). Both of the branches are open Monday to Friday from 9am to 5pm, with money-changing services ending at 4pm.

Baby-sitters   Institut Catholique, 21 rue d'Assas, 6e (☎ **01-45-48-31-70),** runs a service staffed by students. The price is 35F ($5.95) per hour, plus 10F ($1.70) for insurance. The main office is open Monday through Friday from 9am to noon and 2 to 5:30pm, and Saturday 9am to noon.

Business Hours   Most **banks** in Paris are open Monday to Friday from 9am to 4:30pm; only a few are open on Saturday. The *grands magasins* (**department stores**) are generally open Monday to Saturday 9:30am to 6:30pm; **smaller shops** close for lunch and reopen around 2pm, but this has become rarer. Many stores stay open to 7pm in summer; others are closed Monday, especially in the morning. Large **offices** remain open all day, but some also close for lunch.

Currency   American Express (see above) can fill most banking needs. For the best exchange rate, cash your traveler's checks at banks or foreign-exchange offices, not at shops and hotels. The **French franc (F)** is divided into 100 **centimes.** There are coins of 5, 10, 20, and 50 centimes (the latter is usually referred to as a half-franc coin), and 1, 2, 5, 10, and 20 francs. Bills come in 20, 50, 100, 200, and 500-franc denominations, although the 20-franc bill is increasingly

Paris Métro

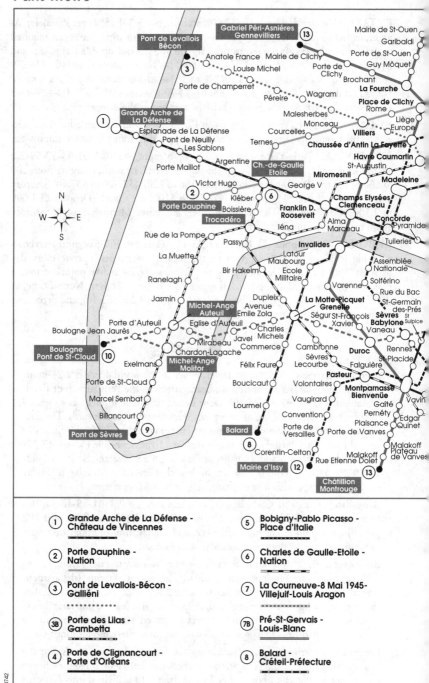

Lines:

1. Grande Arche de La Défense - Château de Vincennes
2. Porte Dauphine - Nation
3. Pont de Levallois-Bécon - Galliéni
3B. Porte des Lilas - Gambetta
4. Porte de Clignancourt - Porte d'Orléans
5. Bobigny-Pablo Picasso - Place d'Italie
6. Charles de Gaulle-Etoile - Nation
7. La Courneuve-8 Mai 1945- Villejuif-Louis Aragon
7B. Pré-St-Gervais - Louis-Blanc
8. Balard - Créteil-Préfecture

3-0742

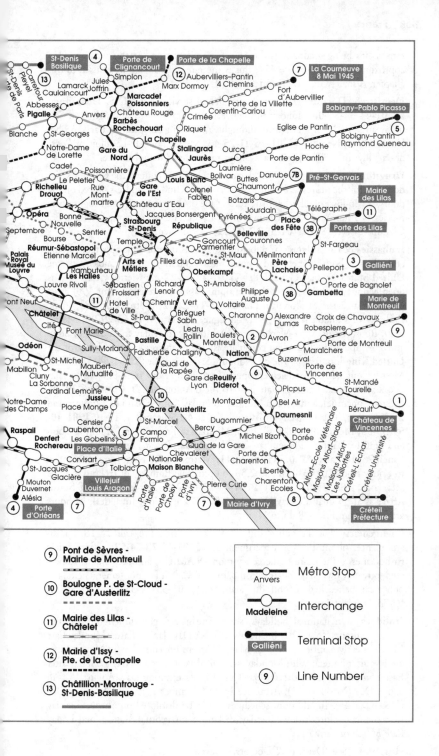

rare, as it's being gradually withdrawn from circulation. At this writing, $1 = approximately 5.8F or 1F = 17¢; this is the rate of exchange we've used in this chapter. Also, 1EUR = 6.5F and £1 = 9.9F.

Dentists & Doctors For emergency dental service, call **S.O.S. Dentaire** at ☎ **01-43-37-51-00** Monday through Friday from 8pm to midnight and Saturday and Sunday from 8am to midnight. **American Hospital of Paris,** 63 bd. Victor-Hugo, Neuilly (☎ **01-46-41-25-43;** Métro: Pont-de-Levallois or Pont-de-Neuilly; Bus: 82), operates a 24-hour medical and dental service.

Drugstores After regular hours, have your concierge contact the Commissariat de Police for the nearest 24-hour *pharmacie.* You'll find the address posted on the doors or windows of all other drugstores. One of the most central all-night pharmacies is **Pharmacy "les Champs,"** in La Galerie Les Champs, 84 av. des Champs-Élysées, 8e (☎ **01-45-62-02-41;** Métro: George V).

Embassies & Consulates Call before you go, as they often keep strange hours and observe both French and home-country holidays. The Embassy of the **United States,** at 2 av. Gabriel, 8e (☎ **01-43-12-22-22;** Métro: Concorde), is open Monday to Friday from 9am to 6pm. Passports are issued (for $55) at its consulate at 2 rue St-Florentin (☎ **01-43-12-22-22;** Métro: Concorde). The Embassy of **Canada** is at 35 av. Montaigne, 8e (☎ **01-44-43-29-00;** Métro: F.-D.-Roosevelt or Alma-Marceau), open Monday to Friday from 9am to noon and 2 to 5pm. The Canadian consulate is at the embassy. The Embassy of the **United Kingdom** is at 35 rue du Faubourg St-Honoré, 8e (☎ **01-44-51-31-00;** Métro: Concorde or Madeleine), open Monday to Friday from 9:30am to 1pm and 2:30 to 5pm. The consulate is at 16 rue d'Anjou, 8e (☎ **01-44-66-29-79;** Métro: Concorde), and is open Monday to Friday from 9:30am to 12:30pm and 2:30 to 5pm. The Embassy of **Australia** is at 4 rue Jean-Rey, 15e (☎ **01-40-59-33-00;** Métro: Bir-Hakeim), open Monday to Friday from 9:15am to noon and 2:30 to 4:30pm. The embassy of **New Zealand** is at 7ter rue Léonard-de-Vinci, 75116 Paris (☎ **01-45-00-24-11;** Métro: Victor Hugo), open Monday to Friday from 9am to 1pm and 2:30 to 6pm. The Embassy of **Ireland** is at 12 ave. Foch, 16e, 75116 Paris (☎ **01-44-17-67-00**). The **Embassy of South Africa** is at 59 quai d'Orsay (☎ **01-53-59-23-23;** Métro: Invalides); its hours are Monday to Friday 8:45 to 11am.

Emergencies For the police, call ☎ **17;** to report a fire, call ☎ **18.** For an ambulance, phone the fire department at ☎ **01-45-78-74-52;** a fire vehicle rushes cases to the nearest emergency room. **S.AM.U** is an independently operated, privately owned ambulance company; call ☎ **15.** For non-emergencies, the police can be reached at 9 bd. du Palais, 4e (☎ **01-53-71-53-71** or 01-53-73-53-73; Métro: Cité).

Holidays On national holidays, shops, businesses, government offices, and most restaurants close. They include New Year's Day (Jan 1); Easter Monday (late March or early April); Labor Day (May 1); Ascension Thursday (in May or June, 40 days after Easter); Whit Monday, also called Pentecost Monday (51st day after Easter, in June or July); Bastille Day (July 14); Assumption Day (August 15); All Saints Day (November 1); Armistice Day (November 11); and Christmas Day (December 25). In addition, schedules might be disrupted on Shrove Tuesday (the Tuesday before Ash Wednesday, in January or February) and Good Friday (late March or early April).

Hospitals See "Dentists & Doctors," above.

Lost & Found The central office is **Objets Trouvés,** Prefecture de Police, 36 rue des Morillons, 15e (☎ **01-515-76-20-00;** Métro: Convention), at the corner of rue de Dantzig. It's open Monday and Wednesday 8:30am to 5pm, Tuesday and Thursday 8:30am to 8pm, and Friday 8:30am to 5:30pm. If the object you're looking for happens to have been lost on the subway or on a city bus, call the same number, but ask the operator there for "Objéts Trouvés R.A.T.P."

Police In an emergency, call ☎ **17.** The principal Prefecture is at 9 bd. du Palais, 4e (☎ **01-53-71-53-71;** Métro: Cité).

Post Office Each of the arrondissements of Paris maintains its own postal headquarters, but the one that remains open longest and is more centrally located than any other in the French capital is the one in the 1st arrondissement. The **Bureau de Poste,** 52 rue du Louvre, 75001 Paris (☎ **01-40-28-20-00;** Métro: Louvre), is open 24 hours a day for the sale of stamps and expedition of faxes and telegrams, with slightly more limited hours—8am to 5pm Monday to Friday and 8am to noon on Saturday—for more esoteric financial services that include the sale of money orders. Your mail can be sent to this post office *poste restante* (general delivery) for a small fee. Take an ID such as a passport. Airmail letters to North America cost 4.40F (75¢); to other European countries, 3F (50¢); to Australia and New Zealand, 5.10F (85¢).

Safety Especially beware of child pickpockets. They roam Paris, preying on tourists around such sites as the Louvre, Eiffel Tower, Notre-Dame, and Montmartre, and they especially like to pick pockets in the Métro, often blocking the entrance and exit to the escalator.

Telephone The **country code** for France is **33.** All phone numbers in France have 10 digits, and this includes the **area code** (or regional prefix). For example, the phone number for the Hôtel Regina—01-42-60-38-09—contains the area code (01) for Paris and the Ile de France. To make a **long-distance call within France,** you would just dial this 10-digit number. **When calling from outside France,** dial the international prefix for your country (**011** for the United States and Canada), the country code for France, and then the last nine digits of the number, dropping the 0 (zero) from the regional prefix. The toll-free international access codes are: **AT&T** ☎ 0800-99-00-11, **Sprint** ☎ 0800-99-0087, and **MCI** ☎ 0-800-99-0019.

   Public phone booths are in cafes, restaurants, Métro stations, post offices, airports, train stations, and sometimes on the streets. Finding a coin-operated phone in France might be an arduous task; a simpler option is to use the *télécarte,* a prepaid calling card available for purchase at most post offices and Métro stations.

Transit Information For information on public transport, stop in at the office of the **Services Touristiques de la RATP,** 53 quai des Grands-Augustins, 6e (Métro: St-Michel), or call ☎ **01-43-46-14-14** for recorded information, in French, about stoppages, subway or bus breakdowns, or exceptionally heavy traffic on any particular bus or Métro line.

Weather Call ☎ **08-36-68-02-75.** The cost is 2.50F (45¢) per minute.

WHERE TO STAY

Many travelers with an early morning flight at Charles de Gaulle (or else those who arrive very late at night) check into the **Hotel Sofitel Paris Aéroport CDG,** Aéroport

Paris Accommodations

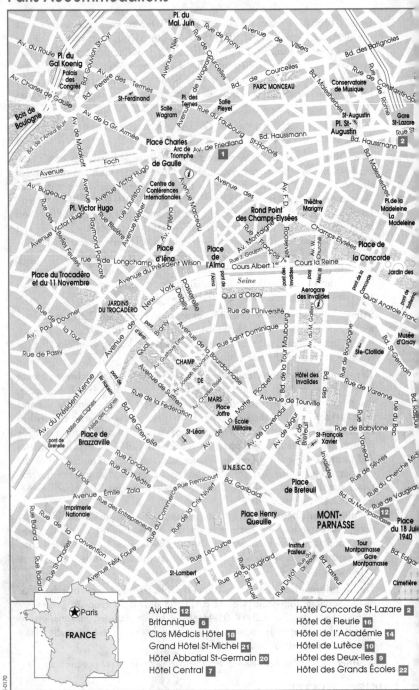

FRANCE
★ Paris

Aviatic **12**	Hôtel Concorde St-Lazare **2**
Britannique **6**	Hôtel de Fleurie **16**
Clos Médicis Hôtel **18**	Hôtel de l'Académie **14**
Grand Hôtel St-Michel **21**	Hôtel de Lutèce **10**
Hôtel Abbatial St-Germain **20**	Hôtel des Deux-Iles **9**
Hôtel Central **7**	Hôtel des Grands Écoles **22**

Moulin Rouge
Bd. de Clichy
MONTMARTRE
Bd. de la Chapelle
Av. Jean Jaurès
Rue Armand Carrel
Place Pigalle
Bd. de Rochechuart
Av. Truddine
Rue Condorc
Gare du Nord
Rue de Magenta
La Fayette
Rue du Faubourg St-Martin
Avenue Secrétan
St-Joseph
St-Georges
PARC DES BUTTES CHAUMONT
Rue Blanche
Rue Pigalle
Rue N.D. de Lorette
asino Paris
Ste-Trinité
St-Vincent de Paul
Rue de Chabrol
Gare de l'Est
St-Laurent
Place du Colonel Fabien
azare
Notre-Dame de Lorette
Rue La Fayette
Folies Bergère
Rue de Paradis
Rue du Faubourg St-Denis
Rue de Strasbourg
Rue du Faubourg St-Martin
Quai de Valmy
Quai de Jemmapes
Rue de la Grange
Rue de la Villette
d. Haussmann
Opéra Garnier
Bd. des Italiens
Bd. Montmartre
Bd. de Bonne Nouvelle
Quai de Jemmapes
Quai de Valmy
Rue St-Maur
upucines
Place de Opéra
Rue St_Augustin
Bourse des Valeurs
Richelieu
Rue de Cléry
Bd. St-Martin
Place de la République
Rue du Faubourg du Temple
St-Joseph
Place endôme
Rue des Petits
St-Roch
Place A. Malraux
Palais Royal
Champs
Rue du Mail
Rue d'Abukir
Rue Réaumur
Conservatoire des Arts et Métiers
Rue St-Martin
Rue de Sébastopol
Turbigo
Rue du Temple
Rue du Temple
Bd. Voltaire
St-Ambroise
uileries
Rue de Rivoli
Bourse du Commerce
Rue du Louvre
Forum des Halles
Rue St-Martin
St-Merri
Rue des Archives
Archives Nationales
Rue de Turenne
St-Denis
Bd. Beaumarchais
LE MARAIS
Bd. Richard Lenoir
Rue du Chemin Vert
Place du Carrousel
Musée du Louvre
Quai des Tuileries
Théâtre du Châtelet
Seine
Hôtel de Ville
Rue St-Antoine
St-Gervais
St-Paul
Place des Vosges
Rue de la Roquette
Théâtre de la Bastille
Royal
Quai Voltaire
Quai Malaquais
pont des Arts
Quai de Conti
pont Neuf
pont au Change
pont N. Dame
Quai de l'Hôtel de Ville
ÎLE DE LA CITÉ
ST-GERMAIN-DES-PRÉS
Bd. St-Germain
Quai des Grands Augustins
Cloître N.Dame
pont St-Louis
Notre-Dame
ÎLE ST-LOUIS
St-Louis
Place de la Bastille
Opéra Bastille
Rue du Faubourg St-Antoi
e du Four
Rue St-Michel
Quai de la Tournelle
pont de la tournelle
Quai Henri IV
Bd. Bourdon
Rue de Charenton
Avenue Doumesnil
Rue de Vaugirard
Rue Jacques
Rue des Ecoles
Bd. St-Germain
pont de Sully
Av. L. Rollin
Rue Bd. Diderot
e d'Assas
Sorbonne
QUARTIER LATIN
Panthéon
Quai Saint Bernard
Université Paris VII
JARDIN DES PLANTES
Gare de Lyon
JARDIN DU LUXEMBOURG
Université Paris V
Rue St. Michel
Rue Gay Lussac
Rue d'Ulm
Rue Claude Bernard
pont d'Austerlitz
Gare d'Austerlitz
Quai de Bercy
u du Montparnasse
net
Montparnasse
Bd. de Port Royal
St-Médard
Rue Censier
Rue Buffon
Université Paris III
Bd. Saint Marcel
Seine
Quai de la Rapée
pont de Bercy

Hôtel du Louvre 5
Hôtel du Quai-Voltaire 13
Hôtel le Colbert 19
Hôtel Regina 4
Hôtel St-Louis 11

Le Ritz 3
L'Hôtel 15
Libertel Quartier Latin 17
Pavillon de la Reine 8
Résidence Lord Byron 1

Information (i) Post Office ⊠

0 .28 Miles
0 .28 Kilometers

311

Charles de Gaulle, Zone Central at Roissy (☎ **800/221-4542** in the U.S. and Canada, or 01-49-19-29-29; fax 01-49-29-00), doubles from 980 to 1,550F ($166.60 to $263.50). International food with French overtones is served at a comfortable first-class restaurant and bar on the hotel's ground floor, and other amenities include 24-hour room service and a swimming pool and sauna.

RIGHT BANK: 1ST ARRONDISSEMENT
Very Expensive

✪ **Le Ritz.** 15 place Vendôme, 75001 Paris. ☎ **800/448-8355** in the U.S. and Canada, or 01-43-16-30-30. Fax 01-43-16-31-78. E-mail: resa@ritzparis.com. 187 units. A/C MINIBAR TV TEL. 3,500–4,300F ($595–$731) double; from 4,700F ($799) suite. AE, DC, MC, V. Parking 220F ($37.40). Métro: Opéra.

Site of Princess Diana's tragic last dinner, Le Ritz is Europe's greatest hotel, an enduring symbol of elegance on one of Paris's most beautiful and historic squares. Rooms are individually decorated with gilt, thick rugs, tapestries, large mirrors, marble fireplaces, double-glazed windows, and brass beds. The spacious marble-clad bathrooms are among the city's most luxurious, filled with deluxe toiletries, hair dryers, scales, a private phone, cords to summon mails and valets, peach robes, full-length and makeup mirrors, and dual basins. (And ever since Edward VII got stuck in a too narrow bathtub with his plump love of the evening, the tubs here have been deep and big.) The Espadon grill room is one of the finest in Paris, and the Ritz Club includes a bar, a salon with a fireplace, a restaurant, and a dance floor. You can order drinks in either the Bar Vendôme or the Bar Hemingway. At ground level is a luxury health club with a pool and massage parlor.

Expensive

Hôtel du Louvre. Place André-Malraux, 75001 Paris. ☎ **01-44-58-38-38** or 800/888-4747 in North America. Fax 01-44-58-38-01. 195 units. A/C MINIBAR TV TEL. 1,650–2,100F ($280.50–$357) double; from 2,800F ($476) suite. AE, DC, MC, V. Ask about midwinter discounts. Parking 100F ($17). Métro: Louvre.

Situated between the Musée du Louvre and the Palais Royal, this hotel is quintessentially Parisian. Many of its smaller bedrooms received a thorough renovation between 1996 and 1998. All with elegant fabrics and upholstery, excellent wool carpeting, double-glazed windows, and traditional wood furniture. Extras include hair dryers, robes, and trouser presses. The newer rooms have shower stalls, but the older rooms are fitted with large tub bathrooms. Le Bar "Defender" is a cozy hideaway, and bistro-style food is served in the French Empire Brasserie du Louvre, with outside terrace tables. Services include 24-hour room service, baby-sitting, laundry, and valet; there's also a business center.

Hôtel Regina. 2 place des Pyramides, 75001 Paris. ☎ **800/448-8355** in the U.S. and Canada or 01-42-60-31-10. Fax 01-40-15-95-16. www.regina/hotel.com. E-mail: reservation@regina/hotel.com. 135 units. A/C MINIBAR TV TEL. 1,350–1,950F ($229.50–$331.50) double; 1,950–3,700F ($331.50–$629) suite. AE, DC, MC, V. Free parking. Métro: Pyramides or Tuileries.

Until a radical renovation upgraded its old-fashioned grandeur in 1995, this hotel slumbered peacefully in a prime location. All that changed when the management added hundreds of thousands of francs' worth of historically appropriate improvements. Bedrooms are richly decorated in such French styles as Directoire, Louis XVI, or art nouveau. Each has a hair dryer, as well as a combination tub and shower. Pluvinel serves a conservative French cuisine in an art deco ambience of deliberate nostalgia.

Inexpensive

✪ **Britannique.** 20 av. Victoria, 75001 Paris. ☎ **01-42-33-74-59.** Fax 01-42-33-82-65. 40 units. MINIBAR TV TEL. 680–950F ($115.60–$161.50) double. AE, DC, MC, V. Parking 120F ($20.40). Métro: Châtelet.

Although the 1st arrondissement has far better hotels, the Britannique is a superior value. The rooms might be small, but they're clean, comfortable, and adequately equipped. Located in the heart of Paris, near Les Halles, the Centre Pompidou, and Notre-Dame, the Britannique was completely renovated in 1998. Bedrooms are cozy and conservatively decorated with traditional furniture. Bathrooms are small but efficiently organized with adequate shelf space and a hair dryer.

RIGHT BANK: 3RD & 4TH ARRONDISSEMENTS

Expensive

✪ **Pavillon de la Reine.** 28 place des Vosges, 75003 Paris. ☎ **01-40-29-19-19.** Fax 01-40-29-19-20. E-mail: pavillon@clus.internet.sr. 55 units. A/C MINIBAR TV TEL. 1,850–2,100F ($314.50–$357) double; 2,000–3,900F ($340–$663) suite or duplex. AE, DC, MC, V. Free parking. Métro: Bastille.

Built in 1986, this neoclassical villa blends into an area that was once home to Victor Hugo. Wing chairs with flame-stitched upholstery combined with iron-banded Spanish antiques create a rustic feel. Each well-furnished and traditional room is different; some are duplexes with sleeping lofts set above cozy salons, but all have a warm decor of weathered beams, reproductions of famous oil paintings, double-glazed windows, and tasteful wool carpets. Bathrooms are generally roomy, with robes and a hair dryer. In the more deluxe rooms, private safes are also provided.

Moderate

Hôtel de Lutèce. 65 rue St-Louis-en-l'Ile, 75004 Paris. ☎ **01-43-26-23-52.** Fax 01-43-29-60-25. 23 units. A/C TV TEL. 850F ($144.50) double; 990F ($168.30) triple. AE, MC, V. Parking nearby 110F ($18.70). Métro: Pont-Marie.

Going into this hotel is much like walking into a country house in Brittany. Each of the individualized rooms is furnished with antiques, and many were renovated in 1998. The hotel is comparable in style and amenities with Deux-Iles (same ownership). Many of the rooms were renovated in 1998 and plush French mattresses were added. Each is traditional and comfortable, with wool carpeting and upholstered chairs. Bathrooms are small but have hair dryers.

Hôtel des Deux-Iles. 59 rue St-Louis-en-l'Ile, 75004 Paris. ☎ **01-43-26-13-35.** Fax 01-43-29-60-25. 17 units. A/C TV TEL. 850F ($144.50) double. AE, MC, V. Parking nearby 130F ($22.10). Métro: Pont-Marie.

This 17th-century hotel is the most appealing on the Ile St-Louis. The collection of bedroom furnishings is eclectic and comfortable, with lots of bamboo and rattan, although none of the pieces is particularly antique-looking. The rooms, which tend to the small side, were renovated during the mid-1990s; their exposed beams lend a sense of old-fashioned charm. Bathrooms are also small, but are tiled and furnished with a hair dryer. In the cellar is a rustic-looking breakfast room whose decor was inspired by a medieval tavern, complete with an open fireplace. Visible from the reception area is a glassed-in courtyard whose landscaping can be admired through glass windows, but not entered. Although the Deux-Iles has nowhere near the style, charm, comfort, and grace of the Pavillon de la Reine, it's a lot cheaper.

✪ **Hôtel St-Louis.** 75 rue St-Louis-en-l'Ile, 75004 Paris. ☎ **01-46-34-04-80.** Fax 01-46-34-02-13. www.paris-hotel.tm.fr. 21 units. TEL. 745–845F ($126.65–$143.65) double. MC, V. Parking nearby 100F ($17). Métro: Pont-Marie.

This small hotel occupies a 17th-century townhouse romantically positioned on Ile St-Louis. Guy Record and his wife Andrée maintain a charming family atmosphere that's increasingly hard to find in Paris. Hôtel St-Louis might not be in the same league as its major rivals, Lutéce and Deux-Iles, but it's an even better value. We prefer the rooms on the fifth floor (no elevator), which have the most atmosphere, views over rooftops, and are decorated with comfortable, attractive old wood furniture. A full renovation in 1998 updated the plumbing.

RIGHT BANK: 8TH ARRONDISSEMENT
Expensive

Hôtel Concorde St-Lazare. 108 rue St-Lazare, 75008 Paris. ☎ **800/888-4747** in the U.S. and Canada, 020/7630-1704 in London, or 01-40-08-44-44. Fax 01-42-93-01-20. 280 units. A/C MINIBAR TV TEL. 1,350–2,300F ($229.50–$391) double; from 3,500F ($595) suite. AE, DC, MC, V. Parking 115F ($19.55). Métro: St-Lazare.

This, the best hotel in the Gare St-Lazare area, sits across from the rail station. In the 1990s, the main lobby, a historic monument, was restored under the supervision of the Concorde chain. The guest rooms and bathrooms underwent a recent multimillion-dollar renovation as well and were elevated to modern standards of comfort, redecorated, and soundproofed. Bedrooms are outfitted in pale-colored marble or tiles, and many, especially those on the lower floors, have high ceilings. Bathrooms have hair dryers. An American bar, Le Golden Black, bears fashion designer Sonia Rykiel's signature decor of black lacquer with touches of gold and amber. Bistrot 108 offers provincial dishes with vintages you can order by the glass.

Moderate

Résidence Lord Byron. 5 rue de Chateaubriand, 75008 Paris. ☎ **01-43-59-89-98.** Fax 01-42-89-46-04. 31 units. MINIBAR TV TEL. 845–945F ($143.65–$160.65) double; 1,295F ($220.15) suite. AE, MC, V. Métro: George-V. RER: Etoile.

Lord Byron, just off the Champs-Élysées on a curving street, might not be as monumentally grand as other hotels of the 8th, but it's a good price performer. No style setter, it's solid and reliable (and maybe a little stuffy). Owner Françoise Benoit has added many personal touches, such as framed prints of butterflies and historic French scenes. The furnishings are good reproductions of antiques or restrained modern pieces. Rooms are very *hotel de charme*, with white walls, plus flowery wallpaper, bedspreads, and curtains. Bathrooms are small with a tub and shower combination (or else only shower) and hair dryers.

LEFT BANK: 5TH ARRONDISSEMENT
Moderate

Grand Hôtel St-Michel. 19 rue Cujas, 75005 Paris. ☎ **01-46-33-33-02.** Fax 01-40-46-96-33. www.123.france.com. E-mail: grand.hotel.st.michel@wanadoo.frweb. 45 units. MINIBAR TV TEL. 890F ($151.30) double. AE, DC, MC, V. Métro: Cluny-La Sorbonne. RER: Luxembourg.

Originally built during the 19th century, this hotel is larger and more businesslike than many of the smaller townhouse-style inns that lie within the same neighborhood. In 1997, the hotel completed a systematic, 2-year renovation. The architectural changes enlarged some rooms and added modern amenities like private safes and minibars; each bedroom was also fitted with a quality French mattress. The bathrooms are as small as ever, but have hair dryers. Fifth-floor rooms (no elevators) have wrought-iron balconies overlooking the surrounding neighborhood, and sixth-floor rooms have interesting views over the surrounding rooftops.

Inexpensive

Hôtel Abbatial St-Germain. 46 bd. St.-Germain, 75005 Paris. ☎ **01-46-34-02-12.** Fax 01-43-25-47-73. E-mail: abbatial@hotellerie.net. 43 units. A/C MINIBAR TV TEL. 680–820F

($115.60–$139.40) double. AE, DC, MC, V. Parking nearby 100F ($17). Métro: Maubert-Mutualité.

Renovations of this hotel have revealed such 17th-century touches as dovecotes and massive oaken beams. In 1996, a radical restoration brought the six stories up to modern, smallish but comfortable standards. Rooms are very much French boudoir in style, with faux-Louis XVI and many well-crafted decorative touches. The towels in the small bathroom are rather thin, but there is a hair dryer. All rooms have double-glazed windows to keep out the intrusive noises of the busy surrounding neighborhood, and many rooms on the fifth and sixth floors enjoy views over the cathedral of Notre-Dame. Fifth-floor rooms have small balconies.

✪ **Hotel des Grandes Écoles.** 75 rue de Cardinal Lemoine, 75005 Paris. ☎ **01-43-26-79-23.** Fax 01-43-25-28-15. 51 units. TEL. 490–670F ($83.30–$113.90) double. MC, V. Parking 100F ($17). Métro: Cardinal-Lemoine, Monge.

Few hotels in the neighborhood offer so much low-key charm at such reasonable prices. This trio of high-ceilinged buildings connected by a sheltered courtyard owes its present look to costly renovations completed in the 1990s. Rooms are artfully old-fashioned with flowered upholsteries, comfortable mattresses, hair dryers, and feminine touches like Laura Ashley-esque ruffles. Many offer views of a bucolic garden whose trellises and flowerbeds evoke the countryside. There are dozens of restaurants in the surrounding rue Mouffetard neighborhood, and weather permitting, breakfast is served in the garden.

LEFT BANK: 6TH ARRONDISSEMENT
Expensive
✪ **L'Hôtel.** 13 rue des Beaux-Arts, 75006 Paris. ☎ **01-44-41-99-00.** Fax 01-43-25-64-81. E-mail: reservation@L-hotel.com. 27 units. A/C MINIBAR TV TEL. 600–2,500F ($102–$425) double; 1,700–3,600F ($289–$612) suite. AE, DC, MC, V. Métro: St-Germain-des-Prés.

L'Hôtel was once a 19th-century fleabag whose major distinction was that Oscar Wilde died here. Throughout the building is an eclectic collection of antiques that includes Louis XV and Louis XVI, Empire, and Directoire pieces. Rooms vary widely in size, style, and price; some are quite small, whereas others are deluxe chambers fit for the occasional movie star guest (Elizabeth Taylor found all the rooms too small for her trunks). Regardless of size, rooms have such extras as decorative fireplaces, private safes, and fabric-covered walls. Clad in marble, the relatively small bathrooms are well equipped with deluxe toiletries, a hair dryer, and a bidet; however, about half of them are tiny tub-less nooks.

Moderate
Clos Médicis Hôtel. 56 rue Monsieur-le-Prince, 75006 Paris. ☎ **01-43-29-10-80.** Fax 01-43-54-26-90. 38 units. A/C MINIBAR TV TEL. 890–990F ($151.30–$168.30) double; 1,200F ($204) duplex suite. AE, DC, MC, V. Métro: Odéon. RER: Luxembourg.

One of this hotel's major advantages is its location adjacent to the Luxembourg Gardens in the heart of the Latin Quarter. You'll find a verdant garden with lattices and exposed stone walls, a lobby with modern spotlights and simple furniture, and a multilingual staff. The warmly colored rooms are uncomplicated and comfortable. Bathrooms are small but have hair dryers. Breakfast is the only meal served.

Hôtel de Fleurie. 32–34 rue Grégoire-de-Tours, 75006 Paris. ☎ **01-53-73-70-00.** Fax 01-53-73-70-20. E-mail: bonjour@hotel-de-fleurie.tm.fr. 29 units. A/C MINIBAR TV TEL. 900–1,200F ($153–$204) double. Small children stay free in parents' room. AE, DC, MC, V. Métro: Odéon.

Just off boulevard St-Germain on a colorful little street, the Fleurie is one of the best of the "new" old hotels. Restored to its former glory in 1988, the facade is studded with statuary spotlit by night, recapturing its 17th-century elegance. The stone walls have been exposed in the reception salon. A 1997 renovation upgraded all the beds and restored the lobby. An elevator takes you to the well-furnished rooms, which, although generally small, have an 18th-century aura with a mixture of antiques and traditional reproductions, wool carpeting, trouser presses, soft lighting, and private safes. Clad in marble, the bathrooms are surprisingly luxurious in a hotel of this rating, and have both hair dryers and deluxe toiletries. Most rooms have a tub and shower combination, but seven come only with a shower. A spiral staircase leads down to the breakfast room.

Libertel Quartier Latin. 9 rue des Ecoles, 75006 Paris. ☎ **800/949-7562,** or 01-44-27-06-45. Fax 01-43-25-36-70. 29 units. MINIBAR TV TEL. 975–1,050F ($165.75–$178.50) double. 1,050–1,200F ($178.50–$204) suites. Nearby parking 100F ($17) per night. AE, DC, MC, V. Métro: Jussieu.

This century-old, six-story building in a neighborhood crowded with *quartier latin* color received a radical upgrade in 1997 that transformed the bedrooms into testimonials to French literature. Expect a hardworking and articulate staff and small, cozy bedrooms where traditional wood furniture is offset with framed portraits of authors or verses of poetry. Bathrooms are small but efficiently organized with adequate shelf space and a hair dryer. Breakfast is the only meal served, but many restaurants lie within the surrounding neighborhood.

Inexpensive

Aviatic. 105 rue de Vaugirard, 75006 Paris. ☎ **01-53-63-25-50.** Fax 01-53-63-25-55. E-mail: welcome@aviatic.fr. 43 units. A/C MINIBAR TV TEL. 680–980F ($115.60–$166.60) double. AE, DC, MC, V. Parking 120F ($20.40). Métro: Montparnasse-Bienvenue.

The Aviatic is a bit of old Paris—it's been a family-run hotel of character and elegance for a century. The reception lounge, with its marble columns, brass chandeliers, antiques, and petit salon, provides an attractive traditional setting. There's also a modest inner courtyard. Although it doesn't have the decorative style and flair of some hotels in the 6th, it offers good comfort and a warm ambience. The rather small bedrooms were renovated in stages throughout the '90s; each has a safe and a rejuvenated bathroom with a hair dryer.

LEFT BANK: 7TH ARRONDISSEMENT

Moderate

Hôtel de l'Académie. 32 rue des Sts-Peres, 75007 Paris. ☎ **01-45-49-80-00.** Fax 01-45-49-80-10. E-mail: aaacademie@aol.com. 34 units. A/C MINIBAR TV TEL. 790–890F ($134.30–$151.30) double; 1,290F ($219.30) junior suite. AE, DC, MC, V. Parking 150F ($25.50). Métro: St-Germain-des-Prés.

The exterior walls and old ceiling beams are all that remain of this 17th-century residence. In 1998, the bedrooms were renovated with strict allegiance to the building's original ceiling beams and exposed stone walls, but with a stylish forest green and bordeaux-colored overlay of paint, fabrics, and accessories inspired by the late 19th-century style known as Napoléon III. Bathrooms are attractive but functional, often trimmed in marble, and have hair dryers. Views from the upper floors sweep out over the historic buildings of the surrounding neighborhood.

Inexpensive

✪ **Hôtel du Quai-Voltaire.** 19 quai Voltaire, 75007 Paris. ☎ **01-42-61-50-91.** Fax 01-42-61-62-26. www.hotelduquaivoltaire.com. 32 units. TV TEL. 650–700F ($110.50–$119) double; 850F ($144.50) triple. AE, DC, MC, V. Parking 110F ($18.70) nearby. Métro: Palais-Royal.

Built in the 1600s as an abbey, then transformed into a hotel in 1856, Quai-Voltaire is best known for its illustrious guests, who have included Wilde, Baudelaire, and Wagner. Twenty-eight of the 32 rooms have views over the Seine. In 1998, double-glazed windows were added to each of the rooms to block out traffic noise, and the carpeting was upgraded and improved. Bedrooms tend to be small, and bathrooms are a bit cramped. You can have drinks in the bar or the small salon, and simple meals can be prepared for those who prefer to eat in.

A GAY HOTEL

Hôtel Central. 33 rue Vieille-du-Temple, 75004 Paris. ☎ **01-48-87-99-33.** Fax 01-42-77-06-27. 7 units (1 with bathroom). TEL. 535F ($90.95) double with or without bathroom. MC, V. Métro: Hôtel-de-Ville.

This is the most visible gay hotel in Paris. The rooms are on the second, third, and fourth floors of this 18th-century building, which contains the Marais's major gay bar, Le Bar Central (see below). If you arrive between 8am and 4pm, you'll find a registration staff one floor above street level; if you arrive at any other time, you'll have to retrieve your key and register at the street-level bar. Accessible via an antique wooden staircase that's as old as the building itself, bedrooms are simple, serviceable, and outfitted with charm and good taste.

WHERE TO DINE
RIGHT BANK: 1ST ARRONDISSEMENT
Very Expensive

✪ **Le Grand Véfour.** 17 rue de Beaujolais, 1er. ☎ **01-42-96-56-27.** Reservations required. Main courses 290–340F ($49.30–$57.80); set-price lunch 345–750F ($58.65–$127.50); set-price dinner 780F ($132.60). AE, DC, MC, V. Mon–Fri 12:30–2:15pm and 7:30–10:15pm. Métro: Louvre. FRENCH.

Dining here is a great gastronomic experience. Specialties, served on Limoges china, include lobster and noisettes of lamb with star anise. An exciting new dish on a menu of delightful surprises is homemade ravioli stuffed with foie gras and served with an emulsion of truffle-flavored crème fraîche. Desserts are often grand, like the gourmandises au chocolat, a richness of chocolate served with chocolate sorbet.

Moderate

Chez Vong. 10 rue de la Grande-Truanderie, 1er. Reservations recommended. Main courses 100–185F ($17–$31.45). AE, DC, MC, V. Mon–Sat noon–2:30pm and 7pm–midnight. Métro: Étienne-Marcel. CANTONESE.

This trend-setter, full of folk from the worlds of entertainment and the arts, is the kind of place you head when you're sick of grand French cuisine and grander culinary pretensions. The decor is a soothing mixture of green and browns, steeped in a Chinese colonial ambience. Menu items include shrimps and scallops served with any degree of spiciness you specify, including a superheated version with garlic and red peppers; "joyous beef" that mingles sliced filet with pepper sauce; chicken in puff pastry with ginger; and a tempting array of fresh fish dishes.

Le Fumoir. 6 rue de l'Amiral Coligny, 1er. ☎ **01-42-92-00-24.** Reservations recommended. Main courses 105–120F ($17.85–$20.40). AE, DC, MC, V. Daily for salads, pastries, and snacks 11am–1am; complete menu daily noon–3pm and 7–11:30pm. AE, DC, MC, V. Métro: Louvre. INTERNATIONAL.

Stylish and breezy, and set in an antique building a few steps from the Louvre, this is an upscale brasserie with ample options for watching hipster denizens of Paris's arts scene come and go. Currently, it's the most fashionable place to be seen eating or drinking in Paris today. In a high-ceilinged ambience of warm but somber browns and indirect lighting, you can order salads, pastries, and drinks during the off-hours noted above, and platters of more substantial food during conventional meal times. Examples include filets of codfish with onions and herbs; sliced rack of veal simmered in its own juices with tarragon; calves' liver with onions; a combination platter of lamb chops with grilled tuna steak; and herring in a mustard-flavored cream sauce.

Inexpensive

✪ **Lescure.** 7 rue de Mondovi, 1er. ☎ **01-42-60-18-91.** Reservations not accepted. Main courses 40–80F ($6.80–$13.60); set-price 4–course menu 100F ($17). MC, V. Mon–Fri noon–2:15pm and 7–10:15pm. Closed 2 weeks in Aug. Métro: Concorde. FRENCH.

This mini-bistro is a major discovery because reasonably priced restaurants near place de la Concorde are difficult to find. The tables on the sidewalk are tiny and there isn't much room inside, but what this place does have is rustic charm. The kitchen is wide-open, and the aroma of drying bay leaves, salami, and garlic hanging from the ceiling fills the room. Don't expect anything overly thrilling, just hearty fare. House specialties include *confit de canard* (duckling) and salmon in green sauce. A favorite dessert is one of the chef's fruit tarts.

RIGHT BANK: 3RD ARRONDISSEMENT

Moderate

L'Ambassade d'Auvergne. 22 rue de Grenier St-Lazare, 3e. ☎ **01-42-72-31-22.** Reservations recommended. Main courses 88–120F ($14.95–$20.40); set-price menu 170F ($28.90). MC, V. Daily noon–2pm and 7:30–11pm. Métro: Rambuteau. FRENCH.

In an obscure district, this rustic tavern serves food derivative of the rib-sticking, hearty, savory cuisine associated with Auvergne. You enter through a busy bar, with heavy oak beams and hanging hams; rough wheat bread is stacked in baskets, and rush-seated ladderback chairs are placed at tables covered with bright cloths, mills to grind your own salt and pepper, and a jug of mustard. Tried-and-true favorites include a parmentier of blood sausage with fried apples; pork sausages served with *aligot* (mashed potatoes with garlic and Cantal cheese); a *potée d'Auvergne* (stewed pork with cabbage, carrots, and white beans); and filet of salmon *à l'Auvergnate*, that's prepared with lard, bacon, garlic, and potatoes.

RIGHT BANK: 4TH ARRONDISSEMENT

Very Expensive

✪ **L'Ambroisie.** 9 place des Vosges, 4e. ☎ **01-42-78-51-45.** Reservations required. Main courses 280–530F ($47.60–$90.10). AE, V. Tues–Sat noon–1:30pm and 8–9:30pm. Métro: St-Paul. FRENCH.

Bernard Pacaud is one of the most talented chefs in Paris, and his restaurant occupies an early 17th-century townhouse built for the duc de Luynes. In summer there's outdoor seating. The dishes change seasonally but may include crayfish tails with sesame seeds and curry sauce; filet of turbot braised with celery and celeriac, served with a julienne of black truffles; fricassée of lobster; and one of our favorites, Bresse chicken roasted with black truffles and truffled vegetables.

Inexpensive

Brasserie de l'Ile St-Louis. 55 quai de Bourbon, 4e. ☎ **01-43-54-02-59.** Reservations recommended. Main courses 65–120F ($11.05–$20.40). MC, V. Thurs–Tues noon–12:30am. Métro: Pont-Marie. FRENCH/ALSATIAN.

This retro-chic brasserie is the perfect place for an impromptu rendezvous. Little about the establishment's patina and paneled decor has changed since it was founded in the 1880s, a fact that adds an allure not equaled in many more modern nearby competitors. Menu items are conservative, flavorful, and well prepared; don't expect cutting-edge culinary fads and trends. Examples include an always-popular version of Alsatian sauerkraut, cassoulet in the old-fashioned style of Toulouse; stingray with a nut and butter sauce; calves' liver; and a succulent version of *jarret* of pork with a warm apple marmalade.

RIGHT BANK: 8TH ARRONDISSEMENT
Expensive

✪ **L'Astor.** In the Hotel Astor, 11 rue d'Astorg, 8e. ☎ **01-53-05-05-20.** Reservations recommended. Main courses 110–240F ($18.70–$40.80); set-price menus 298–520F ($50.65–$88.40). AE, DC, MC, V. Mon–Fri noon–2pm and 7:30–10pm. Métro: St-Augustin. FRENCH.

When culinary guru Joël Robuchon retired from his citadel on avenue Raymond Poincaré (now under the helm of Alain Ducasse; see the next listing), he started dropping in here two or three times a week as a "culinary consultant." L'Astor's current chef is the well-respected Eric Lecerf, who has created his own specialties, such as roasted and braised rack of lamb and a galette of scallops with sea urchins, but those dishes invented by and forever associated with Robuchon are still on the menu. They include truffle tart, Bresse chicken with truffles and macaroni, and a *gelée* of caviar with cauliflower cream sauce.

Spoon Food & Wine. In the Marignan-Élysée Hotel, 14 rue Marignan, 8e. ☎ **01-40-76-34-44.** Reservations required. Appetizers, main courses, vegetable side dishes each 65–180F ($11.05–$30.60). Mon–Fri noon–2:30pm and 7–11:30pm. AE, DC, MC, V. Metro: Franklin-D-Roosevelt. INTERNATIONAL.

Alain Ducasse's newest restaurant has been both praised and condemned by Parisian food critics. Surreal and a bit absurd, the hypermodern, claustrophobic dining room evokes Paris and California. The cuisine roams the world; there are American classics such as macaroni and cheese (rather bland) and barbecued ribs, as well as dishes from Italy, Latin America, or Asia. Sometimes the waitstaff doesn't know the national origin of a dish—*youm loumg,* squid and shellfish in a spicy broth, for example—and some dishes are more successful than others (try the steamed lobster with mango chutney, a real winner). You have great leeway in creating your own meal; for a "vegetable garden," you can mix and match 15 ingredients, including iceberg lettuce, and for the one basic pasta, you have a selection of five different sauces.

Moderate

Androuët. 6 rue Arsene Houssaye, 8e. ☎ **01-42-89-95-00.** Reservations required. Main courses 95–280F ($16.15–$47.60); set-price menus 140–230F ($23.80–$39.10) at lunch, 250–300F ($42.50–$51) at dinner; *dégustation de fromages* 300F ($51). AE, DC, MC, V. Mon–Fri noon–2:30pm and Mon–Sat 7:30–11pm. Métro: Etoile. FRENCH.

Androuët isn't merely chic—it's an institution whose trademark involves combining top-notch, traditional French ingredients with cheeses and cheese sauces from throughout the country. Choices include noisettes of lamb with a Saint-Marcellin sauce (a goat cheese from France's southwest); lobster with Roquefort sauce; sea bass with a soft and sweet *gratte paille* from the Ile de France, and filet steak with Roquefort sauce, flambéed with Calvados. Dishes, if you prefer, can be prepared without cheese as well.

RIGHT BANK: 9TH & 10TH ARRONDISSEMENTS
Moderate

✪ **Au Petit Riche.** 25, rue Le Peletier, 9e. ☎ **01-47-70-68-68.** Reservations recommended. Main courses 92–130F ($15.65–$22.10); set-price lunches 165F ($28.05); set-price dinner 140–180F ($23.80–$30.60). AE, MC, V. Mon–Sat noon–2:15pm and 7pm–midnight. Métro: Le Peletier or Richelieu-Drouot. LOIRE VALLEY (ANJOU).

This bistro serves up simple well-prepared bistro food and a sense of nostalgia. You'll be ushered to one of five different "compartments," each of which was crafted for maximum intimacy, with red velour banquettes, ceilings painted with allegorical themes, and accents of brass and frosted glass. The wine list favors Loire Valley vintages that go well with such dishes as *rillettes* and *rillons* (potted fish or meat, especially pork) in an aspic of Vouvray wine; a platter of poached fish with a buttery white wine sauce; seasonal game dishes; and duck breast with green peppercorns.

Brasserie Flo. 7 cour des Petites-Ecuries, 10e. ☎ **01-47-70-13-59.** Reservations recommended. Main courses 90–168F ($15.30–$28.55); set-price lunch 132F ($22.45); set-price dinner 179F ($30.45); set-price late-night supper (after 10pm) 132F ($22.45). AE, DC, MC, V. Daily noon–3:30pm and 7pm–1:30am. Métro: Château-d'Eau or Strasbourg-St-Denis. ALSATIAN.

This restaurant is in a remote area and a bit hard to find, but once you arrive (after walking through passageway after passageway), you'll see that fin-de-siècle Paris lives on. The restaurant was established in 1860 and has changed its decor very little since. The house specialty is *la formidable choucroute* (a heaping mound of sauerkraut surrounded by boiled ham, bacon, and sausage) for two. It's bountiful in the best tradition of Alsace. The onion soup and sole meunière are always good, as is the warm foie gras and guinea hen with lentils. Look for the *plats du jour* (plates of the day), ranging from roast pigeon to fricassée of veal with sorrel.

RIGHT BANK: 11TH ARRONDISSEMENT
Moderate

Blue Elephant. 43 rue de la Roquette, 11e. ☎ **01-47-00-42-00.** Reservations recommended. Main courses 85–160F ($14.45–$27.20); set-price lunches 150F ($25.50; Mon–Fri only) and 275F ($46.75); set-price dinners 275F ($46.75). AE, DC, MC, V. Sun–Fri noon–2:30pm; Mon–Sat 7pm–midnight; Sun 7–11pm. Métro: Bastille. THAI.

This is the Paris branch of an international chain of Thai restaurants that prides themselves on having the most glamorous, stylish, and best Thai restaurant in whatever city they happen to be in. In this version near the Bastille, the decor is an artful version of the jungles of southeast Asia, with a labyrinth of waterfalls, replicas of garden paths, potted plants, and bridges. Menu items, infused with the lemongrass, coconut milk, coriander, chili, and basil that distinguish Thai cooking, are savory, spicy, and full of deep, intense flavors. Try the salad made with a Thai fruit that's larger and more tart than a grapefruit, a *pomelo*, studded with shrimp and herbs; the salmon soufflé served in banana leaves; or the chicken in green curry sauce.

16TH ARRONDISSEMENT
Very Expensive

✪ **Alain Ducasse.** 59 av. Raymond Poincaré, 16e. ☎ **01-47-27-12-27.** Reservations 2 months in advance. Main courses 350–500F ($59.50–$85); set lunch 480F ($81.60); set dinner 920–1,490F ($156.40–$253.30). AE, DC, MC, V. Mon–Fri 12:30–2pm and 7:30–10pm. Métro: Trocadéro. FRENCH/MEDITERRANEAN.

The celebrated Ducasse has taken Paris by storm since taking over the reins from legendary Joël Robuchon (now semi-retired). This six-star Michelin chef divides his time between Paris and Monaco. In the jaded culinary landscape of Paris, Ducasse spends hours trying to inject new culinary ideas into the restaurant scene. Food has been rarefied to the point where it's so experimental it appears almost hallucinogenic. Examples from the rapidly changing menus include half-dried pasta, creamed and studded with truffles, enriched with sweetbreads and the crest and kidneys of a rooster, slices of crispy lard served with caramelized potatoes, pig's head salad, bitter herbs, and truffles; monkfish with endive and essence of truffles; and chilled crayfish served in a reduction of its own juices and caviar. The food remains sober in presentation, true, precise, and authentic in its flavor. On the ground floor of the restored, four-story mansion is a bar stocked with rare brandies and fine cigars.

LEFT BANK: 5TH ARRONDISSEMENT
Very Expensive
La Tour d'Argent. 15–17 quai de la Tournelle, 5e. ☎ **01-43-54-23-31.** Reservations required. Main courses 250–400F ($42.50–$68); set-price lunch 350F ($59.50). AE, DC, MC, V. Tues–Sun noon–2:30pm and 7:30–10pm. Métro: Maubert-Mutualité or Pont-Marie. FRENCH.

From La Tour d'Argent, a national institution, the view over the Seine and the apse of Notre-Dame is panoramic. Although this penthouse restaurant's long-established reputation as "the best" in Paris has long since faded, dining at this temple of gastronomy remains an unsurpassed theatrical event. The restaurant became famous when it was owned by Frédéric Delair, who began issuing certificates to diners who ordered the house specialty, pressed duck (*caneton*)—it's sensational. A new, lighter dish that is divinely refined is asparagus and lobster in puff pastry. You might also try filet of sole cardinal with a mousse of pike-perch and a crayfish sauce or filet Tour d'Argent with a chive sauce and a slice of warm foie gras resting atop the perfect piece of filet of beef.

Inexpensive
Al Dar. 8 rue Frédéric Sauton, 5e. ☎ **01-43-25-17-15.** Reservations recommended. Main courses 85–92F ($14.45–$15.65). AE, DC, MC, V. Daily noon–midnight. Métro: Maubert-Mutualité. LEBANESE.

This well-respected restaurant works hard to commercialize Lebanon's savory cuisine. In a room lined with photographs of Lebanese architecture and scenery, you can enjoy such dishes as *tabouli*, a refreshing combination of finely chopped parsley, mint, bulgur, tomatoes, onions, lemon juice, olive oil, and salt; baba ganoush (pulverized and seasoned eggplant); and hummus. Any of them can be followed with roasted chicken; minced lamb prepared with mint, cumin, and Mediterranean herbs; or several kinds of tagines and couscous.

Brasserie Balzar. 49 rue des Ecoles, 5e. ☎ **01-43-54-13-67.** Reservations required. Main courses 78–124F ($13.25–$21.10). AE, MC, V. Daily noon–12:30am. Métro: Cluny/La Sorbonne. FRENCH.

Opened in 1898, this brasserie is a bit battered yet cheerful, with some of the friendliest waiters in Paris. It enjoys an increasing reputation as a hip and desirable brasserie with a sense of retro charm. The menu makes almost no concessions to nouvelle cuisine and includes *steak au poivre* (pepper steak), sauerkraut garnished with ham and sausage, pigs' feet, and calves' liver. The food is decently prepared, and who wants to come up with anything new when what has been served for 40 years is just fine?

✪ La Petite Hostellerie. 35 rue de la Harpe (just east of bd. St-Michel), 5e. ☎ **01-43-54-47-12.** All main courses 59F ($10.05); set-price menus 59–89F ($10.05–$15.15). AE, DC, MC, V. Mon–Sat noon–2pm and 6:30–10:45pm. Métro: St-Michel or Cluny/La Sorbonne. FRENCH.

This place has two dining rooms: a usually crowded ground-floor one and a larger (seating 100) upstairs one with attractive 18th-century woodwork. People come for the cozy ambience and decor, decent French country cooking, polite service, and excellent prices. The set-price menu might feature favorites like *coq au vin* (chicken cooked in wine), *canard* (duckling) *à l'orange*, or *entrecôte à la moutarde* (steak with mustard sauce). Start with onion soup or stuffed mussels and finish with cheese or salad and peach Melba or apple tart. The menu and everything else remains virtually unchanged year after year.

LEFT BANK: 6TH ARRONDISSEMENT
Expensive

Jacques Cagna. 14 rue des Grands-Augustins, 6e. ☎ **01-43-26-49-39.** Reservations required. Main courses 180–350F ($30.60–$59.50); set-price menu 270F ($45.90) at lunch, 470F ($79.90) at dinner. AE, DC, MC, V. Tues–Fri noon–2pm and Mon–Sat 7:30–10:30pm. Closed 3 weeks in Aug. Métro: St-Michel. FRENCH.

Both the food and the clientele in this 17th-century townhouse are among the grandest in Paris. Menu items are flavorful and creative, but without the sometimes bizarre experimentation that's become the hallmark of such competitors as Alain Ducasse. Examples include prawns roasted in a lobster sauce with lemon, and snails "surprise-style à la Jacques Cagna" whereby they're removed from their shells and served with butter in a small roasted potato. A particular favorite of ours involves a chicken from Houdan (a town in the Ile de France known for the excellence of its poultry) that's served as a main course in two separate servings: The first part involves the roasted breast *demi-deuil*, in which truffles have stained the white meat dark. The second combines the roasted thigh with garden vegetables.

Moderate

Alcazar Bar & Restaurant. 62 rue Mazarine, 6e. ☎ **01-53-10-19-99.** Reservations recommended. Set-price lunches 140–180F ($23.80–$30.60); main courses 90–190F ($15.30–$32.30). AE, DC, MC, V. Daily noon–5:30pm and 7pm–1am. Métro: Odéon. FRENCH.

One of Paris' newest high-profile, high-style *brasseries de luxe* is this artfully high-tech establishment. It features an all-white, futuristic decor in a large, street-level dining room; a busy and hyper-stylish bar one floor above street level; and a menu that stresses the establishment's role as an upscale bistro and brasserie. Especially good dishes include grilled entrecôte with béarnaise sauce and fried potatoes; Charolais duckling with honey and spices; shashimi and sushi with lime; filet of monkfish with saffron in puff pastry; and a comprehensive collection of shellfish and oysters from the waters of Brittany. Wines are stylish and diverse, and the clientele includes lots of trend-setters wearing lots of black.

Inexpensive

Crèmerie-Restaurant Polidor. 41 rue Monsieur-le-Prince, 6e. ☎ **01-43-26-95-34.** Reservations not accepted. Main courses 60–75F ($10.20–$12.75); set-price lunch (Mon–Fri) 55–100F ($9.35–$17); set-price dinner 100F ($17). No credit cards. Mon–Sat noon–2:30pm and 7pm–12:30am; Sun noon–2:30pm and 7–11pm. Métro: Odéon. FRENCH.

Frequented by students and artists, this is one of the Left Bank's most established literary bistros, and has changed little since opening in 1930. Lace curtains and brass hat racks, drawers in the back where repeat customers lock up their cloth napkins, and clay water pitchers add to the old-fashioned atmosphere. Food is traditional: pumpkin soup, snails from Burgundy, veal in white sauce, confit of duckling, and a supremely old-fashioned holdover from the France of yesterday—roasted guinea fowl with cabbage and ham. The "*crèmerie*" of its name refers to its specialty, frosted crème desserts.

LEFT BANK: 7TH ARRONDISSEMENT
Moderate

La Petite Chaise. 36–38 rue de Grenelle, 7e. ☎ **01-42-22-13-35.** Reservations required. Set-price menus 125–190F ($21.25–$32.30). AE, MC, V. Daily noon–2pm and 7–11pm. Métro: Sèvres-Babylone. FRENCH.

This is Paris's oldest restaurant, established by the baron de la Chaise in 1680. The baron, according to the restaurant's lore, maintained a series of upstairs rooms for afternoon dalliances. The "Little Chair" invites you into a very Parisian world of cramped but attractive tables, old wood paneling, and ornate wall sconces. The only option is a cost-conscious four-course set menu with a large choice of dishes. Choices might include marinated salmon with anise and a creamy mustard sauce, a selection of fresh fish and scallops in saffron sauce with pink potatoes, a salad of leeks and country ham with red-beet vinaigrette, a mignon of pork with figs and honey, and a special dessert of roasted figs with pistachios and vanilla ice cream.

Inexpensive

Chez L'Ami Jean. 27 rue Malar, 7e. ☎ **01-47-05-86-89.** Reservations recommended. Main courses 75–90F ($12.75–$15.30). MC, V. Mon–Sat noon–3pm and 7–10:30pm. Métro: Invalides. BASQUE/SOUTHWESTERN FRENCH.

Ardent fans claim that this is the most authentic and uncompromising Basque restaurant on the Left Bank. You'll dine amid a decor that's as close to an authentic Basque *auberge* (inn) as any other in Paris, with wood panels, sports memorabilia, and red and white woven tablecloths like the ones sold in Bayonne. Menu items include cured Bayonne ham; earthy and herb-laden vegetable soups in the style of Béarn; marinated anchovies and fresh duck liver; confit de canard (duckling); and a succulent omelette (*piperade basque*) laden with peppers, tomatoes, and onions.

GAY RESTAURANTS

Au Rendezvous des Camionneurs. 72 quai des Orfèvres, 1er. ☎ **01-43-54-88-74.** Reservations recommended Sat–Sun. All main courses 98F ($16.65); set-price menu 88–138F ($14.95–$23.45) at lunch, 98–138F ($16.65–$23.45) at dinner. AE, MC, V. Daily noon–2:30pm and 7–11:30pm (last order). Métro: Pont-Neuf. FRENCH.

Set on the Ile de la Cité, adjacent to the Pont-Neuf, this restaurant has the look, feel, and service of a traditional Parisian bistro. It was founded in 1870, and many of the original mirrors and banquettes remain. The food, traditional bistro fare, is reasonably priced and well prepared: terrine of rabbit, *crottin de chavignol* (a traditional appetizer layered with goat's cheese), snails with garlic cream sauce, a ragôut of mussels and shrimp with a fondée of leeks, blanquette de veau (veal in white sauce), and filet mignon. The majority of the regular dinner crowd is gay. This place has an enduring popularity in spite of the rather rude staff.

L'Amazonial. 3 rue Ste-Opportune, 1er. ☎ **01-42-33-53-13.** Reservations recommended. Main courses 65–120F ($11.05–$20.40); set-price menus 85–129F ($14.45–$21.95). AE, MC, V. Daily noon–3pm and 7pm–1am (last order). Métro: Châtelet. SOUTH AMERICAN/FRENCH.

This is one of Paris's busiest and most popular gay restaurants, with an estimated 70% gay clientele (male and female), and a staff that's not in the least reluctant to give off a negative attitude if they happen to be in a bad mood. The decor was inspired by the jungles of South America, with frequent festive overlays based on whatever holiday is timely. Eclectically conceived menu items include a gratin of crayfish tails with Antillean spices; foie gras, smoked salmon, and goat cheese in puff pastry with fried apples and acacia honey; a gigot of monkfish; and sautéed ostrich steak with balsamic vinegar and exotic mushrooms.

CAFES

Brasserie Lipp, 151 bd. St-Germain, 6e (☎ **01-45-48-53-91;** Métro: St-Germain-des-Prés), is known as the "rendezvous for *le tout Paris*." There's an upstairs dining room, but it's more fashionable to sit in the back room. It's open daily from 9am to 1am, although restaurant service is available only from noon to 1am.

Across from the Centre Pompidou, the avant-garde **Café Beaubourg,** 100 rue St-Martin, 4e (☎ **01-48-87-63-96;** Métro: Rambuteau or Hôtel-de-Ville), boasts a minimalist decor by architect Christian de Portzamparc. In summer, tables are set on the terrace, providing a panoramic view of the neighborhood. Open Sunday through Thursday from 8am to 1am and Friday and Saturday from 8am to 2am.

Le Café de la Musique, 212 ave. Jean-Jaurès, 19e (☎ **01-48-03-15-91;** Métro: Porte-de-Pantin), lies within the Cité de la Musique—one of the grandest of Mitterand's *grands travaux.* The site guarantees the presence of a clientele that's passionately devoted to music. Consequently, the recorded sounds that play in the background here are more diverse and more eclectic than in any other cafe in Paris. Its red and green velour setting has a theatricality evocative of a modern opera house (it was designed by decorating superstars Elizabeth and Christian de Portzamparc). You can order *plats du jour.* Views from the windows overlook the lions of the modern fountains in the nearby place de la Fontaine. Open daily from 8am to 2am. There's live jazz every Wednesday between 10pm and 1am.

At **La Coupole,** 102 bd. Montparnasse, 14e (☎ **01-43-20-14-20;** Métro: Vavin), the clientele ranges from artists' models to young men dressed like Rasputin. The dining room looks like a rail station but serves surprisingly good food. Open daily 7:30am to 2am.

The legendary **Deux Magots,** 6 place St-Germain-des-Prés, 6e (☎ **01-45-48-55-25;** Métro: St-Germain-des-Prés), is still the hangout for sophisticated neighborhood residents and is a tourist favorite in summer. Inside are two large oriental statues that give the cafe its name. Open daily 7:30am to 1:30am.

Fouquet's, 99 av. des Champs-Élysées, 8e (☎ **01-47-23-70-60;** Métro: George-V), is the premier cafe on the Champs-Élysées. The outside tables are separated from the sidewalk by a barricade of potted flowers. Throughout, you'll find a decor of leather banquettes, rattan furniture, and a sense of Champs-Élysées bustle. Fouquet's street level is open as a cafe that serves platters of food, salads, tea, omelets, ice cream, and light platters of food every day from 9am till 2am. One floor above street level is a comfortable and relatively formal restaurant that's open daily from noon to 3pm and from 7pm till 1am.

SEEING THE SIGHTS IN THE CITY OF LIGHT

The best way to discover Paris is on foot. Walk along the grand avenue des Champs-Élysées, tour the quays of the Seine, wander around Ile de la Cité and Ile St-Louis, browse through the countless shops and stalls, and wander through the famous squares and parks. Each turn will open a new vista.

SIGHTSEEING SUGGESTIONS FOR FIRST-TIME VISITORS

If you really want to see a lot of sights in a short time, consider taking a 2-hour Cityrama bus tour (see "Organized Tours," below).

If You Have 1 Day   Get up early and find a little cafe for a typical Parisian breakfast of coffee and croissants. If you're a museum and monument junkie, you already know that the two most popular museums are the **Louvre** and the **Musée d'Orsay,** and the three most enduring monuments are the **Eiffel Tower,** the **Arc de Triomphe,** and **Notre-Dame** (which you can save for later in the day). If it's a toss-up between the

Louvre and the d'Orsay, we'd make it the Louvre if you're a first-timer; if it's a toss-up between monuments, we'd make it the Eiffel Tower, for the panoramic view of the city. If you feel your day is too short to visit museums, then spend your time strolling—the streets of Paris are live theater. The most elegant place for a walk in Paris is **Ile St-Louis,** filled with 17th-century mansions. On the **Left Bank,** wander St-Germain-des-Prés or the area around place St-Michel, the heart of the student quarter. As the sun sets over Paris, head for **Notre-Dame,** which stands majestically along the banks of the Seine, and watch the shadows fall over Paris and the lights come on for the night.

If You Have 2 Days   If you explored the Left Bank on your first day, spend your second day taking in the glories of the Right Bank. Begin at the **Arc de Triomphe** and stroll down the grand **Champs-Élysées,** the main boulevard of Paris, until you reach the Egyptian obelisk at the **place de la Concorde.** The place de la Concorde—where some of France's most notable figures met the guillotine—affords terrific views of the **Madeleine,** the **Palais Bourbon,** the Arc de Triomphe, and the Louvre. After all this walking, we'd suggest a rest stop in the **Jardin de Tuileries,** or a long lunch in a Right Bank bistro. After exploring the heart of elegant, monumental Paris, why not go for a walk on the seedy side? Our favorite is a stroll along rue des Rosiers in the **Marais,** a narrow street that's the heart of the Jewish community. After a rest back at your hotel, follow Hemingway's footsteps and head down to **Montparnasse** for a lively dinner.

If You Have 3 Days   This is the day to follow your special interests. Monet fans should head for the **Musée Marmottan-Claude Monet.** Or perhaps you'd rather wander around the sculpture garden of the **Musée National Auguste-Rodin.** If it's the **Picasso Museum** you select, you can use part of the morning to explore some of the art galleries of the Marais. At midday head for the oldest and most charming square of Paris, **place des Vosges,** for lunch. Reserve the afternoon for the **Ile-de-la-Cité,** where you can revisit Notre-Dame and see the **Conciergerie,** where Marie Antoinette and others were held prisoner before beheading, and the **Sainte-Chapelle** in the Palais de Justice with its stunning stained glass. For dinner, we suggest a bistro in Le Marais.

If You Have 4 or 5 Days   On your fourth day, go on your own or take an organized tour to **Versailles.** Then head back to the city for dinner and an evening stroll in the **Latin Quarter.** Some of the livelier streets for wandering include the rue de la Huchette and rue Monsieur-le-Prince.

On your fifth day, devote at least a morning to **Montmartre,** the former artists' community perched on top of the highest of Paris's seven hills. Visit the **Basilica of Sacré-Coeur,** for the view if nothing else.

THE TOP MUSEUMS

✪ **Musée du Louvre.** Pyramid, 1er. ☎ **01-40-20-53-17,** or 01-40-20-51-51 for recorded information; advance credit card sales 01-49-87-54-54. Admission 45F ($7.65) before 3pm, 26F ($4.40) after 3pm and all day Sun; free for children 17 and under. Free first Sun of every month. Mon and Wed 9am–9:45pm (Mon, short tour only); Thurs–Sun 9am–6pm. 90-minute English-language tours leave Mon and Wed–Sat at various times for 17F ($2.90), adults and children alike. Métro: Palais-Royal-Musée-du-Louvre.

More Museum Tips

Museums require that you check shopping bags and book bags, and sometimes those lines can be longer than ticket and admission lines. Visitors who value their time should leave their bags behind or do shopping afterward. Ask if a museum has more than one coat line; if so, avoid the main one and go to the less frequented ones.

The Louvre is the world's largest palace and largest and greatest museum. You have no choice but to miss certain masterpieces since you won't have the time or stamina to see everything—the Louvre's collection is truly staggering. People on one of those "Paris-in-a-day" tours try to break track records to stand with the crowds and see the two most famous ladies here: the *Mona Lisa* and the *Venus de Milo.* Those with an extra 5 minutes go in pursuit of *Winged Victory,* the headless statue discovered at Samothrace and dating from about 200 B.C.

To enter the Louvre, you pass through the 71-foot I. M. Pei glass pyramid in the courtyard, which has received mixed reviews. The collections are divided into departments; those with little time should go on one of the guided tours (in English), lasting about 1½ hours.

Our favorite works include *Ship of Fools* by Hieronymous Bosch (tucked in the Flemish galleries)—no one can depict folly and greed more vividly; *Four Seasons* by Nicolas Poussin, the canonical work of French classicism; Eugène Delacroix's *Liberty Leading the People,* the ultimate endorsement of revolution (Louis-Philippe purchased the painting and hid it during his reign); and Veronese's gigantic *Wedding Feast at Cana,* showing how stunning colors can be when used by a master.

The Richelieu Wing, inaugurated in 1993, houses the museum's collection of northern European and French paintings, along with decorative arts, French sculpture, oriental antiquities (a rich collection of Islamic art), and the grand salons of Napoléon III.

In January of 1998, the museum inaugurated a new site for its splendid collection of Egyptian artifacts, portrait busts, and sarcophagi on the ground floor and first floor of the Sully Wing. Also in the Sully Wing, inaugurated at the same time, is one of the world's largest collections of ancient Greek ceramics.

✪ **Musée d'Orsay.** 1 rue de Bellechasse or 62 rue de Lille, 7e. ☎ **01-40-49-48-14.** Admission 40F ($6.80) adults, 30F ($5.10) ages 18–24 and seniors, free for children 17 and under. Tues–Wed and Fri–Sat 10am–6pm; Thurs 10am–9:45pm; Sun 9am–6pm. June 20–Sept 20, museum opens 9am. Métro: Solférino. RER: Musée-d'Orsay.

The defunct but handsome neoclassical Gare d'Orsay rail station, across the Seine from the Louvre and the Tuileries, has been transformed into a repository of 19th-century art and civilization. The museum houses sculptures and paintings spread across 80 galleries, plus belle époque furniture, photographs, objets d'art, architectural models, and even a cinema.

One of Renoir's most joyous paintings is here—*Moulin de la Galette* (1876). Another celebrated work is by American James McNeill Whistler—*Arrangement in Gray and Black: Portrait of the Painter's Mother.* The most famous piece in the museum is Manet's 1863 *Déjeuner sur l'herbe (Picnic on the Grass),* which created a scandal when it was first exhibited.

✪ **Musée Picasso.** 5 rue de Thorigny, 3e. ☎ **01-42-71-25-21.** Admission 30–38F ($5.10–$6.45) adults, 20–28F ($3.40–$4.75) ages 19–25 and over 60, free for ages 18 and under. Apr–Sept Wed–Mon 9:30am–6pm; Oct–Mar Wed–Mon 9:30am–5:30pm. Métro: St-Paul, Filles-du-Calvaire, or Chemin-Vert.

When it opened in the beautifully restored Hôtel Salé (salt mansion, built in 1656 for Aubert de Fontenay, collector of the dreaded salt tax), a state-owned property in Le Marais, the press hailed it as a "museum for Picasso's Picassos," meaning those he chose not to sell. The greatest Picasso collection in the world, acquired by the state in lieu of $50 million in inheritance taxes, consists of 203 paintings, 158 sculptures,

Bonjour to the New Pompidou

What has been called "the most avant-garde building in the world," the **Centre Pompidou,** place Georges-Pompidou or plateau Beaubourg (☎ **01-44-78-12-33**), closed in late 1997 for extensive renovations, but parts of it remain open. During the lifetime of this edition, the entire complex is scheduled to be fully operational once again (see below).

The dream of former president Georges Pompidou, this center for 20th-century art (designed by Renzo Piano) opened in 1977 and immediately became the focus of loud controversy: Its bold exoskeletal architecture and the brightly painted pipes and ducts crisscrossing its transparent facade were jarring in the old Beaubourg neighborhood. Perhaps the detractors were right all along—within 20 years the building began to deteriorate so badly that a major restoration was called for.

At this writing, the areas of the complex that remain open include the **South Gallery** (*la galerie sud,* site of such temporary exhibitions as a retrospective of the works of British painter David Hockney) and a re-creation of the jazz-age studio of Romanian sculptor Brancusi (*l'Atelier Brancusi*), which is configured as a mini-museum that's separate from the rest of the Centre Pompidou. Both areas are open Monday and Tuesday to Friday from noon to 10pm, Saturday and Sunday from 10am to 10pm. A combined ticket costs 30F ($5.10) for adults, 20F ($3.40) for people under 18.

As a means of providing an insight into the ambitious renovation of the complex, its administrators have erected a steel-and-polyester **"information teepee,"** in the place Igor Stravinsky, adjacent to the center. It's open Sunday to Monday and Wednesday to Friday from 12:30 to 6pm, and Saturday from 2 to 6pm. Although some well-publicized re-inaugurations of the complex are scheduled from December 31, 1999, as a means of ushering in the millennium, you can expect a fully operational Centre Pompidou sometime in the spring of 2000.

What can you expect to see when the Pompidou is going full blast again? The Centre Pompidou encompasses four separate attractions:

The **Musée National d'Art Moderne** (National Museum of Modern Art) offers a large collection of 20th-century art. With some 40,000 works, this is the big attraction, although only some 850 works can be displayed at one time. If you want to view some real charmers, see Alexander Calder's 1926 *Josephine Baker,* one of his earliest versions of the mobile, an art form he invented. Marcel Duchamps's *Valise* is a collection of miniature reproductions of his fabled Dada sculptures and drawings; they're displayed in a carrying case. And every time we visit Paris, we have to see Salvador Dali's *Portrait of Lenin Dancing on Piano Keys.*

In the **Public Information Library** the public has free access to a million French and foreign books, periodicals, films, records, slides, and microfilms in nearly every area of knowledge. The **Center for Industrial Design** emphasizes the contributions made in the fields of architecture, visual communications, publishing, and community planning; and the **Institute for Research and Coordination of Acoustics/Music** brings together musicians and composers interested in furthering the cause of music, both contemporary and traditional.

Paris Attractions

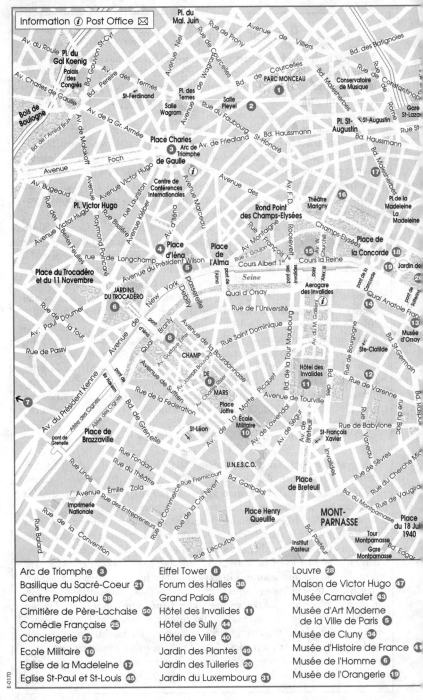

Information ⓘ Post Office ✉

E-0170

328

Musée des Arts d'Afrique et d'Oceanie 48
Musée des Arts Décoratifs 27
Musée d'Orsay 13
Musée National des Arts Asiatiques—Guimet 4
Musée Jacquemart André 2
Musée Marmottan 7
Musée Picasso 42

Musée Rodin 12
Notre-Dame 35
Opéra Garnier 23
Palais Bourbon 14
Palais de l'Elysée 16
Palais du Luxembourg 30
Palais Royal 26
Panthéon 32
Parc du Champ-de-Mars 9

Parc Monceau 1
Place de la Concorde 18
Place des Vosges 46
Place Vendôme 24
Sacré-Cœur 22
Sainte-Chapelle 36
St-Germain-des-Prés 29
Sorbonne 33

16 collages, 19 bas-reliefs, 88 ceramics, and more than 1,500 sketches and 1,600 engravings, along with 30 notebooks. These works span 75 years of Picasso's life and changing styles. The range of paintings includes a remarkable 1901 self-portrait and embraces such masterpieces as *Le Baiser (The Kiss),* painted at Mougins in 1969, and *Reclining Nude* and *The Man with a Guitar. Note:* Higher admission prices (see above) are charged only during special exhibitions.

ON THE CHAMPS-ÉLYSÉES

In late 1995, Paris's most prominent triumphal promenade was augmented with several important improvements. The *contre-allées* (side lanes that had always been clogged with parked cars) have been removed, new lighting and underground parking garages added, the pedestrian sidewalks widened, and new trees planted. Now the Grand Promenade truly is grand again.

Arc de Triomphe. Place Charles-de-Gaulle–Etoile, 16e. ☎ **01-55-37-73-77.** Admission 35F ($5.95) adults, 23F ($3.90) ages 13–25 and over 60, free for children 12 and under. Apr–Sept daily 9:30am–11pm; Oct–Mar daily 10am–10:30pm. Métro: Charles-de-Gaulle–Etoile.

At the western end of the Champs-Élysées, the Arc de Triomphe is the world's largest triumphal arch, about 163 feet high and 147 feet wide. This arch has witnessed some of France's proudest moments and some of its more humiliating defeats, notably those of 1871 and 1940. Commissioned by Napoléon in 1806 to commemorate his Grande Armée's victories, it wasn't completed until 1836, under Louis-Philippe. Four years later Napoléon's remains—brought from his grave on St. Helena—passed under the arch on their journey to his tomb at the Invalides. Since then it has become the focal point for state funerals. It's also the site of the tomb of the unknown soldier, where an eternal flame is kept burning.

THE ILE DE LA CITÉ: WHERE PARIS WAS BORN

Medieval Paris, that architectural blending of grotesquerie and gothic beauty, began on this island in the Seine. Explore as much of it as you can, but if you're in a hurry, try to visit at least Notre-Dame, the Sainte-Chapelle, and the Conciergerie.

Cathédrale Notre-Dame. 6 place du Parvis Notre-Dame, 4e. ☎ **01-42-34-56-10.** Cathedral, free. Towers and crypt 32F ($5.45) for adults, 21F ($3.55) ages 12 to 25 and over 60; free under 12. Museum and treasury 15F ($2.55) adults, 5F (85¢) ages 12 to 25 and over 60, free under 12. Cathedral daily 8am–6:45pm year-round; towers and crypt, Apr–Sept daily 9:30am–6pm, Oct–Mar daily 10am–4:15pm; museum Wed and Sat–Sun 2:30–6pm; treasury Mon–Sat 9:30–11:30am and 12:30–5:30pm. Métro: Cité or St-Michel. RER: St-Michel.

This is the world's most famous Gothic cathedral. From square Parvis, you can view the trio of 13th-century sculptured portals: On the left, the Portal of the Virgin depicts the signs of the Zodiac and the Virgin's coronation. The restored central Portal of the Last Judgment is divided into three levels: The first shows Vices and Virtues; the second, Christ and his Apostles; the third, Christ in triumph after the Resurrection. On the right is the Portal of St. Anne, depicting such scenes as the Virgin enthroned with Child, the most perfect piece of sculpture in Notre-Dame. Equally interesting (although often missed) is the Portal of the Cloisters around on the left.

The interior is typical Gothic, with slender, graceful columns. Over the central portal is the remarkable rose window, 31 feet in diameter. The carved-stone choir screen from the early 14th century depicts such biblical scenes as the Last Supper. Near the altar stands the highly venerated 14th-century Virgin and Child.

To visit those grimy gargoyles (immortalized by Victor Hugo as Quasimodo's hangout), you have to scale steps leading to the twin square towers, rising to a height of 225 feet.

The crypt, lying under the square in the front of the cathedral has been turned into an archaeological museum, containing artifacts from previous churches that have stood on this site. There are even artifacts from the Parisii who lived here some 20 centuries ago. Excavations carried out in the 1960s unearthed many of these relics. You can also view the foundations of a Gallo-Roman rampart from the 3rd century and the foundations of the Merovingian church from the 6th century. The history of Ile de la Cité is revealed in slides and models.

Sainte-Chapelle. Palais de Justice, 4 bd. du Palais, 1er. ☎ **01-53-73-78-50.** Admission 35F ($5.95) adults, 23F ($3.90), students and ages 12–17, free for children under 12. Apr–Sept daily 9:30am–6:30pm; Oct–Mar daily 10am–5pm. Métro: Cité, St-Michel, or Châtelet-Les Halles. RER: St-Michel.

Sainte-Chapelle is Paris's second most important medieval monument after Notre-Dame. It was erected in the flamboyant Gothic style to enshrine relics no longer there, including the Crown of Thorns and two pieces from the True Cross. The walls of the upper chapel consist almost entirely of 15 superb stained-glass windows, and viewed on a bright day with the sun streaming in, they glow with marvelous ruby reds and Chartres blues. The lower level of the chapel is supported by flying buttresses and ornamented with fleurs-de-lis—it was used by the palace servants, the upper chapel by the king and his courtiers.

Conciergerie. 1 quai de l'Horloge, 1er. ☎ **01-53-73-78-50.** Admission 35F ($5.95) adults, 23F ($3.90) ages 12–25 and over 60, free children under 12. Apr–Sept daily 9:30am–6:30pm; Oct–Mar daily 10am–5pm. Métro: Cité, Châtelet-Les Halles, or St-Michel. RER: St-Michel.

The Conciergerie has been called the most sinister building in France. Although it had a long regal history before the revolution, it's visited today chiefly by those wishing to bask in the Reign of Terror's horrors. You approach the Conciergerie through its landmark twin towers, the Tour d'Argent and Tour de César, but the 14th-century vaulted Guard Room is the actual entrance. Also from the 14th century—and even more interesting—is the vast, dark, foreboding Salle des Gens d'Armes (People at Arms), chillingly changed from the days when the king used it as a banqueting hall.

ANOTHER ISLAND IN THE STREAM: ILE ST-LOUIS

As you walk across the iron footbridge from the rear of Notre-Dame, you descend into a world of tree-shaded quays, aristocratic townhouses and courtyards, restaurants, and antique shops.

The sibling island of the Ile de la Cité is primarily residential; its denizens fiercely guard their heritage, privileges, and special position. It was originally two "islets," one named Island of the Heifers. Plaques on the facades make it easier to identify former residents. Madame Curie, for example, lived at 36 quai de Bethune, near ponte de la Tournelle, from 1912 until her death in 1934.

The most exciting mansion is the **Hôtel de Lauzun,** built in 1657, at 17 quai d'Anjou; it's named after a 17th-century rogue, the duc de Lauzun, famous lover and on-again/off-again favorite of Louis XIV. French poet Charles Baudelaire lived here in the 19th century with his "Black Venus," Jeanne Duval. Voltaire resided in the **Hôtel Lambert,** 2 quai d'Anjou, with his mistress, Emilie de Breteuil, the marquise du Châteley (who had an understanding husband).

THE EIFFEL TOWER & ENVIRONS

From place du Trocadéro, you can step between the two curved wings of the Palais de Chaillot and gaze out on a panoramic view. At your feet lie the Jardins du Trocadéro, centered by fountains. Directly in front of you, the pont d'Iéna spans the Seine, leading to the iron immensity of the Tour Eiffel. Beyond, stretching as far as your eye can see, is the Champ-de-Mars, once a military parade ground but now a garden with arches, grottoes, lakes, and cascades.

Tour Eiffel. Champ-de-Mars, 7e. ☎ **01-44-11-23-23.** First landing, 20F ($3.40); second landing, 42F ($7.15); third landing, 59F ($10.05); stairs to second landing, 14F ($2.40). Sept–May daily 9:30am–11pm; June–Aug daily 9am–midnight (in fall and winter the stairs close at 6:30pm). Métro: Trocadéro, Ecole-Militaire, or Bir-Hakeim. RER: Champ-de-Mars/Tour-Eiffel.

Except for the Leaning Tower of Pisa, this is the single most recognizable structure in the world—the symbol of Paris. Weighing 7,000 tons but exerting about the same pressure on the ground as an average-sized person sitting in a chair, the tower was never meant to be permanent. It was built for the Universal Exhibition of 1889 by Gustave-Alexandre Eiffel, the engineer whose fame rested mainly on his iron bridges.

The tower, including its 55-foot TV antenna, is 1,056 feet tall. On a clear day you can see it from some 40 miles away. An open-framework construction, the tower ushered in the almost-unlimited possibilities of steel construction, paving the way for the 20th century's skyscrapers. You can visit the tower in three stages: Taking the elevator to the first landing, you have a view over the rooftops of Paris; the second landing provides a panoramic look at the city; the third gives the most spectacular view, allowing you to identify monuments and buildings.

Hôtel des Invalides (Napoléon's Tomb). Place des Invalides, 7e. ☎ **01-44-42-37-77.** Admission to Musée de l'Armée, Napoléon's Tomb, and Musée des Plans-Reliefs (☎ **01-45-51-95-05**), 37F ($6.30) adults, 27F ($4.60) children 12–18, free for children 11 and under. Oct–Mar daily 10am–5pm; Apr–May and Sept daily 10am–6pm; June–Aug daily 10am–7pm. Closed Jan 1, May 1, Nov 1, and Dec 25. Métro: Latour-Maubourg, Varenne, or Invalides.

The glory of the French military lives on here in the Musée de l'Armée, the world's greatest army museum. It was the Sun King who decided to build the "hotel" to house soldiers who'd been disabled. Among the collections are Viking swords, Burgundian bacinets, 14th-century blunderbusses, Balkan khandjars, salamander-engraved Renaissance serpentines, and American Browning machine guns. As a sardonic touch, there's even General Daumesnil's wooden leg.

To accommodate the Tomb of Napoléon—of red porphyry, with a green granite base—the architect Visconti had to redesign the high altar in 1842. Surounding the tomb are a dozen amazon-like figures representing Napoléon's victories. Almost lampooning the smallness of the man, everything is made awesome: You'd think a real giant were buried here, not a symbolic one.

At the **Musée des Plans-Reliefs,** you'll find detailed sketches and scale models of the many fortresses of France, beginning with the Middle Ages. It's a subcomponent of the Musée de l'Armée.

IN MONTMARTRE

From the 1880s to just before World War I, Montmartre enjoyed its golden age as the world's best-known art colony. *La Vie de bohème* reigned supreme. Following World War I the pseudoartists flocked here in droves, with camera-snapping tourists hot on their heels. The real artists had long gone to such places as Montparnasse.

Before its discovery and subsequent chic, Montmartre was a sleepy farming community, with windmills dotting the landscape. Since it's at the highest point in the city, if you find it too much of a climb you might want to take the miniature train along the steep streets: **Le Petit Train de Montmartre,** which passes all the major landmarks and seats 55 passengers who can listen to the recorded English-language commentary. Board the train at the bottom of the hill, at place Blanche, near the Moulin Rouge, and ride it uphill to the place du Tertre, within a very short walk of the crest of the hill and its monumental basilica. Between June and August, trains run daily from 10am to midnight; otherwise, from 10am to 6pm. The price of 30F ($5.10) for adults, and 18F ($3.05) for those aged 2 to 12, allows you to ascend and descend *la butte* in any of the trains, getting on or off wherever you please en route. Ascents and descents of the hill take about 20 minutes each. For information, contact **Promotrain,** 131 rue de Clignancourt, 18e (☎ **01-42-62-24-00**).

The simplest way to reach Montmartre is to take the Métro to Anvers, and then walk up rue du Steinkerque to the funicular, which runs to the precincts of Sacré-Coeur daily 6am to 11pm.

Basilique du Sacré-Coeur. Place St-Pierre, 18e. ☎ **01-53-41-89-00.** Basilica, free; joint ticket to dome and crypt 30F ($5.10) adults, 16F ($2.70) students and children. Apr–Sept daily 9am–7pm; Oct–Mar daily 9am–6pm. Métro: Abbesses; then take the elevator to the surface and follow the signs to the funiculaire, which goes up to the church for the price of 1 Métro ticket.

Montmartre's crowning achievement is Sacré-Coeur, although the view of Paris from its precincts takes precedence over the basilica itself. In gleaming white, it towers over Paris, its five bulbous domes suggesting some 12th-century Byzantine church and its campanile inspired by Roman-Byzantine art. After France's defeat by the Prussians in 1870, the basilica was planned as an offering to cure the country's misfortunes. Both rich and poor contributed money to build it. Construction began in 1873, but the church was not consecrated until 1919. On a clear day, the vista from the dome can extend for 35 miles.

IN THE LATIN QUARTER

This is the Left Bank precinct of the **University of Paris** (often called the **Sorbonne**). Rabelais called it the Quartier Latin, because of the students and professors who spoke Latin in the classrooms and on the streets. The sector teems with belly dancers, exotic restaurants from Vietnamese to Balkan, sidewalk cafes, bookstalls, and *caveaux*.

A good starting point is **place St-Michel** (Métro: Pont-St-Michel), where Balzac used to get water from the fountain when he was a youth. This center was the scene of much Resistance fighting in the summer of 1944. The quarter centers on **boulevard St-Michel,** to the south (the students call it "Boul Mich").

Musée National du Moyen Age/Thermes de Cluny (Musée de Cluny). 6 place Paul-Painlevé, 5e. ☎ **01-53-73-78-00.** Admission 28F ($4.75) adults, 18F ($3.05) ages 18–25, free for age 17 and under. Wed–Mon 9:15am–5:45pm. Métro: Cluny/La Sorbonne.

There are two reasons to go here: The museum houses the world's finest collection of art from the Middle Ages, including jewelry and tapestries, and it's all displayed in a well-preserved manor house built on top of Roman baths. In the cobblestoned Court of Honor, you can admire the flamboyant Gothic building with its clinging vines, turreted walls, gargoyles, and dormers with seashell motifs. Along with the Hôtel de Sens in Le Marais, this is all that remains in Paris of domestic medieval architecture. Most people come primarily to see the Unicorn Tapestries—all the romance of the age of chivalry lives on in these remarkable yet mysterious tapestries, showing a beautiful princess and her handmaiden, beasts of prey, and just plain pets. They were discovered

---

Sacré-Cake?

One Parisian called Sacré-Coeur "a lunatic's confectionery dream." Zola declared it "the basilica of the ridiculous." But Utrillo never tired of drawing and painting it, and he and Max Jacob came here regularly to pray.

only a century ago in the Château de Boussac in the Auvergne. Downstairs are the ruins of the Roman baths, dating from around A.D. 200. You wander through a display of Gallic and Roman sculptures and an interesting marble bathtub engraved with lions.

HISTORIC GARDENS & SQUARES

GARDENS   Bordering place de la Concorde, the statue-studded **Jardin des Tuileries** (☎ 01-40-20-90-43; Métro: Tuileries) are as much a part of Paris as the Seine. They were designed by Le Nôtre, Louis XIV's gardener and planner of the Versailles grounds. About 100 years before that, Catherine de Médici ordered a palace built here, connected to the Louvre. Twice attacked by enraged Parisians, it was finally burnt to the ground in 1871 and never rebuilt.

Hemingway told a friend that the **Jardin du Luxembourg** (☎ 01-53-35-89-35), 6e (Métro: Odéon; RER: Luxembourg), "kept us from starvation." He related that in his poverty-stricken days in Paris, he wheeled a baby carriage through the gardens because it was known "for the classiness of its pigeons." When the gendarme left to get a glass of wine, the writer would eye his victim, and then lure it with corn and snatch it. "We got a little tired of pigeon that year," he confessed, "but they filled many a void." Before it became a feeding ground for struggling artists in the 1920s, the Luxembourg Gardens knew greater days. But they've always been associated with artists, although students from the Sorbonne and children predominate nowadays. The gardens are the best on the Left Bank (if not in all of Paris). Marie de Médici, the much-neglected wife and later widow of the roving Henri IV, ordered the Palais du Luxembourg built on this site in 1612.

SQUARES   In **place de la Bastille** on July 14, 1789, a mob of Parisians attacked the Bastille and thus sparked the French Revolution. Nothing remains of the historic Bastille, built in 1369, for it was torn down. Many prisoners—some sentenced by Louis XIV for "witchcraft"—were kept within its walls; the best known is the "Man in the Iron Mask." When the fortress was stormed, only seven prisoners were discovered (the marquis de Sade had been transferred to the madhouse 10 days earlier). Bastille Day is celebrated with great festivity on July 14. In the center of the square is the Colonne de Juillet (July Column), but it doesn't commemorate the revolution. It honors the victims of the 1830 July revolution, which put Louis-Philippe on the throne.

✪ **Place des Vosges,** 4e (Métro: St-Paul or Chemin-Vert), is Paris's oldest square and was once the most fashionable. In the heart of the Marais, it was called the Palais Royal in the days of Henri IV, who planned to live here—but his assassin, Ravaillac, had other ideas. Henry II was killed while jousting on the square in 1559. Place des Vosges was one of the first planned squares in Europe. Its *grand siècle* red-brick houses are ornamented with white stone. Its covered arcades allowed people to shop at all times, even in the rain—quite an innovation at the time.

In the east, avenue des Champs-Élysées begins at **place de la Concorde,** an octagonal traffic hub ordered built in 1757 to honor Louis XV and one of the world's grandest squares. The statue of the king was torn down in 1792 and the name of the square changed to place de la Révolution. Floodlit at night, it's dominated now by an Egyptian obelisk from Luxor, the oldest man-made object in Paris; it was carved around 1200 B.C. and presented to France in 1829 by the viceroy of Egypt. During the Reign of Terror, Dr. Guillotin's little invention was erected on this spot and claimed thousands of lives—everybody from Louis XVI, who died bravely, to Mme du Barry, who went kicking and screaming all the way.

For a spectacular sight, look down the Champs-Élysées—the view is framed by Coustou's Marly horses, which once graced the gardens at Louis XIV's Château de Marly (these are copies—the originals are in the Louvre).

HISTORIC PARKS & A CEMETERY

PARKS   One of the most spectacular parks in Europe is the **Bois de Boulogne,** Porte Dauphine, 16e (☎ **01-53-92-82-82;** Métro: Les-Sablons, Porte-Maillot, or Porte-Dauphine). Horse-drawn carriages traverse it, but you can also drive through. Many of its hidden pathways, however, must be discovered by walking. West of Paris, the park was once a forest kept for royal hunts. When Napoléon III gave the grounds to the city in 1852, they were developed by Baron Haussmann. Separating Lac Inférieur from Lac Supérieur is the Carrefour des Cascades (you can stroll under its waterfall). The Lower Lake contains two islands connected by a footbridge.

Parc Monceau, 8e (☎ **01-43-18-70-70;** Métro: Monceau or Villiers), is ringed with 18th- and 19th-century mansions, some of them evoking Proust's *Remembrance of Things Past.* It was built in 1778 by the duc d'Orléans (or Philippe Egalité, as he became known). Parc Monceau was laid out with an Egyptian-style obelisk, a medieval dungeon, a thatched alpine farmhouse, a Chinese pagoda, a Roman temple, an enchanted grotto, various chinoiseries, and a waterfall. The park was opened to the public during Napoléon III's Second Empire.

A CEMETERY   The **Cemetière du Père-Lachaise,** 16 rue de Repos, 20e (☎ **01-43-70-70-33;** Métro: Père-Lachaise), is Paris's largest and contains more illustrious dead than any other. When it comes to name-dropping, this cemetery knows no peer—it's been called the "grandest address in Paris." Everybody from Sarah Bernhardt to Oscar Wilde is buried here. So are Balzac, Delacroix, and Bizet. Colette's body was taken here in 1954, and her pink and black granite slab always sports flowers (legend has it that cats replenish the red roses). In time, the "little sparrow," Edith Piaf, followed. Marcel Proust's black tombstone rarely lacks a tiny bunch of violets. Some tombs are sentimental favorites—Jim Morrison's reportedly draws the most visitors. Another stone is marked Gertrude Stein on one side and Alice B. Toklas on the other. Open Monday through Friday 8am to 6pm, Saturday 8:30am to 6pm, and Sunday 9am to 6pm (closes at 5:30pm November through early March).

ORGANIZED TOURS

BY BUS   A highly visible option for seeing Paris are the get-acquainted tours offered by **Cityrama,** 147–149 rue Saint-Honoré, 1er (☎ **01-44-55-61-00;** Métro: Palais-Royal or Musée-du-Louvre). The company operates a flotilla of double-decker red-and-yellow buses, each with oversized windows and a series of multilingual recorded commentaries that recite an overview of Paris's history and monuments. The most popular tour is a 2-hour affair that departs from the place des Pyramides, adjacent to the rue de Rivoli and the Tuileries Gardens, every day at 9:30am, 10:30am, 1:30pm, and 2:30pm. Throughout the year, there are additional tours every Saturday and Sunday at 11:30am, and between March and October, there are additional tours every day at 3:30 and 4:30pm. The price is 150F ($25.50) per person. Other, more detailed tours are also available. They include a 3½-hour morning tour (Monday, Wednesday, Friday, and Saturday) to the interiors of Notre-Dame and the Louvre, priced at 295F ($50.15) per person. There are 3½-hour morning tours to Versailles at 320F ($54.40) per person, and 3½-hour afternoon tours to Chartres at 275F ($46.75) per person. If you buy tickets for the tours of Versailles and Chartres simultaneously, you'll pay only 500F ($85) for both. And if you're interested in a night tour of Paris as a means of understanding how the City of Light got its name, tours depart every evening at 10pm in summer and at 7pm in winter, at a cost of 150F ($25.50) per person.

BY BOAT   A boat tour on the Seine provides sweeping vistas of the riverbanks and some of the best views of Notre-Dame. Many of the boats have open sundecks, bars, and restaurants. **Bateaux-Mouche** cruises (☎ **01-42-25-96-10** for reservations, 01-40-76-99-99 for schedules; Métro: Alma-Marceau) depart from the Right Bank of the Seine, adjacent to pont de l'Alma, and last about 75 minutes each. Tours leave every day at 20- to 30-minute intervals between May and October, beginning at 10am and ending at 11:30pm. Between November and April, there are at least nine departures every day between 11am and 9pm, with a schedule that changes frequently according to demand and the weather. Fares cost 40F ($6.80) for adults and 20F ($3.40) for children aged 5 to 15. Dinner cruises depart every evening at 8:30pm, last 3 hours, and cost between 500 and 700F ($85 and $119), depending on whch of the set-price menus you order. Aboard dinner cruises, jackets and ties are required for men.

THE SHOPPING SCENE

You don't have to buy anything to appreciate shopping in Paris; just soaking up mass consumerism as the true art form the French have made it is enough. Gawking at the *vitrines* (display windows) will give you a whole new education in style.

THE BEST BUYS   Perfumes and **cosmetics,** including such famous brands as Guerlain, Chanel, Schiaparelli, and Jean Patou, are almost always cheaper in Paris than in the United States. Paris is also a good place to buy Lalique and Baccarat **crystal.** They're expensive but still priced below international market value.

Of course, many people come to Paris just to shop for **fashions.** From Chanel to Yves Saint Laurent, from Nina Ricci to Sonia Rykiel, the city overflows with fashion boutiques, ranging from haute couture to the truly outlandish. Fashion accessories, such as those designed by Louis Vuitton and Céline, are among the finest in the world. Smart Parisians know how to dress in style without mortgaging their condos: They head for discount and resale shops. One of the most visible of these is **Anna Lowe,** 104 rue du Faubourge St-Honoré, 8e (☎ **01-42-66-11-32**; Métro: Miromesnil), one of the busiest fashion discounters for women's clothing in Paris, and located within a few steps of the ultra-exclusive Bristol Hotel. Her inventory includes garments by Thierry Mugler, Chanel, Valentino, Givenchy, Ungaro, and Lacroix from the present or previous season, usually sold at wholesale prices. There's also an inventory of fashion accessories such as belts, shawls, and scarves.

Michel Swiss, 16 rue de la Paix, 2e (☎ **01-42-61-61-11;** Métro: Opéra), looks like the other chic boutiques near place Vendôme. But once you're inside (there's no store-front window), you'll see major brands of luxury perfumes, makeup, leather bags, pens, neckties, accessories, and giftware—all discounted.

Lingerie is another great French export. All the top lingerie designers are represented in boutiques as well as in the major department stores, Galeries Lafayette and Le Printemps.

Paris Shopper's Secret

For bargain cosmetics, try out French dime store (such as **Monoprix** and **Prisunic**) brands. Brands to look for include **Bourjois** (made in the same factories as Chanel cosmetics), **Lierac,** and **Galenic. Vichy,** famous for its water, has a complete skin care and makeup line.

Chocolate lovers will find much to tempt them in Paris. **Christian Constant,** 37 rue d'Assas, 6e (☎ **01-53-63-15-15;** Métro: Rennes), produces some of Paris's most sinfully delicious chocolates. Racks and racks of chocolates are priced individually or by the kilo at **Maison du Chocolat,** 225 rue du Faubourg St-Honoré, 8e (☎ **01-42-27-39-44;** Métro: Ternes), although it'll cost you nearly or over 500F ($85) for a kilo. There are five other branches around Paris.

BUSINESS HOURS   Shops are usually open Monday to Saturday from 9:30am or 10am to 7 or 8pm, but the hours vary greatly and Monday mornings aren't full throttle. Small shops sometimes take a 2-hour lunch break and might not open until after lunch on Monday. Thursday is traditionally devoted to late-night shopping, with stores open until 9 or 10pm.

Sunday shopping is currently limited to tourist areas and flea markets, although there's growing demand for full-scale Sunday hours. The big department stores now open for the five Sundays before Christmas; otherwise, they're dead on Sundays, too.

The **Carrousel du Louvre,** an underground mall adjacent to the Louvre, is open and hopping on Sunday but closed on Monday. The tourist shops lining rue de Rivoli across from the Louvre are all open on Sunday, as are the antiques villages, assorted flea markets and specialty events, and several good food markets in the streets.

GREAT SHOPPING AREAS

1er & 8e   Because these two arrondisements adjoin each other and form the heart of Paris's best Right Bank shopping, they really function as one shopping neighborhood. This area includes the famed **rue du Faubourg St-Honoré,** where the big designer houses are, and **avenue des Champs-Élysées,** where the mass-market and teen scenes are hot.

At one end of the 1st is the **Palais Royal,** where an arcade of boutiques flanks the garden of the former palace. At the other side of town, at the end of the 8th, lies **avenue Montaigne,** 2 blocks of the fanciest shops in the world, where you simply float from big name to big name and in a few hours can see everything from **Louis Vuitton** at no. 54 (☎ 01-45-62-47-00) to **Inès de la Fressange** (Chanel model turned retailer) at no. 14 (☎ 01-47-23-08-94). **Ferragamo** (☎ **01-47-23-36-37**) is at no. 45 in one of the most beautiful apartment buildings in Paris. In addition, you'll find fabulous perfumes at **Parfums Caron** (☎ 01-47-23-40-82). The shop, which was founded in 1904, can be visited at no. 34.

2e   Right behind the Palais Royal lies the **Garment District (Sentier),** as well as very upscale shopping secrets, such as **place des Victoires.** This area hosts a few old-fashioned passages, alleys filled with tiny stores, such as **Galerie Vivienne** on rue Vivienne.

3e & 4e   The difference between these two arrondissements gets fuzzy, especially around **place des Vosges**—center stage of Le Marais. Even so, they offer several dramatically different shopping experiences.

On the surface, the shopping includes the real-people stretch of **rue de Rivoli** (which becomes **rue St-Antoine**). Two department stores are in this area. **La Samaritaine,** 19 rue de la Monnaie (☎ 01-40-41-20-20), occupies four architecturally noteworthy buildings erected between 1870 and 1927. Of special interest are the annual sales that go on here during October and November, when much, but not all, of the merchandise is reduced by between 20% and 40%. **BHZ (Bazar de l'Hôtel de Ville),** which was first opened in 1856, has seven floors loaded with merchandise. It lies adjacent to Paris's City Hall at 52–64 rue de Rivoli (☎ 01-42-74-90-00).

Meanwhile, hidden away in Le Marais is a medieval warren of tiny twisting streets chock-a-block with cutting-edge designers and up-to-the-minute fashions and trends.

Paris's Most Famous Flea Market

The **Marché aux Puces de Clignancourt** (flea market), avenue de la Porte de Clignancourt (Métro: Vanves), has an enormous mixture of vintage bargains and old junk. It's estimated that the complex has 2,500 to 3,000 open stalls spread over half a mile. Monday is traditionally the day for bargain hunters, and negotiating is a must (you can usually find someone who speaks English). Once you arrive at Porte de Clignancourt, turn left and cross boulevard Ney, and then walk north on avenue de la Porte de Clignancourt. You'll pass stalls offering cheap clothing, but continue walking until you see the entrances to the first maze of flea-market stalls on the left.

Start by walking around place des Vosges for art galleries, designer shops, and fabulous little finds, and then dive in and get lost in the area leading to the Musée Picasso.

Place de la Bastille—an up-and-coming area for artists and galleries—is in the 4th arrondissement (leading to the 12th), as is the Ile St-Louis. One of the newest entries to the retail scene, the **Viaduc des Arts,** begins at Bastille but technically stretches to the 12th arrondissement.

6e & 7e   The 6th arrondissement is one of the most famous shopping districts—it's the soul of the Left Bank—but a lot of the really good stuff is hidden in the zone that becomes the wealthy residential 7th. **Rue du Bac,** stretching from the 6th to the 7th in a few blocks, stands for all that wealth and glamour can buy. The street is jammed with art galleries, home-decorating stores, and gourmet-food shops.

9e   To add to the fun of shopping the Right Bank, the 9th arrondissement sneaks in behind the 1st, so if you don't choose to walk toward the Champs-Élysées and the 8th, you can head to the city's big department stores, built in a row along **boulevard Haussmann** in the 9th. These department stores include not only the two mammoth French icons, **Au Printemps,** 64 bd. Haussmann, 9e (☎ **01-42-82-50-00;** Métro: Havre-Caumartin; RER: Auber), and **Galeries Lafayette,** 40 bd. Haussmann, 9e (☎ **01-42-82-34-56;** Métro: Chausée-d'Antin; RER: Auber), but also a large branch of Britain's **Marks & Spencer** at 35 bd. Haussman, 9e (☎ **01-47-42-42-91;** Métro: Chausée-d-Antin; RER: Auber).

PARIS AFTER DARK

Parisians tend to do everything later than their Anglo-American counterparts. Once the workday is over, people head straight to the cafe to meet up with friends, and from there they go to a restaurant or bar, and finally to a nightclub.

THE PERFORMING ARTS

Listings of what's playing can be found in *Pariscope,* a weekly entertainment guide, or the English-language *Boulevard.* Performances start later in Paris than in London or New York City—anywhere from 8 to 9pm—and Parisians tend to dine after the theater. There are many ticket agencies in Paris, but most are found near the Right Bank hotels. *Avoid them if possible*—usually, the cheapest tickets can be purchased at the theater box office.

We do recommend checking a few agencies who sell tickets for cultural events and plays at discounts of up to 50%. One outlet for discount tickets is the **Kiosque Théâtre,** 15 place de la Madeleine, 8e (no phone; Métro: Madeleine), offering leftover tickets for about half-price for tickets sold only on the day of a performance. Tickets for evening performances are sold Tuesday through Friday 12:30 to 8pm and Saturday 2 to 8pm. If you'd like to attend a matinee, buy your ticket Saturday 12:30 to 2pm or Sunday 12:30 to 4pm.

For discounts of 20% to 40% on tickets for festivals, concerts, and theater performances, try one of two locations of the **FNAC** department store chain: 136 rue de Rennes, 6e (☎ **01-49-54-30-00;** Métro: Montparnasse-Bienvenue), or in the Forum des Halles, 1–7 rue Pierre-Lescot, 1er (☎ **01-40-41-40-00;** Métro: Châtelet—Les Halles). To get discounts on tickets, you must purchase a **carte FNAC,** which is valid for 3 years and costs 160F ($27.20).

A particularly charming venue for opera on a smaller scale than the norm in either of Paris' major opera houses is the **Opéra-Comique,** 5 rue Favart, 2e (☎ **01-42-44-45-45;** Métro: Richelieu-Drouot). Built in the late 1890s in an ornate style reminiscent of the Palais Garnier, it's the site of such operas as *Carmen, Don Giovanni, Tosca,* and *Palleas & Melisande.* There are no performances between mid-July and late August. The box office, however, is open year-round, every Monday to Saturday from 11am to 7pm. Tickets cost from 50 to 610F ($8.50 to $103.70) each.

Another worthy musical venue in Paris is **Salle Pleyel,** 232 rue du Faubourg St-Honoré, 8e (☎ **01-45-61-53-00;** Métro: Ternes). Built in 1927 in a conservative art deco style, it's the site of appearances by organizations such as the Orchestre de Paris, the Orchestre Philharmonique de Radio-France, and L'Ensemble Orchestrale de Paris. The ticket office is open Monday to Saturday from 11am to 6pm, with tickets priced at 60 to 320F ($10.20 to $54.40).

For access to some of the most modern and avant-garde music in France, try the **Radio France Salle Oliver Messian,** 116 av. Président-Kennedy, 16e (☎ **01-42-30-15-16;** Métro: Passy-Ranelagh), site of many performances of the Orchestre Philharmonique de Radio-France. A different organization that performs in the same concert hall is the somewhat more conservative Orchestre National de France. The concert hall's box office is open Monday to Saturday from 11am to 6pm. Tickets cost 50 to 100F ($8.50 to $17), depending on the location of your seat and the music event being performed.

Of the half-dozen *grands travaux* conceived by the Mitterrand administration, **Cité de la Musique,** 221 av. Jean Jaurès, 19e (☎ **01-44-84-45-00,** or 01-44-84-44-84 for tickets and information; Métro: Porte de Pantin), has been the most widely applauded, the least criticized, and the most innovative. It incorporates a network of concert halls, a library and research center for the study of all kinds of music from around the world, and a museum. Concerts, presented in any of several of the compound's auditoriums, are presented at 4:30pm and 8pm every day except Monday. Tickets, depending on the concert and the seat, range in price from 80 to 200F ($13.60 to $34) each.

Comédie-Française. 2 rue de Richelieu, 1er. ☎ **01-44-58-15-15.** Tickets 70–190F ($11.90–$32.30). Métro: Palais-Royal-Musée-du-Louvre.

Those with a modest understanding of French can still delight in a sparkling production of Molière at this national theater, established to keep the classics alive and promote the most important contemporary authors. Nowhere else will you see the works of Molière and Racine so beautifully staged. In 1993, a much-neglected wing of the building was renovated and launched as Le Théâtre du Vieux Colombier, specializing in avant-garde productions, with all tickets costing 160F ($27.20). The box office is open daily 11am to 6pm (closed July 21 through September 5).

Opéra Bastille. Place de la Bastille, 120 rue de Lyon, 12e. ☎ **01-43-43-96-96.** Tickets 60–660F ($10.20–$112.20) opera; 60–650F ($10.20–$110.50) dance. Métro: Bastille.

The home of the **Opera National de Paris,** the controversial building was designed by Canadian architect Carlos Ott, with curtains created by Japanese fashion designer Issey Miyake. The showplace was inaugurated in July 1989 (for the Revolution's bicentennial), and on March 17, 1990, the curtain rose for the first time on Hector Berlioz's *Les Troyens.* The main hall is the largest of any French opera house, with 2,700 seats. The building contains two additional concert halls, including an intimate room, usually used for chamber music, with only 250 seats. Both traditional operas and symphony concerts are presented. Several concerts are free, in honor of certain French holidays. Write ahead to the above address for tickets.

Opéra Garnier (Palais Garnier). Place de l'Opéra, 9e. ☎ **01-40-01-17-89.** Tickets 60–650F ($10.20–$110.50) opera; 30–405F ($5.10–$68.85) dance. Métro: Opéra.

Opéra Garnier is the home of the **Ballet National de Paris,** one of the world's great companies, always a leading innovator in the world of dance. This rococo wonder was designed as a contest entry by architect Charles Garnier in the heyday of the empire. Months of painstaking restorations returned the Garnier to its former glory. In mid-1995 the Garnier reopened grandly with Mozart's *Così fan tutte.*

NIGHTCLUBS & CABARETS

✪ **Crazy Horse Saloon.** 12 av. Georges-V, 8e. ☎ **01-47-23-32-32.** Reservations recommended. Cover 450–560F ($76.50–$95.20), including 2 drinks, at a table; or 290F ($49.30) including 2 drinks, for standing room at the bar; dinner spectacle 750F ($127.50). Shows Sun–Fri 8:30pm and 11pm; Sat 7:30, 9:45, and 11:50pm. Métro: Georges-V or Alma-Marceau.

Since it was established in 1951, this sophisticated strip joint has thrived as a staple on the Paris theatrical circuit, thanks to good choreography and a sly, often coquettish philosophy that celebrates and exalts the female form. The theme that binds each of the 5-minute dance numbers together is *La Femme* in her various emotional textures: temperamental, sad, dancing/bouncy, or joyful. Each of the numbers features gorgeous girls, girls, girls, outfitted in the kind of costumes that support Paris's image as one of Europe's erotic capitals. Specific dance numbers that endure season after season include "The Itch" and "The Erotic Lesson," which might end up teaching you a thing or two you might not have known before your visit. If you opt for dinner as part of the show, it will be a tasteful, well-prepared event served with flair at Chez Francis, a restaurant under separate management a few steps from the cabaret itself. Shows last for 1¾ hours each, and are attended by men and, to a lesser extent, women from around Europe and the world.

Folies-Bergère. 32 rue Richer, 9e. ☎ **01-44-79-98-98.** Cover 160–320F ($27.20–$54.40); dinner and show 660–740F ($112.20–$125.80). Performances Tues–Sat 9pm; Sun 3pm. Restaurant opens at 7pm. Reservations at box office window Tues–Sun 10am–6pm. Métro: Rue-Montmartre or Cadet.

The Folies-Bergère is a Paris institution. Since 1886 foreigners have been flocking here for the performances, the excitement, and the scantily clad dancers. Josephine Baker, the African-American singer who used to throw bananas into the audience, became "the toast of Paris" at the Folies-Bergère. The Folies has radically changed its context into a less titillating, more conventional format. It often presents bemused, light-hearted French-language comedies and musical comedies.

Moulin Rouge. Place Blanche, 18e. ☎ **01-53-09-82-82.** Cover including champagne 490–550F ($83.30–$93.50); or dinner and show 770F ($130.90). For seats at the bar, cover 360F ($61.20) includes two drinks, additional drinks 90F ($15.30) each. Dinner nightly at 7pm. Revues presented nightly at 9 and 11pm. Métro: Blanche.

The establishment that Toulouse-Lautrec immortalized in his paintings is still here, but the artist would probably have a hard time recognizing it today. Colette created a scandal here by offering an on-stage kiss to Mme de Morny, but shows today have a harder time shocking audiences. Try to get a table, as the view is much better on the main floor than from the bar. What's the underlying theme that drives spectators back to the Moulin Rouge generation after generation? It's an ongoing emphasis on the strip routines and saucy sexiness of *La Belle Époque,* and of permissive, promiscuous Paris between the World Wars. Handsome men and girls, girls, girls, virtually all of them topless, contribute to the enduring appeal that survives despite an increasing jadedness on the part of both audiences and staff. Dance finales usually include two dozen of the belles ripping loose with a topless can-can in a style that might have been appreciated by Gigi herself.

LE COOL JAZZ

Baiser Salé. 58 rue des Lombards, 1er. ☎ **01-42-33-37-71.** Cover 60–80F ($10.20–$13.60) Wed–Sun. Drinks from 30F ($5.10). Metro: Châtelet.

Set in a cellar lined with jazz-related paintings, with a large central bar and an ongoing roster of videos that show great jazz moments (Charlie Parker, Miles Davis) of the past, this is an appealing, musically varied jazz club. Everything is very, very mellow and laid-back, with an emphasis on grooving to the music of whatever form of jazz happens to be featured on the evening of your arrival. Genres include Afro-Caribbean, Afro-Latino, salsa, merengue, rhythm and blues, and, less frequently, fusion. It's open daily from 6pm to 6am, with music nightly from 10:30 to 3am. Entrance is free every Monday and Tuesday.

Jazz Club La Villa. In the Hotel La Villa, 29 rue Jacob, 6e. ☎ **01-43-26-60-00.** Cover 120–150F ($20.40–$25.50), including first drink. Drinks 60F ($10.20). Mon–Sat 10:30pm–2am. Closed Aug. Métro: St-Germain-des-Prés.

This club is unusual in that it lies in the red-velour cellar of a small but chic four-star hotel in the Latin Quarter. It has a reputation for bringing in famous artists as well as hard-core aficionados of jazz. Much of the music derives from New Orleans, Chicago, or New York, mainly Dixieland or any of the schools that followed. Artists rotate once a week; no food is served.

DANCE CLUBS

Les Bains. 7 rue du Bourg-l'Abbé, 3e. ☎ **01-48-87-01-80.** Cover 100–120F ($17–$20.40), including the first drink. Drinks 50–70F ($8.50–$11.90). Open nightly midnight–6am. Métro: Réaumur.

This chic club has been pronounced "in" and "out" of fashion, but lately it's very "in." The name Les Bains comes from the place's old function as a Turkish bath attracting gay clients, none more notable than Marcel Proust. Today, it's predominantly hetero, with an emphasis on the young, the trendy, and the fashionable, who usually range in age from 20 to around 45. One hideaway in the place is designated as "un coin VIP" (VIP corner), with a velvet rope and a security guard that keeps the paparazzi from disturbing the celebs or their hangers-on. It can be hard to get in if those at the door don't deem you acceptable.

ROCK & ROLL

Bus Palladium. 6 rue Fontaine, 9e. ☎ **01-53-21-07-33.** Cover 100F ($17) for men Tues, Fri, and Sat; 100F ($17) for women Fri–Sat. Tues–Sat 11pm–6am. Métro: Blanche or Pigalle.

This temple to 1960s-style rock and roll—don't expect any techno, punk, jazz, or blues here—has varnished hardwoods and fabric-covered walls that absorb only some of the reverberations of the nonstop recorded music. Straight single clients aged 25 to 35 come here with others of their ilk. An alcoholic drink will set you back a hefty 80F ($13.60), except on Tuesdays, when women drink for free.

WINE BARS

The tiny **Au Sauvignon,** 80 rue des Sts-Pères, 7e (☎ **01-45-48-49-02;** Métro: Sèvres-Babylone), has tables overflowing onto a covered terrace. Wines served range from the cheapest Beaujolais to an expensive white Bordeaux. To go with your wine, choose an Auvergne specialty, such as goat cheese and terrines. Open Monday through Saturday 8:30am to 10:30pm. Closed August and major religious holidays.

A wide assortment of chic Parisians patronize the increasingly popular ♦ **Willi's Wine Bar,** 13 rue des Petits-Champs, 1er (☎ **01-42-61-05-09;** Métro: Bourse, Louvre, or Palais-Royal), in the center of the financial district. About 250 kinds of wine are offered, including a dozen "wine specials" you can taste by the glass for 17 to 80F ($2.90 to $13.60). Lunch is the busiest time—on quiet evenings, you can better enjoy the warm ambience and 16th-century beams. Open for meals Monday to Saturday noon to 2:30pm and 7 to 11pm; the bar is open Monday to Saturday 11am to midnight.

GAY & LESBIAN CLUBS

Le Bar Central, 33 rue Vielle-du-Temple, 4e (☎ **01-48-87-99-33;** Métro: Hôtel-de-Ville), is one of the leading bars for men in the Hôtel-de-Ville area. Open Monday to Thursday 4pm to 2am, Friday and Saturday 2pm to 2am. The club has opened a small hotel upstairs. Both the bar and its hotel are in a 300-year-old building in the heart of the Marais. The hotel caters mostly to gay men, less frequently to lesbians. No cover.

Banana Café, 13 rue de la Ferronnerie, 1er (☎ **01-42-33-35-31;** Métro: Châtelet or Les-Halles), is the most popular gay bar in the Marais, a ritualized stopover for European homosexuals (mostly male and to a much lesser extent, female) visiting or doing business in Paris. Occupying two floors of a 19th-century building, it has dim lighting and a well-publicized policy of raising the price of drinks after 10pm, after the joint starts to become really interesting. There's a street-level bar and a dance floor in the cellar featuring a live pianist and recorded music. On many nights, go-go dancers perform from spotlit platforms. it's open daily 4:30pm to around 5:30am.

Trendy **L'Entr'acte,** 25 bd. Poissonnière, 2e. (☎ **01-40-26-01-93;** Métro: Rue Montmartre), is one of the most visible, popular, and fun lesbian discos in Paris. Outfitted like a replica of a late 19th-century French music hall, it welcomes gay women of all ages. It's best to show up here before midnight. The venue is very cool, with all types of cutting-edge music played in a setting that just happens to discourage the presence of men. The cover of 50F ($8.50) includes the first drink. Open Wednesday to Saturday from midnight until at least 5am.

DAY TRIPS FROM PARIS: THE ILE DE FRANCE

VERSAILLES   Within 50 years the ♦ **Château de Versailles** (☎ **01-39-50-36-22**) was transformed from Louis XIII's simple hunting lodge into an extravagant palace, a monument to the age of absolutism. What you see today is the greatest living museum of a vanished way of life. Begun in 1661, the construction of the château involved 32,000 to 45,000 workmen, some of whom had to drain marshes—often at the cost of their lives—and move forests. Louis XIV set out to create a palace that would awe all Europe, and the result was a symbol of pomp and opulence that was to be copied, yet never quite duplicated, all over Europe and even in America.

The six magnificent **Grands Appartements** are in the Louis XIV style; each takes its name from the allegorical painting on its ceiling. The most famous room is the 236-foot-long **Hall of Mirrors.** Begun by Mansart in 1678 in the Louis XIV style, it was decorated by Le Brun with 17 large arched windows matched by corresponding beveled mirrors in simulated arcades.

Spread across 250 acres, the **Gardens of Versailles** were laid out by the great land-scape artist André Le Nôtre. A long walk across the park takes you to the **Grand Trianon,** in pink-and-white marble, designed by Hardouin-Mansart for Louis XIV in 1687. Traditionally it's been a place where France has lodged important guests. Gabriel, the designer of place de la Concorde in Paris, built the **Petit Trianon** in 1768 for Louis XV; its construction was inspired by Mme de Pompadour, who died before it was completed. In time, Marie Antoinette adopted it as her favorite residence.

The palace is open Tuesday through Sunday 9am to 6:30pm, May 2 through September 30; until 5:30pm the rest of the year. The grounds are open daily from dawn to dusk. Admission to the palace is 45F ($7.65) for adults, 35F ($5.95) for those 18 to 25, and free for those under 18 and over 60. Admission to the Grand Trianon is 25F ($4.25) for adults, 15F ($2.55) for those 18 to 25, and free for those under 18. Admission to the Petit Trianon is 15F ($2.55) for adults, 10F ($1.70) for those 18 to 25, and under 18 free. Admission to both Trianons is 30F ($5.10) for adults, 20F ($3.40) for those 18 to 25, and free for those under 18. Adults pay the reduced rates for all attractions after 3:30pm.

Getting There   To get to Versailles, 13 miles southwest of Paris, catch the RER line C at the Gare d'Austerlitz, St-Michel, Musée d'Orsay, Invalides, Pont-de-l'Alma, Champ-de-Mars, or Javel station and take it to the Versailles Rive Gauche station, from which there's a shuttle bus to the château. The 35F ($5.95) trip takes about 35 to 40 minutes; Eurailpass holders travel free on the train, but pay 20F ($3.40) for a ride on the shuttle bus. Regular SNCF trains also make the run from central Paris to Versailles: One set of trains departs from the Gare St-Lazare for the Versailles Rive Droite RER station; another set of trains departs from the Gare Montparnasse for Versailles Chantiers station, a 15-minute walk from the château. If you don't want to walk the 15-minute trek through town, you can take bus B from Versailles Chantiers to the Château for 8F ($1.35) each way.

As a final resort, you can always go via a combination of Métro and city bus. Travel to the Pont-de-Sèvres stop by Métro, and then transfer to bus 171 for a westward trek that takes from 20 to 45 minutes, depending on traffic. The bus costs you three Métro tickets, and deposits you near the gates of the palace.

If you're driving, take route N-10 and park on the place d'Armes in front of the Château.

FONTAINEBLEAU   Napoléon joined the grand parade of French rulers who used the **Palais de Fontainebleau** (☎ **01-60-71-50-70**) as a resort, hunting in its magnificent forest. Under François I the hunting lodge was enlarged into a royal palace in the Italian Renaissance style that he admired. Artists from the School of Fontainebleau adorned the 210-foot-long **Gallery of François I.**

Fontainebleau found renewed glory under Napoléon. You can wander around much of the palace on your own, but the **Musée Napoléon** and the **Petits Appartements** are accessible by guided tour only. Most impressive are his throne room and his bedroom (look for his symbol, a bee). The furnishings in the grand apartments of Napoléon and Joséphine evoke the imperial heyday.

The interior is open Wednesday to Monday from 9:30am to 12:30pm and 2 to 5pm. In July and August, it's open 9:30am to 6pm. A ticket allowing visits to the *Grands Appartements* costs 35F ($5.95) for adults and 23F ($3.90) for students 18 to 25; under 18 free. A ticket allowing access to the *Petits Appartements* and the Musée Napoléon goes for 16F ($2.70) for adults and 12F ($2.05) for students 18 to 25; under 18 free.

Getting There   Trains to Fontainebleau, 37 miles south of Paris, depart from the Gare de Lyon in Paris, as part of a trip that takes between 45 and 60 minutes each way and that costs 94F ($16) round-trip. Fontainebleau's railway station lies 3 miles from the château, in the suburb of Avon. A local bus (it's marked simply CHÂTEAU) makes the 2-mile trip from the railway station at Avon to the château at 15-minute intervals every Monday to Saturday, and at 30-minute intervals every Sunday, for 10F ($1.70) each way.

CHARTRES   The architectural aspirations of the Middle Ages reached their highest expression in the ✪ **Cathédrale Notre-Dame de Chartres,** 16 Cloître Notre-Dame (☎ 02-37-21-56-33). A mystical light seems to stream through this stained glass, which gave the world a new color—Chartres blue. One of the greatest of the world's high Gothic cathedrals, Chartres contains some of the oldest (some of it created as early as the 12th century) and most beautiful medieval stained glass anywhere. It was spared in both world wars; the glass removed painstakingly piece by piece for storage and safekeeping.

The cathedral you see today dates principally from the 13th century. It was the first to use flying buttresses, giving it a higher and lighter construction. French sculpture in the 12th century broke into full bloom when the Royal Portal was added; the sculptured bodies are elongated and formalized in their long flowing robes, but the faces are amazingly lifelike. Admission free, the cathedral is open Monday to Saturday 7:30am to 7:30pm and Sunday 8:30am to 7:15pm. The crypt can be visited only on a guided tour, costing 11F ($1.85) for adults or 8F ($1.35) for students and children. From April to October, there are five tours daily, curtailed to two per day off-season. Inquire locally about times of tours, as they change frequently.

Getting There   Chartres is 60 miles southwest of Paris. From the Gare Montparnasse, trains run directly to Chartres, taking less than an hour and passing through the sea of wheat fields that characterize Beauce, the granary of France.

2 The Loire Valley Châteaux

Bordered by vineyards, the winding Loire Valley cuts through the land of castles deep in France's heart. When royalty and nobility built châteaux throughout this valley during the French Renaissance, sumptuousness was uppermost in their minds. An era of excessive pomp reigned until Henri IV moved his court to Paris, marking the Loire's decline.

The Loire is blessed with abundant attractions—there's even the castle that inspired the fairy tale *Sleeping Beauty*. Tours is the traditional gateway; once here you can explore either east or west, depending on your interests. From Paris, you can reach Tours by autoroute (take A-10 southwest).

Only in the Loire Valley

Wandering Through the Gardens of Villandry   These are the most splendid gardens in the Loire, containing 10½ miles of boxwood sculpture alone. Borders represent the many facets of love: Pink tulips and dahlias suggest sweet love; red, tragic; and yellow, unfaithful. Crazy love is symbolized by all colors. The vine arbors, citrus hedges, and shady walks keep six men busy full-time. One Renaissance garden contains all the common French vegetables except the potato, which wasn't known in France in the 16th century.

Seeing Where French History Was Made   If you don't like to read books on French history, you can learn about it on the spot. Every château has a juicy story. For

The Loire Valley

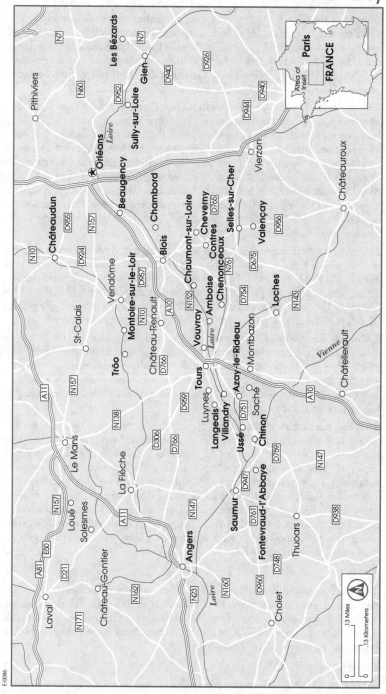

example, at the Château de Blois, you learn about the events of December 23, 1588, when the duc de Guise, a ladies' man in spite of his being called Balafré (Scarface), met his end. Summoned to meet his archrival, Henri III, the duc reluctantly left the bed of one of his loves and was met by the daggers of the guards. Stabbed repeatedly, he fell to the floor in a pool of blood. Only then did Henri emerge from behind the curtains. *"Mon Dieu,"* the king exclaimed, "he's taller dead than alive."

Calling on Les Dames de Chenonceau   The Château de Chenonceau is called the most feminine in the Loire because it's associated with six "lionesses." The most famous was Diane de Poitiers, mistress of Henri II and 20 years his senior. The virtual queen of France, she was presented with the château in 1547. Henri's wife, Catherine de Médici, took over upon her husband's death, sending Diane to Chaumont. The wife of Henri III, Louise de Lorraine, also lived here; she became known as Le Reine Blanche (white queen) after her husband was assassinated. She mourned his death for the rest of her life, even though Henri, who often went about in drag, had preferred his curly haired minions to her. A famous 18th-century occupant was Mme Dupin, grandmother of George Sand.

Following in the Footsteps of Leonardo   The town of Amboise evokes memories of Leonardo da Vinci. He spent his last years here, where his remains were entombed. You can still visit Clos-Lucé, the charming 15th-century manor house that François I, a great patron of the arts, gave to Leonardo after summoning him from Italy in 1514. Obviously Leonardo was happy in these idyllic surroundings, as he left this message: "A well-filled day gives a good sleep. A well-filled life gives a peaceful death."

Calling at the Gates of Chambord   In the middle of a royal game forest, this château is the largest in the Loire, hailed as the most outstanding experience in the valley. There are 440 rooms, plus 365 chimneys. Admittedly, it doesn't have the extravagant beauty of Chenonceau, but it's mammothly impressive. Presumably, you'll arrive at the gates less encumbered than François I—he required 12,000 horses to haul his luggage, servants, and court hangers-on.

Sampling the Cuisine of the Loire   The châteaux district is one of the world's great gastronomic centers. Patricia Wells, author of *The Food Lover's Guide to France,* said that the Loire's cuisine reminds her "of the daffodil days of spring and blue skies of summer." Particularly superb are salmon caught in the Loire River and often served with sorrel. The region's rivers are stocked with other fish as well, like pike, carp, shad, and mullet. Gourmets also prize *pâté d'alouettes* (lark pâté) and *matelote d'anguille* (stewed eel). From the mushroom-rich Sologne comes wild boar, deer, miniature quail, hare, pheasant, and mallard duck. The valley's Atlantic side produces an astonishing variety of grapes used to make wines ranging from dry to lusciously sweet and from still to sparkling and fruity.

TOURS

Tours, 144 miles southwest of Paris and 70 miles southwest of Orléans, is at the junction of the Loire and Cher rivers. The devout en route to Santiago de Compostela in northwest Spain once stopped off here to pay homage at the tomb of St. Martin, the Apostle of Gaul, bishop of Tours in the 4th century. Tours is the traditional place to begin your exploration of the Loire Valley.

ESSENTIALS

GETTING THERE   About ten **trains** make the run from Paris to Tours every day. At least eight of them are TGVs (*trains à grande vitesse*) that roar their way from Paris'

Gare de Montparnasse to Bordeaux, traversing the distance between Paris and Tours in a record-breaking 55 minutes. Each of these TGVs arrives at the railway station in St-Pierre-de-Corps, a hamlet set about 2 miles southeast of Tours that's connected to the city's main railway station (La Gare SNCF de Tours, at the place Maréchal Leclerc) by a free shuttle train that runs on a spur line connecting the two stations. If you're coming into Tours on any of the trains that fan out into the Loire Valley, chances are good that you'll arrive via a conventional (non-TGV) train at the place Maréchal Leclerc, and thereby avoid the need to make the transfer from the TGV station at St-Pierre-de-Corps. For rail information and schedules in Tours, the Loire Valley, and the rest of France, call ☎ **08-36-35-35-35.**

Once you're in Tours, you can rely on public transport to see much of the Loire; you can also rent a **bike** and tour—the region is relatively flat. Try **Amster'Cycle,** 8 rue Édouard Vaillant (☎ **02-47-61-22-23**), which rents both mountain bikes and all-purpose road bikes for 80F ($13.60) per day. A deposit is required in the form of a passport, 1,500F ($255), or a valid credit card. The shop is only 50 yards from the rail station.

VISITOR INFORMATION   The **Office de Tourisme** is at 78 rue Bernard-Palissy (☎ **02-47-70-37-37**).

DEPARTING BY CAR   To reach your first major château in the Loire, follow D-7 for 11 miles west to Villandry.

Exploring Tours

The heart of town is **place Jean-Jaurès. Rue Nationale** is the principal street (the valley's Champs-Élysées), running north to the Loire River. Head along rue du Commerce and rue du Grand-Marché to reach *la vieille ville,* the old town.

Cathédrale St-Gatien, 5 place de la Cathédrale (☎ **02-47-70-21-00**), has a facade in the flamboyant Gothic style, flanked by towers with bases from the 12th century, although the lanterns are Renaissance. The choir is from the 13th century, and each century through the 16th saw new additions. Some of the glorious stained-glass windows are from the 13th century. The cathedral is open daily 9am to 7pm; admission is free.

In the Château Royal, 25 av. André Malraux, is the **Musée de l'Historial de la Touraine** (☎ **02-47-61-02-95**). A perfect, although a bit kitschy, introduction to the region, this museum features 30 scenes and 165 wax figures tracing 1,000 years of Touraine history. The museum is open daily: May 16 through June 30 and September 1 through October 31, 9am to noon and 2 to 6pm; July 1 through August, 31 9am to 6:30pm; and November 1 through May 15, 2 to 5:30pm. Admission is 35F ($5.95) for adults and 20F ($3.40) for children 7 to 16.

Musée des Beaux-Arts, 18 place François-Sicard (☎ **02-47-05-68-73**), is a fine provincial museum housed in the Palais des Archevêques, worth visiting for its lovely rooms and gardens. There are works by Degas, Delacroix, Rembrandt, and Boucher, and sculpture by Houdon and Bourdelle. The museum is open Wednesday to Monday 9am to 12:45pm and 2 to 6pm. Admission is 30F ($5.10) for adults and 15F ($2.55) for students and those over 65. Ages 12 and under are admitted free. You can tour the gardens for free daily from 7am to 8:30pm.

Where to Stay

Best Western Le Central. 21 rue Berthelot, 37000 Tours. ☎ **800/528-1234** in the U.S., or 02-47-05-46-44. Fax 02-47-66-10-26. 40 units (38 with bathroom). MINIBAR TV TEL. 165F ($28.05) double without bathroom; 350–400F ($59.50–$68) double with bathroom. AE, DC, MC, V. Parking 40F ($6.80). Bus: 1, 4, or 5.

Off the main boulevard, this old-fashioned hotel is in walking distance of the river and cathedral, surrounded by gardens, lawns, and trees. Built in 1850, the hotel has just recently been affiliated with Best Western; it's a more modest, but also more economical, choice than others in town. The Tremouilles family offers comfortable rooms at reasonable rates, as well as two salons with reproductions of 18th- and 19th-century pieces. Rooms come in a variety of shapes and sizes; a renovation in 1999 improved them considerably and updated the plumbing in the small bathrooms.

Hôtel Alliance. 292 av. de Grammont, 37200 Tours. ☎ **02-47-28-00-80.** Fax 02-47-27-77-61. 125 units. A/C MINIBAR TV TEL. 350–550F ($59.50–$93.50) double; 600–1,200F ($102–$204) suite. AE, DC, MC, V. Free parking. Bus: 1, 2, 5, 6, 9, or 11.

This is one of the largest and most modern hotels in Tours, about a mile south of the town center. It's decorated in *grand siècle* 18th-century style, and the brightly colored soundproof rooms contain a blend of modern pieces and antique reproductions. Bedrooms are comfortable, but each was last renovated in 1985; the small bathrooms have showers. There's plenty of open space, a French garden, and a pool. Breakfast and drinks are served in a sitting area, and the hotel has a distinguished restaurant with a terrace, plus a tennis court.

Hôtel de l'Univers. 5 bd. Heurteloup, 37000 Tours. ☎ **02-47-05-37-12.** Fax 02-47-61-51-80. 85 units. A/C TV TEL. 860F ($146.20) double. AE, DC, MC, V. Parking 50F ($8.50). Bus 1, 4, or 5.

This hotel on the main artery of Tours is the oldest in town. The rooms, which are decorated partly with modern pieces and partly with art deco pieces, are beginning to look a bit shopworn, although this remains Tours's favorite traditional hotel. On weekdays it's filled mainly with business travelers, and on weekends it hosts many area brides. The small bathrooms have showers and hair dryers. La Touraine, the main dining room, open daily, serves excellent meals from a set-price menu.

WHERE TO DINE

La Rôtisserie Tourangelle. 23 rue du Commerce Tours. ☎ **02-47-05-71-21.** Reservations required. Main courses 90–125F ($15.30–$21.25); set-price menus 85–195F ($14.45–$33.15). AE, DC, MC, V. Tues–Sat 12:15–1:45pm and 7:30–9:30pm; Sun 12:15–1:45pm. Bus: 1, 4, or 5. FRENCH.

This is a local favorite, where you can dine on a terrace in summer (although there's not much to see). It's better to concentrate on the ever-changing menu, which may include homemade foie gras and white fish caught in the Loire served with *beurre blanc* (white butter sauce). Regional ingredients mix well with the local wines, as exemplified by pike-perch with sabayon and *magret de filet de canard* (duckling) served with a "jam" of red Chinon wine. In summer, strawberry parfait with raspberry coulis is a perfect end to the meal. If only the service were a little better.

Le Relais Buré. 1 place de la Résistance. ☎ **02-47-05-67-74.** Main courses 66–115F ($11.20–$19.55); set-price menu (Mon–Fri only) 120F ($20.40). AE, DC, MC, V. Daily noon–2:30pm and 7pm–midnight. Bus: 1 or 5. FRENCH.

A 5-minute walk east of the center of Tours, this brasserie specializes in shellfish and regional recipes, although it's somewhat unimaginative. It has a busy bar and a front terrace, with tables scattered inside on the street level and mezzanine. Menu items include six well-flavored versions of sauerkraut; a wide choice of grilled meats, including steak au poivre; foie gras and smoked salmon; and a tempting array of desserts.

✪ **Parc de Belmont (Jean Bardet).** 57 rue Groison, 37100 Tours. ☎ **02-47-41-41-11.** Fax 02-47-51-68-72. Reservations recommended. Main courses 210–380F ($35.70–$64.60);

set-price menu 250–750F ($42.50–$127.50). AE, DC, MC, V. Nov–Mar, Tues–Sat noon–2pm
and 7:30–10pm, Sun noon–2:30pm; Apr–Oct, Tues–Sun noon–2pm and 7:30–10pm, Mon
7:30–10pm. FRENCH.

Set in three rooms of a 19th-century château and opened in 1987, this fine restaurant
is the creation of the famous, Michelin two-star chef Jean Bardet, who considers all
meals here to be "an orchestration of wines, alcohol, food, and cigars." However, that's
not to say you must partake of all four elements to have one of the best meals in the
region. Specialties of spectacular flavor include a lobster ragôut, sliced sea bass with a
confit of tomatoes and artichoke hearts, and scallops with a purée of shallots and
truffle cream. The duck giblets and lobster accompanied by a red wine and orange
sauce is reason enough to visit.

The rest of the château has been transformed into a luxury hotel and is the domain
of chef Bardet's wife, Sophie. The spacious guest rooms are individually decorated and
have high ceilings, cozy fireplaces, and antique furnishings. Some even have private
balconies that look out onto the gardens. A double room ranges from 750 to 1,050F
($127.50 to $178.50), and suites cost from 1,500 to 1,900F ($255 to $323).

VILLANDRY

The extravagant 16th-century-style gardens of the Renaissance ✪ **Château de Villandry,** 37510 Joué-les-Tours (☎ **02-47-50-02-09**), are celebrated throughout the
Touraine. Forming a trio of superimposed cloisters, with a water garden on the highest
level, the gardens were purchased in a decaying state and restored by Spanish doctor/sci-
entist Joachim Carvallo, the present owner's great-grandfather. The grounds contain 10½
miles of boxwood sculpture, which the gardeners must cut to style in only 2 weeks in September. Every square of the gardens seems like a geometric mosaic. The borders represent
the many faces of love: for example, tender, tragic (with daggers), or crazy, the last evoked
by a labyrinth that doesn't get you anywhere.

Originally a feudal castle stood at Villandry, but in 1536 Jean Lebreton, the chancellor of François I, built the present château; the buildings form a U and are surrounded by a two-sided moat.

Admission to the gardens with a tour of the château is 45F ($7.65) for adults, 38F
($6.45) children. Visiting the gardens separately without a guide costs 32F ($5.45)
adults, 26F ($4.40) children. The château is open mid-February to mid-November,
and guided tours are conducted daily 9am to 6:30pm. The gardens are open year-
round 9am to sunset. Tours are given in French with leaflets in English.

ESSENTIALS

GETTING THERE Unfortunately, Villandry doesn't have train or bus service from
Tours. Rent a **bike** in Tours (see above) and ride along the Cher or go by car (see
above).

DEPARTING BY CAR From Villandry, continue west along D-7, and then take
D-39 south for 7 miles to Azay-le-Rideau.

WHERE TO STAY & DINE

Le Cheval Rouge. Villandry, 37510 Joué-les-Tours. ☎ **02-47-50-02-07.** Fax 02-47-50-
08-77. Reservations recommended. Main courses 80–120F ($13.60–$20.40). Set-price menus
95–170F ($16.15–$28.90). MC, V. Tues–Sun noon–2pm and 7:30–9pm. Closed Feb to mid-
Mar. Open Sun night and Mon if it's a holiday. FRENCH.

This is a well-known lunch stopover near the château, in spite of a stiff, sometimes
unpleasant welcome and a sometimes difficult staff. Set in a conservatively decorated
dining room, about 100 yards from the banks of the Cher, it won't be your most memorable meal in the Loire Valley; the food is competent, but not brilliant. Specialties

include lobster Thermidor, médallions of veal with morels, and turbot with hollandaise sauce. The inn also rents 20 bedrooms, all with bathroom and telephone, with a TV set that plays in the establishment's bar. A double rents for between 230 to 280F ($39.10 to $47.60). Parking is free.

AZAY-LE-RIDEAU

This château's richly detailed towers and blue-slate roof pierced with dormers shimmer in the moat, creating a reflection like a Monet painting. But the defensive medieval look is all for show; the ✪ **Château d'Azay-le-Rideau,** 37190 Azay-le-Rideau (☎ **02-47-45-42-04**), was created as a private residence during the Renaissance at an idyllic spot on the Indre River. Gilles Berthelot, François I's finance minister, commissioned the castle, and his spendthrift wife, Philippa, supervised its construction. So elegant was the creation that the chevalier king grew immensely jealous. In time, Berthelot was forced to flee and the château reverted to the king.

Before entering, circle the château, enjoying the perfect proportions of this crowning achievement of the Renaissance in Touraine. Its most fanciful feature is a bay enclosing a grand stairway with a straight flight of steps. The Renaissance interior is a virtual museum. From the second-floor Royal Chamber, look out at the gardens. This bedroom, also known as the Green Room, is believed to have sheltered Louis XIII.

The château is open daily July to August 9am to 7pm, April through June and October from 9:30am to 6pm, and November through March from 9:30am to 12:30pm and 2 to 5:30pm. Admission is 35F ($5.95) for adults and 23F ($3.90) for children. May to July, *son-et-lumière* (sound and light) performances are staged at 10:30pm; August and September, at 10pm. Tickets cost 60F ($10.20) for adults and 35F ($5.95) for children.

ESSENTIALS

GETTING THERE   Azay-le-Rideau lies astride the railway lines that interconnect Tours with Chinon. The SNCF maintains both **trains** and **buses** that make the transit from both of those towns, a ride of between 25 and 30 minutes from either of them. The SNCF provides about seven transits a day into Azay-le-Rideau, either by bus or by train, depending on their priorities, from both Tours and Chinon. Trains arrive at the railway station a mile west of Azay's center; buses arrive in the town center. For information about either buses or trains, call ☎ **02-47-93-11-04** (the railway station at Chinon) or ☎ **08-36-35-35-35** (the number for SNCF information throughout France).

VISITOR INFORMATION   The **Syndicat d'Initiative** (tourist office) is at place de l'Europe (☎ **02-47-45-44-40**).

DEPARTING BY CAR   After seeing Villandry and Azay-le-Rideau, return to Tours. From Tours, head east for 22 miles to Amboise. To reach Amboise, take either D-751 on the south bank of the Loire or N-152 on the north bank (both good roads). If you take the northern route, you can follow the signs to Vouvray, which turns out the most famous white wine of the Touraine. Vintners post signs if they allow visits and tastings.

WHERE TO DINE

L'Aigle d'Or. 10 av. Adélaïde-Riché. ☎ **02-47-45-24-58.** Reservations recommended. Main courses 75–115F ($12.75–$19.55); set-price lunch 100F ($17); set-price dinner 150–275F ($25.50–$46.75). V. Daily 12:30–2pm and 7:30–9:30pm. Closed Wed and Sun and Tues night in winter; also all of Feb and Dec 10–25. FRENCH.

The service is professional, the welcome often charming, and the food the best in Azay. The selection of appetizers ranges from a mousseline of scallops with a crayfish coulis to foie gras. Main dishes often feature fresh fish from the Loire with sauces made from regional wines. Desserts are made fresh daily and vary with the chef's moods.

AMBOISE

On the banks of the Loire, Amboise is in the center of vineyards known as Touraine-Amboise. Leonardo da Vinci spent his last years in this city.

ESSENTIALS

GETTING THERE   Amboise lies on the main Paris-Blois-Tours rail line, with 14 **trains** per day arriving from both Tours (trip time: 20 minutes) and Blois (trip time: 15 minutes). Five trains arrive daily from Paris (trip time: 2½ hours). For train information and schedules, call ☎ **08-36-35-35-35. Tourisme Verney** (☎ **02-47-57-00-44**), runs five **buses** a day connecting Tours and Amboise (trip time: about 30 minutes). The train station is along Boulevard Gambetta and buses leave from the parking lot adjacent to the tourist office.

VISITOR INFORMATION   The **Office de Tourisme** is on quai du Général-de-Gaulle (☎ **02-47-57-09-28**).

DEPARTING BY CAR   To reach Blois from Amboise, continue along either the south bank (D-751) or the north bank (N-152). Blois is 37 miles northeast of Tours.

EXPLORING AMBOISE

Dominating the town is the ✪ **Château d'Amboise** (☎ **02-47-57-00-98**), the first in France to reflect the Italian Renaissance. A combination of both Gothic and Renaissance, this 15th-century château is mainly associated with Charles VIII, who built it on a rocky spur separating the valleys of the Loire and the Amasse.

You enter via a ramp, opening onto a panoramic terrace fronting the river. At one time this terrace was surrounded by buildings, and *fêtes* were staged in the enclosed courtyard. At the time of the revolution, the castle declined and only a quarter or even less remains of this once-sprawling edifice. First you come to the flamboyant Gothic Chapelle St-Hubert, distinguished by its lacelike tracery. It allegedly contains Leonardo's remains; actually the great artist was buried in the castle's Collegiate Church, which was destroyed between 1806 and 1810. During the Second Empire, excavations here revealed bones "identified" as Leonardo's.

Today the walls of the château are hung with tapestries and the rooms furnished grandly. The Logis du Roi (king's apartment) escaped destruction and can be visited. The château is open daily July and August 9am to 7pm, April to June 9am to 6:30pm, September and October 9am to 6pm, and November to March 9am to noon and 2 to 5pm. Admission is 39F ($6.65) for adults, 27F ($4.60) for students, and 17F ($2.90) for children.

You might also want to visit **Clos-Lucé,** 2 rue de Clos-Lucé (☎ **02-47-57-62-88**), a 15th-century brick-and-stone manor. In what had been an oratory for Anne de Bretagne, François I installed "the great master in all forms of art and science," Leonardo da Vinci. Venerated by the chevalier king, Leonardo lived here for 3 years, dying at the manor in 1519. (Those paintings of Leonardo dying in François's arms are symbolic; the king was supposedly away at the time.) The manor's rooms are well furnished, some with reproductions from Leonardo's time. Clos-Lucé is open March through September daily from 9am to 7pm; off-season, daily from 9am to 6pm. Admission is 38F ($6.45) for adults and 27F ($4.60) for students, 19F ($3.25) ages 6 to 15 (free 5 and under).

WHERE TO STAY

Belle-Vue. 12 quai Charles-Guinot, 37400 Amboise. ☎ **02-47-57-02-26.** Fax 02-47-30-51-23. 32 units. TV TEL. 300–380F ($51–$64.60) double. MC, V. Closed Nov 15–Mar 15.

This modest inn lies at the bridge crossing the Loire at the foot of the château. The bedrooms are furnished in an old-fashioned French style, with low beds and rather thin mattresses. Try to stay in the main building, which has more charm and character than the less convenient annex across the river. Bathrooms are small and have showers. Breakfast is the only meal served.

Hostellerie du Château-de-Pray. Route de Chargé (D-751), 37400 Amboise. ☎ **02-47-57-23-67.** Fax 02-47-57-32-50. 19 units. TV TEL. 590–850F ($100.30–$144.50) double; 850–990F ($144.50–$168.30) suite. Half-board 225F ($38.25) per person extra. AE, DC, V. Closed Jan 2–Feb 10. Free parking.

About a mile east of the town center, this château resembles a tower-flanked castle on the Rhine. Inside, you'll find antlers, hunting trophies, antiques, and a paneled drawing room with a fireplace and a collection of antique oils. Guest rooms in the main building are stylishly conservative and comfortable, and have the added allure of being in a building dating from 1224. Rooms were renovated in 1998 and come in various shapes and sizes; the more spacious chambers are near the ground floor. The small but efficiently organized bathrooms contain hair dryers. Try to avoid the four rooms in the 1990s annex; although they have the same amenities as those in the main building, they are rather impersonally furnished and lack character. The hotel restaurant, open to nonguests, offers set-price menus of excellent quality.

✪ **Le Choiseul.** 36 quai Charles-Guinot, 37400 Amboise. ☎ **02-47-30-45-45.** Fax 02-47-30-46-10. E-mail: choiseul@wanadoo.fr. 32 units. MINIBAR TV TEL. 470–1,400F ($79.90–$238) double; 1,130–1,870F ($192.10–$317.90) suite. AE, DC, MC, V. Closed Dec 8–Jan 24.

There's no better address in Amboise or any better place for cuisine than this 18th-century hotel. This hotel is set in the valley between a hillside and the Loire River, close to the château, and there's a garden with flowering terraces on the grounds. The rooms, 16 of which are air-conditioned, are luxurious; although recently modernized, they've retained their old-world charm. Bathrooms are small but have tub and shower combinations and a hair dryer. The food is better than that in Tours or the surrounding area. The formal dining room has a view of the Loire and welcomes nonguests who phone ahead. It's open daily noon to 2pm and 7 to 9:30pm, with set-price menus ranging from 290 to 500F ($49.30 to $85). The wine list is the best in the area. Facilities include an outdoor pool, a tennis court, and a Ping-Pong table.

WHERE TO DINE

Le Manoir St-Thomas. Place Richelieu. ☎ **02-47-57-22-52.** Reservations required. Main courses 130–150F ($22.10–$25.50); set-price menu 175–295F ($29.75–$50.15). AE, DC, MC, V. Tues–Sat 12:15–2:30pm and 7:15–9:30pm; Sun 12:15–2:30pm. Closed Jan 15–Mar 15. FRENCH.

The best food in town outside of Le Choiseul is served at this Renaissance house in the shadow of the château. The restaurant is in a pleasant garden, and the elegant dining room is richly decorated with a polychrome ceiling and a massive stone fireplace. Owner/chef François Le Coz's specialties include truffles with foie gras, lamb filet with port, and red mullet filet with cream of sweet pepper sauce. The tender saddle of hare is perfectly flavored. Some special culinary delights are the gooseliver pâté wrapped in a combination of truffles and wild black mushrooms, and duck flavored with honey, cinnamon, and ginger.

BLOIS

Blois is the most attractive of the major Loire towns. It rises on the right bank of the Loire, its skyline dominated by its château, where the duc de Guise was assassinated on December 23, 1588, on orders of his archrival, Henri III; it's one of the most famous murders in French history. Several French kings lived here, and the town has a rich architectural history.

ESSENTIALS

GETTING THERE   The Paris-Austerlitz line via Orléans delivers 8 **trains** per day from Paris (trip time: 2 hours). From Tours, 10 trains arrive per day (trip time: 45 minutes), and from Amboise, 10 trains per day arrive (trip time: 20 minutes). For train information and schedules, call ☎ **08-36-35-35-35.** The train station is at place de la Gare. If you'd like to explore the area by **bike,** go to **Cycles Le Blond,** 44 levée des Tuileries (☎ **02-54-74-30-13**), where rentals range from 30 to 120F ($5.10 to $20.40) per day, depending on the model. You have to leave your passport, a credit card, a driver's license, or a deposit of between 500 and 1,500F ($85 and $255), depending on the value of the bike.

VISITOR INFORMATION   The **Office de Tourisme** is at Pavillon Anne-de-Bretagne, 3 av. Jean-Laigret (☎ **02-54-90-41-41**).

DEPARTING BY CAR   To reach Chaumont sur-Loire, take D-751 for 12 miles south of Blois.

EXPLORING THE CHÂTEAU

The murder of the duc de Guise is only one of the memories evoked by the ✪ **Château de Blois** (☎ **02-54-74-16-06**), begun in the 13th century by the comtes de Blois. Charles d'Orléans (son of Louis d'Orléans, assassinated by the Burgundians in 1407) lived at Blois after his release from 25 years of English captivity. He'd married Mary of Cleves and brought a "court of letters" to Blois. In his 70s, Charles became the father of the future Louis XII, who was to marry Anne de Bretagne. Blois was then launched in its new role as a royal château. In time it was to be called the second capital of France, with Blois the city of kings.

However, Blois soon became a palace of banishment. Louis XIII got rid of his interfering mother, Marie de Médici, by sending her here, but this plump matron escaped by sliding into the moat down a mound of dirt left by the builders. Then in 1626 the king sent his conspiring brother, Gaston d'Orléans, here; he stayed.

If you stand in the courtyard, you'll find the château is like an illustrated storybook of French architecture. The Hall of the Estates-General is a beautiful 13th-century work; the Charles d'Orléans gallery was built by Louis XII from 1498 to 1501, who also built the Louis XII wing. The Gaston d'Orléans wing was constructed by Mansart between 1635 and 1638. The most remarkable is the François I wing, a masterpiece of the French Renaissance, containing a spiral staircase with elaborately ornamented balustrades and the king's symbol, the salamander.

The château is open daily mid-October to mid-March from 9am to 12:30pm and 2 to 5pm; mid-March through June and September from 9am to 6:30pm; July and August from 9am to 7:30pm. Admission 35F ($5.95) for adults, 25F ($4.25) for students under 25, and 20F ($3.40) for children under 7. A *son-et-lumière* presentation in French is sponsored nightly between May and September, beginning in most cases at 10:30pm, but in rare instances, including throughout the month of May, at 9:30 or 10:15pm, depending on the school calendar. As a taped lecture is played, colored lights and dramatic readings, in French, evoke the age in which the château was built. Participation in the sound and light show costs 60F ($10.20) for adults and 30F ($5.10) for children 7 to 15; free for children 6 and under.

WHERE TO STAY

Hôtel le Savoie. 6–8 rue du Docteur-Ducoux, 41000 Blois. ☎ **02-54-74-32-21.** Fax 02-54-74-29-58. www.citote.com. 26 units. TV TEL. 230–280F ($39.10–$47.60) double. AE, MC, V.

This modern hotel is both inviting and livable, from its courteous staff to the guest rooms, which though small, are nonetheless quiet and cozy, with flowered upholsteries and a certain French charm. They were last renovated in 1998. Bathrooms are small but have sufficient shelf space. In the morning, a breakfast buffet is set up in the bright dining room.

Mercure Centre. 28 quai St-Jean, 41000 Blois. ☎ **02-54-56-66-66.** Fax 02-54-56-67-00. 96 units. A/C MINIBAR TV TEL. 565F ($96.05) double; 650–680F ($110.50–$115.60) suite. AE, DC, MC, V. Parking 35F ($5.95). Bus: Quayside marked PISCINE.

This is the newest and best-located hotel in Blois—3 stories of reinforced concrete and big windows beside the quays of the Loire, a 5-minute walk from the château. Bedrooms never rise above their chain format and are very roadside motel in look, but are roomy and soundproof and equipped with satellite TV. Bathrooms are excellent, clad entirely in marble with a shower and tub combination and a hair dryer. French and international meals are served daily in the pleasant restaurant.

WHERE TO DINE

Le Médicis. 2 allée François-1er, 41000 Blois. ☎ **02-54-43-94-04.** Fax 02-54-42-04-05. Reservations required. Main courses 80–165F ($13.60–$28.05); set-price menus 110F ($18.70), 165F ($28.05), 275F ($46.75), and 420F ($71.40). AE, DC, MC, V. Daily noon–2pm and 7–10pm. Closed Jan. Bus: 2. FRENCH.

Christian and Annick Garanger maintain one of the most sophisticated inns in Blois—ideal for a gourmet meal or an overnight stop. Fresh fish is the chef's specialty. Typical main courses are asparagus in mousseline sauce, scampi ravioli with saffron sauce, and suprême of perch with morels. Chocolate in many manifestations is the dessert specialty. In addition, the Garangers rent 12 elegant rooms, each with bathroom, air-conditioning, minibar, TV, phone, and hair dryer. The rates are 450 to 550F ($76.50 to $93.50) double; there is one suite that goes for 700F ($119).

✪ Rendezvous des Pêcheurs. 27 rue du Foix. ☎ **02-54-74-67-48.** Reservations recommended. Main courses 96–130F ($16.30–$22.10); set-price menu 145F ($24.65). MC, V. Mon 7:30–10pm; Tues–Sat noon–2pm and 7:30–10pm. Closed 3 weeks in Aug and 1 week in Feb. FRENCH.

This restaurant occupies a small, 16th-century houses that lies within a 5-minute walk from the château. The chefs here, the finest in this part of France, continue to maintain their reputation for quality ingredients, generous portions, and creativity. The chef prepares only two or three meat dishes, including roasted chicken with a medley of potatoes and mushrooms and a confit of garlic, and a fricassée of sweetbreads. They appear alongside a much longer roster of fish and seafood dishes, such as a poached filet of zander served with fresh oysters, and filet of sea bass served with a champagne sauce on a bed of sea urchins.

CHAUMONT-SUR-LOIRE

On the morning when Diane de Poitiers crossed the drawbridge, the ✪ **Château de Chaumont** (☎ **02-54-51-26-26**) looked fiercely grim, with its battlements and pepper-pot turrets crowning the towers. Henri II, her lover, had recently died. The king had given her Chenonceau, but his widow, Catherine de Médici, banished her from her favorite château and sent her into exile at Chaumont. Inside, portraits reveal that Diane truly deserved her reputation as forever beautiful. A portrait of Catherine looking like a devout nun invites unfavorable comparisons.

Chaumont (Burning Mount) was built during the reign of Louis XII by Charles d'Amboise, and spans the period between the Middle Ages and the Renaissance. It was privately owned and inhabited until it was acquired by the state in 1938. Its prize exhibit is a rare collection of medallions by Nini, an Italian artist. A guest of the château for a while, he made medallion portraits of kings, queens, and nobles—even Benjamin Franklin, who once visited. In the bedroom once occupied by Catherine de Médici is a rare portrait, painted when she was young.

The château is open daily January through mid-March and October through December from 10am to 4:30pm; mid-March to September, it's open daily 9:30am to 6pm. Admission is 32F ($5.45) for adults and 21F ($3.55) for children 12 to 17; free for children 11 and under.

ESSENTIALS

GETTING THERE   Seventeen **trains** per day travel from both Blois (trip time: 15 minutes) and Tours (trip time: about 45 minutes). The train station is in Onzain, 1½ miles north of the château, a pleasant walk. For transportation information, call ☎ **02-47-20-50-50.**

From June 15 to September 15, you can take a **bus** in Blois operated by **Point Bus,** 2 place Victor Hugo (☎ **02-54-78-15-66**). The bus leaves Blois at 9:10am, returning at 6pm daily.

VISITOR INFORMATION   The **Office de Tourisme** is on rue du Maréchal-Leclerc (☎ **02-54-20-91-73**).

DEPARTING BY CAR   Blois (above) also makes a perfect launching pad for visiting another important château in the area, that of Chambord, which lies 11 miles east of Blois along D-33 near Bracieux.

WHERE TO STAY & DINE NEARBY

Domaine des Hauts de Loire. Route d'Herbault, 41150 Onzain. ☎ **02-54-20-72-57.** Fax 02-54-20-77-32. E-mail: hauts-loire@relaischateaux.fr. 35 units. MINIBAR TV TEL. 680–1,500F ($115.60–$255) double; from 2,450F ($416.50) suite. AE, DC, MC, V.

Less than 2 miles from the Château de Chaumont, on the opposite side of the Loire, this Relais & Châteaux property is a stately manor house built by the prosperous owner of a Paris-based newspaper in 1840 and named, rather coyly, at the time as a "hunting lodge." It's the most appealing stopover in the neighborhood, with a roster of intensely decorated bedrooms each in the style of Louis Philippe or Empire. About half the accommodations lie in a half-timbered annex that, although originally conceived as stables, was adapted to its present use in the 1960s. Sophisticated and elegant, the site also offers a restaurant that's open to nonresidents who phone in advance. Its well-prepared food served in a stately dining room is a local favorite. Set-price menus ranging from 315 to 620F ($53.55 to $105.40) include a salad of marinated eel with shallot-flavored vinaigrette; oysters on a layered sheet of sardines; filet of sole with black pepper and watercress; roasted filet of Loire Valley whitefish (*sandre*) served with parsley-flavored cream sauce and cabbage stuffed with a compote of snails; and the ultimate Loire valley main course, a filet of smoked eel prepared with Vouvray wine.

CHAMBORD

When François I used to say, "Come on up to my place," he meant the ✪ **Château de Chambord,** 41250 Bracieux (☎ **02-54-50-40-00**), not Fontainebleau or Blois. Some 2,000 workers began to piece together "the pile" in 1519. What emerged after 20 years was the pinnacle of the French Renaissance, the largest château in the Loire Valley. It was ready for the visit of Charles V of Germany, who was welcomed by nymphets in transparent veils gently tossing wildflowers in his path. French monarchs like Henri II and Catherine de Médici, Louis XIV, and Henri III came and went from Chambord, but none developed an affection for it to match François I's. The state acquired Chambord in 1932.

The château is in a park of more than 13,000 acres, enclosed within a wall stretching some 20 miles. Looking out a window in one of the 440 rooms, François is said to have carved these words on a pane with a diamond ring: "A woman is a creature of change; to trust her is to play the fool." Chambord's facade is dominated by four monumental towers. The keep has a spectacular terrace the ladies of the court used to stand on to watch the return of their men from the hunt.

The three-story keep also encloses a corkscrew staircase, superimposed so one person can descend at one end and a second ascend at the other without ever meeting. The apartments of Louis XIV, including his redecorated bedchamber, are also in the keep.

The château is open daily: January through March and October through December from 9:30am to 5:15pm; April through June, it closes at 6:15pm, and July and August it closes at 7:15pm. Admission is 40F ($6.80) for adults and 25F ($4.25) for ages 12 to 25; it's free for children 11 and under. At the tourist office you can pick up tickets for the *son-et-lumière* presentation in summer, called *Jours et Siècles* (Days and Centuries), but check the times. A ticket costs 50F ($8.50).

ESSENTIALS

GETTING THERE   It's best to travel to Chambord by car so you can explore the beautiful countryside on the way there and back. Otherwise, you could rent a **bicycle** in Blois (see above) and cycle to Chambord, or from June 15 to September 15 **Point Bus,** 2 place Victor Hugo (☎ **02-54-78-15-66**), operates a bus service to Chambord, leaving Blois at 9:10am and again at 1:20pm with a return at 1 and 6:10pm.

VISITOR INFORMATION   The **Office de Tourisme** is on place St-Michel (☎ **02-54-20-34-86**).

DEPARTING BY CAR   Back at the launching pad of Blois, you can strike out in another direction for yet another major château. Cheverny lies 12 miles south of Blois, reached by taking D-765.

WHERE TO STAY & DINE

Hôtel du Grand-St-Michel. 103 place St-Michel, 41250 Chambord, near Bracieux. ☎ **02-54-20-31-31.** Fax 02-54-20-36-40. 39 units. TV TEL. 290–450F ($49.30–$76.50) double. MC, V. Closed Nov 14–Dec 20. Free parking.

Across from the château, this inn is really the only one of any substance in town. Try for a front room overlooking the château, which is dramatic when floodlit at night. The rooms are plain but comfortable, with provincial decor. Most visitors arrive for lunch, which in summer is served on an awning-shaded terrace. The regional dishes are complemented by a marvelous collection of Loire wines so good they almost overshadow the cooking itself.

CHEVERNY

The *haut monde* still come to the Sologne area for the hunt as though the 17th century had never ended. However, 20th-century realities, like taxes, are *formidable* here—hence the **Château de Cheverny** (☎ **02-54-79-96-29**) must open some of its rooms for inspection by paying guests. At least that keeps the tax collector at bay and the hounds fed in winter.

Unlike most of the Loire châteaux, Cheverny is actually lived in by the descendants of the original owner, the vicomte de Sigalas. The family's lineage can be traced back to Henri Hurault, the son of the chancellor of Henri III and Henri IV, who built the château here in 1634. Designed in classic Louis XIII style, it boasts square pavilions flanking the central pile.

Inside, the antique furnishings, tapestries, decorations, and objets d'art are quite impressive. A 17th-century French artist, Jean Mosnier, decorated the fireplace with motifs from the legend of Adonis. In the Guards' Room is a collection of medieval armor.

The château is open daily: November through February from 9:30am to noon and 2:15 to 5pm; in March, the last part of September, and October it closes at 5:30pm; in April and May at 6:30pm; and from June to mid-September at 6:45pm. Admission is 34F ($5.80) for adults and 21F ($3.55) for children 7 to 14. It's free for children 6 and under.

ESSENTIALS

GETTING THERE   Cheverny is 12 miles south of Blois, along D-765. It's best reached by car or on an organized **bus tour** from Blois. From the railway station at Blois, there's a bus that departs for Cheverney once a day, at noon, returning to Blois 4 hours later, according to an oft-changing schedule that's dependent on the season and the day of the week. Frankly, most visitors find it a lot easier to take their own car or a taxi from the railway station at Blois.

DEPARTING BY CAR   If after exploring Cheverny you have enthusiasm for one more château, strike out for Valençay. From Cheverny head south on D-102 for 6 miles, crossing the border of the forest of Cheverny. At the town of Contres, connect with the junction of D-956, which traverses the Cher River 12 miles farther south at Selles-sur-Cher. From here, continue the final signposted 9 miles to Valençay.

WHERE TO STAY & DINE

Les Trois Marchands. Place de l'Eglise, 41700 Cour-Cheverny. ☎ **02-54-79-96-44.** Fax 02-54-79-25-60. Main courses 60–180F ($10.20–$30.60); set-price menus 120–240F ($20.40–$40.80). AE, DC, MC, V. Tues–Sun noon–2pm and 7:30–9pm. Closed Feb 1–Mar 15. FRENCH.

This much-renovated coaching inn, more comfortable than Saint-Hubert, has been handed down for many generations. Today Jean-Jacques Bricault owns the three-story building that sports awnings, a mansard roof, a glassed-in courtyard, and sidewalk tables with bright umbrellas. In the large tavern-style dining room, the menu might include foie gras, lobster salad, frogs' legs, fresh asparagus in mousseline sauce, or fish cooked in a salt crust. The inn also rents 38 well-furnished and comfortable rooms, costing 260 to 350F ($44.20 to $59.50) for a double with bathroom; rooms without bathrooms go for 180F ($30.60).

Saint-Hubert. Rue Nationale. 41700 Cour-Cheverny. ☎ **02-54-79-96-60.** Fax 02-54-79-21-17. Main courses 90–160F ($15.30–$27.20); set-price menus 98–280F ($16.65–$47.60). MC, V. Thurs–Tues 12:15–2pm and 7:30–9pm. Closed Jan 10–Feb 17 and Sun night in low season. FRENCH.

About 800 yards from the château, this roadside inn was built in the old provincial style. Chef Jean-Claude Pillaut is the secret of the Saint-Hubert's success. The least expensive menu might include terrine of quail, pike-perch with beurre blanc, a selection of cheeses, and a homemade fruit tart. The most expensive menu might offer lobster, an aiguillette of duckling prepared with grapes, or wild boar with a creamy sauce. Game is featured here in season. The Saint-Hubert offers 19 rooms with bathrooms, charging 200 to 320F ($34 to $54.40) double.

VALENÇAY

One of the Loire's handsomest Renaissance châteaux, 35 miles south of Blois, the **Château de Valençay** (☎ 02-54-00-10-66) was acquired in 1803 by Talleyrand on the orders of Napoléon, who wanted his minister of foreign affairs to receive dignitaries in great style. In 1838, Talleyrand was buried at Valençay, the château passing to his nephew, Louis de Talleyrand-Périgord. Before the Talleyrand ownership, Valençay was built in 1550 by the d'Estampes family. The dungeon and great west tower are of this period, as is the building's main body; other wings were added in the 17th and 18th centuries. The effect is grandiose, almost too much so, with domes, chimneys, and turrets. The private apartments are open to the public; they're sumptuously furnished, mostly in the Empire style but with Louis XV and Louis XVI trappings as well.

Admission to the castle, an antique car museum, and the park is 42F ($7.15) for adults, 34F ($5.80) for seniors and students, and 22F ($3.75) for those 17 and under. It's open daily April through June and September through October from 10am to 6pm; daily July and August from 10am to 7pm; and on Saturday, Sunday, and school holidays November through March 10am to 6pm.

ESSENTIALS

GETTING THERE   There are frequent SNCF rail connections from Blois. Call ☎ 08-36-35-35-35 for **train** information and schedules. The station is near the village center.

VISITOR INFORMATION   The **Office de Tourisme** is on route de Blois (☎ 02-54-00-04-42).

DEPARTING BY CAR   To continue château-hopping, drive north from Valençay until you come to Selles-sur-Cher at the river. This time, head west in the direction of Amboise, taking N-76 along the south bank. Chenonceaux lies 10 miles south of Amboise.

WHERE TO STAY & DINE

✪ **Hôtel d'Espagne.** 9 rue du Château, 36600 Valençay. ☎ **02-54-00-00-02.** Fax 02-54-00-12-63. 16 units. TV TEL. 450–650F ($76.50–$110.50) double; 900F ($153) suite. AE, DC, MC, V. Parking 25F ($4.25). Closed Jan–Feb.

This former coaching inn is maintained by the Fourré family, who offer an old-world ambience. The unique rooms are named after different ancestral manor houses in the region, with names like Belle Etoile and l'Hermitage. Yours might have an authentic Empire, Louis XV, or Louis XVI decor. Bathrooms are exceedingly well maintained, with a tub and shower combination and a hair dryer. Lunch is served in the dining room or gardens Tuesday through Sunday. Specialties include noisettes of lamb with tarragon and sweetbreads with morels. In the hotel's dining room, set-price menus range from 160 to 250F ($27.20 to $42.50), with a special Sunday set menu priced at 300F ($51). In the less formal bistro, set-price menus begin at 110F ($18.70) each.

CHENONCEAUX

A Renaissance masterpiece, the **Château de Chenonceau** (☎ 02-47-23-90-07) is best known for the *dames de Chenonceau* who have occupied it. (Note that the town is spelled with a final *x*, but the château's name is not.) Originally it was owned by the Marqués family, whose members were far too extravagant. Deviously, Thomas Bohier, the comptroller-general of finances in Normandy, began buying up land around the château. The Marqués family was forced to sell to Bohier, who tore down Chenonceau, preserving only the keep and building the rest in the emerging Renaissance style.

Many of the château's walls are covered with Gobelin tapestries, including one depicting a woman pouring water over the back of an angry dragon, another of a three-headed dog and a seven-headed monster. The chapel contains a delicate marble *Virgin and Child,* plus portraits of Catherine de Médici in her traditional black and white. There's even a portrait of the stern Catherine in the former bedroom of her rival, Diane de Poitiers. In François I's Renaissance bedchamber the most interesting portrait is that of Diane de Poitiers as the huntress Diana.

The history of Chenonceau is related in 15 tableaux in the wax museum, which charges 10F ($1.70). Diane de Poitiers, who, among other accomplishments, introduced the artichoke to France, is depicted in three tableaux. One portrays Catherine de Médici tossing out her husband's mistress.

The château is open daily mid-March through mid-September 9am to 7pm; the rest of the year it closes between 4:30 and 6pm. Admission is 45F ($7.65) for adults and 35F ($5.95) for children 7 to 15; children 6 and under free. A *son-et-lumière* spectacle, *In the Old Days of the Dames of Chenonceau,* is staged daily in summer at 10:15pm; admission is 45F ($7.65) for adults and 30F ($5.10) for children.

ESSENTIALS

GETTING THERE   There are 3 daily **trains** from Tours to Chenonceaux (trip time: 45 minutes). The train deposits you near the base of the château. Call ☎ **08-36-35-35-35** for train information and schedules. From June 15 to September 15, **Point Bus,** 2 place Victor Hugo (☎ **02-54-78-15-66**) runs daily buses to Chenonceaux, departing at 9:10am and returning at 6pm.

VISITOR INFORMATION   The **Syndicat d'Initiative** (tourist office) is at rue Bretonneau (☎ **02-47-23-94-45**), open Easter to September.

DEPARTING BY CAR   Continue back to Tours on the N-76, branching out this time for the best of the châteaux in the west. The first stop is Ussé, of *Sleeping Beauty* fame. Follow the directions to the previously visited Azay-le-Rideau. From Tours, it's a short ride down the Indre Valley on D-17 and then D-7 to Ussé.

WHERE TO STAY

Hôtel du Bon-Laboureur et du Château. 6 rue du Dr. Bretonneau, Chenonceaux, 37150 Bléré. ☎ **02-47-23-90-02.** Fax 02-47-23-82-01. 29 units. TV TEL. 350–700F ($59.50–$119) double; 850–1,000F ($144.50–$170) suite. AE, DC, MC, V.

This country inn, with an ivy-covered facade and tall chimneys, is within walking distance of the château and is your best bet for a comfortable night's sleep and good food. The rear garden has a little guesthouse, plus formally planted roses. Founded in 1880, the hotel maintains the flavor of that era, thanks to thick walls, solid masonry, and a scattering of antiques. In 1998, bedrooms received particular attention and upgrades. Most are small, especially those on the upper floors. Bathrooms are also small. The place is noted for its restaurant, which gets notably fewer bus groups than many of its competitors in the region. In fair weather, tables are set up in the courtyard, amid trees and flowering shrubs. Set-price menus in the restaurant cost 170F ($28.90) each. On the premises is a heated outdoor swimming pool.

✪ **La Roseraie.** 7 rue du Dr. Bretonneau, Chenonceaux, 37150 Bléré. ☎ **02-47-23-90-09.** Fax 02-47-23-91-59. 16 units. TV TEL. 280–800F ($47.60–$136) double. AE, DC, MC, V. Closed Dec–Jan.

Thanks to hotelier Laurent Fiorito, who radically upgraded this hotel in 1993, La Roseraie is the most charming and appealing hotel in Chenonceaux. The inviting bedrooms are individually decorated. Well-kept gardens dominate the property, and there's a heated swimming pool. Some of the finest meals in town are served at lunch and dinner in the hotel's restaurant. Set menus range in price from 98 to 170F ($16.65 to $28.90); our favorite dishes include house-style foie gras, magret of duckling with pears and cherries, and an unusual and very delicious invention—emincée of rump-steak with wine-marinated pears.

WHERE TO DINE

Au Gateau Breton. 16 rue du Dr. Bretonneau. ☎ **02-47-23-90-14.** Reservations required July–Aug. Set-price menus 70–115F ($11.90–$19.55). MC, V. May–Sept, Tues 7–9:30pm, Wed 11:30am–2pm, Thurs–Mon 11:30am–2pm and 7–9:30pm; Oct–Apr, Thurs–Tues 11:30am–2pm and 7–9:30pm. FRENCH.

The sun terrace in back of this Breton-type inn, a short walk from the château, is a refreshing place for dinner or tea. Gravel paths run among beds of pink geraniums and lilacs, and the red tables have bright canopies and umbrellas. The chef provides home cooking and cherry liqueur—a specialty of the region. In cool months meals are served in rustic dining rooms. Specialties are small chitterling sausages of Tours, chicken with Armagnac sauce, and *coq au vin* (chicken cooked in wine). The médaillons of veal with mushroom-cream sauce are excellent. Tasty pastries are sold in the front room.

USSÉ

At the edge of the hauntingly dark forest of Chinon, the **Château d'Ussé** (☎ **02-47-95-54-05**) was the inspiration behind Perrault's legend of *Sleeping Beauty (La Belle au Bois Dormant)*. On a hill overlooking the Indre River, it's a complex of steeples, turrets, towers, chimneys, and dormers. Conceived as a medieval fortress, Ussé was erected at the dawn of the Renaissance. Two powerful families, the Bueil and d'Espinay, lived here in the 15th and 16th centuries. The terraces, laden with orange trees, were laid out in the 18th century.

The guided tour begins in the Renaissance chapel, with its sculptured portal and handsome stalls. Then you proceed to the royal apartments, furnished with tapestries and antiques. One gallery displays an extensive collection of swords and rifles. A spiral stairway leads to a tower with a waxwork Sleeping Beauty and a panoramic view of the river.

The château is open daily February to October 9am to 6:30pm; it's closed from November to January. Admission is 59F ($10.05) for adults and 19F ($3.25) for children 8 to 16 (free for those 7 and under).

ESSENTIALS

GETTING THERE   From Tours, motorists can follow D7 into Ussè.

DEPARTING BY CAR   Chinon is easily reached from Ussé via D-7 and D-17. You approach this ancient town with its rock-of-ages castle looming on the horizon.

CHINON

In the film *Joan of Arc,* Ingrid Bergman sought out the dauphin as he tried to conceal himself among his courtiers—an action whose real life equivalent took place at the Château de Chinon, one of the oldest fortress-châteaux in France. Charles VII, mockingly known as the King of Bourges, centered his government at Chinon from 1429 to 1450. In 1429, with the English besieging Orléans, the Maid of Orléans, that "messenger from God," prevailed on the weak dauphin to give her an army. The rest is history. The seat of French power stayed at Chinon until the Hundred Years' War ended.

ESSENTIALS

GETTING THERE   There are three **trains** daily from Tours (trip time: 1 hour). Call ☎ **08-36-35-35-35** for information and schedules. The train station lies at the edge of this very small town. After leaving it, you walk along quai Jeanne d'Arc, taking a right at the Café de la Paix to get to place de l'Hôtel de Ville, the town hall, and the tourist office. There are three **buses** a day from Tours, the trip taking 1½ hours.

VISITOR INFORMATION   The **Office de Tourisme** is at 12 rue Voltaire (☎ 02-47-93-17-85).

DEPARTING BY CAR   Angers is generally considered the western end of the Loire Valley, although the Loire River continues for another 80 miles before reaching Nantes. To reach Angers, continue north from Chinon toward the river. The D-7 connects to the N-152 heading west all the way to Saumur. Once at Saumur, the D-952 continues west into Angers, a distance of 32 miles.

SEEING THE TOWN & CHÂTEAU

On the banks of the Vienne, the town of Chinon retains a medieval atmosphere. It consists of winding streets and turreted houses, many built in the 15th and 16th centuries in the heyday of the court. For the best view, drive across the river, turning right onto quai Danton. From that vantage point you'll have the best perspective, seeing the castle in relation to the village and the river. The gables and towers make Chinon look like a toy village. The most typical street is **rue Voltaire,** lined with 15th- and 16th-century townhouses. At no. 44, Richard the Lion-Hearted died on April 6, 1199, after being mortally wounded while besieging Chalus in Limousin. In the heart of Chinon, the **Grand Carroi** was the crossroads of the Middle Ages.

The most famous son of Chinon, François Rabelais, the earthy and often bawdy Renaissance writer, walked these streets, and lived in a substantial dwelling on the Rue de la Lamproie where today a plaque marks the spot where his father practiced law and maintained a prestigious and prosperous home and office. The isolated (3½ miles west of Chinon) cottage where he was born, maintained solely for the purpose of delivering the children of the Rabelais clan into the world, is the site of the **Musée François Rabelais,** La Devinière, 37500 Seuilly (☎ 02-47-95-91-18). Entrance costs 23F ($3.90) for adults, and 17F ($2.90) for students and those under 24, and it's open as follows: January 1 to March 15 and October 1 to December 31, daily 9:30am to 12:30pm and 2 to 5pm; March 16 to April 30 daily 9:30am to 12:30pm and 2 to 6pm; May 1 to September 30, daily 10am to 7pm. To reach it from Chinon, follow the road signs pointing to Saumur and the D-17.

Château de Chinon (☎ 02-47-93-13-45) is three separate strongholds, once badly ruined, but today at least two of the buildings, the Château du Milieu and Château du Coudray, have been entirely restored, with the exception of their still nonexistent roofs. Some of the grim walls from other dilapidated edifices remain, although many of the buildings—including the Great Hall where Joan of Arc sought out the dauphin—have been torn down. Some of the most destructive owners were the heirs of Cardinal Richelieu. Now gone, the Château de St Georges was built by Henry II of England, who died here in 1189. The Château du Milieu dates from the 11th to the 15th century, containing the keep and the clock tower, where the Musée Jeanne d'Arc has been installed. Separated from the latter by a moat, the Château du Coudray contains the Tour du Coudray, where Joan of Arc stayed during her time at Chinon. In the 14th century the Knights Templar were imprisoned here before meeting their violent deaths.

The château is open daily January 11 through March 14 from 9am to noon and 2 to 5pm, March 15 through June 30 and all of September from 9am to 6pm, July through August from 9am to 7pm, and October from 9am to 5pm. Admission is 28F ($4.75) for adults and 19F ($3.25) for children.

WHERE TO STAY

Chris' Hôtel. 12 place Jeanne-d'Arc, 37500 Chinon. ☎ **02-47-93-36-92.** Fax 02-47-98-48-92. 33 units. TV TEL. 220–380F ($37.40–$64.60) double. AE, DC, MC, V. Free parking.

This well-run hotel is housed in a 19th-century building near the town's historic district. Many of the rooms are small but offer views of the castle and river. Most are furnished in a Louis XV style and all have modern amenities. Bathrooms are quite cramped. Breakfast is the only meal served.

WHERE TO DINE

✪ **Au Plaisir Gourmand.** 2 rue Parmentier. ☎ **02-47-93-20-48.** Reservations required. Main courses 80–150F ($13.60–$25.50); set-price menus 175–340F ($29.75–$57.80). AE, V. Tues–Sat noon–2pm and 7:30–9:30pm; Sun noon–2pm. Closed Feb. FRENCH.

This is the premier restaurant in the area, owned by Jean-Claude Rigollet, who used to direct the chefs at the fabled Les Templiers in Les Bézards. His restaurant offers an intimate dining room with a limited number of tables in a charming 18th-century building. Menu items are likely to include roast rabbit in aspic with foie-gras sauce, oxtail in a Chinon red wine sauce, zander in beurre blanc, and sautéed crayfish with a spicy salad. For dessert, try the prunes stuffed in puff pastry.

ANGERS

Once the capital of Anjou, Angers straddles the Maine River. Although it suffered extensive damage in World War II, it has been considerably restored, somehow blending provincial charm with the suggestion of sophistication. The town is often used as a base for exploring the château district to the west.

ESSENTIALS

GETTING THERE   From Saumur, it's a 30-minute **train** trip to Angers; from Tours, it's 1 hour. Trains also leave Paris-Montparnasse for the 1½-hour trip. The train station at place de la Gare in Angers is a convenient walk from the château. For information and schedules, call ☎ 08-36-35-35-35. There are three **bus** connections from Saumur a day, Monday to Saturday. The trip takes 1½ hours. The buses depart and arrive at place de la République. Call ☎ 02-41-88-59-25 for schedules and information.

VISITOR INFORMATION   The **Office de Tourisme** is on place Kennedy (☎ 02-41-23-51-11).

TOURING THE CHÂTEAU & CATHEDRAL

The moated **Château d'Angers** (☎ 02-41-87-43-47) from the 9th century was once the home of the comtes d'Anjou. After the castle was destroyed, it was reconstructed by St. Louis. From 1230 to 1238 the outer walls and 17 massive towers were built, creating a formidable fortress well prepared to withstand invaders. The château was favored by Good King René; until he was forced to surrender Anjou to Louis XI, a brilliant court life flourished here. Louis XIV turned the château into a prison, dispatching his finance minister, Fouquet, to one of its cells. In the 19th century the castle was also used as a prison, and during World War II it was used by the Nazis as a munitions depot. Allied planes bombed it in 1944.

The castle displays the ✪ **Apocalypse Tapestries,** one of the masterpieces of art from the Middle Ages. (This series of tapestries wasn't always so highly regarded; they once served as a canopy for orange trees to protect the fruit from unfavorable weather and at another time to cover the damaged walls of a church.) The tapestries were created by Nicolas Bataille, master weaver, perhaps in the Parisian workshop of Robert Poinçon, based on cartoons by Hennequin of Bruges. Seventy-seven pieces of them stretch a distance of

335 feet; the series illustrates the book of St. John. One scene is called *La Grande Prosti-tuée*, and another shows Babylon invaded by demons; yet another is a peace scene with two multiheaded monsters holding up a fleur-de-lis.

You can tour the fortress, including the courtyard of the nobles, prison cells, ramparts, windmill tower, 15th-century chapel, and royal apartments. The château is open daily June to September 15 9am to 7pm and September 16 to May 9:30am to 12:30pm and 2 to 6pm. Admission is 35F ($5.95) for adults, 23F ($3.90) ages 13 to 25, and free for children 12 and under.

Cathédrale St-Maurice, place Monsigneur Shappoulie (☎ **02-41-87-58-45**), is mostly from the 12th and 13th centuries; the main tower, however, dates from the 16th century. The statues on the portal represent everybody from the Queen of Sheba to David at the harp. On the tympanum is depicted Christ Enthroned; the symbols, such as the lion for St. Mark, represent the Evangelists. The stained-glass windows from the 12th through the 16th century have made the cathedral famous. The oldest one illustrates the martyrdom of St. Vincent (the most unusual is of former St. Christopher with the head of a dog). Once all the Apocalypse Tapestries were shown here; now only a few remain, and they are mainly exhibited in summer. The 12th-century nave is a landmark in cathedral architecture, a clear, coherent plan that's a work of harmonious beauty, the start of the Plantagenet archi-tecture. It's open daily 9am to 7pm.

WHERE TO STAY

Hôtel d'Anjou. 1 bd. Foch, 49100 Angers. ☎ **800/528-1234** in the U.S., or 02-41-88-24-82. Fax 02-41-87-22-21. 53 units. MINIBAR TV TEL. 370–770F ($62.90–$130.90) double. AE, DC, MC, V. Parking 48F ($8.15).

Situated next to a large park, this hotel is the best choice for overnighting in the area. Although comparable in price to the Hôtel de France, it has more upscale appoint-ments and amenities and a better restaurant than its competitor. The high-ceilinged and more spacious bedrooms are closer to the ground. All the bedrooms were over-hauled in 1998 with new carpets, fabrics, and upholsteries. Bathrooms were also reju-venated, although they remain quite small and have little shelf space. Dining here is also satisfying. Set-price menus from 130 to 210F ($22.10 to $35.70) are served in a setting that includes carefully maintained paneling, a valuable antique tapestry, and a wood-burning fireplace.

Quality Hôtel de France. 8 place de la Gare, 49100 Angers. ☎ **02-41-88-49-42.** Fax 02-41-86-76-70. 57 units. MINIBAR TV TEL. 395–565F ($67.15–$96.05) double. AE, DC, MC, V. Parking 40F ($6.80).

This 19th-century hotel, one of the most respected in town, has been run by the Bouyers since 1893. It's the best choice near the rail station. The rooms are sound-proof, but only four are air-conditioned (it can get hot on a summer night). Many of the bedrooms were renovated in the late 1990s with new upholstery, fresh curtains, and a paint job. Bathrooms are very small, with a shower stall and a hair dryer. The restaurant, Les Plantagenets, serves reliable set-price meals.

WHERE TO DINE

Le Toussaint. 7 place du Président-Kennedy. ☎ **02-41-87-46-20.** Reservations recom-mended. Main courses 85–160F ($14.45–$27.20); set-price menus 140–220F ($23.80–$37.40). AE, MC, V. Tues–Sat noon–2pm and 7:45–9:30pm; Sun noon–2pm. FRENCH.

This restaurant overlooks the town's famous château, and an especially pleasant view can be had from the second-floor dining room. Only fresh ingredients are used on this seasonal menu. Tried-and-true favorites include fried Loire Valley fish served with beurre blanc, and *pied de porc farci et truffe* (stuffed and truffled pig's foot) for more adventurous types. Two more recent delights are partridge roasted with forest mushrooms and filet of rabbit in a peppercorn and rum sauce. You can also enjoy an array of freshly made desserts, many flavored with Cointreau, a liqueur of the region.

Provence Caffè. 9 place du Ralliement. ☎ **02-41-87-44-15.** Reservations recommended. All main courses 85F ($14.45); set-price menus 98–149F ($16.65–$25.35). AE, MC, V. Mon–Sat noon–2pm and 7–10pm. PROVENÇAL.

This restaurant celebrates the herbs, spices, and seafood of Provence. The decor includes bundles of herbs, bright colors, and souvenirs of the Mediterranean; the ambience is casual and sunny. Recommended dishes include a risotto served with asparagus and basil or with snails, grilled salmon with Provençal herbs, and a ballotine of chicken with ratatouille. The chef here continues to delight, perhaps with carpaccio of foie gras or sea wolf grilled with mushrooms and sprinkled with virgin olive oil.

3 Provence & the Côte d'Azur

Provence has been called a bridge between the past and present, where yesterday blends with today in a quiet, often melancholy way. Peter Mayle's best-selling *A Year in Provence* (as well as his other books about the area) has played no small part in the burgeoning popularity that this sunny corner of southern France has enjoyed during recent years.

The Greeks and Romans filled the landscape with cities boasting Hellenic theaters, Roman baths, amphitheaters, and triumphal arches. Romanesque fortresses and Gothic cathedrals followed in the Middle Ages. In the 19th century Provence's light and landscapes attracted illustrious painters, such as Cézanne and van Gogh, to Aix and Arles and other towns.

Provence has its own language and customs. The region is bounded on the north by the Dauphiné, the west by the Rhône, the east by the Alps, and the south by the Mediterranean. We cover the northern area of this region, what's traditionally thought of as Provence, and then head down to the southern part, what's known as the glittering Côte d'Azur, or French Riviera.

The Riviera has been called the world's most exciting stretch of beach and "a sunny place for shady people." Each resort on the Riviera—be it Beaulieu by the sea or eagle's-nest Eze—has a unique flavor and special merits. Glitterati and eccentrics have always been drawn to this narrow strip of fabled real estate. A trail of modern artists, attracted to the brilliant light, have left a rich heritage: Matisse in his chapel at Vence, Cocteau at Menton and Villefranche, Picasso at Antibes and seemingly everywhere else, Léger at Biot, Renoir at Cagnes, and Bonnard at Le Cannet. The best art collection of all is at the Maeght Foundation in St-Paul-de-Vence.

The Riviera's high season used to be winter and spring only. However, with changing tastes, July and August have become the most crowded months, and reservations are imperative. The average summer temperature is 75°F (24°C); the average winter temperature, 49°F (10°C).

The Corniches of the Riviera, depicted in countless films, stretch from Nice to Menton. The Alps drop into the Mediterranean and roads were carved along the way. The lower road, about 20 miles long, is the **Corniche Inférieure.** Along this road are the ports of Villefranche, Cap-Ferrat, Beaulieu, and Cap-Martin. Built between World War I and the beginning of World War II, the **Moyenne Corniche (Middle Road),** 19 miles long, also runs from Nice to Menton, winding spectacularly in and out of tunnels and through mountains. The highlight is at mountaintop Eze. The **Grande Corniche**—the most panoramic—was ordered built by Napoléon in 1806. La Turbie

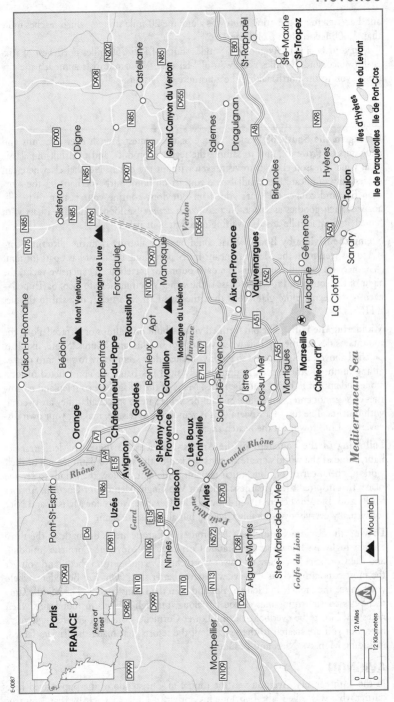

Provence

E-0087

365

and Le Vistaero are the principal towns along the 20-mile stretch, which reaches more than 1,600 feet high at Col d'Eze.

Our tour begins in Avignon, 425 miles south of Paris, 50 miles northwest of Aix-en-Provence, and 66 miles northwest of Marseille. Most motorists approach the city from Lyon in the north, taking the autoroute (A-7) south.

Only in Provence & the Côte d'Azur

Dining in the South of France   Some of the greatest French chefs are sons and daughters of Provence, and to sample the regional produce and to drink the classic local wine is reason enough to visit, even without the beach. No chef elsewhere can successfully duplicate the bouillabaisse you get on home turf—perhaps it's the scorpion fish and conger eel that's added in. But don't confine your tasting to bouillabaisse. Such goodies as salade Niçoise, *fruits de mer* (seafood), grilled sea bass with fennel, and ratatouille are also waiting to tempt your palate.

Seeing the Riviera by Boat   What could be more alluring than the glittering Côte d'Azur as seen from the Mediterranean? Every port along the coast has boats for rent. Whether you join a local fisher on a day's outing or travel on an expensive yacht, the sight of the southern Provençal coast is the same. Villefranche, Monaco, St-Tropez—each name seems more glamorous than the last. Our favorite? A day sail to the Iles d'Hyéres.

Wandering the Hill   The old fortified villages built on hilltops or terraced along the mountainsides are the big bait when you tire of beaches and bikinis. Some, like Eze, perched above the Riviera, are so giddily situated they seem ready to spill into the sea at any minute. Others, such as dramatically sited Les Baux, are constructed of local stone and appear to blend into the rocks. Many of the villages are so steep and narrow that cars cannot enter. Some, like St-Paul-de-Vence, are so spectacular they are overrun with tourists. The fun of a Riviera visit is wandering at leisure, making your own discoveries of hill towns off the beaten track.

Following in the Footsteps of the Artists   Attracted to the clear Mediterranean light, some of the world's greatest artists flocked to the south to paint. Much of their work has been carted off, but much remains to delight. Follow their trails to see the places that inspired their greatness: Arles for Van Gogh, Menton for Cocteau, Antibes for Picasso, Biot for Léger, Aix-en-Provence for Cézanne, Vence for Matisse, and Nice for virtually everybody—notably Chagall, but also Matisse again.

Driving the Riviera Corniches   Few routes in Europe are as dramatic as the three famous highways known as the Grande Corniche, the Moyenne Corniche (middle), and the Corniche Inférieure or Lower Corniche. Of course, from the Grand you get the most panoramic vistas—the view is never better than from Eze Belvedere, where you can see the French and Italian Alps and even the Lerins Islands. The Middle Corniche has coastal panoramas as you zip along, through tunnels in mountains when necessary. Not to be overlooked is the Lower Corniche. You don't get the high vistas here, but you are treated to the sea and all the resorts that made the Riviera fabled, including Monaco, Nice, and Beaulieu.

AVIGNON

In the 14th century, Avignon was the capital of Christendom; the popes lived here during what was called "the Babylonian Captivity." The legacy left by that "court of splendor and magnificence" makes Avignon one of the most interesting and beautiful of Europe's medieval cities.

ESSENTIALS

GETTING THERE Avignon is a junction for bus routes throughout the region. For information about bus routes in the area, call ☎ **04-90-82-07-35;** you'll find the depot to the right of the rail station opening on boulevard St-Roch. Train service from other towns is also frequent. The TGV **trains** from Paris arrive 13 times per day (trip time: 4 hours), and 17 trains per day arrive from Marseille (trip time: 1½ hours). For train information and schedules, call ☎ **08-36-35-35-35;** the Avignon station is at porte de la Rèpublique. If you'd like to explore the area by **bike,** go to **Cycles Peugeot,** 80 rue Guillaume-Puy (☎ **04-90-86-32-49**), which rents all sorts of bikes for 60F ($10.20) per day, including 10-speed road bikes and mountain bikes. A deposit of 1,000F ($170) is required, either in the form of cash or a credit-card imprint.

VISITOR INFORMATION The **Office de Tourisme** is at 41 cours Jean-Jaurès (☎ **04-90-82-65-11**).

DEPARTING BY CAR From Avignon, D-571 continues south to St-Rémy-de-Provence.

EXPLORING THE TOWN

Even more famous than the papal residency is the ditty *"Sur le pont d'Avignon, l'on y danse, l'on y danse,"* echoing through every French nursery and around the world. Ironically, **pont St-Bénézet** was far too narrow for the danse of the rhyme, inspired, according to legend, by a vision a shepherd named Bénézet had while tending his flock. Spanning the Rhône and connecting Avignon with Villeneuve-lèz-Avignon, the bridge is now only a fragmented ruin. Built between 1177 and 1185, it suffered various disasters from then on; in 1669 half of it toppled into the river. On one of the piers is the two-story Chapelle St-Nicolas—one story in Romanesque style, the other Gothic. The bridge is open daily 9am to 6pm. Admission is 15F ($2.55) for adults and 7F ($1.20) for students, children, and seniors.

Dominating Avignon from a hill is the **Palais des Papes,** place du Palais-des-Papes (☎ **04-90-27-50-74**). You're shown through on a guided tour, usually lasting 50 minutes. Most of the rooms have been stripped of their finery; the exception is the Chapelle St-Jean, known for its beautiful frescoes of scenes from the life of John the Baptist and John the Evangelist, attributed to the school of Matteo Giovanetti and painted between 1345 and 1348. The Grand Tinel, or banquet hall, is about 135 feet long and 30 feet wide, and the pope's table stood on the southern side. The pope's bedroom is on the first floor of the Tour des Anges.

From November to March, it's open daily 9:30am to 5:45pm; from April to October, daily 9am to 7pm. During July, it's open daily 9am to 9pm, and during August, daily 9am to 8pm. Admission is 45F ($7.65) for adults and 32F ($5.45) for students, children, and seniors. A guided tour, with a trained staff member or a prerecorded cassette, is included in the price.

Near the palace is the 12th-century **Cathédrale Notre-Dame,** place du Palais-des-Papes (☎ **04-90-86-81-01**), containing the flamboyant Gothic tomb of Pope John XXII, who died at age 90. Benedict XII is also buried here. The cathedral's hours vary, but generally it's open daily 11am to 6pm and admission is free. From the cathedral, enter the promenade du Rocher-des-Doms to stroll through its garden and enjoy the view across the Rhône to Villeneuve-lèz-Avignon.

THE SHOPPING SCENE

Véronique Pichon, place Crillon (☎ **04-90-85-89-00**), is the newest branch of a porcelain manufacturer whose colorful products have been a regional fixture since the

Shopping for Provençal Fabric

The Avignon branch of **Les Olivades,** 28 rue des Marchands (☎ **04-90-86-13-42**), is one of the most visible of a chain of outlets associated in the States with Pierre Deux. Look for fabrics by the yard, bedcovers, slipcovers, draperies, and tablecloths. Fabrics, printed often by hand in a factory only 6 miles from Avignon, tend to feature intricate designs in colors inspired by 19th-century models or, to a somewhat lesser extent, Créole designs with butterflies, pineapples, bananas, and flowers.

The vision that launched **Les Indiens de Nîmes,** 4 rue College de Roure (☎ **04-90-86-32-05**), in the early 1980s involved the duplication of 18th- and 19th-century Provençal fabric patterns. They're sold as fabric by the meter as well as clothing for men, women, and children. Kitchenware and a selection of furniture inspired by originals from Provence and the steamy wetlands west of Marseille are also sold.

All the clothing at **Souleiado,** 5 rue Joseph-Vernet (☎ **04-90-86-47-67**), derives from a Provençal model, and even the Provençal name (which translates as "first ray of sunshine after a storm") evokes a spirit on which the owners want to capitalize. Most, but not all, of the clothing is designed for women; there are some garments—shirts mostly—for men. Fabrics are also sold by the meter.

1700s. Manufactured in the nearby town of Uzès, the tableware, decorative urns, statues, and lamps are cost-effective enough to be shipped virtually anywhere.

WHERE TO STAY

Hôtel d'Angleterre. 29 bd. Raspail, 84000 Avignon. ☎ **04-90-86-34-31.** Fax 04-90-86-86-74. 40 units (39 with bathroom). TV TEL. 190F ($32.30) double without bathroom; 280–390F ($47.60–$66.30) double with bathroom. MC, V. Closed Dec 20–Jan 20. Free parking.

In the heart of Avignon, this classical structure is the city's best budget hotel. The small rooms are comfortably but basically furnished; bathrooms are also small and shower-only. Breakfast is the only meal served.

✪ **La Mirande.** 4 place Amirande, 84000 Avignon. ☎ **04-90-85-93-93.** Fax 04-90-86-26-85. 20 units. A/C MINIBAR TV TEL. 1,700–2,400F ($289–$408) double; 3,200F ($544) suite. AE, DC, V. Parking 80F ($13.60).

This restored 700-year-old townhouse in the heart of Avignon is one of France's grand little luxuries, far better than anything else in town. The exquisite taste of the decorators is reflected in each individually designed bedroom, most of which are quite spacious. Rooms have bedside controls, hand-printed fabrics on the walls, antiques, and art. Bathrooms are also sumptuous, with hair dryers and make-up mirrors. The restaurant earns its one star in Michelin and is among the finest in Avignon. Set-price menus run 210 to 450F ($35.70 to $76.50).

Mercure Palais-des-Papes. Quartier de la Balance, rue Ferruce, 84000 Avignon. ☎ **04-90-85-91-23.** Fax 04-90-85-32-40. 87 units. A/C MINIBAR TV TEL. 550–595F ($93.50–$101.15) double. AE, DC, MC, V. Parking 45F ($7.65). Bus: 11.

This chain hotel is one of the best in Avignon, and is a good value for what it offers. It lies within the city walls, at the foot of the Palace of the Popes. The rooms are well furnished yet functional; what they lack in style they make up for in comfort.

Adjoining bathrooms are small, but often contain a tub/shower combination. There's a small bar, but breakfast is the only meal served.

WHERE TO DINE

✪ **Christian Etienne.** 10 rue Mons. ☎ **04-90-86-16-50.** Reservations recommended. Main courses 170–210F ($28.90–$35.70); set-price lunch (Mon–Fri) 170F ($28.90); set-price dinners 300F ($51), 430F ($73.10), 500F ($85). AE, DC, MC, V. July, daily 12:30–1:30pm and 7:30–9:30pm; the rest of the year, Mon–Fri noon–2:30pm and 8–10:30pm, Sat 8–10:30pm. FRENCH.

This restaurant serves the best food in Avignon. The dining room contains very old ceiling and wall frescoes honoring the marriage of Anne de Bretagne to the French king in 1491. Several of the set-price menus present specific themes, from vegetarian to lobster. À la carte specialties include a filet of red snapper with a coulis of black olives, roasted pigeon with a truffle-enhanced sauce, and a dessert specialty of fennel-flavored sorbet with saffron-flavored English cream sauce.

La Fourchette. 7 rue Racine. ☎ **04-90-85-20-93.** Set-price lunch 100–150F ($17–$25.50); set-price dinner 150F ($25.50). MC, V. Mon–Fri noon–2pm and 7:30–9:30pm. Closed Aug 5–29. Bus: 11. FRENCH.

This bistro offers creative cooking at a moderate price. There are two dining rooms, one like a summer house with walls of glass, the other more like a tavern with oak beams. You might begin with fresh sardines flavored with coriander, ravioli filled with haddock, or parfait of chicken liver with a spinach flan and confiture of onions. Grilled lambs' liver with raisins is a main course specialty.

ST-RÉMY-DE-PROVENCE

Nostradamus, the French physician/astrologer and author of more than 600 obscure verses, was born here in 1503. In 1922, Gertrude Stein and Alice B. Toklas found St-Rémy after "wandering around everywhere a bit," as Ms. Stein once wrote to Cocteau. But mainly St-Rémy is associated with van Gogh, who committed himself to an asylum here in 1889 after cutting off his left ear. Between moods of despair, he painted such works as *Olive Trees* and *Cypresses* here. The town lies 16 miles northeast of Arles and 8 miles north of Les Baux.

ESSENTIALS

GETTING THERE   There are local buses (no trains) from Avignon, which let you off in the center of town (trip time: 45 minutes). Call ☎ **04-90-82-07-35** in Avignon for information and schedules.

VISITOR INFORMATION   The **Office de Tourisme** is at place Jean-Jaurès (☎ **04-90-92-05-22**).

DEPARTING BY CAR   From St-Rémy-de-Provence, head south for 8 miles along the winding D-5 until you reach Les Baux.

EXPLORING ST-RÉMY & ENVIRONS

One interesting activity is visiting the cloisters of the asylum van Gogh made famous in his paintings at the 12th-century **Monastère de St-Paul-de-Mausolée.** Now a psychiatric hospital, the former monastery is east of D-5, a short drive north of Glanum (see below). You can't visit the cell in which van Gogh was confined, but it's still worth coming to explore the Romanesque chapel and cloisters with their circular arches and columns, which have beautifully carved capitals. The cloisters are open daily 9am to 6pm between June and September and daily 9am to 5pm October to May. On your way to the church, you'll see a bust of Van Gogh. Admission costs 10F ($1.70) per person. There's no number that's available to the public in the monastery, but you can call the nearby clinic (☎ 04-90-92-88-01) for information.

In the center of St-Rémy, **Musée Archéologique,** in the Hôtel de Sade, rue du Parage (☎ 04-90-92-64-04), displays both sculptures and bronzes excavated at Glanum. It's open March to September, daily 10am to noon and 2 to 6pm; in February and October, daily 10am to noon and 2 to 5pm; and in November and December, Wednesday, Saturday, and Sunday 10am to noon and from 2 to 5pm. It's closed in January. Admission is 15F ($2.55) for adults, 10F ($1.70) for students, and free for children 11 and under.

A half mile south of St-Rémy on D-5 is **Ruines de Glanum,** avenue Vincent-van-Gogh (☎ 04-90-92-23-79), a Gallo-Roman city (follow the signs to Les Antiques). Its historical monuments include an Arc Municipal, a triumphal arch dating from the time of Julius Caesar, and a cenotaph called the Mausolée des Jules. Garlanded with sculptured fruits and flowers, the arch dates from 20 B.C. and is the oldest in Provence. The mausoleum was raised to honor the grandsons of Augustus and is the only extant monument of its type. In the area are entire streets and foundations of private residences from the 1st-century town. Some remains are from an even earlier Gallo-Greek town dating from the 2nd century B.C. Admission is 32F ($5.45) for adults, 21F ($3.55) for students, and 10F ($1.70) for those 17 and under. The excavations are open daily April to September 9am to 7pm and October to March daily 9am to noon and 2 to 5pm.

WHERE TO STAY

Les Antiques. 15 av. Pasteur, 13210 St-Rémy-de-Provence. ☎ 04-90-92-03-02. Fax 04-90-92-50-40. 27 units. MINIBAR TEL. 370–600F ($62.90–$102) double. AE, DC, MC, V. Closed Oct 20–Apr 4.

This stylish 19th-century villa is in a 7-acre park with a pool. It contains an elegant reception lounge, which opens onto several salons, and Napoléon III furnishings. The handsomely furnished rooms come in a variety of styles and shapes. Although those in the modern pavilion are more comfortable, larger, and have direct access to the garden, they don't have as much character as those in the main building. Bathrooms are small. In summer you're served breakfast (the only meal) in what used to be the Orangerie.

WHERE TO DINE

La Maison Jaune. 15 rue Carnot. ☎ 04-90-92-56-14. Reservations recommended. Set-price lunches 120–285F ($20.40–$48.45); set-price dinners 175–285F ($29.75–$48.45). MC, V. June–Sept Wed–Sun noon–2pm and Tues–Sun 7:30–9:30pm; Oct–May Tues–Sat noon–2pm and Mon–Sat 7:30–9:30pm. FRENCH/PROVENÇAL

One of the most enduringly popular restaurants in St-Remy lies in what was built during the 1700s as the home of a wealthy merchant. Today, in a pair of dining rooms scattered over two floors of the yellow-fronted building, you'll appreciate meals prepared and served with flair. An additional 35 seats are available in nice weather on an outdoor terrace. Good choices include pigeon roasted in wine from Les Baux; grilled sardines with candied lemon and raw fennel; artichoke hearts marinated in white wine; and a succulent roasted rack of lamb served with a black olive and anchovy tapenade.

LES BAUX

What Cardinal Richelieu called "a nesting place for eagles" lies 12 miles north of Arles and 50 miles north of Marseille and the Mediterranean. Once it was the citadel of the powerful *seigneurs* of Les Baux; today, in its lonely position high on a windswept plateau overlooking the southern Alpilles, Les Baux is a ghost of its former self. Still, there is no more dramatically situated town in Provence than this one nestled in a valley surrounded by mysterious, shadowy rock formations.

ESSENTIALS

GETTING THERE   There's no railway station in Les Baux, so most rail passengers get off at the railway station in Arles. From Arles, there are four **buses** daily that stop at Les Baux, after a 25-minute ride, and an additional four or five that originate in Arles and stop in the nearby hamlet of Maussane-les-Alpilles, 2½ miles to the south. The frequency of the bus service is reduced by about half between November and March. For information about buses, call ☎ **04-90-49-38-01** in Arles for information and schedules.

VISITOR INFORMATION   The **Office de Tourisme** is on Ilôt Post Tenebras Lux (☎ **04-90-54-34-39**).

DEPARTING BY CAR   From Les Baux, continue southwest on D-17 for 12 miles to Arles.

EXPLORING LES BAUX

Some one million visitors a year flock here to wander the feudal ruins, inspect the foundation of a demolished castle, and explore the facades of gracefully restored Renaissance homes. The **Château des Baux** (☎ **04-90-54-55-56**) is carved out of the rocky mountain peak; the site of this former castle covers an area at least five times that of Les Baux itself below. As you stand here you can look out over the **Valley of Hell (Val d'Enfer).** Later you might be tempted to drive through its bleak and rugged scenery—access is from the D27 and D78G. At the castle you can enjoy panoramas from Tour Paravel and Tour Sarascenes. The site is open in July and August daily from 9am to 8:30pm; September to February daily 9am to 6pm, March to June daily 9am to 5:30pm. Admisssion is 35F ($5.95) for adults, 27F ($4.60) for students, and 22F ($3.75) for ages 7 to 17 (free 6 and under).

WHERE TO STAY & DINE

✪ **La Riboto de Taven.** Le Val d'Enfer, 13520 Les Baux. ☎ **04-90-54-34-23.** Fax 04-90-54-38-88. Reservations required. Main courses 150–190F ($25.50–$32.30); set-price lunch 220F ($37.40); set-price dinners 300–450F ($51–$76.50). AE, DC, MC, V. Thurs–Mon noon–1:30pm and 7:30–9pm. Closed Jan 15–Mar 1. FRENCH.

This 1835 farmhouse outside the medieval section of town serves food filled with brawny flavors and the heady perfumes of Provençal herbs. In summer, you can sit out at the beautifully laid tables, (one of which is a millstone). Menu items can include sea bass in olive oil, fricassée of mussels flavored with basil, and lamb en croute with olives—plus homemade desserts. It's also possible to rent three double rooms so large they're like suites, each at 1,100F ($187), breakfast included.

ARLES

Arles, 22 miles southwest of Avignon and 55 miles northwest of Marseille, has been called "the soul of Provence," and art lovers, archaeologists, and historians alike are attracted to this town on the Rhône. The great van Gogh left Paris for Arles in 1888 and painted some of his most celebrated works here—*Starry Night, The Bridge at Arles, Sunflowers,* and *L'Arlésienne* among others. Many of these luminous scenes remain to delight visitors today.

Arles isn't quite as charming as Aix-en-Provence, but it has first-rate museums, excellent restaurants, and summer festivals, such as an international photography festival in early June. Although not as lovely as it was when Picasso came here, Arles has enough antique Provençal flavor to keep the appeal alive.

ESSENTIALS

GETTING THERE   Arles lies on the Paris-Marseille and the Bordeaux-St-Raphaël rail lines, so it has frequent connections from most French cities. Ten **trains** arrive daily from Avignon (trip time: 20 minutes) and 10 per day from Marseille (trip time: 1 hour). From Aix-en-Provence, 10 trains arrive per day (trip time: 1¾ hours). Call ☎ **08-36-35-35-35** for details. There are about five **buses** per day from Aix-en-Provence (trip time: 1¾ hours). Call ☎ **04-90-49-38-01** for information and schedules. The bus station is adjacent to the railway station, a 10-minute walk from the center.

VISITOR INFORMATION   The **Office de Tourisme,** where you can buy a *Billet Global* (see below), is on the esplanade des Lices (☎ **04-90-18-41-20**). If you'd like to get around by bicycle, head for the newspaper kiosk immediately next to the town's tourist information office, a site that doubles as the town's only bike rental outfit: **Europbike,** Kiosk à Journaux Le Provençal, Esplanade Charles de Gaulle (☎ **04-90-96-44-20**). A six-speed road bike—all that this emporium stocks—rents for 60F ($10.20) per day, and requires a deposit of 1,000F ($170). **Cycles peugeot,** 15 rue du Pont (☎ **04-90-96-03-77**), rents bikes at comparable rates.

DEPARTING BY CAR   From Arles, head east toward Aix-en-Provence on N-113. Once at Salon-de-Provence, take the autoroute southeast for 23 miles to Aix-en-Provence, the conclusion of your driving tour of Provence. After that, it's south to the French Riviera.

EXPLORING ARLES

At the tourist office you can purchase a ***Billet Global,*** the all-inclusive pass that admits you to the town's museums, Roman monuments, and major attractions; it costs 55F ($9.35) for adults and 35F ($5.95) for children.

The town is full of Roman monuments. The general vicinity of the old Roman forum is occupied by **place du Forum,** shaded by plane trees. Once the Café de Nuit, immortalized by van Gogh, stood on this square. Two Corinthian columns and pediment fragments from a temple can be seen at the corner of the Hôtel Nord-Pinus. South of here is **place de la République** (also known as the place de l'Hotel de Ville), the principal plaza, dominated by a 50-foot-tall blue porphyry obelisk. On the north is the impressive Hôtel-de-Ville or town hall from 1673, built to Mansart's plans and surmounted by a Renaissance belfry.

On the east side of the square is the **Eglise St-Trophime** (☎ **04-90-96-07-38**), noted for its 12th-century portal, one of the finest achievements of southern Romanesque style. In the pediment, Christ is surrounded by the symbols of the Evangelists. The cloister, in both Gothic and Romanesque styles, is noted for its medieval carvings. Admission is free. The church is open Monday to Saturday from 8:30am to 6:30pm, Sunday from 8:30am to 6pm. The cloister's hours are Monday to Saturday from 9am to noon and 2:30 to 6pm. Admission is 15F ($2.55) for adults and 9F ($1.55) for students and children under 12.

Museon Arlaten (☎ **04-90-96-08-23**) is entered at 29 rue de la République (its name is written in old Provençal style.) It was founded by Frédéric Mistral, the Provençal poet and leader of a movement to establish Modern Provençal as a literary language, using the money from his Nobel Prize for literature in 1904. This is really a folklore museum, with regional costumes, portraits, furniture, dolls, a music salon, and one room devoted to mementos of Mistral. The museum is open April through October, daily 9am to noon and 2 to 6:30pm (until 7pm in July and August);

November through March, Tuesday to Sunday 9am to noon and 2 to 5pm. Admission is 20F ($3.40) for adults and 15F ($2.55) for those under 16.

The city's two great classical monuments are the **Théâtre Antique,** rue du Cloître (☎ **04-90-96-93-30**), and the Amphitheater. The Roman theater, begun by Augustus in the 1st century, was mostly destroyed and only two Corinthian columns remain. Now rebuilt, the theater is the setting for an annual drama festival in July. The theater was where the *Venus of Arles* was discovered in 1651. Take rue de la Calade from the town hall. The theater is open daily from 8am to 7pm. Admission is 15F ($2.55) for adults and 9F ($1.55) for children.

Nearby, the **Amphitheater,** Rond-Pont des Arènes (☎ **04-90-49-36-36**), also built in the 1st century, seats almost 25,000 and still hosts bullfights in summer. The government warns you to visit the old monument at your own risk because of the worn and uneven masonry. For a good view, you can climb the three towers that remain from medieval times, when the amphitheater was turned into a fortress. Open daily 8am to 7pm, admission is 15F ($2.55) for adults and 9F ($1.55) 16 and under.

The most memorable sight in Arles is **Les Alyscamps,** rue Pierre-Renaudel (☎ **04-96-49-36-36**), once a necropolis established by the Romans, converted into a Christian burial ground in the 4th century. As the latter, it became a setting for legends in epic medieval poetry and was even mentioned in Dante's *Inferno.* Today it's lined with poplars and the remaining sarcophagi, a cool oasis in hot weather. Open daily June to September 8:30am to 7pm, October and March to May 9am to 12:30pm and 2 to 7pm, and November through February 9am to noon and 2 to 4:30pm. Admission is 15F ($2.55) for adults and 9F ($1.55) for children. Another ancient monument is the **Thermes de Constantin,** rue Dominique-Maisto, near the banks of the Rhône. Today only the baths (*thermae*) remain of a once-grand imperial palace. Visiting hours and admission prices are the same as at Les Alyscamps.

WHERE TO STAY & DINE

Hôtel d'Arlatan. 26 rue du Sauvage, 13631 Arles. ☎ **04-90-93-56-66.** Fax 04-90-49-68-45. 40 units. MINIBAR TV TEL. 541–1,066F ($91.95–$181.20) double; 1,200–1,500F ($204–$255) suite. AE, DC, MC, V. Parking 70F ($11.90).

In the former residence of the comtes d'Arlatan de Beaumont, near place du Forum, this hotel has been managed by the same family since 1920. It was built in the 15th century on the ruins of an old palace—in fact, there's still a 4th-century wall. The rooms (37 of which have air-conditioning) are furnished with authentic Provençal antiques, with walls covered by tapestries in the Louis XV and Louis XVI styles. Try to get a room overlooking the garden. Those on the ground floor are largest. The bathrooms have hair dryers and often a tub/shower combination.

✪ **Hôtel Jules César et Restaurant Lou Marquès.** 7 bd. des Lices, 13200 Arles. ☎ **04-90-93-43-20.** Fax 04-90-93-33-47. 52 units. MINIBAR TV TEL. 700–1,250F ($119–$212.50) double; from 1,450F ($246.50) suite. AE, DC, MC, V. Closed Nov 12–Dec 23. Parking 60F ($10.20).

In the town center, this 17th-century former Carmelite convent is now a stately hotel with the best restaurant in Arles. Although this is a noisy neighborhood, most rooms face the quiet, unspoiled cloister. The decoration is luxurious, with antique Provençal furnishings bought at auctions. The interior rooms are the most tranquil, but also the darkest. Most downstairs rooms are spacious; those upstairs have certain old-world charm that offsets their smaller size. The rooms in the modern extensions, although large and comfortable, lack character. In all cases, the tiled bathrooms are supplied with deluxe toiletries and a hair dryer. Most have a tub/shower combination. You wake to the scent of roses and the sounds of birds singing.

The restaurant, Lou Marquês, has tables outside on the front terrace. The food is extremely fresh. From the à la carte menu, we recomend bourride à la Provençale or Arles lamb. À la carte dinners average 210 to 420F ($35.70 to $71.40).

AIX-EN-PROVENCE

Founded in 122 B.C. by a Roman general, Caius Sextius Calvinus, who named it Aquae Sextiae after himself, Aix was first a Roman military outpost and then a civilian colony. Later roles included the administrative capital of a province of the later Roman Empire, the seat of an archbishop, and the official residence of the medieval comtes de Provence. After the union of Provence with France, Aix remained a judicial and administrative headquarters until the revolution.

The celebrated son of this old capital city of Provence is Paul Cézanne, who immortalized the countryside nearby. Montagne Ste-Victoire looms over the town today just as it did in Cézanne's time, although a string of high rises has cropped up. This faded university town, Provence's most charming center, was once a seat of aristocracy, its streets walked by counts and kings. It's 50 miles southeast of Avignon and 20 miles north of Marseille.

ESSENTIALS

GETTING THERE   As a rail and highway junction, the city is easily accessible, with **trains** arriving hourly from Marseille (trip time: 40 minutes) at the station off rue Gustave Desplace at the end of avenue Victor Hugo. For details, call ☎ **08-36-35-35-35.** There's frequent **bus** service in and out of Aix-en-Provence's **Gare Routière** (☎ **04-42-27-17-91** for information), including four a day to and from Avignon (trip time: 90 minutes). Buses arrive at the station on rue Lapierre at intervals of between 15 and 30 minutes throughout the day from Marseille. If you'd like to explore the region by bike, contact **Cycles Naddeo,** 54 av. de Lattre-de-Tassigny (☎ **04-42-16-11-61**), which rents 10-speeds for 90F ($15.30) per day or mountain bikes for 110F ($18.70) per day. Either a passport or some form of currency representing between 1,000F ($170) and 1,600F ($272), depending on the value of the bike, is required at the time of rental. The shop lies in the heart of town, midway between town hall and the town's main police station.

VISITOR INFORMATION   The **Office de Tourisme** is at 2 place du Général-de-Gaulle (☎ **04-42-16-11-61**).

DEPARTING BY CAR   From Aix-en-Provence, the best way to reach St-Tropez is to take the autoroute (A-8) southeast to the junction with Route 25, then cut south to Ste-Maxime. Once at Ste-Maxime, follow N-98 west to Port Grimaud, at which point you connect with D-98A going east for the final lap to St-Tropez.

EXPLORING THE CITY

✪ **Cours Mirabeau,** the main street, is one of the most beautiful in Europe. Plane trees act like umbrellas, shading the street from the hot Provençal sun and filtering the light into shadows that play on the rococo fountains. On one side are shops and sidewalk cafes, on the other richly embellished sandstone *hôtels particuliers* (mansions) from the 17th and 18th centuries. The street, which honors Mirabeau, the revolutionary and statesman, begins at the 1860 landmark fountain on place de la Libération.

Cathédrale St-Sauveur, place des Martyrs de la Résistance (☎ **04-42-23-45-65**), is dedicated to Christ under the title St-Sauveur (Holy Savior or Redeemer). Its baptistery dates from the 4th and 5th centuries, but the architectural complex as a whole has seen many additions. It contains a brilliant Nicolas Froment triptych, *The Burning Bush,* from the 15th century. One side depicts the Virgin and Child, the other Good King René and his second wife, Jeanne de Laval. It's open daily 7:30am to noon and 2 to 6pm; masses are Sunday at 9am, 10:30am, and 7pm.

Nearby in a former archbishop's palace is the **Musée des Tapisseries,** 28 place de l'Ancien Archeveche (☎ **04-42-23-09-91**). Lining its gilded walls are three series of tapestries from the 17th and 18th centuries collected by the archbishops to decorate the palace: *The History of Don Quixote* by Natoire, *The Russian Games* by Leprince, and *The Grotesques* by Monnoyer. In addition, the museum exhibits rare furnishings from the 17th and 18th centuries. It's open Wednesday to Monday 10am to noon and 2 to 5:45pm; admission is 11F ($1.85).

Up rue Cardinale is the **Musée Granet,** place St-Jean-de-Malte (☎ **04-42-38-14-70**), which owns several Cézannes although not a very typical collection of the great artist's work. Matisse donated a nude in 1941. Housed in the former center of the Knights of Malta, the fine-arts gallery contains work by Van Dyck, Van Loo, and Rigaud; portraits by Pierre and François Puget; and (the most interesting) a *Jupiter and Thetis* by Ingres. Ingres also did an 1807 portrait of the museum's namesake, François Marius Granet. Granet's own works abound. The museum is open Wednesday to Monday 10am to noon and 2:30 to 6pm; closed January. Admission is 18F ($3.05) for adults, and 10F ($1.70) for students and children under 16.

Outside town, at 9 av. Paul-Cézanne, is the **Atelier de Cézanne** (☎ **04-42-21-06-53**), the studio of the painter who was the major forerunner of cubism. Surrounded by a wall, the house was restored by American admirers. Repaired again in 1970, it remains much as Cézanne left it in 1906. It's open daily 10am to noon and from 2:30 to 6pm (until 5pm between October and May). Admission costs 25F ($4.25) for adults and 10F ($1.70) for children.

THE SHOPPING SCENE

Bechard. 12 cours Mirabeau. ☎ **04-42-26-06-78.**

Established a century ago and a standard stop for anyone planning a dinner party in and around Aix, this is the most famous bakery in town. It takes its work so seriously that it refers to its underground kitchens as a *laboratoire* (laboratory). The pastries are truly gorgeous, in most cases made fresh every day.

Girault. 35 rue Bedarrides. ☎ **04-42-27-17-35.**

At another outlet for *santons,* a faithful allegiance to the models of long ago is extremely important. Prices are competitive with those charged by Santons Foque (see below).

La Boutique du Pays d'Aix. 2 place du Général-de-Gaulle (in the Aix-en-Provence Tourist Information Office). ☎ **04-42-16-11-61.**

Few boutiques carry so many *santons* (carved figurines inspired by the Nativity of Jesus), locally woven textiles and carvings, and an assortment of *calissons* (sugared confections made with almonds and a *confit* of melon).

Santons Fouque. 65 cours Gambetta (Route de Nice, RN7). ☎ **04-42-26-33-38.**

Founded in 1934 and set on a busy boulevard about half a mile from the center of Aix, this showroom and factory stocks the largest assortment of *santons* in Aix. More than 1,800 figurines are cast in terra-cotta, finished by hand, and then decorated with oil-based paint according to 18th-century models. Each of the trades practiced in medieval Provence is represented, including grizzled but awestruck shoemakers, barrelmakers, copper and iron smiths, and ropemakers, each poised to welcome the newborn Jesus. Depending on their size and complexity, figurines range from 50 to 5,300F ($8.50 to $901).

WHERE TO STAY

Hôtel Cardinal. 22–24 rue Cardinale, 13100 Aix-en-Provence. ☎ **04-42-38-32-30.** Fax 04-42-26-39-05. 35 units. TV TEL. 270–400F ($45.90–$68) double. MC, V. Parking 60F ($10.20).

Not everything is state of the art, but to many the Cardinal is still the best value in Aix. Lying on the other side of the Cours in the Mazarin quarter, it is distinguished by a lingering air of fragility and nostalgia. Guests stay in simply furnished old rooms either in the main building or in the annex up the street. Some of the bedrooms in the annex have serviceable kitchens. Bathrooms tend to be small but each has a good shower.

✪ **Villa Gallici.** Av. de la Violette (impasse des Grands Pins), 13100 Aix-en-Provence. ☎ **04-42-23-29-23.** Fax 04-42-96-30-45. E-mail: villagallici@relaischateaux.fr. 22 units. A/C MINIBAR TV TEL. 900–1,900F ($153–$323) double; 1,850–2,900F ($314.50–$493) suite. AE, DC, MC, V.

This elegant inn is the most stylishly decorated in Aix. Each large room has a safe and a king-sized bed, often canopied, Some rooms boast a private terrace or garden. Our favorite is room 19, complete with a canopied bed and an antique porcelain stove. Bathrooms are also large with hair dryers and make-up mirrors. The villa sits in a large enclosed garden in the heart of town, close to one of the best restaurants, Le Clos de la Violette. Simple meals can be ordered from this restaurant and eaten beside the pool. The hotel also has its own restaurant, serving a set menu at 380F ($64.60). On the premises are limited spa facilities.

WHERE TO DINE

Le Bistro Latin. 18 rue de la Couronne. ☎ **04-42-38-22-88.** Reservations recommended. Set-price lunch 89F ($15.15); set-price dinner 119–139F ($20.25–$23.65) and 179F ($30.45). MC, V. Mon 7–10:30pm; Tues–Sat noon–2pm and 7–10:30pm. Bus: 27, 42, or 51. FRENCH.

This is the best little bistro in Aix-en-Provence for the price. Provençal music plays in two intimate, antique-decorated dining rooms, and the staff is young and enthusiastic. Try the chartreuse of mussels, one of the meat dishes with spinach-and-saffron cream sauce, or crêpe of hare with basil sauce. We've enjoyed the classic cuisine, particularly the scampi risotto, on all our visits.

✪ **Le Clos de la Violette.** 10 av. de la Violette. ☎ **04-42-23-30-71.** Reservations required. Main courses 185–210F ($31.45–$35.70); set-price lunch 240–500F ($40.80–$85); set-price dinner 400–510F ($68–$86.70). AE, V. Mon 7:30–9:30pm; Tues–Sat noon–1:30pm and 7:30–9:30pm. Closed Nov 1–16. Bus: 27, 42, or 51. FRENCH.

In an elegant residential neighborhood, which most visitors reach by taxi, this is the most innovative restaurant in town. This imposing Provençal villa has an octagonal reception area and several modern dining rooms. The food produced by Jean-Marc and Brigitte Banzo has been called a "song of Provence." Typical dishes—although they change every 2 months—are an upside-down tart of snails with parsley juice, slow-cooked lamb with brown sauce, scallops with artichoke hearts, and a sumptuous array of desserts.

ST-TROPEZ

Sun-kissed lasciviousness is rampant in this carnival town, 47 miles southwest of Cannes, but the true Tropezian resents that the port has such a bad reputation. "We can be classy, too," one native insisted. Creative people in the arts and ordinary folk create a compelling mixture.

Colette lived here for many years. Diarist Anaïs Nin, confidante of Henry Miller, posed on the beach in 1939 in a Dorothy Lamour bathing suit. Earlier, St-Tropez was known to Guy de Maupassant, Matisse, and Bonnard. Today, artists, composers, novelists, and the film colony come to St-Tropez in summer. Trailing them is a line of humanity unmatched anywhere else on the Riviera for sheer flamboyance.

ESSENTIALS

GETTING THERE   The nearest rail station is in St-Raphaël, a neighboring resort; at the Vieux Port, four or five **boats** per day leave the **Gare Maritime de St-Raphaël,** rue Pierre Auble (☎ **04-94-95-17-46**), for St-Tropez (trip time: 50 minutes). Some 15 **Sodetrav buses** per day leave from the **Gare Routière** in St-Raphaël (☎ **04-94-95-24-82**), for St-Tropez (trip time: 1½ to 2¼ hours, depending on the bus). Buses also run directly to St-Tropez from its nearest airport (at Toulon-Hyères 35 miles away.) If you drive, be aware that parking in St-Tropez is extremely difficult, especially in summer, when the carnival atmosphere virtually guarantees a shortage of parking spots. In 1998, some of the situation was relieved with the construction of a multistoried parking lot beneath the place des Lices, **Parc des Lices** (☎ **04-94-97-34-46**), whose entrance is on the Avenue Paul Roussel. Designed for 471 cars, it charges between 8 to 12F ($1.35 to $2.05) for the first hour, and between 8 to 11F ($1.35 to $1.85) for each subsequent hour, depending on the season. Many visitors with expensive cars prefer this site, as it's more carefully supervised and guarded than any other parking lot in St-Tropez.

VISITOR INFORMATION   The **Office de Tourisme** is on quai Jean-Jaurès (☎ **04-94-97-45-21**).

DEPARTING BY CAR   After leaving St-Tropez, take the D-98A northwest again (the same route you traveled to get here), and link up with D-559 at the junction, heading east to Ste-Maxime. This route, which becomes N-98, takes you all the way to Cannes.

EXPLORING ST-TROPEZ & ENVIRONS

Near the harbor is the **l'Annonciade Musée St-Tropez** at place Georges-Grammont (☎ **04-94-97-04-01**), installed in the former chapel of the Annonciade. As a legacy from the artists who loved St-Tropez, the museum shelters one of the finest modern-art collections on the Riviera. Many of the artists, including Paul Signac, depicted the port of St-Tropez. Opened in 1955, the collection includes such works as Van Dongen's yellow-faced *Women of the Balustrade* and paintings and sculpture by Bonnard, Matisse, Braque, Utrillo, Seurat, Derain, Maillol, and Van Dongen. From June to September, the museum is open Wednesday to Monday 10am to noon and from 3 to 7pm. From October to May, it's open Wednesday to Monday 10am to noon and from 2 to 6pm. It's closed in November. Entrance costs 30F ($5.10) for adults and 15F ($2.55) for those under 16.

Two miles from St-Tropez, **Port Grimaud** makes an interesting outing. If you approach the village at dusk, when it's softly bathed in Riviera pastels, it looks like some old hamlet, perhaps from the 16th century, but this is a mirage. Port Grimaud is the dream fulfillment of its promoter, François Spoerry, who carved it out of marshland and dug canals. Flanking these canals, fingers of land extend from the main square to the sea. The homes are Provençal style, many with Italianate window arches. Boat owners can anchor right at their doorsteps. One newspaper called the port "the most magnificent fake since Disneyland."

THE SHOPPING SCENE

Choses. Quai Jean-Jaurès. ☎ **04-94-97-03-44.**

Although better stocked than the norm, Choses is a women's clothing store typical of the hundreds of middle-bracket, whimsically nonchalant emporiums that thrive throughout the Riviera. Its specialty includes clingy and often provocative T-shirt dresses.

Galeries Tropéziennes. 56 rue Gambetta. ☎ **04-94-97-02-21.**

This shop crowds hundreds of unusual gift items, some worthwhile, some rather silly, and textiles into its rambling showrooms near place des Lices. The inspiration is Mediterranean, breezy and sophisticated.

Jacqueline Thienot. 12 rue Georges-Clemenceau. ☎ **04-94-97-05-70.**

In a resort that's increasingly loaded with purveyors of suntan lotion, touristy souvenirs, and T-shirts, Jacqueline Thienot maintains an inventory of Provençal antiques, prized by dealers from as far away as Paris. The one-room shop is housed in a late 18th-century building that shows the 18th- and 19th-century antiques to their best advantage.

HITTING THE BEACH & OTHER OUTDOOR ACTIVITIES

BEACHES St-Tropez has the Riviera's best beaches. The best for families are those closest to the town center, including the amusingly named **Bouillabaisse** and **Plage des Greniers.** The more daring beaches are the 6-mile sandy crescents at **Plage des Salins** and **Plage de Pampellone,** beginning some 2 miles from the town center and best reached by bike (see below) if you're not driving. If you ever wanted to go topless, bottomless, or wear a truly daring bikini, this is the place!

BICYCLING The largest outfitter for bikes and motorscooters is **Louis Mas,** 5 rue Josef-Quaranta (☎ **04-94-97-00-60**). Bikes rent for plus 48F ($8.15) per hour; motorscooters go for 190 to 275F ($32.30 to $46.75) per hour, depending on the size. A deposit of 1,000F ($170), payable with AmEx, MasterCard, or Visa, is also required.

BOATING We recommend **Suncap Company,** 15 Quai de Suffren (☎ **04-94-97-11-23**), which rents boats that range from 18 feet to 40 feet. The smallest can be rented to qualified sailors without a captain, but the larger ones come with a captain at the helm. Prices, per day, start at 3,000F ($510).

GOLF The nearest golf course, at the edge of Ste-Maxime, across the bay from St-Tropez, is the **Golf Club de Beauvallon,** bd. des Collines, Grimaud, 83120 Ste-Maxime (☎ **04-94-96-16-98**), a popular course that brought its complement of holes up to 18 after a massive improvement and enlargement in 1996. No golf carts are available. Greens fees range from 250 to 300F ($42.50 to $51) for 18 holes, and a set of golf clubs rent for 100F ($17) per set.

Sprawling over a rocky, vertiginous landscape that requires a golf cart and a lot of physical labor is the Don Harradine-designed **Golf de Ste-Maxime-Plaza,** Route de Débarquement, B.P. 1, 83120 Ste-Maxime (☎ **04-94-49-26-60**). Built in 1991 and associated with the four-star Plaza de Ste-Maxime, it also welcomes nonguests; phone to reserve tee-off times. Greens fees for 18 holes are 280F ($47.60) per person; renting a cart for two golfers and their equipment costs 125F ($21.25) per 18 holes.

SCUBA DIVING A team of dive enthusiasts who are ready, willing, and able to show you the azure depths off the coast of St-Tropez operate from the **Octopussy I and II,** both of which are aluminum-sided, yellow-painted dive boats, built in the early and mid 1990s, that are based year-round in St-Tropez's Nouveau Port. Experienced divers pay 230F ($39.10) for a one-tank exploration dive, and novices are charged 250F ($42.50) for a *baptême,* that includes one-on-one supervision from a

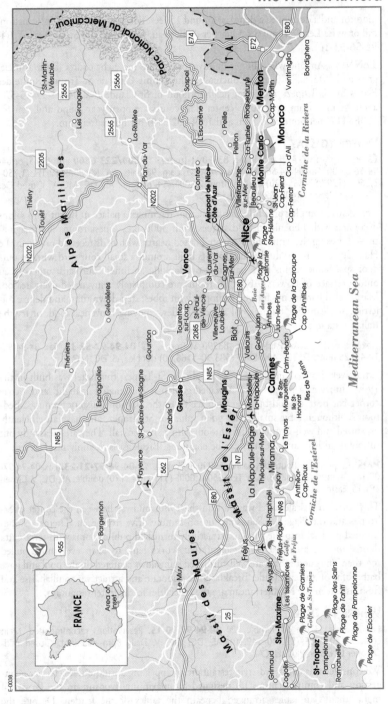

The French Riviera

Parc National du Mercantour

ITALY

St-Martin-Vésuble
2555
2566
Les Granges
2565
La-Rivière
2205
Thiéry
Touët
Plan-du-Var
Sospel
L'Escarène
Peille
Peillon
Contes

N202

Alpes Maritimes

N202

Gréolières

Théniers

Escragnolles

Fayence

Bargemon

955

N85

St-Cézaire-sur-Siagne

Cabris

Gourdon

Tourettes-sur-Loup
2085 St-Paul-de-Vence
Villeneuve-Loubet

Vence

St-Laurent-du-Var

Cagnes-sur-Mer

Grasse

N85

Mougins

Mandelieu-la-Napoule

Biot
Valauris

Golfe-Juan

Ventimiglia
Bordighera

La-Turbie Roquebrune
Menton
Cap-Martin

Monaco

Monte Carlo

Eze Cap d'Ail

Peille

Villefranche-sur-Mer
St-Jean-Cap-Ferrat
Beaulieu
St-Hélène Cap-Ferrat

Corniche de la Riviera

Aéroport de Nice–Côte d'Azur

Nice

Plage Ste-Hélène

Plage la Californie

Baie des Anges

Plage de la Garoupe

Antibes

Juan-les-Pins

Plage d'Antibes

Cap d'Antibes

Cannes

Palm-Beach

Ile Ste-Marguerite
Ile St-Honorat
Iles de Lérins

Mediterranean Sea

N7

La Napoule-Plage

Théoule-sur-Mer
Le Trayas
Miramar
Agay
Anthéor-Cap-Roux

Massif de l'Estérel

Corniche de l'Estérel

562

E80

St-Raphaël
N98

Fréjus-Plage
Golfe de Fréjus
Fréjus

St-Aygulf

Le Muy

25

Massif des Maures

Grimaud

Cogolin

Ste-Maxime

Les Issambres

St-Tropez

Plage de Graniers
Golfe de St-Tropez
Plage des Salins

Pampelonne
Ramatuelle

Plage de Tahiti

Plage de Pampelonne

Plage de l'Escalet

FRANCE
Area of Inset

E-0038

379

monitor and a descent to a depth of around 15 feet. For reservations and information, call or write **Les Octopussys,** Quartier de Berteau, Gassin, 83990 St-Tropez (☎ **04-94-56-53-10**).

TENNIS   Anyone who phones in advance can use the eight courts (both artificial grass and "Quick," a form of concrete) at the **Tennis-Club de St-Tropez,** Route des Plages, in St-Tropez's industrial neighborhood of St-Claude (☎ **04-94-97-15-52**), about ½ mile from the resort's center. The courts are open year-round and rent for 100F ($17) per hour until 5pm and 130F ($22.10) per hour after 5pm.

WHERE TO STAY

✪ **Hôtel Byblos.** Av. Paul-Signac, 83990 St-Tropez. ☎ **800/223-6800** in the U.S. or 04-94-56-68-00. Fax 04-94-56-68-01. www.byblos.com. 98 units. A/C MINIBAR TV TEL. 1,750–3,260F ($297.50–$554.20) double; from 2,800F ($476) suite. AE, DC, MC, V. Closed Oct 15–Easter. Parking 140F ($23.80).

This deluxe complex on a hill over the harbor resembles a palace in Beirut with salons decorated with Phoenician gold statues from 3000 B.C. Guest rooms are imaginative—for example, with a fireplace on a raised hearth with beds recessed on a dais. Le Hameau contains 10 duplex apartments built around a small courtyard with an outdoor spa. Some rooms have balconies overlooking an inner courtyard; others open onto a terrace of flowers. About 10 rooms are completely rejuvenated every season. Marble-clad bathrooms are well equipped with robes, step-down tubs, and deluxe toiletries. You can dine by the pool at Les Arcades, enjoying Provençal food, or try the Italian restaurant.

Hôtel Ermitage. Av. Paul-Signac, 83990 St-Tropez. ☎ **04-94-97-52-33.** Fax 04-94-97-10-43. 26 units. TV TEL. 490–990F ($83.30–$168.30) double. AE, DC, MC, V.

Attractively isolated amid the rocky heights of St-Tropez, this hotel was built in the 19th century as a private villa. A walled garden is illuminated at night, and a cozy corner bar near a wood-burning fireplace takes the chill off blustery evenings. Bedrooms, although a bit small, offer good value for St.-Tropez, and have an efficiently organized and well-maintained bathroom with a shower stall. They are pleasantly but simply furnished, and the staff can be charming. Breakfast is the only meal served.

Hôtel la Tartane. Route des Salins, 83990 St-Tropez. ☎ **04-94-97-21-23.** Fax 04-94-97-09-16. 14 units. A/C MINIBAR TV TEL. 650–1,000F ($110.50–$170) double. AE, DC, V. Closed Oct 15–Easter.

This cozy, small-scale hotel was built in the 1980s midway between the center of St-Tropez and the Plage des Salins, about a 3-minute drive from each. There's a stone-rimmed pool set into the garden, attractively furnished public rooms with terra-cotta floors, and an attentive management that works hard to keep everything pulled together. The guest rooms are well-furnished bungalows centered on the pool and have bathrooms on the small side. Breakfasts are elaborate and attractive; bouillabaisse and fresh fish from the Mediterranean are the specialties in the hotel restaurant.

WHERE TO DINE

La Ramade. 3 rue du Temple. ☎ **04-94-97-00-15.** Reservations recommended. Main courses 120–290F ($20.40–$49.30). AE, DC, MC, V. Daily 8pm–midnight. Closed mid-October to Easter. PROVENÇAL.

We consider this courtyard-style restaurant an appealing antidote to St-Tropez's congestion and commercialism. It's designed for maximum exposure to the Provençal night, thanks to tables arranged beneath the tables of the garden. Despite the charming, albeit a bit disorganized, service, you'll genuinely appreciate the seafood-based specialties that emerge amid clouds of herb-infused steam from the tiny kitchens. Examples include savory versions of both *bourrides* and bouillabaisses, as well as a platter of sea wolf that's slow-roasted over charcoal flames.

L'Echalotte. 35 rue Allard. ☎ **04-94-54-83-26.** Reservations recommended in summer. Main courses 75–140F ($12.75–$23.80); set-price menus 98–160F ($16.65–$27.20). AE, MC, V. Thurs 8–11:30pm; Fri–Wed 12:30–2pm and 8–11:30pm. Closed Nov 15–Dec 15. FRENCH.

This charming restaurant, with a tiny garden, serves consistently good food for moderate prices. You can enjoy lunch on the veranda or dinner indoors. The food is solidly bourgeois, including grilled veal kidneys, crayfish with drawn-butter sauce, and filet of turbot with truffles. The major specialty is several kinds of fish, like sea bass and daurade royale cooked in a salt crust.

Les Mouscardins. 1 rue Portalet. ☎ **04-94-97-29-00.** Reservations required. Main courses 100–300F ($17–$51); set-price menus 135–210F ($22.95–$35.70). AE, MC, V. Daily noon–2:30pm and 7:30–11:30pm. Closed 2 weeks in Nov, and for lunch mid-Nov to mid-Mar. FRENCH.

This restaurant at the end of the harbor has won awards for culinary perfection. The dining room is in formal Provençal style with an adjoining sunroom under a canopy. The menu includes classic Mediterranean dishes; we recommend *moules marinières* (mussels in marinara sauce) as an appetizer. The two celebrated fish stews of the Côte d'Azur are also tempting: *bourride Provençale* and bouillabaisse. The fish dishes, particularly the loup (sea bass), are excellent. For dessert, try a soufflé made with grand Marnier or Cointreau.

ST-TROPEZ AFTER DARK

Les Caves du Roy. In the Hôtel Byblos, av. Paul-Signac. ☎ **04-94-97-16-02.**

Located on the lobby level of this hyperexpensive, hyperelegant hotel, Les Caves is the most prestigious and self-consciously chic nightclub in St-Tropez. Entrance is free, but drinks cost a whopping 120F ($20.40) each. It's open nightly from 11:30pm until dawn, but only from Easter to late September.

Le Papagayo. In the Residence du Nouveau Port, rue Gambetta. ☎ **04-94-97-07-56.** Cover 110F ($18.70), including first drink.

This is one of the largest nightclubs in St-Tropez, with two floors, three bars, and lots of attractive women and men from throughout the Mediterranean eager to pursue their bait. The decor is neo-psychedelic, and the clientele is youthful and high-energy. Between Easter and late September, it's open nightly from 11:30pm till dawn. The rest of the year, it's open only on preselected weekends, usually as part of the celebrations of local charities and sports clubs, events to which the public is welcome.

Le Pigeonnier. 13 rue de la Ponche. ☎ **04-94-97-36-85.** Cover 70F ($11.90), including first drink.

Most of the socializing at this largely gay club revolves around the long and narrow bar, where drinks cost 70F ($11.90). The crowd is composed of some lesbians, but mostly gay men in their 20s or early 30s from all over Europe. There's also a dance floor.

CANNES

When Coco Chanel went here and got a suntan, returning to Paris bronzed, she startled the milk-white ladies of society, but they quickly began copying her. Today the bronzed bodies—in nearly nonexistent swimsuits—still line the sandy beaches of this chic resort.

Popular with celebrities, Cannes is at its most frenzied during the **International Film Festival** at the Palais des Festivals on promenade de la Croisette, held in either

April or May. On the seafront boulevards, flashbulbs pop as the stars emerge. International regattas, galas, *concours d'élégance,* even a Mimosa Festival in February— something is always happening at Cannes, except in November, traditionally a dead month.

Sixteen miles southwest of Nice, Cannes is sheltered by hills. For many it consists of only one street, **promenade de la Croisette** (or just La Croisette), curving along the coast and split by islands of palms and flowers.

A port of call for cruise liners, the seafront of Cannes is lined with hotels, apartment houses, and chic boutiques. Many of the bigger hotels, some dating from the 19th century, claim part of the beaches for the private use of their guests, but there are also public areas.

ESSENTIALS

GETTING THERE   Cannes lies on the major coastal rail line along the Riviera, with **trains** arriving at the station at 1 rue Jean-Laurès throughout the day. Trip time from Antibes is just 15 minutes; from Nice, 35 minutes. The TGV from Paris going via Marseille also services Cannes. For information and schedules, call ☎ **08-36-35-35-35. Bus** service is available from the Nice airport to Cannes every hour during the day (trip time: 35 minutes). For bus information about Cannes routes, call ☎ **04-93-39-18-71;** the station is at place de l'Hôtel de Ville. There's also one bus every half-hour from Antibes. The international airport at Nice is only 20 minutes northeast of Cannes.

VISITOR INFORMATION   The **Office de Tourisme** is in the Palais des Festivals, Esplanade Georges Pompidou (☎ **04-93-39-24-53**).

DEPARTING BY CAR   From Cannes, N-7 heads directly east to the resort of Juan-les-Pins, a distance of 6 miles.

EXPLORING CANNES

Above the harbor, the old town of Cannes sits on Suquet Hill, where you'll see a 14th-century tower, which the English dubbed the **Lord's Tower.**

Nearby is the **Musée de la Castre,** in the Château de la Castre, Le Suquet (☎ **04-93-38-55-26**), containing fine arts, with a section on ethnography. The latter includes relics and objects from everywhere from the Pacific islands to Southeast Asia, including both Peruvian and Mayan pottery. There's also a gallery with relics of ancient Mediterranean civilizations. Five rooms are devoted to 19th-century paintings. The museum is open Wednesday to Monday, April to June from 10am to noon and 2 to 6pm; July to September from 10am to noon and 3 to 7pm; and October to March from 10am to noon and 2 to 5pm (closed in January). Admission is 10F ($1.70) for adults and free for those under 16.

Another museum of note, the **Musée de la Mer,** Fort Royal (☎ **04-93-38-55-26**), displays artifacts from Ligurian, Roman, and Arab civilizations, including paintings, mosaics, and ceramics. You can also see the jail where the "Man in the Iron Mask" was incarcerated. Temporary exhibitions of photography are also shown. It's open July through September from 10:30am to 12:15pm and 2:15 to 6:30pm. The rest of the year it closes at sundown (between 4:30 and 5:30pm). Admission is 10F ($1.70) for adults and free for students and children 12 and under.

THE SHOPPING SCENE

You're likely to find branch outlets of virtually every stylish Paris retailer in Cannes. Most of the big names in designer fashion line **La Croisette.** The best names are closest to the high-rise **Gray-d'Albion,** 17 La Croisette, which is both a mall and a hotel.

At the edge of the Quartier Suquet, **Marché Forville** is the town's primary fruit, flower, and vegetable market. On Monday it's a flea market. There's a somewhat disorganized and invariably busy outdoor flea market every Saturday along the edges of the allée de la Liberté, across from the Palais des Festivals.

Cannes English Bookshop. 11 rue Bivouac Napoléon. ☎ **04-93-99-40-08.**

Richly stocked with books and periodicals from almost every English-speaking country in the world, this shop near the main post office has attracted readers since 1984.

Cannolive. 16–20 rue Vénizelos. ☎ **04-93-39-08-19.**

This distinctive and charmingly old-fashioned shop, owned by the Raynaud family, who founded the place in 1880, sells Provençal olives and all of their by-products—purées (tapenades) that connoisseurs refer to as "Provençal caviar," black "olives de Nice," and green "olives de Provence," as well as three grades of olive oil from several regional producers. Oils and food products are dispensed from no. 16, but gift items (fabrics, porcelain, and Provençal souvenirs) are sold next door.

Maiffret. 31 rue d'Antibes. ☎ **04-93-39-08-29.**

This shop specializes in chocolates and candied fruit, made by culinary processes that must be seen to be fully appreciated. Pâtés and confits of fruit, some of which decorate cakes and tarts, are also sold as desirable confections in their own right. Look for the Provençal national confection, *calissons,* crafted from almonds, a confit of melon, and sugar.

HITTING THE BEACH & OTHER OUTDOOR PURSUITS

BEACHES   The best beach is **Plage du Midi,** west of the old harborfront, with the best sun in the afternoon. **Plage Gazagnaire,** another good beach, is east of the new port, ideal in the morning. Between these two public beaches are many private ones where you can gain entrance by paying a fee that includes a mattress and sun umbrella. Waiters at these private beach clubs come by to take your orders for lunch.

BICYCLING & MOTORSCOOTERING   Despite the roaring traffic, the flat landscapes between Cannes and such satellite resorts as La Napoule are well suited for riding a bike or motorscooter. **Cannes Location Deux Roues,** 11 rue Hélène-Vagliano (☎ 04-93-39-46-15), across from the Gray d'Albion, rents pedal bikes for 62F ($10.55) per day and requires a 1,000F ($170) deposit (payable with American Express, MasterCard, or Visa). Motorscooters cost 160 to 200F ($27.20 to $34) per day and require a deposit of 4,000 to 10,000F ($680 to $1,700), depending on their value. A worthwhile competitor for the rentals of bikes and motorscooters is **Cycles Daniel,** 2 rue du Pont Romain (☎ 04-93-99-90-30), where *vélos tout terrain* (mountain bikes) cost 70F ($11.90) a day. At both of the establishments recommended above, renters of motorized bikes and scooters must be at least 14 years old. For the larger of the scooters, potential renters must present a valid driver's license.

BOATING   Several companies can rent you a boat of any size, with or without a crew, for a day, a week, or a month, depending on your priorities, your bankroll, and your schedule. An outfit known for its short-term rentals of small craft, including motorboats and sailboats, is **Elco Marine,** 106 bd. du Midi (☎ 04-93-47-12-62). Two others that have access to larger boats, including motor-driven and sailing yachts and craft suitable for deep-sea fishing, include **MS Yachts,** 57 La

Croisette (☎ **04-93-99-03-51**); and **Mediterranée Courtage (Agence Y.P)**, 22 quai Saint-Pierre (☎ **04-93-38-30-40**).

GOLF   The dry and rolling landscapes of Provence contribute to memorable golfing. One of the region's most challenging and interesting courses, **Country-Club de Cannes-Mougins**, 175 rte. d'Antibes, Mougins (☎ **04-93-75-79-13**), 4 miles north of Cannes, was a 1976 reconfiguration by Dye & Ellis of an outmoded, under-accessorized course laid out in the 1920s. Noted for olive trees and cypresses that adorn a relatively flat terrain, the par-72 course has many water traps and a deceptively tricky layout loaded with technical challenges. It's the host of the Royal Mougins Open, an important stop on the PGA European Tour. The course is open to anyone with proof of his or her handicap—24 for men, 28 for women—willing to pay greens fees of 380 to 430F ($64.60 to $73.10), depending on the day of the week. An electric golf cart rents for 280F ($47.60), and golf clubs can be rented for 150F ($25.50) per set. Reservations are recommended.

SWIMMING   Most of the larger hotels in Cannes have their own pools. In addition to the tennis courts described below, the **Complexe Sportif Montfleury**, 23 av. Beauséjour (☎ **04-93-38-75-78**), boasts a large modern pool. Entrance fee is 25F ($4.25) for adults, 20F ($3.40) for those under 16.

TENNIS   **Complexe Sportif Montfleury**, 23 av. Beauséjour (☎ **04-93-38-75-78**) has eight hard-surfaced courts that rent for 80F ($13.60) per hour, and two clay-surfaced courts that rent for 100F ($17) per hour.

WHERE TO STAY

Although hotels in Cannes might elect to have their own e-mail address, there is a shared and collective e-mail address for all hotels in the city: infos@cannes.hotel.com.

Very Expensive

Hôtel Carlton Inter-Continental. 58 bd. de la Croisette, 06400 Cannes. ☎ **800/ 327-0200** in the U.S., or 04-93-06-40-06. Fax 04-93-06-40-25. 338 units. A/C MINIBAR TV TEL. 1,030–3,995F ($175.10–$679.15) double; from 3,000F ($510) suite. AE, DC, MC, V. Parking 180F ($30.60). Bus: 11.

Today, except for the Cannes Film Festival, you are more likely to see conventions and groups than the stars and royalty of past years. The guest rooms were renovated in 1990. Special features include double-glazed windows and big combination bathrooms with hair dryers. The most spacious rooms are in the west wing, and many of the upper-floor rooms open onto balconies fronting the sea. The Carlton Casino Club opened in 1989, and La Côte restaurant, open only from June to September, is one of the most distinguished along the Riviera. Otherwise, La Belle Otéro is open for lunch and dinner most of the year. The cuisine here, some of the finest along the entire Riviera, wins two stars from Michelin, and is the only restaurant in Cannes to rival Palme d'Or. There's a private beach, health club with spa facilities, and a glass-roofed indoor pool.

Expensive

Hôtel Gray-d'Albion. 38 rue des Serbes, 06400 Cannes. ☎ **04-92-99-79-79**. Fax 04-93-99-26-10. www.graydalbion@lucienbarriere.com. 189 units. A/C MINIBAR TV TEL. 800–1,900F ($136–$323) double; from 2,800F ($476) suite. AE, DC, MC, V. Bus: 1.

Because it offers a luxurious setting on a scale smaller than the Carlton and the Majestic, we count the Gray d'Albion among the Riviera's more desirable hotels. The bedrooms are fairly standard, blending both contemporary and traditional furnishings along with such amenities as private safes and bedside controls. Each room has a balcony; those on the eighth and ninth floors have views of the Mediterranean, but otherwise the views aren't notable. Bathrooms are well equipped and clad in marble and granite, each with a set of deluxe toiletries, hair dryers, and make-up mirrors. Dining selections include Le Royal Gray (one of Cannes's best), a beach-club restaurant, and a brasserie featuring special dishes from Lebanon.

Moderate

Hôtel le Fouquet's. 2 rond-point Duboys-d'Angers, 06400 Cannes. ☎ **04-92-59-25-00.** Fax 04-92-98-03-39. 10 units. A/C MINIBAR TV TEL. 590–990F ($100.30–$168.30) double. AE, DC, MC, V. Closed Oct to late Mar. Parking 80F ($13.60). Bus: 1.

This is an intimate hotel drawing a discreet clientele, often from Paris, who'd never think of patronizing the grand palace hotels. Very "Riviera French" in design and decor, it's several blocks from the beach. Each of the attractive, airy rooms is decorated in bold colors, containing a loggia and a dressing room. Bathrooms, although small, are efficiently organized, with a shower stall and a hair dryer.

Inexpensive

Hôtel de Provence. 9 rue Molière, 06400 Cannes. ☎ **04-93-38-44-35.** Fax 04-93-39-63-14. 30 units. A/C MINIBAR TV TEL. 300–490F ($51–$83.30) double. AE, DC, MC, V. Parking 35F ($5.95). Bus: 1.

Hôtel de Provence stands in its own walled garden of palms and flowering shrubs on a quiet inner street. Most rooms have private balconies and many overlook the garden. Bedrooms are showing their age but still offer fine comfort, and for Cannes this is a remarkable bargain. Each unit comes with a small bathroom with a shower stall. In warm weather, breakfast is served under the vines and flowers of an arbor.

Hôtel Le Florian. 8 rue Commandant-André, 06400 Cannes. ☎ **04-93-39-24-82.** Fax 04-92-99-18-30. 20 units. A/C TV TEL. 200–350F ($34–$59.50) double. AE, MC, V. Parking 45F ($7.65) per night in a nearby public facility. Bus: 1.

This hotel is set on a busy but narrow, densely commercial street that leads directly into La Croisette, fewer than a hundred yards from both the beach and the city's largest convention hall, Palais des Festivals. Built about a century ago, it has been maintained by three different generations of the Giordano family since the 1950s. In 1992, many much-needed improvements were made to the physical setting. The effect today is basic, but comfortable. Most rooms are rather small but have fine mattresses on the twin or double beds. Bathrooms are compact with a shower stall. No meals are served other than breakfast.

A Gay-Friendly Hotel

Les Charmettes. 47 rue de Grasse, 06400 Cannes. ☎ **04-93-39-17-13.** Fax 04-93-68-08-41. 15 units. 300–450F ($51–$76.50) double. MC, V. No parking available.

This is a modern, somewhat boxy three-story hotel near the center of Cannes, with a laissez-faire attitude, welcoming mainly gays. An 8-minute walk from the Palais des Festivals and a 4-minute walk from the Vieux Port, the hotel was built in the early 1960s but last renovated in 1997. Each room is soundproofed and individually decorated in a tasteful and pleasing style. You can get drinks in the lobby, but breakfast is the only meal served.

WHERE TO DINE
Expensive

Gaston-Gastounette. 7 quai St-Pierre. ☎ **04-93-39-49-44.** Reservations required. Main courses 160–300F ($27.20–$51); set-price lunch 125–170F ($21.25–$28.90); set-price dinner 170F ($28.90). AE, DC, MC, V. Daily noon–2pm and 7–11pm. Closed Nov 30–Dec 19. Bus: 1. FRENCH.

This is the best restaurant to offer views of the marina. Located in the old port, it has a stucco exterior with oak moldings and big windows and a sidewalk terrace surrounded by flowers. Inside you'll be served a delectable bouillabaisse, breast of duckling in garlic-cream sauce, *pot-au-feu de la mer* (a stew of seafood), and perfectly prepared fish platters such as turbot and sole.

✪ **La Palme d'Or.** In the Hôtel Martinez, 73 bd. de la Croisette. ☎ **04-92-98-74-14.** Reservations required. Main courses 250–480F ($42.50–$81.60); set-price lunch 295–580F ($50.15–$98.60); set-price dinner 350–580F ($59.50–$98.60). AE, DC, MC, V. Wed–Sun 12:30–2pm and 7:30–10:30pm; also Tues 7:30–10:30pm mid-June to mid-Sept. Closed Nov 15–Dec 24. Bus: 1. FRENCH.

When this hotel was renovated by the Taittinger family of Champagne fame, one of their primary concerns was to establish a restaurant that could rival the tough competition in Cannes. Well, they've succeeded. The result is a light wood-paneled, art deco marvel overlooking the pool and La Croisette. Chef Christian Willer has worked at some of France's greatest restaurants. Here his sublime specialties include warm foie gras with fondue of rhubarb, filets of fried red mullet with a beignet of potatoes, zucchini, and an olive cream sauce, or a medley of crayfish, clams, and squid marinated in peppered citrus sauce.

Moderate

✪ **La Mère Besson.** 13 rue des Frères-Pradignac. ☎ **04-93-39-59-24.** Reservations required. Main courses 75–120F ($12.75–$20.40); set-price dinners 140–170F ($23.80–$28.90). AE, DC, MC, V. Tues–Fri 12:15–2pm and 7:30–10:30pm; Mon and Sat 7:30–10:30pm (open Sun in summer). Bus: 1. FRENCH.

The culinary traditions of Mère Besson are carried on in one of Cannes' favorite restaurants. The references here are Provençal, set in a venue that's as authentic and nostalgic as you're likely to find anywhere in Cannes. The most appealing of the menu items are the Provençal dishes, such as a savory *bourride* made from monkfish and court bouillon that's featured on Wednesday; and a savory kettle of fish made from a medley of steamed vegetables, mussels, and assorted fish that's offered every Friday with a creamy garlic sauce, aïoli. There's also an *estouffade Provençal* made with braised beef, red wine, and a rich stock flavored with garlic, onions, herbs, and mushrooms, that's the featured dish every Monday. Come with an appetite and a sense of conviviality.

CANNES AFTER DARK

CASINOS The largest and most legendary casino in Cannes is the **Casino Croisette,** in the Palais des Festivals, 1 jetée Albert-Edouard, near promenade de la Croisette (☎ **04-93-38-12-11**). In its glittering confines you'll find all the gaming tables you'd expect. A small subdivision of the casino opens daily at 10am for access to slot machines. The main areas, including the ones with the roulette and baccarat tables, open every day at 7pm and close down at 5am. The Palais des Festivals also contains one of the best nightclubs in town, **Jimmy's de Regine** (☎ **04-93-68-00-07**), outfitted in shades of red. Jimmy's is open Wednesday to Sunday 11pm to dawn. You must present your passport to enter the gambling room. Admission is 100F ($17) and includes a drink.

Considerably smaller than its major competitor, **Le Carlton Casino Club,** in the Carlton Inter-Continental, 50 bd. de la Croisette (☎ **04-92-99-51-00**), nonetheless draws its share of devotees. Jackets are required for men, and a passport or government-issued identity card is necessary for admission. It's open daily 8pm to 4am. Admission is 70F ($11.90).

CLUBS   Jane's, in the cellar of the Gray d'Albion, 38 rue des Serbes (☎ **04-92-99-79-79**), is a stylish and appealing nightclub with an undercurrent of coy permissiveness. The well-dressed crowd (many of the men in jacket and tie) is made up of all ages. The cover ranges from 50 to 100F ($8.35 to $16.70), depending on business; on some slow nights, women enter for free. Open Wednesday to Sunday 11pm to 5am.

JUAN-LES-PINS

This suburb of Antibes is a resort developed in the 1920s by Frank Jay Gould. At that time, people flocked to "John of the Pines" to escape the "crassness" of nearby Cannes. In the 1930s Juan-les-Pins drew a chic crowd during winter. Today, it's often called a honky-tonk town or the "Coney Island of the Riviera" (but anyone who calls it that hasn't seen Coney Island in a long time). One newspaper writer labeled it "a pop-art Monte Carlo, with burlesque shows and nude beaches"—a description much too provocative for such a middle-class resort.

The town has some of the best nightlife on the Riviera, and the action reaches its frenzied height during the **Festival International de Jazz** in July. Many revelers stay up all night in the smoky jazz joints, and then sleep the next day on the beach. For more information on the festival, contact the tourist office (see "Visitor Information," below). The **casino,** in the town center, offers cabaret entertainment, often until daybreak. During the day, skin-diving and waterskiing predominate. The pines sweep down to a good beach, crowded with summer sunbathers, most often in skimpy swimwear.

ESSENTIALS

GETTING THERE   Juan-les-Pins is connected by rail and bus to most other coastal resorts. Frequent **trains** arrive from Nice throughout the day (trip time: 30 minutes). For more information and schedules, call ☎ **08-36-35-35-35.** The station is on avenue l'Esterel. A **bus** leaves from Antibes at place Guynemer (☎ **04-93-34-37-60**), daily every 20 minutes. The trip takes only 10 minutes and costs 7F ($1.20) one way.

VISITOR INFORMATION   The **Office de Tourisme** is at 51 bd. Charles-Guillaumont (☎ **04-92-90-53-05**).

DEPARTING BY CAR   After Juan-les-Pins, ignore the DIRECT TO ANTIBES signs and follow D-2559 around the cape. You'll come first to Cap d'Antibes before approaching the old city of Antibes itself.

WHERE TO STAY

Belles-Rives. Bd. Baudoin, 06160 Juan-les-Pins. ☎ **04-93-61-02-79.** Fax 04-93-67-43-51. 45 units. A/C MINIBAR TV TEL. 990–2,550F ($168.30–$433.50) double; from 3,500F ($595) suite. AE, MC, V. Closed mid-Oct to Mar.

This is one of the fabled addresses on the Riviera. Once it was a holiday villa occupied by Zelda and F. Scott Fitzgerald, and in following years it hosted such illustrious guests as the duke and duchess of Windsor and Edith Piaf. A certain 1930s aura still lingers, and the sea views are as enchanting as ever. A major restoration project was completed in 1990. Rooms range from small to spacious, but each is fitted with a luxurious mattress resting on a double or set of twins. All the tiled bathrooms have a tub/shower combination and a hair dryer. The lower terraces are devoted to garden dining rooms and a waterside aquatic club with a snack bar/lounge and a jetty extending into the water. Also on the premises are a private beach and a landing dock.

✪ **Hôtel Juana.** La Pinède, av. Gallice, 06160 Juan-les-Pins. ☎ **04-93-61-08-70.** Fax 04-93-61-76-60. www.french-riviera.fr. 50 units. A/C TV TEL. 750–2,450F ($127.50–$416.50) double; from 1,600F ($272) suite. MC, V. Closed Nov–Mar. Parking 50F ($8.50).

This balconied art deco building is separated from the sea by a park of pines. The hotel has a private swimming club where guests can rent a "parasol and pad" on the sandy beach. The hotel is constantly being refurbished, and the very attractive rooms come complete with mahogany pieces, well-chosen fabrics, tasteful carpets, and large bathrooms in marble or tile with hair dryers. The rooms also have such extras as safes, and some have balconies. There's a bar in the poolhouse. Also on the premises are a private beach and a heated outdoor pool.

WHERE TO DINE

✪ **La Terrasse.** In the Hôtel Juana, La Pinède, av. Gallice. ☎ **04-93-61-20-37.** Reservations required. Main courses 240–390F ($40.80–$66.30); set-price lunch 280F ($47.60); set-price dinners 480–650F ($81.60–$110.50). AE, MC, V. July–Aug daily 12:30–2pm and 7:30–10:30pm; Apr–June and Sept–Oct Tues and Thurs–Sun 12:30–2pm, Thurs–Mon 7:30–10:30pm. Closed Nov–Mar. FRENCH/MEDITERRANEAN.

The cuisine here is the best in Juan-les-Pins. Bill Cosby is such a fan he's been known to fly chef Christian Morisset to the States to prepare dinner for him. Morisset cooks with a light, precise, and creative hand, interpreting traditional dishes and creating his own. The ideal place to dine in summer is the terrace among a lively, sophisticated crowd. His saddle of lamb is cooked to your taste and served with a rosemary jus, stuffed zucchini flowers, and fresh white beans. Or try the limousine filet of beef—tender and juicy and straight from the charcoal grill. The seafood, including red mullet and sea bass, is caught fresh daily.

ANTIBES & CAP D'ANTIBES

On the other side of the Bay of Angels, 13 miles southwest of Nice, is the port of Antibes. This old Mediterranean town has a quiet charm, unusual for the Côte d'Azur. Its little harbor is filled with fishing boats, the marketplaces with flowers, mostly roses and carnations. If you're in Antibes in the evening, you can watch fishers playing the popular Riviera game of *boule.*

Spiritually, Antibes is totally divorced from Cap d'Antibes, a peninsula studded with the villas and pools of the *haut monde.* In *Tender Is the Night,* F. Scott Fitzgerald described it as a place where "old villas rotted like water lilies among the massed pines."

ESSENTIALS

GETTING THERE   **Trains** from Cannes arrive every 30 minutes (trip time: 16 minutes); trains from Nice also pull in every 30 minutes (trip time: 18 minutes). For rail information, call ☎ **08-36-35-35-35.** The station is on avenue Robert Soleau.

VISITOR INFORMATION   The **Office de Tourisme** is at 11 place du Général-de-Gaulle (☎ **04-92-90-53-00**).

DEPARTING BY CAR   After leaving Antibes, you can take an excursion to the most famous hill towns on the French Riviera: St-Paul-de-Vence and Vence. Follow N-7 to Cagnes-sur-Mer, where you can connect with D-36 heading first to St-Paul-de-Vence, then continuing north to Vence.

TWO MUSEUMS WORTH VISITING

On the ramparts above the port is the Château Grimaldi, place du Château, which contains the ✪ **Musée Picasso** (☎ **04-92-90-54-26** or 04-92-90-54-20 for a recorded message). Once the home of the princes of Antibes of the Grimaldi family, who ruled the city from 1385 to 1608, today it houses one of the greatest Picasso collections in the world. Picasso came to the small town after his bitter war years in Paris and stayed in a hotel at

Golfe-Juan until the museum director at Antibes invited him to work and live at the museum. Picasso then spent 1946 painting at the museum. When he departed he gave the museum all the work he'd done that year—two dozen paintings, nearly 80 pieces of ceramics, 44 drawings, 32 lithographs, 11 oils on paper, 2 sculptures, and 5 tapestries. In addition, a gallery of contemporary art exhibits Léger, Miró, Ernst, and Calder, among others. The museum is open Tuesday to Sunday 10am to noon and 2 to 6pm, except between June and September, when hours are the same, but there's no lunchtime closing. Admission costs 30F ($5.10) for adults, 15F ($2.55) for students 15 to 24 and people over 60, and free for children 14 and under.

Cap d'Antibes has the **Musée Naval et Napoléonien,** Batterie du Grillon, boulevard J-F-Kennedy (☎ **04-93-61-45-32**). This ancient military tower contains an interesting collection of Napoleonic memorabilia, naval models, paintings, and mementos. It's open Monday through Friday 9:30am to noon and 2:15 to 6pm, and Saturday 9:30am to noon. Admission is 30F ($5.10) for adults, 15F ($2.55) for students, and free for children 14 and under.

WHERE TO STAY

Auberge de la Gardiole. Chemin de la Garoupe, 06600 Cap d'Antibes. ☎ **04-93-61-35-03.** Fax 04-93-67-61-87. 21 units. MINIBAR TV TEL. 300–700F ($51–$119) per person. AE, DC, MC, V. Closed Nov–Mar. Free parking. Bus: A2.

M. and Mme. Courtot run this country inn with a delightful personal touch. The large villa, surrounded by gardens and pergola, is in an area of private estates. The charming rooms, on the upper floors of the inn and in the little buildings in the garden, contain personal safes; 15 are air-conditioned. The cheerful dining room has a fireplace and hanging pots and pans, and in good weather you can dine under a wisteria-covered trellis.

✪ **Hôtel du Cap-Eden Roc.** Bd. J-F-Kennedy, 06601 Cap d'Antibes. ☎ **04-93-61-39-01.** Fax 04-93-67-76-04. www.edenroc.hotel.fr. 140 units. A/C TEL. 2,050–4,400F ($348.50–$748) double; from 4,800F ($816) suite. No credit cards. Closed mid-Oct to mid-Apr. Free parking. Bus: A2.

This Second Empire hotel, opened in 1870, is surrounded by 22 splendid acres of gardens. It's like a great country estate, with spacious public rooms, marble fireplaces, scenic paneling, chandeliers, and clusters of richly upholstered armchairs. Rooms are among the most sumptuous on the Riviera, each a testament to the deluxe tastes of another era. Bathrooms are roomy, clad in marble, with posh toiletries, a hair dryer, and a tub/shower combination. The staff is famed for its snobbery. The world-famous Pavillon Eden Roc, near a rock garden apart from the hotel, has a panoramic Mediterranean view.

Hotel Imperial Garoupe. 770 Chemin de la Garoupe, 06600 Antibes. ☎ **800/525-4800** in the U.S., or 04-92-93-31-61. Fax 04-92-93-31-62. www.imperial-garoupe.com. 34 units. A/C MINIBAR TV TEL. 1,250–2,200F ($212.50–$374) double; 2,200–4,500F ($374–$765) suite. AE, DC, MC, V. Free parking. Bus: A2.

One of the Riviera's newest upscale hotels is a very charming pocket of posh that's a bit less intimidating than the more monumental Hotel du Cap. The one-story building is designed around a landscaped patio with architectural elements that evoke both Tudor England and the deserts of Morocco, with a view over a swimming pool. The large, luxurious bedrooms are filled with oversized furniture, padded upholstery, and pastel color schemes. Clad in marble or tile, bathrooms have plenty of shelf space, a hair dryer, and a deluxe set of toiletries. Set within 50 yards of the beach, the hotel is the centerpiece of a 3½-acre park whose rows of pines block some of the views of the sea.

WHERE TO DINE

La Bonne Auberge. Quartier de Brague, route N-7. ☎ **04-93-33-36-65.** Reservations required. Set-price menu 200F ($34). MC, V. Tues–Sun noon–2pm and 7–10:30pm. Closed mid-Nov to mid-Dec. Take the coastal highway (N-7) 2½ miles from Antibes. FRENCH.

For many years after its 1975 opening, this was one of the most famous restaurants on the French Riviera. In 1992, following the death of its famous founder, Jo Rostang, his culinary heir, Philippe Rostang, wisely limited its scope and transformed it into a worthwhile but less ambitious restaurant. The set-price menu offers a wide selection. Choices vary but may include Basque-inspired pipérade with poached eggs, savory swordfish tart, chicken with vinegar and garlic, and perch-pike dumplings Jo Rostang. Dessert might be an enchanting peach soufflé.

✪ **Restaurant de Bacon.** Bd. de Bacon. ☎ **04-93-61-50-02.** Reservations required. Set-price menus 250–400F ($42.50–$68). AE, DC, MC, V. Tues–Sun 12:30–2pm and 8–10pm (open Mon dinner in July–Aug). Closed Nov–Jan. SEAFOOD.

Bouillabaisse aficionados claim, and we agree, that Bacon's offers France's best version. In its deluxe version, saltwater crayfish float atop the savory brew; we prefer the simple version—a waiter adds the finishing touches at your table. You can also try a fish soup with the traditional garlic-laden rouille sauce, or fish terrine, sea bass, John Dory, or one of the exotic fish, such as sar, pageot, or denti, unknown in North America. The venue evokes the chic 1950s, in a low, sprawling, big-windowed building set in a rocky landscape across the coastal highway from the sea.

ST-PAUL-DE-VENCE & VENCE

Of all the perched villages of the Riviera, St-Paul-de-Vence (17 miles east of Cannes and 19 miles north of Nice) is the best known. It was popularized in the 1920s when many noted artists occupied the 16th-century houses flanking the narrow cobblestoned streets. The feudal hamlet grew up on a bastion of rock, almost blending into it. Its ramparts—allow about 30 minutes to encircle them—overlook a peaceful setting of flowers and olive and orange trees. As you make your way through the warren of streets, you'll pass endless souvenir shops, a charming old fountain carved in the form of an urn, and a 13th-century Gothic church. St.-Paul-de-Vence and Vence itself are most often visited as a day trip from either Cannes or Nice; allow at least an afternoon for this jaunt.

ESSENTIALS

GETTING THERE   Some 20 **buses** per day leave from Nice's *gare routière* to drop you in the town center (trip time: 55 minutes).

VISITOR INFORMATION   The **Office de Tourisme** is at Maison Tours, rue Grande (☎ **04-93-32-86-95**).

DEPARTING BY CAR   To reach Nice, take the N-202 south to the junction with the N-7; follow the N-7 east to Nice.

EXPLORING ST-PAUL-DE VENCE & VENCE

The ✪ **Fondation Maeght** (☎ **04-93-32-81-63**) is one of the most modern art museums in Europe. On a hill in pine-studded woods, the Maeght Foundation is like a Shangri-la. Not only is the architecture avant-garde, but the building houses one of the finest collections of contemporary art on the Riviera. Natural and human creations blend harmoniously in this unique achievement of architect José Luís Sert. Its white concrete arcs give the impression of a giant pagoda.

A stark Calder rises like some futuristic monster on the grassy lawns. In a courtyard, the elongated bronze works of Giacometti form a surrealistic garden, creating a hallucinatory mood. Sculpture is also displayed inside, but it's at its best in a natural setting of surrounding terraces and gardens.

A library (open only by appointment), cinema, and cafeteria (open April to September only) are also here. In one showroom, original lithographs by artists like Chagall and Giacometti and limited-edition prints are for sale. Admission is 45F ($7.65) for adults and 35F ($5.95) for students and children 10 to 18. It's open daily July to September 10am to 7pm, and October to June 10am to 12:30pm and 2:30 to 6pm.

North of St-Paul, you can visit the sleepy old town of Vence, with its **Vieille Ville (Old Town).** If you're wearing solid, comfortable shoes, the narrow, steep streets are worth exploring. The **cathedral** on place Godeau is unremarkable except for some 15th-century choir stalls. If it's a Tuesday or Thursday, however, most visitors pass quickly through the narrow gates of this once-fortified walled town on their way to the **Chapelle du Rosaire,** 466 av. Henri-Matisse (☎ **04-93-58-03-26**), created by Henri Matisse.

Matisse was 77 when, after a turbulent time of introspection, he set out to create this masterpiece—in his own words, "the culmination of a whole life dedicated to the search for truth." From the front you might find the chapel of the Dominican nuns of Monteils unremarkable—until you spot a 40-foot crescent-adorned cross rising from a blue-tiled roof.

The light inside picks up the subtle coloring in the simply rendered leaf forms and abstract patterns: sapphire blue, aquamarine, and lemon yellow. In black-and-white ceramics, St. Dominic is depicted in a few lines. The Stations of the Cross are also black-and-white tile, with Matisse's self-styled "tormented and passionate" figures. The bishop of Nice himself came to bless the chapel in the late spring of 1951, when the artist's work was completed. Matisse died 3 years later. Admission is 13F ($2.20); donations are welcomed. In October and from December to June, it is open Tuesday and Thursday from 10am to 11:30am and 2:30 to 5:30pm. From July to September, it is open on those above-mentioned days but also on Wednesday, Friday, and Saturday from 2:30 to 5:30pm. Closed in November.

NICE

The Victorian upper class and tsarist aristocrats loved Nice in the 19th century, but it's solidly middle class today. Of all the major resorts, from Deauville to Biarritz to Cannes, Nice is the least expensive. It's also the best excursion center on the Riviera, especially if you're dependent on public transportation. For example, you can go to San Remo, "the queen of the Italian Riviera," returning to Nice by nightfall. From the Nice airport, the second largest in France, you can travel by bus along the entire coast to resorts like Juan-les-Pins and Cannes, the latter only 20 miles to the west.

Nice is the capital of the Riviera, the largest city between Genoa and Marseille (also one of the most ancient, having been founded by the Greeks, who called it Nike, or Victory). Because of its brilliant sunshine and relaxed living, Nice has attracted artists and writers, among them Matisse, Dumas, Nietzsche, Apollinaire, Flaubert, Hugo, Stendhal, and Mistral.

ESSENTIALS

GETTING THERE   You can take an airport bus (bus no. 23) that travels at 20-minute intervals throughout the day and evening between the **Aéroport Nice-Côte d'Azur** (☎ **04-93-21-30-30**) and the city's **Gare Routière,** promenade du Paillon (☎ **04-93-85-61-81**), in the city center. Buses run daily from 6am to 10:30pm, and cost 8.50F ($1.45) per person. A somewhat more luxurious mode of transport involves a specially conceived *navette de l'aeroport* (airport shuttle bus) that charges 20F ($3.40) for a ride from the airport to Nice's main railway station. A taxi ride into the city center costs at least 150 to 200F ($25.50 to $34) for a carload of up to four passengers. **Trains** arrive at **Gare Nice-Ville,** avenue Thiers (☎ 08-36-35-35-35). From here you can take frequent trains to Cannes, Monaco, and Antibes, among other destinations.

VISITOR INFORMATION Thanks to its status as the tourist centerpiece of the Côte d'Azur, Nice maintains three tourist information offices; the largest and most central one is at 5 Promenade des Anglais (☎ 04-92-14-48-00), near the place Massena. Additional tourist offices are in the arrivals hall of the **Aèroport Nice-Côte d'Azur** (☎ 04-93-21-44-11) and at the railway station (☎ 04-93-87-07-07). Any of the three can make you a hotel reservation (but only for the night of the day you happen to show up), charging a modest fee that varies according to the classification of the hotel you book.

You can rent bicycles and mopeds from **Nicea Rent,** 9 av. Thiers (☎ 04-93-82-42-71), or from a competitor, **Arnaud,** 4 place Grimaldi (☎ 04-93-87-88-55). Both are open daily from 9am to noon and 2 to 6pm, with a Sunday closing between October and April. Rentals begin at around 125F ($21.25) per day, plus a deposit of at least 1,500F ($255) or more, depending on the value of the machine you rent.

DEPARTING BY CAR Leaving Nice, drive east along the Corniche Inférieure until reaching Villefranche; turn right onto D-25, which takes you in a very short distance to the wooded peninsula of St-Jean-Cap-Ferrat, 6 miles east of Nice.

EXPLORING THE TOWN

The wide **boulevard des Anglais** fronts the bay. Split by "islands" of palms and flowers, it stretches for about 4 miles. Fronting the beach are rows of grand cafes, the Musée Masséna, villas, and hotels—some good, others decaying.

In the east, the promenade becomes **quai des Etats-Unis,** the original boulevard, lined with some of the best restaurants in Nice, each specializing in bouillabaisse. Rising sharply on a rock is the site known as **Le Château,** the spot where the ducs de Savoie built their castle, which was torn down in 1706. The steep hill has been turned into a garden of pines and exotic flowers. To reach the site, many prefer to take an elevator; actually, many prefer to take the elevator up, and then walk down. The park is open daily 8am to 7:30pm.

The center of Nice is **place Masséna,** with pink buildings in the 17th-century Genoese style and the **Fontaine du Soleil (Fountain of the Sun)** by Janoit. Stretching from the main square to the promenade is the **Jardin Albert-Ier,** with an open-air terrace and a Triton Fountain. Palms and exotic flowers make this the most relaxing oasis at the resort.

A TRIO OF MUSEUMS WORTH A LOOK

Musée d'Art et d'Histoire Palais Masséna. 65 rue de France. ☎ 04-93-88-11-34. Admission 25F ($4.25) adults, 15F ($2.55) children, free first Sunday every month. Tues–Sun 10am–noon and 2–6pm. Bus: 3, 7, 8, 9, 10, 12, 14, or 22.

The fabulous villa housing this museum was built in 1900 in the style of the First Empire as a residence for Victor Masséna, the prince of Essling and grandson of Napoléon's marshal. The city of Nice has converted the villa, next door to the Négresco, into a museum of local history and decorative art. A remarkably opulent drawing room, with mahogany-veneer pieces and ormolu mounts, is on the ground floor.

✪ **Musée des Beaux-Arts.** 33 av. des Baumettes. ☎ 04-93-44-50-72. Admission 25F ($4.25) adults, 15F ($2.55) children. Tues–Sun 10am–noon and 2–6pm. Bus: 9, 12, 22, 23, or 38.

Nice Beach?

Some of the world's most attractive (and skimpily dressed) people cross the boulevard des Anglais heading for the beach, or "on the rocks," as it's called here. Tough on tender feet, the beach is shingled, one of the least attractive—and least publicized—aspects of this cosmopolitan resort. Many bathhouses provide mattresses for a charge.

Housed in the former residence of Ukrainian Princess Kotchubey, this museum has an important gallery devoted to the masters of the Second Empire and belle époque, with an extensive collection of the 19th-century French experts. The gallery of sculptures includes works by J. B. Carpeaux, Rude, and Rodin. Note the important collection by a dynasty of painters, the Dutch Van Loo family. A fine collection of 19th- and 20th-century art is displayed, including works by Ziem, Raffaelli, Boudin, Renoir, Monet, Guillaumin, and Sisley.

Musée des Arts Asiatiques. 405 promenade des Anglais. ☎ **04-92-29-37-00.** Admission 35F ($5.95) adults, 20F ($3.40) children and students. May to mid-Oct, Wed–Mon 10am–6pm; mid-Oct to Apr, Wed–Mon 10am–5pm.

Set very close to Nice's airport, this museum opened in 1998 as a tribute to the sculpture and paintings of Cambodia, China, India, Tibet, and Japan. Inside are some of the best ceramics and devotional carvings ever found, many of them hauled back to France by colonials during the 19th and early 20th centuries. Of special interest are the accoutrements associated with Japan's tea-drinking ceremony, and several monumental representations of Buddha.

WHAT TO SEE IN NEARBY CIMIEZ

Founded by the Romans, who called it Cemenelum, Cimiez, a hilltop suburb, was the capital of the Maritime Alps province. Recent excavations have uncovered the ruins of a Roman town, and you can wander around the digs. To reach this suburb, take bus no. 15 or 17 from place Masséna.

Monastère de Cimiez (Cimiez Convent), place du Monastère (☎ 04-93-81-00-04), embraces a church that owns three of the most important works from the primitive painting school of Nice by the Bréa brothers. The most stunning is a 1475 Pietà to the right of the entrance as you come in. A Crucifixion on the left in the choir is a later work dating from 1512. Finally, in the third chapel, is a Deposition. In addition, note the huge altarpiece, half in the Renaissance style, half in the baroque, carved in wood and decorated with gold-leaf screens.

In a restored part of the convent where some Franciscan friars still live, **Musée Franciscain** is decorated with 17th-century frescoes. Some 350 documents and works of art from the 15th to the 18th century are displayed, and a monk's cell has been re-created.

In the gardens you can get a panoramic view of Nice and the Bay of Angels. Matisse and Dufy are buried in the cemetery. The museum is open Monday to Saturday from 10am to noon and 3 to 6pm; the church is open daily 8am to 12:30pm and 2 to 7pm. There is no admission charge.

Musée Matisse, in the Villa des Arènes-de-Cimiez, 164 av. des Arènes-de-Cimiez (☎ 04-93-81-08-08), honors the great artist who spent the last years of his life in Nice; he died here in 1954. The museum has several permanent collections, many donated by Matisse and his heirs. These include *Nude in an Armchair with a Green*

Plant (1937), *Nymph in the Forest* (1935/1942), and a chronologically arranged series of paintings from 1890 to 1919. The most famous of these is *Portrait of Madame Matisse* (1905), usually displayed near another portrait of the artist's wife, by Marquet, painted in 1900. The museum is open Wednesday through Monday 10am to 6pm (closes at 5pm off-season). Admission is 25F ($4.25) for adults and free for children 17 and under; it's free for everyone the first Sunday of every month.

THE SHOPPING SCENE

You might want to begin with a stroll through the streets and alleys of Nice's historic core. The densest concentrations of boutiques are along **rue Masséna, place Magenta,** and **rue Paradis,** as well as on the streets funneling into and around them. Nice is also known for its colorful street markets. The **flower market,** Marché aux Fleurs, cours Saleya, is open 6am to 5:30pm except Monday and Sunday afternoon. The main Nice **flea market,** Marché à la Brocante, also at cours Saleya, takes place every Monday. There's another flea market on the port, Les Puces de Nice, place Robilante, open Tuesday through Saturday.

Confiserie Florian du Vieux-Nice. 14 quai Papacino. ☎ **04-93-55-43-50.**

Established in 1949 by the grandfather, Georges Fuchs, of the present English-speaking owners, this shop near the historic center's Old Port specializes in glazed fruits crystallized in sugar or artfully arranged into chocolates. Look for exotic jams (rose-petal preserves or mandarin marmalade) as well as candied violets, verbena leaves, and rosebuds.

Confiserie/Salon de Thé Auer. 7 rue St-François-de-Paule. ☎ **04-93-85-77-98.**

One of the oldest *chocolatiers* in Nice was established five generations ago, in 1820, in a position near the opera house. Since then, few of the original decorative accessories have been changed, allowing tea drinkers to wax nostalgic for an era when taking tea was an integral part of the Niçois afternoon ritual. Today, tea is served Tuesday to Sunday from 8am to 12:30pm and 2:30 to 7pm. Hot chocolate is made the old-fashioned way, by melting bars of chocolate directly into hot milk; and the array of *confits de fruits* is almost comprehensive.

Façonnable. 7–9 rue Paradis. ☎ **04-93-87-88-80.**

This is the site that sparked the creation of what is today several hundred Façonnable menswear stores around the world. Here you'll find one of the largest Façonnable stores, with a wide range of men's suits, raincoats, overcoats, sportswear, and jeans. The look is youthful and conservatively stylish.

Nicola Alziari. 14 rue St-François de Paule. ☎ **04-93-85-76-92.**

If you're thinking of indulging in a Provençal *pique-nique,* you'll find everything you need here, from olives, anchovies, and pistous to aïolis and tapenades. It's one of the oldest stores of its kind in Nice. The house brand of olive oil comes in two strengths, a light version that aficionados claim is vaguely perfumed with Provence and a stronger version well suited to the earthy flavors and robust ingredients of a Provençal winter. Also look for a range of objects crafted from olive wood.

HITTING THE LINKS & OTHER OUTDOOR PURSUITS

GOLF   The oldest golf course on the Riviera is about 10 miles from Nice: **Golf Bastide du Roi** (also known as the Golf de Biot), avenue Jules-Grec, Biot (☎ **04-93-65-08-48**). This is a flat, not particularly challenging, and much-used sea-fronting course. Regrettably, you have to cross over a highway midway through the course to complete the full 18 holes. Open daily throughout the year, tee-off times begin at 8am and continue until 6pm, with the understanding that players then continue their rounds as long as the daylight allows. Reservations aren't necessary, although on weekends you should expect a delay. Greens fees are 240F ($40.80) for 18 holes, and clubs can be rented for 100F ($17). No carts are available.

SCUBA DIVING   The best-respected underwater outfitter is the **Centre International de Plongée de Nice,** 2 Ruelle des Moulins (☎ **04-93-55-59-50**). Adjacent to the city's old port, it lies midway between quai des Docks and boulevard Stalingrad. A *Baptême* (initiatory dive for first-timers) costs 200F ($34), and a one-tank dive for experienced divers, with all equipment included, is 190F ($32.30). This outfitter is open only from mid-March to mid-November.

TENNIS   The oldest tennis club in Nice is the **Nice Lawn Tennis Club,** Parc Impérial, 5 av. Suzanne-Lenglen (☎ **04-93-96-17-70**), located near the rail station. It's open daily 8:30am to 9pm, and charges 120F ($20.40) per person for 2 noncontiguous hours of court time, or a reduced rate of 250F ($42.50) per person for unlimited access to the courts for a 1-week period. The club has a cooperative staff, 13 clay courts, and 6 hard-surfaced courts. Reservations should be made the evening before.

WHERE TO STAY
Very Expensive
Hôtel Négresco. 37 promenade des Anglais, 06007 Nice CEDEX. ☎ **04-93-16-64-00.** Fax 04-93-88-35-68. E-mail: negresco@nicematin.fr. 141 units. A/C MINIBAR TV TEL. 1,350–2,550F ($229.50–$433.50) double; from 3,400F ($578) suite. AE, DC, MC, V. Parking 160F ($27.20). Bus: 8.

This Victorian wedding-cake hotel is one of the many superglamorous hotels along the French Riviera. It was built on the seafront, in the French château style, with a mansard roof and domed tower, and its interior design was inspired by the country's châteaux and museums. The staff wears 18th-century costumes. The guest rooms contain antiques, tapestries, paintings, and art, and come in the widest range of styles and shapes of any hotel in town. Least desirable are the streetside units on the ground floors, where in spite of double-glazed windows, you can still hear traffic noises. The most expensive rooms have balconies and face the Mediterranean. Bathrooms are spacious and clad in marble and handmade tiles; each has a hair dryer, deluxe toiletries, and dual basins. Reasonably priced meals are served in La Rotonde, although the featured restaurant—one of the greatest on the Riviera—is Chantecler (see "Where to Dine," below).

Expensive
✪ **Chateau des Ollières.** 39 avenue des Baumettes, 06000 Nice. ☎ **04-92-15-77-99.** Fax 04-92-15-77-98. 6 units. A/C MINIBAR TV TEL. 800–2,000F ($136–$340) double; 1,900–3,000F ($323–$510) suite. AE, MC, V. Bus: 38.

The most appealing and unusual hotel to open in Nice in many years made its debut as a hotel in 1996 and as a French restaurant a year later. It lies within a 5-minute walk from the Négresco and the Promenade des Anglais, in a 20-acre park loaded with exotic trees and shrubs. Its centerpiece is a Beaux-Arts villa built in the 1870s. Inside, you'll find a noteworthy collection of oil paintings and "neo-Napoléonienne" and Empire-insired antiques. Bedrooms are outfitted in the same high-ceilinged, richly ornate style as the public areas, and have supremely comfortable mattresses and the kind of decorative porcelain and accessories you'd expect in an impeccably upscale private home. Marble- and tile-clad bathrooms are quite luxurious, with generous shelf space, a tub/shower combination, and a hair dryer.

Moderate

Grand Hôtel Aston. 12 av. Félix-Faure, 06000 Nice. ☎ **04-92-17-53-00.** Fax 04-93-80-40-02. 156 units. A/C MINIBAR TV TEL. 650–1,300F ($110.50–$221) double. AE, DC, MC, V. Parking 100F ($17). Bus: 12.

One of the most alluring in its price bracket, this elegantly detailed 19th-century hotel has been radically renovated. Bedrooms are outfitted in monochromatic, pastel-derived color schemes, with comfortable mattresses and price scales that vary according to their views over the street, the splashing fountains of the place Masséna, or the panorama over the coastline from the uppermost floor. Bathrooms have tub/shower combinations and hair dryers. On summer evenings, visit the garden-style bar on the top floor. The hotel is associated with Holland's Golden Tulip chain.

Hotel Windsor. 11 rue Dalpozzo, 06000 Nice. ☎ **04-93-88-59-35.** Fax 04-93-88-94-57. www.windsor@webstore.fr. 57 units. A/C MINIBAR TV TEL. 420–700F ($71.40–$119) double. AE, DC, MC, V. Parking 60F ($10.20).

One of the most arts-conscious hotels in Provence is set in what was built by disciples of Gustav Eiffel as a *maison bourgeoise,* near the Hotel Négresco and the Promenade des Anglais, in 1895. Inside, you'll find an artsy, somewhat claustrophobic, environment that nonetheless is very appealing to artists or those with ties to the artistic community. Bedrooms have good mattresses, and small, tidily maintained bathrooms. High points include a complicated fifth-floor superstructure, site of a health club, steamroom, and sauna, that's considered highly unusual by local architects, and a one-of-a-kind series of frescoes that adorn each of the bedrooms. The dining room is open only to residents of the hotel. There's a swimming pool and a garden with scores of tropical and exotic plants.

Inexpensive

Flots d'Azur. 101 promenade des Anglais, 06000 Nice. ☎ **04-93-86-51-25.** Fax 04-93-97-22-07. 21 units. A/C TEL. 270–500F ($45.90–$85) double. MC, V. Bus: 8.

This three-story villa-hotel is located next to the sea, a short walk from the more elaborate and costlier promenade hotels. While the bedrooms vary in size and decor, all have good views and sea breezes, with 12 containing TVs and minibars. Double-glazed window panes were recently added to cut down on the noise. There's a small sitting room and sun terrace in front, where a continental breakfast is served.

Hôtel Villa Eden. 99 bis promenade des Anglais, 06000 Nice. ☎ **04-93-86-53-70.** Fax 04-93-97-67-97. 10 units. A/C TV TEL. 270–390F ($45.90–$66.30) double. AE, DC, MC, V. Free parking. Bus: 3, 9, 10, 22, 23, or 24 from the center or 12 from the train station.

In 1925, an exiled Russian countess built this art deco villa on the seafront, surrounded it with a wall, and planted a tiny garden. The villa still remains, despite the construction of much taller modern buildings on both sides. You can enjoy the ivy and roses in the garden and stay in old-fashioned partly modernized rooms whose sizes vary greatly. Bathrooms are old-fashioned, but function smoothly. The owner maintains a wry sense of humor and greets guests at breakfast, the only meal served.

WHERE TO DINE

Brasserie Flo. 2-4 rue Sacha-Guitry. ☎ **04-93-13-38-38.** Reservations recommended. Main courses 80–120F ($13.60–$20.40); set-price menus 119F ($20.25) served only at lunch and after 10:30pm; 159F ($27.05) served anytime. AE, DC, MC, V. Daily noon–3pm and 7pm–12:30am. Bus: 1, 2, or 5. FRENCH.

In 1991, a France-based restaurant chain (the Jean-Paul Bucher group), noted for its skill at restoring historic brasseries, bought the premises of a faded but historic turn-of-the-century restaurant near place Masséna and injected it with new life. It's now a stylish, reasonably priced, and fun place, where patrons dine beneath the high ceilings that are covered with their original frescoes. Menu items include an array of grilled fish, *choucroute* (sauerkraut) in the Alsatian style, steaks with brandied pepper sauce, and fresh oysters and shellfish.

✪ **Chantecler.** In the Hôtel Négresco, 37 promenade des Anglais. ☎ **04-93-16-64-00.** Reservations required. Main courses 210–350F ($35.70–$59.50); set-price lunch 245F ($41.65); set-price dinner 415–590F ($70.55–$100.30). AE, DC, MC, V. Daily 12:30–2:30pm and 7:30–10:30pm. Closed mid-Nov to mid-Dec. Bus: 9, 10, or 11. FRENCH.

This restaurant, with its beautifully restored setting—the panels that line the walls were taken from a château in Puilly-Fusse—is the most prestigious in Nice, and chef Alain Llorca offers the most sophisticated and creative dishes. Menu items change almost weekly, but may include filet of turbot served with a purée of broad beans, sun-dried tomatoes, and fresh asparagus; roasted suckling lamb served with beignets of fresh vegetables and ricotta-stuffed ravioli; and a melt-in-your-mouth fantasy of marbled hot chocolate drenched in an almond-flavored cream sauce.

Chez Michel (Le Grand Pavois). 11 rue Meyerbeer. ☎ **04-93-88-77-42.** Reservations required. Main courses 135–160F ($22.95–$27.20); bouillabaisse from 350F ($59.50); set-price menus 195–255F ($33.15–$43.35); *menu gastronomique* 300F ($51). AE, DC, MC, V. Daily noon–2:30pm and 7–11pm. Bus: 8. SEAFOOD.

Chez Michel is nestled under an art deco apartment building near the water. One of the partners, Jacques Marquise, is from Golfe-Juan, where for 25 years he managed the famous fish restaurant Chez Tétou. His bouillabaisse has been widely celebrated. Other recommended specialties are baked sea bass in white wine, herbs, and lemon sauce and grilled flambé lobster.

✪ **Le Safari.** 1 cours Saleya. ☎ **04-93-80-18-44.** Reservations recommended. Main courses 65–150F ($11.05–$25.50); set-price menu 150F ($25.50). AE, DC, MC, V. Daily noon–2:30pm and 7–11:30pm. PROVENÇAL/NIÇOISE.

The decor couldn't be simpler, outfitted as it is with a black ceiling, white walls, and an old-fashioned terra-cotta floor, and the youthful staff is mellow. Expect mobs of clients here, many of whom prefer the outdoor terrace overlooking the nearby *Marché aux Fleurs,* and all of whom appreciate the earthy, unpretentious, reasonably priced, and generously proportioned meals. Examples include a pungent *bagna cauda,* where vegetables are immersed in a sizzling brew of hot oil and anchovy paste; grilled peppers bathed in olive oil; *daube* (stew) of beef; fresh pasta with basil; an omelette with *blettes* (tough but flavorful greens); and the unfortunately named *merda de can* (dogshit), which is gnocchi stuffed with spinach—it's a lot more appetizing than it sounds.

NICE AFTER DARK

Nice has some of the most active nightlife along the Riviera; pick up a copy of *La Semaine de Spectacles,* which outlines the week's nighttime diversions, for clues on what's hot.

THE PERFORMING ARTS   The major cultural center along the Riviera is the **Opéra de Nice,** 4 rue St-François-de-Paule (☎ **04-92-17-40-40**), with a busy season in winter. A full repertoire is presented, including both operas and the popular French Opéra Comique. In one season you might see *La Bohème, Tristan und Isolde,* and *Carmen,* as well as a *saison symphonique,* dominated by the Orchestre Philharmonique de Nice. The opera hall is also the major venue for concerts and recitals. The box office is open Tuesday to Saturday 10am to 5pm, with tickets ranging from 40F ($6.80) all the way to 700F ($119), depending on the event.

CLUBS & BARS   Near the Hôtel Ambassador, **L'Ambassade,** 18 rue de Congrés (☎ **04-93-88-88-87**), was deliberately designed in a mock-Gothic style that includes the wrought-iron accents you'd expect to find in a château. It has two bars and a dance floor and attracts a mostly straight clientele. Cover is 100F ($17), including the first drink.

Near the Négresco and the promenade des Anglais, **Le Blue Boy,** 9 rue Spinetta (☎ **04-93-44-68-24**), is the oldest gay disco on the Riviera. With two bars and two floors, it's a vital nocturnal stopover for passengers aboard the dozens of all-gay cruises that make regular stops at Nice. Cover is 60F ($10.20) on Saturday or 30F ($5.10) otherwise. Ask the tourist office for a free copy of two of their periodicals, *L'X* and *L'Exces,* that list the entertainment and nightlife options for gay travelers in Nice.

ST-JEAN-CAP-FERRAT

This has been called Paradise Found. Of all the oases along the Côte d'Azur, no place has the snob appeal of Cap-Ferrat. It's a 9-mile promontory sprinkled with luxurious villas, outlined by sheltered bays, beaches, and coves. The vegetation is lush. In the port of St-Jean, the harbor accommodates yachts and fishing boats.

The Italianate **Musée Ile-de-France,** avenue Denis-Séméria (☎ **04-93-01-33-09**), allows you to visit one of the most legendary villas along the Côte d'Azur, built by the Baronne Ephrussi Rothschild. She died in 1934, leaving the building and its magnificent gardens to the Institut de France on behalf of the Académie des Beaux-Arts. The wealth of her collection is preserved: 18th-century furniture; Tiepolo ceilings; Savonnerie carpets; screens and panels from the Far East; tapestries from Gobelins, Aubusson, and Beauvais; original drawings by Fragonard; canvases by Renoir, Sisley, and Boucher; rare Sèvres porcelain; and more. Covering 12 acres, the gardens contain fragments of statuary from churches, monasteries, and torn-down palaces.

Between mid-February and October, the museum and its gardens are open daily 10am to 6pm. From November to mid-February, they're open Monday to Friday 2pm to 6pm and Saturday and Sunday 10am to 6pm. The entrance fee is 48F ($8.15) for adults and 30F ($5.10) for children and students 18 to 24. A 14F ($2.40) supplement is charged for anyone who wants to participate in a guided tour. They are conducted in English every day at 11:30am and 2:30, 3:30, and 4:30pm.

ESSENTIALS

GETTING THERE   Most visitors drive or take the hourly bus or a taxi from the rail station at nearby Beaulieu. There's also **bus** service from Nice (no. 111). For bus information and schedules, call ☎ **04-93-85-61-81,** or 04-93-85-61-81. Buses pull into the center of town, but there's no station.

VISITOR INFORMATION   The **Office de Tourisme** is at 54 avenue Denis-Séméria (☎ **04-93-76-08-90**).

DEPARTING BY CAR   From St-Jean-Cap-Ferrat, you can head east toward Monaco by taking D-25 along the coast to the resort of Beaulieu, which is almost as chic as Cap-Ferrat. Continue along N-98 for about 7 miles into Monaco.

WHERE TO STAY

✪ **Grand Hôtel du Cap-Ferrat.** Bd. du Général-de-Gaulle, 06230 St-Jean-Cap-Ferrat. ☎ **04-93-76-50-50.** Fax 04-93-76-04-52. www.grand-hotel-cap-ferrat.com. E-mail: reserve@grand-hotel-cap-ferrat.com. 57 units. A/C MINIBAR TV TEL. 950–6,500F ($161.50–$1,105) double; from 3,400F ($578) suite. Parking is from 150F ($25.50). AE, DC, MC, V.

This turn-of-the-century palace is at the tip of the peninsula in the midst of a 14-acre garden of semitropical trees and manicured lawns. Parts of the exterior have open loggias and big arched windows, and guests enjoy the views from the elaborate flowering terrace over the sea. Rates include admission to the pool, Club Dauphin. Most rooms are quite spacious, and elegantly appointed with wool carpeting, fabric wall coverings, and antique or reproduction furnishings. Each comes with a sumptuously fitted bed containing the town's most comfortable mattressses. The marble bathrooms feature power showerheads, robes, a hair dryer, and dual basins. The indoor/outdoor restaurant's cuisine is based on market-fresh ingredients.

Hôtel Clair Logis. 12 av. Centrale, 06230 St-Jean-Cap-Ferrat. ☎ **04-93-76-04-57.** Fax 04-93-76-11-85. 18 units. TEL. 400–680F ($68–$115.60) double. AE, DC, MC, V. Closed Jan–Feb and Nov–Dec 15. Free parking.

In an otherwise pricey resort strip of deluxe hotels and homes, this 19th-century former villa surrounded by semitropical gardens is a rare find. The pleasant rooms are scattered over three buildings in the confines of the garden. The most romantic and spacious accommodations are in the main building; the units in the annex are the most modern but have the least character. Bedrooms come in a variety of shapes and sizes; bathrooms are small but well-organized.

WHERE TO DINE

Le Provençal. 2 av. Denis-Séméria. ☎ **04-93-76-03-97.** Reservations required. Main courses 230–360F ($39.10–$61.20); set-price menus 280–350F ($47.60–$59.50). MC, V. Apr–Oct 14, daily noon–2:30pm and 7:30–11pm; Oct 15–Mar, Fri–Sun noon–2:30pm and 7:30–11pm. FRENCH.

This restaurant, one of the finest in the area, occupies what was a 2-century-old stone-sided farmhouse above the center of St-Jean-Cap-Ferrat. The venue is very much in the old Provençal style. You can enjoy marinated artichoke hearts with half a lobster, a tart fine of potatoes served with deliberately undercooked foie gras; rack of lamb with local herbs and tarragon sauce; and crayfish served with asparagus and black olive tapenade. A dessert sampler, "les cinq desserts du Provençal," includes five luscious sweets, such as macaroons with chocolate or crème brûlée. The food is solemnly served, as if part of a grand ritual.

MONACO

Monaco—or rather its capital of Monte Carlo—has for a century been a symbol of glamour. Its legend was further enhanced by the 1956 marriage of the man who was at that time the world's most eligible bachelor, Prince Rainier III, to American actress Grace Kelly. Although not always happy in her role, Princess Grace soon won the respect and adoration of her people. The Monégasques still mourn her death in a 1982 car accident.

Monaco became a property of the Grimaldi clan, a Genoese family, as early as 1297. With shifting loyalties, it has maintained something resembling independence ever since. In a fit of impatience, the French annexed it in 1793, but the ruling family recovered it in 1814, although the prince at the time couldn't bear to tear himself away from the pleasures of Paris for "dreary old Monaco."

ESSENTIALS

GETTING THERE   Monaco has rail, bus, and highway connections from other coastal cities, especially Nice. There are no border formalities for anyone entering Monaco from mainland France. **Trains** arrive at the station on avenue Prince Pierre every 30 minutes from Cannes, Nice, Menton, and Antibes. For rail information and schedules, call ☎ **08-36-35-35-35.** For **bus** information, call ☎ **377/93-85-61-81.** Most buses leave from place du Casino (no station).

Phone Tips

On June 21, 1996, Monaco's **phone system** underwent drastic changes. It's now a separate entity from France, which means that calls to and from such nearby places as Nice are long-distance. If you're calling Monaco from France, dial **00** followed by Monaco's new country prefix, **377,** and then the eight-digit local phone number. To call from the United States, use the international access code, **011,** and then 377 plus the eight-digit local number.

VISITOR INFORMATION   The **Direction du Tourisme** is at 2A bd. des Moulins (☎ **377/92-16-61-16**).

Exploring Monaco

The second-smallest state in Europe (Vatican City is the tiniest), Monaco consists of four parts: The old town, **Monaco-Ville,** on a promontory, The Rock, 200 feet high, is the seat of the royal palace and the government building, as well as the home of the Oceanographic Museum. To the west of the bay, **La Condamine,** the 19th-century home of the Monégasques, is at the foot of the old town, forming its harbor and port sector. Up from the port (walking is steep in Monaco) is **Monte Carlo,** once the playground of European royalty and still the center for wintering wealthy, the setting for the casino and its gardens and the deluxe hotels. The fourth part, **Fontvieille,** is a neat industrial suburb.

Ironically, **Monte-Carlo Beach,** at the far frontier, is on French soil. It attracts a chic crowd, including movie stars. The resort has a freshwater pool, an artificial beach, and a sea-bathing establishment.

The Italianate home of Monaco's royal family, the **Palais du Prince,** dominates the principality from "The Rock." When touring Les Grands Appartements du Palais, place du Palais (☎ **377/93-25-18-31**), you're shown the Throne Room and allowed to see some of the art collection, including works by Brueghel and Holbein, as well as Princess Grace's stunning state portrait. The palace was built in the 13th century and part of it is from the Renaissance. The ideal time to arrive is 11:55am to watch the 10-minute changing of the guard. The palace is open daily June to September from 9:30am to 6:30pm and in October from 10am to 5pm. Admission is 30F ($5.10) for adults, 15F ($2.55) for children ages 8 to 14, and free for children 7 and under.

Jardin Exotique, boulevard du Jardin-Exotique (☎ **377/93-15-29-80**), was built on the side of a rock and is known for its cactus collection. The gardens were begun by Prince Albert I, who was both a naturalist and a scientist. He spotted some succulents growing in the palace gardens, and knowing that these plants were normally found only in Central America or Africa, he created the garden from them. You can also explore the grottoes here, as well as the **Musée d'Anthropologie Préhistorique** (☎ **377/93-15-80-06**). The view of the principality is splendid. The site is open daily June to September from 9am to 7pm and October to May daily 9am to 6pm. Admission is 39F ($6.65) for adults and 18F ($3.05) for children 6 to 18; admission is free for children 5 and under.

Musée de l'Océanographie, avenue St-Martin (☎ **377/93-15-36-00**), was founded by Albert I, great-grandfather of the present prince. In the main rotunda is a statue of Albert dressed as a sea captain. Displayed are specimens he collected during 30 years of expeditions aboard his oceanographic boats. The aquarium, one of the finest in Europe, contains more than 90 tanks. The museum is open daily, July and August from 9am to 8pm; April to June and September 9am to 7pm; March and

October 9:30am to 7pm; and November to February 10am to 6pm. Admission is 60F ($10.20) for adults, 30F ($5.10) for children 6 to 18, and free for children 5 and under.

Two Shops Worth a Look

Rising costs and an increase in crime have changed women's tastes in jewelry. **Bijoux Cascio,** Les Galeries du Metropole, 207 av. des Spélugues (☎ **377/93-50-17-57**), sells imitation gemstones, copies of the real McCoys sold by Cartier and Van Cleef & Arpels. Made in Italy of gold-plated silver, cubic zirconia, and glittering chunks of Austrian-made Swarovski crystal, the fake jewelry costs between 200F ($34) and 2,000F ($340) per piece, many thousands of francs less than what you might have paid for the authentic gems.

Boutique du Rocher, 1 av. de la Madone (☎ **377/93-30-91-17**), a short walk from place du Casion, is the larger of two roughly equivalent boutiques opened in 1966 by Princess Grace as the official retail outlets of the charitable foundation that was established by the Grimaldis in her name. Today the foundation is directed by Princess Caroline. The organization merchandises Monégasque and Provençal handcrafts, including carved frames; gift items crafted from porcelain, textiles, and wood; children's toys; and dolls. On the premises are workshops where local artisans produce the goods you'll find for sale.

Taking a Dip & Other Outdoor Activities

BEACHES/SWIMMING   Monaco, in its role as the quintessential kingdom by the sea, offers sea bathing at its most popular beach, **La Plage de Larvetto,** off avenue du Princesse-Grace (☎ **377/93-15-28-76**). There's no charge for bathing on this strip of beach, whose sands are frequently replenished with sand hauled in by barge. The beach is open to public access at all hours.

If a pool is more to your tastes, most of the large hotels in town boast pools, but the dowager empress, across the border in neighboring France, is **Le Monte Carlo Beach Club,** av. du Princesse-Grace, Roquebrune—St-Roman (☎ **377/93-28-66-66**). Founded in 1929, it's one of the most famous beach, pool, and social clubs on the Riviera. Some privileges and perks are reserved for members, but nonmembers who pay 175F ($29.75) can use the facilities on a day pass. An additional 800F ($136) gets you a striped private cabana. Most of the socializing occurs around the edges of the Olympic-sized pool. On the premises are bars and three restaurants. From April to October, windsurfing and water-skiing are popular diversions conducted from the stony beach of this club.

GOLF   The **Monte Carlo Golf Club,** Route N-7, La Turbie (☎ **04-93-41-09-11**), lying within France, is a par-72 golf course with equal parts prestige, scenic panoramas, and local history. Certain perks, including use of electric golf buggies, are reserved exclusively for members. Before they're allowed to play, nonmembers are asked to show proof of membership in another golf club and evidence of their handicap ratings. Greens fees for 18 holes are 375F ($63.75) Monday through Friday and 475F ($80.75) Saturday and Sunday. Clubs can be rented for 150F ($25.50). The course is open daily 8am to sunset.

TENNIS & SQUASH   In addition to 23 tennis courts (21 clay and 2 concrete), the **Monte Carlo Country Club,** av. du Princesse-Grace, Roquebrune—St-Roman (☎ **04-93-41-30-15**), has enough other warm-weather distractions to keep you amused for a week. An entrance fee of 215F ($36.55) gets you access to a restaurant, a health club with Jacuzzi and sauna, a putting green, a beach, squash courts, and the above-mentioned roster of well-maintained tennis courts. Residents of the hotels administered by the Societé des Bains de Mer (the Hotel de Paris, the Hermitage, the Mirabeau, and the Monte Carlo Beach Club) pay half-price. It's open daily 8am to 8 or 9pm, depending on the season.

WHERE TO STAY

Hôtel Alexandra. 33 bd. Princesse-Charlotte, 98000 Monaco. ☎ **377/93-50-63-13.** Fax 377/92-16-06-48. 56 units. A/C TV TEL. 615–850F ($104.55–$144.50) double. AE, DC, MC, V. Parking 40F ($6.80).

This hotel is in the center of the business district, on a busy and often noisy street corner. Its comfortably furnished guest rooms aren't that exciting, but they're reliable and respectable. The Alexandra knows it can't compete with the giants of Monaco and doesn't even try, but if you want to visit the principality without spending a fortune, it's a good deal.

Hôtel Cosmopolite. 4 rue de la Turbie, 98000 Monaco. ☎ **377/93-30-16-95.** Fax 377/ 93-30-23-05. 24 units (none with bathroom). 240–320F ($40.80–$54.40) double. No credit cards.

This century-old three-story hotel is down a set of steps from the train station. Madame Gay Angèle, the English-speaking owner, is proud of her "Old Monaco" establishment. Her more expensive rooms have showers, but the cheapest way to stay here is to request a room without shower—there are adequate facilities in the hall.

Hôtel de Paris. Place du Casino, 98000 Monaco. ☎ **377/92-16-30-00.** Fax 377/92-16-38-50. www.montecarloresort.com. E-mail: hp@sdm.mc. 200 units. A/C MINIBAR TV TEL. 2,100–3,400F ($357–$578) double; from 6,000F ($1,020) suite. AE, DC, MC, V. Parking 130F ($22.10).

On the main plaza, this is one of the most famous hotels in the world and the choicest address in Monaco. The hotel is furnished with a dazzling decor of marble pillars, statues, crystal chandeliers, sumptuous carpets, Louis XVI chairs, and a wall-sized fin-de-siècle mural. The guest rooms are, in many cases, sumptuous, each with an elaborate period decor or a stylish contemporary one. Elegant tasteful fabrics, rich carpeting, and classic accessories make it a continuing favorite among the world's most discerning quests. The marble bathrooms are large, and come with hair dryers, dual basins, robes, and deluxe toiletries. On top of the Hôtel de Paris, the Louis XIV royal galley–style Le Grill has an impressive sliding roof. The elegant Le Louis XV is recommended under "Where to Dine," below. Thermes Marins spa, connected to the hotel, offers complete cures of thalassic therapy under medical supervision.

Hôtel Mirabeau. 1 av. du Princesse-Grace, MC 98000 Monaco. ☎ **377/92-16-65-65.** Fax 377/93-50-84-85. 103 units. A/C MINIBAR TV TEL. 1,400–2,450F ($238–$416.50) double; from 2,250F ($382.50) suite. AE, DC, MC, V. Parking 125F ($21.25).

In the heart of Monte Carlo, next to the casino, the contemporary Mirabeau combines modern design with refined atmosphere. Large mirrors, spacious lighted closets, private safes, elegant fabrics and upholstery, and sumptuous beds with luxurious mattresses make living here idyllic; many rooms also have terraces with romantic views over the pool and Mediterranean. The newest rooms are in the Costa and Excelsior wings. Although as fine as those in the main building are, many prefer the latter for their old-fashioned French decor and streetfront exposures. The marble bathrooms are roomy and well appointed with robes, deluxe toiletries, dual basins, and a hair dryer. La Coupole restaurant is highly praised among restaurants of the Riviera for its inventive yet classical cooking (closed in August).

WHERE TO DINE

Café de Paris. Place du Casino. ☎ **377/92-16-20-20.** Main courses 98–210F ($16.65–$35.70). AE, DC, MC, V. Daily 8am–4am. INTERNATIONAL.

This is the best positioned cafe and restaurant in Monaco, close to both the casino and the Hôtel de Paris, and so close to the tourist center of things that you might get more of a dose of Las Vegas than you care for. But why not revel in the crowds and the hurly-burly? This site offers a front-row seat to the never-ending spectacle of Monte Carlo. Food is professional and well-prepared: About a half-dozen *plats du jour* are available, including fried trout with almonds, pepper steak, osso bucco, and turbot with hollandaise.

✪ **Le Louis XV.** In the Hôtel de Paris, place du Casino. ☎ **377/92-16-30-01.** Reservations recommended. Jacket/tie for men. Main courses 310–590F ($52.70–$100.30); set-price menus 840–950F ($142.80–$161.50). AE, DC, MC, V. July–Aug, Wed 8–10pm; Thurs–Mon noon–2pm and 8–10pm; Sept–June, Thurs–Mon noon–2pm and 8–10pm. Closed Feb 2–17. FRENCH/ITALIAN.

On the lobby level of the five-star Hôtel de Paris, Le Louis XV offers what one critic called "down-home Riviera cooking within a Fabergé egg." In these regal trappings the chef, the great six-star Alain Ducasse, creates a cuisine that is light and attuned to the seasons, with an intelligent modern interpretation of both Provençal and northern Italian courses. Always count on Ducasse for delightful surprises. He stopped being a very good chef a long time ago and became a great one. He commands the finest ingredients in Europe, and his menu is ever-changing to take advantage of what's best in any season. The service is superb.

GAMBLING & OTHER AFTER-DARK DIVERSIONS

The **Sun Casino,** in the Monte Carlo Grand Hotel, 12 av. des Spélugues (☎ **377/93-50-65-00**), is a huge room filled with the one-armed bandits. It also features blackjack, craps, and American roulette. Additional slot machines are available on the roof starting at 11am—for those who want to gamble with a wider view of the sea. It's open daily 4pm to 4am (until 5am for slot machines). Admission is free.

A speculator, François Blanc, made the **Monte Carlo Casino,** place du Casino, (☎ **377/92-16-21-21**) the most famous in the world, attracting Sarah Bernhardt, Mata Hari, King Farouk, and Aly Khan (Onassis used to own a part-interest). The architect of Paris's Opéra Garnier, Charles Garnier, built the oldest part of the casino, and it remains an extravagant example of period architecture.

The **Salle Américaine,** containing only Vegas-style slot machines, opens at noon, as do doors for roulette and trente-quarante. A section for roulette and chemin-de-fer opens at 3pm. Everything heats up at 4pm when the full casino swings into action with more roulette, craps, and blackjack. Gambling continues until very late, and closing time depends on the crowd. To enter the casino, you must be at least 21 and have a passport, driver's license, or identity card. Admission to private rooms is 50 to 100F ($8.50 to $17).

The foremost winter establishment, under the same ownership, is the **Cabaret** in the Casino Gardens, where you can dance to the music of a smooth orchestra. A good cabaret with feathers, glitter, and Riviera-style semi-nudity is presented at 10pm Wednesday to Monday, from mid-September until the end of June. From 9pm you can enjoy dinner for 450F ($76.50). Drinks ordered separately begin at 150F ($25.50). For reservations, call ☎ **377/92-16-36-36.**

In the **Salle Garnier** of the casino, concerts are held periodically; for information, contact the tourist office (see "Visitor Information," above). The music is usually classical, featuring the Orchestre Philharmonique de Monte Carlo.

The casino also contains the **Opéra de Monte-Carlo,** whose patron is Prince Rainier. This world-famous house, opened in 1879 by Sarah Bernhardt, presents a winter and spring repertoire that traditionally includes Puccini, Mozart, and Verdi. The famed Ballets Russes de Monte-Carlo, starring Nijinsky and Karsavina, was created in 1918 by Sergei Diaghilev. The national orchestra and ballet company of Monaco appear here. Tickets might be hard to come by; your best bet is to ask your hotel concierge. You can make inquiries about tickets on your own at the **Atrium du Casino** (☎ **377/92-16-22-99,** open Tuesday to Sunday 10am to 12:15pm and 2 to 5pm. Standard tickets generally cost 125 to 800F ($21.25 to $136).

Germany

by Darwin Porter & Danforth Prince

Berlin is almost, but not quite yet, the capital of unified Germany; here you can see history in the making. What was once the city's biggest tourist attraction, the Berlin Wall, is now a bicycle path where Berliners push baby strollers. Restored baroque Munich, in the south, known as Germany's "secret capital," is the gateway to the Bavarian Alps and the colorful alpine villages. For a taste of medieval Germany, explore the untouched towns of the Romantic Road and Ludwig II's fairy-tale castle of Neuschwanstein.

1 Berlin

When Heinrich Heine arrived in Berlin in 1819, he exclaimed, "Isn't the present splendid!" Were he to arrive today, he might make the same remark. Visitors who come by plane to Berlin see a splendid panorama. Few metropolitan areas are blessed with as many lakes, woodlands, and parks—they cover one-third of the city's area, and small farms with fields and meadows still exist within the city limits.

Berlin today is an almost completely modern city. Regrettably, it's hardly the architectural gem that old-time visitors remember from the pre-Nazi era; it wasn't rebuilt with the same kind of care lavished on Munich and Cologne. But in spite of its decades-long "quadripartite status," it's a vibrant city, always receptive to new ideas, a major economic and cultural center, and a leader in development and research. Because of its excellent facilities, it's a favored site for trade fairs, congresses, and conventions, attracting 6 million visitors a year.

It hasn't been long since the Berlin Wall came down, but change within the city has been so rapid that the government has resorted to painting a red line through its central district so that baffled visitors can tell where it stood. The city still seems to have two of everything—two zoos, two opera companies, two major international airports, to name a few. However, there are also new problems for the reunited Berlin. Economic devastation has affected the eastern sector, and panhandling and crime on the streets have become major problems in some areas of the city.

Only in Berlin

Strolling the Kurfürstendamm Launched by Bismarck in 1870 to surpass the Champs-Elyseés in Paris, this bustling neon-lit boulevard celebrates the victory of capitalism from the heart of Eastern Europe. Two miles of pure consumerism, the Ku'damm is glitzy, showy, and great for a shopping stroll. Stop in at one of the grand cafes, such as Kranzler or Möhring, for a *Milchkaffee* and a slice of *Apfel Strudel.*

Walking Unter den Linden   By all means, stroll along Berlin's second great street. This is the architectural showpiece of the old East Berlin, where you follow in the footsteps of Prussian emperors, under linden trees that were replanted to replace the ones Hitler had removed. Be awed by the imposing Deutsches Historisches Museum, designed by Germany's most famous baroque architect, Andreas Schlüter, and relax in the Lustgarten before walking across Schlossbrücke, Berlin's most beautiful bridge.

Exploring the Gemäldegalerie   Berlin's top-notch museums are reason enough to visit the city. The German capital is a treasure trove of world art, even if some of it, at times, was acquired by what some may view as illegal means. In its new home, the Gemäldegalerie (Picture Gallery) is the city's richest museum, home to some 3,000 world-class paintings. It's a virtual encyclopedia of the great periods of European art, even if its most famous painting, *Man with the Golden Helmet,* is no longer attributed to Rembrandt.

Looking at the Past at the Pergamon   Dedicated to ancient times, this museum shelters the altars, gates, and gathering places of antiquity—none more enthralling than the Hellenistic Pergamon Altar from 180 to 160 B.C. Built of white marble, it's carved with figures of the gods. And that's only one of the attractions here at one of the major architectural museums of the world. The two-story Market Gate of Miletus was erected in A.D. 120, and a dazzling Babylonian Processional Street leads to the Gate of Ishtar.

Taking a Kneipe Crawl Through the Heart of Town   Forget pub crawling; Berliners have their own brand of this nighttime tradition. Every neighborhood is filled with *Kneipen* (bars and taverns) waiting to lure you. These are cozy rendezvous where patrons meet their friends, and you can easily get caught up in the old-time atmosphere and conviviality. Our favorite is **Gaststätte Hoeck,** Wilmersdorferstrasse 149 (☎ **030/3-41-31-10**), the oldest Kneipe in Charlottenburg (1892).

Calling on Marlene   Gone but hardly forgotten, Marlene Dietrich was the seductive femme fatale of the 20th century, a legend ever since she appeared as prostitute Lola-Lola in *The Blue Angel.* Born in Berlin on Christmas 1904, she stood for ambiguously erotic glamour, and her sultry voice singing her signature tune, "Lili Marlene," added to her mystique. Actually, the song is spelled "Lili Marleen," but Dietrich's personality was so great that fans started misspelling it "Marlene" instead. This great personality, the most famous German woman of the 20th century, died in 1992. Loyal fans can buy some of her favorite red roses and lay them on her grave in Berlin-Friedenau cemetery, along Stubenrauchstrasse.

Picnicking in the Tiergarten   What better place for a picnic than the former hunting grounds of the Prussian electors since the 1500s? No longer the bare and denuded forest it was in 1946, the Tiergarten today blossoms with trees from all over the world, including some contributed by Queen Elizabeth II and many towns from throughout Germany. The Tiergarten is ideal for strolling, including crossing the Löwenbrücke or Lion Bridge. Wander at leisure through the 412-acre park until you find a suitable oasis. But first stop at the sixth-floor food emporium of KaDeWe at Wittenbergplatz, the major department store, to secure the makings of one of life's memorable picnics—everything from fresh bread to grilled chicken, sausages, salads, and wine.

ORIENTATION

ARRIVING   By Plane   Tegel Airport (☎ **030/41-01-1**) is the city's busiest, serving most flights from the west. Historic **Tempelhof Airport** (☎ **030/69-51-0**), made famous as the city's lifeline during the Berlin Airlift, has declined in importance. **Schönefeld** (☎ **030/60-91-0**), the airport in the eastern sector, is used primarily by Russian and Eastern European airlines. Private bus shuttles among the three airports operate constantly so you can make connecting flights at a different airport. Buses from each airport also take you into the center of Berlin.

Lufthansa (☎ **800/645-3880** in the U.S., or 020/8750-3300 in London) is the premier airline flying into Berlin, followed closely by **Delta** (☎ **800/221-1212**). **British Airways** (☎ **0345/222-111** in the U.K., 800/247-9297 in the U.S. and Canada) offers direct flights into Berlin from London's Heathrow and Gatwick airports and from Birmingham.

By Train   Frankfurt and Hamburg, among other cities, have good rail connections to Berlin. From Frankfurt to Berlin takes about 7 hours. Eurailpass and GermanRail passes are valid. Most arrivals from western European and western German cities are at the **Bahnhof Zoologischer Garten** (☎ **030/194-19**), the main train station, called "Bahnhof Zoo," in western Berlin. In the center of the city, close to the Kurfürstendamm, it's well connected for public transportation. Facilities include a tourist information counter dispensing free maps and tourist brochures open daily from 5am to 11pm. The staff can also make same-day hotel reservations for a fee of 5DM ($3).

Berlin has two other train stations, the **Berlin Hauptbahnhof** and **Berlin Lichtenberg.** Call the main station at ☎ **030/194-19** for information.

By Bus   The operations center for several independent bus operators, many of them originating within what was at the time two independent Germanies, are headquartered within a central arrivals and departures point, the **ZOB Omnibusbahnhof am Funkturm,** Messedamm 8 (☎ **030/301-80-28**). The information service here (☎ **030/301-80-28** or 030/302-52-94) supplies departure times and fare information for routes to and from Berlin from other parts of Europe.

By Car   From Frankfurt, take the A-66 to Bad Herzfeld, and either go east on the A-4 to pick up A-9 to Berlin or continue on the A-7 to Braunschweig and east on the A-2 toward Berlin. North of Nürnberg, the A-9 leads to Berlin. From Leipzig take A-14 in the direction of Halle; at the intersection of A-9, head northeast into Berlin. From Dresden, head northeast on A-13 all the way into Berlin. Expect heavy traffic delays on Autobahnen, especially on weekends and sunny days when everybody is out touring.

VISITOR INFORMATION   For tourist information and hotel bookings, head for the **Berlin Tourist Information Center,** Europa-Center near Memorial Church, entrance on the Budapesterstrasse side (☎ **030/25-00-25**), open Monday to Saturday 8am to 10pm and Sunday 9am to 9pm. Hotel information and more data can be obtained by calling **Berlin Hotline** at (☎ **030/27-00-25**). You can learn about Berlin on the Internet at www.berlin.de, and the address for e-mail is information@btm.de. For reservations, the e-mail address is reservations@btm.de.

CITY LAYOUT   The center of activity in the western part of Berlin is the 2-mile-long **Kurfürstendamm,** called the *Ku'damm* by Berliners. Along this wide boulevard, you'll find the best hotels, restaurants, theaters, cafes, nightclubs, shops, and department stores. The huge **Tiergarten,** the city's largest park, is crossed by Strasse des 17 Juni, which leads to the famed **Brandenburger Tor (Gate);** just north of here is the Reichstag. On the southwestern fringe of the Tiergarten is the **Berlin Zoo**

If you're going to be in Berlin for 3 days, you can buy a **WelcomeCard** for 29DM ($17.40), which entitles holders to 72 free hours on public transportation in Berlin and Brandenburg. You also get free admission or price reductions up to 50% on sightseeing tours, museums, and other attractions. Reductions of 25% are granted at ten of the city's theaters as well. It's valid for one adult and up to three children 13 or younger.

(Zoologischer Garten). From the Ku'damm you can take Hardenbergstrasse, crossing Bismarckstrasse and traversing Otto-Suhr-Allee, which leads to **Schloss Charlottenburg** and museums, one of your major sightseeing goals. The Dahlem Museums are on the southwestern fringe, often reached by going along Hohenzollerndamm.

The **Brandenburger Tor,** which once separated the two Berlins, is the start of eastern Berlin's most celebrated street, **Unter den Linden,** the cultural heart of Berlin before World War II. The famous street runs from west to east, cutting a path through the city. It leads to **Museumsinsel (Museum Island),** where the most outstanding museums of eastern Berlin, including the Pergamon, are situated. As it courses along, Unter den Linden crosses another major eastern Berlin artery, **Friedrichstrasse.** If you continue south along Friedrichstrasse, you'll reach the former location of **Checkpoint Charlie,** the most famous site of the Cold War days.

Unter den Linden continues east until it reaches **Alexanderplatz,** the center of eastern Berlin, with its TV tower (Fernsehturm). A short walk away is the restored **Nikolai Quarter (Nikolaiviertel),** a neighborhood of bars, restaurants, and shops that evoke life in the prewar days.

GETTING AROUND

BY PUBLIC TRANSPORTATION   The Berlin transport system consists of buses, trams, and U-Bahn and S-Bahn trains. The network is run by the **BVG,** or Public Transport Co. Berlin-Brandenburg (☎ **030/1-94-49**), which operates an information booth outside the Bahnhof Zoo on Hardenbergplatz, open daily from 8am to 10pm. The staff here can provide details about which U-Bahn (underground) or S-Bahn (inner-city railway) line to take to various locations and the ticket options possible. You can also purchase tickets, including discounted cards.

The **BVG standard ticket** (Einzelfahrschein) costs 3.90DM ($2.35) and is valid for 2 hours of transportation in all directions, transfers included. Also available at counters and vending machines is a 24-hour ticket for the whole city; the price is 7.80DM ($4.70). On buses only standard tickets can be purchased, and tram tickets must be purchased in advance. Tickets should be kept until the end of the journey; otherwise, you'll be liable for a fine of 60DM ($36).

BY TAXI   Taxis are available throughout Berlin. The meter starts at 4DM to 6DM ($2.40 to $3.60), with additional kilometers adding D-marks according to a complicated tariff system. The longer the ride, the cheaper the price per kilometer. For short distances, either 5 minutes or 2 kilometers, the fare is 5DM ($3). Visitors can flag down taxis that have a T-sign illuminated. For a taxi, call ☎ **21-02-02,** 6-90-22, or 26-10-26.

BY CAR   Touring Berlin by car isn't recommended. Free parking places are difficult to come by.

Fast Facts: Berlin

American Express   The main office at Uhlandsdtrasse 173 (☎ **030/88-45-88-21**) is open Monday to Friday 9am to 5:30pm and Saturday 9am to noon. Branch offices are at Bayreuthstrasse 23 (☎ **030/21-49-83-63**) and Friedrichstrasse 172 (☎ **030/20-17-40-12**).

Business Hours   Most **banks** are open Monday through Friday from 9am to 1 or 3pm. Most other **businesses** and **stores** are open Monday through Friday from 9 or 10am to 6 or 6:30pm and Saturday from 9am to 2pm. On *langer Samstag*, the first Saturday of the month, shops stay open until 4 or 6pm. Some stores observe late closing on Thursday, usually at 8:30pm.

Currency   The German monetary unit is the **deutsche mark (DM),** which is divided into 100 **pfennig.** Bills exist in denominations of 5, 10, 20, 50, 100, 200, 500, and 1,000DM; coins come in denominations of 1, 2, and 5DM, and in 1, 2, 5, 10, and 50 pfennig. The rate of exchange for the deutsche mark used throughout this chapter was $1 = 1.67DM or 1DM = 60¢. Also, 1EUR = 1.95DM and £1 = 2.90DM.

Currency Exchange   You can exchange money at all airports, at major department stores, at any bank, and at the American Express office (see above).

Dentists & Doctors   The Berlin tourist office in the Europa-Center (see "Visitor Information," above) keeps a list of English-speaking dentists and doctors in Berlin. In case of a medical emergency, call ☎ **030/31-00-31** any time.

Drugstores   If you need a pharmacy (*Apotheke*) at night, go to one on any corner. There you'll find a sign in the window giving the address of the nearest drugstore open at night; such posting is required by law. Otherwise, call ☎ **030/0-11-89** to find out what's open. A central pharmacy is **Europa-Apotheke,** Tauentzienstrasse 9–12 (☎ **030/2-61-41-42**), by the Europa-Center. It's open Monday through Friday 9am to 8pm and Saturday 9am to 4pm.

Embassies & Consulates   There is an embassy office at Neustaedtische Kirchstrasse 4–5 (☎ **030/2-38-51-74**) and a consulate at Clayallee 170 (☎ **030/8-32-92-33**). The U.S. consular information hotline is ☎ **0130/82-63-64.** The **British Embassy's** Berlin office is at Unter den Linden 32–34 (☎ **030/20-18-40**). The Berlin office of the **Embassy of Australia** is on Kempinski Plaza, at Uhlandstrasse 181–183 (☎ **030/8-80-08-80**). The **Embassy of Canada** maintains a consulate at Friedrichstrasse 95 (☎ **030/2-61-11-61**). The **Embassy of New Zealand** is at Bundeskanzlerplatz 2–10 in Bonn (☎ **0228/22-80-70**), with no consulate office in Berlin. The **Consulate of Ireland** is at Ernst-Reuter-Platz 10 (☎ **030/34-80-08-22**) in Berlin. The **South African Consulate** is at Douglasstrasse 9 (☎ **030/82-50-11**). Some time in the year 2000, the full embassy staffs of the countries above may have moved to Berlin and taken larger offices than those listed here. Therefore, if you have business with your home country embassy, check for its exact location before going there. The tourist office promises to keep an up-to-date list.

Emergencies   Call the police at ☎ **110;** dial **112** to report a fire or to summon an ambulance.

Internet Access   If you're feeling out of touch, visit the **Virtuality Café,** Lewishamstrasse 1 (☎ **030/32-75-143**), for Internet access and e-mail. Its Web site is www.vrcafe.de.

Berlin U-Bahn & the S-Bahn

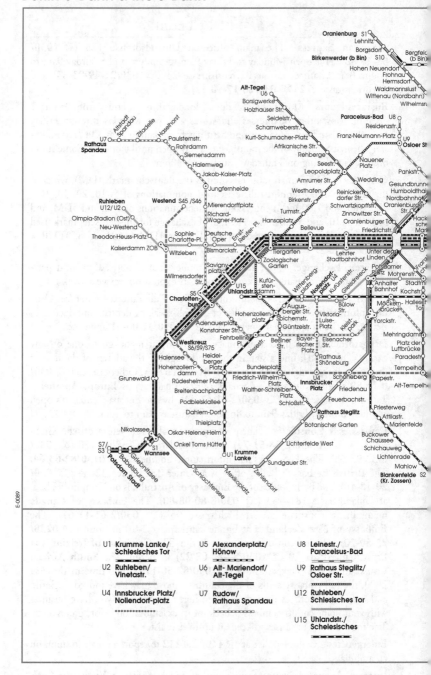

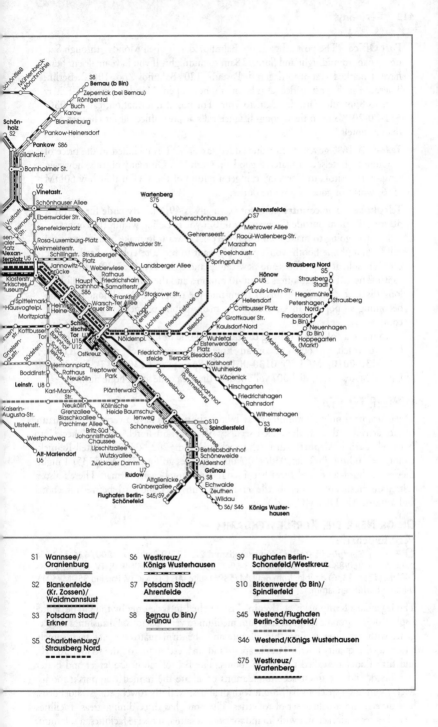

S1 **Wannsee/**
    Oranienburg

S2 **Blankenfelde**
    (Kr. Zossen)/
    Waidmannslust

S3 **Potsdam Stadt/**
    Erkner

S5 **Charlottenburg/**
    Strausberg Nord

S6 **Westkreuz/**
    Königs Wusterhausen

S7 **Potsdam Stadt/**
    Ahrenfelde

S8 **Bernau (b Bin)/**
    Grünau

S9 **Flughafen Berlin-**
    Schonefeld/Westkreuz

S10 **Birkenwerder (b Bin)/**
    Spindlerfeld

S45 **Westend/Flughafen**
    Berlin-Schonefeld/

S46 **Westend/Königs Wusterhausen**

S75 **Westkreuz/**
    Wartenberg

Post Office   The post office at the Bahnhof Zoo is open Monday through Saturday 6am to midnight and Sunday 8am to midnight. If you have mail sent here, have it marked Hauptpostlagernd, Postamt 120, Bahnhof Zoo, 10612, Berlin. There's also a post office at Hauptbahnhof, open Monday through Friday 7am to 8pm and Saturday 8am to 1pm. For postal information, call ☎ **030/ 311-00-20.** You can make long-distance calls at post offices at far cheaper rates than at hotels.

Taxes   A 16% government value-added tax or VAT is included in the price of restaurants, hotels, and material goods in Germany. On many objects, however, temporary visitors to Germany can get a refund of the VAT if they buy 60DM ($36) worth of goods from one outlet.

Telephone   The **country code** for Germany is **49;** the **city code** for Berlin is **30** for calls from outside Germany or **030** if you're calling within the country.

If you're going to make a lot of phone calls or want to make an international call from a phone booth, you'll probably want to buy a **telephone card.** Phone cards are sold at post offices and newsstands and cost 12DM ($7.20) and 50DM ($30). The 12DM card offers about 40 minutes and the 50DM card is useful for long-distance calls. Simply insert them into the telephone slot. Phone cards are becoming so popular in Germany that many public phones no longer accept coins.

To make a **collect or calling card call,** dial one of the following access numbers to reach an operator or an English-language voice prompt: **AT&T** (☎ **0130-0010**), **MCI** (☎ **0130-0012**), or **Sprint** (☎ **0130-0013**). To call the United States direct, dial **001** followed by the area code and phone number.

WHERE TO STAY

Tegel Airport is only 20 minutes away by taxi, but if you have a very early departure or late arrival and want the added security of an airport hotel, you can check into **Novotel Berlin Airport,** Kurt-Schumacher-Damm 202, 03405 Orsteil-Reinickendorf (☎ **030/41060;** fax 030/4106700). Doubles go for 225DM ($135) a night; they're medium-sized and furnished in standard motel-chain format. There's also a restaurant on site, plus a free shuttle service that runs back and forth between the hotel and airport. AE, DC, MC, and V are accepted.

On or Near the Kurfürstendamm
Very Expensive

✪ **Bristol Kempinski Berlin.** Kurfürstendamm 27, 10719 Berlin. ☎ **800/426-3135** in the U.S., or 030/88-43-40. Fax 030/8-33-60-75. 301 units. A/C MINIBAR TV TEL. 425DM–560DM ($255–$336) double; from 660DM ($396) suite. AE, DC, MC, V. Parking 35DM ($21). U-Bahn: Kurfürstendamm.

The legendary Kempinski, or "Kempi," is matched in style only by the Grand Hotel Esplanade. Bedrooms range in size from medium to very spacious. Furnishings are elegant, with art deco styling throughout, and the firm mattresses are handsomely adorned with quality linens. The cheapest (and smallest) rooms on the second, fourth, and fifth floors are called the Berlin rooms. The Bristol rooms are larger and better appointed, and the finest accommodations of all are the refined Kempinski rooms. Each room has a spacious bathroom with dual basins, fluffy towels, scales, shoehorns, hair dryers, and a deluxe set of toiletries. The hotel has three dining areas. Facilities include a recreation center with an indoor pool, a sauna, massage facilities, a solarium, and a fitness center.

Grand Hotel Esplanade. Lützowufer 15, 10785 Berlin. ☎ **030/25-47-80.** Fax 030/ 2-65-11-71. www.esplanade.de. E-mail: info@esplanade.de. 402 units. A/C MINIBAR TV TEL. 430DM–550DM ($258–$330) double; from 750DM ($450) suite. AE, DC, MC, V. Parking costs 24DM ($14.40). U-Bahn: Kurfürstenstrasse, Nollendorfplatz, or Wittenbergplatz.

The Esplanade rivals the Kempinski for supremacy in Berlin. Bedrooms are spacious, bright, and cheerfully decorated, with such extras as cable TV, VCR, sound insulation, and superb lighting. Beds are large with quality mattresses and duvets. Bathrooms are among the city's most spacious and luxurious, with fluffy towels (and plenty of them), hair dryers, and robes. When reserving, ask for one of the corner rooms, as they're the biggest and have the best views of Berlin. Thirty-three rooms are reserved for non-smokers. The gourmet restaurant, Harlekin, is recommended separately in "Where to Dine," below. Facilities include an indoor pool, a whirlpool, a solarium, and a sauna.

Expensive
✪ **Brandenburger Hof Relais & Châteaux.** Eislebener Strasse 14, 10789 Berlin. ☎ **030/ 21-40-50.** Fax 030/21-40-51-00. www.brandenburger-hof.com. E-mail: info@branden-burger-hof.com. 82 units. A/C MINIBAR TV TEL. 330DM–445DM ($198–$267) double; from 725DM ($435) suite. Rates include breakfast. AE, DC, MC, V. Parking 20DM ($12). U-Bahn: Kurfürstendamm or Augsburger Strasse. S-Bahn: Zoologischer Garten.

Guest rooms at this white-fronted classic, although perhaps too severe and minimalist for some tastes, are among the most stylish in the city. This is authentic Bauhaus—torchère lamps, black leather upholstery, and platform beds with deluxe mattresses. French doors open to small balconies, but not on the top floors. Original art adorns the walls, and there is state-of-the-art security. Bathrooms are spacious, with large combination tub and showers, scales, hair dryers, and plenty of shelf space. House-keeping is among the finest in Berlin. The hotel features two restaurants, including its gourmet Die Quadriga.

Kronprinz Berlin. Kronprinzendamm 1, 10711 Berlin. ☎ **030/89-60-30.** Fax 030/ 8-93-12-15. www.kronprinz-hotel.de. E-mail: reception@kronprinzhotel.de. 67 units. MINIBAR TV TEL. 250DM–295DM ($150–$177) double; from 380DM ($228) suite. Children 12 and under stay free in parents' room. Rates include buffet breakfast. AE, DC, MC, V. Free parking. Bus: 104, 110, 119, 129, or 219.

Kronprinz is at the far western edge of the Ku'damm, about half an hour walk from the Gedächtniskirche (although linked by bus). Rooms range from medium to large, with fine appointments (often tasteful reproductions of antiques). Mattresses are firm, high quality, and renewed every other year. Bathrooms have a generous assortment of fluffy towels, a tub and shower combination, a deluxe set of toiletries, and adequate shelf space. The rooms accommodate one or two and include a balcony. Many guests congregate in the cozy in-room bar, or in summer gather in the garden under the chestnut trees for draft beer and wine.

✪ **Savoy.** Fasanenstrasse 9–10, 10623 Berlin. ☎ **800/223-5652** in the U.S. and Canada, or 030/3-11-0-30. Fax 030/3-11-03-333. 140 units. MINIBAR TV TEL. 289DM–389DM ($173.40–$233.40) double; 520DM–900DM ($312–$540) suite. Children under 12 stay free in parents' room. AE, DC, MC, V. Parking 18DM ($10.80). U-Bahn: Kurfürstendamm.

If you don't demand the full-service facilities of the grander choices, this might be the hotel for you. In general guest rooms are a bit small, but they are comfortable nonetheless, with such amenities as private safes, double glazed windows, trouser presses, and quality mattresses on comfortable, large beds. Bathrooms are decently sized, maintained spotlessly, and contain a shower and tub combination, with toi-letries, fluffy towels, and adequate shelf space. Try the restaurant, Belle Époque, and its cozy Times Bar. There's also a sauna and a fitness club.

Western Berlin

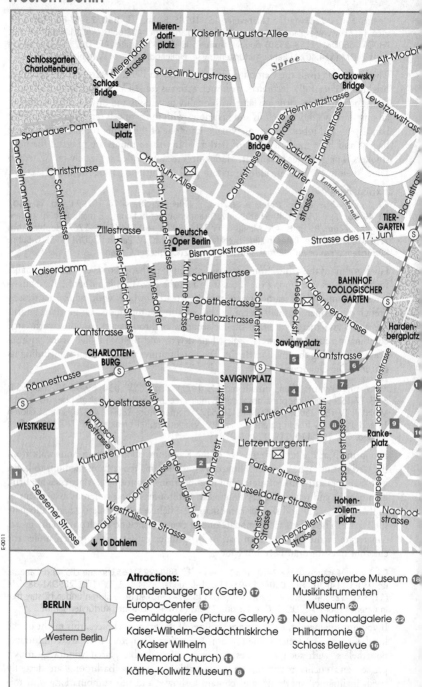

Attractions:

Brandenburger Tor (Gate) 🅬
Europa-Center 🅭
Gemäldgalerie (Picture Gallery) 🅲
Kaiser-Wilhelm-Gedächtniskirche
   (Kaiser Wilhelm
    Memorial Church) 🅫
Käthe-Kollwitz Museum 🅰

Kungstgewerbe Museum 🅮
Musikinstrumenten
   Museum 🅴
Neue Nationalgalerie 🅶
Philharmonie 🅳
Schloss Bellevue 🅪

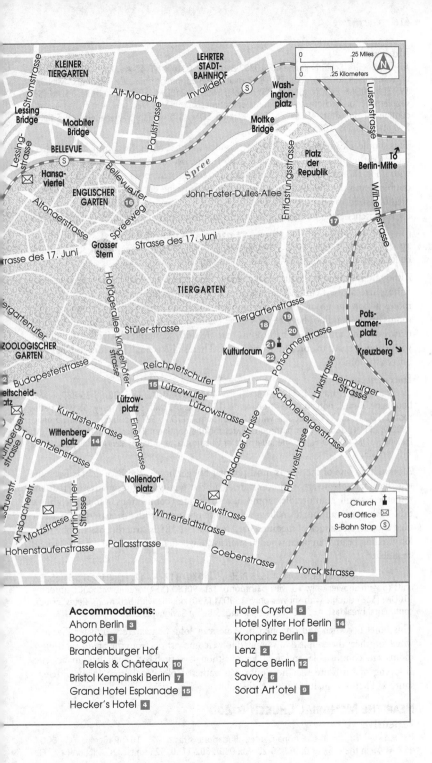

Accommodations:

Ahorn Berlin **3**
Bogotá **3**
Brandenburger Hof
 Relais & Châteaux **10**
Bristol Kempinski Berlin **7**
Grand Hotel Esplanade **15**
Hecker's Hotel **4**

Hotel Crystal **5**
Hotel Sylter Hof Berlin **14**
Kronprinz Berlin **1**
Lenz **2**
Palace Berlin **12**
Savoy **6**
Sorat Art'otel **9**

Moderate

Ahorn Berlin. Schlüterstrasse 40, 10707 Berlin. ☎ **030/8-81-43-44.** Fax 030/8-81-65-00. www.members.aol.com/dglau55015. E-mail: hotel-adhorn@t-online.de. 28 units. MINIBAR TV TEL. 140DM–210DM ($84–$126) double; 160DM–240DM ($96–$144) triple; 15DM ($9) supplement for kitchenette. Discounts sometimes granted in Dec and Aug. Rates include continental breakfast. AE, DC, MC, V. Parking 5DM ($3). U-Bahn: Adenauerplatz; S-Bahn: Savignyplatz; Bus: 109, 119, or 219.

This simple, clean, cost-conscious hotel is near a corner of the Ku'damm. You stay here more for the price than any grand comfort, but bedrooms are inviting nonetheless, with good though much-used furnishings, excellent mattresses on the beds (twins or doubles), and tidy maintenance. Bathrooms are routine but have renewed plumbing, medium-sized towels, and adequate shelf space. Families often book in here, not only for the kitchenettes, but because so many rooms are suitable for three or four guests.

Lenz. Xantenerstrasse 8, 10707 Berlin. ☎ **030/8-81-51-58.** Fax 030/8-81-55-17. 28 units. TV TEL. 160DM–180DM ($96–$108) double; 220DM ($123.20) family room. Rates include buffet breakfast. AE, DC, MC, V. U-Bahn: Adenauerplatz.

Although it might be a bit creaky, many appreciate the old-fashioned, homelike atmosphere of the Lenz. Accommodations vary in size and decor; the most spacious rooms are on the ground floor. Try to book 103, the largest and best furnished. The rooms on the top floor have better views of Berlin, but are small. All rooms have firm mattresses and rather small bathrooms that are tidily kept and efficiently maintained with enough space to spread out your stuff. There's also a small but convivial bar and breakfast room.

Inexpensive

Bogatà. Schlüterstrasse 45, 10707 Berlin. ☎ **030/881-50-01.** Fax 030/88-35-887. www. bogota.de. E-mail: hotel.bogota@t-online.de. 130 units (12 with shower only, 65 with bathroom). TEL. 125DM ($75) double without bathroom; 145DM ($87) double with shower only; 190DM ($114) double with bathroom. Rates include continental breakfast. AE, DC, MC, V. Parking 15DM ($9). U-Bahn: Adenauerplatz or Uhlandstrasse; S-Bahn: Savignyplatz; Bus: 109, 119, or 129.

Although it's one of the town's most popular budget hotels, the Bogotà's facilities are less than state-of-the-art. Bedrooms are small but tidy with aging mattresses that are nonetheless still comfortable. Some have computer connections. Housekeeping is tidy. Bathrooms, although small, are efficiently organized with adequate shelf space, a tiled shower, and a rack of medium-sized towels. The 1890s structure has a lobby with lofty ceiling beams, an open wooden staircase, a wooden balcony, and a heavy bronze chandelier.

Hotel Crystal. Kantstrasse 144, 10623 Berlin. ☎ **030/312-90-47.** Fax 030/312-64-65. 33 units (5 with shower only, 16 with bathroom). TEL. 90DM ($54) double without bathroom; 110DM ($66) double with shower only; 150DM ($90) double with bathroom. Rates include continental breakfast. AE, MC, V. Free parking. S-Bahn: Savignyplatz.

This hotel is owned and operated by American John Schwarzrock and his German wife Dorothée; the couple is always glad to welcome visitors from the States. The guest rooms are comfortable and well kept, although very basic. Each has an eclectic grouping of furniture that no doubt was gathered piecemeal from many different sources. There's a small bar just off the lobby.

NEAR THE MEMORIAL CHURCH & ZOO

Expensive

Palace Berlin. In the Europa-Center, Budapesterstrasse 41, 10789 Berlin. ☎ **800/ 457-4000** in the U.S., or 030/2-50-20. Fax 030/2502-1160. 325 units. A/C MINIBAR TV TEL.

330DM–530DM ($198–$318) double; from 650DM ($390) suite. AE, DC, MC, V. Parking 30DM ($18). U-Bahn: Zoologischer Garten.

The stylish and comfortable Palace is much improved over recent years; however, in some rooms the double glazing on the windows is unable to deafen the noise from the adjacent Europa-Center. All of the seventh floor and some of the sixth is set aside for nonsmokers. The best rooms are in the more recently built Casino Wing, with marble bathrooms and separate showers and tubs. Bedrooms range from medium to spacious in size, each with a deluxe bed, a quality mattress, and a trouser press. The bathrooms are medium in size, most often with a combination tub and shower (sometimes with shower stalls only), but always with a set of good toiletries and a generous rack of fluffy towels. Each bathroom also contains a hair dryer. The hotel's elegant dining room, First Floor, is recommended separately in "Where to Dine," below. The Thermen am Europa-Center, a large health club, offers indoor and outdoor pools, exercise equipment, and a sauna.

✪ **Sorat Art'otel.** Joachimstalerstrasse 28–29, 10719 Berlin. ☎ **030/88-44-70.** Fax 030/ 88-44-77-00. 133 units. A/C MINIBAR TV TEL. 220DM–415DM ($132–$249) double. Rates include buffet breakfast. AE, DC, MC, V. U-Bahn: Kurfürstendamm.

Those partial to the more famous and highly regarded Brandenburger Hof (above) also like this tasteful, discreet hotel. Both chic and avant-garde, the Sorat is unlike any other hotel in Berlin. The bedrooms, all medium in size, are minimalist, with a touch of industrial design. Although they won't please clients seeking a traditional Berlin hotel, modernists will be at home with the pedestal tables evoking cable spools and chrome-legged furnishings, and everyone will appreciate the deluxe mattresses on the large beds, private safes, and tasteful lighting. Bathrooms are generously proportioned and contain deluxe toiletries, hair dryers, state-of-the-art plumbing, and a set of fluffy towels.

Moderate

Hecker's Hotel. Grolmanstrasse 35, 10623 Berlin. ☎ **030/8-89-00.** Fax 030/8-89-02-60. www.heckers-hotel.com. E-mail: info@heckers-hotel.com. 76 units. A/C MINIBAR TV TEL. 370DM ($222) double; 390DM ($234) junior suite. AE, DC, MC, V. Parking 15DM ($9). U-Bahn: Uhlandstrasse; Bus: 109 from Tegel Airport to Uhlandstrasse or 119, 129, or 219.

This conveniently located hotel is near the Ku'damm and the many bars, cafes, and restaurants around the Savignyplatz. Bedrooms range from small to medium sized, but are fairly routine despite the good beds and frequently renewed mattresses. There's a sterility here, but also up-to-date comfort and top-notch maintenance. Bathrooms, although small, still have enough shelf space to spread out your things, plus constantly updated plumbing and a generous rack of medium-sized towels. Some rooms are exclusively for nonsmokers. There's also a bar and a little cafe in the lobby. In summer, guests sit on the rooftop terrace, enjoying the lights of Berlin at night.

Hotel Sylter Hof Berlin. Kurfürstenstrasse 114–116, 10787 Berlin. ☎ **030/2-12-00.** Fax 030/214-28-26. 161 units. MINIBAR TV TEL. 282DM ($169.20) double; from 293DM ($175.80) suite. Rates include buffet breakfast. AE, DC, MC, V. Parking 16DM ($9.60). U-Bahn: Wittenbergplatz; Bus: 100 or X9.

Sylter Hof offers rich trappings at good prices. The main lounges are warmly decorated in an old-world style, with chandeliers, Louis XV-style and provincial chairs, and antiques, such as an armoire and a grandfather clock. The well-maintained rooms, most of which are singles, might be too small for most tastes, but the staff pays special attention to your comfort. Bathrooms are small but efficiently arranged with shelf space, a set of toiletries, and a rack of medium-sized towels. The Friesenstube is a conservative dining room serving Prussian and continental cuisine.

IN BERLIN-MITTE (EASTERN BERLIN)
Very Expensive

✪ **Hotel Adlon.** Unter den Linden 77, 10117 Berlin. ☎ **800/426-3135** or 030/22-61-0. Fax 030/22-61-11-16. www.hotel-adlon.de. E-mail: adlon@kempinski.com. 337 units. A/C MINIBAR TV TEL. 490DM–660DM ($294–$396) double; from 800DM ($480) suite. AE, DC, MC, V. Parking 40DM ($24). S-Bahn: Unter den Linden.

Only steps from the Brandenburg Gate, this hotel is situated at the edge of the former "Death Strip" between East and West Berlin, and considered one of Berlin's premier addresses. The large, beautifully appointed bedrooms contain CD players, fax machines, and king-sized or twin beds with luxury mattresses. Bathrooms are also spacious with deluxe toiletries, a hair dryer, a phone, tiled shower stalls, and a generous rack of fluffy towels. There are two restaurants, two bars, and a coffee shop. Facilities include a spa, health club with indoor and outdoor swimming pools, jogging path that begins across the street, and access to bicycling, golf, and horseback riding on the city limits of Berlin.

✪ **The Westin Grand.** Friedrichstrasse 158–164, 10117 Berlin. ☎ **800/843-3311** in the U.S., or 030/2-02-70. Fax 030/20-27-33-62. 358 units. A/C MINIBAR TV TEL. 295DM–475DM ($177–$285) double; from 550DM ($330) junior suite; from 900DM ($540) apt suite. AE, DC, MC, V. Parking 30DM ($18). U-Bahn: Französische Strasse; S-Bahn: Friedrichstrasse.

Many hotels call themselves grand—this one truly is. In Berlin the Westin Grand is rivaled only by the Kempinski. Since taking over this hotel, Westin has spent a fortune in making the bedrooms among the finest in the city. All are tastefully decorated, with deluxe mattresses, elegant fabrics, and comfortable chairs. Bathrooms are among the most spacious in town, with large tubs, a hair dryer, and a set of deluxe toiletries. Your dining choices are the posh Peacock Bar or the more traditional Goldene Gans (see "Where to Dine," below). Facilities include a fitness club, whirlpool, marble pool, saunas, and solarium.

Expensive

Radisson SAS Hotel Berlin. Karl-Liebknecht-Strasse 5, 10178 Berlin. ☎ **800/333-3333** in the U.S. or 030/23828. Fax 030/2382-7590. 564 units. A/C MINIBAR TV TEL. 360DM–520DM ($216–$312) double; 650DM ($390) suite. AE, DC, DISC, MC, V. Parking 30DM ($18). S-Bahn: Alexanderplatz.

In 1992, the Inter-Hotel Group poured $43 million into a renovation, and the hotel now ranks near the top of the four-star choices. Most rooms open onto a view and are medium to large in size. They have been carefully planned with built-in desks, torchère lamps, breakfast tables, carpet-covered luggage benches, private safes, mirrored closets, and either queen-sized or twin beds with comfortable mattresses. The bathrooms feature private phones, deluxe toiletries, and hair dryers. The Orangerie is an intimate restaurant serving international cuisine. The hotel has a gymnasium with the biggest hotel pool in Berlin.

Moderate

✪ **Hotel Luisenhof.** Köpenicker Strasse 92, 10179 Berlin. ☎ **030/2-41-59-06.** Fax 030/2-79-29-83. 28 units. MINIBAR TV TEL. 195DM ($117) double; 230DM ($138) suite. Rates include breakfast. AE, DC, MC, V. U-Bahn: Märkisches Museum.

One of the most desirable small hotels in Berlin's eastern district, the Luisenhof occupies a dignified 1822 house. Five floors of high-ceilinged rooms will appeal to those desiring to escape modern Berlin's sterility. As befits a former private home, bedrooms range greatly in size, but each is equipped with a good bed or beds (either one queen or two twins) and firm mattresses. Bathrooms, although small, are beautifully appointed and tiled, with a rack of plentiful fluffy towels, toilet articles, shower stalls (often with a large tub), and spotless maintenance. Beneath vaulted ceilings in the cellar, you'll find a very appealing restaurant, the Alexanderkeller.

IN GRÜNEWALD
Very Expensive

✪ **Ritz Carlton.** Brahmsstrasse 10, 14193 Berlin-Grunewald. ☎ **030/89-58-40.** Fax 030/89-58-48-00. 52 units. MINIBAR TV TEL. 595DM–780DM ($357–$468) double; from 950DM ($570) suite. AE, DC, MC, V. Parking 30DM ($18). Bus: 219.

This Italian Renaissance–style palace was built in 1912 and is a good choice for those who gravitate to German castle hotels. In 1994 it reopened after a 3-year renovation by German-born fashion superstar Karl Lagerfeld, who added grand touches such as rich brass and beautiful mahogany woodwork throughout. Rooms are larger and more elegant than the average hotel room, and come with extras like VCRs, CD players, fax machines, data ports—even "Do Not Disturb" switches on the doors. Bathrooms are just as fine; each is roomy, with marble surfaces, makeup mirrors, robes, phones, radiantly heated floors, lots of fluffy towels, and even bedroom slippers. The hotel has two restaurants; the more unusual and better one is Vivaldi's.

WHERE TO DINE

For food on the run, try one of the dozens of kebab stalls (Imbiss) that dot the streets. Some 200,000 Turks live in Berlin and the food that they've introduced—meat- or Scharfskäse-stuffed (sheep's cheese, virtually identical to feta) pitas—make a filling, cheap meal, but watch out for the cascades of cabbage. Good sit-down Turkish restaurants are harder to find, but one of the best is Hitit (Knobelsdorffstrasse 35, ☎ **030/322-45-57,** near Charlottenburg Schloss), with a full array of Turkish specialities, some 150 dishes in all. It's open daily from noon to 1am.

ON OR NEAR THE KURFÜRSTENDAMM
Very Expensive

✪ **Bamberger Reiter.** Regensburgerstrasse 7. ☎ **030/218-42-82.** Reservations required. Main courses 52DM–58DM ($31.20–$34.80); 6- or 7-course set-price menu 165DM–195DM ($99–$117). AE, DC, MC, V. Tues–Sat 6pm–1am (last order 10pm). U-Bahn: Spichernstrasse. CONTINENTAL.

Bamberger Reiter is the city's best restaurant, serving French, German, and Austrian dishes. Only Rockendorf's or Alt Luxemburg can pretend to have better fare. Don't judge it by its location in an undistinguished 19th-century apartment house. Excellent in its forthright approach to fresh ingredients and meticulous in its preparation and service, the restaurant enjoys a loyal following among Berlin's business elite. The decor evokes old Germany, with lots of mirrors and fresh flowers. The menu changes daily according to the availability of fresh ingredients and the chef's inspiration, but might include a roulade of quail, bass with Riesling sauce, lamb with beans and potato croutons, and a date strudel with almond ice cream.

Expensive

✪ **Harlekin.** In the Grand Hotel Esplanade, Lützowufer. ☎ **030/254-78-858.** Reservations recommended. Main courses 44DM–49DM ($26.40–$29.40); 4- to 6-course set-price menu 130DM–165DM ($78–$99). AE, DC, MC, V. Tues–Sat 6–11pm. Closed 3½ weeks in July (dates vary). U-Bahn: Nollendorfplatz or Wittenbergplatz. FRENCH/INTERNATIONAL.

Chefs at traditional favorites like the Kempinski were chagrined at this restaurant's success. The menu is perfectly balanced between tradition and innovation. Appetizers are likely to include such dishes as calves' consommé with crayfish or osso buco consommé with lobster spätzle. For your main course, you might be won over by the saddle of lamb baked in a spring roll or turbot roasted with mixed root vegetables.

Paris Bar. Kantstrasse 152. ☎ **030/313-80-52.** Reservations recommended. Main courses 36DM–45DM ($21.60–$27); set-price lunch 20DM ($12). AE. Daily noon–1am. U-Bahn: Uhlandstrasse. FRENCH.

This French bistro has been a local favorite since the postwar years, when two expatriate Frenchmen established the restaurant to bring a little Parisian cheer to the dismal gray of bombed-out Berlin. The place is just as crowded with elbow-to-elbow tables as a Montmartre tourist trap, but you'll find it a genuinely pleasing little eatery. It's a true restaurant on the see-and-be-seen circuit between Savignyplatz and Gedächtniskiche. The food is invariably fresh and well prepared but not particularly innovative.

Moderate

Hardtke's. Meinekestrasse 27A. ☎ **030/881-98-27.** Reservations required. Main courses 15DM–32DM ($9–$19.20); set-price menu 16.50DM–18.90DM ($9.90–$11.35) available Mon–Fri until 8pm. No credit cards. Sun–Thurs 11am–midnight; Fri–Sat 11am–1am. U-Bahn: Kurfürstendamm. BERLINER.

These Teutonic recipes haven't changed during the 40 years of Hardtke's operation. German retirees like dining here; they're fond of the cuisine they enjoyed in the 1940s and 1950s before the "new German cookery" became all the rage. You can overdose on all the potatoes and sauerkraut, the blood-and-liver sausage (from the in-house butcher shop), and the monstrous bockwurst. The true Berliner asks for the *grosse Schlachteplatte*—fresh black pudding and liver sausage, small pickled knuckle of pork, liver dumpling, shredded pickled white cabbage, mashed peas, and boiled potatoes.

Istanbul. Knesebeckstrasse 77. ☎ **030/883-27-77.** Reservations recommended. 12DM–26DM ($6.85–$14.80). AE, DC, MC, V. Open daily noon–midnight. S-Bahn: Savignyplatz. TURKISH

Vegetarians patronize Istanbul, Berlin's oldest Turkish restaurant, for its selection of hot and cold appetizers. The dark and lavishly decorated interior evokes old Constantinople (as do the belly-dancers performing in a back room). Try the stuffed grape leaves or the hummus (chickpeas with garlic), or even the meat-topped Turkish pizza. Shish kebab is the most popular item, and there is also a wide array of succulent lamb dishes. A chef's speciality is veal grilled on a roasting spit.

✪ **Marjellchen.** Mommsenstrasse 9. ☎ **030/883-26-76.** Reservations required. Main courses 19.50DM–39.50DM ($11.70–$23.70). AE, DC, MC, V. Mon–Sat 5pm–midnight. Closed Dec 23, 24, and 31. U-Bahn: Adenauerplatz or Uhlandstrasse. Bus: 109, 119, or 129. EAST PRUSSIAN.

This is the only restaurant in Berlin specializing in the cuisine of Germany's long-lost province of East Prussia, along with the cuisines of Pomerania and Silesia. Deriving its unusual name from an East Prussian word meaning "young girl," the establishment divides its space among three rooms, the first dominated by a German-style bar. Amid a Bismarckian ambience of still lifes, vested waiters, and oil lamps, you can enjoy a savory version of red-beet soup with strips of beef, East Prussian potato soup with crabmeat and bacon, *falscher Gänsebraten* (pork spareribs stuffed with prunes and bread crumbs), and *mecklenburger Kümmelfleisch* (lamb with chives and onions).

Restaurant Mario. Carmerstrasse 2. ☎ **030/312-31-15.** Reservations recommended. Main courses 15DM–35DM ($9–$21); set-price menus 25DM–70DM ($15–$42). AE, MC, V. Mon–Fri noon–midnight; Sat 4pm–1am. S-Bahn: Savignyplatz. NORTHERN ITALIAN.

Named for its owner, this restaurant serves some of the most imaginative Northern Italian food in Berlin. Originally called Fioretto Bei Cramer, it was created by an East Berliner who'd never been to Italy but wanted to "cook Italian," nevertheless. Today the chefs are fully grounded in the repertoire of Italy, and use the best market-fresh ingredients in creating their culinary offerings. The innovative and refreshing dishes might include platters of the most delectable antipasti in town or carpaccio. At least two different kinds of pastas are offered nightly, including a favorite made with a green pepper pesto. Savory ravioli and rigatoni appear several different ways.

Zlata Praha. Meinekestrasse 4. ☎ **030/881-97-50.** Reservations recommended. Main courses 20DM–35DM ($12–$21). AE, MC, V. Daily 5–11:30pm. U-Bahn: Joachimstaler Strasse. BOHEMIAN/HUNGARIAN.

Zlata Praha serves the best Bohemian cuisine of any restaurant in Berlin. German, French, and Austrian wines are featured. However, the pièce de résistance is the special tap beer, Pilsner Urquell das Echte. Many of the food items spark an instant recognition (paprika lovers take note) and evoke childhood memories from the restaurant's many regular clients. The *Szegendiner goulash* is as fine as any we've had during our tours of Hungary.

Inexpensive

Karavan. Kurfürstendamm 11. ☎ **303/881-05-05.** Reservations not necessary. Most plates 10DM ($6). No credit cards. U-Bahn to Kürfurstendamm. TURKISH.

The chefs claim (with some justification) to make the best Turkish pizza in Berlin. Sandwiches, salads, spinach-filled pastries, and even Turkish-style burgers fill out the bill of fare. There are a few bar stools inside for dining, or you can go sit on one of the benches on the square outside.

La Table. Damaschkestrasse 26. ☎ **030/323-14-04.** Reservations required. Main courses 18.50DM–36DM ($11.10–$21.60). MC, V. Mon–Sat 5pm–midnight. U-Bahn: Adenauerplatz. GERMAN.

West of the center, La Table has gained a reputation as a select dining spot and social center. Savor the recipes that much of Berlin craves, including the *Kohlroulade,* a stuffed cabbage roll, which is the best in town, but served only in winter. The *Tafelspitz,* boiled beef with vegetables, would have pleased Emperor Josef of Austria (it was his favorite dish). Look also for the market-fresh daily specials, especially if fresh fish is featured. Diners enjoy these dishes in a charmingly cluttered Berlin bistro ambience, with kitsch from all over the world.

NEAR THE MEMORIAL CHURCH & ZOO

Very Expensive

✪ **First Floor.** In the Palace Berlin Hotel, Budapesterstrasse 42. ☎ **030/25-02-10-20.** Reservations recommended. Main courses 46DM–75DM ($27.60–$45). Set-price menus 78DM ($46.80) at lunch only; 130DM–158DM ($78–$94.80) at lunch and dinner. AE, DC, MC, V. Mon–Sat noon–3pm and 6–11pm. U-Bahn: Zoologischer Garten. REGIONAL GERMAN/FRENCH.

This is the showcase restaurant within one of the most spectacular hotels ever built near the Tiergarten. Set one floor above street level, it features a perfectly orchestrated service and setting that revolves around the cuisine of master chef Rolf Schmidt. All the carefully rehearsed staff members (wine stewards and a battalion of waiters) that you might expect are on hand to smooth over the logistics and details of an upscale meal. Menu items include a terrine of veal with arugula-flavored butter; sophisticated variations of Bresse chicken; guinea fowl stuffed with foie gras and served with a truffled vinaigrette sauce; a cassolette of lobster and broad beans in a style vaguely influenced by the culinary precepts of southwestern France; filet of sole with champagne sauce; and a mascarpone mousse with lavender-scented honey.

Inexpensive

Alt Nürnberg. Berlin Europa-Center. ☎ **030/2-61-43-97.** Reservations recommended weekends. Main courses 10.50DM–30DM ($6.30–$18). AE, DC, MC, V. Daily 11:30am–11:30pm. U-Bahn: Kurfürstendamm or Zoologischer Garten. GERMAN/BAVARIAN.

This ground-level restaurant handsomely captures the ambience of an old Bavarian tavern. The food is solid German fare, standard and reliable, although hardly exciting. The house specialty is *Nürnberger Rostbratwürstl* (little finger sausages). You might begin with a typical Berlin pea soup with croutons or Hungarian *Goulashsouppe*. The Wiener schnitzel is always reliable, as are the herring salad and the pork filet in pepper sauce with broccoli. Inexpensive platters are usually a meal in themselves.

Schwejk-Prager Gasthaus. Ansbacherstrasse 4. ☎ **030/213-78-92.** Reservations recommended. Main courses 15DM–28DM ($9–$16.80). AE, DC, V. Daily 6pm–1am. U-Bahn: Wittenbergplatz. CZECH.

The taste of Eastern Europe is alive and flourishing at this bistro, where Bohemian specialties are served in generous portions. It's almost as though, at any moment, you expect to see the Hapsburg emperor, Ferdinand the gracious, arriving to proclaim, "I am the emperor and I want dumplings." There's a small bar for drinking. Try Pilsner Urquell or the original Tschech Budweiser with your food. Most of the dishes are quite decent, including specialties like crackling broiled pork shanks (*Schweinehaxen*) and large bowls of thick borscht.

IN GREATER CHARLOTTENBURG

Expensive

✪ Alt-Luxemburg. Windscheidstrasse 31. ☎ **030/323-87-30.** Reservations required. Set-price 3-course menu 95DM ($57); set-price 4-course menu 108DM ($64.80); set-price 5-course menu 118DM ($70.80); set-price 6-course menu 135DM ($81). AE, DC, MC, V. Mon–Sat 7–11pm. U-Bahn: Sophie-Charlotteplatz. CONTINENTAL.

The Bamberger Reiter might be the leader among Berlin restaurants, but the Alt-Luxemburg is nipping at its heels. Chef Karl Wannemacher is one of the most outstanding in eastern Germany. Known for his quality and market-fresh ingredients, he prepares a seductively sensual plate. Everything shows his flawless technique, especially the stuffed and stewed oxtail or the saddle of venison with elderberry sauce. Taste his excellent lacquered duck breast with honey sauce or saddle of lamb with stewed peppers. Alt-Luxemburg offers a finely balanced wine list. The service is both unpretentious and gracious.

Moderate

Ernst-August. Sybelstrasse 16. ☎ **030/324-55-76.** Reservations required. Main courses 25DM–32DM ($15–$19.20). No credit cards. Wed–Sun 6:30pm–1am (kitchen stops serving hot food at midnight). Closed July 15–Aug 15. U-Bahn: Adenauerplatz. FRENCH/INTERNATIONAL.

This unprepossessing restaurant is the type of place a local might take a friend from out of town. The setting is as quiet and unobtrusive as the antique bric-a-brac that adorns its walls. If you don't opt for the filet steak, the chef might prepare one of two variations of hare, or pork filet with gorgonzola sauce. Even the simple rumpsteak gets the care and attention of a fresh herb and green pepper sauce. This restaurant, although outclassed by dozens of establishments, still maintains a special niche.

Ponte Vecchio. Spielhagenstrasse 3. ☎ **030/342-19-99.** Reservations required. Main courses 28DM–46DM ($16.80–$27.60). DC. Wed–Mon 6:30–11pm. Closed 4 weeks in summer. U-Bahn: Bismarckstrasse. TUSCAN.

Although we've dined here many times and were moderately pleased, that impression has improved. We now view this as one of Berlin's finest Italian restaurants. It's not the most elaborately decorated restaurant, but it caters to patrons primarily concerned with what's on the plate. Market-fresh ingredients result in winning dishes with a Tuscan focus. If you don't (wisely) opt for the fresh fish of the day, you'll find any number of other dishes to tempt the palate, especially several variations of veal. Assorted shellfish is always deftly handled according to Tuscan style, with fresh basil and olive oil.

Inexpensive

Bierhaus Luisen-Braü. Luisenplatz 1, Charlottenburg. ☎ **030/341-93-88.** Reservations recommended on weekends. Salads, snacks, and platters 5DM–15DM ($3–$9). V. Sun–Thurs 9am–1am; Fri–Sat 9am–2am. U-Bahn: Richard-Wagner-Platz. GERMAN.

One of the city's largest breweries, Luisen-Bräu opened this restaurant, close to Charlottenburg Castle, in 1987. The decor includes enormous stainless-steel vats of the fermenting brew, from which the waiters happily refill your mug. There's no subtlety of cuisine here: It's robust, traditional fare, the kind Germans enjoyed "between the wars." Victuals are displayed on a long buffet table from which you serve yourself. The seating is indoor or outdoor, depending on the season, at long picnic tables that encourage a sense of beer hall camaraderie.

IN BERLIN-MITTE (EASTERN BERLIN)

Expensive

✪ **Restaurant Vau.** Jägerstrasse 54 (near the Four Seasons Hotel and the Gendamenmarkt). ☎ **030/202-9730.** Reservations recommended. Main courses 40DM–56DM ($24–$33.60). Set-price lunches 60DM ($36); set-price dinners 90DM–150DM ($54–$90). AE, DC, MC, V. Mon–Sat noon–2:30pm and 7–10:30pm. S-Bahn: Hausvoigteiplatz. CONTINENTAL.

This restaurant is the culinary showcase of up-and-coming chef Kolja Kleeberg. Menu choices, which are based on fresh and seasonal ingredients, include terrine of salmon and morels with rocket salad; aspic of suckling pig with sauerkraut; salad with marinated red mullet, mint, and almonds; crisp-fried duck with marjoram; ribs of suckling lamb with thyme-flavored polenta; and desserts such as woodruff soup with champagne-flavored ice cream. The wine list is international and well chosen.

Moderate

Französischer Hof. Jagerstrasse 56. ☎ **030/204-35-70.** Reservations recommended. Main courses 28DM–42DM ($16.80–$25.20). AE, DC, MC, V. May–Oct, daily 10am–1am; Nov–Apr, 10am–midnight. Closed Dec 24. U-Bahn: Hausvogteiplatz. GERMAN.

Französischer Hof opened its art nouveau doors in 1989. It fills two floors connected by a belle époque staircase, evoking a turn-of-the-century Paris bistro. One recent memorable dinner included roast duck breast with Calvados along with zucchini and potato pancakes. The cookery is hardly the finest in eastern Berlin, but the ingredients are fresh and deftly handled. Many guests begin with the terrific selection of fish canapés, and then proceed to the main courses. Saddle of lamb is always admirably done, as is the saddle of venison with juniper berry sauce (served with red cabbage). The white fish, zander, is grilled and appears with an herb sauce. The soups are also a delight here, especially on a winter day and especially the potato and leek.

Goldene Gans. In The Westin Grand, Friedrichstrasse 158. ☎ **030/2027-3246.** Reservations recommended. Main courses 16DM–30DM ($9.60–$18). AE, DC, MC, V. Daily 6pm–midnight. S-Bahn: Friedrichstrasse. GERMAN.

The "Golden Goose" is a deliberate contrast to the beaux arts glamour of the hotel containing it. This rustic *Stube* is one flight above the lobby. It has a wooden ceiling, colorfully embroidered napery, and an open-to-view kitchen. The cuisine is based on Thuringian recipes vividly evocative of old Germany. Although cholesterol counters shun it, the special appetizer of the kitchen (it doesn't appear on the menu) is goose fat with mixed pickles and freshly baked rolls. Goose appears in three other preparations that are very much delicacies. A host of other regional dishes is also offered, but since this place prepares the premier goose dishes in all Berlin, why order anything else?

Restaurant Borchardt. Französische Strasse 47. ☎ **030/2038-7110.** Reservations recommended. Daily specials 20DM ($12); main courses 30DM–42DM ($18–$25.20). AE, V. Daily noon–midnight. U-Bahn: Französische Strasse. FRENCH.

This restaurant is elegant, lighthearted, and fashionable among the city's artistic movers and shakers. It occupies a monumental dining area, complete with marble accents and partially gilded columns. You can order anything from a simple salad (as supermodel Claudia Schiffer often does) to the more substantial cream of potato soup with bacon and croutons; filet of carp prepared with Riesling and herbs, and finished with champagne; foie gras served with caramelized apples; chicken stuffed with morels and served with cream-and-herb sauce; and a pistachio mousse garnished with essence of fresh fruit.

Inexpensive

Keller Restaurant im Brecht-Haus. Chausseestrasse 125. ☎ **030/28-23-843.** Reservations recommended. Main courses 16DM–32DM ($9.60–$19.20). AE, DC, MC, V. Daily 11am–midnight. U-Bahn: Oranienblurger Tor. SOUTH GERMAN/AUSTRIAN.

This unusual restaurant occupies the cellar of a building where Bertolt Brecht and his wife once lived. The restaurant is trimmed with white plaster and exposed stone and has scores of photographs of the playwright's theatrical productions. It serves copious portions of traditional south German and Austrian food, including *Fleisch Laberln*— tasty meatballs made with minced pork, beef, green beans, and bacon, served with dumplings. No one will mind if you just stop for a glass of one of the restaurant's many wine offerings.

Zur Letzten Instanz. Waisenstrasse 14–16. ☎ **030/242-55-28.** Main courses 19DM–36DM ($11.40–$21.60); set-price menu 25DM–35DM ($15–$21). AE, DC, V. Mon–Sat noon–1am; Sun noon–11pm. S-Bahn: Kloster Strasse. GERMAN.

Reputedly Berlin's oldest restaurant, dating from 1525, Zur Letzten Instanz in its day was frequented by everybody from Napoléon to Beethoven. Prisoners used to stop off here for one last beer before going to jail. It occupies two floors of a baroque building whose facade is ornamented with a row of stone bas-reliefs of medieval faces. Double doors open on a series of small woodsy rooms, one with a bar and ceramic stove. At the back a circular staircase leads to another series of rooms, where every evening at 6pm, only food and wine (no beer) are served. On both floors you can select from a limited and old-fashioned menu of Berlin staples.

IN WAIDMANNSLUST

Very Expensive

✪ **Rockendorf's Restaurant.** Düsterhauptstrasse 1. ☎ **030/402-27-42.** Reservations required. Set-price lunch 110DM–175DM ($66–$105); set-price dinner 175DM–198DM ($105–$118.80). AE, DC, MC, V. Tues–Sat noon–2pm and 7–9:30pm. Closed Dec 22–Jan 6 and July. S-Bahn: Waidmannslust. CONTINENTAL.

Rockendorf's occupies a 19th-century art nouveau villa near the Englischer Garten in north Berlin, a 20-minute taxi ride from the center. Chef Siegfried Rockendorf achieves a happy marriage between modern cuisine and classic specialties. The restaurant mounts a serious challenge to the Bamberger Reiter or the Alt-Luxemburg, the only one in Berlin to do so. Try such dishes as filet of turbot in Ricard sauce, which succeeds despite being neither new nor exciting. The same could be said of the goosemeat pâté in sauterne with cranberries. The service is exquisitely refined—attentive without being cloying.

SEEING THE SIGHTS

On the Kurfürstendamm in the western part of the city, Berliners often glance at a sobering reminder of less happy days. At the end of the street stands the **Kaiser-Wilhelm-Gedächtniskirche (Kaiser Wilhelm Memorial Church),** Breitscheidplatz (☎ **030/218-5023**), with only the shell of its neo-Romanesque bell tower (1895) remaining. (You can wander through the ruins Monday to Saturday 10am to 4:30pm.) Admission is free. In striking contrast is the new church, constructed west of the old tower in 1961, and nicknamed "lipstick and powder box" by the Berliners. Its octagonal hall is lit solely by thousands of colored-glass windows set into the honeycomb framework and can hold 1,200 people. Ten-minute services are held in the church daily at 5:30 and 6pm for those going home from work. There's a Saturday concert at 6pm, and an English-language service is held daily at 9am from June to August. The church is open daily 9am to 7pm. This remarkable combination of old and new is what Berlin is all about. Although there's more new than old in this city, which was almost flattened in World War II, Berlin offers a multitude of sights for the visitor.

SIGHTSEEING SUGGESTIONS FOR FIRST-TIME VISITORS

If You Have 1 Day   Get up early and visit the **Brandenburg Gate,** that symbol of Berlin, and then walk down **Unter den Linden** and have coffee and pastry at the Operncafé. Then visit the **Gemäldegalerie** to see some of the world's greatest masterpieces. Afterward, go to **Charlottenburg Palace** and its museums to view the celebrated bust of Queen Nefertiti in the **Egyptian Museum.** In the evening, walk along the Kurfürstendamm, visit the **Kaiser Wilhelm Memorial Church,** and dine in a local restaurant.

If You Have 2 Days   On day 2, return to eastern Berlin and visit the **Pergamon Museum** on Museum Island, seeing the Pergamon Altar. Explore the **National Gallery** and the **Bode Museum,** and then head for Alexanderplatz. Take the elevator up for a view from its TV tower before exploring the **Nikolai Quarter** on foot.

If You Have 3 Days   On day 3, go to **Potsdam** (see "Day Trips from Berlin," below).

If You Have 4 or 5 Days   On day 4, visit the museums of **Dahlem,** especially the **Sculpture Gallery** and **Ethnographical Museum.** In the afternoon return to Charlottenburg Palace and explore the **Historical Apartments,** and in the evening visit the modern **Europa-Center** for drinks and dinner. On day 5, see some of the sights you might have missed. Take some walks through Berlin and stop at the cold war's **Checkpoint Charlie,** with its Museum Haus am Checkpoint Charlie. If time remains, visit the **Berlin Zoo,** stroll through the **Tiergarten,** and attend a cabaret in the evening.

THE TOP MUSEUMS
In the Tiergarten

✪ **Gemäldgalerie (Picture Gallery).** Mattäiskirchplatz 4. ☎ **030/20-90-5555.** Admission 8DM ($4.80) adults, 4DM ($2.40) children. Tues–Fri 9am–6pm; Sat–Sun 10am–5pm. U-Bahn: Kurfürstenstrasse, then bus 148. Bus 129 from Ku'damm (plus a 4-minute walk).

Opening in its new home in 1998, this is one of Germany's greatest galleries. Of the nearly 3,000 paintings it owns, some 600 or more are on display. Several rooms are devoted to early German masters, with panels from altarpieces dating from the 13th, 14th, and 15th centuries. Note the panel of *The Virgin Enthroned with Child* (1350), surrounded by angels that resemble the demons so popular in the later works of

Hieronymus Bosch. Eight paintings make up the Dürer collection in the adjacent rooms, including several portraits.

Another gallery is given over to Italian painting. Here are five Raphael Madonnas, works by Titian (*The Girl with a Bowl of Fruit*), Fra Filippo Lippi, Botticelli, and Correggio (*Leda with the Swan*). There are early Netherlands paintings from the 15th and 16th centuries (van Eyck, van der Weyden, Bosch, and Brueghel) as well.

Several galleries are devoted to Flemish and Dutch masters of the 17th century, with no fewer than 20 works by Rembrandt. Among the most famous of the great painter's works here is the *Head of Christ*. One painting, famous for years as a priceless Rembrandt, *The Man with the Golden Helmet*, was proved by radioactive testing in 1986 to have been painted in Rembrandt's era by an imitator of his style. This remarkable painting is now accepted as an independent original.

Neue Nationalgalerie (New National Galerie). Potsdamerstrasse 50 (just south of the Tiergarten). ☎ **030/2-66-26-62.** Permanent collection, 8DM ($4.80) adults, 4DM ($2.40) children; temporary exhibitions, 12DM ($7.20). Tues–Fri 10am–6pm; Sat–Sun 11am–6pm. Closed Jan 1, Dec 24–25 and 31, and the Tues after Easter and Whitsunday. U-Bahn: Kurfürstenstrasse. S-Bahn: Potsdamer Platz.

In its modern glass-and-steel home designed by Ludwig Mies van der Rohe (1886–1969), the Neue Nationalgalerie is a sequel of sorts to the art at Dahlem. It contains a continually growing collection of modern European and American art. Here you'll find works of 19th-century artists, with a concentration on French impressionists. German art starts with Adolph von Menzel's paintings from about 1850. The 20th-century collection includes works by Max Beckmann, Edvard Munch, and E. L. Kirchner's *Brandenburger Tor* (1929), as well as a few paintings by Bacon, Picasso, Ernst, Klee, and American artists such as Barnett Newman. There's food service in the cafe on the ground floor. Hot meals are served from 10:30am to 6pm.

In Charlottenburg

Charlottenburg is in the quarter of Berlin of the same name, just west of the Tiergarten. In addition to viewing the exhaustive collections in the palace buildings, you can enjoy a relaxing ramble through Schlossgarten Charlottenburg. The gardens have been restored and landscaped much as they were in the days of Friedrich Wilhelm II.

✪ **Schloss Charlottenburg (Charlottenburg Palace).** Luisenplatz. ☎ **030/32091-275.** Combined ticket for all buildings and historical rooms 15DM ($9) adults, 10DM ($6) children under 14. Guided tours of the Historical Rooms (in German), Tues–Fri 9am–5pm; Sat–Sun 10am–5pm (last tour at 4pm). U-Bahn: Sophie-Charlotte-Platz or Richard-Wagner-Platz. Bus: 109, 121, 145, or 204.

Napoléon exaggerated a bit in comparing Schloss Charlottenburg to the great Versailles when he invaded Berlin in 1806, but in its heyday this palace was the most elegant residence for the Prussian rulers outside the castle in Potsdam. Begun in 1695 as a summer palace for the Electress Sophie Charlotte, patron of philosophy and the arts and wife of King Frederick I (Elector Frederick III), the little residence got out of hand

Sightseeing Tip

The **Bodesmuseum,** Monbijoubrücke, is one of Germany's greatest museums. After a major restoration, it should reopen sometime during the life of this edition, with its vast array of Egyptian art, early Christian art, late-Gothic sculptures, and Byzantine masterpieces and huge treasure trove of masterpieces from the 1600s to the 1900s. For information on the status of this world-class museum, call ☎ **030/266-21-47.**

Charlottenburg

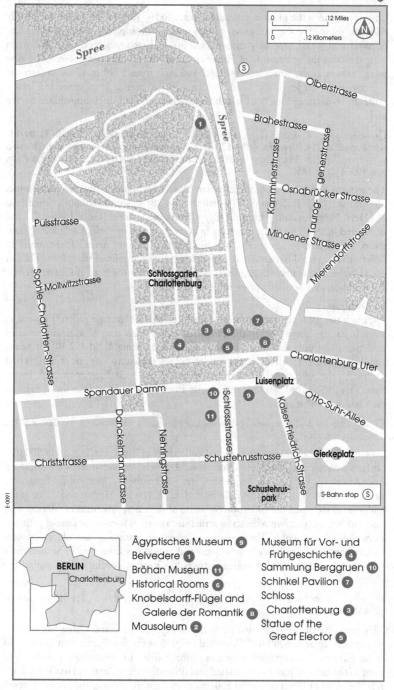

0 .12 Miles
0 .12 Kilometers

Spree

Olberstrasse

Brahestrasse

Kamminerstrasse

Osnabrücker Strasse

Taurog-generstrasse

Mindener Strasse

Mierendorffstrasse

Pulsstrasse

Sophie-Charlotten-Strasse

Mollwitzstrasse

Schlossgarten Charlottenburg

Charlottenburg Ufer

Spandauer Damm

Luisenplatz

Otto-Suhr-Allee

Danckelmannstrasse

Nehringstrasse

Schlossstrasse

Kaiser-Friedrich-Strasse

Gierkeplatz

Christstrasse

Schustehrusstrasse

Schustehrus-park

S-Bahn stop Ⓢ

E-0001

BERLIN
Charlottenburg

Ägyptisches Museum ⑨
Belvedere ①
Bröhan Museum ⑪
Historical Rooms ⑥
Knobelsdorff-Flügel and
    Galerie der Romantik ⑧
Mausoleum ②

Museum für Vor- und
    Frühgeschichte ④
Sammlung Berggruen ⑩
Schinkel Pavilion ⑦
Schloss
    Charlottenburg ③
Statue of the
    Great Elector ⑤

427

until it grew into the massive structure you see today. Parts of the palace were badly damaged during the war, but most of it has now been completely restored. Many furnishings were saved, especially the works of art, and are again on display. The main wing contains the apartments of Frederick I and his "philosopher queen." The **new wing,** known as the Knobelsdorff-Flügel and built from 1740 to 1746, shelters the apartments of Frederick the Great, which have in essence been converted into a museum of paintings, many of which were either collected or commissioned by the king.

✪ **Ägyptisches Museum (Egyptian Museum).** Schloss-strasse 70. ☎ **030/32-09-11.** Admission 8DM ($4.80) adults, 4DM ($2.40) children; free the first Sun of the month. Tues–Fri 9am–6pm; Sat–Sun 11am–6pm. U-Bahn: Sophie-Charlotte-Platz or Richard-Wagner-Platz. Bus: 109, 110, or 145.

The western Berlin branch of the Egyptian Museum is housed in the east guardhouse, built for the king's bodyguard. It's worth the trip just to see the famous colored bust of Queen Nefertiti, dating from the Egyptian Amarna period (about 1340 B.C.) and discovered in 1912. The bust, stunning in every way, is all by itself in a dark first-floor room, illuminated by a spotlight. It is believed that the bust never left the studio in which it was created but served as a model for other portraits of the queen. The left eye of Nefertiti was never drawn in. In addition, look for the head of Queen Tiy and the world-famous head of a priest in green stone.

In Dahlem

Although the greatest museum here, Gemäldegalarie (or "picture gallery") moved in 1998 to its new home (see "In the Tiergarten," above), an array of museums remains to delight. Not only that, but a combination ticket costing 4DM ($2.40) for adults and 2DM ($1.20) for children gets you into all the museums—it's one of Berlin's best values. All the collections, unless otherwise noted, are open Tuesday through Friday from 9am to 5pm and Saturday and Sunday from 10am to 5pm. Take the U-Bahn to the Dahlem-Dorf station.

✪ **Museum für Völkerkunde (Ethnological Museum).** Lansstrasse 8. ☎ **030/83011.** Admission, see above.

This is one of the greatest ethnological collections of earth, totaling some 500,000 artifacts from all continents, even prehistoric America. Art and artifacts are displayed from Africa, the Far East, the South Seas, and South America. Many of the figures are ritualistic masks and are grotesquely beautiful. The Incan, Mayan, and Aztec stone sculpture alone equal the collections of some of the finest museums of Mexico. The best part is the collections of boats in actual size as well as homes and facades gathered from around the globe. The museum displays an intriguing assemblage of pre-Columbian relics, including gold objects and antiquities from Peru. The museum's Department of Music allows visitors to hear folk music recordings from around the globe.

Museum für Ostasiatische Kunst (Museum of Far Eastern Art). Lansstrasse 8. ☎ **030/8301-382.** Admission, see above.

This gem of a museum devoted primarily to Japan, Korea, and China has artifacts dating back as far as 3000 B.C. Launched in 1906 as the first Far Eastern museum of art in Germany, this museum is one of Europe's finest in presenting an overview of some of the most exquisite ecclesiastical and decorative art to come out of the Far East. It is the equal or better of similar collections in Paris. In essence, the museum represents the loot acquired during a massive "shopping expedition" the Germans took to the Orient, where they even managed to garner the 17th-century imperial throne of China, all lacquered and inlaid with mother-of-pearl. The Japanese woodblock prints, each seemingly more exquisite than the next, are reason enough to visit.

Museum for Islamische Kunst (Museum of Islamic Art). Lansstrasse 8. ☎ **030/ 209-0540-1.** Admission 8DM ($4.80) adults, 4DM ($2.40) children under 18. Tues–Sun 10am–6pm.

This collection, one of the most impressive in all of Europe, traces the culture of Islam around the world. Artifacts and art from most Islamic countries from the 8th to the 18th centuries are on display. A virtual Arabian Nights fantasy-land comes alive here, with carpets, glass, jewelry, pottery, examples of Arabic script, whatever. Some of the Persian carpets are among the finest extant in the world. Some exhibits, including a 9th-century Koran parchment, are nearly priceless. There are also rare illuminated manuscripts and tapestries hang from the ceiling to floor.

Museum für Indische Kunst (Museum of Indian Art). Lansstrasse 8. ☎ **030/ 8301-361.** Admission, see above.

Germany's greatest collection of Indian art is on exhibit here, covering a span of 40 centuries. It's an international parade of some of the finest art and artifacts from the world of Buddhism; countries represented include Burma, Thailand, Indonesia, Nepal, and Tibet.

Museum für Deutsche Volkskunde (Museum of German Ethnology). Im Winkel 6–8. ☎ **030/839-0101.** Admission, see above.

Outside the Dahlem museum complex, but only a 5-minute walk away, this museum is devoted to the German people themselves—not the aristocrats but the middle class and the peasant stock who built the country. It is a true "museum of the people." The exhibits go back 4 centuries, tracing how artisans and homemakers lived and worked. Household items are displayed, along with primitive industrial equipment such as a utensil for turning flax into linen. Furnishings, clothing, pottery, and even items used in religious observances are displayed, along with some fun and whimsical exhibits, including depictions of pop culture from the 1950s through the '80s.

Museumsinsel (Museum Island)

✪ **Pergamon Museum.** Kupfergraben, Museumsinsel. ☎ **030/2090-50.** Admission 8DM ($4.80) adults, 4DM ($2.40) children; free the first Sun of the month. Tues–Sun 9am–5pm. U-Bahn/S-Bahn: Friedrichstrasse. Tram: 1, 2, 3, 4, 5, 13, 15, or 53.

The Pergamon Museum complex houses several departments, but if you have time for only one exhibit, go to the central hall of the U-shaped building to see the **Pergamon Altar.** This Greek altar (180–160 B.C.) is so large it has a huge room all to itself. Some 27 steps lead from the museum floor up to the colonnade. Most fascinating is the frieze around the base, tediously pieced together over a 20-year period. Depicting the struggle of the Olympian gods against the Titans as told in Hesiod's *Theogony,* the relief is strikingly alive, with its figures projected as much as a foot from the background. This, however, is only part of the attraction of the **Department of Greek and Roman Antiquities,** housed in the north and east wings. You'll also find a Roman market gate discovered in Miletus and sculptures from many Greek and Roman cities, including a statue of a goddess holding a pomegranate (575 B.C.), found in southern Attica. The **Near East Museum,** in the south wing, contains one of the largest collections anywhere of antiquities discovered in the lands of ancient Babylonia, Persia, and Assyria. Among the exhibits is the Processional Way of Babylon with the Ishtar Gate, from 580 B.C.

Altes Museum. Bodestrasse. Museumsinsel. ☎ **030/20-90-5555.** Admission 8DM ($4.80), 4DM ($2.40) children. Tues–Sun 9am–5pm. S-Bahn: Hackescher Markt or Friedrichstrasse, followed by a 10-minute walk. Bus: 100 to Lustgarten.

Karl Friedrich Schinkel, the city's greatest architect, designed this structure which resembles a Greek Corinthian temple. It first opened its doors to the public in 1876. On its main floor is the **Antikensammlung,** or Museum of Greek and Roman Antiquities. This great collection of world-famous works of antique decorative art was inaugurated in 1960. It's rich in pottery from ancient Greece and Italy; Greek, Etruscan, and Roman bronze statuettes and implements; ivory carvings, glassware, objects in precious stone, and jewelry of the Mediterranean region, as well as gold and silver treasures; mummy portraits from Roman Egypt; wood and stone sarcophagi; and a few marble sculptures. The collection includes some of the finest Greek vases of the black-and red-figures style dating from the 6th to the 4th centuries B.C. The best known is a large Athenian wine jar (*amphora*) found in Vulci, Etruria, dating from 490 B.C., which shows a satyr with a lyre and the god Hermes.

The **Alte Nationalgalerie** above is presently closed for renovation, but some of its major art works—approximately 150—are still on display. Created as a museum of contemporary art, the gallery displays paintings and sculpture from the end of the 18th to the beginning of the 20th centuries, including works by van Gogh, Manet, Monet, Renoir, and Cézanne. The gallery is especially proud to own the world's largest collection of Adolph von Menzel, a famous Berlin artist. The full gallery is scheduled to reopen in 2002.

OTHER MUSEUMS

Deutsche Guggenheim Berlin. Unter den Linden 13–15. ☎ **030/2020-930.** Admission 8DM ($4.80) adults, 5DM ($3) children. Daily 11am–8pm. S-Bahn: Unter den Linden.

Opened in the autumn of 1997, this state-of-the-art museum is a joint venture of the Deutsche Bank and the Solomon R. Guggenheim Foundation, and is devoted to organizing and presenting exhibitions of modern and contemporary art. At the intersection of Unter den Linden and Charlottenstrasse, two of the most historic streets of Berlin, the exhibition space on the ground floor of the newly restored Berlin branch of Deutsche Bank was designed by Richard Gluckman.

The Guggenheim Foundation conceives, organizes, and installs several exhibitions at this site annually, and also presents exhibitions of newly commissioned works created specifically for this exhibition space by world-renowned artists. The bank is also a major player, supporting young artists from the German-speaking world by purchasing their works and displaying them throughout the company's offices and public spaces. In addition to modern artists, exhibitions in the past have ranged from everybody from Picasso and Cézanne to Andy Warhol.

✪ Die Sammlung Berggruen: Picasso und Seine Zeit (The Berggruen Collection: Picasso and his Era). Schlosstrasse 1. ☎ **030/830-1466.** Admission 8DM ($4.80) adults, 4DM ($2.40) students and children. Tues–Fri 9am–6pm; Sat–Sun 11am–6pm. U-Bahn: Sophie-Charlotte-Platz, followed by a 10-minute walk. Bus: 109 or 145.

One of the most unusual private museums in Berlin has accumulated the awesome private collection of respected art and antiques dealer Heinz Berggruen. A native of Berlin who fled the Nazis in 1936, he later established a mini-empire of antique dealerships in Paris and California before returning, with his collection, to his native home in 1996. There's a distinct likelihood that octogenarian Mr. Berggruen himself, who maintains an apartment adjacent to his museum, might be conducting a lecture on his favorite painter or strolling among his paintings sometime during your visit. The setting, which was provided after extensive negotiations by the city of Berlin, is a

Berlin-Mitte (Eastern Berlin)

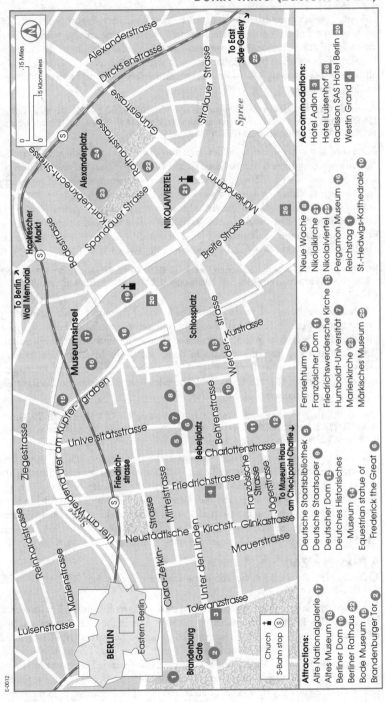

Attractions:
Alte Nationalgalerie 17
Altes Museum 18
Berliner Dom 19
Berliner Rathaus 22
Bode Museum 15
Brandenburger Tor 2
Deutsche Staatsbibliothek 5
Deutsche Staatsoper 9
Deutscher Dom 12
Deutsches Historisches
Museum 11
Equestrian statue of
Frederick the Great 6
Fernsehturm 24
Französischer Dom 1
Friedrichswerdersche Kirche 13
Humboldt-Universität 7
Marienkirche 23
Märkisches Museum 25
Neue Wache 8
Nikolaikirche 21
Nikolaiviertel 25
Pergamon Museum 16
Reichstag 1
St.-Hedwigs-Kathedrale 10

Accommodations:
Hotel Adlon 3
Hotel Luisenhof 26
Radisson SAS Hotel Berlin 20
Westin Grand 4

431

renovated former army barracks designed by noted architect August Stüler in 1859. Although most of the collection is devoted to Picasso, there are also works by such artists as Cézanne, Braque, Klee, and van Gogh. Some 60 or more works in all, the Picasso collection alone is worth the trip, with art ranging from his teenage efforts to all of his major "periods." You'll find its entrance across from the Egyptian Museum, in Charlottenburg.

Käthe-Kollwitz-Museum. Fasanenstrasse 24. ☎ **030/882-52-10.** Admission 8DM ($4.80) adults, 4DM ($2.40) children and students. Wed–Mon 11am–6pm. U-Bahn: Uhland-strasse or Kurfürstendamm. Bus: 109, 119, 129, 219, or 249.

More than any other museum in Germany, this one reflects the individual sorrow of the artist whose work it contains. Some visitors call it a personalized revolt against the agonies of war, as well as a welcome change from the commercialism of the nearby Ku'damm. Established in 1986, it was inspired by Berlin-born Käthe Kollwitz, an ardent socialist, feminist, and pacifist whose stormy social commentary led to the eventual banning of her works by the Nazis. Many Kollwitz works show the agonies of wartime separation of mother and child, inspired in part by her loss of a son in Flanders during World War I and a grandson during World War II.

Märkisches Museum. Am Källnischen Park 5. ☎ **030/30-86-60.** Admission 3DM ($1.80) adults, 1DM (60¢) children. Tues–Sun 10am–6pm. U-Bahn: Märkisches Museum. Bus: 147, 240, or 265.

The full cultural history of Berlin is displayed in one of the most prominent buildings on the banks of the Spree; 42 rooms contain collections of artifacts from excavations, plus such art treasures as Slav silver items and Bronze Age finds. You can learn about Berlin's theaters and literature, the arts in Berlin and in the March of Brandenburg, and the life and work of Berlin artists. Most visitors like the array of mechanical musical instruments that can be played Wednesday from 3 to 4pm and Sunday from 11am to noon, for an extra 2DM ($1.20).

Museum Haus am Checkpoint Charlie. Friedrichstrasse 44. ☎ **030/253-72-50.** Admission 8DM ($4.80) adults, 5DM ($3) children. Daily 9am–10pm. U-Bahn: Kochstrasse or Stadt-mitte. Bus: 129.

This small building houses exhibits depicting the tragic events leading up to and following the erection of the former Berlin Wall. You can see some of the instruments of escape used by East Germans. Photos document the construction of the wall, the establishment of escape tunnels, and the postwar history of both parts of Berlin from 1945 until today, including the airlift of 1948–49. One of the most moving exhibits is the display on the staircase of drawings by schoolchildren who, in 1961–62, were asked to depict both halves of Germany in one picture.

A PARK & A ZOO

✪ **Tiergarten.** From the Bahnhof Zoo to the Brandenburger Tor. Bus: 100, 141, or 341 to Grosser Stern.

Tiergarten, the largest green space in central Berlin, covers just under 1 square mile, with more than 14 miles of meandering walkways. Late in the 19th century, partially to placate growing civic unrest, it was opened to the public, with a layout formalized by one of the leading landscape architects of the era, Peter Josef Lenné. The park was devastated during World War II, and the few trees that remained were chopped down for fuel as Berlin shuddered through the winter of 1945–46. Beginning in 1955, trees were replanted and alleyways, canals, ponds, and flower beds rearranged in their orig-inal patterns through the cooperative efforts of many landscape architects.

The park's largest monuments include the Berlin Zoo, described below, and the **Golden Goddess of Victory** (*Die Siegessäule*), which perches atop a soaring red-granite pedestal from a position in the center of the wide boulevard (Strasse des 17 Juni) that neatly bisects the Tiergarten into roughly equivalent sections.

✪ **Zoologischer Garten Berlin (Berlin Zoo).** Hardenbergplatz 8. ☎ **030/25-40-10.** Zoo, 12DM ($7.20) adults, 6DM ($3.60) children. Aquarium, 12DM ($7.20) adults, 6DM ($3.60) children. Combined ticket 19DM ($11.40) adults, 9.50DM ($5.70) children. Zoo, Apr–Oct daily 9am–6:30pm; Nov–Mar daily 9am–5pm. Aquarium, year-round, daily 9am–6pm. S-Bahn/U-Bahn: Zoologischer Garten.

Occupying most of the southwest corner of Tiergarten is Germany's oldest and finest zoo. Founded in 1844, it's a short walk north from the Ku'damm. Until World War II, the zoo boasted thousands of animals of every imaginable species and description—many familiar to Berliners by nicknames. The tragedy of the war struck here as well, and by the end of 1945, only 91 animals remained. Since the war the city has been rebuilding its large and unique collection; today more than 13,000 animals are housed here, some to prevent their extinction. The zoo has Europe's most modern birdhouse, with more than 550 species. The most valuable inhabitants here are giant pandas.

ORGANIZED TOURS

BUS & BOAT TOURS   Some of the best tours are operated by **Severin + Kühn,** Kurfürstendamm 216 (☎ **030/880-41-90**), which offers half a dozen tours of Berlin and its environs. Their 2-hour **"12 Stops City Tour"** departs at 30-minute intervals every day of the year between 10am and 3pm November to April, and 10am and 4pm May to October. Priced at 30DM ($18) per person, the tour passes most of the important attractions using buses equipped with taped commentaries in eight languages of the sights en route. Among the attractions visited are the Europa-Center, the Brandenburg Gate, and Unter den Linden.

You can supplement this bus tour with a 3-hour boat ride on the Spree, which carries you past the riverbanks and among some of the backwater harbors that are difficult to access except by water. The boat-tour supplement is available only between May and October, with departures every day from 10:30am to 1pm, for a cost of 42DM ($25.20) each. The Severin & Kühn drivers and staff, at the end of the bus tour portion of the experience, deposit you at the appropriate quays (either adjacent to the Berliner Dom or in the Nicolaiviertel, depending on the day of your visit) in time for the boat's departure.

More appealing and personalized is the 3-hour **"Big Berlin Tour,"** which departs at 10am and 2pm daily, costs around 39DM ($23.40) per person, and—depending on the itinerary—usually incorporates sights not included on the shorter tour. Among the attractions is a section of the Grünewald Forest.

One interesting tour lasts 4 hours and visits Potsdam, especially Sans Souci Palace, former residence of Frederick the Great. The price is 59DM ($35.40) per person. Departures are at 10am every Tuesday through Sunday throughout the year. Between May and October, there are additional departures every Friday, Saturday, and Sunday at 2:15pm.

THE SHOPPING SCENE

The central shopping destinations are **Kurfürstendamm, Tauentzienstrasse, Am Zoo,** and **Kantstrasse.** You might also want to walk up streets that intersect with Tauentzienstrasse: Marburger, Ranke, and Nürnberger. Most stores are open Monday through Friday from 9 or 10am until 6 or 6:30pm. Many stores stay open late on

Thursday evening, usually until about 8:30pm. Saturday hours for most stores are 9 or 10am until 2pm.

Berlin's largest indoor shopping center, topped by the Mercedes-Benz star, is the **Europa-Center,** Breitscheidplatz Tauentzienstrasse (☎ **030/348-0088**), in the heart of the western city. Take the U-Bahn to Kurfürstendamm. You'll find the Berlin casino and a number of restaurants and cafes, in addition to an array of shops offering wide-ranging merchandise.

THREE STORES WORTH A LOOK

Kaufhaus des Westens. Wittenbergplatz. ☎ **030/21-21-0.**

Known popularly as KaDeWe (pronounced "kah-day-vay"), this luxury department store is about 2 blocks from the Kurfürstendamm. The huge store, whose name means "department store of the west," was established some 75 years ago. Displaying extravagant items, it's known mainly for its sixth-floor food department. It's been called the greatest food emporium in the world. More than 1,000 varieties of German sausages are displayed, and delicacies from all over the world are shipped in.

✪ **KPM.** Kurfürstendamm 26A. ☎ **030/88-67-21-10.**

Despite its abbreviated name, this is one of Europe's most prestigious emporiums of luxury dinnerware. Königliche Porzellan Manufaktur was founded in 1763 when Frederick the Great invested his personal funds in a lackluster porcelain factory and elevated it to royal status. Each item is hand-painted, hand-decorated, and hand-packed in almost unbreakable formats that can be shipped virtually anywhere.

Wertheim. Kurfürstendamm 231. ☎ **030/8800-3206.**

Located in the heart of the city near the Kaiser Wilhelm Memorial Church and the Europa-Center, this is a good all-around store for travel aids and general basics. It sells a number of perfumes, clothing for the entire family, jewelry, electrical devices, household goods, photography supplies, and souvenirs. It also has a shoe-repair section. Shoppers can fuel up at a large restaurant with a grand view over half the city.

BERLIN'S MARKETS

Berliner Antik & Flohmarkt, in the S-Bahn station on Friedrichstrasse (☎ **030/208-2645**), is one of Berlin's latest flea markets. Some 100 vendors try to tempt buyers with porcelain, brassware, and assorted bric-a-brac. Some have new or used clothing and others might even be selling World War II mementos. The market is open Monday and Wednesday to Sunday 11am to 6pm. The **Turkish Bazaar** is held on the bank of the Maybachufer in Kreuzberg. This area adjacent to the Maybachufer Canal has been converted by Germany's "guest workers." Although much of the merchandise involves food, especially grilled kebabs, there's also a good selection of jewelry, glassware, onyx, and copper items. To reach the bazaar, take the U-Bahn to Kottbusser Tor, followed by a 5-minute walk. The market is open Tuesday and Friday noon to 6:30pm. The Friday market is busier and is the best time to attend if you have a choice.

BERLIN AFTER DARK

The German *Zitty* and *Tip* include some listings in English, and keep you informed about nightlife and cultural venues. Both *Berlin Programm* and *Kultur!news* also contain theater listings and other diversions. Performance arts are also covered in *Berlin,* a quarterly published in both English and German. These pamphlets and magazines are available at news kiosks.

THE PERFORMING ARTS

✪ **Berliner Philharmonisches Orchester (Berlin Philharmonic).** Matthäikirchstrasse 1. ☎ **030/254-88-0.** Tickets 26DM–80DM ($15.60–$48); special concerts 40DM–250DM ($24–$150). Bus: 148.

The Berlin Philharmonic is one of the world's premier orchestras. Claudio Abbado is music director. Its home, the **Philharmonie,** is a significant piece of modern architecture; you might want to visit even if you do not attend a performance. None of the 2,218 seats is more than 100 feet from the rostrum. The box office is open in the main lobby Monday through Friday 3:30 to 6pm and Saturday and Sunday 11am to 2pm. You can't place orders by phone. If you're staying in a first-class or deluxe hotel, you can usually get the concierge to obtain seats for you. Located in the Tiergarten sector, the hall can be reached from the center of the Ku'damm by taking bus no. 129.

✪ **Deutsche Oper Berlin.** Bismarckstrasse 35. ☎ **030/34-384-01.** Tickets 17DM–142DM ($10.20–$85.20). U-Bahn: Deutsche Oper and Bismarckstrasse. S-Bahn: Charlottenburg. Bus: 101 or 109.

The famed Berlin Opera performs in one of the world's great opera houses, built on the site of the prewar opera house in Charlottenburg. The present structure is a notable example of modern theater architecture that seats 1,885. A ballet company performs once a week. Concerts, including Lieder evenings, are also presented on the opera stage.

Deutsche Staatsoper (German State Opera). Unter den Linden 7. ☎ **030/ 20-35-45-55.** Tickets, concerts 12DM–65DM ($7.20–$39); opera 12DM–145DM ($7.20–$87). U-Bahn: Französische Strasse.

Because of the east-west split, Berlin has two famous opera companies. The Deutsche Staatsoper presents some of the finest opera in the world, along with a regular repertoire of ballet and concerts. Its home is a reproduction of the original 1740s Staatsoper, destroyed in World War II. The box office generally sells tickets Monday through Friday 10am to 6pm and Saturday and Sunday noon to 6pm. The opera closes from late June to the end of August.

Komische Oper Berlin. Behrensstrasse 55–57. ☎ **030/479-974-0.** Tickets 15DM–108DM ($9–$64.80). S-Bahn: Friedrichstrasse or Unter den Linden. U-Bahn: Französische Strasse.

Komische Oper lies in the middle of the city near Brandenburger Tor. Over the years, the opera has become one of the most innovative theater ensembles in Europe, presenting many avant-garde productions. The box office is open Monday through Saturday 11am to 7pm, and Sunday 1pm until 1½ hours before the performance.

CABARET

Die Stachelschweine. Tauentzienstrasse and Budapester Strasse (in the basement of Europa-Center). ☎ **030/261-47-95.** Cover 20DM–38DM ($12–$22.80). U-Bahn: Kurfürstendamm.

If you know how to sing "Life is a cabaret, old chum," in German no less, you may enjoy an evening in this postwar "Porcupine." Like its namesake, it pokes prickly fun at German and often American politicians. Get a ticket early because the Berliners love this one. Tickets can be purchased at the box office Tuesday to Friday 10am to 2pm and 3 to 7:30pm and Saturday 10am to 2pm and 3 to 8:45pm. Shows are presented Tuesday to Friday at 7:30pm and Saturday at 6 and 8:45pm. The cabaret is closed during the month of July.

Wintergarten. Potsdamer Strasse 96. ☎ **030/230-88-230.** Cover Fri–Sat 59DM–98DM ($35.40–$58.80), Sun–Thurs 35DM–80DM ($21–$48), depending on the seat. Price includes first drink. U-Bahn: Kurfürstenstrasse.

Opened in 1893 as one of the most popular purveyors of vaudeville in Europe, the Wintergarten operated in fits and starts throughout the war years, until it was demolished in 1944 by Allied bombers. In 1992 a modernized design reopened. Today, it's the largest and most nostalgic Berlin cabaret, laden with schmaltzy reminders of yesteryear and staffed with chorus girls; magicians from America, Britain, and countries of the former Soviet bloc; circus acrobats; political satirists; and musician/dancer combos. Shows begin Monday through Friday at 8pm, Saturday 6pm and 10pm, and Sunday at 6pm. Shows last around 2¼ hours.

MUSIC CLUBS

A-Trane. Bleibtreustrasse 1. ☎ **030/313-25-50.** Cover 10DM–20DM ($6–$12), depending on whoever happens to be playing. S-Bahn: Savignyplatz.

The name is a hybrid of the old big-band standard "Take the A-Train," with the *e* derived from the name of the legendary John Coltrane. At this small and smoky jazz house, virtually everyone seems to have a working familiarity with great names from the jazz world's past and present. It's open Wednesday through Saturday at 9pm, with musicians from all over the world. Music begins around 10pm. Closing hours vary.

Ewige Lampe. Niebuhrstrasse 11A. ☎ **030/324-39-18.** Wed–Sun 8pm–2am, live music from 9pm. Cover 10DM–20DM ($6–$12). S-Bahn: Savignyplatz.

Popular, well managed, and noted for its revolving array of international jazz acts, this place was originally established in 1964 as a working-class restaurant near the Savignyplatz. In 1988, the owners abandoned their preoccupation with food and transformed the place into a hard-drinking enclave of jazz—blues, boogie-woogie, New Orleans, and traditional.

Far Out. Kurfürstendamm 156. ☎ **030/320-00-717.** Tues–Sun 10am–4 to 6am. Cover 6DM–10DM ($3.60–$6). U-Bahn: Adenauerplatz.

Large and artfully drab, this industrial-looking disco plays danceable rock from the '70s to the '90s that manages to get hundreds of high-energy dancers up and out on the floors. Clientele includes lots of students and artists, who dress up in artfully bizarre clothing that has lots of punk-rock overtones. The place really comes alive only after midnight.

Knaack-Klub. Greifswalderstrasse 224. ☎ **030/442-7060.** Nightly from 10pm. Cover 5DM–10DM ($3–$6). S-Bahn: Hackescher Markt.

This four-story club features a live music venue, two floors of dancing, and a floor dedicated to games. They usually have four live rock shows a week, with a fairly even split between German and international touring bands. The music ranges from techno to hip-hop to '80s. Disco music is played on Wednesday, Friday, and Saturday nights.

Opernschänke. In the Opernpalais, Unter den Linden 5. ☎ **030/20-26-83.** Thurs–Sat 6pm–1am, Sun 11pm–8am. No cover. U-Bahn: Friedrichstrasse. Bus: 100.

The premises that contain this popular jazz club were built in 1762, a fact that seems to add a certain importance to a setting that's undeniably historic and to the artists who perform their music live. The venue is big-band swing, something many Berliners remember from childhood, which gets lots of acclaim.

DANCE CLUBS

E-Werk. Wilhelmstrasse 43. ☎ **030/617-93-70.** Open Fri–Sat 11pm–5 to 8am. Cover, Fri–Sat 15DM–20DM ($9–$12). U-Bahn: Mohrenstrasse.

Local clubbies define this former power station as "the apotheosis of techno," complete with industrial machines and colored strobe lights. Several bars and nonstop beats keep the place lively—that is, if you show up after 1am. The largest dance floor is in the cavernous main hall. The old power station machinery is still scattered about, which adds to the offbeat ambience but doesn't make room for any chill-out area. To wind down, you have to escape to the outside courtyard. A lot of gays show up on Saturday.

Metropole. Nollendorfplatz 5, Schöneberg. ☎ **030/217-36-80.** Fri–Sat 9pm–6am. Cover 20DM ($12). U-Bahn: Nollendorfplatz.

One of the leading dance clubs in Berlin opens only on weekends and attracts patrons aged 18 to 38. Built as a theater around the turn of the century, Metropole hosts live concerts and offers special events (by special arrangement only) for gay people.

SO 36. Oranienstrasse 190. ☎ **030/61-40-13-06.** Cover 8DM–10DM ($4.80–$6). U-Bahn: Görlitzer Bahnhof.

Gays, straights, and everybody in between show up here for wild action and frantic dancing into the wee hours. A young, vibrant Kreuzberg crowd is attracted to this joint where the scene changes nightly. On Wednesday it's strictly gay and lesbian disco. On Friday and Saturday the parties "get really wild, man," as the bartender accurately promised. Thursday, however, is for devotees of hard-core, ska, and metal. Open Wednesday through Saturday from 11pm until "we feel like closing," and on Sunday from 5 to 11pm.

Tresor Globus. Leipzigerstrasse 8. ☎ **030/229-06-11.** Cover, Wed 5DM ($3), 10DM ($6) Fri, 15DM–20DM ($9–$12) Sat–Sun. U-Bahn: Mohrenstrasse.

One of Berlin's most rocking techno venues, this club has been packing 'em in since 1991. The building had once been part of Globus Bank. Downstairs there's still a bunkerlike atmosphere with prison-type metal bars and harsh acoustics. However, the spacious dance floor upstairs has lighter house sounds. There's also a bar in the back when you want to chill out. In summer tables are placed outside, with lights strung among the shrubbery. Grilled food is served here, and DJs keep the music blasting. The club is open from 10pm Wednesday and from 11pm Friday through Sunday. It often closes at 6am.

POPULAR BARS

In the heart of old East Berlin, a complex of about 30 bars, shops, and restaurants, called **Die Hackeschen Höfe,** is one of the best places to drink in the evening. Take the S-Bahn to Hackescher Markt. The stylish and hip mini-mall attracts counterculture denizens. You can wander through the galleries, boutiques, and cafes; the most happening spot is **Oxymoron,** in the courtyard of the complex at Rosenthaler Strasse 40–41 (☎ **030/283-91-88-5**), whose red-velvet decor evokes Jazz Age decadence. The site is primarily a restaurant and bar rather than a night club, although some form of live music begins most evenings at 8pm. Menu items are international, and themes range from "gangster nights" to just dancing and jazz. The club is open daily from 11am to 1am (dining), although the bar doesn't shut down until 3am.

Hip, multinational, and breezy, **Madonna Bar,** Weiner Strasse 22 (☎ **030/ 611-69-42**), is a regular fixture with the city's musicians and artists, and is known to virtually every student in the German capital. The building housing it once functioned as a police station. Few vestiges of that original function still remain, a fact that's appreciated by the counterculture crowd that makes this place sociable. They kibbutz, hobknob, and flirt in a large space that's capped with a ceiling fresco inspired by the Italian Renaissance, in the middle of which a Madonna reigns—that is, the original one. There's a limited roster of food items available, including chili, which costs 6.50DM ($3.90) a bowl. More visible are at least 100 brands of scotch, many of them single malts, and 20 North American bourbons. The focal point of the place is a crowded square-shaped bar, which is ringed with only about a dozen tables. Open daily 1pm to 3am. U-Bahn: Görlitzer Bahnhof or bus 129.

CAFES

At the turn of the century, the **Café Adlon,** Kurfürstendamm 69 (☎ **030/883-76-82;** U-Bahn: Adenauerplatz), was one of the most prestigious cafes in its neighborhood. It still offers charming summer vistas from its sidewalk tables and a view of Berlin kitsch from its interior. You'll find a huge selection of cakes. Open daily 8am to 11pm.

The family-owned **Café/Bistro Leysieffer,** Kurfürstendamm 218 (☎ **030/885-74-80;** U-Bahn: Kurfürstendamm), opened in the early 1980s in what had been the Chinese embassy. The street level contains a pastry and candy shop, but most clients climb the flight of stairs to a marble- and wood-sheathed cafe with a balcony overlooking the busy Ku'damm. The breakfast menu is one of the most elegant in town: Parma ham, smoked salmon, a fresh baguette, French butter, and—to round it off—champagne. Open Sunday to Thursday 10am to 8pm, Friday and Saturday 10am to 10pm, and Sunday 10am to 7pm.

✪ **Café Kranzler,** Kurfürstendamm 18–19 (☎ **030/882-69-11;** U-Bahn: Kurfürstendamm), one of Berlin's most famous and visible cafes, opened in 1825 on the eastern side of Berlin, near Unter den Linden. About a century later, it moved to the then less-imposing district around the Kürstendamm. Today owned by Swiss investors, the cafe/restaurant offers a variety of Swiss specialties, among them shredded veal Zurich style. Also available are ice creams, pastries, coffee, and drinks. Open daily 8am to midnight.

GAY & LESBIAN BERLIN

Andreas Kneipe. Ansbacher Strasse 29. ☎ **030/218-32-57.** Daily 11am–4am. U-Bahn: Wittenbergplatz.

It's as warm, cozy, and convivial as many of the other traditional bars scattered throughout Berlin, with a distinct appeal for the many gay men and women who consider it their neighborhood hangout. It's been in business since 1938, making it the oldest gay bar in Berlin. Few of the clients dance, and there's no food served, so this is a place just to talk and drink in a convivial setting.

Begine Café-und-Kulturzentrum für Frauen. Potsdamerstrasse 139. ☎ **030/215-43-25.** No cover. Daily 6pm–1am. U-Bahn: Bülowstrasse. Bus: 119 or 48.

The Café-und-Kulturzentrum für Frauen, established in 1986, is one of Berlin's most visible headquarters for feminists and the most obvious place for women seeking to meet other women. Within its inner sanctums is a changing array of art exhibitions, poetry readings, German-language discussions, lectures, and social events. You can phone in advance for the schedule. The premises are occasionally transformed into a disco.

KitKat Klub. Glogauerstrasse 2. ☎ **030/611-3833.** Cover 10DM–20DM ($6–$12). U-Bahn: Hermannplatz.

This dance club is popular with both heteros and gays, and it's renowned for its uninhibited SEXSEXSEX, including copulation between couples of various persuasions. Some people actually wear clothing; others prefer more immodest garb. In this fluorescent joint, you're told to check your inhibitions at the door. There's a party on Sunday from 8am to 7pm when more clothing is worn. For some hard-core male action, show up for the homoerotic Naked Sex Party night on Thursday—for men only! The club is open Tuesday through Sunday from 11pm.

Kumpelnest 3000. Lützowstrasse 23. ☎ **030/2616-918.** U-Bahn: Kurfürstenstrasse.

Both gays and heteros are welcomed here. All that's asked is that you enjoy a kinky nightclubbing good time in what used to be a Berlin brothel. It's really a bar, but there's dancing to disco classics. Berliners often show up here for early-morning fun after they've exhausted the action at the other hot spots. It's crowded and chaotic. Open daily from 5pm to 5am, but if the house crowd merits it, they'll stay open even later on weekends.

DAY TRIPS FROM BERLIN

POTSDAM   Of all the tours possible from Berlin, the three-star attraction is the baroque town of Potsdam, 15 miles southwest of Berlin on the Havel River, often called Germany's Versailles. From the beginning of the 18th century, it was the residence and garrison town of the Prussian kings. Soviet propagandists once called it a "former cradle of Prussian militarism and reactionary forces." World attention focused on Potsdam from July 17 to August 2, 1945, when the Potsdam Conference shaped postwar Europe.

The center of town is **Sans Souci Park,** with palaces and gardens, which lies to the west of the historic core. In the northern part of the town is the New Garden, on the Heiliger See, a mile northwest of Sans Souci. This garden contains the Cecilienhof Palace.

Getting There   There are 29 daily connections with the rail stations of Berlin, taking 23 minutes to/from the Bahnhof Zoo in Berlin and 54 minutes to/from the Berliner Hauptbahnhof. For rail information in Potsdam, call ☎ **0331/322-386.** Potsdam can also be reached by S-Bahn lines S3, S4, and S7 of the Berlin rapid-transit system, connecting at Wannsee station with lines R1, R3, and R4 (trip time: 30 minutes). Car access is via the E-30 autobahn east and west or the E-53 north and south.

Visitor Information   For tourist information, contact **Potsdam-Information,** Friedrich-Ebert-Strasse 5 (☎ **0331/275580**). Its hours are April to October Monday to Friday 9am to 8pm, Saturday 10am to 6pm, and Sunday 10am to 4pm; November to March Monday to Friday 10am to 6pm and Saturday to Sunday 10am to 2pm.

Exploring Potsdam   With its palaces and gardens, ✪ **Sans Souci** (or Sanssouci) **Park,** Zur historischen Mühle (☎ **0331/96-94-202**), was the work of many architects and sculptors. The park covers an area of about a square mile. Once at Potsdam, you might consider an organized tour of the park and palaces: 10DM ($6) adults, 5DM ($3) children. Take tram no. 94 or 96 or bus no. 612, 614, 631, 632, 692, or 695.

Frederick II ("the Great") chose Potsdam rather than Berlin as his permanent residence. The style of the buildings he ordered erected is called Potsdam rococo, an achievement primarily of Georg Wenzeslaus von Knobelsdorff. Knobelsdorff built **Sans Souci** (or Sanssouci) **Palace,** with its terraces and gardens, as a summer residence for Frederick II. The palace, inaugurated in 1747, is a long one-story building crowned by a dome and flanked by round pavilions. The music salon is the supreme example of the rococo style, and the elliptical Marble Hall is the largest in the palace. As a guest of the king, Voltaire visited in 1750. Sans Souci is open April to October, daily from 9am to 5pm; November to January, daily from 9am to 3pm; and in February and March, daily from 9am to 4pm; closed every Monday. Admission is 10DM ($6) for adults and 5DM ($3) for children.

Schloss Charlottenhof, south of Okonomieweg (☎ **0331/969-42-28;** Tram: 1 or 4), was built between 1826 and 1829 to the designs of Karl Friedrich Schinkel, the greatest master of neoclassical architecture in Germany. He erected the palace in the

A Fabulous Place to Dine in Potsdam

In 1878, one of the courtiers in the service of the Prussian monarchs built an elegant villa on the shore of the Heiliger See. During the 1920s it was used by author Bernhardt Kellerman as the place where he wrote some of his best work. After a Cold War stint as a base for Russian officers, it now functions as the most talked-about restaurant in Potsdam: **Villa Kellerman,** Mangerstrasse 34–36 (☎ **0331/29-15-72;** Bus: 695). The classical Italian cuisine might include marinated carpaccio of seawolf; a mixed platter of antipasti; spaghetti with scampi, herbs, and garlic; or John Dory in butter-and-caper sauce. Reservations are recommended. American Express and Visa accepted. Open Tuesday to Sunday noon to midnight.

style of a villa and designed most of the furniture inside. Open daily May through October 10am to 5pm. Admission is 6DM ($3.60) adults and 3DM ($1.80) children.

North of the 200-acre park, the ✪ **Cecilienhof Palace,** Im Neuer Garten (☎ **0331/ 969-42-44;** Bus: 695), was ordered built by Kaiser Wilhelm II between 1913 and 1917 and was completed in the style of an English country house. The 176-room mansion became the new residence of Crown Prince Wilhelm of Hohenzollern. It was occupied as a royal residence until March 1945, when the crown prince and his family fled to the West, taking many of their possessions. Cecilienhof was the headquarters of the 1945 Potsdam Conference. Hours are daily 9am to 5pm. Admission is 6DM ($3.60) for adults and 4DM ($2.40) for children.

THE SPREEWALD   This landmass southeast of Berlin is flat and water-soaked—but celebrated for its eerie beauty. For at least a thousand years, residents of the region have channeled the marshlands here into a network of canals, streams, lakes, and irrigation channels and built unusual clusters of houses, barns, and chapels on the high points of otherwise marshy ground. Ethnologists consider it one of central Europe's most distinctive adaptations of humans to an unlikely landscape, and botanists appreciate the wide diversity of bird and animal life that flourishes, according to the seasons, on its lush and fertile terrain. And legends of the spirits that inhabit the thick forests of the Spreewald abound.

Many of the people you'll meet here belong to a linguistic subdivision of the German-speaking people, the Sorbs, descendants of Slavic tribes who settled in the region around 600 B.C. Most modern-day Sorbs remain fiercely proud of their dialect and traditions and continue to till the soil of the Spreewald using labor-intensive methods, producing crops of mostly cucumbers and radishes.

The Spreewald is at its most appealing in early spring and autumn, when the crowds of sightseers depart and a spooky chill descends with the fog over these primeval forests and shallow medieval canals.

Getting There   The Spreewald lies 60 miles southeast of Berlin, and the best gateway is Lübben, 60 minutes by train from the Berlin-Lichtenberg station. Once at the Lübben train station, head straight out the front exit and walk in the same direction on a tree-lined street leading into the center of town. Once here, follow the signs directing you to *Kahfahrten* (boat rides) or *Paddlebooten* (paddleboats) and you're off to discover Spreewald.

Visitor Information   The tourist office in Lübben, the main point of departure for most Spreewald cruises, is on Ernst von Huwald Damm 16 (☎ **03546/3090**). The tourist office in the hamlet of Lübbenau, 6 miles away, and a secondary point of departure for Spreewald tours, is at Ehm-Welk-Strasse 15 (☎ 03542/3668).

Exploring the Spreewald   The shallow, nutrient-rich waters of the Spreewald seem ideally suited to boat tours along its timeless surface. If you're interested, several companies offer boat tours from the piers in the hamlet of Lübben. Each charges equivalent rates of 9.50DM ($5.70) for a 3-hour boat tour. Your best bet involves wandering down to the piers near the hamlet's center and hopping aboard the next departure, as virtually no one will speak English (although in addition to their dialect, they speak German). Each of the companies operates only between April and the end of October, with departures scheduled every day between 9am and 4pm. If you're interested in renting a canoe or rowboat and paddling around the Spreewald on your own, head for **Bootsverleih Gebauer,** Lindenstrasse (☎ 03546/7194), where canoes can be rented for 7DM ($4.20) per person hourly.

2 Munich & the Bavarian Alps

Sprawling Munich, home of some 1.3 million people and such industrial giants as Siemens and BMW, is the pulsating capital and cultural center of Bavaria. One of Germany's most festive cities, Munich exudes a hearty Bavarian *Gemütlichkeit.*

Longtime resident of Munich, Thomas Mann, wrote: "Munich sparkles." Although the city he described was swept away by two world wars and some of the most severe bombing in the history of Europe, Munich continues to sparkle, as it introduces itself to thousands of new visitors annually.

The Munich cliché as a beer-drinking town of folkloric charm is marketed by the city itself. Despite a roaring gross national product, Munich likes to present itself as a large, agrarian village peopled by jolly beer drinkers who cling to rustic origins despite the presence on all sides of symbols of the computer age, high-tech industries, a sophisticated business scene, a good deal of Hollywood-style glamour, and fairly hip night action. Bavarians themselves are in danger of becoming a minority in Munich— more than two-thirds of the population comes from outside Germany or from other parts of the country—but everybody buys into the folkloric charm and schmaltz.

Only in Munich

Nude Sunbathing in the Englischer Garten   On any summery sunny day, it seems that half of Munich can be seen letting it all hang out in the Volksgarten (People's Park), much to the delight of camera-toting tourists. The sentimental founding fathers of this park with their Romantic-era ideas surely had no idea they were creating a public nudist colony. If you're not much of a voyeur, and feel that most people look better with their clothes on, you can still come here to enjoy the park's natural beauty.

Snacking on Weisswürst   This sausage is the classic street food of Munich. Traditionally the freshly made "white sausage" of calf's head, veal, and seasoning, about the size of a hot dog, must be consumed before you hear the chimes of midday. Even in this day of refrigeration, that tradition is maintained. Smooth and light in flavor, it is eaten with pretzels and beer—nothing else. Weisswürst etiquette calls for you to remove the sausage from a bowl of hot water, cut it crosswise in half, dip the cut end in sweet mustard, then suck the sausage out of the casing in a single gesture. When you learn to do this properly, you will have become a true Münchener.

Attending Oktoberfest   It's called the "biggest keg party" in the world. Müncheners had so much fun in 1810 celebrating the wedding of Prince Ludwig to Princess

Therese von Sachsen-Hildburghausen that they've been rowdying it up ever since—16 full days from September 21 to October 6. The festival becomes a tent city at the Theresienwiese. The Middle Ages live on as oxen are roasted on open spits, brass bands oompah-pah you into oblivion, and some 750,000 kegs of the brew are tapped.

Spending a Day at Nymphenburg Just northwest of the city center lies Nymphenburg Palace, begun in 1664, an exquisite baroque extravaganza that was the summer home of the Bavarian kings. Nowhere in Munich will you experience such grandeur—a 495-acre park with lakes and hunting lodges and a spectacular palace. We prefer to visit when the summer outdoor concerts are presented, or else in May or June when the rhododendrons are in bloom. Have a look at the painted ceiling in the Great Hall; here Bavarian rococo reached its apogee.

Enjoying Market Day at Viktualienmarkt The most characteristic scene in Munich is a Saturday morning at the food market at the south end of Altstadt. Since 1807 Viktualienmarkt has been the center of Munich life, dispensing fresh vegetables, fruit from the Bavarian countryside, just-caught fish, dairy produce, poultry, rich grainy breads, and farm-fresh eggs. Naturally, there's a beer garden. Even more interesting than the market produce are the stall holders themselves—many evocative of Professor Higgins' "squashed cabbage leaf," Eliza Doolittle in the London's Covent Garden of yore.

Walking and Rafting Along the Isar Admittedly, it doesn't rival the Seine in Paris, but if you can't make it for a country walk in the Bavarian Alps, a walk along the left bank of the Isar is an alternative. Begin at Höllriegelskreuth and follow the scenic path along the Isar's high bank. Your trail will carry you through the Römerschanze into what Müncheners call "The Valley of the Mills" (Mühltal). After passing the Bridge Inn (Brückenwirt), you eventually reach Kloster Schäftlarn where you'll find—what else?—a beer garden. After a mug, you'll be fortified to continue along signposted paths through the Isar River Valley until you reach Wolfrathausen. Instead of walking back, you can often board a raft made of logs and "drift" back to the city, enjoying beer (what else?) and often the oompah-pah sound of a brass band as you head toward Munich.

Having a Night at the Hofbräuhaus Not just the city's major tourist attraction, it's the world's most famous beer hall, with room for 4,500 drinkers. Established in 1589, at first it was for members of the royal court only, but in 1828 the citizens of Munich were allowed to drink "the court's brew." A popular song, "In München steht ein Hofbräuhaus," spread the brewery's fame. For real authenticity, drink in the ground-floor *Schwemme* where some 1,000 beer buffs down their brew at wooden tables while listening to the sounds of an oompah-pah band. More rooms are upstairs, and in summer beer is served in a colonnaded courtyard patio with a lion fountain.

Getting a Bavarian Blast of Culture With all this beer drinking and having fun, it's easy to forget Munich is a great cultural capital of Germany. Its Alte Pinakothek holds one of Germany's most important art collections; the Deutsches Museum is the largest technological museum in the world, and Munich's opera and its three orchestras are internationally renowned.

ORIENTATION

GETTING THERE By Plane The **Franz Josef Strauss Airport** (☎ **089/ 97-52-13-13**), inaugurated in 1992, is among the most modern in the world. It lies 17 miles northeast of central Munich at Erdinger Moos.

S-Bahn (☎ **089/22-33-12-56**) trains connect the airport with the Hauptbahnhof (main railroad station) in downtown Munich. Departures are every 20 minutes for the

40-minute trip. The fare is 14DM ($8.40); Eurailpass holders ride free. A taxi into the center costs about 100DM ($60). Airport buses also run between the airport and the center.

By Train   Munich's main rail station, the **Hauptbahnhof,** on Bahnhofplatz, is one of Europe's largest. Located near the city center, it contains a hotel, restaurants, shopping, car parking, and banking facilities. All major German cities are connected to this station, most with a train arriving and departing almost every hour. Some 20 daily trains connect Munich to Frankfurt, and there are about 23 trains daily to Berlin. For information about long-distance trains, call ☎ **089/194-19.**

By Bus   Munich is a focal point for bus service that fans out across Bavaria and the rest of Germany. The nerve center for this service, and the point of arrivals and departures of most of the bus lines servicing the city, lies on the Arnulfstrasse, within a wing of the Hauptbahnhof, the West-wing-Starnberger Bahnhof. For bus schedules, information, and reservations, call ☎ **089/545-8700.**

VISITOR INFORMATION   You can get tourist information at the Franz Josef Strauss Airport in the central area (☎ **089/233-03-00**), open Monday to Saturday 8:30am to 10pm, Sunday 1 to 9pm. The main tourist office, **Fremdenverkehrsamt,** (☎ **089/23-33-02-56**), is at the Hauptbahnhof at the south exit opening onto Bayerstrasse. Open Monday through Saturday 9am to 10pm and Sunday 10am to 6pm, it offers a free map of Munich and also reserves hotel rooms.

CITY LAYOUT   Munich's Hauptbahnhof lies just west of the town center and opens onto Bahnhofplatz. From the square you can take Schützenstrasse to Karlsplatz (nicknamed Stachus), one of the major centers of Munich. Many tram lines converge on this square. From Karlsplatz, you can continue east along the pedestrians-only Neuhauserstrasse and Kaufingerstrasse until you reach Marienplatz, where you'll be deep in the Altstadt (old town) of Munich.

From **Marienplatz,** the center and heart of the city, you can head north on Dienerstrasse, which leads you to Residenzstrasse and finally to **Max-Joseph-Platz,** a landmark square, with the National Theater and the former royal palace, the Residenz. East of this square runs **Maximilianstrasse,** the most fashionable shopping and restaurant street of Munich. Between Marienplatz and the National theater is the **Platzl** quarter, where you'll want to head for nighttime diversions, as it's the seat of some of the finest (and some of the worst) restaurants in Munich, along with the landmark Hofbräuhaus, the most famous beer hall in Europe.

North of the old town is **Schwabing,** the university and former Bohemian section whose main street is Leopoldstrasse. The large, sprawling municipal park grounds, the Englischer Garten, are due east of Schwabing.

GETTING AROUND

BY PUBLIC TRANSPORTATION   The city's efficient rapid-transit system is the **U-Bahn,** or Untergrundbahn, one of the most modern subway systems in Europe. The **S-Bahn** rapid-transit system, a 260-mile network of tracks, provides service to various city districts and outlying suburbs. The city is also served by a network of **trams** and **buses.** The same ticket entitles you to ride the U-Bahn and the S-Bahn, as well as trams (streetcars) and buses. For more information, call ☎ **089/21-03-30.**

Money-Saving Tip

Munich's S-Bahn is covered by Eurail, so if you have a rail pass, don't buy a separate ticket.

A single-journey ticket for a ride within the city's central zone—a large area that few tourists ever leave—costs 3.40DM ($2.05). If you go to the outermost zones of the subway system, your ride could cost as much as 16DM ($9.60). One of the best things about Munich's transit system is that you can make as many free transfers between subways, buses, and trams as you need to reach your destination.

More economical than single-journey tickets is the *Streifenkarte,* a strip-ticket with 11 units, two of which are annulled for each zone of the system you travel through. A Streifenkarte costs 15DM ($9) for adults (children ages 4 to 14 can purchase a *Kinderstreifenkarte* for 8.50DM/$5.10). With this type of ticket, you can travel in one continuous direction during any 2-hour period with unlimited transfers. You can also use it for multiple passengers (for two people to ride two zones, simply stamp four strips).

An even better deal may be the **Tageskarte (Day Ticket),** which for 8DM ($4.80) gives you unlimited access within the central zone for a full day (double the price for access to all of Greater Munich—a 50-mile radius).

BY TAXI   Cabs are relatively expensive—you'll pay 5DM ($3) when you get inside, plus 2.20DM ($1.30) per kilometer. In an emergency, call ☎ **089/2161-0** or 089/194-10 for a radio-dispatched taxi.

BY CAR   Driving in the city, which has an excellent public transportation system, is not advised. The streets around Marienplatz in the Altstadt are pedestrian only. If you are interested in renting a car locally, try **Sixt/Budget Autovermietung,** Einstein-strasse 106 (☎ **089/550-24-47**), or look under *Autovermietung* in the yellow pages of the Munich phone book.

ON FOOT & BY BICYCLE   Of course, the best way to explore Munich is on foot, since it has a vast pedestrian zone in the center. Many of its attractions can, in fact, be reached only on foot. Pick up a good map and set out.

The tourist office also sells a pamphlet called *Radl-Touren für unsere Gäste,* costing only .50DM (30¢). It outlines itineraries for touring Munich by bicycle. One of the most convenient places to rent a bike is **Radius Bikes** (☎ **089/59-61-13**), at the far end of the Hauptbahnhof, near lockers opposite tracks 30 and 31. The charge is 10DM ($6) for 2 hours, or 25DM ($15) from 10am to 6pm. Mountain bikes are rented for about 25% more. There's a deposit of 100DM ($60); students and Eurail-pass holders are granted a 10% discount. Open April to early October daily 10am to 6pm.

Fast Facts: Munich

American Express   American Express, Promenadeplatz 6 (☎ **089/290-900**), is open for mail pickup and check cashing Monday through Friday 9am to 5:30pm and Saturday 9:30am to 12:30pm. Unless you have an American Express card or traveler's checks, you'll be charged 2DM ($1.20) for picking up your mail.

Business Hours   Most **banks** are open Monday through Friday from 8:30am to 12:30pm and 1:30 to 3:30pm (many stay open until 5:30pm on Thursday). Most **businesses** and **stores** are open Monday through Friday 9am to 6pm and Saturday 9am to 2pm. On *langer Samstag* (first Saturday of the month) stores remain open until 6pm. Many observe a late closing on Thursday, usually 8 or 9pm.

Munich U-Bahn & S-Bahn

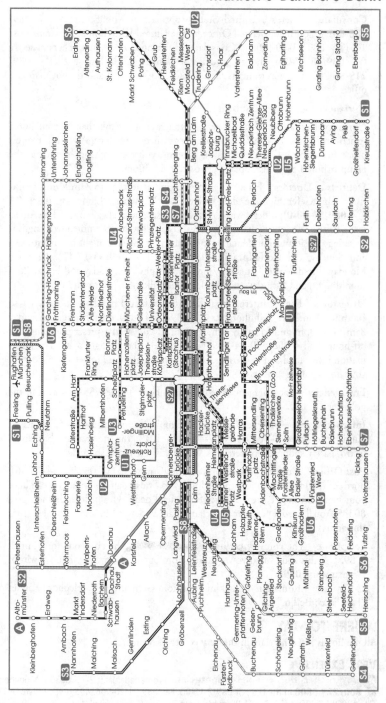

Consulates   There's a **United States** consulate at Königstrasse 5 (☎ **089/ 288-80**); a Consulate General Office for the **United Kingdom** at Bürkleinstrasse 10 (☎ **089/21-10-90**); a Consulate of **Ireland** at Mauerkircherstrasse 1a (☎ **089/98-57-23**); and a consulate of **Canada** at Tal Strasse 29 (☎ **089/ 219-95-70**). The governments of Australia and New Zealand do not maintain offices in Munich.

Currency   See "Fast Facts: Berlin."

Currency Exchange   You can get a better rate at a bank than at your hotel. American Express traveler's checks are best cashed at the local American Express office (see above). On weekends or at night, you can exchange money at the Hauptbahnhof exchange, open daily 6am to 11:30pm.

Dentists & Doctors   For an English-speaking dentist, go to **Klinik und Poliklinik für Kieferchirurgie der Universität München,** Lindwurmstrasse 2A (☎ **089/51-60-0**); it deals with emergency cases and is always open. The American, British, and Canadian consulates keep a list of recommended English-speaking physicians. For dental or medical emergencies at night or on Saturday and Sunday, call **Notfallpraxis,** Elisenstrasse (☎ **089/55-17-17**). It's open Monday, Tuesday, and Thursday 7pm to midnight, Wednesday and Friday 2pm to midnight, and Saturday and Sunday, plus holidays, 7pm to midnight.

Drugstores   For an international drugstore where English is spoken, go to **Bahnhof Apotheke,** Bahnhofplatz (☎ **089/59-41-19**), open Monday to Friday 8am to 6:30pm and Saturday 8am to 2pm. If you need a prescription filled in off-hours, call ☎ **089/59-44-75** for information about what's open. The information is recorded and in German only, so you might need to get someone from your hotel staff to assist you.

Emergencies   For emergency medical aid, phone ☎ **089/55-17-71.** Call the police at ☎ **110.**

Internet Access   **Internet-Café** is at Nymphenburger Strasse 145, corner of Landshutter Allee (☎ **089/129-47-44**). This is also the site of a cafe, bar, disco, bistro, pastry shop, and pizzeria. Its Web site is www.icafe.space.de.

Post Office   A central post office is at Arnulfstrasse 32 (☎ **089/54-54-23-36**), north of the Hauptbahnhof, open Monday to Friday 8am to 8pm. You can have your mail sent here Poste Restante (for general delivery), but include the zip of 80335. You'll need a passport to reclaim mail. Packages can also be mailed from this address.

Telephone   The **country code** for Germany is **49.** The **city code** for Munich is **89.** Use this code when you're calling from outside Germany; if you're within Germany, use **089.**

For more information on making calls from Germany, see "Telephone" under "Fast Facts: Berlin."

WHERE TO STAY

All the hotels listed here are in the very center of Munich.

VERY EXPENSIVE

✪ **Bayerischer Hof & Palais Montgelas.** Promenadeplatz 2–6, 80333 München. ☎ **800/223-6800** in the U.S., or 089/2-12-00. Fax 089/21-20-906. 495 units. MINIBAR TV TEL. 430DM–520DM ($258–$312) double; from 780DM ($468) suite. AE, DC, MC, V. Parking 30DM ($18). Tram: 19.

A Bavarian version of New York's Waldorf-Astoria, this hotel is in a swank loca opening onto a little tree-filled square. Rooms range from medium to extremely sp cious, each with plush duvets topping firm mattresses; many of the beds are four-posters. The decor ranges from Bavarian provincial to British country house chintz. The large bathrooms are marbled with a private phone and plenty of shelf space. The major dining room, the Garden-Restaurant, evokes the grandeur of a small palace. A clubby bar serves generous drinks and grilled specialties, and there's Trader Vic's for Polynesian nights. Facilities include a rooftop pool and garden with bricked sun terrace, sauna, and massage rooms.

✪ **Hotel Vier Jahreszeiten München.** Maximilianstrasse 17, 80539 München. ☎ **800/426-3135** in the U.S., or 089/2125-0. Fax 089/2125-2000. www.kempinski.com. E-mail: reservations.hvj@kempinski.com. 366 units. A/C MINIBAR TV TEL. 510DM–810DM ($306–$486) double; from 1,320DM ($792) suite. AE, DC, MC, V. Parking 30DM ($18). Tram: 19.

This grand hotel with a tradition going back to 1858 is the most elegant place to stay in Munich. Most rooms are decorated with well-preserved antiques or reproductions, and range from medium to very spacious. Bedside controls, luxury mattresses and oriental rugs, plus spacious bathrooms with soft towels, hair dryers, robes, and deluxe toiletries will keep any guest comfortable. Vier Jahreszeiten Restaurant, the hotel's finest dining spot, is open daily, or try the completely refurnished Bistro Eck. There's an indoor pool and sauna, solarium, and sun terrace.

EXPENSIVE

Eden-Hotel-Wolff. Arnulfstrasse 4–8, 80335 München. ☎ **089/55-11-50.** Fax 089/551-15-555. 211 units. MINIBAR TV TEL. 280DM–460DM ($168–$276) double; from 380DM ($228) suite. One child up to age 6 stays free in parents' room. Rates include buffet breakfast. AE, DC, MC, V. Parking 20DM ($12). U-Bahn or S-Bahn: Hauptbahnhof.

The Eden-Hotel-Wolff's sedate, stone exterior belies an interior decorated in a richly traditional style with chandeliers and dark-wood paneling. If you must stay near the train station, this is your best bet. With some exceptions, most rooms are spacious, their styles ranging from modern to rustic Bavarian. Beds offer fine linens and luxurious mattresses, and the bathrooms are large, marble-clad, and furnished with hair dryers. Private safes and double-glazed windows are added features. Some units are hypo-allergenic with special beds and a private ventilation system. The main dining room, with its natural-pine ceiling, gleaming brass lantern sconces, and thick stone arches, serves excellent Bavarian dishes.

MODERATE

Adria. Liebigstrasse 8a, 80538 München. ☎ **089/29-30-81.** Fax 089/22-70-15. 47 units. MINIBAR TV TEL. 190DM–280DM ($114–$168) double. Rates include buffet breakfast. AE, MC, V. Closed Dec 23–Jan 6. U-Bahn: 4 or 5. Tram: 17.

Adria's lobby sets the stylish contemporary look for guest rooms that range from fairly small to medium in size. Each has excellent mattresses and such extras as armchairs, small sofas, and desks. Bathrooms were renewed recently; most have showers and a hair dryer. A buffet breakfast, which includes sparkling wine, is served in the garden room. Services include money exchange, laundry, theater tickets, and arrangements for sightseeing tours. For 50DM ($30) the hotel will give you a "license" allowing you to park free in the neighborhood; when you return the license at checkout time, the fee is returned.

An der Oper. Falkenturmstrasse 11, 80331 München. ☎ **089/290-02-70.** Fax 089/290-02-729. 68 units. TV TEL. 260DM–320DM ($156–$192) double. Rates include buffet breakfast. AE, MC, V. Tram: 19.

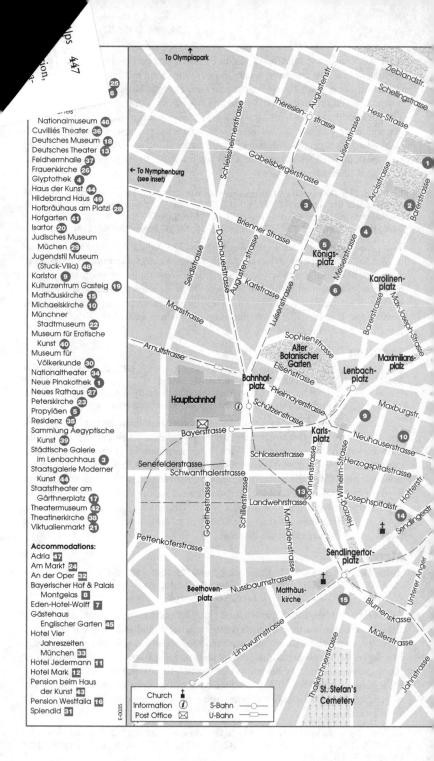

E-0035

Church ✝
Information ⓘ
Post Office ✉
S-Bahn —○—
U-Bahn —□—

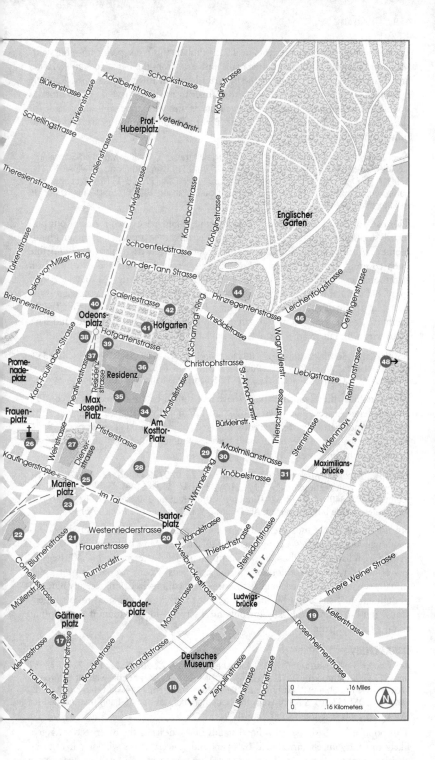

449

Located just off Maximilianstrasse, near Marienplatz, this is a superb choice for sightseeing or shopping in the traffic-free malls, just steps from the Bavarian National Theater. Built in the '70s, it's one of the best-run hotels in this price category. Recently renovated guest rooms, which range from small to medium, have such amenities as double-glazed windows, firm beds, a small sitting area with armchairs, and a table for those who want breakfast in their rooms. Bathrooms are medium in size and beautifully maintained with many towels.

✪ **Gästehaus Englischer Garten.** Liebergesellstrasse 8, 80802 München-Schwabing. ☎ **089/38-39-41-0.** Fax 089/38-39-41-33. 25 units (19 with bathroom). MINIBAR TV TEL. 130DM ($78) double without bathroom; 156DM–194DM ($93.60–$116.40) double with bathroom; from 200DM ($120) apt. No credit cards. Parking 10DM ($6). U-Bahn: U3 or U6 to Münchner Freiheit.

This oasis of charm and tranquility close to the Englischer Garten is one of our preferred stopovers. The decor of the bedrooms might be termed "Bavarian grandmother." Antiques and old-fashioned but comfortable beds (with duvets and fine linen covering firm mattresses) evoke coziness; Oriental carpets add extra warmth. Bathrooms are small and not one of the hotel's stronger features, as they lack shelf space, but the maintenance is first-rate and the towels adequate. In an annex across the street are 15 small apartments, each with a bathroom and tiny kitchenette. Try for room 16, 23, 26, or especially 20; all are more spacious, better furnished, and have better views. In fair weather, breakfast is served in a rear garden for 12DM ($7.20).

Hotel Mark. Senefelderstrasse 12, 80336 München. ☎ **089/55-98-20.** Fax 089/559-82-333. 90 units. MINIBAR TV TEL. 190DM–220DM ($114–$132) double. Rates include buffet breakfast. AE, DC, MC, V. Parking 15DM ($9). S-Bahn or U-Bahn: Hauptbahnhof.

This hotel near the Hauptbahnhof's south exit should be considered for its comfort and moderate prices. The guest rooms are functionally furnished, although a bit cramped, and mattresses were recently renewed, so you should sleep in peace. Bathrooms are small but tidily maintained with a good supply of medium-sized towels. Breakfast is the only meal served.

Splendid. Maximilianstrasse 54, 80538 München. ☎ **089/29-66-06.** Fax 089/29-131-76. 41 units (30 with bathroom). TV TEL. 205DM–315DM ($123–$189) double without bathroom; 230DM–340DM ($138–$204) double with bathroom; 350DM–520DM ($210–$312) suite. Rates include buffet breakfast. AE, DC, MC, V. U-Bahn: 4 or 5. Tram: 17 or 19.

Splendid is one of the most attractive old-world hotels in Munich, with antiques, Oriental rugs, and chandeliers decorating the public rooms. Most bedrooms are decorated in "Bavarian baroque," although two recently remodeled ones are Louis XVI. Regardless of decor, you'll be comfortable on the firm beds. Room size ranges from small (usually singles) to quite spacious. Bathrooms are medium-sized with recently renewed plumbing. Shelf space is a bit inadequate, but the rack of good-sized towels is generous. You can order breakfast—the only meal served—in your room if you want, or sit on a trellised patio.

INEXPENSIVE

Am Markt. Heiliggeistrasse 6, 80331 München. ☎ **089/22-50-14.** Fax 089/22-40-17. 32 units (12 with bathroom). TV TEL. 112DM–120DM ($67.20–$72) double without bathroom; 165DM ($99) double with bathroom. Rates include continental breakfast. No credit cards. Parking 12DM ($7.20). S-Bahn: From the Hauptbahnhof, take any S-Bahn train headed for Marienplatz, a two-stop ride from the station.

This popular but basic Bavarian hotel stands in the heart of the older section. You're likely to find yourself surrounded by opera and concert artists who stay here to be close to where they perform. The guest rooms are trim, neat, and small—space to store your stuff is at a minimum. Mattresses are well worn, but with enough life for comfort. Private bathrooms are also small but have an adequate set of towels. Corridor bathrooms are kept quite fresh.

Hotel Jedermann. Bayerstrasse 95, 80335 München. ☎ **089/53-32-67.** Fax 089/53-65-06. www.hotel-jedermann.de E-mail: hotel-jedermann@cube.net 55 units (34 with bathroom). TEL TV. 95DM–140DM ($57–$84) double without bathroom; 130DM–220DM ($78–$132) double with bathroom; 110DM–185DM ($66–$111) triple without bathroom; 155DM–265DM ($93–$159) triple with bathroom. Rates include buffet breakfast. MC, V. Parking 10DM ($6). Ten-minute walk from Hauptbahnhof (turn right on Bayerstrasse from south exit).

This pleasant spot's central location and value make it a good choice. It's especially good for families as both cribs and cots are available. Rooms are generally small and old-fashioned, but are cozy and comfortable, with firm mattresses. Private bathrooms are also small, but have adequate medium-sized towels and a hair dryer. Corridor bathrooms are numerous enough so you don't usually have to wait in line. Most rooms also have a private safe. A generous breakfast buffet is served in a charming room.

Pension beim Haus der Kunst. Bruderstrasse 4, 80802 München. ☎ **089/22-21-27.** Fax 089/2226. 10 units (1 with bathroom). 90DM ($54) double; 200DM ($120) apt for 4. Rates include breakfast. No credit cards. Parking, when available, is free on the street. U-Bahn: Lehel.

Noted for an ideal location near the Englischer Garten, copious breakfasts, and warm hospitality, this pension is one of Munich's best. Early reservations are important. It's really like an old-fashioned Bavarian boarding house, so don't expect much in the way of amenities, although each of the small and tidily maintained bedrooms has a firm bed with a good mattress. There's only one private bathroom—it's in the apartment—but corridor bathrooms are adequate, and there's rarely a line waiting to get in. You're given a couple of rather thin towels—ask for more or bring your own.

Pension Westfalia. Mozartstrasse 23, 80336 München. ☎ **089/53-03-77.** Fax 089/54-39-120. 19 units (11 with bathroom). TV TEL. 85DM–95DM ($51–$57) double without bathroom; 115DM–130DM ($69–$78) double with bathroom. Rates include buffet breakfast. AE, V. Parking, when available, is free on the street. U-Bahn: 3 or 6 to Goetheplatz. Bus: 58 from the Hauptbahnhof.

Facing the meadow where the annual Oktoberfest takes place, this four-story townhouse near Goetheplatz is another of Munich's top pensions. Rooms range from small to medium, but the owner takes great pride in seeing that they are well maintained and comfortable, renewing mattresses as needed. There are few extras, although some rooms have a TV—that is, if you like watching German TV. Private bathrooms are small with shower stalls, but each has a set of medium-sized towels. If you don't have a private bathroom, you can grab one of those towels and head for the corridor bathrooms, which are well maintained and do the job just as well.

WHERE TO DINE

As with the hotels, most of the restaurants listed are in the heart of the city.

VERY EXPENSIVE

Gasthaus Glockenbach. Kapuzinerstrasse 29, corner of Maistrasse. ☎ **089/53-40-43.** Reservations recommended. Main courses 36DM–55DM ($21.60–$33); set-price menus 40DM–150DM ($24–$90). AE, MC, V. Tues–Fri noon–1:30pm (last order); Tues–Sat 7–9:30pm (last order). Closed for 2 weeks in August, 1 week at Christmas. U-Bahn: U3 or U6 to Goetheplatz. MODERN CONTINENTAL.

The setting is a 200-year-old building, close to a tributary (the Glockenbach) of the nearby Isar. The dignified country-baroque interior is accented with vivid modern paintings, and the most elegant table settings in town, including a lavish array of porcelain by a company not well known in the New World, Hutchenreuther. Cuisine changes with the season and according to the inspiration of the chef. Examples include imaginative preparations of venison and pheasant in autumn, lamb and veal dishes in springtime, preparations of whatever shellfish is seasonal at the time, and a medley of ultra-fresh vegetables and exotica imported from local farms and from sophisticated purveyors throughout Europe and the world.

Hilton Grill. In the Hilton Munich Park, Am Tucherpark 7. ☎ **089/38-450.** Reservations recommended. Set-price lunch 62DM ($37.20); set-price dinners 92DM–145DM ($55.20–$87); main courses 42DM–65DM ($25.20–$39). AE, DC, MC, V. Sun and Tues–Fri noon–2:30pm and 7–10:30pm. U-Bahn: U3 or U6 to Giselastrasse, then bus 54. CONTINENTAL.

Realizing the stiff competition they faced from other restaurants on the northern outskirts of Munich, the developers of the Hilton used their imagination in transforming a corner of its modern premises into one of the most sophisticated and well-conceived restaurants in Bavaria. The impressive result is a replica of a richly paneled private club that is open to the public, and just happens to be a place with charm, panache, and flair. Tables are elaborately decorated; dishes combine both traditional and modern European and North American cuisine. Despite the set luncheon's elegance, management offers a free bottle of champagne if the meal is not completed within an hour of a patron's arrival. A meal might include salmon carpaccio with a white asparagus vinaigrette, spaghettini with morels in an herb sauce, monkfish on lentils with crispy Parma ham, or one of Munich's best Bavarian-style duck dishes on white cabbage with dumplings. Dinners are even more elaborate, including wood pigeon with foie gras and artichokes set in Madeira-flavored aspic, followed by a lavish tray of desserts.

Restaurant Königshof. In the Hotel Königshof, Karlsplatz 25 (Am Stachus). ☎ **089/55-13-60.** Reservations required. Main courses 46DM–68DM ($27.60–$40.80); set-price menus 144DM–174DM ($86.40–$104.40). AE, DC, MC, V. Daily noon–2:30pm and 6:45pm–midnight. S-Bahn: S3, S7, or S8 to Karlsplatz. Tram: 19. INTERNATIONAL.

The owners of this deluxe hotel want the Königshof to surface near the top in culinary delights. This is no longer the finest hotel dining room in Munich, that honor having passed to others, but it still holds on near the top. The Geisel family has made major renovations to the dining room, with its oyster-white oak panels, polished bronze chandeliers, silver candelabra, and porcelain. The chefs here are both inventive and creative. "Culinary masterpieces" depend on their whims, and, almost as important, on what's available in season. Extremely fresh ingredients are used in all the dishes. Perhaps you'll get to try the foie gras with sauternes, loin of lamb with *fines herbes,* lobster with vanilla butter, or sea bass suprême.

✪ **Tantris.** Johann-Fichte-Strasse 7, Schwabing. ☎ **089/3-61-95-90.** Reservations required. Set-price 5-course lunch 158DM ($94.80); set-price dinner 198DM ($118.80) for 5 courses, 225DM ($135) for 8 courses. AE, DC, MC, V. Tues–Sat noon–3pm and 6:30pm–1am. Closed public holidays; annual holidays in Jan and May. U-Bahn: U6 to Dietlindenstrasse. FRENCH/INTERNATIONAL.

Tantris serves Munich's finest cuisine. Chef Hans Haas was voted the top in Germany in 1994 and, if anything, he has refined and sharpened his culinary technique since winning that honor. His penchant for exotic cookery carries him into greater achievements. There is no restaurant in Munich that comes close to equaling this place. The setting is unlikely—but once you're inside, you're transported into an ultramodern atmosphere with fine service. The food is a treat to the eye as well as to the palate. You might begin with a terrine of smoked fish served with green cucumber sauce, and then follow with classic roast duck on mustard-seed sauce or perhaps a delightful concoction of lobster médallions on black noodles. These dishes show a refinement and attention to detail, plus a quest for technical perfection, that you find nowhere else in Munich.

EXPENSIVE

✪ **Alois Dallmayr.** Dienerstrasse 14–15. ☎ **089/213-51-00.** Reservations required. Main courses 30DM–43DM ($18–$25.80). AE, DC, MC, V. Mon–Wed 9:30am–7pm; Thurs–Fri 9:30am–8pm; Sat 9am–4pm. Tram: 19. CONTINENTAL.

Alois Dallmayr's history can be traced back to 1700. Near the Rathaus, it is Germany's most famous delicatessen. After looking at its tempting array of delicacies from around the globe, you'll think you're lost in a millionaire's supermarket. Dallmayr has been a purveyor to many royal courts.

The upstairs dining room serves a subtle German version of continental cuisine, owing a heavy debt to France. The food array is dazzling, ranging from the best herring and sausages we've ever tasted to such rare treats as perfectly vine-ripened tomatoes flown in from Morocco and papayas from Brazil. The famous French poulet de Bresse, believed by many gourmets to be the world's finest, is also shipped in.

Austernkeller. Stollbergstrasse 11. ☎ **089/29-87-87.** Reservations required. Main courses 33DM–49DM ($19.80–$29.40). AE, DC, MC, V. Daily 5pm–1am. Closed Dec 23–26. U-Bahn: Isartorplatz. SEAFOOD.

Here you can feast on the largest selection of the finest oysters in town; many gourmets make an entire meal of raw oysters here. Others prefer them elaborately prepared. A delectable dish to start is the shellfish platter with fresh oysters, mussels, clams, scampi, and sea snails, or you might begin with a richly stocked fish soup and go on to lobster thermidor or shrimp grilled in the shell. French meat specialties are also offered. The decor, under a vaulted ceiling, relies on everything from plastic lobsters to old porcelain.

Spatenhaus. Residenzstrasse 12. ☎ **089/290-70-60.** Reservations recommended. Main courses 24.50DM–42.50DM ($14.70–$25.50). AE, DC, MC, V. Daily 9:30am–12:30pm. U-Bahn: U3, U4, or U6 to Odeonsplatz or Marienplatz. BAVARIAN/INTERNATIONAL.

One of Munich's best-known beer restaurants has wide windows overlooking the opera house on Max-Joseph-Platz. Of course, to be loyal, you should accompany your meal with the restaurant's own beer, Spaten-Franziskaner-Bier. You can sit in an intimate, semiprivate dining nook or at a big table. The Spatenhaus has old traditions, offers typical Bavarian food, and is known for generous portions and reasonable prices. If you want to know what the fabled Bavarian gluttony is all about, order the "Bavarian plate," which is loaded down with various meats, including lots of pork and sausages.

MODERATE

Buon Gusto (Talamonti). Hochbruckenstrasse 3. ☎ **089/296-383.** Reservations recommended. Main courses 25DM–40DM ($15–$24). AE, MC, V. Mon–Sat noon–11pm. U-Bahn or S-Bahn: Marienplatz. Closed Dec 24–Jan 15. ITALIAN.

Its interior offers two dining areas that include a simple, rustic-looking bistro whose sightlines extend over an open kitchen, and a more formal and more upscale-looking dining room. Menu items and prices are identical in both areas. Owned and managed by an extended family, the Talamontis, whose members are likely not to speak anything except Italian and German, the restaurant emphasizes fresh ingredients, strong and savory flavors, and food items inspired by the Italian provinces of the Marches and Tuscany. Examples include ravioli stuffed with mushrooms and herbs, roasted lamb with potatoes, lots of different forms of scallopini, and fresh fish that seems to taste best when served simply, with oil or butter and lemon. Especially flavorful are the array of risottos whose ingredients change with the seasons and the availability of ingredients. During Oktoberfest and trade fairs, the place is mobbed.

✪ **Ratskeller München.** Im Rathaus, Marienplatz 8. ☎ **089/219-98-90.** Reservations required. Main courses 12DM–28DM ($7.20–$16.80). AE, MC, V. Daily 10am–midnight. U-Bahn/S-Bahn: U2 or U3 to Marienplatz. BAVARIAN.

Munich is proud to possess one of the best *ratskellers* (a restaurant in a *Rathaus,* or town hall) in Germany. The decor is typical: lots of dark wood and carved chairs. The most interesting tables, the ones staked out by in-the-know locals, are the semiprivate dining nooks in the rear, under the vaulted painted ceilings. Bavarian music adds to the ambience. The menu, a showcase of regional fare, includes many vegetarian choices, which is unusual for a ratskeller. Some of the dishes are a little heavy and too porky, but you can find lighter fare if you search the menu.

INEXPENSIVE

Andechser am Dom. Weinstrasse 7A. ☎ **089/29-84-81.** Reservations recommended. Main courses 17.50DM–29DM ($10.50–$17.40). AE, DC, MC, V. Daily 10am–midnight. U-Bahn and S-Bahn: Marienplatz. GERMAN.

Set on two floors of a postwar building erected adjacent to the back side of the Frauenkirche, this restaurant and beer hall serves copious amounts of a beer brewed in a monastery near Munich (Andechser) as well as generous portions of German food. Order a snack, a full meal, or just a beer, and enjoy the frothy fun of it all. Menu items are often accompanied with German-style potato salad and green salad, and include such dishes as veal schnitzels, steaks, turkey croquettes, roasted lamb, fish, and several kinds of sausages that taste best with tangy mustard. During clement weather, tables are set up both on the building's roof and on the sidewalk in front, both of which over-look the back side of one of the city's most evocative churches.

✪ **Donisl.** Weinstrasse 1. ☎ **089/22-01-84.** Reservations recommended. Main courses 10.50DM–11.95DM ($6.30–$7.15). AE, DC, MC, V. Daily 9am–midnight. U-Bahn: U2 or U3 to Marienplatz. S-Bahn: All trains. BAVARIAN/INTERNATIONAL.

Donisl is one of Munich's oldest beer halls, dating from 1715. The seating capacity of this relaxed and comfortable restaurant is about 550, and in summer you can enjoy the hum and bustle of Marienplatz while dining in the garden area out front. The standard menu offers traditional Bavarian food as well as a weekly changing specials menu. The little white sausages, Weisswürst, are a decades-long tradition here.

Hundskugel. Hotterstrasse 18. ☎ **089/26-42-72.** Reservations required. Main courses 15DM–37DM ($9–$22.20). No credit cards. Daily 10am–midnight. U-Bahn: U2 or U3 to Marienplatz. BAVARIAN.

The city's oldest tavern, Hundskugel dates back to 1440, and apparently serves the same food as it did back then. If it was good a long time ago, why mess with the menu? Built in an alpine style, it's within easy walking distance of Marienplatz. Perhaps half the residents of Munich have at one time or another made their way here to enjoy the honest Bavarian cookery that has no pretensions. Although the chef specializes in *Spanferkel* (roast suckling pig with potato noodles), you might prefer *Tafelspitz* (boiled beef) in dill sauce, or roast veal stuffed with goose liver.

Nürnberger Bratwurst Glöckl Am Dom. Frauenplatz 9. ☎ **089/29-52-64.** Reservations recommended. Main courses 20DM–30DM ($12–$18). No credit cards. Daily 9am–1am. U-Bahn: U2 or U3 to Marienplatz. S-Bahn: All trains. BAVARIAN.

In the coziest and warmest of Munich's local restaurants, the chairs look as though they were made by some Black Forest woodcarver, and the place is full of memorabilia—pictures, prints, pewter, and beer steins. Upstairs through a hidden stairway is a dining room decorated with reproductions of Dürer prints. The restaurant has a strict policy of shared tables, and service is on tin plates. The homesick Nürnberger comes here just for one dish: *Nürnberger Schweinwurstl mit Kraut* (little sausages with kraut). Last food orders go in at midnight.

Planet Hollywood. Platzl 1. ☎ **089/2903-0500.** Reservations accepted only Mon–Wed and Sun. Main courses 14.95DM–33.90DM ($8.95–$20.35). AE, MC, V. Daily 11:30am–midnight. S-Bahn: Marienplatz or Isartor. AMERICAN.

This is the Munich branch of Planet Hollywood. Memorabilia associated with *Titanic* and seemingly every film ever made by Bruce Willis or Sly Stallone surrounds visitors. Cocktails are served in a commodious bar area. You can eventually gravitate into either the main dining room or a satellite room that immortalizes for a Bavarian clientele the achievements of Hollywood's favorite Teuton, Arnold Schwarzenegger. The staff will be quick to tell you that he was once a resident of Munich. Menu items are firmly grounded in American pop culture and include burgers (with several vegetarian versions), New York strip steaks, chili, club sandwiches, tacos, and ice cream sundaes. For a memorable dessert, try the "famous" *Apfelstrudel*, reputedly made according to a recipe perfected by Arnold's mother. You can have a good time here, even if you find the venue very similar to everything you left America to forget.

BEER GARDENS

Bamberger Haus. Brunnerstrasse 2. ☎ **089/308-89-66.** Main courses 17.50DM–30DM ($10.50–$18). Restaurant, daily noon–midnight; beer hall, daily 5pm–1am. AE, DC, MC, V. U-Bahn: U3 or U6 to Scheidplatz.

In a century-old house northwest of Schwabing at the edge of Luitpold Park, Bamberger Haus is named after the city most noted for the quantity of beer its residents drink. Bavarian and international specialties in the street-level restaurant include well-seasoned soups, grilled steak, veal, pork, and sausages. If you want only to drink, you might visit the rowdier and less expensive beer hall in the cellar. A large beer costs 4.50DM ($2.70). In summer, weather permitting, a beer garden is open daily from 11am to 11pm.

✪ **Biergärten Chinesischer Turm.** Englischer Garten 3. ☎ **089/38-38-730.** Daily 10am–11pm; closed Jan 11–Feb 5. AE, MC, V (in restaurant only). U-Bahn: U3 or U6 to Giselastrasse. Bus: 54 or 154.

Englischer Garten, the park lying between the Isar River and Schwabing is the biggest city-owned park in Europe. It has a main restaurant and several beer gardens, of which the Biergarten Chinesischer Turm is our favorite. It takes its name from its location at the foot of a pagoda-like tower. Beer and Bavarian food, and plenty of it, are what you get here. A large glass or mug of beer (ask for *ein mass Bier*), enough to bathe in, costs 9.50DM ($5.70). The food is very cheap—a simple meal begins at 15DM ($9). Homemade dumplings are a specialty, as are all kinds of tasty sausage. Oompah bands often play, and it's most festive.

SEEING THE SIGHTS
SIGHTSEEING SUGGESTIONS FOR FIRST-TIME VISITORS

If You Have 1 Day   Local tourist tradition calls for a morning breakfast of Weisswürst; head for Donisl (see "Where to Dine," above), which opens at 9am. A true Münchener downs them with a mug of beer. Then walk to **Marienplatz,** with its glockenspiel and **Altes Rathaus** (old town hall). Later stroll along **Maximilianstrasse,** one of Europe's great shopping streets. In the afternoon, visit the **Neue Pinakothek**

and see at least some exhibits at the **Deutsches Museum.** Cap the evening with a night of Bavarian food, beer, and music at the **Hofbräuhaus am Platzl.**

If You Have 2 Days In the morning of day 2, visit the **Bayerisches Nationalmuseum (Bavarian National Museum),** with three vast floors devoted to Bavaria's artistic and historical riches. If the weather's right, plan a lunch in one of the beer gardens of the **Englischer Garten.** In the afternoon, visit the **Nymphenburg Palace,** summer residence of the Wittelsbach dynasty, longtime rulers of Bavaria.

If You Have 3 Days Pass your third day exploring the sights you've missed so far: the **Residenz,** the **Antikensammlungen (Museum of Antiquities),** and the **Glyptothek.** If you have any more time, return to the Deutsches Museum. Have dinner or at least a drink at **Olympiapark,** enjoying a panoramic view of the Alps.

If You Have 4 or More Days As fascinating as Munich is, tear yourself away on day 4 for an excursion to the **Royal Castles** once occupied by the "mad king" Ludwig II (see "Organized Tours" and section 3, "The Romantic Road," below). On day 5, take an excursion to **Dachau,** the notorious World War II concentration camp, and in the afternoon visit **Mittenwald** for a taste of the Bavarian Alps.

Exploring the Altstadt (Old Town)

Marienplatz, dedicated to the patron of the city whose statue stands on a huge column in the center of the square, is the heart of the Altstadt. On its north side is the **Neues Rathaus (New City Hall)** built in 19th-century Gothic style. Each day at 11am, and also at noon and 5pm in the summer, the **Glockenspiel** on the facade performs a miniature tournament, with enameled copper figures moving in and out of the archways. Since you're already at the Rathaus, you might want to climb the 55 steps to the top of its tower (an elevator is available if you're conserving energy) for a good overall view of the city center. The **Altes Rathaus (Old City Hall),** with its plain Gothic tower, is to the right. It was reconstructed in the 15th century, after being destroyed by fire.

Museums & Palaces

✪ **Alte Pinakothek.** Barer Strasse 27. ☎ **089/238-050.** Admission 7DM ($4.20) adults, 4DM ($2.40) students, free for children 14 and under. Tues–Wed and Fri–Sun 10am–5pm; Thurs 10am–8pm. U-Bahn: U2 to Königsplatz. Tram: 27. Bus: 53.

This is not only Munich's most important art museum, but one of the most significant collections in Europe. The nearly 900 paintings on display (many thousands more are in storage) in this huge neoclassical building represent the greatest European artists of the 14th through the 18th centuries. Begun as a small court collection by the royal Wittelsbach family in the early 1500s, the collection has grown and grown. There are only two floors with exhibits, but the museum is immense.

Albrecht Altdorfer, landscape painter *par excellence* of the Danube school, is represented by no fewer than six monumental works. The works of Albrecht Dürer include his greatest—and final—*Self-Portrait* (1500). Here the artist has portrayed himself with almost Christ-like solemnity. Also displayed is the last great painting by the artist, his two-paneled work called *The Four Apostles* (1526).

Antikensammlungen (Museum of Antiquities). Königsplatz 1. ☎ **089/59-83-59.** Admission 6DM ($3.60) adults, 3.50DM ($2.10) students and children. Joint ticket to the Museum of Antiquities and the Glyptothek, 10DM ($6) adults, 5DM ($3) students and children. Tues and Thurs–Sun 10am–5pm; Wed 10am–8pm. U-Bahn: U2 to Königsplatz.

On the south side of Königsplatz, the five main-floor halls house more than 650 Greek vases. The oldest piece is "the goddess from Aegina" from 3000 B.C. Technically not pottery, this pre-Mycenaean figure, carved from a mussel shell, is on display with the Mycenaean pottery exhibits in Room I. Take the stairs down to the lower level to see the collection of Greek, Roman, and Etruscan jewelry.

✪ **Bayerisches Nationalmuseum (Bavarian National Museum).** Prinzregentenstrasse 3. ☎ **089/21-124-1.** Admission 4DM ($2.40) adults, 3DM ($1.80) students and seniors, free for children under 15. No admission on Sun. Tues–Sun 9:30am–5pm. U-Bahn: U4 or U5 to Lehel. Tram: 17. Bus: 53.

Three vast floors of sculpture, painting, folk art, ceramics, furniture, textiles, and scientific instruments demonstrate Bavaria's artistic and historical riches. Entering the museum, turn to the right and go into the first large gallery called the **Wessobrunn Room.** Devoted to early church art from the 5th through the 13th centuries, this room holds some of the oldest and most valuable works. The desk case contains ancient and medieval ivories, including the so-called Munich ivory, from about A.D. 400.

The **Riemenschneider Room** is devoted to the works of the great sculptor Tilman Riemenschneider (ca. 1460–1531) and his contemporaries. The second floor contains a fine collection of stained and painted glass—an art in which medieval Germany excelled—baroque ivory carvings, Meissen porcelain, and ceramics.

✪ **Deutsches Museum (German Museum of Masterpieces of Science and Technology).** Museumsinsel 1. ☎ **089/2-17-91.** Admission 10DM ($6) adults, 7DM ($4.20) seniors, 4DM ($2.40) students, 3DM ($1.80) children 6–12, free for children 5 and under. Daily 9am–5pm (closes at 2pm the second Wed in Dec). Closed major holidays. S-Bahn: Isartor. Tram: 18.

On an island in the Isar River is the largest technological museum of its kind in the world. Its huge collection of priceless artifacts and historic originals includes the first electric dynamo (Siemens, 1866), the first automobile (Benz, 1886), the first diesel engine (1897), and the laboratory bench at which the atom was first split (Hahn, Strassmann, 1938). There are hundreds of buttons to push, levers to crank, and gears to turn, as well as a knowledgeable staff to answer questions and demonstrate how steam engines, pumps, or historical musical instruments work. Among the most popular displays are those on mining, with a series of model coal, salt, and iron mines, as well as the electrical power hall, with high-voltage displays that actually produce lightning. There are many other exhibits, covering the whole range of science and technology.

Glyptothek. Königsplatz 3. ☎ **089/28-61-00.** Admission 6DM ($3.60) adults, 3DM ($1.80) seniors, 1DM (60¢) children. Joint ticket to the Museum of Antiquities and the Glyptothek, 10DM ($6) adults, free for children under 14. Tues–Sun 10am–5pm. U-Bahn: U2 to Königsplatz.

The Glyptothek supplements the pottery and smaller pieces of the main museum with an excellent collection of ancient Greek and Roman sculpture. Included are the famous pediments from the temple of Aegina, two marvelous statues of *kouroi* (youths) from the 6th century B.C., the colossal figure of a *Sleeping Satyr* from the Hellenistic period, and a splendid collection of Roman portraits. The collection is the country's largest assemblage of classical art.

Neue Pinakothek. Barer Strasse 29. ☎ **089/23-80-51-95.** Admission 7DM ($4.20) adults, 4DM ($2.40) students and seniors, free for children 15 and under. Wed–Sun 10am–5pm; Tues 10am–8pm. U-Bahn: U2 to Königsplatz. Tram: 27. Bus: 53.

Neue Pinakothek offers a survey of 18th- and 19th-century art. Across Theresienstrasse from the Alte Pinakothek, the museum has paintings by Gainsborough, Goya, David, Manet, van Gogh, and Monet. Among the more popular German artists represented are Wilhelm Leibl and Gustav Klimt; you'll encounter a host of others whose art is less well known. Note particularly the genre paintings by Carl Spitzweg.

✪ **Residenz.** Max-Joseph-Platz 3. ☎ **089/29-06-71.** Combination ticket for Residenzmuseum and Schatzkammer 12DM ($7.20) adults, 8DM ($4.80) students/seniors, free for ages 15 and under. Ticket for either Schatzkammer or Residenzmuseum 7DM ($4.20) adults, 5DM ($3) seniors/students, free for age 15 and under. Museum and Treasury, Tues–Sun 10am–4:30pm (last tickets sold at 4pm); theater, Mon–Sat 2–5pm, Sun 10am–5pm. U-Bahn: U3, U4, U5, or U6 to Odeonsplatz.

This palace was the official residence of the rulers of Bavaria from 1385 to 1918. Added to and rebuilt over the centuries, the complex is a conglomerate of various styles of art and architecture. Depending on how you approach the Residenz, you might first see a German Renaissance hall (the western facade), a Palladian palace (on the north), or a Florentine Renaissance palace (on the south facing Max-Joseph-Platz). The Residenz has been completely restored since its almost total destruction in World War II and now houses the Residenz Museum, a concert hall, the Cuvilliés Theater, and the Residenz Treasure House.

Residenzmuseum, Max-Joseph-Platz 3 (☎ **089/29-06-71**), comprises the southwestern section of the palace, some 120 rooms of art and furnishings collected by centuries of Wittelsbachs. To see the entire collection, you'll have to take two tours, one in the morning and the other in the afternoon. You can also visit the rooms on your own.

If you have time to view only one item in the **Schatzkammer (Treasure House),** make it the 16th-century Renaissance statue of *St. George Slaying the Dragon.* The equestrian statue is made of gold, but you can barely see the precious metal for the thousands of diamonds, rubies, emeralds, sapphires, and semiprecious stones embedded in it.

From the Brunnenhof, you can visit the **Cuvilliés Theater,** whose rococo tiers of boxes are supported by seven bacchants. The huge box, where the family sat, is in the center. In summer this theater is the scene of frequent concert and opera performances. Mozart's *Idomeneo* was first performed here in 1781.

✪ **Schloss Nymphenburg.** Schloss Nymphenburg 1. ☎ **089/17-908-668.** Admission to all attractions 8DM ($4.80), free for children 14 and under. Nymphenburg Palace, Amalienburg, Marstallmuseum, and museum of porcelain 6DM ($3.60), free for children 14 and under. Apr–Sept Tues–Sun 10am–noon and 1:30–5pm; Oct–Mar Tues–Sun 10am–noon and 1:30–4pm. Parking beside the Marstallmuseum. U-Bahn: U1 to Rotkreuzplatz, then tram no. 17 toward Amalienburgstrasse. Bus: 41.

In summer, the Wittelsbachs would pack up their bags and head for their country house, Schloss Nymphenburg. A more complete, more sophisticated palace than the Residenz in Munich, it was begun in 1664 in Italian villa style and went through more than 150 years and several architectural changes before completion.

Entering the main building, you're in the great hall, decorated in rococo colors and stuccos, with frescoes by Zimmermann (1756). This hall was used for both banquets and concerts in the 18th century. Concerts are still presented here in summer. From the main building, turn left and head for the arcaded gallery connecting the northern pavilions. The first room in the arcade is the Great Gallery of Beauties. More provocative, however, is Ludwig I's Gallery of Beauties in the south pavilion (the apartments of Queen Caroline). Ludwig commissioned no fewer than 36 portraits of the most beautiful women of his day. The paintings by J. Stieler (painted from 1827 to 1850) include the *Schöne Münchnerin* (*Lovely Munich Girl*) and a portrait of Lola Montez, the dancer whose "friendship" with Ludwig I caused a scandal that factored into the Revolution of 1848.

CHURCHES

Peterskirche (St. Peter's Church). Rindermarkt 1. ☎ **089/260-48-28.** Church, free; tower 2.50DM ($1.40) adults, 1.50DM (85¢) students. 50DM (30¢) children. Apr–Oct daily 9am–7pm, Nov–Mar daily 9am–6pm. U-Bahn: Marienplatz.

This is Munich's oldest church (1180). Its tall steeple is worth the climb in clear weather for a view as far as the Alps. In its gilded baroque interior are murals by Johann Baptist Zimmermann. The **Asamkirche,** Sendlinger Strasse, is a remarkable example of rococo, designed by the Asam brothers, Cosmas Damian and Edgar Quirin, in 1733 to 1746. The **Michaelskirche,** Neuhauser Strasse 52, has the distinction of being the largest Renaissance church north of the Alps. The lovely **Theatinerkirche,** Theatinerstrasse 22, with its graceful fluted columns and arched ceilings, is the work of the court architect, François Cuvilliés and his son.

✪ **Frauenkirche (Cathedral of Our Lady).** Frauenplatz 1. Free admission. Daily 7am–7pm. U-Bahn and S-Bahn: Marienplatz.

When the smoke cleared from the 1945 bombings, only a fragile shell remained of Munich's largest church. Workmen and architects who restored the 15th-century Gothic cathedral used whatever remains they could find in the rubble, along with modern innovations. The overall effect of the rebuilt Frauenkirche is strikingly simple yet dignified. The twin towers, which remained intact, have been the city's landmark since 1525. Instead of the typical flying buttresses, huge props on the inside that separate the side chapels support the edifice. The Gothic vaulting over the nave and chancel is borne by 22 simple octagonal pillars.

Entering the main doors at the cathedral's west end, you at first don't notice the windows; other than the tall chancel window, they're hidden by the enormous pillars. According to legend, the devil laughed at the notion of hidden windows and stamped in glee at the stupidity of the architect—you can still see the strange footlike mark called "the devil's step" in the entrance hall.

ORGANIZED TOURS

One of the easiest, and fastest, ways to gain an overview of Munich, one of Germany's largest and most complicated cities, is by means of a guided tour. One of the largest organizers of these tours is **Panorama Tours** (an affiliate of Gray Line), Arnulfstrasse 8 (☎ **089/550-28995**), whose headquarters lie just north of Munich's Hauptbahnhof. At least a half-dozen touring options are available, ranging from a quickie 1-hour overview of the city to full-day excursions to such outlying sites as Berchtesgaden, Oberammergau, and Hohenschwangau, site of three of Bavaria's most stunning palaces.

City tours encompass aspects of both modern and medieval Munich, and depart from the main railway stations aboard blue-sided buses. Departures, depending on the season and the tour, occur between two and eight times a day, and tours are conducted in both German and English. Most tours don't last more than 2½ hours, with the exception of a scientific odyssey that focuses on the technological triumphs of Munich as witnessed by various museums that include the Deutsches Museum. That experience usually lasts a minimum of 4 hours, plus whatever time you spend wandering through museums at the end of your tour.

Depending on the tour, adults pay from 17DM to 39DM ($10.20 to $23.40); children under 12 pay between 9DM to 20DM ($5.40 to $12). Advance reservations for most city tours aren't required, and you can buy your ticket from the bus driver when you board at the city tour departure point near Munich's Hauptbahnhof.

If you want to participate in any tour that covers attractions outside the city limits of Munich, advance reservations are required, especially if you want the bus to pick you up at any of Munich's hotels. Any travel agent in Munich, as well as the concierge or reception staff at any of the hotels, can book a place for you aboard these tours, but if you want to contact Panorama Tours directly, they're open as follows: between November and April, Tuesday, Thursday, and Saturday from 7:30am to 6pm, and Monday, Wednesday, and Friday from 9am to 6pm; between May and October, daily 7:30am to 6pm.

Pedal pushers will want to try Mike Lasher's **Mike's Bike Tour,** St. Bonifatius-strasse 2 (☎ **089/651-4275**). His bike rentals for 29DM ($17.40) include maps and locks, child and infant seats, and helmets at no extra charge. English and bilingual tours of central Munich run March through November, leaving daily at 11:30am and 4pm (call to confirm). The cost of the tour is 35DM ($21).

THE SHOPPING SCENE

The most interesting shops are concentrated on Munich's pedestrians-only streets between **Karlsplatz** and **Marienplatz.**

Handmade crafts can be found on the fourth floor of Munich's major department store, **Ludwig Beck am Rathauseck,** Am Marienplatz 11 (☎ **089/236-91-00**), and ✪ **Wallach,** Residenzstrasse 1 (☎ **089/22-08-71**), a fine place for handcrafts and folk art, both new and antique. Shop here for a memorable object to remind you of your trip. You'll find antique churns, old hand-painted wooden boxes and trays, painted porcelain clocks, and many other items.

✪ **Dirndl-Ecke,** Am Platzl 1/Sparkassenstrasse 10 (☎ **089/22-01-63**), 1 block up from the famed Hofbräuhaus, gets our unreserved recommendation as a stylish place specializing in dirndls, feathered alpine hats, and all the clothing associated with the alpine regions. Everything is of the best quality—there's no tourist junk. Bavarian clothing for children is also available.

The founders of **Hemmerle,** Maximilianstrasse 14 (☎ **089/24-22-600**), made their fortune designing bejeweled fantasies for the Royal Bavarian Court of the fairy-tale king, Ludwig II. Today, all pieces are limited editions, designed and made in-house by Bavarian craftspeople.

On the grounds of Schloss Nymphenburg at Nördliches Schlossrondell 8, you'll find **Nymphenburger Porzellan-manufaktur** (☎ **089/17-91-970**), one of Germany's most famous porcelain makers. You can visit the exhibition and sales rooms; shipments can be arranged if you make purchases. There's also a branch in Munich's center, at Odeonsplatz 1 (☎ **089/28-24-28**).

MUNICH AFTER DARK

To find out what's happening in the Bavarian capital, go to the tourist office and request a copy of *Monats-programm,* costing 2.50DM ($1.50). This pamphlet has complete information about what's going on in Munich and how to purchase tickets.

THE PERFORMING ARTS

Nowhere else in Europe, other than London and Paris, will you find so many musical and theatrical performances. The good news is the low cost of the seats—you'll get good tickets if you're willing to pay anywhere from 15DM to 75DM ($9 to $45).

✪ **Altes Residenztheater (Cuvilliés Theater).** Residenzstrasse 1. ☎ **089/2185-19-40.** Opera tickets, 30DM–255DM ($18–$153); play tickets, 20DM–71DM ($12–$42.60); building tours 3DM ($1.80). U-Bahn: Odeonsplatz.

A part of the Residenz (see "Museums & Palaces," above), this theater is a sightseeing attraction in its own right, and Germany's most outstanding example of a rococo tier-boxed theater. During World War II the interior was dismantled and stored. You can tour it Monday through Friday 2 to 5pm and Sunday 10am to 5pm. The **Bavarian State Opera** and the **Bayerisches Staatsschauspiel (State Theater Company)** perform smaller works here in keeping with the tiny theater's intimate character. Box-office hours are Monday through Friday 10am to 6pm, plus 1 hour prior to performances. On Saturday, it's open from 10am to 1pm only.

Deutsches Theater. Schwanthalerstrasse 13. ☎ **089/552-34-444.** Tickets 40DM–115DM ($24–$69), higher for special events. U-Bahn: Karlsplatz/Stachus.

The regular season of the Deutsches Theater lasts throughout the year. Musicals, operettas, ballets, and international shows are performed here. During carnival season (January to February), the theater becomes a ballroom for more than 2,000 guests.

✪ **Gasteig Kulturzentrum.** Rosenheimer Strasse 5. ☎ **089/48-09-80.** Tickets 15DM–80DM ($9–$48). S-Bahn: take to Rosenheimer Platz, then tram no. 18 to Gasteig. Bus: 51.

The Gasteig Cultural Center is the home of the **Münchner Philharmoniker (Munich Philharmonic Orchestra),** which was founded in 1893. Its present home, which opened in 1985, also shelters the Richard Strauss Conservatory and the Munich Municipal Library. The orchestra performs in Philharmonic Hall, which has the largest seating capacity of the center's five performance halls. In the Haidhausen district, Gasteig stands on the bluffs of the Isar River. You can buy tickets at the ground-level Glashalle Monday through Friday 9am to 6pm and Saturday 9am to 2pm. The Philharmonic season begins in mid-September and runs to July.

✪ **Nationaltheater.** Max-Joseph-Platz 2. ☎ **089/2185-1920.** Tickets 12DM–20DM ($7.20–$12) opera; 8DM–10DM ($4.80–$6) ballet, including standing room. U-Bahn or S-Bahn: Marienplatz.

Practically any night of the year, except August to mid-September, you'll find a performance at the opera house, home of the **Bavarian State Opera,** one of the world's great opera companies. The productions are beautifully mounted and presented and feature famous singers. Hard-to-get tickets can be purchased Monday through Friday 10am to 6pm, plus 1 hour before each performance (during the weekend, only on Saturday from 10am to 1pm). The Nationaltheater is also home to the Bavarian State Ballet.

BEER HALLS

Augustinerbrau. Neuhäuserstrasse 27. ☎ **089/231-83-257.** Open daily 9am–midnight. U-Bahn or S-Bahn: Stachus. Tram: 19.

On the principal pedestrian-only street of Munich, this beer hall offers generous helpings of food, good beer, and a mellow atmosphere. It's been around for only a little less than a century, but beer was first brewed on this spot in 1328. The cuisine is not for dieters: It's hearty, heavy, and starchy, but it sure soaks up that beer.

✪ **Hofbräuhaus am Platzl.** Am Platzl 9. ☎ **089/22-16-76.** Open daily 9:30am–midnight. U-Bahn or S-Bahn: Marienplatz.

The world's most famous beer hall, the Hofbräuhaus is a legend. Visitors with only 1 night in Munich usually target the Hofbräuhaus as their number-one nighttime destination. Owned by the state, the present Hofbräuhaus was built at the end of the 19th century, but the tradition of a beer house on this spot dates from 1589. In the 19th century it attracted artists, students, and civil servants, and was known as the Blue Hall because of its dim lights and smoky atmosphere. When it grew too small to contain everybody, architects designed another in 1897. This one was the 1920 setting for the notorious meeting of Hitler's newly launched German Workers Party.

Today 4,500 beer drinkers can crowd in here on a given night. Several rooms are spread over three floors, including a top-floor room for dancing. The ground floor, with its brass band (which starts playing at 11am), is exactly what you expect of a beer hall—here it's eternal Oktoberfest.

Waldwirtschaft Grosshesslohe. George-Kalb-Strasse 3. ☎ **089/74-99-4030.** Gardens open daily 11am–11pm. Tram: 7.

This popular summertime rendezvous has seats for some 2,000 drinkers. (Note, they have to close early because neighborhood residenst complain.) Music ranging from Dixieland to English jazz to Polish bands is played throughout the week. Entrance is free, and you bring your own food. It's located above the Isar River in the vicinity of the zoo.

THE CLUB & MUSIC SCENE

Bayerischer Hof Night Club. In the Hotel Bayerischer Hof, Promenadeplatz 2–6. ☎ **089/212-09-94.** Piano bar Tues–Sun 7–10pm. Bandstand Tues–Sun 10pm–3am. Cover free to 45DM ($27). Tram: 19.

Here you'll find some of Munich's most sophisticated entertainment. Behind a partition, there's a bandstand for live orchestras. Entrance to the piano bar is free, but there's a cover charge to get into the nightclub. Daily happy hour is from 7 to 8:30pm in the piano bar, with drinks starting at 12DM ($7.20).

Jazzclub Unterfahrt. Kirchenstrasse 96. ☎ **089/448-27-94.** Tues–Sun 8pm–1am. Cover Tues–Sat 15DM–28DM ($9–$16.80); Sun jam session 5DM ($3). U-Bahn or S-Bahn: Ostbahnhof.

This is Munich's leading jazz club for live music, lying near the Ostbahnhof in the Haidhausen district. Wine, small snacks, beer, and drinks are sold as well. Sunday night there's a special jam session for improvisation.

Mister B's. Herzog-Heinrichstrasse 38. ☎ **089/534901.** Tues–Sun doors open at 8pm. Cover 8DM–10DM ($4.80–$6). U-Bahn: Goetheplatz.

Small, dark, and popular with blues and jazz aficionados, this club hosts a slightly older, mellower crowd than the rock and dance clubs. Blues, jazz, and rhythm-and-blues combos take the stage on Thursday through Saturday.

Nachtwerk. Landesbergerstrasse 185. ☎ **089/578-3800.** Thurs 10pm–4am, Fri–Sat doors open at 10:30. Cover 10DM ($6). S-Bahn: Donnersbergerbrücke.

Set in a huge factory warehouse, this is a dance club that also books bands. It's a festive place that's not nearly as pretentious as other more "exclusive" discos (that is, the doorman won't send you away for wearing the wrong shoes or pants).

Parkcafé. Sophienstrasse 7. ☎ **089/59-83-13.** Doors open at 10pm Wed–Sat. Cover 10DM ($6). U-Bahn: Königsplatz.

Male dancers in black leather and feather boas gyrate on elevated platforms, while beautiful people trance out to loud music on the dance floor below them. Who'd ever guess this home to chic freaks was a Nazi hangout in the 1930s?

THE BAR & CAFE SCENE

Once a literary cafe, **Alter Simpl,** Türkenstrasse 57 (☎ **089/272-30-83**), attracts a diverse crowd of locals, including young people. The real fun begins after 11pm, when the iconoclastic artistic ferment becomes more reminiscent of Berlin than Bavaria. Open Sunday to Thursday 11am to 3am, Friday and Saturday 11am to 4am. Take tram no. 18 or bus no. 53.

Nachtcafé, Maximilianplatz 5 (☎ **089/59-59-00**), hums, thrives, and captures the nocturnal imagination of everyone—no other nightspot in Munich attracts such an array of soccer stars, film celebrities, literary figures, and, as one employee put it, "ordinary people, but only the most sympathetically crazy ones." Waves of patrons appear at different times of the evening: at 11pm, when live concerts begin; at 2am, when the restaurants close; and at 4am, when die-hard revelers seek a final drink in the predawn hours. The music is jazz, blues, funk, and soul and the decor is updated 1950s. There's no cover charge. It's open daily from 9pm to 6am. Take tram no. 19.

Schumann's, Maximilianstrasse 36 (☎ **089/22-90-60**), doesn't waste any money on decor—it depends on the local *beau monde* to keep it looking chic. In warm weather the terrace spills out onto the street. Schumann's is known as a "thinking man's bar." Charles Schumann, author of three bar books, wanted a bar that would be an artistic, literary, and communicative social focus of the metropolis. Popular with the film, advertising, and publishing worlds, his place is said to have contributed to a remarkable renaissance of bar culture in the city. It's open Sunday to Friday 5pm to 3am and closed Saturday. Take tram no. 19.

GAY & LESBIAN CLUBS

Much of Munich's gay and lesbian scene takes place in the blocks between the Viktualienmarkt and Gärtnerplatz, particularly on Hans-Sachs-Strasse.

The strident rhythms and electronic sounds of **New York,** Sonnenstrasse 25 (☎ **089/59-10-56**), might just have been imported from New York, Los Angeles, or Paris. The sound system is accompanied by laser-light shows. This is Munich's premier gay (male) disco. Most clients, ranging in age from 20 to 35, wear jeans. There's no cover Monday through Thursday; Friday to Sunday cover is 10DM ($6) including the first drink. It's open daily from 11pm. Take U-Bahn U1, U2, U3, or U6 to Sendlingertorplatz.

Soul City, Maximilianplatz 5 (☎ **089/595272**), is the gay dance club in Munich. Scattered nooks allow conversation sheltered from one of the best sound systems in the city, as well as offering a brief respite from the throng on the dance floor and at the bar. The 10DM ($6) cover charge on Thursday and Friday includes free drinks, and on Saturday you get discounted drink coupons. Open Sunday to Thursday 10pm to 4am, and Friday and Saturday 10pm to 6am. U-Bahn: Karlsplatz.

Teddy Bar, Hans-Sachsstrasse 1 (☎ **089/260-33-59**), is a small, cozy gay bar decorated with teddy bears. It draws a congenial crowd, both foreign and domestic. There's no cover. From October to April, there's a Sunday brunch from 11am to 3pm. The bar is open daily from 6pm to 3am. Take the U-Bahn to Sendlingertor, or tram no. 17, 18 or 27.

Other hot spots include **Mylord,** Ickstattstrasse 2A (☎ **089/260-44-98**), for three decades a lesbian hangout, although drawing a mixed crowd these days, often actors, writers, and musicians, even transvestites and transsexuals. It has a cozy living room atmosphere. Open Sunday to Thursday 6pm to 1am and Friday and Saturday 6pm to 3am. U-Bahn: 6 to Sendlingertorplatz or tram no. 17.

It's said that if Rick (that is, Bogie of Casablanca) were alive today, he'd be operating **Club Morizz,** Klenzestrasse 43 (☎ **089/2-01-67-76**), a stylish gay bar ringed with mirrors. Relax with drinks or food in red leather armchairs clustered around marble-topped tables. The electric menu includes well-prepared Thai dishes, as well as European specialties. Open Sunday to Thursday 7pm to 2am, and Friday and Saturday 7pm to 3am.

DAY TRIPS FROM MUNICH

DACHAU   In 1933, what had once been a quiet little artists' community just 10 miles from Munich became a tragic symbol of the Nazi era. In March, shortly after Hitler became chancellor, Himmler and the SS set up the first German concentration camp on the grounds of a former ammunition factory. Countless prisoners arrived at Dachau between 1933 and 1945. Although the files show a registry of more than 206,000, the exact number of people imprisoned here is unknown.

Entering the camp, **KZ-Gedenkstätte Dachau,** Alte-Römar-Strasse 75 (☎ **08131/1741**), you are faced by three memorial chapels—Catholic, Protestant, and Jewish. Immediately behind the Catholic chapel is the Lagerstrasse, the main camp road lined with poplar trees, once flanked by 32 barracks, each housing 208 prisoners. Two barracks have been rebuilt to give visitors insight into the conditions endured by the prisoners.

The **museum** is housed in the large building that once contained the kitchen, laundry, and shower baths where the SS often brought prisoners for torture. Photographs, documents, and exhibits depict the rise of the Nazi regime and the history of the camp.

Getting There   You can get to the camp by taking the frequent S-Bahn trains (train no. S2) from the Hauptbahnhof to the Dachau station (direction: Petershausen), and then bus no. 724 or 726 from the station to the camp. Admission is free, and the camp is open Tuesday through Sunday 9am to 5pm. The English version of a documentary film, *KZ-Dachau,* is shown at 11:30am and 3:30pm.

HERRENCHIEMSEE & THE NEUES SCHLOSS   Known as the "Bavarian Sea," Chiemsee is one of the Bavarian Alps' most beautiful lakes in a serene landscape. Its main attraction lies on the island of Herrenchiemsee, where "Mad" King Ludwig II built one of his fantastic castles.

✪ **Neues Schloss,** begun by Ludwig II in 1878, was never completed because of the king's death in 1886. The castle was to have been a replica of the grand palace of Versailles that Ludwig so admired. One of the architects of Herrenchiemsee was Julius Hofmann, who the king had also employed for the construction of his alpine castle, Neuschwanstein. When work was halted in 1886, only the center of the enormous palace had been completed. The palace and its formal gardens remain one of the most fascinating of Ludwig's adventures, in spite of their unfinished state.

The splendid Great Hall of Mirrors most authentically replicates Versailles. The 17 door panels contain enormous mirrors reflecting the 33 crystal chandeliers and the 44 gilded candelabra. The vaulted ceiling is covered with 25 paintings depicting the life of Louis XIV. The dining room is a popular attraction for visitors because of the table nicknamed "the little table that lays itself." A mechanism in the floor permitted the table to go down to the room below to be cleared and relaid between courses.

You can visit Herrenchiemsee at any time of the year. From April to September 30, tours are given daily from 9am to 5pm; off-season, daily 10am to 4pm. Admission (in addition to the round-trip boat fare) is 8DM ($4.80) for adults, 5DM ($3) for students, and free for children under 15.

Getting There   You can reach Herrenchiemsee by taking the train to Prien am Chiemsee, about an hour's trip. For train information, call ☎ **08051/28-74.** There is also regional bus service, offered by **RVO Regionalver-kehr Oberbayern** (☎ **08021/948274** for schedules and information). Access by car is via the A-8 Autobahn from Munich.

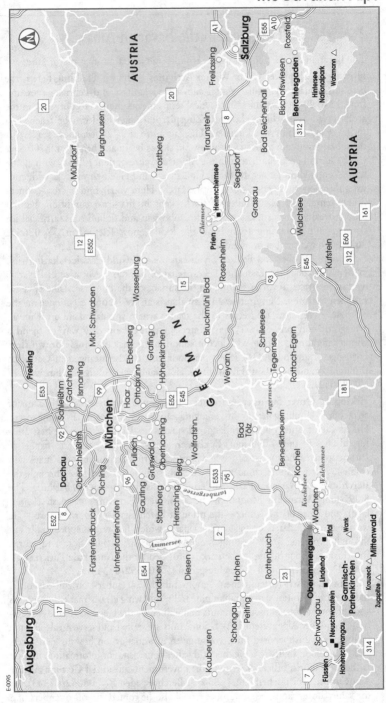

The Bavarian Alps

465

Outdoors in the Bavarian Alps

The Bavarian Alps are both a winter wonderland and a summer playground.

Hitting the Slopes & Other Winter Activities   The winter **skiing** here is the best in Germany. A regular winter snowfall in January and February measures from 12 to 20 inches, which in practical terms means about 6 feet of snow in the areas served by ski lifts. The great **Zugspitzplatt** snowfield can be reached in spring or autumn by a rack railway. The Zugspitze at 9,720 feet above sea level is the tallest mountain peak in Germany. Ski slopes begin at a height of 8,700 feet.

The second great ski district in the Alps is **Berchtesgadener Land,** with alpine skiing centered on Jenner, Rossfeld, Goütschen, and Hochschwarzeck, with consistently good snow conditions until March. Here you'll find a cross-country skiing center and many miles of tracks kept in first-class condition, natural toboggan runs, one artificial ice run for toboggan and skibob runs, artificial ice skating, and ice-curling rinks. Call the local "Snow-Telefon" at ☎ **08652/ 967-297** for current snow conditions.

Between October and February, you can use the world-class **ice-skating** rink in Berchtesgaden (the Eisstadion). Less reliable, but more evocative of Bavaria's wild open spaces, involves skating on the surface of the Hintersee Lake once it's sufficiently frozen. More rare even than that is an ice-skating experience on the Königsee, whose surface freezes to the degree where you can skate on it on an average of only one of every ten winters. A particularly cozy way to spend a winter's night is to huddle with a companion in the back of a **horse-drawn sled.** For a fee of around 90DM ($54) per hour, this can be arranged in Garmisch through **Brandtner, GmbH,** at the Café Waldstein, Königseer Fussweg 17 (☎ **08652/2427**).

Hiking & Other Summer Activities   In summer, **alpine hiking** is a major attraction—climbing mountains, enjoying nature, watching animals in the forest. Hikers can at times observe endangered species firsthand. One of the best areas for hiking is the 4,060-foot **Eckbauer,** lying on the southern fringe of Partenkirchen (the tourist office at Garmisch-Partenkirchen supplies maps and details). Many visitors come to the Alps in summer just to hike through the **Berchtesgaden National Park,** bordering the Austrian province of Salzburg. The 8,091-foot Watzmann Mountain, the Königssee (Germany's cleanest, clearest lake), and parts of the Jenner—the pride of Berchtesgaden's four ski areas—are within the boundaries of the national park, which has well-mapped trails cut through protected areas, leading the hiker along spectacular flora and fauna. Information about hiking in the park is provided by the **Nationale Parkverwaltung,** Doktorberg 6, 83471 Berchtesgaden (☎ **08652/64343**).

From Garmisch-Partenkirchen, serious hikers can embark on full-day or, if they're more ambitious, overnight alpine treks, following clearly marked footpaths and staying in isolated mountain huts maintained by the German Alpine Association (Deutscher Alpenverein/DAV). Some huts are staffed and serve meals. For the truly remote unsupervised huts, you're given information on how to gain access and your responsibility to leave them tidy after your visit. For information, inquire at the local tourist office, or write to the government-subsidized **German Alpine Association,** Am Fischerbichl 1, 83471, Berchtesgaden (☎ **08652/64343**). At the same address and phone number, you'll also be routed to staff members of a privately owned tour operator, the **Summit Club,** an outfit devoted to the organization of high-altitude expeditions throughout Europe and the world.

If you are a true outdoorsperson, you'll briefly savor the somewhat touristy facilities of Garmisch-Partenkirchen, and then use it as a base for exploring the rugged Berchtesgaden National Park, which is within an easy commute of Garmisch. You can also stay at one of the inns in Mittenwald or Oberammergau and take advantage of a wide roster of sporting diversions within the wild open spaces. The outfitter below will provide directions and link-ups with their sports programs from wherever you decide to stay. Street maps of Berchtesgaden and its environs are usually available for free from the **Kurdirektion** (the local tourist office) at Berchtesgaden (☎ **08652/967-0**), and more intricately detailed maps of the surrounding alpine topography are available for a fee.

In addition to hill climbing and rock climbing, summertime activities include **ballooning,** which, weather permitting, can be arranged through Outdoor Club Berchtesgaden, Ludwig-Ganghofer-Strasse 20½ (☎ 08652/50-01). Local enthusiasts warn that ballooning is not a sport for the timid or anyone who suffers unduly in the cold: Warm thermal currents that prevail around Berchtesgaden in summer limit the sport to the cold-weather months. Consequently, the seasonal heyday for ballooning is between December and February. A local variation of **curling** (*Eisstock*) that makes use of wooden, rather than stone, instruments can usually be arranged even when ice and snows have melted on the surrounding slopes at the town's biggest ice rink, Berchtesgaden Eisstadion, An der Schiessstätte (☎ **08652/61405**). If you opted not to carry your ice skates in your luggage during your transatlantic flight, don't worry: A kiosk (☎ **08652/3384**) in the ice stadium rents a wide spectrum of ice skates in all sizes for around 7DM ($4.20) per hour.

Cycling and mountain biking, available through the rental facilities of **Full Stall,** Maximilianstrasse 16 (☎ **08652/948450**), give outdoor enthusiasts an opportunity to simultaneously enjoy the outdoors and exercise their leg muscles.

Anglers will find plenty of **fishing** opportunities (especially salmon, pike-perch, and trout) at Lake Hintersee and the rivers Ramsauer Ache and Königsseer Ache, although in most cases, it's best to get a fishing permit. To acquire one, contact either the Kurdirektion (tourist office) at Berchtesgaden, which directs you to any of four different authorities, based on where you want to fish. For fishing specifically within the Hintersee, contact officials at the **Kurverwaltung,** Im Tal 2 (☎ **08657/98-89-20**) at Ramsau, 7½ miles from Berchtesgaden.

Despite its obvious dangers, **hang-gliding** or **paragliding** from the vertiginous slopes of Mount Jenner can be thrilling. To arrange it, contact the previously recommended Full Stall (see above), or Full Stall's competitor, **Para-Taxi,** Königseestrasse 15 (☎ **08652/948450**). At the same address, you'll find the headquarters for a loosely allied group of parasailing enthusiasts, the **Berchtesgaden Gleitschirmflieger** (☎ **08652/23-63**), whose members sometimes arrange communal paragliding excursions on which qualified newcomers are invited. Practice your **kayaking** or **whitewater-rafting** techniques on one of the many rivers in the area, such as the Ramsauer, Königisser, Bischofswiesener, and the Berchtesgadener Aches. For information and options, contact the above-mentioned Outdoor Club Berchtesgaden.

If you'd like to go **swimming** in an alpine lake—not to everyone's body temperature—there are many "lidos" found in the Bavarian Forest.

From Prien, lake steamers make the trip to Herrenchiemsee. They are operated by **Chiemsee-Schiffahrt Ludwig Fessler** (☎ **08051/60-90** for information). The round-trip fare is 10DM ($6). For visitor information, contact the **Kur und Verkehrsamt,** Alte Rathausstrasse 11, in Prien am Chiemsee (☎ **0851/6-90-50**), open Monday through Friday from 8:30am to 6pm, Saturday 9am to noon.

GARMISCH-PARTENKIRCHEN

In spite of its urban flair, Garmisch-Partenkirchen, Germany's top alpine resort, has maintained the charm of an ancient village. Even today you occasionally see country folk in traditional costumes, and you might be held up in traffic while the cattle are led from their mountain grazing grounds down through the streets of town. Garmisch is about 55 miles southwest of Munich.

ESSENTIALS

GETTING THERE   By Train   The Garmisch-Partenkirchen Bahnhof lies on the major Munich-Weilheim-Garmisch-Mittenwald-Innsbruck rail line with frequent connections in all directions. Twenty trains per day arrive from Munich (trip time: 1 hour, 22 minutes). For rail information and schedules, call ☎ **08821/19-419.**

By Bus   Both long-distance and regional buses through the Bavarian Alps are provided by **RVO Regionalverkehr Oberbayern** in Garmisch-Partenkirchen (☎ **08821/948-274** for information).

By Car   Access is via the A-95 Autobahn from Munich; exit at Eschenlohe.

VISITOR INFORMATION   For tourist information, contact the **Kurverwaltung und Verkehrsamt,** Richard-Strauss-Platz (☎ **08821/18-06**), open Monday through Saturday 8am to 6pm and Sunday 10am to noon.

GETTING AROUND   An unnumbered municipal bus services the town, depositing passengers at Marienplatz or the Bahnhof, from where you can walk to all centrally located hotels. This free bus runs every 15 minutes.

SEEING THE SIGHTS IN TOWN

The symbol of the city's growth and modernity is the **Olympic Ice Stadium,** built for the 1936 Winter Olympics and capable of holding nearly 12,000 people. On the slopes at the edge of town is the much larger **Ski Stadium,** with two ski jumps and a slalom course. In 1936, more than 100,000 people watched the events in this stadium. Today it's still an integral part of winter life in Garmisch—the World Cup Ski Jump is held here every New Year.

Garmisch-Partenkirchen is a center for winter sports, summer hiking, and mountain climbing. In addition, the town environs offer some of the most panoramic views and colorful buildings in Bavaria. The 18th-century pilgrimage **Chapel of St. Anton,** on a pinewood path at the edge of Partenkirchen, is all pink and silver, inside and out. Its graceful lines are characteristic of the time it was built. The **Philosopher's Walk** in the park surrounding the chapel is a delightful spot to enjoy the views of the mountains around the low-lying town.

EXPLORING THE ENVIRONS

One of the most beautiful of the alpine regions around Garmisch is the ✪ **Alpspitz region,** which hikers and hill climbers consider uplifting and healing for both the body and soul. Within its boundaries, you'll find alpine meadows, masses of seasonal wildflowers, and a rocky and primordial geology whose savage panoramas might strick you as Wagnerian. Ranging in altitude from 4,000 to 6,000 feet above sea level, the alps around

Garmisch-Partenkirchen are accessible by more than 30 ski lifts and funiculars, many of which run throughout the year.

The most appealing and panoramic of the lot includes the Alpspitz (Osterfelderkopf) cablecar that runs uphill from the center of Garmisch to the top of the Osterfelderkopf peak, at a height of 6,500 feet. It makes its 9-minute ascent at least every hour, year-round, between 8am and 5pm. The round-trip cost is 37DM ($22.20) for adults, 22DM ($13.20) for children ages 4 to 15, and 26DM ($15.60) for persons aged 16 to 18. After admiring the view at the top, you can either return directly to Garmisch, or continue your journey into the mountains via other cablecars. If you opt to continue, take the Hochalm cablecar across the high-altitude plateaux above Garmisch. At its terminus, you'll have two options, involving treks of either 20 minutes or 75 minutes, both across clearly marked alpine trails. The 20-minute trek takes you to the uppermost station of the Kreuzbergbahn, which carries you back to Garmisch. The 75-minute trek carries you to the upper terminus of the Hausbergbahn, which also carries you back to Garmisch.

Another of the many cablecar options in Garmisch involves an eastwardly cablecar ascent from the center of Partenkirchen to the top of the Wank (5,850 feet) via the Wankbahn, for a round-trip price of 26DM ($15.60). From here, you get a sweeping view of the plateau on which the twin villages of Garmisch and Partenkirchen sit. In winter, the top of the Wank is a favorite departure point for many downhill ski runs. It's also, however, a favorite with the patrons of Garmisch's spa facilities because the plentiful sunshine makes it ideal for the *Liegekur* (deck-chair cure) that's a favorite pastime with many of the resort's midwinter visitors.

If you plan on pursuing any of these options, perhaps in combination with each other, any of several other complicated cablecar/hiking trajectories around Garmisch, it's to your advantage to invest in a day pass, the Classic Garmisch Pass, with which you can ride most of the cablecars in the region (including those to the above-recommended Alpspitz, Kreuzeck, and Wank, and several others that fan out over the Eckbauer and the Ausberg) as many times as you like within the same day. Priced between 47DM ($28.20) and 55DM ($33) per person, depending on the season, the pass is available from any of the town's cablecar stations. For information on all the cablecar schedules and itineraries within the region, call ☎ **08821/7970.**

Another option for exploring the environs of Garmisch involves an ascent to the top of the ✪ **Zugspitze,** the tallest mountain (9,720 feet) in Germany, with a base set astride the Austrian frontier. Ski slopes begin at 8,700 feet. For a panoramic view over both the Bavarian and Tyrolean (Austrian) Alps, go all the way to the summit. The first stage of this ascent begins in the center of Garmisch by taking the cog railway to an intermediary alpine plateau (Zugspitzplatz). Trains depart at hourly intervals throughout the year from 7:39am to 2:39pm, although we recommend that you begin this transit by 1:39pm at the latest (and preferably earlier), and not wait until the cog railway's final ascent from Garmisch. At Zugspitzplatz, you can continue uphill on the same cog railway to the debut of a high-speed, 4-minute ride aboard the Gletscherbahn cablecar, which is the high-altitude conveyance you'll ride to the top of the Zugspitz peak. (The distance between Zugspitzplatz and the debut of the Gletscherbahn can also be transited aboard a secondary cablecar—the Eibsee-Seilbahn, which requires that you walk uphill for part of the route, so be warned in advance, if you're infirm or elderly, that it's advisable to remain aboard the train until its terminus at the debut of the Gletscherbahn.) Regardless of the exact route you follow, round-trip transit between the center of Garmisch and the top of the Zugspitz costs 61DM ($36.60) for adults, 43DM ($25.80) for people 16 to 17, and 37DM ($22.20) for children 5 to 15. Children under 4 ride free. Note that the price of the ascent to the Zugspitz is not included in the above-mentioned Classic Garmisch Pass, as it forms part of an independent network of cablecars that's not associated with the other cablecars within the region. For more information, call the tourist office or ☎ **08821/7920.**

WHERE TO STAY

Gästehaus Trenkler. Kreuzstrasse 20, 82467 Garmisch-Partenkirchen. ☎ **08821/34-39.** Fax 08821/15-67. 9 units (5 with shower). 85DM–90DM ($51–$54) double without shower; 95DM–98DM ($57–$58.80) double with shower. Rates include continental breakfast. No credit cards. Free parking. Bus: Eibsee no. 1.

For a number of years Frau Trenkler has made travelers feel well cared for in her guesthouse, which enjoys a quiet central location. She rents five doubles with showers and toilets and five doubles with hot and cold running water. Each bed is equipped with a good mattress and covered with a duvet. The linens are fresh and crisp. Rooms with private bathrooms have a minimum of medium-sized towels; corridor baths are adequate and tidily maintained. Rooms range from small to medium.

✪ **Post-Hotel Partenkirchen.** Ludwigstrasse 49, 82467 Garmisch-Partenkirchen. ☎ **08821/5-10-67.** Fax 08821/78-568. 59 units. MINIBAR TV TEL. 200DM–280DM ($120–$168) double. Rates include continental breakfast. AE, DC, MC, V.

The Post-Hotel Partenkirchen has emerged as one of the town's most prestigious hotels, especially with the added asset of its unusually fine restaurant (see "Where to Dine," below). The U-shaped rooms are generally medium-sized, with antiques and hand-decorated or elaborately carved furnishings. Duvets rest on comfortable beds with firm mattresses, mostly doubles or twins. Bathrooms are handsomely maintained with adequate shelf space and a hair dryer. The balconies are sun traps; they overlook a garden and offer a view of the Alps. Golf, tennis, swimming, hiking, mountain climbing, skiing, cycling, horseback riding, and paragliding can be arranged.

✪ **Reindl's Partenkirchner Hof.** Bahnhofstrasse 15, 82467 Garmisch-Partenkirchen. ☎ **08821/5-80-25.** Fax 08821/73-401. 65 units. MINIBAR TV TEL. 164DM–260DM ($98.40–$156) double; 260DM–650DM ($156–$390) suite. AE, DC, MC, V. Parking 14DM ($7.85). Closed Nov 10–Dec 15.

This special Bavarian retreat maintains a high level of luxury and hospitality. The annexes have balconies, and the main four-story building has wraparound verandas, giving each room an unobstructed view of the mountains and town. Bedrooms are often furnished with Bavarian artifacts, making for a cozy charm. The best are the suites opening onto panoramic views of mountains or the garden. Fine wool carpeting, rustic pine furniture, and excellent mattresses add to the allure of this place, as do the marble-clad bathrooms with toiletries, hair dryers, and plenty of fluffy towels. The place is also known for Reindl's much-honored restaurant (see "Where to Dine," below). Facilities include a covered pool, sauna, sun room, health club, open terrace for snacks, and two attractive gardens.

✪ **Romantik-Hotel Clausing's Posthotel.** Marienplatz 12, 82467 Garmisch-Partenkirchen. ☎ **08821/7090.** Fax 08821/70-92-05. 43 units. TV TEL. 160DM–300DM ($96–$180) double; 400DM ($240) suite. AE, DC, MC, V. Free parking.

Set behind a florid pink facade in the heart of town, this hotel was originally built in 1512 as a tavern and has retained its *gemütlich* antique charm. In the early 1990s it was radically upgraded. Bedrooms range from rather small and cozy Bavarian nests to spacious rooms with plenty of space to spread out. Bavarian artifacts are used whenever possible, and owners have installed state-of-the-art German mattresses, making for a good night's sleep. Bathrooms are beautifully kept and have hair dryers and an ample supply of soft towels. The Stüberl is an enclave of warmth and carefully presented cuisine.

WHERE TO DINE

Flösserstuben. Schmiedstrasse 2. ☎ **08821/28-88.** Reservations recommended. Main courses 10DM–32DM ($6–$19.20). AE, MC. Daily 11am–2:30pm and 5:30–10pm. Town bus. INTERNATIONAL.

Regardless of the season, a bit of the Bavarian Alps always seems to flower amid the wood-trimmed nostalgia of this intimate restaurant that lies close to the town center. On certain evenings, the weathered beams above the dining tables are likely to reverberate with laughter and good times. You can select a seat at a colorful wooden table or on an ox yoke–inspired stool in front of the spliced saplings that decorate the bar. Moussaka and souvlaki, as well as sauerbraten and all kinds of Bavarian dishes, are abundantly available. You can also order Mexican tacos and tortillas or even *Tafelspitz* (boiled beef) from the Austrian kitchen.

Post-Hotel Partenkirchen. Ludwigstrasse 49, Partenkirchen. ☎ **08821/5-10-67.** Reservations required. Main courses 25DM–50DM ($15–$30); set-price menus 32DM–76DM ($19.20–$45.60). AE, DC, MC, V. Daily noon–2pm and 6–9:30pm. CONTINENTAL.

Post-Hotel Partenkirchen is renowned for its distinguished cuisine. The interior dining rooms are rustic, with lots of mellow, old-fashioned atmosphere. You could imagine meeting Dürer here. Everything seems comfortably subdued, including the guests. The best way to dine is to order one of the set-price menus, which change daily, depending on the availability of seasonal produce. The à la carte menu is extensive, featuring game in the autumn. The Wiener schnitzel served with a large salad is the best we've had in the resort.

۞ Reindl's Restaurant. In the Partenkirchner Hof, Bahnhofstrasse 15. ☎ **08821/5-80-25.** Reservations required. Main courses 27DM–41DM ($16.20–$24.60); set-price lunch 50DM ($30); set-price dinner 120DM ($72). AE, DC, MC, V. Daily noon–2:30pm and 6:30–11pm. Closed Nov 10–Dec 15. CONTINENTAL.

Reindl's is first-class all the way. The seasonal menu is made up of *cuisine moderne* as well as regional Bavarian dishes. The chef de cuisine is Marianne Holzinger, daughter of founding father Karl Reindl. Among main dishes, we recommend *coq au Riesling* (chicken with wine) with noodles, or veal roasted with *Steinpilzen,* a special mushroom from the Bavarian mountains. For dessert, try Grand Marnier sabayon with strawberry and vanilla ice cream or a *Salzburger Nockerl* (a feathery light soufflé made of eggs, flour, butter, and sugar) for two.

MITTENWALD

Seeming straight out of *The Sound of Music,* the year-round resort of Mittenwald lies in a pass in the Karwendel Range, 11 miles southeast of Garmisch-Partenkirchen. Especially noteworthy and photogenic are the painted Bavarian houses with overhanging eaves. Even the baroque church tower is covered with frescoes. On the square stands a monument to Mathias Klotz, who introduced violin making to Mittenwald in 1684. The town is a major international center for this highly specialized craft.

ESSENTIALS

GETTING THERE   By Train   Mittenwald can be reached by almost hourly train service, since it lies on the express rail line between Munich and Innsbruck (Austria). From Munich, trip time is 1½ to 2 hours, depending on the train. Call ☎ **908102/19-419** for information.

By Bus   Regional bus service from Garmisch-Partenkirchen and nearby towns is frequent; call **RVO Regionalverkehr Oberbayern** at Garmisch (☎ **08821/94-82-74** for schedules and information).

By Car   Access by car is via the A-95 Autobahn from Munich.

VISITOR INFORMATION   Contact the **Kurverwaltung und Verkehrsamt,** Dammkarstrasse 3 (☎ **08823/3-39-81**), open Monday through Friday 8am to noon and 1 to 5pm, Saturday 10am to noon.

SEEING THE SIGHTS

The town's museum, with a workshop, has exhibits devoted to violins and other string instruments, from their invention through various stages of their evolution. The **Geigenbau- und Heimatmuseum,** Ballenhausgasse 3 (☎ **08823/25-11**), is open Monday through Friday 10 to noon and 2 to 5pm; Saturday and Sunday 10 to noon. Admission is 3DM ($1.80) for adults and 1DM (60¢) for children. The museum is closed November 1 to December 20.

In the countryside, you are constantly exposed to the changing scenery of the Wetterstein and Karwendel ranges. Horse and carriage trips are available as well as coach tours from Mittenwald to nearby villages. In the evening there is typical Bavarian entertainment, often consisting of folk dancing and singing, zither playing, and yodeling, but you also have your choice of concerts, dance bands, discos, and bars. Mittenwald has good spa facilities, in large gardens landscaped with tree-lined streams and trout pools. Concerts during the summer are held in the music pavilion.

OUTDOOR ACTIVITIES

In winter the town is a skiing center, but it remains equally active throughout the summer. Some 80 miles of paths wind up and down the mountains around the village, with chairlifts making the hiking trails readily accessible. Of course, where there are trails, there is mountain hiking. A biking map is available from the tourist office (see "Visitor Information," above), and mountain climbing expeditions are also available. You can always go swimming to cool off on a hot summer's day—the Lautersee and Ferchensee are brisk waters that, even in summer, might be forfeited by the faint-hearted for the heated adventure pool in Mittenwald.

WHERE TO STAY

Alpenrose. Obermarkt 1, 82481 Mittenwald. ☎ **08823/92-700.** Fax 08823/37-20. 18 units. MINIBAR TV TEL. 124DM–185DM ($74.40–$111) double; 192DM ($115.20) suite. Rates include buffet breakfast. AE, DC, DISC, MC, V. Free parking.

In the village center at the foot of a rugged mountain, the facade of this inn is covered with decorative designs and window boxes hold flowering vines. The main building, a former 14th-century monastery, is much more desirable than the more functionally furnished annex, the Bichlerhof. The bedrooms in the main building are very charming with their finely woven fabrics, old-fashioned farmhouse cupboards, and dark wood paneling. The private bathrooms are well kept, but a bit small with inadequate shelf space.

Gästehaus Franziska. Innsbrucker-Strasse 24, 82481 Mittenwald. ☎ **08823/92030.** Fax 08823/3893. 19 units. MINIBAR TV TEL. 130DM–146DM ($78–$87.60) double; from 144DM–180DM ($86.40–$108) suite. Rates include buffet breakfast. AE, V. Closed Nov 10–Dec 12. Free parking.

When Olaf Grothe built this guesthouse, he named it after the most important person in his life—his wife, Franziska. Both have gone now, and the new owners, the Kufler family, labor to make it the most personalized guesthouse in town. Each room is comfortably furnished and beautifully maintained—first-rate beds feature crisp linen duvets and fine mattresses. All have balconies opening onto mountain views; the suites also have safes and tea or coffee facilities. Bathrooms are a bit small, but are nonetheless inviting and tidy. Breakfast is the only meal served. It's extremely difficult to get bookings June 20 to October 2.

Hotel Post. Obermarkt 9, 82481 Mittenwald. ☎ **08823/10-94.** Fax 08823/10-96. 81 units. TV TEL. 140DM–240DM ($84–$144) double; 220DM–300DM ($132–$180) suite. Rates include buffet breakfast. No credit cards. Parking 8DM ($4.80).

The Post dates from 1632, when stagecoaches carrying mail and passengers across the Bavarian Alps stopped here to refuel. It remains Mittenwald's finest address. A delightful breakfast is served on the sun terrace, with a view of the Alps; in cool weather you can enjoy a beer in the snug lounge-bar with an open fireplace. For a night of hearty Bavarian specialties, head for the wine tavern or the Poststüberl. The guest rooms are comfortable, but standard. Beds (twin or double) and mattresses are among the most comfortable in town, with duvets and beautiful linen. Bathrooms are small. The maids are especially helpful if you need something extra. An indoor pool, massage facilities, and sauna are availble

WHERE TO DINE

Restaurant Arnspitze. Innsbruckerstrasse 68. ☎ **08823/24-25.** Main courses 29DM–43DM ($17.40–$25.80); set–price lunch 43DM ($25.80); set–price dinner 83DM ($49.80). AE. Thurs noon–2pm; daily 6–9pm. Closed Oct 25–Dec 19. Bus: RVO. BAVARIAN.

Housed in a modern chalet hotel on the outskirts of town, Restaurant Arnspitze is the finest dining room in Mittenwald. The restaurant is decorated in the old style; the cuisine is solid, satisfying, and wholesome. You might order sole with homemade noodles or veal steak in creamy smooth sauce, and then finish with one of the freshly made desserts. There's an excellent set-price lunch.

OBERAMMERGAU

In this alpine village, 12 miles north of Garmisch-Partenkirchen, the world-famous **passion play** is presented, usually every 10 years; the next one is scheduled for the year 2000. Surely the world's longest-running show (in more ways than one), it began in 1634 when the town's citizens took a vow after they were spared from the devastating plague of 1633. Lasting about 8 hours, the play is divided into episodes, each introduced by an Old Testament tableau connecting predictions of the great prophets to incidents of Jesus's suffering.

A visit to Oberammergau is ideal in summer or winter. It stands in a wide valley surrounded by forests and mountains, with sunny slopes and meadows. It has long been known for the skill of its woodcarvers. Here in this village right under the Kofel, farms are still intact, and tradition prevails.

ESSENTIALS

GETTING THERE   By Train   The Oberammergau Bahnhof is on the Murnau-Bad Kohlgrum-Oberammergau rail line, with frequent connections in all directions. Murnau has connections to all major German cities. Daily trains from Munich take 2 hours; from Frankfurt, 7 hours. For rail information and schedules, call ☎ **08821/19-419.**

By Bus   Regional bus service to nearby towns is offered by **RVO Regionalverkehr Oberbayern** in Garmisch-Partenkirchen (☎ **08821/948-274**). An unnumbered bus goes back and forth between Oberammergau and Garmisch-Partenkirchen.

By Car   The trip from Munich takes about 1½ hours, and 5½ hours from Frankfurt. Take the A-95 Munich-Garmisch-Partenkirchen Autobahn and exit at Eschenlohe.

VISITOR INFORMATION Contact the **Oberammergau Tourist Information Office,** Eugen-Papst-Strasse 9A (☎ **08822/92310**), open Monday through Friday 8:30am to 6pm and Saturday 8:30am to noon.

SEEING THE SIGHTS

Passionspielhaus, Passionwiese, where the passion play is performed, is at the edge of town. The roofed auditorium holds 4,700 spectators, and the open-air stage is a wonder of engineering, with a curtained center stage flanked by gates opening onto the so-called streets of Jerusalem. In 2000, the play will be presented from May 22 to October 8, daily except Tuesday and Thursday. It begins at 9:30am and continues to 5:30pm, with a 3-hour break for lunch. Tickets can be had by contacting the tourist office's "Passion Play 2000" department, but unfortunately, not many remain. Most tickets are sold as part of complicated hotel packages, but for an indication of price, day tickets cost from 110DM to 165DM ($66 to $99) each.

Aside from the actors, Oberammergau's most respected citizens include another unusual group, the woodcarvers, many of whom have been trained in the village's woodcarver's school. In the **Pilatushaus,** Ludwigthomstrasse (☎ **08822/1682**), you can watch local artists at work, including woodcarvers, painters, sculptors, and potters. Hours are Monday to Friday 1 to 6pm. You'll see many examples of these art forms throughout the town, on the painted cottages and inns and in the churchyard. Also worth seeing when strolling through the village are the houses with frescoes by Franz Zwink (18th century) that are named after fairy-tale characters, such as "Hansel and Gretel House" and the "Little Red Riding Hood House."

Heimatmuseum, Dorfstrasse 8 (☎ **08822/94136**), has a notable collection of Christmas crèches, all hand-carved and painted, and dating from the 18th through the 20th centuries. It's open mid-April to mid-October, Tuesday through Saturday 2 to 6pm; off-season, only on Saturday from 2 to 6pm. Admission is 4DM ($2.40) for adults and 1.50DM (90¢) for children.

NEARBY ATTRACTIONS The Ammer Valley, with Oberammergau in the (almost) center, offers easy access to many nearby attractions. **Schloss Linderhof** (☎ **08822/3512**), designed as a French rococo palace, the smallest and the most successful of Ludwig II's constructions, is open throughout the year. The gardens and smaller buildings here are even more elaborate than the two-story main structure. Especially outstanding is a Hall of Mirrors, set in white and gold panels, decorated with gilded wood carvings. The king's bedchamber overlooks a Fountain of Neptune and the cascades of the garden. The palace is open April to September, daily 9am to 12:15pm and 12:45pm to 5:30pm. From October to March, hours are daily 10am to 12:15pm and 12:45pm to 4pm. Admission is 9DM ($5.40) for adults, or 6DM ($3.60) for children. Buses arrive from Garmisch-Partenkirchen throughout the day. Motorists can leave Oberammergau following the road signs to Ettal, 3 miles away. From Ettal follow the signs for another 3 miles to Draswang, at which point the road into Schloss Linderhof is signposted.

OUTDOOR ACTIVITIES

Numerous **hiking trails** lead through the mountains around Oberammergau to hikers' inns such as the **Kolbenalm** and the **Romanshohe.** You can, however, simply go up to the mountaintops on the Laber cable railway or the Kolben chairlift. Oberammergau also offers opportunities to tennis buffs, minigolf players, cyclists, swimmers, hang-gliding enthusiasts, and canoeists. The recreation center **Wellenberg,** with its large alpine swimming complex with open-air pools, hot water and fountains, sauna, solarium, and restaurant, is one of the Alps' most beautiful recreation centers.

WHERE TO STAY & DINE

Alte Post. Dorfstrasse 19, 82487 Oberammergau. ☎ **08822/91-00.** Fax 08822/910-100. 32 units (28 with bathroom). TV TEL. 120DM ($72) double without bathroom; 140DM ($84) double with bathroom. Rates include continental breakfast. AE, DC, MC, V. Parking 6DM ($3.60). Closed Oct 25–Dec 19. Bus: 30.

A provincial inn in the village center, Alte Post has a wide overhanging roof, green-shuttered windows painted with decorative trim, and tables set on a sidewalk under a long awning. It's the village social hub. The interior has storybook charm, with a ceiling-high green ceramic stove, alpine chairs, and shelves of pewter plates. The rustic guest rooms with their wood-beamed ceilings and wide beds with giant posts range in size from cozy and comfortable to spacious and lovely. Most have views. Bathrooms are medium-sized with a good set of fluffy towels and adequate shelf space. The main dining room is as rustic as the rooms, and there's an intimate drinking bar. The restaurant serves excellent Bavarian dishes.

Hotel Café-Restaurant Friedenshöhe. König-Ludwig-Strasse 31, 82487 Oberammergau. ☎ **08822/35-98.** Fax 08822/43-45. 17 units. TEL. 110DM–170DM ($66–$102) double. Rates include buffet breakfast. AE, DC, MC, V. Closed Nov–Dec 14.

This 1906 villa enjoys a beautiful location, and is among the town's best bargains. Rooms are well maintained and range from rather small singles to spacious doubles. Try to get a corner room, as they're bigger. Each room has a fine bed; bathrooms, however, tend to be too small with a set of thin towels. TVs are available on request. The hotel offers a choice of four dining rooms, including an indoor terrace with a panoramic view and an outdoor terrace. The Bavarian and international cuisine is known for its quality.

Hotel Restaurant Böld. König-Ludwig-Strasse 10, 82487 Oberammergau. ☎ **08822/91-20.** Fax 08822/71-02. 57 units. TV TEL. 180DM–238DM ($108–$142.80) double. Rates include continental breakfast. AE, MC, V. Free outside parking; 10DM–15DM ($6–$9) in the garage.

A stone's throw from the river, this well-designed chalet hotel is one of the town's premier choices. Rooms in both the main building and the annex have equally good beds, usually doubles or twins, each with a firm German mattress and fine bed linen, including crisply ironed duvets. Most rooms open onto balconies. The spotless bathrooms are medium in size and have a rack of fluffy towels. Facilities include a sauna, solarium, and whirlpool. The restaurant features both international and regional cuisine. In the bar (where food is served), you'll find a tranquil atmosphere and attentive service.

3 The Romantic Road

No area of Germany is more aptly named than the Romantische Strasse. Stretching for 180 miles from Würzburg in the north to Füssen in the foothills of the Bavarian Alps in the south, it passes through untouched medieval villages and 2,000-year-old towns.

The best way to see the Romantic Road is by car, stopping whenever the mood strikes you and then driving on through vineyards and over streams until you arrive at the alpine passes in the south. Frankfurt and Munich are convenient gateways. Access is by the A-7 Autobahn from the north and south, or the A-3 Autobahn from the east and west. The A-81 Autobahn has links from the southwest.

You can also explore the Romantic Road by train or bus, or by organized tour.

Only Along the Romantic Road

Visiting the Fairytale Castles   Nothing along the Romantic Road equals the appeal of the two royal castles, Hohenschwangau and the fairytale castle of Neuschwanstein, forever associated with the enduring legend of "Mad King" Ludwig. The most enthralling is the multi-turreted Disney-like Neuschwanstein. From a distance, the castles appear more dreamlike than real. Neuschwanstein is the most photographed and most visited castle in Germany, even though it was never finished after the king's mysterious death.

Walking in "Outer Space"   Before the American Apollo 14 and 17 astronauts headed into outer space, they toured the Ries crater at Nördlingen to give them a preview of the terrain of other planets. This 25-kilometer-wide circular crater resulted from a kilometer-wide meteorite smashing into the earth some 15 million years ago. It had the power of 250,000 atomic bombs and caused massive worldwide environmental havoc. The pressure created a new mineral, *suevite,* similar to rocks found on the moon. Tours of this ancient crater plain are possible.

Wandering the Ancient Streets of Rothenburg   Rothenburg is Europe's most perfectly preserved medieval city and the architectural gem of the Romantic Road. Miraculously, Rothenburg emerged after World War II with its 14th-century fortified walls and towers intact.

Attending a Medieval Banquet   At the Welser Küche, Maximilianstrasse 83 (☎ 0821/33-93-0), in Augsburg, the Middle Ages live on—at least at the banquet staged here. You eat with a dagger and fingers, enjoying recipes from a 16th-century cookbook discovered in 1970.

Escaping the Crowds at Donauwörth   If you want to avoid the hordes who descend on the Romantic Road in summer, head to the old walled town of Donauwörth. Here the Wörnitz River meets the Danube, and time stands still—prosperity and progress left Donauwörth long ago, leaving the town to enchant today's visitor. Explore the Altstadt on an island in the river and stroll down the Reichsstrasse, lined with shops and houses that are centuries old—it's the finest street along the Romantic Road.

ROTHENBURG OB DER TAUBER

Sometimes abbreviated as Rothenburg o.d.T. (ob der Tauber), or just Rothenburg, this city was first mentioned in written records in 804 as Rotinbure, a settlement above (*ob* in German) the Tauber River that grew to be a free imperial city, reaching its apex of prosperity under a famous Burgermeister, Heinrich Toppler, in the 14th century.

The place is such a gem and so well known that its popularity is its chief disadvantage—tourist hordes march through here, especially in summer, and the concomitant souvenir peddlers hawk kitsch. Even so, if your time is limited and you can visit only one town on the Romantic Road, make it Rothenburg.

Contemporary life and industry have made an impact, and if you arrive at the railroad station, the first thing you'll see are factories and office buildings. But don't be discouraged. Inside those undamaged 13th-century city walls is a completely preserved medieval town, relatively untouched by the passage of time.

ESSENTIALS

GETTING THERE   By Train   Daily trains arrive from Frankfurt (trip time: 3 hours), from Hamburg (trip time: 5½ hours), or from Berlin (trip time: 7 hours). Rothenburg lies on the Steinach-Rothenburg rail line, with frequent connections to all major German cities, including Nürnberg and Stuttgart. For information, call ☎ 0821/19-419.

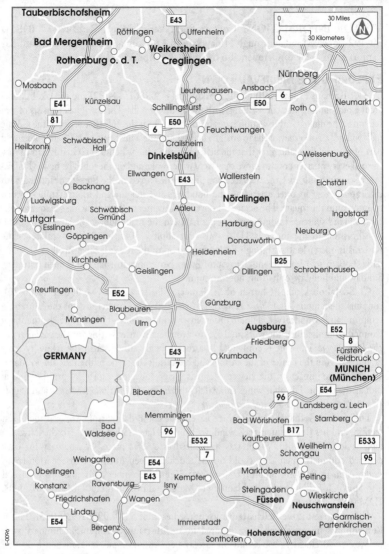

By Bus The bus that traverses the length of the Romantic Road is no. EB189 or EB189E, as operated by Deutsche Touring Frankfurt (☎ **069/790-3281** for information and reservations). Two buses operate along this route every day, but only between April and October. Know in advance that although you'll see a lot of romantic color en route, travel time to Rothenburg from Frankfurt via these buses is 6½ hours because of frequent stops en route. Any travel agent in Germany or abroad can book you a seat on these buses; each stops at sites along the Romantic Road that include Würzburg, Augsburg, Füssen, and Munich.

Regional bus service that's limited to towns and hamlets within the vicinity of Rothenburg and the rest of the Romantic Road is provided by **OVF Omnibusverkehr Franken GmbH,** Kopernikusplatz 14, 90459 Nürnberg (☎ **0911/43-90-60** for information).

VISITOR INFORMATION   Contact **Stadt Verkehrsamt,** Rathaus (☎ **09861/ 40-492**), open Monday through Friday 9am to 12:30pm and 2 to 6pm and Saturday 9am to noon (May to October, also Saturday 2 to 4pm).

EXPLORING THE MEDIEVAL TOWN

The ✪ **Rathaus (Town Hall)** on the Marktplatz (☎ **09861/404-92**) and the Jakobskirche are the outstanding attractions, along with the medieval walls. The town hall consists of two sections. The older, Gothic section dates from 1240. From the 165-foot tower of the Gothic hall, you get an overview of the town. The belfry has quite a history—in 1501, fire destroyed part of the building, and after that the belfry became a fire watchtower. Guards had to ring the bell every quarter hour to prove they were wide awake and on the job. The newer Renaissance section, built in 1572, replaced the portion destroyed in the fire. It's decorated with intricate friezes, an oriel extending the building's full height, and a large stone portico opening onto the square. The octagonal tower at the center of the side facing the square contains a grand staircase leading to the upper hall. On the main floor is the large courtroom.

Admission to the tower is 1DM (60¢) for adults, .50DM (30¢) for children. The Rathaus is open Monday through Friday 8am to 6pm; the tower is open April to October, daily 9:30am to 12:30pm and 1 to 5pm. From November to March, it's open Saturday, Sunday, and holidays only from noon to 3pm.

✪ **St. Jakobskirche (Church of St. James),** Klostergasse 15 (☎ **09861/70-06-20**), contains the famous *Altar of the Holy Blood* (west gallery), a masterpiece of the Würzburg sculptor and woodcarver Tilman Riemenschneider (1460–1531). The Rothenburg Council commissioned the work in 1499 to provide a worthy setting for the *Reliquary of the Holy Blood.* The relic is contained in a rock-crystal capsule set in the reliquary cross (about 1270) in the center of the shrine, and beneath it the scene of the *Last Supper* makes an immediate impact on the viewer—Jesus is giving Judas the morsel of bread, marking him as the traitor. The altar wings show (left) the *Entry of Christ into Jerusalem* and (right) *Christ Praying in the Garden of Gethsemane.*

The vertical Gothic church has three naves. The choir, dating from 1336, is the oldest section, and has fine painted-glass windows from the late Gothic period. To the left is the tabernacle (1390–1400), which was recognized as a "free place," a sanctuary for condemned criminals where they could not be touched. Open April to October Monday to Friday 9am to 5:30pm, Sunday 1:30am to 5:30pm; December daily noon to 2pm and 4 to 5pm. Closed November and January to March. Admission is 2.50DM ($1.50) adults, 1DM (60¢) children.

Also of interest is the **Reichsstadtmuseum,** Klosterhof 5 (☎ **09861/939-043**). This is Rothenburg's historical collection, housed in a 13th-century Dominican nunnery with well-preserved cloisters. You'll find on display here an enormous tankard that holds 3½ liters—more than 6 pints—whose story has echoes all over the city. In 1631, during the Thirty Years' War, the Protestant city of Rothenburg was captured by General Tilly, commander of the armies of the Catholic League. He promised to spare the town from destruction if one of the town burghers would drink the huge tankard full of wine in one draught. Burgermeister Nusch accepted the challenge and succeeded, and so saved Rothenburg. There's a festival every spring at Whitsuntide to celebrate this event. Among the exhibits is the 1494 *Rothenburg Passion* series, 12 pictures by Martinus Schwartz, and works by English painter Arthur Wasse (1854–1930), whose pictures managed to capture in a romantic way the many moods of the city.

Admission to the museum is 4DM ($2.40) for adults, 2DM ($1.20) for children; a family card costs 9DM ($5.40). It's open April to October, daily 10am to 5pm; November to March, daily 1 to 4pm.

The **Kriminal Museum,** Burggasse 3 (☎ **09861/53-59**), is the only museum of its kind in Europe. Housed in a structure built in 1395 with later renovations, it provides insight into the life, laws, and punishments of medieval days. The museum's four floors display 10 centuries of legal history. You'll see chastity belts, shame masks, a shame flute for bad musicians, and a cage for bakers who baked bread too small or too light. It's open April to October, daily 9:30am to 6pm; November and January to March, daily 2 to 4pm; and December, daily 10am to 4pm. Admission is 5DM ($3) for adults and 3DM ($1.80) for children under 13.

WHERE TO STAY
Expensive
✪ **Burg Hotel.** Klostergasse 1–3, 91541 Rothenburg o.d.T. ☎ **09861/94-89-0.** Fax 09861/94-89-40. 19 units. MINIBAR TV TEL. 180DM–300DM ($108–$180) double; from 250DM ($150) suite. Rates include buffet breakfast. AE, DC, MC, V. Parking 10DM ($6).

This old-fashioned timbered house at the end of a cul-de-sac is out of the Brothers Grimm. Its Tauber Valley view, picket fences, and window boxes are a cliché of German charm. Even parking (in the barn of a former Dominican monastery, the most historic garage in Rothenburg) is delightful. Rooms spread across three floors (no elevator), and are decorated with antiques. The mattresses are deluxe German ones, and there are many extras such as private safes and spacious tiled bathrooms with a combination shower and tub, hair dryer, and large mirrors. Any bedroom is likely to please, but if you want a view, ask for numbers 7, 12, or 25.

✪ **Eisenhut.** Herrngasse 3–5, 91541 Rothenburg o.d.T. ☎ **09861/70-50.** Fax 09861/70-545. www.eisenhut.com. E-mail: hotel@eisenhut.rothenburg.de. 80 units. MINIBAR TV TEL. 285DM–385DM ($171–$231) double; 530DM–650DM ($318–$390) suite. AE, DC, MC, V. Parking 15DM ($8.40).

The most celebrated inn on the Romantic Road, Eisenhut is also the finest small hotel in Germany. Four medieval patrician houses, dating from the 12th century, were joined to make this distinctive inn. Demand for rooms is great, and the staff appears forever overworked. No two guest rooms are alike—yours may contain hand-carved, monumental pieces or have a 1940s Hollywood touch with a tufted satin headboard. All, however, are enhanced by well-chosen fabrics, heavy draperies, ample closet space, and comforters and pillows piled high on state-of-the-art German mattresses. Extras include bedside controls, private safes, and spacious marble-clad bathrooms outfitted with hair dryers, a rack of fluffy towels, and often twin basins.

Most impressive is the three-story galleried dining hall, with ornate classic wood paneling and balconies. Other places to dine are richly decorated and furnished, although in sunny weather they're all deserted in favor of the multitiered flagstone terrace on the Tauber.

Goldener Hirsch. Untere Schmiedgasse 16–25, 91541 Rothenburg o.d.T. ☎ **09861/70-80.** Fax 09861/70-81-00. 72 units. MINIBAR TEL. 190DM–320DM ($114–$192) double. Rates include breakfast. AE, DC, MC, V. Parking 6DM ($3.60).

This first-class hotel 3 blocks from the main square is a remake of a 17th-century inn. It looks more austere and institutional and lacks the coziness of some of the other leading inns. Bedrooms are very modern, with built-in furniture more Scandinavia than Bavarian. Bathrooms are tiny and lack adequate shelf space; only the most superior rooms here have hair dryers. Room service and laundry are available. The Blue Terrace, for dining, offers a panoramic view of the Tauber Valley, or you might prefer to take your dinner in the wood-paneled, cozy Ratsherrenstube.

✪ **Hotel Bären.** Hofbronnengasse 9, 91541 Rothenburg o.d.T. ☎ **09861/94-410.** Fax 09861/86-688. 35 units. MINIBAR TV TEL. 250DM–330DM ($150–$198) double. Rates include buffet breakfast. AE, MC, V. Parking 8DM ($4.80). Closed Jan 4–Mar 15.

Opposite the Rathaus, this hotel dates to 1577 and is one of the leading old inns in town. Although modernized by the Müller family, it still has 15-inch oak beams and ornate wainscoting. Duvets cover the firm beds, usually doubles or twins. Only a few rooms have hair dryers in their marble-lined bathrooms. All but five have tubs and complete showers (five have showers only). The owner is a gifted chef who offers some of the best food of any inn in town. Three dining rooms provide both Bavarian and international dishes. There's also a solarium, sauna, and gym.

Hotel Tilman Riemenschneider. Georgengasse 11–13, 91541, Rothenburg o.d.T. ☎ **09861/9790.** Fax 09861/29-79. 65 units. TV TEL. 200DM–340DM ($120–$204) double. Rates include buffet breakfast. AE, DC, MC, V. Parking 10DM ($6).

This hotel's half-timbered facade rises directly above one of Rothenburg's busy historic streets. Its rear courtyard, adorned with geraniums, offers a cool and calm oasis from the heavy pedestrian traffic in front. Most of the bedrooms are medium in size, although a few are small (usually sold to single travelers). All have exceedingly comfortable mattresses and generous bed linens, including duvets. The tiled bathrooms are well maintained. Room service, laundry, and dry cleaning are available, and facilities include a fitness center with a sauna, a turbo-skylab solarium, and two whirlpool baths. For its restaurant, see "Where to Dine," below.

Romantik Hotel Markusturm. Rödergasse 1, 91541 Rothenburg o.d.T. ☎ **09861/9-42-80.** Fax 09861/26-92. 26 units. TV TEL. 200DM–320DM ($120–$192) double. Rates include buffet breakfast. AE, DC, MC, V. Parking 12DM ($7.20).

When this hotel was constructed in 1264, one of Rothenburg's defensive walls was incorporated into the building. Some rooms have four-poster beds; all have firm beds with high-quality mattresses. Tasteful wool carpeting or Oriental rugs are a nice contrast to the many cute and cozily cluttered hotels in town. About half the bathrooms have tubs and showers, and each has a hair dryer. A lot of guests request room 30, a cozy attic retreat. The hotel employs one of the most helpful staffs in town. The hotel is open all year, but its well-regarded restaurant closes from mid-January to mid-February.

Moderate

Hotel Gasthof Glocke. Am Plönlein 1, 91541 Rothenburg o.d.T. ☎ **09861/95899-0.** Fax 09861/95899-22. 25 units. TV TEL. 158DM–188DM ($94.80–$112.80) double. Rates include continental breakfast. AE, DC, MC, V. Parking 8.50DM ($5.10). Closed Dec 24–Jan 6.

South of the town center off Wenggasse, this hotel does not have the charm and style of the premier inns, but it's a good choice for those who want plain, simple, affordable rooms, a family atmosphere, and good food. The mattresses are generally thin but still adequate, and the rooms, although a bit institutional looking, are nonetheless comfortable and a good value for pricey Rothenburg. Bathrooms are exceedingly small. The owners are justifiably proud of their restaurant (see "Where to Dine," below).

Hotel Reichs-Küchenmeister. Kirchplatz 8, 91541 Rothenburg o.d.T. ☎ **09861/9700.** Fax 09861/86-965. 53 units. TV TEL. 140DM–250DM ($84–$150) double; 250DM ($150) suite for 2; 350DM ($210) suite for 5. Rates include buffet breakfast. AE, DC, MC, V. Parking 6DM ($3.60) in lot, 10DM ($6) in garage.

We consider this hotel, one of Rothenburg's oldest structures, near St. Jakobskirche, comparable with Tilman Riemenschneider and the Goldener Hirsch. The owners take special care with the guests' comfort, frequently renewing their firm mattresses and keeping their crisp white bed linens spotless. Rooms are nicely furnished with painted wooden furniture. Bathrooms, however, are a bit small and peas-in-a-pod-ish. This is one of the best-equipped hotels in Rothenburg, with Finnish sauna, whirlpool, solarium, and Turkish bath. Use of the sauna costs 20DM ($12) extra. An extra 17 rooms are available in the duller annex across the street. For its restaurant, see "Where to Dine," below.

Inexpensive

Bayerischer Hof. Ansbacherstrasse 21, 91541 Rothenburg o.d.T. ☎ **09861/60-63.** Fax 09861/86-56-1. 9 units. TV TEL. 120DM–150DM ($72–$90) double. Rates include breakfast. AE, MC, V. Closed Jan.

This little place, midway between the Bahnhof and the medieval walled city, doesn't even try to compete with the grand inns of the town. And why should it? It's found a niche as a B&B, and although the outside looks rather sterile, many cozy warm Bavarian touches, such as painted furniture, grace the interior. Beds are comfortable, although mattresses are a bit thin. Rooms are small, as are the bathrooms, but housekeeping is excellent and the staff is most hospitable. The international/Bavarian food is also very good.

Gasthof Goldener Greifen. Obere Schmiedgasse 5, 91541 Rothenburg o.d.T. ☎ **09861/22-81.** Fax 09861/86-374. 21 units (16 with bathroom). 78DM ($46.80) double without bathroom; 138DM ($82.80) double with shower or bathroom. Rates include buffet breakfast. AE, MC, V. Closed Aug 22–Sept 2 and Dec 22–Feb.

This is one of the very best B&Bs in town if you want Bavarian home-style warmth. Fine mattresses, tidy housekeeping, and a willing staff make this patrician 1374 house off Marktplatz extremely comfortable. Corridor bathrooms are adequate, and generally spruced up after use by a guest. Those in units with a private bathroom will find them small but well maintained and supplied with a set of rather thin towels. You can order your morning coffee in the garden amid roses and geraniums.

WHERE TO DINE

Expensive

✪ **Restaurant Bärenwirt.** In the Hotel Bären, Hofbronnengasse 9. ☎ **09861/94410.** Reservations recommended. Main courses 42DM–80DM ($25.20–$48). AE, MC, V. Daily 6–10pm. FRANCONIAN/INTERNATIONAL.

Many food critics, including the magazine *VIF Gourmet Journal,* cite the "Bear," owned by Fritz and Elisabeth Müller, as one of the finest restaurants in all Germany. The decor is elegantly subdued and the service impeccable. On occasion, the chef is known to serve a historical menu from the Middle Ages. Menu changes are based on the chef's inspiration and use the best seasonal produce.

Moderate

Baumeisterhaus. Obere Schmiedgasse 3. ☎ **09861/94-700.** Reservations required for courtyard tables. Main courses 12.50DM–35DM ($7.50–$21). AE, DC, MC, V. Daily 10am–9pm. FRANCONIAN.

Right off Marktplatz, the Baumeisterhaus is housed in an ancient patrician residence, built in 1596. It has Rothenburg's most beautiful courtyard (which only guests can visit), with colorful murals, serenely draped by vines. Frankly, although the menu is good, the setting is even more romantic. The food, for the most part, is rib-sticking fare beloved of Bavarians, including roast suckling pig with potato dumplings, and one of the chef's best dishes, *sauerbraten* (braised beef marinated in vinegar), served with *spätzle* (small flour dumplings).

Ratsstube. Marktplatz 6. ☎ **09861/55-11.** Reservations recommended. Main courses 18DM–32DM ($10.80–$19.20). MC, V. Mon–Sat 9am–11pm; Sun noon–6pm. Closed Jan 7–Feb. FRANCONIAN.

Ratsstube enjoys a position right on the market square, one of the most photographed spots in Germany. It's a bustling center of activity throughout the day—a day that begins when practically every Rothenburger stops by for a cup of morning coffee. Inside, a true tavern atmosphere prevails with hardwood chairs and tables, vaulted ceilings, and pierced copper lanterns. The à la carte menu of Franconian wines and dishes includes sauerbraten and venison, both served with fresh vegetables and potatoes. For dessert, you can order homemade Italian ice cream and espresso. This is a longtime favorite of those who prefer typical Franconian cookery without a lot of fuss and bother. If you arrive at 9am, the staff will serve you an American breakfast.

Reichs-Küchenmeister. Kirchplatz 8. ☎ **09861/9700.** Reservations required. Main courses 18.80DM–42DM ($11.30–$25.20). AE, DC, MC, V. Daily 11:30am–2pm and 6–9:30pm. FRANCONIAN.

The main dishes served here are the type Bavarians have loved for years, including sauerbraten, or pork tenderloin; white herring and broiled salmon are also available. The *Lebensknodel* (liver dumpling) or goulash soup is perfect for cold days. We recently decided that the chef makes one of the best Wiener schnitzels in town. The restaurant is near St. Jakobskirche and has a typical weinstube decor, along with a garden terrace and a *Konditorei* (cake shop). Service is warm and efficient.

Inexpensive

Hotel Gasthof Glocke. Am Plönlein 1. ☎ **09861/30-25.** Reservations recommended. Main courses 15DM–66DM ($9–$39.60). AE, DC, MC, V. Daily 11am–2pm; Mon–Sat 6–9pm. Closed Dec 24–Jan 6. FRANCONIAN.

This traditional hotel and guesthouse (recommended in "Where to Stay," above) serves regional specialties along with a vast selection of local wine. Meals emphasize seasonal dishes and range from a simple vegetarian plate to lobster. Service is polite and attentive.

Tilman Riemenschneider. Georgengasse 11. ☎ **09861/9790.** Main courses 18.50DM–34DM ($11.10–$20.40); set-price menu 30DM–36DM ($18–$21.60). AE, DC, MC, V. Daily 11:30am–2pm and 6–9pm. FRANCONIAN.

This traditional old weinstube is housed in one of Rothenburg's finest hotels (see "Where to Stay," above). The old-fashioned cookery is served in generous portions. You might begin with air-dried beef or smoked filet of trout, and then follow with poached eel, halibut steak, or loin of pork.

DINKELSBÜHL

Still surrounded by medieval walls and towers, Dinkelsbühl is straight out of a Brothers Grimm story, even down to the gingerbread, which is one of its main products. Behind the ancient 10th-century walls is a town that retains its quiet, provincial ambience in spite of the many tourists who come here. The cobblestoned streets are lined with fine 16th-century houses, many with carvings and paintings depicting biblical and mythological themes. In the center of town, on Marktplatz, is the late Gothic **Georgenkirche,** built between 1448 and 1499. It contains a carved Holy Cross Altar from the same period and pillar sculptures, many from the 15th century.

ESSENTIALS

GETTING THERE By Train The nearest train station is in Ansbach, which has several trains arriving daily from Munich and Frankfurt (trip time: 2½ to 3 hours),

Nürnberg, and Stuttgart. From Ansbach, Dinkelsbhl can be reached by bus. For rail information, call ☎ **0821/19-419.**

By Bus   For long-distance bus service along the Romantic Road, see "Rothenburg," above. Regional buses link Dinkelsbühl with local towns. There are three to five buses a day to Rothenburg and five or six to Nördlingen.

By Car   Take B-25 south from Rothenburg.

VISITOR INFORMATION   Contact **Stadt Verkehrsamt,** Marktplatz (☎ **09851/ 9-02-40**). From April through October, hours are Monday through Friday 9am to noon and 2 to 6pm, Saturday 10am to 1pm and 2 to 4pm, and Sunday 10am to 1pm. From November through March, the office is open only on Saturday from 10am to 1pm.

SPECIAL EVENTS   The **Kinderzeche (Children's Festival),** held for 10 days in July, commemorates the saving of the village by its children in 1632. According to the story, the children pleaded with conquering Swedish troops to leave their town without pillaging and destroying it—and got their wish. The pageant includes concerts given by the local boys' band dressed in historic military costumes.

WHERE TO STAY & DINE

Blauer Hecht. Schweinemarkt 1, 91150 Dinkelsbühl. ☎ **09851/5810.** Fax 09851/581170. 44 units. TV TEL. 150DM–174DM ($90–$104.40) double. Rates include continental breakfast. AE, DC, MC, V. Closed Jan. Free parking.

This inn is the best in town. The elegant ocher building, dating from the 17th century, has three hand-built stories of stucco, stone, and tiles. The hotel was once a brewery tavern, and the owners still brew in the backyard. Although it's centrally located, rooms are tranquil and sunny. The mattresses are the newest and finest in town, and most rooms have controls for bed lights and TVs. Bathrooms are routine but well maintained, with enough shelf space. Good regional food is served in the hotel restaurant.

Deutsches Haus. Weinmarkt 3, 91550 Dinkelsbühl. ☎ **09851/60-58.** Fax 09851/79-11. 15 units. TV TEL. 165DM–210DM ($99–$126) double; 240DM ($144) suite. Rates include continental breakfast. AE, DC, MC, V. Parking 15DM ($9). Closed Dec 23–Jan 6.

The facade of Deutsches Haus, which dates from 1440, is rich in painted designs and festive wood carvings—a niche on the second floor of the arched entrance houses a 17th-century Madonna. The rooms are unique; you may find yourself in one with a ceramic stove or in another with a Biedermeier desk. For the tradition-minded, there are no finer bedrooms in town. Bathrooms are spotless and tiled, often with a shower and tub combination.

Its **Altdeutsches Restaurant** is one of the finest in Dinkelsbühl. It's intimate and convivial, an attractive rendezvous. The restaurant serves Franconian and regional specialties daily from 11:30am to 2pm and 6 to 10pm. In the afternoon, many visitors drop in for coffee and freshly baked pastries.

✪ **Eisenkrug.** Dr.-Martin-Luther-Strasse 1, 91550 Dinkelsbühl. ☎ **09851/57700.** Fax 09851/577070. 23 units. MINIBAR TV TEL. 135DM–170DM ($81–$102) double. Rates include continental breakfast. AE, DC, MC, V. Parking 10DM ($6).

The sienna walls of this centrally located hotel were originally built in 1620. The stylish rooms are wallpapered with flowery prints and filled with engaging old furniture. A newer wing contains the most contemporary guest rooms, all rather standard and modern, each medium in size. The older rooms offer more charm, although some of them tend to be smaller. Some of the beds are canopied, and all have first-class

German mattresses and topnotch housekeeping and maintenance. Bathrooms vary from small to spacious: Some are tiled with cork, and all but one has a shower instead of a tub.

Zum kleinen Obristen serves a gourmet international cuisine—the finest dining along the entire road. The chef invents his own recipes and carefully selects ingredients that go into his market-fresh cuisine. His is an indigenous Franconian-Swabian approach, with many innovative touches. The superior wine cellar has some really unusual vintages. à la carte meals cost 35DM to 65DM ($21 to $39). It's open noon to 2pm and 6 to 10pm; closed Monday and Tuesday evenings.

Goldene Rose. Marktplatz 4, 91550, Dinkelsbühl. ☎ **09851/57-750.** Fax 09851/57-75-75. 34 units. MINIBAR TV TEL. 140DM–220DM ($84–$132) double. Rates include continental breakfast. AE, DC, MC, V. Parking 6DM ($3.60) in lot, 15DM ($9) in garage.

A landmark in the heart of this village since 1450, the intricately timbered Goldene Rose rises three stories, with a steeply pitched roof and overflowing window boxes. Although it doesn't match the impressive standards of the Eisenkrug, it is one of Dinkelsbühl's best values. The small to medium-sized guest rooms have been modernized in a style more often institutional and functional—especially in the use of laminate furnishings—than Bavarian traditional. The more expensive units, however, offer some antiques and more charm. Bathrooms are rather small, but 10 of them have a full tub and shower.

The dining rooms are country-inn style, with an international cuisine (the menu is in English). The à la carte menu offers such tempting items as tenderloin of wild hare flavored with hazelnuts, and rumpsteak. Meals cost 29DM to 58DM ($17.40 to $34.80), and service is daily 11am to 10:30pm.

NÖRDLINGEN

One of the most irresistible and perfectly preserved medieval towns along the Romantic Road, Nördlingen is still completely encircled by its well-preserved 14th- to 15th-century **city fortifications.** You can walk around the town on the covered parapet, which passes 11 towers and 5 fortified gates set into the walls.

Things are rather peaceful around Nördlingen today, and the city still employs sentries to sound the message, *"So G'sell so"* ("All is well"), as they did in the Middle Ages. However, events around here weren't always so peaceful. The valley sits in a gigantic crater, the Ries. Once thought to be the crater of an extinct volcano, it is now known that a meteorite at least half a mile in diameter was responsible. It hit the ground at more than 100,000 miles per hour, the impact having the destructive force of 250,000 atomic bombs of the type that wiped out Hiroshima in 1945. Debris was hurled as far as Slovakia, and all plant and animal life within a radius of 100 miles was destroyed. This momentous event took place some 15 million years ago. Today it is the best preserved and most scientifically researched meteorite crater on earth. The American Apollo 14 and 17 astronauts had their field training in the Ries from August 10 to 14 in 1970.

ESSENTIALS

GETTING THERE **By Train** Nördlingen lies on the main Nördlingen-Aalen-Stuttgart line, with frequent connections in all directions. Call ☎ **0821/19-419** for schedules and more information. Nördlingen can be reached from Stuttgart in 2 hours, from Nürnberg in 2 hours, and from Augsburg in an hour.

By Bus The long-distance bus that operates along the Romantic Road includes Nördlingen; see "Rothenburg," above.

By Car   Take B-25 south from Dinkelsbühl.

VISITOR INFORMATION   Contact the **Verkehrsamt,** Marktplatz 2 (☎ 09081/ 43-80). The office is open Easter to October, Monday through Thursday 9am to 6pm, and Friday 9am to 4:30pm. The rest of the year, hours are Monday through Thursday 9am to 5pm, and Friday 9am to 3:30pm.

SEEING THE SIGHTS

At the center of the circular Altstadt within the walls is **Rübenmarkt.** If you stand in this square on market day, you'll be swept into a world of the past—the country people have preserved many traditional customs and costumes here, which, along with the ancient houses, create a living medieval city. Around the square stand a number of buildings, including the Gothic **Rathaus.** An antiquities collection is displayed in the **Stadtmuseum,** Vordere Gerbergasse 1 (☎ 09081/84-120), open Tuesday through Sunday 1:30 to 4:30pm; closed November through February. Admission is 5DM ($3) for adults and 2.50DM ($1.50) for children.

The Gothic Hallenkirche, the **Church of St. George,** on the square's northern side, is the town's most interesting sight and one of its oldest buildings, dating from the 15th century. Plaques and epitaphs commemorating the town's more illustrious 16th- and 17th-century residents decorate the fan-vaulted interior. Although the original Gothic altarpiece by Friedrich Herlin (1470) is now in the Reichsstadt Museum, a portion of it, depicting the crucifixion, remains in the church. Above the high altar today stands a more elaborate baroque altarpiece. The church's most prominent feature, however, is the 295-foot French Gothic tower, called the "Daniel." At night, the town watchman calls out from the steeple, his voice ringing through the streets. The tower is open daily April to October 9am to 8pm, off-season daily 9am to 5:30pm. Admission is 2.50DM ($1.50) for adults and 1.50DM (90¢) for children.

The **Rieskrater-Museum,** Hintere Gerbergasse (☎ 0981/84-143), documents the impact of the stone meteorite that created the Ries. Examine fossils from Ries Lake deposits and learn about the fascinating evolution of this geological wonder. Hours are Tuesday through Sunday 10am to noon and 1:30 to 4:30pm. Admission is 5DM ($3) for adults and 2.50DM ($1.50) for students, seniors, and large groups. Tours of the crater are possible through the museum.

WHERE TO STAY

Flamberg Hotel Klösterle. Am Klösterle 1, 86720 Nördlingen. ☎ 09081/88-054. Fax 09081/22-740. 90 units. MINIBAR TV TEL. 227DM–257DM ($136.20–$154.20) double; from 246DM ($147.60) suite. Rates include breakfast. AE, DC, MC, V. Parking 15DM ($9).

This is the best place to stay in town. White-sided and red-roofed, this historic building was a monastery in the 1200s. In 1991 the monastery was renovated, a new wing added, and the entire complex transformed into the town's most luxurious hotel. Rated four stars, it offers elevator access, a cozy bar, and a hardworking, polite staff. Under the sloping eaves of its top floor are a sauna, fitness center, and series of conference rooms. The bedrooms have dark-wood fixtures, modern upholstery, excellent mattresses, lots of electronic extras, and large bathrooms with hair dryers. The restaurant serves meals every day from noon to 2pm and 6 to 10pm.

Kaiser Hotel Sonne. Marktplatz 3, 86720 Nördlingen. ☎ **09081/50-67.** Fax 09081/ 23-999. 43 units (35 with bathroom). MINIBAR TV TEL. 125DM ($75) double without bathroom; 175DM ($105) double with bathroom; 230DM ($138) suite. Rates include breakfast. AE, DC, MC, V.

In a bull's-eye position, next to the cathedral and the Rathaus, is the Sonne, an inn since 1405. Among its guests have been Frederick III, Maximilian I, Charles V, and, in more recent times, the American Apollo astronauts. Many of the rooms contain hand-painted four-poster beds to bring out the romantic in you. Others are regular doubles or twins, but each has a firm mattress and quality linens. Goethe might have complained of the lack of comfort he found here, but you'll fare well. Bathrooms are fresh and immaculate. In a choice of dining rooms, you can order the soup of the day, main courses such as rumpsteak Mirabeau, and fattening German desserts. It's all quite casual; the waitresses even urge you to finish the food on your plate.

WHERE TO DINE

Meyer's Keller. Marienhöhe 8. ☎ **09081/44-93.** Reservations required. Main courses 26DM–36DM ($15.60–$21.60); set-price meals 49DM–129DM ($29.40–$77.40). AE, MC, V. Wed–Sun noon–2pm; Tues–Sun 6–10pm. Local bus to Marktplatz. CONTINENTAL.

The conservative, modern decor here seems a suitable setting for the restrained *neue Küche* of the talented chef and owner of this place, Joachim Kaiser, who is adroit with both rustic and refined cuisine. The menu changes according to availability of ingredients and the chef's inspiration; typical selections are likely to include roulade of seawolf and salmon with baby spinach and wild rice, or John Dory with champagne-flavored tomato sauce. The wine list is impressive, with many bottles quite reasonably priced.

EN ROUTE TO AUGSBURG

After Nördlingen, B-25 heads south to Augsburg. After a 12-mile ride you can stop to visit **Schloss Harburg** (it's signposted), one of the best-preserved medieval castles in Germany. It once belonged to the Hohenstaufen emperors and contains treasures collected by the family over the centuries. It is open mid-March to September, Tuesday to Sunday 9am to 5pm; October, Tuesday to Sunday 9:30am to 4:30pm. Admission is 6DM ($3.60) for adults and 4DM ($2.40)for children, including a guided tour. There is no number to call for information.

After exploring the castle, continue 7 miles south to the walled town of **Donauwörth,** where you can stop to walk through the oldest part of the town, on an island in the river, connected by a wooden bridge. Here the Danube is only a narrow, placid stream. The town's original walls overlook its second river, the Woernitz.

After a brief stopover, continue your southward trek for 30 miles to Augsburg, the largest city on the Romantic Road.

AUGSBURG

Augsburg is near the center of the Romantic Road and the gateway to the Alps and the south. Founded 2,000 years ago by the Roman emperor Augustus, for whom it was named, it once was the richest city in Europe. Little remains from the early Roman period. However, the wealth of Renaissance art and architecture is staggering. Over the years, Augsburg has boasted an array of famous native sons, including painters Hans Holbein the Elder and Hans Holbein the Younger and playwright Bertolt Brecht. It was here in 1518 that Martin Luther was summoned to recant his 95 theses before a papal emissary. Only 15% of the city was left standing after World War II, but there is still much here to intrigue. Today Augsburg is an important industrial center on the Frankfurt-Salzburg autobahn, and Bavaria's third largest city after Munich and Nürnberg.

ESSENTIALS

GETTING THERE   **By Train**   Around 90 Euro and InterCity trains arrive here daily from all major German cities. For railway information, call ☎ **0821/1-94-19.**

Exploring the Fuggerei

Throughout its history, Augsburg has been an important city, but during the 15th and 16th centuries, it was one of Europe's wealthiest communities, mainly because of its textile industry and the political and financial clout of its two banking families, the Welsers and the Fuggers. The Welsers, who once owned nearly all of Venezuela, have long since faded from the minds of Augsburgers. But the founders of the powerful Fugger family have established themselves forever in the hearts of townsfolk by an unusual legacy, ✪ **the Fuggerei,** created in 1519 to house poorer Augsburgers. A master mason fallen on hard times, Franz Mozart, once lived at Mittlere Gasse 14—he was the great-grandfather of Wolfgang Amadeus Mozart. The quarter consists of several streets lined with well-maintained Renaissance houses, as well as a church and administrative offices, all enclosed within walls. The Fugger Foundation still owns the Fuggerei.

A house at Mittlere Gasse 13, next to the one once occupied by Mozart's ancestor, is now the Fuggerei's **museum** (☎ **0821/30-868**). The rough 16th- and 17th-century furniture, wood-paneled ceilings and walls, and cast-iron stove, as well as other objects of everyday life, show what it was like to live there in earlier times. Admission is 1DM (60¢). It's open March to October, daily 9am to 6pm. Take tram no. 1.

There are 60 trains a day from Munich (trip time: 30 to 50 minutes), and 35 from Frankfurt (trip time: 3 to 4½ hours).

By Bus Long-distance buses (lines EB190 and 190A, plus line 189) service the Romantic Road. The buses are operated by **Deutsche Touring GmbH** at Am Römerhof in Frankfurt (☎ **069/790-32-56** for reservations and information).

VISITOR INFORMATION Contact **Tourist-Information,** Rathausplatz 7 (☎ **0821/50-20-70**), Monday through Friday 9am to 6pm, Saturday 10am to 4pm, and Sunday 10am to 1pm.

GETTING AROUND The public transportation system in Augsburg consists of four tram lines and 31 bus lines covering the inner city and reaching into the suburbs. Public transportation operates daily 5am to midnight, and service is provided by **Augsburger Verkehrsverband AVV** (☎ **0821/15-70-07**).

SEEING THE SIGHTS IN TOWN

Rathaus. Am Rathausplatz 2. ☎ **0821/5020.** Admission 2DM ($1.20) adults, 1DM (60¢) children 7–14. Daily 10am–6pm. Tram: 1.

In 1805 and 1809, Napoléon visited the Rathaus, built by Elias Holl in 1620. Regrettably, it was also visited by an air raid in 1944, leaving a mere shell of the building that had once been a palatial eight-story monument to the glory of the Renaissance. Its celebrated "golden chamber" was left in shambles. Now, after costly restoration, the Rathaus is open to the public.

Dom St. Maria. Hoher Weg. ☎ **0821/31-66-353.** Free admission. Mon–Sat 7am–6pm; Sun noon–6pm. Tram: 1.

The cathedral of Augsburg has the distinction of containing the oldest stained-glass windows in the world. The Romanesque windows in the south transept, dating from the 12th century, depict Old Testament prophets in a severe but colorful style. They are younger than the cathedral itself, which was begun in 944. You'll find the ruins of the original basilica in the crypt beneath the west chancel. Partially Gothicized in the 14th century, the church stands on the edge of the park, which also fronts the **Episcopal Palace,** where the basic Lutheran creed was presented at the Diet of Augsburg in 1530. The 11th-century bronze doors, leading into the three-aisle nave, are adorned with bas-reliefs of biblical and mythological characters. The cathedral's interior, restored in 1934, contains side altars with altarpieces by Hans Holbein the Elder and Christoph Amberger.

Church of St. Ulrich and St. Afra. Ulrichplatz 19. ☎ **0821/15-60-49.** Free admission. Daily 9am–6pm.

This is the most attractive church in Augsburg. It was constructed between 1476 and 1500 on the site of a Roman temple. The church and the dom, one Protestant, one Catholic, stand side by side, a tribute to the 1555 Peace of Augsburg, which recognized the two denominations, Roman Catholic and Lutheran. Many of the church's furnishings, including the three altars representing the birth and resurrection of Christ and the baptism of the church by the Holy Spirit, are baroque. In the crypt are the tombs of the Swabian saints, Ulrich and Afra.

Schaezlerpalais. Maximilianstrasse 46. ☎ **0821/324-21-71.** Admission 4DM ($2.40) adults, 2DM ($1.20) children. Wed–Sun 10am–4pm. Tram: 1.

Facing the Hercules Fountain is the Schaezlerpalais, which contains the city's art galleries. Constructed as a 60-room mansion between 1765 and 1770, it was willed to Augsburg after World War II. Most of the paintings are from the Renaissance and baroque periods. One of the most famous is Dürer's portrait of Jakob Fugger the Rich, founder of the dynasty that was once powerful enough to influence the elections of the Holy Roman emperors. Other works are by local artists Hans Burgkmair and Hans Holbein the Elder; Rubens, Veronese, and Tiepolo are also represented.

WHERE TO STAY
Very Expensive
✪ **Steigenberger Drei Mohren.** Maximilianstrasse 40, 86150 Augsburg. ☎ **800/223-5652** in the U.S. and Canada, or 0821/5-03-60. Fax 0821/15-78-64. 107 units. MINIBAR TV TEL. 299DM–379DM ($179.40–$227.40) double; 450DM–550DM ($270–$330) suite. Rates include buffet breakfast. AE, DC, MC, V. Parking 22DM ($13.20). Tram: 1.

The original hotel, dating from 1723, was renowned in Germany before its destruction in an air raid. In 1956 it was rebuilt in a modern style, and it remains the premier hotel in town. Decorators worked hard to create a decor that was both comfortable and inviting, with thick carpets, subdued lighting, double glazing at the windows, and such extra amenities as private safes and trouser presses. Rooms vary in size and appointments, however, ranging from some economy specials that are a bit small with narrow twin beds and showers (no tubs) to spacious, luxurious units with full shower and tub. Each has a good mattress, however. Many rooms are nonsmoking, and most bathrooms are fairly spacious. The formal dining room offers an international cuisine. The staff can arrange golf nearby.

Moderate
Dom Hotel. Frauentorstrasse 8, 86152 Augsburg. ☎ **0821/34-39-30.** Fax 0821/34-39-32-00. E-mail: domhotel.augsburg@t-online.de. 43 units. TV TEL. 150DM–210DM ($90–$126) double. Rates include buffet breakfast. AE, DC, MC, V. Free parking or 8DM ($4.80) garage. Tram: 2.

Although it might not have the decorative flair of the more expensive hotels, there is an indoor pool. That, combined with the low rates, makes this one of the most appealing choices in town. The hotel is a half-timbered structure, next to Augsburg's famous cathedral, and was built in the 15th century. Rooms on most floors are medium in size and nicely appointed, although we prefer the smaller attic accommodations where you can rest under a beam ceiling and enjoy a panoramic sweep of the rooftops of the city. Each room, regardless of location, has a good bed with a firm mattress. Bathrooms are small. In warm weather, breakfast—the only meal served—can be enjoyed in a garden beside the town's medieval fortifications.

Hotel Am Rathaus. Am Hinteren Perlachberg 1, 86150 Augsburg. ☎ **082134-64-90.** Fax 0821/346-49-99. 32 units. MINIBAR TV TEL. 240DM ($144) double. Rates include buffet breakfast. AE, DC, MC, V. Parking 12DM ($7.20). Tram: 1.

Many repeat guests consider this hotel's location, just behind Augsburg's famous town hall, to be its best asset. Built in a three-story contemporary format in 1986, the hotel offers comfortable, monochromatic bedrooms accented with darkly stained wood, and a well-stocked breakfast buffet. It might be short on style, but it's long on value. There's no restaurant or bar on the premises.

Romantik Hotel Augsburger Hof. Auf dem Kreuz 2, 86152 Augsburg. ☎ **0821/ 34-30-50.** Fax 0821/343-0555. 36 units. MINIBAR TV TEL. 130DM–250DM ($78–$150) double. Rates include buffet breakfast. AE, DC, MC, V. Parking 10DM ($6). Tram: 1.

Originally built in 1767 in a solid, thick-walled design with exposed beams and timbers, this hotel was carefully restored in 1988. Conveniently located in the town center, it's a favorite for its traditional atmosphere and its excellent food. In spite of the Renaissance interior, the bedrooms are completely up to date and not as romantic as the name of the hotel suggests. They range from cozy to spacious, each with a fine bed, immaculate linen, and a quality mattress. Those overlooking the calm inner courtyard are more expensive than ones facing the street. Some of the bathrooms seemed crowded in as an afterthought, but each is beautifully maintained. On the premises a restaurant serves German and international food.

Inexpensive

Hotel Garni Weinberger. Bismarckstrasse 55, 86391 Stadtbergen. ☎ **0821/24-39-10.** Fax 0821/43-88-31. 31 units (26 with bathroom). 130DM ($78) double without bathroom; 150DM ($90) double with bathroom. Rates include buffet breakfast. No credit cards. Closed Aug 15–30. Tram: 2.

One of the best budget accommodations in the area lies about 2 miles from the heart of Augsburg, along Augsburgerstrasse in the western sector. Bedrooms are small but well kept, with good beds and firm mattresses. The private bathrooms are rather cramped and the towels a bit thin, but housekeeping is excellent. Corridor bathrooms are adequate and kept tidy for those who must share. The place is well patronized by bargain-hunting Germans, and its cafe is one of the most popular in the area for snacks.

WHERE TO DINE

Die Ecke. Elias-Holl-Platz 2. ☎ **0821/51-06-00.** Reservations required. Main courses 25DM– 45DM ($15–$27); set-price dinner 69DM ($41.40) for 4 courses, 98DM ($58.80) for 6 courses. AE, DC, MC, V. Daily 11:30am–2:30pm and 5:30pm–1am. Tram: 2. FRENCH/SWABIAN.

Since Die Ecke was founded in the year Columbus sighted the New World, its guests have included Hans Holbein the Elder, Wolfgang Amadeus Mozart, and, in more contemporary times, Bertolt Brecht, whose sharp-tongued irreverence tended to irritate diners of more conservative political leanings. The weinstube ambience belies the skilled cuisine of the chef, which wins us over year after year. Breast of duckling might be preceded by pâté, and the filet of sole in Riesling is deservedly a classic. Venison dishes in season are a specialty—the best in town.

Fuggerei Stube. Jakoberstrasse 26. ☎ **0821/3-08-70.** Reservations recommended. Main courses 18.50DM–26DM ($11.10–$15.60); set price menu 36DM ($21.60). AE, MC, V. Tues–Sun 11:30am–2pm; Tues–Sat 6:30pm–1:30am. GERMAN/SWABIAN.

The building that contains this carefully maintained restaurant was constructed in 1546 as the home of a local politician and merchant. There's one large dining room, suitable for 60 people at a time, that has welcomed diners since 1946, with little change in the menu, the decor, or the ambience. Expect generous portions of well-prepared food, such as sauerbraten, roasted pork, pork schnitzel; game dishes such as venison, pheasant, and rabbit; and fish such as filet of sole served with boiled potatoes and parsley. The beer foaming out of the taps here is Storchenbräu, and most visitors find that it goes wonderfully with the conservative German specialties.

✪ **Oblinger.** Pfäarrle 14. ☎ **0821/345-83-92.** Reservations required. Main courses 20DM–40DM ($12–$24). AE, DC, MC, V. Tues–Sun 11am–2pm; Tues–Sat 6–11pm. Closed Aug 1–19. Tram: 12. CONTINENTAL.

Near the cathedral, in the heart of the historic section, Oblinger is the best restaurant within the city. It's a charming, intimate 20-seat choice offering a changing array of seasonal specialties. The surroundings are unpretentious, the waiters attentive, and there's a superb collection of wine, more than 200 varieties. You can savor the goose-liver terrine with mushrooms and cabbage, going on to an equally well-prepared sole roulade with crêpes. The turbot with chanterelles and the stuffed Bresse pigeon are also successes—quite simply, the cuisine has personality.

NEUSCHWANSTEIN & HOHENSCHWANGAU: THE ROYAL CASTLES

The 19th century saw a great classical revival in Germany, especially in Bavaria, mainly because of the enthusiasm of Bavarian kings for ancient art forms. Beginning with Ludwig I (1786–1868), who was responsible for many Greek revival buildings in Munich, this royal house ran the gamut of ancient architecture in just 3 short decades. It culminated in the remarkable flights of fancy of Ludwig II, often called "Mad King Ludwig," who died under mysterious circumstances in 1886. In spite of his rather lonely life and controversial alliances, both personal and political, he was a great patron of the arts.

Although the name "Royal Castles" is limited to the castles of Hohenschwangau (built by Ludwig's father, Maximilian II) and Neuschwanstein, the extravagant king was responsible for the creation of two other magnificent castles, Linderhof (near Oberammergau) and Herrenchiemsee (on an island in Chiemsee).

In 1868, after a visit to the great castle of Wartburg, Ludwig wrote to his good friend, composer Richard Wagner: "I have the intention to rebuild the ancient castle ruins of Hohenschwangau in the true style of the ancient German knight's castle." The following year, construction began on the first of a series of fantastic edifices, a series that stopped only with Ludwig's untimely death in 1886, only 5 days after he was deposed because of alleged insanity.

The nearest towns to the castles are **Füssen,** 2 miles away at the very end of the Romantic Road, and **Schwangau,** where accommodations can be found.

ESSENTIALS

GETTING THERE   By Train   There are frequent trains from Munich and Augsburg to Füssen. For information, call ☎ **0821/1-94-19.** The trip time from Munich is 2½ hours; frequent buses travel to the castles.

By Bus   Long-distance bus service into Füssen from other parts of the Romantic Road including Würzburg, Augsburg, and Munich, is provided by the **Deutsche Touring GmbH** along their bus lines EB189 or EB189E. For information and reservations, call their headquarters in Frankfurt (☎ **069/790-3281**). Regional service to villages around Füssen is provided by **RVA Regionalverkehr Allgau GmbH** in Füssen (☎ **08362/37771**). Its most important routing, at least for visitors to Füssen, includes about 14 orange, yellow, or white-sided buses that depart every day from Füssen's railway station for the village of Hohenschwangau, site of both Hohenschwangau Palace and Neuschwanstein Palace, a 10-minute ride. The cost of a one-way ticket to the village or to either of the two palaces is 2.40DM ($1.45). For more information, contact the Füssen tourist office.

By Car   Take B-17 south to Füssen, and then head east from Füssen on B-17.

VISITOR INFORMATION   For information about the castles and the region in general, contact the **Kurverwaltung,** Kaiser-Maximilian-Platz 1, Füssen (☎ **08362/938-50**), open Monday through Friday 8am to noon and 2 to 5pm, and Saturday 10am to noon. Information is also available at the **Kurverwaltung,** Rathaus, Münchenerstrasse 2, in Schwangau (☎ **08362/8-19-80**). It's open Monday through Friday 8am to 5pm.

VISITING THE ROYAL CASTLES

There are often very long lines in summer, especially August. With 25,000 people a day visiting, the wait in peak summer months can be as long as 4 or 5 hours for a 20-minute tour. The telephone number for Neuschwanstein is ☎ **08362/81035;** for Hohenschwangau, ☎ **08362/82127.**

✪ **Neuschwanstein.**

This is the fairytale castle of Ludwig II. Construction went on for 17 years until the king's death, when all work stopped, leaving a part of the interior uncompleted. For a total of about 6 months from 1884 to 1886, Ludwig lived on and off in the rooms that were finished.

The doorway off the left side of the vestibule leads to the king's apartments. The study, like most of the rooms, is decorated with wall paintings showing scenes from the Nordic legends (which also inspired Wagner's operas). The theme of the study is the Tannhäuser saga, painted by J. Aigner. The curtains and chair coverings are in hand-embroidered silk, designed with the gold-and-silver Bavarian coat of arms.

From the vestibule, you enter the throne room through the doorway at the opposite end. This hall, designed in Byzantine style by J. Hofmann, was never completed. The floor, a mosaic design, depicts the animals of the world. The columns in the main hall are the deep copper red of porphyry.

The king's bedroom is the most richly carved and decorated in the entire castle—it took 4½ years to complete this room alone. Aside from the mural showing the legend of Tristan and Isolde, the walls are decorated with panels carved to look like Gothic windows. In the center is a large wooden pillar completely encircled with gilded brass sconces. The ornate bed is on a raised platform with an elaborately carved canopy.

The fourth floor of the castle is almost entirely given over to the **Singer's Hall,** the pride of Ludwig II and all of Bavaria. Modeled after the hall at Wartburg, where the legendary song contest of Tannhäuser supposedly took place, this hall is decorated with marble columns and elaborately painted designs interspersed with frescoes depicting the life of Parsifal.

The castle is open year-round, and in September visitors have the additional treat of hearing Wagnerian concerts and other music in the Singer's Hall. For information and reservations, contact the tourist office in Schwangau, **Verkehrsamt,** at the Rathaus (☎ **08362/8-19-80**). The castle, which is seen by guided tour, is open April to September daily 9am to 5:30pm; October to March daily 10am to 4pm. Admission is 11DM ($6.60) for adults, and 8DM ($4.80) for students and seniors over 65; children 5 and under enter free.

Reaching Neuschwanstein involves a steep half-mile climb from the parking lot of Hohenschwangau Castle, about a 25-minute walk for the energetic, an eternity for anybody else. To cut down on the climb, you can take a bus to Marienbrücke, a bridge that crosses over the Pollat Gorge at a height of 305 feet. From that vantage point you, like Ludwig, can stand and meditate on the glories of the castle and its panoramic surroundings. If you want to photograph the castle, don't wait until you reach the top, where you'll be too close to the edifice. It costs 3.50DM ($2.10) for the bus ride up to the bridge or 2DM ($1.20) if you'd like to take the bus back down the hill. From the Marienbrücke bridge, it's a 10-minute walk to Neuschwanstein over a very steep footpath that is not easy to negotiate for anyone who has trouble walking up or down precipitous hills.

The most colorful way to reach Neuschwanstein is by horse-drawn carriage, costing 8DM ($4.80) for the ascent, 4DM ($2.40) for the descent. However, some readers have objected to the rides, complaining that too many people are crowded in.

✪ Hohenschwangau

Not as glamorous or spectacular as Neuschwanstein, the neo-Gothic Hohenschwangau Castle nevertheless has a much richer history. The original structure dates back to the 12th-century knights of Schwangau. When the knights faded away, the castle began to do so too, helped along by the Napoleonic Wars. When Ludwig II's father, Crown Prince Maximilian (later Maximilian II), saw the castle in 1832, he purchased it and 4 years later he had completely restored it. Ludwig II spent the first 17 years of his life here and later received Richard Wagner in its chambers, although Wagner never visited Neuschwanstein on the hill above.

The rooms of Hohenschwangau are styled and furnished in a much heavier Gothic mode than those in Ludwig's castle, and are typical of the halls of medieval knights' castles. But also unlike Neuschwanstein, this castle has a comfortable look about it, as if it actually were a home at one time, not just a museum. The small chapel, once a reception hall, still hosts Sunday Mass. The suits of armor and the Gothic arches here set the stage. Among the most attractive chambers is the **Hall of the Swan Knight,** named for the wall paintings that tell the saga of Lohengrin.

Hohenschwangau is open March 15 to mid-October daily 8:30am to 5:30pm; off-season, daily 9:30am to 4pm. Admission is 11DM ($6.60) for adults and 8DM ($4.80) for children 6 to 15 and seniors over 65; children 5 and under enter free. Several parking lots nearby enable you to leave your car there while visiting both castles.

PLACES TO STAY NEARBY
In Hohenschwangau

Hotel Lisl and Jägerhaus. Neuschwansteinstrasse 1–3, 87643 Hohenschwangau. ☎ **08362/88-70.** Fax 08362/81-107. 47 units. TV TEL. 180DM–356DM ($108–$213.60) double. AE, DC, MC, V. Closed Jan to mid-Mar. Free parking.

This graciously styled villa and its annex across the street sit in a narrow valley, surrounded by their own gardens. Most rooms have a view of at least one of the two royal castles and some units open onto views of both Schlosses. We prefer the rooms in the main building to the more sterile annex, but all are comfortable and have good, firm mattresses. Bathrooms, although small, are adequate for the job. In the main house, two well-styled dining rooms serve decent meals; the restaurant features both international and local dishes.

Hotel Müller Hohenschwangau. Alpseestrasse 16, 87645 Hohenschwangau. ☎ **08362/ 8-19-90.** Fax 08362/81-99-13. www.online-service.de/hotelmueller. E-mail: hotel-mueller@ t-online.de. 45 units. TV TEL. 220DM–300DM ($132–$180) double; 350DM–450DM ($210– $270) suite. Rates include buffet breakfast. AE, DC, MC, V. Closed Nov–Dec 20. Free parking.

As if the yellow walls, green shutters, and gabled alpine detailing of this hospitable inn weren't incentive enough, its location near the foundation of Neuschwanstein Castle makes it even more alluring. An enlargement and upgrading in 1984 added extra modern conveniences. Bedrooms are inviting and have a bit of Bavarian charm, each with a good bed. The showers-only bathrooms are spotless and tiled. On the premises are two pleasant restaurants. Nature lovers usually enjoy hiking the short distance to nearby Hohenschwangau Castle.

In or Near Füssen
Hotel Christine. Weidachstrasse 31, 87629 Füssen. ☎ **08362/72-29.** Fax 08362/940554. 13 units. TV TEL. 160DM–220DM ($96–$132) double. Rates include continental breakfast. No credit cards. Closed Jan 15–Feb 15.

The Christine, 5 minutes by taxi from the train station in Füssen, is one of the best local choices for accommodation. The staff spends the long winter months refurbishing the rooms so they'll be fresh and sparkling for spring visitors. A Bavarian charm pervades the hotel, and the rooms are cozy, although hardly fit for King Ludwig were he to return. Each is well maintained and supplied with firm German mattresses. The shower-only bathrooms are a bit cramped. Breakfast, the only meal offered, is served on beautiful regional china as classical music plays in the background.

Hotel-Schlossgasthof Zum Hechten. Ritterstrasse 6, 87629 Füssen. ☎ **08362/91-600.** Fax 08362/91-6099. 35 units (29 with bathroom). 95DM ($57) double without bathroom; 130DM ($78) double with bathroom. Rates include buffet breakfast. AE, MC. Free outside parking, 5DM ($3) garage.

Family owners have maintained this impeccable guesthouse for generations—it's one of the oldest (and most comfortable) in town. On a central street with a white-walled facade. In spring, you'll open your window to a flower box of geraniums, and feel like Gretel (or Hansel) getting ready to go milk the cows. Rooms are small to medium in size; the bathrooms spotless but a bit cramped. Guest in rooms without bathrooms will find the corridor bathrooms adequate and well maintained. The guesthouse offers two restaurants. A typical Swabian and Bavarian cuisine is served, with plenty of dishes to please the vegetarian as well.

Seegasthof Weissensee. An der B-310, 87629 Füssen-Weissensee. ☎ **08362/91780.** Fax 08362/917888. 19 units. MINIBAR TEL. 136DM ($81.60) double. Rates include breakfast. Free parking. No credit cards.

The paneled rooms at this hotel have sliding glass doors opening onto a balcony overlooking the lake, 4 miles from central Füssen on B-310. Each room has a minibar stocked with beer, wine, and champagne. Owners are extra careful about the comfort of their guests, maintaining quality mattresses and fresh linens in their small but very well-maintained bedrooms. Bathrooms, also small, are well kept with a shower stall and tiled walls. Breakfast is an appetizing and generous meal of cheese, cold cuts, bread, pastry, eggs, and beverages. The fish that your obliging hosts serve you for dinner might have been caught in the ice-blue waters of the nearby lake, whose far shore you can see from the dining room.

Steig Mühle. Alte Steige 3, 87629 Füssen-Weissensee. ☎ **08362/91-76-0.** Fax 08362/ 31-48. 13 units. TV TEL. 98DM–106DM ($58.80–$63.60) double. Rates include buffet breakfast. No credit cards. Free outside parking, 4.50DM ($2.70) in garage. Closed mid-Nov to mid-Dec. From Füssen, take Route 310 toward Kempten, a 5-minute drive.

Owners and hosts Gunter and Nedwig Buhmann like things to be cozy, and their chaletlike guest house is almost a cliché of Bavarian charm. The rooms open onto a view of the lake or mountains, and many have their own balconies. Each room has been outfitted with either a double or twin bed, on which a good, firm mattress rests. Units are tidily arranged and have well-kept private bathrooms (shower only). There aren't a lot of frills, but the place offers one of the most exceptional hotel values in the area.

WHERE TO DINE

Fischerhütte. Uferstrasse 16, Hopfen am See. ☎ **08362/91-97-0.** Reservations recommended. Main courses 16DM–42DM ($9.60–$25.20). AE, DC, MC, V. Daily 11:30am–2pm and 6–9:30pm. Closed Tues in Jan–Mar. SEAFOOD.

Three miles northwest of Füssen in the hamlet of Hopfen am See, at the edge of the lake within sight of dramatic mountain scenery, lie four gracefully paneled old-fashioned dining rooms, plus a terrace in summer. As the name "Fisherman's Cottage" suggests, the establishment specializes in an array of international fish dishes: half an entire Alaskan salmon (for two); a garlicky version of French bouillabaisse; fresh alpine trout, pan-fried or with aromatic herbs in the style of Provence; North Atlantic lobster; and grilled halibut. A few meat dishes are also offered, as well as tempting desserts.

Zum Schwanen. Brotmarkt 4, Füssen. ☎ **08362/61-74.** Reservations required. Main courses 14DM–32DM ($8.40–$19.20). AE. Tues–Sun 11:30am–2pm; Tues–Sat 5:30–9pm. Closed Nov. SWABIAN/BAVARIAN.

This small, attractively old-fashioned restaurant serves a conservative yet flavorful blend of Swabian and Bavarian specialties. Good-tasting and hearty specialties include homemade sausage, roast pork, lamb, and venison.

OUTDOOR ACTIVITIES IN THE AREA

Most visitors come to Füssen for views of its magnificent Bavarian castles, testimonials to the megalomania of a demented king, but if you want to get away from the grandeur of his dreams, the nearby Forggensee and Hopfensee provide lots of opportunities for windsurfing, swimming, and sailing. The focal points for all of these include the Forggensee's **Yachtschule Forggensee,** Seestrasse 10, 87669 Rieden (☎ **08367/471**), and the Hopfensee's **Selbach Bootsvermietung,** Höhenstrasse 51, 87629 Hopfen (☎ **08362/1487**). At both of these sites, instruction for and rentals of windsurfers and sailboats are available.

Likewise, there's a limited amount of midwinter skiing available in the area, at lower altitudes and with less reliable snowfall than what prevails at more visible resorts, such as Garmisch. About 4 miles from Füssen, the Schigebiet Tegelberg, near the hamlet of Schwangau, provides a half-dozen lifts and a cablecar that ascend the slopes of the Tegelberg. For information about ski passes and instruction, contact the **Schischule Tegelberg-Füssen,** in Schwangau (☎ **08362/8518**).

Frankly, your best bet for recreation, diversion, and distraction will probably involve hiking and hill climbing in the foothills around Füssen and Schwangau. Maps, guide services, and hiking-related information of all kinds are available from the local tourist offices.

A Side Trip to Wieskirche

A fascinating excursion is to the ✪ **Wieskirche** (☎ **08861/8173**), one of the most extravagant and flamboyant rococo buildings in the world, a masterpiece of Dominikus Zimmermann. On the slopes of the Ammergau Alps, between Ammer and Lech, the Wieskirche is a noted pilgrimage church, drawing visitors from all over the globe. It's located in an alpine meadow just off the Romantic Road near Steingaden. Ask at the tourist office for a map and the exact location before setting out. The church, which in German means "in the meadows," was built to honor the memory of Jesus Scourged. With the help of his brother, Johann Baptist, Zimmermann worked on the building from 1746 to 1754. Around the choir the church has "upside-down" arches, and its ceiling is richly frescoed. Hours are daily 8am to 7pm. A bus heading for the church leaves Füssen Monday through Saturday at 11:15am; and on Sunday at 1:05pm. You can return on the 3:50pm bus from the church. The trip takes an hour and costs 15.20DM ($9.10) round-trip.

8

Greece

by Sherry Marker

The "glory that was Greece" continues to lure visitors to see the Acropolis in Athens; Olympia, where the games began; Delphi, with the magnificent temple of Apollo; Mycenae, where Agamemnon met his bloody death when he returned home from Troy; and Epidauros, with its astonishingly well-preserved ancient theater. There is also a profusion of less well-known ancient sites—such as Nemea, home to a newly restored stadium—as well as a wealth of Byzantine monuments, including the churches of Daphni and Osios Loukas. Greece is the quintessential land of mountains and seashore, where you can laze the day away on a perfect beach before dancing the night away on Mykonos or Santorini or one of the other breathtaking beautiful "isles of Greece."

1 Athens

Athens is the city that Greeks love to hate, complaining that it's too expensive, too crowded, too polluted. Some 40% of Greece's population lives here, and with 5 million inhabitants, a rumored 17,000 taxis, and streets so congested you'll suspect that each of those 5 million Athenians has a car, the city is bursting at the seams. Meanwhile, work proceeds at a snail's pace on a new subway line, with the tunneling disrupting traffic in much of central Athens and turning lovely Syntagma Square into a construction site. So, why are you here? Because you, too, will probably soon develop a love-hate relationship with Athens, snarling at the traffic and gasping in wonder at the Acropolis, fuming at the taxi driver who tries to overcharge you and marveling at the stranger who realizes that you're lost and walks several blocks out of his way to take you where you're going.

Allow yourself some time to make haste slowly in Athens. Your best moments may come at a small cafe, sipping a tiny cup of the sweet sludge that Greeks call coffee, or getting hopelessly lost in the Plaka—only to find yourself in the shady courtyard of an old church. With only a little planning, you should find a good hotel, eat well in convivial restaurants, and leave Athens expecting to return, as the Greeks say, *Tou Chronou:* next year.

Only in Athens

Seeing the Ancient Monuments   Head first for the Acropolis and take in the Parthenon, the most famous and beautiful ancient temple in the world. Then stroll through the Agora, the political, civic, and commercial center of ancient Athens.

Exploring the Neighborhoods   Climb Mount Likavitos for a bird's-eye view over much of Athens and down to the Saronic Gulf. Then explore Kolonaki, the chic district below Likavitos. Wander through Plaka, where some streets were laid out in antiquity; in one neighborhood high on the slopes of the Acropolis, Anafiotika, the winding streets may remind you of Cycladic villages.

Spending a Morning at the National Archaeological Museum   See the finest Greek statues, vases, and frescoes, as well as swords, gemstones, and buttons, in this vast warehouse of treasures. Arrive as soon as the doors open to beat the crowds.

Shopping the Flea Market   Explore the area between Plaka and Monastiraki Square, filled with small stores and tourist stalls selling everything from charms to ward off the evil eye to reproductions of ancient vases to sandals to souvlakia.

Reveling in a Night on the Town   Enjoy Athens's lively nightlife into the wee hours at a traditional taverna.

Investigating Sounion   Take a side trip out of town to see the superb 5th century B.C. Temple of Poseidon and swim in the sea below.

ORIENTATION

ARRIVING   By Plane   Athens's **Hellenikon International Airport** is only 7 miles south of central Athens, but traffic to and from the airport is often so heavy that you should allow an hour for the trip. Two terminals share the Hellenikon runways. Most visitors arrive at the **East Air Terminal** (☎ 01/969-4466), on the eastern side of the airport runways. It offers a few convenient facilities, including branches of the major Greek banks (usually open 24 hours). Free luggage carts are available in the baggage area. The information desk, slightly to the left as you come out of customs, usually has tourist pamphlets on Athens. Outside the main exit, there's a managed taxi rank to the right and buses to the left.

All domestic and international flights of the national airline, **Olympic Airways** (☎ 01/926-9111), arrive at the newer **West Air Terminal** (☎ 01/936-3363 or 01/926-9111). Bank offices are located in the arrivals area and are open 7am to 11pm, with ATMs usually operating after hours. Olympic has an information booth, and the **Tourist Police** have a corner office in the building across from the terminal entrance.

Many charter flights now use the **Charter Terminal,** south of the East Air Terminal. The information numbers for the Charter Terminal are ☎ **01/997-2581** or 01/997-2686.

If you arrive at one of these three terminals and have to make connections at another, you can take either the shuttle bus service (200Dr/65¢) or a taxi. The shuttle bus service officially runs once an hour from 8:30am to 8:30pm, but actually runs on an erratic schedule. If you decide to take a taxi, ask an airline official or a policeman what the fare should be, and let the taxi driver know that you have been told the official rate before you begin your journey.

If you are heading into Athens, a **cab** into the center (*kentro*) of town from any of the three terminals should cost about 2,500 to 3,000Dr ($8.35 to $10); double that between midnight and 5am.

All **bus schedules** are erratic, and those posted at the airports are frequently months out of date. Because of ongoing road work between Athens and Piraeus, journey times and routes are subject to change. Buses no. 91 and 91 run from the East and West Terminals into central Athens (200Dr/65¢). Both buses officially run 6am to 9pm; the

Athens

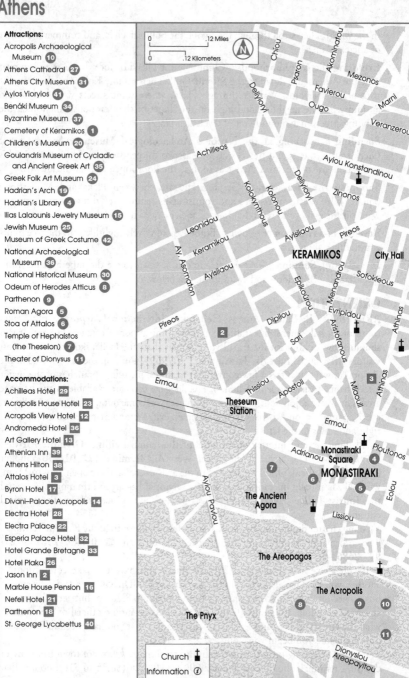

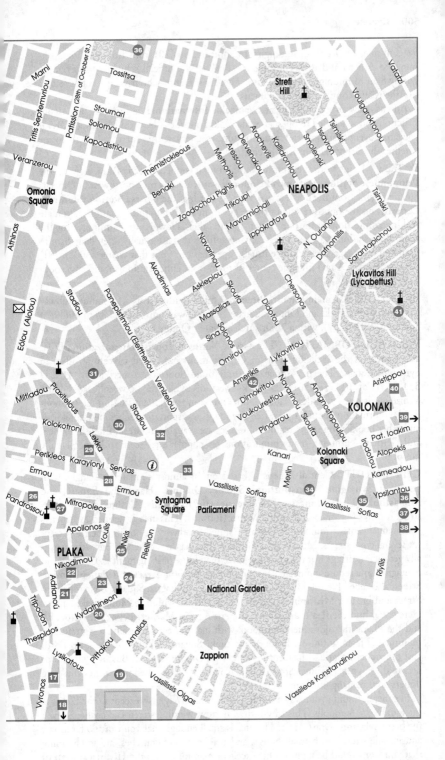

499

91 continues service until midnight. In addition, bus 101 runs from the West Terminal to Athens and then continues to Piraeus; the official schedule for service is hourly 8am to midnight (100Dr/35¢). There is sometimes hourly express bus service to Athens and continuing on to Piraeus.

Athens's new airport, **Eleftherios Venizelos International,** is currently under construction and scheduled to open at Spata, 23km outside Athens, in March of 2001. If you are traveling around this time, be sure to check with your travel agent to see whether the airport has, in fact, opened.

By Train   Trains from the west, including Eurail connections via Patra, arrive at the **Peloponnese Station (Stathmos Peloponnissou),** about a mile northwest of Omonia Square. Trains from the north arrive 3 blocks north at the **Larissa Station (Stathmos Larissis),** on the opposite side of the tracks from the Peloponnese Station. If you are making connections from one station to the other, allow 10 to 15 minutes for the walk. Both stations have currency-exchange offices that are usually open daily 8am to 9pm and a luggage-storage office usually open 6am to 9pm that charges 300Dr ($1) per bag per day. A taxi into the center of town from either station should cost about 1,000Dr ($3.35).

By Boat   Athens's main seaport, **Piraeus,** 7 miles southwest, is a 15-minute subway ride from Monastiraki and Omonia squares. The subway runs about 5am to midnight and costs 75Dr (25¢), with a 75Dr surcharge after Omonia.

VISITOR INFORMATION   The Greek National Tourist Organization (EOT, also known as the Hellenic Tourism Organization) has closed its central office in Syntagma Square. The new office, on the ground floor at 2 Amerikis St. (☎ **01/ 331-0437** or 01/331-0561), 2 blocks west of Syntagma between Stadiou and Venizelou, is open weekdays 9am to 7pm and Saturday 9:30am to 2pm (closed holidays). Information about Athens, free city maps, transportation schedules, hotel lists, and other booklets on many regions of Greece are available in Greek, English, French, and German—although many publications on popular sites seem to be perpetually out of print.

CITY LAYOUT   Central Athens is based on an almost equilateral triangle, with points at **Syntagma (Constitution) Square, Omonia (Harmony) Square,** and **Monastiraki (Little Monastery) Square,** near the **Acropolis.** All three are now construction sites for a new line of the Metro (subway). This area is defined as Athens's commercial center, from which cars are banned (in theory, if not in practice) except for several cross streets. Most Greeks consider Omonia the city center, but visitors usually get their bearings from Syntagma, where the House of Parliament is. Omonia and Syntagma squares are connected by the parallel **Stadiou Street** and **Panepistimiou Street,** also called Eleftheriou Venizelou. West from Syntagma Square, ancient **Ermou Street** and broader **Mitropoleos Street** lead slightly downhill to Monastiraki Square. Here you'll find the **flea market,** the **Ancient Agora (Market)** below the Acropolis, and the **Plaka,** the oldest neighborhood, with many street names and a scattering of monuments from antiquity. From Monastiraki Square, **Athinas Street** leads north past the modern Market (the Central Market) to Omonia Square. Bustling with shoppers in the daytime, Athinas Street is best avoided at night, when prostitutes and drug dealers tend to hang out here.

In general, finding your way around Athens is relatively easy, except in the Plaka, at the foot of the Acropolis. This labyrinth of narrow, winding streets can challenge even the best navigators. Don't panic: The area is small enough that you can't go far astray, and its side streets, with small houses and neighborhood churches, are so charming that you won't mind being lost. One excellent map may help: the **Historical Map of**

Athens, produced by the Greek Archaeological Service, which has maps of Plaka and of the city center showing the major archaeological sites. The map (about 500Dr/$1.65) is sold at many bookstores, museums, ancient sites, and newspaper kiosks.

GETTING AROUND   By Public Transportation   The **blue-and-white buses** run regular routes in Athens and its suburbs every 15 minutes from 5am to midnight. (For the more distant suburbs, you may need to change buses at a transfer station.) The **orange electric trolley buses** serve areas in the city center from 5am to midnight. The **green buses** run between the city center and Piraeus every 20 minutes from 6am to midnight, then hourly until 6am. Tickets cost 100Dr (35¢) and must be purchased in advance, usually in groups of 10, from any news kiosk or special bus ticket kiosks at the main stations.

When you board, validate your ticket in the automatic machine. Hold on to your ticket: Uniformed and plainclothes inspectors periodically check tickets and can levy fines of 1,500Dr ($5) on the spot.

The **Athens map** distributed by the Greek National Tourist Organization indicates major public transportation stops and routes. Keep in mind that the buses are usually very crowded and their schedules are erratic.

The **Metro** currently links Piraeus, the seaport of Athens, and Kifissia, an upscale northern suburb. (A second line is under construction and should be finished before the 2004 Olympic Games in Athens.) In the city center the trains run underground, and the main stops are Monastiraki, Omonia, and Viktorias (Victoria). Trains run about every 5 to 15 minutes from 5am to midnight. Tickets cost 100Dr (35¢), with a 100Dr surcharge after Omonia. Validate your ticket in the machine as you enter the waiting platform or risk a fine. Metro and bus tickets are not interchangeable.

By Taxi   Supposedly there are 17,000 taxis in Athens, but finding one empty is almost never easy. Especially if you have travel connections to make, it's a good idea to reserve a radio taxi.

At press time, the minimum fare was 200Dr (65¢), and the "1" meter rate is 62Dr (20¢) per kilometer, with a surcharge of 150Dr (50¢) for service from a port or rail or bus station, 300Dr ($1) for service from the airport, and a luggage fee of 50Dr (20¢) for every bag over 10kg (22 lb.). These prices may well be higher by the time you visit Greece, as increases were scheduled to go into effect in the summer of 1999.

There are about 15 **radio taxi** companies in Athens, including **Aris** at ☎ 01/346-7137, **Express** at ☎ 01/993-4812, **Kosmos** at ☎ 01/801-9000, **Parthenon** at

---

Traveler's Tip

Fortunately, taxis are inexpensive, and most drivers are honest. However, some, notably those working Piraeus, the airports, and popular tourist destinations, can't resist trying to overcharge the obviously inexperienced. When you get into a taxi, check to see that the meter is turned on and set on "1" rather than "2"; it should be set on "2" (double fare) only between midnight and 5am or if you take a taxi outside the city limits. (If you plan to do this, try to negotiate a flat rate in advance.) Unless your cab is caught in very heavy traffic, a trip to the center of town from the airport between 5am and midnight should not cost more than 4,000Dr ($13.35). Don't be surprised if your driver picks up other passengers en route; he will work out everyone's share, and probably the worst that will happen is that you'll get less of a break than you would if you spoke Greek.

☎ 01/581-4711, and **Piraeus** at ☎ 01/413-5888. If you're trying to make travel connections or traveling during rush hours, the service will be well worth the 300Dr ($1) surcharge.

Keep in mind that your driver may have difficulty understanding your pronunciation of your destination. If you are taking a taxi from your hotel, a staff member can tell the driver your destination or write down the address for you to show to the driver. If you carry a business card from your hotel, you can show it to the driver when you return. If you suspect you have been overcharged, ask for help at your hotel or other destination before you pay the fare. Most restaurants will also call for a taxi at no charge.

The Hellenic Tourism Organization's pamphlet **"Helpful Hints for Taxi Users"** has information on fares as well as a complaint form, which you can send to the Ministry of Transport and Communication, 13 Xenophondos, 101 91 Athens. Replies to complaints should be forwarded to the *Guinness Book of Records.*

On Foot   Most of what you probably want to see and do in Athens is in the city center, allowing you to sightsee mostly on foot. Wheelchair users will find Athens a challenge, although curbs on many streets are being redesigned to accommodate wheelchairs. All visitors should keep in mind that a red traffic light or stop sign is no guarantee that cars will stop for pedestrians. The pedestrian zones in sections of the Plaka, the commercial center, and Kolonaki make strolling, window-shopping, and sightseeing infinitely more pleasant than on other, traffic-clogged streets. Don't relax completely even on pedestrianized streets, though: Athens's multitude of kamikaze motorcycles seldom respects the rules.

By Car   Parking is so difficult and traffic so heavy in Athens that you should use a car only for trips outside the city. Keep in mind that on any day trip (to Sounion or Daphni, for example) you'll spend at least several hours leaving and reentering central Athens.

Not far south of Syntagma Square, **Avis,** 48 Amalias Ave. (☎ 01/322-4951), charges about 16,000Dr ($53.35) per day with unlimited mileage, including insurance and tax. A little farther south, **AutoEurope,** 29 Hatzihristou St., right off Syngrou (☎ 01/924-2206), charges about 12,500Dr ($41.65); **Budget,** 8 Syngrou Ave. (☎ 01/921-4711), charges about 14,000Dr ($46.65); and **Eurodollar Rent a Car,** 29 Syngrou Ave. (☎ 01/922-9672), charges about 12,500Dr ($41.65). You can usually reduce the price considerably by booking from outside Greece; sometimes, especially in the off-season, on-the-spot bargaining is effective.

WARNING: Most companies add, and do not always mention, the hefty surcharge for picking up or dropping off your car at the airport. And be sure to take full insurance; if you are renting with a credit card, check with your company to see exactly what, if any, insurance it provides.

Fast Facts: Athens

American Express   The office at 2 Ermou St., near the southwest corner of Syntagma Square (☎ **01/324-4975;** fax 01/322-7893), offers currency exchange and other services weekdays 8:30am to 4pm and Saturday 8:30am to 1:30pm.

Area Code   The country code for Greece is **30.** The city code for Athens is **1;** use this code when you're calling from outside Greece. If you're within Greece, use **01.**

ATMs   ATM cash dispensers are increasingly common in Athens, and the National Bank of Greece operates a 24-hour ATM next to the tourist information office on Syntagma Square. It's *not* a good idea to rely on using ATMs exclusively in Athens because the machines are often out of service when you need them most: on holidays or during bank strikes.

Banks   Banks are generally open Monday to Thursday 8am to 2pm and Friday 8am to 1:30pm. Most have currency-exchange counters that use the rates set daily by the government, which are usually more favorable than those offered at unofficial exchange bureaus. It's worth doing a little comparison shopping for the best rate of exchange; for example, many hotels offer rates (usually only for cash) that are better than the official bank rates.

Business Hours   In **winter,** shops are generally open Monday and Wednesday 9am to 5pm; Tuesday, Thursday, and Friday 10am to 7pm; and Saturday 8:30am to 3:30pm. In **summer,** shops are generally open Monday, Wednesday, and Saturday 8am to 3pm; and Tuesday, Thursday, and Friday 8am to 1:30pm and 5:30 to 10pm. Note that many shops geared to visitors keep especially long hours, and some close from about 2 to 5pm. Most **food stores** and the **Central Market** are open Monday and Wednesday 9am to 4:30pm, Tuesday 9am to 6pm, Thursday 9:30am to 6:30pm, Friday 9:30am to 7pm, and Saturday 8:30am to 4:30pm.

Currency   The **drachma** (Dr) is the Greek national currency. Coins are issued in 5, 10, 20, 50, and 100Dr; bills are denominated in 50, 100, 500, 1,000, 5,000, and 10,000Dr. At press time, $1 = 300Dr, 1EUR = 324Dr, or £1 = 492Dr, or 100Dr = 33¢, .30EUR, or £.20.

Dentists & Doctors   If you need an English-speaking doctor or dentist, call your embassy for advice or try **SOS Doctor** (☎ 01/331-0310 or 01/331-0311). The English-language *Athens News* lists some American- and British-trained doctors and hospitals offering emergency services. Most of the larger hotels have doctors whom they can call for you in an emergency.

Drugstores   *Pharmakia,* identified by green crosses, are scattered throughout Athens. Hours are usually 8am to 2pm weekdays. In the evening and on weekends most are closed, but they usually post a notice listing the names and addresses of pharmacies that are open or will open in an emergency. Newspapers, including the *Athens News,* list the pharmacies open outside regular hours.

Embassies & Consulates   Australia, 37 Dimitriou Soutsou Ave. (☎ 01/644-7303); **Canada,** 4 Ioannou Yenadiou St. (☎ 01/725-4011); **Ireland,** 7 Leoforos Vasileos Konstantinou (☎ 01/723-2771); **New Zealand** (consulate), 9 Semitelou St. (☎ 01/771-0112); **United Kingdom,** 1 Ploutarchou St. (☎ 01/723-6211); **United States,** 91 Vasilissis Sofias Ave. (☎ 01/721-2951). Embassies are usually closed on their own important national holidays and sometimes on Greek holidays as well.

Emergencies   In an emergency, dial ☎ **100** for fast **police** assistance and ☎ **171** for the **Tourist Police** (see "Police," below). Dial ☎ **199** to report a **fire** and ☎ **166** for an **ambulance** and **hospital**.

Holidays   Major public holidays in Athens include **New Year's Day** (January 1), **Epiphany** (January 6), **Ash Wednesday, Independence Day** (March 25), **Good Friday, Easter** Sunday and Monday (Orthodox Easter can coincide with or vary by 2 weeks from Catholic and Protestant Easter), **Labor Day** (May 1),

Assumption Day (August 15), National Day (October 28), and Christmas (December 25 and 26). Some shops and offices close for at least a week at Christmas and Easter.

Internet Cafes The **Astor Internet Café,** 17 Patission St. (1 block off Omonia Square; ☎ **01/523-8546**), is open Monday to Saturday 10am to 10pm, Sunday 10am to 4pm, and charges 1,500Dr ($5) per hour to use e-mail, Web, and word processing.

Laundry The **National Dry Cleaners and Laundry Service,** 17 Apollonos St. (☎ **01/323-2226**), next to the Hermes Hotel, is open Monday and Wednesday from 7am to 4pm and Tuesday, Thursday, and Friday from 7am to 8pm; laundry costs 1,500Dr ($5) per kilo.

Lost & Found If you lose something on the street or on public transportation, contact the **Police Lost and Found Office,** 173 Alexandras Ave. (☎ **01/642-1616**). It's open Monday to Saturday 9am to 3pm. Lost passports and other documents may be returned by the police to the appropriate embassy, so check there as well. It's a good idea to travel with a photocopy of all important documents.

Police In an emergency, dial ☎ **100.** For help dealing with a troublesome taxi driver, hotel, restaurant, or shop owner, stand your ground and call the **Tourist Police** at ☎ **171.**

Post Office The main **post offices** (no phone) in central Athens are at 100 Eolou St., just south of Omonia Square, and in Syntagma Square on the corner of Mitropoleos Street. They are open weekdays 7:30am to 8pm, Saturday 7:30am to 2pm, and Sunday 9am to 1pm.

Tax **Value-added tax (VAT)** is included in the price of all goods and services in Athens, ranging from 4% on books to 36% on certain luxury items. Some shops attempt to mislead you by quoting you one price and then, when you hand over your credit card, adding on a hefty VAT charge. Be wary. In theory, if you are not a member of a Common Market/European Union country, you can get a refund on major purchases at Hellenikon airport when you leave Greece. In practice, you would virtually have to arrive at the airport a day before your flight to get to the head of the line, do the paper work, get a refund, and catch your flight.

Telephone/Telegrams/Telefaxes Many of the city's public phones now accept only **phone cards,** available at newsstands and OTE offices in several denominations starting at 1,700Dr ($5.65). The card works for 100 short local calls (or briefer long distance or international calls). Some kiosks still have **metered phones;** you pay what the meter records. Local phone calls cost 20Dr (5¢). North Americans can phone home directly by contacting **AT&T** at ☎ **00-800-1311, MCI** at ☎ **00-800-1211,** or **Sprint** at ☎ **00-800-1411;** calls can be collect or billed to your phone charge card. You can send a telegram or fax from offices of the **Telecommunications Organization of Greece (OTE).** At press time, the OTE office at 15 Stadiou, near Syntagma, was temporarily closed, leaving the Omonia Square OTE office and the Victoria Square Office at 85 Patission St. as Athens's most central OTE offices.

Tipping Restaurants include a service charge in the bill, but many visitors add a 10% tip. Most Greeks do not give a percentage tip to taxi drivers, but often round the fare to the nearest 1,000Dr, for example, on a fare of 950Dr.

WHERE TO STAY

Warning: Our hotel prices were accurate at press time, but price increases of 10% to 15% are rumored. Virtually all Greek hotels are clean and comfortable; few are charming or elegant. If shower and tub facilities are important to you, be sure to have a look at the bathroom: Many Greek tubs are tiny, and the showers handheld. Don't assume that just because a hotel says it has air-conditioning, the air-conditioning is working—and check to see if there's functioning central heating in the winter. And keep in mind that very few Greek hotel rooms have hair dryers or coffee- and tea-making facilities.

The area south and west of Syntagma Square and the neighborhoods of Plaka, Kolonaki, Koukaki, **Makriyanni,** and **Monastiraki** offer the most convenient and comfortable choices. For pure convenience, the **Syntagma** hotels and those in the lively **Plaka** area can't be beat. **Kolonaki** is an upscale neighborhood on the slopes of Mount Likavitos—but keep in mind that you'll have an uphill walk to your hotel. The **Koukaki** district, near Philopappos Hill and off the non-Acropolis side of Dionysiou Areopayitou Avenue, offers quiet residential back streets and the feeling of a real Greek neighborhood. Keep in mind that from Koukaki, almost everything you want to do, including buying an English-language newspaper, involves extra walking.

Finally, despite the distance of the airport from Athens, staying in a hotel near the airport is not recommended. Should you have an early morning/late evening, it's easy to get back and forth into Athens at these times.

IN PLAKA

Expensive

Electra Palace. 18 Nikodimou St., Plaka, 105 57 Athens. ☎ **01/324-1401** or 01/324-1407. Fax 01/324-1875. 106 units. A/C MINIBAR TV TEL. 45,000Dr ($150) double. Rates include breakfast. AE, DC, MC, V.

The Electra, just a few blocks southwest of Syntagma Square on a relatively quiet side street, is the most modern and stylish Plaka hotel. The top-floor rooms are smaller, but they're where you want to be, both for the view of the Acropolis and to escape traffic noise. (Ask for a top-floor room when you make your reservation.) The rooms are hardly drop-dead elegant, but they are pleasant, decorated in soft pastels. The rooftop pool is a real plus, and if you're too tired to go out for dinner, the hotel restaurant is quite decent.

Moderate

Acropolis House Hotel. 6–8 Kodrou St., 105 58 Athens. ☎ **01/322-2344.** Fax 01/324-4143. 25 units, 15 with bathroom (3 with tub/shower; 12 with shower); 4 suites. A/C TEL. 15,000Dr($50) double without bathroom; 21,595Dr ($72) double with bathroom. Rates include continental breakfast. Add 4,000Dr ($13) for use of air-conditioning. V.

Planning Ahead

If you're visiting Athens in the summer, **write or fax ahead of time for reservations** because the best-value hotels tend to be full then. If you arrive without a reservation, you can try to book a room at the tourist information booth at the West Air Terminal, run by a private tourist agency and open 7am to 1am; the agency charges a small fee. If you visit Athens in the off-season, especially in the winter, you may be pleasantly surprised at the not-always-publicized low rates available in even the most expensive hotels.

This small hotel in a handsomely restored 150-year-old villa with many of its original classical architectural details offers the convenience of a central location, and the charm of a quiet pedestrian side street. Rooms 401 and 402 have good views and can be requested, but not guaranteed, when making a reservation. The newer wing (only 60 years old) isn't architecturally special and each room's spartan bathroom is across the hall. There's a book-swap spot and a washing machine, free after a 4-day stay.

Byron Hotel. 19 Vyronos St., 105 58 Athens. ☎ **01/325-3554.** Fax 01/323-0327. 20 units, all with bathroom. TEL. 22,000Dr ($74) double. Rates include breakfast. No credit cards.

The Byron has a convenient and reasonably quiet location just off busy Dionissiou Areopagitou St. The small rooms here are spare; those in the back overlooking apartments and gardens are usually quieter than the six in front, but lack balconies and partial views of the Acropolis. Eight rooms have air-conditioning, for which there is a supplemental charge of 2,500Dr ($8.35). As at several smaller Athenian hotels, I've found the staff here to be either very helpful or very preoccupied.

✪ **Hotel Plaka.** 7 Kapnikareas St. and Mitropoleos, 105 56 Athens. ☎ **01/322/2096.** Fax 01/322-2412. 67 units, all with bathroom (32 units with shower only). A/C TV TEL. 28,000Dr ($93) double. Rates include breakfast. AE, DC, EURO, MC, V.

This 10-year-old hotel, popular with Greeks, who prefer its modern conveniences to the old-fashioned charms of most other hotels in the Plaka area, has a teriffic location just off Syntagma Square near the Athens Cathedral on the relatively quiet outskirts of the Plaka. Most bedrooms have bedspreads and rugs in the Greek national colors of blue and white, and many have balconies. Bedrooms on the fifth and sixth floors in the rear (where it's usually quieter) have views of Plaka and the Acropolis, also visible from the roof-garden (snack-bar).

✪ **Nefeli Hotel.** 16 Iperidou St., 105 58 Athens. ☎ **01/322-8044.** Fax 01/322-5800. 18 units, 13 with shower only, 5 with tub/shower. A/C TEL. 23,000Dr ($77) double (considerable off-season reductions). Rates include breakfast. AE, V.

The charming little Nefeli ("Cloud"), steps from the Cultural Center of the Municipality of Athens, is quiet for its central location, with the quietest rooms overlooking pedestrianized Angelikes Hatzimichaelis St. The rooms are small (as are the bathrooms), but I found them to have character, unlike so many Athenian hotels. In late 1998, the hotel completely redecorated, installing all new beds and furniture. The staff is courteous and helpful.

NEAR MONASTIRAKI SQUARE
Moderate

Attalos Hotel. 29 Athinas St., 105 54 Athens. ☎ **01/321-2801.** Fax 01/324-3124. E-mail: atthot@hol.gr. 80 units, all with bathroom. A/C TEL. 18,000Dr ($60) double (ask for the 10% discount for Frommer's readers). Rates include buffet breakfast. AE, V. Walk about 1½ blocks north from Monastiraki Sq. on Athinas St; the hotel (large sign) is on the left.

The excellent value six-story (with elevator) Attalos is only a block from the frenzied comings and goings at the Central Market on Athinas Street, which makes it a great place to stay if you want to be poised to buy anything from oranges to octopuses. The market opens around 5am, which means that the early morning hours on Athinas Street are lively, although the street is usually quiet after the market closes in the late afternoon. (Exercise care when walking along Athinas St. at night, when a certain number of prostitutes and, increasingly, drug dealers work the street.) The rooms here are plain, but there are hair dryers, and many rooms feature framed color photos of archaeological sites and antiquities. One real plus is the roof garden, with its fine views of the city and the Acropolis.

✪ **Jason Inn Hotel.** 12 Ayion Assomaton St., 105 53 Athens. ☎ **01/325-1106.** Fax 01/523-4786. 57 units, all with bathroom. A/C TV TEL. 16,500Dr ($55) double. Rates include American buffet breakfast. DC, MC, V.

This newly renovated hotel (admittedly on a dull street, but just a few blocks from the Agora and Plaka) offers attractive, good-sized comfortable rooms with double-paned windows for extra quiet; bathrooms are on the small side, but the showers are good quality. If you don't mind walking a few extra blocks to Syntagma, this is currently one of the best values in Athens, with an eager-to-help staff. If the Jason Inn is full, staff may be able to find you a room in one of their other hotels: the similarly priced Adrian Hotel, on busy Hadrian St. in the Plaka, or the slightly less expensive King Jason or Jason Hotels, both a few blocks from Omonia Sq.

ON & AROUND SYNTAGMA SQUARE
Very Expensive
Hotel Grande Bretagne. Syntagma Sq., 105 63 Athens. In the U.S. you can make reservations through Sheraton Hotels at ☎ **800/325-3535;** in Greece, 01/321-5555. Fax 01/322-0211. 365 units, 33 suites. A/C MINIBAR TV TEL. 63,000–125,650Dr ($210–$419) double; from 92,000Dr ($307) suite. AE, CB, DC, MC, V.

This venerable 1864 hotel with elegant beaux arts decor is an Athens landmark. Political and social movers and shakers pass through the lobby, with its ornately carved wood paneling, soaring ceilings, and polished marble floors, for power lunches at the popular GB Corner. (So, increasingly, do the tour groups staying here, which doesn't help the ambience.) The bedrooms were renovated in 1992, but many of the courtyard rooms look the worse for wear and utterly lack the elegance of the front rooms, which overlook Syntagma Square (where work on the Metro continues) and the Acropolis. *Note:* If construction on the Metro is still continuing in Syntagma Square, then you might want to consider staying elsewhere; the construction, although relatively quiet, can be dusty.

Expensive
Electra Hotel. 5 Ermou St., 105 63 Athens. ☎ **01/322-3223.** Fax 01/322-0310. 110 units. A/C TV TEL. 36,000–45,000Dr ($120–$150). Rates include buffet breakfast. DC, MC, V.

If Ermou Street remains pedestrianized, the Electra has a location that is both central (steps from Syntagma Square) and quiet. Most bedrooms, although not large, have comfortable armchairs, large windows, and modern bathrooms with hair dryers. The front desk is sometimes understaffed, but the service is generally acceptable.

Esperia Palace Hotel. 22 Stadiou St., 105 61 Athens. In the U.S. call Best Western at ☎ **800/528-1234;** in Greece, 01/323-8001. 185 units. A/C MINIBAR TV TEL. 38,000–46,450Dr ($126–$155) double. Rates include breakfast. AE, DC, MC, V.

This is a good-value hotel with a convenient location near Syntagma Square. The rooms are large and comfortable, although rather plain; some carpets are in need of cleaning. The buffet breakfast is a plus. Many tour groups stay here, which you might find a drawback if you are on your own.

Moderate
✪ **Hotel Achilleas.** 21 Lekka St., 105 62 Athens. ☎ **01/323-3197.** Fax 01/324-1092. 34 units. A/C TEL. 22,000Dr ($74) double. Rates include breakfast. AE, DC, EURO, MC, V.

The Achilleas, on a relatively quiet side street steps from Syntagma Square, was fully renovated in 1995. Although the entrance lacks charm, the central location and fair prices make this a good choice. The pleasant bedrooms are good-sized, cheerful, and light; some rear bedrooms have small balconies. Breakfast is served in the first-floor dining room, which has lots of green plants.

In Kolonaki

Very Expensive

Saint George Lycabettus Hotel. 2 Kleomenous St., 106 75 Athens. ☎ **01/729-0711.** Fax 01/721-0439. 167 units, all with bathroom. A/C TEL TV. 57,000–75,000Dr ($190–$250) double. Rates include breakfast. AE, DC, MC, V.

As yet, the Saint George Lycabettus does not get many tour groups, which helps it maintain its tranquil tone. The nicely appointed rooms look toward Mt. Likavitos or a small park, although the surrounding street traffic keeps it from being a real oasis of calm. The rooftop pool is a real plus, and the hotel is steps from the chic Kolonaki restaurants and shops.

Moderate

✪ **Athenian Inn.** 22 Haritos St., Kolonaki, 106 75 Athens. ☎ **01/723-8097.** Fax 01/724-2268. 28 units, all with bathroom. A/C TEL. 33,000Dr ($110) double. Rates include breakfast. AE, DC, V.

The quiet location 3 blocks from Kolonaki Square is a blessing, as are the clean accommodations and friendly staff. (A quote from Hellenophile Lawrence Durrell in the guest book states: "At last the ideal Athens hotel, good and modest in scale but perfect in service and goodwill.") Some of the balconies look out on Mount Likavitos. Breakfast is served in a small lounge with a fireplace and piano (and, of late, a TV). Between stays, I tend to forget how small the rooms are here, which suggests to me that the staff is doing a good job of making guests feel comfortable.

In the Embassy District

Very Expensive

✪ **Andromeda Hotel.** 22 Timoleontos Vassou St. (off Plateia Mavili), 115 21 Athens. ☎ **01/643-7302.** Fax 01/646-6361. 30 units. A/C MINIBAR TV TEL. 60,000–85,000Dr ($200–$284) double. Special rates sometimes available. AE, DC, EURO, MC, V.

The city's only boutique hotel is easily the most charming in Athens, with a staff that makes you feel that this is your home away from home. Rooms are large and elegantly decorated, with hair dryers, and furniture and paintings you'd be happy to live with. The quiet hotel overlooks the garden of the American ambassador's home. The only drawbacks: It's a serious hike (20 to 30 minutes) or 10-minute taxi ride to Syntagma, and there are few restaurants in this residential neighborhood (although the Andromeda has its own small restaurant). If you're planning a long stay in Athens, check to see whether the Andromeda's planned expansion with service apartments has opened.

Athens Hilton. 46 Vasilissis Sofias Ave., 115 28 Athens. ☎ **800/445-8667** or 01/722-0301. Fax 01/721-3110. 446 units. A/C MINIBAR TV TEL. 114,300–125,400Dr ($381–$418) double. AE, DC, EURO, MC, V.

The Athens Hilton, near the U.S. Embassy, is a brisk 10-minute walk from Syntagma Square. It's something of an Athenian institution, where businessmen and diplomats meet for a drink or a meal. A number of small shops, a beauty parlor, and cafes and restaurants surround the seriously glitzy marble and crystal lobby. The guest rooms (looking toward either the hills outside Athens or the Acropolis) have large marble bathrooms with hair dryers and are decorated in the generic but comfortable international Hilton style, with some Greek touches. The Plaza Executive floor of rooms and suites offers a separate business center and higher level of service. Sports options include a pool and a health club. The Hilton often runs promotions, so check about special rates before booking.

NEAR THE ACROPOLIS (MAKRIYANNI & KOUKAKI DISTRICTS)
Very Expensive
✪ **Divani-Palace Acropolis.** 19–25 Parthenonos St., Makriyanni, 117 42 Athens. ☎ **01/ 92-22-2945.** Fax 01/92-14-993. 253 units. A/C MINIBAR TV TEL. 62,000–72,000Dr ($207–$240) double. AE, DC, MC, V.

For luxury, comfort, and quiet location, you'd have a hard time beating this recently renovated hotel, just 3 blocks south of the Acropolis. The large bedrooms and two-basined bathrooms (with hair dryer) are both elegant and practical, and the service surprisingly personal. The spacious modern lobby has copies of classical sculpture, and there's a small, handsome pool, a bar, a good restaurant, and a lovely roof garden with the view you'd expect. The same hotel group operates the **Divani Caravel Hotel,** near the National Art Gallery and Hilton Hotel at 2 Vas. Alexandrou Ave. (☎ **01/ 725-3725;** fax 01-725-3770).

Moderate
✪ **Acropolis View Hotel.** 10 Webster St., 117 42 Athens. ☎ **01/921-7303.** Fax 01/ 923-0705. 32 units. A/C TV TEL. 32,000Dr ($106) double. Rates include generous breakfast. Substantial reductions Nov 1–Apr 1. AE, EURO, MC, V.

Popular with repeat visitors to Athens, this hotel is on a small winding side street off Rovertou Galli Street, not far from the Herodes Atticus theater. The quiet neighborhood, at the base of Philopappos Hill, is a 10- to 15-minute walk from the heart of Plaka. The rooms (many recently renovated) are small, but clean and pleasant, with good bathrooms. Some rooms, such as 405, overlook Philopappos Hill, and others, such as 407, face the Acropolis. The rooftop bar also has a bead on the Acropolis.

Art Gallery Hotel. 5 Erechthiou St., Koukaki, 117 42 Athens. ☎ **01/923-8376.** Fax 01/ 923-3025. E-mail: ecotec@atenet.gr. 22 units. TEL. 16,800Dr ($56) double. No credit cards.

As you might expect, this small hotel—in a half-century-old house that has been home to several artists—has an artistic flair (and a nice old-fashioned cage elevator). Rooms are plain, but comfortable, with polished hardwood floors and ceiling fans. There's a Victorian-style breakfast room on the fourth floor, with heavy marble-topped tables and several chairs with faded velvet upholstery.

Austria Hotel. 7 Mousson St., Filopappou, 117 42 Athens. ☎ **01/923-5151.** Fax 01/ 924-7350. E-mail: austria@topservice.com or austria@hol.gr. 37 units (9 with shower only). A/C TEL. 20,500Dr ($69) double. Rates include breakfast. AE, DC, EURO, MC, V.

This quiet, well-maintained little hotel at the base of Philopappos Hill is operated by a Greek-Austrian family, who offer guests use of the hotel safe deposit box and fax services, will exchange your foreign money into drachmas (which not all small hotels are prepared to do), and can point you to the convenient neighborhood laundromat. The rooms are rather spartan (the linoleum floors are not enchanting), but tidy. There's a great view over Athens and out to sea from the rooftop, where you can sun or sit under an awning in the shade. Not surprisingly, the hotel has a lot of clients from Austria.

Parthenon. 6 Makri St., 115 27 Athens. ☎ **01/923-4594.** Fax 01/644-1084. 79 units. TEL. 22,500Dr ($75) double. MC, V.

This modern, recently refurbished hotel is in an excellent location just south of Plaka and the Acropolis. The good-sized lobby is more glitzy than at many moderately priced hotels, and there are a bar, restaurant, and small garden. The carpeted bedrooms have bright, cheerful bedspreads and decent-sized bathrooms, and some have TVs. The Parthenon is one of a group of four hotels; if it is full, the management will try to get you a room in the Christina, a few blocks away, or at the Riva or Alexandros, near the Megaron (the Athens Concert Hall).

Inexpensive

✪ **Marble House Pension.** 35 A. Zinni St., Koukaki, 117 41 Athens. ☎ **01/923-4058.** Fax 01/922-6461. 17 units (9 with bathroom). A/C TEL. 13,500Dr ($45) double with bathroom; 12,000Dr ($40) double without bathroom. Oct–May, double rooms can be rented by the month for 100,000Dr ($333). No credit cards.

Named for its marble facade, which is usually covered by fuchsia bougainvillea, this small hotel is on a cul-de-sac just after the church on Zinni Street. It's famous among budget travelers (including many teachers) for its friendly, helpful staff. The rooms are clean, with wood-frame beds, stone floors, ceiling fans, and balconies overlooking the quiet residential neighborhood. If you're spending more than a few days in Athens and don't mind being out of the center, this is a fine, homey base for sightseeing.

WHERE TO DINE

Athens has an astonishing number of restaurants and tavernas (and a growing number of fast-food joints) offering everything from good, cheap Greek food in plain surroundings to fine Greek, French, Asian, and other international cuisines served in luxurious surroundings. Note that many Athenian restaurants do not accept credit cards. If you want to pay with a credit card, double-check to make sure the restaurant will accept your credit card before going there.

Most restaurants have menus in Greek and English, but many don't keep their printed (or handwritten) menus up to date. If a menu is not in English, there's almost always someone working at the restaurant who will either translate or rattle off suggestions for you in English. That may mean you'll be offered some fairly repetitive suggestions because restaurant staff members tend to suggest what most tourists request. In Athens, that means *moussaka* (baked eggplant casserole, usually with ground meat), *souvlakia* (chunks of beef, chicken, pork, or lamb grilled on a skewer), *pastitsio* (baked pasta, usually with ground meat and bechamel sauce), or *dolmadakia* (grape leaves, stuffed usually with rice and ground meat). Although all these dishes can be delicious, all too often restaurants catering to tourists serve profoundly dull moussaka and unpleasantly chewy souvlakia.

Mezedes (appetizers served with bread) are one of the great delights of Greek cuisine, and often can be enjoyed in lieu of a main course. Some perennial favorites include *tzatziki* (garlic, cucumber, dill, and yogurt dip), *melitzanosalata* (eggplant dip), *skordalia* (garlic sauce), *taramosalata* (fish roe dip), *keftedes* (crispy meatballs), *kalamaria* (squid), *gigantes* (large white beans in tomato sauce), *loukanika* (little sausages), and *oktopodi* (octopus).

If you're wondering what to use to wash all this down, you'll want to know that the most popular Greek table wine is *retsina.* It's usually white, although sometime rosé

Eating Well

To avoid the ubiquitous favorites-for-foreigners, you might prefer to tell your waiter you'd like to have a look at the food display case, often positioned just outside the kitchen, and then point out what you'd like to order. Many restaurants are perfectly happy to have you take a look in the kitchen itself, but it's not a good idea to do this without checking first. Not surprisingly, you'll get the best value and the tastiest food at establishments serving a predominantly Greek, rather than a transient tourist, clientele.

or red, and flavored with pine resin. In theory, the European Common Market now controls the amount of resin added, so you're less likely to come across the harsh retsina that some compare to turpentine. If you don't like the taste of retsina, try **aretsinato** (wine without resin).

If you want to find out more about Greek wine, try to pick up a copy of Dimitri Hadjinicolaou's *The A to Z Guide of Greek Wines* (Oenos O Agapitos Publisher). This handy pocket-sized Greek/English guide to wines has illustrations of labels, information on vintages, and sells for about 2,400Dr ($8).

When it comes time for dessert or a mid-afternoon infusion of sugar, Greeks usually head to a **zaharoplastion** (sweet shop). Consequently, most restaurants don't offer a wide variety of desserts. Almost all do serve fruit (stewed in winter, fresh in season), and increasingly, many serve sweets such as **baklava** (pastry and ground nuts with honey), **halva** (sesame, chopped nuts, and honey), and **kataifi** (shredded wheat with chopped nuts and lots of honey). All these sweets are seriously sweet. If you want **coffee** with your dessert, keep in mind that for Greeks, regular coffee usually includes a mere teaspoon of sugar. Sweet coffee seems to be about a 50-50 mixture of coffee and sugar. Watch out for the grounds in the bottom of the cup.

Greek **brandy** is a popular after-dinner drink (although—you guessed it—a bit sweet for non-Greek tastes), but the most popular Greek hard drink is **ouzo.** The anise-flavored liqueur is taken either straight or with water, which turns it cloudy white. You may see Greek men drinking quarter- and even half-bottles of ouzo with their lunch; if you do the same, you'll find out why the after-lunch siesta is so popular. There are many cafes (*ouzeri*) where ouzo, wine, and a selection of mezedes are served from breakfast to bedtime.

IN PLAKA

Some of the most charming old restaurants in Athens are in Plaka—as are some of the worst tourist traps. Here are a few things to keep in mind when you head off for a meal.

Some Plaka restaurants station waiters outside who don't just urge you to come in and sit down, but virtually pursue you down the street with an unrelenting sales pitch. The hard sell is almost always a giveaway that the place caters to tourists.

In general, it's a good idea to avoid places with floor shows; many charge outrageous amounts (and levy surcharges not always openly stated on menus) for drinks and food. If you get burned, stand your ground, phone the **Tourist Police** (☎ **171**), and pay nothing before they arrive. Often the mere threat of calling the Tourist Police has the miraculous effect of causing a bill to be lowered.

Expensive

✪ **Daphne's.** 4 Lysikratous St. ☎ **01-322-7971.** Main courses 4,500–8,500Dr ($15–$28), with some fish priced by the kilo. Daily 1:30pm–6pm and 8pm–2am. No credit cards. ELEGANT GREEK/NOUVELLE.

There are frescoes on the walls of this neo-classical 1830s former home, a shady garden with bits of ancient marble found here when the restaurant was built, and sophisticated Athenians at many tables. The cuisine here gives you all the old favorites (try the zesty eggplant salad) with new distinction, and combines familiar ingredients in innovative ways (delicious hot pepper and feta cheese dip). When I ate here, I could have gone on eating the hors d'oeuvres all night, but am glad I saved room for the *stifado* (stew) of rabbit in *mavrodaphne* (sweet wine) sauce, although I was tempted by my companion's tasty prawns with toasted almonds. Most nights, there's a pair of strolling musicians, whose repertoire ranges from Greek favorites to "My Darling Clementine."

Moderate

Eden Vegetarian Restaurant. 12 Lissiou St. ☎ and fax **01/324-8858.** Main courses 1,600–3,200Dr ($5–$11). AE, D, MC, V. Daily noon–midnight. From Adrianou St., take Mnissikleos up 2 blocks toward Acropolis to Lissiou St. HEALTH/VEGETARIAN.

You can find vegetarian dishes at almost every Greek restaurant, but if you want to experience soy (rather than eggplant) moussaka, mushroom pie with a sturdy whole wheat crust, salads with bean sprouts, and fresh-squeezed juices, join the young Athenians and European students who patronize the Eden. You may or may not be amused to watch Greeks tucking into their healthy fare while smoking nonstop. The decor, with 1920s-style prints and mirrors and wrought-iron lamps, is engaging.

✪ **Platanos Taverna.** 4 Dioyenous St. ☎ **01/322-0666.** Main courses 2,500–3,500Dr ($8–$12). No credit cards. Mon–Sat noon–4:30pm and 8pm–midnight. From Adrianou St., take Mnissikleos up 1 block toward the Acropolis and turn right on Dioyenous. GREEK.

This traditional taverna, on a quiet pedestrian square near the Tower of the Winds, has tables outdoors in good weather beneath a spreading *platanos* (plane tree). Inside, where locals usually congregate to escape the summer sun at midday and the tourists in the evening, you can enjoy looking at the old paintings and photos on the walls. The Platanos has been serving good *spitiko fageto* (home cooking) since 1932, and has managed to keep steady customers happy while enchanting visitors. If artichokes or spinach with lamb are on the menu, you're in luck: They're delicious. The house wine is tasty, and there's a wide choice of bottled wines from many regions of Greece.

Taverna Xinos. 4 Agelou Geronta St. (just off Kidathineon St., and signposted in the cul-de-sac). ☎ **01/322-1065.** Main courses 2,000–4,000Dr ($7–$14). No credit cards. Daily 8pm–11pm (sometimes stays open as late as 1am, depending on season and business); sometimes closed Sun; usually closed part of July and Aug. GREEK.

Despite the forgivable lapse in spelling, Xinos's business card says it best: "In the heart of old Athens there is still a flace [sic] where the traditional Greek way of cooking is upheld." In summer, there are tables outside in the courtyard; in winter, you can warm yourself by the coal-burning stove. Year-round you can enjoy the hearty, generous portions; lamb lovers should try the lamb with artichokes (usually available in the spring), or the lamb with egg, lemon, and dill sauce. The strolling musicians sing wonderful Greek golden oldies, accompanying themselves on the guitar and bouzouki. (If you are serenaded, you might want to give the musicians a small tip. If you want to hear the theme from *Never on Sunday,* ask to hear "Ena Zorbas.") Most evenings, tourists predominate until around 10pm, when locals begin to arrive, as they have since Xinos opened in 1935.

Inexpensive

✪ **Damigos (The Bakaliarakia).** 41 Kidathineon St. ☎ **01/322-5084.** Main courses 1,000–2,500Dr ($3.35–$8). No credit cards. Daily 7pm–11pm (sometimes open as late as 1am, depending on season and business); usually closed June–Sept. From Syntagma Sq., head south on Filellinon or Nikis St. to Kidathineon. GREEK/CODFISH.

Damigos has been serving delicious deep-fried codfish and eggplant, as well as chops and stews, since 1865 in this basement taverna. Don't miss the enormous wine barrels in the back room and an ancient column supporting the roof in the front room. The wine comes from the family vineyards, and there are few pleasures greater than sipping retsina while you watch the cook—who manages to look genial while never smiling—turn out unending meals in his absurdly small kitchen. Try the delicious *skordalia* (garlic sauce), equally good with cod, eggplant, bread—well, you get the idea.

Kouklis Ouzeri (To Yerani). 14 Tripodon St. ☎ **01/324-7605.** Appetizers 600–1,500Dr ($2–$5). No credit cards. Daily 11am–2am. Follow Kidathineon to Thespidos and climb toward Acropolis; Tripodon is first street on right after Adrianou. GREEK.

Besides Kouklis Ouzeri and To Yerani ("geranium"), Greeks also call this popular old favorite "Skolario" because of the nearby school. Find a seat, and a waiter will present a large tray with about a dozen plates of *mezedes*—appetizer portions of fried fish, beans, grilled eggplant, taramosalata, cucumber-and-tomato salad, olives, fried cheese, sausages, and other seasonal specialties. Accept the ones that appeal to you. If you don't order all 12, you can enjoy a tasty and inexpensive meal, washed down with the house *krasi* (wine).

To Tristato. 34 Dedalou St. (near Ayiou Yeronda Sq.). ☎ **01/324-4472.** Light meals 1,000–2,000Dr ($3.35–$7); desserts 800–1,500Dr ($2.70–$5). No credit cards. Mon–Fri 2pm–midnight; Sat 10am–midnight; Sun 11am–midnight. Closed Aug 10–Sept 10. SNACKS/DESSERTS.

This New Age cafe and tearoom by a rose garden serves fresh fruits and yogurt, omelets, fresh-squeezed juices, and scrumptious cakes—everything healthful and homemade. This is an excellent choice for late breakfast, afternoon tea, light supper, or late-night dessert; it's a place where women traveling alone will feel especially comfortable.

NEAR MONASTIRAKI SQUARE
Moderate

✪ **Abyssinia Cafe.** Plateia Abyssinia, Monastiraki. ☎ **01/321-7047.** Appetizers and main courses 1,500–4,000Dr ($5–$13). No credit cards. Tues–Sun 10:30am–6pm. Closed Sundays and usually for about a week at Christmas and Easter and 2 weeks in August. Abyssinia Sq., off Ifaistou (Hephaistos) St., is tucked away behind the entrance to the Ancient Agora. GREEK.

This small cafe in a ramshackle building has a nicely restored interior featuring lots of gleaming dark wood and polished copper. It faces a lopsided square where furniture restorers ply their trade and you can buy anything from gramophones to hubcaps in "antiques" shops. You can sit indoors or outside and have just a coffee, but it's tempting to snack on *saganaki* (fried cheese), fried eggplant, or *keftedes* (meatballs).

Taverna Sigalas. 2 Monastiraki Sq. ☎ **01/321-3036.** Main courses 1,000–2,500Dr ($3.35–$8). No credit cards. Daily 7am–2am. Walk east across the square from the Metro station. GREEK.

This worthy taverna that boasts it is open 365 days a year is in an 1879 commercial building with a newer outdoor pavilion. Inside, there are huge old retsina kegs and dozens of black-and-white photos of Greek movie stars. After 8pm nightly, there's recorded Greek music. At all hours, Greeks and tourists wolf down large portions of stews, moussaka, grilled meatballs, baked tomatoes, gyros, and other tasty dishes.

Inexpensive

Diporto. Athens Central Market. No phone. Main courses 800– 2,000Dr ($2.70–$7). No credit cards. Mon–Sat 6am–6pm. GREEK.

Sandwiched between shops selling olives, this little place serves up salads, stews, and delicious *revithia* (chickpeas, a popular Greek winter dish) to market stall owners, shoppers, and Athenians who make their way here for the cheap and delicious food.

Taverna Ipiros (Epirus). 15 Ayiou Philippou Sq. (2 blocks south of the Monastiraki Metro station. ☎ **01/324-5572.** Main courses 1,200–2,000Dr ($4–$7). No credit cards. Open days vary (call ahead); most days open noon–midnight. GREEK.

Quick Bites

In general, the Syntagma Square area is not known for its food, but it has a number of places to get a snack. The **Apollonion Bakery,** 10 Nikis St., and the **Elleniki Gonia,** 10 Karayioryis tis Servias St., make sandwiches to order and sell croissants, both stuffed and plain. **Ariston** is a small chain of *zaharoplastia* (confectioners), with a branch at the corner of Karayioryis tis Servias and Voulis streets (just off the square) that sells snacks as well as pastries. **Floca** is another excellent chain of pastry shops, with 14 branches; there's one in the arcade on Panepistimiou Street near Syntagma Square and another just south of the Center for Acropolis Studies, at Makriyanni and Hatzihristou streets. As always, you pay extra to be served at a table.

For the quintessential Greek sweet *loukoumades*—round doughnut-center-like pastries deep-fried and then drenched with honey and topped with powdered sugar and cinnamon—nothing beats **Doris,** 30 Praxiteles St. (a continuation of Lekka Street), a few blocks from Syntagma Square. If you're still hungry, Doris serves hearty stews and pasta dishes for absurdly low prices Monday through Saturday until 3:30pm. **Everest** is another chain worth trying; there's a branch 1 block north of Kolonaki Square at Tsakalof and Iraklitou streets. Also in Kolonaki Square, **To Kotopolo** ("the Chicken Place") serves succulent grilled chicken to take out or eat in. In Plaka, you'll find excellent coffee and sweets at the **K. Kotsolis Pastry Shop,** 112 Adrianou St., an oasis of old-fashioned charm in the midst of the souvenir shops. The **Orea Ellada** (Beautiful Greece) cafe is at the Center of Hellenic Tradition, opening onto 36 Pandrossou St. and 59 Mitropoleos St. near the flea market. You can revive yourself with a cappuccino and snack on pastries while you enjoy a spectacular view of the Acropolis.

This is a great budget spot on a crowded little square not far from the entrance to the Ancient Agorain, the heart of the Flea Market. The food is standard Greek, the portions generous, and the prices fair. Be sure to take a table that belongs to unpretentious little Ipiros, rather than a nearby competitor taking advantage of this place's reputation.

✪ **Thanasis.** 69 Mitropoleos St. (just off the northeast corner of Monasteraki Sq.). ☎ **01/ 324-4705.** Main courses 500–2,500Dr ($1.70–$8). No credit cards. Daily 9am–2am. GREEK/ SOUVLAKI.

Thanasis serves very good souvlakia and pita and exceptionally good French fries, both "to go" and at its outdoor and indoor tables; as always, prices are higher if you sit down to eat. On weekends, it often takes the strength and determination of an Olympic athlete to get through the door and place an order here. Yes, it's worth the effort: This is both a great budget choice and a great place to take in the local scene.

NEAR SYNTAGMA SQUARE
Moderate

Gerofinikas. 10 Pindar St. ☎ **01/363-6710.** Reservations strongly recommended. Main courses 3,000–5,200Dr ($10–$17); set-price menu 6,000Dr ($20), not including beverage. AE, DC, MC, V. GREEK/INTERNATIONAL.

For years, this was *the* place to go for a special lunch or dinner, and the food is still very good—which is why tour groups have, alas, discovered it. Still, it's always pleasant to walk down the passageway into Gerofinikas (the name means "the old palm tree"), look at the long display cases of tempting dishes, and try to decide between shrimp with feta cheese, rabbit stew with onions, the tasty eggplant dishes—all the while keeping room for one of the rich desserts..

Inexpensive

Neon. 3 Mitropoleos St. (on the southwest corner of Syntagma Sq.). ☎ **01/322-8155.** Snacks 200–650Dr (70¢–$2.15); sandwiches 450–1,200Dr ($1.50–$4); main courses 1,000– 3,200Dr ($3.35–$11). No credit cards. Daily 9am—midnight. GREEK/INTERNATIONAL.

This new addition to the Neon chain is convenient, although not as charming as the original on Omonia Square. You're sure to find something to your taste—maybe a Mexican omelet, spaghetti Bolognese, the salad bar, or sweets ranging from Black Forest cake to tiramisu. If you're tired of practicing your restaurant Greek, this is a good place to eat, since most things are self-service.

IN KOLONAKI

Expensive

L'Abreuvoir. 51 Xenokratous. ☎ **01/722-9106.** Reservations recommended. Main courses 5,200–8,500Dr ($17–$28). AE, DC, MC, V. Daily 12:30–4:30pm and 8:30pm–midnight. FRENCH/INTERNATIONAL.

A tranquil spot for lunch or dinner, this fine restaurant has been serving excellent food for decades. There are tables indoors and outside under mulberry trees (best avoided when they are dropping their ripe berries whose juice has much in common with indelible ink). From the fluffy spinach tart or smoked trout to the steak au poivre, or *entrecôtes provençals* (a filet cooked in marvelous garlic, mushroom, and parsley sauce), this is an excellent break from Greek food. Try the soufflé au Grand Marnier or chocolate mousse for dessert.

✪ **To Kafeneio.** 26 Loukianou St. ☎ **01/722-9056.** Main courses 1,800–5,200Dr ($6–$17). No credit cards. Mon–Sat 11am–around midnight. GREEK/INTERNATIONAL.

This is hardly a typical rough-and-ready Kafeneio (coffee shop/cafe): There are pictures on the walls, pink tablecloths on the tables, and a clientele of ladies who lunch, as well as staff from the many embassies located in Kolonaki. In short, it's a great people-watching place, where you can easily run up a substantial tab, but where you will also eat elegantly. Try the artichokes à la polita (tender artichokes flanked by carrots and potatoes in an egg-lemon sauce) or leeks in crème fraîche, washed down with draft beer or the house wine—and save room for the delectable profiteroles. I've always found this an especially congenial spot when I'm eating alone (perhaps because I love people-watching and profiteroles).

Moderate

Dimokritos. 23 Dimokritou St. ☎ **01/361-3588.** Main courses 3,200– 4,200Dr ($11–$14). No credit cards. Mon–Sat 1–5pm and 8pm–1am. Off Skoufa St., marked only by the word TAVERNA on the doors. GREEK.

Overlooking the Church of Ayios Dionysios, this cozy taverna serves good food to lots of steady customers. The large menu features grilled veal, rabbit, fish, and lamb, and usually has excellent swordfish souvlaki. A variety of Greek salads and hors d'oeuvres are usually on display in a case by the entrance, and you can usually point out what you want for starters on your way to your table.

Rodia. 44 Aristipou St. ☎ **01/722-9883.** Main courses 2,000–3,500Dr ($7–$12). No credit cards. Mon–Sat 8pm–2am. GREEK.

This long-time taverna in a handsome old Kolonaki house has tables in its small garden in good weather—although the interior, with its tile floor and old prints is so charming that you might be tempted to eat indoors. The Rodia is a favorite of visiting archaeologists from the nearby British and American Schools of Classical Studies, as well as of Kolonaki residents. It may not sound like just what you'd always hoped to have for dinner, but the octopus in mustard sauce is terrific, as are the veal or *dolmades* (stuffed grape leaves) in egg-lemon sauce. The house wine is excellent, as is the halva, which manages to be both creamy and crunchy.

To Ouzadiko. 28 Alopekis (in the Lemos International Shopping Center), Kolonaki. ☎ **01/ 729/5484.** Mezedes and main courses 2,000–4,000Dr ($7–$14). No credit cards. Mon–Sat 12:30pm–12:30am. GREEK.

This cozy ouzo bar has at least 40 kinds of ouzo and as many mezedes, including fluffy *keftedes* (meatballs) that make all others taste leaden. If you can find a seat at this popular hang-out, it's a great place for a snack or a full meal. A serious foody friend of mine goes here especially for the wide variety of *horta* (greens), which she says are the best she's ever tasted.

AROUND OMONIA SQUARE & THE NATIONAL ARCHAEOLOGICAL MUSEUM
Expensive
Restaurant Kostoyannis. 37 Zaimi St. (2 blocks behind the museum). ☎ **01/822-0624.** Main courses 2,500–6,800Dr ($8–$23). No credit cards. Mon–Sat 8pm–2am. GREEK/ SEAFOOD.

It's not easy to simply walk into Kostoyannis and sit down: Just inside the entrance is a show-stopping display of shrimp, mussels, fresh fish, seemingly endless appetizers, tempting stews (*stifada*) in ceramic pots, and yards of chops that could almost make a dedicated vegetarian fall off the wagon. You can choose the items you'd like to sample, or you could make an entire meal just from the *mezedes* (appetizers), which I think are even better than the entrées. Don't be put off by this restaurant's slightly out-of-the way location on a rather uninteresting street: It's well worth the trip.

Moderate
Athinaikon. 2 Themistokleous St., Omonia. ☎ **01/383-8485.** Main courses 2,000– 4,000Dr ($7–$14). No credit cards. Mon–Sat 10am–midnight. Closed Aug. Themistokleous St. intersects Panepistimiou St. at Omonia Sq. GREEK.

This is a favorite haunt of lawyers and businesspeople working in the Omonia Square area. You can have a full meal here, but many customers make their meal from a selection of the excellent appetizers, which include grilled octopus, savory grilled sausages, meatballs, beans in tomato sauce, piquant fried peppers, and a variety of cheeses, including the inevitable feta and the more unusual roquefort.

Inexpensive
Taygetos. 4 Satovriandou St. ☎ **01/523-5352.** Main courses 1,000–2,000Dr ($3.35–$7). No credit cards. Mon–Sat 9am–1am. GREEK/SOUVLAKIA.

This is a great place to stop in on your way to or from the museum. Service is swift, and the souvlakia and fried potatoes are excellent, as are the grilled lamb and chicken (priced by the kilo). The menu sometimes includes delicious *kokoretsia* (grilled entrails). The Ellinikon Restaurant next door is also a good value.

NEAR THE OLYMPIC STADIUM
Very Expensive
✪ **Bajazzo.** 1 Tyrteou & 14 Anapafseos Sts (Corner), Mets. ☎ and fax **01/921-3013.** Dinner only. Reservations required Fri–Sat, and recommended otherwise. Dinner for two from 45,000Dr ($150). Prices vary according to the daily menu. Nonsmoking dining area. AE, DC, MC, V. Mon–Sat 8pm–1am. INTERNATIONAL.

Bajazzo put Greek cuisine on the map when it won its Michelin star in 1998. Chef Klaus Feuerbach rightly says that two can eat here for $150, but I have friends who have eaten at Bajazzo and cheerfully spent almost twice that on the fine food and wine. Specialties include the feta tart, langostino souvlaki, kid with Peloponnesian herbs, and sea bass with mustard sauce—perhaps not to be eaten all at one sitting. The menu changes from night to night, so part of the fun is finding out what's being prepared on any given night.

Myrtia. 32–34 Trivonianou St. ☎ **01/924-7175.** Reservations recommended. Set-price menu 12,000–22,500Dr ($40–$78). AE, DC, EURO, MC, V. Mon–Sat 8:30pm–2am. Closed Aug. GREEK.

Probably the most famous of the set-price menu tavernas in Athens, the Myrtia is a taxi ride from the city center, on the hill behind the Olympic Stadium in Mets. The atmosphere is charmingly bucolic, with tables outdoors in the summer and strolling musicians. You'll be served a full array of mezedes, tender roast chicken, delicious lamb, fruit, sweets, various wines, and much more—all you can eat, prepared to perfection. Unfortunately, this place has become popular with tour groups.

NEAR THE ACROPOLIS
Moderate
✪ **Socrates' Prison.** 20 Mitseon St. ☎ **01/922-3434.** Main courses 1,250–3,200Dr ($4–$11). V. Mon–Sat 7pm–1am. Closed Aug. Mitseon St. is on the non-Acropolis side of Dionysiou Areopayitou St. GREEK/CONTINENTAL.

This is a favorite with both Greeks and American and European expatriates living in Athens, who lounge at tables outdoors in good weather and in the pleasant indoor rooms year-round. Some long tables are communal, and there are also tables for four. The food here is noticeably more imaginative than average Greek fare (try the veggie croquettes), and includes continental dishes such as salade Niçoise and pork roll stuffed with vegetables. The retsina is excellent, and there's a wide choice of bottled wines and beers. This is a good place to head if you don't want to eat in the Plaka but enjoy strolling through on your way to or from dinner.

WORTH A (SHORT) TRIP
Expensive
✪ **Varoulko.** 14 Deligeorgi, Piraeus. ☎ **01/411-2043.** Fax 01/422-1283. Reservations required (make them several days before you plan to eat here). Fish priced by the kilo; prices vary according to what's available. Dinner for two around 30,000Dr ($100). No credit cards. Open for dinner only daily except Sunday. FISH/SEAFOOD.

In an unlikely location on a side street in Piraeus, chef-owner Lefteris Lazarou has created what many consider not just the finest seafood restaurant, but the finest *restaurant* in the greater Athens area. I had one of the best meals in my life here—smoked eel, artichokes with fish roe, crayfish with sundried tomatoes, monkfish livers with soy sauce, honey, and basalmic vinegar—and the best sea bass and monkfish I have ever eaten. Everything is beautifully presented, and everything is delicious. I also like the austere brick walls enlivened by paintings of the old warehouse that Varoulko inhabits, although some, I know, find the style a bit too understated.

Vitrina. 7 Navarchou Apostoli St., Psiri. ☎ **01/321-1200.** Reservations required. Main courses 4,200–9,000Dr ($14–$30). No credit cards. Daily 8pm–late. NOUVELLE GREEK/ INTERNATIONAL.

This drop-dead-fashionable restaurant is one of several new hot spots in the old warehouse district of Psirri off Ermou Street. The walls are pale gold, the tablecloths and chairs are pale gray, and many of the young waiters and waitresses are aspiring actors and writers. The kitchen seems to try too hard with some dishes (shrimp in Muscatel and lavender sauce, for example), but the food is usually both delicious and beautifully presented, and there's a serious wine list. The fashion accessory of choice is a cellular phone—so useful for calling people at the next table—and almost no one arrives before 10pm.

Moderate

Vlassis. 8 Paster St. (off Plateia Mavili), Ilissia. ☎ **01/646-3060** or 01/642-5337. Reservations required. Main courses 1,500–3,600Dr ($5.55–$12). No credit cards. Mon–Sat 8pm–midnight. GREEK.

Greeks call this kind of food *paradisiako*—traditional, but paradisiacal is just as good a description. This is traditional food fit for the gods: delicious fluffy vegetable croquettes, eggplant salad that tastes like no other eggplant salad you've had, hauntingly tender lamb in egg-lemon sauce. It's a sign of Vlassis's popularity with Athenians—the last time I ate there, I was the only obvious foreigner in the place—that there's not even a discreet sign announcing its presence in a small apartment building on hard-to-find Paster Street. Take a taxi; you may feel so giddy with delight after eating that you won't mind the half-hour walk back to Syntagma Square.

SEEING THE SIGHTS
SIGHTSEEING SUGGESTIONS FOR FIRST-TIME VISITORS

If You Have 1 Day Try to be at the **Acropolis** as soon as it opens so that you can take in the site and enjoy seeing the **Parthenon** and the Acropolis Museum before the crowds arrive. Afterward, walk downhill to visit the **Ancient Agora** and then head into **Monastiraki** and **Plaka,** where you can window-shop and relax over lunch or dinner.

Keep an eye out for the **Plaka tram,** which started to offer half-hour tram rides in the summer of 1998. The route begins in Palia Agora Square, loops through the Plaka, and then heads past the Acropolis on Dionissiou Areopayitou Boulevard before heading back into Plaka (10am to 10pm in summer; 1,000Dr/$3.35). This is a great (and relaxing) way to get a sense of what you may want to explore on foot in the Plaka.

If You Have 2 Days On day 1, follow the suggestions above. It's worth spending several hours of day 2 at the **National Archaeological Museum** (again, try to arrive the minute it opens to beat the crowds). Then, visit some of Athens's smaller museums—or, if you need a change of pace, head up **Mount Likavitos,** on the funicular that leaves from the top of Ploutarchou Street (500Dr/$1.70, 8am to 10pm, about every 20 minutes in summer). If the *nefos* (smog) isn't too bad, you'll have a wonderful view of Athens, Piraeus, and the Saronic Gulf. If you have an extra hour, take one of the paths from the summit and stroll down Likavitos, enjoying the scent of the pine trees and the changing views of the city.

If You Have 3 Days or More For days 1 and 2, follow the suggestions above. For the rest of your stay, visit more of the museums listed below, or consider a day trip to one of the great sights of antiquity, such as **Delphi** or **Sounion;** a day excursion to **Corinth, Mycenae,** and **Epidaurus** (best done on a bus tour); or a visit to the Byzantine monasteries of **Daphni** or **Kaisariani** (see "Day Trips from Athens," below). If you don't want to go home without seeing one of the "isles of Greece," take a day trip by boat from Piraeus to one of the islands of the Saronic Gulf. **Aegina (Egina), Poros,** and **Hydra (Idra)** are all feasible day trips—but best not done the day before you leave Athens, lest bad weather strand you on an island.

Whatever else you do, be sure to give yourself time to sit in cafes and watch the world go by.

Strike!

Strikes that close museums and archaeological sites can occur without warning. Decide what you most want to see, and go there as soon as possible after your arrival. The fact that something is open today says nothing about tomorrow. If you're visiting in the off-season, check with the **Greek National Tourist Organization** (☎ **01/331-0437**) for the abbreviated winter hours of sites and museums.

THE TREASURES OF ANTIQUITY

✪ **The Acropolis.** ☎ **01/321-0219.** Admission (includes Acropolis Museum) 2,000Dr ($7) adults, 1,500Dr ($5) seniors, 1,000Dr ($3.35) students with ID; free Sun. Summer, Mon–Fri 8am–6pm, Sat–Sun and holidays 8:30am–3pm; winter, check with Greek National Tourist Organization (☎ 01/331-0437). Museum sometimes closes earlier. Follow Dionysiou Areopayitou St., Theorias St., or path up through Ancient Agora to reach path to ticket booth and Acropolis entrance.

When you climb up the Acropolis—the heights above the city—you'll realize why people seem to have lived here as long ago as 5000 B.C. The sheer sides of the Acropolis make it a superb natural defense, just the place to avoid enemies and to be able to see invaders coming across the sea or the plains of Attica. And, of course, it helped that in antiquity there was a spring here, ensuring a steady supply of water.

In classical times, when Athens's population had grown to around 250,000, people lived on the slopes below the Acropolis, which had become the city's most important religious center. Athens's civic and business center, the Agora, and its cultural center, with several theaters and concert halls, bracketed the Acropolis; when you peer over the sides of the Acropolis at the houses in Plaka and the remains of the ancient Agora and the Theater of Dionysos, you'll see the layout of the ancient city. Syntagma and Omonia squares, the heart of today's Athens, were well out of the ancient city center.

Even the Acropolis's height couldn't protect it from the Persian invasion of 480 B.C., when most of its monuments were burnt and destroyed. You may notice some immense column drums built into the Acropolis's walls. When the great Athenian statesman Pericles ordered the monuments rebuilt, he had the drums from the destroyed Parthenon built into the walls lest Athenians forget what had happened— and so they would remember that they had rebuilt what they had lost. Pericles's rebuilding program began about 448 B.C.; the new Parthenon was dedicated 10 years later, but work on other monuments continued for a century.

The Parthenon—dedicated to Athena Parthenos (the Virgin), patron goddess of Athens—was the most important religious monument here, but there were shrines to many other gods and goddesses on the Acropolis's broad summit. As you climb up, you pass through first the **Beule Gate,** built by the Romans, and now known by the name of the French archaeologist who discovered it in 1852. Next comes the **Propylaia,** the monumental 5th century B.C. entranceway. You'll notice the little **temple of Athena Nike** (Athena of Victory) perched above the Propylaia; the beautifully proportioned Ionic temple was built in 424 B.C. and restored in the 1930s. Off to the left of the Parthenon is the **Erechtheion,** which the Athenians honored as the tomb of Erechtheus, a legendary king of Athens. A hole in the ceiling and floor of the northern porch indicates the spot where Poseidon's trident struck to make a spring (symbolizing control of the sea) gush forth during his contest with Athena to be the city's chief deity. Athena countered with an olive tree (symbolizing control of the rich Attic plain); the olive tree planted beside the Erechtheion reminds visitors of her victory. Give yourself a little time to enjoy the delicate carving on the Erechtheion, and be sure to see the

---

Optical Illusions

If you look over the edge of the Acropolis toward the Temple of Hephaistos in the Ancient Agora, then back up at the Parthenon, you can't help but be struck by how much lighter, how much more graceful, the Parthenon is than the Theseion (as the Temple of Hephaistos is known today). Scholars tell us that this is because Iktinos, the architect of the Parthenon, was something of a magician of optical illusions: the columns and stairs—even the floor—of the Parthenon all appear straight because they are minutely curved. The exterior columns, for example, are slightly thicker in the middle (a device known as *entasis*), which makes the entire column appear straight. That's why the Parthenon, with 17 columns on each side and 8 at each end (creating a **peristyle,** or exterior colonnade, of 46 relatively slender columns), looks so graceful, while the Theseion, with only 6 columns at each end and 13 along each side, seems so stolid.

---

original Caryatids (the monumental female figures who served as columns on the Erechteion's porch) in the Acropolis Museum.

However charmed you are by these elegant little temples, you're probably still heading resolutely toward the **Parthenon,** and you may be disappointed to realize that visitors are not allowed inside, both to protect the monument and to allow restoration work to proceed safely. If you find this frustrating, keep in mind that in antiquity only priests and honored visitors were allowed in to see the monumental—some 36 feet tall—statue of Athena designed by the great Phidias, who supervised Pericles's building program. Nothing of the huge gold-and-ivory statue remains, but there's a small Roman copy in the National Archaeological Museum—and horrific renditions on souvenirs ranging from T-shirts to ouzo bottles. The floor of the room in which the statue stood was covered in olive oil, so that the gold and ivory reflected through the dimly lit room.

The Parthenon's entire roof and much of the interior were blown to smithereens in 1687, when a party of Venetians attempted to take the Acropolis from the Turks. A shell fired from nearby Mouseion Hill struck the Parthenon—where the Turks were storing gunpowder and munitions—and caused appalling damage to the building and its sculptures. Most of the remaining sculptures were carted off to London by Lord Elgin in the first decade of the 19th century. Those surviving sculptures—the **Elgin Marbles**—are on display in the British Museum, causing ongoing pain to generations of Greeks, who continue to press for their return.

The Parthenon originally had sculpture in both its pediments, as well as a frieze running around the entire temple. Alternating *triglyphs* (panels with three incised grooves) and *metopes* (sculptured panels) made up the frieze. The east pediment showed scenes from the birth of Athena, the west pediment Athena and Poseidon's contest for possession of Athens. The long frieze showed the battle of the Athenians (led by the hero Theseus) against the Amazons, scenes from the Trojan War, and the struggles of the Olympian gods against giants and centaurs. The message of most of this sculpture was the triumph of knowledge and civilization (read: Athens) over the forces of darkness and barbarians. An interior frieze showed scenes from the Panathenaic Festival each August, when citizens processed through the streets, bringing a new *peplos* (tunic) for the statue of Athena. Only a few fragments of any of the sculptures remain in place, and every visitor will have to decide whether it's a good or a bad thing that Lord Elgin removed so much before the smog spread over Athens and ate away at the remaining sculpture.

The Acropolis & Ancient Agora

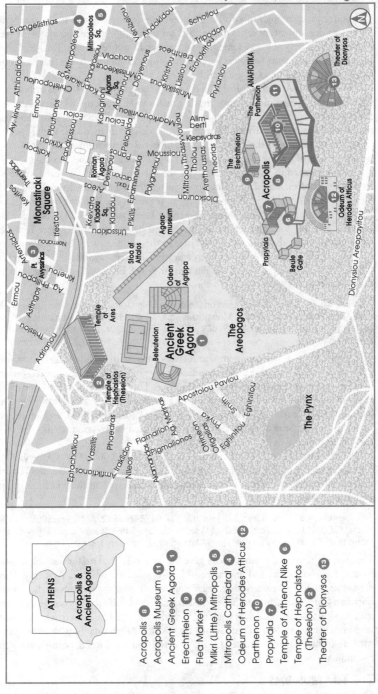

ATHENS

Acropolis & Ancient Agora

Acropolis 8
Acropolis Museum 11
Ancient Greek Agora 1
Erechtheion 9
Flea Market 3
Mikri (Little) Mitropolis 5
Mitropolis Cathedral 4
Odeum of Herodes Atticus 12
Parthenon 10
Propylaia 7
Temple of Athena Nike 6
Temple of Hephaistos (Theseion) 2
Theater of Dionysos 13

521

If you're lucky enough to visit the Acropolis on a smog-free and sunny day, you'll see the golden and cream tones of the Parthenon's handsome Pentelic marble at their most subtle. It may come as something of a shock to realize that the Parthenon, like most other monuments here, was painted in antiquity, with gay colors that have since faded, revealing the tones of the marble.

The **Acropolis Archaeological Museum** hugs the ground to detract as little as possible from the ancient monuments. Inside, you'll see the four original **Caryatids** from the Erechtheion that are still in Athens (one disappeared during the Ottoman occupation, and one is in the British Museum). Other delights here include sculpture from the Parthenon burnt by the Persians, statues of *korai* (maidens) dedicated to Athena, figures of *kouroi* (young men), and a wide range of finds from the Acropolis.

Those interested in learning more about the Acropolis should visit the **Center for Acropolis Studies,** on Makriyanni Street just southeast of the Acropolis (☎ 01/923-9381). It's open daily 9am to 2:30pm; admission is free. On display are artifacts, reconstructions, photographs, drawings—and plaster casts of the Elgin Marbles that Greeks hope will someday return to Athens and be put on display here in a new museum. Work on the museum slowed here in the summer of 1998, when construction unearthed a cluster of houses from an early Christian community. After archaeologists excavate and document the remains, they will be destroyed so that work on the museum can resume.

Ancient Agora. Below the Acropolis on the edge of Monastiraki (entrance on Adrianou St., near Ayiou Philippou Sq., east of Monastiraki Sq.). ☎ **01/321-0185.** Admission (includes museum) 1,200Dr ($4) adults, 900Dr ($3) seniors, 600Dr ($2) students. Tues–Sun 8:30am–3pm.

The Agora was Athens's commercial and civic center, with buildings used for a wide range of political, educational, philosophical, theatrical, and athletic purposes—which may be why what remains seems such a jumble. This is a nice place to wander and enjoy the views up toward the Acropolis, take in the herb garden and flowers planted around the 5th century B.C. **Temple of Hephaistos (the Theseion),** and admire the 2nd century B.C. **Stoa of Attalos,** totally reconstructed by American archaeologists in the 1950s.

The **museum** in the Stoa's ground floor has finds from 5,000 years of Athenian history, including sculpture and pottery, as well as a voting machine and a child's potty seat, all with labels in English. The museum (which has excellent toilet facilities) closes 15 minutes before the site.

The Cemetery of Keramikos. 148 Ermou St. ☎ **01/346-3552.** Admission 500Dr ($1.70) adults, 400Dr ($1.35) seniors, 300Dr ($1) students. Tues–Sun 8:30am–3pm. Walk west from Monastiraki Sq. on Ermou St. past Thisio Metro station; cemetery is on the right.

This ancient cemetery, where Pericles gave his famous funeral oration, is a short walk from the Ancient Agora and not far from the presumed site of Plato's Academy. There are a number of well-preserved funerary monuments and the remains of the colossal **Dipylon Gate,** the main entrance to the ancient city of Athens. This can be a pleasant spot to sit and read because it's seldom crowded. If you like cemeteries, be sure to take in Athens's enormous **First Cemetery,** near the Athens Stadium, where notables such as former Prime Minister George Panandreou are buried beneath elaborate monuments.

THE TOP MUSEUMS

✪ **National Archaeological Museum.** 44 Patission St. ☎ **01/821-7717.** Admission 2,000Dr ($7) adults, 1,000Dr ($3.35) students. Mon 12:30–5pm; Tues–Fri 8am–5pm; Sat–Sun and holidays 8:30am–3pm. Walk about ⅓ mile (10 minutes) north of Omonia Sq. on the road officially named 28 Oktobrio Ave. but usually called Patission.

This is an enormous and enormously popular museum; try to arrive as soon as it opens so you can see the exhibits and not just the other visitors' backs. Early arrival should give you at least an hour before most tour groups turn up. Don't miss the stunning gold masks, cups, dishes, and jewelry unearthed from the site of Mycenae by Heinrich Schliemann in 1876, on display in the first room, and the elegant marble Cycladic figurines (ca. 2000 B.C.) in the adjacent room. Other stars of the collection include the monumental bronzes (especially the mid-5th century B.C. figure variously identified as Zeus or Poseidon), both the black and the red figure vases, and the restored 3500 B.C. frescoes brought here from the island of Santorini.

N.P. Goulandris Foundation Museum of Cycladic Art. 4 Neophytou Douka St. ☎ 01/ **722-8321.** Admission 800Dr ($2.70) adults, 250Dr (85¢) students. Mon, Wed–Fri 10am–4pm; Sat 10am–3pm. From Syntagma Sq., walk 7 blocks east along Vasilissis Sofias, then ½ block north on Neophytou Douka; museum is on right.

This handsome new museum houses the largest collection of Cycladic art outside the National Archaeological Museum, with some 230 stone and pottery vessels and figurines from the 3rd millennium B.C. on display. See if you agree with those who have compared the faces of the Cycladic figurines to the work of Modigliani. Be sure to go through the courtyard into the museum's newest acquisition: an elegant 19th-century house with some of its original furnishings and visiting exhibits.

Benaki Museum. 1 Koumbari St. (at Vasilissis Sofias Ave.). ☎ **01/361-1617.** 5 blocks east of Syntagma Sq. in Kolonaki.

The Benaki Museum has been closed for major alterations. If it has reopened by the time you're here, you're in luck. The costume collection is superb, and the relics of Greece's 1821 War of Independence, including Lord Byron's writing desk and pen, are fascinating.

Byzantine Museum. 22 Vasilissis Sofias Ave. (at Vassileos Konstandinou Ave.). ☎ 01/ **723-1570** or 01/721-1027. Admission 500Dr ($1.70) adults, 250Dr (85¢) students. Tues–Sun 8:30am–3pm. From Syntagma Sq., walk along Vasilissis Sofias Ave. (also known as Venizelou Ave.) for about 15 minutes. The museum is on the right, on the same side of the street as the National Garden.

As its name makes clear, this museum, in a 19th-century Florentine-style former villa, is devoted to the art and history of the Byzantine era. Greece's most important collection of icons and religious art—along with sculptures, altars, mosaics, religious vestments, bibles, and a small-scale reconstruction of an early Christian basilica—are exhibited on several floors around a courtyard.

✪ **Greek Folk Art Museum.** 17 Kidathineon St., Plaka. ☎ **01/322-9031.** Admission 500Dr ($1.70) adults, 400Dr ($1.35) seniors, 300Dr ($1) students. Tues–Sun 10am–2pm.

This endearing small museum has dazzling embroideries and costumes from all over the country. One small room sports zany frescoes of gods and heroes done by the eccentric artist Theofilos Hadjimichael, who painted in the early part of this century.

✪ **Museum of Greek Popular Musical Instruments.** 1–3 Diogenous St. ☎ 01/ **325-0198.** Free admission. Tues, Thurs–Sun 10am–2pm; Wed noon–8pm.

Photos show the musicians, and recordings let you listen to the tambourines, Cretan lyres, lutes, pottery drums, and clarinets on display here. The shop has a wide selection of CDs and cassettes.

Ilias Lalaounis Jewelry Museum. 12 Kalisperi (at Karyatidon). ☎ **01/922-1044.** Admission 800Dr ($2.70). Mon, Thurs, Fri, Sat 9am–4pm; Wed 9am–9pm (entrance free after 3pm); Sun 10am–4pm. Walk 1 block south of the Acropolis between the Theater of Dionysos and the Odeum of Herodes Atticus.

The 3,000 pieces of jewelry on display here are so spectacular that even those with no special interest in baubles will enjoy this glitzy new museum, founded by one of Greece's most successful jewelry designers. The first floor has a coffee shop, boutique, and small workshop. The second and third floors display pieces inspired by ancient, Byzantine, and Cycladic designs, as well as plants and animals.

SOME SMALL MUSEUMS ALSO WORTH A LOOK

Athens has a number of excellent small museums. Some of the nicest include the **Center of Folk Art and Tradition** (also known as the Cultural Center of the Municipality of Athens), 6 Angelikis Hatzimihali St. (☎ 01/324-3987); the **Children's Museum,** 14 Kidathineon St. (☎ 01/331-2995); the **Jewish Museum,** 39 Nikis St. (☎ 01/323-1577); the **Museum of Greek Costume,** 7 Dimokritou St. (☎ 01/362-9513); and the **Athens City Museum,** 7 Paparigopoulou St. (☎ 01/324-6164).

THE NATIONAL GARDEN & MOUNT LIKAVITOS

The National Garden, between Amalias Avenue and Irodou Attikou, south of Vasilissis Sofias Avenue, was once the royal family's palace garden. Today it encompasses a park, garden, and small, rather sad, zoo. It has shade trees, benches, and small lakes and ponds with ducks, swans, and a few peacocks. There are several cafes tucked away, and you can also picnic here. The large neoclassical exhibition and reception hall was built by the brothers Zappas and so is known as the Zappion. The garden is officially open daily 7am to 10pm.

Mount Likavitos (Lycabettus), which dominates the northeast part of the city, is a favorite retreat for Athenians and a great place to get a bird's-eye view of Athens and its environs—if the *nefos* (smog) isn't too bad. Even when the *nefos* is bad, sunsets can be spectacular here. On top, there's a small **chapel of Ayios Yioryios (St. George),** whose name day is celebrated on April 23. There are performances at the **Likavitos Theater** each summer, and the expensive cafes on the summit are usually open all year. You can take the **funicular** from the top of Ploutarchou Street (500Dr/$1.70), 8am to 10pm, about every 20 minutes in summer) or walk up from Dexameni Square, the route preferred by young lovers and the energetic.

ORGANIZED TOURS

Tours of Athens are often no more expensive, and considerably less stressful, than renting a car for the day and driving yourself. You can book through most hotels or any travel agency. A half-day tour of city highlights should cost about 10,500Dr ($35). Night tours can include a sound-and-light show, Greek folk dancing at the Dora Stratou Folk Dance Theater, or dinner and Greek dancing. They range from about 12,000 to 18,000Dr ($40 to $60).

Educational Tours & Cruises, 9 Irving St., Medford, Ma 02111 (☎ 800/275-4109; e-mail: edtours@ars.nep.gr) and 1 Artemídos St., Glyfáda 16674, Athens (☎ 01/898-1741), can arrange tours in Athens and throughout Greece, including individual tours with an emphasis on Greek culture. **CHAT Tours,** 4 Stadiou St. (☎ 01/322-3137); **GO Tours,** 31–33 Voulis St. (☎ 01/322-5951); and **Key Tours,** 4 Kaliroïs St. (☎ 01/923-3166), are all reliable, established companies that offer tours of Athens and various day trips. Destinations include the temple of Apollo at Sounion, Delphi, and the Peloponnese (usually taking in Corinth, Mycenae, and Epidauros).

THE SHOPPING SCENE

If you want to pick up retro clothes or old copper, try the **flea market,** a daily spectacle between Plaka and Monastiraki Square. It's most lively on Sunday, but you can find the usual touristy trinkets, copies of ancient artifacts, jewelry, sandals, and various handmade goods, including embroideries, any day. Keep in mind that not everything sold as an antique is genuine, and that it's illegal to take antiquities and icons more than 100 years old out of the country without a hard-to-obtain export license.

In the Plaka-Monastiraki area, several shops with nicer-than-usual arts and crafts and fair prices include **Stavros Melissinos,** the Poet-Sandalmaker of Athens, 89 Pandrossou St. (☎ 01/321-9247); **Iphanta,** the weaving workshop, 6 Selleu St. (☎ 01/322-3628); **Emanuel Masmanidis' Gold Rose Jewelry** shop, 85 Pandrossou St. (☎ 01/321-5662); and the **Center of Hellenic Tradition,** 59 Mitropoleos and 36 Pandrossou sts. (☎ 01/321-3023), which sells arts and crafts. At the **Hellenic Folk-Art Gallery,** 6 Ipatias and Apollonos sts., Plaka (☎ 01/324-0017), a portion of the proceeds from everything sold (including handsome woven and embroidered carpets), goes to the National Welfare Organization, which encourages traditional crafts. Finally, don't forget that most museums have excellent shops.

The biggest **foreign-language bookstore** in Athens is **Eleftheroudakis,** which has a branch at 4 Nikis St. (☎ 01/322-2255) and a new headquarters at 17 Panepistimiou St. (☎ 01/331-4480). The new store has eight stories filled with a full range of subjects, plus a cafe and a music shop, and stages a series of small concerts and readings by local authors.

Compendium, 28 Nikis St. (☎ 01/322-1248), on the edge of Plaka near Syntagma Square, is a good English-language bookstore, selling new and used fiction and nonfiction, plus magazines and maps. **Reymondos,** 18 Voukourestiou St., a pedestrianized street just off Syntagma Square (☎ 01/364-8189), has a good selection in English, including some dazzling photo books on Greece, and is often open after usual shop hours.

On your way there, you can ogle the window displays at **Zolotas,** 10 Panepistimiou St. (☎ 01/361-3782), and **Lalounis,** 6 Panepistimiou St. (☎ 01/362-1371), Greece's two finest jewelers, which have branches at the foot of Voukourestiou Street.

ATHENS AFTER DARK

Greeks enjoy their nightlife so much that they take an afternoon nap to rest up for it. The evening often begins with a leisurely *volta* (stroll); you'll see it in most neighborhoods, including Plaka and Kolonaki Square. Most Greeks don't think of dinner until at least 9pm—when there's still no hurry. Around midnight the party may move on to a club for music and dancing.

Check the daily *Kathimerini* insert in the *International Herald-Tribune* or the daily *Athens News,* both sold at most major newsstands, for current cultural and entertainment events, including films, lectures, theater, music, and dance. The weekly *Hellenic Times* and *Athenscope* and the monthly *Now in Athens* list nightspots, restaurants, movies, theater, and much else.

THE PERFORMING ARTS

The **Athens Festival** at the Odeon of Herodes Atticus has famous Greek and foreign artists performing music, plays, opera, and ballet from the beginning of June to the beginning of October in a beautiful open-air setting. Find out what's being presented through the English-language press or at the **Athens Festival Office,** 4 Stadiou St. (☎ 01/322-1459, 01/322-3111, or 01/322-3110, ext. 137). The office is open Monday to Saturday 8:30am to 2pm and 5 to 7pm, and Sunday 10am to 1pm. If available—and that's a big "if"—tickets, which range from about $10 to $30, can also be purchased at the **Odeon** (☎ 01/323-2771) several hours before a performance.

The acoustically marvelous new **Megaron Mousikis Concert Hall,** 89 Vasilissis Sofias Ave. (☎ **01/729-0391** or 01/728-2333), hosts a wide range of classical music programs that include quartets, operas in concert, symphonies, and recitals. The box office is open weekdays 10am to 6pm, Saturday 10am to 2pm, and Sunday 6 to 10:30pm on performance nights only. Tickets run from about 1,000 to 22,500Dr ($3.35 to $75), depending on the performance. The Megaron has a limited summer season, but is in full swing most of the rest of the year.

Most major jazz and rock concerts, as well as some classical performances, take place at the **Pallas Theater,** 1 Voukourestiou St. (☎ 01/322-8275).

English-language theater and American-style music are performed at the **Hellenic American Union Auditorium,** 22 Massalias St., between Kolonaki and Omonia squares (☎ **01/362-9886**); you can usually get a ticket for around 3,000Dr ($10). Arrive early and check out the art show or photo exhibition at the adjacent gallery. The **Greek National Opera** performs at the Olympia Theater, 59 Akadimias St., at Mavromihali (☎ **01/361-2461**).

The **Dora Stratou Folk Dance Theater,** which performs on Philopappos Hill, is the best known of the traditional dance troupes. Regional dances are performed in costume with appropriate musical accompaniment nightly at 10:15, with additional shows at 8:15pm on Wednesday and Sunday. You can buy tickets from 8am to 2pm daily from mid-May to mid-September at the box office, 8 Scholio St., Plaka (☎ **01/924-4395,** or 01/921-4650 after 5:30pm). Prices range from about 2,500 to 4,400Dr ($8 to $15).

Sound and Light Shows, seen from the Pnyx, the hill across Dionysiou Areopayitou Street from the Acropolis, illuminate (sorry) Athens's history by focusing on the history of the Acropolis. Try to sit away from the (very) loud speakers, so you won't be deafened by the booming historical narrative and all-too-stirring music and can concentrate instead on the play of lights on the monuments of the Acropolis. Shows are held April to October. Performances in English begin at 9pm and last 45 minutes. Tickets can be purchased at the **Athens Festival Office,** 4 Stadiou St. (☎ **01/322-7944**) or at the entrance to the Sound and Light (☎ **01/922-6210**), which is signposted on the Pnyx. Tickets are 1,800Dr ($6) for adults and 600Dr ($2) students.

THE CLUB, MUSIC & BAR SCENE

Walk the streets of Plaka any night and you'll find plenty of tavernas offering pseudo-traditional live music. Many are clip joints playing the equivalent of Muzak, but some do better. **Taverna Mostrou,** 22 Mnissikleos St. (☎ **01/324-2441**), is one of the largest, oldest, and best known for traditional Greek music and dancing. Shows begin at about 11pm and usually last until 2am. The entrance cost of 6,000Dr ($20) includes a set-menu supper. à la carte fare is available but expensive. Nearby, **Palia Taverna Kritikou,** 24 Mnissikleos St. (☎ **01/322-2809**), is another lively open-air taverna with music and dancing. Other reliable tavernas with live traditional music include **Nefeli,** 24 Panos St. (☎ **01/321-2475**); Dioyenis, 3 Sellei (Shelley) St. (☎ **01/324-7933**); **Stamatopoulou,** 26 Lissiou St. (☎ **01/322-8722**); and **Xinos,** 4 Agelou Geronta St. (☎ **01/322-1065**).

For more intimate and unusual entertainment, climb Mnissikleos Street toward the Acropolis, turn right on Tholou, and find **Apanemia** and **Esperides.** The smoky little cafes are usually filled with hip young Athenians nursing drinks (from 1,500Dr/$5) and enjoying music that's both traditional and innovative, sometimes even humorous.

For Greek pop music, try **Zoom,** 37 Kidathineon St., in the heart of Plaka (☎ **01/322-5920**). Performers, who are likely to have current hit albums, are showered with carnations by adoring fans. The minimum order is 6,000Dr ($20). If you want to check out the local rock and blues scene along with small doses of metal, Athenian popsters play at **Memphis,** 5 Ventiri St., near the Hilton Hotel east of Syntagma Square (☎ **01/722-4104**); it's open Tuesday to Friday 10:30pm to 2:30am.

Those interested in authentic *rebetika* (music of the urban poor and dispossessed) and *bouzoukia* (traditional and pop music featuring the guitarlike bouzouki, almost always loudly amplified) can consult their hotel receptionist or the current issue of *Athenscope* magazine to find out what's going on. Shows usually don't start until nearly midnight, and although there's generally no cover charge, a drink can cost as much as 5,000Dr ($17). Most clubs are closed during the summer, and many are far from the center of town, so budget another 2,500 to 5,000Dr ($8 to $17) for round-trip taxi fare. Among the more distant upscale bouzoukia are the **Dioyenis Palace,** 259 Syngrou (☎ **01/942-4267**)—a lot farther out than you might think—and **Posidonio,** 18 Posidonos, Elliniko, way out by the airport (☎ **01/894-1033**).

One of the more central clubs is the **Stoa Athanaton,** 19 Sofokleous, in the Central Meat Market (☎ **01/321-4362**). It has live rebetika Monday through Saturday 3 to 6pm and after midnight, and serves good food; there's a 3,000Dr ($10) minimum. The smoke-filled **Rebetiki Istoria** (☎ **01/642-4937**), in a neoclassical building at 181 Ippokratous St., features old-style rebetika music, played to a mixed crowd of older regulars and younger students. The music usually doesn't start until at least 11pm, but the seats go earlier. **Taximi,** 29 Odos Isavron, Exarchia (☎ **01/363-9919**), is consistently popular; drinks cost 3,700Dr ($12). It's closed Sunday and July and August. **Frangosyriani,** 57 Odos Arachovis, Exarchia (☎ **01/360-0693**), specializes in the music of rebetika legend Markos Vamvakaris; it's closed Tuesday and Wednesday.

GAY & LESBIAN BARS

The gay scene is fairly low-key; some gay and lesbian groups advertise get-togethers in the English-language press. Information is also available from Greek national gay and lesbian organizations such as **EOK & AKOE-AMPHI,** 21 Patission St., 7th floor (☎ **01/523-9017**). **Granazi,** 20 Lebesi St. (☎ **01/325-3979**), is popular; the best-known alternative is **E . . . Kai?** ("So What?"), off Syngrou Avenue at 12 Iossif ton Rogon (☎ **01/922-1742**). In upscale Kolonaki, **Alexander's,** 44 Anagnostopoulou (☎ **01/364-6660**), is more sedate, with more variety. There's also a lively transvestite cruising scene along Syngrou Avenue in Makriyanni.

DANCE CLUBS

Hidden on the outskirts of Plaka, **Booze,** 57 Kolokotroni St., 2nd floor (☎ **01/324-0944**), blasts danceable rock to a hip student crowd. There's art on every wall, jelled stage lights, and two bars. Admission is 1,500Dr ($5.55), plus 800Dr ($3) per drink. If you crave disco, head east to **Absolut,** 23 Filellinon St. (no phone). If you feel a bit too old there, head north to the **Wild Rose,** in the arcade at 10 Panepistimiou St. (☎ **01/364-2160**). Up the street, **Mercedes Rex,** 48 Panepistimiou St. (☎ **01/361-4591**), has even more diversity.

DAY TRIPS FROM ATHENS
PIRAEUS

You probably won't fall in love with Piraeus, but if you have some time to kill—or want to escape Athens's summer heat—you can find lots to enjoy.

Piraeus has been the port of Athens since antiquity and is still where you catch most island boats and cruise ships. Keep in mind that there are three harbors: the **main harbor** (*Megas Limani*), where you'll see everything from tankers to island boats and cruise ships; **Zea Marina** (also called *Zea Limani*), the port for most of the swift hydrofoils; and **Little Harbor** (*Microlimani,* also called *Turkolimani,* or Turkish Harbor), the location of many fish restaurants. As in antiquity, today's Piraeus has the seamier side of a sailors' port of call and the color and bustle of an active harbor—both aspects, somewhat sanitized, were portrayed in the film *Never on Sunday.* Piraeus also has a sprawling market where you can buy produce shipped in each day, including bread baked that morning on distant islands. There are a number of fish restaurants, but many are overpriced and serve fish that is not as fresh as the bread.

GETTING THERE   By Metro   The fastest and easiest way to Piraeus is to take the Metro from Omonia Square or Monastiraki to the last stop. It costs 100Dr (35¢) and leaves you 1 block from the principal domestic port.

By Bus   From Syntagma Square, take bus no. 40 from the corner of Filellinon Street; it leaves you 1 block from the international port, about a 10-minute walk along the water from the domestic port. From the airport, bus no. 91 goes to Piraeus. The fare is 300Dr ($1).

By Taxi   A taxi from Syntagma Square or the airport costs about 2,400Dr ($8). When tourists headed back to Athens disembark, taxi drivers usually offer flat fees that are wildly out of line. Either insist on the metered rate, or walk away from the harbor and try again.

VISITOR INFORMATION   For boat schedules, transit information, and other tourist information 24 hours a day, dial ☎ **171.**

If you need a travel agency to make reservations or to recommend a particular service, try **Explorations Unlimited,** 2 Kapodistriou St. (☎ **01/411-6395** or 01/ 411-1243), just off Akti Posidonos near the Metro station. It's open weekdays 8am to 7pm and Saturday 9am to 2pm.

FERRIES TO THE ISLANDS   The boats to the islands are opposite the Metro station. Boats to the **Saronic Gulf** and hydrofoils (Flying Dolphins) to **Aegina** are opposite and to the left of the station; the hydrofoils leave from the foot of Gounari Street. Boats to the other islands are around to the right and away from the station. Boats to **Italy** and **Turkey** are a mile or so to the left. Hydrofoils to other destinations leave from Zea Marina, a separate harbor some distance from the Metro station. Very few signs point the way, so try to arrive early.

Ferry **tickets** can be purchased at a ticket office up to 1 hour before departure; after that they can be bought on the boat. To book **first-class cabins** or purchase **advance tickets,** see one of the harborside travel agents around Karaiskaki Square by the domestic ferries and along Akti Miaouli, opposite the Crete ferries. Most open at 6am, and some will hold your baggage for the day (but there's no security). The Greek National Tourist Organization (EOT) publishes a list of weekly sailings, and the **Tourist Police** (☎ 171) or the **Port Authority** (☎ 01/451-1311) can provide schedule information. Keep in mind that all such schedules are tentative.

SEEING THE SIGHTS ON LAND   The **Maritime Museum** at Akti Themistokleous (☎ **01/451-6264**), near the departure pier for the Flying Dolphin hydrofoils, has handsome models of ancient, medieval, and modern ships. The museum is open Tuesday to Saturday 9am to 2pm; admission is 500Dr ($1.70). The nearby **Archaeological Museum,** 32 Harilaou Trikoupi St. (☎ **01/452-1598**), is open Tuesday to Sunday 8:30am to 3pm, and also costs 500Dr ($1.70). The stars of the museum are the three superb monumental bronzes of a youth, the goddess Artemis, and the

---

Traveler's Tip

Whatever your destination from Piraeus, don't be too surprised if your boat leaves late. Schedules depend on the weather, and sailings are often delayed or canceled. It's not a good idea to plan to arrive back in Athens less than 24 hours before your flight home, lest bad weather strand you on an island.

---

goddess Athena. If you have time for only one museum, you'll probably find the Maritime Museum a pleasant departure from what you've seen in other archaeological museums.

WHERE TO DINE   Piraeus has some good restaurants, but the places to eat along the harbor are generally mediocre. If you decide to try one of the seafood restaurants in central Piraeus or Microlimani, make sure you know the price before ordering; if the final tab seems out of line, insist on a receipt, and phone the Tourist Police.

Dourambeis. 29A Dilaveri St., Piraeus. ☎ **01/412-2092.** Reservations recommended. Fish around 9,000–15,000Dr ($30–$50) per kilo; priced daily. No credit cards. Mon–Sat 8:30pm–1am. SEAFOOD.

This taverna near the Delphinario theater in Piraeus is where locals go when they want to splurge on a good fish dinner. The decor is simple, the food excellent. The crayfish soup alone is worth the trip, and the lettuce salad still lingers in my memory, but the whole point of going here is for the excellent grilled fish.

✪ **Vasilainas.** 72 Etolikou, Ayia Sofia. ☎ **01/461-2457.** Reservations recommended Fri–Sat. Meals 6,000Dr ($20). No credit cards. Mon–Sat 8pm–midnight. SEAFOOD/GREEK.

There's no menu at this restaurant in an old grocery store in a suburb just north of Piraeus; for a flat fee of 6,000Dr ($20) per person, you're presented with a steady flow of more than 15 dishes. Even if you come here hungry, you probably won't be able to eat everything set before you. There's plenty of seafood, plus good Greek dishes. Come by taxi; this place can be hard to find.

THE MONASTERY OF DAPHNI & ANCIENT ELEUSIS

THE MONASTERY OF DAPHNI   Laden with dazzling mosaics, the **Monastery of Daphni** (☎ 01/581-1558) is one of the masterpieces of Byzantine art. Sir David Talbot-Rice, the great art historian of Byzantine Greece, has called Daphni "the most perfect monument" of the 11th century. There were shrines on this spot even in antiquity, when Apollo was honored here, as the name "Daphni"—laurel, Apollo's favorite plant—suggests. The present monastery was begun in the late 11th century; in the centuries that followed, it was repeatedly damaged by invaders and earthquakes, and repeatedly rebuilt. After the Crusaders captured Constantinople in 1204, Daphni was used as a Catholic monastery by the Cistercian monks who installed the twin Gothic arches in front of the west entrance to the church. After the Greek War of Independence in the 1820s, the Greek Orthodox Church reclaimed Daphni and restored it to its former glory.

A severe earthquake in the 1980s prompted another round of restoration. The church has been strengthened and its dazzling mosaic cycle restored. The central dome has the commanding mosaic of **Christ Pantocrator (the Almighty).** The image is of an awesome judge rather than the Western conception of a suffering mortal. As is traditional, the **Annunciation, Nativity, Baptism,** and **Transfiguration** are in the squinches (quarter-circles) supporting the dome, and the 16 major **prophets** are displayed between the dome's windows. **The Adoration of the Magi** and the **Resurrection** are in the barrel vault inside the main (southern) entrance of the church, and the

Entry into Jerusalem and the **Crucifixion** are in the northern barrel vault. Mosaics showing scenes from the **life of the Virgin** are in the south bay of the narthex (passage between the entrance and nave).

The monastery is open daily, except major holidays, 8:30am to 3pm. Admission is 800Dr ($2.70).

Getting There   Daphni is 5½ miles west of Athens on the highway to Corinth. Take bus no. 860 from Panepistimiou Street, north of Sina (behind the university); bus no. 853, 862, 873, or 880 from Eleftheria Square off Pireos Avenue (northwest of Monastiraki); or bus no. A 15, "Elefsina," from Sachtouri Street, southeast of Eleftheria Square. The trip should take about half an hour, and the bus stop at Daphni is about 150 yards from the monastery. From Daphni, you can continue by bus to Ancient Eleusis.

ANCIENT ELEUSIS   Eleusis was the site of the most famous and revered of all the ancient Mysteries. The unknown and the famous were initiated into the sacred rites here, yet we know almost nothing about the Eleusinian Mysteries. What we do know is that the Mysteries commemorated the abduction of Demeter's daughter Persephone by the god of the underworld, Hades (Pluto). Demeter was able to strike a bargain with the god, who allowed Persephone to leave the underworld and rejoin her mother for 6 months each year. The mysteries celebrated this—and the cycle of growth, death, and rebirth of each year's crops.

The **Sanctuary of Eleusis** (☎ 01/554-6019), in the modern industrial city of Elefsina, is 14 miles west of central Athens on the highway to Corinth. Despite its substantial remains and glorious past—this was already a religious site in Mycenaean times—the sanctuary's present surroundings are so grim that it's not easy to warm to the spot. You'll see remains of a **Temple of Artemis,** a 2nd century A.D. **Roman propylaia** (monumental entrance), and **triumphal arches** dedicated to the Great Goddesses and to the emperor Hadrian. (Hadrian's arch inspired the Arc de Triomphe, on the Champs-Élysées in Paris.) Nearby is the **Kallichoron Well,** where Demeter wept over the loss of Persephone. The cave here, the **Ploutonion,** was believed to be the entrance to the underworld through which Persephone vanished. Nearby is the **Telesterion,** the Temple of Demeter; only initiates of the cult knew what really happened there.

There's also a small **museum,** with finds from the site, including the greater part of a famous statue of Demeter. The sanctuary and museum are open Tuesday to Sunday and holidays 8:30am to 3pm; admission is 500Dr ($1.70), free on Sunday.

Getting There   Take bus no. 853 or 862 from Eleftheria, a square off Pireos Avenue (northwest of Monastiraki), or bus no. A 15, "Elefsina," from Sachtouri Street, southeast of Eleftheria Square. When you get into Eleusis, tell the bus driver that you want to see *"ta archaia"* (the antiquities).

THE MONASTERY OF KAISARIANI & MT. IMITTOS (HYMETTUS)

Some 10 miles east of central Athens, the beautiful **Kaisariani Monastery** (☎ 01/723-6619) is in a cool, bird-inhabited forest on the lower slopes of Mt. Imittos, famous for its delicious honey and beautiful marble. Alas, the widespread fires of the summer of 1998 devastated many of the trees on Imittos. In antiquity there were a temple to Aphrodite and a sacred spring here. Today the spring water pours forth from the marble goat's head at the monastery's entrance; brides who wish to become pregnant often journey here to drink from the spring, whose waters are believed to speed conception.

The monastery was built in the 11th century over the ruins of a 5th-century Christian church, which in turn probably was built over the temple of Aphrodite. The small

church is in the form of a Greek cross, with four marble columns supporting the dome. Most of the lovely **frescoes** date from the 17th century. On the west side of the paved, flower-filled courtyard are the old kitchen and the refectory, which now house some sculptural fragments. To the south, the old **monks' cells** and a **bathhouse** are being restored. Exploration at your own risk is usually permitted.

The monastery is open Tuesday to Sunday 8:30am to 3pm; admission is 800Dr ($2.70).

GETTING THERE Bus no. 224 leaves from Panepistimiou Street and Vasilissis Sofias Avenue, northeast of Syntagma Square, every 20 minutes. On a cool day, it's a pleasant 1¼-mile walk up the road to the monastery's wooded site.

PICNICKING AT THE TEMPLE OF POSEIDON

One of the most popular, and easiest, day trips from Athens is to the 5th century B.C. **Temple of Poseidon** at **Cape Sounion** (☎ **0292/39-363**), about 2 hours by bus outside Athens. The temple, which was built at about the same time as the Parthenon, occupies a dramatic position on a cliff high above the sea. In antiquity, as today, sailors knew they were nearing Athens when they caught sight of the temple's slender Doric columns. Fifteen of them remain; try to find the spot on one where Lord Byron carved his name. Then you can swim in the sea below and grab a snack at one of the overpriced restaurants. (Better yet, bring a picnic.) This is a good place *not* to go on the weekend, when it is very crowded and the traffic to and from beaches outside Athens is very heavy.

The archaeological site is open daily from 10am to sunset. Admission is 800Dr ($2.70) for adults, 600Dr ($2) for seniors, and 400Dr ($1.35) for students.

GETTING THERE Buses to Sounion leave hourly on the half-hour 6:30am to 6:30pm from the **station** at 14 Mavromateon St. (☎ **01/821-3203**), at the southwest corner of Areos Park, well north of Omonia Square—best reached by taxi.

2 Delphi & the Northern Peloponnese

With the exception of the Acropolis in Athens, the most famous and beautiful ancient sites in Greece bracket the Gulf of Corinth. Apollo's sanctuary at Delphi is on the mainland north of the Gulf of Corinth, and Agamemnon's palace at Mycenae, the Mycenaean fortress of Tiryns, the spectacular 4th century B.C. theater of Epidauros and the birthplace of the Olympic Games at Olympia, are just across the gulf in the northern Peloponnese.

EXPLORING THE REGION BY CAR Thanks to the excellent road linking Athens and the Peloponnese at Corinth, and the frequent ferry service across the Gulf of Corinth between Rio and Anti-Rio, it's easy to combine a visit to Delphi with a tour of the most important ancient sites in the Peloponnese. Try to allow at least 4 days (spending 2 nights at Nafplion and 1 night each at Olympia and Delphi).

Driving Tip

Keep in mind that although most Greek roads are quite good, much of your journey to and around the Peloponnese will be on beautiful, but sometimes vertiginous, winding mountain and coastal roads that make distances deceptive. Therefore, I've indicated how long you should expect each part of the trip to take, rather than giving you a false sense of how quickly you can travel by just telling you how many miles you'll cover.

If traffic is light (and it almost never is), you can drive the 55 miles from Athens to Corinth on the National Road in an hour. After you take a look at the Corinth Canal and the sprawling site of ancient Corinth, an hour's drive (less if you take the new National Road to Argos and double back) through the farmland of Corinthia and Argolis will take you to Mycenae (71 miles southwest of Athens). From Mycenae, it's less than an hour to Nafplion (90 miles southwest of Athens). Generally considered the prettiest town in the Peloponnese, Nafplion is the perfect spot to spend the night before visiting Epidauros.

Although it's only 20 miles from Nafplion to Epidauros, the road is usually clogged with tour buses, especially when there are performances at the ancient theater; allow at least an hour for the drive. From Nafplion and Epicauros, two routes lead across the Peloponnese to Olympia. You can return to Corinth and join the National Road, which runs as far as Patras, where you take the good coast road on to Olympia. (Although there are signs in Patras pointing you toward Olympia, the heavy traffic in Patras means that you can easily spend an hour getting across town).

If you want to avoid Patras, you can join the new National Road at Argos and drive through the Arcadian mountains via Tripolis to Olympia (199 miles west of Athens). Either way, expect to spend at least 4 hours en route—and try to spend more, so that you can enjoy the coastal scenery or the mountain villages of Arcadia. Then, to reach Delphi from Olympia, simply head to Rio, just north of Patras, and catch one of the frequent ferries across the gulf to Anti-Rio, where a new road runs all the way to Delphi (110 miles west of Athens). Allow at least 5 hours for the trip from Olympia to Delphi, and 3 hours to get from Delphi to Athens.

Only at the Classical Sites

Imagining the Ancient Past   Sitting in the shade of the pine trees above the stadium where Greek athletes once raced to win a crown of laurel leaves, you can almost see the famous charioteer of Delphi urging his team of horses around the track. And you can run a lap in the stadium at Olympia and imagine the cheers of spectators.

Attending a Play at Epidauros   After the sun sinks over the horizon, watch a classic Greek tragedy in the acoustically perfect theater of Epidaurus, where a whisper from the stage can be heard in the back row.

Exploring Mount Parnassus   Trek up the slopes of Mount Parnassus to the upland plain of Livadi, which the ancient Greeks thought was the home of Pan and the nymphs—or take the easy way up and drive to the summit.

Enjoying Life in the Towns   Walk under balconies dripping with bougainvillea on the narrow side streets of Nafplion, or have an ouzo in the village square of Arachova, where the waiter will get you a glass of water from one of the springs that gush from marble fountains.

DELPHI

Delphi, which the ancient Greeks believed was the center of the world, is the big enchilada of Greek sites. Even more than Olympia, it has everything: a long and glorious history as the scene of Apollo's famous oracle and the Pythian games; spectacular ancient remains, including the Temple of Apollo and the well-preserved stadium where the ancient games took place; a superb museum; and a heartachingly beautiful location on the slopes of Mount Parnassus. Look up and you see the cliffs and crags of Parnassus; look down at Greece's most beautiful plain of olive trees stretching as far as the eye can see toward the town of Itea on the Gulf of Corinth.

Central Greece & the Northern Peloponnese

0 — 45 Miles
0 — 45 Kilometers

Limni Trichonis

Mt. Parnassus

Delphi Arachova Livadia

Monastery of Ossiu Luka Thiva

Messolongi

Korinthiakos Kolpos

Patras

Megara

Corinth Isthmia

PELOPONNESE Nemea

Mycenae

Epidauros

Tiryns

Pirgos Argos Nafplion

Olympia Tripolis

E-0099

ESSENTIALS

GETTING THERE   By Bus   Depending on the season, as many as five daily buses make the 3-hour trip to Delphi from the Athens station, 260 Liossion St. (☎ 01/831-7096), north of Omnia Square.

By Car   Take the Athens–Corinth National Highway 46 miles west of Athens to the Thebes turnoff and continue 25 miles west to Levadia. If you want to stop at the monastery of Osios Loukas, take the Distomo turnoff for 5½ miles. Return to Distomo and continue via Arachova for 16 miles to Delphi or via the seaside town of Itea for 40 miles to Delphi. The approach from Itea is well worth the time if you aren't in a hurry.

VISITOR INFORMATION   The **tourist office,** on Ods Frederikis Street (☎ 0265/89-920), is usually open daily 8am to 3pm, and in July and August is often open 6 to 8pm as well.

FAST FACTS   The telephone **area code** for Delphi is **0265.** Most services are available on Frederikis Street, Delphi's main thoroughfare. The **post office** is usually open 8am to 4pm, and sometimes also open Sunday 9am to 1pm. The **OTE telephone and telegraph office** is open Monday to Saturday 7:30am to 3pm and Sunday 9am to 1pm. Both banks on Frederikis Street were planning to install ATMs in 1999.

GETTING AROUND   The village of Delphi, with its handful of long, parallel streets connected by stepped side streets, is small enough that most visitors find it easiest to abandon their cars and explore on foot. If you have to drive to the site rather than making the 5- to 10-minute walk from town, be sure to set off early to get one of the few parking places. Whether you walk or drive, keep an eye out for the enormous tour buses that barrel down the center of the road—and for the not-terribly-well-marked one-way streets in the village.

EXPLORING THE SITE

If possible, begin your visit when the site and museum open in the morning (both are sometimes relatively uncrowded in the hour before closing, too). If you begin your visit at the museum, you'll arrive at the site already familiar with many of the works of art that once decorated the sanctuary.

Delphi Museum. ☎ **0265/82-313.** Admission 1,200Dr ($4). Summer, Mon 11am–7pm, Tues–Fri 8am–7pm, Sat–Sun and holidays 8am–3pm; winter, Mon 11am–5:30pm, Tues–Fri 8am–5:30pm, Sat–Sun and holidays 8am–3pm.

Each of the museum's 13 rooms has a specific focus: sculpture from the elegant Sifnian treasury in one room, finds from the Temple of Apollo in two rooms, discoveries from the Roman period (including the Parian marble statue of the epicene youth Antinous, the beloved of the emperor Hadrian) in another. Just outside the first display room stands a 4th century B.C. marble egg, a symbol of Delphi's position as the center of the world. According to legend, when Zeus wanted to determine the earth's center, he released two eagles from Mount Olympus. When the eagles met over Delphi, Zeus had his answer. (You can still see eagles in the sky above Delphi, but as often as not, the large birds circling overhead are the less distinguished Egyptian vultures.)

The star of the museum, with a room to himself, is the famous 5th century B.C. *Charioteer of Delphi,* a larger-than-life bronze figure that was part of a group that originally included a four-horse chariot. It's an irresistible statue—don't miss the handsome youth's delicate eyelashes shading wide enamel and stone eyes or the realistic veins that stand out in his hands and feet.

Although the charioteer is the star of the collection, he's in good company. Delphi was chock-a-block with superb works of art given by wealthy patrons, such as King Croesus of Lydia, who contributed the massive silver bull that's on display. Many of the finest exhibits are quite small, such as the elegant bronzes in the museum's last room, including one that shows Odysseus clinging to the belly of a ram. According to Homer, this is how the wily hero escaped from the cave of the ferocious (but nearsighted) monster Cyclops.

Sanctuary of Apollo, Castalian Spring & Sanctuary of Athena Pronaia. ☎ **0265/82-313.** Admission 1,200Dr ($4). Summer, Mon 11am–7pm, Tues–Fri 8am–7pm, Sat–Sun and holidays 8am–3pm; winter, Mon 11am–5:30pm, Tues–Fri 8am–5:30pm, Sat–Sun and holidays 8am–3pm.

As you enter the **Sanctuary of Apollo,** just past the museum, you'll be on the marble **Sacred Way,** following the route that visitors to Delphi have taken for thousands of years. The Sacred Way twists uphill past the remains of Roman **stoas** and a number

The Delphic Oracle

In antiquity, one of the three priestesses on duty gave voice to Apollo's oracles from a room deep within the **Temple of Apollo.** That much is known, although the details of precisely what happened here are obscure. Did the priestess sit on a tripod balanced over a chasm, breathing in hallucinatory fumes? Did she chew various herbs, including the laurel leaf sacred to Apollo, until she spoke in tongues, while priests interpreted her sayings? Perhaps wisely, the oracle has kept its secrets.

of Greek **treasuries** (including the Siphnian and Athenian treasuries, whose sculpture is in the museum). Just as modern cities compete to see who can construct the tallest skyscraper, ancient cities tried to build the most elegant of these elaborate small temples, storehouses for works of art dedicated to Apollo. Take a close look at the treasury walls: You'll see not only beautiful dry-wall masonry, but countless inscriptions. The ancient Greeks were never shy about using the walls of their buildings as bulletin boards. Alas, so many contemporary visitors have added their own names to the ancient inscriptions that the Greek archaeological service no longer allows visitors inside the massive 4th century B.C. **Temple of Apollo,** which was built here after several earlier temples were destroyed.

From the temple, it's a fairly steep uphill climb to the remarkably well-preserved 4th century B.C. theater and the stadium, which was extensively remodeled by the Romans. In antiquity, contests in the Pythian festivals took place in both venues. Today the theater and stadium are used most summers for the Festival of Delphi—which, on occasion, has featured exceptionally unclassical pop music.

Keep your ticket as you leave the Sanctuary of Apollo and begin the 10-minute walk along the Arachova–Delphi road to the Sanctuary of Athena (also called the Marmaria, which refers to all the marble found here). En route, you'll pass the famous Castalian Spring, where Apollo planted a laurel. Above are the rose-colored cliffs known as the **Phaedriades (the Bright Ones),** famous for the way they reflect the sun's rays. Drinking from the Castalian Spring has inspired legions of poets; however, poets now have to find their inspiration elsewhere because the spring is off-limits to allow repairs to the Roman fountain facade. Poets, be warned: Once an antiquity is closed in Greece, it often stays closed for quite a while.

A path descends from the main road to the **Sanctuary of Athena,** goddess of wisdom, who shared the honors at Delphi with Apollo. The remains here are quite fragmentary, except for the large 4th century B.C. gymnasium, and you might choose simply to wander about and enjoy the site without trying too hard to figure out what's what. The round 4th century B.C. *tholos* with its three graceful standing Doric columns is easy to spot—but no one knows why the building was constructed, why it was so lavishly decorated, or what went on inside. Again, the oracle is silent.

WHERE TO STAY

There's no shortage of hotels in Delphi, and you can usually get a room even in July and August. Still, if you want a room in a specific price category, or with a view, it's best to make a reservation. Finally, consider staying in nearby **Arachova,** where the hotels are usually less crowded (see "Day Trips from Delphi," below). Be sure to check whether your hotel has functioning heating if you visit here in the winter.

Castalia Hotel. 13 Frederikis St. (at Vasileos Pavlou), 33054 Delphi. ☎ **0265/82-205.** 26 units. TEL. 24,000Dr ($80) double. Rates include breakfast. AE, DC, V. Closed weekdays Jan–Feb.

The Castalia, a white stucco building with projecting balconies on Delphi's main street, has been here since 1938 and was completely remodeled in 1986. Most of the good-sized bedrooms have hand-loomed rugs, and the rear bedrooms have fine views over the olive plain.

✪ **Hotel Varonos.** 25 Frederikis St. (at Vasileos Pavlou), 33054 Delphi. ☎ and fax **0265/82-345.** 9 units, 8 with shower only, 1 with tub/shower. TV TEL. 16,000Dr ($54) double. Breakfast supplement 2,000Dr ($7). AE, MC, V.

This small, family-owned hotel has very clean, spare bedrooms; many overlook the olive plain. This is a very welcoming hotel—we once arrived with an ailing gardenia plant, and the entire family pitched in to make sure it was well taken care of.

⭐ **Hotel Vouzas.** 1 Frederikis St. (at Vasileos Pavlou), 33054 Delphi. ☎ **0265/82-232.** Fax 0265/82-033. 59 units. TV TEL. 40,5000Dr ($135) double. AE, DC, MC, V.

If you don't mind not having a swimming pool, this is the place to stay. It has a cozy fireplace in the lobby and spectacular views, and is a short walk from everything you've come to see. The bedrooms and bathrooms are very comfortable, and the balconies have not only a table and chairs, but also, when we stayed there, a welcoming pot of basil.

WHERE TO DINE

You won't starve in Delphi, but there's no really outstanding restaurant, so you may prefer to head to the village of Arachova, 6 miles to the north (see "Day Trips from Delphi," below).

Topiki Gefsi. Odos Pavlou and Frederikis 19. ☎ **0265/82-480.** Main courses 1,800–4,500Dr ($6–$15). AE, DC, MC, V. GREEK.

This large restaurant on the main street has a good view and reasonably good food. Unfortunately, as with most restaurants here, the staff is pretty sure they'll never see you again and the service is consequently haphazard. That said, the stuffed vine leaves are quite tasty, and there are sometimes interesting stews on the menu. A guitar and piano duo occasionally appears in the evening.

DAY TRIPS FROM DELPHI

ARACHOVA   The mountain village of Arachova, 6 miles north of Delphi, clings to Mount Parnassus some 3,100 feet above sea level. Arachova is famous for its hand-loomed *tagari* shoulder bags, heavy blankets, and fluffy *flokakia* rugs. When several tour buses stop here during the daytime, the tiny village can be seriously crowded. Don't despair—come in the evening, when the shops are still open and the cafes and restaurants allow you to escape from the tourist world of Delphi to the village world of Greece. There's usually an energetic evening *volta* (stroll) on the main street, and if you climb the steep stairs to the upper town, you'll find yourself on quiet neighborhood streets where children play and families sit in front of their homes.

On main street, have a look at the weavings in Georgia Charitou's shop, **Anemi** (☎ 0267/31-701), which also offers some nice reproductions of antiques. **Katina Panagakou's shop,** on the main street (☎ 0267/31-743), has examples of local crafts, too.

For lunch or dinner, try the **Taverna Karathanassi** (no phone), by the coffee shops in the main street square with the lovely freshwater springs. The Karathanassi family serves simple, homey fare; expect to pay about $15 for dinner. Just off the square, the **Taverna Dasargyri** (no phone; also known as Barba Iannis) specializes in delicious *loukanika* (sausages), chops, and the *kokoretsi* (stuffed entrails) that are much tastier than they sound. This is a popular local hangout. The meat is usually priced by the kilo, and you can eat well for about $15. Both of these restaurants are usually open from around noon to 4pm and 7pm to midnight; neither takes credit cards.

If you want to stay in Arachova, the **Xenia Hotel** (☎ 0267/31-230; fax 0267/32-175) in town, with 42 rooms, each with a balcony, has doubles at 21,000Dr ($70). The very pleasant **Best Western Anemolia** (☎ 0267/31-640; in the U.S., 800/528-1234), with 52 rooms, on a hill just outside Arachova above the Delphi road, charges 25,000Dr ($83) for a double (prices sometimes are much as $20 higher on the weekend). **The Arachova Inn** (☎ 0267/31-353; fax 0267/31-134), with a cozy fireplace in the lobby, is just outside town on the main road to Delphi. It has 40 rooms, and charges 15,000Dr ($50) for a double. All these hotels are usually full on winter weekends when Greeks flock here to ski Parnassus.

MOUNT PARNASSUS   Parnassus is an odd mountain: Its peaks are difficult to see from Delphi or Arachova, but if you approach from the north, you'll have fine views of its twin summits. You can drive up to the ski resort at Fterolaki in about an hour from either Delphi or Arachova. It's a lively place in winter during the ski season, but usually nothing is open during the summer.

If you want to go **hiking** on Mount Parnassus, there are two possibilities. From Delphi, head uphill on the paved road that runs above the cemetery and stadium, and keep going. Four hours will bring you to the upland meadows known as the **Plateau of Livadi,** where shepherds traditionally pasture their flocks. As always in the mountains, it's not a good idea to make such an excursion alone. If you plan to continue past the meadows to the **Corcyrian Cave** (known locally as *Sarantavli,* or "Forty Rooms"), where Pan and the nymphs once were thought to live, or to the summits, you should check on conditions locally or with the **Hellenic Mountaineering Club** in Athens (☎ **01/323-4555**).

THE MONASTERY OF OSIOS LOUKAS   You can visit Osios Loukas en route to or from Delphi, or make the 60-mile round-trip from Delphi in a day. If you go to Osios Loukas via Levadia, pause at **Schiste (Triodos),** where three roads cross. This is the spot where the ancients believed that Oedipus unknowingly slew his father.

The 10th-century **Monastery of Osios Loukas (Saint Luke)** is a lavishly decorated complex. A wide variety of jewel-like polychrome marbles were used in the monastery's construction. The two churches have superb **mosaics;** along with the mosaics at Daphni, outside Athens (see "Day Trips from Athens" above), and those in the splendid churches of Thessaloniki, these are the finest mosaics in Greece.

Bear in mind that Osios Loukas is not a tourist destination, but a holy spot for Greek Orthodox visitors. This is not the place for sleeveless shirts, shorts, or a casual attitude toward the icons or the tomb of Saint Luke. The monastery is usually open daily 8am to 2pm and 4 to 6pm; admission is 600Dr ($2).

THE NORTHERN PELOPONNESE & THE CLASSICAL SITES

One of the delights of visiting the northern Peloponnese is that it's relatively uncrowded when many of the Aegean islands are sagging under the weight of tourists each summer. That doesn't mean you'll have famous spots like Mycenae, Epidauros, and Olympia to yourself if you arrive at high noon in August. It does mean that if you arrive just as they open or just before they close, you may have an hour under the pine trees at Olympia or Epidauros virtually alone, and be able to stand in Mycenae's Treasury of Atreus with swallows as your only companions.

Because even the most avid tourists do not live by culture alone, it's good to know that one of the great delights of spending time in the northern Peloponnese comes from quiet hours in shady *plateias* (squares), watching fishers mend their nets while local families settle down for a leisurely meal. An hour in a seaside cafe watching the locals watching you watch them is the ideal way to unwind after a day's sightseeing. By the way, if you visit here in the winter, make sure your hotel has functioning heating.

CORINTH

Corinth exported its pottery around the Mediterranean and dominated trade in Greece for much of the 8th and 7th centuries B.C. It experienced a second golden age under the Romans in the 2nd century A.D. Today, as in antiquity, Corinth and Patras are the two major gateways to the Peloponnese. As you pause here, you'll want to leave the main highway to take a look at the Corinth Canal and visit ancient Corinth before heading deeper into the northern Peloponnese.

Essentials

GETTING THERE   By Train   Several trains a day run from Athens's Stathmos Peloponnisou to the Corinth station off Odos Demokratias (☎ **0741/22-522**). The trains are almost invariably late, often taking 3 hours or more. Refreshments sometimes are available on board. For information on schedules and fares, call ☎ **01/512-4913** in Athens.

By Bus   At least 15 buses a day run to Corinth from the Stathmos Leoforia Peloponnisou, 100 Odos Kifissou in Athens. From the Corinth bus station, Ermou and Koliatsou streets (☎ **0741/25-645**), you can catch a bus for the 15- to 20-minute ride to Archaia Korinthos (Ancient Corinth). For schedule and fare information, call ☎ **01/512-8233** in Athens. Buses from Corinth for the Peloponnese leave from the station at the corner of Konstantinou and Aratou streets (☎ **0741/24-403**).

By Car   Corinth is 55 miles west of Athens on the National Highway; the toll is 500Dr ($1.70). Work to widen the highway to seven lanes is almost finished, but there are still a few particularly dangerous three-lane stretches. The highway now continues past the Corinth Canal; just after the canal, you'll see signs for Ancient Corinth (the archaeological site) and Corinth (the uninteresting modern town).

FAST FACTS   The telephone **area code** for Corinth is **0741**. The **police station** is on Ermou Street (☎ **0741/22-143**).

The Corinth Canal

When the main road ran directly past the restaurants and cafes on either side of the canal, almost everyone used to stop here for a coffee, a souvlaki, and a look at the canal that separates the Peloponnese from the mainland. Now buses, trucks, and most cars stay on the new highway, but you can still take the exit for the Canal and Tourist Area to see the canal and have a snack. There's a small post office at the canal, and a kiosk with postcards and English-language newspapers. Most of the large souvlaki places have surprisingly clean toilet facilities (and very tough souvlaki). One word of warning that's necessary here and almost nowhere else in Greece: Be sure to lock your car door. This is a popular spot for thieves to prey on unwary tourists.

The French engineers who built the Corinth Canal between 1881 and 1893 used lots of dynamite, blasting through 285 feet of sheer rock to make this 4-mile-long, 30-yard-wide passageway. The canal utterly revolutionized shipping in the Mediterranean; vessels that previously had spent days making their way around Cape Matapan, at the southern tip of the Peloponnese, could dart through the canal in hours.

Exploring Ancient Corinth

To reach Ancient Corinth, follow the signs after the Corinth Canal for Ancient and Old Corinth.

Ancient Corinth. Old Corinth. ☎ **0741/31-207.** Admission to archaeological site and museum 1,200Dr ($4). Summer, Mon–Fri 8am–7pm, Sat–Sun 8am–3pm; winter, Mon–Fri 8:45am–3pm, Sat–Sun 8:30am–3pm.

The most conspicuous—and the most handsome—surviving building at Ancient Corinth is clearly the 6th century B.C. **Temple of Apollo,** which stands on a low hill overlooking the extensive remains of the **Roman Agora** (marketplace). Only 7 of the temple's 38 monolithic Doric columns are standing, the others having long since been toppled by earthquakes.

Ancient Corinth's main drag, the 40-foot-wide marble-paved road that ran from the port of Lechaion into the heart of the marketplace, is clearly visible from the temple. Along the road, and throughout the Agora, are the foundations of hundreds of the stores that once stocked everything from spices imported from Asia Minor to jugs of wine made from Corinth's excellent grapes.

Two spots in the Agora are especially famous—the **Fountain of Peirene** and the **Bema.** In the 2nd century A.D., the famous Roman traveler, Philhellene, and benefactor Herodes Atticus encased the modest Greek fountain in the elaborate two-story building with arches, arcades, and the 50-square-foot courtyard whose remains you see today. Peirene was a woman who wept so hard when her son died that she dissolved into the spring that still flows here. The Bema (public platform) was where St. Paul had to plead his case when the Corinthians, irritated by his constant criticisms, hauled him in front of the Roman governor Gallo in 52 A.D.

Archaeological Museum. Ancient Corinth, in the town of Old Corinth. ☎ **0741/31-207.** Admission to museum and archaeological site 1,200Dr ($4). Summer, Mon–Fri 8am–7pm, Sat–Sun 8am–3pm; winter, Mon–Fri 8:45am–3pm, Sat–Sun 8:30am–3pm.

As you'd expect, this museum just inside the site entrance has a particularly fine collection of the famous Corinthian pottery, which is often decorated with charming red and black figures of birds and animals. There are also a number of statues of Roman worthies and several mosaics, including one in which Pan is shown piping away to a clutch of cows. The museum courtyard is a shady spot to sit and read up on the ancient site, which has virtually no shade.

Acrocorinth. Old Corinth. Admission 500Dr ($1.70). Summer, daily 8am–7pm; winter, daily 8am–5pm.

A winding dirt road runs from the site of Ancient Corinth to the summit of Acrocorinth, the rugged limestone sugarloaf mountain topped by centuries of fortifications that dominates the plain of Corinth. A superb natural acropolis, Acrocorinth was fortified first by the Greeks and later by the Byzantines, Franks, Venetians, and Turks. Extensive remains of the centuries of walls, turrets, and towers built here still remain. After you roam around enjoying the seemingly endless view over the rich plain below, you can relax at the small cafe just outside the site entrance.

✪ NAFPLION

With two hilltop Venetian fortresses, shady parks, an interesting assortment of small museums, and better-than-average hotels, restaurants, and shops—and even a miniature castle (the Bourtzi) in the harbor—this port town on the northeast coast of the Gulf of Argos is almost everyone's first choice as the most charming town in the Peloponnese. A good deal of Nafplion's appeal comes from the fact that for several years after the Greek War of Independence (1821–28), this was the country's first capital. Although the palace of Greece's young King Otto—a mail-order monarch from Bavaria—burnt down in the 19th century, an impressive number of handsome neoclassical civic buildings and private houses have survived, as have a scattering of Turkish fountains and several mosques.

Essentials

GETTING THERE   By Bus   At least a dozen buses a day run to Nafplion from the **Stathmos Leoforia Peloponnisou,** 100 Odos Kifissou (☎ **01/513-4110** or 01/513-4588), Athens. The trip takes about 4 hours because the bus goes into Corinth and Argos before reaching Nafplion.

By Boat   Flying Dolphin hydrofoil service runs from Marina Zea, Piraeus, to Nafplion, Monday to Saturday, weather permitting. The hydrofoil makes a number of stops and takes almost as long as the bus to reach Nafplion. For fare and schedule information, call ☎ **01/324-2281** or 01/453-6107 in Athens.

By Car From Athens, head south to the Corinth Canal. Take the new Corinth–Tripolis road to the Argos exit and follow signs into Argos and Nafplion. You'll almost certainly get lost at least once in Argos, which has an abysmal system of directional signs. Allow at least 3 hours for the drive from Athens to Nafplion. When you reach Nafplion, park in the large, free municipal lot by the harbor. If you want to stop at Mycenae or Nemea, take the winding old road to Nafplion. If you want to stop at Epidauros, take the signposted turn for Epidauros just after the canal.

VISITOR INFORMATION The **Greek National Tourist Organization (EOT)** office is at 16 Photomara St. (☎ 0752/28-131), cater-corner from the bus station in Plateia Nikitara. It's usually open weekdays 9am to 2pm.

FAST FACTS The telephone **area code** for Nafplion is **0752.** The **post office** is open weekdays 8am to 2pm, and the **OTE telephone and telegraph** office is open weekdays 8am to 7pm. Both are signposted from the bus station. The **National Bank of Greece** has a branch on the main square, Syntagma Square. There are a number of **travel agencies** in Nafplion, including Staikos Travel, by the harbor (☎ 0752/27-950). The best place to swim is at the **beach** beneath the Palamidi, a 15-minute walk (with the sea on your right) from the harborside cafes.

Exploring the Town

Nafplion is a stroller's delight, and one of the great pleasures here is simply walking through the parks, up and down the stepped side streets, and along the harbor. Don't make the mistake of stopping your harborside stroll when you come to the last of the large seaside cafes by the Hotel Agamemnon. If you continue, you can watch fishing boats putting in at the pier and explore several cliffside chapels. Nafplion is so small that you can't get seriously lost, so have fun exploring. Here are some suggestions on how to take in the official sights after you've had your initial stroll.

ACRONAFPLIA & THE PALAMIDI Nafplion's two massive fortresses, Acronafplia and the Palamidi, dominate the skyline. There's no charge to visit the cliffs known as **Acronafplia,** where there are considerable remains of Greek, Frankish, and Venetian fortresses, as well as two modern hotels, the Xenia and Xenia Palace. The easiest way to get up Acronafplia is to drive or hitch a ride on the elevator (signposted) that conveys guests from the lower town to the **Xenia Palace Hotel.** If you want to walk up, follow signs in the lower town to the **Church of Saint Spyridon,** one of whose walls has the mark left by one of the bullets that killed Ianni Kapodistria, the first governor of modern Greece. From Saint Spyridon, follow the signs farther uphill to the **Catholic Church of the Metamorphosis.**

This church is as good a symbol as any for Nafplion's vexed history. Built by the Venetians, it was converted into a mosque by the Turks, and then reconsecrated as a church after the War of Independence. Inside, an ornamental doorway has an inscription listing Philhellenes who died for Greece, including nephews of Lord Byron and George Washington. As you continue to climb to Acronafplia, keep an eye out for several carvings of the winged lion that was the symbol of Saint Mark, the patron saint of Venice.

If you're not in the mood to climb the 800-plus steps to the summit of the **Palamidi,** you can take a taxi up and then walk down. The Venetians spent 3 years building the Palamidi, only to have it conquered the next year (1715) by the Turks. You'll enter the fortress the way the Turkish attackers did, through the main gate to the east. Once inside, you can trace the course of the massive wall that encircled the entire summit and wander through the considerable remains of the five fortresses that failed to stop the Turkish attack. In June, there are sometimes concerts here in the evening. The Palamidi is open weekdays 8am to 7pm in summer, 8:30am to 5pm in winter. Admission is 800Dr ($2.70).

NAFPLION'S MUSEUMS   All four of Nafplion's museums are within easy walking distance of one another. Before closing for renovations, the **Folk Art Museum** (1 Odos V. Alexandrou; ☎ **0752/28-379**) was one of the most delightful museums in Greece; it's hard to imagine that it could be even better when it reopens. It was housed in an elegant 18th-century house with a shady courtyard, a welcome snack bar, and one of the finest collections of costumes in Greece. Throughout, labels were in English as well as Greek, which means you could learn just how cotton was harvested and silk was spun and what kind of loom was used to make what kind of costume. Life-sized photos of women spinning, men shearing sheep, and a wide-eyed bridal couple posing in front of their wedding bed made the exhibits here come alive. The museum is scheduled to reopen in 1999 and to welcome visitors Wednesday to Monday from 9am to 2:30pm. It will be closed in February; admission was not known at press time. Until then, the excellent museum shop (36 Vas Olgas Street; ☎ **0752/25-267**) remains open. Hours are daily from 10am to 1pm and 6 to 10pm.

The **Museum of Childhood,** Stathmos, Kolokotronis Park, an offshoot of the Folk Art Museum, has an eclectic collection of dolls, baby clothes, and toys. It's open year-round, weekdays 4 to 8pm and Saturday 9am to 1pm, with frequent unscheduled closings. Admission is 400Dr ($1.35).

The **Archaeological Museum,** Syntagma Square (☎ **0752/27-502**), is housed in the handsome 18th-century Venetian arsenal that dominates Syntagma Square. The thick walls make it a deliciously cool place to visit on even the hottest day. Displays are from sites in the area and include pottery, jewelry, and some horrific Mycenaean terra-cotta idols, as well as a handsome bronze Mycenaean suit of armor. Open Tuesday to Sunday 8:30am to 1pm; admission is 500Dr ($1.70).

If you like old prints and old photographs, not to mention muskets, you'll enjoy strolling through the exhibits at the **Military Museum,** on Leoforos Amalias (☎ **0752/25-591**). It covers Greek wars from the War of Independence to World War II. Open Tuesday to Sunday 9am to 2pm; admission is free.

Where to Stay

✪ **Byron Hotel.** Plateia Agiou Spiridona, Nafplion 21100. ☎ **0752/22-351.** Fax 0752-26338. E-mail: byronhotel@otenet.gr. 13 units (all with bathroom). TEL. 21,000Dr ($70) double. AE, EURO, MC, V.

This pleasant small hotel, painted a distinctive pink with blue shutters, is in a quiet, breezy location overlooking the Church of Agiou Spiridona, a short, steep hike up from the main plateia. There are a number of nice bits of Victoriana, including marble-topped tables, in the sitting rooms and bedrooms (some of which are quite small for two). Word has gotten out about the Byron's charm, and it's almost impossible to stay here in July or August without a reservation.

Epidauros Hotel. 2 Kokkinou St., Nafplion 21100 (beside the Commercial Bank). ☎ and fax **0752/27-541.** 15 units (all with shower). 12,000Dr ($40) double. No credit cards.

The Epidauros is currently expanding and adding an annex across the street, as well as nearby pension quarters (7,000Dr/$23.35 double). The rooms here are small but pleasant, with good, firm beds. The location, on a quiet street just off the main square, is excellent and the staff, although not wildly welcoming, is helpful.

✪ **Omorphi Poli Pension.** 5 Sofroni St., Nafplion 21100. ☎ **0752/21-565.** 10 units (all with shower). TV TEL. 15,000Dr ($50) double. Rates include breakfast. MC, V.

What a lovely place! This new (1998) small pension/hotel above the charming cafe by the same name (Beautiful City) has gone all-out to restore a building to give guests the sense that they are staying in a Nafplion home—but with privacy. There's nothing to fault here (good beds, nice tile floors, nice prints on the walls); it's a pleasant place to use as a base for touring the area. Families will like the rooms with sleeping lofts for children (18,000Dr/$60 for three).

Xenia Palace Hotel. Acronafplia, 210 00 Nafplion. ☎ **0752/28-981.** Fax 0752/28-987. 51 units, 50 bungalows. A/C MINIBAR TV TEL. 60,000–78,000Dr ($200–$260) double. Rates include breakfast and lunch or dinner. Off-season discounts sometimes available. AE, DC, EURO, MC, V.

The Xenia Palace boasts the best view in town; whether you think it's in the best location depends on whether you want to be in town or up here on the slopes of Acronafplia, looking across the harbor to the Bourtzi and the mountains of the Peloponnese. Unfortunately, the rugs and chairs in many of the bedrooms are showing signs of wear, and the dining room has indifferent "international" and Greek cuisine. One big plus is the swimming pool, the perfect place to cool off after a day's sightseeing. You can sometimes make arrangements to use the pool if you're staying at the nearby **Xenia Hotel** (same phone and fax), the Xenia Palace's less expensive sibling, where rooms are usually at least $25 cheaper.

Where to Dine

Oddly enough, the restaurants in and just off Syntagma Square are not the tourist traps you'd expect. Furthermore, you'll see a good number of Greeks at the big harborside cafes on Akti Miaoulis. In short, Nafplion has lots of good restaurants, as well as one superb pastry shop and any number of ice cream parlors selling elaborate gooey confections.

Hellas Restaurant. Syntagma Sq. ☎ **0752/27-278.** Main courses 1,500–3,500Dr ($6–$12). AE, MC, V. Daily 9am–midnight. GREEK.

Kostas, the host of the Hellas, says that there's been a restaurant here for more than 100 years. Shady trees and awnings make this a cool spot to eat outdoors; there's also an inside dining room, where locals tend to congregate year-round. Excellent dolmades with egg-lemon sauce are usually on the menu, as well as stuffed tomatoes and peppers in season. Just about everyone in town passes through Syntagma Square, so this is a great spot to people-watch.

Karamanlis. 1 Leoforos Bouboulinas. ☎ **0752/27-668.** Main courses 1,500–2,500Dr ($5–$8); fish priced daily by the kilo. AE, EURO, MC, V. Daily 11am–midnight. GREEK.

This simple harborfront taverna several blocks east of the cluster of harborfront cafes tends to get fewer tourists than most of the places in town. It serves good grills and several kinds of meatballs (*keftedes, sousoutakia,* and *yiouvarlakia*). If you like the food here, you'll probably also enjoy the **Kanares Taverna** and the **Hundalos Taverna,** both also on Bouboulinas.

✪ **Noufara.** Plateia Syntagma, Nafplion. ☎ **0752/23-648.** Fax 0752/23-945. Main courses 1,500–4,000Dr ($5–$13). EURO, MC, V. Open daily from about 8am–1am. ITALIAN/GREEK.

If you're not sure you can face another stuffed tomato, head for the Noufara, which has a wide range of Italian dishes as well as the usual Greek favorites. You can sit under the umbrellas and have a cool drink or a full meal—or you can retreat inside to the air-conditioned dining room. The Noufara also has a branch with the same menu (but a wider offering of fish) just outside Nafplion on the shore in Nea Chios (☎ 0752/52-314).

The Pharos. Akti Miaoulis (by the playground). ☎ **0752/26-043.** Ouzo and standard mezedes from 900Dr ($3); ouzo and meal of mezedes from 2,400Dr ($8). No credit cards. Daily 10am–midnight. SNACKS.

It's easy to stop at the Pharos for a drink and a snack and end up eating enough octopus, *keftedes* (meatballs), and *saganaki* (fried cheese) to make up a meal. This is a great spot for enjoying the waterfront away from the main tourist bustle.

Savouras Psarotaverna. 79 Leoforos Bouboulinas. ☎ **0752/27-704.** Fish priced daily by the kilo. AE, EURO, MC, V. Daily noon–11pm. SEAFOOD.

This restaurant has been here more than 20 years, and its fresh fish attracts Greek day-trippers from Tripolis and even Athens. What you eat depends on what was caught that day—and it's always a good idea to check the price before ordering. Expect to pay $50 (and easily more) for two fish dinners, a salad, and some house wine. On summer weekends this restaurant can be terribly crowded.

The Shopping Scene
Nafplion has not escaped the invasion of T-shirt and mass-produced-souvenir shops that threatens to overwhelm Greece, but there are some genuinely fine shops. Many are on or just off Odos Spiliadou, the street immediately above Plateia Syntagma. As in most Greek towns heavily dependent on tourism, many of the shops are closed in the winter.

There are lots of jewelery shops in Nafplion, but one that stands out is **Preludio,** 2 Vas. Constantinou (just off Syntagma Square), Nafplion (☎ **0752/25-277**). Preludio has a surprisingly wide range of handsome earrings, necklaces, bracelets, and rings. Some designs are modern, some traditional, others are replicas of ancient and Byzantine styles (including some nice rings and necklaces with good reproductions of ancient coins). The staff speaks excellent English and is very helpful.

In her shop near the waterfront, **Helene Papadopoulou,** 5 Odos Spiliadou (☎ **0752/25-842**), sells traditional weavings and dolls made from brightly painted gourds. Prices start at 10,000Dr ($33). Next door, her husband has a wide collection of excellent-quality Greek costume dolls (from 12,000Dr/$40), as well as some nice ceramic jewelry of Greek ships and flowers (from 1,500Dr/$5).

Konstantine Beselmes, 6 Athan Siokou St. (☎ **0752/27-274**), sells his own magical paintings of village scenes, sailing ships, idyllic landscapes, and family groups. Although new, the paintings are done on weathered boards, which gives them a pleasantly aged look. Prices begin at around 15,000Dr ($55.55).

The **Komboloi Museum,** 25 Staikopoulou St, Nafplion. ☎ and fax **0752/21-618** (admission 500Dr ($1.70) is a fascinating shop with its own museum of komboloi (usually refered to as "worry beads"). Both the shop and museum have examples of Muslim prayer beads, Catholic rosaries, and the secular Greek worry bead. Prices range from a few dollars to several hundred.

The Corner, Staikopoulou & Koletti, just off Syntagma Square (☎ **0752/21-359**), often has old photographs, prints, wood and copper, and, sometimes, handsome old embroidered aprons and vests from traditional costumes.

The Wine Shop, 5 Amalias, Nafplion (☎ and fax **0752/24-446**), is one of the best wine shops in the Peloponnese and an excellent place to head if you want to browse and learn about Greek wines. Owner Dimitris Karonis is usually happy to talk to browsers about his wide selection of Greek wines, and also stocks wines and spirits from Europe and North America.

The **Odyssey** (no phone) book shop, Syntagma Square, has a wide selection of newspapers, magazines, and books in English, as well as a collection of startling pornographic drink coasters.

Day Trips from Nafplion

TIRYNS   The **archaeological site** of Tiryns is 3 miles outside Nafplion on the Argos road. From the moment you see it, you'll understand why Homer called this **citadel,** which may have been Mycenae's port, "well walled." Tiryns stands on a rocky outcropping 87 feet high and about 330 yards long, girdled by the massive walls that so impressed Homer—but that didn't keep Tiryns from being destroyed around 1200 B.C. Later Greeks thought that only the giants known as Cyclopes could have hefted the 14-ton red limestone blocks into place for the walls that archaeologists still call "cyclopean." Even today, Tiryns's walls stand more than 30 feet high; originally, they were twice as tall—and as much as 57 feet thick. The citadel is crowned by the palace, whose *megaron* (**great hall**) has a well-preserved circular hearth and the base of a throne. This room would have been gaily decorated with frescoes (the surviving frescoes are now in the National Archaeological Museum in Athens). The site is officially open daily, 8am to 7pm in the summer, 8am to 5pm in the winter. Admission is 500Dr ($1.70). Visitors without cars can reach Tiryns from Nafplion by taxi (expect to pay about $20 for a 1-hour round-trip) or the frequent (about every half-hour) Nafplion-Argos-Nafplion bus (about $2; tell the driver you want to get off at Tiryns).

NEMEA   Nemea is signposted on the both the old and new highways from Corinth into the Peloponnese. Throughout antiquity, panhellenic games were held every 4 years at Olympia and Delphi and every 2 years at Isthmia (near Corinth) and Nemea, in a gentle valley in the eastern foothills of the Arcadian mountains. Thanks to the Society for the Revival of the Nemean Games, games were held again at Nemea on June 1, 1996, and are scheduled to be held again on June 5 and 6, 2000. The stadium you visit here is not only the place where athletes once contended, but the site of the new Nemean Games.

The **Nemea Museum,** set on an uncharacteristically Greek green lawn, is one of the most charming small museums in Greece, with helpful labels in English. When you're in the museum, be sure to peer out one of the large picture windows that overlook the shaded ancient site where the coins, vases, athletic gear, and architectural fragments on display were found. A raised stone path tactfully suggests the route from the museum to the site. It passes a carefully preserved early Christian **tomb** and skirts a large Christian **basilica** and Hellenistic bath before arriving at the **Temple of Zeus,** where 3 of the 32 original Doric columns still stand.

The stadium is signposted across the road from the site. Athletes would have stripped down in the locker room, whose foundations are visible just outside the stadium, and then oiled their bodies with olive oil before sprinting into the stadium through the vaulted tunnel. In the stadium, spectators sprawled on earthen benches carved out of the hillside and watched the athletes take their places at the well-preserved stone starting line.

The site is open year-round, Tuesday to Sunday 8:30am to 3pm. Admission to the museum and the ancient site is 500Dr ($1.70), plus another 500Dr ($1.70) for the stadium.

Mycenae

Greek legend and the poet Homer tell us that King Agamemnon of Mycenae was the most powerful leader in Greece at the time of the Trojan War. In about 1250 B.C., Homer says, Agamemnon led the Greeks from Mycenae to Troy, where they fought for 10 years to reclaim fair Helen, the wife of Agamemnon's brother Menelaus, from the Trojan prince Paris. The German archaeologist Heinrich Schliemann, who found and excavated Troy, began to excavate at Mycenae in 1874. Did Schliemann's excavations here prove that what Homer wrote was based on an actual event, not myth and

There's almost no shade at Mycenae, where the terrain is alternately rough and slippery. Be sure to wear a hat, sunscreen, and good shoes.

---

legend? Scholars are suspicious, although most admit that Mycenae could have been built to order from Homer's descriptions of Mycenaean palaces.

Essentials

GETTING THERE   By Bus   Buses run frequently from Athens's **Stathmos Leoforia Peloponnisou,** 100 Odos Kifissou (☎ **01/513-4100**), to Corinth, Argos, and Nafplion. Allow 3 to 4 hours. From any of those places, allow an hour for the trip to Mycenae.

By Car   Mycenae is 71 miles southwest of Athens and 31 miles south of Corinth. From Corinth, take the old Corinth–Argos highway south for about 30 miles, and then take the left turn to Mycenae, which is about 5 miles down the road. From Nafplion, take the road out of town toward Argos. When you reach the Corinth–Argos highway, turn right and then, after about 10 miles, right again at the sign for Mycenae. If you're going to Nafplion when you leave Mycenae, try the pleasant back road that runs through villages and rich farmland. You'll see the sign for Nafplion on your left shortly after you leave Mycenae.

FAST FACTS   The telephone **area code** for the modern village of Mycenae is **0751.** You can buy stamps and change money at the mobile **post office** at the ancient site weekdays 8am to 2pm. This office is sometimes open on weekends and after 2pm, but don't count on it.

Exploring Ancient Mycenae

The Citadel & the Treasury of Atreus. No phone. Admission 1,200Dr ($4). Summer, Mon–Fri 8am–7:30pm, Sat–Sun 8am–3pm; winter, Mon–Fri 8am–5pm, Sat–Sun 8:30am–3pm.

Just as when you visit the Acropolis in Athens, when you walk uphill to Mycenae, you begin to get an idea of why people settled here as long ago as 5000 B.C. Mycenae straddles a low bluff between two protecting mountains and is a superb natural citadel overlooking one of the richest plains in Greece. By the time of the classical era, almost all memory of the Mycenaeans had been lost, and Greeks speculated that places like Mycenae and Tiryns had been built by the Cyclopes. Only such enormous giants, people reasoned, could have moved the huge rocks used to build the ancient citadels' defense walls.

You enter Mycenae through just such a wall, passing under the massive **Lion Gate,** whose two lions probably symbolized Mycenae's strength. The door itself (missing, like the lions' heads) probably was made of wood, covered with bronze for additional protection; cuttings for the door jambs and pivots are clearly visible in the lintel. Soldiers stationed in the round **tower** on your right would have shot arrows down at any attackers who tried to storm the citadel.

One of the most famous spots at Mycenae is immediately ahead of the Lion Gate—the so-called **Grave Circle A,** where Schliemann found the gold jewelry now on display at the National Archaeological Museum in Athens. When Schliemann opened the tombs and found some 30 pounds of gold here, including several solid-gold face masks, he concluded he had found the grave of Agamemnon himself. However, recent scholars have concluded that Schliemann was wrong, and that the kings buried here died long before Agamemnon was born.

From the grave circle, head uphill past the low remains of a number of houses. Mycenae was not merely a palace, but a small village, with administrative buildings and homes on the slopes below the palace. The **palace** had reception rooms, bed-rooms, a throne room, and a large *megaron* (ceremonial hall). You can see the imprint of the four columns that held up the roof in the megaron, as well as the outline of a circular altar on the floor.

If you're not claustrophobic, head to the northeast corner of the citadel and climb down the flight of stairs to have a look at Mycenae's enormous **cistern.** (You may find someone here selling candles, but it's a good idea to bring your own flashlight.) Along with Mycenae's great walls, this cistern, which held a water supply channeled from a spring 500 yards away, helped to make the citadel impregnable for several centuries.

There's one more thing to see before you leave Mycenae. The massive tomb known as the **Treasury of Atreus** is the largest of the *tholos* tombs found here. You'll see signs for the Treasury of Atreus on your right as you head down the modern road away from Mycenae. The Treasury of Atreus may have been built around 1300 B.C., at about the same time as the Lion Gate, in the last century of Mycenae's real greatness. The enor-mous tomb, with its 118-ton lintel, is 43 feet high and 47 feet wide. To build the tomb, workers first cut the 115-foot-long passageway into the hill and faced it with stone blocks. Then the *tholos* chamber itself was built, by placing slightly overlapping courses of stone one on top of the other until a capstone could close the final course. As you look up toward the ceiling of the tomb, you'll see why these are called "beehive tombs." Once your eyes get accustomed to the poor light, you can make out the bronze nails that once held hundreds of bronze rosettes in place in the ceiling. This tomb was robbed even in antiquity, so we'll never know what it contained, although the contents of Grave Circle A give an idea of what riches must have been here. If this was the family vault of Atreus, it's entirely possible that Agamemnon himself was buried here.

Where to Stay

La Belle Helene. Mycenae, 212 00 Argolis. ☎ **0751/76-225.** 8 units (none with bath-room). 18,000–21,000Dr ($60–$70) double. Rates include breakfast. Off-season discounts sometimes available. DC, V. On the main road to Mycenae, on the left as you approach the site.

The real reason to stay here is to add your name to those of Schliemann and other luminaries in the guest book. Tradition aside, this small hotel is usually quiet, and the simple rooms are clean and comfortable. If you stay here, be sure to drive or walk up to the ancient site at night, especially if it's a full moon.

La Petite Planete. Mycenae, 212 00 Argolis. ☎ **0751/76-240.** 30 units. TEL. 22,500Dr ($75) double. Rates include breakfast. Off-season discounts sometimes available. AE, V. On the main road to Mycenae, on the left as you approach the site.

The bright, good-sized bedrooms would make this a nice place to stay even without its swimming pool, which is irresistible after a hot day's trek around Mycenae. We've usually found it quieter here than at La Belle Helene, and friends who stayed here recently praised the restaurant and enjoyed the view over the hills from their window.

Where to Dine

Most of the restaurants specialize in serving set-price meals to groups. If you eat at one of the big, impersonal roadside restaurants, you're likely to be served a bland, luke-warm "European-style" meal of overcooked roast veal, underripe tomatoes, and, even in summer, canned vegetables. You'll have better luck at the smaller restaurants at the hotels listed above. It's sometimes possible to avoid tour groups at the **Achilleus,** Main Street (☎ **0751/76-027**), where you can eat lunch or dinner for around $15.

EPIDAUROS

Epidauros, dedicated to the healing god Asclepios, was one of the most famous shrines in ancient Greece. Greeks came to the shrine of Asclepios in antiquity as they go to the shrine of the Virgin on the island of Tinos today, to give thanks for good health and in hopes of finding cures for their ailments. While at Epidauros, patients and their families could "take the waters" at any one of a number of healing springs and in the superb baths. Visitors could also take in a performance in the theater, just as you can today.

Essentials

GETTING THERE   By Bus   Two buses a day run from the **Stathmos Leoforia Peloponnisou,** 100 Odos Kifissou, Athens (☎ **01/513-4100**). The trip takes about 3 hours. There are three buses a day to Epidauros from the Nafplion bus station, off Plateia Kapodistrias (☎ **0752/27-323**), with extra buses when there are performances at the Theater of Epidauros. The trip takes about an hour.

By Car   Epidauros is 39 miles south of Corinth and 20 miles east of Nafplion. If you're coming from Athens or Corinth, turn left at the sign for Epidauros immediately after the Corinth Canal and take the coast road to the Theatro (ancient theater), not to Nea Epidauvos or Palaia Epidauros. From Nafplion, follow the signs for Epidauros. If you drive to Epidauros from Nafplion for a performance, be alert; the road will be clogged with tour buses and other tourists who are driving the road for the first time.

THEATER PERFORMANCES   There are usually performances at the ancient theater on Saturday and Sunday June to September. Many are given by the National Theater of Greece, some by foreign companies. For information and ticket prices, contact the **Athens Festival Office,** 4 Odos Stadiou (☎ **01/322-1459**). Most of the travel agencies in Nafplion sell tickets, as does the theater itself, from 5pm on the day of a performance. The performance starts around 9pm. The ancient tragedies are usually performed in classical or modern Greek; programs (1,000Dr/$3.35) usually have a full translation or a full synopsis of the play. The excellent Odyssey bookstore on Syntagma Square in Nafplion often has English translations of the plays being performed at Epidauros.

A SPECIAL EVENT   Beginning in 1995, the Society of the Friends of Music have sponsored the **Little Epidauros Music Festival** during the last two weekends of July at the recently restored 4th-century theater at Palea Epidaurus, 7 kilometers from Epidaurus. Check with the Greek National Tourist Office or the **Municipality of Palea Epidauros** (☎ **0753/41-250**) for the schedule of performances. The **Athens Concert Hall,** the Megaron Musikis (☎ **01/728-2333**), also sometimes has information. In 1998, a number of poetry readings were also held in July at the Little Epidauros theater, which seats 4,000, and there are plans to continue this in future summers.

Exploring the Ancient Site

The **excavation museum** at the entrance to the site helps put some flesh on the bones of the confusing remains of the Sanctuary of Asclepios. The museum has an extensive collection of architectural fragments from the sanctuary, including lovely acanthus flowers from the mysterious *tholos,* which you'll see when you visit the site. Also on view are an impressive number of votive offerings that pilgrims dedicated: The terracotta body parts show precisely what part of the anatomy was cured. The display of surgical implements will send you away grateful that you didn't have to go under the knife here, although hundreds of inscriptions record the gratitude of satisfied patients.

It's pleasant to wander through the shady **Sanctuary of Asclepios,** but it's not at all easy to decipher the scant remains. The Asklepion had accommodations for visitors, several large bathhouses, civic buildings, a stadium and gymnasium, and several temples and shrines. The remains are so meager that you might have to take this on faith. Try to find the round *tholos,* which you'll pass about halfway into the sanctuary. The famous 4th century B.C. architect Polykleitos, who built similar round buildings at Olympia and Delphi, was the designer here. If you wonder why the inner foundations of the *tholos* are so convoluted and labyrinthine, you're in good company—scholars still aren't sure what went on here, although some suspect that Asclepios's healing serpents lived in the labyrinth.

The museum and archaeological site are open in summer, weekdays 8am to 7pm and Saturday and Sunday 8:30am to 3:15pm; in winter, weekdays 8am to 5pm and Saturday and Sunday 8:30am to 3:15pm. Admission (also covering the theater; see below) is 1,500Dr ($5). There are several kiosks selling snacks and cold drinks near the ticket booth.

The Theater

If you found the remains of the ancient sanctuary a bit of a letdown, don't worry—the **Theater of Epidauros** is one of the most impressive sights in Greece. Probably built in the 4th century B.C., possibly by Polykleitos, the architect of the *tholos,* the theater seats some 14,000 spectators. Unlike so many ancient buildings, and almost everything at the Sanctuary of Asclepios, the theater was not pillaged for building blocks in antiquity. As a result, it's astonishingly well preserved; restorations have been minimal and tactful.

If you climb to the top, you can look down over the seats, divided into a lower section of 34 rows and an upper section with 21 rows. The upper seats were added when the original theater was enlarged in the 2nd century B.C. The theater's acoustics are famous; you'll almost certainly see someone demonstrating that a whisper can be heard all the way from the round orchestra to the topmost row of seats. Just as the stadium at Olympia brings out the sprinter in many visitors, the theater at Epidauros tempts many to step center stage and recite poetry, declaim the opening of the Gettysburg Address, or burst into song. It's always a magical moment when a performance begins, as the sun sinks behind the orchestra and the first actor steps onto the stage.

Admission to the museum and archaeological site (see above) includes the theater; they keep the same hours.

Where to Stay & Dine

Epidauros Xenia Hotel. Ligourio, Nafplias, Peloponnese. ☎ **0753/22-005.** 26 units (12 with bathroom). TEL. 22,250Dr ($75) double. Rates include breakfast. Off-season discounts sometimes available. No credit cards.

The best place to stay overnight at Epidauros is here, at the site itself. Once everyone leaves, this is a lovely, quiet spot, in a pine grove beside the ancient site. The bungalow-like units (which could use some sprucing up and redecoration) go quickly, so reserve well in advance if you plan to be here the night of a performance. The restaurant serves bland but acceptable food.

OLYMPIA

With its shady groves of pine, olive, and oak trees, the considerable remains of two temples, and the stadium where the first Olympic races were run in 776 B.C., Olympia is the most beautiful major site in the Peloponnese. When you realize that the archaeological museum is one of the finest in Greece, you'll see why you can easily spend a full day or more here. The straggling modern village of Olympia (confusingly known as Ancient Olympia) is bisected by its one main street, Leoforos Kondili. The town has the usual assortment of tourist shops as well as more than a dozen hotels and restaurants.

The ancient site of Olympia lies a 15-minute walk south of the modern village, but if you have a car, you might as well drive; the road teems with tour buses, and the walk is less than relaxing.

Essentials

GETTING THERE   By Train   Several trains a day run from Athens to Pirgos, where you change to the train for Olympia. Information on schedules and fares is available from the **Stathmos Peloponnisou (Railroad Station for the Peloponnese)** in Athens (☎ **01/513-1601**).

By Bus   Three buses a day run to Olympia from the Stathmos Leoforia Peloponnisou, 100 Odos Kifissou, Athens (☎ **01/513-4110**). There are also frequent buses from Patras to Pirgos, with connecting service to Olympia. In Patras, **KTEL** buses leave from the intersection of Zaimi and Othonos streets (☎ **061/273-694**).

By Car   Olympia is at least a 6-hour drive (199 miles) from Athens, whether you take the coast road that links Athens to Corinth, Patras, and Olympia or head inland to Tripolis and Olympia on the new Corinth–Tripolis road. Heavy traffic in Patras (99 miles south) means that the drive from Patras to Olympia can easily take 2 hours.

VISITOR INFORMATION   The office of the Greek National Tourist Organization (EOT) is on the way to the ancient site near the south end of Leoforos Kondili, the main street (☎ **0624/23-100** or 0624/23-125). It's usually open daily, 9am to 10pm in the summer and 11am to 6pm in the winter.

FAST FACTS   The telephone **area code** for Olympia is **0624.** The **OTE telephone and telegraph** office on Odos Praxitelous is open weekdays 7:30am to 10pm. The **train station** is at the north end of town, one street off Leoforos Kondili. You can call ☎ **0624/22-580** for a taxi.

The Museums & the Ancient Site

Archaeological Museum. Admission 1,200Dr ($4). Summer, Mon noon–6pm, Tues–Sat 8am–5pm; winter, Mon noon–6pm, Tues–Sat 11am–5pm. The museum is directly across the road from the Ancient Site (see below).

Even though you'll be eager to see the ancient site, it's a good idea to begin your visit with the museum, whose collection makes clear Olympia's astonishing wealth and importance in antiquity. Every victorious city and almost every victorious athlete dedicated a bronze or marble statue here. Nothing but the best was good enough for Olympia, and many of the superb works of art found since excavations began here more than 150 years ago are on view in the museum. Most of the exhibits are in galleries on either side of the main entrance and follow a chronological sequence, from severe Neolithic vases to baroque Roman imperial statues. The museum's superstars are in the central galleries directly ahead of the entrance.

The monumental images from the **Temple of Zeus** are probably the finest surviving examples of archaic Greek sculpture. The sculpture from the west pediment shows the battle of the Lapiths and Centaurs raging around the magisterial figure of Apollo. On the east pediment, Zeus oversees the chariot race between Oinomaos, king of Pisa, and Pelops, the legendary figure who wooed and won Oinomaos' daughter by the unsporting expedient of loosening his opponent's chariot pins. On either end of the room, sculptured metopes show scenes from the labors of Hercules, including the one he performed at Olympia: cleaning the Augean stables.

Just beyond the sculpture from the Temple of Zeus are the 5th century B.C. **winged victory** done by the artist Paionios and the 4th century B.C. figure of Hermes and the infant Dionysios known as the *Hermes of Praxiteles.* The Hermes has a room to itself—or would, if tourists didn't make a beeline to admire Hermes smiling with amused tolerance at his chubby half-brother Dionysios. If you want to impress your companions, mention casually that many scholars think it's not an original work by Praxiteles, but a Roman copy. In addition to several cases of glorious bronze heads of snarling griffins and the lovely terra-cotta of a resolute Zeus carrying off the youthful Ganymede, the museum has a good deal of **athletic paraphernalia** from the ancient games. You'll see stone and bronze weights used for balance by long jumpers, bronze and stone discuses, and even an enormous stone with an inscription boasting that a weight lifter raised it over his head with only one hand.

Before you leave the museum, have a look at the two excellent **site models** just inside the main entrance. As the models make clear, a low wall divided ancient Olympia into two distinct parts: the *Altis,* or religious sanctuary, containing temples and shrines, and the civic area, with athletic and municipal buildings. Between festivals, Olympia was crowded only with its thousands of statues. Every 4 years, during the games, so many people thronged here that it was said by the time the games began, not even one more spectator could have wedged himself into the stadium. So if the site is crowded when you visit, just remember it would have been much worse in antiquity.

The Ancient Site. Admission 1,200Dr ($4). Summer, Mon–Fri 7:30am–7pm, Sat–Sun 8:30am–3pm; winter, Mon–Fri 8am–5pm, Sat–Sun 8:30am–3pm.

Olympia's setting is magical—pine trees shade the little valley, dominated by the conical Hill of Kronos, that lies between the Alphios and Kladeos rivers. The handsome temples and the famous stadium are not at once apparent as you enter the site. Immediately to the left are the unimpressive low walls that are all that remain of the **Roman baths** where athletes and spectators could enjoy hot and cold plunge baths. The considerably more impressive remains with the slender columns on your right mark the **gymnasium** and **palestra,** where athletes practiced their footracing and boxing skills. The enormous gymnasium had one roofed track, precisely twice the length of the stadium, where athletes could practice in bad weather. Also on the right are the fairly meager remains of a number of structures, including a swimming pool and the large square **Leonidaion,** which served as a hotel for visiting dignitaries until a Roman governor decided it would do nicely as his villa. If you want, you can continue around the outskirts of the site, identifying other civic buildings, but you'll probably want to enter the sanctuary itself.

The **religious sanctuary** is dominated by two shrines: the good-sized Temple of Hera and the massive Temple of Zeus. The **Temple of Hera,** with its three standing columns, is the older of the two, built around 600 B.C. If you look closely, you'll see that the temple's column capitals and drums are not uniform. That's because this temple was originally built with wooden columns, and as each column decayed, it was replaced; inevitably, the new columns had variations. The *Hermes of Praxiteles* was found here, buried under the mud that covered Olympia for so long, caused by the repeated flooding of the rivers. The **Temple of Zeus,** which once had a veritable thicket of 34 stocky Doric columns, was built around 456 B.C. The entire temple—so austere and gray today—was anything but plain in antiquity. Gold, red, and blue paint was everywhere, and inside the temple stood an enormous gold-and-ivory statue of Zeus seated on an ivory-and-ebony throne. The statue was so ornate that it was considered one of the Seven Wonders of the Ancient World—and so large that people joked that if Zeus stood up, his head would go through the temple's roof. In fact, the antiquarian Philo of Byzantium suggested that Zeus had created elephants simply so that the sculptor Phidias would have the ivory to make his statue.

Not only do we know that Phidias made the 42-foot-tall statue, we know where he made it: The **Workshop of Phidias** was on the site of the well-preserved brick building clearly visible west of the temple just outside the sanctuary. How do we know

Olympic Traditions

Ancient tradition makes it clear that the Olympic games began here in 776 B.C. and ended in A.D. 395, but is less clear on why they were held every 4 years. According to one legend, Herakles (Hercules) initiated the games to celebrate completing his 12 labors, one of which took place nearby when the hero diverted the Alphios River to clean the fetid stables that King Augeas had neglected for more than a decade. The stables clean, Herakles paced off the stadium and then ran its entire length—600 Olympic feet (192.27 meters)—without having to take a single breath.

that this was Phidias' workshop? Because a cup with "I belong to Phidias" on it and artists' tools were found here. Between the Temples of Zeus and Hera you can make out the low foundations of a round building: This is all that remains of the shrine that Philip of Macedon, never modest, built here to pat himself on the back after conquering Greece in 338 B.C. Beyond the two temples, built up against the Hill of Kronos itself, are the curved remains of a once-elegant **Roman fountain** and the foundations of 11 **treasuries** where Greek cities stored votive offerings and money. In front of the treasuries are the low bases of a series of bronze statues of Zeus dedicated not by victorious athletes but by those caught cheating in the stadium. The statues would have been the last thing competitors saw before they ran through the vaulted tunnel into the stadium.

Museum of the Olympic Games. Admission 500Dr ($1.70). Mon–Sat 8am–3:30pm; Sun and holidays 9am–2:30pm.

When you head back to town, try to set aside half an hour or so to visit the Museum of the Olympic Games. Not many tourists come here, and the guards are often glad to show visitors around. Displays include victors' medals, commemorative stamps, and photos of winning athletes, such as former King Constantine of Greece and the great African-American athlete Jesse Owens. There's also a photo of the bust of the founder of the modern Olympics, Baron de Coubertin. (The bust itself stands just off the main road east of the ancient site and marks the spot where de Coubertin's heart is buried.)

Where to Stay

Olympia has more than 20 hotels, which means you can almost always find a room, although if you arrive without a reservation in July or August, you might not get your first choice. In the winter, many hotels are closed.

Hotel Europa. 270 65 Ancient Olympia, Peloponnese. ☎ **800/528-1234,** 0624/22-650, or 0624/22-700. Fax 0624/23-166. 80 units. A/C TV TEL. 33,000Dr ($110) double. Rates include breakfast. AE, DC, MC, V.

The Europa is clearly the best hotel in town—and one of the best in the entire Peloponnese. Part of the Best Western chain, it's a few minutes' drive out of town on a hill overlooking both the modern village and the ancient site. Most of the bedrooms overlook a large pool and garden, and several have views of the ancient site. The bedrooms are large, with colorful rugs, extra-firm mattresses, hair dryers, and sliding glass doors opening onto generous balconies.

Hotel Neda. Odos Praxiteles, 270 65 Ancient Olympia, Peloponnese. ☎ **0624/22-563.** Fax 0624/22-206. 43 units. TEL. 22,500Dr ($75.70) double. AE, V.

With a pleasant rooftop cafe, a comfortable lobby, a serviceable restaurant, and a distinctive red-and-white facade, the Neda offers good value. The double rooms, many decorated in shades of pink and rose, are large, with colorful shaggy flokakia rugs on

For a break from Olympia's tourist-oriented commerce, seek out Antonios Kosmopoulos' **Galerie Orphee** bookstore on Leoforos Kondili (☎ **0624/23-555**). With its extensive range of cassettes and CDs of Greek music and frequent displays of contemporary art, it makes a pleasant contrast to Olympia's other shops, which have all too many T-shirts, museum reproductions, and machine-made rugs and embroideries sold as "genuine handmade crafts."

---

the floor and good bedside reading lamps. Some of the double rooms have double beds, but most have twins, so specify which you want. Each room has a good-sized balcony, and the bathrooms are better than those usually found in hotels in this price category (thanks to the presence of shower curtains, which help you to avoid spraying the entire room). The bedrooms here are usually quieter than those at hotels on the main street.

Hotel Praxiteles. 7 Odos Spiliopoulou, 270 65 Ancient Olympia, Peloponnese. ☎ **0624/22-592.** 10 units. 9,000Dr ($30) double. AE, EURO, V.

Just one street back from Olympia's main street, Odos Spiliopoulou has a nice neighborhood feel and is the best bargain in town—if you don't mind a no-frills approach. (Someone may, or may not, always be on duty at the front desk and there's neither air-conditioning nor central heating.) Although the bedrooms are small and spare, with narrow beds, the front rooms have balconies. If you want to avoid the sounds of conversation from the hotel's excellent restaurant on the sidewalk below the balconies, ask for a room at the back (and hope that the neighborhood dogs don't bark too much).

Where to Dine

There are almost as many restaurants as hotels in Olympia. The ones on and just off the main street with large signs in English and German tend to have indifferent food and service, although it's possible to get good snacks of yogurt or *tiropites* (cheese pies) in most of the cafes.

Taverna Ambrosia. Behind the train station. ☎ **0624/23-414.** Main courses 1,500–3,600Dr ($5–$12). AE, MC, V. Daily 7–11pm and some weekends noon–4pm. GREEK.

This large restaurant with a pleasant outside veranda continues to attract locals, although it does a brisk business with tour groups. You'll find the usual grilled chops and souvlakia here, and the vegetable dishes are unusually good, as is the lamb stew with lots of garlic and oregano.

Taverna Kladeos. Behind the train station. ☎ **0624/23-322.** Main courses 1,500–3,600Dr ($5–$12). No credit cards. Daily 7–11pm. GREEK.

The charming Kladeos, with the best food in town, is at the end of the little paved road that runs steeply downhill past the Ambrosia restaurant. You may not be the only foreigner, but you'll probably find lots of locals here. In good weather, tables are set up under canvas awnings and roofs made of rushes. The menu changes according to what's in season. The lightly grilled green peppers, zucchini, and eggplant are especially delicious. The house wine, a light rosé, is heavenly. If you want to buy a bottle to take with you, give your empty water bottle to your waiter and ask him to fill it with *krasi* (wine).

Taverna Praxiteles. In the Hotel Praxiteles, 7 Odos Spiliopoulou. ☎ **0624/23-570** or 0624/22-592. Main courses 900–3,000 ($3–$10). No credit cards. Daily usually noon–2pm and 7pm–midnight. GREEK.

The reputation of the Hotel Praxiteles's excellent and reasonably priced restaurant has spread rapidly. It's packed almost every evening, first with foreigners eating unfashionably early, then with locals, who start showing up around 10pm. Although the entrées are very good—especially the rabbit stew with onions (*stifado*)—it's easy to make a meal of the delicious and varied appetizers. A sampling of mezedes costs about 1,500Dr ($5) and may include octopus, eggplant salad, taramosalata and Russian salad, meatballs stuffed with zucchini, fried cheese, and a handful of olives. In good weather, tables are outside on the sidewalk; the rest of the year, meals are in the pine-paneled dining room.

3 The Cyclades

When most people think of the "Isles of Greece," they're thinking of the Cyclades, the rugged (even barren) chain of Aegean islands whose villages of dazzling white houses look from a distance like so many sugar cubes. The Cyclades got their name from the ancient Greek word meaning "to circle," or surround, because the island chain encircles the sacred island of Delos. Today, especially in the summer, it's the visitors who circle these islands, taking advantage of the swift island boats and hydrofoils that link them.

If you were to describe the best-known Cycladic islands (roughly from north to south), **Tinos** would probably be called the "Lourdes of Greece." Its famous church of the Panagia Evangelistria is Greece's most important pilgrimage destination, especially on the Feast of the Assumption (August 15). **Mykonos'** superior amenities (you can get a margarita as easily as an ouzo) first made it popular in the '60s, and although the Beautiful People might have moved on, Mykonos remains a favorite, although expensive, island—especially in the summer, when reservations are imperative. The crescent of **Santorini (Thira),** with its black sand beaches and blood-red cliffs, is all that remains of the island that was blown apart in antiquity by a volcano that still steams and hisses today. Santorini's exceptional physical beauty, dazzling relics, and elegant restaurants and boutiques cause people to call it "sophisticated." Unfortunately, Santorini's charms draw so many day-trippers from cruise ships that the island almost sinks under the weight of tourists each summer. **Sifnos,** long popular with Athenians, increasingly draws summer visitors to its handsome whitewashed villages, which many consider to have the finest architecture in all the Cyclades. In the spring it's one of the greenest and most fertile of the islands. Finally, some think of **Paros** as the poor man's Mykonos, with excellent windsurfing and a profusion of restaurants and nightspots less pricey than those on its better-known neighbor.

The islands are crowded and expensive in the high season, roughly mid-June to mid-September—and the season seems to get longer every year. If this doesn't appeal to you, visit the Cyclades in the off-season; the best times are spring (mid-April to early June) or fall (mid-September to October). Note that while the restaurant you'd hoped to eat in may be closed, and some of the chic shops shuttered, you'll be able to enjoy the islands without feeling that you're surrounded by other visitors. Should you visit in winter, keep in mind that many island hotels have minimal heating; check ahead of time.

On most of these islands, the capital town has the name of the island itself. It is also sometimes called "Hora," or "Chora," a term meaning "the place" that's commonly used for the most important regional town. The capital of Paros, Parikia, is also called Hora, as is Apollonia, the capital of Sifnos.

One note of explanation: We've dropped our coverage of the island of Ios. Alas, in recent years some visitors have transformed Ios from a lively "party island" into an

Aegean Animal House, complete with food fights in the tavernas. Let's hope that things calm down on the once-lovely island so that we can again recommend visiting.

Only in the Cyclades

Visiting the Panagia Evangelistria   Often called the "Lourdes of Greece," the church of Our Lady of Good Tidings on Tinos is one of the most important religious destinations in Greece. The faithful believe that the church's icon of the Virgin works miracles.

Taking in the View from the Rim of Santorini's Caldera   In a region brimming with spectacular vistas, this is the most stunning. More than 3,500 years ago a volcano erupted here, destroying much of the island and leaving today's crescent of land around the volcano's deep *caldera* (crater). Many scholars believe that legends of Santorini's destruction inspired the legend of the lost continent of Atlantis.

Sailing, Sailing, Over the Deep Blue Sea   Whether on a cruise ship, island ferry, or fisherman's caïque, lounging on deck and watching the Cycladic islands appear on the horizon is one of life's greatest pleasures.

GETTING TO THE CYCLADES

BY AIR   Olympic Airways (☎ **01/926-7593** or 01/966-6666 in Athens) has frequent daily service from Athens to Mykonos, Paros, and Santorini; there's service several times a week from Mykonos or Santorini to Thessaloniki, Iraklio, Crete, and Rhodes. In addition, an increasing number of charter flights from all over Europe fly into the various islands.

BY SEA   Ferries leave daily from Athens's main port of Piraeus and from Rafina, the port east of Athens; contact the Piraeus Port Authority (☎ **01/451-1310** or 01/451-1311) or the Rafina Port Police (☎ **0294/22-300**) for schedules.

It can take an hour for the 17-mile bus ride from Athens to Rafina (the most convenient port for Tinos, Mykonos, and sometimes Paros), but you save about an hour of sailing time and about 20% on the fare. Buses leave every 30 minutes 6am to 10pm from 29 Mavromateon St. (☎ **01/821-0872**), near Areos Park north of the National Archaeological Museum (indicated on most city maps). **Ilio Lines** (☎ **01/422-4772** in Athens or 0294/22-888 in Rafina) offers regular hydrofoil service from Rafina to a number of destinations.

In the summer there's regular ferry service to Iraklio, Crete from Piraeus, the port of Athens. There are also ferry and hydrofoil connections three to four times a week in the summer between Paros and Samos, Ikaria, Karpathos, and Rhodes; several times a week between Mykonos and Kos and Rhodes; twice a week between Mykonos and Skyros, Skiathos, and Thessaloniki; and two or three times a week between Syros and the Dodecanese.

GETTING AROUND THE CYCLADES

There's frequent ferry service between most of the islands. Schedules can be erratic, and service diminishes suddenly at the end of the season. Smaller excursion vessels are easily affected by high winds. To further complicate matters, a line will sometimes authorize only one agent to sell tickets or limit the number of tickets available to an agency, giving other agents little incentive to tout its service. You may want to visit several agents or inquire at the port authority. (For specifics, see "Arriving/Departing" under "Essentials" for each island.)

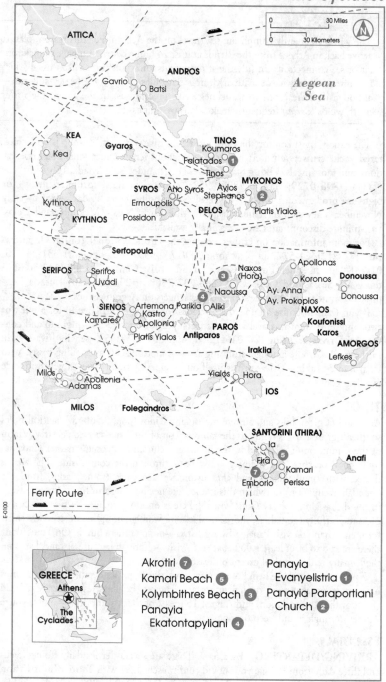

The Cyclades

ATTICA

Aegean Sea

ANDROS
Gavrio
Batsi

KEA
Kea
Gyaros

TINOS
Koumaros
Faiatados 1
Tinos

SYROS
Ano Syros
Ermoupolis
Possidon

MYKONOS
Ayios Stephanos 2
Platis Yialos

DELOS

Kythnos
KYTHNOS

Serfopoula

SERIFOS
Serifos
Livadi

Naxos (Hora) 3
Naoussa 4
Aliki

Apollonas
Koronos

Donoussa
Donoussa

SIFNOS
Artemona Parikia
Kastro
Apollonia
Kamares
Platis Yialos

Antiparos

PAROS

Ay. Anna
Ay. Prokopios

NAXOS

Koufonissi
Karos

AMORGOS
Lefkes

Iraklia

Milos
Apollonia
Adamas

MILOS

Yialos Hora

IOS

Folegandros

SANTORINI (THIRA)
Ia
Fira 5
Emborio 7
Kamari
Perissa

Anafi

Ferry Route

0 — 30 Miles
0 — 30 Kilometers

E-0100

GREECE
Athens
The Cyclades

Akrotiri 7
Kamari Beach 5
Kolymbithres Beach 3
Panayia Ekatontapyliani 4

Panayia Evanyelistria 1
Panayia Paraportiani Church 2

Traveler's Tip

The winds frequently complicate sea travel on the Aegean. For this reason, plan to arrive back in Athens from the islands at least 24 hours before you have to make any air or sea connections. In July the strong winds known as the *meltemi* usually kick up, often playing havoc with hydrofoil schedules. The larger ferries still run—although if you're prone to seasickness, take precautions. In the winter the strong north winds (*vorias*) frequently make sea travel impossible.

The easiest, most comfortable, and most expensive way to island-hop is on a **chartered yacht cruise;** you don't have to worry about ferry connections, hotel reservations, and most meals. **Viking Star Cruises,** 1 Artemidos St., Glyfada, 166 74 Athens (☎ **01/898-0729;** fax 01/894-0952; e-mail: vikings@forum.ars.net.gr or bjgh44a@prodigy.com) offers 7-day cruises beginning every Friday, April to early November. They stop on Tinos, Ios, Santorini, Paros, Naxos, Mykonos, and Delos. Last-minute discount fares are occasionally available.

For more information on cruises, contact the **Greek National Tourist Organization** (☎ **212/421-5777** in New York; 020/7734-5997 in London; 01/331-0437 or 01/331-0561 in Athens) or the **Greek Island Cruise Center** (☎ **800/342-3030** in the U.S.). **Sea Cloud Cruises** (☎ **888/732-2568** or 201/884-0407), uses a four-masted private yacht that take up to 60 passengers on Aegean cruises.

If you want to cruise around the Cyclades (or elsewhere in Greece) for a week or two, and don't want to travel with strangers, put together your own group and contact **Ari Drivas Yachting** (☎ **01/411-3194;** fax 01/411-4459, e-mail: drivasy@ath. forthnet.gr). Choose among a stunning array of motor yachts and sailing vessels with from 2 to 24 cabins. Drivas prides itself on its superbly trained crews, which include excellent cooks.

TINOS

An island of green hills and austere mountains, Tinos (pop. 9,500; 87 nautical miles southeast of Piraeus) is home to the famous icon of the Panagia Evangelistria (Virgin of the Annunciation), housed in the handsome church of the same name. Tinos has some good beaches, and there's good walking through the countryside. The area is dotted with small villages and the distinctive dovecotes (some dating from the Venetian occupation) for which this island, like neighboring Andros, is known. Keep in mind that almost every Greek visiting here is on a pilgrimage. Be sure to act and dress respectfully (no halters, shorts, or slacks for women; no shorts or sleeveless shirts for men) when you visit Panagia Evangelistria—or any other church. On Tinos alone there are said to be at least 1,000 chapels to visit—although because of vandalism and theft, many remain locked except on feast days.

Note: Unless you have firm hotel reservations, don't plan an overnight visit to Tinos on summer weekends or during important religious holidays, especially March 25 (Feast of the Annunciation) and August 15 (Feast of the Assumption)—unless you're willing to rough it and sleep outside.

ESSENTIALS

ARRIVING/DEPARTING   By Boat   There are several ferries daily from Piraeus and three daily from Rafina; you should confirm schedules with **Tourist Information** in Athens (☎ **143**), the **Piraeus Port Authority** (☎ **01/422-6000** or 01/451-1311), or the **Rafina Port Police** (☎ **0294/22-300** or 0294/25-200). **Ilio Lines** (☎ **01/ 422-4772** in Athens or 0294/22-888 in Rafina) runs hydrofoil service from Rafina.

From Tinos, there are connections several times daily with nearby Andros, Mykonos, and Syros, and several daily excursions to Mykonos and Delos from about 12,000Dr ($40).

There are two piers in Tinos harbor, the newer one 600 yards northwest of the main one; be sure to find out from which your ship will depart. The **port authority** can be reached at ☎ **0283/22-348.**

VISITOR INFORMATION   The small tourist information office (☎ **0283/ 22-255**) is near the waterfront at the corner of Kionion and Vlachaki. There are also several helpful travel agents along the waterfront, including **Tinos Mariner** (☎ **0283/ 23-193**), who has information and a good map of the island. The **Nicholas Information Center,** 24 Evangelistria St. (☎ **0283/24-142;** fax 0283/24-049), has information, ferry tickets, and information on renting rooms. It's open 6:30am to midnight. (Evangelistria is the main market street to the left and perpendicular to the port.) **Windmills Travel** (☎ **0283/23-398**), near the new pier, is also a good source of information.

FAST FACTS   The telephone **area code** for Tinos is **0283.** The **banks** are on the waterfront. The **police station** (☎ **0283/22-255**) is signposted on the harbor. The **OTE telephone office** is on Megaloharis Avenue, the main street leading up to the Church of Panagia Evangelistria. It's open Monday through Friday 8am to midnight. The **post office** is at the southeast end of the waterfront.

GETTING AROUND   The **bus station** is at the harbor; check at the KTEL office there for the schedule (which is erratic) and rates. The **taxi stand** is also nearby on the harbor. Several shops on the harborfront rent **mopeds;** rates start at about 5,500Dr ($18) a day. **Nicholas** (☎ **0283/24-142**) and **Moto Mike** (☎ **0283/23-304**) are reliable. Cars can be rented from several harborfront agencies; rates in summer are steep, at about 22,500Dr ($75) a day. Make sure the rate includes full insurance.

EXPLORING THE ISLAND

Each year, the ✪ **Church of Panagia Evangelistria (Our Lady of Good Tidings)** draws thousands of pilgrims seeking the aid of the church's miraculous icon. According to local lore, one night in 1822, a nun named Pelagia dreamed that a miraculous icon was buried nearby. Pelagia led her neighbors to the place she had seen in her dream, and when they began to dig, they discovered the remains of a Byzantine church with the icon. As is the case with many of the most holy icons, the Panagia Evangelistria is believed to be the work of Saint Luke. The massive church—made of marble from the islands of Paros and Tinos, with a distinctive bell tower—was built in 1824 to house the icon.

A broad flight of marble stairs flanked by lovely pebble mosaics leads to the church; inside, hundreds of gold and silver hanging lamps illuminate the holy icon of the Virgin and the gifts—many in gold, silver, and precious jewels—dedicated by the faithful. Even those who do not make a lavish gift customarily light one of the many candles burning inside the church. The pilgrims' devotion is manifest in these gifts—and in the piety of the visitors who crawl on their knees to the church from the dock.

The church is open daily, 8am to 8pm in the summer and noon to 6pm in the winter; the small **museum** (500Dr/$1.70) is usually open Tuesday to Sunday 8:30am to 3pm. To enter the church, men must wear long pants and shirts with sleeves, and women must wear dresses or skirts and blouses with sleeves. If there is a church service while you are here, you will hear the beautiful, resonant chanting that typifies a Greek Orthodox service—but remember that it's not appropriate to explore the church during a service.

On the other hand, the **town** of Tinos, sprawled within eyesight of the inland Venetian fortressof Exomvourgo, is always a pleasant place to explore. There's a lively **flea market** and a great many shops selling religious souvenirs, delicate embroidery, and the special sweet of the island, nougat.

The **Weaving School** on Evangelistrias Street sells handsome hand-loomed fabrics made by its students. Several **ceramics shops** on the waterfront, including Margarita, Bernardo, and Manina, have interesting pottery, jewelry, and copperware at moderate prices. Those interested in contemporary hand-painted icons might ask to be directed to **Maria Vryoni,** off Leoforos Megaloharis, the street from the port to the Panagia Evangelistria. The shop accepts credit cards.

Once you're away from the shops near the harbor, you'll find yourself on quiet residential streets where many of the houses have small gardens—or, at a minimum, some bright geraniums planted in whitewashed metal containers that once held olive oil. The small **Archaeological Museum** (☎ **0283/22-670**) near the Panagia Evangelistria has finds from the Sanctuary of Poseidon at Kionia. It's usually open Tuesday to Sunday 8:30 am to 3pm; admission is 500Dr ($1.70). There's also a **Gallery of Modern Greek Painters** and a **Gallery of Tiniot Artists** near the Panagia Evangelistria.

The famous **Venetian dovecotes** (*peristerionas,* in Greek), many dating from the 17th century, are scattered throughout the island. You can see several, as well as the scattered remains of the **Temple of Poseidon,** by taking the coastal road 1¼ miles west of Tinos to the town of Kionia ("Columns"), a pleasant 30-minute hike past the Hotel Aigli. Another hike, from the village of Xinara, leads 565 meters steeply uphill to the ruins of the **Venetian Fortress of Exomvourgo** (Xombourgo, on some maps). The less energetic may prefer to enjoy some of the island's small villages, such as **Steni** and **Pirgos.**

Tinos has several good **beaches:** The sand beach at Kionia, about 2 miles west of Tinos town, and at Kolimbithra, on the north coast, are especially good. A mile or two east of Tinos town, the beach at Ayios Fokas has a small hotel; hotels are rumored to be in the works for Kionia and Kolimbithria, as well.

There is **bus service** (usually four times a day) from Tinos town to Ayios Fokas and a few miles farther east to the resort of Porto, which has two beaches and several new hotel complexes.

WHERE TO STAY

If you avoid the religious holidays and summer weekends, you'll have no trouble finding a room. People will offer to rent you rooms in their homes, often more politely than elsewhere, at the landing.

✪ **Avra Hotel.** Tinos town, 842 00 Tinos. ☎ **0283/22-242.** 14 units. 15,000Dr ($50) double. Continental breakfast 1,000Dr ($3.35) extra. No credit cards. Turn right from the ferry quay and walk southeast on the waterfront.

This charming century-old neoclassical hotel has simple, spacious, high-ceilinged rooms. Its plant-filled, tiled courtyard is a pleasant place to relax after sightseeing. This is the place to stay in Tinos town if you do not need all the modern conveniences to be happy in a hotel, and don't mind the sometimes noisy bustle of the harbor.

Hotel Eleana. Ierarchon Sq., Tinos town, 842 00 Tinos. ☎ **0283/22-561.** 17 units. 13,500Dr ($45) double. V. Just off the harbor and about 400 yards past the conspicuous Hotel Poseidon.

This excellent value hotel doesn't have harbor views, but the rooms are large, comfortable, and usually quiet.

Tinion. Constantinou Alavanou, off quay, Tinos town, 842 00 Tinos. ☎ **0283/22-261.** 21 units. 15,000Dr ($50) double. MC, V.

If you don't mind not having an elevator and think you'd enjoy sitting on a balcony overlooking the bustling harbor, this is the place to stay. The Tinion has been here since 1925, and has the high-ceilinged rooms, nicely tiled floors, and many of the original solid old furnishings to prove it.

Tinos Beach Hotel. Kionia, 84200 Tinos (4km/2.5 mi. west of Tinos town on the coast road). ☎ **0283/22-626.** Fax 0283/23-153. 180 units. TEL. 30,000Dr ($100) double. Rates include breakfast. AE, DC, MC, V. Usually closed Nov–Mar.

This sprawling beachfront resort hotel with pools, tennis courts, and a restaurant, is a good choice for families (there's a separate childrens' pool). The rooms, all with balconies, are perfectly utilitarian and comfortable, but could use sprucing up.

WHERE TO DINE

Tinos has a number of good restaurants (probably because most of their customers are Greeks). As in most Greek ports, you should (with one exception) avoid harborfront joints; the food is often inferior and expensive, and the service can be rushed.

Lefteris. Harborfront, Tinos town. ☎ **0283/24-213.** Main courses 1000–3,700Dr ($3.35–$12); fish priced daily by the kilo. V. Daily 11am–midnight. GREEK.

This place is an exception to the rule that waterfront restaurants and/or those that cater to tourists (waiters here perform Greek dances and urge diners to join in) are best avoided. Look for a blue sign on the harbor over an arched entrance that leads to a large courtyard decorated with fish plaques. The menu is large and varied; the grilled sea bass, veal *stifado* (stew), and *dolmades* (stuffed grape leaves) in lemon sauce are tasty.

✪ **O Kipos.** Tinos town. ☎ **0283/22-838.** Main courses 900–3,000Dr ($3–$10). No credit cards. Daily noon–midnight. Just off the harbor near the conspicuous Hotel Poseidon. GREEK.

At this small taverna, the cooking is typical down-home Greek, with the usual dishes, including moussaka and souvlakia. You can have a complete meal with good retsina for around 6,000Dr ($20).

Peristerionas. 12 Paksimadi Fraiskou St., Tinos town. ☎ **0283/23-425.** E-mail: tonyk@ mail.otenet.gr. Main courses 2,500–4,000Dr ($8–$13). No credit cards. Daily noon–3pm and 7–11:30pm. Closed in winter. GREEK.

On a small lane uphill behind the Lido Hotel, this restaurant, decorated like one of the island's famous dovecotes, has outdoor tables. You can get good grilled meats and fish here, but also try the delicious fennel pancakes, a house specialty.

Xinari. Plateia Evangelistria, Tinos town. ☎ **0283/23-337.** Reservations recommended. Open 12pm–4pm and 8pm–12am. Closed Oct–Apr. Main courses 2,400–6,000Dr ($8–$20). MC, V. GREEK.

This chic spot serves a combination of traditional dishes with a difference (roast pork—but with plums), nouvelle Greek food (familiar dishes with a less heavy hand pouring out the olive oil), and some Lebanese dishes. Meals aren't cheap, but the food is usually very good and the surroundings charming.

TINOS AFTER DARK

Tinos is not known for its nightlife, but there is a small enclave of music bars off the left (west) side of the port, including **Argonautis,** the **Sibylla Bar,** and **George's Place,** which features Greek dancing. Things usually get going around 10pm.

MYKONOS

If you haven't been to Mykonos (pop. 15,000; 96 nautical miles southeast of Rafina) for a number of years, you'll probably wander around muttering "ruined" when you arrive. Then you'll realize that once you're away from the shops, bars, and restaurants along the harbor, you're pleasantly surprised at how familiar many of the twisting back streets seem. You might even admit that it's not half bad to have such a wide choice of restaurants. If this is your first visit, you'll find lots to enjoy—especially if you avoid July and August, when it seems that every one of the island's 800,000 annual visitors is here.

What makes this small, arid island so popular? At least initially, it was the exceptionally handsome Cycladic architecture—and the fact that many on the poor island were more than eager to rent their houses to visitors, often mainland Greeks who came here to open shops and restaurants. First came the jet-setters, artists, and expatriates (including many sophisticated gay visitors), followed by a curious mixture of wannabes and backpackers. Now, with cruise ships lined up in the harbor all summer and as many as 10 flights each day from Athens, it's easier to say who doesn't come to Mykonos than to define who does. That's why it's *very* important not to arrive here without reservations in the high season, unless you enjoy sleeping outdoors—and don't mind being moved from your sleeping spot by the police, who are not always charmed to find foreigners alfresco.

ESSENTIALS

ARRIVING/DEPARTING　By Air　Olympic Airways has as many as 10 flights daily between Athens and Mykonos. In addition, there is usually one flight daily between Mykonos and Iraklio (Crete), Rhodes, and Santorini, and three flights a week between Mykonos and Ios, Lesvos, and Samos. It's difficult to get a seat on any of these flights, so make reservations early and reconfirm them at the office in Athens (☎ **01/ 961-6161** or 01/966-6666) or Mykonos (☎ **0289/22-490;** 0289/22-237).

By Sea　From Piraeus, **Ventouris Lines** (☎ **01/482-5815**) has departures at least once daily, usually at 8am, with a second on summer afternoons; check schedules in Athens by calling the **Tourist Police** (☎ **171**). From Rafina, **Strintzis Lines** has daily ferry service; schedules can be checked with the **Port Police** (☎ **0294/25-200**). There are daily ferry connections between Mykonos and Andros, Paros, Syros, and Tinos; five to seven trips a week to Ios; four a week to Iraklio, Crete; several a week to Kos and Rhodes; and two a week to Ikaria, Samos, Skiathos, Skyros, and Thessaloniki. **Ilio Lines** (☎ **01/422-4772** in Athens or 0294/22-888 in Rafina) offers daily hydrofoil service to Mykonos from Rafina.

On Myconos, your best bet for getting boat information is to check at individual agents, or to see if either the **tourist police** (☎ **0289/22-482**) at the north end of the harbor, or the **tourist office** (☎ **0289/23-990;** fax 0289/22-229), also on the harbor, has an up-to-date list of sailings.

Check each travel agent's current schedule because most ferry tickets are not interchangeable. **Sea & Sky Travel,** Taxi Square, Mykonos town (Hora) (☎ **0289/ 22-853;** fax 0289/24-753), represents the Strintzis, Ilio, and Agapitos lines, changes money, and offers excursions to Delos. The **Veronis Agency** (☎ **0289/22-687;** fax 0289/23-763), also on the main square, offers information, luggage facilities, and other services.

Hydrofoil service to Crete, Ios, Paros, and Santorini is often irregular. For information, check at the **Port Authority** in Piraeus (☎ **01/451-1311**), Rafina (☎ **0294/ 23-300**), or Mykonos (☎ **0289/22-218**).

VISITOR INFORMATION　The **Mykonos Tourist Office** (☎ **0289/23-990;** fax 0289/22-229) is on the west side of the port near the excursion boats to Delos. Look for a copy of the free *Mykonos Summertime* magazine.

TOWN LAYOUT　Legend has it that the streets of Mykonos town—which locals call Hora—were designed to confuse pirates, so your own confusion will be understandable. As you get off the ferry, you can see the main square south across the harbor beyond the small town beach and a cluster of buildings; we refer to it as **Taxi Square,** although it's officially called Plateia Manto Mavroyennis, after a local heroine. Here you'll find several travel agents, kiosks, snack bars, and of course the town's taxi stand. The map published by **Stamatis Bozinakis** (400Dr/$1.35) is sold at most kiosks and quite decent; the excellent **Mykonos Sky Map** is free at some hotels and shops.

The main street, **Matoyanni,** leads south off Taxi Square behind the church; it's narrow, but you can hardly miss the bars, boutiques, and restaurants. Several "blocks" along it you'll find a "major" cross street, **Kaloyera,** and by turning right, you'll find several of the hotels and restaurants we recommend. If you get lost—and you will— remember that in Mykonos that's part of the fun.

GETTING AROUND   On Foot   One of Hora's greatest assets is the government decree that made the town an architectural landmark and prohibited motorized traffic on its streets. If you don't arrive with your donkey or bicycle, you can walk around town. Much of the rest of the island is served by local buses.

By Bus   Mykonos has one of the best bus systems in the Greek islands; the buses run frequently and on schedule. They cost 200 to 800Dr (70¢ to $2.70) one-way. There are two bus stations in Hora: the **north station,** near the middle of the harbor below the Leto Hotel; and the **south station,** about a 10-minute walk from the harbor, near the Olympic Airways office (follow the helpful blue signs). Schedules are posted, although subject to change. Bus information in English is sometimes available from the **KTEL** office (☎ **0289/23-360**).

By Boat   Weather permitting, excursion boats to **Delos** depart every day at 9am from the west side of the harbor near the tourist office. For more information, see "An Excursion to the Island of Delos," below, or consult a travel agent; guided tours are available. Caïques to the beaches of **Super Paradise, Agrari,** and **Elia** depart from the town harbor every morning, weather permitting. Caïques to **Paradise, Super Paradise, Agrari,** and **Elia** also leave from Plati Yialos every morning, weather permitting. (Caïque service is almost continuous during the high season, when boats also depart from Ornos Bay.)

By Car & Moped   Rental cars and Jeeps are available from travel agents for about 15,000Dr ($50) per day, including full insurance, during the high season, and substantially less at other times if you bargain. Mopeds can be a fun way to get around if you know how to handle one and can negotiate the sometimes-treacherous roads. Mopeds (around 7,600Dr/$25 a day) are available from shops near both bus stations.

Note: If you park in town or in a no-parking area, the police will remove your license plates, and you—not the rental office—will have to find the police station and pay a steep fine to get them back.

By Taxi   Getting a taxi in Hora is easy; walk to Taxi Square, near the statue, and get in line; a notice board gives rates for each destination for both high and low seasons. You can also phone (☎ **0289/22-400,** or 0289/23-700 for late-hours and out-of-town service). You'll be charged the fare from Hora to your pickup point plus the fare to your destination, so before calling, try to find an empty taxi returning to Hora or flag one down along the road.

Fast Facts: Hora

Area Code   The telephone area code for Mykonos is **0289.**

Banks   The Commercial Bank and the National Bank of Greece are on the harbor a couple of blocks west of Taxi Square. Both are open weekdays 8am to

2pm and 6 to 8:30pm. The National Bank is also open Saturday 9am to 12:30pm and 5:30 to 8:30pm, and Sunday 5:30 to 8:30pm, but for currency exchange only. The ATMs usually (but not always) function after hours. Traveler's checks can be cashed at the post office and at many travel agents and hotels, at less than bank rates.

Laundry   The **Ace Laundry** is on Ayios Efthimiou (☎ **0289/28-389**) near the police station. A self-service **launderette** is on Ayion Anaryiron Steet at Scarpa, behind the Church of Paraportiani. Hotel chambermaids often do laundry for a reasonable fee.

Medical Treatment   The **Mykonos Health Center** (☎ **0289/23-994** or 23-996) handles routine medical complaints; serious cases are usually airlifted to the mainland.

Police   The **Tourist Police** office (☎ **0289/22-482**) is on the west side of the port near the ferries to Delos. The **Port Police** office (☎ **0289/22-218**) is on the east side of the harborfront near the post office. The **local police** office (☎ **0289/22-235**) is behind the grammar school.

Post Office   The post office (☎ **0289/22-238**), on the east side of the harbor near the Port Police, is open weekdays 7:30am to 2pm.

Telephones   The **OTE telephone office** (☎ **0289/22-499**), on the east side of the harbor beyond the Hotel Leto, is usually open daily 7:30am to 10pm.

EXPLORING THE ISLAND

Even if you're here for the beaches or to visit the island of Delos, you'll probably want to spend some time exploring Hora and enjoying the twists and turns of the narrow streets—and admiring the harborfront's resident pelican.

The **Archaeological Museum** (☎ **0289/22-325**), near the harbor, has finds from Delos; it's open Monday and Wednesday to Saturday 9am to 3:30pm, Sunday and holidays 10am to 3pm. Admission is 600Dr ($2); free on Sunday. The **Nautical Museum of the Aegean** (☎ **0289/22-700**) across from the park on Enoplon Dinameon St., has just what you'd expect, including some handsome ship models. It's open daily 10:30am to 1pm and 7 to 9pm; admission is 300Dr ($1). The **Museum of Folklore** (☎ **0289/25-591**), in a 19th-century sea captain's mansion near the quay, has examples of local crafts and furnishings and a re-created 19th-century island kitchen. It's usually open Monday to Saturday 4 to 8pm; admission is free.

Hora also has the remains of a small **Venetian Kastro** (fortress) and the island's most famous church, the **Panagia Paraportiani (Our Lady of the Postern Gate),** a thickly whitewashed asymmetrical edifice made up of four small chapels. Beyond the Panagia Paraportiani is the Alefkanda quarter, better known as **Little Venice,** for its cluster of homes built overhanging the sea. Many buildings here have been converted into fashionable bars prized for their sunset views; you can sip a margarita and listen to Mozart most nights at the Montparnasse or Kastro bar (see "Mykonos After Dark," below).

Another nearby watering spot is at the famous **Tria Pigadia (Three Wells).** Local legend says that if a virgin drinks from all three she is sure to find a husband, but it's probably not a good idea to test this hypothesis by drinking the brackish well water. After you visit the Tria Pigadia, you may want to take in the famous **windmills** of Kato Myli and enjoy the views back toward Little Venice.

Mykonos has a lot of shops, mostly selling overpriced souvenirs, clothing, and jewelry. The finest jewelry shop is **Lalaounis,** 14 Polykandrioti St. (☎ **0289/22-444**), associated with the famous Lalaounis museum and shops in Athens. It has superb reproductions of ancient and Byzantine jewelry as well as original designs. If you can't afford Lalaounis, you might have a look at **Delos Dolphins,** Matoyanni at Enoplon Dimameon (☎ **0289/22-765**), which specializes in copies of museum pieces, or **Vildiridis,** 12 Matoyanni St. (☎ **0289/23-245**), which also has designs based on ancient jewelry. **Mykonos Gold,** Ayios Efthimios, in Little Venice (☎ **0289/22-649**), specializes in traditional island designs.

THE BEACHES   If you care who'll be there, take a little time to ask around, because beaches go in and out of favor quickly. Then catch the bus or a caïque to the beach of your choice. If you want a quick swim, the closest beach to Hora is **Megali Ammos (Big Sand),** about a 10-minute walk south of town, and usually crowded. A better but still crowded beach is 2½ miles farther north of Megali Ammos at **Ayios Stephanos,** a major resort center with water sports.

Plati Yialos is another favorite. It's served by bus runs every 15 minutes from 8am to 8pm, then every 30 minutes until midnight during the summer; if Plati Yialos is too crowded, you can catch a caïque there for the more distant beaches of Paradise, Super Paradise, Agrari, and Elia. **Paradise,** the island's most famous nude beach, remains remarkably beautiful, despite the crowds and activity, with especially clear water. Paradise is also easily reached by local bus or taxi.

Super Paradise (Plindri) is accessible only by a very poor road, footpath, or caïque, so it's less crowded. It's predominantly gay and nude, but clothed sunbathing by heterosexuals is tolerated. Farther east across the little peninsula is **Agrari,** a lovely cove sheltered by lush foliage, with a good little taverna.

Elia, a 45-minute caïque ride from Plati Yialos, is one of the island's best and largest beaches. It's usually one of the least crowded, although bus service from the north station will probably soon put an end to that. If it gets too crowded, head back west to Agrari.

The next major beach, **Kalo Livadi (Good Pasture),** a beautiful spot in an idyllic farming valley, is accessible by a scramble over the peninsula east from Elia and by bus from the north station in the summer. There's even a nice restaurant.

The last resort area on the southern coast accessible by bus from the north station is at **Kalafati,** a fishing village that was once the port for the ancient citadel of Mykonos. It's now dominated by the large Aphrodite Beach Hotel complex. Several miles farther east, accessible by a fairly good road from Kalafati, is **Lia,** which has fine sand, clear water, bamboo windbreaks, and a small taverna.

WHERE TO STAY

If you arrive by ferry, you're met by a throng of people hawking rooms, some in small hotels, others in private homes. If you don't have a hotel reservation, one of these rooms may be very welcome. If you're pretty sure that won't suit your needs, be sure you have reserved a room 1 to 3 months in advance of your visit. Many hotels are fully booked all summer by tour groups or regular patrons. The **Mykonos Accommodations Center (MAC),** 46 Odos Matoyanni (☎ **0289/23-160** or 0289/23-408; fax 0289/24-137) or the **Mykonos tourist office** (☎ **0289/22-201**) should be able to advise you. Keep in mind that Mykonos is an easier, more pleasant place to visit in the spring or fall—and off-season hotel rates are sometimes half the quoted high-season rate. The water temperature is cool to cold in spring; warm to cool in fall.

In & Around Hora

✪ **Belvedere Hotel.** Hora, 846 00 Mykonos (Rohari District). ☎ **800/345-8236** or 0289/25-112. Fax 0289/25-126. E-mail: belvedere@myk.forthnet.gr. 47 units. A/C MINIBAR TV TEL. 52,000Dr ($173) double; 81,000Dr ($270) suite. Rates include breakfast. AE, MC, V.

The spiffy new (1998) Belvedere, on the main road into town, has a sauna, Jacuzzi, large pool, and stunning views over the town and harbor, a few minutes' walk away. Rooms are nicely furnished, usually with comfortable chairs, hair dryers, some local decorative touches—and 10 rooms are wired for direct Internet connection. This is the place to stay if you want the amenities of Mykonos's beach resorts, but prefer to be within walking distance of Hora. The in-house Remvi restaurant is excellent (and pricey).

Cavo Tagoo. Hora, 846 00 Mykonos. ☎ **0289/23-692**, 0289/23-693, or 0289/23-694. Fax 0289/24-923. 72 units. A/C TV TEL. 52,500–60,000Dr ($175–$200) double. Rates include buffet breakfast. AE, MC, V. Closed Nov–Mar.

This elegant hotel is hard to resist—its island-style architecture has won awards, and its wooden furniture and local-style weavings are a genuine pleasure. It's only a 10-minute walk to Hora's harbor, although you may find it hard to budge: A pool and a good restaurant are right here. Rooms have hair dryers.

Matina Hotel. 3 Fournakion St., Hora, 846 00 Mykonos. ☎ **0289/22-387.** Fax 0289/24-510. 14 units. 29,300Dr ($98) double. Continental breakfast 2,200Dr($7). No credit cards.

This small hotel is inside a large garden that makes it especially quiet for its central location. The rooms are small, modern, and comfortable, and the owner has been described by several readers as "very helpful."

✪ **Pension Stelios.** 9 Apollonos St., Hora, 846 00 Mykonos. ☎ **0289/24-641.** 12 units (all with shower only). 18,000Dr ($60) double. Rates include breakfast. No credit cards.

This small inn on the hill above the OTE office (take the broad stone steps above the road) has a convenient, central location, and most rooms have terrific views of the harbor. It's especially good for those interested in destinations reached from the north bus stop, including the far east coast beaches. The rooms are clean and modern, with twin beds and balconies.

Philippi Hotel. 25 Kaloyera St., Hora, 846 00 Mykonos. ☎ **0289/22-294.** Fax 0289/24-680. 13 units. 14,000Dr ($47) double. No credit cards.

Each room in this homey little hotel in the heart of Mykonos town is different, so you might want to have a look at several before choosing yours. The owner tends a lush garden that often provides flowers for her son's restaurant, the elegant Philippi's, which can be reached through the garden.

Around the Island

Although most visitors prefer to stay in Hora and commute to the beaches, there are hotels near many of the more popular island beaches.

There are private studios and simple pensions at Paradise and Super Paradise beaches, but rooms are almost impossible to get, and prices more than double in July and August. Contact the **Mykonos Accommodations Center** (☎ 0289/23-160)—or, for Super Paradise, **GATS Travel** (☎ 0289/22-404)—for information on the properties they represent. The tavernas at each beach may also have suggestions.

AT KALAFATI The **Paradise Aphrodite Hotel** (☎ 0289/71-367) has a large pool, two restaurants, and 150 rooms. It's a good value in May, June, and October, when a double costs about 30,000Dr ($100).

AT ORNOS BAY Try elegant new ✪ **Kivotos Clubhouse,** Ornos Bay, 846 00 Mykonos (☎ 800/345-8236 or 0289/25-795; fax 0289/22-844), where most of the 21 units overlook the sea; if you don't like saltwater, head for the freshwater pool, or the

Jacuzzi and sauna. Kivotos Clubhouse is small enough to be intimate and tranquil. Small wonder that this is a popular honeymoon destination. If you ever want to leave (there are several restaurants), the hotel minibus will whisk you into town. Doubles run 45,000 to 120,000Dr ($150 to $400).

AT PLATI YIALOS The 82 units at the **Hotel Petassos Bay,** Plati Yialos, 846 00 Mykonos (☎ **0289/23-737**; fax 0289/24-101; e-mail: petaso@myk.forthnet.gr) all have air-conditioning, minibars, and telephones, and are large and comfortable. Doubles rent for 45,000Dr ($150). Each has a balcony overlooking the beach, which is less than 40 yards away. The hotel has a good-sized pool and sundeck, Jacuzzi, gym, and sauna, and offers free round-trip transportation from the harbor or airport, safety boxes, and laundry service. The new seaside restaurant has a great view and serves a big buffet breakfast (not included in room rate).

The **Hotel Petinos,** Plati Yialos, 846 00 Mykonos (☎ **0289/22-127**; fax 0289/ 23-680), has 66 good, clean, attractive units with air-conditioning, telephones, TVs, and large balconies. The double rate of 45,000Dr ($150) includes breakfast.

AT AYIOS STEPHANOS This popular resort, about 2½ miles north of Hora, has a number of hotels; the 38-unit **Princess of Mykonos,** Ayios Stephanos beach, 846 00 Mykonos (☎ **0289/23-806**; fax 0289/23031) is the most elegant. The Princess has bungalows, a gym, a pool, and an excellent beach; doubles from 45,000Dr ($150). The **Hotel Artemis,** Ayios Stephanos, 846 00 Mykonos (☎ **0289/22-345**), near the beach and bus stop, offers 23 units with bathroom for 27,000Dr ($90), breakfast included. The small **Hotel Mina,** Ayios Stephanos, 846 00 Mykonos (☎ **0289/ 23-024**), uphill behind the Artemis, has 15 doubles with bathroom that go for 18,000Dr ($60). All these hotels are usually closed from November to March.

WHERE TO DINE

Unfortunately, most restaurants here know that you're probably just passing through—hardly an incentive to offer the best in food or service. Restaurants also come and go here, so if possible, check with other travelers or locals as to what's new and good.

As usual on the islands, most of the harborside tavernas are expensive and mediocre, although **Kounelas** on the harbor (no phone; no credit cards) is still a good value.

Antonini's. Plateia Manto, Hora. ☎ **0289/22-319.** Main courses 3,000–5,000Dr ($10–$17). No credit cards. Daily noon–3pm and 7pm–1am in summer. Usually closed Nov–Mar. GREEK.

Antonini's is one of the oldest of Mykonos' restaurants, and it serves consistently good stews, chops, and *mezedes*. Locals still eat here, although in summer, they tend to leave the place to tourists.

✪ **Edem.** Signposted off Matoyanni St. ☎ **0289/22-855.** Reservations recommended July–Aug. Main courses 3,700–6,100Dr ($12–$20). AE, DC, MC, V. Daily noon–3pm and 7pm–midnight in summer (hours are flexible; sometimes open in winter). GREEK.

This restaurant has a lovely garden in a quiet location—unless you have the bad luck to arrive here, as I once did, just before a raucous tour group occupied all the other tables. If that happens, console yourself with the food: excellent appetizers, lots of tasty (and very pricey) seafood, and lamb stews with delicate seasonings.

Philippi. 32 Kalogera, off Matoyanni St. ☎ **0289/22-294.** Reservations recommended July–Aug. Main courses 2,800–6,500Dr ($9–$22). AE, MC, V. Daily 7pm–1am. Walk up the main street, past Kaloyera, and you'll find it on the right. GREEK/CONTINENTAL.

This restaurant in a quiet garden is a nice place to go to escape the hurly-burly of the harbor. Old Greek favorites share space on the menu with French dishes and a more than usually impressive wine list.

Sesame Kitchen. Odos Dinameon, Tria Pigadia Sq. ☎ **0289/24-710.** Main courses 1,500–5,500Dr ($5–$18). V. Daily 7pm–12:30am. Walk up the main street, turn right on Enoplon Dinameon, and it's on the right next to the Nautical Museum. GREEK/ INTERNATIONAL/VEGETARIAN.

This small, health-conscious taverna offers spinach, vegetable, cheese, and chicken pies baked fresh daily. There's a large variety of salads, brown rice, and soy dishes, including a vegetable moussaka, and lightly grilled and seasoned meat dishes.

MYKONOS AFTER DARK

Mykonos has the liveliest, most abundant (and expensive), and most chameleon-like nightlife—especially gay nightlife—in the Aegean. Don't be surprised if the places we suggest have closed, moved, or changed their name or image.

Watching the sunset is a popular sport at the sophisticated bars in Little Venice. The **Kastro** (☎ **0289/23-070**), near the Paraportiani Church, is famous for classical music and frozen daiquiris. This is a great spot to watch handsome young men flirting with each other. If you find it too crowded or tame, sashay along to Le Caprice, which also has a seaside perch and rocks a little harder, or across the street to Diva. The **Montparnasse** (☎ **0289/23-719**), on the same lane, is cozier, with classical music and Toulouse-Lautrec posters. The **Veranda** (☎ **0289/23-290**), in an old mansion overlooking the water with a good view of the windmills, is as relaxing as its name implies.

The decibel level is considerably higher along the harbor, where **Pierro's** (popular with gay visitors) rocks all night long to American and European music. The **Anchor** plays blues, jazz, and classic rock for its 30-something clients, as does **Argo. Stavros Irish Bar,** behind the town hall, is among the wildest places on the island. The **Windmill Disco** draws a younger crowd interested in chatting before anything significant happens. And if you'd like to sample some Greek music and dancing, try **Thalami,** a small club underneath the town hall.

The **City Club Disco** has a nightly drag show, and the **Factory,** near the windmills, is the place for gay striptease.

AN EXCURSION TO THE ✪ ISLAND OF DELOS

According to legend, Delos is the spot where Leto gave birth to the twins Artemis and Apollo. Why did Leto pick this tiny—less than 2 square miles—barren island as her nursery? Because she hoped to escape her lover Zeus's jealous spouse Hera by hiding on the smallest of the Cycladic islands. Although remote and tiny, Delos had an excellent harbor (long since silted up) that made it a vital way station for ancient ships plying the Aegean. The island was also a significant religious shrine in the cult of Apollo, with an oracle second in importance only to Delphi. In addition, the Delian Festival was an important ancient athletic festival. Less endearingly, in Roman times Delos was the most important slave market in the Aegean; there are reports of as many as 10,000 slaves being sold here in a single day. Today, the extensive ruins on Delos make the island rival Delphi and Olympia as one of the most impressive ancient sites in all Greece—although you'll long for the shady pine trees of Delphi and Olympia when you visit virtually shadeless Delos.

ARRIVING/DEPARTING   Delos can be visited only by sea—and many days the sea is too rough for boats to put in here. The site is always closed on Monday. Most people visit on excursion boats from nearby Mykonos, although there are excursions from other neighboring islands, and Delos is a prominent stop for cruise ships and yachts. Spending the night is not allowed. From Mykonos, organized guided and unguided excursions leave Tuesday to Sunday from the west end of the harbor; the trip takes about 40 minutes and costs about 3,000Dr ($10) round-trip for transportation alone. **Yiannakis Tours** (☎ **0289/22-089**) offers guided tours for 12,000Dr ($40) that depart at 9 or 10am and return at 12:30 or 2pm.

Note: Try to leave as early as possible in the morning for Delos, especially in the summer, when both the afternoon heat and the crowds are intense. Be sure to wear sturdy shoes and a hat and bring water and a snack. (There's a cafe near the museum, but the prices are high and the quality is poor.)

Exploring the Island

Delos flourished from the earliest days of Greek history through the Roman era, and the remains here attest to its life as the most important religious, maritime, and commercial center in the Aegean. Still, the 3 hours allotted by most excursion boats should be enough for all except the most avid archaeology enthusiasts to explore the site and museum.

Entrance to the site costs 1,500Dr ($5) unless it was included in your tour; site plans and picture guides are sold at the ticket facility. If you intend to explore the sprawling remains, be sure to get a site plan. If you're energetic enough, climb up **Mount Kythnos,** at 113m (371 ft.), the highest point on the island, for an overview of the site (and a fine view of the neighboring Cyclades).

French archaeologists have been excavating Delos since 1872, and there's a lot to see on and off the **Sacred Way,** the route that runs to the Sanctuary of Apollo. It should be admitted that most visitors are more interested in the marble phalluses in the **Sanctuary of Dionysos** than in the remains of houses, stoas, and religious shrines here—although the marble lions along the **Avenue of the Lions** have their admirers. If you've never seen ancient mosaics, be sure to take in the handsome pebble mosaics in the **House of the Dolphins,** the **House of the Masks,** and the **House of the Tridents.**

✪ SANTORINA (THIRA)

Especially if you arrive by sea, you won't confuse Santorini with any of the other Cyclades—although you might be confused to learn that it's also known as Thira. Ships arrive at Santorini (pop. 8,000; 130 nautical miles southeast of Piraeus) in a spectacular harbor that's part of the enormous *caldera* (crater) formed when a volcano blew out the island's center around 1450 B.C. To this day, some scholars speculate that the destruction gave birth to the myth of the lost continent of Atlantis.

Your first choice upon disembarking will be to decide whether you want to ride the funicular or a donkey 1,100 feet up the sheer sides of the caldera to the island's capital, Fira. Once there, you may decide to reward yourself with a glass of the island's rosé wine before you explore the shops and restaurants of Fira, swim at the black volcanic beach of Kamari, or visit the dazzling site of Akrotiri, an Aegean Pompeii destroyed when the volcano erupted. In case you were wondering, the volcano is now officially dormant, so you don't have to fret about the plumes of steam you might see around the islands of Kamenes in the harbor.

ESSENTIALS

ARRIVING/DEPARTING   By Air   Olympic Airways has several (six in the high season) daily flights between Athens and the airport at Monolithos (☎ **0286/31525**), which also receives European charters. There are also daily connections with Mykonos, three or four a week with Rhodes, two or three a week with Iraklion, Crete, and three a week during the high season with Thessaloniki. For schedule information and reservations, check with the Olympic Airways office on Ayiou Athanassiou Street (☎ **0286/22-490,** or 01/961-6161 or 01/966-6666 in Athens).

By Sea   Several companies operate **ferry service** at least twice daily from Piraeus; the trip takes 10 to 12 hours, and costs about 6,000Dr ($20) one way. If you can book a day sailing, you'll pass many of the Cyclades. In summer, there are often daily ferry connections from Santorini to Ios, Mykonos, and Paros. **Excursion boats** leave Iraklion, Crete, almost daily. The fare is about 4,000Dr ($13) one way. Because this is an open-sea route, the trip can be an ordeal in bad weather. Check the schedules with the **Tourist Police** in Athens (☎ **171**) or the **Port Authority** in Piraeus (☎ **01/451-1310**) or Santorini (☎ **0286/22-239**).

The high-speed **hydrofoil** *Nearchos* connects Santorini with Ios, Paros, Mykonos, and Iraklio, Crete, almost daily in the high season and three times weekly in the low season, if the winds aren't too strong.

VISITOR INFORMATION   There is no official government tourist office, but there are a number of helpful travel agencies. Travel agents, such as **Joint Travel Service** (☎ **0286/24900;** fax 0286/24992), next to the Olympic Airways Office in Fira, or **Nomikos Travel** (☎ **0286/23-660**), with offices in Fira, Karterados, and Perissa, have up-to-date schedule information on ferries and hydrofoils and sell tickets. **Kamari Tours,** 2 blocks south of the main square on the right (☎ **0286/22-666;** fax 0286/22-971), offers day trips to most of the island's sites and can help you find a room and rent a moped. **Damigos Tours,** on the main square (☎ **0286/22-504;** fax 0286/22-266), the first agency established in Fira, offers excellent guided tours at slightly lower prices.

GETTING AROUND   By Bus   Santorini has very good bus service. The island's central bus station is just south of the main square in Fira. Schedules are posted on the wall of the office above it; most routes are serviced every half hour 7am to 11pm in the summer, less frequently in the off-season.

By Car   Most travel agents can help you rent a car. You might find that a local company such as **Zeus** (☎ **0286/24-013**) offers better prices than the big names, although the quality might be a bit lower. Of the better-known agencies, try **Budget Rent-A-Car,** a block below the bus stop square in Fira (☎ **0286/22-900;** fax 0286/22-887), where a four-seat Fiat Panda should cost about 21,000Dr ($70) a day, with unlimited mileage. If you reserve in advance through Budget in the United States (☎ **800/527-0700**), you should be able to beat that price.

By Moped   The roads on the island are notoriously treacherous, narrow, and winding; add local drivers who take the roads at high speed and visiting drivers who aren't sure where they're going, and you'll understand the island's high accident rate. If you're determined to use two-wheeled transportation, expect to pay about 3,000 to 9,000Dr ($10 to $30) per day, depending on car size and season.

By Taxi   The taxi station is just south of the main square. In high season, you should book ahead by phone (☎ **0286/22-555** or 0286/23-700) if you want a taxi for an excursion; prices are standard from point to point. If you call for a taxi outside Fira, you're required to pay the fare from there to your pickup point, although you can sometimes find one that has dropped off a passenger. Taxis are not cheap and not always easy to find, so it's a good idea to book one well in advance if you want to plan a trip around the island by taxi.

Fast Facts: Fira

American Express   The **X-Ray Kilo Travel Service,** on the main square (☎ **0286/22-624;** fax 0286/23-600), is the American Express representative on Santorini.

Area Code   The telephone area code for Santorini is **0286.**

Banks   The **National Bank** (open weekdays 8am to 2pm; ATM machine) is a block south from the main square on the right near the taxi station. Many travel agents also change money; most are open daily 8am to 9:30pm.

Hospital   The small **Health Clinic** is on the southeast edge of town on Ayiou Athanassiou Street (☎ **0286/22-238**), to the left after the playground, near the Santorini Hotel.

Internet Access   The **PC Club** (☎ **0286/24-600**) is in Fira. It's usually open Monday to Saturday 9am to 2pm and 5pm to 8pm; 1,500Dr ($5) per hour for use.

Police   The police station is on Dekigala Street (☎ **0286/22-649**), several blocks south of the main square, on the left. The **port authority** can be reached at ☎ **0286/22-239.**

Post Office   The **post office** (☎ **0286/22-238;** fax 0286/22-698) is off to the right of the bus station. It's open weekdays 8am to 1pm.

Telephone   The **OTE telephone** office is just off Ypapantis Street, up from the post office. It's usually open Monday through Friday 8am to 4pm.

EXPLORING THE ISLAND

FIRA   If you're staying overnight on Santorini, take advantage of the fact that almost all the day-trippers from cruise ships leave in the late afternoon, and explore the capital in the evening. As you stroll, you may be surprised to discover that Fira has a Roman Catholic cathedral and convent in addition to the predictable Greek Orthodox cathedral, a legacy from the days when the Venetians controlled much of the Aegean. The name *Santorini,* in fact, is a Latinate corruption of the Greek for "Saint Irene." The small **Archaeological Museum** (☎ **0286/22-217;** open Tuesday to Sunday 8:30am to 3pm; admission 800Dr/$2.65), with both Minoan and classical finds, is near the cable car station in Fira. You might find it almost deserted, as most visitors head directly for Thira's shops. (A new archaeological museum is rumored to open sometime in 1999.) In addition to the inevitable mass-produced souvenir and T-shirt shops, Fira has a number of nice, small galleries selling watercolors, posters, ceramics, and handcrafted glass—and a great many shops selling jewelry.

It's a good idea to remember the maxim that all that glitters is not necessarily gold as you scout out Fira's seemingly nonstop jewelry shops. The best-known jeweler here is probably **Kostas Antoniou,** on Ayiou Ioannou Street (☎ **0286/22-633;** tel/fax 0296/23-557), north of the cable-car station. **Porphyra,** in the Fabrica Shopping Center near the cathedral (☎ **0286/22-981**), also has some impressive work. Most jewelers will first weigh, then price, what you're interested in—and some will bargain.

VILLAGES   Two island villages well worth visiting are **Pirgos (Tower),** the oldest and highest settlement on the island, and **Oia** (also spelled Ia), on a cliff above the caldera. Badly damaged in a massive earthquake in 1956, Oia was virtually a ghost town until it was rebuilt in the 1960s and '70s and resettled. Now its chic shops and gorgeous sunsets make it an increasingly popular place to stay or to visit—especially with those who find Fira too frenetic. If you travel to either village (local buses run there from Fira, or you can take a taxi), keep a lookout for some of the island's cave dwellings (homes hollowed out of Santorini's soft volcanic stone).

BEACHES   Santorini does not have the soft sand beaches of Mykonos, but the black volcanic sand and pebble beach make **Kamari** a very nice place to swim, especially in the morning, before the all-day sunbathers arrive (and before the black sand gets seriously hot). On the way to or from Kamari from Fira by local bus or taxi, you can stop at the **Antoniou, Roussos,** or **Boutari** vintners to see how wine is made, have a free sample, and perhaps buy a bottle or two to sample later. The **Antoniou winery** (run by the same family who has the Antoniou jewellery in Fira) is especially charming, with the old wine press and barrels on display.

ANCIENT THIRA & AKROTIRI   Above Kamari beach on a rocky promontory are the ruins of **Ancient Thira** (☎ 0286-22217), settled in the 9th century B.C., although most of the scattered remains date from the Hellenistic era. At press time, it was open Tuesday to Friday 8am to 2:30pm, Sunday and holidays 8am to 2:30pm; it was also sometimes open on Saturday 8am to 2:30 pm; admission 500Dr/$1.70). A good, but alarmingly narrow, road now runs almost to the summit, which can also be reached on foot or by donkey (for hire from some travel agents) by a path. The hilltop site is very fine, but if you have to choose between Ancient Thira and Akrotiri, head for Akrotiri.

The excavations at **Akrotiri,** the Minoan settlement destroyed when the volcano erupted around 1450 B.C., have unearthed buildings three stories tall that were lavishly decorated with frescoes (which are now on view in the National Archaeological Museum in Athens). It's still breathtaking to walk down the streets and peek in the windows of houses in a town whose life was extinguished in a torrent of lava and ash so long ago. The site (☎ 0286/81-366) is open Tuesday to Sunday 8:30am to 3pm; admission is 1,200Dr ($4). Akrotiri can be reached by public bus or private bus tour; **Damigos Tours,** on the main square (☎ 0286/22-504), has knowledgeable and entertaining guides.

WHERE TO STAY

Santorini is packed in July and August, so if you plan a summer visit, make a reservation with a deposit at least 2 months in advance or be prepared to accept potluck. Don't accept rooms offered at the port unless you're exhausted and don't care how remote the village is that you wake up in. If you come between April and mid-June or in September or October, when the island is less crowded and far more pleasant, the rates can be nearly half the high-season rates we quote. Most of the hotels recommended below don't have air-conditioning, but with cool breezes blowing through, you won't need it. Many don't have televisions either.

✪ **Astra Apartments.** Imerovigli, 847 00 Santorini. ☎ **0286/23-641.** Fax 0286/24-765. E-mail: astra-ae@oenet.gr. 18 units. A/C TV TEL. 34,000–85,000Dr ($114–$284) double. AE, MC, V.

Perched on a cliffside with spectacular views, looking like a miniature village set within the tiny cliffside hamlet of Imerovigli, the Astra Apartments are quietly elegant, with a drop-dead pool. Each unit has a kitchenette, but breakfast is served on your private terrace or balcony, and there's also a poolside bar that serves delicious snacks. Rooms also have hair dryers. This is an ideal place to escape the hustle and bustle of Fira or Oia and enjoy life. Every detail here is right, the views are spectacular, and the service is outstanding. Not surprisingly, reservations are often hard to come by; this is also a popular place for weddings and honeymoons.

✪ **Katikies.** Oia, 847 02 Santorini. ☎ **800/345-8236** or 0286/71-401. Fax 0286/71-129. E-mail: katikies@otenet.gr. 22 units. A/C MINIBAR TV TEL. 43,000–79,000Dr ($144–$264) double. MC, V.

If you find a more spectacular pool anywhere on the island, let us know: This one runs virtually to the side of the caldera, so that you can paddle about and enjoy an endless view. (There's also a smaller pool intended for the use of guests who have suites.) The hotel's island-style architecture incorporates twists and turns, secluded patios, and antiques. If the people in the next room like to sing in the shower, you might hear them—but most people who stay here treasure the tranquility. The top-of-the-line honeymoon suite has its own Jacuzzi, just in case you can't be bothered going to either outdoor pool.

Loucas Hotel. Fira, 847 00 Santorini. ☎ **0286/22-480** or 0286/22-680. Fax 0286/24-882. 20 units. A/C TV TEL. 34,500Dr ($115) double. Rates include breakfast. MC, V.

This is one of the oldest and best hotels on the caldera, with barrel-ceilinged "caves" built to prevent collapse during an earthquake. The rooms are newly renovated; some were enlarged and furnished with handsome lively blue furniture, and have shared patios overlooking the caldera. It's an excellent value for the location, amenities, and view.

WHERE TO DINE

Aris Restaurant. Ayiou Mina St., Fira. ☎ **0286/22-840.** Main courses 1,500–4,600Dr ($5–$15). MC, V. Daily noon–1am. GREEK/INTERNATIONAL.

This consistently good restaurant is on the lower pedestrian street, south of the donkey path down to Skala, below the Loucas Hotel. The chef was formerly at the Athens Hilton, and although the dishes are mainly Greek, the cooking is more updated and refined. The *mezedes* are delicious, especially the *saganaki* (fried cheese), and the dish-baked moussaka is much better than standard moussaka. Try Aris Ziras' white house wine.

Camille Stephani. Kamari Beach. ☎ **0286/31-716.** Reservations recommended July–Sept. Main courses 3,600–7,500Dr ($12–$25). AE, DC, MC, V. Daily 1–4pm and 6:30pm–midnight. GREEK/INTERNATIONAL.

Even if you're not staying at Kamari, this restaurant on the north end of the beach, 500 yards from the bus stop, will make the trip worthwhile. The house specialty is a tender beef filet with green pepper in Madeira sauce. You can take a moonlight stroll along the beach after dinner.

Katina Fish–Taverna. Port of Oia. ☎ **0286/71-280.** Fish priced daily by the kilo. No credit cards. Daily 11am–1am. SEAFOOD.

One of the best places to eat in Oia isn't in town but down in the port of Ammoudi, which is best reached by donkey (ask in the village about hiring a donkey), or you can walk. Katina Pagoni is considered one of the very best local cooks, and the setting beside the glittering Aegean is romantic.

Kukumavolos. Port of Oia. ☎ **0286/71-413.** Fish priced daily by the kilo. No credit cards. Daily 8pm–midnight. NOUVELLE GREEK.

This elegant restaurant has delicious fresh fish and an adventurous menu of "nouvelle Greek" cuisine (dishes are lighter and less oil-saturated than is customary in Greece). There's a wide selection of island and off-island wines and wonderful views over the sea.

✪ **Selene.** Fira (in the passageway between the Atlantis and Aressana Hotels). ☎ **0286/ 22-249.** Fax 0286/24-395. Reservations recommended. Main courses 3,000–6,000r ($10–$20). AE, MC, V. Mid-Apr to early Oct, Mon–Sat noon–3pm; daily 7pm–midnight. Closed late Oct to early Apr. ELEGANT GREEK.

The best restaurant on Santorini—and one of the best in all Greece—Selene uses local produce to highlight what owners Evelyn and George Hatziyiannakis call the "creative nature of Greek cuisine." The appetizers, including a delicious eggplant salad with octopus and tomato, mushrooms with crabmeat and cheese, and fluffy fava balls with caper sauce, are deservedly famous. Entrees include sea bass grilled with pink peppers, rabbit, quail, and saddle of lamb with yogurt and mint sauce. If you eat only one meal on Santorini, eat it here, in a truly distinguished restaurant with distinctive local architecture—and be sure to try the enormous local capers.

Santorini After Dark

Most people will want to start the evening with a drink on the caldera watching the sunset. **Franco's** (☎ **0286/22-881**) is the most famous place for this magic hour, but drinks are expensive. **Archipelago** (☎ **0286/23-673**) and the **Canava Cafe** (☎ **0286/22-565**) also have good views. For more reasonable prices and the same fantastic view, continue past the Loucas Hotel to the **Renaissance Bar** (☎ **0286/ 22-880**).

Most of the action is north and west of the main square. Underneath the square, the **Kirathira Bar** plays jazz at a level that permits conversation. The **Town Club** appeals to clean-cut rockers, while the **Two Brothers** pulls in the biggest, chummiest crowd on the island. For Greek music, find the **Apocalypse Club,** or **Bar 33** for bouzouki. Discos come and go; follow your ears to find them. The **Koo Club** is the biggest, and **Enigma** is popular with those interested in good music. In Oia, **Melissa's Piano Bar** and **Zorba's** are good spots for a drink at sunset.

None of the places recommended above have specific street addresses; it's best just to ask someone for directions.

SIFNOS

Sifnos (pop. 2,500; 93 nautical miles southeast of Piraeus) is the most beautiful of the western Cyclades, with unusually green hills and valleys, particularly lovely villages, and a reputation for especially good olive oil and distinguished cooking. All this has made the island a favorite summer retreat for Athenians, and now that foreign visitors have discovered Sifnos's charms, the island can be terribly crowded in July (especially around the feast day of the Prophet Elias, the patron saint of the island's most important monastery) and August. If possible, don't visit then, unless you like your restaurants and beaches very busy.

Essentials

ARRIVING/DEPARTING There's at least one boat daily from Piraeus, in addition to daily (twice daily in summer) connections to the other western Cyclades, Serifos and Milos, and less frequently to Kimolos and Kythnos. There are ferry connections four times a week with Santorini; three times a week with Folegand ros, Ios, and Sikinos; and once a week with Andros, Crete, Mykonos, Paros, Rafina, Syros, and Tinos. There's a weekly connection with the Dodecanese islands of Karpathos, Kassos, Rhodes, and Symi. Contact the **Port Authority** in Piraeus (☎ **143** or 01/451-1130) or in Sifnos (☎ **0284/31-617**) for information.

VISITOR INFORMATION You can book a room, buy ferry tickets, rent a car or motorbike, arrange excursions, and leave your luggage at the **Aegean Thesaurus**

Travel and Tourism office on the port (☎ **0284/32-190;** e-mail: thesaurus@ travelling.gr) or at **Siphanto Travel** (☎ **0284/32-034;** fax 0284/31-024), also on the port. Check to see if Aegean Thesaurus has its excellent information packet on Sifnos (400Dr/$1.35) available.

FAST FACTS   The telephone **area code** for Sifnos is **0284.** Tourist services are centered around the main square, Plateia Iroon ("Heroes Square"), in Apollonia, the capital. The **post office** (☎ **0284/31-329**) is open weekdays 8am to 3pm, and in the summer, Saturday and Sunday 9am to 1:30pm. The **National Bank** (☎ **0284/ 31-317**) is open Monday to Thursday 8am to 2pm and Friday 8am to 1:30pm. The **OTE telephone office,** just down the vehicle road, is open daily 8am to 3pm, and in summer 5 to 10pm. The **news kiosk** on the square has a metered phone for after-hours calls. The **police station** (☎ **0284/31-210**), which also functions as an informal information center, is just east of the square, and a first-aid station is nearby; for **medical emergencies,** phone ☎ **0284/31-315.**

GETTING AROUND   Many visitors come to Sifnos just for the wonderful hiking and mountain trails. A car or moped isn't really necessary, but cars can be rented at **FS** (☎ 0284/31-795) and **Aegean Thesaurus** (☎ 0284/32-190) in Apollonia, or in Kamares at **Siphanto Travel** (☎ 0284/32-034) or **Sifnos Car** (☎ 0284/31-793). Apollonia has a few moped dealers; try **Yanni's** (☎ 0284/31-155), on the main square, or **Easy Rider** (☎ 0284/31-001), on the road circling the village. As always, exercise caution if you do decide to rent a car or moped; many drivers, like you, will be unfamiliar with the island roads.

By Bus   Apollonia's Heroes Square is the central bus stop for the island. The system is fairly efficient; buses run regularly to and from the port at Kamares, north to Artemonas, east to Kastro, and south to Faros and Plati Yialos.

By Taxi   Apollonia's Heroes Square is also the main taxi stand, although there aren't many of them on the island. Some mobile phone numbers for taxis are ☎ **094/ 642-680,** 094/444-904, 094/761-210, or 094/936-111.

EXPLORING THE ISLAND

Kamares, on the west coast, is the island's port and will be most visitors' introduction to Sifnos—a pity, because it has none of the charm of the capital, Apollonia, or the inland villages. Still, there's a good **sand beach** at Kamares, and the usual assortment of restaurants and shops, some of which sell the distinctive local pottery, made from island clay.

From Kamares, you can catch a bus for the 3-mile trip to **Apollonia** (also called Hora). En route, you'll begin to get a sense of the island's fecundity and the handsome architecture of the small, cubical, whitewashed houses, almost all with whitewashed containers of geraniums on the doorstep and small gardens.

Apollonia's **Heroes Square (Plateia Iroon)** is the site of a monument to Sifnos's World War II veterans. Home to a number of small cafes, restaurants, and shops, it is the transportation hub of the island, where its vehicular roads converge. There's also a **Museum of Folk Art** (usually open from July until mid-September from 10am to 1pm and 6pm to 10pm; admission 400Dr/$1.35) on the square.

More and more asphalt roads are appearing on Sifnos, but you'll still be able to do most of your walking on the island's distinctive flagstone and marble paths. You'll probably see village women whitewashing the edges of the paving stones, transforming the monochrome paths into elaborate abstract patterns. Apollonia gleams with whitewash, as does the handsome village of Kastro, the former capital, where you can still see remains of the walls of the **medieval fortress (kastro).** Throughout the island, you'll see dovecotes, windmills, and small white chapels in amazingly remote spots.

Most connoisseurs rank **Plati Yialos** on the island's south coast as Sifnos's best beach. Don't expect to be alone: A hotel and a campground are on the popular, long crescent beach. There's also good swimming at **Heronissos, Vroulidia,** and **Faros,** a small resort on the east coast with some good budget accommodations and tavernas. **Apokofto** has a good sand beach, and you can often reach the lovely beach at **Vathy** by one of the caïques that leave from Kamares, or by bus on the new road. **Aegean Thesaurus Travel** (see "Visitor Information," above) has caïque excursions to a number of isolated beaches.

WHERE TO STAY

Many young Athenians vacation on Sifnos, particularly on summer weekends, when it can be very difficult to find a room. If you plan to be in Kamares during the high season, be sure to make reservations by May. If you're here off-season, many of these hotels are closed, but several remain open all year. The efficient Aegean Thesaurus Travel Agency (see "Visitor Information," above) can place you in a room in a private house with your own bathroom, in a studio with a kitchenette, or in other, more stylish accommodations.

Hotel Anthoussa. Apollonia, 840 03 Sifnos. ☎ **0284/31-431.** 15 units. 16,500Dr ($55) double. TV TEL. Continental breakfast 1,500Dr ($5). MC, V.

This hotel is above the excellent and popular Yerontopoulos cafe and patisserie, on the right past Heroes Square. Although the streetside rooms offer wonderful views over the hills, they overlook the late-night sweet-tooth crowd and can be recommended only to night owls. The back rooms are quieter and overlook a beautiful bower of bougainvillea.

✪ **Hotel Petali.** Ano Petali, Apollonia, 840 03 Sifnos. ☎ and fax **0284/33-024.** 11 units. A/C TV MINIBAR. 16,5000–24,000Dr ($55–$80) double. No credit cards. Hotel not always open in winter.

This would be a nice place to stay a week: There are lovely views over Ano Petali (a suburb of Apollonia) to the sea, a large terrace with handsome, comfortable chairs, rooms furnished in Cycladic style, good beds, modern bathrooms, and a small restaurant that serves delicious Sifnian specialties. The hotel offers an American breakfast for 2,000Dr ($6.55). Although the Hotel Petali does not accept credit cards, its managing office, **Aegean Thesaurus Travel Agency** (☎ **0284/33-151;** fax 0284/32-190) accepts MasterCard and Visa.

✪ **Hotel Plati Yialos.** Plati Yialos, 840 03 Sifnos. ☎ **0284/31-324,** or 0831/22-626 in winter. Fax 0284/31-325, or 0831/55-049 in winter. 34 units. A/C TEL. 45,000Dr ($150) double. Rates include breakfast. No credit cards. Hotel usually open in winter.

Thanks to a recent renovation, the island's first beach hotel is still the best. It overlooks the beach on the west side of the cove. Ground-floor rooms have private patios, and all rooms have modern bathrooms and are nicely decorated with ceramics and painted tiles. There are also a number of suites, which are ideal for families. The Plati Yialos's flagstone sundeck extends from the beach to a dive platform at the end of the cove, with a bar and restaurant sharing the same Aegean views.

✪ **Hotel Sifnos.** Apollonia, 840 03 Sifnos. ☎ **0284/31-624.** 9 units. 16,500Dr ($55) double. AE, EURO, MC, V. Usually open in winter.

Many consider this hotel on a quiet pedestrianized street the best in Apollonia. The owners have tried hard to make it reflect island taste, using local pottery and weavings in the good-sized, bright bedrooms. It's usually open year-round and has an excellent restaurant.

WHERE TO DINE

Apostoli's Koutouki Taverna. Apollonia. ☎ **0284/31-186.** Main courses 1,500–4,500Dr ($5–$15). No credit cards. Daily noon–midnight. GREEK.

There are several tavernas in Apollonia, and this one on the main pedestrian street is generally the best for Greek food. The service is usually leisurely at best. All the vegetable dishes, most made from locally grown produce, are tasty, but portions are on the skimpy side.

Sifnos Cafe–Restaurant. Apollonia. ☎ **0284/31-624.** Main courses 1,500–4,600Dr ($5–$15). AE, EURO, MC, V. Daily 8am–midnight. GREEK.

You can start the day here with breakfast, including fresh fruit juice and your choice of a dozen coffees. Stop by later in the day for a snack, light meal, ouzo and mezedes, or dessert. This place often has *rivithia* (chickpeas), a Sifnian specialty, on Sunday.

To Liotrivi (Manganas). Artemona. ☎ **0284/31-246.** Main courses 1,300–4,500Dr ($4.35–$15). No credit cards. Daily noon–midnight. GREEK.

One of the island's favorite tavernas is in the pretty village of Artemona, just over a mile's walk from Apollonia. Taste for yourself why the Sifnians consider Yannis Yiorgoulis one of their best cooks. Try his delectable *kaparosalata* (minced caper leaves and onion salad), *povithokeftedes* (croquettes of ground chickpeas), or *ambelofasoula* (crisp local black-eyed peas in the pod). In short, there are lots of vegetarian delights here, but there's also a very tasty beef filet with potatoes baked in foil. This place usually has the excellent Siphnian specialty of chickpeas *rivithia* on Sundays.

SIFNOS AFTER DARK

In Apollonia, the **Argo Bar, Botzi,** and **Volto,** on the main pedestrian street, are good for the latest European and American pop. In summertime the large **Dolphin Pub** becomes a lively nightspot (it closes in mid-September). At Kamares, you can enjoy the sunset at the picturesque **Old Captain's Bar.** Later, the **Mobilize Dance Club** and the more elegant **Follie-Follie,** right on the beach, start cranking up the volume and become seaside discos.

PAROS

You can catch a boat from Paros (pop. 12,000; 95 nautical miles southeast of Piraeus) to most of the Aegean islands, which means that a lot of people pass through here, especially in summer. Some decide to stay: Paros's good beaches, lovely villages, and increasingly sophisticated nightlife, especially in the village of Naoussa and the capital town Parikia (also known as Hora), have earned it a reputation for being a less expensive Mykonos. In addition, Paros has attractions its better-known neighbor lacks, including extensive vineyards, the substantial remains of a Venetian castle, and the finest Byzantine cathedral in the Cyclades.

ESSENTIALS

ARRIVING/DEPARTING   By Air   Olympic Airlines has five flights daily (10 in summer) between Athens and Paros. For schedule information and reservations, call ☎ **01/961-6161** or 01/961/6666 in Athens or 0284/21-900 in Parikia, or call the **Paros airport** (☎ **0284/91-257**).

By Sea   The main port, Parikia, has ferry service from Piraeus at least once daily and four times daily in the summer. The trip takes 6 hours. Confirm schedules with the

Tourist Police in Athens (☎ **171** or 01/322-2545), the **Port Authority** in Piraeus (☎ **01/451-1310**) or at the **Tourist Office** (☎ **0284/22-079**) in Parikia. **Strintzis Lines** (☎ **01/422-5000** in Athens) and **Ventouris Ferries** (☎ **01/482-8901** in Athens) operate from Piraeus via Syros three or four times a week. **Ilio Lines** (☎ **01/422-4772** in Athens) has hydrofoil service almost daily from Rafina.

Daily ferry service from Parikia links Paros with Ios, Mykonos, Santorini (Thira), and Tinos. Daily excursion tours link Parikia and Naoussa (the north coast port) with Mykonos. Call the **port authority** (☎ **0284/21-240**) or check each travel agent's current schedule. Most ferry tickets are not interchangeable.

VISITOR INFORMATION   The **Paros Information Bureau** is inside the windmill on the harbor (☎ **0284/22-078;** 0284/21-673). In theory, it is open June to September, daily 9am to 11pm; the staff speaks English, provides local schedules, and changes traveler's checks. **Paros Travel** (☎ **0284/21-582;** fax 0284/22-582) is a good, helpful travel agent near the pier.

GETTING AROUND   The capital, Parikia, is best enjoyed by simply strolling about and getting pleasantly lost. Naoussa can also be enjoyed on foot. If you plan to explore the island, however, you may want to rent a car, or take one of the guided tours of the island offered by **Paros Travel** (☎ **0284/21-582**).

By Bicycle   With its rolling, fertile hills, Paros is well suited to exploration by bike, although some of the pebble-and-dirt roads will require strong tires. **Mountain Bike Club Paros,** just off the waterfront (☎ **0284/23-778**), supplies bikes for their organized tours as well as such essentials as a helmet, insurance, repair kits, and water bottles.

By Bus   The **bus station** in Parikia is on the waterfront (☎ **0284/21-395,** left from the windmill. There's hourly public bus service between Parikia and Naoussa. The other public buses from Parikia run hourly. Schedules are posted at the stations.

By Car   There are several agencies along the waterfront, and except in July and August you should be able to bargain. **Rent-A-Car Acropolis,** left from the windmill on the waterfront (☎ **0284/21-830**), has wildly painted dune buggies or Suzuki jeeps. **Budget Rent-a-Car** (☎ **0284/22-320**) and **Paros Europcar S.A.** (☎ **0284/24-408;** fax 0284/22-544 in Parikia) usually have a good selection. Purchasing full insurance is recommended. You'll probably get the best rate if you reserve in advance through **Budget** in the United States (☎ **800/527-0700**). Expect to pay at least $50 per day in the summer.

By Moped   There are several moped dealers along the waterfront. Make sure the cycle is in proper condition before you accept it, and be careful on pebble-and-dirt surfaces. Expect to pay about $15 per day in the summer.

By Taxi   Taxis can be booked (☎ **0284/21-500**) or hailed at the windmill taxi stand. If you're coming off the ferry with lots of luggage and a hotel reservation in Naoussa, it's worth the fee (around 2,000Dr/$7) to take a taxi directly there.

Fast Facts: Parikia

Area Code   The telephone area code for Paros is **0284.**

Banks   The three banks on Mavroyenous Square (to the right behind the windmill) are open Monday to Friday 8am to 2pm and Friday 8am to 1:30pm.

Internet Access   Try **Sindemeno Café** on Market Street in Parikia; the user's fee is 2,500Dr/$8 per hour.

Medical Clinic   The new, private **Medical Center of Paros** (☎ 0284/24-410) is left (west) of Parikia's central square, across from the post office, a block off the port. The public **Parikia Health Clinic** (☎ 0284/22-500) is down the road from the Ekantopyliani Church.

Police   The **police station** is on the central square (☎ 100 or 0284/23-333). The **Tourist Police** are behind the windmill on the port (☎ 0284/21-673). In Marpissa, call ☎ 0284/41-202; in Naoussa, ☎ 0284/51-202.

Post Office   The **post office** (☎ 0284/21-236) is on the waterfront road; it's open Monday to Friday 7:30am to 2pm, with extended hours in July and August. It offers fax service at 0284/22-449.

Telephone   The **OTE telephone office** (☎ 0284/22-135) is to the right of the windmill; it's open Monday through Friday 7:30am to midnight. (If the front door is closed, go around to the back—wind direction determines which door is open.)

EXPLORING THE ISLAND

Parikia, site of the ancient capital, is the main port and largest town on the island, with a busy harborfront whose best-known landmark is the squat, whitewashed windmill just off the main pier. Most of what you'll need—banks, travel agents, several hotels, restaurants, and shops—is clustered nearby in Mavroyenous Square. Things get more interesting when you head inland to Parikia's picturesque **Agora (market)** section, a mixture of food markets and handicraft shops. The nicest part of town is around the 13th-century **Venetian Kastro (fortress).** Like a number of houses and churches here, the Kastro was built of the famous Parian marble originally used to build the temples of Apollo and Demeter.

Today, the churches of Ayios Konstantinos and Ayia Eleni form part of the Kastro, but Parikia's most famous church is the 6th-century **Panayia Ekatondapyliani (Our Lady of a Hundred Doors).** This hyperbolic name simply suggests that the church has more than the usual number of doors. The church is usually open daily 8am to 1pm and 5 to 8pm; admission is free. There is a 500Dr/$1.70 fee for the small **Cathedral Museum.** As on Tinos, many pilgrims come here on the feast of the Virgin on August 15, when finding accommodations on Paros is virtually impossible.

Parikia's **Archaeological Museum** (☎ 0284/21-231) is open Tuesday to Sunday 8:30am to 2:30pm; admission is 500Dr ($1.70). Enter just behind the Panayia Ekatondapyliani. The museum has a lovely statue of a **winged victory** and part of the famous **Parian Chronicle,** a 3rd century B.C. inscription recording important happenings in the history of ancient Greece.

Paros's best-known and most picturesque fishing village, **Naoussa,** with the remains of a Venetian castle, is in the throes of overdevelopment. Much of the construction is concentrated along the shore, and you can still find pleasant old streets in the village itself, as well as a number of new bars, restaurants, boutiques, and hotels. If you want a quieter spot and like butterflies, head for ✪ **Petaloudes,** the **Valley of the Butterflies,** about 4 miles out of Parikia. You can visit the colorful butterflies—actually moths—daily in season (usually May to July) from 9am to 8pm for 800Dr ($2.70). (Take the main coast road south out of Parikia; turn left at the sign for the Convent of Christou sto Dassos, and follow the signs.) The small **Museum of Popular Agean Culture** (free) in the Lefkes Village Hotel in the village of Lefkes has examples of island pottery, furniture, and farm implements.

If you find Paros too crowded for your tastes, you can take a caïque over to **Antiparos,** a small island with some nice beaches, small tavernas (and rapidly increasing touristic development) half a mile offshore. Spelunkers will want to visit the **Cave of Antiparos,** open daily 10am to 4pm (500Dr/$1.65).

OUTDOOR ACTIVITIES   The free booklet *Paros Windsurfing Guide* has a good small map of the island, maps of several beaches, and useful information. It is especially good for those interested in watersports. The free publication *Summer Paros/Antiparos* also has a map of the island, a fairly good map of Parikia, and information.

There are **beaches** north along Parikia Bay, but beach seekers will probably want to head east to Naoussa Bay. One of the island's best and most famous beaches, picturesque **Kolymbithres,** where smooth giant rocks divide the golden sand beach into little coves, is an hour's walk or a 10-minute moped ride west from Naoussa. There are several tavernas and hotels nearby.

North of Kolymbithres, by Ayios Ioannis Church, is **Monastery Beach,** where there's some nudism, and the **Monasteri Club,** a bar and restaurant with music and beach service. Most of the other beaches west of Naoussa are overcrowded because of all the new hotels. **Santa Maria Beach,** on the northeast coast, is particularly popular with windsurfers; the Santa Maria Surf Club rents gear and sometimes gives lessons. There are also a fine beach and windsurfing facilities at **Chrissi Akti (Golden Beach),** half a mile of fine golden sand, which some consider the island's best beach. The frequent stiff winds make it a better spot for windsurfers than for sunbathers. There are small tavernas on all these beaches.

WHERE TO STAY

Most hotels require reservations for July and August; it's advisable to book at least a month in advance. If you arrive without a room, you can often get one in a private house from one of the hawkers who meet ships. If you don't like what you're offered, the **Hotelliers Association of Paros** (☎ **0284/24-555** or 0284/24-556) in Mavroyenous Square may be able to help. Keep in mind that all hotels in Parikia are likely to be noisy in season.

✪ **Astir of Paros.** Kolimbithres Beach, Naoussa, 844 01 Paros. ☎ **0284/51-976.** Fax 0284/51-985. E-mail: astir@prometheus.hol.gr. 61 units. MINIBAR TV TEL. 50,000Dr ($167) double; 56,000–135,000Dr ($187–$450) suite. AE, DC, MC, V.

The Hotel Astir of Paros, on Kolymbithres Beach across from the village of Naoussa, is one of the glamour spots of the Cyclades. There's just about everything you'd expect here: large, quiet suites and rooms, a freshwater pool, miniature golf for the kiddies—in other words, this is as close to a full resort hotel as you'll find in the Aegean. That said, the rooms are comfortable, but not luxurious (although the bathrooms are large and modern). If the Astir is full, you might check out the much larger (191 units), less pleasant, but still excellent **Sunsea Porto Paros Hotel** (☎ **0284/52-010;** fax 0284/51-720), a mile away and also on a fine beach.

Hotel Fotilia. Naoussa, 844 01 Paros. ☎ **0284/51-480.** Fax 0284/51-189. 14 units. TEL. 30,000Dr ($100) double. Rates include breakfast. No credit cards. Climb to the top of the steps at the end of town and to the left of the church you'll see a restored windmill behind a stone archway.

The Fotilia's large rooms are furnished in tasteful country style and have doors opening to balconies overlooking the old harbor and bay. There are also some studio apartments with simple kitchenettes

✪ **Lefkes Village Hotel.** Lefkes 844 00 Paros. ☎ **0284/41-827** and 01/251-6497. Fax 0284/41-827 and 01/675-5019. 25 units. A/C MINIBAR TV TEL. In-season 40,000Dr ($133) double; off-season 24,000–32,000Dr ($80–$107) double. Rates include buffet breakfast.

This handsome new hotel 10km from Parikia is designed to look like a small island village, and is situated in Lefkes, one of Paros's most charming inland villages, with views over the countryside to the sea. Rooms are light and bright, with good bathrooms; some have balconies. There's a restaurant, a handsome swimming pool, a Jacuzzi, and even a small Museum of Popular Aegean Culture.

Lily Apartments. Naoussa, 844 01 Paros. ☎ **0284/51-377,** or 01/958-9314 in Athens. Fax 0284/51-716, or 01/958-9314 in Athens. 17 units. TEL. 22,500Dr ($75) apt for 2. EURO, MC, V.

Lily Ananiadou offers well-kept, efficient apartments. They're simple, pleasantly modern, and fully equipped—with kitchens, telephones, and balconies overlooking dry, scrub-brush hills.

Papadakis Hotel. Naoussa, 84410 Paros. ☎ **0284/51-643.** Fax 0284/51-269. 19 units. 18,000Dr ($60) double. Breakfast 1,800Dr ($6) extra. No credit cards.

This new hotel is comfortable and charming, with lovely views over the village and sea. Ten rooms have satellite TV and minibars, five are air-conditioned, and several have kitchenettes.

WHERE TO DINE

Aligaria Restaurant. Plateia Aligari, Parikia. ☎ **0284/22-026.** Main courses 1,500–3,700Dr ($5–$12). EURO, MC, V. Daily noon–3:30pm and 6:30pm–midnight. Turn left off Mavroyenous Sq. behind the Hotel Kontes. GREEK.

Owner Elizabeth Nikolousou is an excellent cook; her zucchini pie and generous portions of stuffed tomatoes disappear early. There's a good selection of local wines.

Barbarossa Ouzeri. On the waterfront, Naoussa. ☎ **0284/51-391.** Mezedes 600–1,800Dr ($2–$6). No credit cards. Daily 7:30–11:30pm. SNACKS.

This authentic ouzeri is right on the port. Wind-burned fishermen sit for hours nursing their milky ouzo in water and their mini-portions of grilled octopus and olives. This is a good spot to sit and watch the world go by.

✪ **Lalula.** Naoussa. ☎ **0284/51-547.** Reservations recommended July–Aug. Main courses 1,800–5,500Dr ($6–$18). No credit cards. Daily 7–11:45pm. Take a left at the post office; it's across from the Minoa Hotel. GREEK/MEDITERRANEAN/VEGETARIAN.

A gifted German restaurateur is responsible for the delicious and distinctive food, subdued decor, and interesting but unobtrusive music at Lalula. There's a lovely little garden in the back. The cooking is lighter than typical Greek cuisine; the menu depends on what's fresh at the market. Regular items include vegetable quiche, sweet-and-sour chicken with rice and ginger chutney, and fish steamed in herbs. Check to see if there's a set-price menu; it's usually an excellent value.

Levantis Restaurant. Market St., Parikia on island or Paros: ☎ **0284/23-613.** Fax 0284/21-453. http://parosweb.com/levantis. E-mail: levantis@parosweb.com. Reservations recommended July–Aug. Main courses 2,500–4,600Dr ($8–$15). AE, DC, EURO, MC, V. Daily 6pm–1am. GREEK/EASTERN MEDITERRANEAN.

This restaurant serves dinner under a splendid grape arbor that some of the older diners remember being there when they were young. At press time, we learned that

Traveler's Warning

Several places in Paros offer very cheap drinks or "buy one, get one free" deals—usually the locally brewed alcohol that the natives call **bomba.** If you drink it, you'll know why: intoxication and nausea are virtually simultaneous.

the Levantis plans to add an Internet Cafe in 1999, and is adding Asian and Western cuisine to its popular Mediterranean and near Eastern specialties, which include spiced Moroccan lamb and a variety of seafood.

PAROS AFTER DARK

Just behind the windmill is a local landmark, the **Port Cafe,** a basic *kafenio* lit by bare incandescent bulbs and filled day and night with tourists waiting for a ferry, bus, taxi, or fellow traveler. The **Saloon d'Or,** south of the port, is another spot for cheap drinks. If you're not in a mood to party, try the **Pebbles Bar,** where you can usually hear tapes of classical music at sunset, or the **Pirate Bar,** in the Agora, where classical music alternates with jazz and blues. For partiers, there's the **Rendezvous,** where you'll hear rock music, and **Black Bart's,** with loud music and a boisterous, boozy crowd.

In Naoussa, try **Leonardo's, Agosta,** or the **Sofrano Bar,** all on the harbor.

Hungary 9

By *John Mastrini & Hana Mastrini*

Even before the fall of the Iron Curtain in 1989, Hungary was the most progressive of Europe's Communist countries, allowing more foreign investment and attracting more tourism than its neighbors. The head start is now most apparent in Budapest, which has rapidly closed the gap with Western European capitals, offering top-line accommodations and activities, while reviving the best of the Hungarian culture. But to better understand Hungary, you must also get to know the great river that runs through its heart. Take a slow boat (or a fast hydrofoil) up the Danube to the "Bend" towns of Szentendre, Esztergom, or Vác. For pure relaxation, you can sample the resorts at Europe's largest inland pond, Lake Balaton.

1 Budapest

Burgeoning with life after Communism, Budapest is enjoying the post–Cold War world more than any city this side of the former Iron Curtain. Berlin's eastern half is busy being recast into the modern capital of the new Germany, Warsaw is lost in faceless socialist architecture, and Prague broods over its quaint renaissance past, but Budapest is having a party—drawing tourists again with its grandiose 19th-century attitude that built the majestic Magyar capital on the Danube into one of Europe's most cosmopolitan cities.

If you seek one former East Bloc city as a unique destination, we would still suggest Prague, whose baroque palaces and compact Renaissance quarters have no equal in atmosphere. But for pure fun, try Budapest, especially Pest, where wide boulevards, worldly restaurants, and wild nightlife feel much closer to Paris and Rome than Warsaw—and at a fraction of the cost of Western Europe.

The Roman settlements straddling the Danube in what became Buda, Óbuda, and Pest have emerged from many cultures. Having witnessed first conquests of Avars and Huns, the Magyars (Hungarians) settled in the first half of this millennium. After 125 years of Turkish domination until 1686, the cities became part of the Austro-Hungarian Empire dominated by Vienna and the Hapsburgs.

The towns flourished after 1867, when the Hungarians gained autonomy. Budapest was unified in 1873 as the Hungarian identity emerged along with the most magnificent of architecture, including the city's landmark neo-Gothic parliament building, which has lorded over the Danube since the turn of the century.

Now, at the turn of the millennium—after the ravages of two world wars and more than 40 years of Communism—the fin-de-siècle buzz of Budapest's parlors, coffeehouses, and restaurants is back.

Only in Budapest

Living the Spa Life at the Hotel Gellért Nobody should take a trip to Budapest without at least one session in the city's fabled thermal spa. The 80-year-old grand hotel might have lost some of its gleam, but it could still be one of your most memorable stays.

Celebrating at Gundel Budapest's world-renowned restaurant can be enjoyed for the price of a casual lunch in Vienna. The 105-year-old marvel's savior, celebrated New York restaurateur George Lang, wrote the book on Hungarian cuisine, aptly called *The Cuisine of Hungary.*

Spending a Night at the Opera For the price of a baseball ticket, you can sit in the royal box, once the preserve of Hapsburg monarchs.

Nursing an Espresso and People-Watching at Gerbeaud's Hungary's popular 19th-century confectionery buzzes with enough bonhomie to keep you occupied for hours.

Catching the Odd Glimpse of Hungary's Communist Past Budapest has dealt with the relics of Communism in a mind-provoking way at the Statue Park in south Buda. It's a reality check for propaganda of any kind.

Getting to Know the Danube The awesome river dividing Buda from Pest can be seen in many ways; stroll over the stout Chain Bridge or take a boat for a relaxed view of most of the city's riverside skyline.

Discovering the Jewish District Budapest has the largest Jewish population of any city on the European continent, outside Russia. Pest's historic Jewish neighborhood is rundown but relatively unchanged, but the Dohány Synagogue has been lovingly restored.

ORIENTATION

ARRIVING   By Plane Budapest's airport, **Ferihegy** (☎ **1/296-8000**), is in the XVIII district in southeastern Pest. Delta has an alliance with the Hungarian national carrier Malev and usually has two direct flights from New York to Budapest daily. American Airlines, KLM, and Lufthansa have frequent flights to Budapest from connecting hubs in continental Europe.

The easiest and most reliable way into the city is the **Airport Minibus** (☎ **1/296-8555**), a public service of the LRI (Budapest Airport Authority). The minibus, which leaves every 10 or 15 minutes throughout the day, takes you directly to any address in the city. The price is 1,200FT ($5.35) per person.

LRI also runs an Airport-Centrum bus, at 600FT ($2.65) per person, which leaves every half hour from both terminals at Ferihegy airport. Passengers are dropped off at Pest's Erzsébet tér bus station, just off Deák tér, where all three metro lines converge. Tickets are sold aboard the bus for the 30- to 40-minute trip.

Private **taxi** drivers who loiter at the airport are notoriously overpriced. Take taxis only from the recommended fleets (see "Getting Around," below). It's also possible to get to the city by public transport; a **bus** to the metro (subway) takes about 1 hour. From either airport, take the red-lettered bus no. 93 to the last stop, Kóbánya-Kispest.

From there, the **Blue metro line** runs to the Inner City of Pest. The cost is two transit tickets (180FT/80¢); tickets can be bought from any newsstand in the airport.

By Train   Most international trains pull into bustling Keleti pályaudvar (Eastern Station) in Pest's Baross tér. The Red line of the metro is below the station.

Some international trains arrive at **Nyugati pályaudvar** (Western Station) on the Outer Ring. A Blue line metro station is beneath Nyugati. Few international trains arrive at Buda's **Déli pályaudvar** (Southern Station); the terminus of the Red metro line is beneath the train station.

For domestic train information, call ☎ **1/461-5400;** for international train information, call ☎ **1/461-5500,** both 24 hours daily. Purchase tickets at train station ticket offices or from the **Hungarian State Railway (MÁV) Service Office,** VI. Andrássy út 35.

By Bus   Most buses pull into the **Erzsébet tér bus station** (☎ **1/317-2562**), just off Deák tér in central Pest.

By Car   Vienna, 170 miles from Budapest, connects to the Hungarian capital by the Austrian A4 superhighway, which becomes the M1 and feeds into the city via southern Buda. The border crossings from Austria and Slovakia are generally hassle-free. You may be requested to present your driver's license, vehicle registration, and proof of insurance (the number plate and symbol indicating country of origin are acceptable proof). Hungary doesn't require the international driver's license. Cars entering Hungary are required to have a decal indicating country of registration, a first-aid kit, and an emergency triangle.

By Hydrofoil   The **Hungarian State Shipping Agency (MAHART)** operates hydrofoils on the Danube between Vienna and Budapest in the spring and summer. Book your tickets well in advance. In Vienna, contact MAHART at Handelskai 265 (☎ **43-1/729-2161**). The Budapest office of MAHART (☎ **1/318-1704**) is at the dock where the boats arrive, on the Pest side of the Danube at V. Belgrád rakpart, between the Erzsébet Bridge and the Szabadság Bridge.

VISITOR INFORMATION   The city's best information source is **Tourinform** (☎ 1/317-9800; e-mail: tourinform@mail.hungarytourism.hu; www. hungarytourism.hu), at V. Sütő u. 2, just off Deák tér (reached by all three metro lines) in Pest. Open daily 8am to 8pm.

CITY LAYOUT   The city of Budapest was founded in 1873 by joining three cities: Buda, Pest, and Óbuda. Budapest, like Hungary itself, is defined by the River Danube (Duna), along which many historic sites are found. Eight bridges join the two banks; five of them are in the city center.

On the right bank lies **Pest,** the commercial and administrative center. Central Pest is that part of the city between the river and the semicircular **Outer Ring boulevard (Nagykörút),** stretches of which take the names of former monarchs: Ferenc, József, Erzsébet, Teréz, and Szent István. The Outer Ring begins at the Pest side of the Petőfi Bridge in the south and wraps itself around the center, ending at the Margit Bridge in the north. Several of Pest's busiest squares are along the Outer Ring, and Pest's major east–west avenues bisect it at these squares.

Central Pest proper is defined by the **Inner Ring (Kiskörút).** It starts at Szabadság híd (Freedom Bridge) in the south and is alternately named Vámház körút, Múzeum körút, Károly körút, Bajcsy-Zsilinszky út, and József Attila utca before ending at the Chain Bridge (Széchenyi lánchíd). Inside this ring is the **Belváros,** the historic Inner City of Pest.

Váci utca is a popular pedestrian shopping street between the Inner Ring and the Danube. It spills into **Vörösmarty tér,** one of the best-known squares. The **Dunakorzó (Danube Promenade),** a popular evening stroll, runs along the river in Pest, between the Chain Bridge and the Erzsébet Bridge. The **historic Jewish district** of Pest is in the Erzsébetváros, between the two ring boulevards.

Margaret Island (Margit-sziget) is in the middle of the Danube. Accessible by the Margaret Bridge or Árpád Bridge, it's a popular park without vehicular traffic.

On the left bank is **Buda;** to its north, beyond the city center, lies Óbuda. Buda is as hilly as Pest is flat. **Castle Hill** is widely considered the most beautiful part of Budapest. A number of steep paths, staircases, and small streets go up to Castle Hill, but no major roads. The easiest access is from **Clark Ádám tér** (at the head of the Chain Bridge) by funicular, or from **Várfok utca** (near Moszkva tér) by foot or bus. Castle Hill consists of the royal palace itself, home to numerous museums, and the so-called **Castle District,** a lovely neighborhood of small, winding streets, centered on the Gothic Matthias Church.

Below Castle Hill, along the Danube, is a long, narrow neighborhood, historically populated by fishermen and other river workers, known as the **Víziváros (Water-town).**

Central Buda is a collection of low-lying neighborhoods below Castle Hill. The main square is **Moszkva tér,** just north of Castle Hill. Beyond Central Buda, mainly to the east, are the Buda Hills.

Óbuda is on the left bank of the Danube, north of Buda. Although the greater part of Óbuda is modern and drab, it features a beautiful old city center and impressive Roman ruins.

Budapest is divided into 22 districts, called *kerülets* (abbreviated as *ker.*). A Roman numeral followed by a period precedes every written address in Budapest, signifying the kerület; for example, XII. Csörsz utca 9 is in the 12th kerület. Because many street names are repeated in different parts of the city, it's important to know which kerület a certain address is in.

GETTING AROUND

Budapest has an extensive and inexpensive public transportation system. Its biggest disadvantage is that, except for 17 well-traveled bus and tram routes, all forms of transport shut down nightly at around 11:30pm; certain areas of the city, most notably the Buda Hills, are beyond the reach of the limited night service, so you have to take a taxi. Be on the alert for pickpockets when on crowded public transportation. Keep your money and valuables inside your clothing in a money belt.

All forms of public transportation in Budapest require you to validate prepurchased **tickets (*vonaljegy*)** either on board or at the station; you can buy tickets for 90FT (40¢) apiece at metro ticket windows, newspaper kiosks, and the occasional tobacco shop.

Day passes (*napijegy*) cost 700FT ($3.10) and are valid until midnight of the day of purchase. Buy them from metro ticket windows; the clerk validates the pass at the time of purchase. A 3-day *turistajegy* costs 1,400FT ($6.20), and a weekly pass costs 1,750FT ($7.75).

Inspectors frequently check for valid tickets, particularly in metro stations. On-the-spot fines (800FT/$3.55) are assessed to fare dodgers.

All public transport operates on rough schedules, posted at bus and tram shelters and in metro stations. The Budapest Transport Authority produces a more detailed transportation map (BKV térkép), available at most metro ticket windows for 200FT (90¢).

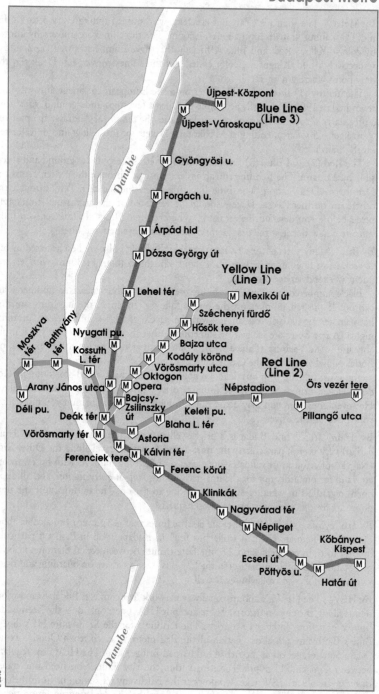

Budapest Metro

Újpest-Központ

Blue Line
(Line 3)

Újpest-Városkapu

Gyöngyösi u.

Forgách u.

Árpád hid

Dózsa György út

Yellow Line
(Line 1)

Lehel tér

Mexikói út

Széchenyi fürdő

Hősök tere

Nyugati pu.

Bajza utca

Moszkva tér

Batthyány tér

Kossuth L. tér

Kodály körönd

Vörösmarty utca

Oktogon

Red Line
(Line 2)

Arany János utca

Opera

Népstadion

Örs vezér tere

Déli pu.

Bajcsy-Zsilinszky út

Keleti pu.

Pillangó utca

Deák tér

Blaha L. tér

Vörösmarty tér

Astoria

Ferenciek tere

Kálvin tér

Ferenc körút

Klinikák

Nagyvárad tér

Népliget

Kőbánya-Kispest

Ecseri út

Pöttyös u.

Határ út

Danube

Danube

E-0015

By Metro The metro is clean and efficient, with trains running every 3 to 5 minutes from about 4:30am until about 11:30pm. The three lines are universally known by color—Yellow, Red, and Blue. Officially they have numbers as well (1, 2, and 3 respectively), but all signs are color-coded. All three lines converge at **Deák tér,** the only point where any meet.

The **Yellow (1) line** is the oldest metro on the European continent, but was fully renovated in 1996. This easily accessible line, just a few steps underground, runs from Vörösmarty tér in the heart of central Pest, out the length of Andrássy út, past the Városliget (City Park), ending at Mexikói út. Tickets for the Yellow line are validated on the train itself.

The **Red (2) and Blue (3) lines** are modern metros, deep under ground and accessible by escalator. The Red line runs from eastern Pest, through the center, across the Danube to Déli Station. The Blue line runs from southeastern Pest, through the center, to northern Pest. Tickets should be validated at the automated timestamp boxes before you descend the escalator. When changing lines at Deák tér, you must validate a new ticket at the orange machines in hallways between lines.

By Bus Many parts of the city, most notably the Buda Hills, are best accessed by bus (*busz*). Most lines are in service from about 4:30am to about 11:30pm, with less frequent weekend service on some.

Black-numbered local buses constitute the majority of bus lines. Red-numbered are express. If the red number on the bus is followed by an *E,* the bus runs nonstop between terminals (whereas an *É*—with an accent mark—signifies *észak,* meaning night). A few buses are labeled by something other than a number; one you'll probably use is the **Várbusz (Palace Bus),** a minibus that runs between Várfok utca, off Buda's Moszkva tér, and the Castle District.

You must validate your bus ticket on board at the mechanical red box found by each door. Tickets cannot be purchased from the driver. You can board the bus by any door. However, after 8pm you may board only through the front door, and you must show your ticket to the driver.

By Tram You'll find Budapest's bright-yellow trams (known as *villamos* in Hungarian) very useful, particularly the **nos. 4 and 6,** which travel along the Outer Ring (Nagykörút). You must validate your ticket on board the tram. As with buses, tickets are valid for one ride, not for the line itself. Trams stop at every station, and all doors open, regardless of whether anyone is waiting to get on. The buttons near the tram doors are for emergency stops, not stop requests.

By Trolleybus Red trolleybuses are electric buses that get power from a cable above the street. There are only 14 trolleybus lines in Budapest, all in Pest. Of particular interest to train travelers is no. 73, the fastest route between Keleti Station and Nyugati Station. All the information in the "By Bus" section above on boarding and ticket validation applies to trolleybuses as well.

By HÉV The HÉV is a suburban railway network that connects Budapest to various points along the city's outskirts. There are four HÉV lines; only one, the **Szentendre line,** is of serious interest to tourists. The terminus for the Szentendre HÉV line is Buda's Batthyány tér, also a station of the Red metro line. To reach Óbuda's Fő tér (Main Square), get off at the Árpád híd (Árpád Bridge) stop. The HÉV runs regularly between 4am and 11:30pm. For trips within the city limits, you need one transit ticket, available at HÉV ticket windows at the Batthyány tér station or from the conductor on board. These tickets are different from the standard transportation tickets and are punched by conductors on board. If you have a valid day pass, you do not need to buy a ticket for trips within the city limits.

Taxi Warning

Beware being taken for a ride by some of the notorious fly-by-night cabs in Budapest. Several fleets have good reputations, honest drivers, and competitive rates. The most highly recommended companies are **Fő Taxi** (☎ 1/222-2222) and **City Taxi** (☎ 1/211-1111). Avoid non-fleet cabs, especially those without official nameplates with the taxi company and car registration number. Rogue cabbies have little accountability and you risk being overcharged, or worse.

By Taxi   In 1998, new taxi regulations were imposed to set fare limits and crack down on the all-too-frequent sport of foreigner-fleecing. Drivers can charge a basic fare of up to 200FT (90¢), plus 200FT per kilometer. The fees rises to 280FT ($1.25) after 10pm.

By Car   We don't recommend using a car for sightseeing in Budapest. You might, however, want to rent a car for trips outside the capital. We recommend **Denzel Europcar InterRent,** VIII. Üllői út 60–62, 1082 Budapest (☎ 1/477-1080), where you can find a Suzuki Swift for 9,000FT ($40) per day, insurance and unlimited mileage included. It also has a rental counter at the airport Ferihegy (☎ 1/296-6610).

Fast Facts: Budapest

American Express   Budapest's main American Express office is between Vörösmarty tér and Deák tér in central Pest, at V. Deák Ferenc u. 10, 1052 Budapest (☎ 1/235-4330). It's open Monday through Friday 9am to 6:30pm in summer (9am to 5:30pm in winter) and Saturday 9am to 2pm. There's an American Express cash ATM on the street in front and also at the airport. For lost traveler's checks, call ☎ 00/800-04411 for the U.K. direct operator. Ask to call collect to ☎ 44-273-571600, or to dial direct (you pay), call 00/44-273-571600. For lost AMEX cards, call ☎ 1/235-4311 in Budapest from 8am to midnight; after midnight and on Sundays when the office closes early, your call is automatically transferred to the U.K.

Business Hours   Most **stores** are open Monday through Friday 10am to 6pm and Saturday 9 or 10am to 1 to 2pm. Many shops close for an hour at lunchtime, and only stores in central tourist areas are open Sunday. Many shops and restaurants close for 2 weeks in August. **Banks** are generally open Monday through Thursday 8am to 3pm and Friday 8am to 1pm.

Currency   The basic unit of currency is the **forint (FT).** There are 100 **fillérs** (almost worthless and soon to be taken out of circulation) in a forint. Coins come in denominations of 50 fillérs and 1, 2, 5, 10, 20, 100, and 200FT. Banknotes come in denominations of 100, 500, 1,000, 5,000, and 10,000FT. The rate of exchange used in this chapter is $1 = 225FT or 100FT = 2¢. Also, 1EUR = 238.7FT and 1£ = 363.8FT.

Many hotels and pensions in Budapest list their prices in German marks (DM); a few list them in U.S. dollars, solely as a hedge against forint inflation; all accept payment in Hungarian forints as well as foreign currencies. We have converted the DM prices into dollar prices, basing our calculations on an exchange rate of 1.75DM to $1, the rate at press time. As this exchange rate fluctuates over time, of course, the price of a room in dollars will fluctuate along with it.

Bargain Hunter's Tip

With annual inflation still topping 10%, prices jump with little notice. This is offset by the "crawling peg" that keeps the local currency, the *forint,* moving lower against the dollar, helping Hungarian exporters, but also foreign tourists. Over the past year, the forint slid from around 200 to the dollar to about 225. The crawling peg has roughly the same effect vis-à-vis the British pound, but the actual differential at any given time depends on fluctuations between the dollar and the pound.

Currency Exchange   The best rates for cash and especially for traveler's checks are obtained at banks, not at the exchange booths seen throughout the city center, in train stations, and in most hotels. Especially avoid the *Inter Change* booths where rates can be as much as 20% worse than the prevailing rate. You can also withdraw money in forints from your home bank account by accessing the PLUS or CIRRUS networks through any of the **ATMs** found throughout the city. You're allowed to re-exchange into hard currency up to half the amount of forints you originally purchased; make sure you keep all your exchange receipts.

Doctors & Dentists   IMS, a private outpatient clinic at XIII. Váci út 202 (☎ 1/329-8423), has English-speaking doctors, and is used by many Americans living in Budapest; it's reached via the Blue metro line (Gyöngyös utca). IMS also operates an emergency service after hours and on weekends, III. Vihar u. 29 (☎ 1/250-1899). Many luxury hotels also have a staff or private doctor with rented office space. For further options, ask at Tourinform.

Drugstores   The Hungarian word is *gyógyszertár* or *patika.* Generally, pharmacies carry only prescription drugs. Hotel "drugstores" are just shops with soap, perfume, aspirin, and other nonprescription items. There are several 24-hour pharmacies in the city; each pharmacy posts the address of the nearest 24-hour pharmacy in its window.

Embassies   The embassy of **Australia** is at XII. Királyhágo tér 8–9 (☎ 1/201-8899); the embassy of **Canada** at XII. Budakeszi út 32 (☎ 1/275-1200); the embassy of **Republic of Ireland** at V. Szabadság tér 7 (☎ 1/302-9600); the embassy of the **United Kingdom** at V. Harmincad u. 6 (☎ 1/266-2888); and the embassy of the **United States** at V. Szabadság tér 12 (☎ 1/267-4400). **New Zealand** does not have representation in Hungary.

Emergencies   Dial ☎ **104** for an ambulance, ☎ **105** for the fire department, or ☎ **107** for the police. To reach a 24-hour English-speaking emergency service, dial ☎ 1/318-8212.

Hospitals   See "Doctors & Dentists" above.

Internet Access   A low-key place is **Budapest Net** at Kecskeméti 5 a few blocks from Kálvin tér on the Blue line in the 5th district (☎ 1/328-0292). A dozen loaded PCs are downstairs for 150FT (65¢) per half-hour of usage. The Web address is www.budapestnet.hu/index.en.

Lost Property   The **BKV (Budapest Transportation Authority)** lost-and-found office is at VII. Akácfa u. 18 (☎ 1/322-6613). For items lost on a train or in a train station, call ☎ 1/329-8037. For items lost on an intercity bus (not on a local BKV bus), call ☎ 1/318-2122.

Luggage Storage   There are luggage storage offices (*ruhatár*) at all three major railroad stations. At Keleti it's in the main waiting room alongside Track 4, open

4am to midnight. At Nyugati it's in the waiting room behind the international ticket office, and it's open 24 hours. Déli Station has an automated locker system in operation in the main ticket-purchasing area; the lockers are large and instructions are provided by a multilingual computer, open Monday through Thursday 6am to 7pm, Friday 6am to 8pm, and Saturday and Sunday 6am to 6pm.

Post Office   The city's main post office (☎ 1/201-7391) is at Petőfi Sándor u. 17–19, not far from Deák tér (all metro lines); it's open Monday through Friday 8am to 8pm and Saturday 8am to 3pm. There are 24-hour post offices near Keleti and Nyugati stations.

Taxes   Taxes are included in all restaurant prices, hotel rates, and shop purchases. For information on refunds of the 25% value-added tax (VAT), which is built into all prices, (available for most consumer goods purchases of more than 25,000FT/$111), see this book's introduction "Planning Your Trip to Europe." In addition to presenting your claim at the airport, you can submit them by mail to **Foreigners' Refund Office** of the APEH Budapest Directorate, XI. Bartók Béla út 156, Budapest (☎ 1/203-0888 or 1/356-9800).

Telephone   The **country code** for Hungary is **36.** The **city code** for Budapest is **1.** For long-distance calls within Hungary, you must first dial **06.** A GTE Hungarian yellow pages phone number search is available in English on the Web at http://www.gte-yellow-pages.com/2Eng.htm. Once you have a number, you'll find the privatized Hungarian phone system Matáv still falls far short of Western standards. Dial slowly and don't be too quick to trust a busy signal—keep trying. For **international and local calls from public phones,** the best procedure is to buy a **telephone card** in 50 or 100 units you can find at post offices, tobacco shops, and some street vendors, from 1,000FT ($4.45) each, and get an international operator. There are many newer card-op phones around town, so the chances of finding a functioning booth are much greater if you have a card than if you depend on coins. To get the international operator from coin-op public phones, a 20FT coin is required to start the call. From card-op phones you are debited a local call. The toll-free international access codes are: **AT&T ☎ 00/ 800-01111, MCI ☎ 00/800-01411,** and **Sprint ☎ 00/800-01877.** Hotels typically add a surcharge, so you're advised to use public booths, the telephone office, or the post office.

Using **direct dial** to the United States and Canada can be as much as twice the charge of calls in the other direction, depending on the time of day. Call **09** for the Hungarian international operator.

If you find that the number you want has changed (you'll hear a recording: *"a hívott szám megváltozott"*). For **local directory assistance** try calling **CoMo Media,** publishers of the English-language phone book, at ☎ 1/266-4916. The **main telecommunications office,** at Petőfi Sándor u. 17 (near Deák tér), is open Monday to Friday 8am to 8pm and Saturday 9am to 3pm. Telephone calls, as well as faxes and telexes, can be made to anywhere in the world. It costs 200FT (90¢) per minute to call the United States from this office. Ask at the main desk for a telephone guide information pamphlet in English.

Phone Alert

Budapest phone numbers are constantly changing as Matáv continues to upgrade its system. All numbers starting with "1" may be subject to change by 2000. In many, but not all, of these cases, the 1 will simply be replaced with 3.

WHERE TO STAY

During a visit to still-Communist Budapest in the late 1980s, we had a desperate time finding a room when arriving by train after 6pm. But even during those days, the state travel bureau Ibusz helped us find a clean, functional room in a workers' hotel for under $10 each. During the post-1989 boom, Budapest has seen the selection and the prices jump, but there still are not enough beds to satisfy the much greater demand. Hotels range from beautiful, historic gems to drab, socialist bed sits. Prices are some of the lowest of any major European city.

When booking, if you want a room with a double bed, be sure to request one; otherwise, you'll get a room with two twin beds. Single rooms are generally available, as are extra beds or cots. Hungarian hotels use the word *apartment* to describe the kind of room we call a suite (that is, connected rooms, without a kitchen). In these listings, we have called a suite a suite, so to speak.

ACCOMMODATIONS AGENCIES   Most accommodations agencies can secure private room rentals, help reserve hotel and pension rooms, and book you into a youth hostel. If you can't get booked into the hotels we list below, your next best bet comes from **Ibusz** (☎ **1/337-0939;** www.ibusz.hu). The main Ibusz reservations office is at Ferenciek tere 10, reached by the Blue metro line. Another number to call if you're interested in booking a room in a private home through Ibusz is ☎ **1/318-1120.**

✪ **PRIVATE ROOMS**   When you book a private room, you get a room in someone's apartment; usually you share the bathroom. Breakfast is usually offered for a fee (400 to 600FT/$1.80 to $2.65). You may also have limited kitchen privileges (ask in advance).

You can book a private room through an accommodation agency (see above). Prices might vary slightly between agencies, but generally speaking, rooms cost 2,500 to 4,500FT ($11.10 to $20), plus 3% tax. Most agencies add a 30% surcharge (to the first night only) for stays of less than 4 nights.

IN THE INNER CITY & CENTRAL PEST

Very Expensive

✪ **K & K Hotel Opera.** VI. Révay u. 24, 1065 Budapest. ☎ **1/269-0222.** Fax 1/269-0230. www.kkhotels.com. E-mail: kk.hotel.opera@kkhotel.hu. 205 units. A/C MINIBAR TV TEL. 270–350DM ($143–$200) double. Rates 5% lower in low season. Rates include breakfast. AE, DC, EURO, MC, V. Parking: 13DM ($7.40). Metro: Opera (Yellow line).

Austria's K & K hotel chain has managed to slip in a top-standard hotel within an old neighborhood just behind the grand Opera House in central Pest. Opened in 1994 and expanded in 1997, this pleasant building has all the standard comforts of a modern western business hotel, but little of the feel of the setting within the historic theater district. Each room has a safe, and guests have use of a sauna and fitness room.

Moderate

King's Hotel. VII. Nagydiófa u. 25–27. ☎ and fax **1/352-7675.** 79 units. TV TEL. 15,750–18,000FT ($70–$80) double; 31,500FT ($140) suite. AE, DC, MC, V. Free parking available on street. Metro: Astoria (Red line).

A good value in the Jewish district, the King's Hotel restored its fin-de-siècle facade in 1995, and updated the rooms, although the modern furniture and floral prints on the bedspreads and curtains will not impress you. the entry and reception areas seem less than inviting, but the rooms are comfortable and have safes. The hotel's Kosher Lemehadrin restaurant has a menu approved by Budapest's chief rabbi, Rabbi Hoffman.

Inexpensive

Hotel MEDOSZ. VI. Jókai tér 9, 1061 Budapest. ☎ **1/353-1700** or 1/374-3000. Fax 1/332-4316. 70 units, all with bathroom. TV TEL. 80DM ($46) double. Rates include breakfast. No credit cards. Parking difficult in neighborhood. Metro: Oktogon (Yellow line).

Most hotels and pensions in Budapest divide the year into three seasons. **High season** is roughly from March or April through September or October and the week between Christmas and New Year's. **Mid-season** is usually considered the months of March and October and/or November. **Low season** is roughly November through February, except Christmas week. Some hotels discount as much as 50% in low season, while others offer no winter discount; be sure to inquire.

Our first taste of Budapest in the 1980s, this hotel used to be one of the perks for members of the MEDOSZ union for agriculture workers. Privatization has not changed the functional Communist veneer much, but it remains a great value in the heart of Pest's theater district, not far from the Opera House. The rooms are simple but clean, if not a bit overwhelmed by the Day-Glo orange fabrics used for curtains and bed covers in many rooms. There's a restaurant and bar in the hotel, and laundry service is available.

✪ **Peregrinus Vendégház.** V. Szerb u. 3, 1056 Budapest. ☎ **1/266-4911.** Fax 1/266-4913. 26 units, all with bathroom. TV TEL MINIBAR. 11,500FT ($51.10) double (10%–15% increase is due by the high season). Rates include breakfast. No credit cards. No parking. Metro: Kálvin tér (Blue line).

Pest's ELTE University runs this guesthouse, which is a sparkling value in the heart of the Inner City. You can't book rooms more than a month in advance, but do call 30 days before your arrival to heighten your chances. Located on a small street just half a block from the Váci utca shopping zone, the building dates from the turn of the century and was renovated in 1994, when the guesthouse was opened. The rooms are simple but comfortable.

JUST BEYOND CENTRAL PEST
Expensive
✪ **Family Hotel.** XIII. Ipoly u. 8/b, 1133 Budapest. ☎ **1/320-1284.** Fax 1/329-1620. 13 units. A/C MINIBAR TV TEL. 80DM ($45.70) double; 240DM ($137) suite. Rates 10%–15% lower in low season. Rates include breakfast. AE, DC, JCB, MC, V. Parking 600FT ($2.65) per day. Trolleybus: 79 from Keleti pu. to Ipoly utca.

This unique hotel is just 3 blocks off the quay across from Margaret Island in Pest. The large maisonette suites with wooden staircases leading to sky-lit sleeping lofts are perfect for families with older children, sleeping four comfortably. The rooms all have tasteful modern wooden furniture, and the dining room is well appointed. Room service is available. Facilities include sauna, massage, hairdresser, and a conference room.

Inexpensive
✪ **Radio Inn.** VI. Benczúr u. 19, 1068 Budapest. ☎ **1/342-8347** or 1/322-0237. Fax 1/322-8284. 32 units. TV TEL. 7,000–14,000FT ($31–$62) apt. for 1 to 3. Breakfast 1,036FT ($4.60) extra. MC, V. Parking available on street. Metro: Bajza utca (Yellow line).

The Radio Inn is the official guesthouse of Hungarian national radio, but is hard to book because of its popularity with visiting bureaucrats and its repeat tourist business. Try to make your reservation months in advance. Beside the affordable rates, the Inn, in a diplomats' neighborhood just off City Park, offers apartments in quiet guest quarters, not a bustling city hotel. The rooms are spacious, with fully equipped kitchens and comfortable, if not stylish, beds. There's a well-kept garden behind the building.

Budapest

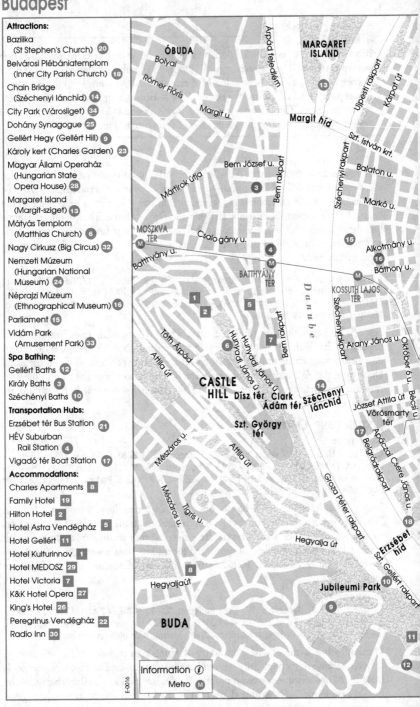

Attractions:

Bazilika
(St Stephen's Church) 20

Belvárosi Plébániatemplom
(Inner City Parish Church) 18

Chain Bridge
(Széchenyi lánchíd) 14

City Park (Városliget) 34

Dohány Synagogue 25

Gellért Hegy (Gellért Hill) 9

Károly kert (Charles Garden) 23

Magyar Állami Operaház
(Hungarian State
Opera House) 28

Margaret Island
(Margit-sziget) 13

Mátyás Templom
(Matthias Church) 6

Nagy Cirkusz (Big Circus) 32

Nemzeti Múzeum
(Hungarian National
Museum) 24

Néprajzi Múzeum
(Ethnographical Museum) 16

Parliament 15

Vidám Park
(Amusement Park) 33

Spa Bathing:

Gellért Baths 12

Király Baths 3

Széchényi Baths 10

Transportation Hubs:

Erzsébet tér Bus Station 21

HÉV Suburban
Rail Station 4

Vigadó tér Boat Station 17

Accommodations:

Charles Apartments 8

Family Hotel 19

Hilton Hotel 2

Hotel Astra Vendégház 5

Hotel Gellért 11

Hotel Kulturinnov 1

Hotel MEDOSZ 29

Hotel Victoria 7

K&K Hotel Opera 27

King's Hotel 26

Peregrinus Vendégház 22

Radio Inn 30

E-0016

Information ⓘ
Metro Ⓜ

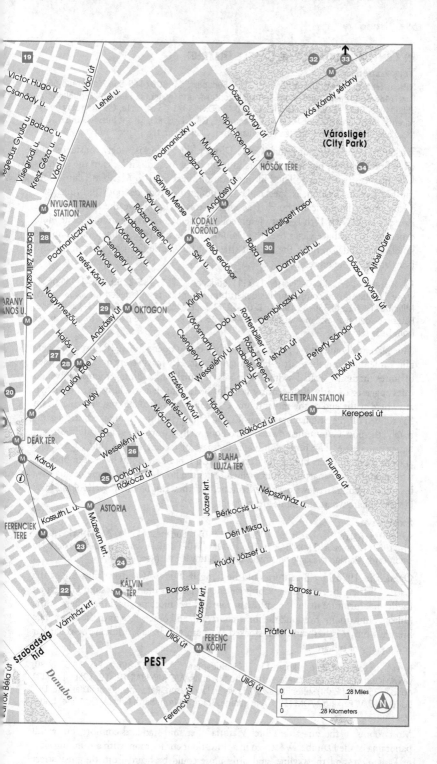

IN CENTRAL BUDA & THE CASTLE DISTRICT
Very Expensive
Hilton Hotel. I. Hess András tér 1–3, 1014 Budapest. ☎ **800/445-8667** or 1/488-6600. Fax 1/488-6644. www.hilton.com. E-mail: hiltonhu@hungary.net. 322 units. A/C MINIBAR TV TEL. 340–530DM ($194–$302) double; 650–900DM ($371–$514) suite. Children stay free in parents' room. Breakfast 29DM ($16.55) extra. AE, CB, DC, EURO, MC, V. Bus: "Várbusz" from Moszkva tér or 16 from Deák tér. Funicular: From Clark Ádám tér.

Tucked into the center of Buda's Castle District, the Hilton is widely considered the city's finest address, but what it offers in luxury and location, it lacks in the Gellért's local nuances (see below). The Hilton's location, next door to Matthias Church and the Fisherman's Bastion, is spectacular. Its design incorporates both the ruins of a 13th-century Dominican church (the church tower rises above the hotel) and the baroque facade of a 17th-century Jesuit college (the hotel's main entrance). The more expensive rooms have views over the Danube, with a full Pest skyline; rooms on the hotel's other side overlook the ancient streets of the Castle District. Hair dryers and irons are available on request.

✪ **Hotel Gellért.** XI. Gellért tér 1, 1111 Budapest. ☎ **1/385-2200.** Fax 1/466-6631. www.danubiusgroup.com/danubius/gellert.html. E-mail: resoff@gellert.hu. 233 units. MINIBAR TV TEL. 46,350–53,100FT ($206–$236) double; 65,700–69,750 ($292–$310) suite. Rates include breakfast. Spa packages available. AE, DC, MC, V. Free parking. Tram: 47 or 49 from Deák tér.

This place really must have been a dandy when it first opened in 1918, just as the curtain came down on the Austro-Hungarian Empire. Its massive art nouveau complex of suites, naturally heated swimming pools, thermal baths, dining rooms, pubs and cafes suggests an early 20th-century taste for hedonism that would be hard to match anywhere at the end of the millennium. Of course, 80 years later, much of the gleam has rubbed off the original brass, marble, and ceramic fixtures lining the hotel. Fortunately, the post-Communist owners have done well to leave the grand lady mostly in her pristine state. The hotel dominates the base of Gellért Hill in Buda, where the ancient thermal waters bubble up next to the Danube. The rooms have been updated with modern, but smart, furniture, which belies the hotel's origins. Some rooms have balconies with great views over the Danube, but they can be noisy overlooking busy Gellért Square where the trams are frequent.

Expensive
✪ **Hotel Astra Vendégház.** I. Vám u. 6, 1011 Budapest. ☎ **1/214-1906.** Fax 1/214-1907. 12 units. A/C MINIBAR TV TEL. 180DM ($102) double. Rates include breakfast. No credit cards. Parking available on street. Metro: Batthyány tér (Red line).

Opened in 1996 in a 3-centuries-old building in Buda's Watertown just under the Castle District, the Astra is an impressive entry. Spacious rooms with solid Hungarian traditional furniture make for a pleasant stay and feel more personal than those at the Hilton. Some rooms overlook the inner courtyard, and others face onto the street. The breakfast buffet is fresh and well-stocked. You can also have a drink at the cellar bar and a game of billiards.

Hotel Victoria. I. Bem rakpart 11, 1011 Budapest. ☎ **1/457-8080.** Fax 1/457-8080. www.victoria.hu. E-mail: victoria@victoria.hu. 27 units. A/C MINIBAR TV TEL. 195DM ($111) double; 350DM ($200) suite. Rates 25% lower in low season. Rates include breakfast. AE, DC, EURO, MC, V. Parking 17DM ($9.70) in garage. Tram: 19 from Batthyány tér (Red line) to the first stop.

Most rooms in the quayside Hotel Victoria offer mid-standard comfort, but a full panorama of the Danube. We stayed in a third-floor corner room with a stunning view of Parliament and the skyline, and little noise could be heard from the busy street below. Two-thirds of the rooms have large double windows with fine Pest views, but you might ask for rooms from the third floor up in this nine-floor building to avoid street noise. The Victoria is a 5-minute walk or one tram stop from Batthyány tér or Clark Ádám tér.

Moderate

◆ Hotel Kulturinnov. I. Szentháromság tér 6, 1014 Budapest. ☎ **1/355-0122.** Fax 1/375-1886. E-mail: mka3@mail.matav.hu. 16 units. TEL. 16,875FT ($75) double. Rates include breakfast. AE, DC, MC, V. Parking 2,000FT ($10). Bus: "Várbusz" from Moszkva tér or 16 from Deák tér. Funicular: From Clark Ádám tér.

As you face the Plague Column in the Castle District, with the Matthias Church just to the left, turn directly around to find this somewhat secret guesthouse in the building run by the Hungarian Culture Foundation. The rooms are not nearly as imposing as the walk up through the dark Gothic entry hall and massive stone staircase. The hotel is open to the public (although once through the main door, the elderly attendant may ask where you're going). Inside you'll find clean, simple furnishings and older standard bathrooms en suite. The atmosphere smacks of a hospital ward, but the price and location are just right.

Inexpensive

◆ Charles Apartments. I. Hegyalja út 23, 1016 Budapest. ☎ **1/201-1796.** Fax 1/212-2584. E-mail: charles@mail.matav.hu. 60 units. TV TEL. 9,000–13,500F ($40–$60) apt. for 1 or 2; 15,750FT ($70) apt. for 3. Rates 10%–15% lower in low season. Rates include buffet breakfast. MC, V. Parking 1,000FT ($4.45) or free on a nearby side street. Bus: 78 from Keleti pu. to Mészáros utca.

Owner Károly Szombati manages these well-equipped apartments in a quiet but convenient Buda neighborhood. All are average Budapest flats, comfortable and clean with full kitchens. Hegyalja út is a very busy street, but only two apartments face out onto it; the rest are in the interior or on the side of the building.

IN THE BUDA HILLS

Moderate

Gizella Panzió. XII. Arató u. 42/b, 1121 Budapest. ☎ **1/249-2282.** Fax 1/249-2281. 14 units. MINIBAR TV TEL. 120DM ($68) double; 140DM ($80) suite. Rates lower in low season. EURO, MC, V. Free parking. Tram: 59 from Moszkva tér to the last stop.

This charming pension is a 10-minute walk from the nearest tram station. Built on the side of a hill, it has a lovely view and a series of terraced gardens leading down to the swimming pool. The pension also features a sauna, solarium, fitness room, and bar.

WHERE TO DINE

You can get more for your money dining in Budapest than probably anywhere else in Europe. The selection of international eateries is wide, and the cuisine more adventurous with spices than, say, that of Czech or Poland. In most restaurants, you have to initiate the paying and tipping ritual by summoning the waiter. The bill is then written out on the spot. If you think the bill is incorrect, don't be embarrassed to call it into question; waiters readily correct the bill when challenged. In all but the fanciest restaurants, the waiter stands there waiting patiently for payment after handing over the bill. The tip (generally about 10%) should be included in the amount you give him. State the full amount you are paying (bill plus tip) and the waiter will make change. Hungarians never leave tips on the table.

DINING BASICS   *Étterem* is the most common word for restaurant; a *vendéglő,* or guesthouse, is a smaller, often folksy restaurant. An *étkezde* is an informal lunchroom.

Önkiszolgáló means self-service cafeteria, typically open only for lunch. A *cukrászda* or *kávéház* is a classic Central European coffeehouse. A *borozó* is a wine bar, a *söröző* is a beer bar, and sandwiches are usually available at both. Finally, a *kocsma* is a sort of roadside tavern; the Buda Hills are filled with them. Most kocsmas serve a full dinner, but the kitchens close early.

IN THE INNER CITY & CENTRAL PEST

Expensive

○ **Faustos.** VII. Dohány u. 5. ☎ **1/269-6806.** Main courses 1,800–2,500FT ($8–11.10). AE, MC, V. Mon–Sat noon–3pm; 7pm–midnight. Metro: Deák tér (all lines) or Astoria (Red line). ITALIAN.

Just down the block from the Dohány Synagogue, this family-run parlor has all the details right. Framed by thick tablecloths and fine silver and elegant but cozy wood furniture, the minestrone and *al dente* pasta are as fresh and plentiful as those served at an Italian Sunday dinner. Fausto himself will join you for a grappa if he's not lording over his kitchen.

Légrádi & Co. Restaurant. V. Magyar u. 23. ☎ **1/318-6804.** Reservations highly recommended. Main courses 1,400–2,600FT ($6.20–$11.55). AE, CB, MC, V. Mon–Sat 6pm–midnight. Metro: Kálvin tér (Blue line). HUNGARIAN.

Small (nine tables) and inconspicuously marked on a sleepy side street in the southern part of the Inner City, this is one of the city's most elegant and formal restaurants. The food is served on Herend china, the cutlery is sterling, and an excellent string trio livens the atmosphere. Try the chicken paprika served with cheese dumplings seasoned with fresh dill, and the veal cavellier, smothered in cauliflower-cheese sauce.

Moderate

○ **Marquis de Salade.** VI. Hajós u. 43. ☎ **1/302-4086.** Main courses 1,300–2,800FT ($5.75–$12.40); set-price meals 700–1,200FT ($3.10–$5.35). V. Daily 9am–midnight. Metro: Arany János utca (Blue line). ASIAN/MIDDLE EASTERN/ECLECTIC.

The cellar in this New Age filling station is a mix of India and Ikea—a sort of Scandinavian raga environment that fits an oddly romantic afternoon or evening meal. The menu is loaded with enough types of salad, chickpeas, curry, and masala to lift your karma to new heights. The eclectic menu has influences ranging from Russian to Bangladeshi, East African to Chinese, with a bit of Hungarian and Italian added for measure. There's additional seating in the upstairs loft, and plans are afoot to expand to the cellar as well.

Inexpensive

○ **Kádár Étkezde.** VII. Klauzál tér 9. ☎ **1/321-3622.** Main courses 200–500FT (80¢–$2.20). No credit cards. Tues–Sat 11:30am–3:30pm. Metro: Astoria (Red line) or Deák tér (all lines). HUNGARIAN.

Uncle Kádár, a neighborhood legend, personally greets guests as they file in past the only small red sign marking the establishment with the single word ÉTKEZDE. By 11:45am, Uncle Kádár's, on a square in the heart of the historic Jewish district, is filled with local regulars—from paint-spattered workers to elderly Jewish couples. Although no more than a neighborhood lunchroom, the place has a great atmosphere: high ceilings, wood-paneled walls with photos (many autographed) of actors and athletes, and old-fashioned seltzer bottles on every table. The food is simple but hearty and the service friendly. Table sharing is the norm.

Tüköry söröző. V. Hold u. 15. ☎ **1/269-5027.** Main courses up to 600FT ($2.65). No credit cards. Mon–Sat noon–midnight. Metro: Arany János (Blue line). HUNGARIAN.

Silvester at Gundel

If you are anywhere near Hungary during the holidays, treat yourself and a partner to the elegant and romantic **New Year's Eve Ball** at **Gundel**. For an all-inclusive price of around $150 per person, the *Szilveszteri Bál* chimes the year in a way to heighten all your senses. In 1999, waiters greeted guests at the entrance with mulled wine. Chef Kálmán Kalla served the packed house eight delicate courses, including smoked salmon with beluga caviar, a chestnut cappuccino cream soup, tournedos with scampi in hollandaise, and then goose-liver-stuffed quail dabbed with Hungarian truffle. A different vintage from Gundel's private vineyards accented each course. Arias from Hungarian soloists were spiced with Gypsy and Hungarian folk dances, all in the beauty of a finely redecorated 19th-century villa. It's entirely worth scheduling your visit to Budapest around this holiday event, which is likely to be similar in amenities and price for the year 2000—it is that good.

A hearty, traditionally Hungarian pub meal is waiting just around the corner from the U.S. Embassy, a few blocks from Parliament. This simple haunt is purely Hungarian, and the daily specials are offered only in the native language, but the wait staff is tolerant and willing to explain the pork, fish, and goulash offerings in English.

JUST BEYOND CENTRAL PEST
Very Expensive

Gundel. XIV. Állatkerti út 2. ☎ **1/321-3550.** Reservations highly recommended. Main courses from 1,800FT ($8). AE, MC, V. Daily noon–4pm; 7pm–midnight. Metro: Hősök tere (Yellow line). HUNGARIAN/CONTINENTAL.

Freshly updated, this 105-year-old Budapest gastronomic marvel has once again become an institution in Budapest. Britain's newspaper *The Independent* gave it top choice in 1998 for holding a celebration dinner if one could go anywhere in the world. We concur. After years of Communist neglect destroyed much of what Budapest's 19th-century gourmand Károly G Gundel had created, the restaurant reopened in 1992 under the patronage of the Hungarian-born restaurateur George Lang, owner of New York's Café des Artistes. Lang has spared no effort in attempting to re-create the original splendor for which Gundel achieved an international reputation. Lamb and wild-game entrées with Hungarian accents are house specialties. Gundel has perhaps the most extensive wine list in town, with selections from its own vineyards.

Robinson. XIV. Városligeti Lake. ☎ **1/343-0955.** Main courses over 1,800FT ($8). AE, MC, V. Open daily noon–4pm; 6pm–midnight. Metro: Hősök tere (Yellow line). CONTINENTAL.

Across the street from Gundel is a fine second choice for a business lunch or formal dinner. Surrounded by the calm waters of the City Park lake and with fare highlighted by daily fresh seafood specials (imported, not from the lake), Robinson offers a more contemporary setting than its more famous neighbor. Continental favorites and Hungarian specialties round out the menu, and the service is sharp and attentive.

IN CENTRAL BUDA
Expensive

Kacsa Vendéglő. I. Fő u. 75. ☎ **1/201-9992.** Reservations recommended. Main courses 1,500–3,000FT ($6.65–$13.35). AE, DC, EURO, MC, V. Daily 6pm–1am; weekdays noon–3pm. Metro: Batthyány tér (Red line). HUNGARIAN.

Kacsa (duck) is located on the main street of Watertown, the Buda neighborhood between Castle Hill and the Danube. Here you'll find an intimate dining atmosphere that's elegant and understated. The service, however, is overbearing. The menu is replete with well-prepared Hungarian specialties.

Moderate

Horgásztanya Vendéglő. I. Fő u. 27. ☎ **1/212-3780.** Main courses 800–1,700FT ($3.55–$7.55). No credit cards. Daily noon–11pm. Metro: Battyhány tér (Red line). HUNGARIAN.

Reminiscent of dinner in a ship's galley, this tavern a block off the river in Watertown delivers a hearty meal for the whole crew. Under nautical kitsch and fish nets, you can get a range of seafood dishes or more terrestrial fare. Hana's roast pork with caramelized sweet cabbage was excellent, and we both enjoyed the button mushroom soup. Avoid the limp, tasteless pasta, however.

Taverna Ressaikos. I. Apor Péter u. 1. ☎ **1/212-1612.** Reservations recommended. Main courses 600FT–1,200FT ($2.65–5.35). AE, EURO, MC. Daily noon–midnight. Bus/tram: Any to Clark Ádám tér, including bus no. 16 from Deák tér. GREEK.

In the heart of Buda's Watertown (Víziváros), next door to the Hotel Alba Budapest, the Ressaikos features generous portions of carefully prepared food at reasonable prices. Try the calamari or the lamb in wine sauce. The menu also features a number of interesting goat dishes. Vegetarians can easily make a meal of the appetizers: stuffed tomatoes, spanikopita, tsatsiki, and the like. The live guitar music in the evenings can get a bit loud, and the service, while attentive, is definitely slow.

IN THE BUDA HILLS

Moderate

Náncsi Néni Vendéglője. II. Ördögárok út 80. ☎ **1/397-2742.** Reservations recommended for dinner. Main courses 600–1,200FT ($2.65–$5.35). AE, CB, DC, DISC, EURO, JCB, MC, V. Daily noon–11pm. Tram: 56 from Moszkva tér to the last stop, and then change to bus no. 63 to Széchenyi utca. HUNGARIAN.

Decorated with photographs of turn-of-the-century Budapest, this popular restaurant is located high in the Buda Hills. There's outdoor garden dining in the summer, with live accordion music at night. The menu features typical Hungarian dishes prepared with care.

Szép Ilona. II. Budakeszi út 1–3. ☎ **1/275-1392.** Main courses 780–1,800FT ($3.45–$8). No credit cards. Daily 11:30am–10pm. Bus: 158 from Moszkva tér (departs from Csaba utca, at the top of the stairs, near the stop from which the Várbusz departs for the Castle District) or by tram 56 from Moszkva tér to Budagyöngye shopping center. HUNGARIAN.

This cheerful, unassuming restaurant serves a mostly local crowd. There's a good selection of specialties: Try the *borjúpaprikás galuskával* (veal paprika) served with *galuska* (a typical Central European style of dumpling). There's a small sidewalk garden for summer dining. The Szép Ilona is located in a pleasant Buda neighborhood; after your meal, have a stroll through the tree-lined streets.

IN NORTHERN BUDA & ÓBUDA

Expensive

✪ **Kis Buda Gyöngye.** III. Kenyeres u. 34. ☎ **1/368-6402.** Reservations highly recommended. Main courses 1,400–2,300FT ($6.20–$10). AE, DC, MC, V. Mon–Sat noon–midnight. Tram: 17 from Margit híd (Buda side). HUNGARIAN.

On a quiet side street in a residential Óbuda neighborhood, Kis Buda Gyöngye (Little Pearl of Buda) is an exotic favorite of Hungarians and visitors. This cheerful place features an interior garden, which sits in the shade of a wonderful old gnarly tree. Inside, an eccentric violin player entertains diners. Standard Hungarian fare is served—try the goose plate, a rich combination platter including roast goose leg, goose cracklings, and goose liver.

COFFEEHOUSES

Imperial Budapest, like Vienna, was famous for its coffeehouse culture. Literary movements and political circles alike were identified in large part by which coffeehouse they met in. You can still go to several classic coffeehouses, all of which offer delicious pastries, coffee, and more in an atmosphere of luxurious splendor. Table sharing is common. The best are **Gerbeaud's,** in the Inner City at V. Vörösmarty tér 7 (☎ 1/429-9000); ✪ **Művész Kávéház,** across the street from the Opera House at VI. Andrássy út 29 (☎ 1/267-0689); the **New York Kávéház,** on the Outer Ring at VII. Erzsébet krt. 9–11 (☎ 1/322-3849), but avoid the overpriced and mediocre dinners here; **Ruszwurm Cukrászda,** in the Castle District at I. Szentháromság u. 7 (☎ 1/375-5284); and ✪ **Angelika Cukrászda,** also in Buda, at I. Batthyány tér 7. (☎ 1/201-4847).

SEEING THE SIGHTS
SIGHTSEEING SUGGESTIONS FOR FIRST-TIME VISITORS

If You Have 1 Day Spend a few hours in the morning exploring the **Inner City** and **central Pest.** Stroll along the **Danube** as far as the neo-Gothic Parliament Building, noting along the way the Chain Bridge. In the afternoon, visit the major sites of **Castle Hill** and meander the cobblestoned streets of the Castle District.

If You Have 2 Days Save the Castle District for the second day, and on the first day in the afternoon, visit the **Statue Park** in south Buda for an eerie glimpse into Communist propaganda before heading for Buda's **Gellért Hotel** and taking a dip in its spa waters. After dinner, use the remaining light to hike up the stairs of **Gellért Hill** for an unparalleled panorama of the city. Devote most of the second day to the Castle District and the sites of **Castle Hill,** and visit some of the smaller museums. Head back to Pest to see **Heroes' Square** and **City Park,** and in the evening, stroll the length of grand **Andrássy út** back to the center of Pest.

If You Have 3 Days or More On day 3, take a boat up the Danube to visit **Szentendre,** a charming riverside town. On days 4 and 5, visit some of the central sites you might have missed, and after lunch cross the Chain Bridge to **Watertown,** to explore Buda's historic riverside neighborhood. See St. Anne's Church, the Capuchin Church, and the Király Baths. Check out Pest's **indoor markethalls,** and visit **Margaret Island.**

THE TOP ATTRACTIONS
In Pest

Néprajzi Múzeum (Ethnographical Museum). V. Kossuth tér 12. ☎ **1/332-6340.** Admission 200FT (90¢). Tues–Sun 10am–6pm. Metro: Kossuth tér (Red line).

Directly across from the Parliament building, this vast museum has an ornate interior equal to that of the Opera House. A ceiling fresco of Justitia, the goddess of justice, by the artist Károly Lotz, dominates the lobby. The exhibits concentrate on the elements of Hungarian life, especially folk art, costumes, furniture, and everyday objects over the past several centuries.

✪ **Nemzeti Múzeum (Hungarian National Museum).** VIII. Múzeum krt. 14. ☎ **1/338-2122.** Admission 250FT ($1.10). Tues–Sun 10am–6pm. Metro: Kálvin tér (Blue line).

The Park of Loathing & Remembering

As permanent residents of another former East Bloc capital, we have found a wide difference in the way Prague and Budapest residents choose to confront their past (or ignore it). Czech writer Milan Kundera sums up Praguers' ignorance-is-bliss approach in his painfully apt tale, *The Book of Laughter and Forgetting,* which may explain why almost all Communist-era monuments have been tossed on the scrap-heap of history.

Budapest's newly elected democratic leaders, however, took a novel approach in the early 1990s by building the **Szoborpark (Statue Park)** in south Buda's 22nd district at Baltoni and Szabadkai út. (☎ **1/227-7446;** www. szoborpark.hu). The park is open daily 10am to dusk, but only on weekends from mid-November to mid-March. Admission is 200FT (90¢). The roughly half-hour bus ride to the park begins by taking the Blue no. 7 bus from Feren-ciek tére about 10 minutes to the end at Kosztolányi Dezso tér, and then changing to the Yellow bus for Szoborpark leaving every 15 minutes from stall 6. It's worth the trip.

Here, an unfinished Potemkin village with a poignantly broken facade sur-rounds the heroic figures who were supposed to inspire Hungarians toward the workers' paradise, whether they wanted to go or not. Scattered in clusters around the largest of ubiquitous Red Stars are many of the cast that played the largest roles setting up Soviet domination. Beyond Marx, Engels, Lenin, and many of the Hungarian heroes of the Communist movement, most striking are the incredibly triumphant workers' statues, suggesting the lock-step agreement that everyone was heading to a better place. For westerners, it's a different view of how manipulative propaganda in any form can be. For residents of the former East Bloc, it's a lasting reminder that often marketing, especially in politics, can also lead you up (or rather down) a slippery slope. The designer of the park, Ákos Eleód, explained its purpose in a way that would have made Jefferson proud: "This park is about dictatorship. And at the same time, because it can be talked about, described, built, this park is about democracy. After all, only democracy is able to give the opportunity to let us think freely about dictatorship. Or about democracy, come to that. Or about anything!"

This enormous neoclassical structure built in 1837–47, played a major role in the beginning of the Hungarian Revolution of 1848–49; on its wide steps on March 15, 1848, the poet Sándor Petőfi and other young radicals are said to have exhorted the people of Pest to revolt against the Hapsburgs. The museum's main attraction is the crown of St. Stephen (King Stephen ruled from 1000 to 1038), ceremoniously returned to Hungary by Secretary of State Cyrus Vance in 1978 from the United States, where it had been stored since the end of World War II.

In Buda

Budapesti Történeti Múzeum (Budapest History Museum). I. In Buda Palace, Wing E, on Castle Hill. ☎ **1/375-7533.** Admission 300FT ($1.30). Guided tours in English available on advance request, 5,000FT ($22.20). May 16–Sept 15 daily 10am–6pm; Sept 16–Oct 31 Wed–Mon 10am–6pm; Nov 1–Feb 28 Wed–Mon 10am–4pm; Mar 1–May 15 Wed–Mon 10am–6pm. Bus: Várbusz from Moszkva tér or 16 from Deák tér to Castle Hill. Funicular: From Clark Ádám tér to Castle Hill.

This museum, also known as the Castle Museum, is the best place to get a sense of the once-great medieval Buda. It's probably worth splurging on a guided tour; even though the museum's descriptions are written in English, the history of the palace's repeated construction and destruction is so arcane that it's difficult to understand what you're really seeing.

✪ **Nemzeti Galéria (Hungarian National Gallery).** I. In Buda Palace, Wings B, C, and D, on Castle Hill. ☎ **1/375-7533.** Admission 300FT ($1.35). Guided tours in English, 2,000FT ($8.90). Mar–Oct Tues–Sun 10am–6pm; Nov–Feb Tues–Sun 10am–4pm. Bus: Várbusz from Moszkva tér or 16 from Deák tér to Castle Hill. Funicular: From Clark Ádám tér to Castle Hill.

Hungary has produced some fine artists, particularly in the late 19th century, and this is the place to view their work. The giants of the time are the brilliant but moody Mihály Munkácsy; László Paál, a painter of village scenes; Károly Ferenczy, a master of light; and Pál Szinyei Merse, the en-plein-air artist and contemporary of the early French impressionists.

MORE ATTRACTIONS

✪ **Vidám Park (Amusement Park).** XIV. Állatkerti krt. 14–16. ☎ **1/343-0996.** No entry fee; rides 100–200FT (45¢–90¢). Apr–Sept daily 10am–8pm; Oct–Mar daily 10am–6pm. Metro: Széchenyi fürdő (Yellow line).

While much of the park has the feel of a prairie state fair, two rides in particular aren't to be missed. The nearly 100-year-old **Merry-Go-Round** (*Körhinta*), constructed almost entirely of wood, was recently restored to its original grandeur. Riders must actively pump to keep the horses rocking and the Wurlitzer playing. As the carousel spins round, it creaks mightily. The **Ferris wheel** (*Óriáskerék*) is also wonderful, although it has little in common with the rambunctious Ferris wheels of the modern age. A gangly bright-yellow structure, it rotates at a liltingly slow pace, gently lifting you high for a remarkable view. The Vidám Park also features Europe's longest wooden roller-coaster.

Historic Buildings

✪ **Magyar Állami Operaház (Hungarian State Opera House).** VI. Andrássy út 22. ☎ **1/353-0170.** Admission (by guided tour only) 600FT ($3). Tours daily at 3 and 4pm. Metro: Opera (Yellow line).

Completed in 1884, Budapest's Opera House boasts a fantastically ornate interior featuring frescoes by two of the best-known Hungarian artists of the day, Bertalan Székely and Károly Lotz. Home to both the State Opera and the State Ballet, the Opera House has a rich and evocative history.

Parliament. V. Kossuth tér. ☎ **1/268-4904.** Guided 30-minute tour in English 900FT ($4), students 500FT ($2.20). Mon–Fri 10am and 2pm; Sat, Sun 10am. **Ibusz** (☎ **1/118-1139** to reserve) offers a 2-hour tour in English for 2,400FT ($12) on Wed, Fri, and Sat. Starting times vary. No tours when Parliament is in session. Metro: Kossuth tér (Red line).

Budapest's great Parliament building, an eclectic design that mixes the predominant neo-Gothic style with a neo-Renaissance dome, was completed in 1902. Standing proudly on the Danube bank, visible from almost any riverside point, it has from the outset been one of Budapest's symbols, although until 1989 a democratically elected government had convened here only once (just after World War II, before the Communist takeover).

Churches & Synagogues

✪ **Dohány Synagogue.** VII. Dohány u. 2–8. ☎ **1/342-2353.** www.synagogue.hu. E-mail: frolich@westel 900.net. Admission by donation. Open Tues–Fri 10am–3pm; Sun 10am–1pm (hours vary). Metro: Astoria (Red line) or Deák tér (all lines).

Built in 1859 and recently restored, it is said to be the largest synagogue in Europe and the second largest in the world. The architecture has striking Moorish elements; the interior is vast and ornate, with two balconies and the unusual presence of an organ. In the garden next to the synagogue is a garden where victims of the Nazi horrors in the Jewish ghetto rest. There's also a Jewish museum next door that traces the origins of Hungarian Judaisim and has exhibits of ceremonial Judaica throughout the centuries, including Torah covers, scholarly writings, and documents.

Bazilika (St. Stephen's Church). V. Szent István tér 33. ☎ **1/317-2859.** Church, free; treasury, 100FT (40¢); tower, 200FT (90¢). Church, daily 7am–7pm, except during services. Treasury and Szent Jobb Chapel, Mon–Sat 9am–5pm, Sun 1–5pm; Oct–May 10am–4pm. Tower, daily 10am–4:30pm. Metro: Arany János utca (Blue line) or Bajcsy-Zsilinszky út (Yellow line).

The basilica took over 50 years to build (the 1868 collapse of the dome caused significant delay) and was finally done in 1906. However, during this time Pest underwent radical growth; while the front of the church dominates sleepy Szent István tér, the rear faces out onto the far busier Inner Ring boulevard. In the Chapel of the Holy Right (Szent Jobb Kápolna), you can see Hungarian Catholicism's most cherished—and bizarre—holy relic: the preserved right hand of Hungary's first Christian king, Stephen. A donation in the box in front of the glass case lights up the hand for a better view.

✪ **Mátyás Templom (Matthias Church).** I. Szentháromság tér 2. ☎ **1/315-5657.** Church, free; exhibition rooms beneath the altar, 100FT (45¢). Daily 9am–5pm. Bus: Várbusz from Moszkva tér or 16 from Deák tér Castle Hill. Funicular: From Clark Ádám tér to Castle Hill.

Officially named the Church of Our Lady, the symbol of Buda's Castle District is popularly known as Matthias Church after the 15th-century king who was twice married here. Although it dates to the mid-13th century, like other old churches in Budapest it has an interesting history of destruction and reconstruction, always being refashioned in the architectural style of the time.

PARKS & PANORAMAS

Gellért Hegy (Gellért Hill), towering 230 meters (750 ft.) above the Danube, offers the single best view of the city. The hill is named after the Italian Bishop Gellért, who assisted Hungary's first Christian king, Stephen I, in converting the Magyars. Gellért became a martyr when he was rolled in a barrel to his death from the side of the hill where his enormous statue now stands. On top of Gellért Hill you'll find the Liberation Monument, built in 1947 to commemorate the Red Army's liberation of Budapest from Nazi occupation. Also atop Gellért Hill is the **Citadella,** built by the Austrians shortly after they crushed the Hungarian War of Independence of 1848–49. To get here, take bus no. 27 from Móricz Zsigmond körtér.

Margaret Island (Margit-sziget) has been a public park since 1908. The long, narrow island, connected to both Buda and Pest by the Margaret and Árpád bridges, is barred to most vehicular traffic. Facilities on the island include the Palatinus Strand open-air baths (see the box "Budapest's Most Popular Thermal Baths,"), which draw upon the famous thermal waters under Margaret Island; the Alfréd Hajós Sport Pool; and the Open Air Theater. Sunbathers line the steep embankments along the river and bicycles are available for rent. Despite all this, Margaret Island is a quiet, tranquil place. It's best reached by bus no. 26 from Nyugati tér, which runs the length of the island, or tram no. 4 or 6, which stops at the entrance to the island midway across the Margaret Bridge. (*Warning:* These are popular lines for pickpockets.)

Budapest's Most Popular Thermal Baths

Budapest's baths have a long and proud history, stretching back to Roman times. Under Turkish occupation the bath culture flourished, and several still-functioning bathhouses—Király, Rudas, and Rac—are among the period's architectural relics. In the late 19th and early 20th centuries, Budapest's "golden age," several fabulous bathhouses were built: the extravagant eclectic Széchenyi Baths in City Park, the splendid art nouveau Gellért Baths, and the solid neoclassical Lukács Baths. All are still in use.

Because thermal bathing is an activity shaped by ritual, and because bathhouse employees tend to be unfriendly relics of the old system, many foreigners find a trip to the baths confusing at first.

The ticket windows with an endless list of prices for different facilities and services now has English translations but just in case look for *uszoda,* pool; *termál,* thermal pool; *fürdő,* bath; *gozfürdő,* steam bath, massage, and sauna. Towel rental is *törülközó* or *lepedő.* An entry ticket generally entitles you to a free locker in the locker room (*öltözo*); you can usually opt to pay an additional fee for a private cabin (*kabin*). A bathing suit is the appropriate attire.

The most spectacular bathhouse, the **Gellért Baths** are located in Buda's Hotel Gellért, at XI. Kelenhegyi út 4 (☎ **1/466-6166**). Go in through the side entrance. The unisex indoor pool is exquisite, with marble columns, majolica tiles, and stone lion heads spouting water. The segregated Turkish-style thermal baths, one off to each side of the pool through badly marked doors, are also glorious, though in need of restoration. The outdoor roof pool attracts great attention for 10 minutes every hour on the hour when the artificial wave machine is turned on.

Admission to the bath is 400FT ($1.80); 15-minute massage is 450FT ($2) plus tip. Lockers are free; a cabin can be rented for 200FT (90¢). Admission to all services costs 1,200FT ($5.35) for adults and 600FT ($2.60) for children. Prices are posted in English. The thermal baths are open year-round, daily 6am to 8pm (last entry 7pm). Take tram no. 47 or 49 from Deák tér to Szent Gellért tér.

The **Király Baths,** at I. Fő u. 84 (☎ **1/201-4392**), are one of Budapest's most important monuments to Turkish rule. Built in the late 16th century, is housed under an octagonal domed roof with stained-glass windows. There are also sauna and steam bath facilities. After your treatment, wrap yourself in a cotton sheet and lounge with a cup of tea in the relaxation room. The Király baths are open on different days for men and women. Reportedly, the men's bath is frequented by a largely gay crowd.

Men can use the baths on Monday, Wednesday, and Friday from 6:30am to 7pm. Women's days are Tuesday and Thursday from 6:30am to 7pm and on Saturday from 6:30am to 1pm. It costs 450FT ($2) to bathe. Take the Red line metro to the Batthyány tér stop.

City Park (Városliget) is an equally popular place to spend a summer day. Heroes' Square, at the end of Andrássy út, is the most logical starting point for a walk in City Park. The lake behind the square is used for boating in summer and ice-skating in winter. The park's Zoo Boulevard (Állatkerti körút), the favorite street of generations of Hungarian children, is where the **zoo,** the **circus,** and the **amusement park** are all found. **Gundel,** Budapest's most famous restaurant, is also here, as are the **Széchenyi Baths.** The Yellow metro line makes stops at Hősök tere (Heroes' Square), at the edge of the park, and Széchenyi Fürdő, in the middle of it.

Károly kert (Charles Garden), a little enclosed park in the southern half of the Inner City, is the location of Budapest's most charming playground. To enter the park, you must pass through a gigantic wrought-iron gate. The equipment here might not be as modern or as varied as at some of the city's other playgrounds, but the place has a distinct old-world charm and its location in the Inner City makes it a convenient destination.

ORGANIZED TOURS

Ibusz, V. Vörösmarty tér (☎ 1/317-7767 or 1/317-8343) offers 11 different boat and bus tours, ranging from basic city tours to special folklore-oriented tours. Bus tours leave from the Erzsébet tér bus station, near Deák tér; boat tours leave from the Vigadó tér landing. There's also a free hotel pickup service 30 minutes before departure time.

The Hungarian company **MAHART** operates daily sightseeing cruises on the Danube. The Budapest office of MAHART is at V. Belgrád rakpart (☎ **1/318-1704,** 1/318-953, and 1/318-1586). Boats depart from Vigadó tér on weekends and holidays in the spring and every day in summer.

Legenda, Fraknó utca 4 (☎ **1/317-2203**), offers boat tours on the Danube. Most of the city's grand sights can be seen from the river. Tours run from mid-April to mid-October; all boats leave from the Vigadó tér port, Pier 6 or 7. Tickets are available through most major hotels, at the dock, or through the Legenda office.

THE SHOPPING SCENE

The packed pedestrian-only **Váci utca,** from the stately Vörösmarty tér, the center of Pest, across the roaring Kossuth Lajos utca, all the way to Vámház krt. Váci utca, and most of the pedestrian streets bisecting it, are lined with shops. Boutiques, not visible from the street, fill the courtyards. The **Castle District** in Buda, with many folk-art boutiques and galleries, is another popular area for souvenir hunters. While locals might window-shop in these two neighborhoods, they tend to do their serious shopping elsewhere. One popular street is Pest's **Outer Ring (Nagykörút);** another is Pest's bustling **Kossuth Lajos utca,** off the Erzsébet Bridge, and its continuation **Rákóczi út,** which extends all the way out to Keleti Station.

BEST BUYS   Folkloric Objects   Hungary's famous folkloric objects are the most popular souvenirs among foreign visitors. The state-owned Folkart shops (Népművészeti Háziipar) have a great selection of handmade goods. Popular items include pillow cases, pottery, porcelain, dolls, dresses, skirts, and sheepskin vests. The main store, **Folkart Centrum,** is at V. Váci u. 14 (☎ 1/318-5840), and is open daily from 9:30am to 7pm. One outstanding private shop on Váci utca is ✪ **Vali Folklór,** in the courtyard of Váci u. 23 (☎ 1/337-6301). This cluttered shop is run by a soft-spoken man named Bálint Ács who travels the villages of Hungary and neighboring countries in search of authentic folk items.

✪ **Holló Folkart Gallery,** at V. Vitkovics Mihály u. 12 (☎ **1/317-8103**), is an unusual gallery selling handcrafted reproductions of folk-art pieces from various regions of the country.

Porcelain & Pottery   Another popular Hungarian item is porcelain, particularly from the country's two best-known producers, Herend and Zsolnay. Although both brands are available in the West, here you'll find a better selection and prices about 50% lower.

You'll find world-renowned hand-painted Herend porcelain (www.herend.com), first produced in 1826 in the town of Herend near Veszprém in western Hungary, at the **Herend Shop,** V. József nádor tér 11 (☎ **1/317-2622**). This shop has the widest Herend selection in the capital, but unfortunately, it can't arrange shipping. If Herend porcelain isn't within your price range, you'll find lovely pottery at ✪ **Herend Village Pottery,** V. Váci u. 23 (☎ **1/318-3240;** fax 1/318-2094). This shop sells Herend porcelain as well as a lovely casual "village-style" pottery. It's also the only shop to date that offers shipping on large orders. Delightfully gaudy Zsolnay porcelain from the southern city of Pécs is Hungary's second-most celebrated brand of porcelain; you'll find it at **Zsolnay Márkabolt,** V. Kígyó u. 4 (☎ 1/318-3712).

Hungarian Foods Connoisseurs generally agree that **Pick Salami** from the southeastern city of Szeged is the best of world-renowned Hungarian salami, and it's easy to carry home without giving your clothes an unforgettable aroma. Chestnut paste (*gesztenye püré*), found in a tin or block wrapped in foil is rare abroad and used primarily as a pastry filling, but can also top desserts and ice cream. Paprika paste (*pirosarany*) is also a rarity, usually in a bright-red tube in hot (*csípős*), deli style (*csemege*), and sweet (*édes*) varieties. All these can be found in grocery stores (*élelmiszer*) and delicatessens (*csemege*). Fine, affordable Hungarian wines from the Szekszárd, Villány, Tokaj, and Eger regions are abundant. The granddaddy of Hungarian "Bulls' Blood" is Kékfrankos or Blaufrankisch in German. A bottle of this full, fierce red wine should be given to your friends back home with adventurous tastes.

MARKETS There are five **vintage market halls (vásárcsarnok),** wonders of steel and glass, built in the 1890s in the ambitious grandiose style of the time. Three are still in use and provide a measure of local color you won't find in the grocery store. The **Központi Vásárcsarnok (Central Market Hall),** on IX. Vámház körút, is the largest and most spectacular market hall. Located on the Inner Ring (Kiskörút), on the Pest side of the Szabadság Bridge, this trilevel hall was impeccably reconstructed in 1995. Other vintage market halls include the **Belvárosi Vásárcsarnok (Inner City Market Hall),** on V. Hold utca, behind Szabadság tér in central Pest, the **Józsefváros Vásárcsarnok,** on VIII. Rákóczi tér, and the **Fehérvári úti Vásárcsarnok,** on XI. Fehérvári út, in front of the Buda Skála department store, just a block from the Móricz Zsigmond körtér transportation hub. The fifth market hall, the **Fény utca Piac** is on II. Fény utca, just off Moszkva tér in Buda.

DEPARTMENT STORES & MALLS Sprawling **Örs Vezér tere,** the eastern terminus of the Red metro line, is home both to Budapest's branch of the internationally known Swedish **Ikea** chain and to the city's first quasi-American–style mall, **Sugár.** On Váci, the **Fortuna Department Store** and a new outlet of Britain's **Marks & Spencer** have the latest in men's and women's fashions. **Made in World Centre,** a mini-mall full of ultratrendy shops, is at Váci utca 30.

OTHER SHOPS OF NOTE Among numerous women's boutiques are **Joker Applied Arts,** VII. Akácfa u. 5/a (☎ 1/341-4281), showcasing original local handmade goods and Asian-accented accessories; ✪ **V50 Design Art Studio,** V. Váci u. 50 (☎ 1/337-5320), featuring Valeria Fazekas's unique, finely tailored clothing and extraordinary hats; **Kaláka Design Studio,** V. Haris köz 2 (☎ 1/318-3313), with gorgeous clothing by hip Hungarian designers.

BUDAPEST AFTER DARK

The most complete schedule of mainstream performing arts is found in the free bimonthly *Koncert Kalendárium* at the Central Philharmonic Ticket Office in

Music for a Summer Evening

During the warm lazy days, you'll find several special venues for classical music. Tickets for them are available at the **National Philharmonic Ticket Office,** V. Vörösmarty tér 1 (☎ 1/317-3222).

The historic outdoor **Dominican Courtyard,** inside the Castle District's Hilton Hotel, I. Hess András tér 1–3 (☎ 1/214-3000), is the site for a series of classical recitals during the summer. The District's beautiful **Matthias Church (Mátyás Templom),** next door at I. Szentháromság tér 2, holds a regular Friday-night series of organ concerts June through September. Concerts start at 7:30pm. Tickets can be purchased before the performance at the church entry.

Organ concerts are also held Monday evenings at 7pm during July and August at **St. Stephen's Basilica,** Hungary's largest church, V. Szent István tér 33 (☎ 1/317-2859). You can buy tickets at the church entry before the performance. Take the Metro to Arany János utca (Blue line) or Bajcsy-Zsilinszky út (Yellow line).

The **Dohány Synagogue** is the venue for occasional concerts from May to September. Concerts begin at 7pm, but days are not regular. Take the Metro to Astoria (Red line). For information and tickets, call the **Central Theater Ticket Office** (☎ 1/312-0000).

Vörösmarty tér. The *Budapest Sun* is a good source, as is the *Budapest Week* Web site (www.budapestweek.hu).

The **Central Theater Ticket Office (Színházak Központi Jegyiroda),** VI. Andrássy út 18 (☎ 1/312-0000), sells tickets to just about everything, from theater and operetta to sports events and rock concerts; it's open Monday to Thursday 9am to 1pm and 1:45 to 6pm (Friday to 5pm). A second branch is at II. Moszkva tér 3 (☎ 1/335-9136), with similar hours except that it opens at 10am. For **classical performances,** go to the National Philharmonic Ticket Office (Filharmónia Nemzeti Jegyiroda), V. Vörösmarty tér 1 (☎ 1/317-6222). For **opera and ballet,** go to the Hungarian State Opera Ticket Office (Magyar Állami Opera Jegyiroda), VI. Andrássy út 20 (entrance inside the courtyard) (☎ 1/353-0170). For events in the **Spring Festival,** go to the Festival Ticket Service, V. 1081 Rákóczi út 65 (☎ 1/210-2795). For **rock and jazz concert** tickets, try Ticket Express, VI. Jókai u. 40 (☎ 1/353-0692).

THE PERFORMING ARTS

Completed in 1884, the **Magyar Állami Operaház (Hungarian State Opera House),** VI. Andrássy út 22 ☎ 1/353-0170; Metro: Opera (Yellow line), is Budapest's most famous performance hall and a tourist attraction in its own right. Hungarians adore opera, and a large percentage of seats are sold on a subscription basis; buy your tickets a few days ahead if possible. The box office is open Monday to Friday 11am to 5pm. With tickets ranging from as little as 300FT ($1.35) in most performances for upper sections, to 4,500FT ($20) for the best box in the house, you can hear big-league opera for the price of cheap seats at a major league baseball game.

Zeneakadémia (Ferenc Liszt Academy of Music). VI. Liszt Ferenc tér 8. ☎ 1/341-4788. Metro: Oktogon (Yellow line).

The Great Hall (Nagyterem) of the Academy of Music is the premier music hall. The Academy was built in the art nouveau style of the early 20th century with the best acoustics in the city. Box office hours are 2pm to showtime on the day of performance.

THE CLUB SCENE

Clubs have found fertile ground since the political changes of 1989—so much so, in fact, that many come in and out of fashion overnight. A few, however, like **Made Inn Mine** and **Piaf**, have had solid staying power since the late 1980s. Check the *Budapest Sun* for up-to-the-minute club listings.

✪ **Fél 10 Jazz Klub.** VIII. Baross u. 30. ☎ **06-60/318-467** (mobile phone). Metro: Kálvin tér (Blue line).

This is a classy, multilevel club—one of the few whose dance floor isn't crammed with teenagers—with live music performances nightly. Techno-free dance parties get going in the wee hours of the morning, Wednesday to Sunday. Open Monday through Friday, noon to dawn and weekends 7pm to dawn; cover is 200FT (90¢).

Made Inn Mine. VI. Andrássy út 112. ☎ **1/311-3437.** Cover 300FT ($1.35); Thurs 500FT ($2.20). Metro: Bajza utca (Yellow line).

This very popular club shares the building of the Young Artists' Club (FMK), another rock club, but the two establishments are completely different. The air-conditioned Made Inn Mine has a subterranean cavelike atmosphere. Wednesday night features a funk dance party and all drinks are half-price. Thursday night is *the* night as the weekend seems to begin for many; you might have to wait in line to enter. Open daily 11am to 3am.

Morrison's Music Pub. VI. Révay u. 25. ☎ **1/269-4060.** Metro: Opera (Yellow line).

A young 20-something crowd packs this casual pub every night of the week. There's a small dance floor and an eclectic variety of loud live music. Open 8pm to 4am (closed Sunday).

Piaf. VI. Nagymező u. 25. ☎ **1/312-3823.** Cover 350FT ($1.55), of which 250FT ($1.10) goes toward your first drink. Metro: Oktogon (Yellow line).

In the heart of Budapest's theater district, Piaf is a sophisticated French-style nightclub, with red velvet chairs and a candlelit atmosphere. Upstairs features live piano music, and downstairs is a bar. Drinks are pricey. Open daily 4pm to 4am.

BARS

Chicago Sörgyár. VII. Erzsébet krt. 2. ☎ **1/269-6753.** Metro: Blaha Lujza tér (Red line).

This bar has a die-hard expatriate crowd that comes not just for the fairly good home-brewed beer, but for the hamburgers, nachos, and French fries. Happy hour is weekdays from 4 to 6pm, with half-price drinks. Open Monday to Friday noon to midnight, Saturday noon to 1am, and Sunday noon to 11pm. Credit cards accepted.

✪ **Fregatt.** V. Molnár u. 26. ☎ **1/318-9997.** Metro: Ferenciek tere (Blue line).

This is the first English-style pub in Hungary, although it's too crowded and noisy to really feel like one. Hungarians make up the better half of the clientele, but American and other English-speaking expatriates frequent Fregatt too. Guinness beer is on draft. Live music includes folk, country, and jazz. Open daily from 5pm to midnight.

✪ **Irish Cat Pub.** V. Múzeum krt. 41. ☎ **1/266-4085.** Metro: Kálvin tér (Blue line).

An Irish-style pub with Guinness on tap and a whiskey bar, Irish Cat is a popular meeting place for expats and travelers. The pub features a full menu. Open daily 11am to 5am.

János Pince söröző. V. Károlyi ut. 11. ☎ **1/328-5704.** Metro: Ferenciek Tere.

An old standby opened in 1872 in southern Pest, this woodsy Hungarian cellar pub keeps the volume low enough for a conversation with friends. A fine selection of local wines and dishes are available.

HUNGARIAN DANCE HOUSES

Recent years have seen the growth of an urban-centered folk revival movement known as the *táncház* (dance house). This interactive evening of **folk music** and **folk dancing,** held in community centers around town, is one of the best cultural experiences you can have in Hungary. The format usually consists of about an hour of dance-step instruction, followed by several hours of dancing accompanied by a live band, which might include some of Hungary's best folk musicians, in an authentic, casual atmosphere.

The leading Hungarian folk band Muzsikás, whose lead singer is the incomparable Márta Sebestyén, hosts a táncház every Wednesday (September to June only) at 8pm (250FT/$1.10) at the **Marczibányi Square Cultural House (Marczibányi Tér Művelődésiház),** II. Marczibányi tér 5/a ☎ 1/212-0803). Take the Red line metro to Moszkva tér. The **FMH Cultural House (Szakszervezetek Fővárosi Művelődési Háza),** XI. Fehérvári út 47 ☎ 1/212-5789), hosts a táncház for kids every Tuesday, from 5:30 to 6:30pm, for 100FT (45¢). It also holds a *csángó* táncház, the oldest and most authentic type of traditional Hungarian folk dance, on Saturday, from 6 to 11pm, for 200FT (90¢). Tram no. 47 from Deák tér gets you there.

DAY TRIPS TO THE DANUBE BEND

The delightful towns along the Bend—Szentendre, Esztergom, and Vác—are easy day trips from Budapest. The great natural beauty of the area, where forested hills loom over the river, makes it a welcome departure for the city weary.

ESSENTIALS

GETTING THERE   By Boat & Hydrofoil   From April to September, **boats** run between Budapest and the towns of the Danube Bend. All boats leave Budapest's Vigadó tér boat landing, stopping to pick up passengers 5 minutes later at Buda's Batthyány tér landing, before continuing up the river.

Schedules and towns served are complicated, so contact **MAHART,** the state shipping company, at the Vigadó tér landing (☎ 1/118-1223) for information. Roundtrip prices are 630FT ($3.15) to Szentendre, 690FT ($3.45) to Vác, and 750FT ($3.75) to Esztergom. Ask about discounts for children. The travel time from Budapest is 1½ hours to Szentendre, 2½ hours to Vác, and 5 hours to Esztergom.

By Train   The HÉV suburban railroad connects Budapest's Batthyány tér with Szentendre. Trains leave daily, year-round, every 20 minutes or so from 4am to 11:30pm. The one-way fare is 109FT (55¢); subtract 60FT (30¢) if you have a valid Budapest public transportation pass. The trip takes 45 minutes. Ten daily trains make the run between Budapest's Nyugati Station and Esztergom. The trip takes about 1¼ hours. Train tickets cost 266FT ($1.35). More than 20 trains a day depart Budapest's Nyugati Station for Vác. The trip takes 45 minutes. Tickets cost 168FT (85¢).

SZENTENDRE   Peopled in medieval times by Serbian settlers, Szentendre (pronouned *Sen*-ten-dreh), 21 kilometers (13 miles) north of Budapest, counts half a dozen Serbian churches among its rich collection of historical buildings. Since the turn of the century, Szentendre has been home to an artist's colony and has a wealth of museums and galleries. The town is an extremely popular tourist destination.

Visitor Information   The information office **Tourinform** is at Dumtsa Jenő u. 22 (☎ 26/317-965 or 26/317-966), and is open Monday through Friday 10am to 4pm.

If you arrive by train, you'll come upon this office as you follow the flow of pedestrian traffic into town on Kossuth Lajos utca. If you arrive by boat, you may find the **Ibusz** office sooner, on the corner of Bogdányi út and Gőzhajó utca (☎ **26/313-597**). It's open April to October, Monday through Friday 9am to 6pm and weekends 10am to 2pm. From November to March, it's open weekdays only, 9am to 4pm. The best source of information, particularly if you are planning to stay in the region more than a day, is **Globe Center**, at Kucsera F. u. 15 (☎ and fax **26/310-030**).

Exploring the Museums & Churches   The ✪ **Margit Kovács Museum,** Vastagh György u. 1, features the work of Hungary's best-known ceramic artist, who died in 1977. We were especially moved by her sculptures of elderly women and by her friezes of village life. Admission is 250FT (90¢). Open April through October, Tuesday through Sunday 10am to 6pm (to 4pm November through March).

The **Blagovestenska church** at Fő tér 4 dates from 1752. A rococo iconostasis features paintings of Mihailo Zivkovic. Notice that the eyes of all the icons are upon you; the effect is extraordinary. Admission is 50FT (25¢). Open Tuesday through Sunday, 10am to 5pm.

Next door is the ✪ **Ferenczy Museum,** dedicated to the art of the prodigious Ferenczy family. The paintings of Károly Ferenczy, one of Hungary's leading impressionists, are featured. Works of his lesser-known children, Noémi (tapestry maker), Valer (painter), and Beni (sculptor and medallion maker), are also on display. Admission is 90FT (45¢). Open April through October, Tuesday through Sunday 10am to 4pm; November through March, Friday through Sunday 10am to 4pm.

Where to Dine If you get hungry, **Aranysárkány Vendéglő (Golden Dragon Inn)**, Alkotmány u. 1/a (☎ **26/311-670**), just east of Fő tér on Hunyadi utca, is always crowded, often with locals (a definite good sign in a tourist town like Szentendre). Choose from such enticing offerings as alpine lamb, roast leg of goose, quail, and venison ragout. A very tasty vegetarian plate is also offered. Various beers are on draft.

   If you walk directly south from Fő tér, you'll find ✪ **Régimodi**, Fűtő u. 3 (☎ **26/311-105**). This elegant restaurant in a former private home serves Hungarian specialties, with an emphasis on game dishes. The wild-boar stew in red wine is particularly sumptuous.

   Be sure to stop in at the **Dobos Museum & Cafe**, Dumtsa Jenő u. 7, for a slice of authentic *dobos torta*, a sumptuously rich layer cake named after pastry chef József Dobos, who experimented with butter frostings in the 19th century. The success of his recipe was immediate, and he was quickly appointed official baker to the Hapsburg emperor.

ESZTERGOM Formerly a Roman settlement, Esztergom (pronounced *Ess*-tair-gome), 46 kilometers (29 miles) northwest of Budapest, was the seat of the Hungarian kingdom for 300 years. Hungary's first king, István I (Stephen I), crowned by the pope in A.D. 1000, converted Hungary to Catholicism, and Esztergom became the country's center of the early church. Although its glory days are long gone, the quiet town remains the seat of the archbishop-primate—the "Hungarian Rome."

Visitor Information **Gran Tours**, centrally located at Széchenyi tér 25 (☎ **33/413-756**), is the best source of information in Esztergom. The office is open Monday through Friday 8am to 4pm and on Saturday from 8am to noon.

Exploring the Town The massive, neoclassical **Esztergom Cathedral** in Szent István tér on Castle Hill, is Esztergom's most popular attraction and one of Hungary's most impressive buildings. It was built in the last century to replace the cathedral ruined during the Turkish occupation. The cathedral **Treasury** (*Kincstár*) contains a stunning array of ecclesiastical jewels and gold works. Since Cardinal Mindszenty's body was moved to the crypt in 1991 (he died in exile in 1975), it has been a place of pilgrimage for Hungarians. If you brave the ascent of the cupola, you're rewarded at the top with unparalleled views of Esztergom and the surrounding Hungarian and Slovak countryside. Admission to the treasury costs 130FT (60¢); cupola, 50FT (20¢). The cathedral is open daily 8am to 8pm in summer, 9am to 3pm in winter. The treasury, crypt, and cupola are open daily 9am to 5pm in summer, and 10am to 3pm in winter.

   It's definitely worth taking a break from the crowds at the cathedral to stroll through the quiet, cobblestoned streets of Esztergom's Víziváros (Watertown). There you'll find the **Keresztény Múzeum (Christian Museum)**, Mindszenty tér 2 (☎ **33/313-880**), in the neoclassical former primate's palace, which houses Hungary's largest collection of religious art and the largest collection of medieval art outside the National Gallery. Admission is 150FT (55¢) for adults. Open Tuesday through Sunday 10am to 5:30pm (closed January through March).

Where to Dine The food at the recently remodeled and enlarged ✪ **Szalma Csárda**, located at Nagy-Duna sétány 2 (☎ **33/315-336**), is absolutely first-rate, with everything made to order and served piping hot. The excellent house soups—fish soup (*halászlé*), goulash (*gulyásleves*), and bean soup (*babgulyás*)—constitute meals in themselves.

VÁC Largely overlooked by tourists, who generally neglect the flatter east bank of the Danube Bend, Vác (pronounced *Vahts*), 34 kilometers (21 miles) north of Budapest, is a quietly charming baroque town, with a historic core dating from the early 18th century. The town's elegant, well-maintained squares and its sleepy Danube-side parks exude an unmistakable charm.

Visitor Information   The best source of information in Vác is **Tourinform,** at Dr. Csányi László krt. 45 (☎ 27/316-160). Open April through September, Monday through Friday 8am to 5pm and Saturday 9am to 1pm (weekdays only October through March). If you arrive in Vác by train, it makes sense to use the **Ibusz** office, at Széchenyi u. 46, for your information-gathering purposes. You can also change money here.

Exploring the Town   Wander around the historic Inner City and its four main squares and admire the baroque architecture. **Március 15 tér** is the town's central square. Here you'll find the Town Hall (*Városház*), with its intricate wrought-iron gate; the Fehérek Church, with its elegant facade dominating the square's southern end; and a row of baroque houses across from the Town Hall. Nearby **Szentháromság tér** features an elaborate Plague Column and the Piarist Church, whose church bell is the favorite of locals. Lush beds of roses ring large, empty **Konstantin tér.** Old-fashioned street lamps line the walkways. The **Bishop's Cathedral,** one of Hungary's earliest (1765–77) examples of neoclassical architecture, dominates Konstantin tér. **Géza király tér,** the center of medieval Vác, was the site of the former fortress and cathedral. Now you can see the baroque Franciscan church here.

Where to Dine   **Halászkert Étterem,** at Liszt Ferenc sétány 9 (☎ 27/315-985), is a large outdoor garden restaurant set right on the Danube Promenade at the northern end of the Inner City. The extensive menu features a number of fish specialties (the restaurant's name means "fish garden"). **Margaréta Kávéház,** Széchenyi u. 19, offers scrumptious pastries, Italian ice cream, and specialty coffees in an upbeat atmosphere on the town's most bustling street.

2 Lake Balaton

Lake Balaton might not be the Mediterranean, but don't tell that to the Hungarians. Somehow, over the years, they have managed to create their own Central European hybrid variety of a Mediterranean culture along the shores of their long, shallow, milky-white lake, Europe's largest at 80 kilometers (50 miles) long and 15 kilometers (10 miles) wide at its broadest stretch.

ESSENTIALS

ARRIVING   By Train   From Budapest, trains to towns along the lake depart from Déli Station. The local trains are interminably slow, so try to get on an express.

By Car   If you're driving from Budapest, take the M-7 motorway south through Székesfehérvár until you hit the lake. Route 71 circles the lake.

By Boat   Passenger boat travel on Lake Balaton lets you travel across the lake as well as between towns on the same shore. It's both extensive and cheap, but considerably slower than surface transportation. All major towns have a dock with departures and arrivals. Children 3 and under travel free, and those 13 and under get half-price tickets. A single ferry (*komp*) running between Tihany and Szántód lets you transport a car across the width of the lake. Boat and ferry information is available from the **MAHART** office in Siófok (☎ 84/310-050). Local tourist offices along the lake also have schedules and information.

STAYING AROUND THE LAKE

Throughout the long summer, swimmers, windsurfers, sailboats, kayaks, and cruisers enjoy the warm and silky-smooth waters; people cast their reels for pike, play tennis, ride horses, and hike in the hills.

The **south shore** towns are as flat as Pest; walk 10 minutes from the lake and you're in farm country. The air here is still and quiet; in summer, the sun hangs heavily in the sky. Teenagers, students, and young travelers tend to congregate in the hedonistic towns of the south shore. Here, huge 1970s-style beachside hotels are filled to capacity all summer long, and disco music pulsates into the early-morning hours.

On the more graceful **north shore,** little villages are neatly tucked away in the rolling countryside, where the grapes of the popular Balaton wines ripen in the strong southern sun. Traveling from Budapest, the northern shore of the lake at first appears every bit as built up and crowded as the southern shore. Beyond Balatonfüred, this impression begins to fade. You'll discover the **Tihany Peninsula,** a protected area whose 12 square kilometers (4¾ square miles) jut out into the lake like a knob. Stop for a swim—or the night—in a small town like **Szigliget.** Moving westward along the coast, you can make forays inland into the rolling hills of the Balaton wine country. The city of **Keszthély,** sitting at the lake's western edge, marks the end of its northern shore.

Because hotel prices are unusually high in the Balaton region, and because just about every local family rents out a room or two in summer, we especially recommend private rooms. You can reserve a room through a local tourist office, or you can just look for the ubiquitous **SZOBA KIADÓ** (or **ZIMMER FREI**) signs along the roads. When you take a room without using a tourist agency as the intermediary, prices are generally negotiable. In the height of the season, you shouldn't have to pay more than $40 (9,000FT)for a double room within reasonable proximity of the lake.

VESZPRÉM

On your way to Lake Balaton, you might want to make a stop in this charming town. Just 10 miles from Lake Balaton, Veszprém (pronounced *Vess*-praym), 116 kilometers (72 miles) southwest of Budapest, surely ranks as one of Hungary's most vibrant small cities, and is often used as a starting point for trips to that popular resort area. In Veszprém you'll find a harmonious mix of old and new: A delightfully self-contained and well-preserved 18th-century baroque Castle District spills effortlessly into a typically modern city center, itself distinguished by lively wide-open, pedestrian-only plazas.

GETTING THERE   Six daily trains depart Budapest's Déli Station for Veszprém, a 1¾-hour trip. Tickets cost 600FT ($3).

VISITOR INFORMATION   The best information sources are **Balatontourist,** at Kossuth u. 21 (☎ **88/429-630;** fax 88/427-062), open Monday through Friday 8:30am to 5pm and Saturday 9am to noon; and **Ibusz,** at Kossuth u. 10 (☎ **88/ 426-492** or 88/427-604), open Monday through Friday 9am to 5:30pm and Saturday 9am to noon. Both offices are apt to close early in the low season.

SEEING THE SIGHTS   Most of Veszprém's main sights are clustered along Vár utca, the street that runs the length of the city's small but lovely **Castle District.**

Housed inside the 18th-century canon's house, the **Exhibition of Religious Art,** Vár u. 35, has a fine collection of religious (Roman Catholic) art. Admission is 20FT (10¢); open daily 9am to 5pm.

At Vár u. 16, the vaulted **Gizella Chapel,** named for King Stephen's wife, was unearthed during the construction of the adjoining Bishop's Palace in the 18th century. Today it houses a modest collection of ecclesiastical art, but is best known for the 13th-century **frescoes** that, in various states of restoration, decorate its walls. Admission is 20FT (10¢); open daily 9am to 5pm.

For a wonderful view of the surrounding Bakony region, climb up the steps to the narrow observation deck at the top of the ✪ **Fire Tower,** at Áváros tér. Although the tower's foundations are medieval, the structure itself was built in the early 19th century.

Enter through the courtyard of Vár u. 17, behind Áváros tér. Admission is 80FT (40¢); open daily 10am to 6pm.

WHERE TO DINE For fast food, try **Mackó Cukrászda,** at Kossuth u. 6. This stand-up eatery, which is somewhat grungy yet always bustling, is popular with young locals. Pizza, hot dogs, French fries, fried chicken, and various sweets are served. **Cserhát Étterem,** housed in the same structure, is an authentic *önkiszólgáló* (self-service cafeteria). You'll find the restaurant behind the Nike store; go up the winding staircase inside the building. A menu is posted.

For something more upscale, try ✪ **Villa Medici Étterem,** next to the zoo at Kittenberger u. 11 (☎ **88/321-273**). Reputedly one of Hungary's best restaurants, it's also relatively expensive. Villa Medici serves Hungarian and continental cuisine, only at lunchtime.

THE TIHANY PENINSULA

The Tihany (pronounced *Tee*-hine) Peninsula is a protected area, and building is heavily restricted. Consequently, it maintains a rustic charm that's unusual in the Balaton region. The peninsula also features a lush, protected interior, accessible by a trail from Tihany Village, with several little inland lakes as well as a lookout tower offering views over the Balaton.

GETTING THERE The rail line that circles Lake Balaton does not serve the Tihany Peninsula. The nearest railway station is in Aszófó, about 3 miles from Tihany Village. A local bus comes to Tihany from the nearby town of Balatonfüred. You can also go by ferry from Szántód or Balatonföldvár, or by boat from Balatonfüred.

VISITOR INFORMATION Visitor information is available at **Balatontourist,** Kossuth u. 20 (☎ and fax **87/448-519**), open March through October, Monday through Friday 8:30am to 4:30pm and Saturday 8:30am to 12:30pm.

SEEING THE SIGHTS The 18th-century baroque ✪ **Abbey Church** is Tihany Village's main attraction. A resident monk carved the exquisite wooden altar and pulpit in the 18th century. The frescoes in the church are by three of Hungary's better-known 19th-century painters: Károly Lotz, Bertalan Székely, and Lajos Deák-Ébner.

Next door to the Abbey Church is the **Tihany Museum,** housed in an 18th-century baroque structure like the church. The museum features exhibitions on the surrounding region's history and culture. You pay a single entry fee of 150FT (75¢) for both church and museum. Both are open daily, 9am to 5:30pm in summer, and 10am to 3pm off-season.

SZIGLIGET

Halfway between Tihany and Keszthély is the scenic little village of Szigliget (pronounced *Sig*-lee-get), with thatched roof houses, lush vineyards, and a lovely Mediterranean quality. Szigliget is marked by the fantastic ruins of the 13th-century ✪ **Szigliget Castle,** which stand above it on **Várhegy (Castle Hill).** In the days of the Turkish invasions, the Hungarian Balaton fleet, protected by the high castle, called Szigliget its home. You can hike up to the ruins for a splendid view of the lake and the surrounding countryside; look for the path behind the white 18th-century church that stands on the highest spot in the village. A good place to fortify yourself for the hike is the **Vár Vendéglő** (on the road up to the castle), a casual restaurant with plenty of outdoor seating, serving traditional Hungarian fare.

The lively **beach** at Szigliget provides a striking contrast to the quiet village. In summer, buses from neighboring towns drop off hordes of beach-goers. The beach area is crowded with fried food and beer stands, ice cream vendors, a swingset, and a volleyball net. Admission to the beach is 100FT (50¢). Szigliget is also home to the **Eszterházy Wine Cellar,**

An Excursion to the Thermal Lake in Hévíz

If you find the water of Lake Balaton warm, just wait until you jump into the lake at Hévíz (pronounced *Hay*-veez), a town about 5 miles northwest of Keszthély.

This is Europe's largest **thermal lake** (and the second largest in the world). The lake's water temperature seldom dips below 85 to 90°F, even in the bitterest storm of winter. Consequently, people swim in the lake year-round. Hévíz has been one of Hungary's leading spa resorts for over 100 years, and it retains some of the 19th-century character that's more typical of the spas in the Czech Republic than of those in Hungary.

You can easily reach Hévíz by bus from Keszthély. Buses depart every half hour or so from the bus station (conveniently stopping to pick up passengers in front of the church on Fő tér). The entrance to the lake is just opposite the bus station. You'll see a whimsical wooden facade and the words TÓ FÜRDŐ (Bathing Lake). Tickets cost 340FT ($1.70) for up to 3 hours or 680FT ($3.40) for a day pass. Your ticket entitles you to a locker. Keep the ticket until exiting, as the attendant needs to see it to determine whether you've stayed a half day or a full day.

---

the largest wine cellar in the region. After a hike in the hills or a day in the sun, a little wine tasting just might be in order.

Natur Tourist, in the village center, is your best (and only) source of information in Szigliget.

KESZTHÉLY

At the western edge of Lake Balaton, Keszthély (pronounced *Kest*-hay), 117 miles southwest of Budapest, is one the largest towns on the lake. Although Keszthély was largely destroyed during the Turkish wars, the town was rebuilt in the 18th century by the Festetics family, an aristocratic family who made Keszthély their home through World War II.

Stop in at **Tourinform,** at Kossuth u. 28 (☎ and fax **83/314-144**), open in summer, Monday through Friday 9am to 6pm and Saturday 9am to 1pm; off-season, Monday through Friday 8am to 4pm and Saturday 9am to 1pm. For private-room bookings, try **Zalatours,** at Kossuth u. 1 (☎ **83/312-560**), or **Ibusz,** at Kossuth u. 27 (☎ **83/314-320**).

The highlight of a visit to Keszthély is the splendid ✪ **Festetics Mansion,** at Szabadsag u. 1 (☎ **83/312-190**), the baroque 18th-century home (with its 19th-century additions) for generations of the Festetics family. Part of the mansion is now open as a museum, the main attraction of which is the ornate library. The museum also features hunting gear and trophies of a bygone era. The museum is open in summer, daily 9am to 6pm (closes at 5pm on Monday in low season). Admission for foreigners is 550FT ($2.75).

The mansion's lovely concert hall is the site of classical music concerts almost every night throughout the summer (two or three times a month in low season). Concerts usually start at 8pm; tickets, at 400FT ($2) apiece, are available at the door or earlier in the day at the museum cashier. Another part of the mansion has in the past—and may again—served as a hotel.

The center of Keszthély's summer scene, just like that of every other settlement on Lake Balaton, is down by the water on the "strand." Keszthély's beachfront is dominated by several large hotels. Regardless of whether you're a guest, you can rent windsurfers, boats, and other water-related equipment from these hotels.

Ireland 10

by Robert Meagher

If you haven't been to Ireland lately, then you haven't been to Ireland. The scale and pace of change here is dizzying. Once the donkey-cart of the European Community, Ireland is now the pace-setter—a young, turbulent, venturesome nation that's slow to look back and quick to outreach itself. If you look for it, the old Ireland lingers here and there, and, to be sure, Ireland remains a land of breathtaking beauty, whose people possess more than their share of wit and welcoming charm. What's new is that Ireland at the millennium is where "it's" happening—a boom, a renaissance, a revolution. No one knows what to call it, because no one knows where it's going. All the same, 5½ million annual visitors come a long way to see it for themselves.

1 Dublin

"Seedy elegance" may have aptly described much, if not most, of Dublin until quite recently, but no longer. Named by *Fortune* magazine as the number one European city in which to do business, and edging out Rome, Venice, and Prague as the fifth most visited city in Europe, Dublin is no backwater. The Liffey may never be potable, but otherwise the sky seems to be the limit. Over 40 new hotels have sprouted up in the past several years alone in what seems a nearly hopeless race to keep up with tourist demand. Dublin is "ground zero" for the new Ireland, the lair of the "Celtic Tiger," and without any contest the hottest spot on the island.

Only in Dublin

Viewing the Book of Kells   This amazing 8th-century, brilliantly illuminated version of the Four Gospels is housed at Trinity College.

Enjoying Dublin's Georgian Landmarks   Dublin is still filled with classic Georgian architecture: Merrion and Fitzwilliam squares, wide Georgian streets and parks lined by rows of restored brick-fronted townhouses; the Custom House, with a long classical facade overlooking the River Liffey; and Leinster House, on Merrion Square, which served as a model for the design of the White House.

Discovering Dublin's Literary Heritage   Make a visit to the Dublin Writers Museum to learn about Dublin's great writers, with books galore, exhibits, paintings, sculptures, and memorabilia. Also visit the Martello tower (described in *Ulysses*), where Joyce lived.

Dublin

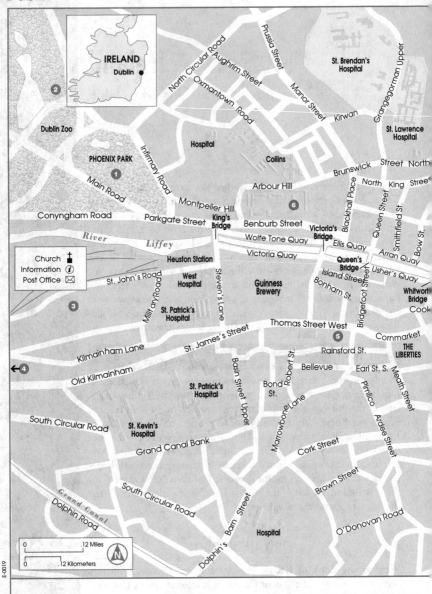

Attractions:

Christ Church Cathedral 18
Collins Barracks 6
Dublin Castle 16
Dublin Writers Museum 8
Dublin Zoo 2

Dvblinia 19
Fitzwilliam Square 33
Garden of Remembrance 9
Guinness Brewery Hop Store/
  Visitor Centre 5
Heraldic Museum/
  Genealogical Office 23

Hugh Lane Municipal Gallery
  of Modern Art 7
Irish Museum of Modern Art 3
James Joyce Cultural Centre 10
Kilmainham Gaol Historical
  Museum 4
Merrion Square 29

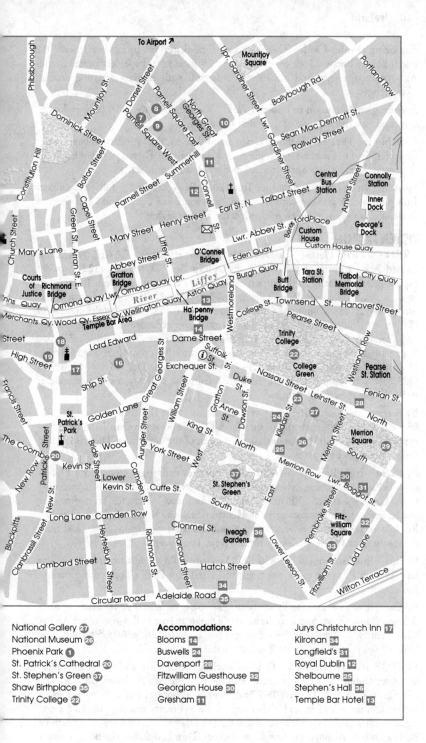

National Gallery 27
National Museum 26
Phoenix Park 1
St. Patrick's Cathedral 20
St. Stephen's Green 37
Shaw Birthplace 35
Trinity College 22

Accommodations:
Blooms 14
Buswells 24
Davenport 28
Fitzwilliam Guesthouse 32
Georgian House 30
Gresham 11

Jurys Christchurch Inn 17
Kilronan 34
Longfield's 31
Royal Dublin 12
Shelbourne 25
Stephen's Hall 36
Temple Bar Hotel 13

Exploring Dublin Castle   Once the seat of the British government in Ireland, the ancient castle boasts a 13th-century tower, a 19th-century chapel, elaborate ceremonial state apartments, and a medieval undercroft with excavations going back to Viking times.

Spending an Afternoon in Phoenix Park   Wander down the quiet lanes and walkways and visit the zoo, one of the oldest in Europe.

Going to the Theater   Dublin has two major theaters, the legendary Abbey Theater for which Sean O'Casey wrote his plays, now the National Theater of Ireland, and the renowned Gate, known worldwide for its distinguished productions.

Spending an Evening in Dublin's Traditional Pubs   Dublin is full of traditional Irish pubs, where you can have a few pints and some fine conversation and listen to traditional Irish music, which is experiencing a major revival.

ORIENTATION

ARRIVING   By Plane   The **Dublin International Airport** (☎ 01/704-4222) is located 7 miles north of the city center. **Dublin Bus** (☎ 01/873-4222) provides express coach service from the airport into the city's central bus station, **Busaras,** on Store Street. Service runs daily, 7:30am until 7:45pm (8:30pm Sundays), with departures every 20 to 30 minutes. One-way fare is £3.50 ($5.43) for adults and £1.25 ($1.94) for children under age 12. These services are expanded during high season, and a local city bus (no. 41) is also available to the city center for £1.10 ($1.71).

For speed and ease, a **taxi** is the best way to get directly to your hotel or guesthouse. Depending on your destination, fares average between £12 ($18.60) and £15 ($23.25). A 10% tip is standard. Taxis are lined up at a first-come, first-served taxi stand outside the arrivals terminal.

By Ferry   Passenger/car ferries from Britain arrive at the **Dublin Ferryport** (☎ 01/855-2222), on the eastern end of the North Docks, and at the **Dun Laoghaire Ferryport** (☎ 01/661-0511), about 10 miles south of the city center. There is bus and taxi service from both ports.

By Train   **Irish Rail** (☎ 01/836-6222) operates daily train service into Dublin from Belfast in Northern Ireland and all major cities in the Irish Republic, including Cork, Galway, Limerick, Killarney, Sligo, Wexford, and Waterford. Trains from the south, west, and southwest arrive at **Heuston Station,** Kingsbridge, off St. John's Road; from the north and northwest at **Connolly Station,** Amiens Street; and from the southeast at **Pearse Station,** Westland Row, Tara Street.

By Bus   **Bus Eireann** (☎ 01/836-6111) operates daily express coach and local bus services from all major cities and towns in Ireland into Dublin's central bus station, Busaras, on Store Street.

By Car   If you are arriving by car from other parts of Ireland or via car ferry from Britain, all main roads lead into the heart of Dublin and are well signposted to An Lar (City Centre). To bypass the city center, the East Link (toll bridge 60p; 50¢) and West Link are signposted, and the M50 circuits the city on three sides.

VISITOR INFORMATION   Dublin Tourism operates five walk-in visitor centers in greater Dublin. Its principal center is in the converted **St. Andrew's Church,** Suffolk Street, Dublin 2 (☎ 01/605-7700), offering all sorts of free information about Dublin and the rest of Ireland. Other services are a currency exchange counter, a car-rental counter, and a hotel reservations desk. The other four centers are at the Arrivals Hall of **Dublin Airport;** the new ferry terminal, **Dun Laoghaire;** the **Baggot Street Bridge,** Dublin 2; and **The Square,** Tallaght, Dublin 24 (all telephone inquiries should be directed to the Suffolk Street center). All centers are open year-round with at least the following hours: Monday to Friday 9am to 5:30pm and Saturday 9am to 1pm.

In addition, an independent center offers details on concerts, exhibits, and other arts events in the **Temple Bar** section at 18 Eustace Street, Temple Bar, Dublin 2 (☎ 01/671-5717), open year-round Monday to Friday 9:30am to 5:30pm and Saturday 10am to 5:30pm.

At any of these centers you can pick up the free *Tourism News;* the free *Dublin Event Guide,* a biweekly entertainment guide; or *In Dublin,* a biweekly arts-and-entertainment magazine selling for £1.95 ($3).

CITY LAYOUT Compared with other European capitals, Dublin is a relatively small metropolis and easy to get to know. The downtown core of the city, identified in Gaelic on bus destination signs as **AN LAR** (the Center), is shaped somewhat like a pie, with the **River Liffey** cutting across the middle from east to west. The top half of the pie, or north side of the city, is rimmed in a semicircular sweep by the **Royal Canal,** and the bottom half, or south side, is edged in a half-circle shape by the waters of the **Grand Canal.** To the north of the Royal Canal are the suburbs of Drumcondra, Glasnevin, Howth, Clontarf, and Malahide; to the south of the Grand Canal are the suburbs of Ballsbridge, Blackrock, Dun Laoghaire, Dalkey, Killiney, Rathgar, Rathmines, and other residential areas.

GETTING AROUND **By Bus** Dublin Bus operates a fleet of green doubledecker buses, frequent single-deck buses, and minibuses throughout the city and its suburbs. Most buses originate on or near **O'Connell Street, Abbey Street,** or **Eden Quay** on the north side, and from **Aston Quay, College Street,** or **Fleet Street** on the south side. Destinations and bus numbers are posted above the front windows; buses destined for the city center are marked with the Gaelic words **AN LAR.**

Bus service runs daily throughout the city, starting at 6am (10am on Sunday), with the last bus at 11:30pm; Friday and Saturday there's a Nitelink service from the city center to the suburbs running midnight to 3am. Schedules are posted on revolving notice boards at each bus stop. Fares are calculated on the distances traveled. Buy your tickets from the driver as you enter the bus; exact change is not required. One-day, 4-day, and weekly passes are available at reduced rates. For more information, contact **Dublin Bus,** 59 Upper O'Connell St. (☎ 01/873-4222).

By DART Although Dublin has no subway in the strict sense, there is an electrifiedtrain rapid-transit system, known as **DART** (Dublin Area Rapid Transit). It travels mostly at ground level or on elevated tracks, linking the city-center stations at **Tara Street, Pearse Street,** and **Amiens Street** with suburbs and seaside communities as far as Howth to the north and Bray to the south. Service operates roughly every 10 to 20 minutes Monday through Saturday from 7am to midnight and Sunday from 9:30am to 11pm. The minimum fare is 65p ($1). One-day, 4-day, and weekly passes, as well as family tickets, are available at reduced rates. For further information, contact **DART,** 35 Lower Abbey St., Dublin 1 (☎ 01/836-6222).

By Taxi Dublin taxis do not cruise the streets looking for fares; instead, they line up at ranks. Ranks are located outside all the leading hotels, at bus and train stations, and on prime thoroughfares, such as Upper O'Connell Street, College Green, and the north side of St. Stephen's Green. You can also phone for a taxi. Some of the companies that operate a 24-hour radio-call service are **Co-Op** (☎ 01/677-7777), **National** (☎ 01/677-2222), and **VIP Taxis** (☎ 01/478-3333). If you need a wake-up call, **VIP** offers that service, along with especially courteous dependability. Taxi rates are fixed by law and posted in each taxi. At peak times in Dublin's often backed-up traffic, it's the minutes and not the miles that are going to add up. The most costly add-ons are for dispatched pick-up and for service from Dublin airport. Some hotel or guest-house staff, when asked to arrange for a taxi, tack on as much as £4 ($6.20) for their services, although this practice violates city taxi regulations.

By Bicycle Riding a bike in Dublin isn't recommended. Traffic is very heavy, the streets are narrow, and pedestrians crowd every corner. For those determined to take to the streets on wheels, a good option is **Dublin Bike Tours** (☎ **01/679-0899**), offering 3-hour tours of the city. The cost is £12 ($18.60) per person; tours depart three times daily (10am, 2pm, and 6pm).

Parking The bottom line here is that you're better off without a car in Dublin, as the city is aggressively discouraging the car as the vehicle of choice for commuters, much less for tourists. During normal business hours, **free parking** on Dublin streets is an endangered option soon to be extinct. Never park in bus lanes or along a curb with double yellow lines. Fines for parking illegally are £15 ($23.25); if a car is towed away, it costs £100 ($155) to retrieve it. What's more, as of May 1998, a new peril faces parked vehicles. The infamous "Texas boot," or wheel clamp, has come to Ireland, and the cost of removing it starts at £65 ($100.75).

Individual **parking meters** in the city center are currently being phased out in favor of multi-bay meters and "pay-and-display" **disc parking.** In Dublin, five discs can be purchased for £4 ($6.20), and each ticket is good for either 1 or 2 hours, depending on the location of the parking site. The most reliable and safest places to park are at surface parking lots or in multistory car parks in central locations, such as Kildare Street, Lower Abbey Street, Marlborough Street, and St. Stephen's Green West. Parking lots charge on average £1.40 ($2.15) per hour and £13 ($20.15) for 24 hours. Night rates vary from £3.50 ($4.45) to £6 ($9.30).

On Foot Small and compact, Dublin is ideal for walking, but be careful to look left and right for oncoming traffic and to obey traffic signals. Each traffic light has timed "walk/don't walk" signals for pedestrians. Pedestrians have the right of way at specially marked, zebra-striped crossings; as a warning, there are usually two flashing lights at these intersections. For some walking-tour suggestions, see "Organized Tours" under "Exploring Dublin," below.

Fast Facts: Dublin

American Express The office is opposite Trinity College, just off College Green, at 41 Nassau St., Dublin 2 (☎ **01/679-9000**). It's open Monday to Friday 9am to 5pm and Saturday 9am to noon. Currency exchange is offered Monday to Saturday 9am to 5pm; June to August the office is also open Sunday 10am to 4pm. There is also an American Express currency exchange desk in the Suffolk Street center of Dublin Tourism.

Baby-sitters With advance notice, most hotels and guesthouses will arrange for baby-sitting.

Banks Two convenient banks are the **National Irish Bank,** 66 Upper O'Connell St., open Monday to Friday 10am to 4pm (to 5pm Thursday), and the **Allied Irish Bank,** 100 Grafton St., open Monday to Friday 10am to 4pm (to 5pm Thursday). Both have ATMs that accept Cirrus network cards as well as MasterCard and Visa.

Business Hours **Banks** are open Monday through Wednesday and on Friday from 10am to 12:30pm and from 1:30 to 3pm, on Thursday from 10am to 12:30pm and from 1:30 to 5pm. Some banks are beginning to stay open through the lunch hour. Most business offices are open from 9am to 5pm, Monday through Friday. **Stores and shops** are open from 9am to 5:30pm Monday through Wednesday and Friday to Saturday, and from 9am to 8pm on Thursday. Some bookshops and tourist-oriented stores also open on Sunday from 11am or noon until 4 or 5pm. During the peak season (May through September), many gift and souvenir shops post Sunday hours.

Currency   The basic unit of currency is the **punt,** or **Irish pound (£).** The punt is divided into 100 **pence (p).** There are 1p, 2p, 5p, 10p, 20p, 50p, and £1 coins, and punt notes of 5, 10, 20, 50, and 100 punts. At press time, $1 = 65p or Irish £1 = $1.55 and that was the rate of exchange used in this chapter. Also, 1EUR = .7 Irish £ and 1 British £ = 1.2 Irish £.

Currency Exchange   Currency-exchange services, signposted as BUREAU DE CHANGE, are in all banks and at many branches of the Irish post office system, known as **An Post.** A bureau de change operates daily during flight arrival and departure times at Dublin airport; a foreign currency note-exchanger machine is also available on a 24-hour basis in the main arrivals hall. Many hotels and travel agencies offer bureau de change services, although the best rate of exchange is usually given at banks or, better yet, when you use your credit card for purchases or expenses.

Dentist   For dental emergencies, contact the **Eastern Health Board Head-quarters,** Dr. Steevens Hospital, Dublin 8 (☎ **01/679-0700**). See also "Dental Surgeons" in the Golden Pages (yellow pages) of the telephone book.

Doctor   In an emergency, most hotels and guesthouses can contact a house doctor for you. You can also call either the Eastern Health Board Headquarters (see "Dentist," above) or the **Irish Medical Organization,** 10 Fitzwilliam Place, Dublin 2 (☎ **01/676-7273**), 9:15am to 5:15pm. See also "Doctors—Medical" in the Golden Pages of the telephone book.

Drugstores   Centrally located drugstores, known locally as *pharmacies* or *chemist shops,* include **Hamilton Long and Co.,** 5 Lower O'Connell St. (☎ **01/ 874-8456**) and **Dame Street Pharmacy,** 16 Dame St., Dublin 2 (☎ **01/ 670-4523**). A late-night chemist shop is **Byrnes Late Night Pharmacy,** 4 Merrion Rd., Dublin 4 (☎ **01/838-6750**).

Embassies & Consulates   The **United States** Embassy is located at 42 Elgin Rd., Ballsbridge, Dublin 4 (☎ **01/668-8777**); **Canadian** Embassy, 65/68 St. Stephen's Green, Dublin 2 (☎ **01/478-1988**); **British** Embassy, 29 Merrion Rd., Dublin 4 (☎ **01/205-3700**); **Australian** Embassy, Fitzwilton House, Wilton Terrace, Dublin 2 (☎ **01/676-1517**); **New Zealand** Consulate-General, 46 Upper Mount St., Dublin 2 (☎ **01/676-2464**).

Emergencies   For the **Garda** (police), fire, or other emergencies, dial ☎ **999.**

Holidays   Dublin holidays are January 1 (New Year's Day), March 17 (St. Patrick's Day), Good Friday and Easter Monday, May Day (the first Monday in May), the first Monday in June and August (Summer Bank Holidays), the last Monday in October (Autumn Bank Holiday), December 25 (Christmas Day), and December 26 (St. Stephen's Day). Most stores remain closed between Christmas and the first Monday after New Year's Day.

Hospitals   For emergency care, two of the most modern health-care facilities are **St. Vincent's Hospital,** Elm Park (☎ **01/269-4533**), on the south side of the city, and **Beaumont Hospital,** Beaumont Road, Dublin 9 (☎ **01/ 837-7755**), on the north side.

Hotlines In Ireland, hotlines are called *helplines.* For **emergencies, police,** or **fire,** dial ☎ **999; Aids Helpline** (☎ **01/872-4277**) Monday to Friday 7 to 9pm and Saturday 3 to 5pm; **Alcoholics Anonymous** (☎ **01/453-8998** and after hours **01/679-5967**); **Narcotics Anonymous** (☎ **01/830-0944**); **Rape Crisis Centre** (☎ **01/661-4911** and FreeFone (1800/778-888; after 5:30pm and weekends ☎ 01/661-4564); and **Samaritans** (☎ **01/872-7700** and 1850/ 609-090).

Internet Access In cyber-literate Dublin, public access terminals are no longer hard to find, appearing in shopping malls, hotels, and hostels throughout the city center. Fast transmission rates are assured at **Cyberia Cafe,** Eustace Street, Temple Bar, Dublin 2 (☎ **01/679-7607;** www.cyberiacafe.net), where 15 minutes online is £1.50 ($2.35), or £1.25 ($1.95) for students. It's open Monday to Saturday 10am to 11pm and Sunday noon to 8pm. At the **Planet Cybercafe** (☎ **01/679-0583**), 23 S. Great Georges St., Dublin 2, half an hour online costs £2.75 ($4.25).

Laundry In the city center, try **Suds,** 60 Upper Grand Canal St., Dublin 2 (☎ **01/668-1786**). Take your dry cleaning to **Craft Cleaners,** 12 Upper Baggot St., Dublin 4 (☎ **01/668-8198**).

Lost Property Most hotels have a lost-property service, usually under the aegis of the housekeeping department. For items lost in public places, contact the **Dublin Garda Siochana (Police) Headquarters,** Harcourt Square, Dublin 2 (☎ **475-5555**).

Police Dial ☎ **999** in an emergency. The metropolitan headquarters for the **Dublin Garda Siochana** (Police) is in Phoenix Park, Dublin 8 (☎ **01/ 677-1156**).

Post Office The **General Post Office** (GPO) is located on O'Connell Street, Dublin 1 (☎ **01/705-7000**). Hours are Monday through Saturday 8am to 8pm, Sunday and holidays 10:30am to 6:30pm. Branch offices, identified by the sign OIFIG AN POST/POST OFFICE, are open Monday through Saturday only, 9am to 6pm.

Telephone The **country code** for the Republic of Ireland is **353.** The **city code** for Dublin is **01.** If you're calling from outside Ireland, drop the initial 0 (zero) from the city code. Thus, to call the Georgian House from the United States, you would dial ☎ 011-353-1/661-8832. For direct-dial calls *to* the United States, dial the international access code (**00** from Ireland), and then the country code (**1**), followed by area code and number. To place a collect call to the United States from Ireland, dial ☎ **1-800/550-000** for USA Direct service. The toll-free international access codes are: **AT&T** ☎ 1-800-550-000, **Sprint** ☎ 1-800-552-001, and **MCI** ☎ 1-800-55-1001.

Ireland has one of Europe's most sophisticated phone systems, and the quality of international connections is exceptional. Throughout the city you can find pay phones that accept coins, both on the street and in pubs; a **local call** costs 20p (30¢). If you want to use one of the many yellow Callcard phones, almost as common as coin phones, you have to buy a **Callcard** (available at post offices, newsstands, and many convenience stores). The Callcard is available in denominations of 10, 20, 50, and 100 units, priced at £2 ($3.10), £3.50 ($5.45), £8 ($12.40), and £16 ($24.80), respectively. There's a local and international phone center at the General Post Office on O'Connell Street. Pay phones accept a variety of coins or a phone card (available at post offices). For information on finding a telephone number, dial ☎ **1190.**

Tipping & Service Charges   Most hotels and guesthouses add a service charge to the bill, usually 12.5% to 15%, although some places add only 10% or nothing at all. For restaurants, the policy is usually printed on the menu—either a gratuity of 10% to 15% is added to your bill, or in some cases, no service charge is added, in which case it is up to you to decide how much tip you want to leave. As a rule, bar staff do not expect a tip, except when table service is provided. Taxi drivers don't expect a tip, but if you want to give one, 10% is appropriate.

VAT   All goods and services in Ireland are subject to a 17.36% tax, known as the **VAT (value-added tax).** For non-European visitors to Ireland, it's relatively easy to arrange a **refund** of all VAT tax paid on goods (the tax paid on services is non-refundable). See "Money" in the "Introduction: Planning a Trip to Europe" for more information, or contact the tourist office.

Weather   Phone ☎ 1-850-241-222.

WHERE TO STAY
HISTORIC OLD CITY & TEMPLE BAR/TRINITY COLLEGE AREA
Expensive
Temple Bar Hotel. Fleet St., Temple Bar, Dublin 2. ☎ **800/44-UTELL** from the U.S., or 01/677-3333. Fax 01/677-3088. 108 units. TV TEL. £110–£190 ($170.50–$294.50) double. Rates include full breakfast. No service charge. MC, V. On-street parking. DART to Tara St. Station. Bus: 78A or 78B.

If you want to be in the heart of the action in the Temple Bar district, then this is a prime place to stay. Opened in summer 1993, this five-story hotel was developed from a row of townhouses and great care was taken to preserve the Georgian brick-front facade with Victorian mansard roof. Guest rooms are modern with traditional furnishings, including amenities such as a garment press, towel warmer, hair dryer, and tea/coffeemaker. Facilities include a skylit garden-style restaurant, the Terrace Cafe, and an Old Dublin–theme pub, Buskers, as well as access to a nearby health club.

Moderate
Blooms. Anglesea St., Dublin 2. ☎ **800/44-UTELL** from the U.S., or 01/671-5622. Fax 01/671-5997. www.blooms.ie. 86 units. TV TEL. £110 ($170.50) double. Service charge 12.5%. AE, DC, MC, V. DART to Tara St. Station. Bus: 21A, 46A, 46B, 51B, 51C, 68, 69, or 86.

Lovers of Irish literature will feel at home at Blooms. Named after Leopold Bloom, a character in James Joyce's *Ulysses,* this hotel is in the heart of Dublin, near Trinity College and on the edge of the artsy Temple Bar district. The bedrooms are modern and functional, with useful extras such as garment presses and hair dryers. The hotel has concierge service, 24-hour room service, and valet/laundry service. The formal restaurant is the Bia restaurant, or for more casual fare, try the Anglesea Bar. Late-night entertainment is available in the basement-level nightclub, known simply as M.

Traveler's Tip

In general, rates for Dublin hotels don't vary as greatly with the seasons as they do in the Irish countryside. Hotels often charge higher prices, however, during special events, such as the Dublin Horse Show. For the best deals, try to reserve a room in Dublin over a weekend, and ask if there's a reduction or a weekend package in effect. Some Dublin hotels cut their rates by as much as 50% on Friday and Saturday nights, when business traffic is low. Also, significant reductions are sometimes available when rooms are booked from the States using the 800 numbers listed in this book.

Inexpensive

Jurys Christchurch Inn. Christ Church Place, Dublin 8. ☎ **800/44-UTELL** from the U.S., or 01/454-0000. Fax 01/454-0012. www.jurys.com. 183 units. A/C TV TEL. £62–£65 ($96.10–$100.75) double. No service charge. AE, CB, DC, MC, V. Bus: 21A, 50, 50A, 78, 78A, or 78B.

Across from Christ Church Cathedral, this relatively new four-story hotel was designed in keeping with the area's Georgian/Victorian architecture. Geared to the cost-conscious traveler, it's the first of its kind in the city's historic district, offering quality hotel lodgings at guesthouse prices. The bedrooms, decorated with contemporary furnishings, can accommodate up to three adults or two adults and two children—all for the same price. Facilities include a moderately priced restaurant, a pub lounge, and an adjacent multistory parking area. There are 38 nonsmoking rooms available.

ST. STEPHEN'S GREEN/GRAFTON STREET AREA

Very Expensive

✪ Shelbourne. 27 St. Stephen's Green, Dublin 2. ☎ **800/225-5843** from the U.S., or 01/676-6471. Fax 01/661-6006. www.shelbourne.ie. 190 units. MINIBAR TV TEL. £419.36–£487.36 ($650–$755.40) double. Rates include full breakfast. Service charge 15%. AE, CB, DC, MC. DART to Pearse Station. Bus: 10, 11A, 11B, 13, or 20B.

With a fanciful red-brick and white-trimmed facade enhanced by wrought-iron railings and window boxes brimming with flowers, this grand six-story hostelry stands out on the north side of St. Stephen's Green. Built in 1824, it has played a significant role in Irish history (the new nation's constitution was signed in Room 112 in 1921) and often been host to international leaders, stars of stage and screen, and literary giants. The public areas, replete with glowing fireplaces, Waterford chandeliers, and original art, are popular rendezvous spots for Dubliners. The guest rooms vary in size, but all offer up-to-date comforts and are furnished with antique and period pieces. The front units overlook the bucolic setting of St. Stephen's Green. In 1996, nearly $2.5 million was spent refurbishing the Shelbourne's bedrooms and meeting rooms. Needless to say, you don't stay here just for the beds, which represent the Irish preference for a mattress somewhere beyond soft and short of firm.

Stephen's Hall. Earlsfort Centre, 14–17 Lower Leeson St., Dublin 2. ☎ **01/638-1111.** Fax 01/638-1122. www.premgroup.com. 37 units. TV TEL. £160–£250 ($248–$387.50) double. No service charge. AE, DC, MC, V. DART to Pearse Station. Bus: 14A, 11A, 11B, 13, 46A, 46B, or 86.

On the southeast corner of St. Stephen's Green, with a gracious Georgian exterior and entranceway, this is Dublin's first all-suite hotel. It's ideal for visitors who plan an extended stay or want to entertain. Newly renovated and furnished in a contemporary motif, each suite contains a hallway, sitting room, dining area, kitchen, bathroom, and one or two bedrooms, with orthopedic beds. The luxury suites on the upper floors offer city views, while the ground-level townhouse suites have private entrances. Twelve suites have computers.

Expensive

Buswells. 25 Molesworth St., Dublin 2. ☎ **800/473-9527** from the U.S., or 01/676-4013. Fax 01/676-2090. 72 units. TV TEL. £150 ($232.50) double. Rates include full breakfast. No service charge. MC, V. DART to Pearse Station. Bus: 10, 11A, 11B, 13, or 20B.

Situated on a quiet street 2 blocks from Trinity College and opposite the National Museum, Library, and Art Gallery and Leinster House, this vintage four-story hotel has long been a meeting point for artists, poets, scholars, and politicians. Originally two Georgian townhouses (dating back to 1736), it was launched as a hotel in 1928 and has been managed by three generations of the Duff family. The public rooms have period furniture, intricate plasterwork, Wedgwood flourishes, old prints, and memorabilia. All the bedrooms, completely refurbished in 1997, have been updated in a contemporary decor with Victorian touches and come with such amenities as tea/coffeemakers and hair dryers. Nonsmoking rooms are available; one room is specially designed for handicapped guests. Facilities include a restaurant, two bars, concierge, and room service.

Moderate

Georgian House Hotel. 18–22 Lower Baggot St., Dublin 2. ☎ **01/661-8832.** Fax 01/661-8834. E-mail: hotel@georgianhouse.ie. 30 units. TV TEL. £90–£160 ($139.50–$248) double. Rates include full breakfast. No service charge. AE, DC, MC, V. DART to Pearse Station. Bus: 10.

Located less than 2 blocks from St. Stephen's Green, this four-story, 200-year-old brick townhouse sits in the heart of Georgian Dublin, within walking distance of most major attractions. The smallish older bedrooms are to be fully renovated in 1999. The hotel's restaurant, the Ante Room, specializes in seafood, and there's a lively in-house pub, Maguire's, in the basement. Current plans call for 50 new executive rooms, a leisure center and indoor pool, an underground garage, and a new dining room by the spring of 2000.

FITZWILLIAM/MERRION SQUARE AREA

Very Expensive

Davenport Hotel. Merrion Sq., Dublin 2. ☎ **800/327-0200** from the U.S., or 01/661-6800. Fax 01/661-5663. E-mail: davenporthotel@tinet.ie. 116 units. A/C TV TEL. £170–£240 ($263.50–$372) double. Rates include full breakfast. Service charge 12.5%. AE, DC, MC, V. DART to Pearse Station. Bus: 5, 7A, 8, or 62.

The hotel building incorporates the neoclassical facade of Merrion Hall, an 1863 church. Inside is an impressive domed entranceway, with a six-story atrium lobby. The guest rooms, in a new section, have traditional furnishings, orthopedic beds, textured wall coverings, and brass accessories. There are three telephone lines in each room plus a computer data line, work desk, personal safe, garment press, tea/coffee welcome tray, mirrored closet, and hair dryer. It's a sister hotel to the Mont Clare, which is across the street and shares valet car-parking arrangements.

Expensive

✪ **Longfield's.** 10 Lower Fitzwilliam St., Dublin 2. ☎ **01/676-1367.** Fax 01/676-1542. 26 units. MINIBAR TV TEL. £70–£160 ($108.50–$248) double. Rates include full breakfast. No service charge. AE, DC, MC, V. DART to Pearse Station. Bus: 10.

Created from two 18th-century Georgian townhouses, this small, classy hotel is named after Richard Longfield, also known as Viscount Longueville, who originally owned this site and was a member of the Irish Parliament 2 centuries ago. Totally restored and recently refurbished, it combines Georgian decor and reproduction period furnishings of dark woods and brass trim. Bedrooms offer extras such as hair dryers. Like the eye of a storm, Longfield's is in the midst but remarkably quiet, an elegant yet unpretentious getaway 5 minutes' walk from St. Stephen's Green. Facilities include a restaurant with bar, room service, and foreign currency exchange.

Moderate

✪ **Fitzwilliam Guesthouse.** 41 Upper Fitzwilliam St., Dublin 2. ☎ **01/662-5155.** Fax 01/676-7488. 12 units, all with bathroom. TV TEL. £60–£80 ($93–$124) double. Rates include full breakfast. AE, DC, MC, V. DART to Pearse Station (then a 10-minute walk southeast). Bus: 10.

This guesthouse occupies a meticulously restored 18th-century townhouse on Fitzwilliam Street, the best-preserved Georgian thorougfare in Dublin and a convenient location for exploring the city. The entrance parlor has a homey atmosphere, with a carved marble fireplace and antique furnishings. The bright bedrooms have high ceilings; bathrooms are somewhat small, but impeccably clean. Tea/coffeemakers are available just outside each room. A full Irish breakfast is served in the vaulted basement restaurant.

Kilronan House. 70 Adelaide Rd., Dublin 2. ☎ **01/475-5266.** Fax: 01/478-2841. 15 units, 12 with bath/shower. TV TEL. £60–£95 ($93–$147.25) double. Children under 7 free. Rates include full breakfast. MC, V. Bus: 14, 15, 19, 20, or 46A.

Noel Comer is the outgoing proprietor at this comfortable guesthouse, located within 5 minutes' walk of St. Stephen's Green, just north of the Royal Canal. The sitting room on the ground floor is small and intimate, with a fire glowing through the cold months of the year. The rooms are very well kept, and those facing the front have commodious bay windows; each comes equipped with tea and coffee facilities. If you don't like stairs, request a room on the second floor because there isn't an elevator. The front rooms, facing Adelaide Street, are also preferable to those in back, which face onto office buildings and a parking lot. When you book, ask about a reduction for Frommer's readers.

O'CONNELL STREET AREA
Very Expensive
Gresham. 23 Upper O'Connell St., Dublin 1. ☎ **01/874-6881.** Fax 01/878-7175. 288 units. AC TV TEL. £160–£200 ($248–$310) double; from £250 ($387.50) suite. Service charge 12.5%. AE, CB, DC, MC, V. DART to Connolly Station. Bus: 40A, 40B, 40C, or 51A.

Centrally located on the city's main business thoroughfare, this Regency-style hotel is one of Ireland's oldest (1817) and best-known lodgings. Although much of the tourist trade in Dublin has shifted south of the River Liffey in recent years, the Gresham is still synonymous with stylish Irish hospitality and provides easy access to the Abbey and Gate Theatres and other northside attractions. The lobby and public areas are a panorama of marble floors, molded plasterwork, and crystal chandeliers. The newly renovated guest rooms vary in size and style, with high ceilings, tiled bathrooms, and period furniture. One-of-a-kind luxury terrace suites grace the upper front floors.

Moderate
Royal Dublin. 40 Upper O'Connell St., Dublin 1. ☎ **800/528-1234** from the U.S., or 01/873-3666. Fax 01/873-3120. E-mail: enq@royaldublin.com. 117 units. TV TEL. £100–£220 ($155–$341) double. Rates include full Irish breakfast and service charge. AE, DC, MC, V. DART to Connolly Station. Bus: 36A, 40A, 40B, 40C, or 51A.

Romantically floodlit at night, this modern five-story hotel is positioned near Parnell Square at the north end of Dublin's main thoroughfare, within walking distance of all the main theaters and northside attractions. It combines a contemporary skylit lobby full of art deco overtones with adjacent lounge areas that were part of an original building, dating back to 1752, with high Georgian ceilings, ornate cornices, crystal chandeliers, gilt-edged mirrors, and open fireplaces. The bedrooms are strictly modern, with light woods and three-sided full-length windows that extend over the busy street below.

BALLSBRIDGE/EMBASSY ROW AREA
Situated south of the Grand Canal, this is Dublin's most prestigious suburb, yet it is within walking distance of downtown. Although primarily a residential area, it is also the home of some of the city's leading hotels, restaurants, and embassies.

Very Expensive
✪ **Berkeley Court.** Lansdowne Rd., Ballsbridge, Dublin 4. ☎ **800/42-DOYLE** from the U.S., or 01/660-1711. Fax 01/661-7238. www.doylehotels.com. 188 units. TV TEL.

£165–£185 ($255.75–$286.75) double; from £250 ($387.50) suite. Breakfast £10.75 ($16.65). Service charge 15%. AE, DC, MC, V. Free valet parking. DART to Lansdowne Rd. Bus: 7, 8, or 45.

The flagship of the Irish-owned Doyle Hotel group, and the first Irish member of Leading Hotels of the World, the Berkeley Court is nestled in a residential area near the American Embassy on well-tended grounds that were once part of the Botanic Gardens of University College. A favorite haunt of diplomats and international business leaders, the hotel is known for its posh lobby decorated with fine antiques, original paintings, mirrored columns, and Irish-made carpets and furnishings. The newly redecorated guest rooms convey an air of elegance, with semicanopy beds and marble bathrooms. Nonsmoking rooms are available. Facilities include a restaurant, conservatory, bar and lounge, mini-gym, hair salon, boutiques, and gift shop.

Jurys Hotel and Towers. Pembroke Rd., Ballsbridge, Dublin 4. ☎ **800/843-3311** from the U.S., or 01/660-5000. Fax 01/660-5540. www.jurys.com. 390 units. TV TEL. Main hotel £195 ($302.25) double; Towers wing (with continental breakfast) £220 ($341) double. Service charge 12.5%. AE, DC, MC, V. DART to Lansdowne Rd. Station. Bus: 5, 7, 7A, or 8.

Setting a progressive tone in a city steeped in tradition, this unique hotel welcomes guests to a skylit, three-story atrium lobby with a marble and teak decor. Situated opposite the American Embassy, this sprawling property is actually two interconnected hotels in one: a modern, eight-story high-rise and a new 100-unit tower with its own check-in desk, separate elevators, and private entrance, as well as full access to all the main hotel's amenities. The guest rooms in the main wing, recently refurbished, have dark wood furnishings, brass trim, and designer fabrics. The Towers section, a first for the Irish capital, is an exclusive wing of oversized concierge-style rooms with bay windows. Each unit has computer-card key access, stocked minibar, three telephone lines, well-lit work area with desk, reclining chair, tile and marble bathroom, walk-in closet, and either a king- or queen-size bed. Decor varies, from contemporary light woods with floral fabrics to dark tones with Far Eastern motifs. Towers guests also enjoy exclusive use of a private hospitality lounge with library, board room, and access to complimentary continental breakfast, daily newspapers, and coffee/tea service throughout the day.

Expensive

Butlers Town House. 44 Lansdowne Rd., Ballsbridge, Dublin 4. ☎ **1-800-44-UTELL** from the U.S., or 01/667-4022. Fax 01/667-3960. 20 units. AC CTV TEL. £80–£160 ($124–$248) double. Rates include full breakfast. AE, DC, MC, V. DART to Lansdowne Road Station. Bus: 7, 7A, 8, 45.

This beautifully restored and expanded Victorian townhouse has a formal yet welcoming elegance—class without the starched collar. The rooms are richly furnished with either four-poster or half-tester beds, and equipped with their own climate control, activated from a hand-held remote. It's hard to elude comfort here, and the staff are especially solicitous. The gem, in our opinion, is the Glendalough Room, which can be requested if you book early. In addition to laundry and dry cleaning, secretarial services are available, and every room has a computer modem. Amenities include free tea or coffee anytime; breakfast, afternoon tea, and high tea served in the atrium dining room; room service, baby-sitting, and one handicapped-equipped room. You'll find that there isn't much Helen Finnegan, the manager, has overlooked here.

Moderate

✪ **Ariel House.** 50/52 Lansdowne Rd., Ballsbridge, Dublin 4. ☎ **01/668-5512.** Fax 01/668-5845. 40 units. TV TEL. £50–£150 ($77.50–$232.50) double (rates vary seasonally). Full Irish breakfast £8.50 ($13.20), continental breakfast £5 ($7.75). MC, V. DART to Lansdowne Rd. Station. Bus: 7, 7A, 8, or 45.

In the age of the generic, Ariel House remains a bastion of distinction and quality. For Dublin guesthouses, this one sets the standard. Michael and Maurice O'Brien are warm and consummate hosts. Guests are welcome to relax in the Victorian-style drawing room with its Waterford glass chandeliers, open fireplace, and delicately carved cornices. The bedrooms are individually decorated, with period furniture, fine paintings and watercolors, and crisp Irish linens, as well as an array of modern extras. Facilities include a conservatory-style dining room where breakfast, morning coffee, and afternoon tea are served; a wine bar; and a private car park.

Mount Herbert. 7 Herbert Rd., Ballsbridge, Dublin 4. ☎ **01/668-4321.** Fax 01/660-7077. E-mail: info@mountherberthotel.ie. 200 units. TV TEL. £70–£99 ($108.50–$153.45) double. Rates include full breakfast. No service charge. AE, DC, MC, V. DART to Lansdowne Rd. Station. Bus: 2, 3, 5, 7, 7A, 8, 18, or 45.

Over 40 years ago, the Loughran family welcomed their first guests to what had once been the family home of Lord Robinson. This gracious residence, with its own mature floodlit gardens, forms the core of a now somewhat sprawling complex. In 4 decades, the Mount Herbert has expanded from 4 guest rooms to 200. The result is a curious mix of family hospitality and large-scale uniformity. The guest rooms are bright, comfortable, and convenient to the city center, although without remarkable charm. Tea/coffee-making facilities, garment presses, and orthopedic beds are standard. Guest facilities include a restaurant, wine bar, sauna, indoor solarium, gift shop, and guest parking for up to 100 cars.

Self-Catering

Lansdowne Village. Newbridge Avenue off Lansdowne Road, Ballsbridge, Dublin 4. ☎ **01/668-3534.** Fax 01/660-6465. 19 units (2 or 3 bedrooms). TV TEL. £400–£595 ($620–$922.25) per week, depending on size of apartment and season. Shorter periods available at reduced rates Oct–Mar. MC, V. DART to Lansdowne Rd. Station. Bus: 2, 3, 5, 7, 7A, 8, 18, 45.

Lansdowne Village is a modest and appealing residential development on the banks of the River Dodder and directly across from Lansdowne Stadium. Within this community, Trident Holiday Homes offers fully equipped two- and three-bedroom rental units, each with an additional pullout double-bed sofa in the living room. They are bright and comfortable, trim and well-maintained so that everything really works. The location is ideal. Not only are you a 5-minute walk from the DART and less than a half-hour's walk from St. Stephen's Green, but the Sandymount Strand, a favorite walking spot for Dubliners, is only 10 minutes away on foot for a pleasant after-dinner stroll. Shops and supermarkets are also nearby, so you can manage here quite well without a car, feeling apart from the city's frenzy and yet not at all cut off. The smaller units are perfect for couples, perhaps with one child; the considerably more spacious three-bedroom units are recommended for larger families or for more than one couple.

WHERE TO DINE
HISTORIC OLD CITY & TEMPLE BAR/TRINITY COLLEGE AREA
Expensive

Les Frères Jacques. 74 Dame St., Dublin 2. ☎ **01/679-4555.** Reservations recommended. Set-price lunch £13.50 ($20.95); set-price dinner £21 ($32.55). à la carte also available. AE, DC, MC, V. Mon–Fri 12:30–2:30pm and 7:30–11pm; Sat 7–11pm. Bus: 50, 50A, 54, 56, or 77. FRENCH.

Well situated between Crampton Court and Sycamore Street opposite Dublin Castle, this restaurant brings a touch of haute cuisine to the lower edge of the trendy Temple Bar district. The menu offers such creative main courses as fillet of beef in red wine and bone marrow sauce; duck suprême on a sweet corn pancake in tangy ginger sauce;

rosette of spring lamb in meat juice sabayon and tomato coulis with crispy potato straws; and grilled lobster from the tank flamed in whiskey.

Lord Edward. 23 Christ Church Place, Dublin 8. ☎ **01/454-2420.** Reservations required. Main courses £9.95–£15.95 ($15.40–$24.70); set-price dinner £20 ($31). AE, DC, MC, V. Mon–Fri noon–10:45pm; Sat 6–10:45pm. Bus: 50, 54A, 56A, 65, 65A, 77, 77A, 123, or 150. SEAFOOD.

Established in 1890, this cozy upstairs dining room claims to be Dublin's oldest seafood restaurant. A dozen different preparations of sole (including au gratin and Véronique) are served, as are seven variations of prawns (from Thermidor to Provençal), and fresh lobster is prepared au naturel or in sauces. There's also fresh fish from salmon and sea trout to plaice and turbot—grilled, fried, or poached. Vegetarian dishes are also available. At lunchtime, light snacks and simpler fare are served in the bar.

Moderate

bruno's. 30 E. Essex St., Dublin 2. ☎ **01/6706767.** Reservations recommended. Main courses £10.95–£13.95 ($16.95–$21.60); set-price lunch £10.95 ($16.95) and £12.95 ($20.05). Service charge 10% on tables over 4. AE, CB, DC, MC, V. Daily noon–midnight. DART to Tara St. Station. Bus: 21A, 46A, 46B, 51B, 51C, 68, 69, 86. FRENCH/MEDITERRANEAN.

This is a sure-fire spot for a flawlessly prepared, interesting lunch or dinner without serious damage to the budget. The atmosphere is light and modern, with the focus on food that is consistently excellent without flourish or pretense. The spinach and goat cheese tart, salad of prawns with honey, lime, sesame seeds, and jalapeno peppers, and the bruscetta of chicken are all worthy of mention.

Café Auriga. Temple Bar Square, Dublin 2. ☎ **01/671-8228.** Main courses £8–£11 ($12.40–$17.05); early bird menu (5:30–7:30pm) £9 ($13.95) for 2 courses. AE, MC, V. Tues–Sat 5:30–11:00pm. Bus: Any city-center bus. CONTEMPORARY IRISH

Café Auriga is a stylish, second-floor cafe whose main dining room overlooks Temple Bar Square. Dinner is served under a ceiling of twinkling stars and is accompanied not by the sweet serenade of a lone violinist, but by the louder melodies of Dublin's top 40. The decor is stylish and simple and the crowd young, sleek, and professional. The food demonstrates the chef's facility in combining simple ingredients to create a piquant surprise for the palate. Subtly spiced, imaginative sauces accompany well-prepared fish and meat dishes, such as salmon in ginger soy sauce or breast of chicken stuffed with basil mousse. Vegetarian offerings include a succulent tagliatelle of goat cheese, cherry tomatoes, spinach, fresh herbs, and cream.

Chameleon. No.1 Fownes Street Lower, Temple Bar, Dublin 2. ☎ **01/671-0362.** Set menus £13.50–£21.50 ($20.95–$33.35); early-bird main courses £6.50–£7 ($10.10–$10.85). MC, V. Tues–Sat 6–11:30pm; Sun 6–10pm. Bus: Any city-center bus. INDONESIAN.

Only a dim candlelit window and an orange sign signal Chameleon, well camouflaged on a small side street off Temple Bar Square. The air is tinged with incense, and rich Indonesian batiks are sumptuous backdrops for the traditional puppets and dark wood carvings that lurk in the corners of the restaurant. The Chameleon offers a variety of menus featuring samplings of seven different dishes and an assortment of condiments. The staff are quick in explaining how to best complement chicken sate with roasted peanuts. *Sambal-badjak,* a red curry paste, gives the rice a robust, pleasantly spicy flavor. Finally, a small morsel of pickled vegetable is suggested as a "palate cleanser"— good advice to swallow if you want to take advantage of the abundance of delicately flavored dishes that Chameleon has to offer.

Dish. 2 Crow St., Dublin 2. ☎ **01/671-1248.** Reservations recommended. Main courses £10.50–13.95 ($16.30–$21.60). Service charge 10% on tables over 5. AE, DC, MC, V. Daily noon–11:30pm. DART to Tara St. Station. Bus: 21A, 46A, 46B, 51B, 51C, 68, 69, or 86. NOU-VEAU INTERNATIONAL.

With expansive floor to ceiling windows, wide-beamed pine floors, light walls, and dark blue linens, Dish offers a relaxed, tasteful atmosphere. The menu is eclectic and enticing, with an emphasis on fresh grilled seafood and Mediterranean flavors that are complex without being confusing. The grilled salmon with avocado, papaya, and tequila-lime dressing, the baked hake, and the char-grilled tiger prawns are particularly outstanding. The desserts we tried—caramelized lemon tart with cassis sauce and the amaretti chocolate cheesecake—were superior. Dish promises to be one of Temple Bar's finest venues, and at a modest price.

Juice. Castle House, 73 S. Great George's St., Dublin 2. ☎ **01/475-7856.** Reservations recommended Fri–Sat. Main courses £8.50–£11 ($13.20–$17.05); early-bird set-price dinner (Mon–Fri 5:30–7pm) £8.95 ($13.85). MC, V. Mon–Fri 9am–10:30pm; Sat–Sun 11am–10:30pm. Fri–Sat late-night light menu 10:30pm–4am. Bus: 50, 50A, 54, 56, or 77. VEGETARIAN.

Juice tempts carnivorous, vegan, macrobiotic, celiac, and yeast-free diners alike, using organic produce to create delicious dressings and entrees among its largely conventional but well-prepared offerings. The avocado filet of blue cheese and broccoli wrapped in filo was superb, and I also highly recommend the spinach-and-ricotta cannelloni. The latter is included in the early-bird dinner—a great deal. Coffees, fresh-squeezed juices, organic wines, and late weekend hours add to the lure of this casual modern place frequented by mature diners who know their food.

Inexpensive

Govinda's. 4 Aungier St., Dublin 2. ☎ **01/475-0309.** Main courses £4.50 ($7); soup and freshly baked bread £1.60 ($2.50). MC, V. Mon–Sat 11am–9pm. Bus: 16, 16A, 19, or 22. VEGETARIAN.

Govinda's serves healthy square meals on square plates for very good prices. The meals are generous, belly-warming concoctions of vegetables, cheese, rice, and pasta. Two main courses are offered cafeteria-style: one East Indian and the other a simple, plainly flavored staple like lasagna or macaroni and cheese. Veggie burgers are also prepared to order. All are accompanied with a choice of two salads (and are unaccompanied by smoke as the restaurant is nonsmoking throughout). Desserts are healthy and huge, like the rich wedge of carob cake with a dollop of cream or homemade ice cream (each £1.25/$1.95).

Leo Burdock's. 2 Werburgh St., Dublin 8. ☎ **01/454-0306.** Main courses £2.50–£4.50 ($3.90–$7). No credit cards. Mon–Fri 12:30–11pm; Sat 2–11pm. Bus: 21A, 50, 50A, 78, 78A, or 78B. FISH-AND-CHIPS.

For three generations, Brian Burdock's family has been serving up the country's best fish-and-chips. Cabinet ministers, university students, poets, Americans who have had the word passed by locals, and almost every other type can be found in the queue, waiting for fish bought fresh that morning and those good Irish potatoes, both cooked in "drippings" (none of that modern cooking oil!). Service is take-out only, but you can sit on a nearby bench or stroll down to the park at St. Patrick's Cathedral. It's located across from Christchurch, around the corner from Jury's Inn.

ST. STEPHEN'S GREEN/GRAFTON STREET AREA

Very Expensive

The Commons. 86 St. Stephen's Green, Dublin 2. ☎ **01/475-2597** or 01/478-0530. Reservations required. Set-price lunch £20 ($31); set-price dinner £35 ($54.25). AE, DC, MC, V. Mon–Fri 12:30–2:15pm and 7–10pm; Sat 7–10pm. DART to Pearse Station. Bus: 10, 11, 13, or 46A. MODERN EUROPEAN.

Nestled on the south side of St. Stephen's Green, this Michelin-starred restaurant occupies the basement level of Newman House, the historic seat of Ireland's major university, composed of two elegant townhouses dating back to 1740. The interior of the dining rooms is a blend of Georgian architecture, cloister-style arches, and original contemporary artworks with Joycean influences. For an aperitif in fine weather, there is a lovely stone courtyard terrace surrounded by a "secret garden" of lush plants and trees. The inventive menu changes daily, but you'll often see dishes such as confit of duck leg on a beetroot boxty, grilled shark with peppered carrot, and loin of rabbit with a stuffing of marinated prune.

Moderate

✪ Fitzers Cafe. 51 Dawson St., Dublin 2. ☎ **01/677-1155.** Reservations recommended. Lunch main courses£7–£9 ($10.85–$13.95); dinner main courses £8–£15 ($12.40–$23.25). AE, DC, MC, V. Daily 9am–3:30pm and 6–10:30pm. DART: Pearse. Bus: 10, 11A, 11B, 13, or 20B. INTERNATIONAL.

In the middle of a busy shopping street, this airy Irish-style bistro has a multi-windowed shopfront facade and a modern Irish decor of light woods. The food is excellent and reasonably priced, contemporary and quickly served, with choices ranging from chicken breast with hot chili cream sauce to brochette of lamb tandoori with mild curry sauce to gratin of smoked cod.

Fitzers has three other locations, each with a different menu and character: in the National Gallery, Merrion Square, Dublin 2 (☎ **01/661-4496**); in the Royal Dublin Society (RDS), Ballsbridge, Dublin 4 (☎ **01/667-1302**); and in Temple Bar Square, Dublin 2 (☎ **01/679-0440**). Consistency is the operative word here. You can count on Fitzers not to disappoint.

✪ Il Primo. 16 Montague St., Dublin 2 (off Harcourt St., 50 yards down from St. Stephen's Green). ☎ **01/478-3373.** Reservations required on weekends. Main courses £8.90– £15.90 ($13.80–$24.65); lunch menu £5.90–£9.80 ($9.15–$22.10). No service charge. AE, DC, MC, V. Mon–Sat 12–3pm and 6–11pm. MODERN ITALIAN.

Word of mouth is what brought me to Il Primo—little else would have, so obscurely is it tucked away off Harcourt Street. From the street all you see are several tables, a bar, an assembly of wooden stools, and a staircase, which happens to lead to some of the most distinguished, innovative Italian cuisine you'll ever meet up with outside Rome or Tuscany. Awaken your palate with a glass of sparkling Venetian prosecco; open with a plate of Parma ham, avocado, and balsamic vinaigrette; and then go for broke with the ravioli Il Primo, an open handkerchief of pasta over chicken, Parma ham, and mushrooms in a light tarragon cream sauce. The proprietor, Dieter Bergman, will assist gladly in selecting appropriate wines, all of which he personally chooses and imports from Tuscany. Wines are by the milliliter, not the bottle. Open any bottle and you pay for only what you drink. Il Primo is full of surprises.

Inexpensive

Bewley's Cafe. 78 Grafton St. (between Nassau St. and St. Stephen's Green). ☎ **01/ 677-6761.** Homemade soup £2.25 ($3.50); main courses £3–£6.50 ($4.65–$10.10); lunch specials from £5 ($7.75). AE, DC, MC, V. Daily 7:30am–11pm (continuous service for breakfast, hot food, and snacks). Bus: Any city-center bus. TRADITIONAL/PASTRIES.

This is Dublin's old reliable, a chain with a 150-year history. The interior is a subdued, mellow mix of dark wood, amber glass, and deep red velvet. Bewley's bustles with the clink of teapots and the satisfied hum of customers sated on scones, almond buns, and baked goods. Less appealing but equally filling are warm suppers of lasagne, sausages and chips, or a variety of casseroles. Most Bewley's are self-service cafeterias, but Bewley's of Grafton Street also has several full-service tearooms. Other locations are at 11 Westmoreland St., Dublin 2; 13 S. Great George's St., Dublin 2; 40 Mary St.,

Dublin 1 (near the ILAC shopping center north of the Liffey); shopping centers in Dundrum, Stillorgan, and Tallaght; and Dublin Airport.

Café Bell. St. Teresa's Courtyard, Clarendon St., Dublin 2. ☎ **01/677-7645.** All items £2–£4 ($3.10–$6.20). No credit cards. Mon–Sat 9am–6pm. Bus: 16, 16A, 19, 19A, 22A, 55, or 83. IRISH/SELF-SERVICE.

In the cobbled courtyard of early 19th-century St. Teresa's Church, this serene little place is one of a handful of dining options springing up in historic or ecclesiastical surroundings. With high ceilings and an old-world decor, Café Bell is a welcome contrast to the bustle of Grafton Street a block away and Powerscourt Town House Centre across the street. The menu changes daily but usually includes homemade soups, sandwiches, salads, quiches, lasagna, sausage rolls, hot scones, and other baked goods.

FITZWILLIAM/MERRION SQUARE AREA
Very Expensive

✪ **Restaurant Patrick Guilbaud.** 21 Upper Merrion St., Dublin 2. ☎ **01/676-4192.** Reservations required. Set-price lunch £20 ($31); main courses around £24 ($37.20). AE, DC, MC, V. Tues–Sat 12:30–2pm and 7:30–10:15pm. DART to Westland Row. Bus: 5, 7A, or 8. FRENCH NOUVELLE.

After being tucked away for many years on James Place, this distinguished restaurant has transferred to new quarters but kept its glowing Michelin-star reputation for fine food and artful service. The menu features such dishes as casserole of black sole and prawns, steamed salmon with orange and grapefruit sauce, fillet of spring lamb with parsley sauce and herb salad, roast duck with honey, and breast of guinea fowl with Madeira sauce and potato crust.

Expensive

✪ **L'Ecrivain.** 109 Lower Baggot St., Dublin 2. ☎ **01/661-1919.** Reservations recommended. 3-course set-price lunch £16.50 ($25.60); early-bird menu (Mon–Thurs 6:30–7:30pm) £17.50 ($27.15); set-price dinner £31.50 ($48.85); main courses £19.50 ($30.25). AE, DC, MC, V. Mon–Fri 12:30–2pm and 7–11pm; Sat 7–11pm. Bus: 10. FRENCH/IRISH.

This is one of Dublin's truly fine restaurants, from start to finish. The atmosphere is relaxed and welcoming, and you can dine on the garden terrace in good weather. The emphasis in the kitchen is on the "best of Irish" ingredients, and each course receives the same devoted attention. The seared sea trout with sweet potato purée and the entrecôte steak with caramelized onion were perfectly prepared on a recent visit. Be sure to leave room for dessert, too, as they get the same special attention as the main courses.

Moderate

Lloyds Brasserie. 20 Upper Merrion St., Dublin 2. ☎ **01/662-7240.** Reservations recommended. Set-price lunch 2-courses £10.50 ($16.30), 3-courses £13.50 ($20.95); main courses £8.95–£15.95 ($13.85–$24.70). No service charge. AE, DC, MC, V. Daily 10am for coffee; lunch Mon–Fri noon–2pm; brunch Sat–Sun 1–4pm; dinner daily 6pm–2am. DART to Westland Row. Bus: 10, 11A, 11B, 13, or 20B. FRENCH NOUVELLE.

This is famed chef Conrad Gallagher's latest venture. The decor is minimalist, contemporary, with hints of art deco—clear, bright, and simple. The food is another matter—bold, often intense, and in presentation nothing less than architectural. The menu, on the page and on the plate, certainly commands attention, although the essential ingredients are often in danger of being taken for granted, even overlooked. A meal here is an adventure, well worth the relatively moderate price, and where else will you find "bubble and squeak" (corned beef, ground lamb, and cabbage), a surprisingly subtle dish?

Inexpensive

Grays. 109 Lower Baggot St. ☎ **01/676-0676.** All items £2.95–£7.50 ($4.55–$11.65). MC, V. Mon–Fri 7:30am–4pm. DART to Pearse Station. Bus: 10. INTERNATIONAL/SELF-SERVICE.

A popular self-service eatery, this cozy converted mews has choir benches, caned chairs, and lots of hanging plants, on both ground and upstairs levels, and an outdoor courtyard for dining in fine weather. The menu choices concentrate on sandwiches and salads made to order, as well as pastas, quiches, curries, and casseroles.

O'CONNELL STREET AREA

Moderate

✪ **101 Talbot.** 100 Talbot St., Dublin 1. ☎ **01/874-5011.** Reservations recommended. Dinner main courses £7.85–£10.75 ($12.15–$16.65). AE, DC, MC, V. Mon–Sat 5–11pm. DART to Connolly Station. Bus: 27A, 31A, 311B, 32A, 32B, 42B, 42C, 43, or 44A. INTERNATIONAL/VEGETARIAN.

Opened in 1991, this second-floor shopfront restaurant features light and healthy foods, with a strong emphasis on vegetarian dishes, including choices for vegans. The setting is bright and casual, with contemporary Irish art on display, big windows, yellow rag-rolled walls, ash-topped tables, and newspapers for browsing. Main courses include jambalaya of lamb, smoked sausage, and black-eyed peas; vegetable satay with rice; and tandoori chicken with mango. The lunch menu changes daily, and the dinner menu weekly. Espresso and cappuccino are always available for sipping, and there's a full bar. It's located at Talbot Lane near Marlborough Street, convenient to the Abbey Theatre.

Inexpensive

Winding Stair. 40 Lower Ormond Quay, Dublin 1. ☎ **01/873-3292.** All items £1.50–£4 ($2.35–$6.20). MC, V. Mon–Sat 10am–6pm; Sun 6pm–10pm. Bus: 70 or 80. IRISH.

Those who resist reading the texts that paper the walls of this cafe's three-storied 18th-century winding stair will soon find themselves in a comforting enclave overlooking the Ha'penny bridge and the River Liffey. Solicitous staff are quick to serve bookish clientele who are as satisfied with the tea, espresso, and healthy sandwiches and cakes as they are with the surrounding shelves filled with new and used books. Thick sandwiches heaped with fresh vegetables and a choice of cheeses and salamis are made to order. Salads include the exotic and the local with both a hearty tabouli and an Irish Brie and Cranberry gracing the chalkboard menu. A banana and honey sandwich as well as carrot cake and lemon-poppyseed loaf make up the "sweet" menu. Soup is also offered—but go early if it's your lunchtime goal as it tends to disappear quickly on rainy Dublin days. Evening events include poetry readings and recitals.

BALLSBRIDGE/EMBASSY ROW AREA

Expensive

Le Coq Hardi. 35 Pembroke Rd., Ballsbridge, Dublin 4. ☎ **01/668-9070.** Reservations required. Set-price lunch £21 ($32.55) for full menu, £13 ($20.15) for 1 course and coffee; dinner main courses £16–£27 ($24.80–$41.85). AE, CB, MC, V. Mon–Fri 12:30–2:30pm and 7–11pm; Sat 7–11pm. DART to Lansdowne Rd. Station. Bus: 18, 46, 63, or 84. FRENCH.

Newly decorated in radiant autumn colors and offering a new cocktail bar, this plush 50-seat restaurant draws a well-heeled local and international business clientele. Chef John Howard has garnered many an award by offering such specialties as Dover sole stuffed with prawns, Irish wild salmon on fresh spinach leaves, fillet of hake roasted on green cabbage and bacon with Pernod butter sauce, and fillet of prime beef flamed in Irish whiskey. The 700-bin wine cellar boasts a complete collection of Château Mouton Rothschild, dating from 1945 to the present.

Moderate

✪ **Roly's Bistro.** 7 Ballsbridge Terrace, Dublin 4. ☎ **01/668-2611.** Reservations required. Main courses £9.50–£14.95 ($14.75–$23.15); set-price lunch £12.50 ($19.40). AE, DC, MC, V. Daily noon–3pm and 6–10pm. DART to Lansdowne Rd. Station. Bus: 5, 6, 7, 8, 18, or 45. IRISH/INTERNATIONAL.

Opened in 1992, this two-story shopfront restaurant quickly skyrocketed to success, thanks to its genial and astute host Roly Saul and its master chef Colin O'Daly. What you get is excellent and imaginatively prepared food at mostly moderate prices. The main dining rooms, with a bright and airy decor and lots of windows, can be noisy when the house is full, but the nonsmoking section has a quiet enclave of booths laid out in an Orient Express style for those who prefer a quiet tête-à-tête. Main courses include roasted venison, pan-fried Dublin Bay prawns, game pie with chestnuts, and wild mushroom risotto. An excellent array of international wines is offered, starting at £9.95 ($15.40) a bottle.

Inexpensive

✪ **Da Vincenzo.** 133 Upper Leeson St., Dublin 4. ☎ **01/660-9906.** Reservations recommended. Main courses £6.50–£10 ($10.40–$16.10); set-price lunch £6.95 ($10.80). AE, DC, MC, V. Mon–Sat 12:30–11:30pm; Sun 1–10pm. Bus: 10, 11A, 11B, 46A, or 46B. ITALIAN.

Occupying a shopfront location within a block of the Hotel Burlington, this informal and friendly owner-run bistro offers ground level and upstairs seating. The casual decor consists of glowing brick fireplaces, pine walls, vases and wreaths of dried flowers, modern art posters, blue and white pottery, and a busy open kitchen. Pizza with a light, pita-style dough, cooked in a wood-burning oven, is a specialty here. Other main courses range from pastas to veal and beef dishes, including an organically produced filet steak.

SEEING THE SIGHTS
SIGHTSEEING SUGGESTIONS FOR FIRST-TIME VISITORS

If You Have 1 Day   Start at the beginning—Dublin's medieval quarter, the area around **Christ Church** and **St. Patrick's Cathedral.** Tour these great churches and then walk the cobblestoned streets and inspect the nearby old city walls at **High Street.** From Old Dublin, take a turn eastward and see **Dublin Castle** and then **Trinity College** with the famous Book of Kells. Cross over the River Liffey to **O'Connell Street,** Dublin's main thoroughfare. Walk up this wide street, passing the landmark General Post Office (GPO), to Parnell Square and the picturesque Garden of Remembrance. If time permits, visit the **Dublin Writers Museum,** and then hop on a double-decker bus heading to the south bank of the Liffey for a visit to **St. Stephen's Green** for a relaxing stroll amid the greenery. Cap the day with a show at the **Abbey Theatre** and maybe a drink or two at a nearby pub.

If You Have 2 Days   On your second day, take a **Dublin Bus city sightseeing tour** to give you an overview of the city—you'll see all the local downtown landmarks, plus some of the leading sites on the edge of the city, such as the **Guinness Brewery,** the **Royal Hospital,** and **Phoenix Park.** In the afternoon, head for **Grafton Street** for some shopping. If time allows, stroll around **Merrion** or **Fitzwilliam squares** to give you a sampling of the best of Dublin's Georgian architecture.

If You Have 3 Days   Make day 3 a day for Dublin's artistic and cultural attractions—visit the **National Museum** and **National Gallery,** the **Guinness Hop Store,** or a special-interest museum, such as the **Writers Museum.** Save time for a walk around **Temple Bar,** the city's Left Bank district, lined with art galleries and film studios, interesting secondhand shops, and casual eateries.

If You Have 4 Days   On day 4, take a ride aboard DART, Dublin's rapid-transit system, to the suburbs, either southward to **Dun Laoghaire** or **Dalkey,** or northward to **Howth.** The DART routes follow the rim of Dublin Bay in both directions, so you'll enjoy a scenic ride and get to spend some time in an Irish coastal village.

DUBLIN'S TOP ATTRACTIONS

✪ **Trinity College and The Book of Kells.** College Green, Dublin 2. ☎ **01/608-2320.** Free admission to college grounds. Old Library/Book of Kells, £4.50 ($7) adults, £4 ($6.20) seniors/students, £9 ($13.95) families, free for children under 12; Dublin Experience, £3 ($4.65) adults, £2.75 ($4.25) seniors/students, free for children under 12. Library, Mon–Sat 9:30am–5pm, Sun noon–4:30pm (opens at 9:30am June–Sept); *Dublin Experience,* May–Sept daily 10am–5pm, closed Oct–Apr. Bus: All city center buses.

The oldest university in Ireland, Trinity was founded in 1592 by Queen Elizabeth I. It sits in the heart of the city on a beautiful 40-acre site just south of the River Liffey, with cobbled squares, gardens, a picturesque quadrangle, and buildings dating from the 17th to the 20th centuries. The college is home to the Book of Kells, an 8th-century version of the four Gospels with elaborate scripting and illumination. This famous treasure and other early Christian manuscripts are on permanent public view in the Colonnades, an exhibition area on the ground floor of the Old Library. Also housed in the Old Library is the *Dublin Experience* (☎ **01/608-1177**), an excellent multimedia introduction to the history and people of Dublin.

✪ **National Museum.** Kildare St., Dublin 2. ☎ **01/677-7444.** Free admission. Tues–Sat 10am–5pm; Sun 2–5pm. DART to Pearse Station. Bus: 7, 7A, 8, 10, 11, or 13.

This important museum reflects Ireland's heritage from 2000 B.C. to the present. It's the home of many of the country's greatest historical finds, including the Ardagh Chalice, Tara Brooch, and Cross of Cong. Other highlights range from the artifacts from the Wood Quay excavations of the Old Dublin Settlements to an extensive exhibition of Irish gold ornaments from the Bronze Age.

Collins Barracks. Benburb Street, Dublin 7. ☎ **01/677-7444.** Free admission. Tours at varying hours, depending on groups, £1 ($1.55). Tues–Sat 10am–5pm; Sun 2–5pm. Bus: 25, 66, 67, or 90.

This is the latest venue of the National Museum, which has already occupied 2 of the 4 blocks available here. Even if it were empty, Collins Barracks—the oldest military barracks in Europe—would be well worth a visit; the structure itself is a splendidly restored early 18th-century masterwork by Colonel Thomas Burgh, Ireland's Chief Engineer and Surveyor General under Queen Anne.

So far, the collection housed here focuses on the decorative arts. Most notable is the extraordinary display of Irish silver and furniture. Collins Barracks also houses a cafe and gift shop.

✪ **Dublin Castle.** Palace St. (off Dame St.), Dublin 2. ☎ **01/677-7129.** Admission £3 ($4.65) adults, £2 ($3.10) seniors and students, £1 ($1.55) children under 12. Mon–Fri 10am–5pm; Sat–Sun and holidays 2–5pm. Guided tours are conducted every 20–25 minutes. Bus: 50, 50A, 54, 56A, 77, 77A, or 77B.

Built between 1208 and 1220, this complex represents some of the oldest surviving architecture in the city and was the center of British power in Ireland for more than 7 centuries until it was taken over by the new Irish government in 1922. Highlights include the 13th-century Record Tower; the State Apartments, once the residence of English viceroys; and the Chapel Royal. The newest developments are the Undercroft, an excavated site on the grounds where an early Viking fortress stood, and the Treasury, built between 1712 and 1715 and believed to be the oldest surviving office building in Ireland. At hand, as well, are a craft shop, heritage center, and restaurant.

Dublin Writers Museum. 18–19 Parnell Sq. N., Dublin 1. ☎ **01/872-2077.** Fax 01/872-2231. Admission £3 ($4.65) adults, £2.55 ($3.95) seniors/students, £1.40 ($2.15) ages 3–11, £8.25 ($12.80) families (2 adults and up to 4 children). Mon–Sat 10am–5pm (6pm June–Aug); Sun and holidays 11am–5pm. DART to Connolly Station. Bus: 11, 13, 16, 16A, 22, or 22A.

Housed in a stunning 18th-century Georgian mansion with splendid plasterwork and stained glass, the museum is itself an impressive reminder of the grandeur of the Irish literary tradition. Yeats, Joyce, Beckett, Shaw, Wilde, Swift, and Sheridan are among those whose lives and works are celebrated here. One of the museum's rooms is devoted to children's literature.

Christ Church Cathedral. Christ Church Place. ☎ **01/677-8099.** Admission: suggested donation £1 ($1.55) adults, 80p ($1.25) students, 50p (78¢) children under 15. Daily 10am–5pm. Closed Dec 26. Bus: 21A, 50, 50A, 78, 78A, or 78B.

Standing on a ridge above the site of the original Norse town, the cathedral was founded in 1038, although the present building dates from around 1172, with substantial renovations from 1871 to 1878. Inside you'll find a monument to Strongbow, the ruler who had the cathedral built. Make sure to look back from the altar and note the leaning wall of Dublin, which has been out of perpendicular by some 18 inches since 1562. The crypt has remained unchanged since the 13th century and is one of the largest medieval crypts in either Britain or Ireland.

St. Patrick's Cathedral. 21–50 Patrick's Close, Patrick St., Dublin 8. ☎ **01/475-4817.** Admission £2 ($3.10) adults, £1.75 ($2.70) students and seniors, £5 ($7.75) family. Mon–Sat 9am–6pm; Sun 9am–4:30pm. Bus: 65, 65B, 50, 50A, 54, 54A, or 56A.

It is said that St. Patrick baptized converts on this site and consequently a church has stood here since A.D. 450, making it the oldest Christian site in Dublin. The present cathedral dates from 1190, but because of a fire and subsequent rebuilding in the 14th century, not much remains from the cathedral's foundation days. It's mainly early English in style, with a square medieval tower that houses the largest ringing peal bells in Ireland, an 18th-century spire, and a 300-foot-long interior, making it the longest church in the country. St. Patrick's is closely associated with Jonathan Swift, who was dean here from 1713 to 1745 and whose tomb lies in the south aisle. St. Patrick's is the national cathedral of the Church of Ireland.

MORE ATTRACTIONS

Dvblinia. St. Michael's Hill, Christ Church, Dublin 8. ☎ **01/679-4611.** Admission £3.95 ($6.10) adults, £2.90 ($4.50) seniors, students, and children, £10 ($15.50) family. Apr–Sept daily 10am–5pm; Oct–Mar Mon–Sat 11am–4pm, Sun 10am–4:30pm. Bus: 50, 78A, or 123.

What was Dublin like in medieval times? Here is a historically accurate presentation of the Old City from 1170 to 1540, re-created through a series of theme exhibits, spectacles, and experiences. Highlights include an illuminated Medieval Maze complete with visual effects, background sounds, and aromas that lead you on a journey through time from the first arrival of the Anglo-Normans in 1170 to the closure of the monasteries in the 1530s. The next segment depicts everyday life in medieval Dublin with a diorama, as well as a prototype of a 13th-century quay along the banks of the Liffey. The finale takes you to The Great Hall for a 360-degree wrap-up portrait of medieval Dublin via a 12-minute cyclorama-style audiovisual.

Guinness Brewery Hop Store/Visitor Centre. James's Gate, Dublin 8. ☎ **01/408-4800.** Admission £5 ($7.75) adults, £4 ($6.20) seniors and students, £1 ($1.55) children under 12. AE, MC, V. Apr–Sept Mon–Sat 9:30am–5pm, Sun 10:30am–4:30pm; Oct–Mar Mon–Sat 9:30am–4pm, Sun 12–4pm. Bus: 51B, 78A, or 123.

Founded in 1759, the Guinness Brewery is one of the world's largest breweries, producing the distinctive dark beer called stout, famous for its thick, creamy head.

Although tours of the brewery itself are no longer allowed, visitors are welcome to explore the adjacent Guinness Hopstore, a converted 19th-century four-story building. It houses the World of Guinness Exhibition, an audiovisual presentation showing how the stout is made, plus a museum and a bar where visitors can sample a glass of the famous brew. The two top floors of the building also serve as a venue for a variety of art exhibits.

Hugh Lane Municipal Gallery of Modern Art. Parnell Sq. N., Dublin 1. ☎ **01/ 874-1903.** Free admission but donations accepted. Tues–Thurs 9:30am–6pm; Fri–Sat 9:30am–5pm; Sun 11am–5pm. DART to Connolly or Tara stations. Bus: 3, 10, 11, or 13.

Housed in a finely restored 18th-century building known as Charlemont House, this gallery is situated next to the Dublin Writers Museum. It is named after Hugh Lane, an Irish art connoisseur who was killed in the sinking of the *Lusitania* in 1915 and who willed his collection (including works by Courbet, Manet, Monet, and Corot) to be shared between the government of Ireland and the National Gallery of London. With the Lane collection as its nucleus, this gallery also contains paintings from the Impressionist and post-Impressionist traditions, sculptures by Rodin, stained glass, and works by modern Irish artists. Bookshop open during museum hours.

James Joyce Centre. 35 N. Great George's St., Dublin 1. ☎ **01/878 8547.** Fax 01/ 878-8488. www.jamesjoyce.ie. Admission £2.75 ($4.25) adult, £2 ($3.10) student/senior, 75p ($1.15) child, £6 ($9.30) family; walking tours and events charged separately. AE, MC, V. Mon–Sat 9:30am–5pm; Sun 12:30–5pm. Closed Dec 24–26. DART to Connolly Station. Bus: 1, 40A, 40B, 40C.

Located near Parnell Square and the Dublin Writers Museum, this newly restored Georgian townhouse, built in 1784, gives literary enthusiasts one more reason to visit Dublin's north side. The house itself was once the home of Denis J. Maginni, a dancing instructor who appears briefly in *Ulysses*. The Ulysses Portrait Gallery on the second floor has a fascinating collection of photographs and drawings of characters from *Ulysses* who had a life outside the novel. A recently opened exhibition room holds the table and writing table used by Joyce in Paris when he was working on Finnegan's Wake. In addition, there are talks and audiovisual presentations daily. The latest addition to the centre is a new coffee shop. Guided walking tours are offered through the neighboring streets of "Joyce Country" in Dublin's northern inner city.

✪ The Joyce Tower Museum. Sandycove, County Dublin. ☎ **01/280-9265.** Admission £2.60 ($4.05) adults, £2.10 ($3.25) seniors and students, £1.30 ($2) children, and £7.75 ($12) family. Apr–Oct Mon–Sat 10am–1pm and 2–5pm; Sun 2–6pm. DART to Sandycove Station. Bus: 8.

No James Joyce fan should miss this small museum housed in the Sandycove Martello Tower where Joyce lived for a while in 1904—it's described in the first chapter of *Ulysses*. The museum contains exhibits on Joyce and Dublin at the time *Ulysses* was written. If you pick up a copy of the "*Ulysses* Map of Dublin," you can make this the starting point of a Joyce tour of the city. Robert Nicholson, the museum's curator, is a great source of information on all topics relating to Joyce, and has published the best guide to Ulysses sites in Dublin, titled simply *The Ulysses Guide*.

Kilmainham Gaol Historical Museum. Kilmainham. ☎ **01/453-5984.** Admission £3 ($4.65) adults, £2 ($3.10) seniors, £1.25 ($1.95) children and students, £7.50 ($11.65) family. Tours Apr–Sept daily 9:30am–4:45pm; Oct–Mar Mon–Fri 9:30am–4pm, Sun 10am–5pm. Bus: 51, 51B, 78, 78A, 78B, or 79 at O'Connell Bridge.

Within these walls political prisoners were incarcerated, tortured, and killed from 1796 until 1924, when the late Pres. Eamon de Valera left as its final prisoner. To walk along these corridors, through the exercise yard, or into the Main Compound is a moving experience that lingers hauntingly in the memory.

Note: The **War Memorial Gardens** (☎ 01/677-0236), located along the banks of the Liffey, are a 5-minute walk from nearby Kilmainham Gaol. The gardens were designed by the famous British architect Sir Edwin Lutyens (1869–1944), who completed a number of commissions for houses and gardens in Ireland. Thankfully, the gardens are fairly well maintained and continue to present a moving testimony to Ireland's war dead. This is one of the finest small gardens in Ireland. The opening times are Monday to Friday 8am to dark and Saturday 10am to dark.

✪ **National Gallery.** Merrion Sq. West, Dublin 2. ☎ **01/661-5133.** www.national-gallery.ie. Free admission. Mon–Wed and Fri–Sat 10am–5:30pm; Thurs 10am–8:30pm; Sun 2–5pm. DART to Pearse Station. Bus: 5, 6, 7, 7A, 8, 10, 44, 47, 47B, 48A, or 62.

Established by an act of Parliament in 1854, this gallery first opened its doors in 1864, with just over 100 paintings. Today the collection of paintings, drawings, watercolors, miniatures, prints, sculpture, and objets d'art is considered one of Europe's finest. Every major European school of painting is represented, including an extensive assemblage of Irish work. Of special note is the new Yeats Museum, dedicated to Jack B. Yeats (1871–1957). The museum features a fine gallery shop and an excellent self-service restaurant. A $14 million refurbishment of the museum was finished in 1996, and a new extension is underway, scheduled to open by 2000. All public areas are wheelchair-accessible.

The Irish Museum of Modern Art. Royal Hospital, Military Road, Kilmainham, Dublin 8. ☎ **01/612-9900.** Fax 01/612-9999. E-mail: info@modernart.ie. Admission free. Tues–Sat 10am–5:30pm; Sun noon–5:30pm. Bus: 68A, 69, 78A, 90, and 123. DART: Feeder bus from Connolly and Tara St. stations to Heuston. Unlimited parking.

One of the city's newest museums is located in its oldest classical building, the stately Kilmainham Hospital. Modeled on Les Invalides in Paris, the old hospital is a quadrangle with chapel and majestic dining hall in the north wing and a row of stables to the south, now converted to artists' studios. Situated in an expansive parkland setting, the building has an elaborate formal garden on its north side and a long, tree-lined ceremonial entrance to the west, extending all the way to the Kilmainham Gaol. The museum occupies the east, west, and south wings of the hospital; the high entrance hall on the south side is adjoined by a fine bookshop and tea house (soup is £1.50/$2.35 and light meals under £5/$7.75). The galleries contain the work of Irish and international artists from the small but impressive permanent collection, with numerous temporary exhibitions at any given time. There's even a drawing room, where kids and parents can record their impressions of the museum with the crayons provided.

PARKS & ZOOS

✪ **St. Stephen's Green,** in the heart of Dublin 2, has been preserved as an open space for Dubliners since 1690. A short walk from most city center locations, this large park is popular for picnics, reading, a quiet stroll, and summertime concerts. The hours are Monday to Saturday 8am to dark and Sunday 10am to dark. While you're here, be sure to visit the **Iveagh Gardens,** a small garden hidden behind the National Concert Hall. Largely neglected by visitors, this is something of a hidden treasure within the city center. The main entrance is from Clonmel Street, off Harcourt Street, less than 5 minutes from Stephen's Green. The hours are the same as those for St. Stephen's Green.

✪ **The Phoenix Park.** Parkgate St., Dublin 7. ☎ **01/677-0095.** Free admission. Daily 24 hours. Visitor Centre: Admission £2 ($3.10) adults, £1.50 ($2.35) seniors, £1 ($1.55) students and children, £5 ($7.75) families. Mid-Mar to end of Mar daily 9:30am–5pm; Apr–May daily 9:30am–5:30pm; June–Sept daily 10am–6pm; Oct daily 9:30am–5pm; Nov to mid-Mar Sat and Sun 9:30am–4:30pm. Bus: 10, 25, or 26.

Dublin's 1,760-acre playground (Europe's largest enclosed urban park) opened in 1747. Situated 2 miles west of the city center, it is traversed by a network of roads and quiet pedestrian walkways, and informally landscaped with ornamental gardens, nature trails, and broad expanses of grassland separated by avenues of trees, including oak, beech, pine, chestnut, and lime. The homes of the Irish president and the U.S. ambassador are on its grounds. Livestock graze peacefully on pasturelands, deer roam the forested areas, and horses romp on polo fields. The new Phoenix Park Visitor Centre, adjacent to Ashtown Castle, has exhibitions and an audiovisual presentation on the history of the Phoenix Park, and houses its own restaurant. The **Dublin Zoo** (☎ **01/677-1425**), also located here, was established in 1830 and is the third-oldest zoo in the world (after London and Paris).

National Botanic Gardens. Botanic Rd., Glasnevin, Dublin 9. ☎ **01/837-4388.** Free admission. Summer Mon–Wed and Fri–Sat 9am–5:15pm, Thurs 9am–3:15pm, and Sun 2–5:45pm; winter Mon–Wed and Fri–Sat 10am–4:15pm, Thurs 10am–3:15pm, and Sun 2–4:15pm. Bus: 13, 19, or 134.

Established by the Royal Dublin Society in 1795 on a rolling 50-acre expanse of land north of the city center, this is Dublin's horticultural showcase. The attractions include more than 20,000 different plants and cultivars, a Great Yew Walk, a bog garden, a water garden, a rose garden, and an herb garden. There are also a variety of Victorian-style glass houses filled with tropical plants and exotic species.

ORGANIZED TOURS

BUS TOURS   For the standard see-it-all-in-under-3-hours tour, climb aboard the **Dublin Bus** open-deck sightseeing coach. Tours leave from the Dublin Bus office at 59 Upper O'Connell St. (☎ **01/873-4222**), departing at 10:15am and 2:15pm. You can purchase your ticket at the office or on the bus: £8 ($12.40) adults and £4 ($6.20) under age 14. This tour takes in most of the important sights but doesn't stop at any.

For more flexible touring, there's the **Dublin City Tour,** a continuous guided bus service connecting 10 major points, such as museums, art galleries, churches and cathedrals, libraries, and historic sites. For £6 ($9.30) adults or £3 ($4.65) under age 14, you can ride the bus for a full day, getting off and on as often as you want. It operates mid-April to September, daily 9:30am to 4:30pm.

WALKING TOURS   You can set out on your own with a map, but the best way to avoid any hassles or missed sights is following one of the four signposted and themed "**tourist trails**": Old City Trail for historic sights; Georgian Trail for the landmark buildings, streets, squares, terraces, and parks; Cultural Trail for a circuit of the top literary sites, museums, galleries, theaters, and churches; and the Rock 'n' Stroll Trail for a tour of contemporary music enclaves, pubs, breweries, nightspots, and more. Each trail is mapped out in a handy booklet, available for £2.50 ($3.90) from the Dublin Tourism Office, Suffolk St., Dublin 2 (☎ **01/605-7700**).

Several firms offer tours led by knowledgeable local guides. Tour times and charges vary, but most last about 2 hours and cost between £4 and £6 ($6.20 and $9.30). **Discover Dublin Tours** (☎ 01/478-0191) offers a musical pub crawl led by two professional musicians. The **Dublin Literary Pub Crawl** (☎ 01/454-0228) departs evenings from the Duke Pub, Duke Street; your guides will recount the stories connecting these pubs with Dublin's literary greats. **Historical Walking Tours of Dublin** (☎ 01/845-0241) departs from the front gate of Trinity College. All guides are history graduates of Trinity College, and participants are encouraged to ask questions.

HORSE-DRAWN CARRIAGE TOURS   If you don't mind being conspicuous, you can tour Dublin in style in a handsomely outfitted horse-drawn carriage while your driver points out the sights. To arrange a ride, consult with one of the drivers stationed with carriages on the Grafton Street side of St. Stephen's Green. Rides range from a short swing around the Green to an extensive half-hour Georgian tour or an hour-long Old City tour. Rides are available on a first-come basis and cost anywhere from £8 to £32 ($12.40–$49.60) for two to five passengers, depending on the duration of the ride. They run from April to October, daily and nightly, depending on the weather.

SPORTS & OUTDOOR ACTIVITIES

SPECTATOR SPORTS   Ireland's national games, **hurling** and **Gaelic football,** are played every weekend throughout the summer at various local fields, culminating in September with the All-Ireland Finals, an Irish version of the Super Bowl. For schedules and admission charges, contact the **Gaelic Athletic Association,** Croke Park, Jones Road, Dublin 3 (☎ **01/836-3222**).

OUTDOOR ACTIVITIES   Beaches   On the outskirts of Dublin are several beaches that offer safe swimming and sandy strands. All can be reached by city buses heading northward: Dollymount, 3½ miles; Sutton, 7 miles; Howth, 9 miles; and Portmarnock and Malahide, each 10 miles away. The southern suburb of Dun Laoghaire, 7 miles away, offers a beach at Sandycove and a long bayfront promenade, ideal for strolling.

Golf   Leading 18-hole courses in the Dublin area are the **Elm Park Golf Club,** Nutley Lane (☎ **01/269-3438**); the **Portmarnock Golf Club,** Portmarnock, County Dublin (☎ **01/846-2968**); and the **Royal Dublin Golf Club,** Bull Island, Dollymount (☎ **01/833-6346**), a top course that has often been compared to St. Andrews in layout, and has hosted several Irish Open tournaments.

Walking   The walk from **Bray to Greystones** along the rocky promontory of Bray Head is a great excursion, with beautiful views back toward Killiney Bay, Dalkey Island, and Howth. Bray, the southern terminus of the DART line, is readily accessible from Dublin. In Bray, follow the beachside promenade south through town; at the outskirts of town the promenade turns left and up, beginning the ascent of Bray Head. Shortly after the beginning of this ascent, a trail branches to the left—this is the cliffside walk, which continues another 3½ miles along the coast to Greystones. From the center of Greystones, there's a train that takes you back to Bray. This is an easy walk, about 2 hours one-way.

THE SHOPPING SCENE

In general, Dublin shops are open Monday to Saturday 9 or 9:30am to 5:30 or 6pm, with late hours Thursday to 8pm. In tourist season, many shops also post Sunday hours.

BOOKS   For books, on the north side go to **Eason & Son Ltd.,** 40–42 Lower O'Connell St. (☎ **01/873-3811**), offering a comprehensive selection of books and maps about Dublin and Ireland. On the south side, you have many choices, including **Hodges Figgis,** 56/58 Dawson St. (☎ **01/677-4754**), a three-story landmark store with great charm and browse appeal and particularly good sections on Irish literature, Celtic studies, and folklore. Just across the street, you'll find **Waterstone's,** 7 Dawson St. (☎ **01/677-4754**), also well worth a browse.

CHINA & CRYSTAL   China Showrooms, 32/33 Abbey St. (☎ **01/878-6211**), is a one-stop source of fine china such as Belleek, Aynsley, Royal Doulton, and hand-cut crystal from Waterford, Tipperary, and Tyrone. The **Dublin Crystal Glass Company,**

Brookfield Terrace, Carysfort Avenue, Blackrock (☎ **01/288-7932**), is Dublin's own distinctive hand-cut crystal business, founded in 1764 and revived in 1968. Visitors are welcome to browse in the factory shop and to see the glass being made and engraved.

CRAFTS & GIFTS   The ✪ **Powerscourt Townhouse Centre,** 59 S. William St. (☎ **01/679-4144**), is a four-story complex with more than 60 boutiques, craft shops, art galleries, snackeries, wine bars, and restaurants. The wares include all kinds of crafts, antiques, paintings, prints, and hand-dipped chocolates and farmhouse cheeses.

If you're searching for contemporary Irish design, head to **The Kilkenny Shop,** 6–10 Nassau St. (☎ **01/677-7066**), a modern multilevel showplace for original Irish designs and quality products including pottery, glass, candles, woolens, pipes, knitwear, jewelry, books, and prints; and **DESIGNyard,** 12 E. Essex St. (☎ **01/677-8453**), a nonprofit gallery for the finest contemporary Irish and European jewelry, furniture, ceramics, glass, lighting, and textiles. Also, the **House of Ireland,** 37–38 Nassau St. (☎ **01/677-7473**), is a happy blend of European and Irish products, from Waterford and Belleek to Wedgwood and Lladro, as well as tweeds, linens, knitwear, Celtic jewelry, mohair capes, shawls, kilts, blankets, and dolls. For quality ceramics, the creations of **Louis Mulcahey,** a noted Kerry potter, now have a Dublin home at 17 Kildare St. (☎ **01/662-8787**).

FASHIONS   **Cleo,** 18 Kildare St. (☎ **01/676-1421**), is the shop for the Joyce family's designer ready-to-wear clothing in a rainbow of vibrant tweed colors. **Pat Crowley,** 3 Molesworth Place (☎ **01/661-5580**), is known for her exclusive line of tweeds and couture evening wear. Men shouldn't miss **Kevin and Howlin,** 31 Nassau St. (☎ **01/677-0257**), a shop that has specialized in men's tweed garments for more than 50 years. There's also a selection of sweaters, scarves, vests, and hats. **Louis Copeland,** 39–41 Capel St. (☎ **01/872-1600**), is known for high-quality work in made-to-measure and ready-to-wear men's suits, coats, and shirts. There are also branches at 30 Pembroke St. and 18 Wicklow St.

HERALDRY   **Heraldic Artists,** 3 Nassau St. (☎ **01/679-7020**), has been known for helping visitors celebrate their family roots for over 20 years. In addition to tracing surnames, it also sells all the usual heraldic items, from parchments and mahogany wall plaques to crests, scrolls, and books on researching ancestry.

KNITWEAR   The **Blarney Woolen Mills,** 21–23 Nassau St. (☎ **01/671-0068**), known for its competitive prices, stocks a wide range of woolen knitwear made at its home base in Blarney, as well as crystal, china, pottery, and souvenirs. The **Dublin Woolen Mills,** 41 Lower Ormond Quay (☎ **01/677-0301**), is on the north side of the River Liffey next to the Ha'penny Bridge, a leading source of Aran handknit sweaters as well as vests, hats, jackets, and tweeds. If you want a cashmere sweater, go to ✪ **Monaghan's,** 15/17 Grafton Arcade, Grafton Street (☎ **01/677-0823**), which has the best selection of colors, sizes, and styles for both men and women anywhere in Ireland. It's also located at 4/5 Royal Hibernian Way, off Dawson Street (☎ **01/679-4451**).

MARKETS   For a walk into the past, don't miss the **Moore Street Market,** Moore Street, full of streetside barrow vendors plus plenty of local color and chatter. It's the principal open-air fruit, flower, fish, and vegetable market of the city. Up and running Monday through Saturday 9am to 6pm—or until supplies run out.

At the **Blackrock Market,** 19a Main St., Blackrock (☎ **01/283-3522**), more than 60 vendors sell a wide variety of old and new goods at great prices in this indoor/outdoor setting; it's open Saturday 11am to 5:30pm and Sunday noon to 5:30pm.

The ✪ **Mother Red Caps Market,** Back Lane, off High Street (☎ **01/454-4655**), is one of Dublin's best, an enclosed market in the heart of Old Dublin. The stalls offer everything from antiques and used books and coins to silver, handcrafts, music tapes, furniture, and even a fortune teller! It's worth a trip here just to sample the farm-made cheeses, baked goods, and jams at the Ryefield Foods stall. Open Friday to Sunday, 10am to 5:30pm.

DUBLIN AFTER DARK

The best way to find out what's going on is to consult *In Dublin,* the leading magazine for upcoming events and happenings. *The Event Guide* also contains a useful and up-to-date listing of events throughout Ireland, with a focus on Dublin.

THE PERFORMING ARTS
Concert & Performance Halls
National Concert Hall. Earlsfort Terrace, Dublin 2. ☎ **01/4751572.** Tickets £8–£55 ($12.40–$85.25). Lunchtime concerts £3 ($4.65).

Dublin's main venue for classical music was originally part of University College, Dublin. The hall stays busy with performances several nights a week for much of the year and is home to the National Symphony Orchestra. The box office is open Monday to Saturday from 11am to 7pm.

Olympia Theatre. 72 Dame St., Dublin 2. ☎ **01/677-7744.** Tickets £7.50–£15 ($11.65–$23.25).

With its Victorian jewel-box facade and garish red lobby, the Olympis Theatre looks as though it should be home to high-stepping cancan girls. However, it's one of Dublin's busier old theaters, hosting everything from contemporary Irish plays to rock concerts. The box office is open Monday to Saturday 10am to 6:30pm.

The Point. East Link Bridge, North Wall Quay. ☎ **01/836-3633.** Tickets £10–£50 ($15.50–$77.50).

With a seating capacity of 3,000, The Point is Ireland's newest large theater/concert venue, attracting top Broadway-caliber shows and international stars. The box office is open Monday to Saturday 10am to 6pm.

The City Arts Centre. 23–25 Moss St., at City Quay. ☎ **01/677-0643.**

The City Arts Centre is an affiliate of Trans Europe Halles, the European network of independent arts centers. It presents a varied program, from local drama groups, theatrical discussions, and readings by local writers to touring companies from abroad.

Theater
Abbey Theatre. Lower Abbey St., Dublin 1. ☎ **01/878-7222.** Tickets £8–£15 ($18.60–$23.25); reduced tickets for students Mon–Thurs.

For more than 90 years, the Abbey has been the national theater of Ireland. The original theater, destroyed by fire in 1951, was replaced in 1966 by this functional-though-uninspired 600-seat house. The Abbey's artistic reputation within Ireland has risen and fallen many times and is at present reasonably strong. The box office is open Monday to Saturday 10am to 6pm; performances begin at 8 or 8:15pm.

Andrews Lane Theatre. 12/16 Andrews Lane, Dublin 2. ☎ **01/679-5720.** Tickets £6–£12 ($9.30–$18.60).

This relatively new venue has an ascending reputation for fine theater. It consists of a 220-seat main theater where contemporary works from home and abroad are presented, and a 76-seat studio geared for experimental productions. The box office is open Monday to Saturday 10:30am to 7pm.

✪ **The Gate.** 1 Cavendish Row, Dublin 1. ☎ **01/874-4368.** Fax 01/874-5373. Tickets £13–£15 ($20.15–$23.25).

Dinner & a Song

There are several venues in Dublin where you can have dinner and listen to traditional music. At the **Abbey Tavern,** Abbey Road, Howth, County Dublin. (☎ **01/839 0307**), a complete four-course meal is accompanied by authentic Irish ballad music, with its blend of fiddles, pipes, tin whistles, and spoons. Tickets for dinner and entertainment are £28–£32 ($43.40–$49.60); entertainment only, £3 ($4.65). The box office is open Monday through Saturday 9am to 5pm; dinner and shows are daily March through October, and Monday to Saturday November through February.

Just north of O'Connell Street off Parnell Square, this recently restored 370-seat theater was founded in 1928 by Hilton Edwards and Michael MacLiammoir to provide a showing for a broad range of plays. This policy prevails today, with a program that includes a blend of modern works and the classics. Although less well known by visitors, the Gate is easily as distinguished as the Abbey. The box office is open Monday to Saturday 10am to 7pm.

Traditional Irish Entertainment

✪ **Culturlann Na heireann.** 32 Belgrave Sq., Monkstown. ☎ **01/280-0295.** http://comhaltas.com. Tickets: Ceilis £4 ($6.20); informal music sessions £2 ($3.10); stage shows £6 ($9.30).

This is the home of Comhaltas Ceoltoiri Eireann, an Irish cultural organization that has been the prime mover in encouraging the renewal of Irish traditional music. An authentic fully costumed show featuring traditional music, song, and dance is staged June through September, Monday to Thursday 9 to 10:30pm. No reservations are necessary. Year-round, ceili dances are performed Friday 9pm to 12:30am; informal music sessions are held Friday and Saturday 9 to 11:30pm.

Jury's Irish Cabaret. Pembroke Road, Ballsbridge. ☎ **01/660-5000.** Dinner and show £36.50 ($56.60); show with two drinks £23 ($35.65).

Ireland's longest-running show (over 30 years) offers a mix of traditional Irish music and Broadway classics, set dancing, humorous monologues, and audience participation. Shows take place May through October, Tuesday to Sunday with dinner at 7:15pm and the show at 8pm.

THE PUB SCENE

Pubs for Conversation & Atmosphere

✪ **Brazen Head.** 20 Lower Bridge St. ☎ **01/679-5186.**

This brass-filled and lantern-lit pub claims to be the city's oldest—and with good reason, considering that it was licensed in 1661 and occupies the site of an earlier tavern dating from 1198. On the south bank of the River Liffey, it's at the end of a cobblestoned courtyard and was once the meeting place of Irish freedom fighters, such as Robert Emmet and Wolfe Tone.

Davy Byrnes. 21 Duke St. (just off Grafton St.). ☎ **01/677-5217.**

Referred to as a "moral pub" by James Joyce in *Ulysses,* this imbibers' landmark has drawn poets, writers, and lovers of literature ever since. Davy Byrnes first opened the doors in 1873; he presided here for more than 50 years and visitors today can still see his likeness on one of the turn-of-the-century murals hanging over the bar.

Flannery's Temple Bar. 47/48 Temple Bar. ☎ **01/497-4766.**

In the heart of the trendy Temple Bar district on the corner of Temple Lane, this small three-room pub was established in 1840. The decor is an interesting mix of crackling fireplaces, globe ceiling lights, old pictures on the walls, and shelves filled with local memorabilia.

The Long Hall. 51 S. Great George's St. ☎ **01/475-1590.**

Tucked into a busy commercial street, this is one of the city's most photographed pubs, with a beautiful Victorian decor of filigree-edged mirrors, polished dark woods, and traditional snugs. The hand-carved bar is said to be the longest counter in the city.

Neary's. 1 Chatham St., Dublin 2. ☎ **01/677-7371.**

Adjacent to the back door of the Gaiety Theatre, this celebrated enclave is a favorite with stage folk and theatergoers. Trademarks here are the pink-and-gray marble bar and the brass hands that support the globe lanterns adorning the entrance.

✪ **W. Ryan.** 28 Parkgate St. ☎ **01/677-6097.**

Three generations of the Ryan family have contributed to the success of this public house, located on the north side of the Liffey near Phoenix Park. The pub has such fine features as a metal ceiling and domed skylight, beveled mirrors, etched glass, brass lamp holders, a mahogany bar, and four old-style snugs.

Pubs with Traditional/Folk Music

✪ **Kitty O'Shea's.** 23–25 Upper Grand Canal St. ☎ **01/660-9965.**

Situated just south of the Grand Canal, this pub is named after the sweetheart of 19th-century Irish statesman Charles Stewart Parnell. The decor reflects the Parnell era, with ornate oak paneling, stained-glass windows, old political posters, cozy alcoves, and brass railings. Traditional Irish music is on tap every night.

O'Donoghue's. 15 Merrion Row, Dublin 2. ☎ **01/660-7194.**

For fans of traditional Irish music, this is a must. The Dubliners, one of Ireland's favorite traditional bands, got their start here, and impromptu music sessions are held almost every night.

Oliver St. John Gogarty. 57/58 Fleet St. ☎ **01/671-1822.**

Situated in the heart of Temple Bar and named for one of Ireland's literary greats, this pub has an inviting old-world atmosphere, with shelves of empty bottles, stacks of dusty books, a horseshoe-shaped bar, and old barrels for seats. There are traditional music sessions every night from 9 to 11pm. A Saturday session is at 4:30pm, and Sunday from noon to 2pm.

Slattery's. 129–130 Capel St. ☎ **01/873-1979.** No cover for Irish-music sessions; £4–£5 ($6.20–$7.75) for rock or blues.

Located on the north side of the Liffey, this pub has a classic facade and an interior of brass trim, dark wood, gas lamps, and church pew benches. On Sunday at 12:30 and 2pm, it's a focal point for traditional Irish music and ballads, with as many as 20 musicians playing in an informal session in the main bar. Rock and blues music are featured in the upstairs lounge Wednesday to Sunday 9 to 11:30pm.

THE CLUB SCENE

The club scene in Dublin is complex and volatile. It's mostly a young crowd at the "in" places. Many of the hottest spots have a strict door policy, admitting only those deemed acceptable. Most trendy clubs have DJs, not live music. Average cover charges range from nominal to £8 ($12.40), and most clubs open between 10pm and

11pm and go on to 2am or later. Trendy clubs include **The Kitchen,** 6/8 Wellington Quay (☎ **01/677-6635**), housed in the basement of the Clarence Hotel in the heart of the Temple Bar district, partly owned by the rock group U2; **Lillie's Bordello,** 45 Nassau St. (☎ **01/679-9204**), a stylish private club, open to members and nonmembers; **POD,** Harcourt Street (☎ **01/478-0166**), which is as loud as it is dazzling to behold; and **Rí-Rá,** 1 Exchequer St. (☎ **01/677-4835**), which has a more friendly door policy.

If uptight door policies aren't your thing and you prefer an orderly crowd, the following clubs might be more to your liking: **Annabel's,** in the Burlington Hotel, Upper Leeson Street (☎ **01/660-5222**), which welcomes a mix of tourists and locals; **Club M,** Blooms Hotel, Anglesea Street (☎ **01/671-5485**); **Court,** in the Harcourt Hotel, Harcourt Street (☎ **01/4783677**); and **Rumours,** in the Gresham Hotel, O'Connell Street (☎ **01/874-1635**).

Three of the principal venues for live music are **Whelans,** 25 Wexford St. (☎ **01/478-0766**); **Eammon Doran's,** 3A Crown Alley, Temple Bar (☎ **01/679-9114**); and **Mean Fiddler,** 26 Wexford St. (☎ **01/475-8555**).

THE GAY & LESBIAN SCENE

New gay and lesbian bars, clubs, and venues appear monthly, it seems, and many clubs and organizations, such as the Irish Film Centre, have special gay events or evenings once a week to once a month, so it's best to check the *Gay Community News* and *In Dublin* for the latest listings.

The **George Bar and Night Club,** 89 S. Great George's St. (☎ **01/478-2983**), was the first gay bar established in Dublin and now houses two bars—one quiet and the other trendy, with dance music—and an after-hours nightclub called The Block upstairs. It's a comfortable mixed-age venue with something for everyone. **Stonewallz,** The Barracks, Griffith College, South Circular Road (☎ **01/872-7770**), is a women-only late-night venue, offering music from the '60s to the '90s.

TWO SIDE TRIPS FROM DUBLIN

✪ **Malahide Castle.** Malahide, County Dublin. ☎ **01/846-2184.** Admission £3.10 ($4.80) adults, £2.60 ($4.05) students and seniors, £1.70 ($2.65) children under 12, £8.50 ($13.20) family; gardens free. Combination tickets available with Fry Model Railway and Newbridge House. Apr–Oct Mon–Sat 10am–5pm, Sun 11am–6pm; Nov–Mar Mon–Fri 10am–5pm, Sat–Sun 2–5pm; gardens May–Sept daily 2–5pm. Closed for tours 12:45–2pm (restaurant remains open). Bus: 42.

About 8 miles north of Dublin, Malahide is one of Ireland's most historic castles, founded in the 12th century by Richard Talbot and occupied by his descendants until 1973. The fully restored interior of the building is the setting for a comprehensive collection of Irish furniture, dating from the 17th through the 19th centuries, and the walls are lined with one-of-a-kind Irish historical portraits and tableaux on loan from the National Gallery. The furnishings and art reflect life in and near the house over the past 8 centuries.

After touring the house, you can explore the 250-acre estate, which includes 20 acres of prized gardens with more than 5,000 species of plants and flowers. The Malahide grounds also contain the Fry Model Railway Museum, an exhibit of rare handmade models of more than 300 Irish trains, from the introduction of rail to the present.

✪ **Newgrange.** Near the village of Donore, County Meath. ☎ **041/24488.** Admission to Newgrange and Brugh na Boinne Centre £3 ($4.65) adults, £2 ($3.10) seniors, £1.25 ($1.95) students and children over 6, £7.50 ($11.65) family. Daily, Nov–Feb 9:30am–5pm, Mar–Apr 9:30am–5:30pm, May 9am–6:30pm, June to mid-Sept 9am–7pm; mid to end Sept 9am–6:30pm; Oct 9:30am–5:30pm.

Newgrange is Ireland's best-known prehistoric monument and one of the archaeological wonders of Western Europe. Built as a burial mound more than 5,000 years ago—long before the Great Pyramids and Stonehenge—it sits atop a hill near the Boyne, massive and impressive. The huge mound, 36 feet tall and approximately 260 feet in diameter, consists of 200,000 tons of stone, a 6-ton capstone, and other stones weighing up to 16 tons each, many of which were hauled from as far away as County Wicklow and the Mountains of Mourne. Each stone fits perfectly in the overall pattern and the result is a watertight structure, an amazing feat of engineering. Carved into the stones are myriad spirals, diamonds, and concentric circles. Inside, a passage 60 feet long leads to a central burial chamber with a 19-foot ceiling. All tickets are issued at the new visitor center. Combined tickets with **Knowth,** another nearby megalithic passage tomb, are available at the center. Because of the great numbers of visitors to Newgrange, especially in the summer, delays are to be expected and access is not guaranteed.

2 Kerry & the Dingle Peninsula

Kerry is a place of disorienting contrasts, where the tackiest tourist attractions coexist with some of Ireland's most spectacular scenic wonders. It's a rugged place for the most part, some of it so rugged that it's seldom visited and remains quite pristine; Ireland's two highest mountains, Carrantuohill and Mount Brandon, are two examples. You could be driving along—say, on the famous and popular Ring of Kerry, which traces the shores of the Iveragh Peninsula—make one little detour from the main road, and be in wild and unfrequented territory. The transition can be startling.

Thanks to its remoteness, County Kerry has always been an outpost of Gaelic culture. Poetry and music are intrinsic to Kerry lifestyle, as is a love of the outdoors and sports. Gaelic football is an obsession in this county, and Kerry wins most of the national championships. You'll also find some of Ireland's best golf courses here, and the fishing for salmon and trout is equally hard to resist.

GETTING TO COUNTY KERRY   By Plane   Aer Lingus offers daily direct flights from Dublin into **Kerry County Airport,** Farranfore, County Kerry (☎ **066/ 64644**), about 10 miles north of Killarney and 15 miles south of Tralee.

By Car   Roads leading into Kerry include N-21 and N-23 from Limerick, N-22 from Cork, N-72 from Mallow, and N-70 from West Cork.

Only in Kerry

Enjoying Killarney's Natural Beauty   Killarney National Park, a 25,000-acre expanse of natural lakeland and mountain scenery, is one of the world's most beautiful spots. Hike to the Gap of Dunloe, and then take a boat across Killarney's lakes, set amid craggy mountains.

Touring the Ring of Kerry and the Dingle Peninsula   Ireland's highest mountains contrast with spectacular views of dramatic coastline on both these panoramic routes. Drive around the Ring of Kerry, but tour the Dingle Peninsula by bicycle.

Exploring Ireland's Archaeological Heritage   Recalling Ireland's rich cultural past as preserver of learning and scholarship are Skellig Michael, a 6th-century monastic settlement; Gallarus Oratory, one of Ireland's best-preserved early Christian buildings; and the ruins of St. Brendan's House, where the saint reputedly set out to discover America long before Columbus.

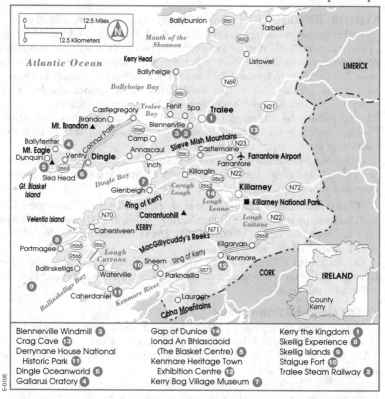

Blennerville Windmill 3   Gap of Dunloe 14   Kerry the Kingdom 1
Crag Cave 13   Ionad An Bhlascaoid   Skellig Experience 8
Derrynane House National   (The Blasket Centre) 5   Skellig Islands 9
  Historic Park 11   Kenmare Heritage Town   Staigue Fort 10
Dingle Oceanworld 6   Exhibition Centre 12   Tralee Steam Railway 2
Gallarus Oratory 4   Kerry Bog Village Museum 7

Shopping for Crafts   County Kerry has many local craftspeople, who produce wonderful weavings, ceramics, leatherwork, and the distinctive colored Kerry glass in Killorglin.

Spending an Evening in a Pub   Most of Kerry's pubs, especially in Killarney and Dingle, have traditional music evenings. Irish music is played every night in any pub in Dingle, sometimes with step dancing.

KILLARNEY TOWN

Killarney is a relatively small town with a population of around 7,000 people. The town is very walkable, although the streets are usually crowded with tourists, especially in summer. The busiest section of town is at the southern tip of Main Street, where it meets East Avenue Road. Here the road curves and heads southward out to Muckross Road and the entrance to Killarney National Park.

ESSENTIALS

GETTING THERE   **By Train**   **Irish Rail** offers daily service from most major Irish cities, arriving at **Killarney Railway Station,** Railway Road, off East Avenue Road (☎ **064/31067**).

By Bus   **Bus Eireann** operates regularly scheduled bus service from all parts of Ireland. The **bus station** is adjacent to the train station at Railway Road, off East Avenue Road, Killarney (☎ **064/34777**).

VISITOR INFORMATION The **Killarney Tourist Office,** Aras Fáilte, is located at the Town Centre Car Park, Beech Road, Killarney (☎ **064/31633**). It's open January to April, Monday to Saturday 9:15am to 1pm and 2:15 to 5:30pm; May, Monday to Saturday 9:15am to 5:30pm; June, Monday to Saturday 9am to 6pm, Sunday 10am to 1pm and 2:15 to 6pm; July to August, Monday to Saturday 9am to 8pm, Sunday 10am to 1pm and 2:15 to 6pm; September, Monday to Saturday 9am to 6pm, Sunday 10am to 1pm and 2:15 to 6pm; October to December, Monday to Saturday 9:15am to 1pm and 2:15 to 5:30pm. It offers many helpful booklets, including the *Tourist Trail* walking-tour guide and the *Killarney Area Guide* with maps.

Useful local publications include *Where: Killarney,* a quarterly magazine distributed free at hotels and guesthouses. It's packed with all types of current information on tours, activities, events, and entertainment.

GETTING AROUND The town is so small and compact that it's best traversed on foot. **Taxis** line up at the rank on College Square (☎ **064/31331**). You can also phone for a taxi from John Burke (☎ **064/32448**), **Dero's Taxi Service** (☎ **064/31251**), or **O'Connell Taxi** (☎ **064/31654**).

You can drive to Killarney National Park, or go by **jaunting car.** The horse-drawn jaunting cars line up at Kenmare Place, offering rides to Killarney National Park sites and other scenic areas.

✪ KILLARNEY NATIONAL PARK

This is Killarney's centerpiece: a 25,000-acre area of natural beauty. You'll find three storied lakes—the Lower Lake (or Lough Leane), the Middle Lake (or Muckross Lake), and the Upper Lake—myriad waterfalls, rivers, islands, valleys, mountains, bogs, and woodlands, and lush foliage and trees, including oak, arbutus, holly, and mountain ash. There's also a large variety of wildlife, including a rare herd of red deer. No automobiles are allowed within the park, so touring is best done on foot, bicycle, or horse-drawn jaunting car. The park offers four signposted walking and nature trails along the lakeshore.

Access is available from several points along the Kenmare road (N71), with the main entrance being at Muckross House, where there is a new visitor center featuring background exhibits on the park and a 20-minute film titled *Mountain, Wood, Water.* Admission is free, and the park is open year-round during daylight hours.

VIEWS & VISTAS The journey through the ✪ **Gap of Dunloe** is a must. The winding and rocky Gap of Dunloe is situated amid mountains and lakelands about 6 miles west of Killarney. The route through the gap passes a kaleidoscope of craggy rocks, massive cliffs, meandering streams, and deep valleys. The road through the gap ends at Upper Lake. One of the best ways to explore the gap is by bicycle. Horse fanciers may want to take one of the horseback excursions offered by **Castlelough Tours,** 7 High St. (☎ **064/31115**); **Corcoran's Tours,** Kilcummin (☎ **064/43151**); and **Dero's Tours,** 22 Main St. (☎ **064/ 31251**).

Aghadoe Heights, on Tralee Road (off N-22) is a spectacular viewing point over the lakes and town. To your left is the ruin of the 13th-century Castle of Parkvonear, erected by Norman invaders and well worth a visit. In the nearby churchyard are the remains of a stone church and round tower dating from 1027.

MORE ATTRACTIONS

✪ **Muckross House and Gardens.** Kenmare Rd. (N-71), Killarney. ☎ **064/31440.** Admission £3.80 ($5.90) adults, £2.70 ($4.20) seniors, £1.60 ($2.50) students and children, £9 ($13.95) family. Daily mid-Mar to June and Sept–Oct 9am–6pm; July–Aug 9am–7pm; Nov to mid-Mar 9am–5:30pm.

The Muckross Estate is the focal point of the Middle Lake. The gracious ivy-covered, Elizabethan-style residence with its colorful and well-tended gardens was built by Henry Arthur Herbert in 1843 and visited by Queen Victoria in 1861. The house is now a folk museum, and the cellars have been converted into craft shops where local artisans demonstrate the traditional trades of bookbinding, weaving, and pottery making. The adjacent gardens are known for their fine collection of rhododendrons and azaleas.

Just across from Muckross House is an attraction you might overlook but which is really quite fascinating, especially for families with children. **Muckross Traditional Farms,** a 70-acre park, is home to displays of traditional farm life and artisans' shops. The farmhouses and buildings are so authentically detailed that visitors feel they are dropping in on working farms and lived-in houses. The animals and household environments are equally fascinating for children and adults. Combined tickets are available with Muckross House.

Ross Castle. Ross Rd., off Kenmare Rd. (N-71). ☎ **064/35851.** Admission £2.50 ($4) adults, £1.75 ($2.80) seniors, £1 ($1.60) students and children, £6 ($9.60) family. Apr daily 11am–6pm; May and Sept daily 10am–6pm; June–Aug daily 9am–6:30pm; Oct Tues–Sun 10am–5pm. Last admission 45 min. before closing.

Built in the 14th century by the O'Donoghue chieftains, this castle was the last significant stronghold in Ireland to fall to Cromwell's armies. All that remains today is a tower house, surrounded by an enclosure with rounded turrets. The castle offers a magnificent view of the lakes and islands from its top, but access is by guided tour only.

Sightseeing Tours

BUS TOURS   Dero's Tours, 7 Main St. (☎ 064/31251), offers a 3-hour Killarney Highlights tour that takes you to Killarney's lakes, Aghadoe, the Gap of Dunloe, Ross Castle, Muckross House, and Torc Waterfall. Tours are given May through September, daily at 10:30am (but schedules do vary, so check in advance); the cost is £8 ($12.40). **Castlelough Tours,** 7 High St. (☎ 064/31115), offers a 3½-hour Lakeland Tour that visits Muckross House and Gardens and includes a tour of the lakes by Killarney Waterbus. Tours are given May through September, daily at 10:30am and 2pm, and the cost is £15 ($23.25).

BOAT TOURS   There is nothing quite like seeing the sights from a boat on the Lakes of Killarney. Two companies operate regular boating excursions lasting just over an hour, with full commentary. One is **M.V. Pride of the Lakes Tours,** Scotts Gardens, Killarney (☎ **064/32638**). The cost is £5 ($7.75) adults, £2.50 ($3.90) children, and £12.50 ($19.40) family. The tours run April to October at 11am, 12:30pm, 2:30pm, 4pm, and 5:15pm. The other company is **M.V. Lily of Killarney Tours,** 3 High St., Killarney (☎ **064/31068**). Tickets cost £5 ($7.75) adults, £2.50 ($3.90) children, and £12 ($18.60) family. Tours run April to October at 10:30am, noon, 1:45pm, 3:15pm, and 4:30pm. Reservations are suggested.

Enjoying the Great Outdoors

BICYCLING   The **Killarney National Park** is a paradise for bikers. Various types of bikes, from 21-speed touring bikes and mountain bikes to tandems, are available. Rental charges average £6 ($9.30) per day or £25 ($38.75) per week. Try one of the following shops: **Killarney Rent-a-Bike,** High Street (☎ 064/32578); **O'Neills Cycle Shop,** 6 Plunkett St., Killarney (☎ 064/31970); and D. O'Sullivan's **The Bike Shop,** High Street, Killarney (☎ **064/31282**). Most shops are open year-round from 9am to 6pm daily, with extended hours until 8 or 9pm in the summer months.

One great ride beginning in Killarney takes you through the Gap of Dunloe along a dirt forest road, where you'll see some of the best mountain scenery in the area; it can be made into a 35-mile loop if you return on N71.

FISHING   Fishing for salmon and brown trout in Killarney's unpolluted lakes and rivers is a big attraction. Brown trout fishing is free on the lakes, but a permit is necessary for the Rivers Flesk and Laune. A trout permit costs £3 to £10 ($4.65 to $15.50) per day.

Salmon fishing anywhere in Ireland requires a license; the cost is £3 ($4.65) per day or £10 ($15.50) for 21 days. In addition, some rivers also require a salmon permit, which costs £8 to £10 ($12.40 to $15.50) per day. Permits and licenses can be obtained at the Fishery Office at the **Knockreer Estate Office,** New Street, Killarney (☎ **064/31246**).

For fishing tackle, bait, rod rental, and other fishing gear, as well as permits and licenses, try **O'Neill's,** 6 Plunkett St., Killarney (☎ **064/31970**). This shop also arranges the hire of boats and ghillies (fishing guides), for £60 ($93) per day on the Killarney Lakes, leaving from Ross Castle. Gear and tackle can also be purchased from Michael O'Brien at **Angler's Paradise,** Loreto Road, Killarney (☎ **064/33818**).

GOLF   Visitors are always welcome at the twin 18-hole championship courses of the **Killarney Golf & Fishing Club,** Killorglin Road, Fossa, Killarney (☎ **064/31034**), located 3 miles west of the town center. Widely praised as one of the most scenic golf settings in the world, these courses, known as "Killeen" and "Mahony's Point," are surrounded by lake and mountain vistas. Greens fees are £38 ($58.90) on either course.

HORSEBACK RIDING   Many trails in the Killarney area are suitable for horseback riding. The cost of hiring a horse ranges from £10 to £15 ($15.50 to $23.25) per hour at the following establishments: **Killarney Riding Stables,** R562, Ballydowney, Killarney (☎ **064/31686**); **O'Donovan's Farm,** Mangerton Road, Muckross, Killarney (☎ **064/32238**); and **Rocklands Stables,** Rockfield, Tralee Road, Killarney (☎ **064/32592**). Lessons and week-long trail rides can also be arranged.

WALKING   Killarney is ideal for walking enthusiasts. On the outskirts of town, the **Killarney National Park** offers four signposted nature trails. Leaflets with maps of these four trails are available at the park's visitor center. For long-distance walkers, there is the 125-mile "Kerry Way," a signposted walking route that extends from Killarney around the Ring of Kerry.

THE SHOPPING SCENE: KERRY GLASS & MORE

Shopping hours are normally Monday through Saturday 9am to 6pm, but May through September, most shops stay open to 9 or 10pm. Although there are more souvenir and craft shops in Killarney than you can shake a stick (or shillelagh) at, here are a few of the best.

The ✪ **Kerry Glass Studio and Visitor Centre,** Killorglin Road, Fossa (☎ **064/44666**), is the studio that produces Killarney's distinctive colored glass. Visitors are welcome to watch—and photograph—the craftspeople firing, blowing, and adding color to the glass. The center includes a factory shop and snack bar.

The **Blarney Woolen Mills,** 10 Main St. (☎ **064/33222**), has everything from handknit or hand-loomed Irish-made sweaters to tweeds, crystal, china, pottery, and souvenirs. **Quill's Woolen Market,** 1 High St. (☎ **064/32277**), is one of the best shops in town for handknit sweaters of all kinds, as well as tweeds, mohair, and sheepskins.

The **Frank Lewis Gallery,** 6 Bridewell Lane (☎ **064/31108**), shows and sells a wide variety of contemporary and traditional paintings, sculptures, and photographs by some of Ireland's most acclaimed emerging artists.

WHERE TO STAY

Expensive

✪ **Killarney Park Hotel.** Kenmare Place, Killarney, County Kerry. ☎ **064/35555.** Fax 064/35266. www.killarneyparkhotel.ie. 75 units. TV TEL. £150–£190 ($232.50–$294.50) double; £220–£450 ($341–$697.50) suite. No service charge. Rates include full breakfast. AE, DC, MC, V.

With a striking yellow neo-Georgian facade, this new four-story property is located on its own grounds on the eastern edge of town. Public rooms are posh and spacious, with brass fixtures, oil paintings, open fireplaces, and a sunlit conservatory-style lounge overlooking the gardens. Guest rooms have dark and light wood furnishings, quilted designer fabrics, and marble-finished bathrooms. Public areas include a restaurant, piano bar, patio, indoor heated swimming pool, gym, and steam room.

Moderate

Castlerosse. Killorglin Rd., Killarney, County Kerry. ☎ **800/528-1234** from the U.S., or 064/31114. Fax 064/31031. 110 units. TV TEL. £70–£104 ($108.50–$161.20) double. Rates include full Irish breakfast and service charge. AE, DC, MC, V. Closed Dec–Feb.

Set on its own parklands between the Lower Lake and surrounding mountains, this modern, rambling, ranch-style inn is 2 miles from the heart of town and next to Killarney's two golf courses. The recently refurbished guest rooms offer contemporary furnishings and views of the lake. Nonsmoking rooms are available on request. Facilities include a new leisure and fitness center, two tennis courts, putting green, walking paths, and jogging trails. New self-catering two-bedroom suites are also available.

Earls Court Guesthouse. Woodlawn Junction, Muckross Rd., Killarney, County Kerry. ☎ **064/34009.** Fax 064/34366. E-mail: castler@iol.ie. 11 units (1 single with shower only). TV TEL. £57–£90 ($88.35–$139.50) double. Rates include full Irish breakfast and service charge. AE, DC, MC, V. Closed Nov 6–Feb. Follow the sign off N-71; it's a 5-minute walk from Killarney center.

Earls Court is among Killarney's newest and most attractive quality guesthouses. The spacious and immaculately clean rooms are furnished with exceptional style and taste. Some have sitting areas, and nearly all have balconies. The second-floor rooms, in particular, have clear views of the mountains. All rooms have firm beds, and all are non-smoking.

✪ **Kathleen's Country House.** Madam's Height, Tralee Rd. (N-22), Killarney, County Kerry. ☎ **064/32810.** Fax 064/32340. 16 units. TV TEL. £59–£79 ($91.45–$122.45) double. No service charge. Rates include full breakfast. AE, MC, V. Closed mid-Nov to early Mar.

Of the many guesthouses in this area, this one really does stand out. It's a two-story contemporary house, on its own 3 acres of gardens. The enthusiastic and efficient hostess, Kathleen O'Regan, has outfitted the bedrooms (all nonsmoking) with ortho-pedic beds, hair dryers, tea/coffeemakers, and cheerful furnishings. All were recently refurbished in antique pine and enhanced with original paintings. A new library/drawing room has also been added.

Inexpensive

✪ **Gleann Fia Country House.** Deerpark, Killarney, County Kerry. ☎ **064/35035.** Fax 064/35000. E-mail: gleanfia@iol.ie. 17 units. TV TEL. £40–£60 ($62–$93) double. No service charge. Rates include full breakfast. AE, MC, V. Closed Dec–Feb.

Although only a mile from town, this modern guesthouse feels pleasantly secluded, tucked away as it is in 26 acres of lawns and woodlands. Amenities include an airy conservatory with tea-making facilities, a guest lounge, and an unusually extensive breakfast menu. There is a nature walk along the stream that runs by one side of the house.

The rooms in the most recent addition are slightly larger and more elegantly furnished than those in the main house, and are correspondingly pricier. All bedrooms are nonsmoking. There's also a spacious family room on the ground floor of the main house with a double bed, single bed, and couch.

WHERE TO DINE

Expensive

✪ **Gaby's Seafood Restaurant.** 27 High St., Killarney. ☎ **064/32519.** Reservations recommended. Main courses £12.90–£28 ($20–$43.40). AE, DC, MC, V. Mon–Sat 6–10pm. Closed mid-Feb to mid-Mar. SEAFOOD.

One of Killarney's longest established restaurants, this nautically themed place is a mecca for lovers of fresh seafood. It's known for its succulent lobster, served grilled or in a house sauce of cognac, wine, cream, and spices. Other choices include turbot, haddock in wine, local salmon, and a giant Kerry shellfish platter, a veritable feast of prawns, scallops, mussels, lobster, and oysters.

Moderate

✪ **Bricín.** 26 High St., Killarney. ☎ **064/34902.** Reservations recommended for dinner. Main courses £8.50–£13.50 ($13.20–$21); snacks £1.60–£5 ($2.50–$7.75). MC, V. Year-round Tues–Sat 10am–4:30pm; Easter–Oct daily 6–10pm. IRISH.

Traditional Kerry boxty dishes (potato pancakes with various fillings, such as chicken, seafood, curried lamb, or vegetables) are the trademark of this upstairs restaurant. The menu also offers a variety of fresh seafood, pastas, Irish stew, and specials. Housed in one of Killarney's oldest buildings, Bricín sports original stone walls, turf fireplaces, and, something very rare in Ireland—a completely nonsmoking room seating 40.

Swiss Barn. 17 High St., Killarney. ☎ **064/36044.** Reservations recommended. Lunch main courses £4–£7.95 ($6.20–$12.30); dinner main courses £8.50–£19.50 ($13.20–$30.25); 4-course early-bird special 5:30–7:30pm £8.50 ($13.20); 5-course tourist menu £13.65 ($21.15). AE, DC, MC, V. Mid-Mar to Jun daily 6–9:30pm; July–Sept daily 5:30–10pm; Oct–Dec Thurs–Mon 6–9pm. Closed Jan to mid-Mar.SWISS/CONTINENTAL.

With a rustic alpine decor, this restaurant aims to bring the taste of Switzerland and the Continent to Killarney. The menu offers Swiss favorites such as émincé of veal Zurichoise, pork fillet in morel sauce, and fondue bourguignonne, as well as veal cordon bleu, beef Stroganoff, steaks, seafood, and vegetarian platters.

THE RING OF KERRY

Undoubtedly Ireland's most popular scenic drive, the Ring of Kerry is a 110-mile panorama of seacoast, mountain, and lakeland vistas. Bicyclists usually avoid this route, since the scores of tour buses that thunder through here every day in the summer aren't always generous about sharing the road.

ESSENTIALS

MAKING THE DRIVE   By Bus   Bus Eireann (☎ 064/34777) provides limited daily service from Killarney to Caherciveen, Waterville, Kenmare, and other towns on the Ring of Kerry.

By Car   This is by far the best way to get around the Ring. For the most part, the route follows N-70.

VISITOR INFORMATION   For year-round information, stop in at the **Killarney Tourist Office,** Town Centre Car Park, Beech Road, Killarney (☎ 064/31633), before you begin your drive. June through September, **The Barracks Tourist Office,** Caherciveen (☎ 066/72589), is open; Easter through September, the **Kenmare**

Tourist Office, Market Square, Kenmare (☎ **064/41233**), is open. Most telephone numbers on the Ring of Kerry use the 064 or 066 code.

EXPLORING THE RING

The drive can be undertaken in either direction, but we strongly recommend a counterclockwise route for the most spectacular views. It's worth noting that the farther you get along the road, the more the signs tend to be in Gaelic only. Since the maps are all in English, this can be somewhat confusing. Careful study of the maps is suggested when exploring away from N-20. You can buy an Ordnance Survey map (sheet 83) from the tourist office, which gives names in both English and Gaelic.

Leave Killarney and follow the signs for **Killorglin.** Be sure to make the detour to visit **Ballymalis Castle.** Probably built by the Ferris family at the end of the 16th century, this ruin is typical of the tower houses built by wealthy landlords to protect their households from unwelcome intruders. Climbing the narrow, winding staircase, you're rewarded with splendid views over mountains, rivers, and fields. Backtrack to the main road and continue.

When you arrive in **Killorglin,** you might want to stop and walk around this spot, known far and wide for its annual mid-August horse, sheep, and cattle fair. Its official name is Puck Fair. The locals capture a wild goat from the mountains and enthrone it in the center of town as a sign to begin unrestricted merrymaking—although not necessarily for the goat.

Continuing on N-70, follow the signs for **Glenbeigh,** with views of Ireland's tallest Mountain, **Carrantuohill** (3,414 ft.), to your left. Open bogland is a constant companion on this stretch, and locals dig peat, or turf, to burn in their fireplaces. On your right just before you reach Glenbeigh is the **Kerry Bog Village Museum** (☎ **066/ 69184**), where a cluster of thatched cottages illustrates Kerry life in the early 1800s. As you explore the blacksmith's forge, the turf cutter's house, and the laborer's cottage, the smell of burning peat hangs heavy in the air. The village is also home to the Kerry Bog pony, a breed that has been saved from extinction and is now unique to this museum.

The next town on the Ring is **Glenbeigh,** a palm tree–lined fishing resort with a lovely duney beach called Rossbeigh Strand. You may want to stop here, or continue on the Ring, with the first sightings of the Atlantic appearing away to your right. The views on the next section of the Ring are breathtaking, although the drive can be a bit hair-raising since the road twists and winds around the cliffs. There's a gorgeous view down over **Kells Bay,** best viewed from the road, instead of making the drive down to it. The route then moves inland with mountains to your right and a patchwork of fields in many shades of green to your left.

When you reach **Cahersiveen,** follow the signs right for the two forts, reached along a scenic though narrow road. You need to park a little way past the first fort, **Cahergeal,** and walk back along a rough track. The fort is made from gray stones and boulders piled one on top of the other. Staircases and walkways snake their way up and around ramparts, and the view across the bay is magical. The second fort can be reached along a narrow road to the right a little farther along. This is **Leacanabuaile Fort,** one of the few stone forts to have been excavated. The objects found suggest that the fort was in use until the 9th or 10th century. The castle that can be seen from both forts is Ballycarbery, but isn't really worth a visit, being best viewed from the distance.

Return to Cahersiveen and rejoin N-70, and then follow the signs right marked VALENTIA VIA FERRY. **Valentia** (also spelled Valencia) can also be reached by road, following the signs for Port Magee farther along N-70, but the ferry crossing saves a good deal of time and costs just £3 ($4.65) for the car. Valentia Island, 7 miles long, is one of the most westerly points in Europe. It has the distinction of being the place from which the first telegraph cable was laid across the Atlantic, in 1866.

Once ashore at Knightstown, follow the signs for **Glanleam Gardens,** Glanleam House (☎ **066/76176**). Created over 150 years ago by the Knights of Kerry, the gardens are justly famous for a unique collection of southern hemisphere plants. Broad walks weave through junglelike plantings of South American palms, Australian tree ferns, bananas, giant groves of bamboo, and rust-colored myrtles from Chile.

Leaving the gardens, follow the signs for **Portmagee,** stopping on the outskirts to visit **The Skellig Experience,** Skellig Heritage Centre (☎ **066/76306**). This attraction blends right in with the terrain, with a stark, stone facade, framed by grassy mounds. The center gives you a detailed look at the bird and plant life of the Valentia area. In particular it tells the story of the **Skellig rocks**—Skellig Michael and Little Skellig—two rocky islands sitting off the coast in the Atlantic. In the 6th century, Skellig Michael, the larger of the two, became home to a group of monks who founded a monastery that survived for more than 600 years. Today, the other Skellig is one of the largest breeding grounds for the gannet in Western Europe. Admission to the Skellig Experience, for the exhibition and audiovisual, is £3 ($4.65) for adults, £2.70 ($4.20) for seniors and students, £1.50 ($2.35) for children under 12, and £7 ($10.85) for a family of two adults and up to four children; for the exhibition, audiovisual, and sea cruise circuiting the Skelligs, the fee is £15 ($23.25) for adults, £13.50 ($20.95) for seniors and students, £7.50 ($11.65) for children under 12, £40 ($62) for a family. It's open April through October, 10am to 7pm.

It's well worth making the 8-mile sea journey to the Skelligs, if only to climb the "stairway to Heaven," leading to the remains of the monastic settlement where you can marvel at the lifestyle of the monks who once lived here. Thanks to the degree to which the place has been preserved, little imagination is needed to picture those early years of Irish Christianity. Ferries leave daily from Ballyferriter, usually between 9am and noon; call **Joe Roddy** (☎ **066/74268**) or **Sean Feehan** (☎ **066/79182**). Ferries departing from Portmagee are run by **Murphy's** (☎ **066/77156**). The cost is £20 ($31) per person.

In the 18th century Valentia harbor was famous as a refuge for smugglers and privateers; tradition has it that John Paul Jones, the Scottish-born American naval officer in the War of Independence, anchored here frequently.

The route now continues into **Portmagee** and on through the **Coomanaspig Pass,** with dramatic views across St. Finan's Bay. This remote Irish-speaking area is an outpost of Gaelic culture and has an Irish college to which children come in the summer months to learn their native language. Continue through the glen, passing miles of golden, sandy beaches. When you reach Ballinskelligs, follow the road around the bay to **Waterville.** An overnight at this idyllic spot is highly recommended. There are many excellent restaurants, and from 9pm on, almost every bar on the seafront comes alive with the singing of traditional Irish songs.

Leaving Waterville, continue along N-70. If time allows (you'll need a good 50 minutes), take the first left turn, signposted CLUB MED (yes, you'll pass their only branch in Ireland) and enjoy a spectacular drive along the shores of **Lough Currane.** This is a very narrow and little-used road, but the dramatic views are well worth the effort. To your left, the dark waters of the lough and the towering ruggedness of the purple mountains suddenly give way to a patchwork of green fields. Take your time and take it all in. The road ends at a cottage, where you'll need to turn around and backtrack to N-70.

Continuing on N-70 through the Coomakista Pass, you arrive at another viewpoint at the crest of the road, where there's a statue of the Virgin Mary looking down onto the mouth of the Kenmare River and back along the pass to Waterville.

The next village is **Caherdaniel,** where a right turn leads to **Derrynane House** (☎ 066/75113), the home, for most of his life, of Daniel O'Connell, the liberator. The house is now a museum dedicated to his struggle, with documents, maps, and memorabilia. Nature trails twist and turn through the 320-acre grounds and an explanatory booklet is available.

Return to N-70 and continue on until you reach signs to the left for the **Staigue Fort,** which possibly dates from around 1000 B.C. Forts such as this, with massive stone walls, were built as centers for communal refuge. The fort is nestled between the hills and mountains, and the views down over the tree tops across the bay and estuary are magnificent.

Back on N-70, you'll arrive at the pretty, colorful village of **Sneem,** its houses painted in vibrant shades of blue, pink, yellow, and purple. There's a memorial commemorating General de Gaulle's visit in 1969, and don't miss, to the right of the Catholic church, *The Way the Fairies Went,* a creation by James Scanlon, with four pyramid-shaped natural-stone structures with stained glass panels.

Once through Sneem, you have a choice. You can continue on the Ring to Kenmare, a route that's pretty but at times tedious and uneventful. Or for a truly awe-inspiring scenic drive, follow the signs left to **Killarney,** on a route that takes you through the mountains. At every twist and turn of the road, a spectacular new vista opens out before you—myriad shades of green, surrounded on all sides by the moody, purple mountains, and babbling brooks that trickle into dark roadside lakes. When you reach Molls Gap, turn right for a visit to **Kenmare,** an enchanting place originally called Neidin, meaning "Little Nest." Well laid out and immaculately maintained by its proud residents (population 1,200), Kenmare more than rivals Killarney as a base for County Kerry sightseeing.

However, our last section of the Ring and the grand finale beckons. Backtrack to Molls Gap and then follow the signs for **Killarney.** Soon you're crossing the boundary of the national park, and every viewpoint is well worth the time it takes to stop and gaze across the Lakes of Killarney. Most popular is **Ladies View,** so called because of the pleasure expressed by Queen Victoria's ladies in waiting when they visited this picturesque spot in 1861. Farther on, don't miss the **Torc Waterfall,** signposted from the road and located in a peaceful woodland setting. From here it's a short distance to Muckross House and then back to Killarney.

WHERE TO STAY AROUND THE RING
Very Expensive
✪ **The Park Hotel.** Kenmare, County Kerry. ☎ 800/223-6764 from the U.S., or 064/41200. Fax 064/41402. 48 units. TV TEL. £232–£460 ($359.60–$713) double. No service charge. Rates include full breakfast. AE, DC, MC, V. Closed Nov–Dec 23 and Jan 2 to mid-Apr.

Ensconced amid palm tree–lined gardens beside Kenmare Bay, this 1897 Victorian-style château is a haven of impeccable service and luxurious living. The interior is rich with high-ceilinged sitting rooms and lounges, fireplaces, original oil paintings, tapestries, plush furnishings, and museum-worthy antiques. The individually decorated bedrooms are decked out in a mix of Georgian and Victorian styles, many with four-poster or canopy beds, hand-carved armoires, and china lamps. Most have views of the river and mountains. Nonsmoking rooms are available; 100% are wheelchair accessible. The dining room is one of the most highly acclaimed hotel restaurants in Ireland, meriting a Michelin star. Facilities include an 18-hole golf course, joggers' trail, tennis court, croquet lawn, and salmon fishing. In 1998, the Park Hotel was named the Conde Nast "Best Hotel in Ireland."

Expensive

Parknasilla Great Southern Hotel. Ring of Kerry Rd. (N-70), Parknasilla, County Kerry. ☎ **064/45122.** Fax 064/45323. E-mail: res@parknasilla.gsh.ie. 84 units. TV TEL. £146–£204 ($226.30–$316.20) double. Service charge 12.5%. AE, DC, MC, V. Closed Jan to mid-Mar.

Facing one of the loveliest seascape settings in Ireland, this château-style hotel is set amid 300 acres of lush, subtropical palm trees and flowering shrubs. George Bernard Shaw stayed here and was inspired to write much of his play *Saint Joan.* The hotel has a private nine-hole golf course, a heated indoor saltwater swimming pool, saunas, and tennis courts, and offers riding, fishing, and boating. The bedrooms are individually furnished, and most look out onto broad vistas of the Kenmare River and the Atlantic.

Moderate

Towers. Ring of Kerry Rd. (N-70), Glenbeigh, County Kerry. ☎ **066/976-8212.** Fax 066/976-8260. 28 units. TV TEL. £76–£94 ($117.80–$145.70) double. Service charge 12.5%. Rates include full breakfast. AE, DC, MC, V. Closed Jan–Mar.

If you'd like to be right in the heart of one of the Ring of Kerry's most delightful towns, then this vintage brick-faced country inn is for you. Shaded by ancient palms, it sits in the middle of a small fishing village, yet is within a mile of the sandy Rossbeigh Strand. Recently refurbished and updated, most of the guest rooms are in a contemporary-style new wing with lovely views of the nearby waters. Facilities include a lively old-fashioned pub and a good seafood restaurant.

WHERE TO DINE AROUND THE RING

The Huntsman. The Strand, Waterville. ☎ **066/947-4124.** Reservations recommended. Main courses £9–£18 ($13.95–$27.90); lunch/bar food items from £4 ($6.20). AE, DC, MC, V. Mar–Oct daily 10am–10pm; Nov–Feb daily noon–8pm. INTERNATIONAL.

It's worth a trip to Waterville just to dine at this contemporary restaurant on the shores of Ballinskelligs Bay. Owner/chef Raymond Hunt takes the time to circulate and chat with diners, offering suggestions as to the extensive menu, which uses only the freshest local catch and produce. Skellig lobster fresh from the tank and Kenmare Bay scampi are among the seafood dishes; meat dishes include rack of lamb, seasonal pheasant, rabbit, duck, and Irish stew.

✪ **Lime Tree.** Shelbourne Rd., Kenmare. ☎ **064/41225.** Reservations recommended. Main courses £9.95–£13.50 ($15.40–$21). MC, V. Apr–Oct daily 6:30–10:30pm. IRISH.

Innovative cuisine is the focus at this restaurant in an 1821 landmark renovated schoolhouse next to the grounds of the Park Hotel. The decor includes a skylit gallery and stone walls lined with paintings by local artists, and the menu offers such dishes as goat's cheese potato cake with balsamic glaze, oak planked wild salmon, filet of Irish beef with colcannon, and oven-roasted Kerry lamb.

The Vestry. Templenoe, Kenmare. ☎ **064/41958.** Reservations recommended for dinner. Main courses £9.95–£17.95 ($15.40–$27.80). DC, MC, V. Apr–Oct daily 10am–10pm. MODERN IRISH/INTERNATIONAL.

As its name implies, this building is a former Church of Ireland edifice, constructed between 1790 and 1816, and in use for services until 1987. In 1993, it was tastefully converted into a restaurant, retaining many of its original decorations and fixtures. Recently, the modern Irish menu, highlighting fresh local seafood and vegetables, was expanded to include more exotic items such as kangaroo, ostrich, and wild boar. A current favorite is the shark steak with ratatouille.

SHOPPING IN KENMARE

Cleo, 2 Shelbourne Rd. (☎ **064/41410**), is a branch of the long-established Dublin store of the same name. This trendy women's wear shop is known for its colorful tweed and linen fashions, as well as specialty items like Kinsale cloaks. **The Green Note,** 18 Henry St. (☎ **064/41212**), is a traditional Irish-music store selling banjos, harps, and tin whistles. You can also purchase a bodhran, the Irish hand drum, at an attractive price. The **Kenmare Bookshop,** Shelbourne Street (☎ **064/41578**), specializes in books on Ireland, particularly Irish biographies and books by Irish writers, as well as maps and guides to the surrounding area, including ordinance survey maps, walking and specialist guides, and marine charts. **Nostalgia Linen and Lace,** 27 Henry St. (☎ **064/41669**), specializes in Irish linens and sells lace by the meter. Finally, you can't miss stumbling into **Quills Woolen Market,** Market Square and Main Street (☎ **064/41078**), one of the many Quills branch stores known for Aran handknits, Donegal tweed jackets, Irish linen, Celtic jewelry, and colorful hand-loomed knitwear.

TRALEE

Tralee, with its population of 22,000, is County Kerry's chief town and the gateway to the Dingle Peninsula. A busy, bustling, and not particularly attractive place, its greatest claim to fame is that it was the inspiration for the song "The Rose of Tralee," composed by local resident William Mulninock more than 100 years ago. Consequently, Tralee is now the setting for the Rose of Tralee festival, the country's largest annual festival, held in August. It's also the permanent home of the National Folk Theatre of Ireland, Siamsa Tire.

ESSENTIALS

GETTING THERE   By Air   Aer Lingus operates daily nonstop flights from Dublin into **Kerry County Airport,** Farranfore, County Kerry (☎ **066/64644**), about 15 miles south of Tralee.

By Train   Trains from major cities arrive at the **Tralee Railway Station** on John Jo Sheehy Road (☎ **066/712-3522**).

By Bus   Buses from all parts of Ireland arrive daily at the **Bus Eireann Depot** on John Jo Sheehy Road, near the train station (☎ **066/712-3566**).

VISITOR INFORMATION   The **Tralee Tourist Office,** in Ashe Memorial Hall, Denny Street, Tralee (☎ **066/712-1288**), is open year-round Tuesday through Saturday 9am to 1pm and 2 to 5pm, with extended hours in the summer season. There is also a first-rate cafe on the premises.

SEEING THE SIGHTS

One of Ireland's largest indoor heritage centers, **Kerry the Kingdom,** Ashe Memorial Hall, Denny Street, Tralee (☎ **066/712-7777**), offers three separate attractions that give an in-depth look at 7,000 years of life in County Kerry. A 10-minute video, *Kerry in Colour,* presents the seascapes and landscapes of Kerry; the **Kerry County Museum** chronologically examines the county's music, history, legends, and archaeology through interactive and hands-on exhibits; and the exhibit on Gaelic football is unique. Many items of local origin that were previously on view at the National Museum in Dublin are now here. Complete with lighting effects and aromas, a theme park–style ride called "Geraldine Tralee" takes you through a re-creation of Tralee's streets, houses, and abbeys during the Middle Ages. Admission is £4 adults ($6.20), £2.50 ($3.90) children. Open March to October, daily 10am–6pm, and November to December, daily 2 to 5pm; closed January to February.

The restored ✪ **Tralee Steam Railway** (☎ **066/712-8888**) offers 2-mile narrated scenic trips from Tralee's Ballyard Station to Blennerville. It uses equipment that was once part of the Tralee & Dingle Light Railway, one of the world's most famous narrow-gauge railways. Trains run on the hour from Tralee and on the half hour from

Blennerville, and the trip costs £3 ($4.65) for adults and £1.75 ($2.70) for children. It operates daily April through September; closed on the second Monday of each month for maintenance.

WHERE TO STAY

Abbey Gate Hotel. Maine St., Tralee, County Kerry. ☎ **066/712-9888.** Fax 066/712-9821. 100 units. TV TEL. £76–£100 ($117.80–$155) double. No service charge. AE, DC, MC, V.

This modern three-story hotel is located in the center of Tralee. The bedrooms are spacious and tastefully decorated, and the public areas are modern and functional. Nonsmoking rooms are available, and all beds are orthopedic.

Ballyseede Castle Hotel. Tralee-Killarney Road, Tralee, County Kerry. ☎ **066/712-5799.** Fax 066/712-5287. 12 units. TV TEL. £130–£190 ($201.50–$294.50) double. Service charge 12.5%. AE, DISC, MC, V.

This turreted four-story castle was once the chief garrison of the legendary Fitzgeralds, the earls of Desmond. The lobby has Doric columns and a hand-carved oak staircase. The two drawing rooms are warmed by marble fireplaces. Residents can feel like royalty in the elegant bedrooms (nonsmoking available), a feeling that's reiterated in the Regency restaurant with its huge oil paintings and fabric-lined walls. It goes without saying that the castle is haunted.

The Shores. Cappatigue, Castlegregory, County Kerry. ☎ **066/713-9196.** 5 units (4 with bathroom). £32–£40 ($49.60–$62) double. Rates include full breakfast. MC, V. Closed Dec–Jan. ½ mile west of Stradbally on the Conor Pass Rd.

The Shores, a modern house on the south side of Brandon Bay, commands good views of Tralee Bay and Mount Brandon. Annette O'Mahoney is an avid interior decorator, and she has done a great job of giving each room a unique ambience. Furnishings are lavish, with a canopy bed in one of the upstairs rooms and writing desks in three of the rooms. The downstairs room has a private entrance and a fireplace. Breakfast options are particularly extensive, with smoked salmon and waffles given as alternatives to the standard fry.

WHERE TO DINE

In addition to the recommendation below, you can get excellent pub grub, especially steaks, at **Kirby's Olde Brogue Inn,** Rock Street, Tralee (☎ **066/712-3357**). This pub has a barnlike layout, with an interior that incorporates agricultural instruments, farming memorabilia, and rush-work tables and chairs. Sometimes traditional music and folk ballads are served up, too.

✪ **Larkins.** Princes St., Tralee. ☎ **066/712-1300.** Main courses £7.90–£16 ($12.25–$24.80); set-price menu £13.90 ($21.55) May–Sept. DC, MC, V. Mon–Fri 12:30– 2pm and 6:30–9:30pm; Sat 6:30–9:30pm (Sun hours June–Sept). IRISH/SEAFOOD/VEGETARIAN.

This bright, welcoming Irish-country restaurant is widely acclaimed for its catch of the day and its roast rack of Irish lamb. Modestly priced and immodestly tasty, Larkins' offerings are well worth a stop.

The Tankard. Kilfenora, Fenit. ☎ **066/713-6164.** Reservations recommended. Main courses £8–£15 ($12.40–$23.25). AE, DC, MC, V. Daily 6–10pm. SEAFOOD/IRISH.

Six miles northwest of Tralee, this is one of the few restaurants in the area that capitalizes on sweeping views of Tralee Bay. Situated right on the water's edge, it is outfitted with wide picture windows and a sleek contemporary decor. The straightforward menu primarily features local shellfish and seafood such as lobster, scallops, prawns, and black sole, but also includes rack of lamb, duck, quail, and a variety of steaks. Bar food is available all day, but this restaurant is at its best in the early evening, especially at sunset.

TRALEE AFTER DARK

Siamsa Tire, the National Folk Theatre of Ireland, is located at Town Park, Tralee (☎ **066/712-3055;** fax 066/27246). Founded in 1974, Siamsa (pronounced *Sheem*-sha) offers a mixture of music, dance, and mime, and its programs focus on three different themes: Fado Fado/The Long Ago; Sean Agus Nua/Myth and Motion; and Ding Dong Dedero/Forging the Dance. The scenes depict old folk tales and farmyard activities such as thatching a cottage roof, flailing sheaves of corn, and twisting a sugan (straw) rope.

In addition to these folk theater entertainments, Siamsa presents a full program of drama and musical concerts (from traditional to classical) performed by visiting amateur and professional companies. Admission is £10 ($15.50) for adults, £8 ($12.40) for seniors, students, and children, £34 ($52.70) for a family of two adults and up to four children. The schedule is Tuesday, Thursday, and Saturday in May; Monday, Tuesday, Thursday, and Saturday in June and September; and Monday through Saturday in July and August; curtain time is 8:30pm (8pm Octto Apr).

PUBS   Tralee pubs can be a little crowded and impersonal. **Olde Macs,** The Mall (☎ **066/712-1572**), is an exception. From the delightful flowers in the hanging baskets outside to the dark-wood interior, the pub exudes atmosphere. Conversation is lighthearted, and the regulars are extremely friendly.

THE DINGLE PENINSULA

While the Dingle Peninsula is an ideal drive, it also makes a fine bicycling tour. Dingle village is a delightful place to stay (see below) while exploring the peninsula.

The best route to the Dingle Peninsula is to follow the camp road (N-86) from Tralee. Three miles to the west you'll pass the **Blennerville Windmill** (☎ **066/712-1064**). This is the largest working windmill in Ireland and was built in 1850. After years of neglect, it was recently restored and now produces 5 tons of whole-meal flour per week. The visitors complex has an emigration exhibition center, craft workshops, and a cafe. Admission is £3 ($4.65) for adults, £2.50 ($3.90) for seniors and students, and £1.75 ($2.70) for children over 5; it's open April through October, Monday through Saturday 10am to 6pm, and Sunday 11am to 6pm.

The route continues with delightful vistas over Tralee Bay, passing through the town of **Camp.** From here on the road hugs the shore with vistas of **Brandon Mountain,** Ireland's second highest. Follow the signs for the **Conor Pass,** a spectacular drive through the mountains that reaches a height of 1,500 feet. Rising steeply, the often very narrow road passes through a landscape of rocky mountain slopes, dark lakes, and cliffs. On a clear day, the views of Tralee and Brandon Bays are superb. Be sure to stop at the viewpoint when you reach the top of the pass. The final descent offers views over Dingle Bay and an enticing glimpse of Dingle itself (see below).

From **Dingle,** follow the signs for **Slea Head Drive,** a route that takes you on a spectacular, often rugged trip, returning eventually to Dingle. The **Beehive Huts** that stand to the right of the road past **Ventry** are worth a stop. These unmortared, prehistoric cells or huts owe their shape to the ancient method of construction known as drystone corbelling, in which the circular walls are constructed of overlapping stones and curve gradually inward until they can be covered with a capstone at the top.

Also worth a visit is the **Dunbeg Fort,** situated on an oceanside site with beautiful sea views. A viewpoint at **Slea Head** overlooks a mountainous curve at the end of the peninsula; it's been the setting for many a picture postcard and sea-splashed landscape painting. You also have a view of the seven **Blasket Islands,** sitting out in the Atlantic. Until 1953 the largest of these, Great Blasket, was still inhabited. Great Blasket was once an outpost of Irish civilization and nurtured a small band of Irish-language writers. The quite splendid **Blasket Centre,** on the westerly tip of the Dingle Peninsula near Dunquin (☎ **066/915-6371**), has a series of displays, exhibits, and a video presentation that celebrate the cultural and literary traditions of the Blaskets. Admission is £2.50 ($3.90) for adults, £1.75 ($2.70) for seniors, £1 ($1.55) for children and students, and £6 ($9.30) for families; it's open Easter through June and September through October daily 10am to 6pm; July through August daily 10am to 7pm.

The route now continues to **Ballyferriter,** a largely Gaelic-speaking village. From here you head east and follow the signs to the **Gallarus Oratory,** one of the best-preserved early Christian church buildings in Ireland. Constructed of unmortared stone and shaped like an upturned boat, it's still watertight even after a thousand years.

Continue following the signs marked SLEA HEAD DRIVE until you arrive at the **Kilmalkedar Church,** dating from the 12th century. Inside the ruined church is an abecedarian stone, with the Latin alphabet crudely carved, a relic of a 7th-century school and probably the oldest-surviving Irish relic of Roman script. Don't miss the 15th-century ruins of **St. Brendan's House,** hidden among the bushes a little way past the church, once a substantial priests' dwelling.

Continue on the road and turn right, following the signs to **Brandon Creek.** It was from here, in the 6th century, that St. Brendan reputedly set out for the Islands of Paradise in the Western Ocean, a 7-year voyage that led him, it has been claimed, to discover America. The life of the saint and the story of his voyage, *Navigation Sancti Brendai Abbatis,* was written in the 9th century. The Latin narrative was popular reading in medieval Europe and the inspiration for many voyagers and explorers, including Christopher Columbus.

Backtrack to Slea Head Drive and follow it on a picturesque route back to Dingle. From here take R-561 eastward along Dingle Bay, through the villages of Lispole and Annascaul to **Inch,** one of Dingle's most beautiful seascapes, a 4-mile stretch of sandy beach, with distant views of the Ring of Kerry and Killarney. From here you can return to Camp or Tralee or continue to Castlemaine (where the Wild Colonial Boy was born) and onward to Limerick or other parts of Kerry and Cork.

DINGLE TOWN

With a charter dating back many centuries, Dingle was Kerry's principal harbor in medieval times. Even though it's just a small town (pop. 1,500), Dingle has more fine restaurants than many of Ireland's major cities, and is known for the traditional Irish music in its pubs.

EXPLORING THE TOWN

The new gem in Dingle town is ✪ **Dingle Oceanworld,** Dingle Harbour, Dingle (☎ **066/915-2111;** fax 066/52155; e-mail marabeo@iol.ie). Admission is £4.50 ($7) adults, £3.50 ($5.45) seniors and students, £2.75 ($4.25) children, and £12 ($18.60) family. It's open September and June daily 9:30am to 7pm, July to Aug daily 9:30am to 8:30pm, and October to May daily 9:30am to 6pm. This new harborside aquarium, which is dedicated to the exploration and understanding of the nearby ocean's depths and its critters, is already a main family attraction. All but the sharks are indigenous to local waters. In addition, there are exhibits on Brendan the Navigator and the Spanish Armada, as well as a cafe and gift shop.

Just west of the Dingle Marina is **Ceardlann Na Coille** (☎ **066/915-1797**), a cluster of traditional cottages in a circular craft village. Each craft worker produces and sells his or her own wares, which include knitwear, leather goods, handweaving, and wood turning. It's open daily 10am to 6pm.

In 1984 Fungie, an adult male bottlenosed dolphin, swam solo into the waters of Dingle harbor. Since then a whole industry has grown up around him. **Fungie the Dolphin Tours**

(☎ **066/915-1967**) will ferry you out to find him (if there's no sighting, you don't pay). Fungie happily swims alongside the boats, although his enthusiasm has abated slightly in recent years. Fares for the 1-hour boat trip are £6 ($9.30) for adults and £3 ($4.65) for children 11 and under. More adventurous visitors can swim with him on a dolphin encounter, arranged by Bridgit Flannery at ☎ **066/915-1967** or 066/915-1163, most any day from 8am to 8pm. The procedure is to book a swim the day before, when you rent your gear (semi-dry suit, mask, snorkel, boots and fins—all in one duffel). The full overnight outfitting coast is £14 ($21.70) per person. Then you show up in your gear early the next morning to be brought out by boat to your aquatic rendezvous. The 2-hour escorted swim period costs an additional £10 ($15.50). If you prefer, you can use your rented outfit and swim out on your own. Fungie also welcomes drop-ins. This outing is for teenagers on up, although smaller children will certainly enjoy watching.

ORGANIZED TOURS

Celtic Nature Expeditions, under the direction of Capt. Michael O'Connor, The Old Stone House, Cliddaun, Dingle (☎ **066/915-9882;** www.oconnor.ie), offers a range of sailing adventures aboard the *Kimberly Laura,* a 41-foot cutter-rigged sailing yacht, including 1–3-day explorations—with your own geologist and naturalist aboard—of Dingle Bay, the Iveragh Peninsula, and the Blasket Islands. No sailing experience needed, just a love of the sea. Capt. O'Connor and his wife Becky also offer inexpensive B&B accommodations (entirely nonsmoking and with orthopedic beds) in their restored and renovated 1864 stone farmhouse.

ENJOYING THE GREAT OUTDOORS

BICYCLING   Rentals begin at £5 ($7.75) per day or £25 ($38.75) per week. Contact **Foxy John's Hardware Store,** Main Street (☎ **066/915-1316**). Mountain bikes can be rented at **The Mountain Man,** Strand Street, Dingle (☎ **066/915-1868**), for £6 ($9.30) per day or £30 ($46.50) per week.

HORSEBACK RIDING   At **Dingle Horse Riding,** Ballinaboula House, Dingle (☎ **066/915-2018;** fax 066/915-2099), rides are available along nearby beaches or through the mountains; the cost is £15 ($23.25) for a 1-hour ride. Half-day, full-day, and 3- to 5-day packages including accommodation, meals, and riding can be arranged.

SAILING   Sailing the beautiful waters of Dingle Bay is a relaxing way to enjoy the coastline. **John Doyle,** 3 John St., Dingle (☎ **066/915-1174**), offers skippered sailing trips from Dingle Marina on board his 32-foot sailing cruiser, *Canna.* The price is £65 ($100.75) for a half day and £125 ($193.75) for a full day, for up to four people. All cruises depend on the weather, and advance reservations are required.

WALKING   The **Dingle Way** begins in Tralee and circles the peninsula, covering 95 miles of gorgeous mountain and coastal landscape. The most rugged section is along Brandon Head, where the trail passes between Mount Brandon and the ocean; the views are tremendous, but the walk is long (about 15 miles/9 hours) and strenuous, and should be attempted only when the sky is clear. The section between Dunquin and Ballyferriter (15 miles) follows an especially lovely stretch of coast. For more information see *The Dingle Way Map Guide,* available in local tourist offices and shops.

WHERE TO STAY

✪ **Doyle's Townhouse.** 5 John St., Dingle, County Kerry. ☎ **800/223-6510** from the U.S., or 066/915-1174. Fax 066/915-1816. 16 units. TV TEL. £68 ($105.40) double. Service charge 10%. Rates include full breakfast. DC, MC, V. Closed mid-Nov to mid-Mar.

This old-world guesthouse is just a few minutes' walk away from Dingle's main street. It has a lovely Victorian fireplace in the main sitting room area and many of the antique furnishings date back 250 years or more. Period pieces and country pine predominate in the bedrooms, although the fixtures and fittings are modern and include semi-orthopedic beds. Some back rooms face a garden with mountain vistas in the background.

✪ **Greenmount House.** John St., Dingle, County Kerry. ☎ **066/915-1414.** Fax 066/915-1974. 12 units. TV TEL. £40–£70 ($62–$108.50) double. No service charge. Rates include full breakfast. MC, V. Closed Dec 20–26.

Perched on a hill overlooking Dingle Bay and town, this modern bungalow-style bed-and-breakfast home is a standout in its category. It has all the comforts of a hotel at bargain prices, including bedrooms decorated with contemporary furnishings and orthopedic beds, a public sitting room with an open fireplace, and a sunlit conservatory filled with plants. No smoking is allowed in the bedrooms or dining room.

✪ **Milltown House.** Dingle, County Kerry. ☎ **066/915-1372.** Fax 066/915-1095. 10 units. TV TEL. £45–£75 ($69.75–$116.25). Rates include full breakfast. MC, V.

You couldn't wish for a more picturesque Dingle setting than this bayside haven. A narrow road leads to it and, once inside, you'll see why much of their business is repeat. The guest rooms are tastefully and individually furnished, several offering bay windows that gaze out onto a bay and harbor panorama. The public areas include a peaceful lounge with an open fire and a bright, airy conservatory. The owners, John and Angela Gill, go out of their way to leave you wanting for nothing. A four-course evening meal is offered with a full wine list. There are also on-site stables for riding and trekking.

WHERE TO DINE

✪ **Doyle's Seafood Bar.** 4 John St., Dingle. ☎ **066/915-1174.** Reservations required. Main courses £12–£20 ($18.60–$31). DC, MC, V. Mon–Sat 6–10pm. Closed mid-Nov to mid-Mar. SEAFOOD.

Owned by John and Steela Doyle, this excellent establishment has won international acclaim and is the benchmark of all Dingle's restaurants. The atmosphere is homey with stone walls and floors, sugan (a kind of straw) chairs, and old Dingle sketches. All the ingredients come from the sea, the Doyles' own garden, or nearby farms. Specialties include the Doyles' own smoked salmon, baked fillet of lemon sole with prawn sauce, hot poached lobster, and a signature platter of seafood (sole, salmon, lobster, oysters, and crab claws).

✪ **Waterside Cafe.** Strand St., Dingle. ☎ **066/9151458.** Reservations recommended for dinner. Cafe items £2–£10 ($3.10–$15.50); restaurant main courses £9–£13 ($13.95–$20.15). MC, V. Easter–Sept, cafe daily 10am–6pm; restaurant June–Aug, 7–10pm. Closed Oct–Easter. INTERNATIONAL.

For a daytime snack with a Dingle ambience, this restaurant offers a setting opposite the busy town marina. It's a bright and airy place with a decor of blue and white, enhanced by seasonal flowers and plants. There is seating in a sunlit conservatory-style room as well as on an outdoor patio. It operates as a cafe by day and as a full-service restaurant on summer nights. The choices include oysters on the half-shell, cockles and mussels sandwiches, prawn and crab seafood salads, and soups, as well as quiches, omelets, crêpes, and pastries. The evening menu concentrates on local seafood and steaks.

THE SHOPPING SCENE

Brian De Staic, The Wood (☎ **066/915-1298**), is considered by many to be Ireland's leading goldsmith. His workshop is just west of the Dingle Pier. He specializes in unusual Irish jewelry, handcrafted and engraved with the letters of the Ogham alphabet, an ancient Irish form of writing dating back to the 3rd century.

At **Holden Dingle,** Main Street (☎ **066/915-1896**), Jackie and Conor Holden offer beautiful handcrafted leather handbags lined with suede and silk pockets as well as duffle and travel bags and briefcases.

At **The Weavers Shop,** Green Street (☎ **066/915-1688**), Lisbeth Mulcahy, one of Ireland's leading weavers, creates fabrics and tapestries inspired by seasonal changes in the Irish land- and seascapes. Pure Irish wool, linen/cotton, and alpaca are used in weaving wall hangings and tapestries, as well as scarves, shawls, and knee rugs.

DINGLE AFTER DARK

At night virtually every pub in Dingle offers live music from 9pm on.

An Droichead Beag/The Small Bridge. Lower Main St. ☎ 066/915-1723.

One of Dingle's most atmospheric pubs, it has a dark, cavernous interior that's filled with banter and laughter. Traditional Irish music takes place every night at 9pm. But be warned: It's popular, so get there early if you want a seat.

Dick Mack's "Haberdashery." Green St. ☎ 066/915-1070.

Although Richard "Dick" Mack died a few years ago, his family keeps up the traditions of this unique pub where Dick handcrafted leather boots, belts, and other items in between pub chores. Corridors lined with old pictures and mugs lead into tiny snug bars where locals and visitors stand around sipping stout and exchanging jokes and gossip. It's been a favorite pub with celebrities such as Robert Mitchum, Timothy Dalton, and Paul Simon, whose names are now commemorated with stars on the sidewalk just outside.

Kruger's Guest House and Bar. Ballinaraha, Dunquin. ☎ 066/915-6127.

Deep in the outer reaches of the Dingle Peninsula, this pub is a social center of the Irish-speaking district, and an entertainment hub, with nightly performances of the "sean-nos" Irish singing (an old, unaccompanied style), plus traditional music and step dancing on weekends. Guesthouse is open March through October

11

Italy

by Darwin Porter & Danforth Prince

Italy is a feast for the senses and the intellect, and Rome will be the center of the revelry for the celebration of the millennium. All roads won't lead just to Rome, however, but to Florence, Venice, Assisi, and countless other destinations. Any mention of Italy has forever conjured visions of Pompeii, the Renaissance, and Italy's rich treasury of art and architecture. But some of the country's best experiences can involve the simple act of living in the Italian style, eating the regional cuisines, and enjoying the countryside.

1 Rome

The city of Rome, the city of the millennium, is simultaneously strident, romantic, and sensual. And although the romantic poets would probably be horrified at today's traffic, pollution, overcrowding, crime, political discontent, and the barely controlled chaos of modern Rome, the city endures and thrives in a way that is called "eternal."

It would take a lifetime to know a city filled with 27 centuries of artistic achievement. A cradle of western civilization, Rome is timeless with its ancient history, art, and architecture, containing more treasures per square foot than any other city in the world. Caesar was assassinated here, Charlemagne crowned, and the list of the major events goes on and on. While you're trying to absorb all that Rome has to offer, however, make sure you take the time to relax and meet the Romans.

Only in Rome

Walking Through Ancient Rome There is a vast, almost unified archaeological park that cuts through the center of Rome—all the way from the Rome of the Caesars to Via Appia Antica. You can wander at will through the very streets where Julius Caesar's carriage once rolled or (much later) that of Lucrezia Borgia. A slice of history unfolds at every turn—an ancient fountain, a long-forgotten statue, the ruins of a temple dedicated to some long-faded goddess. The Roman Forum and the Palatine Hill are the most rewarding targets for your archaeological probe, but the glory of Rome is hardly confined to these dusty fields.

Strolling at Sunset in the Pincio Gardens Above the landmark Piazza del Popolo, this terraced and lushly planted hillside is the most romantic place for a twilight walk. The ancient Romans turned this hill into gardens, but today's look came from the design of Giuseppe

Valadier in the 1800s. The main square, Piazzale Napoleone I, offers a spectacular city view that stretches from the Janiculum to Monte Mario. The Egyptian-style obelisk you see was erected by Hadrian on the tomb of his great love, Antinous, a beautiful male slave who died prematurely.

Hanging Out at the Pantheon   The world's best-preserved ancient monument at Piazza della Rotunda is now a hot spot—especially at night. Find a cafe table on the square and observe what a young Fellini should be recording on film. First a Roman temple to "all the gods," then a church since the Middle Ages, this behemoth, built on the foundations of Agrippa's temple, has become a symbol of Rome itself.

Wandering Through Campo de' Fiori at Mid-Morning   In an incomparable setting of medieval houses, this is the liveliest fruit and vegetable market in Rome. It's best viewed after 9am Monday to Saturday; by 1pm, the stalls are closing down. We come here every day we're in Rome for a lively view of local life. Often you'll spot your favorite trattoria chef bargaining for the best and freshest produce—from fresh cherries to the perfect vine-ripened tomato.

Touring the Janiculum   On the Trastevere side of the river, where in 1849 Garibaldi held off the attacking French troops, Janiculum Hill (*Gianicolo*) was always strategic in Rome's defense. Today a walk in this park at the top of the hill is a much-needed retreat from the traffic-filled and often hot streets of Trastevere. Filled with monuments to Garibaldi and his brave men, the hill is no longer peppered with monasteries as it was in the Middle Ages. The best view is from the Villa Lante, a Renaissance summer residence.

Spending a Day on the Appian Way   Dating from 312 B.C., the Appian Way once traversed the whole peninsula of Italy, the road on which Roman legions marched to Brindisi and their conquests in the East. One of its darkest moments was the crucifixion of the rebellious slave army of Spartacus in 71 B.C., when bodies lined the road from Rome to Capua. Fashionable Romans were buried here, and early Christians dug catacombs to flee their persecutors. Begin at the Tomb of Cecilia Metella and proceed up Via Appia Antica past a series of tombs and monuments, including the Tomb of Marcus Servilius. You can go all the way to the Church of Domine Quo Vadis.

Listening to Music in the Churches   Concerts in the churches are advertised all over Rome. Top professionals such as Plácido Domingo and Luciano Pavarotti play at the "big name" churches, but don't overlook those smaller, hard-to-find ones; some of the best music we've ever heard has been by up-and-coming musicians getting their start in little-known churches. By decree of Pope John Paul II, music in the churches must be sacred—no pop music allowed.

Visiting the Campidoglio at Night   There is no more splendid place to be at night than Piazza del Campidoglio, where Michelangelo designed both the geometric paving and the building facades. A broad flight of steps, the Cordonata, takes you up to this panoramic site, the citadel of ancient Rome from which traitors to the empire were once tossed to their deaths. Home during the day to the Capitoline museums, it

Jubilee 2000

The jubilee year, originally a Jewish tradition in which every 50th year was set aside for God, was adapted in 1300 by Pope Boniface VIII for Christian use. Since then, the church has begun every century with a Holy Year urging Christians to do penance—and, if possible, to visit Rome. The jubilee will run from Christmas Eve 1999 to early 2001.

feels different at night when it's dramatically lit, the measured Renaissance facades glowing like jewel boxes. The views of the brilliantly lit Forum and Palatine Hill at night are worth the long trek up those stairs.

ORIENTATION

ARRIVING   By Plane   Chances are you'll arrive in Italy at Rome's **Leonardo da Vinci International Airport** (☎ **06/65951** or 06/65953640 for information), popularly known as Fiumicino, 18½ miles from the city center. Domestic flights arrive at one terminal, international ones at the other. If you're flying by charter, you might arrive at Ciampino Airport.

To get into the city, there's a **shuttle service** directly from Fiumicino to the main train station, Stazione Termini. Upon leaving Customs, follow the signs marked TRENI. Trains go back and forth between the airport and the rail station daily from 7am to 10pm. A one-way ticket costs 15,000L ($9). Trains arrive at Track 22 at Stazione Termini. A local **train,** costing 7,000L ($4.20), also runs between the airport and Tiburtina Station, from which you can go the rest of the way to Rome's Termini by subway line B (go down the stairs at the back of the train); the subway to Termini costs another 1,000L (60¢), but this is an inconvenient connection.

Taxis from Fiumicino to city center are expensive—75,000L ($45) and up.

Should you arrive on a charter flight at **Ciampino Airport** (☎ **06/794941**), take a COTRAL bus, departing every 30 minutes or so, which delivers you to the Anagnina stop of Metropolitana Line A. At Anagnina you can take Line A to the Stazione Termini, the rail station in the heart of Rome, where your final connections can be made. The trip takes about 45 minutes and costs 1,500L (90¢).

By Train   Trains arrive in the center of old Rome at the **Stazione Termini,** Piazza dei Cinquecento (☎ **1478/880881**), the train and subway transportation hub for the city. Many hotels lie near the station, and you can walk to your hotel if you don't have too much luggage. Otherwise, an array of taxi, bus, and subway lines awaits you.

If you're taking the **Metropolitana** (Rome's subway network), follow the illuminated M sign in red that points the way. To catch a bus, go straight through the outer hall of the Termini and enter the sprawling bus lot of Piazza dei Cinquecento. You can also find taxis here.

By Bus   Arrivals are at the **Stazione Termini** (see "By Train," above).

By Car   From the north, the main access route is **A-1 (Autostrada del Sole),** cutting through Milan and Florence, or you can take the coastal route, SSI Aurelia, from Genoa. If you're driving north from Naples, you take the southern lap of the **Autostrada del Sole (A-2).** All these autostrade join with the **Grande Raccordo Anulare,** a ring road that encircles Rome, channeling traffic into the congested city.

VISITOR INFORMATION   Tourist information is available at the **Ente Provinciale per il Turismo,** Via Parigi 5, 00185 Roma (☎ **06/48899253**), open Monday through Friday from 8:15am to 7:15pm and Saturday from 8:15am to 2:15pm, but the information dispensed here is meager. There's another information bureau at the **Stazione Termini** (☎ **06/4871270**), open daily 8:15am to 7:15pm.

CITY LAYOUT   The drive into the city from the airport is rather uneventful until you pass through the city wall, the still remarkably intact **Great Aurelian Wall,** started in A.D. 271 to calm Rome's barbarian jitters. Suddenly, ruins of imperial baths loom on one side and great monuments can be seen in the middle of blocks.

Stazione Termini, the modern railroad station, faces a huge piazza, **Piazza dei Cinquecento,** named after 500 Italians who died heroically in a 19th-century battle in Africa.

The bulk of ancient, Renaissance, and baroque Rome lies on the east side of the **Fiume Tevere (Tiber River),** which meanders between 19th-century stone embankments. However, several important monuments are on the other side: **St. Peter's Basilica** and the **Vatican,** the **Castel Sant' Angelo** (formerly the tomb of the emperor Hadrian), and the colorful section of town known as **Trastevere.** The city's quarters are linked by large boulevards—large at least in some places—that have mostly been laid out since the late 19th century.

Starting from the **Vittorio Emmanuele monument,** a highly controversial pile of snow-white Brescian marble, there's a street running practically due north to **Piazza del Popolo** and the city wall. This is **Via del Corso,** one of Rome's main streets—noisy, congested, always crowded with buses and shoppers, called simply "Il Corso." Again from the Vittorio Emmanuel monument, the major artery going west—and ultimately across the Tiber to St. Peter's—is **Corso Vittorio Emanuele.** To go in the other direction, toward the Colosseum, you take **Via dei Fori Imperiali,** named for the excavated ruins of the imperial forums that flank this avenue. Yet another central conduit is **Via Nazionale,** running from **Piazza della Repubblica** (also called **Piazza Esedra**) and ending near the Victor Emmanuel monument at **Piazza Venezia,** which lies in front of it. The final lap of Via Nazionale is called **Via Quattro Novembre.**

GETTING AROUND

Much of the inner core of Rome is traffic-free, so you need to walk whether you like it or not. However, walking in many parts of the city is hazardous and uncomfortable because of overcrowded streets, heavy traffic, and very narrow sidewalks.

BY SUBWAY The **Metropolitana,** or **Metro** for short, is the fastest means of transportation in Rome. It has two underground lines: **Line A** and **Line B.** A big red letter M indicates the subway entrance. The fare is 1,500L (90¢). Tickets are available from vending machines at all stations. These machines accept 50L, 100L, and 200L coins. Ticket booklets are available at *tabacchi* (tobacco) shops and in some terminals. Some machines change 1,000L (60¢) notes into coins. *A tip:* Avoid riding the trains when the Romans are going to or from work or you'll be mashed flatter than fettuccine.

BY BUS/TRAM Roman buses are operated by **ATAC (Azienda Tramvie e Autobus del Comune di Roma),** Via Volturno 65 (☎ **06/46951** for information). For only 1,500L (90¢), you can ride to most parts of Rome on quite good bus service. The ticket is valid for 1¼ hours, and you can get on as many buses during that time period as you want, using the same ticket.

BY TAXI Don't count on hailing a taxi on the street or even getting one at a stand. If you're going out, have your hotel call one. At a restaurant, ask the waiter or cashier to dial for you. If you want to call yourself, try one of these numbers: **06/6645, 06/3570,** or **06/4994.** The meter begins at 4,500L ($2.70) for the first 3 kilometers, then 1,300L (80¢) per kilometer. On Sunday a 2,000L ($1.20) supplement is assessed, plus another 5,000L ($3) supplement from 10pm to 7am. There's yet another 2,000L ($1.20) supplement for every suitcase. The driver expects a 10% tip.

BY CAR You can rent a car from **Hertz,** near the parking lot of the Villa Borghese, Via Vittorio Veneto 156 (☎ **06/3216831**); **Budget,** Via Ludovisi 60

Travel Tip

At the Stazione Termini, you can buy a special **tourist bus pass,** which costs 6,000L ($3.60) for 1 day or 24,000L ($14.40) for a week. The tourist pass is valid on the subway, too.

Rome Metro

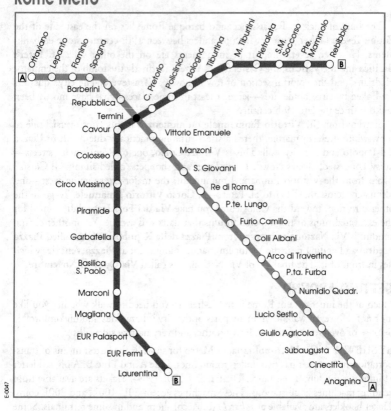

(☎ **06/4820966**); or the local Italian company **Maggiore,** Via di Tor Cervara 225 (☎ **06/229351**).

BY BICYCLE   You can rent bicycles at many places throughout Rome. Ask at your hotel for the nearest rental location, or else go to **I Bike Rome,** Via Vittorio Veneto 156 (☎ **06/3225240**), which rents bicycles from the underground parking garage at the Villa Borghese. Most bikes cost 4,000L ($2.40) per hour or 10,000L ($6) per day. Open daily from 8:30am to 7:30pm.

Fast Facts: Rome

American Express   The offices are at Piazza di Spagna 38 (☎ **06/67641**). The travel service and tour desk are open Monday to Friday 9am to 5:30pm and Saturday 9am to 12:30pm. Hours for the financial and mail services are Monday to Friday 9am to 5pm and Saturday 9am to noon.

Baby-sitters   Most hotel desks in Rome can help you secure a baby-sitter. Inquire as far in advance as possible, and make another request for an English-speaking sitter. You won't always get one, but it pays to ask.

Business Hours   In general, **banks** are open Monday through Friday 8:30am to 1:30pm and 3 to 4pm. Most **stores** are open year-round, Monday through Saturday 9am to 1pm and 3:30 or 4pm to 7:30 or 8pm.

Currency The Italian unit of currency is the lira, almost always used in the plural form, **lire** (abbreviated as "L" in this guide). The lowest unit of currency these days is the silver 50-lire coin. There is also a silver 100-lire piece, a gold 200-lire coin, and a combination of silver-and-gold 500-lire coin and 1,000-lire coin. Notes come in 1,000, 2,000, 5,000, 10,000, 50,000, 100,000, and 500,000L. The rate of exchange used in this chapter was $1 = 1,667L. Also, 1EUR = 1,936L and £1 = 2,950L.

Dentist For an English-speaking dentist, call the U.S. Embassy in Rome, Via Vittorio Veneto (☎ **06/46741**). There's also the 24-hour **G. Eastman Dental Hospital,** Viale Regina Elena 287 (☎ **06/844831**).

Doctor Call the U.S. Embassy (see "Dentist," above), which will provide a list of English-speaking doctors. All big hospitals in Rome have a 24-hour first-aid service (go to the emergency room). You'll find English-speaking doctors at the **Rome American Hospital,** Via Emilio Longoni 69 (☎ **06/22551**).

Drugstores A reliable pharmacy is **Farmacia Internazionale,** Piazza Barberini 49 (☎ **06/4871195**), open day and night. Most pharmacies are open 8:30am to 1pm and 4 to 7:30pm. In general, pharmacies follow a rotation system so that several are always open on Sunday.

Embassies & Consulates The Embassy of the **United States,** Via Vittorio Veneto 121 (☎ **06/46741**), is open Monday through Friday 8:30am to noon and 2 to 4pm. Consular and passport services for **Canada,** Via Zara 30 (☎ **06/445981**), are open Monday through Friday 10am to 12:30pm. The office of the **United Kingdom,** Via XX Settembre 80A (☎ **06/4825441**), is open Monday through Friday 9:15am to 1:30pm. The Embassy of **Australia,** Via Alessandria 215 (tel **06/852721**), is open Monday through Thursday 8:30am to 12:30pm and 1:30 to 5:30pm and Friday 8:30am to 1:15pm. The **New Zealand** office, Via Zara 28 (☎ **06/4402928**), is open Monday through Friday 8:30am to 12:45pm and 1:45 to 5pm. In case of emergency, embassies have a 24-hour referral service.

Emergencies The police "hotline" number is **212121.** Usually, however, dial **113** for the police, **115** to report a fire, or **5510** to summon an ambulance.

Internet Access Stop in at the **Internet Café,** Via dei Marrucini 12 (☎ **06/445953**), in the San Lorenzo district. The cafe boasts 22 positions for navigators or video game fans. The e-mail address is info@internetcafe.it.

Post Office The **central post office,** on Piazza San Silvestro 19, behind the Rinascente department store on Piazza Colonna (☎ **06/6771**), is open Monday through Friday 9am to 6pm and on Saturday 9am to 3pm.

Safety Purse snatching is commonplace in Rome. Young men on Vespas or whatever ride through the city looking for victims. To avoid trouble, stay away from the curb and hold on tightly to your purse. Don't lay anything valuable on tables or chairs where it can be grabbed up easily. Gypsy children are a particular menace. You have to practically fight them off, if they completely surround you. They often approach you with pieces of cardboard hiding their stealing hands.

Taxes A value-added tax (called IVA in Italy) is added to all consumer products and most services, including restaurants and hotels. The tax is not the same for all goods and services. The average tax on most items is 19%, but it could rise as much as 35% on certain luxury goods.

Telephone   The **country code** for Italy is **39.** The **city code** for Rome is **06,** which is the code you use every time you dial a party in Rome, regardless of whether you're within the city limits. Note that phone numbers in Italy can have anywhere from four to eight digits, although efforts are being made for a more unified system.

To call **from one city code to another** within Italy, dial the city code, complete with the initial zero, and then the local number. To **dial direct internationally,** dial 00, then the country code for the country you are calling, then the area or city code, and then the local number. Direct-dial calls from the United States to Italy are usually cheaper than calls placed from an Italian hotel to most phones in North America, so if possible, try to arrange for friends and acquaintances to call you at your hotel.

To ring national **telephone information** (in Italian) in Italy, dial **12.** International information is available at **176,** but costs 1,200L (70¢) per request.

To make a **collect or calling-card call** from a public phone, drop in 200L or insert a prepaid phone card (available from most *tabacchi*/tobacco shops) and dial one of the following access numbers to reach an American operator or an English-language voice prompt: **AT&T,** ☎ 172-10-11 (if calling a country other than the U.S., after the access code, dial 01, the country code of the country you are calling, the city code, and the local number); **MCI,** ☎ 172-1022; and **Sprint,** ☎ 172-1877.

WHERE TO STAY
NEAR STAZIONE TERMINI
Expensive

Hotel Artemide. Via Nazionale 22, 00184 Roma. ☎ **06/489911.** Fax 06/48991700. www.spacehotels.it or www.travel.it. E-mail: artemide@spacehotels.it. 79 units. A/C MINIBAR TV TEL. 490,000–540,000L ($294–$324) double; 630,000L ($378) suite. Prices include breakfast. AE, MC, DC, V. Parking 30,000L ($18). Metro: Piazza della Repubblica.

A refined four-star hotel, this establishment was transformed from a 19th-century palazzetto and turned into an elegant hotel named for Artemide, the Greek goddess. Near the Stazione Termini, close to the Opera, the Artemide combines stylish simplicity with modern comforts against a backdrop of art nouveau motifs. The original stained-glass skylight dome was retained in the lobby. Bedrooms are furnished in natural color schemes and have good furnishings, and extras such as room safes. The spacious bathrooms are adorned in marble and have hair dryers and generous towels. The restaurant, called Caffè Caffeteria Nazionale, serves a Mediterranean cuisine along with international dishes. There's also an American bar.

Hotel Diana. Via Principe Amedeo 4, 00185 Roma. ☎ **06/4827541.** Fax 06/486998. www.venere.it/roma/diana.html. E-mail: diana@venere.it. 186 units. A/C MINIBAR TV TEL. 320,000L ($192) double; 400,000L ($240) suite. Rates include breakfast. AE, DC, MC, V. Parking 35,000L ($21).

Close to the Stazione Termini, the Diana has been given a renewed lease on life, totally renovated in an inviting art deco style. It has recaptured the flavor of its heyday at the turn of the century, when both the aristocracy and the bourgeoisie would drop in for a drink after the opera. The Diana offers an elegant, yet comfortable, atmosphere. Rooms are tastefully furnished in colorful floral fabrics, and walls are covered in English-style striped tapestry in soft greens and creamy tones. Bathrooms are tiled with attractive ceramics, offering hair dryers, heated towel racks, and a choice between a tub or shower. The hotel restaurant offers a menu selection of classic Italian dishes and daily seasonal specialties. In the summer, the American Bar moves to the panoramic rooftop terrace where lunch and dinner can also be served.

Moderate

Aberdeen Hotel. Via Firenze 48, 00184 Roma. ☎ **06/4823920.** Fax 06/4821092. www. travel.it/roma/aberdeen. E-mail: hotel.aberdeen@travel.it. 26 units. A/C MINIBAR TV TEL. 180,000–270,000L ($108–$162) double. Rates include buffet breakfast. AE, DC, MC, V. Bus: 64 or 170.

This completely renovated hotel near the Rome Opera House is centrally located for landmarks and rail and bus connections. Rooms range in size from small to medium, and although the furnishings are uninspired, the value here is good. Bathrooms are on the small side, but are well appointed, with hair dryers and great towels. The breakfast buffet is the only meal served.

Hotel Ranieri. Via XX Settembre 43, 00187 Roma. ☎ **06/4814467.** Fax 06/4818834. www. hotelranieri.com. E-mail: hotelranieri@italyhotel.com. 47 units. A/C MINIBAR TV TEL. 220,000–240,000L ($132–$144) double. Rates include breakfast. Weekend discounts granted in Dec, Jan, and Feb; daily discounts in Aug. AE, MC, V. Parking 30,000–40,000L ($18–$24). Metro: Piazza della Repubblica.

Ranieri is a winning three-star hotel in a very old, newly restored building, and seven rooms were added in 1998. The Ranieri's location is good; from the hotel you can stroll to the Rome Opera, Piazza della Repubblica, and Via Vittorio Veneto. The public rooms are attractively decorated, and the bedrooms are small but comfortable. Beds have firm mattresses, and bathrooms have a spacious shower, a hair dryer, medium-sized towels, and shampoos and soaps. You can arrange for a home-cooked meal—both regional or national—in the dining room.

Medici. Via Flavia 96, 00187 Roma. ☎ **06/4827319.** Fax 06/4740767. E-mail: megahotel-sroma@mclink.it. 68 units. MINIBAR TV TEL. 200,000–320,000L ($120–$192) double. Rates include breakfast. AE, DC, MC, V. Parking 35,000–40,000L ($21–$24). Metro: Piazza della Repubblica.

The Medici, built in 1906, is a substantial hotel near the railway terminal and the shops along Via XX Settembre. Many rooms overlook an inner patio garden, with Roman columns and benches. Bedrooms, renovated in 1997, are a generous size. The cheapest rooms are a good buy here (being only a bit smaller than the other rooms), although superior units are better furnished and have air conditioning. All beds have first-class mattresses, and bathrooms have shower/tub combinations and plenty of medium-sized towels. Hair dryers are available on request.

Inexpensive

Hotel Pavia. Via Gaeta 83, 00185 Roma. ☎ **06/483801.** Fax 06/4819090. E-mail: hotel-paviaroma@hotmail.com. 25 units. A/C MINIBAR TV TEL. 240,000L ($144) double. Rates include breakfast. AE, DC, MC, V. Parking 20,000L ($12). Metro: Stazione Termini.

Hotel Pavia is a popular choice on this quiet street near the gardens of the Baths of Diocletian. The hotel, established in the 1980s, occupies a much-renovated century-old building. Front rooms tend to be noisy, but that's the curse of all Termini hotels. Nevertheless, the rooms are comfortable, with firm mattresses, and the medium-sized bathrooms have hair dryers and good towels.

NEAR VIA VENETO & PIAZZA BARBERINI

Very Expensive

✪ **Hotel Eden.** Via Ludovisi 49, 00187 Roma. ☎ **800/225-5843** in the U.S. or 06/478121. Fax 06/4821584. www.hotel-eden.it. 112 units. A/C MINIBAR TV TEL. 790,000–900,000L ($474–$540) double; from 1,900,000L ($1,140) suite. AE, DC, MC, V. Parking 45,000L ($27). Metro: Piazza Barberini.

Rome Accommodations

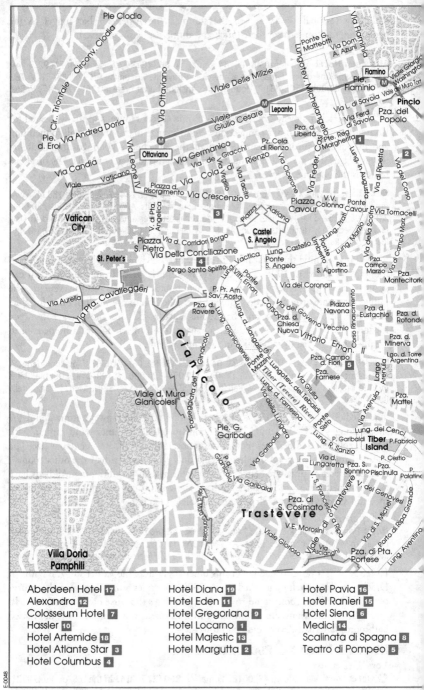

Aberdeen Hotel **17**	Hotel Diana **19**	Hotel Pavia **16**
Alexandra **12**	Hotel Eden **11**	Hotel Ranieri **15**
Colosseum Hotel **7**	Hotel Gregoriana **9**	Hotel Siena **6**
Hassler **10**	Hotel Locarno **1**	Medici **14**
Hotel Artemide **18**	Hotel Majestic **13**	Scalinata di Spagna **8**
Hotel Atlante Star **3**	Hotel Margutta **2**	Teatro di Pompeo **5**
Hotel Columbus **4**		

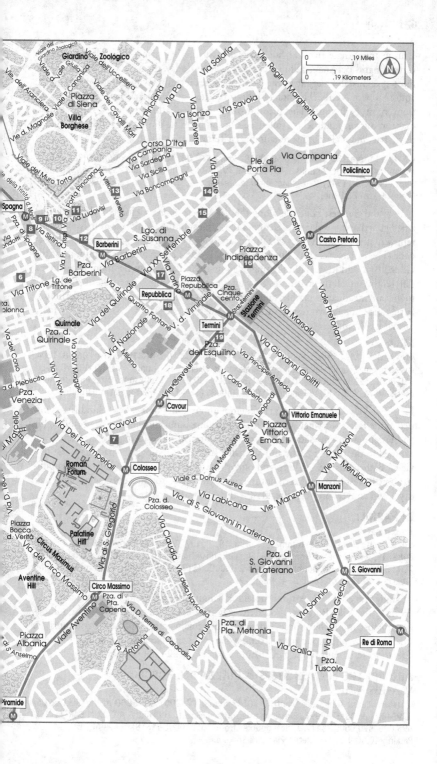

During this ornate five-star hotel's heyday, all the big names—Hemingway, Maria Callas, Ingrid Bergman, Fellini—checked in here. Today, the bedrooms are among the most spacious and elegant in the city. Amenities include fax machines, private safes, and TVs with VCRs. The hotel's hilltop position guarantees a panoramic city view from most bedrooms. The medium-sized marble bathrooms offer fluffy towels, makeup mirrors, and deluxe toiletries. On the premises are a gym and health club, a piano bar, and a glamorous restaurant, La Terrazza.

✪ **Hotel Majestic.** Via Veneto 50, 00187 Roma. ☎ **06/486841.** Fax 06/4880984. E-mail: alexandra@venere.it. 94 units. A/C MINIBAR TV TEL. 635,000–720,000L ($381–$432) double; from 900,000L ($540) suite. Rates include breakfast. AE, DC, MC, V. Parking 40,000L ($24). Metro: Piazza Barberini.

One of the grandest buildings along the Via Veneto sports a Liberty-style facade and a pedigree that has welcomed Eleonora Duse, most of the politicians of Italy and trade representatives from the rest of Europe, and George Bush during his tenure as president. The ornate, six-story hotel opened in 1889 as an architectural triumph of the Gilded Age, and it was radically upgraded in 1990. Each plush bedroom is decorated differently, and all the mattresses are supremely comfortable. The medium-sized bathrooms are sheathed in marble, and have plush towels, hair dryers, and wonderful toiletries. The hotel's two restaurants include the brasserie-style La Ninfa and the more formal La Veranda.

Moderate
Alexandra. Via Vittorio Veneto 18, 00187 Roma. ☎ **06/4881943.** Fax 06/4871804. www.venere.it/roma/alexandra. E-mail: alexandra@venere.it.45 units. A/C MINIBAR TV TEL. 350,000L ($210) double; 430,000L ($258) triple; 500,000L ($300) suite. Rates include buffet breakfast. AE, DC, MC, V. Parking 40,000–50,000L ($24–$30). Metro: Piazza Barberini.

Here's where you can stay on Via Veneto without going broke. Set behind the dignified stone facade of what was a 19th-century mansion, this hotel offers comfortable and tasteful accommodations. Mattresses are firm. (Rooms facing the Via Veneto are exposed to the roaring traffic and animated street, but those in the back have less of a view.) Bathrooms are smallish, and only the largest rooms have a tub/shower combination (the rest have showers), but the towels are fluffy. You must bring your own hair dryer and conversion plug. Breakfast is the only meal served.

In Parioli
Inexpensive
Hotel delle Muse. Via Tommaso Salvini 18, 00197 Roma. ☎ **06/8088333.** Fax 06/8085749. www.venere.it/roma/muse. E-mail: hmuse@flashnet.it. 61 units. TV TEL. 150,000–220,000L ($90–$132) double; 200,000–290,000L ($120–$174) triple. Rates include buffet breakfast. AE, DC, MC, V. Bus: 4. Tram: 19.

A family-run establishment, this hotel is a winning but unheralded choice, half a mile north of the Villa Borghese. You don't stay here for grand comfort, but the value is good. Most rooms have been renovated but remain rather Spartan. Bathrooms are small but tidy, with good towels. Bring your own hair dryer. In the summer, the hotel operates a restaurant in the garden, and a bar is open 24 hours a day.

Around the Spanish Steps & Piazza del Popolo
Very Expensive
Hassler. Piazza Trinità dei Monti 6, 00187 Roma. ☎ **800/223-6800** in the U.S., or 06/699340. Fax 06/6789991. E-mail: hasslerroma inclink.it. 100 units. A/C MINIBAR TV TEL. 695,000–810,000L ($417–$486) double; from 1,030,000L ($618) suite. AE, DC, MC, V. Parking 40,000L ($24). Metro: Piazza di Spagna.

The only deluxe hotel in this old part of Rome, it uses the Spanish Steps as its grand entrance; the crown worn by the Hassler is still in place after all these years. The bedrooms, some of which are small, are furnished to give each room its own character. The nicest touch is the bowls of fresh flowers. Some rooms (on the upper floors) have balconies with views of the city. The medium-sized bathrooms come complete with soft, fluffy towels, hair dryers, and a wide range of deluxe toiletries. The Hassler Roof Restaurant, on the top floor, is a favorite with visitors and Romans alike for its fine cuisine and view.

Expensive

Hotel Locarno. Via della Penna 22, 00186 Roma. ☎ **06/3610841.** Fax 06/3215249. E-mail: locarno@venere.it. 52 units. MINIBAR TV TEL. 330,000–360,000L ($198–$216) double; 390,000L ($234) suite. Rates include buffet breakfast. AE, DC, MC, V. Metro: Flamino.

This little charmer, near the Piazza del Popolo, is said to be haunted by the imperial ghost of Nero, although that isn't expected to disturb your night's sleep: You can count on Rome's heavy traffic to do that. The Liberty-style hotel occupies four floors of a six-story building, and a 1920s aura pervades the hotel. Bedrooms and bathrooms are completely up to date, decorated in bright colors with good furnishings (mattresses are new and firm) and a bit of style. Bathrooms offer hair dryers and medium-sized towels. Electronic safes are provided.

You can sit in the garden and enjoy the orchids in cachepots, or, if you'd like to go exploring, the Locarno even supplies you with a bike. There's also a wonderful roof terrace where you can take your breakfast and enjoy some of the major sights of Rome's skyline.

✪ Scalinata di Spagna. Piazza Trinità dei Monti 17, 00187 Roma. ☎ **06/6793006.** Fax 06/69940598. www.venere.it/home/roma/scalinata/scalinata.html. 16 units. A/C MINIBAR TV TEL. 380,000–430,000L ($228–$258) double; from 560,000L ($336) suite. AE, MC, V. Parking 45,000L ($27). Metro: Piazza di Spagna.

This upscale B&B at the top of the Spanish Steps has always been one of the most sought-after hotels in Rome. This delightful little building—only two floors are visible from the outside—is painted mustard yellow and burgundy red. The decor varies radically from one room to the next; some rooms have low, beamed ceilings and ancient-looking wood furniture, and others offer loftier ceilings and more average appointments. (For some of the best views in Rome, request room 10 or 12.) All the bedrooms and bathrooms were renovated in 1998. The medium-sized tiled bathrooms have hair dryers and a wide array of fluffy towels. In season, breakfast is served on the rooftop garden terrace with its sweeping view of the dome of St. Peter's across the Tiber.

Moderate

Hotel Gregoriana. Via Gregoriana 18, 00187 Roma. ☎ **06/6794269.** Fax 06/6784258. 20 units. A/C TV TEL. 340,000–380,000L ($204–$228) double. Rates include breakfast. No credit cards. Parking 30,000–40,000L ($18–$24). Metro: Piazza di Spagna.

Although surrounded by much more expensive neighbors, the small Gregoriana (in a former 17th-century convent) has its own fans—mainly members of the Italian fashion industry. The door to each bedroom has a reproduction of an Erté print whose fanciful characters indicate the letter designating that room. The smallish rooms are comfortable, and the beds have firm mattresses. Bathrooms are a bit small, but have medium-sized towels and hair dryers.

Hotel Siena. Via S. Andrea delle Fratte 33, 00187 Roma. ☎ **06/796121.** Fax 06/67875509. E-mail: hotelsiena@flashnet.it. 21 units. A/C MINIBAR TV TEL. 290,000L ($174) double. Rates include breakfast. AE, DC, MC, V. Parking 40,000L ($24) per day. Metro: Piazza di Spagna.

This hotel could survive on its location alone: It's between the Spanish Steps and the Piazza Navona, and close to the Trevi Fountain. A major remodeling will occur sometime in 1999. The hotel is decorated simply, with hardwood floors and light-wood furnishings in the main lobby. Many of the double rooms are larger than others (smaller units are called "standard"), but since there's no difference in price, request a more spacious room. Rooms facing the street tend to be noisy, so if you're a light sleeper, ask for a unit in the rear. Bathrooms are on the small side and offer adequate-quality towels. You can request a hair dryer from the main desk.

The staff is helpful in offering advice about where to go in monumental Rome. A large buffet is served every morning in the breakfast room.

Inexpensive
Hotel Margutta. Via Laurina 34, 00187 Roma. ☎ **06/3223674.** Fax 06/3200395. 21 units. TEL. 156,000–190,000L ($93.60–$114) double; 210,000L ($126) triple. Rates include breakfast. AE, DC, MC, V. Metro: Flaminio.

Located in an 18th-century building on a cobblestoned street near Piazza del Popolo, this hotel offers attractively decorated rooms and a helpful staff. The best rooms are on the top floor; two of them share a terrace, and another larger bedroom has a private terrace. Beds are comfortable, and bathrooms (most of which don't have a tub/shower combination) have sets of soft, fluffy towels and hair dryers.

NEAR CAMPO DE' FIORI
Moderate
Teatro di Pompeo. Largo del Pallaro 8, 00186 Roma. ☎ **06/68300170.** Fax 06/68805531. 13 units. A/C TV TEL. 290,000L ($174) double. Rates include breakfast. AE, DC, MC, V. Bus: 46, 62, or 64.

Built on top of the ruins of the Theater of Pompey, this small charmer lies near the spot where Julius Caesar met his final fate. Intimate and refined, it's on a quiet piazzetta near the Palazzo Farnese and Campo de' Fiori. The bedrooms are decorated in an old-fashioned Italian style with hand-painted tiles, and the beamed ceilings date from the days of Michelangelo. There's no restaurant, but breakfast is served.

NEAR VATICAN CITY
Very Expensive
Hotel Atlante Star. Via Vitelleschi 34, 00193 Roma. ☎ **06/6873233.** Fax 06/6872300. E-mail: atlante.star@atlantelhotels.com. 90 units. A/C MINIBAR TV TEL. 480,000L ($288) double; from 650,000L ($390) suite. Rates include breakfast. AE, DC, MC, V. Parking 40,000L ($24). Metro: Ottaviano. Tram: 19 or 30.

The Atlante Star is a first-class hotel a short distance from St. Peter's Basilica and the Vatican. You have the the the impression of being inside a luxurious ocean liner here: Even the door handles are art deco inspired. The small but posh bedrooms are outfitted with comfy beds. A royal suite features a Jacuzzi. The hotel has the most striking views of St. Peter's of any hotel in Rome. The restaurant, Les Étoiles, is an elegant roof-garden choice at night, offering a 360-degree panoramic view of Rome.

Expensive
Hotel Columbus. Via della Conciliazione 33, 00193 Roma. ☎ **06/6865435.** Fax 06/6864874. 92 units. MINIBAR TV TEL. 370,000L ($222) double; 460,000L ($276) suite. Rates include breakfast. AE, DC, MC, V. Hotel has 30 free parking spaces. Bus: 64.

In an impressive 15th-century palace, Hotel Columbus is a few minutes' walk from St. Peter's. It was once the private home of the wealthy cardinal who later became Pope Julius II (who had Michelangelo paint the Sistine Chapel). The building looks much as it must have those long centuries ago—a severe, time-stained facade, small windows, and heavy wooden doors leading from the street to the colonnades and arches of the inner courtyard. The bedrooms are simpler than the tiled and tapestried salons, but they are spacious. A few rooms are enormous and have original details, such as decorated wood ceilings and frescoed walls. The medium-sized bathrooms offer hair dryers, good towels, and a set of toiletries. La Veranda restaurant serves good Roman and international cuisine. In summer, meals are served in a garden.

NEAR ANCIENT ROME
Inexpensive
Colosseum Hotel. Via Sforza 10, 00184 Roma. ☎ **06/4827228.** Fax 06/4827285. 50 units. TEL TV. 226,000L ($135.60) double. Rates include breakfast. AE, DC, MC, V. Parking 30,000L ($18). Metro: Cavour.

Not far from the Santa Maria Maggiore Basilica, the Colosseum offers baronial living on a miniature scale. The tasteful hotel reflects the best of Italy's design heritage. The white-walled bedrooms are furnished with well-conceived antique reproductions (beds of heavy carved wood, dark-paneled wardrobes, leatherwood chairs). Some of the units are air-conditioned. The drawing room, with its long refectory table, white walls, red tiles, and provincial armchairs, invites lingering.

WHERE TO DINE
NEAR STAZIONE TERMINI
Expensive
Agata e Romeo. Via Carlo Alberto 45. ☎ **06/4466115.** Reservations recommended. Main courses 40,000–50,000L ($24–$30). AE, DC, MC, V. Mon–Sat 1–3pm and 8–10:30pm. Metro: Piazza Vittorio. ROMAN.

Named after the husband-wife team who run the place (Romeo Caraccio) and cook (Agata), this small-scale, charming enclave of culinary creativity sits in the shadow of the Church of Santa Maria Maggiore. Menus, while based on mainline culinary traditions, change with the seasons and the whims and inspiration of both the kitchen and wine cellar. Examples of the fare include a purée of eggplant capped with slices of rabbit filet, or a deceptively simple version of white beans topped with fried cuttlefish. Spaghetti is often prepared with shellfish, especially clams. Breast of duck with porcini and herb sauce, or rack of lamb with rosemary sauce, are perennial favorites. One of the establishment's most enduring dessert specialties is its version of *millefiori*— chantilly cream laced with liqueur and served in puff pastry.

Moderate
Scoglio di Frisio. Via Merulana 256. ☎ **06/4872765.** Reservations recommended. Main courses 18,000–32,000L ($10.80–$19.20). AE, DC, MC, V. Mon–Fri 12:30–3pm and 7:30–11pm; Sat–Sun 7:30–11pm. Bus: 714 from Stazione Termini. NEAPOLITAN/PIZZA.

South of the Stazione Termini, Scoglio di Frisio is the choice *suprême* to introduce yourself to Neapolitan cuisine. While here, you should get reacquainted with pizza— this is the genuine article. At night, you can begin with a plate-size Neapolitan pizza (crunchy, oozy, and excellent) with clams and mussels. After a medley of stuffed vegetables and antipasti, you might then settle for chicken cacciatore or veal scaloppine. Scoglio di Frisio also presents Neapolitan songs, so it makes for an inexpensive night on the town.

Inexpensive
Il Dito e La Luna. 47–51 Via dei Sabelli, San Lorenzo. ☎ **06/4940726.** Reservations recommended. Main courses 19,000–24,000L ($11.40–$14.40). No credit cards. Daily 8pm–midnight. Metro: Termini. SICILIAN/ITALIAN.

At this small, charming restaurant the menu is equally divided between traditional Sicilian recipes and more creative, up-to-date recipes prepared with gusto and flair.

Menu items include fresh orange-infused anchovies served on orange segments; a creamy flan of mild onions and mountain cheese; seafood couscous loaded with shell-fish; and such succulent pastas as square-cut spaghetti (*tonnarelli*) prepared with mus-sels, bacon, tomatoes, and exotic mushrooms.

NEAR VIA VENETO & PIAZZA BARBERINI

Very Expensive

✿ **Sans Souci.** Via Sicilia 20. ☎ **06/4821814.** Reservations required. Main courses 35,000–68,000L ($21–$40.80). AE, DC, MC, V. Tues–Sun 8pm–1am. Closed Aug 10–30. Metro: Piazza Barberini. FRENCH/ITALIAN.

Sans Souci, which was getting a little tired, has bounced back, and Michelin has restored its coveted star. It's now the market leader for glitz, glamour, and nostalgia for *la dolce vita*. This is a major stop on the see-and-be-seen circuit and might be your best bet for spotting a movie star, albeit a faded one. The menu is ever-changing, as "new creations" are devised. You might begin with a terrine of goose liver with truffles, the chef's special creation. The fish soup, according to one Rome restaurant critic, is "a legend to experience." The soufflés are also deservedly popular; artichoke, asparagus, and spinach are our favorites.

Expensive

Colline Emiliane. Via Avignonesi 22. ☎ **06/4817538.** Reservations required. Main courses 45,000–60,000L ($27–$36). MC, V. Sat–Thurs 12:45–2:45pm and 7:45–10:45pm. Closed Aug. Metro: Piazza Barberini. EMILIANA-ROMAGNOLA.

This small restaurant right off Piazza Barberini serves *classica cucina bolognese*. It's a family-run place where everybody helps out. The owner is the cook and his wife makes the pasta, which, incidentally, is about the best you'll encounter in Rome. The house specialty is an inspired *tortellini alla panna* (cream sauce) with truffles. To start your meal, we suggest *culatello di Zibello*, a delicacy from a small town near Parma that's known for having the finest prosciutto in the world. An excellent main course is *braciola di maiale*—boneless rolled pork cutlets that have been stuffed with ham and cheese, breaded, and sautéed. *Bollito misto* (mixed boiled meats) is another specialty. *Note:* Emiliana-Romagnola cuisine is named for Emilia-Romagna, a district of central Italy centering around Bologna and known for such specialties as tagliatelle, tortellini, and lasagne.

Moderate

Césarina. Via Piemonte 109. ☎ **06/4880828.** Reservations recommended. Main courses 18,000–26,000L ($10.80–$15.60). AE, DC, MC, V. Mon–Sat 12:30–3pm and 7:30–11pm. Bus: 52, 53, 56, 58, or 95. EMILIANA-ROMAGNOLA/ROMAN.

This restaurant has grown since it was established by Cesarina Masi, a well-meaning matriarch. Although Masi died in the mid-1980s, the restaurant continues her culi-nary traditions in a new version of the original hole-in-the-wall: Today, there are three dining rooms and more than 200 seats. The restaurant serves excellent versions of *bollito misto* (an array of well-seasoned boiled meats) and a *misto Cesarina*—three kinds of pasta, each handmade and served with a different sauce. Equally appealing is the *saltimbocca* (veal with ham) and the *cotoletta alla bolognese* (veal cutlet baked with ham and cheese).

✿ **Girarrosto Toscano.** Via Campania 29. ☎ **06/4823835.** Reservations required. Main courses 25,000–35,000L ($15–$21). AE, DC, MC, V. Thurs–Tues 12:30–2:30pm and 7:30–11pm. Bus: 90B, 95, 490, or 495. TUSCAN.

You might have to wait for a table at this popular place facing the walls of the Borghese Gardens. Under vaulted ceilings in a cellar setting, fine Tuscan specialties are served. Begin with an enormous selection of antipasti: succulent little meatballs, vine-ripened melon with prosciutto, mozzarella, and especially savory Tuscan salami. You're then given a choice of pasta. The *bistecca alla fiorentina* (grilled steak seasoned with oil, salt, and pepper) is the best item to order. Oysters and fresh fish from the Adriatic are also served every day. Meat and fish dishes are priced according to weight, and costs can run considerably higher than the prices quoted above.

IN PARIOLI
Very Expensive
Relais Le Jardin. In the Hotel Lord Byron, Via G. de Notaris 5. ☎ **06/3613041.** Reservations required. Main courses 45,000–53,000L ($27–$31.80). AE, DC, MC, V. Mon–Sat 1–3pm and 8–10:30pm. Closed Aug. Bus: 26 or 52. ITALIAN/INTERNATIONAL.

For both a traditional and creative cuisine in an elegantly romantic setting, Relais Le Jardin is the place to go. A chi-chi crowd with demanding palates patronizes this place. Inside one of Rome's most elite small hotels, the restaurant sports a decor that's almost aggressively lighthearted. Relais Le Jardin serves a frequently changing array of seasonal dishes. The pasta and soups are among the best in town—the *tonnarelli* (square-cut spaghetti) pasta with asparagus and smoked ham served with *concassé* tomatoes is delectable, as is the pasta with ricotta sauce, black olives, corn, and oregano. For your main course, choose the loin of lamb with artichoke romana, the pork filet stuffed with crab, or the grilled beef sirloin with hot chicory and sautéed potatoes.

Moderate
Al Ceppo. Via Panama 2. ☎ **06/8419696.** Reservations recommended. Main courses 19,000–32,000L ($11.40–$19.20). AE, DC, MC, V. Tues–Sun 12:30–3pm and 8–11pm. Closed the last 3 weeks of Aug. Bus: 4, 52, or 53. ROMAN.

This restaurant's somewhat hidden location (although it's only 2 blocks from the Villa Borghese, near Piazza Ungheria) means that the clientele is likely to be Roman rather than foreign. At this longtime and enduring favorite, the cuisine is as good as ever. "The Log" features an open fireplace where the chef prepares lamb chops, liver, and bacon to charcoal perfection. The beefsteak, which hails from Tuscany, is also succulent. Other dishes include *linguine monteconero* (made with clams and fresh tomatoes) and a savory version of spaghetti with pepperoni, fresh basil, and pecorino cheese.

NEAR THE SPANISH STEPS & PIAZZA DEL POPOLO
Expensive
El Toulà. Via della Lupa 29B. ☎ **06/6873498.** Reservations required for dinner. Main courses 40,000–46,000L ($24–$27.60); set-price menus 100,000–120,000L ($60–$72). AE, DC, MC, V. Tues–Fri noon–3pm and Mon–Fri 7:30–11pm. Closed Aug. Bus: 81, 90, 90b, 628, or 913. ROMAN/VENETIAN.

El Toulà offers quintessential Roman haute cuisine with a creative flair in an elegant setting of vaulted ceilings and large archways. Guests stop in the charming bar to order a drink while deciding what to order from the impressive menu, which changes every month. One section of the menu is devoted exclusively to culinary specialties of Venice, including Venice's classic dish, *fegato* (liver) *alla Veneziana;* calamari stuffed with vegetables; a *baccalà* (codfish) mousse with polenta; and another Venetian classic, *broetto* (fish soup made with monkfish and clams). El Toulà usually isn't crowded at lunchtime.

Moderate
Dal Bolognese. Piazza del Popolo 1–2. ☎ **06/3611426.** Reservations required. Main courses 22,000–28,000L ($13.20–$16.80). AE, DC, MC, V. Tues–Sun 12:30–3pm and 8:15–1am. Closed 20 days in Aug. Metro: Flaminio. BOLOGNESE.

If *La Dolce Vita* were being filmed now, this restaurant would be used as a backdrop, its patrons photographed in the latest Fendi drag. It's one of those rare dining spots that's not only chic, but noted for its food as well. Young actors, models, artists from nearby Via Margutta, even industrialists on an off-the-record evening on the town show up here. To begin your meal, we suggest a *misto di pasta*—four forms of pasta, each flavored with a different sauce, arranged on the same plate. For your main course, specialties include *lasagne verdi, tagliatelle alla bolognese,* and a most recommendable *cotoletta alla bolognese* (veal cutlet topped with cheese). Although almond cake is the house specialty, it's hard to resist the fresh strawberry tart.

Otello alla Concordia. Via della Croce 81. ☎ **06/6791178.** Main courses 14,000–30,000L ($8.40–$18); set-price menu 36,000L ($21.60). AE, DC, MC, V. Mon–Sat 12:30–3pm and 7:30–11pm. Closed 2 weeks in Feb. Metro: Piazza di Spagna. ROMAN.

This is a popular and reliable restaurant on a side street amid the glamorous boutiques near the northern edge of the Spanish Steps. Diners enter through a stone corridor leading from the street into a dignified building and then choose a table (space permitting) in either an arbor-covered courtyard or in a cramped but convivial series of inner dining rooms. The *spaghetti alle vongole veraci* (spaghetti with clams) and the pasta with chickpeas are excellent, as are Roman-style *abbacchio arrosto* (roasted baby lamb), a selection of grilled or sautéed fish dishes, and classic eggplant parmagiana.

Ristorante Nino. Via Borgognona 11. ☎ **06/6795676.** Reservations recommended. Main courses 20,000–50,000L ($12–$30). AE, DC, MC, V. Mon–Sat 12:30–3pm and 7:30–11pm. Closed Aug. Metro: Piazza di Spagna. TUSCAN.

Ristorante Nino, off Via Condotti (a short walk from the Spanish Steps), is a tavern mecca for writers, artists, and an occasional model from one of the nearby fashion houses. Nino's enjoys deserved acclaim for its Tuscan dishes, such as pasta with hare sauce, and the hearty cooking is completely unpretentious. The restaurant is particularly known for its steaks, shipped in from Florence and charcoal broiled (priced according to weight). Cannelloni Nino is one of the chef's specialties.

Near Campo de' Fiori & the Jewish Ghetto
Moderate
Da Giggetto. Via del Portico d'Ottavia 21–22. ☎ **06/6861105.** Reservations recommended. Main courses 16,000–24,000L ($9.60–$14.40). AE, DC, MC, V. Tues–Sun 12:30–3pm and 7:30–11pm. Closed Aug 1–15. Bus: 62, 64, 75, 90, or 170. ROMAN.

Da Giggetto, in the old ghetto, is a short walk from the Theater of Marcellus. Not only is it right next to these ruins, but old Roman columns extend practically to its doorway. The Romans flock to this bustling trattoria for their special traditional dishes. No dish is more traditional than *carciofi alla giudea,* baby-tender fried artichokes. This is a true delicacy! The cheese concoction, mozzarella in *carrozza,* is another good choice, as are the zucchini flowers stuffed with mozzarella and anchovies, and even the dried salted cod filet. Also sample *fettuccine al 'Amatriciana,* with shrimp sautéed in garlic and olive oil.

Il Drappo. Vicolo del Malpasso 9. ☎ **06/6877365.** Reservations required. Set-price menus (including Sardinian wine) 65,000–70,000L ($39–$42). AE, MC, V. Mon–Sat 8pm–midnight. Closed Aug. Bus: 46, 62, or 64. SARDINIAN.

Il Drappo, on a narrow, hard-to-find street off a square near the Tiber, is operated by a woman known to her regulars only as "Valentina." The facade is graced with a modernized trompe-l'oeil painting above the stone entrance, flanked with potted plants. Inside, you have your choice of two tastefully decorated dining rooms. Set-price dinners may include a wafer-thin appetizer called *carte di musica* (sheet-music paper), topped with tomatoes, green peppers, parsley, and olive oil, followed by fresh spring lamb in season, or a changing selection of strongly flavored regional specialties that are otherwise difficult to find in Rome. Among these is roast suckling Sardinian pig with an herb sauce.

Vecchia Roma. Via della Tribuna di Campitelli 18. ☎ **06/6864604.** Reservations recommended. Main courses 24,000–40,000L ($14.40–$24). AE, DC. Thurs–Tues 1–3:30pm and 8–11pm. Closed 10 days in Aug. Bus: 64, 90, 90b, 97, or 774. ITALIAN.

Vecchia Roma is a charming, moderately priced trattoria in the heart of the Jewish ghetto (a short walk from Michelangelo's Campidoglio). The owners are known for their selection of fresh seafood, and the minestrone of the day is made with fresh vegetables. An interesting selection of antipasti is always presented, including salmon and a vegetable antipasto. The pastas and risottos are also excellent; the "green" risotto with porcini mushrooms is invariably good. Lamb is one of the chef's specialties.

NEAR PIAZZA NAVONA & THE PANTHEON
Very Expensive
✪ **Quinzi & Gabrileli.** Via delle Coppelle 5/6, 00185 Roma. ☎ **06/6879389.** Reservation required as far in advance as possible. Main courses 40,000–60,000L ($24–$36). AE, DC, MC, V. Mon–Sat 7:30–11:30pm. Closed Aug. Bus: 44, 46, 55, 60, 61, 62, 64, or 65. SEAFOOD.

We've never found better seafood—or fresher—than the creatures of the sea served in this 15th-century building. Don't be put off by the rough-and-ready service; this restaurant attracts Rome's most discriminating fish fanciers. Be forewarned, however; fresh seafood is extremely expensive in Rome. Partners Alberto Quinzi and Enrico Gabrieli have earned their reputation on their simply cooked and presented fish. Everything tastes natural and fresh, and heavy sauces aren't used to disguise old fish as they are in many restaurants. In fact, the restaurant is known for its raw seafood, such as a delicate carpaccio of swordfish, sea bass, and deep-sea shrimp. The house specialty is spaghetti with lobster, but all sorts of fish are served, including sea urchins, octopus, sole, and red mullet. You can check out what's available in a special display on ice at the entrance. Sometimes the headwaiters prepare wriggling crab or scampi right on the grill before you—that way you know it's fresh. In summer, French doors lead to a small dining terrace.

Expensive
Il Convivio. Via dei Soldati 28. ☎ **06/6869432.** Reservations recommended. Main courses 20,000–43,000L ($12–$25.80). AE, DC, MC, V. Tues–Sat 1–2:30pm and Tues–Sun 8–10:30pm. Bus: 70, 87, or 90. ITALIAN.

In a new location that's a great improvement over the former cramped setting, Chef Angelo Troiana still is on the A-list of Roman chefs, even though he now has a lot more diners to feed. Seasonal Italian cooking and creative culinary innovation make for solid good taste. Since 1989, Angelo, along with his two brothers, has excited the discriminating palates of Rome. Launch yourself into the excitement with a warm seafood salad made with clams, mussels, white fish, and a giant prawn with al dente vegetables and a "mayonnaise of the sea," a fragrant lemony sauce. Even the ravioli is stuffed creatively, with ingredients and inspiration that change with the seasons. Worthy main courses include saddle of rabbit that might be stuffed with porcini mushrooms and served with an onion marmalade, or a boned rack of lamb cooked in an herb and vegetable crust. For dessert, consider a slice of almond and bitter chocolate cake accented with fresh currants.

Moderate
Bramante. Via della Pace 25, Roma. ☎ **06/68803916.** Reservations recommended. Main courses 20,000–30,000L ($12–$18). AE, DC, MC, V. Daily 5pm–2am. Closed Dec 24. Bus: 44, 46, 55, 60, 61, 62, 64, 65. ROMAN.

In an exquisite 18th-century structure on a cobblestoned street behind the Piazza Navona, this cafe-restaurant opens onto a delightful small square of vine-draped taverns. The establishment is named for the 16th-century church on the square, designed by the architect Bramante. Behind the ivy-covered facade is a frescoed interior where white candles illuminate the marble bar, creating a cozy, inviting atmosphere. The owner, Mr. Giuseppe, tries to make visitors appreciate Italian food and traditions, and succeeds admirably. Almost all his dishes are handmade, and the cooks use only the freshest ingredients. The simple recipes are rich in Mediterranean flavor. You can taste wonderful pastas made with fresh tomato sauce and garlic, or something heavier, such as braised beef or tender grilled steak flavored with herbs and served with potatoes. They don't serve fish, however.

La Carbonara. Piazza Campo de' Fiori 23. ☎ **06/6864783.** Reservations recommended. Main courses 16,000–24,000L ($9.60–$14.40). AE, MC, V. Wed–Mon noon–2:30pm and 6:30–10:30pm. Closed 3 weeks in Aug. Bus: 64. ROMAN.

In an antique palazzetto at the edge of the market square, this amicable trattoria claims to be the home of the original spaghetti carbonara. The much-disputed legend claims that the dish was invented when American GIs donated their K-rations of powdered eggs and salted bacon to the chef—the result was that tempting concoction of egg, cheese, and bacon-enriched pasta that has become well-loved throughout the world. Actually, the name of the restaurant comes from the fact that in 1800 this place served meals to the *Carbonari*, the people who brought coal into the houses for heating. The owner's father was a *carbonaro*, so he dedicated the restaurant to his memory. The current chef still prepares the dish as his predecessor did, as well as succulent antipasti, grilled meats, and fresh seasonal vegetables. A dish that is truly *divino* is the sautéed artichokes with pumpkin flowers.

L'Eau Vive. Via Monterone 85. ☎ **06/68801095.** Reservations recommended. Main courses 25,000–70,000L ($15–$42); set-price menus 22,000L ($13.20), 30,000L ($18), and 50,000L ($30). AE, MC, V. Mon–Sat 12:30–2:30pm and 8–10:30pm. Closed Aug 1–20. Bus: 46, 62, 64, 78, or 492. FRENCH/INTERNATIONAL.

L'Eau Vive is run by lay missionaries who wear the dress of their native countries. The restaurant occupies the cellar and ground floor of a 17th-century palace, and it is filled with monumental paintings. In this formal atmosphere, the waitresses sing religious hymns and "Ave Marias" at 10pm each evening. Your gratuity for service will be turned over for religious purposes. Pope John Paul II used to dine here when he was still archbishop of Kraków. Specialties include hors d'oeuvres and frogs' legs. Main dishes range from guinea hen with onions and grapes in a wine sauce to couscous. Other selections include salad niçoise, several kinds of homemade pâté, and beefsteak in wine sauce. The chocolate mousse is a smooth finish to the meal.

Osteria dell'Antiquario. Piazzetta di S. Simeone 26/27, Via dei Coronari. ☎ **06/6879694.** Reservations recommended. Main courses 18,000–40,000L ($10.80–$24). AE, DC, MC, V. Tues–Sat 12:30–2:30pm and 8–11pm; Mon 8–11pm. Closed 15 days in mid-Aug, Christmas, Jan 1–15. Bus: 70, 87, or 90. INTERNATIONAL/ROMAN.

A virtually undiscovered osteria, but with a good location, this little restaurant lies a few blocks down the Via dei Coronari as you leave the Piazza Navona and head toward St. Peter's. Set in a stone stable built in the 1500s, this restaurant has three dining rooms—although in fair weather, diners prefer to retreat outdoors for a table on the terrace. Shaded by umbrellas, tables face a view of the Palazzo Lancillotti. We like to begin with the delectable sautéed shellfish (usually mussels and clams), although you might opt for the risotto with porcini mushrooms. For a main course, you can be a bit daring and have the filet of ostrich covered by a slice of ham and grated Parmesan, or else opt for shellfish flavored with saffron. The fish soup with fried bread is excellent, as is an array of freshly made soups and pastas. Roman-style veal rolls and turbot flavored with fresh tomatoes and basil are other excellent choices. This is dining in the classic Roman style.

Tre Scalini. Piazza Navona 30. ☎ **06/6879148.** Reservations recommended. Main courses 22,000–32,000L ($13.20–$19.20). AE, DC, MC, V. Thurs–Tues 12:15–3pm and 7–11pm. Closed Dec–Feb. Bus: 70, 87, or 90. ROMAN.

Established in 1882, this is the most famous and respected restaurant on Piazza Navona—a landmark for ice cream as well as more substantial meals. Yes, it's literally crawling with tourists, but the waiters are friendly and helpful. Although there's a cozy bar on the upper floor, outfitted with simple furniture with a view over the piazza, most visitors opt for a seat either in the ground-floor cafe or restaurant, or, during warm weather, at tables on the piazza. House specialties include risotto with porcini mushrooms, spaghetti with clams, roast duck with prosciutto, a carpaccio of sea bass, and roast lamb in the Roman style. No one will object if you order just a pasta and salad, unlike at other restaurants nearby. Their famous *tartufi* (ice cream disguised with a coating of bittersweet chocolate, cherries, and whipped cream) and other ice creams cost 10,000L ($6) each.

NEAR VATICAN CITY
Very Expensive
✪ **Les Étoiles.** In the Hotel Atlante Star, Via Vitelleschi 34. ☎ **06/6893434.** Reservations required. Main courses 45,000–80,000L ($27–$48). AE, DC, MC, V. Daily 12:30–2:30pm and 7:30–11pm. Metro: Ottaviano. MEDITERRANEAN.

Les Étoiles deserves all the stars it receives, both for its cuisine and for its panoramic view of Rome. At this garden in the sky, you'll have an open window over the rooftops of Rome—a 360-degree view of landmarks, especially the floodlit dome of St. Peter's. In summer everyone wants a table outside, but in winter almost the same view can be seen through the picture windows. Refined Mediterranean cuisine, with perfectly balanced flavors, is served here. Dishes include quail cooked either with radicchio or in a casserole with mushrooms and herbs, artichokes stuffed with ricotta and pecorino cheese, Venetian-style risotto with squid ink, and roast suckling lamb with mint.

Moderate
Ristorante Il Matriciano. Via dei Gracchi 55. ☎ **06/3212327.** Reservations required. Main courses 14,000–26,000L ($8.40–$15.60). AE, DC, MC, V. Daily 12:30–3pm and 8pm–midnight. Closed Aug 5–25. Metro: Ottaviano. ROMAN.

Il Matriciano is a family restaurant with a devoted following, many from the Italian stage. The food is good, but it's mostly country fare—nothing fancy. The decor is also fairly simple. In summer, try to sit at a sidewalk table behind a green hedge under a shady canopy. For starters, we suggest the *tagliolini con tartufi* (truffles), and for the main course, try the *abbacchio al forno* (oven-roasted lamb) or the *trippa alla romana* (tripe). The house specialty is based on that Roman favorite, *Amatriciana* sauce. Here, it's prepared with *bucatini* pasta and richly flavored with bacon, tomatoes, and basil.

Inexpensive
Ristorante Giardinaccio. Via Aurelia 53. ☎ **06/631367.** Reservations recommended, especially on weekends. Main courses 10,000–40,000L ($6–$24). AE, DC, MC, V. Daily 12:15–3:15pm and 7:15–11:15pm. Bus: 46, 62, or 98. ITALIAN/MOLISIAN/INTERNATIONAL.

This popular restaurant is only 200 yards from St. Peter's. It's unique because it offers specialties from the provincial Molise region in southeast Italy, and is appropriately decorated in rustic country-tavern style. Flaming grills provide succulent versions of perfectly done quail, goat, and other dishes, but you might want to be adventurous and try the mutton goulash. Many pastas are featured, including *taconelle*, a home-made pasta with lamb sauce. There's also a large self-service selection of antipasti.

IN ANCIENT ROME
Inexpensive

Abruzzi. Via del Vaccaro 1. ☎ **06/6793897.** Reservations recommended. Main courses 9,000–20,000L ($5.40–$12). AE, DC, MC, V. Sun–Fri 12:30–3pm and 7–10:30pm. Closed 2 weeks in Aug (dates vary). Bus: 57, 64, 70, or 17. ABRUZZESE.

Abruzzi takes its name from a little-explored region east of Rome known for its haunting beauty and curious superstitions. The restaurant is located at one side of Piazza SS. Apostoli, just a short walk from Piazza Venezia. The good food here at reasonable prices makes it popular among students. The chef is justly praised for his satisfying assortment of cold antipasti. For a starter, you'll find a good *stracciatella* (an egg-and-Parmesan cheese soup). A typical main dish is *vitello tonnato con capperi*, a veal in tuna fish sauce with capers.

Alvaro al Circo Massimo. Via dei Cerchi 53. ☎ **06/6786112.** Reservations required. Main courses 16,000–35,000L ($9.60–$21). AE, MC, V. Tues–Sat 12:30–3:30pm and 7:30–11pm; Sun 12:30–3:30pm. Closed Aug. Metro: Circo Massimo. ITALIAN.

Alvaro al Circo Massimo, at the edge of the Circus Maximus, is the closest thing in Rome to a genuine provincial inn. Here is all the decor associated with Italian taverns, including corncobs hanging from the ceiling and rolls of fat sausages. The antipasti and pasta dishes are fine, the meat courses are well prepared, and there's an array of fresh fish—never overcooked. Other specialties include *tagliolini* with mushrooms and truffles, and roasted turbot with potatoes. They're especially well stocked with exotic seasonal mushrooms, including black truffles so good you'd have to go directly to Spoleto to find better.

IN TRASTEVERE
Expensive

Alberto Ciarla. Piazza San Cosimato 40. ☎ **06/5818668.** Reservations required. Main courses 20,000–45,000L ($12–$27); set-price menus 75,000–110,000L ($45–$66). AE, DC, MC, V. Mon–Sat 8:30pm–12:30am. Closed 1 week in Jan and 1 week in Aug. Bus: 44, 75, 170, 280, or 718. SEAFOOD.

Alberto Ciarla is the best and most expensive restaurant in Trastevere. Some critics still consider it one of Rome's finest, although it's not as chic as it was in the late 1980s, and Michelin no longer awards it a star. It serves some of the most elegant fish dishes in the city. Specialties include a handful of ancient recipes subtly improved by Signor Ciarla, such as soup of pasta and beans with seafood. Original dishes include a delectable salmon Marcel Trompier with lobster sauce, as well as well-flavored sushi, a full array of shellfish, and filet of sea bass prepared at least three different ways, including an award-winning version with almonds.

Moderate

La Cisterna. Via della Cisterna 13. ☎ **06/5812543.** Reservations recommended. Main courses 20,000–32,000L ($12–$19.20). AE, DC, MC, V. Mon–Sat 7pm–1:30am. Bus: 44, 75, 170, 280, or 710. ROMAN.

La Cisterna lies deep in the heart of Trastevere. For more than half a century, it has been run by the Simmi family, who are interested in serving only the best and providing a good time for all guests. The restaurant's name comes from the ancient Roman well discovered in the cellar. No one's ever awarded any stars to this place—and food critics probably never will—but if you like traditional cookery based on the best regional produce, come here. In summer you can inspect the antipasti right out on the street before going in. House specialties include Roman-style suckling lamb (*abbacchio*), *rigatoni a l'Amatriciana* (with diced bacon, olive oil, garlic, tomatoes, red peppers, and onions), and fresh fish—especially sea bass baked with herbs.

SEEING THE SIGHTS IN THE ETERNAL CITY

Rome is studded with ancient monuments that silently evoke its history as one of the greatest centers of Western civilization—once all roads led to Rome, with good reason. It became the first cosmopolitan city in Europe, importing everything from slaves and gladiators to great art from the far corners of the empire. With all its carnage and mismanagement, Rome left a legacy of law and order and an uncanny lesson in how to conquer enemies by absorbing their cultures. But ancient Rome is only part of the spectacle. The papacy also made the city a center of the world in art as well as religion: Although Vatican architects rifled much of the glory of the past for their projects, they also created the great Renaissance treasures we come to see today.

SIGHTSEEING SUGGESTIONS FOR FIRST-TIME VISITORS

If You Have 1 Day   Rome wasn't built in a day and you aren't likely to see it in a day either, but make the most of your limited time. You'll basically have to decide on the legacy of imperial Rome—the Roman Forum, the Imperial Forum, and the Colosseum—or else St. Peter's and the Vatican. Walk along the Spanish Steps at sunset. At night go to Piazza del Campidoglio for a fantastic view of the Forum below. Have a nightcap on Via Veneto, which, although past its prime, is still appealing. Toss a coin in the Trevi fountain and promise yourself a return visit.

If You Have 2 Days   If you elected to see the Roman Forum and the Colosseum on your first day, then spend the second day exploring St. Peter's and the Vatican Museums (or vice versa). Have dinner in a restaurant in Trastevere.

If You Have 3 Days   In the morning go to the Pantheon in the heart of Old Rome, and then, after lunch, try to explore the Castel Sant'Angelo and the Etruscan Museum. Have dinner at a restaurant in or around Piazza Navona.

If You Have 4 or 5 Days   On day 4 head for the environs, notably Tivoli, where you can see the Villa d'Este and Hadrian's Villa. On day 5 explore the ruins of Ostia Antica, return to Rome for lunch, and visit the Capitoline Museum and Basilica di San Giovanni in Laterano in the afternoon.

ST. PETER'S & THE VATICAN

✪ **Basilica di San Pietro (St. Peter's Basilica).** Piazza San Pietro. ☎ **06/69884466.** Basilica (including the sacristy, treasury, and grottoes), free; guided tour of excavations around St. Peter's tomb, 10,000L ($6), children under 15 are not admitted; stairs to the dome 5,000L ($3) adults, 4,000L ($2.40) students; elevator to the dome 6,000L ($3.60) adults, 5,000L ($3) students. Basilica (including the sacristy and treasury), Oct–Mar daily 7am–6pm; Apr–Sept daily 7am–7pm. Grottoes, daily 7am–5pm. Dome, Oct–Mar daily 8am–5pm; Apr–Sept 8am–6pm. Bus: 23, 30, 32, 49, 51, or 64. *Note:* To be admitted to St. Peter's, women must wear skirts that cover the knees or pants. Men cannot wear shorts. Sleeveless tops are not allowed for either gender. You *will* be turned away. To tour the area around St. Peter's tomb, you must apply several days in advance to the excavations office (☎ **06/69885318**), open Mon–Sat 9am–noon and 2–5pm. Pass under the arch to the left of the facade of St. Peter's to find it.

As you stand in Bernini's **Piazza San Pietro (St. Peter's Square),** you'll be in the arms of an ellipse; like a loving parent, the Doric-pillared colonnade reaches out to embrace the faithful. Holding 300,000 is no problem for this square.

Inside, the size of this famous church is awe-inspiring—although its dimensions (about two football fields long) are not apparent at first. St. Peter's is said to have been

Rome Attractions

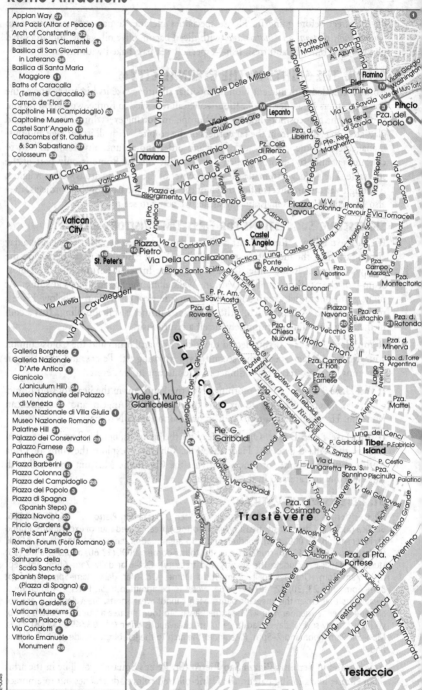

Appian Way 37
Ara Pacis (Altar of Peace) 5
Arch of Constantine 32
Basilica di San Clemente 34
Basilica di San Giovanni
  in Laterano 36
Basilica di Santa Maria
  Maggiore 11
Baths of Caracalla
  (Terme di Caracalla) 38
Campo de'Fiori 22
Capitoline Hill (Campidoglio) 28
Capitoline Museum 27
Castel Sant'Angelo 15
Catacombs of St. Calixtus
  & San Sabastiano 37
Colosseum 33

Galleria Borghese 2
Galleria Nazionale
  D'Arte Antica 9
Gianicolo
  (Janiculum Hill) 24
Museo Nazionale del Palazzo
  di Venezia 25
Museo Nazionale di Villa Giulia 1
Museo Nazionale Romano 10
Palatine Hill 31
Palazzo dei Conservatori 29
Palazzo Farnese 23
Pantheon 21
Piazza Barberini 8
Piazza Colonna 13
Piazza del Campidoglio 28
Piazza del Popolo 3
Piazza di Spagna
  (Spanish Steps) 7
Piazza Navona 20
Pincio Gardens 4
Ponte Sant'Angelo 14
Roman Forum (Foro Romano) 30
St. Peter's Basilica 16
Santuario della
  Scala Sancta 35
Spanish Steps
  (Piazza di Spagna) 7
Trevi Fountain 12
Vatican Gardens 19
Vatican Museums 17
Vatican Palace 16
Via Condotti 6
Vittorio Emanuele
  Monument 26

E-0048

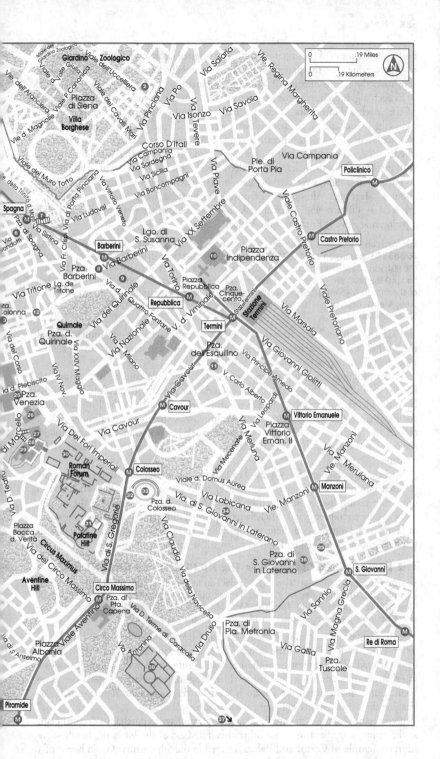

built over the tomb of the crucified saint. The original church was erected on the order of Constantine, but the present structure is essentially Renaissance and baroque; it showcases the talents of some of Italy's greatest artists.

In such a grand church, don't expect subtlety, but the basilica is rich in art. Under Michelangelo's dome is the celebrated **baldacchino** by Bernini. In the nave on the right (the first chapel) is the best-known piece of sculpture, the *Pietà* that Michelangelo sculpted while still in his early twenties. You can visit the sacristy and treasury, filled with jewel-studded chalices, reliquaries, and copes and the **Vatican grottoes,** with their tombs, both ancient and modern (Pope John XXII gets the most adulation).

The grandest sight is yet to come: the climb to **Michelangelo's dome,** which towers about 375 feet high. Although you can walk up the steps, we recommend the elevator for as far as it'll carry you. You can walk along the roof, where you'll be rewarded with a panoramic view of Rome and the Vatican.

✪ **Vatican Museums and the Sistine Chapel.** Viale Vaticano, Vatican City. ☎ **06/69883333.** Admission 15,000L ($9) adults, 10,000L ($6) children under 17, free for everyone the last Sun of each month (be ready for a crowd). Mar 16–Oct 30 Mon–Fri 8:45am–3:45pm, Sat and the final Sun of the month 8:45am–12:45pm; off-season, Mon–Sat and the final Sun of the month 8:45am–12:45pm. Last admission 1 hour before closing. Closed religious holidays. Metro: Ottaviano. The museum entrance is a long walk around the Vatican walls from St. Peter's Square.

In 1929 the Lateran Treaty between Pope Pius XI and the Italian government created the world's smallest independent state. Although tiny, this state contains a gigantic repository of treasures.

You can follow one of four itineraries—A, B, C, or D—according to the time you have at your disposal (from 1½ to 5 hours) and your special interests. You can choose from the picture gallery, which houses paintings from the 11th to the 19th centuries, the Egyptian collection, the Etruscan museum, Greek and Roman sculpture, and, of course, the Sistine Chapel. Consult the large panels at the entrance, and then follow the letter and color of the itinerary chosen. Facilities for people with disabilities are available.

Michelangelo labored for 4 years (1508–12) over the epic Sistine Chapel, now restored (although not without controversy) to its original glory. The work was so physically taxing that it permanently damaged his eyesight. Glorifying the human body as only a sculptor could, Michelangelo painted nine panels taken from the pages of Genesis and surrounded them with prophets and sibyls. Also, visit the Stanze di Raphael, rooms decorated by Raphael when still a young man.

THE FORUM, THE COLOSSEUM & THE HIGHLIGHTS OF ANCIENT ROME

✪ **Foro Romano (Roman Forum).** Via dei Fori Imperiali. ☎ **06/6990110.** Admission 12,000L ($7.20) adults, free for children 17 and under and seniors 60 and over. Apr–Sept Mon–Sat 9am–6pm, Sun 9am–1pm; Oct–Mar Mon–Sat 9am–3pm, Sun 9am–1pm; last admission 1 hour before closing. Closed Jan 16–Feb 15. Metro: Colosseo.

The Roman Forum was built in the marshy land between the Palatine and the Capitoline Hills. It flourished as the center of Roman life in the days of the Republic, before it gradually lost prestige to the Imperial Forum. By day the columns of now-vanished temples and the stones from which long-forgotten orators spoke are mere shells. But at night, when the Forum is silent in the moonlight, it isn't difficult to imagine that vestal virgins still guard the sacred temple fire.

If you want the stones to have some meaning, you have to purchase a detailed plan, as the temples are hard to locate otherwise. The best of the lot is the handsomely adorned **Temple of Castor and Pollux,** erected in the 5th century B.C. in honor of a battle triumph. The **Temple of Faustina,** with its lovely columns and frieze (griffins

Ancient Rome & Attractions Nearby

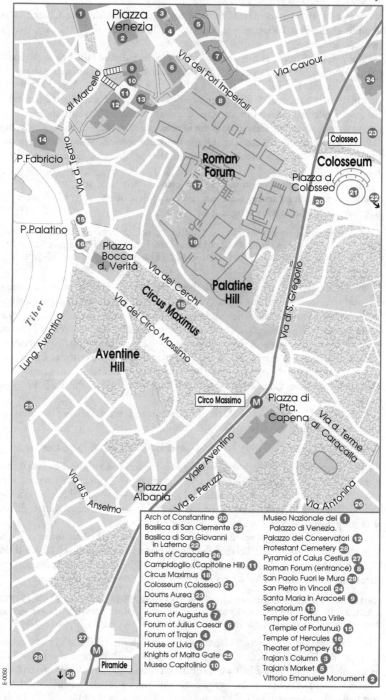

Piazza Venezia

Via dei Fori Imperiali

Via Cavour

di Marcello

Via d. Teatro

P.Fabricio

Roman Forum

Colosseo

Colosseum

Piazza d. Colosseo

P.Palatino

Piazza Bocca d. Verità

Via del Cerchi

Palatine Hill

Via di S. Gregorio

Tiber

Circus Maximus

Via dei Circo Massimo

Lung. Aventino

Aventine Hill

Circo Massimo

Piazza di Pta. Capena

Via d. Terme di Caracalla

Via di S. Anselmo

Piazza Albania

Viale Aventino

Via B. Peruzzi

Via Antonina

Piramide

E-0050

689

and candelabra), was converted into the San Lorenzo in Miranda Church. The **Temple of the Vestal Virgins** is a popular attraction; some of the statuary, mostly headless, remains.

A long walk up from the Roman Forum leads to the **Palatine Hill,** one of the seven hills of Rome; your ticket from the Forum will admit you to this attraction (it's open the same hours). The Palatine, tradition tells us, was the spot on which the first settlers built their huts, under the direction of Romulus. In later years the hill became a patrician residential district that attracted citizens like Cicero. It's worth the climb for the panoramic, sweeping view of both the Roman and Imperial Forums, as well as the Capitoline Hill and the Colosseum. Of the ruins that remain, none is finer than the so-called **House of Livia** (the "abominable grandmother" of Robert Graves's *I, Claudius*).

When the glory that was Rome has completely overwhelmed you, you can enjoy a respite in the cooling **Farnese Gardens,** laid out in the 16th century, which incorporate some of Michelangelo's designs.

✪ **Colosseo (Colosseum).** Piazzale del Colosseo, Via dei Fori Imperiali. ☎ **06/7004261.** Admission 10,000L ($6) all levels. Oct–Jan 15 daily 9am–3pm; Jan 16–Feb 15 daily 9am–4pm; Feb 16–Mar 17 daily 9am–4:30pm; Mar 18–Apr 16 daily 9am–5pm; Apr 17–Sept daily 9am–6pm. Metro: Colosseo.

In spite of the fact that it's a mere shell, the Colosseum remains the greatest architectural inheritance from ancient Rome. Vespasian ordered the construction of the elliptically shaped bowl, called the Amphitheatrum Flavium, in A.D. 72; it was inaugurated by Titus in A.D. 80 with a many-weeks-long bloody combat between gladiators and wild beasts. At its peak, the Colosseum could seat 50,000 spectators, and exotic animals—humans also—were shipped in from the far corners of the empire to satisfy jaded tastes. Many historians now believe that one of the most enduring legends linked to the Colosseum—that Christians were fed to the lions here—is unfounded.

Next to the Colosseum is the **Arch of Constantine,** erected in honor of Constantine's defeat of the pagan Maxentius (A.D. 306).

Campidoglio (Capitoline Hill). Piazza del Campidoglio. Bus: 46, 89, 92, 94, or 716.

Of the Seven Hills of Rome, the *Campidoglio* is the most sacred; legends about this hill stretch way back into antiquity (an Etruscan temple to Jupiter once stood on this spot). The approach to the Capitoline Hill is dramatic—climbing the long, sloping steps designed by Michelangelo. At the top is a perfectly proportioned square, Piazza del Campidoglio, also laid out by the Florentine artist.

One side of the piazza is open; the others are bounded by the **Senatorium** (Town Council), the statuary-filled **Palazzo dei Conservatori,** and the **Museo Capitolinio** (Capitoline Museum; see "More Attractions," below). The Campidoglio is dramatic at night (walk around to the back for a regal view of the floodlit Roman Forum).

Castel Sant'Angelo. Lungotevere Castello 50. ☎ **06/6875036.** Admission 8,000L ($4.80) adults, free for children 17 and under and seniors 60 and over. Daily 9am–7pm. Closed second and last Wed of each month. Metro: Ottaviano. Bus: 23, 46, 49, 62, 64, 87, 98, 280, or 910.

This overpowering structure, in a landmark position on the Tiber just east of Vatican City (see the "Rome Attractions" map), was originally built in the 2nd century A.D. as a tomb for the emperor Hadrian; it continued as an imperial mausoleum until the time of Caracalla. It's an imposing, grim castle with thick walls and a cylindrical shape. If it looks like a fortress, it should, as that was its function in the Middle Ages. In the 14th century it became a papal residence. Its legend rests largely on its link with Pope

Alexander VI, whose mistress bore him two children—Cesare and Lucrezia Borgia. Today, the highlight of the castle is a trip through the Renaissance apartments with their coffered ceilings and lush decoration. Their walls have witnessed plots and intrigues that make up some of the arch-treachery of the High Renaissance.

Now an art museum, the castle halls display the history of the Roman mausoleum, along with a wide-ranging selection of ancient arms and armor. You can climb to the top terrace for another one of those dazzling views of the Eternal City.

✪ **Pantheon.** Piazza della Rotonda. ☎ **06/68300230.** Free admission. Mon–Sat 9am–6pm; Sun 9am–1pm. Bus: 46, 62, 64, 170, or 492 to Largo di Torre Argentina; then walk up Via di Torre Argentina or Via dei Cestari.

Of all the great buildings of ancient Rome, only the Pantheon (literally, "All the Gods") remains intact today. It was built in 27 B.C. by Marcus Agrippa, and later reconstructed by the emperor Hadrian in the first part of the 2nd century A.D. This remarkable building is among the architectural wonders of the world because of its dome and its concept of space (see the "Rome Attractions" map).

The Pantheon was once ringed with white marble statues of Roman gods in its niches. Animals were sacrificed and burned in the center, and the smoke escaped through the only means of light, an opening at the top 27 feet in diameter. Michelangelo came here to study the dome before designing the cupola of St. Peter's (whose dome is only 2 feet smaller than the Pantheon's).

THE CATACOMBS OF THE APPIAN WAY

Of all the roads that led to Rome, **Via Appia Antica**—built in 312 B.C.—reigned as the leader. It eventually stretched all the way from Rome to the seaport of Brindisi, through which trade with the colonies in Greece and the East was funneled.

Along the Appian Way the patrician Romans built great monuments above the ground, whereas Christians met in the catacombs beneath. The remains of both can be visited today. In some dank, dark grottoes (never stray too far from either your party or one of the exposed lightbulbs), you can still discover traces of early Christian art.

Of the catacombs open to the public, the Catacombs of St. Callixtus and those of St. Sebastian are the most important. Both can be reached by taking bus no. 118, which leaves from near the Colosseum close to the Metro station.

Catacombe di San Sebastiano is at Via Appia Antica 136 (☎ 06/7887035). Today the tomb of the martyr is in the basilica (church), but it was originally in the catacomb under the building. From the reign of the emperor Valerian to the reign of Constantine, the bodies of Saint Peter and Saint Paul were hidden in this catacomb. The tunnels here, if stretched out, would reach a length of 7 miles. Admission is 8,000L ($4.80) for adults, 4,000L ($2.40) for children 6 to 15, and free for children under 6. Open April to October Monday to Saturday, from 9am to noon and 2:30 to 5:30pm; November to March Monday to Saturday, from 8:30am to noon and 2:30 to 5pm.

The **Catacombs di San Callisto,** Via Appia Antica 110 (☎ 06/51301580), are the first cemetery of Rome's Christian community; they were the burial place of 16 popes in the 3rd century. These catacombs bear the name of St. Callixtus, the deacon who was put in charge of them by the pope, St. Zephyrinus. Callixtus himself was later elected pope (217–222). The complex is made up of a network of galleries stretching for nearly 12 miles, structured in five different levels, reaching a depth of about 65 feet. Admission is 8,000L ($4.80) for adults, 4,000L ($2.40) for children 6 to 15, and free for children under 6. From April to October, hours are Thursday to Tuesday 8:30am to noon and 2:30 to 5:30pm. November to January, and in March, Thursday to Tuesday from 8:30am to noon and 2:30 to 5pm. Closed in February for restoration.

PIAZZA DI SPAGNA (SPANISH STEPS)

The Spanish Steps were the last part of the outside world that Keats saw before he died in a house at the foot of the stairs. The steps are filled, in season, with flower vendors, jewelry dealers, and photographers snapping pictures of tourists. Both the steps and the square take their names from the Spanish Embassy, which used to have its head-quarters here. At the foot of the steps is a nautically shaped fountain, designed by Pietro Bernini, papa of the more famous Giovanni Lorenzo Bernini.

MORE ATTRACTIONS

Terme di Caracalla (Baths of Caracalla). Via delle Terme di Caracalla 52. ☎ **06/5758626.** Admission 8,000L ($4.80), free for children under 12. Apr–Sept Tues–Sat 9am–6pm, Sun–Mon 9am–1pm; Oct–Mar Tues–Sat 9am–3pm, Sun–Mon 9am–1pm. Bus: 90 or 118.

Named for the emperor Caracalla, Terme di Caracalla were completed in the early part of the 3rd century. The richness of decoration has faded, and the lushness can be judged only from the shell of brick ruins that remain.

Basilica di San Clemente. Piazza San Clemente, Via Labicana 95. ☎ **06/70451018.** Church, free; grottoes, 4,000L ($2.40). Mon–Sat 9:30am–12:30pm and 3–6pm; Sun 10am–12:30pm and 3–6pm. Metro: Colosseo. Bus: 81, 85, 87, or 186. Tram: 13 or 30.

From the Colosseum, head up Via di San Giovanni in Laterano, which leads to the Basilica of Saint Clement. In this church-upon-a-church, centuries of history peel away: A 4th-century church was built over a secular house from the 1st century A.D., beside which stood a pagan temple dedicated to Mithras (god of the sun); the Normans destroyed the lower church, and a new one was built in the 12th century. Down in the eerie grottoes (which you can explore on your own—unlike the catacombs on the Appian Way), you'll discover well-preserved frescoes from the 1st to the 3rd centuries A.D.

Basilica di San Giovanni in Laterano. Piazza San Giovanni in Laterano 4. ☎ **06/69886433.** Basilica, free; cloisters, 4,000L ($2.40). Daily 9am–5pm. Metro: San Giovanni.

This church—not St. Peter's—is the cathedral of the diocese of Rome. Catholics all over the world refer to it as their "mother church." Originally built in A.D. 314 by Constantine, the cathedral has suffered many vicissitudes and was forced to rebuild many times. The present structure is characterized by the 18th-century facade by Alessandro Galilei (statues of Christ and the Apostles ring the top). Borromini gets the credit—some say blame—for the interior, built for Innocent X. It's said that in the misguided attempt to redecorate, frescoes by Giotto were destroyed.

The most unusual sight is across the street at the "Palace of the Holy Steps," called the **Santuario della Scala Sancta,** Piazza San Giovanni in Laterano (☎ **06/70494619**). It's alleged that these were the actual steps that Christ climbed when he was brought before Pilate. These steps are supposed to be climbed only on your knees, which you're likely to see the faithful doing throughout the day. Visiting hours are daily 6:15am to noon and 3:30 to 6:30pm. Admission is free.

Basilica di Santa Maria Maggiore (Saint Mary the Great). Piazza Santa Maria Maggiore. ☎ **06/4881094.** Free admission. Daily 7am–7pm (until 8pm in summer). Metro: Stazione Termini.

This great church was originally founded by Pope Liberius in A.D. 358 but was rebuilt by Pope Sixtus III in 432–440. Its campanile, erected in the 14th century, is the loftiest in the city. Much doctored in the 18th century, the facade is not an accurate reflection of the treasures inside. The basilica is especially noted for the 5th-century Roman mosaics in its nave, as well as for its coffered ceiling, said to have been gilded with gold brought from the New World. In the 16th century Domenico Fontana built a now-restored "Sistine Chapel." The church contains the tomb of Bernini, Italy's most important architect during the flowering of the baroque in the 17th century.

✪ **Museo Capitolino and Palazzo dei Conservatori.** Piazza del Campidoglio. ☎ **06/67102071.** Admission to both museum and palace 10,000L ($6) adults, 5,000L ($3) children 18 and under and seniors 60 and over. Tues–Sun 9am–7pm. Bus: 46, 89, 92, 94, or 716.

The Capitoline Museum was built in the 17th century, based on an architectural sketch by Michelangelo. In the first room is *The Dying Gaul*, a work of majestic skill; in a special gallery all her own is *The Capitoline Venus*, who demurely covers herself—this statue (a Roman copy of the Greek original) was the symbol of feminine beauty and charm down through the centuries.

The famous statue of *Marcus Aurelius* is the only bronze equestrian statue to have survived from ancient Rome. It was retrieved from the Tiber where it had been tossed by marauding barbarians. For centuries it was thought to be a statue of Constantine the Great; this mistake protected it further, since papal Rome respected the memory of the first Christian emperor.

The **Palazzo dei Conservatori,** across the way, is rich in classical sculpture and paintings. One of the most notable bronzes—a work of incomparable beauty—is *Lo Spinario* (the little boy picking a thorn from his foot), a Greek classic that dates from the 1st century B.C. In addition, you'll find *Lupa Capitolina* (the Capitoline Wolf), a rare Etruscan bronze that may go back to the 5th century B.C. (Romulus and Remus, the legendary twins that the wolf suckled, were added at a later date.)

✪ **Galleria Borghese.** Piazza Scipione Borghese, off Via Pinciano. ☎ **06/32010** for reservations, 06/8417645 for information. Admission 12,000L ($7.20). Tues–Sun 9am–10pm; Sun 9am–8pm. Bus: 56 or 910. *Note:* No more than 300 visitors at a time are allowed on the ground floor, no more than 90 on the upper floor. Reservations are essential (call Mon–Fri 9am–6pm).

Closed for 14 years, this jewelbox collection of masterworks is finally back. The masterpieces are displayed in what was once Borghese's summer residence. However, in the spring of 1997, after a complete restoration, it was reopened in all its fabulous glory. The bad news is that it might be hard to get in because of limited access (see above). The Italian state purchased the museum in 1902 but, as it turned out, it was resting on an unstable honeycomb of subterranean grottoes and watercourses.

A whole new generation has come into adulthood in Rome without sampling this treasure trove of art, ranging from such masterpieces as Bernini's *David, The Rape of Persephone,* and *Apollo and Daphne;* Titian's *Sacred and Profane Love;* Raphael's *Deposition;* even Caravaggio's *Jerome.*

The collection began with the gallery's founder, Scipione Borghese, who by the time of his death in 1633 had accumulated some of the greatest art of all time, even managing to acquire Bernini's most spectacular sculptures (see above). Scipione even had Raphael's *Deposition* stolen in the night from a church in Perugia. He actually paid for a Caravaggio, *Madonna dei Palafrenieri,* one of the artist's most famous paintings. But Scipione got it for half of what it was worth at the time. When he wanted more Caravaggios, he had his uncle, Pope Paul V, confiscate them from another painter. Some paintings were spirited out of Vatican museums, and even confiscated when their rightful owners were hauled off to prison until they become "reasonable" about turning over their art. The great collection suffered at the hands of Napoléon's sister,

Pauline, who married Camillo Borghese in 1807 and sold most of the ancient collection (many works now in the Louvre in Paris). One of the most viewed pieces of sculpture in today's gallery, ironically, is Canova's life-size sculpture of Pauline in the pose of "Venus Victorious." When Pauline was asked if she felt uncomfortable about posing in the nude, she replied, "Why should I? The studio was heated."

Galleria Nazionale d'Arte Antica. Via delle Quattro Fontane 13. ☎ **06/4814430.** Admission 10,000L ($6) adults, free for children 17 and under and seniors 60 and over. Tues–Sun 9am–10pm. Metro: Piazza Barberini.

Palazzo Barberini, right off Piazza Barberini, is one of Rome's most magnificent baroque palaces. It was begun by Carlo Maderno in 1627 and completed in 1633 by Bernini, whose lavishly decorated rococo apartments, called the Gallery of Decorative Art, are on view. The palace houses the Galleria Nazionale. On the first floor of the palace, a splendid array of paintings includes works that date back to the 13th and 14th centuries, notably the *Mother and Child* by Simone Martini. Art from the 15th and 16th centuries include works by Filippo Lippi, Andrea Solario, Francesco Francia, Il Sodoma (Giovanni Antonio Bazzi), and Raphael. You can also visit a newly restored 18th-century apartment decorated with frescoes from the school of Barberini. Admission is 2,000L ($1.20), and hours are Tuesday to Sunday 9am to 10pm.

✪ **Museo Nazionale di Villa Giulia (Etruscan).** Piazzale di Villa Giulia 9. ☎ **06/3201951.** Admission 8,000L ($4.80) adults, free for children 18 and under and seniors 60 and over. Tues–Sat 9am–7pm; Sun 9am–2pm. Metro: Flaminio.

A 16th-century papal palace in the Villa Borghese Gardens shelters this priceless collection of art and artifacts of the mysterious Etruscans, who predated the Romans. Little is known about these people except for their sophisticated art and design. If you have time only for the masterpieces, head for Sala 7, which has a remarkable *Apollo* from Veio from the end of the 6th century B.C. (clothed, for a change). The other two widely acclaimed pieces of statuary in this gallery are *Dea con Bambino* (a goddess with a baby) and a greatly mutilated, but still powerful, *Hercules* with a stag. In the adjoining room, Sala 8, you'll see the lions' sarcophagus from the mid-6th century B.C. which was excavated at Cerveteri, north of Rome. Finally, in Sala 9, is one of the world's most important Etruscan art treasures, the bride and bridegroom coffin from the 6th century B.C., also dug out of the tombs of Cerveteri.

ORGANIZED TOURS

One of the leading tour operators (among the zillions of possibilities) is **American Express,** Piazza di Spagna 38 (☎ **06/67641**), open Monday to Friday 9am to 5:30pm and Saturday 9am to 12:30pm. One popular tour is a 4-hour orientation tour of Rome and the Vatican, which departs most mornings at 9:30am and costs 70,000L ($42) per person. Another 4-hour tour, which focuses on the Rome of antiquity (including visits to the Colosseum, the Roman Forum, the ruins of the Imperial Palace, and the Church of San Pietro in Vincoli), costs 60,000L ($36). Outside Rome, a popular excursion April to October is a 5-hour bus tour to Tivoli, where visits are conducted of the Villa d'Este and its spectacular gardens and the ruins of the Villa Adriana, for 70,000L ($42) per person.

If your time in Italy is really limited, you might opt for 1-day excursions to points farther afield on tours that are marketed (but not conducted) by American Express. A series of 1-day tours is offered to Pompeii, Naples, and Sorrento for 160,000L ($96) per person; to Florence for 190,000L ($114); and to Capri and Sorrento for 210,000L ($126). These trips, which include lunch, depart from Rome around 7am and return to your hotel sometime after 9 or 10pm.

To Market, to Market

At Rome's sprawling **Porta Portese** open-air flea market, held every Sunday morning in Trastevere, every peddler from Trastevere and the surrounding Castelli Romani sets up a temporary shop. The vendors sell merchandise ranging from secondhand paintings of Madonnas to pseudo-Etruscan hairpins. The flea market is near the end of Viale Trastevere (bus no. 75 to Porta Portese), then a short walk to Via Portuense. By 10:30am the market is full of people. As you would at any street market, beware of pickpockets. Open Sunday 7am to 1pm.

THE SHOPPING SCENE
Shopping hours are generally Monday from 3:30 to 7:30pm and Tuesday to Saturday from 9:30 or 10am to 1pm and 3:30 to 7 or 7:30pm. Some shops are open on Monday mornings, however, and some shops don't close for the afternoon break.

THE BEST SHOPPING STREETS
Via Borgognona & Via Condotti   Both of these posh shopping streets begin near Piazza di Spagna. For the most part, the merchandise on both streets is very, very chic.

Via del Corso   This street doesn't have the image or the high prices of Via Condotti and Via Borgognona; the styles here are aimed at younger consumers. There are, however, some gems scattered amid the shops selling jeans and sporting equipment. The most interesting shops are on the section of the street nearest the fashionable cafes of Piazza del Popolo.

Via Francesco Crispi   Most shoppers reach this street by following Via Sistina (see below) 1 long block from the top of the Spanish Steps. Near the intersection of these streets are several shops full of unusual and less expensive gifts.

Via Frattina   This street begins at Piazza di Spagna and runs parallel to Via Condotti, its more famous sibling. Part of its length is closed to traffic; here, the concentration of shops is densest.

Via Nazionale   This traffic-clogged shopping street—just crossing the street is no small feat—begins at Piazza della Repubblica and runs almost to the 19th-century monuments of Piazza Venezia. Here you'll find an abundance of leather stores—more reasonable in price than those in many other parts of Rome—and a welcome handful of stylish boutiques.

Via Sistina   Beginning at the top of the Spanish Steps, Via Sistina runs to Piazza Barberini. The shops are small, stylish, and based on the personalities of their owners. The pedestrian traffic is less dense here than on other major streets.

Via Vittorio Veneto & Via Barberini   Evocative of *La Dolce Vita* fame, Via Veneto is filled these days with cafes, luxurious hotels, and an array of stores selling shoes, gloves, and leather goods.

Via dei Coronari   Buried in a colorful section of the Campus Martius, this street is an antiquer's dream, literally lined with magnificent vases, urns, chandeliers, breakfronts, chaises, refectory tables, and candelabra. To find the entrance to the street, turn left out of the north end of Piazza Navona, pass the excavated ruins of Domitian's Stadium, and the street will be just ahead of you. There are more than 40 antiques stores in the next 4 blocks.

SOME SHOPS WORTH SEEKING OUT

Anatriello del Regalo. Via Frattina 123. ☎ **06/6789601.**

This shop stocks new and antique silver, some of it quite unusual. The new items are made by Italian silversmiths, in designs ranging from the whimsical to the severely formal.

E. Fiore. Via Ludovisi 31. ☎ **06/4819296.**

E. Fiore sells a wide assortment of charms, bracelets, necklaces, rings, brooches, and cameos. The store also carries elegant watches, silverware, and goldware.

Emporio Armani. Via del Babuino 140. ☎ **06/3600-2197.**

This boutique stocks moderately priced men's wear crafted by the couturier who has dressed more stage and screen stars than any other designer in Italy. The designer's more expensive line—sold at prices that are sometimes 30% less than what you'd pay in the United States—lies a short walk away, at **Giorgio Armani,** Via Condotti 77 (☎ **06/6991460**).

Farnese. Piazza Farnese 52. ☎ **06/6896109.**

Here is Rome's most evocative collection of floor tile patterns, which can be used as wall or floor inserts, as borders, or even as complete floor coverings. Various designs depict everything from the scenes of ancient Roman mosaics to the glazed tiles of Capodimonte in Naples.

La Rinascente. Via del Corso 189. ☎ **06/6797691** at the Piazza Colonna.

This is Rome's most famous department store. Rather upscale, it has a little bit of everything: clothing, hosiery, perfume, cosmetics, housewares, and even furniture, plus its own line of clothing (Ellerre) for men, women, and children.

Saddlers Union. Via Condotti 26. ☎ **06/6798050.**

Here's a great place to look for well-crafted leather accessories—handbags, belts, wallets, shoes, briefcases, and other high-quality items.

Salvatore Ferragamo. Via Condotti 73–74. ☎ **06/6798402.**

Head here for Ferragamo's elegant and fabled footwear, plus ties and women's clothing and accessories in an atmosphere full of Italian style. Figure on a 30-minute wait outside.

ROME AFTER DARK

There are few evening diversions quite as pleasurable as a stroll past the solemn pillars of old temples or the cascading torrents of Renaissance fountains glowing under the blue-black sky. Of the **fountains,** the Naiads (Piazza della Repubblica), the Tortoises (Piazza Mattei), and, of course, the Trevi are particularly beautiful at night. The **Capitoline Hill** is magnificently lit after dark, with its measured Renaissance facades glowing like jewel boxes. Behind the Senatorial Palace is a fine view of the **Roman Forum.** If you're staying across the Tiber, **Piazza San Pietro,** in front of St. Peter's Basilica, is impressive at night without the tour buses and crowds. And a combination of illuminated architecture, Renaissance fountains, and, frequently, sidewalk shows and art expositions is at **Piazza Navona.** If you're ambitious and have a good sense of direction, try exploring the streets west of Piazza Navona, which look like a stage set when they're lit at night.

The little guide (in English), *Enjoy Rome,* will help you with all the information concerning how to get in and out of Rome and where to find information offices; it also has an entertainment section. You can get the guide for free from Enjoy Rome,

---

A Meal & a Song

Roman rusticity is combined with theatrical flair at **Fantasie di Trastevere,** Via di Santa Dorotea 6 (☎ **06/5881671**), the "people's theater," where the famous actor Petrolini made his debut. Waiters dressed in regional garb serve with drama. The cuisine isn't subtle, but it's bountiful. Expect to pay 80,000 to 120,000L ($48 to $72) for a full meal. Your first drink will cost 35,000L ($21). Some two dozen folk singers and musicians in regional costumes perform, making it a festive affair. Meals are served daily beginning at 8pm, and piano bar music is offered from 8:30 to 9:30pm, followed by the show, lasting until 10:30pm.

Via Varese 39 (☎ **04/4451-843**). Even if you don't speak Italian, you can generally follow the listings featured in *La Repubblica,* a leading Italian newspaper. The Paris editon of the *International Herald Tribune* is also available at news kiosks, and it has a good entertainment section, too.

THE PERFORMING ARTS

If you're in the capital for the opera season, which usually runs from December to June, you can attend a performance at the historic **Teatro dell'Opera (Rome Opera House),** located off Via Nazionale, at Piazza Beniamino Gigli 1 (☎ **06/481601**). In the summer, the venue switches to Piazza di Siena. The **Rome Opera Ballet** also performs at the Teatro dell'Opera. Look for announcements in newspapers, or check with your hotel desk, for classical concerts that take place in churches and other venues.

THE CLUB & MUSIC SCENE

Clubs are generally open Monday through Saturday from 9 or 10pm to 2 to 4am.

Nightclubs

Arciliuto. Piazza Monte Vecchio 5. ☎ **06/6879419.** Cover (including 1 drink) 35,000L ($21).

Arciliuto, reputedly the former studio of Raphael, is one of the most romantic candlelit spots in Rome. From 10pm to 2am Monday through Saturday, guests enjoy a musical salon ambience, listening to a guitarist, a pianist, and a violinist. The evening's presentation also includes live Neapolitan songs and new Italian madrigals, even current hits from Broadway or London's West End. Closed July 20 through September 3.

Jazz, Soul & Funk

Alexanderplatz. Via Ostia 9. ☎ **06/39742171.** 2-month membership 12,000L ($7.20).

Every night but Sunday, Alexanderplatz features live jazz music. There's also a good restaurant here that serves everything from gnocchi alla romana to Japanese cuisine.

Big Mama. Vicolo San Francesco a Ripa 18. ☎ **06/5812551.** No cover for minor shows, 20,000–30,000L ($12–$18) for big acts, plus 20,000L ($12) for a seasonal membership.

Big Mama is a hangout for jazz and blues musicians; you're likely to meet the up-and-coming jazz stars of tomorrow. Sometimes the big names appear as well. Closed June to September.

Gilda. Via Mario dei Fiori 97. ☎ **06/6784838.** Cover (including 1 drink) 40,000L ($24).

Gilda is an adventurous combination of nightclub, disco, and restaurant known for the glamorous acts it books. The artistic direction ensures first-class shows, a well-run restaurant, and disco music played between the musical acts. The restaurant and pizzeria open at 9:30pm and occasionally offer shows. The nightclub, opening at midnight, plays music of the 1960s as well as modern recordings.

Gay Clubs

Angelo Azzuro. Via Cardinal Merry del Val 13. ☎ **06/5800472.** Cover (including 1 drink) 10,000L ($6) Fri and Sun, 20,000L ($12) Sat.

This gay "hot spot," deep in the heart of Trastevere, is open Friday to Sunday from 11pm to 4am. No food is served, nor is live music presented. Friday is for women only.

The Hangar. Via in Selci 69. ☎ **06/4881397.** No cover, but card membership of 3,000L ($1.80) needed.

This is the premier gay bar in Rome, on one of the city's oldest streets, adjacent to the Roman Forum. Women are welcome any night except Monday, when videos and entertainment for gay men are featured. The busiest nights are Saturday, Sunday, and Monday, when as many as 500 clients cram inside. The Hangar is closed for 3 weeks in August.

New Joli Coeur. Via Sirte 5. ☎ **06/86215827.** Cover (including 1 drink) 15,000–20,000L ($9–$12).

Open on Saturday and Sunday from 11pm to 3am only, this bar in a seedy neighborhood caters mainly to lesbians. Saturday night is reserved for women only, although Sunday the crowd can be mixed.

THE CAFE SCENE

Caffè de Paris. Via Vittorio Veneto 90. ☎ **06/4885284.**

This cafe rises and falls in popularity depending on the decade. In the 1950s it was a haven for the fashionable, and now it's a popular restaurant in summer, when the tables spill out onto the sidewalk. Open daily 8am to 3am.

Canova Café. Piazza del Popolo. ☎ **06/3612231.**

Canova has a sidewalk terrace for pedestrian-watching, plus a snack bar, a restaurant, and a wine shop inside. In summer you'll have access to a courtyard with ivy-covered walls. Meals cost 20,000L ($12) and up.

Caffè Sant'Eustachio. Piazza Sant'Eustachio 82. ☎ **06/6861309.**

This is one of the city's most celebrated espresso shops, on a small square near the Pantheon. The water supply comes from a source outside Rome, which the emperor Augustus funneled into the city with an aqueduct in 19 B.C. Rome's most experienced espresso judges claim that the water plays an important part in the coffee's flavor, although steam forced through ground Brazilian coffee roasted on the premises has an important effect as well.

Antico Caffè Greco. Via Condotti 86. ☎ **06/6791700.**

Since 1760 this has been Rome's most posh and fashionable coffee bar. For years, it has enjoyed a reputation as the gathering place of the *literati*. In the front is a wooden bar, and beyond that a series of small salons, decorated in a 19th-century style.

SIDE TRIPS FROM ROME

TIVOLI   Tivoli, known as Tibur to the ancient Romans, was the playground of emperors. Today its reputation continues unabated: It's the most popular half-day jaunt from Rome.

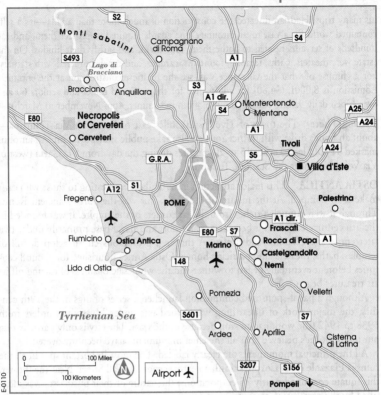

Monti Sabatini

S2

Campagnano di Roma

S4

A1

S493

Lago di Bracciano

Bracciano Anquillara

S3

A1 dir.

S4

Monterotondo

Mentana

A25

A24

E80

Necropolis of Cerveteri

Cerveteri

G.R.A.

A1

S5

Tivoli

A24

Villa d'Este

Palestrina

A12 S1

Fregene

ROME

A1 dir.

Frascati

Rocca di Papa A1

Fiumicino Ostia Antica

E80 S7

Marino

Castelgandolfo

Nemi

Lido di Ostia

148

Velletri

Pomezia

Tyrrhenian Sea

S601

S7

Ardea Aprilia

Cisterna di Latina

0   100 Miles

0   100 Kilometers

Airport ✈

S207 S156

Pompeii ↓

E-0110

While the ✪ **Villa d'Este,** Piazza Trento, Viale delle Centro Fontane (☎ **077 4/312070**), is just a dank Renaissance palace with second-rate paintings that's hardly worth the trek from Rome, its gardens—designed by Pirro Ligorio—dim the luster of Versailles. Visitors descend a cypress-studded slope and are treated to everything from lilies to gargoyles spouting water, torrential streams, and waterfalls. The loveliest fountain—on this there is some agreement—is the **Fontana del'Ovato,** designed by Ligorio. But nearby is the most spectacular achievement—the **hydraulic organ fountain,** dazzling visitors with its water jets in front of a baroque chapel, with four maidens who look tipsy. The best walk is along the promenade, which has 100 spraying fountains. Admission is 10,000L ($6). The villa opens daily at 9am; closing times vary according to the season. From November to January it closes at 4pm; closing times may be as late as 6:45pm in high season.

The Villa d'Este dazzles with artificial glamour, but **Villa Gregoriana,** Largo Sant'Angelo (☎ **0774/334522**), relies more on nature. The gardens were built by Pope Gregory XVI in the 19th century. At one point on the circuitous walk carved along a slope, visitors stand and look out onto Tivoli's most panoramic waterfall (Aniene). The trek to the bottom on the banks of the Anio is studded with grottoes and balconies that open onto the chasm. From one belvedere there's a panoramic view of the Temple of Vesta on the hill. Admission is 3,500L ($2.10). It's open daily from 9am to 1 hour before sunset.

Of all the Roman emperors dedicated to *la dolce vita,* the globe-trotting Hadrian spent the last 3 years of his life in the grandest style. Less than 4 miles from Tivoli he built his great estate—the ✪ **Villa Adriana (Hadrian's Villa),** Via di Villa Adriana (☎ **0774 /530203**)—and filled acre after acre with some of the architectural wonders he'd seen on his many trips. Hadrian directed the construction of much more than a villa—it's a self-contained world for a vast royal entourage, the guards required to protect them, and the hundreds of servants needed to bathe them, feed them, and satisfy their libidos. On the estate were theaters, baths, temples, fountains, gardens, and canals bordered with statuary. For a glimpse of what the villa once was, see the plastic reconstruction at the entrance. Admission is 8,000L ($4.80) for adults, free for those 17 and under and seniors 60 and over. Open daily 9am to sunset (about 6:30pm in summer, 4pm November to March).

Getting There   The town of Tivoli is 20 miles east of Rome on Via Tiburtina—about an hour's drive with traffic. You can also take public transportation: An autobus marked TIVOLI leaves every 15 to 20 minutes during the day from Via Gaeta (west of Via Volturno), near the Stazione Termini.

OSTIA ANTICA   This major attraction is particularly interesting to those who can't make it to Pompeii. At the mouth of the Tiber, this was the port of ancient Rome. Through it were funneled riches from the far corners of the empire. It was founded in the 4th century B.C., and it became a major port and naval base primarily under two later emperors: Claudius and Trajan. A thriving, prosperous city developed, full of temples, baths, theaters, and patrician homes. Ostia Antica flourished for about 8 centuries before it eventually began to wither and the wholesale business of carting off its art treasures began.

Although a papal-sponsored commission launched a series of digs in the 19th century, the major work of unearthing was carried out under Mussolini's orders from 1938 to 1942 (the work had to stop because of the war). The city is only partially dug out today, but it's believed that all the chief monuments have been uncovered.

All the principal monuments are clearly labeled. The most important spot in all the ruins is **Piazzale delle Corporazioni,** an early version of Wall Street. Near the theater, this square contained nearly 75 corporations; the nature of their businesses was identified by the patterns of preserved mosaics.

Ostia Antica is entered on Viale dei Romagnoli 717 (☎ **06/56358099**). Admission is 12,000L ($7.20) for adults and free for children 17 and under. Open Tuesday to Sunday 9am to 4pm.

Getting There   To get here on public transportation, take the Metropolitana (subway) Line B from the Stazione Termini to the Magliana stop, and then change for the Lido train to Ostia Antica, about 16 miles from Rome. Departures are about every half hour, and the trip takes 20 minutes. The Metro lets you off across the highway that connects Rome with the coast. It's just a short walk to the excavations.

HERCULANEUM & POMPEII   Both these ancient sights are more easily visited from Naples; however, many organized tours go here from Rome. American Express, Piazza di Spagna (☎ **06/67641**), offers day tours to Pompeii, leaving Rome around 7am and returning between 9 and 10pm. You can also explore one—but rarely both—attraction on a day's drive here and back from Rome. Naples is about 2½ hours from Rome by frequent trains. The Circumvesuviana Railway in Naples departs every half hour from Piazza Garibaldi; the trip takes 45 minutes each way. At the railway station in Pompeii, bus connections take you to the entrance to the excavations.

The builders of ✪ **Herculaneum** (*Ercolano* in Italian) were still working to repair the damage caused by an A.D. 62 earthquake when Vesuvius erupted on that fateful August day in A.D. 79. Herculaneum, a much smaller town (about one-fourth the size of Pompeii), didn't start to come to light again until 1709, when Prince Elbeuf launched the unfortunate fashion of tunneling through it for treasures. The prince was more intent on profiting from the sale of objets d'art than in uncovering a dead Roman town.

Subsequent excavations at the site, **Ufficio Scavi di Ercolano,** Corso Resina, Ercolano (☎ **081/7390963**), have been slow. Herculaneum is not completely dug out today.

All the streets and buildings of Herculaneum hold interest, especially the baths (*terme*), divided between those at the forum and those on the outskirts (Terme Suburbane, near the more elegant villas). The municipal baths, which segregated the sexes, are larger, but the ones at the edge of town are more lavishly adorned. Important private homes to see include the **House of the Bicentenary,** the **House of the Wooden Cabinet,** the **House of the Wooden Partition,** and the **House of Poseidon (Neptune) and Amphitrite,** the last containing the best-known mosaic discovered in the ruins. The finest example of how the aristocracy lived is provided by a visit to the **Casa dei Cervi,** named the House of the Stags because of sculpture found inside.

The ruins may be visited daily from 9am to 1 hour before sunset. Admission is 12,000L ($7.20). To reach the archaeological zone, take the regular train service from Naples on the Circumvesuviana Railway, a 20-minute ride leaving about every half hour from Corso Garibaldi 387, or take bus no. 255 from Piazza Municipio. Otherwise, it's a 4½-mile drive on the autostrada to Salerno (turn off at **Ercolano**).

When Vesuvius erupted in A.D. 79, Pliny the Younger, who later recorded the event, thought the end of the world had come. Lying 15 miles south of Naples, the ruined Roman city of ✪ **Pompeii** (*Pompei* in Italian) has been dug out from the inundation of volcanic ash and pumice stone. At the excavations, the life of 19 centuries ago is vividly experienced.

The **Ufficio Scavi di Pompei** is entered at Piazza Esedra (☎ **081/8610744**). The most elegant of the patrician villas, the **House of Vettii** has a courtyard, statuary (such as a two-faced Janus), paintings, and a black-and-red Pompeiian dining room frescoed with cupids. The second important villa, near the Porto Ercolano (Herculaneum Gate), lies outside the walls. The **House of Mysteries** (Villa dei Misteri) is reached by going out Viale alla Villa dei Misteri. What makes the villa exceptional, aside from its architectural features, are its remarkable frescoes. The **House of the Faun** (Casa del Fauno), so called because of a bronze statue of a dancing faun found there, takes up a city block and has four different dining rooms and two spacious peristyle gardens. In the center of town is the **Forum;** although rather small, it was the heart of Pompeiian life.

The excavations may be visited daily from 9am to 1 hour before sunset. Admission is 12,000L ($7.20).

2 Florence & Tuscany

No other city in Europe, with the exception of Venice, lives off its past in the way Florence does. The Renaissance began here, and Florence is a bit foreboding and architecturally severe. Many of its *palazzi* (palaces), built in the Medici style, look like fortresses. But remember, when these structures were built, the aim was to keep foreign enemies at bay. These facades guard treasures within.

Ever since the 19th century, it seems as if Florence has been visited by half the world. The city has managed to impress some hard-to-impress people, including Mark Twain, who found it overwhelmed with "tides of color that make all the sharp lines dim and faint and turn the old city to a city of dreams."

Florence might appear as though it's caught in a time warp—a Medici returning to the city would have no trouble finding his way around. But Florence virtually pulsates with modern life. Students racing to and from the university quarter add vibrance to the city, and it's amusing to watch the way many local businesspeople avoid the city's impossible traffic today: They whiz by on Vespas, while cars are stalled in traffic.

Florentines like to present *una bella figura* (a good appearance) to the rest of the world and are incredibly upset when that appearance is attacked, as in the case of the May 1993 bombing of the Uffizi that cost them many treasures. The entire city rallied to reopen this treasure trove of Renaissance and other works of art.

Try to visit this city, even on the most rushed of European itineraries. There's nothing like it anywhere else. Venice and Rome are too different from Florence to invite meaningful comparisons.

Florence is also an ideal base from which to explore the district of Tuscany. Although increasingly built up, Tuscany still has enough old towns and rolling hills studded with olives and grapevines to attract the romantic. Tuscany is the heart of Italy, and its Tuscan dialect, the speech of Dante and Petrarch, is the country's textbook Italian. Florence and Siena are the chief drawing cards, but Fiesole, right outside Florence, and Pisa also have their allure.

Only in Florence

Sipping Coffee on Piazza della Signoria Find a cafe table and order a cappuccino and the day is yours. This ancient center of city life is one of the world's most dramatic squares and the setting for many epic moments in Florence's history, including Savonarola's "bonfire of the vanities," in which Florentines burned such precious items as paintings to "purify" themselves. The reformer ended up getting set afire himself. Today the square is home to the Loggia dei Lanzi, with Cellini's *Perseus* holding a beheaded Medusa. Michelangelo's *David* on the square is a copy, however.

Checking Out Piazza del Duomo's Architectural Wonders In the heart of Florence, this treasure of Renaissance architecture falls within the shadow of the Duomo, the Cathedral of Santa Maria del Fiore. Capped by Brunelleschi's dome—an amazing architectural feat—the Duomo dominates the skyline. Visitors also flock here to see the neighboring bell tower, one of the most beautiful in all of Italy, and the Baptistry across the way with its famous doors, jewels among Italian Renaissance sculpture.

Shopping for Gold on the Ponte Vecchio The oldest of Florence's bridges is flanked by jewelry stores and will carry you across the Arno. The shops peddle exquisite jewelry at an unprecedented rate. Many of the great artists of Florence began as goldsmiths, including Ghiberti, Donatello, and Cellini. The Corridoio Vasariano runs the length of the Ponte Vecchio—built by Vasari in just 5 months. Stand on the bridge at sunset, when it becomes a stream of molten gold itself.

Staring in Awe at Michelangelo's *David* The world's most reproduced statue resides at the Galleria dell'Accademia. The artist's study of the male anatomy has been hailed as "flawless," although Michelangelo had hardly turned 26 when he began the 4-year project. The statue has never met with universal approval and has been the subject of cruel jeers and even rotten egg attacks over the years; one historian called David "an awkward overgrown actor at one of our minor theaters, without his clothes." But most art lovers view David as an enduring legacy of the ideals of the High Renaissance.

Spending a Day at the Uffizi When the last grand duchess of the Medici family died, she bequeathed to the people of Tuscany a wealth of Renaissance and classical art that had been accumulated over 3 centuries. It's waiting for you today in a palace from the 16th century that Vasari designed for Cosimo I. Everyone has his or her favorites—ours is Botticelli's *Allegory of Spring* or *Primavera*. It's a gem.

Escaping to Fiesole This ancient town is on a hill overlooking Florence and offers the greatest panoramic views of the city of the Renaissance and the Arno Valley.

Founded by the Etruscans as early as the 7th century B.C., it lures you to its Piazza Mino da Fiesole, the center of local life. The air is always fresh and clean here and you don't have to visit any special sights—just enjoy Fiesole for itself.

ORIENTATION

ARRIVING   By Plane   If you're flying from New York, the best air connection is Rome, where you can board a domestic flight to the **Galileo Galilei Airport** at Pisa (☎ **050/500707**), 58 miles west of Florence. You can then take an express train for the hour-long trip to Florence. There's also a small domestic airport, **Amerigo Vespucci,** on Via del Termine, near A-11 (☎ **055/30615**), 3½ miles (and a 15-minute drive) northwest of Florence. This airport can be reached by city bus service available on the ATAF line (no. 62), departing from the main Santa Maria Novella rail terminal. Domestic air service is provided by **Alitalia,** with offices at Lungarno degli Acciaiuoli 10–12 in Florence (☎ **055/27881**).

By Train   If you're coming north from Rome, count on a 2- to 3-hour trip, depending on your connection. **Santa Maria Novella rail station,** in Piazza della Stazione, adjoins Piazza di Santa Maria Novella. For railway information, call ☎ **055/ 2351.** Some trains into Florence stop at the **Stazione Campo di Marte,** on the eastern side of Florence. A 24-hour bus service (no. 91) runs between the two rail terminals.

By Bus   Long-distance buses service Florence, run by **SITA,** Viale Cadorna 105 (☎ **055/483651**), and **Lazzi Eurolines,** Piazza della Stazione 4–6 (☎ **055/215155**). Both SITA and Lazzi Eurolines offer transfers from Florence to Siena, Arezzo, Pisa, and San Gimignano. A one-way ticket from Florence to Siena, for example, costs 11,000L ($6.60). If you're traveling on SITA, and you want to go to Pisa, the one-way fare is 20,000L ($12), but you'll have to call SITA 3 days in advance to reserve a seat.

By Car   Autostrada A-1 connects Florence with both the north and the south of Italy. It takes about an hour to reach Florence from Bologna and about 3 hours from Rome. The Tyrrhenian coast is only an hour from Florence on **A-11** heading west. Florence lies 172 miles north of Rome, 65 miles west of Bologna, and 185 miles south of Milan. Use a car only to get to Florence. Don't even contemplate its use once there.

VISITOR INFORMATION   Contact the **Azienda Promozione Turistica,** Via A. Manzoni 16 (☎ **055/2346284**), open Monday to Friday 8:15am to 1pm. Another helpful office, with information about both Florence and Tuscany, is **APT** at Via Cavour 1R (☎ **055/290832**). Hours here are March to November, Monday to Saturday 8:15am to 7:15pm; November to February, Monday to Saturday 8:15am to 1:45pm.

CITY LAYOUT   The city is split by the **Arno River,** which usually looks serene and peaceful but can turn ferocious with floodwaters on rare occasions. The major monumental and historical core lies on the north ("right") side of the river. But the "left" side—called the **Oltrarno**—is not devoid of attractions. Many long-time visitors frequent the Oltrarno for its tantalizing trattoria meals; they also maintain that the shopping here is less expensive. Even the most hurried visitor will want to cross over the Arno to see the Pitti Palace, with its many art treasures, and walk through the Giardini di Boboli, a series of formal gardens.

The Arno is spanned by eight bridges; the **Ponte Vecchio,** lined with jewelry stores, is the most celebrated. **Ponte S. Trinità** is the second-most important bridge spanning the Arno. After crossing it, you can continue along **Via dei Tornabuoni,** the most important right-bank shopping street. At the Ponte Vecchio you can walk along **Via Por Santa Maria,** which becomes Via Calimala. This leads you into **Piazza della Repubblica,** a commercial district known for its cafes.

Florence

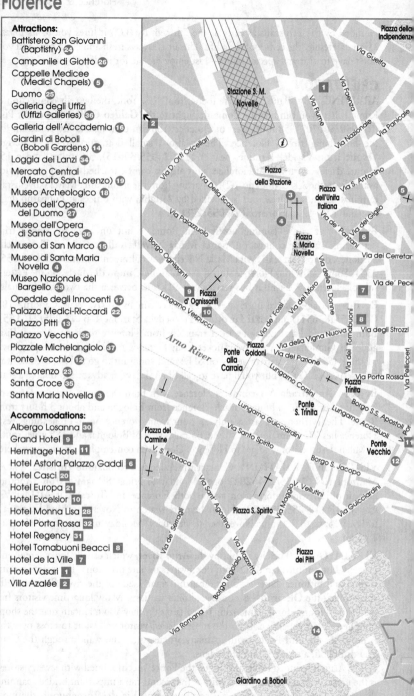

Attractions:

E-0111

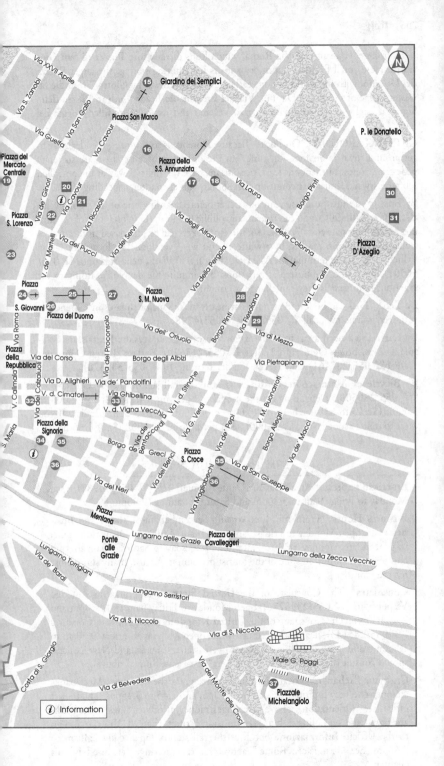

Via XXVII Aprile

Via S. Zanobi

Via S. Gallo

Via San Gallo

Via Cavour

Via Guelfa

15 Giardino dei Semplici

Piazza San Marco

P. le Donatello

16

Piazza della S.S. Annunziata

Piazza del Mercato Centrale

19

Via de' Ginori

20 ⓘ Via Cavour **21**

17 **18** Via Laura

Borgo Pinti

30

Piazza S. Lorenzo

22

Via Ricasoli

Via dei Servi

Via degli Alfani

Via della Colonna

31

Via de' Martelli

Via dei Pucci

Piazza D'Azeglio

23

Via della Pergola

Via L. C. Farini

Piazza S. Giovanni

24 ✚ **25**

26

Piazza del Duomo

27

Piazza S. M. Nuova

28

Borgo Pinti

Via Fiesolana

29 Via di Mezzo

Via Roma

Via del Proconsolo

Via dell' Oriuolo

Piazza della Repubblica

Via del Corso

Borgo degli Albizi

Via Pietrapiana

Via Calimala

Via D. Alighieri

Via de' Pandolfini

Via Calzaiuoli

V. d. Cimatori ✚

Via Ghibellina

32

Via i. d. Stinche

33

V. d. Vigna Vecchia

V. M. Buonarroti

S. Maria

Piazza della Signoria

Via de' Bentaccorai

Via G. Verdi

34 **35**

Borgo de' Greci

Via de' Benci

Piazza S. Croce

35 Via di San Giuseppe

Via de' Pepi

Borgo Allegri

Via de' Macci

ⓘ

36

36

Via del Neri

Via Magliabechi

Piazza Mentana

Ponte alle Grazie

Lungarno delle Grazie

Piazza dei Cavalleggeri

Lungarno Torrigiani

Via de' Bardi

Lungarno della Zecca Vecchia

Lungarno Serristori

Via di S. Niccolo

Via di S. Niccolo

Costa di S. Giorgio

Viale G. Poggi

Via del Monte alle Croci

37

Piazzale Michelangiolo

Via di Belvedere

ⓘ Information

From here, you can take **Via Roma,** which leads directly into **Piazza di San Giovanni.** Here you'll find the Baptistery and its neighboring sibling, the larger **Piazza del Duomo,** with the world-famous cathedral and bell tower by Giotto. From the far western edge of Piazza del Duomo, **Via del Proconsolo** heads south to **Piazza della Signoria,** sight of the landmark Palazzo Vecchio and its sculpture-filled Loggia dei Lanzi.

GETTING AROUND   On Foot   Because Florence is so compact, the ideal way to get around town is on foot—at times it's the only way because there are so many pedestrian zones. In theory at least, pedestrians have the right of way at uncontrolled zebra crosswalks, but don't count on that should you encounter a speeding Vespa.

By Bus   You must purchase your bus ticket before boarding one of the public vehicles. For 1,500L (90¢), you can ride on any public bus in the city for a total of 60 minutes. A 24-hour pass costs 7,500L ($4.50). Bus tickets can be purchased from *tabacchi* (tobacconists' shops, marked by a white T) and news vendors. The local bus station (which serves as the terminal for ATAF city buses) is at Piazza della Stazione (☎ **055/56501**). Bus routes are posted at bus stops, but inquire the day you're riding to get exact bus numbers, as they can change overnight.

By Taxi   Taxis can be found at stands at nearly all the major squares in Florence. If you need a radio taxi, call ☎ **055/4390** or **055/4798.**

By Car   You'll need a car to really explore Tuscany's countryside. Rentals are available at **Avis,** Borgo Ognissanti 128R (☎ **055/213629**); **Budget,** Borgo Ognissanti 134R (☎ **055/287161**); and **Hertz,** Via del Termine 1 (☎ **055/307370**).

By Bicycle or Motorscooter   **Alinari** is near the rail station at Via Guelfa 85R (☎ **055/280500**). Depending on the model of bike you rent, it will cost 4,000 to 5,000L ($2.40 to $3) per hour or 20,000 to 30,000L ($12 to $18) per day. If you want to rent a scooter, it costs 15,000L ($9) per hour or 50,000L ($30) for 5 hours.

Fast Facts: Florence

American Express   Amex is at Via Dante Alighieri 22R (☎ **055/50981**), open Monday to Friday 9am to 5:30pm and Saturday 9am to 12:30pm.

Business Hours   From mid-June to mid-September, most **shops** and **businesses** are open Monday to Friday 9am to 1pm and 4 to 8pm. Off-season hours, in general, are Monday 3:30 to 7:30pm and Tuesday to Saturday 9am to 1pm and 3:30 to 7:30pm. In spite of the tourist invasion in August, many shops close for the month.

Consulates   The Consulate of the **United States** is at Lungarno Amerigo Vespucci 46 (☎ **055/2398276**), open Monday to Friday 9am to 12:30pm and 2 to 3:30pm. The Consulate of the **United Kingdom** is at Lungarno Corsini 2 (☎ **055/284133**), near Piazza Santa Trinità, open Monday to Friday 9:30am to 12:30pm and 2:30 to 4:30pm. Citizens of Australia, Canada, and New Zealand should consult their missions in Rome (see "Fast Facts: Rome," above).

Currency Exchange   Local banks in Florence grant the best rates. Most banks are open Monday to Friday 8:30am to 1:30pm and 2:45 to 3:45pm. The tourist office (see "Orientation," above) exchanges money at official rates when banks are closed and on holidays, but a commission is often charged. You can also go to the **Ufficio Informazione** booth at the rail station, open daily 7:30am to 7:40pm. See "Fast Facts: Rome," above, for the exchange rate used in this chapter.

Dentists & Doctors   For a list of English-speaking dentists, consult your consulate, if possible, or contact **Tourist Medical Service,** Via Lorenzo il Magnifico 59 (☎ 055/475411). Visits without an appointment are possible only Monday to Friday 11am to noon and 5 to 6pm and Saturday 11am to noon.

Emergencies   For fire, call **115;** for an ambulance, call **055/212222;** for the police, **113;** and for road service, **116.**

Hospitals   Call the **General Hospital of Santa Maria Nuova,** Piazza Santa Maria Nuova 1 (☎ 055/27581).

Internet Access   Cyber Cafe in Florence is called **Internet Train,** via Guelfa, 24A (☎ 055/214794; e-mail: info@fionline.it). Open Monday to Saturday 10am to 8pm.

Lost Property   The lost-and-found office, **Oggetti Smarriti,** is at Via Circondaria 19 (☎ 055/32831), near the rail terminal.

Luggage Storage   This is available at the Santa Maria Novella train station, in the center of the city at Piazza della Stazione (☎ 055/2351). It's open daily 4:15am to 1:45am.

Police   Dial **113** in an emergency. Foreigners who want to see and talk to the police should go to the **Ufficio Stranieri** station at Via Zara 2 (☎ 055/49771), where English-speaking personnel are available daily 9am to 2pm.

Post Office   The **Central Post Office** is at Via Pellicceria 3, off Piazza della Repubblica (☎ 055/2774539 or 055/211838; **055/2774322** for English-speaking operators). It's open Monday to Saturday from 8:15am to 7pm. Stamps are purchased in the main post office at windows 21–22. If you want your mail sent to Italy general delivery (*fermo postal*), have it sent in care of this post office (use the **50100 Firenze** postal code). Mail can be picked up at windows 23–24.

Safety   Violent crimes are rare in Florence; crime consists mainly of pickpockets who frequent crowded tourist centers, such as the corridors of the Uffizi Galleries. Members of group tours who cluster together are often singled out as victims. Car thefts are relatively common: Don't leave your luggage in an unguarded car, even if it's locked in the trunk. Women should be especially careful in avoiding purse snatchers, some of whom grab a purse while whizzing by on a Vespa, often knocking the woman down. Documents such as passports and extra money are better stored in the safe at your hotel.

Telephone   The **country code** for Italy is **39.** The **city code** for Florence is **055,** which is the code you'll use every time you dial a party in Florence, regardless of whether you're within the city limits. For additional information, see "Fast Facts: Rome," above.

Transit Information   For international flights from Galileo Galilei Airport, call ☎ 050/500707; for domestic flights at Peretola, call ☎ 055/30615; for rail information, dial ☎ 055/288785; for long-distance bus information, call ☎ 055/483651; and for city buses, dial ☎ 055/56501.

WHERE TO STAY
NEAR THE DUOMO
Expensive

✪ **Hotel J and J.** Via di Mezzo 20, 50121 Firenze. ☎ **055/2345005.** Fax 055/240282. E-mail: jandj@dada.it. 19 units. A/C MINIBAR TV TEL. 400,000L ($240) double; 500,000L ($300) junior suite; 550,000–600,000L ($330–$360) suite. Rates include breakfast. AE, DC, MC, V. Parking 35,000–45,000L ($21–$27).

This charming hotel was built in the 16th century as a monastery. A 5-minute walk from the church of Santa Croce, it underwent a massive restoration in 1990. You'll find many sitting areas throughout, including a flagstone-covered courtyard with stone columns and a salon with vaulted ceilings and several preserved ceiling frescoes. The rooms combine an unusual mixture of modern furniture with the monastery's original beamed ceilings. The suites usually contain sleeping lofts and, in some cases, rooftop balconies overlooking Florence's historic center.

Hotel Monna Lisa. Borgo Pinti 27, 50121 Firenze. ☎ **055/2479751.** Fax 055/2479755. E-mail: monnalis@ats.it. 30 units. A/C MINIBAR TV TEL. 300,000–480,000L ($180–$288) double; 390,000–570,000L ($234–$342) triple. Rates include breakfast. AE, DC, MC, V. Parking 20,000L ($12).

Hotel Monna Lisa (yes, that's the right spelling) is a privately owned Renaissance palazzo, 4 blocks east of the Duomo. On a narrow street where carts were once driven, the palace's facade is forbiddingly severe, in keeping with the style of its day. But when you enter the reception rooms, you'll find an inviting atmosphere. Most of the great old rooms overlook either an inner patio or a modest rear garden. Each of the salons is handsomely furnished with fine antiques and oil paintings. The rooms vary greatly—some are quite large, although no two are alike.

Hotel Porta Rossa. Via Porta Rossa 19. 50123 Firenze. ☎ **055/287551.** Fax 055/282179. 80 units. A/C MINIBAR TV TEL. 264,000L ($158.40) double; 308,000–484,000L ($184.80–$290.40) suite. Rates include breakfast. AE, DC, MC, V. Parking 40,000–55,000L ($24–$33).

If you're tired of Italian modernity and would like—at least in Florence—to settle into an antique palace, this is the place to stay. It even still has frescoes in some of its bedrooms. The hotel occupies the top three floors of a six-story building. The place is a bit dark, as buildings were back then, but on a hot Tuscan summer day you welcome that in lieu of air-conditioning. Since the hotel isn't as well known or publicized as some of its competitors, such as the Hermitage or Tornabuoni, you stand a better chance for getting a reservation. In spite of its antiquity, the hotel has kept abreast of the times, installing modern conveniences, good beds, and ample bathrooms. What we like about this place is that the managers have resisted making two new rooms out of one of the old spacious ones from centuries ago. Breakfast is the only meal served, and a little terrace offers a panoramic view of Florence. No buses run to the hotel, but you are in the town center.

NEAR THE PONTE VECCHIO
Moderate
Hermitage Hotel. Vicolo Marzio 1, Piazza del Pesce I, 50122 Firenze. ☎ **055/287216.** Fax 055/212208. E-mail: florence@hermitagehotel.com. 29 units. A/C TV TEL. 290,000–330,000L ($174–$198) double; 350,000–390,000L ($210–$234) triple; 450,000L ($270) family room. Rates include breakfast. MC, V. Parking 30,000–40,000L ($18–$24).

The offbeat, intimate Hermitage is a charming place, with a roof sun terrace providing a view of much of Florence. You can take your breakfast under a leafy arbor surrounded by potted roses and geraniums. The extremely small rooms are pleasantly furnished, many with Tuscan antiques, rich brocades, and good beds. Rooms overlooking the Arno have the most scenic view, and they've been fitted with double-glazed windows, which reduces the traffic noise by 40%. The tiled bathrooms are superb and contain lots of toiletries. Some restored bathrooms have hydro massage bathtubs.

NEAR PIAZZA SANTA TRÍNITA
Moderate
Hotel Tornabuoni Beacci. Via Tornabuoni 3, 50123 Firenze. ☎ **055/212645.** Fax 055/283594. E-mail: tornabuoni_beacci@italyhotel.com. 34 units. A/C MINIBAR TV TEL. 300,000–340,000L ($180–$204) double. Rates include breakfast. AE, DC, MC, V. Parking 40,000L ($24).

Near the Arno and Piazza S. Trinità, on the principal shopping street, this pensione occupies the top three floors of a 14th-century palazzo. The public rooms have been furnished in a tatty provincial style, with bowls of flowers, parquet floors, a formal fireplace, and old paintings. The hotel was recently renovated, but it still bears an air of old-fashioned gentility. The rooms are moderately well furnished. The roof terrace, surrounded by potted plants and flowers, is for breakfast or late-afternoon drinks. Dinner, typically Florentine and Italian dishes, is served here in summer.

NEAR PIAZZA SAN LORENZO & THE MERCATO CENTRALE
Inexpensive
Hotel Casci. Via Cavour 13, 50129 Firenze. ☎ **055/211686.** Fax 055/2396461. www.hotelcasci.com. E-mail: casci@pn.itnet.it. 25 units. TV TEL. 190,000L ($114) double; 240,000L ($144) triple; 306,000L ($183.60) quad. Rates include buffet breakfast. AE, DC, MC, V. Parking 35,000–40,000L ($21–$24).

Casci is a well-run little hotel in the historic district, 100 yards from Piazza del Duomo and 200 yards from the main rail station. The building dates from the 14th century, and some of the public rooms feature the original frescoes. The hotel is both traditional and modern, and the English-speaking reception staff is attentive. The medium-sized rooms are comfortably furnished, and the beds have firm mattresses. The bathrooms are small, but have plush towels, toiletries, and hair dryers.

Hotel Europa. Via Cavour 14, 50129 Firenze. ☎ **055/210361.** Fax 055/210361. 13 units. TV TEL. 170,000L ($102) double; 220,000L ($132) triple. Rates include breakfast. AE, MC, V.

Two long blocks north of the Duomo, this 16th-century building has functioned as a family-run hotel since 1925. Despite the facade's antique appearance, much of the interior has been modernized, but many homey touches remain. All but four of the rooms open onto a view of the Duomo. Rooms facing the street are noisier, but they do have double-glazed windows that keep out at least some of the traffic noises.

NEAR PIAZZA SANTA MARIA NOVELLA & THE TRAIN STATION
Expensive
Hotel Astoria Palazzo Gaddi. Via del Giglio 9, 50123 Firenze. ☎ **055/2398095.** Fax 055/214632. 102 units. A/C MINIBAR TV TEL. 530,000L ($318) double; 700,000L ($420) suite. Rates include buffet breakfast. AE, DC, MC, V. Parking 40,000L ($24) nearby.

In spite of its location among cheap railroad station hotels, this impressive Renaissance palace still contains original 16th-century frescoes painted by Luca Giordano. In the 17th century, John Milton wrote parts of *Paradise Lost* in one of these rooms. The Astoria has been renovated and turned into an enduring choice with a helpful staff. From the rooms on the upper floors, you'll have a view over the terra-cotta rooftops. Most of the smallish bedrooms have stylish traditional furnishings and excellent mattresses. The tiled, medium-sized bathrooms have fluffy towels and hair dryers. The hotel also has a well-known restaurant, Palazzo Gaddi, that offers excellent Tuscan and Italian dishes. Sometimes the hotel will organize a costume dinner in which the wait-staff wears 15th-century clothing.

Hotel de la Ville. Piazza Antinori 1, 50123 Firenze. ☎ **055/2381805.** Fax 055/2381809. 79 units. A/C MINIBAR TV TEL. 490,000L ($294) double; 800,000L ($480) suite. Rates include buffet breakfast. AE, DC, MC, V. Parking 45,000–50,000L ($27–$30).

On the most elegant street of the historic center, close to the Arno and the rail station, this recently refurbished hotel has a loyal following among Italian business travelers. It has a conservatively contemporary appearance and an elegant decor. The rooms are soundproof, with private safes and contemporary furnishings in muted colors. There's an American-style bar, a breakfast room, and a parking area reserved for guests, and laundry and baby-sitting are available.

Moderate

Villa Azalée. Viale Fratelli Rosselli 44, 50123 Firenze. ☎ **055/214242.** Fax 055/268264. E-mail: villaazalee@firenze.flashnet.it. 24 units. A/C MINIBAR TV TEL. 250,000L ($150) double; 340,000L ($204) triple. Rates include buffet breakfast. AE, DC, MC, V. Parking from 35,000L ($21).

Villa Azalée, a handsome structure set on a street corner with a big garden, is a remake of a private home built in the 1860s and transformed into a hotel in 1964, when an annex was added. Go for the rooms in the old villa, if possible—they are cozier and more elegant. The rooms have distinction (one boasts a flouncy canopy bed). My favorite is number 24, with the huge 19th-century fresco on the ceiling. Most of the smallish tiled bathrooms have tub/shower combinations and plush towels and bathrobes. Hair dryers are available on request. The hotel is a 5-minute walk from the rail station. You can rent bicycles at the hotel for 5,000L ($3) per day.

Inexpensive

Hotel Vasari. Via B. Cennini 9–11, 50123 Firenze. ☎ **055/212753.** Fax 055/294246. 30 units. A/C MINIBAR TV TEL. 150,000–230,000L ($90–$138) double. Rates include breakfast. AE, DC, MC, V. Parking 15,000L ($9).

Built in the 1840s as a private home, this was a rundown two-star hotel until 1993, when its owners poured money into a renovation and upgraded it to one of the most fairly priced three-star hotels in town. Its three stories are connected by an elevator. Bedrooms are comfortable and clean, albeit somewhat Spartan, and the tiled bathrooms offer medium-sized towels and hair dryers.

ON PIAZZA OGNISSANTI

Piazza Ognissanti is a fashionable—albeit car-clogged—Renaissance square opening onto the Arno. It's home to two of the most legendary hotels in the city.

Very Expensive

Grand Hotel. Piazza Ognissanti 1, 50123 Firenze. ☎ **800/325-3589** in the U.S. and Canada, or 055/288781. Fax 055/217400. 107 units. A/C MINIBAR TV TEL. 750,000–950,000L ($450–$570) double; from 1,518,000L ($910.80) suite. AE, DC, MC, V. Parking from 60,000L ($36). Bus: 6 or 17.

The Grand Hotel is a bastion of luxury, although it's not as exclusive as the Hotel Regency (see below). A hotel of history and tradition, the Grand is known for its halls and salons. Its rooms and suites have a refined elegance, and the best rooms overlook the Arno. Rooms are spacious, and the mattresses here are among the best in the world. Bathrooms are quite large with delux fluffy towels, hair dryers, and lots of amenities (showercaps, plush bathrobes, separate phone line, bidets). A highlight of the hotel is the Winter Garden, an enclosed court lined with arches where regional and international dishes are served.

Hotel Excelsior. Piazza Ognissanti 3, 50123 Firenze. ☎ **800/325-3535** in the U.S. and Canada, or 055/264201. Fax 055/210278. www.deluxurycollection.firenze.net. 191 units.

A/C MINIBAR TV TEL. 680,000–750,000L ($408–$450) double; from 1,100,000L ($660) junior suite. AE, DC, MC, V. Parking 60,000L ($36). Bus: 6 or 17.

The Excelsior is the ultimate in luxury. Cosmopolitan and sophisticated, it has the best-trained staff in town, but in recent years more tranquil and less commercial establishments, including the Regency, have distracted customers from its positive attributes. If you like glamour and glitz, stay here. The opulent rooms have 19th-century Florentine antiques and sumptuous fabrics. In these old palaces, expect the accommodations to come in a variety of configurations. Il Cestello, the hotel's deluxe restaurant, attracts an upper-crust clientele.

ON OR NEAR PIAZZA MASSIMO D'AZEGLIO

Piazza Massimo d'Azeglio is a 12-minute walk northeast of Florence's historic center.

Very Expensive

✪ **Hotel Regency.** Piazza Massimo d'Azeglio 3, 50121 Firenze. ☎ **055/245247.** Fax 055/2346735. www.regency-hotel.com. E-mail: info@regency-hotel.com. 34 units. A/C MINIBAR TV TEL. 470,000–620,000L ($282–$372) double; from 850,000L ($510) suite. Rates include breakfast. AE, DC, MC, V. Parking 50,000L ($30).

The Regency is an intimate villa of taste and exclusivity. It's only a 15-minute stroll to the cathedral. This well-built old-style villa, a member of Relais & Châteaux, has its own garden across from a park in a residential area of the city. The hotel is a luxurious hideaway, and you'll find no better bedrooms in all of Florence. Mattresses are deluxe, and the rooms are exquisitely furnished. The large bathrooms are extremely luxurious, with a wide range of toiletries, a bidet, robes, plush towels, and hair dryers. The dining room, Relais le Jardin, is renowned for its *alta cucina*.

Inexpensive

Albergo Losanna. Via Vittorio Alfieri 9, 50121 Firenze. ☎ and fax **055/245840.** 8 units (3 with bathroom). TEL. 95,000L ($57) double without bathroom; 130,000L ($78) double with bathroom; 210,000L ($126) suite. Rates include breakfast. AE, MC, V. Parking 30,000–35,000L ($18–$21). Bus: 6.

A good choice, Albergo Losanna is a tiny family-run place off Viale Antonio Gramsci, between Piazzale Donatello and Piazza Massimo d'Azeglio. The rooms are small and the mattresses aren't so firm, but the hotel offers utter simplicity and cleanliness. The private bathrooms are tiny, but the towels are good. The large corridor bathrooms are kept very clean.

WHERE TO DINE
NEAR THE DUOMO
Inexpensive

Il Cavallino. Via della Farine 6R. ☎ **055/215818.** Reservations recommended. Main courses 14,000–28,000L ($8.40–$16.80); set-price menu 32,000L ($19.20). AE, DC, MC, V. Mar–Oct daily noon–3pm and 7–10:30pm; off-season Thurs–Tues noon–3pm and Thurs–Mon 7–10:30pm. TUSCAN/ITALIAN.

Il Cavallino is the kind of discreetly famous restaurant where Florentines invariably go just to be with one another. The place has been a local favorite since the 1930s. It's on a tiny street (which probably won't even be on your map) that leads off Piazza della Signoria at its northern end, not far from the equestrian statue. There's usually a gracious reception at the door, especially if you've called ahead for a reservation. Two of the three dining rooms have vaulted ceilings and peach-colored marble floors. The main room looks out over the piazza. Menu items are typical hearty Tuscan fare, including an assortment of boiled meats in green herb sauce, grilled filet of steak, breast of chicken Medici style, and the inevitable Florentine spinach.

Paoli. Via dei Tavolini 12R. ☎ **055/216215.** Reservations required. Main courses 16,000–32,000L ($9.60–$19.20); set-price menu 40,000L ($24). AE, DC, MC, V. Wed–Mon noon–2:30pm and 7–10:30pm. Closed 3 weeks in Aug. TUSCAN/ITALIAN.

Paoli, between the Duomo and Piazza della Signoria, is one of Florence's finest restaurants. Housed in a building from 1824, the restaurant turns out a host of specialties, but could be recommended almost solely for its medieval-tavern atmosphere, with arches and ceramics stuck into the walls like medallions. All pastas are homemade, and the fettuccine alla Paoli is served piping hot and full of flavor. The chef also does a superb *rognoncino trifolato* (thinly sliced kidney cooked with oil, garlic, and parsley) and sole meunière. A recommendable side dish is *piselli* (garden peas) in the Florentine style.

NEAR THE PONTE VECCHIO
Inexpensive
Buca dell'Orafo. Via Volta dei Girolami 28R. ☎ **055/213619.** Main courses 12,000–30,000L ($7.20–$18). No credit cards. Tues–Sat 12:30–2:30pm and 7:30–10:30pm. Closed Aug and 2 weeks in Dec. FLORENTINE.

Buca dell'Orafo is a little dive (one of the many cellars or *buca*-type establishments beloved by Florentines). The trattoria is usually stuffed with regulars, so if you want a seat, go early. Over the years the chef has made little concession to the foreign palate, turning out genuine Florentine specialties, like tripe and mixed boiled meats with a green sauce and *stracotto e fagioli* (beef braised in a sauce of chopped vegetables and red wine), served with beans in a tomato sauce.

NEAR PIAZZA SAN LORENZO & THE MERCATO CENTRALE
Inexpensive
Le Fonticine. Via Nazionale 79R. ☎ **055/282106.** Reservations recommended for dinner. Main courses 18,500–30,000L ($11.10–$18). AE, DC, MC, V. Tues–Sat noon–2:30pm and 7–10pm. Closed Jan 1–15 and Aug. TUSCAN/BOLOGNESE.

Le Fonticine used to be part of a convent until owner Silvano Bruci converted both it and its adjoining garden into one of the most hospitable restaurants in Florence. The richly decorated interior contains the second passion of Signor Bruci's life, his collection of original modern paintings. The first passion, as a meal here reveals, is the cuisine he and his wife produce from recipes she collected from her childhood in Bologna. The food, served in plentiful portions, is both traditional and delectable. Begin with a platter of fresh antipasti, and then enjoy samplings of three of the most excellent pasta dishes of the day. This might be followed by veal scaloppine.

Trattoria Antellesi. Via Faenza 9R. ☎ **055/216990.** Reservations recommended. Main courses 18,000–26,000L ($10.80–$15.60). AE, DC, MC, V. Nov–Aug Mon–Sat noon–3pm and 7–10:30pm; Sept–Oct daily noon–3pm and 7–10:30pm. TUSCAN.

On the ground floor of a 15th-century historic monument, a few steps from the Medici Chapel, this restaurant is devoted almost exclusively to Tuscan recipes that have stood the test of time. Owned by the Italian-American team of Enrico Verrecchia and his Arizona-born wife, Janice, the restaurant prepares at least seven *piatti del giorno* that change according to the availability of the ingredients. Menu items may include *tagliatelle* with porcini mushrooms or braised arugula, *crespelle alla fiorentina* (a Tuscan Renaissance cheesy spinach crêpe introduced to France by Catherine de Medici's kitchen staff), market-fresh fish (generally on Friday), and delicious Valdostana chicken.

NEAR PIAZZA SANTA MARIA NOVELLA & THE TRAIN STATION
Expensive
I Quattro Amici. Via degli Orti Oricellari 29. ☎ **055/215413.** Reservations recommended. Main courses 30,000–60,000L ($18–$36). AE, DC, MC, V. Daily noon–2:30pm and 7–10:30pm. SEAFOOD.

Opened in 1990 by four Tuscan entrepreneurs, this restaurant occupies the street level of a modern building near the rail station. Amid a vaguely neoclassical decor, the place serves endless quantities of fish. Specialties include such dishes as pasta with fish sauce and fragments of sausage; fish soup; fried shrimp and squid in the style of Livorno; and grilled, stewed, or baked versions of all the bounty of the Mediterranean. The roast sea bass and roast snapper, flavored with Mediterranean herbs, are among the finest dishes.

Moderate
Buca Lapi. Via del Trebbio 1R. ☎ **055/213768.** Reservations required for dinner. Main courses 22,000–36,000L ($13.20–$21.60). AE, DC, MC, V. Mon–Fri 12:30–2:30pm; Wed–Fri 7:30–10:30pm. Closed 2 weeks in Aug. TUSCAN.

Buca Lapi, a cellar restaurant, is big on glamour, good food, and the enthusiasm of fellow diners. Its decor alone—under the Palazzo Antinori—makes it fun: Vaulted ceilings are covered with travel posters from all over the world. There's a long table of interesting fruits, desserts, and vegetables. The cooks know how to turn out the most classic dishes of the Tuscan kitchen with superb finesse. Specialties include pâté, cannelloni, *scampi giganti alla girglia* (a super-size shrimp), and *bistecca alla fiorentina* (local beefsteak), still cooked over coals in the old-fashioned way. In season, the *fagioli toscani all'olio* (Tuscan beans in the native olive oil) are a delicacy.

✪ **Don Chisciotte.** Via Ridolfi 4R. ☎ **055/475430.** Reservations recommended. Main courses 28,000–35,000L ($16.80–$21); set-price menu 90,000L ($54). AE, DC, MC, V. Mon 8–10:30pm; Tues–Sat 1–2:30pm and 8–10:30pm. ITALIAN/SEAFOOD.

One floor above street level in a Florentine palazzo, this restaurant is known for its creative cuisine and changing array of very fresh fish. Menu items are produced with a flourish from the kitchens. Examples include red *taglierini* with clams, pesto, and cheese; risotto of broccoli and baby squid; and black ravioli colored with squid ink and stuffed with a purée of shrimp and crayfish.

Sabatini. Via de'Panzani 9A. ☎ **055/211559.** Reservations recommended. Main courses 35,000–60,000L ($21–$36). AE, DC, MC, V. Tues–Sun 12:30–2:30pm and 7:30–10:30pm. FLORENTINE.

Despite its less-than-chic location near the rail station, Sabatini has long been extolled by Florentines and visitors alike as the finest of the restaurants characteristic of the city. To celebrate our return visit every year, we order the same main course—boiled Valdarno chicken with savory green sauce. Other main courses are also delicious, especially the veal scaloppine with artichokes. Of course, you can always order a good sole meunière and the classic beefsteak Florentine.

Inexpensive
Ristorante Otello. Via degli Orti Oricellari 36R. ☎ **055/216517.** Reservations recommended. Main courses 16,000–32,000L ($9.60–$19.20). AE, DC, MC, V. Daily noon–3pm and 7:30–11pm. FLORENTINE.

Beside the train station, Ristorante Otello is a long-established, comfortable Florentine dining room. Its *antipasto Toscano* is one of the best in town, an array of appetizing hors d'oeuvres that practically becomes a meal in itself. The waiter urges you to

"*Mangi, mangi, mangi!*" ("Eat, eat, eat!"). The truly stoic go on to order one of the succulent pasta dishes, such as spaghetti with baby clams or pappardelle with garlic sauce.
The meat and poultry dishes are equally delectable, including sole meunière and veal
pizzaiola with lots of garlic.

✪ **Sostanza.** Via del Porcellana 25R. ☎ **055/212691.** Reservations recommended. Main
courses 15,000–29,000L ($9–$17.40). No credit cards. Mon–Fri noon–2:10pm and
7:30–9:30pm. Closed Aug and 2 weeks at Christmas. FLORENTINE.

Sostanza is a tucked-away little trattoria where working people have gone since 1869
to get excellent, reasonably priced food. It's the city's oldest and most revered trattoria.
The small dining room has crowded family tables. The rear kitchen is open, its secrets
exposed to diners. Specialties include breaded chicken breast and a succulent T-bone
steak. You might also want to try tripe the Florentine way—cut into strips and baked
in a casserole with tomatoes, onions, and parmesan.

NEAR PIAZZA GOLDONI
Moderate
Harry's Bar. Lungarno Vespucci 22R. ☎ **055/2396700.** Reservations required. Main
courses 18,000–36,000L ($10.80–$21.60). AE, MC, V. Mon–Sat noon–3pm and 7–11pm.
Closed 1 week in Aug and Dec 18–Jan 8. INTERNATIONAL/ITALIAN.

Harry's Bar, in a prime position on the Arno, is an enclave of expatriate and well-
heeled visiting Yankees that deserves its reputation. Patrons can order from an international menu—small, but select, and beautifully prepared, featuring fresh fish on its
menu every day. A specialty is risotto or tagliatelle with ham, onions, and cheese.
Harry has created his own tortellini, but Harry's hamburger and his club sandwich are
the most popular items. The chef also prepares about a dozen specialties every day, like
breast of chicken "our way," grilled, giant-size scampi, and lean broiled sirloin.

Trattoria Coco Lezzone. Via del Parioncino 26R. ☎ **055/287178.** Reservations accepted
only for groups of 10 or more. Main courses 16,000–70,000L ($9.60–$42). No credit cards.
Mon–Sat noon–2:30pm and 7–10pm. Closed last week of July–Aug and Dec 25–Jan 6. Bus: 27
or 31. FLORENTINE.

In Florentine dialect, the establishment's name refers to the sauce-stained apron of the
chef who established this place more than a century ago. Today, it remains a good
place to sample the food of the nearby Tuscan countryside. Florentine "blue bloods"
wait with workers crowding in on their lunch hours for a seat at one of the long tables.
Go before the rush begins if you want a seat in this bustling trattoria. The rib-sticking
fare includes generous portions of boiled meats with a green sauce, pasta *fagiole*
(beans), *osso buco* (beef or veal knuckle braised in wine, butter, garlic, and lemon),
tripe, and beefsteak Florentine.

NEAR PIAZZA SANTA CROCE
Expensive
Alle Murate. Via Ghibellina, 52R. ☎ **055/240618.** Reservations recommended. Main
courses 45,000–70,000L ($27–$42). AE, DC, MC, V. Tues–Sun 7:30–11:30pm. Closed 15 days
at Christmas. Bus: 14. TUSCAN/SOUTHERN ITALIAN.

This sophisticated eatery with its uncluttered dining room, wood floors, and soft
lighting, prepares some of the most creative and classic Tuscan dishes in town. Yet it
allows you to take a night off from Tuscan fare by offering some of the classics of the
south, including the famous pasta, *orecchiette* sauced with broccoli, fish poached *acqua
pazza* (tomatoes, garlic, and parsley), or five-bean purée topped with cooked chicory.
The chefs make the best lasagne in town. Several soufflés are prepared with seasonal
vegetables, such as leeks or artichokes. Handmade *tortelli* (a kind of ravioli) is stuffed

with small eggplants and served with a butter and thyme sauce. *Brasato di chianina* is veal braised with Brunello di Montalcino red wine. There's nothing finer here than the baked sea bream with crunchy potatoes. In an adjacent smaller room, Vineria, the menu is different, the service is not as good, but the food's slightly cheaper.

Moderate

Cibreo. Via dei Macci 118R. ☎ **055/2341100.** Reservations recommended in the restaurant, not accepted in the trattoria. Main courses 45,000L ($27) in the restaurant; 20,000L ($12) in the trattoria. AE, DC, MC, V (restaurant only). Tues–Sat 12:30–3pm and 7:30–11pm. Closed late July–early Sept. MEDITERRANEAN.

Despite its lack of pretensions, Cibreo is one of the largest eateries in the neighborhood. From a small and impossibly old-fashioned kitchen, it prepares food for a restaurant, a less formal tavern-style trattoria, and a cafe-bar across the street. The kitchens are noteworthy for not containing a grill and not serving pastas. They specialize in foodstuffs cooked in a wood-burning oven and cold marinated dishes, especially vegetables. Menu items include a *sformato* (a soufflé made from potatoes and ricotta, served with Parmesan and tomato sauce) and a flan of Parmesan, veal tongue, and artichokes. One of the chef's favorite dishes is the roast pigeon flavored with a fruity mustard.

ACROSS THE ARNO

Moderate

Mamma Gina. Borgo Sant'Jacopo 37R. ☎ **055/2396009.** Reservations required for dinner. Main courses 20,000–32,000L ($12–$19.20). AE, DC, MC, V. Mon–Sat noon–2:30pm and 7–10pm. Closed Aug 7–21. TUSCAN.

Mamma Gina is a rustic left-bank restaurant in a 15th-century building that's a winner for fine foods prepared in the traditional bustling manner. This restaurant is named after its founding matriarch (Mamma Gina), whose legend has continued despite her death in the 1980s. This exceptional trattoria, well worth the trek across the Ponte Vecchio, is a center for hearty Tuscan fare. The menu items are rich, savory, and tied to the seasons and include dishes such as *cannelloni Mamma Gina* (stuffed with a purée of minced meats, spices, and vegetables); tagliolini with artichoke hearts or mushrooms and whatever else is in season; and chicken breast Mamma Gina, baked in the northern Italian style, with prosciutto and Emmenthaler cheese.

SEEING THE SIGHTS IN THE RENAISSANCE CITY

Florence was the fountainhead of the Renaissance, the city of Dante and Boccaccio. Florentines are noted for their cunning, as represented by Machiavelli. For three centuries, Florence was dominated by the Medici family—patrons of the arts and masters of assassination—but it's chiefly through its artists that we know of the apogee of the Renaissance: Ghiberti, Fra Angelico, Donatello, Brunelleschi, Botticelli, and the incomparable Leonardo da Vinci and Michelangelo.

✪ **Piazza della Signoria,** although never completed, is one of the most beautiful squares in Italy. In the square's center is the Fountain of Neptune, the sea god surrounded by creatures from the deep, as well as frisky satyrs and nymphs. Near the fountain is the spot where Savonarola walked his last mile. This zealous monk was a fire-and-brimstone reformer who rivaled Dante in conjuring up the punishment hell would inflict on sinners. For centuries Michelangelo's *David* stood in this piazza, but it was moved to the Academy Gallery in the 19th century. The figure you see here today is an inferior copy.

On the piazza, the 14th-century **Loggia dei Lanzi** (sometimes called the Loggia della Signoria) is a gallery of sculpture that often depicts fierce, violent scenes. The best piece is a rare work by Benvenuto Cellini, the goldsmith and tell-all autobiographer.

Critics have said that his exquisite *Perseus,* who holds the severed head of Medusa, is the most significant Florentine sculpture since Michelangelo's *Night* and *Day.*

For a view of the wonders of Florence below and Fiesole above, climb aboard bus no. 13 from the central station and head for **Piazzale Michelangelo,** a 19th-century belvedere with a view seen in many a Renaissance painting. It's best at dusk, when the purple-fringed Tuscan hills frame Giotto's bell tower, Brunelleschi's dome, and the towering stones sticking up from the Palazzo Vecchio. Another copy of Michelangelo's *David* dominates the square.

SIGHTSEEING SUGGESTIONS FOR FIRST-TIME VISITORS

If You Have 1 Day   You'll have to accept the inevitable—you can visit only a small fraction of Florence's stellar attractions. Go to the Uffizi Galleries as soon as they open and concentrate on only some of the masterpieces or your favorite artists. Have lunch on **Piazza della Signoria,** which is dominated by the Palazzo Vecchio, and admire the statues in the Loggia dei Lanzi. After lunch, visit the **Duomo** and **Baptistery,** before continuing north to see Michelangelo's *David* at the **Accademia.** Next, head back south toward the Arno and the Ponte Vecchio. On the way, do a little shopping at the fabled **Straw Market,** Mercato Nuovo. Sunset should find you at the landmark **Ponte Vecchio.** Finish your very busy day with a hearty Tuscan dinner in one of Florence's many *bucas* (cellar restaurants).

If You Have 2 Days   Spend your first day as suggested above. On day 2, return to the Uffizi Galleries for a more thorough look at this museum—the most important museum in Italy. In the afternoon, visit the **Pitti Palace,** on the other side of the Arno, and wander through the Galleria Palatina, with its 16th- and 17th-century master-pieces, including 11 works by Raphael. After a visit, stroll through the adjoining **Boboli Gardens.** At sunset, return to the Duomo and the Baptistery for a much better look.

If You Have 3 Days   Spend your first 2 days as suggested above. In the morning of day 3, visit the **Palazzo Vecchio** on Piazza della Signoria, and then walk to the nearby **Museo Nazionale del Bargello,** which contains the most important works of Tuscan and Florentine sculpture from the Renaissance era. After lunch, visit the **Museo del-l'Opera del Duomo,** with its sculptural masterpieces from the Duomo, including Donatello's *Mary Magdalene.*

If You Have 4 Days or More   Spend days 1 to 3 as suggested above. On day 4, con-tinue your exploration of Renaissance masterpieces with a visit to the **Medici Chapels,** home to Michelangelo's tomb for Lorenzo de Medici, which includes the fig-ures of *Dawn* and *Dusk.* Later in the morning, go to the **Museo di San Marco,** a small museum that's a monument to the work of Fra Angelico. Before it closes at 6:30pm, visit the **Basilica di Santa Croce,** with its two restored chapels by Giotto.

On day 5, leave Florence and head south to yet another fascinating art city, **Siena,** the most important of the Tuscan hill towns.

THE TOP MUSEUMS

✪ **Galleria degli Uffizi.** Piazzale degli Uffizi 6. ☎ **055/23885.** Admission 12,000L ($7.20). Mon–Sat 8:30am–7pm; Sun and holidays 8:30am–1:50pm (last entrance 45 minutes before closing).

This is one of the world's outstanding museums and Italy's finest collection of art; to see and absorb all the paintings would take at least 2 weeks. The Uffizi is nicely grouped into periods or schools to show the progress of Italian and European art. The first room begins with classical sculpture. A special treasure is a work by Masaccio, who died at an early age but is credited as the father of modern painting. In his madonnas and bambini you can see the beginnings of the use of perspective. The Botticelli rooms contain his finest works, including *The Birth of Venus* (what's commonly called "Venus on the Half Shell"). In another room you'll see Leonardo da Vinci's unfinished but brilliant *Adoration of the Magi* and Verrocchio's *Baptism of Christ*, not a very important painting but noted because Leonardo painted one of the angels when he was 14. Also in this salon hangs Leonardo's *Annunciation*.

In the rooms that follow are works by Perugino, Dürer, Mantegna, Bellini, Giorgione, and Correggio. Finally, you can view Michelangelo's *Holy Family*, as well as Raphael's *Madonna of the Goldfinch*, plus his portraits of Julius II and Leo X. There is also what might be dubbed the Titian salon, which has two of his interpretations of Venus (one depicted with Cupid).

✪ **Galleria dell'Accademia.** Via Ricasoli 60. ☎ **055/2388609.** Admission 12,000L ($7.20). Tues–Sat 8:30am–7pm; Sun 8:30am–2pm.

This museum contains Michelangelo's colossal *David*, unveiled in 1504, which overshadows everything else. In the connecting picture gallery is a collection of Tuscan masters, such as Botticelli, and Umbrian works by Perugino (Raphael's teacher).

✪ **Palazzo Pitti and the Giardini di Boboli (Boboli Gardens).** Piazza de'Pitti. ☎ **055/23885.** Palatina, 12,000L ($7.20); Modern Art Gallery, 8,000L ($4.80); Argenti, 8,000L ($4.80); Boboli Gardens, 4,000L ($2.40). Galleria Palatina and Appartamenti Reali, Mar–Oct, Tues–Sat 8:30am–10pm and Sun 8:30am–8pm; off-season, Tues–Sat 8:30am–6:50pm and Sun 8:30am–1:50pm. Museo degli Argenti Tues–Sat 8:30am–1:30pm; Modern Art Gallery, Tues–Sat 8:30am–2pm. Boboli Gardens, June–Sept daily 8:30am–6:30pm; Apr–May and Oct daily 8:30am–5:30pm; Nov–Mar daily 9am–4:30pm. Ticket office closes 1 hour before the gardens.

The Pitti Palace, on the left bank (a 5-minute walk from the Ponte Vecchio), actually contains several museums, the most important of which is the **Galleria Palatina,** a repository of old masters. This gallery houses one of Europe's great art collections, with masterpieces hung one on top of the other, as in the days of the Enlightenment. If for no other reason, come here for the Raphaels. In the **Sala di Saturno,** look to the left of the entrance wall to see Raphael's *Madonna of the Canopy.* On the third wall near the door is the greatest Pitti prize, Raphael's *Madonna of the Chair,* his best-known interpretation of the Virgin, and what is one of the six most celebrated paintings in all Europe. The Pitti, built in the mid-15th century (Brunelleschi was the original architect), was once the residence of the powerful Medici family.

Other museums are the **Appartamenti Reali,** which the Medici family once called home; the **Museo degli Argenti,** 16 rooms devoted to displays of the "loot" acquired by the Medici dukes; the **Coach and Carriage Museum;** the **Galleria d'Arte Moderna;** the **Museo delle Porcellane** (porcelain); and the **Galleria del Costume.** The Museo degli Argenti has a separate number to call for information (☎ 055/2388-709), as does the Modern Art Gallery (☎ 055/2388-601).

Behind the Pitti Palace are the **Boboli Gardens,** Piazza de'Pitti 1 (☎ 055/218741), through which the Medici romped. The gardens were laid out by Triboli, a great landscape artist, in the 16th century. The Boboli is a popular spot for strolling or for an idyllic interlude. The gardens are filled with fountains and statuary, such as a Giambologna *Venus* in the "Grotto" of Buontalenti. You can climb to the top of the Fortezza di Belvedere for a dazzling city view.

Cappelle Medicee (Medici Chapels). Piazza Madonna degli Aldobrandini 6. ☎ **055/23885.** Admission 12,000L ($7.20); free ages 5 and under. Tues–Sat 8:30am–1:15pm; Sun 8:30am–1:50pm.

The Medici tombs are adjacent to the Basilica of San Lorenzo (see "Other Churches," below). You enter the tombs, housing the "blue-blooded" Medici, in back of the church by going around to Piazza di Madonna degli Aldobrandini. The "New Sacristy" was designed by Michelangelo. Working from 1521 to 1534, he created the Medici tomb in a style that foreshadowed the baroque. Lorenzo the Magnificent—a ruler who seemed to embody the qualities of the Renaissance itself—was buried near Michelangelo's uncompleted *Madonna and Child* group, a simple monument that evokes a promise unfulfilled. Ironically, the finest groups of sculpture were reserved for two Medici "clan" members, who (in the words of Mary McCarthy) "would better have been forgotten." They're represented by Michelangelo as armored, idealized princes. The other two figures on Lorenzo's tomb are most often called *Dawn* and *Dusk*, with morning represented as woman and evening as man. The best-known figures—Michelangelo at his most powerful—are *Night* and *Day* at the feet of Giuliano, the duke of Nemours. *Night* is chiseled as a woman in troubled sleep; *Day* is a man of strength awakening to a foreboding world.

Museo Nazionale del Bargello. Via del Proconsolo 4. ☎ **055/2388606.** Admission 8,000L ($4.80). Tues–Sat 8:30am–1:50pm; 2nd and 4th Sun of the month 8:30am–1:50pm; 1st and 3rd Mon of the month 8:30am–1:50pm.

The National Museum, a short walk from Piazza della Signoria, is a 13th-century fortress palace whose dark underground chambers once resounded with the cries of the tortured. Today it's a vast repository of some of the most important Renaissance sculptures, including works by Michelangelo and Donatello.

Here you'll see another Michelangelo *David* (referred to in the past as *Apollo*), chiseled perhaps 25 to 30 years after the statuesque figure in the Accademia. The Bargello *David* is totally different—even effete when compared to its stronger brother. Among the more significant sculptures is Giambologna's *Winged Mercury.* The Bargello displays two versions of Donatello's *John the Baptist*—one emaciated, the other a younger and much kinder edition. Look for at least one more notable work, another *David*—this one by Andrea del Verrocchio, one of the finest of the 15th-century sculptors. The Bargello contains a large number of terra-cottas by the della Robbia clan.

Museo di San Marco. Piazza San Marco 1. ☎ **055/2388608.** Admission 8,000L ($4.80). Daily 8:30am–1:50pm. Closed 1st, 3rd, and 5th Sun of the month, and 2nd and 4th Mon of the month.

This state museum is a handsome Renaissance palace whose walls are decorated with frescoes by the mystical Fra Angelico, one of Europe's greatest 15th-century painters. In the days of Cosimo dei Medici, San Marco was built by Michelozzo as a Dominican convent. It originally contained bleak, bare cells, which Angelico and his students then brightened considerably with some of the most important works of this pious artist from Fiesole, who portrayed recognizable landscapes in vivid colors. One of his better-known paintings here is *The Last Judgment,* which depicts people with angels on the left dancing in a circle and lordly saints towering overhead. On the second floor—at the top of the hall—is Angelico's masterpiece, *The Annunciation.*

THE DUOMO, CAMPANILE & BAPTISTERY

✪ **Cattedrale di Santa Maria del Fiore (Duomo).** Piazza del Duomo. ☎ **055/2302885.** Cathedral, free; excavations, 5,000L ($3); cupola, 10,000L ($6). Mar–Oct, Mon–Sat 8:30am–6:20pm, Sun 1–5pm; off-season, Mon–Sat 8:30am–3:20pm, Sun 1–5pm.

The Duomo, graced by Brunelleschi's dome, is the crowning glory of Florence. But don't rush inside too quickly, as the view of the exterior, with its geometrically patterned bands of white, pink, and green marble, is, along with the dome, the best feature. One of the world's largest churches, the Duomo represents the flowering of the "Florentine Gothic" style. Begun in 1296, it was finally consecrated in 1436, yet finishing touches on the facade were applied as late as the 19th century. The cathedral was designed by Arnolfo di Cambio in the late 13th century.

Inside, the overall effect of the cathedral is bleak, except when you stand under the cupola, frescoed in part by Vasari. Some of the stained-glass windows in the dome were based on designs by Donatello (Brunelleschi's friend) and Ghiberti (Brunelleschi's rival). If you resist scaling Giotto's bell tower (below), you may want to climb Brunelleschi's ribbed dome. The view is well worth the trek.

Campanile (Giotto's Bell Tower). Piazza del Duomo. ☎ 055/2302885. Admission 10,000L ($6). Nov–Mar daily 9am–4:20pm; Apr–Oct daily 9am–6:50pm.

Giotto left to posterity the most beautiful bell tower, or *campanile,* in Europe, rhythmic in line and form. He designed the campanile in the last 2 or 3 years of his life and died before its completion. The final work was admirably carried out by Andrea Pisano, one of the greatest Gothic sculptors in Italy (see his bronze doors on the nearby Baptistery). The 274-foot tower, a "Tuscanized" Gothic, with bands of colored marble, can be scaled for a panorama of the sienna-colored city. The view will surely rank among your most memorable—it encompasses the enveloping hills and Medici villas.

Battistero San Giovanni (Baptistery). Piazza S. Giovanni. ☎ 055/2302885. Admission 5,000L ($3). Mon–Sat noon–6:30pm; Sun 8:30am–1:30pm.

Named after the city's patron saint, Giovanni (John the Baptist), the present octagonal Battistero dates from the 11th and 12th centuries. The oldest structure in Florence, the Baptistery is a highly original interpretation of the Romanesque style, with its bands of pink, white, and green marble. Visitors from all over the world come to gape at its three sets of bronze doors. The east door is a copy; the other two are originals. In his work on two sets of doors, Lorenzo Ghiberti reached the pinnacle of his artistry in *quattrocento* Florence. The gilt panels—representing scenes from the New Testament, including the *Annunciation,* the *Adoration,* and Christ debating the elders in the temple—make up a flowing, rhythmic narration in bronze.

After his long labor, the Florentines gratefully gave Ghiberti the task of sculpting the east doors (directly opposite the entrance to the Duomo). Upon seeing the doors, Michelangelo is said to have exclaimed, "The Gateway to Paradise!"

OTHER CHURCHES

Basilica di San Lorenzo. Piazza San Lorenzo. ☎ 055/216634. Free admission. Library, Mon–Sat 7:30–11:45am and 3:30–5:30pm.

This is Brunelleschi's 15th-century Renaissance church, where the Medici used to attend services from their nearby palace on Via Larga, now Via Camillo Cavour. Most visitors flock to see Michelangelo's "New Sacristy" with his *Night* and *Day* (see the Medici Chapels under "The Top Museums," above), but Brunelleschi's handiwork deserves some time, too. Built in the style of a Latin cross, the church is distinguished by harmonious grays and rows of Corinthian columns.

Biblioteca Medicea Laurenziana (☎ 055/210760) is entered separately at Piazza San Lorenzo 9 and was designed by Michelangelo to shelter the Medici family's expanding library. Beautiful in design and concept, and approached by exquisite stairs, the library is filled with some of Italy's greatest manuscripts—many of which are handsomely illustrated. Hours are Monday to Saturday 9am to 1pm. Admission is free; the only time you'll be charged is if some special exhibition is mounted.

Basilica di Santa Croce. Piazza Santa Croce 16. ☎ 055/244619. Church, free; cloisters and church museum, 5,000L ($3). Church, Mon–Sat 8am–6:30pm, Sun 3–6:30pm; museum and cloisters, Thurs–Tues 10am–12:30pm and 3–5pm.

The Pantheon of Florence, this church shelters the tombs of everyone from Michelangelo to Machiavelli, from Dante (he was actually buried at Ravenna) to Galileo. Santa Croce was the church of the Franciscans, said to have been designed by Arnolfo di Cambio. In the right nave (first tomb) is the Vasari-executed monument to Michelangelo, whose body was smuggled back to his native Florence from its original burial place in Rome. The Trecento frescoes are reason enough for visiting Santa Croce—especially those by Giotto to the right of the main chapel.

Basilica di Santa Maria Novella. Piazza Santa Maria Novella. ☎ **055/210113.** Church, free; Spanish Chapel and cloisters, 5,000L ($3). Church, Mon–Fri 7am–noon and 3–6pm; Sat–Sun 3–5pm; Spanish Chapel and cloisters, Sat–Thurs 8am–2pm.

Near the railway station is one of Florence's most distinguished churches, begun in 1278 for the Dominicans. Its geometric facade, with bands of white and green marble, was designed in the late 15th century by Leon Battista Alberti, a true Renaissance man. The church borrows from and harmonizes the Romanesque, Gothic, and Renaissance styles.

In the left nave as you enter (the third large painting) is the great Masaccio's *Trinity*, a curious work that has the architectural form of a Renaissance stage setting, but whose figures—in perfect perspective—are like actors in a Greek tragedy. Head straight up the left nave to the Gondi Chapel for a look at Brunelleschi's wooden *Christ on the Cross*, which is said to have been carved to compete with Donatello's same subject in Santa Croce.

PALACES

Palazzo Vecchio. Piazza della Signoria. ☎ **055/2768325.** Admission 10,000L ($6) or 7,500L ($4.50) ages 9–14 (free 8 and under). Mon–Wed and Fri–Sat 9am–7pm; Thurs 9am–2pm; Sun 8am–1pm. Ticket office closes 1 hour before palace.

The secular "Old Palace" is without doubt the most famous and imposing palace in Florence. It dates from the closing years of the 13th century. Its remarkable architectural feature is its 308-foot tower, an engineering feat that required supreme skill. Once home to the Medici, the Palazzo Vecchio (also called the Palazzo della Signoria) is occupied today by city employees, but much of it is open to the public.

The 16th-century "Hall of the 500" (Dei Cinquecento), the most outstanding part of the palace, is filled with frescoes and sculpture done by Vasari and his workshop. As you enter the hall, look for Michelangelo's *Victory*. Later you can stroll through the rest of the palace, through its apartments and main halls. You can also visit the private apartments of Eleanor of Toledo, wife of Cosimo I, and a chapel that was begun in 1540 and frescoed by Bronzino.

Palazzo Medici-Riccardi. Via Camillo Cavour 1. ☎ **055/2760340.** Admission 6,000L ($3.60) adults, 4,000L ($2.40) children 6–12 (free 5 and under). Mon–Tues and Thurs–Sat 9am–1pm and 3–6pm; Sun 9am–noon.

This palace, a short walk from the Duomo, was the home of Cosimo dei Medici before he moved his household to the Palazzo Vecchio. Built by palace architect Michelozzo in the mid-15th century, the brown stone building was also the scene, at times, of the court of Lorenzo the Magnificent. Art lovers visit today chiefly to see the mid-15th-century frescoes by Benozzo Gozzoli in the Medici Chapel. Gozzoli's frescoes, which depict the *Journey of the Magi*, form his masterpiece—in fact, they're a hallmark in Renaissance painting in that they abandoned ecclesiastical themes to celebrate emerging man (he peopled his work with the Medici, the artist's master Fra Angelico, and even himself).

OTHER MUSEUMS

Museo Archeologico. Via della Colonna 38. ☎ **055/23575.** Admission 8,000L ($4.80). Tues–Sat 9am–2pm; Sun 9am–1pm.

The Archaeological Museum, a short walk from Piazza della Santissima Annunziata, houses one of Europe's most outstanding Egyptian and Etruscan collections. Its Egyptian mummies and sarcophagi are on the first floor, along with some of the better-known Etruscan works. Pause to look at the lid to the coffin of a fat Etruscan. Three bronze Etruscan masterpieces are among the rarest objets d'art of these relatively unknown people; one is the Chimera, a lion with a goat sticking out of its back.

Museo dell'Opera del Duomo. Piazza del Duomo 9. ☎ **055/2302885.** Admission 10,000L ($6). Apr–Oct, Mon–Sat 9am–6:50pm; Nov–Mar, Mon–Sat 9am–5:20pm.

Museo dell'Opera del Duomo, across the street but facing the apse of Santa Maria del Fiore, is beloved by connoisseurs of Renaissance sculptural works. It shelters the sculpture removed from the campanile and the Duomo. A major attraction of this museum is the unfinished *Pietà* by Michelangelo, which is in the middle of the stairs. It was carved between 1548 and 1555, when the artist was in his seventies.

A good reason for visiting the museum is to see the marble choirs—*cantorie*—of Donatello and Luca della Robbia (the works face each other, and are in the first room you enter after climbing the stairs). The Luca della Robbia choir is more restrained, but it still "praises the Lord" in marble, with clashing cymbals and sounding brass that constitute a reaffirmation of life.

THE SHOPPING SCENE

Skilled craftsmanship and traditional design unchanged since the days of the Medici have made Florence a destination for serious shoppers. Florence is noted for its hand-tooled **leather goods** and its **straw merchandise,** as well as superbly crafted **gold jewelry.** Its reputation for fashionable custom-made clothes is no longer what it was, having lost its position of supremacy to Milan.

Florence is not a city for bargain shopping, and merchandise is generally rather high-priced. Most visitors interested in gold or silver jewelry head for the **Ponte Vecchio** and its tiny shops. It's difficult to tell one shop from the other, but you really don't need to since the merchandise is similar. If you're looking for a charm or souvenir, these shops are fine. But the heyday of finding gold jewelry bargains on the Ponte Vecchio is long gone.

The street for antiques in Florence is **Via Maggio;** some of the furnishings and objets d'art here are from the 16th century. Another major area for antiques shopping is **Borgo Ognissanti.**

Florence's Fifth Avenue is **Via dei Tornabuoni.** This is the place to head for the best-quality leather goods, for the best clothing boutiques, and for very stylish shoes. Here you'll find everyone from Giorgio Armani to Salvatore Ferragamo.

The better shops are for the most part along Tornabuoni, but there are many on **Via Vigna Nuova, Via Porta Rossa,** and **Via degli Strozzi.** You might also stroll along the Arno on the Lungarno.

For some of the best buys in leather, check out **Via del Parione,** a short, narrow street off Tornabuoni.

Shopping hours are generally Monday from 4 to 7:30pm and Tuesday to Saturday from 9 or 10am to 1pm and 3:30 or 4 to 7:30pm. During the summer, some shops are open Monday mornings. However, don't be surprised if shops close for several weeks in August, if not for the entire month.

Florence's Famous Markets

After checking into their hotels, the most intrepid shoppers head for **Piazza del Mercato Nuovo** (the Straw Market), called "Il Porcellino" by the Italians because of the bronze statue of a reclining wild boar in the square. (It's a copy of the one in the Uffizi.) Tourists pet its snout (which is well worn) for good luck. The market stands in the monumental heart of Florence, an easy stroll from the Palazzo Vecchio. It sells not only straw items, but leather goods as well, along with an array of typically Florentine merchandise—frames, trays, hand embroidery, table linens, and hand-sprayed and painted boxes in traditional designs. Open Monday to Saturday from 9am to 7pm.

However, even better bargains await those who make their way through pushcarts to the stalls of the open-air **Mercato Centrale** (also called the Mercato San Lorenzo), in and around Borgo San Lorenzo, near the train station. If you don't mind bargaining, which is imperative here, you'll find an array of merchandise, including raffia bags, Florentine leather purses, salt-and-pepper shakers, straw handbags, and art reproductions.

SOME SHOPS WORTH A LOOK

Balatresi Gift Shop. Lungarno Acciaiuoli 22R. ☎ **055/287851.**

Among the many treasures found here are Florentine mosaics created for the shop by Maestro Metello Montelatici, who is arguably one of the greatest mosaicists alive today. The store also sells original ceramic figurines by the sculptor Giannitrapani, and a fine selection of hand-carved alabaster, enamel ware, and Tuscan glass.

Befani E Tai. Via Vacchereccia 13R. ☎ **055/287825.**

In front of the Palazzo Vecchio, this is one of the most unusual jewelry stores in Florence—some of its pieces date back to the 19th century. The store was established, right after World War II, by expert goldsmiths who were childhood friends. Some of their clients design their own jewelry and have the store's artisans handcraft their creations.

Bojola. Via dei Rondinelli 25R. ☎ **055/211155.**

Sergio Bojola, a leading name in leather, has distinguished himself in Florence by the variety of his selections, in both synthetic materials and beautiful leathers. Here you'll find first-class quality and craftsmanship. You might be especially interested in their beautiful leather suitcases.

Galleria Masini. Piazza Goldoni 6R. ☎ **055/294000.**

This is the oldest art gallery in Florence. The selection of modern and contemporary paintings by top artists is extensive, representing the work of more than 700 Italian painters. Even if you're not a collector, this is a good place to select a picture that will be a lasting reminder of your visit to Italy—you can take it home duty-free.

Menegatti. Piazza del Pesce, Ponte Vecchio 2R. ☎ **055/215202.**

The wide inventory here includes pottery from Florence, Faenza, and Deruta. There are also della Robbia reproductions made in red clay like the originals. Items can be sent home if you arrange it at the time of your purchase.

Officina Profumo Farmaceutica di Santa Maria Novella. Via della Scala 16N. ☎ **055/216276.**

This is the most fascinating pharmacy in Italy. Located northwest of the Church of Santa Maria Novella, it opened its doors to the public in 1612, offering a selection of herbal remedies that were created by Dominican friars. Those closely guarded secrets have been retained, and many of the same elixirs are still sold today. A wide selection of perfumes, scented soaps, shampoos, and of course potpourris, along with creams and lotions, is also sold. The shop is closed on Saturday afternoon in July and August.

FLORENCE AFTER DARK

For theatrical and concert listings, pick up a free copy of *Welcome to Florence*, available at the tourist office and at most hotels. This helpful publication contains information on recitals, concerts, theatrical productions, and other cultural presentations.

Many cultural presentations are performed in churches. These might include open-air concerts in the cloisters of the Badia Fiesolana in Fiesole (the hill town above Florence) or at the Ospedale degli Innocenti, the foundling "hospital of the innocents" (on summer evenings only).

THE PERFORMING ARTS

Teatro Comunale di Firenze/Maggio Musicale Fiorentino. Corso Italia 16. ☎ **055/211158.** Tickets, 40,000–200,000L ($24–$120) for opera; 35,000–45,000L ($21–$27) for concerts; 35,000–50,000L ($21–$30) for ballet.

This is the main theater in Florence, with an opera and ballet season presented from September to December and a concert season from January until April. This is also the venue for the Maggio Musicale Fiorentino, Italy's oldest and most prestigious festival. It takes place from May until July and offers opera, ballet, concerts, recitals, and cinema productions. The theater's box office is open Tuesday to Friday from 11am to 4:30pm and Saturday from 9am to 1pm. It also opens 1 hour before the curtain goes up.

Teatro della Pergola. Via della Pergola 18. ☎ **055/2479651.** Tickets 22,000–44,000L ($13.20–$26.40); 14,500–28,500L ($8.70–$17.10) ages 24 and under.

You'll have to understand Italian to appreciate most of the plays presented here. Plays are performed year-round except during the Maggio Musicale, when the theater becomes the setting for the festival's many musical presentations. Performances are Tuesday to Saturday at 8:45pm. The box office is open Tuesday to Saturday from 9:30am to 1pm and 3:30 to 6:45pm and on Sunday from 10am to noon.

MUSIC & DANCE CLUBS

Full-Up. Via della Vigna Vecchia 23–25R. ☎ **055/293006.** Cover (including 1 drink) 15,000–25,000L ($9–$15).

Contained in the cellar of an antique building in the historic heart of town, this well-known establishment attracts college students from the city's many universities, although older clients usually feel at ease, too. One section contains a smallish dance floor and recorded dance music; another is devoted to the somewhat more restrained ambience of a piano bar. Open Wednesday to Monday from 9pm to 3am.

Meccanó. Viale degli Olmi 1. ☎ **055/331371.** Cover (including 1 drink) 25,000L ($15).

Set within a 20-minute bus ride from Piazza Duomo, near the Parco della Cascine, this is one of the few discos in Italy to offer an indoor-outdoor setting that includes century-old trees, a terrace, and three dance floors on two different levels. Gays mix with mostly hetero people, and the average age of patrons is from 18 to 32. Dancing reigns supreme every night except Sunday, Monday, and Wednesday, from 11:30pm until 4am.

Yab Yum. Via Sassetti 5R. ☎ **055/215161.** Cover (including 1 drink) 15,000–22,000L ($9–$13.20).

This popular dance club is located in the heart of Florence's historic core. Owned and operated by the same entrepreneurs who maintain the larger, more fun, and less inhibited Meccanó, it offers much the same kind of scene, albeit in a smaller and more cramped setting. It's open Wednesday through Saturday from 11pm to 4am and is closed between May and October.

IRISH PUBS

Dublin Pub. Via Faenza 27R. ☎ **055/293049.**

If you ask whether this is an Italian pub, the all-Italian staff will respond rather grandly that such a concept doesn't exist, and that pubs are by definition Irish. And once you get beyond the fact that virtually no one on the staff here has ever been outside of Tuscany, and that there's very little to do here except drink and perhaps practice your Italian, you might settle down and have a rollicking old (very Latin) time. Beers, at least, are appropriately Celtic and include, on tap, such brands as Harp, Guinness, Kilkenny, and Strong's. It's near the Santa Maria Novella train station.

Fiddler's Elbow. Piazza Santa Maria Novella 7R. ☎ **055/215056.**

After an initial success in Rome, Fiddler's Elbow, near the train station, has now invaded the city of Donatello and Michelangelo. It has quickly become one of the most popular bars in Florence.

CAFES

Café Rivoire, Piazza della Signoria 4R (☎ **055/214412**), offers a classy and amusing old-world ambience with a direct view of the statues of one of our favorite squares. Try the hot chocolate.

Behind three Tuscan arches on a fashionable shopping street in the center of the old city, **Giacosa,** Via Tornabuoni 83R (☎ **055/2396226**), has a warmly paneled interior, a lavish display of pastries and sandwiches, and a reputation as the birthplace of the Negroni, a drink that's a combination of gin, Campari, and red vermouth.

Gilli, Piazza della Repubblica 39R (☎ **055/213896**), a few minutes' walk from the Duomo, is the oldest and most beautiful cafe in Florence, founded in 1733. The interior is all wood and brass, and tables are placed outside in summer.

The waiters at **Giubbe Rosse,** Piazza della Repubblica 13–14R (☎ **055/212280**), still wear red coats, as they did when it was founded in 1888. Originally a beerhall, it's now an elegant cafe/bar/restaurant filled with turn-of-the-century chandeliers and polished granite floors.

TUSCANY DAY TRIPS

TOURING TUSCANY   If you love to walk or bike, **I Bike Italy** (☎ **055/2342371** Monday to Friday or 0368/459123 weekends) books guided bike rides through the countryside from March to November. **Country Walks in Italy** can be booked with the same outfit year-round. If you want to see Italy as did the Romans and the Renaissance condottieri, you can book a horseback trek through **Equitour** (☎ **800/ 545-0019** in the U.S.).

FIESOLE   This town—once an Etruscan settlement—is the most popular outing from Florence. Bus no. 7, which leaves from Piazza San Marco, brings you here in 25 minutes and offers a panoramic view along the way. You'll pass fountains, statuary, and gardens strung out over the hills like a scrambled jigsaw puzzle.

Exploring Fiesole   You won't find anything as dazzling here as the Renaissance treasures of Florence—the charms of Fiesole are more subtle. Fortunately, all major sights branch out within walking distance of the main piazza, beginning with the **Cattedrale di San Romolo.** Dating from A.D. 1000, it was much altered during the Renaissance. In the Salutati Chapel are important sculptural works by Mino da Fiesole. It's open daily 7:30am to noon and 4 to 7pm.

The ecclesiastical **Bandini Museum,** Via Dupre (☎ **055/59477**), around to the side of the Duomo, belongs to the Fiesole Cathedral Chapter. On the ground floor are della Robbia terra-cotta works, as well as art by Michelangelo and Nino Pisano. From March to October, hours are daily 9:30am to 7pm; off-season, daily 9:30am to 5pm. It's always closed the first Tuesday of every month. Admission is 10,000L ($6) adults or 6,000L ($3.60) children under 17 and seniors 65 and over. The ticket also includes admission to the Teatro Romano e Museo Civico (see below).

The hardest task you'll have in Fiesole is to take the steep trail up to the **Museo Missionario Francescano Fiesole,** Via San Francesco 13 (☎ **055/59175**), where you can visit the Franciscan church. Built in the Gothic style in the first years of the 1400s, the church was not consecrated until 1516. Inside are many paintings by well-known Florentine artists. In the basement of the church is the ethnological museum. Begun in 1906, the collection has a large section of Chinese artifacts, including ancient bronzes. An Etruscan-Roman section contains some 330 archaeological pieces, and an Egyptian section also has numerous objects. Admission is free (donation expected). It's open Monday to Saturday 9:30am to noon and 3 to 6pm and Sunday 3 to 6pm.

On the site of the **Teatro Romano e Museo Civico,** Via Portigiani 1 (☎ **055/ 59477**), is the major surviving evidence that Fiesole was an Etruscan city 6 centuries before Christ, then later a Roman town. In the 1st century B.C. a theater was built, the restored remains of which you can see today. Near the theater are the skeleton-like ruins of the baths, which may have been built at the same time. The Etruscan-Roman museum contains many interesting finds that date from the days when Fiesole—not Florence—was supreme (a guide is on hand to show you through). For admission and hours, see the Bandini Museum above.

SIENA   In Rome you see classicism and the baroque; in Florence, the Renaissance; but in the walled city of Siena, you stand solidly planted in the Middle Ages. On three sienna-colored hills in the center of Tuscany, Sena Vetus lies in Chianti country, 21 miles south of Florence. Preserving its original character more markedly than any other Italian city, today it's still a showplace of the Italian Gothic.

Had Siena continued to expand and change after reaching the zenith of its power in the 14th century, chances are it would be markedly different today, influenced by the rising tides of the Renaissance and the baroque (represented here only to a small degree). But Siena retained its uniqueness (certain Sienese painters were still showing the influence of Byzantium in the late 15th century).

Getting There   Trains arrive hourly from both Florence and Pisa, and **TRAIN,** Piazza San Domenico 1 (☎ **0577/204245**), in Siena, offers bus service to all of Tuscany, with air-conditioned coaches. The one-way fare between Florence and Siena is 11,000L ($6.60). **Motorists** can head south from Florence along the Firenze-Siena autostrada, a superhighway linking the cities, going through Poggibonsi.

The **tourist information office** is at Piazza del Campo 56 (☎ **0577/280551**), open Monday to Saturday 8:30am to 7:30pm. From November to February, hours are Monday to Saturday 8:30am to 1pm and 3 to 7pm.

Exploring Siena   Start in the heart of Siena, described by Montaigne as "the finest of any city in the world," in the shell-shaped **Piazza del Campo.** Pause to enjoy the

Tuscany & Umbria

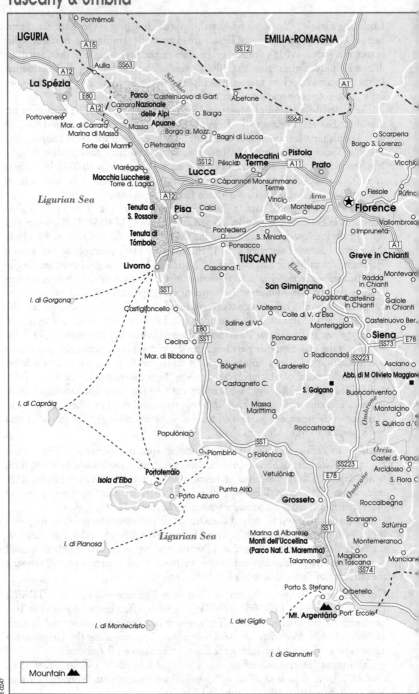

LIGURIA

EMILIA-ROMAGNA

La Spézia

Ligurian Sea

I. di Gorgona

I. di Capráia

I. di Pianosa

Ligurian Sea

Isola d'Elba

I. di Montecristo

I. del Giglio

I. di Giannutri

TUSCANY

Mountain ▲▲

E-0247

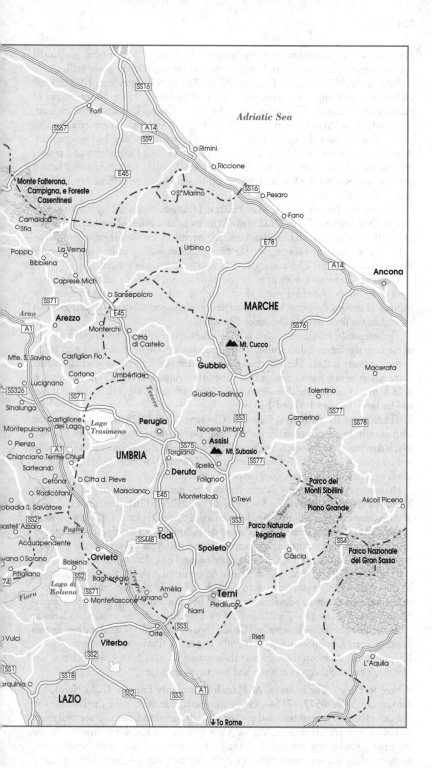

Fonte Gaia, with embellishments by Jacopo della Quercia (the present sculptured works are reproductions; the badly worn originals are found in the town hall).

Palazzo Pubblico, Piazza del Campo (☎ 0577/292263), dates from 1288 to 1309 and is filled with important artworks by some of the leaders in the Sienese school of painting and sculpture. This collection is the Museo Civico. Upstairs in the museum is the **Sala della Pace,** frescoed from 1337 to 1339 by Ambrogio Lorenzetti; the allegorical frescoes show the idealized effects of good government and bad government. Admission is 8,000L ($4.80) for adults and 4,000L ($2.40) for students and seniors 65 and over. From March to October, hours are Monday to Saturday 9:30am to 6:30pm and Sunday 9:30am to 1:30pm; off-season, Monday to Saturday 10am to 4pm and Sunday 10am to 1:30pm.

At Piazza del Duomo, southeast of Piazza del Campo, stands the architectural fantasy of ✪ **Il Duomo** (☎ 0577/283048). With its colored bands of marble, the Sienese cathedral is an original and exciting building, erected in the Romanesque and Italian Gothic styles during the 12th century. The dramatic facade—designed in part by Giovanni Pisano—dates from the 13th century, as does the Romanesque bell tower.

The zebra-like interior, with its black and white stripes, is equally stunning. The floor consists of various embedded works of art, many of which are roped off to preserve the richness in design, depicting both biblical and mythological subjects. Numerous artists worked on the floor, notably Domenico Beccafumi.

The octagonal 13th-century pulpit is by Nicola Pisano (Giovanni's father), who was one of the most significant Italian sculptors before the dawn of the Renaissance (see his pulpit in the Baptistery at Pisa). The Siena pulpit is his masterpiece; it reveals in relief such scenes as the slaughter of the innocents and the Crucifixion. Admission is free. The cathedrals is open March 17 to October, daily 7:30am to 7:30pm; the rest of the year, it closes at sunset and for lunch between 1:30 and 2:30pm.

The facade of the **Battistero,** Piazza San Giovanni (☎ 0577/283048), dates from the 14th century. In the center of the interior is the baptismal font by Jacopo della Quercia, which contains some bas-reliefs by Donatello and Ghiberti. Admission is 3,000L ($1.80), and it's open March 16 to October, daily 9am to 7:30pm; November to March 15, daily 10am to 1pm and 3 to 5pm; closed January 1 and December 25.

Housed in the 14th-century Palazzo Buonsignori, near Piazza del Campo, **Pinacoteca Nazionale (Picture Gallery),** Via San Pietro 29 (☎ 0577/281161), contains a collection of the Sienese school of painting, which once rivaled that of Florence. Displayed are some of the giants of the pre-Renaissance. Most of the paintings cover the period from the late 12th to the mid-16th century. The principal treasures are on the second floor, where you'll contemplate the artistry of Duccio in the early salons. The gallery is rich in the art of the two Lorenzetti brothers, Ambrogio and Pietro, who painted in the 14th century. Ambrogio is represented by an *Annunciation* and a *Crucifix,* but one of his most celebrated works is an almond-eyed *Madonna e Bambino* surrounded by saints and angels. Pietro's most important work is an altarpiece—*The Madonna of the Carmine*—made for a church in Siena in 1329. Simone Martini's *Madonna and Child,* although damaged, is one of the best-known paintings here. Admission is 8,000L ($4.80). Hours are Tuesday to Saturday 8:30am to 1:30pm; in the afternoon there are only three guided visits, at 2:30, 4, and 5:30pm. On Monday, it's open 8:30am to 1:30pm, and Sunday, 8am to 1pm.

Where to Dine The beautiful **Al Marsili (Ristorante Enoteca Gallo Nero),** Via del Castoro 3 (☎ 0577/47154), the best in Siena, stands between the Duomo and Via della Città in a neighborhood packed with medieval and Renaissance buildings. You dine beneath crisscrossed ceiling vaults whose russet-colored brickwork was designed centuries ago. Specialties of the chef include roast boar with tomatoes and herbs, *ribollita* (a savory vegetable soup in the Sienese style), spaghetti with a sauce of

Siena

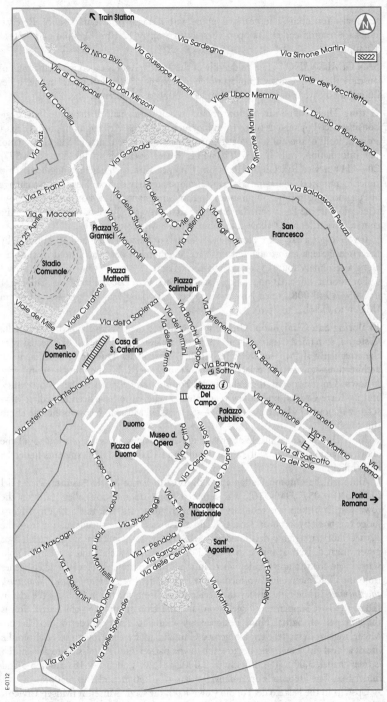

seasonal mushrooms, and veal scaloppine with tarragon and tomato sauce. Reservations are recommended. It's open Tuesday to Sunday 12:30 to 2:30pm and 7:30 to 10:30pm.

SAN GIMIGNANO The golden lily of the Middle Ages is called the Manhattan of Tuscany since it preserves 13 of its noble towers, giving it a skyscraper skyline. It lies 26 miles northwest of Siena and 34 miles southwest of Florence.

Getting There The **rail station** nearest to San Gimignano is the station at Poggibonsi, serviced by regular trains from Florence and Siena. At Poggibono, buses depart from in front of the rail station at frequent intervals to the center of San Gimignano. For information, call ☎ **0577/204-111. Buses** operated by TRAIN (☎ **0577/204-111**) service San Gimignano from Florence with a change at Poggibonsi (trip time: 75 minutes). The same company also operates service from Siena, with a change at Poggibonsi (trip time: 50 minutes). In San Gimignano, buses stop at Piazzale Montemaggio, outside Porta San Giovanni, the southern gate. You'll have to walk into the center, as vehicles aren't allowed in most of the town's core.

If you've got a **car,** leave Florence (1½ hours) or Siena (1 hour and 10 minutes) by the Firenze-Siena autostrada and drive to Poggibonsi, where you'll need to cut west along a secondary route (S324) to San Gimignano.

For tourist information, go to **Associazione Pro Loco,** Piazza del Duomo 1 (☎ **0577/940-008**), open November to February daily 9am to 1pm and 2 to 6pm (March to October to 7pm).

Exploring San Gimignano In the town center is the palazzo-flanked **Piazza della Cisterna,** so named because of the 13th-century cistern in its heart. Connected with the irregularly shaped square is its satellite, **Piazza del Duomo,** whose medieval architecture—towers and palaces—is almost unchanged. It's the most beautiful spot in town. On the square, the **Palazzo del Popolo** was designed in the 13th century, and its **Torre Grossa,** built a few years later, is believed to have been the tallest "skyscraper" (about 178 feet high) in town—see the Civil Museum below for how to climb this tower.

Note: One ticket, available at any of the sites below, allows admission to all the above attractions for 16,000L ($9.60) adults and 12,000L ($7.20) students under 18 and children.

Although the **Duomo Collegiata o Basilica di Santa Maria Assunta,** Piazza del Duomo (☎ **0577/940-316),** was demoted from "duomo" to "collegiata" after the town lost its bishop, the residents of San Gimignano still call this a Duomo. Don't judge this book by its cover (facade): Plain and austere on the outside, dating from the 12th century, it's richly decorated inside. Actually, for some reason the facade was never finished. Retreat inside to a world of tiger-striped arches and a galaxy of gold stars. Head for the north aisle, where in the 1360s Bartolo di Fredi depicted scenes from the Old Testament. Two memorable images are *The Trials of Job* and *Noah with the Animals.* In the right aisle, panels trace scenes from the life of Christ—the kiss of Judas, the Last Supper, the Flagellation, and the Crucifixion. The chief attraction is the **Chapel of Santa Fina,** designed by Giuliano and Benedetto da Maiano. Michelangelo's fresco teacher, Domenico Ghirlandaio, frescoed it with scenes from the life of a local girl, Fina, who became the town's patron saint. Admission to the church is free; chapel, 3,000L ($1.80) adults, 2,000L ($1.20) students 6–18; children 5 and under free. The Duomo is open daily, 9:30am to 12:30pm and 3 to 5:30pm.

Upstairs in the Palazzo del Popolo (town hall), the **Civic Museum (Museo Civico),** Piazza del Duomo 1 (☎ **0577/940-340),** the most notable attraction here is the **Sala di Dante,** where Dante, a supporter of White Guelph, spoke out for his cause in

1300. While you're here, look for one of the masterpieces of San Gimignano—the *Maestà* (Madonna enthroned) by Lippo Memmi (later touched up by Gozzoli). The first large room upstairs contains the other masterpiece: a *Madonna in Glory*, with Sts. Gregory and Benedict, painted by Pinturicchio. On the other side of it are two depictions of the *Annunciation* by Filippino Lippi. Admission is 7,000L ($4.20) adults, 5,000L ($3) students, and 3,500L ($2.10) children. The museum is open daily from April to October, 9:30am to 7pm; from November to March, Tuesday to Sunday, 9:30am to 1pm and 2:30 to 4:30pm.

Passing through the Museo Civico, you can scale the **Torre Grossa** and be rewarded with a bird's-eye view of this most remarkable town. The tower, the only one in town you can climb, is open March to October daily 9:30am to 7:30pm; off-season, Tuesday to Saturday 9:30am to 1:30pm and 2:30 to 4:30pm. Admission is 8,000L ($4.80) adults and 6,000L ($3.60) students under 18 and children.

Where to Dine   Most day trippers from Florence end up at San Gimignano for lunch. Here are your best bets.

At the **Ristorante Bel Soggiorno,** in the Hotel Bel Soggiorno, Via San Giovanni 91 (☎ 0577/940-375), you'll get a strong sense of Tuscany's agrarian bounty, thanks to windows looking out on the countryside and the chef's devoted use of fresh ingredients from nearby farms. Two of the most appealing specialties (available only late summer to late winter) are roasted wild boar with red wine and mixed vegetables and pappardelle pasta garnished with a savory ragôut of pheasant. Other pastas are pappardelle with roasted hare and risotto with herbs and seasonal vegetables. Reservations are recommended. The restaurant is open Thursday to Tuesday, 12:30 to 2:30pm and 7:30 to 10pm. Credit cards are accepted.

Another good choice is the **Ristorante Le Terrazze,** in La Cisterna, Piazza della Cisterna 24 (☎ 0577/940-328). One of this restaurant's two dining rooms boasts stones laid in the 1300s. The newer dining room (added in 1969) has lots of rustic accessories and large windows overlooking the old town and the Val d'Elsa. The setting is one of a country inn, and the food features an assortment of produce from the surrounding Tuscan farms. The soups and pastas make fine beginnings, and specialties of the house include delectable items like sliced filet of wild boar with polenta and Chianti, breast of goose with walnut sauce, *vitello* (veal) *alla Cisterna* with buttered beans, and Florence-style steaks. Reservations are required. The restaurant is closed from November through February; the rest of the year, hours are Wednesday from 7:30 to 10pm, and Thursday to Monday from 12:30 to 2:30pm and 7:30 to 10pm.

PISA   Few buildings in the world have captured imaginations as much as the **Leaning Tower of Pisa.** It's one of the most instantly recognizable buildings in the Western world. Visitors are drawn to it as a symbol of the fragility of people—or at least the fragility of their work. The Leaning Tower is a landmark powerful enough to entice visitors to stop at Pisa, and once here, they find many other sights to explore as well.

Getting There   Trains connect Pisa and Florence, running every hour. The trip takes 1 hour, and one-way fare is 7,500L ($4.50). From Florence, motorists take the autostrada west (A-11) to the intersection (A-12) going south to Pisa.

The **tourist information office** is at Piazza del Duomo 3 (☎ 050/560464), open March to October, Monday to Saturday 9:30am to 1pm and 3 to 7pm; off-season, Monday to Saturday 9:30am to 1pm and 2:30 to 5:30pm.

Seeing the Sights   In the Middle Ages, Pisa reached the apex of its power as a maritime republic before eventually falling to its rivals, Florence and Genoa. Its greatest legacy remains at ✪ **Piazza del Duomo,** which D'Annunzio labeled Piazza dei Miracoli (miracles). Here you'll find an ensemble of the top three attractions—original "Pisan-Romanesque" buildings, including the Duomo, the Baptistery, and the Leaning Tower itself.

Construction of the ✪ **Leaning Tower,** an eight-story campanile, was begun in 1174 by Bonanno, and a persistent legend is that the architect deliberately intended the bell tower to lean (that claim is undocumented). Another legend is that Galileo let objects of different weights fall from the tower, and then timed their descent to prove his theories on bodies in motion.

Unfortunately, the tower is in serious danger of collapse. The government is taking measures to keep it from falling, including clamping five rings of half-inch steel cable around its lower stones and pouring tons of lead around its base to keep it stabilized. The tower is said to be floating on a sandy base of water-soaked clay; it leans at least 14 feet from the perpendicular. If it stood up straight, the tower would measure about 180 feet tall. In 1990 the government suspended visits inside the tower. In years gone by, one of the major attractions in Europe was to climb the Tower of Pisa—taking all 294 steps.

✪ **Il Duomo,** Piazza del Duomo 17 (☎ 050/560547), dating from 1063, was designed by Buschetto, although Rainaldo in the 13th century erected the unusual facade with its four layers of open-air arches that diminish in size as they ascend. The cathedral is marked by three bronze doors—rhythmic in line—that replaced the originals, destroyed in a fire in 1596. The south door, the most notable, was designed by Bonanno in 1180. In the restored interior, the chief art treasure is the pulpit by Giovanni Pisano, which was finished in 1310. There are other treasures, too: Galileo's lamp (according to unreliable tradition, the Pisa-born astronomer used the chandelier to formulate his laws of the pendulum), mosaics in the apse said to have been designed by Cimabue, the tomb of Henry VII of Luxembourg, *St. Agnes* by Andrea del Sarto, *Descent from the Cross* by Il Sodoma, and a crucifix by Giambologna. Admission is 3,000L ($1.80) from March to October; from November to February, it's free. The Duomo is open May to October, Monday to Saturday from 10am to 8pm and Sunday from 1 to 7:40pm. The rest of the year, it's open Monday to Saturday from 10am to 1pm and 3 to 5pm and Sunday from 3 to 4:45pm.

Begun in 1153, the **Battistero,** Piazza del Duomo (☎ 050/560547), is like a Romanesque crown. Although it's most beautiful on the exterior, with its arches and columns, venture inside to see the hexagonal pulpit made by Nicola Pisano in 1260. Supported by pillars resting on the backs of three marble lions, the pulpit contains bas-reliefs of the Crucifixion, the Adoration of the Magi, the presentation of the Christ Child at the temple, and the Last Judgment (many angels have lost their heads over the years). Admission (including entry to another monument) is 10,000L ($6). The Battistero opens daily at 9am, closing at 8pm from June to August, 1 to 2 hours earlier the rest of the year. Closed December 31 and January 1.

Near Piazza Mazzini, **Museo Nazionale di San Matteo,** Piazzetta San Matteo 1 (☎ 050/541865), contains a good assortment of paintings and sculpture, many dating from the 13th to the 16th centuries. In the museum are statues by Giovanni Pisano; Simone Martini's *Madonna and Child with Saints,* a polyptych (a many-paneled alterpiece); Nino Pisano's *Madonna de Latte,* a marble sculpture; Masaccio's *St. Paul,* painted in 1426; Domenico Ghirlandaio's two *Madonna and Saints* depictions; works by Strozzi and Alessandro Magnasco; and old copies of works by Jan and Pieter Bruegel. You enter from Piazza San Matteo. Admission is 8,000L ($4.80). It's open Tuesday to Saturday 9am to 7pm and Sunday 9am to 1pm.

Where to Dine Near Piazzetta di Vecchi Macelli, ✪ **Al Ristoro dei Vecchi Macelli,** Via Volturno 49 (☎ 050/20424), is the best restaurant in Pisa. After selecting from a choice of two dozen varieties of seafood antipasti, you can enjoy a homemade pasta with scallops and zucchini or fish-stuffed ravioli in shrimp sauce. Other dishes are gnocchi with pesto and shrimp and roast veal with a velvety truffle-flavored cream sauce. Reservations are required. The restaurant is open Monday, Tuesday, and Thursday to Saturday from 1 to 3pm and 8 to 10:30pm; closed 2 weeks in August.

LUCCA　In 56 B.C., Caesar, Crassus, and Pompey met in **Lucca** and agreed to rule Rome as a triumvirate. By the time of the Roman Empire's collapse, it was virtually the capital of Tuscany. Periodically in its valiant, ever-bloody history, Lucca was an independent principality, similar to Genoa. This autonomy attests to the fame and prestige it enjoyed. Now, however, Lucca is largely neglected by visitors, although it offers great rewards to the discriminating few who take the time to stop here.

By the late 1600s, Lucca had gained its third and final set of city walls. This girdle of ramparts is largely intact and is one of the major reasons to visit the town, with its medley of architecture ranging from Roman to Liberty (the Italian term for art nouveau).

Today, Lucca is best known for its *olio d'oliva lucchese,* the quality olive oil produced in the region outside the town's walls. Lucca is a sort of Switzerland of the south: The banks have latticed Gothic windows, the shops look like well-stocked linen cupboards, children play in landscaped gardens, and geraniums bloom from the roofs of medieval tower houses.

Getting There　At least 20 **trains** travel daily between Florence and Lucca. The trip takes 1¼ hours. The rail station lies about a quarter-mile south of Lucca's historic center, a short walk from the city's ramparts. For **rail information** in Lucca, call ☎ **0583/47-013.** The **Lazzi bus company** (☎ **0583/584-877**) operates buses traveling between Florence and Lucca. They take less time than the train (50 minutes to an hour). If you've got a **car,** leave Florence and take A11 through Prato, Pistoia, and Montecatini before reaching the outskirts of Lucca. (If you're traveling from Pisa, take SS12.)

The Lucca **tourist office** is on Piazzale Verdi (☎ **0583/419-689**), open daily 9:30am to 6:30pm April to October (off-season to 3:30pm).

Seeing the Sights　The objects of greatest visitor interest, ✪ **Le Mura** enclose the old town. The Lucchesi are fiercely proud of these city walls, which are the best-preserved Renaissance defense ramparts in Europe. The present walls, measuring 115 feet at the base and soaring 40 feet high, replaced crumbling ramparts built during the Middle Ages. If you'd like to join in one of the grand promenades of Tuscany, you can gain access to the ramparts from one of 10 bastions, the most frequently used of which is in back of the tourist office at **Piazzale Verdi.** For orientation, you may want to walk completely around the city on the tree-shaded ramparts, a distance of 2½ miles.

On Piazza San Martino, the **Cattedrale di San Martino (Duomo)** (☎ **0583/ 494-726**) is the town's most visible monument. The Duomo dates back to 1060, although the present structure was mainly rebuilt during the following centuries. The facade is exceptional, evoking the Pisan-Romanesque style with enough originality and idiosyncrasies to distinguish it from the Duomo at Pisa. Designed mostly by Guidetto da Como in the early 13th century, the west front contains three wide, ground-level arches surmounted by three scalloped galleries with twisting columns. The main relic inside—in some ways the religious symbol of Lucca—is the *Volto Santo,* a crucifix carved by Nicodemus (so tradition has it) from the Cedar of Lebanon. The face of Christ was supposedly chiseled onto the statuary. Admission to the cathedral is free, but for the sacristy and inner sanctum, it's 3,000L ($1.80) adults, 1,500L (90¢) children under 14; children under 6 are free. The church and sacristy are open from April to October, daily 10am to 6pm; November to March, Monday through Friday 10am to 2pm, and Saturday to Sunday 10am to 5pm.

The Romanesque **Chiesa San Frediano,** Piazza San Frediano (☎ **0583/493-627**), is one of Lucca's most important and famous churches. Built in the 12th and 13th centuries, when the town enjoyed its greatest glory, the church's severe white facade is relieved by a 13th-century mosaic of the Ascension, and the campanile, or bell tower, rises majestically above. Inside, the bas-reliefs on the Romanesque font add a note of comic relief: Supposedly depicting the story of Moses, among other themes, they show Egyptians in medieval armor chasing after the Israelites. Admission is free, and the church is open Monday to Saturday, 7:30am to noon and 3 to 6pm, and Sunday, 9am to 1pm and 3 to 6pm.

The **National Picture Gallery and Palazzo Mansi Museum (Pinacoteca Nazionale e Museo di Palazzo Mansi),** Via Galli Tassi 43 ☎ **0593/55-570**), is where the Lucchesi horde their art treasures. This palace was built for the powerful Mansi family, whose descendants are still some of the movers and shakers in town; today its most notable treasure is a portrait of Princess Elisa by Marie Benoist. Elisa Bonaparte (1777–1820), who married into a wealthy local family (the Bacceocchis), was "given" the town by her brother Napoléon in 1805, when he made her princess of Lucca and Piombino. The collection also has works by Lanfranco, Luca Giordano, and Tintoretto, among others, though they are not their greatest works. Admission is 8,000L ($4.80) adults, 4,000L ($2.40) children 6 to 18; children 5 and under free. The palace is open Tuesday to Saturday, 9am to 7pm, and Sunday, 9am to 2pm.

Where to Dine On a difficult-to-find alley near Piazza san Michele, ✪ **Buca di Sant'Antonio,** Via della Cervia 1 (☎ **0583/55-881**), is Lucca's finest restaurant. The 1782 building was constructed on the site of a chapel (Buca di Sant'Antonio) believed to be favorable for invoking the protective powers of St. Anthony. The cuisine here is refined and inspired, respecting traditional methods but also daring to be innovative. Menu items include homemade ravioli stuffed with ricotta and pulverized zucchini, grilled meat and fish dishes, and roast Tuscan goat with roast potatoes and braised greens. Reservations are recommended. The restaurant is open Tuesday to Sunday, noon to 3pm, and Tuesday to Saturday, 7:30 to 10:30pm; closed 2 weeks in July.

3 Highlights of the Tuscan & Umbrian Countryside

Rome may rule Italy, but Tuscany presides over its heart. The Tuscan landscapes, little changed since the days of the Medicis, look just like Renaissance paintings, with cypress trees, olive groves, evocative hill towns, and those fabled Chianti vineyards.

Tuscany was the place where the Etruscans first appeared in Italy. The Romans followed, absorbing and conquering them, and by the 11th century, the region had evolved into a collection of independent city-states, such as Florence and Siena, each trying to dominate the other. Although the Renaissance was immensely popular in Florence, it was slow to spread into the surrounding region.

When the Renaissance did arrive, however, with its titans of art, such as Giotto, Michelangelo, and Leonardo, critics claim that Western civilization was "rediscovered" in Tuscany. According to D.H. Lawrence, Tuscany became "the perfect center of man's universe." Art flourished under the patronage of the powerful Medicis, and the legacy remains of Masaccio, della Francesca, Signorelli, Raphael, Donatello, Botticelli, and countless others. Tuscany also became known for its men of letters, such as Dante, Petrarch, and Boccaccio (who wrote in the vernacular rather than in Latin).

Umbria, a small region at the heart of the Italian peninsula, is associated mainly with saints, such as St. Francis of Assisi, founder of the Franciscan order, but Umbrian painters (such as Il Perugino) also contributed to the glory of the Renaissance. The landscape is as alluring as that of Tuscany, with fertile plains of olive groves and vineyards.

Some suggestions for shorter visits (you can find these cities on the Tuscany & Umbria map) are offered in the following sections.

AREZZO

The most landlocked of all towns or cities of Tuscany, Arezzo, 50 miles southeast of Florence, was originally an Etruscan settlement and later a Roman center. The city flourished in the Middle Ages before its capitulation to Florence.

The walled town grew up on a hill, but large parts of the ancient city, including Petrarch's house, were bombed during World War II. Apart from Petrarch, the other famous son of Arezzo was Vasari, the painter/architect remembered chiefly for his history of the Renaissance artists.

Today, Arezzo looks a little rustic, but it really isn't. The city has one of the biggest jewelry industries in Western Europe; little firms on the city outskirts turn out an array of rings and chains, and bank vaults are overflowing with gold ingots. Because of the lack of any really good hotels, you might want to return to Florence for the night, or stop here on your way to Gubbio.

Getting There   A **train** comes from Florence at intervals of 20 to 60 minutes throughout the day, and the trip takes between 40 and 60 minutes. In Arezzo, trains depart and arrive at the **Stazione Centrale,** Piazza della Repubblica (☎ **0575/22-663**). Because of complicated transfers required en route and travel time of as much as 2 ½ hours each way, a trip by **bus** from Florence to Arezzo isn't a good idea. If you have a **car** and are in Rome, head north on A1; from Florence, head south on A1. In both directions, the turn-off for Arezzo is clearly marked.

The **tourist office,** at Piazza della Repubblica 28 (☎ **0575/377-678**), is open April to September every Monday to Saturday 9am to 1:15pm and 3 to 7pm and Sunday 9am to 1pm; October to May, it's open Monday to Saturday 9am to 1:15pm and 3 to 7pm, and Sunday 9am to 1pm.

EXPLORING AREZZO

The biggest event on the Arezzo calendar is the **Giostra del Saraceno,** staged the third Sunday of June and the first Sunday of September on Piazza Grande. Horsemen in medieval costumes reenact the joust ritual—with balled whips cracking in the air—as they have since the 13th century. But you should visit **Piazza Grande** at any time of the year for the medieval and Renaissance palaces and towers that flank it, including the 16th-century loggia by Vasari.

If you have only an hour for Arezzo, race to the ✪ **Basilica di San Francesco,** Piazza San Francesco (☎ **0575/20-630**), a Gothic church finished in the 14th century for the Franciscans. Inside is a Piero della Francesca masterpiece, a fresco cycle called *Legend of the True Cross.* His frescoes are remarkable for their grace, clearness, dramatic light effects, well-chosen colors, and ascetic severity. The frescoes depict the burial of Adam, Solomon receiving the queen of Sheba at the court (the most memorable scene), the dream of Constantine with the descent of an angel, and the triumph of the Holy Cross with Heraclius, among other subjects. You can visit daily 8:30am to noon and 2 to 6:30pm. Admission is free. *Warning:* The frescoes are being restored until 2000, and only limited sightseeing is possible.

Santa Maria della Pieve, Corso Italia (☎ **0575/22-629**), is a Romanesque church with a west-end face consisting of three open-air loggias (each pillar designed uniquely). The 14th-century bell tower is known as "the hundred holes," as it's riddled with windows. Inside, the church is bleak and austere, but there's a notable polyptych, *The Virgin with*

Saints, by one of the Sienese Lorenzetti brothers (Pietro), painted in 1320. The church is open Monday to Saturday 8am to 1pm and 3 to 7pm, and Sunday 8am to 1pm and 3 to 6:30pm. Admission is free.

A short walk away is **Petrarch's House,** Via dell'Orto 28A (☎ **0575/24-700**), which was rebuilt after World War II. Born at Arezzo in 1304, Petrarch was a great Italian lyrical poet and humanist who immortalized his love, Laura, in his sonnets. His house is open Monday to Saturday 10am to noon and Monday to Friday 3 to 5pm; admission is free. Ring the bell to enter.

SHOPPING

Arezzo hosts one of Europe's biggest gold jewelry industries. In the very center of town, around **Piazza Grande,** are dozens of antique shops that have earned Arezzo the title "ye olde curiosity shop of Tuscany." They spill out onto the piazza during the **Antiques Fair,** held the first weekend of every month.

WHERE TO DINE

✪ The city's finest dining choice is **Buca di San Francesco,** Via San Francesco 1 (☎ **0575/23-271**), where reservations are recommended. The restaurant is housed in the historic core of Arezzo in the cellar of a 14th-century building; it's decorated with medieval references and strong Tuscan colors of sienna and blue. The food here is of an extremely high quality. Menu items include pollo del Valdarno arrosto (roast chicken from the valley of the Arno) flavored with anise, homemade tagliolini with tomatoes and ricotta, and calves' liver with onions. All ingredients are fresh, many of the staples are produced in-house, and even the olive oil is from private sources not shared by other restaurants.

GUBBIO

Lying 57 miles southeast of Arezzo, Gubbio is one of the best-preserved medieval towns in Italy. It has modern apartments and stores on its outskirts, but once you press through that, you're firmly back in the Middle Ages. The best-known streets of its medieval core are **Via XX Settembre, Via dei Consoli, Via Galeotti,** and **Via Baldassini.** All these are in the old town (*Città Vecchia*), set against the steep slopes of Monte Ingino.

Since Gubbio is off-the-beaten track, it remains a fairly sleepy backwater today, except for intrepid shoppers who drive here to shop for ceramics (see below). Gubbio is almost as well known for ceramics as is Deruta. Today, the central **Piazza dei Quaranta Martiri** is named for and honors victims of Nazi atrocities in 1944.

Getting There Gubbio doesn't have a rail station of its own, so **train** passengers headed for Gubbio from other parts of Italy get off at the nearby railway station of Fossato di Vico, 12 miles away, and then transfer to one of the frequent buses that make the short trip on to Gubbio. Fosato di Vico lies astride the rail lines stretching between Rome and Ancona. If you're **driving** from Florence, take the A1 south to Orte, and then take SS3 north 88 miles to its intersection with SS298 at Schéggia. Go southwest on SS298 for 8 miles to Gubbio.

The **tourist office** is at Piazza Oderisi 6 (☎ **075/922-0693**), open Monday to Saturday 8:30am to 1:30pm and 3:30 to 6:30pm and Sunday 9:30am to 12:30pm.

EXPLORING THE OLD TOWN

Begin exploring Gubbio, whose golden age was in the 1300s, at **Piazza Grande,** the most important square. Here you can visit the **Palazzo dei Consoli** (☎ 075/927-4298), a Gothic edifice housing the famed bronze *tavole eugubine,* a series of tablets as old as Christianity, discovered in the 15th century. The tablets contain writing in the mysterious Umbrian language. It's open April to September, daily 10am to 1pm and 3 to 6pm and October to March 10am to 1pm and 2 to 5pm. Admission is 5,000L ($3) adults; children under 12 free.

The other major sight is the **Ducal Palace (Palazzo Ducale),** Via Ducale (☎ 075/927-5872). This palace is associated with the memories (not always good ones) of the ruling dukes of Urbino. Today the palace houses some baroque paintings by Zoi and Manetti, although the view of the Gubbio might be more compelling. The palace was built for Federico of Montefeltro and is open Monday to Saturday 9am to 1pm and 2:30 to 7pm and Sunday 9am to 1pm; admission is 4,000L ($2.40). After visiting the palace, you can go inside **Il Duomo,** Via Ducale (☎ 075/927-3980), across the way. The cathedral is a relatively unadorned pink Gothic building with a single nave and some stained-glass windows from the 12th century. It's open daily 9am to 12:30pm and 3:30 to 8:30pm, and admission is free.

If the weather is right, you can take a cable car up to **Monte Ingino,** at a height of 2,690 feet, for a panoramic view of the area. Service is daily June to August 8:30am to 8pm (to 7:30pm April, May, and September to March). A round-trip ticket is 6,500L ($3.90).

SHOPPING

Shopping is the major reason many visitors flock here. Gubbio's fame as a ceramics center had its beginnings in the 14th century. Two of the best ceramics outlets are in the town center. Head for **Ceramica Rampini,** Via Leonardo da Vinci 94 (☎ 075/927-2963), or its largest competitor, **La Mastro Giorgio,** 3 Piazza Grande (☎ 075/927-1574). La Mastro Giorgio opens its factory, at Via Tifernate 10 (☎ 075/927-3616), about half a mile from the center, to well-intentioned visitors who phone in advance for a convenient hour.

WHERE TO STAY

Palace Hotel Bosone. Via XX Settembre 22, 06024 Gubbio. ☎ **075/922-0698.** Fax 075/922-0552. 30 units. MINIBAR TV TEL. 125,000–140,000L ($75–$84) double; 220,000–295,000L ($132–$177) suite. AE, DC, MC, V. Closed 3 weeks in Feb. Free self-parking nearby.

This hotel is in the town's most scenic location. It also has something of a history, as it once housed Dante Alighieri. The house was built in the 1300s and enlarged during the Renaissance, and the three-story stone building was converted into a hotel in 1974. Rooms are spacious and elegant, and the beds have great mattresses. Bathrooms are also spacious and have fluffy towels and hair dryers. Room 212 is the most elegant room, with frescoes in the bedroom and bathroom. Breakfast is the only meal served.

✪ **Villa Montegranelli.** 2 miles SW of Gubbio (reached along Via Buozzi). ☎ **075/922-20-185.** Fax 075/927-33-72. 20 units. TV TEL. 175,000L ($105) double. DC, MC, V.

The area's most tranquil retreat isn't in Gubbio itself but in this lovely restored 18th-century manor house in a panoramic setting. The rooms are beautifully furnished, and the mattresses are new and firm. The full bathrooms have been completely updated. The staff is among the most helpful and efficient in the area, providing such thoughtful extras as placing a basket of fresh fruit in your room every day. Even if you can't stay here, consider calling ahead and visiting for a meal.

WHERE TO DINE

Gubbio has many taverns, but the most authentically medieval is the one recommended below.

Taverna del Lupo. Via Giovanni Ansidei 21. ☎ **075/927-4368.** Reservations recommended. Main courses 18,000–32,000L ($10.80–$19.20). AE, DC, MC, V. Tues–Sun 12:15–3pm and 7pm–midnight. Closed Jan. ITALIAN/UMBRIAN.

Built in the 1200s, with unusual rows of tiles, this restaurant contains ceilings supported by barrel vaults and stone ribbing. For such a relatively modest place, the menu is sophisticated and filled with the rich bounty from this part of Italy. Menu items include a terrine of duck studded with truffles, suprême of pheasant, rich minestrone, and many of the pork, veal, and beef dishes that are distinctly Tuscan.

ASSISI

Ideally placed on the rise to Mt. Subasio, watched over by the medieval **Rocca Maggiore,** this purple-fringed Umbrian hill town retains a mystical air. The site of many a pilgrimage, Assisi is forever linked in legend with is native son, St. Francis. The gentle saint founded the Franciscan order and shares honors with St. Catherine of Siena as the patron saint of Italy, but he's remembered by many as a lover of nature (his preaching to an audience of birds is one of the legends of his life). Dante compared him to John the Baptist. St. Francis put Assisi on the map, and making a pilgrimage here is one of the highlights of a visit to Umbria.

Assisi is still recovering from twin earthquakes that struck in the autumn of 1997. Its major attraction, the Basilica di San Francesco, is being restored, but much of the damage that occurred to its art cannot be fully recovered.

GETTING THERE   Although there is no rail station in Assisi, the town, which lies 110 miles north of Rome and 15 miles southeast of Perugia, is but a 30-minute bus or taxi ride from the rail station in the nearby hamlet of **Santa Maria degli Angeli.** The cab ride costs about $9 (15,000L). From Santa Maria degli Angeli, buses depart at 30-minute intervals for Piazza Matteotti, in the heart of Assisi. **Trains** between Florence and Assisi usually require a transfer in the junction of Terontola. Frequent **buses** connect Perugia with Assisi; the trip takes 1 hour. One bus a day arrives from Rome. Two buses pull in from Florence, taking 2½ hours.

If you have a **car,** it takes 30 minutes from Perugia to reach Assisi (take S3 southwest). At the junction of Route 147, just follow the signs toward Assisi. But you'll have to park outside the town's core, as those neighborhoods are usually closed to traffic.

The **tourist office** is at Piazza del Commune 12 (☎ **075/812-534**), open Monday to Friday 8am to 2pm and 3:30 to 6:30pm, Saturday 9am to 1pm and 3:30 to 6:30pm, and Sunday 9am to 1pm. Closed December 25 and January 1.

EXPLORING ASSISI

In the heart of Assisi, **Piazza del Comune** is a dream for a lover of architecture. On the square is a pagan structure, with six Corinthian columns, called the **Temple of Minerva (Tempio di Minerva),** from the 1st century B.C. With Minerva-like wisdom, the people of Assisi turned it into a baroque church inside so as not to offend the devout. Adjoining the temple is the 13th-century **Tower** (*Torre*), built by Ghibelline supporters. The site is open daily 7am to noon and 2:30pm to dusk. In the wake of the earthquakes, the tower can no longer be visited.

✪ **Basilica di San Francesco.** Piazza San Francesco. ☎ **075/819-001.** Free admission. Apr–Oct daily 6:30am–7pm; Nov–Mar daily 6:30am–6pm.

This important church, with both an upper and a lower church, houses some of the most important fresco cycles in Italy, including works by such pre-Renaissance giants as Cimabue and Giotto. The lower basilica is from 1228 to 1230 and the upper basilica from 1230 to 1253. The basilica and its paintings form the most significant monument to St. Francis. The lower basilica is open to the public and has been restored, but the upper church with the Giotto frescoes is not anticipated to open until December 1999.

Until the restoration is complete, you can enjoy Giotto's most celebrated frescoes, of St. Francis preaching to the birds, only on video. In the nave are the cycle of 27 additional frescoes, some by Giotto, although the authorship of the entire cycle is a subject of controversy. Many frescoes are almost surrealistic (in architectural frameworks), like a stage set that strips away the walls and allows you to see the actors inside. In the cycle you can see pictorial evidence of the rise of humanism that led to Giotto's and Italy's split from the rigidity of Byzantium.

The upper church also contains the damaged masterpiece by Cimabue, his *Crucifixion*. Time and quakes have robbed the fresco of its former radiance, but its power and ghostlike drama remain at least on video. The cycle of badly damaged frescoes in the transept and apse are other works by Cimabue and his helpers. Rather tragically, art experts spend hours daily sorting through boxes of rubble, trying to piece together the jigsaw puzzle caused by the quakes. There's a debate about whether the Cimabue and Giotto frescoes will ever be in good enough condition to be restored to their historic place.

From the transept of the upper church, proceed down the stairs through the two-tiered cloisters to the lower church; this will put you in the south transept, which is open to the public. Look for Cimabue's faded but masterly *Virgin and Child* with four angels and St. Francis looking on from the far right; it's often reproduced in detail as one of Cimabue's greatest works. You'll also find works here by Giotto, Pietro Lorenzetti, and Simone Martini.

Prisons' Hermitage (Eremo delle Carceri). Via Eremo delle Carceri. ☎ **075/812-301.** Free admission (donations accepted). Apr–Oct daily 7am–7pm; Nov–Mar daily 7am–5pm. About 2½ miles east of Assisi (out Via Eremo delle Carceri).

Eremo delle Carceri dates from the 14th and 15th centuries. The "prison" isn't a penal institution but rather a spiritual retreat. It's believed that St. Francis retired to this spot for meditation and prayer. Out back is a gnarled, moss-covered *ilex* (live oak) more than 1,000 years old, where St. Francis is believed to have blessed the birds, after which they flew in the four major compass directions to symbolize that Franciscans, in coming centuries, would spread from Assisi all over the world. The friary also contains some faded frescoes. One of the handful of friars who still inhabit the retreat will show you through.

Basilica di Santa Chiara (Clare). Piazza di Santa Chiara. ☎ **075/812-282.** Basilica, free; however, the custodian turns away visitors in shorts, miniskirts, plunging necklines, and backless or shoulderless attire. Nov–Mar daily 8:30am–noon and 3–5pm; Apr–Oct daily 8:30am–12:05pm and 2–6:55pm.

The basilica is dedicated to "the little plant of Blessed Francis," as St. Clare liked to describe herself. Born in 1193 into one of the noblest families of Assisi, Clare gave all her wealth to the poor and founded, together with St. Francis, the Order of the Poor Clares. She was canonized by Pope Alexander IV in 1255. Pope Pius XII declared her Patroness of Television in 1958. It was decided to entrust to her this new means of social communication based on a vision she had on Christmas Eve 1252, while bedridden in the Monastery of San Damiano: She saw the manger and heard the friars sing in the Basilica of St. Francis. Although many of the frescoes that once adorned the basilica have been completely or partially destroyed (not as a result of the quakes), much remains that's worthy of note. The basilica also houses the remains of St. Clare as well as the crucifix under which St. Francis received his command from above.

Before going here, check the status of this attraction with the tourist office, as it may be closed for parts of 1999 to repair damage caused by the earthquakes.

WHERE TO STAY

Space in Assisi tends to be tight—so reservations are vital. For such a small town, however, it has a good number of accommodations.

Albergo Ristorante del Viaggiatore. Via San Antonio 14, 06081 Assisi. ☎ **075/816-297** or 075/812-424. Fax 075/813-051. 16 units. TEL. 110,000L ($66) double. Rates include breakfast. Half-board 75,000L ($45) per person extra. DC, MC, V.

If it's not the most luxurious hotel in town, this is a great hotel for value. This ancient townhouse has been totally renovated, although the stone walls and arched entryways of the lobby hint at its age. The high-ceilinged rooms are spacious and very contemporary, and mattresses are firm. Bathrooms are very small but have soft towels. There are no hair dryers. The restaurant offers excellent local and regional fare and wines.

Hotel del Priori. Corso Mazzini 15, 0601 Assisi. ☎ **075/812-237.** Fax 075/816-804. www.assind.perugia.it/hotel/dpriori. E-mail: hpriori@edisons.it. 34 units. TEL. 140,000–188,000L ($84–$112.80) double; 248,000–300,000L ($148.80–$180) suite. Rates include breakfast. AE, DC, MC, V. Parking 12,000–18,000L ($7.20–$10.80).

This frequently renovated hotel opened in 1923, and it occupies one of the town's most historic buildings, dating back to the 17th century. A homey, somewhat old-fashioned Umbrian atmosphere prevails, with terra-cotta, vaulted ceilings, and stone-arched doorways remaining from its heyday as an aristocratic palace. Many of the rooms are a bit small (others are quite spacious), and the mattresses are firm. Bathrooms are also small but have fluffy towels (no hair dryers). The hotel's bar serves Umbrian dishes such as green gnocchi with gorgonzola sauce.

Hotel Sole. Corso Mazzini 35, 06081 Assisi. ☎ **075/812-373** or 075/812-922. Fax 075/813-706. www.umbria.org/Hotel/sole. E-mail: sole@technonet.it. 35 units. TV TEL. 120,000L ($72) double; 150,000L ($90) triple. Rates include breakfast. Half-board (Apr–Nov only) 85,000L ($51) extra. AE, DC, MC, V.

For Umbrian hospitality and a general down-home feeling, the Sole is a winner in the heart of medieval Assisi—comfortable but traditional, a bit tattered but affordable. The severe beauty of rough stone walls and ceilings and terra-cotta floors pay homage to the past. Bedrooms are in the main building and in the annex across the street (rooms are the same in either location). The medium-sized bedrooms have firm mattresses, and bathrooms are small but offer soft towels. Bring your own hair dryer. The owners also offer some of the town's best cuisine under the 15th-century vaults of their restaurant.

WHERE TO DINE

Il Medioevo. Via Arco dei Priori 48. ☎ **075/813-068.** Reservations recommended. AE, DC, MC, V. Thurs–Tues noon–2:30pm and 7:30–9:45pm. Closed Jan 7–Feb 7 and July 1–20. UMBRIAN/INTERNATIONAL.

Assisi's best restaurant is one of the architectural oddities of the town's historic center, with foundations that are at least 1,000 years old. Alberto Falsinotti and his family prepare superb versions of Umbrian recipes whose origins are as old as Assisi itself. Specialties are tortelloni stuffed with minced turkey, veal, and beef, served with butter and parmigiano reggiano; gnocchi stuffed with ricotta and spinach and sprinkled with parmigiano reggiano; roasted rabbit with red-wine sauce and truffles; roast lamb with rosemary, potatoes, and herbs; homemade pasta stuffed with black truffles; and grilled filet of veal with herb sauce.

Ristorante Buca di San Francesco. Via Brizi 1. ☎ **075/812-204.** Reservations recommended. Main courses 28,000–40,000L ($16.80–$24). AE, DC, MC, V. Tues–Sun noon–2:30pm and 7:30–9:30pm. Closed July 1–15. UMBRIAN/ITALIAN.

Hospitable and evocative of the Middle Ages, this restaurant occupies the premises of a cave near the foundation of a 12th-century palace. Menu items change frequently and are based on the availability of ingredients: What you're likely to find are *spaghetti alla buca,* with exotic mushrooms and meat sauce; *umbricelli* (big noodles) with asparagus sauce; *cannelloni* (crèpes) with ricotta, spinach, and tomatoes; *carlacca* (baked crèpes stuffed with cheese, prosciutto, and roasted veal); and *piccione alla sisana* (roasted pigeon with olive oil, capers, and aromatic herbs).

4 Venice

Venice is a preposterous monument to both the folly and the obstinacy of humankind. It shouldn't exist, but it does, much to the delight of thousands of tourists, gondoliers, lacemakers, hoteliers, restaurateurs, and glassblowers.

Fleeing the barbarians centuries ago, Venetians left drydock and drifted out to a flotilla of "uninhabitable" islands in the lagoon. Survival was difficult enough, but no Venetian has ever settled for mere survival. The remote ancestors of today's inhabitants created the world's most beautiful and unusual city.

However, it's sinking at a rate of about 2½ inches per decade, and it's estimated that one-third of the city's art will have deteriorated hopelessly within the next decade, if action isn't taken to save it. Clearly, Venice is in peril, under assault by uncontrolled tides, pollution, atmospheric acid, and old age. Efforts are being made to address these problems, but it's possible that to your children or their children, Venice may become a legend from the past.

This is one of the most enchantingly evocative cities on earth, but you must pay a price for all this beauty. In the sultry heat of the Adriatic in summer, the canals become a smelly stew. Steamy, overcrowded July and August are the worst times to visit; May and June or September and October are much more ideal.

Only in Venice

Viewing Giorgione's *Tempest* at the Accademia   One of the world's most famous paintings, the *Tempest* depicts a baby suckling from the breast of its mother, while a man with a staff looks on. What might have emerged as a simple pastoral scene on the easel of a lesser artist comes forth as a picture of exceptional beauty. Summer lightning pierces the sky, but the tempest seems to be in the background—far away from the figures in the foreground, who are menaced without knowing it. In a city filled with art, no painting has captured our endless fascination as much as this one.

Wandering the Narrow Streets of Dorsoduro   This southernmost section of the historic district is the least populated of Venice's six *sestieri* (quarters), filled with old homes and half-forgotten churches. Its major attractions are the Gallerie dell'Accademia and the Guggenheim Foundation. Dorsoduro's heyday came in the 19th century, when it was the most fashionable area in which to live. Its most famous church is La Salute, whose first stone was laid in 1631. The Zattere is a broad quay built after 1516 and is one of Venice's favorite promenades. Cafes, trattorie, and pensiones abound in the area.

Hanging Out on Piazza San Marco   Called "the drawing room of Europe" by Napoléon, this piazza has been the heart of Venetian life for more than a thousand years. It's the address of St. Mark's Basilica and the campanile (bell tower). Around the corner is the Palazzo Ducale (Doge's Palace), with its Bridge of Sighs. Although the square has become a gaudy tourist belt filled with fanfare, sitting on the square at a cafe table as a string quartet plays "As Time Goes By" is still one of the highlights of Europe.

Spending a Day at the Lido   This slim, sandy island cradles the Venetian lagoon. Italy's most fashionable bathing resort, it's 7½ miles long and about half a mile wide, reaching 2½ miles at its broadest point. The Lido was "discovered" back in the mid-1800s, when Musset, Byron, and Shelley, among others, sang its praises, although few traces of that past remain. It has some of the most fashionable and expensive hotels in Venice along its Lido Promenade, but there are cheaper ones as well. The best way to get around is by bike or tandem, which you can rent on the spot at Via Zara and Gran Viale.

Exploring Torcello, the Gem of the Lagoon   Lying 6½ miles northeast of Venice, Torcello is called "the mother of Venice," having been settled between the 9th and the 17th centuries. Once it was the most populous of the islands in the lagoon, but since the 18th century it has been nearly deserted. If you ever hope to find solitude in Venice, you'll find it here. A ghost of its former self, it was once a flourishing island until it degenerated into a malarial swamp after the 14th century. It's visited chiefly today by those wanting to see the Cattedrale di Torcello with stunning Byzantine mosaics and to lunch at the Locanda Cipriani.

Riding in a Gondola   In *Death in Venice,* Thomas Mann wrote: "Is there anyone but must repress a secret thrill, on arriving in Venice for the first time—or returning thither after long absence—and stepping into a Venetian gondola? That singular conveyance, come down unchanged from ballad times, black as nothing else on earth except a coffin—what pictures it calls up of lawless, silent adventures in the plashing night; or even more, what visions of death itself, the bier and solemn rites and last soundless voyage!" It's estimated that in the heyday of the Renaissance there were some 15,000 gondolas afloat in Venice. What a sight it must have been, like a giant festive regatta. Now there are only about 350 gondolas, serving tourists.

ORIENTATION

GETTING THERE   All roads lead not necessarily to Rome but, in this case, to the docks of mainland Venice. The arrival scene at the unattractive Piazzale Roma is filled with nervous expectation, and even the most veteran traveler can become confused. Whether you arrive by train, bus, car, or airport limousine, there's one common denominator—everyone walks to the nearby docks to select a method of transport to his or her hotel. The cheapest way is by *vaporetto* (water bus), the more expensive by gondola or motor launch.

By Plane   You'll land at Mestre, with its **Marco Polo Aeroporto** (☎ **041/ 2606111**). **Boats** depart every 30 minutes directly from the airport, taking you to a terminal near Piazza San Marco. The fare is 17,000L ($10.20).

It's less expensive to take a **bus** from the airport to Piazzale Roma, a trip of less than 5 miles; a one-way fare is 1,500L (90¢). The trip takes half an hour, and departures are usually on the hour. Once at Piazzale Roma, you can make transportation connections to most parts of Venice, including the Lido.

By Train   Trains pull into the **Stazione di Santa Lucia**, at Piazzale Roma. Travel time by train from Rome is about 5¼ hours; from Milan, 3½ hours; from Florence, 4 hours; and from Bologna, 2 hours. For information about rail connections, call

☎ **04178/88088.** The best and least expensive way to get from the station to the rest of town is to take a *vaporetto*, which departs near the main entrance to the station.

By Bus   Buses arrive from points on the mainland of Italy at **Piazzale Roma.** For information about schedules, call the office of **ACTV** at Piazzale Roma (☎ **041/ 5287886**). If you're coming from a distant city in Italy, it's better to take the train.

By Car   Venice has autostrada links with the rest of Italy, with direct routes from such cities as Trieste (driving time: 1½ hours), Milan (driving time: 3 hours), and Bologna (driving time: 2 hours). Bologna is 94 miles southwest of Venice; Milan, 165 miles west of Venice; and Trieste, 97 miles east. Rome is 327 miles to the southwest.

If you arrive by car, there are several multitiered parking areas at the terminus where the roads end and the canals begin. One of the most visible is the **Garage San Marco,** Piazzale Roma (☎ **041/5235101**), near the *vaporetto*, gondola, and motorlaunch docks. You'll be charged 35,000 to 46,000L ($21 to $27.60) per day, maybe more, depending on the size of your car.

VISITOR INFORMATION   You can get information at the **Azienda di Pro-mozione Turistica,** Palazzetto Selva-Giardinetti Reali (Molo S. Marco) (☎ **041/ 5226356**). Summer hours are daily from 9:30am to 6:30pm; off-season, the office is open Monday through Saturday 9:30am to 3:30pm.

CITY LAYOUT   Venice, 2½ miles from the Italian mainland and 1¼ miles from the Adriatic, is an archipelago of some 117 islands. Most visitors, however, concern themselves only with Piazza San Marco and its vicinity. In fact, the entire city has only one piazza: San Marco. Venice is divided into six quarters that locals call *sestieri,* including San Marco, Santa Croce, San Paolo, Castello, Cannaregio, and Dorsoduro, the last of which has been compared to New York's Greenwich Village.

Many of the so-called streets of Venice are actually **canals,** some 150 in all. A canal is called a *rio,* and a total of 400 bridges span these canals. If Venice has a main street, it's the **Grand Canal,** which is spanned by three bridges: the Rialto, the Academy Bridge, and the stone Railway Bridge (the last dating from the 20th century). The canal splits Venice into two unequal parts.

South of the section called Dorsoduro, which is south of the Grand Canal, is the **Canale della Giudecca,** a major channel separating Dorsoduro from the large island of La Giudecca. At the point where the Canale della Giudecca meets the Canale di San Marco, you'll spot the little **Isola di San Giorgio Maggiore,** with a church by Palladio. The most visited islands in the lagoon, aside from the **Lido,** are **Murano, Burano,** and **Torcello.**

Once you land and explore Piazza San Marco and its satellite, Piazzetta San Marco, you can head down **Riva degli Schiavoni,** with its deluxe and first-class hotels, or follow the signs along the **Mercerie,** the major shopping artery, which leads to the Rialto, site of the market area.

Maps & Finding an Address   The system of addresses in Venice is so confusing it's probably known only to the postman. The best thing to do is to arm yourself with a good map, such as the **Falk** map of Venice, which is pocket-sized and available in many kiosks and bookstores.

GETTING AROUND
ON FOOT   This is the only way to explore Venice unless you plan to see it from a boat on the Grand Canal. Everybody walks in Venice—there's no other way.

BY VAPORETTO   The motorboats, or *vaporetti,* of Venice provide inexpensive and frequent, if not always fast, transportation in this canal-riddled city. An *accelerato* is a vessel that makes every stop and a *diretto* makes only express stops. The average fare is 4,500L ($2.70). In summer the vaporetti are often fiercely crowded. Pick up a map of the system from the tourist office. There is frequent service daily 7am to midnight, then hourly midnight to 7am.

Visitors to Venice may avail themselves of a 24-hour 15,000L ($9) *biglietto turistico* (tourist ticket), which allows them to travel all day long on any of the many routes of the city's boat services. This all-inclusive ticket is a bargain, as is the 3-day ticket that goes for 30,000L ($18).

BY WATER TAXI/MOTOR LAUNCH   The city's many private motor launches are called *taxi acquei.* You may or may not have the cabin of one of these sleek vessels to yourself, since the captains fill their boats with as many passengers as the law allows before taking off. The price of a transit by water taxi from Piazzale Roma (the road and rail terminus) to Piazza San Marco begins at 80,000L ($48) for one to six passengers. You can also call for a taxi acquei—try **Cooperativa San Marco** at **041/5222303.**

BY GONDOLA   When riding in a gondola, two major agreements have to be reached: the price of the ride and the length of the trip. The official rate is 100,000L ($60), but virtually no one pays that amount; prices really start at about 150,000L ($90) for up to 50 minutes. Two major stations at which you can hire gondolas are Piazza San Marco (☎ **041/5200685**) and the Ponte Rialto (☎ **041/5224904**). Both organize gondola tours, lasting about 40 minutes and costing from 120,000 to 150,000L ($72 to $90) per person.

Fast Facts: Venice

American Express   The American Express office is at San Marco 1471 (☎ **041/5200844**), in the San Marco area. City tours and mail handling can be obtained here. The office is open May to October, Monday to Saturday 8am to 8pm for currency exchange and 9am to 5:30pm for all other transactions. From November to April, Saturday hours are 9am to 12:30pm; weekday hours, the same.

Consulates   There's no U.S. consulate in Venice; the closest is in Milan, at Via Prìncipe Amedeo 2 (☎ **02/290351**). The British consulate is at Dorsoduro 1051 (☎ **041/5227207**), open Monday to Friday 10am to noon and 2 to 3pm.

Currency   See "Fast Facts: Rome" above.

Currency Exchange   There are many banks in Venice where you can exchange money. Try the **Deutsch Bank SPA,** San Marco 2216 (☎ **041/5207024**). Hours are Monday to Friday 8:30am to 1:30pm and 2:45 to 4pm. Many travelers find that **Guetta Viaggi,** San Marco 1261 (☎ **041/5285101**), offers the best rates in Venice. Hours are Monday to Friday 9am to 12:30pm and 3 to 6:30pm. From April to October, open Saturday 9am to noon, too.

Dentists & Doctors   Your best bet is to have your hotel call and set up an appointment with an English-speaking dentist or doctor. The American Express office and the British Consulate also have a list.

Drugstores   If you need a drugstore in the middle of the night, call **192** for information about which one is open. Pharmacies take turns staying open late. A well-recommended, centrally located one is the **International Pharmacy,** Via XXII Marzo 2067 (☎ **041/5222311**).

Emergencies   Emergency phone numbers are **113** for the police, **118** for an ambulance, and **115** to report a fire.

Hospitals   Get in touch with the **Ospedale Civile Santi Giovanni e Paolo,** Campo Santi Giovanni e Paolo in Castello (☎ **041/5294111**).

Luggage Storage & Lockers   These services are available at the main rail station, **Stazione di Santa Lucia,** at Piazzale Roma (☎ **041/715555**). The cost is 5,000L ($3) per item.

Post Office   The main post office is at Fondaco dei Tedeschi (☎ **041/ 2717111**), in the vicinity of the Rialto Bridge. It's open Monday to Saturday from 8:15am to 5pm.

Safety   The curse of Venice is the pickpocket. Violent crime is rare, but because of the overcrowding on *vaporetti* and even on the small, narrow streets, it's easy to pick pockets. Purse snatchings are commonplace as well. A purse snatcher seemingly darts out of nowhere, grabs a purse, and in seconds seems to have disappeared down some narrow, dark alley. Secure your valuables, and if your hotel has safes, keep them locked there when not needed.

Telephone   The **country code** for Italy is **39.** The **city code** for Venice is **041,** which is the code you use every time you dial a party in Venice, regardless of whether you're within the city limits. For additional information, see "Fast Facts: Rome," above.

Transit Information   For flights, call ☎ **041/2606111;** for rail information, ☎ **147/888-088;** and for bus schedules, ☎ **041/5287886.**

WHERE TO STAY
NEAR PIAZZA SAN MARCO
Very Expensive

✪ **Gritti Palace.** Campo Santa Maria del Giglio, San Marco 2467, 30124 Venezia. ☎ **800/ 325-3535** in the U.S., 416/947-4864 in Canada, or 041/794611. Fax 041/5200942. E-mail: reso73grittipalace@ittsheraton.com. 99 units. A/C MINIBAR TV TEL. 1,056,000–1,342,000L ($633.60–$805.20) double; from 2,398,000L ($1,438.80) suite. Rates include buffet breakfast. AE, DC, MC, V. Vaporetto: Santa Maria del Giglio.

Gritti Palace, in a stately setting on the Grand Canal, is the renovated four-story palazzo of the 15th-century doge Andrea Gritti. It's a bit starchy, and there's something of a museum aura to the place. The range and variety of the rooms seems almost limitless, from elaborate suites to relatively small singles, but in every case, the stamp of glamour is evident (the mattresses are deluxe). Most bathrooms are sumptuous, stocked with robes, large fluffy towels, and hair dryers. For a splurge, ask for Hemingway's old suite or the Doge Suite, once occupied by W. Somerset Maugham.

Expensive

Hotel Concordia. Calle Larga, San Marco 367, 30124 Venezia. ☎ **041/5206866.** Fax 041/ 5206775. E-mail: hotelconcordia@shineline.it. 55 units. A/C MINIBAR TV TEL. 290,000– 620,000L ($174–$372) double. Rates include buffet breakfast. AE, DC, MC, V. Vaporetto: San Marco.

The Concordia is the only hotel in Venice that has rooms overlooking St. Mark's Square. Completely renovated and awarded four stars, the hotel is housed in a russet-colored building with stone-trimmed windows. A series of gold-plated marble steps takes you to the lobby, where you'll find a comfortable bar area and elevators to whisk you to the labyrinthine corridors upstairs. The rooms are decorated in a Venetian antique style and contain an electronic safe and hair dryer in addition to other amenities. Light meals and Italian snacks are available in the bar.

Venice

Attractions:

Accademia ⑯
Basilica di San Marco ①
Bridge of Sighs ⑥
Campanile di San Marco ②
Ca' d'Oro ㉓
Ca' Rezzonico ⑲
Collezione Peggy Guggenheim ⑭
Museo Civico Correr ⑥
Palazzo Ducale ③
Piazza San Marco ④
Ponte di Rialto ㉕
Santa Maria della Salute ⑬
Scuola di San Rocco ㉑

Accommodations:

American Hotel ⑮
Boston Hotel ⑧
Cipriani ⑫
Gritti Palace ⑪
Hotel Carpaccio ⑳
Hotel Concordia ⑦
Hotel do Pozzi ⑩
Hotel la Fenice et des Artistes ⑨
Hotel San Cassiano Ca'Favretto ㉒
Locanda ai Santi Apostoli ㉔
Locanda Montin ⑰
Pensione Accademia ⑱

E-0058

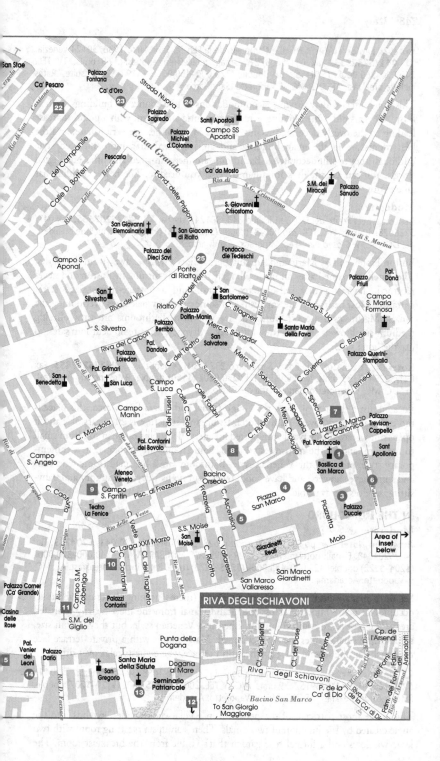

Hotel la Fenice et des Artistes. Campiello de la Fenice, San Marco 1936, 30124 Venezia. ☎ **041/5232333.** Fax 041/5203721. E-mail: fenice@fenicehotels.it. 69 units. TV TEL. 240,000–360,000L ($144–$216) double; 320,000–480,000L ($192–$288) suite. Rates include breakfast. AE, DC, MC, V. Vaporetto: San Marco.

This hotel offers widely varying accommodations in two connected buildings, each at least 100 years old. One building is rather romantic and worn, with a grand staircase leading to the overly decorated rooms. Rooms in the annex are very ornate, and the best rooms are in the main building and are furnished in a more subdued style (although they're still decorative). Bathrooms are medium-sized and offer good-sized towels. You can ask the desk for a hair dryer if you need to. The newer building has an elevator.

Moderate

Boston Hotel Ponte dei Dai, San Marco 848, 30124 Venezia. ☎ **041/5287665.** Fax 041/ 5226628. 42 units. A/C TEL. 250,000–310,000L ($150–$186) double. Rates include breakfast. AE, DC, MC, V. Closed Nov–Feb. Vaporetto: San Marco.

Boston Hotel, run by Mario and Adriana Bernardi, is a whisper away from St. Mark's. The hotel was named after an uncle who left to seek his fortune in Boston and never returned. There's a tiny self-operated elevator and a postage-stamp–sized street entrance. Most bedrooms are smallish, and some have tiny balconies overlooking the canals. Mattresses are a bit worn but are still firm. Bathrooms are tiny, offering medium-sized towels and toiletries, but no hair dryers. There are no bedroom safes, so use the hotel safe.

Hotel Do Pozzi. Corte do Pozzi, San Marco 2373, 30124 Venezia. ☎ **041/5207855.** Fax 041/5229413. 35 units. MINIBAR TV TEL. 250,000L ($150) double. Rates include breakfast. AE, DC, MC, V. Vaporetto: Santa Maria del Giglio.

Located just a short stroll from the Grand Canal and Piazza San Marco, this place is more like a country tavern than a hotel. Its original structure is 200 years old, and it opens onto a paved courtyard with potted greenery. Bedrooms range in size from small to medium, and all the mattresses are firm. Some rooms are decorated in a contemporary style, others in the Venetian style. Bathrooms are a bit small (some have tubs and some have showers) and have good towels, but no hair dryers. Laundry and baby-sitting services are available.

IN THE DORSODURO

Moderate

American Hotel. Campo San Vio, Dorsoduro 628, 30123 Venezia. ☎ **041/5204733.** Fax 041/5204048. E-mail: hotelameri@tin.it. 29 units. A/C MINIBAR TV TEL. 340,000–370,000L ($204–$222) double; 425,000–455,000L ($255–$273) triple. Rates include breakfast. AE, MC, V. Vaporetto: Accademia.

Set on a small waterway, the American Hotel (there's nothing American about it) occupies an ochre building across the Grand Canal from the most heavily touristed areas. The rooms are comfortably furnished in a Venetian style, but they vary in size; some of the smaller ones are a bit cramped. Many rooms with a private terrace face the canal. On the second floor is a beautiful terrace where guests relax over drinks.

✪ **Pensione Accademia.** Fondamenta Bollani, Dorsoduro 1058, 30123 Venezia. ☎ **041/ 5237846.** Fax 041/5239152. 29 units. A/C TV TEL. 200,000–345,000L ($120–$207) double. Rates include breakfast. AE, DC, MC, V. Vaporetto: Accademia.

This is the most patrician of the pensioni, in a villa whose garden extends into the angle created by the junction of two canals. There's an upstairs sitting room with two large windows and a formal rose garden that's visible from the breakfast room. The rooms are spacious and decorated with original 19th-century furniture, and some are air-conditioned and recently renovated (with new mattresses). The medium-sized bathrooms contain plush towels, and hair dryers are available in only a few rooms. There are no private safes, but the hotel has an electronic safe you can use.

Inexpensive

✪ **Locanda Montin.** Fondamenta di Borgo, Dorsoduro 1147, 31000 Venezia. ☎ **041/5227151.** Fax 041/5200255. 10 units (5 with bathroom). 150,000L ($90) double without bathroom; 190,000L ($114) double with bathroom. AE, DC, MC, V. Vaporetto: Accademia.

The Locanda Montin is an old-fashioned Venetian inn whose adjoining restaurant is one of the most loved in the area. The hotel is in the Dorsoduro section, across the Grand Canal from the most popular tourist zones. Marked only by a small carriage lamp etched with the name of the establishment extending over the pavement, the inn is a little difficult to locate but worth the search. Rooms are small and cozy, and the mattresses are comfortable (although they've seen better days). The private bathrooms are very cramped, and you might find yourself waiting to use the hall bathrooms if the house is full. Towels are a bit thin here. There are no hair dryers and no private safes.

In San Polo

Moderate

Hotel Carpaccio. San Tomà, San Polo 2765, 30125 Venezia. ☎ **041/5235946.** Fax 041/5242134. 17 units. MINIBAR TV TEL. 320,000L ($192) double. Rates include breakfast. MC, V. Closed mid-Nov to Mar. Vaporetto: San Tomà.

Don't be put off by the narrow, winding alleys leading up to the wrought-iron entrance of this hotel—the building was meant to be approached by gondola. This building used to be the Palazzo Barbarigo della Terrazza, and part of it is still reserved for private apartments. The hotel offers tasteful and spacious rooms filled with serviceable furniture (mattresses are comfortable and firm). Bathrooms are cramped and offer medium-sized towels. There are no hair dryers and no room safes.

In Santa Croce

Moderate

Hotel San Cassiano Ca'Favretto. Calle della Rosa, Santa Croce 2232, 30135 Venezia. ☎ **041/5241768.** Fax 041/721033. www.sancassiano.it. E-mail: cassiano@sancassiano.it. 36 units. A/C MINIBAR TV TEL. 200,000–361,000L ($120–$216.60) double. Rates include breakfast. AE, DC, MC, V. Vaporetto: San Stae.

San Cassiano Ca'Favretto was once the studio of 19th-century painter Giacomo Favretto, although the hotel was built as a palace in the 14th century. The present owner has worked closely with Venetian authorities to preserve the original details. Fifteen of the conservatively decorated rooms overlook a canal, and the small- and medium-sized rooms have beds with firm mattresses. Bathrooms are small but have generous towels (but no hair dryers).

In Cannaregio

Expensive

Locanda ai Santi Apostoli. Strada Nuova, Canaregio 4991, 30123 Venezia. ☎ **041/5212612.** Fax 041/5212611. 11 units. TV TEL. 320,000–360,000L ($192–$216) double; 460,000L ($276) double with view on the Canal Grande; 650,000L ($390) suite. Rates include breakfast. AE, DC, MC, V. Vaporetto: Ca d'Oro.

If you can't afford the Gritti Palace (and few can), but still fantasize about living in a palazzo overlooking the Grande Canal, here is an opportunity: You're still going to pay for the location, but it's a lot less expensive than the grand palaces. The hotel is situated on the top floor of a 15th-century building (there's an elevator to take you to the top), and the pastel-decorated rooms, although simple, are roomy and inviting (with good beds). The bathrooms are small and have medium-sized towels. (There are no hair dryers nor room safes.) Naturally, the two rooms actually opening onto the Grand Canal are the most requested. This is one of three 14th- or 15th-century palaces in Venice still owned by the original family that built it. Breakfast is the only meal served.

ON ISOLA DELLA GIUDECCA
Very Expensive

✪ **Cipriani.** Isola della Giudecca 10, 30133 Venezia. ☎ **800/992-5055** in the U.S., or 041/5207744. Fax 041/5207745. www.orient-expresshotels.com. E-mail: cipriani@gipnet.it. 104 units. A/C MINIBAR TV TEL. 2,250,000–2,500,000L ($1,350–$1,500) double; from 2,850,000L ($1,710) suite. Rates include breakfast. AE, DC, MC, V. Closed Nov–Mar. Vaporetto: Zitelle.

Isolated, security-conscious, and elegant, the Cipriani occupies a 16th-century cloister on the residential island of Giudecca. This refined, tranquil, and luxurious resort hotel was established in 1958 by the late Giuseppe Cipriani, the founder of Harry's Bar and the one real-life character in Hemingway's Venetian novel. The rooms have different decors—ranging from tasteful contemporary to an antique design—but all have splendid views. Lunch is served at Il Gabbiano, and more formal meals are served at night in the restaurant. There's an Olympic-size pool with filtered salt water, tennis courts, a sauna, and a fitness center.

WHERE TO DINE
NEAR PIAZZA SAN MARCO
Very Expensive

Harry's Bar. Calle Vallaresso, San Marco 1323. ☎ **041/5285777.** Reservations required. Main courses 75,000–90,000L ($45–$54). AE, DC, MC, V. Daily 10:30am–11pm. Vaporetto: San Marco. VENETIAN.

Harry's Bar (whose fame was spread by Ernest Hemingway) serves the best food in Venice, although Quadri and the Antico Martini (see below) have more elegant atmospheres. A. E. Hotchner, in *Papa Hemingway,* quoted the writer as saying, "We can't eat straight hamburger in a Renaissance palazzo on the Grand Canal." So he ordered a 5-pound "tin of beluga caviar" to, as he said, "take the curse off it." Hemingway would avoid the place today, fleeing from the foreign visitors, and the prices would come as a shock even to him. You choose between dining in the bar downstairs or in the room with a view upstairs. We recommend the Venetian fish soup, followed by scampi Thermidor with rice pilaf or seafood ravioli.

Expensive

✪ **Antico Martini.** Campo San Fantin, San Marco 1983. ☎ **041/5224121.** Reservations required. Main courses 35,000–50,000L ($21–$30); set-price menu 45,000–55,000L ($27–$33) at lunch; 75,000–126,000L ($45–$75.60) at dinner. AE, DC, MC, V. Wed 7–11:30pm; Thurs–Mon noon–2:30pm and 7–11:30pm. Vaporetto: San Marco or Santa Maria del Giglio. VENETIAN/INTERNATIONAL.

As the city's leading traditional restaurant, Antico Martini, located near La Fenice, elevates Venetian cuisine to its highest level. The walls are paneled, elaborate chandeliers glitter overhead, and gilt-framed oil paintings adorn the walls. The courtyard is favored in summer. An excellent beginning to your meal is the creamy, Venetian-style *risotto di frutti di mare,* with plenty of fresh seafood. For a main dish, try the *fegato alla veneziana,* which is tender liver fried with onions and served with polenta, a yellow cornmeal mush. The chefs are best at creating the regional dishes.

Da Ivo. Calle dei Fuseri, San Marco 1809. ☎ **041/5285004.** Reservations required. Main courses 40,000–55,000L ($24–$33). AE, DC, MC, V. Mon–Sat noon–2:40pm and 7pm–midnight. Closed Jan 6–31. Vaporetto: San Marco. TUSCAN/VENETIAN.

Da Ivo has such a faithful clientele that you'll think at first you're in a semiprivate club. The rustic atmosphere is cozy and relaxing, with candles on the well-set tables. Homesick Florentines go here for fine Tuscan cookery; regional Venetian dishes are also served. In season, game, according to an ancient tradition, is cooked over an open charcoal grill. On one cold day, our hearts and plates were warmed when we ordered homemade tagliatelle. It came topped with slivers of tartufi bianchi, the pungent white truffle from the Piedmont district that's unforgettable to the palate. Dishes change according to the season and the availability of ingredients.

Quadri. Piazza San Marco, San Marco 120–124. ☎ **041/5289299.** Reservations required. Main courses 42,000–75,000L ($25.20–$45). AE, DC, MC, V. Wed–Sun noon–2:30pm and Tues–Sun 7–10:30pm. Vaporetto: San Marco. INTERNATIONAL.

One of Europe's famous restaurants, the deluxe Quadri is on the second floor, overlooking the "living room" of Venice. The setting is one of gilt and rosy velvet, evoking the world of its former patrons, Proust and Stendhal. Many diners come here just for the setting and are often surprised when they're treated to high-quality cuisine and impeccable service. You pay for all this nostalgia, however. The Venetian cuisine has been acclaimed—at least by one food critic—as "befitting a doge," though we doubt if those old doges ate as well. The chef is likely to tempt you with such dishes as octopus in fresh tomato sauce, salt codfish with polenta, or sea bass with crab sauce. Try the "baked" ice cream for dessert.

Moderate

Ristorante da Raffaele. Calle Larga XXII Marzo (Fondamenta delle Ostreghe), San Marco 2347. ☎ **041/5232317.** Reservations recommended Sat–Sun. Main courses 25,000–38,000L ($15–$22.80). AE, DC, MC, V. Fri–Wed noon–3pm and 7–10:30pm. Closed Dec 10 to mid-Feb. Vaporetto: San Marco or Santa Maria del Giglio. ITALIAN/VENETIAN.

This place, a 5-minute walk from Piazza San Marco and a minute from the Grand Canal, has long been a favorite canalside stop. It's often overrun with tourists, but the veteran kitchen staff holds up well. The restaurant offers the kind of charm and special atmosphere that are unique to the city. The huge inner sanctum has a high-beamed ceiling, 17th- to 19th-century pistols and sabers, exposed brick, wrought-iron chandeliers, a massive fireplace, and hundreds of copper pots. The food is excellent, beginning with a choice of tasty antipasti or well-prepared pastas. Seafood specialties include scampi, squid, or a platter of deep-fried fish from the Adriatic. The grilled meats are also succulent and can be followed by rich, tempting desserts.

Taverna la Fenice. Campiello de la Fenice, San Marco 1938. ☎ **041/5223856.** Reservations required. Main courses 20,000–36,000L ($12–$21.60). AE, DC, MC, V. Mon–Sat noon–2pm and 7–11pm. Closed 2nd week in Jan. Vaporetto: San Marco. ITALIAN/VENETIAN.

Opened in 1907, when Venetians were flocking in record numbers to hear the *bel canto* performances in the opera house nearby, this restaurant is one of Venice's most romantic dining spots. Gabriele D'Annunzio himself provided the name for this historic place. The interior is suitably elegant, but the preferred spot in mild weather is out beneath a canopy, a few steps from the burned Teatro La Fenice, where Stravinski introduced works that included *The Rake's Progress*. The service is smooth and efficient. You might enjoy risotto with scampi and arugula, freshly made tagliatelle with cream and exotic mushrooms, or John Dory filets with artichokes.

Trattoria La Colomba. Piscina Frezzeria, San Marco 1665. ☎ **041/5221175.** Reservations recommended. Main courses 35,000–65,000L ($21–$39). AE, DC, MC, V. Daily noon–3pm and 7–11pm. Closed Wed June 19–Aug and Nov–Apr. Vaporetto: San Marco or Rialto. VENETIAN/INTERNATIONAL.

This is one of the most distinctive and popular *trattorie* in town, with a history going back at least a century and a by-now legendary association with some of Venice's leading painters. In 1985, a $2-million restoration improved the infrastructure, making it a more attractive foil for the dozens of modern paintings that hang on its walls. Menu items are likely to include at least five daily specials based exclusively on the time-honored cuisine of Venice. Otherwise, you can order *risotto di funghi del Montello* (risotto with mushrooms from the local Montello hills) or *baccalà alla vicentina* (milk-simmered dry cod seasoned with onions, anchovies, and cinnamon, then served with polenta).

Vini da Arturo. Calle degli Assassini, San Marco 3656. ☎ **041/5286974.** Reservations recommended. Main courses 26,000–40,000L ($15.60–$24). No credit cards. Mon–Sat noon–2:30pm and 7–10:30pm. Closed Aug. Vaporetto: San Marco or Rialto. VENETIAN.

Vini da Arturo attracts many devoted regulars, including artists and writers. Here you get some of the most delectable local cooking—and not just the standard cliché Venetian dishes and not seafood, which may be unique for a Venetian restaurant. Instead of ordering plain pasta, try a tantalizing dish called *spaghetti alla gorgonzola.* The beef is also good, especially when prepared with a cream sauce flavored with mustard and freshly ground pepper. The salads are made with crisp, fresh ingredients, often in unusual combinations. The place is small and contains only seven tables; it's between the Fenice Opera House and St. Mark's Square.

Inexpensive

Restaurant da Bruno. Calle del Paradiso, Castello 5731. ☎ **041/5221480.** Main courses 14,000–22,000L ($8.40–$13.20); set-price menu 25,000L ($15). AE, DC, MC, V. Wed–Mon noon–3pm and 7–11pm. Closed 1 week in Jan. Vaporetto: San Marco or Rialto. VENETIAN.

Da Bruno is like a country tavern in the center of Venice. On a narrow street about halfway between the Rialto Bridge and Piazza San Marco, this restaurant attracts its crowds by grilling meats on an open-hearth fire. Get your antipasti at the counter and watch your prosciutto being prepared—paper-thin slices of spicy flavored ham wrapped around breadsticks (*grissini*). In the right season, da Bruno does some of the finest game specialty dishes in Venice. If it's featured, try *capriolo* (roebuck) or *fagiano* (pheasant). Another great dish is veal scaloppine with wild mushrooms.

Sempione. Ponte Beretteri, San Marco 578. ☎ **041/5226022.** Reservations recommended. Main courses 18,000–30,000L ($10.80–$18). AE, DC, MC, V. Daily 11:30am–3pm and 6:30–10pm. Closed Tues and/or Thurs Nov–Dec, depending on business. Vaporetto: Rialto. VENETIAN.

This restaurant has done an admirable job of feeding local residents and visitors for 90 years. Set adjacent to a canal, within a 15th-century building near St. Mark's Square, it contains three dining rooms outfitted in a traditional style, a well-trained staff, and a kitchen that prepares mainly traditional Venetian cuisine. Examples include grilled fish, spaghetti with crabmeat, risotto with fish, fish soup, and a timeless and delectable version of Venetian calf's liver. Try for a table by the window so you can watch the gondolas slide by.

Trattoria alla Madonna. Calle de la Madonna, San Pollo 594. ☎ **041/5223824.** Reservations recommended but not always accepted. Main courses 18,000–22,000L ($10.80–$13.20).

AE, MC, V. Thurs–Tues noon–3pm and 7:15–10pm. Closed Jan 7–Feb 7 and Aug 1–15. Vaporetto: Rialto. VENETIAN.

This restaurant was opened in 1954 in a 300-year-old building of historic distinction. Named after *another* famous Madonna, it's one of the most popular and characteristic *trattorie* of Venice, specializing in traditional recipes and an array of grilled fresh fish. A suitable beginning may be the antipasto *frutti di mare.* Pastas, polentas, risottos, meats (including *fegato alla veneziana,* liver with onions), and many kinds of irreproachably fresh fish are widely available.

EAST OF PIAZZA SAN MARCO
Moderate
Ristorante Corte Sconta. Calle del Pestrin, Castello 3886. ☎ **041/5-22-70-24.** Reservations required. Main courses 20,000–35,000L ($12–$21); set-price menu 70,000–85,000L ($42–$51). AE, DC, MC, V. Tues–Sat 12:30–2:30pm and 7:30–9:30pm. Closed Jan 7–Feb 7 and July 15–Aug 15. Vaporetto: Arsenale. SEAFOOD.

Ristorante Corte Sconta is located near the Arsenale behind a narrow storefront that you'd probably ignore if you didn't know about this place; it's in a narrow alley whose name is shared by at least three other streets in Venice (this particular one is near Campo Bandiere Moro and San Giovanni in Bragora). The modest restaurant, whose name in Italian means "hidden courtyard," has a multicolored marble floor, plain wooden tables, and no serious attempt at decoration. It has become well known, however, as a sophisticated gathering place for artists, writers, and filmmakers. This fish restaurant serves a variety of grilled creatures (much of the "catch" is largely unknown in North America). The fish is flawlessly grilled, and it's also flawlessly fresh—the gamberi, for example, is placed live on the grill. Begin with marinated salmon with arugula and pomegranate seeds in rich olive oil. If you don't like fish, a tender filet of beef is available.

Inexpensive
Nuova Rivetta. Campo San Filippo, Castello 4625. ☎ **041/5287302.** Reservations required. Main courses 18,000–32,000L ($10.80–$19.20). AE, MC, V. Tues–Sun 10am–10pm. Closed July 23–Aug 20. Vaporetto: San Zaccaria. SEAFOOD.

Nuova Rivetta is an old-fashioned Venetian trattoria where you eat well without having to pay a lot. The restaurant stands in the monumental heart of the old city. Many find it best for lunch during a stroll around Venice. The most representative dish to order is *frittura di pesce,* a mixed fish fry from the Adriatic that includes squid or other sea creatures that turned up at the market that day. Other specialties are gnocchi stuffed with Adriatic spider crab, pasticcio of fish (a main course), and spaghetti flavored with squid ink.

NEAR THE PONTE DI RIALTO
Moderate
"Al graspo de ua". Calle dei Bombaseri, San Marco 5094. ☎ **041/5200150.** Reservations required. Main courses 26,000–36,000L ($15.60–$21.60). AE, DC, MC, V. Tues–Sun noon–3pm and 8–11pm. Closed Aug 5–20. Vaporetto: Rialto. SEAFOOD/VENETIAN.

"Al graspo de ua" is one bunch of grapes you'll want to pluck. For that special meal, it's a winner. Decorated in the old tavern style, it offers several air-conditioned dining rooms. One has a beamed ceiling, hung with garlic and copper bric-a-brac. Among the best fish restaurants in Venice, this place has been patronized by such celebs as Elizabeth Taylor, Jeanne Moreau, and even Giorgio de Chirico. You can help yourself to all the hors d'oeuvres you want—known on the menu as "self-service mammoth."

The wonderful *gran fritto dell'Adriatico* is a mixed treat of deep-fried fish from the Adriatic.

✪ **Poste Vechie.** Pescheria Rialto, San Polo 1608. ☎ **041/721822.** Reservations recommended. Main courses 24,000–36,000L ($14.40–$21.60). AE, DC, MC, V. Wed–Mon noon–3:30pm and 7–10:30pm. Vaporetto: Rialto. SEAFOOD.

This is one of Venice's most charming restaurants, near the Rialto fish market and connected to the rest of the city with a small, privately owned bridge. It was established in the early 1500s as the local post office—food was served to the mail carriers to fortify them for their deliveries. Today it's one of the oldest restaurants in town, with two intimate dining rooms and a verdant courtyard. Menu items include a super fresh array of fish from the nearby markets; a salad of shellfish and exotic mushrooms; a spicy soup of Adriatic fish; tagliolini flavored with squid ink, crabmeat, and fish sauce; and the restaurant's pièce de résistance, *seppie* (cuttlefish) *alla veneziana* with polenta. If you don't like fish, calf's liver or veal shank with ham and cheese are also well prepared. The desserts come rolling to your table on a trolley and are usually sumptuous.

Ristorante à la Vecia Cavana. Rio Terà SS. Apostoli, Cannaregio 4624. ☎ **041/5287106.** Main courses 40,000–60,000L ($24–$36); set-price menu 50,000L ($30). AE, DC, MC, V. Fri–Wed noon–2:30pm and 7:30–10:30pm. Vaporetto: Ca' d'Oro. SEAFOOD.

This restaurant is off the tourist circuit and well worth the trek through the winding streets to find it. When you enter, you're greeted with brick arches, stone columns, terra-cotta floors, framed modern paintings, and a photograph of 19th-century fishermen relaxing after a day's work. It's an appropriate introduction to a menu that specializes in seafood, including a mixed grill from the Adriatic, fresh sole, three types of risotto (each prepared with seafood), and spicy *zuppa di pesce* (fish soup). Another specialty is *antipasti di pesce Cavana,* which includes just about every sea creature.

IN SAN POLO
Moderate

Osteria da Fiore. Calle del Scaletèr, San Polo 2202. ☎ **041/72-13-08.** Reservations required. Main courses 36,000–42,000L ($21.60–$25.20). AE, DC, MC, V. Tues–Sat 12:30–2:30pm and 8–10:30pm. Closed 3 weeks in Aug and Dec 25–Jan 14. Vaporetto: San Tomà. SEAFOOD.

The breath of the Adriatic seems to blow through this place, although how the wind finds this little restaurant tucked away in a labyrinth is a mystery. The restaurant serves only fish, and has done so since 1910. An imaginative and changing fare is offered, depending on the availability of fresh fish and produce. You'll find everything from scampi (a sweet Adriatic prawn, cooked in as many different ways as there are chefs) to granzeola, a type of spider crab. Try such dishes as *capelunghe alla griglio* (razor clams opened on the grill), *masenette* (tiny green crabs that you eat shell and all), and *canoce* (mantis shrimp). For your wine, we suggest Prosecco, which has a distinctive golden-yellow color and a bouquet that's refreshing and fruity.

IN THE DORSODURO
Moderate

La Furatola. Calle Lunga San Barnaba, Dorsoduro 2870A. ☎ **041/5208594.** Reservations recommended for dinner. Main courses 26,000–45,000L ($15.60–$27). AE, DC, MC, V. Fri–Tues 12:30–2:30pm and 7:30–10:30pm. Closed Aug. Vaporetto: Ca' Rezzonico. SEAFOOD.

La Furatola (an old Venetian word meaning "restaurant") is very much a Dorsoduro neighborhood hangout, but it has captured the imagination of local foodies. It's in a 300-year-old building, along a narrow flagstone-paved street that you'll need a good map and a lot of patience to find. Perhaps you'll have lunch here after a visit to the Church of San Rocco, only a short distance away. The specialty is fish brought to your table in a wicker basket so you can judge its size and freshness by its bright eyes and red gills. A display of seafood antipasti is set out near the entrance. A standout is the baby octopus boiled and eaten with a drop of red-wine vinegar.

Inexpensive

⭐ **Locanda Montin.** Fondamenta di Borgo, Dorsoduro 1147. ☎ **041/5227151.** Reservations recommended. Main courses 16,000–36,000L ($9.60–$21.60). AE, DC, MC, V. Tues 12:30–2:30pm; Thurs–Mon 12:30–2:30pm and 7:30–9:30pm. Closed 10 days in mid-Aug and 20 days in Jan. Vaporetto: Accademia. INTERNATIONAL/ITALIAN.

Since this restaurant opened just after World War II, its famous patrons have included Ezra Pound, Jackson Pollock, Mark Rothko, and many of the assorted artist friends of the late Peggy Guggenheim. The inn is owned and run by the Carretins, who have covered the walls with paintings donated by or purchased from their many friends and diners. Today the arbor-covered garden courtyard of this 17th-century building is filled with regulars, many of whom allow their favorite waiter to select most of their dishes. The frequently changing menu includes a variety of salads, grilled meats, and fish caught in the Adriatic. Specialties include fresh crab with virgin olive oil and lemon, tortelloni (a kind of dumpling) stuffed with artichokes and covered in a scampi cream sauce, and seasonal fish often served in a Barolo red wine sauce.

SEEING THE SIGHTS IN VENICE

Ahead, we'll explore the city's great art and architecture. But, unlike Florence, Venice would reward you with treasures even if you never ducked inside a museum or church. In the city on the islands, the frame eternally competes with the picture inside.

SIGHTSEEING SUGGESTIONS FOR FIRST-TIME VISITORS

If You Have 1 Day   Get up early and watch the sun rise over **Piazza San Marco** as the city wakes up. The pigeons will already be here to greet you. Have an early-morning cappuccino on the square, and then visit the **Basilica of San Marco** and the **Palazzo Ducale** later. Ride the **Grand Canal** in a gondola 2 hours before sunset and spend the rest of the evening wandering the narrow streets of this strangely unreal and most fascinating city. Apologize to yourself for such a short visit and promise to return.

If You Have 2 Days   Spend your first day as above. On day 2 it's time for more concentrated sightseeing. Begin at **Piazza San Marco** (viewing it should be a daily ritual, regardless of how many days you have in Venice), and then head for the major museum, the **Accademia,** in the morning. In the afternoon, visit the **Collezione Peggy Guggenheim** (modern art) and perhaps the **Ca' d'Oro** and **Ca' Rezzonico.**

If You Have 3 Days   Spend your first 2 days as above. Begin day 3 by having a cappuccino on Piazza San Marco, and then inspect the **Campanile di San Marco.** Later in the morning visit the **Museo Correr.** In the afternoon, go to the **Scuola Grande di San Rocco** to see the works of Tintoretto. Spend the rest of the day strolling the streets of Venice and ducking into shops that capture your imagination. Even if you get lost, you'll eventually return to a familiar landmark, and you can't help but see the signs pointing you back to Piazza San Marco. Have dinner in one of the most typical of Venetian trattorias, such as Locanda Montin.

If You Have 4 or 5 Days   Spend days 1 to 3 as above. On day 4 plan to visit the islands of the lagoon, including **Murano, Burano,** and **Torcello.** All three can be covered—at least briefly—in 1 busy day. On day 5, relax, wander around the streets, and take in some of the many attractions you might have missed.

THE GRAND CANAL

Peoria may have its Main Street, Paris its Champs-Elysées—but Venice, for unique-ness, tops them all with its ✪ **Canal Grande (Grand Canal).** Lined with *palazzi* (palaces)—many designed in an elegant Venetian-Gothic style—today this great road of water is filled with vaporetti, motorboats, and gondolas. Along the canal the boat moorings look like peppermint sticks. The canal begins at Piazzetta San Marco on one side and Longhena's Salute Church on the opposite bank. At midpoint, it's spanned by the Rialto Bridge. Eventually the canal winds its serpentine course to the railway station. We can guarantee that there's not a dull sight en route.

THE BASILICA, DOGES' PALACE & CAMPANILE

✪ **Piazza San Marco** (St. Mark's Square) was the heartbeat of La Serenissima (the Serene Republic) in its heyday, when it was a seafaring state. If you have only 1 day for Venice, you need not leave the square, as the city's major attractions, such as the Basilica of St. Mark and the Doges' Palace, are centered here or nearby. Thanks to Napoléon, the square was unified architecturally. The emperor added the Fab-brica Nuova, thus bridging the Old and New Procuratie. Flanked with medieval-looking palaces, Sansovino's Library, elegant shops and colonnades, the square is now finished—unlike Piazza della Signoria in Florence.

If Piazza San Marco is the drawing room of Europe, then its satellite, **Piazzetta San Marco,** is the antechamber. Hedged in by the Doges' Palace, Sansovino's Library, and one side of St. Mark's Basilica, the tiny square faces the Grand Canal. One of the two tall granite columns in the piazzetta is surmounted by a winged lion, which represents St. Mark. On top of the other column is a statue of a man taming a dragon, suppos-edly the dethroned patron saint Theodore. Both columns came from the East in the 12th century.

✪ **Basilica di San Marco.** Piazza San Marco. ☎ **041/5225205.** Basilica, free; treasury, 4,000L ($2.40); presbytery, 3,000L ($1.80); Marciano Museum, 3,000L ($1.80). Basilica and presbytery, Apr–Sept Mon–Sat 9:30am–5:30pm, Sun 2–5:30pm; Oct–Mar Mon–Sat 9:30am–5pm, Sun 1:30–4:30pm. Treasury, Mon–Sat 9:30am–5pm, Sun 2–5pm. Marciano Museum, Apr–Sept Mon–Sat 10am–5:30pm, Sun 2–4:30pm; Oct–Mar Mon–Sat 10am–4:45pm, Sun 2–4:30pm. Warning: Visitors must wear appropriate clothing (no tank tops, shorts, or cut-off jeans) and remain silent during their visit. Photography is forbidden. Vaporetto: San Marco.

This "Church of Gold" dominating Piazza San Marco is one of the world's greatest and most richly embellished churches—in fact, it looks as though it were moved here from Istanbul. The basilica is a conglomeration of styles, yet it's particularly indebted to Byzantium. It incorporates other schools of design, such as Romanesque and Gothic, with freewheeling abandon. Like Venice itself, it's adorned with booty from every corner of the city's once far-flung mercantile empire—capitals from Sicily, columns from Alexandria, porphyry from Syria, sculpture from Constantinople. The basilica is capped by a dome that—like a spider plant—sends off shoots, in this case a quartet of smaller-scale cupolas. Spanning the facade is a loggia, surmounted by replicas of the four famous St. Mark's horses—the *Triumphal Quadriga.*

If you look back at the aperture over the entryway, you can see a mosaic, the dance of Salome before Herod and his court. Wearing a star-studded russet-red dress and three white fox tails, Salome dances under a platter holding John the Baptist's head. Her glassy face is that of a Madonna, not an enchantress. Proceed up the right nave to the doorway to the **treasury** (*tesoro*). The entrance to the **presbytery** is nearby. On the high altar, the alleged sarcophagus of St. Mark rests under a green marble blanket and is held up by four sculptured alabaster Corinthian columns. The **Pala d'Oro,** from

Constantinople, is a masterpiece of Byzantine and Venetian goldsmith work studded with hundreds of precious gems.

On leaving the basilica, head up the stairs in the atrium for the **Marciano Museum** and the Loggia dei Cavalli. The museum's star attraction is the world-famous *Quadriga,* four horses looted from Constantinople when it was sacked by Venetian crusaders in 1204. This is the only *quadriga* (a quartet of horses yoked together) that has survived from the classical era.

✪ **Palazzo Ducale.** Piazzetta San Marco. ☎ **041/5224951.** Admission 17,000L ($10.20) adults, 10,000L ($6) students 15–29 years old, 6,000L ($3.60) ages 7–14 (free 6 and under). Apr–Oct daily 9am–5:30pm; off-season daily 9am–3:30pm. Vaporetto: San Marco.

You enter the Palace of the Doges through the magnificent 15th-century Porta della Carta on the piazzetta. It's somewhat like a frosty birthday cake in pinkish red marble and white Istrian stone. The Venetian-Gothic palazzo—with all the architectural intricacies of a doily—gleams in the tremulous Venetian light. The grandest civic structure in Italy, it dates back to 1309, although a fire in 1577 destroyed much of the original.

After climbing the Sansovino stairway of gold, proceed to the Anti-Collegio salon, which houses the palace's greatest artworks—notably Veronese's *Rape of Europa,* to the far left on the right wall. Tintoretto is well represented with his *Three Graces* and *Bacchus and Ariadne,* which some critics consider his supreme achievement.

Now trek downstairs through the once-private apartments of the doges to the grand Maggior Consiglio, with its allegorical *Triumph of Venice* on the ceiling, painted by Veronese. What makes the room outstanding, however, is Tintoretto's *Paradise,* over the Grand Council chamber—said to be the largest oil painting in the world.

Reenter the Maggior Consiglio and follow the arrows across the **Bridge of Sighs,** linking the Doges' Palace with the Palazzo delle Prigioni. In the Palazzo, you'll find the cells that held the prisoners who felt the quick justice of the Terrible Ten. The "sighs" in the bridge's name stemmed from the sad laments of the numerous victims led across it to certain torture and possible death.

Campanile di San Marco. Piazza San Marco. ☎ **041/5224064.** Admission 8,000L ($4.80). Oct–Feb daily 9:30am–4pm; Mar–June daily 9am–7pm; July–Sept daily 9am–9pm. Closed Jan 7–31. Vaporetto: San Marco.

One summer night back in 1902, the bell tower of the Basilica of St. Mark on Piazza San Marco gave out a warning sound that sent the fashionable crowd scurrying from the Florian Caffè in a dash for their lives. The campanile, which was suffering from years of decay in the damp Venetian climate, graciously waited until the next morning—July 14—before tumbling into the piazza. The Venetians rebuilt their belfry, and it's now safe to ascend. A modern elevator takes you up for a pigeon's view of the city. It's a particularly good vantage point for seeing St. Mark's cupolas.

MUSEUMS & GALLERIES

✪ **Accademia.** Campo della Carità, Dorsoduro. ☎ **041/5222247.** Admission 12,000L ($7.20) adults, free for children 12 and under. Tues–Fri 9am–8pm; Sun–Mon 9am–2pm. Vaporetto: Accademia.

The pomp and circumstance, the glory that was Venice, lives on in this remarkable collection of paintings spanning the 14th to the 18th century. The hallmark of the Venetian school is color and more color. From Giorgione to Veronese, from Titian to Tintoretto, with a Carpaccio cycle thrown in, the Accademia has works by its most famous sons.

You'll see works by such 14th-century artists as Paolo and Lorenzo Veneziano, who bridged the gap from Byzantine art to Gothic (see the latter's *Annunciation*). You'll also view Giovanni Bellini's *Madonna and Saint* (poor Sebastian, not another arrow) and Carpaccio's fascinating (yet gruesome) work of mass crucifixion. Two of the most important works with secular themes are Mantegna's armored *St. George*, with the dragon slain at his feet, and Hans Memling's 15th-century portrait of a young man. Giorgione's *Tempest* is the most famous painting at the Accademia.

Collezione Peggy Guggenheim. Ca' Venier dei Leoni, Dorsoduro 701, Calle San Cristoforo. ☎ **041/5206288.** Admission 12,000L ($7.20) adults, 8,000L ($4.80) students, free children 10 and under. Wed–Mon 11am–6pm. Vaporetto: Accademia.

This is one of the most comprehensive and brilliant modern-art collections in the Western world, and it reveals the foresight and critical judgment of its founder. The collection is housed in an unfinished palazzo, the former home of Peggy Guggenheim, who died in 1979. In the tradition of her family, Guggenheim was a lifelong patron of contemporary painters and sculptors. As her private collection increased, she decided to find a larger showcase and selected Venice. Displayed here are works not only by Pollock and Ernst but also by Picasso (see his cubist *The Poet* of 1911), Duchamp, Chagall, Mondrian, Brancusi, Delvaux, and Dalí, plus a garden of modern sculpture that includes works by Giacometti.

Ca' d'Oro. Cannaregio 3931–3932. ☎ **041/5238790.** Admission 6,000L ($3.60). Sept–Nov Tues–Sat 9am–6:30pm, Sun–Mon 9am–1:30pm; Dec–Aug daily 9am–1:30pm. Closed Jan 1, May 1, and Dec 25. Vaporetto: Ca' d'Oro.

This is one of the most handsomely embellished palaces along the Grand Canal. Although it contains the important **Galleria Giorgio Franchetti,** the House of Gold (its facade was once gilded) competes with its own paintings. Built in the first part of the 15th century in the ogival (pointed arch) style, it has a lacy look. Baron Franchetti, who restored the palace and filled it with his collection of paintings, sculpture, and furniture, left the palace to Italy in his will. In a special niche is Andrea Mantegna's icy-cold *St. Sebastian,* the masterpiece of the Franchetti collection.

Museo Civico Correr. In the Procuratie Nuove, Piazza San Marco. ☎ **041/5225625.** Admission 17,000L ($10.20) adults, 10,000L ($6) ages 14–29, 6,000L ($3.60) children 6–14, free for children under 6. Apr–Oct daily 9am–7pm; Nov–Mar daily 9am–5pm. Vaporetto: San Marco.

This museum traces the development of Venetian painting from the 14th to the 16th century. On the second floor are the red and maroon robes once worn by the doges, plus some fabulous street lanterns. There's also an illustrated copy of *Marco Polo in Tartaria.* You can see Cosmé Tura's *La Pietà,* a miniature of renown from the genius in the Ferrara School. This is one of his more gruesome works, depicting a bony, gnarled Christ sprawled on the lap of the Madonna. Farther on, search out a Schiavone *Madonna and Child* (no. 545), our candidate for ugliest bambino ever depicted on canvas (no wonder the mother looks askance). One of the most important rooms at the Correr is filled with three masterpieces: *La Pietà* by Antonello da Messina, *The Crucifixion* by the Flemish painter Hugo van der Goes, and *Madonna and Child* by Dieric Bouts, who depicted the baby suckling his mother in a sensual manner. The star attraction of the Correr is the Bellini salon, which includes works by founding padre Jacopo and his son, Gentile. But the real master of the household was the other son, Giovanni.

Ca' Rezzonico. Fondamenta Rezzonico, Dorsoduro 3136. ☎ **041/2410100.** Admission 14,000L ($8.40) adults, 8,000L ($4.80) children 12–18, 4,000L ($2.40) children under 12. Oct–Apr Sat–Thurs 10am–4pm; May–Sept daily 10am–5pm. Vaporetto: Ca' Rezzonico.

This 17th- and 18th-century palace along the Grand Canal is where Robert Browning set up his bachelor headquarters. Pope Clement XIII also stayed here. It's a virtual treasure house, known for its baroque paintings and furniture. You first enter the Grand Ballroom with its allegorical ceiling, then proceed through lavish rooms with Venetian chandeliers, brocaded walls, portraits of patricians, tapestries, gilded furnishings, and touches of chinoiserie. At the end of the first walk is the Throne Room, with its allegorical ceiling by Giovanni Battista Tiepolo.

Upstairs you'll find a survey of 18th-century Venetian art. As you enter the main room from downstairs, head for the first salon on your right (facing the canal), which contains the best works of all, paintings from the brush of Pietro Longhi. His most famous work, *The Lady and the Hairdresser,* is the first canvas to the right on the entrance wall.

Warning: This museum will be closed for restoration for much of 2000; call to check on its status or ask at the tourist office before heading here.

THE SCUOLE

Scuola di San Rocco. Campo San Rocco, San Polo. ☎ **041/5234864.** Admission 8,000L ($4.80) adults, 6,000L ($3.60) students, 3,000L ($1.80) children. Mar 28–Nov 2 daily 9am–5:30pm; Nov 3–30 and Mar 1–27 daily 10am–4pm; Dec–Feb Mon–Fri 10am–1pm, Sat–Sun 10am–4pm. Closed Easter and Dec 25–Jan 1. Vaporetto: San Tomà; from the station, walk straight onto Ramo Mondoler, which becomes Larga Prima; then take Salizzada San Rocco, which opens into Campo San Rocco.

Of Venice's *scuole* (in the Renaissance, *scuole* were centers used by social and religious organizations affiliated with the local parish), none is as richly embellished as the Scuola di San Rocco, filled with epic canvases by Tintoretto. Through a clever trick, he won the competition to decorate the darkly illuminated early 16th-century building. He began painting in 1564, and the work stretched on until his powers as an artist waned. The paintings sweep across the upper and lower halls, mesmerizing the viewer with a kind of passion play. In the grand hallway are scenes from the New Testament, devoted largely to episodes in the life of Mary (the *Flight into Egypt* is among the best). In the top gallery are works illustrating scenes from the Old and the New Testament, the most renowned of which are those devoted to the life of Christ. In a separate room is what's considered Tintoretto's masterpiece—a mammoth *Crucifixion,* one of the world's most celebrated paintings.

Scuola di San Giorgio degli Schiavoni. Calle dei Furiani, Castello. ☎ **041/5228828.** Admission 5,000L ($3). Nov–Mar Tues–Sat 10am–12:30pm and 3–6pm, Sun 10am–12:30pm; Apr–Oct Tues–Sat 9:30am–12:30pm and 3:30–6:30pm, Sun 9:30am–12:30pm. Vaporetto: San Zaccaria.

At the St. Antonino Bridge (*Fondamenta dei Furlani*) is the second important scuola to visit in Venice. Between 1502 and 1509, Vittore Carpaccio painted a pictorial cycle here of exceptional merit and interest. Of enduring fame are his works of St. George and the Dragon—these are our favorite pieces of art in all of Venice. In one frame, St. George charges the dragon on a field littered with half-eaten bodies and skulls. Gruesome? Not at all. Any moment you expect the director to call "Cut!"

ORGANIZED TOURS

Daily at 9:10am, **American Express,** San Marco 1471 (☎ 041/5200844), offers a 2-hour guided tour of the city, costing 40,000L ($24). Sights include St. Mark's Square, the basilica, the Doges' Palace, the prison, the bell tower, and in some cases, a demonstration of the art of Venetian glassblowing. Daily between 3 and 5pm, a 2-hour

Tips on Shopping for Venetian Glass & Lace

Venice is literally crammed with **glass** shops. It's estimated that there are at least 1,000 of them in the *sestiere* of San Marco alone. Unless you go to an absolutely top-quality and reliable dealer, such as those we recommend, most stores sell both shoddy and high-quality glassware. Only the most trained eye can tell the difference. The big secret (which is becoming less of a secret all the time) is that a lot of so-called Venetian glass isn't Venetian at all, but comes from former Eastern Bloc countries, including the Czech Republic. Of course, the Czech Republic has some of the finest glassmakers in Europe, so that may not be bad either. If you're looking for an heirloom, stick to such award-winning houses as **Pauly & Co.** or **Venini** (see "Some Shops Worth a Look," below).

Most of the **lace** vendors are around Piazza San Marco. Although high, prices of Venetian lace are still reasonable, considering the painstaking work that goes into it. Much of the lace is shoddy, and some of it—a lot of it, really—isn't Venetian lace but machine made in who knows what country. *The* name in Venetian lace is **Jesurum** (see below), which has stood for quality since the last century.

guided tour incorporates visits to the exteriors of several palaces along Campo San Benetto and other sights of the city. The tour eventually crosses the Grand Canal to visit the Church of Santa Maria dei Frari, which contains Titian's *Assumption.* The tour continues by gondola down the canal to visit the Ca' d'Oro and ends at the Rialto Bridge. The afternoon tour costs 45,000L ($27). A combined purchase of the morning and afternoon tour is just 75,000L ($45).

The **Evening Serenade Tour,** at 55,000L ($33) per person, allows a nocturnal view of Venice accompanied by the sound of singing musicians in gondolas. From May to October, there are two daily departures, at 7:30 and 9:30pm, leaving from Campo Santa Maria del Giglio. Five to six occupants fit in each gondola as a singer and a handful of musicians perform throughout the Venetian evening. The experience lasts 50 minutes.

THE SHOPPING SCENE

Venetian **glass** and **lace** are known throughout the world. However, selecting quality products in either craft requires a shrewd eye, as there's much that is tawdry and shoddily crafted. Some of the glassware hawked isn't worth the cost of shipping it home. Yet other pieces represent some of the world's finest artistic and ornamental glass. Murano is the island famous for its handmade glass. However, you can find little glass animal souvenirs in shops all over Venice.

For lace, head out to Burano, where the last of a long line of women put in painstaking hours to produce some of the finest lace in the world.

SHOPPING STROLLS All the main shopping streets of Venice, even the side streets, are touristy and overrun. The greatest concentration of shops is around Piazza San Marco and the Rialto Bridge. Prices are much higher at San Marco, but the quality of merchandise is also higher. There are two major shopping strolls in Venice. First, from Piazza San Marco you can stroll through Venice toward the spacious square of **Campo Morosini.** You just follow one shop-lined street all the way to its end (although the name will change several times along the way). You begin at Salizzada

San Moisè, which becomes Via 22 Marzo, and then Calle delle Ostreghe, before it opens onto Campo Santa Maria Zobenigo. The street then narrows again and changes its name to Calle Zaguri before widening once more into Campo San Maurizio, finally becoming Calle Piovan before it reaches Campo Morosini. The only deviation from this tour is a detour down Calle Vallaressa, between San Moisè and the Grand Canal, a major shopping artery with some of the biggest designer names in the business.

The other great shopping stroll in Venice wanders from Piazza San Marco to the Rialto in a succession of streets collectively known as **The Mercerie.** It's virtually impossible to get lost because each street name is preceded by the word *merceria,* such as Merceria dell'Orologio, which begins near the clock tower in Piazza San Marco. Many commercial establishments—mainly shops—line the Mercerie before it reaches the Rialto, which then explodes into one vast shopping emporium.

SOME SHOPS WORTH A LOOK

Il Papiro. Calle del Piovan, San Marco 2764. ☎ **041/5223055.** Vaporetto: Accademia.

Il Papiro is mainly noted for its stationery supplies, but it also carries and sells many textures and colors of writing paper and cards. In addition to hand-printed paper, the store stocks any number of easy-to-pack gift items.

Jesurum. Mercerie del Capitello, San Marco 4857. ☎ **041/5206177.** Vaporetto: San Zaccaria or Rialto.

This elegant shop, the best place in Venice for serious lace purchases, has been in a 12th-century church since 1868. You'll find Venetian hand- or machine-made lace and embroidery on table, bed, and bathroom linens, and hand-printed bathing suits.

Laboratorio Artigiano Maschere. Barbaria delle Tole, Castello 6657. ☎ **041/5223110.** Vaporetto: Rialto.

This is one of the best places to purchase carnival masks handcrafted in papier-mâché or leather. The masks carry names and symbols, the best known being the birdlike luck bringer, called *Buonaventura* in Italian.

Pauly & Co. Ponte Consorzi, San Marco. ☎ **041/5209899.** Vaporetto: San Zaccaria.

You can wander through 21 salons, enjoy an exhibition of artistic glassware, and later see a furnace in full action. Pauly's production, which is mainly made-to-order, consists of continually renewed patterns, subject to change and alteration based on customer desire.

Venini. Piazzetta Leoncini, San Marco 314. ☎ **041/5224045.** Vaporetto: San Zaccaria.

Venini's Venetian glass has won collector fans all over the globe. It sells lamps, bottles, and vases, but not ordinary ones. Many are works of art, representing the best of Venetian craftsmanship in design and manufacture. Their best-known glass has a distinctive swirl pattern in several colors, which is called a *venature.*

VENICE AFTER DARK

The tourist office distributes a free pamphlet (part in English, part in Italian), called *Un Ospite di Venezia.* A section of this useful publication lists events, including any music and opera or theatrical presentations, along with art exhibitions and local special events.

In addition, classical concerts are often at various churches, such as the Chiesa di Vivaldi. To see if any **church concerts** are being presented at the time of your visit, call ☎ **041/5208722** for information.

Sipping a Bellini at Harry's Bar

The single most famous of all the watering holes of Ernest Hemingway, **Harry's Bar,** Calle Vallaresso, San Marco 1323 (☎ **041/5285777;** vaporetto: San Marco), is known for inventing its own drinks and exporting them around the world. It's also said that *carpaccio,* the delicate raw-beef dish, was invented here. Devotees say that Harry's makes the best Bellini of any bar in the world. In Venice, this bar is a tradition and landmark, not quite as famous as the Basilica di San Marco—but almost.

THE PERFORMING ARTS

In January 1996, a dramatic fire left the fabled **La Fenice** at Campo San Fantin, the city's main venue for performing arts, a blackened shell. The Italian government has pledged $12.5 million for the reconstruction of the theater, one of the most beautiful in Italy. However, you can still see performances of the Orchestra and Caro della Fenice in a temporary venue, PalaFenice in the Tronchetto parking facilities near Piazzale Roma. Tickets for most events range from 30,000 to 150,000L ($18 to $90), but prices sometimes vary. For more information, call ☎ **041/5205422.**

Teatro Goldoni, Calle Goldoni, near Campo San Luca (☎ **041/5207583**), close to the Ponte Rialto in the San Marco district, honors Carlo Goldoni (1707–93), the most prolific—critics say the best—Italian playwright. The theater presents a changing repertoire of productions, often plays in Italian, but musical presentations as well. The box office is open Monday to Saturday 10am to 1pm and 4:30 to 7pm. Tickets are 20,000 to 45,000L ($12 to $27).

PIANO BARS & DANCE CLUBS

Il Piccolo Mondo. Calle Contarini Corfu 1056A. ☎ **041/520-0371.** Cover (including the first drink) 12,000L ($7.20) Thurs–Fri, 18,000L ($10.80) Sat; otherwise free. Vaporetto: Accademia.

This pub, near the Accademia, is open during the day, and at night it features disco dancing and organized parties. The crowd is often young, and dance music prevails. It's open from Thursday to Tuesday from 10pm to 4am, but the action actually doesn't begin until after midnight.

Martini Scala Club. Campo San Fantin, San Marco 1980. ☎ **041/5224121.** Vaporetto: San Marco or Santa Maria del Giglio

This elegant restaurant with a piano bar has functioned as some kind of an inn, in one manifestation or another, since 1724. You can enjoy its food and wine until 2am—it's the only kitchen in Venice that stays open late. After 10pm you can come here to enjoy the piano bar. The restaurant is open year-round, Thursday to Monday noon to 2:30pm and 7pm to 11:30pm and on Wednesday from 7 to 11:30pm. The bar, which offers a piano bar and food, is open daily 10pm to 3am, but closed in July and August.

CAFES

Venice's most famous cafe is the ✪ **Florian,** Piazza San Marco, San Marco 56–59 (☎ **041/5285338;** vaporetto: San Marco). It was built in 1720 and remains romantically and elegantly decorated, with red plush banquettes, elaborate murals, and art-nouveau lamps. The Florian sells wonderful pastries and cakes. It's open Thursday to Tuesday 9:30am to midnight. Closed the first week in December and the first week in January.

✪ **Quadri,** Piazza San Marco, San Marco 120–124 (☎ **041/5222105;** vaporetto: San Marco), was founded in 1638. It's elegantly decorated in an antique style, and the food here is quite excellent. Wagner used to drop in for a drink when he was working on *Tristan und Isolde.* The cafe here is open April to October daily 9am to midnight; off-season, Tuesday to Sunday 9am to midnight.

CASINOS

If you want to risk your luck and your lire, you can take a vaporetto ride on the **Casino Express,** which leaves from the rail station's stops, Piazzale Roma, and Piazzetta San Marco, and delivers you to the landing dock of the **Casino Municipale,** Lungomare G. Marconi 4, Lido (☎ **041/5297111**). Admission is 10,000L ($6); bring your passport to get in. The building itself is foreboding, almost as though it could have been inspired by Mussolini-era architects. However, the action gets hotter once you step inside. At the casino, you can play blackjack, roulette, baccarat, or whatever. You can also dine, drink at the bar, or enjoy a floor show. It's open July to September daily from 3pm to 2:30am.

From October to June the casino action moves to the **Vendramin-Calergi Palace,** Strada Nuova, Cannaregio 2040 (☎ **041/5297111;** vaporetto: San Marcuola). Incidentally, in 1883 Wagner died in this house, which opens onto the Grand Canal. The casino is open daily 3pm to 2:30am. Admission is 10,000L ($6).

DAY TRIPS FROM VENICE

MURANO   On this island, **glassblowers** have been producing fantastic creations for centuries. They have crafted amazing chandeliers (the kind Victorian ladies prized) and they also make heavily ornamented glasses so ruby red or indigo blue you can't quite tell what you're drinking. Happily, the glassblowers are still plying their trade, although increasing competition—notably from Sweden—has compelled a greater degree of sophistication in design. You can combine a tour of Murano with a trip along the lagoon. To reach the island, take vaporetto no. 5 at Riva degli Schiavoni, a short walk from Piazzetta San Marco. The boat docks at the landing platform at Murano where—lo and behold—the first furnace conveniently awaits. It's best to go Monday through Friday 10am to noon if you want to see some glassblowing action.

BURANO   Burano is a world-famous center of **lacemaking,** a craft that reached its pinnacle in the 18th century (recall Venetian point?). If you can spare a morning to visit this island, you'll be rewarded with a charming little fishing village far removed in spirit from the grandeur of Venice, but lying only half an hour away by ferry. Boats leave from Fondamente Nuove, overlooking the Venetian graveyard (which is well worth the trip all on its own). Take vaporetto no. 12 or 52 from Riva degli Schiavoni, get off at Fondamente Nuove, and catch a separate boat, Line 12, marked Burano.

Once at Burano, you'll discover that the houses of the islanders come in varied colors—sienna, robin's-egg or cobalt blue, barn red, butterscotch, grass green. **Scuola Merietti** stands in the center of the fishing village on Piazza Baldassare Galuppi. The Burano School of Lace was founded in 1872 as part of a resurgence movement aimed at restoring the age-old craft that had earlier declined, giving way to other lacemaking centers, such as Chantilly and Bruges. By going up to the second floor, you can see the lacemakers, mostly young women, at painstaking work and can purchase hand-embroidered or handmade lace items.

After visiting the lace school, you can walk across the square to the **Duomo** and its leaning campanile (inside, look for the *Crucifixion* by Tiepolo). However, walk quickly; the bell tower is leaning so precariously it looks as though it might topple at any moment.

TORCELLO   Of all the islands of the lagoon, Torcello—the "Mother of Venice"—offers the most charm. If Burano is behind the times, Torcello is positively antediluvian. You can follow in Hemingway's footsteps and stroll across a grassy meadow, traverse an ancient stone bridge, and step back into that time when the Venetians first fled from invading barbarians to create a city of Neptune in the lagoon. To reach Torcello, take vaporetto no. 12 from Fondamenta Nuova on Murano. The trip takes about 45 minutes.

Cattedrale di Torcello, also called the Church of Santa Maria Assunta Isola di Torcello (☎ **041/730084**), was founded in A.D. 639 and subsequently rebuilt. It stands in a lonely, grassy meadow beside a campanile dating from the 11th century. It's visited chiefly because of its Byzantine mosaics. Clutching her child, the weeping Madonna in the apse is a magnificent sight, and on the opposite wall is a powerful *Last Judgment*. It's open daily April to October, 10am to 12:30pm and 2:30 to 6:30pm; November to March, 10am to 12:30pm and 2:30 to 5pm. Admission is 1,500L (90¢).

While on the island, you can dine in Venice's most idyllic luncheon stopover, ✪ **Locanda Cipriani,** Piazza San Fosca 29 (☎ **041/730150**), operated by Bonifacio Brass, nephew of Harry Cipriani of Hotel Cipriani and Harry's Bar fame. This low-key, deliberately rustic *locanda* (inn) serves authentic Venetian cuisine—everything from succulent risotto made from fresh vegetables and herbs from the family garden to filet of John Dory in the style of Carla, a late and much-revered matriarch here (the fish is flavored with tomatoes and capers). Main courses run from 30,000 to 40,000L ($18 to $24) and hours are Wednesday to Monday noon to 3pm and Friday and Saturday 7 to 10pm. Closed January 15 to February 15. American Express, Diners Club, MasterCard, and Visa are accepted.

THE LIDO   Near the turn of the century, the Lido began to blossom into a fashionable beachfront resort, complete with deluxe hotels and its Casino Municipale.

Today the Lido is past its heyday. The fashionable and chic of the world still patronize the **Excelsior Palace** and the **Hotel des Bains,** but the beach strip is overtouristed and opens onto polluted waters. It's not just the beaches around Venice that are polluted—the entire Adriatic is reputedly polluted. For swimming, guests use their hotel pools. They can, however, still enjoy the sands along the Lido. Try the **Lungomare G. d'Annunzio Public Bathing Beach** at the end of the Gran Viale (Piazzale Ettore Sorger), a long stroll from the vaporetto stop. You can book cabins—called *camerini*—and enjoy the sand. Rates change seasonally.

To reach the Lido, take vaporetto no. 6 (the ride takes about 15 minutes). The boat departs from a landing stage near the Doges' Palace.

Where to Stay   The ✪ **Excelsior Palace,** Lungomare Marconi 41, 30126 Venezia Lido (☎ **800/325-3535** in the U.S. and Canada, or 041/5260201; fax 041/5267276; vaporetto: Lido, then bus A, B, or C), is a monument to *la dolce vita* and did much to make the Lido fashionable. Today it is the Lido's most luxurious hotel. Rooms range in style and amenities from cozy singles to suites. Most of the social life takes place around the angular pool or on the flowered terraces leading up to the cabanas on the sandy beach. All rooms—some big enough for tennis games—have been modernized, often with vivid colors. On the premises is one of the most elegant dining rooms of the Adriatic, the Tropicana. Rates, including breakfast, are 688,000 to 950,000L ($412.80 to $570) for a double and from 2,100,000L ($1,260) for a suite. American

Express, Diners Club, MasterCard, and Visa are accepted. The hotel is closed November to March 15.

○ **Hotel des Bains,** Lungomare Marconi 17, 30126 Venezia Lido (☎ **800/ 325-3535** in the U.S. and Canada, or 041/5265921; fax 041/5260113; vaporetto: Lido, then bus A, B, or C), was built in the grand era of European resort hotels. It has its own wooded park and private beach with individual cabanas along with a kind of confectionary facade from the turn of the century. Thomas Mann stayed here several times before making it the setting for *Death in Venice,* and later it was used as a set for the film of the same name. The hotel has fairly large, well-furnished rooms. Many resort-type amenities are offered, including tennis courts, a large pool, a private pier, and a park. Rates are 581,000 to 870,000L ($348.60 to $522) for a double; suites begin at 1,285,000L ($771). American Express, Diners Club, MasterCard, and Visa are accepted. It's closed November to March.

12

The Netherlands

by George McDonald

This chapter mainly covers easy-going and prosperous Amsterdam, full of canals, bridges, and world-class museums. It also includes day trips to historic Haarlem; the seaside resort Zandvoort; Delft, famous for its blue-and-white earthenware; the flower centers; and two IJsselmeer lakeside villages, Volendam and Marken.

Amsterdam

Amsterdam has never entirely shed its reputation as a hippie haven of peace, love, pot, and tulips, even with an economy that has become the envy of Europe. Fueled more by free trade than free love, prosperity has settled like a protective cloak over a graceful cityscape of canals and 17th-century townhouses. The historic city center recalls Amsterdam's golden age as the command post of a vast trading network and colonial empire, when wealthy merchants constructed gabled residences along neatly laid-out canals. Now a new generation of entrepreneurs is revitalizing old neighborhoods such as the Jordaan, turning some of the distinctive houses into bustling shops, cafes, hotels, and restaurants.

A delicious irony is that the placid 17th-century structures also host brothels, smoke shops, and Europe's wildest nightlife. The Dutch are proud of their live-and-let-live attitude, which is based on pragmatism as much as the country's long history of tolerance. Deciding to control what they cannot effectively outlaw, they permit prostitution in the red light district and the sale of marijuana and hashish in designated "coffee shops."

But don't think Amsterdammers drift around in a drug-induced haze. They are too busy whizzing around the city on bicycles, jogging through Vondelpark, feasting on arrays of ethnic dishes, or simply watching the parade of streetlife from the terrace of an outdoor cafe. Their zest for living is infectious. Between dips into Amsterdam's trove of artistic and historical treasures, take time out to absorb the free-wheeling spirit of Europe's most vibrant city.

Only in Amsterdam

Cruising the Canals Hop aboard a glass-topped canal boat for a cruise through Amsterdam's beautiful canals. A canal-boat cruise is the best way to view the gabled golden age merchants' houses and picturesque bridges, including the famous Magere Brug (Skinny Bridge) over the Amstel.

Admiring Rembrandt   Stand in front of Rembrandt's *The Night Watch* at the Rijksmuseum, and then explore the 200-plus rooms displaying works by Dutch and other European masters.

Visiting van Gogh   In the outstanding Van Gogh Museum you can trace this great impressionist's artistic and psychological development. Then head next door to the always challenging Stedelijk Museum of Modern Art.

Remembering Anne Frank   Spend a reflective moment amid the surroundings of her World War II hideaway, now the Anne Frankhuis, where she kept her famous diary.

Visiting the Flower Centers   There's nothing like the burst of color come spring as millions of bulbs in bloom make the greatest flower show on earth. Narcissi, daffodils and hyacinths, bluebells, crocuses, lilies, amaryllis, and, of course, tulips carpet the ground in a blaze of color.

Biking Around Town   Rent a bicycle and join the flow of cyclists for a classic Amsterdam experience. Or pedal yourself through the canals for an hour or two on your own private boat. (Amsterdammers scoff at these water bikes, but let them!) Either way, ride carefully.

Listening to Classical Music   To hear how classical music sounds in one of the world's most acoustically superlative halls, take in a concert by the Royal Concertgebouw Orchestra at the Concertgebouw.

Strolling the Red Light District   Examine the quaint gabled architecture along its narrow canals—Oh, yes, and you might also notice certain ladies watching the world go by through their red-fringed windows.

Spending an Evening in a Brown Cafe   Even if you're not a beer lover, an evening spent in a traditional Amsterdam watering hole gives you a peek into the city's everyday life, and you'll feel the centuries of conviviality the minute you walk in the door.

ORIENTATION

ARRIVING   By Plane   Amsterdam's **Schiphol Airport** (☎ **0900/0141** for flight information), is served by Dutch national carrier KLM in association with Northwest Airlines, in addition to American Airlines, United Airlines, and many other international carriers. You emerge from baggage retrieval into Schiphol Plaza, a combined arrivals hall, railway station, and shopping mall.

The **KLM hotel shuttle bus** operates between the airport and city center on a circular route directly connecting 16 top hotels, with stops close to many others. The one-way fare is 17.50Dfl ($9.20); no reservations are needed, and buses leave from in front of Schiphol Plaza every 20 minutes from 7am to 6pm and every 30 minutes from 6 to 9:30pm.

Trains leave from Schiphol Station, downstairs from Schiphol Plaza, for Amsterdam's Centraal Station. Departures range from one per hour at night to six per hour at peak times. The fare is 6.25Dfl ($3.30) one-way, and the trip takes about 20 minutes. Other stations—which include Amsterdam Zuid (South) and RAI—are also served, so be sure to check which one is best (including any tram or bus connection) for your hotel.

From the airport to the city center, **taxis** charge about 60Dfl ($31.60).

By Train   International trains arrive at Amsterdam's Centraal Station from Brussels, Paris (including the Thalys high-speed train), and several German cities, as well as

Amsterdam

Attractions:

E-0003

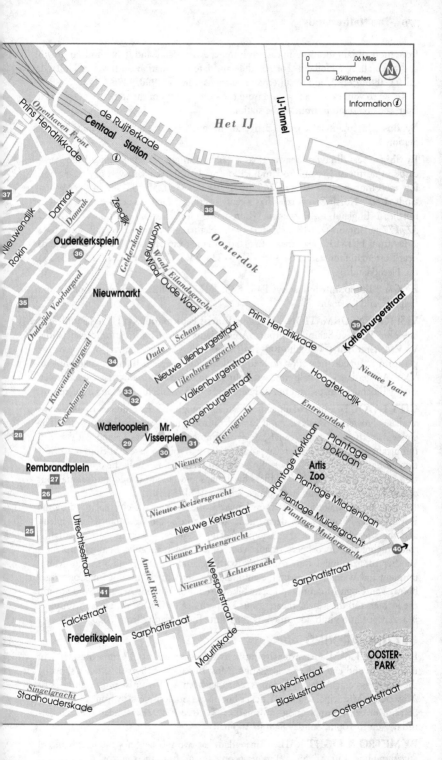

from more distant locations in eastern Europe, Switzerland, and Italy, and from towns and cities all over Holland. For schedule and fare information on travel in Holland, call ☎ **0900/9292,** and for international trains, call ☎ **0900/9296.**

To get to your hotel, take a tram from the stops in front of the station, or take a taxi from the taxi stand in front of the station.

By Bus   International coaches arrive at the main bus terminal opposite Centraal Station.

By Ship   Scandinavian Seaways has a daily overnight car ferry service from Newcastle in northeast England to IJmuiden on the North Sea coast west of Amsterdam; for reservations, call ☎ **01255/240240** in Britain; ☎ 0255/534-546 in the Netherlands. **P&O North Sea Ferries** has a daily overnight car ferry service from Hull in northeast England to Rotterdam (Europoort); for reservations, call ☎ **01482/ 377177** in Britain; ☎ 0181/255-555 in the Netherlands. **Stena Line** sails four times a day from Harwich in southeast England to Hoek van Holland (Hook of Holland) near Rotterdam; for reservations, call ☎ **01233/647047** in Britain, 0174/389-333 in the Netherlands.

By Car   European expressways E19, E35, E231, and E22 reach Amsterdam from Belgium and Germany.

VISITOR INFORMATION   Holland Tourist Information (HTI) has an office in Schiphol Plaza at Schiphol Airport. Amsterdam's tourist information organization, **VVV Amsterdam** (☎ **0900/400-4040**), has offices inside Centraal Station beside platform 1, outside the station on Stationsplein, at Leidseplein 1, and on Stadionplein. VVV Amsterdam can help you with almost any question about the city, and can supply brochures, maps, and more. There are separate desks for reserving hotel rooms.

CITY LAYOUT   Amsterdam center is small enough that its residents think of it as a village. However, as villages go, it can be confusing until you get the hang of it. The concentric rings of major canals are its defining characteristic, along with several important squares that act as focal points. It's easy to think you're headed in one direction along the canal ring, only to find out you're going in exactly the opposite direction. A map is essential. VVV offices have maps and guides, including the small but detailed VVV Amsterdam map, which sells for 4Dfl ($2.10).

There are six major squares. Dam Square is the heart of the city, encircled by the Royal Palace, Nieuwe Kerk, department stores, hotels, and restaurants. Leidseplein, and the streets around it, is Amsterdam's Times Square, glittering with restaurants, cafes, nightclubs, discos, performance centers, and movie theaters. Rembrandtplein is another entertainment center, bustling with restaurants, cafes, and a casino. Museumplein and Waterlooplein are the cultural hubs, with the Rijksmuseum, Concertgebouw, Van Gogh Museum, and Stedelijk Museum of Modern Art all in and around the former, and the Muziektheater (plus a superb flea market) at the latter. Muntplein is a transportation hub, identified by the Munt Tower, dating from 1620.

GETTING AROUND

BY BUS & TRAM   An extensive bus network complements 17 tram routes; 11 of them begin and end at Centraal Station. Most bus/tram shelters have maps showing the entire system. A detailed map is available from VVV tourist offices and GVB/ Amsterdam Municipal Transport ticket booths on Stationsplein in front of Centraal Station, or call transportation information (☎ **0900/9292**), Monday through Saturday 7am to 10pm, Sunday 8am to 10pm.

BY METRO & LIGHT RAIL   Amsterdam has two subway lines and four light rail (*sneltram*) lines (50, 51, 53, 54) to get people to and from the suburbs.

Fare Information   A single-journey **ticket** (an *enkeltje*) costs 3 to 7.50Dfl ($1.60 to $3.95) depending on how many zones you travel through. There are 11 fare zones in greater Amsterdam, although tourists rarely travel beyond the city center zone 5700 (Centrum). Make sure your ticket is validated for the number of zones you plan to travel through. Several types of tickets are valid on buses, trams, metro, and light rail. You can buy a **day ticket** (*dagkaart*), valid for the day of purchase and the night following, from any bus or tram driver, conductor, or ticket dispenser for 12Dfl ($6.30). Also available are tickets valid for 2 to 9 days, priced from 16 to 42.25Dfl ($8.40 to $22.25); they have to be purchased at the GVB/Amsterdam Municipal Transport ticket booths. Bear in mind that you need to take a lot of trams for day and multiday cards to be worthwhile

If you plan to do a lot of walking and take trams only around the city center, you're probably better off with a *strippenkaart* (strip card) that you can use throughout your stay. You can buy an eight-strip card for 12Dfl ($6.30) from drivers and conductors, or a 15-strip card (11.50Dfl, or $6.05) or a 45-strip card (33.75Dfl, or $17.75) from railway and metro stations, GVB/Amsterdam Municipal Transport ticket booths, post offices, and many news vendors. The card is easy to use: Fold at the line and punch it in the validating machine aboard the tram. On some trams a conductor at the rear validates the card; on buses, the driver does it.

Validated cards can be used for any number of transfers between lines and modes of transportation, within 1 hour of the time stamped on them at validation and within the paid-for number of zones. The fare system is based on canceling one strip more than the number of zones you travel within—two strips for one zone, three strips for two zones, and so on.

BY TAXI   Officially, you can't simply hail a cab, but often they stop if you do. Otherwise, call **Taxi Centrale** (☎ 020/677-7777) or find one of the taxi stands sprinkled around the city, generally near the luxury hotels and at major squares such as Dam Square, Centraal Station, Spui, Rembrandtplein, Westermarkt, and Leidseplein. Taxis are metered and fares—which include the tip—begin at 5.80Dfl ($3.05) when you get in and run up at the rate of 2.85Dfl ($1.50) per kilometer. For a **water taxi,** call ☎ **020/622-2181.**

BY CAR   Don't rent a car to get around Amsterdam—you'll regret the expense and hassle. The city is a jumble of one-way streets, narrow bridges, and no-parking zones. In addition, car break-ins are not uncommon, especially at night.

Outside the city, driving is another story; you may want to rent a car for a trip into the countryside. Call **Avis,** Hogehilweg 7 (☎ **020/430-9611**); **Budget,** Overtoom 121 (☎ **020/612-6066**); or **Hertz,** Overtoom 333 (☎ **020/612-2441**).

BY BICYCLE   Follow the Dutch example and cycle. Sunday, when the city is quiet, is a good day to pedal through the parks and to practice riding on cobblestones and dealing with trams before venturing forth into the fray of rush hour. Bike-rental rates average 12Dfl ($6.30) per day or 60Dfl ($31.60) per week, with a deposit required. You can rent bikes from **MacBike,** Mr. Visserplein 2 (☎ **020/620-0985**); **MacBike Too,** Gravesandestraat 49 (☎ **020/693-2104**) and Marnixstraat 220 (☎ **020/626-6964**); and **Bike City,** Bloemgracht 70 (☎ **020/626-3721**).

BY WATER BICYCLE   Rent a water bicycle (pedal boat) to pedal along the canals; they seat two or four and cost 19.50Dfl ($10.25) for a 1-hour jaunt for two and 29.50Dfl ($15.55) for four. Moorings are at Leidseplein; Westerkerk, near the Anne Frankhuis; Stadhouderskade, between the Rijksmuseum and Heineken Reception Center; and Toronto Bridge on the Keizersgracht, near Leidsestraat. You can rent a water bike at one mooring and leave it at another.

Fast Facts: Amsterdam

American Express   Offices are at Damrak 66 (☎ **020/520-7777**) and Van Baerlestraat 39 (☎ **020/673-8550**). Both are open Monday to Friday 9am to 5pm and Saturday 9am to noon. The Damrak office books tours and excursions and offers a full range of services, including currency exchange. The Van Baerlestraat office only books tours and excursions.

Business Hours   Banks are open Monday through Friday 9am to 4 or 5pm (some until 7pm on Thursday). Regular shopping hours are Monday 11am to 6pm, Tuesday, Wednesday, and Friday 9am to 6pm, Thursday 9am to 9pm, Saturday 9am to 5pm, and Sunday (some stores only) noon to 5pm.

Currency   Holland's monetary unit is the guilder, yet you see it written as Dutch florins (abbreviated "f," "fl," "Hfl", or "Dfl"); since this is a holdover from the past, ignore the written symbol and read all prices as guilders. There are 100 Dutch cents to a guilder. The exchange rate used in this chapter is $1 = 1.90Dfl or 1Dfl = 55¢. Also, 1EUR = 2.2Dfl or £1 = 3.3Dfl.

Currency Exchange   Change your money at **VVV tourist offices,** or if you carry American Express traveler's checks, at **American Express,** Damrak 66 (☎ **020/520-7777**), open Monday through Friday from 9am to 5pm, where there's no commission charge. Other fair-dealing options are the **GWK exchanges** at Schiphol Airport and Centraal Station, which also handle money transfers via Western Union.

Doctors & Dentists   Contact the Central Medical Service (☎ **020/ 592-3434**).

Drugstores   In Holland a pharmacy is called an *apotheek.* Try **Dam Apotheek** at Damstraat 2 (☎ **020/624-4331**). All pharmacies have the name of an all-night pharmacy posted on the door.

Embassies & Consulates   The United States Consulate is at Museumplein 19 (☎ **020/575-5309**); the American Embassy is at Lange Voorhout 102, The Hague (☎ **070/310-9209**). The Consulate-General of the United Kingdom is at Koningslaan 44 (☎ **020/676-4343**); the British Embassy is at Lange Voorhout 10, Den Haag (**070/364-5800**).

Emergencies   In an emergency, dial ☎ **112** to call the police, to report a fire, or to summon an ambulance.

Internet Access   **Waag,** in the castle in the middle of the Nieuwmarket, is a popular cybercafe and restaurant, with free terminals. **Cyber C@fé,** Nieuwendijk 19 (☎ **020/623-5146**), is an Internet cafe and smoking coffee shop.

Post Office   The main post office/PTT is at Singel 250–256 (☎ **020/ 556-3311**), at the corner of Radhuisstraat. It's open Monday through Friday 9am to 6pm and Saturday 9am to 3pm.

Taxes   Citizens from outside the European Union can shop tax free. If you spend more than 300Dfl ($157.90)in one store, you can ask for a Tax Free Shopping Cheque, which is stamped by Customs when you leave the European Union. A refund of 13.5% can be paid to your credit card account.

Telephone   The country code for the Netherlands is **31.** The city code for Amsterdam is **20** from outside the Netherlands, **020** inside the country (no code at all if you're in the city).

A local call in Amsterdam costs .50Dfl (25¢) for 3 minutes. Most pay phones in the Netherlands accept only phone cards, which are sold at newsstands, post offices, tobacconists, and train stations for 10Dfl ($5.25), 25Dfl ($13.15), and 50Dfl ($26.30). Coin phones take 0.25, 1, 2.50, or 5Dfl. On both coin and card phones, watch the digital reading, which tracks your decreasing deposit so you'll know when to add more coins or another card. For directory assistance within the country, call ☎ **0900/8008;** for international assistance, dial ☎ **0900/8418.**

To charge a call to your calling card, dial **AT&T** (☎ 0800/022-9111); **MCI** (☎ 0800/022-9122); **Sprint** (☎ 0800/022-9119); **Canada Direct** (☎ 0800/022-9116); or **British Telecom** (☎ 0800/022-9944).

WHERE TO STAY

Most Amsterdam hotels, whatever their cost, are clean and tidily furnished, and in many cases they've been recently renovated or redecorated. Booking ahead is always advised. The Dutch hotel industry runs a free hotel-booking service: the **NRC/ Netherlands Reservations Center,** P.O. Box 404, 2260 AK Leidschendam (☎ **070/ 419-5500;** fax 070/419-5519).

If you arrive in Amsterdam without a reservation, the **VVV tourist offices** inside and outside Centraal Station will help you for the moderate charge of 5Dfl ($2.65) per person. Another possibility is the **Dutch Tourist Information Office,** Damrak 35 (☎ **020/638-2800;** fax 020/625-0974). Hotels with unsold rooms often sell them at the last minute through this office at a substantial discount. The reservation fee is 2.50Dfl ($1.30) per person. The office is open Monday through Saturday 8am to 10pm, and Sunday 9am to 10pm.

If you need to stay near the airport, try the **Sheraton Amsterdam Airport** (☎ **800/ 325-3535** or 020/316-4300), or the less expensive **Dorint Schiphol Amsterdam** (☎ **020/658-8111).**

VERY EXPENSIVE

✪ **American Hotel.** Leidsekade 97 (facing Leidseplein), 1017 PN Amsterdam, Netherlands. ☎ **020/624-5322.** Fax 020/625-3236. www.interconti.com. E-mail: american@interconti. com. 188 units. A/C MINIBAR TV TEL. 550Dfl ($289.45) double; 750Dfl ($394.75) suite; add 5% city tax. AE, CB, DC, JCB, MC, V. Parking at nearby lot 60Dfl ($31.60). KLM Hotel Shuttle from Schiphol Airport stops nearby. Tram: 1, 2, 5, 6, 7, or 10 to Leidseplein.

Art nouveau, neo-Gothic, and castle-like, the American has been a city landmark and meeting place since the turn of the century. Its location is one of the best in town if you want to be where the action is—some rooms overlook kaleidoscopic Leidseplein; others, the tranquil Singelgracht canal. Rooms are decorated in art deco style, with clean lines and subtle lighting. All have hair dryers. Dine in the magnificent, art deco Café Américain, and watch the street life from the Nightwatch Bar's glassed-in sidewalk terrace. Amenities include concierge, 24-hour room service, dry cleaning and laundry, and health center with sauna and solarium.

Grand Hotel Krasnapolsky. Dam 9 (facing the Royal Palace), 1012 JS Amsterdam, Netherlands. ☎ **020/554-9111.** Fax 020/622-8607. 539 units. www.krasnapolsky.nl. E-mail: book@krasnapolsky.nl. A/C MINIBAR TV TEL. 660Dfl ($347.35) double; 1,300–1,500Dfl ($684.20–$789.45) suite; add 5% city tax. Children under 5 stay free in parents' room; children 6–12 charged half-price. AE, CB, DC, MC, V. Valet and self-parking 45Dfl ($23.70). KLM Hotel Shuttle from Schiphol Airport. Tram: 4, 9, 14, 16, 20, 24, or 25 to Dam Square.

One of the city's landmarks, the "Kras," as it's known locally, began life in 1866 as the Wintertuin (Winter Garden) restaurant, which still dominates the hotel's ground floor. The size and shape of the rooms vary, with some tastefully converted into individually decorated mini-apartments. All have hair dryers and coffeemakers. Recent enhancements include a new wing with a Japanese garden and Dutch roof garden. The Winter Garden is complemented by the French Brasserie Reflet, Japanese Edo and Kyo restaurants, and the Bedouin Shibli. Amenities include concierge, 24-hour room service, dry cleaning and laundry, health club, beauty salon, and boutiques.

Hôtel de l'Europe. Nieuwe Doelenstraat 2–8 (facing Muntplein), 1012 CP Amsterdam, Netherlands. ☎ **800/223-6800** in the U.S. and Canada, or ☎ 020/531-1777. Fax 020/531-1778. www.leurope.nl. E-mail: hotel@leurope.nl. 100 units. A/C MINIBAR TV TEL. 630Dfl ($357.90) double; suites from 870Dfl ($457.90); add 5% city tax. AE, DC, MC, V. Valet parking 50Dfl ($26.30). Tram: 4, 9, 14, 16, 20, 24, or 25 to De Munt.

Built in 1896, the Hôtel de l'Europe has a grand style and sense of ease. Its pastel-red and white facade overlooks the River Amstel where it runs into the city's canal network. Guest rooms and bathrooms are spacious and bright, furnished with classic good taste. Some have mini-balconies on the river, and all have hair dryers and marble bathrooms. An extensive renovation program began in 1998, updating about 20 units a year. Dine in the elegant Excelsior restaurant or in the less formal Le Relais. Le Bar and La Terrasse (summer only) serve drinks and hors d'oeuvres daily. There's a waterside cafe terrace in summer. Amenities include concierge, 24-hour room service, heated indoor pool, and health club with sauna and massage.

Pulitzer ITT Sheraton. Prinsengracht 315–331 (near Westermarkt), 1016 GZ Amsterdam, Netherlands. ☎ **800/325-3535** or ☎ 020/523-5235. Fax 020/627-6753. www.sheraton.com. 224 units. MINIBAR TV TEL. 495–585Dfl ($260.55–$307.90) double; 1,570Dfl ($826.30) suite; add 5% city tax. Extra person 95Dfl ($50). AE, CB, DC, MC, V. Valet and self-parking 49.50Dfl ($26.05). KLM Hotel Shuttle from Schiphol Airport. Tram: 13, 14, 17, or 20 to Westermarkt.

A real prize-winner, constructed within the walls of 24 adjoining canal houses, most of which are between 200 and 400 years old. You walk between two houses to enter the lobby, or climb the steps of a former merchant's house to enter the crowded and cheerful bar. Rooms are spacious and modern, with wicker furnishings, and have been renovated in the past 2 years. They have views on one of two historic canals, Prinsengracht and Keizersgracht, or on the hotel garden. All have hair dryers. Dine in the tony De Goudsbloem restaurant, or snack in the chic cafe or bar. A restored saloon cruiser from 1909 awaits your pleasure at the hotel's jetty. Amenities include concierge, 24-hour room service, laundry, and dry cleaning.

EXPENSIVE

Dikker & Thijs Fenice. Prinsengracht 444 (at Leidsestraat), 1017 KE Amsterdam, Netherlands. ☎ **020/626-7721.** Fax 020/625-8986. www.dikkerenthijsfenice.nl. E-mail: info@dikkerenthijsfenice.nl. 26 units. MINIBAR TV TEL. 315–450Dfl ($165.80–$236.85) double. Rates include continental breakfast. Children 12 and under stay free in parents' room. AE, DC, JCB, MC, V. Parking at nearby lot 50Dfl ($26.30). Tram: 1, 2, or 5 to Prinsengracht.

Small and homey, this hotel reveals a cozy character behind its stylish facade. Spacious rooms, tastefully styled in a modern version of art deco, are clustered in groups of two or four around small lobbies, which makes the hotel feel more like an apartment building. Double-glazed windows eliminate the noise from Leidsestraat. All rooms were renovated during 1997 and 1998 and have hair dryers and in-room movies. Those at the front have a great view of Prinsengracht. The Prinsenkelder restaurant serves fine French and Italian cuisine. Amenities include a concierge, room service, and dry cleaning and laundry.

Estheréa. Singel 303–309 (near Spui), 1012 WJ Amsterdam, Netherlands. ☎ **020/ 624-5146.** Fax 020/623-9001. 70 units. MINIBAR TV TEL. 355–425Dfl ($186.85–$223.70) double. One child 12 and under may stay free in parents' room; extra person 50Dfl ($26.30). Rates include breakfast. AE, DC, JCB, MC, V. Limited parking available on street. Tram: 1, 2, or 5 to Spui.

This large, family-owned hotel occupying neighboring 17th-century canal houses has the intimacy and personality of a much smaller establishment. Most rooms are a good size, as are the bathrooms, closets, and beds. All have hair dryers, and several have extra beds, making them ideal for families. Furnishings are discreetly classic, but an enthusiastic new generation is redecorating and adding a lighter, fresher look. There's an elevator as well as a comfortable lounge and bar. As an added touch, the hotel offers guests free coffee and tea. The Greek Traîterie Grekas restaurant next door delivers room-service meals. Other amenities include a concierge, limited-hours room service, and dry cleaning and laundry.

Jan Luyken. Jan Luykenstraat 54–58 (near Van Gogh Museum), 1071 CS Amsterdam, Netherlands. ☎ **020/573-0730.** Fax 020/676-3841. www.janluyken.nl. E-mail: info@ janluyken.nl. 63 units. MINIBAR TV TEL. 330–435Dfl ($165–$217.50) double. Children 4–12 are charged half-price; children under 4 stay free in parents' room; extra person 85Dfl ($42.50). Rates include Dutch buffet breakfast. AE, DC, MC, V. Limited parking available on street. Tram: 2, 5, or 20 to Paulus Potterstraat; 3 or 12 to Eerste Constantijn Huygensstraat.

One block from the P. C. Hooftstraat shopping street, this is best described as a small hotel with many of the amenities and facilities of a big one. It maintains a balance between sophistication and an intimate, personalized approach appropriate to a residential neighborhood. Guest rooms are classically furnished with period furniture and fabrics; the modern bathrooms have hair dryers. The owners are proud of the setting they've created and are constantly improving the hotel's facilities. Amenities include a health center with Jacuzzi, steambath, and solarium.

✪ Schiller. Rembrandtplein 26–36, 1017 CV Amsterdam, Netherlands. ☎ **020/554-0700.** Fax 020/624-0098. www.krasnapolsky.nl. 92 units. TV TEL. 385–495Dfl ($202.65–$260.55) double; suite from 525Dfl ($276.30). AE, DC, MC, V. Limited parking available on street. Tram: 4, 9, 14, or 20 to Rembrandtplein.

A blend of Jugendstil (art nouveau) and art deco, whose sculpted facade, wrought-iron balconies and stained glass windows stand out on brash Rembrandtplein, the Schiller was constructed by painter/hotelier Frits Schiller during the 1890s, and no fewer than 600 of his works are on view inside. Tastefully decorated, the rooms were totally renovated in 1997, refurnished and reappointed with such amenities as trouser presses, coffeemakers, and hair dryers. One in three has a minibar. Dine in the oak-paneled Brasserie Schiller, and join the in crowd for a drink in the art deco Café Schiller. Amenities include 24-hour room service, laundry, and dry cleaning.

MODERATE

Canal House. Keizersgracht 148 (near Leliegracht), 1015 CX Amsterdam, Netherlands. ☎ **020/622-5182.** Fax 020/624-1317. www.canalhouse.nl. E-mail: canalhousehotel@ compuserve.com. 26 units. TEL. 225–290Dfl ($118.40–$152.65) double. Rates include continental breakfast. AE, DC, MC, V. Limited parking available on street. Tram: 13, 14, 17, or 20 to Westermarkt.

A contemporary approach to reestablishing the elegant canal-house atmosphere has been taken by the American owner of this small hotel in an effort to create a home away from home. Three adjoining houses dating from 1630 were rebuilt to provide private bathrooms, and then filled with antiques, quilts, and Chinese rugs. Room 26 has a panoramic view of the canal. There is an elevator, a staircase with a beautifully carved old balustrade, an elegant breakfast room seemingly unchanged since the 17th century overlooking the back garden, and a cozy Victorian-style saloon.

Cok City. Nieuwezijds Voorburgwal 50 (between Centraal Station and Dam Square), 1012 SC Amsterdam, Netherlands. ☎ **800/44-UTELL** in the U.S. and Canada, or 020/422-0011. Fax 020/420-0357. 106 units. TV TEL. 280Dfl ($147.35) double. Extra person 55Dfl ($28.95). Rates include buffet breakfast. AE, DC, MC, V. Tram: 1, 2, 5, 13, 17, or 20 to Nieuwezijds Voorburgwal.

If you like modern comforts with the personal touch of a small, locally owned chain, this six-floor hotel in a converted printing house 5 minutes from Centraal Station and Dam Square could be right for you. Rooms are modern, comfortable, and decorated with flair, and have trouser presses and hair dryers. You'll be staying in a kind of art gallery, as owners Ger and Jaap Cok are keen artists, and their paintings grace guest rooms and public spaces. Amenities include dry cleaning and laundry and an ironing room on every floor.

✪ **De Filosoof.** Anna van den Vondelstraat 6 (beside Vondelpark), 1054 GZ Amsterdam. ☎ **020/683-3013.** Fax 020/685-3750. www.xs4all.nl/~filosoof. E-mail: filosoof@xs4all.nl. 25 units. TV TEL. 155–185Dfl ($81.60–$97.35) double. Rates include buffet breakfast. AE, MC, V. Limited parking available on street. Tram: 1 or 6 to Overtoom.

On a quiet street of brick houses, this extraordinary hotel is an open challenge to cookie-cutter hotel rooms. One of the owners is a philosophy professor who has expressed her passion for ideas in imaginatively decorated rooms. Posters, painted ceilings, framed quotes, and unusual objects are carefully chosen visual representations of philosophical or cultural themes. You can ponder the meaning of life in rooms dedicated to Goethe, Wittgenstein, Nietzsche, Marx, and Einstein, and rooms based on motifs such as Eros, the Renaissance, astrology, or women. You can consult philosophical works or join in one of the weekly philosophy roundtables. Rooms are larger in the annex across the street and some open onto a private terrace. Beds are firm; bathrooms vary in size but are well equipped. The hotel was installing an elevator in 1999.

✪ **Die Port van Cleve.** Nieuwezijds Voorburgwal 176–180 (behind the Royal Palace), 1012 SJ Amsterdam, Netherlands. ☎ **020/624-4860.** Fax 020/622-0240. E-mail: dieportvancleve. amsterdam@wxs.nl. 120 units. TV TEL. 415Dfl ($218.40) double; 625–750Dfl ($328.95–$394.75) suite; extra person 95Dfl ($50). Rates include buffet breakfast. AE, CB, DC, MC, V. Nearby parking lot 40Dfl ($21.05). KLM Hotel Shuttle from Schiphol Airport. Tram: 1, 2, 5, 13, 17, or 20 to Dam Square.

Oozing history and class, this is one of the city's oldest hotels; it began its life in 1864 as the first Heineken brewery. The ornamental facade, complete with turrets and alcoves, is original and was restored in 1997. The interior, too, has been completely renovated, and the rooms, though on the small side, are comfortably furnished in modern yet cozy style. All have hair dryers and in-room movie channels, and some have minibars. You won't eat better Dutch food than in the Brasserie de Poort, and you can drink in the Bodega de Blauwe Parade watched over by Delft Blue tiles.

Seven Bridges. Reguliersgracht 31, 1017 LK Amsterdam. ☎ **020/623-1329.** 11 units, 6 with bathroom. 155Dfl ($81.60) double without bathroom; 260Dfl ($136.85) double with bathroom. Rates include full breakfast. AE, MC, V. Limited parking available on street. Tram: 16, 24, or 25 to Keizersgracht.

Owners Pierre Keulers and Gunter Glaner have made this one of the city's gems. Rooms are individually decorated, with antique furnishings and Impressionist art posters. The biggest room, sleeping four, is on the second floor and has a huge bathroom with wood paneling, double sinks, a fair-sized shower, and a separate area for the toilet. There are some attic rooms with sloped ceilings and exposed wood beams, plus big, bright basement rooms done almost entirely in white. The latest update includes handmade Italian drapes, hand-painted tiles, and wood-tiled floors.

Wiechmann. Prinsengracht 328–330 (at Looiersgracht), 1016 HX Amsterdam, Netherlands. ☎ **020/626-3321.** Fax 020/626-8962. 40 units. TV TEL. 200–250Dfl ($105.25–$131.60) double. Rates include breakfast. No credit cards. Limited parking available on street. Tram: 1, 2, or 5 to Prinsengracht.

It takes only a moment to feel at home in the antique-adorned lobby of the Amsterdam Wiechmann. Owned for years by American T. Boddy and his Dutch wife, Nicky, the Wiechmann is comfortable and casual. Like a good wine, it gets better with age, and the location is one of the best you'll find in this or any price range. Most of the rooms are standard, with good-sized twin or double beds, and some have big bay windows. Furnishings are elegant, with oriental rugs gracing many floors. Higher-priced doubles have antique furnishings, and many have a view of the canal. There's a breakfast room with white linen cloths on the tables, a lounge, and a bar.

INEXPENSIVE

✪ **Acacia.** Lindengracht 251 (off Prinsengracht and Brouwersgracht), 1015 KH, Amsterdam, Netherlands. ☎ **020/622-1460.** Fax 020/638-0748. E-mail: acacia.nl@wxs.nl. 18 units. TV TEL. 145Dfl ($76.30) double; 175Dfl ($92.10) houseboat double. Rates include full breakfast. MC, V. Parking 35Dfl ($18.40). Tram: 3 to Nieuwe Willemstraat.

Fronting a canal in the Jordaan, this clean, well-kept hotel is run by Hans and Marlene van Vliet, a friendly young couple who have worked hard to make it welcoming. Rooms, recently furnished with new beds, tables, and chairs, are simple but clean and comfortable, and all have writing tables. Breakfast is served in a triangular breakfast room, with windows on both sides giving a nice view of the canal. Two houseboats on nearby Lijnbaansgracht add an authentic local touch.

Amstel Botel. Oosterdokskade 2–4 (beside Centraal Station), 1011 AE Amsterdam, Netherlands. ☎ **020/626-4247.** Fax 020/639-1952. 176 units. TV TEL. 159Dfl ($83.70) double. AE, DC, JCB, MC, V. Limited parking available on quayside. Turn left out of Centraal Station, pass the bike rental, and you'll see it floating in front of you. Tram: Any tram to Centraal Station.

Where better to experience a city built on water than on a boat-hotel? The boat, launched in 1993 to serve as a hotel, has become very popular because of its location, adventurous quality, and comfort at reasonable rates. Four decks connected by an elevator accommodate 176 cabins. Be sure to ask for a room with a view on the water side, not on the uninspiring quayside. There's a concierge, in-room movie channel, and dry cleaning.

Casa Cara. Emmastraat 24 (at Koninginneweg), 1075 HV Amsterdam, Netherlands. ☎ **020/662-3135.** Fax 020/676-8119. www.com-all.nl/hotels/casa-cara. 9 units, 6 with bathroom. TEL. 85Dfl ($44.75) double without bathroom; 130–155Dfl ($68.40–$81.60) double with bathroom. Summer rates include continental breakfast. No credit cards. Limited parking available on street. Tram: 2 or 16 to Koninginneweg.

Gradually and faithfully trying to meet the demands of the 1990s traveler, the Casa Cara, near Vondelpark, is a simple but well-crafted conversion of a residential house in a neighborhood with deep front lawns. The hotel has two large rooms with a private shower and toilet on each floor (they also have a TV), and a trio of rooms without bathrooms that, as a result, have the hall facilities almost to themselves.

⊕ **De Admiraal.** Herengracht 563 (at Thorbeckeplein), 1071 CD Amsterdam, Netherlands. ☎ **020/626-2150.** Fax 020/623-4625. 9 units. TV. 125–185Dfl ($65.80–$97.35) double; 200–320Dfl ($105.25–$168.40) family room. MC, V (5% surcharge). Limited parking available on street. Tram: 4, 9, 14, or 20 to Rembrandtplein.

Occupying a building from 1666, part of which was a spice warehouse for the East Indies trade, this hotel still has a nautical feel, with a bar and breakfast room that looks like an old sailing-ship officer's quarters. The simply furnished but clean and comfortable rooms—three of which are family rooms—are reached by a narrow staircase and have a fine view of the canal or adjacent Thorbeckeplein. Room 6 is the best, with two double beds, a panoramic view, and a balcony.

Piet Hein. Vossiusstraat 52–53 (facing Vondelpark), 1071 AK Amsterdam, Netherlands. ☎ **020/662-7205.** Fax 020/662-1526. www.hotelpiethein.com. E-mail: info@ hotelpiethein.nl. 36 units. TV TEL. 135–205Dfl ($71.05–$107.90) double. Rates include continental breakfast. AE, DC, JCB, MC, V. Parking at nearby lot 20Dfl ($10.55). Tram: 2 or 5 to Paulus Potterstraat.

The Piet Hein is a well-kept hotel in a villa near the city's most important museums. It's named after a Dutch folk hero, a 17th-century admiral who captured a Spanish silver shipment. Rooms are spacious and well furnished, and the staff friendly and professional. Half the rooms overlook the park; two second-floor doubles have semicircular balconies; and there is a honeymoon suite with waterbed. Lower-priced rooms are in the annex. Hair dryers are available on request, and the hotel provides concierge, room service for drinks, dry cleaning and laundry, baby-sitting, and in-room movies.

Prinsenhof. Prinsengracht 810 (at Utrechtsestraat), 1017 JL Amsterdam, Netherlands. ☎ **020/623-1772.** Fax 020/638-3368. www.xs4all.nl/~prinshof. E-mail: prinshof@xs4all.nl. 10 units, 2 with bathroom. TEL. 125Dfl ($65.80) double without bathroom; 165Dfl ($86.85) double with bathroom. Rates include continental breakfast. AE, MC, V. Limited parking available on street. Tram: 4 to Keizersgracht.

A modernized canal house near the River Amstel. Most rooms are large, with beamed ceilings and basic yet reasonably comfortable beds. The hotel has recently been redecorated, and new showers and carpets installed. Front rooms look out onto the Prinsengracht, where colorful houseboats are moored. Breakfast is served in an attractive blue-and-white decorated dining room. The owner, Ives Molin, takes pride in his hotel and will make you feel welcome. There's no elevator, but a pulley hauls your luggage up and down the stairs.

WHERE TO DINE

As a trading city, a gateway city, and one that positively revels in its status as a melting pot, Amsterdam has absorbed culinary influences from far and wide. Just about any international cuisine can be found on the city's restaurant roster.

In general, with the exception of late-night restaurants, kitchens in Amsterdam take their last dinner orders at 10 or 11pm. Restaurants with outside terraces are always in big demand on pleasant summer evenings, and few take reservations.

One way to combat escalating dinner tabs is to take advantage of the low-cost tourist menu offered by some restaurants and the *dagschotel* (dish of the day) offered by many.

VERY EXPENSIVE

⊕ **La Rive.** In the Amstel Intercontinental Hotel, Professor Tulpplein 1 (off Weesperstraat). ☎ **020/622-6060.** Jacket/tie required for men. Main courses 45–130Dfl ($23.70–$68.40); set-price menus 135–195Dfl ($71.05–$102.65). AE, DC, MC, V. Mon–Fri noon–2pm; Mon–Sat 6:30–10:30pm. Tram: 6, 7, 10, or 20 to Sarphatistraat. FRENCH.

Earning the restaurant in his charge two Michelin stars, chef Robert Kranenborg has created a menu that combines the finesse of classical French cuisine with the modern trend toward lighter, healthier eating. Luxury is not forgotten either. The freshest seasonal fish and game is enhanced by sauces of truffles, cêpes, and foie gras. The setting is intimate but formal, and several tables are next to the tall French windows that overlook the water.

EXPENSIVE

De Silveren Spiegel. Kattengat 4–6 (off Singel). ☎ **020/624-6589.** Main courses 47.50–55Dfl ($25–$28.95); set-price menus 75–85Dfl ($39.45–$44.75). AE, MC, V. Daily 6–11pm (open for lunch on reservation). Tram: 1, 2, 5, 13, 17, or 20 to Martelaarsgracht. DUTCH/FRENCH.

The two houses that form the premises were constructed in 1614 for a wealthy soapmaker, Laurens Jansz Spieghel. It's typically Old Dutch inside, with the bar downstairs and more dining rooms where the bedrooms used to be. There's a garden in back, and the whole place emanates a traditionally Dutch tidiness that's very welcoming. The menu has been updated, with finely prepared seafood and meat dishes, such as baked sole fillets with wild spinach, and Texel lamb with ratatouille, and traditional Zaanse mustard is always available.

✪ **D'Vijff Vlieghen.** Spuistraat 294–302 (entrances on Singel and Spuistraat). ☎ **020/624-8369.** Main courses 44–62.50Dfl ($23.15–$32.90); set-price menus 75–97.50Dfl ($39.45–$51.30). AE, DC, MC, V. Daily 5:30pm–midnight. Tram 1, 2, or 5 to Spui. DUTCH.

Yes, it's touristy, but at the "Five Flies" the food is authentic stick-to-the-ribs Dutch fare. The menu offers a selection of seasonal fish and game often marinated with fresh herbs and served with unusual vegetables such as chard, wild spinach, and brussels sprout leaves. If you're feeling adventurous, try the wild boar with sweet chestnuts and gin sauce. Occupying five canal houses, the restaurant is a kind of Dutch theme park with seven separate dining rooms decorated with artifacts from Holland's golden age. Don't miss the four original Rembrandt etchings and the collection of handmade glass. The chef is passionate about an updated form of Dutch cuisine he calls "the new Dutch kitchen."

Mangerie de Kersentuin. In the Bilderberg Garden Hotel, Dijsselhofplantsoen 7 (off Apollolaan). ☎ **020/664-2121.** Reservations recommended on weekends. Main courses 42.50–49Dfl ($22.35–$25.80); set-price menus 57.50–67.50Dfl ($30.25–$35.55). AE, DC, MC, V. Mon–Fri noon–2pm; Mon–Sat 6–11pm. Tram: 5 or 24 to Apollolaan; 16 to De Lairessestraat. INTERNATIONAL.

All cherry red and gleaming brass, the "Cherry Orchard" has floor-to-ceiling windows overlooking the residential street outside and semi-screened interior windows looking into the glimmering kitchen inside. It follows its own unique culinary concept, based on regional recipes from around the world, using fresh ingredients from Dutch waters and farmlands. The menu changes every two months, but these samples give some idea of what to expect: lamb fillet prepared in goose fat with creamy salsifies and coriander-scented vanilla sauce; or sea bass sautéed with peppers, garlic, sea salt, and sesame seeds, served on stir-fried pak-choi and tofu, with lemongrass butter.

't Swarte Schaep. Korte Leidsedwarsstraat 24 (at Leidseplein). ☎ **020/622-3021.** Main courses 45–52.50Dfl ($23.70–$27.65); set-price menu 77.50Dfl ($40.80). AE, DC, JCB, MC, V. Daily noon–11pm. Tram: 1, 2, 5, 6, 7, or 10 to Leidseplein. DUTCH.

In a house that dates from 1687, the "Black Sheep" still seems like an old Dutch home. You climb a steep flight of tiled steps to reach the second-floor dining room, where the beams and ceiling panels are dark with age. It's a cozy, almost crowded place made both fragrant and inviting by the fresh flowers on every table and those that spill from the polished brass buckets hanging from the ceiling beams. The "Black Sheep" is well known for its wine list and its crêpes Suzette. Other menu items might include sole meunière with asparagus or grilled salmon with fresh thyme.

MODERATE

✪ **Amsterdam.** Watertorenplein 6 (off Haarlemmerweg). ☎ **020/682-2666.** Reservations recommended on weekends. Main courses 16.50–40Dfl ($8.70–$21.05). AE, DC, MC, V. Daily 11:30am–1am. Tram: 10 to Van Halstraat. CONTINENTAL.

This restaurant in a century-old water-pumping station was deservedly an instant hit when it opened a few years ago in the redeveloping Westerpark district. It's a little bit out of the way, but easily worth the tram ride. You dine amid a buzz of conviviality in the big, brightly lit former pumping hall, which had been so carefully tended by the water workers that some of its elegant decoration didn't need repainting. Service is breezy, the food is good, and the menu long. The emphasis is on seafood, but lots of meat and vegetarian dishes are offered too. If you're feeling flush, you could spring for a double starter of a half lobster with six Zeeland oysters.

Bodega Keyser. Van Baerlestraat 96 (beside the Concertgebouw). ☎ **020/671-1441.** Main courses 39.50–68.50Dfl ($20.80–$36.05); set-price menu 63Dfl ($33.15). AE, DC, MC, V. Mon–Sat 9am–midnight; Sun 11am–midnight. Tram: 2 to Willemsparkweg; 3, 5, 12, or 20 to Van Baerlestraat; 16 to De Lairessestraat. DUTCH.

Whether or not you attend a concert at the Concertgebouw, you may want to plan a visit to its next-door neighbor. An Amsterdam landmark since 1903, the Keyser has enjoyed a colorful joint heritage with the world-famous concert hall. There's an elegance here that combines traditional dark-and-dusky decor and highly starched pink linens. The menu leans heavily toward local fish and, in season, game specialties, such as hare and venison.

Brasserie Schiller. In the Hotel Schiller, Rembrandtplein 26–36. ☎ **020/554-0700.** Main courses 29.50–35Dfl ($15.55–$18.40); set-price menu 49.50Dfl ($26.05). AE, DC, MC, V. Daily 7am–11pm. Tram: 4, 9, 14, or 20 to Rembrandtplein. DUTCH.

Beamed and paneled in well-aged oak and graced with etched-glass panels and stained-glass skylights, this century-old Jugendstil landmark is a splendid sight. Paintings by Frits Schiller, the artist who constructed the hotel (see "Where to Stay," above), adorn the walls, and the menu harks back to the turn of the century. (Elderly former chefs were even consulted on old recipes and cooking styles.) Among the classic dishes are stewed eel and potato-and-cabbage casserole, T-bone steak, roast leg of lamb with mint sauce, and spaghetti bolognese.

Café Américain. In the American Hotel, Leidsekade 97 (at Leidseplein). ☎ **020/624-5322.** Main courses 35–52Dfl ($18.40–$27.35). AE, DC, MC, V. Daily 7am–midnight (lunch noon–3pm; dinner 5–10:30pm). Tram: 1, 2, 5, 6, 7, or 10 to Leidseplein. INTERNATIONAL.

The lofty Café Américain is a national monument of Dutch Jugendstil and art deco. Mata Hari held her wedding reception here in her pre-espionage days, and since its 1900 opening the place has been a haven for Dutch and international artists, writers, dancers, and actors. Leaded windows, newspaper-littered reading tables, bargello-patterned velvet upholstery, frosted-glass chandeliers from the 1920s, and tall carved columns are all part of the dusky sit-and-chat setting. Menu dishes include monkfish, perch, rack of Irish lamb, and rosé breast of duck with creamed potatoes. Jazz lovers can stock up on good music at a Sunday jazz brunch.

De Belhamel. Brouwersgracht 60 (at Herengracht). ☎ **020/622-1095.** Reservations recommended on weekends. Main courses 28.50–45Dfl ($15–$23.70); set-price menu 49.50Dfl ($26.05). AE, MC, V. Daily 6pm–midnight. Bus: 18 or 22 to Haarlemmerstraat. CONTINENTAL.

Classical music compliments art nouveau in a graceful setting overlooking the Herengracht and Brouwersgracht canals. The menu changes seasonally and game is a specialty. You can also expect such dishes as puffed pastries layered with salmon, shellfish, crayfish tails, and chervil beurre-blanc to start; and beef tenderloin in Madeira sauce with zucchini rösti and puffed garlic for a main course. Vegetarian dishes are served, too.

De Oesterbar. Leidseplein 10. ☎ **020/623-2988.** Main courses 38.50–85Dfl ($20.25–$44.75). AE, DC, MC, V. Daily noon–1am. Tram: 1, 2, 5, 6, 7, or 10 to Leidseplein. SEAFOOD/DUTCH.

The decor at this 50-year-old restaurant is a delight: White tiles with fish tanks bubbling at your elbows on the street level, and Victorian brocades and etched glass in the more formal dining room upstairs. The menu is a regular compendium of the variety of fish available in Holland and the variety of ways they can be prepared, but it also includes a few meat selections. Choices include sole Danoise with tiny North Sea shrimp, sole Véronique with muscadet grapes, stewed eel in wine sauce, and the assorted fish plate of turbot, halibut, and fresh salmon.

Haesje Claes. Spuistraat 275 (beside Spui). ☎ **020/624-9998.** Main courses 22.25–34.50Dfl ($11.70–$18.15). AE, DC, MC, V. Daily noon–midnight. Tram: 1, 2, or 5 to Spui. DUTCH.

If you're yearning for a cozy Old Dutch environment and hearty Dutch food at moderate prices, go to Haesje Claes. It's an inviting, intimate place with lots of nooks and crannies and with brocaded benches and traditional Dutch hanging lamps. The menu covers a lot of ground, ranging from canapés to caviar, but you'll be happiest with such Dutch stalwarts as omelets, tournedos, *hutspot* (stew), *stampot* (mashed potatoes and cabbage), or various fish stews, including those with IJsselmeer *paling* (eel).

Kantjil en de Tijger. Spuistraat 291 (beside Spui). ☎ **020/620-0994.** Main courses 21.50–29.50Dfl ($11.30–$15.55); *rijsttafel* 75–95Dfl ($39.45–$50). AE, DC, MC, V. Daily 4:30–11pm. Tram: 1, 2, or 5 to Spui. INDONESIAN.

Unlike Indonesian restaurants that wear their ethnic origins on their sleeve, the "Antelope and the Tiger" is chic, modern, and cool. Two best-sellers are *nasi goreng Kantjil* (fried rice with pork kebabs, stewed beef, pickled cucumbers, and mixed vegetables) and the 20-item *rijsttafel* (rice with meat, seafood, and vegetables)for two. Other choices include stewed chicken in soja sauce, tofu omelet, shrimp with coconut dressing, Indonesian pumpkin, and mixed steamed vegetables with peanut-butter sauce. Finish off your meal with the multi-layered cinnamon cake or the coffee with ginger liqueur and whipped cream.

✪ **Kort.** Amstelveld 12 (at Prinsengracht). ☎ **020/626-1199.** Reservations required for sidewalk terrace. Main courses 25–40Dfl ($13.15–$21.05); set-price menu 49.50Dfl ($26.05). AE, CB, DC, MC, V. Wed–Mon 11:30am–midnight. Tram: 4 to Prinsengracht. CONTINENTAL.

This is one of the few restaurants that take reservations for evening dining outdoors in good weather— when such facilities fill up instantly. On the edge of a canal and a wide, open square, the tree-shaded terrace is far enough away from traffic to be unaffected by noise. Service is friendly, and menu dishes include excellent vegetarian choices, such as grilled goat's cheese with spinach and salad. Look also for the Eastern spiced fish, a house specialty. Dining indoors in the restored 17th-century Amstelkerk is recommended, too, with fancier table sets than outside.

INEXPENSIVE

✪ **Café Luxembourg.** Spuistraat 22–24 (beside Spui). ☎ **020/620-6264.** Snacks 9.50–19.50Dfl ($5–$10.25). MC, V. Sun–Fri 9am–1am; Fri–Sat 9am–2am. Tram: 1, 2, or 5 to Spui. GRAND CAFE.

The *New York Times* called Café Luxembourg "one of the world's great cafes." The large portions of food at reasonable prices in a stylish and relaxing setting attract all kinds of people. Soup, club sandwiches, and such menu dishes as meat loaf join with specialties taken from other well-known restaurants in the city. Between 5 and 7pm the bar is packed with tired nine-to-fivers, and in summer there's sidewalk dining. International newspapers are provided to encourage lingering.

Café-Restaurant Blincker. Sint-Barberenstraat 7 (off Rokin and Nes, near Theater Frascati). ☎ **020/627-1938.** Main courses 10–30Dfl ($5.25–$15.80). AE, DC, MC, V. Mon–Sat 4pm–1am. Tram: 4, 9, 16, 20, 24, or 25 to Rokin. CONTINENTAL.

This intimate restaurant in the Frascati Theater building, on a small side street off Rokin, attracts actors, journalists, artists, and other assorted bohemians. At night the place is jammed with people who cluster around the bar. The food is simple but tasty, including lamb chops with garlic, pancakes with cheese and mushrooms, homemade pasta, and cheese fondue.

De Jaren. Nieuwe Doelenstraat 20–22 (near Muntplein). ☎ **020/625-5771.** Main courses 16–30Dfl ($8.40–$15.80); set-price menus 20–28Dfl ($10.55–$14.75). No credit cards. Daily 10am–1am (Fri, Sat until 2am). Tram: 4, 9, 16, 20, 24, or 25 to the Munt. GRAND CAFE.

De Jaren is a big cafe, with 300 seats inside and 150 on the terrace beside the River Amstel. Students from the nearby campus often lunch here, contributing to its informality. Originally a bank, the renovated building has unusually high ceilings and a tiled mosaic floor. You can enjoy everything from a cup of coffee or a glass of *jenever* (potent Dutch gin) to spaghetti bolognese and rib-eye steak.

De Prins. Prinsengracht 124 (at Leliegracht). ☎ **020/624-9382.** Reservations not accepted. Main courses 12–25Dfl ($6.30–$13.15); dish of the day 19.50Dfl ($10.25); specials 23.50–27.50Dfl ($12.35–$14.45). AE, MC, V. Daily 10am–midnight. Tram: 13, 14, 17, or 20 to Westermarkt. DUTCH/FRENCH.

This companionable, brown cafe/restaurant serves the kind of food you'd expect from a much more expensive place. The clientele is loyal, so the relatively few tables fill up quickly. It's a quiet neighborhood restaurant—nothing fancy or trendy, but quite appealing, housed in a 17th-century canal house, with the bar on a slightly lower level than the restaurant, and a sidewalk terrace for drinks in summer.

Keuken van 1870. Spuistraat 4 (at Martelaarsgracht). ☎ **020/624-8965.** Reservations not accepted. Main courses 9–18.50Dfl ($4.75–$9.75). AE, DC, MC, V. Mon–Fri 12:30pm–8pm; Sat–Sun 4–9pm. Tram: 1, 2, 5, 13, 17, or 20 to Martelaarsgracht. DUTCH.

One of the cheapest and plainest places to eat in Amsterdam. Opened in 1870 as a public soup kitchen, it serves meals cafeteria-style. Tables are bare, and menu dishes are basic, but the food is good. Pork chops, fish, and chicken—all accompanied by vegetables and potatoes—are some of the main courses on the menu. It's a good place to go if you're on a tight budget.

La Place. Rokin 160 (near Muntplein). ☎ **020/622-0171.** Main courses 7.50–17.50Dfl ($3.95–$9.20). AE, MC, V. Mon–Sat 9:30am–8pm; Sun 11am–8pm. Tram: 4, 9, 14, 16, 20, 24, or 25 to Muntplein. DUTCH.

A vast, multilevel food depot with something for everyone. The ground floor offers thick slabs of quiche, an assortment of pizzas, and deliciously flavored fresh breads— the cheese-onion loaf is a meal in itself. An airy, glass-topped cafeteria covers the three upstairs floors. Menu dishes include a meat or fish of the day, often with an Indonesian touch, along with vegetables and potatoes. Vegetarians love the soup and salad selection, and there's an assortment of freshly squeezed fruit juices.

SEEING THE SIGHTS

SIGHTSEEING SUGGESTIONS FOR FIRST-TIME VISITORS

If You Have 1 Day   For the perfect introduction to the city, take a cruise on its canals and admire the many gabled merchants' houses and almost 1,200 bridges. (The canals are even more special after dark, when the glow of street and house lights shimmers on the water). In the afternoon, visit the Rijksmuseum to see Rembrandts and works by other golden age masters. In the evening, dine at a traditional restaurant or opt for an Indonesian *rijsttafel,* and end your day by dropping into a brown cafe.

If You Have 2 Days   Day 1 as above. On day 2, visit the Anne Frank house in the morning. In the afternoon, explore the historic center on foot, visiting Dam Square and the Royal Palace and other major squares. In the evening attend a concert at the Concertgebouw, or opera or dance at the Muziektheater (book ahead).

If You Have 3 Days   Days 1 and 2 as above. On day 3, take in the Van Gogh Museum in the morning. Relax over coffee at the Café Américain, with its stunning art nouveau interior. Look into some street markets, either the Albert Cuyp market, the floating Flower Market, or the Waterlooplein flea market. In the evening, take a walk in the Red Light District. (If this isn't your idea of an edifying experience, consider the alternative dining option from Day 1.)

THREE MUST-SEE ATTRACTIONS

✪ **Anne Frankhuis.** Prinsengracht 263 (beside Westermarkt). ☎ **020/556-7100.** Admission 10Dfl ($5.25) adults, 5Dfl ($2.65) children 10–17, free for children under 10. Apr–Aug daily 9am–9pm; Sept–Mar daily 9am–5pm. Tram: 13, 14, 17, or 20 to Westermarkt.

Anne Frank's famous diary was written in a secret annex of this house, where eight Jewish refugees from three separate families lived together in nearly total silence for more than 2 years during World War II. The hiding place Otto Frank found for his family and some friends kept them safe until they were betrayed and their refuge was raided by pro-Nazi police, tragically close to the war's end. Anne and six of the other *onderduikers* (divers or hiders) died in concentration camps. The rooms are still as bare as they were when Anne's father, the only survivor, returned—nothing has been changed.

✪ **Rijksmuseum.** Stadhouderskade 42 (behind Museumplein). ☎ **020/674-7000** or ☎ 0900/8898-1212 for taped information in English and Dutch. Admission 15Dfl ($7.90) adults, 7.50Dfl ($3.95) children 6–18, free for children under 6. Daily 10am–5pm. Tram: 2, 5, or 20 to Hobbemastraat; 6, 7, or 10 to Spiegelgracht.

The architectural legacy of Holland's 17th-century golden age is all around you in Amsterdam. For the artistic lowdown, head to the neo-Gothic Rijksmuseum, opened in 1885. It holds the world's largest collection of paintings by the Dutch masters, including the most famous: Rembrandt's 1642 *The Night Watch*. Rembrandt, Jacob van Ruysdael, Maerten van Heemskerck, Frans Hals, Paulus Potter, Jan Steen, Jan Vermeer, Pieter de Hooch, Gerard Terborch, and Gerard Dou are all represented, as are Fra Angelico, Tiepolo, Goya, Rubens, Van Dyck, and later artists of the Hague School and the Amsterdam Impressionist movement. You'll also find prints and sculpture, furniture, Asian and Islamic art, china and porcelain, trinkets and glassware, armaments and ship models, 17th-century dollhouses, costumes, screens, badges, and laces.

✪ **Van Gogh Museum.** Paulus Potterstraat 7 (at Museumplein). ☎ **020/570-5200.** Admission 12.50Dfl ($6.60) adults, 5Dfl ($2.65) children 13–17, free for children under 13. Daily 10am–5pm. Tram: 2, 5, or 20 to Paulus Potterstraat; 3, 12, or 16 to Museumplein.

This three-story museum houses the world's largest van Gogh collection—more than 200 paintings displayed chronologically according to the seven distinct periods that defined his short career. They include a progression of 18 paintings produced during the 2 years the artist spent in the south of France, generally considered his artistic high point. The ground floor displays paintings by Van Gogh's contemporaries—Toulouse-Lautrec, Gauguin, Monet, Sisley, and others. One flight up is one of the most famous paintings of modern times, *Still Life Vase with Fourteen Sunflowers,* best known simply as *Sunflowers,* and van Gogh's last painting, *Cornfield with Crows,* whose mood seems to presage his suicide in 1890 at the age of 37. Upper floors contain Van Gogh drawings, a library, and temporary exhibits. The museum was totally refurbished in 1998–99, with the addition of a new wing designed by Japanese architect Kisho Kurokawa.

CANALS & CANALSIDE HOUSES

A canal-boat cruise is the best way to see old Amsterdam and its large and busy harbor. A typical itinerary includes Centraal Station; the Harlemmersluis floodgates; the Cat Boat (a houseboat—one of around 2,400 in the city—with a permanent population of as many as 150 wayward felines); and both the narrowest building in the city and one of its largest houses still in use as a single-family residence. You may also see the burgomaster's (mayor's) official residence; the "Golden Bend" on Herengracht, traditionally the best address in town; picturesque bridges, including the famous Magere Brug (Skinny Bridge) over the Amstel; and Amsterdam Drydocks.

Trips depart at regular intervals from *rondvaart* (canal circuit) piers in key locations around town and last approximately 1 hour. The majority of launches are docked along Damrak and Prins Hendrikkade near Centraal Station, on Rokin near Muntplein, and near Leidseplein. They leave every 15 to 30 minutes during summer (9am–9:30pm) and every 45 minutes in winter (10am–4pm). Average fare is 12 to 18Dfl ($6.30–$9.45) for adults, 10 to 12Dfl ($5.25–$6.30) for children 4 to 13. Numerous canal-boat cruise operators offer comparable prices and trips.

MORE ATTRACTIONS
Historic Buildings & Monuments
Begijnhof. Gedempte Begijnensloot (at Spui). No telephone. Free admission. Daily until sunset. Tram: 1, 2, or 5 to Spui.

Formerly an almshouse for *begijns,* pious lay women involved in religious and charitable work, this beautiful cloister of small homes around a 14th-century garden courtyard makes for a perfect escape from the city's bustle. In the southwest corner is one of two surviving wooden houses in Amsterdam, dating from the 15th century. (Construction of wooden houses was prohibited in 1452 after a series of disastrous fires.) Most of the tiny 17th- and 18th-century buildings still house the city's elderly poor, and you should respect their privacy, especially after sunset.

Koninklijk Paleis (Royal Palace). Dam Square. ☎ **020/620-4060.** Admission 7Dfl ($3.70) adults, 5Dfl ($2.65) seniors and children 13–18, 2.50Dfl ($1.30) children 5–12, free for children under 5. Easter and June–July daily 10am–5:30pm, Aug–Oct daily 12:30–5pm; otherwise, generally Tues–Thurs 12:30–5pm, closed mid-Dec to mid Feb. (Opening days and hours are highly variable, and it's best to check before going.) Tram: 1, 2, 4, 5, 9, 13, 14, 16, 17, 20, 24, or 25 to Dam Square.

The 17th-century, neoclassical Royal Palace was Amsterdam's town hall for 153 years. It was first used as a palace during Napoleon's 5-year rule of the city in the early 19th century, when the French emperor's brother, Louis Bonaparte, was King of the Netherlands. You can visit its high-ceilinged Citizens' Hall, Burgomasters' Chambers, and Council Room, as well as the Vierschaar—a marble tribunal where death sentences were pronounced during the 17th century. Although this is the monarch's official palace, Queen Beatrix rarely uses it for more than occasional receptions or official ceremonies.

Museums & Galleries

✪ **Amsterdams Historisch Museum.** Kalverstraat 92 and Nieuwezijds Voorburgwal 359. ☎ **020/523-1822.** Admission 9Dfl ($4.75) adults, 4.50Dfl ($2.35) children 6–16, free for children under 6. Mon–Fri 10am–5pm; Sat–Sun 11am–5pm. Tram: 1, 2, 4, 5, 9, 16, 20, 24, or 25 to Spui.

In a huge 17th-century former city orphanage that has been beautifully restored, this fascinating museum gives you a better understanding of everything you see as you explore the city. Gallery by gallery, century by century, you learn how a small fishing village became a major world power. You can also view many famous paintings by Dutch masters in the context of their time and place. Next to the museum is the Schuttersgalerij (Civic Guard Gallery), a narrow, two-story skylit chamber bedecked with a dozen large 17th-century group portraits of militiamen. The hours are the same as for the museum, and admission is free.

Holland Experience. Waterlooplein 17. ☎ **020/422-2233.** Admission 17.50Dfl ($9.20) adults, 15Dfl ($7.90) seniors and children under 13. Daily 10am–5:30pm (6:30pm in summer). Tram: 9, 14, or 20 to Waterlooplein.

A multidimensional film and theater show takes you through Holland's landscapes and culture at different historical periods up to the present. Exhibitions include farming and fishing scenes, and there's an exciting simulated dike collapse.

Joods Historisch Museum (Jewish Historical Museum). Jonas Daniël Meijerplein 2–4 (facing Waterlooplein). ☎ **020/626-9945.** Admission 8Dfl ($4.20) adults, 4Dfl ($2.10) children 10–16, free for children under 10. Daily 11am–5pm. Tram: 9, 14, or 20 to Waterlooplein.

This museum, in the restored Ashkenazi Synagogue complex, tells the intertwining stories of Jewish identity, religion, culture, and history in the Netherlands through objects, photographs, artworks, and interactive displays. Take time to appreciate the beauty of the buildings, which include Europe's oldest public synagogue.

Museum Het Rembrandthuis. Jodenbreestraat 4–6 (at Waterlooplein). ☎ **020/520-0400.** Admission 7.50Dfl ($3.95) adults, 5Dfl ($2.65) children 10–15, free for children under 10. Mon–Sat 10am–5pm; Sun and holidays 1–5pm (main museum closed until Sept 1999; Saskia House remains open). Tram: 9, 14, or 20 to Waterlooplein.

Rembrandt had to leave his home of 19 years in 1658 because of bankruptcy. Based on an inventory made for his creditors, architect Karel Petrus de Bazel attempted to restore the house in 1906, but gave it more of a 19th-century look. A new restoration to be completed in September 1999 should return it to the way it looked when Rembrandt lived and worked here. About 120 of the museum's 250 Rembrandt etchings hang on the walls at any one time, including self-portraits and landscapes, and you can see the artist's printing press. In 1998, a new wing opened in the adjacent former house of Rembrandt's wife Saskia; it's mainly used for temporary exhibitions.

Nederlands Scheepvaartmuseum (Netherlands Maritime Museum). Kattenburgerplein 1 (in the Eastern Dock). ☎ **020/523-2222.** Admission 12.50Dfl ($6.60) adults, 8Dfl ($4.20) children 17 and under. Tues–Sat 10am–5pm (also Mon mid-June to mid-Sept); Sun noon–5pm. Bus: 22 or 32 to Kattenburgerplein.

A former Amsterdam Admiralty arsenal overlooking Amsterdam harbor provides the backdrop for rooms and rooms of ships, ship models, and seascapes. Old maps include a 15th-century Ptolemaic atlas and a sumptuously bound edition of the *Great Atlas,* or *Description of the World,* by Jan Blaeu, master cartographer of Holland's golden age. Among the historic papers on display are several pertaining to the Dutch colonies Nieuwe Amsterdam (New York City) and Nieuwe Nederland (New York State). A full-size replica of the Dutch East India Company sailing ship *Amsterdam,* which foundered off Hastings in 1749, is moored at the wharf, and a replica of an 1854 iron clipper with the same name is under construction.

Stedelijk Museum of Modern Art. Paulus Potterstraat 13 (at Museumplein). ☎ **020/ 573-2911.** Admission 9Dfl ($4.75) adults, 4.50Dfl ($2.35) children 7–16, free for children under 7. Daily 11am–5pm. Tram: 2, 5, or 20 to Paulus Potterstraat; 3, 12, or 16 to Museumplein.

The Stedelijk centers its collection around De Stijl, CoBrA (an expressive, abstract style from the 1950s) and post-CoBrA painting, nouveau réalisme, pop art, color-field painting, zero and minimal art, and conceptual art. On display are works by such Dutch painters as Karel Appel, Willem de Kooning, and Piet Mondrian; French artists Chagall, Cézanne, Picasso, Renoir, Monet, and Manet; and Americans Calder, Oldenburg, Rosenquist, and Warhol. The museum houses the largest collection outside Russia of abstract painter Kasimir Malevich.

Tropenmuseum (Tropical Museum). Linnaeusstraat 2 (at Mauritskade). ☎ **020/ 568-8215.** Admission 12.50Dfl ($6.60) adults, 7.50Dfl ($3.95) children 18 and under. Mon–Fri 10am–5pm; Sat–Sun and holidays noon–5pm. Tram: 6, 9, 10, or 14 to Mauritskade; 20 to Sarphatistraat.

Built by the Royal Tropical Institute in the 19th century, this museum is devoted to contemporary culture and problems in tropical areas. Its most interesting exhibits are walk-through model villages that capture daily life in such places as India and Indonesia (minus the inhabitants); displays of tools and techniques used to produce *batik,* the distinctively dyed Indonesian fabric; and displays of the instruments and ornaments one would find in a tropical residence. A new permanent exhibition covers West Asia and North Africa. A section of the museum, Kindermuseum TM Junior (☎ 020/568-8300), is open only to children 6 to 12 (one adult per child is allowed).

Churches & a Synagogue
The most important places of worship in Amsterdam are the 14th-century Nieuwe Kerk, Holland's coronation church, on Dam Square; 17th-century Westerkerk, on Prinsengracht at Westermarkt, which has the tallest, most beautiful tower in Amsterdam and is the burial place of Rembrandt; 14th-century Oude Kerk, at Oudekerksplein on Oudezijds Voorburgwal in the Red Light District, surrounded by almshouses turned into prostitutes' rooms; and the 17th-century Portuguese Synagogue, on Mr. Visserplein, facing the Jewish Historical Museum.

A Great Zoo
✪ **Artis Zoo.** Plantage Kerklaan 38–40. ☎ **020/523-3400.** Admission 25Dfl ($13.15) adults, 17.50Dfl ($9.20) children 4–11, free for children under 4. Daily 9am–5pm. Tram: 9, 14, or 20 to Plantage Middenlaan.

Diamond-Cutting Demonstrations

Although a diamond-cutting demonstration will probably just consist of a lone polisher working at a small wheel in the back of a jewelry store or in the lobby of a factory building, it will still give you an idea of how a diamond is cut and polished.

The main diamond factories and showrooms in the city are **Amsterdam Diamond Center,** Rokin 1, off Dam Square (☎ 020/624-5787); **Coster Diamonds,** Paulus Potterstraat 2–6, near the Rijksmuseum (☎ 020/676-2222); **Gassan Diamonds,** Nieuwe Uilenburgerstraat 173–175 (☎ 020/622-5333); **Holshuijsen Stoeltie,** Wagenstraat 13–17 (☎ 020/623-7601); **Van Moppes Diamonds,** Albert Cuypstraat 2–6, at the street market (☎ 020/676-1242); and **Reuter Diamonds,** Kalverstraat 165 or Singel 526 (☎ 020/623-3500).

Established in 1838, this is the oldest zoo in the Netherlands, housing more than 6,000 animals. Also on the property are a planetarium, aquarium, geological and zoological museum, and a children's farm. The aquarium, constructed in 1882 and recently renovated, is well presented, particularly the exhibits on the Amazon River, coral reefs, and Amsterdam's canals, with their fish and garbage.

The Red Light District (De Wallen/Rosse Buurt)

The warren of streets around Oudezijds Achterburgwal and Oudezijds Voorburgwal by the Oude Kerk is one of Amsterdam's most famous destinations. It's extraordinary to see women of all nationalities dressed in exotic underwear and perched in windows, knitting, brushing their hair or just slinking, enticingly, in their seats, waiting for customers. The district has become a major tourist attraction, not only for customers of storefront sex but for sightseers. If you choose to go there, you need to exercise caution. Stick to the busy streets, particularly at night, and be wary of pickpockets at all times. In a neighborhood where anything seems permissible, the one no-no is taking pictures. Violate this rule and your camera could be removed from you and broken. To get there, take tram 4, 9, 16, 20, 24, or 25 to Dam Square, and then pass behind the Grand Hotel Krasnapolsky.

ORGANIZED TOURS

A 3-hour bus tour costs 35 to 40Dfl ($18.40 to $21.05) and includes tickets for a canal cruise. Children 4 to 13 are usually charged half-price. Companies offering tours include **The Best of Holland,** Damrak 34 (☎ **020/623-1539**); **Holland International Excursions,** Dam 6 (☎ **020/551-2800**); **Holland Keytours,** Dam Square 19 (☎ **020/624-7304**); and **Lindbergh Excursions,** Damrak 26 (☎ **020/622-2766**).

A clever way of putting all that water to use, and a great time-saver for anyone in a hurry, the **Museum Boat,** Stationsplein 8 (☎ **020/622-2181**), motors between major museums close to the canals and harbor and offers as good a view as a regular canal-boat cruise. Stops are made every 30 minutes at seven key spots, providing access to 16 museums. The fare for the whole day, including a discount on museum admissions, is 25Dfl ($13.15) for adults, 20Dfl ($10.55) for children 13 and under. Half-day tours after 1pm cost 15Dfl ($7.90), no reduction for children; single round-trip tours cost 20Dfl ($10.55) for adults, 15Dfl ($7.90) for children 13 and under.

THE SHOPPING SCENE

Regular shopping hours are Monday 11am to 6pm, Tuesday, Wednesday, and Friday 9am to 6pm, Thursday 9am to 9pm, and Saturday 9am to 5pm. Shops in the Magna

Plaza mall, some large department stores, and some other stores are open on Sunday from noon to 5pm and shops in the Museum quarter are open every first Sunday of the month.

Best buys include special items the Dutch produce to perfection, or produced to perfection in the past and now retail as antiques—Delftware, pewter, crystal, and old-fashioned clocks—or commodities in which they have significantly cornered a market, like diamonds. If cost is an important consideration, remember the Dutch also have inexpensive specialties, such as cheese, flower bulbs, and chocolate.

For jewelry, trendy clothing, or athletic gear, try the department stores around Dam Square and shops on Kalverstraat and Leidsestraat. For fashion, antiques, and art, shop on Van Baerlestraat, P. C. Hooftstraat, and Nieuwe Spiegelstraat. For fashion boutiques and funky little specialty shops, or a good browse through a flea market or secondhand store, Reestraat, Hartenstraat, Wolvenstraat, and Runstraat are particularly good choices. Amsterdam's top department store, with the best selection and a great cafe, is **De Bijenkorf,** Dam 1 (☎ **020/621-8080**).

MARKETS

You'll find all types of foods, clothing, flowers, plants, and textiles at the **Albert Cuyp Markt,** Albert Cuypstraat, open 6 days a week. Every Friday there's a secondhand book market on the Spui, with about 25 booths.

The ✪ **Floating Flower Market,** a row of barges permanently moored on the Singel at Muntplein, sells fresh-cut flowers, plants, ready-to-travel packets of tulip bulbs, and home gardening accessories. Buying flowers here is an Amsterdam ritual.

The **Sunday Art Market,** at Thorbeckeplein, runs from March to December, with sculptures, paintings, jewelry, and mixed-media pieces by local artists.

You'll find everything and anything at the **Waterlooplein Flea Market,** at Waterlooplein. On Sunday during summer (late May to September), the junk is replaced for a day by antiques and books.

✪ **Kunst & Antiekcentrum de Looier,** Elandsgracht 109 (☎ **020/624-9038**), is a big indoor antiques market that spreads through several old warehouses along the Jordaan canals. Individual dealers rent booths and corners to show their best wares: antique jewelry, prints, and engravings.

SHOPS

A van der Meer. P. C. Hooftstraat 112. ☎ **020/662-1936.**

A landmark amid P. C. Hooftstraat's fashionable stores, this is a quiet place to enjoy antique maps, prints, and engravings, including 17th- and 18th-century Dutch world maps.

ABK Gallery for Sculpture. Zeilmakersstraat 15. ☎ **020/625-6332.**

Call before you head out to this cooperative gallery for modern sculpture, since it's open only by appointment, Thursday to Sunday noon to 6pm.

American Book Center. Kalverstraat 185. ☎ **020/625-5537.**

A big array of best-sellers, paperbacks, hardcover editions, and magazines is available here.

Blue Gold Fish. Rozengracht 17. ☎ **020/623-3134.**

The crafts and curios on sale here cover a wide range of ceramics, jewelry, household items (including colorful lamps), and textiles, running the gamut from chic to kitsch.

✪ **Focke & Meltzer.** P.C. Hooftstraat 65–67. ☎ **020/664-2311.**

The best one-stop shop for authentic Delft Blue and Makkumware porcelain, as well as Hummel figurines, Leerdam crystal, and a world of other fine china, porcelain, silver, glass, and crystal.

H. P. de Vreng en Zonen. Nieuwendijk 75. ☎ **020/624-4581.**

This distillery creates Dutch liqueurs and gins using old-fashioned methods. Try Old Amsterdam *jenever* or some of the more flamboyantly colored brews, like the brilliant green *Pruimpje prik in.*

Heinen. Prinsengracht 440, off Leidsestraat. ☎ **020/627-8299.**

Unless you simply must have brand-name articles, you can save considerably on hand-painted pottery here, and even watch the product being made.

Jacob Hooy & Co. Kloveniersburgwal 10–12. ☎ **020/624-3041.**

Opened in 1743, this wonderland of fragrant smells offers more than 500 different herbs and spices, along with 30 different teas, sold loose by weight. Everything is stored in wooden drawers and barrels with the name hand-scripted in gold. Lining the counter are fishbowl jars with 30 different types of *dropjes* (drops or lozenges).

P. G. C. Hajenius. Rokin 92–96. ☎ **020/623-7494.**

P. G. C. Hajenius has been the city's leading purveyor of cigars and smoking articles since 1826. Cigars are the house specialty, and there's a room full of Havanas. They also sell long, handmade clay pipes of the kind you see in old Dutch paintings, as well as ceramic pipes.

AMSTERDAM AFTER DARK

Amsterdam has highly regarded orchestras, ballet, and opera companies, a strong jazz tradition, and a thriving club and dance-bar scene. Its brown cafes—typical Amsterdam pubs—are a highlight of any visit. Cabarets and theaters can be counted on for English-language shows on a regular basis.

Your best source of information on nightlife and culture is the VVV tourist office's monthly *What's On in Amsterdam.* Many hotels have copies for guests, or you can pick up one at VVV offices for 4Dfl ($2.10). *De Uitkrant,* a free monthly paper in Dutch, has an even more thorough listing of events and is available in performance venues, clubs, and VVV offices.

For tickets to theatrical and musical events (including rock concerts), contact **Amsterdam Uit Buro (AUB) Ticketshop,** Leidseplein 26 (☎ **020/621-1211**), which can book tickets for almost every venue in town. VVV Amsterdam also books tickets, for a 5Dfl ($2.65) fee.

THE PERFORMING ARTS
Music & Ballet
Classical music in Amsterdam centers on the world-famous **Royal Concertgebouw Orchestra,** based in the superb Concertgebouw, Concertgebouwplein 2–6 (☎ **020/671-8345**). Throughout the musical season (Sept to May) and annual Holland Festival (June to July), the world's greatest orchestras, ensembles, conductors, and soloists travel to Amsterdam to perform here. The **Netherlands Philharmonic Orchestra** and **Netherlands Chamber Orchestra** perform at the Beurs van Berlage, Damrak 243 (☎ **020/627-0466**).

From September to March, the **Netherlands Opera** produces classics at the Muziektheater, Waterlooplein 22 (☎ **020/625-5455**). Also performing at the Muziektheater are two dance companies: **The Dutch National Ballet** and The

Hague–based **Netherlands Dance Theater,** whose artistic director/choreographer, Jirí Kylián, has enjoyed great success. Dance performances are occasionally held at the **Felix Meritis Theater,** Keizersgracht 324 (☎ **020/626-2321**).

Theater

Amsterdammers speak English so well that Broadway road shows and English-language touring companies often make the city a stop on their European itineraries. Broadway and London musicals also come to Amsterdam.

Look for touring shows at **Koninklijke Theater Carré,** Amstel 115–125 (☎ **020/622-5225**), but get tickets as far in advance as possible—hot shows sell out fast. The **Stadsschouwburg,** Leidseplein 26 (☎ **020/624-2311**), is the city's main venue for Dutch theater as well as Dutch and, occasionally, English versions of international plays.

Comedy Theater

✪ **Boom Chicago Theater.** Leidsepleintheater, Leidseplein 12. ☎ **020/530-7300.**

Compared by *Time* to Chicago's famous Second City troupe, Boom Chicago puts on great improvisational comedy, and Dutch audiences have no problem with the English sketches. You can have dinner and a drink while enjoying the show at a candlelit table. It's open daily in summer, closed Sunday in winter. Tickets are 27.50Dfl ($14.45); the restaurant opens at 7pm, with meals from 20 to 25Dfl ($10.55 to $13.15).

THE CLUB & MUSIC SCENE

Most big-name touring rock and pop acts perform at Ajax soccer club's **Amsterdam Arena,** Arena Boulevard, Amsterdam Zuid-Oost (☎ **020/311-1313**).

Alto Jazz Café. Korte Leidsedwarsstraat 115. ☎ **020/626-3249.** No cover.

There's a regular crowd and regular and guest combos in this small, comfortable cafe.

Bimhuis. Oudeschans 73–77. ☎ **020/623-1361.** Cover Thurs–Sun 15–25Dfl ($7.90–$13.15); no cover other days.

Bimhuis is relaxed, but serious about jazz. Top musicians, including European and American stars, often perform here. Closed Tuesdays for jazz workshops.

De IJsbreker. Weesperzijde 23. ☎ **020/693-9093.** Cover 15–25Dfl ($7.90–$13.15).

This place offers the latest in electronic music and anything else that goes out on a musical limb. It has a good cafe with a terrace beside the River Amstel.

Gay & Lesbian Clubs

Amsterdam is the gay capital of Europe, proud of its open and tolerant attitude toward homosexuality. There are lots of bars and dance clubs for gay men all over the city, but fewer lesbian nightspots. Generally the trendier spots are on Reguliersdwarsstraat. You'll find a more casual atmosphere on Kerkstraat near Leidseplein and leather bars on Warmoesstraat.

Some of the more popular places for men are **C-Ring,** Warmoesstraat 96 (☎ 020/623-9604), a gay music-cafe where the music tends toward raunchy; **Café April,** Reguliersdwarsstraat 37 (☎ 020/623-4254) and associated **April's Exit,** Reguliersdwarsstraat 42 (☎ 020/625-8788), a disco that attracts a young crowd; **iT,** Amstelstraat 24 (☎ 020/625-0111), a flashy disco with a mixed gay and straight crowd; and **Argos,** Warmoesstraat 95 (☎ 020/622-6572), Europe's oldest leather bar. **Saarein,** Elandstraat 119 (☎ 020/623-4901) is a women-only bar, and **Vive la Vie,** Amstelstraat 7 (☎ 020/624-0114) is a lively lesbian bar that hosts occasional parties.

Dance Clubs

As long as your attire and behavior suit the management's sensibilities, you should have no problem getting past the bouncer in these clubs. Drinks can be expensive—a beer or Coke averages 10Dfl ($5.25), and a whisky or cocktail, 15Dfl ($7.90).

Escape, Rembrandtplein 11 (☎ **020/622-1111**), is big and popular, with several dance floors and a capacity of 2,000. Cover is 10 to 20Dfl ($5.25 to $10.55), free for students on Thursday.

Melkweg, Lijnbaansgracht 234a (☎ **020/624-1777**), is a former hippie hangout turned multipurpose venue that includes a dance club. Temporary membership (required) is 5Dfl ($2.65) for a month; cover is 12 to 35Dfl ($6.30 to $18.40).

At ✪ **Odeon,** Singel 460 (☎ **020/624-9711**), you can dance to jazz, funk, house, techno, R&B, or classic disco amid graceful surroundings in a 17th-century canal house. Cover is 7.50 to 12.50Dfl ($3.95 to $6.60).

Paradiso, Weteringschans 6–8 (☎ **020/626-4521**), presents an eclectic variety of music in a former church. Theme nights range from jazz to raves to disco. Cover is 5 to 35Dfl ($2.65 to $18.40).

Membership policy is strict at **RoXY,** Singel 465–467 (☎ **020/620-0354**), one of the hippest places in town, and it's usually hard to get in. Some nights, the membership rules are dropped and anyone can enter. Wednesday is gay night for men; Sunday's Pussy Lounge is women-only. Cover is 10 to 20Dfl ($5.25 to $10.55).

BROWN CAFES

You haven't tasted Dutch beer until you've tasted it in a *bruine kroeg,* or brown cafe (what Americans would call a bar). Even if you're not a beer lover, brown cafes afford you a peek into the city's everyday life. You find them on almost every corner in old neighborhoods. There is no mistaking them: The smoky, mustard brownness inside comes from centuries of thick smoke and heated conversation. Some have been around since Rembrandt's time. The best are on Prinsengracht, below Westermarkt; at Dam Square; Leidseplein; Spui; and, with a bit of looking, on tiny streets between canals.

Café Chris. Bloemstraat 42. ☎ **020/624-5942.**

Said to be where the builders of the Westerkerk were paid, it opened in 1624 and has some curious old features, including a toilet that flushes from outside the bathroom door.

De Druif. Rapenburg 83. ☎ **020/624-4530.**

"The Grape," on the waterfront behind the Eastern Dock, is mainly frequented by friendly locals.

De Vergulde Gaper. Prinsenstraat 30. ☎ **020/624-8975.**

In bad weather you can retreat into the warm, cozy interior and in good you can sit on a terrace beside the Prinsengracht—in the unlikely event you get a seat. (There's an unseemly dash whenever a table becomes free.)

Hoppe. Spui 18–20. ☎ **020/420-4420.**

Hoppe, which dates from 1670, has become a tourist attraction, but locals love it too, often stopping for a drink on their way home. It's usually standing-room only, and the crowds overflow onto the street.

In de Wildeman. Kolksteeg 3. ☎ **020/638-2348.**

This wood-paneled tavern in a medieval alley serves more than 200 kinds of beer. The tile floor and rows of bottles and jars behind the counters are remnants from its early days as a distillery's retail shop. ✪ **'t Smalle.** Egelantiersgracht 12. ☎ **020/623-9617.** Opened by Pieter Hoppe in 1786 as a liquor distillery and tasting house, this place is wonderfully cozy, although you probably won't find a seat here, or even be able to see one. In good weather, a boat moored on the canal alongside serves as a terrace.

Other Cafes
The Grand Cafe concept, combining drinks and fine food in elegant surroundings, has won plenty of devotees, tired of cramped and crowded brown cafes. Among the best are **Café Luxembourg,** Spuistraat 24 (☎ **020/620-6264**), a chic rendezvous that takes some of its menu dishes from top eateries around town; and ✪ **Royal Cafe De Kroon,** Rembrandtplein 15 (☎ **020/625-2011**), a mix of Louis XVI and tropical decor, overlooking the square.

Other chic cafes are **Café Dante,** Spuistraat 320 (☎ **020/638-8839**) whose owners' love of modern art shows itself in a different exhibition every month; ✪ **Café Schiller,** Rembrandtplein 26 (☎ **020/624-9846**), whose bright glassed-in terrace on the square and finely carved art deco interior makes it popular with artists and writers.

Another notable hangout is **Café Schuim,** Spuistraat 189 (☎ **020/638-9357**), attracting an assortment of creative types. On summer evenings trendies head to the terrace of ✪ **Café Vertigo,** Vondelpark 3 (☎ **020/612-3021**), on the edge of the park, for the liveliest scene in town. Inside, low arched ceilings, subtle lighting, and unobtrusive music set a mood of casual sophistication.

DAY TRIPS FROM AMSTERDAM
HAARLEM

Haarlem is a city of music and art just 20km (12 miles) west of Amsterdam, traditionally considered the capital's little sister city.

GETTING THERE From Amsterdam, Haarlem is 20 minutes by hourly train from Centraal Station. It can also be reached by frequent bus from outside Centraal Station. By car, take the N5 west.

VISITOR INFORMATION VVV **Haarlem** is at Stationsplein 1 (☎ **0900/ 616-1600;** fax 023/534-0537), outside the train station.

EXPLORING HAARLEM Haarlem is where Frans Hals, Jacob van Ruysdael, and Pieter Saenredam lived and painted portraits, landscapes, and church interiors while Rembrandt was living and working in Amsterdam. Handel and Mozart made special visits to the city to play the magnificent organ of **St. Bavokerk** (St. Bavo's Church), also known as the Grote Kerk (Great Church), Oude Groenmarkt 23 (☎ **023/ 532-4399**). Look for Frans Hals's tombstone, and for a cannonball imbedded in the wall during the 1572–73 Spanish siege. Don't miss the 1738 Christian Müller Organ, which has 5,068 pipes and is nearly 30m (98 feet) tall; you can hear it at free concerts on Tuesdays and Thursdays, April through October. The church is open Monday through Saturday from 10am to 4pm. Admission is 2.50Dfl ($1.30) for adults, 1.50Dfl (80¢) for children under 14.

From St. Bavo's, it's a short walk to Holland's oldest and perhaps most unusual museum, the **Teylers Museum,** Spaarne 16 (☎ **023/531-9010**). It houses drawings by Michelangelo, Raphael, and Rembrandt; fossils, minerals, and skeletons; and an odd assortment of inventions, including the world's biggest electrostatic generator, dating from 1784, and a 19th-century radarscope. The museum is open Tuesday through Saturday 10am to 5pm and Sunday 1 to 5pm. Admission is 8Dfl ($4.20) for adults, 4Dfl ($2.10) for students, seniors, and children 5 to 15, free for children under 5.

Be sure to visit the ✪ **Frans Halsmuseum,** Groot Heiligland 62 (☎ **023/516-4200**), whose galleries are halls and chambers of a former seniors' home. Famous paintings by Haarlem School masters hang in settings that look like the 17th-century homes they were originally intended to adorn. Open Monday through Saturday from 11am to 5pm, Sunday 1 to 5pm. Admission is 8Dfl ($4.20) for adults, 4Dfl ($2.10) for children 10 to 17, free for children under 10.

An ideal way to view the city is by hourly **canal boat cruise,** operated by Woltheus Cruises from their River Spaarne jetty at Gravensteenbrug (☎ **023/535-7723**). Cruises are from April through October, at 10:30am, noon, 1:30, 3, and 4:30pm.

ZANDVOORT

If you feel like a breath of sea air, do what Amsterdammers do: Head for Zandvoort on the North Sea coast.

GETTING THERE   Trains leave Amsterdam Centraal Station every hour; transfer at Haarlem. During summer, extra trains go direct from Centraal Station. Journey time is 30 minutes. Buses leave every 30 minutes from outside Amsterdam Centraal Station. You can go by car via Haarlem on the N5 west, but during summer, there are frequent traffic jams.

VISITOR INFORMATION   VVV Zandvoort is at Schoolplein 1 (☎ **023/ 571-7947;** fax 023/571-7003), opposite the bus station.

EXPLORING ZANDVOORT   There's not much more than a beach, but what a beach. Seemingly endless sands are lined in summertime with beach cafes and discos, and the conditions are good for sailboarding. Down from the mainstream beaches are gay and nudist beaches.

Holland Casino Zandvoort, Badhuisplein 7 (☎ **023/571-8044**), is one of ten legal casinos in Holland, with roulette, blackjack and more. Dress code is "correct" (collar and tie for men), the minimum age is 18, and you'll need your passport. It's open daily from 1:30pm until 2am. Admission is 6Dfl ($3.15).

You can find tranquillity in the **Kennemer Duinen** and **Amsterdamse Waterleiding Duinen,** protected zones of sand dune and vegetation that play an important role in sea defense. Stroll along paths through woods on the eastern side and across dunes leading west toward the sea. There's beachy shopping and plenty of eating and drinking possibilities in town.

DELFT

Delft is the home of the famous blue-and-white porcelain, but don't let Delftware be your only reason to visit. The small, handsome city is quiet and intimate, with flowers in its flower boxes and linden trees bending over gracious canals. The cradle of the Dutch Republic, Delft is still the burial place of the royal family, and the birthplace and inspiration of artist Jan Vermeer, the 17th-century master of light and subtle emotion.

GETTING THERE   There are trains at least hourly from Amsterdam, Rotterdam, and The Hague. By car, Delft is off the A13, the main The Hague–Rotterdam expressway.

VISITOR INFORMATION   VVV Delft is at Markt 83–85 (☎ **015/212-6100;** fax 015/215-8695).

EXPLORING DELFT   Vermeer's house is long gone from Delft, as are his paintings. But you can visit the **Oude Kerk,** Roland Holstlaan 753 (☎ **015/212-3015**), where he's buried, open April through October, Monday to Saturday 10am to 5pm.

You can also visit the ✪ **Nieuwe Kerk,** Markt (☎ **015/212-3025**), where Prince William of Orange (Willem van Oranje) and the other members of the House of Oranje-Nassau are buried. Open April through October, Monday to Saturday 9am to 6pm, November through March Monday to Saturday 11am to 4pm.

The **Prinsenhof Museum,** Sint-Agathaplein 1 (☎ **015/260-2358**), on Oude Delft canal, is where William I of Orange (William the Silent) lived and had his headquarters when he helped found the Dutch Republic. He was assassinated here in 1584, and you can see the musket-ball holes in the stairwell. The Prinsenhof is now a museum of paintings, tapestries, silverware, and pottery. It's open Tuesday through Saturday from 10am to 5pm and Sunday from 1 to 5pm (also Monday from 1 to 5pm June through August). Admission is 5Dfl ($2.65).

A fine collection of Delft tiles graces the wood-paneled setting of the 19th-century mansion that's now the **Lambert van Meerten Museum,** Oude Delft 199 (☎ **015/260-2358**). It's open Tuesday through Saturday from 10am to 5pm, Sunday 1 to 5pm (closed Sunday November through March). Admission is 3.50Dfl ($1.85).

To view brand-new **Delftware,** and see how it's hand painted, visit the factory showroom of ✪ **De Porceleyne Fles,** Rotterdamseweg 196 (☎ **015/256-0234**). It's open April through October, Monday to Saturday from 9am to 5pm and Sun 9:30am to 4pm; November through March, Monday to Saturday 9am to 5pm. Admission is free.

THE FLOWER CENTERS

Flowers at **Keukenhof Gardens,** Lisse (☎ **025/465-555**), have a short but glorious season. You'll never forget a visit to this meandering 70-acre wooded park in the heart of the bulb-producing region, planted each fall by major Dutch growers. Each spring the bulbs burst forth and produce millions (almost eight million at last count) of tulips, narcissi, daffodils, hyacinths, bluebells, crocuses, lilies, amaryllis, and more. A blaze of color is everywhere in the park and greenhouses, beside brooks and shady ponds, along paths and in neighboring fields, in neat little plots and helter-skelter on lawns. By its own report, it's the greatest flower show on earth.

The park is open from late March to late May only, daily 8am to 7:30pm. There are special train-bus connections via Haarlem and the nearby town of Leiden. Admission is 17Dfl ($8.95) for adults, 15Dfl ($7.90) for seniors, and 8.50Dfl ($4.45) for children 4 to 12.

Flowers are a billion-guilder-per-year business at **Aalsmeer Flower Auction** (☎ **0297/393-939**), held in lakeside Aalsmeer near Schiphol Airport. Every year, three billion flowers and 400 million plants from 8,000 nurseries are auctioned off. Get there early to see the biggest array of flowers and to have as much time as possible to watch the computerized auctioning. As flower lots go by on carts, the first bid to stop the auction "clock" as it works down from 100 to 1 wins the posies. The auction is held Monday through Friday from 7:30 to 11am. Bus no. 172 takes you there from Amsterdam's Centraal Station. Admission is 5Dfl ($2.65) for adults, free for children 12 and under.

VOLENDAM & MARKEN

One of these neighboring villages on the IJsselmeer lake is on the mainland, the other on a former island; one is Catholic, the other Protestant; in one, women wear white caps with wings, and in the other, caps with ribbons—but they are often combined on bus-tour itineraries.

GETTING THERE There are separate, hourly buses to Volendam and Marken from outside Amsterdam's Centraal Station.

VISITOR INFORMATION   VVV Volendam is at Zeestraat 37 (☎ **0299/363-747;** fax 0299/368-484). Marken has no VVV office.

EXPLORING VOLENDAM & MARKEN   Volendam is geared for tourism, with souvenir shops, boutiques, and restaurants. Its boat-filled harbor, tiny streets, and traditional houses have an undeniable charm. If you want a snapshot of yourself surrounded by fishermen wearing little caps and balloon-legged pants, Volendammers will gladly pose. They understand that the traditional costume is worth preserving, as is the economy of a small town that lost most of its fishing industry when the Zuiderzee enclosure dam cut it off from the North Sea. You can see such attractions as the fish auction, diamond cutter, clog maker, and the house with a room entirely wall-papered in cigar bands.

✪ **Marken** was an island until a causeway connected it with the mainland, and it remains as insular as ever. Quieter than Volendam, with a village of green-painted houses on stilts around a tiny harbor, it is also more rural. Clusters of farmhouses dot the polders (the reclaimed land from the sea that makes up two-thirds of Holland), and a candy-striped lighthouse stands on the IJsselmeer shore. Marken does not gush over tourists, but it will feed and water them, and let them wander around its pretty streets. Villagers wear traditional costume, as much to preserve the custom as to appease the tourists who pour in daily. The **Marken Historisch Museum,** Kerkbuurt 44 (☎ **0299/601-904**) is a typical house open as a museum from Good Friday to the end of October, Monday through Saturday 10am to 5pm, and Sunday noon to 4pm. Admission is 4Dfl ($2.10) for adults, 2Dfl ($1.05) for children. A clog maker works in the parking lot during the summer.

13 Norway

by Darwin Porter & Danforth Prince

Norway is a land of tradition, as exemplified by its rustic stave churches—look for these mysterious dark structures with steep gables surmounted by dragon heads and pointed steeples—and folk dances stepped to the airs of a fiddler. But Norway is also modern, a technologically advanced nation that's rich in petroleum and hydroelectric energy. One of the last great natural frontiers of the world, Norway is a land of astonishing beauty; its steep and jagged fjords, salmon-teeming rivers, glaciers, mountains, and meadows invite exploration. In winter, the shimmering Northern Lights beckon; in summer, the midnight sun shines late and warm.

Oslo, Bergen & the Fjords

Our tour begins in the Norwegian capital of Oslo and continues west to the capital of the fjord district, Bergen. Then we discuss the many options for exploring the spectacular fjords.

OSLO

Today, Oslo is one of the 10 largest capitals in the world in sheer area, if not in urban buildup. After World War II, Oslo grew to 175 square miles. The city is one of the most heavily forested on earth, and fewer than half a million Norwegians live and work here.

One of the oldest Scandinavian capital cities, founded in the mid-11th century, Oslo has never been a mainstream tourist site. But the city is a culturally rich capital with many diversions—enough to fill at least 3 or 4 busy days. It's also the center for many easy excursions along the Oslofjord or to towns and villages in its environs, both north and south.

In recent years Oslo has grown from what even the Scandinavians viewed as a Nordic backwater to one of Europe's happening cities. Restaurants, nightclubs, cafes, shopping complexes, and other venues keep on opening. A kind of Nordic *joie de vivre* permeates the city; the only drawback is that all this fun is going to cost you—Oslo ranks as one of Europe's most expensive cities.

Only in Oslo

Experiencing Life on the Water In summer, head for the harbor, where boats wait to take you sightseeing, fishing, or to the beaches.

Hanging Out in Students' Grove   Summer is short in Oslo, but locals savor its warmth and long, late hours. Late-night drinkers sit in open-air beer gardens, enjoying the pale nights that have no end.

Enjoying Fresh Shrimp off the Boats   In Oslo, head for the harbor in front of the Rådhuset and buy a bag of freshly caught and cooked shrimp from a shrimp fisher. Get a beer at an Aker Brygge cafe and shell and eat your shrimp along the harbor.

Listening to the Street Musicians   Hundreds of musicians flock to Oslo in summer. You can enjoy their music along Karl Johans Gate and at the Marketplace.

Taking the Ferry to Bygdøy   The Bygdøy peninsula is a treasure trove of Viking ships, Thor Heyerdahl's *Kon-Tiki,* seafood buffets, a sailboat harbor, bathing beaches, and a folk museum with old farmsteads, houses, and often folk dancing.

ESSENTIALS

GETTING THERE   By Plane   Most arrivals are at **Fornebu** (☎ **67-59-33-40**) at Snaroya, 5½ miles from Oslo. Fornebu services both domestic and international flights of SAS and other intra-European airlines, including British Airways and Icelandair.

SAS operates a **bus service** from both terminals to the Sentralstasjon train station and other points in Oslo every 10 minutes. The fare for the 20- to 30-minute trip is 40NOK ($5.20).

A cab ride into the city from the airport costs from 120 to 150NOK ($15.60 to $19.50) for up to four passengers.

By Train   Trains from the Continent and from Sweden or Copenhagen pull into **Oslo Sentralstasjon (Central Station),** Jernbanetorget 1 at the beginning of Karl Johans Gate (☎ **81-50-08-88** for train information), in the city center. The station is open daily 7am to 11pm. From the Central Station, you can catch trains heading for Bergen and all other rail links in Norway. From the station, you can also take trams to all major parts of Oslo.

By Car   If you're driving from mainland Europe, the fastest way to reach Oslo is to take the car ferry from Frederikshavn, Denmark (see below); the drive from Copenhagen to Frederikshavn takes about 4½ hours. You can also take a car ferry from Copenhagen (see below) or drive from Copenhagen by crossing over to Helsingborg, Sweden, from Helsingør, Denmark. Once at Helsingborg, take E-6 north all the way to Stockholm. If you're driving from Stockholm to Oslo, follow E-18 west all the way; the trip takes about 7 hours. Once you near the outskirts of Oslo from any direction, follow the signs into the SENTRUM, or city center.

By Ferry   Ferries from Europe arrive at the Oslo port, a 15-minute walk or a short taxi ride from the city center. From Denmark, car ferries depart for Oslo from Copenhagen (trip time: 12 hours), Hirtshals (trip time: 9 hours), and Frederikshavn (trip time: 8½ hours). From Strømstad, Sweden, there's a daily crossing in summer to Sandefjord, Norway, which takes 2½ hours; from Sandefjord, it's an easy drive or train ride north to Oslo. Call ☎ **22-41-90-90** or 22-33-50-00 for schedules and information. Reservations are required.

VISITOR INFORMATION   Assistance and information for visitors are available at the **Tourist Information Office,** Vestbaneplassen 1, 0250 Oslo (☎ **22-83-00-50**). Free maps, brochures, sightseeing tickets, and guide services are available. The office is open in June, daily 9am to 6pm; in July and August, daily 9am to 7pm; in May and September, Monday to Saturday 9am to 4pm; January to April and October to December, Monday to Friday 9am to 4pm.

There's also an Oslo-only **information office** at the Oslo Sentralstasjon (Central Station), Jernbanetorget 1, at the beginning of Karl Johans Gate (no telephone), open daily 8am to 11pm.

Once you're in Norway, it might be quicker to call the Norway-only telephone number (☎ **82-06-01-00**) for information about Oslo or any other Norwegian destination. If you're calling, expect to be placed in a telephone queue for up to 30 minutes. If you are calling only to inquire about a telephone number, you get much quicker service by contacting the **national operator** (☎ **55-96-60-00**).

CITY LAYOUT   Oslo is at the mouth of the 60-mile-long Oslofjord. Opening onto the harbor is **Rådhusplassen (City Hall Square),** dominated by the modern City Hall, a major attraction. Guided bus tours leave from this square, and the launches that cruise the fjords depart from the pier facing the municipal building. (You can catch ferries to the Bygdøy Peninsula from the quay at Rådhusplassen.)

Out on a promontory to the east is the **Akershus Castle.** At **Bygdøy,** the much larger peninsula that juts out to the west, are four of Oslo's major attractions: the Viking ships, the Polar Ship *Fram* Museum, the *Kon-Tiki* Museum, and the Folk Museum.

Karl Johans Gate, Oslo's main street (especially for shopping and strolling) is north of City Hall Square. This boulevard begins at Oslo **Sentralstasjon** (Central Station) and stretches all the way to the 19th-century **Royal Palace** at the western end.

A short walk from the palace is the famed **Student's Grove** (the University of Oslo is nearby), where everybody gathers on a summer day to socialize. Dominating this area is the **National Theater.** South of the theater and near the harbor is **Stortings-gaten,** another shopping street.

The main city square is **Stortorvet,** although it's no longer the center of city life, which has now shifted to Karl Johans Gate.

At a subway stop near the National Theater you can catch an electric train to **Try-vannstårnet,** the loftiest lookout in Scandinavia, and to the **Holmenkollen Ski Jump.**

GETTING AROUND   A 24-hour **Tourist Ticket (Turistkort)** lets you travel anywhere in Oslo whenever you want, by bus, tram, subway, local railway, or boat, including the Bygdøy ferries in summer. The Tourist Ticket costs 40NOK ($5.20) for adults and half-price for children 4 to 15; children under 4 travel free. The ticket is stamped when it's used for the first time and is then good for the next 24 hours.

An even better deal, especially for short-term visitors, might be the **OsloCard,** which allows unlimited travel by public transportation, free parking validation, and free admission to all museums and major tourist attractions. A 1-day pass costs 150NOK ($19.50) for adults and 50NOK ($6.50) for children up to 15; a 2-day pass costs 220NOK ($28.60) for adults and 60NOK ($7.80) for children; and a 3-day pass costs 250NOK ($32.50) for adults and 70NOK ($9.10) for children.

By Bus, Tram & Subway   Jernbanetorget, in front of the Central Station, is the major bus and tram terminal stop in Oslo. Most buses and trams passing through the heart of town stop at Wessels Plass, next to the Parliament (Stortinget), or at Stortorvet, the main marketplace. Many also stop at the National Theater or University Square on Karl Johans Gate.

The **T-banen (subway)** has four main lines running to the east of Oslo and four lines running to the west. The most heavily traveled routes by tourists are the eastern lines, which cut through the major districts of interest to visitors. The western lines take in Holmenkollen and residential and recreational areas west and north of the city.

Single-journey tickets cost 18NOK ($2.35) for adults; children travel for half-fare. You can buy tickets on-board from bus and tram drivers, or you can purchase them in advance at Trafikanten in front of Oslo Sentralstasjon (☎ 22-17-70-30). You must cancel your ticket in the automated machines located in subway stations and on buses and trams.

An eight-coupon "Maxi" card costs 110NOK ($14.30), half-price for children. Maxi cards can be used for unlimited transfers within 1 hour of the time the ticket is stamped. For information about timetables and fares, call **Trafikanten** (☎ 22-17-70-30).

By Taxi   The cheapest and most spontaneous way to get a taxi is either hailing one on the street or waiting your turn at any of the city's taxi stands. In either case, the initial meter reading ranges from 24.50 to 29.50NOK ($3.20 to $3.85), depending on the time of day. If you call for a cab and ask that it pick you up at a specific address, the initial meter reading ranges from 37 to 44NOK ($4.80 to $5.70), depending on the time of day. In either case, after your initial charge is noted, you pay between 7.75NOK ($1) and 11.20NOK ($1.45) per kilometer you travel, depending on the time of day and how far you travel.

If you need to order a taxi, call ☎ **22-38-80-90,** 24 hours a day. Reserve at least an hour in advance, and be prepared to be placed on hold indefinitely.

By Ferry   In warmer months, usually from mid-April until late September, ferries depart for Bygdøy from Pier 3 in front of the Oslo Rådhuset. For schedule information, call **Båtservice** (☎ 22-20-07-15). We recommend using a ferry or bus to Bygdøy since parking conditions there are crowded. Other ferries leave for various parts of the Oslofjord; ask at the **Tourist Information Office** at Vestbaneplassen 1 (☎ 22-83-00-50). One-way fare to Bygdøy or any destination in Oslo is 25NOK ($3.25).

By Bicycle   **Den Rustne Eike,** Vestbaneplassen 2 (☎ 23-11-51-08), rents bikes at moderate rates, complete with free maps of interesting routes in Oslo and its environs. The cost is 85 to 135NOK ($11.05 to $17.55) per day or 465 to 835NOK ($60.45 to $108.55) per week, with a 1,000NOK ($130) deposit required. Helmets are included at no charge, and a child's seat is available for 50NOK ($6.50). It's open May to October, daily 10am to 6:30pm; off-season, Monday to Friday 10am to 6pm.

Fast Facts: Oslo

American Express   American Express Reisebyrå, Karl Johans Gate (☎ 22-98-37-00), is open Monday through Friday 9am to 6pm and Saturday 10am to 3pm.

Currency   You pay your way in Norway in Norwegian **kroner (NOK).** There are 100 øre in 1 krone. Banknotes are issued in denominations of 5, 10, and 20 kroner. The exchange rate used in this chapter was $1 = 7.6NOK or 1NOK = 13¢. Also, 1EUR = 8.1NOK and £1 = 12.3NOK.

Dentists   In an emergency, contact the **Tøyen Senter,** Kolstadgate 18 (☎ 22-67-78-00), open daily 11am to 2pm and 7 to 10pm. For private dentists, look under *Tannleger* ("tooth doctors") in volume 1B of the telephone directory; there's rarely a language barrier.

Doctors   Oslo's most prominent emergency clinic is the 24-hour **Oslo Municipal Casualty Clinic (Legavakten)** at Storgata 40 (☎ **22-11-70-70** or

Oslo

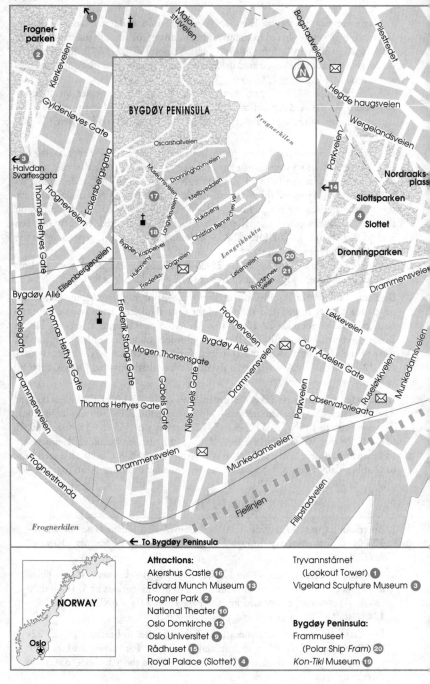

BYGDØY PENINSULA

Attractions:
Akershus Castle **16**
Edvard Munch Museum **13**
Frogner Park **2**
National Theater **10**
Oslo Domkirche **12**
Oslo Universitet **9**
Rådhuset **15**
Royal Palace (Slottet) **4**

Tryvannstårnet
(Lookout Tower) **1**
Vigeland Sculpture Museum **3**

Bygdøy Peninsula:
Frammuseet
(Polar Ship *Fram*) **20**
Kon-Tiki Museum **19**

NORWAY

Oslo ★

800

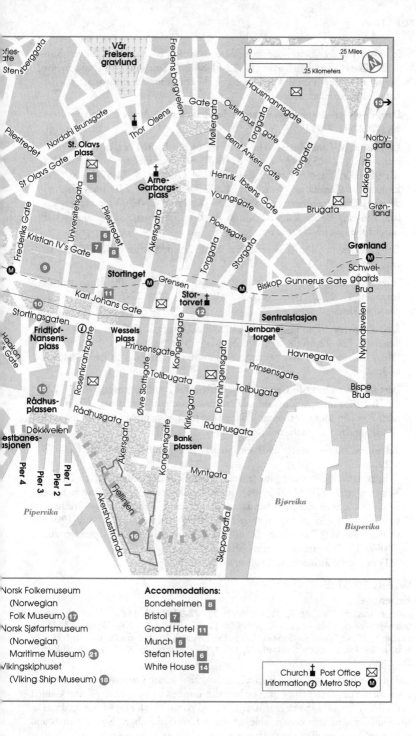

Norsk Folkemuseum
  (Norwegian
  Folk Museum) **17**
Norsk Sjøfartsmuseum
  (Norwegian
  Maritime Museum) **21**
Vikingskiphuset
  (Viking Ship Museum) **18**

Accommodations:

Bondeheimen **8**
Bristol **7**
Grand Hotel **11**
Munch **5**
Stefan Hotel **6**
White House **14**

Church ✝ Post Office ✉
Information ⓘ Metro Stop Ⓜ

22-00-81-60). For more routine medical assistance, contact Oslo's biggest hospital, **Ullavel,** Kirkeveien 166 (☎ **22-11-80-80**). To consult a private doctor (nearly all of whom speak English), check the telephone directory or ask at your hotel for a recommendation.

Drugstores   A 24-hour pharmacy is **Jernbanetorvets Apotek,** Jernbanetorget 4A (☎ **22-41-24-82**).

Embassies & Consulates   The Embassy of the **United States** is at Drammensveien 18, 0255 Oslo 2 (☎ **22-44-85-50**); the Embassy of the **United Kingdom,** at Thomas Heftyes Gate 8, 0264 Oslo 2 (☎ **22-55-24-00**); the Embassy of **Canada,** at Oscarsgate 20, 0244 Oslo 3 (☎ **22-46-69-55**); and **South Africa,** Drammensveien 88C, 0255 (☎ **22-44-79-10**). Visitors from Ireland and New Zealand should contact the British Embassy. Australians should contact the Canadian Embassy.

Emergencies   Dial the Oslo **police** at ☎ **112;** report a **fire** at ☎ **110;** call an **ambulance** at ☎ **113.**

Internet Access   If you want to check your e-mail, try the **Underworld-Internet Café & Bar,** Akersgata 39, Oslo (☎ **22-33-38-98;** www. netcafeguide.com/norge.htm).

Lost Property   The Lost and Found Office, Hittegodskontoret, at Grølandsleiret 44 (☎ **22-66-98-65**), is open May 15 to September 15, Monday to Friday 8:15am to 1:45pm; September 16 to May 14, Monday to Friday 8:15am to 3pm.

Post Office   The **Oslo General Post Office** is at Dronningensgate 15 (☎ **22-40-78-10** for information), although the entrance is at the corner of Prinsensgate. It's open Monday through Friday 8am to 6pm, Saturday 9am to 3pm; it's closed Sunday and public holidays.

Telephone   The country code for Norway is **47,** and the city code for Oslo is **22.**

International calls can be made from **Telenor's Telecommunications Office,** Kongensgate 21 (☎ **22-40-55-09**), open Monday through Friday 9am to 8pm, Saturday 10am to 5pm, and Sunday noon to 6pm. The entrance is on Prinsensgate. To make a long-distance **collect or calling card call,** dial ☎ **800/19011** to reach an AT&T operator; ☎ **800/19912** to reach an MCI operator; and ☎ **800/19877** to reach a Sprint operator.

For operator assistance in English, dial ☎ **115.**

WHERE TO STAY
Expensive
Bristol. Kristian IV's Gate 7, 0164 Oslo 1. ☎ **22-82-60-00.** Fax 22-82-60-01. E-mail: bristol@online.no. 145 units. A/C MINIBAR TV TEL. 920–1,750NOK ($119.60–$227.50) double; 2,800–3,500NOK ($364–$455) suite. Children 14 and under stay free in parents' room. Rates include breakfast. AE, DC, MC, V. Parking 130NOK ($16.90). T-banen: Stortinget.

In the heart of the city, on a side street north of Karl Johans Gate, this 1920s-era hotel is warm, inviting, and luxurious. The Moorish-inspired lobby, with its Winter Garden and Library Bar, sets the elegant tone. The bedrooms, which range from medium to spacious, are especially comfortable, generally furnished in light Nordic pastels and with excellent, firm mattresses. Although the plumbing in some of the rooms is a bit antiquated, you'll find hair dryers, first-class toilet articles, and a generous assortment of towels. Some units are nonsmoking. The Bristol's meal options range from sand-wiches and lighter fare to the more formal intimacy of the Bristol Grill.

✪ **Grand Hotel.** Karl Johans Gate 31, 0159 Oslo 1. ☎ **800/223-5652** in the U.S., or 22-42-93-90. Fax 22-42-12-25. E-mail: reservation@grand-hotel.no. 327 units. MINIBAR TV TEL. Summer, 1,090NOK ($141.70) double, 2,050–10,000NOK ($266.50–$1,300) suite; rest of the year, 1,875NOK ($243.75) double, 2,675–10,000NOK ($347.75–$1,300) suite. Rates include buffet breakfast. AE, DC, MC, V. Parking 120NOK ($15.60). T-banen: Stortinget.

Norway's leading hotel, on the wide boulevard that leads to the Royal Palace, is a stone-walled building from 1874, with mansard gables and a copper tower. Now com-pletely renovated, all the bedrooms, ranging in size from medium to large, have new furniture, including excellent beds with firm mattresses, carpeting, and wallpaper. Most bathrooms have plenty of room to spread out your stuff, a hair dryer, and big fluffy towels. High-ceilinged rooms in the 19th-century core are decorated in a classic style with heavy draperies and furniture in somber tones. Newer rooms, although fea-turing brighter color schemes and light woods, still manage to reflect both the hotel's history and its sense of luxury. Some rooms are air-conditioned. The hotel has several restaurants, serving both international and Scandinavian food. The Palmen and the Grand Café offer live entertainment, as does the nightclub, Bonanza. Facilities include an indoor swimming pool, sauna, and solarium.

Moderate

Bondeheimen. Rosenkrantzgate 8 (entrance on Kristian IV's Gate), 0159 Oslo 1. ☎ **800/528-1234** in the U.S., or 22-42-95-30. Fax 22-41-94-37. www.bestwestern.com. 81 units. MINIBAR TV TEL. 1,020NOK ($132.60) double Mon–Thurs; 750NOK ($97.50) double Fri–Sun. Rates include breakfast. AE, DC, MC, V. Parking 125NOK ($16.25). Tram: 7 or 11.

In the city center, Bondeheimen has been associated with the Best Western hotel chain for the past 9 years. The medium-sized rooms are comfortable, often adorned with Norwegian pine pieces, including excellent beds with firm, frequently renewed mat-tresses. Many of the bathrooms have a minimum of shelf space and are small, but they are well maintained. Towels are medium in size. There's an inexpensive cafeteria serving homemade Norwegian dishes. Unfortunately for hotel guests, this makes the place popular with bus tours, so be warned that large groups frequent the place almost daily. The hotel does not have a license to serve alcohol.

Stefan Hotel. Rosenkrantzgate 1, 0159 Oslo 1. ☎ **22-42-92-50.** Fax 22-33-70-22. E-mail: stefan@os.telia.no. 138 units. A/C MINIBAR TV TEL. 1,015NOK ($131.95) double Mon–Thurs; 755NOK ($98.15) double Fri–Sun. Rates include breakfast. AE, DC, MC, V. Parking 130NOK ($16.90). Tram: 11, 17, or 18.

This clean, comfortable hotel boasts an excellent location in the city center. Built in 1952, it has been modernized and much improved since then, with a complete reno-vation in 1990 and further updates in 1996. The bedrooms are well furnished and maintained. Renovations again in 1997 brought warmer, brighter tones throughout the hotel. Two bedrooms have facilities for travelers with disabilities, and all but eight of the rooms are air-conditioned. The Restaurant Stefan is recommended separately under "Where to Dine," below. There is also a cozy hotel bar.

Inexpensive

Munch. Munchsgaten 5, 0130 Oslo 1. ☎ **22-42-42-75.** Fax 22-20-64-69. 180 units. MINIBAR TV TEL. 870NOK ($113.10) double Mon–Thurs; 690NOK ($89.70) double Fri–Sun. Rates include breakfast. AE, DC, MC, V. Parking 100NOK ($13). T-banen: Stortinget. Tram: 7 or 11. Bus: 37.

Built in 1983, this solid, nine-floor hotel offers good-value accommodations (at least by Oslo standards), and each floor reached by elevator. Bedrooms are comfortably furnished, well maintained, and functional in a streamlined Nordic style. As a grace note, they are decorated with reproductions of Edvard Munch's paintings. Although not overly large, rooms are cozy and well heated, the mattresses firm and frequently renewed. Bathrooms tend to be tiny, with showers or a shower and tub combination, with tidy maintenance and a minimum of towels (although you can ask for more if needed).

White House. President Harbitz Gate 18, 0259 Oslo 2. ☎ **22-44-19-60.** Fax 22-55-04-30. 21 units. MINIBAR TV TEL. 820NOK ($106.60) double Mon–Thurs; 695NOK ($90.35) double Fri–Sun. Rates include breakfast. AE, DC, MC, V. Free parking. Tram: 1.

One of the smallest hotels in Oslo, the White House was originally built around 1900 as a private home. It lies in the forested residential district of Breskeby, a short walk from the rear of the Royal Palace. Set on a steeply sloping lot and greatly modernized since its original construction, it attracts a loyal clientele that appreciates the hotel's small scale and sense of intimacy. Bedrooms have a cozy Norwegian charm, almost like something encountered in the countryside. They range in size from small to medium, but you'll enjoy the comfort of good beds and firm mattresses, great housekeeping, and snug but adequate bathrooms (mostly with shower units) with a generous supply of medium-sized towels. The in-house restaurant, Den Lelle Sondue, has an outdoor wooden deck looking down over the street in front.

WHERE TO DINE

Norwegians are as fond of smørbrød as the Danes (you'll see it offered everywhere for lunch), except they spell it differently. Basically, it means bread and butter, but it's really an open-faced sandwich that can be stacked with practically anything, including ham with a slice of peach resting on top or perhaps a mound of dill-flavored shrimp.

Expensive

D'Artagnan. Øvre Slottsgate 16. ☎ **22-41-50-62.** Reservations required. Main courses 250–285NOK ($32.50–$37.05); 5-course set-price menu 595NOK ($77.35). AE, DC, MC, V. Mon–Fri (also Sat Oct to Christmas) 4:30–11pm. Closed July–Aug 5 and Dec 22–Jan 3. Bus: 27, 29, 30, 41, or 61. FRENCH.

D'Artagnan is one of Oslo's most elegant and upscale restaurants. Amid flickering candles and bouquets of flowers, you'll enjoy menu items that change with the seasons but might include a salad of king crab from Finnmark with avocado and grapefruit segments, yogurt-marinated reindeer with a boysenberry sauce, wild duck served with roasted mixed nuts and a port wine sauce, and one of the most unusual dishes of all—wild lamb from the mountains of central Norway, served with a herb-flavored mustard sauce. Always featured, in salads and main dishes, is salmon smoked on the premises using different types of wood and tea leaves.

✪ **Statholdergaarden.** Rådhusgate 11. ☎ **22/41-88-00.** Reservations recommended. Main courses 230–330NOK ($29.90–$42.90); set-price menu 630NOK ($81.90). Mon–Sat 6–10pm. Tram 11, 15, or 18. NOUVELLE NORWEGIAN.

One of the most richly historic restaurant settings in Oslo is directed by one of the capital's most fêted and successful chefs, Bent Stiansen, whose interpretations of Norwegian nouvelle cuisine have attracted the attention and admiration of gastronomes throughout the country. The setting is beneath the stucco-covered and frescoed ceilings of what was built in 1640 as the governor's headquarters. Menu items change frequently, according to whatever is in season at the time of your visit. Examples include grilled crayfish served with a scallop and salmon tartare, and thyme-infused codfish with a crabmeat mousse and two sauces. (One is a simple white wine sauce; the other is based on a rare vanilla bean imported from Thailand.) One of the most appealing and all-time favorite dishes we've enjoyed was a lightly fried Arctic char with sautéed savoy cabbage, and a lime beurre blanc. Don't confuse this upscale and prestigious site with the less expensive bistro, Statholderstueakroen, that occupies the building's vaulted cellar.

Moderate

Grand Café. In the Grand Hotel, Karl Johans Gate 31. ☎ **22-42-93-90.** Reservations recommended. Main courses 175–266NOK ($22.75–$34.60). AE, DC, MC, V. Mon–Sat 11am–midnight; Sun noon–11pm. T-banen: Stortinget. NORWEGIAN.

This is the grand old cafe of Oslo, steeped in legend and tradition—in fact, atmosphere and tradition are a more compelling reason to visit here than the cuisine. A large mural depicts, among many others, Ibsen, who once enjoyed whale steaks here, and Edvard Munch. (A postcard sold at the reception desk identifies these diners).

The menu relies on the best of Norwegian country traditions (after all, how many places still serve elk stew?). Choices range from a Napoléon with coffee to a full meal; you'll find fried stingray, standard veal and beef dishes, and reindeer steaks. Sandwiches for 70NOK ($9.10) are also available. This is tasty, unpretentious cooking that will win you over if you like solid, honest, and earthy flavors, but more important, this is the place to be seen.

✪ Restaurant Stefan. In the Stefan Hotel, Rosenkrantzgate 1. ☎ **22-42-92-50.** Reservations recommended. Main courses 178–200NOK ($23.15–$26); lunch smörgåsbord 175NOK ($22.75); evening smörgåsbord 225NOK ($29.25). Mon–Fri 11:30am–2:30pm and 4:30–10:30pm; Sat noon–2:30pm and 4:30–10:30pm. Smörgåsbord daily at lunch and Thurs–Fri at dinner. Tram: 7 or 11. NORWEGIAN.

This bustling, unpretentious restaurant is better known than the hotel that houses it. It's especially popular at lunchtime, when the locals come for the city's best smörgåsbord, a buffet laden with traditional Norwegian foods. Samplings usually include cucumber salad, fish and meat salads, sausages, meatballs, potato salad, smoked fish, assorted Norwegian cheeses, and breads. Selections from the à la carte menu include "Stefan's special platter," an old-fashioned but flavorful dish that incorporates slices of reindeer, moose meat, and ox tongue, with lingonberries and potatoes.

Inexpensive

Brasserie 45. Karl Johans Gate 45. ☎ **22/41-34-00.** Reservations recommended. Main courses 68–179NOK ($8.85–$23.25). AE, DC, MC, V. Mon–Thurs noon–midnight; Fri–Sat noon–2am; Sun 1pm–9pm. T-banen: Centrum. CONTINENTAL.

Airy, artful, and stylish, this bistro lies one floor above street level of a building overlooking the biggest fountain along the showplace promenade of downtown Oslo. Within a setting that's mostly red, you're attended by uniformed staff wearing black and white, bearing steaming platters of dishes that include especially flavorful versions of fried catfish with lemon-garlic sauce; fried chicken in a spicy tomato-based sweet-and-sour sauce; pork schnitzels with béarnaise sauce and shrimp; and a tartare of salmon with dill-enriched boiled potatoes. Dessert might include a chocolate terrine with cloudberry-flavored sorbet. The cuisine is ambitious, but lives up to its promise.

Det Gamla Rådhus (Old Town Hall). Nedre Slottsgate 1. ☎ **22-42-01-07.** Reservations recommended. Main courses 120–220NOK ($15.60–$28.60); smørbrød at lunch 45–65NOK ($5.85–$8.45). AE, DC, MC, V. Mon–Fri 11am–3pm; Sat 4–11pm. (Kroen Bar Mon–Sat 4pm–midnight.) Bus: 27, 29, 30, 41, or 61. NORWEGIAN.

The oldest restaurant in Oslo, Gamla Rådhus is located in what was Oslo's Town Hall in 1641. At noon you can sit in the spacious dining room and choose from an array of open-faced sandwiches (smørbrød). À la carte dinner selections include fresh fish, game, and Norwegian specialties. Ingredients are fresh, and the service accommodating.

Engebret Café. Bankplassen 1. ☎ **22-33-66-94.** Reservations recommended. Main courses 198–289NOK ($25.75–$37.55) ; smørbrød 55–87NOK ($7.15–$11.30). AE, DC, MC, V. Mon–Sat 11am–11pm. Bus: 27, 29, or 30. NORWEGIAN.

An enduring Oslovian favorite since 1857, this restaurant is housed in two 400-year-old joined landmark buildings directly north of Akershus Castle. It has an old-fashioned atmosphere and good food. During lunch, a tempting selection of open-faced sandwiches is available. The menu grows more elaborate in the evening when you might begin with a terrine of game with blackberry–port-wine sauce or fish soup. You can then order such traditional dishes as trout in sour cream with boiled potatoes and pickled cucumber, red wild boar with whortleberry sauce, or smoked or roast reindeer filets.

SEEING THE SIGHTS

In the Bygdøy Peninsula

✪ **Vikingskiphuset (Viking Ship Museum).** Huk Aveny 35, Bygdøy. ☎ **22-43-83-79.** Admission 30NOK ($3.90) adults, 10NOK ($1.30) children. May–Aug daily 9am–6pm; Sept daily 11am–5pm; Apr daily 11am–4pm; Nov–Mar daily 11am–3pm; Oct daily 11am–6pm. Ferry: In summer, leaves from Pier 3 facing the Rådhuset. Bus: 30 from the National Theater to polar ship *Fram* and *Kon-Tiki* Museum (see below).

Displayed here are three Viking burial vessels that were excavated on the shores of the Oslofjord and preserved in clay. The most spectacular find is the 9th-century *Oseberg*, discovered near Norway's oldest town. This 64-foot dragon ship features a wealth of ornaments and is the burial chamber of a Viking queen and her slave. The *Gokstad* find is an outstanding example of Viking vessels because it's so well preserved. The smaller *Tune* ship was never restored. Look for the *Oseberg* animal-head post, the elegantly carved sleigh used by Viking royalty, and the *Oseberg* four-wheeled cart.

Frammuseet (Polar Ship *Fram*). Bygdøynesveien. ☎ **22-43-83-70.** Admission 25NOK ($3.25) adults, 10NOK ($1.30) students and children. May 1–15 daily 10am–4:45pm; May 16–Aug daily 9am–5:45pm; Sept daily 10am–4:45pm; Mar–Apr Mon–Fri 11am–3:45pm, Sat–Sun 11am–3:45pm; Oct–Nov Mon–Fri 11am–2:45pm, Sat–Sun 11am–3:45pm; Dec–Feb Sat–Sun 11am–3:45pm. Ferry: In summer, leaves from Pier 3 facing the Rådhuset. Bus: 30 from the National Theater.

A long walk from the Viking ships, the Frammuseet contains the sturdy polar exploration ship *Fram*, which Fridtjof Nansen sailed across the Arctic (1893–96). The vessel was later used by Norwegian explorer Roald Amundsen, the first man to reach the South Pole (1911).

Kon-Tiki Museum. Bygdøynesveien 36. ☎ **22-43-80-50.** Admission 30NOK ($3.90) adults, 10NOK ($1.30) children. Apr–May and Sept daily 10:30am–5pm; June–Aug daily 9:30am–5:45pm; Oct–Mar daily 10:30am–4pm. Ferry: In summer, leaves from Pier 3 facing the Rådhuset. Bus: 30 from the National Theater.

Kon-Tiki is the world-famed balsa-log raft that the young Norwegian scientist Thor Heyerdahl and his five comrades sailed in for 4,300 miles in 1947—all the way from Callao, Peru, to Raroia, Polynesia. Besides the raft, there are other exhibits from Heyerdahl's subsequent visit to Easter Island, including an Easter Island family cave, with a collection of sacred lava figurines.

Norsk Sjøfartsmuseum (Norwegian Maritime Museum). Bygdøynesveien 37. ☎ **22-43-82-40.** Admission (museum and boat hall) 30NOK ($3.90) adults, 15NOK ($1.95) children. May–Sept daily 10am–7pm; Oct–Apr Mon, Wed, Fri–Sat, 10:30am–4pm, Tues and Thurs 10:30am–7pm. Ferry: In summer, leaves from Pier 3 facing the Rådhuset. Bus: 30 from the National Theater.

This museum, which contains a complete ship's deck with helm and chart house, and a three-deck-high section of the passenger steamer *Sandnaes*, chronicles the maritime history and culture of Norway. The Boat Hall features a fine collection of original small craft. The fully restored polar vessel *Gjoa*, used by Roald Amundsen in his search for America's Northwest Passage, is also on display. The three-masted schooner *Svanen* (Swan) is moored at the museum, too.

Norsk Folkemuseum (Norwegian Folk Museum). Museumsveien 10. ☎ **22-12-37-00.** Admission 50NOK ($6.50) adults, 10NOK ($1.30) children 7–16. Jan 1–May 14 and Sept 15–Dec 31, Fri–Sat 11am–3pm, Sun 11am–4pm; May 15–June 14 and Sept 1–Sept 14, daily 10am–5pm; June 15–Aug 31, 10am–6pm. Ferry: In summer, leaves from Pier 3, facing the Rådhuset. Bus: 30.

From all over Norway, 140 original buildings have been transported and reassembled on 35 acres on the Bygdøy Peninsula. This open-air folk museum includes a number of medieval buildings, such as the Raulandstua, one of the oldest wooden dwellings still standing in Norway, and a stave church from about 1200. The rural buildings are grouped together by region of origin, and the urban houses have been laid out in the form of an old town.

In Western Oslo

✪ **Vigeland Sculpture Museum.** Frogner Park, Nobelsgata 32. ☎ **22-54-25-30.** Park, free; museum, 30NOK ($3.90) adults, 15NOK ($1.95) students and children. Park, daily 24 hours. Museum, May–Sept, Tues–Sat 10am–6pm, Sun noon–7pm; Oct–Apr, Tues–Sat noon–4pm, Sun noon–6pm. Tram: 12 or 15. Bus: 20.

The lifetime work of Gustav Vigeland, Norway's greatest sculptor, is displayed inside the museum as well as throughout the nearby 75-acre Frogner Park in western Oslo. Nearly 211 sculptures in granite, bronze, and iron can be admired. See in particular his four granite columns, symbolizing the fight between humanity and evil (a dragon, the embodiment of evil, embraces a woman). The angry boy is the most photographed statue in the park, but the really celebrated work is the 52-foot-high monolith, composed of 121 figures of colossal size—all carved into one piece of stone.

In Eastern Oslo

✪ **Edvard Munch Museum.** Tøyengate 53. ☎ **22-67-37-74.** Admission 50NOK ($6.50) adults, 20NOK ($2.60) students and children under 15. June to mid-Sept daily 10am–6pm; mid-Sept to May Tues–Wed and Fri–Sat 10am–4pm, Thurs and Sun 10am–6pm. T-banen: Tøyen. Bus: 20.

Devoted exclusively to the works of Edvard Munch (1863–1944), Scandanivia's leading painter, this exhibit (Munch's gift to the city), traces his work from early realism to his latter-day expressionism. The collection comprises 1,100 paintings, some 4,500 drawings, around 18,000 prints, numerous graphic plates, six sculptures, and important documentary material.

In the City Center

Akershus Castle. Festnings-Plassen. ☎ **22-41-25-21.** Admission 20NOK ($2.60) adults, 10NOK ($1.30) students and children. May–Sept 15, Mon–Sat 10am–4pm, Sun 12:30–4pm; Apr 15–30 and Sept 16–Oct, Sun 12:30–4pm. Closed Nov–Apr 14. Tram: 1, 2, or 10.

One of the oldest historical monuments in Oslo, Akershus Castle was built in 1300 by King Haakon V Magnusson. It was a fortress and a royal residence for several centuries. A fire in 1527 devastated the northern wing, and the castle was rebuilt and transformed into a royal Renaissance palace under the Danish-Norwegian king

Christian IV. Now it's used by the Norwegian government for state occasions. A few rooms of the castle, including its chapel, are open to the public. In the rectangular court, markings show where the massive medieval keep used to stand. You can wander through two large halls (Olav's Hall and Christian IV's Hall), which occupy the top floor of the north and south wings, respectively. For many, the most interesting part is the dungeon, which includes an "escape-proof room" built for a prisoner, Ole Pedersewn Hoyland. After he was placed in the chamber and realized there was no way he could ever escape, he killed himself.

Attractions Nearby

Tryvannstårnet (Lookout Tower). Voksenkollen. ☎ **22-14-67-11.** Admission 30NOK ($3.90) adults, 15NOK ($1.95) children. May and Sept daily 10am–5pm; June daily 9am–7pm; July daily 9am–10pm; Aug daily 9am–8pm; Oct–Apr Mon–Fri 10am–3pm. T-banen: Holmenkollen SST Line 1 from near the National Theater to Voksenkollen, a 30-minute ride, then a 15-minute walk uphill.

This is the loftiest lookout tower in Scandinavia—the gallery is approximately 1,900 feet above sea level and offers a view of the Oslofjord with Sweden to the east. A walk down the hill takes you back to the famous restaurant Frognerseteren. You can take another 20-minute walk down the hill to the Holmenkollen ski jump, the site of the 1952 Olympic competitions as well as the Holmenkollen Ski Festival, when skiers compete in downhill, slalom, giant slalom, cross-country ski races, and jumping.

Henie-Onstad Kunstsenter (Henie-Onstad Art Center). Høvikodden, Baerum. ☎ **67-54-30-50.** Admission 50NOK ($6.50) adults, 30NOK ($3.90) ages 25 and under. June–Aug Mon 11am–5pm, Tues–Fri 9am–9pm, Sat–Sun 11am–7pm; Sept–May Tues 9am–9pm, Sat–Mon 11am–5pm. Bus: 151, 152, 251, or 261 for Høvikodden.

On a site beside the Oslofjord 7 miles west of Oslo, ex-movie star and skating champion Sonja Henie and her husband, Niels Onstad, a shipping tycoon, opened a museum to display their art collection. This especially good 20th-century collection includes some 1,800 works by Munch, Picasso, Matisse, Léger, Bonnard, and Miró. Ms. Henie's Trophy Room is impressive with 600 trophies and medals, including three Olympic gold medals—she was the star at the 1936 competition—and 10 world skating championships.

ORGANIZED TOURS

H. M. Kristiansens Automobilbyrå, Hegdehaugsveien 4 (☎ **22-20-82-06**), known as H.M.K. tours, has been showing visitors around Oslo for more than a century. All year the agency offers a full-day Oslo sightseeing tour, leaving daily at 10am and 1:30pm. It costs 210NOK ($27.30) for adults and 110NOK ($14.30) for children, not including lunch. The tour passes through the city center and makes stops at the Vigeland Sculpture Park, the Holmenkollen Ski Jump, the Viking Ship Museum, the *Kon-Tiki* Museum, and the Vikingland theme park. A shorter 2-hour tour departs daily at 10am and 5:30pm, costing 140NOK ($18.20) for adults and 75NOK ($9.75) for children. Tours leave from the Norway information center, Vestbaneplassen 1; you should arrive 15 minutes before departure. Authorized guides speak English.

THE SHOPPING SCENE

Near the marketplace and the cathedral (Oslo Domkirche), **Den Norske Husflidsforening,** Møllergata 4 (☎ **22-42-10-75**)—or *Husfliden,* as it's called—is the display and retail center for the Norwegian Association of Home Arts and Crafts, founded in 1891. Today it's almost eight times larger than any of its competitors, with two floors displaying the very finest of Norwegian design in ceramics, glassware, furniture, and

Exploring the Fjords from Oslo

The scenery around Bergen is even more spectacular than that found around Oslo, but if the Oslo area is your only chance to see Norwegian fjord country, then go for it. The eastern side of the fjord is sunny and preferable for touring. Along the way, you pass old Viking ruins, once-fortified towns, woodlands, and endless blue waters. Quaint cottages pose on rolling hills that suddenly plunge downward to the deeply blue, narrow depths that dramatically snake their way inland.

Oslofjord links the capital with the open sea. It's studded with islets and sheltered waters. Regrettably, industry has blighted some of the shoreline, but there is much that's still pristine, beautiful, and unspoiled, a perfect combination of mountain scenery and fjord waters.

Departing from Pier 3 in front of the Oslo Rådhuset (City Hall), **Båtservice Sightseeing,** Rådhusbrygge 3, Rådhusplassen (☎ **22-20-07-15**), offers a 50-minute mini-cruise boat tour, with a view of the harbor and the city, including the ancient fortress of Akershus and the islands in the inner part of the Oslofjord. Cruises depart mid-May to late August, on the hour daily 11am to 8pm (limited sailing at the season's beginning and end). Adults pay 70NOK ($9.10); children, 35NOK ($4.55).

An evening fjord cruise, including a maritime buffet at the Norwegian restaurant Lanternen, leaves late June through August, daily at 3:30 and 5:45pm. The 3½-hour cruise costs 325NOK ($42.25) for adults and 120NOK ($15.60) for children.

If you have more time, take the 2-hour fjord cruise through the maze of islands and narrow sounds in the Oslofjord. Departures are May to September, daily at 10:30am and 1, 3:30, and 5:45pm; the cost is 140NOK ($18.20) for adults, and 70NOK ($9.10) for children. Refreshments are available on board. There are variations of this cruise, such as the fjord cruise with lunch, also 2 hours, leaving May to mid-September, daily at 10:30am, and costing 240NOK ($31.20) for adults, 120NOK ($15.60) for children. After the 2-hour fjord cruise, the boat anchors so that passengers can go ashore for lunch at Lanternen Restaurant.

---

woodworking. You can also purchase souvenirs, gifts, textiles, rugs, knotted rya rugs, embroidery, wrought iron, and fabrics by the yard. Goods are shipped all over the world.

Norway's largest department store, **Steen & Strøm,** Kongensgate 23 (☎ **22-00-40-00**), is a treasure house with hundreds of Nordic items spread through 58 individual departments. Look for handknit sweaters and caps, hand-painted wooden dishes reflecting traditional Norwegian art, and pewter dinner plates made from old molds.

Heimen Husflid, Rosenkrantzgate 8 (☎ **22-41-40-50**), about a block from Karl Johans Gate, carries folk costumes, antiques, and reproductions. Handknit sweaters in traditional Norwegian patterns are a special item, as are pewter and brass items.

William Schmidt, Karl Johans Gate 41 (☎ **22-42-02-88**), established in 1853, is a leading purveyor of unique souvenirs, including pewter items (everything from Viking ships to beer goblets), Norwegian dolls in national costumes, wood carvings (the troll collection is the most outstanding in Oslo), and sealskin moccasins. The shop specializes in handknit cardigans, pullovers, gloves, and caps; sweaters are made from moth-proofed 100% Norwegian wool.

OSLO AFTER DARK

To find out what's happening when you're visiting, pick up *What's On in Oslo,* which details concerts and theaters and other useful information.

Theater, ballet, and opera tickets are sold at various box offices and also at **Billettsentralen,** Karl Johans Gate 35 (☎ **22-17-05-05**), although this service costs quite a bit more than your typical box office. Tickets to sports and cultural events can now be bought easily and more cheaply via computer linkup at any post office in the city, so when you buy a stamp you can also buy a voucher for a ticket to the ballet, theater, or hockey game.

The Performing Arts

Home to the National Theater Company, the **National Theater,** Johans Eidvolls Plass 1 (☎ **22-41-27-10**), stages dramatic performances 6 nights a week (Monday through Saturday) every month except June to August. Ticket prices range from 107 to 190NOK ($13.90 to $24.70).

Two blocks from the National Theater, **Oslo Konserthus,** Munkedamsveien 14 (☎ **23-11-31-00**), is the home of the widely acclaimed Oslo Philharmonic. Performances are given on Thursday and Friday evenings except in June and July, and ticket prices range from 225 to 250NOK ($29.25 to $32.50). Big-name jazz and pop acts show up regularly; ticket prices depend on the act.

The 1931 building, originally a movie theater, at Storgaten 23, was adapted for better acoustics and dedicated in 1959 to the **Den Norske Opera (Norwegian National Opera)** (☎ **22-42-94-75**). It's also the venue for the National Ballet. Productions of both companies are staged between September and mid-June. Between the two companies, there are generally three performances a week, with the only set performance night being Saturday. Tickets range from 170 to 320NOK ($22.10 to $41.60).

Summer Cultural Entertainment

Det Norske Folkloreshowet (Norwegian Folklore Show) performs from July to early September at the Oslo Konserthus, Munkedamsveien 15 (☎ **23-11-31-11** for reservations). The 1-hour performances are Monday and Thursday at 8:30pm, and tickets cost 160NOK ($20.80) for adults, 110NOK ($14.30) for children.

The **Norwegian Folk Museum,** on Bygdøy, often presents folk-dance performances by its own ensemble on summer Sunday afternoons at the museum's open-air theater (see *What's On in Oslo* for details). Admission is free, as the performance is included in the museum's entrance price. Take the ferry from Pier 3 near the Rådhuset.

The Club & Music Scene

Smuget, Rosenkrantzgate 22 (☎ **22-42-52-62**), is the most talked-about nightlife joint in the city, and has the long lines (especially on weekends) to prove it. It's in a 19th-century building in back of the City Hall and has a restaurant, an active dance floor, and a stage where live bands from throughout Europe and the world perform. It's open Monday through Saturday 8pm to 3am; the cover is 50NOK ($6.50) on weekdays and 70NOK ($9.10) on Saturday and Sunday.

With a capacity of 1,200 patrons, the **Rockefeller Music Hall,** Torggata 16 (☎ **22-20-32-32**), a combination concert hall and nightclub, is one of the largest establishments of its kind in Oslo. There are live concerts every night, everything from reggae to rock to jazz. Cover runs 60 to 300NOK ($7.80 to $39). It's usually open Sunday to Thursday 8pm to 2:30am and Friday to Saturday 9pm to 3:30am. Show time is about an hour after the doors open.

A labyrinth of hallways, dance areas, and bars, **Dixie,** Universitetsgata 26 (☎ **22-41-36-33**), is one of Oslo's busiest clubs. Inside, you'll find the **New Orleans Restaurant** (☎ **22-42-44-20**) and the high-energy **Barock Disco** (☎ **22-42-44-20**). Barock is open as a bar on Wednesday night, and as a disco every Thursday through Saturday 9pm to 3:30am. Entrance on disco nights is 50NOK ($6.50).

Set immediately behind the Bristol Hotel, **Club Castro,** Kristians IV Gate 7 (☎ **22-41-51-08**), is the largest, most visible, and most popular gay bar and disco in Norway. It's open Tuesday through Sunday 9pm to 3:30am.

DAY TRIPS FROM OSLO

The best 1-day excursion from Oslo includes visits to Fredrikstad and Tønsberg, which gives you a chance to explore the scenic highlights of the Oslofjord. A trip to Fredrikstad, in Østfold on the east bank of the Oslofjord, can easily be combined in 1 day with a visit to the port of Tønsberg on the west bank, by crossing over on the ferry from Moss to Horten, and then heading south.

To reach the first stop, Fredrikstad, take E-6 south from Oslo toward Moss. Continue past Moss until you reach the junction of Route 110, which is signposted south of Fredrikstad. About six buses per day depart for the town from the Central Station in Oslo.

FREDRIKSTAD   In recent years Fredrikstad, 60 miles south of Oslo, has become a major tourist center, thanks to its Old Town and 17th-century fortress. Across the river on the west is a modern industrial section, and although a bridge links the two sections, the best way to reach Old Town is by ferry, which costs 5NOK (65¢). The departure point is about 4 blocks from the Fredrikstad railroad station; simply follow the crowd out the main door of the station, make an obvious left turn, and continue down to the shore of the river. It's also possible to travel between the two areas by bus (no. 360 or 362), although most pedestrians opt for the ferry.

Fredrikstad was founded in 1567 as a marketplace at the mouth of the River Glomma. **Gamlebyen (Old Town)** became a fortress in 1663 and continued in that role until 1903, boasting some 200 guns in its heyday. It still serves as a military camp. The main guardroom and old convict prison are now the **Fredrikstad Museum,** Gamleslaveri (☎ **69-32-09-01**), open May through September, Monday through Friday 11am to 5pm, Saturday and Sunday noon to 5pm. Admission is 30NOK ($3.90) for adults and 10NOK ($1.30) for children.

Outside the gates of Old Town is **Kongsten Fort,** on what was first called Gallows Hill, an execution site. When Fredrikstad Fortress was built, it was provisionally fortified in 1677, becoming known as Svenskeskremme (Swede Scarer). Present-day Kongsten Fort with its 20 cannons, underground chambers, passages, and countermines, eventually replaced it.

Since Fredrikstad's heyday as a trading port and merchant base, Old Town has attracted craftspeople and artisans, many of whom create their products in the Old Town's historic houses and barns. Many of these glassblowers, ceramic artists, and silversmiths choose not to display or sell their products at their studios, preferring instead to leave the sales aspect to local shops.

En Route to Tønsberg   You can drive back north from Fredrikstad to the town of Moss, where you can take a ferry to Horten. Once at Horten, signs point the way south for the short drive to Tønsberg.

TØNSBERG Bordering the western bank of the Oslofjord, Tønsberg, 64 miles south of Oslo, is Norway's oldest town. It's divided into a historic area, filled with old clapboard-sided houses, and the commercial center, where the marketplace is located.

Tønsberg was founded a year before King Harald Fairhair united parts of the country in 872, and this Viking town became a royal coronation site. Svend Foyn, who invented modern whaling and seal hunting, was born here.

Slottsfjellet, a huge hill fortress directly ahead of the train station, is touted as "the Acropolis of Norway." But it has only some meager ruins, and people mostly come here for the view from the lookout tower. Built in 1888, the **Slottsfjelltårnet** (☎ 33-31-18-72) is open May 18 to June 23, Monday through Friday 10am to 3pm; June 24 to August 18, daily 11am to 6pm; August 19 to September 15, Saturday and Sunday noon to 5pm; and September 16 to 29, Saturday and Sunday noon to 3pm. Admission is 10NOK ($1.30) for adults and 5NOK (65¢) for children.

Nordbyen is the old and scenic part of town, with well-preserved houses. **Haugar** cemetery, at Møllebakken, is right in the town center, with the Viking graves of King Harald's sons, Olav and Sigrød.

Sem Church, Hageveien 32 (☎ 33-36-93-99), the oldest in Vestfold, was built of stone in the Romanesque style around 1100. It's open Tuesday through Friday 9am to 2pm; ask at the vestry. Admission is free.

You should also see **Fjerdingen,** a street of charming restored houses. Tønsberg was also a Hanseatic town during the Middle Ages, and some houses have been redone in typical Hanseatic style.

In the **Vestfold Folk Museum,** Frammannsveien 30 (☎ 33-31-29-19), there are many Viking and whaling treasures. One of the biggest (literally) thrills is the skeleton of a blue whale. There's also a real Viking ship displayed, the *Klastad* from Tjolling, built about A.D. 800. Admission is 20NOK ($2.60) for adults, 15NOK ($1.95) for seniors and students, and 5NOK (65¢) for children. It's open mid-May to mid-September, Monday through Saturday 10am to 5pm, Sunday and holidays noon to 5pm; mid-September to mid-May, Monday through Friday 10am to 2pm.

BERGEN: GATEWAY TO THE FJORDS

In western Norway the landscape takes on an awesome beauty, with iridescent glaciers, deep fjords that slash into rugged, snowcapped mountains, roaring waterfalls, and secluded valleys that lie at the end of corkscrew-twisting roads. From Bergen, the most beautiful fjords to visit are the **Hardanger** (best at blossom time, May and early June), to the south; the **Sogne,** Norway's longest fjord, immediately to the north; and the **Nordfjord,** north of that. A popular excursion on the Nordfjord takes visitors from Loen to Olden along rivers and lakes to the Brixdal Glacier.

If you have time, on the Hardangerfjord you can stop over at one of the fjord resorts, such as Ulvik or Lofthus. From many vantage points, it's possible to see the Folgefonn Glacier, Norway's second-largest ice field, which spans more than 100 square miles.

Bergen, with its many sightseeing attractions, good hotels and restaurants, and excellent boat, rail, and coach connections, is the best center for touring the fjord district. This ancient city looms large in Viking sagas. Until the 14th century it was the seat of the medieval kingdom of Norway. The Hanseatic merchants established a major trading post here, holding sway until the 18th century.

ESSENTIALS

GETTING THERE   By Plane   The **Bergen Airport** at Flesland, 12 miles south of the city, offers frequent flights to such larger cities as Copenhagen and London,

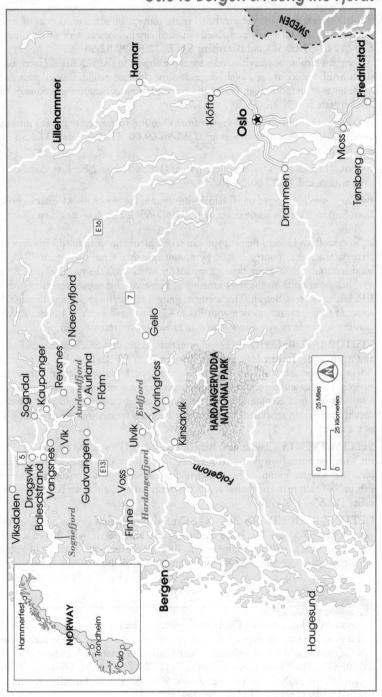

through which most international flights are routed. In addition, dozens of direct flights leave here for nearly every medium-sized city in Norway with such airlines as **SAS** (☎ 67-59-60-50) and **Braathens SAFE** (☎ 55-99-82-50).

Frequent airport bus service circles from the airport to the SAS Royal Hotel, Braathens SAFE's office at the Hotel Norge, and the city bus station. Buses depart every 20 minutes Monday through Friday and every 30 minutes Saturday and Sunday. The one-way fare is 40NOK ($5.20).

By Train   Day and night trains arrive from Oslo and stations en route. For information, call the Bergen train station at ☎ **55-96-69-00.** The trip from Oslo can take 6 to 8½ hours.

By Bus   Express buses travel to Bergen from Oslo in 11 hours. For long-distance bus information, call ☎ **22-00-24-40.**

By Car   A toll is charged on all vehicles driven into the city center Monday to Friday from 6am to 10pm. A single ticket costs 5NOK (65¢); a book of 20 tickets, 90NOK ($11.70).

To cross from Oslo to Bergen, you can take a mountain drive filled with dramatic scenery. Since the country is split by mountains, there's no direct road. Take the southern route, E76, going through mountain passes until the junction with Route 47; then head north to the ferry crossing at Kinsarvik that goes across the fjords to E16 leading west to Bergen. The northern route is via Highway 7, going through the resort of Geilo, to the junction with Route 47; then head south to Kinsarvik. After crossing on the ferry, you arrive at E16 and head west to reach Bergen.

VISITOR INFORMATION   For information, maps, and brochures about Bergen and its environs, **Tourist Information,** Bryggen 7 (☎ 55-32-14-80), is open June to August, daily from 8:30am to 10pm; October to April, Monday to Saturday from 9am to 4pm. In May and September it's open from 9am to 8pm. Tourist Information can also help you find accommodations, exchange foreign currency, and cash traveler's checks when banks are closed. You can also buy tickets for city sightseeing or for tours of the fjords.

SPECIAL EVENTS   The annual **Bergen Festival,** held for 12 days in late May, features performances by regional, national, and international orchestras, dance ensembles, and theater groups. The complete festival schedule is usually available by February of each year. For festival and ticket information, contact the **Bergen Festival office** (☎ 55-21-61-50).

GETTING AROUND   By Bus   The **Central Bus Station** (Bystasjonen), Strømgaten 8 (☎ 55-55-90-70), is the terminal for all buses serving the Bergen and the Hardanger area, as well as the airport bus. Bergen Sporvei runs a network of yellow-sided **city buses** (☎ 55-59-32-00 for information) that also serve the city center.

Traveler's Tip

To cut costs, buy a **Bergen Card,** which gives you free bus transport and usually free museum entrance throughout Bergen, plus discounts on car rentals, parking, and some cultural and leisure activities. Ask at Tourist Information. A 24-hour card costs 130NOK ($16.90) for adults and 60NOK ($7.80) for children 3 to 15. A 48-hour card sells for 200NOK ($26) for adults and 90NOK ($11.70) for children. Children 2 and under generally travel or enter free.

By Taxi   Taxis are readily available at the airport, or call ☎ **55-99-70-00.** A ride to the center costs 235NOK ($30.55). Sightseeing by taxi costs about 325NOK ($42.25) per hour.

WHERE TO STAY
Expensive
Clarion Admiral Hotel. Christian Sundts Gate 9, 5004 Bergen. ☎ **55-23-64-00.** Fax 55-23-64-64. 205 units. MINIBAR TV TEL. Mon–Thurs 1,495NOK ($194.35) double, 2,300–3,800NOK ($299-$494) suite; Fri–Sun 790NOK ($102.70) double, 1,495–2,500NOK ($194.35-$325) suite. AE, DC, MC, V. Parking is 70NOK ($9.10). Bus: 2, 4, or 11.

When it was originally built in 1906, this building was one of the largest warehouses in Bergen, with six sprawling floors peppered with massive trusses and beams. In 1987, it was transformed into a comfortable, tastefully appointed hotel, and in 1998, it was enlarged and renovated into the bustling establishment you see today. Rooms are a bit small, but comfortable and filled with vague touches of art nouveau styling and attractively tiled, but relatively small, bathrooms. The most desirable units open onto flower-bedecked balconies with the best harbor views in town. The in-house restaurant, Emily, offers set-price menus at lunch and dinner, each priced at 198NOK ($25.75).

✪ **Radisson-SAS Hotel Norge.** Ole Bulls Plass 4, 5001 Bergen. ☎ **800/333-3333** in the U.S., or 55-57-30-00. Fax 55-57-30-01. www.radisson.com. 359 units. A/C MINIBAR TV TEL. June 25–Aug 18, 1,050NOK ($136.50) double, 2,000–5,000NOK ($260–$650) suite; Aug 19–June 24 1,395NOK ($181.35) double, 2,500NOK ($325) suite. Rates include breakfast. Children 17 and under stay free in parents' room. DC, MC, V. Parking 100NOK ($13). Book your parking spot along with your room, as space is limited. Bus: 2, 3, or 4.

In the city center, the Norge has been a tradition since 1885. In September 1996, it became part of the SAS Radisson chain. Some rooms have oversized bathtubs big enough for two, and other units open onto private balconies overlooking the flower-ringed borders of a nearby park. The hotel offers the widest array of drinking and dining establishments in Bergen, including its gourmet restaurant, Grillen, and Ole Bull, an informal place for lunch and light meals. Facilities include a swimming pool, solarium, sauna, Jacuzzi, gym, and garage.

Moderate
Hotell Hordaheimen. C. Sundtsgate 18, 5004 Bergen. ☎ **55-23-23-20.** Fax 55-23-49-50. 64 units. TV TEL MINIBAR. May 15–Sept 15, 790NOK ($102.70) double; Sept 16–May 14, Mon–Thurs 1,030NOK ($133.90) double, Fri–Sun 700NOK ($91) double; year-round 1,130NOK ($146.90) junior suite. Rates include breakfast. AE, DC, MC, V. Free parking (limited spaces). Bus: 1, 5, or 9.

Operated by the Bondeungdomslaget i Bergen, an association that sponsors cultural and folklore programs, the hotel has long been a Bergen base for many young people from nearby districts, yet it still considers itself primarily a business hotel. However, school and civic groups traveling together sometimes fill up nearly all the rooms. The hotel was built at the turn of the century, but renovated in stages between 1989 and 1995. Traditional Norwegian furniture dating to 1913 fills the reception area and public rooms, but contemporary pieces are used in the simple, immaculate guest rooms. The restaurant serves traditional Norwegian dishes.

Rosenkrantz. Rosenkrantzgate 7, 5003 Bergen. ☎ **55-31-50-00.** Fax 55-31-14-76. 129 units. MINIBAR TV TEL. May 15–Sept 15, 810NOK ($105.30) double; Sept 16–May 14, 1,080NOK ($140.40) double Sun–Thurs, 710NOK ($92.30) double Fri–Sat. Rates include breakfast. AE, DC, MC, V. Parking 60NOK ($7.80). Bus: 1, 5, or 9.

This simple, unpretentious choice stands near Bryggen in the city center. The lobby, with white marble floors, leads to a comfortable dining room and bar. The rooms, decorated in light, bright colors, are pleasantly furnished. The hotel was recently renovated. Facilities include a TV lounge, a piano bar, and a restaurant serving traditional dishes. A covered parking garage is located beside the hotel.

Inexpensive

Fagerheim Pensjonat. Kalvedalsveien 49A, 5018 Bergen. ☎ **55-31-01-72.** Fax 55-31-58-49. 15 units (none with bathroom). 450NOK ($58.50) double. MC, V. Free parking. Bus: 2, 4, 7, or 11 from the post office.

This attractively old-fashioned 1900 hillside house is about a 15-minute walk from the town center. A few of the homey bedrooms have small kitchens, and most open onto a view of the water and city. A garden surrounds the house. Although breakfast can be arranged, there is no restaurant or bar on the premises.

Myklebust Pensiojat. Rosenbergsgate 19, 5015 Bergen. ☎ **55-90-16-70.** Fax 55-23-18-01. 6 units (2 with bathroom). 470NOK ($61.10) double without bathroom; 520NOK ($67.60) double with bathroom. No credit cards. Free parking on the street. Bus: 2, 3, or 4.

This stone-built, century-old house is near the heart of Bergen, about a 15-minute walk from the railroad station. All the bedrooms are furnished in a contemporary Norwegian style, with hot and cold running water; shower and toilet facilities are close by. All but one has a TV set. Breakfast, costing extra, will be brought to your room whenever you request it.

WHERE TO DINE

Bryggeloftet/Stuen. Bryggen 11. ☎ **55-31-06-30.** Main courses 130–235NOK ($16.90–$30.55); lunch smørbrød 48–72NOK ($6.25–$9.35). AE, DC, MC, V. Mon–Sat 11am–11:30pm; Sun 1–11:30pm. Bus: 1, 5, or 9. NORWEGIAN.

This is the best established restaurant along the harborfront. At street level, the Stuen has low ceiling beams, carved banquettes, and 19th-century murals of old Bergen, along with dozens of clipper-ship models. For a more formal meal, head upstairs to the Bryggeloftet, with its high ceilings and wood paneling. A dinner in either section might include fried porbeagle (a form of whitefish) served with shrimp, mussels, and a white-wine sauce; roast reindeer with cream sauce; or pepper steak with a salad. Several different preparations of salmon and herring are featured, along with roast pork with Norwegian sour cabbage. This is a quintessential Norwegian type of place; come here if you're seeking authentic flavors, the type sea captains might have enjoyed a long time ago when they sailed into Bergen harbor.

✪ **Finnegaardstuene.** Rosenkrantzgate 6. ☎ **55-55-03-00.** Reservations recommended. Main courses 220–275NOK ($28.60–$35.75); set-price menu 520NOK ($67.60). AE, DC, MC, V. Mon–Sat 4:30–11pm. Closed 1 week at Easter and Dec 22–Jan 8. Bus: 5, 21. NORWEGIAN/FRENCH.

The foundations of this restaurant were laid around 1400, when it was used by merchants of the Hanseatic League as a warehouse. Today, you'll find a richly timbered, partially paneled environment where some of the woodwork dates from the 1700s; four small-scale dining rooms create a cozy atmosphere of welcome intimacy. Cuisine revolves around Norwegian ingredients, especially very fresh fish, and classical French methods of preparation. Menus change with the season and the inspiration of the chef, but are likely to include platters of crayfish served with filets of French foie gras in a cider and foie gras sauce; a gratin of monkfish with sea scallops; filets of venison with juniperberry sauce; and breast of duck with lime and fig sauce. We really like the way the chefs have created some culinary magic in sleepy Bergen. The menu is well thought out with carefully prepared dishes.

✪ **To Kokker.** Enhjørninggården. ☎ **55-32-28-16.** Reservations required. Main courses 205–275NOK ($26.65–$35.75). AE, DC, MC, V. Mon–Sat 5–10pm. NORWEGIAN.

Favored by celebrities who have included Britain's Prince Andrew, this restaurant occupies a building that was reconstructed in 1703 after a fire the year before. Set one floor above street level, it has scarlet walls, a collection of old paintings, and a solidly grounded staff that work competently under pressure. Menu items include such time-tested favorites as lobster soup; whitebait roe with chopped onions, sour cream, and fresh-baked bread; and a filet of lamb with mustard sauce and pommes Provençal. Savvy local foodies are increasingly gravitating to this restaurant because of the competence of its cuisine and the use of first-rate ingredients.

SEEING THE SIGHTS

In addition to the sights below, take a stroll around **Bryggen (the Quay).** This row of Hanseatic timbered houses, rebuilt along the waterfront after the disastrous fire of 1702, is what remains of medieval Bergen. The northern half burned to the ground as recently as 1955. Bryggen is on UNESCO's World Heritage List as one of the world's most significant cultural and historical re-creations of a medieval settlement. It's a center for arts and crafts, where painters, weavers, and craftspeople have their workshops.

✪ **Det Hanseatiske Museum.** Finnegårdsgaten 1A, Bryggen. ☎ **55-31-41-89.** Admission May–Sept 35NOK ($4.55) adults, Oct–Apr 20NOK ($2.60) adults; free for children. June–Aug daily 9am–5pm; Sept–May daily 11am–2pm. Bus: 1, 5, or 9.

In one of the best-preserved wooden buildings at Bryggen, this museum illustrates Bergen's commercial life on the wharf centuries ago. German merchants, representatives of the Hanseatic League centered in Lübeck, lived in these medieval houses built in long rows up from the harbor. With dried cod, grain, and salt as articles of exchange, fishers from northern Norway met German merchants during the busy summer season. The museum is furnished with authentic articles dating from 1704.

Mariakirke (St. Mary's Church). Dreggen. ☎ **55-31-59-60.** Admission 15NOK ($1.95) adults, free for children. May 18–Sept 10, Mon–Fri 11am–4pm; Sept 11–May 17, Tues–Fri noon–1:30pm. Bus: 1, 5, or 9.

The oldest building in Bergen (its exact date is unknown, but perhaps from the mid-12th century) is this Romanesque church, one of the most beautiful in Norway. Its altar is the oldest ornament in the church, and there's a baroque pulpit, donated by Hanseatic merchants, with carved figures depicting everything from Chastity to Naked Truth. Church-music concerts are given May to August several nights a week.

Fløibanen. Vetrlidsalm 23A. ☎ **55-31-48-00.** Round-trip ticket 30NOK ($4.30) adults, 14NOK ($2) children. May 25–Aug, Mon–Fri 7:30am–midnight, Sat 8am–midnight, Sun 9am–midnight; Sept–May 24, Mon–Thurs 7:30am–11pm, Fri 7:30am–11:30pm, Sat 8am–11:30pm, Sun 9am–11pm. Bus: 6.

A short walk from the fish market is the station where the funicular heads up to Fløien, the most famous of Bergen's seven hills. At 1,050 feet, the view of the city, the neighboring hills, and the harbor is worth every øre.

Gamle Bergen. Elsesro, Sandviken. ☎ **55-25-78-50.** Admission 40NOK ($5.20) adults, 20NOK ($2.60) children and students. Houses, mid-May–Aug, guided tours daily every hour 11am–5pm. Park and restaurant, daily noon–10pm. Bus: 1 or 9 from the city center, leaving every 10 minutes.

At Elsesro and Sandviken is a collection of houses from the 18th and 19th centuries set in a park. Old Town is complete with streets, an open square, and narrow alleyways. Some of the interiors are exceptional, including a merchant's living room in the typical style of the 1870s—padded sofas, heavy curtains, potted plants—a perfect setting for Ibsen's *A Doll's House*.

✪ **Troldhaugen (Troll's Hill).** Troldhaugveien 65, Hop. ☎ **55-91-17-91.** Admission 40NOK ($5.20) adults, free for children under 16. Apr 21–Sept, daily 9am–6pm; Oct–Nov, Mon–Fri 10am–2pm, Sat–Sun 10am–4pm; Jan–Apr 20, Mon–Fri 10am–2pm. Closed Dec. Bus: 20, 21, 30, and 50 leave from the bus station at Bergen (platforms 18–20); once the bus lets you off, turn right, walk about 200 yards, turn left at Hopsvegen, and from here follow the signs to Troldhaugen, a 20- to 30-minute walk.

This Victorian house, in beautiful rural surroundings at Hop, near Bergen, was the summer villa of composer Edvard Grieg. The house still contains Grieg's own furniture, paintings, and other mementos. His Steinway grand piano is frequently used at concerts given in the house during the annual Bergen festival, as well as at Troldhaugen's own summer concerts. Grieg and his wife, Nina, are buried in a cliff grotto on the estate.

ORGANIZED TOURS

A 1-hour **tram tour** uses the city tram lines and specially designed red-sided tramcars equipped with multilingual headsets. The tour departs every hour on the hour from Bryggen and costs 70NOK ($9.10) for adults and 35NOK ($4.55) for children. It operates May through September daily 10am to 7pm.

The most popular and most highly recommended **bus tour** of Bergen is the 3-hour city tour, which departs daily at 10am and covers all major sightseeing attractions, including Troldhaugen and Old Bergen. It also runs May through September and costs 200NOK ($26) for adults and 100NOK ($13) for children. For information and tickets for either tour, contact the tourist office at Bryggen 7 (☎ **55-32-14-80**).

THE SHOPPING SCENE

Bergen's pedestrian shopping area includes the streets **Gamle Strandgaten, Torgalmenningen,** and **Marken.** Shops are open weekdays from 9am until 4:30pm, except on Thursday, when they close at 7pm. Saturday hours are 9am to 3pm. Shopping centers are open weekdays 9am to 8pm, and close at 4pm on Saturday. When cruise ships are anchored in the harbor, most shops extend their hours to take advantage of the tourist trade.

You'll find the widest selection of national handcrafts at **Husfliden I Bergen,** Vågsalmenningen 3 (☎ **55-31-78-70**)—the finest handmade knitwear from the western district, along with woodwork, brass, pewterware, and national costumes. Especially popular are the selection of hand-turned wooden bowls and ceramics featuring a traditional hand-painted rose motif.

The leading outlet for glassware and ceramics, **Prydkunst-Hjertholm,** Olav Kyrres Gate 7 (☎ **55-31-70-27**), purchases much of its merchandise directly from the studios of Norwegian and other Scandinavian artisans who turn out quality goods not only in glass and ceramics, but also in pewter, brass, wood, and textiles.

BERGEN AFTER DARK

Opened in mid-1978, the modern **Grieg Hall (Grieghallen),** Lars Hillesgate 3A (☎ **55-21-61-50**), is Bergen's monumental showcase for music, drama, and a host of other cultural events. The Bergen Symphony Orchestra, founded in 1765, performs here from August to May on Thursday and some Fridays.

Norway's oldest theater performs September to June at **Den National Scene,** Engen 1 (☎ **55-54-97-10**). Its repertoire consists of classical Norwegian and international drama and contemporary plays, as well as visiting productions of opera and ballet in conjunction with the annual Bergen Festival. Performances are held Monday through Saturday.

In summer, the **Bergen Folklore dancing troupe** (☎ **55-31-67-10**), arranges a 1-hour folklore program at the Bryggens Museum on Tuesday and Thursday at 9pm. Tickets, which cost 95NOK ($12.35), are on sale at the tourist information center or at the door. **Ulriken Mountain Concerts** offers free folk and classical concerts weekdays at 7pm between June and August. A round-trip ticket to reach this mountaintop show costs 70NOK ($9.10) for adults and 35NOK ($4.55) for children; it includes rides on a shuttle bus from the Bergen tourist office (leaving at a quarter past the hour from 9:15am until 8:15pm) and the Ulriken cable car.

EXPLORING THE FJORDS

Norway's fjords can be explored from both Oslo and Bergen by ship and car or by a scenic train ride. Here are the details.

BY CAR FROM BERGEN

Bergen is the best departure point for trips to the fjords: To the south lies the famous **Hardangerfjord** and to the north the **Sognefjord,** cutting 111 miles inland. We've outlined a driving tour of the fjords, starting in Bergen and heading east on Route 7 to Ulvik, a distance of 93 miles.

ULVIK   Ulvik is that rarity—an unspoiled resort. It lies like a fist at the end of an arm of the Hardangerfjord that's surrounded in summer by misty peaks and fruit farms. The village's 1858 church is attractively decorated in the regional style. It's open June through August daily 9am to 5pm, and presents concerts.

From Ulvik, you can explore the **Eidfjord** district, which is the northern tip of the Hardangerfjord, home to some 1,000 people and a paradise for hikers. Anglers are attracted to the area because of its mountain trout.

The district contains nearly one-quarter of ✪ **Hardangervidda National Park,** which is on Europe's largest high-mountain plateau. It's home to 20,000 wild reindeer, and well-marked hiking trails connect a series of 15 tourist huts.

Several canyons, including the renowned **Måbø Valley,** lead down from the plateau to the fjords. Here you'll see the famous 550-foot **Voringfoss** waterfall; the Valurefoss in Hjømo Valley has a free fall of almost 800 feet.

Part of the 1,000-year-old road across Norway, traversing the Måbø Valley, has been restored for hardy hikers.

En Route to Voss   From Ulvik, take Highway 20 to Route 13. Follow Route 13 to Voss, 25 miles west of Ulvik and 63 miles east of Bergen.

VOSS   Between the Sogne and Hardanger fjords, Voss is a famous year-round resort, also known for its folklore and as the birthplace of football hero Knute Rockne. Maybe the trolls don't strike fear into the hearts of farm children anymore, but they're still called out of hiding to give visitors a little fun.

Voss is a natural base for exploring the two largest fjords in Norway, the Sognefjord to the north and the Hardangerfjord to the south. In and around Voss are glaciers, mountains, fjords, waterfalls, orchards, rivers, and lakes.

A ride on the **Hangursbanen cable car** (☎ **56-51-12-12**) offers panoramic views of Voss and the environs. The hardy take the cable car up, and then spend the rest of the afternoon strolling down the mountain. A round-trip ride costs 50NOK ($6.50) for adults, 25NOK ($3.25) for children 8 to 16, and it's free for children under 8. The cable-car entrance is on a hillside that's a 10-minute walk north of the town center. It's open in summer and winter, but closed May and September to November.

Built in 1277, the **Vangskyrkje,** Vangsgata 3 (☎ **56-51-22-78**), with a timbered tower, contains a striking Renaissance pulpit, a stone altar and triptych, fine wood carvings, and a painted ceiling. It's a 5-minute walk east of the railroad station. We recommend that you call in advance to reserve an English-speaking guide. Admission is 10NOK ($1.30) for adults, 5NOK (65¢) for children, and free for children 6 and under. The church is open only June through August, daily 10am to 4pm. If you arrive when the church is closed, it's possible to arrange a private tour by calling the parsonage at ☎ **56-51-22-78.**

Voss Folkemuseum, Mølster (☎ **56-51-15-11**), is a collection of authentically furnished houses that shows what early farm life was like. Lying half a mile north of Voss on a hillside overlooking the town, the museum consists of more than a dozen farmhouses and other buildings, ranging in age from the 1500s to around 1870. Admission is 30NOK ($3.90) for adults, and it's free for children. It's open May and September, daily 10am to 5pm; June to August, daily 10am to 7pm; and October through April, Monday to Friday 10am to 3pm and Sunday noon to 3pm.

About a mile west of Voss in Finne, **Finnesloftet** (☎ **56-51-11-00**) is one of Norway's oldest timbered houses, dating from the mid-13th century. It's a 15-minute walk west of the railway station. Admission is 30NOK ($3.90) for adults and 15NOK ($1.95) for children. It's open June 15 to August 15, daily 10:30am to 4:30pm.

An Excursion to the Sognefjord   If you have time, you may want to visit the Sognefjord district, the largest of all Norwegian fjords. From Voss continue north on Route 13 to **Vik.** The scenery is beautiful, and the road goes along for miles across a desolate tableland at 3,000 feet above sea level. The lakes on a summer day appear green, and on the distant slopes is snow.

In Vik, see the stave church, one of the most attractive in Norway; then take the road to **Vangsnes,** where you can make the short car ferry connection across the Sognefjord to Balestrand or Dragsvik. Once across, take Route 5 north. The highway is steep, bringing you through rolling countryside with waterfalls until you reach **Viksdalen,** about 40 miles from Dragsvik.

BALESTRAND   Long known for its arts and crafts, Balestrand lies on the northern rim of the Sognefjord, at the junction of the Vetlefjord, the Esefjord, and the Fjaerlandsfjord.

Kaiser Wilhelm II, a frequent visitor to Balestrand, presented the district with two statues of old Norse heroes, King Bele and Fridtjof the Bold, which stand in the town center.

You can explore by setting out in nearly any direction, on scenic country lanes with little traffic, or a wide choice of marked trails and upland farm tracks. You can buy a touring map at the **tourist office** in the town center (☎ **57-69-12-55**). There's good sea fishing, as well as lake and river trout fishing. Fishing tackle, rowboats, and bicycles can all be rented in the area.

En Route to Flåm   From Balestrand, follow Route 55 east along the Sognefjord, crossing the fjord via ferry at Dragsvik and by bridge at Sogndal. At Sogndal, drive east to Kaupanger, where you cross the Ardalsfjord by ferry, south to Revsnes. In Revsnes, pick up Route 11 heading southeast. Drive east until you connect with a secondary road heading southwest through Kvigno and Aurland. When you arrive in Aurland, take Route 601 southwest to the town of Flåm, 60 miles southeast of Balestrand and 103 miles east of Bergen.

What a Ride: Exploring the Fjords by Scenic Train

One of the great train rides of Europe is the ✪ **Bergensbanen** (☎ **55-96-69-00** for schedule information), with five daily departures from Oslo, plus an additional train on Sunday. The most popular routing is Oslo to Bergen, although you can also take the train from Bergen to Oslo, depending on where you land in Norway. We think it's the most scenic and beautiful train ride in the world. Departures are from Oslo Central Station, and the trip takes 7½ to 8½ hours to cut across some of the most panoramic fjord and mountain scenery in Europe. The cost of a one-way ticket is 500NOK ($65) but a 20NOK ($2.60) seat reservation is required.

If your time is more limited, you can take a brief train ride from Bergen that covers the most panoramic part of the journey.

The most exciting rail journey in Norway is a 12-hour tour from Bergen, encompassing two arms of the Sognefjord. The main feature of this journey—and the reason most passengers take the ride—is the 12-mile route from Myrdal to Flåm (see below). An electric train "drops" 2,900 feet, past seemingly endless waterfalls. In summer, the tour leaves from the Bergen railroad station daily at 7:33am and 8:50am, and Monday through Friday at 11:48am. Guests may have lunch at Flåm, and then board a river steamer for Gudvangen, where they hop on a bus to Voss, then a train back to Bergen. The round-trip fare, excluding meals, is 480NOK ($62.40) for adults, 240NOK ($31.20) for children under 12, and 285NOK ($37.05) for those over 67. Holders of Eurail or Scandinavian Rail Passes get a reduced fare. For more information, contact the Bergen tourist office (☎ **55-32-14-80**).

FLÅM   Flåm (pronounced "Flawm") lies on the Aurlandsfjord, a tip of the more famous Sognefjord. In the village you can visit the old church dating from 1667, with painted walls done in typical Norwegian country style.

Flåm is an excellent starting point for excursions by car or boat to other well-known centers on the Sognefjord, Europe's longest and deepest fjord. Worth exploring are two of the wildest and most beautiful fingers of the Sognefjord: Nærøyfjord and Aurlandfjord. Ask at the **tourist office,** near the rail station (☎ **57-63-21-06**), about a summer-only cruise from Flåm, where you can experience the dramatic scenery of both of these fjords. From Flåm by boat, you can disembark either in Gudvangen or Aurland and continue the tour by coach, or you can return to Flåm by train.

There are also a number of easy walks in the Flåm district. The tourist office has a map outlining these walks.

BY SHIP/TOUR FROM BERGEN

There are several ways to visit Sognefjord, Norway's longest fjord, from Bergen. One way is to cross the fjord on an express steamer that travels from Bergen to **Gudvangen.** From Gudvangen, passengers go to Voss (see above), and from Voss a train runs back to Bergen. You can go by boat, bus, and then train for 495NOK ($64.35) round-trip. Details about this and other tours are available from the Tourist Information office in Bergen, Bryggen 7 (☎ **55-32-14-80**).

If you have more than a day to see the fjords in the environs of Bergen, you can take the grandest fjord cruise in the world, a **coastal steamer** going all the way to the North Cape and beyond. The coastal steamers are elegantly appointed ships that travel along the western coast of Norway from Bergen to Kirkenes, carrying passengers and cargo to 34 ports along the Norwegian coast. Eleven ships in all make the journey year-round. The ships sail through Norway's more obscure fjords, providing panoramic scenery and many opportunities for adventure. Along the way, sightseeing excursions to the surrounding mountains and glaciers are offered, as well as sails on smaller vessels through some of the more obscure fjords.

The chief operator of these coastal cruises is the **Bergen Line,** 405 Park Ave., New York, NY 10022 (☎ **800/323-7436** or 212/319-1300 in the U.S.). Tours may be booked heading north from Bergen, south from Kirkenes, or round-trip. The 7-day northbound journey costs $636 to $2,688 per person, including meals and taxes. Visitors opting for the southbound trip from Kirkenes pay $539 to $2,275. The round-trip voyage lasts 12 days and costs $975 to $4,133 per person.

Portugal 14

by Darwin Porter & Danforth Prince

Today tourists are realizing that Portugal, previously written off as a "poor man's Spain," has been unjustly overlooked. The word is out about its sandy beaches, art treasures, unique architecture, friendly people, flavorful cuisine, and relatively low prices. Lisbon presides over a country that has one of Europe's fastest-growing economies, much of it fueled by European Union investments. About 160 miles south of Lisbon, the maritime province of the Algarve, often called the "garden of Portugal," was once considered the edge of the earth. Its coastline stretches 100 miles and is dotted with hundreds of beaches—the finest in Portugal.

1 Lisbon & Environs

Lisbon has blossomed into a cosmopolitan city—Europe's smallest capital is no longer a backwater at the far corner of Iberia. Sections along Avenida da Liberdade, the main street, at times evoke Paris in miniature. Sidewalk portrait painters beg to sketch your likeness, artisans offer you jewelry claiming it's gold (you both know it isn't), and vendors peddle handcrafts from embroidery to leatherwork. Some of the formerly clogged streets of the Baixa have been closed to traffic, and cobblestoned pedestrian malls have been created.

Today, after a long slumber, there's excitement again in this city of seven hills. The world dropped in on Lisbon as it celebrated Expo '98, marking the 500th anniversary of Vasco da Gama's journey to India. Not since the aftermath of the 1755 earthquake was there such a building boom. In the spring of 1998 a new bridge—Ponte Vasco da Gama—opened that spans the Tagus; this addition to the city's infrastructure has speeded access to Spain and to other areas of Portugal, including the Alentejo province.

In Lisbon, there's life after Expo '98. The site of the last great World's Fair of this century will not become a ghost town. Many of the attractions and facilities remain, including the Oceanarium, the largest aquarium in Europe. The Utopia Pavilion—an indoor stadium with advanced theatrical equipment—has become Lisbon's first multimedia arena for concerts, sporting events, theatrical shows, and international congresses. The Lisbon Exhibition Center today holds dozens of international affairs every year, and the recreational harbor now has a capacity for 700 to 900 moorings for leisure craft.

Some 1.6 million people now call Lisbon home, and many Lisboetas (Lisbonites), having drifted in from the far corners of the world, don't even speak Portuguese.

Consider an off-season visit, especially in spring or fall, when the city is at its most glorious, avoiding the hot and humid days of July and August. Lisbon isn't infested with visitors then, and you can wander about without fear of being trampled underfoot.

Only in Lisbon

Getting Lost in the Alfama Maze   The houses are so close together in the Alfama that in many places it's impossible to stretch your arms to their full length. Streamers of laundry wave from the smallest houses, and the fishwives make early-morning appearances on their iron balconies to water pots of geraniums. In the street markets, you can wander through a maze of stacks of brightly colored vegetables from the country, bananas from Madeira, pineapples from the Azores, and fish from the Atlantic. Armies of cats protect the street from rats. Occasionally a black-shawled old woman, stooped over a brazier grilling sardines in front of her house, will toss one of these felines a fish head.

Following the Trail of Fado in the Bairro Alto   *Fado,* an authentic Portuguese musical genre, means "fate" or "destiny." Its sad lament to lost love and glory is heard nightly in the little houses of the Bairro Alto. Women swathed in black (called *fadistas,* as are male fado singers) are accompanied by 12-stringed guitars. Listening to these melancholy songs is the quintessential Lisbon experience.

Shopping for Handcrafts   The shopping in Lisbon is irresistible. Artisans from all over the country display their finest wares in the capital: ceramics, embroidery (from the Azores and Madeira), silver, elegant porcelain, gleaming crystal, *azulejos* (tiles), handwoven rugs, and handknit sweaters.

Spending an Afternoon in Sintra   Some savvy travelers claim that after they've visited Sintra, the rest of Europe seems like a footnote. Follow in the footsteps of Portuguese kings and queens of yesteryear and head for Byron's "glorious Eden." Byron wasn't alone in proclaiming this village "perhaps the most delightful in Europe." Even the sometimes skeptical Spanish proclaim: "To see the world and yet leave Sintra out/ Is, verily, to go blindfold about."

Witnessing Relics of a Vanished Empire   At Belém, where the river Tagus (*Tejo* in Portuguese) meets the sea, the Portuguese caravels (three-masted sailing ships) that charted the world unknown to the West were launched on their missions: Vasco da Gama to India, Ferdinand Magellan to circumnavigate the globe, and Bartolomeu Dias to round the Cape of Good Hope. Belém flourished as riches poured back into Portugal. Great monuments, including the Belém Tower and Jerónimos Monastery, were built and embellished in the Manueline style. Much of the district's character still remains, including those monuments to former glory.

Shopping on Market Day   The big market of Ribeira Nova is as close as you can get to the heart of Lisbon. Near the Cais do Sodré, where trains leave for the Costa del Sol, an enormous roof shelters stalls offering the produce used in Lisbon's fine restaurants. Foodstuffs are brought in each morning in wicker baskets bulging with oversize carrots, cabbages as big as shrubbery, and stalks of bananas. Some arrives by donkey, some by truck, some balanced on the heads of Lisboan women in quintessential Mediterranean fashion. "Seeing-eye" fishing boats (believed to have been based on Phoenician designs) dock at dawn with their catch. Soon the *varinas,* balancing wicker baskets of the fresh catch on their heads, climb the cobbled streets of the Alfama or the Bairro Alto to sell fish from door to door.

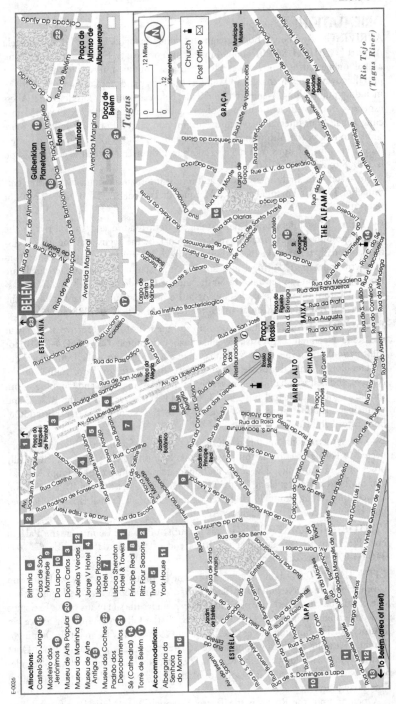

Lisbon

Attractions:
Castelo São Jorge 15
Mosteiro dos Jerónimos 19
Museu de Arts Popular 20
Museu da Marinha 18
Museu de Arte Antiga 13
Museu dos Coches 22
Padrão dos Descobrimentos 21
Sé (Cathedral) 14
Torre de Belém 17

Accommodations:
Albergaria da Senhora do Monte 16
Britania 6
Casa de São Mamede 9
Da Lapa 10
Dom Carlos 3
Janelas Verdes 12
Jorge V Hotel 4
Lisboa Plaza, Hotel 7
Lisboa Sheraton Hotel & Towers 1
Príncipe Real 8
Ritz Four Seasons 2
Tivoli 5
York House 11

E-0026

ORIENTATION

ARRIVING   By Plane   Both foreign and domestic flights land at Lisbon's **Portela Airport** (☎ **01/841-50-00**), about 4 miles north of the city. Daily from 7am to 9pm, a small orange-sided Airbus carries passengers at 20-minute intervals from the airport into the town center. It charges 430$ ($2.45) each way and stops at several key places, including points along Avenida da Liberdade, before arriving at Cais do Sodre. A less expensive but less efficient option involves catching municipal bus no. 44 or 45, traveling at half-hour intervals between the airport and central Lisbon. It follows a route similar to that of the Airbus for a one-way fare of 160$ (95¢), but it makes an interminable number of stops. You can also take a taxi; the average fare into central Lisbon is 2,000$ to 2,200$ ($11.60 to $12.75).

For ticket sales, flight reservations, and tourist information, contact the polite personnel of **TAP Air Portugal** at Praça Marquês de Pombal 3A (☎ **01/317-91-00** for reservations).

By Train   Most international rail passengers from Madrid and Paris arrive at the **Santa Apolónia Rail Station,** the major terminal, by the Tagus near the Alfama district. Two daily trains make the 10-hour run from Madrid to Lisbon. Rail lines from northern and eastern Portugal also arrive at this station. Other rail terminals are **Rossio,** where you can get trains to Sintra, and the **Cais do Sodré,** with trains to Cascais and Estoril on the Costa del Sol. At **Sul e Sueste,** you can board trains to the Algarve. For **rail information** at any of the terminals, call ☎ **01/888-40-25.**

By Bus   Buses from throughout Portugal, and the rest of Europe, arrive in Lisbon at the **Rede Nacional Expressos,** Avenida João Crisostomo (☎ **01/314-77-10** for information), near the Praça Saldanha, about a 30-minute walk from Praça dos Restauradores. Many buses depart and arrive from here for Faro, capital of the Algarve, and at least a half-dozen buses head northward for Porto and Coimbra. From the bus station, municipal buses no. 1, 21, and 32 deliver you to the Rossio, and municipal bus no. 1 carries you to Cais do Sodré, the site of public transportation to both Estoril and Cascais.

By Car   International motorists must arrive through Spain, the only nation connected to Portugal via road. You have to cross Spanish border points, which usually poses no great difficulty. The roads are moderately well maintained. From Madrid, you can head southwest along Route 90, through the border town of Badajoz (Spain) and continue along Route 90 via Estremoz into Lisbon. The final lap of the journey into Lisbon is along express highway A2.

VISITOR INFORMATION   The main tourist office in Lisbon is at the **Palácio Foz,** Praça dos Restauradores, at the Baixa end of Avenida da Liberdade (☎ **01/346-63-07**), open daily 9am to 8pm.

CITY LAYOUT   Lisbon is best approached through its gateway, **Praça do Comércio (Commerce Square** or **Black Horse Square),** bordering the Tagus. This is one of Europe's most perfectly planned squares, and it's the site of the Stock Exchange and government ministries. Directly west stands the City Hall, fronting **Praça do Município.** The building was erected in the late 19th century by architect Domingos Parente. Heading north from Commerce Square, you enter the bustling Praça Dom Pedro IV, popularly known as the **Rossio.** The "drunken" undulation of the tiled sidewalks, with their checkered arabesques of black and white, have led to the appellation "the dizzy praça."

Opening onto the Rossio is the Teatro Nacional Dona Maria II, a freestanding building whose facade has been preserved. If you arrive by train, you'll enter the

Estação do Rossio, whose exuberant Manueline architecture is worth seeing. Separating the Rossio from Avenida da Liberdade is **Praça dos Restauradores,** named in honor of the Restoration, when the Portuguese chose their own king, thus freeing themselves from 60 years of Spanish rule. The event is marked by an obelisk.

Lisbon's main street is handsomely laid out. **Avenida da Liberdade (Avenue of Liberty),** dating from 1880 and once called the "antechamber of Lisbon," is like a mile-long park, with shade trees, gardens, and center walks for the promenading crowds. Flanking it are fine shops, headquarters for many major airlines, travel agents, coffeehouses with sidewalk tables, and hotels, including the Tivoli. At the top of the avenue is **Praça Marquês de Pombal,** with a statue honoring Pombal, the 18th-century prime minister credited with Lisbon's reconstruction in the aftermath of the 1755 earthquake. Proceeding north, you'll enter **Parque Eduardo VII,** named in honor of the son of Queen Victoria, who paid a state visit to Lisbon. In the park is the Estufa Fria, a greenhouse well worth a visit.

GETTING AROUND   Tickets valid for travel on the trams, the Metro, the buses, the funicular, and the Santa Justa Elevator cost 1,640$ for 4 days or 2,320$ for 7 days ($9.50 or $13.45). These discount passes may be purchased from 8am to 8pm daily at CARRIS booths, which are in most Metro and network train stations. You must show a passport to buy a pass.

By Metro   Metro stations are designated by large M signs, and the system has 24 stations. The subway runs daily 6:30am to 1am. A single ticket costs 100$ (60¢) per ride. You can buy 10 tickets at one time for 800$ ($4.65).

By Bus & Tram   They are among the cheapest in Europe. The electric trams, **eléctricos,** make the steep run up to the Bairro Alto and are usually painted a rich Roman gold. You pay a flat fare of 160$ (95¢) on a bus if you buy the ticket from the driver. The transportation system within the city limits is divided into zones ranging from one to five, and your fare depends on how many zones you traverse. Buses and eléctricos run daily 6am to 1am.

By Electric Train   Lisbon is connected to all the towns and villages along the Portuguese Riviera by a smooth-running modern electric train system. You can board at the waterfront **Cais do Sodrè Station** in Lisbon and head up the coast all the way to Cascais. Only one class of seat is offered, and the rides are cheap and generally comfortable. Sintra can't be reached by the electric train. You must go to the **Estação do Rossio,** opening onto Praça Dom Pedro IV, where frequent connections can be made. On the Lisbon-Cascais, Lisbon-Estoril, and Lisbon-Sintra run, the one-way fare is 190$ ($1.10).

By Taxi   The taxis, usually diesel-engine Mercedes, charge a basic fare of 250$ ($1.45) for the first 480 yards. Most fares in the city average 700$ ($4.05), with 20% extra 10pm to 6am. The driver is allowed by law to tack on another 50% if your luggage weighs more than 66 pounds. Portuguese tip about 20% of an already modest fare. Make sure the meter has been activated the moment you step into a cab. For a **Radio Taxi,** call ☎ **01/815-50-61** or 01/793-27-56.

By Car   Car-rental kiosks are at the airport as well as in the city center. They include **Avis,** Avenida Praia da Vitoria 12C (☎ **01/346-26-76**); **Hertz,** Rua Castillo 72, near the Ritz Hotel (☎ **01/381-24-30**); and **Budget,** whose only office is at the airport. *Be warned:* Driving in congested Lisbon is extremely difficult and potentially dangerous; the city has an alarmingly high accident rate and parking is impossible. It's best to wait and rent a car for excursions from the capital.

Fast Facts: Lisbon

American Express This agency is represented by Top Tours, Av. Duque de Loulé 108 (☎ **01/315-58-77**), open Monday to Friday 9:30am to 1pm and 2:30 to 6:30pm.

Baby-sitters Most first-class hotels can provide baby-sitters from lists the concierge keeps. At small places, the sitter is likely to be a relative of the proprietor. Rates are low. You need to request a baby-sitter early in the day.

Business Hours Typically, **shops** are open Monday to Friday 9am to 1pm and 3 to 7pm (although some stay open through lunch), and Saturday 9am to 1pm; some are also open Saturday afternoon. **Banks** are open Monday to Friday 8:30am to 3pm; some offer a foreign-exchange service Monday to Saturday 6 to 11pm.

Currency The Portuguese currency unit is the **escudo,** written **1$00.** Fractions of an escudo (**centavos**) follow the "$"; for example, 100 escudos and 50 centavos is written "100$50." Coins are minted in 50 centavos and 1, 5, 10, 20, 50, 100, and 200 escudos. Notes are printed in 500, 1,000, 2,000, 5,000, and 10,000 escudos. The exchange rate used in this chapter was $1 = 172 escudos and 1 escudo = 5.8¢. Also, 1EUR = 200.4 escudos or £1 = 305.4 escudos.

Dentists & Doctors Contact **Clinica Medical Espanha,** Rua Dom Luis de Navona 32 (☎ **01/796-74-57**), where some dentists speak English. Almost every hotel maintains a list of doctors and dentists who can be called on in emergencies.

Drugstores A central and well-stocked one is **Farmácia Vall,** Avenida Visconde Valmor 60B (☎ **01/797-30-43**). Pharmacies that are closed post a notice indicating the nearest one that's open.

Embassies & Consulates If you lose your passport or have some other pressing problem, you need to get in touch with the **U.S. Embassy,** Avenida das Forças Armadas (Sete Rios), 1600 Lisboa (☎ **01/727-33-00**). Hours are Monday to Friday 8am to 12:30pm and 1:30 to 5pm. If you've lost a passport, the embassy can take photos for you and help you to obtain the proof of citizenship needed to get a replacement. The **Canadian Embassy** is at Avenida da Liberdade 144, 4th floor, 1250 Lisboa (☎ **01/347-48-92**); hours are Monday to Friday 8:30am to 12:30pm and 1:30 to 5pm (in July and August, the embassy closes at 1pm on Fridays). The **British Embassy,** Rua São Bernardo 33, 1200 Lisboa (☎ **01/ 392-40-00**), is open Monday to Friday 10am to 12:30pm and 3 to 4:30pm. **Australians** and **New Zealanders** can refer to the British Embassy (see above). The **Republic of Ireland Embassy,** Rua de Imprensa à Estrêla 1, 1200 Lisboa (☎ **01/392-94-40**), is open Monday to Friday 9:30am to noon and 2:30 to 4:30pm.

Emergencies For any emergency, including one that calls for the police, an ambulance, or a fire, call ☎ **112,** or you can reach the police by calling ☎ **01/ 342-16-23,** an ambulance by calling ☎ **01/853-73-53,** and the fire department by dialing ☎ **01/392-47-00.**

Hospitals In case of a medical emergency, inquire at your hotel or call your embassy and ask the staff there to recommend an English-speaking physician, or try the **British Hospital,** Rua Saraiva de Carvalho 49 (☎ **01/395-50-67**), where the telephone operator, staff, and doctors all speak English.

Internet Access   Travelers can get online at **Cyberbica,** Rua Duques de Bragança 7 (☎ **01/342-1707;** e-mail: Cyberbica@telepac.pt), in the Chiado district, open Monday to Saturday 10:30am to 2am.

Lost Property   Go in person to the **Policia de Estrangeiros,** in the Palacio Foz, Praça dos Restauradores (☎ **01/342-16-23**). The department dealing with lost property is open Monday to Saturday 9am to noon and 2 to 6pm. For items lost on public transportation, inquire at **Seção de Achados da PSP,** Olivais Sul, Praça Cidade Salazar Lote 180 (☎ **01/853-54-03**), open Monday to Friday 9am to 5pm.

Luggage Storage & Lockers   They can be found at the Estação Rossio station. Lockers cost 450$ to 600$ ($2.60 to $3.50) for up to 48 hours.

Photographic Needs   A convenient place to develop film or buy photo-related equipment is **Fotosport,** Centro Comercial Amoreiras, Shop 2149 (☎ **01/383-21-01**). It's open Monday to Friday 10am to 11pm.

Post Office   The general post office is on Praça do Comércio (☎ **01/346-32-31**), open Monday to Friday 8:30am to 6:30pm.

Telephone   The **country code** for Portugal is **351.** The **city code** for Lisbon is **1;** use this code when you're calling from outside Portugal. If you're within Portugal but not in Lisbon, use **01.** If you're calling within Lisbon, simply leave off the code and dial only the regular phone number.

You can make a **local call** in Lisbon in one of the many telephone booths. For most **long-distance calls,** particularly transatlantic calls, go to the central post office (see above). Give an assistant there the number you want, and he or she can make the call, billing you at the end. Some phones are equipped for using calling cards, including American Express and Visa. You can also buy phone cards from the post office in denominations of 50 units for 800$ ($4.65) or 120 units for 1,850$ ($10.75). The phone debit cards are used only in public phones in public places. These debit cards bear one of two different names: T.L.P. cards and CrediFone cards. Both are sold at the cashier's desk of most hotels as well as at post offices.

To make an international call using your calling card, and thereby bypassing many of the add-on charges imposed by your hotel, dial the appropriate access number to reach a North American operator or an English-language voice prompt. For **AT&T,** call ☎ 05/017-12-88; for **MCI,** call ☎ 05/017-12-34; for **Sprint,** call ☎ 05/017-18-77.

WHERE TO STAY
The closest hotel to the airport is the **Radisson SAS Lisboa,** recommended in the section "In the Campo Grande District," below.

IN THE CENTER
Very Expensive

✪ **Da Lapa.** Rua do Pau de Bandeira 4, 1200 Lisboa. ☎ **800/237-1236** in the U.S., 01/395-00-05. Fax 01/395-06-65. www.orient/expresshotels.com. 94 units. A/C MINIBAR TV TEL. 50,000$–68,000$ ($255–$522) double; from 59,000$ ($522) suite. AE, DC, MC, V. Free parking. Bus: 13 or 27.

We never thought we'd see a hotel replace the Ritz as the premier address, but Da Lapa has done it. Its lushly manicured gardens (huge by urban standards) lie close to the Tagus, south of the city center. All but about 20 of the units are in a six-story modern wing, and each balconied room contains reproductions of French and English furniture, classic late 18th-century design, luxurious beds, and marbled bathrooms. The public areas have multicolored ceiling frescoes and patterned marble floors in sometimes startling geometric patterns. Embaixada is one of Lisbon's most elegant restaurants. Facilities include an outdoor pool.

✪ **Hotel Dom Pedro.** Avenida Engenheiro. Duarte Pacheco, 1070 Lisboa. ☎ **01/389-66-00.** Fax 01/389-66-01. E-mail: dp.lisboa@mail.telepac.pt. 263 units. A/C MINIBAR TV TEL. 40,000$–60,000$ ($232–$348) double; 80,000$–500,000$ ($464–$2,900) suite. AE, DC, MC, V. Metro: Rotonda or Rato.

Lisbon's newest hotel opened in the spring of 1998 and quickly showed signs of surpassing its older and more staid rivals. Rated five stars by the Portuguese government, it's set within the very central Amoreiras district, across from one of the city's biggest shopping centers. It rises 21 stories behind a hyper-modern sheathing of reflective glass. The interior is as conservative and opulent as the exterior is futuristic: Bedrooms are richly furnished, usually with heraldic symbols or medallions woven subtly through the fabrics and wallpapers. The more upscale of the hotel's two restaurants is the separately recommended II Gatto Pardo, an Italian restaurant with a leopardskin theme. Its services are supplemented by an upscale bistro, Le Café.

Ritz Four Seasons. Rua Rodrigo Fonseca 88, 1200 Lisboa. ☎ **800/332-3442** in the U.S. and Canada, or 01/383-20-20. Fax 01/383-17-83. E-mail: ritzfourseasons@mail.telepac.pt. 284 units. A/C MINIBARS TV TEL. 50,000$–65,000$ ($290–$377) double; 120,000$–475,000$ ($696–$2,755) suite. AE, DC, MC, V. Free parking. Metro: Rotunda. Bus 2 or 12.

One of the most famous and legendary hotels in Lisbon was built by dictator Antonio Salazar in the late 1950s. In 1998, its management contract was taken over by the well-respected Four Seasons group, who immediately embarked on a sweeping upgrade of the premises. An army of decorators retained the marble floors, but added a pale gray color scheme and an English Victorian theme to the lobby. The supremely comfortable bedrooms, with upgraded carpets, mattresses, and upholsteries, have an English country house look that emphasizes the marquetry and the mahogany. Each of the bedrooms has its own terrace, about half of them overlooking the Edward VII park; each has a marble bathroom with a double basin, hair dryer, and lots of electronic extras. Service, especially among the concierge staff, is superb. Meals are served in an upscale bistro, the Ritz Coffee Shop, and an airy and formal restaurant, Verandah. There's a business center and room service, both open 24 hours a day. Guests receive temporary memberships in a modern health and exercise club within the nearby park.

Expensive

Hotel Lisboa Plaza. Travessa do Salitre 7, Av. da Liberdade, 1250 Lisboa. ☎ **800/448-8355** in the U.S., or 01/346-39-22. Fax 01/347-16-30. E-mail: heritage.hotels@mail.telepac.pt. 118 units. A/C MINIBAR TV TEL. 23,300$–32,900$ ($135.15–$190.80) double; 34,000$–48,000$ ($197.20–$278.40) suite. Rates include buffet breakfast. Children under 12 stay free in parents' room. AE, DC, MC, V. Parking 2,300$ ($13.35) nearby. Metro: Avenida. Bus: 1, 2, 36, or 44.

This family-owned and -operated hotel in the heart of the city is a charmer, with many appealing art nouveau touches, including its facade. When the hotel was overhauled in 1988, a well-known Portuguese designer lent it a contemporary classic style. The guest rooms—boasting well-stocked marble bathrooms (with hair dryers) and in-room VCRs—are nicely decorated and comfortable. Try for a room in the rear, overlooking the botanical gardens. Quinta d'Avenida restaurant specializes in traditional Portuguese cuisine.

Hotel Tivoli. Av. da Liberdade 185, 1298 Lisboa Codex. ☎ **01/319-89-00.** Fax 01/319-89-50. 329 units. A/C MINIBAR TV TEL. 24,000$–42,000$ ($139.20–$243.60) double; from 56,000$ ($324.80) suite. Rates include continental breakfast. AE, DC, MC, V. Parking 1,700$ ($9.85). Metro: Avenida. Bus: 1, 2, 9, or 32.

A much-needed renovation in 1998 made this hotel sparkle once again. The Tivoli boasts extensive facilities, including the only hotel pool in central Lisbon. Best of all, its prices aren't extravagant, considering the amenities. The rooms contain a mix of modern and traditional furniture; the largest and best rooms face the front, although those in the rear are quieter. Some are better appointed and more spacious than others. The wood-paneled O Zodíaco restaurant serves lunch and dinner buffets. The top-floor O Terraço offers a view of Lisbon as well as à la carte meals. Facilities include access to the Tivoli Club, surrounded by a lovely garden, with a pool that can be heated when necessary, a tennis court, and a solarium.

✪ **Janelas Verdes Inn.** Rua das Janelas Verdes 47, 1200 Lisboa. ☎ **01/396-81-43.** Fax 01/396-81-44. 17 units. A/C TV TEL. 24,200$–35,200$ ($140.35–$204.15) double. Rates include continental breakfast. AE, DC, MC, V. Bus: 27, 40, 49, or 60.

Owned by the proprietors of the Hotel Lisboa Plaza (see above), this aristocratic 18th-century mansion was the home of Portuguese novelist Eça de Queiros. Near the Museum of Ancient Art, its large, luxurious, and marvelously restored rooms have abundant closet space and generous tile bathrooms. The lounges are evocative of a comfortable bourgeois house in turn-of-the-century Lisbon.

Lisboa Sheraton Hotel & Towers. Rua Latino Coelho 1, 1097 Lisboa. ☎ **800/325-3535** in the U.S., or 01/312-00-00. Fax 01/354-71-64. E-mail: sherlis@ittsheraton.com. 381 units. A/C MINIBAR TV TEL. 26,000$–44,000$ ($150.80–$255.20) double; from 80,000$ ($464) suite. AE, DC, MC, V. Parking 1,900$ ($11). Bus: 1, 2, 9, or 32.

This 25-floor skyscraper is at a traffic-clogged intersection a bit removed from the center, a few blocks north of Praça Marquês de Pombal. The guest rooms don't match the grandeur of the public rooms, but they're generally spacious, and each was renovated in the late '90s. The understated decor includes thick wool carpeting, print fabrics, and traditional, if a bit chunky, wood furniture. Marble bathrooms are a highlight, and the most desirable rooms are in the tower, opening onto views of the longest bridge in Europe. The hotel's restaurants include the glamourous Alfama Grill. A rooftop bar features live music nightly, and there's an outdoor pool and a health club.

Moderate
Britania. Rua Rodrigues Sampaio 17, 1150 Lisboa. ☎ **01/315-50-16.** Fax 01/315-50-21. E-mail: britaniahotel@mail.telepac.pt. 30 units. A/C MINIBAR TV TEL. 21,300$–27,300$ ($123.55–$158.35) double. Rates include buffet breakfast. AE, DC, MC, V. Metro: Avenida. Bus: 1, 2, 11, 21, 32, or 36.

In its own way, the Britania is one of Lisbon's most traditional and refreshingly con-servative hotels, designed by well-known Portuguese architect Cassiano Branco in 1944. About a block from Avenida da Liberdade, it boasts a distinguished and loyal clientele and an old-fashioned, almost courtly, staff. In 1995 the hotel was refurbished, making the pastel-colored rooms on all five of its floors more comfortable. Each bed-room has a hair dryer and a safety deposit box.

Dom Carlos. Av. Duque de Loulé 121, 1050 Lisboa. ☎ **01/353-97-69.** Fax 01/352-07-28. 76 units. A/C MINIBAR TV TEL. 14,700$–17,500$ ($85.25–$101.50) double; 16,000$–18,000$ ($92.80–$104.40) triple. Rates include buffet breakfast. AE, DC, MC, V. Metro: Rotunda. Bus: 36, 44, 45, 83, or 90.

Just off Praça Marquê de Pombal, the Dom Carlos faces its own triangular park dedi-cated to the partially blind Camilo Castelo Branco, a 19th-century "eternity poet."

The curvy all-glass facade creates an outdoorsy feel reinforced by the park's green trees and beds of orange and red canna. The hotel was completely renovated in early 1995. The guest rooms are paneled in reddish Portuguese wood. In a neighborhood of similar competitors, this is the best three-star hotel of the lot, with more spacious bedrooms and a higher standard of maintenance.

Príncipe Real. Rua de Alegria 53, 1200 Lisboa. ☎ **800/223-1356** or 01/346-01-16. Fax 01/342-21-04. 24 units. A/C MINIBAR TV TEL. 17,200$–19,900$ ($99.75–$115.40) double. Rates include buffet breakfast. AE, DC, MC, V. Metro: Rotunda or Avenida. Bus: 2.

This modern five-story hotel is reached after a long, steep climb from Avenida da Liberdade. Selectivity and care are apparent in the individualized guest rooms, which are small but tasteful. The beds, reproductions of fine antiques, have excellent mattresses. The hotel's restaurant opens onto panoramic views of Lisbon and serves excellent Portuguese cuisine. There's also a bar on the premises.

✪ **York House.** Rua das Janelas Verdes 32, 1200 Lisboa. ☎ **01/396-24-35.** Fax 01/397-27-93. E-mail: yorkhouse@mail.telepac.pt. 34 units. TV TEL. 22,000$–32,200$ ($127.60–$186.75) double. Rates include buffet breakfast. AE, DC, MC, V. Bus: 27, 40, 49, 54, or 60.

York House mixes the color of the past with the conveniences of the present. Once a 16th-century convent, it's located outside the center of traffic-filled Lisbon, almost opposite the National Art Gallery. York House was tastefully furnished by one of the most distinguished Lisbon designers. All guest rooms, which come in various sizes, have antique beds, good mattresses, and 18th- and 19th-century bric-a-brac. Book well in advance.

Inexpensive

Casa de São Mamede. Rua da Escola Politécnica 159, 1200 Lisboa. ☎ **01/396-31-66.** Fax 01/395-1896. 28 units. TEL. 12,000$–15,000$ ($69.60–$87) double. Rates include continental breakfast. No credit cards. Bus: 9 or 49. Metro: Rato.

Constructed in the 1800s as a villa for the count of Coruche, this building, behind the Botanical Gardens, was transformed into a hotel in 1945. The Marquês family manages the hotel, about midway between Avenida da Liberdade and the Amoreiras shopping center. Although renovated, the rooms retain a somewhat frayed charm, accented by the original high ceilings. Breakfast is served in a sunny second-floor dining room decorated with antique yellow-and-blue tiles.

Jorge V Hotel. Rua Mouzinho da Silveira 3, 1200 Lisboa. ☎ **01/356-25-25.** Fax 01/315-03-19. E-mail: info@hoteljorgeV.com. 49 units. A/C TV TEL. 12,000$–18,000$ ($69.60–$104.40) double; 15,000$–24,000$ ($87–$139.20) suite. Rates include continental breakfast. AE, DC, MC, V. Metro: Avenida or Rotunda.

The Jorge V, a neat little hotel with a 1960s design, is an inexpensive place to stay in a choice location a block off noisy Avenida da Liberdade. Its facade contains rows of balconies, roomy enough for guests to have breakfast or afternoon refreshments. A tiny elevator takes guests to a variety of aging rooms, which are comfortable but compact; all have small tile bathrooms. There's no on-site restaurant, but the in-house bar serves sandwiches and light snacks.

Residência Nazareth. Av. António Augusto de Aguiar 25, 1000 Lisboa. ☎ **01/354-20-16.** Fax 01/356-08-36. 32 units. A/C MINIBAR TV TEL. 8,500$–15,000$ ($49.30–$87) double. Rates include continental breakfast. AE, DC, MC, V. Metro: São Sebastião. Bus: 31, 41, or 46.

You'll recognize this place by its dusty-pink facade and windows, some surrounded with decorative arches raised in low relief. Take an elevator to the fourth-floor landing, where, far from the beauticians, hair stylists, and offices below, there's a medieval vaulting you might find in a romanticized Portuguese fortress. The old-looking plaster and the wrought-iron lanterns are obvious facsimiles. Even the spacious bar/TV lounge looks like a vaulted cellar. Some guest rooms, which are very basic, contain platforms, requiring guests to step up or down to the bathroom or to the comfortable bed. A little refurbishing is in order here.

IN THE GRAÇA DISTRICT
Moderate
✪ **Hotel Albergaria da Senhora do Monte.** Calçada do Monte 39, 1100 Lisboa. ☎ **01/886-60-02.** Fax 01/887-77-83. 28 units. A/C TV TEL. 19,000$–28,000$ ($110.20–$162.40) double; 28,000$–30,000$ ($162.40–$174) suite. Rates include continental breakfast. AE, DC, MC, V. Metro: Socorro. Tram: 28. Bus: 12, 17, or 35.

This little hilltop hotel, last renovated in 1995, has a unique character. It's perched near a belvedere (a type of gazebo), the Miradouro Senhora do Monte, with a memorable nighttime view of the city, St. George's Castle, and the Tagus. The intimate living room features tufted sofas and oversized tables and lamps. Multilevel corridors lead to the excellent guest rooms, all with verandas. The rooms reveal a decorator's touch, especially the gilt-edged door panels, grass-cloth walls, and tile bathrooms with bronze fixtures. There's a panoramic bar on site, but other than breakfast, no meals are served.

IN THE CAMPO GRANDE DISTRICT
Expensive
Radisson SAS Lisboa. Avenida Marechal Craveiro Lopes, 1700 Lisbon. ☎ **800/333-3333** in the U.S., or 01/759-9639. Fax 01/758-6949. 237 units. A/C MINIBAR TV TEL. 35,000$–40,000$ ($203–$232) double; from 43,000$ ($249.40) suite. AE, DC, MC, V. Parking 1,000$ ($5.80). Metro: Campo Grande

One of the city's most visible hotels—formerly a Holiday Inn Crowne Plaza—was taken over by the Radisson/SAS group in 1996. It rises 12 floors above the Campo Grande residential district, 2 miles north of Rossio Square. Sheathed in a soft pink shade of stone, it has a stylish but conservative lobby marked by hundreds of slabs of gray-and-white marble, and bedrooms whose predominant color is a dusty shade of pink. Each has a hair dryer, big windows, and comfortable furnishings running toward bland international themes that appeal to a clientele of mostly business travelers. The in-house restaurant, Bordal Pinheiro, serves international cuisine, and there's also a health club.

WHERE TO DINE
IN THE CENTER
Very Expensive
Casa da Comida. Travessa de Amoireiras 1. ☎ **01/388-53-76.** Reservations required. Main courses 3,500$–8,000$ ($20.30–$46.40). AE, DC, MC, V. Mon–Fri 1–3pm; Mon–Sat 8pm–midnight. Metro: Rato. PORTUGUESE/FRENCH.

Casa da Comida, off Rua Alexandre Herculano, is touted by local gourmets as having some of the finest food in Lisbon. The dining room is handsomely decorated, the bar done in period style, and the walled garden charming. Specialties include roast kid with herbs, a medley of shellfish Casa da Comida, and bass Alentejo style (that is, seasoned with cilantro), and house-style codfish with onions and potatoes. One speciality is stewed pheasant that has been marinated in port; the recipe for this dish dates from the Middle Ages. An excellent selection of wines is available. The food is often more imaginative here than at some of the other top-rated choices.

✪ **Embaixada.** In the Da Lapa, Rua do Pau de Bandeira 4. ☎ **01/395-00-05.** Reservations recommended. Main courses 2,700$–8,500$ ($15.65–$49.30); set-price lunch buffet 4,750$ ($27.55) per person; *menu dégustation* 7,500$ ($43.50). AE, DC, MC, V. Daily noon–3pm and 7:30–10:30pm. Bus: 13 or 27. INTERNATIONAL/PORTUGUESE.

This dignified dining room, with flowered curtains and a view of one of the most lavish gardens in this exclusive neighborhood, is a favorite with diplomats from the foreign embassies and consulates nearby. Especially popular is the set-price lunch buffet with an array of international choices. The à la carte menu available at lunch and dinner could include, depending on the season, fresh salmon fried with sage, lamb chops with mint sauce, a succulent version of a traditional *feijoada* (casserole of white beans and meats), and duck breast with pears. Although you might not run to phone *Gourmet* magazine, you'll be amply rewarded with deluxe ingredients perfectly handled by the staff.

Restaurante Tavares. Rua da Misericórdia 37. ☎ **01/342-11-12.** Reservations required. Main courses 2,800$–8,000$ ($16.25–$46.40). AE, DC, MC, V. Mon–Fri 12:30–3pm and 8–10:30pm; Sun 8–10:30pm. Bus: 15. PORTUGUESE/CONTINENTAL.

Lisbon's oldest restaurant, Tavares is a nostalgic favorite, still serving competently prepared food with flawless service. It may be one of the capital's more glittering settings, but it's beginning to show a little wear. Your meal may begin with crêpes de marisco prepared with shellfish. For a main-course, there might be sole in champagne, stuffed crab Tavares style, or tournedos Grand Duc. Many continental dishes are on the menu, including the classic scallops of veal viennoise. The restaurant nearly always serves such basic Portuguese dishes as sardines and salted codfish.

Expensive

✪ **António Clara.** Av. da República 38. ☎ **01/799-42-80.** Reservations required. Main courses 2,800$–3,500$ ($16.25–$20.30). AE, DC, MC, V. Mon–Sat noon–3pm and 7–11pm. Metro: Entre Campos. PORTUGUESE/INTERNATIONAL.

This turn-of-the-century art nouveau villa is the former home of one of Portugal's most revered architects. Although it is no longer as chic and glamorous as it was in the early '90s, it still offers first-rate cuisine in romantic surroundings. It was built in 1890 by Miguel Ventura Terra (1866–1918), whose photograph hangs amid polished antiques and gilded mirrors. Meals include specialties such as smoked swordfish, paella for two, pork with prunes and prawns, codfish Margarida da Praça, and tournedos of beef with asparagus. These dishes may be familiar, but only the highest-quality ingredients go into them.

Bachus. Largo da Trindade 8–9. ☎ **01/342-28-28.** Reservations recommended. Main courses 2,680$–8,000$ ($15.55–$46.40). AE, DC, MC, V. Mon–Fri noon–midnight; Sat 7pm–1am. Bus: 58. INTERNATIONAL.

Amusing murals cover the wood-paneled facade of this restaurant; inside, the decor is elaborate and sophisticated. The ambience is an eclectic mix of a Russian Tsarist salon, a turn-of-the-century English club, and a stylized Manhattan bistro. Specialties change frequently, depending on market availability. Full meals might include mixed grill Bachus, chateaubriand with béarnaise sauce, mountain goat, beef Stroganoff, shrimp Bachus, or other daily specials. The chef has a conservative approach and rarely gets any complaints. The wine list is extensive.

Clara. Campo dos Mártires da Pátria 49. ☎ **01/885-30-53.** Reservations required. Main courses 2,900$–3,500$ ($16.80–$20.30). AE, DC, MC, V. Mon–Fri noon–3:30pm and 7pm–midnight. Closed Aug 1–15. Metro: Avenida. PORTUGUESE/INTERNATIONAL.

On a hillside amid decaying villas and city squares, this green tile house contains an elegant restaurant. During lunch, you might prefer to sit near the garden terrace's plants and fountain. At night, an indoor seat—perhaps near the large marble fireplace—is more appealing. A piano plays softly through dinner. Specialties include tournedos Clara, stuffed rabbit with red-wine sauce, sea bass cooked in wine, filet of sole with orange, and pheasant with grapes. Shellfish dishes are often lethal in price, ranging from 5,600$ ($32.50) for a shrimp platter to 9,000$ ($52.20) for a lobster. Prices are based on daily market value. As in many top Lisbon restaurants, these dishes aren't creative or innovative, but they're often prepared flawlessly. The wine list is very selective, containing mostly Portuguese wines from small scale and prestigious wineries.

Escorial. Rua das Portas de Santo Antão 47. ☎ **01/346-44-29.** Reservations recommended. Main courses 2,300$–9,000$ ($13.35–$52.20). AE, DC, MC, V. Daily noon–4pm and 7pm–midnight. Metro: Rossio. INTERNATIONAL.

Near Praça dos Restauradores, this Spanish-owned place offers classic Spanish dishes in an inviting rosewood-paneled dining room. A menu is printed in English (always look for the course of the day). For an appetizer, you might enjoy Portuguese oysters or squid on a skewer. The chef's specialties are barbecued baby goat, beef Stroganoff, and partridge casserole. In spite of its neighborhood, which grows increasingly sleazy at night, Escorial has stood the test of time and remains an enduring, although not incredibly innovative, favorite.

✪ **Gambrinus.** Rua das Portas de Santo Antão 25. ☎ **01/342-14-66.** Reservations required. Main courses 3,000$–6,500$ ($17.40–$37.70). AE, MC, V. Daily noon–2am. Metro: Rossio. SEAFOOD.

One of Lisbon's premier restaurants since 1936, Gambrinus is the finest choice for fish and shellfish. It's in the congested heart of the city, off the Rossio on a little square behind the National Theater. Have your meal in the severely macho dining room with leather chairs under a cathedral-beamed ceiling, or select a little table beside a fireplace on the raised end of the room. Gambrinus offers a diversified à la carte menu accompanied by specialties of the day. Specials might include conch and shellfish Thermidor or sea bass minhota. Crustaceans can go for as high as 20,000$ ($116), so check the market price before ordering. If you don't fancy fish and like your dishes spicy *hot,* ask for chicken piri-piri.

Il Gatto Pardo. in the Hotel Dom Pedro, Avenida Eng. Duarte Pacheco. ☎ **01/389-6600.** Reservations recommended. Main courses 2,200$–3,200$ ($12.75–$18.55); set-price menus 6,000$–8,000$ ($34.80–$46.40). AE, DC, MC, V. Daily 12:30–3:30pm and 8–11pm. Metro: Rotonda or Rato. ITALIAN.

The most appealing and stylish Italian restaurant in Lisbon is worlds apart from the pasta and pizza joints that until now have passed for Italian restaurants within the Portuguese capital. Set on the third floor of the previously recommended hotel (see "Where to Stay," above), it has lots of exposed hardwoods, bas-relief sculptures, and a leopardskin theme that's defined by the boldly patterned carpets. Virtually everything was imported from Italy, including many members of the staff, who prepare ultra-fresh versions of pasta with clams; risotto with forest mushrooms; veal cutlets Milanese-style; sea wolf coated in breadcrumbs; grilled swordfish steak in parsley sauce; roasted veal cooked in heady Barolo wine; and *saltimbocca* (veal with ham). When the weather is nice, an outdoor terrace that's ringed with potted shrubs and vines provides sweeping views over the surrounding neighborhood.

Sua Excelência. Rua do Conde 34. ☎ **01/390-36-14.** Reservations required. Main courses 2,900$–3,500$ ($16.80–$20.30). AE, DC, MC, V. Mon–Tues and Thurs–Fri 1–3pm; Thurs–Tues 8–10:30pm. Closed Sept. Bus: 27 or 49. PORTUGUESE.

Sua Excelência is the creation of Francisco Queiroz, who has created an atmosphere somewhat like that of a fashionable drawing room, with colorful tables in an intimate Portuguese provincial decor. Some dishes are uncommon for Portugal, including Angolan chicken cooked in palm oil with a medley of vegetables. Specialties include prawns piri-piri (not unreasonably hot); *lulas a moda da casa* (squid stewed in white wine, crème fraîche, and cognac); what Queiroz proclaims the "best smoked swordfish in Portugal"; and clams cooked at least five ways. One unusual specialty is "little jacks," a small fish eaten whole, served with a well-flavored "paste" made from 2-day-old bread. The restaurant is just a block up the hill from the entrance to the National Art Gallery.

Moderate

✪ **A Gôndola.** Av. de Berna 64. ☎ **01/797-04-26.** Reservations required. Main courses 3,000$–4,000$ ($17.40–$23.20). AE, DC, MC, V. Mon–Fri 12:30–3pm and 7:30–10pm; Sat 12:30–3pm. Metro: Praça de Espanha. Bus: 16 or 26. ITALIAN/PORTUGUESE.

Although the decor isn't inspired, the food more than makes up for it. The cooking here is old-fashioned and robust Italian. A full dinner is quite a buy considering what you get. A first-course selection might be Chaves ham with melon and figs, followed by filet of sole meunière or grilled sardines with pimientos. This is followed by yet another course, ravioli or cannelloni Roman style, or veal cutlet Milanese. This feast is topped off by fruit or dessert. A Gôndola has both indoor seating and alfresco meals in the courtyard.

Bonjardim. Travessa de Santo Antão 10–12. ☎ **01/342-74-24.** Main courses 1,500$–3,000$ ($6–$16). AE, DC, MC, V. Daily noon–11:30pm. Metro: Restauradores. PORTUGUESE.

Owner-manager Henrique Castanheira caters mostly to families, offering wholesome meals at good prices. The restaurant, one of the most popular in town, is just east of Avenida da Liberdade near the grimy Praça dos Restauradores. In the main restaurant, the second-floor air-conditioned dining room is designed in rustic Portuguese style, with a beamed ceiling and a tile mural depicting farm creatures. The street-floor dining room, with an adjoining bar, has walls of decorative tiles. During your dinner, the aroma of chickens roasting to a golden brown on the charcoal spit can easily persuade you to try one. An order of this house specialty, called *frango no espeto,* is adequate for two, with a side dish of French fries. The cook also bakes hake in the Portuguese style; an alternative dish is pork fried with clams.

✪ **Conventual.** Praça das Flores 45. ☎ **01/390-91-96.** Reservations required. Main courses 2,300$–5,000$ ($13.35–$29); set-price menus 5,500$–6,000$ ($31.90–$34.80). AE, DC, MC, V. Mon–Fri 12:30–3:30pm and 7:30–11:00pm; Sat 7:30–11:30pm. Metro: Avenida. Bus: 100. PORTUGUESE.

In many ways this is one of our favorite Lisbon restaurants, because of the taste and sensitivity of its gracious owner, Dina Marquês. Many of its admirers (including the prime minister of Portugal) rank it as the best place to dine in Lisbon today, even though its prices are about a quarter less than at many of its competitors. Inside, you're treated to a display of old panels from baroque churches, religious statues, and bric-a-brac from Mrs. Marquês's private collection. The owner invented a few of the delectably flavored recipes, including creamy coriander soup, stewed partridge in port, duck in champagne sauce, grilled monkfish in herb-flavored cream sauce, and dried cod with olive oil and coriander.

Restaurant 33. Rua Alexandre Herculano 33A. ☎ **01/354-60-79.** Reservations recommended. Main courses 2,700$–3,800$ ($15.65–$22.05); set-price menu 5,000$ ($29). AE, DC, MC, V. Mon–Fri 12:30–3pm; Mon–Sat 8–10pm. Metro: Rotunda. Tram: 20 or 25. Bus: 6 or 9. PORTUGUESE/INTERNATIONAL.

Restaurant 33 is a treasure. Decorated like an English hunting lodge, it lies near many recommended hotels, including the Ritz. Specialties include shellfish rice served in a crab shell, smoked salmon or stuffed Dover sole filets, and pepper steak. Large portions, tasty stews, and strong-flavored ingredients characterize the food. You can order a glass of port in the small bar and enjoy the pianist who performs during dinner.

Sancho. Travessa da Glória 14. ☎ **01/346-97-80.** Reservations recommended. Main courses 1,300$–2,800$ ($7.55–$16.25). AE, MC, V. Mon–Sat noon–3pm and 7–10:30pm. Metro: Avenida. PORTUGUESE/INTERNATIONAL.

Sancho is a cozy rustic-style restaurant just off Avenida da Liberdade, close to Praça dos Restauradores. The decor is classic Iberian, with a beamed ceiling, a fireplace, leather-and-wood chairs, and stuccoed walls. Fish gratinée soup is a traditional way to begin. Shellfish, always expensive, is the specialty. Main dishes may be the chef's special hake, grilled veal, or pan-broiled Portuguese steak. If your palate is fireproof, order *churrasco de cabrito* (goat) au piri-piri. For dessert, try the crêpes Suzette or chocolate mousse. This is a long-time local favorite, and the recipes never change.

Inexpensive

António Ribeiro. Rua Tomás Ribiero 63. ☎ **01/353-87-80.** Main courses 900$–1,100$ ($5.20–$6.40). AE, DC, MC, V. Daily noon–4pm and 7–10:30pm. Metro: Picoas. Bus: 55. PORTUGUESE/INTERNATIONAL.

This place was created for Portuguese businesspeople looking for a relaxing ambience and good food. Just a bit away from the din of central traffic, it's a refreshing oasis with blue-and-white glazed earthenware tiles and a freeform blue ceiling. Fish dishes are garnished with vegetables, and the filets of baked sole are served with tomato sauce. Polvo à lagareira (octopus with broiled potatoes, olive oil, and garlic) is a specialty. From among the fowl and meat dishes, try the *frango na prata* (chicken broiled in foil with potatoes) or pork with clams Alentejana style. The owner-manager recommends his *açorda de marisco*, a stewlike breaded shellfish-and-egg dish that's a treat.

Cervejaria Brilhante. Rua das Portas de Santo Antão 105. ☎ **01/346-14-07.** Main courses 1,300$–3,500$ ($7.55–$20.30); tourist menu 1,850$ ($10.75). AE, DC, MC, V. Daily noon–midnight. Metro: Rossio. Bus: 1, 2, 36, 44, or 45. SEAFOOD.

Lisboans from every walk of life stop here for a beer and *mariscos* (seafood). The tavern is decorated with stone arches, wood-paneled walls, and pictorial tiles of sea life. The front window is packed with an appetizing array of king crabs, oysters, lobsters, baby clams, shrimp, and even barnacles. Prices change every day, depending on the market; you pay by the kilo. This is hearty, robust eating. It's a challenge to attract a waiter's attention.

Cervejaria Ribadoura. Av. da Liberdade 155. ☎ **01/354-94-11.** Main courses 1,000$–3,500$ ($6–$20). AE, DC, MC, V. Daily 9am–2am. Metro: Avenida. Bus: 1, 2, 44, or 45. SEAFOOD.

Cervejaria Ribadoura is one of central Lisbon's typical shellfish-and-beer places, midway along the major boulevard at the corner of Rua do Salitre. The decor is simple; the emphasis is all on fish. The classic *bacalhau* (codfish) a Bras is a good choice; for a lighter bite, try the shrimp omelet. Many diners follow fish with a meat dish. Beware the sautéed pork cutlets with piri-piri, made with red-hot peppers from Angola—only those who've been trained on the most mouth-wilting Indian curries should order this blazing dish.

Cervejaria Trindade. Rua Nova de Trindade 20C. ☎ **01/342-35-06.** Main courses 1,400$–3,200$ ($8.10–$18.55). AE, DC, MC, V. Daily 10am–1:30am. Metro: Rossio. Tram: 24. Bus: 15, 20, or 100. PORTUGUESE.

Cervejaria Trindade is a German beer hall/Portuguese tavern. In operation since 1836, it's the oldest tavern in Lisbon, built on the site of the 13th-century Convento dos Frades Tinos, destroyed in the 1755 earthquake. You can order tasty little steaks and heaps of crisp French-fried potatoes. Many Portuguese prefer *bife na frigideira*—steak with mustard sauce and a fried egg, served in a clay frying pan. The tavern features shellfish, which come from private fish ponds, and the house specialties are *ameijoas* (clams) à Trindade and giant prawns.

Pastelaria Sala de Cha Versailles. Av. da República 15A. ☎ **01/354-63-40.** Sandwiches 265$ ($1.55); pastries 130$–160$ (75¢–95¢); plats du jour 1,150$–2,400$ ($7–$14). No credit cards. Daily 7:30am–10pm. Métro: Salenña. SANDWICHES/PASTRIES.

Lisbon's most famous teahouse, this place has been declared part of the "national patrimony." In older days, the specialty was Licungo, Mozambique's famed black tea; you can still order it, but nowadays many drinkers have switched to English brands. The Portuguese claim they (not the English) introduced the custom of tea drinking to the English court, after Catherine of Bragança married Charles II in 1662. The decor is rich, with chandeliers, gilt mirrors, stained-glass windows, tall stucco ceilings, and black-and-white-marble floors. You can also order milk shakes, mineral water, and fresh orange juice, along with beer and liquor. Snacks come in many varieties, including codfish balls and toasted ham-and-cheese sandwiches. They now serve a limited choice of Portuguese dishes that are simple but wholesome.

IN THE CHIADO DISTRICT

West of Baixa, and traversed by Rua Garrett, this is Lisbon's main shopping area.

Expensive

✪ **Tágide.** Largo da Académia Nacional de Belas Artes 18–20. ☎ **01/342-07-20.** Reservations required. Main courses 3,900$–4,200$ ($22.60–$24.35). AE, DC, MC, V. Mon–Fri 12:30–2:30pm and 7–10pm. Metro: Alvaro. Tram: 20. Bus: 15. PORTUGUESE/INTERNATIONAL.

Tágide has had an interesting past—once the townhouse of a diplomat, then a major nightclub, and now one of Lisbon's leading restaurants. It's up from the docks, atop a steep hill overlooking the old part of Lisbon and the Tagus. The Louis XIV–style dining room's windows look down on the ships moored in the port. Specialties include suprême of halibut with coriander, pork with clams and coriander, and grilled baby goat with herbs. Regulars from the world of Lisbon finance and government, including Portugal's president, are given preferential seating and treatment.

Inexpensive

A Brasileira. Rua Garrett 120. ☎ **01/346-95-41.** Sandwiches 300$–400$ ($1.75–$2.30); pastries 150$–180$ (85¢–$1.05); meals in restaurant 1,500$–5,000$ ($8.70–$29). AE, MC, V (restaurant only). Daily 7:30am–2pm. Metro: Rossio. SANDWICHES/PASTRIES.

One of Lisbon's oldest coffeehouses, A Brasileira boasts an art nouveau facade and was once a gathering place of Lisbon literati. Guests sit at small tables on chairs made of tooled leather, amid mirrored walls and marble pilasters. A statue of the great Portuguese poet Fernando Pessoa sits on a chair side by side with the customers. The restaurant here serves basic fare such as omelets, steaks, and fish. Note that you'll pay more for sandwiches and pastries in the restaurant than in the coffee bar.

IN THE ALCÂNTARA

This area is South of Bairro Alto along the Rio Tejo.

Expensive

Café Alcântara. Rua Maria Luisa Holstein 15. ☎ **01/363-71-76.** Reservations recommended. Main courses 2,600$–7,500$ ($15.10–$43.50). AE, DC, MC, V. Daily 8pm–1am. Bus: 57. FRENCH/PORTUGUESE.

One of Lisbon's most fun and hip dining-and-entertainment complexes attracts an international crowd. A 600-year-old warehouse for storing timber, the vast building has forest-green and bordeaux walls, exposed marble, ceiling fans, burgeoning plants, and simple wooden tables and chairs. Menu items include filet of salmon with lemon sauce, fresh fish, steak tartare, three different preparations of duck, and a Portuguese platter of the day, which might include fried *bacalhau* (codfish) or a hearty *feijoada*, a bean-and-meat stew. The Disco Alcântara adjoins.

SEEING THE SIGHTS IN LISBON
SIGHTSEEING SUGGESTIONS FOR FIRST-TIME VISITORS

If You Have 1 Day   This is just enough time to take a walking tour of the **Alfama,** Lisbon's most interesting district. Visit the 12th-century **Sé** (cathedral) and take in a view of the city and the river Tagus from the **Santa Luzia Belvedere.** Climb up to the **Castelo São Jorge (St. George's Castle).** Then take a taxi or bus to **Belém** to see the **Mosteiro dos Jerónimos (Jerónimos Monastery)** and the **Torre de Belém.** While at Belém, explore the **Museu Nacional dos Coches (National Coach Museum).** End your day at a **fado café.**

If You Have 2 Days   On day 2, head for **Sintra,** the single most visited sight in the environs—Byron called it "glorious Eden." You can spend the day here, exploring the castle and other palaces in the panoramic area. Try to visit at least the **Palácio Nacional de Sintra** and the **Palácio Nacional da Pena.** Return to Lisbon for a night at a **fado café.**

If You Have 3 Days   Spend the morning of day 3 at the **Museu Calouste Gulbenkian,** one of Europe's artistic treasure troves. Have lunch at a *típico* restaurant in the Bairro Alto. In the afternoon, see the **Museu Nacional de Art Antiga (National Museum of Ancient Art).** At the day's end, wander through **Parque Eduardo VII.**

If You Have 4 Days   On day 4, take an excursion from Lisbon (perhaps an organized tour) to visit the fishing village of **Nazaré** and the walled city of **Óbidos.** Those interested in Roman Catholic sights might also want to go to the shrine at **Fátima,** although it would be hectic to see it on the same day.

✪ THE ALFAMA

Old Lisbon lives on in the Alfama district. The wall built by the Visigoths and incorporated into some of the houses is testimony to its ancient past. The Alfama was the Saracen sector for centuries before its conquest by the Christians. Some of the buildings survived the devastating 1755 earthquake, and the Alfama has retained much of its original charm—narrow cobblestoned streets, cages of canaries chirping in the afternoon sun, strings of garlic and pepper inviting you inside *típico* taverns, old street markets, and charming balconies.

One of the best views is from the **Largo das Portas do Sol,** near the Museum of Decorative Art. It's a balcony opening onto the sea, overlooking the houses as they sweep down to the Tagus. One of the oldest churches is **Santo Estevão (St. Stephen),** at Largo de Santo Estevão. It was first built in the 13th century; the present marble structure dates from the 18th. Also of medieval origin is the **Church of São Miguel (St. Michael),** at Largo de São Miguel, deep in the Alfama on a palm tree–shaded square. **Rua da Judiaria (Street of the Jews)** is another reminder of the past. It was settled largely by Jewish refugees fleeing Spain's Inquisition.

✪ **Castelo São Jorge (St. George's Castle).** Rua Costa do Castelo. ☎ **01/887-17-22.** Free admission. Daily 10am–6pm. Bus: 37.

It's believed that this hilltop was used as a fortress to guard the Tagus and its settlement below even before the arrival of the Romans. Beginning in the 5th century A.D.,

---

Traveler's Tip

If your time is limited, explore the National Coach Museum, the Jerónimos Monastery, and the Alfama with St. George's Castle. At least two art museums merit attention: the Museu Nacional de Art Antiga and the Museu Calouste Gulbenkian.

The Alfama

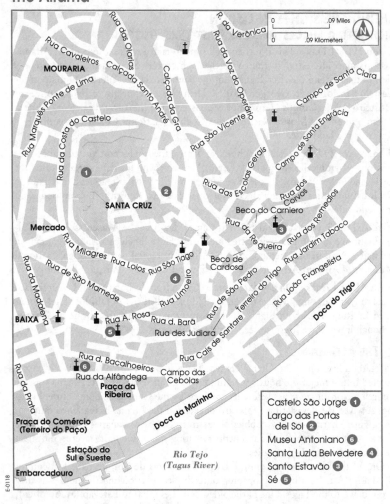

MOURARIA

Rua Cavaleiros
Rua das Olarias
Calçada Santo André
Calçada da Gra
R. da Verônica
Rua da Voz do Operário
Rua Marquês Ponte de Lima
Rua da Costa do Castelo
Calçada da Gra
Rua São Vicente
Campo de Santa Clara

SANTA CRUZ

Mercado
Rua Milagres
Rua de São Mamede
Rua Loios
Rua São Tiago
Rua das Escolas Gerais
Campo de Santa Engrácia
Rua dos Corvos
Beco do Carniero
Rua da Regueira
Rua dos Remedios
Rua Jardim Tabaco

BAIXA
Rua da Madalena
Rua A. Rosa
Rua d. Barã
Beco de Cardosa
Rua de São Pedro
Rua Limoeiro
Terreiro do Trigo
Rua João Evangelista
Doca do Trigo

Rua des Judiara
Rua Cais de Santare
Rua d. Bacalhoeiros
Rua da Alfândega
Praça da Ribeira
Campo das Cebolas

Rua da Prata
**Praça do Comércio
(Terreiro do Paço)**
Estação do Sul e Sueste
Embarcadouro
Doca da Marinha
*Rio Tejo
(Tagus River)*

Castelo São Jorge	1
Largo das Portas del Sol	2
Museu Antoniano	6
Santa Luzia Belvedere	4
Santo Estavão	3
Sé	5

F-0118

the site was a Visigothic fortification; it fell in the early 8th century to the Saracens. Many of the walls still standing were erected during the centuries of Moorish domination, which lasted until 1147, when Afonso Henríques, the country's first king, chased them out and extended his kingdom south. Even before Lisbon was made the capital of the newly emerging nation, the site was used as a royal palace. For the finest view of the Tagus and the Alfama, walk the esplanades and climb the ramparts of the old castle, named in commemoration of an Anglo-Portuguese pact dating from as early as 1371. On the grounds you can stroll through a setting of olive, pine, and cork trees, inhabited by swans and rare white peacocks.

Cathedral São Largo da Sé. ☎ **01/86-67-52.** Cathedral, free; cloister, 100$ (60¢). Treasury Museum, 400$ ($2.30) adults, 200$ ($1.15) students and senior citizens, children under 13 free. Cathedral and cloister daily 9am–noon and 2–6pm; Treasury Museum Mon–Sat 10am–5pm. Tram: 28 (Graça). Bus: 37.

Characterized by twin towers flanking its entrance, the Sé represents an architectural wedding of Romanesque and Gothic. The facade is severe enough to resemble a medieval fortress. When the city was captured early in the 12th century by Christian Crusaders, led by Portugal's first king, Afonso Henríques, the Sé became the first church in Lisbon. It was damaged in the earthquakes of 1344 and 1755.

Inside the rough exterior are many treasures, including the font where St. Anthony of Padua is said to have been christened in 1195. The cloister, built in the 14th century by King Dinis, is of Gothic construction, with garlands, a Romanesque wrought-iron grille, and tombs with inscription stones. In the sacristy, or Treasury Museum, are marbles, relics, valuable images, and pieces of ecclesiastical treasure from the 15th and 16th centuries.

Museu Antoniano. Largo de Santo António de Sé. ☎ **01/886-04-47.** Admission 170$ ($1). Daily 10am–1pm and 2–6pm. Metro: Rossio. Bus: 37. Tram: 28 or 28B.

St. Anthony of Padua, an itinerant Franciscan monk who became Portugal's patron saint, was born in 1195 in a house that once stood here. The original church was destroyed by the 1755 earthquake, and the present building was designed by Mateus Vicente in the 18th century. In the crypt, a guide will show you the spot where the saint was allegedly born (he's buried in Padua, Italy). The devout come to this little church to light candles under his picture. He's known as a protector of young brides and also has a special connection with the children of Lisbon.

THE BAIRRO ALTO

Like the Alfama, the Bairro Alto (Upper City) preserves the characteristics of an older Lisbon. It once was called the heart of the city, probably referring to both its location and its inhabitants. Many of its buildings survived the 1755 earthquake. Today it's a center of nightlife, with some of the finest fado cafés. The Bairro Alto is also a fascinating place to visit during the day, when its charming narrow cobblestoned streets and alleys, lined with ancient buildings, can be appreciated in the warm light coming off the sea.

From the windows and balconies, streamers of laundry hang out to dry, and the air is filled with the chirping of canaries, parrots, parakeets, and other birds. In the morning, the street scene is made up of housewives emerging from their homes to shop, following the cries of the *varinas* (fishmongers) and other food vendors. At night, the area comes alive with fado clubs, discos, and small bars; the people leisurely stroll along the streets lit by Victorian lights.

BELÉM

At Belém, the most southwestern district of Lisbon, the Tagus meets the sea. From here, the caravels that charted the unknown world were launched on their missions: Vasco da Gama to India, Ferdinand Magellan to circumnavigate the globe, and Bartolomeu Dias to round the Cape of Good Hope. Belém emerges from the Restelo, the point of land from which the ships set sail across the so-called Sea of Darkness. From these explorations, wealth flowed into Belém, especially from the spice trade with the far east.

In time, the royal family established a summer palace here. Wealthy Lisboans began moving out of the city center and building townhouses here, establishing the character of the district. For many years Belém was a separate municipality, but is now incorporated into Lisbon as a parish.

A tram to Belém (no. 150) leaves from the Praça do Comércio every 20 minutes, taking 20 minutes and costing 150$ (85¢). You can also take a train from the Estaçao Cais do Sodré, departing every 15 minutes during the day; the ride takes 15 minutes and costs 110$ (65¢).

Torre de Belém. Praça do Imperio. ☎ **01/362-00-34.** Admission 400$ ($2.30) adults, 200$ ($1.15) children and seniors. June–Sept Tues–Sun 10am–6pm; Oct–May Tues–Sun 10am–5pm. Bus: 43 or 49. Tram: 15 or 17.

The quadrangular Tower of Belém is a monument to Portugal's Age of Discovery. Erected between 1515 and 1520 in Manueline style (flamboyant Gothic and Moorish influences with elements of the nascent Renaissance), the tower is Portugal's classic landmark. It stands on or near the spot where the caravels once set out to sea. Its architect, Francisco de Arruda, blended Gothic and Moorish elements, using such architectural details as twisting ropes carved of stone. The coat-of-arms of Manuel I rests above the loggia, and balconies grace three sides. Along the balustrade of the loggias, stone crosses symbolize the Portuguese Crusaders.

Padrão dos Descobrimentos (Memorial to the Discoveries). Praça da Boa Esperança. ☎ **01/301-62-28.** Admission 330$ ($1.90) adults, 165$ (95¢) children under 12. Tues–Sun 9:30am–7pm. Bus: 43 or 49. Tram: 15 or 17.

Like the prow of a caravel from the Age of Discovery, this memorial stands on the Tagus, as if ready at any moment to strike out across the Sea of Darkness. Memorable explorers, chiefly Vasco da Gama, are immortalized in stone along the ramps. At the point where the two ramps meet is a representation of Henry the Navigator, whose genius opened up new worlds. One of the stone figures is that of a kneeling Philippa of Lancaster, Henry's English mother; other figures symbolize crusaders, navigators, monks, cartographers, and cosmographers.

Beneath the heroic representations, the memorial contains a series of exposition rooms that include a permanent exhibit on the role of the Portuguese in exploring the world, as well as temporary exhibits on the Portuguese experience.

✪ **Mosteiro dos Jerónimos (Jerónimos Monastery).** Praça do Império. ☎ **01/362-00-34.** Church, free. Cloisters, June–Sept 400$ ($2.30), Oct–May 250$ ($1.45); children and seniors free. Tues–Sun 10am–5pm. Bus: 27, 28, 29, 43, or 49. Tram: 15 or 17.

In an expansive mood of celebration, Manuel I, the Fortunate, ordered this monastery built in 1502 to commemorate Vasco da Gama's voyage to India and to give thanks to the Virgin Mary for its success. Manueline, the style of architecture to which the king contributed his name, combines flamboyant Gothic and Moorish influences with elements of the nascent Renaissance in Portugal. The 1755 earthquake damaged the monastery, and extensive restoration, some ill-conceived, was carried out.

The church interior is divided into three naves, noted for their fragile-looking pillars. Some of the ceilings, like those in the monks' refectory, have a ribbed barrel vault. The "palm tree" in the sacristy is exceptional.

Museu da Marinha (Maritime Museum). Praça do Império. ☎ **01/362-00-19.** Admission 400$ ($2.30) adults, 200$ ($1.15) students; children under 10 and seniors free. June–Sept Tues–Sun 10am–6pm; Oct–May Tues–Sun 10am–5pm. Bus: 27, 28, 29, 43, 49, or 51. Tram: 15 or 17.

The pageant and the glory that characterized Portugal's domination of the high seas is evoked for posterity in the Maritime Museum, one of the most important in Europe. Appropriately, it's installed in the west wing of the Mosteiro dos Jerónimos. These royal galleys re-create an age of opulence that never feared excess, as exemplified by dragon heads dripping with gilt and sea monsters coiling with abandon.

The museum contains hundreds of models, from 15th-century sailing ships to 20th-century warships. In a special room is a model of the queen's stateroom on the royal yacht of Carlos I, the Bragança king who was assassinated at Praça do Comércio in 1908.

✪ **Museu Nacional dos Coches (National Coach Museum).** Praça Afonso de Albuquerque. ☎ **01/361-08-85.** Admission 530$ ($3.05) adults, 225$ ($1.30) students 14–25; children under 14 free. Tues–Sun 10am–5:30pm. Closed holidays. Bus: 28, 29, 43, 49, or 51. Tram: 15.

The most popular attraction in Lisbon, the National Coach Museum is the finest of its type in the world. The coaches stand in a former 18th-century riding academy connected to the Belém Royal Palace; most date from the 17th to the 19th century. Of interest is a trio of opulently gilded baroque carriages once used by the Portuguese ambassador to the Vatican at the time of Pope Clement XI (1716). Also displayed is a 17th-century coach in which the Spanish Hapsburg king, Phillip II, journeyed from Madrid to Lisbon to see his new possession.

Museu de Arte Popular (Folk Art Museum). Av. de Brasília. ☎ **01/301-16-75.** 300$ ($1.75) adults; 150$ (85¢) children 12 and under. Tues–Sun 10am–12:30pm and 2–5pm. Closed holidays. Bus: 27, 28, 29, 43, 49, or 51. Tram: 15 or 17.

This is the most dramatic exhibition of the folk arts and customs of Portugal. The walls of the building are painted by contemporary artists, including Carlos Botelho, Eduardo Anahory, Estréla Faria, Manuel Lapa, Paulo Ferreira, and Tomás de Melo. The 1948 opening of the Folk Art Museum was a result of the campaign for ethnic revival directed by António Ferro. The collections—including ceramics, furniture, wickerwork, clothes, farm implements, and paintings—are displayed in five rooms that correspond more or less to the provinces, each of which maintains its own distinct personality.

ELSEWHERE IN LISBON

✪ **Museu Nacional de Arte Antiga (National Museum of Ancient Art).** Rua das Janelas Verdes 9. ☎ **01/396-41-51.** Admission 500$ ($2.90) adults, 250$ ($1.45) students; children under 14 free. Tues 2–6pm; Wed–Sun 10am–6pm. Bus: 27, 40, 49, or 60. Tram: Alcântara.

This museum occupies two connected buildings: a 17th-century palace and an added edifice built on the site of the old Carmelite Convent of Santo Alberto. The museum has many notable paintings, including the famous polyptych from St. Vincent's monastery attributed to Nuno Gonçalves between 1460 and 1470. Other outstanding works are Hieronymus Bosch's triptych *The Temptation of St. Anthony,* Hans Memling's *Mother and Child,* Albrecht Dürer's *St. Jerome,* and paintings by Velázquez, Zurbarán, Poussin, and Courbet. Paintings from the 15th through the 19th century trace the development of Portuguese art, and the museum also exhibits a remarkable collection of gold- and silversmiths' work.

✪ **Museu de Fundação Calouste Gulbenkian.** In Parque de Palhavã, Av. de Berna 45. ☎ **01/795-02-36.** Admission 500$ ($2.90) adults; children under 10 and seniors free. Free for everyone on Sun. June–Sept Tues, Thurs–Sat 10am–5pm, Wed and Sun 10am–7pm; Oct–May Tues–Sun 10am–5pm. Metro: Sebastião or Palhava. Bus: 16, 26, 31, 41, 46, or 56. Tram: 24.

Opened in 1969, this museum, part of the Fundação Calouste Gulbenkian, houses what one critic called "one of the world's finest private art collections." It was deeded by Armenian oil tycoon Calouste Gulbenkian, who died in 1955.

The collection covers Egyptian, Greek, and Roman antiquities; a remarkable set of Islamic art; and vases, prints, and lacquerwork from China and Japan. The European displays feature medieval illuminated manuscripts and ivories, 15th- to 19th-century painting and sculpture, important collections of 18th-century French decorative works, French impressionist paintings, and Lalique jewelry and glassware. Notable are Gulbenkian's two Rembrandts, Rubens's *Portrait of Hélène Fourment,* and *Portrait of Madame Claude Monet* by Pierre-Auguste Renoir.

✪ **Oceanario de Lisboa.** Parque das Naçoñas (right off Avenida Marechal Gomes Costa). ☎ **01/891-7002.** Admission 1,500$ ($8.70) adults, 800$ ($4.65) students and children under 13. Daily 10am–6pm. Metro: Estação do Oriente.

In 1998, most of Portugal waited expectantly for the opening of Expo '98, a well-publicized PR and marketing event meant to propel Portugal into the consciousness of Europe and the world. After the event ended, this world-class aquarium remains as the most enduring and impressive achievement of that busy hubbub, and one that will endure for many generations to come. Considered the second-biggest aquarium in the world, exceeded in size only by a facility in Osaka, Japan, it's in a stone and glass building whose centerpiece is a 1.3-million gallon (5-million liter) holding tank. (The facilities in Osaka and Lisbon were both designed by Boston-born engineer and architect Peter Chermayeff.) Its waters are divided into four distinct ecosystems that replicate the Atlantic, Pacific, Indian, and Antarctic Oceans, and each is supplemented with dry land on which birds, amphibians, and reptiles also flourish. Look for otters in the Pacific waters, penguins in the Antarctic section, trees and flowers of Polynesia in the Indian Ocean division, and puffins, terns, and seagulls in the Atlantic subdivision. The Portuguese take a lot of pride in this huge facility, a latter-day reminder of their former mastery of the seas.

ORGANIZED TOURS

Cityrama (☎ 01/386-4322), with tours departing from Avenida Sidónio Pais, offers the best tours of Lisbon and its environs. Its half-day tour of Lisbon, costing 5,250$ ($30.45), takes in all the major sights in the city center, including the Alfama, and also ventures out to the Coach Museum and Belém Tower. Departures are daily year-round at 9am and again at 2:30pm. A full-day tour, departing daily at 9am, includes not only the major sights of Lisbon but also the scenic highlights of Sintra, Estoril, and Cabo da Roca (the westernmost point of Europe). A Lisbon by night tour is offered only on Monday, Wednesday, and Friday, costing 12,500$ ($72.50). You go in a bus to see the major monuments floodlit at night, including Jerónimos Monastery. Later you eat at a traditional restaurant with fado singing and folkloric dances. The price includes dinner at the restaurant.

THE SHOPPING SCENE

Baixa, between the Rossio and the Tagus, is a major shopping area. **Rua do Ouro (Street of Gold), Rua da Prata,** and **Rua Augusta** are the principal shopping streets. Another major upscale shopping artery is **Rua Garrett,** in the Chiado; to reach the area, you can take the Santa Justa elevator near the Rossio.

The most unusual buys in Lisbon are *azulejos,* the decorated glazed tiles sought by collectors, and pottery from all over Portugal. Pottery with brightly colored roosters from Barcelos is legendary, and blue-and-white pottery is made in Coimbra. Our favorites come from Caldas da Rainha, including yellow-and-green dishes in the shape of vegetables, fruit, and animals. Vila Real is known for its black pottery, and polychrome pottery comes from Aceiro. The red-clay pots from the Alentejo region are based on designs that go back to the Etruscans.

One of the very best buys in Portugal is gold. Gold is strictly regulated by the government, which requires jewelers to put a minimum of 19¼ karats in the jewelry they sell. Filigree jewelry, made of fine gold or silver wire, is an art that dates back to ancient times.

Along both sides of **Rua de S. José** are treasure troves of shops packed with antiques from all over the world. **Rua Dom Pedro V** is another street of antiques shops.

SELECT SHOPS   Near the Ritz Hotel, the **Galleria Sesimbra,** Rua Castilho 77 (☎ 01/387-02-91), is a top art gallery, mainly displaying Portuguese artists. It was established in the 1970s by an expatriate Scotsman.

Casa Quintão, Rua Serpa Pinto 12A (☎ **01/346-58-37**), is the showcase for Arraiolos carpets. Rugs sold here are priced by the square foot, according to the density of the stitching. Casa Quintão can reproduce intricate Oriental or medieval designs in rugs and tapestries or create any customized pattern. The shop, dating from 1880, also sells materials and gives instructions on how to make your own carpets and tapestry-covered pillows.

✪ **Vista Alegre,** Largo do Chiado 18 (☎ **01/347-54-81**), turns out some of the finest porcelain dinner services in the country, along with objets d'art and limited editions, as well as a range of practical day-to-day tableware.

For something typically Portuguese, try **Casa das Cortiças,** Rua da Escola Politécnica 4–6 (☎ **01/342-58-58**). "Mr. Cork," the original owner, became somewhat of a legend in Lisbon for offering "everything conceivable" that could be made of cork; Portugal controls a hefty part of its world market. He's long gone now, but the store carries on.

In the same building as the Hotel Avenida Palace, **Casa Bordados da Madeira,** Rua 1 de Dezembro 137 (☎ **01/342-14-47**), offers handmade embroideries from Madeira and Viana. If you want to place an order, the staff will mail it to you.

Casa Regional da Ilha Verde, Rua Paiva de Andrade 4 (☎ **01/342-59-74**), specializes in handmade items, especially embroideries from the Azores—that's why it's called the "Regional House of the Green Island." You can get some good buys here.

✪ **Madeira House,** Rua Augusta 131–135 (☎ **01/342-68-13**), specializes in high-quality regional cottons, linens, and gift items.

If you're looking for fado recordings, **Valentim de Carvalho,** Rossio (☎ **01/322-44-00**), is the largest outlet in Portugal for records and tapes, with a staggering collection of fado music. At the **Feira da Ladra,** you can experience the fun of haggling for bargains at an open-air street market. The vendors peddle their wares on Tuesday and Saturday from 6:30am to 2 or 3pm. About a 5-minute walk from the waterfront in the Alfama, the market sits behind the Maritime Museum, adjoining the Pantheon of São Vicente. Start your browsing at Campo de Santa Clara in the Alfama. Portable stalls and individual displays are lined up on this hilly street with its tree-lined center.

Well on its way to being a century old, the **Joalharia do Carmo,** Rua do Carmo 87B (☎ **01/342-42-00**), is one of the best shops in Lisbon for gold filigree work.

✪ **W. A. Sarmento,** Rua Áurea 251 (☎ **01/342-67-74**), is the most distinguished silver- and goldsmith in Portugal, specializing in lacy filigree jewelry, including charm bracelets.

Founded in 1741 in the Chiado, ✪ **Sant'Anna,** Rua do Alecrim 95–97 (☎ **01/ 342-25-37**), is Portugal's leading ceramic center, famous for its *azulejos* (glazed tiles). The showroom is on Rua do Alecrim, but you can also visit the factory at Calçada da Boa Hora 96; however, you should make an appointment by calling ☎ **01/363-82-92.** The factory is open Monday to Friday 9am to 6pm.

LISBON AFTER DARK

Consult *What's On in Lisbon,* available at most newsstands, for the latest listings. The local newspaper, *Diário de Notícias,* also carries cultural listings, but in Portuguese. No special discount tickets are offered, except that students get 50% off on tickets purchased for the national theater. Also of interest is *Agenda Cultural,* an English- and Portuguese-language seasonal periodical that's available without charge at cafes, hotels, and the Lisbon branch of the Portuguese tourist office. Inside, you'll find an abbreviated listing of musical, theatrical, and cultural choices available throughout the city.

THE PERFORMING ARTS

Museu da Fundação Calouste Gulbenkian. Av. de Berna 45. ☎ **01/795-02-36.** Metro: Sebastião or Palhava. Bus: 16, 26, 31, 46, or 56. Tram: 24.

From October to June, concerts, recitals, and occasionally ballet are performed here; sometimes there are also jazz concerts. You have to inquire locally about what's happening at the time of your visit.

Teatro Municipal de São Luís. Rua António Maria Cardoso 40. ☎ **01/346-12-60.** Métro: Estação Cais do Sodré. Tram: 10, 28, or 28B.

Chamber-music and symphony concerts and ballet are presented at this municipal theater. Check locally to see if anything is featured when you are in Lisbon.

Teatro nacional Doña Maria II. Plaza Dom Piedro IV (Rossio). ☎ **01/347-2246.** Metro: Rossio.

Originally built in the 1840s, and restored after a disastrous fire in 1964, this publicly funded theater ranks along with the Teatro San Carlos and the Teatro San Luis as the most important cultural venue in Lisbon. Despite its funding by the Ministry of Culture, it does not limit its repertoire to just Portuguese-language productions, although those are the most common. There are occasional ballets, as well as the classic plays of the Italian, German, Spanish, and English-speaking worlds. Thanks to government funding, tickets are reasonably priced, costing from 1,500$ to 3,500$ ($8.70 to $20.30) each.

Teatro Nacional de São Carlos. Rua Serpa Pinto 9. ☎ **01/346-84-08.** Tram: 24, 28, or 28B. Bus: 15 or 100.

This theater attracts opera and ballet aficionados from all over Europe. Top companies from around the world perform at this 18th-century theater, and the season begins in mid-September and extends through July. The box office is open daily from 1 to 7pm. There are no special discounts.

PORT WINE TASTING

Solar do Vinho do Porto. Rua de São Pedro de Alcântara 45. ☎ **01/347-57-07.** Bus: 58 or 100.

A bar devoted exclusively to drinking and enjoying port in all its variations, Solar lies near the Bairro Alto and its fado clubs. You enter what appears to be a private living room that offers a relaxing atmosphere enhanced by an open stone fireplace. Owned and sponsored by the Port Wine Institute, Solar displays many artifacts related to the industry. But the real reason for dropping by is for its *lista de vinhos*—there are more than 200 wines from which to choose. Solar is about 50 yards from the upper terminus of the Gloria funicular. It's open Monday to Friday 10am to 11:30pm and Saturday 11am to 10:30pm.

BARS

Bachus. Largo da Trindade 9. ☎ **01/342-28-28.** No cover. Bus: 15.

Bachus is a restaurant and a friendly watering hole. Amid Oriental carpets, fine hardwoods, bronze statues, and intimate lighting, you can hobnob with some of the most glamorous people in Lisbon. Late-night candlelit suppers are served in the bar.

Bora-Bora. Rua da Madalena 201. ☎ **01/887-20-43.** No cover. Metro: Rossio. Tram: 12 or 28.

You might find the Polynesian theme unexpected and even a bit surreal, but despite that, the concept is all the rage in Lisbon today. Amid an artfully re-created jungle that's filled with images of the South Pacific, you can hear recorded versions of

The Quintessential Lisbon Experience: Fado

Fado is Portugal's most vivid art form; no visit to Lisbon is complete without at least one night in a tavern where this traditional music is played. Fado is typically sung by women, called *fadistas,* accompanied by guitar and viola. The songs express romantic longing and sadness, *saudade,* capturing the country's sense of nostalgia for the past.

Adega Machado, Rua do Norte 91 (☎ 01/322-46-40; Bus: 58 or 100), located in Barrio Alto, has passed the test of time and is still one of Portugal's most popular fado clubs. Alternating with the *fadistas* are folk dancers whirling, clapping, and singing their native songs in colorful costumes. Dinner is à la carte, and the cuisine is mostly Portuguese, with a number of regional dishes. Dining starts at 8:30pm, and the doors don't close until 3am. The first show starts at 9:15pm. Cover (including two drinks) is 2,750$ ($15.95). It's open Tuesday to Sunday.

Every night at Barrio Alto's **A Severa,** Rua das Gaveas 51 (☎ 01/346-40-06; Bus: 20 or 24), top *fadistas* sing, both male and female, alternating with folk dancers. In a niche you'll spot a statue honoring the club's namesake, Maria Severa, the legendary 19th-century Gypsy *fadista* who made fado famous. The kitchen turns out regional dishes based on recipes from the north of Portugal. Cover (including two drinks) is 3,500$ ($20.30), and the club is open Friday to Wednesday 8pm to 3:30am.

Try to catch the tempestuous Fernanda Maria, the owner of **Lisboa a Noite,** Rua das Gaveas 69 (☎ 01/346-85-57; Bus: 58 or 100), when she's about to make her first appearance of the evening. The 17th-century–style setting is rustic yet luxurious (this Bairro Alto club was once a stable). In the rear is an open kitchen and charcoal grill. Cover (including two drinks) is 3,000$ ($17.40), and hours are Monday to Saturday 8pm to 3am; shows begin at 9:30pm.

Seemingly every *fadista* worth her shawl has sung at the old-time **Parreirinha da Alfama,** Beco do Espirito Santo 1 (☎ 01/886-82-09; Bus: 39 or 46), just a minute's walk from the docks of the Alfama. It's fado and fado only here, and it's open daily 8:30pm to 2:30am; music begins at 9:30pm. In the first part of the program, *fadistas* get all the popular songs out of the way, and then settle in to their more classic favorites. Cover (credited toward drinks) is 2,000$ ($11.60).

ukelele music as you sip a tropical cocktail. Drinks are fruited, flaming, sunset-colored, and potent. In the late 1990s, based on the success of this place, management opened a second, somewhat larger, branch within the Alameda district, which more or less duplicated the original's style. It's **Bora Bora,** Avenida Almirante Reis 197C (☎ 01/ 840-5873; Metro: Alameda). Although doors for both places open nightly at 8pm, they're sort of sleepy till around 10pm, when the trendy crowd tends to wake the place up.

Panorama Bar. In the Lisboa Sheraton Hotel, Rua Latino Coelho 1. ☎ 01/357-57-57. No cover. Bus: 1, 2, 9, or 32.

This bar occupies the top floor of one of Portugal's tallest buildings, the 30-story Lisboa Sheraton. From this perch you can look out over the old and new cities, the mighty Tagus, and many towns on the river's far bank. Amid a decor of chiseled stone and stained glass, a polite uniformed staff serves you.

Procópio Bar. Alto de San Francisco 21A. ☎ **01/385-28-51.** No cover. Closed Aug 1–15. Bus: 9.

A long-time favorite of journalists, politicians, and foreign actors, the once-innovative Procópio has become a tried-and-true staple. It might easily become your favorite bar—if you can find it. It lies just off Rua de João Penha, which is off the landmark Praça das Amoreiras.

Gay & Lesbian Bars

The collapse of Salazar's dictatorship in 1974 paved the way for a new openness of Lisbon nightlife; at least eight gay bars have sprung up in the district known as **Príncipe Real.**

Agua No Bico Bar. Rua de São Marçal 170. ☎ **01/347-28-30.** No cover. Bus: 58 or 100.

This dark pink place is lined with movie posters and filled mainly with men. You won't see any sign out in front—instead, a discreet brass plaque marks this place on a steeply sloping street lined with dignified 18th-century villas. Recorded music plays in an atmosphere that might remind you—because of its lack of a dance floor—of an English pub.

Kings & Queens. Rua de Cintura do Porto de Lisboa, Warehouse 8, Naves A&B, Doca de Alcântara Norte. ☎ **01/395-58-70.** Cover 1,000$ ($6). Tram: 15.

This is one of the most frequented gay nightclubs in Lisbon, larger than any of its competitors and outfitted with an enormous dance floor that's flooded with the latest music from a sophisticated sound system. Most of the crowd is gay, male, and under 35. It's open Monday to Saturday 10pm to 6am, or sometimes later, depending on the energy level of the dance floor.

Memorial Bar. Rua Gustavo de Matos Sequeira 42A. ☎ **01/396-88-91.** Cover 1,000$ ($5.80). Bus: 58 or 100.

In the narrow streets of the Bairro Alto, Memorial is a "household word" among lesbians, who consider it one of the premier networking sites in Portugal. This small and rather cramped disco with ample bar space welcomes newcomers. There's an occasional round of live entertainment; otherwise, the place is low-key and unpretentious.

DANCE CLUBS

The Bar of the Café Alcântara/Disco Alcântara Mar. Rua da Cozinha Económica 11. ☎ **01/363-71-76.** No cover for bar. Cover for disco 1,000$–2,500$ ($5.80–$14.50). Bus: 14, 22, 27, or 32.

Although the sophisticated restaurant is popular, many people come here for the bar and dance club. The bar is long and curvy, with a turn-of-the-century feel. The opportunity for adventure increases for those who cross an interior footbridge into the Disco Alcântara Mar, an all-green high-tech enclave pumping British and American techno. The bar is open nightly 8pm to 3 or 4am; the dance club, Thursday to Sunday 11:30pm to 7 or 8am.

Docks. Avenida 24 de Julio, at Centro Mare. ☎ **01/395-0868.** No cover. Tram: 15 or 18.

As its name implies, this place is adjacent to the Tagus in Alcântara and has windows overlooking the river. Sophisticated and stylish, with a decor that's one of the most beautiful in the neighborhood, it has a 30-ish crowd. It's open nightly at 9pm.

Kremlin. Escadinhas da Praia 5. ☎ **01/60-87-68.** Cover 1,000$ ($5.80). Bus: 27, 28, 32, or 43.

Kremlin, the most energetic and iconoclastic of Lisbon discos, welcomes a very hip crowd of techno and garage music lovers into an angular and metallic-looking setting that's an artfully surreal take-off on the trappings of Soviet dictatorship. It's open Tuesday and Thursday from 1am to 7am, Friday and Saturday from 1am to 8am.

Model's. Travessa Teixeira Junior 6. ☎ **01-363-39-59.** Cover 1,200$ ($6.95). Bus 4, 27, 28, 32. Tram 15, 18.

If you're up for late-night, high-energy partying with students and club kids who love to dance, this is the place to go. Within a large and echoing space, with virtually indestructible bartops and dance floors, the music changes nightly. The DJs spin tribal underground, techno, garage, house, and on some nights, a scattering of salsa and merengue. It's open from 11:30pm till 4am every Tuesday to Sunday.

A DAY TRIP TO THE COSTA DEL SOL: THE PORTUGUESE RIVIERA

Lisbon's environs are so intriguing that many fail to see the capital itself, lured instead by Guincho (near the westernmost point in continental Europe), the Mouth of Hell, and Lord Byron's "glorious Eden" at Sintra. You could spend a day drinking in the wonders of the pretty pink rococo palace at Queluz or enjoying seafood at the Atlantic beach resort of Cascais.

The **Costa del Sol** is the string of beach resorts forming the Portuguese Riviera on the northern bank of the mouth of the Tagus. If you arrive in Lisbon when the sun is shining and the air balmy, consider heading for this cabana-studded shoreline. So near to Lisbon is Estoril that it's easy to dart in and out of the capital to see the sights or visit the fado clubs, while you spend your nights in a hotel by the sea. An inexpensive electric train leaving from the Cais do Sodré in Lisbon makes the trip frequently throughout the day and evening, ending its run in Cascais.

The Riviera is a microcosm of Portugal. Ride out on the train, even if you don't plan to stay there. Along the way, you pass pastel-washed houses with red-tiled roofs and facades of antique blue-and-white tiles; miles of modern apartment dwellings; rows of canna, pines, mimosa, and eucalyptus; and, in the background, green hills studded with villas, chalets, and new homes. The sun coast is sometimes known as the Costa dos Reis, the "coast of kings," because of all the deposed royalty who have settled there—everybody from exiled kings to pretenders, marquesses from Italy, princesses from Russia, and baronesses from Germany.

ESTORIL   The first stop is 15 miles west of Lisbon. This chic resort has long basked in its reputation as a playground of monarchs.

The **Parque Estoril,** in the town center, is a well-manicured piece of landscaping, a subtropical setting with plants swaying in the breeze. At night, when it's floodlit, it's great for a stroll. The palm trees studding the grounds have prompted many to call it "a corner of Africa." At the top of the park sits the **casino,** offering not only gambling, but also international floor shows, dancing, and movies.

Across the railroad tracks is the **beach,** where some of Europe's most fashionable women sun themselves on the peppermint-striped canvas chairs along the Tamariz Esplanade. The atmosphere is cosmopolitan and the beach sandy, unlike the pebbly strand at that other Riviera in France. If you don't want to swim in the polluted ocean, you can check in at an oceanfront pool for a plunge.

CASCAIS   Just 4 miles west of Estoril and 19 miles west of Lisbon, Cascais has more of a Portuguese atmosphere than Estoril, even though it has been increasingly over-built. That Cascais is growing is an understatement: It's leapfrogging! Apartment houses, new hotels, and the finest restaurants along the Costa del Sol draw a never-ending stream of visitors every year.

However, the life of the simple fisher folk still goes on. Auctions, called *lotas,* at which the latest catch is sold, still take place on the main square, though a modern hotel has sprouted up in the background. In the small harbor, rainbow-colored fishing boats share space with pleasure craft owned by an international set that flocks to Cascais from early spring until autumn.

The most popular excursion outside Cascais is to the ✪ **Boca de Inferno (Mouth of Hell).** Reached by heading out on the highway to Guincho, then turning left toward the sea, the Boca deserves its ferocious reputation. At their peak, thundering waves sweep in with such power and fury they long ago carved a wide hole (*boca*) in the cliffs. However, if you should arrive when the sea is calm, you might be wondering what all the fuss is about. The Mouth of Hell can be a windswept roar if you don't stumble over too many souvenir hawkers.

The three sandy **beaches** at Cascais are almost as overcrowded as those at Estoril, and the waters here are less polluted, but still contaminated. Hotel pools remain the safer choice. Although there's a dangerous undertow, the best beach—at least for sunbathing—is Praia do Guincho, around Cabo da Roca, right outside Cascais. The sand-duned beach is mostly uncrowded and relatively pollution free. The continental winds make it a favorite for surfers.

QUELUZ   At the Estação Rossio in Lisbon, take the Sintra line train 9 miles northwest to Queluz. Trains depart every 15 minutes, and the trip takes half an hour, costing 120$ (70¢) one-way. After leaving the train station in Queluz, take a left turn and follow the signs for half a mile to the ✪ **Palácio de Queluz,** Largo do Palácio (☎ **01/436-38-61**), a brilliant example of the rococo style in Portugal. Pedro III ordered its construction in 1747, and the work dragged on until 1787. What you see now isn't quite what it was in the 18th century. Queluz suffered a lot during the French invasions, and almost all its belongings were transported to Brazil with the royal family. A 1934 fire destroyed a great deal of Queluz, but tasteful reconstruction has restored the lighthearted aura of the original. Inside, you can wander through the queen's dressing room, lined with painted panels depicting children playing; the Don Quixote Chamber (Dom Pedro was born here and returned from Brazil to die in the same bed); the Music Room, complete with a French grande pianoforte and an 18th-century English harpsichord; and the mirrored throne room adorned with crystal chandeliers.

The palace is open Wednesday to Monday (except holidays) from 10am to 1pm and 2 to 5pm. Admissions costs 500$ ($2.90) for adults, and 250$ ($1.45) for students. It's always free for anyone under 14, and free for general admission every Sunday morning.

SINTRA   Sintra, 18 miles northwest of Lisbon, is a 45-minute train ride from the Estação Rossio in Lisbon, costing 180$ ($1.05) each way. Lord Byron called it a "glorious Eden," and so it remains. Visitors flock here not only to absorb the town's beauty and scenic setting but also to visit two major sights.

Opening onto the central town square, the ✪ **Palácio Nacional de Sintra,** Largo da Rainha D. Amélia (☎ **01/923-00-85**), was a royal palace until 1910. Much of it was constructed in the early 16th century, during the days of the first Manuel, the Fortunate. Two conical chimney towers form the most distinctive landmark on the Sintra skyline. The Swan Room was a favorite of João I, one of the founding kings, father of Henry the Navigator and husband of Philippa of Lancaster. The Room of the Sirens or Mermaids is one of the most elegant in the palace. In the Heraldic or Stag Room, coats-of-arms of aristocratic Portuguese families and hunting scenes are depicted. The palace is rich in paintings and Iberian and Flemish tapestries, but it's truly at its best when you wander around a tree- and plant-shaded patio, listening to the fountain.

Admission costs 400$ ($2.30) for adults, half-price for students, and free for anyone 13 and under. The palace is open Thursday to Tuesday 10am to 1 and 2 to 5pm.

Towering over Sintra, the **Palácio Nacional da Pena,** Estrada de Pena (☎ **01/923-02-27**), sits on a plateau about 1,500 feet above sea level. At the top of the castle is a soaring agglomeration of towers, cupolas, and battlemented walls. Crossing over a drawbridge, you enter the palace proper, whose last royal occupant was Queen Amélia in 1910. Pena has remained much as Amélia left it, which is part of its fascination; it emerges as a rare record of European royal life in the halcyon days preceding World War I. Admission costs 400$ ($2.30) for adults, half-price for students, and free for anyone 13 and under. The palace is open Tuesday to Sunday 10am to 1pm and 2 to 5pm.

2 The Algarve

The maritime province of the Algarve, often called the "garden of Portugal," is the southwesternmost part of Europe. Its coastline stretches 100 miles—all the way from Henry the Navigator's Cape St. Vincent to the town of Vila Real de Santo António on the Spanish border. The varied coastline contains sluggish estuaries, sheltered lagoons, low-lying marshes, long sandy spits, and promontories jutting out into the white-capped foam.

Called *Al-Gharb* by the Moors, the land south of the *serras* (hills) of Monchique and Caldeirão remains a spectacular anomaly, more like a transplanted section of the North African coastline than Europe. The countryside abounds in vegetation: almonds, lemons, oranges, carobs, pomegranates, and figs.

Many Moorish and even Roman ruins remain. In the character of its fret-cut chimneys, mosquelike cupolas, and cubist houses, a distinct Oriental flavor prevails. Phoenicians, Greeks, Romans, Visigoths, Moors, and Christians all touched this land. However, much of the historic flavor is gone forever, swallowed by a sea of dreary high-rise apartment blocks surrounding most towns.

Many former fishing villages—now summer resorts—dot the Algarvian coast: Carvoeiro, Albufeira, Olhão, Portimão. The sea is still the source of life, as it always has been. The marketplaces in the villages sell esparto (made out of tough, wiry grass) mats, copperwork, pottery, and almond and fig sweets sometimes shaped like birds and fish.

Our tour stretches along the coast, beginning at Lagos, 164 miles south of Lisbon and 21 miles east of Sagres, the most southwestern point. From Sagres the road to Lagos (N-125) generally has minor traffic, unlike in the rest of the Algarve.

Only in the Algarve

Seeing the Almond Blossoms   There's no more dramatic sight in Portugal than the burgeoning white almond blossoms that bloom and blanket the Algarve in late January and early February. Legend has it that a vizier who married a Nordic princess ordered the trees planted to remind his homesick bride of her snow-covered native land.

Experiencing Algarvian Beach Life   The coast is dotted with literally hundreds of beaches—the finest in Portugal. The best cove beaches are at Lagos, especially Praia Dona Ana, and at Albufeira. Praia da Rocha, a creamy-yellow beach, has become the most popular seaside resort, and Praia dos Três Irmãos offers 9 miles of lustrous sand lying 3 miles southwest of Portimão.

Travel Tip

The best way to visit towns along the Algarve—that is, if you don't have a car—is on one of the buses run by EVA. Their headquarters are in Faro at Avenida República (☎ **089/89-97-00** for information, fares, and schedules).

Visiting Sagres   Portugal's southwesternmost point was once considered the end of the world. Four miles from Sagres, the dramatic promontory of Cabo de São Vicente forms a rugged, wind-swept landscape. Ancients believed it was the meeting place of the gods, and Prince Henry the Navigator established a school of geography and navigation here.

Golfing in the Algarve   Since around 1965, vast stretches of terrain have been bulldozed, landscaped, irrigated, and reconfigured into golf courses that stretch like strands in a necklace all along the coast. Many are associated with real-estate developments or major resorts, such as the 2,000-acre Quinta del Lago, where retirement villas nestle amid vegetation at the edges of the fairways. Most are open to qualified golfers, who should inquire in advance about tee times.

Seeking Out the Famous Chimneys   If you never thought that chimneys could excite you, you haven't seen the ones on the Algarve. The best parade of these chimneys is at Loulé, 9½ miles north of Faro. These fret-cut plaster towers rise from many of the houses and cottages here. They resemble fine lacework or filigree in stone; others are delicately contrived, like snow crystals blown against glass.

Discovering the Whitewashed Fishing Villages   Not many fishing villages remain, but of those that do, our favorite is Praia do Carvoeiro, 3 miles south of the wine-rich town of Lagoa. Now an expatriate colony, it offers a sandy beach nestled between two rock masses. The shadows of the cliffs are cooling, the seas calm. East of the beach on a steep slope, a belvedere provides a panoramic view. Nearby, you can explore Algar Seco, a collection of huge reddish stones carved by the sea into interesting shapes, plus a number of sea caves, often underwater. The local fishers will take you out in their boats.

LAGOS

Lagos, known to the Lusitanians and Romans as Locobriga and to the Moors as Zawaia, became an experimental shipyard of caravels during the time of Henry the Navigator. Edged by the Costa do Ouro (Golden Coast), the Bay of Sagres at one point in its epic history was big enough to allow 407 warships to maneuver with ease. An ancient port city (one historian traced its origins back to the Carthaginians 3 centuries before the birth of Christ), Lagos was well known centuries later to the sailors of Admiral Nelson's fleet.

Actually, not that much has changed since Nelson's day. The principal pleasures of Lagos remain those of table and beach. In winter, the almond blossoms match the whitecaps on the water and the climate is often warm enough for sunbathing. In town, the flea market sprawls through narrow streets, with vendors selling rattan baskets, earthenware pottery, fruits, vegetables, crude furniture, cutlery, knitted shawls, and leather boots.

Less than a mile down the coast, the hustle and bustle of market day is forgotten as the rocky headland of the Ponta da Piedade (Point of Piety) appears. This spot is the most beautiful on the entire coast. Amid the colorful cliffs and secret grottoes carved by the waves are the most flamboyant examples of Manueline architecture.

ESSENTIALS

ARRIVING   By Ferry & Train   From Lisbon, take the ferryboat at Praça do Comércio across the Tagus to Barreiro. There, you can make connections to Lagos on the Southern Line Railway. Five trains per day arrive from Lisbon, taking 6½ hours and costing 2,000$ ($11.60) each way. For information and schedules, call ☎ **01/ 888-40-25** in Lisbon or ☎ **082/76-29-87** in Lagos.

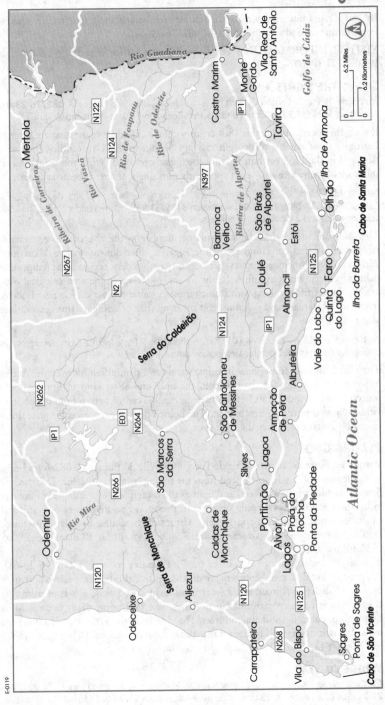

The Algarve

E-0119

By Bus   Eight buses a day make the run between Lisbon and Lagos, taking 5 hours. For information and schedules, call ☎ **082/76-29-44.**

VISITOR INFORMATION   The **Lagos Tourist Office** is at Largo Marquês de Pombal (☎ **082/76-30-31**).

SEEING THE SIGHTS

Igreja de Santo António (Church of St. Anthony). Rua Silva Lopes. ☎ **082/76-23-01.** Admission 340$ ($1.95), children under 5 free. Tues–Sun 9:30am–noon and 2–5pm.

Just off the waterfront sits this 18th-century church. Decorating the altar are some of Portugal's most notable rococo gilt carvings. Begun in the 17th century, they were damaged in the 1755 earthquake but subsequently restored. What you see represents the work of many artisans—each apparently pursuing a different theme at times.

Museu Municipal Dr. José Formosinho (Municipal Museum). Rua General Alberto Carlos Silveira. ☎ **082/76-23-01.** Admission 340$ ($1.95), children under 5 free. Tues–Sun 9:30am–noon and 2–5pm. Closed holidays.

This museum, which has the same phone number as the church above, contains replicas of the fret-cut chimneys of the Algarve, three-dimensional cork carvings, 16th-century vestments, ceramics, 17th-century embroidery, ecclesiastical sculpture, a painting gallery, weapons, minerals, and a coin collection. In the archaeological wing are Neolithic artifacts, along with Roman mosaics found at Boca do Rio near Budens, fragments of statuary and columns, and other remains of antiquity from excavations along the Algarve.

Antigo Mercado de Escravos (Old Customs House). Praça Infante Dom Henríques. No phone. Free admission. Open for viewing any time.

The Old Customs House, now in ruins, stands as a painful reminder of the Age of Exploration. The arcaded slave market, the only one of its kind in Europe, looks peaceful today, but under its four Romanesque arches captives taken from their homelands were sold to the highest bidders. The house opens onto a peaceful square dominated by a statue of Henry the Navigator.

PLAYING GOLF

Parque da Floresta, Budens, Vale do Poco, 8650 Vila do Bispo (☎ **082/69-53-33**), is 9 miles west of Lagos, just inland from the fishing hamlet of Salema. Designed by Spanish architect Pepe Gancedo and built as the centerpiece of a complex of holiday villas, this course offers sweeping views. Some shots must be driven over vineyards and others over ravines, creeks, and gardens. Critics of the course have cited its rough grading and rocky terrain. Greens fees are 7,900$ ($45.80) for 18 holes and 4,900$ ($28.40) for 9.

Some 2½ miles west of Lagos is the par-71 **Palmares** course (☎ **082/76-29-61**), designed by Frank Pennink, with many differences in altitude. Some fairways require driving a ball across railroad tracks, over small ravines, or around groves of palms. Its landscaping is more evocative of North Africa than of Europe, partly because of its hundreds of palm, fig, and almond trees. The view from the 17th green is among the most dramatic of any golf course on the Algarve. Greens fees for 18 holes are 7,300$ to 9,500$ ($42.35 to $55.10), depending on the season.

WHERE TO STAY

✪ **Casa de São Gonçalo da Lagos.** Rua Cândido dos Reis 73, 8600 Lagos. ☎ **082/76-21-71.** Fax 082/76-39-27. 13 units. TEL. June–Aug, 15,000$–17,000$ ($87–$98.60) double; otherwise, 7,500$–10,500$ ($43.50–$60.90) double. AE, DC, MC, V. Closed Nov–Mar. Free parking.

Sagres: Sunset at the End of the Earth

The rocky escarpment of **Sagres,** the southwesternmost point in Europe, was considered by the ancients to be the end of the world. It was here that Henry the Navigator founded his school of navigation and launched Portugal and the rest of Europe headlong into the Age of Exploration. Three miles away is the windswept promontory of **Cabo de São Vicente,** named for St. Vincente, whose body, according to legend, arrived at the cape in a boat guided by ravens. A lighthouse, the second most powerful in Europe, shines 60 miles out into the Atlantic. Get permission from the gatekeeper before climbing it.

Both the cape and Sagres have wonderful vantage points to watch the sunset. You can imagine Magellan, Diaz, and Vasco de Gama standing in the same spot centuries before, contemplating their journeys into the unknown.

The most dramatic place to dine, and the one offering the best cuisine, is **Fotaleza do Belixe,** Fortaleza do Belixe, Vila do Bipso 8650 Sagres (☎ **082/62-41-24**), which serves Portuguese and international cuisine in the remnants of a medieval fortress. From Sagres, drive west for 3 miles along the coastal road, following the signs to Cabo de São Vicente.

From Lagos, about 10 buses a day make the 1-hour trip to Sagres, with a one-way trip costing 445$ ($2.60). By car, drive west from Lagos along N-125 to Vila do Bispo, then head south on N-268 to Sagres. Cabo de São Vicente can be reached only by car..

This pink villa, with its fancy iron balconies, dates from the 18th century. At the core of Lagos, the antiques-filled home is almost an undiscovered gem. Most of the public lounges and guest rooms are oriented, in the Iberian fashion, toward the inward peace of a sun-filled patio. All the furnishings are individualized: hand-embroidered linens, period mahogany tables, silver candlesticks, chests with brass handles, inlaid tables, and ornate beds from Angola. Street-level rooms can be noisy.

Hotel de Lagos. Rua Nova da Aldeia 1, 8600 Lagos. ☎ **082/76-99-67.** Fax 082/76-99-20. 315 units. A/C TV TEL. 10,640$–26,500$ ($61.70–$153.70) double; 15,999$–36,800$ ($92.80–$213.45) suite. AE, DC, MC, V. Free parking.

A 20th-century castle of Moorish and Portuguese design, Hotel de Lagos has its own ramparts and moats (a pool and a paddling pool). Standing at the eastern side of the old town, far removed from the beach, this first-class hotel is spread over 3 hilltop acres overlooking Lagos; no matter which room you get, you have a view, even if it's a courtyard with semitropical greenery. Some guest rooms have ground-level patios, but most are on the upper six floors; you have a choice of standard or deluxe rooms. A 31-room wing, complete with pool and health club, was added in 1989, and the hotel has its own beach club a mile away.

WHERE TO DINE

Alpendre. Rua António Barbosa Viana 17. ☎ **082/76-27-05.** Reservations recommended. Main courses 1,800$–3,800$ ($10.45–$22.05). AE, DC, MC, V. Daily noon–11pm. PORTUGUESE.

Alpendre offers one of the most elaborate and sophisticated menus along the Algarve, but, considering the lackluster competition, that's not saying too much. The food is tasty, but the portions aren't large. Service tends to be slow, so don't come here if you're rushed. House specialties include shellfish rice, steak Diane, and filet of sole sautéed in butter, flambéed with cognac, and served with a sauce of cream, orange and lemon juices, vermouth, and secret seasonings.

PRAIA DA ROCHA

En route to Praia da Rocha, off N-125 between Lagos and Portimão, 11 miles away, you'll find several good beaches and rocky coves, particularly at **Praia dos Três Irmãos** and **Alvor.** But the most popular seaside resort on the Algarve is the creamy yellow beach of Praia da Rocha. At the outbreak of World War II, there were only two small hotels on the Red Coast, but nowadays Praia da Rocha is booming, as many have fallen under the spell cast by its shoreline and climate.

It's named the Beach of the Rock because of its beautiful sculptural rock formations. At the end of the mussel-encrusted cliff, where the Arcade flows into the sea, are the ruins of the **Fort of St. Catarina,** whose location offers many views of Portimão's satellite, Ferragudo, and of the bay.

To reach Praia da Rocha from Portimão, you can catch a bus for the 1½-mile trip south. Algarve buses aren't numbered but are marked by their final destination, such as Praia da Rocha. Frequent trains run throughout the day between Lagos (see above) and Portimao. The main highway across the southern coast (N-125) has a cut-off for Portimao that is well signposted.

PLAYING GOLF

Vale de Pint and Quinta do Gramacho, Praia do Carvoeiro (☎ **082/34-09-00**), are twin par-71 courses, sharing a clubhouse and staff. They're set amid a landscape of tawny rocks and arid hillocks. Both of them route their players through groves of twisted olive, almond, carob, and fig trees. Views from the fairways, designed in 1992 by Californian Ronald Fream, sweep over the low masses of the Monchique mountains, close to the beach resort of Carvoeiro. Experts consider these two to be among the most challenging courses in Portugal. Clusters of bunkers, barrier walls, and abrupt changes in elevation complicate the course. Greens fees are 10,000$ ($58) for 18 holes.

WHERE TO STAY

✪ **Bela Vista.** Av. Tómas Cabreira, Praia da Rocha, 8500 Portimão. ☎ **082/42-40-55.** Fax 082/41-53-69. 14 units. MINIBAR TV TEL. 10,000$–23,000$ ($58–$133.40) double; 15,000$–34,000$ ($87–$197.20) suite. AE, DC, MC, V.

The Bela Vista is an artfully rustic Moorish-style mansion built during the past century as a summer home for a wealthy family. It's set atop its own palisade, with a minaret-type tower at one end of its facade; you have access to a sandy cove below where you can swim. The villa is ideal for those who enjoy architecture of the past and who remember to make a reservation way in advance. It's flanked by the owner's home and a simple cliff-edge annex shaded by palm trees. The entry hall has an art nouveau bronze torchère and a winding staircase, with walls almost covered with 19th-century blue-and-white tiles. The guest rooms facing the sea, the former master bedrooms, are the most desirable, although all rooms have character. Decorations vary from an inset tile shrine to the Virgin Mary to crystal sconces.

Residencial Sol. Av. Tomás Cabreira 10, Praia da Rocha, 8500 Portimão. ☎ **082/42-40-71.** Fax 082/41-71-99. 40 units. TEL. 8,400$–9,200$ ($48.70–$53.35) double; from 10,000$ ($58) suite. AE, DC, MC, V.

The painted concrete facade of this hotel appears somewhat bleak, in part because of its location near the noisy main street. In this case, however, appearances are deceiving, since the guest rooms offer some of the cleanest, most attractive, and unpretentious accommodations in town. Each unit is designed for two. The rooms in back are quieter, but the terrace-dotted front units look across the traffic toward a bougainvillea-filled park.

WHERE TO DINE

Titanic. Edifício Colúmbia, Rua Engenheiro Francisco Bivar. ☎ **082/42-23-71.** Reservations recommended, especially in summer. Main courses 1,500$–3,490$ ($8.70–$20.25). AE, DC, MC, V. Daily 7–11pm. Closed Nov 27–Dec 27. INTERNATIONAL.

Complete with gilt and crystal, the 100-seat air-conditioned Titanic is the most elegant restaurant in town. From its open-view kitchen, it serves the best food, including shellfish and flambé dishes. Even though it's named after the ill-fated luxury liner, it's not on the water, but in a modern residential complex. You can dine very well here on such appealing dishes as the fish of the day, pork filet with mushrooms, prawns *à la plancha* (grilled), Chinese fondue, and sole Algarve.

PRAIA DOS TRÊS IRMÃOS & ALVOR

At **Praia dos Três Irmãos** (the Beach of the Three Brothers), you get 9 miles of burnished golden sand, broken only by an occasional crag riddled with arched passages. Just 3 miles southwest of Portimão, this beach has been discovered by skin divers who explore its undersea grottoes and shoreside cave. You can visit Praia dos Três Irmãos for its beach, even if you prefer not to stay here. From Portimão, you can reach it or the tourist development at Alvor by public bus service leaving from the center of Portimão. Service is frequent throughout the day.

Its neighbor is the whitewashed fishing village of **Alvor,** where Portuguese and Moorish arts and traditions have mingled since the Arabs surrendered after 500 years of occupation. Alvor was a favorite coastal haunt of João II. The summer hordes descend on the long strip of sandy beach here. It's not the best in the area, but at least you have space.

PLAYING GOLF

Penina, Apartado 146 (☎ 082/41-54-15), lies 3 miles west of Portimão, farther west than many of the other great golf courses of the Algarve. Completed in 1966, it was one of the first courses here and the universally acknowledged masterpiece of British designer Sir Henry Cotton. It occupies what was once a network of marshy rice paddies, on level terrain that critics said was unsuited for anything except wetlands. The solution involved planting groves of eucalyptus (350,000 trees in all), which grew quickly in the muddy soil, eventually drying it out enough to create a labyrinth of fairways and greens with dozens of water traps. The course wraps itself around a luxury hotel (the Meridien Penina). Greens fees are 12,500$ to 13,500$ ($72.50 to $78.30) for 18 holes.

WHERE TO STAY

✪ **Alvor Praia.** Praia dos Três Irmãos, Alvor, 8500 Portimão. ☎ **082/45-89-00.** Fax 082/45-89-99. E-mail: pestana.hotels@mail.telepac.pt. 198 units. A/C MINIBAR TV TEL. Summer 42,850$–49,300$ ($248.55–$285.95) double; 48,200$–81,300$ ($279.55–$471.55) suite. Off-season, 15,570$–25,900$ ($90.30–$150.20) double; 17,700$–29,900$ ($102.65–$173.40) suite. Rates include breakfast. AE, DC, MC, V. Free parking.

This citadel of hedonism is so self-contained you might never stray from the premises. On a landscaped crest, the luxury hotel has many of its guest rooms and public rooms exposed to the ocean view, gardens, and Olympic-size pool. The guest rooms are decorated in a classically modern style; most have oversized beds, long desk-and-chest combinations, and well-designed bathrooms with double basins and lots of towels. Many have private balconies where you can eat breakfast with a view of the Bay of

Lagos. Rooms to avoid are those in the rear with so-so views, small balconies, and Murphy beds. The bi-level main dining room boasts three glass walls so every guest has an ocean view. The Grill Maisonette is your best bet. Facilities include a health club.

Le Meridien Penina Golf & Resort. Montes de Alvor, 8502 Portimão. ☎ **800/ 225-5843** in the U.S., or 082/41-54-15. Fax 082/41-50-00. 196 units. A/C MINIBAR TV TEL. 30,000$–55,000$ ($174–$319) double; 59,000$–101,000$ ($342.20–$585.80) suite. Children 3–13 stay free in parents' room. AE, DC, MC, V. Free parking.

The first deluxe hotel on the Algarve was this major sporting mecca located between Portimão and Lagos. Most guest rooms contain picture windows and honeycomb balconies, with views of the course and pool, or vistas of the Monchique hills. The spacious rooms are pleasantly furnished, combining traditional pieces with Portuguese provincial spool beds; the so-called attic rooms have the most charm, with French doors opening onto terraces. You can dine at any of four restaurants. Facilities include three championship golf courses (one 18-hole and two 9-hole), a private beach with its own snack bar and changing cabins reached by shuttle bus, a pool, and six floodlit hard tennis courts.

WHERE TO DINE

Restaurante O Búzio. Aldeamento da Prainha, Praia dos Três Irmãos. ☎ **082/45-87-72.** Reservations recommended. Main courses 2,800$–4,500$ ($16.25–$26.10); set-price dinner 3,600$ ($20.90). AE, DC, MC, V. Daily 7–10:30pm. Closed Nov–Feb. INTERNATIONAL.

This restaurant stands at the end of a road encircling a resort development dotted with exotic shrubbery. Lunch and dinner are served in separate locations; dinner is in a room where blue curtains reflect the color of the shimmering ocean visible at the bottom of the cliffs. Your dinner might include fish soup, gazpacho, carre de borrego Serra da Estrela (grantinée of roast lamb with garlic, butter, and mustard), Italian pasta dishes, or lamb kebabs with saffron-flavored rice. The wine cellar is extensive.

SILVES

When you pass through the Moorish-inspired entrance of this hillside town, you'll quickly realize that Silves is unlike other Algarve towns and villages. It lives in the past, recalling its heyday when it was known as Xelb, the seat of Muslim culture in the south before it fell to the crusaders. Since then, Christian warriors and earthquakes have been rough on the town.

To reach Silves from Portimão, take N-125 east for 5 miles to Lagoa, a market town. This is the junction with the road (124) leading 4½ miles north to Silves.

EXPLORING SILVES

The red-sandstone **Castle of Silves,** crowning the hilltop, may date back to the 9th century. From its ramparts, you can look down on the saffron-mossed tile roofs of the village houses and the narrow cobbled streets where roosters strut and scrappy dogs sleep peacefully in the doorways. Once the blood of the Muslims, staging their last stand in Silves, "flowed like red wine," as one Portuguese historian wrote, and the cries and screams of women and children resounded over the walls. Inside the walls, the government has planted a flower garden, adorning it with golden chrysanthemums and scarlet poinsettias. In the fortress, water rushes through a huge cistern and a deep well made of sandstone. Below are dungeon chambers and labyrinthine tunnels where the last of the Moors hid out before the crusaders found them. The castle at Silves is free, and open daily from 9am to 1pm and 2:30 to 5:30pm.

The 13th-century former **cathedral of Silves** (now a church), below the castle, was built in the Gothic style. You can wander through its aisles and nave, noting the beauty in their simplicity. The flamboyant Gothic chancel and transept date from a later period. The Christian architects who originally constructed it may have torn down an old mosque. Many of the tombs here are believed to have been the graves of crusaders who took the town in 1244. The structure is one of the most outstanding religious monuments in the Algarve. The cathedral is also free; it's open June to September daily from 8:30am to 1pm and 2:30 to 6pm, closes at 5:30pm October through May.

WHERE TO DINE

Ladeira. Ladeira de São Pedro 1. ☎ **082/44-28-70.** Main courses 950$–3,000$ ($5.50–$17.40); tourist menu 1,400$ ($8.10). AE, MC, V. Mon–Sat noon–3pm and 6–10pm. PORTUGUESE.

This rustic restaurant is a well-known neighborhood spot on the western outskirts of Silves. It features grilled fish, home cooking, and regional specialties. Steak Ladeira and mixed-fish *cataplana* (a local stew) are especially good. In season, game such as partridge or rabbit is often served.

ARMAÇÃO DE PÊRA

Squat fishers' cottages make up the core of this ancient village that rests almost at water's edge on a curvy bay near **Golden Beach,** one of the largest along Portugal's southern coast. Near the center of the village is a wide beach where fishing boats are drawn up on the sand when a fish auction (*lota*) is held. In the direction of Portimão are rolling low ridges, while Albufeira's rosy cliffs rise to the east. Once used by the Phoenicians as a trading post and stopping-off point, Armação de Pêra has almost become engulfed in a sea of high-rise buildings, which have virtually eliminated its once rather charming character.

From Silves, head 9 miles southeast along N-125 and follow the signs to Alcantar-ilha, where you'll see the first signs pointing to Armação de Pêra, 5 miles away. You can also reach the resort by bus from Lisbon, a trip of about 4 hours, or by train to the village of Alcantarilha.

While at the resort, you may want to walk out to **Nossa Senhora da Rocha (Our Lady of the Rock),** a Romanesque chapel on a 95-foot-high stone that sticks out into the ocean like the prow of a boat. Underneath are cathedral-size **sea grottoes** (*furnas*). Unique in the Algarve, the sea caves are entered through a series of arches that frame the sky and ocean from the inside. In their galleries and vaults, where pigeons nest, the splashing and cooing reverberate in the upper stalactite-studded chambers.

The **tourist office,** on Avenida Marginal (☎ **082/31-21-45**), open Monday to Friday 9:30am to 12:30pm and 2 to 5:30pm and Saturday 9:30am to 12:30pm, can offer advice about how to visit these sea caves. Basically, all you need to do is walk down to any local beach and negotiate with a group of fishers to take you to the caves. There's no formal tour operator for this. A 2-hour excursion generally costs 2,500$ ($14.50) per person.

WHERE TO STAY

Hotel Viking. Praia da Nossa Senhora da Rocha, 8365 Armação de Pêra. ☎ **082/31-48-76.** Fax 082/31-48-52. 186 units. A/C MINIBAR TV TEL. Apr–Oct, 22,400$–25,800$ ($129.90–$149.65) double; 35,000$ ($203) suite. Nov–Mar, 6,800$–7,600$ ($39.45–$44.10) double; 10,800$ ($62.65) suite. Rates include breakfast. AE, DC, MC, V. Free parking.

About a mile southwest of the resort, this hotel rises in a mass of gray stone and buff-colored concrete between two spits of land jutting into the sea. A 1997 renovation made it competitive with many of the newer hotels nearby. The hotel has contemporary guest rooms with wall-to-wall carpeting, marble-sheathed bathrooms, and private balconies angled toward the sea. Drinking and dining choices include a cocktail lounge, a large bar leading into an enormous dining room, and a snack bar. There's also a replica of a 19th-century cafe set in a sheltered courtyard. Facilities include use of nearby tennis courts, a watersports staff, and two clifftop pools.

WHERE TO DINE

Panorama Sol Grill. Alporchinos. ☎ **082/31-24-24.** Reservations recommended. Main courses 950$–2,400$ ($5.50–$13.90). No credit cards. Daily noon–3pm and 6–10:30pm. Closed mid-Nov to Jan. PORTUGUESE/INTERNATIONAL.

On the road west of town leading to the Hotel Viking, this restaurant occupies an expanded 300-year-old former mill that's 300 yards from the edge of the sea. You can dine in an outdoor walled-in terrace, but if you continue to climb past an outdoor grill to the top of the stairs, you'll find a baronial dining hall with its own stone fireplace and a relatively dignified ambience. The catch of the day, as well as an array of meats, is usually displayed in a refrigerated case. Menu choices might include sea bass, fresh asparagus, giant prawns with garlic, and several preparations of beef, veal, and pork.

Santola. Largo da Fortaleza. ☎ **082/31-23-32.** Reservations recommended. Main courses 2,800$–6,500$ ($16.25–$37.70). AE, MC, V. Daily noon–3pm and 6:30–11pm. Closed mid-Nov to Jan. PORTUGUESE/SEAFOOD.

This popular restaurant was thriving back when Armação de Pêra was only a sleepy fishing village. It's in the heart of the resort adjacent to the sea in a building that's at least a century old. "The Spider Crab" specializes in fresh seafood dishes that always seem to focus with justifiable pride on a wonderful version of *cataplana,* a local stew with onions, tomatoes, shellfish, and fish. Other worthy choices are filets of hake in white sauce with mushrooms and shrimp; sea bass or monkfish in garlic sauce; and grilled swordfish. Grilled meats such as steak and pork filets are also on the menu. In chilly weather, the blazing fireplace alleviates the cold dampness.

ALBUFEIRA

The cliffside town of Albufeira, formerly a fishing village, is the Saint-Tropez of the Algarve. The lazy life, sunshine, and beaches make it a haven for young people and artists. Although the old-timers still regard the foreign invasion that began in the late 1960s with some ambivalence, some residents open the doors of their cottages to those seeking a place to stay. Travelers without the money often sleep in tents on the cliff or under the sky.

The big, bustling resort retains characteristics more closely associated with a North African seaside community. Its streets are steep, and the villas are staggered up and down the hillside. Albufeira rises above a sickle-shaped **beach** that shines in the bright sunlight. A rocky grottoed bluff separates the strip used by the sunbathers from the working beach, where brightly painted fishing boats are drawn up on the sand. Beach access is provided by a passageway tunneled through the rock.

ESSENTIALS

ARRIVING   By Train   Trains connect Albufeira with Faro (see below), which has good connections to and from Lisbon. The train station is 4 miles north of the center, but frequent buses run back and forth to the resort every 30 minutes. The fare is 200$ ($1) one-way. Call ☎ **089/57-16-16** for information and schedules.

By Bus   Buses run between Albufeira and Faro every hour; the trip takes 1 hour and costs 625$ ($3.60) one-way. Seven buses per day link Portimão with Albufeira, also a 1-hour trip. This trip costs 500$ to 700$ ($2.90 to $4.05). Call ☎ **089/58-97-55** for information and schedules.

By Car   Continue east from Armação de Pêra for 8½ miles along N-125.

VISITOR INFORMATION   The **Tourist Information Office** is on Rua 5 de Outubro (☎ 089/58-52-79).

WHERE TO STAY

Estalagem do Cerro. Rua Samora Barros, 8200 Albufeira. ☎ **089/58-61-91.** Fax 089/58-61-91. 95 units. A/C TV TEL. 10,000$–16,000$ ($58–$92.80) double. AE, DC, MC, V.

Estalagem do Cerro manages to capture Algarvian charm without neglecting modern amenities. This "Inn of the Craggy Hill" is half a mile east of the center at the top of a hill overlooking Albufeira's bay, about a 10-minute walk down to the beach. The older regional-style building has been renovated, but its character has been maintained; it's joined to a modern structure in a similar Moorish style. The tasteful guest rooms have verandas overlooking the sea, pool, or garden. A panoramic dining room provides good meals. On most nights, the hotel hosts some type of entertainment, often dancing. The inn has an outdoor heated pool in a garden setting.

Hotel Montechoro. Av. Dr. Francisco Sá Carneiro, Montechoro (Apartado 928), 8200 Albufeira. ☎ **089/58-94-23.** Fax 089/58-99-47. E-mail: reservas@grupomontechoro.com. 362 units. A/C TV TEL. June–Aug, 22,400$–25,800$ ($130–$150) double; 35,000$ ($203.50) suite. Off-season, 6,800$–7,600$ ($39.50–$44.20) double; 10,800$ ($62.80) suite. Rates include buffet breakfast. AE, V. Parking 250$ ($1.45).

This is the largest hotel in and around Albufeira, a four-star resort set in the vacation-oriented suburb of Montechoro, about a mile northeast of Albufeira's center. The modern, somewhat streamlined guest rooms open onto views of the sunbaked countryside. The hotel's only drawback is its lack of an adjacent beach, although management supplies frequent minivans to Oura Beach, about a mile away, and the bar-packed center of Albufeira. Dining choices include the Restaurant Montechoro and the more formal Grill das Amendoeiras, on the panoramic fifth floor. Facilities include two pools, eight professional tennis courts, two squash courts, a sauna, and a gym.

WHERE TO DINE

O Cabaz da Praia. Praça Miguel Bombarda 7. ☎ **089/51-21-37.** Reservations recommended. Main courses 2,500$–5,000$ ($14.50–$29). AE, MC, V. Fri–Wed noon–2:30pm and 6:30–11pm. FRENCH/PORTUGUESE.

The 32-year-old "Beach Basket" sits on a colorful little square near the Church of São Sebastião, now a museum. In a former fisher's cottage, the restaurant has an inviting ambience and good food. With its large sheltered terrace, it offers diners a view over the main Albufeira beach. Main courses, including favorites such as cassoulet of seafood, salade océane, and papillotte of salmon, are served with fresh vegetables. The restaurant is renowned for its lemon meringue pie. If you're visiting in winter, call first.

VALE DO LOBO

Almancil, 8 miles west of Faro and 15 miles east along N-125 from Albufeira, is a small market town of little interest, yet it's a center for two of the most exclusive tourist developments along the Algarve: **Vale do Lobo,** 4 miles southeast of Almancil, and **Quinta do Lago,** 6 miles southeast of town. Both are a golfer's paradise.

PLAYING GOLF

Vale do Lobo, Vale do Lobo, 8135 Almancil (☎ **089/39-39-39**), has played an important role in establishing Portugal's image as a golfer's paradise. Its name, which means valley of the wolf, suggests some forlorn spot set amid bleak terrain—but this course is hardly that. It was originally designed by British golfer Henry Cotton as three 9-hole courses, but a recent addition of another 9-hole course has allowed the management to create two 18-hole courses, the Oceanfront and the Royal. Some of the long shots along both of these courses require driving the ball over ravines, where variable winds make a straight shot difficult.

Although both courses are equally desirable and, in most respects, equally challenging, greens fees at the newer Royal Course cost 18,000$ ($104.40) for 18 holes of play, as opposed to 15,000$ ($87) for the Oceanfront Course.

Since its opening in 1991, **Vila Sol,** Alto do Semino (☎ 089/30-05-05), has been judged as having the best fairways and the boldest and most inventive contours of any course in the Algarve. Designed by English architect Donald Steel, it's part of a 362-acre residential estate. Great care was taken in allowing the terrain's natural contours to determine the layout of the fairways and greens. Vila Sol was selected as host to the Portuguese Open 2 years in a row (1992 and 1993). Golfers especially praise holes 6, 7, and 8, which manage to funnel golf balls around and over ponds, creek beds, and pine groves in nerve-racking order. Par is 72, and greens fees for 18 holes are 14,250$ ($82.65).

The most famous and sought-after of this complex's trio of golf courses is the **Vilamoura Old Course,** sometimes called Vilamoura I (☎ 089/31-03-41), laid out in 1969 by noted English architect Frank Pennink. The most English of south Portugal's golf courses, it's invariably praised for its beauty, lushness, and landscaping. Although some of its holes are almost annoyingly difficult (four par-fives), the course is among the most consistently crowded on the Algarve. Its par is 73, and greens fees are 18,000$ ($104.40) for 18 holes.

Adjacent to the Old Course are a pair of newer, less sought-after courses. They include the **Pinhal Golf Course,** formerly known as Vilamoura II (☎ 089/32-15-62), noted for the challenging placement of its many pines. Greens fees cost between 5,750$ and 11,500$ ($33.35 to $66.70), depending on the season and the time of day. Nearby is the newest of the three, **Laguna Golf Course,** Vilamoura III (☎ 089/31-01-80), with a labyrinth of water traps and lakes. Greens fees range from 5,250$ to 10,500$ ($30.45 to $60.90), depending on the season and the time of day. Tee-offs in the heat of noon are less expensive than the more sought-after early morning slots. Pars for both Pinhal and Laguna are 72.

Quinta do Lago also has superb facilities and is one of the most elegant "tourist estates" on the Algarve. This pine-covered beachfront property has been the retreat of everybody from movie stars to European presidents. The resort's 27 superb holes of golf are also a powerful lure.

Of the four golf courses that undulate across the massive Quinta do Lago development, the par-72 ✪ **São Lourenço** (☎ 089/39-65-22) is the most interesting, challenging, and prestigious. Set amid the grassy wetlands of the Rio Formosa Nature Reserve, home to millions of waterfowl, its contours were crafted by American golf designers William (Rocky) Roquemore and Joe Lee. In 1997, *Golf World* magazine voted it the second most-desirable course in continental Europe. Ironically, although the hotel lies within the confines of Quinto do Logo, it's closely associated with the Meridien Doña Felipa Hotel in Vale do Lobo, 4½ miles to the west. Residents of that hotel pay 7,000$ ($40.60) for 18 holes of golf. Greens fees for everyone else cost 24,500$ ($142.10) for 18 holes. The most panoramic hole on this course is the 6th; the most frustrating are the 8th and 18th. Many long drives, especially those on the 17th and 18th holes, soar over the waters of a saltwater lagoon.

Quinta do Lago (☎ 089/39-07-00), the namesake course of the massive development, is actually composed of four 9-hole golf courses identified as A, B, C (designed by American William Mitchell), and D (designed by American Joe Lee). Together they comprise more than 600 acres of sandy terrain abutting the Rio Formosa Wildlife Sanctuary. Very few long drives here are over open water; instead, the fairways undulate through cork forests, groves of pine trees, and terrain with sometimes abrupt changes in elevation. Golfers can combine any of the course's four quadrants into different 18-hole combinations, all par 72. Greens fees run 15,000$ ($87) for 18 holes and 7,500$ ($43.50) for 9.

Pinheiros Altos, Quinta do Lago (☎ **089/39-43-40**), is one of the most deceptive golf courses on the Algarve, with contours that even professional golfers have misplayed. Abutting the wetland refuge of the Rio Formosa National Park, its 250 acres of terrain, designed by U.S. architect Ronald Fream, are dotted with pines and small lakes. Carts navigate their way around the terrain on cobble-covered paths. The par is 73. Greens fees are 16,000$ ($92.80) for 18 holes and 9,000$ ($52.20) for 9.

WHERE TO STAY

Hotel Meridien Dona Filipa. Vale de Lobo, 8136 Almancil. ☎ **800/237-2747** in the U.S., or 089/39-41-41. Fax 089/39-42-88. 162 units. A/C MINIBAR TV TEL. June–Aug, 44,000$–47,500$ ($255.20–$275.50) double; from 68,500$ ($397.30) suite. Off-season, 33,500$–37,000$ ($194.30–$214.60) double; from 53,000$ ($307.40) suite. Rates include breakfast. AE, DC, MC, V. Free parking.

Dona Filipa is a deluxe golf hotel with impressive grounds embracing 450 acres of rugged coastline. The exterior is somewhat uninspired, but a greater thoughtfulness was brought to the interior with green-silk banquettes, marble fireplaces, Portuguese ceramic lamps, and old prints over baroque-style love seats. The well-furnished guest rooms have balconies. The hotel includes a grill restaurant serving an à la carte menu and, by the pool, a coffee shop offering lunch. Facilities include three tennis courts and discounts on greens fees at nearby golf courses.

✪ **Quinta do Lago.** Quinta do Lago, 8135 Almancil. ☎ **800/223-6800** in the U.S., or 089/39-66-66. Fax 089/39-63-93. 141 units. A/C MINIBAR TV TEL. 40,000$–79,000$ ($232–$458.20) double; from 80,000$ ($464) suite. AE, DC, MC, V. Free parking.

This is the hotel associated with the massive Quinta do Lago resort development, a sprawling, 1,600-acre estate that incorporates private villas, golf courses, beachfront, swimming pools, and a host of resort-oriented amenities. The contemporary buildings in Mediterranean style rise three to six floors. The guest rooms are generally spacious, with tile or marble bathrooms and balconies that open onto views of the estuary. The Navegadores is an informal grill room overlooking a pool. Facilities include a riding center, one of the best in southern Europe; a 27-hole golf course, designed by American William F. Mitchell, that's among the top six in Europe; tennis courts; indoor and outdoor pools; and a health club.

WHERE TO DINE

Montinho's Casa Velha. Quinta do Lago. ☎ **089/39-49-83.** Reservations recommended. Main courses 3,500$–4,300$ ($20.30–$24.95); set-price menu 7,500$ ($43.50). AE, MC, V. Mon–Sat 7–10:30pm. Closed mid-Dec to Jan. FRENCH.

Casa Velha is an excellent choice that's not part of the massive Quinta do Lago resort but overlooks the resort's lake from a century-old farmhouse. The menu is French, with a scattering of Portuguese and international dishes. Specialties include a salad of chicken livers and gizzards with leeks and vinaigrette, and roasted duck *en service* (the staff presents different parts of the bird throughout the meal, beginning with the thighs *en confit* and ending with the breast *en magret*). Other choices are carefully flavored sea bass, sole, and rack or saddle of lamb.

✪ **Restaurant Ermitage.** Estrada Almancil-Vale de Lobo. ☎ **089/39-43-29.** Reservations recommended. Main courses 3,500$–4,800$ ($20.30–$27.85); set menu 8,000$–9,700$ ($46.40–$56.25). AE, MC, V. Tues–Sat 7–10:30pm. Closed 3 weeks in Dec, 2 weeks in Jan, and 1 week in June. From Almancil, drive 2 miles south, following the signs to Vale de Lobo. ITALIAN/SWISS/INTERNATIONAL.

Our favorite restaurant in the region occupies an 18th-century farmhouse surrounded by gardens and flowering vines. Built from locally quarried stone, its focal point is a cozy dining room whose fireplaces add warmth in winter and whose outdoor terrace adds beauty in summer. Starters include goose-liver terrine with blackberry sauce and a "symphony of homemade pastas," shrimp and spinach-stuffed ravioli with four other pastas and sauces. Main courses, which change with the season and the chef's inspiration, include grilled fish of the day with herb-flavored hollandaise sauce and filet of monkfish with prawn-and-curry sauce. A favorite dessert is a walnut-flavored parfait with freshly made ice cream and mocha sauce. Your hosts, and the restaurant's manager and chef, are the Dutch-born Willemina Gilhooley and her husband, Vincent.

FARO

Loved by the Romans and later by the Moors, Faro is the main city of the Algarve. Since Afonso III drove out the Moors for the last time in 1266, Faro has been Portuguese. On its outskirts an international airport brings in thousands of visitors every summer. The airport has done more than anything else to speed tourism not only to Faro, but also to the entire Algarve.

ESSENTIALS

ARRIVING   By Plane   You can fly to Faro from Lisbon in 45 minutes. For **flight information,** call ☎ **089/80-08-01.** You can then take bus no. 14 or 16 to the railway station in Faro. The bus operates daily 7:20am to 9:40pm, leaving every 45 minutes. The one-way fare is 160$ (95¢).

By Train   Trains arrive in Faro from Lisbon six times a day, taking between 4 and 7 hours for the one-way transit. One-way fares costs 2,600$ ($15.10) in second class and around 3,600$ ($20.90) in first. For rail information in Faro, call the **railway station** at Largo Estação (☎ **089/80-17-26**).

By Bus   Buses arrive seven times a day from Lisbon after a 4½-hour journey. The **bus station** is on Avenida da República (☎ **089/89-97-60**), adjacent to the railway station.

By Car   After leaving Vale do Lobo, continue east along N-125 directly into Faro.

VISITOR INFORMATION   The **Tourist Office** is at Rua da Misericórdia 8–12 (☎ **089/80-36-04**). Open June to September daily 9:30am to 7pm; otherwise, Monday to Friday 9:30am to 7pm, Saturday and Sunday 9:30am to 5:30pm.

SEEING THE SIGHTS

The most bizarre attraction in Faro is the **Capela d'Ossos (Chapel of Bones),** entered via a courtyard from the rear of the **Igreja (Church) de Nossa Senhora do Monte do Carmo do Faro,** on Largo do Carmo. Erected in the 19th century, this chapel is completely lined with the skulls and bones of human skeletons, an extraordinarily ossicular rococo. In all, it's estimated that there are 1,245 skulls. The chapel is open Monday to Friday 10am to 1pm and 2:30 to 5pm, and Saturday 10am to 1pm. Entrance is free to the church but 250$ ($1.45) to the chapel.

Other religious monuments include the old **Sé (cathedral),** Largo da Sé, built in the Gothic and Renaissance styles (originally a Muslim mosque stood on this site); and the **Igreja de São Francisco,** Largo de São Francisco, with panels of glazed earthenware tiles in milk white and Dutch blue depicting the life of the patron saint. The church is open Monday to Friday 10am to 5pm, and Saturday 10am to 1:30pm. Entrance to the church costs 250$ ($1.45). Yes, they charge admission to enter the church, somewhat of a rarity in Portugal. Sunday masses are conducted at 10am and 11am (no charge then).

But most visitors don't come to Faro to look at churches. Rather, they take the harbor ferry to the wide white-sand beaches of **Praia de Faro,** on an islet. The ride is available only in summer. The beach is also connected to the mainland by bridge, 4 miles from the town center. Once here, you can water-ski, fish, or just rent a deck chair and umbrella and lounge in the sun.

WHERE TO STAY

Eva. Av. da República, 8000 Faro. ☎ **089/80-33-54.** Fax 089/80-23-04. 148 units. A/C TEL. 16,700$–24,100$ ($96.85–$139.80) double; 24,500$–33,000$ ($142.10–$191.40) suite. AE, DC, MC, V. Free Parking.

Eva dominates the harbor like a fortress. This modern five-story hotel occupies an entire side of the yacht-clogged harbor. It was beginning to look worn and tired, but a recent rejuvenation has perked it up. There are direct sea views from most guest rooms, which are furnished in a restrained, even austere, style and equipped with new mattresses and tiny bathrooms; some contain minibars. The better rooms open onto the water with large balconies. The Eva's best features are its penthouse restaurant and rooftop pool.

WHERE TO DINE

Dois Irmãos. Largo do Terreiro do Bispo 13–15. ☎ **089/82-33-37.** Reservations recommended. Main courses 900$–3,200$ ($5.20–$18.55); set-price menu 1,800$ ($10.45). AE, MC, V. Daily noon–11pm. PORTUGUESE.

This popular Portuguese bistro, founded in 1925, has a no-nonsense atmosphere appreciated by its devotees. The menu and the prices are as modest as the place, but you get a good choice of fresh fish and shellfish. Ignore the paper napkins and concentrate on the fine kettle of fish placed before you. Clams in savory sauce is a favorite, and sole is regularly featured—of course, everything depends on the catch of the day. Service is slow but amiable.

Restaurante Cidade Velha. Rua Domingos Guieiro 19. ☎ **089/82-71-45.** Reservations recommended. Main courses 1,780$–2,750$ ($10.30–$15.95). AE, DC, V. Mon–Fri 12:30–2pm and 7:30–10:30pm; Sat 7:30–10:30pm. PORTUGUESE/INTERNATIONAL.

The leading restaurant in town is the Cidade Velha, which used to be one of the best private homes in Faro. You'll find it behind the cathedral, with thick stone walls built at least 250 years ago. Meals are served in a pair of rooms, each with a vaulted brick ceiling. The cooking is first-rate, as you'll agree as you feast on smoked mackerel mousse, mushroom pâté en brioche, filet of sole in cream sauce, or filet of pork stuffed with dates and walnuts and flavored with port wine.

DAY TRIPS FROM FARO

OLHÃO   Olhão, described as the living re-creation of a Georges Braque collage, is the famous cubist town of the Algarve, so long beloved by painters. In its heart, white blocks stacked one on the other, with flat red-tiled roofs and exterior stairs on the stark walls, evoke the casbahs of North Africa. But let us not paint too romantic a portrait. Many readers have found it disappointing—dirty, dusty, and too commercial.

If you do go here, try to attend the **fish market** near the waterfront when a *lota* (auction) is underway. Olhão is also known for its bullfights of the sea, in which fishermen wrestle with struggling tuna trapped in nets and headed for the smelly warehouses along the harbor.

For the best view, climb **Cabeça Hill,** its grottoes punctured with stalagmites and stalactites, or **St. Michael's Mount,** offering a panorama of the casbah-like Barreta. Finally, for one of the most idyllic beaches on the Algarve, take a 10-minute motorboat ride to the **Ilha de Armona,** a nautical mile away. Olhão, 6½ miles west of Faro, is reached by going east on N-125.

SÃO BRAS DE ALPORTEL   Traveling north from Faro for 12½ miles, you'll pass through groves of figs, almonds, and oranges, and through pine woods where resin collects in wooden cups on the tree trunks. At the end of the run, you come upon isolated São Bras de Alportel, one of the Algarve's most charming and least-known spots.

Far from the crowded beaches, it attracts those wanting pure air, peace, and quiet—a bucolic setting filled with flowers pushing through nutmeg-colored soil. Northeast of Loulé, this whitewashed, tile-roofed town rarely gets lively except on **market days.** Like its neighbor, Faro, it's noted for its perforated plaster chimneys. Lying at the foot of the Serra do Caldeirão, the whole area has been called one vast garden.

A change of pace from the seaside accommodations is offered at **Pousada de Sao Bras,** Estrada de Lisboa, N2, 8150 Saoñ Bras de Alportel (☎ **089/84-23-05**). The government-owned inn built in 1942 is a hilltop villa, with fret-cut limestone chimneys and a crow's-view of the surrounding serras. Many visitors come just for lunch or dinner (daily 12:30 to 2:30pm and 7:30 to 9:30pm). The 3,600$ ($20.90) table d'hôte menu offers soup, a fish course, a meat dish, vegetables, and dessert. The cuisine is plain but good. The Pousada, the third one built in Portugal, also offers 33 well-furnished bedrooms, each with air conditioning, minibar, and TV. The cost ranges from 16,000$ to 24,600$ ($92.80 to $142.70) a day with breakfast included. American Express, Mastercard, and Visa are accepted.

VILA REAL DE SANT ANTÓNIO/MONTE GORDO

Twenty years after the Marquês de Pombal rebuilt Lisbon, which had been destroyed in the 1755 earthquake, he sent architects and builders to Vila Real de Santo António to reestablish the frontier town on the bank opposite Spain. It took only 5 months. Pombal's motivation was jealousy of Spain. Much has changed, of course, although Praça de Pombal remains. An obelisk stands in the center of the square, which is paved with inlays of black-and-white tiles radiating outward like the sun. Separated from its Iberian neighbor by the Guadiana River, Vila Real de Santo António offers a car-ferry between Portugal and Ayamonte, Spain.

Today, Vila Real is a mostly residential and industrial community that prides itself on its royal and historical associations. It's supplemented today by Monte Gordo. Set 2 miles to the east, it's the site of most of the region's tourist facilities and hotels, with easier access to the sandy beaches that attract tourists every summer from as far away as Northern Europe.

ESSENTIALS

ARRIVING   By Train   The railway facilities in Vila Real are bigger, better accessorized, and more convenient than those in Monte Gordo, which has a railway stopping point but not a bona-fide station. In Vila Real, however, 11 trains per day arrive from Faro, a 90-minute ride. Tickets costs 500$ ($2.90) each way. Four direct trains arrive from Lagos (many more require transfers en route), each taking 4½ hours and costing 980$ ($5.70) each way. For railway information and schedules, call ☎ **081/ 54-32-42.**

By Bus   It's faster to take the bus from Faro to Vila Real. Five *espressos* per day arrive from Faro, taking 1 hour. The cost is 710$ ($4.10). Eight buses arrive from Lagos (a 4-hour trip), and four buses a day pull in from Lisbon (a 6-hour trip). Call ☎ **089/ 51-18-07** for information. Buses pull into Vila Real at the bus station on the Avenida Da República.

By Car   From Faro, take N-125 53 miles east to reach your final destination, at the Spanish frontier.

VISITOR INFORMATION   The **tourist office** is on Avenida Infante Henrique in Monte Gordo (☎ 081/54-44-95). Open June to September daily 9:30am to 7pm; otherwise, Monday to Friday 9:30am to 7pm, and Saturday and Sunday 9:30am to 5:30pm.

EXPLORING VILA REAL

A long esplanade, **Avenida da República,** lines the river, and from its northern extremity, you can view the Spanish town across the way. Gaily painted **horse-drawn carriages** take you sightseeing past the shipyards and the lighthouse.

A short drive north on the road to Mertola takes you to the gull-gray castle-fortress of **Castro Marim.** This formidable structure, with its walls and ramparts, is a legacy of the old border wars between Spain and Portugal. Afonso III, who expelled the Moors from this region, founded the original fortress, which was razed by the 1755 earthquake. Inside the walls are the ruins of the **Church of São Tiago,** dedicated to St. James.

Directly southwest of Vila Real is the emerging resort of **Monte Gordo,** which has the greatest concentration of hotels in the eastern Algarve after Faro. Monte Gordo is the last in a long line of Algarvian resorts; it's 2 miles southwest of the frontier town of Vila Real de Santo António at the mouth of the Guadiana River. Its wide beach, one of the finest along the southern coast of Portugal, is backed by lowlands.

Sadly, this was once a sleepy little fishing village. Now young men tend to work in the hotels instead of on the sea, fishing for tips instead of tunny. It has many good hotels, and a number of Europeans use it as their place in the Algarvian sun.

WHERE TO STAY

In Vila Real

Hotel Apolo. Av. dos Bombeiros Portugueses, 8900 Vila Real de Santo António. ☎ **081/51-24-48.** Fax 081/51-24-50. 42 units. A/C TV TEL. 7,500$–16,000$ ($43.50–$92.80) double. Rates include breakfast. AE, DC, MC, V. Free parking.

Built in the mid-1980s on the western edge of town, near the beach and the river, Hotel Apolo attracts vacationers as well as travelers who don't want to cross the Spanish border at night. The hotel is a marginal choice, with a spacious marble-floored lobby leading into a large bar scattered with comfortable sofas and flooded with sunlight. The simply furnished guest rooms have comfortable beds, cramped bathrooms, and balconies.

✪ **Hotel Guadiana.** Av. da República 94, 8900 Vila Real de Santo António. ☎ **081/51-14-82.** Fax 081/51-14-78. 37 units. A/C TV TEL. 8,000$–12,000$ ($46.40–$69.60) double; 12,000$–16,000$ ($69.60–$92.80) suite. AE, DC, MC, V.

This is the best hotel in town (which isn't saying a lot), housed in a mansion classified as a historic national monument. Close to the river and the Spanish border, it's ideally located for exploring the town, less than a mile from Santo António beach. The guest rooms are traditional and old-fashioned but have modern amenities, including comfortable beds, plus small but well-maintained private bathrooms—most often with a shower instead of a tub. There's a cozy bar, and breakfast is the only meal served.

In Monte Gordo

Hotel Alcázar. Rua de Ceuta, Monte Gordo, 8900 Vila Real de Santo António. ☎ **081/51-21-84.** Fax 081/51-22-42. 95 units. A/C MINIBAR TV TEL. 7,500$ ($43.50) double; 9,500$ ($55.10) suite. AE, DC, MC, V.

Hotel Alcázar, last renovated in 1994, is the best hotel at the resort. A freeform pool is built on terraces into the retaining walls that shelter it from the wind and extend the hot-weather season late into autumn. The interior design is a vaguely Arabesque series of repetitive arches and vaults. Each rather austere unit has its own sun terrace. The basement disco is open in summer. An alluring spot is under the soaring ceiling of the in-house restaurant, where formal meals (rather standard fare) are served.

Hotel dos Navegadores. Monte Gordo, 8900 Vila Real de Santo António. ☎ **081/51-24-90.** Fax 081/51-28-72. E-mail: tanginsor@mail.telepac.pt. 344 units. TEL. 10,500$–26,000$ ($60.90–$150.80) double; 14,400$–34,250$ ($83.50–$198.65) suite. Rates include breakfast. AE, DC, MC, V.

This hotel is popular with vacationing Portuguese and British families, who congregate under the dome covering the atrium's pool. The public rooms are clean and functional, and about three-quarters of the standardized guest rooms have balconies. The bedrooms are far from glamorous, but most are rather airy and roomy, each with a decent and rather comfortable mattress. The beach is only a 5-minute walk away. There are dull boutiques in a corridor near the pool, along with a hairdresser and a coffee shop. The hotel restaurant serves Portuguese and international dishes (dinner only).

Hotel Vasco Da Gama. Av. Infante D. Henríque, Monte Gordo, 8900 Vila Real de Santo António. ☎ **081/51-13-21.** Fax 081/51-16-22. 169 units. TV TEL. 10,500$–24,650$ ($60.90–$142.95) double. AE, DC, MC, V.

The entrepreneurs here know what their guests seek—lots of sunbathing and swimming. Although this hotel enjoys a position on a long, sandy beach, it also offers an Olympic-sized pool with a high-dive board and nearly an acre of flagstoned sun terrace. All the spartan guest rooms are furnished conservatively, and glass doors open onto balconies. There's an oceanfront dining room.

WHERE TO DINE

Edmundo. Av. da República 55. ☎ **081/51-15-39.** Reservations recommended. Main courses 1,400$–2,800$ ($8.10–$16.25). AE, DC, MC, V. Mon–Sat noon–3pm and 7–10pm; Sun 7–10pm. PORTUGUESE.

Edmundo has long been known in the Algarve, attracting Spaniards who often visit just for the day. It overlooks the river and Spain across the water—try to get a sidewalk table. The people who run this place are friendly and proud of their local cuisine, especially fresh seafood. You might begin with shrimp cocktail, and then follow with fried sole, crayfish, or sautéed red mullet. You can also order such meat dishes as lamb cutlets and veal filet.

by Darwin Porter & Danforth Prince

Whether you go to Scotland to seek out your ancestral roots, explore ancient castles, drive the whisky trail, or partake in the internationally acclaimed Edinburgh Festival, you'll find a country rich in history, legend, and romance. If it's the outdoors you love, Scotland offers great salmon fishing, peaceful walks in heather-covered Highland hills, and some of the best (and the oldest) golf courses in the world.

1 Edinburgh & Environs

One of Europe's fairest cities, "the Athens of the North," Edinburgh is the second most visited city in Britain after London. It is a "whitecollar" city in contrast to industrialized bastions such as Aberdeen or Glasgow. Edinburgh has played a large role in Scottish and British history. John Knox, Mary Queen of Scots, Robert Louis Stevenson, Sir Arthur Conan Doyle, Alexander Graham Bell, Sir Walter Scott, and Bonnie Prince Charlie are all part of the city's past; you can walk in their footsteps along Prince Street and the Royal Mile, and explore the sights associated with them. But today Edinburgh is as hip as it is historic. Home of the ever-growing Edinburgh Festival, and its alternative Fringe offspring, this city has exploded onto the scene as one of Europe's cultural capitals.

Only in Edinburgh

Contemplating Edinburgh from Arthur's Seat You'll visit the Highlands in miniature from Arthur's Seat, a volcanic hill, 823 feet above sea level (reached by a climb that begins in the surrounding Holyrood Park). The view of Endinburgh twinkling below is "magical," and Scots congregate here to await the summer solstice.

Visiting Dean Village About 100 feet below the level of the rest of the city, Dean Village is an 800-year-old grain-milling town on the Water of Leith. Take in the local color from its woodland walk along the river. Exotic denizens of nearby Stockbridge village amuse with their zany makeup and dress.

Shopping Along Princes Street This is Edinburgh's main street, the local equivalent of New York's Fifth Avenue. Flower-filled gardens stretch along the street's south side. You can browse and buy among the country's finest merchandise—from kilts to Scottish crystal.

Edinburgh

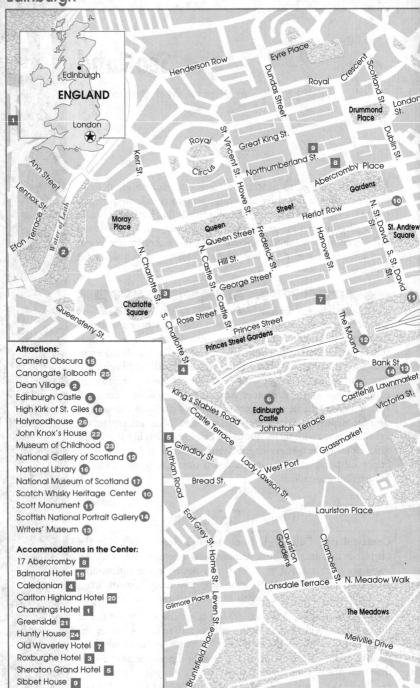

Attractions:
Camera Obscura **15**
Canongate Tolbooth **25**
Dean Village **2**
Edinburgh Castle **6**
High Kirk of St. Giles **18**
Holyroodhouse **26**
John Knox's House **22**
Museum of Childhood **23**
National Gallery of Scotland **12**
National Library **16**
National Museum of Scotland **17**
Scotch Whisky Heritage Center **10**
Scott Monument **11**
Scottish National Portrait Gallery **14**
Writers' Museum **13**

Accommodations in the Center:
17 Abercromby **8**
Balmoral Hotel **19**
Caledonian **4**
Carlton Highland Hotel **20**
Channings Hotel **1**
Greenside **21**
Huntly House **24**
Old Waverley Hotel **7**
Roxburghe Hotel **3**
Sheraton Grand Hotel **5**
Sibbet House **9**

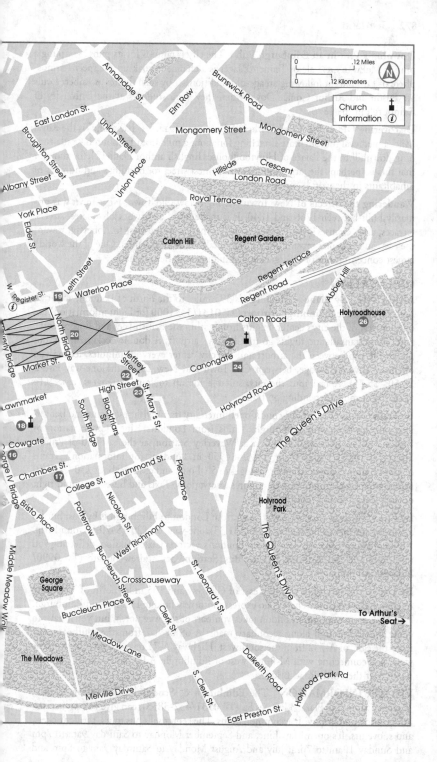

Downing a Pint in an Edinburgh Pub   The city is famous for its pubs. Sampling a pint of McEwan's real ale or Tennent's lager is a chance to soak up the special atmosphere of Edinburgh, following an age-old tradition set by such figures as Robert Louis Stevenson and Arthur Conan Doyle when they were students at the University of Edinburgh in the 1870s.

Discovering Old Town   This is where Edinburgh began. Its "backbone" is the Royal Mile, a medieval thoroughfare stretching for about a mile from Edinburgh Castle running downhill to the Palace of Holyroodhouse. English author Daniel Defoe thought that this is "perhaps the largest, longest, and finest street for buildings and number of inhabitants in the world."

Wandering the Streets of New Town   Lying below Old Town, New Town was primarily built between 1766 and 1840. It is made up of a network of squares, streets, terraces, and "circuses" that reaches from Haymarket in the west to Abbeyhill toward the east, and occupies most of the northern half of the city's center. One of the world's largest concentrations of Georgian-style buildings can be seen here.

ORIENTATION

ARRIVING   By Plane   Edinburgh is 393 miles to the north of London, about an hour's flying time. **Edinburgh Airport** (☎ 0131/3331000 for flight information) lies 6 miles west of the city's center. Flights from within the British Isles and Europe come here; most transatlantic flights go to Glasgow's airport. A double-decker Airlink bus makes the trip between the airport and the city center every 20 minutes, letting you off near Waverley Bridge, between Old Town and New Town; the one-way fare is £3.50 ($5.75). A taxi into the city, suitable for up to four passengers, costs £14 ($23.10) or more, depending on traffic.

By Train   Fast, efficient, air-conditioned InterCity trains with restaurant and bar service link London with Edinburgh. Trains from London's King's Cross Station or Euston Station arrive in Edinburgh at **Waverley Station,** at the east end of Princes Street (☎ 0131/5562477 or 0345/484950 in London, for information). Trains depart London every hour or so, taking 4 to 5½ hours and costing about £50 ($82.50) round-trip. An overnight sleeper requires reservations. Taxis and buses are found right outside the station in Edinburgh.

By Bus   The least expensive way to go from London to Edinburgh is by bus, but it's a 9-hour journey. The fare is £19 ($31.35) one-way or £29 ($47.85) round-trip. National Express coaches depart from London's Victoria Coach Station, delivering you to Edinburgh's **St. Andrew Square Bus Station,** St. Andrew Square (☎ 0990/808080 in Edinburgh).

By Car   Edinburgh lies 46 miles east of Glasgow and 105 miles north of Newcastle upon Tyne in England. There is no express motorway linking London and Edinburgh. The M-1 motorway from London takes you part of the way north, but you'll have to come into Edinburgh along secondary roads: A-68 or A-7 from the southeast, A-1 from the east, or A-702 from the southwest. Highway A-71 or A-8 comes in from the west, A-8 connecting with M-8 just west of Edinburgh; A-90 comes down from the north over the Forth Road Bridge.

VISITOR INFORMATION   The **Edinburgh & Scotland Information Centre,** Waverley Shopping Plaza, 3 Princes St. (☎ 0131/437-3855), can give you sightseeing information and help with accommodations. The center sells bus tours, theater tickets, and souvenirs. It's open May, June, and September Monday to Saturday 9am to 7pm and Sunday 10am to 7pm; July and August Monday to Saturday 9am to 8pm and

Sunday 10am to 8pm; April and October Monday to Saturday 9am to 6pm and Sunday 10am to 6pm; and November to March Monday to Wednesday 9am to 5pm, Thursday to Saturday 9am to 6pm, and Sunday 10am to 5pm. There's also an **information and accommodation desk** at Edinburgh Airport (☎ **0131/3332167**), which is open according to the frequency of incoming flights.

CITY LAYOUT   Edinburgh is divided into an **Old Town** and a **New Town.** Chances are, you'll find lodgings in New Town and visit Old Town for dining, drinking, shopping, and sightseeing.

New Town, with its world-famous **Princes Street,** came about in the 18th century in the "Golden Age" of Edinburgh. The first building went up in New Town in 1767, and by the end of the century, classical squares, streets, and rows of townhouses had been added. Princes Street runs straight for about a mile; it's known for its shopping and also for its beauty, as it opens onto the **Princes Street Gardens** with stunning views of Old Town.

North of Princes Street, and running parallel to it, is the second great street of New Town, **George Street.** It begins at Charlotte Square and runs east to St. Andrew Square. Directly north of George Street is another impressive thoroughfare, **Queen Street,** opening onto Queen Street Gardens on its north side.

You'll also hear a lot about **Rose Street,** directly north of Princes Street. It has more pubs per square block than any other place in Scotland, and is also filled with shops and restaurants.

Everyone seems to have heard of the **Royal Mile,** the main thoroughfare of Old Town, beginning at Edinburgh Castle and running all the way to the Palace of Holyroodhouse. A famous street to the south of the castle (you have to descend to it) is **Grassmarket,** where convicted criminals were hung on the dreaded gallows that once stood here.

GETTING AROUND   **Walking** is the best way to explore Edinburgh, particularly Old Town with its narrow lanes, wynds, and closes. Most attractions are along the Royal Mile, Princes Street, or on one of the major streets of New Town.

By Bus   This will probably be your chief method of transport within the Scottish capital. The fare you pay depends on the distance you ride, based on a confusing system that derives from "stages" that usually incorporate between two and five bus stops and a distance of about a half-mile. The minimum fare you pay depends on the distance you intend to travel; the driver determines the fare, sells you your ticket, and even makes change. The minimum bus fare is 50p (85¢) per adult, for one or two stages, going up to a maximum of £1.60 ($2.65) per adult for travel between 28 or more stages. Children 5 to 15 pay a flat rate of 50p (85¢), regardless of how many stages they travel, and children 4 and under ride free and must be accompanied by an adult.

The **Edinburgh Freedom Ticket** allows 1 day of unlimited travel on city buses at a cost of £2.40 ($3.95) for adults and £1.50 ($2.45) for children aged 5 to 15. (Any adult can be accompanied by up to two children aged 4 or under for free.) A **Tourist Card,** providing unlimited bus transit during the period of its validity, plus discounts on some museum entrances, is available in increments of 2 to 7 days. A 2-day pass costs £12 ($19.80) for adults and £6 ($9.90) for children, and a 7-day pass sells for £22 ($36.30) for adults and £13.50 ($22.30) for children. For daily commuters or diehard Scottish enthusiasts, a **RidaCard** season ticket allows unlimited travel on all buses at a cost of £10.50 ($17.35) for adults for 1 week, and £30.50 ($50.30) for 4 weeks. The validity of the RidaCard, regardless of its duration, always begins on a Sunday and requires the presentation of a passport-sized photograph. For children aged 5 to 15, the cost is £6.50 ($10.75) for 1 week, and £18 ($29.70) for 4 weeks.

These tickets and further information can be obtained from the Edinburgh Tourist Office or the **Lothian Region Transport Office,** 14 Queen St. (☎ 0131/555-6363).

By Taxi Cabs can be hailed on the street or met at any of several taxi stands, each of which lie at important intersections throughout the city. Fares are prominently displayed in the front of each taxi. The meter begins ticking at £1.30 ($2.15) between 6am and 6pm, and at £1.80 ($2.95) between 6pm and 6am. Regardless of the time of day, you're charged 20p (35¢) per 300 yards (about a quarter-mile). If you phone for a cab at any time, you pay a surcharge of 60p ($1). To call a taxi, dial **City Cabs** (☎ 0131/228-1211) or **Central Radio Taxi** (☎ 0131/229-2468).

By Car Car rentals are relatively expensive, and driving in Edinburgh is a tricky business, with plenty of one-way streets—and few parking spots. However, a car is convenient, and sometimes a must, for touring the countryside. Most companies will accept your U.S. or Canadian driver's license, provided you have held it for more than a year and are over 21.

Most of the major rental car agencies maintain offices at the Edinburgh airport: Try **Avis** (☎ 0990/900500), **Hertz** (☎ 0131/556-8311), or **Eurodollar** (☎ 0131/337-8686).

By Bicycle You can rent bikes by the day or by the week from a number of outfits. Nevertheless, bicycling is not a good idea for most visitors because the city is constructed on a series of high ridges and terraces.

You might, however, want to rent a bike for exploring the flatter countryside. Try **Central Cycle Hire,** 13 Lochrin Place (☎ 0131/228-6333), off Home Street in Tollcross, near the Cameo Cinema. Depending on the type of bike, rates range from £10 to £15 ($16.50 to $24.75) per day. A deposit of £50 to £100 ($82.50 to $165) is imposed. The shop is open Monday through Saturday from 10am to 5:30pm; June through August it also opens Sunday noon to 5pm. Another outfitter charging basically the same rates is **Edinburgh Cycle Hire,** 29 Blackfriars St. (☎ 0131/556-5560).

Fast Facts: Edinburgh

American Express The office is at 139 Princes St. (☎ 0131/2257881), 5 blocks from Waverley Station. Open Monday to Wednesday and Friday 9am to 5:30pm, Thursday 9:30am to 5:30pm, and Saturday 9am to 4pm.

Baby-sitters The most reliable service is **Guardians,** 13 Eaton Terrace (☎ 0131/343-3870).

Business Hours In Edinburgh, **banks** are usually open Monday to Friday 9am to 5pm. **Shops** are generally open Monday to Saturday 9am to 5pm.

Currency The basic unit of currency is the **pound sterling** (£), which is divided into 100 **pence** (p). There are 1p, 2p, 10p, 20p, 50p, £1, and £2 coins; banknotes are issued in £1, £5, £10, £20, £50, and £100 denominations. The exchange rate used in this chapter was $1 = 61p or £1 = $1.65. Also, 1EUR = .65£.

Currency Exchange There's a **Bureau de Change** at 3 Princes St., the top floor of the Waverley Shopping Plaza (☎ 0131/557-3953).

Dentists For a dental emergency, go to the **Edinburgh Dental Institute,** 39 Lauriston Place (☎ 0131/536-4900), open Monday through Friday from 9am to 3pm. For an alternative, with a schedule that fluctuates according to the season and the staff, try the emergency dental services at the **Western General Hospital,** Crewe Road South (☎ 0131/537-1000).

Doctors   In a medical emergency, you can seek help from the **Edinburgh Royal Infirmary,** 1 Lauriston Place (☎ **0131/536-1000**). Medical attention is available 24 hours.

Drugstores   There are no 24-hour drugstores (called "chemists" or "pharmacies") in Edinburgh. The major drugstore is **Boots,** 48 Shandwick Place (☎ **0131/225-6757**), open Monday through Saturday 8am to 9pm and Sunday 10am to 5pm.

Embassies & Consulates   The Consulate of the **United States** is at 3 Regent Terrace (☎ **0131/556-8315**), which is an extension of Princes Street beyond Nelson's Monument. The **Canadian** consulate is at Standard Life House, 30 Lothian Rd. (☎ **0131/220-4333**). Visitors from other countries should contact their embassies in London.

Emergencies   Call ☎ **999** in an emergency to summon the police, an ambulance, or firefighters.

Eyeglasses   Your best bet is **Boots Opticians,** 101–103 Princes St. (☎ **0131/225-6397**), Monday through Saturday 9am to 6pm; Thursday until 7:30pm.

Hospital   The best and most convenient is the **Edinburgh Royal Infirmary,** 1 Lauriston Place (☎ **0131/536-1000**).

Internet Access   Try **Cyberia Edinburgh,** 88 Hanover St. (☎ **0131/220-4405;** e-mail: edinburgh@cybersurf.co.uk).

Lost Property   If you've lost property (or had it stolen), go to Police Headquarters on Fettes Avenue (☎ **0131/311-3131**).

Luggage Storage & Lockers   You can store luggage at **Waverley Station,** at Waverley Bridge (☎ **0131/556-2477**), open daily from 6:10am to 11pm.

Photographic Needs   **Edinburgh Cameras,** 55 Lothian Rd. (☎ **0131/229-4416**), is open Monday through Saturday 9am to 5:30pm.

Post Office   The Edinburgh Branch **Post Office,** St. James's Centre (☎ **0131/5508232**), is open Monday 9am to 5:30pm, Tuesday to Friday 8:30am to 5:30pm, and Saturday 8:30am to 6pm.

Taxes   A 17.5% value-added tax (known as VAT) is added to all goods and services in Edinburgh, as elsewhere in Britain. There are no special city taxes.

Telephone   The United Kingdom's **country code** is **44.** The city code for **Edinburgh** is **0131.** If you're calling from inside the U.K. but outside the city code area, dial the complete area code; if you're calling from outside the U.K., drop the zero. As in the United States, if you're calling from inside the code area, dial just the seven-digit number.

   Public phones cost 10p (16¢) for the first 3 minutes and accept coins of various denominations. You can also purchase at post offices and newsstands a phone card for use in special phones. A 3-minute phone call to the United States costs about £4.50 ($7.45). Or you can reach an **AT&T** operator and get U.S. rates for collect or credit card calls by dialing toll free ☎ **0800/890011.** To reach an **MCI** operator, dial ☎ **0800/890222.** To reach a **Sprint** operator, dial ☎ **0800/890877** or 0500/890877.

WHERE TO STAY

One of the most convenient hotels to the airport is the **Swallow Royal Scot,** 111 Glasgow Rd. (☎ **0131/334-9191**), lying off the A8 on the western outskirts of Edinburgh. Doubles, including breakfast, range from £125 to £185 ($206.25 to $305.25).

VERY EXPENSIVE

✪ **Balmoral Hotel.** Princes St., Edinburgh, Lothian EH2 2EQ. ☎ **800/223-6800** in the U.S. or 0131/5562414. Fax 0131/5578740. www.rfhotels.com. E-mail: ijones@balmoral-rf. demon.co.uk. 186 units. A/C MINIBAR TV TEL. May–Sept £215–£265 ($354.75–$437.25) double, from £350 ($577.50) suite; Oct–Apr £175–£205 ($288.75–$338.25) double, from £260 ($429) suite. AE, DC, MC, V. Parking £15 ($24.75). Bus: 15 or 17.

This legendary establishment was originally opened in 1902 as the largest, grandest, and most impressive hotel in the north of Britain. After its sale to the Rocco Forte group in 1998, the hotel benefited from a renovation of some eight million pounds. Its soaring clock tower is a city landmark. Furnished with reproduction pieces, the bedrooms are distinguished, conservative, and rather large, a graceful reminder of Edwardian sprawl with a contemporary twist. Rooms today are often in neutral or pastel-tinged monochromes, with a Scottish baronial theme. Rounded or oversized windows and the many original Victorian/Edwardian quirks that survived renovations contribute to this monument's indelible charm. The hotel's most elegant restaurant is Number 1 Princes Street (see "Where to Dine," below). Facilities include a large and well-equipped health club with Jacuzzi, sauna, exercise equipment, and a pool.

Caledonian Hotel. Princes St., Edinburgh, Lothian EH1 2AB. ☎ **800/223-6800** in the U.S., or 0131/459-9988. Fax 0131/225-6632. 247 units. MINIBAR TV TEL. £220–£299 ($363–$493.35) double; from £275 ($453.75) suite. Children 15 and under stay free in parents' room. AE, DC, MC, V. Bus: 3, 31, 36, or 69.

"The Caley" is Edinburgh's most visible hotel, with commanding views over Edinburgh Castle and the Princes Street Gardens. It's built of Dumfriesshire stone, a form of deep red sandstone used in only three other buildings in town. Completely renovated in 1991, the hotel remains a city landmark. The pastel-colored public rooms evoke the age of Edwardian splendor, and the often spacious bedrooms are conservatively but individually styled with reproduction furniture. The fifth-floor rooms are the smallest. Although the accommodations are comparable to other first-class hotels in Edinburgh, the Caledonian lacks the leisure facilities of its major competitor, the Balmoral. Of the hotel restaurants, the formal La Pompadour Restaurant (see "Where to Dine," below) serves the best food.

EXPENSIVE

Carlton Highland Hotel. 19 North Bridge, Edinburgh, Lothian EH1 1SD. ☎ **0131/ 556-7277.** Fax 0131/556-2691. 197 units. MINIBAR TV TEL. £184 ($303.60) double; from £250 ($412.50) suite. Children 14 and under stay free in parents' room. AE, DC, MC, V. Bus: 4, 15, 35, or 44.

The Victorian turrets, Flemish-style gables, and severe gray stonework of this hotel rise imposingly from a street corner on the Royal Mile, a few steps from Waverley Station. A former department store, the hotel was converted into a bright and airy space with hardwood paneling, pastel colors, and modern conveniences. Each bedroom has a kind of Scandinavian simplicity, with matching tartan draperies and spreads, and coffeemakers, hair dryers, and trouser presses. Bathrooms tend to be quite small. The hotel's restaurant, Quills, resembles a private 19th-century library, and offers an international and Scottish regional menu. Facilities include an exercise room with a swimming pool, solarium, whirlpool, sauna, two squash courts, and an aerobics studio.

Channings Hotel. South Learmonth Gardens, Edinburgh, Lothian EH4 1EZ. ☎ **0131/ 315-2226.** Fax 0131/3329631. 48 units. TV TEL. Apr–Oct £155 ($255.75) double; Nov–Mar £130 ($214.50) double. Rates include breakfast. Children 14 and under stay free in parents' room. AE, DC, MC, V. Bus: 18, 19, 41, or 81.

Seven blocks north of Dean Village, in a tranquil residential area that's a 5-minute drive from the city center, sits one of Edinburgh's leading townhouse hotels. Five Edwardian terrace houses were combined to create this hotel that maintains the atmosphere of a Scottish country house with oak paneling, ornate fireplaces, molded ceilings, and antiques. The bedrooms are tastefully modern; the front units overlook a cobblestoned street lined with townhouses with lovely window boxes full of greenery and flowers in the summer. The units in back are quieter. The most desirable rooms are labeled "Executive," and they often have bay windows and wingback chairs; standard rooms are a bit cheaper, but are much smaller. In the downstairs bar and brasserie, Scottish/French cuisine is served.

Old Waverley Hotel. 43 Princes St., Edinburgh, Lothian EH2 2BY. ☎ **0131/5564648.** Fax 0131/5576316. 66 units. TV TEL. Apr–Oct £160 ($264) double; Nov–Mar £152 ($250.80) double. AE, DC, MC, V. Parking £4 ($6.60) for 8 hours. Bus: 4, 15, or 44.

Opposite Waverley Station, the Old Waverley Hotel dates back to 1848, when the seven-floor structure was built to celebrate the then-newfangled railroads. The hotel has completed a major redecorating of its bedrooms, and they look brighter and fresher than ever. Some units look onto Princes Street and, at night, the floodlit Edinburgh Castle; units have satellite TVs, trouser presses, and hair dryers. A good carvery-style restaurant serves à la carte and table d'hôte meals. Twenty-four-hour room service is available.

Roxburghe Hotel. 38 Charlotte Sq., Edinburgh, Lothian EH2 4HG. ☎ **0131/240-5300.** Fax 0131/240-5656. 201 units. A/C TV TEL. £180–£195 ($297–$321.75) double; £230 ($379.50) suite. Children 13 and under stay free in parents' room. AE, DC, MC, V. Parking £5 ($8.25). Bus: 3, 21, 26, 31, or 85.

Originally a stately four-story Adam townhouse of dove-gray stone, the hotel stands on a tree-filled square at the corner of noisy George Street, a short walk from Princes Street. In 1999 it reopened with a new wing, more than doubling the original size of the hotel. The new wing offers four-star hotel comfort, completely contemporary styling, and up-to-date furnishings, including better mattresses. The old wing of the hotel remains much as it was before, with ornate ceilings and woodwork, antique furnishings, and tall arched windows opening toward the park in front. All rooms have thoughtful extras, such as trouser presses and tea/coffeemakers. There are two restaurants, the Consult, offering fine à la carte Scottish cuisine, and the more informal Melrose, a bistro with light fare. There are also three bars.

✪ **Sheraton Grand Hotel.** 1 Festival Sq., Edinburgh, Lothian EH3 9SR. ☎ **800/325-3535** in the U.S. and Canada, or 0131/229-9131. Fax 0131/228-4510. 261 units. A/C MINIBAR TV TEL. June–Sept £230–245 ($379.50–$404.25) double; from £340 ($561) suite; off-season, £145 ($239.25) double, £215 ($355) suite. Children 18 and under stay free in parents' room. AE, DC, MC, V. Bus: 4, 15, or 44.

Town leaders still praise the development of a former railway siding, a short walk from Princes Street, into a six-story postmodern structure that houses a glamorous hotel and office complex. The hotel is elegantly appointed and run by a team of helpful concierges. The spacious, well-upholstered guest rooms offer double-glazed windows. The hotel has two restaurants: the brasserie-style Terrace, with castle views and a conservatory atmosphere, where chefs prepare specialties before you, and the Grill Room, small and intimate with traditional warm wood paneling, providing the best of Scottish produce. A leisure center offers a swimming pool (too small for lap swimming), whirlpool, sauna, and fully equipped gym.

MODERATE

17 Abercromby Place. 17 Abercromby Place, Edinburgh, Lothian EH3 6LB. ☎ **0131/557-8036.** Fax 0131/558-3453. E-mail: eirlyslloyd@virgin.net. 6 units. TV TEL. £90–£100 ($148.50–$165) double. Rates include breakfast. MC, V.

Eirlys Lloyd runs this fine B&B, just a 5-minute walk north of Princes Street. Although designed by a less-well-known architect, the five-story gray stone terrace house was the home in the 1820s of William Playfair, who designed many of Edinburgh's most visible landmarks, including the Royal Scottish Academy and Surgeon Hall on the campus of the Royal College of Surgeons. Two rooms are in what was originally a separate mews house, now connected to the main house. Evening meals can be arranged.

Ellersly Country House Hotel. 4 Ellersly Rd., Edinburgh, Lothian EH12 6HZ. ☎ **0131/337-6888.** Fax 0131/313-2543. 57 units. TV TEL. £95–£119 ($156.75–$196.35) double; £114–£134 ($188.10–$221.10) executive rm. AE, DC, MC, V. Take A-8 2½ miles west of the city center.

Surrounded by walled gardens, this three-story Edwardian country house offers the privacy of a home. It's in a dignified west-end residential section near the Murrayfield rugby grounds, about a 5-minute ride from the center, and is one of Edinburgh's best moderately priced hotels. The well-equipped bedrooms vary in size and are in either the main house or a less desirable annex. After recent renovations, the hotel is better than ever, and service is first-class. The hotel has a well-stocked wine cellar and offers good-tasting Scottish and French meals. A fitness center is nearby.

✪ **Sibbet House.** 26 Northumberland St., Edinburgh, Lothian EH3 6LS. ☎ **0131/556-1078.** Fax 0131/557-9445. www.sibbet-house.co.uk. E-mail: sibbet.house@net.co.uk. 4 units. TV TEL. £90–£100 ($148.50–$165) double; from £100–£120 ($165–$198) suite. Rates include breakfast. MC, V. Bus: 13, 23, or 27.

Set on a residential terrace a 10-minute walk from Princes Street, this sandstone-fronted, three-story Georgian house is the cheerful domain of James Sibbet and his French-born wife, Aurora, who do everything they can to distinguish their family home from "just another hotel." If asked, James (proud of his Lowland Scottish origins) will play the bagpipes. Rooms are small to medium, but comfortably cozy with fine linens and mattresses. There's a drawing room/salon where glasses are supplied for those who bring their own liquor.

INEXPENSIVE

A Haven. 180 Ferry Rd., Edinburgh, Midlothian EH6 4NS. ☎ **0131/554-6559.** Fax 0131/554-5252. www.ahaven.co.uk. E-mail: reservations@a-haven.co.uk. 12 units. TV TEL. £64–£90 ($105.60–$148.50) double. Rates include breakfast. AE, MC, V. Bus: 1, 6, 7, 14, 14A, 14B, CE.

This is a semidetached gray stone, four-story Victorian house, built in 1862, within a 15-minute walk or a 5-minute bus ride north of the rail station. The traditionally furnished rooms were completely refurbished in 1997. The bedrooms on the lower floors are more spacious and noisy; those upstairs are small, snug havens. Some rooms in back overlook the Firth of Forth, and those in the front have views of Arthur's Seat. Moira and Ronnie Murdock extend a Scottish welcome in this family-type place, and often offer their guests sightseeing advice. They have a licensed bar, but the only meal served is breakfast.

Greenside Hotel. 9 Royal Terrace, Edinburgh, Midlothian EH7 5AB. ☎ **0131/557-0022.** Fax 0131/557-0022. 15 units. TV TEL. £50–£100 ($82.50–$165) double; £22.50–£45 ($37.15–$74.25) per person triple. Rates include breakfast. AE, DC, MC, V. Bus: 4, 15, or 44.

Set behind a smooth, chiseled sandstone façade, on the back side of Carlton Hill, this is a four-story Georgian house originally built in 1786. During a long-running renovation, every effort was made to retain its Georgian features, including the high ceilings, the original cove moldings, and the elaborate trim. Bedrooms are larger than you might have imagined—so large that 10 of the 15 contain a double bed and two singles as well. Bathrooms are small and compact with a shower stall. The Firth of Forth, as well as the royal yacht *Britannia* are visible from the uppermost floors of the hotel's front side, and a sloping, tiered garden is visible from the rear. Breakfast is served in a formal dining room.

✪ **Teviotdale House.** Grange Loan, Edinburgh, Lothian EH9 2ER. ☎ **0131/667-4376.** Fax 0131/667-4376. E-mail: teviotdale.house@btinternet.com. 7 units. TV TEL. May–Sept £60–£76 ($99–$125.40) double; Oct–Apr £52–£70 ($85.80–$115.50) double. AE, MC, V. Bus: 42.

Some visitors rate this three-story 1848 house as the finest B&B in Edinburgh. Located south of the center, it's on a main bus route about 10 minutes from Princes Street, Waverley Station, and Edinburgh Castle. Jane E. Coville's attention to detail has earned her an enviable reputation. Each of the bedrooms is individually decorated. The house is completely nonsmoking and furnished with antiques. The home-cooked breakfast may be the highlight of your day's dining, and can include smoked salmon, kippers, and home-baked bread and scones.

WHERE TO DINE
IN THE CENTER: NEW TOWN
Expensive
✪ **The Atrium.** 10 Cambridge St. (beneath Saltire Ct.). ☎ **0131/228-8882.** Reservations recommended (for Fri–Sat evenings 2 weeks in advance). Main courses £8.50–£13 ($14–$21.45) lunch; £12.50–£20 ($20.65–$33) dinner. AE, MC, V. Mon–Fri noon–2:30pm and 6–10:30pm; Sat 6–10:30pm. Closed for 1 week at Christmas. MODERN MEDITER-RANEAN.

Since its opening in 1993, the Atrium has been one of the most analyzed and emu-lated restaurants in Edinburgh. No more than 60 diners can be accommodated in the "deliberately moody" dining room that's a fusion of Argentinean hacienda and stylish Beverly Hills bistro. Flickering oil lamps cast shadows on the dark-colored walls while patrons enjoy dishes prepared by chef Alan Metheison. Although offerings vary according to the whim of the chef and his manager, our favorites include grilled salmon or roasted seabass. The latter comes with Dauphinois potatoes, baby spinach, chargrilled eggplant, and baby fennel. Whether it's game or lamb from the Scottish Highlands, dishes have taste, style, and flair. The desserts are equally superb, especially the warm date pudding with caramelized dates and crème fraîche.

Bonars. 56 St. Mary's St. ☎ **0131/5565888.** Reservations required. Main courses £16.95 ($27.95); set-price lunch £10.80–£12.95 ($17.80–$21.35); set-price dinner £24.95 ($41.15). AE, MC, V. Daily noon–2pm and 5–10pm. Bus: 1, 6, 34, or 35. CLASSIC FRENCH/SCOTTISH.

Just off the Royal Mile, between Cowgate and Canongate, this restaurant is ranked among the top 60 in Scotland, and the service is the most polished in town, with crystal and fine bone china. Only the finest Scottish ingredients are used in its classic French cuisine, which is backed up by a carefully chosen wine list. Game and fish are specialties, and each dish—whether from the moors, lochs, or sea—is individually pre-pared. The menu changes frequently but has included confit of duck in a cassis sauce, Scottish salmon, and saddle of hare. The lunch menu is changed monthly, and the dinner menu is adjusted daily, depending on what is fresh at the market.

Café Royal Oyster Bar. 17 W. Register St. ☎ **0131/556-4124.** Reservations recom-mended year-round, but essential during the Edinburgh Festival. Main courses £14–£26 ($23.10–$42.90). AE, DC, MC, V. Daily noon–2pm and 7–10pm. Bus: 42 or 44. SEAFOOD/GAME.

Its physical space is one of the most dramatic in Edinburgh, thanks to its richly ornate Victorian bar and its soaring windows inset with stained-glass depictions of 19th-century

Scotsmen in full Highland dress. This intimate and quiet restaurant specializes in seafood and game dishes. Try the salmon with mussels, shrimp with Camembert and white wine, or oak-smoked haddock poached in cream and topped with spinach. The emphasis here is on freshness; daily deliveries include seafood that's still alive. Caviar and lobster are specialties.

La Pompadour Restaurant. In the Caledonian Hotel, Princes St. ☎ **0131/459-9988.** Reservations required. Main courses £12–£27 ($19.80–$44.55). AE, DC, MC, V. Tues–Sat 7:30–10:15pm. Bus: 4, 15, or 44. SCOTTISH/FRENCH.

On the mezzanine floor of the famous Caledonian Hotel, this restaurant serves fine Scottish and French cuisine. The restaurant has been refurbished, with gray wall panels interspersed with floral-patterned silk in a sort of Louis XV decor—after all, the restaurant is named for his mistress. The chef blends *cuisine moderne* with more traditional approaches in this intimate, luxurious place. The à la carte menu features fresh produce from both local and French markets—dishes such as goose liver with wild mushrooms, pan-fried scallops in a sesame seed vinaigrette, poached lobster with summer vegetables and a tarragon butter sauce, and lamb with a rosemary and garlic sauce. There is a nonsmoking area. The wine list is lethal in price and strangely absent of bottles from the New World.

Number 1 Princes Street. In the Balmoral Hotel, 1 Princes St. ☎ **0131/556-2414.** Reservations recommended. Main courses £19.50–£22 ($32.15–$36.30); set-price lunch £15.95–£18.95 ($26.30–$31.25); set-price 5-course dinner £50 ($82.50). AE, DC, MC, V. Mon–Fri noon–2pm; Sun–Thurs 7–10pm; Fri–Sat 7–10:30pm. SCOTTISH/CONTINENTAL.

This, the premier restaurant in the Balmoral Hotel, is an intimate, crimson-colored enclave one floor below the reception area. The decor is just informal enough to be interesting and just formal enough to be very, very elegant. This is very much the grand-style hotel dining room, and it offers good food if you don't mind paying high prices. There's always a delightful culinary surprise or two on the menu—perhaps a minestrone of Scottish seafood with an herb-laden tortellini. For a main course, opt for such dishes as roast Bresse pigeon in a Madeira dressing, pan-seared Isle of Skye monkfish with a saffron and mussel broth, or perhaps braised osso bucco with a variety of mushrooms. Tables are placed far apart, and the continental staff provides refined and polished service.

Moderate

Café Saint-Honoré. 34 NW Thistle Street Lane. ☎ **0131/226-2211.** Reservations recommended. Lunch main courses £7.75–£12.10 ($12.80–$19.95); dinner main courses £15.10–£16.40 ($24.90–$27.05). AE, DC, MC, V. Mon–Fri noon–2pm and Mon–Sat 7–10pm. Bus 12. FRENCH/SCOTTISH.

Between Frederick and Hanover Streets, this is a French-inspired bistro that transforms during the week from a deliberately rapid lunchtime spot to a much more formal and expensive affair in the evening. The menu is completely revised each day, based on whatever's fresh in the market and whatever the chefs feel inspired to cook. An upbeat and usually enthusiastic staff serves a combination of Scottish and French cuisine that includes venison with juniper berries and wild mushrooms, local pheasant in wine and garlic sauce, or lamb kidneys with broad beans. Fish is very fresh.

✪ **Peevers.** 167 Roe St. ☎ **0131/225-1546.** Reservations recommended. Set-price lunch £8 ($13.20); dinner main courses £7.95–£17 ($13.10–$28.05); set-price dinners £10–£15 ($16.50–$24.75). AE, MC, V. Daily noon–3pm and 5–10:30pm. Bus: 31 or 33. SCOTTISH.

One of the newest and most promising restaurants in the neighborhood was established in 1998 behind the somber-looking stone facade of what was a private house built around 1830. Inside, Steven Levey, head chef and owner, has created a decor based on hopscotch ("peevers"), a game close to the hearts of all Scottish children. You'll find an artfully simple patchwork decor with walls painted in solid tones of magnolia, yellow, and blue; a hopscotch board built into the wooden floor of one of the two dining rooms; paintings with evocative or nostalgic Scottish themes; and a menu and corporate logo designed by Mr. Levey's 7-year-old son. The menu focuses exclusively on Scottish produce prepared according to the traditional tenets of French cuisine. Examples include fresh West Coast mussels in a creamy herb sauce with wine, and haggis pâté, a mousse made from fresh sea trout and smoked salmon. Main courses include a highly unusual version of haggis Wellington (filet steak that's coated with a layer of the above-mentioned haggis pâté, flavored with Glayva, a whisky-based liqueur, and then wrapped in honey-glazed puff pastry). Other choices, depending on the inspiration of the French-trained chefs, include wine-poached fresh Scottish salmon with mushrooms and a white wine cream sauce, and pan-fried duck breast with apples and Calvados.

Inexpensive

Far Pavilions. 10 Craigleith Rd., Comely Bank. ☎ **0131/332-3362.** Reservations recommended. Lunch main courses £8.50–£12 ($14–$19.80); lunch buffet £7.95 ($13.10) per person; dinner main courses £7.90–£14 ($13.05–$23.10); children's menu £5.95 ($9.80). AE, DC, MC, V. Mon–Sat noon–2pm and 5:30–11:30pm. Bus: 21. INDIAN/CONTINENTAL.

Established in 1987, this authentic Indian restaurant offers finely tuned service. The long menu includes dishes from the Portuguese colony of Goa and the north Indian province of Punjab. Highly recommended is the house specialty, Murgi Massalam, with slow-cooked tandoori chicken in a garlic-based butter sauce that literally falls off the bone. All the British-influenced curry dishes are suitably piquant, whether lamb, seafood, vegetables, or beef.

✪ **Henderson's Salad Table.** 94 Hanover St. ☎ **0131/2252131.** Main courses £2.75–£4.75 ($4.55–$7.85). AE, DC, MC, V. Mon–Sat 8am–10:30pm. Bus: 23 or 27. VEGETARIAN.

This is a Shangri-la for health-food lovers. At this self-service place, you can pick and choose among eggs, carrots, grapes, nuts, yogurt, cheese, potatoes, cabbage, watercress—you name it. Hot dishes such as peppers stuffed with rice and pimiento are served on request, and a vegetarian twist on the national dish of Scotland—haggis—is usually available. Other well-prepared and flavorful dishes include cheese and onion potato croquet, vegetable lasagna, and a broccoli and cheese crumble. The homemade desserts include fresh-fruit salad and a cake with double-whipped cream and chocolate sauce. The wine cellar offers 30 wines. Live music, ranging from classical to jazz to folk, is played every evening.

Indian Cavalry Club. 3 Atholl Place. ☎ **0131/2283282.** Reservations required. Main courses £6–£13 ($9.90–$21.45); 2-course buffet lunch £6.95 ($11.45); 5-course table d'hôte dinner £16 ($26.40). AE, DC, MC, V. Daily noon–2:30pm and 5:30–11:30pm. Bus: 3, 21, 23, or 26. INDIAN.

Vegetarians flock here to enjoy the elegant atmosphere that evokes the golden age of the Raj. Here you'll find the expected Indian dishes, although much of it steamed, as well as Burmese and Nepalese specialties. The restaurant is divided into different sections, including the ground-floor Officers' Mess and the marquee-style Club Tent downstairs. The Indian Calvary Club is many cuts above the ordinary curry houses of Edinburgh.

IN THE CENTER: OLD TOWN

Expensive

Witchery by the Castle. Castlehill, the Royal Mile. ☎ **0131/225-5613.** Reservations recommended. Main courses £16.95–£21.95 ($27.95–$36.20); set-price 3-course lunch £14.95 ($24.65); set-price dinner £23.95 ($39.50); theater supper menu £9.95 ($16.40) 5:30–6:30pm. AE, DC, MC, V. Daily noon–4pm and 5:30–11:30pm. Bus: 1, 34, or 35. SCOTTISH.

This place bills itself as the "oldest, most haunted" restaurant in town and as the medieval meeting spot for the Hellfire Club. The building has been linked with witchcraft since the period between 1470 and 1722 when more than 1,000 people were burned alive on Castlehill. One of the victims, Old Mother Long Nose, once a practitioner of herbal medicine, allegedly haunts the Witchery. James Thomson, the owner and chef, uses his creative flair to make the restaurant, a member of the "Taste of Scotland" program, a good spot for genuine and unfussy Scottish food and hospitality. Menus change seasonally and might include Skye prawns or Tay salmon. Angus steak is a specialty. Vegetarian dishes are also offered; try the spinach fettuccine.

Moderate
Jackson's Restaurant. 209 High St., the Royal Mile. ☎ **0131/225-1793.** Reservations recommended. Main courses £11–£16.50 ($18.15–$27.20). AE, MC, V. Daily noon–2:30pm and 6–11pm. Bus: 35. SCOTTISH/FRENCH.

Serving a cuisine described as "Scottish with a French flair," this bustling, popular restaurant is in the austere but cozy stone cellar of a 300-year-old building. You select from a "Taste of Scotland" menu featuring local ingredients. The charming staff can help you translate such items as "beasties of the glen" (a poetic designation for haggis with a whisky-cream sauce); noisettes of venison served in a blackberry, red currant, and port wine sauce; and kilted salmon pan-fried in a green ginger and whisky sauce. The menu items sound so cute you might think it's a tourist trap, but it isn't.

Inexpensive
Baked Potato Shop. 56 Cockburn St. ☎ **0131/225-7572.** Reservations not accepted. Food items 80p–£3.20 ($1.30–$5.30). No credit cards. Daily 9am–9pm. Bus: 5. VEGETARIAN/ WHOLE FOOD.

This is the least expensive restaurant in a very glamorous neighborhood, and it attracts mobs of office workers every day. Many carry their food away. Place your order at the countertop, and it's served in ecology-conscious recycled cardboard containers. Only free-range eggs, whole foods, and vegetarian cheeses are used. Vegetarian cakes are a specialty.

Pierre Victoire. 10 Victoria St. ☎ **0131/225-1721.** Reservations recommended. Main courses £7.50–£9.50 ($12.40–$15.65); set-price lunch £5.90 ($9.75). MC, V. Daily noon–3pm and 6–11pm. Bus: 1, 34, or 35. FRENCH.

This is the original of six franchises, each named Pierre Victoire, that have sprouted up in recent years across Edinburgh. Many residents still prefer the original to the newer versions. It's an ideal, if chaotic, stop if you're antique shopping and climbing Victoria Street. Its long hours make it one of the most popular evening gathering places in the city. Wine specials are posted on the chalkboard. In a bistro setting with crowded tables, you can order grilled mussels in garlic with Pernod butter, scallops with salmon, or roast pheasant with cassis. Vegetarians will also find selections to suit their taste.

SOUTH OF THE CENTER
Expensive
Kelly's. 46 W. Richmond St. ☎ **0131/6683847.** Reservations recommended. Set-price 2- or 3-course dinner £21–£25 ($34.65–$41.25); 2- to 3-course lunch £12–£15 ($19.80–$24.75). DC, MC, V. Wed–Sat noon–2pm and 7–9:30pm. Bus: 11, 12, or 14. MODERN BRITISH/MODERN FRENCH.

Catering to a crowd of barristers, artists, financiers, and employees of the nearby university, this stylish restaurant is a 20-minute walk south of the center in a residential neighborhood. The place offers an intimate setting decorated with flowers, watercolors, and unusual ceramics. Focusing on fresh ingredients, the menu includes such dishes as galantine of duck with Cumberland sauce, loin of lamb, wild mushroom lasagna, and roast breast of duck with garlic. All desserts are homemade.

LEITH

In the northern regions of Edinburgh, Leith is the old port town, opening onto the Firth of Forth. Once it was a city of its own until it (and its harbor facilities) was slowly absorbed into Edinburgh.

Expensive

Vintners Room. The Vaults, 87 Giles St., Leith. ☎ **0131/554-6767.** Reservations recommended. Main courses £15–£18.50 ($24.75–$30.55); 2- to 3-course lunch £11.50–£14.50 ($18.95–$23.90). AE, MC, V. Mon–Sat 12:30–3pm and 6:30–11pm. Closed for 2 weeks at Christmas. Bus: 7 or 10. FRENCH/SCOTTISH.

This stone-fronted building was originally constructed around 1650 as a warehouse for the barrels of bordeaux (claret) and port that came in from Europe's mainland. Near the entrance, beneath a time-tested ceiling of oak beams, a wine bar serves food and drink beside a large stone fireplace. Most diners, however, head for the small but elegant dining room, illuminated by flickering candles. Here, elaborate Italianate plasterwork decorates a 300-year-old room formerly used for wine auctions. A robust cuisine includes seafood salad with mango mayonnaise, a terrine of smoked salmon and rabbit, loin of pork with mustard sauce, and venison in a bitter chocolate sauce.

SEEING THE SIGHTS
SIGHTSEEING SUGGESTIONS FOR FIRST-TIME VISITORS

If You Have 1 Day   Visit Edinburgh Castle as soon as it opens in the morning, and then walk the Royal Mile to the Palace of Holyroodhouse, former abode of Mary, Queen of Scots. Look out over the city from the vantage point of Arthur's Seat, and stroll through Princes Street Gardens, capping your day with a walk along the major shopping thoroughfare, Princes Street.

If You Have 2 Days   In the morning of your second day, head for Old Town again, but this time explore its narrow streets, wynds, and closes, and visit the John Knox House, the High Kirk of St. Giles, and the small museums. After lunch, climb the Scott Monument for a good view of Old Town and the Princes Street Gardens. Spend the rest of the afternoon exploring the National Gallery of Scotland.

If You Have 3 Days   Spend day 3 getting acquainted with the major attractions of New Town, including the National Museum of Scotland, National Portrait Gallery, Georgian House, and Royal Botanic Garden.

If You Have 4 Days   On the fourth day, take a trip west to Stirling Castle and see some of the dramatic scenery of the Trossachs.

THE ROYAL MILE

The Royal Mile stretches from Edinburgh Castle all the way to the Palace of Holyroodhouse. Walking along, you'll see some of the most interesting and oldest structures in Edinburgh, with their turrets, gables, and towering chimneys. Take bus no. 1, 6, 23, 27, 30, 34, or 36 to reach the various spots along the Royal Mile.

At 354 Castlehill, Royal Mile, the **Scotch Whisky Heritage Center** (☎ **0131/ 220-0441**) is privately funded by a conglomerate of Scotland's biggest whisky distillers. It highlights the economic effect of whisky on both Scotland and the world and illuminates the centuries-old traditions associated with whisky making, as well as the art and science of distilling. There's a 7-minute audiovisual show and an electric car ride past 13 theatrical sets showing historic moments in the whisky industry. Admission is £4.95 ($8.15) for adults, £3.50 ($5.75) for senior citizens and students with

ID, £2.50 ($4.15) for children under 17, and free for children under 6. For a supplement of £10 ($16.50), you can sample two whiskies during the tour. A tasting tour costs £18 ($29.70) per person, entitling you to sample five whiskies and take away a miniature bottle to enjoy later. Open daily 9:30am to 6pm.

The **Writer's Museum** lies in a close off Lawnmarket (☎ 0131/5294901). It was built in 1622 by a prominent merchant burgess and was once known as Lady Stair's House, taking its name from a former owner, Elizabeth, the dowager countess of Stair. Today it's a treasure house of portraits, relics, and manuscripts relating to three of Scotland's greatest men of letters—Robert Burns, Sir Walter Scott, and Robert Louis Stevenson. It's open Monday through Saturday from 10am to 5pm. Admission is free.

Inside the **High Kirk of St. Giles** on High Street (☎ 0131/225-9442), one outstanding feature is its **Thistle Chapel,** designed by Sir Robert Lorimer. It houses beautiful stalls and notable heraldic stained-glass windows. The church is open Monday through Saturday from 9am to 5pm (until 7pm in summer), and on Sunday from 1 to 5pm. Of course, you're welcome to join in the cathedral's services; they are conducted Sunday at 8am, 10am, 11:30am, and 6 and 8pm; Monday to Saturday 8am and noon. Cathedral guides are available at all times to conduct tours. Admission is free, but a £1 ($1.65) donation is suggested.

At 43–45 High Street is the **John Knox House** (☎ 0131/556-9579), with a history dating back to the late 15th century. Even if you're not interested in the reformer who founded the Scottish Presbyterian Church, you may want to visit his house, as it is characteristic of the "lands" that used to flank the Royal Mile. All of them are gone now, except Knox's house, with its timbered gallery. Inside, you'll see the tempera ceiling in the Oak Room, along with exhibitions of Knox memorabilia. The house is open Monday through Saturday from 10am to 4:30pm; admission is £1.95 ($3.20) for adults, 75p ($1.25) for children.

Museum of Childhood, 42 High St. (☎ 0131/529-4142), stands just opposite John Knox's House, the first museum in the world of its kind. The contents of its four floors range from antique toys and games to exhibits on health, education, and costumes. Because of the youthful clientele it naturally attracts, it also ranks as the "noisiest museum in the world." It's open Monday through Saturday from 10am to 5pm, and also from 2 to 5pm on Sunday during the Edinburgh Festival. Admission is free.

Continue along Canongate toward the Palace of Holyroodhouse. At 163 Canongate stands one of the handsomest buildings along the Royal Mile. **Canongate Tolbooth** was constructed in 1591 and was once the courthouse, prison, and center of municipal affairs for the burgh of Canongate.

Across the street at 142 Canongate is **Huntly House** (☎ 0131/529-4143), an example of a restored 16th-century mansion. Now it's Edinburgh's principal museum of local history. You can stroll through period rooms and reconstructions Monday through Saturday from 10am to 5pm and, during the festival, also on Sunday from 2 to 5pm. Admission is free.

HISTORIC SITES

✪ **Edinburgh Castle.** Castlehill. ☎ 0131/225-1012. Admission £6.50 ($10.75) adults, £5 ($8.25) seniors, £2 ($3.30) children 15 and under. Apr–Oct daily 9:30am–6pm; Nov–Mar daily 9:30am–5pm. Bus: 1, 6, or 34.

Although its early history is vague, it's believed that Edinburgh was built on the dead volcano, Castle Rock. It is known that in the 11th century, Malcolm III (Canmore) and his Saxon queen, later venerated as St. Margaret, founded a castle on this same spot. The only fragment left of their original castle—in fact, the oldest structure in Edinburgh—is **St. Margaret's Chapel.** Built in the Norman style, the oblong structure dates principally from the 12th century.

Inside the castle you can visit the **State Apartments,** particularly Queen Mary's bedroom, where Mary Queen of Scots gave birth to James VI of Scotland (later James I of England). The highlight is the Crown Chamber, which houses the Honours of Scotland (Scottish Crown Jewels), used at the coronation of James VI, along with the scepter and the sword of state of Scotland.

You can also view the Stone of Scone or "Stone of Destiny," on which Scottish kings had been crowned since time immemorial. Edward I of England carried the stone off to Westminster Abbey in 1296, where it rested under the British coronation chair. It was finally returned to its rightful home in Scotland in November 1996, where it was welcomed with much pomp and circumstance.

✪ **Palace of Holyroodhouse.** Canongate, at the eastern end of the Royal Mile. ☎ **0131/ 556-7371.** Admission £5.30 ($8.75) adults, £3.70 ($6.10) seniors, £2.60 ($4.30) children 15 and under; £13 ($21.45) family pass for 2 adults and 2 children. Apr–Oct daily 9:30am–6pm; Nov–Mar daily 9:30am–4pm. Closed Jan 1–3, 2 weeks in May (dates vary), the last week in June, the first week of July, and Dec 25–26. Bus: 1 or 6.

This palace was built adjacent to an Augustinian abbey established by David I in the 12th century. The nave, now in ruins, remains today. James IV founded the neighboring palace in the early part of the 16th century, but only the north tower is left. Much of what you see today was ordered built by Charles II.

The most dramatic incident in the history of Holyroodhouse occurred in the old wing when Mary Queen of Scots was in residence. Her Italian secretary, David Rizzio, was murdered (with 56 stab wounds) in the audience chamber by Mary's husband, Lord Darnley, and his accomplices. The palace suffered long periods of neglect, although it returned to glory at the ball thrown by Bonnie Prince Charlie in the mid-18th century. The present queen and Prince Philip live at Holyroodhouse whenever they visit Edinburgh. When they're not in residence, the palace is open to visitors.

Visitors are allowed to see the Throne Room and other richly furnished drawing rooms, which are used for state occasions. The Picture Gallery has a large portrait collection depicting Scottish monarchs. Don't take all the portraits too seriously. Some of these "royal figures" might never have existed, and the likenesses of some Scottish monarchs aren't known. The portraits were the work of a Dutch artist, Jacob De Witt, who signed a contract in 1684 to turn out one "potboiler" portrait after another at the rate of one a week for 2 years.

MORE ATTRACTIONS

Camera Obscura. Castlehill. ☎ **0131/2263709.** Admission £3.95 ($6.50) adults, £2.50 ($4.15) senior citizens, £3.15 ($5.20) students, £1.95 ($3.20) children. Apr–Oct daily 9:30am–6pm; Nov–Mar daily 10am–5pm. Bus: 1 or 6.

This landmark is at the top of the Outlook Tower, where you can take in a panorama of the surrounding city. Trained guides point out the landmarks and talk about Edinburgh's fascinating history. In addition, there are several entertaining exhibits, all with an optical theme, and a well-stocked shop selling books, crafts, and compact discs.

✪ **National Gallery of Scotland.** 2 The Mound. ☎ **0131/556-8921.** Free admission. Mon–Sat 10am–5pm, Sun 2–5pm; during the festival, Mon–Sat 10am–6pm, Sun 11am–6pm. Bus: 3, 21, or 26.

This museum is located in the center of Princes Street Gardens. The gallery is rather small, but the collection was chosen with great care and has been expanded considerably by bequests, gifts, and loans. The Duke of Sutherland has lent the museum some paintings, including two Raphaels, Titian's two Diana canvases and his Venus rising from the sea, and the *Seven Sacraments,* a work of the great 17th-century Frenchman Nicolas Poussin. The Spanish masters are represented as well.

You can also see excellent examples of English painting: Gainsborough's *The Hon. Mrs. Graham* and Constable's *Dedham Vale,* along with works by Turner, Reynolds, and Hogarth. Naturally, the work of Scottish painters is prominent, including Alexander Naysmith and Henry Raeburn, whose most famous work, *The Reverend Walker,* can be seen here.

National Museum of Scotland (NMS). Chambers St. ☎ **0131/225-7534.** £3 ($4.95) adults, £1.50 ($2.45) seniors and students, free ages 17 and under. Mon and Wed–Sat 10am–5pm; Tues 10am–8pm; Sun noon–5pm. Bus: 7, 8, 14, or 87.

In 1998, two long-established museums, the Royal Museum of Scotland and the National Museum of Antiquities, were united into this single institution behind a Venetian Renaissance facade 2 blocks south of the Royal Mile. The museum showcases exhibits in the decorative arts, ethnography, natural history, geology, archaeology, technology, and science. The museum's five modern galleries distill billions of years of Scottish history, with a total of 10,000 items ranging from rocks found on the island of South Uist dating back 2.9 billion years to a Hillman Imp, one of the last 500 cars manufactured at the Linwood plant near Glasgow before it closed in 1981. One gallery is devoted to Scotland's role as an independent nation before it merged with the United Kingdom in 1707. Another, devoted to industry from 1707 to 1914, includes exhibits on shipbuilding, whisky distilling, the railways, and such textiles as the tartan and paisley.

Royal Observatory Visitor Centre. Blackford Hill (southern Edinburgh). ☎ **0131/668-8405.** Admission £3 ($4.95) adults; £2 ($3.30) students and seniors; £1.50 ($2.45) children 5–16, free for children under 5. Mon–Sat 10am–5pm; Sun noon–5pm. Bus: 41 or 42.

On display here are the works of the Scottish National Observatory, featuring the finest images of astronomical objects, Scotland's largest telescope, and antique instruments. There's also a panoramic view of the city from the balcony. An exhibit, *The Universe,* uses photographs, videos, computers, and models to take you on a cosmic whirlwind tour from the beginning of time to the farthest depths of space in a couple of hours.

✪ **Scottish National Gallery of Modern Art.** Belford Rd. ☎ **0131/624-6200.** Free admission, except for some temporary exhibits. Mon–Sat 10am–5pm; Sun 2–5pm. Bus: 13, or take 18, 20, or 41; ask the driver for the stop closest to the museum and then take the 5-minute walk up Queensferry Terrace and Belford Rd. to the gallery.

In 1984, Scotland's national collection of 20th-century art moved into a gallery set on 12 acres of grounds, just a 15-minute walk from the west end of Princes Street. The collection is international in scope and high in quality, despite its modest size.

Major sculptures outside the building include pieces by Henry Moore and Barbara Hepworth. Inside, the collection ranges from fauvism (Derain) to cubism (Braque and Picasso) to recent works by Paolozzi. There's a strong representation of English and Scottish artists—William Turner, John Constable, Henry Raeburn, and David Wilkie, to name a few. Works by Matisse, Miró, Kirchner, Kokoschka, Ernst, Ben Nicholson, Nevelson, Balthus, Lichtenstein, Kitaj, and Hockney are also on view.

Scottish National Portrait Gallery. 1 Queen St. ☎ **0131/624-6200.** Free admission, except for some temporary exhibits. Mon–Sat 10am–5pm; Sun 2–5pm. Bus: 18, 20, or 41.

Housed in a red stone Victorian Gothic building designed by Rowand Anderson, this portrait gallery gives you a chance to see what the famous people of Scottish history looked like. The portraits, several by Ramsay and Raeburn, include everybody from Mary Queen of Scots to Sean Connery, from Flora Macdonald to Irvine Welsh.

Britannia: The People's Yacht

So the Queen never invited you sailing on her 412-foot yacht either? Well, there is still a chance to go aboard this world-famous vessel. Launched on April 16, 1953, the luxury yacht was decommissioned December 11, 1997. Today, the yacht—technically a Royal Navy ship—which has sailed more than a million miles, rests at anchor in the port of Leith, 2 miles from the center of Edinburgh. The gangplank is now lowered for the public, who in the past had been shunned for such world leaders as Mahatma Gandhi, Tony Blair, and Nelson Mandela.

British taxpayers spent $160 million maintaining the yacht throughout most of the '90s, but because of budgetary constraints, a decision was made to put it in dry dock. Even a major refit would have prolonged the vessel's life for only a few more years. The public reaches the ship by going through a visitor center designed by Sir Terence Conran. At its centerpiece is the yacht's 41-foot tender floating in a pool.

Once on board, you can walk the decks where Prince Charles took his beautiful, blushing bride, the late Princess of Wales. You can also visit the drawing room and the Royal Apartments, once occupied by the Queen and Prince Philip, as well as other members of the royal family (William, Harry, Edward, Andrew, Anne, and Margaret). Even the engine room, the galleys, and the captain's cabin can be checked out.

All tickets should be booked as far in advance as possible by calling ☎ **0131/ 555-5566.** The yacht is open daily except Christmas, with the first tour beginning at 10:30am and the last tour at 3:50pm. Lasting 90 to 120 minutes, each tour is a self-guided audio tour of the five decks with headsets lent to participants. Adults pay £6.50 ($10.75), seniors £5 ($8.25), and children ages 5–15 £3.75 ($6.20). Those 4 and under visit for free; a family ticket, good for two adults and up to two children, pay £18 ($29.70). From Waverley Bridge, take either city bus (Lothian Transport) X50, or else the Guide Friday tour bus, which is marked all over its sides with the word BRITANNIA.

Scott Monument. In the East Princes Street Gardens. ☎ **0131/5294068.** Admission £2.50 ($4.15). Apr–Sept Mon–Sat 9am–6pm; Oct–Mar Mon–Sat 9am–3pm. Bus: 2. 3. 4, 4A, 10, 11, 15, 15A, 16, 43, 80, or 80A.

Completed in the mid-19th century, the Gothic-inspired Scott Monument is the most famous landmark in Edinburgh. Sir Walter Scott's heroes are carved as small figures in the monument, and you can climb to the top. You can also see the first-ever **floral clock** (bed of flowers arranged in the shape of a clock), which was constructed in 1904, in the West Princes Street Gardens. The monument reopened in the spring of 1999 following a major restoration.

A GARDEN

Gardeners and nature lovers in general will admire the **Royal Botanic Garden,** Inverleith Row (☎ **0131/552-7171**). Hours are daily April to August 9:30am to 7pm, September and March 9:30am to 6pm, October and February 9:30am to 5pm, and November to January 9:30am to 4pm. Of special interest are the Exhibition Plant Houses, which have displays ranging from the fern forests of the southern hemisphere to desert succulents from arid areas. It's open year-round daily 9am to 1 hour before sunset. See also Inverleith House, Exhibition Hall, Alpine House, the Demonstration Garden, the Heath Garden, and many others. Admission is free.

Take a Step Back in Time at Historic Dean Village

Set in a valley about 100 feet below the rest of Edinburgh is charming and nostalgic Dean Village. How charming? The village is possibly the most photographed sight in the city. The settlement dates from the 12th century, and for many centuries it was a grain-milling center. The current residents worked hard to restore the old buildings—many of which were converted into flats and houses—and managed to resuscitate the original Brigadoon-like atmosphere. A few minutes from the West End, it's located at the end of Bell's Brae, off Queensferry Street, on the Water of Leith. You can enjoy a celebrated view by looking downstream under the high arches of Dean Bridge, designed by Telford in 1833. The most scenic walk is along the water in the direction of St. Bernard's Well.

ORGANIZED TOURS

If you want a quick introduction to the principal attractions in and around Edinburgh, consider one or more of the tours offered by **Lothian Region Transport,** 27 Hanover St. (☎ **0131/554-4494**). You won't find a cheaper way to hit the highlights. The buses leave from Waverley Bridge, near the Scott Monument. The tours are given from April to late October; a curtailed winter program is also offered.

You can see most of the major sights of Edinburgh, including the Royal Mile, the Palace of Holyroodhouse, Princes Street, and Edinburgh Castle, by double-deck motorcoach for £6 ($9.90) for adults and £2 ($3.30) for children. This ticket is valid all day on any LRT Edinburgh Classic Tour bus, which allows passengers to get on and off at any of the 15 stops along its routes. Buses start from Waverley Bridge every day beginning at 9:10am, departing every 15 minutes in summer and about every 30 minutes in winter, and then embark on a circuit of Edinburgh, which—if you remain on the bus without ever getting off—takes about 2 hours. Commentary is offered along the way.

Tickets for any of these tours can be bought at LRT offices at Waverley Bridge, at 27 Hanover St., or at the tourist information center in Waverley Market. Advance reservations are a good idea. For more information, call ☎ **0131/555-6363,** 24 hours a day.

THE SHOPPING SCENE

The best buys are in tartans and woolens, along with bone china and Scottish crystal. Princes Street, George Street, and the Royal Mile are the major shopping arteries. Here are a few suggestions.

Looking for a knitted memento? Moira-Anne Leask, owner of the **Shetland Connection,** 491 Lawnmarket (☎ **0131/225-3525**), promotes the skills of the Shetland knitter, and her shop is packed with sweaters, hats, and gloves in colorful Fair Isle designs. She also offers handknitted mohair, Aran, and Icelandic sweaters. Her oldest knitter is 90 years old!

If you've ever suspected that you might be Scottish, **Tartan Gift Shops,** 54 High St. (☎ **0131/558-3187**), has a chart indicating the place of origin—in Scotland—of your family name. You're then faced with a bewildering array of hunt-and-dress tartans. The high-quality wool is sold by the yard, as well as in the form of kilts for both men and women.

Clan Tartan Centre, 70–74 Bangor Rd., Leith (☎ **0131/553-5100**), is one of the leading specialists in Edinburgh, regardless of which clan you claim as your own. If you want help in identifying a particular tartan, the staff at this shop will assist you. There's also the **James Pringle Woollen Mill,** 70–74 Bangor Rd., Leith (☎ **0131/553-5161**), which produces a large variety of top-quality wool items, including a range of Scottish knitwear—cashmere sweaters, tartan and tweed ties, travel rugs, tweed hats, and tam o'shanters. In addition, the mill has the only Clan Tartan Centre in Scotland, where more than 2,500 sets and trade designs are accessible through their research facilities.

Edinburgh Crystal factory, Eastfield, Penicuik (☎ **01968/675128**), lies about 10 miles south of Edinburgh, just off A-701 to Peebles; take bus 62, 64, 65, 81, or 87. It's devoted entirely to handmade crystal glassware, and you can take tours to watch glassmakers at work Monday to Friday from 9am to 3:30pm. At the Visitor Centre is a factory shop where the world's largest collection of Edinburgh crystal is on view and for sale. You can also find inexpensively priced factory seconds.

For beautiful wall hangings, you can make your own brass rubbings or buy them ready-made from the **Scottish Stone and Brass Rubbing Centre,** Trinity Apse, Chalmers Close, near the Royal Mile (☎ **0131/556-4364**). You can visit the center's collection of replicas molded from ancient Pictish stones, rare Scottish brasses, and medieval church brasses.

The two best department stores in Edinburgh are **Debenham's,** 109–112 Princes St. (☎ **0131/2251320**), and **Jenners,** 48 Princes St. (☎ **0131/2252442**). Both stock Scottish and international merchandise.

Other shops worth checking out include **Old Town Weaving Company,** 555 Castlehill (☎ **0131/226-1555**), where you can converse with craftspeople and purchase some of their work. If you're interested in old-fashioned Scottish crafts, this is the place. Established in 1866, **Hamilton & Inches,** 87 George St. (☎ **0131/ 225-4898**), is a gold- and silversmith with both modern and antique designs. It has a stunning late Georgian interior as well.

EDINBURGH AFTER DARK

For a thorough list of entertainment options, pick up a copy of *The List,* a biweekly entertainment paper available at the Tourist Information Office for £1.90 ($3.15).

FESTIVALS

The highlight of Edinburgh's year—some would say the only time when the real Edinburgh emerges—comes in the last weeks of August during the ✪ **Edinburgh International Festival.** Since 1947 the festival has attracted world-class artists and companies in all fields of the arts, including music, opera, dance, theater, exhibition, poetry, and prose. During the festival, "Auld Reekie" takes on a cosmopolitan air.

One of the most exciting spectacles is the Military Tattoo on the floodlit esplanade in front of Edinburgh Castle, high on its rock above the city. Huge audiences watch the precision marching of Scottish regiments and military units from all parts of the world and, of course, the stirring skirl of the bagpipes and the swirl of the kilt.

Less predictable in quality but greater in quantity (and risk) is the **Edinburgh Festival Fringe,** a more egalitarian opportunity for literally anybody to put on a performance wherever they can find an empty stage or street corner. Late-night reviews, outrageous and irreverent contemporary drama, avant-garde works, university theater presentations, the amazing, the shocking, and the plain bad—Edinburgh gives them all free rein. A **Film Festival,** a **Jazz Festival,** a **Television Festival,** and a **Book Festival** (every second year) all overlap at varying times during August.

Ticket prices range from £5 ($8.25) up to about £50 ($82.50) a seat. Information can be obtained at **Edinburgh International Festival,** 21 Market St., Edinburgh EH1 1BW (☎ **0131/4732000;** fax 0131/4732003). The office is open Monday through Friday from 9:30am to 5:30pm.

Other sources of event information include **Edinburgh Festival Fringe,** 180 High St., Edinburgh EH1 1BW (☎ **0131/226-5257**); **Edinburgh Book Festival,**

137 Dundee St., Edinburgh EH1 1BG (☎ **0131/228-5444**); **Edinburgh Film Festival,** 88 Lothian Rd., Edinburgh EH3 9BZ (☎ **0131/228-4051**); and **Edinburgh Military Tattoo,** 32 Market St., Edinburgh EH1 1QB (☎ **0131/225-4783**). The festival also has a Web site: www.go-edinburgh.co.uk.

THEATER

Edinburgh has a lively theater scene. In 1994, the ✪ **Edinburgh Festival Theatre,** 13–29 Nicolson St. (☎ **0131/662-1112** for administration, ☎ **0131/529-6000** for tickets during the Edinburgh Festival), opened in time to take part in some of the Edinburgh Festival. Set on the eastern edge of Edinburgh, near the old campus of the University of Edinburgh, it has since been called "Britain's *de facto* Dance House" because of its sprung floor, its enormous stage (the largest in Britain), and its suitability for opera presentations of all kinds.

Another major theater is the **King's Theatre,** 2 Leven St. (☎ **0131/529-6000**), a 1,600-seat Victorian theater offering a wide repertoire of classical entertainment, including ballet, opera, and West End productions. The **Netherbow Arts Centre,** 43 High St. (☎ **0131/556-9579**), is more informal, and productions here are often excellent and experimental—new Scottish theater at its best. Ask about lunchtime performances.

The resident company of **Royal Lyceum Theatre,** Grindlay Street (☎ **0131/248-4848**), also has an enviable reputation; its presentations range from the works of Shakespeare to new Scottish playwrights. The **Traverse Theatre,** Cambridge Street (☎ **0131/228-1404**), is one of the few theaters in Britain funded solely to present new plays by British writers and first translations into English of international works. In a modern location, it now offers two theaters under one roof: Traverse 1, with a seating capacity of 250, and Traverse 2, with a smaller capacity of 100.

Ballet, Opera & Classical Music

The **Scottish Ballet** and the **Scottish Opera** perform at the **Playhouse Theatre,** 18–22 Greenside Place (☎ **0131/557-2590**), which, with 3,100 seats, is the town's largest theater. The **Scottish Chamber Orchestra** makes its home at the **Queen's Hall,** Clerk Street (☎ **0131/668-2019**), also a major venue for the Edinburgh International Festival.

The **Royal Scottish National Orchestra** plays at **Usher Hall,** Lothian Road, near Princes Street (☎ **0131/228-8616**), Edinburgh's chief venue for orchestral and choral music.

FOLK MUSIC & CEILIDHS

Folk music is presented in many clubs and pubs in Edinburgh, but these strolling players tend to be somewhat erratic or irregular in their appearances. It's best to read notices in pubs and talk to the tourist office to see where the *ceilidh* (Scottish hoedown) will be on the night of your visit.

Some hotels regularly feature traditional Scottish music in the evenings. You might check with the **Carlton Highland Hotel** on North Bridge (☎ **0131/556-7277**) or the **George Hotel** 19–21 George Street (☎ **0131/225-1251**). **Jamie's Scottish Evening** is presented at the King James Hotel on Leith Street (☎ **0131/556-0111**) Tuesday through Sunday at 7pm.

DANCE CLUBS & ROCK

Club Mercado. 36–39 Market St. ☎ **0131/226-4224.** Cover £5–£10 ($8.25–$16.50).

This popular dance club attracts an 18- to 35-year-old clientele. On Fridays the '70s and '80s are revisited from 5pm to 3am. Admission is £5 ($8.25). On Saturday, the

A Wee Dram for Fans of Malt Whisky

It requires a bit of an effort to reach it (take bus no. 10A, 16, or 17 from Princes Street to Leith), but for fans of malt whisky, the **Scotch Malt Whisky Society** has been called "The Top of the Whisky Pyramid" by distillery-industry magazines in Britain. It's on the second floor of a 16th-century warehouse at 87 Giles St., Leith (☎ **0131/554-3451**), and was originally designed to store bordeaux and port wines from France and Portugal. All you can order are single-malt whiskies, served neat, usually in a dram (unless you want yours watered down with branch water), and selected from a staggering choice of whiskies from more than 100 distilleries throughout Scotland. Hours are Monday to Friday 9am to 7pm, Saturday 10am to 3pm.

popular and funky Alternaclub (part of the Mercado) draws a cultural cross-section of Edinburgh between 9pm and 3am, with a cover ranging from £8 to £10 ($13.20 to $16.50). Wednesday is students' night from 10:30pm to 3am, with a £5 ($8.25) cover. Also popular is a techno party on Sunday from 10pm to 3am when the cover is lowered to £5 ($8.25).

Revolution. 31 Lothian Rd. ☎ **0131/2297670.** Wed–Thurs £3–£4 ($4.95–$6.60); Fri–Sat £5–£7 ($8.25–$11.55); Sun £4–£5 ($6.60–$8.25).

This is the largest nightclub in Edinburgh, and it's also one of the most popular. The under-25 crowd gathers here in droves. There are also three bars around the dance floor and one above it. It's open Wednesday through Sunday from 10pm to 3am.

The Venue. 15 Calton Rd. ☎ **0131/557-3073.** Cover £6–£7 ($9.90–$11.55).

Behind the main Post Office and Waverley Station is the city's principal venue for live music, with different bands featured every week. Some of the biggest bands in the U.K. perform here, and when they aren't appearing, you're entertained by Scottish wannabees. Posters and flyers throughout the town let you know what's on at any given time. Open daily 10:30am to 3am.

Whynot. 14 George St. ☎ **0131/624-8633.** Cover £3–£7.50 ($4.95–$12.40).

In the basement of The Dome Bar & Grill, this club is a hot entertainment complex that opened in 1997 in the former Bank of Scotland building. It has low ceilings with curtains hanging like waves of veils above the dance floor and lots of seating coves tucked away for privacy. The club is open Thursday through Sunday from 10pm to 3am. On Thursday night, dance to the music of the '60s, '70s, and '80s for a £3 ($4.95) cover. Friday night features chart music, with a £5 ($8.25) cover before 11pm and a £7.50 ($12.40) cover after 11pm. Saturday the club pumps with the best dance music, with a £7.50 ($12.40) cover all night. On Sunday, a local radio station hosts a party with a £5 ($8.25) cover.

PUBS & BARS

Located on a shop-lined street below the Royal Mile, the **Black Bull,** 12 Grassmarket (☎ **0131/225-6636**), is often overlooked by visitors. The pub is decorated like a scarlet version of a Victorian railway car, with an attention-grabbing black bull's head. The place rocks at night to chart-topping pop. There's a chance this place will change its name during the life of this edition, following a refurbishment, but the address will be the same.

Edinburgh's most famous pub—**Café Royal Circle Bar,** 17 W. Register St. (☎ **0131/556-1884**)—is a long-enduring favorite. One part is now occupied by the Oyster Bar of the Café Royal, but life in the Circle Bar continues at its old pace. The opulent trappings of the Victorian era are still on display. Go up to the serving counter, an island in a sea of drinkers, and place your order.

Established in 1806, **Deacon Brodie's Tavern,** 435 Lawnmarket (☎ **0131/ 225-6531**), is the neighborhood pub along the Royal Mile. It perpetuates the memory of Deacon Brodie, good citizen by day, robber by night. The tavern and wine cellars contain a restaurant and lounge bar.

GAY & LESBIAN BARS & CLUBS

C.C. Bloom's, 23–24 Greenside Place (☎ **0131/556-9331**), is one of the most popular gay bars in Edinburgh. The upstairs bar offers drinks and same-sex camaraderie. The downstairs club features dancing to a wide range of music, and one night a week is set aside for karaoke.

Attracting a larger female clientele than most other gay bars in Edinburgh is **Route 66,** 6 Baxters Place (☎ **0131/524-0061**). It's mainly a place to sit and enjoy a drink, but once a month there's a theme night with drink specials and activities.

Other gay spots include **Casekudas,** 22 Greenside Place (☎ **0131/558-1270**), where the local joke is that this pub answers the eternal question of what's under the kilt. Gays enjoy the cafe downstairs and the disco upstairs on Friday and Saturday nights.

DAY TRIPS FROM EDINBURGH

LINLITHGOW   Mary Queen of Scots was born in this royal burgh, a county town in West Lothian, 18 miles west of Edinburgh. From Edinburgh direct trains (☎ **0345/484950**) run every 15 minutes during the day to Linlithgow (trip time: 20 minutes). The round-trip fare is £4.70 ($7.75) for adults, £2.35 ($3.90) for children. Buses also leave from St. Andrew's Square in Edinburgh (☎ **01324/613-777** for schedules), every 20 minutes (trip time: 1 hour). The round-trip fare is £4.15 ($6.85) for adults, £2.10 ($3.45) for children. Motorists can take A902 to Corstorphine, then A8 to M9, getting off at the signposted junction (no. 3) to Linlithgow.

The roofless ✪ **Linlithgow Palace** (☎ **01506/842896**), birthplace of Mary Queen of Scots in 1542, can still be explored today, even if it's but a shell of its former self. The queen's suite was in the north quarter, but was rebuilt for the homecoming of James VI (James I of Great Britain) in 1620. The palace burned to the ground in 1746. The Great Hall is on the first floor, and a small display shows some of the more interesting architectural relics. The ruined palace is half a mile from Linlithgow Station. Admission is £2.30 ($3.80) for adults, £1.75 ($2.90) for seniors, £1 ($1.65) for children. From April to September, hours are daily 9:30am to 6:30pm; from October to March, they're Monday to Saturday 9:30am to 4:30pm and Sunday 2 to 4pm.

South of the palace stands the medieval kirk of **St. Michael's Parish Church** (☎ **01506/842188**), open only April to October from 10am to 4pm. Many a Scottish monarch has worshiped here since its consecration in 1242. Despite being ravaged by the disciples of John Knox and transformed into a stable by Cromwell, it's one of Scotland's best examples of a parish church.

In the midst of beautifully landscaped grounds, laid out along the lines of Versailles, sits ✪ **Hopetoun House** (☎ **0131/331-2451**), 10 miles from Edinburgh. This is Scotland's greatest Adam mansion and a fine example of 18th-century architecture. The splendid reception rooms are filled with 18th-century furniture, paintings, statues, and other artwork. From a rooftop viewing platform you get a panoramic view of the Firth of Forth. You can take the nature trail, explore the deer parks, investigate the Stables

Museum, or stroll through the formal gardens, all on the grounds. The house is 2 miles from the Forth Road Bridge near South Queensferry, off A-904. If you don't have a car, take a cab from the rail station in Linlithgow for about £7 to £9 ($11.55 to $14.85). Admission is £4.70 ($7.75) for adults, £4.20 ($6.95) for seniors, and £2.60 ($4.30) for children; a family ticket (for up to six) is £14.50 ($23.90). Open Easter weekend to September, daily from 10am to 4:30pm. It's closed October through April.

NORTH BERWICK   This royal burgh, created in the 14th century, was once an important Scottish port. In East Lothian, 24 miles east from Edinburgh, it is today a popular Scottish holiday spot. Visitors are drawn here, on the Firth of Forth, for its golf courses, beaches, and harbor life. You can climb the rocky shoreline or enjoy the heated outdoor swimming pool in July and August.

Trains (☎ 0345/484950) leave from Edinburgh about every half hour for the 30-minute trip, a round-trip costing £5.50 ($9.05) for adults or £2.75 ($4.55) for children. Buses (☎ 0131/366-39233) also leave from Charlotte Square in Edinburgh at 33 minutes past the hour daily from 8:03am to 5:33pm, taking 1¼ hours and costing £2.75 ($4.55) round-trip for adults or £1.40 ($2.30) for children. Motorists follow A-198 from Edinburgh to North Berwick (it's signposted all the way).

At the **information centre,** Quality Street (☎ 01620/892197), you can pick up information on boat trips to the offshore islands, including **Bass Rock,** a volcanic island that is a breeding ground for about 10,000 gannets. Hours are Monday to Saturday 9am to 1:30pm and 2:30 to 5pm.

Some 2 miles east of North Berwick, and 25 miles east of Edinburgh on A-198, stand the ruins of the 14th-century diked and rose-colored **Tantallon Castle** (☎ 01620/892727). This was the ancient stronghold of the Douglases until their defeat by Cromwell's forces in 1650. Overlooking the Firth of Forth, the castle ruins are still formidable, with a square, five-story central tower and a dovecote, plus the shell of its east tower, a D-shaped structure with a wall from the central tower. The best way to get to the castle is by car, but there are buses that run every 2 hours from North Berwick. You can visit the castle April to September, daily from 9:30am to 6:30pm; the rest of the year it's open Monday through Wednesday and Saturday 9:30am to 4:30pm, Thursday 9:30am to 12:30pm, and Sunday 2 to 4:30pm. Admission is £2.50 ($4.15) for adults, £1.75 ($2.90) for seniors, and £1 ($1.65) for children.

DIRLETON   This little town, a preservation village, vies for the title of "prettiest village in Scotland." The town plan, drafted in the early 16th century, is essentially unchanged today. Dirleton has two greens shaped like triangles, with a pub opposite Dirleton Castle, placed at right angles to a group of cottages. It's on the Edinburgh–North Berwick road (A-198). North Berwick (see above) is 5 miles to the east and Edinburgh 19 miles to the west. Buses (☎ 0131/663-9233) leave from St. Andrew's Square station in Edinburgh at 10 past the hour and 20 to the hour (trip time: 1 hour). The last bus departs at 5:10pm. A one-way fare costs £1.50 ($2.45) for adults or 75p ($1.25) for children.

A rose-tinted 13th-century castle with surrounding gardens, once the seat of the wealthy Anglo-Norman de Vaux family, **Dirleton Castle** (☎ 01620/850330) looks like a fairy-tale fortification, with towers, arched entries, and oak ramp. Ruins of the Great Hall and kitchen can be seen, as well as what's left of the lord's chamber where the de Vaux family lived. The 16th-century main gate has a hole through which boiling tar or water could be poured to discourage unwanted visitors. The castle's country garden and bowling green are still in use. Admission is £2.50 ($4.15) for adults, £1.75 ($2.90) for seniors, and £1 ($1.65) for children. You can tour the castle daily April to October 9:30am to 6pm, and October to March, Monday to Saturday 9:30am to 4pm and Sunday 2 to 4pm.

2 Tayside & Grampian

Tayside and Grampian, two history-rich sections in northeast Scotland, offer a vast array of sights, even though they're relatively small areas. Tayside, for example, is about 85 miles east to west, and some 60 miles south to north. The two regions share the North Sea coast between the Firth of Tay in the south and the Firth of Moray farther north. The so-called Highland Line, separating the Lowlands in the south from the Highlands in the north, crosses both regions. The Grampians, the highest mountain range in Scotland, are to the west of this line.

Carved out of the old counties of Perth and Angus, **Tayside** is named for its major river, the 119-mile-long Tay. The region is easy to explore, and its tributaries and dozens of lochs and Highland streams are among the best salmon and trout waters in Europe. One of the loveliest regions of Scotland, Tayside is filled with heather-clad Highland hills, long blue lochs under tree-lined banks, and miles and miles of walking trails. Tayside's Perth and Dundee are among the six leading cities of Scotland. The region provided the backdrop for many novels by Sir Walter Scott, including *The Fair Maid of Perth, Waverley,* and *The Abbot.* Its golf courses are world famous, ranging from the trio of 18-hole courses at Gleneagles to the open championship links at Carnoustie.

The **Grampian region** is home to Aberdeen, Scotland's third-largest city, and Braemar, site of the most famous of the Highland gatherings. The queen herself comes here to holiday at Balmoral Castle, her private residence, a tradition dating back to the days of Queen Victoria and her consort, Prince Albert. As you journey along the scenic roads of Scotland's northeast, you pass heather-covered moorland and peaty lochs, wood glens and salmon-filled rivers, granite-stone villages and ancient castles, and fishing harbors as well as North Sea beach resorts.

After exploring Edinburgh, you can tour Tayside and Grampian. Perth, 44 miles north of Edinburgh, makes the best "gateway" to the region.

Only in Tayside & Grampian

Exploring Glamis Castle   Balmoral Castle draws more visitors, but Glamis also has its links with the crown. Princess Margaret was born here, the first royal princess born in Scotland in 3 centuries, and the Queen Mother grew up here. Dating from the early 15th century, the castle contains Duncan's Hall, allegedly the setting for Shakespeare's *Macbeth* (he was the Thane of Glamis).

Golfing at St. Andrew's   Only 15 miles northeast of Edinburgh, you can play golf in this ancient university town where the rules of golf were first codified and arbitrated; even Mary Queen of Scots herself enjoyed a game in 1567. All six of St. Andrew's world-class golf courses are open to the public, and The Old Course is a 6,566-yard, 18-hole course billed as "the Home of Golf."

Calling on the Queen at Balmoral   The Queen won't actually be there if you're allowed to visit, but you can see where the royal family lives when they head this far north. Balmoral Castle, near Ballater, was "this dear paradise" to Queen Victoria and has been a private residence of British sovereigns ever since. Only the ballroom is open to the public, but you can enjoy walking through some of the most beautiful and well-manicured grounds in Scotland.

Sampling the Wares Along the Whisky Trail   The Malt Whisky Trail of Scotland stretches for some 70 miles through the glens of Speyside. Here distilleries turn out what locals call *uisge breatha* or the "water of life," enjoyed by connoisseurs around the

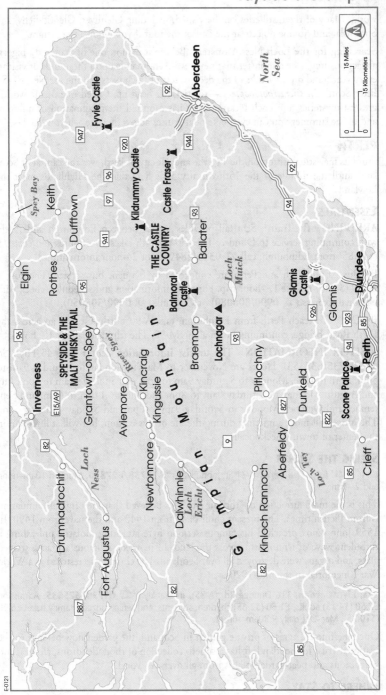

North Sea

Spey Bay

Fyvie Castle

Aberdeen

Kildrummy Castle

Castle Fraser

Keith

Dufftown

Elgin

Rothes

THE CASTLE COUNTRY

Ballater

Loch Muick

Glamis Castle

Dundee

SPEYSIDE & THE MALT WHISKY TRAIL

Balmoral Castle

Glamis

Inverness

Grantown-on-Spey

Lochnagar

Perth

Aviemore

Kincraig

Braemar

Scone Palace

Kingussie

Pitlochry

Dunkeld

Crieff

Drumnadrochit

Newtonmore

Aberfeldy

Loch Ness

Dalwhinnie

Loch Ericht

Kinloch Rannoch

Loch Tay

Fort Augustus

Grampian Mountains

River Spey

15 Miles

15 Kilometers

world. Many of the distilleries can be visited, including Glenlivet, Glenfiddichy, and Strathisla, and no one objects at the end of the tour if you enjoy a "wee dram."

Searching for the Loch Ness Monster   Believe it or not, one of Scotland's biggest attractions might be a monster that never was. Thousands upon thousands of visitors every year stand on the banks of the deep waters of Loch Ness waiting for Nessie—Sir Peter Scott's *Nessitera rhombopteryx*—to stick her head up. Called one of the world's greatest mysteries, the Loch Ness monster has captured the imagination of millions, and in the summer you can even take boat cruises across the lake—if you dare!

PERTH

From its majestic position on the Tay, the ancient city of Perth was the capital of Scotland until the middle of the 15th century. It is here that the Highlands meet the Lowlands.

ESSENTIALS

ARRIVING   By Train   ScotRail provides service between Edinburgh and Perth, with continuing service to Dundee. The trip to Perth takes 90 minutes and costs £9 ($14.85) from Edinburgh; call ☎ **0345/484950** for 24-hour information.

By Bus   Edinburgh and Perth are connected by frequent bus service. The cost is £4.50 ($7.45) for the 1½-hour trip. For more information and schedules, check with National Express (☎ **0990/808080**) or CityLink (☎ **0990/505050**).

By Car   To reach Perth from Edinburgh, take A-90 northwest and go across the Forth Road Bridge, continuing north along M-90. The trip takes about 1½ hours.

VISITOR INFORMATION   The **tourist information center** is at 45 High St. (☎ **01738/638353**). Hours are November to March, Monday to Saturday 9am to 5pm; April to June, Monday to Saturday 9am to 6pm and Sunday 11am to 4pm; July and August, Monday to Saturday 9am to 8pm and Sunday 11am to 6pm; and September and October, Monday to Saturday 9am to 6pm and Sunday 11am to 4pm. The office will move sometime during the life of this edition, but will still remain in the center of town. Check locally.

SEEING THE SIGHTS

Kirk of St. John the Baptist. 31 St. John Place. ☎ **01738/627820.** Mon–Fri 10am–noon and 2–4pm.

This is the main attraction of "the fair city." It's believed that the original foundation is from Pictish times. The present choir dates from 1440 and the nave from 1490. In 1559 John Knox preached his famous sermon here attacking idolatry, unleashing a turbulent wave of iconoclasm across the land. In its wake, religious artifacts, stained glass, and organs were destroyed all over Scotland. The church was restored as a World War I memorial in the mid-1920s.

Branklyn Garden. 116 Dundee Rd. (A-85), in Branklyn. ☎ **01738/625535.** Admission £2.50 ($4.15) adults, £1.60 ($2.65) children, students, and senior citizens; family ticket £6.20 ($10.25). Mar–Oct daily 9:30am–sunset.

Once the finest 2 acres of private garden in Scotland, the garden now belongs to the National Trust for Scotland. It has a superb collection of rhododendrons, alpines, and herbaceous and peat-garden plants from all over the world.

WHERE TO STAY

Dupplin Castle. Near Aberdalgie, Perth, Perthshire PH2 0PY. ☎ **01738/623224.** Fax 01738/444140. www.dupplin.co.uk. 6 units. TEL. £55 ($90.75) per person based on double occupancy. Rates include breakfast. MC, V. From Perth, follow the main highway (M-90) to Glasgow, turning left onto B-9112 toward Aberdalgie and Forteviot.

Only a 1-hour drive from Edinburgh, this modern, severely dignified mansion with sandstone mullions was built in 1968 by well-known architect Schomber Scott to replace the last of the three castles that had once risen proudly from the site. The last of them was visited by Queen Victoria in 1842. Surrounded by 30 acres of forest and spectacular gardens (some of its specimens are 250 years old), this spot is one of the most beautiful near Perth. Views from many of the bedrooms overlook the valley of the River Earn. Meals, which must be booked 24 hours in advance, cost £28 ($46.20).

Hunting Tower. Crieff Rd., Perth, Perthshire PH1 3JT. ☎ **01738/583771.** Fax 01738/583777. 34 units. MINIBAR TV TEL. £95 ($156.75) double; £125 ($206.25) suite. Rates include breakfast. AE, DC, MC, V. Drive 3½ miles west on A-85.

This late-Victorian country house, about a 10-minute drive from the city center, is set on 3½ acres of well-manicured gardens, with a modern wing of rooms added in 1998. Taste and concern are apparent in the interior decoration. The bedrooms are distinguished, although they range from rather large to rather compact, and all have hair dryers and trouser presses. Seven of the rooms have spa bathrooms. The fine Scottish cuisine served in the Oak Room is reason enough to stay here.

✪ **Parklands Hotel & Restaurant.** 2 St. Leonard's Bank, Perth, Perthshire PH2 8EB. ☎ **01738/622451.** Fax 01738/622046. www.centuryhousehotels@compuserve.com. 14 units. TV TEL. £95–£109.50 ($156.75–$180.65) double. Rates include breakfast. AE, DC, MC, V. Free parking.

Luxuriously overhauled, this is a country-house hotel in the middle of the city. The beautifully decorated bedrooms are filled with wood paneling and cornices, and overlook the South Inch Park. All the rooms are spacious and contain teamakers and hair dryers. Light traditional fare is served in country-house style.

WHERE TO DINE

✪ **Let's Eat.** 77 Kinnoul St. ☎ **01738/643377.** Reservations recommended. Lunch main courses £6.50–£9.95 ($10.75–$16.40); dinner main courses £7.95–£14.75 ($13.10–$24.35). AE, MC, V. Tues–Sat noon–2pm and 6:30–9:30pm. BRITISH/INTERNATIONAL.

The most visually striking, and most appealing, restaurant in Perth occupies a former theater built in 1822. Today tables are interspersed amid the soaring white columns of its original construction. A particularly cozy lounge, with log-burning iron stove and comfortable sofas, is a great place for a pre-dinner drink. The frequently changing menu is among the best in town, and might include a warm salad of pigeon breast with avocado slices and pine kernels; wild mushroom risotto with truffle oil; and a salad of prawns, mango, and avocado. Main courses may feature roasted rack of lamb with gratin potatoes *dauphinoise* (blended with eggs, seasonings, and grated Gruyère cheese, then baked), pea purée, and fried Parma ham, or a succulent version of monkfish and king prawn gumbo with saffron-flavored rice. Be careful not to confuse this restaurant with its less grand, less expensive sibling, Let's Eat Again, which operates in a different part of town under the same management.

Let's Eat Again. 33 George St. ☎ **1738/633771.** Reservations recommended. Main courses £5–£9 ($8.25–$14.85). AE, MC, V. Tues–Sat noon–2pm and 6:30–9:30pm. BRITISH/INTERNATIONAL.

Set behind the bright-yellow-with-lime-green trim of what was originally a 19th-century home, this is an upbeat bistro that caters to the young-at-heart with well-prepared but relatively inexpensive versions of Mediterranean and international cuisine. Your meal might include char-grilled Mediterranean vegetables with mozzarella; smoked haddock and chive-laced risotto; smoked local venison with spicy pears; salmon and codfish cakes with lemon-flavored butter sauce; or Thai-style chicken curry with noodles. Be careful not to confuse this restaurant with the more upscale Let's Eat, which is under the same management but in another neighborhood.

Littlejohn's. 24 St. John's St. ☎ **01738/639888.** Main courses £6–£9 ($9.90–$14.85). AE, DC, MC, V. Daily 10am–11pm. INTERNATIONAL.

Set on one of Perth's busiest commercial streets, behind a century-old facade, this restaurant has one large dining room with old-fashioned wood paneling, antique signs, and lots of Scottish charm. Despite the conservative nature of the setting, the food offerings are eclectic, including pizzas, pastas, Mexican tortillas, burgers, steaks, and an occasional lobster dish.

A DAY TRIP TO SCONE

Old Scone, 2 miles from Perth on the River Tay, was the ancient capital of the Picts. On a lump of sandstone called the "Stone of Destiny," the early Scottish monarchs were enthroned. In 1296, Edward I, the "Hammer of the Scots," moved the stone to Westminster Abbey, and for hundreds of years it rested under the chair on which British monarchs were crowned. The Scots have always bitterly resented this theft, and at last it has been returned to Scotland, finding a permanent home in Edinburgh Castle, where it can be viewed by the public.

The seat of the earls of Mansfield and birthplace of David Douglas of fir-tree fame, **Scone Palace,** along A-93 (☎ **01738/552300**), was largely rebuilt in 1802, incorporating the old palace of 1580. Inside is an impressive collection of French furniture, china, ivories, and 16th-century needlework, including bed hangings executed by Mary Queen of Scots. A fine collection of rare conifers is found on the grounds in the Pinetum. Rhododendrons and azaleas grow profusely in the gardens and woodlands around the palace. To reach the palace, head 2 miles northeast of Perth on A-93. The site is open from Good Friday to mid-October only, daily from 9:30am to 5pm. Admission is £5.20 ($8.60) for adults, £2.80 ($4.60) for children, including entrance to both house and grounds. Admission to the grounds only is £2.50 ($4.15) for adults and £1.40 ($2.30) for children.

Where to Stay & Dine

✪ **The Murrayshall.** New Scone, Perthshire PH2 7PH. ☎ **01738/551171.** Fax 01738/552595. 26 units. TV TEL. £120 ($198) double; from £150 ($247.50) suite. Rates include Scottish breakfast. AE, DC, MC, V. Take A-94 1½ miles east of New Scone.

Murrayshall, an elegant country-house hotel and restaurant set in 300 acres of parkland, was completely refurbished in 1987 and reopened as one of the showpieces of Perthshire. The Victorian mansion has its own 18-hole, par-73 golf course, interspersed with trees, water hazards, and white-sand bunkers. The hotel offers traditionally decorated public rooms and bedrooms, as well as the finest dining in the area in its Old Masters restaurant.

GLENEAGLES

This famous golfing center and sports complex is on a moor between Strathearn and Strath Allan. Gleneagles has four **18-hole golf courses,** open only to residents of the Gleneagles Hotel: King's Course, the longest one; Queen's Course, next in length; Prince's Course, shortest of all; and Glendevon, the newest of the quartet, built in 1980. They're among the best in Scotland, and the sports complex is one of the best equipped in Europe.

ESSENTIALS

ARRIVING   By Train   The 15-minute ride from Perth costs £3 ($4.95), and departs every 3 or 4 hours. Eight trains per day make the 1 hour and 40-minute trip from Edinburgh, costing £7.90 ($13.05). For information, call ☎ **0345/484950.**

By Bus   The only service departs from Glasgow. The trip takes slightly more than an hour and costs £5.80 ($9.55). For information and schedules, call ☎ **01738/26847.**

By Car   Gleneagles is on A-9, about halfway between Perth and Stirling to the south-west, a short distance from the village of Auchterarder. It lies 55 miles from Edinburgh and 45 miles from Glasgow.

VISITOR INFORMATION   The year-round tourist information center is at 90 High St., Auchterarder (☎ **01764/663450**). Open July and August, Monday to Saturday 9am to 7pm and Sunday 11am to 6pm; April to June, September, and October, Monday to Saturday 9:30am to 5:30pm and Sunday 11am to 4pm; November to March, Monday to Friday 9:30am to 5pm and Saturday 11am to 3pm.

WHERE TO STAY & DINE

Gleneagles Hotel. Auchterarder, Perthshire PH3 1NF. ☎ **01764/662231.** Fax 01764/662134. 229 units. MINIBAR TV TEL. £225–£260 ($371.25–$429) double; from £305 ($503.25) suite. Rates include Scottish breakfast. AE, DC, MC, V. Take A-9 1½ miles southwest of Auchterarder.

Gleneagles Hotel stands on its own 830-acre estate. Built in isolated grandeur in 1924, it was then the only five-star hotel in Scotland. The hotel's legendary golf course, its main attraction, is open only to guests of Gleneagles, who pay £80 ($132) per person to play the famous 18 holes in summer or £55 ($90.75) off-season.

The service and elegant decor here are among the finest in the country. Each of the luxurious bedrooms offers views of hills and glens. The chef uses fresh Scottish and French produce, combining traditional flair and imagination with a lighter, more modern touch. Service is impeccable. The hotel's country club, enclosed in a glass dome to provide a year-round tropical climate, offers members and guests use of a swimming pool, whirlpool, Turkish bath, saunas, plunge pool, and children's pool.

CRIEFF

At the edge of the Perthshire Highlands, with good fishing and golf, Crieff makes a pleasant stopover. This small burgh was the seat of the court of the earls of Strathearn until 1747, and the gallows in its marketplace were once used to execute Highland cattle rustlers.

You can take a "day trail" into **Strathearn,** the valley of the River Earn, the very center of Scotland. Here highland mountains meet gentle lowland slopes, and moorland mingles with rich green pastures. North of Crieff, the road to Aberfeldy, A-822, passes through the narrow pass of the **Sma' Glen,** a famously beautiful spot, with hills rising on either side to 2,000 feet.

ESSENTIALS

ARRIVING   By Train   There is no direct service. The nearest rail stations are at Gleneagles, 9 miles away, and at Perth, 18 miles away (see above). Call ☎ **0345/484950** for information and schedules.

By Bus   Once you arrive in Perth, you'll find regular connecting bus service hourly during the day. The one-way bus fare is £2.30 ($3.80). For information about times and schedules, call **Stagecoach** at ☎ **01738/629339.** However, the bus service from Gleneagles is too poor to recommend.

By Car   From Perth, head west on A-85 for 18 miles to Crieff.

By Taxi   From Gleneagles, a taxi costs from £15 to £20 ($24.75 to $33).

VISITOR INFORMATION   The year-round **tourist information office** is in the Town Hall on High Street (☎ **01764/652578**). Open July and August, Monday to Saturday 9am to 7pm and Sunday 11am to 6pm; April to June, September, and October, Monday to Saturday 9:30am to 5:30pm and Sunday 11am to 4pm; and November to March, Monday to Friday 9:30am to 5pm and Saturday 11am to 3pm.

SEEING THE SIGHTS

Glenturret Distillery Ltd. Hwy. A-85, Glenturret. ☎ **01764/656565.** Guided tours £3.50 ($5.75) adults, £3 ($4.95) seniors and students, £2.30 ($3.80) youths 12–17, free for children 11 and under. Mar–Dec Mon–Sat 9:30am–6pm, Sun noon–6pm; Jan Mon–Fri 11:30am–4pm; Feb Mon–Sat 11:30am–4pm, Sun noon–4pm. Closed Jan 1–2 and Dec 25–26. Take A-85 northwest toward Comrie; ¾ of a mile from Crieff, turn right at the crossroads; the distillery is ¼ mile up the road.

Scotland's oldest distillery, Glenturret was established in 1775 on the banks of the River Turret. Visitors can see the milling of malt, mashing, fermentation, distillation, and cask filling, followed by a free "wee dram" dispensed at the end of the tour. Guided tours leave at frequent intervals—sometimes as often as every 10 minutes when there's a demand for it—and take about 25 minutes each. They can be followed or preceded by a 20-minute video, "The Water of Life," that's presented next to a small museum devoted to the implements of the whisky trade.

Drummond Castle Gardens. Grimsthorpe, Crieff. ☎ **01764/681257.** Admission £3 ($4.95) adults, £2 ($3.30) seniors, £1.50 ($2.45) children. May–Sept daily 2–6pm. Closed Oct–Apr. Take A-822 for 3 miles south of Crieff.

The gardens of Drummond Castle, first laid out in the early 17th century by John Drummond, second earl of Perth, are among the finest formal gardens in Europe. There's a panoramic view from the upper terrace, overlooking an early Victorian *parterre* (ornamental garden with paths among the beds) in the form of St. Andrew's Cross. The multifaceted sundial by John Mylne, master mason to Charles I, has been the centerpiece since 1630.

PLAYING GOLF

Crieff Golf Club (☎ **01764/652909**) has two courses—both are set in Perthshire with panoramic views and excellent facilities. The most challenging is the 18-hole Fern Tower, a par-71 course with three par-5 holes. The Dornock is a 32-par, 9-hole course with three par-3 holes. It's not quite as difficult as the Fern Tower, but a test nonetheless. Greens fees for the Fern Tower are £21 ($34.65) per round Monday through Friday, and £29 ($47.85) on weekends. Greens fees for the Dornock are £8 ($13.20) for 9 holes and £12 ($19.80) for 18 holes. Carts cost £15 ($24.75) per round. From April to October, the golf club is open 8am to 11pm; November to March, open Monday to Friday 11am to 6pm and Saturday and Sunday 11am to 11pm.

WHERE TO STAY & DINE

Murraypark Hotel. Connaught Terrace, Crieff, Perthshire PH7 3DJ. ☎ **01764/653731.** Fax 01764/655311. 20 units. TV TEL. £75 ($123.75) double or suite. Rates include breakfast. AE, DC, MC, V.

This stone-fronted house lies in a residential neighborhood about a 10-minute walk from Crieff's center. In 1993 a new wing was opened, enlarging the public rooms and the number of simply furnished guest accommodations. All the rooms have the same amenities, including comfortable beds; those in the main house have more character, but the rooms in the new wing are more spacious. Bathrooms are small but adequate, with a tub and shower combination. The restaurant's cuisine is based on Scottish, French, and international inspirations.

ABERFELDY

The "Birks o' Aberfeldy" are among the beauty spots made famous by the poet Robert Burns. Once a Pictish center, this small town makes a fine base for touring Perthshire's glens and lochs. Loch Tay lies 6 miles to the west; Glen Lyon, 15 miles west; and Kinloch Rannoch, 18 miles northwest. The town's shops offer good buys in tweeds and tartans, plus other types of Highland dress.

ESSENTIALS

ARRIVING   By Train   There is no direct service into Aberfeldy. You can take a train to either Perth (see above) or Pitlochry, and then continue the rest of the way by bus. Call ☎ **0345/484950** for schedules.

By Bus   Buses connect Perth or Pitlochry with Aberfeldy at the rate of 10 per day. The cost of a one-way bus fare from either Perth or Pitlochry to Aberfeldy is £3 ($4.95). The private bus line **Stagecoach** (☎ **01738/629339**) handles much of the bus travel to the smaller towns and villages in the area.

By Car   From Crieff, take A-822 on a winding road north to Aberfeldy. The 30-mile drive from Perth takes 30 to 45 minutes.

VISITOR INFORMATION   The **tourist information office** is at The Square (☎ **01887/820276**). Hours are July and August, daily 9:30am to 5pm; April to June and September and October, daily 9am to 5:30pm; and October to March, Monday to Saturday 9am to 5:30pm.

PLAYING GOLF

Aberfeldy Golf Club, at Aberfeldy (☎ **01887/820535**), is a flatland course on the banks of the River Tay. It's an 18-hole par 68 that the local pro called a "challenge." The River Tay comes into play on several holes, and if you're not careful, you'll be making trips back to the pro shop for more golf balls. Greens fees are £14 ($23.10) for 18 holes and £16 ($26.40) on weekends. Cart fees are £2 ($3.30) per round (pull carts). From April to October the club is open daily 8am to 11pm. During other months, call first to see if they are open; it depends on the weather.

WHERE TO STAY & DINE

Farleyer House Hotel. Hwy. B-846, Aberfeldy, Perthshire PH15 2JE. ☎ **01887/820332.** Fax 01887/829430. 19 units, 1 family suite. TV TEL. £150 ($247.50) double; £170 ($280.50) suite. Rates include Scottish breakfast. AE, DC, MC, V. Take B-846 for 2 miles west of Aberfeldy.

A tranquil oasis, this hotel stands on 70 acres of grounds in the Tay Valley. Although restored and altered over the years, the building dates back to the 1500s. The staff entertains guests as though they were in a private home. The public rooms are immaculate and beautifully furnished, and the bedrooms are well maintained and comfortable. The internationally renowned Menzies Restaurant offers a set-price menu of five courses that changes daily.

DUNKELD

A cathedral town, Dunkeld lies in a thickly wooded valley of the Tay River at the edge of the Perthshire Highlands. Once a major ecclesiastical center, it's one of the seats of ancient Scottish history and an important center of the Celtic church.

ESSENTIALS

ARRIVING   By Train   There are four trains a day going between Edinburgh and Dunkeld, costing £9.20 ($15.20) for a one-way ticket. Trip time is 1½ hours. Trains from Perth cost £4.20 ($6.95). Call ☎ **0345/484950** for information and schedules.

By Bus   Pitlochry-bound buses leaving from Perth make a stopover in Dunkeld after 50 minutes, letting you off at the Dunkeld Car Park, which is at the train station. The cost is £2.20 ($3.65). Contact **Stagecoach** at ☎ **01738/629339.**

By Car   From Aberfeldy, take the A-827 east until you reach the junction of A-9 heading south to Dunkeld.

VISITOR INFORMATION   A **tourist information office** is at The Cross (☎ 01350/727688). It is open July 1 through September 8, Monday through Saturday 9am to 7:30pm and Sunday 11am to 7pm; April through June and September 9 through October 27, Monday through Saturday from 9:30am to 5:30pm and Sunday 11am to 4pm; October 28 through December, Monday through Saturday from 9:30am to 1:30pm (closed January through March).

EXPLORING THE TOWN

Founded in A.D. 815, the **Cathedral of Dunkeld** was converted from a church to a cathedral in 1127 by David I. It stands on scenic Cathedral Street along the River Tay. The cathedral was first restored in 1815, and traces of the 12th-century structure remain today. Admission is free, and the cathedral is open April to September, Monday to Saturday 9:30am to 6:30pm and Sunday 2 to 6:30pm; October to March, Monday to Saturday 9:30am to 4pm and Sunday 2 to 4pm.

The National Trust for Scotland has restored many of the old houses and shops around the marketplace and cathedral. The trust owns 20 houses on High Street and Cathedral Street as well. Many of these houses were constructed in the closing years of the 17th century after the rebuilding of the town following the Battle of Dunkeld. One of these, the **Ell Shop,** The Cross (☎ **01350/727460**), specializes in Scottish handcrafts. From June to August, it is open daily 10am to 5:30pm. Off-season hours are Monday to Saturday 10am to 4:30pm. Closed January through Easter.

The **Scottish Horse Museum,** The Cross (no phone), has exhibits tracing the history of the Scottish Horse Yeomanry, a cavalry force first raised in 1900. The museum is open from Easter to the end of October only, Saturday to Wednesday from 10am to noon and 1:50 to 5pm. Admission is free.

Shakespeare fans may want to seek out the oak and sycamore in front of the destroyed Birnam House, a mile to the south. It was believed to be a remnant of the **Birnam Wood** in *Macbeth;* as you may recall, Macbeth could be defeated only when "Birnam Wood came to Dunsinane."

The **Hermitage,** lying off A-9 about 2 miles west of Dunkeld, was called a "folly" when it was constructed in 1758 above the wooded gorge of the River Braan. Today it makes for one of the most scenic woodland walks in the area.

PLAYING GOLF

Dunkeld & Birnam, at Dunkeld (☎ **01350/727524**), with sweeping views of the surrounding environs, is touted as the best in the area. The 18-hole course is not too long, but can be quite difficult to play. It's edged in many areas with bracken, and many a golfer has had to take a drop (along with the mandatory extra stroke) instead of searching for an errant ball. Greens fees are £11 ($18.15) for 18 holes Monday through Friday, and £16 ($26.40) for 18 holes Saturday and Sunday. There are no electric carts; pull carts are available for £2 ($3.30) per round. Hours are daily 7am to 11pm April to September. From October to March, greens fees are reduced to £5

($8.25), and hours are daily 8am to 4pm. There is no official dress code, although if the starter feels you are not dressed "appropriately," you're asked to "smarten up" the next time you play the course.

WHERE TO STAY & DINE

✪ **Kinnaird.** Kinnaird, Kinnaird Estate, Dunkeld, Perthshire PH8 0LB. ☎ **01796/482440.** Fax 01796/482289. 10 units. TV TEL. £255–£315 ($420.75–$519.75) double; £350 ($577.50) suite. Rates include breakfast. AE, MC, V. No children under 12 accepted.

On a 9,000-acre private estate, this small hotel offers great warmth, charm, and comfort. Built in 1770 as a hunting lodge, the house has been restored to its previous grandeur. All the beautifully furnished bedrooms have king-size beds, private bathrooms, and great views. Some rooms overlook the valley of the River Tay; others open onto gardens and woodlands. Kinnaird House Restaurant brings high-caliber cuisine to the area. The chef cooks in the modern, post-nouvelle British and continental style, depending on fresh ingredients, with changing menus based on the season. Sporting facilities on the estate include salmon and trout fishing and hunting.

Stakis Dunkeld House Resort Hotel. Dunkeld, Perthshire PH8 0HX. ☎ **01350/727771.** Fax 01350/728924. 86 units. MINIBAR TV TEL. £130 ($214.50) double; from £180 ($297) suite. Rates include Scottish breakfast. AE, DC, MC, V.

This hotel, offering a taste of the quiet dignity of life in a Scottish country house, is ranked as one of the leading leisure and sports hotels in the area. On the banks of the Tay, the surrounding grounds—280 acres in all—make an idyllic setting. The house is beautifully kept, and the accommodations come in a wide range of styles, space, and furnishings. In the life of this edition, new rooms will be added. Its restaurant is one of the finest in the area, paying homage to its "Taste of Scotland" dishes, but also serving international selections. Salmon and trout fishing are possible right on the grounds, and facilities include an indoor swimming pool and all-weather tennis courts.

DUNDEE & GLAMIS CASTLE

This royal burgh and old seaport is an industrial city on the north shore of the Firth of Tay. When steamers took over the whaling industry from sailing vessels, Dundee became the leading home port from the 1860s until World War I. Long known for its jute and flax operations, we think today of the rich Dundee fruitcakes, marmalades, and jams. This was also the home of the man who invented stick-on postage stamps, James Chalmers. Dundee has a raffish charm and is a good base for a trip to Glamis Castle.

Spanning the Firth of Tay is the **Tay Railway Bridge,** opened in 1888. Constructed over the tidal estuary, the bridge is some 2 miles long, one of the longest in Europe. There's also a road bridge 1¼ miles long, with four traffic lanes and a walkway in the center.

ESSENTIALS

ARRIVING   By Train   ScotRail offers frequent service between Perth, Dundee, and Aberdeen. Phone ☎ 0345/484950 for schedules and departure times. A round-trip ticket between Edinburgh and Dundee costs £17.40 ($28.70).

By Bus   National Express buses offer frequent bus service from Edinburgh and Glasgow. The 2 hour trip from Edinburgh costs £5.50 ($9.10). Call ☎ 0990/080080 for information.

By Car   The fastest way to reach Dundee is to cut south back to Perth along A-9 and link up with the A-85 going east.

VISITOR INFORMATION   The **tourist information office** is at 21 Castle St. (☎ **01382/434664**). Hours are April to September Monday to Saturday 9am to 6pm, Sunday 10am to 4pm. From October to March, Monday to Saturday 9am to 5pm.

SEEING THE SIGHTS

For a panoramic view of Dundee, the Tay bridges, and mountains to the north, go to **Dundee Law,** a 572-foot hill a mile north of the city. The hill is an ancient volcanic plug.

HMS *Unicorn*. Victoria Dock. ☎ **01382/200900**. Admission £3 ($4.95) adults, £2 ($3.30) seniors and children; £8 ($13.20) family ticket. Easter–Oct daily 9am–5pm, Nov–Easter Mon–Fri 10am–4pm. Bus: 6, 23, or 78.

This 46-gun wooden ship of war commissioned in 1824 by the Royal Navy, now the oldest British-built ship afloat, has been restored so visitors can explore all four decks: the quarterdeck with 32-pound cannonades; the gun deck with its battery of 18-pound cannons and the captain's quarters; the berth deck with officers' cabins and crews' hammocks; and the orlop deck and hold. Various displays portraying life in the sailing navy and the history of the *Unicorn* make this a rewarding visit.

Broughty Castle. Castle Green, Broughty Ferry. ☎ **01382/436916**. Free admission. July–Sept Mon 11am–5pm, Tues–Thurs 10am–1pm and 2–5pm, Sun 2–5pm; Oct–June Mon 11am–5pm, Tues–Thurs 10am–1pm and 2–5pm. Bus: 7, 9, 11, or 24.

This 15th-century estuary fort lies about 4 miles east of the city center on the seafront, at Broughty Ferry, a little fishing hamlet and once the terminus for ferries crossing the Firth of Tay before the bridges were built. Besieged by the English in the 16th century, and attacked by Cromwell's army under General Monk in the 17th, it was eventually restored as part of Britain's coastal defenses in 1861. Its gun battery was dismantled in 1956, and it's now a museum with displays on local history, arms and armor, and Dundee's whaling story. The observation area at the top of the castle provides fine views of the Tay estuary and northeast Fife.

PLAYING GOLF

Caird Park, at Dundee (☎ **01382/434706**), is an 18-hole, par-72 course that presents most golfers with an average challenge. The course is quite flat, but there are more than a few bunkers to navigate. There is also a restaurant and bar on the premises. Greens fees are £14.70 ($24.25) for 18 holes, or £24.30 ($40.10) for a day ticket. No carts of any sort are allowed on the course, and there is no particular dress code. The park is open April to October daily 7am to 8pm.

WHERE TO STAY

Invercarse Hotel. 371 Perth Rd., Dundee, Angus DD2 1PG. ☎ **01382/669231**. Fax 01382/644112. 32 units. TV TEL £90 ($148.50) double; £100 ($165) suite. Rates include breakfast. AE, MC, V.

In landscaped gardens overlooking the River Tay, this privately owned hotel lies 3 miles west of the heart of Dundee. Many prefer it for its fresh air, tranquil location, and Victorian country-house aura. The guest rooms open onto views across the Tay to the hills of the Kingdom of Fife. Accommodations come in a variety of sizes, but all are well maintained. Guests can enjoy drinks in the bar, and later order continental or Scottish cuisine.

Stakis Earl Grey Hotel. Earl Grey Place, Dundee, Angus DD1 4DE. ☎ **01382/229271**. Fax 01382/200072. www.stakis.plc.uk. 132 units. TV TEL. £121 ($199.65) double; from £170 ($280.50) suite. AE, DC, MC, V. Bus: 1A, 1B, or 20.

This chain hotel helped rejuvenate the once-seedy waterfront of Dundee. Built in a severe modern style, it takes its name from the famous English tea, which most often accompanies marmalade and Dundee fruitcakes, the city's two most famous products. Some of the well-furnished bedrooms overlook the Firth, the river, or the Tay Bridge. Guests can dine at the Unicorn Restaurant, featuring buffet-style meals along with table d'hôte lunches and dinners. Facilities include a heated indoor swimming pool, exercise equipment, sauna, and whirlpool.

WHERE TO DINE

Jahangir Tandoori. 1 Sessions St. (at the corner of Hawk Hill). ☎ **01382/202022.** Reservations recommended. Main courses £7–£15 ($11.55–$24.75). AE, MC, V. Sun–Thurs 5pm–midnight; Fri–Sat 5pm–1am. INDIAN.

Built around an indoor fish pond in a dining room draped with the soft folds of an embroidered tent, this is one of the most exotic restaurants in the region. Meals are prepared with fresh ingredients and cover the gamut of recipes from both north and south India. Some preparations are slow-cooked in clay pots (tandoori) and spiced according to your preference. Both meat and vegetarian dishes are available.

A DAY TRIP TO GLAMIS

The little village of Glamis (pronounced without the "i") grew up around **Glamis Castle,** Estate Office, Glamis (☎ **01307/840393**). With its link to the British crown, Glamis Castle is second only to Balmoral Castle in visitors. For six centuries it has been connected to members of the British royal family. The Queen Mother was brought up here; and Princess Margaret was born here, becoming the first royal princess born in Scotland in three centuries. The present owner is the queen's great-nephew. The castle contains Duncan's Hall, supposedly the setting for Shakespeare's *Macbeth,* who was thane of Glamis.

The present Glamis Castle dates from the early 15th century, but there are records of a castle on the site from the 11th century. Glamis Castle has been in the possession of the Lyon family since 1372, and it contains some fine plaster ceilings, furniture, and paintings.

The castle is open to the public, with access to the Royal Apartments and many other rooms, as well as the fine gardens, from the end of March to the end of October only, daily from 10:30am to 5:30pm. Admission to the castle and gardens is £5.40 ($8.90) adults, £2.80 ($4.60) children. If you wish to visit the grounds only, the charge is £2.50 ($4.15) adults, £1.40 ($2.30) children. Buses run between Dundee and Glamis. The ride is about 35 minutes; cost is £3.70 ($6.10) one way. Buses don't run on Sunday, and they also don't stop in front of the castle which lies 1 mile from the bus stop.

Where to Stay

Castleton House. Eassie by Glamis, Forfar, Tayside DD8 1SJ. ☎ **01307/840340.** Fax 01307/840506. 6 units. TV TEL. Apr–Oct £140 ($231) double, Nov–Mar £110 ($181.50) double. Children stay free in parents' room. Rates include half board. MC, V. Drive 3 miles west of Glamis on A-94.

This Victorian hotel has been restored with love and care by its owners, Anthony and Sheila Lilly. In cool weather you're greeted by welcoming coal fires in both the bar and public lounge; the youthful staff is the most considerate we've encountered in the area. Bedrooms of various sizes are furnished with reproduction antiques. The chef features a set luncheon and a set-price dinner. The menu changes daily but is always based on the freshest seasonal produce.

Where to Dine

Strathmore Arms. Glamis. ☎ **01307/840248.** Reservations recommended. Main courses £5.50–£12 ($9.05–$19.80). MC, V. Apr–Aug Mon–Fri 11am–9pm, Sat–Sun noon–9pm. Sept–Mar daily noon–3pm and 5–9pm. CONTINENTAL/SCOTTISH.

Playing the World's Oldest Course

At St. Andrew's, 14 miles southeast of Dundee and 51 miles northeast of Edinburgh, the rules of golf in Britain and the world were codified and arbitrated. Golf was played for the first time in the 1400s, probably on the site of St. Andrew's Old Course, and Mary Queen of Scots teed up here in 1567. All six of St. Andrew's golf courses are open to the public on a more-or-less democratic basis—ballots are drawn one day in advance. To participate in the balloting, you must be staying in St. Andrews for a minimum of two days and you must be able to present a current handicap certificate issued by the governing golf body of your home country. If you meet these requirements, you can enter the ballot in person at the golf course, or by phone at ☎ **01334/466666,** before 1:45pm on the day prior to the one on which you wish to play. At 2pm each day, the balloting is drawn, and the following day's players are announced at 4pm. Bear in mind that your wait to play will most likely be from 4 to 6 days; however, some lucky players get on the course the next day. Players who call the golf course several weeks in advance to make reservations can often circumvent the balloting system, depending on demand.

The Old Course, St. Andrews, Golf Place, St. Andrew's, Fife (☎ **01334/ 466666**), is a 6,566-yard 18-hole course billed as "the Home of Golf." Greens fees are £75 ($123.75) per round April to September or £34 ($56.10) otherwise. A caddy will cost £27 ($44.55) plus tip. Golf clubs rent for £15 ($24.75) per round. Electric carts are not allowed, and you can rent a trolley only on afternoons between May through September for £3 ($4.95). The course is a par 72.

To reach St. Andrews from Edinburgh, travel north along the A90 to Dunfermline. From there continue northeast along A910, which becomes A915 at Leven. From Leven, drive northeast on A915 directly to St. Andrews. Expect your total trip time to be at least 1 hour.

Try this place near the castle for one of the best lunches in the area. You might begin with a freshly made soup of the day or Cheddar-filled mushrooms wrapped in bacon and grilled. Grilled lamb cutlets are regularly featured, as is poached sole with prawns and mushrooms in a light curry sauce. You might also try filet of Angus beef in a whisky sauce.

BRAEMAR

In the heart of some of Grampian's most beautiful countryside, Braemar is not only known for its own castle, but it also makes a good center from which to explore Balmoral Castle (see "Ballater & Balmoral Castle," below). In this Highland village, set against a massive backdrop of hills covered with heather in summer, Clunie Water joins the River Dee. The massive **Cairn Toul** towers over Braemar, reaching a height of 4,241 feet.

ESSENTIALS

ARRIVING   By Train   Take the train to Aberdeen, then continue the rest of the way by bus. For information and schedules, call ☎ **0345/484950.**

By Bus   Buses run daily from Aberdeen to Braemar. The 2 hour, 10 minute trip costs £6.50 ($10.75). The bus and train stations in Aberdeen are next to each other on Guild Street (call ☎ **01224/212266** for information about schedules).

By Car To reach Braemar from Dundee, return west toward Perth, then head north along A-93, following the signs into Braemar. The 70-mile drive will take 70 to 90 minutes.

VISITOR INFORMATION The year-round **Braemar Tourist Office** is in The Mews, Mar Road (☎ **013397/41600**). In June hours are daily 10am to 6pm; July and August daily 9am to 7pm, and in September daily 10am to 1pm and 2 to 6pm. In off-season hours are Monday to Saturday 10am to 1pm and 2 to 5pm, Sunday noon to 5pm.

SPECIAL EVENTS The spectacular ✪ **Royal Highland Gathering** takes place annually in late August or early September in the Princess Royal and Duke of Fife Memorial Park. The queen herself often attends the gathering. It is believed that these ancient games were created by King Malcolm Canmore. This chieftain ruled much of Scotland at the time of the Norman conquest of England, and he selected his hardiest warriors from all the clans for a "keen and fair contest."

Call the tourist office (see "Visitor Information," above) for more information. Braemar is overrun with visitors during the gathering—anyone thinking of attending would be wise to reserve accommodations anywhere within a 20-mile radius of Braemar no later than early April.

SEEING THE SIGHTS

If you're a royal family watcher, you might be able to spot members of the family, even the queen, at **Crathie Church,** 9 miles east of Braemar on A-93 (☎ **013397/42208**), where they attend Sunday services when in residence. Services are at 11:30am; otherwise the church is open to view April to October, Monday through Saturday from 9:30am to 5pm and on Sunday 12:30 to 5pm.

Nature lovers may want to drive to the **Linn of Dee,** 6 miles west of Braemar, a narrow chasm on the River Dee, which is a local beauty spot. Other beauty spots include Glen Muick, Loch Muick, and Lochnagar. A **Scottish Wildlife Trust Visitor Centre,** reached by a minor road, is located in this Highland glen, off the South Deeside road. An access road joins B-976 at a point 16 miles east of Braemar. The tourist office (see above) will give you a map pinpointing these beauty spots.

Braemar Castle. On the Aberdeen–Ballater–Perth Rd. (A-93). ☎ **013397/41219.** Admission £2.50 ($4.15) adults, £2 ($3.30) seniors and students, £1 ($1.65) children. Easter weekend to June and Sept–Oct Sat–Thurs 10am–6pm. July–Aug daily 10am–6pm. Closed Nov–Good Friday. Take A-93 half a mile northeast of Braemar.

This romantic 17th-century castle is a fully furnished private residence with architectural grace, scenic charm, and historical interest. The castle has barrel-vaulted ceilings, an underground prison, and is known for its remarkable star-shaped defensive curtain wall.

PLAYING GOLF

Braemar Golf Course, at Braemar (☎ **013397/41618**), is the highest golf course in the country. The green of the second hole is 1,250 feet above sea level—this is the trickiest hole on the course. Pro golf commentator Peter Alliss has deemed it "the hardest par 4 in all of Scotland." Greens fees are as follows: Monday through Friday £13 ($21.45) for 18 holes and £18 ($29.70) for a day ticket; Saturday and Sunday £16 ($26.40) for 18 holes and £21 ($34.65) for a day ticket. Pull carts can be rented for £2 ($3.30) per day and sets of clubs can be borrowed for £5 ($8.25) per day. The only dress code is "be reasonable." The course is open only April to October daily (hours can vary—so call in advance).

WHERE TO STAY & DINE

Braemar Lodge Hotel. 6 Glenshee Rd., Braemar, Aberdeenshire AB35 5YQ. ☎ and fax **013397/41627.** 7 units. TV. £50–£80 ($82.50–$132) double. Rates include breakfast. MC, V. Closed Nov. Bus: 201.

This hotel, popular with skiers who frequent the nearby Glenshee slopes, is set on 2 acres of grounds at the head of Glen Clunie. The bedrooms have a strikingly modern decor. Dinner, served in the restaurant from 7pm, includes Scottish regional dishes on the à la carte menu. The food is excellent. The chef's specialties include venison with red wine, bacon, mushroom, and onion sauce; steaks served in a creamy pepper sauce; and sautéed filet of trout with hollandaise sauce. The hotel is on the road to the Glenshee ski slopes, near the cottage where Robert Louis Stevenson wrote *Treasure Island.*

Invercauld Arms Thistle Hotel. Braemar, Aberdeenshire AB35 5YR. ☎ **013397/41605.** Fax 013397/41428. 68 units. £110 ($181.50) double. Rates include breakfast. AE, DC, MC, V. Bus: 201.

This hotel is in an old granite building, with parts dating back to the 18th century. The bedrooms are comfortably furnished, if rather uninspired. In cool weather a roaring log fire will greet you after a walk in the hills that are home to deer, golden eagles, and other wildlife. Fishing and, in winter, skiing are other pursuits in the nearby area. In the pub close by, you can meet the local "ghilles" and "stalkers" (hunting and fishing guides) before returning to the hotel for the Scottish and international fare.

BALLATER & BALMORAL CASTLE

Ballater is a holiday resort center on the Dee River, with the Grampian Mountains in the background. The town still centers around its Station Square, where the royal family used to be photographed as they arrived to spend holidays. The railway is now closed.

ESSENTIALS

ARRIVING   By Train   Go to Aberdeen and continue the rest of the way by connecting bus. For rail schedules and information, call ☎0345/484950.

By Bus   Buses run hourly from Aberdeen to Ballater. The bus station in Aberdeen is on Guild Street (☎ 01224/212266 for information about schedules), beside the train station. Bus no. 201 from Braemar runs to Ballater. Travel time is 1 hour and 15 minutes; cost is £5 ($8.25).

By Car   From Braemar, go east along A-93.

VISITOR INFORMATION   The **tourist information office** is at Station Square (☎ 013397/55306). Hours are July and August, daily 10am to 1pm and 2 to 6pm; September and October, and May and June, Monday through Saturday 10am to 1pm and 2 to 5pm, Sunday 1 to 5pm. Closed November through April.

THE CASTLE

Balmoral Castle. Balmoral, Ballater. ☎ **013397/42334.** Admission £4 ($6.60) adults, £3 ($4.95) senior citizens, £1 ($1.65) for children 5–16, free 4 and under. Apr 12–July 31 Mon–Sat 10am–5pm. Crathie bus from Aberdeen to the Crathie station; Balmoral Castle is signposted from there (a quarter-mile walk).

"This dear paradise" is how Queen Victoria described Balmoral Castle, rebuilt in the Scottish baronial style by her "beloved" Albert and completed in 1855. Today Balmoral, 8 miles west of Ballater, is still a private residence of the British sovereign, and its principal feature is a 100-foot tower. On the grounds are many memorials to the royal family. In addition to the gardens there are country walks, pony trekking, souvenir shops, and a refreshment room. Of the actual castle, only the ballroom is open to the public; it houses an exhibition of pictures, porcelain, and works of art.

PLAYING GOLF

Ballater Golf Club, at Ballater (☎ **013397/55567**), is one of the more scenic courses in the area. Set in a bowl of mountains and situated on the banks of the River Dee, this is a 5,638-yard, par-67 course. Greens fees are as follows: Monday through Friday, £18 ($29.70) for 18 holes or £27 ($44.55) for a day ticket; Saturday and Sunday, £21 ($34.65) for 18 holes or £31 ($51.15) for a day ticket. There are no electric carts for hire; pull-carts rent for £2 ($3.30) per day. Dress should be smart but casual. The course is open daily April to September, 7:30am to sunset. From October to March, hours are daily 9am to sunset, but only if the weather permits.

WHERE TO STAY

Craigendarroch Hotel and Country Club. Braemar Rd., Ballater, Aberdeenshire AB35 5XA. ☎ **013397/55858.** Fax 013397/55447. www.stakis.co.uk. 44 units. TV TEL. £142–£162 ($234.30–$267.30) double; £217–£237 ($358.05–$391.05) suite. Rates include half-board (breakfast and dinner) in the Club House Bistro. AE, DC, MC, V.

This hotel, built in the Scottish baronial style, is set amid old trees on a 28-acre estate. Although modern comforts have been added, the owners try to maintain a 19th-century atmosphere. The luxurious public rooms include a regal oak staircase and a large sitting room. The oak-paneled study is complete with a log fire and book-lined shelves. The fair-sized bedrooms open onto views of the village of Ballater and the River Dee. Each of the rooms is individually furnished; all have hair dryers, trouser presses, private bathrooms with showers, and small refrigerators (not minibars). Facilities include the Leisure Club with a spa pool, two swimming pools, a sauna, and a solarium.

Monaltrie Hotel. 5 Bridge Sq., Ballater, Aberdeenshire AB35 5QJ. ☎ **013397/55417.** Fax 013397/55180. E-mail: monaltrie.hotel@virgin.net. 25 units. TV TEL. £70–£84 ($115.50–$138.60) double. Rates include Scottish breakfast. AE, DC, MC, V.

This hotel, the first in the region, was built in 1835 of Aberdeen granite to accommodate the clients of a now-defunct spa. Today it bustles with a clientele who come for the live music in its pub and for the savory food served in its two restaurants. The more unusual of the two is a Thai restaurant, which serves dinner only, Thursday through Tuesday from 7 to 10pm. Each of the bedrooms has an unobtrusive monochromatic decor and comfortable beds.

WHERE TO DINE

Green Inn. 9 Victoria Rd., Ballater, Aberdeenshire AB35 5QQ. ☎ **013397/55701.** Reservations required. Set-price menu £21 ($34.65) for 2 courses; £25 ($41.25) for 3 courses. Apr–Oct daily 7–9:30pm, Sun 7–9pm; Nov–Mar Tues–Sat 7–9:30pm. Closed 2 weeks in Oct. SCOTTISH.

In the heart of town, this establishment was once a temperance hotel. Now the pink-granite inn is one of the finest dining rooms in town, especially for traditional Scottish dishes. The chef emphasizes local produce, including home-grown vegetables when available. In season, loin of venison is served with a bramble sauce, and you can always count on fresh salmon and the best of Angus beef.

Three very simply furnished double bedrooms are rented here, all with private bathrooms (with shower) and TV. B&B costs £55 ($90.75) per person.

Oaks Restaurant. In the Craigendarroch Hotel and Country Club, Braemar Rd. ☎ **013397/55858.** Reservations strongly recommended. Set-price 4-course dinner £27.50 ($45.40). AE, DC, MC, V. Daily 6:30–9:30pm. BRITISH.

The most glamorous restaurant in the region, the Oaks is in the century-old mansion that was originally built by the "marmalade kings" of Britain, the Keiller family. (The company's marmalade is still a household name throughout the U.K.) This is the most upscale of the three restaurants in a resort complex that includes hotel rooms, time-share villas, and access to a nearby golf course. To start, try the venison and duck ter-rine flavored with orange and brandy and served with a warm black conch vinaigrette. Main courses include roast rack of lamb, breast of Grampian chicken, loin of venison, or filet of Aberdeen Angus beef.

THE CASTLE COUNTRY

The city of Aberdeen, Scotland's "third city," is bordered by fine sandy beaches (if you're a polar bear) and is filled with buildings constructed largely of pink and gray granite. The harbor is one of the largest fishing ports in the country, and Aberdeen is home base for the oil workers of six North Sea oilfields. However, far more interesting to visitors with limited time are the 40 inhabited castles all lying within a 40-mile radius of the city, which has earned the area the title of "castle country." Since time is limited for most motorists, we've spotlighted only the most intriguing.

ESSENTIALS

ARRIVING   By Train   Scotrail runs trains from Edinburgh (3½ hours) at the rate of 9 per day Monday to Saturday and 10 per day on Sunday, costing £31 ($51.15) for a one-way ticket. For information, call ☎ **0345/484950.**

By Bus   Scottish Citylink (☎ **0990/505050**) arrives in Aberdeen from Edinburgh at the rate of at least one bus per hour during the day, costing £13 ($21.45) one-way.

CASTLING

Castle Fraser. Sauchen, near Kemnay. ☎ **01330/833463.** Admission £4 ($6.60) adults, £2.70 ($4.45) children, free for children 4 and under. July–Aug daily 11am–5:30pm; May–June and Sept daily 1:30–5:30pm; Easter weekend and Oct Sat–Sun 1:30–5:30pm; closed Nov–Mar. 3 miles south of Kemnay, 16 miles west of Aberdeen, off A-944.

One of the most impressive of the fortress-like castles of Mar, Castle Fraser stands in a 25-acre parkland setting. The sixth laird, Michael Fraser, began construction in 1575, and his son finished it in 1636. Its Great Hall is spectacular, and you can wander around the grounds, which include an 18th-century walled garden.

Kildrummy Castle. Hwy. A-97, Kildrummy. ☎ **019755/71331.** Admission £1.80 ($2.95) adults, £1 ($1.65) seniors, 75p ($1.25) children. Easter–Sept Mon–Sat 9:30am–6pm, Sun 2–6pm; Oct–Nov Mon–Sat 9:30am–4pm, Sun 2–4pm. Closed Dec–Easter. Take A-944 for 35 miles west of Aberdeen; it's signposted off A-97, 10 miles west of Alford.

This is the most extensive example of a 13th-century castle in Scotland. Once the ancient seat of the earls of Mar, the four round towers, the hall, and the chapel remain from the original structure. The great gatehouse and other parts date from the 16th century. The castle played a major role in Scottish history up to 1715, when it was dis-mantled.

Fyvie Castle. Turriff, on the Aberdeen–Banff road. ☎ **01651/891266.** Admission £4.40 ($7.25) adults, £2.90 ($4.80) seniors and children. July–Aug daily 11am–5:30pm; Apr–June and Sept daily 1:30–5:30pm; Oct Sat–Sun 1:30–5:30pm. Closed Nov–Mar. Take A947 for 23 miles northwest of Aberdeen.

The National Trust for Scotland opened this castle to the public in 1986. The oldest part, dating from the 13th century, is the grandest existing example of Scottish baro-nial architecture. There are five towers, named after Fyvie's five families—the Prestons, Melddrums, Setons, Gordons, and Leiths—who lived here over 5 centuries. Originally built in a royal hunting forest, Fyvie means "deer hill" in Gaelic. The interior, created by the first Lord Leith of Fyvie, a steel magnate, reflects the opulence of the Edwardian era. His collections contain arms and armor, 16th-century tapestries, and important artworks by Raeburn, Gainsborough, and Romney. The castle is rich in ghosts, curses, and legends.

WHERE TO STAY

✪ **The Jays Guest House.** 422 King St., Aberdeen, Aberdeenshire AB24 3BR. ☎ or fax **01224/638295.** 10 units. TV. £50–£60 ($82.50–$99) double. MC, V. Rates include Scottish breakfast. Bus: 1, 2, 3, 4, or 7.

Near the university and the Offshore Survival Centre, this is one of the nicer guesthouses in Aberdeen, mainly because of the high standards of the owners, Alice and George Jennings. Everything runs smoothly, and the rooms are bright and airy, each newly renovated. The small- to medium-sized rooms are attractively furnished, with comfortable Scottish beds. All rooms have double-glazed windows, and units are reserved for nonsmokers. Ironing facilities and hair dryers can be made available.

✪ **Marcliffe at Pitfodels.** N. Deeside Rd., Aberdeen, Aberdeenshire AB1 9YA. ☎ **01224/ 861000.** Fax 01224/868860. www.nettrak.co.uk/marcliffe/. E-mail: enquiries@marcliffe.com. 42 units. MINIBAR TV TEL. £165–£195 ($272.25–$321.75) double; from £235 ($387.75) suite. Rates include breakfast. AE, DC, MC, V.

On the western edge of the city, lying about a mile off A92 at the Aberdeen ring road and less than half an hour from the airport, this deluxe hotel is clearly the best in Aberdeen today. The newly built, traditionally styled three-story manor house surrounds a courtyard and stands on 6 acres of landscaped grounds. The oriental rugs, stone floors, and tartan sofas set the decor in the public rooms; a scattering of antiques add a grace note. The rather spacious bedrooms are furnished in Chippendale and reproduction pieces, with armchairs and desks, plus a host of extras (even fresh milk in the minibar). The beautifully appointed guest rooms contain elegant fabrics, quality mattresses, and well-maintained bathrooms with a hair dryer and a rack of thick towels.

The Conservatory Restaurant offers such regional dishes as Highland lamb and freshly caught Scottish salmon. There's also a more expensive restaurant, The Invery Room, favored by corporate execs. In the library lounge, guests can choose from more than 100 scotch whiskies.

WHERE TO DINE

Gerard's. 50 Chapel St. ☎ **01224/639600.** Reservations recommended. Cafe: Main courses £5.95–£14.35 ($9.80–$23.70); set price 2-course dinner £9.50 ($15.70); set price 3-course dinner £12.50 ($20.65). Restaurant: Main courses £10–£19 ($16.50–$31.35); set-price 2-course dinner £18.75 ($30.95) or £23.75 ($39.20) for 3 courses. AE, DC, MC, V. Restaurant: Daily noon–2:30pm and 6–10:45pm. Cafe: Daily 10am–midnight; meals noon–2:30pm and 5:30–10:30pm. FRENCH/INTERNATIONAL.

Restaurateur Gerard Flechers' popular eatery is inspired by the cuisine of France, but often makes a nod to other regions as well. The restaurant is split into the more formal dining room and the relaxed Café Colmar, which has a separate entrance at the rear of the building. Expect such dishes as pan-fried maigrette of duck, Cumberland sausage with a five-bean fricassée served on cabernet sauvignon jus, or médaillons of Aberdeen Angus fillet on a potato crostini with oyster mushrooms, Provençal salsa, and stuffed tomato served with a pepper sauce. In the cafe, dishes include roasted Mediterranean vegetables with lemongrass and a Thai sauce in a pastry case on a bed of rice pilaf, or breast of chicken filled with creamed lemon cheese in a leek cream sauce. The cooking in both the restaurant and the cafe is first-rate, with a reliance on top-quality ingredients and regional produce whenever available. The chefs here know their stuff and have the confidence to be original. The bar stocks a wide range of single-malts and ports, along with French wines unavailable anywhere else in the region.

SPEYSIDE & THE MALT WHISKY TRAIL

Much of the Speyside region covered in this section is in the Moray district, on the southern shore of the Moray Firth, a great inlet cutting into the northeastern coast of Scotland. The district stretches in a triangular shape south from the coast to the wild heart of the Cairngorm Mountains near Aviemore. It's a land steeped in history, as its many castles, battle sites, and ancient monuments testify. It's also a good place to fish and, of course, play golf. Golfers can purchase a 5-day ticket from tourist information centers that allow them to play at more than 11 courses in the area.

One of the best of these courses is **Boat of Garten,** Speyside (☎ 01479/831282). Relatively difficult, the almost 6,000-yard course is dotted with many bunkers and wooded areas. From April to October, greens fees are £21 ($34.65) Monday to Friday and hours are 9:20am to sunset. On Saturday greens fees are £31 ($51.15), and hours are 10am to 4pm. In winter, you should call to see if the course is open. Greens fees are then reduced to £10 ($16.50) for a round of golf. Pull-carts can be rented for £2 ($3.30), and electric carts are available for £5 ($8.25). Dress reasonably; blue jeans are not acceptable.

The valley of the second-largest river in Scotland, the Spey, lies north and south of Aviemore. It's a land of great natural beauty. The Spey is born in the Highlands above Loch Laggan, which lies 40 miles south of Inverness. Little more than a creek at its inception, it gains in force, fed by the many "burns" that drain water from the surrounding hills. It's one of Scotland's great rivers for salmon fishing, and it runs between the towering Cairngorms on the east and the Monadhliath Mountains on the west. Its major center is Grantown-on-Spey.

The major tourist attraction in the area is the **Malt Whisky Trail,** 70 miles long, running through the glens of Speyside. Distilleries here, many of which can be visited, are known for their production of *uisge beatha,* or "water of life." Whisky (note the spelling without the *e*) is its more familiar name.

Half the malt distilleries in the country lie along the River Spey and its tributaries. Here peat smoke and Highland water are used to turn out single-malt (unblended) whisky. There are five malt distilleries in the area: **Glenlivet, Glenfiddich, Glenfarclas, Strathisla,** and **Tamdhu.** Allow about an hour each to visit them.

The best way to reach Speyside from Aberdeen is to take A-96 northwest, signposted Elgin. If you're traveling north on the A-9 road from Perth and Pitlochry, your first stop might be at Dalwhinnie, which has the highest whisky distillery in the world at 1,888 feet. It's not in the Spey Valley but, at the northeastern end of Loch Ericht, it has great views of lochs and forests.

KEITH

Keith, 11 miles northwest of Huntly, grew up because of its strategic location, where the main road and rail routes between Inverness and Aberdeen cross the River Isla. It has an ancient history, but owes its present look to the "town planning" of the late 18th and early 19th centuries. Today it's a major stopover along the Malt Whisky Trail.

The oldest operating distillery in the Scottish Highlands, the **Strathisla Distillery,** on Seafield Avenue (☎ 01542/783044), was established in 1786. From Easter to late October the facilities are open Monday to Saturday from 9:30am to 5pm and Sunday from 12:30 to 5pm for self-guided tours. The price is £4 ($6.60) per person. Note that the tours are self guided; the tours at Glen Grant (see below) are much more organized and informative.

Where to Stay & Dine

Royal Hotel. Church Rd., Keith, Banffshire AB5 5BQ. ☎ 01542/882528. Fax 01542/886101. 16 units (3 with bathroom). £38 ($62.70) double without bathroom; £45 ($74.25) double with bathroom. Rates include breakfast. AE, MC, V.

In addition to being a cozy and comfortable hotel, this stone establishment, a quarter mile north of town beside A-96, serves as the village pub and social center. Built in 1883, it has probably welcomed the grandparents and parents of virtually every longtime resident of Keith. A handful of the more expensive bedrooms contain TV sets and tea-making facilities. On the premises is a restaurant; inexpensive platters are served as bar snacks in the lounge.

DUFFTOWN

James Duff, the fourth earl of Fife, founded this town in 1817. The four main streets of town converge at the battlemented **clock tower,** which is also the tourist information center. A center of the whisky-distilling industry, Dufftown is surrounded by seven malt distilleries. The family-owned **Glenfiddich Distillery** is on A-941, half a mile north of Dufftown (☎ 01340/820373). It's open Monday to Friday from 9:30am to 4:30pm; from Easter to October, it's also open on Saturday from 9:30am to 4:30pm and on Sunday from noon to 4:30pm. Guides in kilts show visitors around the plant and explain the process of distilling. A film of the history of distilling is also shown. At the finish of the tour, you're given a dram of malt whisky to sample. The tour is free, but there's a souvenir shop where the owners hope you'll spend a few pounds.

Other sights include **Balvenie Castle,** along A-941 (☎ 01340/668860), the ruins of a moated stronghold from the 14th century on the south side of the Glenfiddich Distillery. During her northern campaign against the earl of Huntly, Mary Queen of Scots spent 2 nights here. It's open April to September, daily 9:30am to 6:30pm. Admission is £1.20 ($2) for adults and 50p (85¢) for children 15 and under.

Mortlach Parish Church in Dufftown is one of the oldest places of Christian worship in the country. It's reputed to have been founded in 566 by St. Moluag. A Pictish cross stands in the graveyard. The present church was reconstructed in 1931 and incorporates portions of an older building.

Where to Dine

Taste of Speyside. 10 Balvenie St. ☎ 01340/820860. Reservations recommended in the evening. Main courses £8.50–£13.50 ($14–$22.30); Speyside platter £8.50 ($14) at lunch, £10.50 ($17.35) at dinner. AE, MC, V. Daily 11am–5:30pm and 6–9pm. Closed Nov–Feb. SCOTTISH.

True to its name, this restaurant in the town center, just off the main square, avidly promotes a Speyside cuisine as well as Speyside malt whiskies. In the bar you can buy the product of each of Speyside's 46 distilleries. A platter including a slice of smoked salmon, smoked venison, smoked trout, pâté flavored with malt whisky, locally made cheese (cow or goat), salads, and homemade oat cakes is offered at noon and at night. Soup is made fresh daily and is served with homemade bread. There's also a choice of meat pies, including venison with red wine and herbs or rabbit. For dessert, try Scotch Mist, which contains fresh cream, malt whisky, and crumbled meringue.

ROTHES

A Speyside town with five distilleries, Rothes, on A-941 north of Dufftown, is just to the south of the Glen of Rothes, 62 miles northwest of Aberdeen. Founded in 1766, the town lies between Ben Aigan and Conerock Hill. A little settlement, the basis of the town today, grew up around **Rothes Castle,** ancient stronghold of the Leslie family, who lived here until 1622. Only a single massive wall of the castle remains.

Among the several distilleries launched by the Grant family is the **Glen Grant Distillery** (☎ 01542/783318), opened in the mid-19th century. It's located right outside town (signposted from the center). Admission is £2.50 ($4.15), which includes a tour of both the gardens and distillery, a taste of whisky, plus a £2 ($3.30) voucher applied against one of the large bottles of whisky on sale here. From June to September, hours are Monday to Saturday 10am to 5pm and Sunday 11:30am to 5pm. From March to May and in October, hours are Monday to Saturday 9:30am to 4pm. Closed November through February.

Where to Stay & Dine
Rothes Glen Hotel. Rothes, Morayshire AB38 7AQ. ☎ **01340/831254.** Fax 01340/831566. E-mail: rothesglen@compuserve.com. 16 units. TV TEL. £100–£160 ($165–$264) double. Rates include breakfast. AE, MC, V. Take A-941 3 miles north of Rothes.

This old turreted house was designed by the same architect who built Balmoral. It's surrounded by about 40 acres of fields with grazing Highland cattle. The historic building retains many of its original pieces of furniture. The dining room serves good, wholesome meals in true Scottish tradition. A set-price four-course dinner is offered for £30 to £35 ($49.50 to $57.75).

GRANTOWN-ON-SPEY
This holiday resort, with its gray granite buildings, is 34 miles southeast of Inverness, in a wooded valley from which it commands views of the Cairngorm Mountains. It's a key center of winter sports in Scotland, and the Spey is renowned for its salmon fishing. One of Scotland's many 18th-century planned towns, it was founded on a heather-covered moor in 1765 by Sir James Grant and became the seat of that ancient family.

From a base here, you can explore the valleys of the Don and Dee, the Cairngorms, and Culloden Moor, scene of the historic battle in 1746, when Bonnie Prince Charlie and his army were defeated.

Grantown-on-Spey is reached by taking the A939, 24 miles south of the city of Nairn.

A year-round **tourist information office** is on High Street (☎ **01479/872773**). Hours April to October are daily 9am to 7pm, Sunday 10am to 5pm; from November to March, Monday to Friday 9am to 5pm, Saturday 10am to 5pm.

The Great Outdoors
Grantown-on-Spey is the best center for touring the Cairngorms, which stretch 50 miles and encompass over 50 peaks. It's excellent for skiing in the winter, or cycling, golf, and fishing during warmer months. The road up Glen More past Loch Morlick leads to a chairlift going all the way to the summit. The cost is £6 ($9.90), and it is open daily from 9am to 4:30pm; later in midsummer if the weather holds. For information, call ☎ **01479/861-261.** This is a popular lift in the ski season, lasting from December to April. For information about rock and ice climbing, bike tours, and guided walks, call Ron Walker of Talisman Activities at ☎ **01479/841576.** The local tourist office (see above) can also offer advice about watersports on Loch Morlick and Lock Insh nearby.

Where to Stay
Garth Hotel. The Square, Castle Rd., Grantown-on-Spey, Morayshire PH26 3HN. ☎ **01479/872836.** Fax 01479/872116. 18 units. TV TEL. £54–£64 ($89.10–$105.60) double. Half-board £69–£79 ($113.85–$130.35) per person. MC, V.

The elegant, comfortable Garth stands on 4 acres of grounds beside the town square. Guests enjoy the use of a spacious upstairs lounge, whose high ceilings, wood-burning stove, and vine-covered veranda make it an attractive place for morning

coffee or afternoon tea. This pleasant hotel features comfortable and handsomely furnished bedrooms, with all the necessary amenities. Extensive and selective meals with
a French slant favor "Taste of Scotland" dishes, with emphasis on fresh local produce,
including seafood, salmon, venison, game, and beef.

Tulchan Lodge. Advie, Grantown-on-Spey, Morayshire PH26 3PW. ☎ **01807/510200.** Fax
01807/510234. 13 units. TEL. £350–£500 ($577.50–$825) double. Rates include full board.
No credit cards. Closed Feb–Mar. Drive 9 miles northeast of Grantown on B-9102.

Tulchan Lodge is the greatest sporting lodge in all of Europe. Built in 1906 to serve as
the 23,000-acre Tulchan Estate's fishing and shooting lodge, it's a splendid retreat for
both sports-oriented visitors and travelers who are able and willing to splurge. In
return, guests get to immerse themselves in the elegance demanded by Edward VII,
who used to come here for sports. The lodge has panoramic views of the Spey Valley,
and each of the bedrooms is unique in size and furnishings. Tulchan Lodge is open
from April to January. In the two beautiful dining rooms, Scottish and international
dishes are served, with particular attention to Scottish beef, lamb, game, and fresh
local seafood. The vegetables are grown in the lodge's garden. Only full-board residents
are accepted. Facilities include a tennis court, nature trails, and a golf course nearby.

Where to Dine

Craggan Mill. Hwy. A-95 ¾ of a mile south of Grantown-on-Spey. ☎ **01479/872288.**
Reservations recommended. Main courses £6.95–£13.50 ($11.45–$22.30). MC, V. June–Sept
daily noon–2pm and 6–10pm; Oct–May Tues–Sun 7–10pm. BRITISH/ITALIAN.

This licensed restaurant and lounge bar, a 10-minute walk south of the town center,
is housed in a restored ruined granite mill whose waterwheel is still visible. The
owners offer British and Italian cuisine at attractive prices. Your appetizer might be
smoked trout in deference to Scotland, or ravioli, inspired by sunny Italy. Main
courses might be breast of chicken with cream or chicken cacciatore, followed by a
dessert of rum-raisin ice cream or peach Melba. You've probably had better versions
of all the dishes offered here, but what you get isn't bad. A good selection of Italian
wines is also offered.

GLENLIVET

As you leave Grantown-on-Spey, head east along A-95 until you come to the junction
with B-9008; go south along this route and you won't miss the **Glenlivet Distillery.**
The location of the **Glenlivet Reception Centre** (☎ **01542/783220**) is 10 miles
north of the nearest town, Tomintoul. Near the River Livet, a Spey tributary, this distillery is one of the most famous in Scotland. From May to June, it is open Monday
to Saturday 10am to 4pm; July and August, Monday to Saturday 10am to 6pm; and
September and October, Monday to Saturday 10am to 4pm. Closed otherwise.
Admission is £2.50 ($4.15); however, if you purchase a bottle of whisky in the gift
shop you get a £2 ($3.30) reduction with the admission voucher.

   Back on A-95, you can visit the **Glenfarclas Distillery** at Ballindalloch (☎ **01807/
500245**), one of the few malt whisky distilleries that's still independent of the giants.
Founded in 1836, Glenfarclas is managed by the fifth generation of the Grant family.
It's open all year, Monday through Friday from 9am to 5pm; from June to September,
it's also open Saturday from 10am to 4pm and Sunday from 12:30 to 4:30pm. There's
a small craft shop, and each visitor is offered a dram of Glenfarclas Malt Whisky.
Guided tours cost £3.50 ($5.75); children under 18 free.

Where to Stay

Minmore House Hotel. Glenlivet, Ballindalloch, Banffshire AB37 9DB. ☎ **01807/590378.**
Fax 01807/590472. 10 units. TEL. £150 ($247.50) double. Rates include breakfast, afternoon
tea, and 5-course dinner. MC, V. Closed end of Oct to Apr.

Spotting Nessie

Sir Peter Scott's *Nessitera rhombopteryx* continues to elude her pursuers. "Nessie," as she's more familiarly known, has captured the imagination of the world, drawing thousands of visitors yearly to Loch Ness. The Loch Ness monster is still described as one of the world's greatest mysteries. Half a century ago, A82 was built alongside the banks of the loch's western shores. Since that time, many sightings have been recorded.

All types of high-tech underwater contraptions have searched for the Loch Ness monster, but no one can find her in spite of the photographs that have been taken. Dr. Robert Rines and his associates at the Academy of Applied Science in Massachusetts maintain an all-year watch with sonar-triggered cameras and strobe lights suspended from a raft in Urquhart Bay.

The loch is 24 miles long, a mile wide, and some 755 feet deep. Even if the monster doesn't put in an appearance, you can enjoy the loch seascape. In summer, you can take boat cruises across Loch Ness from both Fort Augustus and Inverness.

Buses from either Fort Augustus or Inverness traverse A82, taking you to Drumnadrochit. Call ☎ **0990/808080** for schedules and more information. The bucolic hamlet of Drumnadrochit lies a mile from Loch Ness at the entrance to Glen Urquhart. It's the village closest to the part of the loch where sightings of the monster have been reported most frequently.

Driving Directions from Grantown-on-Spey to Loch Ness   From Grantown-on-Spey, take the A938 west until you merge with northwest-bound Highway E15/A9, which leads to Inverness on the north tip of Loch Ness. From Inverness, you can travel on the A82 south, which runs the length of the western shoreline. The eastern shoreline can be traveled by following signposted rural roads from Inverness.

Standing on 5 acres of private grounds adjacent to the Glenlivet Distillery, this impressive country house was the home of the distillery owners before becoming a hotel. The hotel operators have elegantly furnished their drawing room, which opens onto views of the Ladder Hills and an outdoor swimming pool. The well-furnished bedrooms have tea/coffeemakers, and drinks can be enjoyed in the oak-paneled lounge bar, which has an open log fire on chilly nights. The Scottish food is excellent, served in a Regency-style dining room with mahogany tables and matching chairs.

KINCRAIG

Kincraig enjoys a scenic spot at the northern end of Loch Insh, overlooking the Spey Valley to the west and the Cairngorm Mountains to the east.

Near Kincraig, the most notable sight is the **Highland Wildlife Park** (☎ **01540/651280**), a natural area of parkland with a collection of wildlife, some of which is extinct elsewhere in Scotland. Herds of European bison, red deer, shaggy Highland cattle, wild horses, St. Kilda Soay sheep, and roe deer range the park. In enclosures are wolves, polecats, wildcats, beavers, badgers, and pine martens. Protected birds to see are golden eagles and several species of grouse—of special interest is the capercaillie ("horse of the woods"), a large Eurasian grouse that's a native of Scotland's pine forests. There's a visitor center with a gift shop, cafe, and exhibition areas. Ample parking and a picnic site are also available.

You need a car to go through the park; walkers are discouraged and are picked up by park rangers. From April to October, adults pay £6.30 ($10.40), students and children £4.20 ($6.95), and seniors £5.25 ($8.65). From November to March, adults pay £4 ($6.60), students and children £2.50 ($4.15), and seniors £3 ($4.95). The park opens every day, year-round, at 10am. Between April and October, the last entrance is 4pm, except in July and August when the last entrance is 5pm. Between November and March, the last entrance is at 2pm. All people and vehicles are expected to vacate the park within 2 hours of the day's last admission.

KINGUSSIE

Your next stop along the Spey might be at the little summer holiday resort and winter ski center of Kingussie (it's pronounced "King-*you*-see"), just off A-9. The resort is the capital of Badenoch, a district known as "the drowned land" because the Spey can flood the valley when the snows of a severe winter melt in the spring.

Kingussie practically adjoins Newtonmore (see below), directly southwest along A-86. The resort is 117 miles northwest of Edinburgh, 41 miles south of Inverness, and 11 miles southwest of Aviemore.

Five trains per day arrive from Edinburgh, taking 2 hours and 45 minutes, costing £27.70 ($45.70) one-way. Trains also arrive from Aberdeen at the rate of one per hour (with a change at either Perth or Inverness). The trip takes 4 hours and costs £21.60 ($35.65) one-way.

A summer-only **tourist information center** is on King Street (☎ **01540/661297**). It is open only from May 22 through September 22, Monday through Saturday from 10am to 1pm and 2 to 6pm, and on Sunday from 10am to 1pm and 2 to 5pm.

A Folk Museum

Highland Folk Museum. Duke St. ☎ **01540/661307.** Admission £3 ($4.95) adults, £2 ($3.30) children and senior citizens, £8 ($13.20) family ticket. Apr–Oct Mon–Fri 10:30am–5:30pm; also Sat–Sun 10:30am–5:30pm June–Sept. Tours Nov–Mar Mon–Fri 11am and 1pm.

This is the first folk museum established in Scotland (1934), and its collections are based on the life of the Highlanders. You'll see domestic, agricultural, and industrial items. Open-air exhibits are a turf *kailyard* (kitchen garden), a Lewis "black house," and old vehicles and carts. Traditional events such as spinning, music-making, and handcraft fairs are held throughout the summer.

The Great Outdoors

Kingussie is also set in one of the most scenic areas of Scotland, and you can take tours in many directions. For example, directly south of town, the A9 passes through some of the area's most panoramic scenery set against a backdrop of moor, woodlands, and hills. The highway passes through Glen Trim to Dalwhinnie, going through the Pass of Drumochter. This is an isolated and unpopulated area and, for that reason, all the more dramatic. You can also take the A86 west from Kingussie to Glen Roy and Spean Bridge, going through lush glens set off by towering hills. The road dips and climbs beside Loch Laggan, one of the region's most beautiful lakes. At several points along this route, you might want to get out of your car and go for long walks in the country, past secret lochans and hidden glens. Perhaps you'll stumble upon Brigadoon.

If you'd like to go **hiking** in the area, the local tourist office (see above) will help you plan a trip into the Monadhiath Mountains (the word in Gaelic meaning "gray moors"). They loom over Kingussie, separating Speyside from the Great Glen. Athough the Cairngorm mountains are far better known, the Monadhliath mountains are equally as beautiful and far less crowded in summer.

Insh Marshes, 2 miles from Kingussie along B970, is a nature reserve with much more than just birds to see. Along a marked trail, going through meadow and marshland, you can see some of the area's more beautiful and lush scenery. Six types of wild orchids alone grow here. At two lookout points, high above the marshes, you have a good vantage point to spot birds of prey, hundreds of waterfowl, and even wild Scottish deer and otters.

Where to Stay

Homewood Lodge. Newtonmore Rd., Kingussie, Inverness-shire PH21 1HD. ☎ **01540/ 661507.** E-mail: homewoodlodge.fraaserve.co.uk. 4 units. TV. £36–£42 ($59.40–$69.30) double. Rates include breakfast. No credit cards.

One of the best B&Bs in the area, this small Highland house offers large, simply furnished rooms for either two travelers or families. Set on a half acre of garden and woodland, the house has a sitting room with an open fire. Good traditional local fare is served in the evening; reservations are recommended. Summer barbecues are also offered, and children are welcome.

Osprey Hotel. Ruthven Rd. (at High St.), Kingussie, Inverness-shire PH21 1EN. ☎ and fax **01540/661510.** 8 units. £48–£58 ($79.20–$95.70) double. Rates include breakfast. AE, MC, V.

This 1895 Victorian structure, 300 yards from the rail station, is a convenient place to stay, with comfortable, although very plain, bedrooms, all with electric blankets and electric fires. The hotel has a licensed bar, residents' lounge, and a TV lounge. Babysitting and baby-listening service is provided, and laundry and ironing facilities are available. The place is known for its completely homemade meals. Prime Scottish meats are served; in summer, salmon and trout from local rivers are offered either fresh or peat-smoked.

Where to Dine

The Cross. Tweed Mill Brae, off the Ardbroilach road, Kingussie, Inverness-shire PH21 1TC. ☎ **01540/661166.** Fax 01540/661080. Reservations recommended. Set-price 5-course dinner £35 ($57.75). MC, V. Wed–Mon 7–9pm. Closed Dec–Feb. SCOTTISH.

This chic restaurant comes as a major surprise: In an out-of-the-way setting in a remote Highland village, it serves superlative meals that involve theater as much as they do fine food. The restaurant stands on 4 acres, with the Gynack Burn running through the grounds. The main building is an old tweed mill with an open-beam ceiling. French doors lead out onto a terrace over the water's edge where alfresco dinners are served. Specialties depend on the produce in the local markets and might include venison cooked in white wine, wild pigeon with grapes, or Highland lamb with sorrel.

Nine rooms are rented in a new building. Each room is different in size and style—for example, two rooms have canopied beds, and another has a balcony overlooking the mill pond. Doubles, including half-board, cost £190 ($313.50). Ruth and Tony Hadley run this place with a commitment to personal service and attention to detail, and Ruth's cooking has put it on the gastronomic map of Scotland.

NEWTONMORE

This Highland resort, directly southeast of Kingussie on A-86, in Speyside is a good center for exploring the Grampian and Monadhliath mountains, and it offers excellent fishing, golf, pony trekking, and hill walking. A track from the village climbs past the Calder River to Loch Dubh and the massive **Carn Ban** (3,087 ft.), where eagles fly. **Castle Cluny,** ancient seat of the MacPherson chiefs, is 6 miles west of Newtonmore.

You may want to stop and have a look at **Clan Macpherson House & Museum,** Main Street (☎ **01540/673332**). Displayed are clan relics and memorials, including the Black Chanter and Green Banner, a "charmed sword," and the broken fiddle of the freebooter, James MacPherson—a Scottish Robin Hood. Relics associated with Bonnie Prince Charlie are also here. An annual clan rally is held in August. Admission is free, but donations are accepted. It's open Monday to Saturday 10am to 5pm, Sunday 2:30 to 5:30pm, but only April to October.

There is no local tourist office to go to for information, but if you're staying at one of the little inns or guesthouses in the area, the reception desks at your hotel can hook you up with any activities.

Where to Stay

Pines Hotel. Station Rd., Newtonmore, Inverness-shire PH20 1AR. ☎ **01540/673271.** 6 units. TV. £70 ($115.50) double. Rates include dinner and breakfast. No credit cards. Closed Nov–May.

This granite house sits on a hill overlooking the Spey Valley, a quarter-mile west of the hamlet's center. Your hosts are John and Fran Raw, émigrés from Liverpool, who maintain a half-dozen cozy bedrooms with an ambience that says "you can put your feet up and relax." Almost everyone here opts for half-board because of the wholesome, straightforward British cuisine made from ultra-fresh ingredients. Examples include roast lamb with mint sauce; poached salmon steak in white wine sauce; venison casserole with red wine and onions; and dessert specialties such as sherry trifle or lemon meringue pie. Regrettably, the dining room is usually closed to non-residents.

16

Spain

by Darwin Porter & Danforth Prince

The fascinating history of Spain is perceptible in towns small and large, but this country of 40 million is no relic mired in the past. Spain today is a vital and exciting place. This land of sun-drenched beaches, terraced vineyards, sleepy villages, and jeweled Moorish palaces is undergoing a remarkable cultural renaissance. Contemporary art, literature, cinema, and fashion are the tools of new and original expression, and cafes and bars hum with animated discussion about politics, society, and Spain's newfound prosperity.

1 Madrid

Landlocked Madrid lies on a windswept and often arid plain, beneath a sky that has been described as Velázquez blue. Poetically, Madrid has been called the "gateway to the skies": *de Madrid al cielo.* The city is populated by adopted sons and daughters from virtually every region of Spain, adding to its cosmopolitan gloss. Despite its influence as the cultural beacon of the Spanish-speaking world and its quintessentially Spanish nature, Madrid lacks the features that for many bespeak Spain: a beach, an ancient castle or cathedral, and an archbishop. Madrileños long ago learned how to compensate: They substituted long strolls through the city's verdant parks and along its *paseos,* and they built an elegant palace and erected countless churches, many with baroque ornamentation and gilt.

Artists and writers gravitate to the newly revitalized capital and its fertile artistic climate. The city itself was a central character in Pedro Almodóvar's films, such as *Women on the Verge of a Nervous Breakdown* and *Tie Me Up! Tie Me Down!* Spaniards—and particularly Madrileños—pursue nightlife with a passion; they party until the wee hours and then greet the dawn over hot chocolate and *churros* (fried fingerlike doughnuts). But despite the city's many pleasures, Madrid is also a place for work, evidenced by the spate of emerging local industries, services, and products.

Only in Madrid

Sitting in the Sol or Sombra at the Bullfights Bullfighting is more entwined with the temperament and passions of the land than any other pastime in Iberia. Aficionados view bullfighting as an art form—a microcosm of death, catharsis, and rebirth—and defend it as one of the most evocative and memorable events in Spain. Detractors claim the sport is cruel, bloody, violent, and savage. Head for the *plaza de toros* (bullring) and decide for yourself. A "sol" seat puts you in the baking afternoon sun, while the more expensive "sombra" offers shade.

Visiting the Prado   It's one of the world's supreme art museums, ranking up there with the Louvre. The Prado is the artistic repository of some 4,000 universal masterpieces, many of them acquired by Spanish kings. The wealth of Spanish painters is staggering—everything from Goya's *Naked Maja* to the celebrated *Las Meninas* by Velázquez. Masterpiece after masterpiece unfolds before your eyes. It would take a lifetime to savor all the Prado's wonders.

Feasting on Tapas in the Tascas   Tapas bars (*tascas*) are the quintessential Madrileño experience, and tapas are reason enough to go to Madrid. While tapas bars have sprung up the world over, their little treats always taste better here. The *tapeo* is the equivalent of the pub crawl in London; make your way from one tasca to the next, sampling from the bar anything from *gambas* (deep-fried shrimp) and *pulpo* (octopus) to stuffed peppers and chorizo (spicy sausage). To really go native, try lamb's sweetbreads or bull's testicles. These dazzling spreads will fortify you until the fashionably late dining hour (10pm or later). The best streets for your tasca crawl are Ventura de la Vega, the area around Plaza de Santa Ana or Plaza de Santa Bárbara, Cava Baja, and Calle de Cuchilleros.

Checking Out the Rastro   This is Madrid's biggest flea market, a tradition dating back 500 years. Savvy shoppers arrive before 7am every Sunday to beat the rush and be the first to get their hands on the best merchandise. The teeming place doesn't really get going until about 9am, and then it's shoulder-to-shoulder stretching down Calle Ribera de Curtidores. Real or fake antiques, secondhand clothing, porno films, Franco-era furniture, paintings (endless copies of Velázquez), bullfight posters, old books, and religious relics, as well as a splendid collection of junk, are sold here. Women who have lost their purse to a mugger the day before often report that they can find it here for resale—sans contents, of course.

ORIENTATION

GETTING THERE   By Plane   Nine miles east of the city center, **Barajas** (☎ **91-305-83-43** for airport information), Madrid's international airport, has two terminals—one international, the other domestic. A conveyor belt connects the two.

Air-conditioned yellow airport buses take you from the arrivals terminal to the bus depot under Plaza de Colón, a central point. You can also get off at stops along the way, provided that your baggage isn't stored in the hold. The fare is 380ptas. ($2.65), and the buses leave every 15 minutes, either to or from the airport.

If you go into town by taxi, expect to pay 2,800ptas. ($19.60) and up, plus surcharges for the trip to or from the airport and for baggage handling. If you take an unmetered limousine, negotiate the price in advance.

By Train   Madrid has three major railway stations: **Atocha,** Avenida Ciudad de Barcelona (Metro: Atocha RENFE), for trains to and from Lisbon, Toledo, Andalusia, and Extremadura; **Chamartín,** in the northern suburbs at Augustín de Foxá (Metro: Chamartín), for trains to and from Barcelona, Asturias, Cantabria, Castille-León, the Basque country, Aragón, Catalonia, Levante (Valencia), Murcia, and the French border; and **Estación Príncipe Pío** or Norte, Po. del Rey 30 (Metro: Norte), for trains to and from northwest Spain (Salamanca and Galicia). For information about connections from any of these stations, call **RENFE,** Spanish State Railways (☎ **91-328-90-20** daily 7am to 11pm). For tickets, go to the principal office of RENFE, Alcalá 44 (Metro: Banco de España), open Monday to Friday 9am to 8pm.

Bilbao & the Guggenheim

The world is flocking to Bilbao, that "ugly, gray, decaying smokestack" city, 246 miles north of Madrid. The capital of the Basque country, and Spain's sixth largest city, Bilbao is the home of the new $100 million **Guggenheim Museum,** designed by American architect Frank Gehry. If this new art mecca is on your Spain or Europe itinerary, here are some details:

The easiest way to get to Bilbao is to fly into **Bilbao Airport** (☎ 94-486-93-00), 5 miles north of the metropolis in the small town of Sandica. From the airport, yellow bus A-3247 runs into the heart of the city. Flights on Iberia arrive frequently from both Barcelona and Madrid, plus other key cities in Spain, as well as from London, Paris, Milan, and Zurich. Two trains arrive daily from both Barcelona (trip time: 11 hours) and Madrid (trip time: 6 or 7 hours); phone ☎ 94-423-86-23 for rail information.

Once in Bilbao, you can pick up information and a city map at the **Bilbao Tourist Office,** Plaza Arriaga (☎ 94-416-00-22), open Monday through Friday 9am to 1:30pm and 4 to 7:30pm, Saturday 9am to 2pm, and Sunday 10am to 2pm.

Inaugurated in October 1997, the ✪ **Guggenheim Museum** at Muella Evaristo Churruca 1 (☎ 94-423-27-99) stands at the intersection of the Puente de la Salve bridge and the Nervión River. The museum is devoted to American and European art of the 20th century, including works by Kandinsky, Mondrian, Picasso, Ernst, Pollock, Lichtenstein, Oldenburg, Serra, and others. Admission is 800 pesetas ($5.60) for adults and 400 pesetas ($2.80) for students and seniors; free for children age 12 and under. It's open Tuesday through Sunday 11am to 8pm.

While in Bilbao, also visit the **Museum de Bellas Artes,** Plaza del Museo 2 (☎ 94-439-60-60), one of Spain's most important art museums, containing both medieval and modern works, including paintings by Velásquez, Goya, Zurbarán, and El Greco.

Since Bilbao up to now has mainly attracted business travelers, its hotels lack the charm of those found in art cities such as Barcelona and Seville. We consider the **Hotel López de Haro,** Obispo Orueta 2 (☎ 94-423-55-00), the finest in town. Although sterile looking, it has the most efficient staff and polished service. It's major competitor is the also-sterile **Gran Hotel Ercilla,** Ercilla 37–39 (☎ 94-410-20-00). A good moderately priced choice is **Hotel Avenida,** Zumalacárregui 40 (☎ 94-412-43-00). For a bargain, head for **Roquefer,** Lotería 2–4 (☎ 94-415-07-55).

Basque cuisine is the finest in Spain, featuring *pintxos* (pronounced *Peen-*chohz), or tapas. The best place for tapas bars is Calle Licenciado Poza, between Alameda del Doctor Areilza and Calle Iparraguirre. The most enticing bar, however, is **Victor,** Plaza Nueva 2 (☎ 94-415-16-78), which specializes in seafood tapas. Other favorites include **Atlanta,** Calle Rodríguez 28 (☎ 94-427-64-72), famous for their prosciutto sandwiches, and **Busterri,** Calle Licenciado Poza 42 (☎ 94-441-50-67), known for their grilled anchovies.

By Bus Madrid has at least eight major bus terminals, including the large **Estación Sur de Autobuses,** Calle Méndez Alvaro (☎ 91-468-42-00; Metro: Alvaro). Most buses pass through this station.

By Car   The following are the major highways into Madrid, with information on driving distances to the city: Rte. NI from Irún, 315 miles; NII from Barcelona, 389 miles; NIII from Valencia, 217 miles; NIV from Cádiz, 388 miles; NV from Badajoz, 254 miles; and NVI from Galicia, 374 miles.

VISITOR INFORMATION   The most convenient **tourist office** is on the ground floor of the 40-story Torre de Madrid, Plaza de España (☎ **91-429-31-77;** Metro: Plaza de España); it's open Monday to Friday 9am to 7pm and Saturday 9:30am to 1pm. Ask for a street map of the next town on your itinerary, especially if you're driving.

CITY LAYOUT   In modern Spain all roads, rails, and phone lines lead to Madrid. The capital has outgrown all previous boundaries and is branching out in all directions.

Every new arrival ought to find the **Gran Vía,** which cuts a winding pathway across the city beginning at **Plaza de España,** where you'll find one of Europe's tallest skyscrapers, Edificio España. On this principal avenue is the largest concentration of shops, hotels, restaurants, and movie houses. **Calle de Serrano,** in the Salamanca neighborhood, is a runner-up in terms of importance.

South of the **Gran Vía** lies the **Puerta del Sol.** All road distances in Spain are measured from this square. However, today its significance has declined, and it's prime hunting ground for pickpockets and purse snatchers. Here **Calle de Alcalá** begins its 2½-mile run.

Plaza Mayor is the heart of Old Madrid, its mix of French and Georgian architecture an attraction in itself. (Again, be wary, especially late at night.) Pedestrians pass under the arches of the huge square onto the narrow streets of the old town, where you can find some of the capital's most intriguing restaurants and tascas.

The area south of Plaza Mayor—known as **barrios bajos**—merits exploration. The narrow cobblestoned streets are lined with 16th- and 17th-century buildings. Directly south of the plaza is the **Arco de Cuchilleros,** a street packed with markets, restaurants, flamenco clubs, and taverns.

Gran Vía meets Calle de Alcalá at **Plaza de la Cibeles,** with its fountain to Cybele, "the mother of the gods," and what has become known as "the cathedral of post offices." From Cibeles, the wide **Paseo de Recoletos** begins a short run to **Plaza de Colón.** From this latter square rolls the serpentine **Paseo de la Castellana,** flanked by expensive shops, apartment buildings, luxury hotels, and foreign embassies.

Heading south from Cibeles is **Paseo del Prado,** where you'll find Spain's major attraction, the Museo del Prado, as well as the Jardín Botánica (Botanical Garden). The paseo also leads to the Atocha Rail Station. To the east of the garden lies the **Parque del Retiro,** once reserved for royalty, with restaurants, nightclubs, a rose garden, and two lakes.

GETTING AROUND

Getting around spread out Madrid isn't easy. Even many Madrileño taxi drivers, often new arrivals, are unfamiliar with their own city once they're off the main boulevards.

ON FOOT   This is the perfect way to see Madrid, especially the narrow streets of the old town. If you're going to another district (and chances are that your hotel will be outside the old town), you can take the bus or Metro. For such a large city, Madrid can be covered amazingly well on foot, because so much of what will interest a visitor lies in clusters.

BY SUBWAY (METRO) The Metro system is easy to learn and convenient. The central converging point is the Puerta del Sol, and the fare is 130ptas. (90¢) for a one-way trip. The Metro operates daily 6am to 1:30am; avoid rush hours if possible. For information, call ☎ **91-429-31-77.** You can save money on public transportation by purchasing a 10-trip ticket known as a *bonos*—for the Metro it costs 670ptas. ($4.70).

BY BUS A bus network also services the city and suburbs, with routes clearly shown at each stop on a schematic diagram. Buses are fast and efficient because they travel along special lanes. Both red and yellow buses charge 130ptas. (90¢) per ride.

For 670ptas. ($4.70), you can purchase a 10-trip ticket (but without transfers) for Madrid's bus system. It's sold at **Empresa Municipal de Transportes,** Plaza de la Cibeles (☎ **91-406-88-00**), where you can also purchase a guide to the bus routes. The office is open daily 8am to 8:30pm.

BY TAXI Even though cab fares have risen recently, they're still reasonable. When you flag down a taxi, the meter should register 170ptas. ($1.20); for every kilometer thereafter, the fare increases by 80ptas. (55¢). A supplement is charged for trips to the rail station or the bullring. The ride to Barajas Airport carries a 350-pta. ($2.45) surcharge, and there's a 160-pta. ($1.10) supplement for trips from the rail stations. In addition, there's a 150-pta. ($1.05) supplement on Sundays and holidays, plus a 150-pta. ($1.05) supplement at night. It's customary to tip about 10% of the fare. To call a taxi, dial ☎ **91-445-32-32** or 91-447-51-80.

BY CAR Driving is nightmarish and potentially dangerous in congested Madrid—it always feels like rush hour. It's not a good idea to rent a car while staying in the city. It is near impossible to park, and thieves frequently target rentals. If you want to rent a car in Madrid to tour the environs, however, you'll have several choices. In addition to its office at Barajas Airport (☎ **91-393-72-22**), **Avis** has a main office downtown at Gran Vía 60 (☎ **91-205-42-73**). **Hertz,** too, has an office at Barajas Airport (☎ **91-393-72-28**) and another in the heart of Madrid in the Edificio España, Gran Vía 18 (☎ **91-541-99-24**). **Budget Rent-a-Car** maintains an office at Juan Hurtado de Mendoza 7 (☎ **91-457-59-68**), with another office at Barajas Airport (☎ **91-393-72-16**).

BY BICYCLE Ever wonder why you see so few people riding bikes in Madrid? Those who tried were overcome by the traffic pollution. Plus, the traffic is very difficult to contend with. It's better to walk.

Fast Facts: Madrid

American Express For your mail or banking needs, you can go to the American Express office at the corner of Marqués de Cubas and Plaza de las Cortes 2, across the street from the Palace Hotel (☎ **91-322-55-00;** Metro: Gran Vía). Open Monday to Friday 9am to 5:30pm and Saturday 9am to noon.

Baby-sitters Most major hotels can arrange for baby-sitters, called *canguros* (kangaroos!) in Spanish. Usually the concierge keeps a list of reliable nursemaids and will contact them for you, provided that you give adequate notice. Rates vary

Telephone Changes

All over Spain, the city codes have now been incorporated directly into the local phone number, meaning that whether you're calling a number within the same city or in a different city, you must dial the city code.

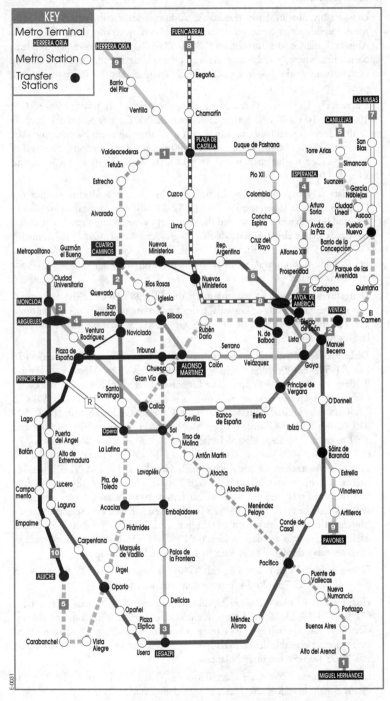

Madrid Metro

KEY

Metro Terminal
HERRERA ORIA

Metro Station ○

Transfer Stations ●

FUENCARRAL 8

HERRERA ORIA 9

Barrio del Pilar

Ventilla

Chamartín

Begoña

Valdeacederas 1

Tetuán

Estrecho

Alvarado

Cuzco

Lima

PLAZA DE CASTILLA

Duque de Pastrana

Pio XII

Colombia

Concha Espina

Cruz del Rayo

Rep. Argentina

Torre Arias

LAS MUSAS 7

CANILLEJAS 5

San Blas

Simancas

ESPERANZA 4

Suanzes

García Noblejas

Arturo Soria

Ciudad Lineal

Ascao

Avda. de la Paz

Pueblo Nuevo

Alfonso XIII

Barrio de la Concepción

Prosperidad

Parque de las Avenidas

Metropolitano

Guzmán el Bueno

CUATRO CAMINOS

Nuevos Ministerios

Ciudad Universitaria

Quevedo

Ríos Rosas

2

Iglesia

Nuevos Ministerios

6

8

7 Cartagena

Quintana

AVDA. DE AMÉRICA

El Carmen

MONCLOA 3

ARGÜELLES 4

San Bernardo

Bilbao

Rubén Darío

Serrano

N. de Balboa

Lista

VENTAS 2

Ventura Rodríguez

Noviciado

Tribunal

Diego de León

Manuel Becerra

Plaza de España

Chueca

ALONSO MARTÍNEZ

Colón

Velázquez

Goya

PRINCIPE PIO

Gran Vía

Santo Domingo

Callao

R

Príncipe de Vergara

O'Donnell

Lago

Puerta del Angel

Opera

Sol

Sevilla

Banco de España

Retiro

Ibíza

Batán

Alto de Extremadura

La Latina

Tirso de Molina

Antón Martín

Sáinz de Baranda

Campamento

Lucero

Pta. de Toledo

Lavapiés

Atocha

Estrella

Atocha Renfe

Vinateros

Laguna

Acacias

Embajadores

Menéndez Pelayo

Artilleros

Empalme

Pirámides

Conde de Casal

Carpentana

Marqués de Vadillo

Palos de la Frontera

PAVONES 9

10

Urgel

Pacífico

ALUCHE

Oporto

Puente de Vallecas

5

Opañel

Delicias

Nueva Numancia

Plaza Elíptica

3

Méndez Alvaro

Portazgo

Carabanchel

Vista Alegre

Usera

LEGAZPI

Buenos Aires

Alto del Arenal

1

MIGUEL HERNÁNDEZ

E-0031

considerably but are fairly reasonable. Although some baby-sitters in Madrid speak English, don't count on it. You might also want to contact **La Casa de la Abuela,** Calle Condes Torreanas 4 (☎ **91-574-30-94**), in the prestigious Barrio Salamanca, where "grandmother's house" offers childcare combined with creative exercises and workshops in a child-friendly environment. It's open year-round; prices vary.

Currency   The unit of currency is the Spanish **peseta (pta.),** with coins of 1, 5, 10, 25, 50, 100, 200, and 500 pesetas. Be aware that the 500-peseta coin is easily confused with the 100-peseta coin. Learn to distinguish them by size. Notes are issued in 1,000, 2,000, 5,000, and 10,000-peseta denominations. The rate of exchange used in this chapter was $1 = 145ptas. Also, 1EUR = 166.3ptas. and £1 = 253.5ptas.

Dentists & Doctors   For an English-speaking dentist or doctor, contact the U.S. Embassy, Calle Serrano 75 (☎ **91-587-22-00**); they maintain a list of dentists and doctors who have offered their services to Americans abroad. For dental services, consult also **Unidad Médica Anglo-Americana,** Conde de Arandá 1 (☎ **91-435-18-23**), in back of Plaza de Colón; office hours are Monday to Friday 9am to 8pm and Saturday 10am to 1pm, although there's a 24-hour answering service.

Drugstores   For a late-night pharmacy, dial ☎ **098** or look in the daily newspaper under "Farmacias de Guardia" to learn what drugstores are open after 8pm. Every pharmacy, even if it's closed, posts a list of nearby pharmacies that are open late on that date.

Embassies & Consulates   The Embassy of the **United States,** Calle Serrano 75 (☎ **91-587-22-00;** Metro: Núñez de Balboa), is open Monday to Friday 9:30am to noon and 3 to 5pm. The Embassy of **Canada,** Núñez de Balboa 35 (☎ **91-431-43-00;** Metro: Velázquez), is open Monday to Friday 9am to 12:30pm. The **United Kingdom** Embassy, Calle Fernando el Santo, 16 (☎ **91-319-02-00;** Metro: Colón), is open Monday to Friday from 9am to 2pm and 3:30 to 6pm. The **Republic of Ireland** has an embassy at Claudio Coello, 73 (☎ **91-576-35-00;** Metro: Serrano); it's open Monday to Friday from 10am to 2pm. The **Australian** Embassy, Paseo de la Castellana, 143 (☎ **91-579-04-28;** Metro: Cuzco), is open Monday through Thursday 8:30am to 1:30pm and 2:30 to 5pm, and Friday 8:30am to 2pm. Citizens of **New Zealand** have an embassy at Plaza de la Lealtad, 2 (☎ **91-523-02-26;** Metro: Banco de España); it's open Monday through Friday 9am to 1:30pm and 2:30 to 5:30pm. The **South African** Embassy is at Claudio Coello 91 (☎ **91-435-66-88;** Metro: Serrano), open Monday through Friday 9am to 1:30pm and 2:30 to 5pm.

Emergencies   In an emergency, call ☎ **080** to report a **fire,** ☎ **091** to reach the **police,** or ☎ **734-25-54** to request an **ambulance.**

Hospitals & Clinics   Unidad Médica Anglo-Americana, Conde de Arandá 1 (☎ **91-435-18-23;** Metro: Usera), is a private outpatient clinic offering the services of various specialists. It isn't an emergency clinic, although someone on the staff is always available. It's open daily 9am to 8pm. For a real medical emergency, call ☎ **734-25-54** for an ambulance.

Internet Access   Net Café, San Bernardo 81, 28015 Madrid (☎ **91-594-0999;** e-mail: netcafe@netcafe.es), is open daily 11am to 2am.

Lost Property   If you've lost something on a bus, go to the office at Alcántra 26 (☎ **91-406-88-43;** Metro: Goya), open Monday to Friday 9am to 2pm. If you've lost something on the Metro, go at any time to the Cuatro Caminos station (☎ **91-552-49-00**). For objects lost in a taxi, go to Plaza de Chamberí (☎ **91-448-79-26;** Metro: Chamberí), open Monday to Friday 9am to 2pm and Saturday 9am to 1pm. For items lost anywhere else, go to the Palacio de Comunicaciones at Plaza de la Cibeles (Metro: Banco de España), open Monday to Friday 9am to 2pm and Saturday 9am to 1pm. Don't call; show up in person.

Luggage Storage/Lockers   You can find them at both the Atocha and Chamartín railway terminals, as well as the major bus station at the Estación Sur de Autobuses, Calle Méndez Alvaro (☎ **91-468-42-00;** Metro: Alvaro). Storage is also provided at the air terminal underneath Plaza de Colón.

Police   In an emergency, dial ☎ **091.**

Post Office   If you don't want to receive your mail at your hotel or the American Express office, direct it to *Lista de Correos* at the central post office in Madrid. To pick up mail, go to the window marked LISTA, where you're asked to show your passport. Madrid's central office is at Plaza de la Cibeles (☎ **396-20-00**).

Safety   Because of an increasing crime rate in Madrid, the U.S. Embassy has warned visitors to leave their valuables in a hotel safe or other secure place when going out. Your passport could be needed, however, as the police may stop foreigners for identification checks. Carry only enough cash for the day's needs. Purse snatching is common, and criminals often work in pairs, using a variety of well-known scams. Even a friendly "Do you know the time?" can be used to establish that you are a foreigner and distract you.

Taxes   There are no special city taxes for tourists.

Telephone   To call Spain from the United States, dial **011** followed by **34** (Spain's country code) and the city code (for example, 1 for Madrid, 3 for Barcelona) plus the seven-digit number. When calling in Spain from one city to another, the city prefix begins with a **9.** Therefore, to call Barcelona from Madrid, dial 93 followed by the number.

For **long-distance calls,** especially transatlantic ones, it may be best to go to the main phone exchange, Locutorio Gran Vía, at Gran Vía 30, or Locutorio Recoletos, at Paseo de Recoletos 37–41. You might not be lucky enough to find an English-speaking operator, but you can fill out a simple form that facilitates placing a call. The toll-free international access codes are: **AT&T** ☎ 900-99-00-11, **Sprint** ☎ 900-99-0013, **MCI** ☎ 900-99-0014.

WHERE TO STAY

If you need to stay near the airport, a decent option is the **Best Western Villa de Barajas,** av. De Logroño 331 (☎ **91-329-2818;** fax 91-329-2704). The cost of a double room is 13,400ptas. ($93.80). The hotel runs a free shuttle bus to and from the airport. The trip takes about 5 minutes.

NEAR PLAZA DE LAS CORTES
Very Expensive
Palace. Plaza de las Cortes 7, 28014 Madrid. ☎ **800/325-3535** in the U.S., 800/325-3589 in Canada, or 91-360-80-00. Fax 91-360-81-00. 440 units. A/C MINIBAR TV TEL. 51,000–67,000ptas. ($357–$469) double; from 90,000ptas. ($630) suite. AE, DC, MC, V. Metro: Banco de España.

The Palace, an ornate Victorian "wedding cake," covers a city block, facing the Prado and Neptune Fountain. When this elegant, grand hotel first opened its doors in 1912, it was the largest hotel in Europe. Everyone from Dalí to Picasso, from Sarah

Madrid Accommodations

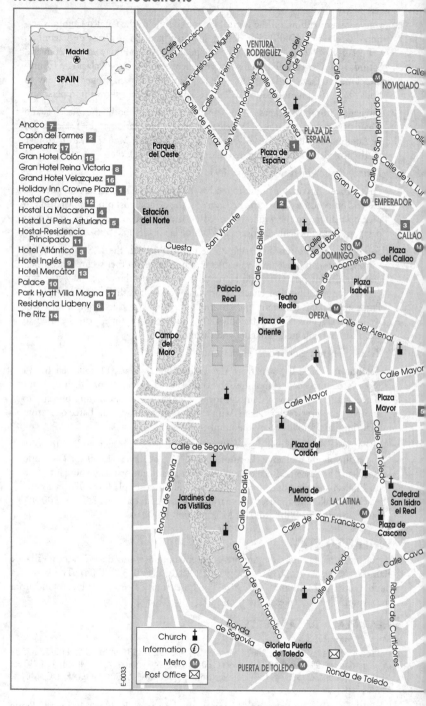

Church †
Information (*i*)
Metro (M)
Post Office ⊠

E-0033

928

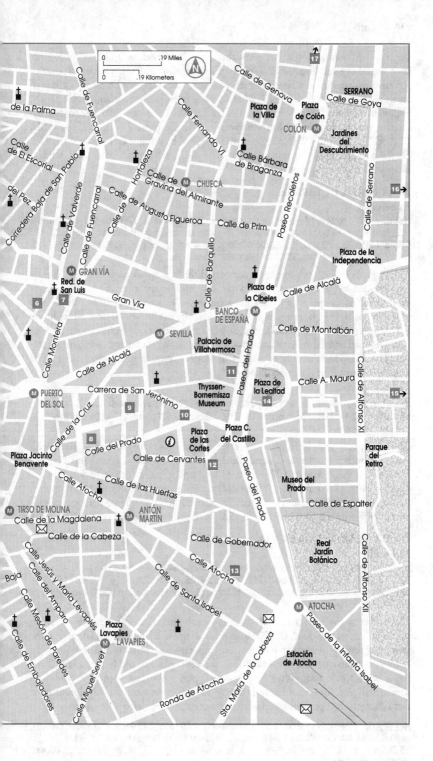

Bernhardt to Sophia Loren, has spent the night. Nevertheless, it doesn't achieve the snob appeal of its sibling, the Ritz (under the same management). The rooms are conservative and traditional, boasting plenty of space and large bathrooms with lots of amenities. As was the style when the hotel was built, the accommodations vary widely, although each was completely renovated in 1997. The elegant dining choice is La Cupola, serving Italian and Spanish specialties. Less expensive is the buffet-style La Rotonda. In the mid-1990s, the hotel was acquired by an upscale branch of the ITT Sheraton chain. Club Neptuno, a new, state-of-the-art fitness center commands a panoramic rooftop location.

NEAR PLAZA DE ESPAÑA
Expensive
Holiday Inn Crowne Plaza. Plaza de España 8, 28013 Madrid. ☎ **800/465-4329** in the U.S., or 91-547-12-00. Fax 91-548-23-89. E-mail: reservas@crowneplaza.es. 306 units. A/C MINIBAR TV TEL. 29,500ptas. ($206.50) double; from 38,000ptas. ($266) suite. AE, DC, MC, V. Parking 1,200ptas. ($8.40). Metro: Plaza de España.

The Plaza, built in 1953, might be considered the Waldorf-Astoria of Spain. A massive rose-and-white structure, it soars to a central 26-story tower. One of the tallest skyscrapers in Europe, it's a landmark visible for miles around. Once one of the best hotels in Spain, the Plaza no longer enjoys such lofty distinction, as new deluxe hotels have sprung up around Madrid. The hotel's accommodations include both conventional doubles and luxurious suites; the latter have sitting rooms and abundant amenities. The furniture is usually of a standard modern style, in harmonized colors. The quieter rooms are on the upper floors.

Moderate
Casón del Tormes. Calle del Río 7, 28013 Madrid. ☎ **91-541-97-46.** Fax 91-541-18-52. 63 units. A/C TV TEL. 12,500ptas. ($87.50) double; 15,800ptas. ($110.60) triple. MC, V. Parking 1,400ptas. ($9.80). Metro: Plaza de España.

The attractive 3-star Casón del Tormes, set behind a four-story red-brick facade with stone-trimmed windows, is around the corner from the Royal Palace and Plaza de España. The long, narrow lobby contains wood paneling, a marble floor, and a bar opening onto a separate room. The guest rooms, generally roomy and comfortable, have color-coordinated fabrics and dark wood furnishings, including mahogany headboards crowning the firm beds. Bathrooms, with shower stalls, are very small.

ON OR NEAR THE GRAN VÍA
Moderate
Anaco. Tres Cruces 3, 28013 Madrid. ☎ **91-522-46-04.** Fax 91-531-64-84. 40 units. A/C TV TEL. 9,500–10,500ptas. ($66.50–$73.50) double; 12,825–14,175ptas. ($89.80–$99.25) triple. AE, DC, MC, V. Parking 1,400ptas. ($9.80). Metro: Gran Vía, Callao, or Puerta del Sol.

Modest yet modern, with a simple boxy design, Anaco is just off the main shopping thoroughfare, the Gran Vía. Opening onto a tree-shaded plaza, it attracts those seeking a resting place that features contemporary amenities and cleanliness. The rooms are compact, with built-in headboards, reading lamps, and lounge chairs. Each has a comfortable bed with a firm mattress, plus a compact tiled bathroom with shower stall. Ask for one of the five terraced rooms on the top floor, which rent at no extra charge. The hotel has a bar/cafeteria/restaurant open daily.

Hotel Atlántico. Gran Vía 38, 28013 Madrid. ☎ **800/528-1234** in the U.S. and Canada, or 91-522-64-80. Fax 91-531-02-10. www.bestwestern.com. 80 units. A/C MINIBAR TV TEL. 13,305ptas. ($93.15) double. Rates include breakfast. AE, DC, MC, V. Parking 2,000ptas. ($14). Metro: Gran Vía.

The most startling thing about this hotel is the difference between its grand, turn-of-the-century exterior and its more basic, somewhat stripped-down modern interior. Refurbished in stages between the late 1980s and 1994, it occupies six floors on a prominent street corner of one of Madrid's central avenues. Bedrooms are clean and quiet, but simple, compact, and relatively unadorned. There's an English-inspired bar near the functional-looking reception area, and a diligent English-speaking staff who work hard at offsetting some of the hotel's sterility.

Residencia Liabeny. Salud 3, 28013 Madrid. ☎ **91-531-90-00.** Fax 91-532-74-21. 222 units. A/C MINIBAR TV TEL. 9,600–14,000ptas. ($67.20–$98) double; 16,000–21,000ptas. ($112–$147) triple. AE, MC, V. Parking 1,500ptas. ($10.50). Metro: Puerta del Sol, Callao, or Gran Vía.

This hotel, behind an austere stone-sheathed facade, is in a prime location midway between the tourist highlights of the Gran Vía and the Puerta del Sol. Named after the original owner, it contains seven floors of comfortable, contemporary rooms that, even though newly redecorated, are a bit too pristine for our tastes. The masculine cocktail bar is more warming, but the functional-looking dining room is strictly for convenience. A coffee shop is also on the premises, and good laundry service and personalized attention from the staff add to the allure of the place.

NEAR THE PUERTA DEL SOL
Expensive

✪ **Gran Hotel Reina Victoria.** Plaza de Santa Ana 14, 28012 Madrid. ☎ **91-531-45-00.** Fax 91-522-03-07. 201 units. A/C MINIBAR TV TEL. 25,000ptas. ($175) double; from 60,000ptas. ($420) suite (includes breakfast). AE, DC, MC, V. Parking 1,750ptas. ($12.25). Metro: Tirso de Molina or Puerta del Sol.

Since a recent renovation and upgrading by Spain's Tryp Hotel Group, this hotel is less staid and more impressive than ever. The hotel boasts an ornate and eclectic stone facade that the Spanish government protects as a historic monument. Although it's in a congested and noisy neighborhood in the center of town, Reina Victoria opens onto its own sloping plaza, a meeting place of intellectuals during the 17th century. Each room contains sound-resistant insulation, a safe, and a private bathroom with many amenities. The lobby bar, Manuel Rodriguez Manolete, displays bullfighting memorabilia, and there's a good in-house restaurant, El Ruedo.

Moderate

✪ **Hotel Inglés.** Calle Echegaray 8, 28014 Madrid. ☎ **91-429-65-51.** Fax 91-420-24-23. 58 units. TV TEL. 11,100ptas. ($77.70) double; 15,000ptas. ($105) suite. AE, DC, MC, V. Parking 1,300ptas. ($9.10). Metro: Puerta del Sol or Sevilla.

On a central street lined with lively tascas, this hotel has welcomed overnight guests since it opened in 1853. It's more modern and impersonal than it was when Virginia Woolf made it her address in Madrid. Behind its red-brick facade you'll find unpretentious and contemporary rooms, with comfortable beds and small, tiled bathrooms, all well maintained. Rooms aren't air-conditioned, and guests who open their windows at night are likely to hear noise from the enclosed courtyard, so light sleepers beware. There's a simple cafeteria on the premises, serving drinks and uncomplicated platters daily from 7:30am to 11pm.

Inexpensive

✪ **Hostal la Macarena.** Cava de San Miguel 8, 28005 Madrid. ☎ **91-365-92-21.** Fax 91-364-27-57. 18 units. TV TEL. 6,300ptas. ($44.10) double; 7,500ptas. ($52.50) triple; 8,500ptas. ($59.50) quad. MC, V. Metro: Puerta del Sol, Opera, or La Latina.

Known for its reasonable prices and praised by readers for the warmth of its reception, this unpretentious, clean hostel is run by the Ricardo González family. Its 19th-century facade, accented with belle époque patterns and individual balconies, offers an ornate contrast to the chiseled simplicity of the ancient buildings facing it. The location is one of the hostel's assets: It's on a street (an admittedly noisy one) immediately behind Plaza Mayor, near one of the best clusters of tascas in Madrid. Windows facing the street have double panes. No breakfast is served on site, but there's an array of neighborhood cafes.

Hostal la Perla Asturiana. Plaza de Santa Cruz 3, 28012 Madrid. ☎ **91-366-46-00.** Fax 91-366-46-08. E-mail: perlaasturiana@mundivia.es. 33 units. TV TEL. 5,000ptas. ($35) double; 7,200ptas. ($50.40) triple. AE, MC, V. Parking: 2,000ptas. ($14). Metro: Puerta del Sol.

Ideal for those who want to stay in the heart of Old Madrid (1 block off Plaza Mayor and 2 blocks from the Puerta del Sol), this small family-run establishment has a courteous staff member at the desk 24 hours a day for security and convenience. You can socialize in the small, comfortable lobby that's adjacent to the reception desk. The rooms are clean and comfortable but simple and often cramped, with fresh towels supplied daily. Many inexpensive restaurants and tapas bars are nearby. No breakfast is served.

NEAR THE PRADO
Very Expensive

✪ **Hotel Ritz.** Plaza de la Lealtad 5, 28014 Madrid. ☎ **800/225-5843** in the U.S. and Canada, or 91-521-28-57. Fax 91-532-87-76. www.ritz.es. 183 units. A/C MINIBAR TV TEL. 52,000–63,550ptas. ($364–$444.85) double; from 92,500ptas. ($647.50) suite. AE, DC, MC, V. Parking 4,000ptas. ($28). Metro: Banco de España.

Spain's most famous and prestigious hotel is encased in a turn-of-the-century shell of soaring ceilings and graceful columns. Billions of pesetas have been spent on renovations since the British-based Forte chain acquired it in the 1980s. The result is a bastion of glamour. The Ritz was built at the command of Alfonso XIII, with the aid of César Ritz, in 1908. The rooms contain fresh flowers, well-accessorized marble bathrooms, and TVs with video movies and satellite reception. In the hotel's formal restaurant, Goya, the chefs present an international menu featuring Madrid's most elaborate paella.

Moderate

Hotel Mercátor. Calle Atocha 123, 28012 Madrid. ☎ **91-429-05-00.** Fax 91-369-12-52. 92 units. MINIBAR TV TEL. 11,900ptas. ($83.30) double; 13,250ptas. ($92.75) suite. AE, DC, MC, V. Parking 1,650ptas. ($11.55). Metro: Atocha or Antón Martín.

Only a 3-minute walk from the Prado, the Mercátor draws a clientele seeking an orderly, well-run, and clean hotel, with enough comforts and conveniences to please the weary traveler. The public rooms are simple and minimalistic. Some of the guest rooms are more inviting than others, especially those with desks and armchairs. Twenty-one units are air-conditioned. It has a bar and cafeteria serving light meals.

Inexpensive

Hostal Cervantes. Cervantes 34, 28014 Madrid. ☎ and fax **91-429-27-45.** 12 units. 6,000ptas. ($42) double. No credit cards. Metro: Banco de España.

One of Madrid's most pleasant family-run hotels, the much-restored, circa 1940s Cervantes has been toasted by our readers for years. You'll take a tiny birdcage-style elevator to the immaculately maintained second floor of this stone-and-brick building. Each accommodation contains a comfortable bed and rather spartan furniture; each unit also comes with a tiny bathroom with a shower stall and thin towels. No breakfast is served, but the owners, the Alfonsos, will direct you to one of several nearby cafes. The hotel is convenient to the Prado, Retiro Park, and the older sections of Madrid.

Hostal-Residencia Principado. Zorrilla 7, 28014 Madrid. ☎ and fax **91-429-81-87.** 15 units. TV. 6,000ptas. ($42) double. AE, MC, V. Parking: 2,200ptas. ($15.40). Metro: Sevilla or Banco de España. Bus: 5, 9, or 53.

The two-star Principado is a real find. Located one floor above street level in a well-kept, turn-of-the-century townhouse, it's run by a gracious owner who keeps everything clean and inviting. New tiles, attractive bedspreads, and curtains give the rooms a fresh look. Safety boxes are provided. No meals are served, but most guests retreat to a nearby cafe for breakfast.

NEAR RETIRO & SALAMANCA
Very Expensive
Park Hyatt Villa Magna. Paseo de la Castellana 22, 28046 Madrid. ☎ **800/223-1234** in the U.S. and Canada, or 91-587-12-34. Fax 91-431-22-86. www.travelweb.com/hyatt.html. 182 units. A/C MINIBAR TV TEL. 55,000ptas. ($385) double; from 90,000ptas. ($630) suite. AE, DC, MC, V. Parking 2,500ptas. ($17.50). Metro: Rubén Darío.

One of Europe's finest hotels, the nine-story Park Hyatt is set behind a bank of pines and laurels on the city's most fashionable boulevard. Today it's an even finer choice than the Palace and is matched in luxury, ambience, and tranquility only by the Ritz. A contemporary facade of rose-colored granite contrasts with an interior that recaptures the style of Carlos IV, with paneled walls, marble floors, and fresh flowers. This luxury palace offers plush but dignified rooms decorated in Louis XVI, English Regency, or Italian provincial style. The Berceo Le Divellec, a branch of the famous Paris restaurant, serves international seafood in a glamorous setting. There's also Tse-Yang, an upscale Chinese restaurant, and a lavish English-style bar. The hotel is known for its summer terraces, set in the gardens.

Expensive
Emperatriz. López de Hoyos 4, 28006 Madrid. ☎ **91-563-80-88.** Fax 91-563-98-04. 158 units. A/C MINIBAR TV TEL. 26,500ptas. ($185.50) double; 65,000ptas. ($455) suite. AE, DC, MC, V. Parking 1,500ptas. ($10.50) nearby. Metro: Rubén Darío.

This eight-story hotel, just off the wide Paseo de Castellana, charges relatively reasonable rates. Last renovated in 1995, the guest rooms, classically styled and comfortable, with both traditional and modern furniture, remain much finer than the somewhat unimaginative public rooms. If one is available, ask for a seventh-floor room, where you get a private terrace at no extra charge. There's a bar and restaurant on site, serving both Spanish and international food, plus 24-hour room service.

Grand Hotel Velázquez. Calle de Velázquez 62, 28001 Madrid. ☎ **91-575-28-00.** Fax 91-575-28-09. 146 units. A/C MINIBAR TV TEL. 21,970ptas. ($153.80) double; from 29,160ptas. ($204.10) suite. AE, DC, MC, V. Parking 1,700ptas. ($11.90). Metro: Retiro.

On an affluent residential street near the center of town, this hotel has an art deco facade and a 1940s interior filled with well-upholstered furniture and richly grained paneling. This is a very Spanish hotel with less international exposure than some of its more cosmopolitan competitors. Several public rooms lead off a central oval area; one of them includes a bar area. As in many hotels of its era, the rooms vary; some are large enough for entertaining, with a small but separate sitting area. Elegantly striped fabrics, built-in closets, and private safes are some of the amenities. This is one of the most attractive medium-sized hotels in Madrid, with plenty of comfort and convenience.

Moderate
Gran Hotel Colón. Pez Volador 11, 28007 Madrid. ☎ **91-573-59-00.** Fax 91-573-08-09. 380 units. A/C MINIBAR TV TEL. 8,000–12,700ptas. ($56–$88.90) double. AE, DC, MC, V. Parking 1,800ptas. ($12.60). Metro: Sainz de Baranda.

West of Retiro Park, Gran Hotel Colón is a few minutes from the city center by subway. It offers comfortable yet moderately priced accommodations, with good beds and adequate bathrooms. More than half the rooms have private balconies, and all contain traditional furniture, much of it built-in. Two dining rooms and a bar are on the premises.

WHERE TO DINE
NEAR PLAZA DE LAS CORTÉS
Moderate
El Espejo. Paseo de Recoletos 31. ☎ **91-308-23-47.** Reservations required. Menú del día 2,850ptas. ($19.95); main courses 1,200–2,800ptas. ($8.40–$19.60). AE, DC, MC, V. Sun–Fri 1–4pm and 9pm–1am; Sat 9pm–1am. Metro: Banco de España or Colón. Bus: 27. INTERNATIONAL.

Here you'll find good-tasting food and one of the most perfectly crafted art nouveau decors in Madrid. If the weather is good, grab an outdoor table, served by uniformed waiters who carry food across the busy street to a green area flanked by trees and strolling pedestrians. There's also a charming cafe/bar. The menu includes grouper ragôut with clams, steak tartare, guinea fowl with Armagnac, and lean duck meat with pineapple.

Inexpensive
La Trucha. Manuel Fernández González 3. ☎ **91-429-58-33.** Reservations recommended. Main courses 1,600–3,200ptas. ($11.20–$22.40). AE, MC, V. Mon–Sat 12:30–4pm and 7:30pm–midnight. Metro: Sevilla. SPANISH/SEAFOOD.

La Trucha offers Andalusian tavern ambience in a street-level bar and a small dining room. The arched ceiling and whitewashed walls are festively hung with braids of garlic, dried peppers, and onions; on the lower level is a second bustling area. The specialty is fish, and the à la carte menu includes *trucha* (trout), *verbenas de ahumados* (smoked delicacies), *fabada* (a stew made with beans, Galician ham, black sausage, and smoked bacon), and *comida casera rabo de toro* (home-style oxtail). No one should miss nibbling on the *tapas variadas* in the bar.

ON OR NEAR THE GRAN VÍA
Expensive
Arce. Augusto Figueroa 32. ☎ **91-522-59-13.** Reservations recommended. Main courses 2,500–5,750ptas. ($17.50–$40.25). AE, DC, MC, V. Mon–Fri 1:30–4pm and 9pm–midnight; Sat 9pm–midnight. Closed the week before Easter and Aug 15–31. Metro: Colón. BASQUE.

Arce has brought some of the best modern interpretations of Basque cuisine to Madrid, thanks to the enthusiasm of owner/chef Iñaki Camba and his wife, Theresa. In a comfortably decorated dining room, you can enjoy simple preparations that allow the natural flavors to dominate your taste buds. Examples include a salad of fresh scallops, an oven-baked casserole of fresh, lightly-seasoned boletus mushrooms, unusual preparations of hake, and seasonal variations of such game dishes as pheasant and woodcock.

Moderate
El Mentidero de la Villa. Santo Tomé 6. ☎ **91-308-12-85.** Reservations required. Main courses 1,950–2,400ptas. ($13.65–$16.80); menú del día 2,200ptas. ($15.40). AE, DC, MC, V. Mon–Fri 1:30–4pm and 9pm–midnight; Sat 9pm–midnight. Closed last 2 weeks of Aug. Metro: Alonso Martínez, Colón, or Gran Vía. Bus: 37. SPANISH/FRENCH.

This "Gossip Shop" is certainly a multicultural experience. The owner describes the cuisine as "modern Spanish with Japanese influence; the cooking technique is French." The result is usually a graceful achievement. The kitchen prepares such adventuresome dishes as squid ink spaghetti served with lobster sauce, mussels, and médaillons of crayfish; an avocado, crabmeat, watercress, and bacon salad; and rack of lamb stuffed with minced leg of lamb, enhanced with a pepper/white wine/potato sauce. Despite many new desserts, the most popular remains a sherry trifle.

NEAR THE PUERTA DEL SOL
Very Expensive
Lhardy. Carrera de San Jerónimo 8. ☎ **91-521-33-85.** Reservations recommended in the upstairs dining room. Main courses 6,000–8,000ptas. ($42–$56). AE, DC, MC, V. Mon–Sat 1–3:30pm and 9–11:30pm. Closed Aug. Metro: Puerta del Sol. SPANISH/INTERNATIONAL.

Lhardy has been a Madrileño legend since it opened in 1839 as a gathering place for the city's literati and political leaders. Its street level contains what might be the most elegant snack bar in Spain. In a dignified setting of marble and varnished hardwoods, cups of steaming consommé are dispensed from silver samovars into delicate porcelain cups. To taste the real culinary skill of the place, head up to Lhardy's second floor, where you'll find a formal restaurant decorated in the ornate style of Isabel Segunda. Specialties include fresh fish; tripe in a garlicky tomato-and-onion/wine sauce; and *cocido,* the chickpea stew of Madrid, made with sausage, pork, and vegetables. *Soufflé sorpresa* (baked Alaska) is the dessert specialty.

Expensive
Casa Paco. Plaza de la Puerta Cerrada 11. ☎ **91-366-31-66.** Reservations required. Main courses 1,100–3,800ptas. ($7.70–$26.60); set-price menu 3,600ptas. ($25.20). DC. Mon–Sat 1:30–4pm and 8:30pm–midnight. Closed Aug. Metro: Puerta del Sol, Opera, or La Latina. Bus: 3, 21, or 65. STEAK.

Madrileños defiantly name Casa Paco, beside Plaza Mayor in the old town, when someone has the nerve to put down Spanish steaks. Here you can get the thickest, juiciest steaks in Spain, priced according to weight. Señor Paco was the first in Madrid to sear steaks in boiling oil before serving them on plates so hot that the almost-raw meat continues to cook, preserving the natural juices. Although this two-story restaurant offers three dining rooms, reservations are imperative—otherwise, you face a long wait. Casa Paco isn't just a steak house. You can start with a fish soup, and other entrees include grilled sole, lamb, or Casa Paco cocido, the famous chickpea/ meat stew of Madrid.

Platerías Comedor. Plaza de Santa Ana 11. ☎ **91-429-70-48.** Reservations recommended. Main courses 4,000–5,000ptas. ($28–$35). AE, DC, MC, V. Mon–Fri 2:30–4pm and 9pm–midnight; Sat 9pm–midnight. Metro: Puerta del Sol. SPANISH.

One of the most charming dining rooms in Madrid, Platerías Comedor has richly brocaded walls and a graceful setting dating from 1862. Despite the busy socializing on the plaza outside, this serene oasis makes few concessions to modernity in its food, decor, or formally attired waiters. Specialties are beans with clams, stuffed partridge with cabbage and sausage, hake, magret of duckling with orange sauce or pomegranates, and duck liver with white grapes. You might finish with passionfruit sorbet.

Moderate
Café de Oriente. Plaza de Oriente 2. ☎ **91-541-39-74.** Reservations recommended (in formal restaurant only). In cafe, tapas 850ptas. ($5.95), coffee 650ptas. ($4.55); in restaurant, main courses 1,700–3,950ptas. ($11.90–$27.65). AE, DC, MC, V. Cafe daily 8:30am–12:30am (till 2:30am Fri–Sat); restaurant daily 1–4pm and 9pm–1:30am. Metro: Opera. FRENCH/ SPANISH.

Set on one of Madrid's most historic and regal-looking squares, the Oriente manages both bistro-style informality and grand dining. The more formal area is in a richly accessorized cellar, where intricate, stylish Basque cuisine is served at 10 tables suitable for Spanish royalty. High-powered corporate groups dine in the private dining rooms nestled off to the side. On the street level, you'll find a less intense, more workaday crowd of cafe patrons who appreciate the rich array of tapas, coffee, wine, and beer, as well as the set-price menu that's one of the true bargains in this gilt-edged neighborhood.

Inexpensive

Casa Alberto. Huertas 18. ☎ **91-429-93-56.** Reservations recommended. Main courses 650–2,250ptas. ($4.55–$15.75). AE, DC, MC, V. Tues–Sun 11:30am–12am. Metro: Antón Martín. CASTILIAN.

One of the oldest tascas in the neighborhood, Casa Alberto occupies the street level of the house where Miguel de Cervantes lived briefly in 1614. It contains an appealing mixture of bullfighting memorabilia, engravings, and reproductions of old master paintings. Tapas are continually replenished from platters on the bartop, but there's also a sit-down dining area in the back for more substantial meals. Specialties include fried squid, shellfish in vinaigrette sauce, *chorizo* (sausage) in cider sauce, and several versions of baked or roasted lamb. If you're not that hungry, it's also a great place to sit down and have a cold beer or glass of *vino tinto* and a wedge of tortilla española.

Hylogui. Ventura de la Vega 3. ☎ **91-429-73-57.** Reservations recommended. Main courses 1,000–2,200ptas. ($7–$15.40); set-price menu 1,400–1,700ptas. ($9.80–$11.90). AE, MC, V. Mon–Sat 1–4:30pm and 9pm–midnight; Sun 1–4:30pm. Metro: Sevilla. SPANISH.

Hylogui, a local legend since the 1930s, is a humongous dining room along Ventura de la Vega, broken up by many arches and nooks that allow for privacy. One globe-trotting American wrote enthusiastically that he took all his Madrid meals here, finding the soup pleasant and rich, the flan soothing, the regional wine dry, and the prices affordable. The food is old-fashioned Spanish home-style cooking.

NEAR RETIRO & SALAMANCA

Very Expensive

Alkalde. Jorge Juan 10. ☎ **91-576-33-59.** Reservations required. Main courses 5,000–5,600ptas. ($35–$39.20); set-price menu from 4,750ptas. ($33.25). AE, DC, MC, V. Daily 1–4:30pm and 8:30pm–midnight. Closed Sat–Sun July–Aug. Metro: Retiro or Serrano. Bus: 8, 21, 29, or 53. BASQUE/INTERNATIONAL.

Alkalde serves top-quality Spanish food in an old Basque tavern setting, with beamed ceilings and hams hanging from the rafters. Upstairs is a large *típico* tavern; downstairs is a maze of stone-sided cellars that are pleasantly cool in summer. Basque cuisine is the best in Spain, and Alkalde honors that tradition nobly. You might begin with the cream-of-crabmeat soup, followed by *gambas a la plancha* (grilled shrimp), chicken cutlets, or *cigalas* (crayfish). Other well-recommended dishes are *mero en salsa verde* (brill in a green sauce), trout Alkalde, stuffed peppers, and chicken steak.

Horcher. Alfonso XII 6. ☎ **91-532-35-96.** Reservations required. Jackets and ties required for men. Main courses 3,400–8,000ptas. ($23.80–$56). AE, DC, MC, V. Mon–Fri 1:30–4pm and 8:30pm–midnight; Sat 8:30pm–midnight. Metro: Retiro. GERMAN/INTERNATIONAL.

Horcher originated in Berlin in 1904. Prompted by a tip from a high-ranking German officer that Germany was losing the war, Herr Horcher moved his restaurant to Madrid in 1943. R. W. Apple, Jr., writing for *The New York Times,* found the "old fascist air" still lingering, with such dishes as *kartoffelpuffers* or potato pancakes remaining on the menu. The restaurant has continued its grand European traditions, including excellent service, ever since. You might try the skate, shrimp tartare, or the distinctive warm hake salad. The venison stew in green pepper with orange peel and the crayfish with parsley and cucumber are excellent; game dishes like wild boar or roast wild duck are offered in autumn.

Viridiana. Juan de Mena 14. ☎ **91-523-44-78.** Reservations recommended. Main courses 4,000–9,000ptas. ($28–$63). AE, MC, V. Mon–Sat 1:30–4pm and 9pm–midnight. Closed Aug and 1 week at Easter. Metro: Banco. INTERNATIONAL.

Praised as one of Madrid's top restaurants, Viridiana is known for the creative imagination of chef and part-owner Abraham García, a cinema historian and self-taught chef who named his restaurant after the 1961 Luís Bruñuel classic. Menu specialties are usually contemporary adaptations of traditional recipes and change frequently according to the availability of the ingredients. Examples are tuna tartare, a salad of exotic lettuces with smoked salmon, filet steak with truffles, guinea fowl stuffed with herbs and wild mushrooms, and roast lamb in puff pastry with fresh basil. A delectable dish is vineyard snails cooked in vine leaves, rosemary, tomato sauce, and pimentos.

Expensive

El Amparo. Callejón de Puígcerdá 8 (at the corner of Jorge Juan). ☎ **91-431-64-56.** Reservations required. Main courses 3,000–5,000ptas. ($21–$35); set-price menu 10,000ptas. ($70). AE, MC, V. Mon–Fri 1:30–3:30pm and 9:30–11:30pm; Sat 9:30–11:30pm. Closed the week before Easter and 1 week in Aug. Metro: Goya. Bus: 21 or 53. BASQUE.

Behind the cascading vines of its facade lies one of Madrid's most elegant gastronomic enclaves, a pioneer in inventive cuisine. It introduced (some 16 years ago) cod cheeks with smooth purées of red peppers. A sloping skylight floods the interior of this former carriage house with sun by day; at night, pinpoints of light from the high-tech hanging lanterns create intimate shadows. A battalion of polite uniformed waiters serves well-prepared nouvelle-cuisine versions of cold marinated salmon with tomato sorbet, delectable fish salads, bisque of shellfish with Armagnac, ravioli stuffed with seafood, and a platter of steamed fish of the day.

✪ **La Gamella.** Alfonso XII 4. ☎ **91-532-45-09.** Reservations required. Main courses 2,300–4,200ptas. ($16.10–$29.40). AE, DC, MC, V. Mon–Fri 1:30–4pm and 9pm–midnight; Sat 9pm–midnight. Closed 2 weeks around Easter and 2 weeks in Aug. Metro: Retiro. Bus: 19. CALIFORNIAN/CASTILIAN.

In 1988, La Gamella's Illinois-born owner, former choreographer Dick Stephens, moved his restaurant into this 19th-century building where Spanish philosopher Ortega y Gasset was born. The legendary Horcher is across the street, but the food here is somehow more creative, more spontaneous, and, in its own quirky way, more appealing than at its older neighbor. Mr. Stephens has even prepared his food for the king and queen of Spain. Low-key, glamorous, and soothing, the restaurant serves a roster of staples, plus some dishes that in North America might be referred to as *fusion*. Examples include "the only edible hamburger in Madrid" and steak tartare spiked with Jack Daniels, as well as more upscale food, such as sliced duck liver in truffle sauce, spicy Thai chicken, and a perennial favorite, quiche with Spanish sausage and red peppers. Also look for increasingly creative dishes, such as monkfish and scallops in a poblano chile sauce, served on a bed of corn pudding.

Moderate

Gran Café de Gijón. Paseo de Recoletos 21. ☎ **91-521-54-25.** Reservations required for restaurant. Main courses 3,000–5,000ptas. ($21–$35); set-price menu 1,500ptas. ($10.50). MC, V. Daily 8am–2am. Metro: Banco de España, Colón, or Recoletos. SPANISH.

Each European capital has a coffeehouse steeped in literary tradition. In Madrid it's the Gijón, which opened in 1888. Artists and writers still patronize this venerated cafe; many spend hours over one cup of coffee. Hemingway made the place famous for Americans. Gijón has open windows looking out onto the wide paseo, as well as a large terrace for sun worshipers and bird-watchers. Along one side is a stand-up bar and on the lower level is a restaurant. The cuisine is the "way it used to be" in Madrid.

CHAMBERÍ
Very Expensive

Jockey. Amador de los Ríos 6. ☎ **91-319-24-35.** Reservations required. Main courses 3,500–5,500ptas. ($24.50–$38.50). AE, DC, MC, V. Mon–Sat 1–4pm and 9–11:30pm. Closed Aug. Metro: Colón. INTERNATIONAL.

Since 1945 this has been Spain's premier restaurant, although competition is more severe today. At any rate, it's still a favorite of international celebrities, and some of the more faithful patrons look on it as their private club. Wood-paneled walls are decorated with a dozen prints of horses and jockeys—hence the name of the place. The chef prides himself on coming up with new and creative dishes. Try his fatted duck with ginger and citrus sauce, or slices of Jabugo ham. His cold melon soup with shrimp is soothing on a hot day, especially when followed by grill-roasted young pigeon cooked in its own juice or monkfish en papillotte with Mantua sauce. Stuffed small chicken "Jockey style" is a specialty.

Expensive

Las Cuatro Estaciones. General Ibémñez Ibero 5. ☎ **91-553-63-05.** Reservations required. Main courses 1,600–5,000ptas. ($11.20–$35); set-price dinner 4,500ptas. ($31.50). AE, DC, MC, V. Mon–Fri 1:30–4pm and 9pm–midnight; Sat 9–11:30pm. Closed Aug. Metro: Guzmán el Bueno. MEDITERRANEAN.

Praised by gastronomes and horticulturists, Las Cuatro Estaciones has become the main rival of the prestigious Jockey. Each person involved in food preparation spends a prolonged apprenticeship at one of the great restaurants of France. In addition to superb food, the restaurant prides itself on its masses of flowers, changed seasonally, which accentuate the modern and softly inviting decor. Specialties include a petite marmite of fish and shellfish, imaginative preparations of salmon, black rice with squid ink and squid, hake with a tomato and garlic butter sauce, and a three-fish platter with fine herbes.

Inexpensive

La Bola. Calle de la Bola 5. ☎ **91-547-69-30.** Reservations required. Main courses 1,400–3,000ptas. ($9.80–$21); set-price menu 2,125ptas. ($14.90). No credit cards. Mon–Sat 1–4pm; daily 9pm–midnight. Metro: Plaza de España or Opera. Bus: 1 or 2. MADRILEÑA.

Just north of the Teatro Real, this taberna is one of the few restaurants (if not the only one) left in Madrid with a blood-red facade; at one time, nearly all fashionable restaurants were so coated. La Bola hangs on to tradition like a tenacious bull. Time has passed, but not inside this restaurant: The soft, traditional atmosphere; the gentle and polite waiters; the Venetian crystal; the Carmen-red draperies; and the aging velvet preserve the 1870 ambience. Ava Gardner, with her entourage of bullfighters, used to patronize this spot, but that was long before La Bola became so well known to tourists. A host of refreshing appetizers include grilled shrimp, red-pepper salad, and lobster cocktail. Grilled sole, filet of veal, and roast veal are regularly featured. Basque-style hake and grilled salmon are also well recommended.

OFF PLAZA MAYOR
Moderate

✪ **Sobrino de Botín.** Calle de Cuchilleros 17. ☎ **91-366-42-17.** Reservations required. Main courses 950–3,000ptas. ($6.65–$21); set-price menu 3,860ptas. ($27). AE, DC, MC, V. Daily 1–4pm and 8pm–midnight. Metro: La Latina, Puerto del Sol, or Opera. SPANISH.

Ernest Hemingway made Sobrino de Botín famous. In the final pages of *The Sun Also Rises*, Jake invites Lady Brett there for the Segovian specialty of roast suckling pig, washed down with Rioja Alta. By merely entering its portals you step back to 1725, the year the restaurant was founded. You'll see an open kitchen with a charcoal hearth, hanging copper pots, an 18th-century tile oven for roasting the suckling pig, and a big pot of regional soup whose aroma wafts across the room. The other house specialty is roast Segovian lamb, and the filet steak is excellent and robust. You can wash down your meal with Valdepeñas or Aragón wine, or even sangría.

CHAMARTIN

Very Expensive

✪ **Zalacaín.** Alvarez de Baena 4. ☎ **91-561-48-40.** Reservations required. Main courses 9,500–11,000ptas. ($66.50–$77). AE, DC, MC, V. Mon–Fri 1:30–3:30pm; Mon–Sat 9–11:30pm. Closed week before Easter and in Aug. Metro: Rubén Darío. INTERNATIONAL.

Outstanding in both food and decor, Zalacaín opened in 1973 and introduced nouvelle cuisine to Spain. It is reached by an illuminated walk from Paseo de la Castellana and housed in the garden end of a modern apartment complex. The name of the restaurant comes from the intrepid hero of Basque author Pío Baroja's 1909 novel, *Zalacaín El Aventurero.* Zalacaín is small, exclusive, and expensive. It has the atmosphere of an elegant old mansion: The walls are covered with textiles, and some are decorated with Audubon-type paintings. Men should wear jackets and ties.

The menu features many Basque and French specialties, often with nouvelle cuisine touches. It might offer a superb sole in a green sauce or grilled pig's feet. Among the most recommendable main dishes are oysters with caviar and sherry jelly; crêpes stuffed with smoked fish; ravioli stuffed with mushrooms, foie gras, and truffles; and Spanish bouillabaisse. For dessert, we'd suggest one of the custards, perhaps raspberry or chocolate.

Expensive

✪ **El Olivo Restaurant.** General Gallegos 1. ☎ **91-359-15-35.** Reservations recommended. Main courses 2,950–3,700ptas. ($20.65–$25.90); set-price meals 3,850–5,700ptas. ($26.95–$39.90). AE, DC, MC, V. Tues–Sat 1–4pm and 9pm–midnight. Closed Aug 15–31 and 4 days around Easter. Metro: Plaza de Castilla. MEDITERRANEAN.

Locals praise the success of a non-Spaniard (in this case, French-born Jean Pierre Vandelle) in recognizing the international appeal of two of Spain's most valuable culinary resources: olive oil and sherry. Located in northern Madrid, his likable restaurant, designed in tones of green and amber, pays homage to the glories of the Spanish olive. From a trolley wheeled from table to table, diners select from among 40 varieties of olives to soak up with chunks of rough-textured bread that is, according to your taste, seasoned with a dash of salt.

Menu specialties include grilled filet of monkfish marinated in herbs and olive oil, and then served with black-olive sauce over a compote of fresh tomatoes, and four preparations of codfish arranged on a single platter and served with a pil-pil sauce. (Named after the sizzling noise it makes as it bubbles on a stove, *pil-pil* sauce is composed of codfish gelatin and herbs that are whipped into a mayonnaiselike consistency with olive oil.) For dessert, try one of several different chocolate pastries. A wide array of reasonably priced Bordeaux and Spanish wines are available.

SEEING THE SIGHTS

Madrid has changed drastically in recent years. It is no longer fair to say that in this lively European capital, only the Prado is worth a visit. As you'll discover, Madrid has something to amuse and delight everyone.

SIGHTSEEING SUGGESTIONS FOR FIRST-TIME VISITORS

If You Have 1 Day If you have just arrived in Spain after a long flight, don't tackle too much on your first day. Spend the morning seeing a few of the masterpieces at the **Prado,** one of the world's great art museums. It's best to arrive when it opens at 9am

Madrid Attractions

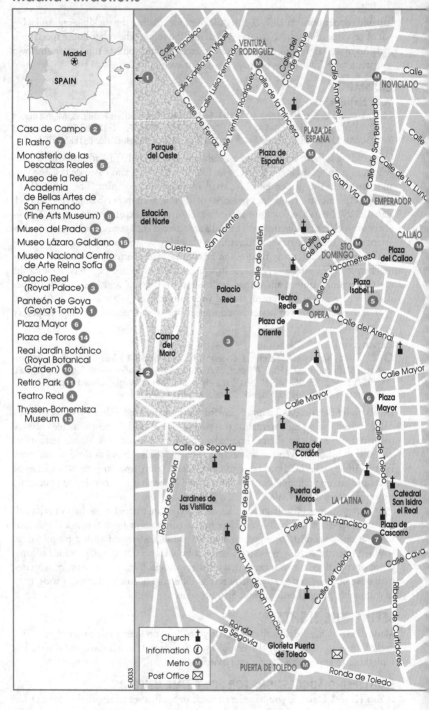

Casa de Campo ②
El Rastro ⑦
Monasterio de las Descalzas Reales ⑤
Museo de la Real Academia de Bellas Artes de San Fernando (Fine Arts Museum) ⑧
Museo del Prado ⑫
Museo Lázaro Galdiano ⑮
Museo Nacional Centro de Arte Reina Sofía ⑨
Palacio Real (Royal Palace) ③
Panteón de Goya (Goya's Tomb) ①
Plaza Mayor ⑥
Plaza de Toros ⑭
Real Jardín Botánico (Royal Botanical Garden) ⑩
Retiro Park ⑪
Teatro Real ④
Thyssen-Bornemisza Museum ⑬

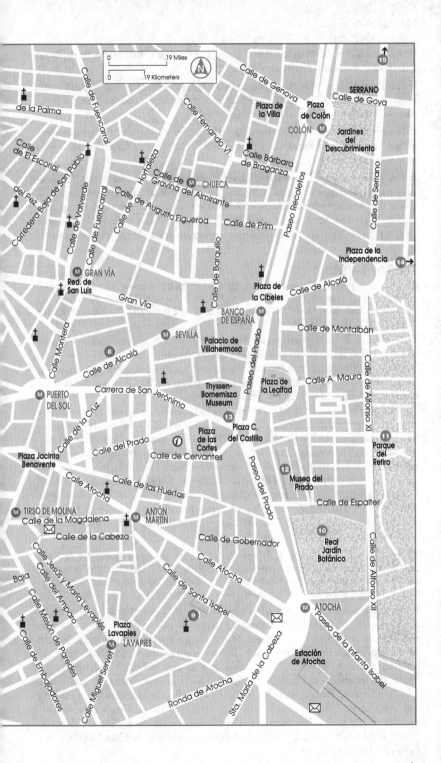

(remember, it's closed Monday). Have lunch and then visit the **Palacio Real (Royal Palace).** Have an early dinner near **Plaza Mayor.**

If You Have 2 Days   On day 2 take a trip to **Toledo,** where you can visit El Greco's House and Museum, the Santa Cruz Museum, the Church of Santo Tomé, and the Alcázar. Return to Madrid in the evening.

If You Have 3 Days   On your third day, take a 1-hour train ride to the **Monastery of San Lorenzo de El Escorial,** in the foothills of the Sierra de Guadarrama. Return to Madrid in the evening.

If You Have 4 Days   Day 4 would be very busy indeed if you visited the **Thyssen-Bornemisza Museum** in the morning, strolled around **Madrid's medieval area,** and visited the **Museo Nacional Centro de Arte Reina Sofía** in the late afternoon or early evening (it closes at 9pm most nights). Here you can see Picasso's *Guernica* plus other great art of the 20th century. Have dinner once again at one of the many restaurants off Plaza Mayor.

THE TOP MUSEUMS

✪ **Museo del Prado.** Paseo del Prado. ☎ **91-330-28-00.** Admission 500ptas. ($3.50), 250ptas. ($1.75) students, free children 11 and under and seniors. Tues–Sat 9am–7pm; Sun and holidays 9am–2pm. Closed Jan 1, Good Fri, May 1, and Dec 25. Metro: Banco de España or Atocha. Bus: 10, 14, 27, 34, 37, 45, or M6.

With more than 7,000 paintings, the Prado is one of the most important repositories of art in the world. It began as a royal collection, frequently enhanced by the Hapsburgs. In paintings of the Spanish school the Prado has no equal, so on your first visit, concentrate on the Spanish masters: Velázquez, Goya, and El Greco, as well as Zurbarán and Murillo. Most major works are on the first floor.

The Prado is a treasure trove of the work of El Greco (1524–1614), the Crete-born artist who spent much of his life in Toledo. You'll also find a splendid array of works by the incomparable Diego Velázquez (1599–1660); the museum's most famous painting is his *Las Meninas,* a triumph in the use of light. The Prado also contains an outstanding collection of the work of Hieronymus Bosch (1450?–1516), the Flemish genius; his best-known work, *The Garden of Earthly Delights,* is here. Francisco de Goya (1746–1828) ranks along with Velázquez and El Greco in the trio of great Spanish artists. Hanging here are his unflattering portraits of his patron, Charles IV, and his family, as well as the *Clothed Maja,* the *Naked Maja,* and pictures from his black period.

✪ **Thyssen-Bornemisza Museum.** Palacio de Villahermosa, Paseo del Prado 8. ☎ **91-369-01-51.** Admission 700ptas. ($4.90) adults, 450ptas. ($3.15) seniors and students, free children 11 and under. Tues–Sun 10am–7pm. Metro: Banco de España. Bus: 1, 2, 5, 9, 10, 14, 15, 20, 27, 34, 45, 51, 52, 53, 74, 146, or 150.

An almost unrivaled private collection was amassed over a period of about 60 years by the Thyssen-Bornemisza family, scions of a shipping/banking/mining fortune. Baron von Thyssen is married to a Spaniard, who desperately wanted to see the collection permanently reside in her native Spain. When it went on the market, Spain acquired it for $350 million. To house the collection, an 18th-century building adjacent to the Prado, the Villahermosa Palace, was retrofitted and the rooms arranged numerically (nos. 1–48, spread over three floors), so that by following the order European painting can be traced from the 13th through the 20th centuries. The nucleus of the collection consists of 700 world-class paintings. They include works by El Greco, Velázquez, Dürer, Rembrandt, Watteau, Canaletto, Caravaggio, Frans Hals, Hans Memling, and Goya, among many others.

Museo Nacional Centro de Arte Reina Sofía. Santa Isabel 52. ☎ **91-467-50-62.** Admission 500ptas. ($3.50) adults, 250ptas. ($1.75) students and children 11 and under. Mon and Wed–Sat 10am–9pm; Sun 10am–2:30pm. Metro: Atocha. Bus: 6, 14, 26, 27, 32, 45, 57, or C.

This is Madrid's greatest repository of 20th-century art. The museum is a high-ceilinged showplace named after the Greek-born wife of Spain's present king. One of Europe's largest museums, it was designated as "the ugliest building in Spain" by the Catalán architect Oriol Bohigas, although many are thrilled with the huge glass-enclosed elevators on the outside of the structure. Special emphasis is paid to the great 20th-century artists of Spain: Juan Gris, Dalí, and Miró. Picasso's masterpiece, *Guernica,* now rests here after a long and troubling nomadic history. (During the reign of Generalissimo Franco, it was housed in New York's Museum of Modern Art, per Picasso's request.) This antiwar piece immortalizes the German blanket bombing during the Spanish Civil War of the village of Guernica, cradle of the Basque nation.

✪ **Palacio Real (Royal Palace).** Plaza de Oriente, Calle de Bailén 2. ☎ **91-542-00-59.** Guided tour 950ptas. ($6.65) adults, 350ptas. ($2.45) seniors, students, and children 11 and under. Mon–Sat 9am–6pm; Sun 9am–3pm. Metro: Opera or Plaza de España.

This huge palace was begun in 1738 on the site of the Madrid Alcázar, which burned in 1734. Some of its 2,000 rooms are open to the public, but others are still used for state business. The guided tour includes the Reception Room, the State Apartments, the Armory, and the Royal Pharmacy. The rooms are literally stuffed with art treasures and antiques—salon after salon of monumental grandeur, with no apologies for the damask, mosaics, stucco, Tiepolo ceilings, gilt and bronze, chandeliers, and paintings. In the Armory you'll see a fine collection of weaponry.

MORE ATTRACTIONS

Museo de la Real Academia de Bellas Artes de San Fernando (Fine Arts Museum). Alcalá 13. ☎ **91-522-14-91.** Tues–Fri 300ptas. ($2.10) adults, 150ptas. ($1.05) students, free for children and seniors 60 and over; Sat–Sun free for everyone. Tues–Fri 9am–7pm; Sat–Mon 9am–2:30pm. Metro: Puerta del Sol or Sevilla. Bus: 15, 20, 51, 52, or M12.

An easy stroll from the Puerta del Sol, the Fine Arts Museum is located in the restored and remodeled 17th-century baroque palace of Juan de Goyeneche. The collection—more than 1,500 paintings and 570 sculptures, ranging from the 16th century to the present—was started in 1752 during the reign of Fernando VI (1746–59). It emphasizes works by Spanish, Flemish, and Italian artists. Masterpieces by El Greco, Rubens, Velázquez, Zurbarán, Ribera, Cano, Coello, Murillo, and Sorolla are here. The Goya collection in itself is worth the trip. Goya was a member of the academy since 1780, and the museum houses two of his self-portraits; a full-sized portrait of the actress, La Tirana, and the royal "favorite," Manuel Godoy; the carnival scene, *Burial of the Sardine;* and eight more oils.

Panteón de Goya (Goya's Tomb). Glorieta de San António de la Florida. ☎ **91-542-07-22.** Admission 300ptas. ($2.10) adults, 150ptas. ($1.05) seniors and children 17 and under. Tues–Fri 10am–2pm and 4–8pm; Sat–Sun 10am–2pm. Metro: Norte. Bus: 41, 46, 75, or C.

In a remote part of town beyond the North Station lies Goya's tomb, which contains one of his masterpieces: an elaborately beautiful fresco depicting the miracles of St. Anthony on the dome and cupola of the little hermitage of San António de la Florida. This has been called Goya's Sistine Chapel. Already deaf when he began the painting, Goya labored from dawn to dusk for 16 weeks, painting with sponges rather than brushes. In depicting common street life—stone masons, prostitutes, and beggars—Goya raised the ire of the nobility. However, when Carlos IV viewed it and approved, the formerly "outrageous" painting was deemed acceptable.

✪ **Museo Lázaro Galdiano.** Serrano 122. ☎ **91-561-60-84.** Admission 300ptas. ($2.10) adults, 150ptas. ($1.05) students, free for seniors and children 11 and under. Tues–Sun 10am–2pm. Closed holidays and Aug. Metro: Av. de América. Bus: 9, 16, 19, 51, or 89.

This well-preserved 19th-century mansion bulges with artworks of all kinds. You can take the elevator to the top floor and work your way down; there are 15th-century hand-woven vestments, swords and daggers, royal seals, 16th-century crystal from Limoges, Byzantine jewelry, Italian bronzes from ancient times to the Renaissance, and medieval armor. There are also works by the Old Masters El Greco, Velázquez, Zurbarán, Ribera, Murillo, and Valdés-Leal, as well as Tiepolo and Guardi. A section is devoted to works by the English artists Reynolds, Gainsborough, and Constable.

✪ **Monasterio de las Descalzas Reales.** Plaza de las Descalzas Reales. ☎ **91-542-00-59.** Admission 650ptas. ($4.55) adults, 350ptas. ($2.45) seniors and children 11 and under. Tues–Thurs and Sat 10:30am–12:30pm and 4–5pm; Fri 10:30am–12:30pm; Sun 11am–1:15pm. Bus: 1, 2, 5, 20, 46, 52, 53, 74, M1, M2, M3, or M5. From Plaza del Callao, off Gran Vía, walk down Postigo de San Martín to Plaza de las Descalzas Reales; the convent is on the left.

In the mid-16th century, aristocratic women came to this convent to take the veil. Each of them brought a dowry, making this one of the richest convents in the land, although by the mid-20th century the convent sheltered mostly poor women. The convent contained a priceless collection of art treasures, which the sisters were forbidden to auction off; in fact, they were literally starving. The state eventually intervened, and the pope granted special dispensation to open the convent as a museum.

In the Reliquary are the noblewomen's dowries, one of which is said to include bits of wood from the Cross; another, bones of St. Sebastian. The most valuable painting is Titian's *Caesar's Money.* The Flemish Hall shelters other fine works, including paintings by Hans de Beken and Breughel the Elder, and tapestries based on Rubens's cartoons.

PARKS & GARDENS

Casa de Campo, the former royal hunting grounds, consists of miles of parkland south of the Royal Palace across the Manzanares River. You can see the gate through which the kings rode out of the palace grounds—either on horseback or in carriages—on their way to the park. Casa de Campo has a variety of trees and a lake, usually filled with rowers. You can have drinks and light refreshments around the water or go swimming in a municipal pool. The park can be visited daily 8am to 9pm. Take the Metro to the Lago or Batán stop.

Retiro Park, originally a playground for the Spanish monarchs and their guests, extends over 350 acres. The huge palaces that once stood here were destroyed in the early 19th century and only the former dance hall, Casón del Buen Retiro (housing the modern works of the Prado; Picasso's *Guernica* used to hang here before being moved to the Reina Sofia), and the building containing the Army Museum remain. The park boasts numerous fountains and statues, plus a large lake. There are also two exposition centers, the Velásquez and Crystal Palaces (built to honor the Philippines in 1887), and a lakeside monument, erected in 1922 in honor of Alfonso XII. In summer the rose gardens are worth a visit, and you'll find several places where you can have inexpensive snacks and drinks. The park is open daily 24 hours, but it's safest, like most public parks, during the day (7am to 8:30pm). Take the Metro to the Retiro stop.

Across Calle de Alfonso XII, at the southwest corner of Retiro Park, is the **Real Jardín Botánico (Royal Botanical Garden),** Plaza de Murillo 2 (☎ **91-420-30-17**). Founded in the 18th century, the garden contains more than 100 species of trees and 3,000 types of plants. Also on the premises are an exhibition hall and a library specializing in botany. The park is open daily 10am to 9pm; admission is 200ptas.

($1.40) for adults and 100ptas. (70¢) for children. Take the Metro to the Atocha stop or take bus no. 10, 14, 19, 32, or 45.

ORGANIZED TOURS

One of Spain's largest tour operators is **Pullmantours,** Plaza de Oriente 8 (☎ **91-541-18-07**). Regardless of its destination or duration, virtually every tour departs from the Pullmantour terminal at that address. Half-day tours of Madrid include an artistic tour at 5,100ptas. ($35.70) per person, which provides entrance to a selection of the city's museums, and a panoramic half-day tour for 2,500ptas. ($17.50).

Southward treks to **Toledo** are the most popular full-day excursions. They cost 8,000ptas. ($56), including lunch. These tours depart daily at 9:30am from the above-mentioned departure point, last all day, and include ample opportunities for wandering at will through the city's narrow streets. You can take an abbreviated morning tour of Toledo, without stopping for lunch, for 5,300ptas. ($37.10). Between May and September, these half-day visits to Toledo are conducted in both the morning and afternoon; the rest of the year, they depart only in the afternoon.

Another popular tour stops briefly in Toledo and continues on to visit both the monastery at **El Escorial** and **Valle de los Caídos (the Valley of the Fallen)** before returning the same day to Madrid. With lunch included, this all-day excursion costs 11,300ptas. ($79.10).

A final touring option is a full-day Pullmantour excursion from Madrid that incorporate both **Segovia** and **Avila**—both focal points of Spanish culture and history—on the same day. Departing every day at 8:45am, and returning the same day at 6:30pm, they cost 6,800ptas. ($47.60); from 8,900ptas. ($62.30) for those who opt for lunch.

THE SHOPPING SCENE

Tirso de Molina, the 17th-century playwright, called Madrid "a shop stocked with every kind of merchandise." Its estimated 50,000 stores sell everything from high-fashion clothing to flamenco guitars to art and ceramics.

THE MAIN SHOPPING AREAS

THE CENTER   The sheer diversity of shops in Madrid's center is staggering. Their densest concentration lies immediately north of Puerta del Sol, radiating out from Calle del Carmen, Calle Montera, and Calle Preciados.

GRAN VÍA   Conceived, designed, and built in the 1910s and 1920s as a showcase for the city's best shops, hotels, and restaurants, the Gran Vía has since been eclipsed by other shopping districts, and yet its art nouveau/art deco glamour still survives. The bookshops here are among the best in the city, as are outlets for fashion, shoes, jewelry, and handcrafts from all regions of Spain.

PLAZA MAYOR   Under the arcades of the square itself are exhibitions of lithographs and oil paintings, and within 3 or 4 blocks in every direction you'll find tons of souvenir shops.

SALAMANCA DISTRICT   It's known throughout Spain as the quintessential upper-bourgeois neighborhood. Here you'll find exclusive furniture, fur, and jewelry shops, as well as several department stores. The main streets are Calle de Serrano and Calle de Veláquez. The district lies northeast of the center of Madrid, a few blocks north of Retiro Park. Its most central Metro stops are Serrano and Veláquez.

SOME NOTEWORTHY SHOPS

Antigua Casa Talavera. Isabel la Católica 2. ☎ **91-547-34-17.** Metro: Santo Domingo. Bus: 1, 2, 46, 70, 75, or 148.

Spain's Biggest Flea Market

Foremost among Madrid flea markets is **El Rastro,** Plaza Cascorro and Ribera de Curtidores (Metro: La Latina; bus: 3 or 17), which occupies a roughly triangular district of streets and plazas a few minutes' walk south of Plaza Mayor. This market will delight anyone who loves digging through a mishmash of fascinating junk interspersed with bric-a-brac and paintings. But thieves are rampant here (hustling more than just antiques), so secure your wallet carefully, be alert, and proceed with caution. Open Saturday and Sunday 9:30am to 1:30pm and, to a lesser extent, from 5 to 8pm.

Established in 1904 as the "first house of Spanish ceramics," this place offers a sampling of regional styles from every major area of Spain. Sangría pitchers, dinnerware, tea sets, plates, and vases are all handmade. Inside one of the showrooms is an interesting selection of tiles painted with scenes from bullfights, dances, and folklore. One series depicts famous paintings at the Prado.

Casa de Diego. Puerto del Sol 12. ☎ **91-522-66-43.** Metro: Puerto del Sol.

Here you'll find a wide inventory of fans, ranging from plain to fancy, from plastic to exotic hardwood, from cost-conscious to lavish.

El Arco de los Cuchilleros Artesanía de Hoy. Plaza Mayor 9 (basement level). ☎ **91-365-26-80.** Metro: Puerta del Sol or Opera.

This shop is devoted to unusual craft items from throughout Spain. The merchandise is one-of-a-kind, Spanish, and, in most cases, contemporary. Items include a changing array of pottery, leather, textiles, wood carvings, glassware, wickerwork, papier-mâché, and silver jewelry.

El Corte Inglés. Preciados 3. ☎ **91-379-80-00.** Metro: Puerta del Sol.

El Corte Inglés is the mother of all Spanish department stores, and this is the flagship store in Madrid. It sells Spanish handcrafts as well as glamorous fashion articles, such as Pierre Balmain designs, for about a third less than in most European capitals.

Lasarte. Gran Vía 44. ☎ **91-521-49-22.** Metro: Callao.

This is Madrid's, and Spain's, largest outlet for Lladró porcelain—the most characteristic and memorable fine porcelain made in Spain. You'll find at least 1,500 styles of figurines here, priced from 3,300ptas. ($23.10) for a small plate. Anything you buy here can be shipped.

Loewe. Gran Vía 8. ☎ **91-522-68-15.** Metro: Gran Vía.

Since 1846, Loewe has been Spain's most elegant leather store. Its designers have always kept abreast of changing tastes and styles, but the inventory still retains a timeless chic. The store sells luggage, handbags, and jackets for men and women (in leather or suede).

MADRID AFTER DARK

In summer Madrid sponsors a series of plays, concerts, and films, and the city takes on the air of a virtual free festival. Pick up a copy of *Guía del Ocio* (available at most newsstands) for listings of these events. This guide also has information about occasional discounts for commercial events, such as the concerts given in Madrid's parks. Also check the program of the **Fundación Juan March,** Calle Castello 77

(☎ 91-435-42-40; Metro: Núñez de Balboa), which frequently stages free classical and chamber music concerts.

Flamenco in Madrid is geared mainly to tourists with fat wallets, and nightclubs are expensive. But since Madrid is preeminently a city of song and dance, you can often be entertained at very little cost—in fact, for the price of a glass of wine or beer, if you sit at a bar with live entertainment.

Tickets to dramatic and musical events usually range from 700 to 3,000ptas. ($4.90 to $21), with discounts of up to 50% on certain days (usually Wednesday and early performances on Sunday). In the event your choice is sold out, you may be able to get tickets (with a reasonable markup) at **Localidades Galicia,** Plaza del Carmen 1 (☎ 91-531-27-32; Metro: Puerta del Sol). This agency, however, mainly markets tickets to bullfights and sports events. It's open Tuesday to Sunday, 9:30am to 1pm and 4:30 to 7:30pm.

THE PERFORMING ARTS

For those who speak Spanish, **Compañía Nacional de Nuevas Tendencias Escénicas** is an avant-garde troupe that performs new—and often controversial—works by undiscovered writers. **Compañía Nacional de Teatro Clásico,** as its name suggests, is devoted to the Spanish classics, including works by the ever-popular Lope de Vega or Tirso de Molina.

Ballet Nacional de España is devoted exclusively to Spanish dance; its performances are always well attended. The national ballet company is the **Ballet Lírico Nacional.** Also look for performances by choreographer Nacho Duato's **Compañía Nacional de Danza.**

World-renowned flamenco sensation António Canales and his troup, **Ballet Flamenco António Canales,** offer high-energy, spirited performances. Productions are centered on Canales's impassioned *Torero*—his interpretation of a bullfighter and the physical and emotional struggles within the man. For tickets and information, call ☎ 91- 531-27-32.

Classical Music

Madrid's opera company is the **Teatro de la Opera,** and its symphony orchestra is the outstanding **Orquesta Sinfónica de Madrid.**

Auditorio Nacional de Música. Príncipe de Vergara 146. ☎ **91-337-01-00.** Tickets 1,000–6,000ptas. ($7–$42). Metro: Cruz del Rayo.

This hall is the ultramodern home of both the **National Orchestra of Spain,** which emphasizes the music of Spanish composers, and the **National Chorus of Spain.** Just north of Madrid's Salamanca district, it ranks as a major addition to the competitive circles of classical music in Europe.

Teatro Real. Plaza Isabel II. ☎ **91-516-06-60.** Tickets 4,000–60,000ptas. ($28–$420). Metro: Opera.

Reopened in 1997 after a massive $157 million renovation, this theater is one of the world's finest stage and acoustic settings for opera. Its extensive state-of-the-art equipment affords elaborate stage designs and special effects. Luís Antonio García Navarro, the internationally heralded maestro from Valencia, is the musical and artistic director of the Royal Opera House, at least until 2002. He'll be working with leading Spanish lyric talents, including Plácido Domingo. Today, the building is the home of the Compañía del Teatro Real, a company specializing in opera, as well as a major venue for classical music and opera. On November 19, 1850, under the reign of Queen Isabel II, the Royal Opera house opened its doors with Donizetti's *La Favorita*.

FLAMENCO

Café de Chinitas. Torija 7. ☎ **91-559-51-35.** Dinner and show from 9,500ptas. ($66.50); show and 1 drink 4,300ptas. ($30.10). Metro: Santo Domingo. Bus: 1 or 2.

One of the best flamenco clubs in town, Café de Chinitas is one floor above street level in a 19th-century building midway between the Opera and the Gran Vía. It features an array of (usually) Gypsy-born flamenco artists from Madrid, Barcelona, and Andalusia, whose acts and performers change about once a month. You can arrange for dinner before the show. Open Monday to Saturday, with dinner served 9 to 11pm and the show lasting 10:30pm to 2am. Reservations are recommended.

Casa Patas. Calle Cañizares 10. ☎ **91-369-04-96.** Admission 2,500ptas. ($17.50). Metro: Tirso de Molina.

Following an upswing of interest in flamenco after a decline in the 1980s, this club is now one of the best places to see "true" flamenco as opposed to the more tourist-oriented version. It's also a bar/restaurant, with space reserved in the rear for flamenco. Shows are presented at midnight Thursday through Saturday and during Madrid's major fiesta month of May. The club itself is open daily from 9pm to 5am.

CABARET

Café de Foro. Calle San Andres 38. ☎ **91-445-37-52.** Free admission (but cover might be imposed for a specially booked act). Metro: Bilbao. Bus: 40, 147, 149, or N19.

Since the mid-1990s, this cabaret favorite in the Malasaña district has been one of the most fashionable places to hang out after dark. Patronizing the club are members of the literati along with a large student clientele. You never know exactly what the program for the evening will be, but live pop, rock, merengue, salsa, or flamenco generally starts at 11pm. Cabaret is often featured. It's open daily 7pm to 3am.

Scala Melía Castilla. Calle Capitán Haya 43 (entrance at Rosario Pino 7). ☎ **91-571-44-11.** Dinner and show, 10,200ptas. ($71.40); show and 1 drink, 5,300ptas. ($37.10). Metro: Cuzco.

Madrid's most famous dinner show is a major Las Vegas–style spectacle. The program is varied—you might see international or Spanish ballet, magic acts, ice skaters, whatever. Most definitely you'll be entertained by a live orchestra. It's open Tuesday through Saturday 8:30pm to 3am. Dinner is served beginning at 9pm; the show is presented at 10:30pm. Reservations are needed for the 90-minute show, which is changed annually.

JAZZ

Café Central. Plaza del Angel 12. ☎ **91-369-41-43.** Cover 1,100ptas. ($7.70). Metro: Antón Martín.

Off Plaza de Santa Ana, Café Central has a vaguely art deco interior, with an unusual series of stained-glass windows. The marble-topped tables are filled with people reading newspapers and talking during the day, but the ambience is far more animated during the nightly jazz sessions. It's open Sunday to Thursday 1:30pm to 2:30am and Friday and Saturday 1:30pm to 3:30am; live jazz is offered daily 10pm to midnight.

Clamores. Albuquerque 14. ☎ **91-445-79-38.** Cover Tues–Sat 600–1,200ptas. ($4.20–$8.40), depending on the act. Metro: Bilbao.

With dozens of small tables and a huge bar, dark and smoky Clamores is the largest and one of the most popular jazz clubs in Madrid. It has thrived by bringing in talented American and Spanish jazz bands. The place is open daily 6pm to 3am or so, but jazz is presented only Tuesday to Saturday. Tuesday through Thursday, sets are at 11pm and again at 1am; Saturday sets begin at 11:30pm, with an additional show at 1:30am. There are no live performances Sunday or Monday nights.

DANCE CLUBS

Bocaccio. Calle Marqués de la Ensenada 16. ☎ **91-308-49-81.** Cover 600–1,000ptas. ($4.20–$7). Metro: Colón.

A copycat of the hot clubs of London and New York, this bi-leveled spot caters to Madrid's beautiful and trendy. Low-key during the week, this club lets its hair down on the weekends. The lower level, *Infierno* (or Hell), is the more intense, awash in sex, drugs, alcohol, and the techno beats of British pop, with scarlet velour couches completing the atmosphere. The upstairs is trés chic—you can sip drinks on antique chairs and couches, while admiring the collection of art and tapestries that adorn the walls. Open Monday to Thursday from 7 to 11pm, Friday and Saturday 7pm to 6am, and Sunday 7pm to 3am.

Kapital. Atocha 125. ☎ **91-420-29-06.** Cover, with first drink included, 2,000ptas. ($14). Metro: Antón Martín.

Kapital is the most sprawling, labyrinthine, and multicultural dance club in Madrid. In what was formerly a theater, it covers seven levels, each with at least one bar and its own, sometimes radically different, ambience and musical theme. If you grow tired of the frenetic dancing on the lower levels, keep climbing: Things get calmer and more laid-back as you rise. In warm weather, the seventh floor opens onto an outdoor terrace. It's open Thursday to Sunday from 11:30pm to 5:30am.

Kathmandu. Señores de Luzón 3. ☎ **91-541-52-53.** Cover 1,000ptas. ($7), including first drink. Metro: Sol.

This is Madrid's club of the moment, where the cutting-edge music hits on reggae, jungle, hip-hop, and funk. At this alternative, Soho-esque disco, be prepared for a dizzy psychedelic experience. The crowd is decidedly androgynous at this Oriental-inspired, ultra-modern scoff at normalcy. The bar on the top floor is a curious retreat with Tibetan textiles draped from the ceiling. Nepalese art decorates part of the downstairs. At times the floor becomes so overcrowded you think the club will sink, but it carries on with wild abandon. Open Thursday from 10am to 5am, Friday and Saturday from 10am until 6am.

PUBS & BARS

Bar Cock. De la Reina 16. ☎ **91-532-28-26.** Metro: Gran Vía.

It attracts some of the most visible artists, actors, models, and filmmakers in Madrid, among them the award-winning Spanish director Pedro Almódovar. The name comes from the word *cocktail,* or so they say. The decoration is elaborately unique, in contrast to the hip clientele. It's open daily 7pm to 3am; closed December 24 to 31.

✪ **Chicote.** Gran Vía 12. ☎ **91-532-67-37.** Metro: Gran Vía.

Beloved by Hemingway, who had quite a few drinks here, this is Madrid's most famous cocktail bar. It's a classic, with the same 1930s interior design it had when the foreign press sat out the Civil War here. Even the seats are original. Long a favorite of artists and writers, the bar became a haven for prostitutes in the late Franco era. No more. It's back in the limelight again, a sophisticated and much-frequented rendezvous. It's open daily 4pm to 3am.

Palacio Gaviria. Calle del Arenal 9. ☎ **91-526-60-69.** Cover 1,500ptas. ($10.50), including the first drink. Metro: Puerta del Sol or Opera.

The 1847 construction of the Gaviria Palace was heralded as the architectural triumph of one of the era's most flamboyant aristocrats, the Marqués de Gaviria. Famous as one of the paramours of Isabel II, he outfitted his palace with the ornate jumble of neoclassical and baroque styles that later became known as Isabelino. In 1993, after extensive renovations, the building was opened to the public as a concert hall for the occasional presentation of classical music and as a late-night cocktail bar. Guests wander and dance through the ten richly decorated, high-ceilinged rooms in what is the most kitschy and rococo disco in Madrid. Open Monday to Friday 9am to 3pm, Saturday and Sunday 9pm to 5am.

GAY & LESBIAN CLUBS & CAFES

Black and White, Gravina, at the corner of Libertad (☎ **91-531-11-41;** Metro: Chueca), Madrid's major gay bar, is located in the center of the Chueca district. A guard opens the door to a large room painted, as you might expect, black and white. There's a dance club in the basement, but the street-level bar is the premier gathering spot, featuring drag shows Thursday to Sunday, male striptease, and videos. Old movies are shown against one wall. It's open Monday to Friday 8pm to 5am and Saturday and Sunday 8pm to 6am.

Plaza de Chueca (Metro: Chueca) has no fewer than four gay cafes lining the square's edges and something approaching a gay living room (with a healthy number of lesbians as well) is created every evening from 8pm to early the next morning.

Open daily 1:30pm to 4am, both **Café Figueroa,** Calle Augusto Figueroa 17 (☎ **91-521-16-73**), and **Café Aquarella,** Calle Gravina 10 (☎ **91-570-6907**), have elevated table-hopping to a fine art. A diverse clientele includes both gay men and lesbians. Lesbians frequent **Truco,** a *bar de copas* at Gravina 10 (☎ **91-532-89-21**). All three can be reached by taking the Metro to Chueca.

CAVE CRAWLING

To capture a glimpse of the unique Madrid joie de vivre, visit some *mesones* and *cuevas,* many found in the *barrios bajos*. From Plaza Mayor, walk down Arco de Cuchilleros until you find one of the Gypsy-like caves that fits your fancy.

The bartenders at the **Mesón del Champiñón,** Cava de San Miguel 17 (no phone; Metro: Puerta del Sol or Opera), keep a brimming bucket of sangría behind the long stand-up bar as a thirst quencher for the crowd. The name of the establishment means mushroom, and that's exactly what you'll see depicted along sections of the vaulted ceilings. A more appetizing way to experience a champiñón is to order a *ración* (serving) of grilled, stuffed, and salted mushrooms, served with toothpicks. Open daily 7pm to 1:30am. Our favorite cueva in the area, the **Mesón de la Guitarra,** Cava de San Miguel 13 (☎ **91-559-95-31;** Metro: Puerta del Sol or Opera), is loud and exciting any night of the week, and it's as warmly earthy as anything you'll find in Madrid. The decor combines terra-cotta floors, antique brick walls, hundreds of sangría pitchers clustered above the bar, murals of gluttons, old rifles, and faded bullfighting posters. Like most things in Madrid, the place doesn't get rolling until around 10:30pm. Open daily 7pm to 1:30am.

DAY TRIPS FROM MADRID
TOLEDO

If you have only 1 day for an excursion outside Madrid, go to Toledo, 42 miles to the southwest, a place made special by its blending of Arab, Jewish, Christian, and even Roman and Visigothic elements. Declared a national landmark, the city that inspired El Greco in the 16th century has remained relatively unchanged in parts of its central core. You can still stroll through streets barely wide enough for a man and his donkey.

GETTING THERE   RENFE trains run here frequently every day. Those departing Madrid's Atocha Rail Station for Toledo run daily 7:25am to 8:25pm; those leaving Toledo for Madrid run daily 7am to 9pm. Travel time is approximately 2 hours, and a one-way fare costs 630ptas. ($4.40). For train information in Madrid, call ☎ **91-328-90-20;** in Toledo, call ☎ **925-22-30-99.**

Bus transit between Madrid and Toledo is faster and more convenient than travel by train. Buses, operated by several companies, the largest of which include Continental and Galiano, depart from Madrid's South Bus Station (Estacíon Sur de Autobuses), Calle Méndez Alvaro (☎ **91-468-42-10** for tickets and information), daily 6:30am to 10pm. Buses depart at 30-minute intervals throughout the day, and a oneway ticket costs 580ptas. ($4.05).

Motorists exit Madrid via Cibeles (Paseo del Prado) and take N-401 south.

The **tourist information office** is at Puerta de Bisagra (☎ **925-22-08-43**), open Monday to Friday 9am to 6pm, Saturday 9am to 7pm, and Sunday 9am to 3pm.

EXPLORING TOLEDO　Ranked among the greatest of Gothic structures, the ✪ **cathedral,** Arcos de Palacio (☎ **925-22-22-41;** bus: 5 or 6), actually reflects a variety of styles because it took more than 2½ centuries (from 1226 to 1493) to construct. The portals have witnessed many historic events, including the proclamation of Joanna the Mad and her husband, Philip the Handsome, as heirs to the throne of Spain. Among its art treasures, the *transparente* stands out—a wall of marble and florid baroque alabaster sculpture overlooked for years because of the cathedral's poor lighting. The sculptor Narciso Tomé cut a hole in the ceiling, much to the consternation of Toledans, and now light touches the high-rising angels, a *Last Supper* in alabaster, and a Virgin in ascension. The 16th-century Capilla Mozárabe, containing works by Juan de Borgona, is another curiosity. The Treasure Room has a 500-pound, 15th-century gilded monstrance—allegedly made with gold brought back from the New World by Columbus—that's still carried through the streets of Toledo during the feast of Corpus Christi. Admission to the cathedral is free; admission to the Treasure Room is 500ptas. ($3.50). Open Monday to Saturday 10:30am to 1pm and 3:30 to 7pm, Sunday 10:30am to 1:30pm and 4 to 7pm.

Alcázar, Calle General Moscardó 4, near Plaza de Zocodover (☎ **925-22-30-38;** bus: 5 or 6), at the eastern edge of the old city, dominates the Toledo skyline. It became famous at the beginning of the Spanish Civil War when it underwent a 70-day siege that almost destroyed it. Today it has been rebuilt and turned into an army museum, housing such exhibits as a plastic model of what the fortress looked like after the Civil War, electronic equipment used during the siege, and photographs taken during the height of the battle. A walking tour gives a realistic simulation of the siege. Admission is 150ptas. ($1.05). Entrance is free on Wednesday and always free for children 9 and under. It's open Tuesday to Sunday 10am to 1:30pm and 4 to 5:30pm (6:30pm July to September).

Today a museum of art and sculpture, the ✪ **Museo de Santa Cruz,** Miguel de Cervantes 3 (☎ **925-22-10-36;** bus: 5 or 6), was originally a 16th-century Spanish Renaissance hospice, founded by Cardinal Mendoza—"the third king of Spain"—who helped Ferdinand and Isabella gain the throne. The facade is almost more spectacular than any of the exhibits inside. It's a stunning architectural achievement in the classical plateresque style, with elaborate ornamentation. The major artistic treasure inside is El Greco's *The Assumption of the Virgin,* his last known work. Paintings by Goya and Ribera are also on display. Admission is 250ptas. ($1.75) for adults and free for children. Open Tuesday to Saturday 10am to 6:30pm, Sunday 10am to 2pm, and Monday 10am to 2pm and 4 to 6:30pm. To get here, pass beneath the granite archway on the eastern edge of Plaza de Zocodover and walk about 1 block.

SAN LORENZO DE EL ESCORIAL

The second most important excursion from Madrid is the austere Royal Monastery of San Lorenzo de El Escorial, 30 miles to the west. Philip II ordered the construction of this rectangular granite-and-slate monster in 1563, 2 years after he moved his capital to Madrid. Once the haunt of aristocratic Spaniards, El Escorial is now a resort where hotels and restaurants flourish in summer, as hundreds flock here to escape the heat of the capital.

GETTING THERE More than two dozen trains depart daily from Madrid's Atocha, Nuevos Ministerios, and Chamartín train stations. During summer extra coaches are added. Trains take 1 hour and cost 780 pesetas ($5.45) round-trip. For schedules and information, call ☎ **91-328-90-20.**

The Office of Empresa Herranz, Calle Reina Victoria 3 in El Escorial (☎ **91-890-41-22**), runs some 40 buses per day back and forth between Madrid's Moncloa Station and El Escorial; on Sunday, service is curtailed to 10 buses. Trip time is 1 hour, and a round-trip fare is 740ptas. ($5.20).

Motorists can follow NVI (marked on some maps as A-6) from the northwest perimeter of Madrid toward Lugo, La Coruña, and El Escorial. After about half an hour, fork left onto C-505 toward San Lorenzo. Driving time from Madrid is about an hour.

The **tourist information office** is at Floridablanca 10 (☎ **91-890-59-03**), open Monday to Friday 10am to 2pm and 3 to 5pm and Saturday 10am to 2pm.

EXPLORING THE MONASTERY The huge granite fortress of the ✪ **Real Monasterio de San Lorenzo de El Escorial,** Calle San Lorenzo de El Escorial 1 (☎ **91-890-59-03**), houses a wealth of paintings and tapestries and serves as a burial place for Spanish kings. Foreboding both inside and out because of its sheer size and institutional look, El Escorial took 21 years to complete. Philip II, who collected many of the paintings exhibited here in the New Museums, didn't appreciate El Greco and favored Titian. But you'll still find El Greco's *The Martyrdom of St. Maurice,* rescued from storage, and his *St. Peter.* Other superb works are Titian's *Last Supper* and Velázquez's *The Tunic of Joseph.* The Royal Library houses a priceless collection of 60,000 volumes—one of the most significant in the world. The displays range from the handwriting of St. Teresa of Avila to medieval instructions on playing chess.

You can also visit the Philip II Apartments; they are strictly monastic, and Philip called them the "cell for my humble self" in this "palace for God." The Apartments of the Bourbon Kings are lavishly decorated, in contrast to Philip's preference for the ascetic.

A comprehensive ticket costs 850ptas. ($5.95) for adults and 350ptas. ($2.45) for children. The monastery is open Tuesday to Sunday; April to September 10am to 7pm, and October to March 10am to 6pm.

SEGOVIA

Less commercial than Toledo, Segovia, 54 miles northwest of Madrid, typifies the glory of Old Castile. Wherever you look, you'll see reminders of a golden era—whether it's the most spectacular Alcázar on the Iberian Peninsula or the well-preserved and still-functioning Roman aqueduct. Segovia lies on the slope of the Guadarrama Mountains, where the Eresma and Clamores rivers converge. This ancient city stands in the center of the most castle-rich part of Castile. Isabella was proclaimed queen of Castile here in 1474.

GETTING THERE Fifteen trains leave Madrid's Chamartín Rail Station every day and arrive 2 hours later at the station in Segovia, on Paseo Obispo Quesada (☎ **921-42-07-74**), a 20-minute walk southeast of the town center. A one-way rail fare from Madrid costs 765ptas. ($5.35). Bus no. 3 departs every quarter hour for Plaza Mayor.

Buses arrive and depart from the Estacionamiento Municipal de Autobuses, Paseo de Ezequile González 10 (☎ **921-42-77-25**), near the corner of Avenida Fernández

Ladreda and the steeply sloping Paseo Conde de Sepúlveda. There are 10 to 15 buses a day to and from Madrid (which depart from Paseo de la Florida 11; Metro: Norte). A one-way bus fare from Madrid to Segovia sells for 765ptas. ($5.35).

Motorists can take NVI (on some maps it's known as A-6) or the Autopista del Nordeste northwest from Madrid, toward León and Lugo. At the junction with Rte. 110 (signposted SEGOVIA), turn northeast.

The **tourist information office** is at Plaza Mayor 10 (☎ **921-46-03-34**), open daily 10am to 2pm and 5 to 8pm.

EXPLORING SEGOVIA   Your first glimpse of the castle ✪ **El Alcázar,** Plaza de la Reina Victoria Eugenia (☎ **921-46-07-59;** bus: 3), is from below, at the junction of the Clamores and Eresma rivers. It's on the west side of Segovia, and you might not spot it when you first enter the city. But that's part of the surprise. The castle dates back to the 12th century, and royal romance is inextricably associated with it. Isabella first met Ferdinand here, and today you can see a facsimile of her dank bedroom. Walk the battlements of this once-impregnable castle, from which its defenders poured boiling oil onto the enemy below. Brave the hazardous stairs of the tower, built by Isabella's father as a prison, for a panoramic view of Segovia. Admission is 375ptas. ($2.65) for adults, 175ptas. ($1.25) for children 8 to 14, and free for children under 8. The castle is open daily, April to September 10am to 7pm and October to March 10am to 6pm. Take either Calle Vallejo, Calle de Velarde, Calle de Daoiz, or Paseo de Ronda.

The ✪ **Roman aqueduct,** Plaza del Azoguejo, is an architectural marvel built by the Romans more than 2,000 years ago. Until 50 years ago, it was still used to carry water. Constructed of mortarless granite, it consists of 118 arches, and in one two-tiered section it soars 95 feet to its highest point. The Spanish call it simply *El Puente.* Stretching nearly 800 yards, it spans the old market square, Plaza del Azoguejo. When the Moors took Segovia in 1072, they destroyed 36 arches, which were rebuilt under Ferdinand and Isabella in 1484.

Constructed between 1515 and 1558, the ✪ **Cabildo Catedral de Segovia,** Plaza de la Catedral, Marqués del Arco (☎ **921-46-22-05**), is the last Gothic cathedral built in Spain. Fronting historic Plaza Mayor, it stands on the spot where Isabella I was proclaimed queen of Castile. Affectionately called La Dama de las Catedrales ("the Lady of Cathedrals"), it contains numerous treasures, such as the Blessed Sacrament Chapel (created by the flamboyant Churriguera), stained-glass windows, elaborately carved choir stalls, and 16th- and 17th-century paintings, including a reredos (the ornamental screen behind the altar) portraying the deposition of Christ from the cross by Juan de Juni. Admission to the cathedral is free; admission to the cloisters, museum, and chapel room is 250ptas. ($1.75) for adults and 50ptas. (35¢) for children. Open daily spring and summer 9am to 7pm and off-season 9am to 6pm.

2 Barcelona & Environs

Hardworking Barcelona enjoys the most diversified and prosperous economy of any region in Spain. Culturally, it is as rich as any. Its roster of natives and longtime residents—the *modernista* architect Antoni Gaudí, artists Pablo Picasso, Salvador Dalí, and Joan Miró, as well as the opera star Montserrat Caballé—have been instrumental in defining Catalán culture.

As one local newspaper critic put it, "If there were an award for the city that has done the most in the last few years to rebuild, reclaim, and expand, while maintaining its elegance and charm, Barcelona would win hands down." The years that led up to and immediately following the 1992 Olympics made a huge difference to the city. Residual benefits from the games have included a roster of impressive new hotels, top-notch sporting facilities, the refurbishing of an airport capable of funneling 18 million annual visitors into Catalonia, and new ring roads that have alleviated some crucial traffic problems. And Barcelona, despite its dearly protected Catalán cultural and linguistic identity, continues in its proud role as Spain's literary and publishing headquarters.

With a reputation as the savviest business center in Spain, Barcelona boasts buildings by I. M. Pei, Arata Isozaki, Richard Meier, Norman Foster, Victorio Gregotti, and native son Ricardo Bofill. Miles of grimy industrial waterfronts have been returned to clean and sandy beaches. In fact, the entire city, which had once seemed to turn its back to the Mediterranean, has now been reoriented toward the sea. Flower stalls, bird cages, and decorative pavements line the gorgeous and rejuvenated pedestrian boulevard Les Rambles, and a state-of-the-art transportation network carries visitors past monuments that look better than when they were first erected. Unlike its landlocked competitors, Seville and Madrid, Barcelona can—and does—welcome the newest phenomena in tourism, the cruise-ship industry.

Despite the city's burgeoning population (and the regrettable growth in both drug addiction and street crime), people are flocking to the newly revived Barcelona. Nearly 40% of tourists to Spain go to Catalonia, and many are repeat visitors.

Only in Barcelona

Walking Through the Barri Gòtic Following in the footsteps of Miró (who was born in this barrio), Dalí, and Picasso, you can wander for hours in the Gothic Quarter. You'll get lost, of course, but that's part of the fun. There's much more here than a great cathedral. Gurgling fountains, vintage stores, charcuteries, wall-to-wall cobblestones, and literary cafes like Els Quatre Gats make it all worthwhile.

Watching (or Dancing) the Sardana Catalonia's national dance is performed at noon at Plaça de San Jaume, a block east of the cathedral (in front of the Palau de la Generalitat). Nothing is more folkloric than the sardana, which, to Cataláns, has great cultural pride and meaning. Against the backdrop of a *cobla* (brass band), men and women join a circle, placing their bags in the center, and begin the light-footed ritual. The dance may have originated on one of the Greek islands and was brought here by sailors. It might even have come from Sardinia—hence its name—but Cataláns have made it uniquely their own.

Strolling Along Les Rambles Victor Hugo called it "the most beautiful street in the world." Les Rambles cuts through the heart of Barcelona'a oldest district beginning at Plaça de Catalunya and running toward the sea. This tree-lined boulevard, the most famous street in Spain, is really composed of five Rambles (*Ramblas* in Spanish). Street performers, shop owners, tourists, drag queens, drug dealers, and prostitutes share this street lined with hotels, cafes, porno houses, newsstands, and endless flower stalls.

Making a Toast of Cava in a *Xampanyería* Enjoy a glass of bubbly—Barcelona style. The wines are excellent, and Cataláns swear that their *cavas* taste better than French champagne. After the Franco years, *xampanyerías* literally burst into bloom all over Barcelona, many staying open until the early hours of the morning. You can select *brut* or *brut nature* (brut is slightly sweeter). Try any of these popular brands: Mestres, Parxet, Torello, Recaredo, Gramona, or Mont-Marçal.

Exploring the Museu Picasso—One of Barcelona's most popular attractions, this museum housed in three Gothic mansions spans the artist's multifaceted career, including his Blue Period, cubism, and more. Of special interest is the Barcelona section from the years 1895 to 1897, when Picasso lived in the Catalán capital before journeying to Paris. You can even see Picasso the copyist (he re-created Velázquez's famous portrait of Philip IV) and see the depictions of his family, especially his aunt, *Retrato de la Tipa Pepa* (Portrait of Aunt Pepa). Two rooms are devoted to the fabled *Les Meninas,* a series Picasso produced in Cannes in 1957 as a tribute to Velázquez's most famous painting (now in Madrid's Prado).

Going Gaga over Gaudí   No architect in Europe was as fantastical as Antoni Gaudí y Cornet. The city of Barcelona is studded with modernist architectural gems created by this extraordinary artist—in fact, UNESCO lists all his creations as World Trust Properties. In 1997, his masterpiece apartment building on Paseo de Gracia, La Pedrera (Casa Milá), was lovingly restored. No two buildings of this eccentric genius are alike; he conceived the buildings as "visions." A recluse and celibate bachelor, he died in penury, run over by a tram in 1926. Nothing is more stunning than his Templo Expiatorio de la Sagrada Familia, Barcelona's best-known landmark, a church on which Gaudí labored for the last 43 years of his life. It was never completed, although work is being performed on it and the debate over its propriety (Gaudí left no detailed plans) rages. If it's ever finished, La Sagrada Familia will be Europe's largest church.

ORIENTATION
GETTING THERE   By Plane   Even post-Olympics, most transatlantic passengers are obliged to change aircraft in Madrid before continuing on to Barcelona. The only exception is **TWA** (☎ **800/892-4141**), which maintains nonstop transatlantic service to Barcelona from New York. Within Spain, **Iberia** (☎ **800/772-4642**) is the most likely carrier, offering a string of peak-hour shuttle flights at 15-minute intervals between Madrid and Barcelona. Service from Madrid to Barcelona at less congested times of the day averages around one flight every 30 to 40 minutes. **Air Europa** (☎ **93-298-33-28**) and **Spanair** (☎ **93-298-33-62**) also run shuttles between Madrid and Barcelona. These flights are generally cheaper than Iberia; frequency of shuttle flights depends on demand, with more occurring in the early morning and late afternoon.

The **Aeropuerto de Barcelona,** 08820 Prat de Llobregat (☎ **93-298-38-38**), lies 7½ miles southwest of the city. A train runs at 30-minute intervals between the airport and Barcelona's Estació Central de Barcelona-Sants daily 6:14am to 10:44pm (10:14pm is the last city departure, 6:14am the first airport departure). The 21-minute trip costs 305ptas. ($2.15) Monday to Friday or 350ptas. ($2.45) Saturday and Sunday. If your hotel lies near Plaça de Catalunya, you might opt for an Aerobús that runs daily every 15 minutes from 5:30am to 10pm. The fare is 475ptas. ($3.35). A taxi from the airport into central Barcelona costs about 3,000ptas. ($21).

By Train   A train called *Barcelona Talgo* provides rail service between Paris and Barcelona in 11½ hours. For many other connections from the mainland of Europe, it's necessary to change trains at Port Bou. Most trains issue seat and sleeper reservations.

Trains departing from the **Estació de Franca,** Avenida Marqués de l'Argentera, cover long distances in Spain as well as international routes. There are express night trains from Paris, Zurich, Milan, and Geneva. All the international routes served by the state-owned RENFE rail company use the Estació de Franca, including some of its most luxurious express trains, such as the *Pau Casals* and *Talgo Catalán.* From this station you can book tickets to the major cities: Madrid (five *talgos,* 7 hours; three *rápidos,* 10 hours), Seville (two per day, 10½ hours), and Valencia (11 per day, 4 hours). For general **RENFE information,** call ☎ **93-490-02-02.**

By Bus Bus travel to Barcelona is cheaper than the train, faster than all but the *talgos,* and very popular among Spaniards who travel frequently between the two main cities. **Enatcar,** Estació del Nord (☎ **93-245-25-28**), operates five buses per day from Madrid (trip time: 8 hours) and 10 buses per day from Valencia (trip time: 4½ hours). A one-way ticket to Madrid costs 2,140ptas. ($15); a one-way ticket to Valencia is 2,900ptas. ($20.30).

By Car From France (the usual road approach to Barcelona), the major access route is at the eastern end of the Pyrenees. You have a choice of the express highway (E-15) or the more scenic coastal road. From France, it's possible to approach Barcelona via Toulouse. Cross the border into Spain at Puigcerdá (frontier stations are there), near the principality of Andorra. From here, take N-152 to Barcelona. From Madrid, take N-2 to Zaragoza, then A-2 to El Vendrell, followed by A-7 to Barcelona.

VISITOR INFORMATION A conveniently located tourist office is the **Oficina de Informacio de Turisme de Barcelona,** Plaça de Catalunya, 17-S (☎ **93-304-31-35;** Metro: Plaça de Catalunya). It's open daily from 9am to 9pm.

CITY LAYOUT **Plaça de Catalunya** (*Plaza de Cataluña* in Spanish) is the city's heart; the world-famous Rambles (Ramblas) and the grand boulevard Passeig de Gracia its arteries. Les Rambles begins at Plaça Portal de la Pau, with its 164-foot-high monument to Columbus and a panoramic view of the port, and stretches north to Plaça de Catalunya, with its fountains and trees.

At the end of Les Rambles is the **Barri Xinés** (Barrio Chino, the "Chinese Quarter"), which in the past was a notorious haven of prostitution and drugs. It is being cleaned up, but is still not a terribly safe district; it's best viewed during the day. Off Les Rambles is **Plaça Reial** (*Plaza Real* in Spanish), Barcelona's most harmoniously proportioned square.

The major wide boulevards are **Avinguda Diagonal, Passeig de Colom,** and the elegant shopping street **Passeig de Gràcia (Paseo de Gracia).** A short walk from Les Rambles takes you to **Passeig del Moll de la Fusta,** a waterfront promenade developed for the Olympic renewal with some of the finest (but not the cheapest) restaurants in Barcelona. To the east is the old port of the city, **La Barceloneta,** from the 18th century.

Barri Gótic (Barrio Gótico, the Gothic Quarter) lies to the east of Les Rambles. This is the site of the city's oldest buildings, including the cathedral and many gorgeous palaces with central courtyards. North of Plaça de Catalunya, the **Eixample** unfolds. An area of wide boulevards, in contrast to the Gothic Quarter, it contains two major roads leading out of Barcelona, Avinguda Diagonal and Gran Vía de les Corts Catalánes. Another major area, **Gràcia,** lies north of the Eixample. **Montjuïc,** one of the mountains of Barcelona, begins at Plaça d'Espanya, a traffic rotary. This was the setting for the 1992 Summer Olympic Games and is today the site of Vila Olimpica. The other mountain, **Tibidabo,** in the northwest, offers fine views of the city and the Mediterranean and has an amusement park.

Traveler's Tip

To save money on sightseeing tours during summer, take a ride on **Bus Turistic,** which passes by a dozen of the most popular sights. You can get on and off the bus as you please and ride the Tibidabo funicular and the Montjuïc cable car and funicular for the price of a single ticket. Tickets, which can be purchased on the bus or at the transportation booth at Plaça de Catalunya, cost 1,700ptas. ($11.90) for 1 day or 2,300ptas. ($16.10) for 2 days.

Barcelona Metro

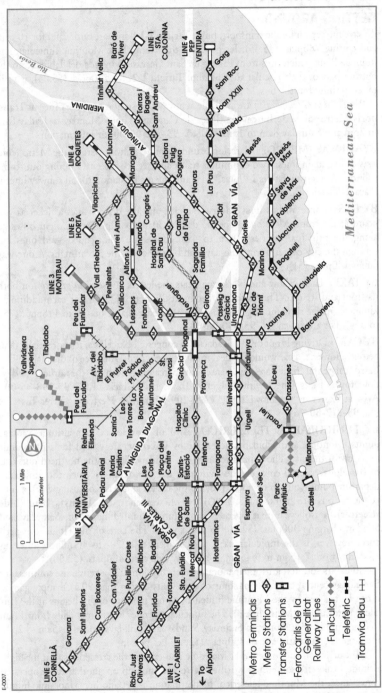

E-0007

957

GETTING AROUND

To save money on public transport, buy a **Tarjeta T-1** transport card, valid for 10 trips and costing 780ptas. ($5.45). It's good for the Metro, bus, Montjuïc funicular, and Tramvía Blau, which runs from Passeig de Sant Gervasi/Avinguda del Tibidabo to the bottom part of the funicular to Tibidabo. **Tarjeta T-2,** for 720ptas. ($5.05), is valid on everything but the bus.

Passes (*abonos temporales*) are available at any Metro station or at the office of **Transports Metropolita de Barcelona,** Plaça de Catalunya, open Monday to Friday 8am to 7pm and Saturday 8am to 1pm. Call ☎ **93-412-00-00** for information.

BY SUBWAY (METRO) Barcelona's underground railway system, the Metro, consists of five main lines. Two commuter trains also service the city, fanning out to the suburbs. A one-way fare is 140ptas. ($1), and the major station for all subway lines is Plaça de Catalunya.

BY BUS Some 50 bus lines traverse the city, and the driver issues a ticket as you board at the front. Most buses operate daily 6:30am to 10pm; some night buses go along the principal arteries 10pm to 4am. Buses are color-coded—red ones cut through the city center during the day, and blue ones do the job at night. A one-way fare is 140ptas. ($1).

BY TAXI Each yellow-and-black taxi bears the letters SP (*servicio público*) on both its front and its rear. The basic rate begins at 295ptas. ($2.05). For each additional kilometer in the slow-moving traffic, you're assessed a charge of 110 to 118ptas. (75¢ to 85¢). For a taxi, call ☎ **93-330-08-04.**

BY CAR Driving is not only a headache in congested Barcelona, it's potentially dangerous. However, a car would be ideal to tour the environs. All three of the major U.S.-based car-rental firms are represented in Barcelona, both at the airport and at downtown offices. Check with **Budget,** at Travesera de Gràcia 71 (☎ **93-298-35-00**); **Avis,** at Carrer de Casanova 209 (☎ **93-209-95-33**); or **Hertz,** at Carrer Tuset 10 (☎ **93-217-80-76**).

BY FUNICULAR & TELEFÉRICO Two of Barcelona's high-altitude vantage points, Montjuïc and Tibidabo, accessible by funicular, are visited for a panoramic overview of the city. The departure point for Tibidabo lies on the northern outskirts of Barcelona's central core, on the **Avinguda del Tibidabo.** To reach the funicular's departure point, you can take a taxi (by far the easiest and least confusing way), a conventional bus (it's marked TIBIDABO), or, on weekends, the **Tramvía Blau (blue streetcar),** a trolleycar that operates only during limited hours on Saturday and Sunday, charging 300ptas. ($2.10) to hop aboard. The core of the Tibidabo experience, however, is the funicular itself, which operates at 20- to 30-minute intervals every day from 7:15am to 9:45pm. A one-way ride costs 400ptas. ($2.80).

Tibidabo's counterpart is the panoramic eyrie of Montjuïc, a gentle rise southeast of Barcelona's central core. Site of some of the events during the 1992 Olympic games, it can be reached by the Montjuïc funicular, whose point of origin begins at the Parallel Metro station (Metro line 3). The funicular operates in summer daily from 11am to 8pm, and in winter only on Saturday, Sunday, and holidays from 10:45am to 2pm. It charges a round-trip fare of 350ptas. ($2.45) per person.

You can get off the funicular at Montjuïc and explore the attractions, but for high-altitude freaks, it's sometimes worthwhile to continue up on another cable-operated conveyance, the Montjuïc teleférico. Its destination is yet another panoramic hilltop and the Castell de Montjuïc. Operating daily in summer from 11am to 10pm, and in winter daily from 10:45am to 8pm, it charges a one-way fare of 400ptas. ($2.80), and a round-trip fare of 600ptas. ($4.20).

For another spectacular aerial view of Barcelona—not for those afraid of heights—book a ride aboard the **Transbordador Aeri del Puerto.** This aerial cable car lifts passengers hundreds of feet above the port between Barceloneta and Montjuïc hill. The ride's a bit scary, so be warned. The cable car runs between July and September daily from 11am to 9pm; off-season hours are Sunday and Tuesday from noon to 5:45pm and Saturday from noon to 6:15pm. Departures are every 15 minutes; a one-way passage ranges from 800 to 1,200ptas. ($5.60 to $8.40). For more information, call ☎ 93-412-00-00.

Fast Facts: Barcelona

American Express   The American Express office is at Passeig de Gràcia 101 (☎ 93-217-00-70; Metro: Diagonal), near the corner of Carrer del Rosselló. It's open Monday to Friday 10am to 6pm and Saturday 9:30am to noon.

Consulates   The Consulate of the **United States,** at Reina Elisenda 23 (☎ 93-280-22-27; train: Reina Elisenda), is open Monday to Friday 9am to 12:30pm and 3 to 5pm. The **Canadian Consulate,** Travessera de les Corts 265 (☎ 93-215-07-04), is open Monday to Friday 10am to noon. The Consulate of the **United Kingdom,** Av. Diagonal 477 (☎ 93-419-90-44; Metro: Hospital Clínic), is open Monday to Friday 9am to 1:30pm and 4 to 5pm. The Consulate of **Australia** is at Gran Vía Carlos III 98, 9th floor (☎ 93-330-94-96; Metro: María Cristina), open Monday to Friday 10am to noon.

Currency   See "Fast Facts: Madrid."

Currency Exchange   Most banks exchange currency Monday to Friday 8:30am to 2pm and Saturday 8:30am to 1pm. A major *oficina de cambio* (exchange office) operates at the Estació Central de Barcelona-Sants, the principal rail station; it's open Monday to Saturday 8:30am to 10pm and Sunday 8:30am to 2pm and 4:30 to 10pm. There are three major banks at Plaça de Catalunya, including La Caixa, with currency exchange windows frequented by tourists.

Dentists   Call **Clinica Dental Beonadex,** Paseo Bona Nova 69, third floor (☎ 93-418-44-33), for an appointment. It is open Monday from 3 to 9pm and Tuesday through Friday from 8am to 3pm.

Drugstores   The most central one is **Farmacia Manuel Nadal i Casas,** Rambla de Canaletes 121 (☎ 93-317-49-42; Metro: Plaça de Catalunya), open daily 9am to 1:30pm and 4:30 to 10pm. After hours, pharmacies take turns staying open at night. All pharmacies that are not open post the names and addresses of after-hours pharmacies in the area.

Emergencies   In an emergency, phone **080** to report a **fire, 092** to call the **police,** and **061** to request an **ambulance.**

Hospitals   Barcelona has many hospitals and clinics, including **Hospital Clínic,** Casanova 143 (☎ 93-454-60-00) and **Hospital de la Santa Creu i Sant Pau,** at the intersection of Carrer Cartagena and Carrer Sant Antoni Maria Claret (☎ 93-291-90-00; Metro: Hospital de Sant Pau).

Internet Access   **El Café de Internet,** Avenida de las Corts Catalanas 656 (☎ 34-93-412-1915; e-mail: JordiCarcellaChoia@sevicom.es), is open daily 9am to midnight.

Lost Property   To recover lost property, go to **Objects Perduts,** Carrer Ciutat 9 (☎ 93-317-38-79; Metro: Jaume I), Monday to Friday 9am to 12pm. If you've lost property on public transport, contact the office in the Metro station at Plaça de Catalunya (☎ **93-318-70-74**).

Luggage Storage/Lockers The train station, **Estació Central de Barcelona-Sants** (☎ **93-491-44-31**), has lockers for 400 to 600ptas. ($2.80 to $4.20) per day. You can find locker space daily 7am to 10pm.

Post Office The main post office is at Plaça d'Antoni López (☎ **93-219-71-97;** Metro: Jaume I). It's open Monday to Friday 8am to 10pm and Saturday 8am to 8pm.

Safety Be particularly careful with cameras, purses, and wallets, all favorite targets of thieves and pickpockets in Barcelona—particularly on the world-famous Rambles. The southern part of Les Rambles, near the waterfront, is the most dangerous section, especially at night. Use common sense and be cautious.

Telephone The **country code** for Spain is **34.** The **city code** for Barcelona is **3;** use this code when calling from outside Spain. If you're within Spain, use **93.**

To make an **international call,** dial ☎ **07,** wait for the tone, and dial the country code, the area code, and the number. Note that an international call from a public phone requires stacks and stacks of 100 peseta coins. As an alternative, buy a **phone card** from a tobacco shop (*estanco*), the post office, or other authorized dealer.

For more information on making calls from Spain, see "Telephone" under "Fast Facts: Madrid."

WHERE TO STAY
CIUTAT VELLA (OLD CITY)
Very Expensive

✪ **Le Meridien Barcelona.** Rambles 111, 08002 Barcelona. ☎ **800/543-4300** in the U.S., or 93-318-62-00. Fax 93-301-77-76. 214 units. A/C MINIBAR TV TEL. 26,000–42,000ptas. ($182–$294) double; from 53,000ptas. ($371) suite. AE, DC, MC, V. Parking 2,000ptas. ($14). Metro: Liceu or Plaça de Catalunya.

This nine-story tower is the finest hotel in the old town, thanks in large part to a major refurbishment of the bedrooms in 1997. It's superior in both amenities and comfort to its closest old town rival, the Colón. The guest rooms are spacious and comfortable, with such amenities as extra-large beds, heated bathroom floors, 18 TV channels, three in-room VCRs, hair dryers, and two phones; all rooms have double-glazed windows. The hotel contains a comfortable bar and an excellent restaurant, Le Patio.

Expensive

Hotel Colón. Av. de la Catedral 7, 08002 Barcelona. ☎ **800/845-0636** in the U.S., or 93-301-14-04. Fax 93-317-29-15. E-mail: colon@nexus.es. 147 units. A/C MINIBAR TV TEL. 23,000–36,500ptas. ($161–$255.50) double; from 41,500ptas. ($290.50) suite. AE, DC, MC, V. Bus: 16, 17, 19, or 45.

Blessed with one of the most dramatic locations in Barcelona, opposite the cathedral's main entrance, this postwar hotel boasts a neoclassical facade with carved pilasters and ornamental wrought-iron balustrades. Inside you'll find conservative and slightly old-fashioned public rooms, a helpful staff, and guest rooms filled with comfortable furniture and (despite recent renovations) an appealingly dowdy kind of charm. Although lacking views, the rooms in back are quieter. The sixth-floor rooms with balconies overlooking the square are the most desirable; some lower rooms are dark. The hotel maintains two well-recommended restaurants, the Grill (continental specialties) and the Carabela (Catalán specialties).

Moderate

✪ **Duques de Bergara.** Bergara 11. ☎ **93-301-51-51.** Fax 93-317-34-42. 150 units. A/C MINIBAR TV TEL. 20,900ptas. ($146.30) double; 39,500ptas. ($276.50) triple. AE, DC, MC, V. Parking in nearby public garage 3,000ptas. ($21) per night. Metro: Catalunya.

Barcelona's newest upscale hotel occupies the former turn-of-the-century private townhouse of the Duke of Bergara. In 1998, the original five-story structure more than doubled in size with the addition of a new seven-story tower. Bedrooms here are outfitted with the same conservatively traditional comforts that characterize units in the older wing. Public areas contain most of the paneling, stained glass, and decorative accessories originally installed by the architect, Emilio Salas I Cortes, a professor of the modernist school's greatest luminary, Gaudí. Within the hotel's reception area, look for the stained glass panels that contain the heraldic coat of arms of the building's original occupant and namesake, the Duke of Bergara.

On the premises are a restaurant (El Duc), a bar, a cafe one floor above the lobby, and an outdoor swimming pool.

Hotel Regencia Colón. Carrer Sagristans 13–17, 08002 Barcelona. ☎ **93-318-98-58.** Fax 93-317-28-22. 55 units. A/C MINIBAR TV TEL. 16,700ptas. ($116.90) double; 20,800ptas. ($145.60) triple. Rates include breakfast. AE, DC, MC, V. Metro: Jaume 1 or Urquinaona.

This stately stone 6-story building stands behind the more prestigious and expensive Hotel Colón—both are in the shadow of the cathedral. The formal lobby seems a bit dour, but the well-maintained rooms are comfortable and often roomy, albeit worn. The rooms are insulated against sound, and 40 of them have full tub bathrooms, the remainder with shower. The hotel is a good value for Barcelona.

Montecarlo. Ramble dels Estudis 124, 08002 Barcelona. ☎ **93-412-04-04.** Fax 93-318-73-23. E-mail: montecarlobcn@abaforum.es. 75 units. A/C MINIBAR TV TEL. 16,000ptas. ($112) double; 19,000ptas. ($133) triple. AE, DC, MC, V. Parking 2,000ptas. ($14). Metro: Plaça de Catalunya.

This hotel, beside the wide and sloping promenade of Les Rambles, was built around 200 years ago as an opulent private home. In the 1930s, it was transformed into the comfortably unpretentious hotel you'll find today. Each of the rooms is efficiently decorated; most were renovated around 1989. Double-glazed windows help keep out some of the noise. The public areas include some of the building's original accessories, with carved doors, a baronial fireplace, and crystal chandeliers.

Inexpensive

Hostal Levante. Baïxada de Sant Miguel 2, 08002 Barcelona. ☎ **93-317-95-65.** Fax 93-317-05-26. E-mail: hostallevante@mx3.redestb.es. 38 units (7 with bathroom). 4,000ptas. ($28) double without bathroom; 5,000ptas. ($35) double with bathroom. No credit cards. Metro: Liceu or Jaume 1.

The small and very simple rooms here are scattered over two floors of a 200-year-old building connected by a cramped and creaking elevator. The drawback is that you're likely to be confronted with lots of screaming children, relatives of the family who owns the place, during your stay. Benefits include a position in the heart of the historic Barri Gótic, near the Plaça de Sant Jaume, and clean, simple bedrooms. No meals are served, and the place is strictly laissez-faire, but a worthy choice for its location and rock-bottom prices.

Hostal Neutral. Rambla de Catalunya 42, 08007 Barcelona. ☎ **93-487-63-90.** Fax 93-487-40-28. 35 units (28 with full bathroom, 7 with shower only [no toilet]). TEL. 4,550ptas. ($31.85) double with shower only (no toilet); 5,510ptas. ($38.55) double with bathroom. MC, V. Metro: Aragón.

Barcelona

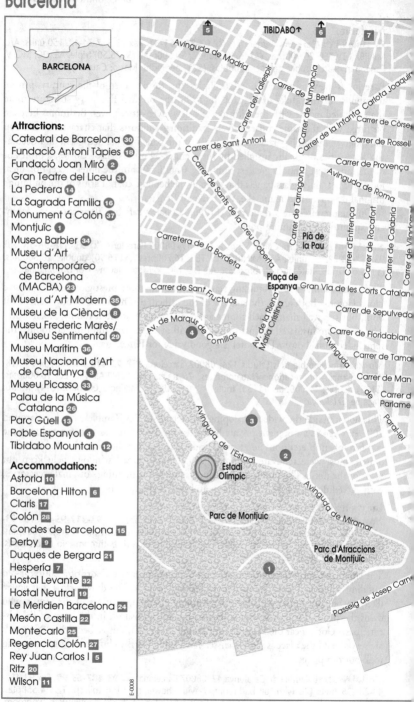

BARCELONA

E-0008

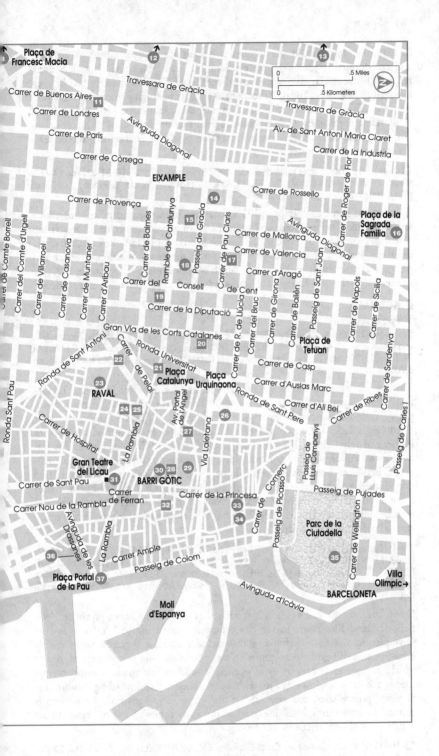

Plaça de
Francesc Macia

Carrer de Buenos Aires 11

Carrer de Londres

Carrer de Paris

Carrer de Còrsega

Travessara de Gràcia

Avinguda Diagonal

EIXAMPLE

Carrer de Provença

Carrer de Comte Borrell

Carrer del Comte d'Urgell

Carrer de Villarroel

Carrer de Casanova

Carrer de Muntaner

Carrer d'Aribau

Carrer de Balmes

Ramble de Catalunya

Carrer del

Consell

Carrer de la Diputació

Gran Via de les Corts Catalanes

Ronda de Sant Antoni

Carrer

de Pelai

Ronda Universitat

Passeig de Gracia

Carrer de Pau Claris

Carrer de Mallorca

Carrer de Valencia

Carrer d'Aragó

de Cent

Travessara de Gràcia

Av. de Sant Antoni Maria Claret

Carrer de la Industria

Carrer de Rossello

Avinguda Diagonal

Carrer de Roger de Flor

Plaça de la
Sagrada
Familia 16

Carrer de Napols

Carrer de Sicilia

Carrer de R. de Llúcia

Carrer del Bruc

Carrer de Girona

Carrer de Bailén

Passeig de Sant Joan

Plaça de
Tetuan

Carrer de Casp

Ronda Sant Pau

Ronda de Sant Antoni

22

Plaça
Catalunya 21

Plaça
Urquinaona

Carrer d'Ausias Marc

Carrer d'Ali Bei

Ronda de Sant Pere

RAVAL 23

Carrer de Hospital

Carrer de Sant Pau

Gran Teatre
del Licau 31

La Rambla

24 25

Av. Portal
de l'Angel

27

26

Via Laietana

30 28

BARRI GOTIC 29

Carrer
de Ferran

32

Carrer de la Princesa

33

34

Carrer de Comerç

Passeig de Picasso

Passeig de
Lluis Companys

Carrer de Sardenya

Passeig de Carles I

Passeig de Pujades

Parc de la
Ciutadella

35

Carrer de Wellington

Villa
Olimpic→

BARCELONETA

Carrer Nou de la Rambla

Avinguda de les
Drassanes

36

Plaça Portal
de la Pau 37

La Rambla

Carrer Ample

Passeig de Colom

Avinguda d'Icàvia

Moll
d'Espanya

0   .5 Miles

0   .5 Kilometers

In 1917, the original innkeeper acquired two floors of a six-floor, circa 1890 building and transformed it into a simple pension. The name he chose, Hostal Neutral, reflected his neutrality during the armed conflict of World War I that had by then engulfed all of Europe. Today, it functions as an older but highly recommendable pension; the affordable rooms are "neutral" in their decor, but clean, high-ceilinged, and comfortable nonetheless. Colorful antique floor tiles brighten some of them. Breakfast, the only meal available, is served in a salon with a coffered ceiling, and there's a TV lounge on the premises.

✪ **Mesón Castilla.** Carrer Valldoncella 5, 08002 Barcelona. ☎ **93-318-21-82.** Fax 93-412-40-20. 56 units. A/C MINIBAR TV TEL. 11,700ptas. ($81.90) double. V. Parking 2,000ptas. ($14). Metro: Plaça de la Universitat.

This two-star hotel, established in 1952, occupies a former apartment building with a severely simple Castilian facade and an interior with occasional touches of art nouveau detailing. Owned and operated by the Spanish hotel chain HUSA, the Castilla is clean, charming, and well maintained. Its nearest rival is the Regencia Colón, to which it is comparable in atmosphere. The rooms, which benefited from a renovation in 1997, are comfortable—the beds have ornate headboards—and some open onto large terraces.

DIAGONAL
Very Expensive

Barcelona Hilton. Av. Diagonal 589–591, 08014 Barcelona. ☎ **800/445-8667** in the U.S. and Canada, or 93-495-77-77. Fax 93-495-77-00. www.hilton.com. 290 units. A/C MINIBAR TV TEL. 32,000ptas. ($224) double; from 40,000ptas. ($280) suite. AE, DC, MC, V. Parking 3,200ptas. ($22.40). Metro: María Cristina.

This five-star property is opposite the gates to the fairgrounds of Barcelona (beyond that, to the Olympic Stadium). It's a huge 11-floor corner structure, with a contemporary, cosmopolitan facade. Even so, it lacks the glamour of the Palace and Claris. The lobby is sleek with lots of marble, and the public lounges are furnished with black leather and velvet chairs. Most rooms are rather large and finely equipped. The furnishings are Hilton-standardized, but with amenities such as private safes. The Restaurant Cristal Garden serves well-prepared international and Spanish menus in a relaxed but polished setting. Less expensive meals are served at the informal Le Bistro. There's a small and somewhat cramped exercise room on the hotel's sixth floor, but serious exercise buffs will head for a health club a half mile away, with which the Hilton maintains a cooperative relationship.

Claris. Carrer de Pau Claris 150, 08009 Barcelona. ☎ **800/888-4747** in the U.S., or 93-487-62-62. Fax 93-487-87-36. www.derbyhotels.es. E-mail: info@derbyhotels.es. 158 units. A/C MINIBAR TV TEL. 40,900ptas. ($286.30) double; 50,000ptas. ($350) suite. Ask about possible holiday and weekend discounts. AE, DC, MC, V. Parking 2,000ptas. ($14). Metro: Passeig de Gràcia.

One of the most unusual hotels in Barcelona, the postmodern Claris is one of only two five-star grand luxe hotels in the city center. It opened in 1992, in time for the Olympics, in a seven-story building that includes a pool and garden on its roof, a mini-museum of Egyptian antiquities on its second floor, and two restaurants, one of which, Beluga, specializes in—you guessed it—caviar. The spacious bedrooms are among the most opulent in town, with wood marquetry and paneling, custom furnishings, private safes, and some of the city's most sumptuous beds. Each room is painted an iconoclastic blue-violet and incorporates copies of ancient Egyptian art with state-of-the-art electronic accessories.

✪ **Hotel Ritz.** Gran Vía de les Corts Catalanes 668, 08010 Barcelona. ☎ **93-318-52-00.** Fax 93-318-01-48. 161 units. A/C MINIBAR TV TEL. 35,000–43,000ptas. ($245–$301) double;

80,000ptas. ($560) suite. AE, DC, MC, V. Parking 3,500ptas. ($24.50). Metro: Passeig de Gràcia.

Acknowledged as the finest, most prestigious, and most architecturally distinguished hotel in Barcelona, the Ritz was built in art deco style in 1919. Richly remodeled in 1996 and 1997, it has welcomed more millionaires, celebrities, and aristocrats than any other hotel in northeastern Spain. One of the finest features is its cream-and-gilt neoclassical lobby, with marble floors and potted palms. The guest rooms are as formal and richly furnished, sometimes with Regency furniture; bathrooms are accented with mosaics and tubs inspired by ancient Rome. The elegant Restaurant Diana serves French and Catalán cuisine amid soaring ceilings and crystal chandeliers.

Rey Juan Carlos I/Conrad International Barcelona. Av. Diagonal 661, 08028 Barcelona. ☎ **800/445-8355** in the U.S., or 93-448-08-08. Fax 93-448-06-07. www.lhw.com. 412 units. A/C MINIBAR TV TEL. Mon–Thurs 38,000ptas. ($266) double, 60,000ptas. ($420) suite; Fri–Sun 23,000ptas. ($161) double, 52,500ptas. ($367.50) suite. AE, DC, MC, V. Free parking for guests. Metro: Zona Universitaria.

Named for the Spanish king who attended its opening and who has visited it several times since, this is the only five-star choice that competes effectively against the Ritz and Claris. Opened in 1992, in time for the Olympics, it rises 17 stories above the northern end of the Diagonal. The design includes a soaring inner atrium, at one end of which a bank of glass-sided elevators glide silently up and down. Bedrooms contain many electronic extras, conservatively comfortable furnishings, and in many cases, views out over Barcelona to the sea. The hotel's most elegant restaurant is Chez Vous, a glamorous and panoramic locale with impeccable service and French/Catalán specialties. Amenities include a swimming pool, health club, and business center.

Expensive

Hotel Condes de Barcelona. Passeig de Gràcia 73–75, 08008 Barcelona. ☎ **93-488-22-00.** Fax 93-488-06-14. www.condesdebarcelona.com. E-mail: cbhotel@condesdebarcelona.com. 183 units. A/C MINIBAR TV TEL. 20,500ptas. ($143.50) double; 32,000–50,000ptas. ($224–$350) suite. AE, DC, MC, V. Parking 2,000ptas. ($14). Metro: Passeig de Gràcia.

No longer looking as fresh as it did for the 1992 Olympics, this hotel has fallen some but still has quite a bit of charm, and its public areas contain more references to medieval Barcelona than any other hotel in town. Business has been so good that it opened a 74-room extension, which regrettably lacks the élan of the original. It boasts a unique neomedieval facade, influenced by Gaudí's modernist movement. Hints of high-tech furnishings were added, but much of the original opulence remains. The curved lobby-level bar and its adjacent restaurant add a touch of art deco. All the comfortable guest rooms contain marble bathrooms and soundproof windows, although some are beginning to show wear and tear. The hotel has a Jacuzzi on the fifth floor.

Moderate

Hotel Derby/Hotel Gran Derby. Loreto 21–25, and Loreto 28, 08029 Barcelona. ☎ **93-322-32-15.** Fax 93-410-08-62. www.derbyhotels.es. E-mail: info@derbyhotels.es. 151 units. A/C MINIBAR TV TEL. 14,500–18,500ptas. ($101.50–$129.50) double; 16,500–20,400ptas. ($115.50–$142.80) suite. AE, DC, MC, V. Parking 1,800ptas. ($12.60). Metro: Hospital Clínic.

These twin hotels occupy two separate buildings in a tranquil neighborhood about 2 blocks south of the busy intersection of Avinguda Diagonal and Avinguda Sarría. The Derby offers conventional rooms, and the Gran Derby (across the street) contains suites, many of which have small balconies overlooking a flowered courtyard. (All drinking, dining, and entertainment facilities are in the Derby.) A team of English-inspired designers have imported a British aesthetic, and the pleasing results include well-oiled hardwood panels, soft lighting, and comfortably upholstered armchairs. Guest rooms and suites are comfortable and quiet. Less British in feel, they're outfitted with simple furniture in a variety of decorative styles. A coffee shop and bistro in the Hotel Derby serves sandwiches and light platters throughout the day.

Hotel Hespería. Los Vergós 20, 08017 Barcelona. ☎ **93-204-55-51.** Fax 93-204-43-92. www.hoteles-hesperia.es. 134 units. A/C MINIBAR TV TEL. Mon–Thurs 15,400ptas. ($107.80) double; Fri–Sun 9,500ptas. ($66.50) double. AE, DC, MC, V. Parking 1,650ptas. ($11.55). Metro: Tres Torres.

This six-story hotel, on the northern edge of the city, a 12-minute taxi ride from the center, is surrounded by the verdant gardens of one of Barcelona's most pleasant residential neighborhoods. Built in the late 1980s, it was renovated before the 1992 Olympics. You'll pass a Japanese rock garden to reach the stone-floored reception area, with its adjacent bar. Sunlight floods the monochromatic interiors of the rooms, which—although no great style-setters—emphasize comfort and convenience. The uniformed staff offers fine service. A restaurant on the premises serves a regional cuisine.

Inexpensive

Hotel Astoria. París 203, 08036 Barcelona. ☎ **93-209-83-11.** Fax 93-202-30-08. www.derbyhotels.es. E-mail: info@derbyhotels.es. 114 units. A/C MINIBAR TV TEL. 9,500–16,800ptas. ($66.50–$117.60) double. AE, DC, MC, V. Metro: Diagonal.

One of our favorites, the 1954 Astoria has an art deco facade that makes it appear older than it is. The high ceilings, geometric designs, and brass-studded detailings in the public rooms could be Moorish or Andalusian. Last renovated in the mid-1980s, each of the comfortable guest rooms is soundproofed. The more old-fashioned rooms have exposed cedar and elegant modern accessories. There's a bar on the premises, but the only meal served is breakfast.

Hotel Wilson. Av. Diagonal 568, 08021 Barcelona. ☎ **93-209-25-11.** Fax 93-200-83-70. www.husa.es. E-mail: depcomcen@husa.es. 57 units. A/C MINIBAR TV TEL. 14,000ptas. ($98) double; from 22,000ptas. ($154) suite. AE, DC, MC, V. Metro: Diagonal.

Set within a neighborhood rich with architectural, especially modernist, curiosities, this hotel was originally conceived as a dormitory for employees—particularly pilots—of Iberia Airlines. In 1974, it was transformed into the appealing three-star hotel you'll see today. Managed by the nationwide HUSA chain, its seven floors focus on a small, not particularly impressive lobby, and a large, sunny coffee shop and bar one floor above street level. Guest rooms are simple, clean, and well maintained, and laundry services can be arranged.

VILA OLÍMPICA

Very Expensive

Hotel Arts. Carrer de la Marina 19–21, 08005 Barcelona. ☎ **800/241-3333** in the U.S., or 93-221-10-00. Fax 93-221-10-70. www.ritzcarlton.com. 453 units. A/C MINIBAR TV TEL. Mon–Thurs 40,000ptas. ($280) double, from 45,000ptas. ($315) suite; Fri–Sun 27,500ptas. ($192.50) double, from 37,500ptas. ($262.50) suite. AE, DC, MC, V. Parking 3,200ptas. ($22.40). Metro: Ciutadella–Vila Olímpica.

This hotel, managed by the luxury-conscious Ritz-Carlton chain, occupies 33 floors of one of Spain's tallest buildings, a 44-floor postmodern tower about 1½ miles southwest of Barcelona's historic core, adjacent to the sea and the Olympic Village. Its decor is contemporary and elegant, including a lobby sheathed in slabs of soft gray and yellow marble and guest rooms outfitted in pastel yellow or blue. Views from the rooms sweep out over the skyline and the Mediterranean. Bedrooms are spacious and well equipped, with generous desk space, private safes, and large, comfortable beds. Clad in pink marble, the deluxe bathrooms have both tubs and stall showers, along with hair dryers, dual basins, and separate phones. The food and drink facilities are the best of any hotel in Barcelona, including a summer-only bar set beside the pool. Other facilities include a fitness center.

WHERE TO DINE
CIUTAT VELLA (OLD CITY)
Expensive

Agut d'Avignon. Carrer Trinitat 3. ☎ **93-302-60-34.** Reservations required. Main courses 1,900–5,000ptas. ($13.30–$35). AE, MC, V. Daily 1–4:30pm and 9pm–12:30am. Metro: Jaume I or Liceu. CATALÁN.

One of our favorite restaurants in Barcelona is near Plaça Reial, in a tiny alleyway (the cross street is Calle d'Avinyó 8). The restaurant explosion here has toppled Agut d'Avignon from its once preeminent position, but partly because of its nostalgic charm it's still going strong. A small 19th-century vestibule leads to the multilevel dining area, with two balconies and a main hall that's evocative of a hunting lodge. Specialties range from the strictly traditional to the culinary avant-garde and are likely to include local shrimp with aïoli (garlicky mayonnaise), acorn-squash soup served in its shell, fisher's soup with garlic toast, duck with figs, and haddock stuffed with shellfish, the latter a Catalonian specialty.

Casa Leopoldo. Carrer Sant Rafael 24. ☎ **93-441-30-14.** Reservations required. Main courses 1,250–5,500ptas. ($8.75–$38.50); set-price menu 4,750ptas. ($33.25). AE, DC, MC, V. Tues–Sun 1–4pm and Tues–Sat 9–11pm. Closed 1 week in Aug and at Easter. Metro: Liceu. SEAFOOD.

An excursion through the streets of the Barri Xinés only adds to the adventure of finding this warm and surprisingly sophisticated restaurant. It has thrived here since 1929, within a building erected in 1780, by offering its loyal clientele some of the freshest seafood in town. There's a popular stand-up tapas bar in front, then two dining rooms, one slightly more formal than the other. Specialties include oxtail stew; fried sea bass with chives, lemon, olive oil, and garlic; shellfish soup; and deep-fried eels. An enduring specialty is an enormous platter of fish and shellfish for two.

✪ Los Caracoles. Escudellers 14. ☎ **93-302-31-85.** Reservations required. Main courses 1,500–8,000ptas. ($10.50–$56). AE, DC, MC, V. Daily 1pm–midnight. Metro: Drassanes. CATALÁN/SPANISH.

Set in a labyrinth of narrow cobblestoned streets, Los Caracoles is the port's most colorful restaurant—and it has been since 1835. It has won acclaim for its spit-roasted chicken, roast suckling pig, roast suckling lamb, and its namesake, snails. In summer tables are placed outside. The excellent food features all sorts of Spanish and Catalán specialties, especially a mixed grill of seafood. Although a number-one tourist stop, it delivers the same aromatic and robust food it always did.

Moderate

Brasserie Flo. Jonqueras 10. ☎ **93-319-31-02.** Reservations recommended. Main courses 1,900–3,750ptas. ($13.30–$26.25); set-price menu 2,090ptas. ($14.65). AE, DC, MC, V. Mon–Thurs 1–4pm and 8:30pm–midnight; Fri–Sun 1–4pm and 8:30pm–1am. Metro: Urquinaona. FRENCH/INTERNATIONAL.

The art deco dining room here is spacious, palm-filled, comfortable, and air-conditioned. Installed in a handsomely restored warehouse, it's as close as Barcelona gets to offering an Alsatian brasserie. The menu items borrow equally from the bistro traditions of both France and Catalonia. French-derived items include fresh foie gras and large platters of *choucroute* (sauerkraut) served with sausages, pork chops, and a steamed ham hock. Catalán specialties include *mariscado* (shellfish stew), *parillada de mariscos* (mixed grilled shellfish), *caldereta* of lobster, and fresh seasonal oysters.

Egipte. Carrer Jerusalem 3. ☎ **93-317-74-80.** Reservations recommended. Main courses 1,200–2,500ptas. ($8.40–$17.50); set-price menu (Mon–Sat) 1,000–3,000ptas. ($7–$21). AE, DC, MC, V. Mon–Sat 1–4pm and 8pm–midnight. Metro: Liceu. CATALÁN/SPANISH.

A favorite among locals, this tiny place, set amid narrow medieval streets behind the central marketplace, is lively day and night. The excellent menu includes spinach *vol-au-vent* (spinach and sauce baked in a shell, traditionally served with an egg on top), *lengua de ternera* (tongue), and *berengeras* (stuffed eggplant), a chef's specialty. The local favorite is codfish prepared several ways. A savory starter is baked bread layered with ham and a salty Catalán cheese. Expect hearty market-fresh food and a total lack of pretension.

Els Quatre Gats. Montsió 3. ☎ **93-302-41-40.** Reservations required Sat–Sun. Main courses 1,200–2,800ptas. ($8.40–$19.60); set-price lunch 1,800ptas. ($12.60). AE, MC, V. Restaurant, Mon–Sat 1–4pm and 9pm–midnight; cafe, daily 8am–2am. Metro: Plaça de Catalunya. CATALÁN.

A Barcelona legend since 1897, the "Four Cats" was the favorite of Picasso and other artists. In their heyday, their works decorated the walls of this fin-de-siécle cafe on a narrow cobblestoned street near the cathedral. Today a *tertulia* (clublike) bar in the heart of the Barri Gótic, it retains its fine old look, despite restoration. The good Catalán cooking is prepared *cuina de mercat* (based on whatever looked fresh at the market that day).

✪ **Restaurant Hoffman.** Argenteria 74–78. ☎ **93-319-58-89.** Reservations required. Main courses 1,300–3,300ptas. ($9.10–$23.10); set lunch (wine and coffee included) 4,800ptas. ($33.60). AE, DC, MC, V. Mon–Fri 1:30–4pm and 9pm–midnight. Metro: Jaume I. CATALÁN/FRENCH/INTERNATIONAL.

This restaurant in the Barri Gótic has suddenly become one of the most famous in Barcelona, partially because of its creative cuisine, partly because of its close association with a well-respected hotel and restaurant training school. The decor here is eclectic—expect to find masses of verdant plants and fresh flowers, old photographs, and dramatic oil paintings. When the weather's nice, tables are also set up outside. Menu items change every 2 months and are often concocted from ingredients acquired in nearby France. Examples include a superb version of *fine tarte* with deboned sardines; foie gras wrapped in puff pastry; a ragôut of crayfish with green risotto; and a succulent version of pig's feet with eggplant. Especially flavorful is a filet steak cooked in Rioja wine and served with a confit of shallots and a gratin of potatoes. Fondant of chocolate makes a worthy dessert.

Inexpensive

Biocenter. Pintor Fortuny 25. ☎ **93-301-45-83.** Set-price menu 1,125ptas. ($7.90). Main courses 625–1,000ptas. ($4.40–$7). No credit cards. Mon–Sat 9am–5pm; bar, Mon–Sat 9am–11pm. Metro: Plaça de Catalunya. VEGETARIAN.

Funky and alternative, this is Barcelona's largest and best-known vegetarian restaurant. Meals are served in two ground-floor dining rooms whose walls are decorated with the paintings and artworks of the owner and his colleagues. There's a salad bar, an array of vegetarian casseroles, soups such as gazpacho and lentil, and a changing selection of seasonal vegetables.

Can Culleretes. Quintana 5. ☎ **93-317-64-85.** Reservations recommended. Main courses 950–2,000ptas. ($6.65–$14). DC, V. Tues–Sun 1:30–4pm; Tues–Sat 9–11pm. Closed 3 weeks in July. Metro: Liceu. Bus: 14 or 59. CATALÁN.

Founded in 1786 as a *pastelería* (pastry shop) in the Barri Gótic, this oldest of Barcelona restaurants still retains many architectural features. All three dining rooms are decorated in Catalán style, with tile dadoes and wrought-iron chandeliers. The well-prepared food, mostly seafood, features authentic dishes of northeastern Spain, including sole Roman style, *zarzuela à la marinara* (shellfish medley), *canalones* (cannelloni), filet of sole with clams, and paella. October to January, special game dishes are available, including *perdiz* (partridge).

Garduña. Mercado La Boquería, Morera 17–19. ☎ **93-302-43-23.** Reservations recommended. Main courses 1,000–4,000ptas. ($7–$28); set-price menu 1,375ptas. ($9.65). AE, MC, V. Daily 1–4pm and 8pm–midnight. Metro: Liceu. CATALÁN.

This is the most famous restaurant in La Boquería, the covered food market. Battered and somewhat ramshackle, it nonetheless enjoys a fashionable reputation among actors, sculptors, writers, and painters who appreciate the blue-collar atmosphere. It's near the back of the market, so you have to pass endless rows of fresh produce, cheese, and meats that whet your appetite before you even reach it. You can dine downstairs, near a crowded bar, or a bit more formally upstairs. The food is ultra-fresh and might include "hors d'oeuvres of the sea," *canalones* (cannelloni) Rossini, grilled hake with herbs, seafood rice, filet steak with green peppercorns, or zarzuela of fresh fish.

Nou Celler. Princesa 16. ☎ **93-310-47-73.** Reservations required. Main courses 750–1,800ptas. ($5.25–$12.60); set-price menus 1,000–1,300ptas. ($7–$9.10). MC, V. Sun–Fri 8am–midnight. Closed June 15–July 15. Metro: Jaume I. CATALÁN/SPANISH.

Near the Museu Picasso, this spot is perfect for either a bodega-type meal or just a cup of coffee. Country artifacts hang from the beamed ceiling and plaster walls. The back entrance, at Barra de Ferro 3, is at the quieter end of the place, where dozens of original artworks are arranged in a collage. The dining room offers such "Franco-era" food as fish soup, Catalán soup, *zarzuela* (a medley of seafood), paella, Catalán-style chicken, and a well-prepared version of fried squid with onion, almond, and garlic sauce.

Pitarra. Avinyó 56. ☎ **93-301-16-47.** Reservations required. Main courses 1,100–2,000ptas. ($7.70–$14); set-price lunch 1,200ptas. ($8.40). AE, DC, MC, V. Mon–Sat 1–4pm and 8:30–11pm. Metro: Liceu. CATALÁN.

This restaurant in the Barri Gótic was named after the 19th-century Catalán playwright who lived and wrote his plays and poetry in the back room. Menu items read like a roster of traditional Catalán specialties, and most of them are flavorful. Examples include mushroom crêpes layered with strips of duck meat; pork chops smothered with morel mushrooms; and an ultra-traditional version of sea bass baked with tomatoes, peppers, onions, and garlic. There are also two forms of paella served here: the Valencian version with fish, shellfish, and assorted meats, and an all-seafood version beloved by Catalonians.

SUR DIAGONAL
Very Expensive

Beltxenea. Mallorca 275. ☎ **93-215-30-24.** Reservations recommended. Main courses 2,500–5,500ptas. ($17.50–$38.50); menú degustación 6,900ptas. ($48.30). AE, DC, MC, V. Mon–Fri 1:30–4pm and Mon–Sat 8:30–11:30pm. Closed 2 weeks in Aug. Metro: Passeig de Gràcia. BASQUE/INTERNATIONAL.

In a late-19th–century modernist apartment building, this restaurant celebrates the nuances and subtleties of Basque cuisine. Since the Basques are known as the finest chefs in Spain, the cuisine is amazing, and the restaurant is also one of the most elegantly and comfortably furnished in Barcelona. Save a visit for that special night—it's worth the money. The menu reflects the inspiration of the chef and the availability of ingredients. Examples are hake, either fried with garlic or garnished with clams and served with fish broth. Roast lamb, grilled rabbit, and pheasant are well prepared and succulent, as are the desserts. Summer dining is possible in the formal garden.

⭐ **La Dama.** Av. Diagonal 423. ☎ **93-202-06-86.** Reservations required. Main courses 6,000–8,000ptas. ($42–$56); set-price menu 6,000–8,500ptas. ($42–$59.50). AE, DC, MC, V. Daily 1–4pm and 8:30–11:30pm. Metro: Provença. CATALÁN/INTERNATIONAL.

Located one floor above street level in one of the grand, iconoclastic, 19th-century buildings for which Barcelona is famous, this stylish and well-managed restaurant is one of the few in Barcelona to deserve—and get—a Michelin star. La Dama serves a clientele of local residents and civic dignitaries with impeccable taste. The succulent specialties may include warm scampi salad with orange zest, tenderloin of beef layered with foie gras, salmon steak served with vinegar derived from cava and onions, and an abundant seasonal platter of autumn mushrooms. The building, designed by modernist architect Manuel Sayrach, is 3 blocks west of the intersection of Avinguda Diagonal and Passeig de Gràcia.

Expensive

T Les Flors 12. ☎ **93-441-11-39.** Reservations required. Main courses 2,200–3,800ptas. ($15.40–$26.60). AE, MC, V. Mon–Sat 1:30–4pm and 8:30–11:30pm. Closed Aug. Metro: Paral.lel. CATALÁN.

This is the most sophisticated Catalán bistro in Barcelona, drawing such patrons as King Juan Carlos and Queen Sofía. Flowers and artwork decorate the restaurant, and the array of food is beautifully prepared and served. Try spider crabs and shrimp, roast goat with vegetables, filet of beef in wine sauce, filet of pork with cider, a medley of autumnal mushrooms, sweetbreads with port and flap mushrooms, or carpaccio of veal Harry's Bar style.

Inexpensive

Ca La María. Tallers 77 bis. ☎ **93-318-89-93.** Reservations recommended. Main courses 950–1,600ptas. ($6.65–$11.20). AE, DC, MC, V. Daily 1:30–4pm; Tues–Sat 8:30–11pm. Metro: Plaça de la Universitat. CATALÁN.

This small, family-operated, good-natured, and charming restaurant can accommodate only 36 guests at a time, who dine in cozy intimacy on a quiet square opposite a Byzantine-style church near Plaça de la Universitat. With some recent exceptions, menu items are endearingly homey—provided you grew up in a family of Catalán cooks. Examples include anglerfish with brown garlic sauce, filet of sole with mushrooms and prawns, tournedos with cêpe mushrooms, and a veal filet "Café de Paris."

NORTE DIAGONAL

Very Expensive

⭐ **Botafumiero.** Gran de Gràcia 81. ☎ **93-218-42-30.** Reservations recommended for meals in the dining rooms. Main courses 2,600–5,800ptas. ($18.20–$40.60); set-price menus 8,000–9,000ptas. ($56–$63). AE, DC, MC, V. Mon–Sat 1pm–1am; Sun 1–5pm. Metro: Enrique Cuiraga. SEAFOOD.

Although the competition is fierce, this well-managed *restaurante marisquería* (seafood restaurant) consistently serves Barcelona's finest seafood. Much of its allure comes from the attention to detail paid by the white-jacketed staff. You can dine at the bar or in one of the attractive dining rooms with light-grained panels, polished brass, and paintings by Galician artists. The menu includes grilled sea bass with a paprika, garlic, olive oil, and lemon sauce; braised grouper with cider and cava sauce; and baked hake with a tomato-herb sauce. The restaurant prides itself on its fresh and saltwater fish, clams, mussels, lobster, crayfish, scallops, and several varieties of crustaceans that you may never have seen before.

Expensive

Neichel. Pedralbes 16. ☎ **93-203-84-08.** Reservations required. Main courses 2,300–3,800ptas. ($16.10–$26.60). AE, DC, MC, V. Mon–Sat 1:30–3:30pm and 8:30–11pm. Closed Aug and holidays. Metro: Palau Reial or María Christina. MEDITERRANEAN.

Alsatian-born Jean Louis Neichel has been called "the most brilliant ambassador French cuisine has ever had in Spain." Focusing on a delicate culinary display that uses olive oil instead of butter and cream, Neichel prepares such dishes as fresh foie gras with a confit of figs; crayfish salad with a truffle-studded vinaigrette; a salad of wild mushrooms with a carpaccio of wild duck; John Dory with pulverized shellfish suspended in an emulsion of olive oil; and filet of beef stuffed with foie gras and served with a sauce made from the heady Spanish red wine, *merlap*. In 1996, the dessert trolley at this glamorous restaurant won an award as the most appealing dessert choices in Spain.

MOLL DE LA FUSTA & BARCELONETA
Expensive

Can Costa. Passeig Don Joan de Borbò 70. ☎ **93-221-59-03.** Reservations recommended. Main courses 2,000–4,200ptas. ($14–$29.40). AE, MC, V. Daily 12:30–4pm; Mon–Sat 8–11:30pm. Metro: Barceloneta. SEAFOOD.

One of the most enduring seafood restaurants in this seafaring town is Can Costa, whose big windows overlook the water. Originally established in the late 1930s, it contains two busy dining rooms, a uniformed and well-seasoned staff, and an outdoor terrace where diners can enjoy the streaming sunlight and harborfront breezes. Fresh seafood rules the menu here, prepared according to traditional recipes. They include the best baby squid in town—it's sautéed in a flash so that it has an almost grilled flavor, and is almost never overcooked or too rubbery. A chef's specialty of many years is *fideuá de piex*, a classic Valencian shellfish paella, except in this case, noodles are used in lieu of rice. All the desserts are homemade daily.

Moderate

Siete Puertas (also known as 7 Portes). Passeig d'Isabel II, 14. ☎ **93-319-30-33.** Reservations required. Main courses 950–3,320ptas. ($6.65–$23.25). AE, DC, MC, V. Daily 1pm–midnight. Metro: Barceloneta. SEAFOOD.

This is a lunchtime favorite for businesspeople (the Stock Exchange is across the way) and an evening favorite for in-the-know diners who have made it their preferred restaurant in Catalonia. It's been going since 1836. The enormous regional dishes include fresh herring with onions and potatoes, a different paella daily (sometimes with shellfish, or possibly with rabbit), an herb-laden stew of black beans with pork or white beans with sausage, and a wide array of fresh fish and succulent oysters.

SEEING THE SIGHTS
Spain's second-largest city is also its most cosmopolitan and avant-garde. Barcelona is filled with landmark buildings and world-class museums offering many sightseeing opportunities. They include Antoni Gaudí's **Sagrada Familia, Museu Picasso,** Barcelona's **Gothic cathedral,** and **Les Rambles,** the famous tree-lined promenade cutting through the heart of the old quarter.

SIGHTSEEING SUGGESTIONS FOR FIRST-TIME VISITORS

If You Have 1 Day Spend the morning exploring the Barri Gótic. In the afternoon visit Antoni Gaudí's unfinished cathedral masterpiece, La Sagrada Familia, before returning to the heart of the city for a walk down Les Rambles. To cap your day, take the funicular to the fountains at Montjuïc or go to the top of Tibidabo for a panoramic view of Barcelona and its harbor.

If You Have 2 Days On day 2 visit the Museu Picasso in the Gothic Quarter. Then stroll through the surrounding district, the Barri de la Ribera, which is filled with Renaissance mansions and the gorgeous church, Santa María del Mar. Follow this with a ride to the top of the Columbus Monument for a panoramic view of the harborfront.

Have a seafood lunch at La Barceloneta, and in the afternoon, stroll up Les Rambles again. Explore Montjuïc and visit the Museu d'Art de Catalunya if time remains. End the day with a meal at Los Caracoles, a famous restaurant in the old city, just off Les Rambles.

If You Have 3 Days   On day 3, make a pilgrimage to the monastery of Montserrat, about 45 minutes outside of Barcelona, to see the venerated Black Virgin and a host of artistic and scenic attractions. Try to time your visit to hear the 50-member boys' choir.

If You Have 4 or 5 Days   On day 4 take a morning walk along the harborfront, or in the modernist Eixample section of Barcelona, the planned urban expansion area from 1860. Have lunch on the pier. In the afternoon visit Montjuïc again to tour the Fundació Joan Miró and walk through the Poble Espanyol, a miniature village with reproductions of representative regional architecture, created for the 1929 World's Fair. On day 5 take another excursion from the city. If you're interested in history, visit the former Roman city of Tarragona to the south. If you want to unwind on a beach, head south to Sitges.

THE TOP ATTRACTIONS

✪ **Catedral de Barcelona.** Plaça de la Seu. ☎ **93-315-15-54.** Cathedral, free; museum, 100ptas. (70¢); cloisters, 50ptas. (35¢). Cathedral, daily 8am–1:30pm and 4–7:30pm; museum and cloisters, daily 10am–1pm. Metro: Jaume I.

Barcelona's cathedral is a celebrated example of Catalonian Gothic. Except for the 19th-century west facade, the basilica was begun at the end of the 13th century and completed in the mid-15th century. The three naves, cleaned and illuminated, have splendid Gothic details. With its large bell towers, blending of medieval and Renaissance styles, beautiful cloister, high altar, side chapels, sculptured choir, and Gothic arches, it ranks as one of Spain's most impressive cathedrals. The cloister, illuminated on Saturday and fiesta days, contains a museum of medieval art.

Fundació Joan Miró. Plaça de Neptú, Parc de Montjuïc. ☎ **93-329-19-08.** Admission 700ptas. ($4.90) adults, 400ptas. ($2.80) students, free for children 14 and under. Tues–Wed and Fri–Sat 10am–8pm (July–Sept) or 10am–7pm (Oct–June); Thurs 10am–9:30pm; Sun 10am–2:30pm. Bus: 61 from Plaça d'Espanya.

Joan Miró (1893–1983) is one of Spain's greatest painters, known for his whimsical abstract forms and brilliant colors. Some 10,000 works by this Catalán surrealist, including paintings, graphics, and sculptures, have been collected here. The building has been greatly expanded in recent years, following the design of the Catalán architect Josep Lluís Sert, a close friend of Miró's. An exhibition charts (in a variety of media) Miró's complete artistic evolution, from his first drawings at the age of 8 to his last works. Touring international shows of considerable interest are also held at the Fundació Miró.

✪ **La Sagrada Familia.** Mallorca 401. ☎ **93-455-02-47.** Church, 800ptas. ($5.60), including a 12-minute video about Gaudí's religious and secular works; elevator to the tower (about 200 ft.), 200ptas. ($1.40). Apr–Aug, daily 9am–8pm; Mar and Sept, daily 9am–7pm; Oct–Feb, daily 9am–6pm. Metro: Sagrada Familia.

Gaudí's incomplete masterpiece is one of the most idiosyncratic works of architecture in the world. If you have time to see only one Catalán landmark, make it this one. Begun in 1882 and still incomplete at Gaudí's death in 1926, this incredible church— the Temple of the Holy Family—is a bizarre wonder. The languid, amorphous structure embodies the essence of Gaudí's style, which some have described as art nouveau run rampant. The spires—Gaudí planned to construct a total of 12 to reflect the 12 disciples—look a bit like dripping candles. Work continues on the structure, but, without any sure idea of what Gaudí intended, disagreements are constant. The newest sculptures have provoked outrage among many art critics. Still, some predict that the church will be completed in the mid-21st century.

✪ **Museu Picasso.** Montcada 15–19. ☎ **93-319-63-10.** Admission 600ptas. ($4.20) adults, 300ptas. ($2.10) students, free for children 17 and under. Tues–Sat 10am–8pm; Sun 10am–3pm. Metro: Jaume I.

Two converted palaces on a medieval street house works by Pablo Picasso, who donated some 2,500 of his paintings, engravings, and drawings to this museum in 1970. Picasso was particularly fond of Barcelona, where he spent much of his formative youth—some of the paintings were done when Picasso was 9. One portrait, from 1896, depicts his stern aunt, Tía Pepa. Another, completed at the turn of the century, when Picasso was 16, depicts *Science and Charity* (his father was the model for the doctor). Many of the works, especially the early paintings, show the artist's debt to van Gogh, El Greco, and Rembrandt; a famous series, *Las Meninas* (1957), is said to "impersonate" the work of Velázquez. From his Blue Period, the *La Vie* drawings are perhaps the most interesting.

Parc Güell. Carretera del Carmen (no number). ☎ **93-424-38-09.** Free admission. May–Sept, daily 10am to 9pm; Oct–Apr, daily 10am to 6pm. Bus: 24, 25, 31, or 74.

This fanciful park on the northern tier of Barcelona's inner core is much more than green space. It was begun by Antoni Gaudí as a real-estate venture for a wealthy friend, Count Eusebi Güell, a well-known Catalán industrialist, but never completed. Only two houses were constructed, but Gaudí's whimsical creativity is on abundant display, especially in the soaring columns that impersonate trees and splendid winding benches of broken mosaics. The city took over the property in 1926 and turned it into a public park. The panoramic views are excellent.

OTHER ATTRACTIONS

Monument à Colom (Columbus Monument). Portal de la Pau. ☎ **93-302-52-34.** Admission 250ptas. ($1.75) adults, 150ptas. ($1.05) children 4–12, free for children under 4. June 1–Sept 24, daily 9am–8:30pm; Sept 25–May 31, Mon–Fri 10am–2pm and 3:30–6:30pm, Sat–Sun and holidays 10am–6:30pm. Closed Jan 1, Jan 6, and Dec 25–26. Metro: Drassanes. Bus: 14, 18, 36, 57, 59, or 64.

This monument to Christopher Columbus was erected at Barcelona's harborfront on the occasion of the Universal Exhibition of 1888. It's divided into four parts: a plinth with bronze bas-reliefs depicting the principal feats of Columbus; the base of the column, consisting of an eight-sided polygon; the column itself, rising 167 feet; and finally a 25-foot-high bronze statue of Columbus himself by Rafael Ataché. Inside the iron column, an elevator ascends to the mirador, where a panoramic view of Barcelona and its harbor unfolds.

A Neighborhood to Explore

The ✪ **Barri Gótic** is Barcelona's old aristocratic quarter, parts of which have survived from the Middle Ages. Spend at least 2 or 3 hours exploring the Gothic Quarter's narrow streets and squares. Start by walking up Carrer del Carme, east of Les Rambles. A nighttime stroll takes on added drama, but exercise extreme caution. The buildings, for the most part, are austere and sober, the cathedral being the crowning achievement. Roman ruins and the vestiges of 3rd-century walls further entice. This area is intricately detailed and filled with many attractions that are easy to miss.

Poble Espanyol. Marqués de Comilias, Parc de Montjuïc. ☎ **93-325-78-66.** Village, 950ptas. ($6.65) adults, 525ptas. ($3.70) seniors, students, and children 7–11, free for children 6 and under; audiovisual hall, free. Mon 9am–8pm; Tues–Thurs 9am–2am; Fri–Sat 9am–4am; Sun 9am–midnight. Bus: 61.

In this re-created Spanish village, built for the 1929 World's Fair, regional architectural styles are reproduced. The infrastructure is crumbling a bit and the format has grown stale and a bit corny, but it remains an enduring attraction nonetheless. There are 115 life-sized reproductions of buildings and monuments, ranging from the 10th to the 20th centuries. The center of the village has an outdoor cafe. Shops sell crafts from all the provinces, and in some of them can see artists at work, printing fabric or blowing glass. The village has 14 restaurants, a dance club, and eight musical bars. The whole attraction is a lot more appealing at night.

MORE MUSEUMS

Fundació Antoni Tápies. Aragó 255. ☎ **93-487-03-15.** Admission 500ptas. ($3.50) adults, 350ptas. ($2.45) students and children 10–18, free for children under 10. Tues–Sun 11am–8pm. Metro: Passeig de Gràcia.

When it opened in 1990, this became Barcelona's third museum devoted to the work of a single artist. Antoni Tàpies probably has the greatest international renown of any living artist in Spain. In 1984, Tàpies set up the foundation bearing his name, and the city of Barcelona donated an ideal site near the Passeig de Gràcia in Eixample. One of Barcelona's landmark buildings, the splendid brick-and-iron structure was built between 1881 and 1884 by the Catalán modernist, Lluís Doménech i Montaner. The core of the museum is a collection of works by Tàpies (most contributed by the artist), covering the stages of his career as it evolved into abstract expressionism.

Museu Barbier-Mueller Art Precolombí. Carrer de Montcada 14. ☎ **93-319-76-03.** Admission 500ptas. ($3.50) adults, 250ptas. ($1.75) students, free children under 12. Free admission on the first Sat of every month. Tues–Sat 10am–8pm; Sun and holidays 10am–3pm. Metro: Jaume. Bus: 14, 17, 19, 39, 40, 45, and 51.

Opened by Queen Sofia in the spring of 1997, this is one of the most prominent collections of pre-Columbian art in the world. Encased in the Palacio Nadal, built during the Middle Ages and restored, the collection contains almost 6,000 pieces of tribal and ancient art. Pre-Columbian cultures created religious, funerary, and ornamental objects of great stylistic variety with relatively simple means. Especially outstanding are the stone sculptures and ceramic objects. For example, the Olmecs, who settled on the coast of the Gulf of Mexico at the beginning of the first millennium B.C., executed notable monumental sculpture in stone and magnificent jade figures. Many exhibits display Mayan cultural artifacts, some dating back to 1000 B.C.

Museu d'Art Contemporáreo de Barcelona (MACBA). Plaça dels Angels. ☎ **93-412-08-10.** Admission 700ptas. ($4.90) adults, 500ptas. ($3.50) seniors and students, free ages 12 and under. Tues–Fri noon–8pm; Sat 10am–8pm; Sun 10am–3pm. Metro: Plaça de Catalunya.

A soaring, glistening edifice in Barcelona's Raval district, the Museum of Contemporary Art is to Barcelona what the Pompidou Center is to Paris. Designed by American architect Richard Meier, the building itself is a work of art, manipulating sunlight to create brilliant natural interior lighting. On display in the 74,000 square foot space is the work of such modern luminaries as Tápies, Klee, Miró, and many others. The museum contains a library, bookshop, and cafeteria.

Museu d'Art Modern. Plaça d'Armes, Parc de la Ciutadella. ☎ **93-319-57-28.** Admission 500ptas. ($3.50) adults, 250ptas. ($1.75) students and seniors 65 and over, free for children 6 and under. Tues–Sat 10am–7pm; Sun 10am–2:30pm. Closed Jan 1 and Dec 25. Metro: Arc de Triomf. Bus: 14, 16, 17, 39, or 40.

This museum shares a wing of the Palau de la Ciutadella with the Catalonian Parliament. Constructed in the 1700s, this former arsenal was once part of Barcelona's defenses. Its collection of art focuses on the early 20th century and features the work of Catalán artists, including Martí Alsina, Vayreda, Casas, Fortuny, and Rusiñol. The collection also encompasses modernist furniture, including designs by architect Puig i Cadafalch.

Museu de la Ciéncia (Science Museum). Teodor Roviralta, 55. ☎ **93-212-60-50.** Admission to museum and planetarium, 750ptas. ($5.25) adults, 650ptas. ($4.55) children 16 and under; museum only 550ptas. ($3.85) adults, 350ptas. ($2.45) children; planetarium only 200ptas. ($1.40). Tues–Sun 10am–8pm. Bus: 17, 22, 58, or 73.

The science museum's modern design and hands-on activities have made it a major cultural attraction. You can touch, listen, watch, and participate in a variety of exhibits designed to stir a sense of wonder about science and technology. From the beauty of life in the sea to the magic of holograms, the museum offers a world of science to discover. Watch the world turn beneath the Foucault pendulum, ride on a human gyroscope, hear a friend whisper from 20 yards away, feel an earthquake, or use the tools of a scientist to examine intricate life forms with microscopes and video cameras.

Museu Frederic Marés/Museu Sentimental. Plaça de Sant lú 5–6. ☎ **93-310-58-00.** Admission (to both museums) 300ptas. ($2.10), free for children 15 and under. Tues–Sat 10am–5pm; Sun 10am–2pm. Metro: Jaume I. Bus: 17, 19, or 45.

One of the biggest repositories of medieval sculpture in the region is the Frederic Marès Museum, just behind the cathedral. It's housed in an ancient palace whose interior courtyards, chiseled stone, and soaring ceilings are impressive in their own right— an ideal setting for the hundreds of polychrome sculptures. The sculpture section dates from pre-Roman times to the 20th century. Also housed here is the Museu Sentimental, a collection of everyday items that help to illustrate life in Barcelona during the past 2 centuries.

Museu Marítim. Av. de las Drassanes. ☎ **93-318-32-45.** Admission 800ptas. ($5.60), 400ptas. ($2.80) seniors and children 14 and under. Apr–Oct Tues–Sun 10am–7pm; Nov–Mar Tues–Sat 10am–6pm, Sun 10am–2pm. Closed holidays. Metro: Drassanes. Bus: 14, 18, 36, 38, or 57.

In the formal Royal Shipyards of the Drassanes Reials, this 13th-century civil Gothic complex was used for the construction of ships for the Catalán-Aragonese rulers. The most outstanding exhibition here is a reconstruction of *La Galería Real* of Don Juan of Austria, a lavish royal galley. Another special exhibit features a map by Gabriel de Vallseca that was once owned by explorer Amerigo Vespucci.

Museu Nacional d'Art de Catalunya. Palau Nacional, Parc de Montjuïc. ☎ **93-423-71-99.** Admission 800ptas. ($5.60) adults, 400ptas. ($2.80) children 7–20, free children under 7. Tues–Wed and Fri–Sat 10am–7pm; Thurs 10am–9pm; Sun 10am–2:30pm. Metro: Espanya.

This recently reopened and redesigned (1997) museum is the world's major depository of Gothic and Romanesque Catalán art. More than 100 pieces, including sculptures, icons, and frescoes, are on display. The highlight of the museum is the collection of murals from Romanesque churches throughout Catalonia.

PARKS & GARDENS

While Barcelona is not a city of abundant green space, most people head to the hills for a respite from the density and activity of the city below. The mountain park of **Montjuïc** has splashing fountains, gardens, outdoor restaurants, and museums. This is where the principal Olympic stadiums are located. The re-created village, the Poble Espanyol, and the Joan Miró Foundation are also in the park. There are many walks and vistas over the Barcelona skyline.

Another attraction, **Tibidabo Mountain,** offers the finest panoramic view of Barcelona. A funicular takes you up 1,600 feet to the summit. The funicular runs daily 7:15am to 9:45pm and costs 400ptas. ($2.80) each way. The ideal time to visit this summit north of the port (the culmination of the Sierra de Collcerola) is at sunset, as the city lights begin to flicker below. A slightly kitschy amusement park—with Ferris wheels that spin over Barcelona—has been here for years. There's also a church, Santa Creu ("Sacred Heart"), in this carnival-like setting, plus restaurants and mountaintop hotels. From Plaça John Kennedy take the funicular uphill, or catch any of the buses from central Barcelona labeled Tibidabo.

ORGANIZED TOURS

Pullmantur, Gran Vía de les Corts Catalánes 635 (☎ **93-317-12-97**), offers a morning tour departing from the terminal at the above address at 9:30am, which takes in the cathedral, the Gothic Quarter, the Rambles, the monument to Columbus, the Spanish Village, and the Olympic Stadium. It costs 4,575ptas. ($32.05). An afternoon tour leaves at 3:30pm, with visits to some of the most outstanding buildings in the Eixample, including Gaudí's Sagrada Familia, Parc Güell, and a stop at the Picasso Museum. This tour costs 4,575ptas. ($32.05). Pullmantur also offers several excursions into the environs. The daily tour of the monastery of Montserrat departs at 9:30am and returns to the city at 2:30pm. Tours include a visit to the Royal Basilica to view the famous sculpture of the Black Virgin. The tour returns to Barcelona to the harbor, where passengers have the option to remain for the afternoon. Tours cost 5,800ptas. ($40.60).

Another company that offers tours of Barcelona and the surrounding countryside is **Juliatours** (☎ **93-317-64-54**). Itineraries are similar to those above, with similar prices. One, the Visita Ciudad Artistica, offers a tour of Barcelona focusing on the city's artistic significance. Tours pass many of Gaudí's brilliant buildings, including La Sagrada Familia. Also included are visits to the Museu Picasso or Museu d'Art Modern, depending on the day of your tour. Tours cost 4,500ptas. ($31.50) and leave at 3:30pm and again at 6:30pm.

THE SHOPPING SCENE
THE BEST SHOPPING STREETS

The main shopping street in Barcelona is **Passeig de Gràcia.** Stroll this street from the Avinguda Diagonal to the Plaça de Catalunya, and you'll pass some of Barcelona's most elegant boutiques.

In the **old quarter** the principal shopping streets are the Ramblas, Carrer del Pi, Carrer de la Palla, and Avenguda Portal de l'Angel. Moving north to the Eixample are Passeig de Catalunya, Passeig de Gràcia, and Rambla de Catalunya. Going even farther north, Avinguda Diagonal is a major shopping boulevard. Via Augusta is another prominent street.

Another shopping expedition is to the **Mercat de la Boquería,** Rambla 101, near Carrer del Carme. Here you'll see a wide array of straw bags and regional products, along with handsome displays of fruits, vegetables, cheeses, meats, and fish.

THE BEST BUYS

This city of design and fashion offers a wealth of shopping opportunities. In addition to modern, attractively designed, and stylish clothing, shoes and decorative objects are often good buys. Designs for both women and men are sold at **Groc,** Ramble de Catalunya 100 (☎ **93-215-74-74;** Metro: Plaça de Catalunya). One of the most fashionable shops in Barcelona, the Catalán designer Antonio Miró's shop is expensive but filled with high-quality apparel made from the finest of natural fibers. The men's store is downstairs, the women's store one flight up. Miró has a newer, fancier, and bigger store a few blocks down the Ramble, Consejo de Ciento 349 (☎ **93-487-06-70**).

For designer housewares and the best in Spanish contemporary furnishings, your best bet is **Vinçón,** Passeig de Gràcia, 96 (☎ **93-215-60-50**), housed in the former home of artist Ramón Casas.

In the city of Miró, Tàpies, and Picasso, **art** is a major business. You'll find dozens of galleries, especially in the Barri Gótic and around the Picasso Museum. In business since 1840, **Sala Parés,** Petritxol 5 (☎ **93-318-70-20;** Metro: Plaça de Catalunya), is one of the city's finest art galleries. Paintings are displayed in a two-story amphitheater; exhibitions change about once a month. Petritxol is one of the nicest shopping and strolling streets in the Gothic Quarter. At **Art Picasso,** Tapineria 10 (☎ **93-310-49-57;** Metro: Jaume I), you can get good lithographs of works by Picasso, Miró, and Dalí, as well as T-shirts and books. Tiles sold here often carry their provocatively painted scenes.

Unless you're seeking some specialty item, one of your best bets for **antiques** is **El Bulevard des Antiquarius,** Passeig de Gràcia 55 (no central phone). This 70-unit complex, just off one of the city's most aristocratic avenues, has a huge collection of art and antiques assembled in a series of boutiques. There's also a cafe-bar on the upper level.

Most shoppers from abroad are on the lookout for **handcrafts,** and Barcelona is rich in offerings, ranging from simple pottery to handmade furniture. Named after the Victorian English illustrator, **Beardsley,** Petritxol 12 (☎ **93-301-05-76;** Metro: Plaça de Catalunya), is on the same street where the works of Picasso and Dalí were exhibited before they became world-famous. The wide array of gifts includes a little bit of everything from everywhere—dried flowers, writing supplies, silver dishes, unusual bags, and lots more.

At **Itaca,** Carrer Ferran 26 (☎ **93-301-30-44;** Metro: Liceu), you'll find a wide array of handmade pottery, not only from Catalonia but also from Spain, Portugal, Mexico, and Morocco. The merchandise has been selected for its basic purity, integrity, and simplicity.

If your time and budget are limited, you may want to check out Barcelona's major department store, **El Corte Inglés,** Plaça de Catalunya (☎ **93-302-12-12;** Metro: Plaça de Catalunya). The store sells everything from Spanish handcrafts to high-fashion items to Catalán records and food. The store also has restaurants and cafes and offers a number of consumer-related services, such as a travel agent. It will arrange for mailing purchases back home.

BARCELONA AFTER DARK

Your best source of information about the cornucopia known as Barcelona nightlife appears in either of two magazines, *Guia del Ocio,* and its less comprehensive counterpart, *La Semana de Barcelona.* Both publications are available at virtually every news kiosk along Les Rambles, and each costs 125ptas. (90¢). Both are in Spanish, but the listings seem to be worded in ways that even non-native speakers can sort of understand.

Culture and the arts are deeply ingrained in the Catalán soul. The performing arts are strong here—this is the city, after all, that produced the opera legends Plácido Domingo, José Carreras, and Montserrat Caballé. Other, more popular arts take place on the street, especially along Les Rambles, where crowds often gather around a singer or mime.

THE PERFORMING ARTS

Gran Teatre del Liceu. Rambla de Caputxins 61. ☎ **93-485-99-13.**

Founded in 1847, this was once one of the world's leading opera stages until fire destroyed it on January 31, 1997. When it burned, distraught crowds gathered outside on the Ramblas, and the singer Montserrat Caballé wept. Following a complete restoration, the theater is scheduled to reopen in 1999, but there could be delays because of construction. Check its status when you arrive in Barcelona.

Mercat de Les Flors. Lleida 59. ☎ **93-426-18-75.** Tickets 2,000–3,000ptas. ($14–$21). Metro: Plaça de Espanya.

Housed in a building constructed for the 1929 International Exhibition at Montjuïc, this is the other major Catalán theater. Peter Brook used it for a 1983 presentation of *Carmen*. Innovators in drama, dance, and music are showcased here, as are modern dance companies from across Europe. The 999-seat house also contains a restaurant overlooking the rooftops of the city.

✪ **Palau de la Música Catalán.** Sant Francesc de Paula 2. ☎ **93-268-10-00.** Ticket prices depend on the presentation, usually 1,000–3,500ptas. ($7–$24.50). Metro: Urquinaona.

In a city of architectural highlights, this fantastical modernist monument, recently named a UNESCO World Heritage site, stands out. In 1908, Lluís Doménech i Montaner, a Catalán architect, designed this structure, adorning it with stained glass, ceramics, statuary, and ornate lamps. It stands today—restored—as a classic example of modernism. Classical concerts, leading recitals, and the occasional jazz and pop performance are presented here. The box office is open Monday to Friday 10am to 9pm and Saturday 3 to 9pm.

FLAMENCO

El Tablao de Carmen. Poble Espanyol de Montjuïc. ☎ **93-325-68-95.** Dinner and show, 7,800ptas. ($54.60); show and 1 drink, 4,200ptas. ($29.40). Metro: Plaça de Espanya, then a 10-minute walk.

This is the most enduring of Barcelona's flamenco shows, with a reputation for authenticity and dancers from Andalusia. It's set on the panoramic highlands of Montjuïc, within the Poble Espanyol compound. You can either eat dinner—traditional Catalán specialties—at tables set up in front of the stage, or opt for a drink or two as the dancers clap and stamp. The club is open Tuesday to Sunday from 8pm. During the week they sometimes close around 1am, often staying open until 2 or 3am on weekends (everything depends on business). The first show is always at 9:30pm, and the second show Tuesday through Thursday and Sunday is at 11:30pm and on Friday and Saturday at midnight. Reservations are encouraged.

Tablao Flamenco Cordobés. Les Rambles 35. ☎ **93-317-66-53.** Dinner and show, 7,800ptas. ($54.60); show and 1 drink, 4,200ptas. ($29.40). Metro: Drassanes or Liceu.

At the southern end of Les Rambles, you'll hear the strum of the guitar, the sound of rhythmic hand clapping punctuated by staccato heels, and the haunting sound of the flamenco, a tradition here since 1968. Head upstairs to an Andalusian-style room for the traditional *cuadro flamenco* performance—singers, dancers, and guitarist. Cordobés is said to be the best showcase for flamenco in Barcelona. From November 1 to March 15 (except for 1 week in December), the show begins at 10pm. From March 15 through October, two shows are offered nightly at 9:30 and 11:15, with meals beginning about an hour before show time. Reservations are required.

A CABARET

✪ **Bodega Bohemia.** Lancaster 2. ☎ **93-302-50-61.** Metro: Liceu.

This cabaret extraordinaire, off Les Rambles, is a Barcelona institution. The Bodega Bohemia rates as high camp—a talent showcase for theatrical personalities whose joints aren't so flexible but who perform with bracing dignity. Curiously, most audiences are filled with young people, who cheer, boo, catcall, and scream with laughter—the old-timers on stage love it. In all, it's an incredible entertainment bargain if your tastes lean slightly to the bizarre. The street outside is none too safe; take a taxi right to the door. Open daily 11pm to 4am.

DANCE CLUBS

Bikini. Deu I Mata 105. ☎ **093-322-00-05.** Cover 1,000–2,500 ptas ($7–$17.50). Metro: Les Corts.

Set within the basement of a commercial-looking shopping center, this is one of the most comprehensive and wide-ranging nightlife compounds in the city, with at least two venues for dancing to every type of music, including funk, rock, golden-oldies, and even tango. There's a separate room for Puerto Rican salsa (the owners refer to it as a "salsoteca") and a very large area where young (and green) bands play to enthusiastic and supportive crowds. Open Monday to Thursday 7pm to 4:30am and Friday and Saturday 7pm to 6am.

Up and Down. Numancia Diagonal 179. ☎ **93-280-29-22.** Cover 1,800–3,000ptas. ($12.60–$21), including first drink. Metro: María Cristina.

This fashionable and trendy disco attracts the elite of Barcelona, from across the generations. The more mature patrons, specifically the black-tie, post-opera crowd, head for the upstairs section, leaving the downstairs to the loud music and hip, young crowd. Up and Down is the most cosmopolitan disco in Barcelona, with a carefully planned ambience, impeccable service, and a welcoming atmosphere. Technically, this is a private club, and you can be turned away at the door. The disco is open Tuesday through Saturday from 12:30am to anytime between 5am and 6:30am, depending on business.

JAZZ & BLUES

Barcelona Pipa Club. Plaça Reial 3. ☎ **93-302-47-32.** Cover 1,030ptas. ($7.20). Metro: Liceu.

Long beloved by jazz aficionados, this is for pure devotees. Ring the buzzer and you'll be admitted (at least we hope you will) to the club, two flights up in a seedy rundown building. A series of five rooms are decorated with displays or photographs of pipes—naturally Sherlock Holmes gets in on the act. Depending on the performer, music ranges from New Orleans jazz to Brazilian rhythms. Jazz is featured Thursday through Sunday from 10pm to 5am, although the club with its comfortable bar is open daily during the same hours.

Jamboree. Plaça Reial 17. ☎ **93-301-75-64.** Cover 1,550ptas. ($10.85). Metro: Liceu.

In the heart of the Barri Gótic, this has long been one of the city's premier venues for good blues and jazz. Performances here tend to vary, sometimes featuring even Latin dance bands. World-class performers appear here, but most likely it'll be a younger group. Shows are at midnight, and the club is open daily from 9pm to 5am.

XAMPANYERÍAS (CHAMPAGNE BARS)

The Cataláns have their own version of champagne cava. In Spanish, champagne bars are called *champanerías,* and in Catalán the name is *xampanyerías.* These Spanish wines are often excellent, said by some to be better than their French counterparts.

La Cava del Palau. Verdaguer I Callis 10. ☎ **93-310-07-22.** Metro: Urquinaona.

Located in an old part of Barcelona, this large champagne bar is a favorite of the after-concert crowd. Live music is sometimes presented, accompanied by a wide assortment of cheeses, cold cuts, pâtés, and fresh anchovies. Open Monday through Friday from 1:30 to 4pm and 8pm to 2am and Saturday from 8pm to 2am.

Xampanyería Casablanca. Bonavista 6. ☎ **93-237-63-99.** Metro: Passeig de Gràcia.

Someone had to fashion a champagne bar after the Bogart-Bergman film, and this is it. Four kinds of house *cava* are served by the glass. The staff also serves a good selection of tapas, especially pâtés. The Casablanca is close to the Passeig de Gràcia. Open Sunday through Thursday from 6:45pm to 2:30am and Friday and Saturday from 6:45pm to 3am.

GAY & LESBIAN CLUBS

Gay residents of Barcelona refer to **Chaps,** Av. Diagonal 365 (☎ **93-215-53-65;** Metro: Diagonal), a saloon-style watering hole, as Catalonia's premier leather bar. However, the dress code usually steers more toward boots and jeans than leather and chains. Set behind a pair of swinging doors evocative of the old American West, Chaps contains two bar areas and is open daily 7pm to 3am.

Behind a pair of unmarked doors, in a neighborhood of art nouveau buildings, **Martín's Disco,** Passeig de Gràcia 130 (☎ **93-218-71-67;** Metro: Passeig de Gràcia), is one of the more popular gay dance clubs in Barcelona. In a series of all-black rooms, you'll wander through a landscape of men's erotic art, upended oil drums (used as cocktail tables), and the disembodied front-end chassis of yellow cars set amid the angular surfaces of the drinking and dancing areas. Another bar supplies drinks for a large room where films are shown. Open daily midnight to 5am. Cover, including the first drink, is 1,000ptas. ($7).

Santanassa, Carrer Aribau 27 (no phone; Metro: Universidad), is a regular staple on Barcelona's gay circuit, with a bar and dance floor, as well as provocative art. Although gay women have greatly increased their presence here in the past several years, gay males still dominate the scene. Open nightly 11pm to 3am, it has a cover of 1,000ptas. ($7) on Friday and Saturday. The cover includes your first drink.

DAY TRIPS FROM BARCELONA
PENEDÉS WINERIES

From the Penedés wineries come the famous *cava* (Catalán champagne), which you can sample in Barcelona's champagne bars. You can see where this wine originates by driving 25 miles from Barcelona via highway A-2, Exit 27. There are also daily trains to Sant Sadurní d'Anoia, home to 66 cava firms, departing from Barcelona-Sants station.

The winery best equipped to receive visitors is **Codorníu** (☎ **93-818-32-32**), the largest producer of cava—some 40 million bottles a year. Your best bet is to visit Codorniu by car because public transportation is unreliable. Tours are presented in English and take 1½ hours; you visit some of the 10 miles of underground cellars by electric cart. Take a sweater, even on a hot day. The tour ends with a cava tasting. Tours are conducted Monday to Friday from 9am to 5pm. Call for more information. Codorníu is closed in August.

SITGES

One of the most frequented resorts of southern Europe, Sitges, 25 miles south of Barcelona, is the brightest spot on the Costa Dorada. It's crowded in summer, mostly with affluent young northern Europeans, many of them gay. For years the resort was patronized largely by prosperous middle-class industrialists from Barcelona, but those rather staid days have gone; Sitges is as lively today as Benidorm and Torremolinos down the coast, but it's nowhere near as tacky. It has earned a reputation as a gay resort, but the attitude is hardly in-your-face.

Sitges has long been known as a city of culture, thanks in part to resident artist/playwright/Bohemian mystic Santiago Rusiñol. The 19th-century modernist movement largely began here, and the town remained the scene of artistic encounters and demonstrations long after modernism waned. Sitges continued as a resort of artists, attracting such giants as Salvador Dalí and the poet Federico García Lorca, until the Spanish Civil War (1936–39) erased what has come to be called the "golden age" of Sitges.

RENFE runs trains from Barcelona-Sants or from the Passeig de Gràcia to Sitges; the 40-minute trip runs along the coast. Between 5:45am and 10pm daily, there's a train from Barcelona to Sitges every 10 to 15 minutes. Call ☎ 93-894-98-89 in Barcelona for information about schedules. A one-way ticket costs 305ptas. ($2.15).

Sitges is a 45-minute drive from Barcelona along C-246, a coastal road. An express highway, A-7, opened in 1991. The coastal road is more scenic, but it can be extremely slow on weekends because of the heavy traffic, as all of Barcelona seemingly heads for the beaches.

The **tourist information office** is at Carrer Sínis Morera 1 (☎ 93-894-42-51). It's open June to September 15 daily 9am to 9pm; September 16 to May, Monday to Friday 9am to 2pm and 4 to 6:30pm, Saturday 10am to 1pm.

EXPLORING SITGES   Most visitors head straight to the beaches. They have showers, bathing cabins, and stalls. Kiosks rent such items as motorboats and air cushions for fun on the water. Beaches on the eastern end and those inside the town center are the most peaceful, including **Aiguadoiç** and **Els Balomins. Playa San Sebastián, Fragata Beach,** and **"Beach of the Boats"** (under the church and next to the yacht club) are the area's family beaches. Most young people go to the **Playa de la Ribera,** to the west.

Beaches aside, Sitges has a handful of interesting museums. The Catalán artist Santiago Rusiñol combined two 16th-century cottages to make the **Museu Cau Ferrat,** Carrer del Fonollar (☎ 93-894-03-64). He lived and worked here, and upon his death in 1931, he willed it to Sitges along with his art collection. The museum collection includes two paintings by El Greco and several small Picassos, including *The Bullfight.* A number of Rusiñol's works are displayed. Admission is 400ptas. ($2.80) for adults, 200ptas. ($1.40) for students, and free for children 15 and under. A combination ticket granting admission to this museum and the two below is 700ptas. ($4.90) for adults or 350ptas. ($2.45) for students and children. All three museums keep the same hours: Open June 22 to September 10 Tuesday to Saturday 9:30am to 2pm and 4 to 9pm, Sunday 9:30am to 2pm. The rest of the year, hours are Tuesday to Friday 9:30am to 2pm and 4 to 6pm, Saturday 9:30am to 2pm and 4 to 8pm, and Sunday 9:30am to 2pm.

Opened by the king and queen of Spain, the **Museu Maricel,** Carrer del Fonallar (☎ 93-894-03-64), contains art donated by Dr. Jesús Pérez Rosales. The palace, owned by American Charles Deering when it was built right after World War I, is in two parts connected by a small bridge. The museum has a good collection of Gothic and Romantic paintings and sculptures, as well as many fine Catalán ceramics. There are also three noteworthy works by Rebull and an allegorical painting of World War I by Sert. Admission is 500ptas. ($3.50) for adults, 250ptas. ($1.75) for students, and free for children 15 and under. Admission is included in the combination ticket (above). For museum hours, see above.

Museu Romàntic ("Can Llopis"), Sant Gaudenci 1 (☎ 93-894-29-69), re-creates the daily life of a Sitges landowning family in the 18th and 19th centuries. The family rooms, furniture, and household objects are most interesting. You'll also find wine cellars and an important collection of antique dolls (upstairs). Admission is 300ptas. ($2.10) for adults, 150ptas. ($1.05) for students, and free for children 15 and under. Admission is included in the combination ticket (above). For museum hours, see above.

MONTSERRAT

Lying 35 miles northwest of Barcelona, Montserrat ("the serrated mountain") is the most popular day excursion, although it's too crowded for Sunday visits. The winds blow cold at Montserrat, even in summer, so take along a warm sweater, jacket, or coat; in winter, thermal underwear might not be a bad idea.

The best and most exciting way to go is via the Catalán railway—Ferrocarrils de la Generalitat de Catalunya (Manresa line), with five trains a day leaving from Plaça de Espanya in Barcelona. The central office is at Plaça de Catalunya 1 (☎ **93-205-15-15**). The train connects with an aerial cableway (Aeri de Montserrat), included in the rail passage. Expect to spend 1,720ptas. ($12.05), including the funicular. Motorists can take N-2 southwest of Barcelona toward Tarragona, turning west at the junction with N-11. The signposts and exit to Montserrat will be on your right. From the main road, it's 9 miles to the monastery through dramatic scenery, with eerie rock formations.

The **tourist information office** is at Plaça de la Creu (☎ **93-835-02-51**), open daily 10am to 1:45pm and 3 to 5:30pm.

EXPLORING MONTSERRAT Sitting atop a 4,000-foot mountain 7 miles long and 3½ miles wide, Montserrat is one of the most important pilgrimage spots in Spain. Thousands travel here every year to see and touch the 12th-century statue of **La Moreneta (The Black Virgin),** the patron saint of Catalonia. The 50-member ✪ **Escolanía** (boys' choir) is one of Europe's oldest and most renowned, dating from the 13th century. At 1pm daily you can hear them sing "Salve Regina" and the "Virolai" (hymn of Montserrat) in the Nostra Senyora de Montserrat. The basilica is open daily 8 to 10:30am and noon to 6:30pm. Admission is free. To view the Black Virgin (12th- or 13th-century) statue, enter the church through a side door to the right. At Plaça de Santa María you can also visit the **Museu de Montserrat** (☎ **93-835-02-51**), known for its collection of ecclesiastical paintings, including works by Caravaggio and El Greco. The museum is open Monday to Friday 10am to 6pm, Saturday and Sunday 9:30am to 6:30pm, charging 500ptas. ($3.50) for adults or 300ptas. ($2.10) for children and students.

Trains from Barcelona stop at the base of the mountain, where a 9-minute funicular ride takes you the final leg of the journey to the 4,119-foot peak, Sant Jeroni. The funicular operates every 20 minutes April through October, daily from 10am to 6:40pm. The cost is included in the price of the train ride to Montserrat. From the top, you'll see not only all Catalonia but also the Pyrenees and the islands of Majorca and Ibiza.

3 Andalusia & the Costa del Sol

This once-great stronghold of Muslim Spain is incredibly rich in history and tradition, containing some of the country's most celebrated sightseeing treasures: the **Mezquita** (mosque) in Córdoba, the **Alhambra** in Granada, and the great **Gothic cathedral** in Seville. This is also the land of the famed *pueblos blancos* ("white villages"), such as **Ronda,** and interminable, undulating olive groves. Give Andalusia at least a week, and you'll still have only skimmed the surface of its many offerings.

This dry, mountainous region also embraces the **Costa del Sol** (Málaga, Marbella, and Torremolinos are covered here), a popular beach strip of Spain. Go to the Costa

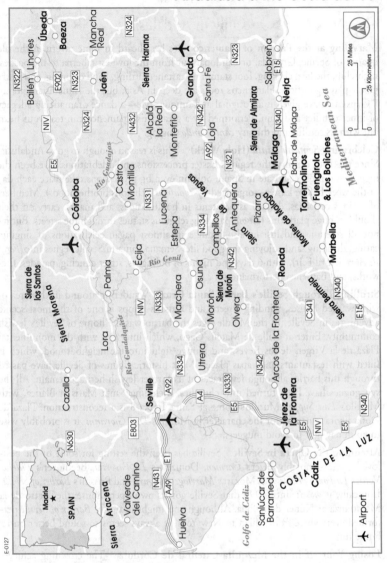

del Sol for resorts, after-dark fun, and relaxation; visit Andalusia for its architectural wonders, beauty, and relaxed way of life.

The mild winter climate and almost-guaranteed sunshine in summer have made the razzle-dazzle Costa del Sol shoreline a year-round attraction. It begins at the western frontier harbor city of Algeciras and stretches east to the port city of Almería. Sandwiched between these points is a steep, rugged coastline, with poor-to-fair beaches, set against the Sierra Nevada. You'll find sandy coves, whitewashed houses, olive trees, lots of new apartment houses, fishing boats, golf courses, souvenir stands, fast-food outlets, and widely varied flora—both human and vegetable. From June to October the coast is mobbed, so make sure you've nailed down a reservation.

Only in Andalusia

Marveling at the Passion of Flamenco It's best heard in some tavern in the old quarter of Seville, Granada, or Córdoba. But from the lowliest taberna to the poshest nightclub, the heel clicking, foot stamping, castanet rattling, hand clapping, and sultry guitar playing entices. Flamenco's roots are deep in Asia, but the Andalusian gitanos ("Gypsies") have given it an original and unique style—a dance dramatizing a legacy of inner conflict and pain. Performed by a great artist, flamenco can tear your heart out with its soulful and throaty *canto hondo* singing.

Celebrating *Semana Santa* (Holy Week) This is reason enough to go to Andalusia. Since the 16th century, the region's Easter processions and celebrations have been the biggest and most elaborate in Spain. Solemn evening processions take place each day of the week before Easter—organized by *codafrías* (religious brotherhoods). Members of various codafrías, dressed as penitents in hoods, capes, and masks, carry on their shoulders huge platforms (*pasos*), parading religious statues through the streets. But it's not all solemn. Andalusians also indulge in almost pagan celebrations of singing, eating, drinking, and enjoying the good life. Semana Santa in Seville segues into *Feria de Abril* (April Fair), with 6 days and nights of bullfights, street dancing, parades, fireworks, and flamenco performances.

Strolling Through Seville's Barrio Santa Cruz Wandering around in this area of whitewashed houses, winding streets, and artisans' shops is one of the most scenic adventures in Seville. In the Middle Ages the barrio was the home of Seville's Jewish community. Enter at Calle de Mateus Gago, which intersects with the monumental Plaza de la Virgen de los Reyes, and plunge right into the neighborhood, which is filled with restaurants and tapas places. Most historic figures of Seville have passed through this barrio, although few traces of its former Jewish heritage remain. All the synagogues have been turned into churches, including Santa Maris la Blanca, with Murillo's *Last Supper*. Murillo's home at Santa Teresa 8 is a reconstruction. Plaza de Doña Elvira is named for the character in Mozart's *Don Giovanni*. It is probably wise to go in daylight to avoid muggers.

Attending the Opera in Seville Seville has been the setting for some of the best-loved operas—notably Bizet's *Carmen,* Donizetti's *La Favorita,* Beethoven's *Fidelio,* Verdi's *La Forza del Destino,* Mozart's *Marriage of Figaro,* and Rossini's *Barber of Seville.* Ironically, it wasn't until 1991 that Seville got its own opera house: the Teatro de la Maestranza at Núñez de Balboa. Although you might hear *The Barber of Seville* performed everywhere from Milan to New York, it always seems to sound better on its home turf.

Losing Yourself in the Mezquita-Catedral de Córdoba The crowning achievement of Muslim architecture in the West, rivaled only by the mosque at Mecca, the Mezquita, in the words of its biggest admirers, is reason enough to visit Andalusia. This 1,200-year-old masterpiece by a series of caliphs is so vast you can easily get lost in it. In the center is an enormous Catholic cathedral. You can wander through the "forest" of Moorish horseshoe-shaped arches, all in red and white "candy stripes"—there's nothing like this in all of Europe.

Reliving *The Arabian Nights* at the Alhambra Girded by nearly a mile of ramparts, the last remaining fortress-palace of the caliphs stands atop the Alhambra. Behind the walls is a former "royal city," straight from the pages of *The Arabian Nights.* At the core is the Casa Real (Royal Palace), where the Moorish rulers were entertained nightly by their "favorites." The sultans of yore once conducted state business here and also housed their harems and families. Fanciful halls, fountained courtyards, and scalloped windows framing picture-postcard views are just part of the attraction of this monument, the single most visited tourist attraction in Spain. Many consider the Alhambra one of the top attractions in all of Europe.

CÓRDOBA

Ten centuries ago Córdoba was one of the world's greatest cities. The capital of Muslim Spain, it was Europe's largest city (with a population of 900,000) and a cultural and intellectual center. As the seat of the Western Caliphate, the city flourished, with public baths, mosques, a great library, and palaces. But barbarian invasions from the north descended on the city, sacking ancient buildings and carting off art treasures. Despite these assaults, Córdoba retains traces of its former glory, rivaling Seville and Granada as the most fascinating city in Andalusia.

Today this provincial capital is known chiefly for its mosque, but it abounds in other artistic and architectural riches, especially its domestic dwellings. The old Arab and Jewish quarters are famous for their narrow streets lined with whitewashed homes and flower-filled patios and balconies; it's perfectly acceptable to walk along gazing into the courtyards.

ESSENTIALS

GETTING THERE   Córdoba is a railway junction for routes to the rest of Andalusia and the rest of Spain. There are about 22 *talgo* and AVE **trains** daily between Córdoba and Madrid (1½ to 2 hours). Other trains (*tranvías*) take 5 to 8 hours for the same trip. Train fare from Madrid, depending on the train, ranges from 5,900 to 7,000 ptas ($41.30 to $49) one-way. There are also 25 trains from Seville every day (1½ hours). The main rail station is on the town's northern periphery, at Av. de América 130, near the corner of Avenida de Cervantes. For information about RENFE services in Córdoba, call ☎ **957-49-02-02.**

There are several different **bus** companies, each of which maintains a separate terminal. The town's most important bus terminal is at Calle Diego Serrano 14 (☎ **957-23-64-74**), 1 block south of Avenida Medina Azahara, on the western outskirts of town (just west of the gardens beside Paseo de la Victoria). From the bus terminal operated by Empresa Bacoma, Avenida de Cervantes 22 (☎ **957-45-64-14**), a short walk south of the railway station, there are three buses per day to and from Seville (a 2-hour and 3-hour trip, respectively) and five daily buses to Jaén (3 hours). Buses arrive here from Madrid (5½ hours); a one-way fare costs 1,550 ptas ($10.85).

A **driving** tour of Andalusia and the Costa del Sol can begin at the "gateway" city of Córdoba, 260 miles southwest of Madrid (about 4 hours). The city lies astride NIV (E-5) connecting Madrid with Seville. From Córdoba take NIV toward Seville, but try to stop over in Carmona, 65 miles to the southwest. Partially surrounded by its Roman walls, this is one of the most scenic towns in all of Andalusia. You can lunch here at the parador. After lunch, continue on NIV for another 24 miles into Seville.

VISITOR INFORMATION   Córdoba's **tourist information office** is at Calle Torrijos 10 (☎ **957-47-12-35**). Open Monday to Saturday 9:30am to 8pm and Sunday 9am to 2pm.

SEEING THE SIGHTS

✪ **Alcázar de los Reyes Cristianos.** Amador de los Ríos. ☎ **957-42-01-51.** Admission 425ptas. ($3) adults, 150ptas. ($1.05) children. May–Sept, Tues–Sat 10am–2pm and 6–8pm, Sun 10am–3pm; Oct–Apr, Tues–Sat 9:30am–3pm and 4:30–6:30pm, Sun 9:30am–3pm. Bus: 3 or 12.

Commissioned in 1328 by Alfonso XI (the "Just"), the Alcázar de los Reyes Cristianos (Alcázar of the Christian Kings), is a fine example of military architecture. Ferdinand

and Isabella governed Castile from this fortress on the river as they prepared to recon-quer Granada, the last Moorish stronghold in Spain. Columbus journeyed here to fill Isabella's ears with his plans for discovery. Two blocks southwest of the mosque, the quadrangular building was defended by powerful walls and a trio of towers: the Tower of the Lions, the Tower of Allegiance, and the Tower of the River. The Tower of the Lions contains intricately decorated ogival ceilings that are the most notable example of Gothic architecture in Andalusia. The beautiful gardens (illuminated May to September, Tuesday to Saturday 10pm to 1am) and the Moorish baths are celebrated attractions. The Patio Morisco is a lovely spot, its pavement decorated with the arms of León and Castile.

✪ **Mezquita-Catedral de Córdoba.** Calle Cardenal Herrero. ☎ **957-47-05-12.** Admission 750ptas. ($5.25) adults, 375ptas. ($2.65) children 12 and under. Daily May–Sept 10am–7pm; Oct–Apr 10am–6pm.

Dating from the 8th century, the mosque was the crowning Muslim architectural achievement in the West, rivaled only by the one at Mecca. Córdoba's is a fantastic labyrinth of red-and-white-striped pillars. To the astonishment of visitors, a cathedral sits awkwardly in the middle of the mosque, disturbing the purity of the lines. The 16th-century cathedral, a blend of many styles, is impressive in its own right, with an intricately carved ceiling and baroque choir stalls. Additional ill-conceived annexes later turned the mezquita into an architectural oddity. Its most interesting feature is the mihrab, a domed shrine of Byzantine mosaics that once housed the Koran. After exploring the interior, stroll through the Courtyard of the Orange Trees, which has a beautiful fountain.

Museo de Bellas Artes de Córdoba. Plazuela del Potro 1. ☎ **957-47-33-45.** Admission 250ptas. ($1.75), free for children 11 and under. June 15–Sept 15, Tues–Sat 10am–2pm and 6pm–8pm, Sun 10am–1:30pm; Sept 16–June 14, Tues–Sat 10am–2pm and 5–7pm, Sun 10am–1:30pm. Bus: 3 or 4.

Housed in an old hospital, the Fine Arts Museum contains medieval Andalusian paintings, examples of Spanish baroque art, and works by many of Spain's important 19th- and 20th-century painters, including Goya. The museum is east of the Mezquita, about a block south of the Church of St. Francis (San Francisco).

Museo Municipal de Arte Taurino. Plaza de las Bulas (also called Plaza Maimónides. ☎ **957-20-10-56.** Admission 425ptas. ($3), free for children 17 and under. May–Sept, Tues–Sat 10:30am–2pm and 6–8pm, Sun 9:30am–3pm; Oct–Apr, Mon–Sat 10am–2pm and 5–7pm, Sun 9:30am–3pm. Bus: 3 or 12.

Memorabilia of great bullfights are housed in this museum, a 16th-century building in the Jewish Quarter, inaugurated in 1983. Its ample galleries recall Córdoba's great bullfighters with "suits of light," pictures, trophies, posters, and even stuffed bulls' heads. You'll see Manolete in repose and the blood-smeared uniform of El Cordobés—both of these famous matadors came from Córdoba.

THE SHOPPING SCENE

The largest and most comprehensive association of craftspeople in Córdoba is **Arte Zoco,** on Calle de los Júdios (no phone). Opened in the Jewish quarter as a business cooperative in the mid-1980s, it assembles the creative output of about a half-dozen artisans, whose media include leather, wood, silver, crystal, terra-cotta, and iron. Some of the artisans maintain on-premises studios, which you can visit to check out the techniques and tools they use to produce their crafts. The center is open Monday to Friday 9:30am to 8pm and Saturday and Sunday 9:30am to 2pm. The workshops and studios of the artisans open and close according to the whims of their occupants, but are usually open Monday to Friday 10am to 2pm and 5:30 to 8pm.

At **Meryan,** Calleja de las Flores 2 (☎ **957-48-71-65**), you can see artisans plying their ancient craft of leather-making in a 250-year-old building. Most items must be custom-ordered, but there are some ready-made pieces for sale, including cigarette boxes, jewel cases, attaché cases, book and folio covers, and ottoman covers. Meryan is open Monday to Friday 9am to 8pm and Saturday 9am to 2pm.

WHERE TO STAY

Expensive

El Conquistador Hotel. Magistral González Francés 15, 14003 Córdoba. ☎ **957-48-11-02.** Fax 957-47-46-77. 102 units. A/C TV TEL. 16,585ptas. ($116.10) double; from 23,100ptas. ($161.70) suite. AE, DC, MC, V. Parking 1,500ptas. ($10.50). Bus: 12.

Benefiting from one of the most evocative locations in Córdoba, just across a narrow street from the Mezquita, this hotel opened in 1986 within the much renovated premises of an interconnected pair of 19th-century villas. Triple rows of stone-trimmed windows and ornate iron balustrades shelter a marble-and-granite lobby that opens into an interior courtyard filled with seasonal flowers, a pair of splashing fountains, and a symmetrical stone arcade. The quality, size, and comfort of the rooms—each with a black-and-white marble floor—have earned the hotel four stars from the government.

Parador Nacional de la Arruzafa. Av. de la Arruzafa 33, 14012 Córdoba. ☎ **957-27-59-00.** Fax 957-28-04-09. 96 units. A/C MINIBAR TV TEL. 17,500ptas. ($122.50) double; 21,500ptas. ($150.50) suite. AE, DC, MC, V. Free parking.

Lying 2½ miles outside town in the suburb of El Brillante, this circa 1960 *parador* (named after an Arab word meaning "palm grove") offers the conveniences and facilities of a luxurious resort hotel at reasonable rates. Built atop the foundations of a former caliphate palace, it's one of the finest paradors in Spain, with a view, a pool, and a tennis court. The spacious rooms have been furnished with fine dark-wood pieces, and some have balconies. The restaurant serves regional specialties.

Moderate

Hotel González. Manríquez 3, 14003 Córdoba. ☎ **957-47-98-19.** Fax 957-48-61-87. 17 units. A/C TV TEL. 9,850–11,000ptas. ($68.95–$77) double; 13,000ptas. ($91) triple; 17,000ptas. ($119) quad. Rates include breakfast. AE, DC, MC, V. Parking 1,400ptas. ($9.80).

Within walking distance of Córdoba's major monuments, the González is clean and decent but not a lot more. The hotel's the result of a radical reconstruction of a crumbling antique house that was so comprehensive that very little of the original core remains. The rooms are functionally furnished and comfortable. In the hotel restaurant you can sample both regional and national specialties. Readers have praised the staff's attitude.

Sol Inn Gallos. Medina Azahara 7, 14005 Córdoba. ☎ **800/336-3542** in the U.S., or 957-23-55-00. Fax 957-23-16-36. 114 units. A/C TV TEL. 11,000ptas. ($77) double; 13,200ptas. ($92.40) triple. AE, DC, MC, V.

Half a block from a wide, tree-shaded boulevard on the western edge of town, this aging 1977 hotel stands eight floors high, crowned by an informal roof garden. The blandly international hotel is a favorite of groups and commercial travelers. The comfortable but small rooms have many extra amenities, including balconies, and the outdoor pool is a pleasure during summer. The hotel also offers a restaurant, a drinking lounge, and a spacious lobby.

Inexpensive

Hostal el Triunfo. Corregidor Luís de la Cerda 79, 14003 Córdoba. ☎ **957-47-55-00.** Fax 957-48-68-50. 58 units. A/C TV TEL. 6,200ptas. ($43.40) double; 7,300ptas. ($51.10) triple. AE, DC, MC, V. Parking 1,500ptas. ($10.50). Bus: 12.

Opposite the mosque and a block from the northern bank of the Guadalquivir River, this simple hotel, with a polite and efficient staff, is a real find. Beyond its formal entrance, you'll find a pleasant, white-walled lounge and comfortable, well-furnished rooms, renovated in 1992. The three-floor hotel has no elevator; its only other drawback is that the bells of the Mezquita cathedral might make it difficult to sleep.

Hotel Riviera. Plaza de Aladreros 5, 14001 Córdoba. ☎ **957-47-30-00.** Fax 957-47-60-18. 30 units. A/C TV TEL. 5,500–6,500ptas. ($38.50–$45.50) double; 7,000–8,000ptas. ($49–$56) triple. AE, DC, V. Parking 7,000ptas. ($49) nearby.

The genial owner of this 1978 hotel is likely to be behind the reception desk when you arrive. His establishment—on a triangular plaza in a commercial section of town, a short walk south of the train station—offers very clean, "no-frills" accommodations. No meals are served, but many cafes are within walking distance.

WHERE TO DINE

✪ **El Caballo Rojo.** Cardinal Herrero 28, Plaza de la Hoguera. ☎ **957-47-53-75.** Reservations required. Main courses 1,600–3,000ptas. ($11.20–$21). AE, DC, MC, V. Daily 1–4:30pm and 8pm–midnight. Bus: 12. SPANISH.

This restaurant is the most popular in Andalusia, often overrun by tourists, and except for La Almudaina, it's Córdoba's best. The place has a noise level matched by no other restaurant in town, but the skilled waiters seem to cope with all demands. Within walking distance of the Mezquita in the old town, it's down a long open-air passage flanked with potted geraniums and vines. Try a variation on the usual gazpacho—almond-flavored broth with apple pieces. In addition to Andalusian dishes, the chef offers Sephardic and Mozarabic specialties, such as monkfish with pine nuts, currants, carrots, and cream. Real aficionados come for the *rabo de toro* (stew made with the tail of an ox or a bull).

✪ **La Almudaina.** Plaza de los Santos Mártires 1. ☎ **957-47-43-42.** Reservations required. Main courses 3,000–5,000ptas. ($21–$35); set-price menu 3,000ptas. ($21). AE, DC, MC, V. Mon–Sat noon–5pm and 8:30pm–midnight; Sun noon–5pm. Closed Sun July–Aug. Bus: 12. SPANISH/FRENCH.

Fronting the river in what used to be the Jewish Quarter, La Almudaina is one of the most attractive restaurants in Andalusia. You can dine in one of the lace-curtained salons or in a glass-roofed central courtyard. Specialties include salmon crêpes; a wide array of fish, such as hake with shrimp sauce; and meats, such as pork loin in wine sauce. For dessert, try the not-too-sweet chocolate crêpe. Very fresh ingredients deftly handled by the kitchen ensure a wonderful meal.

Restaurante Da Vinci. Plaza de los Chirinos 6. ☎ **957-47-75-17.** Reservations required. Main courses 1,300–1,900ptas. ($9.10–$13.30); menú del día 1,600ptas. ($11.20). V. Daily 1:30–4:30pm and 8pm–midnight. ITALIAN/INTERNATIONAL.

This ranks as one of the leading restaurants in town. Although it's not as highly rated as those above, for value it has both of them beat. Both the cuisine and the decor are a blend of Andalusian, international, and Italian influences. Dishes include a choice of roast meats (veal, pork, beefsteak, and lamb), a selection of pastas and salads, and many kinds of seafood, especially hake, monkfish, squid, and salmon. There is no real innovation and little flair, but it's still good.

SEVILLE

Seville, the capital of Andalusia, is justly famous for its beauty and romance. It lies 341 miles southwest of Madrid and 135 miles northwest of Málaga. In spite of the sultry (some would say oppressive) heat in summer and its many problems, such as rising unemployment and street crime, it remains one of the most charming Spanish cities.

Don Juan and Carmen—aided by Mozart and Bizet—have given Seville a romantic reputation it seems unable to live down. If a visitor can see only two Spanish cities in a lifetime, they ought to be Seville and Toledo.

Unlike most Spanish cities, Seville has fared well under most of its conquerors—the Romans, Arabs, and Christians. When Spain entered its 16th-century golden age, Seville funneled gold from the New World into the rest of the country. Columbus docked here after his journey to America.

ESSENTIALS

GETTING THERE From Seville's **San Pablo Airport,** Calle Almirante Lobo (☎ 95-467-29-81), 6 miles north of the center of Seville, beside the highway leading to and signposted to Carmona, Iberia flies several times a day to and from Madrid and Barcelona. A bus, identified by the sign AE (*Aeropuerto*), runs at frequent intervals between the airport, the bus station, and strategic points in the city center. Train service into Seville is now centralized into the **Estación Santa Justa,** Avenida Kansas City (☎ 95-454-02-02 for information and reservations). Buses no. C1 and C2 travel between the railway station and the town's bus station at Prado de San Sebastian.

The high-speed AVE train, charging between 7,000 and 9,500ptas. ($49 and $66.50) each way, depending on when you travel, has reduced travel time from Madrid to Seville to 2½ hours. It makes 14 cross-country runs a day, with a stop in Córdoba. In addition, 10 less rapid trains connect Seville with Córdoba; the AVE train takes 50 minutes, the *talgo* train takes 1½ hours, and conventional trains, which charge 980ptas. ($6.85) each way between the two Andalusian cities, take about 2 hours, with many stops en route.

Most buses arrive and depart from the city's largest **bus terminal,** on the southeast edge of the old city, at Prado de San Sebastián, Calle José María Osborne 11 (☎ 95-441-71-11). Many lines also converge on Plaza de la Encarnación; on Plaza Nueva, in front of the cathedral on Avenida Constitución; and at Plaza de Armas (across the street from the old train station, Estación de Córdoba). From here, buses from several companies make frequent runs to and from Córdoba (2½ hours). For information and prices, calle Alsina Graells at ☎ 95-441-88-11.

If you're driving from Córdoba, take the NIV (E-5) for another 90 miles southwest into Seville (about 2½ hours).

VISITOR INFORMATION The tourist office, **Oficina de Información del Turismo,** at Av. de la Constitución 21B (☎ 95-422-14-04), is open Monday to Saturday 9am to 7pm and Sunday and holidays 10am to 2pm.

SEEING THE SIGHTS

✪ **Alcázar.** Plaza del Triunfo. ☎ 95-422-71-63. Entrance is north of the cathedral. Admission 600ptas. ($4.20). Apr–Sept, Tues–Sat 9:30am–8pm, Sun 9:30am–6pm; Oct–Mar, Tues–Sat 9:30am–6pm, Sun 9:30am–2:30pm.

A magnificent 14th-century Mudéjar palace, the Alcázar, the oldest royal residence in Europe still in use, was built by Pedro the Cruel. From the Dolls' Court to the Maidens' Court and through the domed Ambassadors' Room, it contains some of the finest work of Sevillian artisans. In many ways it evokes the Alhambra at Granada. Former residents Ferdinand and Isabella welcomed Columbus here on his return from America. On the top floor, the Oratory of the Catholic Monarchs has a fine altar of polychrome tiles made by Pisano in 1504.

✪ **Catedral.** Plaza del Triunfo, Av. de la Constitución. ☎ 95-421-49-71. Admission, including Giralda Tower, 700ptas. ($4.90), 200ptas. ($1.40) children and students (free 12 and under). Mon–Sat 10:30am–5pm; Sun 2–7pm.

Don't-Miss Strolls: Barrio de Santa Cruz & Parque María Luisa

What was once a ghetto for Spanish Jews, who were forced out of Spain in the 15th century in the wake of the Inquisition, the ✪ **Barrio de Santa Cruz** today is Seville's most colorful district. Near the old walls of the Alcázar, winding medieval streets with names like Vida (Life) and Muerte (Death) open onto pocket-sized plazas. Balconies with draping bougainvillea and potted geraniums jut out over this labyrinth, and through numerous wrought-iron gates you can glimpse patios filled with fountains and plants. To enter the Barrio Santa Cruz, turn right after leaving the Patio de Banderas exit of the Alcázar. Turn right again at Plaza de la Alianza and go down Calle Rodrigo Caro to Plaza de Doña Elvira. Use caution when strolling through the area, particularly at night; many robberies have occurred here.

Parque María Luisa, dedicated to María Luisa, sister of Isabella II, was once the grounds of the Palacio de San Telmo, Avenida de Roma. Its baroque facade visible behind the deluxe Alfonso XIII Hotel, the palace today houses a seminary. The former private royal park is now open to the public. Running south along the Guadalquivir River, the park attracts those who want to take boat rides, walk along paths bordered by flowers, jog, or go biking. The most romantic way to traverse it is by rented horse and carriage, but this can be expensive depending on your negotiating skills.

The largest Gothic building in the world, Seville's cathedral was designed by builders with a stated goal—that "those who come after us will take us for madmen." Construction began in the late 1400s and took centuries to complete. Built on the site of an ancient mosque, the cathedral claims to contain the remains of Columbus, with his tomb mounted on four statues.

Works of art abound, many of them architectural, such as the 15th-century stained-glass windows, the iron screens (*rejas*) closing off the chapels, the elaborate 15th-century choir stalls, and the Gothic reredos above the main altar. Emerge into the sunlight in the Patio of Orange Trees, with its fresh citrus scents and chirping birds.

✪ **La Giralda.** Plaza del Triunfo. Entrance through the cathedral (admission is included with cathedral).

Just as Big Ben symbolizes London, La Giralda conjures up Seville. This Moorish tower, next to the cathedral, is the city's most famous monument. Erected as a minaret in the 12th century, it has seen later additions, such as 16th-century bells. To climb it is to take the walk of a lifetime. There are no steps—you ascend an endless ramp. If you make it to the top, you'll have a dazzling view of Seville.

Museo Provincial de Bellas Artes de Sevilla. Plaza del Museo 9. ☎ **95-422-18-29.** Admission 250ptas. ($1.75), free for students. Tues 3–8pm; Wed–Sat 9am–8pm; Sun 9am–3pm. Bus: 21, 24, 30, or 31.

In a lovely old convent off Calle de Alfonso XII, this museum houses an important Spanish art collection. Some art experts claim that after the two leading art museums of Madrid, this is the most valuable and significant repository of art in Spain. A whole gallery is devoted to two paintings by El Greco, and works by Zurbarán are exhibited; however, the devoutly religious paintings of the Seville-born Murillo are the highlights. An entire wing is given over to macabre paintings by the 17th-century artist Valdés-Leál. The top floor, which displays modern paintings, is less interesting.

Seville

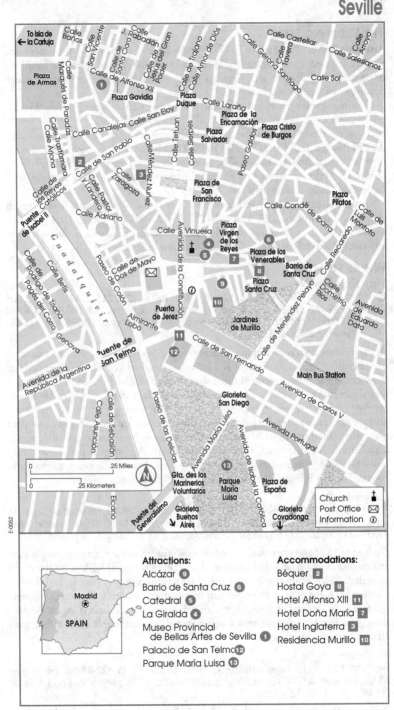

Attractions:

Alcázar ⑨
Barrio de Santa Cruz ⑥
Catedral ⑤
La Giralda ④
Museo Provincial de Bellas Artes de Sevilla ①
Palacio de San Telmo ⑫
Parque María Luisa ⑬

Accommodations:

Béquer ②
Hostal Goya ⑧
Hotel Alfonso XIII ⑪
Hotel Doña María ⑦
Hotel Inglaterra ③
Residencia Murillo ⑩

Church ✝
Post Office ⊠
Information ⓘ

E-0052

THE SHOPPING SCENE

Artesanía Textil, Calle Sierpes 70 (☎ 95-456-28-40), specializes in the nubbly and roughly textured textiles, including linens and embroidery, that reflect the earthiness of contemporary Spanish art. Weavings (some of which use linen, others the rough Spanish wool) are the specialty here.

Close to Seville's town hall, **Ceramics Martian,** Calle Sierpes 74 (☎ 95-421-34-13), sells a wide selection of painted tiles and ceramics, all made in or near Seville. Many of the pieces exhibit ancient geometric patterns of Andalusia. Near the cathedral, **El Postigo,** Calle Arfe (☎ 95-456-00-13), offers one of the biggest selections in town of famous Andalusian ceramics. Some of the pieces are much, much too big to fit into your suitcase; others—especially the hand-painted tiles—make charming souvenirs that can be packed with your luggage.

Carmen fluttered her fan and broke hearts as Andalusian maidens have done for centuries. **Casa Rubio,** Calle Sierpes 56 (☎ 95-422-68-72), stocks a large collection of fans and castanets that range from the austere or dramatic to some of the most florid and fanciful aids to coquetry (or cooling) available in Spain.

WHERE TO STAY

Very Expensive

✪ **Hotel Alfonso XIII.** San Fernando 2, 41004 Sevilla. ☎ **800/221-2340** in the U.S. and Canada, or 95-422-28-50. Fax 95-421-60-33. www.ittsheraton.com. 148 units. A/C MINIBAR TV TEL. 48,000–64,000ptas. ($336–$448) double; from 90,000ptas. ($630) suite. AE, DC, MC, V. Parking 2,250ptas. ($15.75).

At the southwestern corner of the gardens fronting Seville's famous Alcázar, this turn-of-the-century rococo monument is a legendary hotel and Seville's premier address. Now under the management of the luxury division of Sheraton, the ITT group, it reigns supreme in Seville as a bastion of glamour. Built in the Mudéjar/Andalusian Revival style, its halls glitter with hand-painted tiles, acres of marble and mahogany, antique furniture embellished with intricately embossed leather, and a spacious floor plan that is nothing short of majestic. The spacious bedrooms come in Moorish, Castilian, or Baroque styles, each with luxury carpeting, elegant upholstery, heavy wood furnishings, many antiques, mainly twin beds, and old-fashioned, marble bathrooms. The San Fernando restaurant offers Italian/continental cuisine.

Expensive

Hotel Inglaterra. Plaza Nueva 7, 41001 Sevilla. ☎ **95-422-49-70.** Fax 95-456-13-36. 116 units. A/C TV TEL. May–Mar, 18,000–22,000ptas. ($126–$154) double; Apr, 21,000–23,700ptas. ($147–$165.90) double. AE, DC, MC, V. Parking 1,500ptas. ($10.50).

Opened in 1857 and since modernized into a glossy seven-story contemporary design, this eminently respectable and rather staid hotel lies a 5-minute walk southwest of the cathedral. Much of its interior is sheathed with white-and-gray marble, and the furnishings are made of Spanish leather and floral-patterned fabrics. The rooms still have old-fashioned touches of Iberian gentility; the best accommodations are on the fifth floor. The sunny restaurant serves well-prepared set-price meals from a frequently changing international menu.

Moderate

Bécquer. Calle de los Reyes Católicos 4, 41001 Sevilla. ☎ **95-422-89-00.** Fax 95-421-44-00. 118 units. A/C TV TEL. 13,000ptas. ($91) double. AE, DC, MC, V. Parking 1,400ptas. ($9.80). Bus: 21, 31, 32, or 33.

A short walk from the action of the Seville bullring (Maestranza) and only 2 blocks from the river, the Bécquer lies on a street of cafes where you can order tapas (appetizers) and Andalusian wine. The Museo de Bellas Artes also is nearby. The hotel occupies the site of a mansion and retains many objets d'art rescued before that building was demolished. Rooms are all functionally furnished, well kept, and reasonably comfortable.

Hotel Doña María. Don Remondo 19, 41004 Sevilla. ☎ **95-422-49-90.** Fax 95-421-95-46. 69 units. A/C TV TEL. Mar–June and Sept–Dec 18,000–26,000ptas. ($126–$182) double; Jan–Feb and July–Aug 13,000ptas. ($91) double. AE, DC, MC, V. Parking 2,000ptas. ($14).

Doña María's rooftop terrace affords a dramatic view of the cathedral only a few steps away. Originally built in 1978, this well-conceived, four-star, four-story hotel was radically upgraded in 1992 and has received broad-based renovations since. Tasteful Iberian antiques fill the stone lobby and upper halls. The ornate neoclassical entry is offset by a pure-white facade and iron balconies. Amid the flowering plants on the upper floor, you'll find a pool ringed with garden-style lattices and antique wrought-iron railings. Each of the one-of-a-kind rooms is well furnished and comfortable, although some are rather small. A few have four-poster beds; others, a handful of antique reproductions.

Inexpensive

Hostal Goya. Mateus Gago 31, 41004 Sevilla. ☎ **95-421-11-70.** Fax 95-456-02-88. 20 units (10 with bathroom). Jan–Mar and May–Dec, 5,990ptas. ($41.95) double without bathroom, 6,400ptas. ($44.80) double with bathroom; Apr, 7,000ptas. ($49) double without bathroom, 8,000ptas. ($56) double with bathroom. No credit cards.

The location of this 1960s-era hotel, within a narrow-fronted building in the oldest part of the barrio, is one of the Goya's strongest virtues. The building's ornate iron railings and old-fashioned Andalusian-style facade conceal bedrooms which, although extremely simple and spartan (no TV or phone), can be cozy nonetheless. Guests congregate in the marble-floored salon, where a skylight floods the slightly battered couches and chairs with sunlight. There's no restaurant on the premises, but lots of cafes nearby serve morning coffee.

Residencia Murillo. Calle Lope de Rueda 7–9, 41004 Sevilla. ☎ **95-421-60-95.** Fax 95-421-96-16. 27 units. TEL. 6,200–7,800ptas. ($43.40–$54.60) double; 7,700–9,800ptas. ($53.90–$68.60) triple. AE, DC, MC, V. Parking 2,000ptas. ($14) nearby.

Tucked away on a narrow street in the heart of Santa Cruz, the old quarter, the 1950s-style Murillo (named after the artist who used to live in this district) is almost next to the Alcázar's gardens. Inside, the lounges have some fine architectural characteristics and faux antique reproductions; behind a grilled screen is a retreat for drinks. Many of the rooms we inspected were cheerless and gloomy, so have a look before checking in. Like all of Seville's hotels, the Murillo is in a noisy area.

WHERE TO DINE

Very Expensive

Egaña Oriza. San Fernando 41. ☎ **95-422-72-11.** Reservations required. Main courses 2,700–5,900ptas. ($18.90–$41.30); set-price tasting menus 5,200–9,600ptas. ($36.40–$67.20). AE, DC, MC, V. Mon–Fri 1:30–3:30pm and 9–11:30pm; Sat 9–11:30pm; bar, daily 9am–midnight. Closed Aug. BASQUE/INTERNATIONAL.

Seville's best restaurant occupies a mansion built as a showplace for the city's 1929 international exposition. The restaurant is one of the few that specializes in game in Andalusia—a province that's otherwise devoted to seafood. The restaurant was established by Basque-born owner/chef José Mari Egaña, who managed to combine his passion for hunting with his flair for cooking his catch. Try the salad of wild partridge, casserole of wild boar with cherries and raisins, quenelles of duck in a potato nest with apple purée, rice with stewed thrush, hake cooked in a salt crust, or even woodcock flamed in Spanish brandy.

Expensive

Casa Robles. Calle Alvarez Quintero 58. ☎ **95-421-31-50.** Reservations recommended. Main courses 1,200–2,200ptas. ($8.40–$15.40); set-price menus 4,800–10,500ptas. ($33.60–$73.50). AE, DC, MC, V. Daily 1–4:30pm and 8pm–1am. ANDALUSIAN.

This restaurant began its life as an unpretentious bar/bodega in 1954 and developed into a courteous but bustling dining hall on two floors of a building a short walk from the cathedral. Amid an all-Andalusian decor, you can enjoy some surprisingly complicated dishes, most of them flavorful and well prepared, in a setting that retains touches of old-fashioned formality. Menu items include Andalusian fish soup; *lubina con naranjas* (sea bass with Sevillana oranges); a suprême of hake garnished with clams, shrimp, and strips of Serrano ham; and filet of beef layered with foie gras.

Moderate

✪ **Enrique Becerra.** Gamazo 2. ☎ **95-421-30-49.** Reservations recommended. Main courses 1,900–2,400ptas. ($13.30–$16.80). AE, DC, MC, V. Mon–Sat 1–5pm and 8pm–midnight. ANDALUSIAN.

Off Plaza Nueva and near the cathedral, this restaurant has flourished since 1979 by providing some of the best meals in Seville. The restaurant takes its name from its owner, a smart and helpful host. A popular tapas bar and Andalusian dining spot, it offers an intimate setting and a hearty welcome. The gazpacho here is among the city's best, and the sangría is served ice cold. Specialties include hake real, sea bream Bilbaon style, rockfish cooked in Amontillada sherry, and oxtail braised in red wine. Many vegetarian dishes are also featured.

Inexpensive

Hostería del Laurel. Plaza de los Venerables 5, 41001 Sevilla. ☎ **95-422-02-95.** Reservations recommended. Main courses 850–2,500ptas. ($5.95–$17.50). AE, DC, MC, V. Daily noon–4pm and 7:30pm–midnight. ANDALUSIAN.

In one of the most charming buildings on tiny, difficult-to-find Plaza de los Venerables, in the labyrinthine Barrio de Santa Cruz, this hideaway restaurant has iron-barred windows stuffed with plants. Some kind of inn has been functioning within these antique walls since the 1600s, and as such, it's one of the oldest restaurants in the city. Many diners delay their entrance into the plant-filled dining room until after a round of drinks—preferably sherry—at the beamed and smoke-stained tapas bar. Fish and grilled meats, typical of the region, are served in generous portions.

SEVILLE AFTER DARK

In the 1990s Seville finally got its own opera house, **Teatro de la Maestranza,** Núñez de Balboa (☎ **95-422-65-73**), which quickly became a premier venue for world-class operatic performances. Jazz, classical music, and even the quintessentially Spanish *zarzuelas* (operettas) are also performed here. The opera house can be visited only during performances. Tickets, which vary in cost depending on the attraction, can be purchased daily from 11am to 2pm and 5 to 8pm at the box office in front of the theater.

In central Seville on the riverbank between two historic bridges, ✪ **El Patio Sevillano,** Paseo de Cristóbal Colón 11 (☎ **95-421-41-20**), is a showcase for Spanish folk song and dance, performed by exotically costumed dancers. The presentation includes a wide variety of Andalusian flamenco and songs, as well as classical pieces by composers like Falla, Albéniz, Granados, and Chueca. Three shows are given nightly at 7:30, 10, and 11:45pm. From November to February, there are only two shows nightly at 7:30 and 10pm. Admission, including one drink, is 3,800ptas. ($26.60).

RONDA

This little town, high in the Serranía de Ronda Mountains (2,300 feet above sea level), is one of the oldest and most aristocratic places in Spain. The main tourist attraction is a 500-foot **gorge,** spanned by a Roman stone bridge, Puente San Miguel, over the Guadelevín River. On both sides of this hole in the earth are cliff-hanging houses, which look as though, with the slightest push, they would plunge into the chasm.

The road here, once difficult to navigate, is now a wide highway with guard rails. The town and the surrounding mountains were legendary hideouts for bandits and smugglers, but today the Guardia Civil has almost put an end to that occupation.

The gorge divides the town into an older part, the Moorish and aristocratic quarter, and the newer section south of the gorge, built principally after the Reconquest. The old quarter is by far the more fascinating; it contains narrow, rough streets and buildings with a marked Moorish influence (watch for the minaret). After the lazy resort living of Costa del Sol, make a side excursion to Ronda; its unique beauty and refreshing mountain air are a tonic.

Ronda is great for the explorer. Local children may attach themselves to you as guides. For a few pesetas it might be worth it to hire one, since it's difficult to weave your way in and out of the narrow streets.

GETTING THERE   By Train   There are four trains daily from Málaga (2 hours), three per day from Seville (3½ hours), and three per day from Granada (3 hours). Most rail routes into Ronda require a change of train in the railway junction of Bobadilla, several miles to the northeast. Ronda's railway station lies in the western edge of the new city, on Avenida Andalucía (☎ **95-287-16-73**).

By Bus   The main bus company in Ronda is Los Amarillos, running daily bus service to both Málaga and Seville. Buses depart from the bus station on the western edge of the new town, at Plaza Concepcion Garcia Redonda 2 (☎ **95-218-7061**). From Málaga, there are six buses a day Monday to Friday and four on weekends. From Seville, there are five buses a day Monday to Friday, three on Saturday, and four on Sunday.

By Car   Five highways converge on Ronda from all parts of Andalusia. All five head through mountainous scenery, but the road south to Marbella, through the Sierra Palmitera, is one of the most winding and dangerous. Ronda lies 63 miles northeast of Algeciras, 60 miles west of Málaga, 91 miles southeast of Seville, and 367 miles south of Madrid.

VISITOR INFORMATION   The **tourist information office** is at Plaza de España, 1 (☎ **95-287-12-72**), open Monday through Friday from 9am to 2pm and 4 to 7pm, Saturday and Sunday 10am to 2pm.

SEEING THE SIGHTS

The still-functioning **Baños Árabes** are reached from the turnoff to Puente San Miguel. Dating from the 13th century, the baths have glass roof-windows and hump-shaped cupolas. They are generally open Tuesday through Sunday from 9am to 2pm and 4 to 6pm. Admission is free, but you should tip the caretaker who shows you around.

Palacio de Mondragón, El Campillo (☎ **95-287-84-50**), was once the private home of one of the ministers to Charles III. Flanked by two Mudéjar towers, it now has a baroque facade. Inside are Moorish mosaics. Open Monday through Friday from 10am to 7pm and Saturday and Sunday from 10am to 3pm; admission is 250 pesetas ($1.75), but free for children under 14.

Casa del Rey Moro, Marqués de Parada 17, is misnamed, as this House of the Moorish King was actually built in the early 1700s. However, it is believed to have been constructed over Moorish foundations. The interior is closed, but from the garden you can take an underground stairway of 365 steps, called La Mina, which leads you to the river. Christian slaves cut these steps in the 14th century to guarantee a steady water supply in case Ronda came under siege.

On the same street you'll see the 18th-century **Palacio del Marqués de Salvatierra** (☎ 95-287-12-06). Still inhabited by a private family, this Renaissance-style mansion is open for guided tours, operating every 30 minutes, provided that half a dozen people are present. It's open Monday through Wednesday and Friday and Saturday from 11am to 2pm and 4 to 7pm, Thursday and Sunday from 11am to 2pm. Admission is 400 pesetas ($2.80).

Ronda has the oldest bullring in Spain. Built in the 1700s, **Plaza de Toros** is the setting for the yearly Goyesque Corrida in honor of Ronda native son Pedro Romero, one of the greatest bullfighters of all time. If you want to know more about Ronda bullfighting, head for the **Museo Taurino** (☎ 95-287-41-32), reached through the ring. It is open June through September, daily from 10am to 8pm; October through May, daily 10am to 6pm. Admission is 300 pesetas ($2.10).

Exhibits document the exploits of the noted Romero family. Francesco invented the killing sword and the muleta, and his grandson, Pedro (1754–1839), killed 5,600 bulls during his 30-year career. Pedro was the inspiration for Goya's famous Tauromaquia series. There are also exhibits devoted to Cayetano Ordóñez, the matador immortalized by Hemingway in *The Sun Also Rises*.

A NEARBY ATTRACTION

Near Benaoján, **Cueva de la Pileta** (☎ 95-216-72-02), 15½ miles southwest of Ronda, plus a 1¼-mile hard climb, has been compared to the Caves of Altamira in northern Spain, where prehistoric paintings were discovered toward the end of the 19th century. In a wild, beautiful area known as the Serranía de Ronda, José Bullón Lobato, grandfather of the present owners, discovered this cave in 1905. More than a mile in length and filled with oddly and beautifully shaped stalagmites and stalactites, the cave was found to contain five fossilized human and two animal skeletons.

In the mysterious darkness, prehistoric paintings have been discovered, depicting animals in yellow, red, black, and ochre, as well as mysterious symbols. One of the highlights of the tour is a trip to the chamber of the fish, containing a wall painting of a great black seal-like creature about 3 feet long. This chamber, the innermost heart of the cave, ends in a precipice that drops vertically nearly 250 feet.

In the valley just below the cave lives a guide who will conduct you around the chambers, carrying artificial light to illuminate the paintings. Plan to spend at least an hour here. Tours are given daily from 10am to 1pm and 4 to 5pm. Admission, including the 1-hour tour, is 800 pesetas ($5.60) adults, 500 pesetas ($3.50) children.

You can reach the cave most easily by car from Ronda, but those without private transport can take the train to Benaoján. The cave, whose entrance is at least 4 miles uphill, is located in the rocky foothills of the Sierra de Libar, midway between two tiny villages: Jimera de Libar and Benaoján. The valley that contains the cave is parallel to the valley holding Ronda, so the town of Ronda and the cave are separated by a steep range of hills, requiring a rather complicated detour either to the south or north of Ronda, then a doubling back.

WHERE TO STAY

Hostal Residencia Royal. Virgen de la Paz, 42, 29400 Ronda. ☎ **95-287-11-41.** Fax 95-287-81-32. 29 units. A/C TEL. 5,700ptas. ($39.90) double. AE, DC, MC, V.

An adequate stopover for those who want to spend the night in the modern section of town, the Residencia Royal stands near the old bull arena. Each of the basic guest rooms is reasonably comfortable; rooms in the rear, however, tend to be noisy. Most rooms are small, mattresses are a bit thin, and the bathrooms are cramped, but the place is clean and well maintained, and the bargain of the town if your demands are not too great. No breakfast is served, but clients head for any of the town's several cafes for their morning caffeine.

Hotel Reina Victoria. Paseo Dr. Fleming 25, 29400 Ronda. ☎ **95-287-12-40.** Fax 95-287-10-75. 89 units. A/C TV TEL. 17,600ptas. ($123.20) double; 23,000ptas. ($161) suite. AE, DC, MC, V. Free parking.

On the eastern periphery of town, a short walk from the center, this country-style hotel was built in 1906 by an Englishman. It's near the bullring, with terraces that hang right over a 490-foot precipice. Hemingway frequently visited the hotel, but the Reina Victoria is known best as the place where poet Rainer Maria Rilke wrote *The Spanish Trilogy.* His third-floor room has been set aside as a museum, with first editions, manuscripts, photographs, and even a framed copy of his hotel bill. A life-sized bronze statue of the poet stands in a corner of the hotel garden.

Bedrooms are big, airy, and comfortable, some with complete living rooms containing sofas, chairs, and tables. Many also have private terraces with garden furniture. The beds are sumptuous, but in general the furnishings look a bit dowdy; bathrooms are compact and tiled. Opt for one of the rooms in front if at all possible, as those in the rear have no views.

The dining room offers well-prepared food. The hotel also has an outdoor pool and a well-stocked bar.

✪ Parador de Ronda. Plaza de España, 29400 Ronda. ☎ **95-287-75-00.** Fax 95-287-81-88. 78 units. A/C MINIBAR TV TEL. 15,000–18,500ptas. ($105–$129.50) double; 20,000–25,000ptas. ($140–$175) suite. AE, DC, MC, V. Parking 1,200ptas. ($8.40).

When this parador opened in 1994, it surpassed the Reina Victoria (see above) to become the finest accommodation in the area. It sits on a high cliff overlooking the Tajo, a fantastic gorge that cuts a swath more than 500 feet deep and 300 feet wide through the center of this mountain town. Stretching along the edge of the gorge to a bridge, Puente Nuevo, built over the Tajo in 1761, the parador is surrounded by a footpath with scenic overlooks of the gorge and the torrents of the Guadalevín River below. The parador fronts the old food market and the original Town Hall on the town's most historic square. The guest rooms are beautifully furnished, often opening onto views of the rugged peaks that surround Ronda. Bedrooms are generally spacious, with very sleek and contemporary furnishings. Bathrooms, with Andalusian tiles, have combination tub and shower and a hair dryer.

Overlooking the gorge, the parador dining room (open to the public) features typically regional cuisine. There is also a bar-cafeteria. The grounds include a swimming pool.

WHERE TO DINE

Don Miguel Restaurant. Plaza de España 3. ☎ **95-287-10-90.** Main courses 1,400–2,200ptas. ($9.80–$15.40). AE, DC, MC, V. Daily 12:30–4pm and 7:30–10:30pm. Reservations not required. Closed Jan 10–24. SPANISH.

At the end of the bridge, facing the river, this restaurant offers diners views of the upper gorge. It has enough tables set outside to seat 300 people, and in summer this is a bustling place. The food is good, and the waiters are polite and speak enough English to get by. There is also a pleasant bar for drinks and tapas. Try one of the seafood selections or the house specialty, stewed bull's tail.

Mesón Santiago. Marina 3. ☎ **95-287-15-59.** Main courses 1,000–2,000ptas. ($7–$14); set-price menus 1,200–1,600ptas. ($8.40–$11.20). AE, DC, MC, V. Daily noon–5pm. Reservations not required. SPANISH.

Santiago Ruíz Gil operates one of the best inexpensive restaurants in Ronda, serving lunch only. A three-course *menú del día*, with bread and wine, is not a bad deal, considering the price. If you order from the *especialidades de la casa,* count on spending more. Try the *caldo de cocido,* a savory stew with large pieces of meat cooked with such vegetables as garbanzos and white beans, a meal in itself. All the servings are generous. The more expensive à la carte menu is likely to include partridge, lamb, mountain trout, and regional meats. Fresh asparagus and succulent strawberries are also available in season. Mesón Santiago is located near Plaza del Socorro.

MARBELLA

Although it's packed with tourists, ranking just behind Torremolinos in popularity, Marbella is still the most exclusive resort along the Costa del Sol. Despite the hordes, Marbella remains a pleasant Andalusian town at the foot of the Sierra Blanca, 50 miles east of Gibraltar, 47 miles east of Algeciras, and 373 miles south of Madrid.

Traces of the past are found in its palatial town hall, its medieval ruins, and its ancient Moorish walls. Marbella's most charming area is the **old quarter,** with narrow cobblestoned streets and Arab houses, centering around Plaza de los Naranjos.

The biggest attractions in Marbella, however, are **El Fuerte** and **La Fontanilla,** the two main beaches. There are other, more secluded beaches, but you need your own transportation to get to them.

ESSENTIALS

GETTING THERE Twenty buses run between Málaga and Marbella daily, plus three buses that come in from Madrid and another three from Barcelona.

From Seville, take A-4 (E-5) south toward Cádiz, bypassing the city by going along NIV, where you connect with N340 heading southeast. This coastal road takes you past Algeciras and Gibraltar and through the resort of Estepona until you reach Marbella.

VISITOR INFORMATION The **tourist information office** is on Glorieta de la Fontanilla (☎ **95-277-14-42**), open April to October, Monday to Friday 9:30am to 8pm and Saturday 9:30am to 2pm. Another **tourist office** is on Plaza Naranjos (☎ **95-282-35-50**), keeping the same hours.

WHERE TO STAY

Very Expensive

✪ **Marbella Club.** Bulevar Príncipe Alfonso von Hohenlohe, 29600 Marbella. ☎ **800/448-8355** in the U.S., or 95-282-22-11. Fax 95-282-98-84. 130 units. A/C MINIBAR TV TEL. 25,000–55,000ptas. ($175–$385) double; 41,000–58,500ptas. ($287–$409.50) suite; 120,000–250,000ptas. ($840–$1,750) bungalow. AE, DC, MC, V. Free parking.

This exclusive enclave, established in 1954, sprawls over a landscaped property that slopes from its roadside reception area down to the beach. It's composed of small, ecologically conscious clusters of garden pavilions, bungalows, and small-scale annexes (none taller than two stories). The spacious rooms are among the most sumptuous on the coast; all have private balconies or terraces. The Marbella Club Restaurant moves from indoor shelter to an outdoor terrace according to the season. There are two pools and a beach with a lunch restaurant. Golf can be arranged nearby, and tennis courts are available within a 2-minute walk.

Expensive

Los Monteros. Carretera de Cádiz, km 187, 29600 Marbella. ☎ **95-277-17-00.** Fax 95-282-58-46. 180 units. A/C MINIBAR TV TEL. 24,200–29,000ptas. ($169.40–$203) double; from 32,500ptas. ($227.50) suite. Rates include breakfast. AE, DC, MC, V. Free parking.

Los Monteros, 400 yards from the beach and 2½ miles east of Marbella, is one of the most tasteful resort complexes along the Costa del Sol. The complex, built in 1963, was getting a bit tired and battered, so it closed late in 1997, reopening in the spring of 1998 after a radical upgrade. Situated between the coastal road and its own private beach, it attracts those seeking intimacy and luxury. No cavernous lounges exist here; instead, many small public rooms, Andalusian/Japanese in concept, are the style. Guests can relax in various salons with open fireplaces, a library, or on terraces. The guest rooms are brightly decorated, with light-colored lacquered furniture and terraces. The hotel has a bar and four restaurants that open onto flower-filled patios, gardens, and fountains. Grill El Corzo is one of the finest grill rooms along the coast. Other facilities include several pools, a beach club with a heated indoor pool, 10 tennis courts, and a riding club. The tennis courts and riding club are operated independently of the hotel.

Moderate

Hotel El Fuerte. Av. del Fuerte, 29600 Marbella. ☎ **800/448-8355** in the U.S., or 95-286-15-00. Fax 95-282-44-11. 263 units. A/C MINIBAR TV TEL. 12,600–19,500ptas. ($88.20–$136.50) double; from 26,000ptas. ($182) suite. AE, DC, MC, V. Parking 650ptas. ($4.55).

The largest and most recommendable hotel in the center of Marbella, El Fuerte is directly on the waterfront. The hotel, which consists of two six-story towers, lies across an all-pedestrian traffic-free promenade from the beach; an underground tunnel leads beneath the promenade directly to the sand. The hotel was last renovated in 1994. It caters to a sedate clientele of conservative northern Europeans. There's a palm-fringed pool across the street from a sheltered lagoon and a wide-open beach. Rooms, ranging from small to medium in size, are rather bandboxy and functionally furnished, but comfortable. The hotel offers a handful of terraces, some shaded by flowering arbors.

Inexpensive

Hostal El Castillo. Plaza San Bernabé 2, 29600 Marbella. ☎ **95-277-17-39.** 26 units. 4,000–4,500ptas. ($28–$31.50) double. MC, V.

At the foot of the castle, in the narrow streets of the old town, this small 1960s hotel opens onto a minuscule triangular area used by the adjoining convent and school as a playground. There's a small, covered courtyard, and the simple second-floor rooms have only inner windows. The spartan rooms are scrubbed clean and contain white-tiled bathrooms and writing desks, but not a lot more. No meals are served, but many cafes, suitable for breakfast, lie nearby.

WHERE TO DINE

Balcón de la Virgen. Remedios 2. ☎ **95-277-60-92.** Reservations recommended. Main courses 1,500–3,000ptas. ($10.50–$21). AE, MC, V. Daily 7pm–midnight. Closed Tues Nov–May. SPANISH.

Set in the historic core of old Marbella, this restaurant is named after a 200-year-old statue of the Virgin that adorns a wall niche surrounded by flowers and vines—the focal point of this antique house. Only a short walk from the Plaza de los Naranjos, it's almost always bustling with people drawn by the floral charm, good food, attentive service, and reasonable prices. The menu—mostly Andalusian and partially Spanish—features Málaga-style meat stew, baked hake with olive oil and herbs, marinated swordfish, roasted pork, and grilled filets of beef.

✪ **La Hacienda.** Urbanización Hacienda Las Chapas, Carretera de Cádiz, km 193. ☎ **95-283-12-67.** Reservations recommended. Main courses 2,200–3,200ptas. ($15.40–$22.40); set-price menu 6,815ptas. ($47.70). AE, DC, MC, V. Summer, daily 8:30–11:30pm; winter, Wed–Sun 1–3:30pm and 8:30–11:30pm. Closed Nov 15–Dec 20. INTERNATIONAL.

La Hacienda, a tranquil choice 8 miles east of Marbella, enjoys a reputation for serving some of the best food along the Costa del Sol. In cooler months you can dine in the rustic tavern before an open fireplace; in fair weather, meals are served on a patio partially encircled by open Romanesque arches. The chef is likely to offer foie gras with lentils, lobster croquettes (as an appetizer), and roast guinea hen with cream, minced raisins, and port. Dishes have a great deal of flavor, are presented with style, and prepared with the freshest ingredients available. Although the food is admirable, the service is sometimes lacking.

MARBELLA AFTER DARK

Near Puerto Banús, **Casino Nueva Andalucía Marbella,** Urbanización Nueva Andalucía (☎ **95-281-40-00**), is on the lobby level of the Andalucía Plaza Hotel, 4½ miles from Marbella's center beside the road leading to Cádiz. Games include French and American roulette, blackjack, punto y banco, craps, and chemin de fer. Entrance to the casino is 600ptas. ($4.20), and you have to present a valid passport. You can dine before or after gambling in the Casino Restaurant. The casino is open daily 8pm to 4 or 5am. La Caseta Bar offers flamenco shows at 11pm Friday to Saturday. Entrance is free, but drinks cost 1,800ptas. ($12.60) and up.

TORREMOLINOS

The most famous Mediterranean beach resort in Spain is a veritable melting pot of Europeans and Americans. International travelers relax here after a whirlwind tour of Europe—the living's easy, the people are fun, and there are no historic monuments to visit. Thus, the sleepy fishing village of Torremolinos has been engulfed in a cluster of concrete-walled resort hotels. Prices are on the rise, but it nevertheless remains one of Europe's vacation bargains. The sands along the beachfront tend to be gritlike and grayish. The best beaches are **El Bajondillo** and **La Carihuela,** the latter bordering an old fishing village. All beaches here are public, but don't expect changing facilities. Although it's technically not allowed, many women go topless on the beaches.

ESSENTIALS

GETTING THERE   Torremolinos is served by the nearby Málaga airport, 9 miles west. There are also frequent rail departures from the terminal at Málaga; for information, call ☎ **95-236-02-02.** Buses run frequently between Málaga and Torremolinos; for information, call ☎ **95-235-00-61.**

Torremolinos is 7 miles west of Málaga along E-15/N340, or a short drive east of Fuengirola along E-15/N340.

VISITOR INFORMATION   The **tourist information office** at Plaza de las Comunidades Autonomas (☎ **95-237-19-09**) is open daily 8am to 3pm.

WHERE TO STAY

Hotel Las Palomas. Carmen Montes 1, 29620 Torremolinos. ☎ **95-238-50-00.** Fax 95-238-64-66. 345 units. TEL. 6,510–13,178ptas. ($45.55–$92.25)double. AE, DC, MC, V.

Built during Torremolinos's construction boom (1968), this well-managed low-rise hotel surrounded by gardens is one of the town's most attractive. A 1-minute walk from the beach and a 10-minute walk south of the center of town, it has an Andalusian decor that extends into the rooms, a formal entrance, and a clientele of repeat visitors. Each room has a private balcony, a tiled bathroom, and furniture inspired by southern Spain. None is air-conditioned, but guests can open their windows and balcony doors to catch the sea breezes. Three pools are on-site.

Sol Don Pablo. Paseo Marítimo, s/n, 29620 Torremolinos. ☎ **95-238-38-88.** Fax 95-238-37-83. 443 units. A/C MINIBAR TV TEL. 15,200–19,560ptas. ($106.40–$136.90) double. Rates include buffet breakfast. AE, DC, MC, V.

One of the most desirable hotels in Torremolinos is housed in a modern building that's a minute from the beach and surrounded by its own garden and playground areas. The surprise is the glamorous interior, which borrows heavily from Moorish palace and medieval castle themes. Splashing fountains are found in the arched-tile arcades, and niches with life-sized stone statues of nude figures line the grand staircase. The comfortably furnished bedrooms have sea-view terraces and private bathrooms. In addition to having several places where you can order a drink, the hotel's restaurant serves buffet-only lunches and dinners. The hotel has a full day and night entertainment program, including fitness classes, dancing to a live band, and a disco.

Sol Élite Aloha Puerto. Calle Salvador Allende 45, 29620 Torremolinos. ☎ **800/336-3542** in the U.S., or 95-238-70-66. Fax 95-238-57-01. 430 units. A/C MINIBAR TV TEL. 11,500–17,690ptas. ($80.50–$123.85) double. Rates include buffet breakfast. AE, DC, MC, V.

Heralded as one of the most modern hotels along the Costa del Sol when it was built in 1972, this now-aging hotel stands on the seashore in the residential suburb of El Saltillo, on the southwestern edge of Torremolinos, beside the coastal road leading to Marbella. Away from the noise of the town center, it offers spacious rooms, all defined by the hotel as mini-suites. Each faces the sea, the Benalmádena marina, or the beach, and each has a separate sitting area. Amid all the amenities of a resort, guests are given a choice of two restaurants and four bars. The most popular lunchtime option is an all-you-can-eat poolside buffet. The two swimming pools are heated.

WHERE TO DINE

Casa Juan. Calle Mar 14, La Carihuela. ☎ **95-238-4106.** Reservations recommended. Main courses 1,500–2,800ptas. ($10.50–$19.60). AE, DC, MC, V. Tues–Sun 12:30–4:30pm and 7:30pm–midnight. Closed Dec. SEAFOOD.

This seafood restaurant is set within a modern-looking building in the old-timey satellite hamlet of La Carihuela, about a mile west of Torremolinos's center. Menu items include selections from a lavish display of fish and shellfish prominently positioned near the entrance. Dishes include a fried platter of mixed fish, several different versions of codfish, meat or fish kebabs, and paella. Of special note is *lubina a la sal*—sea bass that's packed in layers of roughly textured salt, which is then broken open at your table and deboned in front of you. Whenever it gets busy (which is frequently), the staff is likely to rush around hysterically and at times even brusquely, although many of the restaurant's local fans think this only adds to its charm.

El Gato Viudo. La Nogalera 8. ☎ **95-238-51-29.** Main courses 800–1,900ptas. ($5.60–$13.30). AE, DC, MC, V. Nov–Apr Thurs–Tues 1–4pm and 6–11:30pm; May–Oct daily 1–4pm and 6–11:30pm. SPANISH.

Simple and amiable, this old-fashioned tavern with sidewalk seating occupies the street level and cellar of a building off Calle San Miguel. The menu includes tasty dishes such as platters of grilled fish; marinated hake; roasted pork, steak, and veal; calamari with spicy tomato sauce; grilled shrimp; and shellfish or fish soup.

TORREMOLINOS AFTER DARK

One of the major casinos along the Costa del Sol, **Casino Torrequebrada,** Carretera de Cádiz 220, Benalmádena Costa (☎ **95-244-25-45**), is on the lobby level of the Hotel Torrequebrada. The Torrequebrada combines a nightclub/cabaret, a restaurant, and an array of tables devoted to blackjack, chemin de fer, punto y banco, and two kinds of roulette. The nightclub presents a flamenco show every Tuesday to Saturday at 10:30pm. Many visitors prefer to attend just the show, paying 4,000ptas. ($28) for entrance (includes the first drink). Dinner is served Wednesday to Saturday at 9pm and costs 7,600ptas. ($53.20), which includes admission to the show. The casino is especially lively in midsummer. The casino, its facilities, and its gaming tables are open daily 9pm to 4am. The entrance fee to the gaming rooms is 600ptas. ($4.20).

MÁLAGA

Málaga is a bustling commercial and residential center whose economy doesn't depend exclusively on tourism. Its chief attraction is the mild off-season climate—summer can be sticky. Málaga's most famous native son is Pablo Picasso, born in 1881 at Plaza de la Merced, in the center of the city.

ESSENTIALS

GETTING THERE Iberia, the national airline of Spain, has flights every 2 hours into Málaga from Madrid. To make reservations, call ☎ **800/772-4642** in the United States. Málaga maintains good rail connections with Madrid (at least five trains a day); the trip takes around 4½ hours. For rail information in Málaga, call **RENFE** at ☎ **95-221-31-22.** Buses from all over Spain arrive at the terminal on Paseo de los Tilos, behind the RENFE office. Málaga is linked by bus to all the major cities of Spain, including Madrid (eight buses per day) and Seville (10 per day). Trip time from Madrid is 7 hours; from Sevilla, 13 hours. Call ☎ **95-235-00-61** in Málaga for bus information. From Málaga, N-340, a curving, winding road, heads east to Nerja, and E-15/N340 leads east to Torremolinos, Fuengirola, and Marbella.

VISITOR INFORMATION   The **tourist information office** at Pasaje de Chinitas 4 (☎ **95-221-34-45**) is open Monday to Friday 9am to 7pm and Saturday and Sunday 9am to 2pm. Keeping longer hours is **Municipal,** Avenida Cervantes 1 (☎ **95-260-44-10**), open Monday to Friday 8:15am to 2:45pm and 4:30 to 7pm, Saturday 9:30am to 1:30pm.

EXPLORING MÁLAGA

The remains of the ancient Moorish **Alcazaba,** Plaza de la Aduana, Alcazabilla (☎ **95-221-60-05;** bus: 4, 18, 19, or 24), are within easy walking distance of the city center, off Paseo del Parque (plenty of signs point the way up the hill). The fortress was erected in the 9th or 10th century, although there have been later additions and reconstructions. Ferdinand and Isabella stayed here when they reconquered the city. The Alcazaba now houses an archaeological museum, with exhibits of cultures ranging from Greek to Phoenician to Carthaginian. Admission to the museum is 30ptas. (20¢).

The 16th-century Renaissance **cathedral,** Plaza Obispo (☎ **95-221-59-17;** bus: 14, 18, 19, or 24), in Málaga's center, was built on the site of a great mosque. Although it suffered damage during the Civil War, it remains vast and impressive. Its most notable attributes are the richly ornamented choir stalls by Ortiz, Mena, and Michael. The cathedral has been declared a national monument. Admission is 200ptas. ($1.40). It's open daily 10am to 12:45pm and 4 to 6:30pm; closed holidays.

WHERE TO STAY

Parador de Málaga-Gibralfaro. Monte Gibralfaro, 29016 Málaga. ☎ **95-222-19-02.** Fax 95-222-19-04. 38 units. A/C MINIBAR TV TEL. 16,500–18,000ptas. ($115.50–$126) double. AE, DC, MC, V. Free parking.

Originally established in 1948, and renovated between 1992 and 1994, this is one of Spain's oldest paradors. It's immediately adjacent to the foundations of a medieval castle. Although the interior is modern and streamlined, it enjoys a scenic position overlooking the city and the Mediterranean, with views of the bullring, mountains, and beaches. The guest rooms, with their own entrances, have living-room areas and wide glass doors opening onto private sun terraces with garden furniture. They're tastefully decorated with modern furnishings and reproductions of Spanish antiques. On the premises are two dining rooms with a reputation for good food served in generous portions.

Parador Nacional del Golf. Carretera de Málaga, Torremolinos, 29080 Apartado 324, Málaga. ☎ **95-238-12-55.** Fax 95-238-09-63. 60 units. A/C MINIBAR TV TEL. 16,500ptas. ($115.50) double. AE, DC, MC, V. Free parking.

A resort hotel created by the Spanish government, this hacienda-style parador is flanked by a golf course on one side and the Mediterranean on another. It's less than 2 miles from the airport, 6½ miles from Málaga, and 2½ miles from Torremolinos. Each room has a balcony with a view of the golfing greens, the circular pool, or the water; some rooms are equipped with Jacuzzis. Long tiled corridors lead to the air-conditioned public rooms—graciously furnished lounges and a restaurant.

WHERE TO DINE

Café de Paris. Vélez Málaga 8. ☎ **95-222-50-43.** Reservations required. Main courses 2,800–3,500ptas. ($19.60–$24.50); menú del día 2,000ptas. ($14). AE, DC, MC, V. Mon–Sat 1–4pm and 8:30pm–midnight. Closed July 1–15. Bus: 13. FRENCH/SPANISH.

Málaga's best restaurant is in La Malagueta, the district surrounding the Plaza de Toros (bullring). This is the domain of proprietor/chef de cuisine José García Cortés, who worked at many important dining rooms before carving out his own niche. Some critics have said that the cuisine is pitched too high for the taste and budget of the average Malagueño—particularly when it comes to caviar, game (including partridge), and foie gras, which are often featured. Much of the Cortés's cuisine has been adapted from classic French dishes to please the Andalusian palate. Menus are changed frequently, reflecting the chef's imagination and the availability of produce. You might be served crêpes gratinées (filled with baby eels) or local white fish baked in salt (it doesn't sound good, but is excellent). Stroganoff is made here with ox meat instead of beef. Other specialties include artichokes Café de Paris stuffed with foie gras and a succulent version of hake that's stuffed with pulverized shellfish and served with a fish-based tomato sauce.

NERJA

Nerja, 32 miles east of Málaga, is known for its good beaches and small coves, its seclusion, its narrow streets and courtyards, and its whitewashed, flat-roofed houses. Nearby is one of Spain's greatest attractions, the Cave of Nerja (see "Exploring a Cave," below).

At the mouth of the Chillar River, Nerja gets its name from an Arabic word, *narixa*, meaning "bountiful spring." Its most dramatic spot is the **Balcón de Europa,** a palm-shaded promenade that juts out into the Mediterranean. The sea-bordering walkway was built in 1885 in honor of a visit from the Spanish king Alfonso XIII in the wake of an earthquake that had shattered part of nearby Málaga. The phrase "Balcón de Europa" is said to have been coined by the king during one of the speeches he made in Nerja praising the beauty of the panoramas around him. To reach the best beaches, head west from the Balcón and follow the shoreline.

ESSENTIALS

GETTING THERE There is no railway station in Nerja, so railway passengers get off in Málaga and then go by bus. Nerja is well-serviced by buses from Málaga—at least 10 per day make the 90-minute run. Buses depart from a point immediately adjacent to the railway station. For bus information in both Málaga and Nerja, call ☎ **95-235-00-61.** Nerja is 32 miles east of Málaga along N-340. From Granada, take N-323 south to N-340 west to Nerja.

VISITOR INFORMATION The **tourist information office** is at Puerta del Mar 2 (☎ **95-252-15-31**). Open Monday to Friday 10am to 2pm and 5:30 to 8:30pm and Saturday 10am to 1pm.

EXPLORING A CAVE

The most popular outing from either Málaga or Nerja is to the ✪ **Cueva de Nerja (Cave of Nerja),** Carretera de Maro (☎ **95-252-96-35**), which scientists believe was inhabited from 25,000 to 2,000 B.C. This prehistoric stalactite and stalagmite cave lay undiscovered until 1959, when it was found by chance by a handful of boys. When fully opened, it revealed a wealth of treasures, including Paleolithic paintings. They depict horses and deer, but as of this writing they're not open to public viewing. The archaeological museum in the cave contains a number of prehistoric artifacts. You can walk through its stupendous galleries, where the ceiling soars to a height of 200 feet.

The cave is open daily 10am to 2pm and 4 to 6:30pm. (During July and August, the evening closing is at 8pm.) Admission is 650ptas. ($4.55) for adults, 300ptas. ($2.10) for children 6 to 12, and free for children 5 and under. If you want to visit the Nerja caves directly from Málaga, buses depart from Málaga's railway station, stopping en route at Málaga's Muelle de Heredia, at intervals of between 60 and 90 minutes every day between 7am and 8:15pm. The trip takes about an hour.

WHERE TO STAY

✪ **Parador Nacional de Nerja.** Calle Almuñecar 8, Playa de Burriana–Tablazo, 29780 Nerja. ☎ **95-252-00-50.** Fax 95-252-19-97. 73 units. A/C MINIBAR TV TEL. 14,500–18,000ptas. ($101.50–$126) double. AE, DC, MC, V. Free parking.

A 5-minute walk from the center of town, this government-owned hotel takes the best of modern motel designs and blends them with a classic Spanish decor of beamed ceilings, tiled floors, and hand-loomed draperies. It was built in the 1960s on the edge of a cliff, around a flower-filled courtyard with a splashing fountain. Social life revolves around the large pool and tennis courts. There's a sandy beach below, reached by an elevator, plus lawns and gardens. The rooms are spacious and furnished in an understated but tasteful style. International and Spanish meals are served in the hotel restaurant.

WHERE TO DINE

Restaurante Rey Alfonso. Paseo Balcón de Europa. ☎ **95-252-09-58.** Reservations recommended. Main courses 850–2,100ptas. ($5.95–$14.70). AE, DC, MC, V. Thurs–Tues 11am–4pm and 7–11pm. Closed Nov. SPANISH/INTERNATIONAL.

Few visitors to the Balcón de Europa realize they're standing directly above one of the most unusual restaurants in town. You enter from the bottom of a flight of stairs that skirts the rocky base of a late 19th-century *miradore* (viewing station), which juts seaward as an extension of the town's main square. The restaurant's menu and interior decor don't hold many surprises, but the close-up view of the crashing waves makes dining here worthwhile. Specialties include a well-prepared paella Valenciana, tournedos Nerja (flambéed with mushrooms), entrecôte Rey Alfonso with a red wine and cream sauce, five preparations of sole (from grilled to meunière), and crayfish in whisky sauce.

GRANADA

Granada, 76 miles northeast of Málaga, is 2,200 feet above sea level. This beautiful city sprawls over two main hills, the Alhambra and the Albaicín, and is crossed by two rivers, the Genil and the Darro. The **Cuesta de Gomérez** is one of the most important streets in Granada, climbing uphill from Plaza Nueva, the center of the modern city, to the Alhambra, Spain's major tourist attraction. This former stronghold of Moorish Spain, in the foothills of the snowcapped Sierra Nevada range, is replete with romance and folklore. In his *Tales of the Alhambra,* Washington Irving used the symbol of the city, the pomegranate (*granada*), to conjure up a spirit of romance.

ESSENTIALS

GETTING THERE **Iberia** flies to Granada once or twice daily from both Barcelona and Madrid. Granada's airport (☎ **958-24-52-00**) is 10 miles west of the city center, in the hamlet of Chauchina. Airline ticketing problems and airline information is more easily handled at the **Iberia** ticketing office in the city center, at Plaza Isabel la Católica 2 (☎ **958-22-75-92**). A shuttle bus makes runs several times a day between the airport and the city center, at hours timed to coincide with the arrival and departures of flights. The buses meander through the city center before heading out to the airport, but the most convenient and central place to catch one is on the Gran Vía de Colón, immediately in front of the city's cathedral. Passage costs 425ptas. ($3) each way.

Two **trains** daily connect Granada with Madrid's Atocha Railway Station (trip time: 5 hours). Granada's railway station is on Calle Dr. Jaime García Royo (☎ **958-27-12-72**), at the end of Avenida Andaluces.

Most **buses** pull into the station on the fringe of Granada at Carretera de Madrid. **Alsina Graells** (☎ **958-18-50-10**) is the most useful company here, offering 6 buses per day to Córdoba (3 hours), 12 per day from Jaén (1½ hours), 9 per day from Madrid (5 hours), 15 from Málaga (2 hours), and 6 from Seville (3 hours).

From the Costa del Sol, follow N340/E-15 east to N-323 north into Granada. To reach Granada from Córdoba, head south along N331 to the junction with N342, at which point you drive east.

VISITOR INFORMATION   The **tourist information office** is at Plaza de Mariana Pineda 10 (☎ **958-22-66-88**), open Monday to Friday 9am to 7pm and Saturday 10am to 2pm.

SEEING THE SIGHTS

✪ **Alhambra.** Palacio de Carlos V. ☎ **958-22-09-12.** Comprehensive ticket, including Alhambra and Generalife (below), 725ptas. ($5.10); Museo Bellas Artes, 250ptas. ($1.75); Museo Hispano-Musulman, 250ptas. ($1.75); illuminated visits, 725ptas. ($5.10). Mar–Oct, daily 9am–7:45pm, floodlit visits daily 10pm–midnight; Nov–Feb, daily 9am–5:45pm, floodlit visits daily 8–10pm. Bus: 2. Note: Crowds can be overwhelming at the Alhambra. Some visitors arriving after 10am might not be admitted until 1:30pm, and if you arrive after 4pm, there's a chance you won't get in at all.

The last remaining fortress-palace in Spain, built for the conquering caliphs of Islam, the Alhambra is a once-royal city surrounded by walls—it's actually a series of three interconnected palaces. You'll enter a world of *The Arabian Nights,* where sultans of old conducted state business, raised their families, and were entertained by their harems.

You may be surprised by its somewhat somber exterior. You have to walk across the threshold to discover the true delights of this Moorish palace. The most-photographed part is the Court of Lions, named after its highly stylized fountain. This was the heart of the palace, the most private section. Opening onto the court are the Hall of the Two Sisters, where the "favorite" of the moment was kept, and the Gossip Room, a factory of intrigue. In the dancing room in the Hall of Kings, entertainment was provided nightly to amuse the sultan's party.

You can see the room where Washington Irving lived (in the chambers of Charles V) while he was compiling his *Tales of the Alhambra.*

Charles V may have been horrified when he saw the cathedral placed in the middle of the great mosque at Córdoba, but he's responsible for his own architectural meddling here, building a Renaissance palace at the Alhambra; although it's quite beautiful, it's terribly out of place. Today, it houses the **Museo de la Bellas Artes en la Alhambra** (☎ **958-22-48-43**), devoted to painting and sculpture from the 16th to the 19th centuries, and the **Museo de l'Alhambra** (☎ **958-22-62-79**), which focuses more intensely on the region's breathtaking traditions of Hispanic-Muslim art and architecture. Both museums are open Monday to Saturday 9am to 2pm.

✪ **Generalife.** Alhambra, Cerro de Sol. ☎ **958-22-09-12.** Comprehensive ticket, including Alhambra and Generalife, 725ptas. ($5.10). For hours, see the Alhambra above.

The sultans used to spend their summers in this palace (pronounced "hay-nay-rahl-*ee*-fay"), safely locked away with their harems. Built in the 13th century to overlook the Alhambra, the Generalife's glory is its gardens and courtyards. Don't expect an Alhambra in miniature: The Generalife was always meant to be a retreat, even from the splendors of the Alhambra.

Catedral and Capilla Real. Plaza de la Lonja, Gran Vía de Colón 5. ☎ **958-22-29-59.** Admission to cathedral, 250ptas. ($1.75); chapel, 200ptas. ($1.40). Cathedral and chapel, daily 10:30am–1:30pm and 4–7pm (closes at 6:30pm in winter).

The richly ornate Spanish Renaissance cathedral, with its spectacular altar, is one of the country's great architectural highlights, acclaimed for its beautiful facade and gold-and-white decor. It was begun in 1521 and completed in 1714. Behind the cathedral (entered separately) is the flamboyant Gothic **Royal Chapel** where lie the remains of Isabella and Ferdinand. It was their wish to be buried in recaptured Granada, not Castile or Aragón. The coffins are remarkably tiny—a reminder of how short they must have been. Accenting the tombs is a masterful wrought-iron grill. Occupying much larger tombs are the remains of their daughter, Joanna the Mad, and her husband, Philip the Handsome. The Capilla Real abuts the cathedral's eastern edge.

Albaicín

This old Arab quarter, on one of the two main hills of Granada, doesn't belong to the city of 19th-century buildings and wide boulevards. It, and the surrounding Gypsy caves of Sacromonte, are holdovers from the past. The Albaicín once flourished as the residential section of the Moors, even after the city's reconquest, but it fell into decline when the Christians drove them out. This narrow labyrinth of crooked streets escaped the fate of much of Granada, which was torn down in the name of progress. Fortunately, its plazas, whitewashed houses, villas, and the decaying remnants of the old city gate have all been preserved. Here and there you can catch a glimpse of a private patio filled with fountains and plants, a traditional and graceful way of life that still flourishes today. To reach the Albaicín from the medieval and 19th-century center of Granada, take bus no. 7 to Calle de Pagés. Alternatively, you can hop aboard any of the small red-and-white buses marked ALBAICÍN that make runs at 15-minute intervals from the Plaza Isabel la Católica. The free buses operate daily from 7am to 11pm.

The Gypsy Caves of Sacromonte

The Gypsy Caves of Sacromonte, where gypsies have installed homes with kitchens, bedrooms, and living rooms, are a tourist trap, one of the most obviously commercial and shadowy rackets in Spain. Yet visitors seem to flock to them in spite of the warnings. It's safer to go on an organized tour. A visit to the caves is almost always included as part of the morning and (more frequently) afternoon city tours offered every day by such companies as **Grana Vision** (☎ **958-13-58-04**). A tour of Granada, including not only the caves but the cathedral, the monastery, the royal chapel, and the Albaicín, costs 4,000ptas. ($28) per person. Tours depart daily at 4:30pm, ending at 7pm. Night tours of the caves (when they're at their most eerie, evocative, and, unfortunately, larcenous) are usually offered only to those who can assemble 10 or more people into a group. Before agreeing to a tour, negotiate the price carefully.

THE SHOPPING SCENE

The **Alcaicería,** once the Moorish silk market, is next to the cathedral in the lower city. The narrow streets of this rebuilt village of shops are filled with vendors selling the arts and crafts of the province. The Alcaicería offers you one of Spain's most splendid assortments of tiles, castanets, and wire figures of Don Quixote chasing windmills. The jewelry found here compares favorably with the finest Toledan work. For the window shopper, in particular, it's a great place for a stroll.

Artesanía Albaicín (Tienda Eduardo Ferrer Lucena), Calle del Agua 19 (☎ 958-27-90-56), is one of the Arab Quarter's most enduring outlets for the intricately tooled leather for which Andalusia is famous. Also in the Arab quarter, **Céramica Aliatar,** Plaza de Aliatar 18 (☎ 958-27-80-89), is the place to head for a wide assortment of charming ceramic water and wine pitchers, serving platters, dinner plates, and garden pots.

WHERE TO STAY
Very Expensive

✪ **Parador Nacional de San Francisco.** Alhambra, 18009 Granada. ☎ **800-343-0020** in the U.S., or 958-22-14-40. Fax 958-22-22-64. 36 units. A/C MINIBAR TV TEL. 33,000ptas. ($231) double. AE, DC, MC, V. Free parking. Bus: 13.

Spain's most famous parador—and the hardest to get a room at—is housed in an old brick building with a new annex, set on the grounds of the Alhambra. The decor is tasteful, evoking a rich Andalusian past. The parador is a former convent founded by the Catholic monarchs immediately after they conquered the city in 1492. One side of the parador opens onto its own lovely gardens and the other fronts the Alhambra. From its terrace, you have views of the Generalife gardens and the Sacromonte caves. The rooms, generally spacious and comfortable, had their last major renovation in 1992, with subsequent upgrades.

Expensive

Hotel Alhambra Palace. Peña Partida 2, 18009 Granada. ☎ **958-22-14-68.** Fax 958-22-64-04. 132 units. A/C MINIBAR TV TEL. 20,500ptas. ($143.50) double; 31,000ptas. ($217) suite. AE, DC, MC, V. Free parking. Bus: 2.

Reminiscent of a Moorish fortress, complete with a crenellated roofline, a crowning dome, geometric tilework, and a suggestion of a minaret, this is Granada's best known and most dramatic hotel. Last renovated in 1996, it's one of the last grand palace hotels of Andalusia that hasn't been commandeered by an international chain. It's still owned by descendants of its original founders. It was built in 1910 in a sort of Mudéjar Revival style in a shady, secluded spot, midway up the slope to the Alhambra. The guest rooms don't live up to the richness of the public areas, which include an *Arabian Nights* dining room and a glassed-in dining terrace. Try for a room with a balcony opening onto a view of the Alhambra and the old city; the court rooms lack double-glazed windows and can be noisy at night. Many rooms are spacious and comfortable, but others are small and without much style. Ask to see the room before accepting it.

Moderate

Hotel América. Real de la Alhambra 53, 18009 Granada. ☎ **958-22-74-71.** Fax 958-22-74-70. 14 units. A/C TEL. 14,660ptas. ($102.60) double; 16,900ptas. ($118.30) suite. AE, DC, MC, V. Closed Dec–Feb. Bus: 2.

Located within the ancient Alhambra walls, this small hotel was built during the 19th-century administration of Napoléon's brother. Walk through the covered entry of this former villa into a shady patio that's lively yet intimate, with large trees, potted plants, and ferns. Other plants cascade down the white plaster walls and entwine with the ornate grillwork. Garden chairs and tables are set out for home-cooked Spanish meals. The living room of this intimate retreat is graced with a collection of regional decorative objects; some of the rooms have Andalusian reproductions. The rather small rooms are old-fashioned and homey, with comfortable beds and small bathrooms.

Hotel Rallye. Camino de Ronda 107, 18003 Granada. ☎ **958-27-28-00.** Fax 958-27-28-62. 79 units. A/C MINIBAR TV TEL. 15,800ptas. ($110.60) double. AE, DC, MC, V. Parking 1,400ptas. ($9.80). Bus: 1 or 5.

Some locals consider this one of the best hotels in town, and it's a relatively good value for the price. Built as a three-star hotel in 1964, it was thoroughly upgraded into a four-star choice in 1990. It's a 15-minute walk from the cathedral, on the northern perimeter of Granada's urban center. The rooms are comfortable and well maintained, and the in-house restaurant, the Rallye, serves very good meals.

Inexpensive

Hotel Residencia Cóndor. Constitución 6, 18012 Granada. ☎ **958-28-37-11.** Fax 958-28-38-50. 104 units. A/C TV TEL. 10,300–13,000ptas. ($72.10–$91) double. AE, DC, MC, V. Parking 1,300ptas. ($9.10). Bus: 6, 8, 9, or 10.

The attractive 1987 design of this hotel helps make it one of Granada's best in its price range. In 1997, following renovations, it was upgraded to four-star status. It's in the center of town, a 5-minute walk from the Alhambra and the cathedral. Many of the pleasant rooms have terraces, and all have light-grained contemporary furniture. The hotel's restaurant serves both Spanish and international cuisine, and there's also a cafeteria for snacks; room service is available 24 hours a day.

WHERE TO DINE

Cunini. Plaza de la Pescadería 14. ☎ **958-25-07-77.** Reservations recommended. Main courses 2,200–5,500ptas. ($15.40–$38.50); set-price menu 5,000ptas. ($35). AE, DC, MC, V. Tues–Sun noon–4pm and 8pm–midnight. SEAFOOD.

The array of seafood specialties offered here, perhaps a hundred selections, extends even to the tapas served at the long, stand-up bar. After a drink or two, patrons move on to the paneled ground-floor restaurant, where the cuisine reflects the whole of Spain. Meals often begin with soup, such as *sopa sevillana* (with ham, shrimp, and whitefish). Also popular is a deep fry of small fish called a *fritura Cunini*. Other specialties are rice with seafood, *zarzuela* (fish stew), smoked salmon, and grilled shrimp. Plaza de la Pescadería is adjacent to the Gran Vía de Colón, just below the cathedral.

Restaurante Sevilla. Calle Oficios 12. ☎ **958-22-12-23.** Reservations recommended. Main courses 1,000–3,000ptas. ($7–$21); set-price menu 2,500ptas. ($17.50). AE, DC, MC, V. Mon–Sat 1–4pm and 8–11pm; Sun 1–4pm. SPANISH/ANDALUSIAN.

Attracting a crowd of all ages, the Sevilla was the favorite restaurant of such hometown boys as García Lorca and Manuel de Falla. Our most recent meal included gazpacho, Andalusian veal, and caramel custard and fresh fruit. To break the gazpacho monotony, try *sopa virule*, made with pine nuts and chicken breasts. For a main course, we recommend the *cordero à la pastoril* (lamb with herbs and paprika). The best dessert is bananas flambé. You can dine inside, where it's pleasantly decorated, or on the terrace.

✪ **Ruta del Valleta.** Carretera de la Sierra Nevada, km 5.5, Cenés de la Vega. ☎ **958-48-61-34.** Reservations recommended. Main courses 2,500–3,200ptas. ($17.50–$22.40); set-price menus 4,000–7,000ptas. ($28–$49). AE, DC, MC, V. Mon–Sat 1–4:30pm and 8pm–midnight; Sun 1–4:30pm. ANDALUSIAN/INTERNATIONAL.

Despite its 1976 origins as an unpretentious roadhouse restaurant, this place rapidly evolved into what's usually acclaimed as the best restaurant in or around Granada. It's in the hamlet of Cenés de la Vega, about 3½ miles northwest of Granada's center. Inside are six dining rooms of various sizes, all decorated with a well-planned mix of English and Andalusian furniture and accessories. Menu items change with the seasons but are likely to include roast suckling pig, breast of duck in a sweet-and-sour sauce, roasted game birds such as pheasant and partridge (often served with Rioja wine sauce), and preparations of fish and shellfish.

GRANADA AFTER DARK

The best **flamenco** show in Granada is staged at the **Jardines Neptuno,** Calle Arabial (☎ **958-25-11-12**), nightly at 10:15pm. The acts are a bit racy, although they've been toned down. In addition to flamenco, performers attired in regional garb perform folk dances and present guitar concerts. The show takes place in a garden setting. There's a high cover charge of 3,500ptas. ($24.50), including your first drink. It's located about a mile south of the center; it's best to take a taxi here .

Several neighborhoods of Granada are lively at night. But as a university city, Granada attracts the most boisterous and fun crowds at the bars and pubs flanking **Calle Pedro Antonio de Alarcón,** running from Calle Perogidas to Plaza Albert Einstein. The street is also filled with disco bars and late-night pizza joints.

17

Sweden

by Darwin Porter & Danforth Prince

Although it was founded 7 centuries ago, Stockholm didn't become Sweden's capital until the mid-17th century. Today it's the capital of a modern welfare state with a strong focus on leisure activities and access to nature only a few minutes away.

Stockholm & Environs

Stockholm (pop. 1.4 million) is built on 14 islands in Lake Mälaren, marking the beginning of an archipelago of 24,000 islands, skerries, and islets that stretches all the way to the Baltic Sea. It's a city of bridges and islands, towers and steeples, cobblestoned squares and broad boulevards, Renaissance splendor and steel-and-glass skyscrapers. The medieval walls of Gamla Stan (the Old Town) no longer stand, but the winding streets have been preserved. You can even go fishing in downtown waterways, thanks to a long-ago decree from Queen Christina.

Once an ethnically homogeneous society, Stockholm has experienced a vast wave of immigration in the past several years. More than 10% of Sweden's residents are immigrants or children of immigrant parents, with most coming from other Scandinavian countries. Because of Sweden's strong stance on human rights, the country has also become a major destination for political and social refugees from Africa and the Middle East and the former Yugoslavia.

An important aspect of Stockholm today is a growing interest in cultural activities. Over the past 20 years, attendance at live concerts has grown, book sales are up, and more and more people are visiting museums.

Only in Stockholm

Experiencing Skansen This is the world's oldest open-air museum, where you can get a glimpse of Swedish life of days gone by. Be it butter churning or folk dancing, there's always something to amuse people of all ages as you wander the 75 acres of parkland.

Strolling Through Gamla Stan at Night It's like going back in time to walk the narrow cobblestone alleys of the Old Town at night. Most of the buildings are illuminated, and the look is almost that of a hollywood stage set rather than a real town. It takes little imagination to envision what everyday life must have been like in this "city between the bridges

Taking the Baths   Swedes, both men and women, are fond of roasting themselves on wooden platforms like chickens on a grill, and then plunging into a shower of Arctic-chilled water. After this experience, bathers emerge lighthearted and light-headed into the fresh northern air, fortified for an evening of revelry.

Watching the Summer Dawn   In midsummer at 3am, you can get out of bed, as many Stockholmers do, and sit out on balconies to watch the eerie blue sky—pure, crystal, exquisite. Gradually it's bathed in peach as the early dawn of a too-short summer day approaches. Locals don't like to miss a minute of their summer, even if they have to get up early to enjoy it.

Going Aboard the Royal Flagship *Vasa*   This recovered 17th-century man-of-war is Scandinavia's number-one sight-seeing attraction. The world's oldest identified and complete ship, it sank in 1628 in Stockholm harbor on its maiden voyage. It was raised from its seabed in 1961 after its discovery in 1956; the hull was found largely intact. Now restored to its former (but brief) glory, the *Vasa* is a monument to a vanished life—displaying everything from 700 original sculptures to sailor's pants in Lübeck gray.

Attending a Performance at Drottningholm   This 18th-century court theater was constructed for Queen Lovisa Ulrika in 1766 as a wedding present for her son, Gustavus III. Regrettably, he was assassinated at a masked ball in 1792 and the theater wasn't used. But in 1922 it was rediscovered, and now it has a season running from late May to early September. The original stage machinery and settings are still in use. Mozart is a perennial favorite here. *Tip:* The seats are hard, so take a cushion.

ORIENTATION

ARRIVING   By Plane   You'll arrive at **Stockholm Arlanda Airport,** about 28 miles north of Stockholm on the E-4 highway. A long, covered walkway connects the international and domestic terminals. For information on flights, call ☎ **08/797-61-00. SAS** (☎ **800/221-2350**) is the most common carrier, but **TWA** (☎ **800/221-2000** also flies daily from New York to Stockholm, and **American Airlines** (☎ **800/443-7300**) offers daily flights to Stockholm from Chicago. **Delta** (☎ **800/241-4141**) has daily flights to Stockholm from New York.

A **bus** outside the terminal building goes to the City Terminal, Klarabergsviadukten, in the city center every 10 to 15 minutes, for 60SEK ($7.70). It's about a 35-minute trip. For more information, call ☎ **08/600-10-00.** Or you can take the **Flight Taxi limousine service.** Go to the limousine-service desk in the arrivals hall at Arlanda; the limousine takes you to central Stockholm for 300 to 350SEK ($38.40 to $44.80). For advance reservations or information, call ☎ **08/ 686-10-10.** A taxi to or from the airport costs 435SEK ($55.70).

By Train   Trains arrive at Stockholm's **Centralstationen (Central Station)** on Vasagatan, in the city center (☎ **020/75-75-75**), where connections can be made to Stockholm's subway, the T-bana. Follow the sign marked TUNNELBANA.

By Bus   Buses arrive at the **Centralstationen** on Vasagatan, and from here you can catch the T-bana (subway) to your final Stockholm destination. For bus information or reservations in the Stockholm area, call the bus system's ticket offices at ☎ **08/440-85-70.** For information or reservations on buses departing Stockholm for other destinations, call ☎ **08/762-5997.** Ticket office hours are Monday through Friday and Sunday 9am to 6pm; Saturday 9am to 4pm.

By Car   Getting into Stockholm by car is relatively easy because the major national expressway from the south, E-4, joins with the national express highway E-3 coming in from the west and leads right into the heart of the city. Stay on the highway until you see the turnoff for Central Stockholm or Centrum.

Stockholm

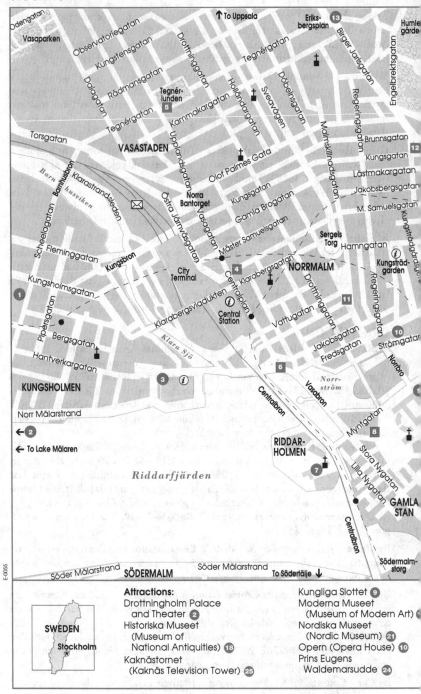

Attractions:

Drottningholm Palace and Theater ②
Historiska Museet (Museum of National Antiquities) ⑱
Kaknästornet (Kaknäs Television Tower) ㉕

Kungliga Slottet ⑨
Moderna Museet (Museum of Modern Art) ⑯
Nordiska Museet (Nordic Museum) ㉑
Opern (Opera House) ⑩
Prins Eugens Waldemarsudde ㉔

E-0055

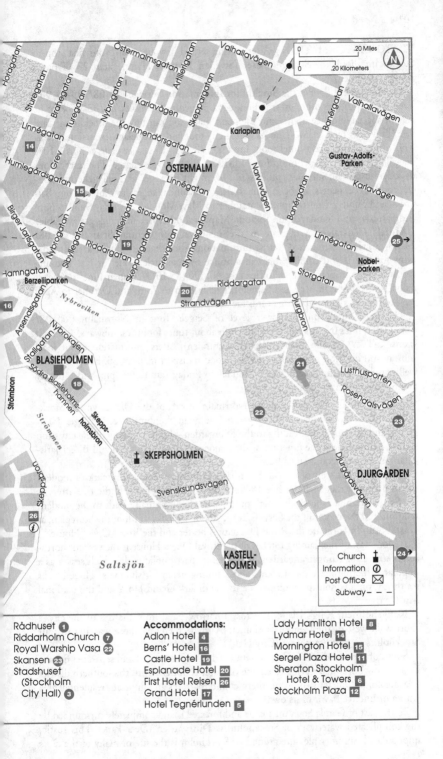

VISITOR INFORMATION   After getting settled in your room, your first stop in Stockholm should be **Sverige Huset (Sweden House),** Hamnagatan 27 (T-Bana: Kungsträdgården).

On the ground floor is the **Stockholm Information Service** (☎ 08/789-24-90). Even if you need no other information, get a free copy of *Stockholm This Week* for its lists of special and free events and the good map. You can buy the Stockholm Card (see "Traveler's Tip," below) here, as well as city tour and archipelago-excursion tickets. This office can reserve a hotel room for a 40SEK ($5.10) service charge, plus a 10% deposit, or a youth hostel room for a 15SEK ($1.90) service charge. The reservations desk can also book summer cottages and overnight packages and sell tickets to concerts and soccer games. It's open June to August, Monday to Friday 9am to 7pm, Saturday and Sunday 9am to 5pm; September to May, Monday to Friday 9am to 6pm and Saturday and Sunday 10am to 3pm. Maps and other free materials are available.

Hotell Centralen, Vasagatan in the main hall of Central Station (☎ 08/24-08-84), is an authorized tourist information office that also books accommodations for free if you contact them in advance by mail, telephone, or fax. Booking requests made in person at the office cost 40SEK ($5.10). It's open June to August daily 7am to 9pm; in May and September daily 8am to 7pm, and October to April 9am to 6pm. Credit and charge cards are accepted.

The **SL Center,** on the lower level of Sergels Torg in Norrmalm (☎ 08/686-11-97; if it's busy or you need only info about times for buses, subways, and local trains, call ☎ 08/686-10-00; T-bana: Centralen), offers information about local subway and bus transportation and sells a good transport map for 35SEK ($4.50), as well as tickets for the system. Open Monday to Friday 7am to 6:30pm, and Saturday and Sunday 10am to 5pm.

CITY LAYOUT   On the island of Norrmalm north of the Old Town are Stockholm's major streets, such as **Kungsgatan** (the main shopping street), **Birger Jarlsgatan,** and **Strandvägen** (leading to the Djurgården—home of many of the city's top sights). **Stureplan,** at the junction of the major avenues Kungsgatan and Birger Jarlsgatan, is the city's commercial hub.

About 4 blocks west of the Stureplan rises **Hötorget City,** a landmark of modern urban planning that includes five 18-story skyscrapers. Its main traffic-free artery is the **Sergelgatan,** a 3-block shopper's promenade that eventually leads to the modern sculptures in the center of the **Sergels Torg.** About 9 blocks south of the Stureplan, at **Gustav Adolfs Torg,** are the Royal Dramatic Theater and the Royal Opera House.

A block east of the flaming torches of the Royal Opera House is the verdant north-south stretch of **Kungsträdgården,** part avenue, part public park, which serves as a popular gathering place for students and a resting perch for shoppers. Three blocks southeast, on a famous promontory, lie the landmark Grand Hotel and the National Museum.

Kungsholmen, King's Island, is across a narrow canal from the rest of the city, a short walk west of the Central Station. It's visited chiefly by those wanting to tour Stockholm's elegant Stadshuset (City Hall).

South of the island where **Gamla Stan** (Old Town) is located and separated from it by a narrow but much-navigated stretch of water is **Södermalm,** the southern district of Stockholm. Quieter than its northern counterpart, it's an important residential area with a distinctive flavor of its own.

To the east of Gamla Stan, on a large and forested island completely surrounded by the complicated waterways of Stockholm, is **Djurgården** (Deer Park). This rustic, unpopulated, summer pleasure ground of Stockholm is the site of many of the city's

Costing just 199SEK ($25.45) for 1 day, 350SEK ($44.80) for 2 days, or 470SEK ($60.15) for 3 days, the **Stockholmskortet (Stockholm Card)** is a personal discount card that includes unlimited travel on Stockholm's public transport network (except airport buses), admission to most museums, and a guidebook to the city. You can also take a free sight-seeing tour with **City Sightseeing,** which allows you to get on and off as often as you choose, looking at the sights according to your own schedule. You get boat sight-seeing at half price, too, plus a one-way ticket to Drottningholm Palace. Cards are sold at the tourist information counter at Sweden House and at Hotell Centralen at Central Station, and each is valid for one adult and two children 17 and under.

most popular attractions: the open-air museums of Skansen, the *Vasa* man-of-war, Gröna Lund's Tivoli, the Waldemarsudde estate of the "painting prince" Eugen, and the Nordic Museum.

GETTING AROUND

Walking is the best way to get to know the city. In any case, you have to explore Gamla Stan on foot, as cars are banned from most of the streets. Djurgården and Skeppsholmen are other popular haunts for strolling.

BY SUBWAY (TUNNELBANA OR T-BANA)   Subways (called Tunnelbana or T-bana) and buses are operated by **SL,** the city transportation network, and charge according to a zone system—the price increases the farther you go. Most places you visit in central Stockholm cost 14SEK ($1.80), payable at the Tunnelbana and bus entrance. The subway system is fast, efficient, and far-reaching. Color-coded maps are on station walls and printed in most tourist publications. Timetables for each train are also posted. Subway entrances are marked with a blue *T* on a white background. For information about schedules, routes, and fares, call ☎ **08/600-10-00.**

One ticket costs 14SEK ($1.80) and is good for 1 hour (use it as often as you want), or you can get a strip of 20 coupons for 95SEK ($12.15). Your best transportation bet is to purchase a **tourist season ticket.** A 1-day card, costing 60SEK ($7.70), is valid for 24 hours of unlimited travel by T-bana, bus, and commuter train in Stockholm. It also includes passage on the ferry to Djurgården. Most visitors will probably want the 3-day card for 120SEK ($15.35), valid for 72 hours in both Stockholm and the adjacent county. The 3-day card is also valid for admission to Skansen, Kaknästornet, and Gröna Lund. Children under 18 pay 36SEK ($4.60) for a 1-day card or 72SEK ($9.20) for a 3-day card, but children up to age 7 can travel free with an adult. Tickets are sold at tourist-information offices, in subway stations, and at most news vendors. You can buy day passes at the SL center (see "Visitor Information," above).

If you're paying with cash or using a strip ticket, pass through the gate and tell the person in the ticket booth where you're going. He or she either asks for your fare or stamps your ticket. If you have a Stockholm Card, just flash it. Sometimes the ticket collector is absent; in these instances, few commuters wait for the collector to return—they just walk through.

BY BUS   A bus fills the need when the T-bana isn't convenient. The two systems have been coordinated to complement each other. Many visitors use a bus to reach Djurgården (although you can walk there), since the T-bana doesn't go there. Enter through the front door and pay the driver, show your Stockholm Card, or have your strip ticket stamped. For a list of bus routes, buy the *SL Stockholmskartan*, available for 42SEK ($5.40) at the Stockholm Information Service in the Sweden House or the SL Center (see "Visitor Information," above). Many buses depart from Normalmstorg, cater-corner to Kungsträdgården and 2 blocks from Sweden House.

BY FERRY Ferries run between Gamla Stan (near the bridge to Södermalm) and Djurgården year-round, providing the best link between these two. In summer, boats depart every 15 minutes 9am to midnight (to 10:40pm Sunday); in winter, daily 9am to 6pm. The ride costs 20SEK ($2.55) adults, half price for seniors and children 7 to 18. Passage is free for ages 6 and under. Ferries also run between Nybroplan and Djurgården (summer only) and between Slussen and Djurgården (year-round). Contact **Vaxholmsbolaget** (☎ 08/679-58-30) for more information.

An offbeat experience that you might want to try if you're fond of ocean voyages is the overnight ferryboats between Stockholm and Helsinki, across the Gulf of Bothnia. **Silja Line** (☎ 08/22-21-40), whose itineraries and prices are closely matched by **Viking Line** (☎ 08/452-40-00), operates ships that depart from both Stockholm and Helsinki every evening at 6pm; they pull into Helsinki or Stockholm after a 13½-hour east- or west-bound transit. If you opt to visit Helsinki from Stockholm for the day, you'll enjoy about 9 hours of touring the city before the departure of your ship back to Stockholm. Depending on the season, your cabin, and the day of the week, round-trip fares for two people sharing a cabin range from 1,570 to 3,800SEK ($200.95 to $486.40). Meals and drinks on board cost extra.

BY TAXI Taxis are expensive in Stockholm—in fact, they're among the most expensive in the world, with a double-tiered charge that applies both for the distance you travel and for the time your ride takes. The meter begins at 28SEK ($3.60); after that, the per-kilometer charge ranges from 6.60SEK (85¢) to 9.80SEK ($1.25), and the per-minute charge ranges from 4.60SEK (60¢) to 4.95SEK (65¢). Both of those variables depend on the time of day or night and the day of the week you travel, but the outcome is that taxi rides within Stockholm can easily cost as much as 100SEK ($12.80). If you're heading from anywhere in downtown Stockholm to Arlanda airport, there's a set-price charge of 435SEK ($55.70) that's valid for up to four passengers with their luggage. Taxis whose dome lights display the word *ledig* aren't otherwise engaged and can be hailed on the street. If you want to call for a taxi, the most reputable taxi companies include **Taxi Stockholm** (☎ 08/15-00-00 or 08/15-04-00), **Taxi Kurir** (☎ 08/30-00-00), and **Taxicard** (☎ 08/97-00-00). Note that there are some occasional independent, unmetered taxis within Stockholm, which tend to be frowned on by local authorities. If you opt to travel in one of them, negotiate a reasonable fare with the driver before leaving the curb.

BY CAR Each of the major car-rental firms is represented in Stockholm, including Avis and Hertz, both of which maintain offices at Arlanda Airport (**Hertz:** ☎ 08/797-9900; **Avis:** ☎ 08/797-9970) and in locations a few steps from Stockholm's main railway station. Hertz's downtown office is at Vasagatan 26 (☎ 08/240-720); Avis's downtown office is at Vasagatan 10B (☎ 08/20-20-60). Rentals at both organizations are usually cheaper if you reserve them by phone before leaving North America. For reservations and information within the United States and Canada, call Avis at ☎ 800/331-2112 or Hertz at ☎ 800/654-3001.

BY BICYCLE The best place to go cycling is on Djurgården. You can rent bicycles from **Skepp o Hoj,** Djurgårdsbron (☎ 08/660-57-57), for about 150SEK ($19.20) per day or 500SEK ($64) per week. A valid credit-card number is held on deposit on any bicycle rental. The shop is open May through August, daily 9am to 9pm.

Fast Facts: Stockholm

American Express American Express is at Norrlandsgatan 21 (☎ **08/ 679-78-80**), open Monday to Friday 9am to 6pm (until 5pm in winter) and Saturday 10am to 3pm (until 1pm in winter).

Currency You pay your way in Stockholm in Swedish Kr **(KR)** or crowns (singular **krona**), internationally abbreviated **SEK,** which are divided into 100 **öre.** Bills come in denominations of 10, 20, 50, 100, and 1,000KR. Coins are issued in 50 öre, as well as 1, 5, and 10KR. The exchange rate used in this chapter was $1 = 7.80SEK or 1SEK = 13¢. Also, 1EUR = 8.7SEK and £1 = 13.2SEK.

Dentists Emergency dental treatment is offered at **St. Eriks Hospital,** Fleminggatan 22 (☎ **08/654-11-17**), open daily 8am to 8pm.

Doctors If you need emergency medical care, check with **Medical Care Information** (☎ **08/644-10-00**). There's also a private clinic, **City Akuten,** at Hölländargartan 3 (☎ **08/412-29-61**).

Drugstores One 24-hour pharmacy is **C. W. Scheele,** Klarabergsgatan 64 (☎ **08/454-81-00**).

Embassies & Consulates The **U.S. Embassy** is at Strandvägen 101, 115 89 Stockholm (☎ **08/783-53-00**); the **British Embassy** (☎ **08/671-90-00**) is at Skarpögatan 6–8 (mailing address: P.O. Box 27819, 115 93 Stockholm); the **Canadian Embassy** is at Tegelbacken 4, 103 23 Stockholm (☎ **08/453-30-00**); the **Irish Embassy** (☎ **08/661-80-05**) is at Östermalmsgatan 97 (mailing address: P.O. Box 10326, 100 55 Stockholm); the **Australian Embassy** (☎ **08/613-29-00**) is at Sergels Torg 12 (mailing address: P.O. Box 7003, 103 86 Stockholm), and the **South Africa Embassy** is at Linnég 76, 115 00 Stockholm (☎ **08/24-39-50**). **New Zealand** doesn't maintain an embassy in Sweden.

Emergencies Call ☎ **90-000** anywhere in Sweden if you need an ambulance, the police, or the fire department.

Hospitals Call **Medical Care Information** at ☎ **08/463-91-00** and an English-speaking operator will inform you of the hospital closest to you.

Internet Access Stockholm's first Internet cafe is **Café Access,** Kulturhuset (☎ **08/700-01-53**), in the Stockholm Culture House in the heart of the city. It is open Monday 11am to 6pm, Tuesday to Thursday 11am to 7pm, Friday 11am to 6pm, Saturday and Sunday noon to 5pm. E-mail: cafe. accessexpressen.se.

Post Office The main post office is at Vasagatan 28–34 (☎ **08/781-20-00**), open Monday to Friday 8am to 6pm and Saturday 9am to 1pm. Mail can be sent % general delivery as follows: Post Restante, % Postens Huyudkontor (Main Post Office), Vasagatan 28–34, 10 430 Stockholm, Sweden.

Telephone The **country code** for Sweden is **46.** The **city code** for Stockholm is **8;** use this code when you're calling from outside Sweden. If you're within Sweden but not in Stockholm, use **08.** If you're calling within Stockholm, simply leave off the code and dial the regular phone number.

Instructions in English are posted in **public phone boxes,** which can be found on street corners. Very few phones in Sweden are coin operated; most require the purchase of a phone card (called a **Telekort**). You can get phone cards at most newspaper stands and tobacco shops.

You can make international calls from the **TeleCenter Office** on the Central Station's ground floor (☎ **08/456-74-94**), open daily 8am to 9pm, except major holidays. Long-distance rates are posted. To make a collect or calling-card call, dial one of the following access numbers to reach an American operator or an English-language voice prompt: **AT&T,** ☎ 020/795-611 (if calling a country other than the U.S., after the access code dial 01, the country code of the country you are calling, city code, and local number); **MCI,** ☎ 020/795-9222; and **Sprint,** ☎ 020/799-011.

For **directory assistance,** dial ☎ **0018.** For directory listings or other information for Stockholm or other parts of Sweden only, dial ☎ **07975;** for other parts of Europe, dial ☎ **07977.**

Transit Information   For information on all services, including buses and subways (Tunnelbana), even suburban trains (*pendeltåg*), call ☎ **08/689-10-00.** Or else visit the SL Center (see "Visitor Information," above) on the lower level of Sergels Torg. It provides information about transportation and also sells a map of the city's system, as well as tickets and special discount passes.

WHERE TO STAY

If you want to stay in a hotel convenient to your flight, there is nothing closer than the **Radisson SAS SkyCity Hotel,** Stockholm/Arlanda Airport, 190 45 Stockholm/Arlanda (☎ **08/59077300;** fax 08/59378100). With 230 modernized and tastefully styled bedrooms, it's right in the airport complex. As you check out of your hotel, you're virtually at the check-in for your flight, as this hotel lies midway between two of the busiest terminals (numbers 4 and 5) at the airport. Doubles cost 1,195SEK ($152.95) every Friday to Sunday; for any night in July the price is 1,895SEK ($242.55) each. There's also a bar, fitness center, and international restaurant.

Nearby, accessible from the main airport terminals via yellow-sided airport bus 14, but not accessible by covered walkway, is the SkyCity Hotel's twin, the nearly identical, 300-room **SAS Arlandia Hotel,** Bernstocksvägen 1, 190 45 Stockholm/Arlanda (☎ **08/59361-800;** fax 08/59361-970), charging comparable rates.

A silver shuttle bus marked **FLYGBUS** runs between the hotels and Stockholm's main railway station, and charges 60SEK ($7.70) per person each way.

IN THE CITY CENTER
Very Expensive

✪ **Grand Hotel.** Södra Blaisieholmshamnen 8, 103 27 Stockholm. ☎ **800/223-5652** in the U.S. and Canada, or 08/679-35-00. Fax 08/611-86-86. E-mail: guest@grandhotel.se. 321 units. MINIBAR TV TEL. 2,410–3,275SEK ($308.50–$419.20) double; 4,370–9,785SEK ($559.35–$1,252.50) suite. Rates include breakfast. AE, DC, MC, V. Parking 290SEK ($37.10). T-bana: Kungsträdgården. Bus: 46, 55, 62, or 76.

Traveler's Tip

Most European capitals experience high season in summer, when hordes of tourists arrive, but the situation is different in Stockholm. Although most tourists arrive in summer, the city's hotels are more dependent on business travelers than tourists. Consequently, hotels sometimes lower their prices when their business clients desert the capital in summer. Even during the busier winter season, hotels often lower prices on Friday, Saturday, and possibly Sunday nights, when most business travelers have packed up and headed for home. It always pays to ask if any discounts are being granted.

Opposite the Royal Palace, this hotel is grand indeed, the only five-star hotel in Sweden. Built in 1874, it has been continuously renovated (most recently in 1996), but its old-world style has been maintained. Rooms come in all shapes and sizes, but each is elegant, and some have air-conditioning. Pale-blue fabrics and light woods predominate, and the mattresses and level of comfort are the finest in town. The spacious bathrooms are decorated with Italian marble and tiles and have heated floors, fluffy towels, and hair dryers. The Grand Veranda specializes in traditional food served from a buffet, and the Franska Matsalen is the hotel's gourmet restaurant.

Expensive

Berns' Hotel. Näckströmsgatan 8, 111 47 Stockholm. ☎ **08/614-07-00.** Fax 08/566-32-201. 68 units. A/C MINIBAR TV TEL. 2,340–2,740SEK ($299.50–$350.70) double; from 3,240SEK ($414.70) suite. Rates include breakfast. AE, DC, MC, V. Parking 260SEK ($33.30). T-bana: Östermalmstorg.

During its 19th-century heyday, this was Sweden's most elegant hotel, with a lush gilded-age interior. In 1989, after years of neglect, the premises were rebuilt in their original style. The upstairs bedrooms are soundproofed and comfortably isolated from the activities downstairs. Bedrooms range from medium to spacious; each has a satellite TV, CD player, and a good-sized bathroom sheathed in Italian marble and containing such amenities as fluffy towels, hair dryers, a separate phone, and a makeup mirror. Some units are nonsmoking. The open-air terrace on the hotel's rooftop offers views over the city's historic core. The Salonger is the hotel's major restaurant.

Lydmar Hotel. Sturegatan 10, 114 36 Stockholm. ☎ **08/566-11-300.** Fax 08/566-11-301. E-mail: info@lydmar.se. 58 units. MINIBAR TV TEL. 1,700–1,950SEK ($217.60–$249.60) double; 2,600SEK ($332.80) junior suite. Rates include buffet breakfast. AE, DC, MC, V. Parking 250SEK ($32). T-bana: Östermalmstorg. Bus: 41, 46, 56, or 91.

Opposite the garden of the King's Library, in what looks like an office building, the Lydmar opened in 1930. The bedrooms (renovated in the mid-'90s) are cozy and traditionally furnished and come in many shapes and sizes, ranging from small singles to medium-sized doubles. They're exceptionally well maintained, with wool carpeting and tasteful Nordic furnishings. Mattresses are firm and frequently renewed, and bathrooms are state of the art, with a generous supply of good towels and adequate space. Both Swedish and international cuisines are served in the hotel's restaurant; there's a rooftop terrace where you can enjoy drinks in summer, and a popular lobby bar.

Sergel Plaza. Brunkebergstorg 9, 103 27 Stockholm. ☎ **800/THE-OMNI** in the U.S., or 08/22-66-00. Fax 08/21-50-70. E-mail: sergel.plaza.hotel@provobis.se. 418 units. A/C TV TEL. 1,950–2,800SEK ($249.60–$358.40) double; 6,500SEK ($832) suite. Rates include breakfast. AE, DC, MC, V. Parking 210SEK ($26.90). T-bana: Centralen. Bus: 47, 52, or 69.

This hotel at the entrance to Drottninggatan, the main shopping street, is one of the city's best. The elegant decor includes 18th-century artwork and antiques. It's a bastion of comfort and good taste, as reflected by the beautifully decorated bedrooms, which are generally spacious. All units contain firm mattresses, good double-glazed windows, and average-sized tiled bathrooms that are immaculately maintained, with plenty of soft towels and a hair dryer. Some rooms are nonsmoking, and some are wheelchair accessible. The Anna Rella gourmet restaurant offers both Swedish and international specialties. Facilities include saunas, solariums, and Jacuzzis.

Sheraton Stockholm & Towers. Tegelbacken 6, 101 23 Stockholm. ☎ **800/325-3535** in the U.S. and Canada, or 08/412-34-00. Fax 08/412-34-09. E-mail: sheraton-stockholm@ittsheraton.com. 470 units. A/C MINIBAR TV TEL. 1,200–2,650SEK ($153.60–$339.20) double; from 3,500SEK ($448) suite. Rates include breakfast. AE, DC, MC, V. Parking 160SEK ($20.50). T-bana: Centralen.

Across the street from Stockholm's City Hall, this hotel rises eight stories and is sheathed with Swedish granite. Short on charm, it is, however, excellent by chain hotel standards. The most recent upgrades were in 1996 and 1997. The bedrooms are the largest in the city; mirrored closets, one king or two double beds (good firm mattresses) with bedside controls, and medium-sized tile bathrooms with such amenities as hair dryers and fluffy towels add to the allure. Some units have bidets and all offer heated racks with plenty of fluffy towels. Most have sweeping views over the city. A pair of ethnic brasseries, Die Ecke and Le Bistro, serve German and French specialties, respectively.

Moderate

Castle Hotel. Riddargatan 14, 114 35 Stockholm. ☎ **08/679-57-00.** Fax 08/611-20-22. www.castle/hotel.se. E-mail: receptionen@castle/hotel.se. 49 units. TV TEL. 850–1,400SEK ($108.80–$179.20) double; 1,450–2,400SEK ($185.60–$307.20) suite. Rates include breakfast. AE, DC, MC, V. T-bana: Östermalmstorg.

In an expensive neighborhood a short walk east of the center, this house was originally constructed in 1920 as a private apartment building. The good-sized bedrooms are adorned with gilded accents and art deco accessories, twin beds with excellent mattresses are common throughout, and the tidy, medium-sized bathrooms have lots of towels and enough shelf room to spread out your stuff. Discounts are offered on certain weekends throughout the year.

Esplanade Hotel. Strandvägen 7A, 114 56 Stockholm. ☎ **08/663-07-40.** Fax 08/662-59-92. E-mail: hotel@esplanadesto.se. 34 units. TV TEL. 1,195–1,795SEK ($152.95–$229.75) double. Rates include breakfast. AE, DC, MC, V. T-bana: Östermalmstorg. Bus: 47 or 69.

This informal hotel was constructed in 1910 as a simple boarding house. The single rooms are minuscule, but the doubles, for the most part, are more spacious, with double-glazed windows, trouser presses, extra-long beds with comfortable mattresses, and medium-sized tiled bathrooms with a generous set of fluffy towels. Many rooms have minibars, and four have a water view. The English lounge has a balcony with a view of the Djurgården. Breakfast is the only meal served.

Mornington Hotel. Nybrogatan 53, 102 44 Stockholm. ☎ **800/528-1234** in the U.S., or 08/663-12-40. Fax 08/662-21-79. E-mail: mornington.hotel-sth@wmhotels.se. 141 units. TV TEL. June 26–Aug 9, 800SEK ($102.40) double; Aug 10–June 25, 1,595–1,695SEK ($204.15–$216.95) double; 1,800SEK ($230.40) suite. Rates include breakfast. AE, DC, MC, V. Closed Dec 23–26. Parking 150SEK ($19.20). T-bana: Östermalmstorg. Bus: 49, 54, or 62.

This efficiently modern establishment has a concrete exterior brightened with rows of flower boxes. Rooms, many quite small, are kept in tiptop shape, with excellent mattresses on their comfortable beds. The hotel offers nonsmoking rooms and units for guests with disabilities. Bathrooms are medium sized and tiled, although many have showers and no tubs. Each has a generous supply of medium-sized towels. The lobby is enhanced with a small rock garden and modern versions of Chesterfield armchairs. The hotel's sauna and Turkish bath are free, and the Restaurant Eleonora serves international and Swedish cuisine.

Stockholm Plaza. Birger Jarlsgatan 29, 103 95 Stockholm. ☎ **08/566-22-00.** Fax 08/566-22-020. E-mail: stockholm.plaza@elite.se. 151 units. TV TEL. 990–1,495SEK ($126.70–$191.35) double; 2,900SEK ($371.20) suite. Rates include breakfast. AE, DC, MC, V. Parking 185SEK ($23.70). T-bana: Hötorget or Östermalmstorg.

This is an inviting choice in the city center, which was upgraded into a first-class hotel in 1984. The small to medium-sized bedrooms have light, fresh interiors with firm beds, good wool carpeting, adequate desk space, and excellent lighting. The medium-sized tiled bathrooms are kept immaculately and provided with hair dryers and a generous supply of fluffy towels. On the premises is an elegant upscale French-style brasserie serving Gallic and Swedish specialties.

Inexpensive

Adlon Hotel. Vasagatan 42, 111 20 Stockholm. ☎ **08/402-65-00.** Fax 08/20-86-10. www.adlon.se. E-mail: hotel@adlon.se. 72 units. TV TEL. 525–1,330SEK ($67.20–$170.25) double. Rates include breakfast. AE, DC, MC, V. Parking 195SEK ($24.95). T-bana: Centralen.

Adlon Hotel was originally built in the 1890s, but a 1990 renovation created a more comfortable look, and improvements have been frequent ever since. The rather small but beautifully maintained bedrooms are comfortably furnished, with good carpeting, adequate desk space, and new mattresses. The bathrooms, although small, contain such amenities as hair dryers and medium-sized towels in generous supply. Some 70% of the bedrooms are designated for nonsmokers. Adlon is near the Central Station and subway and is convenient to buses heading for Arlanda Airport.

Hotel Tegnérlunden. Tegnérlunden 8, 113 59 Stockholm. ☎ **08/34-97-80.** Fax 08/32-78-18. E-mail: info.tegener@swedenhotels.se. 103 units. TV TEL. 760–1,120SEK ($97.30–$143.35) double. Rates include breakfast. AE, DC, MC, V. Parking 80SEK ($10.25). Bus: 47, 53, or 69 from the Central Station.

In a 19th-century building at the edge of a city park, this hotel's best feature is its tasteful rooms, each blissfully quiet, opening onto the rear. They come in a variety of sizes and shapes, with most on the small to medium side. Each is well maintained but furnished in a somewhat functional Scandinavian style evocative of a good motel. Nonetheless, you'll be comfortable here (especially on the excellent Swedish mattresses). Bathrooms, although tidy, are small with only adequate medium-sized towels. There's a sauna, too.

IN GAMLA STAN (OLD TOWN)

Expensive

⭘ **Lady Hamilton Hotel.** Storkyrkobrinken 5, 111 28 Stockholm. ☎ **08/23-46-80.** Fax 08/411-11-48. E-mail: info@lady-hamilton.se. 34 units. MINIBAR TV TEL. 1,350–1,990SEK ($172.80–$254.70) double. Rates include breakfast. AE, DC, MC, V. T-bana: Gamla Stan. Parking 220SEK ($28.15). Bus: 48.

This historic hotel on a quiet street scatters dozens of antiques in its medium-sized bedrooms, most of which rest under beamed ceilings. The beds have firm, frequently renewed mattresses. Bathrooms come in a variety of sizes, ranging from spacious to cramped. All, however, have heated racks with plenty of fluffy towels, heated floors, and a hair dryer, although only some have complete tub bathrooms (the rest offer showers). The top-floor rooms have skylights and memorable views, and some non-smoking rooms are available. Simple food, such as sandwiches, along with beer and wine, are served in the breakfast room throughout the day. There's also a sauna.

Moderate

First Hotel Reisen. Skeppsbron 12, 111 30 Stockholm. ☎ **08/22-32-60.** Fax 08/20-15-59. 114 units. MINIBAR TV TEL. 1,225–1,695SEK ($156.80–$216.95) double; from 2,500SEK ($320) suite. Rates include breakfast. AE, DC, MC, V. Bus: 43, 46, 55, 59, or 76.

This Old Town hotel facing the water has benefited from a 1997 renovation. Dating from the 17th century, the three-building structure attractively combines the old and the new. The medium-sized bedrooms are comfortably furnished and stylishly modern, although inspired by traditional Swedish design. Mattresses are frequently renewed, and bathrooms are generously sized and equipped with massaging shower-heads, scales, marble floors, heated towel racks, lots of fluffy towels, and a separate phone. Some nonsmoking units are available, and the top-floor accommodations open onto small balconies. The main restaurant is the warm and nautical Quarter Deck; the Clipper Club piano bar specializes in simple snacks.

WHERE TO DINE
IN THE CITY CENTER
Very Expensive

Operakällaren. Operahuset, Kungsträdgården. ☎ **08/676-58-00.** Reservations required. Main courses 260–310SEK ($33.30–$39.70); set-price menu 570SEK ($72.95) for 3 courses; 900SEK ($115.20) for 7-course *menu dégustation.* AE, DC, MC, V. Mon–Fri 11:30am–2pm and 5–11:30pm; Sat 11:30am–11:30pm; Sun 5–10pm. Closed July. T-bana: Kungsträdgarden. FRENCH/SWEDISH.

Opposite the Royal Palace, this is Sweden's most famous and luxurious restaurant. Its elegant classic decor and style are reminiscent of a royal court banquet at the turn of the century. Dress formally (the dress code is not strictly enforced, but men are encouraged to wear jackets and ties) to enjoy its impeccable service and house special-ties, including the platter of northern delicacies, with everything from smoked eel to smoked reindeer along with Swedish red caviar.

You might want to sip a drink in the Café Opera, with its magnificent crystal chan-deliers and a ceiling painted by Vicke Andrén, or smoke an after-dinner cigar in the new cigar bar. A glass-enclosed outer room has a lofty ceiling and is brightly sunlit during the day. After midnight, the cafe turns into a popular disco (see "Stockholm After Dark," below). There is also a cigar bar.

✪ **Paul & Norbert.** Strandvägen 9. ☎ **08/663-81-83.** Reservations required. Main courses 250–340SEK ($32–$43.50); 8-course *grand menu de frivolité* 1,050SEK ($134.40). AE, DC, MC, V. Mon–Fri noon–3pm and 5:30–10:30pm. Closed July and Dec 23–Jan 6. T-bana: Östermalmstorg. CONTINENTAL.

In a patrician residence dating from 1873, this is Stockholm's most innovative restau-rant. Seating only 30 people at nine tables, it has a vaguely art deco decor, with beamed ceilings and dark paneling. Owners Paul Beck and Norbert Lang worked in many of the top restaurants of Europe before opening this establishment. Lang's foie gras is the finest in town. Main courses, which change seasonally, tend to favor game and game birds; examples include juniper-marinated noisettes of reindeer with cheese, and escargot-filled breast of guinea fowl in rosemary sauce with garlic and onion. The seafood menu offers sole and salmon dishes along with a daily catch.

Wedholms Fisk. Nybrokajen 17. ☎ **08/611-78-74.** Reservations required. Main courses 235–360SEK ($30.10–$46.10); set-price lunch 220SEK ($28.15); set-price dinner 295SEK ($37.75). AE, DC, MC, V. Mon–Sat 5–11pm. Closed July. T-bana: Östermalmstorg. SWEDISH/FRENCH.

This is one of the classic—and one of the best—restaurants in Stockholm. Housed in an old Swedish building whose decor has been stripped down to its basics, it has no curtains in the windows and no carpets, but the display of modern paintings by Swedish artists is riveting. You might begin with marinated herring with garlic and bleak roe, or tartare of salmon with salmon roe. The chef has reason to be proud of such dishes as perch poached with clams and saffron sauce; prawns marinated in herbs and served with Dijon hollandaise; and grilled filet of sole with a Beaujolais sauce. For dessert, try the homemade vanilla ice cream with cloudberries. The cuisine is both innovative and traditional. How many places today would prepare a chevre mousse to accompany a simple tomato salad? (On the other hand, they dare serve grandmother's favorite: cream stewed potatoes.)

Expensive

Teatergrillen. Nybrogatan 3. ☎ **08/611-70-44.** Reservations recommended. Main courses 160–300SEK ($20.50–$38.40). AE, DC, MC, V. Mon–Fri 11:30am–2:30pm; Mon–Sat 5–11:30pm. Closed July. T-bana: Östermalmstorg. Bus: 46. SWEDISH/FRENCH.

Near the Royal Dramatic Theater, this restaurant is appropriately decorated with theatrical memorabilia. It's divided into two rooms—a small, windowless grill room and a spacious main room that's filled with fresh flowers and has views of the surrounding neighborhood. Many traditional, home-style Swedish dishes are offered at lunch. Each noon features a different specialty—perhaps sautéed fish in a tarragon sauce with rice or pork schnitzel with thyme-flavored fried potatoes. At dinner the cuisine is considerably upgraded with the likes of halibut with chanterelles in a curry sauce or pikeperch appearing with mussels in a citrus-flavored tomato broth. Increasingly, the chefs have become more innovative, offering such appetizers as deep-fried chicken in a peanut sauce accompanied by a coriander and mint salad.

Moderate

Akvarium. Kungsträdgården. ☎ **08/100-626.** Reservations recommended. Main courses 150–175SEK ($19.20–$22.40); set-price lunches 53–99SEK ($6.80–$12.65). AE, DC, MC, V. Mon–Fri 11:30am–2:30pm and 5pm–midnight; Sat–Sun 11:30am–midnight. T-bana: Kungsträdgården. CONTINENTAL.

Don't expect bubbling fishtanks as a background for this hip and stylish restaurant: Its name derives from its former incarnation as a seafood restaurant, not from any aquariums it contains. You'll find a bustling kitchen that's open to view, a bar dotted with colored lamps, and a big veranda that accommodates diners who appreciate the light of midsummer. Menu items include "duck espresso" that consists of breast of duck with port wine sauce and plums; veal saltimbocca (with ham); tagliatelle with mussels, clams, and squid ink; grilled butterfish with pesto sauce; and an all-vegetarian version of ravioli stuffed with porcini mushrooms.

✪ **Eriks Bakfica.** Fredrikshovsgatan 4. ☎ **08/660-15-99.** Reservations recommended. Main courses 100–230SEK ($12.80–$29.45); 3-course entrecôte dinner 210SEK ($26.90). AE, DC, MC, V. Mon–Fri 11:30am–11pm; Sat 5–11pm; Sun 4–10pm. Bus: 47. SWEDISH.

Although there are other restaurants here bearing the name Eriks, this one is relatively moderate and offers particularly good value. It features two dining rooms. One is a small, bustling bistro with a bar and background music; the main dining room is quieter, with muted yellow walls and antique wooden furnishings. The menu features a handful of Swedish dishes from the tradition of *husmanskost* (wholesome home cooking). There's a daily choice of herring appetizers. Main courses include grilled char with lobster sauce, and grilled veal schnitzel with mushrooms and a red wine sauce. We suggest you try the archipelago stew, a ragôut of fish flavored with tomatoes and served with garlic mayonnaise. If none of these strike your fancy, stick to the cheeseburger with a special secret sauce.

KB Restaurant. Smålandsgatan 7. ☎ **08/679-60-32.** Reservations recommended. Main courses 150–255SEK ($19.20–$32.65); set-price lunch 150SEK ($19.20); set-price dinner 175SEK ($22.40). AE, DC, MC, V. Mon–Fri 11:30am–11pm, Sat 5–11:30pm; bar Mon–Sat 11:30am–midnight. Closed June 23–Aug 7. T-bana: Östermalmstorg. SWEDISH/CONTINENTAL.

This has been a traditional artists' rendezvous since opening on New Year's Eve, 1931. It still features the original dark wood furniture; the dark red and green color scheme and wall-to-wall carpeting were added more recently. Located in the center of town, KB offers good Swedish cookery as well as continental dishes. The fish dishes are especially recommended. You might begin with any of a number of herring starters followed by baked North Sea cod with broad beans and lobster in lemon sauce, or perhaps fried pigeon with onion marmalade, potato terrine, and currant-pepper sauce.

Inexpensive

✪ **Bakfickan.** Jakobs Torg 12. ☎ **08/676-58-09.** Reservations not accepted. Main courses 85–149SEK ($10.90–$19.05). AE, DC, MC, V. July, Mon–Sat 5–11:30pm; Aug–June, Mon–Sat 11:30am–11:30pm. T-bana: Kungsträdgården. SWEDISH.

Tucked away in the back of the swanky Operakällaren restaurant (see above), the "Hip Pocket" is a chic place to get a moderately priced meal. It's a small art nouveau room, and its features have been meticulously maintained since 1904. There's seating for 30 diners at tables surrounding a horseshoe-shaped bar. Although it's located within the Operakällaren, it has its own kitchen and a separate menu. Main courses might include grilled marinated filet of cod with mustard sabayon, or perhaps sautéed roulades of pork stuffed with Swedish cheese in cider sauce and served with mashed vegetables and lingonberries. You'll always find salmon butterfly with béarnaise sauce and fried parsley, or thinly sliced beef tenderloin with horseradish, egg yolk, and mashed potatoes.

Lisa Elmquist. Östermalms Saluhall, Nybrogatan 31. ☎ **08/660-92-32.** Reservations recommended. Main courses 100–165SEK ($12.80–$21.10). AE, DC, MC, V. Mon 10am–6pm; Tues–Fri 9am–6pm; Sat 9am–3pm. T-bana: Östermalmstorg. SEAFOOD.

Under the soaring roof and amid the food stalls of Stockholm's produce market (the Östermalms Saluhall) sits this likable cafe/oyster bar. The menu varies daily according to the catch, but might include fried monkfish with scampi and mixed vegetables, and boiled lemon sole with tarragon sauce and trout roe. Some people just order a portion of shrimp with bread and butter for 85 to 115SEK ($10.90 to $14.70). On Saturday, when only the bar is open, only cold and raw seafood items are available.

Prinsens. Mäster Samuelsgatan 4. ☎ **08/611-13-31.** Reservations recommended. Main courses 100–210SEK ($12.80–$26.90); set-price lunch 85SEK ($10.90). AE, DC, MC, V. Mon–Sat 11am–10:30pm; Sun 5–9:30pm. T-bana: Östermalmstorg. SWEDISH.

A 2-minute walk from the Stureplan, this favorite haunt of artists has been feeding people since 1897. Diners are seated on one of two levels, and in summer some tables are placed outside. The cuisine is fresh and flavorful and includes daily dishes and traditional Swedish menu items such as veal patty with homemade lingonberry preserves, sautéed fjord salmon, and roulades of beef. The most popular item on the menu is a filet of beef, served with fried potatoes and onions, marinated cucumbers, and egg yolk and mayonnaise on the side. For dessert, try the homemade vanilla ice cream.

IN GAMLA STAN (OLD TOWN)
Very Expensive
Eriks. Österlånggatan 17. ☎ **08/23-85-00.** Reservations required 2 days in advance. Main courses 262–338SEK ($33.55–$43.25); luncheon plates 75–125SEK ($9.60–$16); 10-course *menu dégustation* 1,050SEK ($134.40). AE, DC, MC, V. Mon–Fri 11:30am–11pm; Sat 1–11pm. Closed July and Dec 25–Jan 1. T-bana: Gamla Stan. FRENCH.

This restaurant, which occupies two floors of a building dating from the 1600s in the Old Town, has a warmly autumnal color scheme and English country-house decor. It's the domain of Erik Lallerstedt, one of the great master chefs of Stockholm. You can select from such appetizers as a warm lobster salad with leeks, tomatillos, and a lobster dressing, or perhaps goose-liver terrine with truffle soufflé. The chef's top specialty is fried duckling served in two courses—the breast in cider sauce is followed by the leg in green-pepper sauce. Fish selections include the catch of the day, or perfectly prepared lobster, turbot, and halibut with a chervil-and-champagne sauce, accompanied by wild rice.

Expensive
Den Gyldene Freden. Österlånggatan 51. ☎ **08/24-97-60.** Reservations recommended. Main courses 98–265SEK ($12.55–$33.90). AE, DC, MC, V. Mon–Sat 6–11pm. Closed July 2–Aug 2, bank holidays. T-bana: Gamla Stan. SWEDISH.

The "Golden Peace" is Stockholm's oldest tavern, opened in 1722. Its building is owned by the Swedish Academy, and members frequent the place on Thursday night.

The cozy dining rooms, named for Swedish historic figures, are divided between the rooms of the traditional 18th-century pub and the medieval cellar vaults below. You get good traditional Swedish cooking here, and the chefs are especially fond of fresh Baltic fish and game from the forests of Sweden. Specials include roast reindeer in juniperberry sauce with a timbale of black grouse; fried sole served with lemon, horseradish, and butter; and breast of pigeon and leg of guinea hen stuffed with duck liver and asparagus in sherry sauce.

Fem Små Hus. Nygrånd 10. ☎ **08/10-87-75.** Reservations required. Main courses 195–245SEK ($24.95–$31.35). AE, DC, MC, V. Tues–Sat 5pm–midnight; Sun–Mon 5–11pm. T-bana: Gamla Stan. SWEDISH/FRENCH.

This historic restaurant, whose cellars date from the 17th century, is furnished like the interior of a private castle, with European antiques and oil paintings. It is actually five houses built together, and has a total of nine dining rooms. After being shown to a candlelit table somewhere in the labyrinthine interior, you can order seasonal classic Swedish cuisine—fried filet of reindeer served with a juniperberry sauce, half an artichoke filled with vegetable ragôut, and a French potato gratinée. The most popular dish on the menu, named after a woman who at one time ran a speakeasy in the cellars of these buildings, is veal Anna Lynberg, in a morel cream sauce flavored with gorgonzola. Fish dishes include fresh salmon slightly oven-baked, then served in a Chablis sauce with fresh asparagus, trout caviar, and boiled potatoes, or grilled turbot with ratatouille and basil butter.

Moderate
Cattelin Restaurant. Storkyrkobrinken 9. ☎ **08/20-18-18.** Reservations recommended. Main courses 90–200SEK ($11.50–$25.60); set-price lunch (Mon–Fri 11am–2pm only) 50SEK ($6.40). AE, DC, MC, V. Mon–Fri 11am–10pm; Sat–Sun noon–10pm. T-bana: Gamla Stan. SWEDISH.

Don't expect genteel service at this boisterous restaurant where the clattering of china can be almost deafening at times. Opened in 1927, the restaurant has been deemed a historic property by the government. Furniture, paintings—everything but the paint—is part of the original decor. Economical menu items include fried brill with mushrooms and pressed potatoes, sliced beef with mushrooms and fried potatoes, and Swedish meatballs. The swordfish with lobster sauce, filet mignon black and white, and trout with white wine sauce and spinach are other options.

SEEING THE SIGHTS
Everything from the *Vasa* Ship Museum to the changing of the guard at the Royal Palace to the Gröna Tivoli amusement park will keep you intrigued. Even just window shopping for well-designed Swedish crafts can be a great way to spend an afternoon.

SIGHTSEEING SUGGESTIONS FOR FIRST-TIME VISITORS
If You Have 1 Day   Take a ferry to Djurgården to visit the **Royal Warship *Vasa,*** Stockholm's most famous attraction, and to explore the open-air **Skansen** folk museum. In the afternoon, walk through **Gamla Stan** (Old Town) and have dinner at one of its restaurants.

If You Have 2 Days   On day 2, get up early and visit the **Kaknästornet** TV tower for a panoramic view of Stockholm, its many islands, and the archipelago. Go to the **Nordic Museum** for insight into 5 centuries of life in Sweden. After lunch, visit the **Millesgården** of Lidingö, the sculpture garden and former home of Carl Milles.

If You Have 3 Days   Spend your third morning walking through the center of Stockholm and doing some shopping. At noon (1pm on Sunday), return to Gamla Stan to see the **changing of the guard at the Royal Palace.** View this French-inspired building that has been the residence of Swedish kings for more than 700 years. In the afternoon, see the attractions at the **National Museum.**

If You Have 4 or 5 Days On day 4, take one of the many tours of the **Stockholm archipelago.** Return to Stockholm and spend the evening at the **Gröna Tivoli** amusement park on Djurgården. On your last day, visit **Drottningholm Palace** and its 18th-century theater. In the afternoon, explore the university town of **Uppsala,** north of Stockholm, easily reached by public transportation.

THE TOP ATTRACTIONS
At Djurgården

✪ **Royal Warship *Vasa*.** Galärvarvet, Djurgården. ☎ **08/666-48-00.** Admission 50SEK ($6.40) adults, 30SEK ($3.85) students, 10SEK ($1.30) children 7–15, free for children under 7. June 10–Aug 20 daily 9:30am–7pm; Aug 21–June 9 Wed 10am–8pm, Thurs–Tues 10am–5pm. Closed Jan 1, May 1, and Dec 24–25 and 31. Bus: 44 or 47. Ferry from Slussen all year, from Nybroplan in summer only.

This 17th-century man-of-war is the number-one attraction in Scandinavia—and for good reason. Housed in a museum specially constructed for it at Djurgården near Skansen, the *Vasa* is the world's oldest identified and complete ship.

In 1628, on its maiden voyage and in front of thousands of horrified onlookers, the Royal Warship *Vasa* capsized and sank almost instantly to the bottom of Stockholm harbor. When it was salvaged in 1961 more than 4,000 coins, carpenters' tools, and other items of archaeological interest were found on board. Best of all, 97% of the 700 original sculptures were retrieved. Carefully restored and preserved, they're back aboard the ship, which looks stunning now that it once again carries grotesque faces, lion masks, fish-shaped bodies, and other carvings, some with their original paint and gilt.

✪ **Skansen.** Djurgården 49–51. ☎ **08/442-80-00.** Admission 30–55SEK ($3.85–$7.05) adults, 10SEK ($1.30) children 7–14, free for children under 7. Historic buildings, May–Aug daily 11am–5pm; Sept–Apr daily 11am–3pm. Bus: 47 from central Stockholm. Ferry from Slussen to Djurgården.

Often called "Old Sweden in a Nutshell," this 75-acre open-air museum, near Gröna Lund's Tivoli, contains more than 150 dwellings, most from the 18th and 19th centuries. Exhibits range from a windmill to a manor house to a complete town quarter. Browsers can explore the old workshops and see where the early book publishers, silversmiths, and pharmacists plied their trades. Handcrafts (glass blowing, for example) are demonstrated here, along with peasant crafts such as weaving and churning. Folk dancing and open-air symphonic concerts are also featured.

Nordiska Museet (Nordic Museum). Djurgårdsvägen 6–16, Djurgården. ☎ **08/666-46-00.** Admission 60SEK ($7.70) adults, 50SEK ($6.40) seniors, 30SEK ($3.85) students, 10SEK ($1.30) children 7–15, free for children under 7. Tues–Sun 11am–5pm. Bus: 44, 47, or 69.

This museum houses an impressive collection of implements, costumes, and furnishings of Swedish life from the 1500s to the present. Highlights are period costumes ranging from matching garters and ties for men to purple flowerpot hats from the 1890s. In the basement is an extensive exhibit of the tools of the Swedish fishing trade, plus relics from nomadic Lapps.

Prins Eugens Waldemarsudde. Prins Eugens Väg 6, Djurgården. ☎ **08/662-18-33.** Admission 50SEK ($6.40) adults, 30SEK ($3.85) students and seniors, free for children under 17. June–Aug Tues and Thurs 11am–8pm, Wed and Fri–Sun 11am–5pm; Sept–May Tues–Sun 11am–4pm. Bus: 47 to the end of the line.

The Changing of the Royal Guard

Even the most hurried traveler will want to see the **changing of the Royal Guard.** You can watch the parade of the military guard daily in summer and on Wednesday and Sunday in winter (on all other days, you can see only the changing of the guard). The parade route on weekdays begins at Sergels Torg and proceeds along Hamngatan, Kungsträdgårdsgatan, Strömgatan, Gustav Adolfs Torg, Norrbro, Skeppsbron, and Slottsbacken. On Sunday the guard departs from the Army Museum, going along Riddargatan, Artilerigatan, Strandvägen, Hamngatan, Kungsträdgårdsgatan, Strömgatan, Gustav Adolfs Torg, Norrbro, Skeppsbron, and Slottsbacken. For information on the time of the march, ask at the Information Service in the Sweden House (see "Visitor Information," above). The actual changing of the guard takes place at noon Monday to Saturday (at 1pm on Sunday) in front of the Royal Palace in Gamla Stan.

This once-royal residence is today an art gallery and a memorial to one of the most famous royal artists in recent history, Prince Eugen (1865–1947). The youngest of King Oscar II's four children, he was credited with making innovative contributions to the techniques of Swedish landscape paintings, specializing in depictions of his favorite regions in central Sweden. Among his most visible works are the murals on the inner walls of the Stadshuset.

On Gamla Stan & Neighboring Islands

✪ **Kungliga Slottet (Royal Palace).** Kungliga Husgeradskammaren (☎ **08/402-61-32** for Royal Apartments and Treasury; ☎ **08/666-42-50** for Royal Armoury; ☎ **08/402-61-30** for Museum of Antiquities. Royal Apartments, 45SEK ($5.75) adults, 25SEK ($3.20) students, 10SEK ($1.30) children 7–18. Royal Armoury, 40SEK ($5.10) adults, 30SEK ($3.85) students, 15SEK ($1.90) children. Museum of Antiquities, 30SEK ($3.85) adults, 20SEK ($2.55) students. Treasury 40SEK ($5.10) adults, 25SEK ($3.20) seniors and students. Children under 7 are admitted free to all. Apartments and Treasury, July–Aug daily 10am–4pm, Sept–June Tues–Sun noon–3pm. Royal Armoury, year-round Tues–Sun 11am–4pm, May 1–Aug 30 Mon 11am–4pm. Royal Apartments off-limits during official government receptions. Museum of Antiquities, June–Aug daily 10am–4pm, Sept–May daily noon–3pm. T-bana: Gamla Stan. Bus: 43, 46, 59, or 76.

Severely dignified, even cold-looking, on the outside, this palace has a lavish interior designed in the Italian baroque style. Kungliga Slotta is one of the few official residences of a European monarch that's open to the public. Although the Swedish king and queen prefer to live at Drottningholm, this massive 608-room showcase, built between 1691 and 1754, remains their official address.

The most popular rooms include the **State Apartments;** look for at least three magnificent baroque ceiling frescoes and fine tapestries. In the building's cellar is the **Stattkammaren (Treasury),** the repository for Sweden's crown jewels. Most intriguing to any student of war and warfare is the **Royal Armoury,** whose entrance is on the castle's rear side, at Slottsbacken 3. Gustavas III's collection of sculpture from the days of the Roman Empire can be viewed in the **Antikmuseum** (Museum of Antiquities).

Riddarholm Church. Riddarholmen. ☎ **08/402-61-30.** Admission 20SEK ($2.55) adults, 10SEK ($1.30) students and children. May and Sept Wed and Sat–Sun noon–3pm; June–Aug daily noon–4pm. Closed Oct–Apr. T-bana: Gamla Stan.

The second-oldest church in Stockholm is on the tiny island of Riddarholmen, next to Gamla Stan. It was founded in the 13th century as a Franciscan monastery. Almost all the royal heads of state are entombed here, except for Christina, who is buried in Rome. There are three principal royal chapels, including one—the Bernadotte wing—that belongs to the present ruling family.

In the City Center

Historiska Museet (Museum of National Antiquities). Narvavägen 13–17. ☎ **08/ 783-94-00.** Admission 60SEK ($7.70) adults, 50SEK ($6.40) seniors and students, 35SEK ($4.50) children 7–15, free for children under 7. Apr–Sept Tues–Sun 11am–5pm; Oct–Mar Tues–Sun 11am–5pm (until 8pm on Thurs). T-bana: Karlaplan or Östermalmstorg. Bus: 44, 47, 54, 56, 69, or 76.

If you're interested in Swedish history, especially the Viking era, here you'll find the nation's finest repository of relics left by those legendary conquerors who once terrorized Europe. Many relics have been unearthed from ancient burial sites. The collection of artifacts ranges from prehistoric to medieval times, including Viking stone inscriptions and coins minted in the 10th century. The Gold Room features authentic Viking silver and gold jewelry, large ornate charms, elaborate bracelet designs found nowhere else in the world, and a unique neck collar from Färjestaden.

National Museum (National Museum of Fine Arts). Blasieholmskajen. ☎ **08/519- 54-300.** Admission 60SEK ($7.70) adults, 40SEK ($5.10) seniors and students, free for children under 16. Tues and Thurs 11am–8pm; Wed and Fri–Sun 11am–5pm. T-bana: Kungsträdgården. Bus: 46, 62, 65, or 76.

At the tip of a peninsula, a short walk from the Royal Opera House and the Grand Hotel, is Sweden's state treasure house of paintings and sculpture, one of the oldest museums in the world. The first floor is devoted to applied arts (silverware, handcrafts, porcelain, furnishings), but first-time visitors might want to head directly to the second floor where the painting collection contains works by Rembrandt and Rubens, Lucas Cranach's most amusing *Venus and Cupid,* and a rare collection of Russian icons from the Moscow School of the mid-16th century. The most important room in the gallery has one whole wall devoted to Rembrandt—*Portrait of an Old Man* and *Portrait of an Old Woman,* along with his *Kitchen Maid.*

Moderna Museet (Museum of Modern Art). Skeppsholmen. ☎ **08/519-55-200.** Admission 60SEK ($7.70) adults, 40SEK ($5.10) seniors and students, free for children 15 and under. Tues–Thurs 11am–10pm; Fri–Sun 11am–6pm. T-bana: Rådmansgatan. Bus: 65 to Skeppsholmen.

This museum focuses on contemporary works by Swedish and international artists, including kinetic sculptures. Highlights are a small but good collection of cubist art by Picasso, Braque, and Léger; Matisse's *Apollo* découpage; the famous *Enigma of William Tell* by Salvador Dalí; and works by Brancusi, Max Ernst, Giacometti, and Arp, among others.

Stadshuset (Stockholm City Hall). Hantverkargatan 1. ☎ **08/785-90-74.** Admission 30SEK ($3.85) adults, seniors, students; free for children under 12. Tower, May–Sept daily 10am–4pm. City Hall tours (subject to change), June–Sept daily at 10am, 11am, noon, and 2pm; Oct–May daily at 10am and noon. T-bana to Central Station or Rådhuset. Bus: 48 or 62.

Built in what's called the "National Romantic Style," the Stockholm City Hall, on the island of Kungsholmen, is one of Europe's finest examples of modern architecture. Designed by Ragnar Ostberg, the red-brick structure is dominated by a lofty square tower 348 feet high, topped by three gilt crowns and the national coat-of-arms. The Nobel Prize banquet takes place here in the Blue Hall. About 18 million pieces of gold and colored mosaics made of special glass cover the walls, and the southern gallery contains murals by Prince Eugen, the painter prince.

Just Outside Stockholm

✪ **Drottningholm Palace and Theater.** Ekerö, Drottningholm. ☎ **08/402-62-80.** Palace, 40SEK ($5.10) adults, 20SEK ($2.55) students and people under 26. Theater, 40SEK ($5.10) adults, 10SEK ($1.30) students and people under 26. Chinese Pavilion, 40SEK ($5.10) adults, 10SEK ($1.30) students and people under 26. All 3 are free for children under 16. Palace, May daily 11am–4:30pm, June–Aug 10am–4:30pm, Sept noon–3:30pm; closed Oct–Apr. Theater, guided tours in English, May–Aug 12:30, 1:30, 2:30, 3:30, and 4:30pm, and Sept 1:30, 2:30, and 3:30pm; closed Oct–Apr. Chinese Pavilion, May–Aug 11am–4:30pm, Sept noon–3:30pm, Oct 1–3:30pm; closed Nov–Mar. All hours are daily. There are two ways of reaching Drottningholm. The first is by steamboat, which takes 50 min. and costs 75SEK ($9.60) round-trip adults or 50SEK ($6.40) children 6–11. Boats leave from Stadshusbron, beside Stockholm's City Hall, daily, early June to mid-Aug on the hour 10am–4pm and at 6pm and May to early June and mid-August to early September 10am–2pm (to 4pm on weekends). Contact **Strömma Kanalbolaget** at **08/23-33-75** (fax 08/20-50-31) for more information. **Stockholm Sightseeing** (☎ **08/24-04-70**) offers round-trips to Drottningholm in turn-of-the-century boats. You can also take the T-bana to Brommaplan, and then connect to any Mälarö bus for Drottningholm.

Originally conceived as the centerpiece of Sweden's royal court, this regal complex of stately buildings sits on an island in Lake Mälaren. Dubbed the "Versailles of Sweden," Drottningholm, or Queen's Island, is about 7 miles west from Stockholm. The palace—loaded with courtly art and furnishings—is surrounded by fountains and parks, and still functions as one of the official residences of the country's royal family. On the grounds is one of the most perfectly preserved 18th-century theaters in the world, **Drottningholm Court Theater** (☎ **08/759-04-06**), with 30 annual performances (mostly 18th-century operas) between May and September. The theater seats only 450, and performances often sell out long in advance. (For ticket information, see "Stockholm After Dark," below.)

✪ **Millesgården.** Carl Milles Väg 2, Lidingö. ☎ **08/446-75-90.** Admission 50SEK ($6.40) adults, 35SEK ($4.50) seniors and students, 15SEK ($1.90) children 7–16, free for children under 7. May–Sept, daily 10am–5pm; Oct–Apr, Tues–Sun noon–4pm. T-bana to Ropsten and a bus from there to Torsviks torg or a train to Torsvik.

On the island of Lidingö, northeast of Stockholm, is Carl Milles's former villa and sculpture garden beside the sea, now a museum. Many of his best-known works are displayed here (some are copies), as are works of other artists. Milles (1875–1955), who relied heavily on mythological themes, was Sweden's most famous sculptor.

A VIEW ON HIGH

Kaknästornet (Kaknäs Television Tower). Ladugårdsvägen 60. ☎ **08/789-24-35.** Admission 20SEK ($2.55) adults, 12SEK ($1.55) children 7–15, free for children under 7. May–Aug daily 9am–10pm; Sept–Apr daily 10am–9pm. Closed Dec 24–25. Bus: 69 from Central Station.

The tallest man-made structure in Scandinavia, this radio/television tower stands 508 feet high. Two elevators take visitors to an observation platform, where you can see everything from the cobblestoned streets of the Old Town to the city's modern concrete-and-glass structures and the archipelago beyond.

AN AMUSEMENT PARK

Gröna Lunds Tivoli. Djurgården. ☎ **08/670-76-00.** Admission 40SEK ($5.10) adults, free for children under 13. Apr–Aug daily noon–11pm or midnight (hours are subject to change; call for exact hours). Bus: 44 or 47. Djurgården ferry from Nybroplan.

Unlike its Copenhagen namesake, this is an amusement park, not a fantasyland. For those who like Coney Island–type thrills, it's a good nighttime adventure.

ORGANIZED TOURS

Stockholm Sightseeing (☎ 08/24-04-70) operates 3-hour bus tours of Stockholm year-round, leaving daily from the Opera House at 2pm, and also at 5pm mid-April to early October. The cost is 220SEK ($28.15) for adults and half price for children 6 to 11. From early June to early August, 1-hour tours leave from the Opera House at 10 and 11am, noon, and 2 and 3pm; the cost is 125SEK ($16) for adults and half price for children 6 to 11. Ask about the combination excursions that include walking, touring by bus, and/or taking a boat.

Also offered are boat tours of the city, departing from Strömkajen, in front of the Grand Hotel. (Locals insist that the best way to explore their city is by boat.) Get tickets at the kiosk topped with yellow flags with a red *S* on them. The company's "Under the Bridges of Stockholm" tour takes 2 hours and costs 130SEK ($16.65) for adults and half price for children 6 to 15; it's offered mid-April to mid-December. The hour-long "Royal Canal Tour" runs mid-May to early September for 80SEK ($10.25).

THE SHOPPING SCENE

A whopping 25% goods tax makes shopping in Sweden expensive, and you can get most items at home for less money. On the positive side, Swedish stores usually stock items of the highest quality. Favorite buys include crystal, clothing, and Scandinavian-design furniture.

For the best shopping and window-shopping, stroll along the streets of **Gamla Stan** (especially **Västerlånggatan**), filled with boutiques, art galleries, and jewelry stores. Attractive shops and galleries can also be found along the **Hornsgats-Puckeln** (the Hornsgatan-Hunchback, a reference to the shape of the street), on **Södermalm.** Other good browsing streets are **Hamngatan, Birger Jarlsgatan, Biblioteksgatan,** and **Kungsgatan,** all in **Norrmalm.**

Blås & Knåda, Hornsgatan 26 (☎ 08/642-77-67; T-bana: Slussen), sells the products of a cooperative of 50 Swedish ceramic artists and glassmakers. Prices begin at 160SEK ($20.50) for small functional pieces, and go way up for museum-quality works of art.

Bone china, stoneware dinner services, and other fine table and decorative ware are made at **Keramiskt Centrum Gustavsberg** (Gustavsberg Ceramics Center; ☎ 08/570-356-58; bus: 422 or 24400), on Värmdö Island, about 13 miles east of Stockholm.

In the center of Stockholm, the largest department store in Sweden is **Åhlesns City,** Klarabergsgatan 50 (☎ 08/676-60-00; T-bana: T-Centralen), with a gift shop, restaurant, and famous food department. Also seek out the fine collection of home textiles and Orrefors and Kosta crystal ware. **Nordiska Kompanient,** NK for short, at

Traveler's Tip

Many stores offer tax rebates to visitors spending over 200SEK ($25.60). When you make your purchase, ask the retailer for a Tax Free Check (valid for 1 month) and leave your purchase sealed until you leave the country. At any border crossing on your way out of Sweden (or at repayment centers in Denmark, Finland, or Norway), show both the check (to which you've added your name, address, and passport number) and the purchase to an official at the tax-free desk. You'll get a cash refund of about 16% to 18% in U.S. dollars (or seven other currencies) after the service charge has been deducted (remember not to check the purchase in your luggage until after you receive the refund). For more information, call ☎ 0410/613-01.

Hamngatan 18–20 (☎ **08/762-80-00;** T-bana: Kungsträdgården), is another high-quality department store. Most of the big names in Swedish glass are displayed at NK, including Orrefors (see the Nordic Light collection) and Kosta. Swedish handcrafted items are in the basement. Stainless steel is also a good buy in Sweden. Greta Garbo got her start in the millinery department at **PUB,** Hötorget 13 (☎ **08/239-915;** T-bana: Hötorget), a popular department store that sells middle-bracket clothing and good-quality housewares.

At **Loppmarknaden I Skärholmen (Skärholmen Shopping Center),** Skärholmen (☎ **08/710-00-60;** T-bana: 13 or 23 to Skärholmen, a 20-minute ride), the biggest flea market in northern Europe, you might find *anything.* Try to go on Saturday or Sunday (the earlier the better) when the market is at its peak. Weekend admission is 10SEK ($1.30), but weekdays are free.

Geocity, Tysta Marigången 5, Tegélbacken (☎ **08/411-11-40;** T-bana: T-Centralen), offers exotic mineral crystals, jewelry, Scandinavian gems, Baltic amber, and lapidary equipment. Its staff includes two certified gemologists who can cut and set any gem you select, as well as appraise jewelry you already own. Its inventory includes stones from Scandinavia and around the world, including Greenland, Madagascar, Siberia, and South America.

An unusual outlet, **Slottsbodarna (Royal Gift Shop),** in the south wing of the Royal Palace, Slottsbacken (☎ **08/402-60-48;** T-bana: Gamla Stan), sells items related to or copied from the collections in the Royal Palace, re-created in silver, gold, brass, pewter, textiles, and glass. Every item is made in Sweden.

Svensk Hemslojd (Society for Swedish Handcrafts), Sveavägen 44 (☎ **08/ 23-21-15;** T-bana: Hötorget), has a wide selection of glass, pottery, gifts, and wooden and metal handcrafts, the work of some of Sweden's best artisans. You'll also see a display of handwoven carpets, upholstery fabrics, tapestries, lace, and embroidered items; you can even find beautiful yarns for your own weaving and embroidery.

STOCKHOLM AFTER DARK

Pick up a copy of *Stockholm This Week,* distributed at the Stockholm Information Service in the Sweden House (see "Visitor Information," above), to see what's on.

THE PERFORMING ARTS

All the major opera, theater, and concert performances begin in autumn, except for special summer festival performances. Fortunately, most of the major opera and theatrical performances are funded by the state, which keeps the ticket price reasonable.

✪ **Drottningsholm Slottsteater.** Drottningholm. ☎ **08/660-82-25.** Tickets 100–470SEK ($12.80–$60.15). T-bana: Brommaplan.

Founded by King Gustavus III in 1766, this unique theater stands on an island in Lake Mälaren, 7 miles from Stockholm. It stages operas and ballets with full 18th-century regalia, complete with period costumes and wigs. The theater, a short walk from the royal residence, seats only 450 patrons, which makes tickets hard to come by. Eighteenth-century music performed on antique instruments is a perennial favorite. The season is May through September and most performances begin at 7:30pm, lasting 2½ to 4 hours. Tickets should be ordered at least 2 months in advance by phoning the number above and giving your American Express card number (only American Express is accepted).

Filharmonikerna I Konserthuset (Concert Hall). Hötorget 8. ☎ **08/10-21-10** or 08/457-02-11. Tickets 110–400SEK ($14.10–$51.20). T-bana: Hötorget.

Home of the **Stockholm Philharmonic Orchestra,** this is the principal place to hear classical music in Sweden. (The Nobel Prizes are also awarded here). Constructed in 1920, the building houses two concert halls—one, seating 1,600, is better suited for major orchestras; the other, seating 450, is suitable for chamber music groups. Box office hours are Monday through Friday noon to 6pm, Saturday 11am to 3pm.

Operan (Royal Opera House). Gustav Adolfs Torg. ☎ **08/24-82-40.** Tickets 100–400SEK ($12.80–$51.20); many tickets are discounted 10%–20% for seniors and students. T-bana: Kungsträdgården.

Founded in 1773 by King Gustavus III, who was assassinated here at a masked ball, the Operan is the home of the **Royal Swedish Opera** and the **Royal Swedish Ballet.** The present building dates from 1898. Performances are usually Monday through Saturday at 7:30pm (closed mid-June to August). The box office is open Monday through Friday noon to 7:30pm (closes at 6pm if no performance is scheduled) and Saturday noon to 3pm.

LOCAL CULTURAL ENTERTAINMENT

Skansen. Djurgården 49–51. ☎ **08/442-80-00.** Admission 55SEK ($7.05) adults, 10SEK ($1.30) children 7–14, free for children under 7. Bus: 44 or 47, or Djurgården ferry lines.

Skansen arranges traditional seasonal festivities, various special events, autumn market days, and a Christmas Fair. In summer there are concerts, sing-alongs, and guest performances. Folk-dancing performances are staged June through August, Monday through Saturday at 7pm and Sunday at 2:30 and 4pm. Live music accompanies outdoor dancing June through August, Monday through Friday 8:30 to 11:30pm.

NIGHTCLUBS

Café Opera. Operahuset, Kungsträdgården. ☎ **08/676-58-07.** Cover free before 11pm, 80SEK ($10.25) after 11pm. T-bana: Kungsträdgården.

This cafe—Swedish beaux arts at its best—functions as a bistro, brasserie, and tearoom during the day and as one of the most popular nightclubs in Stockholm at night. (Don't confuse this spot with the opera's main dining room, the Operakällaren, whose entrance is through a different door). Near the entrance of the cafe is a stairway leading to one of the Opera House's most beautiful corners, the clublike Operabaren (Opera Bar). It's open Monday to Saturday 11:30am to 3am and Sunday 1pm to 3am.

Göta Källare. In the Medborgplatsen subway station, Södermalm. ☎ **08/642-08-28.** Cover 55SEK ($7.05) before 9:30pm; 85SEK ($10.90) after 9:30pm. T-bana: Medborgplatsen.

This is the largest and most successful supper-club–style dance hall in Stockholm, with a long list of clients who have met here, and subsequently fallen in love and gotten married. Large, echoing, and paneled with lots of wood in a *faux-espanol* style, it has a restaurant and a large terrace that surrounds an enormous tree. Expect a crowd of people aged 45 and older, and music from a live orchestra (performing *Strangers in the Night* a bit too frequently). The place is open every night from 8:30pm.

ROCK & JAZZ CLUBS

Fasching. Kungsgatan 63. ☎ **08/21-62-67.** Cover 90–225SEK ($11.50–$28.80). T-bana: T-Centralen.

Some of Sweden's and the world's best-known jazz musicians regularly play here. It's so small, you almost feel like you're in the band. Weekend late nights are for dancing, and after midnight on Friday there's salsa; Saturday late is dedicated to soul. Hours can be irregular, so it's best to call in advance, but it's usually open nightly from 7pm to at least 2am.

Hard Rock Café. Sveavägen 75. ☎ **08/16-03-50.** No cover.

The Swedish branch of this chain is fun and gregarious. Sometimes an American, British, or Scandinavian band gives a live concert; otherwise, it's the sound system. Club sandwiches, hamburgers, T-bone steaks, and barbecued spareribs are available. Open Sunday to Thursday from 11am to 1am and Friday and Saturday from 11am to 3am.

Pub Engelen/Nightclub Kolingen. Kornhamnstorg 59B. ☎ 08/20-10-92. Cover after 8pm to pub and nightclub, Sun–Thurs 40SEK ($5.10), Fri–Sat 60SEK ($7.70). T-bana: Gamla Stan.

This three-in-one combination consists of the Engelen Pub, the Restaurant Engelen, and the Nightclub Kolingen in the cellar. The restaurant, which serves some of the best steaks in town, is open Sunday to Thursday 5 to 11:30pm and Friday to Saturday 5pm to 1:30am. Swedish groups (mostly) perform live in the pub daily from 8:30pm to midnight—usually soul, funk, and rock. The pub is open Tuesday to Thursday 4pm to 1am, Friday and Saturday 4pm to 2am, and Sunday 5pm to 1am. In the cellar (which dates from the 15th century), the Nightclub Kolingen is a disco nightly from 10pm to about 3am. You must be 23 or over to enter.

Stampen. Stora Nygatan 5. ☎ **08/20-57-93.** Cover 50–100SEK ($6.40–$12.80). T-bana: Gamla Stan.

The name of this club is an informal Swedish term for a pawnshop—an appropriate name since this place is crammed full of an eclectic mix of secondhand items. The club is mainly a hangout for jazz and blues lovers who come to hear the sounds of live bands playing Dixieland, swing, blues, and soul. In summer an outdoor veranda is open when the weather permits. The club has two stages, with dancing upstairs and downstairs almost every night. Hours are Monday 8pm to midnight, Tuesday 8pm to 12:30am, Wednesday and Thursday 8pm to 1am, Friday 8pm to 2am, and Saturday 1 to 5pm and 8pm to 2am.

BARS

One of the hippest and most talked-about bars in Stockholm, **Tiger Bar/Havana Bar,** 18 Kungsgatan (☎ **08-244-700;** T-bana: Östermalmstorg), attracts a bevy of super-models and TV actors. It's divided into a street-level site (the Tiger Bar) that's outfitted in black leather upholstery and a postmodern kind of cool, and a basement-level re-creation of pre-Castro Cuba (the Havana Bar) that's outfitted with plastic palms and the deliberately garish colors associated with Old Havana's most raunchy 1950s-era excesses. You're likely to hear anything from recorded disco (every Friday and Saturday beginning at midnight) to live salsa and merengue (every Wednesday from 9pm to 5am). The place is open Wednesday and Thursday 7pm to 3am, and Friday and Saturday 7pm to 4am.

Named after the builder of the deluxe Grand Hotel, the **Cadier Bar,** Södra Blasieholmshamnen 8 (☎ **08/679-35-00;** T-bana: Kungsträdgården), offers a view of the harbor and Royal Palace. It's one of the most sophisticated places for a rendezvous in Stockholm. You can also enjoy light meals at any time of day in the extension over-looking the waterfront. Open Monday to Saturday noon to 2am and Sunday noon to 12:30am; a piano player performs Monday to Saturday 9:30pm to 1:30am.

If you're gay, consider slugging back a round or two at **Sidetrack,** Wollmar Yxkulls-gatan 7 (☎ **08/641-1688;** T-bana: Mariatorget). Small and committed to shunning any semblance of trendiness, it was named after its founder's favorite gay bar in Chicago. It's open every night from 6pm to 1am. Tuesdays here seem to be something of an institution in gay Stockholm. Other nights, however, it's fine too—something like a Swedish version of a bar and lounge at your local bowling alley where everyone happens to be into same-sex encounters.

DAY TRIPS FROM STOCKHOLM

SKOKLOSTER CASTLE **Skokloster,** 746 96 Skokloster (☎ **018/38-60-77**), is a splendid 17th-century castle and one of the most interesting baroque museums in Europe. It's next to Lake Mälaren, 40 miles west of Stockholm and 31 miles south of Uppsala. Original interiors aside, the castle is noted for its rich collections of paintings, furniture, applied art, tapestries, arms, and books. Admission is 60SEK ($7.70) for adults, 50SEK ($6.40) for seniors, and 30SEK ($3.85) for students and children. Guided tours are conducted May through August every hour from 11am to 4pm daily; in September at noon daily; and in April and October at noon on Saturday and Sunday only. The site is completely closed November through March.

Skokloster Motor Museum (☎ **018/38-61-00**), on the palace grounds, contains the largest collection of vintage automobiles and motorcycles in the country. One of the most notable cars is a 1905 8-horsepower De Dion Bouton. Unlike the castle, the museum is open all year. It costs 40SEK ($5.10) for adults, 10SEK ($1.30) for children 7 to 14, and it's free for children under 7. It's open May through September daily, 11am to 5pm, and October through April on Saturday and Sunday, 11am to 5pm.

Getting There   From Stockholm, take a train to the hamlet of Bålsta, 12 miles from the castle. At the village train station, you can either take bus no. 894 directly to Skokloster or call for a taxi from a direct telephone line that's prominently positioned just outside the railway station.

UPPSALA   The major university city of Sweden, Uppsala, 42 miles northwest of Stockholm, is the most popular destination of day-trippers from Stockholm, and for good reason. Uppsala has not only a great university, but also a celebrated 15th-century cathedral. Even in the time of the Vikings, it was a religious center, the scene of animal and human sacrifices in honor of the old Norse gods, and was once the center of royalty as well. Queen Christina occasionally held court here. The church is still the seat of the archbishop, and the first Swedish university was founded here in 1477.

Getting There   You can easily reach the town by train in about 45 minutes from Stockholm's Central Station. Trains leave about every hour during the peak daylight hours. Boats from Stockholm to Uppsala (or vice versa) also stop at Skokloster and Sigtuna. Check with the tourist office in Stockholm or Uppsala for details.

Visitor Information   The **Tourist Information Office** is at Fyris Torg 8 (☎ **018/ 27-48-00**), open Monday through Friday 10am to 6pm and Saturday 10am to 3pm.

Exploring Uppsala   At the end of Drottninggatan is the **Carolina Rediviva (University Library)** (☎ **018/471-00-00;** bus: 6, 7, or 22), with its more than 5 million volumes and 40,000 manuscripts, among them many rare works from the Middle Ages. But the manuscript that really draws visitors is the *Codex Argenteus* (Silver Bible), translated into the old Gothic language in the middle of the 3rd century and copied in about A.D. 525. It's the only book extant in the old Gothic script. Also worth seeing is *Carta Marina,* the earliest map (1539), a fairly accurate map of Sweden and its neighboring countries. Admission is free. The library's exhibition room is open Monday through Friday 9am to noon.

Linnaeus Garden and Museum, Svartbäcksgatan 27 (☎ **018/13-65-40** for the museum, or 018/10-94-90 for the garden; walk straight from the rail station to Kungsgatan, and go for about 10 minutes to Svartbäcksgatan), is the former home of Swedish botanist Carl von Linné. Von Linné, known as Carolus Linnaeus, developed a classification system for the world's plants and flowers. This museum is on the spot where he restored Uppsala University's botanical garden, which resembles a miniature baroque garden. Linnaeus's detailed sketches and descriptions of the garden have been faithfully followed. Admission to the museum is 20SEK ($2.55) for adults and free for children. Admission to the gardens is 10SEK ($1.30) for adults and free for children under 12. The gardens are open May to August daily 9am to 9pm and September daily 9am to 7pm. The museum is open June to mid-September, Tuesday through Sunday noon to 4pm.

The largest cathedral in Scandinavia at nearly 400 feet tall, the twin-spired Gothic ✪ **Uppsala Domkyrka,** Domkyrkoplan 5 (☎ **018/18-72-01;** bus: 1 and 2), was founded in the 13th century. It was severely damaged in 1702 in a disastrous fire that swept over Uppsala, and then was restored near the turn of this century. Among the regal figures buried in the crypt is Gustav Vasa. The remains of St. Erik, patron saint of Sweden, are entombed in a silver shrine. Botanist Linnaeus and philosopher-theologian Swedenborg are also buried here. A small museum displays ecclesiastical relics of Uppsala. Admission to the cathedral is free; museum admission is 20SEK ($2.55) for adults and 10SEK ($1.30) for children 7 to 15 (free for children under 7). The cathedral is open daily from 8am to 6pm.

✪ **GRIPSHOLM CASTLE** On an island in Lake Mälaren, Gripsholm Castle (Gripsholm Slottsfervaltning), P.O. Box 14, 64721 Mariefred (☎ **0159/101-94**)— the fortress built by Gustavus Vasa in the late 1530s—is one of the best-preserved castles in Sweden. It lies near Mariefred, an idyllic small town known for its vintage narrow-gauge railroad.

Even though Gripsholm was last occupied by royalty (Charles XV) in 1864, it's still a royal castle. Its outstanding features include a large collection of portrait paintings depicting obscure branches of the Swedish monarchy, its brooding architecture, and its 18th-century theater built for the amusement of the 18th-century actor-king Gustavus III. It's open May to August, daily 10am to 4pm; in April and September, Tuesday to Friday 10am to 3pm and Saturday and Sunday 10am to 3pm; October to March, only on Saturday and Sunday from noon to 3pm. Admission is 40SEK ($5.10) for adults and 20SEK ($2.55) for children under 12.

Getting There The castle is 42 miles southwest of Stockholm, easily reached by the E-20 south or by taking the fast X-2000 train from Stockholm's main railway station for a 35-minute ride. In summertime, you might also opt to take a ferryboat from Stockholm's Klara Malarstrand Pier, near Stadshuset. Your best best is to take one of the ferries that departs every Monday to Friday at 10am for an arrival at Mariefred at 1:30pm. It's a 5-minute stroll from the Mariefred pier to the castle.

18 Switzerland

by Darwin Porter & Danforth Prince

Switzerland evokes images of towering peaks, mountain lakes, lofty pastures, and alpine villages, but it also offers a rich cultural life in cities such as sophisticated Geneva and perfectly preserved medieval Bern.

1 Geneva

Geneva is in the Rhône Valley at the southwestern corner of Lake Geneva (Lac Léman in French), between the Jura Mountains and the Alps. It's the capital of the canton of Geneva, the second-smallest canton in the Swiss confederation.

Switzerland's second-largest city is truly cosmopolitan. The setting is idyllic, on one of the biggest alpine lakes and within view of the glorious pinnacle of Mont Blanc. Filled with parks and promenades, the city becomes a virtual garden in summer. It's also one of the world's healthiest cities because the prevailing north wind blows away any pollution.

The yachts bobbing in the harbor and the Rolls-Royces cruising the promenades testify that Geneva is home to some of the richest people in the world. Its state religion is said to be banking—half of Switzerland's are located here.

Geneva has long held a position as a center of enlightenment and humane tolerance. Over the years it has offered a refuge to such controversial figures as Voltaire, Lenin, and native son Jean-Jacques Rousseau. Geneva also hosted Knox and Calvin, the religious reformers, and provided a safe haven for many artists. Today the headquarters of the International Red Cross and the World Health Organization are here, and it attracts many other international organizations.

At the end of the '90s, the traditional role of Swiss tolerance came under increasing attack, as more and more revelations exposed Switzerland's wartime role as a banker of Nazi gold. In August of 1998 large Swiss banks agreed to pay $1.25 billion to Holocaust survivors for pain and suffering they endured. Sadly, studies have shown that this move has led to a rise in anti-Semitism in Switzerland, although it seems more prevalent in the German-speaking west than in the French-speaking eastern part of the country.

Only in Geneva

Tasting Wine in the Countryside   Winding your way through the rolling vineyards just outside Geneva makes for a lovely day's outing. Many of the best Swiss wines never leave the country, and grapes grow on slopes overlooking Lake Geneva and the Rhône. Pick up the "Discover Geneva and Its Vineyards" brochure from the tourist office and set out.

Sailing Lake Geneva   The crescent-shaped lake gives Geneva a resortlike ambience. In summer it hums with activity—and you can join in the fun.

Wandering Through Old Town   Geneva's Vieille Ville has been called Europe's best-kept secret. Exploring its ancient streets brings you to art galleries, antiques shops, booksellers, and tiny bistros. Follow the Grand' Rue, where Jean-Jacques Rousseau was born, and wander back into time.

Discovering Les Pâquis District   One of Geneva's most animated and elegant districts, Les Pâquis faces the harbor from the Right Bank. To reach it, head north along quai des Bergues, which leads into quai du Mont-Blanc. On your left, at the intersection of quai du Mont-Blanc and Gare Routière, stands the Brunswick Monument, the tomb of Charles II of Brunswick, who died in Geneva in 1873. Les Pâquis boasts cozy bistros, nightclubs, ateliers, boutiques, and banks. After wandering through the district, you can tour Lake Geneva in one of the steamers leaving from quai du Mont-Blanc.

Seeing the Fountain & the Flower Clock   There are no two more delightful sights in Geneva. The Jet d'Eau on quai Gustave-Ador is the city's trademark. Visible for miles from April through September, it throws water 460 feet into the air above the lake. The Genevese call the fountain the *jeddo*. It dates from 1891 but was improved in 1951. Many cities have sent engineers here to study the secret workings of the fountain, but it remains a carefully guarded secret. The fountain pumps 132 gallons of water per second into the air. The Flower Clock in the Jardin Anglais (English Garden), another Geneva landmark, is directly off quai Général-Guisan. Its face is made of beds of flowers, and it keeps perfect time!

Following in the Footsteps of Rousseau   In the middle of the Rhône, the lovely Ile Rousseau boasts a statue of the philosopher sculpted by Pradier in 1834. Rousseau's former stamping ground, and the site of many of his reveries, is now home to ducks, swans, grebes, and other aquatic fowl. Rousseau was born in Geneva on June 28, 1712, and he became one of the controversial figures of his era, advocating a "return to nature" to escape the corruption of civilization. His writings helped pave the way for the French Revolution, and he's the father of the Romantic movement.

ORIENTATION

ARRIVING   By Plane   The **Geneva-Cointrin Airport** (☎ **022/717-71-11**), although busy, is compact and easily negotiated. **Swissair** (☎ **800/221-4750** in the U.S.) has the most frequent flights from North America to Geneva. **American Airlines** (☎ **800/433-7300**) makes daily nonstop flights from Chicago to Zurich, where planes fly frequently into Geneva. Connections can also be made on **United Airlines** (☎ **800/241-6522**) with a daily nonstop flight from Washington to Zurich with a connection to Geneva. Finally, **Air Canada** (☎ **800/776-3000**) flies nonstop daily from Toronto to Zurich, where passengers then wing their way to Geneva on one of several frequent flights.

Geneva

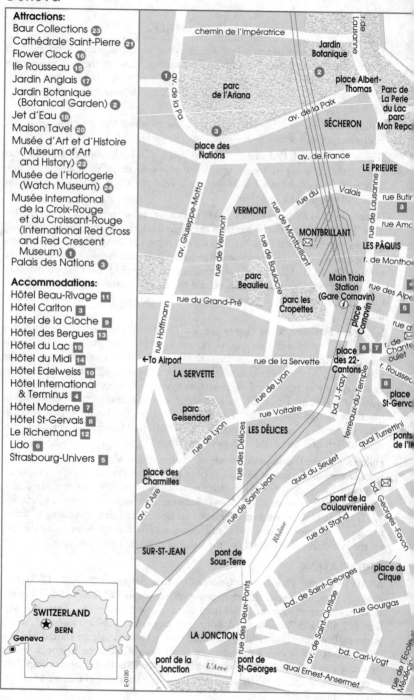

Attractions:
Baur Collections ㉓
Cathédrale Saint-Pierre ㉑
Flower Clock ⑯
Ile Rousseau ⑮
Jardin Anglais ⑰
Jardin Botanique
(Botanical Garden) ②
Jet d'Eau ⑱
Maison Tavel ⑳
Musée d'Art et d'Histoire
(Museum of Art
and History) ㉒
Musée de l'Horlogerie
(Watch Museum) ㉔
Musée International
de la Croix-Rouge
et du Croissant-Rouge
(International Red Cross
and Red Crescent
Museum) ①
Palais des Nations ③

Accommodations:
Hôtel Beau-Rivage ⑪
Hôtel Carlton ③
Hôtel de la Cloche ⑨
Hôtel des Bergues ⑬
Hôtel du Lac ⑲
Hôtel du Midi ⑭
Hôtel Edelweiss ⑩
Hôtel International
& Terminus ④
Hôtel Moderne ⑦
Hôtel St-Gervais ⑧
Le Richemond ⑫
Lido ⑥
Strasbourg-Univers ⑤

E-0120

SWITZERLAND

★ BERN

Geneva

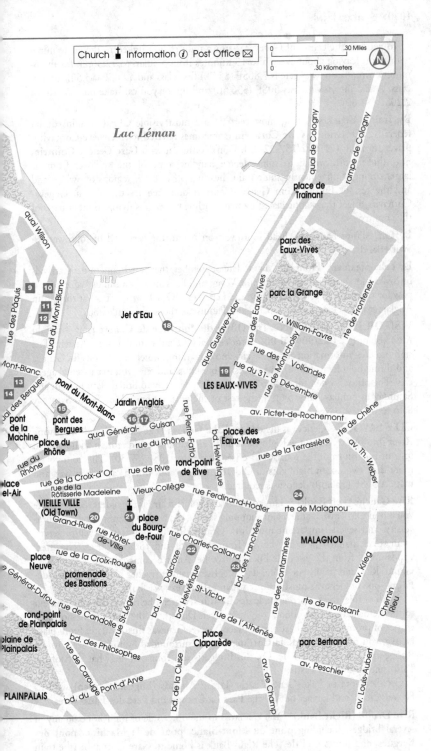

Church ✚ Information ⓘ Post Office ⊠

Lac Léman

quai Wilson

quai de Cologny

rampe de Cologny

place de Traînant

parc des Eaux-Vives

parc la Grange

Jet d'Eau **18**

9 **10**

rue des Pâquis

11

12

quai du Mont-Blanc

rue des Eaux-Vives

quai Gustave-Ador

av. William-Favre

rue des Montcholsy

rte de Frontenex

Vollandes

Mont-Blanc

13

14

quai des Bergues

pont du Mont-Blanc

Jardin Anglais

15

pont de la Machine

pont des Bergues

place du Rhône

16 **17** Guisan

quai Général-

rue du 31- de Décembre

LES EAUX-VIVES **19**

av. Pictet-de-Rochemont

rte de Chêne

rue du Rhône

rue Pierre-Fatio

bd. Helvétique

place des Eaux-Vives

rue de la Terrassière

av. Th. Weber

rue du Rhône

rue de la Croix-d'Or

rue de Rive

rond-point de Rive

place el-Air

rue de la Rôtisserie Madeleine

Vieux-Collège

rue Ferdinand-Hodler

rte de Malagnou

24

VIEILLE VILLE (Old Town) **20**

Grand-Rue

rue Hôtel-de-Ville

21 place du Bourg-de-Four

rue Charles-Galland

22

bd. des Tranchées

MALAGNOU

av. Krieg

place Neuve

rue de la Croix-Rouge

Dalcroze

23

rue St-Victor

rue des Contamines

Chemin Rieu

promenade des Bastions

e Général-Dufour

rue de Candolle

rue St-Léger

bd. J.-F.

bd. Helvétique

rte de Florissant

rond-point de Plainpalais

plaine de Plainpalais

bd. des Philosophes

rue de Carouge

place Claparède

rue de l'Athénée

parc Bertrand

av. de Champ

av. Peschier

av. Louis-Aubert

PLAINPALAIS

bd. du Pont-d'Arve

bd. de la Cluse

To get into the center of Geneva, there's a train station linked to the air terminal with trains leaving about every 5 to 15 minutes from 5:30am to 12:36pm for the 6-minute trip; the one-way fare is 7.80SF ($5.70) first-class and 4.80SF ($3.50) second-class. A taxi into town costs 50SF ($36.50) and up, or you can take bus no. 10 for 2.20SF ($1.60).

By Train   Geneva's busiest, most central, and most visible CFF (Chemins de fer fédéraux) rail station is **Gare Cornavin** (sometimes referred to as Genève-Cornavin), place Cornavin (☎ **022/157-22-22**). Don't confuse it with **Gare Genève-Cointrin**, near the airport, which to some degree handles some of the spillover from its larger sibling. Conveniently, some trains heading off to other regions of Switzerland and the rest of Europe from Genève-Cointrin don't require transfers in Genève-Cornavin, a fact that's appreciated by many airline passengers flying to other parts of the country.

By Car   From Lausanne, head southwest on N1 to the very end of southwestern Switzerland.

By Lake Steamer   From late May to late September, there are frequent daily arrivals by Swiss lake steamer from Montreaux, Vevey, and Lausanne (you can use your Eurailpass for the trip). If you're staying in the Left Bank (Old Town), get off at the Jardin Anglais stop in Geneva; Mont Blanc and Pâquis are the Right Bank stops.

VISITOR INFORMATION   The **Office du Tourisme de Genève** is at 3 rue du Mont-Blanc (☎ **022/909-70-00**), at the central CFF rail station, Gare Cornavin. The staff provides information about the city and can arrange hotel reservations (in Geneva and throughout Switzerland) and excursion bookings and refer you to car-rental agencies. The office is open June 15 to September 15, Monday to Friday 8am to 8pm and Saturday to Sunday 8am to 6pm; the rest of the year, it's open Monday to Saturday 8am to 6pm.

CITY LAYOUT   Geneva is divided by **Lake Geneva (Lac Léman)** and the **Rhône River** into two sections: the Right Bank and Left Bank. You can rent an audio-guided tour in English from the tourist office (see above) for 10SF ($7.30). This tour covers more than two dozen highlights in Old Town and comes with a cassette, player, and map. A 50SF ($36.50) deposit is required.

Rive Gauche (Left Bank)   This compact and colorful area is the oldest section. Here you'll find Old Town, some major shopping streets, the famous Flower Clock, the university, and several important museums. **Grand' Rue** is Old Town's well-preserved main street, flanked by many houses from the 15th and 18th centuries. The street winds uphill from the ponts de l'Ile; at place Bel-Air it becomes rue de la Cité, then Grand' Rue, and finally rue Hôtel-de-Ville. Eventually it reaches **place du Bourg-de-Four**—one of Geneva's most historic squares (Rousseau was born in no. 40).

South of this street is **promenade des Bastions**, a green-belt area with a monument to the Reformation; it overlooks the Arve River. Directly to the west, in the northern corner of promenade des Bastions, is **place Neuve**, Geneva's finest square. From place Neuve, you can take **rue de la Corraterie**, once surrounded by the city wall, to the Rhône and the **ponts de l'Ile.** On this bridge is the Tour de l'Ile, what's left of the 13th-century bishops' castle.

On the shore of Lake Geneva is the **Jardin Anglais (English Garden)** with its Flower Clock, and farther out are the **Parc La Grange** and **Parc des Eaux-Vives.**

Rive Droite (Right Bank)   You can cross to the other side of the Rhône on any of several bridges, including **pont du Mont-Blanc, pont de la Machine, pont des Bergues,** and **ponts de l'Ile.** The Right Bank is home to **Gare Cornavin** (the train station), the major international organizations, and several attractive parks. **Place**

St-Gervais is in the St-Gervais district; since the 18th century, it has been an area for jewelers and watchmakers. Along the northern shore of Lake Geneva is **quai du Président-Wilson,** named for the U.S. president who helped found the League of Nations.

The Right Bank is surrounded by parks, from the tree-shaded promenades along the Rhône to the **Parc de la Perle du Lac, Parc Barton,** and **Parc Mon-Repos** on the outskirts.

GETTING AROUND

BY PUBLIC TRANSPORTATION   For the most part, all of Geneva's transportation lines begin at place Cornavin, in front of the main rail station. From here, you can take bus F, 5, or 8 to the Palais des Nations. Tickets for **Zone 10,** the urban area, are sold from automatic vending machines at each stop, operated by coins or magnetic cards (free cards are available from Geneva public transport agencies). Tickets for other zones, including Geneva's suburbs and France, are sold by drivers on the corresponding buses.

Four **basic tickets** are provided: free transfers for 1 hour in Zone 10, with as many changes as you want on any vehicle, for 2.20SF ($1.60); a trip limited to three stops, valid for half an hour, allowing a return trip, at 1.50SF ($1.10); free transportation for 1½ hours in all zones of the network of Geneva, at 4SF ($2.90); and a ride for 1 hour in Zone 10 for children 6 to 12 as well as seniors (women over 62 and men over 65), at 1.50SF ($1.10); children 5 and under ride free.

You can buy **multiuse tickets** and **daily cards** from agents whose addresses are listed on posts at the various stops. A wide range of them is available, and often you can adapt the system to your needs. For example, a daily ticket for unlimited transportation in Zone 10 is 5SF ($3.65) for as many trips and changes as you need; it's valid from the time you stamp it up to the termination of the day's service, around midnight. There's also a daily ticket at 8.50SF ($6.20), including transportation not only in Zone 10 but in Zones 21, 31, and 41, taking in practically the whole network of greater Geneva. Many worthy attractions and restaurants are in the suburbs.

These tickets and many other kinds, including combined bus/cable-car tickets to climb to the top of Mont Salève, are available from the Geneva public transport systems agencies or from official dealers. For customer service and more information, call ☎ **022/308-34-34.**

BY TAXI   Cab fares start at 6.30SF ($4.60), plus 3.10SF ($2.25) for each kilometer in the city. The fare from the airport is about 50SF ($36.50). No tipping is required; for a taxi, call ☎ **022/331-41-33** or 022/320-20-20.

BY CAR   Driving isn't recommended—parking is too difficult and the many one-way streets make navigation complicated. However, should you want to rent a car and tour Lake Geneva, you'll find many rental companies at the airport or in the city center. Major offices include **Avis,** 44 rue de Lausanne (☎ **022/731-90-00); Budget,** 37 rue de Lausanne (☎ **022/732-52-52); Europcar,** 35 rue de Zurich (☎ **022/731-51-50);** and **Hertz,** 60 rue de Berne (☎ **022/731-12-00).**

BY BICYCLE OR MOTORSCOOTER   Touring the city by bicycle isn't practical because of the steep cobblestoned streets and general congestion. However, you might want to rent a bike to visit the nearby countryside. The major rental outlet is at the *bagages* desk at Gare Cornavin (☎ **022/791-02-50),** where city bikes are 21SF ($15.35) per day and mountain bikes 29SF ($21.15) per day.

If you're interested in renting a motorscooter, try **Horizon Motos,** 22 rue des Pâquis (☎ **022/738-36-96),** where rentals begin at 45SF ($32.85) per day.

Fast Facts: Geneva

American Express   The American Express office at 7 rue du Mont-Blanc (☎ **022/731-76-00;** fax 022/732-72-11), is open Monday to Friday 8:30am to 5:30pm and Saturday 9am to noon.

Baby-sitters   A list of agencies is available at the tourist office. Hotels can also secure an English-speaking sitter for you, or you can call **Service de Placement de l'Université,** 4 rue de Candolle (☎ **022/329-39-70**). Call this office before 11am if you want a sitter at night.

Business Hours   Most **banks** are open Monday to Friday 8:30am to 4:30pm (to 5:30pm on Wednesday). Most **offices** are open Monday to Friday 8am to noon and 2 to 6pm, although this can vary. It's always best to call first.

Consulates   If you lose your passport or have other business with your home government, go to your nation's consulate: **United States,** Route de Près Bois 29 (☎ **022/798-16-15**); **Australia,** 56–58 rue Moillebeau (☎ **022/918-29-00**); **Canada,** 1 chemin du Pré-de-la-Bichette (☎ **022/733-90-00**); **Ireland,** Kirchenfelderstrasse 68 (☎ **022/352-14-42**); **New Zealand,** 28A chemin du Petit-Saconnex (☎ **022/734-95-30**); the **United Kingdom,** 37–39 rue de Vermont (☎ **022/734-38-00**); or **South Africa,** rue de Rhône 65 (☎ **022/849-54-54**).

Currency   The basic unit of currency is the **Swiss franc (SF),** made up of 100 centimes. Banknotes are in denominations of 10, 20, 50, 100, 500, and 1,000 francs, and coin denominations are 5, 10, 20, and 50 centimes and 1, 2, and 5 francs. The rate of exchange used in this chapter was \$1 = 1.37SF or 1SF = 73¢. Also, 1EUR = 1.6SF and £1 = 2.4SF.

Currency Exchange   The money exchange at **Gare Cornavin,** place Cornavin (☎ **022/715-23-89**), is open daily 6:45am to 9pm. For other financial transactions, the **Société de Banque Suisse (Swiss Bank Corporation)** is at 2 rue de la Confédération (☎ **022/375-75-75**).

Dentists   English-speaking dentists are available at one of the *cliniques dentaires* at 5 rue Malombré (☎ **022/346-64-44**), Monday to Friday 7:30am to 8pm and Saturday to Sunday 8am to 6pm.

Doctors   In a medical emergency, call ☎ **022/320-25-11,** or arrange an appointment with an English-speaking doctor at the **Hôpital Cantonal,** 24 rue Micheli-du-Crest (☎ **022/372-3311**).

Drugstores   One of the world's biggest drugstores, **Pharmacie Principale,** Confédération-Centre, rue de la Confédération (☎ **022/311-31-30**), offers everything from medicine to clothing, perfumes, optical equipment, cameras, and photo supplies. It's open Monday to Friday 9am to 7pm and Saturday 9am to 5pm.

Emergencies   In an emergency, dial ☎ **117** for the police, ☎ **142** for an ambulance, and ☎ **118** to report a fire.

Hospitals   You can go to the **Hôpital Cantonal,** 24 rue Micheli-du-Crest (☎ **022/372-3311**).

Internet Access   Global Café, 71 rue des Rois (☎ **022/328-2619;** e-mail: info@globalcafe.ch), is open Monday 2 to 11pm and Tuesday to Saturday 10am to 11pm.

Post Office   The city's main post office, **Bureau de Poste Montbrillant,** rue de Gares (☎ **022/739-21-11**), offers a full range of telephone, telegraph, and mail-related services Monday to Friday 8am to 10:45pm, Saturday 8am to 10pm, and Sunday noon to 8pm. There's a branch offering less extensive services at **Gare Cornavin,** 16 rue de Gares (☎ 022/739-24-15), open Monday to Friday 6am to 10:45pm, Saturday 6am to 8pm, and Sunday noon to 8pm.

Taxes   Geneva has no special city tax. All goods and services throughout Switzerland have a 6.5% value-added tax (VAT) attached, however.

Telephone/Telex/Fax   The **country code** for Switzerland is **41.** The **city code** for Geneva is **22;** use this code when you're calling from outside Switzerland. If you're within Switzerland but not in Geneva, use **022.** If you're calling within Geneva, simply leave off the code and dial the regular phone number.

A big **long-distance phone center** is at the main train station, Gare Cornavin, place Cornavin; it's open 24 hours. It's much cheaper to make your long-distance calls here than at your hotel—some Geneva hotels add a 40% surcharge to long-distance calls. Telegrams and faxes can be sent at the post office at 18 rue du Mont-Blanc (☎ 022/739-21-11), 2 blocks from the train station. The toll-free international access codes are: **AT&T** ☎ 888/288-4685, **Sprint** ☎ 800/877-4646, and **MCI** ☎ 800/444-4141.

WHERE TO STAY
ON THE RIGHT BANK
Very Expensive

Hôtel Beau-Rivage. 13 quai du Mont-Blanc, 1201 Genève. ☎ **022/716-66-66.** Fax 022/716-60-60. E-mail: insoo@beaurivage.ch. 97 units. MINIBAR TV TEL. 520–740SF ($379.60–$540.20) double; from 880SF ($642.40) junior suite. AE, DC, MC, V. Parking 30SF ($21.90). Bus: 6 or 33.

This landmark 1865 hotel gets our highest recommendation for its traditional Victorian charm and impeccable service. However, you pay dearly for them. The "romantic" rooms are bigger than the "classical," and some contain frescoes. Double-glazed windows cut down on street noise, and each unit has a roomy bathroom, clad in marble or tile, with robes and a hair dryer. Some rooms are air-conditioned; those in front open onto views of the Right Bank. The more elegant of the hotel's two restaurants is Le Chat-Botté (see "Where to Dine," below).

Hôtel des Bergues. 33 quai des Bergues, 1211 Genève. ☎ **022/908-70-00.** Fax 022/732-19-89. www.hoteldesbergues.com. E-mail: gml289@forte-hotel.com. 138 units. A/C MINIBAR TV TEL. 470–730SF ($343.10–$532.90) double; from 1,950SF ($1,423.50) suite. AE, DC, MC, V. Parking 35SF ($25.55) per night. Bus: 7.

This elegant four-story hotel, a historic monument, once catered to the monarchs of Europe. It has long been ranked by *Institutional Investor* as one of the world's top hotels, grandly memorable from its central position at the edge of the Rhône. The 110-person staff is the most hospitable in Geneva. The guest rooms have Directoire and Louis-Philippe furnishings and a marble-clad combination bathroom (tub and shower) with a private phone, hair dryer, full-length mirrors, and thick towels. Those ranked superior on the Bel Etage floor are the finest choices, although lake view rooms are more expensive. The two restaurants and bar are highly recommended.

✪ **Le Richemond.** Jardin Brunswick, 1211 Genève. ☎ **022/731-14-00.** Fax 022/731-67-09. E-mail: reservation@richemond.ch. 98 units. A/C MINIBAR TV TEL. 640–740SF ($467.20–$540.20) double; from 990SF ($722.70) suite. AE, DC, MC, V. Parking 45SF ($32.85). Bus: 1 or 9.

Le Richemond, which counts some of the world's most prominent people among its guests, is Geneva's greatest hotel. Erected in 1875, the neoclassical building has wrought-iron balustrades and is near the lake, across from a small park. Its public rooms look like those in a museum, with dozens of valuable engravings and an array of furniture from the days of Louis XII. Nearly half of the units here are suites. A large number are renovated every year, but even those between rehabs look as good as new. This is true Grand Hotel living, with elegant fabrics, tasteful upholstery, luxurious beds, and spacious marble bathrooms with hair dryers, robes, and a basket of expensive toiletries. Some of the accommodations are reserved for nonsmokers. Gentilhomme is among the finest dining rooms in Geneva, and Le Jardin is the city's most fashionable cafe.

Moderate

Hôtel Carlton. 22 rue Amat, 1202 Genève. ☎ **022/908-68-50.** Fax 022/908-68-68. E-mail: carlton gva@swissonline.ch. 123 units. TV TEL. 200–268SF ($146–$195.65) double; 311SF ($227.05) studio. Free for children under 12. Rates include buffet breakfast. AE, DC, MC, V. Parking 10SF ($7.30). Bus: 4 or 44.

This hotel is about 7 city blocks east of the rail station and 300 yards from the waterfront views of quai du Président-Wilson. The facade combines weathered vertical slats and smooth stones decoratively cemented into rectangular patterns beneath the modern windows. Bedrooms, most often decorated in neutral tones, have minimal sitting areas but good beds and fine linen. Bathrooms feature both shower and tubs. Lunch and dinner are served in the restaurant/grill, Le Carlton, with an international menu that includes an extensive salad buffet and fresh fish.

Hôtel du Midi. 4 place Chevelu, 1211 Genève. ☎ **022/731-78-00.** Fax 022/731-00-20. www.hotel du midi.ch. E-mail: midihotel@irponink.ch. 90 units. MINIBAR TV TEL. 210–230SF ($153.30–$167.90) double; 425SF ($310.25) suite for four. AE, DC, MC, V. Bus: 7.

On a tree-lined square near the center of Geneva, this salmon-colored eight-story hotel resembles an apartment building. A complete renovation in 1994 moved the reception area to the street level and added half a dozen rooms. The windows are double-glazed to keep out traffic noise, and there's wall-to-wall carpeting, warming racks for towels, and safes in every room. Bedrooms, although not spectacular, are well maintained and comfortable. Bathrooms are a bit cramped but have adequate shelf space. The hotel maintains a small restaurant at street level.

Hôtel Edelweiss. 2 place de la Navigation, 1201 Genève. ☎ **022/731-36-58.** Fax 022/738-85-33. 39 units. MINIBAR TV TEL. 180-225SF ($131.40–$164.25) double. Rates include continental breakfast. AE, DC, MC, V. Parking across the street 12SF ($8.75). Bus: 1.

This brown-and-white eight-story hotel towers above its neighbors near quai du Président-Wilson. Built in the early 1960s, the hotel was last renovated in 1993; its rustic interior decor contrasts with its modern exterior. The rooms, cozy with pinewood furniture crafted in country-Swiss style, have sitting areas and desk space, but bathrooms are small and devoid of many amenities. Its little restaurant is patronized by locals and is inexpensively priced.

Hôtel Moderne. 1 rue de Berne, 1211 Genève. ☎ **022/732-81-00.** Fax 022/738-26-58. 55 units. TV TEL. 180–200SF ($131.40–$146) double. Rates include buffet breakfast. AE, DC, MC, V. Bus: 6 or 33.

Near the rail station and the lake, this hotel is a white seven-story rectangle, with a low-lying glassed-in extension containing the breakfast room. The public rooms are modern, with Nordic furniture and abstract angles and curves. The guest rooms, with soundproof windows, are modern, clean, and sunny, although predictably furnished and a bit sterile. Some are reserved for nonsmokers. You'll probably wish the bathrooms had more room to spread out your stuff. Baby-sitting, room service, and laundry facilities are available. The hotel's restaurant serves only breakfast, but there's an Italian restaurant in the building. There's no parking; the public lot next door charges 25SF ($18.25) for the night

Strasbourg-Univers. 10 rue J.-J.-Pradier, 1201 Genève. ☎ **800/528-1234** in the U.S. or 022/906-58-00. Fax 022/738-42-08. 53 units. TV TEL. 200–240SF ($146–$175.20) double; 250–500SF ($182.50–$365) suite. Rates include continental breakfast. AE, DC, MC, V. Bus: 1, 2, 3, 4, 8, 12, 13, or 44. Tram: 16.

Close to the rail station, this building was constructed around 1900, although many renovations both outside and in have kept it looking fresh. The most spacious rooms tend to be those on the lower floors. Some of the more recently renovated rooms have wooden surfaces and pastels. The compact, tiled bathrooms are minimally equipped. Most rooms contain a minibar. On the premises is a pleasant restaurant.

Inexpensive

✪ **Hôtel de la Cloche.** 6 rue de la Cloche, 1211 Genève. ☎ **022/732-94-81.** Fax 022/738-16-12. 8 units (3 with bathroom). TV. 80SF ($58.40) double without bathroom; 120SF ($87.60) double with bathroom; 95SF ($69.35) triple without bathroom; 130SF ($94.90) quad without bathroom. AE, DC, MC, V. Parking across the street at a public garage costs 25SF ($18.25). Bus: 1.

This small hotel, one of Geneva's best deals, occupies the second floor of a 19th-century apartment building on a narrow street behind the Noga Hilton. Unpretentious despite a glamorous location, it's run by an elderly widow, Mme Chabbey. The rooms are spacious, well cared for, and designed with an eye to old-fashioned comfort. Many have high-ceilings, often with ornate plasterwork, elegant moldings, and simple furniture; some have views over a quiet inner courtyard and others open onto views over the lake. Those with private bathrooms will find rather cramped shower stalls; corridor bathrooms are well maintained, and there's rarely a wait. Breakfast is the only meal served.

Hôtel International & Terminus. 20 rue des Alpes, 1201 Genève. ☎ **022/732-80-95.** Fax 022/732-18-43. 53 units. TV TEL. 99–220SF ($72.25–$160.60) double. Rates include continental breakfast. AE, DC, MC, V. Bus: 6, 10, or 33.

This hotel lies across from the main entrance of Geneva's railway station and has been run by three generations of the Cottier family. Built around 1900, it was radically upgraded in 1993 and 1994, with pairs of smaller rooms reconfigured into larger units. Don't expect grand style; the allure of this place is its exceedingly good value. Bathrooms seem to have been added as an afterthought in areas not designed for them, and are a bit cramped. The restaurant, La Veranda, serves some of the most reasonable meals in Geneva.

Hôtel St-Gervais. 20 rue des Corps-Saints, 1201 Genève. ☎ and fax **022/732-45-72.** 26 units (24 with sink only, 1 with shower only, 1 with bathroom). 78SF ($56.95) double without bathroom; 98SF ($71.55) double with shower only; 105SF ($76.65) double with bathroom. Rates include continental breakfast. Parking at a public garage costs 25–26SF ($18.25–$19) for the night. AE, MC, V. Tram: 13.

This simple, good-value hotel lies in an old-fashioned, vaguely nondescript building within Geneva's medieval core, a 3-minute walk from Gare Cornavin. Although it has the kind of quirky idiosyncrasies that appeal to architects and historic renovators, its minimalist furnishings and conservative decor are a bit lackluster. Most rooms have a sink, but the shared hall bathrooms are frequently tidied for the next guest's use. There's a convivial pub on the ground floor.

ON THE LEFT BANK
Moderate

Hôtel Touring-Balance. 13 place Longemalle, 1204 Genève. ☎ **022/310-40-45.** Fax 022/310-40-39. 58 units. MINIBAR TV TEL. 250SF ($182.50) double; 350SF ($255.50) suite. Rates include buffet breakfast. AE, DC, MC, V. Parking 15SF ($10.95). Bus 6, 8, or 9.

Previously two hotels across the street from each other, the Touring-Balance is in the heart of the Left Bank's shopping district. The Balance is a recognized historic monument. The buildings are comparable in style and amenities; both have brightly colored interiors and comfortable rooms. Those on the upper floors are more modern than those on the lower levels. Bathrooms are compact, neat, and well kept. There's a coffee shop adjacent to the lobby in the Touring.

Inexpensive
Hôtel du Lac. 15 rue des Eaux-Vives, 1207 Genève. ☎ **022/735-45-80.** 26 units (none with bathroom). 80SF ($58.40) double; 110SF ($80.30) triple. Rates include continental breakfast. No credit cards. Free parking on street. Bus: 9 from the train station to place des Eaux-Vives.

This small-budget hotel in the old city occupies the sixth and seventh floors of an apartment building. The Swiss-Italian managers don't pretend to offer first-class service, but they make up for it with their hospitality. Although the rooms (most have a phone and a balcony) are small and the mattresses somewhat thin and used, this minimalist place is one of the best values in a very expensive city. There are no private bathrooms, but the public bathrooms are quite decent.

WHERE TO DINE
On the Right Bank
Very Expensive
✪ **Le Chat-Botté.** In the Hôtel Beau-Rivage, 13 quai du Mont-Blanc. ☎ **022/716-69-20.** Reservations required. Main courses 32–53SF ($23.35–$38.70); set-price menu 60–135SF ($43.80–$98.55) at lunch, 110–135SF ($80.30–$98.55) at dinner. AE, DC, MC, V. Daily noon–2pm and 7–10pm. Closed 15 days in late Dec (dates vary). Bus: 6 or 33. FRENCH.

"Puss in Boots" is in one of Geneva's grandest hotels. Decorated with tapestries, sculpture, and rich upholstery, and graced by a polite staff, it serves delectable food. In nice weather you can dine on the flower-bedecked terrace, overlooking the Jet d'Eau. The cuisine, although inspired by French classics, is definitely contemporary. The large selection includes filets of red mullet vinaigrette, cutlets of salmon pan-fried with spices, and breast of chicken stuffed with vegetables. Highly recommended is delicate perch filet from Lake Geneva, sautéed until it's golden and sometimes served with fava beans. In the autumn gourmets flock here for the roast saddle of roebuck, prepared only for two or more diners.

Le Cygne. In the Noga Hilton, 19 quai du Mont-Blanc. ☎ **022/908-90-85.** Reservations required. Main courses 34–64SF ($24.80–$46.70); set-price menu 59SF ($43.05) at lunch, 75SF ($54.75) at dinner; all-fish menu 108SF ($78.85); *menu dégustation* 145SF ($105.85). AE, DC, MC, V. Daily noon–2:30pm and 7–10pm. Closed 1 week in Jan, 11 days at Easter, and the first 3 weeks of July. Bus: 1. FRENCH.

Le Cygne overlooks the harbor with the famous Jet d'Eau and, in the distance, the Alps. A refined cuisine is offered, with impeccable service. The menu changes seasonally and may offer such choices as terrine of blackened chicken in crayfish- and anise-flavored aspic. Also good are the smoked filet of sea bass with truffle-flavored vinaigrette and the roasted lamb with coriander and tomatoes stuffed with moussaka. Five elaborate trolleys, each laden with a different selection, make one of the most spectacular arrays of desserts in Switzerland.

Le Neptune. In the Hôtel du Rhône, 1 quai Turrettini. ☎ **022/731-98-31.** Reservations required. Main courses 50–68SF ($36.50–$49.65); set-price lunch 65SF ($47.45); set-price dinner 95–125SF ($69.35–$91.25). AE, DC, MC, V. Mon–Fri noon–2pm and 7:30–10pm. Bus: 6, 8, 10, or 15. SEAFOOD.

At one of Geneva's finest seafood restaurants, the decor is intimate, intensely floral, and graced with an enormous fresco displaying an inside view of Neptune's kingdom. Although the menu changes based on market conditions, you're likely to be offered such dishes as herbed vichyssoise with hazelnut oil and a dollop of foie gras, cassolette of oysters seasoned with algae-flavored butter sauce, or Atlantic sea bass roasted in a salt crust with thyme. If you're not in the mood for fish, try rack of Scottish lamb in puff pastry with spices or partridge roasted en casserole with autumn herbs.

Expensive

La Mère Royaume. 9 rue des Corps-Saints. ☎ **022/732-70-08.** Reservations required. Brasserie, main courses 16–28SF ($11.70–$20.45); set-price menu 36–48SF ($26.30–$35.05). Restaurant, main courses 28–48SF ($20.45–$35.05); set-price menus 50–98SF ($36.50–$71.55). AE, DC, MC, V. Mon–Fri noon–2pm and 7–10:30pm; Sat 7–10:30pm. Closed July 20–Aug 15. Bus: 4, 6, or 7. Tram: 13. FRENCH.

Opened around the turn of the century, this is one of the oldest restaurants in town. It's named after a heroine who in 1602 poured boiling stew over a Savoyard soldier's head and cracked his skull with the kettle. With an antecedent like that, you'd expect some of the heartiest fare in Geneva, but instead the kitchen offers perfectly cooked French specialties such as *omble chevalier*, the delicate white fish of Lake Geneva that is known as the world's most divine trout. Less expensive meals are served in the brasserie.

Moderate

✪ **Chez Jacky.** 9–11 rue Necker. ☎ **022/732-86-80.** Reservations recommended. Main courses 38–39SF ($27.75–$28.45); business lunch 38SF ($27.75); set-price menus 54–84SF ($39.40–$61.30). AE, DC, MC, V. Mon–Fri 11am–2pm and 6–10pm. Closed first week of Jan and 3 weeks in Aug. Bus: 5, 10, or 44. SWISS.

Now main couses are 38 to 39SF ($27.75 to $28.45). As to your question, why so little variation, the owner said, "That's how I choose to do it!"

This French provincial bistro should be better known, although it already attracts everyone from grandmothers to young skiers en route to Verbier. It's the domain of Jacky Gruber, an exceptional chef from Valais. There's a subtlety in M Gruber's cooking that suggests the influence of his mentor, Frédy Giradet, once hailed as the world's greatest chef. You might begin with Chinese cabbage and mussels and continue with filet of turbot roasted with thyme or beautifully prepared pink duck on spinach with onion confit. Be prepared to wait for each course.

ON THE LEFT BANK

Very Expensive

Restaurant du Parc des Eaux-Vives. 82 quai Gustave-Ador. ☎ **022/735-41-40.** Reservations required. Main courses 40–65SF ($29.20–$47.45); set-price menu 55–138SF ($40.15–$100.75) at lunch, 88–110SF ($64.25–$80.30) at dinner. AE, MC, V. Apr–Oct Tues–Sun noon–2pm, Tues–Sat 7–10pm; Nov–Mar Tues–Sat noon–2pm and 7–10pm. Bus: 2. FRENCH/SWISS.

To reach this restaurant, you pass through a wrought-iron gate and proceed along a winding drive that leads to the dining room of an 18th-century château owned by the city of Geneva. Excellent meals are prepared by chefs who adjust the menu seasonally but tend to concentrate on classical French cuisine. The local trout is superb; in autumn, the menu offers many game dishes. Of course, everything tastes better with truffles, including lobster salad, foie gras, and sea bass flambé with fennel.

Expensive

Le Béarn. 4 quai de la Poste. ☎ **022/321-00-28.** Reservations required. Main courses 30–60SF ($21.90–$43.80); set-price menu 53–165SF ($38.70–$120.45) at lunch, 90–165SF ($65.70–$120.45) at dinner. AE, DC, MC, V. Mon–Fri noon–2pm; Mon–Sat 7:15–10pm. Closed mid-July to mid-Aug and Sat night June–Sept. Bus: 2, 10, or 22. FRENCH.

Jean-Paul Goddard and his excellent staff have created the best restaurant in Geneva's business center. With only 10 tables, everything is on a small scale, and the service is personal. There are two dining areas in the Empire style. The chefs prepare dishes such as morels stuffed with fresh asparagus tips, roasted Scottish thrush (one of the world's most expensive birds), and a platter called "three terrines of autumn" (rabbit, partridge, and thrush).

Moderate

Au Pied de Cochon. 4 place du Bourg-de-Four. ☎ **022/310-47-97.** Reservations recommended. Main courses 23.50–39.50SF ($17.15–$28.85). AE, DC, MC, V. Mon–Fri 7am–midnight; Sat–Sun noon–midnight. Bus: 2 or 22. Tram: 12. LYONNAISE/SWISS.

Come here for hearty Lyonnaise fare if you don't mind smoke and noise. A lot of young people are attracted to this place, as well as lawyers from the Palais de Justice across the way, artists, and local workers. The cooking is like grandma's—provided she came from Lyon. Naturally, the namesake *pieds de cochon* (pigs' feet) is included on the menu, along with *petit salé* (lamb), tripe, and some of the best grilled andouillettes (sausages made of chitterlings) in Geneva.

Brasserie Lipp. Confédération-Centre, 8 rue de la Confédération. ☎ **022/311-10-11.** Reservations recommended. Main courses 25–41SF ($18.25–$29.95); set-price menus 50–72SF ($36.50–$52.55). AE, DC, MC, V. Daily 7am–2am. Bus: 7 or 12. SWISS.

This bustling place is named after the famous Parisian brasserie, and when you enter (especially at lunch) and see the waiters in black jackets with long white aprons rushing about, you'll think you've been transported to France. The impossibly long menu contains a sampling of the repertoire of bistro dishes, but like its namesake, the Geneva Lipp specializes in several versions of charcuterie. You can also order three kinds of pot-au-feu and such classics as Toulousain cassoulet with confit de canard (duckling), available in autumn and winter. The fresh oysters are among the best in the city, and tables are placed outside in summer.

La Coupole. 116 rue du Rhône. ☎ **022/787-50-10.** Plats du jour 22–36SF ($16.05–$26.30). Mon–Sat 11:30am–2:15pm and 7–11:30pm. Bus: 2, 9, or 22. Tram: 12. SWISS.

This is a true brasserie, and far more elegant than its Parisian namesake. The place is most popular at noon, especially with shoppers and office workers. Fanciful and fun, it's dotted with grandfather clocks, a bronze *Venus*, Edwardian palms, and comfortable banquettes. The menu is limited but well selected; the *cuisine du marché* (cooking based on market-fresh ingredients) is some of the finest in this part of town. Chefs search the market in the early morning for the freshest and best of ingredients, and then quickly compose a day's menu based on their purchases.

L'Aïoli. 6 rue Adrien-Lachenal. ☎ **022/736-79-71.** Main courses 29.50–40SF ($21.55–$29.20); *menu dégustation* 69SF ($50.35). AE, DC, MC, V. Tues–Sat 11am–2pm and 7–10pm. Closed Aug and Sat–Sun June–July. Bus: 1 or 6. Tram: 12. FRENCH/PROVENÇAL.

This popular neighborhood restaurant stands opposite Le Corbusier's Maison de Verre. Something of a local secret, it offers personalized service and the finest Provençal cooking in town. An evening meal includes an appetizer, a first plate, a main dish, cheese, a dessert, coffee, and wine (you can spend more by ordering à la carte). Frogs' legs Provençal are simmered in a savory tomato, onion, and garlic sauce; also recommended is the lamb gigot, in which the meat is infused with fresh herbs and garlic and baked to a tender perfection. The chefs also prepare a delectable pot-au-feu, a perfect stew of broth, meat, and vegetables.

✪ **La Favola.** 15 rue Jean-Calvin. ☎ **022/311-74-37.** Reservations required. Main courses 25–45SF ($18.25–$32.85). AE, MC, V. Mon–Fri noon–2pm and 7:15–10pm. Closed 1 week at Christmas, 2 weeks between July and Aug, and Sat–Sun. Tram: 12. TUSCAN/ITALIAN.

This is the best Italian dining spot in Geneva, and its most devoted habitués go even further, hailing it as the best restaurant in Geneva. Within a few steps of the Cathédrale St-Pierre, it contains only two cramped dining rooms and boasts a family-managed staff. The menu is small and short but choice, varying with the availability of ingredients and the season. Look for such dishes as carpaccio of beef; *vitello tonnato* (paper-thin veal with a tuna sauce); lobster salad; potato salad with cèpe mushrooms; and ravioli made on-site.

Le Lyrique. 12 bd. du Théâtre. ☎ **022/328-00-95.** Reservations recommended. Restaurant, main courses 23–45SF ($16.80–$32.85); set lunch 45–55SF ($32.85–$40.15); set dinner 55SF ($40.15). Brasserie, main courses 20–40SF ($14.60–$29.20); set menus (lunch or dinner) 35–45SF ($25.55–$32.85). AE, DC, MC, V. Mon–Fri noon–2pm and 6:30–10pm. Bus: 2 or 22. SWISS/FRENCH.

Le Lyrique contains both a formal restaurant and a brasserie. The brasserie, which has a terrace, is open all day but serves hot meals only during the hours above. The restaurant turns out some of the most perfect steaks in the city, flavored with oils, herbs, and fresh garlic and grilled to your specification. A delight is fresh eggplant "caviar," in which eggplant is chopped fine and combined with black olives. One unusual pairing is grapefruit and fillet of sea wolf, a dish that packs a lot of punch. A roulade of rabbit is served with a succulent pasta, but an even better pasta dish is the tagliatelle with delectable, perfectly cooked prawns.

Inexpensive

Taverne de la Madeleine. 20 rue Toutes-Ames. ☎ **022/310-60-70.** Reservations recommended. Main courses 15–18SF ($10.95–$13.15); plat du jour 14SF ($10.20). MC, V. Mon–Fri 7:30am–6:30pm (last food order at 4pm); Sat 9:30–4pm (last food order at 2:30pm). Bus: 2. Tram 12. SWISS.

This very good restaurant is set against the old city wall beside the Eglise de la Madeleine. The building is a century old, and the restaurant was opened about 80 years ago. The brusquely efficient staff caters to a lunchtime business crowd, and the place is operated by a philanthropic organization that forbids the consumption of alcohol (alcohol-free beer is available). You can order a variety of well-prepared dishes or specials, such as four types of pasta, vegetarian sandwiches, and a big plate of *osso buco* (braised veal shank) with *pommes frites*. The kitchen prides itself on its filet of lake perch meunière style (in butter sauce) or Vevey style with exotic mushrooms.

SEEING THE SIGHTS

You can see most of Geneva on foot, which is the best way to familiarize yourself with the city.

SIGHTSEEING SUGGESTIONS FOR FIRST-TIME VISITORS

If You Have 1 Day Begin the day by viewing the spectacular water fountain, **Jet d'Eau,** and the **Flower Clock** in the Jardin Anglais. Then take a **steamer cruise** of Lake Geneva. Return in the early afternoon and explore the Left Bank's **Old Town.** Have dinner at a restaurant on or around place du Bourg-de-Four.

If You Have 2 Days Spend day 1 as above. On day 2, visit some of the most important museums, each completely different. It'll take a full day of sightseeing to absorb the **Musée d'Art et d'Histoire,** the **Musée International de la Croix-Rouge et du Croissant-Rouge (Red Cross Museum),** and the **Palais des Nations.**

If You Have 3 Days Spend days 1 and 2 as above. On day 3, take a stroll along the **quays** of Geneva in the morning, and in the afternoon go on an organized excursion to the **Alps,** including Mont Blanc, for a panoramic view.

If You Have 4 or 5 Days Spend days 1 to 3 as above. On day 4, take a lake steamer to **Lausanne.** You'll have time to explore its old town and walk its lakeside quays at Ouchy before returning to Geneva in the evening. On day 5, take another lake steamer, this time to **Montreux;** after visiting this lakeside resort, take a trip outside the town to see the **Château de Chillon,** immortalized by Lord Byron.

THE TOP ATTRACTIONS

In addition to the sights below, Geneva's top attractions are the ✪ **Jet d'Eau,** the famous fountain that has virtually become the city's symbol; the **Flower Clock,** in the Jardin Anglais; and the **Old Town,** the oldest part of the city.

Baur Collections. 8 rue Munier-Romilly. ☎ **022/346-17-29.** Admission 5SF ($3.65) adults, 4SF ($2.90) students, children under 12 free. Tues–Sun 2–6pm. Bus: 1, 8, or 17.

The collections, housed in a 19th-century mansion with a garden, constitute a private exhibit of artworks from China (10th to 19th centuries) and Japan (17th to 20th centuries). On display are jade, ceramics, lacquer, ivories, and delicate sword fittings.

Maison Tavel. 6 rue du Puits-St-Pierre. ☎ **022/310-29-00.** Free admission. Tues–Sun 10am–5pm. Bus: 3, 5, 12, 17, or 23.

Built in 1303 and partially reconstructed after a fire in 1334, this is the city's oldest house and one of its newest museums. The museum exhibits historical collections from Geneva dating from the Middle Ages to the mid-19th century. The Magnin relief in the attic is outstanding, as is the copper-and-zinc model of 1850s Geneva, which is accompanied by a light-and-tape commentary. Objects of daily use are displayed in the old living quarters.

Musée Ariana. 10 av. de la Paix. ☎ **022/734-29-50.** Free admission, but 5SF ($3) for special exhibits. Wed–Mon 10am–5pm. Bus: 5, 8, 14, F, or Z.

To the west of the Palais des Nations, this Italian Renaissance building was constructed by Gustave Revilliod, the 19th-century Genevese patron who began the collection. Today it's one of the top porcelain, glass, and pottery museums in Europe. Here you'll see Sèvres, Delft faïence, and Meissen porcelain, as well as pieces from Japan and China. It's also the headquarters of the International Academy of Ceramics.

✪ **Musée d'Art et d'Histoire (Museum of Art and History).** 2 rue Charles-Galland. ☎ **022/418-26-00.** Free admission. Tues–Sun 10am–5pm. Bus: 5, 8, or 17.

Geneva's most important museum is between boulevard Jacques-Dalcroze and boulevard Helvétique. Displays include prehistoric relics, Greek vases, medieval stained glass, 12th-century armor, Swiss timepieces, and Flemish and Italian paintings. The Etruscan pottery and medieval furniture are quite impressive. A 1444 altarpiece by Konrad Witz depicts the "miraculous" draught of fishes. Many galleries also contain works by such artists as Rodin, Renoir, Le Corbusier, Picasso, Chagall, Corot, Monet, and Pissarro.

Musée de l'Horlogerie (Watch Museum). 15 route de Malagnou. ☎ **022/418-64-70.** Free admission. Wed–Mon 10am–5pm. Bus: 6 or 8. Tram: 12.

This townhouse chronicles the history of watches and clocks from the 16th century. It displays everything from sand timers to sundials, although most of the exhibits are concerned with Geneva's watches, usually from the 17th and 18th centuries. The enameled watches of the 19th century are particularly intriguing (many play chimes when you open them).

✪ **Musée International de la Croix-Rouge et du Croissant-Rouge (International Red Cross and Red Crescent Museum).** 17 av. de la Paix. ☎ **022/734-52-48.** Admission 10SF ($7.30) adults, 5SF ($3.65) seniors, students, and children. Wed–Mon 10am–5pm. Bus: 8 or F.

Here you can experience the legendary past of the Red Cross in the city where it started; it's across from the visitors' entrance to the European headquarters of the United Nations. The dramatic story from 1863 to the present is revealed through displays of rare documents and photographs, films, multiscreen slide shows, and cycloramas. You're taken from the battlefields of Europe to the plains of Africa to see the Red Cross in action. When Henry Dunant founded the Red Cross in Geneva in 1863, he needed a recognizable symbol to suggest neutrality. The Swiss flag (a white cross on a red field), with the colors reversed, ended up providing the perfect symbol for one of the world's greatest humanitarian movements.

✪ **Palais des Nations.** Parc de l'Ariana, 14 av. de la Paix. ☎ **022/907-48-96.** Admission 8.50SF ($6.20) adults, 6.50SF ($4.75) students, children under 6 free. July–Aug daily 9am–6pm; Sept–June daily 10am–noon and 2–4pm. Bus: 2, 5, 11, 14, or F.

Surrounded by ancient trees and modern monuments, these buildings form the second-largest complex in Europe after Versailles. Until 1936, the League of Nations met at the Palais Wilson, when the League's headquarters were transferred to the Palais des Nations. The international organization continued minor activities through the war years until it was dissolved in 1946, just as the newly created United Nations met in San Francisco. Today the Palais des Nations is the headquarters of the United Nations in Europe, with a modern wing added in 1973.

Inside is a **philatelic museum** and the **League of Nations Museum,** although the building itself is the most interesting attraction. Daily tours leave from the visitors' entrance at 14 av. de la Paix, opposite the Red Cross building. For information, contact the **Visitors' Service,** United Nations Office, 14 av. de la Paix (☎ **022/907-45-60**).

RELIGIOUS MONUMENTS

The old town, **Vieille Ville,** on the Left Bank, is dominated by the ✪ **Cathédrale St-Pierre,** Cour St-Pierre (☎ **022/738-56-50**), built in the 12th and 13th centuries and partially reconstructed in the 15th century. Recent excavations have disclosed that a Christian sanctuary was here as early as A.D. 400. In 1536, the people of Geneva gathered in the cloister of St-Pierre's and voted to make the cathedral Protestant. The church has a modern organ with 6,000 pipes. The northern tower was reconstructed at the end of the 19th century, with a metal steeple erected between the two stone towers. If you don't mind the 145 steps, you can climb to the top of the north tower for a panoramic view. The tower is open daily 11:30am to 5:30pm. Admission is 2.50SF ($1.85).

To enter the St-Pierre archaeological site, called **Site Archéologique de St-Pierre,** go through the entrance in the Cour St-Pierre, at the right corner of the cathedral steps. The underground passage extends under the present cathedral and the High Gothic (early 15th century) **Chapelle des Macchabées,** which adjoins the church's southwestern corner. The chapel was restored during World War II, after having been used as a storage room following the Reformation. Excavations have revealed baptisteries, a crypt, the foundations of several cathedrals, the bishop's palace, 4th-century mosaics, and sculptures and geological strata.

The cathedral and chapel are open June through September, daily 9am to 7pm; March through May and October, daily 9am to noon and 2 to 6pm; November through February, daily 9am to noon and 2 to 3pm. There's no admission fee, but donations are welcome. The archaeological site is open Tuesday to Saturday 10am to 1pm and 2 to 6pm; admission is 5SF ($3.65).

PARKS, GARDENS & SQUARES

If you walk along the quays, heading north as if to Lausanne, you'll come to some of the lushest parks in Geneva. **Parc Mon-Repos** is off avenue de France, and **La Perle du Lac** lies off rue de Lausanne. Directly to the right is the **Jardin Botanique**

(Botanical Garden), opened in 1902. It has an alpine garden, a little zoo, greenhouses, and exhibitions; you can visit it free daily October through April, 9:30am to 5pm, and May through September, 8am to 7:30pm.

Back at lakeside, you can take a boat to the other bank, getting off at quai Gustave-Ador. From here you can explore two more lakeside parks—**Parc la Grange,** which has the most extravagant rose garden in Switzerland (especially in June), and, next to it, **Parc des Eaux-Vives.**

When you leave the Botanical Garden on the Left Bank, you can head west, along avenue de la Paix, about a mile north from pont du Mont-Blanc, to the Palais des Nations in **Parc de l'Ariana.**

ORGANIZED TOURS

A 2-hour city tour is operated daily by **Key Tours S.A.,** 7 rue des Alpes, square du Mont-Blanc (☎ **022/731-41-40**). The tour starts from the Gare Routière, the bus station at place Dorcière, near the Key Tours office. From November through March, a tour is offered only once a day at 2pm; the rest of the year, two tours leave daily, at 10am and 2pm.

A bus will drive you through the city to see the monuments, landmarks, and lake promenades. In the Old Town you can take a walk down to the Bastions Park to the Reformation Wall. After an English-language tour through the International Center—where you'll be shown the headquarters of the International Red Cross—the bus returns to its starting place. Adults pay 32SF ($23.35), children 4 to 12 accompanied by an adult are 16SF ($11.70), and children 3 and under go free.

THE SHOPPING SCENE

As one might suspect, watches, knives, cheese, and chocolate are among Geneva's best buys. Check prices carefully; many Swiss watches are currently cheaper in the United States than in Switzerland. Swiss army knives are still a good deal, and as for chocolate, well, it's incomparable and just not the same when you buy it in another country.

Geneva's Left Bank shopping area is along the exclusive **rue du Rhône** and adjacent streets. Here you'll find shop after shop of designer fashions and expensive watches. Along the winding streets of the **Old City** you can explore antiques stores and galleries. For Swiss army knives and watches, stroll along the pedestrians-only **rue du Mont-Blanc** on the Right Bank. You'll find an endless assortment of watches, knives, and other souvenirs, all priced similarly.

Colorful **outdoor markets,** overflowing with flowers and fruit, take place several times a week at places Rive, Coutance, Carouge, and others. A **flea market** is held every Wednesday and Saturday on the Plaine de Plainpalais; markets for books take place on place de la Madeleine on most days during summer.

SELECT SHOPS Virtually all the inventory at **Antiquorum,** 2 rue du Mont-Blanc (☎ **022/738-85-85**), consists of antique jewelry and antique watches—a sure attraction for a city that derives so much of its income from selling timepieces. The array includes some of the world's most historically important watches.

The aroma of chocolate from the **Confiserie Rohr,** 3 place du Molard (☎ **022/343-32-77**), practically pulls you in off the street. You'll find chocolate-covered truffles, "gold" bars with hazelnuts, and *poubelles au chocolat* (chocolate "garbage pails"). There's another branch at 42 rue du Rhône (☎ **022/311-68-76**).

On place du Molard, **Bon Genie,** 34 rue du Marché (☎ **022/818-11-11**), is a department store selling high-fashion women's clothing and a limited selection of men's. Its windows display art objects from local museums alongside designer clothes. Geneva's largest department store, **Globus,** 48 rue du Rhône (☎ **022/319-50-50**), has just about everything: a travel bureau, an agency selling theater tickets, a hairdresser, a newsstand, a handful of boutiques, a restaurant, and a sandwich shop. **Bruno Magli,** 47 rue du Rhône (☎ 022/311-53-77), is one of Geneva's best-stocked shoe stores, with an elegant variety of Italian shoes, purses, and accessories. This outlet of the Bologna-based chain stocks mainly women's shoes.

Opposite pont du Mont-Blanc, the chrome-and-crystal **Bucherer,** 26 quai du Général-Guisan (☎ 022/319-62-66), sells expensive watches and diamonds. The store offers such name brands as Rolex, Piaget, Baume & Mercier, Tissot, Rado, and Swatch. The third floor is filled with relatively inexpensive watches. Once you're on that floor, you'll also find a large selection of cuckoo clocks, music boxes, embroideries, and souvenirs, as well as porcelain pill boxes and other gift items.

Established over a century ago, **Leinen Langenthal,** 13 rue du Rhône (☎ 022/310-65-10), boasts an enviable reputation for good-quality merchandise and a showroom on the city's most prestigious shopping street, across from the Union des Banques Suisses. The merchandise includes napery, towels, bed linens, and "table suites," some of it embroidered by hand in the Swiss lace center of St-Gallen.

At the corner of rue de la Fontaine, **Jouets Weber (Franz Carl Weber),** 12 rue de la Croix-d'Or (☎ 022/310-42-55), is the best toy store in the city. It has all kinds of children's toys, from slide shows to cartoon characters, as well as dolls and sports equipment.

GENEVA AFTER DARK

For a preview of events at the time of your visit, pick up a copy of the monthly **"List of Events"** issued by the tourist office.

THE PERFORMING ARTS

Grand Théâtre de Genève. Place Neuve. ☎ **022/418-30-00.** Tickets 37–127SF ($92.70) for opera; 19–87SF ($13.85–$63.50) for ballet.

Modeled on Paris's Opéra Garnier, this building was opened in 1879, and is often included in lists of the world's ten best opera houses. It burned down in 1951 and was subsequently rebuilt in the same style, except for the modern auditorium, which has seating for 1,488. From September to July, it presents about eight operas and two ballets, as well as recitals and chamber-music concerts.

Orchestre de la Suisse Romande. 14 rue du Général-Dufour. ☎ **022/317-00-17.** Tickets 20–75SF ($14.60–$54.75)).

This celebrated orchestra's home is the 1,866-seat **Victoria Hall.** The orchestra is Geneva's most famous musical institution. For 50 years its conductor was Ernst Ansermet and, through this maestro, it was closely associated with Igor Stravinsky.

THE CLUB & MUSIC SCENE

Arthur's Club. Centre I.C.C., Rte. des Près-Bois 20. ☎ **022/788-16-00.** Cover 20SF ($14.60), including first drink.

This fun, unpretentious club is committed to preserving a healthy balance of clients between the ages of 18 and 45. Inside, each of the ten different bars manages to attract a mini-subculture all its own, so regardless of your age or preferences, you'll eventually find something or someone that appeals to you. On busy nights, expect as many as 2,500 clients, many of whom dance, dance, dance, crammed inside. It's open Friday and Saturday 10am to 5am.

Au Chat Noir. 13 rue Vautier, Carouges. ☎ **022/343-49-93.** Cover 10–15SF ($7.30–$10.95).

In the suburb of Carouges, this is the current hot spot in town, a venue for funk, rock, salsa, jazz, and some good old New Orleans blues. It's crowded on weekends but the club will take reservations. A changing repertoire of concerts is presented nightly at either 9 or 10pm. The club itself is open Monday to Thursday 6pm to 4am, Friday 6pm to 5am, Saturday 9pm to 5am, and Sunday 9am to 4am. After a few drinks, you begin to fear that the car suspended from the ceiling might fall on you. Take tram 12 from Place Bel-Air in central Geneva.

Club 58. 15 Glacis de Rive. ☎ **022/735-15-15.** Cover 15–20SF ($10.95–$14.60).

This private club does allow nonmembers to enter, although men are required to wear jackets. It's mainly a disco, but there's an attached restaurant. Occasionally the club presents some top names in show business. It opens daily at 10pm; the restaurant opens at 8pm. Drinks in the club cost 25SF ($18.25); restaurant drinks are 12SF ($8.75).

Griffin's Club. 36 bd. Helvétique. ☎ **022/735-12-18.** No cover.

Griffin's is the chicest club in Geneva. Technically, it's private—you may or may not get in, depending on the mood of the management at the time of your visit. On Friday and Saturday, precedence is usually given to members. Jackets are required for men. The decor of the place, much of which is in a basement, is gilt and gray, with lots of live plants and large paintings in the restaurant. The restaurant serves à la carte and set-price meals, beginning at 130SF ($94.90) without wine. It's open Monday through Saturday from 8pm to at least 2:30am. The disco opens at 11pm and closes between 4 and 5am, depending on the night of the week.

L'Interdit. Quai du Seujet 18. ☎ **022/738-90-91.** Cover 20SF ($14.60), including first drink.

This club isn't as difficult to get into as other clubs in Geneva. It's hip, heterosexual, and worthy of a visit if you want to meet attractive strangers of the opposite sex. There's also a restaurant here, but the main appeal is the dancing, which starts every night at 10pm and lasts until around 5am.

Velvet. 7 rue de Jeu-de-l'Arc. ☎ **022/735-00-00.** Sun–Thurs no cover; Fri–Sat 16SF ($11.70) cover.

If you're into disco dancing and barside flirting, it's a nonstop party at Velvet. There are two stages where seminaked women dance, frug, boogaloo, and pose as appealingly as they can to a sometimes appreciative, sometimes blasé audience. There's likely to be a working woman or two waiting for an unaccompanied male to buy her a drink; the place is very heterosexual and relatively permissive. Drinks begin at a steep 22SF ($16.05). The *artistes*—as many as 30 are employed by this place—begin dancing at 11pm and continue in ongoing shifts until 4 or 5am. You'll find the place on the Left Bank of the commercial heart of Geneva, in the Quartier des Eaux-Vives.

BARS

Bar des Bergues. In the Hôtel des Bergues, 33 quai des Bergues. ☎ **022/731-50-50.**

Sheathed in mahogany, brass, and dark-green upholstery, this fashionable bar is decorated with a series of late 19th-century menus from the Cercle des Arts et des Lettres. Although most people come just for a drink or two, the place also serves lunches and platters from the hotel's top-notch kitchen. Ask the barman for the list of daily specials. Beginning in the early evening, there's an international array of pianists.

Le Gentilhomme Bar. In the Hôtel Richemond, Jardin Brunswick. ☎ **022/731-14-00.**

Although this is technically the apéritif bar for the hotel's elegant Restaurant Le Gentilhomme, many visitors consider the venue an attractive and stylish option in its own right. It attracts a chic crowd, ranging from U.S.-based beneficiaries of corporate mergers to Zurich bankers to glamorous women in $50,000 furs.

GAY GENEVA

Centre Femmes Nathalie Barney (Le Maison). 30 av. Peshier. ☎ **022/789-26-00.**

Many lesbian groups meet at this center in the Champel district. It's the best-organized outlet for gay women in French-speaking Switzerland and is named for Nathalie Barney, a well-known lesbian liberationist who ran a salon in Paris at the turn of the century. Different social and political gatherings take place several nights a week. The center maintains a restaurant open for group dinners only on designated nights of the week and a women's bar open only Friday and Saturday nights.

Dialogai. 57 av. de Wendt. ☎ **022/340-00-00.**

In the district of Servette, this place provides multilingual information and advice. On the basement-level premises are a library, a cafe and bar, and meeting rooms for Wednesday-night dinners and Saturday-night dancing parties. The organization publishes a list—free to anyone who asks—of the gay bars of Geneva and French-speaking Switzerland, and is the best conduit to Geneva's male homosexual network.

Le Loft and Le Backside. 20 quai du Seujet. ☎ **022/738-28-28.**

This began as a large and amicable gay bar, but so many straight people flocked here that a separate area (Le Backside; ☎ **022/732-13-13**) was installed for gays; it's a darkened area with a prominent bar at the rear of the ground floor. Regardless of where you opt to congregate, you'll find a convivial site, usually with a distinct sense of humor, and shows that begin every night at 11pm. The place functions as a cafe throughout the day, serving croissants and café au lait to office workers as early as 6am, but its most amusing times are nightly beginning around 10pm and lasting till around 3am.

DAY TRIPS FROM GENEVA

MONT SALÈVE   The limestone ridge of Mont Salève (House Mountain) is 4 miles south of Geneva in France, so you'll need your passport. Its peak is at 4,000 feet. If you have a car, you can take a road that goes up the mountain; it's also popular with rock climbers. Bus no. 8 will take you to Veyrier, on the French border, where there's a passport and Customs control. A 6-minute cable-car ride carries you to a height of 3,750 feet on Mont Salève. From the top you'll have a panoramic sweep of the Valley of the Arve, with Geneva and Mont Blanc in the background.

✪ **MONT BLANC & CHAMONIX**   We highly recommend a Mont Blanc excursion, an all-day trip to Chamonix, France, by bus and a cable-car ride to the summit of the Aiguille du Midi (12,610 ft.). The tour leaves Geneva at 8am and returns at 6pm daily. Buses leave from Gare Routière, and you must take your passport.

Other climbs on this tour are Vallée Blanche by télécabin, an extension of the Aiguille du Midi climb, April through October; to Mer de Glâce via electric rack railway to the edge of the glacier, from which you can descend to the ice grotto (the climb isn't available in winter); and to Le Brevent, an ascent by cable car to a rocky belvedere at 7,900 feet, facing the Mont Blanc range.

An English-speaking guide will accompany your bus tour. **Key Tours S.A.,** 7 rue des Alpes (place du Mont-Blanc), Case Postale 1745, 1211 Genève (☎ **022/731-41-40**), requires a minimum of eight people per trip. Tours begin at 193SF ($140.90) for adults and 113SF ($82.50) for children.

LAKE GENEVA CRUISES   Two companies offer cruises on Lac Léman. The smaller one, **Mouettes Genevoises Navigation,** 8 quai du Mont-Blanc (☎ **022/732-29-44**), specializes in small-scale boats carrying only about 100 passengers. Each features some kind of guided (recorded) commentary, in French and English. An easy promenade that surveys the landscapes and bird life along the uppermost regions of the Rhône draining the lake is the company's "Tour du Rhône" (Rhône River Tour). The trip originates at a point adjacent to Geneva's pont de l'Ile and travels downstream for about 9 miles to the Barrage de Verbois (Verbois Dam) and back. From April through October, departures are daily at 2:15pm and also Wednesday, Thursday, Saturday, and Sunday at 10am. It costs 22SF ($16.05) for adults and 15SF ($10.95) for children 4 to 12; free for children under 4. The same company also offers 1¼-hour tours (four times a day) and 2-hour tours (two times a day) out onto the lake. The longer tour includes a recorded commentary on the celebrity residences and ecology of the lake. It's 12SF ($8.75) for the shorter tour and 20SF ($14.60) for the longer tour; no stops are made en route.

Bateaux de la Mouette's largest competitor, **CGN (Compagnie General de Navigation),** quai du Mont-Blanc (☎ **022/312-52-21**), offers roughly equivalent tours, May through September, that last an hour and depart four times a day from the company's piers along the quai du Mont-Blanc. Known as " Mouettes Genevoises Navigation," they charge 12SF ($8.75) for adults and 6SF ($4.40) for children 6 to 16 (children under 6 free). Tours include recorded commentaries and last about as long as many short-term visitors to the city want.

2 Bern & the Berner Oberland

Dating from the 12th century, Bern is one of the loveliest and oldest cities in Europe. Since much of its medieval architecture has remained untouched, the United Nations declared it a world landmark in 1983. As the capital of Switzerland, it's also a city of diplomats and the site of many international organizations and meetings.

Bern is a convenient center for exploring the lakes and peaks of the Berner Oberland—a vast recreation area only minutes from the capital, sprawling between the Reuss River and Lake Geneva. It's an important center for winter sports, one of the best-equipped areas for downhill skiers, and a challenging place for hikers and mountain climbers. The Jungfrau (13,642 ft.) and the Finsteraarhorn (14,022 ft.) are the highest alpine peaks. The canton of Bern, encompassing most of the area, is Switzerland's second-largest, and contains 100 square miles of glaciers.

The best center for exploring the Berner Oberland is Interlaken, a popular summer resort. Summer and winter playgrounds are at Gstaad, Grindelwald, Kandersteg, and Mürren. You can ski in the mountains in winter and surf, sail, and water-ski on Lake Thun in summer.

Only in the Berner Oberland

Hiking in and Around Bern   After a walk through the old heart of medieval Bern (allow about 2½ hours), you should be ready for an even greater hike in the environs. The most popular day trip is to Bern's own mountain, Gurten, 25 minutes by tram. Here you'll find walks in many directions and can enjoy a panorama over the Alps. But that's not all: Walks in and around Bern include 155 miles of marked rambling paths, one of the most scenic being along the banks of the Aare through the English Gardens.

Bicycling Through the Berner Oberland   There are some 1,860 miles of roadway in the Berner Oberland. The tourist office will give you a map outlining the routes, and you can rent a bike at the main rail station—and then set off on your adventure.

Getting Around the Oberland   In this section of Switzerland, getting here is half the fun. To compensate for the region's almost impossible geography, Swiss engineers have crisscrossed the Oberland with cogwheel railways (some still driven by steam), aerial cableways, and sinuous mountain roads. When you tire of all this high-altitude travel, you can take more relaxing ferries across the lakes, including Thun and Brienz. Regardless of where you travel, panoramic scenery unfolds at every turn.

Taking a Rail Trip to Jungfraujoch   This ranks as one of the top rail trips of a lifetime. After leaving Interlaken, you change at Kleine Scheidegg to the highest rack railway in Europe, the Jungfraubahn. You have 6 miles to go, 4 of them through a tunnel carved between 1896 and 1912. You stop twice, at Eigerwand and Eismeer, to view a sea of ice from windows in the rock. The Eigerwand is at 9,400 feet, the Eismeer at 10,368 feet. When the train emerges from the tunnel, the daylight is momentarily blinding. Once here, the eerie ice world of Jungfrau awaits you.

Following the Trail of Sherlock Holmes   A 50-minute train ride from Interlaken delivers you to Meiringen, a resort known to devotees of Holmesiana. From here, you can take an excursion to Reichenbachfall, where the rivers of the Rosenlaui valley meet. The beauty of the falls so impressed Conan Doyle that he described it in *The Final Problem,* in which the villain, Professor Moriarty, struggles with the detective before tossing him into the falls. From mid-May to mid-September, a funicular takes you to a point at 2,779 feet, near terraces overlooking the water.

Skiing at Gstaad   One of the world's great ski resorts, attracting the rich and famous, Gstaad is set against a dramatic backdrop of glaciers and peaceful alpine pastures in a district known as Saanenland, one of the most beautiful parts of Switzerland. From mountain railroads to gondolas, Gstaad is well served by public transport to take you to the ski action, including a mountain at 6,550 feet with a vertical drop of 3,555 feet. There's even skiing in summer, and when darkness falls the après-ski life of Gstaad is legendary.

BERN

The modern mingles harmoniously with the old in this charming city. Contemporary buildings are discreetly designed to blend in with the historic environment. The city stands on a thumb of land that's bordered on three sides by the Aare River, and several bridges connect the old part of the city with the newer sections.

Market days in Bern are Tuesday and Saturday, when people from the outlying areas come to town to sell their produce and wares. If you're fortunate enough to arrive on the fourth Monday of November, you'll witness the centuries-old Zwiebelmarkt (Onion Market). This is the city's last big event before the onset of winter, as residents traditionally stock up on onions in anticipation of the first snows.

ORIENTATION

ARRIVING   By Plane   The **Bern-Belp Airport** (☎ 031/960-21-11) is 6 miles south of the city in Belpmoos. International flights arrive from London, Paris, and Nice, but transatlantic jets are not able to land here. Fortunately, it's a short hop to Bern from the international airports in Zurich and Geneva.

Taxis are about 40SF ($29.20) to the city center, so it's better to take the shuttle bus that runs between the airport and the Bahnhof (train station), costing 17SF ($12.40) one way.

By Train   Bern has direct connections to the continental rail network that includes France, Italy, Germany, and the Benelux countries, even Scandinavia and Spain. The superfast TGV train connects Paris with Bern in just 4½ hours. Bern also lies on major Swiss rail links, particularly those connecting Geneva and Zurich; each city is only 90 minutes away.

The **Bahnhof,** on Bahnhofplatz, is in the center of town near all the major hotels. If your luggage is light, you can walk to your hotel; otherwise, take one of the taxis waiting outside the station. For **information** about tickets and train schedules for the Swiss Federal Railways, call ☎ **157-22-22** (no area code).

VISITOR INFORMATION The **Bern Tourist Office,** in the Bahnhof, on Bahnhofplatz (☎ **031/311-66-11**), is open June through September, daily 9am to 8:30pm; October through May, Monday to Saturday 9am to 6:30pm and Sunday 10am to 5pm. If you need help finding a hotel room, the tourist office can make a reservation for you.

GETTING AROUND

BY BUS & TRAM The public transportation system, the **Stadtische Verkehrsbetriebe (SVB),** is a reliable 48-mile network of buses and trams. Before you board, buy a ticket from the self-service automatic machines at each stop (conductors don't sell tickets). If you're caught traveling without one, you're fined 50SF ($36.50). A short-range ticket (six stations) costs 1.50SF ($1.10); a regular ticket, valid for 45 minutes one-way only, is 2.40SF ($1.75).

BY TAXI You can catch a taxi at the public cab ranks, or you can call a dispatcher. Try **Nova Taxi** at ☎ **031/301-11-11** or **Bären Taxi** at ☎ **031/371-11-11.** The meter registers at 6SF ($4.40) when you get in, and then goes up to 3.10SF ($2.25) per kilometer. After 8pm and until 6am daily, the per kilometer rate rises to 3.50SF ($2.55).

BY CAR Don't try to drive in the city; use your car for exploring the environs. Car-rental companies in Bern include **Hertz,** Casinoplatz at Kochergasse 1 (☎ **031/318-21-60**), and **Avis,** Wabernstrasse 41 (☎ **031/372-13-13**).

BY BICYCLE The Altstadt is compressed into such a small area that it's better to cover it on foot rather than on a bike. Bicycles aren't allowed on the many pedestrians-only streets anyway. However, in Greater Bern and its environs there are 248 miles of cycling paths. They are marked on a special cycling map available at the tourist office (see "Visitor Information," above). Bicycle lanes are indicated by yellow marked lanes on parts of the road network. The point of departure for most official cycling routes is Bundesplatz (Parliament Square). Special red signs guide you through a wide variety of landscapes. For 22SF ($16.05) per day, you can rent bicycles at the **SBB Railway Station,** Bahnhofplatz (☎ **051/220-23-74**). Call the day before for a reservation.

SEEING THE SIGHTS

The **Zutgloggeturm (Clock Tower)** on Kramgasse was built in the 12th century and restored in the 16th. Four minutes before every hour, crowds gather for the world's oldest (since 1530) and biggest horological puppet show: Mechanical bears, jesters, and emperors put on an animated performance. The tower marked the west gate of Bern until 1250.

The ✪ **Bärengraben (Bear Pits),** on the opposite side of the river, is a deep moon-shaped den where bears, Bern's mascots, have been kept since 1480. According

---

Traveler's Tip

To save time, and possibly money, you can purchase a **1-day ticket** for 7.50SF ($5.50), entitling you to unlimited travel on the SVB network. Just get the ticket stamped at the automatic machine before you begin your first trip. One-day tickets are available at the ticket offices at Bubenbergplatz 5 (☎ **031/321-86-31**) and in the underpass of the Bahnhof (☎ **031/321-86-41**), as well as at other outlets in the city.

Bern

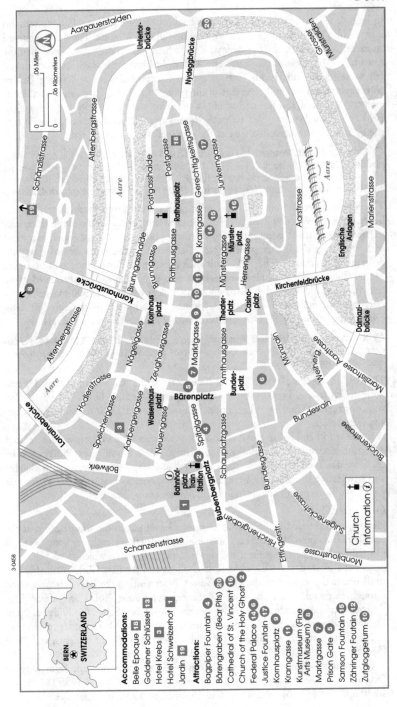

Accommodations:
Belle Epoque 18
Goldener Schlüssel 13
Hotel Krebs 3
Hotel Schweizerhof 1
Jardin 19

Attractions:
Bagpiper Fountain 4
Bärengraben (Bear Pits) 20
Cathedral of St. Vincent 16
Church of the Holy Ghost 2
Federal Palace 14, 6
Justice Fountain 17
Kornhausplatz 9
Kramgasse 11
Kunstmuseum (Fine Arts Museum) 8
Marktgasse 7
Prison Gate 5
Samson Fountain 15
Zähinger Fountain 12
Zytgloggeturm 10

SWITZERLAND
BERN

3-0458

to legend, when the duke of Zähringen established the town in 1191, he sent his hunters into the encircling woods, which were full of wild game. The duke promised to name the city after the first animal slain, which was a Bär (bear). Since then the town has been known as Bärn, or Bern. Today, the bears are beloved, pampered, and fed by residents and visitors (carrots are most appreciated). The **Nydegg Bridge (Nydeggbrücke)** was built over one of the gorges of the Aare River; its central stone arch has a span of 180 feet and affords a sweeping view of the city from its center. Below the Bear Pits, you can visit the **Rosengarten (Rose Gardens)**, from which there's a much-photographed view of the medieval sector and the river.

✪ **Cathedral of St. Vincent.** Münsterplatz. ☎ **031/311-05-72.** Cathedral, free; viewing platform, 3SF ($2.20) adults, 1SF (75¢) children under 12. Easter Sun–Oct, Tues–Sat 10am–5pm, Sun 11am–5pm; off-season, Tues–Fri 10am–noon and 2–4pm, Sat 10am–noon and 2–5pm, Sun 11am–2pm. Viewing platform closes half an hour before cathedral. Bus: 12.

The Münster, dating from 1421, is one of Switzerland's newer Gothic churches; the belfry, however, was completed in 1893. The most exceptional feature of this three-aisle pillared basilica is the tympanum over the main portal, depicting the Last Judgment with more than 200 figures, some painted. Mammoth 15th-century stained-glass windows are in the chancel. The 1523 choir stalls brought the Renaissance to Bern. In the Matter Chapel is a remarkable stained-glass window, the *Dance of Death,* created in the last year of World War I, but based on a much older design. The 300-foot-tall belfry offers a panoramic sweep; to get to the viewing platform, you must climb 270 steps. Outside the basilica on Münsterplatz is the Moses Fountain, constructed in 1545.

✪ **Kunstmuseum (Fine Arts Museum).** Hodlerstrasse 12. ☎ **031/311-09-44.** Permanent collection, 6SF ($4.40); special exhibit, 10–18SF ($7.30–$13.15) extra. Tues 10am–9pm; Wed–Sun 10am–5pm. Bus: 20.

The world's largest collection of Paul Klee works is the star attraction here. He was born in Switzerland in 1879, the same year that the building housing the collection was constructed. The Klee collection includes 40 oils and 2,000 drawings, gouaches, and watercolors.

Other works emphasize the 19th and 20th centuries. The important 20th-century collection has works by Kandinsky, Modigliani, Matisse, Soutine, and Picasso, and by the Surrealist and Constructivist schools as well as contemporary Swiss artists. There's also a collection of Italian 14th-century primitives, notably Fra Angelico's *Virgin and Child,* and Swiss primitives, including the *Masters of the Carnation.*

Organized Tours

Highly recommended is the **2-hour bus tour** leaving from the tourist office at the Bahnhof, at Bahnhofplatz. An English-speaking guide takes you through the city's residential quarters, past museums, and down to the Aare River, which flows below the houses of Parliament. You'll see the Rose Gardens and the Late Gothic cathedral and stroll under the arcades to the Clock Tower. After visiting the Bear Pits, you're led through medieval streets and back to the railroad station. Tours are offered June through September daily at 2pm; October and November, Sunday to Friday at 2pm; December through March, Saturday at 2pm; and April and May Monday to Saturday at 2pm. The cost is 22SF ($16.05) for adults, 20SF ($14.60) for students, and 11SF ($8.05) for children 6 to 16; children 5 and under are free.

The tourist office also conducts 2-hour **walking tours** of Bern from May to October. Tours leave daily at 11:15am from Zutglogge. The cost is 12SF ($8.75) for adults and 6SF ($4.40) for children 6 to 16; children 5 and under are free.

Taking a Cable-Train to Mont Gurten

The most panoramic attraction in the immediate vicinity is the ✪ **belvedere atop Mont Gurten,** where there's also a children's fairyland and a walking area. The belvedere is connected to Bern by the Gurtenbahn cable-train, one of the fastest in all Europe. The train departs from a station beside the Monbijoustrasse, about 1½ miles from Bern's center. Round-trip passage on the cable-train is 7.50SF ($5.50). The train operates year-round, daily 7:30am to sunset. For details, contact **Gurtenbahn Bern,** Eigerplatz 3 (☎ **031/961-23-23**). To reach the departure platform, take tram no. 9 (2.50SF ($1.85) each way) to the Gurtenbahn station. If you're driving, follow the road signs to Thun. There's a parking lot in the hamlet of Wabern, a short walk from the cable-train station.

WHERE TO STAY
Very Expensive
Hotel Schweizerhof. Bahnhofplatz 11, 3001 Bern. ☎ **031/311-45-01.** Fax 031/312-21-79. E-mail: info@schweizerhof bern.ch. 90 units. MINIBAR TV TEL. 360–450SF ($262.80–$328.50) double; from 620SF ($452.60) suite. Rates include buffet breakfast. AE, DC, MC, V. Parking 25SF ($18.25). Tram: 3, 9, or 12.

Built in 1859, this central hotel managed by the Gauer family is popular with diplomats and remains the grandest hotel in the Swiss capital. It contains many antiques and some of the best decorative art in Bern: 18th-century drawing-room pieces, wall-sized tapestries, and crystal chandeliers. Some units are quite contemporary, others more antique, but all offer comfortably upholstered chairs and sofas, with a fairly good chest, desk, or table; some are air-conditioned. Clad in marble, the luxurious bathrooms contain cosmetics bars, hair dryers, tubs with shower, and robes. There are several formal restaurants, including the Schultheissenstube, our favorite, which offers attentive service.

Expensive
✪ **Belle Epoque.** Gerechtigkeitsgasse 18, 3001 Bern. ☎ **031/311-43-36.** Fax 031/311-39-36. 18 units. MINIBAR TV TEL. 220–285SF ($160.60–$208.05) double; from 350SF ($255.50) suite. AE, DC, MC, V. Parking 24SF ($17.50). Bus: 12.

One of the highlights of this renovated medieval home in Bern's historic core is a bar outfitted like an art and antiques gallery, lined with late-19th- and early-20th-century oil paintings and filled with Jugendstil (German art nouveau) furnishings and comfortable settees. Each guest room boasts reproduction turn-of-the-century furniture accented with century-old artifacts, period light fixtures from the 1920s, and engravings. Many bathrooms have both tubs and showers.

Innere Enge. Engestrasse 54, 3012 Bern. ☎ **031/309-61-11.** Fax 301/309-61-12. 26 units. TV TEL. 230–390SF ($167.90–$284.70) double. Rates include continental breakfast. AE, DC, MC, V. Bus: 21.

When you tire of impersonal bandboxes, head for this 18th-century building and the small, choice hotel it contains. From your light spacious, and airy bedroom, you are likely to have a view of the Bernese Alps. Bedrooms have style and character, with traditional (if not antique) beds and roomy bathrooms, sometimes with a tub and shower combination. Swiss regional and international dishes are served in the restaurant, and jazz acts are booked in the Louis Armstrong Bar.

Moderate

Hotel Ambassador. Seftigenstrasse 99, 3007 Bern. ☎ **031/371-41-11.** Fax 031/371-41-17. E-mail: ambassador@ping.ch. 97 units. MINIBAR TV TEL. 179–190SF ($130.65–$138.70) double. AE, DC, MC, V. Tram: 9.

This nine-story hotel in a neighborhood of older houses with red-tile roofs, is about a mile from the train station, but easily reached by tram. The guest rooms come with refrigerators, and many have a view of the Bundeshaus. They tend to be smallish and furnished somewhat impersonally, but they're well maintained. Dining choices include the Restaurant Pavilion Café and the Japanese Teppan Restaurant, and there's a sauna, fitness center, and 24-hour indoor pool.

Hotel Krebs. Genfergasse 8, 3011 Bern. ☎ **031/311-49-42.** Fax 031/311-10-35. www.hotelonline.de. E-mail: hotel-krebs thenet.ch. 46 units (41 with bathroom). TV TEL. 158SF ($115.35) double without bathroom; 173SF ($126.30) double with bathroom. Rates include buffet breakfast. AE, DC, MC, V. Parking 32SF ($23.35). Tram: 3 or 9.

This three-star hotel is near the train station and shares its ground floor with a store. The rooms are rather Spartan but occasionally sunny, and wood paneling adds more warmth. Some of the rooms can be converted for families. The few singles, without bathroom, are among the more reasonably priced in the area. Private bathrooms are small, and a little short of shelf space; those in the hall are tidily kept.

Inexpensive

✪ **Goldener Schlüssel.** Rathausgasse 72, 3011 Bern. ☎ **031/311-02-16.** Fax 031/311-56-88. 29 units (20 with bathroom). TV TEL. 110SF ($80.30) double without bathroom, 139SF ($101.45) double with bathroom; 149SF ($108.75) triple without bathroom, 185SF ($135.05) triple with bathroom. Rates include buffet breakfast. MC, V. Parking 14SF ($10.20). Bus: 12. Tram: 9.

In the heart of Altstadt, opening onto Rathausgasse, the building housing this little inn dates from the 13th century, when it was used as a stable. It's beautifully maintained today. Some of the carpeted guest rooms have wood-paneled walls. As it's fairly busy on the street outside, ask for one of the rear rooms if you want less noise. Immaculate linens on the beds and fresh tiles in the bathroom speak of good housekeeping. If you're a bargain hunter, ask for a room without bathroom—the hallway plumbing is adequate. The hotel's sidewalk cafe does a thriving business throughout summer, and the restaurant offers reasonably priced meals.

Jardin. Militarstrasse 38, 3014 Bern. ☎ **031/333-01-17.** www.hotelonline.de. 20 units. TV TEL. 133SF ($97.10) double. Rates include breakfast. AE, DC, MC, V. Tram: 9 to Breitenrainplatz.

In 1985, this building about half a mile north of the city center was converted from a restaurant and apartment building into a modern and warmly appealing hotel. The guest rooms here are larger than virtually any others in their price range. The hotel is run by identical twins Andy and Daniel Balz, whose similarities may confuse you; one or the other is almost always available to help guests. Joggers and nature lovers appreciate the verdant areas across the street; they're part of the land surrounding Bern's largest military academy.

WHERE TO DINE

Expensive

Della Casa. Schauplatzgasse 16. ☎ **031/311-21-42.** Reservations recommended. Main courses 28–44SF ($20.45–$32.10); set-price menu 22SF ($16.05). AE, DC, MC, V (downstairs only). Mon–Fri 11am–2pm and 6–9:30pm; Sat 9:30am–3pm. Upstairs level closed in July (downstairs dining room remains open). Tram: 3, 5, or 9. CONTINENTAL.

From under an arcade, you enter a low-ceilinged paneled room that's often crowded with chattering diners. For those eager to follow the latest political trends and opinions, an inner room has all the day's newspapers—indeed, the place has been called Switzerland's "unofficial Parliament headquarters." Upstairs is a quieter, somewhat more formal dining room. The menu features continental and Italian dishes. Two of our favorites are the ravioli maison and the fried zucchini; a popular meat specialty is filet mignon à la bordelaise with Créole rice. More typical, however, is the Berner platter with sauerkraut, sausages, ham, bacon, and pork.

Räblus. Zeughausgasse 3. ☎ **031/311-59-08.** Reservations required. Main courses 20–35SF ($14.60–$25.55). AE, DC, MC, V. Mon–Sat 4pm–1am. Tram: 3 or 9. FRENCH.

Centrally located near the Clock Tower, this 200-year-old restaurant has a ground-floor bar where you can stop for an apéritif before proceeding up to the richly paneled, sculpture-filled dining room. The kitchen prepares a French cuisine with a definite Swiss/German influence. Try such dishes as tender pieces of veal in a creamy sauce, lamb chops in the Provençal style (that is, with tomatoes and garlic), or a classic beef Stroganoff.

Moderate

Commerce. Gerechtigkeitsgasse 74. ☎ **031/311-11-61.** Reservations required. Main courses 12–45SF ($8.75–$32.85). AE, DC, MC, V. Tues–Sat 11am–2pm; Mon–Sat 5–10pm. Closed last 3 weeks in July. Tram: 12. SPANISH.

This small Spanish tavern near the Fountain of Justice (Gerechtigkeitsbrunnen) attracts many expatriate Spaniards, some of whom work at the Spanish Embassy. The decor is Iberian, and the paella is popular, even if it isn't as authentic as that served in Valencia. The specialty is scampi prepared in several ways; we also recommend the *zarzuela,* Spanish-style bouillabaisse.

Goldener Schlüssel. Rathausgasse 72. ☎ **031/311-02-16.** Reservations recommended. Main courses 16.50–33.50SF ($12.05–$24.45). MC, V. Daily 11:30am–2pm and 6–10pm. Bus: 12. Tram: 9. SWISS.

You'll relish both the food and the bustling atmosphere at this very Swiss restaurant, where the old planking and stonework of a 13th-century building can be seen overhead. Serving wholesome food in ample portions, the restaurant is on the street level of a budget-priced hotel of the same name (see "Where to Stay," above). Specialties include a roulade of lamb filets with guinea fowl that's served with a homemade cornmeal croquette, sauerbraten that's marinated in red wine sauce and served with mashed potatoes and four different vegetables, and butter-fried sausage with onion sauce and a succulent version of rösti.

Ratskeller. Gerechtigkeitsgasse 80. ☎ **031/311-17-71.** Reservations recommended. Main courses 18–43SF ($13.15–$31.40); set-price lunch 16.50–25SF ($12.05–$18.25). AE, DC, MC, V. Daily 11:30am–2pm and 6–10pm. Tram: 9. SWISS.

This historic place has old masonry, modernized paneling, and a battalion of busy waitresses serving ample portions. Although there's a fondness for artful presentations, such as a traditional omelet radically altered by the addition of fresh fruits, much of the cookery has a charming simplicity, as evoked by that longtime Swiss favorite, a perfectly sautéed and grilled calf's liver dusted with fresh herbs and given the old salt-and-pepper treatment. Exceptionally good are the tender veal cutlets with a butter sauce and a marinated rack of lamb for two.

Inexpensive

Jardin. Militärstrasse 38. ☎ **031/333-01-17.** Reservations recommended. Main courses 15–35SF ($10.95–$25.55); set-price menu 15SF ($10.95). AE, DC, MC, V. Mon–Sat 11am–2pm and 5–10pm. Tram: 9 to Breitenrainplatz. INTERNATIONAL.

Set in the previously recommended hotel of the same name, this stately looking restaurant flourished long before the hotel was established in 1985. Part of its appeal derives from its ability to be as formal or informal as you want; consequently, it serves snacks such as cheese croquettes to accompany your foaming mugfuls of beer, as well as more substantial grilled steaks, minced Zürich-style veal with rösti potatoes, and schnitzels of pork with braised cabbage.

BERN AFTER DARK

This Week in Bern, distributed free by the tourist office, has a list of cultural events.

The Performing Arts

The **Bern Symphony Orchestra,** one of Switzerland's finest, is directed by the widely acclaimed Russian-born Dmitrij Kitajenko; famous guest conductors also frequently appear. Performances are usually at the concert facilities in the **Bern Casino,** Herrengasse 25 (☎ 031/311-42-42).

Major opera and ballet performances are usually staged in the century-old **Stadttheater,** Kornhausplatz 20 (☎ 031/311-07-77). Plays and dance programs are presented in the **Theater am Käfigturm,** Spitalgasse 4 (☎ 031/311-61-00). Plays are usually in German and, to a lesser degree, French. Contemporary German-language theater is featured in the **Kleintheater,** Kramgasse 6 (☎ 031/320-26-26).

Wine Cellars & Traditional Music

✪ **Klötzlikeller.** 62 Gerechtigkeitsgasse. ☎ 031/311-74-56.

The oldest wine tavern in Bern is near the Gerechtigkeitsbrunnen (Fountain of Justice), the first fountain you see on your walk from the Bear Pits to the Clock Tower. Watch for the lantern outside an angled cellar door. The tavern, dating from 1635, is owned by the city and leased to an independent operator (by tradition, an unmarried woman). Some 20 wines are sold by the glass, with prices at 3.80 to 7SF ($2.75 to $5.10). The traditional kitchen serves various dinner plates (20 to 40SF/$14.60 to $29.20) that change every 6 weeks, but reflect regional specialties. The bar is open Tuesday to Saturday 4pm to 12:30am.

Kornhaus Keller. Kornhausplatz 18. ☎ 031/311-11-33.

This former grain warehouse in the Altstadt is the city's best-known wine cellar. The symmetrical stone building, with an arcade on the ground floor, seats 462 diners in a baronial atmosphere; musical acts are often performed in the evening. Main courses— go for the classic, a plate of smoked meats and sauerkraut—range from 18 to 45SF ($32.85); the set-price menu costs 18SF ($13.15) but is served only at lunch. Food service is daily 11:30am to 1:45pm and 6 to 9:45pm, but guests usually linger over their drinks till around midnight.

Swiss Chalet Restaurant. In the Hotel Glocke, Rathausgasse 75. ☎ 031/311-37-71.

The dining room is brick with beamed ceilings and red-checkered tablecloths; oversized cowbells and alpine farm implements hang on the walls. Oompah bands appear Monday to Saturday beginning at 8:30pm, and when a big group shows up, there are also yodelers on the program. The kitchen stays open until 12:45am (perfect for after-theater snacks.) Fondues, fish, steak, and chicken are all available, and main courses range from 10 to 30SF ($7.30 to $21.90). Beer is 3.20 to 5SF ($2.35 to $3.65). Admission is free, but they expect you to at least have a drink. Hours are Monday to Wednesday 11am to 1am, Thursday 11am to 2am, Friday and Saturday 11am to 3am, and Sunday 3 to 10pm.

A Gay Bar

Samurai Club. Aarbergergasse 35. ☎ 031/311-88-03.

This gay bar draws many people who work in the local embassies, as well as Bern locals and young men from the Bernese Oberland in for a night on the town. Women are also welcome. The club is open Sunday to Thursday 5pm to 2:30am and Friday and Saturday 5pm to 3:30am; on weekdays 5 to 8pm, a beer is 3.50SF ($2.55); at other times, 4.50SF ($3.30).

THE BERNER OBERLAND

The Berner Oberland is a Valhalla for walkers, hikers, and skiers. Here nature's scenery satisfies both the most ambitious adventurer and the slowest stroller. It's one of the world's best-equipped regions for winter sports, and walking trails branch out from almost every junction. Most of them are paved and signposted, with distances and esti-mated walking times posted. Most tourist offices, including those at Interlaken (see below), can provide guidance and suggested itineraries.

EXPLORING THE AREA BY TRAIN & BICYCLE   If you're not driving, you'll find that public transport is quite adequate for exploring the area. The **Regional Pass** is valid on most rail lines, including all mountain trains, cable cars, chairlifts, steamers on Lake Thun and Lake Brienz, and most postal-bus lines. The ticket qualifies you for a 25% reduction on the Kleine Scheidegg-Eigergletscher-Jungfraujoch railway, the Mürren-Schilthorn aerial cable line, and the bus to Grosse Scheidegg and Bussalp. It's valid for 15 days and allows you to travel free on 5 days, paying reduced fares the rest of the time. The pass is 245SF ($178.85) in first-class and 200SF ($146) in second.

Cycling tours through the Berner Oberland often begin at Interlaken. Hundreds of miles of cycling paths cover the area. Separate from the network of hiking paths, the bicycle routes are signposted and marked on rental maps distributed at bike-rental agencies. Some 13 rail stations in the Berner Oberland offer bike-rental services, and rates are reasonable. For example, families can rent two city bikes for the parents and a mountain bike for two children under 16 for an all-inclusive 44SF ($32.10) per day or 220SF ($160.60) per week. You must make reservations at least by the evening before the tour at any of the rail stations providing the service. Call ☎ **033/822-21-38** or fax 033/822-27-51 for reservations.

INTERLAKEN

Interlaken is the Berner Oberland's tourist capital. Cableways and cog railways designed for steeply inclined hills and mountains connect it with most of the region's villages. A dazzling sight is the snowy heights of the Jungfrau, which rises a short dis-tance to the south.

The "town between the lakes" (Thun and Brienz) has been a holiday resort for more than 300 years. Although it was once a summer resort, it has developed into a year-round playground. Interlaken charges low-season prices in January and February, when smaller resorts at higher altitudes charge their highest rates. The most expensive time to visit is midsummer, when high-altitude ski resorts often charge their lowest rates.

Essentials
ARRIVING   By Train   There are several trains daily between Zurich and Inter-laken (trip time: 2 hours) and between Bern and Interlaken (40 minutes). Frequent

---

Traveler's Tip

You must buy your **Regional Pass** at least a week before you arrive. For informa-tion about the pass, call ☎ **212/757-5944** in New York City, ☎ **310/640-8900** in Los Angeles, ☎ **312/332-9900** in Chicago, ☎ **416/695-2090** in Toronto, or ☎ **020/7734-1921** in England.

Glaciers in the Sky: A Trip to Jungfraujoch

A trip to ✪ **Jungfraujoch,** at 11,333 feet, can be the highlight of your visit. Since the 1860s it has been the highest rail station in Europe. It's also one of the most expensive: A round-trip tour is 168.60SF ($123.10) first-class or 158.20SF ($115.50) second. However, families can fill out a Family Card form, available at the rail station; it allows children 16 and under to ride free. There are departures from Interlaken's **East Railway Station (Bahnhof Interlaken Ost)** every hour in winter, and every half hour in summer, but for true aficionados of the experience, the area is at its panoramic best if you depart at 8:05am and return to Bahnhof Interlaken Ost at 4pm. You get to see the mountain when it is most dazzlingly lit, and have enough time for a leisurely lunch. To check times, contact the sales office of **Jungfrau Bahnen (Jungfrau Railways),** Höheweg 37 (☎ **033/828-72-33).**

Once at the Jungfraujoch terminus, you might feel a little giddy until you get used to the air. You'll find much to do in this eerie world high up Jungfrau, but take it slowly—your metabolism will be affected and you may tire quickly.

Within a 5-minute, well-marked walk from the Jungfraujoch railway terminus is an elevator that leads to the famed ✪ **Eispalast (Ice Palace).** Here you'll be walking within what's called "eternal ice"—caverns hewn out of the slowest-moving section of the glacier. Cut 65 feet below the glacier's surface, they were begun in 1934 by a Swiss guide and subsequently enlarged and embellished with additional sculptures. The cost of entrance to the Ice Palace is included in the price of a railway ticket to the Jungfraujoch. Hours of the Ice Palace coincide with the arrival of the first train in the morning and the departure of the last train in the evening.

After returning to the station, you can take the **Sphinx Tunnel** to another elevator. This one takes you up 356 feet to an observation deck called the **Sphinx Terraces,** overlooking the saddle between the Mönch and Jungfrau peaks. You can also see the **Aletsch Glacier,** a 14-mile river of ice—the longest in Europe. The snow melts into Lake Geneva and eventually flows into the Mediterranean.

train service also connects Geneva and Interlaken (2½ hours). Although the town has two rail stations, about 2 miles apart, **Interlaken East** and **Interlaken West,** most of the city center lies near or around Interlaken West. Call ☎ **157-22-22** (no area code) for schedules and fares.

By Car To reach Interlaken from Bern, drive south on N6 to Spiez, and then continue west on N8 to Interlaken.

VISITOR INFORMATION The **Tourism Organization Interlaken** is at Höheweg 37 (☎ **033/822-21-21),** in the Hotel Metropole, and will provide itineraries for hikers. It's open July and August, Monday to Friday 8am to noon and 1:30 to 6:30pm, Saturday 8am to 5pm, and Sunday 5 to 7pm; the rest of the year, hours are Monday to Friday 8am to noon and 2 to 6pm and Saturday 8am to noon.

Exploring Interlaken

What you do in Interlaken is walk. You can walk at random, as there are panoramic views in virtually all directions, or, if you'd like some guidance, go to the tourist office for a copy of "What to Do in Interlaken"; it maps out walks of all levels of difficulty.

The **Höheweg** covers 35 acres in the middle of town, between the west and east train stations. Once the property of Augustinian monks, it was acquired in the mid-19th century by Interlaken's hotel keepers, who turned it into a park. As you stroll

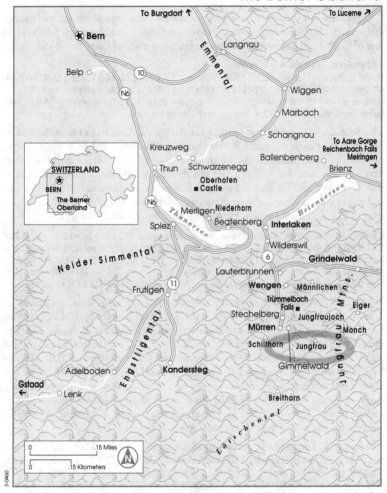

along **Höhenpromenade,** admire the famous view of the Jungfrau. Another beautiful sight is the **flower clock** at the Kursaal (casino), and you'll also see **fiacres** (horse-drawn cabs). The promenade is lined with hotels, cafes, and gardens.

Cross over the Aare River to **Unterseen,** built in 1280 by Berthold von Eschenbach. Here you can visit the **parish church,** with its Late Gothic tower from 1471. This is one of the most photographed sights in the Berner Oberland. The Mönch mountain appears on the left of the tower, the Jungfrau on the right.

Back in Interlaken, visit the **Touristik-Museum der Jungfrau-Region,** am Stadthausplatz, Obere Gasse 26 (☎ **033/22-98-39**), the country's first regional museum of tourism, showing its development over the past 2 centuries. It's open May to mid-October, Tuesday to Sunday 2 to 5pm. Admission is 3SF ($2.20), or 2SF ($1.45) with a Visitor's Card. Children 12 and under pay 1.50SF ($1.10).

For a sightseeing fiacre ride, go to the Westbahnhof. The half-hour round-trip is 30SF ($21.90) for one or two, plus 9SF ($6.55) for each extra person; children 7 to 16 are charged half fare, and those 6 and under ride free.

Other attractions include animal parks, afternoon concerts, and the luscious pastries sold in cafes. During summer, you can sit in covered grandstands and watch Schiller's version of the William Tell story. Steamers carry passengers across Lakes Brienz and Thun.

Expensive Accommodations

Hotel Bellevue. Marktgasse 59, 3800 Interlaken. ☎ **033/822-44-31.** Fax 033/822-92-50. 40 units. MINIBAR TV TEL. 148–218SF ($108.05–$159.15) double. Half-price reduction for children up to 12 sharing parents' room. Half-board 35SF ($25.55) per person. Rates include buffet breakfast. AE, DC, MC, V. Free parking. Closed Nov–Mar.

The Bellevue, in a central spot opening directly on the Aare, retains something of its original 1789 design as a mock fortified castle and is surrounded by an English-style garden. The modernized rooms, which come in a variety of shapes and sizes, often have balconies with a view of the river and the distant mountains. All contain a mixture of modern and traditional furniture. Bathrooms are compact, often with a tub and shower. Breakfast and dinner are served in the formal dining room, and guests relax in a nicely furnished salon facing the garden and a view of the Alps.

✪ **Victoria-Jungfrau Grand Hotel & Spa.** Höheweg 41, 3800 Interlaken. ☎ **800/223-6800** in the U.S. or 033/828-28-28. Fax 033/828-28-86. www.victoria-jungfrauch. E-mail: victoria@bluewin.ch. 215 units. MINIBAR TV TEL. Summer 620SF ($452.60) double, 860SF ($627.80) suite; winter 470SF ($343.10) double, from 780SF ($569.40) suite. Half-board 95SF ($69.35) per person extra. AE, DC, MC, V. Parking 18SF ($13.15) in garage.

Since 1865 this has been one of Switzerland's most important resort properties. In richly ornate Victorian styling, it sits in the town center at the foot of rigidly symmetrical gardens. The hotel boasts one of the best-trained staffs in the country. The most deluxe rooms open onto views of the Jungfrau. Nearly all bedrooms are spacious and feature amenities such as bedside controls, irons, and ironing boards. Bathrooms have tub and shower combinations and hair dryers. Dining choices include La Terrasse, a gourmet restaurant with a pianist and a winter garden, and Jungfraustube, a rustic restaurant with traditional Swiss dishes and charcoal-grilled specialties. Facilities include a pool, indoor and outdoor tennis courts, a sauna, a solarium, whirlpools, steambaths, and one of Switzerland's best spas.

Moderate & Inexpensive Accommodations

Hotel Beau-Site. Seestrasee 16, 3800 Interlaken. ☎ **033/826-75-75.** Fax 033/826-75-85. 50 units (42 with bathroom). TEL. 110SF ($80.30) double without bathroom; 180–240SF ($131.40–$175.20) double with bathroom. Rates include continental breakfast. AE, DC, MC, V. Free parking outside, 20SF ($14.60) in garage.

A short walk from the Interlaken West train station, this hotel is surrounded by spacious gardens with parasol-shaded card tables and chaise longues in summer, and provides a pleasant, relaxing oasis. The rooms are modern; some open onto mountain views, and most have TVs and minibars. Rooms on the upper floors are a bit small and often rented as singles. The spotless bathrooms, although a bit small, have adequate shelf space. The hotel has two fine restaurants, the budget-priced Stübli and the more elegant and expensive Veranda.

Hotel de la Paix. Bernastrasse 24, 3800 Interlaken. ☎ **033/822-70-44.** Fax 033/822-87-28. 22 units. TEL. 98–170SF ($71.55–$124.10) double. Rates include buffet breakfast. AE, DC, MC, V. Closed mid-Oct to mid-Mar. Free parking.

This family-run hotel is a block from the Westbahnhof (Interlaken West). You'll recognize it by its ornate roofline, which is gabled and tiled like a house in a Brothers Grimm fairy tale. Gillian and Georges Etterli offer a pleasant, relaxed atmosphere. The rooms are simply furnished; some have TVs. Those downstairs are quite spacious. The bathrooms are small.

Park-Hotel Mattenhof. Hauptstrasse, Matten, 3800 Interlaken. ☎ **033/821-61-21.** Fax 033/822-28-88. www.park/mattenhof.ch. 70 units. TV TEL. June–Sept and Dec 26–Jan 1, 250–330SF ($182.50–$240.90) double; off-season, 220–290SF ($160.60–$211.70) double. Rates include buffet breakfast. AE, DC, MC, V. Free parking. Bus: 5.

This old-fashioned hotel is in a secluded area at the edge of a forest 1 mile south of the center; you can reach it by heading away from the center toward Wilderswil. Originally a simple 19th-century pension, it adopted a mock-medieval look complete with high pointed roof, tower, loggias, and balconies after a massive 1908 enlargement. The Bühler family offers a calm retreat, with terraces, manicured lawns, and panoramic views of the Alps. Bedrooms come in a variety of sizes, and bathrooms are compact, with suitable shelf space. Facilities include a pool, a tennis court, play areas, terraces, bars, and restaurants.

Swiss Inn. Général-Guisan-Strasse 23, 3800 Interlaken. ☎ **033/822-36-26.** Fax 033/823-23-03. E-mail: swissinn@bluewin.ch. 60 units. TV TEL. 90–130SF ($65.70–$94.90) double; 130–170SF ($94.90–$124.10) apt for 2; 180–250SF ($131.40–$182.50) apt for 4. MC, V.

This is a small-scale Edwardian-era inn with balconies, gables, and a sense of economy. Mrs. Vreny Müller Lohner offers conventional double rooms that are simply decorated and a bit spare, but they benefit from daily maid service. Bathrooms are very small and have a shower stall. There are also some self-contained apartments with kitchens that get clean-up service only once a week. Guests have access to a lounge, a sitting area with a fireplace, a laundry, and, in the garden, a barbecue grill.

Where to Dine

Gasthof Hirschen. Hauptstrasse, Matten. ☎ **033/822-15-45.** Reservations recommended. Main courses 18–82SF ($13.15–$59.85). AE, DC, MC, V. Thurs–Mon 11:30am–2pm and 6–10pm; Wed 6–10pm. Closed Nov 1 to mid-Dec. SWISS.

This hotel restaurant offers some of the best and most reasonably priced meals in town, and the menu is varied. The potato soup with mountain cheese is the finest we've ever tasted. Other appetizers include salmon-filled ravioli. For a main dish, try sautéed calves' liver, filet of beef bordelaise, broiled trout, or chateaubriand. The Hirschen operates its own farm, and many of the items it features are home-grown, including Bio-Angus beef, veal, cheese, and fresh vegetables and herbs.

Il Bellini. In the Hotel Metropole, Höheweg 37. ☎ **033/828-66-66.** Reservations recommended Fri–Sun. Main courses 25–40SF ($18.25–$29.20); pastas 15–20SF ($10.95–$14.60). AE, DC, MC, V. Daily 11:30am–2pm and 6:30–10pm. ITALIAN.

This is the finest Italian restaurant in the area, with food that evokes some of the best trattorie south of the border. One floor above the lobby of the tallest hotel in Interlaken, it's done in a graceful 19th-century rendition of pale pinks and greens. An assortment of antipasti from the buffet or a homemade minestrone is followed by such main courses as beefsteak Florentine, *saltimbocca* (veal with ham), or a small chicken flavored with fresh basil. The fish selections are limited but well chosen, and can be grilled on request.

Schun. Höheweg 56. ☎ **033/822-94-41.** Main courses 21–32SF ($15.35–$23.35); set-price menu 38SF ($27.75). AE, DC, MC, V. Tues–Sun 8am–11pm. Closed Oct 26–Dec 5. SWISS/CONTINENTAL.

This attractive restaurant and tearoom in the center of town has a sunny terrace with a view of the Jungfrau. The calf's liver is excellent, perfectly grilled and seasoned, and their daily soups are pure homemade goodness. Salads rely on market fresh ingredients, and the desserts often incorporate locally grown berries and fruits. Their pastries are justifiably acclaimed as the finest in the area.

MÜRREN

At 5,414 feet above the Lauterbrunnen Valley, Mürren is the highest permanently inhabited village in the Berner Oberland. It's an exciting excursion from Interlaken in summer and a major ski resort in winter. Downhill skiing was developed and the slalom invented here in the 1920s, and Mürren is also the birthplace of modern alpine racing.

Essentials

ARRIVING   By Train   Trains from Interlaken to Mürren's train station in town center, require a change of equipment in both Lauterbrunen and Grutschalp. The combined trip takes an hour from Interlaken, and a round-trip fare costs 16.80SF ($12.25).

By Bus & Car   A regular postal-bus service departs once an hour from Lauterbrunnen to the hamlet of Stechelberg, the last town along the Lauterbrunnen Valley road, the end of the line for cars and buses, and the departure point for a cable car that runs uphill to Mürren. The cable car that continues from Stechelberg on to Mürren departs at 30-minute intervals, costs 28SF ($20.45) round-trip, and takes about 10 minutes each way.

VISITOR INFORMATION   The **Mürren Tourist Information Bureau** at the Sportzentrum (☎ **033/856-86-86**) is open Monday to Friday 9am to noon and 2 to 5pm.

Hitting the Slopes & Other Active Endeavors

There are 30 miles of prepared ski runs, including 16 downhills; the longest run measures 7½ miles. For cross-country skiers there's a 7½-mile track in the Lauterbrunnen Valley, 10 minutes by railway from Mürren.

The alpine **Sportzentrum (Sports Center)** (☎ **033/856-86-86**), in the middle of Mürren, is one of the finest in the Berner Oberland. The modern building has an indoor pool, a lounge, a snack bar, an outdoor skating rink, a tourist information office, and a children's playroom and library. There are facilities for playing squash, outdoor tennis, and curling. Hotel owners subsidize the operation, tacking the charges onto your hotel bill. Supplemental charges include 21SF ($15.35) per hour for tennis or per 45-minute session for squash and 13SF ($9.50) per hour for use of the sauna. The facility is usually open Monday to Friday 9am to noon and 2 to 5pm, but check locally, as these times can vary.

Nearby Excursions

The famous **Mürren-Allmendhubel Cableway** leaves from the northwestern edge of Mürren. From the high destination there's a panoramic view of the Lauterbrunnen Valley as far as Wengen and Kleine Scheidegg, and between mid-June and late August the alpine meadows are covered with wildflowers. A hill walk in this region might be a highlight of your trip. The cable car operates daily 8am to 5pm. However, there are annual closings for maintenance in May and in November. It costs 12SF ($8.75) per person round-trip.

The most popular excursion from Mürren is a cable-car ride to the ✪ **Schilthorn,** famous for its 360-degree view. The panorama extends from the Jura to the Black Forest and includes the Eiger, Mönch, and Jungfrau. The Schilthorn is also called "Piz Gloria" after the James Bond film *On Her Majesty's Secret Service,* partly filmed at this dramatic location. Today Piz Gloria is the name of the revolving restaurant here, and the summit is the start of the world's longest downhill ski race. The cable car to Schilthorn leaves every 30 minutes. A round-trip ticket is 58SF ($42.35), and the journey to the top takes 20 minutes. For details, call ☎ **033/823-14-44.**

Where to Stay

Hotel Alpenruh. 3825 Mürren. ☎ **033/856-88-00.** Fax 033/856-88-88. 26 units. MINIBAR TV TEL. 180–250SF ($131.40–$182.50) double. 50% discount for children 12 and under sharing parents' room. Half-board 30SF ($21.90) per person. Rates include breakfast. AE, MC, V.

In the most congested, yet still charming, section of the village, the Alpenruh has a plusher interior than its chalet-style facade implies. The old building was upgraded in 1986 to three-star status without sacrificing any of its small-scale charm. The rooms have pine paneling and a mix of antique and contemporary furniture, and most have a view of the Jungfrau. The tidy bathrooms are small, compact, and efficiently organized.

Hotel Blumental. 3825 Mürren. ☎ **033/855-18-26.** Fax 033/855-36-86. www.muerren. ch/blumental. E-mail: blumental@muerren.ch. 20 units. MINIBAR. 120–170SF ($87.60–$124.10) double. Half-board 25SF ($18.25) per person. Rates include buffet breakfast. AE, DC, V.

Centrally located and redecorated and remodeled, this is a small chalet-type hotel, with stone masonry and wood-paneled public areas. Run by the von Allmen family, it offers a cozy atmosphere inspired by the nearby mountains. The wood walls of the rooms contrast with new pine furnishings and attractive colors; several rooms have private balconies. The small bathrooms have shower stalls. The hotel also operates a French restaurant.

Hotel Eiger. 3825 Mürren. ☎ **033/855-13-31.** Fax 033/855-39-31. www.muerren.ch/eiger. E-mail: hoteleiger@iben.net. 33 units. MINIBAR TEL. Summer 190–220SF ($138.70–$160.60) double; winter 300–350SF ($219–$255.50) double; year-round 400SF ($292) suite. Rates include buffet breakfast. AE, DC, MC, V. Closed May and Nov.

This chalet is Mürren's best-established hotel. First built in 1898, it was later torn down and completely rebuilt in 1981 and turned into an eminently reliable three-star hotel. The public rooms are warmly decorated, and many windows have panoramic views. The guest rooms, small and cozy, are decorated in typical alpine style. The small bathrooms have showers. The hotel has a fine restaurant (see below) and a popular après-ski bar, plus an indoor heated pool with a glassed-in view of the ice and snow outside.

Where to Dine

✪ **Eigerstübli.** In the Hotel Eiger. ☎ **033/855-13-31.** Reservations recommended. Main courses 13–52SF ($9.50–$37.95). AE, DC, MC, V. Daily 11:30am–2pm and 6–10pm. Closed Easter to mid-June and mid-Sept to Christmas. SWISS.

Here you'll find Mürren's best food, served in a festive ambience. The cuisine includes fondue as well as an international range of hearty specialties well suited to the alpine heights and chill. Try, for example, roast lamb shoulder with lentils, roast breast of duck with orange sauce, or poached filet of trout with a sauce flavored with alpine herbs. All main dishes can be ordered with rösti.

WENGEN

The Mönch, Jungfrau, and Eiger loom above this sunny resort, built on a sheltered terrace high above the Lauterbrunnen Valley, at about 4,160 feet. Wengen (pronounced *Ven*-ghen) is one of the more chic and better-equipped ski and mountain resorts in the Berner Oberland. It has 30 hotels in all price categories, as well as 500 apartments and chalets for rent.

In the 1830s, the International Lauberhorn Ski Race was established here. At that time, Wengen was a farm community, but the Brits popularized the resort after World

War I. Parts of the area retain their rural charm, but the main street is filled with cafes, shops, and restaurants. No cars are allowed in Wengen, but the streets still bustle with service vehicles and electric luggage carts.

Essentials

ARRIVING By Train Take the train (frequent service) from Interlaken East to Lauterbrunnen. For information, call ☎ 157-22-22 (no area code). From here, the journey to Wengen is by cog railway, a 15-minute trip. A one-way fare is 5.40SF ($3.95).

By Car Unlike Mürren, Wengen, 16 miles south of Interlaken, can be reached by car—at least for part of the trip. From Interlaken, head south in the direction of Wilderswil, following the minor signposted road to Lauterbrunnen, where there are garages or open-air spaces for parking. After that, it's cog railway the rest of the way to Wengen.

VISITOR INFORMATION The **Wengen Tourist Information Office** (☎ 033/855-14-14) is in the center of the resort and is signposted. It's open Monday to Friday 8am to noon and 2 to 6pm, and Saturday 8:30 to 11:30am only.

Exploring the Area

The ski area around Wengen is highly developed, with both straight and serpentine trails carved into the sides of such sloping geological formations as Männlichen, Kleine Scheidegg, Lauberhorn, and Eigergletscher. A triumph of alpine engineering, the town and its region contain three mountain railways, two aerial cableways, one gondola, five chairlifts, nine ski lifts, and three practice lifts. You'll also find a branch of the Swiss ski school, more than 7 miles of trails for cross-country skiing, an indoor and outdoor skating rink, a curling hall, an indoor pool, and a day nursery.

In summer, the district attracts hill climbers from all over Europe. Hiking trails are well maintained and carefully marked, with dozens of unusual detours to hidden lakes and panoramas.

Nearby Attractions

In winter, skiers take the cableway to **Männlichen,** at 7,335 feet, which opens onto a panoramic vista of the treacherous Eiger. From here, there's no direct run back to Wengen; however, skiers can enjoy an uninterrupted ski trail stretching 4½ miles to Grindelwald.

There are many sights you can visit up and down the Lauterbrunnen Valley from either Wengen or Grindelwald. **Trümmelbach Falls** plunges in five powerful cascades through a gorge. An elevator built through the rock leads to a series of galleries; the last stop is at a wall where the upper fall descends (bring a raincoat). You can visit the falls daily May through June and September through October 9am to 5pm and July through August 8:30am to 6pm. Admission is 10SF ($7.30) adults and 4SF ($2.90) children 6 to 16. It takes about 45 minutes to reach the falls on foot. For information, call ☎ 033/855-32-32. The postal bus from Lauterbrunnen departs once an hour and stops at Trümmelbach Falls; fares are 10SF ($7.30) adults and 4SF ($2.90) children.

You might also want to visit the base of the **Staubbach Waterfall,** which plunges nearly 1,000 feet in a sheer drop over a rock wall in the valley above Lauterbrunnen. Lord Byron compared this waterfall to the "tail of the pale horse ridden by Death in the Apocalypse."

Where to Stay

Hotel Eden. 3823 Wengen. ☎ **033/855-16-34.** Fax 033/855-39-50. 30 units (6 with bathroom). Summer 116SF ($84.70) double without bathroom, 154SF ($112.40) double with bathroom; winter 150SF ($109.50) double without bathroom, 180SF ($131.40) double with bathroom. Half-board 30SF ($21.90) per person. Rates include breakfast. AE, DC, MC, V.

You'll feel comfortable and at home in this economy oasis that stands among guesthouses and private chalets above the commercial center of town. Kerstin Bucher directs a cooperative staff. Meals are served in a simple modern room with a few frivolous touches. There's a small TV lounge and a tiny Jägerstübli, where guests mix with locals over Swiss wine and specialties. Although the rooms are a bit spartan, the beds are comfortable. Only a few units have a private bathroom, and they are quite small without much room for your stuff.

Hotel Eiger. 3823 Wengen. ☎ **800/528-1234** in the U.S. and Canada, or 033/855-11-31. Fax 033/855-10-30. www.wengen.com/hotel/eiger. E-mail: eiger@wengen.com. 37 units. MINIBAR TV TEL. Summer 206–228SF ($150.40–$166.45) double; winter 298–320SF ($217.55–$233.60) double; suite for 2, 1,500SF ($1,095) per week. Half-board 21SF ($15.35) per person. Rates include breakfast. AE, DC, MC, V.

Rustic timbers cover the walls and ceilings of this attractive hotel behind the cog-railway station. Karl Fuchs and his family offer spacious attractive rooms with balconies. A modern dining room has views of the Jungfrau massif and the Lauterbrunnen Valley. Bedrooms have cozy, alpine styling, but bathrooms are small and cramped. In the lobby is an inviting sitting area with a fireplace, and there's also a bar reserved for hotel guests.

Where to Dine

Hotel Hirschen Restaurant. In the Hotel Hirschen. ☎ **033/855-15-44.** Reservations recommended. Main courses 18–52SF ($13.15–$37.95); set-price menu 19–36SF ($13.85–$26.30). DC, MC, V. Mon–Fri 5–11pm; Sat–Sun 11:30am–2:30pm and 5–11pm. Closed mid-Apr to May and Sept–Dec 15. SWISS.

This quiet retreat at the foot of the slopes has true alpine flavor. The rear dining room is decorated with hunting trophies, pewter, and wine racks. The restaurant is noted especially for its fondues, which include Fondue Bacchus, made with two kinds of cheese and a generous dose of kirsch (folks tend to get smashed a bit more quickly with this combination than with any other kind of fondue); Fondue Bourguignonn made with chunks of beef and red wine; and Fondue Chinois with a vegetable, herb, and meat-flavored bouillon base for dipping meat. The restaurant is also known for its homemade rösti, which gourmets acclaim as Europe's finest version of what Americans might call hash-brown potatoes.

GRINDELWALD

The "glacier village" of Grindelwald, both a summer and a winter resort, is set against a backdrop of the Wetterhorn and the towering north face of the Eiger. Grindelwald is surrounded with folkloric hamlets, swift streams, and as much alpine beauty as you're likely to find anywhere in Switzerland. It's also easier to reach from Interlaken than either Wengen or Mürren. Although at first the hiking options and cable-car networks might seem baffling, the tourist office can provide helpful maps.

Essentials

ARRIVING   By Train   The Berner Oberland Railway (BOB) leaves from the Interlaken East station. The trip takes 35 minutes. Call ☎ **157-22-22** (no area code) for information.

VISITOR INFORMATION   Grindelwald's **tourist office** is at Sportszentrum, Hauptstrasse, 3818 Grindelwald (☎ 033/854-12-12), open mid-June to late September Monday to Friday 8am to 7pm, Saturday 8am to 5pm, and Sunday 9 to 11am and 3 to 5pm. Otherwise, hours are Monday to Friday 8am to 6pm, Saturday 8am to noon, and Sunday 10am to noon and 3 to 5pm.

Seeing the Glaciers

Adjacent to the base of the **Lower Grindelwald Glacier (Untere Gletscher)** is a sheltered observation gallery offering a look at the rock-strewn ravine formed by the glacier and its annual snowmelt. The half-mile gallery stretches past deeply striated rocks, which include formations of colored marble worn smooth by the glacier's erosion. Don't expect a view of the glacier from this point, as you'll have to go to a higher altitude, at least in summer, to see the actual ice. The gallery is easy to reach on foot or by car from the center of Grindelwald. Yellow-sided buses labeled GLETSCHER-SCHLUCHT depart from a point in front of Grindelwald's rail station at least four times a day, year-round, for the lower glacier and points beyond. Passage to the lower glacier costs 4.80SF ($3.50) each way, but since the distance from the center of Grindelwald is about 2½ miles, in nice weather, many hardy souls opt to trek across well-marked hiking trails instead.

A more exotic destination farther afield is the **Blue Ice Grotto,** whose frozen mass is part of the Upper Grindelwald Glacier (Obere Gletscher). Popular with hill climbers, it's a 3-hour hike (which includes navigating up an 890-step alpine staircase) or a 15-minute bus ride from the Lower Grindelwald Glacier. The upper and lower glaciers are separated by rocky cliffs and flow in different valleys. At midday the 150-foot-thick ice walls of the grotto take on an eerie blue tinge. Local guides assure you that although the grotto—and the glacier containing it—are moving slowly downhill, you're perfectly safe. The grotto is open daily mid-June to October 9am to 6pm. If you don't want to make the uphill trek on foot from Grindelwald, a yellow-sided bus marked GROSSE SCHEIDEGG departs at approximately 1-hour intervals, year-round, during daylight hours. One-way fares from Grindelwald to the Obere Gletscher and its grotto cost 4.40SF ($3.20) each way.

Hiking & Mountain Climbing

Grindelwald and environs offer dozens of challenging paths and mountain trails that are well marked and maintained. Outdoor adventures range from an exhilarating ramble across the gentle incline of an alpine valley to a dangerous trek with ropes and pitons along the north face of Mount Eiger. The choice depends on your inclination, degree of experience, and mountaineering skills. Maps showing the paths, trails, and their various elevations are available at the town's tourist office.

You can reach the high-altitude plateau known as **First Mountain** (at 7,113 ft.) from Grindelwald after a 30-minute ride on a six-passenger gondola ("bubble car"). The round-trip transport is 45SF ($32.85). You can stop at such intermediate stations as Bort and Grindel (a site that some locals refer to as Scheckfeld) on your way to **First Mountain terminal and sun terrace.** From First, where there are dining facilities, you have many hiking possibilities into the neighboring Bussalp or Grosse Scheidegg area. Also from First, an hour's brisk hike takes you to the still high-altitude waters of **Bachalpsee (Lake Bachalp).** Buses depart from Grindelwald from both Bussalp and Grosse Scheidegg if you opt not to walk all the way back.

Faulhorn, at 8,796 feet, is a historic vantage point with a panorama of untouched alpine beauty. Near the summit is the Faulhorn Hotel (☎ **033/853-27-13**), which has been here for more than 150 years. Faulhorn is a 6½-hour hike from Grindelwald. For a shorter climb, take either the bus to Bussalp, the cable car to First, or the train to Schynige Platte. From any of these intermediate points, climbers can continue their treks on to Faulhorn. Hikes from Bussalp take 3 hours; from First, 2½ hours; and from Schynige Platte, 4 hours.

Grosse Scheidegg, at 6,434 feet, is a famous pass between the Grindelwald and Rosenlaui valleys. You can hike here in 3 hours from Grindelwald or can take a

40-minute bus ride from Grindelwald to Grosse Scheidegg and begin hill walking at a point that's far from the village traffic and crowds. Round-trip bus passage from Grindelwald to Grosse Scheidegg is 31SF ($22.65).

Where to Stay

✪ **Grand Hotel Regina.** 3818 Grindelwald. ☎ **800/223-6800** in the U.S. or 033/854-54-55. Fax 033/853-47-17. 90 units. MINIBAR TV TEL. 410SF ($299.30) double; from 600SF ($438) suite. AE, DC, MC, V. Closed mid-Oct to Dec 20.

Across from the Grindelwald train station, this turn-of-the-century hotel is part rustic, part urban slick. The facade of the hotel's oldest part has an imposing set of turrets with red-tile roofs. Antiques blend with modern furnishings into a harmonious whole, and the beds are exceedingly comfortable. Bathrooms are tiled and well maintained, with robes and a hair dryer. A steel-and-glass extension houses sports facilities, and live music is performed at the disco. Both set-price and à la carte menus are served in the restaurant. There's an indoor and outdoor pool, a sauna, a solarium, and two tennis courts.

Hotel Eiger. 3818 Grindelwald. ☎ **033/853-21-21.** Fax 033/853-21-01. www. eiger-grindelwald.ch. E-mail: eiger-grindelwald@swissonline.ch. 50 units. MINIBAR TV TEL. Summer 190–260SF ($138.70–$189.80) double; winter 250–290SF ($182.50–$211.70) double. Half-board 35SF ($25.55) per person. Rates include buffet breakfast. AE, DC, MC, V. Free parking outdoors; 6–15SF ($4.40–$10.95) in garage.

This hotel appears to be a collection of interconnected balconies, each on a different plane, angled toward the alpine sunshine and built of contrasting shades of white stucco and natural wood. The interior is attractive and unpretentious, with lots of warmly tinted wood, hanging lamps, and contrasting lights. Bedrooms range from small to medium; each has cozy alpine comfort with a soft, snug bed, and a compact bathroom with adequate shelf space. The Gepsi-Bar offers live music, recently released songs, and "evergreen" (mountain) tunes. The Heller family offers a bar and restaurant, including a steakhouse, and the facilities include a sauna and a steam bath.

Hotel Hirschen. 3818 Grindelwald. ☎ **033/854-84-84.** Fax 033/854-84-80. 28 units. TV TEL. 150–215SF ($109.50–$156.95) double. Half-board 28SF ($20.45) per person. Rates include continental breakfast. AE, DC, MC, V. Closed Nov–Dec 19. Free parking outside; 7.50SF ($5.50) garage.

In the three-star Hirschen, the Bleuer family offers one of the resort's best values. Bedrooms are a bit small, but each is cozy, warm, and a great place to retreat on a cold winter's night. The bathrooms are tiny but tidy. It has a respectable dining room as well as a popular bowling alley in the cellar.

Where to Dine

Il Mercato. In the Hotel Spinne. ☎ **033/854-88-88.** Reservations recommended. Main courses 18–48SF ($13.15–$35.05). AE, DC, MC, V. Daily 11am–2pm and 6:30–10:30pm. Closed mid-Oct to mid-Dec and mid-Apr to mid-May. ITALIAN/SWISS.

The decor is elegant and alpine, with Italian touches. The dining room's centerpiece is a large window with a sweeping view over the mountains; during warm weather, tables are set on the terrace. Menu items include virtually everything Italian, with an emphasis on cold-weather dishes from the Val d'Aosta (northern Italy's milk and cheese district). A tempting array of dishes based on market-fresh ingredients changes daily. Especially good are the risottos; these simmered rice dishes come in infinite varieties. The chefs also specialize in grilled meats and homemade salads, which even in the dead of winter use fresh, crisp ingredients. Their pizzas are the best in town. Daily pastas are featured, each with a succulent sauce.

⭐ **Restaurant Français.** In the Hotel Belvedere. ☎ **033/854-54-54.** Reservations recommended. Main courses 39–48SF ($28.45–$35.05); set-price menu 55–68SF ($40.15–$49.65). AE, DC, MC, V. Daily noon–1pm and 6:45–9pm. Closed late-Oct to mid-Dec. INTERNATIONAL.

Special buffets are featured at Grindelwald's best restaurant. After you study the ever-changing menu to the soothing sounds of a live pianist, you may decide on an appetizer of game terrine, Grindewald air-dried meat, or thinly sliced lamb carpaccio. On recent visits, dishes have included poached turbot filet on zucchini, peppercorn-coated lamb entrecôte, and breast of guinea fowl with red wine and prunes.

KANDERSTEG

Between Grindelwald and Gstaad, Kandersteg is a popular resort at one of the southern points of the Berner Oberland. It's a tranquil and lovely mountain village with rust- and orange-colored rooftops and green Swiss meadows. The summer and winter resort is spread over 2½ miles, so nothing is crowded. The village itself is at the foot of the Blumlisalp chain (12,000 ft.) and provides access to six remote alpine hamlets.

Kandersteg developed as a resting point on the road to the Gemmi Pass, which long ago linked the Valais with the Berner Oberland. The village still has many old farmhouses and a tiny church from the 16th century.

Essentials

ARRIVING By Train Kandersteg is at the northern terminus of the 9-mile-long Lotschberg Tunnel, which, ever since the beginning of World War I, has linked Bern with the Rhône Valley. The railroad that runs through the tunnel can transport cars. Trains leave every 30 minutes; no reservations are necessary. The resort is also served by the Bern-Lotschberg-Simplon railway. Call ☎ **157-22-22** (no area code) for information. The station is in the center of town.

By Car Kandersteg is 27 miles southwest of Interlaken. Take N8 east to where the Kandersteg road heads south into the mountains. The journey from Spiez to Kandersteg along a well-built road takes only 20 minutes.

VISITOR INFORMATION The **Kandersteg Tourist Office,** Hauptstrasse 3718 Kandersteg (☎ **033/675-80-80**), is open Monday to Friday 8am to noon and 2 to 6pm.

Outdoor Activities

Around Kandersteg is an extensive network of level footpaths and strategically located benches; these paths are open year-round. In summer, qualified riders in proper clothes can rent horses at the local riding school. In winter, the resort attracts cross-country skiers and downhill novices (top-speed skiers go elsewhere). It has a cable car, two chairlifts, and four ski tows; the National Nordic Ski Center offers a ski-jumping station. The 1½-mile cross-country ski trail is floodlit in the evening, and other facilities include an indoor and outdoor ice rink.

Excursions Nearby

The most popular excursion from Kandersteg is to **Oeschinensee (Lake Oeschinen),** high above the village. The lake is surrounded by the snow-covered peaks of the Blumlisalp, towering 6,000 feet above the extremely clear water. You can walk to it from the Victoria Hotel or take a chairlift, costing 16SF ($11.70), to the Oeschinen station and walk down from that point. If you opt to walk, allow about 1½ hours, or 2 hours if you'd like to stroll. Many visitors who take the chairlift decide to hike back to Kandersteg. Be aware, however, of the steep downhill grade.

Another popular excursion is to **Klus Gorge.** Park your car at the cable station's lower platform at Stock and walk 2 miles to the gorge, which was formed by the abrasive action of the Kander River. The rushing water creates a romantic, even primeval, setting. However, you must watch your step, as the path gets very slippery in places, and the spray coats the stones and pebbles and has fostered a layer of moss. There's a tunnel over the gorge, but in winter the access route is dangerous and icebound.

Where to Stay & Dine

Hotel Adler. 3718 Kandersteg. ☎ **033/675-80-10.** Fax 033/675-80-11. E-mail: chale-tadler@bluewin.ch. 24 units. MINIBAR TV TEL. Feb–Mar and July–Sept 170-250SF ($124.10–$182.50) double; off-season, 160–240SF ($116.80–$175.20) double. Rates include breakfast. AE, DC, MC, V. Closed Nov 22–Dec 18.

An open fire crackling in the foyer sets the tone at this cozy inn, a wood-sided chalet on the main street near the town center. The fourth-generation owner, Andreas Fetzer, and his Finnish-born wife, Eija, offer comfortable rooms paneled in pinewood, a few with Jacuzzis. Almost all open onto a private balcony. The small, neat bathrooms are inviting and have adequate shelf space. The Adler-Bar is one of the most popular après-ski hangouts, and there's also a brasserie (the Adlerstube) as well as a relatively formal restaurant.

GSTAAD

Against a backdrop of glaciers and mountain lakes, Gstaad is a haven for the rich and famous. Built at the junction of four quiet valleys near the southern tip of the Berner Oberland, Gstaad was once only a place to change horses on the grueling trip by carriage through the Berner Oberland. As the rail lines developed, it grew into a resort for the wealthy who flocked to the Palace Hotel, which promised the ultimate in luxury.

The town retains much of its turn-of-the-century charm. Some first-time visitors, however, say that the resort is a bore if you can't afford to stay at the Gstaad Palace or mingle with the stars in their private chalets. Yet the town has many moderately priced hotels, taverns, and guesthouses with an allure of their own.

Essentials

ARRIVING   By Train   Gstaad is on the local train line connecting Interlaken with Montreux and several smaller towns in central-southwest Switzerland. About a dozen trains come into Gstaad's centrally located station every day from both cities, each of which is a rail junction with good connections to the rest of Switzerland. Travel time from Montreux can be as little as 1⅓ hours; from Interlaken, about 30 minutes, sometimes with a change of train at the hamlet of Zweisimmen. Call ☎ **157-22-22** (no area code) for information.

By Car   From Spiez, follow Route 11 southwest to Gstaad.

VISITOR INFORMATION   The **Gstaad-Saanenland Tourist Association,** 3780 Gstaad (☎ **033/748-81-81**), can help you find hotels, restaurants, and attractions if the signposts don't point you in the right direction. It's open Monday to Friday 8am to noon and 1:30 to 6pm and Saturday 9am to noon only.

Skiing & Hiking

The resort is rich in **sports facilities.** Many skiers stay in Gstaad and go to one of the nearby ski resorts in the daytime. Cable cars take passengers to altitudes of 5,000 and 10,000 feet—at the higher altitude, there's skiing even in summer. Other facilities include tennis courts, heated indoor and outdoor pools, and some 200 miles of hiking trails. Many of these scenic trails are possible to walk or hike year-round (the tourist office can advise you). The Gstaad International Tennis Tournament, held the second week in July, is the most important tennis event in Switzerland.

Skiers setting off from Gstaad have access to 70 lifts, mountain railroads, and gondolas. The altitude of Gstaad's highest skiable mountain is 6,550 feet, with a vertical drop of 3,555 feet. Most beginner and intermediate runs are east of the village in **Eggli,** a sunny, south-facing ski area that's reached by cable car.

Wispellan-Sanetch is good for afternoon skiing, and has lots of runs down to the village. At the summit is the Glacier des Diablerets, at 9,900 feet. **Wasserngrat,** prized by skilled skiers for its powder skiing on steep slopes, is reached from the south side of the resort.

Where to Stay

✪ **Hostellerie Alpenrose.** Hauptstrasse, 3778 Schönried Gstaad. ☎ **033/744-67-67.** Fax 033/744-67-12. www.hotelalpenrose.ch. E-mail: alpenrose@bluewin.ch. 19 units. MINIBAR TV TEL. Summer 250–580SF ($182.50–$423.40) double; winter 330–650SF ($240.90–$474.50) double. Rates include breakfast and dinner. AE, DC, MC, V. Closed Easter–May 20 and Nov–Dec 15. Parking 15SF ($10.95) in garage.

For those who like the charm of a small inn, this is the preferred choice, the only Relais & Châteaux listing within 30 miles. Its owner, Michel von Siebenthal, is a memorable host, setting the fashionable tone of the chalet, which is famous for its restaurants. The pine-paneled public rooms are exquisitely decorated with rustic furnishings. The guest rooms are tastefully appointed and have mountain views and private safes. Bathrooms have hair dryers and showers, but no tubs. Although the original house has more character, the accommodations in the contemporary annex are more spacious and luxurious—some are fireplace suites, quite romantic on a wintry night. Facilities include a sauna, whirlpool, and solarium.

✪ **Hotel Olden.** Hauptstrasse, 3780 Gstaad. ☎ **033/744-34-44.** Fax 033/744-61-64. 15 units. MINIBAR TV TEL. Summer 230–290SF ($167.90–$211.70) double; winter 290–380SF ($211.70–$277.40) double. Rates include buffet breakfast. AE, DC, MC, V. Closed late Apr to late May. Parking 20SF ($14.60) in garage.

This is a low-key and gracefully unpretentious hotel, a sort of Victorian country inn set amid a sometimes chillingly glamorous landscape. The facade is painted with regional floral designs and pithy bits of folk wisdom, with embellishments carved or painted into the stone lintels around many of the doors. The folkloric alpine-style bedrooms are very cozy. The small bathrooms don't have a lot of extras, but maintenance is spotless. Rooms in the chalet wing are generally roomier and more up to date.

✪ **Palace Hotel Gstaad.** 3780 Gstaad. ☎ **800/223-6800** in the U.S., or 033/748-50-00. Fax 033/748-50-01. 124 units. MINIBAR TV TEL. Winter 480–1,120SF ($350.40–$817.60) double; off-season (including summer) 450–790SF ($328.50–$576.70) double; year-round from 900SF ($657) junior suite. AE, DC, MC, V. Parking 18SF ($13.15) in garage. Closed end of Mar to mid-June and mid-Sept to mid-Dec.

This landmark hotel is on a wooded hill overlooking the center of Gstaad. It's one of the most sought-after luxury hideaways in the world, attracting corporation heads, film stars, jet-setters, and the titled. The nerve center of this chic citadel is an elegantly paneled main salon, with an eternal flame burning in the baronial stone fireplace. Radiating halls lead to superb restaurants, bars, discos, and sports facilities. Bedrooms (some large enough for Elizabeth Taylor and all her husbands, dead or alive) are country deluxe with regional artifacts, cheerful print wallpaper and rustic pine furnishings. Bathrooms are exceedingly luxurious with fluffy robes, dual basins, and hair dryers. Facilities include an indoor pool with an underwater sound system, a fitness center, a sauna, a solarium, and tennis courts.

Where to Dine

Olden Restaurant. In the Hotel Olden, Hauptstrasse. ☎ **033/744-34-44.** Reservations recommended. Main courses 35–60SF ($25.55–$43.80). AE, DC, MC, V. Daily noon–2pm and 7–10pm. Closed mid-Apr to mid-May and 2 weeks in Nov. MEDITERRANEAN/SWISS.

This most elegant of the several dining areas in the above-recommended hotel attracts visiting celebrities. The service is formal and refined, and the food as good as, or better than, anything in the area. Although local ingredients are used whenever possible, the kitchen also imports some of its finest products from all over Europe, including a tender Scottish lamb fed on heather, which emerges well seasoned and flavorful from the kitchen's ovens. The fresh goose-liver terrine is comparable to what's found in central France, and the soups, especially the shrimp bisque with green peppercorns, are rich and well seasoned. The kitchen also prepares old-fashioned *raclette*, where a wheel of mountain cheese is brought out and melted before you. One of the finest meat courses is médaillons of veal fried extremely tender and given an added zest by a confit of lemon.

✪ **Restaurant Chesery.** Lauenenstrasse. ☎ **033/744-24-51.** Reservations required. Main courses 40–60SF ($29.20–$43.80); set-price lunch 60SF ($43.80); set-price dinner 155SF ($113.15). AE, DC, MC, V. Tues–Sun 11:30am–2:30pm and 7pm–midnight. INTERNATIONAL.

One of Switzerland's 10 best restaurants perches at an elevation of 3,600 feet. Natural stone floors and polished pine walls pair naturally with a menu that changes daily, but is always based on the freshest of ingredients—grouse from Scotland, Charolais beef from France, truffles from Umbria. Try the salt-crusted sea bass with wild rice or chicken Houban (a special breed from France). In the basement bar, Casino, a piano player entertains nightly; the bar is open 6pm to around 3am.

Appendix

A European Tourist Offices

Here are the addresses, phone numbers, e-mail addresses, and Internet Web sites for the tourist offices of the countries covered in this guide.

Note that the official Web site of the **European Travel Commission** is **www.visiteurope.com**.

AUSTRIAN NATIONAL TOURIST OFFICE

IN THE U.S. P.O. Box 1142, New York, NY 10108-1142 (☎ **212/944-6880**); 500 N. Michigan Ave., Suite 1950, Chicago, IL 60611 (☎ **312/644-8029**); P.O. Box 491938, Los Angeles, CA 90049 (☎ **310/478-8376**).

IN CANADA 1010 Sherbrooke St. W., Suite 1410, Montréal, PQ H3A 2R7 (☎ **514/849-3709**); 2 Bloor St. E., Suite 3330, Toronto, ON M4W 1A8 (☎ **416/967-3381**); Suite 1380, Granville Square, 200 Granville St., Vancouver, BC V6C 1S4 (☎ **604/683-5808**).

IN THE U.K. 30 St. George St., London W1R 0AL (☎ **020/7629-0461**).

E-MAIL None.

WEB SITE www.anto.com

BELGIAN TOURIST OFFICE

IN THE U.S. 780 Third Ave., New York, NY 10017 (☎ **212/758-8130**).

IN CANADA P.O. Box 760 NDG, Montréal, PQ H4A 3S2 (☎ **514/489-8965**).

IN THE U.K. 29 Prince St., London W1R 7RG (☎ **020/7629-3777**).

E-MAIL belinfo@nyxfer.blythe.org

WEB SITE www.visitbelgium.com

BRITISH TOURIST AUTHORITY

IN THE U.S. 551 Fifth Ave., Suite 701, New York, NY 10176 (☎ **800/462-2748** or 212/986-2200); 625 N. Michigan Ave., Suite 1510, Chicago, IL 60611 (☎ **800/462-2748**).

IN CANADA 111 Avenue Rd., Suite 450, Toronto, ON M5R 3J8 (☎ **416/961-8124**).

IN AUSTRALIA Level 16, Gateway, 1 Macquarie Place, Sydney, NSW 2000 (☎ **02/9377-4400**).

IN NEW ZEALAND Suite 305, Dilworth Bldg., Customs and Queen streets, Auckland 1 (☎ **09/303-1446**).

E-MAIL travelinfo@bta.org.uk

WEB SITE www.vistibritain.com

CZECH TOURIST AUTHORITY
IN THE U.S. 1109 Madison Ave., New York, NY 10028 (☎ **212/288-0830**).

IN CANADA P.O. Box 198, Exchange Tower, 130 King St. W, Suite 715, Toronto, ON M5X 1A6 (☎ **416/367-3432**).

IN THE U.K. 95 Great Portland St., London W1M 5RA (☎ **020/7291-9920**).

E-MAIL nycenter@ny.czech.cz

WEB SITE wwwczech.cz/new_york

FRENCH GOVERNMENT TOURIST OFFICE
IN THE U.S. 444 Madison Ave., 16th Floor, New York, NY 10022 (☎ **212/838-7800**); 676 N. Michigan Ave., Suite 3360, Chicago, IL 60611 (☎ **312/751-7800**); 9454 Wilshire Blvd., Suite 715, Beverly Hills, CA 90212 (☎ **310/271-6665**). To request information at any of these offices, call the **France on Call hotline** at ☎ **900/990-0040** (50¢ per minute).

IN CANADA Maison de la France/French Government Tourist Office, 1981 av. McGill College, Suite 490, Montréal, PQ H3A 2W9 (☎ **514/288-4264**).

IN THE U.K. Maison de la France/French Government Tourist Office, 178 Piccadilly, London, W1V 0AL (☎ **0891/244-123**).

IN AUSTRALIA French Tourist Bureau, 25 Bligh St., Sydney, NSW 2000 (☎ **02/9231-5244**).

E-MAIL info@francetourism.com

WEB SITE www.fgtousa.org or www.francetourism.com

GERMAN NATIONAL TOURIST OFFICE
IN THE U.S. 122 E. 42nd St., 52nd Floor, New York, NY 10168 (☎ **212/661-7200**); 11766 Wilshire Blvd., Suite 750, Los Angeles, CA 90025 (☎ **310/575-9799**).

IN CANADA 175 Bloor St. E., North Tower, 6th Floor, Toronto, ON M4W 3R8 (☎ **416/968-1570**).

IN THE U.K. Nightingale House, 65 Curzon St., London, W1Y 8NE (☎ **020/7495-0081**).

IN AUSTRALIA Lufthansa House, 143 Macquarie St., 12th Floor, Sydney, NSW 2000 (☎ **02/9367-3890**).

E-MAIL gntony@aol.com

WEB SITE www.germany-tourism.de

GREEK NATIONAL TOURIST ORGANIZATION

IN THE U.S. 645 Fifth Ave., 5th Floor, New York, NY 10022 (☎ **212/421-5777**); 168 N. Michigan Ave., Suite 600, Chicago, IL 60601 (☎ **312/782-1084**); 611 W. 6th St., Suite 2198, Los Angeles, CA 90017 (☎ **213/626-6696**).

IN CANADA 2 Bloor St. W., Cumberland Terrace, Toronto, ON M4W 3E2 (☎ **416/968-2220**); 1233 rue de la Montagne, Suite 101, Montréal, PQ H3G 1Z2 (☎ **514/871-1535**).

IN THE U.K. 4 Conduit St., London W1R D0J (☎ **020/7734-5997**).

IN AUSTRALIA 51–57 Pitt St., Sydney, NWS 2000 (☎ **02/9241-1663**).

E-MAIL None.

WEB SITE www.hellas.de or www.greektourism.com

HUNGARIAN NATIONAL TOURIST OFFICE

IN THE U.S. 150 E. 58th St., New York, NY 10155 (☎ **212/355-0240**).

IN THE U.K. ℅ Embassy of the Republic of Hungary, Trade Commission, 46 Eaton Place, London, SW1 X8AL (☎ **020/7823-1032**).

E-MAIL huntour@idt.net

WEB SITE www.hungarytourism.hu

IRISH TOURIST BOARD

IN THE U.S. 345 Park Ave., New York, NY 10154 (☎ **800/223-6470** or 212/418-0800).

IN CANADA 160 Bloor St. E., Suite 1150, Toronto, ON M4W 1B9 (☎ **416/929-2777**).

IN THE U.K. 150 New Bond St., London W1Y OAQ (☎ **020/7493-3201**).

IN AUSTRALIA 36 Carrington St., 5th Level, Sydney, NSW 2000 (☎ **02/9299-6177**).

E-MAIL info@irishtouristboard.com

WEB SITE www.ireland.travel.ie

ITALIAN GOVERNMENT TOURIST BOARD

IN THE U.S. 630 Fifth Ave., Suite 1565, New York, NY 10111 (☎ **212/245-4822**); 401 N. Michigan Ave., Suite 3030, Chicago, IL 60611 (☎ **312/644-0990**); 12400 Wilshire Blvd., Suite 550, Beverly Hills, CA 90025 (☎ **310/820-0098**).

IN CANADA 1 place Ville-Marie, Suite 1914, Montréal, PQ H3B 2C3 (☎ **514/866-7667**).

IN THE U.K. 1 Princes St., London W1R 8AY (☎ **020/7408-1254**).

E-MAIL None.

WEB SITE None.

MONACO GOVERNMENT TOURIST OFFICE

IN THE U.S. 565 Fifth Ave., New York, NY 10017 (☎ **800/753-9696** or 212/286-3330); 542 S. Dearborn St., Suite 550, Chicago, IL 60605 (☎ **312/939-7836**).

IN THE U.K. 3–8 Chelsea Garden Market, Chelsea Harbour, London, SW10 0XE (☎ **020/7352-9962**).

E-MAIL mgto@monaco1.org

WEB SITE www.monaco.mc/usa

NETHERLANDS BOARD OF TOURISM
IN THE U.S. 355 Lexington Ave., 21st Floor, New York, NY 10017 (☎ **212/370-7360**); 225 N. Michigan Ave., Suite 1854, Chicago, IL 60601 (☎ **312/819-0300**).

IN CANADA 25 Adelaide St. E., Suite 710, Toronto, ON M5C 1Y2 (☎ **416/363-1577**).

IN THE U.K. 18 Buckingham Gate, London, SW1E 6LB (☎ **020/ 7828-7900**).

E-MAIL go2holland@aol.com

WEB SITE www.goholland.com

PORTUGUESE NATIONAL TOURIST OFFICE
IN THE U.S. 590 Fifth Ave., New York, NY 10036 (☎ **212/354-4403**).

IN CANADA 600 Bloor St. W., Suite 1005, Toronto, ON M4W 3B8 (☎ **416/921-7376**).

IN THE U.K. 1–5 New Bond St., London, W1Y 0NP (☎ **020/ 7493-3873**).

E-MAIL aavila@portugal.org

WEB SITE www.portugal.org

SCANDINAVIAN TOURIST BOARDS
IN THE U.S. P.O. Box 4649, Grand Central Station, New York, NY 10163 (☎ **212/949-2333** or 212/885-9700); 8929 Wilshire Blvd., Beverly Hills, CA 90211 (☎ **213/854-1549**).

IN THE U.K. The Danish Tourist Board, 55 Sloane St., London SW1X 95Y (☎ **020/7259-5959**); the Swedish Travel and Tourism Council, 73 Welbeck St., London W1M 8AN (☎ **020/7724-5869**).

E-MAIL info@gosweden.org

WEB SITES www.visitdenmark.com or www.gosweden.org

SWITZERLAND TOURISM
IN THE U.S. 608 Fifth Ave., New York, NY 10020 (☎ **212/757-5944**); 150 N. Michigan Ave., Suite 2930, Chicago, IL 60601 (☎ **312/630-5840**); 222 N. Sepulveda Blvd., Suite 1570, El Segundo, CA 90245 (☎ **310/335-5980**).

IN CANADA 154 University Ave., Suite 610, Toronto, ON M5H 3Y9 (☎ **416/971-9734**).

IN THE U.K. Swiss Centre, Swiss Court, London, W1V 8EE (☎ **020/ 7734-1921**).

E-MAIL stnewyork@switzerlandtourism.com

WEB SITE www.switzerlandtourism.com

TOURIST OFFICE OF SPAIN
IN THE U.S. 666 Fifth Ave., 35th Floor, New York, NY 10103 (☎ **212/ 265-8822**); 845 N. Michigan Ave., Suite 915E, Chicago, IL 60611 (☎ **312/ 642-1992**); 8383 Wilshire Blvd., Suite 960, Beverly Hills, CA 90211 (☎ **213/658-7188**); 1221 Brickell Ave., Suite 1850, Miami, FL 33131 (☎ **305/358-1992**).

IN CANADA   102 Bloor St. W., 14th Floor, Toronto, ON M5S 1M9 (☎ **416/961-3131**).

IN THE U.K.   57 St. James's St., London SW1 (☎ **020/7499-0901**).

IN AUSTRALIA   203 Castlereagh St., Suite 21A (P.O. Box 675), Sydney, NSW 2000 (☎ **02/9264-7966**).

E-MAIL   oetny@here-i.com

WEB SITE   www.okspain.org

Airline Toll-Free Numbers & Web Sites

NORTH AMERICAN AIRLINES WITH FREQUENT SERVICE TO EUROPE

For the latest on airline Web sites, check airlines-online.com or www.itn.com.

Air Canada
☎ 800/776-3000 in the U.S.
800/555-1212 in Canada
  for local number
www.aircanada.ca

American Airlines
☎ 800/433-7300
www.americanair.com

Canadian Airlines
☎ 800/426-7000 in U.S.
800/665-1177 in Canada
www.cdnair.ca

Continental Airlines
☎ 800/231-0856
www.flycontinental.com

Delta Airlines
☎ 800/241-4141
www.delta-air.com

Northwest Airlines
☎ 800/447-4747
www.nwa.com

Tower Air
☎ 800/221-2500
www.towerair.com

TWA
☎ 800/892-4141
www.twa.com

US Airways
☎ 800/622-1015
www.usairways.com

MAJOR NATIONAL & COUNTRY-AFFILIATED EUROPEAN AIRLINES

AUSTRIA

Austrian Airlines
☎ 800/843-0002 in the U.S. and
  Canada
☎ 020/7434-7300 in the U.K.
☎ 02/9241-4277 in Australia
www.aua.com

BELGIUM

Sabena
☎ 800/955-2000 in the U.S. and
  Canada
☎ 020/7494-2629 in the U.K.
www.sabena-usa.com

CZECH REPUBLIC

CSA Czech Airlines
☎ 800/223-2365 in the U.S. and
  Canada
☎ 020/7255-1898 in the U.K.

☎ 02/9247-6196 in Australia
www.csa.cz

FRANCE

Air France
☎ 800/237-2747 in the U.S.
☎ 514/847-1106 in Canada
☎ 020/8742-6600 in the U.K.
☎ 02/9321-1000 in Australia
☎ 068/725-8800 in New Zealand
www.airfrance.com

GERMANY

Lufthansa
☎ 800/645-3880 in the U.S.
☎ 800/563-5954 in Canada
☎ 0345/737-747 in the U.K.
☎ 02/9367-3888 in Australia
☎ 09/303-1529 in New Zealand
www.lufthansa.com

GREECE
Olympic Airways
- ☎ 800/223-1226 in the U.S. or 212/735-0200 in New York State
- ☎ 514/878-3891 in Canada (Montréal) or 416/920-2452 (Toronto)
- ☎ 020/7409-2400 in the U.K.
- ☎ 02/9251-2044 in Australia

agn.hol.gr/info/olympic1.htm

HUNGARY
Malev Hungarian Airlines
- ☎ 800/262-5380 in the U.S.
- ☎ 416/9440-093 in Canada
- ☎ 020/7439-0577 in the U.K.
- ☎ 02/9321-9111 in Australia
- ☎ 09/379-4455 in New Zealand

www.malev-airlines.com

IRELAND
Aer Lingus
- ☎ 800/IRISH-AIR in the U.S.
- ☎ 020/8899-4747 in the U.K. in London, or 0645/737-747 in all other areas
- ☎ 02/9321-9123 in Australia
- ☎ 09/379-4455 in New Zealand

www.aerlingus.ie

ITALY
Alitalia
- ☎ 800/223-5730 in the U.S.
- ☎ 514/842-8241 in Canada (Montréal) or 416/363-1348 (Toronto)
- ☎ 020/8745-8200 in the U.K.
- ☎ 02/9247-1307 in Australia
- ☎ 09/379-4457 in New Zealand

www.alitalia.com

THE NETHERLANDS
KLM Royal Dutch Airlines
- ☎ 800/374-7747 in the U.S.
- ☎ 514/939-4040 in Canada (Montréal) or 416/204-5100 (Toronto)
- ☎ 0990/750-9900 in the U.K.
- ☎ 02/9231-6333 in Australia
- ☎ 09/309-1782 in New Zealand

www.klm.nl

PORTUGAL
TAP Air Portugal
- ☎ 800/221-7370 in the U.S.
- ☎ 020/7828-0262 in the U.K.

www.tap-airportugal.pt

SCANDINAVIA (DENMARK, NORWAY, SWEDEN)
Icelandair
- ☎ 800/223-5500 in the U.S. and Canada
- ☎ 020/7388-5599 in the U.K.

www.icelandair.is

SAS Scandinavian Airlines
- ☎ 800/221-2350 in the U.S.
- ☎ 020/7734-6777 in the U.K.
- ☎ 02/9299-6688 in Australia

www.flysas.com

SPAIN
Iberia
- ☎ 800/772-4642 in the U.S.
- ☎ 800/363-4534 in Canada
- ☎ 020/7830-0011 in the U.K.
- ☎ 02/9283-3660 in Australia
- ☎ 09/379-3076 in New Zealand

www.iberia.com

SWITZERLAND
Swissair
- ☎ 800/221-4750 in the U.S. and Canada
- ☎ 020/7434-7300 in the U.K.
- ☎ 02/9232-1744 in Australia

www.swissair.com

UNITED KINGDOM
British Airways
- ☎ 800/247-9297 in the U.S. and Canada
- ☎ 020/8897-4000 or 034/522-2111 in the U.K.
- ☎ 02/9258-3300 in Australia

www.british-airways.com

Virgin Atlantic Airways
- ☎ 800/862-8621 in the U.S. and Canada
- ☎ 01293/747-747 in the U.K.
- ☎ 02/9352-6199 in Australia

www.fly.virgin.com

C Average Travel Times by Rail

Amsterdam to
Berlin 8 hr. 30 min.
Cologne 3 hr.
Copenhagen 11 hr. 30 min.
Frankfurt 6 hr.
Munich 8 hr. 30 min.
Paris 4 hr. 15 min.
Zurich 10 hr.

Athens to
Munich 42 hr. 30 min.
Vienna 43 hr.

Avignon to
Barcelona 6 hr. 30 min.
Paris 3 hr. 30 min.

Barcelona to
Madrid 7 hr.
Paris 11 hr. 30 min.

Bath to
London 1 hr. 11 min.

Berlin to
Frankfurt 6 hr.
Munich 7 hr.
Paris 11 hr.
Prague 6 hr. 30 min.

Bern to
Interlaken 1 hr.
Milan 4 hr. 30 min.
Paris 4 hr. 30 min.
Zurich 1 hr. 30 min.

Bordeaux to
Paris 3 hr.

Brussels to
Frankfurt 5 hr. 30 min.
London 2 hr. 45min
Paris 1 hr. 25 min.

Budapest to
Frankfurt 15 hr. 30 min.
Prague 9 hr. 30 min.
Vienna 4 hr.

Cannes to
Paris 6 hr.

Copenhagen to
Oslo 10 hr. 30 min.
Paris 15 hr.
Stockholm 8 hr.

Edinburgh to
London 4 hr.

Florence to
Geneva 8 hr.
Milan 3 hr.
Paris 12 hr. 30 min.

Rome 1 hr. 30 min.
Venice 3 hr.
Zurich 8 hr.

Frankfurt to
Munich 3 hr. 30 min.
Paris 6 hr. 15 min.
Prague 8 hr.
Salzburg 5 hr.
Vienna 8 hr.
Zurich 5 hr.

Geneva to
Milan 4 hr. 15 min.
Paris 3 hr. 30 min.
Venice 8 hr.

Glasgow to
London 5 hr. 5 min.

Granada to
Madrid 6 hr. 30 min.

Helsinki to
Stockholm 10 hr.

Innsbruck to
Munich 3 hr.
Vienna 8 hr.
Zurich 5 hr.

Lausanne to
Milan 4 hr. 30 min.
Paris 3 hr. 45 min.

Lillehammer to
Oslo 2 hr. 30 min.

Lisbon to
Madrid 10 hr.

London to
Paris 3 hr.

Luxembourg to
Paris 4 hr.

Luzerne to
Paris 7 hr. 30 min.
Venice 8 hr.

Lyon to
Nice 5 hr.
Paris 2 hr.

Madrid to
Malaga 7 hr.

Marseille to
Paris 4 hr. 15 min.

Milan to
Nice 5 hr.
Paris (day) 6 hr. 40 min.
Rome 5 hr.
Venice 3 hr.
Zurich 4 hr. 30 min.

Munich to
Paris   8 hr. 30 min.
Prague   7 hr. 30 min.
Rome   11 hr.
Salzburg   2 hr.
Venice   9 hr.
Vienna   4 hr. 45 min.
Zurich   5 hr.

Nantes to
Paris   2 hr.

Naples to
Rome   2 hr.

Nice to
Paris   6 hr. 30 min.
Rome   10 hr.
Venice   10 hr.

Oslo to
Stockholm   6 hr. 30 min.

Paris to
Rome   15 hr.
Salzburg   10 hr.
Strasbourg   4 hr.
Toulouse   5 hr.
Tours   1 hr.
Venice   12 hr. 15 min.
Vienna   13 hr. 30 min.
Zurich   6 hr.

Pisa to
Rome   4 hr.

Prague to
Vienna   5 hr.

Rome to
Siena   3 hr.
Venice   4 hr. 30 min.
Zurich   8 hr. 30 min.

Salzburg to
Vienna   4 hr.

Venice to
Vienna   8 hr.

Vienna to
Zurich   12 hr.

Frommer's Online Directory

By Michael Shapiro

Michael Shapiro is the author of *Internet Travel Planning* (The Globe Pequot Press). Bruce Gerstman and Karen Pojmann contributed listings for some European countries to this directory.

Frommer's Online Directory is a new feature designed to help you take advantage of the Internet to better plan your trip. Part 1 lists general Internet resources that can make any trip easier, such as sites for booking airline tickets. In Part 2, you'll find some top online guides for Europe. It's not meant to be a comprehensive list—it's a discriminating selection of useful sites to get you started, with stars for the best. Finally, remember this is a press-time snapshot of leading Web sites; some undoubtedly will have evolved, changed, or moved by the time you read this.

1 Top Travel-Planning Web Sites

Among the most popular travel sites are online travel agencies. The top agencies, including Expedia, Preview Travel, and Travelocity, offer an array of tools that are valuable even if you don't book online. You can check flight schedules, hotel availability, and car rental prices, or get paged if your flight is delayed.

Although online agencies have come a long way over the past few years, they don't always yield the best prices. Unlike a travel agent, for example, they're unlikely to tell you that you can save money by flying a day earlier or a day later. On the other hand, if you're looking for a bargain fare, you might find something online that an agent wouldn't take the time to dig up. Because airline commissions have been cut, a travel agent may not find it worthwhile spending half an hour trying to find you the best deal. On the Net, you can be your own agent and take all the time you want.

Online booking sites aren't the only places to book airline tickets. All major airlines have their own Web sites and often offer incentives, such as bonus frequent flyer miles or Net-only discounts, for buying online. These incentives have helped airlines capture the majority of the online booking market. According to Jupiter Communications, online agencies such as Travelocity booked about 80% of tickets purchased online in 1996, but by 1999 airline sites (such as **www. ual.com**) were projected to own more than half of the online market, with online agencies' share of the pie dwindling each year.

LEADING BOOKING SITES

Cheap Tickets. www.cheaptickets.com
Essentials: Discounted rates on domestic and international airline tickets and hotel rooms.

Playing It Safe

Far more people look online than book online, partly because of the fear of putting their credit cards through on the Net. Although secure encryption has made this fear less justified, there's no reason you can't find a flight online and then book it by calling a toll-free number or contacting your travel agent. To be sure you're in secure mode when you book online, look for a little icon of a key (in Netscape) or a padlock (Internet Explorer) at the bottom of your Web browser's screen.

Sometimes discounters, such as Cheap Tickets, have exclusive deals that aren't available through more mainstream channels. Registration at Cheap Tickets requires entering a credit card number before getting started, which is one reason many people elect to call the company's toll-free number instead of booking online. One of the most frustrating things about the Cheap Tickets site is that it offers fare quotes for a route, and later shows this fare is not valid for your dates of travel. Other Web sites, such as Preview Travel, consider your dates of travel before showing what fares are available. Despite its problems, Cheap Tickets can be worth the effort because its fares can be lower than those offered by its competitors.

✪ Expedia. **expedia.com**

Essentials: Domestic and international flight, hotel, and rental car booking; late-breaking travel news; destination features and commentary from travel experts; and deals on cruises and vacation packages. Free registration is required for booking.

Expedia makes it easy to handle flight, hotel, and car booking on one itinerary, so it's a good place for one-stop shopping. Expedia's hotel search offers crisp, zoomable maps to pinpoint most properties; click on the camera icon to see images of the rooms and facilities. But like many online databases, Expedia focuses on the major chains, such as Hilton and Hyatt, so don't expect to find too many one-of-a-kind resorts or B&Bs here.

Once you're registered (it's necessary to do this only once from each computer you use), you can start booking with the Roundtrip Fare Finder box on the home page, which expedites the process. After selecting a flight, you can hold it until midnight the following day or purchase online. If you think you might do better through a travel agent, you'll have time to try to get a lower price; you might do better with a travel agent because Expedia's computer reservation system does not include all airlines.

Preview Travel. **www.previewtravel.com**

Essentials: Domestic and international flight, hotel, and rental car booking; Travel Newswire lists fare sales; and deals on cruises and vacation packages. Free (one-time) registration is required for booking. Preview offers express booking for members, but at press time this feature was buried below the fold on Preview's reservation page.

Preview features the most inviting interface for booking trips, but the wealth of graphics can make the site somewhat slow to load. Use Farefinder to quickly find the lowest current fares on flights to dozens of major cities. Carfinder offers a similar service for rental cars, but you can search only airport locations, not city pick-up sites. To see the lowest fare for your itinerary, enter the dates and times for your route and see what Preview comes up with.

For More Information

See "Airline Toll-Free Numbers & Web Sites," in the Appendix for airline contact information.

When Should You Book Online?

Online booking works best for trips within North America. For international tickets, it's usually cheaper and easier to use a travel agent or consolidator. But if you want to know as much as possible about your options, the Net is a good place to start, especially for bargain hunters, who can take advantage of last-minute specials, such as American Airlines' weekend deals or other Internet-only fares that must be purchased online. Another advantage is that you can cash in on incentives for booking online, such as rebates or bonus frequent flyer miles.

Online booking is also not for those with a complex international itinerary. If you require follow-up services, such as itinerary changes, use a travel agent. Although Expedia and some other online agencies employ travel agents available by phone, these sites are geared primarily for self-service.

In recent years Preview and other leading booking services have added features such as Best Fare Finder, so after Preview searches for the best deal on your itinerary, it checks flights that are a bit later or earlier to see if it might be cheaper to fly at a different time. While these searches have become quite sophisticated, they still occasionally overlook deals that might be uncovered by a top-notch travel agent. If you have the time, see what you can find online and then call an agent to see if you can get a better price.

With Preview's Fare Alert feature, you can set fares for up to three routes and get e-mail notices when the fare drops below your target amount. For example, you could tell Preview to alert you when the round-trip fare from New York to Paris drops below $450. If it does, you'll get an e-mail telling you the current fare.

Note to AOL Users: You can book flights, hotels, rental cars, and cruises on AOL at keyword **Travel.** The booking software is provided by Preview Travel and is similar to Preview on the Web. Use the AOL Travelers Advantage program to earn a 5% rebate on flights, hotel rooms, and car rentals.

Priceline. www.priceline.com

Even people who aren't familiar with too many Web sites have heard about Priceline.com. Launched in 1998 with a $10 million ad campaign featuring William Shatner, Priceline lets you "name your price" for domestic and international airline tickets and hotel rooms. In other words, you select a route and dates, guarantee with a credit card, and make a bid for what you're willing to pay. If one of the airlines in Priceline's database has a fare that's lower than your bid, your credit card is automatically charged for a ticket.

You can't say what time you want to fly—you have to accept any flight leaving between 6 a.m. and 10 p.m. on the dates you choose, and you might have to make one stopover. No frequent flyer miles are awarded, and tickets are non-refundable and can't be exchanged for another flight. So if your plans change, you're out of luck. Priceline can be good for travelers who have to take off on short notice (and who are thus unable to qualify for advance purchase discounts). But be sure to shop around first; if you overbid, you're required to buy the ticket and Priceline pockets the difference.

Travelocity. www.travelocity.com

Essentials: Domestic and international flight, hotel, and rental car booking; and deals on cruises and vacation packages. Travel Headlines spotlights latest bargain airfares. Free (one-time) registration is required for booking.

Take a Look at Frommer's Site

We highly recommend Arthur Frommer's Budget Travel Online (**www.frommers.com**) as an excellent travel-planning resource. Of course, we're a little biased, but you will find indispensable travel tips, reviews, monthly vacation giveaways, and online booking.

Subscribe to Arthur Frommer's Daily Newsletter (**www.frommers.com/newsletters**) to get the latest travel bargains and inside travel secrets in your mailbox every day. You'll read daily headlines and articles from the dean of travel himself, highlighting last-minute deals on airfares, accommodations, cruises, and package vacations. You'll also find great travel advice by checking the Tip of the Day or Hot Spot of the Month.

Search the Destinations archive (**www.frommers.com/destinations**) of more than 200 domestic and international destinations for great places to stay, tips for traveling there, and what to do while you're there. Once you've researched your trip, you might try the online reservation system (**www.frommers.com/booktravelnow**) to book your dream vacation at affordable prices.

Travelocity almost got it right. Its Express Booking feature enables travelers to complete the booking process more quickly than they could at Expedia or Preview, but Travelocity gums up the works with a page called "Featured Airlines." Big placards of several featured airlines compete for your attention. If you want to see the fares for all available airlines, click the much smaller box at the bottom of the page labeled "Book a Flight."

Some have worried that Travelocity, which is owned by American Airlines' parent company AMR, directs bookings to American. This doesn't seem to be the case—I've booked there dozens of times and have always been directed to the cheapest listed flight, for example, on Tower or ATA. But this "Featured Airlines" page seems to be Travelocity's way of trying to cash in with ads and incentives for booking certain airlines. There are rewards for choosing one of the featured airlines. You get 1,500 bonus frequent flyer miles if you book through United's site, for example, but the site doesn't tell you about other airlines that might be cheaper. If the United flight costs $150 more than the best deal on another airline, it's not worth spending the extra money for a relatively small number of bonus miles.

On the plus side, Travelocity has some leading-edge techie tools for modern travelers. Exhibit A is Fare Watcher Email, an "intelligent agent" that keeps you informed of the best fares offered for the city pairs (round-trips) of your choice. Whenever the fare changes by $25 or more, Fare Watcher alerts you by e-mail. Exhibit B is Flight Paging—if you own an alphanumeric pager with national access that can receive e-mail, Travelocity's paging system can alert you if your flight is delayed.

FINDING LODGINGS ONLINE

The services listed above offer hotel booking, but it can be best to use a site devoted primarily to lodging because you might find properties that aren't listed on more general online travel agencies. Some lodging sites specialize in a particular type of accommodations, such as B&Bs, that you won't find on the more mainstream booking services. Other services, such as TravelWeb, offer weekend deals on major chain properties, which cater to business travelers and have more empty rooms on weekends.

All Hotels on the Web. www.all-hotels.com

Well, this site *doesn't* include all the hotels on the Web, but it does have tens of thousands of listings throughout the world. Bear in mind that each hotel listed has paid a small fee ($25 and up) for placement, so it's not an objective list, but more like a book of online brochures.

Hotel Reservations Network. www.180096hotel.com

Bargain room rates at hotels in more than two dozen U.S. and international cities. The cool thing is that HRN books blocks of rooms in advance, so sometimes it has rooms—at discount rates—at hotels that are "sold out." Select a city, enter your dates, and you get a list of the best prices for a selection of hotels. Descriptions include an image of the property and a locator map; to book online click the "Book Now" button. HRN is notable for some deep discounts, even in cities where hotel rooms are expensive. The toll-free number is printed all over this site; call it if you want more options than are listed online.

InnSite. www.innsite.com

B&B listings for inns in dozens of countries around the globe. Find an inn at your destination, have a look at images of the rooms, check prices and availability, and then send e-mail to the innkeeper if you have further questions. This is an extensive directory of bed-and-breakfast inns but includes listings only if the proprietor submitted one (*note:* it's free to get an inn listed). The descriptions are written by the innkeepers, and many listings link to the inn's own Web sites, where you can find more information and images. Also see Bed and Breakfast Channel (**bedandbreakfast.com**).

Places to Stay. www.placestostay.com

Mostly one-of-a-kind places in the United States and abroad that you might not find in other directories, with a focus on resort accommodations. Again, listing is selective—this isn't a comprehensive directory, but can give you a sense of what's available at different destinations.

✪ TravelWeb. www.travelweb.com

TravelWeb lists more than 16,000 hotels worldwide, focusing on chains such as Hyatt and Hilton, and you can book almost 90% of them online. TravelWeb's Click-It Weekends, updated each Monday, offers weekend deals at many leading hotel chains. TravelWeb is the online home for Pegasus Systems, which provides transaction processing systems for the hotel industry.

LAST-MINUTE DEALS & OTHER ONLINE BARGAINS

There's nothing airlines hate more than flying with lots of empty seats (well, maybe they hate competition more, but that's another story). The Net has allowed airlines to offer last-minute bargains to entice travelers to fill those seats. Most of them are announced on Tuesday or Wednesday and are valid for travel the following weekend, but some can be booked weeks or months in advance. You can sign up for weekly e-mail alerts at airlines' sites (for airlines' Web site addresses, see "Airline Toll-Free Numbers & Web Sites" in the Appendix) or check sites such as WebFlyer (see below) that compile lists of these bargains. To make it easier, visit a site listed in this section that rounds up all the deals and sends them in one convenient weekly e-mail. But last-minute deals aren't the only online bargains—other sites can help you find value even if you can't wait until the eleventh hour.

✪ 1travel.com. www.1travel.com

Deals on domestic and international flights, cruises, hotels, and all-inclusive resorts such as Club Med. 1travel.com's Saving Alert compiles last-minute air deals so you don't have to scroll through multiple e-mail alerts. A feature called "Drive a little using low-fare airlines" helps map out strategies for using alternative airports to find lower fares. Farebeater searches a database that includes published fares, consolidator bargains and special deals exclusive to 1travel.com. *Note:* The travel agencies listed by 1travel.com have paid for placement.

BestFares. www.bestfares.com

Budget-seeker Tom Parsons lists some great bargains on airfares, hotels, rental cars, and cruises, but the site is poorly organized. News Desk is a long list of hundreds of bargains, but they're not broken down into cities or even countries, so it's not easy trying to find what you're looking for. If you have time to wade through it, you might find a good deal. Some material is available only to paid subscribers.

Go4less.com. www.go4less.com

Specializing in last-minute cruise and package deals, Go4less has some eye-popping offers. You can avoid sifting through all this material by using the Search box and entering vacation type, destination, month, and price.

LastMinuteTravel.com. www.lastminutetravel.com

Suppliers with excess inventory distribute unsold airline seats, hotel rooms, cruises, and vacation packages through this online agency.

Moment's Notice. www.moments-notice.com

As the name suggests, Moment's Notice specializes in last-minute vacation and cruise deals. You can browse for free, but if you want to purchase a trip you have to join Moment's Notice, which costs $25.

Smarter Living. www.smarterliving.com

Best known for its e-mail dispatch of weekend deals on 20 airlines, Smarter Living also keeps you posted about last-minute bargains on everything from Windjammer Cruises to flights to Iceland.

✪ WebFlyer. www.webflyer.com

WebFlyer is the ultimate online resource for frequent flyers and has an excellent listing of last-minute air deals. Click on "Deal Watch" for a round-up of weekend deals on flights, hotels, and rental cars from domestic and international suppliers.

TRAVELER'S TOOLKIT

Veteran travelers usually carry some essential items to make their trips easier. Following is a selection of online tools to smooth your journey.

ATM LOCATORS

Visa (www.visa.com/pd/atm/),
MasterCard (www.mastercard.com/atm)
Find ATMs in hundreds of cities in the United States and around the world. Both sites include maps for some locations and list airport ATM locations, some with maps.

Handy Tip

While most people learn about last-minute air specials from e-mail dispatches, it can be best to find out precisely *when* these deals become available and check airlines' Web sites at that time. To find out when deals become available, check the pages devoted to these specials on airlines' Web pages. Because these deals are limited, they can vanish within hours, sometimes even minutes, so it pays to log on as soon as they're available.

Checking E-Mail on the Road

Until a few years ago, most travelers who checked their e-mail while traveling carried a laptop, but this posed some problems. Not only are laptops expensive, but they can be difficult to configure, incur expensive connection charges, and are attractive to thieves. Thankfully, Web-based free e-mail programs have made it much easier to check your mail.

Just open an account at a free mail provider, such as Hotmail (**hotmail.com**) or Yahoo! Mail (**mail.yahoo.com**) and all you'll need to check your mail is a Web connection, easily available at Net cafes and copy shops around the world. After logging on, just point the browser to www.hotmail.com, for example, enter your username and password, and you'll have access to your mail.

Internet cafes have become ubiquitous, so for a few dollars an hour, you can check your mail and send messages back to colleagues, friends, and family. If you already have a primary e-mail account, you can set it to forward mail to your free mail account while you're away. Free mail programs have become enormously popular (Hotmail claims more than 10 million members) because they enable everyone, even those who don't own a computer, to have an e-mail address they can check wherever they log on to the Web.

✪ CultureFinder. www.culturefinder.com
Up-to-date listings for plays, opera, classical music, dance, film, and other cultural events in more than 1,300 U.S. cities. Enter the dates you'll be in a city and get a list of events happening then; you can also purchase tickets online. Also see FestivalFinder (**www.festivalfinder.com**) for the latest on more than 1,500 rock, folk, reggae, blues, and bluegrass festivals throughout North America.

✪ Foreign Languages for Travelers. www.travlang.com
Learn basic terms in more than 70 languages and click on any underlined phrase to hear what it sounds like. (*Note:* Free audio software and speakers are required.)

Intellicast. www.intellicast.com
Weather forecasts for cities around the world. Note that temperatures are in Celsius for many international destinations, so don't think you'll need that winter coat for your next trip to Athens.

Net Café Guide. www.netcafeguide.com/mapindex.htm
Locate Internet cafes at hundreds of locations around the globe. Catch up on your e-mail, log on to the Web, and stay in touch with the home front, usually for just a few dollars per hour.

Tourism Offices Worldwide Directory. www.towd.com
An extensive listing of tourism offices, some with links to these offices' Web sites.

Trip.com: Airport Maps and Flight Status. www.trip.com
A business travel site where you can find out when an airborne flight is scheduled to arrive. Click on "Guides and Tools" to peruse airport maps for more than 40 domestic cities.

Universal Currency Converter. www.xe.net/currency
See what your dollar or pound is worth in more than a hundred other countries.

U.S. Customs Service Traveler Information. www.customs.ustreas.gov/ travel/index.htm

Wondering what you're allowed to bring in to the United States? Check at this thorough site, which includes maximum allowance and duty fees.

2 Top Web Sites for Planning a Trip to Europe

The first section includes sites that cover the continent, and successive sections list sites for specific countries. Please bear in mind that some of the best sites are listed in the first category covering Europe in general. So if you're looking for information on Italy, don't just check the Italy section—also see sites such as Europe and TimeOut.com.

GENERAL SITES FOR EUROPE

About.com: Europe. about.com/travel/europe/index.htm
Formerly known as Miningco.com, this site rounds up some of the best Web sites by country, culled by "human guides" hired for each subject. Although some countries have better selections than others, About.com is worth a look for its extensive sets of links.

Europe. www.visiteurope.com
An all-encompassing planning site with advice by country and updated planning information, including passports, visas, international phone codes, and more. The site has a form you can use to request a free brochure.

Europe Online. www.europeonline.com
Similar to About.com, this site has personal guides for each country, who select the best links for travel categories. Some sections are very strong; others, well, need improvement.

✪ RailEurope. www.raileurope.com
This is a one-stop shopping site for European train travel, whether you're looking for fares and schedules, a Eurail pass, or a ride through the Chunnel.

Rail Pass Express. www.eurail.com
A good source for Eurail pass information, purchasing, and deals. Also see Rick Steves' Europe Through the Back Door (**www.ricksteves.com**) for insider tips on Eurail passes.

✪ Rick Steves' Europe Through the Back Door. www.ricksteves.com
The man who's made a cottage industry writing about Europe offers a tremendous amount of information here, from Eurail pass comparisons to recommendations for that quaint little inn on the Italian Riviera. In "Travel Tips and Tricks," he shares the wisdom he's gained from more than 2 decades of European travel.

✪ Subway Navigator. metro.ratp.fr:10001/bin/cities/english
An amazing site with detailed subway route maps for dozens of European cities. Select a city and enter your departure and arrival points. Subway Navigator maps your route and tells you how long the trip should take. It even shows your route on a subway map.

✪ TimeOut.com. www.timeout.com
An outstanding guide to more than a dozen European cities, with a focus on entertainment listings. The advice here is hip and savvy, and includes listings for hotels, restaurants, shops, galleries, museums, and music venues.

UK Golf. www.uk-golf.com/index.shtml
A listing of 3,000 courses throughout Europe with greens fees and directions to help you get there. Although the name implies it's just for the UK, you'll also find listings for France, Spain, and Portugal.

Yahoo Destination Guides. dir.yahoo.com/Recreation/Travel/ Destination_Guides/By_Country

You'll find more than 100 countries listed here, including all the countries of Europe. Just click on the country you're interested in for a treasure trove of links to Web sites on that country. Or just visit (**yahoo.com**) and search for the name of a country, and you'll most likely be directed to the Yahoo Travel page with listings for that country.

COUNTRY SITES
AUSTRIA

Austria National Tourist Office. www.anto.com
This official site is geared for North Americans and other English speakers, and has late-breaking information on culture and events. The tour finder includes advice for all sorts of vacations, from brewery tours to trips for the physically challenged. You'll also find magazine-style features and city guides for nine Austrian cities.

LiveCam Vienna. rhwcam.markant.at
This site is in German, but it doesn't matter—you're here for the live views of Vienna. No special software is required, but keep in mind the views are much better during Vienna's daylight hours.

Mozart Concerts. www.mozart.co.at/concerts
Learn about where and when to see performances, such as recitals by the Vienna Mozart Orchestra.

Tourist.net: Austria. www.tourist-net.co.at/main1e.htm
A region-by-region guide to Austria, including plenty of captivating photos, updated events listings, and advice on dining and attractions, such as the basket-weaving community of Piringsdorf.

Vienna Tourist Board. info.wien.at/e/index.htm
An up-to-date guide with listings for cultural events, museum exhibitions, and more. The 72-hour guide is a fine whirlwind tour for those who have only 3 days in this city. You'll also find advice on getting around Vienna.

BELGIUM

Art Events. www.art-events.be
A listing of cultural events throughout the country, including dates, a short synopsis, and links to the event's own Web site when available.

Belgium: Official Travel Guide. www.visitbelgium.com/bxhome.htm
Sure this site is boosterish, but what would you expect from the country's tourism office? It's still a fine place to research tours, see images of attractions, and find out what's new (such as museum exhibitions) in "Europe's best-kept secret."

Brussels. www.trabel.com/brussels.htm
A solid round-up of attractions, cultural events, and museums, complete with insider advice for tourists. Some of the categories are whimsical, such as "City of Beer" and "Brussels Lace."

Hotels Belgium. www.hotels-belgium.com
A good place to research hotels, where you can compare prices, see images of the rooms, and use e-mail to get in touch with proprietors.

✪ **Welcome to Belgium. www.trabel.com/index2.htm**
An extensive overview of the country, including tourism advice, airport information, and a search feature. If you like, you can sign up for a free e-mail newsletter.

CZECH REPUBLIC

CzechSite. **www.czechsite.com**
A clean, well-designed site offering tips on getting around, attractions, museums, galleries, and restaurants. You'll also find an online message board where you can communicate with others about your visit.

Czech Tourism Pages. **czech-tourism.com**
An extensive round-up of links to other Web sites, culled by Net veteran Marcus Endicott, who awards a Czech flag icon to his favorite sites.

Everyday Prague. **www.everydayprague.com**
Want to live like the locals? Then this is the guide for you—it includes everything from the latest fashion and shopping advice to a section on shipping home the treasures you find.

✪ HotelsCzech. **www.HotelsCzech.com**
A well-organized site showing hotels by the number of stars they receive. Click on a hotel to find prices by date, photos of the buildings and rooms, and reservation forms. *Note:* Reservations are not instant—you must fill out a form and the site promises an agent will get back to you within 48 hours.

DENMARK

Budget Accommodation in Copenhagen. **www.mdb.ku.dk/tarvin/copenhagen**
Lodging in Denmark's capital isn't cheap, but this site can help direct you to its most affordable accommodations.

Welcome to Denmark. **www.visitdenmark.com**
A wide-ranging site from the Danish Tourist Board. The lodging section, for example, ranges from "Castles and Manor Houses" to "Farm Holidays." You'll also find late news and transportation tips.

Wonderful Copenhagen. **www.woco.dk**
A product of Copenhagen's official visitors bureau, this jazzed-up site takes a long time to load, but can be worth the wait. Click on "Copenhagen A-Z" for all the basics on dining, lodging, and attractions.

ENGLAND

✪ Automobile Association UK. **www.theaa.co.uk**
This outstanding guide includes extensive lodging listings, ranked by price and quality. Many accept online bookings. You'll also find restaurant information with ratings based on food, service, atmosphere, and price.

The British Museum. **www.british-museum.ac.uk**
At press time, the first page of this site informed visitors "There are currently no Egyptian mummies on display." Shame. Still, the British Museum is well worth visiting and the Web site can tell you what's on (and what's happening in the mummy-less Egyptian Galleries) during the dates of your visit.

Buckingham Palace. **www.royal.gov.uk/palaces/bp.htm**
The official site from the British monarchy offers history, images, and descriptions of the "working palace" and "visitors' palace."

Hotels England. **www.hotelsengland.com**
Promising up to 50% off, this site has some reasonably good deals, but I checked a hotel where I paid about $120 for a room last year and the best Hotels England could do was $154. If you do find a good deal, you can book online.

Houses of Parliament. www.parliament.uk
A matter-of-fact visitors' guide to the House of Commons and the House of Lords, which includes tour times and a schedule of when Parliament is in session. See **www.parliament.uk/parliament/TOURS.HTM** for more about touring.

London Airports. www.heathrow.co.uk
A guide and terminal maps for Heathrow, Gatwick, Stansted, and other lesser airports, including flight arrival times, duty free shops, airport restaurants, and information on getting from airports to downtown London. Also see **www.heathrowexpress.co.uk** for information about the train that takes just 15 minutes to get from Heathrow to downtown London.

London Transport. www.londontransport.co.uk
London Transport is the agency that operates the Underground subway and city bus systems. This extensive and well-designed site includes maps, fare information, and advice to help you get around London as easily and cheaply as possible. Also see London Transport Museum (**www.ltmuseum.co.uk**).

The National Trust: Travel. www.nationaltrust.org.uk/travel.htm
The National Trust maintains more than 200 cottages and other unusual lodgings throughout the UK. The proceeds help support the work of this preservation organization.

✪ **Natural History Museum. www.nhm.ac.uk/museum**
A remarkably lively and extensive site offering a preview of the exhibitions and special programs. Click on the gallery guide where the sections include Dinosaurs, Creepy Crawlies, Wonders, and many more.

Official London Theater Guide. www.officiallondontheatre.co.uk
An extensive theater guide with information on the booth that sells half-price, day-of-show tickets. Search for plays by type of show, title, theater name, or date.

✪ **Original London Walks. www.walks.com**
London's most established walking tour company posts a schedule of walks by day of the week. Click on a day and get a list of more than a dozen distinct tours, such as "In the Footsteps of Sherlock Holmes" or "Jack the Ripper Haunts."

✪ **Tower of London Tour. www.toweroflondontour.com**
An extensive and illuminating photographic tour of one of London's oldest and most intriguing attractions.

✪ **Westminster Abbey. www.westminster-abbey.org**
A superb historical tour with lots of photos of one of the world's most magnificent churches. Includes basic visitor information such as tours of the nave, sanctuary, Henry VII Chapel, and a section on the coronations that have occurred at the abbey.

FRANCE

Aeroports de Paris. www.paris-airports.com
For the Charles de Gaulle and Orly airports, find listings of hotels, restaurants, and car rental agencies. The parking map and accessibility information for disabled travelers could help out upon landing.

Beyond the French Riviera. www.beyond.fr
The Travel section of this regional guide explains the trains, buses, air, and sea travel in detail. A directory of towns brings users to photos, history, and excursions.

Brittany Holiday Guide. www.brittany-guide.com
Thorough descriptions with photos of hotels and guesthouses, transportation information, history, and an events calendar for the region.

Chateau Versailles. www.chateauversailles.com
Before visiting the old digs of Louis the 14th, print out pages from this reference full of history, pictures of the grounds, and the works of art that hang from the palace walls.

Eiffel Tower. www.tour-eiffel.fr
Read history of the tower and download a free version of QuickTime VR software for virtual views from the top.

✪ FranceWay. www.franceway.com
Full of suggestions for your trip to France. Especially heavy on information about Paris, this guide covers dining, lodging, and transportation. The detailed listings of restaurants in Paris don't appear to be paid ads.

✪ Giverny and Vernon. giverny.org
Visitors to the old stomping grounds of Claude Monet will find loads of useful travel and transportation information at this basic, non-high-tech site. Find details on the area's castles, museums, and places of archeological interest.

The Louvre. mistral.culture.fr/louvre/louvrea.htm
After checking out descriptions of the guided tours, permanent collections, and temporary exhibitions, download the free QuickTime VR software to take a virtual stroll through the museum. Venus de Milo and Mona Lisa await your visit.

✪ Paris Pages. www.paris.org
The lodging reviews are organized by area of the city and which monuments stand nearby. The city guide includes an events calendar, shop listings, a map of attractions with details about each, and a photo tour.

✪ Provence Touristic Guide. www.provence.guideweb.com
Dig into the Leisure and Culture section for pictures, exhibit descriptions, and contact information for museums. A directory of hotels and guesthouses includes photos and some online reservations.

Region Bretagne. www.region-bretagne.fr
Go straight to the Tourism section, and then to the Leisure section, which includes outdoor activities, such as hiking and horseback riding. Otherwise, this glitzy site offers little substance in its dining and lodging sections.

Travel France. www.bonjour.com
Pick one of the country's regions and peruse a directory of links to attractions, tour operators, and city visitors bureaus. Check out the hints for getting around Paris.

GERMANY

Bavaria Alpine Net Guide. www.bavaria.com
All things Bavarian, such as an Oktoberfest raft, beer, and music ride down the River Isar. You'll also find advice that covers shopping, getting around, and enjoying the Alps, among lots of other nuggets.

Berlin Info. www.berlin-info.de/index_e.html
Take a virtual tour of Berlin's sights through this Web page, but beware that some of the links go to German-only pages.

Eat Germany. www.eat-germany.net/english.htm
A definitive dining guide that lets you search the site or view its Top 10 for each city. The restaurants are selected by site users who rate them, making the listings quite objective.

German Castles. www.germancastles.com
A guide to 48 castles and manors, complete with lots of photos and suggestions about lodging.

German National Tourist Board. **www.us.germany-tourism.de**
A solid and informative site including basics on lodging, getting around, and upcoming events, such as Expo 2000 in Hanover.

The Germany Way. **www.german-way.com/german**
Although this site isn't solely devoted to travel, it does have a nice travel section with lots of links. But don't just visit the travel section; the rest of the site is a solid background resource on Germany, covering topics from cinema to museums.

Hotels and Travel in Germany. **www.hotelstravel.com/germany.html**
This site not only provides some listings for hotels in Germany, but also has links to many other sites, such as Relais & Chateaux, that offer lodging and general travel information.

Oktoberfest. **www.munich-tourist.de/english/o.htm**
Updated for each year's festival, this site from the Munich Tourist Office includes a program of events, a guide to beer tents, and images from past festivals.

GREECE

✪ Aegean. **agn.hol.gr/main.htm**
A well-designed and easy-to-use travel guide to the Greek islands, including detailed hotel information, travel agencies, special offers (such as Net-only discounts), and more. Use the "Map of Greece" link for in-depth guides to various islands.

Athens Guide. **www.athensguide.com**
A wide-ranging yet personal guide that includes getting around, walking tours, dining, nightlife, and more. You'll find topics on Athens's outdoor markets, public gardens, and Internet cafes.

GoGreece.com. **www.gogreece.com**
A search site for Greece, including destination advice, maps, news, and much more.

Greek National Tourism Office. **www.vacation.net.gr/p/gnto.html**
Taxi fares, museum hours, ferry schedules—you name it: There's a good chance you'll find it here.

GreekNet. **www.greeknet.com/index2.htm**
A picturesque guide to the Greek islands; use the clickable map to learn more about the islands you plan to visit.

RodosNet. **www.rodosnet.gr/TouristGuide**
A lively guide to dining, shops, bars, sports, lodging, and more on the island of Rhodes.

Vacation in Greece. **www.vacation.net.gr/p/index.html**
An image-rich guide including archeology, history, and guides to Greek cities and islands.

HUNGARY

Budapest.com. **www.budapest.com**
View a virtual slideshow, consult the shopping guide, or see what the city looked like a century ago. Use the forum link for online discussions.

Hungarian Cultural and Information Center. **hungary.org**
Use the extensive collection of links as a jumping-off point for learning more about Hungary's history, culture, cuisine, and more. Of course, there's also a travel section.

✪ Hungarian National Tourist Office. **gotohungary.com**
This U.S.-based Web sites loads far more quickly than sites based in Europe and has a wealth of information for the Hungary traveler. Especially useful is the up-to-date

events calendar and special-interest guide, with links to spas and thermal baths, for example.

IRELAND

✪ Go Ireland. www.goireland.com
The breadth of this guide is almost overwhelming: More than 11,000 lodging listings (many with pictures) and thousands of restaurants (some with menus) are listed, but in some cases the information is pretty thin. Still, this is an extraordinary resource, especially if you're planning to visit more out-of-the-way places.

✪ Heritage of Ireland. www.heritageireland.ie
Use this Web site to get visitor information and view images of historic sites, parks, gardens, and cultural attractions, such as the Irish Museum of Modern Art.

Ireland Tourism. www.shamrock.org
Learn about package vacations and find some special deals, such as off-peak fares on Aer Lingus, through this site.

Irish Tourist Board. www.ireland.travel.ie
Use this well-designed site for tips on getting around, places to stay, and things to do. You'll also find a listing of major events, such as the Guinness Jazz Festival and Galway Art Festival.

Virtual Tour of Ireland. www.iol.ie/tip
With this site, it's not such a long way to Tipperary. See images of towns, peruse the destination information, and find tips for getting around, lodging, and dining.

ITALY

Carnival of Venice. www.carnivalofvenice.com/uk
Find out what's afoot for the carnival celebration of the year 2000 in the city of gondolas. There's also information about transportation, city services, and other Venice basics.

Dolce Vita. www.dolcevita.com
The self-proclaimed "insider's guide to Italy" is all about style—as it pertains to fashion, cuisine, design, and travel. While clearly driven by consumers and advertisers, Dolce Vita is a good place to stay up to date on trends in modern Italian culture.

✪ In Italy Online. www.initaly.com
This extensive site helps you find all sorts of accommodations (including country villas, historic residences, and gay-friendly hotels) and includes tips on shopping, dining, driving, and viewing works of art.

Italian Tourist Web Guide. www.itwg.com
The site features a searchable directory of accommodations, transportation tips, and city-specific lists of restaurants and attractions.

ItalyTour.com. www.italytour.com
This vast directory covers arts, culture, business, tours, entertainment, restaurants, lodging, real estate, news and media, shopping, sports, transportation, and major Italian cities. See photo collections and videos in the Panorama section.

Jubilee 2000. www.xibalba.com/solt/jubilee
If you're planning to be there when Rome bursts into jubilation for the beginning of Christianity's third millennium, be sure to first pay a visit to this site, which lists accommodations, artistic events, and celebrations.

Know It All: Know Tuscany. www.knowital.com
As the name suggests, this travel guide does seem to know it all about lodging, dining, and wine in the Italian region of Tuscany.

Traveling with Ed and Julie. www.twenj.com/romevisit.htm
Seasoned travelers advise green-footed wanderers on what to do when in Rome. Musing romantically about the ancient city, the pair guides tourists to hotels, restaurants, excursions, kids' activities, and major attractions such as the Vatican and the Coliseum.

THE NETHERLANDS

✪ **Amsterdam Channels. www.channels.nl**
This is one of the best virtual tours on the Net—the images are clear, and you can direct your own tour and chat with others about Amsterdam.

Go Amsterdam. www.go-amsterdam.org
This cleanly designed site includes an extensive "A-Z Index" with listings for museums, restaurants, hotels, transportation, and many other categories.

Hollandlinks. www.regiolicht.nl/homepages/fkleuve1/holland.htm
This ungainly Web address is worth typing in for the extensive and well-organized list of links, including sites for Webcams, newspapers, dining, Amsterdam, and many others.

Welcome to Holland. www.visitholland.com
The official site from the Netherlands Board of Tourism is awkwardly designed (maximizing your browser to its full size helps), but it does have useful advice for upcoming events, cycling, and culture, and even lets you know when the tulips bloom.

NORWAY

✪ **Coastal Route Norway. www.rv17.no**
This beautifully illustrated guide includes ferry schedules, a virtual tour, and a form to order a free print guide to the coast.

Norway Info. www.cyberclip.com/Katrine/NorwayInfo/index.html
Thousands of interesting tidbits appear on this personal site, produced by a woman named Katrine. Click on "A Year in Norway" to learn more about festivals, holidays, traditions, and folklore.

Norway Online Information Service. www.norway.org
Take a 13-photo virtual tour or get up to speed on current events and visa regulations.

✪ **Visiting Norway. www.norway.org/travel**
This well-designed site offers a wide-ranging introduction to the country's cities and regions, with information on lodging, attractions, cruises, shopping, and much more.

PORTUGAL

Nancy's Portugal Site. home.sol.no/~nancys/portugal
No, Nancy's not Portuguese (she's actually Norwegian, which might account for her love of this sun-soaked land), but she's put together a refreshingly personal love letter to her second home. Coverage of Lisbon and Madeira is strong.

O Chefe (Portugal Restaurant Guide). restaurantes.netopia.pt/chefe/en/
Use the search site to zoom in on restaurants by cuisine type, price, and location, and then see specialties for the places that meet your criteria.

Portugal Web. www.portugal-web.com
This site isn't devoted solely to travel, but it has sections on sightseeing, restaurants, car rental, and lodging (including vacation rentals and villas).

Virtual Portugal. www.portugalvirtual.pt
A remarkably extensive collection of Web links for exploring Portugal. Main categories include Tourism, Shopping, Accommodation, and Restaurants.

SCOTLAND

Discover Scotland. www.discover-scotland.com
This site from the *Daily Record* and *Sunday Mail* combines news headlines with travel advice ranging from fine dining to golf.

Golf Courses of Scotland. www.uk-golf.com/courses/scotland/index.shtml
Some say you haven't played golf until you've teed up in Scotland. This site, which lists locations and greens fees, will help you find a course wherever you plan to be.

Holidays in Scotland. www.holiday.scotland.net
This official site from the Scottish Tourist Board is an excellent source for events, lodgings, getting around, and outdoor activities. However, the Special Offers section requires a lot of clicks for very little payoff.

Scotland Holiday Net. www.aboutscotland.co.uk
This site combines a nice collection of information on dining, lodging, and sightseeing, with some personal accounts, such as a letter from an author who lives in the West Coast Highlands.

✪ Travel Scotland. www.travelscotland.co.uk
Curious about Scotland's top 20 free attractions? Interested in restaurant reviews from other diners? This site has all that and much more.

SPAIN

✪ All About Spain. www.red2000.com
A very deep and well-organized travel guide encompassing all sorts of attractions, from museums to fiestas. A section called Yellow Pages offers quick and easy access to topics.

CyberSpain. www.cyberspain.com
If you're not afraid of almost too much information, this is the site for you. Sure, it has the basics on lodging and dining, but you'll find much more, like background on Spanish traditions, such as La Tuna, and an extensive section on artists, including Goya.

Go Spain. www.clark.net/pub/jumpsam
Another extensive site that ranges from Jewels of Spain (Picasso, La Alhambra, etc.) to Spanish cooking. You'll also find a photo archive, links to news outlets, and a search engine for other resources covering Spain.

Tourist Office of Spain. www.okspain.org
This official site can help plan your trip with listings of lodging options, attractions, and tour operators and packages. You'll also find handy tips on getting around.

SWEDEN

Guide to Sweden. www.guidetosweden.com
If you're ever on "Jeopardy" and have to take "Famous Swedes for $400," you'll be glad you visited this site. In addition to trivia, look for practical advice and images of Swedish attractions.

Stockholm Information Service. www.stoinfo.se/england
Check this site just before you go for updated events listings. You'll also find advice for dining, lodging, and museums, as well as links to media outlets.

Swedish Information Smorgasbord. www.sverigeturism.se/smorgasbord
Interested in a steamship ride to the islands in Storsjön? This site will help you learn about this and thousands of other intriguing ways to spend your time in the land of the midnight sun.

SWITZERLAND

GoSki: Switzerland. **www.goski.com/switz.htm**
Get the low-down on skiing the high country here. This site will help you find a resort, tell you the best time to go, and keep you posted about conditions.

Switzerland.com. **www.switzerland.com/travel.html**
Not so much a destination in itself as a launching pad to other Web sites, Switzerland.com can point the way to museums, hotels, restaurants, and other attractions.

Switzerland Tourism. **www.switzerlandtourism.com**
Although this site is poorly designed, it does have useful travel advice on hotels and travel packages. The aerial video tour is very cool, but takes a minute or two to get started and requires Real Video software.

Index

Page numbers in *italics* refer to maps.

Index

Index

Index

FROMMER'S® COMPLETE TRAVEL GUIDES

THE UNOFFICIAL GUIDES®

SPECIAL-INTEREST TITLES

TAXS1076

10% Off*
AUSTIN REED

Find smart ladies' and men's fashions at one of the largest department stores in the heart of Regent Street. Also visit our convenient location in Knightsbridge.

103 Regent Street, London
Phone: (0) 171 734 6789

163 Brompton Road, London
Phone: (0) 171 584 4407

Code 20

TAXS1076

10% Off*
CREST OF LONDON

One of the most popular souvenir shops in London. Buy all your gifts and keepsakes at any of our 8 convenient locations.

Oxford Street, Piccadilly, Leicester Square, Whitehall, Queensway
Phone: (0) 171 935 0044

TAXS1076

10% Off*
MAX MARA

The best in smart and stylish Italian designer clothing for ladies.

32 Sloane Street, London
Phone: (0) 171 235 7941

153 New Bond Street, London
Phone: (0) 171 491 4748

TAXS1076

5% Off*
BRENTANA

Luxurious boutique with fashionable furs, quality leather and accessories from top designers like Brentana, Fendi Fourrure and more.

362, rue St. Honore, Paris 75001
(angle cour Vendôme)
Phone: 01.40.15.01.51

TAXS1076

5% Off*
ISA PARVEX

Located in the heart of St. Germain des Près, this beautiful boutique offers precious jewelry designed by Isa Parvex.

15, rue du Dragon, Paris 75006
Phone: 01.45.44.88.00

TAXS1076

5% Off*
TINTORETTO

Where youthful women get the latest chic fashions from this Spanish designer.

51, rue de Rennes, Paris 75006
Phone: 01.45.48.20.47

TAXS1076

5% Off*
CERIZE

The most sophisticated shop for beautiful jewelry, hats, gloves, scarves, and accessories by the world's top designers.

380, rue St. Honore, Paris, 75001
Phone: 01.42.60.84.84

TAXS1076

10% Off*
PLANET HOLLYWOOD

Visit this store in the Planet Hollywood restaurant and find a wide range of Planet Hollywood products such as T-shirts, fleece jackets, beer glasses, caps, and more

Reguliersbreestraat 35, 1017 CM Amsterdam
Phone: 020-4277827

SHOP Tax Free Where You See This Sign ▶ 🏷️ TAX FREE SHOPPING

1 Ask for your Global Refund Cheques when making purchases.

2 Get your Global Refund Cheques stamped at customs.

3 Claim your cash refund at any Cash Refund Desk.

For more information, call 800-566-9828.

10% Off*
CREST OF LONDON

*Phone cards and postage stamps excluded.
Void where prohibited, taxed, or restricted by law. Offer not available to citizens of European Union Countries.
© 1999, Cendant Membership Services, Inc.

Valid through 12/31/00

10% Off*
AUSTIN REED

*Minimum purchase required: £100. Only on full-price merchandise. Excludes factory outlets.
Void where prohibited, taxed, or restricted by law. Offer not available to citizens of European Union Countries.
© 1999, Cendant Membership Services, Inc.

Valid through 12/31/00

5% Off*
BRENTANA

*Minimum purchase required: 1200 FF.
Void where prohibited, taxed, or restricted by law. Offer not available to citizens of European Union Countries.
© 1999, Cendant Membership Services, Inc.

Valid through 12/31/00

10% Off*
MAX MARA

*Off full retail price only. Already discounted items excluded.
Void where prohibited, taxed, or restricted by law. Offer not available to citizens of European Union Countries.
© 1999, Cendant Membership Services, Inc.

Valid through 12/31/00

5% Off*
TINTORETTO

*Excluding sale items. Minimum purchase required: 1200 FF.
Void where prohibited, taxed, or restricted by law. Offer not available to citizens of European Union Countries.
© 1999, Cendant Membership Services, Inc.

Valid through 12/31/00

5% Off*
ISA PARVEX

*Minimum purchase required: 1200 FF.
Void where prohibited, taxed, or restricted by law. Offer not available to citizens of European Union Countries.
© 1999, Cendant Membership Services, Inc.

Valid through 12/31/00

10% Off*
PLANET HOLLYWOOD

*Not valid in conjunction with any other offer.
Void where prohibited, taxed, or restricted by law. Offer not available to citizens of European Union Countries.
© 1999, Cendant Membership Services, Inc.

Valid through 12/31/00

5% Off*
CERIZE

*Minimum purchase required: 1200 FF.
Void where prohibited, taxed, or restricted by law. Offer not available to citizens of European Union Countries.
© 1999, Cendant Membership Services, Inc.

Valid through 12/31/00

10% Off*
ZWILLING J.A. HENCKELS

Specializing in cutlery, scissors, manicure sets, pocket knives, and designer kitchen products, this store carries top brands such as Victorinox, Solingen, and more.

P.C. Hooftstraat 43, 1071 BM, Amsterdam
Phone: 020-6714220

5% Off*
GALTRUCCO

Browse through three floors of high fashion textiles, men's and ladies' fashions including top brands such as Brioni, Burini, Longhi, Moschino, Valentino, and Ungaro.

Piazza Duomo 2, Milan
Phone: 02-876256

5% Off*
CALZADOS BRAVO

Men's and women's shoes, leather goods, and travel gear.

Gran Via, 31 and 68, Madrid
Phone: 091 541 12 11

Serrano, 42, Madrid
Phone: 091 435 27 29

7% Off*
KASTORIA

Conveniently located by the Cathedral, this store sells fine Spanish leather, fur, and accessories, and has one of the best gift shops in town!

Avenida Catedral, 6-8, Barcelona
Phone: 093 310 04 11

10% Off*
ARTESANIA REYES

A fine jewelry shop dedicated to Spain's famous Majorica pearls.

Gran Via, 59, Madrid
Phone: 091 542 30 71

10% Off*
SAINT-PHIL

Located in prime areas of Zurich, these shops are renowned for day and evening fashions for men and women.

Charmant Bahnhofstrasse 26, Zurich
Phone: 211 94 55

Cocktail Bahnhofstrasse 14, Zurich
Phone: 211 40 25

2 éme Saison Kappelergasse 15, Zurich
Phone: 211 79 97

Homme et Femme Bahnhofstrasse 20, Zurich
Phone: 211 79 10

5% Off*
MAJESTIC CHAUSSURES

In the heart of Geneva, this store sells shoes and accessories including such brands as Bally, Christian Pellet, and Forlini.

21, rue Mont Blanc, Geneva
Phone: 741 00 50

5% Off*
HORLOGERIE R. RASCHLE

Near the Jet d'eau, this store sells watches and souvenirs including such brands as Casio, Swiss Army, and Victorinox.

15, rue Mont Blanc, Geneva
Phone: 901 19 05

1 Ask for your Global
Refund Cheques when
making purchases.

2 Get your Global Refund
Cheques stamped at customs.

3 Claim your cash
refund at any
Cash Refund Desk.

For more information, call 800-566-9828.

5% Off*
GALTRUCCO

Valid through 12/31/00

10% Off*
ZWILLING J.A. HENCKELS

Valid through 12/31/00

7% Off*
KASTORIA

Valid through 12/31/00

5% Off*
CALZADOS BRAVO

Valid through 12/31/00

10% Off*
SAINT-PHIL

Valid through 12/31/00

10% Off*
ARTESANIA REYES

Valid through 12/31/00

5% Off*
HORLOGERIE R. RASCHLE

Valid through 12/31/00

5% Off*
MAJESTIC CHAUSSURES

Valid through 12/31/00

WHEREVER
YOU TRAVEL,
*H*ELP IS NEVER
FAR AWAY.

From planning your trip to

providing travel assistance along

the way, American Express®

Travel Service Offices

are always there to help

you do more.

American Express Travel Service
Offices are found in central locations
throughout Europe.

Travel

www.americanexpress.com/travel